GRAND PRIX DATA BOOK 1997

A Complete Record of the Formula 1 World Championship from 1950

Published in 1996 by
Duke Marketing Ltd
PO Box 46
Douglas
Isle of Man
British Isles
IM99 1DD

Designed by
David Hayhoe,
Shaun Earnshaw
& Mark Green
(Words & Spaces)
and
Duke Marketing

ISBN 0 9529325 0 4

Printed and bound in Great Britain by
Butler & Tanner Ltd, Frome and London

CONTENTS

FOREWORD BY JOHN WATSON

I was very pleased to be asked to write this foreword to the third edition of the *Grand Prix Data Book.*

Having been a Grand Prix winner during the 70s and 80s and more recently a member of Eurosport's television team, I can see that this excellent book will be an invaluable tool for myself and anyone with an interest in the sport.

From a very early age, I have been fascinated with Formula 1 and now, with the *Grand Prix Data Book*, you too can join me in reminiscing over the great history of my sport. 1997 sees a new era of Formula 1 broadcasting, where the demand for knowledge and information will be even greater. That's where this book comes in, for David Hayhoe and David Holland have covered the subject in tremendous depth and for any Formula 1 motor racing enthusiast, or indeed newcomer to the sport, it will be a must have.

John Watson

Welcome to the third edition of the *Grand Prix Data Book*, a volume that we hope will be regarded as the most reliable reference source for the Formula 1 World Championship. *Grand Prix Data Book 2* was very well received with all 2,000 copies sold out during 1995. This new version has brought the story bang up to date and given us the opportunity to correct any errors that slipped in last time. More importantly, further research has enabled us to put right many anomalies and come up with further ideas to make the work even more valuable. As always though, there are still gaps in the framework and we would be grateful to any readers who can assist with more information to help us compile future editions.

Due to the nature of this reference work there are many great racing drivers who are missing, but our story is confined to those drivers who participated in the Formula 1 World Championship and helped develop this sport into the global attraction that it is today. Hopefully this book will not just help you follow the current racing scene but also to dip into its myriad history. Our comprehensive race results section which shows car numbers, will provide ideal reference material when viewing the races on DUKE's seasonal review videos and other film.

Our very special thanks go to Eurosport television's Formula 1 expert John Watson, for sparing valuable time and having sufficient confidence in us to write a foreword, and to Alain Baudouin, Dave Cox (D & S Classic Sportscars), Peter Duke (Duke Marketing), Anthony Hayes (British Racing Green), Shaun Earnshaw, Mark Green (Words & Spaces), Christopher Hilton, Henry Hope-Frost (Autosport), Colin Lane, Maureen Magee, Bruce Malcolm (Fotosouvenirs), Thomas Moulton, Doug Nye, David Phipps, John Ross, Steve Small, Christer Svensson, Dave Webb and everybody else who has taken time to contribute information and ideas since the last edition.

Performance records in this book are taken up to the end of the 1996 season.

INTRODUCTION

Throughout the *Grand Prix Data Book*, distances and average speeds have been recalculated to remove obvious previously published errors. There may be apparent discrepancies, because of rounding.

Drivers are referred to by their most commonly used names or nicknames, although a table in Chapter 3 details drivers' proper names.

Happy reading...

DAVID HAYHOE and DAVID HOLLAND

ABOUT THE AUTHORS

DAVID HAYHOE

David Hayhoe was born in Beckenham in 1954, currently lives in Surrey and has been following motorsport and particularly the Grand Prix scene closely since the early 80s. A career Civil Servant, his full-time job takes him to airports for the Department of Transport. Apart from an appreciation of music and travel, most of his time is dedicated to researching, working on his computer database and attending race meetings. His first *Grand Prix Data Book* started him off on his part-time journalistic career in 1989, he has been *Autocourse* statistician since 1990 and contributed motorsport articles and photographs to newspapers, magazines and sponsors. The 2nd Edition of the *Grand Prix Data Book* was the outcome of a collaboration with David Holland and the pair continue to work closely together in developing their output.

DAVID HOLLAND

David Holland was born in Peterborough in 1961 and now lives in King's Lynn with wife Carolyn and children Jonathan and Jessica. In his limited spare time, he enjoys fishing, football and music and is still in the process of restoring his 1963 Triumph TR4. A childhood interest has developed into detailed research of Formula 1, its personalities and its history which has culminated in contributing his knowledge and enthusiasm into the *Grand Prix Data Book* project.

ABBREVIATIONS

NATIONALITIES / COUNTRIES

A	Austria *
AUS	Australia *
B	Belgium *
BR	Brazil *
CDN	Canada *
CH	Switzerland *
CO	Colombia
D	Germany *
DK	Denmark
E	Spain *
F	France *
FIN	Finland
FL	Liechtenstein
GB	Britain *
H	Hungary *
I	Italy *
IRL	Ireland
J	Japan *
MA	Morocco *
MC	Monaco *
MEX	Mexico *
NL	Netherlands *
NZ	New Zealand
P	Portugal *
RA	Argentina *
RCH	Chile
RSM	San Marino *
RSR	South Rhodesia (now Zimbabwe)
S	Sweden *
T	Thailand
U	Uruguay
USA	United States of America *
YV	Venezuela
ZA	South Africa *

** Countries hosting a Championship race*

OTHER RACES

DAL	Dallas (USA)
DET	Detroit (USA)
EUR	Europe
INDY	Indianapolis 500 (USA)
LV	Caesars Palace, Las Vegas (USA)
PAC	Pacific
PES	Pescara (Italy)
USAE	USA East
USAW	USA West

GP OF EUROPE HELD IN

Britain	(1983, 85 & 93)
Germany	(1984, 95 & 96)
Spain	(1994)

Pacific GP held in Japan
San Marino GP held in Italy
Swiss GP held in France.

ENGINES

Climax	Coventry Climax
Weslake	Gurney Weslake

all Castellotti engines are rebadged Ferrari, whilst all Megatron engines are rebadged BMW.

INTERIOR

1996 DRIVERS
Jean Alesi
Rubens Barrichello
Gerhard Berger
Martin Brundle
David Coulthard
Johnny Herbert
Damon Hill
Eddie Irvine
Ukyo Katayama
Andrea Montermini
Jos Verstappen
David Hayhoe / Fast Action Photos

Luca Badoer
Pedro Diniz
Giancarlo Fisichella
Heinz-Harald Frentzen
Mika Häkkinen
Pedro Lamy
Olivier Panis
Ricardo Rosset
Mika Salo
Michael Schumacher
Jacques Villeneuve
Bruce Malcolm / Fotosouvenirs

1996 CARS
Benetton B196-Renault
Ferrari F310
Footwork FA17 (TWR Arrows)-Ford Cosworth
Forti FG01-95B-Ford Cosworth
Jordan 196-Peugeot
Ligier JS43-Mugen Honda
McLaren MP4/11-Mercedes Benz
Minardi M195B-Ford Cosworth
Sauber C15-Ford Cosworth
Tyrrell 024-Yamaha
Williams FW18-Renault
Bruce Malcolm / Fotosouvenirs

HISTORIC CAR PAINTINGS
Ferrari 375 (1951)
Maserati A6GCM (1953)
Mercedes-Benz W196 str. (1954-55)
Lancia-Ferrari D50 (1956)
Vanwall (1957)
Ferrari D246 (1958-60)
BRM P25 (1959)
Cooper T53-Climax (1960)
Ferrari 156 (1961)
Porsche 804 (1962)
Brabham BT7-Climax (1964)
Ferrari 312 (1966)
Honda RA300 (1967)
Lotus 49B-Ford Cosworth (1968)
BRM P153 (1970)
Tyrrell 002-Ford Cosworth (1971)
Lotus 72D-Ford Cosworth (1972)
Ferrari 312B3 (1974)
Hesketh 308-Ford Cosworth (1975)
Tyrrell P34-Ford Cosworth (1976)
Wolf WR1-Ford Cosworth (1977)
Brabham BT46-Alfa Romeo (1978)
Ligier JS11-Ford Cosworth (1979-80)
Renault RE30 (1981)
Ferrari 126C2 (1982)
Tyrrell 011-Ford Cosworth (1983)
McLaren MP4/2-TAG Porsche (1984)
Brabham BT54-BMW (1985)
Benetton B186-BMW (1986)
Williams FW13-Renault (1989)
Benetton B191-Ford Cosworth (1991)
Williams FW15C-Renault (1993)
Ferrari 412T1B (1994)
Benetton B195-Renault (1995)
Williams FW17-Renault (1995)
Ferrari 412T2 (1995)
Alain Baudouin

LIST OF ILLUSTRATIONS

Giovanni Lavaggi
Anthony Hayes / British Racing Green

Tarso Marques
Martyn Elford

Other photographs
Dave Cox
David Hayhoe / Fast Action Photos
David Phipps
Footwork Arrows
Geoff Goddard Photo Library
ICN UK
John Ross
Maureen Magee
Proaction Media Relations

All photographs supplied by FOTOSOUVENIRS and FAST ACTION PHOTOS, whilst printed in this book in black & white, are available in colour for purchase. See information elsewhere in this book

DRIVERS

Jean ALESI
Luca BADOER
Rubens BARRICHELLO
Gerhard BERGER
Martin BRUNDLE
David COULTHARD
Pedro DINIZ
Giancarlo FISICHELLA
Heinz-Harald FRENTZEN
Mika HÄKKINEN
Johnny HERBERT
Damon HILL
Eddie IRVINE
Ukyo KATAYAMA
Pedro LAMY
Giovanni LAVAGGI
Tarso MARQUES
Andrea MONTERMINI
Olivier PANIS
Ricardo ROSSET
Mika SALO
Michael SCHUMACHER
Jos VERSTAPPEN
Jacques VILLENEUVE

1996 SCENE

TEAMS

ARROWS
BENETTON
FERRARI
FORTI
JORDAN
LIGIER
McLAREN
MINARDI
SAUBER
TYRRELL
WILLIAMS

SPONSORS

Jean ALESI

PERSONAL DATA

Nationality: French
Date of Birth: 11 June 1964
Place of Birth: Montfavet, nr Avignon, France
Home: Nyon, nr Geneva, Switzerland / Avignon
Marital Status: Divorced. Girlfriend: Kumiko
Children: Daughter - Charlotte Marcelle

FORMULA 1 CAREER

1996 Team / Car Number: Benetton / 3 (GPs: all)
Formula 1 Teams: Tyrrell (1989 to 90)
Ferrari (1991 to 95)
Benetton (1996)

First Entry: F 89 (Paul Ricard) Tyrrell-Ford Cosworth
Races: 118
First Race: F 89 (Paul Ricard) Tyrrell-Ford Cosworth
Most Recent Race: J 96 (Suzuka) Benetton-Renault

World Championships: —
Best World Championship: 4th, 1996 Benetton-Renault

Wins: 1
First Win: CDN 95 (Montréal) Ferrari
2nd: 12
3rd: 13
4th: 11
5th: 9
6th: 4

Pole Positions: 1
First Pole Position: I 94 (Monza) Ferrari

Front Rows: 6
First Front Row: CDN 94 (Montréal) Ferrari
Most Recent Front Row: J 95 (Suzuka) Ferrari

Fastest Laps: 4
First Fastest Lap: USA 91 (Phoenix) Ferrari
Most Recent Fastest Lap: MC 96 (Monte Carlo) Benetton-Renault

Points: I 89
First Point: F 89 (Paul Ricard) Tyrrell-Ford Cosworth
Most Recent Point: P 96 (Estoril) Benetton-Renault

Races Led: 17
Laps Led: 233
Distance Led: 1,101.6 km, 684.5 miles
First Lap Led: USA 90 (Phoenix) Tyrrell-Ford Cosworth
Most Recent Lap Led: P 96 (Estoril) Benetton-Renault

NON-FORMULA 1 CAREER HIGHLIGHTS

Coupe Renault 5	(1983):	1st at Nogaro *(First win in a racing car)*, 1 x 4th, 1 x 5th, 2 x 6th, 7th in Championship
Formula Renault Turbo	(1984):	6th at Albi, 10th in Championship
	(1985):	2nd at Bugatti, 4 x 3rd, 2 x 5th, 2nd in Championship
French Formula 3	(1986):	1st at Albi & Bugatti, 2nd at Rouen *(disqualified)*, Nogaro & Magny Cours, 3 x 3rd, pole at Rouen, Albi & Bugatti, 2 x fastest laps, 2nd in Championship (Dallara-Alfa Romeo) 7 x 1st, 1 x 2nd, 2 x 3rd, 5 x poles, 3 x fastest laps, 1st in Championship (Martini/ Dallara-Alfa Romeo)
FIA F3 Nations Cup, Imola	(1986):	10th (Dallara-Alfa Romeo)
FIA Formula 3 'Macau GP'	(1986):	8th (Dallara-Alfa Romeo)
	(1988):	2nd in heat 1, 11th overall (Dallara-Alfa Romeo)
Monaco Formula 3 race	(1987):	2nd (Dallara-Alfa Romeo)
FIA Formula 3000	(1988):	2nd at Pau, 5th at Silverstone & Dijon, 6th at Enna-Pergusa, 10th in Championship (March & Reynard-Ford Cosworth)
	(1989):	1st at Pau, Birmingham & Spa, 2nd at Brands Hatch, 1 x 4th, 1 x 5th, 1 x 6th, pole at Enna-Pergusa & Birmingham, fastest lap at Birmingham, 1st in Championship (Reynard-Mugen Honda)
IMSA Camel GT	(1989):	3rd at Laguna Seca (Ferrari F40)

Luca BADOER

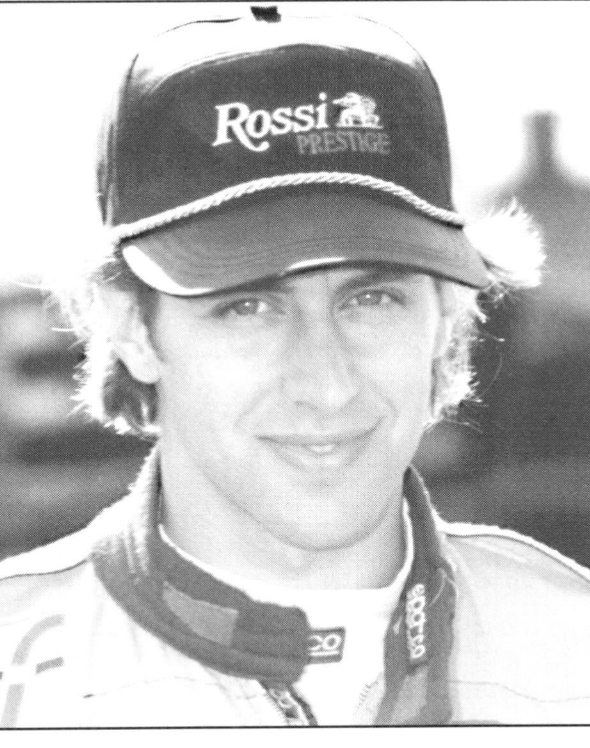

PERSONAL DATA

Nationality: Italian
Date of Birth: 25 January 1971
Place of Birth: Montebelluna, Treviso, Italy
Home: Monte Carlo, Monaco
Marital Status: Unmarried

FORMULA 1 CAREER

1996 Team / Car Number: Forti / 22 (GPs: AUS to GB)
Formula 1 Teams: BMS Scuderia Italia Lola (1993)
Minardi Scuderia Italia (1995)
Forti (1996)

First Entry: ZA 93 (Kyalami) Lola-Ferrari
Races: 34
First Race: BR 93 (Interlagos) Lola-Ferrari
Most Recent Race: F 96 (Magny-Cours) Forti-Ford Cosworth

World Championships: —
Best World Championship: —

Wins: —

Best placing: 8th, CDN 95 (Montréal) & H 95 (Hungaroring) Minardi-Ford Cosworth

Pole Positions: —

Front Rows: —

Best Grid Position: 12th, H 95 (Hungaroring) Minardi-Ford Cosworth

Fastest Laps: —

Points: —

Races Led: —

NON-FORMULA 1 CAREER HIGHLIGHTS

Italian F3	(1989):	(Dallara-Alfa Romeo)
	(1990):	1st at Vallelunga, 9th in Championship (Ralt-Alfa Romeo)
	(1991):	1st at Imola, Varano, Monza & Mugello (disqualified), 1 x 3rd, 1 x 5th, 1 x 6th, 2 x fastest laps, 4th in Championship (Dallara-Alfa Romeo)
Marlboro Masters of F3, Zandvoort	(1991):	4th (Dallara-Alfa Romeo)
FIA Formula 3000	(1992):	1st at Enna-Pergusa, Hockenheim, Nürburgring & Nogaro, 2nd at Albacete, 1 x 5th, 2 x 6th, 5 x poles, 3 x fastest laps, 1st in Championship (Reynard-Ford Cosworth)

Rubens BARRICHELLO

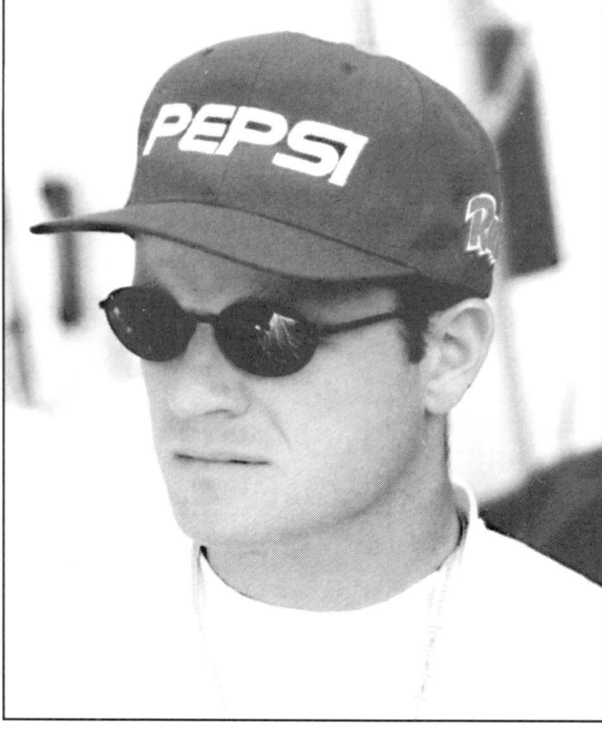

PERSONAL DATA

Nationality:	Brazilian
Date of Birth:	23 May 1972
Place of Birth:	Sâo Paulo, Brazil
Home:	Cambridge, England / Sâo Paulo
Marital Status:	Unmarried

FORMULA 1 CAREER

1996 Team / Car Number:	Jordan / 11 (GPs: all)
Formula 1 Teams:	Jordan (1993 to 96)
First Entry:	ZA 93 (Kyalami) Jordan-Hart
Races:	64
First Race:	ZA 93 (Kyalami) Jordan-Hart
Most Recent Race:	J 96 (Suzuka) Jordan-Peugeot
World Championships:	—
Best World Championship:	6th, 1994 Jordan-Hart
Wins:	—
Best placing:	2nd, CDN 95 (Montréal) Jordan-Peugeot
2nd:	1
3rd:	1
4th:	8
5th:	4
6th:	4
Pole Positions:	1
First Pole Position:	B 94 (Spa-Francorchamps) Jordan-Hart
Front Rows:	2
First Front Row:	B 94 (Spa-Francorchamps) Jordan-Hart
Most Recent Front Row:	BR 96 (Interlagos) Jordan-Peugeot
Fastest Laps:	—
Points:	46
First Point:	J 93 (Suzuka) Jordan-Hart
Most Recent Point:	I 96 (Monza) Jordan-Peugeot
Races Led:	2
Laps Led:	4
Distance Led:	18.9 km, 11.7 miles
First Lap Led:	P 94 (Estoril) Jordan-Hart
Most Recent Lap Led:	I 95 (Monza) Jordan-Peugeot

NON-FORMULA 1 CAREER HIGHLIGHTS

Brazilian F. Ford 1600	(1989):	4th in Championship
Formula Vauxhall-Lotus	(1990):	2 x 3rd, 1 x pole, 11th in Championship
GM Lotus Euroseries	(1990):	1st at Zandvoort, Silverstone, Hockenheim (x2), Spa & Jerez, 2nd at Imola & Estoril, 7 x poles, 7 x fastest laps,1st in Championship
British Formula 3	(1991):	4 x 1st, 2 x 2nd, 2 x 3rd, 9 x poles, 7 x fastest laps,1st in Championship (Ralt-Mugen Honda)
Marlboro Masters of F3, Zandvoort	(1991):	6th, pole & fastest lap (Ralt-Mugen Honda)
FIA Formula 3 'Macau GP'	(1991):	5th (Ralt-Mugen Honda)
	(1992):	7th (Ralt-Vauxhall)
FIA Formula 3000	(1992):	2nd at Silverstone & Montmeló, 3rd at Pau & Nürburgring, 3rd in Championship (Reynard-Judd & -Ford Cosworth)

Gerhard BERGER

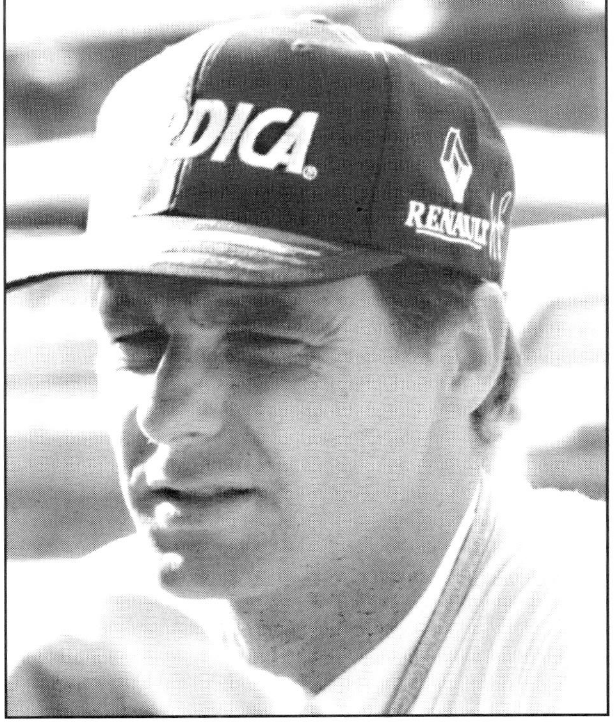

PERSONAL DATA

Nationality: Austrian
Date of Birth: 27 August 1959
Place of Birth: Wörgl, nr Innsbruck, Austria
Home: Monte Carlo, Monaco / Söll, nr Wörgl, Austria
Marital Status: Married to Ana
Children: Daughters - Cristina & Sarah Maria

FORMULA 1 CAREER

1996 Team / Car Number: Benetton / 4 (GPs:all)
Formula 1 Teams: ATS (1984)
Arrows (1985)
Benetton (1986)
Ferrari (1987 to 89)
McLaren (1990 to 92)
Ferrari (1993 to 95)
Benetton (1996)

First Entry: A 84 (Österreichring) ATS-BMW
Races: 196
First Race: A 84 (Österreichring) ATS-BMW
Most Recent Race: J 96 (Suzuka) Benetton-Renault

World Championships: —
Best World Championship: 3rd, 1988 Ferrari &
3rd, McLaren-Honda/
3rd, 1994 Ferrari

Wins: 9
First Win: MEX 86 (Mexico City) Benetton-BMW
Most Recent Win: D 94 (Hockenheim) Ferrari

2nd: 16
3rd: 21
4th: 23
5th: 8
6th: 11

Pole Positions: 11
First Pole Position: P 87 (Estoril) Ferrari
Most Recent Pole Position: B 95 (Spa-Francorchamps) Ferrari

Front Rows: 31
First Front Row: B 86 (Spa-Francorchamps) Benetton-BMW
Most Recent Front Row: D 96 (Hockenheim) Benetton-Renault

Fastest Laps: 19
First Fastest Lap: D 86 (Hockenheim) Benetton-BMW
Most Recent Fastest Lap: B 96 (Spa-Francorchamps) Benetton-Renault

Points: 359
First Point: I 84 (Monza) ATS-BMW
Most Recent Point: J 96 (Suzuka) Benetton-Renault

Races Led: 31
Laps Led: 713
Distance Led: 3,445.5 km, 2,140.9 miles
First Lap Led: A 86 (Österreichring) Benetton-BMW
Most Recent Lap Led: D 96 (Hockenheim) Benetton-Renault

NON-FORMULA 1 CAREER HIGHLIGHTS

Alfasud Trophy	(1979):	First win in a racing car, Österreichring (Ford Escort)
German Alfasud Trophy	(1981):	1st in Championship
German Formula 3	(1982):	1 x 1st, 3rd in Championship (Martini-Alfa Romeo & -Toyota)
FIA European Formula 3	(1983):	2nd at Österreichring & Knutstorp, 1 x 3rd, 7th in Championship (Ralt-Alfa Romeo)
	(1984):	1st at Österreichring & Monza, 2nd at Mugello, 4 x 3rd, 3rd in Championship (Ralt-Alfa Romeo)
Austrian GP, F3 race	(1983):	4th (Ralt-Alfa Romeo)
FIA Formula 3 'Macau GP'	(1983):	3rd (Ralt-Alfa Romeo)
Monaco Formula 3 race	(1984):	2nd (Ralt-Alfa Romeo)
European Touring Car	(1985):	1st at Spa, 3rd at Brno & Estoril (BMW 635CSi)
	(1986):	1st at Misano & Nogaro, 2nd at Donington & Zolder, 7th= in 2,500cc+ Class (BMW 635CSi)

Martin BRUNDLE

PERSONAL DATA:

Nationality:	British
Date of Birth:	1 June 1959
Place of Birth:	King's Lynn, Norfolk, England
Home:	Gayton, King's Lynn
Marital Status:	Married to Liz (Elizabeth)
Children:	Son - Alexander; Daughter - Charlotte

FORMULA 1 CAREER

1996 Team / Car Number:	Jordan / 12 (GPs: all)
Formula 1 Teams:	Tyrrell (1984 to 86) Zakspeed (1987) Williams (1988) Brabham (1989, 1991) Benetton (1992) Ligier (1993, 1995) McLaren (1994) Jordan (1996)
First Entry:	BR 84 (Rio de Janeiro) Tyrrell-Ford Cosworth
Races:	158
First Race:	BR 84 (Rio de Janeiro) Tyrrell-Ford Cosworth
Most Recent Race:	J 96 (Suzuka) Jordan-Peugeot
World Championships:	—
Best World Championship:	6th, 1992 Benetton-Ford Cosworth
Wins:	—
Best placing:	2nd, I 92 (Monza) Benetton-Ford Cosworth/ MC 94 (Monte Carlo) McLaren-Peugeot
2nd:	2
3rd:	7
4th:	8
5th:	12
6th:	10
Pole Positions:	—
Front Rows:	—
Best Grid Position:	3rd, F 93 (Magny-Cours) Ligier-Renault
Fastest Laps:	—
Points:	98
First Point:	BR 86 (Rio de Janeiro) Tyrrell-Renault
Most Recent Point:	J 96 (Suzuka) Jordan-Peugeot
Races Led:	—

NON-FORMULA 1 CAREER HIGHLIGHTS

British Saloon Car	(1977):	pole in debut, 1st in second race, 3rd in class (Toyota Celica)
	(1978):	7th in Championship
BMW County	(1980):	1st (Norfolk) in Championship
Motorcraft British F. Ford 2000	(1980):	5th in Championship (Reynard)
Imperial Leather British F. Ford	(1980):	7th in Championship (Reynard)
Willhire 24-hours,Snetterton	(1980):	1st in 1601-2300cc class
Marlboro British Formula 3	(1982):	1st at Oulton Park & Thruxton, 3 x 2nd, 2 x 3rd, 4th in Championship (Ralt-Volkswagen)
	(1983):	7 x 1st, 10 x 2nd, 2 x 3rd, 5 x fastest laps, 2nd in Championship (Ralt-Toyota)
Grovewood Award	(1982):	1st
European Formula 3	(1983):	1st at Silverstone & Donington, 7th= in Championship (Ralt-Toyota)
Austrian GP, F3 race	(1983):	1st (Ralt-Toyota)
FIA Formula 3 'Macau GP'	(1983):	10th (Ralt-Toyota)
World Endurance/ FIA Sports-Prot.	(1985):	3rd at Mosport (Jaguar)
	(1987):	1st at Spa, 24th= in Championship (Jaguar)
	(1988):	1st at Jarama, Monza, Silverstone, Brands Hatch & Fuji, 3 x 2nd, 1st in Championship (Jaguar)
	(1990):	1st at Silverstone, 2 x 3rd, 1 x fastest lap, 8th in Championship (Jaguar)
	(1991):	1st at Monza, 3rd at Silverstone (Jaguar)
IMSA Camel GT	(1988):	1st at Daytona 24-hours & Del Mar, 3 x 2nd, 1 x 3rd, fastest lap at Del Mar, 5th in Championship (Jaguar)
	(1990):	2nd at Daytona 24-hours (Jaguar)
Le Mans 24-hours	(1990):	1st (Jaguar)

David COULTHARD

PERSONAL DATA

Nationality: British
Date of Birth: 27 March 1971
Place of Birth: Twynholm, Dumfries, Scotland
Home: Monte Carlo, Monaco / Twynholm
Marital Status: Girlfriend - Andrea

FORMULA 1 CAREER

1996 Team / Car Number: McLaren / 8 (GPs: all)
Formula 1 Teams: Williams (1994 to 95)
McLaren (1996)

First Entry: E 94 (Montmeló) Williams-Renault
Races: 41
First Race: E 94 (Montmeló) Williams-Renault
Most Recent Race: J 96 (Suzuka) McLaren-Mercedes Benz

World Championships: —
Best World Championship: 3rd, 1995 Williams-Renault

Wins: 1
First Win: P 95 (Estoril) Williams-Renault

2nd: 6
3rd: 4
4th: 3
5th: 4
6th: 2

Pole Positions: 5
RA 95 (Buenos Aires) Williams-Renault
PAC 95 (Aida) Williams-Renault

Front Rows: 7
RA 95 (Buenos Aires) Williams-Renault
AUS 95 (Adelaide) Williams-Renault

Fastest Laps: 4
First Fastest Lap: D 94 (Hockenheim) Williams-Renault
Most Recent Fastest Lap: P 95 (Estoril) Williams-Renault

Points: 81
First Point: CDN 94 (Montréal) Williams-Renault
Most Recent Point: D 96 (Hockenheim) McLaren-Mercedes Benz

Races Led: 16
Laps Led: 233
Distance Led: 1,060.4 km, 658.9 miles
First Lap Led: B 94 (Spa-Francorchamps) Williams-Renault
Most Recent Lap Led: B 96 (Spa-Francorchamps) McLaren-Mercedes Benz

NON-FORMULA 1 CAREER HIGHLIGHTS

Dunlop/Autosport F. Ford 1600	(1989):	10 x 1st, 1st in Championship (13 races)
P & O Ferries Junior F. Ford 1600	(1989):	1st in debut Formula Ford race (Thruxton), 9 x 1st, 1st in Championship (14 races)
F. Ford Festival, Brands Hatch	(1989):	3rd (Van Diemen)
McLaren/Autosport 'Young Driver Of The Year'	(1989):	1st
Formula Vauxhall-Lotus	(1990):	1st at Silverstone & Brands Hatch, 1 x 2nd, 1 x 3rd, pole at Brands Hatch, 4th in Championship
GM Lotus Euroseries	(1990):	1st at Knutstorp, 3rd at Hockenheim, 2 x 4th, 1 x 5th, 5th in Championship
British Formula 3	(1991):	5 x 1st, 1 x 2nd, 2 x 3rd, 2nd in Championship (Ralt-Mugen Honda)
FIA Formula 3 'Macau GP'	(1991):	1st (Ralt-Mugen Honda)
Marlboro Masters of F3, Zandvoort	(1991):	1st (Ralt-Mugen Honda)
Euro-Macau-Fuji Formula 3	(1991):	2nd & pole (Ralt-Mugen Honda)
	(1992):	8th (Reynard-Mugen Honda)
FIA Formula 3000	(1992):	3rd at Nogaro & Magny-Cours, 9th in Championship (Reynard-Judd)
	(1993):	1st at Enna-Pergusa, 2nd at Silverstone & Pau, 1 x 3rd, 3rd in Championship (Reynard-Ford Cosworth)
	(1994):	2nd at Silverstone, 9th in Championship (Reynard-Ford Cosworth) (1 race)
Le Mans 24-hours	(1993):	15th (Jaguar)(1st in GT class)

Pedro DINIZ

PERSONAL DATA

Nationality:	Brazilian
Date of Birth:	22 May 1970
Place of Birth:	Sâo Paulo, Brazil
Home:	Monte Carlo, Monaco / Sâo Paulo
Marital Status:	Unmarried

FORMULA 1 CAREER

1996 Team / Car Number:	Ligier / 10 (GPs: all)
Formula 1 Teams:	Forti (1995) Ligier (1996)
First Entry:	BR 95 (Interlagos) Forti-Ford Cosworth
Races:	33
First Race:	BR 95 (Interlagos) Forti-Ford Cosworth
Most Recent Race:	J 96 (Suzuka) Ligier-Mugen Honda
World Championships:	—
Best World Championship:	15th, 1996 Ligier-Mugen Honda
Wins:	—
Best placing:	6th, I 96 (Monza) / E 96 (Montmeló) Ligier-Mugen Honda
6th:	2
Pole Positions:	—
Front Rows:	—
Best Grid Position:	11th, F 96 (Magny-Cours) / D 96 (Hockenheim) Ligier-Mugen Honda
Fastest Laps:	—
Points:	2
First Point:	E 96 (Montmeló) Ligier-Mugen Honda
Most Recent Point:	I 96 (Monza) Ligier-Mugen Honda
Races Led:	—

NON-FORMULA 1 CAREER HIGHLIGHTS

Brazilian Formula Ford 1600	(1989):	6th in Championship
South American Formula 3	(1990):	1 x 3rd
British Formula 3	(1991):	6th at Silverstone, 11th= in Championship (Ralt-Mugen Honda)
	(1992):	3rd at Thruxton & Brands Hatch, 12th= in Championship (Reynard & Ralt-Mugen Honda)
FIA Formula 3000	(1993):	7th at Enna-Pergusa (Reynard-Ford Cosworth)
	(1994):	4th at Estoril, 12th= in Championship (Reynard-Ford Cosworth)

Giancarlo FISICHELLA

PERSONAL DATA

Nationality:	Italian
Date of Birth:	14 January 1973
Place of Birth:	Rome, Italy
Home:	Monte Carlo, Monaco / Rome
Marital Status:	Unmarried. Girlfriend: Luna

FORMULA 1 CAREER

1996 Team / Car Number:	Minardi Scuderia Italia / 21 (GPs: AUS, EUR to GB)
Formula 1 Teams:	Minardi Scuderia Italia (1996)
First Entry:	AUS 96 (Melbourne) Minardi-Ford Cosworth
Races:	8
First Race:	AUS 96 (Melbourne) Minardi-Ford Cosworth
Most Recent Race:	GB 96 (Silverstone) Minardi-Ford Cosworth
World Championships:	—
Best World Championship:	—
Wins:	—
Best placing:	8th, CDN 96 (Montréal) Minardi-Ford Cosworth
Pole Positions:	—
Front Rows:	—
Best Grid Position:	16th, AUS 96 (Melbourne) / CDN 96 (Montréal) Minardi-Ford Cosworth
Fastest Laps:	—
Points:	—
Races Led:	—

NON-FORMULA 1 CAREER HIGHLIGHTS

Italian Formula 3	(1992):	1st at Imola, 1 x 5th, 8th in Championship (Ralt-Alfa Romeo)
	(1993):	1st at Enna-Pergusa & Monza, 3rd at Varano & Imola, 1 x 4th, 2 x 5th, 1 x 6th, 1 x fastest lap, 2nd in Championship (Dallara-Fiat)
	(1994):	10 x 1st, 6 x 2nd, 1 x 3rd, 1 x 4th, 3 x poles, 6 x fastest laps, 1st in Championship (Dallara-Opel)
British Formula 3	(1994):	4th at Silverstone, 16th= in Championship (Dallara-Opel)
Monaco Formula 3 race	(1993):	2nd and pole (Dallara-Fiat)
	(1994):	1st and pole (Dallara-Opel)
Marlboro Masters of F3, Zandvoort	(1994):	9th (Dallara-Opel)
FIA Formula 3 'Macau GP'	(1994):	pole (Dallara-Opel)
International Touring Car	(1995):	2nd at Mugello, 4th at Estoril, 5th at Donington, 10th in Championship (Alfa Romeo)
	(1996):	2nd at Estoril & Magny-Cours, 3rd at Diepholz, Magny-Cours & Mugello, 1 x 4th, 4 x 5th, 2 x fastest laps, 8th (provisional) in Championship (Alfa Romeo)
German Touring Car	(1995):	4th at AVUS, 6th at Hockenheim, Diepholz & Nürburgring, 15th in Championship (Alfa Romeo)

Heinz-Harald FRENTZEN

PERSONAL DATA

Nationality:	German
Date of Birth:	18 May 1967
Place of Birth:	Mönchengladbach, Germany
Home:	Monte Carlo, Monaco
Marital Status:	Girlfriend - Tanja

FORMULA 1 CAREER

1996 Team / Car Number:	Sauber / 15 (GPs: all)
Formula 1 Teams:	Sauber (1994 to 96)
First Entry:	BR 94 (Interlagos) Sauber-Mercedes Benz
Races:	48
First Race:	BR 94 (Interlagos) Sauber-Mercedes Benz
Most Recent Race:	J 96 (Suzuka) Sauber-Ford Cosworth
World Championships:	—
Best World Championship:	9th, 1995 Sauber-Ford Cosworth
Wins:	—
Best placing:	3rd, I 95 (Monza) Sauber-Ford Cosworth
3rd:	1
4th:	4
5th:	3
6th:	7
Pole Positions:	—
Front Rows:	—
Best Grid Position:	3rd, J 94 (Suzuka) Sauber-Mercedes Benz
Fastest Laps:	—
Points:	29
First Point:	PAC 94 (Aida) Sauber-Mercedes Benz
Most Recent Point:	J 96 (Suzuka) Sauber-Ford Cosworth
Races Led:	—

NON-FORMULA 1 CAREER HIGHLIGHTS

German Formula Ford 2000	(1987):	2nd in Championship
GM Lotus Euroseries	(1988):	1st at Estoril & Jerez, 2nd at Nürburgring, 2 x poles, 1 x fastest lap, 6th in Championship
German Opel/Lotus Challenge	(1988):	4 x 1st, 1st in Championship
German Formula 3	(1989):	2 x 1st, 2nd= in Championship (Dallara & Reynard-Volkswagen)
FIA Formula 3000	(1990):	5th at Enna-Pergusa, 6th at Hockenheim,16th= in Championship (Reynard-Mugen Honda)
	(1991):	5th at Enna-Pergusa & Spa, 6th at Mugello, 14th in Championship (Lola-Mugen Honda)
FIA World Sports-Prototype	(1990):	2nd at Donington, 17th= in Championship (Mercedes-Benz)
FIA World Sports Car	(1992):	4th at Donington, 13th at Le Mans 24-hours, 14th in Championship (Lola-Judd)
All-Japan Sports-Prototype	(1992):	3rd at Mine
All-Japan Formula 3000	(1992):	3rd at Suzuka, 1 x 6th, 14th= in Championship (Lola-Mugen Honda)
	(1993):	2nd at Fuji, 1 x 5th, 1 x pole, 9th= in Championship (Lola-Mugen Honda)

Mika HÄKKINEN

PERSONAL DATA

Nationality:	Finnish
Date of Birth:	28 September 1968
Place of Birth:	Helsinki, Finland
Home:	Monte Carlo, Monaco
Marital Status:	Girlfriend - Erja

FORMULA 1 CAREER

1996 Team / Car Number:	McLaren / 7 (GPs: all)
Formula 1 Teams:	Lotus (1991 to 92) McLaren (1993 to 96)
First Entry:	USA 91 (Phoenix) Lotus-Judd
Races:	79
First Race:	USA 91 (Phoenix) Lotus-Judd
Most Recent Race:	J 96 (Suzuka) McLaren-Mercedes Benz
World Championships:	—
Best World Championship:	4th, 1994 McLaren-Peugeot
Wins:	—
Best placing:	2nd, B 94 (Spa-Francorchamps) McLaren-Peugeot I 95 (Monza) / J 95 (Suzuka) McLaren-Mercedes Benz
2nd:	3
3rd:	10
4th:	5
5th:	7
6th:	4
Pole Positions:	—
Front Rows:	1
First Front Row:	MC 94 (Monte Carlo) McLaren-Peugeot
Fastest Laps:	—
Points:	91
First Point:	RSM 91 (Imola) Lotus-Judd
Most Recent Point:	J 96 (Suzuka) McLaren-Mercedes Benz
Races Led:	6
Laps Led:	17
Distance Led:	89.5 km, 55.6 miles
First Lap Led:	RSM 94 (Imola) McLaren-Peugeot
Most Recent Lap Led:	B 96 (Spa-Francorchamps) McLaren-Mercedes Benz

NON-FORMULA 1 CAREER HIGHLIGHTS

Finnish, Swedish & Nordic Formula Ford 1600	(1987):	First win in a racing car at Ahvenisto, Finland, 9 x 1st, 1st in each Championship (Reynard)(15 races)
EFDA Bridgestone F. Ford 1600 Euroseries	(1987):	7th= in Championship (Reynard)
GM Lotus Euroseries	(1988):	1st at Zandvoort, Paul Ricard, Spa, Knutstorp, 1 x 2nd, 1 x 3rd, 2 x poles, 6 x fastest laps, 1st in Championship
Vauxhall/Lotus Challenge	(1988):	1st at Silverstone, Mondello & Thruxton, 3 x 2nd, 1 x 3rd, 4 x poles, 7 x fastest laps, 2nd in Championship
British Formula 3	(1989):	1 x 2nd, 1 x 3rd, 2 x fastest laps, 7th in Championship (Reynard-Toyota)
	(1990):	9 x 1st, 5 x 2nd, 1 x 3rd, 11 x poles, 10 x fastest laps, 1st in Championship (Ralt-Mugen Honda)
Monaco Formula 3 race	(1989):	16th (Reynard-TOM'S Toyota)
Cellnet Super Prix, Brands	(1989):	1st, pole & fastest lap (Ralt-Mugen Honda)
Italian Formula 3	(1990):	1st at Imola (Ralt-Mugen Honda)
German Formula 3	(1990):	1st & fastest lap at Hockenheim (Ralt-Mugen Honda)
FIA Formula 3 'Macau GP'	(1990):	pole & fastest lap (Ralt-Mugen Honda)

H

Johnny HERBERT

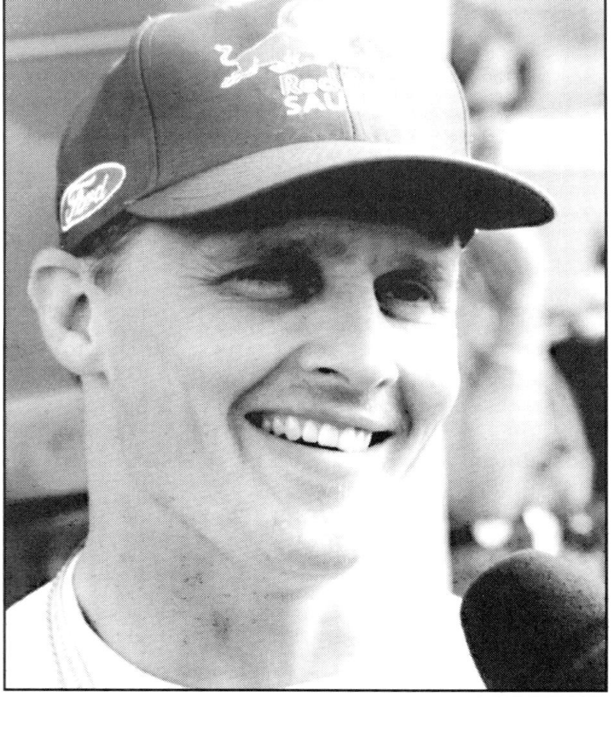

PERSONAL DATA

Nationality:	British
Date of Birth:	25 June 1964
Place of Birth:	Brentwood, Essex, England
Home:	Monte Carlo, Monaco
Marital Status:	Married to Becky (Rebecca)
Children:	Daughters - Chloe-Ann & Aimelia

FORMULA 1 CAREER

1996 Team / Car Number:	Sauber / 14 (GPs: all)
Formula 1 Teams:	Benetton (1989) Tyrrell (1989) Lotus (1990 to 94) Ligier (1994) Benetton (1994 to 95) Sauber (1996)
First Entry:	BR 89 (Rio de Janeiro) Benetton-Ford Cosworth
Races:	96
First Race:	BR 89 (Rio de Janeiro) Benetton-Ford Cosworth
Most Recent Race:	J 96 (Suzuka) Sauber-Ford Cosworth
World Championships:	—
Best World Championship:	4th, 1995 Benetton-Renault
Wins:	2
First Win:	GB 95 (Silverstone) Benetton-Renault
Most Recent Win:	I 95 (Monza) Benetton-Renault
2nd:	1
3rd:	2
4th:	8
5th:	3
6th:	3
Pole Positions:	—
Front Rows:	—
Best Grid Position:	4th, I 94 (Monza) Lotus-Mugen Honda/ BR 95 (Interlagos) / B 95 (Spa-Francorchamps) Benetton-Renault
Fastest Laps:	—

Points:	67
First Point:	BR 89 (Rio de Janeiro) Benetton-Ford Cosworth
Most Recent Point:	MC 96 (Monte Carlo) Sauber-Ford Cosworth
Races Led:	3
Laps Led:	27
Distance Led:	149.4 km, 92.8 miles
First Lap Led:	GB 95 (Silverstone) Benetton-Renault
Most Recent Lap Led:	I 95 (Monza) Benetton-Renault

NON-FORMULA 1 CAREER HIGHLIGHTS

Dunlop-Autosport 'Star of Tomorrow' FF 1600	(1984):	2 x 3rd, pole at Mallory Park, 6th in Championship (Sparton)
BP 'Superfind' Junior FF 1600	(1984):	1st at Silverstone, 1 x 3rd, 8th in Championship (Sparton)
RAC FF 1600	(1985):	4 x 2nd, 1 x 3rd, 2 x pole, 8th in Championship (Quest)
Esso FF 1600	(1985):	4 x 2nd, 1 x 3rd, 1 x pole, 3 x f laps, 5th in Championship (Quest)
EFDA Euroseries FF	(1985):	1st, pole & f lap at Brands Hatch (Quest)
F. Ford Festival, Brands Hatch	(1985):	1st (Quest)
Racing Displays Brit. FF 2000	(1986):	1 x 4th, 1 x 5th, 2 x 6th (Quest)
Grovewood Award	(1986):	2nd
Lucas British Formula 3	(1986):	4th at Donington on debut & Silverstone (x2), 15th in Championship (Ralt-Volkswagen)
	(1987):	5 x 1st, 2 x 2nd, 3 x 3rd, 6 x poles, 5 x fastest laps, 1st in Championship (Reynard-Volkswagen)
Cellnet F3 Super Prix, Brands	(1986):	3rd (Ralt-Volkswagen)
	(1987):	1st & pole (Reynard-Volkswagen)
Monaco Formula 3 race	(1987):	3rd (Reynard-Volkswagen)
FIA Formula 3 'Macau GP'	(1987):	18th (Reynard-Volkswagen)
FIA European Formula 3	(1987):	3rd in Championship (Reynard-Volkswagen) *
FIA Formula 3000	(1988):	1st at Jerez, 1 x 3rd, pole at Jerez & Brands,1 x fastest lap, 8th= in Championship (Reynard-Ford Cosworth)
Fuji 1000 Challenge	(1989):	6th (Porsche)
All-Japan Formula 3000	(1990):	5th at Fuji, 6th at Suzuka, 16th= in Championship (Reynard-Ford Cosworth)
	(1991):	2nd at Mine, 1 x 5th, 1 x 6th, 10th in Championship (Ralt-Mugen Honda)
All-Japan Sports-Prototype	(1990):	4th at Fuji, 16th= in Championship (Mazda)
	(1991):	2 x 4th at Fuji, 16th= in Championship
FIA World Sports Car	(1991):	1st at Le Mans 24-hours, 16th= in Championship (Mazda)
	(1992):	2nd at Silverstone, 4th at Le Mans 24-hours, 9th in Championship (Mazda)

* points scored at Brands Hatch in Cellnet Super Prix

Damon HILL

PERSONAL DATA

Nationality: British
Date of Birth: 17 September 1960
Place of Birth: Hampstead, London, England
Home: Killiney, Dublin, Ireland
Marital Status: Married to Georgie
Children: Sons - Oliver & Joshua; Daughter - Tabitha

FORMULA 1 CAREER

1996 Team / Car Number: Williams / 5 (GPs: all)
Formula 1 Teams: Brabham (1992)
Williams (1993 to 96)

First Entry: E 92 (Montmeló) Brabham-Judd
Races: 67
First Race: GB 92 (Silverstone) Brabham-Judd
Most Recent Race: J 96 (Suzuka) Williams-Renault

World Championships: 1 - 1996 Williams-Renault

Wins: 21
First Win: H 93 (Hungaroring) Williams-Renault
Most Recent Win: J 96 (Suzuka) Williams-Renault

2nd: 14
3rd: 5
4th: 3
5th: 1
6th: 1

Pole Positions: 20
First Pole Position: F 93 (Magny-Cours) Williams-Renault
Most Recent Pole Position: P 96 (Estoril) Williams-Renault

Front Rows: 47
First Front Row: BR 93 (Interlagos) Williams-Renault
Most Recent Front Row: J 96 (Suzuka) Williams-Renault

Fastest Laps: 19
First Fastest Lap: GB 93 (Silverstone) Williams-Renault
Most Recent Fastest Lap: H 96 (Hungaroring) Williams-Renault

Points: 326
First Point: BR 93 (Interlagos) Williams-Renault
Most Recent Point: J 96 (Suzuka) Williams-Renault

Races Led: 42
Laps Led: 1,274
Distance Led: 5,906.9 km, 3,670.4 miles
First Lap Led: BR 93 (Interlagos) Williams-Renault
Most Recent Lap Led: J 96 (Suzuka) Williams-Renault

NON-FORMULA 1 CAREER HIGHLIGHTS

Moto 'Champion of Brands'	(1984):	over 40 x 1st, 1st (Yamaha TZ 350cc motorcycle)
BP British Formula Ford 1600	(1984):	1st win in a racing car (at Brands), 10th in Championship (Van Diemen)
Esso British Formula Ford 1600	(1985):	5 x 1st, 3rd in Championship (Van Diemen)
RAC/Townsend Thoresen British Formula Ford 1600	(1985):	1st at Donington, 5th in Championship (Van Diemen)
F. Ford Festival, Brands Hatch	(1985):	3rd (Van Diemen)
Grovewood Award	(1985):	3rd
TV 'Rally-Sprint'	(1986):	1st
Lucas British Formula 3	(1986):	2nd at Snetterton, 9th= in Championship (Ralt-Volkswagen)
	(1987):	1st at Zandvoort & Spa, 2 x 2nd, 2 x 3rd, 2 x poles, 2 x F. laps, 5th in Championship (Ralt-TOMS Toyota)
	(1988):	1st at Thruxton & Silverstone, 2 x 2nd, 4 x 3rd, 2 x poles, 1 x F lap, 3rd in Championship (Ralt-TOMS Toyota)
Cellnet F3 Super Prix, Brands	(1987):	10th (Ralt-TOM'S Toyota)
Monaco Formula 3 race	(1988):	6th (Ralt-TOM'S Toyota)
FIA Formula 3 'Macau GP'	(1988):	2nd (Ralt-TOM'S Toyota)
FIA Formula 3000	(1988):	8th at Dijon (Lola-Ford Cosworth) (2 races)
	(1989):	14th at Spa (Footwork-Mugen Honda) (6 races)
	(1990):	led 5 races, 2nd at Brands, pole at Monza, Estoril & Hockenheim, 2 x fastest laps, 13th= in Championship (Lola-Ford Cosworth)
	(1991):	3rd at Nogaro, 4th at Vallelunga & Bugatti, 7th in Championship (Lola & Reynard-Ford Cosworth)
British Touring Car	(1989):	4th at Donington (1 race)
British Formula 3000	(1989):	3rd at Oulton Park, 11th in Championship (Reynard-Ford Cosworth) (2 races)

Eddie IRVINE

PERSONAL DATA

Nationality: British
Date of Birth: 10 November 1965
Place of Birth: Conlig, nr Newtownards, Co. Down, Northern Ireland
Home: Dalkey, Dublin, Ireland / Bologna, Italy
Marital Status: Unmarried

FORMULA 1 CAREER

1996 Team / Car Number: Ferrari / 2 (GPs: all)
Formula 1 Teams: Jordan (1993 to 95)
Ferrari (1996)

First Entry: J 93 (Suzuka) Jordan-Hart
Races: 48
First Race: J 93 (Suzuka) Jordan-Hart
Most Recent Race: J 96 (Suzuka) Ferrari

World Championships: —
Best World Championship: 10th, 1996 Ferrari

Wins: —

Best placing: 3rd, CDN 95 (Montréal)
Jordan-Peugeot / AUS 96 (Melbourne) Ferrari

3rd: 2
4th: 3
5th: 4
6th: 3

Pole Positions: —

Front Rows: —

Best Grid Position: 3rd, AUS 96 (Melbourne) Ferrari

Fastest Laps: —

Points: 28
First Point: J 93 (Suzuka) Jordan-Hart
Most Recent Point: P 96 (Estoril) Ferrari

Races Led: —

NON-FORMULA 1 CAREER HIGHLIGHTS

Irish Formula Ford 1600	(1983):	(Crosslé)
	(1984):	(Crosslé & Mondiale)
	(1985):	(Mondiale & Quest)
EFDA Formula Ford 1600	(1984):	2nd at Mondello (Mondiale)
Champion of Brands F.Ford 1600	(1984):	1 x 1st, 1 x 2nd (3 races)
F. Ford Festival, Brands Hatch	(1984):	7th (Mondiale)
	(1986):	8th (Van Diemen)
	(1987):	1st (Van Diemen)
British Formula Ford 1600	(1985 & 86):	(Mondiale, Quest & Van Diemen)
RAC British & Esso Formula Ford 1600	(1987):	14 x 1st,1st in both Championships (Van Diemen)
Lucas British Formula 3	(1988):	5 x 2nd, 3 x 3rd, 5th in Championship (Ralt-Alfa Romeo)
Cellnet Super Prix, Brands	(1988):	fastest lap (Ralt-Alfa Romeo)
FIA Formula 3 'Macau GP'	(1988):	1st in Heat 1, pole & fastest lap (Ralt-Alfa Romeo)
	(1990):	3rd (Ralt-Mugen Honda)
FIA Formula 3000	(1989):	3rd at Enna-Pergusa, 9th in Championship (Reynard-Mugen Honda)
	(1990):	1st at Hockenheim, 2nd at Monza, 3rd at Brands & Bugatti, pole at Brands Hatch, 3rd in Championship (Reynard-Mugen Honda)
Euro-Macau-Fuji Formula 3	(1990):	3rd (Ralt-Mugen Honda)
All-Japan Formula 3000	(1991):	1st at Mine, 1 x 4th, 1 x 5th, 7th in Championship (Lola-Mugen Honda)
	(1992):	1st at Mine, 2 x 4th, 1 x 5th, 8th in Championship (Lola-Mugen Honda)
	(1993):	1st at Suzuka, 2 x 2nd, 2 x 3rd, 2nd in Championship (Lola-Mugen Honda)
All-Japan Sports-Prototype	(1992):	5th in Atmo Class (Toyota)
Le Mans 24-hours	(1992):	9th (Toyota)
	(1993):	4th & fastest lap (Toyota)
	(1994):	2nd (Toyota)

Ukyo KATAYAMA

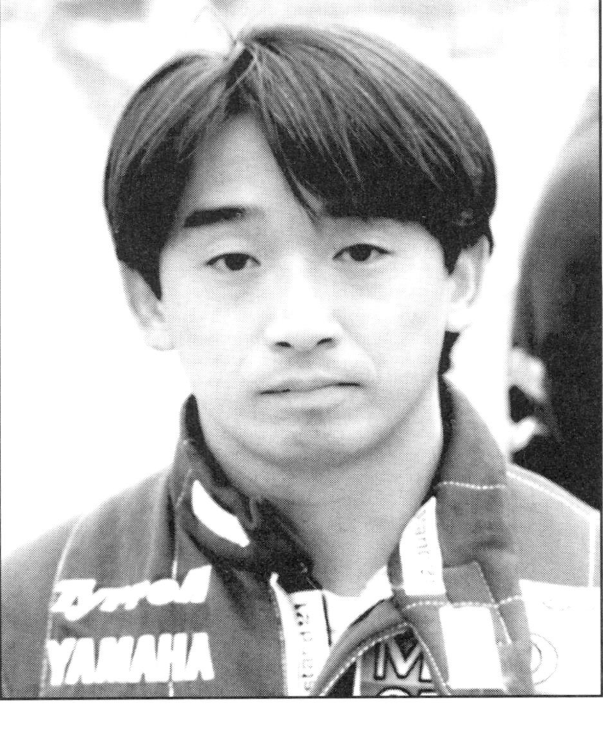

PERSONAL DATA

Nationality:	Japanese
Date of Birth:	29 May 1963
Place of Birth:	Tokyo, Japan
Home:	Monte Carlo, Monaco / Outwood, Surrey
Marital Status:	Married to Rumiko
Children:	Son - Ryui, Daughter - Risa

FORMULA 1 CAREER

1996 Team / Car Number:	Tyrrell / 18 (GPs: all)
Formula 1 Teams:	Venturi Larrousse (1992) Tyrrell (1993 to 96)
First Entry:	ZA 92 (Kyalami) Venturi-Lamborghini
Races:	78
First Race:	ZA 92 (Kyalami) Venturi-Lamborghini
Most Recent Race:	J 96 (Suzuka) Tyrrell-Yamaha
World Championships:	—
Best World Championship:	17th, 1994 Tyrrell-Yamaha
Wins:	—
Best placing:	5th, BR 94 (Interlagos) / RSM 94 (Imola) Tyrrell-Yamaha
5th:	2
6th:	1
Pole Positions:	—
Front Rows:	—
Best Grid Position:	5th, D 94 (Hockenheim) / H 94 (Hungaroring) Tyrrell-Yamaha
Fastest Laps:	—
Points:	5
First Point:	BR 94 (Interlagos) Tyrrell-Yamaha
Most Recent Point:	GB 94 (Silverstone) Tyrrell-Yamaha
Races Led:	—

NON-FORMULA 1 CAREER HIGHLIGHTS

Tsukuba FJ 1600	(1983):	1st & pole in first race, 1st in Class B of Championship
Suzuka FJ 1600	(1984):	2 x 1st, 1st in Class A of Championship
All-Japan Formula 3	(1985):	6th in Championship (Nissan)
Formula Renault Turbo	(1986):	1 x 2nd, 1 x pole
All-Japan Formula 3000	(1988):	10th in Championship (March & Lola-Mugen Honda)
	(1990):	2nd at Fuji, 3rd at Fuji & Suzuka, 2 x 5th, 5th in Championship (Lola-Ford Cosworth)
	(1991):	2 x 1st at Suzuka, 2 x 2nd, 1 x 4th, 1 x 6th, 3 x poles, 1 x fastest lap, 1st in Championship (Lola-Mugen Honda)
FIA Formula 3000	(1989):	18th at Jerez (Mooncraft-Mugen Honda)

*Champion

L

Pedro LAMY

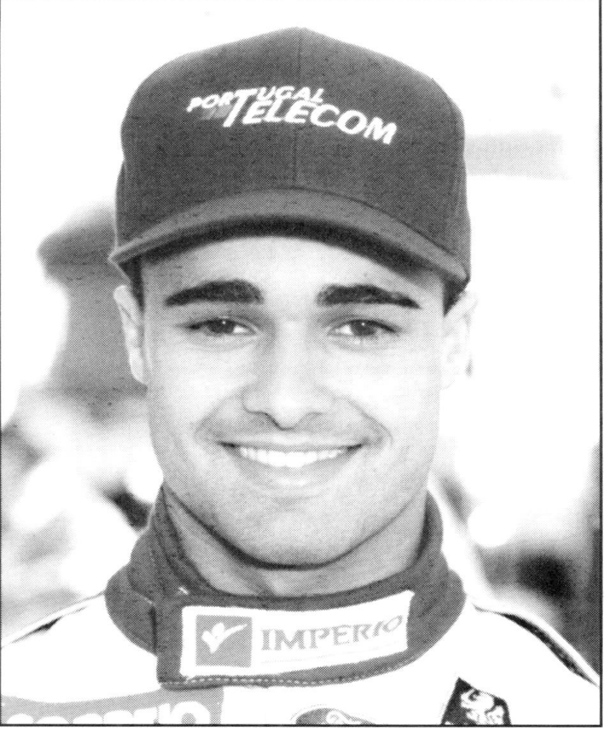

PERSONAL DATA

Nationality:	Portuguese
Date of Birth:	20 March 1972
Place of Birth:	Aldeia Galega, Portugal
Home:	Paiol, Portugal
Marital Status:	Unmarried

FORMULA 1 CAREER

1996 Team / Car Number:	Minardi Scuderia Italia / 20 (GPs: all)
Formula 1 Teams:	Lotus (1993 to 94) Minardi Scuderia Italia (1995 to 96)
First Entry:	I 93 (Monza) Lotus-Ford Cosworth
Races:	32
First Race:	I 93 (Monza) Lotus-Ford Cosworth
Most Recent Race:	J 96 (Suzuka) Minardi-Ford Cosworth
World Championships:	—
Best World Championship:	17th=, 1995 Minardi-Ford Cosworth
Wins:	—
Best placing:	6th, AUS 95 (Adelaide) Minardi-Ford Cosworth
6th:	1
Pole Positions:	—
Front Rows:	—
Best Grid Position:	14th, PAC 95 (Aida) Minardi-Ford Cosworth
Fastest Laps:	—
Points:	1
First Points:	AUS 95 (Adelaide) Minardi-Ford Cosworth
Races Led:	—

NON-FORMULA 1 CAREER HIGHLIGHTS

Portuguese Motocross	(1979):	1st in Championship
Portuguese Formula Ford 1600	(1989):	3 x 1st, 4 x poles, 1st in Championship (6 races)
Formula Vauxhall-Lotus	(1990):	pole at Silverstone
GM Lotus Euroseries	(1990):	3rd at Estoril, 10th in Championship
	(1991):	4 x 1st, 4 x 2nd, 1st in Championship
GM Lotus Nations Cup	(1990):	1st
German Formula 3	(1992):	11 x 1st, 1st in Championship
Marlboro Masters of F3, Zandvoort	(1992):	1st (Reynard-Opel)
FIA Formula 3 'Macau GP'	(1992):	2nd & fastest lap (Reynard-Opel)
Euro-Macau-Fuji Formula 3	(1992):	3rd (Reynard-Opel)
FIA Formula 3000	(1993):	1st at Pau, 2nd at Donington & Hockenheim, 1 x 3rd, pole at Pau & Hockenheim, 2nd in Championship (Reynard-Ford Cosworth)

Giovanni LAVAGGI

PERSONAL DATA

Nationality:	Italian
Date of Birth:	18 February 1958
Place of Birth:	Augusta, Sicily, Italy
Home:	Monte Carlo, Monaco / Syracuse, Italy
Marital Status:	Unmarried

FORMULA 1 CAREER

1996 Team / Car Number:	Minardi / 21 (GPs: D to J)
Formula 1 Teams:	Pacific (1995) Minardi (1996)
First Entry:	D 95 (Hockenheim) Pacific-Ford Cosworth
Races:	7
First Race:	D 95 (Hockenheim) Pacific-Ford Cosworth
Most Recent Race:	P 96 (Estoril) Minardi-Ford Cosworth
World Championships:	—
Best World Championship:	—
Wins:	—
Best placing:	10th, H 96 (Hungaroring) Minardi-Ford Cosworth
Pole Positions:	—
Front Rows:	—
Best Grid Position:	20th, H 96 (Hungaroring) / I 96 (Monza) / P 96 (Estoril) Minardi-Ford Cosworth
Fastest Laps:	—
Points:	—
Races Led:	—

NON-FORMULA 1 CAREER HIGHLIGHTS

Italian Formula 3	(1986)	
World Sports-Prototype	(1988)	
	(1989):	3rd at Nurburgring, 25th in Championship (Porsche)
	(1990)	
FIA Formula 3000	(1991):	12th at Nogaro (Reynard & Ralt-Ford Cosworth)
Le Mans 24-hour race	(1992):	7th (Porsche)
	(1993):	12th (Porsche)
IMSA Camel GT	(1995):	1st at Daytona 24-hours (Porsche Spyder)

Tarso MARQUES

PERSONAL DATA

Nationality: Brazilian
Date of Birth: 19 January 1976
Place of Birth: Curitiba (Paranà), Brazil
Home: Curitiba
Marital Status: Unmarried

FORMULA 1 CAREER

1996 Team / Car Number: Minardi Scuderia Italia / 21 (GPs: BR to RA)
Formula 1 Teams: Minardi Scuderia Italia (1996)

First Entry: BR 96 (Interlagos) Minardi-Ford Cosworth
Races: 2
First Race: BR 96 (Interlagos) Minardi-Ford Cosworth
Most Recent Race: RA 96 (Buenos Aires) Minardi-Ford Cosworth

World Championships: —
Best World Championship: —

Wins: —

Best placing: —

Pole Positions: —

Front Rows: —

Best Grid Position: 14th, RA 96 (Buenos Aires) Minardi-Ford Cosworth

Fastest Laps: —

Points: —

Races Led: —

NON-FORMULA 1 CAREER HIGHLIGHTS

Brazilian Formula Opel	(1992):	1st win in a car
FIA Formula 3000	(1994):	4th at Magny-Cours, 8th at Spa, fastest lap at Spa, 10th at Hockenheim, 2th= in Championship (Reynard-Ford Cosworth)
	(1995):	1st at Estoril, 3rd at Montmeló, 5th at Spa pole at Pau & Estoril fastest lap at Silverstone & Magny-Cours. 5th= in Championship (Reynard-Ford Cosworth)

Andrea MONTERMINI

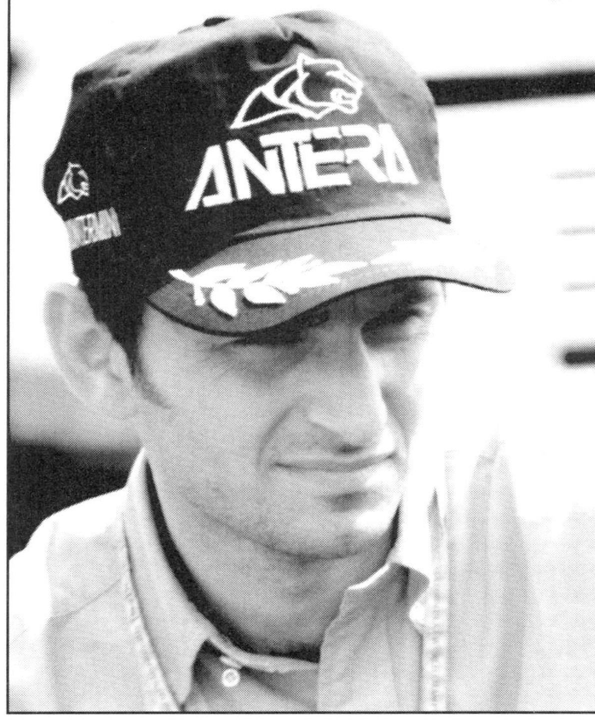

PERSONAL DATA

Nationality:	Italian
Date of Birth:	30 May 1964
Place of Birth:	Sassuolo, Modena, Italy
Home:	Monte Carlo, Monaco
Marital Status:	Unmarried

FORMULA 1 CAREER

1996 Team / Car Number:	Forti / 23 (GPs: AUS to GB)
Formula 1 Teams:	Simtek (1994) Pacific (1995) Forti (1996)
First Entry:	E 94 (Montmeló) Simtek-Ford Cosworth
Races:	21
First Race:	BR 95 (Interlagos) Pacific-Ford Cosworth
Most Recent Race:	F 96 (Magny-Cours) Forti-Ford Cosworth
World Championships:	—
Best World Championship:	—
Wins:	—
Best placing:	8th, D 95 (Hockenheim) Pacific-Ford Cosworth
Pole Positions:	—
Front Rows:	—
Best Grid Position:	19th, J 95 (Suzuka) Pacific-Ford Cosworth
Fastest Laps:	—
Points:	—
Races Led:	—

NON-FORMULA 1 CAREER HIGHLIGHTS

Italian Formula Alfa Boxer	(1987):	First win in a racing car, 3 x 1st, 2 x 2nd, 3rd in Championship
Italian Formula 3	(1989):	1st at Rome, 2 x 2nd, 1 x 3rd, 3 x poles, 4th in Championship (Reynard-Alfa Romeo)
Monaco Formula 3 race	(1989):	2nd & fastest lap (Reynard-Alfa Romeo)
FIA Formula 3000	(1990):	2nd at Bugatti, 3rd at Jerez, pole at Donington, 8th in Championship (Reynard-Mugen Honda)
	(1991):	3rd at Jerez & Bugatti, pole at Hockenheim, 2 x fastest laps, 10th in Championship (Ralt-Ford Cosworth)
	(1992):	1st at Montmeló, Spa & Albacete, 3rd at Enna-Pergusa, pole at Pau, Montmeló & Spa, 2 x fastest laps, 2nd in Championship (Reynard-Judd & -Ford Cosworth)
IndyCar World Series	(1993):	4th at Detroit, 18th= in Championship (Lola-Chevrolet)
	(1994):	7th at Toronto, 9th at Laguna Seca 24th in Championship (Lola-Ford Cosworth)

P

Olivier PANIS

PERSONAL DATA

Nationality:	French
Date of Birth:	2 September 1966
Place of Birth:	Oullins, nr Lyon, France
Home:	Pont de Claix, nr Grenoble, France
Marital Status:	Married to Anne
Children:	son - Aurélien

FORMULA 1 CAREER

1996 Team / Car Number:	Ligier / 9 (GPs: all)
Formula 1 Teams:	Ligier (1994 to 96)
First Entry:	BR 94 (Interlagos) Ligier-Renault
Races:	49
First Race:	BR 94 (Interlagos) Ligier-Renault
Most Recent Race:	J 96 (Suzuka) Ligier-Mugen Honda
World Championships:	—
Best World Championship:	8th, 1995 Ligier-Mugen Honda
Wins:	1
First Win:	MC 96 (Monte Carlo) Ligier-Mugen Honda
2nd:	2
3rd:	—
4th:	2
5th:	3
6th:	4
Pole Positions:	—
Front Rows:	—
Best Grid Position:	6th, I 94 (Monza) Ligier-Renault F 95 (Magny-Cours) Ligier-Mugen Honda
Fastest Laps:	—
Points:	38
First Point:	D 94 (Hockenheim) Ligier-Renault
Most Recent Point:	H 96 (Hungaroring) Ligier-Mugen Honda
Races Led:	1
Laps Led:	16
Distance Led:	53.2 km, 33.1 miles
First Lap Led:	MC 96 (Monte Carlo) Ligier-Mugen Honda

NON-FORMULA 1 CAREER HIGHLIGHTS

Volant Elf au Paul Ricard	(1987):	1st
Formula Renault Turbo	(1988):	4th in Championship
	(1989):	5 x 1st, 9 x top 3, 1st in Championship French Formula 3
	(1990):	2 x 2nd, 2 x 3rd, 4th in Championship (Dallara-Alfa Romeo)
	(1991):	1st at Magny-Cours, Pau, Albi, Croix & Pau-Arnos, 1 x 2nd, 6 x poles, 2nd in Championship (Ralt-Alfa Romeo)
Monaco Formula 3 race	(1990):	7th (Dallara-Alfa Romeo)
FIA Formula 3000	(1992):	2nd at Magny-Cours, 3rd at Silverstone, 10th in Championship (Lola-Ford Cosworth)
	(1993):	1st at Hockenheim, Nürburgring & Spa, 1 x 3rd, pole at Nürburgring & Spa, 1st in Championship (Reynard-Ford Cosworth)

Ricardo ROSSET

PERSONAL DATA

Nationality:	Brazilian
Date of Birth:	27 July 1968
Place of Birth:	Sâo Paulo, Brazil
Home:	Cambridge, England / Sâo Paulo
Marital Status:	Girlfriend - Michelle

FORMULA 1 CAREER

1996 Team / Car Number:	Arrows *Footwork* / 16 (GPs: all)
Formula 1 Teams:	Arrows *Footwork* (1996)
First Entry:	AUS 96 (Melbourne) Footwork-Hart
Races:	16
First Race:	AUS 96 (Melbourne) Footwork-Hart
Most Recent Race:	J 96 (Suzuka) Footwork-Hart
World Championships:	—
Best World Championship:	—
Wins:	—
Best placing:	8th, BR 96 (Interlagos) / P 96 (Estoril) Footwork-Hart
Pole Positions:	—
Front Rows:	—
Best Grid Position:	17th, BR 96 (Interlagos) / P 96 (Estoril) Footwork-Hart
Fastest Laps:	—
Points:	—
Races Led:	—

NON-FORMULA 1 CAREER HIGHLIGHTS

Brazilian F Ford 1600	(1991):	3 x 1st, 2 x poles. 5th in Championship
Brazilian F Ford 2000	(1991):	10th in Championship
Vauxhall Lotus Euroseries	(1992):	15th in Championship
British Formula 3	(1993):	2nd at Silverstone, 3rd at Silverstone & Snetterton, 4 x 6th at Brands Hatch, 6th= in Championship (Ralt & Dallara-Mugen Honda)
	(1994):	1st at Snetterton, 2nd at Silverstone, 3rd at Pembrey, Silverstone & Thruxton, 2 x 4th, 2 x 5th, 3 x 6th, pole at Snetterton, fastest lap at Donington & Snetterton, 5th in Championship (Dallara-Mugen Honda)
FIA Formula 3 'Macau GP'	(1994):	8th (Dallara-Mugen Honda)
FIA Formula 3000	(1995):	1st at Silverstone & Enna-Pergusa, 2nd at Montmeló, 1 x 4th, 1 x 5th, pole at Silverstone, fastest lap at Enna-Pergusa & Hockenheim, 2nd in Championship (Reynard-Ford Cosworth)

Mika SALO

PERSONAL DATA

Nationality:	Finnish
Date of Birth:	30 November 1966
Place of Birth:	Helsinki, Finland
Home:	Chelsea, London, England / Helsinki
Marital Status:	Girlfriend - Noriko

FORMULA 1 CAREER

1996 Team / Car Number:	Tyrrell / 19 (GPs: all)
Formula 1 Teams:	Lotus (1994) Tyrrell (1995 to 96)
First Entry:	J 94 (Suzuka) Lotus-Mugen Honda
Races:	35
First Race:	J 94 (Suzuka) Lotus-Mugen Honda
Most Recent Race:	J 96 (Suzuka) Tyrrell-Yamaha
World Championships:	—
Best World Championship:	13th, 1996 Tyrrell-Yamaha
Wins:	—
Best placing:	5th, I 95 (Monza) / AUS 95 (Adelaide) / BR 96 (Interlagos) / MC 96 (Monte Carlo) Tyrrell-Yamaha
5th:	4
6th:	2
Pole Positions:	—
Front Rows:	—
Best Grid Position:	7th, RA 95 (Buenos Aires) Tyrrell-Yamaha
Fastest Laps:	—
Points:	10
First Points:	I 95 (Monza) Tyrrell-Yamaha
Most Recent Points:	MC 96 (Monte Carlo) Tyrrell-Yamaha
Races Led:	—

NON-FORMULA 1 CAREER HIGHLIGHTS

Finnish & Scandinavian FF1600	(1987):	2nd in each Championship
Finnish, Scandinavian & European FF1600	(1988):	1st in all 14 races, 10 x poles, 1st in each Championship (Van Diemen)
British Formula 3	(1989):	5 x 5th, 1 x 6th, 14th in Championship (Reynard-Alfa Romeo)
	(1990):	6 x 1st, 5 x 2nd, 1 x 3rd, 6 x fastest laps, 2nd in Championship (Ralt-Mugen Honda)
Cellnet Super Prix, Brands	(1989):	5th (Reynard-Alfa Romeo)
FIA Formula 3 'Macau GP'	(1990):	2nd (Ralt-Mugen Honda)
Euro-Macau-Fuji Formula 3	(1990):	8th (Ralt-Mugen Honda)
All-Japan Formula 3000	(1991):	1 x 6th, 22nd= in Championship (Lola & Reynard-Mugen Honda)
	(1992):	4th at Mine, 1 x 5th, 14th= in Championship (Reynard-Mugen Honda)
	(1993):	1 x 6th, 19th= in Championship (Lola-Mugen Honda)

Michael SCHUMACHER

PERSONAL DATA

Nationality:	German
Date of Birth:	3 January 1969
Place of Birth:	Hürth-Hermühlheim, Germany
Home:	Geneva, Switzerland / Kerpen, nr Cologne, Germany
Marital Status:	Married to Corinna

FORMULA 1 CAREER

1996 Team / Car Number:	Ferrari / 1 (GPs: all)
Formula 1 Teams:	Jordan (1991) Benetton (1991 to 95) Ferrari (1996)
First Entry:	B 91 (Spa-Francorchamps) Jordan-Ford Cosworth
Races:	85
First Race:	B 91 (Spa-Francorchamps) Jordan-Ford Cosworth
Most Recent Race:	J 96 (Suzuka) Ferrari
World Championships:	2 - 1994 Benetton-Ford Cosworth / 1995 Benetton-Renault
Wins:	22
First Win:	B 92 (Spa-Francorchamps) Benetton-Ford Cosworth
Most Recent Win:	I 96 (Monza) Ferrari
2nd:	14
3rd:	10
4th:	4
5th:	2
6th:	2
Pole Positions:	14
First Pole Position:	MC 94 (Monte Carlo) Benetton-Ford Cosworth
Most Recent Pole Position:	H 96 (Hungaroring) Ferrari
Front Rows:	29
First Front Row:	E 92 (Montmeló) Benetton-Ford Cosworth
Most Recent Front Row:	H 96 (Hungaroring) Ferrari
Fastest Laps:	25
First Fastest Lap:	B 92 (Spa-Francorchamps) Benetton-Ford Cosworth
Most Recent Fastest Lap:	I 96 (Monza) Ferrari
Points:	362
First Point:	I 91 (Monza) Benetton-Ford Cosworth
Most Recent Point:	J 96 (Suzuka) Ferrari
Races Led:	35
Laps Led:	1,271
Distance Led:	5,831.3 km, 3,623.4 miles
First Lap Led:	B 92 (Spa-Francorchamps) Benetton-Ford Cosworth
Most Recent Lap Led:	I 96 (Monza) Ferrari

NON-FORMULA 1 CAREER HIGHLIGHTS

German Formula König	(1988):	9 x 1st (First win in a racing car at Hockenheim, 24 April), 1 x 2nd, pole & fastest lap at Nürburgring, 1st in Championship (Fiat)
European Formula Ford 1600	(1988):	1st at Zandvoort, 2 x 2nd, pole at Zolder, 2nd in Championship (Van Diemen) (4 races)
German Formula Ford 1600	(1988):	6th in Championship (Van Diemen)
Non-Championship F3	(1989):	1st & 2nd & fastest lap at Hockenheim (Reynard-Volkswagen)
	(1990):	1st at Hockenheim (Reynard-Volkswagen)
German Formula 3	(1989):	1st at Zeltweg & Nürburgring, 5 x 3rd, 2 x poles, 2nd= in Championship (Reynard-Volkswagen)
	(1990):	5 x 1st, 2 x 2nd, 6 x poles, 4 x fastest laps, 1st in Championship (Reynard-Volkswagen)
FIA Formula 3 'Macau GP'	(1989):	1st in heat 1 (Reynard-Volkswagen)
	(1990):	1st (Reynard-Volkswagen)
European F3 Cup, Bugatti	(1990):	1st & fastest lap (*disqualified*), pole (Reynard-Opel)
Euro-Macau-Fuji Formula 3	(1990):	1st (Reynard-Volkswagen)
FIA World Sports-Prototype	(1990):	1st & fastest lap in Mexico City, 2nd at Dijon & Nürburgring.
FIA World Sports Car	(1991):	1st at Autopolis, 2nd at Silverstone, 1 x 5th, fastest lap at Le Mans 24-hours, 9th= in Championship (Mercedes-Benz)
All-Japan Formula 3000	(1991):	2nd at Sugo (in only race), 12th= in Championship (Ralt-Mugen Honda)

Jos VERSTAPPEN

PERSONAL DATA

Nationality: Dutch
Date of Birth: 4 March 1972
Place of Birth: Montfort, Netherlands
Home: Monte Carlo, Monaco / Maaseik, Belgium
Marital Status: Unmarried

FORMULA 1 CAREER

1996 Team / Car Number: Arrows *Footwork* / 17 (GPs: all)
Formula 1 Teams: Benetton (1994)
Simtek (1995)
Arrows *Footwork* (1996)

First Entry: BR 94 (Interlagos) Benetton-Ford Cosworth
Races: 31
First Race: BR 94 (Interlagos) Benetton-Ford Cosworth
Most Recent Race: J 96 (Suzuka) Footwork-Hart

World Championships: —
Best World Championship: 10th, 1994 Benetton-Ford Cosworth

Wins: —

Best placing: 3rd, H 94 (Hungaroring) /
B 94 (Spa-Francorchamps) Benetton-Ford Cosworth

3rd: 2
4th: —
5th: 1
6th: 1

Pole Positions: —

Front Rows: —

Best Grid Position: 6th, B 94 (Spa-Francorchamps) Benetton-Ford Cosworth

Fastest Laps: —

Points: 11
First Point: H 94 (Hungaroring) Benetton-Ford Cosworth
Most Recent Point: RA 96 (Buenos Aires) Footwork-Hart

Races Led: —

NON-FORMULA 1 CAREER HIGHLIGHTS

Benelux & Dutch Opel Lotus	(1992):	8 x 1st, 1st in both Championships (9 races)
Vauxhall-Lotus Euroseries	(1992):	2 x 1st at Zolder, 6th at Magny-Cours & Spa, 7th in Championship
Dutch Driver Of The Year	(1992):	1st
New Zealand Formula Atlantic	(1992/3):	3 x 1st, 4th in Championship (Swift-Toyota)
German Formula 3	(1993):	8 x 1st, 5 x 2nd, 1 x 3rd, 1st in Championship (Dallara-Opel)
Monaco Formula 3 race	(1993):	3rd (Dallara-Opel)
Marlboro Masters of F3, Zandvoort	(1993):	1st & pole (Dallara-Opel)

Jacques VILLENEUVE

PERSONAL DATA

Nationality:	Canadian
Date of Birth:	9 April 1971
Place of Birth:	St-Jean-sur-Richelieu, Chambly, Québec, Canada
Home:	Monte Carlo, Monaco
Marital Status:	Unmarried

FORMULA 1 CAREER

1996 Team / Car Number:	Williams / 6 (GPs: all)
Formula 1 Teams:	Williams (1996)
First Entry:	AUS 96 (Melbourne) Williams-Renault
Races:	16
First Race:	AUS 96 (Melbourne) Williams-Renault
Most Recent Race:	J 96 (Suzuka) Williams-Renault
World Championships:	—
Best World Championship:	2nd, 1996 Williams-Renault
Wins:	—
First Win:	EUR 96 (Nürburgring) Williams-Renault
Most Recent Win:	P 96 (Estoril) Williams-Renault
2nd:	4
3rd:	5
4th:	2
5th:	—
6th:	—
Pole Positions:	3
First Pole Position:	AUS 96 (Melbourne) Williams-Renault
Most Recent Pole Position:	J 96 (Suzuka) Williams-Renault
Front Rows:	9
First Front Row:	AUS 96 (Melbourne) Williams-Renault
Most Recent Front Row:	J 96 (Suzuka) Williams-Renault
Fastest Laps:	6
First Fastest Lap:	AUS 96 (Melbourne) Williams-Renault
Most Recent Fastest Lap:	J 96 (Suzuka) Williams-Renault
Points:	78
First Point:	AUS 96 (Melbourne) Williams-Renault
Most Recent Point:	P 96 (Estoril) Williams-Renault
Races Led:	9
Laps Led:	285
Distance Led:	1,369.8 km, 851.2 miles
First Lap Led:	AUS 96 (Melbourne) Williams-Renault
Most Recent Lap Led:	P 96 (Estoril) Williams-Renault

NON-FORMULA 1 CAREER HIGHLIGHTS

Italian Group N Saloon	(1988):	10th at Enna-Pergusa in first race (Alfa Romeo) (3 races)
Italian Formula 3	(1989):	10th at Enna-Pergusa (Reynard-Alfa Romeo)
	(1990):	1st at Vallelunga (*but penalised 1 minute*), 2nd at Binetto, 5th and fastest lap at Imola, 6th at Enna-Pergusa, 14th in Championship (Reynard-Alfa Romeo)
	(1991):	2nd at Monza, 3rd at Monza and Vallelunga, 4th at Magione & Imola, 3 x poles, 6th in Championship (Reynard & Ralt-Alfa Romeo)
FIA Formula 3 'Macau GP'	(1991):	8th (Ralt-Alfa Romeo)
	(1992):	3rd (TOM's Toyota)
Euro-Macau-Fuji Formula 3	(1991):	8th (Ralt-Alfa Romeo)
Monaco Formula 3 race	(1992):	9th (Dallara-Alfa Romeo)
All-Japan Formula 3	(1992):	1st win in a car at Nishi-Sendai (other wins at Mine & Suzuka), 2 x poles, 2nd in Championship (TOM'S Toyota)
All-Japan Sports-Prototype	(1992):	2nd at Mine (Toyota)
Players Ltd./Toyota Atlantic	(1992):	3rd at Trois-Rivières (Swift)
	(1993):	1st at Road Atlanta, Montréal, Mid Ohio, Laguna Seca (x 2), 7 x poles, 3rd in Championship (Ralt-Toyota), 'Rookie of the Year'
IndyCar World Series	(1994):	1st at Road America, 2nd at Indianapolis, 3rd at Laguna Seca, 4th at Cleveland, 6th in Championship (Reynard-Ford Cosworth), IndyCar & Indy 500 'Rookie Of The Year'
	(1995):	1st at Miami, Indianapolis, Road America & Cleveland, 2nd at Nazareth, 3rd at Toronto & Mid Ohio, 1 x 4th, 1 x 5th, 1 x 6th, 6 x poles, 1st in Championship (Reynard-Ford Cosworth)

ARROWS

ADDRESS:
TWR Arrows
Arrows Grand Prix International Limited
Leafield Technical Centre
Witney
Oxfordshire OX8 5PF
ENGLAND

PHONE: +44 (0)1993-871000
FAX: +44 (0)1993-871100
DRIVERS: 16 - Ricardo ROSSET (Nat: BR) (GPs: all)
17 - Jos VERSTAPPEN (Nat: NL) (GPs: all)

MANAGEMENT:

Chairman & Chief Executive Officer:	Tom WALKINSHAW
Sporting Director:	Jackie OLIVER
Racing Director:	Tony DOWE
Technical Director:	Frank DERNIE
Operations Director:	Roger SILMAN
Chief Enginer:	David BOWEN
Team Manager:	John WATSON
Chief Mechanic:	Ken SIBLEY
Race Engineer (car 16):	Rod NELSON
(car 17):	Allen McDONALD

CHASSIS: Footwork FA17
TYRES: Goodyear
ENGINE: make - Hart Type 830
type - 3 litre, V8
weight - 115 kg

SPONSORS:
Power Horse Energy-Drink
Philips Car Systems (car stereo)
TWR (Tom Walkinshaw Racing)

Bauducco (clothing)
Carin Navigation Systems
Castrol (lubricants)
Goodyear (tyres)
Hype (energy drink)
Lectra Systèmes (composite & textile automated cutting systems)
Lycra Marca Exclusiva Dupont (textile)
Parmalat (foods)
Quest International (fragrances & food additives)
Ricardo (engine design, development & research)
Track & Field Designed For A Better Performace (sports shop)
Vittoria Coffee

Amik Societa' Chimica (chemicals)
Bell South (telecommunications)
CADCentre (computer-aided design)
Cricket & Co (men's clothing)
Enkei (race wheels)
Footwork (parcel delivery, real estate etc)
Glasurit (car paint)
Hewlett Packard (information technology products)
I.B.S. Industria Bulloneria Spectale
Lobo Bolts and Nuts
Packplast (plastics for furniture)
Sally Ferries (car ferries)
Sergio Tacchini (sports clothing & shoes)
Silicon Graphics Computer Systems
Thrifty Location d'autos
Topware (CD ROM production & distribution)

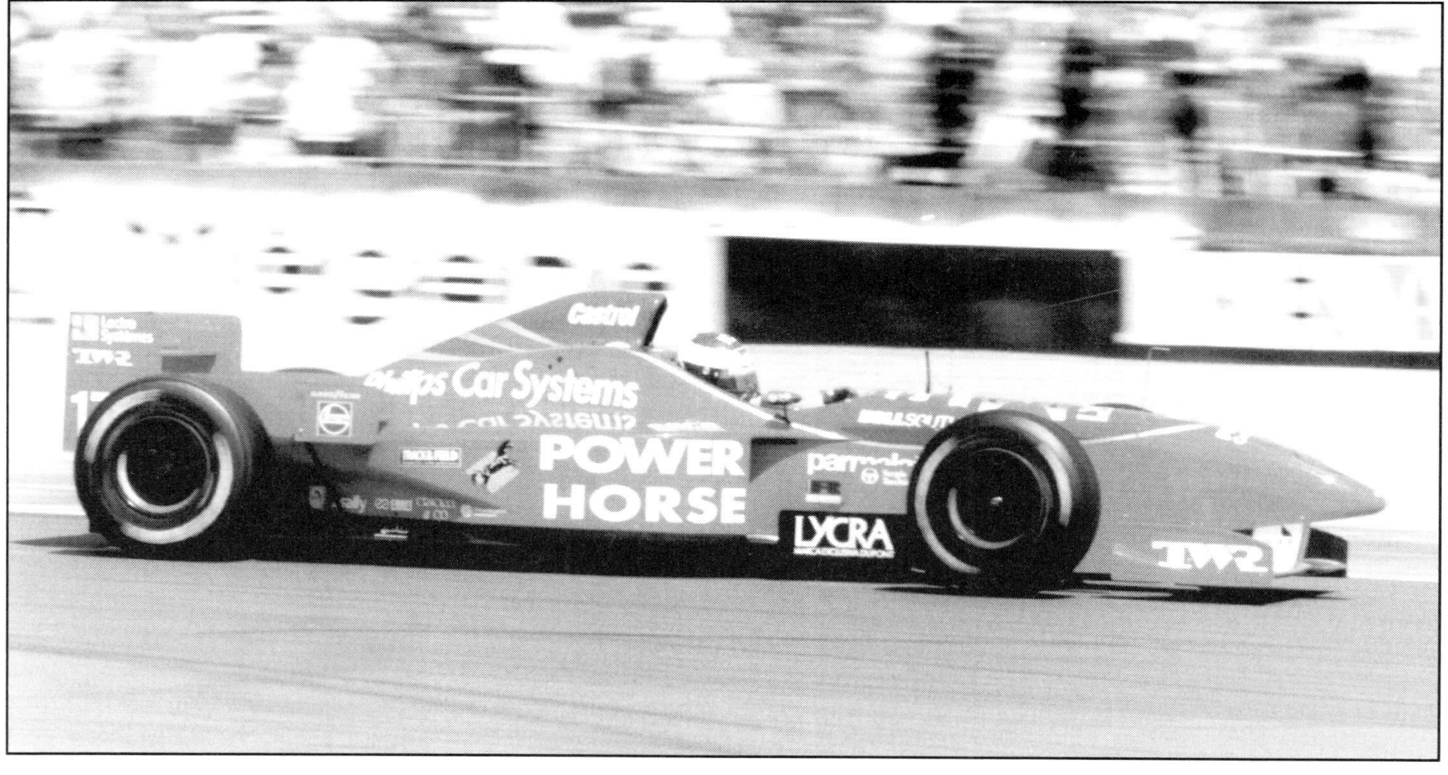

BENETTON

ADDRESS:
Mild Seven Benetton Renault
Benetton Formula Limited
Whiteways Technical Centre
Enstone, Chipping Norton
Oxfordshire OX7 4EE
ENGLAND

PHONE: +44 (0)1608-678000
FAX: +44 (0)1608-678514 (Technical)
+44 (0)1608-678609 (Marketing)
+44 (0)1608-678800 (General)

DRIVERS: 3 - Jean ALESI (Nat: F) (GPs: all)
4 - Gerhard BERGER (Nat: A) (GPs: all)

MANAGEMENT:

President:	Alessandro BENETTON
Managing Director:	Flavio BRIATORE
Technical Director:	Ross BRAWN
Operations Director:	Joan VILLADELPRAT
Financial Director:	Michael BOON
Marketing Director:	John POSTLETHWAITE
Chief Designer:	Rory BYRNE
Design Office Manager:	Graham HEARD
Electronics Engineer:	Tad CZAPSKI
Chief Mechanic:	Mick AINSLEY-COWLISHAW
Production Controller:	John MARDLE
Sub-Assembly Manager:	Dave CAMPBELL
Team Co-ordinator:	Greg FIELD
Special Projects Engineer:	Nick WIRTH
Race Engineer (car 3):	Pat SYMONDS
(car 4):	Christian SILK
Test Engineer:	Malcolm TIERNEY
Press Officers:	Patrizia SPINELLI & Giselle DAVIS

CHASSIS: Benetton B196
TYRES: Goodyear
ENGINE: make - Renault RS08
type - 3 litre, V10
weight - 132 kg

SPONSORS:
Benetton Sportsystem (sports equipment)
Nordica (ski-boots)
Prince (tennis, squash & badminton products)
Rollerblade (in-line skates, skating equipment & accessories)
Mild Seven (Japan Tobacco)
Renault (motor vehicles & engines)
Elf (fuels & lubricants)
Kingfisher Premium Lager Beer

APE (home & car cleaning products)
Cesare Paciotti (footwear)
Fondmetal Group (light alloy wheels & aerodynamic systems)
Hype (energy drink)
Kickers (designer footwear)
Minichamps Model Cars
PI.SA Ceramica (ceramic tiles)
The UB Group (United Breweries-lager beer)

BBS (alloy wheels)
Brembo (disc brake systems)
Compaq (computer hardware)
Goodyear (tyres)
Magneti Marelli (telemetry & data acquisition systems)
Schössmetall/ Schösstec (sliding doors)
Typhoon (scooters)

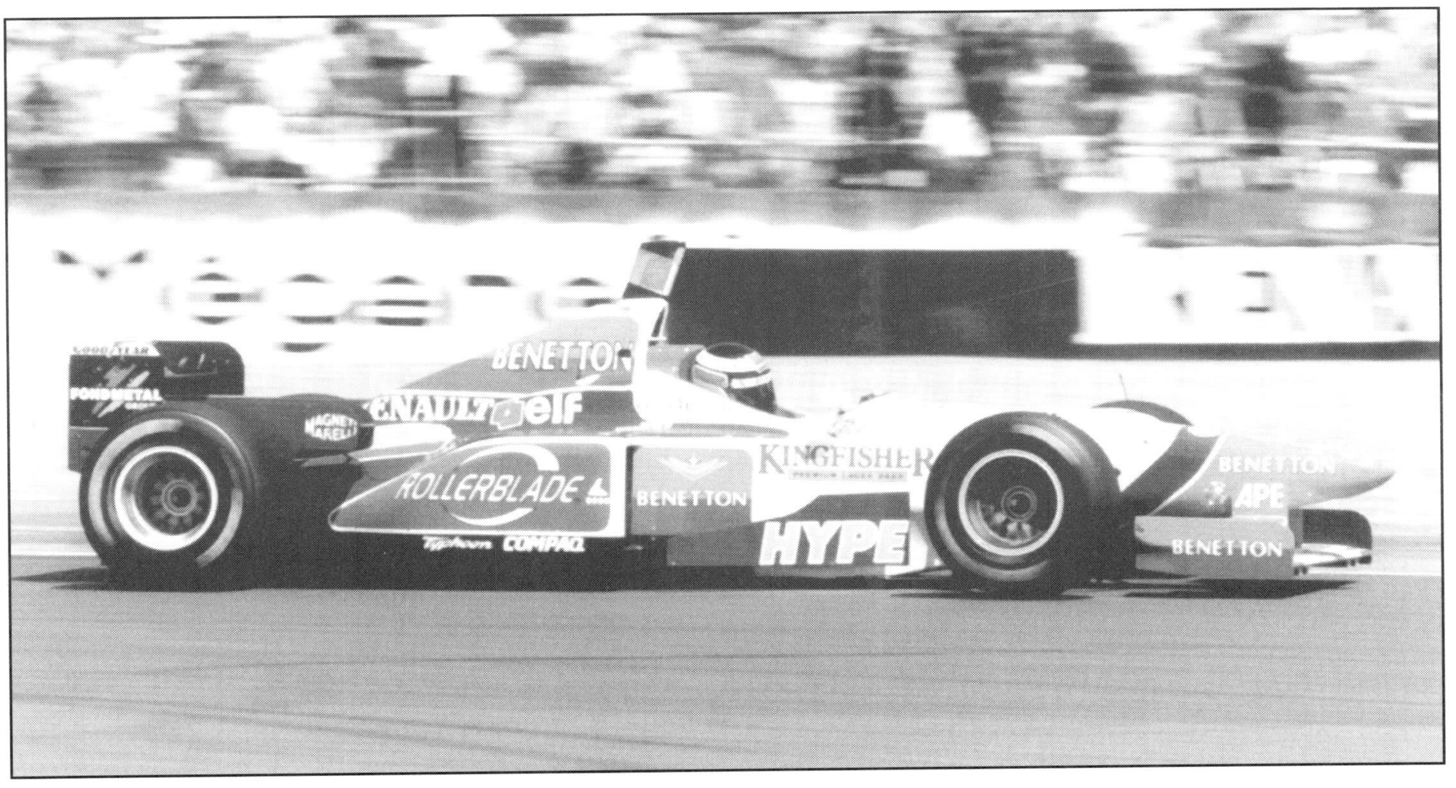

FERRARI

ADDRESS:
Ferrari S.p.A.
Gestione Sportiva
via Ascari, 55 / 57
I-41053 Maranello (Modena)
ITALY

PHONE: +39 (0)536-949111
FAX: +39 (0)536-946488
DRIVERS: 1 - Michael SCHUMACHER (Nat: D) (GPs: all)
2 - Eddie IRVINE (Nat: GB) (GPs: all)

MANAGEMENT:

Ferrari S.p.A. President:	Luca di MONTEZEMOLO
Ferrari Gestione Sporting Director:	Jean TODT
Logistics Engineer:	Claudio BERRO
Planning & Quality Engineer:	Bernard NICLOT
Purchasing Manager:	Rino CAMPANA
Administration Manager:	Fausto CAPPI
Personnel & Organisation & Sponsorship Manager:	Stefano DOMENICALI
Press & PR Manager:	Giancarlo BACCINI
Chief Designer:	John BARNARD
Chassis & Track Engineer:	Giorgio ASCANELLI
Engine Designer:	Paolo MARTINELLI
Electronics Engineer:	Roberto DALLA
Production Engineer:	Mario ALMONDO
Research & Development Engineer:	Gustav BRUNNER
Team Coordinator:	Nigel STEPNEY
Race Engineer (car 1):	Ignazio LUNETTA
(car 2):	Luca BALDISSERR
Chief Mechanic:	Gianni PETTERLINI
Mechanics:	Gianluca SOCIALI & Giuliano TACCONI
Consultant:	Niki LAUDA

CHASSIS: Ferrari F310
TYRES: Goodyear
ENGINE: make - Ferrari 046/1
type - 3 litre, V10
weight - 142 kg

SPONSORS:
Marlboro (Philip Morris tobacco)

Asprey (jewellery, gold, silver & leather goods)
Pioneer (audio & video)
Shell (fuels & lubricants)

Arexons (car care & technical products)
BBS (alloy wheels)
Brembo (disc brake systems)
Fiat (motor vehicles)
General Electric (aeroplane engines)
Goodyear (tyres)
Magneti Marelli (telemetry & data acquisition systems)
SKF (rolling bearings & seals)
Telecom Italia - a STET Company (telecommunications & information technology)

FORTI

ADDRESS:
Forti Grand Prix
Forti Corse F1
via Eiunaudi 33
15100 Alessandria
ITALY

PHONE: +39 131-24-82-20
FAX: +39 131-24-68-91
DRIVERS: 22 - Luca BADOER (Nat: I) (GPs: AUS to GB)
23 - Andrea MONTERMINI (Nat: I) (GPs: AUS to GB)

MANAGEMENT:

Chairmen:	Guido FORTI & Carlo GANCIA
Team Principal:	Guido FORTI
Commercial & Marketing Director:	Guido FORTI
Managing Director:	Daniele CARONNA
Team Manager:	Cesare FIORIO
Technical Director & Race Engineer (car 22):	Bruno PETRINI
(car 23):	Paolo GUERCI
Chief Mechanic:	Loreto SANFRATELLO
PR & Press Officer:	Franco LIISTRO
Car Designer:	Sergio RINLAND
Aerodynamics Engineer:	Hans FOUCHÉ
Team Co-ordinator:	Daniele MORELLI

CHASSIS: Forti FG01-95B/ FG03-96
TYRES: Goodyear
ENGINE: make - Ford Cosworth ED
type - 3 litre, V8
weight - 130kg

SPONSORS:
Hudson
Roces inline skates
Shannon (financial services)
Kaiser (beer)

Antera (alloy wheels)
Aron (hydraulics)
Bettina Sponge
Fin First group
Foster Advertising
GAIERO Prodotti Siderurgici (metal)
ITS Ceramiche (ceramics)
JAS International
Parmalat (foods)
Replay Jeans
Sokol Helicopters
Studio Industrial Automation
TAT Tiles & Trading International

ACI (Italian Automobile Club)
Beta Utensili (handtools)
Blitz
Camozzi (pneumatic systems for factory automation)
Credicard Advantage MasterCard (credit card)
Ford (electronic management systems)
FZA
Goldenflat
Goodyear (tyres)
Hewlett Packard (information technology products)
Jotas
Morse (open systems computer reseller)
Pagnossin (ceramics)
Promodesign
RCM
Rossi Prestige (furniture)
STP (lubricants)

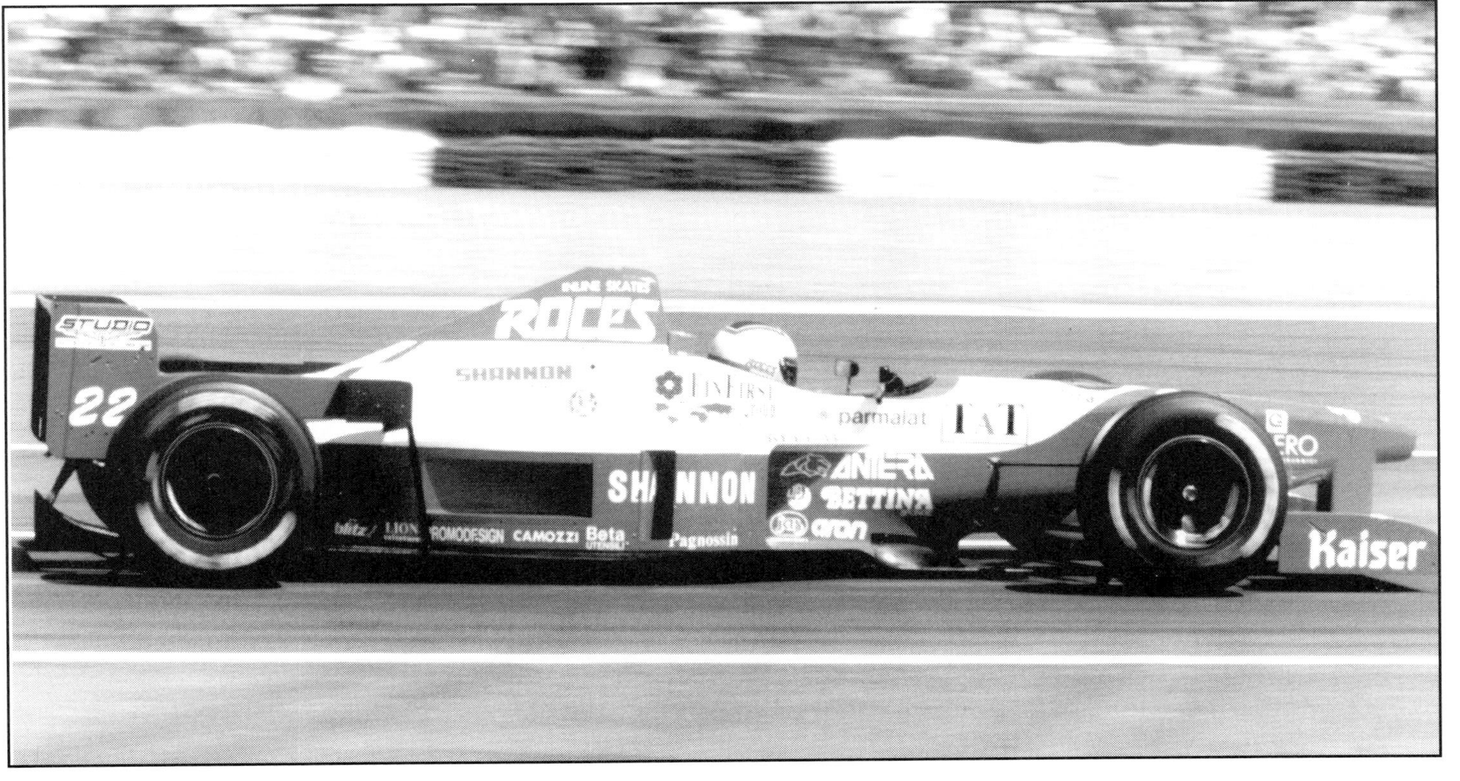

JORDAN

ADDRESS:
Benson & Hedges Total Jordan Peugeot
Jordan Grand Prix Limited
Buckingham Road
Silverstone
Northamptonshire NN12 8TJ
ENGLAND

PHONE: +44 (0)1327-857153
FAX: +44 (0)1327-858120 (office) 858210 (press)
DRIVERS: 11 - Rubens BARRICHELLO (Nat: BR) (GPs: all)
12 - Martin BRUNDLE (Nat: GB) (GPs: all)

MANAGEMENT:

Team Principal:	Eddie JORDAN
Technical Director:	Gary ANDERSON
Commercial Manager:	Ian PHILLIPS
General Manager:	Trevor FOSTER
Team Manager:	vacant
Race Engineer (car 11):	Andrew GREEN
(car 12):	Paul WHITE
Chief Mechanic:	Jim VALE
Sponsorship Managers:	Paul JORDAN & Mark GALLAGHER
Press Officer:	Louise GOODMAN

CHASSIS: Jordan 196
TYRES: Goodyear
ENGINE: make - Peugeot A12 EV5
type - 3 litre, V10
weight - 133 kg

SPONSORS:
Benson & Hedges (tobacco)
Peugeot (motor vehicles & engines)
Total (fuels and lubricants)
Serra mono ceramic (ceramics)
Corona (Mexican beer)
Davene (cosmetics)
Diavia (car air conditioning)
Fox (petroleum)
G de Z Capital (investments)
Globe Communications S.R.L. (telecommunications)
Hewlett Packard (information technology products)
Polimor (plastic furniture components)
Tecnotest/ Visa (garage equipment)
TIE (telecommunications)
Uliveto (mineral water)
Auto Parts International (car parts)
Cellular Line - leader in accessories (telecommunications)
Control Techniques Worldwide (electronic drives & controls)
FBL furniture
FIAMM batteries, horns
Goodyear (tyres)
Hutchinson (graphic design)
IMASAF Marmitte (exhaust systems)
Jolly Motor (motors for shutters & sun-blinds)
Kremlyovskaya Vodka
Lampo zippers
Metagal (mirrors)
Osama Writing Instruments
O.Z. Wheels
Sally Freight (shipping)
Scania (commercial vehicles)
Sports Cafe (London restaurant)
Star Graphics
S.T.M. A.Vidale Group (freight forwarder)
Startek - Electronic Tools by Stark
Unipart (car parts & accessories)

LIGIER

ADDRESS:
Equipe Ligier Gauloises Blondes
Ligier Sports SA
Technopole du Circuit
58470 Magny-Cours
FRANCE

PHONE: +33 (0)86-60-62-00
FAX: +33 (0)86-21-22-97
DRIVERS: 9 - Olivier PANIS (Nat: F) (GPs: all)
10 - Pedro DINIZ (Nat: BR) (GPs: all)

MANAGEMENT:

President:	Flavio BRIATORE
General Manager:	Bruno MICHEL
Technical Director:	André DE CORTANZE
Sporting Director:	Cesare FIORIO
Operations Manager:	Didier PERRIN
Aerodynamics & R & D Engineer:	Loïc BIGOIS
Drawing Office Manager:	Claude DELBET
Test Team Manager:	Jean-Pierre CHATENET
Assistant Team Manager:	Eric VUILLEMIN
Race Engineer (car 9):	Paolo CATONE
(car 10):	Humphrey CORBETT
PR & Press Liaison Manager:	Chris WILLIAMS

CHASSIS: Ligier JS43
TYRES: Goodyear
ENGINE: make - Mugen Honda MF 301HA
type - 3 litre, V10
weight - 134-6 kg

SPONSORS:
Gauloises (tobacco)
Parmalat (foods)

Arisco (condiments & food)
Kickers (designer footwear)
Power Horse Energy-Drink

Amik Societa' Chimica (chemicals)
Brembo (disc brake systems)
BBS (alloy wheels)
Cricket & Co (men's clothing)
EDS Unigraphics (CAD/ CAM software)
Fontana Bullonerie (nuts & bolts)
Giordana (cycling wear)
Goodyear (tyres)
GUAM (cosmetic creme)
Kibon (ice cream)
Mugen Honda (engines)
NGK spark plugs
TWR (Tom Walkinshaw Racing)

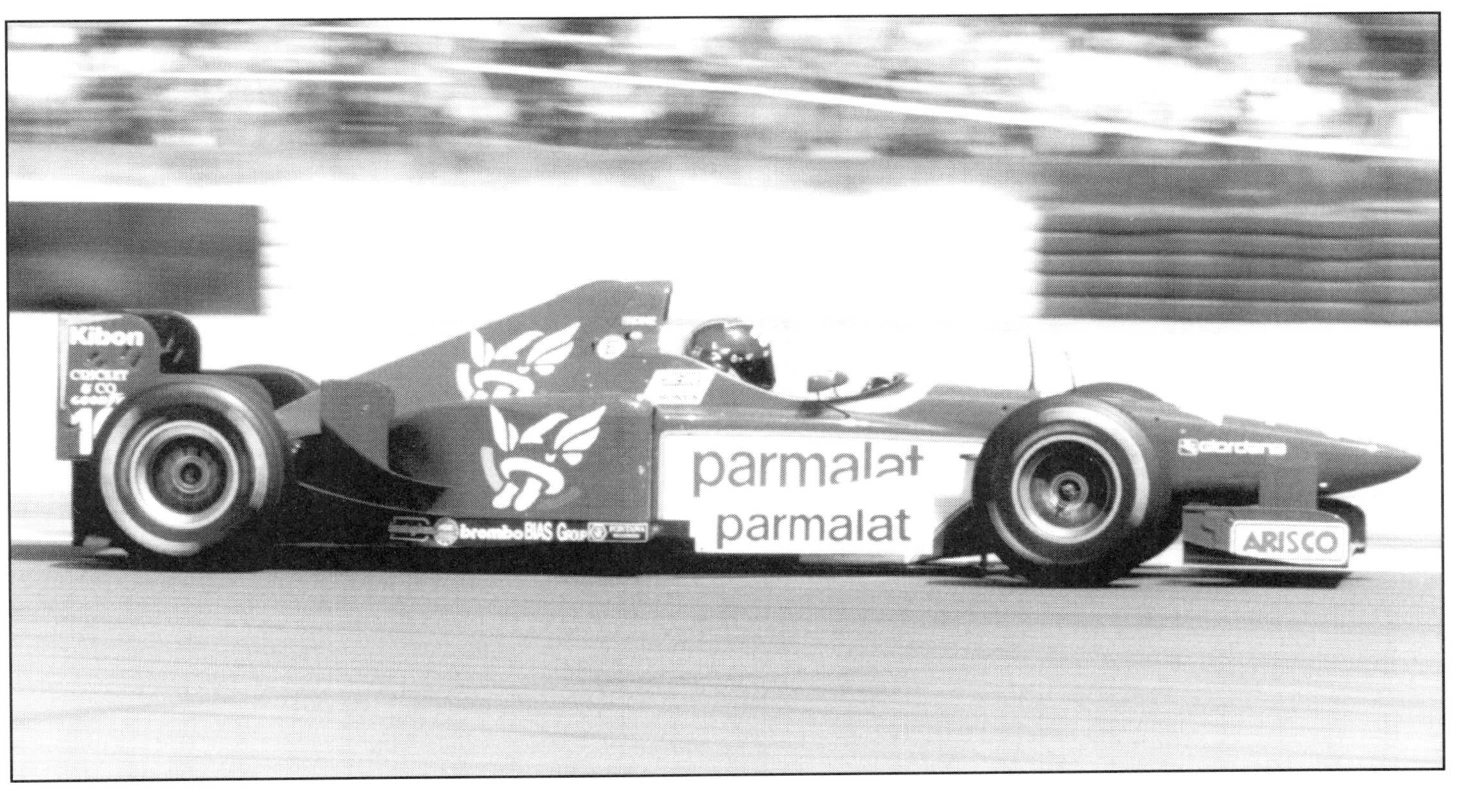

M

McLAREN

ADDRESS:
Marlboro McLaren Mercedes
McLaren International Ltd.
Unit 22, Woking Business Park
Albert Drive, Woking
Surrey GU21 5JY
ENGLAND

PHONE: +44 (0)1483-728211
FAX: +44 (0)1483-720157
DRIVERS: 7 - Mika HÄKKINEN (Nat: SF) (GPs: all)
8 - David COULTHARD (Nat: GB) (GPs: all)

MANAGEMENT:

Managing Director:	Ron DENNIS
Financial Director:	Bob ILLMAN
Commercial & Marketing Director:	Ekrem SAMI
Team Co-ordinator:	Jo RAMIREZ
Team Manager:	Dave RYAN
Special Projects Manager:	Tyler ALEXANDER
Chief Designer:	Neil OATLEY
Head of Aerodynamics:	Henri DURAND
Head of Systems Engineering:	Dieter GUNDEL
Head of Research & Development:	Patrick LOWE
Head of Vehicle Engineering:	Steve NICHOLS
Chassis Project Leader:	Matthew JEFFREYS
Transmisson Project Leader:	David NORTH
Suspension Project Leader:	David NEILSON
Engine Installation Project Leader:	Mark INGHAM
Race Engineer (car 7):	Steve HALLAM
(car 8):	David BROWN
Chief Mechanic:	Michael NEGLINE
Marketing Co-ordinators:	Peter STAYNER & Matthew WINTER
Media Relations:	Jocelyne BIA

CHASSIS: McLaren MP4/11 & MP4/11B
TYRES: Goodyear
ENGINE: make - Mercedes-Benz FO110 phase 3
type - 3 litre, V10
weight - 133 kg

SPONSORS:
Marlboro (Philip Morris tobacco)
Mercedes-Benz (motor vehicles & engines)
Mobil 1 (lubricants)

Camozzi (pneumatic systems for factory automation)
Loctite (adhesives, sealants & specialised chemicals)

Boss Men's Fashion
Cisco Systems (computer networking hardware)
Enkei (race wheels)
Goodyear (tyres)
Sun (Unix workstations & servers)

MINARDI

ADDRESS:
Minardi-Scuderia Italia
Minardi Team S.p.A.
via Spallanzani 21 (z.i.)
I-48018 Faenza (Ravenna)
ITALY

PHONE: +39 (0)546-62-04-80
FAX: +39 (0)546-62-09-98
DRIVERS: 20 - Pedro LAMY (Nat: P) (GPs: all)
21 - Giovanni LAVAGGI (Nat: I)(GPs: D to J)
21 - Giancarlo FISICHELLA (Nat: I) (GPs: AUS, EUR to GB)
21 - Tarso MARQUES (Nat: BR)(GPs: BR to RA)

MANAGEMENT:

President:	Gian Carlo MINARDI
Sports Director:	Frédéric DHAINAUT
Technical Coordinator & Race Engineer (car 20):	Gabriele TREDOZI
(car 21):	Renato MOSCATI
Chief Mechanic:	Gabriele PAGLIARINI
Aerodynamics Engineer:	Mariano ALPERIN
Project Engineer:	Mauro GENNARI
Servo-Control Engineer:	Lorenzo VINCENTI
Manufacturing Director:	Bruno FAGNOCCHI
Telemetry Engineer:	Alessandro IACOPONI
Marketing Manager:	Federico GAETANO
Press Manager:	Roberta LEONARDI
PR & Sponsorship Liaison Officer:	Jane PARISI
PR & Press Liaison Officer:	Renato CAPPUCCI
Contracts Manager:	Rodolfo INTELISANO
Logistics Manager:	Domenico SANGIORGI
Financial Director:	Stefano SANGIORGI

CHASSIS: Minardi M195B
TYRES: Goodyear
ENGINE: make - Ford Cosworth ED2 & ED3
type - 3 litre, V8
weight - 130 kg

SPONSORS:
Doimo Industrie Mobili (house & office furniture)
Bossini (bathroom accessories)
Clearly Canadian (mineral water)
Magnum (watches)
Valleverde (shoes)
Brum's kids and sportswear

Correio da Manha (Portuguese newspaper)
Império (insurance)
Mercatone Uno (hardware supermarkets)
IREM Group (off-shore platforms)

Berco (earth moving machine components)
Beta (handtools)
Brembo (disc brake systems)
Cimatron (CAD-CAM computer software)
Fondmetal (light alloy wheels & aerodynamic systems)
Goodyear (tyres)
Itali Avera La Radio Doc (radio communications)
JVC (electronics)
Magneti Marelli (telemetry & data acquisition systems)
Milpass (accident prevention institute)
Motorquality (dampers & springs)
New Line F1 sportswear by Minardi
RBM (components for hydro-thermal plants)
Setrans Societa' Europea di Trasporti (transporting)
Veglia (watches)

SAUBER

ADDRESS:
Red Bull Sauber Ford
Team Sauber Formel 1
Wildbachstrasse 9
CH-8340 Hinwil
SWITZERLAND

PHONE: +41 (0)1-938-1400
FAX: +41 (0)1-938-1670
DRIVERS: 14 - Johnny HERBERT (Nat: GB) (GPs: all)
15 - Heinz-Harald FRENTZEN (Nat: D) (GPs: all)

MANAGEMENT:

Team Principal:	Peter SAUBER
Team Director:	Max WELTI
Team Manager:	Beat ZEHNDER
Chief Designer:	Leo RESS
Aerodynamics Engineer:	René HILHORST
Composites Engineer:	Ian THOMSON
Race Engineer (car 14):	Gilles ALEGOET
(car 15):	Willy RAMPF
Press Officer:	Gustav BÜSING

CHASSIS: Sauber C15
TYRES: Goodyear
ENGINE: make - Ford Cosworth Zetec-R
type - 3 litre, V10
weight - 130 kg

SPONSORS:
Red Bull energy drink
Petronas Malaysia (fuels & lubricants)

AMIK Societa' Chimica (chemicals)
Bäumler (men's fashion)
Brembo (disc brake systems)
Catamaran Watches
Ford (electronic management systems)
Goodyear (tyres)

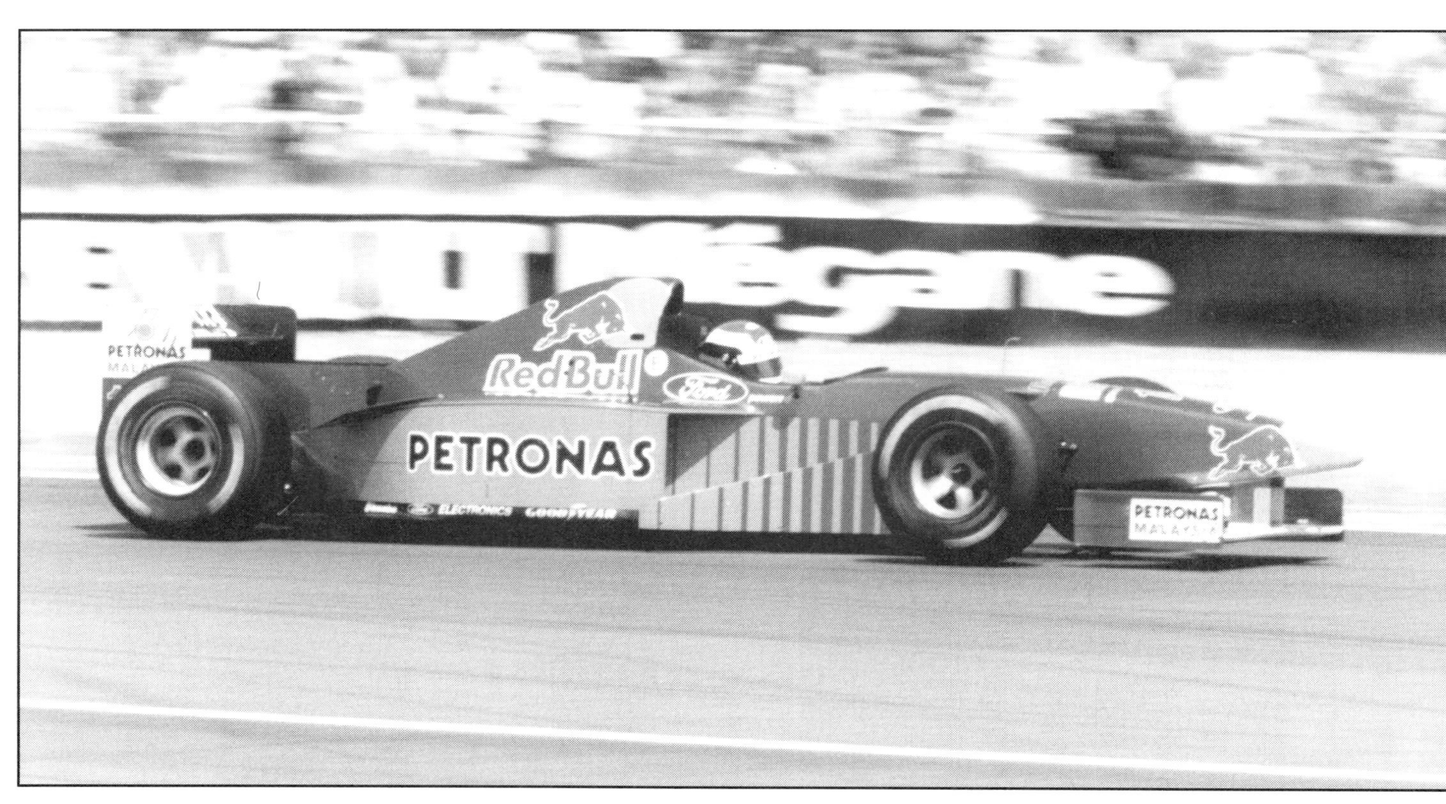

TYRRELL

ADDRESS:
Tyrrell Yamaha
Tyrrell Racing Organisation Ltd.
Long Reach, Ockham
Woking, Surrey GU23 6PE
ENGLAND

PHONE: +44 (0)1483-284955
FAX: +44 (0)1483-284892
DRIVERS: 18 - Ukyo KATAYAMA (Nat: J) (GPs: all)
19 - Mika SALO (Nat: SF) (GPs: all)

MANAGEMENT:

Chairman:	Ken TYRRELL
Managing Director-Commercial:	Bob TYRRELL
Managing Director-Engineering:	Dr Harvey POSTLETHWAITE
Deputy Technical Director:	Mike GASCOYNE
Marketing & Communications Director:	Noel STANBURY
Commercial Director:	Rupert MANWARING
Financial Director:	George KOOPMAN
Team Manager:	Steve NIELSEN
Chief Mechanic:	Nigel STEER
Race Engineers (car 18):	Tim DENSHAM
(car 19):	David BROWN
Press Officer:	Vincent FRANCESCHINI

CHASSIS: Tyrrell 024
TYRES: Goodyear
ENGINE: make - Yamaha OX-11A
type - 3 litre, V10
weight - 125 kg

SPONSORS:
Mild Seven (Japan Tobacco)
Korean Air (international airline)
Yamaha (motorcycles & engines)
Morse (open systems computer reseller)

Apan 777 by Zent (amusement centre)
Catamaran Watches
Cell Star (telecommunications)
Elf (fuels & lubricants)
Fondmetal (light alloy wheels & aerodynamic systems)
Goodyear (tyres)

Auto Express (magazine)
FIAMM (automotive & industrial batteries & horns)
Hoxsin Futures - Bussa (futures commission merchant)
Koni (shock absorbers)
MiTech Europe Ltd (network & cabling)
Motion (ball drive actuators)
Motorola (car stereo)
Parametric Technology Corporation
(software tools for CAD/CAM/CAE)

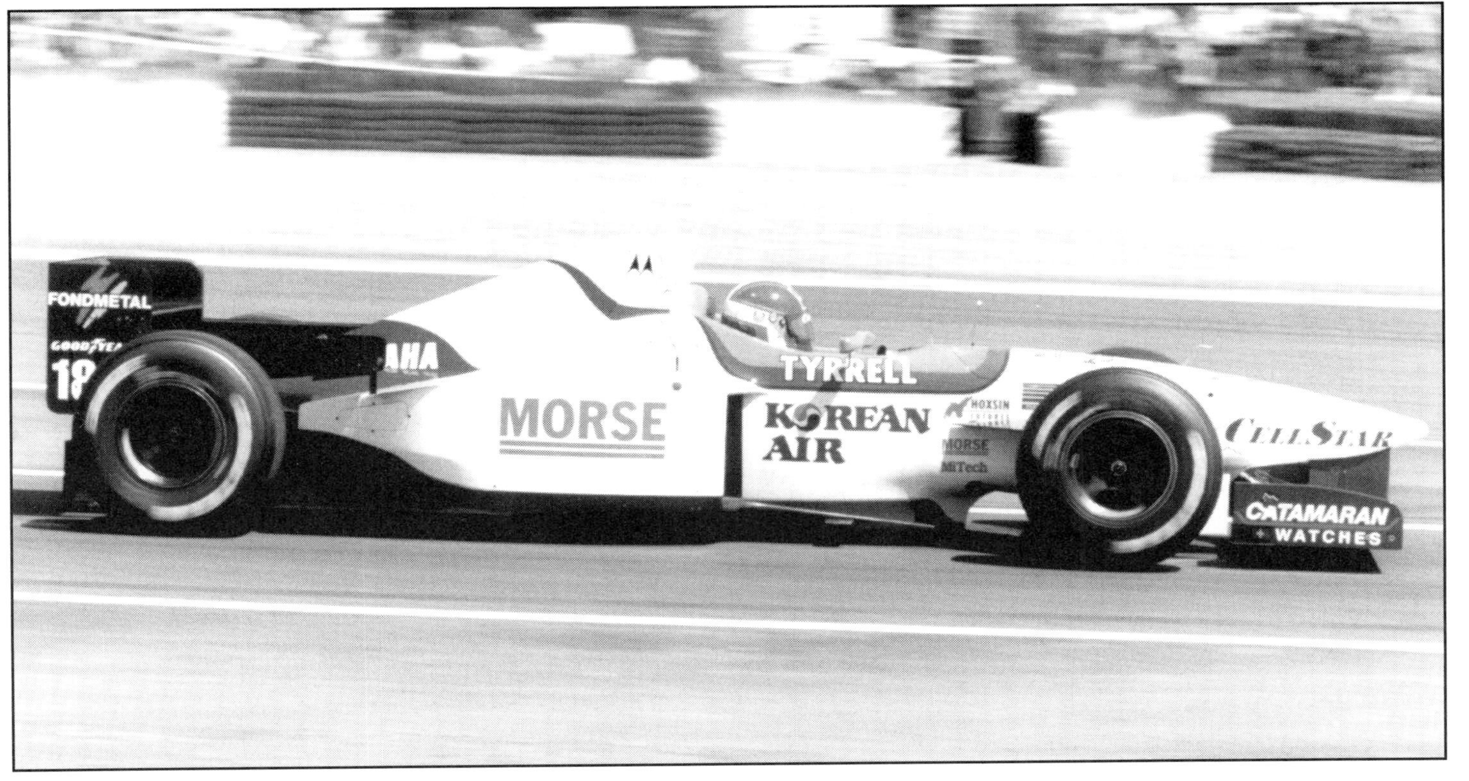

WILLIAMS

ADDRESS:
Rothmans Williams Renault
Williams Grand Prix Engineering Ltd
Station Road
Grove
Wantage
Oxfordshire
OX12 0DQ
ENGLAND

PHONE: +44 (0)1235-777700
FAX: +44 (0)1235-764705 (General)
+44 (0)1235-777739 (Media office)
+44 (0)1235-777733 (Race office)
+44 (0)1235-777731 (Marketing)

DRIVERS: 5 - Damon HILL (Nat: GB) (GPs: all)
6 - Jacques VILLENEUVE (Nat: CDN)(GPs: all)

MANAGEMENT:

Managing Director:	Frank WILLIAMS, CBE
Technical Director:	Patrick HEAD
General Manager:	David WILLIAMS
Senior Acquisitions Manager:	Jim WRIGHT
Account Managers:	Iain CUNNINGHAM
	Victoria KING
	Pierpaolo GARDELA
	David OWEN
	Christian VINE
Chief Designer:	Adrian NEWEY
Race Team Manager:	Dickie STANFORD
Test Team Manager:	Bryan LAMBERT
Senior Operations Engineer:	James ROBINSON
Race Engineer (car 5):	Tim PRESTON
(car 6):	Jock CLEAR
Chief Mechanic:	Carl GADEN
Support Systems Manager:	Alan CHALLIS
Electronics Engineer:	Steve WISE
Prototype Engineer:	Ian ANDERSON
Chief Mechanic (car 5):	Bob DAVIS
(car 6):	Stewart PRATTLEY
(spare):	Colin WATTS
Motorsport Press Officer:	Ann BRADSHAW
Media Manager:	Jane GORARD
Media Assistant:	Lindsay MORLE

CHASSIS: Williams FW18
TYRES: Goodyear
ENGINE: make - Renault RS08 & RS08B
type - 3 litre, V10
weight - 132 kg approx

SPONSORS:
Rothmans (tobacco)
Renault (motor vehicles & engines)
Elf (fuels & lubricants)
Sanyo (consumer electronics)
Black Tower (German white wine)

Mirage Granito Ceramico (ceramics)
Sonax (car polishes)

Goodyear (tyres)
Daniel Hechter menswear
Komatsu (construction equipment & industrial machinery)
Magneti Marelli (telemetry & data acquisition systems)
O.Z. Wheels

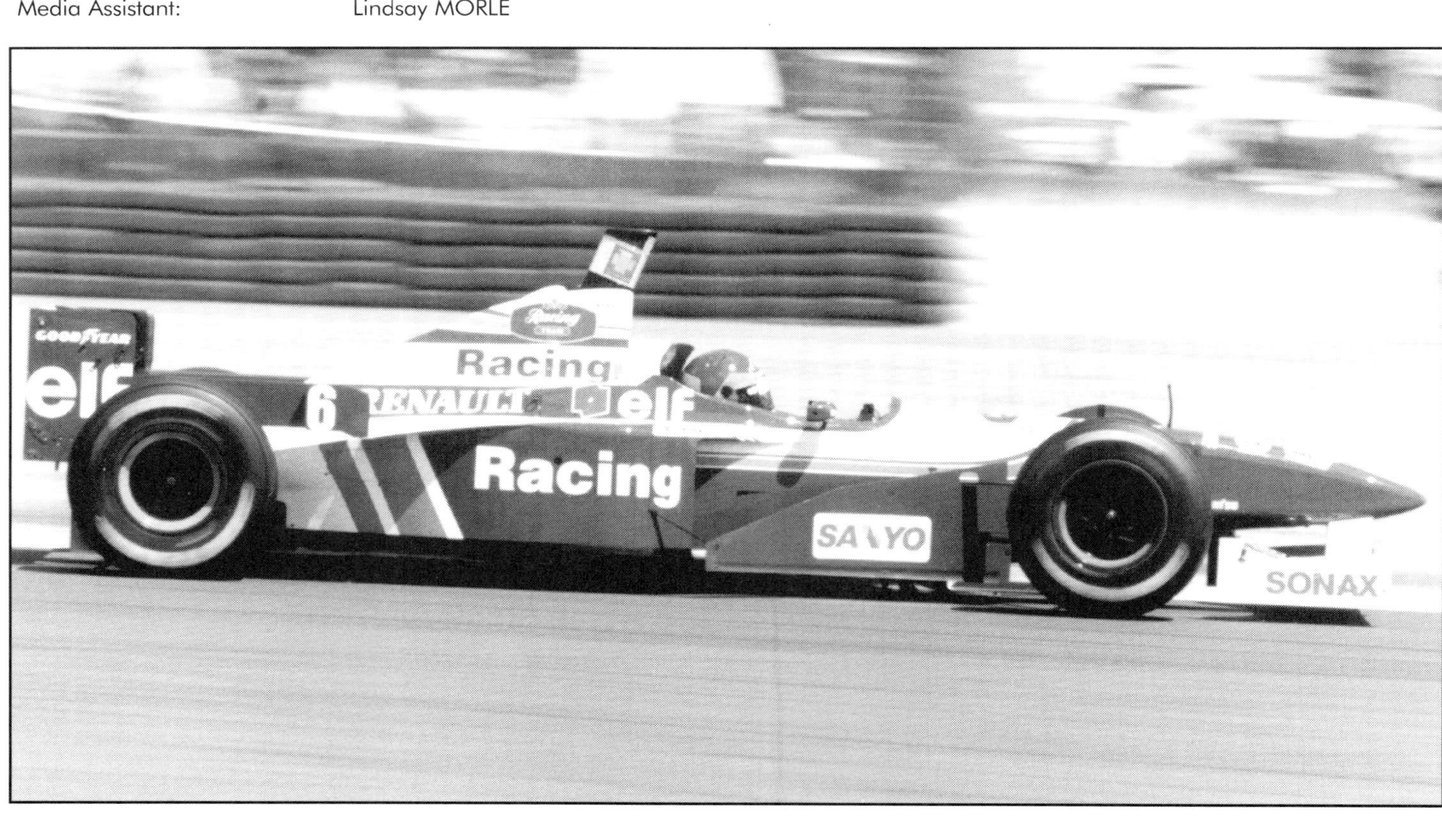

SPONSORS

SPONSOR (PRODUCT) - TEAM

ACI (Italian Automobile Club) - Forti
Amik Societa' Chimica (chemicals) - Arrows, Ligier, Sauber
Antera (alloy wheels) - Forti
Apan 777 by Zent (amusement centre) - Tyrrell
APE (home & car cleaning products) - Benetton
Arexons (car care & technical products) - Ferrari
Arisco (condiments & food) - Ligier
Aron (hydraulics) - Forti
Asprey (jewellery, gold, silver & leather goods) - Ferrari
Auto Express (magazine) - Tyrrell
Auto Parts International (car parts) - Jordan
Bauducco (clothing) - Arrows
Bäumler (men's fashion) - Sauber
BBS (alloy wheels) - Benetton, Ferrari, Ligier
Bell South (telecommunications) - Arrows
Benetton Sportsystem (sports equipment) - Benetton
Benson & Hedges (tobacco) - Jordan
Berco (earth moving machine components) - Minardi
Beta Utensili (handtools) - Forti, Minardi
Bettina Sponge - Forti
Black Tower (German white wine) - Williams
Blitz - Forti
Boss Men's Fashion - McLaren
Bossini (bathroom accessories) - Minardi
Brembo
(disc brake systems) - Benetton, Ferrari, Ligier, Minardi, Sauber
Brum's kids and sportswear - Minardi
CADCentre (computer-aided design) - Arrows
Camozzi (pneumatic systems for factory automation)
- Forti, McLaren
Carin Navigation Systems - Arrows
Castrol (lubricants) - Arrows
Cell Star (telecommunications) - Tyrrell
Catamaran Watches - Sauber, Tyrrell
Cellular Line - leader in accessories
(telecommunications) - Jordan
Cesare Paciotti (footwear) - Benetton
Cimatron (CAD-CAM computer software) - Minardi
Cisco Systems (computer networking hardware) - McLaren
Clearly Canadian (minaeral water) - Minardi
Compaq (computer hardware) - Benetton
Control Techniques Worldwide
(electronic drives & controls) - Jordan
Corona (Mexican beer) - Jordan
Correio da Manha (Portuguese newspaper) - Minardi
Credicard Advantage MasterCard (credit card) - Forti
Cricket & Co (men's clothing) - Arrows, Ligier
Daniel Hechter menswear - Williams
Davene (cosmetics) - Jordan
Diavia (car air conditioning) - Jordan
Doimo Industrie Mobili (house & office furniture) - Minardi
EDS Unigraphics (CAD/ CAM software) - Ligier
Elf (fuels & lubricants) - Benetton, Tyrrell, Williams
Enkei (race wheels) - Arrows, McLaren
FBL furniture - Jordan
FIAMM batteries, horns - Jordan, Tyrrell
Fiat (motor vehicles) - Ferrari
Fin First group - Forti
Fondmetal (light alloy wheels & aerodynamic systems)
- Benetton, Minardi, Tyrrell
Fontana Bullonerie (nuts & bolts) - Ligier
Footwork (parcel delivery, real estate etc)) - Arrows
Ford (electronic management systems) - Forti, Sauber
Foster Advertising - Forti
Fox (petroleum) - Jordan
FZA - Forti
G de Z Capital (investments) - Jordan
GAIERO Prodotti Siderurgici (metal) - Forti
Gauloises (tobacco) - Ligier
General Electric (aeroplane engines) - Ferrari
Giordana (cycling wear) - Ligier
Glasurit (car paint) - Arrows
Globe Communications S.R.L. (telecommunications) - Jordan
Goldenflat - Forti
Goodyear (tyres) - all teams
GUAM (cosmetic creme) - Ligier
Hewlett Packard
(computer equipment) - Arrows, Forti, Jordan
Hoxsin Futures - Bussan (futures commission merchant) - Tyrrell
Hudson - Forti
Hutchinson (graphic design) - Jordan
Hype (energy drink) - Arrows, Benetton
I.B.S. Industria Bulloneria Spectale - Arrows
IMASAF Marmitte (exhaust systems) - Jordan
Império (insurance) - Minardi
IREM Group (off-shore platforms) - Minardi
Itali Avera La Radio Doc (radio communications) - Minardi
ITS Ceramiche (ceramics) - Forti
JAS International - Forti
Jolly Motor (motors for shutters & sun-blinds) - Jordan
Jotas - Forti
JVC (electronics) - Minardi
Kaiser (beer) - Forti
Kibon (ice cream) - Ligier
Kickers (designer footwear) - Benetton, Ligier
Kingfisher Premium Lager Beer - Benetton
Komatsu (construction equipment & industrial machinery)
- Williams
Koni (shock absorbers) - Tyrrell
Korean Air (international airline) - Tyrrell
Kremlyovskaya Vodka - Jordan
Lampo zippers - Jordan
Lectra Systèmes (composite & textile automated cutting systems)
- Arrows
Lobo Bolts and Nuts - Arrows
Loctite (adhesives, sealants & specialised chemicals) - McLaren
Lycra Marca Exclusiva Dupont (textile) - Arrows
Magneti Marelli (telemetry & data acquisition systems)
- Benetton, Ferrari, Minardi, Williams
Magnum (watches) - Minardi
Marlboro (Philip Morris tobacco) - Ferrari, McLaren
Mercatone Uno (hardware supermarkets) - Minardi
Mercedes-Benz (motor vehicles & engines) - McLaren
Metagal (mirrors) - Jordan
Mild Seven (Japan Tobacco) - Benetton, Tyrrell
Milpass (accident prevention institute) - Minardi
Minichamps Model Cars - Benetton
Mirage Granito Ceramico (ceramics) - Williams
MiTech Europe Ltd (network & cabling) - Tyrrell
Mobil 1 (lubricants) - McLaren
Morse (open systems computer reseller) - Forti, Tyrrell
Motion (ball drive actuators) - Tyrrell
Motorola (car stereo) - Tyrrell
Motorquality (dampers & springs) - Minardi
Mugen Honda (engines) - Ligier
New Line F1 sportswear by Minardi - Minardi
NGK spark plugs - Ligier
Nordica (ski boots) - Benetton
O.Z. Wheels - Jordan, Williams
Osama Writing Instruments - Jordan
Packplast (plastics for furniture) - Arrows
Pagnossin (ceramics) - Forti
Parametric Technology Corporation
(software tools for CAD/CAM/CAE) - Tyrrell
Parmalat (foods) - Arrows, Forti, Ligier
Petronas Malaysia (fuels & lubricants) - Sauber
Peugeot (motor vehicles & engines) - Jordan
Philips Car Systems (car stereo) - Arrows
PI.SA Ceramica (ceramic tiles) - Benetton
Pioneer (audio & video) - Ferrari
Polimor (plastic furniture components) - Jordan
Power Horse Energy-Drink - Arrows, Ligier
Prince (tennis, squash & badminton products) - Benetton
Promodesign - Forti

Quest International
(fragrances & food additives) - Arrows
RBM (components for hydro-thermal plants) - Minardi
RCM - Forti
Red Bull energy drink - Sauber
Renault (motor vehicles & engines) - Benetton, Williams
Replay Jeans - Forti
Ricardo (engine design, development & research) - Arrows
Roces inline skates - Forti
Rollerblade
(in-line skates, skating equipment & accessories) - Benetton
Rossi Prestige (furniture) - Forti
Rothmans (tobacco) - Williams
S.T.M. A.Vidale Group (freight forwarder) - Jordan
Sally Ferries (car ferries) - Arrows
Sally Freight (shipping) - Jordan
Sanyo (consumer electronics) - Williams
Scania (commercial vehicles) - Jordan
Schössmetall/ Schösstec (sliding doors) - Benetton
Sergio Tacchini (sports clothing & shoes) - Arrows
Serra mono ceramic (ceramics) - Jordan
Setrans Societa' Europea di Trasporti (transporting) - Minardi
Shannon (financial services) - Forti
Shell (fuels & lubricants) - Ferrari
Silicon Graphics Computer Systems - Arrows
SKF (rolling bearings & seals) - Ferrari
Sokol Helicopters - Forti
Sonax (car polishes) - Williams
Sports Cafe (London restaurant) - Jordan
Star Graphics - Jordan
Startek - Electronic Tools by Stark - Jordan
STP (lubricants) - Forti
Studio Industrial Automation - Forti
Sun (Unix workstations & servers)
TAT Tiles & Trading International - Forti
Tecnotest/ Visa (garage equipment) - Jordan
Telecom Italia - a STET Company
(telecommunications & information technology) - Ferrari
The UB Group (United Breweries-lager beer) - Benetton
Thrifty Location d'autos - Arrows
TIE (telecommunications) - Jordan
Topware (CD ROM production & distribution) - Arrows
Total (fuels and lubricants) - Jordan
Track & Field Designed For A Better Performance
(sports shop) - Arrows
TWR (Tom Walkinshaw Racing) - Arrows, Ligier
Typhoon (scooters) - Benetton
Uliveto (mineral water) - Jordan
Unipart (car parts & accessories) - Jordan
Valleverde (shoes) - Minardi
Veglia (watches) - Minardi
Vittoria Coffee - Arrows
Yamaha (motorcycles & engines) - Tyrrell

Damon Hill, 1996 Formula 1 World Champion.

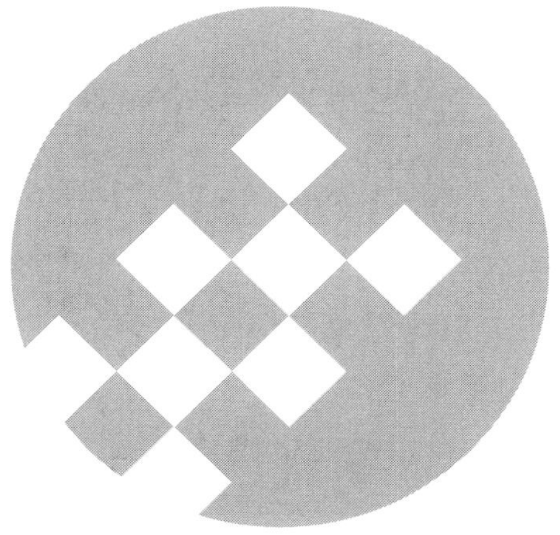

RACES 1950-96

RACE ENTRANTS AND RESULTS

LAP LEADERS

DRIVER POINTS

CONSTRUCTOR POINTS
( ) - points scored but not counted towards final Championship total

SEASON SUMMARY

Grands Prix

KEY TO ABBREVIATIONS & SYMBOLS

=	shared
dq	disqualified
ew	entry withdrawn
exc	excluded
f	fastest lap
nc	not classified
npq	non pre-qualified
nq	non qualified
ns	non started
r	retired
+	driver died during the year
-1 laps	retired on parade lap (officially a starter)

KEY TO ENGINE CONFIGURATIONS

4, 6, 8	straight/in-line
F4, F8, F12	'Flat' or 'Boxer'
H16	Double 'Flat'
V2, V6, V8, V10, V12, V16	'V' formation
W12	'W' formation
s	supercharged
t	turbocharged
tbn	turbine

number denotes how many cylinders

PARADE LAPS

All drivers who set off from the dummy grid on the parade lap are regarded as starters, even if they retired on that non-racing lap. Examples would be M Schumacher in France, 1996, and A Prost in San Marino, 1991 (these are all designated in the laps completed column as -'1').

Drivers who do not leave the dummy grid under their own power are regarded as non-starters, as would be expected. Examples would be M Donnelly in USA 1990 and L Badoer in Australia, 1995.

Full listings of these instances are given in the Records & Trivia chapter.

RETIREMENTS

In the early years of the World Championship, classifications were somewhat haphazard. Drivers who retired were generally not classified unless they pushed their car over the line after the winner took the flag. For instance G Hill in Belgium, 1960 completed enough laps to be classified 3rd, but retired in the pits as opposed to pushing the car over the line. Conversely, H Schell was classified 7th in Germany, 1959, despite his car failing 11 laps from the end of the 60 lap race.

This anomaly has now been cleared up with the advent of the rule requiring cars to complete 90% of the race distance to be classified.

SHARED DRIVES

It was common practice in the 50s for drivers to share a car, either by taking over from a team-mate or by swapping cars. In most cases points were shared.

RESTARTED RACES

Races that have been restarted within the first two laps are regarded as a new race under current legislation, but this leads to confusion concerning drivers who then didn't take the restart.

To this end these drivers are regarded as race starters who have retired. It would be wrong to claim N Lauda in Germany 76 and J Laffite in Britain 86 were non-starters when considering their severe injuries at the start of these races.

FORMULA 2

Formula 2 cars have often been raced in World Championship Grands Prix. In 1952 and 1953 the formula only permitted Formula 2 cars due to the lack of quality Formula 1 entrants. On occasion, F2 cars were included on equal terms with F1 entrants to simply make up the numbers, as in Italy 1960. However, in six races (D57, 58, 66, 67 & 69 and MA 58). Formula 2 cars raced simultaneously for separate honours and although not eligible for points were regarded as starters.

INDIANAPOLIS

From 1950 until 1960, the Indy 500 featured as part of the World Championship. Very few drivers crossed from one discipline to the other, which was the original intention. Although points were awarded in a similar manner, the final point was awarded for fastest 'leading' lap.

These were not regarded as Grands Prix, the first United States Grand Prix in the championship being held at Sebring in 1959.

The Fédération Internationale de l'Automobile decided to create a new World Championship for drivers, similar to the European championships of the 1930s and the motorcycle championship of 1949. Motor Racing was getting back to normal after the turmoil of war and the new formula was made up of the cars that were available. This meant the basic pre-war designs of 1.5 litre supercharged or blown engines (voiturette cars) and the 4.5 litre unblown cars, formed a parallel and equivalent formula. Alfa Romeo had resumed racing after a year off and were firm favourites.

ALFA ROMEO
SA Alfa Romeo: Farina, Fangio, Fagioli, Parnell, Sanesi, Taruffi

FERRARI
Scuderia Ferrari: Ascari, Villoresi, Sommer, Serafini
Privateers: Whitehead, Biondetti

MASERATI
Officine Alfieri Maserati: Chiron, Rol
Scuderia Ambrosiana: Murray, Hampshire, Parnell
Enrico Platé: de Graffenried, Bira
Scuderia Achille Varzi: Gonzàlez, (Piàn), Pagani, Branca
Scuderia Milano: Bonetto, Comotti
Privateers: Fry, Shawe-Taylor, Branca, Pietsch

TALBOT LAGO
Automobiles Talbot-Darracq SA: Giraud-Cabantous, Martin, Rosier (CH,B,F), Êtançelin (B), Sommer (F)
Ecurie Rosier: Rosier, Louveau
Ecurie Belge: Claes
Ecurie Bleue: Schell
Ecurie Lutetia: Chaboud
Privateers: Êtançelin, Sommer, Levegh, Pozzi, Mairesse

SIMCA GORDINI
Equipe Gordini: Manzon, Trintignant

ERA
ERA Ltd: Johnson
Privateers: Harrison, Gerard, Walker, Rolt

ALTA
Privateers: Kelly, Crossley

COOPER
Horschell Racing Corp: Schell

(Drivers whose names are in brackets, were non-starters. Race codes are shown, where a driver was with more than one entrant of the same constructor during the season).

13 May 1950 — BRITAIN: Silverstone (Round: 1) (Race: 1)

70 laps x 4.649 km, 2.889 miles = 325.458 km, 202.230 miles

POS.	NO	DRIVER	CAR	MODEL	ENGINE		LAPS	TIME/REASON FOR RETIREMENT	GRID:POS	ROW
1	2	G Farina	Alfa Romeo	158	Alfa Romeo	8s	70	2h 13m 23.600s	1	1
2	3	L Fagioli	Alfa Romeo	158	Alfa Romeo	8s	70	2h 13m 26.200s	2	1
3	4	R Parnell	Alfa Romeo	158	Alfa Romeo	8s	70	2h 14m 15.600s	4	1
4	14	Y Giraud-Cabantous	Talbot Lago	T26C-DA	Talbot	6	68		6	2
5	15	L Rosier	Talbot Lago	T26C	Talbot	6	68		9	3
6	12	B Gerard	ERA	B/C	ERA	6s	67		13	4
7	11	C Harrison	ERA	B	ERA	6s	67		15	5
8	16	P Êtançelin	Talbot Lago	T26C	Talbot	6	65		14	4
9	6	D Hampshire	Maserati	4CLT/48	Maserati	4s	64		16	5
10=	10	J Fry	Maserati	4CL	Maserati	4s			20	6
10=	10	B Shawe-Taylor	Maserati	4CL	Maserati	4s	64			
11	18	J Claes	Talbot Lago	T26C	Talbot	6	64		21	6
r	1	J M Fangio	Alfa Romeo	158	Alfa Romeo	8s	62	oil line/ connecting rod	3	1
nc	23	J Kelly	Alta	GP	Alta	4s	57		19	6
r	21	B Bira	Maserati	4CLT/48	Maserati	4s	49	fuel injection	5	2
r	5	D Murray	Maserati	4CLT/48	Maserati	4s	44	engine	18	5
r	24	G Crossley	Alta	GP	Alta	4s	43	transmission	17	5
r	20	E de Graffenried	Maserati	4CLT/48	Maserati	4s	36	connecting rod	8	3
r	19	L Chiron	Maserati	4CLT/48	Maserati	4s	24	clutch	11	3
r	17	E Martin	Talbot Lago	T26C-DA	Talbot	6	8	oil pressure	7	2
r=	9	P Walker	ERA	E	ERA	6s			10	3
r=	9	T Rolt	ERA	E	ERA	6s	5	gearbox		
r	8	L Johnson	ERA	E	ERA	6s	2	supercharger	12	4

Winning Speed: 146.390 km/h, 90.963 mph
Pole Position speed: 151.063 km/h, 93.866 mph (G Farina, 1 min:50.800 sec)
Fastest Lap speed: 151.337 km/h, 94.036 mph (G Farina, 1 min:50.600 sec on lap 2)
Lap Leaders: G Farina 1-9, 6-37, 9-70 (63); L Fagioli 10-14, 8 (6); J M Fangio 15 (1).

Also the Grand Prix of Europe.

21 May 1950 — MONACO: Monte Carlo (Round: 2) (Race: 2)

100 laps x 3.180 km, 1.76 miles = 318.000 km, 197.596 miles

POS.	NO	DRIVER	CAR	MODEL	ENGINE		LAPS	TIME/REASON FOR RETIREMENT	GRID:POS	ROW
1	34	J M Fangio	Alfa Romeo	158	Alfa Romeo	8s	100	3h 13m 18.700s	1	1
2	40	A Ascari	Ferrari	125	Ferrari	V12s	99		7	3
3	48	L Chiron	Maserati	4CLT/48	Maserati	4s	98		8	3
4	42	R Sommer	Ferrari	125	Ferrari	V12s	97		9	4
5	50	B Bira	Maserati	4CLT/48	Maserati	4s	95		15	6
6	26	B Gerard	ERA	A	ERA	6s	94		16	7
7	6	J Claes	Talbot Lago	T26C	Talbot	6	94		19	8
r	38	L Villoresi	Ferrari	125	Ferrari	V12s	63	rear axle	6	3
r	14	P Étançelin	Talbot Lago	T26C	Talbot	6	36	oil line	4	2
r	2	F González	Maserati	4CLT/48	Maserati	4s	1	accident/ fire	3	1
r	36	L Fagioli	Alfa Romeo	158	Alfa Romeo	8s	0	accident	5	2
r	32	G Farina	Alfa Romeo	158	Alfa Romeo	8s	0	accident	2	1
r	16	L Rosier	Talbot Lago	T26C	Talbot	6	0	accident	10	4
r	10	R Manzon	Simca Gordini	T15	Gordini	4s	0	accident	11	5
r	8	H Schell	Cooper	T12	JAP	V2	0	accident	20	8
r	52	E de Graffenried	Maserati	4CLT/48	Maserati	4s	0	accident	12	5
r	12	M Trintignant	Simca Gordini	T15	Gordini	4s	0	accident	13	5
r	24	C Harrison	ERA	B	ERA	6s	0	accident	14	6
r	44	F Rol	Maserati	4CLT/48	Maserati	4s	0	accident	17	7
ns	4	A Piàn	Maserati	4CLT/48	Maserati	4s		accident	18	7
ns	28	P Whitehead	Ferrari	125	Ferrari	V12s		engine		

Winning speed: 98.701 km/h, 61.330 mph
Pole Position speed: 103.884 km/h, 64.550 mph (J M Fangio, 1 min:50.200 sec)
Fastest Lap speed: 103.135 km/h, 64.085 mph (J M Fangio, 1 min:51.000 sec)
Lap Leaders: J M Fangio 1-100 (100).

First two rows of the grid determined by first day's practice.

30 May 1950 — INDIANAPOLIS: 500 (Round: 3) (Race: 3)

138 laps x 4.023 km, 2.500 miles = 555.224 km, 345.000 miles

POS.	NO	DRIVER	CAR	MODEL	ENGINE		LAPS	TIME/REASON FOR RETIREMENT	GRID:POS	ROW
1	1	J Parsons	Kurtis Kraft		Offenhauser	4	138	2h 46m 55.970s	5	2
2	3	B Holland	Deidt		Offenhauser	4	137	2h 48m 47.367s	10	4
3	31	Rose	Deidt		Offenhauser	4	137		3	1
4	54	C Green	Kurtis Kraft	3000	Offenhauser	4	137		12	4
5=	17	J Chitwood	Kurtis Kraft	2000	Offenhauser	4			9	3
5=	17	T Bettenhausen	Kurtis Kraft	2000	Offenhauser	4	136			
6	8	L Wallard	Moore		Offenhauser	4	136		23	8
7	98	W Faulkner	Kurtis Kraft	2000	Offenhauser	4	135		1	1
8	5	G Connor	Lesovsky		Offenhauser	4	135		4	2
9	7	P Russo	Nichels		Offenhauser	4	135		19	7
10	59	P Flaherty	Kurtis Kraft	3000	Offenhauser	4	135		11	4
11	2	M Fohr	Marchese		Offenhauser	4	133		16	6
12	18	D Carter	Stevens		Offenhauser	4s	133		13	5
13	15	M Hellings	Kurtis Kraft	2000	Offenhauser	4	132		26	9
14r	49	J McGrath	Kurtis Kraft	3000	Offenhauser	4	131	spin	6	2
15	55	T Ruttman	Lesovsky		Offenhauser	4	130		24	8
16	75	G Hartley	Langley		Offenhauser	4	128		31	11
17	22	J Davies	Ewing		Offenhauser	4	128		27	9
18	62	J McDowell	Kurtis Kraft	2000	Offenhauser	4	128		33	11
19	4	W Brown	Kurtis Kraft	2000	Offenhauser	4	127		20	7
20	21	S Webb	Maserati	8CTF	Offenhauser	4	126		14	5
21	81	J Hoyt	Kurtis Kraft	2000	Offenhauser	4	125		15	5
22	27	W Ader	Rae		Offenhauser	4s	123		29	10
23r	77	J Holmes	Olson		Offenhauser	4	123	spin	30	10
24	76	J Rathmann	Wetteroth		Offenhauser	4	122		28	10
25r=	12	H Banks	Maserati	8CTF	Offenhauser	4s			21	7
25r=	12	F Agabashian	Maserati	8CTF	Offenhauser	4s	112	oil line		
26r	67	B Schindler	Snowberger		Offenhauser	4	111	universal joint	22	8
27r=	24	B Levrett	Adams		Offenhauser	4			17	6
27r=	24	B Cantrell	Adams		Offenhauser	4	108	oil pressure		
28r	28	F Agabashian	Kurtis Kraft	3000	Offenhauser	4s	64	oil line	2	1
29r	61	J Jackson	Kurtis Kraft		Cummins	6s	52	supercharger	32	11
30r	23	S Hanks	Kurtis Kraft	2000	Offenhauser	4	42	oil pressure	25	9
31r	14	T Bettenhausen	Deidt		Offenhauser	4	30	wheel bearing	8	3
32r	45	D Rathmann	Watson		Offenhauser	4	25	stalled	18	6
33r	69	D Dinsmore	Kurtis Kraft	2000	Offenhauser	4	10	oil leak	7	3

Winning speed: 199.562 km/h, 124.002 mph
Pole Position speed: 216.206 km/h, 134.344 mph (W Faulkner, 1 min: 6.992 sec)
Fastest Lap speed: not available (J Parsons)

Stopped early because of rain.

4 Jun 1950 — SWITZERLAND: Bremgarten (Round: 4) (Race: 4)

42 laps x 7.280 km, 4.524 miles = 305.760 km, 189.990 miles

POS.	NO	DRIVER	CAR	MODEL	ENGINE		LAPS	TIME/REASON FOR RETIREMENT	GRID:POS	ROW
1	16	G Farina	Alfa Romeo	158	Alfa Romeo	8s	42	2h 02m 53.700s	2	1
2	12	L Fagioli	Alfa Romeo	158	Alfa Romeo	8s	42	2h 02m 54.100s	3	1
3	10	L Rosier	Talbot Lago	T26C-DA	Talbot	6	41		10	4
4	30	B Bira	Maserati	4CLT/48	Maserati	4s	40		8	3
5	34	F Bonetto	Maserati Milano	4CLT/50	Maserati Milano	4s	40		12	5
6	32	E de Graffenried	Maserati	4CLT/48	Maserati	4s	40		11	5
7	2	N Pagani	Maserati	4CLT/48	Maserati	4s	39		15	6
8	44	H Schell	Talbot Lago	T26C	Talbot	6	39		18	7
9	26	L Chiron	Maserati	4CLT/48	Maserati	4s	39		16	7
10	4	J Claes	Talbot Lago	T26C	Talbot	6	39		14	6
11	40	T Branca	Maserati	4CL	Maserati	4s	35		17	7
r	14	J M Fangio	Alfa Romeo	158	Alfa Romeo	8s	33	electrics	1	1
r	42	P Étançelin	Talbot Lago	T26C	Talbot	6	25	gearbox	6	3
r	20	R Sommer	Ferrari	166	Ferrari	V12	19	suspension	13	5
r	8	E Martin	Talbot Lago	T26C-DA	Talbot	6	19	accident	9	4
r	22	L Villoresi	Ferrari	125	Ferrari	V12s	9	transmission	4	2
r	18	A Ascari	Ferrari	125	Ferrari	V12s	4	oil line	5	2
r	6	Y Giraud-Cabantous	Talbot Lago	T26C-DA	Talbot	6	0	accident	7	3

Winning speed: 149.279 km/h, 92.757 mph
Pole Position speed: 161.678 km/h, 100.462 mph (J M Fangio, 2 min:42.100 sec)
Fastest Lap speed: 162.178 km/h, 100.773 mph (G Farina, 2 min:41.600 sec on lap 8)
Lap Leaders: J M Fangio 1-6,21-22 (8); G Farina 7-20,24-42 (33); L Fagioli 23 (1).

18 Jun 1950 — BELGIUM: Spa-Francorchamps (Round: 5) (Race:5)

35 laps x 14.120 km, 8.774 miles = 494.200 km, 307.082 miles

POS.	NO	DRIVER	CAR	MODEL	ENGINE		LAPS	TIME/REASON FOR RETIREMENT	GRID:POS	ROW
1	10	J M Fangio	Alfa Romeo	158	Alfa Romeo	8s	35	2h 47m 26.000s	2	1
2	12	L Fagioli	Alfa Romeo	158	Alfa Romeo	8s	35	2h 47m 40.000s	3	1
3	14	L Rosier	Talbot Lago	T26C-DA	Talbot	6	35	2h 49m 45.000s	8	3
4	8	G Farina	Alfa Romeo	158	Alfa Romeo	8s	35	2h 51m 31.000s	1	1
5	4	A Ascari	Ferrari	125/275	Ferrari	V12	34		6	3
6	2	L Villoresi	Ferrari	125	Ferrari	V12s	33		4	2
7	22	P Levegh	Talbot Lago	T26C	Talbot	6	33		10	4
8	24	J Claes	Talbot Lago	T26C	Talbot	6	32		14	6
9	26	G Crossley	Alta	GP	Alta	4s	30		12	5
10	30	T Branca	Maserati	4CL	Maserati	4s	29		11	5
r	20	E Chaboud	Talbot Lago	T26C	Talbot	6	22	engine	13	5
r	6	R Sommer	Talbot Lago	T26C	Talbot	6	20	engine	5	2
r	16	P Étançelin	Talbot Lago	T26C-DA	Talbot	6	15	engine overheating	7	3
r	18	Y Giraud-Cabantous	Talbot Lago	T26C-DA	Talbot	6	2	engine	9	4

Winning speed: 177.097 km/h, 110.043 mph
Pole Position speed: 183.509 km/h, 114.027 mph (G Farina, 4 min:37.000 sec)
Fastest Lap speed: 185.451 km/h, 115.234 mph (G Farina, 4 min:34.100 sec on lap 18)
Lap Leaders: J M Fangio 1-6,20-35 (22); G Farina 7-11,18-19 (7); L Fagioli 12 (1); R Sommer 13-17 (5).

2 Jul 1950 — FRANCE: Reims-Gueux (Round: 6) (Race: 6)

64 laps x 7.816 km, 4.857 miles = 500.224 km, 310.825 miles

POS.	NO	DRIVER	CAR	MODEL	ENGINE		LAPS	TIME/REASON FOR RETIREMENT	GRID:POS	ROW
1	6	J M Fangio	Alfa Romeo	158	Alfa Romeo	8s	64	2h 57m 52.800s	1	1
2	4	L Fagioli	Alfa Romeo	158	Alfa Romeo	8s	64	2h 58m 18.500s	3	1
3	14	P Whitehead	Ferrari	125	Ferrari	V12s	61		19	8
4	44	R Manzon	Simca Gordini	T15	Gordini	4s	61		13	5
5=	16	P Étançelin	Talbot Lago	T26C-DA	Talbot	6			4	2
5=	16	E Chaboud	Talbot Lago	T26C-DA	Talbot	6	59			
6=	26	C Pozzi	Talbot Lago	T26C	Talbot	6			16	7
6=	26	L Rosier	Talbot Lago	T26C	Talbot	6	56			
7r	2	G Farina	Alfa Romeo	158	Alfa Romeo	8s	55	fuel pump	2	1
8	18	Y Giraud-Cabantous	Talbot Lago	T26C-DA	Talbot	6	52		5	2
r	22	P Levegh	Talbot Lago	T26C	Talbot	6	37	engine	9	4
r	40	F Bonetto	Maserati Milano	4CLT/50	Maserati Milano	4s	15	engine	11	5
r	42	J Claes	Talbot Lago	T26C	Talbot	6	12	engine overheating	15	6
r	20	L Rosier	Talbot Lago	T26C-DA	Talbot	6	11	engine overheating	6	3
r	32	R Parnell	Maserati	4CLT/48	Maserati	4s	10	engine	12	5
r	28	F Rol	Maserati	4CLT/48	Maserati	4s	7	engine	7	3
r	30	L Chiron	Maserati	4CLT/48	Maserati	4s	7	engine	14	
r	34	D Hampshire	Maserati	4CLT/48	Maserati	4s	6	engine	18	7
r	12	R Sommer	Talbot Lago	T26C-GS	Talbot	6	5	engine	17	7
r	36	F González	Maserati	4CLT/48	Maserati	4s	4	engine	8	3
ns	24	E Chaboud	Talbot Lago	T26C	Talbot	6		shared with Étançelin instead	10	4
ns	8	L Villoresi	Ferrari	175/275	Ferrari	V12		drove in different race		
ns	10	A Ascari	Ferrari	175/275	Ferrari	V12		drove in different race		

Winning speed: 168.729 km/h, 104.843 mph
Pole Position speed: 186.837 km/h, 116.095 mph (J M Fangio, 2 min:30.600 sec)
Fastest Lap speed: 180.833 km/h, 112.364 mph (J M Fangio, 2 min:35.600 sec on lap 52)
Lap Leaders: G Farina 1-16 (16); J M Fangio 17-64 (48).

3 Sep 1950 — ITALY: Monza (Round: 7) (Race: 7)

80 laps x 6.300 km, 3.915 miles = 504.000 km, 313.171 miles

POS.	NO	DRIVER	CAR	MODEL	ENGINE		LAPS	TIME/REASON FOR RETIREMENT	GRID:POS	ROW
1	10	G Farina	Alfa Romeo	158	Alfa Romeo	8s	80	2h 51m 17.400s	3	1
2=	48	D Serafini	Ferrari	375	Ferrari	V12			6	2
2=	48	A Ascari	Ferrari	375	Ferrari	V12	80	2h 52m 36.000s		
3	36	L Fagioli	Alfa Romeo	158	Alfa Romeo	8s	80	2h 52m 53.000s	5	2
4	58	L Rosier	Talbot Lago	T26C	Talbot	6	75		13	4
5	24	P Étançelin	Talbot Lago	T26C	Talbot	6	75		16	4
6	38	E de Graffenried	Maserati	4CLT/48	Maserati	4s	72		17	5
7	8	P Whitehead	Ferrari	125	Ferrari	V12s	72		18	5
r	50	D Murray	Maserati	4CLT/48	Maserati	4s	56	gearbox/ valve	24	6
r	32	C Harrison	ERA	B	ERA	6s	51	radiator	21	6
r	12	R Sommer	Talbot Lago	T26C	Talbot	6	48	gearbox	8	2
r	40	G Mairesse	Talbot Lago	T26C	Talbot	6	42		11	3
r	4	F Rol	Maserati	4CLT/48	Maserati	4s	39		9	3
r=	60	P Taruffi	Alfa Romeo	158	Alfa Romeo	8s			7	2
r=	60	J M Fangio	Alfa Romeo	158	Alfa Romeo	8s	34	valve		
r	56	P Levegh	Talbot Lago	T26C	Talbot	6	29		20	5
r	18	J M Fangio	Alfa Romeo	158	Alfa Romeo	8s	23	gearbox	1	1
r	2	J Claes	Talbot Lago	T26C	Talbot	6	22	engine overheating	22	6
r	16	A Ascari	Ferrari	375	Ferrari	V12	21	engine	2	1
r	22	C Biondetti	Ferrari	166S	Jaguar	6	17	engine	25	7
r	64	H Louveau	Talbot Lago	T26C-GS	Talbot	6	16		14	4
r	62	F Comotti	Maserati Milano	4CLT/50	Maserati Milano	4s	15		26	7
r	6	L Chiron	Maserati	4CLT/48	Maserati	4s	13	oil pressure	19	5
r	42	M Trintignant	Simca Gordini	T15	Gordini	4s	13	water pipe	12	3
r	46	C Sanesi	Alfa Romeo	158	Alfa Romeo	8s	11	engine	4	1
r	44	R Manzon	Simca Gordini	T15	Gordini	4s	7	transmission	10	3
r	30	B Bira	Maserati	4CLT/48	Maserati	4s	1	engine	15	4
r	28	P Pietsch	Maserati	4CLT/48	Maserati	4s	0	engine	27	7
ns	52	F Bonetto	Milano		Maserati	4s			23	6

Winning speed: 176.543 km/h, 109.699 mph
Pole Position speed: 191.231 km/h, 118.825 mph (J M Fangio, 1 min:58.600 sec)
Fastest Lap speed: 189.000 km/h, 117.439 mph (J M Fangio, 2 min: 0.000 sec on lap 7)
Lap Leaders: G Farina 1-13,16-80 (78); A Ascari 14-15 (2).

Lap Leaders 1950

POS	DRIVER	CAR-ENGINE	GPS	LAPS	KM	MILES
1	G Farina	Alfa Romeo	5	197	1,248.4	775.7
2	J M Fangio	Alfa Romeo	5	179	1,066.7	662.8
3	L Fagioli	Alfa Romeo	3	8	49.3	30.6
4	R Sommer	Talbot Lago	1	5	70.6	43.9
5	A Ascari	Ferrari	1	2	12.6	7.8
			6	**391**	**2,447.6**	**1,520.9**

Driver Points 1950

		GB	MC	INDY	CH	B	F	I	TOTAL	
1	G Farina	9	-	-	9	4	-	8	30	
2	J M Fangio	-	9	-	-	8	9	1	27	
3	L Fagioli	6	-	-	6	6	6	(4)	24	(4)
4	L Rosier	2	-	-	4	4	-	3	13	
5	A Ascari	-	6	-	-	2	-	3	11	
6	J Parsons	-	-	9	-	-	-	-	9	
7	B Holland	-	-	6	-	-	-	-	6	
8	B Bira	-	2	-	3	-	-	-	5	
9	R Parnell	4	-	-	-	-	-	-	4	
	L Chiron	-	4	-	-	-	-	-	4	
	M Rose	-	-	4	-	-	-	-	4	
	P Whitehead	-	-	-	-	-	4	-	4	
13	Y Giraud-Cabantous	3	-	-	-	-	-	-	3	
	R Sommer	-	3	-	-	-	-	-	3	
	C Green	-	-	3	-	-	-	-	3	
	R Manzon	-	-	-	-	-	3	-	3	
	D Serafini	-	-	-	-	-	-	3	3	
	P Étançelin	-	-	-	-	-	1	2	3	
19	F Bonetto	-	-	-	2	-	-	-	2	
20	T Bettenhausen	-	-	1	-	-	-	-	1	
	J Chitwood	-	-	1	-	-	-	-	1	
	E Chaboud	-	-	-	-	-	1	-	1	

8, 6, 4, 3 and 2 points awarded to the first five finishers. The driver setting the fastest lap scored a point also. Points shared for shared drives. Best 4 scores.

The formula continued into its second year with the promise of stiffer competition from the 4.5 litre Ferrari and the long awaited V16 BRM. The Talbot entries were now in private hands and sadly missing from their number would be the popular Raymond Sommer, killed in a minor French race at the end of the previous season.

ALFA ROMEO
SA Alfa Romeo: Farina, Fangio, Sanesi, Bonetto, de Graffenried, Fagioli, Pietsch

FERRARI
Scuderia Ferrari: Ascari, Villoresi, Taruffi, González
G A Vandervell: Parnell, Whitehead (GB), (Shaure-Taylor)
Ecurie Espadon: Fischer
Privateers: Whitehead, Landi

MASERATI
Enrico Platé: de Graffenried, Schell, Chiron
Scuderia Ambrosiana: Murray
Scuderia Milano: Marimón, Godia, (Jover)
Ecurie Siam: Bira
Privateers: Fotheringham-Parker, James, Branca

OSCA
OSCA Automobili: Rol

TALBOT LAGO
Ecurie Rosier: Rosier, Chiron, Louveau
Ecurie Belgique: Mairesse, Swaters, Pilette
Ecurie Belge: Claes
Privateers: Giraud-Cabantous, Étançelin, Levegh, Hamilton, González, Chaboud, Grignard

SIMCA GORDINI
Equipe Gordini: Manzon, Trintignant, Simon, Gordini

ERA
Privateers: Gerard, Shawe-Taylor

ALTA
Privateer: Kelly

HWM
HW Motors: Abecassis, Moss

BRM
BRM Ltd: Parnell, Walker, (Richardson, Stuck)

VERITAS
Ecurie Espadon: Hirt

Ascari at Reims-Gueux France, 1951.

27 May 1951 — SWITZERLAND: Bremgarten (Round: 1) (Race: 8)

42 laps x 7.280 km, 4.524 miles = 305.760 km, 189.990 miles

POS.	NO	DRIVER	CAR	MODEL	ENGINE		LAPS	TIME/REASON FOR RETIREMENT	GRID:POS	ROW
1	24	J M Fangio	Alfa Romeo	159	Alfa Romeo	8s	42	2h 07m 53.640s	1	1
2	44	P Taruffi	Ferrari	375	Ferrari	V12	42	2h 08m 48.880s	6	3
3	22	G Farina	Alfa Romeo	159	Alfa Romeo	8s	42	2h 09m 12.950s	2	1
4	28	C Sanesi	Alfa Romeo	159	Alfa Romeo	8s	41		4	2
5	26	E de Graffenried	Alfa Romeo	159	Alfa Romeo	8s	40		5	2
6	20	A Ascari	Ferrari	375	Ferrari	V12	40		7	3
7	30	L Chiron	Maserati	4CLT/48	Maserati	4s	40		19	8
8	14	S Moss	HWM	(51)	Alta	4	40		14	6
9	8	L Rosier	Talbot Lago	T26C-DA	Talbot	6	39		8	3
10	4	P Étançelin	Talbot Lago	T26C-DA	Talbot	6	39		12	5
11	38	R Fischer	Ferrari	212	Ferrari	V12	39		10	4
12	32	H Schell	Maserati	4CLT/48	Maserati	4s	38		17	7
r	16	P Whitehead	Ferrari	125	Ferrari	V12s	36	accident	9	4
13	2	J Claes	Talbot Lago	T26C-DA	Talbot	6	35		18	7
14	40	G Mairesse	Talbot Lago	T26C	Talbot	6	31		21	9
r	10	H Louveau	Talbot Lago	T26C	Talbot	6	30	accident	11	5
r	12	G Abecassis	HWM	(51)	Alta	4	23	magneto	20	8
r	6	Y Giraud-Cabantous	Talbot Lago	T26C	Talbot	6	14	ignition	15	6
r	18	L Villoresi	Ferrari	375	Ferrari	V12	12	accident	3	1
r	42	F González	Talbot Lago	T26C-GS	Talbot	6	10	oil pump	13	5
r	52	P Hirt	Veritas	Meteor	Veritas	6	0	fuel pump	16	7

Winning speed: 143.444 km/h, 89.132 mph
Pole Position speed: 168.108 km/h, 104.457 mph (J M Fangio, 2 min:35.900 sec)
Fastest Lap speed: 153.174 km/h, 95.178 mph (J M Fangio, 2 min:51.100 sec on lap 33)
Lap Leaders: J M Fangio 1-23,29-42 (37); G Farina 24-28 (5).

30 May 1951 — INDIANAPOLIS: 500 — (Round: 2) (Race: 9)

200 laps x 4.023 km, 2.500 miles = 804.672 km, 500.000 miles

POS.	NO	DRIVER	CAR	MODEL	ENGINE		LAPS	TIME/REASON FOR RETIREMENT	GRID:POS	ROW
1	99	L Wallard	Kurtis Kraft		Offenhauser	4	200	3h 57m 38.050s	2	1
2	83	M Nazaruk	Kurtis Kraft		Offenhauser	4	200	3h 59m 25.293s	7	3
3=	9	J McGrath	Kurtis Kraft	3000	Offenhauser	4			3	1
3=	9	M Ayulo	Kurtis Kraft	3000	Offenhauser	4	200			
4	57	A Linden	Sherman		Offenhauser	4	200		31	11
5	52	B Ball	Schroeder		Offenhauser	4	200		29	10
6	1	H Banks	Moore		Offenhauser	4	200		17	6
7	68	C Forberg	Kurtis Kraft	3000	Offenhauser	4	193		24	8
8	27	D Carter	Deidt		Offenhauser	4	180		4	2
9r	5	T Bettenhausen	Deidt		Offenhauser	4	178	spin	9	3
10r	18	D Nalon	Kurtis Kraft	Novi		8s	151	stalled	1	1
11r	69	G Force	Kurtis Kraft	2000	Offenhauser	4	142	oil pressure	22	8
12r	25	S Hanks	Kurtis Kraft	3000	Offenhauser	4	135	connecting rod/ spin	12	4
13r	10	B Schindler	Kurtis Kraft	2000	Offenhauser	4	129	connecting rod	16	6
14r	16	M Rose	Deidt		Offenhauser	4	126	wheel collapsed/ spin	5	2
15r	2	W Faulkner	Kuzma		Offenhauser	4	123	crankshaft	14	5
16r	76	J Davies	Pawl		Offenhauser	4	110	rear end drive gears	27	9
17r	59	F Agabashian	Kurtis Kraft	3000	Offenhauser	4	109	clutch	11	4
18r	73	C Scarborough	Kurtis Kraft	2000	Offenhauser	4	100	front axle	15	5
19r	71	B Mackey	?		Offenhauser	4	97	clutch shaft	33	11
20r	8	C Stevenson	Marchese		Offenhauser	4	93	fire	19	7
21r	3	J Parsons	Kurtis Kraft	3000	Offenhauser	4	87	magneto	8	3
22r	4	C Green	Kurtis Kraft	3000	Offenhauser	4	80	connecting rod	10	4
23r	98	T Ruttman	Kurtis Kraft	2000	Offenhauser	4	78	crankshaft	6	2
24r	6	D Dinsmore	Schroeder		Offenhauser	4	73	engine overheating	32	11
25r	32	C Miller	Kurtis Kraft		Novi	8s	56	ignition	28	10
26r	44	W Brown	Kurtis Kraft	3000	Offenhauser	4	55	magneto	13	5
27r	48	R Ward	Bromme		Offenhauser	4	34	oil line	25	9
28r	23	C Griffith	Kurtis Kraft	2000	Offenhauser	4	30	rear axle	18	6
29r	81	B Vukovich	Trevis		Offenhauser	4	29	oil tank	20	7
30r	22	G Connor	Lesovsky		Offenhauser	4	29	universal joint	21	7
31r	19	M Hellings	Deidt		Offenhauser	4	18	piston	23	8
32r	12	J McDowell	Maserati	8CTF	Offenhauser	4s	15	fuel tank	26	9
33r	26	J James	Watson		Offenhauser	4	8	drive shaft	30	10

Winning speed: 203.171 km/h, 126.244 mph
Pole Position speed: 219.672 km/h, 136.498 mph (D Nalon, 1 min: 5.935 sec)
Fastest Lap speed: 215.345 km/h, 133.809 mph (L Wallard, 1 min: 7.260 sec on lap 23)
Fastest qualifier: W Faulkner (220.274 km/h, 136.872 mph).

17 Jun 1951 — BELGIUM: Spa-Francorchamps — (Round: 3) (Race: 10)

36 laps x 14.120 km, 8.774 miles = 508.320 km, 315.855 miles

POS.	NO	DRIVER	CAR	MODEL	ENGINE		LAPS	TIME/REASON FOR RETIREMENT	GRID:POS	ROW
1	4	G Farina	Alfa Romeo	159	Alfa Romeo	8s	36	2h 45m 46.200s	2	1
2	8	A Ascari	Ferrari	375	Ferrari	V12	36	2h 48m 37.200s	4	2
3	10	L Villoresi	Ferrari	375	Ferrari	V12	36	2h 50m 08.100s	3	1
4	14	L Rosier	Talbot Lago	T26C-DA	Talbot	6	34		7	3
5	22	Y Giraud-Cabantous	Talbot Lago	T26C	Talbot	6	34		8	3
6	24	A Pilette	Talbot Lago	T26C	Talbot	6	33		12	5
7	16	J Claes	Talbot Lago	T26C-DA	Talbot	6	33		11	5
8	26	P Levegh	Talbot Lago	T26C	Talbot	6	32		13	5
9	2	J M Fangio	Alfa Romeo	159	Alfa Romeo	8s	32		1	1
r	18	L Chiron	Talbot Lago	T26C	Talbot	6	28	piston	9	4
r	6	C Sanesi	Alfa Romeo	159	Alfa Romeo	8s	11	radiator	6	3
r	12	P Taruffi	Ferrari	375	Ferrari	V12	8	rear axle	5	2
r	20	P Étançelin	Talbot Lago	T26C-DA	Talbot	6	0	transmission	10	4

Winning speed: 183.985 km/h, 114.323 mph
Pole Position speed: 191.819 km/h, 119.191 mph (J M Fangio, 4 min:25.000 sec)
Fastest Lap speed: 193.941 km/h, 120.510 mph (J M Fangio, 4 min:22.100 sec on lap 10)
Lap Leaders: L Villoresi 1-2 (2); G Farina 3-14,16-36 (33); J M Fangio 15 (1).

1 Jul 1951 — FRANCE: Reims-Gueux (Round: 4) (Race: 11)

77 laps x 7.816 km, 4.857 miles = 601.832 km, 373.961 miles

POS.	NO	DRIVER	CAR	MODEL	ENGINE		LAPS	TIME/REASON FOR RETIREMENT	GRID:POS	ROW
1=	8	L Fagioli	Alfa Romeo	159	Alfa Romeo	8s			7	3
1=	8	J M Fangio	Alfa Romeo	159	Alfa Romeo	8s	77	3h 22m 11.000s		
2=	14	F González	Ferrari	375	Ferrari	V12			6	3
2=	14	A Ascari	Ferrari	375	Ferrari	V12	77	3h 23m 09.200s		
3	10	L Villoresi	Ferrari	375	Ferrari	V12	74		4	2
4	26	R Parnell	Thin Wall Ferrari	375 tw	Ferrari	V12	73		9	4
5	2	G Farina	Alfa Romeo	159	Alfa Romeo	8s	73		2	1
6	42	L Chiron	Talbot Lago	T26C	Talbot	6	71		8	3
7	46	Y Giraud-Cabantous	Talbot Lago	T26C	Talbot	6	71		11	5
8	44	E Chaboud	Talbot Lago	T26C-GS	Talbot	6	69		14	6
9	48	G Mairesse	Talbot Lago	T26C	Talbot	6	66		19	8
10	6	C Sanesi	Alfa Romeo	159	Alfa Romeo	8s	58		5	2
11=	4	J M Fangio	Alfa Romeo	159	Alfa Romeo	8s			1	1
11=	4	L Fagioli	Alfa Romeo	159	Alfa Romeo	8s	55			
r	28	J Claes	Talbot Lago	T26C-DA	Talbot	6	54	accident	12	5
r	40	L Rosier	Talbot Lago	T26C-DA	Talbot	6	43	rear axle	13	5
r	38	P Étançelin	Talbot Lago	T26C-DA	Talbot	6	37	inlet manifold	10	4
r	36	A Gordini	Simca Gordini	T11	Gordini	4s	27	valve gear	17	7
r	20	H Schell	Maserati	4CLT/48	Maserati	4s	24	engine overheating	22	9
r	32	M Trintignant	Simca Gordini	T15	Gordini	4s	11	valves	18	7
r	12	A Ascari	Ferrari	375	Ferrari	V12	10	gearbox	3	1
r	34	A Simon	Simca Gordini	T15	Gordini	4s	7	engine	21	9
r	30	R Manzon	Simca Gordini	T15	Gordini	4s	3	engine	23	9
r	50	O Marimón	Maserati Milano	4CLT/50	Maserati Milano	4s	2	piston	15	6
r	18	E de Graffenried	Maserati	4CLT/48	Maserati	4s	1	transmission	16	7
r	24	P Whitehead	Ferrari	125	Ferrari	V12s	1	gasket	20	8
ns	26	B Shawe-Taylor	Thin Wall Ferrari	375 tw	Ferrari	V12		car raced by Parnell		

Winning speed: 178.600 km/h, 110.977 mph
Pole Position speed: 193.120 km/h, 119.999 mph (J M Fangio, 2 min:25.700 sec)
Fastest Lap speed: 190.376 km/h, 118.294 mph (J M Fangio, 2 min:27.800 sec on lap 32)
Lap Leaders: A Ascari 1-8,45-50 (14); J M Fangio 9,51-77 (28); G Farina 10-44 (35).

Also the Grand Prix of Europe.

14 Jul 1951 — BRITAIN: Silverstone (Round: 5) (Race: 12)

90 laps x 4.649 km, 2.889 miles = 418.446 km, 260.010 miles

POS.	NO	DRIVER	CAR	MODEL	ENGINE		LAPS	TIME/REASON FOR RETIREMENT	GRID:POS	ROW
1	12	F González	Ferrari	375	Ferrari	V12	90	2h 42m 18.200s	1	1
2	2	J M Fangio	Alfa Romeo	159	Alfa Romeo	8s	90	2h 43m 09.200s	2	1
3	10	L Villoresi	Ferrari	375	Ferrari	V12	88		5	2
4	4	F Bonetto	Alfa Romeo	159	Alfa Romeo	8s	87		7	2
5	6	R Parnell	BRM	P15	BRM	V16s	85		20	6
6	3	C Sanesi	Alfa Romeo	159	Alfa Romeo	8s	84		6	2
7	7	P Walker	BRM	P15	BRM	V16s	84		19	6
8	9	B Shawe-Taylor	ERA	B	ERA	6s	84		12	4
9	14	P Whitehead	Thin Wall Ferrari	375 tw	Ferrari	V12	83		8	3
10	22	L Rosier	Talbot Lago	T26C-DA	Talbot	6	83		9	3
11	8	B Gerard	ERA	B/C	ERA	6s	82		10	3
12	18	D Hamilton	Talbot Lago	T26C	Talbot	6	81		11	3
13	25	J Claes	Talbot Lago	T26C-DA	Talbot	6	80		14	4
r	1	G Farina	Alfa Romeo	159	Alfa Romeo	8s	75	clutch/ fire	3	1
nc	5	J Kelly	Alta	GP	Alta	4s	75		18	5
r	11	A Ascari	Ferrari	375	Ferrari	V12	56	gearbox	4	1
r	17	P Fotheringham-Parker	Maserati	4CL	Maserati	4s	46	oil line	16	5
r	15	D Murray	Maserati	4CLT/48	Maserati	4s	45	valve spring	15	5
r	23	L Chiron	Talbot Lago	T26C	Talbot	6	41	brakes	13	4
r	16	J James	Maserati	4CLT/48	Maserati	4s	23	radiator	17	5

Winning speed: 154.690 km/h, 96.120 mph
Pole Position speed: 161.874 km/h, 100.584 mph (F González, 1 min:43.400 sec)
Fastest Lap speed: 160.941 km/h, 100.004 mph (G Farina, 1 min:44.000 sec on lap 38)
Lap Leaders: F Bonetto 1 (1); F González 2-9,39-47,49-90 (59); J M Fangio 10-38,48 (30).

29 Jul 1951 - GERMANY : Nürburgring (Round: 6) (Race: 13)

20 laps x 22.810 km, 14.173 miles = 456.200 km, 283.470 miles

POS.	NO	DRIVER	CAR	MODEL	ENGINE		LAPS	TIME/REASON FOR RETIREMENT	GRID:POS	ROW
1	71	A Ascari	Ferrari	375	Ferrari	V12	20	3h 23m 03.300s	1	1
2	75	J M Fangio	Alfa Romeo	159	Alfa Romeo	8s	20	3h 23m 33.800s	3	1
3	74	F González	Ferrari	375	Ferrari	V12	20	3h 27m 42.300s	2	1
4	72	L Villoresi	Ferrari	375	Ferrari	V12	20	3h 28m 53.500s	5	2
5	73	P Taruffi	Ferrari	375	Ferrari	V12	20	3h 30m 52.400s	6	2
6	91	R Fischer	Ferrari	212	Ferrari	V12	19		8	3
7	82	R Manzon	Simca Gordini	T15	Gordini	4s	19		9	3
8	84	L Rosier	Talbot Lago	T26C-DA	Talbot	6	19		15	5
9	90	P Levegh	Talbot Lago	T26C	Talbot	6	18		19	6
10	93	J Swaters	Talbot Lago	T26C	Talbot	6	18		22	7
r	87	Y Giraud-Cabantous	Talbot Lago	T26C	Talbot	6	17	accident	11	3
11	94	J Claes	Talbot Lago	T26C-DA	Talbot	6	17		18	5
r	81	M Trintignant	Simca Gordini	T15	Gordini	4s	13	engine	14	4
r	77	F Bonetto	Alfa Romeo	159	Alfa Romeo	8s	12	magneto	10	3
r	88	D Hamilton	Talbot Lago	T26C	Talbot	6	12	oil pressure	20	6
r	83	A Simon	Simca Gordini	T15	Gordini	4s	11	engine	12	4
r	78	P Pietsch	Alfa Romeo	159	Alfa Romeo	8s	11	accident	7	2
r	76	G Farina	Alfa Romeo	159	Alfa Romeo	8s	8	engine overheating	4	1
r	86	P Étançelin	Talbot Lago	T26C-DA	Talbot	6	4	gearbox	21	6
r	92	T Branca	Maserati	4CLT/48	Maserati	4s	3	engine	17	5
r	85	L Chiron	Talbot Lago	T26C	Talbot	6	3	engine	13	4
r	79	E de Graffenried	Maserati	4CLT/48	Maserati	4s	2	engine	16	5
ns	89	D Murray	Maserati	4CLT/48	Maserati	4s		accident		

Winning speed: 134.801 km/h, 83.761 mph
Pole Position speed: 137.825 km/h, 85.640 mph (A Ascari, 9 min:55.800 sec)
Fastest Lap speed: 137.825 km/h, 85.640 mph (J M Fangio, 9 min:55.800 sec on lap 12)
Lap Leaders: J M Fangio 1-4,11-14 (8); A Ascari 5-9,15-20 (11); F González 10 (1).

16 Sep 1951 ITALY: Monza (Round: 7) (Race: 14)

80 laps x 6.300 km, 3.915 miles = 504.000 km, 313.171 miles

POS.	NO	DRIVER	CAR	MODEL	ENGINE		LAPS	TIME/REASON FOR RETIREMENT	GRID:POS	ROW
1	2	A Ascari	Ferrari	375	Ferrari	V12	80	2h 42m 39.300s	3	1
2	6	F González	Ferrari	375	Ferrari	V12	80	2h 43m 23.900s	4	1
3=	40	F Bonetto	Alfa Romeo	159	Alfa Romeo	8s			7	2
3=	40	G Farina	Alfa Romeo	159	Alfa Romeo	8s	79			
4	4	L Villoresi	Ferrari	375	Ferrari	V12	79		5	2
5	8	P Taruffi	Ferrari	375	Ferrari	V12	78		6	2
6	48	A Simon	Simca Gordini	T15	Gordini	4s	74		11	3
7	18	L Rosier	Talbot Lago	T26C-DA	Talbot	6	73		15	4
8	24	Y Giraud-Cabantous	Talbot Lago	T26C	Talbot	6	72		14	4
9	44	F Rol	OSCA	4500G	OSCA	V12	67		18	5
r	38	J M Fangio	Alfa Romeo	159	Alfa Romeo	8s	39	piston	1	1
r	46	R Manzon	Simca Gordini	T15	Gordini	4s	29	engine	13	4
r	50	M Trintignant	Simca Gordini	T15	Gordini	4s	29	piston	12	3
r	20	L Chiron	Talbot Lago	T26C	Talbot	6	23	ignition	17	5
r	22	P Levegh	Talbot Lago	T26C	Talbot	6	9	engine	20	5
r	28	J Swaters	Talbot Lago	T26C	Talbot	6	7	engine overheating	22	6
r	34	G Farina	Alfa Romeo	159	Alfa Romeo	8s	6	lubrication	2	1
r	26	J Claes	Talbot Lago	T26C-DA	Talbot	6	4	oil scavenge pump	21	6
r	36	E de Graffenried	Alfa Romeo	159	Alfa Romeo	8s	1	supercharger	9	3
r	16	P Whitehead	Ferrari	125	Ferrari	V12s	1	piston	19	5
r	12	C Landi	Ferrari	375	Ferrari	V12	1	transmission	16	4
ns	30	R Parnell	BRM	P15	BRM	V16s		engine/ gearbox	8	2
ns	32	K Richardson	BRM	P15	BRM	V16s		incorrect licence	10	3
ns	32	H Stuck	BRM	P15	BRM	V16s		engine/ gearbox		
ns	14	R Fischer	Ferrari	212	Ferrari	V12		accident		

Winning speed: 185.915 km/h, 115.522 mph
Pole Position speed: 200.353 km/h, 124.494 mph (J M Fangio, 1 min:53.200 sec)
Fastest Lap speed: 194.678 km/h, 120.967 mph (G Farina, 1 min:56.500 sec on lap 64)
Lap Leaders: J M Fangio 1-3,8-13 (9); A Ascari 4-7,14-80 (71).

28 Oct 1951 — SPAIN: Pedralbes (Round: 8) (Race: 15)

70 laps x 6.316 km, 3.925 miles = 442.120 km, 274.721 miles

POS.	NO	DRIVER	CAR	MODEL	ENGINE		LAPS	TIME/REASON FOR RETIREMENT	GRID:POS	ROW
1	22	J M Fangio	Alfa Romeo	159	Alfa Romeo	8s	70	2h 46m 54.100s	2	1
2	6	F González	Ferrari	375	Ferrari	V12	70	2h 47m 48.380s	3	1
3	20	G Farina	Alfa Romeo	159	Alfa Romeo	8s	70	2h 48m 39.640s	4	1
4	2	A Ascari	Ferrari	375	Ferrari	V12	68		1	1
5	24	F Bonetto	Alfa Romeo	159	Alfa Romeo	8s	68		8	3
6	26	E de Graffenried	Alfa Romeo	159	Alfa Romeo	8s	66		6	2
7	28	L Rosier	Talbot Lago	T26C-DA	Talbot	6	64		20	6
8	34	P Étançelin	Talbot Lago	T26C-DA	Talbot	6	63		13	4
9	14	R Manzon	Simca Gordini	T15	Gordini	4s	63		9	3
10	44	C Godia	Maserati	4CLT/48	Maserati	4s	60		17	5
r	4	L Villoresi	Ferrari	375	Ferrari	V12	48	ignition	5	2
r	16	A Simon	Simca Gordini	T15	Gordini	4s	48	engine	10	3
r	36	J Claes	Talbot Lago	T26C-DA	Talbot	6	37	accident	15	5
r	8	P Taruffi	Ferrari	375	Ferrari	V12	30	wheel lost	7	2
r	12	M Trintignant	Simca Gordini	T15	Gordini	4s	25	engine	11	3
r	38	G Grignard	Talbot Lago	T26C-DA	Talbot	6	23	engine	16	5
r	32	Y Giraud-Cabantous	Talbot Lago	T26C	Talbot	6	7	accident	14	4
r	30	L Chiron	Talbot Lago	T26C	Talbot	6	4	rocker	12	4
r	18	B Bira	Maserati	4CLT/48	OSCA	V12	1	engine	19	6
ns	46	J Jover	Maserati	4CLT/48	Maserati	4s		engine	18	5

Winning speed: 158.939 km/h, 98.760 mph
Pole Position speed: 174.114 km/h, 108.190 mph (A Ascari, 2 min:10.590 sec)
Fastest Lap speed: 166.053 km/h, 103.180 mph (J M Fangio, 2 min:16.930 sec on lap 3)
Lap Leaders: A Ascari 1-3 (3); J M Fangio 4-70 (67).

Revised fastest lap time as issued by race organisers.

Lap Leaders 1951

POS	DRIVER	CAR-ENGINE	GPS	LAPS	KM	MILES
1	J M Fangio	Alfa Romeo	7	180	1,304.1	810.4
2	A Ascari	Ferrari	4	99	826.6	513.6
3	G Farina	Alfa Romeo	3	73	775.9	482.1
4	F González	Ferrari	2	60	297.1	184.6
5	L Villoresi	Ferrari	1	2	28.2	17.5
6	F Bonetto	Alfa Romeo	1	1	4.6	2.9
			7	415	3,236.6	2,011.2

Driver Points 1951

		CH	INDY	B	F	GB	D	I	E	TOTAL	
1	J M Fangio	9	-	(1)	(5)	6	7	-	9	31	(6)
2	A Ascari	-	-	6	3	-	8	8	(3)	25	(3)
3	F González	-	-	-	(3)	8	4	6	6	24	(3)
4	G Farina	4	-	8	(2)	(1)	-	3	4	19	(3)
5	L Villoresi	-	-	4	4	4	3	(3)	-	15	(3)
6	P Taruffi	6	-	-	-	-	2	2	-	10	
7	L Wallard	-	9	-	-	-	-	-	-	9	
8	F Bonetto	-	-	-	-	3	-	2	2	7	
9	M Nazaruk	-	6	-	-	-	-	-	-	6	
10	R Parnell	-	-	-	3	2	-	-	-	5	
11	L Fagioli	-	-	-	4	-	-	-	-	4	
12	C Sanesi	3	-	-	-	-	-	-	-	3	
	A Linden	-	3	-	-	-	-	-	-	3	
	L Rosier	-	-	3	-	-	-	-	-	3	
15	E de Graffenried	2	-	-	-	-	-	-	-	2	
	M Ayulo	-	2	-	-	-	-	-	-	2	
	B Ball	-	2	-	-	-	-	-	-	2	
	J McGrath	-	2	-	-	-	-	-	-	2	
	Y Giraud-Cabantous	-	-	2	-	-	-	-	-	2	

8, 6, 4, 3 and 2 points awarded to the first five finishers. The driver setting the fastest lap scored a point also. Points shared for shared drives. Best 4 scores.

With Alfa's withdrawal and BRM's unreliability, race organisers had little option but to turn to the existing F2 category for closer racing. The FIA agreed to move the World Championship to this formula, which at the time consisted of 2 litre unblown and 750cc supercharged. This would provide larger entries and prepare teams for the forthcoming 2.5 litre formula. Ferrari remained favourites, especially as their main opponent, Maserati was weakened by the absence of Fangio, seriously injured at Monza in June.

FERRARI
Scuderia Ferrari: Ascari, Farina, Taruffi, Villoresi, Simon
Ecurie Espadon: R Fischer, Hirt, Schoeller, (Stuck)
Scuderia Marzotto: Carini, Comotti
Ecurie Francorchamps: de Tornaco, Laurent
Ecurie Rosier: Rosier, Trintignant
G Caprara: Salvadori
Privateer: P Whitehead

MASERATI
Officine Alfieri Maserati: Bonetto, Rol, González
Enrico Platé: de Graffenried, Schell, (Crespo)
Escuderia Bandeirantes: Bianco, Cantoni, Landi, Étançelin, Flinterman

CISITALIA
Privateer: (Dusio)

OSCA
Privateer: Bayol

GORDINI
Equipe Gordini: Manzon, Behra, Trintignant, Bira, Claes (B)
Ecurie Belge: Claes, Frère
Alfred Dattner: de Terra
Privateer: O'Brien

ERA
ERA Ltd: Moss

ALTA
Privateers: G Whitehead, P Whitehead

COOPER
Ecurie Richmond: Brandon, Brown
L D Hawthorn: Hawthorn
A H M Bryde: Hawthorn (F), Parnell
Scuderia Franera: Wharton
Ecurie Ecosse: Murray

HWM
HW Motors: Collins, Macklin, Frère, Hamilton, Laurent, Abecassis, Moss, Giraud-Cabantous, Claes, van der Lof
Privateer: Gaze

FRASER NASH
Scuderia Franera: Wharton
Privateer: Crook

ASTON
W S Aston: Aston, Montgomerie-Charrington

CONNAUGHT
Connaught Engineering: McAlpine, Poore, Thompson, Downing, Moss
Privateer: Downing (NL)

VERITAS
Motor-Presse-Verlag: Pietsch
Privateers: Ulmen, Riess, Helfrich, Brudes, Klenk, Peters, Legat

AFM
AFM: Stuck
Privateers: Heeks, Niedermayr, (L Fischer, Krakau)

BMW
Privateers: Balsa, Nacke, Klodwig, Krause, (Merkel)

18 May 1952 — SWITZERLAND: Bremgarten (Round: 1) (Race: 16)
62 laps x 7.280 km, 4.524 miles = 451.360 km, 280.462 miles

POS.	NO	DRIVER	CAR	MODEL	ENGINE		LAPS	TIME/REASON FOR RETIREMENT	GRID:POS	ROW
1	30	P Taruffi	Ferrari	500	Ferrari	4	62	3h 01m 46.100s	2	1
2	42	R Fischer	Ferrari	500	Ferrari	4	62	3h 04m 23.300s	5	2
3	6	J Behra	Gordini	T16	Gordini	6	61		7	3
4	22	K Wharton	Frazer Nash	FN48	Bristol	6	60		13	5
5	26	A Brown	Cooper	T20	Bristol	6	59		15	6
6	38	E de Graffenried	Maserati Platé	4CLT	Maserati Platé	4	58		8	3
7	44	P Hirt	Ferrari	212	Ferrari	V12	56		19	8
8	24	E Brandon	Cooper	T20	Bristol	6	55		17	7
r	10	B Bira	Simca Gordini	T15	Gordini	4	52	engine	11	5
r=	32	A Simon	Ferrari	500	Ferrari	4			4	2
r=	32	G Farina	Ferrari	500	Ferrari	4	51	magneto		
r	40	H Schell	Maserati Platé	4CLT	Maserati Platé	4	31	engine	18	7
r	46	S Moss	HWM	(52)	Alta	4	24	withdrew	9	4
r	20	L Macklin	HWM	(52)	Alta	4	24	withdrew	12	5
r	8	R Manzon	Gordini	T16	Gordini	6	20	cooling damper	3	1
r	28	G Farina	Ferrari	500	Ferrari	4	16	magneto	1	1
r	18	P Collins	HWM	(52)	Alta	4	12	drive shaft/ accident	6	3
r	16	G Abecassis	HWM	(52)	Alta	4	12	drive shaft/ accident	10	4
r	4	T Ulmen	Veritas	Meteor	Veritas	6	4	fuel tank	16	7
r	2	H Stuck	AFM		Küchen	V8	4	piston	14	6
r	12	L Rosier	Ferrari	500	Ferrari	4	2	accident	20	8
r	50	M de Terra	Simca Gordini	T11	Gordini	4	1	magneto	21	9
ns	14	M Trintignant	Ferrari	166	Ferrari	V12		engine		

Winning speed: 148.990 km/h, 92.578 mph
Pole Position speed: 156.466 km/h, 97.223 mph (G Farina, 2 min:47.500 sec)
Fastest Lap speed: 154.985 km/h, 96.303 mph (P Taruffi, 2 min:49.100 sec on lap 46)
Lap Leaders: G Farina 1-16 (16); P Taruffi 17-62 (46).

30 May 1952 — INDIANAPOLIS: 500 (Round: 2) (Race: 17)

200 laps x 4.023 km, 2.500 miles = 804.672 km, 500.000 miles

POS.	NO	DRIVER	CAR	MODEL	ENGINE		LAPS	TIME/REASON FOR RETIREMENT	GRID:POS	ROW
1	98	T Ruttman	Kuzma		Offenhauser	4	200	3h 52m 41.880s	7	3
2	59	J Rathmann	Kurtis Kraft	3000	Offenhauser	4	200	3h 56m 44.209s	10	4
3	18	S Hanks	Kurtis Kraft	3000	Offenhauser	4	200		5	2
4	1	D Carter	Lesovsky		Offenhauser	4	200		6	2
5	33	A Cross	Kurtis Kraft	4000	Offenhauser	4	200		20	7
6	77	J Bryan	Kurtis Kraft	3000	Offenhauser	4	200		21	7
7	37	J Reece	Kurtis Kraft	4000	Offenhauser	4	200		23	8
8	54	G Connor	Kurtis Kraft	3000	Offenhauser	4	200		14	5
9	22	C Griffith	Kurtis Kraft	2000	Offenhauser	4	200		9	3
10	5	J Parsons	Kurtis Kraft		Offenhauser	4	200		31	11
11	4	J McGrath	Kurtis Kraft	3000	Offenhauser	4	200		3	1
12	29	J Rigsby	Watson		Offenhauser	4	200		26	9
13	14	J James	Kurtis Kraft	4000	Offenhauser	4	200		16	6
14	7	B Schindler	Stevens		Offenhauser	4	200		15	5
15	65	G Fonder	Sherman		Offenhauser	4	197		13	5
16	81	E Johnson	Trevis		Offenhauser	4	193		24	8
17r	26	B Vukovich	Kurtis Kraft	500A	Offenhauser	4	191	steering pin/ accident	8	3
18	16	C Stevenson	Kurtis Kraft	4000	Offenhauser	4	187		11	4
19	2	H Banks	Lesovsky		Offenhauser	4	184		12	4
20	8	M Ayulo	Lesovsky		Offenhauser	4	184		28	10
21	31	J McDowell	Kurtis Kraft		Offenhauser	4	182		33	11
22r	48	S Webb	Bromme		Offenhauser	4	162	oil leak	29	10
23r	34	R Ward	Kurtis Kraft	4000	Offenhauser	4	130	oil pressure	22	8
24r	27	T Bettenhausen	Deidt		Offenhauser	4	93	starter	30	10
25r	36	D Nalon	Kurtis Kraft		Novi	8s	84	supercharger shaft	4	2
26r	73	B Sweikert	Kurtis Kraft	2000	Offenhauser	4	77	differential	32	11
27r	28	F Agabashian	Kurtis Kraft		Cummins	6s	71	supercharger clogged	1	1
28r	67	G Hartley	Kurtis Kraft	4000	Offenhauser	4	65	exhaust	18	6
29r	93	B Scott	Kurtis Kraft	2000	Offenhauser	4	49	drive shaft	25	9
30r	21	C Miller	Kurtis Kraft		Novi	8s	41	supercharger shaft	27	9
31r	12	A Ascari	Ferrari	375	Ferrari	V12	40	hub flange/ spin	19	7
32r	55	B Ball	Stevens		Offenhauser	4	34	gear case	17	6
33r	9	A Linden	Kurtis Kraft	4000	Offenhauser	4s	20	oil pump	2	1

Winning speed: 207.481 km/h, 128.922 mph
Pole Position speed: 222.108 km/h, 138.011 mph (F Agabashian, 1 min: 5.212 sec)
Fastest Lap speed: 217.479 km/h, 135.135 mph (B Vukovich, 1 min: 6.600 sec on lap 8)
Fastest qualifier: C Miller (223.754 km/h, 139.034 mph).

22 Jun 1952 — BELGIUM: Spa-Francorchamps (Round: 3) (Race: 18)

36 laps x 14.120 km, 8.774 miles = 508.320 km, 315.855 miles

POS.	NO	DRIVER	CAR	MODEL	ENGINE		LAPS	TIME/REASON FOR RETIREMENT	GRID:POS	ROW
1	4	A Ascari	Ferrari	500	Ferrari	4	36	3h 03m 46.300s	1	1
2	2	G Farina	Ferrari	500	Ferrari	4	36	3h 05m 41.500s	2	1
3	14	R Manzon	Gordini	T16	Gordini	6	36	3h 08m 14.700s	4	2
4	8	M Hawthorn	Cooper	T20	Bristol	6	35		6	3
5	28	P Frère	HWM	(52)	Alta	4	34		8	3
6	10	A Brown	Cooper	T20	Bristol	6	34		9	4
7	34	C de Tornaco	Ferrari	500	Ferrari	4	33		13	5
8	18	J Claes	Gordini	T16S	Gordini	6	33		19	8
9	12	E Brandon	Cooper	T20	Bristol	6	33		12	5
10	20	B Bira	Simca Gordini	T15	Gordini	4	32		18	7
11	24	L Macklin	HWM	(52)	Alta	4	32		14	6
12	30	R Laurent	HWM	(52)	Alta	4	32		20	8
13	38	A Legat	Veritas	Meteor	Veritas	6	31		21	9
14	44	R O'Brien	Simca Gordini	T15	Gordini	4	30		22	9
15	42	T Gaze	HWM	(51)	Alta	4	30		16	7
r	40	R Montgomerie-Charrington	Aston	NB	Butterworth	F4	17	misfire	15	6
r	16	J Behra	Gordini	T16	Gordini	6	13	accident	5	2
r	6	P Taruffi	Ferrari	500	Ferrari	4	13	accident	3	1
r	36	K Wharton	Frazer Nash	FN48	Bristol	6	10	accident	7	3
r	22	L Rosier	Ferrari	500	Ferrari	4	6	transmission	17	7
r	26	P Collins	HWM	(52)	Alta	4	3	drive shaft	11	5
r	32	S Moss	ERA	G	Bristol	6	0	gudgeon pin / accident	10	4

Winning speed: 165.962 km/h, 103.124 mph
Pole Position speed: 183.509 km/h, 114.027 mph (A Ascari, 4 min:37.000 sec)
Fastest Lap speed: 172.312 km/h, 107.070 mph (A Ascari, 4 min:55.000 sec on lap 2 & 7)
Lap Leaders: J Behra 1 (1); A Ascari 2-36 (35).

Also the Grand Prix of Europe.

6 Jul 1952 FRANCE: Rouen-les-Essarts (Round: 4) (Race: 19)

76 laps x 5.100 km, 3.169 miles = 386.874 km, 240.393 miles

POS.	NO	DRIVER	CAR	MODEL	ENGINE		LAPS	TIME/REASON FOR RETIREMENT	GRID:POS	ROW
1	8	A Ascari	Ferrari	500	Ferrari	4	77	3h 00m 00.000s	1	1
2	10	G Farina	Ferrari	500	Ferrari	4	76		2	1
3	12	P Taruffi	Ferrari	500	Ferrari	4	75		3	1
4	2	R Manzon	Gordini	T16	Gordini	6	74		5	2
5	44	M Trintignant	Simca Gordini	T15	Gordini	4	72		6	3
6	22	P Collins	HWM	(52)	Alta	4	70		8	3
7	4	J Behra	Gordini	T16	Gordini	6	70		4	2
8	28	P Étançelin	Maserati	A6GCM	Maserati	6	70		18	7
9	20	L Macklin	HWM	(52)	Alta	4	70		14	6
10	24	Y Giraud-Cabantous	HWM	(52)	Alta	4	68		10	4
11=	34	R Fischer	Ferrari	212	Ferrari	V12			17	7
11=	34	P Hirt	Ferrari	212	Ferrari	V12	66			
12	38	F Comotti	Ferrari	166	Ferrari	V12	63		16	7
r	6	B Bira	Gordini	T16	Gordini	6	56	rear axle	7	3
r	42	M Hawthorn	Cooper	T20	Bristol	6	51	ignition	15	6
r=	16	E de Graffenried	Maserati Platé	4CLT	Maserati Platé	4			12	5
r=	16	H Schell	Maserati Platé	4CLT	Maserati Platé	4	34	brakes		
r	26	P Whitehead	Alta	F2	Alta	4	26	clutch	13	5
r	14	L Rosier	Ferrari	500	Ferrari	4	17	engine	9	4
r	32	J Claes	Simca Gordini	T15	Gordini	4	15	connecting rod	20	8
r	18	H Schell	Maserati Platé	4CLT/48	Maserati Platé	4	7	gearbox	11	5
r	40	P Carini	Ferrari	166	Ferrari	V12	2	cylinder head gasket	19	8

Winning speed: 128.958 km/h, 80.131 mph
Pole Position speed: 136.202 km/h, 84.632 mph (A Ascari, 2 min:14.800 sec)
Fastest Lap speed: 133.722 km/h, 83.091 mph (A Ascari, 2 min:17.300 sec on lap 28)
Lap Leaders: A Ascari 1-76 (76).

Race stopped at 3 hours. Cars on rows 3, 5 and 7 did not line up exactly according to their practice times, those affected being: B Bira (qualified 8), P Collins (7), H Schell (12), E de Graffenried (11), F Comotti (18), P Étançelin (16).

19 Jul 1952 BRITAIN: Silverstone (Round: 5) (Race: 20)

85 laps x 4.711 km, 2.927 miles = 400.397 km, 248.795 miles

POS.	NO	DRIVER	CAR	MODEL	ENGINE		LAPS	TIME/REASON FOR RETIREMENT	GRID:POS	ROW
1	15	A Ascari	Ferrari	500	Ferrari	4	85	2h 44m 11.000s	2	1
2	17	P Taruffi	Ferrari	500	Ferrari	4	84		3	1
3	9	M Hawthorn	Cooper	T20	Bristol	6	83		7	2
4	6	D Poore	Connaught	A	Lea Francis	4	83		8	3
5	5	E Thompson	Connaught	A	Lea Francis	4	82		9	3
6	16	G Farina	Ferrari	500	Ferrari	4	82		1	1
7	8	R Parnell	Cooper	T20	Bristol	6	82		6	2
8	14	R Salvadori	Ferrari	500	Ferrari	4	82		19	6
9	4	K Downing	Connaught	A	Lea Francis	4	82		5	2
10	21	P Whitehead	Ferrari	125	Ferrari	V12	81		20	6
11	26	B Bira	Gordini	T16	Gordini	6	81		10	3
12	1	G Whitehead	Alta	F2	Alta	4	80		12	4
13	19	R Fischer	Ferrari	500	Ferrari	4	80		15	5
14	27	J Claes	Simca Gordini	T15	Gordini	4	79		23	7
15	31	L Macklin	HWM	(52)	Alta	4	79		29	9
16	3	K McAlpine	Connaught	A	Lea Francis	4	79		17	5
17	33	H Schell	Maserati Platé	4CLT	Maserati Platé	4	78		32	9
18	34	G Bianco	Maserati	A6GCM	Maserati	6	77		28	8
19	32	E de Graffenried	Maserati Platé	4CLT	Maserati Platé	4	76		31	9
20	10	E Brandon	Cooper	T20	Bristol	6	76		18	5
21	23	T Crook	Frazer Nash	421	Bristol	6	75		25	7
r	29	P Collins	HWM	(52)	Alta	4	73	misfire	14	4
22	11	A Brown	Cooper	T20	Bristol	6	69		13	4
r	30	D Hamilton	HWM	(52)	Alta	4	44	engine	11	3
r	12	S Moss	ERA	G	Bristol	6	36	cylinder head	16	5
r	25	M Trintignant	Gordini	T16	Gordini	6	21	gearbox	21	6
r	28	T Gaze	HWM	(52)	Alta	4	20	cylinder head gasket	26	8
r	7	D Murray	Cooper	T20	Bristol	6	14	spark plugs	22	7
r	24	R Manzon	Gordini	T16	Gordini	6	9	clutch	4	1
r	20	P Hirt	Ferrari	212	Ferrari	V12	3	brakes	24	7
r	35	E Cantoni	Maserati	A6GCM	Maserati	6	1	brakes	27	8
ns	2	B Aston	Aston	NB	Butterworth	F4		withdrew	30	9

Winning speed: 146.323 km/h, 90.921 mph
Pole Position speed: 154.163 km/h, 95.793 mph (G Farina, 1 min:50.000 sec)
Fastest Lap speed: 151.411 km/h, 94.082 mph (A Ascari, 1 min:52.000 sec on lap 9)
Lap Leaders: A Ascari 1-85 (85).

3 Aug 1952 GERMANY: Nürburgring (Round: 6) (Race: 21)

18 laps x 22.810 km, 14.173 miles = 410.580 km, 255.123 miles

POS.	NO	DRIVER	CAR	MODEL	ENGINE		LAPS	TIME/REASON FOR RETIREMENT	GRID:POS	ROW
1	101	A Ascari	Ferrari	500	Ferrari	4	18	3h 06m 13.300s	1	1
2	102	G Farina	Ferrari	500	Ferrari	4	18	3h 06m 27.400s	2	1
3	117	R Fischer	Ferrari	500	Ferrari	4	18	3h 13m 23.400s	6	2
4	103	P Taruffi	Ferrari	500	Ferrari	4	17		5	2
5	108	J Behra	Gordini	T16	Gordini	6	17		11	3
6	119	R Laurent	Ferrari	500	Ferrari	4	16		17	5
7	121	F Riess	Veritas	RS	Veritas	6	16		12	4
8	125	T Ulmen	Veritas	RS	Veritas	6	16		15	5
9	124	H Niedermayr	AFM		BMW	6	15		22	7
10	113	J Claes	HWM	(52)	Alta	4	15		32	9
11	128	H Klenk	Veritas	Meteor	Veritas	6	14		8	3
12	135	E Klodwig	BMW	Heck	BMW	6	14		29	9
r	107	R Manzon	Gordini	T16	Gordini	6	8	wheel lost	4	1
r	123	W Heeks	AFM		BMW	6	7		9	3
r	120	T Gaze	HWM	(52)	Alta	4	6	gearbox	14	4
r	110	M Balsa	BMW	Speciale	BMW	6	5		25	7
r	126	A Brudes	Veritas	Meteor	Veritas	6	5	engine	19	6
r	130	B Nacke	BMW	Eigenbau	BMW	6	5	spark plugs	30	9
r	116	E Cantoni	Maserati	A6GCM	Maserati	6	4	rear axle	26	8
r	136	R Krause	BMW	Greifzu	BMW	6	3		23	7
r	118	R Schoeller	Ferrari	212	Ferrari	V12	3	suspension	24	7
r	114	B Aston	Aston	NB	Butterworth	F4	2	oil pressure	21	6
r	104	P Carini	Ferrari	166	Ferrari	V12	1	brakes	27	8
r	127	P Pietsch	Veritas	Meteor	Veritas	6	1	gearbox	7	2
r	122	T Helfrich	Veritas	RS	Veritas	6	1		18	5
r	112	P Frère	HWM	(52)	Alta	4	1	de Dion tube	13	4
r	129	J Peters	Veritas	RS	Veritas	6	1		20	6
r	109	M Trintignant	Gordini	T16	Gordini	6	1	gearbox/ accident	3	1
dq	105	F Bonetto	Maserati	A6GCM	Maserati	6	1	push start after spin	10	3
r	115	G Bianco	Maserati	A6GCM	Maserati	6	0		16	5
ns	133	W Krakau	AFM		BMW	6			28	8
ns	131	L Fischer	AFM		BMW	6			31	9
ns	134	H Merkel	BMW	Eigenbau	BMW	6				
ns	111	P Collins	HWM	(52)	Alta	4		crankshaft		

Winning speed: 132.288 km/h, 82.200 mph
Pole Position speed: 135.864 km/h, 84.422 mph (A Ascari, 10 min: 4.400 sec)
Fastest Lap speed: 135.706 km/h, 84.324 mph (A Ascari, 10 min: 5.100 sec on lap 5)
Lap Leaders: A Ascari 1-18 (18).

17 Aug 1952 NETHERLANDS: Zandvoort (Round: 7) (Race: 22)

90 laps x 4.193 km, 2.605 miles = 377.370 km, 234.487 miles

POS.	NO	DRIVER	CAR	MODEL	ENGINE		LAPS	TIME/REASON FOR RETIREMENT	GRID:POS	ROW
1	2	A Ascari	Ferrari	500	Ferrari	4	90	2h 53m 28.500s	1	1
2	4	G Farina	Ferrari	500	Ferrari	4	90	2h 54m 08.600s	2	1
3	6	L Villoresi	Ferrari	500	Ferrari	4	90	2h 55m 02.900s	4	2
4	32	M Hawthorn	Cooper	T20	Bristol	6	88		3	1
5	10	R Manzon	Gordini	T16	Gordini	6	87		8	3
6	12	M Trintignant	Gordini	T16	Gordini	6	87		5	2
7	28	D Hamilton	HWM	(52)	Alta	4	85		10	4
8	26	L Macklin	HWM	(52)	Alta	4	84		9	4
9=	16	C Landi	Maserati	A6GCM	Maserati	6			16	7
9=	16	J Flinterman	Maserati	A6GCM	Maserati	6	83			
r	34	K Wharton	Frazer Nash	421	Bristol	6	76	rear axle	7	3
r	36	S Moss	ERA	G	Bristol	6	73	engine	18	7
nc	30	D van der Lof	HWM	(52)	Alta	4	70		14	6
r	22	K Downing	Connaught	A	Lea Francis	4	27	oil pressure	13	5
r	24	C de Tornaco	Ferrari	500	Ferrari	4	19	valve	17	7
r	14	P Frère	Simca Gordini	T15	Gordini	4	15	gearbox/ clutch	11	5
r	8	J Behra	Gordini	T16	Gordini	6	10	carburettor	6	3
r	20	J Flinterman	Maserati	A6GCM	Maserati	6	7	differential	15	6
r	18	G Bianco	Maserati	A6GCM	Maserati	6	4	rear axle	12	5

Winning speed: 130.521 km/h, 81.102 mph
Pole Position speed: 141.735 km/h, 88.070 mph (A Ascari, 1 min:46.500 sec)
Fastest Lap speed: 137.475 km/h, 85.423 mph (A Ascari, 1 min:49.800 sec on lap 89)
Lap Leaders: A Ascari 1-90 (90).

7 Sep 1952 — ITALY: Monza (Round: 8) (Race: 23)

80 laps x 6.300 km, 3.915 miles = 504.000 km, 313.171 miles

POS.	NO	DRIVER	CAR	MODEL	ENGINE		LAPS	TIME/REASON FOR RETIREMENT	GRID:POS	ROW
1	12	A Ascari	Ferrari	500	Ferrari	4	80	2h 50m 45.600s	1	1
2	26	F González	Maserati	A6GCM	Maserati	6	80	2h 51m 47.400s	5	2
3	16	L Villoresi	Ferrari	500	Ferrari	4	80	2h 52m 49.800s	2	1
4	10	G Farina	Ferrari	500	Ferrari	4	80	2h 52m 57.000s	3	1
5	22	F Bonetto	Maserati	A6GCM	Maserati	6	79		13	4
6	8	A Simon	Ferrari	500	Ferrari	4	79		8	2
7	14	P Taruffi	Ferrari	500	Ferrari	4	77		6	2
8	48	C Landi	Maserati	A6GCM	Maserati	6	76		18	5
9	40	K Wharton	Cooper	T20	Bristol	6	76		15	4
10	62	L Rosier	Ferrari	500	Ferrari	4	75		17	5
11	50	E Cantoni	Maserati	A6GCM	Maserati	6	75		23	6
12	30	D Poore	Connaught	A	Lea Francis	4	74		19	5
13	36	E Brandon	Cooper	T20	Bristol	6	73		20	5
14	2	R Manzon	Gordini	T16	Gordini	6	71		7	2
15	38	A Brown	Cooper	T20	Bristol	6	68		21	6
r	32	S Moss	Connaught	A	Lea Francis	4	60	push rod	9	3
r	46	G Bianco	Maserati	A6GCM	Maserati	6	46	engine	24	6
r	6	J Behra	Gordini	T16	Gordini	6	42	valve	11	3
nc	42	M Hawthorn	Cooper	T20	Bristol	6	38		12	3
r	24	F Rol	Maserati	A6GCM	Maserati	6	24	engine	16	4
r	4	M Trintignant	Gordini	T16	Gordini	6	5	valve gear	4	1
r	28	K McAlpine	Connaught	A	Lea Francis	4	4	rear suspension	22	6
r	18	R Fischer	Ferrari	500	Ferrari	4	3	engine	14	4
r	34	É Bayol	OSCA	20	OSCA	6	0	gearbox	10	3
nq	70	C de Tornaco	Ferrari	500	Ferrari	4				
nq	58	A Crespo	Maserati Platé	4CLT	Maserati Platé	4				
nq	60	E de Graffenried	Maserati Platé	4CLT	Maserati Platé	4				
nq	54	P Collins	HWM	(52)	Alta	4				
nq	68	P Whitehead	Ferrari	125	Ferrari	V12				
nq	56	T Gaze	HWM	(52)	Alta	4				
nq	64	B Aston	Aston	NB	Butterworth	F4				
nq	52	L Macklin	HWM	(52)	Alta	4				
nq	20	H Stuck	Ferrari	212	Ferrari	V12				
nq	66	J Claes	Simca Gordini	T15	Gordini	4				
nq	44	P Dusio	Cisitalia	D46	BPM					

Winning speed: 177.091 km/h, 110.039 mph
Pole Position speed: 180.430 km/h, 112.114 mph (A Ascari, 2 min: 5.700 sec)
Fastest Lap speed: 179.857 km/h, 111.758 mph (A Ascari/ F González, 2 min: 6.100 sec on lap 56 / 57 & 60)
Lap Leaders: F González 1-36 (36); A Ascari 37-80 (44).

Lap Leaders 1952

POS	DRIVER	CAR-ENGINE	GPS	LAPS	KM	MILES
1	A Ascari	Ferrari	6	348	2,347.4	1,458.6
2	P Taruffi	Ferrari	1	46	334.9	208.1
3	F González	Maserati	1	36	226.8	140.9
4	G Farina	Ferrari	1	16	116.5	72.4
5	J Behra	Gordini	1	1	14.1	8.8
			7	447	3,039.7	1,888.8

Driver Points 1952

		CH	INDY	B	F	GB	D	NL	I	TOTAL	
1	A Ascari	-	-	9	9	9	9	(9)	(8.5)	36	(17.5)
2	G Farina	-	-	6	6	-	6	6	(3)	24	(3)
3	P Taruffi	9	-	-	4	6	3	-	-	22	
4	R Fischer	6	-	-	-	-	4	-	-	10	
	M Hawthorn	-	-	3	-	4	-	3	-	10	
6	R Manzon	-	-	4	3	-	-	2	-	9	
7	T Ruttman	-	8	-	-	-	-	-	-	8	
	L Villoresi	-	-	-	-	-	-	4	4	8	
9	F González	-	-	-	-	-	-	-	6.5	6.5	
10	J Rathmann	-	6	-	-	-	-	-	-	6	
	J Behra	4	-	-	-	-	2	-	-	6	
12	S Hanks	-	4	-	-	-	-	-	-	4	
13	K Wharton	3	-	-	-	-	-	-	-	3	
	D Carter	-	3	-	-	-	-	-	-	3	
	D Poore	-	-	-	-	3	-	-	-	3	
16	A Brown	2	-	-	-	-	-	-	-	2	
	A Cross	-	2	-	-	-	-	-	-	2	
	P Frère	-	-	2	-	-	-	-	-	2	
	M Trintignant	-	-	-	2	-	-	-	-	2	
	E Thompson	-	-	-	-	2	-	-	-	2	
	F Bonetto	-	-	-	-	-	-	-	2	2	
20	B Vukovich	-	1	-	-	-	-	-	-	1	

8, 6, 4, 3 and 2 points awarded to the first five finishers. The driver setting the fastest lap scored A point also. Points shared for shared drives. Best 4 scores.

The second year of the Formula 2 World Championship continued with Ferrari setting the pace, although Maserati produced a revised version of their car and Fangio was back as team leader. During the two year period of this stop-gap formula there wasn't a single world championship entry based on the 750cc supercharged category.

FERRARI
Scuderia Ferrari: Ascari, Farina, Villoresi, Hawthorn, Maglioli, Carini
Ecurie Espadon: Adolff, Hirt, de Terra
Ecurie Francorchamps: Swaters, (de Tornaco)
Ecurie Rosier: Rosier

MASERATI
Officine Alfieri Maserati: Fangio, Bonetto, González, Marimón, Gálvez, Claes, Lang, Mantovani, Musso
Scuderia Milano: Landi, Bira
Privateers: de Graffenried, Landi (CH)

OSCA
Privateers: Chiron, Bayol

GORDINI
Equipe Gordini: Behra, Trintignant, Schell, Manzon, Mières, Menditéguy, Birger, Wacker
Privateer: Berger

COOPER
Cooper Car Co: Moss, Wharton (GB), Brown (RA), Barber, Schwelm Cruz
Equipe Anglaise: Brown, (Glöckler)
RJ Chase: Brown (GB)
Atlantic Stable: Whitehead
Ecurie Ecosse: J Stewart
Privateers: Wharton, Gerard, Crook, Nuckey

HWM
HW Motors: Macklin, Collins, Frère, Giraud-Cabantous,
Hamilton, Fairman, Scherrer, Fitch

CONNAUGHT
Connaught Engineering: McAlpine, Salvadori, Bira, Moss, Fairman
Ecurie Belge: Claes, Pilette
R RC Walker Racing Team: Rolt
Ecurie Ecosse: I Stewart

VERITAS
H Klenk: Herrmann
Privateers: Seidel, Heeks, Helfrich, Karch, Loof, Bauer, Legat

AFM
H Niedermayr: Fitzau
Privateers: Stuck, Bechem

BMW
Dora Greifzu: Krause
Privateer: Klodwig

EMW
EMW Rennkollectiv: Barth

18 Jan 1953 — ARGENTINA: Buenos Aires No.2 (Round: 1) (Race: 24)
97 laps x 3.912 km, 2.431 miles = 379.464 km, 235.788 miles

POS.	NO	DRIVER	CAR	MODEL	ENGINE		LAPS	TIME/REASON FOR RETIREMENT	GRID:POS	ROW
1	10	A Ascari	Ferrari	500	Ferrari	4	97	3h 01m 04.600s	1	1
2	14	L Villoresi	Ferrari	500	Ferrari	4	96		3	1
3	4	F González	Maserati	A6GCM	Maserati	6	96		5	2
4	16	M Hawthorn	Ferrari	500	Ferrari	4	96		6	2
5	8	O Gálvez	Maserati	A6GCM	Maserati	6	96		9	3
6	30	J Behra	Gordini	T16	Gordini	6	94		11	3
7=	28	M Trintignant	Gordini	T16	Gordini	6			7	2
7=	28	H Schell	Gordini	T16	Gordini	6	91			
8	22	J Barber	Cooper	T23	Bristol	6	90		16	5
9	20	A Brown	Cooper	T20	Bristol	6	87		12	4
r	26	R Manzon	Gordini	T16	Gordini	6	67	wheel lost	8	3
r	2	J M Fangio	Maserati	A6GCM	Maserati	6	36	propellor shaft	2	1
r	6	F Bonetto	Maserati	A6GCM	Maserati	6	31	transmission	15	5
r	12	G Farina	Ferrari	500	Ferrari	4	30	accident (spectator killed)	4	1
r	32	C Menditéguy	Gordini	T16	Gordini	6	24	gearbox	10	3
r	34	P Birger	Simca Gordini	T15	Gordini	4	21	crown wheel & pinion	14	4
r	24	A Schwelm Cruz	Cooper	T20	Bristol	6	20	wheel lost	13	4

Winning speed: 125.736 km/h, 78.129 mph
Pole Position speed: 122.038 km/h, 75.831 mph (A Ascari, 1 min:55.400 sec)
Fastest Lap speed: 129.919 km/h, 80.728 mph (A Ascari, 1 min:48.400 sec)
Lap Leaders: A Ascari 1-97 (97).

Connaught A-T in the pits (No. Bira, No.50: Salvadori, No.48: Claes). Reims, France, 1953.

30 May 1953 — INDIANAPOLIS: 500 (Round: 2) (Race: 25)

200 laps x 4.023 km, 2.500 miles = 804.672 km, 500.000 miles

POS.	NO	DRIVER	CAR	MODEL	ENGINE		LAPS	TIME/REASON FOR RETIREMENT	GRID:POS	ROW
1	14	B Vukovich	Kurtis Kraft	500A	Offenhauser	4	200	3h 53m 01.690s	1	1
2	16	A Cross	Kurtis Kraft	4000	Offenhauser	4	200	3h 56m 32.562s	12	4
3=	3	S Hanks	Kurtis Kraft	4000	Offenhauser	4			9	3
3=	3	D Carter	Kurtis Kraft	4000	Offenhauser	4	200			
4=	59	F Agabashian	Kurtis Kraft	500B	Offenhauser	4			2	1
4=	59	P Russo	Kurtis Kraft	500B	Offenhauser	4	200			
5	5	J McGrath	Kurtis Kraft	4000	Offenhauser	4	200		3	1
6	48	J Daywalt	Kurtis Kraft	3000	Offenhauser	4	200		21	7
7=	2	J Rathmann	Kurtis Kraft	500B	Offenhauser	4			25	9
7=	2	E Johnson	Kurtis Kraft	500B	Offenhauser	4	200			
8	12	E McCoy	Stevens		Offenhauser	4	200		20	7
9r=	98	T Bettenhausen	Kuzma		Offenhauser	4			6	2
9r=	98	C Stevenson	Kuzma		Offenhauser	4				
9r=	98	G Hartley	Kuzma		Offenhauser	4	196	axle/ accident		
10	53	J Davies	Kurtis Kraft	500B	Offenhauser	4	193		32	11
11r	9	D Nalon	Kurtis Kraft		Novi	8s	191	spin avoiding Bettenhausen	26	9
12=	73	C Scarborough	Kurtis Kraft	2000	Offenhauser	4		(died later of heat exhaustion)	19	7
12=	73	B Scott	Kurtis Kraft	2000	Offenhauser	4	190			
13r	88	M Ayulo	Kuzma		Offenhauser	4	184	connecting rod	4	2
14	8	J Bryan	Schroeder		Offenhauser	4	183		31	11
15r=	49	B Holland	Kurtis Kraft	500B	Offenhauser	4			28	10
15r=	49	J Rathmann	Kurtis Kraft	500B	Offenhauser	4	177	cam gear		
16r=	92	R Ward	Kurtis Kraft		Offenhauser	4	177	rear axle	10	4
16r=	92	A Linden	Kurtis Kraft		Offenhauser	4				
16r=	92	D Dinsmore	Kurtis Kraft		Offenhauser	4				
17=	23	w Faulkner	Kurtis Kraft	500A	Offenhauser	4			14	5
17=	23	J Mantz	Kurtis Kraft	500A	Offenhauser	4	176			
18r	22	M Teague	Kurtis Kraft	4000	Offenhauser	4	169	oil leak	22	8
19r=	62	S Webb	Kurtis Kraft	3000	Offenhauser	4			18	6
19r=	62	J Thomson	Kurtis Kraft	3000	Offenhauser	4				
19r=	62	J Holmes	Kurtis Kraft	3000	Offenhauser	4	166	oil leak		
20r	51	B Sweikert	Kuzma		Offenhauser	4	151	suspension radius rod	29	10
21r	83	M Nazaruk	Turner		Offenhauser	4	146	stalled	23	8
22r	77	P Flaherty	Kurtis Kraft	3000	Offenhauser	4	115	accident	24	8
23r=	55	J Hoyt	Kurtis Kraft	4000	Offenhauser	4			7	3
23r=	55	C Stevenson	Kurtis Kraft	4000	Offenhauser	4				
23r=	55	A Linden	Kurtis Kraft	4000	Offenhauser	4	107	cockpit too hot		
24r	4	D Carter	Lesovsky		Offenhauser	4	94	ignition	27	9
25r	7	P Russo	Kurtis Kraft	3000	Offenhauser	4	89	magneto	17	6
26r	21	J Parsons	Kurtis Kraft	500B	Offenhauser	4	86	crankshaft	8	3
27r	38	D Freeland	Watson		Offenhauser	4	76	accident	15	5
28r	41	G Hartley	Kurtis Kraft	4000	Offenhauser	4	53	accident	13	5
29r	97	C Stevenson	Kuzma		Offenhauser	4	42	fuel leak	16	6
30r	99	C Niday	Kurtis Kraft		Offenhauser	4	30	magneto	30	10
31r	29	B Scott	Bromme		Offenhauser	4	14	oil leak	11	4
32r	56	J Thomson	Del Roy		Offenhauser	4	6	ignition	33	11
33r	32	A Linden	Stevens		Offenhauser	4	3	accident	5	2

Winning speed: 207.187 km/h, 128.740 mph
Pole Position speed: 222.723 km/h, 138.393 mph (B Vukovich, 1 min: 5.032 sec)
Fastest Lap speed: 218.661 km/h, 135.870 mph (B Vukovich, 1 min: 6.240 sec on lap 27)

7 Jun 1953 — NETHERLANDS: Zandvoort (Round: 3) (Race: 26)

90 laps x 4.193 km, 2.605 miles = 377.370 km, 234.487 miles

POS.	NO	DRIVER	CAR	MODEL	ENGINE		LAPS	TIME/REASON FOR RETIREMENT	GRID:POS	ROW
1	2	A Ascari	Ferrari	500	Ferrari	4	90	2h 53m 35.800s	1	1
2	6	G Farina	Ferrari	500	Ferrari	4	90	2h 53m 46.200s	3	1
3=	16	F Bonetto	Maserati	A6GCM	Maserati	6			13	5
3=	16	F González	Maserati	A6GCM	Maserati	6	89			
4	8	M Hawthorn	Ferrari	500	Ferrari	4	89		6	3
5	18	E de Graffenried	Maserati	A6GCM	Maserati	6	88		7	3
6	24	M Trintignant	Gordini	T16	Gordini	6	87		12	5
7	10	L Rosier	Ferrari	500	Ferrari	4	86		8	3
8	36	P Collins	HWM	(53)	Alta	4	84		16	7
9	34	S Moss	Connaught	A	Lea Francis	4	83		9	4
r	4	L Villoresi	Ferrari	500	Ferrari	4	67	throttle control	4	2
r	28	K McAlpine	Connaught	A	Lea Francis	4	63	engine	14	6
r	20	H Schell	Gordini	T16	Gordini	6	59	transmission	10	4
nc	30	J Claes	Connaught	A	Lea Francis	4	52		17	7
r	12	J M Fangio	Maserati	A6GCM	Maserati	6	36	rear axle	2	1
r	22	R Mières	Gordini	T16	Gordini	6	28	transmission	19	8
r	14	F González	Maserati	A6GCM	Maserati	6	22	rear axle	5	2
r	32	K Wharton	Cooper	T23	Bristol	6	19	rear suspension	18	7
r	26	R Salvadori	Connaught	A	Lea Francis	4	14	valves	11	5
r	38	L Macklin	HWM	(53)	Alta	4	7	throttle control	15	6
ns	40	F Wacker	Gordini	T16	Gordini	6		engine used by Schell		

Winning speed: 130.430 km/h, 81.045 mph
Pole Position speed: 135.867 km/h, 84.424 mph (A Ascari, 1 min:51.100 sec)
Fastest Lap speed: 133.819 km/h, 83.151 mph (G Villoresi, 1 min:52.800 sec on lap 59)
Lap Leaders: A Ascari 1-90 (90).

21 Jun 1953 BELGIUM: Spa-Francorchamps (Round: 4) (Race: 27)

36 laps x 14.120 km, 8.774 miles = 508.320 km, 315.855 miles

POS.	NO	DRIVER	CAR	MODEL	ENGINE		LAPS	TIME/REASON FOR RETIREMENT	GRID:POS	ROW
1	10	A Ascari	Ferrari	500	Ferrari	4	36	2h 48m 30.300s	2	1
2	8	L Villoresi	Ferrari	500	Ferrari	4	36	2h 51m 18.500s	5	2
r=	6	J Claes	Maserati	A6GCM	Maserati	6			10	4
r=	6	J M Fangio	Maserati	A6GCM	Maserati	6	35	steering/ accident		
3	28	O Marimón	Maserati	A6GCM	Maserati	6	35		6	3
4	30	E de Graffenried	Maserati	A6GCM	Maserati	6	35		9	4
5	18	M Trintignant	Gordini	T16	Gordini	6	35		8	3
6	14	M Hawthorn	Ferrari	500	Ferrari	4	35		7	3
7	20	H Schell	Gordini	T16	Gordini	6	33		12	5
8	32	L Rosier	Ferrari	500	Ferrari	4	33		13	5
9	38	F Wacker	Gordini	T16	Gordini	6	32		15	6
10	24	P Frère	HWM	(53)	Alta	4	30		11	5
11	40	A Pilette	Connaught	A	Lea Francis	4	29		18	7
r	22	L Macklin	HWM	(53)	Alta	4	19	engine	17	7
r	12	G Farina	Ferrari	500	Ferrari	4	16	engine	4	2
r	4	J M Fangio	Maserati	A6GCM	Maserati	6	13	engine	1	1
r	2	F González	Maserati	A6GCM	Maserati	6	11	throttle	3	1
r	16	J Behra	Gordini	T16	Gordini	6	9	cylinder head gasket	14	6
r	26	P Collins	HWM	(53)	Alta	4	4	clutch	16	7
r	34	G Berger	Simca Gordini	T15	Gordini	4	3	engine	20	8
r	36	A Legat	Veritas	Meteor	Veritas	6	0	transmission	19	8
ns	42	J Swaters	Ferrari	500	Ferrari	4		withdrew		
ns	44	C de Tornaco	Ferrari	500	Ferrari	4		withdrew		

Winning speed: 180.999 km/h, 112.467 mph
Pole Position speed: 188.267 km/h, 116.983 mph (J M Fangio, 4 min:30.000 sec)
Fastest Lap speed: 185.518 km/h, 115.276 mph (F González, 4 min:34.000 sec on lap 2, 3, 9 & 11)
Lap Leaders: F González 1-11 (11); J M Fangio 12-13 (2); A Ascari 14-36 (23).

5 Jul 1953 FRANCE: Reims (Round: 5) (Race: 28)

60 laps x 8.347 km, 5.187 miles = 500.820 km, 311.195 miles

POS.	NO	DRIVER	CAR	MODEL	ENGINE		LAPS	TIME/REASON FOR RETIREMENT	GRID:POS	ROW
1	16	M Hawthorn	Ferrari	500	Ferrari	4	60	2h 44m 18.600s	7	3
2	18	JM Fangio	Maserati	A6GCM	Maserati	6	60	2h 44m 19.600s	4	2
3	20	F González	Maserati	A6GCM	Maserati	6	60	2h 44m 20.000s	5	2
4	10	A Ascari	Ferrari	500	Ferrari	4	60	2h 44m 23.200s	1	1
5	14	G Farina	Ferrari	500	Ferrari	4	60	2h 45m 26.200s	6	3
6	12	L Villoresi	Ferrari	500	Ferrari	4	60	2h 45m 34.500s	3	1
7	46	E de Graffenried	Maserati	A6GCM	Maserati	6	58		9	4
8	44	L Rosier	Ferrari	500	Ferrari	4	56		10	4
9	22	O Marimón	Maserati	A6GCM	Maserati	6	55		8	3
10	2	J Behra	Gordini	T16	Gordini	6	55		22	9
11	38	B Gerard	Cooper	T23	Bristol	6	55		12	5
12	48	J Claes	Connaught	A	Lea Francis	4	53		21	9
13	28	P Collins	HWM	(53)	Alta	4	52		17	7
14	30	Y Giraud-Cabantous	HWM	(53)	Alta	4	50		18	7
15	32	L Chiron	OSCA	20	OSCA	6	43		25	10
r	24	F Bonetto	Maserati	A6GCM	Maserati	6	42	engine	2	1
r	36	S Moss	Cooper	Spl.	Alta	4	38	clutch	13	5
r	42	B Bira	Connaught	A	Lea Francis	4	29	differential	11	5
r	34	É Bayol	OSCA	20	OSCA	6	18	engine	15	6
r	40	K Wharton	Cooper	T23	Bristol	6	17	bearings	14	6
r	4	M Trintignant	Gordini	T16	Gordini	6	14	transmission	23	9
r	26	L Macklin	HWM	(53)	Alta	4	9	clutch	16	7
r	8	R Mières	Gordini	T16	Gordini	6	4	rear axle	24	10
r	6	H Schell	Gordini	T16	Gordini	6	4	connecting rod	20	8
r	50	R Salvadori	Connaught	A	Lea Francis	4	2	ignition	19	8

Winning speed: 182.881 km/h, 113.637 mph
Pole Position speed: 186.409 km/h, 115.829 mph (A Ascari, 2 min:41.200 sec)
Fastest Lap speed: 186.525 km/h, 115.901 mph (J M Fangio/ A Ascari, 2 min:41.100 sec on lap 25 / 37)
Lap Leaders: F González 1-29 (29); J M Fangio 30-31,35-36,39-41,45-47,49-53,55-56 (17); M Hawthorn 32-34,37-38,42-44,48,54,57-60 (14).

18 Jul 1953 — BRITAIN: Silverstone (Round: 6) (Race: 29)

90 laps x 4.711 km, 2.927 miles = 423.949 km, 263.430 miles

POS.	NO	DRIVER	CAR	MODEL	ENGINE		LAPS	TIME/REASON FOR RETIREMENT	GRID:POS	ROW
1	5	A Ascari	Ferrari	500	Ferrari	4	90	2h 50m 00.000s	1	1
2	23	J M Fangio	Maserati	A6GCM	Maserati	6	90	2h 51m 00.000s	4	1
3	6	G Farina	Ferrari	500	Ferrari	4	88		5	2
4	24	F González	Maserati	A6GCM	Maserati	6	88		2	1
5	8	M Hawthorn	Ferrari	500	Ferrari	4	87		3	1
6	25	F Bonetto	Maserati	A6GCM	Maserati	6	82		16	5
7	10	B Bira	Connaught	A	Lea Francis	4	82		19	6
8	16	K Wharton	Cooper	T23	Bristol	6	80		11	3
r	18	J Stewart	Cooper	T20	Bristol	6	79	accident	15	5
9	20	P Whitehead	Cooper	T24	Alta	4	79		14	4
10	9	L Rosier	Ferrari	500	Ferrari	4	78		24	7
r	14	T Rolt	Connaught	A	Lea Francis	4	71	half shaft	10	3
r	7	L Villoresi	Ferrari	500	Ferrari	4	67	rear axle	6	2
r	26	O Marimón	Maserati	A6GCM	Maserati	6	67	engine	7	2
r	2	P Collins	HWM	(53)	Alta	4	56	accident	23	7
r	19	A Brown	Cooper	T23	Bristol	6	56	fan belt	21	6
r	4	J Fairman	HWM	(53)	Alta	4	54	clutch	27	8
r	12	R Salvadori	Connaught	A	Lea Francis	4	50	suspension radius rod	28	8
r	31	E de Graffenried	Maserati	A6GCM	Maserati	6	34	clutch	26	8
r	1	L Macklin	HWM	(53)	Alta	4	31	clutch	12	4
r	30	J Behra	Gordini	T16	Gordini	6	30	fuel pump	22	7
r	15	I Stewart	Connaught	A	Lea Francis	4	26	engine	20	6
r	29	M Trintignant	Gordini	T16	Gordini	6	15	rear axle	8	3
r	3	D Hamilton	HWM	(53)	Alta	4	14	clutch	17	5
r	17	B Gerard	Cooper	T23	Bristol	6	8	front suspension	18	5
r	28	H Schell	Gordini	T16	Gordini	6	5	magneto	9	3
r	22	T Crook	Cooper	T20	Bristol	6	0	fuel injection	25	7
r	11	K McAlpine	Connaught	A	Lea Francis	4	0	split hose	13	4
ns	27	L Chiron	OSCA	20	OSCA	6				

Winning speed: 149.629 km/h, 92.975 mph
Pole Position speed: 157.018 km/h, 97.567 mph (A Ascari, 1 min:48.000 sec)
Fastest Lap speed: 154.163 km/h, 95.793 mph (A Ascari/ F González, 1 min:50.000 sec)
Lap Leaders: A Ascari 1-90 (90).

2 Aug 1953 — GERMANY: Nürburgring (Round: 7) (Race: 30)

18 laps x 22.810 km, 14.173 miles = 410.580 km, 255.123 miles

POS.	NO	DRIVER	CAR	MODEL	ENGINE		LAPS	TIME/REASON FOR RETIREMENT	GRID:POS	ROW
1	2	G Farina	Ferrari	500	Ferrari	4	18	3h 02m 25.000s	3	1
2	5	J M Fangio	Maserati	A6GCM	Maserati	6	18	3h 03m 29.000s	2	1
3	3	M Hawthorn	Ferrari	500	Ferrari	4	18	3h 04m 08.600s	4	1
4	7	F Bonetto	Maserati	A6GCM	Maserati	6	18	3h 11m 13.600s	7	2
5	17	E de Graffenried	Maserati	A6GCM	Maserati	6	17		11	3
6	19	S Moss	Cooper	T23	Alta	4	17		12	4
7	18	J Swaters	Ferrari	500	Ferrari	4	17		19	6
8=	1	A Ascari	Ferrari	500	Ferrari	4			1	1
8=	1	L Villoresi	Ferrari	500	Ferrari	4	17			
9	31	H Herrmann	Veritas	Meteor	Veritas	6	17		14	4
10	20	L Rosier	Ferrari	500	Ferrari	4	17		22	7
11	40	R Nuckey	Cooper	T23	Bristol	6	16		20	6
12	24	T Helfrich	Veritas	RS	Veritas	6	16		28	8
13	16	K McAlpine	Connaught	A	Lea Francis	4	16		16	5
14	36	R Krause	BMW	Greifzu	BMW	6	16		26	8
r=	4	L Villoresi	Ferrari	500	Ferrari	4			6	2
r=	4	A Ascari	Ferrari	500	Ferrari	4	15	engine		
r	38	A Brown	Cooper	T23	Bristol	6	15	misfire/ accident	17	5
15	37	E Klodwig	BMW	Heck	BMW	6	15		32	9
16	22	W Seidel	Veritas	RS	Veritas	6	14		29	9
r	8	O Marimón	Maserati	A6GCM	Maserati	6	13	suspension	8	3
r	12	J Claes	Connaught	A	Lea Francis	4	12		25	7
r	35	E Barth	EMW		EMW	6	12	exhaust	24	7
r	26	O Karch	Veritas	RS	Veritas	6	10		34	10
r	23	W Heeks	Veritas	Meteor	Veritas	6	8		18	5
r	9	J Behra	Gordini	T16	Gordini	6	7	gearbox	9	3
r	11	H Schell	Gordini	T16	Gordini	6	6	cylinder head gasket	10	3
r	14	B Bira	Connaught	A	Lea Francis	4	6	rocker	15	5
r	28	T Fitzau	AFM		BMW	6	3		21	6
r	34	K Adolff	Ferrari	166	Ferrari	V12	3		27	8
r	41	G Bechem	AFM		BMW	6	2		30	9
r	15	R Salvadori	Connaught	A	Lea Francis	4	1	rocker	13	4
r	32	E Bauer	Veritas	RS	Veritas	6	1		33	10
r	10	M Trintignant	Gordini	T16	Gordini	6	1	differential	5	2
r	21	H Stuck	AFM		Bristol	6	0		23	7
r	30	E Loof	Veritas	Meteor	Veritas	6	0	fuel pump	31	9
ns	39	H Glöckler	Cooper	T23	Bristol	6		engine		

Winning speed: 135.047 km/h, 83.914 mph
Pole Position speed: 136.906 km/h, 85.069 mph (A Ascari, 9 min:59.800 sec)
Fastest Lap speed: 137.779 km/h, 85.612 mph (A Ascari, 9 min:56.000 sec on lap 12)
Lap Leaders: A Ascari 1-4 (4); M Hawthorn 5-7 (3); G Farina 8-18 (11).

23 Aug 1953 — SWITZERLAND: Bremgarten (Round: 8) (Race: 31)

65 laps x 7.280 km, 4.524 miles = 473.200 km, 294.033 miles

POS.	NO	DRIVER	CAR	MODEL	ENGINE		LAPS	TIME/REASON FOR RETIREMENT	GRID:POS	ROW
1	46	A Ascari	Ferrari	500	Ferrari	4	65	3h 01m 34.400s	2	1
2	24	G Farina	Ferrari	500	Ferrari	4	65	3h 02m 47.330s	3	1
3	26	M Hawthorn	Ferrari	500	Ferrari	4	65	3h 03m 10.360s	7	3
4=	32	J M Fangio	Maserati	A6GCM	Maserati	6			1	1
4=	32	F Bonetto	Maserati	A6GCM	Maserati	6	64			
5	34	H Lang	Maserati	A6GCM	Maserati	6	62		11	5
6	28	L Villoresi	Ferrari	500	Ferrari	4	62		6	3
7	20	K Wharton	Cooper	T23	Bristol	6	62		9	4
r	4	C Landi	Maserati	A6GCM	Maserati	6	54	gearbox	20	8
8	40	M de Terra	Ferrari	166	Ferrari	V12	51		19	8
9	18	A Scherrer	HWM	(53)	Alta	4	49		18	7
r	42	E de Graffenried	Maserati	A6GCM	Maserati	6	48	camshaft	8	3
r	36	O Marimón	Maserati	A6GCM	Maserati	6	46	oil line	5	2
r	8	M Trintignant	Gordini	T16	Gordini	6	43	rear axle	4	2
r	6	J Behra	Gordini	T16	Gordini	6	37	oil pressure	12	5
r=	30	F Bonetto	Maserati	A6GCM	Maserati	6			10	4
r=	30	J M Fangio	Maserati	A6GCM	Maserati	6	29	valve		
r	16	L Macklin	HWM	(53)	Alta	4	29	valve	15	6
r	38	P Hirt	Ferrari	500	Ferrari	4	17	oil loss	17	7
r	14	P Frère	HWM	(53)	Alta	4	1	connecting rod	16	7
r	10	L Rosier	Ferrari	500	Ferrari	4	0	accident	14	6
r	2	J Swaters	Ferrari	500	Ferrari	4	0	accident	13	5
ns	12	L Chiron	OSCA	20	OSCA	6				
ns	22	É Bayol	OSCA	20	OSCA	6				
ns	44	F Wacker	Gordini	T16	Gordini	6		accident/ injury		

Winning speed: 156.367 km/h, 97.162 mph
Pole Position speed: 163.698 km/h, 101.717 mph (J M Fangio, 2 min:40.100 sec)
Fastest Lap speed: 162.480 km/h, 100.960 mph (A Ascari, 2 min:41.300 sec on lap 50)
Lap Leaders: A Ascari 1-40,54-65 (52); G Farina 41-53 (13).

13 Sep 1953 — ITALY: Monza (Round: 9) (Race: 32)

80 laps x 6.300 km, 3.915 miles = 504.000 km, 313.171 miles

POS.	NO	DRIVER	CAR	MODEL	ENGINE		LAPS	TIME/REASON FOR RETIREMENT	GRID:POS	ROW
1	50	J M Fangio	Maserati	A6GCM	Maserati	6	80	2h 49m 45.900s	2	1
2	6	G Farina	Ferrari	500	Ferrari	4	80	2h 49m 47.300s	3	1
r	4	A Ascari	Ferrari	500	Ferrari	4	79	accident	1	1
3	2	L Villoresi	Ferrari	500	Ferrari	4	79		5	2
4	8	M Hawthorn	Ferrari	500	Ferrari	4	79		6	2
5	36	M Trintignant	Gordini	T16	Gordini	6	79		8	3
r	52	F Bonetto	Maserati	A6GCM	Maserati	6	77	out of fuel	7	3
6	40	R Mières	Gordini	T16	Gordini	6	77		16	6
7=	56	S Mantovani	Maserati	A6GCM	Maserati	6			12	4
7=	56	L Musso	Maserati	A6GCM	Maserati	6	76			
r	54	O Marimón	Maserati	A6GCM	Maserati	6	75	accident	4	2
8	10	U Maglioli	Ferrari	553	Ferrari	4	75		11	4
9	38	H Schell	Gordini	T16	Gordini	6	75		15	5
10	32	L Chiron	OSCA	20	OSCA	6	72		25	9
11	44	B Bira	Maserati	A6GCM	Maserati	6	72		23	8
r	58	E de Graffenried	Maserati	A6GCM	Maserati	6	70	engine	9	3
12	46	A Brown	Cooper	T23	Bristol	6	70		24	8
13	28	S Moss	Cooper	T23	Alta	4	70		10	4
14	48	H Stuck	AFM		Bristol	6	67		29	10
15	16	Y Giraud-Cabantous	HWM	(53)	Alta	4	67		28	10
16	64	L Rosier	Ferrari	500	Ferrari	4	65		17	6
nc	20	J Fairman	Connaught	A	Lea Francis	4	61		22	8
nc	30	K Wharton	Cooper	T23	Bristol	6	57		19	7
nc	24	K McAlpine	Connaught	A	Lea Francis	4	56		18	6
r	12	P Carini	Ferrari	553	Ferrari	4	40	engine	20	7
r	22	R Salvadori	Connaught	A	Lea Francis	4	33	throttle linkage	14	5
r	42	C Landi	Maserati	A6GCM	Maserati	6	18	piston	21	7
r	34	É Bayol	OSCA	20	OSCA	6	17	engine	13	5
r	18	J Fitch	HWM	(53)	Alta	4	14	engine	26	9
r	26	J Claes	Connaught	A	Lea Francis	4	7	fuel line	30	10
r	14	L Macklin	HWM	(53)	Alta	4	6	engine	27	9

Winning speed: 178.129 km/h, 110.684 mph
Pole Position speed: 184.841 km/h, 114.855 mph (A Ascari, 2 min: 2.700 sec)
Fastest Lap speed: 182.169 km/h, 113.194 mph (J M Fangio, 2 min: 4.500 sec on lap 39)
Lap Leaders: A Ascari 1-6,9,14-24,29-33,36-40,42-45,47-49,53-79 (62); J M Fangio 7-8,11,25,27-28,34-35,41,50-52,80 (13); G Farina 10,12-13,26,46 (5).

Jean Behra in a Maserati 250F at the British Grand Prix 1957, which was held in Aintree. *Refer to page 85.*

Lap Leaders 1953

POS	DRIVER	CAR-ENGINE	GPS	LAPS	KM	MILES
1	A Ascari	Ferrari	7	418	2,366.0	1,470.2
2	F González	Maserati	2	40	397.4	246.9
3	J M Fangio	Maserati	3	32	252.0	156.6
4	G Farina	Ferrari	3	29	377.1	234.3
5	M Hawthorn	Ferrari	2	17	185.3	115.1
			8	**536**	**3,577.7**	**2,223.1**

Driver Points 1953

		RA	INDY	NL	B	F	GB	D	CH	I	TOTAL	
1	A Ascari	9	-	8	(8)	(3.5)	8.5	(1)	9	-	34.5	(12.5)
2	J M Fangio	-	-	-	-	6.5	6	6	(1.5)	9	27.5	(1.5)
3	G Farina	-	-	6	-	(2)	(4)	8	6	6	26	(6)
4	M Hawthorn	3	-	(3)	-	8	(2)	4	4	(3)	19	(8)
5	L Villoresi	6	-	1	6	-	-	-	-	4	17	
6	F González	4	-	2	(1)	4	3.5	-	-	-	13.5	(1)
7	B Vukovich	-	9	-	-	-	-	-	-	-	9	
8	E de Graffenried	-	-	2	3	-	-	2	-	-	7	
9	F Bonetto	-	-	2	-	-	-	3	1.5	-	6.5	
10	A Cross	-	6	-	-	-	-	-	-	-	6	
11	O Marimón	-	-	-	4	-	-	-	-	-	4	
	M Trintignant	-	-	-	2	-	-	-	-	2	4	
13	O Gálvez	2	-	-	-	-	-	-	-	-	2	
	S Hanks	-	2	-	-	-	-	-	-	-	2	
	D Carter	-	2	-	-	-	-	-	-	-	2	
	J McGrath	-	2	-	-	-	-	-	-	-	2	
	H Lang	-	-	-	-	-	-	-	2	-	2	
18	F Agabashian	-	1.5	-	-	-	-	-	-	-	1.5	
	P Russo	-	1.5	-	-	-	-	-	-	-	1.5	

8, 6, 4, 3 and 2 points awarded to the first five finishers. The driver setting the fastest lap scored a point also. Points shared for shared drives. Best 4 scores.

The year saw the return of true Formula 1 cars with the introduction of the 2.5 litre formula. With this stability, major manufacturers committed themselves to racing at the top level, Mercedes and Lancia re-entered Grand Prix racing, signing the two big names Fangio and Ascari who were free to race for others until the cars were available.

FERRARI
Scuderia Ferrari: González, Hawthorn, Trintignant, Farina, Taruffi, Maglioli, Ascari, Manzon (CH)
Ecurie Rosier: Rosier, Manzon
Ecurie Francorchamps: Swaters
Scuderia Ambrosiana: Parnell

MASERATI
Officine Alfieri Maserati: Marimón, Fangio, Musso, Mantovani, Mières, Bira (RA), Moss (CH-E), Ascari, Villoresi, Schell (CH), Rosier (I), Godia
Prince Bira: Bira, Flockhart
Gilby Engineering Ltd: Salvadori
Owen Racing Organisation: Wharton
Baron de Graffenried: de Graffenried, Volonterio
Ecurie Rosier: Rosier
O Marimón: (Menditéguy),
Privateers: Moss, Mières (RA-D), Schell, Daponte, (de Riu)

LANCIA
Scuderia Lancia: Ascari, Villoresi

GORDINI
Equipe Gordini: Behra, Pilette, Bayol, Loyer, Frère, Pollet, Bucci, Wacker
Privateer: Berger

COOPER
Ecurie Richmond: Brandon, (Nuckey)
Gould's Garage (Bristol): Gould
R J Chase: (Brown)
Privateers: Gerard, Whitehead

HWM
HW Motors: Macklin

CONNAUGHT
R. R. C. Walker Racing Team: Riseley-Prichard
Ecurie Ecosse: Thorne
Sir Jeremy Boles: Beauman
Privateers: Marr, Whitehouse

VANWALL
G A Vandervell: Collins

MERCEDES-BENZ
Daimler Benz AG: Fangio, Kling, Herrmann, Lang

KLENK
Hans Klenk: Helfrich

17 Jan 1954 ARGENTINA: Buenos Aires No.2 (Round: 1) (Race: 33)
87 laps x 3.912 km, 2.431 miles = 340.344 km, 211.480 miles

POS.	NO	DRIVER	CAR	MODEL	ENGINE		LAPS	TIME/REASON FOR RETIREMENT	GRID:POS	ROW
1	2	J M Fangio	Maserati	250F	Maserati	6	87	3h 00m 55.800s	3	1
2	10	G Farina	Ferrari	625	Ferrari	4	87	3h 02m 14.800s	1	1
3	12	F González	Ferrari	625	Ferrari	4	87	3h 02m 56.800s	2	1
4	26	M Trintignant	Ferrari	625	Ferrari	4	86		5	2
5	20	É Bayol	Gordini	T16	Gordini	6	85		14	4
6	28	H Schell	Maserati	A6GCM	Maserati	6	84		10	3
7	8	B Bira	Maserati	A6GCM	Maserati	6	83		9	3
8	30	E de Graffenried	Maserati	A6GCM	Maserati	6	83		12	4
9	16	U Maglioli	Ferrari	625	Ferrari	4	82		11	3
dq	14	M Hawthorn	Ferrari	625	Ferrari	4		push start after spin	4	1
dq	18	J Behra	Gordini	T16	Gordini	6		push start after spin	16	5
r	4	O Marimón	Maserati	250F	Maserati	6	5	accident	6	2
r	32	R Mières	Maserati	A6GCM	Maserati	6		engine	8	3
r	34	J Daponte	Maserati	A6GCM	Maserati	6		oil pressure	17	5
r	22	R Loyer	Gordini	T16	Gordini	6		oil pressure	15	5
r	24	L Rosier	Ferrari	500	Ferrari	4	2	accident	13	4
ns	6	L Musso	Maserati	A6GCM	Maserati	6		engine	7	2
ns	36	C Menditéguy	Maserati	A6GCM	Maserati	6		engine		

Winning speed: 112.865 km/h, 70.131 mph
Pole Position speed: 134.382 km/h, 83.501 mph (G Farina, 1 min:44.800 sec)
Fastest Lap speed: 130.159 km/h, 80.877 mph (F González, 1 min:48.200 sec)
Lap Leaders: G Farina 1-14,63-64 (16)*; F González 15-32,47-58,61-62 (32)*; M Hawthorn 33-34 (2); J M Fangio 35-46,59-60,65-87 (37)*.

* estimated from contemporary text

Peter Collins in action at the British Grand Prix. He led from start to finish in the Ferrari D246.

31 May 1954 INDIANAPOLIS: 500 (Round: 2) (Race: 34)

200 laps x 4.023 km, 2.500 miles = 804.672 km, 500.000 miles

POS.	NO	DRIVER	CAR	MODEL	ENGINE	LAPS	TIME/REASON FOR RETIREMENT	GRID:POS	ROW
1	14	B Vukovich	Kurtis Kraft	500A	Offenhauser 4	200	3h 49m 17.270s	19	7
2	9	J Bryan	Kuzma		Offenhauser 4	200	3h 50m 27.221s	3	1
3	2	J McGrath	Kurtis Kraft	500C	Offenhauser 4	200		1	1
4=	34	T Ruttman	Kurtis Kraft	500A	Offenhauser 4	200		11	4
4=	34	D Carter	Kurtis Kraft	500A	Offenhauser 4				
5	73	M Nazaruk	Kurtis Kraft	500C	Offenhauser 4	200		14	5
6	77	F Agabashian	Kurtis Kraft	500C	Offenhauser 4	200		24	8
7	7	D Freeland	Phillips		Offenhauser 4	200		6	2
8=	5	P Russo	Kurtis Kraft	500A	Offenhauser 4			32	11
8=	5	J Hoyt	Kurtis Kraft	500A	Offenhauser 4	200			
9	28	L Crockett	Kurtis Kraft	3000	Offenhauser 4	200		25	9
10	24	C Niday	Stevens		Offenhauser 4	200		13	5
11=	45	A Cross	Kurtis Kraft	4000	Offenhauser 4			27	9
11=	45	J Parsons	Kurtis Kraft	4000	Offenhauser 4				
11=	45	S Hanks	Kurtis Kraft	4000	Offenhauser 4				
11=	45	A Linden	Kurtis Kraft	4000	Offenhauser 4				
11=	45	J Davies	Kurtis Kraft	4000	Offenhauser 4	200			
12=	98	C Stevenson	Kuzma		Offenhauser 4			5	2
12=	98	W Faulkner	Kuzma		Offenhauser 4	199			
13	88	M Ayulo	Kuzma		Offenhauser 4	197		22	8
14	17	B Sweikert	Kurtis Kraft	4000	Offenhauser 4	197		9	3
15=	16	D Carter	Kurtis Kraft	4000	Offenhauser 4			8	3
15=	16	J Jackson	Kurtis Kraft	4000	Offenhauser 4	196			
15=	16	T Bettenhausen	Kurtis Kraft	4000	Offenhauser 4				
15=	16	M Teague	Kurtis Kraft	4000	Offenhauser 4				
16	32	E McCoy	Kurtis Kraft	500B	Offenhauser 4	194		20	7
17	25	J Reece	Pankratz		Offenhauser 4	194		7	3
18=	27	E Elisian	Stevens		Offenhauser 4			31	11
18=	27	B Scott	Stevens		Offenhauser 4	193			
19=	71	F Armi	Kurtis Kraft		Offenhauser 4	193		33	11
19=	71	G Fonder	Kurtis Kraft		Offenhauser 4				
20r=	1	S Hanks	Kurtis Kraft	4000	Offenhauser 4			10	4
20r=	1	J Davies	Kurtis Kraft	4000	Offenhauser 4				
20r=	1	J Rathmann	Kurtis Kraft	4000	Offenhauser 4	191	crankshaft/ spin		
21r	35	P O'Connor	Kurtis Kraft	500C	Offenhauser 4	181	spin	12	4
22r=	12	R Ward	Pawl		Offenhauser 4	172	stalled	16	6
22r=	12	E Johnson	Pawl		Offenhauser 4				
23r=	31	G Hartley	Kurtis Kraft	4000	Offenhauser 4			17	6
23r=	31	M Teague	Kurtis Kraft	4000	Offenhauser 4	168	clutch		
24r=	43	J Thomson	Nichels		Offenhauser 4			4	2
24r=	43	A Linden	Nichels		Offenhauser 4				
24r=	43	B Homeier	Nichels		Offenhauser 4	165	stalled		
25r=	74	A Linden	Schroeder		Offenhauser 4			23	8
25r=	74	B Scott	Schroeder		Offenhauser 4	165	torsion bar		
26r	99	J Hoyt	Kurtis Kraft		Offenhauser 4	130	engine	30	10
27r	19	J Daywalt	Kurtis Kraft	500C	Offenhauser 4	111	spin/ hit wall & Flaherty	2	1
28r=	38	J Rathmann	Kurtis Kraft	500C	Offenhauser 4			28	10
28r=	38	P Flaherty	Kurtis Kraft	500C	Offenhauser 4	110	accident		
29r	10	T Bettenhausen	Kurtis Kraft	500C	Offenhauser 4	105	connecting rod	21	7
30r=	65	S Webb	Bromme		Offenhauser 4			29	10
30r=	65	D Kladis	Bromme		Offenhauser 4	104	oil leak		
31r=	33	L Duncan	Schroeder		Offenhauser 4			26	9
31r=	33	G Fonder	Schroeder		Offenhauser 4	101	brake cylinder		
32r	15	J Parsons	Kurtis Kraft	500C	Offenhauser 4	79	stalled in pits	15	5
33r	51	B Homeier	Kurtis Kraft	500C	Offenhauser 4	74	hit wall leaving pits	18	6

Winning speed: 210.566 km/h, 130.840 mph.
Pole Position speed: 226.970 km/h, 141.033 mph (J McGrath, 1 min: 3.815 sec)
Fastest Lap speed: 226.173 km/h, 140.537 mph (J McGrath, 1 min: 4.040 sec on lap 29)

20 Jun 1954 — BELGIUM: Spa-Francorchamps (Round: 3) (Race: 35)

36 laps x 14.120 km, 8.774 miles = 508.320 km, 315.855 miles

POS.	NO	DRIVER	CAR	MODEL	ENGINE		LAPS	TIME/REASON FOR RETIREMENT	GRID:POS	ROW
1	26	J M Fangio	Maserati	250F	Maserati	6	36	2h 44m 42.400s	1	1
2	8	M Trintignant	Ferrari	625	Ferrari	4	36	2h 45m 06.600s	6	3
3	22	S Moss	Maserati	250F	Maserati	6	35		9	4
4=	10	M Hawthorn	Ferrari	625	Ferrari	4			5	2
4=	10	F González	Ferrari	625	Ferrari	4	35			
5	18	A Pilette	Gordini	T16	Gordini	6	35		8	3
6	20	B Bira	Maserati	250F	Maserati	6	35		13	5
7	30	S Mantovani	Maserati	250F	Maserati	6	34		11	5
r	16	P Frère	Gordini	T16	Gordini	6	14	engine	10	4
r	4	G Farina	Ferrari	553	Ferrari	4	14	ignition	3	1
r	12	J Behra	Gordini	T16	Gordini	6	12	rear suspension	7	3
r	28	O Marimón	Maserati	250F	Maserati	6	3	valve	4	2
r	2	J Swaters	Ferrari	500	Ferrari	4	1	engine	14	6
r	6	F González	Ferrari	553	Ferrari	4	1	oil line	2	1
r	24	R Mières	Maserati	A6GCM	Maserati	6	0	fuel on exhaust pipe/ fire	12	5

Winning speed: 185.173 km/h, 115.061 mph
Pole Position speed: 193.941 km/h, 120.510 mph (J M Fangio, 4 min:22.100 sec)
Fastest Lap speed: 191.458 km/h, 118.966 mph (J M Fangio, 4 min:25.500 sec on lap 13)
Lap Leaders: G Farina 1-2,11-13 (5); J M Fangio 3-10,14-36 (31).

E de Graffenried was present in a camera car - Maserati A6GCM-Maserati 6 (50).

4 Jul 1954 — FRANCE: Reims (Round: 4) (Race: 36)

61 laps x 8.302 km, 5.159 miles = 506.422 km, 314.676 miles

POS.	NO	DRIVER	CAR	MODEL	ENGINE		LAPS	TIME/REASON FOR RETIREMENT	GRID:POS	ROW
1	18	J M Fangio	Mercedes-Benz	W196 str.	Mercedes	8	61	2h 42m 47.900s	1	1
2	20	K Kling	Mercedes-Benz	W196 str.	Mercedes	8	61	2h 42m 48.000s	2	1
3	34	R Manzon	Ferrari	625	Ferrari	4	60		12	5
4	46	B Bira	Maserati	250F	Maserati	6	60		6	3
5	14	L Villoresi	Maserati	250F	Maserati	6	58		14	6
6	24	J Behra	Gordini	T16	Gordini	6	56		17	7
r	28	P Frère	Gordini	T16	Gordini	6	50	rear axle	19	8
r	4	M Trintignant	Ferrari	625	Ferrari	4	36	piston	9	4
r	36	L Rosier	Ferrari	500	Ferrari	4	27	engine	13	5
r	12	O Marimón	Maserati	250F	Maserati	6	27	gearbox	5	2
r	16	R Mières	Maserati	A6GCM	Maserati	6	24	piston	11	5
r	42	K Wharton	Maserati	250F	Maserati	6	19	propellor shaft	16	7
r	48	H Schell	Maserati	A6GCM	Maserati	6	19	fuel pump	21	9
r	22	H Herrmann	Mercedes-Benz	W196 str.	Mercedes	8	16	engine	7	3
r	44	R Salvadori	Maserati	250F	Maserati	6	15	half shaft	10	4
r	2	F González	Ferrari	553	Ferrari	4	13	engine	4	2
r	32	L Macklin	HWM	(53)	Alta	4	10	engine	15	6
r	30	G Berger	Gordini	T16	Gordini	6	9	valve	20	8
r	6	M Hawthorn	Ferrari	553	Ferrari	4	9	engine	8	3
r	26	J Pollet	Gordini	T16	Gordini	6	8	engine	18	7
r	10	A Ascari	Maserati	250F	Maserati	6	1	engine	3	1
ns	40	S Mantovani	Maserati	250F	Maserati	6				

Winning speed: 186.644 km/h, 115.975 mph
Pole Position speed: 200.048 km/h, 124.304 mph (J M Fangio, 2 min:29.400 sec)
Fastest Lap speed: 195.469 km/h, 121.459 mph (H Herrmann, 2 min:32.900 sec on lap 3)
Lap Leaders: K Kling 1-2,29-33,38,54-57,60 (13); J M Fangio 3-28,34-37,39-53,58-59,61 (48).

17 Jul 1954 — BRITAIN: Silverstone (Round: 5) (Race: 37)

90 laps x 4.711 km, 2.927 miles = 423.949 km, 263.430 miles

POS.	NO	DRIVER	CAR	MODEL	ENGINE		LAPS	TIME/REASON FOR RETIREMENT	GRID:POS	ROW
1	9	F González	Ferrari	625	Ferrari	4	90	2h 56m 14.000s	2	1
2	11	M Hawthorn	Ferrari	625	Ferrari	4	90	2h 57m 24.000s	3	1
3	33	O Marimón	Maserati	250F	Maserati	6	89		28	8
4	1	J M Fangio	Mercedes-Benz	W196 str.	Mercedes	8	89		1	1
5	10	M Trintignant	Ferrari	625	Ferrari	4	87		8	3
6	4	R Mières	Maserati	A6GCM	Maserati	6	87		32	9
7	2	K Kling	Mercedes-Benz	W196 str.	Mercedes	8	87		6	2
8	8	K Wharton	Maserati	250F	Maserati	6	86		9	3
9	19	A Pilette	Gordini	T16	Gordini	6	86		12	4
10	29	B Gerard	Cooper	T23	Bristol	6	85		18	5
11	25	D Beauman	Connaught	A	Lea Francis	4	84		17	5
12	3	H Schell	Maserati	A6GCM	Maserati	6	83		16	5
13	23	L Marr	Connaught	A	Lea Francis	4	82		22	7
r	7	S Moss	Maserati	250F	Maserati	6	80	transmission	4	1
14	26	L Thorne	Connaught	A	Lea Francis	4	78		23	7
r	22	B Whitehouse	Connaught	A	Lea Francis	4	63	fuel system	19	6
r	17	J Behra	Gordini	T16	Gordini	6	54	rear suspension	5	2
r	5	R Salvadori	Maserati	250F	Maserati	6	53	oil line	7	2
r=	6	B Bira	Maserati	250F	Maserati	6			10	3
r=	6	R Flockhart	Maserati	250F	Maserati	6	44	accident		
15	28	H Gould	Cooper	T23	Bristol	6	44		20	6
r=	32	L Villoresi	Maserati	250F	Maserati	6			27	8

POS.	NO	DRIVER	CAR	MODEL	ENGINE		LAPS	TIME/REASON FOR RETIREMENT	GRID:POS	ROW
r=	32	A Ascari	Maserati	250F	Maserati	6	40	oil pressure		
r	24	J Riseley-Prichard	Connaught	A	Lea Francis	4	40	accident	21	6
r	12	R Parnell	Ferrari	500	Ferrari	4	25	water jacket	14	4
r	31	A Ascari	Maserati	250F	Maserati	6	21	dropped valve	30	9
r	18	C Bucci	Gordini	T16	Gordini	6	18	accident	13	4
r	20	P Collins	Vanwall	Spl.	Vanwall	4	16	cylinder head gasket	11	3
r	14	R Manzon	Ferrari	625	Ferrari	4	16	cylinder block	15	5
r	21	P Whitehead	Cooper	T24	Alta	4	4	oil line	24	7
r	15	L Rosier	Ferrari	500	Ferrari	4	2	engine	31	9
r	30	E Brandon	Cooper	T23	Bristol	6	2		25	7
ns	27	A Brown	Cooper	T23	Bristol	6			26	8
ns	30	R Nuckey	Cooper	T23	Bristol	6		car raced by Brandon	29	9

Winning speed: 144.337 km/h, 89.687 mph
Pole Position speed: 161.505 km/h, 100.354 mph (J M Fangio, 1 min:45.000 sec)
Fastest Lap speed: 154.163 km/h, 95.793 mph (Ascari/Behra/Fangio/González/Hawthorn/Marimón/Moss, 1 min:50.000 sec)
Lap Leaders: F González 1-90 (90).

1 Aug 1954 GERMANY: Nürburgring (Round: 6) (Race: 38)
22 laps x 22.810 km, 14.173 miles = 501.820 km, 311.816 miles

POS.	NO	DRIVER	CAR	MODEL	ENGINE		LAPS	TIME/REASON FOR RETIREMENT	GRID:POS	ROW
1	18	J M Fangio	Mercedes-Benz	W196	Mercedes	8	22	3h 45m 45.800s	1	1
2=	1	F González	Ferrari	625	Ferrari	4			5	2
2=	1	M Hawthorn	Ferrari	625	Ferrari	4	22	3h 47m 22.300s		
3	2	M Trintignant	Ferrari	625	Ferrari	4	22	3h 50m 54.400s	7	3
4	19	K Kling	Mercedes-Benz	W196	Mercedes	8	22	3h 51m 52.300s	23	9
5	7	S Mantovani	Maserati	250F	Maserati	6	22	3h 54m 36.300s	15	6
6	4	P Taruffi	Ferrari	625	Ferrari	4	21		13	5
7	15	H Schell	Maserati	A6GCM	Maserati	6	21		14	6
8	25	L Rosier	Ferrari	500	Ferrari	4	21		18	7
9	24	R Manzon	Ferrari	625	Ferrari	4	20		12	5
10	9	J Behra	Gordini	T16	Gordini	6	20		9	4
r	14	B Bira	Maserati	250F	Maserati	6	18	steering	19	8
r	21	H Lang	Mercedes-Benz	W196	Mercedes	8	10	spin	11	5
r	11	C Bucci	Gordini	T16	Gordini	6	8	wheel lost	16	7
r	22	T Helfrich	Klenk	Meteor	BMW	6	8	engine	21	9
r	20	H Herrmann	Mercedes-Benz	W196 str.	Mercedes	8	7	fuel line	4	2
r	10	P Frère	Gordini	T16	Gordini	6	4	wheel lost	6	3
r	3	M Hawthorn	Ferrari	625	Ferrari	4	3	rear axle	2	1
r	8	R Mières	Maserati	250F	Maserati	6	2	fuel tank	17	7
r	16	S Moss	Maserati	250F	Maserati	6	1	big end	3	1
r	12	A Pilette	Gordini	T16	Gordini	6	0	gearbox	20	8
ns	6	O Marimón	Maserati	250F	Maserati	6		fatal accident	8	3
ns	5	L Villoresi	Maserati	250F	Maserati	6		withdrew after Marimon accident	10	4
ns	17	K Wharton	Maserati	250F	Maserati	6		withdrew	22	9

Winning speed: 133.366 km/h, 82.870 mph
Pole Position speed: 139.156 km/h, 86.468 mph (J M Fangio, 9 min:50.100 sec)
Fastest Lap speed: 137.987 km/h, 85.741 mph (K Kling, 9 min:55.100 sec on lap 16)
Lap Leaders: J M Fangio 1-14,17-22 (20); K Kling 15-16 (2).

Also the Grand Prix of Europe.

22 Aug 1954 SWITZERLAND: Bremgarten (Round: 7) (Race: 39)
66 laps x 7.280 km, 4.524 miles = 480.480 km, 298.556 miles

POS.	NO	DRIVER	CAR	MODEL	ENGINE		LAPS	TIME/REASON FOR RETIREMENT	GRID:POS	ROW
1	4	J M Fangio	Mercedes-Benz	W196	Mercedes	8	66	3h 00m 34.500s	2	1
2	20	F González	Ferrari	625	Ferrari	4	66	3h 01m 32.300s	1	1
3	6	H Herrmann	Mercedes-Benz	W196	Mercedes	8	65		7	3
4	30	R Mières	Maserati	250F	Maserati	6	64		12	5
5	28	S Mantovani	Maserati	250F	Maserati	6	64		9	4
6	18	K Wharton	Maserati	250F	Maserati	6	64		8	3
7	24	U Maglioli	Ferrari	553	Ferrari	4	61		11	5
8	2	J Swaters	Ferrari	500	Ferrari	4	58		16	7
r	8	K Kling	Mercedes-Benz	W196	Mercedes	8	38	fuel injection pump	5	2
r	26	M Trintignant	Ferrari	625	Ferrari	4	33	engine	4	2
r	22	M Hawthorn	Ferrari	625	Ferrari	4	30	oil pump	6	3
r	34	H Schell	Maserati	250F	Maserati	6	23	oil pump	13	5
r	32	S Moss	Maserati	250F	Maserati	6	21	oil pump	3	1
r	14	F Wacker	Gordini	T16	Gordini	6	10	transmission	15	6
r	10	J Behra	Gordini	T16	Gordini	6	8	clutch	14	6
r	12	C Bucci	Gordini	T16	Gordini	6	0	fuel pump	10	4
ns	24	R Manzon	Ferrari	553	Ferrari	4		accident		

Winning speed: 159.650 km/h, 99.202 mph
Pole Position speed: 164.313 km/h, 102.100 mph (F González, 2 min:39.500 sec)
Fastest Lap speed: 164.108 km/h, 101.972 mph (J M Fangio, 2 min:39.700 sec on lap 34)
Lap Leaders: J M Fangio 1-66 (66).

5 Sep 1954 — ITALY: Monza (Round: 8) (Race: 40)

80 laps x 6.300 km, 3.915 miles = 504.000 km, 313.171 miles

POS.	NO	DRIVER	CAR	MODEL	ENGINE		LAPS	TIME/REASON FOR RETIREMENT	GRID:POS	ROW
1	16	J M Fangio	Mercedes-Benz	W196 str.	Mercedes	8	80	2h 47m 47.900s	1	1
2	40	M Hawthorn	Ferrari	625	Ferrari	4	79		7	3
3=	38	U Maglioli	Ferrari	625	Ferrari	4			13	5
3=	38	F González	Ferrari	625	Ferrari	4	78			
4	12	H Herrmann	Mercedes-Benz	W196	Mercedes	8	77		8	3
5	30	M Trintignant	Ferrari	625	Ferrari	4	75		11	4
6	42	F Wacker	Gordini	T16	Gordini	6	75		18	6
7	10	P Collins	Vanwall	Spl.	Vanwall	4	75		16	6
8	26	L Rosier	Maserati	250F	Maserati	6	74		20	7
9	18	S Mantovani	Maserati	250F	Maserati	6	74		9	3
10	28	S Moss	Maserati	250F	Maserati	6	71		3	1
11	8	J Daponte	Maserati	A6GCM	Maserati	6	70		19	7
r	34	A Ascari	Ferrari	625	Ferrari	4	48	valves	2	1
r	22	L Villoresi	Maserati	250F	Maserati	6	42	clutch spring	6	2
r	14	K Kling	Mercedes-Benz	W196 str.	Mercedes	8	36	accident	4	2
r	24	R Mières	Maserati	250F	Maserati	6	34	suspension	10	4
r	20	L Musso	Maserati	250F	Maserati	6	33	transmission	14	5
r	6	R Manzon	Ferrari	625	Ferrari	4	16	engine	15	5
r	32	F González	Ferrari	553	Ferrari	4	16	gearbox oil seal	5	2
r	46	C Bucci	Gordini	T16	Gordini	6	13	transmission	17	6
r	44	J Behra	Gordini	T16	Gordini	6	2	engine	12	4
ns	2	G de Riu	Maserati	A6GCM	Maserati	6				

Winning speed: 180.216 km/h, 111.981 mph
Pole Position speed: 190.588 km/h, 118.426 mph (J M Fangio, 1 min:59.000 sec)
Fastest Lap speed: 187.748 km/h, 116.661 mph (F González, 2 min: 0.800 sec on lap 2)
Lap Leaders: K Kling 1-3 (3); J M Fangio 4-5,23,68-80 (16); A Ascari 6-22,24-44,46-48 (41); S Moss 45,49-67 (20).

24 Oct 1954 — SPAIN: Pedralbes (Round: 9) (Race: 41)

80 laps x 6.316 km, 3.925 miles = 505.280 km, 313.966 miles

POS.	NO	DRIVER	CAR	MODEL	ENGINE		LAPS	TIME/REASON FOR RETIREMENT	GRID:POS	ROW
1	38	M Hawthorn	Ferrari	553	Ferrari	4	80	3h 13m 52.100s	3	1
2	14	L Musso	Maserati	250F	Maserati	6	80	3h 15m 05.300s	7	2
3	2	J M Fangio	Mercedes-Benz	W196	Mercedes	8	79		2	1
4	10	R Mières	Maserati	250F	Maserati	6	79		11	3
5	4	K Kling	Mercedes-Benz	W196	Mercedes	8	79		12	4
6	16	C Godia	Maserati	250F	Maserati	6	76		13	4
7	26	L Rosier	Maserati	250F	Maserati	6	74		20	6
8	28	K Wharton	Maserati	250F	Maserati	6	74		14	4
9	18	B Bira	Maserati	250F	Maserati	6	68		15	5
r	12	S Mantovani	Maserati	250F	Maserati	6	58	brakes/ accident	10	3
r=	22	E de Graffenried	Maserati	A6GCM	Maserati	6			21	6
r=	22	O Volonterio	Maserati	A6GCM	Maserati	6	57	engine		
r	6	H Herrmann	Mercedes-Benz	W196	Mercedes	8	50	fuel injection pump	9	3
r	40	M Trintignant	Ferrari	625	Ferrari	4	47	gearbox	8	3
r	48	J Pollet	Gordini	T16	Gordini	6	37	engine	16	5
r	24	H Schell	Maserati	250F	Maserati	6	29	rear axle	4	1
r	8	S Moss	Maserati	250F	Maserati	6	20	oil scavenge pump	6	2
r	46	J Behra	Gordini	T16	Gordini	6	17	brakes	18	5
r	30	J Swaters	Ferrari	500	Ferrari	4	16	engine	19	6
r	34	A Ascari	Lancia	D50	Lancia	V8	10	clutch	1	1
r	36	L Villoresi	Lancia	D50	Lancia	V8	2	brakes	5	2
r	20	R Manzon	Ferrari	625	Ferrari	4	2	engine	17	5
ns	42	P Collins	Vanwall	Spl.	Vanwall	4		accident		

Winning speed: 156.378 km/h, 97.169 mph
Pole Position speed: 164.646 km/h, 102.306 mph (A Ascari, 2 min:18.100 sec)
Fastest Lap speed: 161.949 km/h, 100.630 mph (A Ascari, 2 min:20.400 sec on lap 3)
Lap Leaders: H Schell 1-2,10,13,15-17,19,21,23 (10); A Ascari 3-9 (7); M Trintignant 11-12,14,18,20 (5); M Hawthorn 22,24-80 (58).

Lap Leaders 1954

POS	DRIVER	CAR-ENGINE	GPS	LAPS	KM	MILES
1	J M Fangio	Maserati	*2	68	582.5	361.9
		Mercedes-Benz	4	150	1,436.0	892.3
			6	218	2,018.5	1,254.2
2	F González	Ferrari	*2	122	549.2	341.2
3	M Hawthorn	Ferrari	2	60	374.2	232.5
4	A Ascari	Ferrari	1	41	258.3	160.5
		Lancia	1	7	44.2	27.5
			2	48	302.5	188.0
5	G Farina	Ferrari	*2	21	133.2	82.8
6	S Moss	Maserati	1	20	126.0	78.3
7	K Kling	Mercedes-Benz	3	18	172.4	107.2
8	H Schell	Maserati	1	10	63.2	39.2
9	M Trintignant	Ferrari	1	5	31.6	19.6
* lap totals include estimates			8	522	3,770.7	2,343.0

Driver Points 1954

		RA	INDY	B	F	GB	D	CH	I	E	TOTAL	
1	J M Fangio	8	-	9	8	(3*)	8	9	(8)	(4)	42	(15.14)
2	F González	5	-	(1.5)	-	8*	3	6	3	-	25.14	(1.5)
3	M Hawthorn	-	-	1.5	-	6*	3	-	6	8	24.64	
4	M Trintignant	3	-	6	-	2	4	-	2	-	17	
5	K Kling	-	-	-	6	-	4	-	-	2	12	
6	B Vukovich	-	8	-	-	-	-	-	-	-	8	
	H Herrmann	-	-	-	1	-	-	4	3	-	8	
8	G Farina	6	-	-	-	-	-	-	-	-	6	
	J Bryan	-	6	-	-	-	-	-	-	-	6	
	L Musso	-	-	-	-	-	-	-	-	6	6	
	R Mières	-	-	-	-	-	-	3	-	3	6	
12	J McGrath	-	5	-	-	-	-	-	-	-	5	
13	S Moss	-	-	4	-	*	-	-	-	-	4.14	
	O Marimón	-	-	-	-	4*	-	-	-	-	4.14	
15	R Manzon	-	-	-	4	-	-	-	-	-	4	
	S Mantovani	-	-	-	-	-	2	2	-	-	4	
17	B Bira	-	-	-	3	-	-	-	-	-	3	
18	E Bayol	2	-	-	-	-	-	-	-	-	2	
	M Nazaruk	-	2	-	-	-	-	-	-	-	2	
	A Pilette	-	-	2	-	-	-	-	-	-	2	
	L Villoresi	-	-	-	2	-	-	-	-	-	2	
	U Maglioli	-	-	-	-	-	-	-	2	-	2	
23	T Ruttman	-	1.5	-	-	-	-	-	-	-	1.5	
	D Carter	-	1.5	-	-	-	-	-	-	-	1.5	
25	A Ascari	-	-	-	-	*	-	-	-	1	1.14	
26	J Behra	-	-	-	-	*	-	-	-	-	0.14	

8, 6, 4, 3 and 2 points awarded to the first five finishers.
*The driver setting the fastest lap scored a point also. Points shared for shared drives. Best 5 scores. * Point for fastest lap shared by seven drivers.*

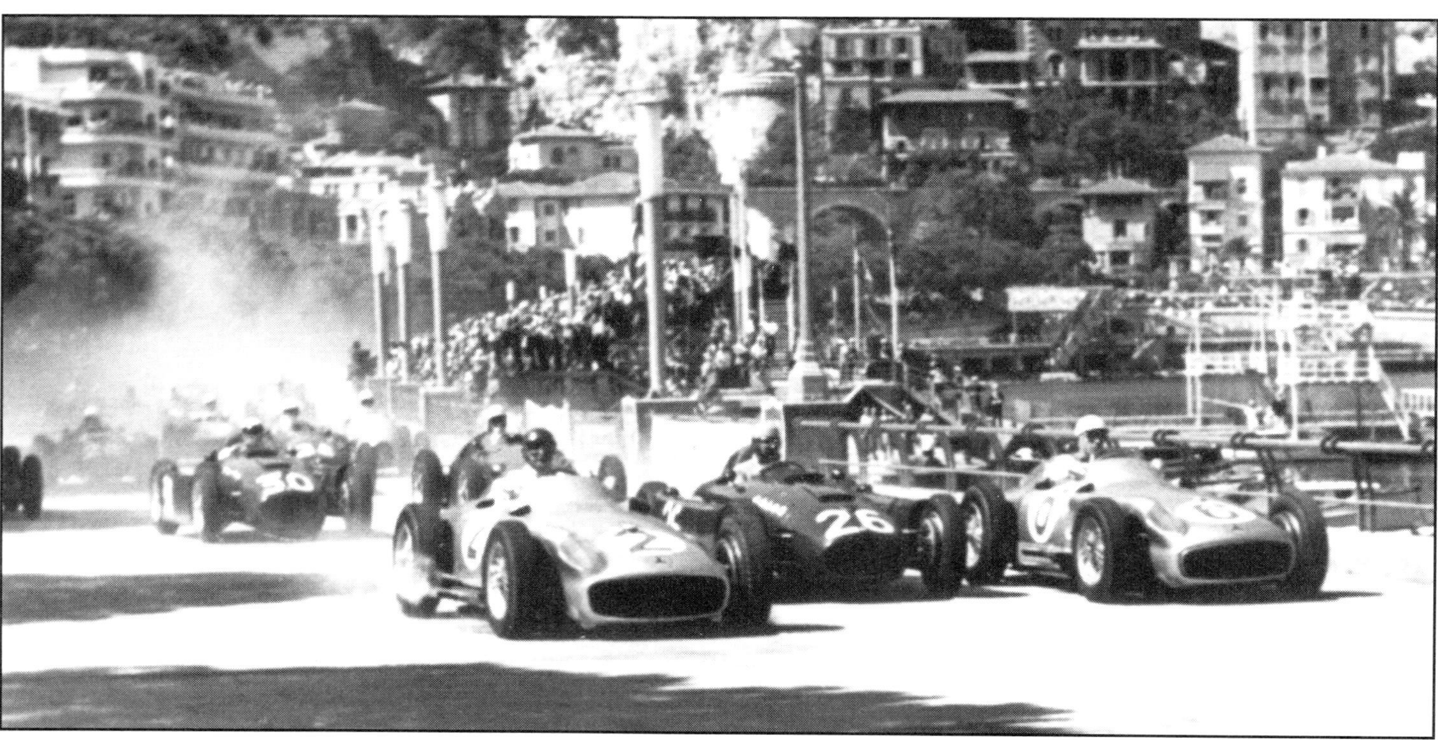

The original post-war start on the quayside at Monaco in 1955. J M Fangio was on pole, but retired with transmission problems on lap 49. *Refer to page 76.*

Mercedes dominance continued into 1955, with Moss moving into the big time as Fangio's team-mate. Ascari was killed at Monza while trying out a Ferrari sportscar, just days after surviving a ducking in the Monaco harbour.

Worse was to come with the Le Mans tragedy that took the life of more than 80 spectators and resulted in many cancelled World Championship races. This led to a temporary motorsport ban in France and a ban of all circuit racing in Switzerland (which still remains). In July, Lancia handed over their complete racing team to Ferrari.

FERRARI
Scuderia Ferrari: Trintignant, Farina, Castellotti, Taruffi, González, Frère, Maglioli, Hawthorn, Schell Equipe Nationale Belge: Claes

LANCIA
Scuderia Lancia: Ascari, Villoresi, Castellotti, Chiron
Scuderia Ferrari: Farina, Villoresi (I)

MASERATI
Officine Alfieri Maserati: Behra, Musso, Mières, Perdisa, Menditéguy, Schell, Mantovani, Bucci, Simon, Collins (I), Gould (I)
Stirling Moss Ltd: Macklin, Walker, Fitch (Claes)
Ecurie Rosier: Rosier
Gould's Garage (Bristol): Gould
Gilby Engineering Ltd: Salvadori
Owen Racing Organisation: Collins
Privateer: Uria

ARZANI VOLPINI
Privateer: (Piotti)

GORDINI
Equipe Gordini: Manzon, Pollet, da Silva Ramos, Bayol, Sparken, Lucas, Birger, Iglesias

CONNAUGHT
Connaught Engineering: McAlpine, (Fairman)
R. R. C. Walker Racing Team: Rolt, Walker
Privateer: Marr

COOPER
Cooper Car Co: Brabham

VANWALL
Vandervell Products Ltd: Hawthorn, Wharton, Schell

MERCEDES-BENZ
Daimler Benz AG: Fangio, Moss, Kling, Herrmann, Taruffi, Simon

HWM
Privateer: (Whiteaway)

16 Jan 1955 — ARGENTINA: Buenos Aires No.2 (Round: I) (Race: 42)

96 laps x 3.912 km, 2.431 miles = 375.552 km, 233.357 miles

POS.	NO	DRIVER	CAR	MODEL	ENGINE		LAPS	TIME/REASON FOR RETIREMENT	GRID:POS	ROW
1	2	J M Fangio	Mercedes-Benz	W196	Mercedes	8	96	3h 00m 38.600s	3	1
2=	12	F González	Ferrari	625	Ferrari	4			1	1
2=	12	G Farina	Ferrari	625	Ferrari	4	96	3h 02m 08.200s		
2=	12	M Trintignant	Ferrari	625	Ferrari	4				
3=	10	G Farina	Ferrari	625	Ferrari	4			5	2
3=	10	U Maglioli	Ferrari	625	Ferrari	4	94			
3=	10	M Trintignant	Ferrari	625	Ferrari	4				
4=	8	H Herrmann	Mercedes-Benz	W196	Mercedes	8			10	3
4=	8	K Kling	Mercedes-Benz	W196	Mercedes	8				
4=	8	S Moss	Mercedes-Benz	W196	Mercedes	8	94			
5	18	R Mières	Maserati	250F	Maserati	6	91		16	5
6=	28	H Schell	Maserati	250F	Maserati	6			7	2
6=	28	J Behra	Maserati	250F	Maserati	6	88			
7=	22	L Musso	Maserati	250F	Maserati	6			18	5
7=	22	S Mantovani	Maserati	250F	Maserati	6				
7=	22	H Schell	Maserati	250F	Maserati	6	83			
r=	26	C Bucci	Maserati	250F	Maserati	6			20	6
r=	26	H Schell	Maserati	250F	Maserati	6				
r=	26	C Menditéguy	Maserati	250F	Maserati	6	54	fuel pressure		
r=	20	S Mantovani	Maserati	250F	Maserati	6			19	6
r=	20	L Musso	Maserati	250F	Maserati	6				
r=	20	J Behra	Maserati	250F	Maserati	6	54	engine		
r	42	J Iglesias	Gordini	T16	Gordini	6	38	transmission	17	5
r	14	M Trintignant	Ferrari	625	Ferrari	4	36	valve	14	4
r=	36	E Castellotti	Lancia	D50	Lancia	V8			12	4
r=	36	L Villoresi	Lancia	D50	Lancia	V8	35	accident		
r	6	S Moss	Mercedes-Benz	W196	Mercedes	8	29	fuel vaporisation	8	3
r	30	A Uria	Maserati	A6GCM	Maserati	6	22	fuel pressure	21	6
r	32	A Ascari	Lancia	D50	Lancia	V8	21	accident	2	1
r	38	É Bayol	Gordini	T16	Gordini	6	7	transmission	15	5
r	34	L Villoresi	Lancia	D50	Lancia	V8	2	fuel line	11	3
r	16	J Behra	Maserati	250F	Maserati	6	2	accident	4	1
r	4	K Kling	Mercedes-Benz	W196	Mercedes	8	2	accident	6	2
r	40	P Birger	Gordini	T16	Gordini	6	1	accident	9	3
r	24	C Menditéguy	Maserati	250F	Maserati	6	1	accident	13	4

Winning speed: 124.738 km/h, 77.509 mph
Pole Position speed: 136.597 km/h, 84.878 mph (F González, 1 min:43.100 sec)
Fastest Lap speed: 130.039 km/h, 80.802 mph (J M Fangio, 1 min:48.300 sec on lap 45)
Lap Leaders: J M Fangio 1-2,26-34,43-96 (65)*; A Ascari 3-4,11-20 (12)*; F González 5-10,21-25 (11)*; H Schell 35-38 (4)*; R Mières 39-42 (4)*.

* estimated from contemporary text

22 May 1955 — MONACO: Monte Carlo (Round: 2) (Race: 43)

100 laps x 3.145 km, 1.954 miles = 314.500 km, 195.421 miles

POS.	NO	DRIVER	CAR	MODEL	ENGINE		LAPS	TIME/REASON FOR RETIREMENT	GRID:POS	ROW
1	44	M Trintignant	Ferrari	625	Ferrari	4	100	2h 58m 09.700s	9	4
2	30	E Castellotti	Lancia	D50	Lancia	V8	100	2h 58m 30.000s	4	2
3=	34	J Behra	Maserati	250F	Maserati	6			5	2
3=	34	C Perdisa	Maserati	250F	Maserati	6	99			
4	42	G Farina	Ferrari	625	Ferrari	4	99		14	6
5	28	L Villoresi	Lancia	D50	Lancia	V8	99		7	3
6	32	L Chiron	Lancia	D50	Lancia	V8	95		19	8
7	10	J Pollet	Gordini	T16	Gordini	6	91		20	8
r=	40	C Perdisa	Maserati	250F	Maserati	6			11	5
r=	40	J Behra	Maserati	250F	Maserati	6	86	spin		
8=	48	P Taruffi	Ferrari	555	Ferrari	4			15	6
8=	48	P Frère	Ferrari	555	Ferrari	4	86			
9	6	S Moss	Mercedes-Benz	W196	Mercedes	8	81		3	1
r	26	A Ascari	Lancia	D50	Lancia	V8	80	accident	2	1
r	46	H Schell	Ferrari	555	Ferrari	4	68	engine	18	7
r	36	R Mières	Maserati	250F	Maserati	6	64	rear axle	6	3
r	12	É Bayol	Gordini	T16	Gordini	6	63	rear axle	16	7
r	2	J M Fangio	Mercedes-Benz	W196	Mercedes	8	49	transmission	1	1
r	8	R Manzon	Gordini	T16	Gordini	6	38	gearbox	13	5
r	4	A Simon	Mercedes-Benz	W196	Mercedes	8	24	valve	10	4
r	18	M Hawthorn	Vanwall	VW (55)	Vanwall	4	22	throttle linkage	12	5
r	14	L Rosier	Maserati	250F	Maserati	6	8	fuel tank	17	7
r	38	L Musso	Maserati	250F	Maserati	6	7	transmission	8	3
nq	22	L Macklin	Maserati	250F	Maserati	6				
nq	24	T Whiteaway	HWM	(53)	Alta	4				
ns	4	H Herrmann	Mercedes-Benz	W196	Mercedes	8		accident/ injury		

Winning speed: 105.915 km/h, 65.813 mph
Pole Position speed: 111.988 km/h, 69.586 mph (J M Fangio, 1 min:41.100 sec)
Fastest Lap speed: 110.566 km/h, 68.703 mph (J M Fangio, 1 min:42.400 sec on lap 27)
Lap Leaders: J M Fangio 1-49 (49); S Moss 50-80 (31); M Trintignant 81-100 (20).

Also the Grand Prix of Europe.

30 May 1955 — INDIANAPOLIS: 500 (Round: 3) (Race: 44)

200 laps x 4.023 km, 2.500 miles = 804.672 km, 500.000 miles

POS.	NO	DRIVER	CAR	MODEL	ENGINE		LAPS	TIME/REASON FOR RETIREMENT	GRID:POS	ROW
1	6	B Sweikert	Kurtis Kraft	500C	Offenhauser	4	200	3h 53m 59.530s	14	5
2=	10	T Bettenhausen	Kurtis Kraft	500C	Offenhauser	4	200	3h 56m 43.088s	2	1
2=	10	P Russo	Kurtis Kraft	500C	Offenhauser	4				
3	15	J Davies	Kurtis Kraft	500B	Offenhauser	4	200		10	4
4	44	J Thomson	Kuzma		Offenhauser	4	200		33	11
5=	77	W Faulkner	Kurtis Kraft	500C	Offenhauser	4	200		7	3
5=	77	B Homeier	Kurtis Kraft	500C	Offenhauser	4				
6	19	A Linden	Kurtis Kraft	4000	Offenhauser	4	200		8	3
7	71	A Herman	Kurtis Kraft		Offenhauser	4	200		16	6
8	29	P O'Connor	Kurtis Kraft	500D	Offenhauser	4	200		19	7
9	48	J Daywalt	Kurtis Kraft		Offenhauser	4	200		17	6
10	89	P Flaherty	Kurtis Kraft	500B	Offenhauser	4	200		12	4
11	98	D Carter	Kuzma		Offenhauser	4	197		18	6
12	41	C Weyant	Kurtis Kraft	3000	Offenhauser	4	196		25	9
13	83	E Johnson	Trevis		Offenhauser	4	196		32	11
14	33	J Rathmann	Epperly		Offenhauser	4	191		20	7
15r	12	D Freeland	Phillips		Offenhauser	4	178	transmission	21	7
16r	22	C Niday	Kurtis Kraft	500B	Offenhauser	4	170	accident/ fire	9	3
17r	99	A Cross	Kurtis Kraft	500C	Offenhauser	4	168	connecting rod	24	8
18r	81	S Templeman	Trevis		Offenhauser	4	142	transmission	31	11
19r	8	S Hanks	Kurtis Kraft	500C	Offenhauser	4	134	transmission	6	2
20r	31	K Andrews	Schroeder		Offenhauser	4	120	ignition	28	10
21r	16	J Parsons	Kurtis Kraft	500C	Offenhauser	4	119	magneto	27	9
22r	37	E Russo	Pawl		Offenhauser	4	112	ignition	13	5
23r	49	R Crawford	Kurtis Kraft	500B	Offenhauser	4	111	valve	23	8
24r	1	J Bryan	Kuzma		Offenhauser	4	90	fuel pump	11	4
25r	4	B Vukovich	Kurtis Kraft	500C	Offenhauser	4	56	fatal accident	5	2
26r	3	J McGrath	Kurtis Kraft	500C	Offenhauser	4	54	magneto	3	1
27r	42	A Keller	Kurtis Kraft	2000	Offenhauser	4	54	accident	22	8
28r	27	R Ward	Kuzma		Offenhauser	4	53	accident	30	10
29r	39	J Boyd	Kurtis Kraft	500D	Offenhauser	4	53	accident	26	9
30r	68	E Elisian	Kurtis Kraft	4000	Offenhauser	4	53	stopped to help Vukovich	29	10
31r	23	J Hoyt	Stevens		Offenhauser	4	40	oil leak	1	1
32r	14	F Agabashian	Kurtis Kraft	500C	Offenhauser	4	39	spin	4	2
33r	5	J Reece	Pankratz	Offenhauser	4	10		connecting rod/ spin	15	5

Winning speed: 206.333 km/h, 128.209 mph
Pole Position speed: 225.381 km/h, 140.045 mph (J Hoyt, 1 min: 4.265 sec)
Fastest Lap speed: 227.487 km/h, 141.354 mph (B Vukovich, 1 min: 3.670 sec on lap 27)
Fastest qualifier: J McGrath (229.460 km/h, 142.580 mph).

5 Jun 1955 — BELGIUM: Spa-Francorchamps (Round: 4) (Race: 45)

36 laps x 14.120 km, 8.774 miles = 508.320 km, 315.855 miles

POS.	NO	DRIVER	CAR	MODEL	ENGINE		LAPS	TIME/REASON FOR RETIREMENT	GRID:POS	ROW
1	10	J M Fangio	Mercedes-Benz	W196	Mercedes	8	36	2h 39m 29.000s	2	1
2	14	S Moss	Mercedes-Benz	W196	Mercedes	8	36	2h 39m 37.100s	3	1
3	2	G Farina	Ferrari	555	Ferrari	4	36	2h 41m 09.500s	4	2
4	6	P Frère	Ferrari	555	Ferrari	4	36	2h 42m 54.500s	8	3
5=	24	R Mières	Maserati	250F	Maserati	6			13	5
5=	24	J Behra	Maserati	250F	Maserati	6	35			
6	4	M Trintignant	Ferrari	555	Ferrari	4	35		10	4
7	22	L Musso	Maserati	250F	Maserati	6	34		7	3
8	26	C Perdisa	Maserati	250F	Maserati	6	33		11	5
9	28	L Rosier	Maserati	250F	Maserati	6	33		12	5
r	12	K Kling	Mercedes-Benz	W196	Mercedes	8	21	oil line	6	3
r	30	E Castellotti	Lancia	D50	Lancia	V8	16	gearbox	1	1
r	40	M Hawthorn	Vanwall	VW (55)	Vanwall	4	8	gearbox	9	4
r	20	J Behra	Maserati	250F	Maserati	6	3	accident	5	2
ns	38	J Claes	Maserati	250F	Maserati	6		engine		

Winning speed: 191.238 km/h, 118.829 mph
Pole Position speed: 196.947 km/h, 122.377 mph (E Castellotti, 4 min:18.100 sec)
Fastest Lap speed: 195.058 km/h, 121.203 mph (J M Fangio, 4 min:20.600 sec on lap 18)
Lap Leaders: J M Fangio 1-36 (36).

19 Jun 1955 — NETHERLANDS: Zandvoort (Round: 5) (Race: 46)

100 laps x 4.193 km, 2.605 miles = 419.300 km, 260.541 miles

POS.	NO	DRIVER	CAR	MODEL	ENGINE		LAPS	TIME/REASON FOR RETIREMENT	GRID:POS	ROW
1	8	J M Fangio	Mercedes-Benz	W196	Mercedes	8	100	2h 54m 23.800s	1	1
2	10	S Moss	Mercedes-Benz	W196	Mercedes	8	100	2h 54m 24.100s	2	1
3	18	L Musso	Maserati	250F	Maserati	6	100	2h 55m 20.900s	4	2
4	16	R Mières	Maserati	250F	Maserati	6	99		7	3
5	6	E Castellotti	Ferrari	555	Ferrari	4	97		9	4
6	14	J Behra	Maserati	250F	Maserati	6	97		6	3
7	2	M Hawthorn	Ferrari	555	Ferrari	4	97		5	2
8	22	N da Silva Ramos	Gordini	T16	Gordini	6	92		14	6
9	28	L Rosier	Maserati	250F	Maserati	6	92		13	5
10	24	J Pollet	Gordini	T16	Gordini	6	90		12	5
11	30	J Claes	Ferrari	500	Ferrari	4	88		16	7
r	4	M Trintignant	Ferrari	555	Ferrari	4	65	gearbox	8	3
r	20	R Manzon	Gordini	T16	Gordini	6	44	rear axle	11	5
r	32	H Gould	Maserati	250F	Maserati	6	23	accident	15	6
r	12	K Kling	Mercedes-Benz	W196	Mercedes	8	21	spin	3	1
r	26	P Walker	Maserati	250F	Maserati	6	2	wheel bearing	10	4

Winning speed: 144.257 km/h, 89.637 mph
Pole Position speed: 150.948 km/h, 93.795 mph (J M Fangio, 1 min:40.000 sec)
Fastest Lap speed: 149.602 km/h, 92.958 mph (R Mières, 1 min:40.900 sec on lap 3)
Lap Leaders: J M Fangio 1-100 (100).

16 Jul 1955 — BRITAIN: Aintree (Round: 6) (Race: 47)

90 laps x 4.828 km, 3.000 miles = 434.523 km, 270.000 miles

POS.	NO	DRIVER	CAR	MODEL	ENGINE		LAPS	TIME/REASON FOR RETIREMENT	GRID:POS	ROW
1	12	S Moss	Mercedes-Benz	W196	Mercedes	8	90	3h 07m 21.200s	1	1
2	10	JM Fangio	Mercedes-Benz	W196	Mercedes	8	90	3h 07m 21.400s	2	1
3	14	K Kling	Mercedes-Benz	W196	Mercedes	8	90	3h 08m 33.000s	4	2
4	50	P Taruffi	Mercedes-Benz	W196	Mercedes	8	89		5	2
5	4	L Musso	Maserati	250F	Maserati	6	89		9	4
6=	16	M Hawthorn	Ferrari	625	Ferrari	4			12	5
6=	16	E Castellotti	Ferrari	625	Ferrari	4	87			
7	26	M Sparken	Gordini	T16	Gordini	6	81		23	9
8	46	L Macklin	Maserati	250F	Maserati	6	79		16	7
9=	28	K Wharton	Vanwall	VW (55)	Vanwall	4			15	6
9=	28	H Schell	Vanwall	VW (55)	Vanwall	4	72			
r	18	M Trintignant	Ferrari	625	Ferrari	4	59	engine overheating	13	5
r	6	R Mières	Maserati	250F	Maserati	6	47	piston	6	3
r	40	J Brabham	Cooper	T40	Bristol	6	30	valve	25	10
r	32	K McAlpine	Connaught	B str.	Alta	4	30	oil line	17	7
r	42	P Collins	Maserati	250F	Maserati	6	28	clutch	24	10
r	24	N da Silva Ramos	Gordini	T16	Gordini	6	26	engine	18	7
r	44	R Salvadori	Maserati	250F	Maserati	6	23	gearbox	20	8
r	48	H Gould	Maserati	250F	Maserati	6	22	brakes	22	9
r	30	H Schell	Vanwall	VW (55)	Vanwall	4	20	throttle	7	3
r=	36	T Rolt	Connaught	B	Alta	4			14	6
r=	36	P Walker	Connaught	B	Alta	4	19	throttle control		
r	38	L Marr	Connaught	B str.	Alta	4	18	brakes/ accident	19	8
r	20	E Castellotti	Ferrari	625	Ferrari	4	16	transmission	10	4
r	8	A Simon	Maserati	250F	Maserati	6	9	gearbox	8	3
r	2	J Behra	Maserati	250F	Maserati	6	9	oil line	3	1
r	22	R Manzon	Gordini	T16	Gordini	6	4	transmission	11	5
ns	34	J Fairman	Connaught	B	Alta	4		engine	21	9

Winning speed: 139.156 km/h, 86.468 mph
Pole Position speed: 144.360 km/h, 89.701 mph (S Moss, 2 min: 0.400 sec)
Fastest Lap speed: 144.360 km/h, 89.701 mph (S Moss, 2 min: 0.400 sec on lap 88)
Lap Leaders: J M Fangio 1-2,18-25 (10); S Moss 3-17,26-90 (80).

11 Sep 1955 — ITALY: Monza — (Round: 7) (Race: 48)

50 laps x 10.000 km, 6.214 miles = 500.000 km, 310.686 miles

POS.	NO	DRIVER	CAR	MODEL	ENGINE		LAPS	TIME/REASON FOR RETIREMENT	GRID:POS	ROW
1	18	J M Fangio	Mercedes-Benz	W196 str.	Mercedes	8	50	2h 25m 04.400s	1	1
2	14	P Taruffi	Mercedes-Benz	W196	Mercedes	8	50	2h 25m 05.100s	9	4
3	4	E Castellotti	Ferrari	555	Ferrari	4	50	2h 25m 50.600s	4	2
4	36	J Behra	Maserati	250F str.	Maserati	6	50	2h 29m 01.900s	6	3
5	34	C Menditéguy	Maserati	250F	Maserati	6	49		16	7
6	12	U Maglioli	Ferrari	555	Ferrari	4	49		12	5
7	28	R Mières	Maserati	250F	Maserati	6	48		7	3
8	8	M Trintignant	Ferrari	555	Ferrari	4	47		15	6
9	40	J Fitch	Maserati	250F	Maserati	6	46		20	8
r	6	M Hawthorn	Ferrari	555	Ferrari	4	38	gearbox mounting	14	6
r	20	K Kling	Mercedes-Benz	W196	Mercedes	8	32	gearbox	3	1
r	30	L Musso	Maserati	250F	Maserati	6	31	gearbox	10	4
r	38	H Gould	Maserati	250F	Maserati	6	31	oil sump	21	9
r	16	S Moss	Mercedes-Benz	W196 str.	Mercedes	8	27	engine	2	1
r	26	J Pollet	Gordini	T16	Gordini	6	26	engine	19	8
r	22	N da Silva Ramos	Gordini	T16	Gordini	6	23	fuel pump	18	7
r	32	P Collins	Maserati	250F	Maserati	6	22	rear suspension	11	5
r	42	H Schell	Vanwall	VW (55)	Vanwall	4	7	de Dion tube	13	5
r	24	J Lucas	Gordini	T32	Gordini	8	7	engine	22	9
r	44	K Wharton	Vanwall	VW (55)	Vanwall	4	0	fuel injection pump	17	7
ns	2	G Farina	Lancia	D50	Lancia	V8		tyres	5	2
ns	10	L Villoresi	Lancia	D50	Lancia	V8		tyres	8	3
ns	46	L Piotti	Arzani Volpini		Maserati	4		engine		

Winning speed: 206.792 km/h, 128.495 mph
Pole Position speed: 216.216 km/h, 134.351 mph (J M Fangio, 2 min:46.500 sec)
Fastest Lap speed: 215.698 km/h, 134.029 mph (S Moss, 2 min:46.900 sec on lap 21)
Lap Leaders: J M Fangio 1-7,9-50 (49); S Moss 8 (1).

Lap Leaders 1955

POS	DRIVER	CAR-ENGINE	GPS	LAPS	KM	MILES
1	J M Fangio	Mercedes-Benz	*6	309	1,874.3	1,164.6
2	S Moss	Mercedes-Benz	3	112	493.7	306.8
3	M Trintignant	Ferrari	1	20	62.9	39.1
4	A Ascari	Lancia	*1	12	46.9	29.2
5	F González	Ferrari	*1	11	43.0	26.7
6	H Schell	Maserati	*1	4	15.6	9.7
	R Mières	Maserati	*1	4	15.6	9.7
* lap totals include estimates			**6**	**472**	**2,552.2**	**1,585.9**

Driver Points 1955

		RA	MC	INDY	B	NL	GB	I	TOTAL	
1	J M Fangio	9	(1)	-	9	8	6	8	40	(1)
2	S Moss	1	-	-	6	6	9	1	23	
3	E Castellotti	-	6	-	-	2	-	4	12	
4	M Trintignant	3.33	8	-	-	-	-	-	11.33	
5	G Farina	3.33	3	-	4	-	-	-	10.33	
6	P Taruffi	-	-	-	-	-	3	6	9	
7	B Sweikert	-	-	8	-	-	-	-	8	
8	R Mières	2	-	-	1	4	-	-	7	
9	L Musso	-	-	-	-	4	2	-	6	
	J Behra	-	2	-	1	-	-	3	6	
11	K Kling	1	-	-	-	-	4	-	5	
12	J Davies	-	-	4	-	-	-	-	4	
13	T Bettenhausen	-	-	3	-	-	-	-	3	
	P Russo	-	-	3	-	-	-	-	3	
	J Thomson	-	-	3	-	-	-	-	3	
	P Frère	-	-	-	3	-	-	-	3	
17	F González	2	-	-	-	-	-	-	2	
	C Perdisa	-	2	-	-	-	-	-	2	
	L Villoresi	-	2	-	-	-	-	-	2	
	C Menditéguy	-	-	-	-	-	-	2	2	
21	U Maglioli	1.33	-	-	-	-	-	-	1.33	
22	H Herrmann	1	-	-	-	-	-	-	1	
	W Faulkner	-	-	1	-	-	-	-	1	
	B Homeier	-	-	1	-	-	-	-	1	
	B Vukovich	-	-	1	-	-	-	-	1	

8, 6, 4, 3 and 2 points awarded to the first five finishers. The driver setting the fastest lap scored a point also. Points shared for shared drives. Best 5 scores.

Mercedes withdrew at the end of 1955 just as British cars were beginning to be more prominent with the reappearance of BRM and the success of Connaught in the non-championship Syracuse Grand Prix in October 1955. Fangio moved to the Ferrari team which continued to modify the Lancia cars. Disc brakes became more evident.

FERRARI
Scuderia Ferrari: Fangio, Collins, Castellotti, Musso, de Portago, Gendebien, Frère, Pilette, (von Trips)
Scuderia Centro Sud: Scarlatti

MASERATI
Officine Alfieri Maserati: Moss, Behra, Godia, Perdisa, Villoresi (I), Maglioli (D,I), Landi, Gerini (RA), F González, Menditéguy, Taruffi, Bonnier
Scuderia Centro Sud: Villoresi (B), Schell, de Graffenried, (Chiron)
Scuderia Guastella: Maglioli (GB), Gerini (I)
Owen Racing Organisation: Hawthorn
Gilby Engineering Ltd: Salvadori
Ecurie Rosier: Rosier
L Piotti: Piotti, Villoresi
A Uria: Uria, O González
Gould's Garage (Bristol): Gould
Privateers: Volonterio, Simon, Halford, Brabham

GORDINI
Equipe Gordini: Manzon, da Silva Ramos, Pilette, Bayol, Milhoux, Simon

BUGATTI
Automobiles Bugatti: Trintignant

BRM
Owen Racing Organisation: Hawthorn, Brooks, Flockhart

COOPER
Privateer: Gerard

CONNAUGHT
Connaught Engineering: Fairman, Flockhart, Scott-Brown, Leston, Titterington
Privateer: Scotti

EMERYSON
Emeryson Cars: Emery

VANWALL
Vandervell Products Ltd: Schell, Trintignant, Hawthorn, F González, Taruffi, (Chapman)

22 Jan 1956 — ARGENTINA: Buenos Aires No.2 (Round: 1) (Race: 49)

98 laps x 3.912 km, 2.431 miles = 383.376 km, 238.219 miles

POS.	NO	DRIVER	CAR	MODEL	ENGINE		LAPS	TIME/REASON FOR RETIREMENT	GRID:POS	ROW
1=	34	L Musso	Lancia Ferrari	D50	Lancia Ferrari	V8			3	1
1=	34	J M Fangio	Lancia Ferrari	D50	Lancia Ferrari	V8	98	3h 00m 03.700s		
2	4	J Behra	Maserati	250F	Maserati	6	98	3h 00m 28.100s	4	1
3	14	M Hawthorn	Maserati	250F	Maserati	6	96		8	3
4=	10	C Landi	Maserati	250F	Maserati	6			11	3
4=	10	G Gerini	Maserati	250F	Maserati	6	92			
5	38	O Gendebien	Ferrari	555	Lancia Ferrari	V8	91		10	3
6=	16	A Uria	Maserati	A6GCM	Maserati	6			13	4
6=	16	O González	Maserati	A6GCM	Maserati	6	88			
r	2	S Moss	Maserati	250F	Maserati	6	81	engine	7	2
r	36	P Collins	Ferrari	555	Ferrari	4	58	accident	9	3
r	8	L Piotti	Maserati	250F	Maserati	6	57	accident	12	4
r	6	C Menditéguy	Maserati	250F	Maserati	6	42	half shaft	6	2
r	32	E Castellotti	Lancia Ferrari	D50	Lancia Ferrari	V8	40	gearbox	2	1
r	12	F González	Maserati	250F	Maserati	6	24	valve	5	2
r	30	J M Fangio	Lancia Ferrari	D50	Lancia Ferrari	V8	22	fuel pump	1	1

Winning speed: 127.748 km/h, 79.379 mph
Pole Position speed: 137.397 km/h, 85.375 mph (J M Fangio, 1 min:42.500 sec)
Fastest Lap speed: 133.744 km/h, 83.104 mph (J M Fangio, 1 min:45.300 sec)
Lap Leaders: F González 1-3 (3); C Menditéguy 4-42 (39); S Moss 43-66 (24); J M Fangio (32).

13 May 1956 — MONACO: Monte Carlo (Round: 2) (Race: 50)

100 laps x 3.145 km, 1.954 miles = 314.500 km, 195.421 miles

POS.	NO	DRIVER	CAR	MODEL	ENGINE		LAPS	TIME/REASON FOR RETIREMENT	GRID:POS	ROW
1	28	S Moss	Maserati	250F	Maserati	6	100	3h 00m 32.900s	2	1
2=	26	P Collins	Lancia Ferrari	D50	Lancia Ferrari	V8			9	4
2=	26	J M Fangio	Lancia Ferrari	D50	Lancia Ferrari	V8	100	3h 00m 39.000s		
3	30	J Behra	Maserati	250F	Maserati	6	99		4	2
4=	20	J M Fangio	Lancia Ferrari	D50	Lancia Ferrari	V8			1	1
4=	20	E Castellotti	Lancia Ferrari	D50	Lancia Ferrari	V8	94			
5	6	N da Silva Ramos	Gordini	T16	Gordini	8	93		14	6
r	2	R Manzon	Gordini	T16	Gordini	6	90	brakes/ accident	12	5
6=	4	É Bayol	Gordini	T32	Gordini	8			11	5
6=	4	A Pilette	Gordini	T32	Gordini	8	88			
7	32	C Perdisa	Maserati	250F	Maserati	6	86		7	3
8	18	H Gould	Maserati	250F	Maserati	6	85		16	7
r	8	L Rosier	Maserati	250F	Maserati	6	72	engine	15	6
r	22	E Castellotti	Lancia Ferrari	D50	Lancia Ferrari	V8	14	clutch	3	1
r	14	M Trintignant	Vanwall	VW (56)	Vanwall	4	13	engine overheating	6	3
r	16	H Schell	Vanwall	VW (56)	Vanwall	4	2	accident	5	2
r	24	L Musso	Lancia Ferrari	D50	Lancia Ferrari	V8	2	accident	8	3
ns	10	M Hawthorn	BRM	P25	BRM	4		engine	10	4
ns	12	T Brooks	BRM	P25	BRM	4		valve	13	5
ns	34	L Chiron	Maserati	250F	Maserati	6		engine		
nq	36	G Scarlatti	Ferrari	500	Ferrari	4				

Winning speed: 104.515 km/h, 64.943 mph
Pole Position speed: 108.865 km/h, 67.646 mph (J M Fangio, 1 min:44.000 sec)
Fastest Lap speed: 108.448 km/h, 67.387 mph (J M Fangio, 1 min:44.400 sec on lap 100)
Lap Leaders: S Moss 1-100 (100).

30 May 1956 — INDIANAPOLIS: 500 (Round: 3) (Race: 51)

200 laps x 4.023 km, 2.500 miles = 804.672 km, 500.000 miles

POS.	NO	DRIVER	CAR	MODEL	ENGINE		LAPS	TIME/REASON FOR RETIREMENT	GRID:POS	ROW
1	8	P Flaherty	Watson		Offenhauser	4	200	3h 53m 28.840s	1	1
2	4	S Hanks	Kurtis Kraft	500C	Offenhauser	4	200	3h 53m 49.290s	13	5
3	16	D Freeland	Phillips		Offenhauser	4	200		26	9
4	98	J Parsons	Kuzma		Offenhauser	4	200		6	2
5	73	D Rathmann	Kurtis Kraft	500C	Offenhauser	4	200		4	2
6	1	B Sweikert	Kuzma		Offenhauser	4	200		10	4
7	14	B Veith	Kurtis Kraft	500C	Offenhauser	4	200		23	8
8	19	R Ward	Kurtis Kraft	500C	Offenhauser	4	200		15	5
9	26	J Reece	Lesovsky		Offenhauser	4	200		21	7
10	27	C Griffith	Stevens		Offenhauser	4	199		30	10
11	82	G Hartley	Kuzma		Offenhauser	4	196		22	8
12	42	F Agabashian	Kurtis Kraft	500C	Offenhauser	4	196		7	3
13	57	B Christie	Kurtis Kraft	500D	Offenhauser	4	196		25	9
14	55	A Keller	Kurtis Kraft	4000	Offenhauser	4	195		28	10
15	81	E Johnson	Kuzma		Offenhauser	4	195		32	11
16	41	B Garrett	Kuzma		Offenhauser	4	194		29	10
17	64	D Dinsmore	Kurtis Kraft	500A	Offenhauser	4	191		33	11
18	7	P O'Connor	Kurtis Kraft	500D	Offenhauser	4	187		3	1
19	2	J Bryan	Kuzma		Offenhauser	4	185		19	7
20r	24	J Rathmann	Kurtis Kraft	500C	Offenhauser	4	175	oil pressure	2	1
21r	34	J Tolan	Kurtis Kraft	500C	Offenhauser	4	173	engine	31	11
22r	99	T Bettenhausen	Kurtis Kraft	500C	Offenhauser	4	160	tyre blow-out/ accident	5	2
23r=	10	E Elisian	Kurtis Kraft	500C	Offenhauser	4			14	5
23r=	10	E Russo	Kurtis Kraft	500C	Offenhauser	4	160	stalled		
24r	48	J Daywalt	Kurtis Kraft	500D	Offenhauser	4	134	accident	16	6
25r	54	J Turner	Kurtis Kraft	500B	Offenhauser	4	131	engine	24	8
26r	89	K Andrews	Kurtis Kraft	500B	Offenhauser	4	94	spin	20	7
27r	5	A Linden	Kurtis Kraft	500C	Offenhauser	4	90	oil leak	9	3
28r	12	A Herman	Kurtis Kraft	500B	Offenhauser	4	74	tyre blow-out/ accident	27	9
29r	49	R Crawford	Kurtis Kraft	500B	Offenhauser	4	49	accident	17	6
30r	15	J Boyd	Kurtis Kraft	500E	Offenhauser	4	35	engine	12	4
31r	53	T Ruttman	Kurtis Kraft	500C	Offenhauser	4	22	spin	11	4
32r	88	J Thomson	Kuzma		Offenhauser	4	22	spin in pits/ struck mechanic	18	6
33r	29	P Russo	Kurtis Kraft		Novi	8s	21	tyre blow-out/ accident	8	3

Winning speed: 206.785 km/h, 128.490 mph
Pole Position speed: 234.314 km/h, 145.596 mph (P Flaherty, 1 min: 1.815 sec)
Fastest Lap speed: 232.415 km/h, 144.416 mph (P Russo, 1 min: 2.320 sec on lap 19)

3 Jun 1956 — BELGIUM: Spa-Francorchamps (Round: 4) (Race: 52)

36 laps x 14.120 km, 8.774 miles = 508.320 km, 315.855 miles

POS.	NO	DRIVER	CAR	MODEL	ENGINE		LAPS	TIME/REASON FOR RETIREMENT	GRID:POS	ROW
1	8	P Collins	Lancia Ferrari	D50	Lancia Ferrari	V8	36	2h 40m 00.300s	3	1
2	6	P Frère	Lancia Ferrari	D50	Lancia Ferrari	V8	36	2h 41m 51.600s	8	3
3=	34	C Perdisa	Maserati	250F	Maserati	6			9	4
3=	34	S Moss	Maserati	250F	Maserati	6	36	2h 43m 16.900s		
4	10	H Schell	Vanwall	VW (56)	Vanwall	4	35		6	3
5	22	L Villoresi	Maserati	250F	Maserati	6	34		11	5
6	20	A Pilette	Lancia Ferrari	D50	Lancia Ferrari	V8	33		15	6
7	32	J Behra	Maserati	250F	Maserati	6	33		4	2
8	24	L Rosier	Maserati	250F	Maserati	6	33		10	4
r	2	J M Fangio	Lancia Ferrari	D50	Lancia Ferrari	V8	23	transmission	1	1
r	12	M Trintignant	Vanwall	VW (56)	Vanwall	4	11	engine	7	3
r	28	P Scotti	Connaught	B	Alta	4	10	oil pressure	12	5
r	30	S Moss	Maserati	250F	Maserati	6	10	wheel lost	2	1
r	4	E Castellotti	Lancia Ferrari	D50	Lancia Ferrari	V8	10	transmission	5	2
r	26	H Gould	Maserati	250F	Maserati	6	2	gearbox	14	6
r	36	C Godia	Maserati	250F	Maserati	6	0	accident	13	5
ns	38	M Hawthorn	Maserati	250F	Maserati	6		withdrew		

Winning speed: 190.614 km/h, 118.442 mph
Pole Position speed: 203.491 km/h, 126.443 mph (J M Fangio, 4 min: 9.800 sec)
Fastest Lap speed: 199.576 km/h, 124.011 mph (S Moss, 4 min:14.700 sec on lap 30)
Lap Leaders: S Moss 1-4 (4); J M Fangio 5-23 (19); P Collins 24-36 (13).

1 Jul 1956 — FRANCE: Reims (Round: 5) (Race: 53)

61 laps x 8.302 km, 5.159 miles = 506.422 km, 314.676 miles

POS.	NO	DRIVER	CAR	MODEL	ENGINE		LAPS	TIME/REASON FOR RETIREMENT	GRID:POS	ROW
1	14	P Collins	Lancia Ferrari	D50	Lancia Ferrari	V8	61	2h 34m 23.400s	3	1
2	12	E Castellotti	Lancia Ferrari	D50	Lancia Ferrari	V8	61	2h 34m 23.700s	2	1
3	4	J Behra	Maserati	250F	Maserati	6	61	2h 35m 53.300s	7	3
4	10	J M Fangio	Lancia Ferrari	D50	Lancia Ferrari	V8	61	2h 35m 58.500s	1	1
5=	6	C Perdisa	Maserati	250F	Maserati	6			13	5
5=	6	S Moss	Maserati	250F	Maserati	6	59			
6	36	L Rosier	Maserati	250F	Maserati	6	58		12	5
7	40	C Godia	Maserati	250F	Maserati	6	57		17	7
8	32	N da Silva Ramos	Gordini	T32	Gordini	8	57		14	6
9	30	R Manzon	Gordini	T32	Gordini	8	56		15	6
10=	24	M Hawthorn	Vanwall	VW (56)	Vanwall	4			6	3
10=	24	H Schell	Vanwall	VW (56)	Vanwall	4	56			
11	34	A Pilette	Gordini	T16	Gordini	6	55		19	8
r	42	A Simon	Maserati	250F	Maserati	6	41	engine	20	8
r	8	P Taruffi	Maserati	250F	Maserati	6	40	engine	16	5
r	44	O Gendebien	Lancia Ferrari	D50	Lancia Ferrari	V8	38	clutch	11	5
r	38	L Villoresi	Maserati	250F	Maserati	6	23	brakes	10	4
r	16	A de Portago	Lancia Ferrari	D50	Lancia Ferrari	V8	20	gearbox	9	4
r	28	M Trintignant	Bugatti	T251	Bugatti	8	18	throttle	18	7
r	2	S Moss	Maserati	250F	Maserati	6	12	gear lever	8	3
r	22	H Schell	Vanwall	VW (56)	Vanwall	4	5	engine	4	2
ns	26	C Chapman	Vanwall	VW (56)	Vanwall	4		accident	5	2

Winning speed: 196.809 km/h, 122.291 mph
Pole Position speed: 208.564 km/h, 129.596 mph (J M Fangio, 2 min:23.300 sec)
Fastest Lap speed: 204.988 km/h, 127.373 mph (J M Fangio, 2 min:25.800 sec on lap 61)
Lap Leaders: P Collins 1,47-48,50-61 (15); E Castellotti 2-3,39-46,49 (11); J M Fangio 4-38 (35).

C Chapman's qualifying time was set by H Schell.

14 July 1956 — BRITAIN: Silverstone (Round: 6) (Race: 54)

101 laps x 4.711 km, 2.927 miles = 475.766km, 295.627 miles

POS.	NO	DRIVER	CAR	MODEL	ENGINE		LAPS	TIME/REASON FOR RETIREMENT	GRID:POS	ROW
1	1	J M Fangio	Lancia Ferrari	D50	Lancia Ferrari	V8	101	2h 59m 47.000s	2	1
2=	4	A de Portago	Lancia Ferrari	D50	Lancia Ferrari	V8			12	4
2=	4	P Collins	Lancia Ferrari	D50	Lancia Ferrari	V8	100			
3	8	J Behra	Maserati	250F	Maserati	6	99		13	4
4	21	J Fairman	Connaught	B	Alta	4	98		21	6
5	31	H Gould	Maserati	250F	Maserati	6	97		14	4
6	11	L Villoresi	Maserati	250F	Maserati	6	96		19	6
7	9	C Perdisa	Maserati	250F	Maserati	6	95		15	5
8	10	C Godia	Maserati	250F	Maserati	6	94		25	7
9	15	R Manzon	Gordini	T32	Gordini	8	94		18	5
r	7	S Moss	Maserati	250F	Maserati	6	94	rear axle	1	1
10=	3	E Castellotti	Lancia Ferrari	D50	Lancia Ferrari	V8			8	3
10=	3	A de Portago	Lancia Ferrari	D50	Lancia Ferrari	V8	92			
11	26	B Gerard	Cooper	T23	Bristol	6	88		22	7
r	16	H Schell	Vanwall	VW (56)	Vanwall	4	86	fuel line	5	2
r	20	D Titterington	Connaught	B	Alta	4	74	connecting rod	11	3
r	14	N da Silva Ramos	Gordini	T32	Gordini	8	71	rear axle	26	8
r	17	M Trintignant	Vanwall	VW (56)	Vanwall	4	70	fuel line	16	5
r	2	P Collins	Lancia Ferrari	D50	Lancia Ferrari	V8	64	oil pressure	4	1
r	28	R Salvadori	Maserati	250F	Maserati	6	59	fuel pressure	7	2
r	24	T Brooks	BRM	P25	BRM	4	39	throttle/ accident	9	3
r	23	M Hawthorn	BRM	P25	BRM	4	24	oil leak	3	1
r	27	L Rosier	Maserati	250F	Maserati	6	23	carburettor union	27	8
r	29	B Halford	Maserati	250F	Maserati	6	22	piston	20	6
r	12	U Maglioli	Maserati	250F	Maserati	6	21	gearbox	24	7
r	19	A Scott-Brown	Connaught	B	Alta	4	16	wheel lost	10	3
r	32	P Emery	Emeryson	(56)	Alta	4	12	ignition	23	7
r	30	J Brabham	Maserati	250F	Maserati	6	3	engine	28	8
r	25	R Flockhart	BRM	P25	BRM	4	2	engine	17	5
r	18	F González	Vanwall	VW (56)	Vanwall	4	0	drive shaft	6	2

Winning Speed: 158.780 km/h, 98.661 mph
Pole Position speed: 167.901 km/h, 104.329 mph (S Moss, 1 min:41.000 sec)
Fastest Lap speed: 164.322 km/h, 102.105 mph (S Moss, 1 min:43.200 sec on lap 71)
Lap Leaders: M Hawthorn 1-15 (15); S Moss 16-68 (53); J M Fangio 69-101 (33).

5 Aug 1956 — GERMANY: Nürburgring (Round: 7) (Race: 55)

22 laps x 22.810 km, 14.173 miles = 501.820 km, 311.816 miles

POS.	NO	DRIVER	CAR	MODEL	ENGINE		LAPS	TIME/REASON FOR RETIREMENT	GRID:POS	ROW
1	1	J M Fangio	Lancia Ferrari	D50	Lancia Ferrari	V8	22	3h 38m 43.700s	1	1
2	7	S Moss	Maserati	250F	Maserati	6	22	3h 39m 30.100s	4	1
3	6	J Behra	Maserati	250F	Maserati	6	22	3h 46m 22.000s	8	3
4	20	C Godia	Maserati	250F	Maserati	6	20		16	5
dq	21	B Halford	Maserati	250F	Maserati	6	20	push start after spin	11	3
5	15	L Rosier	Maserati	250F	Maserati	6	19		14	4
nc	22	O Volonterio	Maserati	A6GCM	Maserati	6	16		19	6
r	11	A Milhoux	Gordini	T32	Gordini	8	15	misfire	21	6
r=	5	A de Portago	Lancia Ferrari	D50	Lancia Ferrari	V8			10	3
r=	5	P Collins	Lancia Ferrari	D50	Lancia Ferrari	V8	14	accident		
r	18	L Villoresi	Maserati	250F	Maserati	6	13	engine	20	6
r	12	H Schell	Maserati	250F	Maserati	6	13	engine overheating	12	4
r=	4	L Musso	Lancia Ferrari	D50	Lancia Ferrari	V8			5	2
r=	4	E Castellotti	Lancia Ferrari	D50	Lancia Ferrari	V8	11	accident		
r	2	P Collins	Lancia Ferrari	D50	Lancia Ferrari	V8	8	fuel line/ leak	2	1
r	3	E Castellotti	Lancia Ferrari	D50	Lancia Ferrari	V8	5	magneto	3	1
r	8	U Maglioli	Maserati	250F	Maserati	6	3	steering	7	2
r	19	H Gould	Maserati	250F	Maserati	6	3	oil pressure	13	4
r	16	R Salvadori	Maserati	250F	Maserati	6	2	rear suspension	9	3
r	10	R Manzon	Gordini	T32	Gordini	8	0	suspension	15	5
r	14	G Scarlatti	Ferrari	500	Ferrari	4	0	engine	17	5
ns	8	C Perdisa	Maserati	250F	Maserati	6		accident/ injury	6	2
ns	11	A Pilette	Gordini	T32	Gordini	8		accident/ injury	18	5
ns	18	L Piotti	Maserati	250F	Maserati	6		car raced by Villoresi		

Winning Speed: 137.656 km/h, 85.535 mph
Pole Position speed: 138.897 km/h, 86.307 mph (J M Fangio, 9 min:51.200 sec)
Fastest Lap speed: 141.190 km/h, 87.731 mph (J M Fangio, 9 min:41.600 sec on lap 14)
Lap Leaders: J M Fangio 1-22 (22).

2 Sep 1956 — ITALY: Monza (Round: 8) (Race: 56)

50 laps x 10.000 km, 6.214 miles = 500.000 km, 310.686 miles

POS.	NO	DRIVER	CAR	MODEL	ENGINE		LAPS	TIME/REASON FOR RETIREMENT	GRID:POS	ROW
1	36	S Moss	Maserati	250F	Maserati	6	50	2h 23m 41.300s	6	2
2=	26	P Collins	Lancia Ferrari	D50	Lancia Ferrari	V8			7	3
2=	26	J M Fangio	Lancia Ferrari	D50	Lancia Ferrari	V8	50	2h 23m 47.000s		
3	4	R Flockhart	Connaught	B	Alta	4	49		23	8
4	38	C Godia	Maserati	250F	Maserati	6	49		17	6
r	28	L Musso	Lancia Ferrari	D50	Lancia Ferrari	V8	46	steering	3	1
5	6	J Fairman	Connaught	B	Alta	4	47		15	5
6	40	L Piotti	Maserati	250F	Maserati	6	47		14	5
7	14	E de Graffenried	Maserati	250F	Maserati	6	46		18	6
8=	22	J M Fangio	Lancia Ferrari	D50	Lancia Ferrari	V8			1	1
8=	22	E Castellotti	Lancia Ferrari	D50	Lancia Ferrari	V8	46			
9	12	A Simon	Gordini	T16	Gordini	6	45		24	8
r=	46	U Maglioli	Maserati	250F	Maserati	6			12	4
r=	46	J Behra	Maserati	250F	Maserati	6	42	steering		
10	42	G Gerini	Maserati	250F	Maserati	6	42		16	6
11	44	R Salvadori	Maserati	250F	Maserati	6	41		13	5
r	18	H Schell	Vanwall	VW (56)	Vanwall	4	32	transmission	10	4
r	32	J Behra	Maserati	250F	Maserati	6	23	magneto	5	2
r	48	B Halford	Maserati	250F	Maserati	6	16	engine	21	7
r	20	M Trintignant	Vanwall	VW (56)	Vanwall	4	13	rear suspension	11	4
r	16	P Taruffi	Vanwall	VW (56)	Vanwall	4	12	suspension	4	2
r	24	E Castellotti	Lancia Ferrari	D50	Lancia Ferrari	V8	9	puncture	2	1
r	10	R Manzon	Gordini	T32	Gordini	8	7	gearbox	22	8
r=	34	L Villoresi	Maserati	250F	Maserati	6			8	3
r=	34	J Bonnier	Maserati	250F	Maserati	6	7	engine		
r	30	A de Portago	Lancia Ferrari	D50	Lancia Ferrari	V8	6	puncture	9	3
r	2	L Leston	Connaught	B	Alta	4	6	torsion bar	19	7
r	8	N da Silva Ramos	Gordini	T32	Gordini	8	3	engine	20	7
ns	4	A Scott-Brown	Connaught	B	Alta	4		refused race entry		
ns	50	W von Trips	Lancia Ferrari	D50	Lancia Ferrari	V8		accident		

Winning speed: 208.785 km/h, 129.733 mph
Pole Position speed: 221.402 km/h, 137.573 mph (J M Fangio, 2 min:42.600 sec)
Fastest Lap speed: 217.523 km/h, 135.162 mph (S Moss, 2 min:45.500 sec on lap 47)
Lap Leaders: E Castellotti 1-4 (4); S Moss 5-10,12-45,48-50 (43); H Schell 11 (1); L Musso 46-47 (2).

Also the Grand Prix of Europe.

Lap Leaders 1956

POS	DRIVER	CAR-ENGINE	GPS	LAPS	KM	MILES
1	S Moss	Maserati	5	224	1,144.6	711.2
2	J M Fangio	Ferrari	5	141	1,341.3	833.5
3	C Menditéguy	Maserati	1	39	152.6	94.8
4	P Collins	Ferrari	2	28	308.1	191.4
5	E Castellotti	Ferrari	2	15	131.3	81.6
	M Hawthorn	BRM	1	15	70.7	43.9
7	F González	Maserati	1	3	11.7	7.3
8	L Musso	Ferrari	1	2	20.0	12.4
9	H Schell	Vanwall	1	1	10.0	6.2
			7	**468**	**3,190.2**	**1,982.3**

Driver Points 1956

		RA	MC	INDY	B	F	GB	D	I	Total	
1	J M Fangio	5	4	-	-	4	8	9	(3)	30	(3)
2	S Moss	-	8	-	3	1	(1)	6	9	27	(1)
3	P Collins	-	3	-	8	8	3	-	3	25	
4	J Behra	6	4	-	-	4	4	4	-	22	
5	P Flaherty	-	-	8	-	-	-	-	-	8	
6	E Castellotti	-	1.5	-	-	6	-	-	-	7.5	
7	S Hanks	-	-	6	-	-	-	-	-	6	
	P Frère	-	-	-	6	-	-	-	-	6	
	C Godia	-	-	-	-	-	-	3	3	6	
10	J Fairman	-	-	-	-	-	3	-	2	5	
11	M Hawthorn	4	-	-	-	-	-	-	-	4	
	L Musso	4	-	-	-	-	-	-	-	4	
	D Freeland	-	-	4	-	-	-	-	-	4	
	R Flockhart	-	-	-	-	-	-	-	4	4	
15	J Parsons	-	-	3	-	-	-	-	-	3	
	H Schell	-	-	-	3	-	-	-	-	3	
	A de Portago	-	-	-	-	-	3	-	-	3	
	C Perdisa	-	-	-	2	1	-	-	-	3	
19	O Gendebien	2	-	-	-	-	-	-	-	2	
	N da Silva Ramos	-	2	-	-	-	-	-	-	2	
	D Rathmann	-	-	2	-	-	-	-	-	2	
	L Villoresi	-	-	-	2	-	-	-	-	2	
	H Gould	-	-	-	-	-	2	-	-	2	
	L Rosier	-	-	-	-	-	-	2	-	2	
25	G Gerini	1.5	-	-	-	-	-	-	-	1.5	
	C Landi	1.5	-	-	-	-	-	-	-	1.5	
27	P Russo	-	-	1	-	-	-	-	-	1	

8, 6, 4, 3 and 2 points awarded to the first five finishers. The driver setting the fastest lap scored a point also. Points shared for shared drives. Best 5 scores. J M Fangio was classified both 2nd and 4th in shared drives at Monaco. He only received points for his 2nd place.

Italian GP 1957. Stirling Moss went on to win, with Fangio second.

Gordini withdrew from racing and Connaught followed soon after the Monaco Grand Prix. Formula 2 re-emerged with rearengine Coopers showing the way forward. Ferrari, Maserati and Vanwall dominated the races; the highlight of which was Fangio's stunning performance at the Nürburgring, often regarded as the championship's finest race.

FERRARI
Scuderia Ferrari: Musso, Hawthorn, Collins, Trintignant, von Trips, Castellotti, Perdisa, González, de Portago
Scuderia Centro Sud: de Tomaso

MASERATI
Officine Alfieri Maserati: Fangio, Behra, Schell, Menditéguy, Scarlatti, Moss, (Herrmann)
Scuderia Centro Sud: Gregory, Bonnier, Schell (MC), Herrmann (D), (Simon)
Gilby Engineering Ltd: Bueb
Ottorino Volonterio: Volonterio, Simon (I)
Privateers: Godia, Gould, Halford, Piotti, Bonnier (GB)

BRM
Owen Racing Organisation: Flockhart, MacKay-Fraser, Leston, Fairman, (Salvadori)

COOPER
Cooper Car Co: Brabham, Salvadori, MacDowel, (Leston)
Privateer: Gerard

CONNAUGHT
Connaught Engineering: Lewis-Evans, Bueb

VANWALL
Vandervell Products Ltd: Moss, Brooks, Lewis-Evans, Salvadori
(Entries for the F2 section are not included above)

13 Jan 1957 — ARGENTINA: Buenos Aires No. 2 (Round: 1) (Race: 57)
100 laps x 3.912 km, 2.431 miles = 391.200 km, 243.080 miles

POS.	NO	DRIVER	CAR	MODEL	ENGINE		LAPS	TIME/REASON FOR RETIREMENT	GRID:POS	ROW
1	2	J M Fangio	Maserati	250F	Maserati	6	100	3h 00m 55.900s	2	1
2	6	J Behra	Maserati	250F	Maserati	6	100	3h 01m 14.200s	3	1
3	8	C Menditéguy	Maserati	250F	Maserati	6	99		8	3
4	22	H Schell	Maserati	250F	Maserati	6	98		9	3
5=	20	F González	Lancia Ferrari	801	Lancia Ferrari	V8			10	3
5=	20	A de Portago	Lancia Ferrari	801	Lancia Ferrari	V8	98			
6=	18	C Perdisa	Lancia Ferrari	801	Lancia Ferrari	V8			11	3
6=	18	P Collins	Lancia Ferrari	801	Lancia Ferrari	V8				
6=	18	W von Trips	Lancia Ferrari	801	Lancia Ferrari	V8	98			
7	24	J Bonnier	Maserati	250F	Maserati	6	95		13	4
8	4	S Moss	Maserati	250F	Maserati	6	93		1	1
9	26	A de Tomaso	Ferrari	500	Ferrari	4	91		12	4
10	28	L Piotti	Maserati	250F	Maserati	6	90		14	4
r	14	E Castellotti	Lancia Ferrari	801	Lancia Ferrari	V8	75	hub shaft	4	1
r	16	M Hawthorn	Lancia Ferrari	801	Lancia Ferrari	V8	35	clutch	7	2
r	12	L Musso	Lancia Ferrari	801	Lancia Ferrari	V8	31	clutch	6	2
r	10	P Collins	Lancia Ferrari	801	Lancia Ferrari	V8	26	clutch	5	2

Winning Speed: 129.729 km/h, 80.610 mph
Pole Position speed: 137.263 km/h, 85.291 mph (S Moss, 1 min:42.600 sec)
Fastest Lap speed: 134.510 km/h, 83.581 mph (S Moss, 1 min:44.700 sec on lap 75)
Lap Leaders: J Behra 1-2,9-12,81,84 (8); E Castellotti 3-8 (6); P Collins 13-25 (13); J M Fangio 26-80,82-83,85-100 (73).

19 May 1957 — MONACO: Monte Carlo (Round: 2) (Race: 58)
105 laps x 3.145 km, 1.954 miles = 330.225 km, 205.192 miles

POS.	NO	DRIVER	CAR	MODEL	ENGINE		LAPS	TIME/REASON FOR RETIREMENT	GRID:POS	ROW
1	32	J M Fangio	Maserati	250F	Maserati	6	105	3h 10m12.800s	1	1
2	20	T Brooks	Vanwall	VW (57)	Vanwall	4	105	3h 10m 38.000s	4	2
3	2	M Gregory	Maserati	250F	Maserati	6	103		10	4
4	10	S Lewis-Evans	Connaught	B	Alta	4	102		13	5
5	30	M Trintignant	Lancia Ferrari	801	Lancia Ferrari	V8	100		6	3
6	14	J Brabham	Cooper	T43	Climax	4	100		15	6
7r=	24	W von Trips	Lancia Ferrari	801	Lancia Ferrari	V8			9	4
7r=	24	M Hawthorn	Lancia Ferrari	801	Lancia Ferrari	V8	95	engine/ accident		
r=	34	G Scarlatti	Maserati	250F	Maserati	6			14	6
r=	34	H Schell	Maserati	250F	Maserati	6	64	oil leak		
r	6	R Flockhart	BRM	P25	BRM	4	60	timing gear	11	5
r	36	C Menditéguy	Maserati	250F	Maserati	6	51	accident	7	3
r	12	I Bueb	Connaught	B	Alta	4	47	fuel tank	16	7
r	38	H Schell	Maserati	250F	Maserati	6	23	suspension	8	3
r	22	H Gould	Maserati	250F	Maserati	6	10	accident	12	5
r	28	M Hawthorn	Lancia Ferrari	801	Lancia Ferrari	V8	4	accident	5	2
r	26	P Collins	Lancia Ferrari	801	Lancia Ferrari	V8	4	accident	2	1
r	18	S Moss	Vanwall	VW (57)	Vanwall	4	4	accident	3	1
nq	40	H Herrmann	Maserati	250F	Maserati	6				
nq	4	A Simon	Maserati	250F	Maserati	6				
nq	8	R Salvadori	BRM	P25	BRM	4				
nq	42	L Piotti	Maserati	250F	Maserati	6				
nq	16	L Leston	Cooper	T43	Climax	4				

Winning Speed: 104.165 km/h, 64.725 mph
Pole Position speed: 110.243 km/h, 68.502 mph (J M Fangio, 1 min:42.700 sec)
Fastest Lap speed: 107.216 km/h, 66.621 mph (J M Fangio, 1 min:45.600 sec)
Lap Leaders: S Moss 1-4 (4); J M Fangio 5-105 (101).

30 May 1957 — INDIANAPOLIS: 500 (Round: 3) (Race: 59)

200 laps x 4.023 km, 2.500 miles = 804.672 km, 500.000 miles

POS.	NO	DRIVER	CAR	MODEL	ENGINE		LAPS	TIME/REASON FOR RETIREMENT	GRID:POS	ROW
1	9	S Hanks	Epperly		Offenhauser	4	200	3h 41m 14.250s	13	5
2	26	J Rathmann	Epperly		Offenhauser	4	200	3h 41m 35.711s	32	11
3	1	J Bryan	Kuzma		Offenhauser	4	200		15	5
4	54	P Russo	Kurtis Kraft		Novi	8s	200		10	4
5	73	A Linden	Kurtis Kraft	500G	Offenhauser	4	200		12	4
6	6	J Boyd	Kurtis Kraft	500G	Offenhauser	4	200		5	2
7	48	M Teague	Kurtis Kraft	500D	Offenhauser	4	200		28	10
8	12	P O'Connor	Kurtis Kraft	500G	Offenhauser	4	200		1	1
9.	7	B Veith	Phillips		Offenhauser	4	200		16	6
10	22	G Hartley	Lesovsky		Offenhauser	4	200		14	5
11	19	J Turner	Kurtis Kraft	500G	Offenhauser	4	200		19	7
12	10	J Thomson	Kuzma		Offenhauser	4	199		11	4
13	95	B Christie	Kurtis Kraft	500C	Offenhauser	4	197		33	11
14	82	C Weyant	Kuzma		Offenhauser	4	196		25	9
15	27	T Bettenhausen	Kurtis Kraft		Novi	8s	195		22	8
16	18	J Parsons	Kurtis Kraft	500G	Offenhauser	4	195		17	6
17	3	D Freeland	Kurtis Kraft	500D	Offenhauser	4	192		21	7
18r	5	J Reece	Kurtis Kraft	500C	Offenhauser	4	182	throttle	6	2
19r	92	D Edmunds	Kurtis Kraft	500G	Offenhauser	4	170	spin	27	9
20r	28	J Tolan	Kuzma		Offenhauser	4	138	clutch	31	11
21r	89	A Herman	Dunn		Offenhauser	4	111	accident	30	10
22r	14	F Agabashian	Kurtis Kraft	500G	Offenhauser	4	107	fuel leak	4	2
23r	88	E Sachs	Kuzma		Offenhauser	4	105	piston	2	1
24r	77	M Magill	Kurtis Kraft	500G	Offenhauser	4	101	accident	18	6
25r	43	E Johnson	Kurtis Kraft	500G	Offenhauser	4	93	front wheel bearing	20	7
26r	31	B Cheesbourg	Kurtis Kraft	500G	Offenhauser	4	81	fuel leak	23	8
27r	16	A Keller	Kurtis Kraft	500G	Offenhauser	4	75	accident	8	3
28r	57	J Daywalt	Kurtis Kraft	500C	Offenhauser	4	53	accident	29	10
29r	83	E Elisian	Kurtis Kraft	500C	Offenhauser	4	51	timing gear	7	3
30r	8	R Ward	Lesovsky		Offenhauser	4s	27	supercharger bearing	24	8
31r	52	T Ruttman	Watson		Offenhauser	4	13	piston	3	1
32r	55	E Russo	Kurtis Kraft	500C	Offenhauser	4	0	accident	26	9
33r	23	E George	Kurtis Kraft	500B	Offenhauser	4	0	accident	9	3

Winning Speed: 218.228 km/h, 135.601 mph
Pole Position speed: 231.664 km/h, 143.949 mph (P O'Connor, 1 min: 2.522 sec)
Fastest Lap speed: 230.822 km/h, 143.426 mph (J Rathmann, 1 min: 2.750 sec on lap 127)
Fastest qualifier: P Russo (233.060 km/h, 144.817 mph)

7 Jul 1957 — FRANCE: Rouen-les-Essarts (Round:4) (Race: 60)

77 laps x 6.542 km, 4.065 miles = 503.734 km, 313.006 miles

POS.	NO	DRIVER	CAR	MODEL	ENGINE		LAPS	TIME/REASON FOR RETIREMENT	GRID:POS	ROW
1	2	J M Fangio	Maserati	250F	Maserati	6	77	3h 07m 46.400s	1	1
2	10	L Musso	Lancia Ferrari	801	Lancia Ferrari	V8	77	3h 08m 37.200s	3	1
3	12	P Collins	Lancia Ferrari	801	Lancia Ferrari	V8	77	3h 09m 52.400s	5	2
4	14	M Hawthorn	Lancia Ferrari	801	Lancia Ferrari	V8	76		7	3
5	4	J Behra	Maserati	250F	Maserati	6	70		2	1
6	6	H Schell	Maserati	250F	Maserati	6	70		4	2
7=	24	M MacDowel	Cooper	T43	Climax	4			15	6
7=	24	J Brabham	Cooper	T43	Climax	4	68			
r	18	S Lewis-Evans	Vanwall	VW (57)	Vanwall	4	30	steering	10	4
r	8	C Menditéguy	Maserati	250F	Maserati	6	30	engine	9	4
r	20	R Salvadori	Vanwall	VW (57)	Vanwall	4	25	valve spring	6	3
r	28	H MacKay-Fraser	BRM	P25	BRM	4	24	transmission	12	5
r	16	M Trintignant	Lancia Ferrari	801	Lancia Ferrari	V8	23	magneto	8	3
r	30	H Gould	Maserati	250F	Maserati	6	4	rear axle	14	6
r	22	J Brabham	Cooper	T43	Climax	4	4	accident	13	5
r	26	R Flockhart	BRM	P25	BRM	4	2	accident	11	5

Winning Speed: 160.960 km/h, 100.016 mph
Pole Position speed: 166.440 km/h, 103.421 mph (J M Fangio, 2 min:21.500 sec)
Fastest Lap speed: 165.388 km/h, 102.767 mph (L Musso, 2 min:22.400 sec on lap 65)
Lap Leaders: L Musso 1-3 (3); J M Fangio 4-77 (74).

There is an element of doubt as to the respective positions of J Behra and H Schell. Some contemporary reports suggest that Behra's final lap was completed slower than the minimum time allowed, after he had pushed his car across the line.

20 Jul 1957 — BRITAIN: Aintree (Round: 5) (Race: 61)

90 laps x 4.828 km, 3.000 miles = 434.523 km, 270.000 miles

POS.	NO	DRIVER	CAR	MODEL	ENGINE		LAPS	TIME/REASON FOR RETIREMENT	GRID:POS	ROW
1=	20	T Brooks	Vanwall	VW (57)	Vanwall	4			3	1
1=	20	S Moss	Vanwall	VW (57)	Vanwall	4	90	3h 06m 37.800s		
2	14	L Musso	Lancia Ferrari	801	Lancia Ferrari	V8	90	3h 07m 03.400s	10	4
3	10	M Hawthorn	Lancia Ferrari	801	Lancia Ferrari	V8	90	3h 07m 20.600s	5	2
4=	16	M Trintignant	Lancia Ferrari	801	Lancia Ferrari	V8			9	4
4=	16	P Collins	Lancia Ferrari	801	Lancia Ferrari	V8	88			
5	36	R Salvadori	Cooper	T43	Climax	4	85		15	6
6	38	B Gerard	Cooper	T44	Bristol	6	82		18	7
7	22	S Lewis-Evans	Vanwall	VW (57)	Vanwall	4	82		6	3

POS.	NO	DRIVER	CAR	MODEL	ENGINE		LAPS	TIME/REASON FOR RETIREMENT	GRID:POS	ROW
r	34	J Brabham	Cooper	T43	Climax	4	74	clutch	13	5
8	32	I Bueb	Maserati	250F	Maserati	6	71		19	8
r	4	J Behra	Maserati	250F	Maserati	6	69	clutch	2	1
r	12	P Collins	Lancia Ferrari	801	Lancia Ferrari	V8	53	radiator pipe	8	3
r=	18	S Moss	Vanwall	VW (57)	Vanwall	4			1	1
r=	18	T Brooks	Vanwall	VW (57)	Vanwall	4	51	engine		
r	2	J M Fangio	Maserati	250F	Maserati	6	49	engine	4	2
r	24	J Fairman	BRM	P25	BRM	4	46	engine	16	7
r	26	L Leston	BRM	P25	BRM	4	44	engine	12	5
r	6	H Schell	Maserati	250F	Maserati	6	39	water pump	7	3
r	8	C Menditéguy	Maserati	250F	Maserati	6	35	transmission	11	5
r	28	J Bonnier	Maserati	250F	Maserati	6	18	transmission	17	7
ns	30	H Gould	Maserati	250F	Maserati	6		accident/ injury	14	6

Winning Speed: 139.696 km/h, 86.803 mph
Pole Position speed: 144.600 km/h, 89.850 mph (S Moss, 2 min: 0.200 sec)
Fastest Lap speed: 145.813 km/h, 90.604 mph (S Moss, 1 min:59.200 sec)
Lap Leaders: S Moss 1-22,70-90 (43); J Behra 23-69 (47).

Also the Grand Prix of Europe.

4 Aug 1957 — GERMANY: Nürburgring (Round: 6) (Race: 62)
22 laps x 22.810 km, 14.173 miles = 501.820 km, 311.816 miles

POS.	NO	DRIVER	CAR	MODEL	ENGINE		LAPS	TIME/REASON FOR RETIREMENT	GRID:POS	ROW
1	1	J M Fangio	Maserati	250F	Maserati	6	22	3h 30m 38.300s	1	1
2	8	M Hawthorn	Lancia Ferrari	801	Lancia Ferrari	V8	22	3h 30m 41.900s	2	1
3	7	P Collins	Lancia Ferrari	801	Lancia Ferrari	V8	22	3h 31m 13.900s	4	1
4	6	L Musso	Lancia Ferrari	801	Lancia Ferrari	V8	22	3h 34m 15.900s	8	3
5	10	S Moss	Vanwall	VW (57)	Vanwall	4	22	3h 35m 15.800s	7	2
6	2	J Behra	Maserati	250F	Maserati	6	22	3h 35m 16.800s	3	1
7	3	H Schell	Maserati	250F	Maserati	6	22	3h 37m 25.800s	6	2
8	16	M Gregory	Maserati	250F	Maserati	6	21		10	3
9.	11	T Brooks	Vanwall	VW (57)	Vanwall	4	21		5	2
10	4	G Scarlatti	Maserati	250F	Maserati	6	21		13	4
11	15	B Halford	Maserati	250F	Maserati	6	21		16	5
12	21	E Barth	* Porsche	RS550	Porsche	F4	21	(1st F2 Section)	12	4
13	28	B Naylor	* Cooper	T43	Climax	4	20		17	5
14	27	C G de Beaufort	* Porsche	RS550	Porsche	F4	20		20	6
15	25	T Marsh	* Cooper	T43	Climax	4	17		22	7
r	17	H Herrmann	Maserati	250F	Maserati	6	14	engine	11	3
r	20	U Maglioli	* Porsche	RS550	Porsche	F4	13	engine	15	5
r	18	C Godia	Maserati	250F	Maserati	6	11	steering	21	6
r	23	R Salvadori	* Cooper	T43	Climax	4	11	suspension	14	4
r	12	S Lewis-Evans	Vanwall	VW (57)	Vanwall	4	10	gearbox	9	3
r	24	J Brabham	* Cooper	T43	Climax	4	6	transmission	18	5
r	26	P England	* Cooper	T41	Climax	4	4	distributor	23	7
r	29	D Gibson	* Cooper	T43	Climax	4	3	steering	24	7
r	19	H Gould	Maserati	250F	Maserati	6	1	crown wheel	19	6

Winning Speed: 142.943 km/h, 88.820 mph
Pole Position speed: 145.184 km/h, 90.213 mph (J M Fangio, 9 min:25.600 sec)
Fastest Lap speed: 147.320 km/h, 91.540 mph (J M Fangio, 9 min:17.400 sec on lap 20)
Lap Leaders: M Hawthorn 1-2,15-20 (8); J M Fangio 3-11,21-22 (11); P Collins 12-14 (3).

*Formula 2 cars raced simultaneously with F1, and are marked thus *.*

18 Aug 1957 — PESCARA : Pescara (Round: 7) (Race: 63)
18 laps x 25.579 km, 15.894 miles = 460.422 km, 286.093 miles

POS.	NO	DRIVER	CAR	MODEL	ENGINE		LAPS	TIME/REASON FOR RETIREMENT	GRID:POS	ROW
1	26	S Moss	Vanwall	VW (57)	Vanwall	4	18	2h 59m 22.700s	2	1
2	2	J M Fangio	Maserati	250F	Maserati	6	18	3h 02m 36.600s	1	1
3	6	H Schell	Maserati	250F	Maserati	6	18	3h 06m 09.500s	5	2
4	14	M Gregory	Maserati	250F	Maserati	6	18	3h 07m 39.200s	7	3
5	30	S Lewis-Evans	Vanwall	VW (57)	Vanwall	4	17		8	3
6	8	G Scarlatti	Maserati	250F	Maserati	6	17		10	4
7	24	J Brabham	Cooper	T43	Climax	4	15		16	7
r	10	C Godia	Maserati	250F	Maserati	6	10	engine	12	5
r	20	B Halford	Maserati	250F	Maserati	6	9	differential	14	6
r	34	L Musso	Lancia Ferrari	801	Lancia Ferrari	V8	9	oil tank	3	1
r	16	J Bonnier	Maserati	250F	Maserati	6	7	engine overheating	9	4
r	4	J Behra	Maserati	250F	Maserati	6	4	oil line	4	2
r	22	R Salvadori	Cooper	T43	Climax	4	3	accident/suspension	15	6
r	12	L Piotti	Maserati	250F	Maserati	6	1	engine	13	5
r	18	H Gould	Maserati	250F	Maserati	6	1	accident	11	5
r	28	T Brooks	Vanwall	VW (57)	Vanwall	4	1	engine	6	3

Winning Speed: 154.006 km/h, 95.695 mph
Pole Position speed: 157.517 km/h, 97.876 mph (J M Fangio, 9 min:44.600 sec)
Fastest Lap speed: 157.517 km/h, 97.876 mph (S Moss, 9 min:44.600 sec on lap 9)
Lap Leaders: L Musso 1 (1); S Moss 2-18 (17).

8 Sep 1957 — ITALY: Monza (Round: 8) (Race: 64)

87 laps x 5.750 km, 3.573 miles = 500.250 km, 310.841 miles

POS.	NO	DRIVER	CAR	MODEL	ENGINE		LAPS	TIME/REASON FOR RETIREMENT	GRID:POS	ROW
1	18	S Moss	Vanwall	VW (57)	Vanwall	4	87	2h 35m 03.900s	2	1
2	2	J M Fangio	Maserati	250F	Maserati	6	87	2h 35m 45.100s	4	1
3	36	W von Trips	Lancia Ferrari	801	Lancia Ferrari	V8	85		8	3
4	26	M Gregory	Maserati	250F	Maserati	6	84		11	3
5=	8	G Scarlatti	Maserati	250F	Maserati	6			12	4
5=	8	H Schell	Maserati	250F	Maserati	6	84			
6	34	M Hawthorn	Lancia Ferrari	801	Lancia Ferrari	V8	83		10	3
7	22	T Brooks	Vanwall	VW (57)	Vanwall	4	82		3	1
8	32	L Musso	Lancia Ferrari	801	Lancia Ferrari	V8	82		9	3
9	10	C Godia	Maserati	250F	Maserati	6	81		15	5
10	14	H Gould	Maserati	250F	Maserati	6	78		18	5
11=	28	A Simon	Maserati	250F	Maserati	6			16	5
11=	28	O Volonterio	Maserati	250F	Maserati	6	72			
r	30	P Collins	Lancia Ferrari	801	Lancia Ferrari	V8	62	valve	7	2
r	6	J Behra	Maserati	250F	Maserati	V12	50	engine overheating	5	2
r	20	S Lewis-Evans	Vanwall	VW (57)	Vanwall	4	49	header tank	1	1
r	16	B Halford	Maserati	250F	Maserati	6	47	engine	14	4
r	4	H Schell	Maserati	250F	Maserati	6	34	oil line	6	2
r	24	J Bonnier	Maserati	250F	Maserati	6	31	engine overheating	13	4
r	12	L Piotti	Maserati	250F	Maserati	6	3	engine	17	5

Winning speed: 193.564 km/h, 120.275 mph
Pole Position speed: 202.148 km/h, 125.609 mph (S Lewis-Evans, 1 min:42.400 sec)
Fastest Lap speed: 199.614 km/h, 124.035 mph (T Brooks, 1 min:43.700 sec on lap 74)
Lap Leaders: S Moss 1-3,5,11,21-87 (72); J Behra 4,6 (2); J M Fangio 7-10 (4); T Brooks12-15 (4); S Lewis-Evans 16-20 (5).

Lap Leaders 1957

POS	DRIVER	CAR-ENGINE	GPS	LAPS	KM	MILES
1	J M Fangio	Maserati	5	263	1,361.2	845.8
2	S Moss	Vanwall	4	136	1,069.0	664.3
3	J Behra	Maserati	3	57	269.7	167.6
4	P Collins	Ferrari	2	16	119.3	74.1
5	M Hawthorn	Ferrari	1	8	182.5	113.4
6	E Castellotti	Ferrari	1	6	23.5	14.6
7	S Lewis-Evans	Vanwall	1	5	28.7	17.9
8	L Musso	Ferrari	2	4	45.2	28.1
	T Brooks	Vanwall	1	4	23.0	14.3
			7	**499**	**3,122.2**	**1,940.0**

Driver Points 1957

		RA	MC	INDY	F	GB	D	PES	I	TOTAL	
1	J M Fangio	8	9	-	8	-	9	6	(6)	40	(6)
2	S Moss	1	-	-	-	5	2	9	8	25	
3	L Musso	-	-	-	7	6	3	-	-	16	
4	M Hawthorn	-	-	-	3	4	6	-	-	13	
5	T Brooks	-	6	-	-	4	-	-	1	11	
6	M Gregory	-	4	-	-	-	-	3	3	10	
7	S Hanks	-	-	8	-	-	-	-	-	8	
	J Behra	6	-	-	2	-	-	-	-	8	
	P Collins	-	-	-	4	-	4	-	-	8	
	H Schell	3	-	-	-	-	-	4	1	8	
11	J Rathmann	-	-	7	-	-	-	-	-	7	
12	S Lewis-Evans	-	3	-	-	-	-	2	-	5	
	M Trintignant	-	2	-	-	3	-	-	-	5	
14	C Menditéguy	4	-	-	-	-	-	-	-	4	
	J Bryan	-	-	4	-	-	-	-	-	4	
	W von Trips	-	-	-	-	-	-	-	4	4	
	P Russo	-	-	3	-	-	-	-	-	3	
17	A Linden	-	-	2	-	-	-	-	-	2	
18	R Salvadori	-	-	-	-	2	-	-	-	2	
	F González	1	-	-	-	-	-	-	-	1	
20	A de Portago	1	-	-	-	-	-	-	-	1	
	G Scarlatti	-	-	-	-	-	-	-	1	1	

8, 6, 4, 3 and 2 points awarded to the first five finishers. The driver setting the fastest lap scored a point also. Points shared for shared drives.

Best 5 scores. P Collins received no points for a shared 4th place in Britain, because he covered insufficient distance (3 laps)(M Trintignant awarded all 3 points).

New fuel regulations were announced. Cars were to run on commercial petrol, which meant Aviation fuel to 130 octane (Avgas). Race distances were reduced to 300 km or 2 hours and there would be no points awarded for shared drives. The Constructors' Championship was inaugurated. The factory Maserati team withdrew, as rear engined cars emerged the quickest.

FERRARI
Scuderia Ferrari: Hawthorn, Collins, Musso, von Trips, Gendebien, P Hill

MASERATI
Scuderia Centro Sud: Gerini, Shelby, Gregory, Ruttman, Seidel, Herrmann (D), Trintignant, Allison, Bonnier
Scuderia Sud Americana: Fangio (RA), Menditéguy
Temple Buell: Gregory (I,MA) Shelby (P)
Joakim Bonnier: Bonnier, Herrmann, P Hill, Cabianca, Schell
Ken Kavanagh: (Kavanagh, Taramazzo), Behra
Privateers: Gould, Godia, Fangio, Scarlatti, de Filippis, (Testut, Chiron)

OSCA
Automobili OSCA: (Piotti, Cabianca)

BRM
Owen Racing Organisation: Schell, Behra, Bonnier, Trintignant, Flockhart

CONNAUGHT
B C Ecclestone: Bueb, Fairman, (Kessler, Emery, Ecclestone)

COOPER
Cooper Car Co: Salvadori, Brabham, Burgess, Fairman
R. R. C. Walker Racing Team: Trintignant, Moss, (Flockhart)

LOTUS
Team Lotus: Allison, G Hill, Stacey

VANWALL
Vandervell Products Ltd: Moss, Brooks, Lewis-Evans

PORSCHE
Ecurie Maarsbergen: de Beaufort

(Entries for the F2 section are not included)

19 Jan 1958 — ARGENTINA: Buenos Aires No.2 (Round: 1) (Race: 65)
80 laps x 3.912 km, 2.431 miles = 312.960 km, 194.464 miles

POS.	NO	DRIVER	CAR	MODEL	ENGINE		LAPS	TIME/REASON FOR RETIREMENT	GRID:POS	ROW
1	14	S Moss	Cooper	T43	Climax	4	80	2h 19m 33.700s	7	2
2	16	L Musso	Ferrari	D246	Ferrari	V6	80	2h 19m 36.400s	5	2
3	20	M Hawthorn	Ferrari	D246	Ferrari	V6	80	2h 19m 46.300s	2	1
4	2	J M Fangio	Maserati	250F	Maserati	6	80	2h 20m 26.700s	1	1
5	4	J Behra	Maserati	250F	Maserati	6	78		4	1
6	8	H Schell	Maserati	250F	Maserati	6	77		8	3
7	6	C Menditéguy	Maserati	250F	Maserati	6	76		6	2
8	10	C Godia	Maserati	250F	Maserati	6	75		9	3
9	12	H Gould	Maserati	250F	Maserati	6	71		10	3
r	18	P Collins	Ferrari	D246	Ferrari	V6	0	rear axle	3	1

Winning Speed: 134.547 km/h, 83.604 mph
Pole Position speed: 138.071 km/h, 85.793 mph (J M Fangio, 1 min:42.000 sec)
Fastest Lap speed: 138.342 km/h, 85.962 mph (J M Fangio, 1 min:41.800 sec on lap 30)
Lap Leaders: J Behra 1 (1); M Hawthorn 2-9 (8); J M Fangio 10-34 (25); S Moss 35-80 (46).

S Moss's victory was the first in a rear-engined car.

18 May 1958 — MONACO : Monte Carlo (Round: 2) (Race: 66)
100 laps x 3.145 km, 1.954 miles = 314.500 km, 195.421 miles

POS.	NO	DRIVER	CAR	MODEL	ENGINE		LAPS	TIME/REASON FOR RETIREMENT	GRID:POS	ROW
1	20	M Trintignant	Cooper	T45	Climax	4	100	2h 52m 27.900s	5	2
2	34	L Musso	Ferrari	D246	Ferrari	V6	100	2h 52m 48.100s	10	4
3	36	P Collins	Ferrari	D246	Ferrari	V6	100	2h 53m 06.700s	9	4
4	16	J Brabham	Cooper	T45	Climax	4	97		3	1
5	8	H Schell	BRM	P25	BRM	4	91		12	5
r	40	W von Trips	Ferrari	D246	Ferrari	V6	91	engine	11	5
6	24	C Allison	Lotus	12	Climax	4	87		13	5
r	58	J Bonnier	Maserati	250F	Maserati	6	71	accident	16	7
r	26	G Hill	Lotus	12	Climax	4	69	engine	15	6
r	18	R Salvadori	Cooper	T45	Climax	4	56	gearbox	4	2
r	38	M Hawthorn	Ferrari	D246	Ferrari	V6	47	fuel pump	6	3
r	28	S Moss	Vanwall	VW (57)	Vanwall	4	38	engine	8	3
r	6	J Behra	BRM	P25	BRM	4	30	brakes	2	1
r	46	G Scarlatti	Maserati	250F	Maserati	6	27	engine	14	6
r	30	T Brooks	Vanwall	VW (57)	Vanwall	4	22	spark plug	1	1
r	32	S Lewis-Evans	Vanwall	VW (57)	Vanwall	4	12	steering	7	3
nq	22	R Flockhart	Cooper	T43	Climax	4				
nq	4	C Godia	Maserati	250F	Maserati	6				
nq	50	K Kavanagh	Maserati	250F	Maserati	6				
nq	50	L Taramazzo	Maserati	250F	Maserati	6				
nq	48	G Gerini	Maserati	250F	Maserati	6				
nq	12	B Kessler	Connaught	B	Alta	4				
nq	14	P Emery	Connaught	B	Alta	4				
nq	44	M T de Filippis	Maserati	250F	Maserati	6				
nq	56	A Testut	Maserati	250F	Maserati	6				
nq	56	L Chiron	Maserati	250F	Maserati	6				
nq	52	G Cabianca	OSCA		OSCA	4				
nq	54	L Piotti	OSCA		OSCA	4				
nq	42	H Gould	Maserati	250F	Maserati	6				
nq	12	B Ecclestone	Connaught	B	Alta	4				

Winning Speed: 109.414 km/h, 67.986 mph
Pole Position speed: 113.447 km/h, 70.493 mph (T Brooks, 1 min:39.800 sec)
Fastest Lap speed: 112.545 km/h, 69.932 mph (M Hawthorn, 1 min:40.600 sec on lap 36)
Lap Leaders: J Behra 1-27 (27); M Hawthorn 28-32,39-47 (14); S Moss 33-38 (6); M Trintignant 48-100 (53).

26 May 1958 — NETHERLANDS: Zandvoort (Round: 3) (Race: 67)

75 laps x 4.193 km, 2.605 miles = 314.475 km, 195.406 miles

POS.	NO	DRIVER	CAR	MODEL	ENGINE		LAPS	TIME/REASON FOR RETIREMENT	GRID:POS	ROW
1	1	S Moss	Vanwall	VW (57)	Vanwall	4	75	2h 04m 49.200s	2	1
2	15	H Schell	BRM	P25	BRM	4	75	2h 05m 37.100s	7	3
3	14	J Behra	BRM	P25	BRM	4	75	2h 06m 31.500s	4	2
4	7	R Salvadori	Cooper	T45	Climax	4	74		9	4
5	5	M Hawthorn	Ferrari	D246	Ferrari	V6	74		6	3
6	17	C Allison	Lotus	12	Climax	4	73		11	5
7	6	L Musso	Ferrari	D246	Ferrari	V6	73		12	5
8	8	J Brabham	Cooper	T45	Climax	4	73		5	2
9	9	M Trintignant	Cooper	T45	Climax	4	72		8	3
10	11	J Bonnier	Maserati	250F	Maserati	6	71		15	6
11	18	C G de Beaufort	Porsche	RSK	Porsche	F4	69		17	7
r	10	G Scarlatti	Maserati	250F	Maserati	6	51	rear axle	16	7
r	3	S Lewis-Evans	Vanwall	VW (57)	Vanwall	4	45	valve	1	1
r	16	G Hill	Lotus	12	Climax	4	41	gasket	13	5
r	4	P Collins	Ferrari	D246	Ferrari	V6	32	spin	10	4
r	12	M Gregory	Maserati	250F	Maserati	6	16	fuel pump	14	6
r	2	T Brooks	Vanwall	VW (57)	Vanwall	4	13	rear axle	3	1
ns	12	H Gould	Maserati	250F	Maserati	6		car raced by Gregory		

Winning Speed: 151.166 km/h, 93.930 mph
Pole Position speed: 155.456 km/h, 96.596 mph (S Lewis-Evans, 1 min:37.100 sec)
Fastest Lap speed: 154.660 km/h, 96.101 mph (S Moss, 1 min:37.600 sec)
Lap Leaders: S Moss 1-75 (75).

30 May 1958 — INDIANAPOLIS: 500 (Round: 4) (Race: 68)

200 laps x 4.023 km, 2.500 miles = 804.672 km, 500.000 miles

POS.	NO	DRIVER	CAR	MODEL	ENGINE		LAPS	TIME/REASON FOR RETIREMENT	GRID:POS	ROW
1	1	J Bryan	Epperly		Offenhauser	4	200	3h 44m 13.800s	7	3
2	99	G Amick	Epperly		Offenhauser	4	200	3h 44m 41.429s	25	9
3	9	J Boyd	Kurtis Kraft	500G	Offenhauser	4	200		8	3
4	33	T Bettenhausen	Epperly		Offenhauser	4	200		9	3
5	2	J Rathmann	Epperly		Offenhauser	4	200		20	7
6	16	J Reece	Watson		Offenhauser	4	200		3	1
7	26	D Freeland	Phillips		Offenhauser	4	200		13	5
8	44	J Larson	Watson		Offenhauser	4	200		19	7
9.	61	E Johnson	Kurtis Kraft	500G	Offenhauser	4	200		26	9
10	54	B Cheesbourg	Kurtis Kraft		Novi	8s	200		33	11
11	52	A Keller	Kurtis Kraft	500G-2	Offenhauser	4	200		21	7
12	45	J Parsons	Kurtis Kraft		Offenhauser	4	200		6	2
13	19	J Tolan	Kuzma		Offenhauser	4	200		30	10
14r	65	B Christie	Kurtis Kraft	500C	Offenhauser	4	189	spin	17	6
15r	59	D Wilson	Kuzma		Offenhauser	4	151	refuelling fire	32	11
16r	29	A J Foyt	Kuzma		Offenhauser	4	148	spin	12	4
17r	77	M Magill	Kurtis Kraft	500G	Offenhauser	4	136	red flagged	31	11
18r	15	P Russo	Kurtis Kraft		Novi	8s	122	throttle	14	5
19r	83	S Templeman	Kurtis Kraft	500D	Offenhauser	4	116	brakes	23	8
20r	8	R Ward	Lesovsky		Offenhauser	4	93	magneto	11	4
21r	43	B Garrett	Kurtis Kraft	500G	Offenhauser	4	80	cam gear	15	5
22r	88	E Sachs	Kuzma		Offenhauser	4	68	universal joint	18	6
23r	7	J Thomson	Kurtis Kraft		Offenhauser	4	52	steering damaged	22	8
24r	89	C Weyant	Dunn		Offenhauser	4	38	brakes locked/ accident	29	10
25r	25	J Turner	Lesovsky		Offenhauser	4	21	fuel pump	10	4
26r	14	B Veith	Kurtis Kraft	500G	Offenhauser	4	1	accident	4	2
27r	97	D Rathmann	Watson		Offenhauser	4	0	accident	1	1
28r	5	E Elisian	Watson		Offenhauser	4	0	accident	2	1
29r	4	P O'Connor	Kurtis Kraft	500G	Offenhauser	4	0	fatal accident	5	2
30r	31	P Goldsmith	Kurtis Kraft	500G	Offenhauser	4	0	accident	16	6
31r	92	J Unser	Kurtis Kraft	500G	Offenhauser	4	0	accident	24	8
32r	68	L Sutton	Kurtis Kraft	500G	Offenhauser	4	0	accident	27	9
33r	57	A Bisch	Kuzma		Offenhauser	4	0	accident	28	10

Winning Speed: 215.316 km/h, 133.791 mph
Pole Position speed: 234.922 km/h, 145.974 mph (D Rathmann, 1 min: 1.655 sec)
Fastest Lap speed: 232.229 km/h, 144.300 mph (T Bettenhausen, 1 min: 2.370 sec on lap 55)

15 Jun 1958 — BELGIUM: Spa-Francorchamps (Round: 5) (Race: 69)

24 laps x 14.100 km, 8.761 miles = 338.400 km, 210.272 miles

POS.	NO	DRIVER	CAR	MODEL	ENGINE		LAPS	TIME/REASON FOR RETIREMENT	GRID:POS	ROW
1	4	T Brooks	Vanwall	VW (57)	Vanwall	4	24	1h 37m 06.300s	5	2
2	16	M Hawthorn	Ferrari	D246	Ferrari	V6	24	1h 37m 27.000s	1	1
3	6	S Lewis-Evans	Vanwall	VW (57)	Vanwall	4	24	1h 40m 07.200s	11	5
4	40	C Allison	Lotus	12	Climax	4	24	1h 41m 21.800s	12	5
5	10	H Schell	BRM	P25	BRM	4	23		7	3
6	20	O Gendebien	Ferrari	D246	Ferrari	V6	23		6	3
7	28	M Trintignant	Maserati	250F	Maserati	6	23		16	7
8	24	R Salvadori	Cooper	T45	Climax	4	23		13	5
9	36	J Bonnier	Maserati	250F	Maserati	6	22		14	6
10	26	M T de Filippis	Maserati	250F	Maserati	6	22		19	8
r	38	C Godia	Maserati	250F	Maserati	6	22	engine	18	7

POS.	NO	DRIVER	CAR	MODEL	ENGINE		LAPS	TIME/REASON FOR RETIREMENT	GRID:POS	ROW
r	22	J Brabham	Cooper	T45	Climax	4	16	gasket/engine overheating	8	3
r	42	G Hill	Lotus	12	Climax	4	12	engine	15	6
r	18	L Musso	Ferrari	D246	Ferrari	V6	5	accident	2	1
r	8	J Behra	BRM	P25	BRM	4	5	oil pressure/engine	10	4
r	14	P Collins	Ferrari	D246	Ferrari	V6	5	engine overheating	4	2
r	32	W Seidel	Maserati	250F	Maserati	6	4	engine	17	7
r	30	M Gregory	Maserati	250F	Maserati	6	0	engine	9	4
r	2	S Moss	Vanwall	VW (57)	Vanwall	4	0	valves	3	1
ns	34	K Kavanagh	Maserati	250F	Maserati	6		engine		

Winning Speed: 209.093 km/h, 129.925 mph
Pole Position speed: 214.087 km/h, 133.027 mph (M Hawthorn, 3 min:57.100 sec)
Fastest Lap speed: 213.009 km/h, 132.358 mph (M Hawthorn, 3 min:58.300 sec on lap 24)
Lap Leaders: T Brooks 1,3,5-24 (22); P Collins 2,4 (2).

Also the Grand Prix of Europe. Front row of the grid reversed by request of M Hawthorn (pole). Different numbers were worn by some cars during practice.

6 Jul 1958 — FRANCE: Reims (Round: 6) (Race: 70)
50 laps x 8.302 km, 5.159 miles = 415.100 km, 257.931 miles

POS.	NO	DRIVER	CAR	MODEL	ENGINE		LAPS	TIME/REASON FOR RETIREMENT	GRID:POS	ROW
1	4	M Hawthorn	Ferrari	D246	Ferrari	V6	50	2h 03m 21.300s	1	1
2	8	S Moss	Vanwall	VW (57)	Vanwall	4	50	2h 03m 45.900s	6	3
3	6	W von Trips	Ferrari	D246	Ferrari	V6	50	2h 04m 21.000s	21	9
4	34	J M Fangio	Maserati	250F	Maserati	6	50	2h 05m 51.900s	8	3
5	42	P Collins	Ferrari	D246	Ferrari	V6	50	2h 08m 46.200s	4	2
6	22	J Brabham	Cooper	T45	Climax	4	49		12	5
7	36	P Hill	Maserati	250F	Maserati	6	49		[illegible]	5
8	38	J Bonnier	Maserati	250F	Maserati	6	48		[illegible]	7
9	32	G Gerini	Maserati	250F	Maserati	6	47		[illegible]	6
10	30	T Ruttman	Maserati	250F	Maserati	6	45		[illegible]	7
r	14	J Behra	BRM	P25	BRM	4	41	fuel [illegible]	[illegible]	4
r	16	H Schell	BRM	P25	BRM	4	41	engi[illegible]	[illegible]	1
11	20	R Salvadori	Cooper	T45	Climax	4	37		[illegible]	6
r=	12	S Lewis-Evans	Vanwall	VW (57)	Vanwall	4			[illegible]	4
r=	12	T Brooks	Vanwall	VW (57)	Vanwall	4	35	engi[illegible]		
r	24	G Hill	Lotus	16	Climax	4	33	engi[illegible]	[illegible]	8
r	40	C Godia	Maserati	250F	Maserati	6	28	accid[illegible]	[illegible]	5
r	18	M Trintignant	BRM	P25	BRM	4	23	oil lin[illegible]	[illegible]	3
r	10	T Brooks	Vanwall	VW (57)	Vanwall	4	16	gearb[illegible]	[illegible]	2
r	28	C Shelby	Maserati	250F	Maserati	6	9	engine	17	7
r	2	L Musso	Ferrari	D246	Ferrari	V6	9	fatal accident	2	1
r	26	C Allison	Lotus	12	Climax	4	6	engine	20	8

Winning Speed: 201.905 km/h, 125.458 mph
Pole Position speed: 210.919 km/h, 131.059 mph (M Hawthorn, 2 min:21.700 sec)
Fastest Lap speed: 206.261 km/h, 128.165 mph (M Hawthorn, 2 min:24.900 sec on lap 45)
Lap Leaders: M Hawthorn 1-50 (50).

C Godia's qualifying time was set by J M Fangio.

19 Jul 1958 — BRITAIN: Silverstone (Round: 7) (Race: 71)
75 laps x 4.711 km, 2.927 miles = 353.291 km, 219.525 miles

POS.	NO	DRIVER	CAR	MODEL	ENGINE		LAPS	TIME/REASON FOR RETIREMENT	GRID:POS	ROW
1	1	P Collins	Ferrari	D246	Ferrari	V6	75	2h 09m 04.200s	6	2
2	2	M Hawthorn	Ferrari	D246	Ferrari	V6	75	2h 09m 28.400s	4	1
3	10	R Salvadori	Cooper	T45	Climax	4	75	2h 09m 54.800s	3	1
4	9	S Lewis-Evans	Vanwall	VW (57)	Vanwall	4	75	2h 09m 55.000s	7	2
5	20	H Schell	BRM	P25	BRM	4	75	2h 10m 19.000s	2	1
6	11	J Brabham	Cooper	T45	Climax	4	75	2h 10m 27.400s	10	3
7	8	T Brooks	Vanwall	VW (57)	Vanwall	4	74		9	3
8	4	M Trintignant	Cooper	T43	Climax	4	73		12	4
9	5	C Shelby	Maserati	250F	Maserati	6	72		15	5
r	3	W von Trips	Ferrari	D246	Ferrari	V6	59	engine bearings	11	3
r	22	J Bonnier	Maserati	250F	Maserati	6	49	gearbox	13	4
r	6	G Gerini	Maserati	250F	Maserati	6	43	gearbox	18	5
r	12	I Burgess	Cooper	T45	Climax	4	40	clutch	16	5
r	7	S Moss	Vanwall	VW (57)	Vanwall	4	25	engine	1	1
r	17	C Allison	Lotus	12	Climax	4	21	engine bearings	5	2
r	15	I Bueb	Connaught	B	Alta	4	19	gearbox oil pump	17	5
r	19	J Behra	BRM	P25	BRM	4	19	puncture	8	3
r	18	A Stacey	Lotus	16	Climax	4	19	engine overheating	20	6
r	16	G Hill	Lotus	16	Climax	4	17	engine overheating	14	4
r	14	J Fairman	Connaught	B	Alta	4	7	engine	19	6

Winning Speed: 164.232 km/h, 102.049 mph
Pole Position speed: 170.603 km/h, 106.008 mph (S Moss, 1 min:39.400 sec)
Fastest Lap speed: 168.234 km/h, 104.536 mph (M Hawthorn, 1 min:40.800 sec on lap 50)
Lap Leaders: P Collins 1-75 (75).

3 Aug 1958 — GERMANY: Nürburgring (Round: 8) (Race: 72)

15 laps x 22.810 km, 14.173 miles = 342.150 km, 212.602 miles

POS.	NO	DRIVER	CAR	MODEL	ENGINE		LAPS	TIME/REASON FOR RETIREMENT	GRID:POS	ROW
1	8	T Brooks	Vanwall	VW (57)	Vanwall	4	15	2h 21m 15.000s	2	1
2	10	R Salvadori	Cooper	T45	Climax	4	15	2h 24m 44.700s	6	2
3	11	M Trintignant	Cooper	T45	Climax	4	15	2h 26m 26.200s	7	2
4	4	W von Trips	Ferrari	D246	Ferrari	V6	15	2h 27m 31.300s	5	2
5	20	B McLaren	* Cooper	T45	Climax	4	15	2h 27m 41.300s (1st F2 Section)	12	4
6	21	E Barth	* Porsche	RSK	Porsche	F4	15	2h 27m 47.400s	13	4
7	26	I Burgess	* Cooper	T43	Climax	4	15	2h 28m 14.300s	11	3
8	30	T Marsh	* Cooper	T45	Climax	4	15	2h 28m 24.900s	14	4
9	23	P Hill	* Ferrari	D156	Ferrari	V6	15	2h 29m 00.500s	10	3
10	12	C Allison	Lotus	16	Climax	4	13	(5th F1 Section)	24	7
11	28	I Bueb	* Lotus	12	Climax	4	13		16	5
r	3	M Hawthorn	Ferrari	D246	Ferrari	V6	11	clutch	1	1
r	2	P Collins	Ferrari	D246	Ferrari	V6	10	fatal accident	4	1
r	6	H Schell	BRM	P25	BRM	4	9	brakes	8	3
r	22	W Seidel	* Cooper	T43	Climax	4	9	suspension	17	5
r	5	J Behra	BRM	P25	BRM	4	4	suspension	9	3
r	25	G Hill	* Lotus	16	Climax	4	4	oil line	22	7
r	27	C Goethals	* Cooper	T43	Climax	4	4	fuelpump	23	7
r	17	H Herrmann	Maserati	250F	Maserati	6	3	engine	20	6
r	7	S Moss	Vanwall	VW (57)	Vanwall	4	3	magneto	3	1
r	18	C G de Beaufort	* Porsche	RS550	Porsche	F4	3	engine	15	5
r	19	D Gibson	* Cooper	T43	Climax	4	2	engine	18	5
r	24	J Brabham	* Cooper	T45	Climax	4	1	accident	19	6
r	29	B Naylor	* Cooper	T45	Climax	4	1	fuelpump	25	7
r	16	J Bonnier	Maserati	250F	Maserati	6	1	accident	21	6
ns	14	T Ruttman	Maserati	250F	Maserati	6		engine		

Winning Speed: 145.338 km/h, 90.309 mph
Pole Position speed: 148.224 km/h, 92.102 mph (M Hawthorn, 9 min:14.000 sec)
Fastest Lap speed: 149.519 km/h, 92.907 mph (S Moss, 9 min: 9.200 sec on lap 3)
Lap Leaders: S Moss 1-3 (3); M Hawthorn 4 (1); P Collins 5-10 (6); T Brooks 11-15 (5).

*Drivers on rows 6 and 7 were relegated to these positions due to infringements during practice. F2 cars raced simultaneously with F1,and are marked thus *.*
B McLaren finished 5th, but was not eligible for points due to being in the F2 section of the race.

24 Aug 1958 — PORTUGAL: Porto (Round: 9) (Race: 73)

50 laps x 7.407 km, 4.602 miles = 370.350 km, 230.125 miles

POS.	NO	DRIVER	CAR	MODEL	ENGINE		LAPS	TIME/REASON FOR RETIREMENT	GRID:POS	ROW
1	2	S Moss	Vanwall	VW (57)	Vanwall	4	50	2h 11m 27.800s	1	1
2	22	M Hawthorn	Ferrari	D246	Ferrari	V6	50	2h 16m 40.550s	2	1
3	6	S Lewis-Evans	Vanwall	VW (57)	Vanwall	4	49		3	1
4	8	J Behra	BRM	P25	BRM	4	49		4	2
5	24	W von Trips	Ferrari	D246	Ferrari	V6	49		6	3
6	10	H Schell	BRM	P25	BRM	4	49		7	3
7	14	J Brabham	Cooper	T45	Climax	4	48		8	3
8	12	M Trintignant	Cooper	T43	Climax	4	48		9	4
r	28	C Shelby	Maserati	250F	Maserati	6	47	brakes/ accident	10	4
9	16	R Salvadori	Cooper	T45	Climax	4	46		11	5
r	4	T Brooks	Vanwall	VW (57)	Vanwall	4	36	accident	5	2
r	20	G Hill	Lotus	16	Climax	4	25	accident	12	5
r	18	C Allison	Maserati	250F	Maserati	6	15	engine	13	5
r	32	J Bonnier	Maserati	250F	Maserati	6	9	driver ill	14	6
r	30	M T de Filippis	Maserati	250F	Maserati	6	6	engine	15	6

Winning Speed: 169.028 km/h, 105.029 mph
Pole Position speed: 172.915 km/h, 107.444 mph (S Moss, 2 min:34.210 sec)
Fastest Lap speed: 175.003 km/h, 108.742 mph (M Hawthorn, 2 min:32.370 sec on lap 36)
Lap Leaders: S Moss 1,8-50 (44); M Hawthorn 2-7 (6).

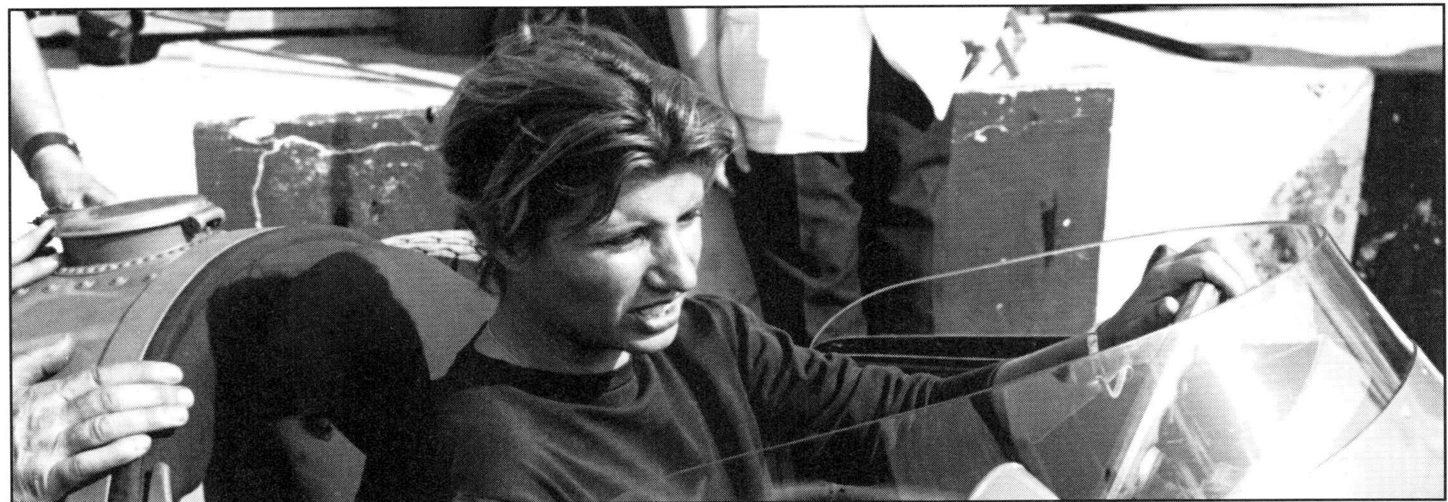

Maria-Teresa de Filippis, the first lady of Formula 1 – Italy 1958.

7 Sep 1958 — ITALY: Monza (Round: 10) (Race: 74)

70 laps x 5.750 km, 3.573 miles = 402.500 km, 250.102 miles

POS.	NO	DRIVER	CAR	MODEL	ENGINE		LAPS	TIME/REASON FOR RETIREMENT	GRID:POS	ROW
1	28	T Brooks	Vanwall	VW (57)	Vanwall	4	70	2h 03m 47.800s	2	1
2	14	M Hawthorn	Ferrari	D246	Ferrari	V6	70	2h 04m 12.000s	3	1
3	18	P Hill	Ferrari	D246	Ferrari	V6	70	2h 04m 16.100s	7	2
4=	32	M Gregory	Maserati	250F	Maserati	6			11	3
4=	32	C Shelby	Maserati	250F	Maserati	6	69			
5	6	R Salvadori	Cooper	T45	Climax	4	62		14	4
6	38	G Hill	Lotus	16	Climax	4	62		12	4
7	36	C Allison	Lotus	12	Climax	4	61		16	5
r	42	M T de Filippis	Maserati	250F	Maserati	6	57	connecting rod	21	6
r	22	G Cabianca	Maserati	250F	Maserati	6	51	engine	20	6
r	8	J Behra	BRM	P25	BRM	4	42	brakes/ clutch	8	3
r	24	H Herrmann	Maserati	250F	Maserati	6	32	valve	18	5
r	30	S Lewis-Evans	Vanwall	VW (57)	Vanwall	4	30	engine overheating	4	1
r	2	M Trintignant	Cooper	T45	Climax	4	24	gearbox	13	4
r	26	S Moss	Vanwall	VW (57)	Vanwall	4	17	gearbox	1	1
r	12	J Bonnier	BRM	P25	BRM	4	14	transmission/ fire	10	3
r	20	O Gendebien	Ferrari	D246	Ferrari	V6	4	de Dion tube	5	2
r	40	G Gerini	Maserati	250F	Maserati	6	2	accident	19	6
r	34	C Shelby	Maserati	250F	Maserati	6	1	engine	17	5
r	10	H Schell	BRM	P25	BRM	4	0	accident	9	3
r	16	W von Trips	Ferrari	D246	Ferrari	V6	0	accident	6	2
r	4	J Brabham	Cooper	T45	Climax	4	0	accident	15	5

Winning Speed: 195.078 km/h, 121.216 mph
Pole Position speed: 205.970 km/h, 127.984 mph (S Moss, 1 min:40.500 sec)
Fastest Lap speed: 201.166 km/h, 124.999 mph (P Hill, 1 min:42.900 sec on lap 26)
Lap Leaders: P Hill 1-4,35-37 (7); M Hawthorn 5-6,9,15-34,38-60 (46); S Moss 7-8,10-14 (7); T Brooks 61-70 (10).

M Gregory and C Shelby were originally disqualified for sharing a car but later reinstated, although they received no points.

19 Oct 1958 — MOROCCO: Ain-Diab (Round: 11) (Race: 75)

53 laps x 7.618 km, 4.734 miles = 403.754 km, 250.881 miles

POS.	NO	DRIVER	CAR	MODEL	ENGINE		LAPS	TIME/REASON FOR RETIREMENT	GRID:POS	ROW
1	8	S Moss	Vanwall	VW (57)	Vanwall	4	53	2h 09m 15.100s	2	1
2	6	M Hawthorn	Ferrari	D246	Ferrari	V6	53	2h 10m 39.800s	1	1
3	4	P Hill	Ferrari	D246	Ferrari	V6	53	2h 10m 40.600s	5	2
4	18	J Bonnier	BRM	P25	BRM	4	53	2h 11m 01.800s	8	3
5	16	H Schell	BRM	P25	BRM	4	53	2h 11m 48.800s	10	4
6	22	M Gregory	Maserati	250F	Maserati	6	52		13	5
7	30	R Salvadori	Cooper	T45	Climax	4	51		14	6
8	32	J Fairman	Cooper	T45	Climax	4	50		11	5
9	24	H Herrmann	Maserati	250F	Maserati	6	50		18	7
10	34	C Allison	Lotus	12	Climax	4	49		16	7
11	50	J Brabham	* Cooper	T45	Climax	4	49	(1st F2 Section)	19	8
12	28	G Gerini	Maserati	250F	Maserati	6	48	(11th F1 Section)	17	7
13	52	B McLaren	* Cooper	T45	Climax	4	48		21	9
14	58	R La Caze	* Cooper	T45	Climax	4	48		23	9
15	60	A Guelfi	* Cooper	T45	Climax	4	48		25	10
16	36	G Hill	Lotus	16	Climax	4	45		12	5
r	12	S Lewis-Evans	Vanwall	VW (57)	Vanwall	4	41	engine/ fatal accident	3	1
r	54	F Picard	* Cooper	T43	Climax	4	31	accident	24	10
r	56	T Bridger	* Cooper	T45	Climax	4	30	accident	22	9
r	10	T Brooks	Vanwall	VW (57)	Vanwall	4	29	engine	7	3
r	2	O Gendebien	Ferrari	D246	Ferrari	V6	29	accident	6	3
r	14	J Behra	BRM	P25	BRM	4	26	engine	4	2
r	26	W Seidel	Maserati	250F	Maserati	6	15	accident	20	8
r	20	R Flockhart	BRM	P25	BRM	4	15	camshaft	15	6
r	38	M Trintignant	Cooper	T45	Climax	4	9	engine	9	4

Winning speed: 187.427 km/h, 116.462 mph
Pole Position speed: 191.648 km/h, 119.084 mph (M Hawthorn, 2 min:23.100 sec)
Fastest Lap speed: 192.455 km/h, 119.586 mph (S Moss, 2 min:22.500 sec on lap 21)
Lap Leaders: S Moss 1-53 (53).

*Formula 2 cars raced simultaneously with F1, and are marked thus *.*
During practice, some cars had different numbers from those in the race.

Far left: S Moss, T Brooks and S Lewis-Evans at the Italian Grand Prix, 1958.

Left: One minute to go at the British Grand Prix, 1958.

Lap Leaders 1958

POS	DRIVER	CAR-ENGINE	GPS	LAPS	KM	MILES
1	S Moss	Cooper-Climax	*1*	*46*	*180.0*	*111.8*
		Vanwall	*6*	*188*	*1,171.7*	*728.1*
			7	234	1,351.7	839.9
2	M Hawthorn	Ferrari	6	125	822.2	510.9
3	P Collins	Ferrari	3	83	518.4	322.1
4	M Trintignant	Cooper-Climax	1	53	166.7	103.6
5	T Brooks	Vanwall	3	37	481.8	299.3
6	J Behra	BRM	*1*	*27*	*84.9*	*52.8*
		Maserati	*1*	*1*	*3.9*	*2.4*
			2	28	88.8	55.2
7	J M Fangio	Maserati	1	25	97.8	60.8
8	P Hill	Ferrari	1	7	40.2	25.0
			10	**592**	**3,567.5**	**2,216.8**

Driver Points 1958

		RA	MC	NL	INDY	B	F	GB	D	P	I	MA	TOTAL	
1	M Hawthorn	(4)	(1)	(2)	-	7	9	7	-	7	6	6	42	(7)
2	S Moss	8	-	9	-	-	6	-	1	8	-	9	41	
3	T Brooks	-	–	-	-	8	-	-	8	-	8	-	24	
4	R Salvadori	-	-	3	-	-	-	4	6	-	2	-	15	
5	P Collins	-	4	-	-	-	2	8	-	-	-	-	14	
	H Schell	-	2	6	-	2	-	2	-	-	-	2	14	
7	M Trintignant	-	8	-	-	-	-	-	4	-	-	-	12	
	L Musso	6	6	-	-	-	-	-	-	-	-	-	12	
9	S Lewis-Evans	-	-	-	-	4	-	3	-	4	-	-	11	
10	P Hill	-	-	-	-	-	-	-	-	-	5	4	9	
	J Behra	2	-	4	-	-	-	-	-	3	-	-	9	
	W von Trips	-	-	-	-	-	4	-	3	2	-	-	9	
13	J Bryan	-	-	-	8	-	-	-	-	-	-	-	8	
14	J M Fangio	4	-	-	-	-	3	-	-	-	-	-	7	
15	G Amick	-	-	-	6	-	-	-	-	-	-	-	6	
16	T Bettenhausen	-	-	-	4	-	-	-	-	-	-	-	4	
	J Boyd	-	-	-	4	-	-	-	-	-	-	-	4	
18	J Brabham	-	-	3	-	-	-	-	-	-	-	-	3	
	C Allison	-	-	-	-	3	-	-	-	-	-	-	3	
	J Bonnier	-	-	-	-	-	-	-	-	-	-	3	3	
21	J Rathmann	-	-	-	2	-	-	-	-	-	-	-	2	

8, 6, 4, 3 and 2 points awarded to the first five finishers. The driver setting the fastest lap scored a point also.
Points only awarded to drivers who handled the car throughout the race. Best 6 scores.
M Gregory and C Shelby (Maserati) were ineligible for points in Italy, because of their shared drive.

Constructor Points 1958

		RA	MC	NL	INDY	B	F	GB	D	P	I	MA	TOTAL	
1	Vanwall	-	-	8	-	8	(6)	(3)	8	8	8	8	48	(9)
2	Ferrari	6	6	(2)	-	6	8	8	(3)	6	(6)	(6)	40	(17)
3	Cooper-Climax	8	8	3	-	-	-	4	6	-	2	-	31	
4	BRM	-	2	6	-	2	-	2	-	3	-	3	18	
5	Maserati	3	-	-	-	-	3	-	-	-	-	-	6	
6	Lotus-Climax	-	-	-	-	3	-	-	-	-	-	-	3	

8, 6, 4, 3 and 2 points awarded to the first five finishers. Indianapolis excluded. Points only for highest placed car. Best 6 scores.

The new world Champion Mike Hawthorn announced his retirement but was sadly killed when his Jaguar saloon left the road near Guildford in January. Vanwall withdrew from serious competition citing ill health, but the many racing fatalities of the previous season were regarded as the true reason. A new formula based on the existing Formula 2 was announced for the 1961 season.

FERRARI
Scuderia Ferrari: Brooks, P Hill, Allison, Gurney, Behra, Gendebien, von Trips

MASERATI
Scuderia Centro Sud: d'Orey (Bayardo)
Scuderia Ugolini: Scarlatti, de Beaufort Ottorino
Volonterio: Cabianca
Monte Carlo Auto Sport: (Testut)
Privateer: (Cade)

BRM
Owen Racing Organisation: Bonnier, Schell, Flockhart
British Racing Partnership: S Moss, Herrmann

COOPER
Cooper Car Co: Brabham, McLaren, Gregory, Scarlatti
R. R. C. Walker Racing Team: Trintignant, S Moss
Scuderia Centro Sud: Burgess, Davis, de Cabral, Herrmann
High Efficiency Motors: Salvadori Fairman
British Racing Partnership: Bueb, Bristow
Alan Brown Equipe: Ashdown, M Taylor
R. H. H. Parnell: H Taylor, (Parnell)
Ecurie Bleue: Schell
Automobili OSCA: de Tomaso
Mike Taylor: Constantine
Privateer: (Lucienbonnet)
Gilby Engineering Co Ltd: (Greene);
Ace Garage (Rotherham): (T Taylor)
Equipe Nationale Belge: (Bianchi, de Changy)
United Racing Stable: (B Moss)

CONNAUGHT
Paul Emery Connaught Cars: Said

LOTUS
Team Lotus: G Hill, Ireland, Stacey, (Lovely)
Dorchester Service Station: Piper
John Fisher: Halford
Privateer: (D Taylor)

ASTON MARTIN
David Brown Corporation: Salvadori, Shelby

VANWALL
Vandervell Products Ltd: Brooks

JBW
J B Naylor: Naylor

FRY
David Fry: (Parkes)

PORSCHE
Dr Ing F Porsche KG: von Trips, (de Filippis)
Ecurie Maarsbergen: de Beaufort
Blanchard Automobile Co: Blanchard
Privateer: (Behra)

TEC MEC
Camoradi USA/Gordon Pennington Jr: d'Orey

KURTIS KRAFT
Leader Cards Inc.: Ward

10 May 1959 — MONACO: Monte Carlo (Round: 1) (Race: 76)
100 laps x 3.145 km, 1.954 miles = 314.500 km, 195.421 miles

POS.	NO	DRIVER	CAR	MODEL	ENGINE		LAPS	TIME/REASON FOR RETIREMENT	GRID:POS	ROW
1	24	J Brabham	Cooper	T51	Climax	4	100	2h 55m 51.300s	3	1
2	50	T Brooks	Ferrari	D246	Ferrari	V6	100	2h 56m 11.700s	4	2
3	32	M Trintignant	Cooper	T51	Climax	4	98		6	3
4	48	P Hill	Ferrari	D246	Ferrari	V6	97		5	2
5	22	B McLaren	Cooper	T51	Climax	4	96		13	5
6r	38	R Salvadori	Cooper	T45	Maserati	4	83	transmission	8	3
r	30	S Moss	Cooper	T51	Climax	4	81	transmission	1	1
r	20	R Flockhart	BRM	P25	BRM	4	64	brakes/ spin	10	4
r	16	H Schell	BRM	P25	BRM	4	48	fuel tank	9	4
r	18	J Bonnier	BRM	P25	BRM	4	44	brakes/ accident	7	3
r	46	J Behra	Ferrari	D246	Ferrari	V6	24	engine	2	1
r	40	G Hill	Lotus	16	Climax	4	21	fire	14	6
r	26	M Gregory	Cooper	T51	Climax	4	6	gearbox	11	5
r	44	B Halford	Lotus	16	Climax	4	1	accident	16	7
r	52	C Allison	Ferrari	D156	Ferrari	V6	1	accident	15	6
r	6	W von Trips	Porsche	718	Porsche	F4	1	accident	12	5
nq	34	I Bueb	Cooper	T51	Climax	4				
nq	54	G Scarlatti	Maserati	250F	Maserati	6				
nq	10	L Bianchi	Cooper	T51	Climax	4				
nq	12	A de Changy	Cooper	T51	Climax	4				
nq	4	M T de Filippis	Behra	Porsche	Porsche	F4				
nq	42	P Lovely	Lotus	16	Climax	4				
nq	14	J Lucienbonnet	Cooper	T45	Climax	4				
nq	56	A Testut	Maserati	250F	Maserati	6				

Winning Speed: 107.304 km/h, 66.676 mph
Pole Position speed: 113.675 km/h, 70.634 mph (S Moss,1 min:39.600 sec)
Fastest Lap speed: 112.769 km/h, 70.071 mph (J Brabham,1 min:40.400 sec on lap 83)
Lap Leaders: J Behra 1-21 (21); S Moss 22-81 (60); J Brabham 82-100 (19).

30 May 1959 — INDIANAPOLIS: 500 (Round: 2) (Race: 77)
200 laps x 4.023 km, 2.500 miles = 804.672 km, 500.000 miles

POS.	NO	DRIVER	CAR	MODEL	ENGINE		LAPS	TIME/REASON FOR RETIREMENT	GRID:POS	ROW
1	5	R Ward	Watson		Offenhauser	4	200	3h 40m 49.200s	6	2
2	16	J Rathmann	Watson		Offenhauser	4	200	3h 41m 12.477s	3	1
3	3	J Thomson	Lesovsky		Offenhauser	4	200		1	1
4	1	T Bettenhausen	Epperly		Offenhauser	4	200		15	5
5	99	P Goldsmith	Epperly		Offenhauser	4	200		16	6
6	33	J Boyd	Epperly		Offenhauser	4	200		11	4
7	37	D Carter	Kurtis Kraft		Offenhauser	4	200		12	4
8	19	E Johnson	Kurtis Kraft	500G	Offenhauser	4	200		8	3
9	45	P Russo	Kurtis Kraft	500G	Offenhauser	4	200		27	9
10	10	A J Foyt	Kuzma		Offenhauser	4	200		17	6
11	88	G Hartley	Kuzma		Offenhauser	4	200		9	3
12	74	B Veith	Moore		Offenhauser	4	200		7	3
13	89	A Herman	Dunn		Offenhauser	4	200		23	8
14	66	J Daywalt	Kurtis Kraft		Offenhauser	4	200		13	5

15	71	C Arnold	Kurtis Kraft		Offenhauser	4	200		21	7
16	58	J McWithey	Kurtis Kraft	500C	Offenhauser	4	200		33	11
17r	44	E Sachs	Kuzma		Offenhauser	4	182	gear tower bolt/ spin	2	1
18r	57	A Keller	Kuzma		Offenhauser	4	163	pistons	28	10
19r	64	P Flaherty	Watson		Offenhauser	4	162	accident	18	6
20r	73	D Rathmann	Watson		Offenhauser	4	150	caught fire in pits	4	2
21r	53	B Cheesbourg	Kuzma		Offenhauser	4	147	magneto	30	10
22r	15	D Freeland	Kurtis Kraft	500G	Offenhauser	4	136	magneto	25	9
23r	49	R Crawford	Elder		Offenhauser	4	115	accident	32	11
24r	9	D Branson	Phillips		Offenhauser	4	112	torsion bar	10	4
25r	65	B Christie	Kurtis Kraft	500C	Offenhauser	4	109	rod bolt	24	8
26r	48	B Grim	Kurtis Kraft	500G	Offenhauser	4	85	magneto	5	2
27r	24	J Turner	Christensen		Offenhauser	4	47	fueltank	14	5
28r	47	C Weyant	Kurtis Kraft	500G	Offenhauser	4	45	accident	29	10
29r	7	J Larson	Kurtis Kraft		Offenhauser	4	45	accident	19	7
30r	77	M Magill	Sutton		Offenhauser	4	45	accident	31	11
31r	87	R Amick	Kurtis Kraft	500C	Offenhauser	4	45	accident	26	9
32r	8	L Sutton	Lesovsky		Offenhauser	4s	34	accident	22	8
33r	6	J Bryan	Epperly		Offenhauser	4	1	clutch/ cam gear	20	7

Winning Speed: 218.641 km/h, 135.857 mph
Pole Position speed: 234.815 km/h, 145.907 mph (J Thomson, 1 min: 1.683 sec)
Fastest Lap speed: 234.030 km/h, 145.419 mph (J Thomson, 1 min: 1.890 sec on lap 64)

31 May 1959 NETHERLANDS: Zandvoort (Round: 3) (Race: 78)
75 laps x 4.193 km, 2.605 miles = 314.475 km, 195.406 miles

POS.	NO	DRIVER	CAR	MODEL	ENGINE		LAPS	TIME/REASON FOR RETIREMENT	GRID:POS	ROW
1	7	J Bonnier	BRM	P25	BRM	4	75	2h 05m 26.800s	1	1
2	8	J Brabham	Cooper	T51	Climax	4	75	2h 05m 41.000s	2	1
3	9	M Gregory	Cooper	T51	Climax	4	75	2h 06m 49.800s	7	3
4	12	I Ireland	Lotus	16	Climax	4	74		9	4
5	1	J Behra	Ferrari	D246	Ferrari	V6	74		4	2
6	3	P Hill	Ferrari	D246	Ferrari	V6	73		12	5
7	14	G Hill	Lotus	16	Climax	4	73		5	2
8	10	M Trintignant	Cooper	T51	Climax	4	73		11	5
9	16	C Allison	Ferrari	D246	Ferrari	V6	71		15	6
10	15	C G de Beaufort	Porsche	RSK	Porsche	F4	68		14	6
r	11	S Moss	Cooper	T51	Climax	4	63	gearbox	3	1
r	6	H Schell	BRM	P25	BRM	4	46	engine	6	3
r	2	T Brooks	Ferrari	D246	Ferrari	V6	42	oil leak	8	3
r	5	C Shelby	Aston Martin	DBR4	Aston Martin	6	25	engine	10	4
r	4	R Salvadori	Aston Martin	DBR4	Aston Martin	6	3	engine overheating	13	5

Winning Speed: 150.411 km/h, 93.461 mph
Pole Position speed: 157.238 km/h, 97.703 mph (J Bonnier, 1 min: 36.000 sec)
Fastest Lap speed: 156.099 km/h, 96.996 mph (S Moss, 1 min:36.700 sec on lap 42)
Lap Leaders: J Bonnier 1, 12-29, 34-59,63-75 (58); M Gregory 2-11 (10); J Brabham 30-33 (4); S Moss 60-62 (3).

5 Jul 1959 FRANCE: Reims (Round: 4) (Race: 79)
50 laps x 8.302 km, 5.159 miles = 415.100 km, 257.931 miles

POS.	NO	DRIVER	CAR	MODEL	ENGINE		LAPS	TIME/REASON FOR RETIREMENT	GRID:POS	ROW
1	24	T Brooks	Ferrari	D246	Ferrari	V6	50	2h 01m 26.500s	1	1
2	26	P Hill	Ferrari	D246	Ferrari	V6	50	2h 01m 54.000s	3	1
3	8	J Brabham	Cooper	T51	Climax	4	50	2h 03m 04.200s	2	1
4	22	O Gendebien	Ferrari	D246	Ferrari	V6	50	2h 03m 14.000s	11	5
5	12	B McLaren	Cooper	T51	Climax	4	50	2h 03m 14.200s	10	4
6	44	R Flockhart	BRM	P25	BRM	4	50	2h 03m 32.200s	13	5
7	6	H Schell	BRM	P25	BRM	4	47		9	4
dq	2	S Moss	BRM	P25	BRM	4	42	push start after spin	4	2
8	40	G Scarlatti	Maserati	250F	Maserati	6	41		21	9
9	42	C G de Beaufort	Maserati	250F	Maserati	6	40		20	8
10	38	F d'Orey	Maserati	250F	Maserati	6	40		18	7
11	14	M Trintignant	Cooper	T51	Climax	4	36		8	3
r	30	J Behra	Ferrari	D246	Ferrari	V6	31	piston	5	2
r	16	R Salvadori	Cooper	T45	Maserati	4	20	piston	16	7
r	28	D Gurney	Ferrari	D246	Ferrari	V6	19	radiator	12	5
r	34	I Ireland	Lotus	16	Climax	4	14	wheel bearing	15	6
r	18	I Burgess	Cooper	T51	Maserati	4	13	engine	19	8
r	10	M Gregory	Cooper	T51	Climax	4	8	driver exhausted	7	3
r	32	G Hill	Lotus	16	Climax	4	7	radiator	14	6
r	20	C Davis	Cooper	T51	Maserati	4	7	oil line	17	7
r	4	J Bonnier	BRM	P25	BRM	4	6	cylinder head gasket	6	3
nq	36	A Bayardo	Maserati	250F	Maserati	6				

Winning Speed: 205.086 km/h, 127.435 mph
Pole Position speed: 214.399 km/h, 133.221 mph (T Brooks, 2 min:19.400 sec)
Fastest Lap speed: 209.294 km/h, 130.049 mph (S Moss, 2 min:22.800 sec on lap 40)
Lap Leaders: T Brooks 1-50 (50).

Also the Grand Prix of Europe. S Moss's fastest lap was allowed to stand, despite being disqualified.

18 Jul 1959 — BRITAIN: Aintree (Round: 5) (Race: 80)

75 laps x 4.828 km, 3.000 miles = 362.102 km, 225.000 miles

POS.	NO	DRIVER	CAR	MODEL	ENGINE		LAPS	TIME/REASON FOR RETIREMENT	GRID:POS	ROW
1	12	J Brabham	Cooper	T51	Climax	4	75	2h 30m 11.600s	1	1
2	6	S Moss	BRM	P25	BRM	4	75	2h 30m 33.800s	7	3
3	16	B McLaren	Cooper	T51	Climax	4	75	2h 30m 34.000s	8	3
4	8	H Schell	BRM	P25	BRM	4	74		3	1
5	18	M Trintignant	Cooper	T51	Climax	4	74		4	2
6	2	R Salvadori	Aston Martin	DBR4	Aston Martin	6	74		2	1
7	14	M Gregory	Cooper	T51	Climax	4	73		5	2
8	30	A Stacey	Lotus	16	Climax	4	71		12	5
9	28	G Hill	Lotus	16	Climax	4	70		9	4
10	48	C Bristow	Cooper	T51	Borgward	4	70		16	7
r	4	C Shelby	Aston Martin	DBR4	Aston Martin	6	69	magneto	6	3
11	58	H Taylor	Cooper	T51	Climax	4	69		21	9
12	52	P Ashdown	Cooper	T45	Climax	4	69		23	9
13	46	I Bueb	Cooper	T51	Borgward	4	69		18	7
r	40	F d'Orey	Maserati	250F	Maserati	6	57	accident	20	8
r	42	R Flockhart	BRM	P25	BRM	4	53	spin	11	5
r	38	J Fairman	Cooper	T45	Climax	4	39	gearbox	15	6
r	10	J Bonnier	BRM	P25	BRM	4	37	throttle linkage	10	4
r	22	I Burgess	Cooper	T51	Maserati	4	31	gearbox	13	5
r	24	H Herrmann	Cooper	T51	Maserati	4	21	gearbox	19	8
r	64	D Piper	Lotus	16	Climax	4	19	cylinder head gasket	22	9
r	36	B Naylor	JBW	(59)	Maserati	4	18	transmission	14	6
r	50	M Taylor	Cooper	T45	Climax	4	17	transmission	24	10
r	20	T Brooks	Vanwall	VW (59)	Vanwall	4	13	misfire	17	7
ns	30	I Ireland	Lotus	16	Climax	4		driver ill/ car raced by Stacey		
nq	56	B Moss	Cooper	T51	Climax	4				
nq	60	M Parkes	Fry		Climax	4				
nq	44	T Taylor	Cooper	T51	Climax	4				
nq	54	K Greene	Cooper	T45	Climax	4				
nq	66	T Parnell	Cooper	T45	Climax	4				
nq	62	D Taylor	Lotus	12	Climax	4				

Winning Speed: 144.655 km/h, 89.884 mph
Pole Position speed: 147.296 km/h, 91.525 mph (J Brabham, 1 min:58.000 sec)
Fastest Lap speed: 148.555 km/h, 92.308 mph (S Moss/ B McLaren, 1 min:57.000 sec on lap 69 / 75)
Lap Leaders: J Brabham 1-75 (75).

2 Aug 1959 — GERMANY: AVUS (Round: 6) (Race: 81)

60 laps x 8.300 km, 5.157 miles = 498.000 km, 309.443 miles

POS.	NO	DRIVER	CAR	MODEL	ENGINE		LAPS	TIME/REASON FOR RETIREMENT	GRID:POS	ROW
1	4	T Brooks	Ferrari	D246	Ferrari	V6	60	2h 09m 31.600s	1	1
2	6	D Gurney	Ferrari	D246	Ferrari	V6	60	2h 09m 33.500s	3	1
3	5	P Hill	Ferrari	D246	Ferrari	V6	60	2h 10m 36.400s	6	2
4	8	M Trintignant	Cooper	T51	Climax	4	59		12	4
5	9	J Bonnier	BRM	P25	BRM	4	58		7	2
6	18	I Burgess	Cooper	T51	Maserati	4	56		15	5
7r	10	H Schell	BRM	P25	BRM	4	49	clutch (pushed over line)	8	3
r	2	B McLaren	Cooper	T51	Climax	4	37	clutch	9	3
r	11	H Herrmann	BRM	P25	BRM	4	35	accident	11	3
r	3	M Gregory	Cooper	T51	Climax	4	23	engine	5	2
r	1	J Brabham	Cooper	T51	Climax	4	15	clutch	4	1
r	16	G Hill	Lotus	16	Climax	4	10	oil radiator	10	3
r	15	I Ireland	Lotus	16	Climax	4	7	gear selection	13	4
r	17	C Allison	Ferrari	D246	Ferrari	V6	2	clutch	14	4
r	7	S Moss	Cooper	T51	Climax	4	1	gearbox	2	1
ns	12	J Behra	Behra Porsche		Porsche	F4		fatal accident in support race		
ns	14	W von Trips	Porsche	718	Porsche	F4		withdrew after Behra accident		

Winning speed: 230.686 km/h, 143.342 mph
Pole Position speed: 237.331 km/h, 147.471 mph (T Brooks, 2 min: 5.900 sec)
Fastest Lap speed: 240.000 km/h, 149.129 mph (T Brooks, 2 min: 4.500 sec on lap 18)
Lap Leaders: T Brooks 1-2,5-13,15,18-22,24-30,32-35,37,40,42,46-47,52-60 (42); M Gregory 3-4,23 (3); D Gurney 14,16-17,41,43-44,50-51 (8); P Hill 31,36,38-39,45,48-49 (7).

Race staged in 2 heats of 30 laps each, with results being on aggregate.
C Allison set a time quick enough for pole position, but being a reserve driver, had to start from the back of the grid.

23 Aug 1959 — PORTUGAL: Monsanto Park (Round: 7) (Race: 82)

62 laps x 5.440 km, 3.380 miles = 337.280 km, 209.576 miles

POS.	NO	DRIVER	CAR	MODEL	ENGINE		LAPS	TIME/REASON FOR RETIREMENT	GRID:POS	ROW
1	4	S Moss	Cooper	T51	Climax	4	62	2h 11m 55.410s	1	1
2	2	M Gregory	Cooper	T51	Climax	4	61		3	1
3	16	D Gurney	Ferrari	D246	Ferrari	V6	61		6	3
4	5	M Trintignant	Cooper	T51	Climax	4	60		4	2
5	6	H Schell	BRM	P25	BRM	4	59		9	4
6	10	R Salvadori	Aston Martin	DBR4	Aston Martin	6	59		12	5
7	8	R Flockhart	BRM	P25	BRM	4	59		11	5
8	9	C Shelby	Aston Martin	DBR4	Aston Martin	6	58		13	5
9	14	T Brooks	Ferrari	D246	Ferrari	V6	57		10	4
10	18	M de Cabral	Cooper	T51	Maserati	4	56		14	6
r	3	B McLaren	Cooper	T51	Climax	4	38	transmission	8	3
r	1	J Brabham	Cooper	T51	Climax	4	23	accident	2	1
r	7	J Bonnier	BRM	P25	BRM	4	10	engine	5	2
r	15	P Hill	Ferrari	D246	Ferrari	V6	5	accident	7	3
r	11	G Hill	Lotus	16	Climax	4	5	accident	15	6
r	12	I Ireland	Lotus	16	Climax	4	3	gearbox	16	7

Winning Speed: 153.398 km/h, 95.317 mph
Pole Position speed: 159.362 km/h, 99.023 mph (S Moss, 2 min: 2.890 sec)
Fastest Lap speed: 156.584 km/h, 97.297 mph (S Moss, 2 min: 5.070 sec on lap 28)
Lap Leaders: S Moss 1-62 (62).

13 Sep 1959 — ITALY: Monza (Round: 8) (Race: 83)

72 laps x 5.750 km, 3.573 miles = 414.000 km, 257.248 miles

POS.	NO	DRIVER	CAR	MODEL	ENGINE		LAPS	TIME/REASON FOR RETIREMENT	GRID:POS	ROW
1	14	S Moss	Cooper	T51	Climax	4	72	2h 04m 05.400s	1	1
2	32	P Hill	Ferrari	D246	Ferrari	V6	72	2h 04m 52.100s	5	2
3	12	J Brabham	Cooper	T51	Climax	4	72	2h 05m 17.900s	3	1
4	36	D Gurney	Ferrari	D246	Ferrari	V6	72	2h 05m 25.000s	4	2
5	34	C Allison	Ferrari	D246	Ferrari	V6	71		8	3
6	38	O Gendebien	Ferrari	D246	Ferrari	V6	70		6	3
7	2	H Schell	BRM	P25	BRM	4	70		7	3
8	6	J Bonnier	BRM	P25	BRM	4	70		11	5
9	16	M Trintignant	Cooper	T51	Climax	4	70		13	5
10	26	C Shelby	Aston Martin	DBR4	Aston Martin	6	70		19	8
11	40	C Davis	Cooper	T51	Maserati	4	68		18	7
12	10	G Scarlatti	Cooper	T51	Climax	4	68		12	5
13	4	R Flockhart	BRM	P25	BRM	4	67		15	6
14	42	I Burgess	Cooper	T51	Maserati	4	67		16	7
15	28	G Cabianca	Maserati	250F	Maserati	6	64		21	9
r	24	R Salvadori	Aston Martin	DBR4	Aston Martin	6	44	engine	17	7
r	8	B McLaren	Cooper	T51	Climax	4	22	engine	9	4
r	22	J Fairman	Cooper	T45	Maserati	4	18	piston	20	8
r	20	I Ireland	Lotus	16	Climax	4	14	brakes	14	6
r	18	G Hill	Lotus	16	Climax	4	1	engine	10	4
r	30	T Brooks	Ferrari	D246	Ferrari	V6	0	piston	2	1

Winning Speed: 200.177 km/h, 124.384 mph
Pole Position speed: 207.623 km/h, 129.011 mph (S Moss,1 min:39.700 sec)
Fastest Lap speed: 206.175 km/h, 128.111 mph (P Hill,1 min:40.400 sec on lap 32)
Lap Leaders: S Moss1,4,15,33-72 (43); P Hill 2-3,5-14,16-32 (29).

12 Dec 1959 — USA: Sebring (Round: 9) (Race: 84)

42 laps x 8.369 km, 5.200 miles = 351.481 km, 218.400 miles

POS.	NO	DRIVER	CAR	MODEL	ENGINE		LAPS	TIME/REASON FOR RETIREMENT	GRID:POS	ROW
1	9	B McLaren	Cooper	T51	Climax	4	42	2h 12m 35.700s	10	4
2	6	M Trintignant	Cooper	T51	Climax	4	42	2h 12m 36.300s	5	2
3	2	T Brooks	Ferrari	D246	Ferrari	V6	42	2h 15m 36.600s	4	2
4	8	J Brabham	Cooper	T51	Climax	4	42	2h 17m 33.000s	2	1
5	10	I Ireland	Lotus	16	Climax	4	39		9	4
6	4	W von Trips	Ferrari	D246	Ferrari	V6	38		6	3
7	17	H Blanchard	Porsche	RSK	Porsche	F4	38		16	7
r	12	R Salvadori	Cooper	T45	Maserati	4	23	transmission	11	5
r	3	C Allison	Ferrari	D246	Ferrari	V6	23	clutch	7	3
r	1	R Ward	Kurtis Kraft	Midget	Offenhauser	4	20	clutch	19	8
r	14	A de Tomaso	Cooper	T43	OSCA	4	13	brakes	14	6
r	5	P Hill	Ferrari	D246	Ferrari	V6	8	clutch	8	3
r	15	F d'Orey	Tec Mec	F415	Maserati	6	6	oil leak	17	7
r	19	H Schell	Cooper	T51	Climax	4	5	clutch	3	1
r	16	G Constantine	Cooper	T45	Climax	4	5	cylinder head gasket	15	6
r	7	S Moss	Cooper	T51	Climax	4	5	gearbox	1	1
r	11	A Stacey	Lotus	16	Climax	4	1	clutch	12	5
r	18	B Said	Connaught	C	Alta	4	0	engine/ accident	13	5
ns	22	P Cade	Maserati	250F	Maserati	6		engine	18	7

Winning Speed: 159.047 km/h, 98.827 mph
Pole Position speed: 167.372 km/h, 104.000 mph (S Moss, 3 min: 0.000 sec)
Fastest Lap speed: 162.848 km/h, 101.189 mph (M Trintignant, 3 min: 5.000 sec on lap 39)
Lap Leaders: S Moss 1-5 (5); J Brabham 6-41 (36); B McLaren 42 (1).

Lap Leaders 1959

POS	DRIVER	CAR-ENGINE	GPS	LAPS	KM	MILES
1	S Moss	Cooper-Climax	5	173	827.7	514.3
2	J Brabham	Cooper-Climax	4	134	739.9	459.8
3	T Brooks	Ferrari	2	92	763.7	474.5
4	J Bonnier	BRM	1	58	243.2	151.1
5	P Hill	Ferrari	2	36	224.8	139.7
6	J Behra	Ferrari	1	21	66.0	41.0
7	M Gregory	Cooper-Climax	2	13	66.8	41.5
8	D Gurney	Ferrari	1	8	66.4	41.3
9	B McLaren	Cooper-Climax	1	1	8.4	5.2
			8	**536**	**3,007.0**	**1,868.4**

Driver Points 1959

		MC	INDY	NL	F	GB	D	P	I	USA	TOTAL	
1	J Brabham	9	-	6	4	8	-	-	4	(3)	31	(3)
2	T Brooks	6	-	-	8	-	9	-	-	4	27	
3	S Moss	-	-	1	1	6.5	-	9	8	-	25.5	
4	P Hill	3	-	-	6	-	4	-	7	-	20	
5	M Trintignant	4	-	-	-	2	3	3	-	7	19	
6	B McLaren	2	-	-	2	4.5	-	-	-	8	16.5	
7	D Gurney	-	-	-	-	-	6	4	3	-	13	
8	J Bonnier	-	-	8	-	-	2	-	-	-	10	
	M Gregory	-	-	4	-	-	-	6	-	-	10	
10	R Ward	-	8	-	-	-	-	-	-	-	8	
11	J Rathmann	-	6	-	-	-	-	-	-	-	6	
12	J Thomson	-	5	-	-	-	-	-	-	-	5	
	I Ireland	-	-	3	-	-	-	-	-	2	5	
	H Schell	-	-	-	-	3	-	2	-	-	5	
15	T Bettenhausen	-	3	-	-	-	-	-	-	-	3	
	O Gendebien	-	-	-	3	-	-	-	-	-	3	
17	P Goldsmith	-	2	-	-	-	-	-	-	-	2	
	J Behra	-	2	-	-	-		-	-	-	2	
	C Allison	-	-	-	-	-	-	-	2	-	2	

8, 6, 4, 3 and 2 points awarded to the first five finishers.
The driver setting the fastest lap scored a point also. Points only awarded to drivers who handled the car throughout the race. Best 5 scores.

Constructor Points 1959

		MC	INDY	NL	F	GB	D	P	I	USA	TOTAL	
1	Cooper-Climax	8	-	(6)	(4)	8	(3)	8	8	8	40	(13)
2	Ferrari	6	-	(2)	8	-	8	4	6	(4)	32	(6)
3	BRM	-	-	8	-	6	2	2	-	-	18	
4	Lotus-Climax	-	-	3	-	-	-	-	-	2	5	

8, 6, 4, 3 and 2 points awarded to the first five finishers. Indianapolis excluded. Points only for highest placed car. Best 5 scores.

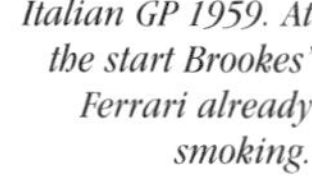
Italian GP 1959. At the start Brookes' Ferrari already smoking.

Top Left: Innes Ireland, Italian Grand Prix 1959.

Top Right: J M Fangio and P Collins — 'The Master and the Pupil', at the 1957 British Grand Prix.

Left: Masten Gregory preparing for British Grand Prix 1959, in a Cooper T51.

Below: Maurice Tinitignant (No. 44) and Giuseppe Farina (No. 42) in Ferrari 625s at Monaco in 1955.

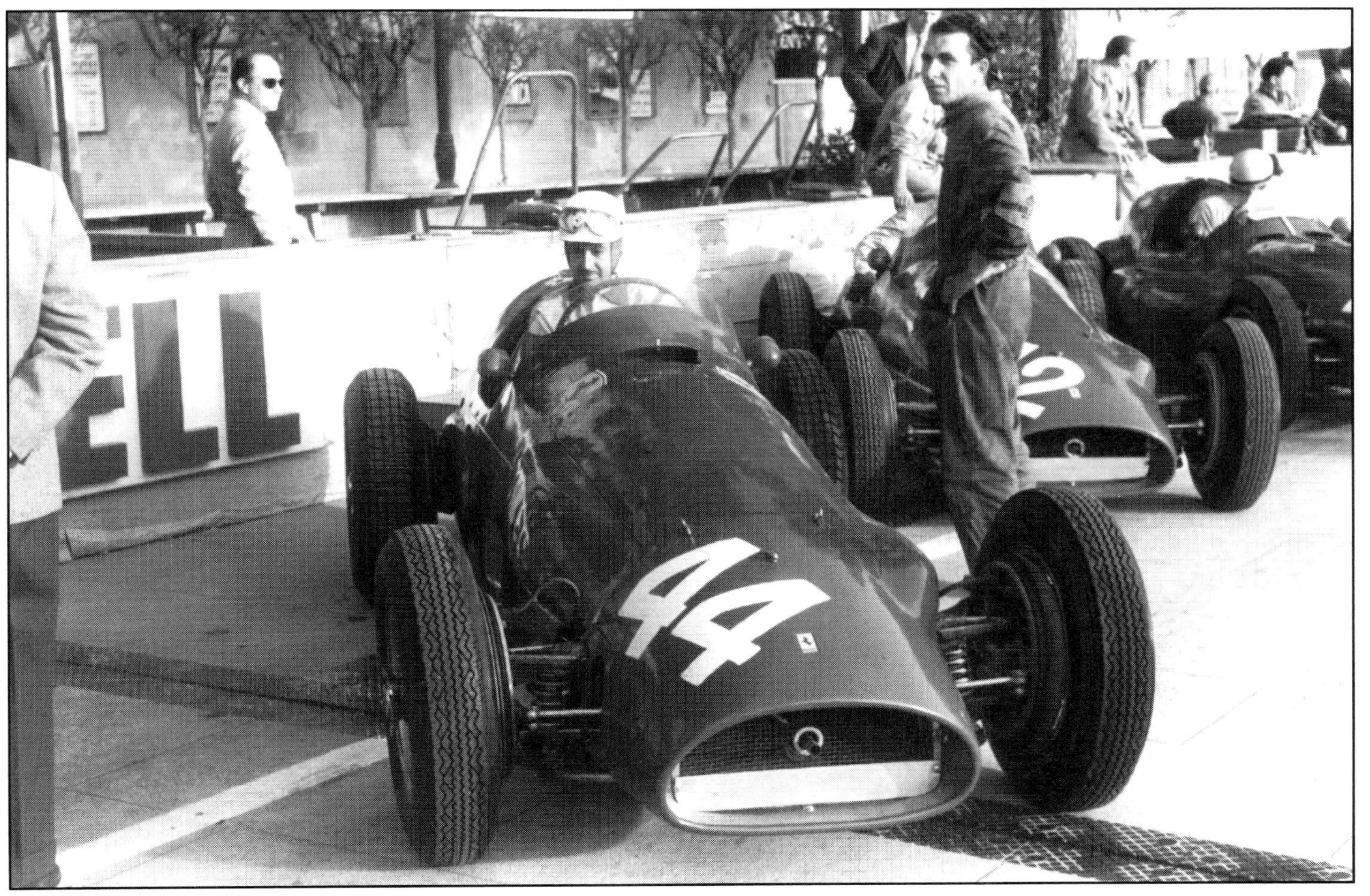

The point for fastest lap was dropped and replaced by a point for sixth place. Lotus, BRM and even the traditionalist Ferrari turned to rear engined cars. This was the last year for a front engine victory and the new Scarab and Aston Martin were soon outdated. The Belgian Grand Prix meeting was a black weekend for racing with two drivers killed and two seriously injured.

FERRARI
Scuderia Ferrari: P Hill, von Trips, Ginther, Mairesse, Allison, González

MASERATI
Joe Lubin: Drake
Privateers: Chimeri, Creus, Estefano, Munaron, Scarlatti, (Gould)

ASTON MARTIN
David Brown Corporation: Salvadori, Trintignant

BRM
Owen Racing Organisation: G Hill, Bonnier, Gurney

COOPER
Cooper Car Co: Brabham, McLaren, Flockhart, Daigh
R R C Walker Racing Team: Moss, Trintignant (RA), (Reventlow)
Yeoman Credit Racing Team: Brooks, Gendebien.
H Taylor, Bristow, P Hill, Halford (F)
Scuderia Centro Sud: Gregory, Trintignant, Burgess
Bonomi, de Cabral, Thiele, von Trips, Menditéguy
Scuderia Castellotti: Munaron, Scarlatti, Cabianca
High Efficiency Motors: Salvadori
C T Atkins: Fairman
Fred Tuck Cars: Bianchi, (Halford)
Equipe Nationale Belge: Bianchi (B)
Ecurie Maarsbergen: de Beaufort
Scuderia Colonia: Drogo
Gilby Engineering Co Ltd: Greene
Fred Armbruster: Lovely
Ecurie Bleue: Schell
Eqipe Prideux/Dick Gibson: Wilson
Privateers: Owen, Seidel

JBW
J B Naylor: Naylor

LOTUS
Team Lotus: Ireland, Clark, Stacey, Surtees, Flockhart, Larreta
R R C Walker Racing Team: Moss
Robert Bodle Ltd: Piper
Taylor-Crawley Racing Team: (M Taylor)
Privateer: Hall

VANWALL
Vandervell Products Ltd: Brooks

PORSCHE
Dr Ing F Porsche KG: Barth
Porsche System Engineering: Herrmann
Camoradi International: Gregory, Gamble

SCARAB
Reventlow Automobiles Inc.: Reventlow, Daigh, (Ginther)

7 Feb 1960 — ARGENTINA: Buenos Aires No.2 (Round: 1) (Race: 85)
80 laps x 3.912 km, 2.431 miles = 312.960 km, 194.464 miles

POS.	NO	DRIVER	CAR	MODEL	ENGINE		LAPS	TIME/REASON FOR RETIREMENT	GRID:POS	ROW
1	16	B McLaren	Cooper	T51	Climax	4	80	2h 17m 49.500s	13	4
2	24	C Allison	Ferrari	D246	Ferrari	V6	80	2h 18m 15.800s	7	2
3=	38	M Trintignant	Cooper	T51	Climax	4			8	3
3=	38	S Moss	Cooper	T51	Climax	4	80	2h 18m 26.400s		
4	6	C Menditéguy	Cooper	T51	Maserati	4	80	2h 18m 42.800s	12	4
5	30	W von Trips	Ferrari	D246	Ferrari	V6	79		5	2
6	20	I Ireland	Lotus	18	Climax	4	79		2	1
7	40	J Bonnier	BRM	P25	BRM	4	79		4	1
8	26	P Hill	Ferrari	D246	Ferrari	V6	77		6	2
9	46	R Larreta	Lotus	16	Climax	4	77		15	5
10	32	F González	Ferrari	D246	Ferrari	V6	77		11	3
11	4	R Bonomi	Cooper	T51	Maserati	4	76		17	5
12	2	M Gregory	Behra Porsche		Porsche	F4	76		16	5
13	14	G Munaron	Maserati	250F	Maserati	6	72		19	6
14	10	N Estefano	Maserati	250F	Maserati	6	70		20	6
r	34	H Schell	Cooper	T51	Climax	4	63	fuel pump	9	3
r	18	J Brabham	Cooper	T51	Climax	4	42	gearbox	10	3
r	36	S Moss	Cooper	T51	Climax	4	40	suspension	1	1
r	42	G Hill	BRM	P25	BRM	4	37	engine overheating	3	1
r	22	A Stacey	Lotus	16	Climax	4	24	driver exhausted	14	4
r	44	E Chimeri	Maserati	250F	Maserati	6	23	driver exhausted	21	6
r	12	A Creus	Maserati	250F	Maserati	6	16	driver exhausted	22	7
r	8	G Scarlatti	Maserati	250F	Maserati	6	10	engine overheating	18	5

Winning speed: 136.242 km/h, 84.657 mph
Pole Position speed: 145.337 km/h, 90.309 mph (S Moss, 1 min:36.900 sec)
Fastest Lap speed: 142.398 km/h, 88.482 mph (S Moss, 1 min:38.900 sec on lap 37)
Lap Leaders: I Ireland 1 (1); J Bonnier 2-15,21-36,41-67 (57); S Moss 16-20,37-40 (9); B McLaren 68-80 (13).

29 May 1960 — MONACO: Monte Carlo (Round: 2) (Race: 86)
100 laps x 3.145 km, 1.954 miles = 314.500 km, 195.421 miles

POS.	NO	DRIVER	CAR	MODEL	ENGINE		LAPS	TIME/REASON FOR RETIREMENT	GRID:POS	ROW
1	28	S Moss	Lotus	18	Climax	4	100	2h 53m 45.500s	1	1
2	10	B McLaren	Cooper	T53	Climax	4	100	2h 54m 37.600s	11	5
3	36	P Hill	Ferrari	D246	Ferrari	V6	100	2h 54m 47.400s	10	4
4	18	T Brooks	Cooper	T51	Climax	4	99		3	1
5	2	J Bonnier	BRM	P48	BRM	4	83		5	2
6	34	R Ginther	Ferrari	D246P	Ferrari	V6	70		9	4
7r	6	G Hill	BRM	P48	BRM	4	66	accident	6	3
8r	38	W von Trips	Ferrari	D246	Ferrari	V6	61	clutch	8	3
9	22	I Ireland	Lotus	18	Climax	4	56		7	3
nc	4	D Gurney	BRM	P48	BRM	4	44		14	6
dq	8	J Brabham	Cooper	T53	Climax	4	40	push start after spin	2	1
r	14	R Salvadori	Cooper	T51	Climax	4	29	engine overheating	12	5
r	24	A Stacey	Lotus	18	Climax	4	23	engine mounting	13	5
r	26	J Surtees	Lotus	18	Climax	4	17	transmission	15	6
r	16	C Bristow	Cooper	T51	Climax	4	17	gearbox	4	2
r	44	M Trintignant	Cooper	T51	Maserati	4	4	gearbox	16	7
nq	12	B Halford	Cooper	T51	Climax	4				
nq	20	B Naylor	JBW	(59)	Maserati	4				
nq	30	G Scarlatti	Cooper	T51	Castellotti	4				
nq	32	C Allison	Ferrari	D246	Ferrari	V6		accident/ injury		
nq	40	M Gregory	Cooper	T51	Maserati	4				
nq	42	I Burgess	Cooper	T51	Climax	4				
nq	46	C Daigh	Scarab		Scarab	4				

POS.	NO	DRIVER	CAR	MODEL	ENGINE		LAPS	TIME/REASON FOR RETIREMENT	GRID:POS	ROW
nq	48	L Reventlow	Scarab		Scarab	4				
nq	30	G Munaron	Cooper	T51	Castellotti	4				

Winning speed: 108.599 km/h, 67.480 mph
Pole Position speed: 117.570 km/h, 73.055 mph (S Moss, 1 min:36.300 sec)
Fastest Lap speed: 117.692 km/h, 73.131 mph (B McLaren, 1 min:36.200 sec on lap 11)
Lap Leaders: J Bonnier 1-16,61-67 (23); S Moss 17-33,41-60,68-100 (70); J Brabham 34-40 (7).

30 May 1960 — INDIANAPOLIS 500 — (Round: 3) (Race: 87)

200 laps x 4.023 km, 2.500 miles = 804.672 km, 500.000 miles

POS.	NO	DRIVER	CAR	MODEL	ENGINE		LAPS	TIME/REASON FOR RETIREMENT	GRID:POS	ROW
1	4	J Rathmann	Watson		Offenhauser	4	200	3h 36m 11.360s	2	1
2	1	R Ward	Watson		Offenhauser	4	200	3h 36m 24.109s	3	1
3	99	P Goldsmith	Epperly		Offenhauser	4	200		26	9
4	7	D Branson	Phillips		Offenhauser	4	200		8	3
5	3	J Thomson	Lesovsky		Offenhauser	4	200		17	6
6	22	E Johnson	Trevis		Offenhauser	4	200		7	3
7	98	L Ruby	Watson		Offenhauser	4	200		12	4
8	44	B Veith	Meskowski		Offenhauser	4	200		25	9
9	18	B Tingelstad	Trevis		Offenhauser	4	200		28	10
10	38	B Christie	Kurtis Kraft	500C	Offenhauser	4	200		14	5
11	27	R Amick	Epperly		Offenhauser	4	200		22	8
12	17	D Carter	Kuzma		Offenhauser	4	200		27	9
13	39	B Homeier	Kuzma		Offenhauser	4	200		31	11
14	48	G Hartley	Kurtis Kraft	500G	Offenhauser	4	196		24	8
15	65	C Stevenson	Watson		Offenhauser	4	196		9	3
16	14	B Grim	Meskowski		Offenhauser	4	194		21	7
17	26	S Templeman	Kurtis Kraft	500C	Offenhauser	4	191		19	7
18r	56	J Hurtubise	Christensen		Offenhauser	4	185	connecting rod	23	8
19r	10	J Bryan	Epperly		Offenhauser	4	152	fuel pump drive	10	4
20r	28	T Ruttman	Watson		Offenhauser	4	134	rear axle	6	2
21r	6	E Sachs	Ewing		Offenhauser	4	132	magneto	1	1
22r	73	D Freeland	Kurtis Kraft		Offenhauser	4	129	magneto	11	4
23r	2	T Bettenhausen	Watson		Offenhauser	4	125	connecting rod	18	6
24r	32	W Weiler	Epperly		Offenhauser	4	103	accident	15	5
25r	5	A J Foyt	Kurtis Kraft		Offenhauser	4	90	clutch	16	6
26r	46	E Russo	Kurtis Kraft	500G	Offenhauser	4	84	accident	29	10
27r	8	J Boyd	Epperly		Offenhauser	4	77	piston	13	5
28r	37	G Force	Kurtis Kraft	500G	Offenhauser	4	74	brakes	20	7
29r	16	J McWithey	Epperly		Offenhauser	4	60	brakes	32	11
30r	9	L Sutton	Watson		Offenhauser	4	47	piston ring	5	2
31r	97	D Rathmann	Watson		Offenhauser	4	42	brake line	4	2
32r	76	A Herman	Ewing		Offenhauser	4	34	clutch	30	10
33r	23	D Wilson	Kurtis Kraft	500G	Offenhauser	4	11	magneto point spring	33	11

Winning speed: 223.324 km/h, 138.767 mph
Pole Position speed: 235.917 km/h, 146.592 mph (E Sachs, 1 min: 1.395 sec)
Fastest Lap speed: 235.170 km/h, 146.128 mph (J Rathmann, 1 min: 1.590 sec on lap 197)
Fastest qualifier: (J Hurtubise 239.882 km/h, 149.056 mph).

6 Jun 1960 — NETHERLANDS: Zandvoort — (Round: 4) (Race: 88)

75 laps x 4.193 km, 2.605 miles = 314.475 km, 195.406 miles

POS.	NO	DRIVER	CAR	MODEL	ENGINE		LAPS	TIME/REASON FOR RETIREMENT	GRID:POS	ROW
1	11	J Brabham	Cooper	T53	Climax	4	75	2h 01m 47.200s	2	1
2	4	I Ireland	Lotus	18	Climax	4	75	2h 02m 11.200s	3	1
3	16	G Hill	BRM	P48	BRM	4	75	2h 02m 43.800s	5	2
4	7	S Moss	Lotus	18	Climax	4	75	2h 02m 44.900s	1	1
5	2	W von Trips	Ferrari	D246	Ferrari	V6	74		15	6
6	3	R Ginther	Ferrari	D246	Ferrari	V6	74		12	5
7	10	H Taylor	Cooper	T51	Climax	4	70		14	6
8	20	C G de Beaufort	Cooper	T51	Climax	4	69		17	7
r	5	A Stacey	Lotus	18	Climax	4	57	transmission	8	3
r	1	P Hill	Ferrari	D246	Ferrari	V6	54	engine	13	5
r	14	J Bonnier	BRM	P48	BRM	4	54	engine/ accident	4	2
r	6	J Clark	Lotus	18	Climax	4	42	transmission	11	5
r	18	M Trintignant	Cooper	T51	Maserati	4	39	gearbox	16	7
r	15	D Gurney	BRM	P48	BRM	4	11	brakes/ accident	6	3
r	8	C Bristow	Cooper	T51	Climax	4	9	engine	7	3
r	12	B McLaren	Cooper	T53	Climax	4	8	universal joint	9	4
r	9	T Brooks	Cooper	T51	Climax	4	4	gearbox	10	4
ns	22	C Daigh	Scarab		Scarab	4		starting money dispute		
ns	21	L Reventlow	Scarab		Scarab	4		starting money dispute		
ns	17	R Salvadori	Aston Martin	DBR4	Aston Martin	6		starting money dispute		
ns	19	M Gregory	Cooper	T51	Maserati	4		starting money dispute		

Winning speed: 154.931 km/h, 96.270 mph
Pole Position speed: 161.961 km/h, 100.638 mph (S Moss, 1 min: 33.200 sec)
Fastest Lap speed: 160.925 km/h, 99.994 mph (S Moss, 1 min: 33.800 sec on lap 75)
Lap Leaders: J Brabham 1-75 (75).

19 Jun 1960 BELGIUM: Spa-Francorchamps (Round: 5) (Race: 89)

36 laps x 14.100 km, 8.761 miles = 507.600 km, 315.408 miles

POS.	NO.	DRIVER	CAR	MODEL	ENGINE		LAPS	TIME/REASON FOR RETIREMENT	GRID:POS	ROW
1	2	J Brabham	Cooper	T53	Climax	4	36	2h 21m 37.300s	1	1
2	4	B McLaren	Cooper	T53	Climax	4	36	2h 22m 40.600s	13	5
r	10	G Hill	BRM	P48	BRM	4	35	engine	5	2
3	34	O Gendebien	Cooper	T51	Climax	4	35		4	2
4	24	P Hill	Ferrari	D246	Ferrari	V6	35		3	1
5	18	J Clark	Lotus	18	Climax	4	34		9	4
6	32	L Bianchi	Cooper	T51	Climax	4	28		14	6
r	16	A Stacey	Lotus	18	Climax	4	24	fatal accident	16	7
r	22	W Mairesse	Ferrari	D246	Ferrari	V6	23	transmission	12	5
r	26	W von Trips	Ferrari	D246	Ferrari	V6	22	transmission	10	4
r	36	C Bristow	Cooper	T51	Climax	4	19	fatal accident	8	3
r	30	C Daigh	Scarab		Scarab	4	16	engine	17	7
r	6	J Bonnier	BRM	P48	BRM	4	14	engine	6	3
r	14	I Ireland	Lotus	18	Climax	4	13	spin	7	3
r	8	D Gurney	BRM	P48	BRM	4	4	engine	11	5
r	38	T Brooks	Cooper	T51	Climax	4	2	gearbox	2	1
r	28	L Reventlow	Scarab		Scarab	4	1	engine	15	6
ns	12	S Moss	Lotus	18	Climax	4		accident/ injury		
ns	20	M Taylor	Lotus	18	Climax	4		accident/ injury		

Winning speed: 215.052 km/h, 133.627 mph
Pole Position speed: 220.696 km/h, 137.134 mph (J Brabham, 3 min:50.000 sec)
Fastest Lap speed: 218.887 km/h, 136.010 mph (P Hill/ J Brabham/ I Ireland, 3 min:51.900 sec)
Lap Leaders: J Brabham 1-36 (36).

3 Jul 1960 FRANCE: Reims (Round: 6) (Race: 90)

50 laps x 8.302 km, 5.159 miles = 415.100 km, 257.931 miles

POS.	NO.	DRIVER	CAR	MODEL	ENGINE		LAPS	TIME/REASON FOR RETIREMENT	GRID:POS	ROW
1	16	J Brabham	Cooper	T53	Climax	4	50	1h 57m 24.900s	1	1
2	44	O Gendebien	Cooper	T51	Climax	4	50	1h 58m 13.200s	11	5
3	18	B McLaren	Cooper	T53	Climax	4	50	1h 58m 16.800s	9	4
4	46	H Taylor	Cooper	T51	Climax	4	49		13	5
5	24	J Clark	Lotus	18	Climax	4	49		12	5
6	22	R Flockhart	Lotus	18	Climax	4	49		8	3
7	20	I Ireland	Lotus	18	Climax	4	43		4	2
8r	48	B Halford	Cooper	T51	Climax	4	40	engine	16	7
9	40	M Gregory	Cooper	T51	Maserati	4	37		17	7
10	42	I Burgess	Cooper	T51	Maserati	4	36		20	8
11r	4	W von Trips	Ferrari	D246	Ferrari	V6	31	transmission	6	3
12r	2	P Hill	Ferrari	D246	Ferrari	V6	29	transmission	2	1
r	8	J Bonnier	BRM	P48	BRM	4	22	engine	10	4
r	36	L Bianchi	Cooper	T51	Climax	4	18	transmission	15	6
r	10	D Gurney	BRM	P48	BRM	4	17	engine	7	3
r	30	G Munaron	Cooper	T51	Castellotti	4	15	transmission	19	8
r	6	W Mairesse	Ferrari	D246	Ferrari	V6	14	transmission	5	2
r	14	T Brooks	Vanwall	VW11	Vanwall	4	7	vibration	14	6
r	38	M Trintignant	Cooper	T51	Maserati	4	0	accident	18	7
r	12	G Hill	BRM	P48	BRM	4	0	accident	3	1
ns	28	R Ginther	Scarab		Scarab	4		engine		
ns	34	D Piper	Lotus	16	Climax	4		engine		
ns	26	C Daigh	Scarab		Scarab	4		engine		

Winning speed: 212.119 km/h, 131.805 mph
Pole Position speed: 218.474 km/h, 135.753 mph (J Brabham, 2 min:16.800 sec)
Fastest Lap speed: 217.361 km/h, 135.062 mph (J Brabham, 2 min:17.500 sec on lap 25)
Lap Leaders: J Brabham 1-3,5,7,9-10,12,14,18-50 (42); P Hill 4,6,8,11,13,15-17 (8).

16 Jul 1960 BRITAIN: Silverstone (Round: 7) (Race: 91)

77 laps x 4.711 km, 2.927 miles = 362.712 km, 225.379 miles

POS.	NO.	DRIVER	CAR	MODEL	ENGINE		LAPS	TIME/REASON FOR RETIREMENT	GRID:POS	ROW
1	1	J Brabham	Cooper	T53	Climax	4	77	2h 04m 24.600s	1	1
2	9	J Surtees	Lotus	18	Climax	4	77	2h 05m 14.200s	11	3
3	7	I Ireland	Lotus	18	Climax	4	77	2h 05m 54.200s	5	2
4	2	B McLaren	Cooper	T53	Climax	4	76		3	1
5	12	T Brooks	Cooper	T51	Climax	4	76		9	3
6	11	W von Trips	Ferrari	D246	Ferrari	V6	75		7	2
7	10	P Hill	Ferrari	D246	Ferrari	V6	75		10	3
8	15	H Taylor	Cooper	T51	Climax	4	74		16	5
9	14	O Gendebien	Cooper	T51	Climax	4	74		12	4
10	5	D Gurney	BRM	P48	BRM	4	74		6	2
11	19	M Trintignant	Aston Martin	DBR5	Aston Martin	6	72		21	6
12	26	D Piper	Lotus	16	Climax	4	72		23	7
13	25	B Naylor	JBW	(59)	Maserati	4	72		18	5
r	4	G Hill	BRM	P48	BRM	4	71	accident	2	1
14	16	M Gregory	Cooper	T51	Maserati	4	71		14	4
15	21	G Munaron	Cooper	T51	Castellotti	4	68		24	7
16	8	J Clark	Lotus	18	Climax	4	68		8	3
r	24	L Bianchi	Cooper	T51	Climax	4	60	magneto	17	5
r	6	J Bonnier	BRM	P48	BRM	4	59	rear suspension	4	1
r	3	C Daigh	Cooper	T51	Climax	4	56	engine overheating	19	6

POS.	NO.	DRIVER	CAR	MODEL	ENGINE		LAPS	TIME/REASON FOR RETIREMENT	GRID:POS	ROW
r	17	I Burgess	Cooper	T51	Maserati	4	56	engine	20	6
r	23	J Fairman	Cooper	T51	Climax	4	44	fuel pump	15	5
r	18	R Salvadori	Aston Martin	DBR5	Aston Martin	6	44	steering	13	4
r	22	K Greene	Cooper	T45	Maserati	4	12	engine overheating	22	7
ns	3	L Reventlow	Cooper	T51	Climax	4		car raced by Daigh		

Winning speed: 174.928 km/h, 108.695 mph
Pole Position speed: 179.260 km/h, 111.387 mph (J Brabham, 1 min:34.600 sec)
Fastest Lap speed: 179.640 km/h, 111.623 mph (G Hill, 1 min:34.400 sec on lap 56)
Lap Leaders: J Brabham 1-54,72-77 (60); G Hill 55-71 (17).

A Stacey's qualifying time was set by I Ireland.

14 Aug 1960 — PORTUGAL: Porto (Round: 8) (Race: 92)

55 laps x 7.407 km, 4.602 miles = 407.385 km, 253.137 miles

POS.	NO.	DRIVER	CAR	MODEL	ENGINE		LAPS	TIME/REASON FOR RETIREMENT	GRID:POS	ROW
1	2	J Brabham	Cooper	T53	Climax	4	55	2h 19m 00.030s	3	1
2	4	B McLaren	Cooper	T53	Climax	4	55	2h 19m 58.000s	6	3
3	14	J Clark	Lotus	18	Climax	4	55	2h 20m 53.260s	8	3
4	28	W von Trips	Ferrari	D246	Ferrari	V6	55	2h 20m 58.840s	9	4
dq	12	S Moss	Lotus	18	Climax	4	50	drove in wrong direction	4	2
5	6	T Brooks	Cooper	T51	Climax	4	49		12	5
6	16	I Ireland	Lotus	18	Climax	4	48		7	3
7	8	O Gendebien	Cooper	T51	Climax	4	46		14	6
r	32	M de Cabral	Cooper	T51	Maserati	4	37	gearbox	15	6
r	18	J Surtees	Lotus	18	Climax	4	36	radiator	1	1
r	26	P Hill	Ferrari	D246	Ferrari	V6	29	accident	10	4
r	24	D Gurney	BRM	P48	BRM	4	24	engine overheating	2	1
r	30	M Gregory	Cooper	T51	Maserati	4	21	gearbox	11	5
r	22	G Hill	BRM	P48	BRM	4	8	gearbox	5	2
r	20	J Bonnier	BRM	P48	BRM	4	6	head gasket	13	5
ns	10	H Taylor	Cooper	T51	Climax	4		accident/ injury		

Winning speed: 175.849 km/h, 109.268 mph
Pole Position speed: 183.190 km/h, 113.829 mph (J Surtees, 2 min:25.560 sec)
Fastest Lap speed: 180.744 km/h, 112.309 mph (J Surtees, 2 min:27.530 sec on lap 33)
Lap Leaders: D Gurney 1-10 (10); J Surtees 11-35 (25); J Brabham 36-55 (20).

4 Sep 1960 — ITALY: Monza (Round: 9) (Race: 93)

50 laps x 10.000 km, 6.214 miles = 500.000 km, 310.686 miles

POS.	NO.	DRIVER	CAR	MODEL	ENGINE		LAPS	TIME/REASON FOR RETIREMENT	GRID:POS	ROW
1	20	P Hill	Ferrari	D246	Ferrari	V6	50	2h 21m 09.200s	1	1
2	18	R Ginther	Ferrari	D246	Ferrari	V6	50	2h 23m 36.800s	2	1
3	16	W Mairesse	Ferrari	D246	Ferrari	V6	49		3	1
4	2	G Cabianca	Cooper	T51	Castellotti	4	48		4	2
5	22	W von Trips	Ferrari	D246P	Ferrari	V6	48		6	3
6	26	H Herrmann	Porsche	718	Porsche	F4	47		10	4
7	24	E Barth	Porsche	718	Porsche	F4	47		12	5
8	12	P Drogo	Cooper	T43	Climax	4	45		15	6
9	10	W Seidel	Cooper	T45	Climax	4	44		13	5
10	28	F Gamble	Behra Porsche		Porsche	F4	41		14	6
r	6	B Naylor	JBW	(59)	Maserati	4	41	gearbox	7	3
r	34	A Thiele	Cooper	T51	Maserati	4	32	gearbox	9	4
r	4	G Munaron	Cooper	T51	Castellotti	4	27	oil line	8	3
r	36	G Scarlatti	Cooper	T51	Maserati	4	26	throttle linkage	5	2
r	30	V Wilson	Cooper	T43	Climax	4	23	oil sump	16	7
r	8	A Owen	Cooper	T45	Climax	4	0	accident	11	5
ns	14	H Gould	Maserati	250F	Maserati	6		crossed fuel lines		

Winning speed: 212.535 km/h, 132.063 mph
Pole Position speed: 223.048 km/h, 138.596 mph (P Hill, 2 min:41.400 sec)
Fastest Lap speed: 220.049 km/h, 136.732 mph (P Hill, 2 min:43.600 sec on lap 23)
Lap Leaders: R Ginther 1-16,18-25 (24); P Hill 17,26-50 (26).

Also the Grand Prix of Europe.

20 Nov 1960 — USA: Riverside (Round:10) (Race: 94)

75 laps x 5.271 km, 3.275 miles = 395.295 km, 245.625 miles

POS.	NO.	DRIVER	CAR	MODEL	ENGINE		LAPS	TIME/REASON FOR RETIREMENT	GRID:POS	ROW
1	5	S Moss	Lotus	18	Climax	4	75	2h 28m 52.200s	1	1
2	10	I Ireland	Lotus	18	Climax	4	75	2h 29m 30.200s	7	3
3	3	B McLaren	Cooper	T53	Climax	4	75	2h 30m 14.200s	10	4
4	2	J Brabham	Cooper	T53	Climax	4	74		2	1
5	15	J Bonnier	BRM	P48	BRM	4	74		4	2
6	9	P Hill	Cooper	T51	Climax	4	74		13	5
7	24	J Hall	Lotus	18	Climax	4	73		12	5
8	14	R Salvadori	Cooper	T51	Climax	4	73		15	6
9	26	W von Trips	Cooper	T51	Maserati	4	72		16	7
10	23	C Daigh	Scarab		Scarab	4	70		18	7
11	25	P Lovely	Cooper	T45	Castellotti	4	69		20	8

POS.	NO.	DRIVER	CAR	MODEL	ENGINE		LAPS	TIME/REASON FOR RETIREMENT	GRID:POS	ROW
12	7	O Gendebien	Cooper	T51	Climax	4	69		8	3
13	20	B Drake	Maserati	250F	Maserati	6	68		22	9
14	8	H Taylor	Cooper	T51	Climax	4	68		14	6
15	18	M Trintignant	Cooper	T51	Maserati	4	66		19	8
16	12	J Clark	Lotus	18	Climax	4	61		5	2
r	17	G Hill	BRM	P48	BRM	4	34	gearbox	11	5
r	19	I Burgess	Cooper	T51	Maserati	4	29	ignition	23	9
r	21	B Naylor	JBW	(59)	Maserati	4	20	engine	17	7
r	16	D Gurney	BRM	P48	BRM	4	18	engine overheating	3	1
r	4	R Flockhart	Cooper	T51	Climax	4	11	transmission	21	9
r	6	T Brooks	Cooper	T51	Climax	4	6	spin	9	4
r	11	J Surtees	Lotus	18	Climax	4	3	accident	6	3

Winning speed: 159.318 km/h, 98.996 mph
Pole Position speed: 165.858 km/h, 103.059 mph (S Moss, 1 min:54.400 sec)
Fastest Lap speed: 163.148 km/h, 101.376 mph (J Brabham, 1 min:56.300 sec on lap 71)
Lap Leaders: J Brabham 1-4 (4); S Moss 5-75 (71).

Lap Leaders 1960

POS	DRIVER	CAR-ENGINE	GPS	LAPS	KM	MILES
1	J Brabham	Cooper-Climax	7	244	1,644.7	1,021.9
2	S Moss	Cooper-Climax	1	9	35.2	21.9
		Lotus-Climax	2	141	594.4	369.3
			3	150	629.6	391.2
3	J Bonnier	BRM	2	80	295.3	183.5
4	P Hill	Ferrari	2	34	326.4	202.8
5	J Surtees	Lotus-Climax	1	25	185.2	115.1
6	R Ginther	Ferrari	1	24	240.0	149.1
7	G Hill	BRM	1	17	80.1	49.8
8	B McLaren	Cooper-Climax	1	13	50.9	31.6
9	D Gurney	BRM	1	10	74.1	46.0
10	I Ireland	Lotus-Climax	1	1	3.9	2.4
			9	**598**	**3,530.1**	**2,193.5**

Driver Points 1960

		RA	MC	INDY	NL	B	F	GB	P	I	USA	TOTAL	
1	J Brabham	-	-	-	8	8	8	8	8	-	3	43	
2	B McLaren	8	6	-	-	6	4	(3)	6	-	4	34	(3)
3	S Moss	-	8	-	3	-	-	-	-	-	8	19	
4	I Ireland	1	-	-	6	-	-	4	1	-	6	18	
5	P Hill	-	4	-	-	3	-	-	-	8	1	16	
6	O Gendebien	-	-	-	-	4	6	-	-	-	-	10	
	W von Trips	2	-	-	2	-	-	1	3	2	-	10	
8	J Rathmann	-	-	8	-	-	-	-	-	-	-	8	
	R Ginther	-	1	-	1	-	-	-	-	6	-	8	
	J Clark	-	-	-	-	2	2	-	4	-	-	8	
11	T Brooks	-	3	-	-	-	-	2	2	-	-	7	
12	C Allison	6	-	-	-	-	-	-	-	-	-	6	
	R Ward	-	-	6	-	-	-	-	-	-	-	6	
	J Surtees	-	-	-	-	-	-	6	-	-	-	6	
15	P Goldsmith	-	-	4	-	-	-	-	-	-	-	4	
	G Hill	-	-	-	4	-	-	-	-	-	-	4	
	W Mairesse	-	-	-	-	-	-	-	-	4	-	4	
	J Bonnier	-	2	-	-	-	-	-	-	-	2	4	
19	C Menditéguy	3	-	-	-	-	-	-	-	-	-	3	
	D Branson	-	-	3	-	-	-	-	-	-	-	3	
	H Taylor	-	-	-	-	-	3	-	-	-	-	3	
	G Cabianca	-	-	-	-	-	-	-	-	3	-	3	
23	J Thomson	-	-	2	-	-	-	-	-	-	-	2	
24	E Johnson	-	-	1	-	-	-	-	-	-	-	1	
	L Bianchi	-	-	-	-	1	-	-	-	-	-	1	
	R Flockhart	-	-	-	-	-	1	-	-	-	-	1	
	H Herrmann	-	-	-	-	-	-	-	-	1	-	1	

8,6 ,4, 3, 2 and 1 point awarded to the first six finishers. Best 6 scores.

M Trintignant and S Moss (Cooper-Climax) were ineligible for points for their 3rd place in Argentina, because of the shared drive.

Constructor Points 1960

		RA	MC	INDY	NL	B	F	GB	P	I	USA	TOTAL	
1	Cooper-Climax	8	(6)	-	8	8	8	8	8	-	(4)	48	(10)
2	Lotus-Climax	(1)	8	-	6	2	(2)	6	4	-	8	34	(3)
3	Ferrari	6	4	-	2	3	-	(1)	3	8	-	26	(1)
4	BRM	-	2	-	4	-	-	-	-	-	2	8	
5	Cooper-Maserati	3	-	-	-	-	-	-	-	-	-	3	
	Cooper-Castellotti	-	-	-	-	-	-	-	-	3	-	3	

8, 6, 4, 3, 2 and 1 point awarded to the first six finishers. Indianapolis excluded.

Points only for highest placed car. Best 6 scores.

Porsche received no points for their 6th place in Italy, due to entering a Formula 2 car.

The new 1.5 litre formula, although announced some three years earlier, caught most of the British teams off guard. They hoped for a last minute reprise of the existing rules, and had to rely on old four cylinder engines until the V8's were ready. Ferrari on the other hand developed their already successful F2 team and clearly had the early season advantage. Now there would be 9 points for a win.

FERRARI
Scuderia Ferrari SpA SEFAC: P Hill, von Trips, Ginther, Gendebien, Mairesse, Rodriguez
FISA: Baghetti (F)
Scuderia Sant Ambroeus: Baghetti

DE TOMASO
Scuderia Serenissima: Scarlatti, Vaccarella
Scuderia Settecolli: Lippi
Isobele de Tomaso: Bussinello

BRM
Owen Racing Organisation: G Hill, Brooks

COOPER
Cooper Car Co: Brabham, McLaren
Yeoman Credit Racing Team: Surtees, Salvadori
Camoradi International: Gregory, Burgess
Scuderia Centro Sud: Bandini, Natili
Scuderia Serenissima: Trintignant
Pescara Racing Club: Pirocchi
H & L Motors: Lewis
Fred Tuck: Fairman
Momo Corporation: Hansgen
John M Wyatt III: Penske
Privateers: Collomb, Sharp

EMERYSON
Equipe Nationale Belge: (Bianchi, Gendebien, Pilette)

FERGUSON
R R C Walker Racing Team: Fairman, Moss

GILBY
Gilby Engineering Co Ltd: Greene

JBW
JBW Cars: Naylor

LOTUS
Team Lotus: Clark, Ireland, T Taylor, Mairesse (F)
R R C Walker Racing Team: Moss
UDT Laystall Racing Team: H Taylor, Bianchi, Gregory, Allison, Gendebien, (Bordeu)
Scuderia Colonia: May, Seidel
Camoradi International: Burgess
Equipe Nationale Belge: Mairesse, Bianchi (B)
Louise Bryden-Brown: Maggs
J Wheeler Autosport: Ryan
J Frank Harrison: Ruby
Privateers: Parnell, Ashmore, Marsh, Starrabba, Hall

PORSCHE
Porsche System Engineering: Gurney, Bonnier, Herrmann
Ecurie Maarsbergen: de Beaufort, Herrmann (NL)

14 May 1961 — MONACO: Monte Carlo (Round: 1) (Race: 95)

100 laps x 3.145 km, 1.954 miles = 314.500 km, 195.421 miles

POS.	NO.	DRIVER	CAR	MODEL	ENGINE		LAPS	TIME/REASON FOR RETIREMENT	GRID:POS	ROW
1	20	S Moss	Lotus	18	Climax	4	100	2h 45m 50.100s	1	1
2	36	R Ginther	Ferrari	156	Ferrari	V6	100	2h 45m 53.700s	2	1
3	38	P Hill	Ferrari	156	Ferrari	V6	100	2h 46m 31.400s	5	2
4r	40	W von Trips	Ferrari	156	Ferrari	V6	98	engine/ accident	6	3
5	4	D Gurney	Porsche	718	Porsche	F4	98		10	4
6	26	B McLaren	Cooper	T55	Climax	4	95		7	3
7	42	M Trintignant	Cooper	T51	Maserati	4	95		15	6
8	32	C Allison	Lotus	18	Climax	4	93		14	6
9	6	H Herrmann	Porsche	718	Porsche	F4	91		12	5
10	28	J Clark	Lotus	21	Climax	4	89		3	1
11r	22	J Surtees	Cooper	T53	Climax	4	68	fuel pump	11	5
12r	2	J Bonnier	Porsche	787	Porsche	F4	59	fuel injection pump drive	9	4
13r	16	T Brooks	BRM	P48/57	Climax	4	54	valve	8	3
r	8	M May	Lotus	18	Climax	4	42	gearbox	13	5
r	24	J Brabham	Cooper	T55	Climax	4	38	misfire	16	7
r	18	G Hill	BRM	P48/57	Climax	4	11	fuel pump drive	4	2
ns	30	I Ireland	Lotus	21	Climax	4		accident/ injury		
nq	14	M Gregory	Cooper	T53	Climax	4				
nq	10	L Bianchi	Emeryson	(61)	Maserati	4				
nq	34	H Taylor	Lotus	18	Climax	4				
nq	12	O Gendebien	Emeryson	(61)	Maserati	4				

Winning speed: 113.788 km/h, 70.704 mph
Pole Position speed: 114.248 km/h, 70.991 mph (S Moss, 1 min:39.100 sec)
Fastest Lap speed: 117.570 km/h, 73.055 mph (R Ginther/ S Moss, 1 min:36.300 sec on lap 84 / 85)
Lap Leaders: R Ginther 1-13 (13); S Moss 14-100 (87).

22 May 1961 — NETHERLANDS: Zandvoort (Round: 2) (Race: 96)

75 laps x 4.193 km, 2.605 miles = 314.475 km, 195.406 miles

POS.	NO.	DRIVER	CAR	MODEL	ENGINE		LAPS	TIME/REASON FOR RETIREMENT	GRID:POS	ROW
1	3	W von Trips	Ferrari	156	Ferrari	V6	75	2h 01m 52.100s	2	1
2	1	P Hill	Ferrari	156	Ferrari	V6	75	2h 01m 53.000s	1	1
3	15	J Clark	Lotus	21	Climax	4	75	2h 02m 05.200s	10	4
4	14	S Moss	Lotus	18	Climax	4	75	2h 02m 14.300s	4	2
5	2	R Ginther	Ferrari	156	Ferrari	V6	75	2h 02m 14.400s	3	1
6	10	J Brabham	Cooper	T55	Climax	4	75	2h 03m 12.200s	7	3
7	12	J Surtees	Cooper	T53	Climax	4	75	2h 03m 18.800s	9	4
8	4	G Hill	BRM	P48/57	Climax	4	75	2h 03m 21.900s	5	2
9	5	T Brooks	BRM	P48/57	Climax	4	74		8	3
10	7	D Gurney	Porsche	787	Porsche	F4	74		6	3
11	6	J Bonnier	Porsche	787	Porsche	F4	73		11	5
12	11	B McLaren	Cooper	T55	Climax	4	73		13	5
13	16	T Taylor	Lotus	18	Climax	4	73		14	6
14	8	C G de Beaufort	Porsche	718	Porsche	F4	72		15	6
15	9	H Herrmann	Porsche	718	Porsche	F4	72		12	5
ns	17	M Gregory	Cooper	T53	Climax	4		reserve entry		
ns	18	I Burgess	Lotus	18	Climax	4		reserve entry		

Winning speed: 154.827 km/h, 96.205 mph
Pole Position speed: 157.730 km/h, 98.009 mph (P Hill, 1 min:35.700 sec)
Fastest Lap speed: 158.061 km/h, 98.214 mph (J Clark, 1 min:35.500 sec on lap 7)
Lap Leaders: W von Trips 1-75 (75).

18 Jun 1961 — BELGIUM: Spa-Francorchamps (Round: 3) (Race: 97)

30 laps x 14.100 km, 8.761 miles = 423.000 km, 262.840 miles

POS.	NO.	DRIVER	CAR	MODEL	ENGINE		LAPS	TIME/REASON FOR RETIREMENT	GRID:POS	ROW
1	4	P Hill	Ferrari	156	Ferrari	V6	30	2h 03m 03.800s	1	1
2	2	W von Trips	Ferrari	156	Ferrari	V6	30	2h 03m 04.500s	2	1
3	6	R Ginther	Ferrari	156	Ferrari	V6	30	2h 03m 23.300s	5	2
4	8	O Gendebien	Ferrari	156	Ferrari	V6	30	2h 03m 49.400s	3	1
5	24	J Surtees	Cooper	T53	Climax	4	30	2h 04m 30.600s	4	2
6	20	D Gurney	Porsche	718	Porsche	F4	30	2h 04m 34.800s	10	4
7	18	J Bonnier	Porsche	718	Porsche	F4	30	2h 05m 50.900s	9	4
8	14	S Moss	Lotus	18/21	Climax	4	30	2h 06m 59.400s	8	3
9	40	J Lewis	Cooper	T53	Climax	4	29		13	5
10	44	M Gregory	Cooper	T53	Climax	4	29		12	5
11	22	C G de Beaufort	Porsche	718	Porsche	F4	28		14	6
12	34	J Clark	Lotus	21	Climax	4	24		18	7
13	38	T Brooks	BRM	P48/57	Climax	4	24		7	3
r	36	G Hill	BRM	P48/57	Climax	4	24	oil leak	6	3
r	26	M Trintignant	Cooper	T51	Maserati	4	23	transmission	20	8
r	46	L Bandini	Cooper	T53	Maserati	4	20	oil pressure	17	7
r	28	J Brabham	Cooper	T55	Climax	4	12	connecting rod	11	5
r	12	L Bianchi	Lotus	18	Climax	4	9	oil line	21	9
r	32	I Ireland	Lotus	21	Climax	4	9	engine	16	7
r	30	B McLaren	Cooper	T55	Climax	4	9	fuel system	15	6
r	10	W Mairesse	Lotus	18	Climax	4	7	engine	19	8
ns	42	T Marsh	Lotus	18	Climax	4		no starting money		
ns	48	W Seidel	Lotus	18	Climax	4		no starting money		
ns	50	I Burgess	Lotus	18	Climax	4		no starting money		
ns	16	C Allison	Lotus	18	Climax	4		accident/ injury		

Winning speed: 206.235 km/h, 128.149 mph
Pole Position speed: 212.119 km/h, 131.804 mph (P Hill, 3 min:59.300 sec)
Fastest Lap speed: 211.676 km/h, 131.530 mph (R Ginther, 3 min:59.800 sec on lap 20)
Lap Leaders: P Hill 1,3-5,8,11-13,15,17-18,21-23,25-30 (20); O Gendebien 2,6-7 (3); W von Trips 9-10,14,16,19-20,24 (7).

J Clark qualified 16th and I Ireland 18th, but lined up on the grid in reverse order.

2 Jul 1961 — FRANCE: Reims (Round: 4) (Race: 98)

52 laps x 8.302 km, 5.159 miles = 431.704 km, 268.248 miles

POS.	NO.	DRIVER	CAR	MODEL	ENGINE		LAPS	TIME/REASON FOR RETIREMENT	GRID:POS	ROW
1	50	G Baghetti	Ferrari	156	Ferrari	V6	52	2h 14m 17.500s	12	5
2	12	D Gurney	Porsche	718	Porsche	F4	52	2h 14m 17.600s	9	4
3	8	J Clark	Lotus	21	Climax	4	52	2h 15m 18.600s	5	2
4	6	I Ireland	Lotus	21	Climax	4	52	2h 15m 27.800s	10	4
5	4	B McLaren	Cooper	T55	Climax	4	52	2h 15m 59 300s	8	3
6	22	G Hill	BRM	P48/57	Climax	4	52	2h 15m 59.400s	6	3
7	10	J Bonnier	Porsche	718	Porsche	F4	52	2h 17m 32.900s	13	5
8	42	R Salvadori	Cooper	T53	Climax	4	51		15	6
9	16	P Hill	Ferrari	156	Ferrari	V6	50		1	1
10	30	H Taylor	Lotus	18/21	Climax	4	49		25	10
11	46	M May	Lotus	18	Climax	4	48		22	9
12	36	M Gregory	Cooper	T53	Climax	4	43		16	7
13	32	M Trintignant	Cooper	T51	Maserati	4	42		23	9
14	38	I Burgess	Lotus	18	Climax	4	42		24	10
15r	18	R Ginther	Ferrari	156	Ferrari	V6	40	oil pressure	3	1
r	26	S Moss	Lotus	18/21	Climax	4	31	brake pipe	4	2
r	48	W Mairesse	Lotus	21	Climax	4	27	fuel system	20	8
r	14	C G de Beaufort	Porsche	718	Porsche	F4	23	engine	17	7
r	28	L Bianchi	Lotus	18/21	Climax	4	21	clutch	19	8
r	20	W von Trips	Ferrari	156	Ferrari	V6	18	engine	2	1
r	34	G Scarlatti	De Tomaso	F1	OSCA	4	15	engine	26	11
r	2	J Brabham	Cooper	T55	Climax	4	14	oil pressure	14	6
r	52	B Collomb	Cooper	T53	Climax	4	6	valve	21	9
r	40	J Surtees	Cooper	T53	Climax	4	4	accident/ suspension	7	3
r	24	T Brooks	BRM	P48/57	Climax	4	4	engine overheating	11	5
r	44	J Lewis	Cooper	T53	Climax	4	4	engine overheating	18	7
ns	28	J-M Bordeu	Lotus	18/21	Climax	4		car raced by Bianchi		

Winning speed: 192.880 km/h, 119.850 mph
Pole Position speed: 206.261 km/h, 128.165 mph (P Hill, 2 min:24.900 sec)
Fastest Lap speed: 203.176 km/h, 126.248 mph (P Hill, 2 min:27.100 sec)
Lap Leaders: P Hill 1-12,18-37 (32); W von Trips 13-17 (5); R Ginther 38-40 (3); G Baghetti 41-43,45,47,50,52 (7); J Bonnier 44 (1); D Gurney 46,48-49,51 (4).

15 Jul 1961 — BRITAIN: Aintree — (Round: 5) (Race: 99)

75 laps x 4.828 km, 3.000 miles = 362.102 km, 225.000 miles

POS.	NO.	DRIVER	CAR	MODEL	ENGINE		LAPS	TIME/REASON FOR RETIREMENT	GRID:POS	ROW
1	4	W von Trips	Ferrari	156	Ferrari	V6	75	2h 40m 53.600s	4	2
2	2	P Hill	Ferrari	156	Ferrari	V6	75	2h 41m 39.600s	1	1
3	6	R Ginther	Ferrari	156	Ferrari	V6	75	2h 41m 40.400s	2	1
4	12	J Brabham	Cooper	T55	Climax	4	75	2h 42m 02.200s	9	4
5	8	J Bonnier	Porsche	718	Porsche	F4	75	2h 42m 09.800s	3	1
6	36	R Salvadori	Cooper	T53	Climax	4	75	2h 42m 19.800s	13	5
7	10	D Gurney	Porsche	718	Porsche	F4	74		12	5
8	14	B McLaren	Cooper	T55	Climax	4	74		14	6
9	22	T Brooks	BRM	P48/57	Climax	4	73		6	3
10	16	I Ireland	Lotus	21	Climax	4	72		7	3
11	42	M Gregory	Cooper	T53	Climax	4	71		16	7
12	60	L Bandini	Cooper	T53	Maserati	4	71		21	9
13	50	T Maggs	Lotus	18	Climax	4	69		24	10
14	44	I Burgess	Lotus	18	Climax	4	69		25	10
15	54	K Greene	Gilby	(61)	Climax	4	69		23	9
16	56	C G de Beaufort	Porsche	718	Porsche	F4	69		18	7
r	18	J Clark	Lotus	21	Climax	4	62	oil line	8	3
17	52	W Seidel	Lotus	18	Climax	4	58		22	9
dq	26	J Fairman	Ferguson	P99	Climax	4			20	8
dq	26	S Moss	Ferguson	P99	Climax	4	56	push start in pits (Fairman)		
r	32	L Bianchi	Lotus	18/21	Climax	4	45	gearbox	30	12
r	28	S Moss	Lotus	18/21	Climax	4	44	brake pipe	5	2
r	20	G Hill	BRM	P48/57	Climax	4	43	engine	11	5
r	58	G Baghetti	Ferrari	156	Ferrari	V6	27	spin	19	8
r	25	T Marsh	Lotus	18	Climax	4	25	misfire	27	11
r	34	J Surtees	Cooper	T53	Climax	4	23	transmission	10	4
r	38	T Parnell	Lotus	18	Climax	4	12	clutch	29	12
r	46	J Lewis	Cooper	T53	Climax	4	7	handling	15	6
r	40	G Ashmore	Lotus	18	Climax	4	7	misfire	26	11
r	30	H Taylor	Lotus	18/21	Climax	4	5	accident	17	7
r	62	M Natili	Cooper	T51	Maserati	4	0	engine	28	11

Winning speed: 135.034 km/h, 83.907 mph
Pole Position speed: 146.304 km/h, 90.909 mph (P Hill, 1 min:58.800 sec)
Fastest Lap speed: 147.546 km/h, 91.681 mph (T Brooks, 1 min:57.800 sec on lap 72)
Lap Leaders: P Hill 1-6 (6); W von Trips 7-75 (69).

6 Aug 1961 — GERMANY: Nürburgring — (Round: 6) (Race: 100)

15 laps x 22.810 km, 14.173 miles = 342.150 km, 212.602 miles

POS.	NO.	DRIVER	CAR	MODEL	ENGINE		LAPS	TIME/REASON FOR RETIREMENT	GRID:POS	ROW
1	7	S Moss	Lotus	18/21	Climax	4	15	2h 18m 12.400s	3	1
2	3	W von Trips	Ferrari	156	Ferrari	V6	15	2h 18m 33.800s	5	2
3	4	P Hill	Ferrari	156	Ferrari	V6	15	2h 18m 34.900s	1	1
4	14	J Clark	Lotus	21	Climax	4	15	2h 19m 29.500s	8	3
5	18	J Surtees	Cooper	T53	Climax	4	15	2h 20m 05.500s	10	3
6	2	B McLaren	Cooper	T55	Climax	4	15	2h 20m 53.800s	12	4
7	9	D Gurney	Porsche	718	Porsche	F4	15	2h 21m 35.000s	7	2
8	5	R Ginther	Ferrari	156	Ferrari	V6	15	2h 23m 35.500s	14	4
9	28	J Lewis	Cooper	T53	Climax	4	15	2h 23m 36.100s	18	5
10	19	R Salvadori	Cooper	T53	Climax	4	15	2h 30m 23.900s	15	5
11	33	T Maggs	Lotus	18	Climax	4	14		22	7
12	30	I Burgess	Cooper	T53	Climax	4	14		24	7
13	11	H Herrmann	Porsche	718	Porsche	F4	14		11	3
14	31	C G de Beaufort	Porsche	718	Porsche	F4	14		17	5
r	6	W Mairesse	Ferrari	156	Ferrari	V6	13	accident	13	4
15	37	T Marsh	Lotus	18	Climax	4	13		20	6
16	27	G Ashmore	Lotus	18	Climax	4	13		25	7
r	20	M Trintignant	Cooper	T51	Maserati	4	12	engine	21	6
r	38	B Collomb	Cooper	T53	Climax	4	11	engine	26	8
r	32	L Bandini	Cooper	T53	Maserati	4	10	engine	19	6
r	16	T Brooks	BRM	P48/57	Climax	4	6	engine	9	3
r	8	J Bonnier	Porsche	718	Porsche	F4	5	engine	4	1
r	26	W Seidel	Lotus	18	Climax	4	3	steering	23	7
r	15	I Ireland	Lotus	21	Climax	4	1	fire	16	5
r	17	G Hill	BRM	P48/57	Climax	4	1	accident	6	2
r	1	J Brabham	Cooper	T58	Climax	V8	0	throttle jammed/ accident	2	1
ns	25	M May	Lotus	18	Climax	4		accident		

Winning speed: 148.538 km/h, 92.297 mph
Pole Position speed: 153.430 km/h, 95.337 mph (P Hill, 8 min:55.200 sec)
Fastest Lap speed: 152.689 km/h, 94.876 mph (P Hill, 8 min:57.800 sec on lap 10)
Lap Leaders: S Moss 1-15 (15).

Also the Grand Prix of Europe.

10 Sep 1961 — ITALY: Monza — (Round: 7) (Race: 101)

43 laps x 10.000 km, 6.214 miles = 430.000 km, 267.190 miles

POS.	NO.	DRIVER	CAR	MODEL	ENGINE		LAPS	TIME/REASON FOR RETIREMENT	GRID:POS	ROW
1	2	P Hill	Ferrari	156	Ferrari	V6	43	2h 03m 13.000s	4	2
2	46	D Gurney	Porsche	718	Porsche	F4	43	2h 03m 44.200s	12	6
3	12	B McLaren	Cooper	T55	Climax	4	43	2h 05m 41.400s	14	7
4	60	J Lewis	Cooper	T53	Climax	4	43	2h 05m 53.400s	16	8
5	26	T Brooks	BRM	P48/57	Climax	4	43	2h 05m 53.500s	13	7
6	40	R Salvadori	Cooper	T53	Climax	V8	42		18	9
7	74	C G de Beaufort	Porsche	718	Porsche	F4	41		15	8
8	62	L Bandini	Cooper	T53	Maserati	4	41		21	11
9	48	M Trintignant	Cooper	T51	Maserati	4	41		22	11
10	16	T Parnell	Lotus	18	Climax	4	40		27	14
11	20	H Taylor	Lotus	18/21	Climax	4	39		23	12
12	58	R Pirocchi	Cooper	T51	Maserati	4	38		29	15
r	28	S Moss	Lotus	21	Climax	4	36	front wheel bearing	11	6
r	6	R Ginther	Ferrari	156	Ferrari	V6	23	engine	3	2
r	72	G Starrabba	Lotus	18	Maserati	4	19	engine	30	15
r	44	J Bonnier	Porsche	718	Porsche	F4	14	rear suspension	8	4
r	50	N Vaccarella	De Tomaso	F1	Conrero	4	13	engine	20	10
r	32	G Baghetti	Ferrari	156	Ferrari	V6	13	engine	6	3
r	8	R Rodriguez	Ferrari	156	Ferrari	V6	13	fuel pump	2	1
r	22	M Gregory	Lotus	18/21	Climax	4	11	rear suspension	17	9
r	24	G Hill	BRM	P48/57	Climax	4	10	engine	5	3
r	10	J Brabham	Cooper	T58	Climax	V8	8	engine overheating	10	5
r	14	B Naylor	JBW	(61)	Climax	4	6	engine	31	16
r	30	J Fairman	Cooper	T45	Climax	4	5	engine	26	13
r	38	I Ireland	Lotus	18/21	Climax	4	5	chassis	9	5
r	42	J Surtees	Cooper	T53	Climax	4	2	accident	19	10
r	56	W Seidel	Lotus	18	Climax	4	1	engine	28	14
r	54	R Bussinello	De Tomaso	F1	Conrero	4	1	engine	24	12
r	52	R Lippi	De Tomaso	F1	OSCA	4	1	engine	32	16
r	36	J Clark	Lotus	21	Climax	4	1	accident	7	4
r	4	W von Trips	Ferrari	156	Ferrari	V6	1	fatal accident	1	1
r	18	G Ashmore	Lotus	18	Climax	4	0	accident	25	13
nq	68	A Pilette	Emeryson	(61)	Climax	4				
ns	58	M Natili	Cooper	T51	Maserati	4		car raced by Pirocchi		

Winning speed: 209.387 km/h, 130.107 mph
Pole Position speed: 216.476 km/h, 134.512 mph (W von Trips, 2 min:46.300 sec)
Fastest Lap speed: 213.777 km/h, 132.835 mph (G Baghetti, 2 min:48.400 sec on lap 2)
Lap Leaders: P Hill 1-3,5,7,10,14-43 (36); R Ginther 4,6,8-9,11-13 (7).

8 Oct 1961 — USA: Watkins Glen — (Round: 8) (Race: 102)

100 laps x 3.701 km, 2.300 miles = 370.149 km, 230.000 miles

POS.	NO.	DRIVER	CAR	MODEL	ENGINE		LAPS	TIME/REASON FOR RETIREMENT	GRID:POS	ROW
1	15	I Ireland	Lotus	21	Climax	4	100	2h 13m 45.800s	8	4
2	12	D Gurney	Porsche	718	Porsche	F4	100	2h 13m 50.100s	7	4
3	5	T Brooks	BRM	P48/57	Climax	4	100	2h 14m 34.800s	6	3
4	2	B McLaren	Cooper	T55	Climax	4	100	2h 14m 43.800s	4	2
5	4	G Hill	BRM	P48/57	Climax	4	99		2	1
6	11	J Bonnier	Porsche	718	Porsche	F4	98		10	5
r	19	R Salvadori	Cooper	T53	Climax	4	96	engine	12	6
7	14	J Clark	Lotus	21	Climax	4	96		5	3
8	6	R Penske	Cooper	T53	Climax	4	96		16	8
9	16	P Ryan	Lotus	18/21	Climax	4	96		13	7
10	3	H Sharp	Cooper	T53	Climax	4	93		17	9
11	21	O Gendebien	Lotus	18/21	Climax	4			15	8
11	21	M Gregory	Lotus	18/21	Climax	4	92			
r	26	L Ruby	Lotus	18	Climax	4	76	magneto	19	10
r	17	J Hall	Lotus	18	Climax	4	76	fuel leak	18	9
r	7	S Moss	Lotus	18/21	Climax	4	58	engine	3	2
r	1	J Brabham	Cooper	T58	Climax	V8	57	engine overheating	1	1
r	22	M Gregory	Lotus	18/21	Climax	4	23	gear selection	11	6
r	60	W Hansgen	Cooper	T53	Climax	4	14	accident	14	7
r	18	J Surtees	Cooper	T53	Climax	4	0	connecting rod	9	5

Winning speed: 166.032 km/h, 103.167 mph
Pole Position speed: 173.057 km/h, 107.532 mph (J Brabham, 1 min:17.000 sec)
Fastest Lap speed: 170.401 km/h, 105.882 mph (J Brabham, 1 min:18.200 sec on lap 28 & 30)
Lap Leaders: S Moss 1-5,16,24-25,34-35,39-58 (30); J Brabham 6-15,17-23,26-33,36-38 (28); I Ireland 59-100 (42).

Lap Leaders 1961

POS	DRIVER	CAR-ENGINE	GPS	LAPS	KM	MILES
1	W von Trips	Ferrari	4	156	787.8	489.5
2	S Moss	Lotus-Climax	3	132	726.8	451.6
3	P Hill	Ferrari	4	94	936.6	582.0
4	I Ireland	Lotus-Climax	1	42	155.4	96.6
5	J Brabham	Cooper-Climax	1	28	103.6	64.4
6	R Ginther	Ferrari	3	23	135.8	84.4
7	G Baghetti	Ferrari	1	7	58.1	36.1
8	D Gurney	Porsche	1	4	33.2	20.6
9	O Gendebien	Ferrari	1	3	42.3	26.3
10	J Bonnier	Porsche	1	1	8.3	5.2
			8	**490**	**2,988.0**	**1,856.7**

Driver Points 1961

		MC	NL	B	F	GB	D	I	USA	TOTAL	
1	P Hill	4	6	9	-	6	(4)	9	-	34	(4)
2	W von Trips	3	9	6	-	9	6	-	-	33	
3	S Moss	9	3	-	-	-	9	-	-	21	
	D Gurney	2	-	1	6	-	-	6	6	21	
5	R Ginther	6	2	4	-	4	-	-	-	16	
6	I Ireland	-	-	-	3	-	-	-	9	12	
7	J Clark	-	4	-	4	-	3	-	-	11	
	B McLaren	1	-	-	2	-	1	4	3	11	
9	G Baghetti	-	-	-	9	-	-	-	-	9	
10	T Brooks	-	-	-	-	-	-	2	4	6	
11	J Brabham	-	1	-	-	3	-	-	-	4	
	J Surtees	-	-	2	-	-	2	-	-	4	
13	O Gendebien	-	-	3	-	-	-	-	-	3	
	J Lewis	-	-	-	-	-	-	3	-	3	
	J Bonnier	-	-	-	-	2	-	-	1	3	
	G Hill	-	-	-	1	-	-	-	2	3	
17	R Salvadori	-	-	-	-	1	-	1	-	2	

9, 6, 4, 3, 2 and 1 point awarded to the first six finishers. Best 5 scores.

Constructor Points 1961

		MC	NL	B	F	GB	D	I	USA	TOTAL	
1	Ferrari	(6)	8	8	8	8	(6)	8	-	40	(12)
2	Lotus-Climax	8	4	-	4	-	8	-	8	32	
3	Porsche	2	-	(1)	6	2	-	6	6	22	(1)
4	Cooper-Climax	(1)	(1)	2	2	3	(2)	4	3	14	(4)
5	BRM-Climax	-	-	-	1	-	-	2	4	7	

8, 6, 4, 3, 2 and 1 point awarded to the first six finishers. Points only for highest placed car. Best 5 scores.

Stirling Moss was seriously injured at Goodwood before the championship had begun, effectively ending his racing career. The British teams began to dominate as the V8 engines emerged. Lotus re-introduced the monocoque to top line racing with the Type 25 model. Ferrari suffered a mass walk out when many of its leading engineers went on to form the ATS team, while the factory introduced its revised car at the German Grand Prix. The famous twin-nostril Ferrari was consigned to the scrap heap.

FERRARI
Scuderia Ferrari SpA SEFAC: P Hill, Rodriguez, Baghetti, Bandini, Mairesse

DE TOMASO
Scuderia de Tomaso: (Estefano)
Scuderia Settecolli: Lippi

BRM
Owen Racing Organisation: G Hill, Ginther
Ecurie Galloise: (Lewis)
Privateer: Johnstone

BRABHAM
Brabham Racing Organisation: Brabham

COOPER
Cooper Car Co: McLaren, Maggs, Mayer
Ecurie Galloise: Lewis
Anglo-American Equipe: Burgess
Privateers: Collomb, Sharp, Love, Harris

EMERYSON
Emeryson Cars: Settember
Ecurie Maarsbergen: Seidel

GILBY
Gilby Engineering Co Ltd: Greene

LOLA
Bowmaker-Yeoman Racing Team: Surtees, Salvadori

LOTUS
Team Lotus: Clark, T Taylor
Rob Walker Racing Team: Trintignant
UDT Laystall Racing Team: Ireland, Gregory
Brabham Racing Organisation: Brabham
Scuderia SSS Republica di Venezia: Vaccarella
Ecurie Filipinetti: Schiller, Siffert
Emeryson Cars: Campbell-Jones
Equipe Nationale Belge: Bianchi
Autosport Team Wolfgang Seidel: Seidel, (Gurney, Seiffert)
Ecurie Excelsior: Chamberlain
John Dalton: Shelly, (Greene)
Dupont Team Zerex: Penske
John Mecom: Schroeder
Scuderia Jolly Club: (Prinoth)
Ecurie Nationale Suisse: (Siffert (MC))
Privateers: Pieterse, Lederle, Hall, (Ashmore)

PORSCHE
Porsche System Engineering: Bonnier, Gurney, (P Hill)
Ecurie Maarsbergen: de Beaufort, Pon
Ecurie Filipinetti: Walter
Scuderia SSS Republica di Venezia: Vaccarella

ENB
Equipe Nationale Belge: Bianchi

LDS
Otelle Nucci: Serrurier

20 May 1962 — NETHERLANDS: Zandvoort (Round: 1) (Race: 103)

80 laps x 4.193 km, 2.605 miles = 335.440 km, 208.433 miles

POS.	NO.	DRIVER	CAR	MODEL	ENGINE		LAPS	TIME/REASON FOR RETIREMENT	GRID:POS	ROW
1	17	G Hill	BRM	P57	BRM	V8	80	2h 11m 02.100s	2	1
2	5	T Taylor	Lotus	24	Climax	V8	80	2h 11m 29.300s	10	4
3	1	P Hill	Ferrari	156	Ferrari	V6	80	2h 12m 23.200s	9	4
4	2	G Baghetti	Ferrari	156	Ferrari	V6	79		12	5
5	7	T Maggs	Cooper	T55	Climax	4	78		15	6
6	14	C G de Beaufort	Porsche	718	Porsche	F4	76		14	6
7	11	J Bonnier	Porsche	804	Porsche	F8	75		13	5
r	3	R Rodriguez	Ferrari	156	Ferrari	V6	73	spin	11	5
r	18	R Ginther	BRM	P48/57	BRM	V8	71	accident	7	3
8	21	J Lewis	Cooper	T53	Climax	4	70		19	8
9	4	J Clark	Lotus	25	Climax	V8	70		3	1
r	9	I Ireland	Lotus	24	Climax	V8	61	spin	6	3
r	10	M Gregory	Lotus	18/21	Climax	4	54	gearbox	16	7
nc	16	W Seidel	Emeryson	(61)	Climax	4	52		20	8
r	12	D Gurney	Porsche	804	Porsche	F8	47	gearbox	8	3
r	6	B McLaren	Cooper	T60	Climax	V8	21	gearbox	5	2
r	20	R Salvadori	Lola	Mk 4	Climax	V8	12	withdrew	17	7
r	19	J Surtees	Lola	Mk 4	Climax	V8	8	front suspension/ accident	1	1
r	8	J Brabham	Lotus	24	Climax	V8	4	accident	4	2
r	15	B Pon	Porsche	787	Porsche	F4	2	spin	18	7

Winning speed: 153.596 km/h, 95.440 mph
Pole Position speed: 163.187 km/h, 101.400 mph (J Surtees, 1 min:32.500 sec)
Fastest Lap speed: 159.903 km/h, 99.359 mph (B McLaren, 1 min:34.400 sec on lap 5)
Lap Leaders: J Clark 1-11 (11); G Hill 12-80 (69).

Also the Grand Prix of Europe.

3 Jun 1962 — MONACO: Monte Carlo (Round: 2) (Race: 104)

100 laps x 3.145 km, 1.954 miles = 314.500 km, 195.421 miles

POS.	NO.	DRIVER	CAR	MODEL	ENGINE		LAPS	TIME/REASON FOR RETIREMENT	GRID:POS	ROW
1	14	B McLaren	Cooper	T60	Climax	V8	100	2h 46m 29.700s	3	1
2	36	P Hill	Ferrari	156	Ferrari	V6	100	2h 46m 31.000s	9	4
3	38	L Bandini	Ferrari	156	Ferrari	V6	100	2h 47m 53.800s	10	4
4	28	J Surtees	Lola	Mk 4	Climax	V8	99		11	5
5	2	J Bonnier	Porsche	718	Porsche	F4	93		15	6
6r	10	G Hill	BRM	P57	BRM	V8	92	engine	2	1
7r	40	W Mairesse	Ferrari	156	Ferrari	V6	90	oil pressure	4	2
8r	22	J Brabham	Lotus	24	Climax	V8	77	front suspension/ accident	6	3
r	34	I Ireland	Lotus	24	Climax	V8	64	fuel pump	8	3
r	18	J Clark	Lotus	25	Climax	V8	55	clutch	1	1
r	26	R Salvadori	Lola	Mk 4	Climax	V8	44	suspension	12	5
r	16	T Maggs	Cooper	T55	Climax	4	43	gearbox	16	7
r	20	T Taylor	Lotus	24	Climax	V8	24	oil leak	14	6
r	4	D Gurney	Porsche	804	Porsche	F8	0	accident	5	2
r	8	R Ginther	BRM	P48/57	BRM	V8	0	throttle jammed/ accident	13	5
r	30	M Trintignant	Lotus	24	Climax	V8	0	accident	7	3
s	40	R Rodriguez	Ferrari	156	Ferrari	V6		car raced by Mairesse		

POS.	NO.	DRIVER	CAR	MODEL	ENGINE		LAPS	TIME/REASON FOR RETIREMENT	GRID:POS	ROW
nq	44	C G de Beaufort	Porsche	718	Porsche	F4				
nq	46	J Siffert	Lotus	21	Climax	4				
nq	24	J Lewis	BRM	P48/57	BRM	V8				
nq	32	M Gregory	Lotus	24	BRM	V8				
nq	42	N Vaccarella	Lotus	18/21	Climax	4				

Winning speed: 113.337 km/h, 70.424 mph
Pole Position speed: 118.679 km/h, 73.744 mph (J Clark, 1 min:35.400 sec)
Fastest Lap speed: 118.555 km/h, 73.667 mph (J Clark, 1 min:35.500 sec on lap 42)
Lap Leaders: B McLaren 1-6,93-100 (14); G Hill 7-92 (86).

17 Jun 1962 — BELGIUM: Spa-Francorchamps — (Round: 3) (Race: 105)

32 laps x 14.100 km, 8.761 miles = 451.200 km, 280.363 miles

POS.	NO.	DRIVER	CAR	MODEL	ENGINE		LAPS	TIME/REASON FOR RETIREMENT	GRID:POS	ROW
1	16	J Clark	Lotus	25	Climax	V8	32	2h 07m 32.300s	12	5
2	1	G Hill	BRM	P57	BRM	V8	32	2h 08m 16.400s	1	1
3	9	P Hill	Ferrari	156	Ferrari	V6	32	2h 09m 38.800s	4	2
4	12	R Rodriguez	Ferrari	156	Ferrari	V6	32	2h 09m 38.900s	7	3
5	5	J Surtees	Lola	Mk 4	Climax	V8	31		11	5
6	15	J Brabham	Lotus	24	Climax	V8	30		15	6
7	7	C G de Beaufort	Porsche	718	Porsche	F4	30		13	5
8	18	M Trintignant	Lotus	24	Climax	V8	30		16	7
9	19	L Bianchi	Lotus	18/21	Climax	4	29		18	7
10	22	J Siffert	Lotus	21	Climax	4	29		17	7
r	17	T Taylor	Lotus	24	Climax	V8	25	accident	3	1
r	10	W Mairesse	Ferrari	156	Ferrari	V6	25	accident	6	3
r	2	R Ginther	BRM	P57	BRM	V8	22	transmission	9	4
r	26	T Maggs	Cooper	T60	Climax	V8	22	gearbox	10	4
r	25	B McLaren	Cooper	T60	Climax	V8	19	oil pressure	2	1
11	4	J Campbell-Jones	Lotus	18	Climax	4	16		19	8
r	21	M Gregory	Lotus	24	BRM	V8	13	withdrew	8	3
r	20	I Ireland	Lotus	24	Climax	V8	9	rear suspension	5	2
r	11	G Baghetti	Ferrari	156	Ferrari	V6	4	ignition wiring	14	6
ns	23	D Gurney	Lotus	24	BRM	V8		car unraceworthy		

Winning speed: 212.266 km/h, 131.896 mph
Pole Position speed: 214.177 km/h, 133.084 mph (G Hill, 3 min:57.000 sec)
Fastest Lap speed: 215.450 km/h, 133.874 mph (J Clark, 3 min:55.600 sec on lap 15)
Lap Leaders: G Hill 1 (1); T Taylor 2-3,5,7-8 (5); W Mairesse 4,6 (2); J Clark 9-32 (24).

8 Jul 1962 — FRANCE: Rouen-les-Essarts — (Round: 4) (Race: 106)

54 laps x 6.542 km, 4.065 miles = 353.268 km, 219.511 miles

POS.	NO.	DRIVER	CAR	MODEL	ENGINE		LAPS	TIME/REASON FOR RETIREMENT	GRID:POS	ROW
1	30	D Gurney	Porsche	804	Porsche	F8	54	2h 07m 35.500s	6	3
2	24	T Maggs	Cooper	T60	Climax	V8	53		11	5
3	10	R Ginther	BRM	P57	BRM	V8	52		10	4
4	22	B McLaren	Cooper	T60	Climax	V8	51		3	1
5	18	J Surtees	Lola	Mk 4	Climax	V8	51		5	2
6	38	C G de Beaufort	Porsche	718	Porsche	F4	51		17	7
7	28	M Trintignant	Lotus	24	Climax	V8	50		13	5
8	14	T Taylor	Lotus	25	Climax	V8	48		12	5
9r	8	G Hill	BRM	P57	BRM	V8	44	ignition pump mounting	2	1
10r	32	J Bonnier	Porsche	804	Porsche	F8	42	gearbox	9	4
r	12	J Clark	Lotus	25	Climax	V8	33	front suspension	1	1
r	42	J Lewis	Cooper	T53	Climax	4	27	brakes/ accident	16	7
r	20	R Salvadori	Lola	Mk 4	Climax	V8	20	oil pressure	14	6
r	34	M Gregory	Lotus	24	BRM	V8	14	ignition	7	3
r	26	J Brabham	Lotus	24	Climax	V8	10	rear suspension	4	2
r	40	J Siffert	Lotus	24	BRM	V8	5	clutch	15	6
r	36	I Ireland	Lotus	24	Climax	V8	1	puncture/ wheel buckled	8	3

Winning speed: 166.124 km/h, 103.225 mph
Pole Position speed: 174.712 km/h, 108.561 mph (J Clark, 2 min:14.800 sec)
Fastest Lap speed: 172.032 km/h, 106.896 mph (G Hill, 2 min:16.900 sec on lap 32)
Lap Leaders: G Hill 1-29,33-41 (38); J Clark 30-32 (3); D Gurney 42-54 (13).

21 Jul 1962 — BRITAIN: Aintree — (Round: 5) (Race: 107)

75 laps x 4.828 km, 3.000 miles = 362.102 km, 225.000 miles

POS.	NO.	DRIVER	CAR	MODEL	ENGINE		LAPS	TIME/REASON FOR RETIREMENT	GRID:POS	ROW
1	20	J Clark	Lotus	25	Climax	V8	75	2h 26m 20.800s	1	1
2	24	J Surtees	Lola	Mk 4	Climax	V8	75	2h 27m 10.000s	2	1
3	16	B McLaren	Cooper	T60	Climax	V8	75	2h 28m 05.600s	4	2
4	12	G Hill	BRM	P57	BRM	V8	75	2h 28m 17.600s	5	2
5	30	J Brabham	Lotus	24	Climax	V8	74		9	4
6	18	T Maggs	Cooper	T60	Climax	V8	74		13	5
7	34	M Gregory	Lotus	24	Climax	V8	74		14	6
8	22	T Taylor	Lotus	24	Climax	V8	74		10	4
9	8	D Gurney	Porsche	804	Porsche	F8	73		6	3
10	42	J Lewis	Cooper	T53	Climax	4	72		15	6
11	40	T Settember	Emeryson	(61)	Climax	4	71		19	8
12	36	I Burgess	Cooper	T53	Climax	4	71		16	7

POS.	NO.	DRIVER	CAR	MODEL	ENGINE		LAPS	TIME/REASON FOR RETIREMENT	GRID:POS	ROW
13	14	R Ginther	BRM	P57	BRM	V8	70		8	3
14	54	C G de Beaufort	Porsche	718	Porsche	F4	69		17	7
15	46	J Chamberlain	Lotus	18	Climax	4	64		20	8
16	32	I Ireland	Lotus	24	Climax	V8	61		3	1
r	2	P Hill	Ferrari	156	Ferrari	V6	46	distributor	12	5
r	26	R Salvadori	Lola	Mk 4	Climax	V8	34	ignition	11	5
r	10	J Bonnier	Porsche	804	Porsche	F8	26	crown wheel & pinion	7	3
r	44	W Seidel	Lotus	24	BRM	V8	10	brakes/ engine overheating	21	9
r	48	T Shelly	Lotus	18/21	Climax	4	5	engine overheating	18	7
ns	48	K Greene	Lotus	18/21	Climax	4		car raced by Shelly		

Winning speed: 148.457 km/h, 92.247 mph
Pole Position speed: 153.001 km/h, 95.070 mph (J Clark, 1 min:53.600 sec)
Fastest Lap speed: 151.138 km/h, 93.913 mph (J Clark, 1 min:55.000 sec on lap 36)
Lap Leaders: J Clark 1-75 (75).

5 Aug 1962 — GERMANY: Nürburgring — (Round: 6) (Race: 108)

15 laps x 22.810 km, 14.173 miles = 342.150 km, 212.602 miles

POS.	NO.	DRIVER	CAR	MODEL	ENGINE		LAPS	TIME/REASON FOR RETIREMENT	GRID:POS	ROW
1	11	G Hill	BRM	P57	BRM	V8	15	2h 38m 45.300s	2	1
2	14	J Surtees	Lola	Mk 4	Climax	V8	15	2h 38m 47.800s	4	1
3	7	D Gurney	Porsche	804	Porsche	F8	15	2h 38m 49.700s	1	1
4	5	J Clark	Lotus	25	Climax	V8	15	2h 39m 27.400s	3	1
5	9	B McLaren	Cooper	T60	Climax	V8	15	2h 40m 04.900s	5	2
6	3	R Rodriguez	Ferrari	156	Ferrari	V6	15	2h 40m 09.100s	10	3
7	8	J Bonnier	Porsche	804	Porsche	F8	15	2h 43m 22.600s	6	2
8	12	R Ginther	BRM	P57	BRM	V8	15	2h 43m 45.400s	7	2
9	10	T Maggs	Cooper	T55	Climax	4	15	2h 43m 52.100s	23	7
10	2	G Baghetti	Ferrari	156	Ferrari	V6	15	2h 47m 00.000s	13	4
11	25	I Burgess	Cooper	T53	Climax	4	15	2h 47m 00.600s	16	5
12	19	J Siffert	Lotus	21	Climax	4	15	2h 47m 03.800s	17	5
13	18	C G de Beaufort	Porsche	718	Porsche	F4	15	2h 47m 57.100s	8	3
14	32	H Walter	Porsche	718	Porsche	F4	14		14	4
15	26	N Vaccarella	Porsche	718	Porsche	F4	14		15	5
16	21	L Bianchi	ENB	Maserati		4	14		25	7
17r	20	J Lewis	Cooper	T53	Climax	4	10	engine	21	6
r	16	J Brabham	Brabham	BT3	Climax	V8	9	throttle linkage	24	7
r	1	P Hill	Ferrari	156	Ferrari	V6	9	rear suspension	12	4
r	27	K Greene	Gilby	(62)	BRM	V8	7	front suspension	19	6
r	17	M Trintignant	Lotus	24	Climax	V8	4	gear selection	11	3
r	4	L Bandini	Ferrari	156	Ferrari	V6	4	accident	18	5
r	15	R Salvadori	Lola	Mk 4	Climax	V8	4	gearbox	9	3
r	28	H Schiller	Lotus	24	BRM	V8	4	oil pressure	20	6
r	31	B Collomb	Cooper	T53	Climax	4	2	gearbox	22	7
r	6	T Taylor	Lotus	24	Climax	V8	0	accident	26	8
nq	29	T Shelly	Lotus	18/21	Climax	4				
nq	34	W Seidel	Lotus	24	BRM	V8				
nq	30	J Chamberlain	Lotus	18	Climax	4				
nq	34	G Seiffert	Lotus	24	BRM	V8				

Winning speed: 129.312 km/h, 80.351 mph
Pole Position speed: 155.759 km/h, 96.784 mph (D Gurney, 8 min:47.200 sec)
Fastest Lap speed: 134.133 km/h, 83.346 mph (G Hill, 10 min:12.200 sec on lap 3)
Lap Leaders: D Gurney 1-2 (2); G Hill 3-15 (13).

T Taylor qualified 22nd, but was put on back row because he failed to complete 5 laps in practice.

16 Sep 1962 — ITALY: Monza — (Round: 7) (Race: 109)

86 laps x 5.750 km, 3.573 miles = 494.500 km, 307.268 miles

POS.	NO.	DRIVER	CAR	MODEL	ENGINE		LAPS	TIME/REASON FOR RETIREMENT	GRID:POS	ROW
1	14	G Hill	BRM	P57	BRM	V8	86	2h 29m 08.400s	2	1
2	12	R Ginther	BRM	P57	BRM	V8	86	2h 29m 38.200s	3	2
3	28	B McLaren	Cooper	T60	Climax	V8	86	2h 30m 06.200s	4	2
4	8	W Mairesse	Ferrari	156	Ferrari	V6	86	2h 30m 06.600s	10	5
5	2	G Baghetti	Ferrari	156	Ferrari	V6	86	2h 30m 39.700s	18	9
6	18	J Bonnier	Porsche	804	Porsche	F8	85		9	5
7	30	T Maggs	Cooper	T60	Climax	V8	85		12	6
8	6	L Bandini	Ferrari	156	Ferrari	V6	84		17	9
9	24	N Vaccarella	Lotus	24	Climax	V8	84		14	7
10	32	C G de Beaufort	Porsche	718	Porsche	F4	81		20	10
11	10	P Hill	Ferrari	156	Ferrari	V6	81		15	8
12	38	M Gregory	Lotus	24	BRM	V8	77		6	3
13r	16	D Gurney	Porsche	804	Porsche	F8	66	crown wheel & pinion	7	4
14r	4	R Rodriguez	Ferrari	156	Ferrari	V6	63	engine	11	6
r	40	I Ireland	Lotus	24	Climax	V8	45	front suspension	5	3
r	46	J Surtees	Lola	Mk 4A	Climax	V8	42	engine	8	4
r	44	R Salvadori	Lola	Mk 4	Climax	V8	41	engine	13	7
r	22	T Taylor	Lotus	25	Climax	V8	25	transmission	16	8
r	48	T Settember	Emeryson	(61)	Climax	4	18	engine overheating	21	11
r	36	M Trintignant	Lotus	24	Climax	V8	17	electrics	19	10
r	20	J Clark	Lotus	25	Climax	V8	12	transmission	1	1
nq	60	T Shelly	Lotus	24	BRM	V8				
nq	56	K Greene	Gilby	(62)	BRM	V8				
nq	52	G Ashmore	Lotus	18/21	Climax	4				

POS.	NO.	DRIVER	CAR	MODEL	ENGINE		LAPS	TIME/REASON FOR RETIREMENT	GRID:POS	ROW
nq	62	I Burgess	Cooper	T53	Climax	4				
nq	42	J Siffert	Lotus	24	BRM	V8				
nq	54	E Prinoth	Lotus	18	Climax	4				
nq	50	R Lippi	De Tomaso	F1	OSCA	4				
nq	26	J Chamberlain	Lotus	18	Climax	4				
nq	34	N Estefano	De Tomaso	801	De Tomaso	F8				

Winning speed: 198.941 km/h, 123.616 mph
Pole Position speed: 206.278 km/h, 128.175 mph (J Clark, 1 min:40.350 sec)
Fastest Lap speed: 202.346 km/h, 125.732 mph (G Hill, 1 min:42.300 sec on lap 3 & 4)
Lap Leaders: G Hill 1-86 (86).

7 Oct 1962 — USA: Watkins Glen — (Round: 8) (Race: 110)

100 laps x 3.701 km, 2.300 miles = 370.149 km, 230.000 miles

POS.	NO.	DRIVER	CAR	MODEL	ENGINE		LAPS	TIME/REASON FOR RETIREMENT	GRID:POS	ROW
1	8	J Clark	Lotus	25	Climax	V8	100	2h 07m 13.000s	1	1
2	4	G Hill	BRM	P57	BRM	V8	100	2h 07m 22.200s	3	2
3	21	B McLaren	Cooper	T60	Climax	V8	99		6	3
4	17	J Brabham	Brabham	BT3	Climax	V8	99		5	3
5	10	D Gurney	Porsche	804	Porsche	F8	99		4	2
6	16	M Gregory	Lotus	24	BRM	V8	99		7	4
7	22	T Maggs	Cooper	T60	Climax	V8	97		10	5
8	15	I Ireland	Lotus	24	Climax	V8	96		15	8
9	14	R Penske	Lotus	24	Climax	V8	96		12	6
10	26	R Schroeder	Lotus	24	Climax	V8	93		16	8
11	24	H Sharp	Cooper	T53	Climax	4	91		14	7
12	9	T Taylor	Lotus	25	Climax	V8	85		8	4
13	11	J Bonnier	Porsche	804	Porsche	F8	79		9	5
r	5	R Ginther	BRM	P57	BRM	V8	35	gearbox oil leak	2	1
r	6	M Trintignant	Lotus	24	Climax	V8	32	brake fluid leak	17	9
r	23	T Mayer	Cooper	T53	Climax	4	31	gear lever	11	6
r	18	J Surtees	Lola	Mk 4	Climax	V8	19	oil line	18	9
r	12	C G de Beaufort	Porsche	718	Porsche	F4	9	accident	13	7
ns	19	R Salvadori	Lola	Mk 4	Climax	V8		car raced by Surtees		
ns	25	J Hall	Lotus	21	Climax	4		dropped valve		
ns	11	P Hill	Porsche	804	Porsche	F8		not a serious attempt		

Winning speed: 174.576 km/h, 108.476 mph
Pole Position speed: 175.796 km/h, 109.235 mph (J Clark, 1 min:15.800 sec)
Fastest Lap speed: 177.672 km/h, 110.400 mph (J Clark, 1 min:15.000 sec on lap 70)
Lap Leaders: J Clark 1-11,19-100 (93); G Hill 12-18 (7).

29 Dec 1962 — SOUTH AFRICA: East London — (Round: 9) (Race: 111)

82 laps x 3.920 km, 2.436 miles = 321.470 km, 199.752 miles

POS.	NO.	DRIVER	CAR	MODEL	ENGINE		LAPS	TIME/REASON FOR RETIREMENT	GRID:POS	ROW
1	3	G Hill	BRM	P57	BRM	V8	82	2h 08m 03.300s	2	1
2	8	B McLaren	Cooper	T60	Climax	V8	82	2h 08m 53.100s	8	4
3	9	T Maggs	Cooper	T60	Climax	V8	82	2h 08m 53.600s	6	3
4	10	J Brabham	Brabham	BT3	Climax	V8	82	2h 08m 57.100s	3	2
5	11	I Ireland	Lotus	24	Climax	V8	81		4	2
6	20	N Lederle	Lotus	21	Climax	4	78		10	5
7	4	R Ginther	BRM	P57	BRM	V8	78		7	4
8	18	J Love	Cooper	T55	Climax	4	78		12	6
9	5	B Johnstone	BRM	P48/57	BRM	V8	76		17	9
10	14	E Pieterse	Lotus	21	Climax	4	71		13	7
11r	15	C G de Beaufort	Porsche	718	Porsche	F4	70	fuel pump	16	8
r	21	D Serrurier	LDS	Mk 2	Alfa Romeo	4	62	radiator	14	7
r	1	J Clark	Lotus	25	Climax	V8	61	oil leak	1	1
r	7	R Salvadori	Lola	Mk 4	Climax	V8	56	fuel tank	11	6
r	22	M Harris	Cooper	T53	Alfa Romeo	4	31	big end bearings	15	8
r	6	J Surtees	Lola	Mk 4	Climax	V8	26	engine	5	3
r	2	T Taylor	Lotus	25	Climax	V8	11	transmission	9	5

Winning speed: 150.624 km/h, 93.594 mph
Pole Position speed: 158.044 km/h, 98.204 mph (J Clark, 1 min:29.300 sec)
Fastest Lap speed: 155.091 km/h, 96.369 mph (J Clark, 1 min:31.000 sec on lap 3)
Lap Leaders: J Clark 1-61 (61); G Hill 62-82 (21).

Lap Leaders 1962

POS	DRIVER	CAR-ENGINE	GPS	LAPS	KM	MILES
1	G Hill	BRM	8	321	1,721.7	1,069.8
2	J Clark	Lotus-Climax	6	267	1,349.6	838.6
3	D Gurney	Porsche	2	15	130.7	81.2
4	B McLaren	Cooper-Climax	1	14	44.0	27.4
5	T Taylor	Lotus-Climax	1	5	70.5	43.8
6	W Mairesse	Ferrari	1	2	28.2	17.5
			9	**624**	**3,344.7**	**2,078.3**

Driver Points 1962

		NL	MC	B	F	GB	D	I	USA	ZA	TOTAL	
1	G Hill	9	(1)	6	-	(3)	9	9	(6)	9	42	(10)
2	J Clark	-	-	9	-	9	3	-	9	-	30	
3	B McLaren	-	9	-	(3)	4	(2)	4	4	6	27	(5)
4	J Surtees	-	3	2	2	6	6	-	-	-	19	
5	D Gurney	-	-	-	9	-	4	-	2	-	15	
6	P Hill	4	6	4	-	-	-	-	-	-	14	
7	T Maggs	2	-	-	6	1	-	-	-	4	13	
8	R Ginther	-	-	-	4	-	-	6	-	-	10	
9	J Brabham	-	-	1	-	2	-	-	3	3	9	
10	T Taylor	6	-	-	-	-	-	-	-	-	6	
11	G Baghetti	3	-	-	-	-	-	2	-	-	5	
12	L Bandini	-	4	-	-	-	-	-	-	-	4	
	R Rodriguez	-	-	3	-	-	1	-	-	-	4	
14	W Mairesse	-	-	-	-	-	-	3	-	-	3	
	J Bonnier	-	2	-	-	-	-	1	-	-	3	
16	I Ireland	-	-	-	-	-	-	-	-	2	2	
	C G de Beaufort	1	-	-	1	-	-	-	-	-	2	
18	M Gregory	-	-	-	-	-	-	-	1	-	1	
	N Lederle	-	-	-	-	-	-	-	-	1	1	

9, 6, 4, 3, 2 and 1 point awarded to the first six finishers. Best 5 scores.

Constructor Points 1962

		NL	MC	B	F	GB	D	I	USA	ZA	TOTAL	
1	BRM	9	(1)	6	(4)	(3)	9	9	(6)	9	42	(14)
2	Lotus-Climax	6	-	9	-	9	3	-	9	(2)	36	(2)
3	Cooper-Climax	(2)	9	-	6	4	(2)	4	(4)	6	29	(8)
4	Lola-Climax	-	3	2	2	6	6	-	-	-	19	
5	Porsche	1	2	-	9	-	4	(1)	2	-	18	(1)
	Ferrari	4	6	4	-	-	1	3	-	-	18	
7	Brabham-Climax	-	-	-	-	-	-	-	3	3	6	
8	Lotus-BRM	-	-	-	-	-	-	-	1	-	1	

9, 6, 4, 3, 2 and 1 point awarded to the first six finishers. Points only for highest placed car. Best 5 scores.

Right: Trevor Taylor, the Lotus Driver, still looking dazed after his violent accident with Willy Mairesse talks to Colin Chapman. Belgium Grand Prix 1962.

Far right: Graham Hill on his lap of honour after the Netherlands Grand Prix 1962.

Surtees joined Ferrari, which along with BRM, produced its first semi-monocoque. The factory Porsche effort closed with Gurney moving to the emerging Brabham team. Drivers now had to cover two thirds race distance to be classified.

FERRARI
Scuderia Ferrari SpA SEFAC: Surtees, Bandini, Mairesse, Scarfiotti

ATS
Automobili Turismo e Sport: P Hill, Baghetti

DE TOMASO
Scuderia Settecolli: (Lippi)

BRABHAM
Brabham Racing Organisation: Brabham, Gurney
Privateer: Prophet

BRM
Owen Racing Organisation: G Hill, Ginther
Scuderia Centro Sud: Bandini, Trintignant, Solana

BRP
British Racing Partnership: Ireland

COOPER
Cooper Car Co: McLaren, Maggs
R. R. C. Walker Racing Team: Bonnier
Scuderia Centro Sud: de Cabral, (Brambilla)
Scuderia Lupini: Blokdyk
Privateers: Love, (Dochnal)

GILBY
Ian Raby (Racing): Raby

LOLA
Reg Parnell (Racing): Amon, Gregory, Trintignant, Bianchi, Hailwood
Tim Parnell: Campbell-Jones
DW Racing Enterprises: Anderson

LOTUS
Team Lotus: Clark, Taylor, Rodriguez, Spence, (Arundell)
British Racing Partnership: Hall, Ireland
Reg Parnell (Racing): Sharp, Trintignant, Hailwood, Amon, Ward, Gregory (GB)
Tim Parnell: Gregory, (Pilette, Parnell)
Brabham Racing Organisation: Brabham
Ecurie Filipinetti: P Hill
Siffert Racing Team: Siffert
Ted Lanfear: Niemann
Selby Auto Spares: (Driver)
Privateers: Collomb, Pieterse, (Kuhnke, Pilette (I))

SCIROCCO
Scirocco-Powell (Racing Cars): Settember, Burgess

STEBRO
Canadian Stebro Racing: Broeker

PORSCHE
Ecurie Maarsbergen: de Beaufort, Mitter

ALFA SPECIAL
Otelle Nucci: de Klerk

LDS
Otelle Nucci: Serrurier
Privateer: Tingle

26 May 1963 — MONACO: Monte Carlo (Round: 1) (Race: 112)

100 laps x 3.145 km, 1.954 miles = 314.500 km, 195.421 miles

POS.	NO.	DRIVER	CAR	MODEL	ENGINE		LAPS	TIME/REASON FOR RETIREMENT	GRID:POS	ROW
1	6	G Hill	BRM	P57	BRM	V8	100	2h 41m 49.700s	2	1
2	5	R Ginther	BRM	P57	BRM	V8	100	2h 41m 54.300s	4	2
3	7	B McLaren	Cooper	T66	Climax	V8	100	2h 42m 02.500s	8	4
4	21	J Surtees	Ferrari	156	Ferrari	V6	100	2h 42m 03.800s	3	2
5	8	T Maggs	Cooper	T66	Climax	V8	98		10	5
6	10	T Taylor	Lotus	25	Climax	V8	98		9	5
7	11	J Bonnier	Cooper	T60	Climax	V8	94		11	6
8r	9	J Clark	Lotus	25	Climax	V8	78	gear selection/ accident	1	1
9r	3	J Brabham	Lotus	25	Climax	V8	77	gearbox	15	8
r	14	I Ireland	Lotus	24	BRM	V8	40	gearbox/ accident	5	3
r	20	W Mairesse	Ferrari	156	Ferrari	V6	37	clutch	7	4
r	17	M Trintignant	Lola	Mk 4A	Climax	V8	34	oil loss	14	7
r	4	D Gurney	Brabham	BT7	Climax	V8	25	crown wheel & pinion	6	3
r	12	J Hall	Lotus	24	BRM	V8	20	gearbox	13	7
r	25	J Siffert	Lotus	24	BRM	V8	3	engine	12	6
ns	15	C Amon	Lola	Mk 4A	Climax	V8		car raced by Trintignant		
nq	24	B Collomb	Lotus	24	Climax	V8		too slow		

Winning speed: 116.605 km/h, 72.455 mph
Pole Position speed: 120.064 km/h, 74.604 mph (J Clark, 1 min:34.300 sec)
Fastest Lap speed: 119.810 km/h, 74.446 mph (J Surtees, 1 min:34.500 sec on lap 100)
Lap Leaders: G Hill 1-17,79-100 (39); J Clark 18-78 (61).

Also the Grand Prix of Europe.

9 Jun 1963 — BELGIUM: Spa-Francorchamps (Round: 2) (Race: 113)

32 laps x 14.100 km, 8.761 miles = 451.200 km, 280.363 miles

POS.	NO.	DRIVER	CAR	MODEL	ENGINE		LAPS	TIME/REASON FOR RETIREMENT	GRID:POS	ROW
1	1	J Clark	Lotus	25	Climax	V8	32	2h 27m 47.600s	8	3
2	14	B McLaren	Cooper	T66	Climax	V8	32	2h 32m 41.600s	5	2
3	18	D Gurney	Brabham	BT7	Climax	V8	31		2	1
4	8	R Ginther	BRM	P57	BRM	V8	31		9	4
5	12	J Bonnier	Cooper	T60	Climax	V8	30		13	5
6	29	C G de Beaufort	Porsche	718	Porsche	F4	30		18	7
7r	15	T Maggs	Cooper	T66	Climax	V8	27	spin	4	2
8r	24	T Settember	Scirocco	SP	BRM	V8	25	spin	19	8
r	9	J Surtees	Ferrari	156	Ferrari	V6	19	fuel pressure	10	4
r	7	G Hill	BRM	P57	BRM	V8	17	gearbox	1	1
r	22	L Bianchi	Lola	Mk 4	Climax	V8	17	accident	16	7
r	5	J Hall	Lotus	24	BRM	V8	16	accident	12	5
r	28	J Siffert	Lotus	24	BRM	V8	16	spin	14	6
r	26	P Hill	ATS	100	ATS	V8	13	transmission	17	7
r	17	J Brabham	Brabham	BT3	Climax	V8	12	fuel injection pump	6	3
r	21	C Amon	Lola	Mk 4A	Climax	V8	10	oil leak	15	6
r	4	I Ireland	BRP	Mk 1	BRM	V8	9	gear selection	7	3
r	27	G Baghetti	ATS	100	ATS	V8	7	gearbox	20	8
r	10	W Mairesse	Ferrari	156	Ferrari	V6	7	dropped valve	3	1
r	2	T Taylor	Lotus	25	Climax	V8	5	oil pressure	11	5

Winning speed: 183.175 km/h, 113.819 mph
Pole Position speed: 216.830 km/h, 134.732 mph (G Hill, 3 min:54.100 sec)
Fastest Lap speed: 213.188 km/h, 132.469 mph (J Clark, 3 min:58.100 sec on lap 16)
Lap Leaders: J Clark 1-32 (32).

23 Jun 1963 — NETHERLANDS: Zandvoort (Round: 3) (Race: 114)

80 laps x 4.193 km, 2.605 miles = 335.440 km, 208.433 miles

POS.	NO.	DRIVER	CAR	MODEL	ENGINE		LAPS	TIME/REASON FOR RETIREMENT	GRID:POS	ROW
1	6	J Clark	Lotus	25	Climax	V8	80	2h 08m 13.700s	1	1
2	18	D Gurney	Brabham	BT7	Climax	V8	79		14	6
3	2	J Surtees	Ferrari	156	Ferrari	V6	79		5	2
4	30	I Ireland	BRP	Mk 1	BRM	V8	79		7	3
5	14	R Ginther	BRM	P57	BRM	V8	79		6	3
6	4	L Scarfiotti	Ferrari	156	Ferrari	V6	78		11	5
7	36	J Siffert	Lotus	24	BRM	V8	77		17	7
8	42	J Hall	Lotus	24	BRM	V8	77		18	7
9	32	C G de Beaufort	Porsche	718	Porsche	F4	75		19	8
r	12	G Hill	BRM	P57	BRM	V8	69	engine	2	1
r	16	J Brabham	Brabham	BT7	Climax	V8	68	spin/ chassis	4	2
10	8	T Taylor	Lotus	25	Climax	V8	66		10	4
11	28	J Bonnier	Cooper	T60	Climax	V8	56		8	3
r	10	C Amon	Lola	Mk 4A	Climax	V8	29	water pump	12	5
r	26	G Baghetti	ATS	100	ATS	V8	17	ignition	15	6
r	24	P Hill	ATS	100	ATS	V8	15	rear hub	13	5
r	22	T Maggs	Cooper	T66	Climax	V8	14	engine overheating	9	4
r	20	B McLaren	Cooper	T66	Climax	V8	7	gearbox	3	1
r	34	G Mitter	Porsche	718	Porsche	F4	2	clutch	16	7

Winning speed: 156.958 km/h, 97.529 mph
Pole Position speed: 164.790 km/h, 102.396 mph (J Clark, 1 min:31.600 sec)
Fastest Lap speed: 161.097 km/h, 100.101 mph (J Clark, 1 min:33.700 sec on lap 56)
Lap Leaders: J Clark 1-80 (80).

30 Jun 1963 — FRANCE: Reims (Round: 4) (Race: 115)

53 laps x 8.302 km, 5.159 miles = 440.006 km, 273.407 miles

POS.	NO.	DRIVER	CAR	MODEL	ENGINE		LAPS	TIME/REASON FOR RETIREMENT	GRID:POS	ROW
1	18	J Clark	Lotus	25	Climax	V8	53	2h 10m 54.300s	1	1
2	12	T Maggs	Cooper	T66	Climax	V8	53	2h 11m 59.200s	8	3
3	2	G Hill	BRM	P61	BRM	V8	53	2h 13m 08.200s	2	1
4	6	J Brabham	Brabham	BT7	Climax	V8	53	2h 13m 09.500s	5	2
5	8	D Gurney	Brabham	BT7	Climax	V8	53	2h 13m 27.700s	3	1
6	36	J Siffert	Lotus	24	BRM	V8	52		10	4
7	30	C Amon	Lola	Mk 4A	Climax	V8	51		15	6
8	28	M Trintignant	Lotus	24	Climax	V8	50		14	6
9	32	I Ireland	BRP	Mk 1	BRM	V8	49		9	4
10	46	L Bandini	BRM	P57	BRM	V8	45		19	8
11	34	J Hall	Lotus	24	BRM	V8	45		16	7
12r	10	B McLaren	Cooper	T66	Climax	V8	42	ignition	6	3
13r	20	T Taylor	Lotus	25	Climax	V8	41	crown wheel & pinion	7	3
r	42	P Hill	Lotus	24	BRM	V8	34	fuel pump	13	5
r	44	J Bonnier	Cooper	T60	Climax	V8	32	ignition/ gearbox	11	5
r	48	M Gregory	Lotus	24	BRM	V8	30	gearbox	17	7
r	16	J Surtees	Ferrari	156	Ferrari	V6	12	fuel pump	4	2
r	38	T Settember	Scirocco	SP	BRM	V8	5	rear hub bearing	18	7
r	4	R Ginther	BRM	P57	BRM	V8	4	radiator	12	5
ns	14	L Scarfiotti	Ferrari	156	Ferrari	V6		accident/ injury		
ns	22	P Arundell	Lotus	25	Climax	V8		drove in different race		

Winning speed: 201.676 km/h, 125.315 mph
Pole Position speed: 213.175 km/h, 132.461 mph (J Clark, 2 min:20.200 sec)
Fastest Lap speed: 211.068 km/h, 131.151 mph (J Clark, 2 min:21.600 sec on lap 12)
Lap Leaders: J Clark 1-53 (53).

20 Jul 1963 — BRITAIN: Silverstone — (Round: 5) (Race: 116)

82 laps x 4.711 km, 2.927 miles = 386.265 km, 240.014 miles

POS.	NO.	DRIVER	CAR	MODEL	ENGINE		LAPS	TIME/REASON FOR RETIREMENT	GRID:POS	ROW
1	4	J Clark	Lotus	25	Climax	V8	82	2h 14m 09.600s	1	1
2	10	J Surtees	Ferrari	156	Ferrari	V6	82	2h 14m 35.400s	5	2
3	1	G Hill	BRM	P57	BRM	V8	82	2h 14m 47.200s	3	1
4	2	R Ginther	BRM	P57	BRM	V8	81		9	3
5	3	L Bandini	BRM	P57	BRM	V8	81		8	3
6	12	J Hall	Lotus	24	BRM	V8	80		13	4
7	19	C Amon	Lola	Mk 4A	Climax	V8	80		14	4
8	20	M Hailwood	Lotus	24	Climax	V8	78		17	5
9	7	T Maggs	Cooper	T66	Climax	V8	78		7	2
10	23	C G de Beaufort	Porsche	718	Porsche	F4	76		21	6
11	21	M Gregory	Lotus	24	BRM	V8	75		22	7
12	22	B Anderson	Lola	Mk 4	Climax	V8	75		16	5
13	24	J Campbell-Jones	Lola	Mk 4	Climax	V8	74		23	7
r	25	J Siffert	Lotus	24	BRM	V8	66	gearbox	15	5
r	14	J Bonnier	Cooper	T66	Climax	V8	65	oil pressure	12	4
r	9	D Gurney	Brabham	BT7	Climax	V8	59	engine	2	1
r	26	I Raby	Gilby	(62)	BRM	V8	59	gearbox	19	6
r	16	I Burgess	Scirocco	SP	BRM	V8	36	ignition	20	6
r	8	J Brabham	Brabham	BT7	Climax	V8	27	engine	4	1
dq	11	I Ireland	BRP	Mk 1	BRM	V8	26	push start in pits	11	3
dq	5	T Taylor	Lotus	25	Climax	V8	23	push start in pits	10	3
r	15	T Settember	Scirocco	SP	BRM	V8	20	ignition	18	5
r	6	B McLaren	Cooper	T66	Climax	V8	6	engine	6	2

Winning speed: 172.748 km/h, 107.341 mph
Pole Position speed: 179.640 km/h, 111.623 mph (J Clark, 1 min:34.400 sec)
Fastest Lap speed: 176.646 km/h, 109.763 mph (J Surtees, 1 min:36.000 sec on lap 3)
Lap Leaders: J Brabham 1-3 (3); J Clark 4-82 (79).

4 Aug 1963 — GERMANY: Nürburgring — (Round: 6) (Race: 117)

15 laps x 22.810 km, 14.173 miles = 342.150 km, 212.602 miles

POS.	NO.	DRIVER	CAR	MODEL	ENGINE		LAPS	TIME/REASON FOR RETIREMENT	GRID:POS	ROW
1	7	J Surtees	Ferrari	156	Ferrari	V6	15	2h 13m 06.800s	2	1
2	3	J Clark	Lotus	25	Climax	V8	15	2h 14m 24.300s	1	1
3	2	R Ginther	BRM	P57	BRM	V8	15	2h 15m 51.700s	6	2
4	26	G Mitter	Porsche	718	Porsche	F4	15	2h 21m 18.300s	15	5
5	20	J Hall	Lotus	24	BRM	V8	14		16	5
6	16	J Bonnier	Cooper	T66	Climax	V8	14		12	4
7	9	J Brabham	Brabham	BT7	Climax	V8	14		8	3
8	4	T Taylor	Lotus	25	Climax	V8	14		18	5
9r	18	J Siffert	Lotus	24	BRM	V8	10	transmission	9	3
10	28	B Collomb	Lotus	24	Climax	V8	10		21	6
r	17	C G de Beaufort	Porsche	718	Porsche	F4	9	wheel lost	17	5
r	6	T Maggs	Cooper	T66	Climax	V8	7	camshaft	10	3
r	10	D Gurney	Brabham	BT7	Climax	V8	6	gearbox	13	4
r	22	M de Cabral	Cooper	T60	Climax	V8	6	gearbox	20	6
r	24	I Burgess	Scirocco	SP	BRM	V8	5	steering arm	19	6
r	23	T Settember	Scirocco	SP	BRM	V8	5	accident	22	7
r	5	B McLaren	Cooper	T66	Climax	V8	3	accident	5	2
r	21	C Amon	Lola	Mk 4A	Climax	V8	2	steering/ accident	14	4
r	1	G Hill	BRM	P57	BRM	V8	2	gearbox	4	1
r	8	W Mairesse	Ferrari	156	Ferrari	V6	1	accident	7	2
r	14	I Ireland	Lotus	24	BRM	V8	1	accident	11	3
r	15	L Bandini	BRM	P57	BRM	V8	0	accident	3	1
nq	29	A Pilette	Lotus	18/21	Climax	4				
nq	25	I Raby	Gilby	(62)	BRM	V8				
nq	30	T Parnell	Lotus	18/21	Climax	4				
nq	27	K Kuhnke	Lotus	18	Borgward	4				

Winning speed: 154.222 km/h, 95.829 mph
Pole Position speed: 156.173 km/h, 97.042 mph (J Clark, 8 min:45.800 sec)
Fastest Lap speed: 155.818 km/h, 96.821 mph (J Surtees, 8 min:47.000 sec on lap 9)
Lap Leaders: R Ginther 1 (1); J Surtees 2-3,5-15 (13); J Clark 4 (1).

8 Sep 1963 — ITALY: Monza — (Round: 7) (Race: 118)

86 laps x 5.750 km, 3.573 miles = 494.500 km, 307.268 miles

POS.	NO.	DRIVER	CAR	MODEL	ENGINE		LAPS	TIME/REASON FOR RETIREMENT	GRID:POS	ROW
1	8	J Clark	Lotus	25	Climax	V8	86	2h 24m 19.600s	3	2
2	10	R Ginther	BRM	P57	BRM	V8	86	2h 25m 54.600s	4	2
3	18	B McLaren	Cooper	T66	Climax	V8	85		8	4
4r	32	I Ireland	BRP	Mk 1	BRM	V8	84	engine	10	5
5	22	J Brabham	Brabham	BT3	Climax	V8	84		7	4
6	20	T Maggs	Cooper	T66	Climax	V8	84		13	7
7	58	J Bonnier	Cooper	T66	Climax	V8	84		11	6
8	30	J Hall	Lotus	24	BRM	V8	84		16	8
9	66	M Trintignant	BRM	P57	BRM	V8	83		19	10
10	40	M Hailwood	Lola	Mk 4	Climax	V8	82		17	9
11	16	P Hill	ATS	100	ATS	V8	79		14	7
12	48	B Anderson	Lola	Mk 4	Climax	V8	79		18	9
13r	6	M Spence	Lotus	25	Climax	V8	73	oil pressure	9	5

POS.	NO.	DRIVER	CAR	MODEL	ENGINE		LAPS	TIME/REASON FOR RETIREMENT	GRID:POS	ROW
14r	24	D Gurney	Brabham	BT7	Climax	V8	64	fuel injection	5	3
15	14	G Baghetti	ATS	100	ATS	V8	63		20	10
16r	12	G Hill	BRM	P61	BRM	V8	59	clutch	2	1
r	54	J Siffert	Lotus	24	BRM	V8	40	oil pressure	15	8
r	2	L Bandini	Ferrari	156	Ferrari	V6	37	gearbox	6	3
r	42	M Gregory	Lotus	24	BRM	V8	26	cam follower	12	6
r	4	J Surtees	Ferrari	156	Ferrari	V6	16	engine	1	1
ns	38	C Amon	Lola	Mk 4A	Climax	V8		accident/ injury		
nq	64	M de Cabral	Cooper	T60	Climax	V8				
nq	50	I Raby	Gilby	(62)	BRM	V8				
nq	34	T Settember	Scirocco	SP	BRM	V8				
nq	28	C G de Beaufort	Porsche	718	Porsche	F4				
nq	62	T Brambilla	Cooper	T53	Maserati	4				
nq	46	A Pilette	Lotus	18/21	Climax	4				
nq	44	R Lippi	De Tomaso	F1	Ferrari	V6				

Winning speed: 205.575 km/h, 127.739 mph
Pole Position speed: 212.744 km/h, 132.193 mph (J Surtees, 1 min:37.300 sec)
Fastest Lap speed: 209.302 km/h, 130.054 mph (J Clark, 1 min:38.900 sec on lap 60)
Lap Leaders: G Hill 1-3,24-26,29-30,32,34-35,39,41 (13); J Surtees 4-16 (13);
J Clark 17-22,28,36,40,42-43,45,47-51,53-54,56-86 (50); D Gurney 23,27,31,33,37-38,44,46,52,55 (10).

6 Oct 1963 — USA: Watkins Glen (Round: 8) (Race: 119)

110 laps x 3.701 km, 2.300 miles = 407.164 km, 253.000 miles

POS.	NO.	DRIVER	CAR	MODEL	ENGINE		LAPS	TIME/REASON FOR RETIREMENT	GRID:POS	ROW
1	1	G Hill	BRM	P57	BRM	V8	110	2h 19m 22.100s	1	1
2	2	R Ginther	BRM	P57	BRM	V8	110	2h 19m 56.400s	4	2
3	8	J Clark	Lotus	25	Climax	V8	109		2	1
4	5	J Brabham	Brabham	BT7	Climax	V8	108		5	3
5	24	L Bandini	Ferrari	156	Ferrari	V6	106		9	5
6	12	C G de Beaufort	Porsche	718	Porsche	F4	99		19	10
7	21	P Broeker	Stebro	Mk IV	Ford	4	88		21	11
8	11	J Bonnier	Cooper	T66	Climax	V8	85		12	6
9r	23	J Surtees	Ferrari	156	Ferrari	V6	82	piston	3	2
10r	16	J Hall	Lotus	24	BRM	V8	76	gearbox	16	8
11r	3	B McLaren	Cooper	T66	Climax	V8	74	fuel injection	11	6
r	14	J Siffert	Lotus	24	BRM	V8	56	gearbox	14	7
r	18	R Ward	Lotus	24	BRM	V8	44	gearbox	17	9
r	4	T Maggs	Cooper	T66	Climax	V8	44	engine	10	5
r	6	D Gurney	Brabham	BT7	Climax	V8	42	chassis	6	3
r	10	P Rodriguez	Lotus	25	Climax	V8	36	camshaft	13	7
r	9	T Taylor	Lotus	25	Climax	V8	24	ignition	7	4
r	17	M Gregory	Lola	Mk 4A	Climax	V8	14	oil pressure/ engine overheating	8	4
r	22	H Sharp	Lotus	24	BRM	V8	6	tappet	18	9
r	25	P Hill	ATS	100	ATS	V8	4	oil pump	15	8
r	26	G Baghetti	ATS	100	ATS	V8	0	oil pump	20	10

Winning speed: 175.290 km/h, 108.920 mph
Pole Position speed: 181.545 km/h, 112.807 mph (G Hill, 1 min:13.400 sec)
Fastest Lap speed: 178.864 km/h, 111.141 mph (J Clark, 1 min:14.500 sec on lap 50, 59 & 61)
Lap Leaders: G Hill 1-6,32,35,83-110 (36); J Surtees 7-31,33-34,36-82 (74).

27 Oct 1963 — MEXICO: Mexico City (Round: 9) (Race: 120)

65 laps x 5.000 km, 3.107 miles = 325.000 km, 201.946 miles

POS.	NO.	DRIVER	CAR	MODEL	ENGINE		LAPS	TIME/REASON FOR RETIREMENT	GRID:POS	ROW
1	8	J Clark	Lotus	25	Climax	V8	65	2h 09m 52.100s	1	1
2	5	J Brabham	Brabham	BT7	Climax	V8	65	2h 11m 33.200s	10	5
3	2	R Ginther	BRM	P57	BRM	V8	65	2h 11m 46.800s	5	3
4	1	G Hill	BRM	P57	BRM	V8	64		3	2
5	11	J Bonnier	Cooper	T66	Climax	V8	62		8	4
6	6	D Gurney	Brabham	BT7	Climax	V8	62		4	2
7	22	H Sharp	Lotus	24	BRM	V8	61		16	8
8	16	J Hall	Lotus	24	BRM	V8	60		15	8
9	14	J Siffert	Lotus	24	BRM	V8	59		9	5
10	12	C G de Beaufort	Porsche	718	Porsche	F4	58		18	9
11r	13	M Solana	BRM	P57	BRM	V8	57	cam follower	11	6
r	25	P Hill	ATS	100	ATS	V8	40	rear suspension	17	9
r	24	L Bandini	Ferrari	156	Ferrari	V6	36	misfire	7	4
r	3	B McLaren	Cooper	T66	Climax	V8	30	camshaft	6	3
r	10	P Rodriguez	Lotus	25	Climax	V8	26	suspension	20	10
r	17	M Gregory	Lola	Mk 4A	Climax	V8	23	suspension	14	7
r	9	T Taylor	Lotus	25	Climax	V8	19	cam follower	12	6
dq	23	J Surtees	Ferrari	156	Ferrari	V6	19	push start in pits	2	1
r	26	G Baghetti	ATS	100	ATS	V8	12	carburation	21	11
r	18	C Amon	Lotus	24	BRM	V8	9	gearbox	19	10
r	4	T Maggs	Cooper	T66	Climax	V8	7	engine	13	7
ns	20	F Dochnal	Cooper	T53	Climax	4		accident		

Winning speed: 150.152 km/h, 93.300 mph
Pole Position speed: 151.515 km/h, 94.147 mph (J Clark, 1 min:58.800 sec)
Fastest Lap speed: 152.413 km/h, 94.705 mph (J Clark, 1 min:58.100 sec)
Lap Leaders: J Clark 1-65 (65).

28 Dec 1963 SOUTH AFRICA: East London (Round:10) (Race: 121)

85 laps x 3.920 km, 2.436 miles = 333.231 km, 207.060 miles

POS.	NO.	DRIVER	CAR	MODEL	ENGINE		LAPS	TIME/REASON FOR RETIREMENT	GRID:POS	ROW
1	1	J Clark	Lotus	25	Climax	V8	85	2h 10m 36.900s	1	1
2	9	D Gurney	Brabham	BT7	Climax	V8	85	2h 11m 43.700s	3	1
3	5	G Hill	BRM	P57	BRM	V8	84		6	3
4	10	B McLaren	Cooper	T66	Climax	V8	84		9	4
5	4	L Bandini	Ferrari	156	Ferrari	V6	84		5	2
6	12	J Bonnier	Cooper	T66	Climax	V8	83		11	5
7	11	T Maggs	Cooper	T66	Climax	V8	82		10	4
8	2	T Taylor	Lotus	25	Climax	V8	81		8	3
9	19	J Love	Cooper	T55	Climax	4	80		13	5
10	14	C G de Beaufort	Porsche	718	Porsche	F4	79		20	8
11	16	D Serrurier	LDS	Mk 2	Alfa Romeo	4	78		18	7
12	23	T Blokdyk	Cooper	T51	Maserati	4	77		19	8
13r	8	J Brabham	Brabham	BT7	Climax	V8	70	accident	2	1
14	21	B Niemann	Lotus	22	Ford	4	66		15	6
r	18	P de Klerk	Alfa Special		Alfa Romeo	4	53	gearbox	16	7
r	22	D Prophet	Brabham	BT6	Ford	4	49	oil pressure	14	6
r	6	R Ginther	BRM	P57	BRM	V8	43	half shaft	7	3
r	3	J Surtees	Ferrari	156	Ferrari	V6	43	engine	4	2
r	7	E Pieterse	Lotus	21	Climax	4	3	engine	12	5
r	20	S Tingle	LDS	Mk 1	Alfa Romeo	4	2	half shaft	17	7
ns	15	P Driver	Lotus	24	BRM	V8		accident		

Winning speed: 153.075 km/h, 95.116 mph
Pole Position speed: 158.755 km/h, 98.646 mph (J Clark, 1 min:28.900 sec)
Fastest Lap speed: 158.398 km/h, 98.424 mph (D Gurney, 1 min:29.100 sec on lap 33)
Lap Leaders: J Clark 1-85 (85).

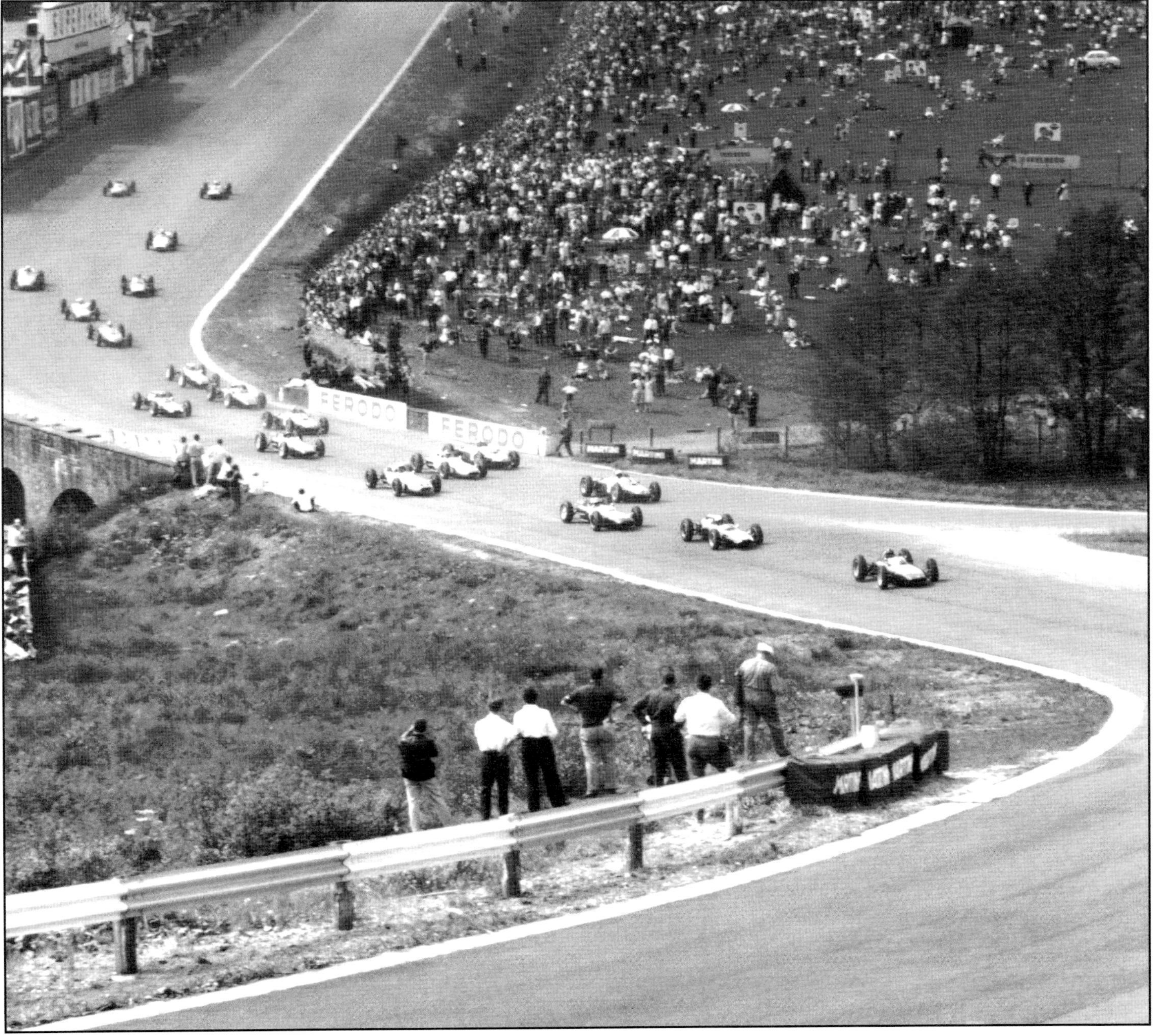

The awesome 'Eau Rouge' on first lap. Belgium Grad Prix 1962.
Refer to page 111

Lap Leaders 1963

POS	DRIVER	CAR-ENGINE	GPS	LAPS	KM	MILES
1	J Clark	Lotus-Climax	9	506	2,759.2	1,714.5
2	J Surtees	Ferrari	3	100	645.2	400.9
3	G Hill	BRM	3	88	330.6	205.5
4	D Gurney	Brabham-Climax	1	10	57.5	35.7
5	J Brabham	Brabham-Climax	1	3	14.1	8.8
6	R Ginther	BRM	1	1	22.8	14.2
			10	**708**	**3,829.4**	**2,379.5**

Driver Points 1963

		MC	B	NL	F	GB	D	I	USA	MEX	ZA	Total	
1	J Clark	-	9	9	9	9	(6)	9	(4)	9	(9)	54	(19)
2	G Hill	9	-	-	-	4	-	-	9	3	4	29	
	R Ginther	6	3	(2)	-	(3)	4	6	6	4	-	29	(5)
4	J Surtees	3	-	4	-	6	9	-	-	-	-	22	
5	D Gurney	-	4	6	2	-	-	-	-	1	6	19	
6	B McLaren	4	6	-	-	-	-	4	-	-	3	17	
7	J Brabham	-	-	-	3	-	-	2	3	6	-	14	
8	T Maggs	2	-	-	6	-	-	1	-	-	-	9	
9	I Ireland	-	-	3	-	-	-	3	-	-	-	6	
	L Bandini	-	-	-	-	2	-	-	2	-	2	6	
	J Bonnier	-	2	-	-	-	1	-	-	2	1	6	
12	G Mitter	-	-	-	-	-	3	-	-	-	-	3	
	J Hall	-	-	-	-	1	2	-	-	-	-	3	
14	C G de Beaufort	-	1	-	-	-	-	-	1	-	-	2	
15	T Taylor	1	-	-	-	-	-	-	-	-	-	1	
	L Scarfiotti	-	-	1	-	-	-	-	-	-	-	1	
	J Siffert	-	-	-	1	-	-	-	-	-	-	1	

9, 6, 4, 3, 2 and 1 point awarded to the first six finishers. Best 6 scores.

G Hill (BRM) was classified 3rd in France, but awarded no points because he was push-started on the grid.

Constructor Points 1963

		MC	B	NL	F	GB	D	I	USA	MEX	ZA	TOTAL	
1	Lotus-Climax	(1)	9	9	9	9	(6)	9	(4)	9	(9)	54	(20)
2	BRM	9	(3)	(2)	-	4	4	6	9	4	(4)	36	(9)
3	Brabham-Climax	-	4	6	3	-	-	(2)	3	6	6	28	(2)
4	Ferrari	3	-	4	-	6	9	-	2	-	2	26	
5	Cooper-Climax	4	6	-	6	-	(1)	4	-	2	3	25	(1)
6	BRP-BRM	-	-	3	-	-	-	3	-	-	-	6	
7	Porsche	-	1	-	-	-	3	-	1	-	-	5	
8	Lotus-BRM	-	-	-	1	1	2	-	-	-	-	4	

9, 6, 4, 3, 2 and 1 point awarded to the first six finishers. Points only for highest placed car. Best 6 scores.

New for this season was a full monocoque for BRM, with the P261 and the debut of Honda, with its transverse mounted V12 engine. John Surtees became the first man to win a world title on four as well as two wheels. A new 3 litre formula for 1966 was announced.

FERRARI
Scuderia Ferrari SpA SEFAC: Surtees, Bandini, Scarfiotti
North American Racing Team: Surtees, Bandini, Rodriguez (USA,MEX)

ATS
Derrington-Francis Racing Team: de Cabral

BRABHAM
Brabham Racing Organisation: Brabham, Gurney
R. R. C. Walker Racing Team: Bonnier, Siffert (USA,MEX), Sharp, Rindt, (Geki)
DW Racing Enterprises: Anderson
John Willment Automobiles: Gardner
Privateers: Siffert, Raby

BRP
British Racing Partnership: Ireland, T Taylor

BRM
Owen Racing Organisation: G Hill, Ginther, (Attwood)
Scuderia Centro Sud: Baghetti, Maggs
Privateer: Trintignant

COOPER
Cooper Car Co: McLaren, P Hill, (Love)
R. R. C. Walker Racing Team: Bonnier, Barth
Bob Gerard Racing: J Taylor
Fabre Urbain: (Rudaz)

LOTUS
Team Lotus: Clark, Spence, Arundell, Mitter, Hansgen, Solana
Reg Parnell (Racing): Hailwood, Amon, Revson (B, F)
British Racing Partnership: T Taylor, (Ireland)
Privateers: Revson, Siffert, (Collomb)

PORSCHE
Ecurie Maarsbergen: de Beaufort

SCIROCCO
Equipe Scirocco Belge: Pilette

HONDA
Honda R & D Co: Bucknum

10 May 1964 — MONACO: Monte Carlo — (Round: 1) (Race: 122)

100 laps x 3.145 km, 1.954 miles = 314.500 km, 195.421 miles

POS.	NO.	DRIVER	CAR	MODEL	ENGINE		LAPS	TIME/REASON FOR RETIREMENT	GRID:POS	ROW
1	8	G Hill	BRM	P261	BRM	V8	100	2h 41m 19.500s	3	2
2	7	R Ginther	BRM	P261	BRM	V8	99		8	4
3	11	P Arundell	Lotus	25	Climax	V8	97		6	3
4r	12	J Clark	Lotus	25	Climax	V8	96	engine	1	1
5	19	J Bonnier	Cooper	T66	Climax	V8	96		11	6
6	18	M Hailwood	Lotus	25	BRM	V8	96		15	8
7r	16	B Anderson	Brabham	BT11	Climax	V8	86	gearbox mounting	12	6
8	24	J Siffert	Lotus	24	BRM	V8	78		16	8
9r	9	P Hill	Cooper	T73	Climax	V8	70	rear suspension	9	5
10r	20	L Bandini	Ferrari	156	Ferrari	V6	67	gearbox	7	4
r	6	D Gurney	Brabham	BT7	Climax	V8	61	gearbox	5	3
r	4	M Trintignant	BRM	P57	BRM	V8	53	driver exhausted	13	7
r	5	J Brabham	Brabham	BT7	Climax	V8	29	fuel injection	2	1
r	10	B McLaren	Cooper	T66	Climax	V8	17	oil leak	10	5
r	21	J Surtees	Ferrari	158	Ferrari	V8	14	gearbox	4	2
r	15	T Taylor	BRP	Mk 1	BRM	V8	7	fuel leak	14	7
ns	14	I Ireland	Lotus	24	BRM	V8		accident/ injury		
nq	17	C Amon	Lotus	25	BRM	V8				
nq	2	P Revson	Lotus	24	BRM	V8				
nq	3	B Collomb	Lotus	24	Climax	V8				

Winning speed: 116.969 km/h, 72.681 mph
Pole Position speed: 120.447 km/h, 74.842 mph (J Clark, 1 min:34.000 sec)
Fastest Lap speed: 120.575 km/h, 74.922 mph (G Hill, 1 min:33.900 sec on lap 53)
Lap Leaders: J Clark 1-36 (36); D Gurney 37-52 (16); G Hill 53-100 (48).

24 May 1964 — NETHERLANDS: Zandvoort — (Round: 2) (Race: 123)

80 laps x 4.193 km, 2.605 miles = 335.440 km, 208.433 miles

POS.	NO.	DRIVER	CAR	MODEL	ENGINE		LAPS	TIME/REASON FOR RETIREMENT	GRID:POS	ROW
1	18	J Clark	Lotus	25	Climax	V8	80	2h 07m 35.400s	2	1
2	2	J Surtees	Ferrari	158	Ferrari	V8	80	2h 08m 29.000s	4	2
3	20	P Arundell	Lotus	25	Climax	V8	79		6	3
4	6	G Hill	BRM	P261	BRM	V8	79		3	1
5	10	C Amon	Lotus	25	BRM	V8	79		13	5
6	34	B Anderson	Brabham	BT11	Climax	V8	78		11	5
7	24	B McLaren	Cooper	T73	Climax	V8	78		5	2
8	22	P Hill	Cooper	T73	Climax	V8	76		9	4
9	26	J Bonnier	Brabham	BT11	BRM	V8	76		12	5
10	32	G Baghetti	BRM	P57	BRM	V8	74		16	7
11	8	R Ginther	BRM	P261	BRM	V8	64		8	3
12r	12	M Hailwood	Lotus	25	BRM	V8	57	crown wheel & pinion	14	6
13	36	J Siffert	Brabham	BT11	BRM	V8	55		18	7
r	14	J Brabham	Brabham	BT7	Climax	V8	44	ignition	7	3
r	4	L Bandini	Ferrari	158	Ferrari	V8	25	fuel injection pump	10	4
r	16	D Gurney	Brabham	BT7	Climax	V8	23	steering wheel	1	1
r	28	C G de Beaufort	Porsche	718	Porsche	F4	8	engine	17	7
ns	30	T Maggs	BRM	P57	BRM	V8		accident	15	6

Winning speed: 157.743 km/h, 98.017 mph
Pole Position speed: 165.513 km/h, 102.845 mph (D Gurney, 1 min:31.200 sec)
Fastest Lap speed: 162.659 km/h, 101.072 mph (J Clark, 1 min:32.800 sec on lap 6)
Lap Leaders: J Clark 1-80 (80).

14 Jun 1964 — BELGIUM: Spa-Francorchamps (Round: 3) (Race: 124)

32 laps x 14.100 km, 8.761 miles = 451.200 km, 280.363 miles

POS.	NO.	DRIVER	CAR	MODEL	ENGINE		LAPS	TIME/REASON FOR RETIREMENT	GRID:POS	ROW
1	23	J Clark	Lotus	25	Climax	V8	32	2h 06m 40.500s	6	3
2	20	B McLaren	Cooper	T73	Climax	V8	32	2h 06m 43.900s	7	3
3	14	J Brabham	Brabham	BT7	Climax	V8	32	2h 07m 28.600s	3	1
4	2	R Ginther	BRM	P261	BRM	V8	32	2h 08m 39.100s	8	3
5r	1	G Hill	BRM	P261	BRM	V8	31	out of fuel	2	1
6r	15	D Gurney	Brabham	BT7	Climax	V8	31	out of fuel	1	1
7	4	T Taylor	BRP	Mk 2	BRM	V8	31		12	5
8	6	G Baghetti	BRM	P57	BRM	V8	31		17	7
9	24	P Arundell	Lotus	25	Climax	V8	28		4	2
10	3	I Ireland	BRP	Mk 1	BRM	V8	28		16	7
dq	29	P Revson	Lotus	24	BRM	V8	27	push start after engine cut	10	4
r	17	J Siffert	Brabham	BT11	BRM	V8	13	piston	13	5
r	21	P Hill	Cooper	T73	Climax	V8	13	connecting rod	15	6
r	11	L Bandini	Ferrari	158	Ferrari	V8	11	oil loss/ engine	9	4
r	28	A Pilette	Scirocco	SP	Climax	V8	10	engine	18	7
r	16	J Bonnier	Brabham	BT11	BRM	V8	7	driver ill	14	6
r	27	C Amon	Lotus	25	BRM	V8	3	connecting rod	11	5
r	10	J Surtees	Ferrari	158	Ferrari	V8	3	piston	5	2
ns	7	T Maggs	BRM	P57	BRM	V8		engine		
ns	18	B Anderson	Brabham	BT11	Climax	V8		ignition		

Winning speed: 213.712 km/h, 132.795 mph
Pole Position speed: 219.835 km/h, 136.599 mph (D Gurney, 3 min:50.900 sec)
Fastest Lap speed: 221.466 km/h, 137.613 mph (D Gurney, 3 min:49.200 sec on lap 27)
Lap Leaders: D Gurney 1-2,4-29 (28); J Surtees 3 (1); G Hill 30-31 (2); J Clark 32 (1).

28 Jun 1964 — FRANCE: Rouen-les-Essarts (Round: 4) (Race: 125)

57 laps x 6.542 km, 4.065 miles = 372.894 km, 231.706 miles

POS.	NO.	DRIVER	CAR	MODEL	ENGINE		LAPS	TIME/REASON FOR RETIREMENT	GRID:POS	ROW
1	22	D Gurney	Brabham	BT7	Climax	V8	57	2h 07m 49.100s	2	1
2	8	G Hill	BRM	P261	BRM	V8	57	2h 08m 13.200s	6	3
3	20	J Brabham	Brabham	BT7	Climax	V8	57	2h 08m 14.000s	5	2
4	4	P Arundell	Lotus	25	Climax	V8	57	2h 08m 59.700s	4	2
5	10	R Ginther	BRM	P261	BRM	V8	57	2h 10m 01.200s	9	4
6	12	B McLaren	Cooper	T73	Climax	V8	56		7	3
7	14	P Hill	Cooper	T73	Climax	V8	56		10	4
8	6	M Hailwood	Lotus	25	BRM	V8	56		13	5
9	26	L Bandini	Ferrari	158	Ferrari	V8	55		8	3
10	34	C Amon	Lotus	25	BRM	V8	53		14	6
11	28	M Trintignant	BRM	P57	BRM	V8	52		16	7
12	19	B Anderson	Brabham	BT11	Climax	V8	50		15	6
r	16	I Ireland	BRP	Mk 1	BRM	V8	31	spin	11	5
r	2	J Clark	Lotus	25	Climax	V8	31	engine	1	1
r	24	J Surtees	Ferrari	158	Ferrari	V8	6	engine	3	1
r	18	T Taylor	BRP	Mk 2	BRM	V8	6	brakes/ accident	12	5
r	30	J Siffert	Brabham	BT11	BRM	V8	4	clutch	17	7
ns	36	P Revson	Lotus	25	BRM	V8		car raced by Hailwood		

Winning speed: 175.042 km/h, 108.766 mph
Pole Position speed: 181.722 km/h, 112.917 mph (J Clark, 2 min: 9.600 sec)
Fastest Lap speed: 179.233 km/h, 111.370 mph (J Brabham, 2 min:11.400 sec on lap 44)
Lap Leaders: J Clark 1-30 (30); D Gurney 31-57 (27).

11 Jul 1964 BRITAIN: Brands Hatch (Round: 5) (Race: 126)

80 laps x 4.265 km, 2.650 miles = 341.181 km, 212.000 miles

POS.	NO.	DRIVER	CAR	MODEL	ENGINE		LAPS	TIME/REASON FOR RETIREMENT	GRID:POS	ROW
1	1	J Clark	Lotus	25	Climax	V8	80	2h 15m 07.000s	1	1
2	3	G Hill	BRM	P261	BRM	V8	80	2h 15m 09.800s	2	1
3	7	J Surtees	Ferrari	158	Ferrari	V8	80	2h 16m 27.600s	5	2
4	5	J Brabham	Brabham	BT7	Climax	V8	79		4	2
5	8	L Bandini	Ferrari	156	Ferrari	V6	78		8	3
6	10	P Hill	Cooper	T73	Climax	V8	78		15	6
7	19	B Anderson	Brabham	BT11	Climax	V8	78		7	3
8	4	R Ginther	BRM	P261	BRM	V8	77		14	6
9	2	M Spence	Lotus	25	Climax	V8	77		13	5
10	11	I Ireland	BRP	Mk 2	BRM	V8	77		10	4
11	20	J Siffert	Brabham	BT11	BRM	V8	76		16	7
12	18	G Baghetti	BRM	P57	BRM	V8	76		21	9
13	6	D Gurney	Brabham	BT7	Climax	V8	75		3	1
14	22	J Taylor	Cooper	T73	Ford	4	56		20	8
r	16	J Bonnier	Brabham	BT11	BRM	V8	46	brake pipe	9	4
r	24	P Revson	Lotus	24	BRM	V8	43	differential	22	9
r	23	I Raby	Brabham	BT3	BRM	V8	37	rear hub	17	7
r	17	T Maggs	BRM	P57	BRM	V8	37	gearbox	23	9
r	12	T Taylor	Lotus	24	BRM	V8	22	driver unfit (practice accident)	18	7
r	14	M Hailwood	Lotus	25	BRM	V8	16	oil line	12	5
r	15	C Amon	Lotus	25	BRM	V8	9	clutch	11	5
r	9	B McLaren	Cooper	T73	Climax	V8	6	gearbox	6	3
r	26	F Gardner	Brabham	BT10	Ford	4	0	accident	19	8
ns	21	D Attwood	BRM	P67	BRM	V8		withdrew		
nq	25	M Trintignant	BRM	P57	BRM	V8				

Winning speed: 151.505 km/h, 94.141 mph
Pole Position speed: 156.505 km/h, 97.248 mph (J Clark, 1 min:38.100 sec)
Fastest Lap speed: 155.396 km/h, 96.559 mph (J Clark, 1 min:38.800 sec on lap 73)
Lap Leaders: J Clark 1-80 (80).

Also the Grand Prix of Europe.

2 Aug 1964 GERMANY: Nürburgring (Round: 6) (Race: 127)

15 laps x 22.810 km, 14.173 miles = 342.150 km, 212.602 miles

POS.	NO.	DRIVER	CAR	MODEL	ENGINE		LAPS	TIME/REASON FOR RETIREMENT	GRID:POS	ROW
1	7	J Surtees	Ferrari	158	Ferrari	V8	15	2h 12m 04.800s	1	1
2	3	G Hill	BRM	P261	BRM	V8	15	2h 13m 20.400s	5	2
3	8	L Bandini	Ferrari	156	Ferrari	V6	15	2h 16m 57.600s	4	1
4	19	J Siffert	Brabham	BT11	BRM	V8	15	2h 17m 27.900s	10	3
5r	22	M Trintignant	BRM	P57	BRM	V8	14	battery	14	4
6	26	T Maggs	BRM	P57	BRM	V8	14		16	5
7	4	R Ginther	BRM	P261	BRM	V8	14		11	3
8	2	M Spence	Lotus	33	Climax	V8	14		17	5
9	23	G Mitter	Lotus	25	Climax	V8	14		19	6
10	5	D Gurney	Brabham	BT7	Climax	V8	14		3	1
11r	14	C Amon	Lotus	25	BRM	V8	12	suspension	9	3
12r	6	J Brabham	Brabham	BT11	Climax	V8	11	crown wheel & pinion	6	2
13r	20	R Bucknum	Honda	RA271	Honda	V12	11	spin	22	7
14r	27	P Revson	Lotus	24	BRM	V8	10	accident	18	5
r	1	J Clark	Lotus	33	Climax	V8	7	valve gear	2	1
r	9	B McLaren	Cooper	T73	Climax	V8	4	valve spring	7	2
r	16	B Anderson	Brabham	BT11	Climax	V8	4	suspension	15	5
r	12	E Barth	Cooper	T66	Climax	V8	3	clutch	20	6
r	18	G Baghetti	BRM	P57	BRM	V8	2	throttle control	21	6
r	10	P Hill	Cooper	T73	Climax	V8	1	engine	8	3
r	15	M Hailwood	Lotus	25	BRM	V8	0	engine	13	4
r	11	J Bonnier	Brabham	BT11	BRM	V8	0	ignition	12	4
ns	29	C G de Beaufort	Porsche	718	Porsche	F4		fatal accident		
nq	28	A Pilette	Scirocco	SP	Climax	V8				

Winning speed: 155.429 km/h, 96.579 mph
Pole Position speed: 158.403 km/h, 98.427 mph (J Surtees, 8 min:38.400 sec)
Fastest Lap speed: 158.220 km/h, 98.313 mph (J Surtees, 8 min:39.000 sec on lap 11)
Lap Leaders: J Clark 1 (1); J Surtees 2-3,5-15 (13); D Gurney 4 (1).

23 Aug 1964 AUSTRIA: Zeltweg (Round: 7) (Race: 128)

105 laps x 3.200 km, 1.988 miles = 336.000 km, 208.781 miles

POS.	NO.	DRIVER	CAR	MODEL	ENGINE		LAPS	TIME/REASON FOR RETIREMENT	GRID:POS	ROW
1	8	L Bandini	Ferrari	156	Ferrari	V6	105	2h 06m 18.230s	7	2
2	4	R Ginther	BRM	P261	BRM	V8	105	2h 06m 24.410s	5	2
3	22	B Anderson	Brabham	BT11	Climax	V8	102		14	4
4	19	T Maggs	BRM	P57	BRM	V8	102		19	6
5	14	I Ireland	BRP	Mk 2	BRM	V8	102		11	3
6	11	J Bonnier	Brabham	BT7	Climax	V8	101		10	3
7	18	G Baghetti	BRM	P57	BRM	V8	96		15	5
8	17	M Hailwood	Lotus	25	BRM	V8	95		18	5
9	6	J Brabham	Brabham	BT11	Climax	V8	76		6	2
r	12	J Rindt	Brabham	BT11	BRM	V8	58	steering	13	4
r	10	P Hill	Cooper	T66	Climax	V8	58	accident/ fire	20	6

POS.	NO.	DRIVER	CAR	MODEL	ENGINE		LAPS	TIME/REASON FOR RETIREMENT	GRID:POS	ROW
r	5	D Gurney	Brabham	BT7	Climax	V8	47	front suspension	4	1
r	9	B McLaren	Cooper	T73	Climax	V8	43	valve spring	9	3
r	2	M Spence	Lotus	33	Climax	V8	41	drive shaft	8	3
r	1	J Clark	Lotus	33	Climax	V8	40	drive shaft	3	1
r	15	T Taylor	BRP	Mk 1	BRM	V8	21	rear suspension	16	5
r	20	J Siffert	Brabham	BT11	BRM	V8	18	spin	12	4
r	7	J Surtees	Ferrari	158	Ferrari	V8	8	rear suspension	2	1
r	16	C Amon	Lotus	25	Climax	V8	7	engine	17	5
r	3	G Hill	BRM	P261	BRM	V8	5	distributor	1	1

Winning speed: 159.615 km/h, 99.180 mph
Pole Position speed: 164.948 km/h, 102.494 mph (G Hill, 1 min: 9.840 sec)
Fastest Lap speed: 163.265 km/h, 101.448 mph (D Gurney, 1 min:10.560 sec on lap 32)
Lap Leaders: D Gurney 1,8-46 (40); J Surtees 2-7 (6); L Bandini 47-105 (59).

6 Sep 1964 — ITALY: Monza — (Round: 8) (Race: 129)

78 laps x 5.750 km, 3.573 miles = 448.500 km, 278.685 miles

POS.	NO.	DRIVER	CAR	MODEL	ENGINE		LAPS	TIME/REASON FOR RETIREMENT	GRID:POS	ROW
1	2	J Surtees	Ferrari	158	Ferrari	V8	78	2h 10m 51.800s	1	1
2	26	B McLaren	Cooper	T73	Climax	V8	78	2h 11m 57.800s	5	2
3	4	L Bandini	Ferrari	158	Ferrari	V8	77		7	3
4	20	R Ginther	BRM	P261	BRM	V8	77		9	4
5	46	I Ireland	BRP	Mk 2	BRM	V8	77		13	5
6	10	M Spence	Lotus	33	Climax	V8	77		8	3
7	12	J Siffert	Brabham	BT11	BRM	V8	77		6	3
8	30	G Baghetti	BRM	P57	BRM	V8	77		15	6
9	6	L Scarfiotti	Ferrari	156	Ferrari	V6	77		16	7
10	16	D Gurney	Brabham	BT7	Climax	V8	75		2	1
11	22	B Anderson	Brabham	BT11	Climax	V8	75		14	6
12	34	J Bonnier	Brabham	BT7	Climax	V8	74		12	5
13	38	P Revson	Lotus	24	BRM	V8	72		18	7
14r	14	J Brabham	Brabham	BT11	Climax	V8	59	connecting rod	11	5
r	8	J Clark	Lotus	25	Climax	V8	27	piston	4	2
r	50	M de Cabral	Derrington Francis (D-F)		ATS	V8	24	ignition	19	8
r	48	M Trintignant	BRM	P57	BRM	V8	21	fuel injection	20	8
r	28	R Bucknum	Honda	RA271	Honda	V12	12	brakes/ oil leak	10	4
r	40	M Hailwood	Lotus	25	BRM	V8	4	cam follower	17	7
r	18	G Hill	BRM	P261	BRM	V8	0	clutch	3	1
ns	60	J-C Rudaz	Cooper	T60	Climax	V8		piston		
nq	44	T Taylor	BRP	Mk 1	BRM	V8				
nq	36	Geki	Brabham	BT11	BRM	V8				
nq	24	J Love	Cooper	T73	Climax	V8				
nq	56	I Raby	Brabham	BT3	BRM	V8				

Winning speed: 205.634 km/h, 127.775 mph
Pole Position speed: 212.526 km/h, 132.057 mph (J Surtees, 1 min:37.400 sec)
Fastest Lap speed: 209.514 km/h, 130.186 mph (J Surtees, 1 min:38.800 sec on lap 63 & 67)
Lap Leaders: D Gurney 1,6-7,10,12-14,16,22,25-26,29,32,37-38,45,47-48,50-52,55 (22);
J Surtees 2-5,8-9,11,15,17-21,23-24,27-28,30-31,33-36,39-44,46,49,53-54,56-78 (56).

4 Oct 1964 — USA: Watkins Glen — (Round: 9) (Race: 130)

110 laps x 3.701 km, 2.300 miles = 407.164 km, 253.000 miles

POS.	NO.	DRIVER	CAR	MODEL	ENGINE		LAPS	TIME/REASON FOR RETIREMENT	GRID:POS	ROW
1	3	G Hill	BRM	P261	BRM	V8	110	2h 16m 38.000s	4	2
2	7	J Surtees	Ferrari	158	Ferrari	V8	110	2h 17m 08.500s	2	1
3	22	J Siffert	Brabham	BT11	BRM	V8	109		12	6
4	4	R Ginther	BRM	P261	BRM	V8	107		13	7
5	17	W Hansgen	Lotus	33	Climax	V8	107		17	9
6	12	T Taylor	BRP	Mk 2	BRM	V8	106		15	8
7r=	2	M Spence	Lotus	33	Climax	V8			6	3
7r=	2	J Clark	Lotus	33	Climax	V8	102	fuel pump		
8r	14	M Hailwood	Lotus	25	BRM	V8	101	oil line	16	8
r	6	D Gurney	Brabham	BT7	Climax	V8	69	oil pressure	3	2
nc	23	H Sharp	Brabham	BT11	BRM	V8	65		18	9
r	8	L Bandini	Ferrari	1512	Ferrari	F12	58	engine	8	4
r=	1	J Clark	Lotus	25	Climax	V8			1	1
r=	1	M Spence	Lotus	25	Climax	V8	54	fuel injection		
r	28	R Bucknum	Honda	RA271	Honda	V12	50	cylinder head gasket	14	7
r	15	C Amon	Lotus	25	BRM	V8	47	starter motor	11	6
r	16	J Bonnier	Brabham	BT7	Climax	V8	37	stub axle	9	5
r	9	B McLaren	Cooper	T73	Climax	V8	26	valve	5	3
r	5	J Brabham	Brabham	BT11	Climax	V8	14	piston	7	4
r	10	P Hill	Cooper	T73	Climax	V8	4	ignition	19	10
r	11	I Ireland	BRP	Mk 2	BRM	V8	2	gear lever	10	5

Winning speed: 178.799 km/h, 111.100 mph
Pole Position speed: 183.419 km/h, 113.971 mph (J Clark, 1 min:12.650 sec)
Fastest Lap speed: 183.293 km/h, 113.893 mph (J Clark, 1 min:12.700 sec)
Lap Leaders: J Surtees 1-12,44 (13); J Clark 13-43 (31); G Hill 45-110 (66).

25 Oct 1964 — MEXICO: Mexico City (Round:10) (Race: 131)

65 laps x 5.000 km, 3.107 miles = 325.000 km, 201.946 miles

POS.	NO.	DRIVER	CAR	MODEL	ENGINE		LAPS	TIME/REASON FOR RETIREMENT	GRID:POS	ROW
1	6	D Gurney	Brabham	BT7	Climax	V8	65	2h 09m 50.320s	2	1
2	7	J Surtees	Ferrari	158	Ferrari	V8	65	2h 10m 59.260s	4	2
3	8	L Bandini	Ferrari	1512	Ferrari	F12	65	2h 10m 59.950s	3	2
4	2	M Spence	Lotus	25	Climax	V8	65	2h 11m 12.180s	5	3
5r	1	J Clark	Lotus	33	Climax	V8	64	oil leak/ engine	1	1
6	18	P Rodriguez	Ferrari	156	Ferrari	V6	64		9	5
7	9	B McLaren	Cooper	T73	Climax	V8	64		10	5
8	4	R Ginther	BRM	P261	BRM	V8	64		11	6
9r	10	P Hill	Cooper	T73	Climax	V8	63	piston	15	8
10	17	M Solana	Lotus	33	Climax	V8	63		14	7
11	3	G Hill	BRM	P261	BRM	V8	63		6	3
12	11	I Ireland	BRP	Mk 2	BRM	V8	61		16	8
13	23	H Sharp	Brabham	BT11	BRM	V8	60		19	10
r	15	C Amon	Lotus	25	BRM	V8	45	gearbox	12	6
r	5	J Brabham	Brabham	BT11	Climax	V8	44	electrics	7	4
r	14	M Hailwood	Lotus	25	BRM	V8	11	engine overheating	17	9
r	22	J Siffert	Brabham	BT11	BRM	V8	10	fuel pump	13	7
r	16	J Bonnier	Brabham	BT7	Climax	V8	9	suspension	8	4
r	12	T Taylor	BRP	Mk 2	BRM	V8	5	engine overheating	18	9

Winning speed: 150.186 km/h, 93.321 mph
Pole Position speed: 153.531 km/h, 95.400 mph (J Clark, 1 min:57.240 sec)
Fastest Lap speed: 152.066 km/h, 94.489 mph (J Clark, 1 min:58.370 sec)
Lap Leaders: J Clark 1-63 (63); D Gurney 64-65 (2).

Graham Hill

Lap Leaders 1964

POS	DRIVER	CAR-ENGINE	GPS	LAPS	KM	MILES
1	J Clark	Lotus-Climax	8	322	1,452.8	902.7
2	D Gurney	Brabham-Climax	7	136	909.1	564.9
3	G Hill	BRM	3	116	423.4	263.1
4	J Surtees	Ferrari	5	89	699.9	434.9
5	L Bandini	Ferrari	1	59	188.8	117.3
			10	**722**	**3,674.0**	**2,282.9**

Driver Points 1964

		MC	NL	B	F	GB	D	A	I	USA	MEX	TOTAL	
1	J Surtees	-	6	-	-	4	9	-	9	6	6	40	
2	G Hill	9	3	(2)	6	6	6	-	-	9	-	39	(2)
3	J Clark	3	9	9	-	9	-	-	-	-	2	32	
4	L Bandini	-	-	-	-	2	4	9	4	-	4	23	
	R Ginther	6	-	3	2	-	-	6	3	3	-	23	
6	D Gurney	-	-	1	9	-	-	-	-	-	9	19	
7	B McLaren	-	-	6	1	-	-	-	6	-	-	13	
8	P Arundell	4	4	-	3	-	-	-	-	-	-	11	
	J Brabham	-	-	4	4	3	-	-	-	-	-	11	
10	J Siffert	-	-	-	-	-	3	-	-	4	-	7	
11	B Anderson	-	1	-	-	-	-	4	-	-	-	5	
12	T Maggs	-	-	-	-	-	1	3	-	-	-	4	
	M Spence	-	-	-	-	-	-	-	1	-	3	4	
	I Ireland	-	-	-	-	-	-	2	2	-	-	4	
15	J Bonnier	2	-	-	-	-	-	1	-	-	-	3	
16	C Amon	-	2	-	-	-	-	-	-	-	-	2	
	M Trintignant	-	-	-	-	-	2	-	-	-	-	2	
	W Hansgen	-	-	-	-	-	-	-	-	2	-	2	
19	M Hailwood	1	-	-	-	-	-	-	-	-	-	1	
	P Hill	-	-	-	-	1	-	-	-	-	-	1	
	T Taylor	-	-	-	-	-	-	-	-	1	-	1	
	P Rodriguez	-	-	-	-	-	-	-	-	-	1	1	

9, 6, 4, 3, 2 and 1 point awarded to the first six finishers. Best 6 scores.

Constructor Points 1964

		MC	NL	B	F	GB	D	A	I	USA	MEX	TOTAL	
1	Ferrari	-	6	-	-	(4)	9	9	9	6	6	45	(4)
2	BRM	9	(3)	(3)	6	6	6	6	(3)	9	-	42	(9)
3	Lotus-Climax	4	9	9	3	9	-	-	(1)	(2)	3	37	(3)
4	Brabham-Climax	-	1	4	9	3	-	4	-	-	9	30	
5	Cooper-Climax	2	-	6	1	1	-	-	6	-	-	16	
6	Brabham-BRM	-	-	-	-	-	3	-	-	4	-	7	
7	BRP-BRM	-	-	-	-	-	-	2	2	1	-	5	
8	Lotus-BRM	1	2	-	-	-	-	-	-	-	-	3	

9, 6, 4, 3, 2 and 1 point awarded to the first six finishers. Points only for highest placed car. Best 6 scores.

Tyre development increased dramatically, with treads becoming wider. Clark totally dominated, and also won the Indy 500 for good measure. Surtees was seriously injured at Mosport at the end of the season. Coventry Climax announced an end to its Formula 1 involvement with the final season of the 1.5 litre formula.

FERRARI
Scuderia Ferrari SpA SEFAC: Surtees, Bandini, Vaccarella, (Scarfiotti)
North American Racing Team: Rodriguez, Bondurant

BRABHAM
Brabham Racing Organisation: Brabham, Gurney, Hulme, Baghetti

R. R. C. Walker Racing Team: Bonnier, Siffert
John Willment Automobiles: Gardner, Hawkins
DW Racing Enterprises: Anderson
Ian Raby (Racing): Raby, (Amon)
Privateer: Prophet

BRM
Owen Racing Organisation: Hill, Stewart
Scuderia Centro Sud: Gregory, Bussinello, Bassi, Bianchi, (Mairesse)

COOPER
Cooper Car Co: McLaren, Rindt
Gerard Racing: Rhodes, (Rollinson)
Privateers: Love, (Blokdyk)

LOTUS
Team Lotus: Clark, Spence, Solana, Mitter, Geki
Reg Parnell (Racing): Attwood, Ireland, Amon, Maggs, Hailwood, Bondurant
DW Racing Enterprises: Hawkins
Lawson Organisation: (Pieterse)
Scuderia Scribante: (Lederle)
Ted Lanfear: (Niemann)
Privateers: (Gubby, Puzey, Charlton)

HONDA
Honda R & D Co: Ginther, Bucknum

ALFA SPECIAL
Otelle Nucci: de Klerk

LDS
Otelle Nucci: (Serrurier)
Privateers: Tingle, (Pretorius)

1 Jan 1965 — SOUTH AFRICA: East London (Round: 1) (Race: 132)
85 laps x 3.920 km, 2.436 miles = 333.231 km, 207.060 miles

POS.	NO.	DRIVER	CAR	MODEL	ENGINE		LAPS	TIME/REASON FOR RETIREMENT	GRID:POS	ROW
1	5	J Clark	Lotus	33	Climax	V8	85	2h 06m 46.000s	1	1
2	1	J Surtees	Ferrari	158	Ferrari	V8	85	2h 07m 15.000s	2	1
3	3	G Hill	BRM	P261	BRM	V8	85	2h 07m 17.800s	5	2
4	6	M Spence	Lotus	33	Climax	V8	85	2h 07m 40.400s	4	2
5	9	B McLaren	Cooper	T77	Climax	V8	84		8	3
6	4	J Stewart	BRM	P261	BRM	V8	83		11	5
7	12	J Siffert	Brabham	BT11	BRM	V8	83		14	6
8	7	J Brabham	Brabham	BT11	Climax	V8	81		3	1
9	18	P Hawkins	Brabham	BT10	Ford	4	81		16	7
10	20	P de Klerk	Alfa Special		Alfa Romeo	4	79		17	7
11	15	T Maggs	Lotus	25	BRM	V8	77		13	5
12	16	F Gardner	Brabham	BT11	BRM	V8	75		15	6
13	25	S Tingle	LDS	Mk 1	Alfa Romeo	4	73		20	8
14	19	D Prophet	Brabham	BT10	Ford	4	71		19	8
15r	2	L Bandini	Ferrari	1512	Ferrari	F12	66	electrics	6	3
nc	14	B Anderson	Brabham	BT11	Climax	V8	50		12	5
r	11	J Bonnier	Brabham	BT7	Climax	V8	42	clutch/ gearbox	7	3
r	10	J Rindt	Cooper	T73	Climax	V8	39	electrics	10	4
r	17	J Love	Cooper	T55	Climax	4	20	half shaft	18	7
r	8	D Gurney	Brabham	BT11	Climax	V8	11	ignition	9	4
nq	28	T Blokdyk	Cooper	T59	Ford	4				
nq	23	N Lederle	Lotus	21	Climax	4				
nq	21	D Serrurier	LDS	Mk 2	Climax	4				
nq	27	B Niemann	Lotus	22	Ford	4				
nq	22	E Pieterse	Lotus	21	Climax	4				
npq	24	C Puzey	Lotus	18/21	Climax	4				
npq	29	J Pretorius	LDS	Mk 1	Alfa Romeo	4				
npq	32	D Charlton	Lotus	20	Ford	4				

Winning speed: 157.722 km/h, 98.004 mph
Pole Position speed: 161.850 km/h, 100.569 mph (J Clark, 1 min:27.200 sec)
Fastest Lap speed: 161.111 km/h, 100.110 mph (J Clark, 1 min:27.600 sec on lap 80)
Lap Leaders: J Clark 1-85 (85).

30 May 1965 — MONACO: Monte Carlo (Round: 2) (Race: 133)
100 laps x 3.145 km, 1.954 miles = 314.500 km, 195.421 miles

POS.	NO.	DRIVER	CAR	MODEL	ENGINE		LAPS	TIME/REASON FOR RETIREMENT	GRID:POS	ROW
1	3	G Hill	BRM	P261	BRM	V8	100	2h 37m 39.600s	1	1
2	17	L Bandini	Ferrari	1512	Ferrari	F12	100	2h 38m 43.600s	4	2
3	4	J Stewart	BRM	P261	BRM	V8	100	2h 39m 21.500s	3	2
4r	18	J Surtees	Ferrari	158	Ferrari	V8	99	out of fuel	5	3
5	7	B McLaren	Cooper	T77	Climax	V8	98		7	4
6	14	J Siffert	Brabham	BT11	BRM	V8	98		10	5
7	12	J Bonnier	Brabham	BT7	Climax	V8	97		13	7
8	2	D Hulme	Brabham	BT7	Climax	V8	92		8	4
9	9	B Anderson	Brabham	BT11	Climax	V8	85		9	5
10r	10	P Hawkins	Lotus	33	Climax	V8	79	accident	14	7
r	1	J Brabham	Brabham	BT11	Climax	V8	43	engine	2	1
r	15	D Attwood	Lotus	25	BRM	V8	43	accident	6	3
r	19	R Bucknum	Honda	RA272	Honda	V12	33	gear linkage	15	8
r	11	F Gardner	Brabham	BT11	BRM	V8	29	engine mounting	11	6
r	16	M Hailwood	Lotus	25	BRM	V8	11	gearbox	12	6
r	20	R Ginther	Honda	RA272	Honda	V12	1	drive shaft	16	8
nq	8	J Rindt	Cooper	T77	Climax	V8				

Winning speed: 119.688 km/h, 74.371 mph
Pole Position speed: 122.400 km/h, 76.056 mph (G Hill, 1 min:32.500 sec)
Fastest Lap speed: 123.468 km/h, 76.719 mph (G Hill, 1 min:31.700 sec on lap 82)
Lap Leaders: G Hill 1-24,65-100 (60); J Stewart 25-29 (5); L Bandini 30-33,43-64 (26); J Brabham 34-42 (9).

13 Jun 1965 BELGIUM: Spa-Francorchamps (Round: 3) (Race: 134)

32 laps x 14.100 km, 8.761 miles = 451.200 km, 280.363 miles

POS.	NO.	DRIVER	CAR	MODEL	ENGINE		LAPS	TIME/REASON FOR RETIREMENT	GRID:POS	ROW
1	17	J Clark	Lotus	33	Climax	V8	32	2h 23m 34.800s	2	1
2	8	J Stewart	BRM	P261	BRM	V8	32	2h 24m 19.600s	3	1
3	4	B McLaren	Cooper	T77	Climax	V8	31		9	4
4	14	J Brabham	Brabham	BT11	Climax	V8	31		10	4
5	7	G Hill	BRM	P261	BRM	V8	31		1	1
6	10	R Ginther	Honda	RA272	Honda	V12	31		4	2
7	18	M Spence	Lotus	33	Climax	V8	31		12	5
8	21	J Siffert	Brabham	BT11	BRM	V8	31		8	3
9	2	L Bandini	Ferrari	1512	Ferrari	F12	30		15	6
10	15	D Gurney	Brabham	BT11	Climax	V8	30		5	2
11	5	J Rindt	Cooper	T77	Climax	V8	29		14	6
12	27	L Bianchi	BRM	P57	BRM	V8	29		17	7
13	22	I Ireland	Lotus	25	BRM	V8	27		16	7
14r	23	D Attwood	Lotus	25	BRM	V8	26	accident/ fire	13	5
r	29	M Gregory	BRM	P57	BRM	V8	12	fuel pump/ suspension	19	8
r	11	R Bucknum	Honda	RA272	Honda	V12	9	transmission	11	5
r	20	J Bonnier	Brabham	BT7	Climax	V8	9	ignition	7	3
r	1	J Surtees	Ferrari	158	Ferrari	V8	5	ignition	6	3
r	26	F Gardner	Brabham	BT11	BRM	V8	3	ignition	18	7
ns	24	B Anderson	Brabham	BT11	Climax	V8		withdrew		
ns	28	W Mairesse	BRM	P57	BRM	V8				

Winning speed: 188.550 km/h, 117.159 mph
Pole Position speed: 225.200 km/h, 139.933 mph (G Hill, 3 min:45.400 sec)
Fastest Lap speed: 200.712 km/h, 124.716 mph (J Clark, 4 min:12.900 sec on lap 23)
Lap Leaders: J Clark 1-32 (32).

Also the Grand Prix of Europe.

27 Jun 1965 FRANCE: Clermont-Ferrand (Round: 4) (Race: 135)

40 laps x 8.055 km, 5.005 miles = 322.200 km, 200.206 miles

POS.	NO.	DRIVER	CAR	MODEL	ENGINE		LAPS	TIME/REASON FOR RETIREMENT	GRID:POS	ROW
1	6	J Clark	Lotus	25	Climax	V8	40	2h 14m 38.400s	1	1
2	12	J Stewart	BRM	P261	BRM	V8	40	2h 15m 04.700s	2	1
3	2	J Surtees	Ferrari	158	Ferrari	V8	40	2h 17m 11.900s	4	2
4	16	D Hulme	Brabham	BT11	Climax	V8	40	2h 17m 31.500s	6	3
5	10	G Hill	BRM	P261	BRM	V8	39		13	5
6	36	J Siffert	Brabham	BT11	BRM	V8	39		14	6
7	8	M Spence	Lotus	33	Climax	V8	39		10	4
8r	4	L Bandini	Ferrari	1512	Ferrari	F12	36	wheel lost/ accident	3	1
9r	30	B Anderson	Brabham	BT11	Climax	V8	34	electrics	15	6
r	18	B McLaren	Cooper	T77	Climax	V8	23	suspension/ handling	9	4
r	34	J Bonnier	Brabham	BT7	Climax	V8	21	alternator drive	11	5
r	24	C Amon	Lotus	25	BRM	V8	20	fuel injection	8	3
r	22	I Ireland	Lotus	25	BRM	V8	18	gearbox	17	7
r	14	D Gurney	Brabham	BT11	Climax	V8	16	engine	5	2
r	26	R Ginther	Honda	RA272	Honda	V12	9	ignition	7	3
r	28	R Bucknum	Honda	RA272	Honda	V12	4	ignition	16	7
r	20	J Rindt	Cooper	T77	Climax	V8	3	accident	12	5

Winning speed: 143.583 km/h, 89.218 mph
Pole Position speed: 146.233 km/h, 90.865 mph (J Clark, 3 min:18.300 sec)
Fastest Lap speed: 145.792 km/h, 90.591 mph (J Clark, 3 min:18.900 sec on lap 34)
Lap Leaders: J Clark 1-40 (40).

10 Jul 1965 BRITAIN: Silverstone (Round: 5) (Race: 136)

80 laps x 4.711 km, 2.927 miles = 376.844 km, 234.160 miles

POS.	NO.	DRIVER	CAR	MODEL	ENGINE		LAPS	TIME/REASON FOR RETIREMENT	GRID:POS	ROW
1	5	J Clark	Lotus	33	Climax	V8	80	2h 05m 25.400s	1	1
2	3	G Hill	BRM	P261	BRM	V8	80	2h 05m 28.600s	2	1
3	1	J Surtees	Ferrari	1512	Ferrari	F12	80	2h 05m 53.000s	5	2
4	6	M Spence	Lotus	33	Climax	V8	80	2h 06m 05.000s	6	2
5	4	J Stewart	BRM	P261	BRM	V8	80	2h 06m 40.000s	4	1
6	7	D Gurney	Brabham	BT11	Climax	V8	79		7	2
7	15	J Bonnier	Brabham	BT7	Climax	V8	79		14	4
8	17	F Gardner	Brabham	BT11	BRM	V8	78		13	4
9	16	J Siffert	Brabham	BT11	BRM	V8	78		18	5
10	9	B McLaren	Cooper	T77	Climax	V8	77		11	3
11	24	I Raby	Brabham	BT3	BRM	V8	73		20	6
12	12	M Gregory	BRM	P57	BRM	V8	70		19	6
13	22	D Attwood	Lotus	25	BRM	V8	63		16	5
14r	10	J Rindt	Cooper	T77	Climax	V8	63	engine	12	4
r	23	I Ireland	Lotus	25	BRM	V8	41	engine	15	5
r	20	J Rhodes	Cooper	T60	Climax	V8	38	ignition	21	6
r	18	B Anderson	Brabham	BT11	Climax	V8	33	gearbox	17	5
r	14	D Hulme	Brabham	BT7	Climax	V8	29	alternator belt	10	3
r	11	R Ginther	Honda	RA272	Honda	V12	26	ignition	3	1
r	2	L Bandini	Ferrari	158	Ferrari	V8	2	piston	9	3
ns	7	J Brabham	Brabham	BT11	Climax	V8		car raced by Gurney	8	3

POS.	NO.	DRIVER	CAR	MODEL	ENGINE		LAPS	TIME/REASON FOR RETIREMENTGRID:POS	ROW
ns	24	C Amon	Brabham	BT3	BRM	V8		car raced by Raby	
nq	25	A Rolli	nson	Cooper	T71/73	Ford	4		
nq	26	B Gubby	Lotus	24	Climax	V8			

Winning speed: 180.275 km/h, 112.017 mph
Pole Position speed: 186.762 km/h, 116.048 mph (J Clark, 1 min:30.800 sec)
Fastest Lap speed: 183.926 km/h, 114.286 mph (G Hill, 1 min:32.200 sec on lap 80)
Lap Leaders: J Clark 1-80 (80).

18 Jul 1965 — NETHERLANDS: Zandvoort (Round: 6) (Race: 137)

80 laps x 4.193 km, 2.605 miles = 335.440 km, 208.433 miles

POS.	NO.	DRIVER	CAR	MODEL	ENGINE		LAPS	TIME/REASON FOR RETIREMENT	GRID:POS	ROW
1	6	J Clark	Lotus	33	Climax	V8	80	2h 03m 59.100s	2	1
2	12	J Stewart	BRM	P261	BRM	V8	80	2h 04m 07.100s	6	3
3	16	D Gurney	Brabham	BT11	Climax	V8	80	2h 04m 12.100s	5	2
4	10	G Hill	BRM	P261	BRM	V8	80	2h 04m 44.200s	1	1
5	14	D Hulme	Brabham	BT11	Climax	V8	79		7	3
6	22	R Ginther	Honda	RA272	Honda	V12	79		3	1
7	2	J Surtees	Ferrari	1512	Ferrari	F12	79		4	2
8	8	M Spence	Lotus	25	Climax	V8	79		8	3
9	4	L Bandini	Ferrari	158	Ferrari	V8	79		12	5
10	38	I Ireland	Lotus	25	BRM	V8	78		13	5
11	30	F Gardner	Brabham	BT11	BRM	V8	77		11	5
12	34	D Attwood	Lotus	25	BRM	V8	77		17	7
13	28	J Siffert	Brabham	BT11	BRM	V8	55		10	4
r	20	J Rindt	Cooper	T77	Climax	V8	48	oil pressure	14	6
r	18	B McLaren	Cooper	T77	Climax	V8	36	crown wheel & pinion	9	4
r	26	J Bonnier	Brabham	BT7	Climax	V8	16	ignition/ fuel system	15	6
r	36	B Anderson	Brabham	BT11	Climax	V8	11	engine overheating	16	7

Winning speed: 162.329 km/h, 100.867 mph
Pole Position speed: 166.426 km/h, 103.412 mph (G Hill, 1 min:30.700 sec)
Fastest Lap speed: 166.609 km/h, 103.526 mph (J Clark, 1 min:30.600 sec on lap 5)
Lap Leaders: R Ginther 1-2 (2); G Hill 3-5 (3); J Clark 6-80 (75).

1 Aug 1965 — GERMANY: Nürburgring (Round: 7) (Race: 138)

15 laps x 22.810 km, 14.173 miles = 342.150 km, 212.602 miles

POS.	NO.	DRIVER	CAR	MODEL	ENGINE		LAPS	TIME/REASON FOR RETIREMENT	GRID:POS	ROW
1	1	J Clark	Lotus	33	Climax	V8	15	2h 07m 52.400s	1	1
2	9	G Hill	BRM	P261	BRM	V8	15	2h 08m 08.300s	3	1
3	5	D Gurney	Brabham	BT11	Climax	V8	15	2h 08m 13.800s	5	2
4	12	J Rindt	Cooper	T77	Climax	V8	15	2h 11m 22.000s	8	3
5	4	J Brabham	Brabham	BT11	Climax	V8	15	2h 12m 33.600s	14	4
6	8	L Bandini	Ferrari	158	Ferrari	V8	15	2h 13m 01.000s	7	2
7	16	J Bonnier	Brabham	BT7	Climax	V8	15	2h 13m 50.900s	9	3
8	24	M Gregory	BRM	P57	BRM	V8	14		18	5
r	7	J Surtees	Ferrari	1512	Ferrari	F12	11	gearbox	4	1
r	17	J Siffert	Brabham	BT11	BRM	V8	9	engine	11	3
r	3	G Mitter	Lotus	25	Climax	V8	8	water leak	12	4
r	2	M Spence	Lotus	33	Climax	V8	8	drive shaft	6	2
r	20	D Attwood	Lotus	25	BRM	V8	7	water leak	16	5
r	11	B McLaren	Cooper	T77	Climax	V8	7	gear selection	10	3
r	6	D Hulme	Brabham	BT7	Climax	V8	5	fuel leak	13	4
r	22	P Hawkins	Lotus	33	Climax	V8	4	oil leak	19	6
r	19	C Amon	Lotus	25	BRM	V8	3	ignition	15	5
r	10	J Stewart	BRM	P261	BRM	V8	2	suspension	2	1
r	21	F Gardner	Brabham	BT11	BRM	V8	0	gearbox	17	5
ns	18	B Anderson	Brabham	BT11	Climax	V8		accident		
nq	25	R Bussinello	BRM	P57	BRM	V8				
nq	23	I Raby	Brabham	BT3	BRM	V8				

Winning speed: 160.542 km/h, 99.756 mph
Pole Position speed: 163.350 km/h, 101.501 mph (J Clark, 8 min:22.700 sec)
Fastest Lap speed: 162.896 km/h, 101.219 mph (J Clark, 8 min:24.100 sec on lap 10)
Lap Leaders: J Clark 1-15 (15).

12 Sep 1965 — ITALY: Monza — (Round: 8) (Race: 139)

76 laps x 5.750 km, 3.573 miles = 437.000 km, 271.539 miles

POS.	NO.	DRIVER	CAR	MODEL	ENGINE		LAPS	TIME/REASON FOR RETIREMENT	GRID:POS	ROW
1	32	J Stewart	BRM	P261	BRM	V8	76	2h 04m 52.800s	3	1
2	30	G Hill	BRM	P261	BRM	V8	76	2h 04m 56.100s	4	2
3	12	D Gurney	Brabham	BT11	Climax	V8	76	2h 05m 09.300s	9	4
4	4	L Bandini	Ferrari	1512	Ferrari	F12	76	2h 06m 08.700s	5	2
5	16	B McLaren	Cooper	T77	Climax	V8	75		11	5
6	40	D Attwood	Lotus	25	BRM	V8	75		13	5
7	42	J Bonnier	Brabham	BT7	Climax	V8	74		14	6
8	18	J Rindt	Cooper	T77	Climax	V8	74		7	3
9	38	I Ireland	Lotus	25	BRM	V8	74		18	7
10r	24	J Clark	Lotus	33	Climax	V8	63	fuel pump	1	1
11r	26	M Spence	Lotus	33	Climax	V8	62	ignition	8	3
12r	6	N Vaccarella	Ferrari	158	Ferrari	V8	58	engine	15	6
13r	50	R Bussinello	BRM	P57	BRM	V8	58	oil pressure	21	9
14r	20	R Ginther	Honda	RA272	Honda	V12	56	ignition	17	7
r	14	D Hulme	Brabham	BT11	Climax	V8	46	suspension	12	5
r	46	F Gardner	Brabham	BT11	BRM	V8	45	engine	16	7
r	44	J Siffert	Brabham	BT11	BRM	V8	43	gearbox	10	4
r	28	Geki	Lotus	25	Climax	V8	37	crown wheel & pinion	20	8
r	8	J Surtees	Ferrari	1512	Ferrari	F12	34	clutch	2	1
r	22	R Bucknum	Honda	RA272	Honda	V12	27	engine	6	3
r	48	M Gregory	BRM	P57	BRM	V8	22	gearbox	23	9
r	10	G Baghetti	Brabham	BT7	Climax	V8	12	connecting rod	19	8
r	52	G Bassi	BRM	P57	BRM	V8	8	engine	22	9

Winning speed: 209.962 km/h, 130.464 mph
Pole Position speed: 215.850 km/h, 134.123 mph (J Clark, 1 min:35.900 sec)
Fastest Lap speed: 214.730 km/h, 133.427 mph (J Clark, 1 min:36.400 sec on lap 46)
Lap Leaders: J Clark 1-2,4,7,10,18,21,27,33-36,38,44,46,51,53-54,57 (19); G Hill 3,5,25-26,28,40-41,43,45,50,55-56, 64,70-71,73,74 (17); J Stewart 6,8-9,11-17,19-20,22-24,29-32,37,39,42,47-49,52,58-63,65-69,72,75-76 (40).

3 Oct 1965 — USA: Watkins Glen — (Round: 9) (Race: 140)

110 laps x 3.701 km, 2.300 miles = 407.164 km, 253.000 miles

POS.	NO.	DRIVER	CAR	MODEL	ENGINE		LAPS	TIME/REASON FOR RETIREMENT	GRID:POS	ROW
1	3	G Hill	BRM	P261	BRM	V8	110	2h 20m 36.100s	1	1
2	8	D Gurney	Brabham	BT11	Climax	V8	110	2h 20m 48.600s	8	4
3	7	J Brabham	Brabham	BT11	Climax	V8	110	2h 21m 33.600s	7	4
4	2	L Bandini	Ferrari	1512	Ferrari	F12	109		5	3
5	14	P Rodriguez	Ferrari	1512	Ferrari	F12	109		15	8
6	10	J Rindt	Cooper	T77	Climax	V8	108		13	7
7	11	R Ginther	Honda	RA272	Honda	V12	108		3	2
8	15	J Bonnier	Brabham	BT7	Climax	V8	107		10	5
9	24	B Bondurant	Ferrari	158	Ferrari	V8	106		14	7
10	21	D Attwood	Lotus	25	BRM	V8	101		16	8
11	16	J Siffert	Brabham	BT11	BRM	V8	99		11	6
12	18	M Solana	Lotus	25	Climax	V8	95		17	9
13	12	R Bucknum	Honda	RA272	Honda	V12	92		12	6
r	4	J Stewart	BRM	P261	BRM	V8	12	front suspension	6	3
r	9	B McLaren	Cooper	T77	Climax	V8	11	oil pressure	9	5
r	5	J Clark	Lotus	33	Climax	V8	11	engine	2	1
r	22	I Ireland	Lotus	25	BRM	V8	9	driver ill (influenza)	18	9
r	6	M Spence	Lotus	33	Climax	V8	9	engine	4	2

Winning speed: 173.752 km/h, 107.965 mph
Pole Position speed: 187.023 km/h, 116.211 mph (G Hill, 1 min:11.250 sec)
Fastest Lap speed: 185.332 km/h, 115.160 mph (G Hill, 1 min:11.900 sec on lap 105)
Lap Leaders: G Hill 1,5-110 (107); J Clark 2-4 (3).

24 Oct 1965	MEXICO: Mexico City	(Round:10) (Race: 141)
	65 laps x 5.000 km, 3.107 miles = 325.000 km, 201.946 miles	

POS.	NO.	DRIVER	CAR	MODEL	ENGINE		LAPS	TIME/REASON FOR RETIREMENT	GRID:POS	ROW
1	11	R Ginther	Honda	RA272	Honda	V12	65	2h 08m 32.100s	3	2
2	8	D Gurney	Brabham	BT11	Climax	V8	65	2h 08m 34.990s	2	1
3	6	M Spence	Lotus	33	Climax	V8	65	2h 09m 32.250s	6	3
4	16	J Siffert	Brabham	BT11	BRM	V8	65	2h 10m 26.520s	11	6
5	12	R Bucknum	Honda	RA272	Honda	V12	64		10	5
6	21	D Attwood	Lotus	25	BRM	V8	64		16	8
7	14	P Rodriguez	Ferrari	1512	Ferrari	F12	62		13	7
8	2	L Bandini	Ferrari	1512	Ferrari	F12	62		7	4
r	3	G Hill	BRM	P261	BRM	V8	56	engine	5	3
r	18	M Solana	Lotus	25	Climax	V8	55	ignition	9	5
r	15	J Bonnier	Brabham	BT7	Climax	V8	43	suspension	12	6
r	10	J Rindt	Cooper	T77	Climax	V8	39	ignition	15	8
r	7	J Brabham	Brabham	BT11	Climax	V8	38	oil leak	4	2
r	4	J Stewart	BRM	P261	BRM	V8	35	clutch	8	4
r	22	B Bondurant	Lotus	33	BRM	V8	29	rear suspension	17	9
r	9	B McLaren	Cooper	T77	Climax	V8	25	gear selection	14	7
r	5	J Clark	Lotus	33	Climax	V8	8	engine	1	1
ns	24	L Scarfiotti	Ferrari	1512	Ferrari	F12		car raced by Rodriguez		
ns	22	I Ireland	Lotus	25	BRM	V8		dismissed by team		

Winning speed: 151.710 km/h, 94.268 mph
Pole Position speed: 154.945 km/h, 96.279 mph (J Clark, 1 min:56.170 sec)
Fastest Lap speed: 155.387 km/h, 96.553 mph (D Gurney, 1 min:55.840 sec on lap 57)
Lap Leaders: R Ginther 1-65 (65).

Lap Leaders 1965

POS	DRIVER	CAR-ENGINE	GPS	LAPS	KM	MILES
1	J Clark	Lotus-Climax	8	349	2,260.5	1,404.6
2	G Hill	BRM	4	187	695.0	431.9
3	R Ginther	Honda	2	67	333.4	207.2
4	J Stewart	BRM	2	45	245.7	152.7
5	L Bandini	Ferrari	1	26	81.8	50.8
6	J Brabham	Brabham-Climax	1	9	28.3	17.6
			10	**683**	**3,644.7**	**2,264.7**

Driver Points 1965

		ZA	MC	B	F	GB	NL	D	I	USA	MEX	TOTAL	
1	J Clark	9	-	9	9	9	9	9	-	-	-	54	
2	G Hill	4	9	(2)	(2)	6	(3)	6	6	9	-	40	(7)
3	J Stewart	(1)	4	6	6	2	6	-	9	-	-	33	(1)
4	D Gurney	-	-	-	-	1	4	4	4	6	6	25	
5	J Surtees	6	3	-	4	4	-	-	-	-	-	17	
6	L Bandini	-	6	-	-	-	-	1	3	3	-	13	
7	R Ginther	-	-	1	-	-	1	-	-	-	9	11	
8	M Spence	3	-	-	-	3	-	-	-	-	4	10	
	B McLaren	2	2	4	-	-	-	-	2	-	-	10	
10	J Brabham	-	-	3	-	-	-	2	-	4	-	9	
11	D Hulme	-	-	-	3	-	2	-	-	-	-	5	
	J Siffert	-	1	-	1	-	-	-	-	-	3	5	
13	J Rindt	-	-	-	-	-	-	3	-	1	-	4	
14	P Rodriguez	-	-	-	-	-	-	-	-	2	-	2	
	R Bucknum	-	-	-	-	-	-	-	-	-	2	2	
	D Attwood	-	-	-	-	-	-	-	1	-	1	2	

9, 6, 4, 3, 2 and 1 point awarded to the first six finishers. Best 6 scores.

Constructor Points 1965

		ZA	MC	B	F	GB	NL	D	I	USA	MEX	TOTAL	
1	Lotus-Climax	9	-	9	9	9	9	9	-	-	(4)	54	(4)
2	BRM	(4)	9	6	6	6	(6)	(6)	9	9	-	45	(16)
3	Brabham-Climax	-	-	3	(3)	(1)	4	4	4	6	6	27	(4)
4	Ferrari	6	6	-	4	4	-	(1)	3	3	-	26	(1)
5	Cooper-Climax	2	2	4	-	-	-	3	2	1	-	14	
6	Honda	-	-	1	-	-	1	-	-	-	9	11	
7	Brabham-BRM	-	1	-	1	-	-	-	-	-	3	5	
8	Lotus-BRM	-	-	-	-	-	-	-	1	-	1	2	

9, 6, 4, 3, 2 and 1 point awarded to the first six finishers. Points only for highest placed car. Best 6 scores.

The long awaited return to power started with a splutter, with many teams unable to field the new 3 litre engine. Yet again, most of the British teams were unprepared while Ferrari race-readied their sports car engine. Their season was disrupted when Surtees walked out and joined Cooper. BRM introduced another complicated engine design with the unique H16, while Brabham went in the other direction with the simple and reliable Repco units. Firestone entered Grand Prix racing. Giuseppe Farina was killed in a road accident, en route to the French GP. A rule was introduced which required cars to complete 90% of the race distance (rounded down) to be classified.

FERRARI
Scuderia Ferrari SpA SEFAC: Bandini, Surtees, Parkes, Scarfiotti
Reg Parnell Racing Ltd: Baghetti

BRABHAM
Brabham Racing Organisation: Brabham, Hulme, Irwin
R. R. C. Walker Racing Team: Siffert
DW Racing Enterprises: Anderson
David Bridges: J Taylor
Joakim Bonnier Racing Team: Bonnier
Privateer: (Amon)

BRM
Owen Racing Organisation: G Hill, Stewart
Team Chamaco-Collect: Bondurant, (Wilson)
Bernard White Racing: Ireland

COOPER
Cooper Car Co: Rindt, Surtees, Ginther, Amon, Solana
Joakim Bonnier Racing Team: Bonnier
R. R. C. Walker Racing Team: Siffert
J A Pearce Engineering Ltd: Lawrence
Privateer: Ligier

LOTUS
Team Lotus: Clark, Arundell, Rodriguez, Geki
Reg Parnell Racing Ltd: Spence, (Baghetti)

McLAREN
Bruce McLaren Motor Racing: McLaren

SHANNON
Shannon Racing Cars: T Taylor

EAGLE
Anglo American Racers: Gurney, Bondurant, (P Hill)

HONDA
Honda R & D Co: Ginther, Bucknum

(Entries for the F2 section are not included)

22 May 1966 — MONACO: Monte Carlo (Round: 1) (Race: 142)
100 laps x 3.145 km, 1.954 miles = 314.500 km, 195.421 miles

POS.	NO.	DRIVER	CAR	MODEL	ENGINE		LAPS	TIME/REASON FOR RETIREMENT	GRID:POS	ROW
1	12	J Stewart	BRM	P261	BRM	V8	100	2h 33m 10.500s	3	2
2	16	L Bandini	Ferrari	246	Ferrari	V6	100	2h 33m 50.700s	5	3
3	11	G Hill	BRM	P261	BRM	V8	99		4	2
4	19	B Bondurant	BRM	P261	BRM	V8	95		16	8
r	9	R Ginther	Cooper	T81	Maserati	V12	80	drive shaft	9	5
nc	21	G Ligier	Cooper	T81	Maserati	V12	75		15	8
nc	18	J Bonnier	Cooper	T81	Maserati	V12	73		14	7
r	4	J Clark	Lotus	33	Climax	V8	60	rear suspension	1	1
r	10	J Rindt	Cooper	T81	Maserati	V12	56	engine	7	4
r	14	J Siffert	Brabham	BT11	BRM	V8	35	clutch	13	7
r	6	M Spence	Lotus	25	BRM	V8	34	rear suspension	12	6
r	7	J Brabham	Brabham	BT19	Repco	V8	17	gearbox	11	6
r	17	J Surtees	Ferrari	312	Ferrari	V12	16	transmission	2	1
r	8	D Hulme	Brabham	BT22	Climax	4	15	drive shaft	6	3
r	2	B McLaren	McLaren	M2B	Ford	V8	9	oil leak	10	5
r	15	B Anderson	Brabham	BT11	Climax	4	3	engine	8	4

Winning speed: 123.192 km/h, 76.548 mph
Pole Position speed: 125.940 km/h, 78.255 mph (J Clark, 1 min:29.900 sec)
Fastest Lap speed: 126.080 km/h, 78.343 mph (L Bandini, 1 min:29.800 sec on lap 90)
Lap Leaders: J Surtees 1-14 (14); J Stewart 15-100 (86).

12 Jun 1966 — BELGIUM: Spa-Francorchamps (Round: 2) (Race: 143)
28 laps x 14.100 km, 8.761 miles = 394.800 km, 245.317 miles

POS.	NO.	DRIVER	CAR	MODEL	ENGINE		LAPS	TIME/REASON FOR RETIREMENT	GRID:POS	ROW
1	6	J Surtees	Ferrari	312	Ferrari	V12	28	2h 09m 11.300s	1	1
2	19	J Rindt	Cooper	T81	Maserati	V12	28	2h 09m 53.400s	2	1
3	7	L Bandini	Ferrari	246	Ferrari	V6	27		5	2
4	3	J Brabham	Brabham	BT19	Repco	V8	26		4	2
5	18	R Ginther	Cooper	T81	Maserati	V12	25		8	3
nc	22	G Ligier	Cooper	T81	Maserati	V12	24		12	5
nc	27	D Gurney	Eagle	T1G	Climax	4	23		15	6
r	24	B Bondurant	BRM	P261	BRM	V8	0	accident	11	5
r	20	J Bonnier	Cooper	T81	Maserati	V12	0	accident	6	3
r	10	J Clark	Lotus	33	Climax	V8	0	accident	10	4
r	14	G Hill	BRM	P261	BRM	V8	0	accident	9	4
r	4	D Hulme	Brabham	BT22	Climax	4	0	accident	13	5
r	21	J Siffert	Cooper	T81	Maserati	V12	0	engine	14	6
r	16	M Spence	Lotus	25	BRM	V8	0	accident	7	3
r	15	J Stewart	BRM	P261	BRM	V8	0	accident	3	1
ns	24	B McLaren	McLaren	M2B	Serenissima	V8		bearings		
ns	8	V Wilson	BRM	P261	BRM	V8		car raced by Bondurant		
ns	11	P Arundell	Lotus	43	BRM	H16		engine		

Winning speed: 183.360 km/h, 113.935 mph
Pole Position speed: 232.844 km/h, 144.683 mph (J Surtees, 3 min:38.000 sec)
Fastest Lap speed: 196.212 km/h, 121.920 mph (J Surtees, 4 min:18.700 sec on lap 18)
Lap Leaders: J Surtees 1,3,24-28 (7); L Bandini 2 (1); J Rindt 4-23 (20).

P Hill was present in a camera car - McLaren-Ford V8 (28). B Bondurant changed his number on race day from number 8 due to the requirements of the MGM film 'Grand Prix'.

3 Jul 1966 — FRANCE: Reims — (Round: 3) (Race: 144)

48 laps x 8.302 km, 5.159 miles = 398.496 km, 247.614 miles

POS.	NO.	DRIVER	CAR	MODEL	ENGINE		LAPS	TIME/REASON FOR RETIREMENT	GRID:POS	ROW
1	12	J Brabham	Brabham	BT19	Repco	V8	48	1h 48m 31.300s	4	2
2	22	M Parkes	Ferrari	312	Ferrari	V12	48	1h 48m 40.800s	3	1
3	14	D Hulme	Brabham	BT20	Repco	V8	46		9	4
4	6	J Rindt	Cooper	T81	Maserati	V12	46		5	2
5	26	D Gurney	Eagle	T1G	Climax	4	45		14	6
6	44	J Taylor	Brabham	BT11	BRM	V8	45		15	6
7	36	B Anderson	Brabham	BT11	Climax	4	44		12	5
8	8	C Amon	Cooper	T81	Maserati	V12	44		7	3
nc	42	G Ligier	Cooper	T81	Maserati	V12	42		11	5
r	2	P Rodriguez	Lotus	33	Climax	V8	40	oil line	13	5
nc	20	L Bandini	Ferrari	312	Ferrari	V12	37		1	1
nc	30	J Bonnier	Brabham	BT22	Climax	4	32		17	7
r	16	G Hill	BRM	P261	BRM	V8	13	camshaft	8	3
r	38	J Siffert	Cooper	T81	Maserati	V12	10	engine overheating	6	3
r	32	M Spence	Lotus	25	BRM	V8	8	clutch	10	4
r	10	J Surtees	Cooper	T81	Maserati	V12	5	engine overheating	2	1
r	4	P Arundell	Lotus	43	BRM	H16	3	gear selection	16	7
ns	2	J Clark	Lotus	33	Climax	V8		hit in face by bird		

Winning speed: 220.322 km/h, 136.902 mph
Pole Position speed: 233.859 km/h, 145.313 mph (L Bandini, 2 min: 7.800 sec)
Fastest Lap speed: 227.625 km/h, 141.440 mph (L Bandini, 2 min:11.300 sec on lap 30)
Lap Leaders: L Bandini 1-31 (31); J Brabham 32-48 (17).

Also the Grand Prix of Europe.

16 Jul 1966 — BRITAIN: Brands Hatch — (Round: 4) (Race: 145)

80 laps x 4.265 km, 2.650 miles = 341.181 km, 212.000 miles

POS.	NO.	DRIVER	CAR	MODEL	ENGINE		LAPS	TIME/REASON FOR RETIREMENT	GRID:POS	ROW
1	5	J Brabham	Brabham	BT19	Repco	V8	80	2h 13m 13.400s	1	1
2	6	D Hulme	Brabham	BT20	Repco	V8	80	2h 13m 23.000s	2	1
3	3	G Hill	BRM	P261	BRM	V8	79		4	2
4	1	J Clark	Lotus	33	Climax	V8	79		5	2
5	11	J Rindt	Cooper	T81	Maserati	V12	79		7	3
6	14	B McLaren	McLaren	M2B	Serenissima	V8	78		13	5
7	7	C Irwin	Brabham	BT22	Climax	4	78		12	5
8	22	J Taylor	Brabham	BT11	BRM	V8	76		16	7
9	25	B Bondurant	BRM	P261	BRM	V8	76		14	6
10	19	G Ligier	Cooper	T81	Maserati	V12	75		17	7
11	24	C Lawrence	Cooper	T73	Ferrari	V12	73		19	8
nc	20	J Siffert	Cooper	T81	Maserati	V12	70		11	5
nc	21	B Anderson	Brabham	BT11	Climax	4	70		10	4
r	12	J Surtees	Cooper	T81	Maserati	V12	67	rear axle	6	3
r	18	J Bonnier	Brabham	BT7	Climax	V8	42	clutch	15	6
r	2	P Arundell	Lotus	33	BRM	V8	32	gear selection	20	8
r	4	J Stewart	BRM	P261	BRM	V8	17	engine	8	3
r	17	M Spence	Lotus	25	BRM	V8	15	oil leak	9	4
r	16	D Gurney	Eagle	T1G	Climax	4	9	engine	3	1
r	23	T Taylor	Shannon	Mk 1	Climax	V8	0	fuel tank	18	7

Winning speed: 153.658 km/h, 95.479 mph
Pole Position speed: 162.467 km/h, 100.952 mph (J Brabham, 1 min:34.500 sec)
Fastest Lap speed: 158.280 km/h, 98.351 mph (J Brabham, 1 min:37.000 sec on lap 60)
Lap Leaders: J Brabham 1-80 (80).

24 Jul 1966 — NETHERLANDS: Zandvoort — (Round: 5) (Race: 146)

90 laps x 4.193 km, 2.605 miles = 377.370 km, 234.487 miles

POS.	NO.	DRIVER	CAR	MODEL	ENGINE		LAPS	TIME/REASON FOR RETIREMENT	GRID:POS	ROW
1	16	J Brabham	Brabham	BT19	Repco	V8	90	2h 20m 32.500s	1	1
2	12	G Hill	BRM	P261	BRM	V8	89		7	3
3	6	J Clark	Lotus	33	Climax	V8	88		3	1
4	14	J Stewart	BRM	P261	BRM	V8	88		8	3
5	32	M Spence	Lotus	25	BRM	V8	87		12	5
6	2	L Bandini	Ferrari	312	Ferrari	V12	87		9	4
7	30	J Bonnier	Cooper	T81	Maserati	V12	84		13	5
8	38	J Taylor	Brabham	BT11	BRM	V8	84		17	7
9	36	G Ligier	Cooper	T81	Maserati	V12	84		16	7
r	28	J Siffert	Cooper	T81	Maserati	V12	79	engine	11	5
r	34	B Anderson	Brabham	BT11	Climax	4	73	suspension	14	6
r	24	J Surtees	Cooper	T81	Maserati	V12	44	electrics	10	4
r	18	D Hulme	Brabham	BT20	Repco	V8	37	ignition	2	1
r	8	P Arundell	Lotus	33	BRM	V8	28	ignition	15	6
r	10	D Gurney	Eagle	T1G	Climax	4	26	oil line	4	2
r	4	M Parkes	Ferrari	312	Ferrari	V12	10	accident	5	2
r	26	J Rindt	Cooper	T81	Maserati	V12	2	accident	6	3
ns	20	B McLaren	McLaren	M2B	Serenissima	V8		engine		

Winning speed: 161.107 km/h, 100.107 mph
Pole Position speed: 171.337 km/h, 106.464 mph (J Brabham, 1 min:28.100 sec)car
Fastest Lap speed: 166.609 km/h, 103.526 mph (D Hulme, 1 min:30.600 sec on lap 2)
Lap Leaders: J Brabham 1-26,76-90 (41); J Clark 27-75 (49).

7 Aug 1966 — GERMANY: Nürburgring — (Round: 6) (Race: 147)

15 laps x 22.810 km, 14.173 miles = 342.150 km, 212.602 miles

POS.	NO.	DRIVER	CAR	MODEL	ENGINE		LAPS	TIME/REASON FOR RETIREMENT	GRID:POS	ROW
1	3	J Brabham	Brabham	BT19	Repco	V8	15	2h 27m 03.000s	5	2
2	7	J Surtees	Cooper	T81	Maserati	V12	15	2h 27m 47.400s	2	1
3	8	J Rindt	Cooper	T81	Maserati	V12	15	2h 29m 35.600s	9	3
4	5	G Hill	BRM	P261	BRM	V8	15	2h 33m 44.400s	10	3
5	6	J Stewart	BRM	P261	BRM	V8	15	2h 35m 31.900s	3	1
6	9	L Bandini	Ferrari	312	Ferrari	V12	15	2h 37m 59.400s	6	2
7	12	D Gurney	Eagle	T1G	Climax	4	14		8	3
8	34	J-P Beltoise	* Matra	MS5	Cosworth	4	14	(1st F2 section)	18	5
9	26	H Hahne	* Matra	MS5	BRM	4	14		27	8
10	33	J Schlesser	* Matra	MS5	Cosworth	4	14		19	6
11	28	H Herrmann	* Brabham	BT18	Cosworth	4	14		22	7
12	2	P Arundell	Lotus	33	BRM	V8	14	(8th F1 section)	17	5
r	15	M Spence	Lotus	25	BRM	V8	12	alternator	13	4
r	1	J Clark	Lotus	33	Climax	V8	11	accident	1	1
r	20	C Lawrence	Cooper	T73	Ferrari	V12	10	suspension	26	8
r	11	L Scarfiotti	Ferrari	246	Ferrari	V6	9	electrics	4	1
r	10	M Parkes	Ferrari	312	Ferrari	V12	9	accident	7	2
r	4	D Hulme	Brabham	BT20	Repco	V8	8	ignition	15	5
r	31	P Rodriguez	* Lotus	44	Cosworth	4	7	engine	20	6
r	29	A Rees	* Brabham	BT18	Cosworth	4	4	engine	24	7
r	17	J Bonnier	Cooper	T81	Maserati	V12	4	clutch	12	4
r	32	P Courage	* Lotus	44	Cosworth	4	3	accident	23	7
r	14	B Bondurant	BRM	P261	BRM	V8	3	engine	11	3
r	25	K Ahrens	* Brabham	BT18	Cosworth	4	3	gearbox	21	6
r	19	B Anderson	Brabham	BT11	Climax	4	2	transmission	14	4
r	27	J Ickx	* Matra	MS5	Cosworth	4	1	accident	16	5
r	16	J Taylor	Brabham	BT11	BRM	V8	0	fatal accident	25	7
ns	35	S Moser	* Brabham	BT16	Cosworth	4		engine		
ns	30	G Mitter	* Lotus	44	Cosworth	4		driver unfit (earlier accident)		
ns	18	G Ligier	Cooper	T81	Maserati	V12		accident/ injury		

Winning speed: 139.606 km/h, 86.747 mph
Pole Position speed: 165.390 km/h, 102.768 mph (J Clark, 8 min:16.500 sec)
Fastest Lap speed: 155.229 km/h, 96.455 mph (J Surtees, 8 min:49.000 sec on lap 4)
Lap Leaders: J Brabham 1-15 (15).

*Formula 2 cars raced simultaneously with F1, and are marked thus *.*

4 Sep 1966 — ITALY: Monza — (Round: 7) (Race: 148)

68 laps x 5.750 km, 3.573 miles = 391.000 km, 242.956 miles

POS.	NO.	DRIVER	CAR	MODEL	ENGINE		LAPS	TIME/REASON FOR RETIREMENT	GRID:POS	ROW
1	6	L Scarfiotti	Ferrari	312	Ferrari	V12	68	1h 47m 14.800s	2	1
2	4	M Parkes	Ferrari	312	Ferrari	V12	68	1h 47m 20.600s	1	1
3	12	D Hulme	Brabham	BT20	Repco	V8	68	1h 47m 20.900s	10	4
4	16	J Rindt	Cooper	T81	Maserati	V12	67		8	3
5	42	M Spence	Lotus	25	BRM	V8	67		14	6
6	40	B Anderson	Brabham	BT11	Climax	4	66		15	6
7	48	B Bondurant	BRM	P261	BRM	V8	65		18	7
8r	24	P Arundell	Lotus	33	BRM	V8	63	engine	13	5
9	20	Geki	Lotus	33	Climax	V8	63		20	8
nc	44	G Baghetti	Ferrari	246	Ferrari	V6	59		16	7
r	22	J Clark	Lotus	43	BRM	H16	58	gearbox	3	1
r	36	J Siffert	Cooper	T81	Maserati	V12	46	engine	17	7
r	2	L Bandini	Ferrari	312	Ferrari	V12	33	ignition	5	2
r	14	J Surtees	Cooper	T81	Maserati	V12	31	fuel leak	4	2
r	18	R Ginther	Honda	RA273	Honda	V12	16	tyre/ accident	7	3
r	30	D Gurney	Eagle	T1G	Weslake	V12	7	engine	19	8
r	10	J Brabham	Brabham	BT19	Repco	V8	7	oil leak	6	3
r	28	J Stewart	BRM	P83	BRM	H16	5	fuel leak	9	4
r	38	J Bonnier	Cooper	T81	Maserati	V12	3	throttle linkage	12	5
r	26	G Hill	BRM	P83	BRM	H16	0	camshaft	11	5
nq	34	P Hill	Eagle	T1G	Climax	4				
nq	32	C Amon	Brabham	BT11	BRM	V8				

Winning speed: 218.748 km/h, 135.924 mph
Pole Position speed: 226.725 km/h, 140.880 mph (M Parkes, 1 min:31.300 sec)
Fastest Lap speed: 224.026 km/h, 139.203 mph (L Scarfiotti, 1 min:32.400 sec on lap 49)
Lap Leaders: L Bandini 1 (1); M Parkes 2,8-10,12,27 (6); J Brabham 4-7 (4); J Surtees 3 (1); D Hulme 11 (1); L Scarfiotti 13-26,28-68 (55).

G Baghetti also practiced in a Lotus 25-BRM V8, but after an engine failure, was loaned a Ferrari for the race.

2 Oct 1966 — USA: Watkins Glen (Round: 8) (Race: 149)

108 laps x 3.701 km, 2.300 miles = 399.761 km, 248.400 miles

POS.	NO.	DRIVER	CAR	MODEL	ENGINE		LAPS	TIME/REASON FOR RETIREMENT	GRID:POS	ROW
1	1	J Clark	Lotus	43	BRM	H16	108	2h 09m 40.100s	2	1
2	8	J Rindt	Cooper	T81	Maserati	V12	107		9	5
3	7	J Surtees	Cooper	T81	Maserati	V12	107		4	2
4	19	J Siffert	Cooper	T81	Maserati	V12	105		13	7
5	17	B McLaren	McLaren	M2B	Ford	V8	105		11	6
6	2	P Arundell	Lotus	33	Climax	V8	101		19	10
r	10	I Ireland	BRM	P261	BRM	V8	96	alternator	17	9
nc	12	R Ginther	Honda	RA273	Honda	V12	81		8	4
r	18	M Spence	Lotus	25	BRM	V8	74	ignition	12	6
r	14	R Bucknum	Honda	RA273	Honda	V12	58	transmission	18	9
nc	22	J Bonnier	Cooper	T81	Maserati	V12	57		15	8
r	5	J Brabham	Brabham	BT20	Repco	V8	55	engine	1	1
r	4	J Stewart	BRM	P83	BRM	H16	53	engine	6	3
r	3	G Hill	BRM	P83	BRM	H16	52	crown wheel & pinion	5	3
r	9	L Bandini	Ferrari	312	Ferrari	V12	34	engine	3	2
r	6	D Hulme	Brabham	BT20	Repco	V8	18	oil pressure	7	4
r	15	D Gurney	Eagle	T1G	Weslake	V12	13	clutch	14	7
r	11	P Rodriguez	Lotus	33	BRM	V8	13	starter	10	5
dq	16	B Bondurant	Eagle	T1G	Climax	4	5	push start	16	8

Winning speed: 184.977 km/h, 114.939 mph
Pole Position speed: 194.758 km/h, 121.017 mph (J Brabham, 1 min: 8.420 sec)
Fastest Lap speed: 191.264 km/h, 118.846 mph (J Surtees, 1 min: 9.670 sec on lap 31)
Lap Leaders: L Bandini 1-9,20-34 (24); J Brabham 10-19,35-55 (31); J Clark 56-108 (53).

23 Oct 1966 — MEXICO: Mexico City (Round: 9) (Race: 150)

65 laps x 5.000 km, 3.107 miles = 325.000 km, 201.946 miles

POS.	NO.	DRIVER	CAR	MODEL	ENGINE		LAPS	TIME/REASON FOR RETIREMENT	GRID:POS	ROW
1	7	J Surtees	Cooper	T81	Maserati	V12	65	2h 06m 35.340s	1	1
2	5	J Brabham	Brabham	BT20	Repco	V8	65	2h 06m 43.220s	4	2
3	6	D Hulme	Brabham	BT20	Repco	V8	64		6	3
4	12	R Ginther	Honda	RA273	Honda	V12	64		3	2
5	15	D Gurney	Eagle	T1G	Climax	4	64		9	5
6	22	J Bonnier	Cooper	T81	Maserati	V12	63		12	6
7	2	P Arundell	Lotus	33	BRM	V8	61		17	9
8	14	R Bucknum	Honda	RA273	Honda	V12	60		13	7
r	11	P Rodriguez	Lotus	33	Climax	V8	49	crown wheel & pinion	8	4
r	17	B McLaren	McLaren	M2B	Ford	V8	40	engine	14	7
r	19	J Siffert	Cooper	T81	Maserati	V12	33	suspension	11	6
r	8	J Rindt	Cooper	T81	Maserati	V12	32	suspension	5	3
r	10	I Ireland	BRM	P261	BRM	V8	28	transmission	16	8
r	4	J Stewart	BRM	P83	BRM	H16	26	oil leak	10	5
r	16	B Bondurant	Eagle	T1G	Weslake	V12	24	fuel injection	18	9
r	3	G Hill	BRM	P83	BRM	H16	18	engine	7	4
r	9	M Solana	Cooper	T81	Maserati	V12	9	engine overheating	15	8
r	1	J Clark	Lotus	43	BRM	H16	9	gearbox	2	1
ns	18	M Spence	Lotus	25	BRM	V8		accident		

Winning speed: 154.042 km/h, 95.717 mph
Pole Position speed: 159.039 km/h, 98.822 mph (J Surtees, 1 min:53.180 sec)
Fastest Lap speed: 158.242 km/h, 98.327 mph (R Ginther, 1 min:53.750 sec on lap 58)
Lap Leaders: R Ginther 1 (1); J Brabham 2-5 (4); J Surtees 6-65 (60).

Lap Leaders 1966

POS	DRIVER	CAR-ENGINE	GPS	LAPS	KM	MILES
1	J Brabham	Brabham-Repco	7	192	1,154.1	717.1
2	J Clark	Lotus-BRM	*1*	*53*	*196.2*	*121.9*
		Lotus-Climax	*1*	*49*	*205.6*	*127.7*
			2	102	401.6	249.5
3	J Stewart	BRM	1	86	270.5	168.1
4	J Surtees	Cooper-Maserati	*2*	*61*	*305.7*	*190.0*
		Ferrari	*2*	*21*	*142.7*	*88.7*
			4	82	448.4	278.7
5	L Bandini	Ferrari	4	57	366.0	227.4
6	L Scarfiotti	Ferrari	1	55	316.2	196.5
7	J Rindt	Cooper-Maserati	1	20	282.0	175.2
8	M Parkes	Ferrari	1	6	34.5	21.4
9	D Hulme	Brabham-Repco	1	1	5.7	3.6
	R Ginther	Honda	1	1	5.0	3.1
			9	**602**	**3,284.2**	**2,040.7**

Driver Points 1966

		MC	B	F	GB	NL	D	I	USA	MEX	TOTAL	
1	J Brabham	-	(3)	9	9	9	9	-	-	6	42	(3)
2	J Surtees	-	9	-	-	-	6	-	4	9	28	
3	J Rindt	-	6	3	(2)	-	4	3	6	-	22	(2)
4	D Hulme	-	-	4	6	-	-	4	-	4	18	
5	G Hill	4	-	-	4	6	3	-	-	-	17	
6	J Clark	-	-	-	3	4	-	-	9	-	16	
7	J Stewart	9	-	-	-	3	2	-	-	-	14	
8	M Parkes	-	-	6	-	-	-	6	-	-	12	
	L Bandini	6	4	-	-	1	1	-	-	-	12	
10	L Scarfiotti	-	-	-	-	-	-	9	-	-	9	
11	R Ginther	-	2	-	-	-	-	-	-	3	5	
12	D Gurney	-	-	2	-	-	-	-	-	2	4	
	M Spence	-	-	-	-	2	-	2	-	-	4	
14	B Bondurant	3	-	-	-	-	-	-	-	-	3	
	J Siffert	-	-	-	-	-	-	-	3	-	3	
	B McLaren	-	-	-	1	-	-	-	2	-	3	
17	J Taylor	-	-	1	-	-	-	-	-	-	1	
	B Anderson	-	-	-	-	-	-	1	-	-	1	
	P Arundell	-	-	-	-	-	-	-	1	-	1	
	J Bonnier	-	-	-	-	-	-	-	-	1	1	

9, 6, 4, 3, 2 and 1 point awarded to the first six finishers. Best 5 scores.

Constructor Points 1966

		MC	B	F	GB	NL	D	I	USA	MEX	TOTAL	
1	Brabham-Repco	-	(3)	9	9	9	9	(4)	-	6	42	(7)
2	Ferrari	6	9	6	-	1	(1)	9	-	-	31	(1)
3	Cooper-Maserati	-	6	3	(2)	-	6	(3)	6	9	30	(5)
4	BRM	9	-	-	4	6	3	-	-	-	22	
5	Lotus-BRM	-	-	-	-	2	-	2	9	-	13	
6	Lotus-Climax	-	-	-	3	4	-	-	1	-	8	
7	Eagle-Climax	-	-	2	-	-	-	-	-	2	4	
8	Honda	-	-	-	-	-	-	-	-	3	3	
9	McLaren-Ford	-	-	-	-	-	-	-	2	-	2	
10	Brabham-BRM	-	-	1	-	-	-	-	-	-	1	
	McLaren-Serenissima	-	-	-	1	-	-	-	-	-	1	
	Brabham-Climax	-	-	-	-	-	-	1	-	-	1	

9, 6, 4, 3, 2 and 1 point awarded to the first six finishers. Points only for highest placed car. Best 5 scores.

Brabham produced a similar, smaller car, still based on the spaceframe chassis. The Ford Cosworth DFV (Double Four Valve) engine made a dramatic entry to Formula 1 in the Lotus 49, winning the Dutch Grand Prix. Hill returned to Lotus, making a very strong partnership with double champion Clark. Honda turned to Lola for help and won first time out in the new car.

FERRARI
Scuderia Ferrari SpA SEFAC: Bandini, Amon, Parkes, Scarfiotti, Williams

BRABHAM
Brabham Racing Organisation: Brabham, Hulme
DW Racing Enterprises: Anderson
Scuderia Scribante: Charlton
Privateers: Botha, Ligier

BRM
Owen Racing Organisation: Stewart, Spence
Reg Parnell Racing Ltd: Irwin, Courage
Bernard White Racing: Hobbs

COOPER
Cooper Car Co: Rindt, Rodriguez, Ickx, Rees, Attwood
Rob Walker/Jack Durlacher Racing Team: Siffert
Joakim Bonnier Racing Team: Bonnier, de Adamich
Charles Vögele: Moser
Privateers: Ligier, Love, (Jones)

LOLA
Bayerische Motoren Werke AG: Hahne

LOTUS
Team Lotus: Clark, Hill, Solana, Wietzes, Baghetti
Reg Parnell Racing Ltd: Courage, Irwin
Privateer: Fisher

McLAREN
Bruce McLaren Motor Racing: McLaren

MATRA
Matra Sports: Beltoise, Servoz-Gavin

EAGLE
Anglo American Racers: Gurney, McLaren, Scarfiotti, (Ginther)
Castrol Oils Ltd: Pease

HONDA
Honda Racing: Surtees

LDS
Privateer: Tingle

(Entries for the F2 section are not included above)

2 Jan 1967 — SOUTH AFRICA: Kyalami (Round: 1) (Race: 151)

80 laps x 4.094 km, 2.544 miles = 327.534 km, 203.520 miles

POS.	NO.	DRIVER	CAR	MODEL	ENGINE		LAPS	TIME/REASON FOR RETIREMENT	GRID:POS	ROW
1	4	P Rodriguez	Cooper	T81	Maserati	V12	80	2h 05m 45.900s	4	2
2	17	J Love	Cooper	T79	Climax	4	80	2h 06m 12.300s	5	3
3	11	J Surtees	Honda	RA273	Honda	V12	79		6	3
4	2	D Hulme	Brabham	BT20	Repco	V8	78		2	1
5	14	B Anderson	Brabham	BT11	Climax	4	78		10	5
6	1	J Brabham	Brabham	BT20	Repco	V8	76		1	1
nc	19	D Charlton	Brabham	BT11	Climax	4	63		8	4
nc	20	L Botha	Brabham	BT11	Climax	4	60		17	9
r	18	S Tingle	LDS	Mk 3B	Climax	4	56	accident	14	7
r	16	P Courage	Lotus	25	BRM	V8	51	fuel system	18	9
r	9	D Gurney	Eagle	T1G	Climax	4	44	suspension	11	6
r	12	J Siffert	Cooper	T81	Maserati	V12	41	engine	16	8
r	3	J Rindt	Cooper	T81	Maserati	V12	38	engine	7	4
r	6	M Spence	BRM	P83	BRM	H16	31	oil line	13	7
r	15	J Bonnier	Cooper	T81	Maserati	V12	30	engine	12	6
r	7	J Clark	Lotus	43	BRM	H16	22	engine	3	2
r	8	G Hill	Lotus	43	BRM	H16	6	accident	15	8
r	5	J Stewart	BRM	P83	BRM	H16	2	engine	9	5

Winning speed: 156.260 km/h, 97.095 mph
Pole Position speed: 166.920 km/h, 103.719 mph (J Brabham, 1 min:28.300 sec)
Fastest Lap speed: 163.949 km/h, 101.873 mph (D Hulme, 1 min:29.900 sec on lap 3)
Lap Leaders: D Hulme 1-60 (60); J Love 61-73 (13); P Rodriguez 74-80 (7).

7 May 1967 — MONACO: Monte Carlo (Round: 2) (Race: 152)

100 laps x 3.145 km, 1.954 miles = 314.500 km, 195.421 miles

POS.	NO.	DRIVER	CAR	MODEL	ENGINE		LAPS	TIME/REASON FOR RETIREMENT	GRID:POS	ROW
1	9	D Hulme	Brabham	BT20	Repco	V8	100	2h 34m 34.300s	4	2
2	14	G Hill	Lotus	33	BRM	V8	99		8	4
3	20	C Amon	Ferrari	312	Ferrari	V12	98		14	7
4	16	B McLaren	McLaren	M4B	BRM	V8	97		10	5
5	11	P Rodriguez	Cooper	T81	Maserati	V12	96		16	8
6	5	M Spence	BRM	P83	BRM	H16	96		12	6
r	18	L Bandini	Ferrari	312	Ferrari	V12	81	fatal accident	2	1
r	6	P Courage	BRM	P261	BRM	V8	64	spin	13	7
r	12	J Clark	Lotus	33	Climax	V8	42	rear suspension	5	3
r	7	J Surtees	Honda	RA273	Honda	V12	32	engine	3	2
r	17	J Siffert	Cooper	T81	Maserati	V12	31	engine	9	5
r	10	J Rindt	Cooper	T81	Maserati	V12	14	gearbox	15	8
r	4	J Stewart	BRM	P261	BRM	V8	14	crown wheel & pinion	6	3
r	23	D Gurney	Eagle	T1G	Weslake	V12	4	fuel pump drive	7	4
r	2	J Servoz-Gavin	Matra	MS7	Cosworth	4	4	fuel injection	11	6
r	8	J Brabham	Brabham	BT19	Repco	V8	0	engine	1	1
nq	15	B Anderson	Brabham	BT11	Climax	4				
nq	1	J-P Beltoise	Matra	MS7	Cosworth	4				
nq	22	R Ginther	Eagle	T1G	Weslake	V12				

Winning speed: 122.079 km/h, 75.857 mph
Pole Position speed: 129.247 km/h, 80.310 mph (J Brabham, 1 min:27.600 sec)
Fastest Lap speed: 126.503 km/h, 78.605 mph (J Clark, 1 min:29.500 sec on lap 38)
Lap Leaders: L Bandini 1 (1); D Hulme 2-5,15-100 (90); J Stewart 6-14 (9).

4 Jun 1967 — NETHERLANDS: Zandvoort (Round: 3) (Race: 153)

90 laps x 4.193 km, 2.605 miles = 377.370 km, 234.487 miles

POS.	NO.	DRIVER	CAR	MODEL	ENGINE		LAPS	TIME/REASON FOR RETIREMENT	GRID:POS	ROW
1	5	J Clark	Lotus	49	Cosworth	V8	90	2h 14m 45.100s	8	3
2	1	J Brabham	Brabham	BT19	Repco	V8	90	2h 15m 08.700s	3	1
3	2	D Hulme	Brabham	BT20	Repco	V8	90	2h 15m 10.800s	7	3
4	3	C Amon	Ferrari	312	Ferrari	V12	90	2h 15m 12.400s	9	4
5	4	M Parkes	Ferrari	312	Ferrari	V12	89		10	4
6	22	L Scarfiotti	Ferrari	312	Ferrari	V12	89		15	6
7	18	C Irwin	Lotus	25	BRM	V8	88		13	5
8	10	M Spence	BRM	P83	BRM	H16	87		12	5
9	21	B Anderson	Brabham	BT11	Climax	4	86		17	7
10	20	J Siffert	Cooper	T81	Maserati	V12	83		16	7
r	7	J Surtees	Honda	RA273	Honda	V12	73	throttle slides	6	3
r	9	J Stewart	BRM	P83	BRM	H16	51	brakes	11	5
r	12	J Rindt	Cooper	T81B	Maserati	V12	41	suspension	4	2
r	14	P Rodriguez	Cooper	T81	Maserati	V12	39	gearbox	5	2
r	6	G Hill	Lotus	49	Cosworth	V8	11	timing gears	1	1
r	15	D Gurney	Eagle	T1G	Weslake	V12	8	fuel injection	2	1
r	17	B McLaren	McLaren	M4B	BRM	V8	1	accident	14	6

Winning speed: 168.029 km/h, 104.408 mph
Pole Position speed: 178.426 km/h, 110.868 mph (G Hill, 1 min:24.600 sec)
Fastest Lap speed: 171.376 km/h, 106.488 mph (J Clark, 1 min:28.080 sec on lap 67)
Lap Leaders: G Hill 1-10 (10); J Brabham 11-15 (5); J Clark 16-90 (75).

18 Jun 1967 — BELGIUM: Spa-Francorchamps (Round: 4) (Race: 154)

28 laps x 14.100 km, 8.761 miles = 394.800 km, 245.317 miles

POS.	NO.	DRIVER	CAR	MODEL	ENGINE		LAPS	TIME/REASON FOR RETIREMENT	GRID:POS	ROW
1	36	D Gurney	Eagle	T1G	Weslake	V12	28	1h 40m 49.400s	2	1
2	14	J Stewart	BRM	P83	BRM	H16	28	1h 41m 52.400s	6	3
3	1	C Amon	Ferrari	312	Ferrari	V12	28	1h 42m 29.400s	5	2
4	29	J Rindt	Cooper	T81B	Maserati	V12	28	1h 43m 03.300s	4	2
5	12	M Spence	BRM	P83	BRM	H16	27		11	5
6	21	J Clark	Lotus	49	Cosworth	V8	27		1	1
7	34	J Siffert	Cooper	T81	Maserati	V12	27		16	7
8	19	B Anderson	Brabham	BT11	Climax	4	26		17	7
9r	30	P Rodriguez	Cooper	T81	Maserati	V12	25	engine	13	5
10	32	G Ligier	Cooper	T81	Maserati	V12	25		18	7
nc	2	L Scarfiotti	Ferrari	312	Ferrari	V12	24		9	4
r	25	J Brabham	Brabham	BT24	Repco	V8	15	engine	7	3
r	26	D Hulme	Brabham	BT19	Repco	V8	14	engine	14	6
r	39	J Bonnier	Cooper	T81	Maserati	V12	10	fuel feed	12	5
r	22	G Hill	Lotus	49	Cosworth	V8	3	clutch	3	1
r	17	C Irwin	BRM	P261	BRM	V8	1	camshaft	15	6
r	7	J Surtees	Honda	RA273	Honda	V12	1	crankshaft	10	4
r	3	M Parkes	Ferrari	312	Ferrari	V12	0	accident	8	3

Winning speed: 234.944 km/h, 145.987 mph
Pole Position speed: 243.921 km/h, 151.566 mph (J Clark, 3 min:28.100 sec)
Fastest Lap speed: 239.547 km/h, 148.848 mph (D Gurney, 3 min:31.900 sec on lap 19)
Lap Leaders: J Clark 1-12 (12); J Stewart 13-20 (8); D Gurney 21-28 (8).

2 Jul 1967 — FRANCE: Bugatti au Mans (Round: 5) (Race: 155)

80 laps x 4.422 km, 2.748 miles = 353.760 km, 219.816 miles

POS.	NO.	DRIVER	CAR	MODEL	ENGINE		LAPS	TIME/REASON FOR RETIREMENT	GRID:POS	ROW
1	3	J Brabham	Brabham	BT24	Repco	V8	80	2h 13m 21.300s	2	1
2	4	D Hulme	Brabham	BT24	Repco	V8	80	2h 14m 10.800s	6	3
3	10	J Stewart	BRM	P261	BRM	V8	79		10	4
4	18	J Siffert	Cooper	T81	Maserati	V12	77		11	5
5r	15	C Irwin	BRM	P83	BRM	H16	76	engine	9	4
6	14	P Rodriguez	Cooper	T81	Maserati	V12	76		13	5
nc	16	G Ligier	Cooper	T81	Maserati	V12	68		15	6
r	2	C Amon	Ferrari	312	Ferrari	V12	47	throttle linkage	7	3
r	9	D Gurney	Eagle	T1G	Weslake	V12	40	fuel line	3	1
r	12	J Rindt	Cooper	T81B	Maserati	V12	33	piston	8	3
r	8	B McLaren	Eagle	T1G	Weslake	V12	26	ignition	5	2
r	6	J Clark	Lotus	49	Cosworth	V8	23	crown wheel & pinion	4	2
r	17	B Anderson	Brabham	BT11	Climax	4	16	ignition	14	6
r	7	G Hill	Lotus	49	Cosworth	V8	13	crown wheel & pinion	1	1
r	11	M Spence	BRM	P83	BRM	H16	9	transmission	12	5

Winning speed: 159.166 km/h, 98.901 mph
Pole Position speed: 165.480 km/h, 102.825 mph (G Hill, 1 min:36.200 sec)
Fastest Lap speed: 164.625 km/h, 102.293 mph (G Hill, 1 min:36.700 sec on lap 7)
Lap Leaders: G Hill 1,11-13 (4); J Brabham 2-4,24-80 (60); J Clark 5-10,14-23 (16).

15 Jul 1967 — BRITAIN: Silverstone — (Round: 6) (Race: 156)

80 laps x 4.711 km, 2.927 miles = 376.844 km, 234.160 miles

POS.	NO.	DRIVER	CAR	MODEL	ENGINE		LAPS	TIME/REASON FOR RETIREMENT	GRID:POS	ROW
1	5	J Clark	Lotus	49	Cosworth	V8	80	1h 59m 25.600s	1	1
2	2	D Hulme	Brabham	BT24	Repco	V8	80	1h 59m 38.400s	4	1
3	8	C Amon	Ferrari	312	Ferrari	V12	80	1h 59m 42.200s	6	2
4	1	J Brabham	Brabham	BT24	Repco	V8	80	1h 59m 47.400s	3	1
5	12	P Rodriguez	Cooper	T81	Maserati	V12	79		9	3
6	7	J Surtees	Honda	RA273	Honda	V12	78		7	2
7	15	C Irwin	BRM	P261	BRM	V8	77		13	4
8	20	D Hobbs	BRM	P261	BRM	V8	77		14	4
9	14	A Rees	Cooper	T81	Maserati	V12	76		15	5
10	18	G Ligier	Brabham	BT20	Repco	V8	76		21	6
r	19	B Anderson	Brabham	BT11	Climax	4	67	engine	17	5
r	6	G Hill	Lotus	49	Cosworth	V8	64	engine	2	1
r	4	M Spence	BRM	P83	BRM	H16	44	ignition	11	3
r	9	D Gurney	Eagle	T1G	Weslake	V12	34	clutch	5	2
r	22	S Moser	Cooper	T77	ATS	V8	29	oil pressure	20	6
r	11	J Rindt	Cooper	T86	Maserati	V12	26	engine	8	3
r	3	J Stewart	BRM	P83	BRM	H16	20	transmission	12	4
r	10	B McLaren	Eagle	T1G	Weslake	V12	14	engine	10	3
r	17	J Siffert	Cooper	T81	Maserati	V12	10	engine	18	5
r	23	J Bonnier	Cooper	T81	Maserati	V12	0	engine	19	6
ns	16	P Courage	BRM	P261	BRM	V8		car raced by Irwin	16	5

Winning speed: 189.327 km/h, 117.642 mph
Pole Position speed: 198.804 km/h, 123.531 mph (J Clark, 1 min:25.300 sec)
Fastest Lap speed: 194.919 km/h, 121.117 mph (D Hulme, 1 min:27.000 sec on lap 3)
Lap Leaders: J Clark 1-25,55-80 (51); G Hill 26-54 (29).

6 Aug 1967 — GERMANY: Nürburgring — (Round: 7) (Race: 157)

15 laps x 22.835 km, 14.189 miles = 342.525 km, 212.835 miles

POS.	NO.	DRIVER	CAR	MODEL	ENGINE		LAPS	TIME/REASON FOR RETIREMENT	GRID:POS	ROW
1	2	D Hulme	Brabham	BT24	Repco	V8	15	2h 05m 55.700s	2	1
2	1	J Brabham	Brabham	BT24	Repco	V8	15	2h 06m 34.200s	7	2
3	8	C Amon	Ferrari	312	Ferrari	V12	15	2h 06m 34.700s	8	3
4	7	J Surtees	Honda	RA273	Honda	V12	15	2h 08m 21.400s	6	2
5	24	J Oliver	* Lotus	48	Cosworth	4	15	2h 12m 04.900s (1st F2 section)	19	6
6	16	J Bonnier	Cooper	T81	Maserati	V12	15	2h 14m 37.800s (5th F1 section)	16	5
7	22	A Rees	* Brabham	BT23	Cosworth	4	15	2h 14m 43.600s	20	6
8	15	G Ligier	Brabham	BT20	Repco	V8	14		17	5
9	18	C Irwin	BRM	P83	BRM	H16	13		15	5
10	27	D Hobbs	* Lola	T100	BMW	4	13		22	7
11	6	P Rodriguez	Cooper	T81	Maserati	V12	13		10	3
r	9	D Gurney	Eagle	T1G	Weslake	V12	12	drive shaft	4	1
r	29	J Ickx	* Matra	MS7	Cosworth	4	12	suspension	18	6
nc	25	B Hart	* Protos		Cosworth	4	12		25	8
r	14	J Siffert	Cooper	T81	Maserati	V12	11	fuel pump	12	4
r	4	G Hill	Lotus	49	Cosworth	V8	8	rear suspension	13	4
r	17	H Hahne	Lola	T100	BMW	4	6	front suspension	14	4
r	11	J Stewart	BRM	P115	BRM	H16	5	crown wheel & pinion	3	1
r	5	J Rindt	Cooper	T86	Maserati	V12	4	steering	9	3
r	3	J Clark	Lotus	49	Cosworth	V8	4	front suspension/ puncture	1	1
r	26	K Ahrens	* Protos		Cosworth	4	4	radiator	23	7
r	10	B McLaren	Eagle	T1G	Weslake	V12	3	oil line	5	2
r	12	M Spence	BRM	P83	BRM	H16	3	crown wheel & pinion	11	3
r	23	J Schlesser	* Matra	MS5	Cosworth	4	2	clutch	21	6
r	20	G Mitter	* Brabham	BT23	Cosworth	4	0	engine	24	7
ns	28	B Redman	* Lola	T100	Cosworth	4			26	8

Winning speed: 163.200 km/h, 101.408 mph
Pole Position speed: 169.812 km/h, 105.516 mph (J Clark, 8 min: 4.100 sec)
Fastest Lap speed: 166.039 km/h, 103.172 mph (D Gurney, 8 min:15.100 sec on lap 3)
Lap Leaders: J Clark 1-3 (3); D Gurney 4-12 (9); D Hulme 13-15 (3).

*Formula 2 cars raced simultaneously with F1, and are marked thus *.*

J Oliver finished 5th, but was not eligible for points due to being in the F2 section of the race.

27 Aug 1967 — CANADA: Mosport Park — (Round: 8) (Race: 158)

90 laps x 3.957 km, 2.459 miles = 356.164 km, 221.310 miles

POS.	NO.	DRIVER	CAR	MODEL	ENGINE	LAPS		TIME/REASON FOR RETIREMENT	GRID:POS	ROW
1	1	J Brabham	Brabham	BT24	Repco	V8	90	2h 40m 40.000s	7	3
2	2	D Hulme	Brabham	BT24	Repco	V8	90	2h 41m 41.900s	3	1
3	10	D Gurney	Eagle	T1G	Weslake	V12	89		5	2
4	4	G Hill	Lotus	49	Cosworth	V8	88		2	1
5	16	M Spence	BRM	P83	BRM	H16	87		10	4
6	20	C Amon	Ferrari	312	Ferrari	V12	87		4	2
7	19	B McLaren	McLaren	M5A	BRM	V12	86		6	3
8	9	J Bonnier	Cooper	T81	Maserati	V12	85		14	6
9	12	D Hobbs	BRM	P261	BRM	V8	85		12	5
10	8	D Attwood	Cooper	T81B	Maserati	V12	84		13	5
11	6	M Fisher	Lotus	33	BRM	V8	81		17	7
r	3	J Clark	Lotus	49	Cosworth	V8	69	ignition wet	1	1
r	5	E Wietzes	Lotus	49	Cosworth	V8	69	ignition wet	16	7
r	15	J Stewart	BRM	P115	BRM	H16	65	throttle slides	9	4
nc	11	A Pease	Eagle	T1G	Climax	4	47		15	6
r	17	C Irwin	BRM	P83	BRM	H16	18	spin	11	5
r	71	J Rindt	Cooper	T81	Maserati	V12	4	ignition	8	3
ns	14	J Siffert	Cooper	T81	Maserati	V12		starter ring		
nq	41	T Jones	Cooper	T82	Climax	V8				

Winning speed: 133.007 km/h, 82.647 mph
Pole Position speed: 172.895 km/h, 107.432 mph (J Clark, 1 min:22.400 sec)
Fastest Lap speed: 171.439 km/h, 106.527 mph (J Clark, 1 min:23.100 sec on lap 54)
Lap Leaders: J Clark 1-3,58-67 (13); D Hulme 4-57 (54); J Brabham 68-90 (23).

10 Sep 1967 — ITALY: Monza — (Round: 9) (Race: 159)

68 laps x 5.750 km, 3.573 miles = 391.000 km, 242.956 miles

POS.	NO.	DRIVER	CAR	MODEL	ENGINE	LAPS		TIME/REASON FOR RETIREMENT	GRID:POS	ROW
1	14	J Surtees	Honda	RA300	Honda	V12	68	1h 43m 45.000s	9	4
2	16	J Brabham	Brabham	BT24	Repco	V8	68	1h 43m 45.200s	2	1
3	20	J Clark	Lotus	49	Cosworth	V8	68	1h 44m 08.100s	1	1
4	30	J Rindt	Cooper	T86	Maserati	V12	68	1h 44m 41.600s	11	5
5	36	M Spence	BRM	P83	BRM	H16	67		12	5
6	32	J Ickx	Cooper	T81B	Maserati	V12	66		15	6
7	2	C Amon	Ferrari	312	Ferrari	V12	64		4	2
r	22	G Hill	Lotus	49	Cosworth	V8	58	engine	8	3
r	24	G Baghetti	Lotus	49	Cosworth	V8	50	engine	17	7
r	6	J Siffert	Cooper	T81	Maserati	V12	50	accident	13	5
r	4	B McLaren	McLaren	M5A	BRM	V12	46	engine	3	1
r	26	J Bonnier	Cooper	T81	Maserati	V12	46	engine overheating	14	6
r	34	J Stewart	BRM	P115	BRM	H16	45	engine	7	3
r	18	D Hulme	Brabham	BT24	Repco	V8	30	engine overheating	6	3
r	12	G Ligier	Brabham	BT20	Repco	V8	26	valve	18	7
r	38	C Irwin	BRM	P83	BRM	H16	16	fuel injection pump drive	16	7
r	10	L Scarfiotti	Eagle	T1G	Weslake	V12	5	engine	10	4
r	8	D Gurney	Eagle	T1G	Weslake	V12	4	engine	5	2

Winning speed: 226.120 km/h, 140.505 mph
Pole Position speed: 233.898 km/h, 145.338 mph (J Clark, 1 min:28.500 sec)
Fastest Lap speed: 233.898 km/h, 145.338 mph (J Clark, 1 min:28.500 sec on lap 26)
Lap Leaders: D Gurney 1-2 (2); J Clark 3-9,11-12,61-67 (16); D Hulme 10,13-15,17,24-27 (9); J Brabham 16,59-60 (3); G Hill 18-23,28-58 (37); J Surtees 68 (1).

Also the Grand Prix of Europe.

1 Oct 1967 — USA: Watkins Glen — (Round:10) (Race: 160)

108 laps x 3.701 km, 2.300 miles = 399.761 km, 248.400 miles

POS.	NO.	DRIVER	CAR	MODEL	ENGINE	LAPS		TIME/REASON FOR RETIREMENT	GRID:POS	ROW
1	5	J Clark	Lotus	49	Cosworth	V8	108	2h 03m 13.200s	2	1
2	6	G Hill	Lotus	49	Cosworth	V8	108	2h 03m 19.500s	1	1
3	2	D Hulme	Brabham	BT24	Repco	V8	107		6	3
4	15	J Siffert	Cooper	T81	Maserati	V12	106		12	6
5	1	J Brabham	Brabham	BT24	Repco	V8	104		5	3
6	16	J Bonnier	Cooper	T81	Maserati	V12	101		15	8
7	22	J-P Beltoise	Matra	MS7	Cosworth	4	101		18	9
r	3	J Surtees	Honda	RA300	Honda	V12	96	alternator	11	6
r	9	C Amon	Ferrari	312	Ferrari	V12	95	oil pressure	4	2
r	7	J Stewart	BRM	P115	BRM	H16	72	fuel injection pump drive	10	5
r	21	J Ickx	Cooper	T86	Maserati	V12	45	engine overheating	16	8
r	19	G Ligier	Brabham	BT20	Repco	V8	43	camshaft	17	9
r	17	C Irwin	BRM	P83	BRM	H16	41	connecting rod	14	7
r	8	M Spence	BRM	P83	BRM	H16	35	engine	13	7
r	4	J Rindt	Cooper	T81B	Maserati	V12	33	engine	8	4
r	11	D Gurney	Eagle	T1G	Weslake	V12	24	rear suspension	3	2
r	14	B McLaren	McLaren	M5A	BRM	V12	16	water hose	9	5
r	18	M Solana	Lotus	49	Cosworth	V8	7	ignition	7	4

Winning speed: 194.657 km/h, 120.954 mph
Pole Position speed: 203.503 km/h, 126.451 mph (G Hill, 1 min: 5.480 sec)
Fastest Lap speed: 201.900 km/h, 125.455 mph (G Hill, 1 min: 6.000 sec on lap 81)
Lap Leaders: G Hill 1-40 (40); J Clark 41-108 (68).

22 Oct 1967 **MEXICO: Mexico City** **(Round:11) (Race: 161)**

65 laps x 5.000 km, 3.107 miles = 325.000 km, 201.946 miles

POS.	NO.	DRIVER	CAR	MODEL	ENGINE		LAPS	TIME/REASON FOR RETIREMENT	GRID:POS	ROW
1	5	J Clark	Lotus	49	Cosworth	V8	65	1h 59m 28.700s	1	1
2	1	J Brabham	Brabham	BT24	Repco	V8	65	2h 00m 54.060s	5	3
3	2	D Hulme	Brabham	BT24	Repco	V8	64		6	3
4	3	J Surtees	Honda	RA300	Honda	V12	64		7	4
5	8	M Spence	BRM	P83	BRM	H16	63		11	6
6	21	P Rodriguez	Cooper	T81B	Maserati	V12	63		13	7
7	22	J-P Beltoise	Matra	MS7	Cosworth	4	63		14	7
8	12	J Williams	Ferrari	312	Ferrari	V12	63		16	8
9	9	C Amon	Ferrari	312	Ferrari	V12	62		2	1
10	16	J Bonnier	Cooper	T81	Maserati	V12	61		17	9
11	19	G Ligier	Brabham	BT20	Repco	V8	61		19	10
12r	15	J Siffert	Cooper	T81	Maserati	V12	59	engine	10	5
r	14	B McLaren	McLaren	M5A	BRM	V12	45	oil pressure	8	4
r	17	C Irwin	BRM	P83	BRM	H16	33	oil loss	15	8
r	7	J Stewart	BRM	P115	BRM	H16	24	engine	12	6
r	6	G Hill	Lotus	49	Cosworth	V8	18	universal joint	4	2
r	18	M Solana	Lotus	49	Cosworth	V8	12	front suspension	9	5
r	11	D Gurney	Eagle	T1G	Weslake	V12	4	radiator	3	2
r	10	M Fisher	Lotus	33	BRM	V8	1	fuel metering unit	18	9

Winning speed: 163.210 km/h, 101.414 mph
Pole Position speed: 167.348 km/h, 103.986 mph (J Clark, 1 min:47.560 sec)
Fastest Lap speed: 166.466 km/h, 103.437 mph (J Clark, 1 min:48.130 sec on lap 52)
Lap Leaders: G Hill 1-2 (2); J Clark 3-65 (63).

Left: Dan Gurney driving an Eagle Weslake in the British Grand Prix 1967.

Bottom left: John Surtees in the Honda RA273 at the British Grand Prix 1967.

Lap Leaders 1967

POS	DRIVER	CAR-ENGINE	GPS	LAPS	KM	MILES
1	J Clark	Lotus-Cosworth	9	317	1,573.3	977.6
2	D Hulme	Brabham-Repco	5	216	862.6	536.0
3	G Hill	Lotus-Cosworth	6	122	567.0	352.3
4	J Brabham	Brabham-Repco	4	91	394.5	245.2
5	D Gurney	Eagle-Weslake	3	19	329.8	204.9
6	J Stewart	BRM	2	17	141.1	87.7
7	J Love	Cooper-Climax	1	13	53.2	33.1
8	P Rodriguez	Cooper-Maserati	1	7	28.7	17.8
9	J Surtees	Honda	1	1	5.7	3.6
	L Bandini	Ferrari	1	1	3.1	2.0
			11	**804**	**3,959.2**	**2,460.1**

Driver Points 1967

		ZA	MC	NL	B	F	GB	D	CDN	I	USA	MEX	TOTAL	
1	D Hulme	3	9	4	-	6	6	9	6	-	4	4	51	
2	J Brabham	1	-	6	-	9	3	6	9	6	(2)	6	46	(2)
3	J Clark	-	-	9	1	-	9	-	-	4	9	9	41	
4	J Surtees	4	-	-	-	-	1	3	-	9	-	3	20	
	C Amon	-	4	3	4	-	4	4	1	-	-	-	20	
6	P Rodriguez	9	2	-	-	1	2	-	-	-	-	1	15	
	G Hill	-	6	-	-	-	-	-	3	-	6	-	15	
8	D Gurney	-	-	-	9	-	-	-	4	-	-	-	13	
9	J Stewart	-	-	-	6	4	-	-	-	-	-	-	10	
10	M Spence	-	1	-	2	-	-	-	2	2	-	2	9	
11	J Love	6	-	-	-	-	-	-	-	-	-	-	6	
	J Rindt	-	-	-	3	-	-	-	-	3	-	-	6	
	J Siffert	-	-	-	-	3	-	-	-	-	3	-	6	
14	B McLaren	-	3	-	-	-	-	-	-	-	-	-	3	
	J Bonnier	-	-	-	-	-	-	2	-	-	1	-	3	
16	B Anderson	2	-	-	-	-	-	-	-	-	-	-	2	
	M Parkes	-	-	2	-	-	-	-	-	-	-	-	2	
	C Irwin	-	-	-	-	2	-	-	-	-	-	-	2	
19	L Scarfiotti	-	-	1	-	-	-	-	-	-	-	-	1	
	G Ligier	-	-	-	-	-	-	1	-	-	-	-	1	
	J Ickx	-	-	-	-	-	-	-	-	1	-	-	1	

9, 6, 4, 3, 2 and 1 point awarded to the first six finishers. Best 5 scores from first 6 races, best 4 from remaining 5 races.

Constructor Points 1967

		ZA	MC	NL	B	F	GB	D	CDN	I	USA	MEX	TOTAL	
1	Brabham-Repco	3	9	6	-	9	6	9	9	6	(4)	6	63	(4)
2	Lotus-Cosworth	-	-	9	1	-	9	-	3	4	9	9	44	
3	Cooper-Maserati	9	2	-	3	3	2	2	-	3	3	1	28	
4	Honda	4	-	-	-	-	1	3	-	9	-	3	20	
	Ferrari	-	4	3	4	-	4	4	1	-	-	-	20	
6	BRM	-	1	-	6	4	-	-	2	2	-	2	17	
7	Eagle-Weslake	-	-	-	9	-	-	-	4	-	-	-	13	
8	Cooper-Climax	6	-	-	-	-	-	-	-	-	-	-	6	
	Lotus-BRM	-	6	-	-	-	-	-	-	-	-	-	6	
10	McLaren-BRM	-	3	-	-	-	-	-	-	-	-	-	3	
11	Brabham-Climax	2	-	-	-	-	-	-	-	-	-	-	2	

9, 6, 4, 3, 2 and 1 point awarded to the first six finishers. Points only for highest placed car.
Best 5 scores from first 6 races, best 4 from remaining 5 races.

The Racing world was devastated with the death of Jim Clark at a minor F2 race at Hockenheim. Sponsorship arrived at the very next race in Spain, where Lotus appeared in the red and white colours of Gold Leaf cigarettes. The Cosworth engine was now made available to other teams. Aerodynamic aids appeared at the Belgian Grand Prix, initially manually operated wings.

FERRARI
Scuderia Ferrari SpA SEFAC: Amon, Ickx, Bell, de Adamich

BRABHAM
Brabham Racing Organisation: Brabham, Rindt, Gurney
Charles Vögele Racing: Moser
Caltex Racing Team Frankfurt: Ahrens
Team Gunston: Love
Scuderia Scribante: Charlton
Team Pretoria: Pretorius

BRM
Owen Racing Organisation: Rodriguez, Spence, Attwood, Unser Reg Parnell Racing Ltd: Courage
Bernard White Racing: (Gardner)

COOPER
Cooper Car Co: Scarfiotti, Bianchi, Redman, Elford, Servoz-Gavin, Widdows
Rob Walker/Jack Durlacher Racing: Siffert
Joakim Bonnier Racing Team: Bonnier
John Love: van Rooyen

LOLA
Bayerische Motoren Werke AG: Hahne

LOTUS
Team Lotus*: Clark, Hill, Oliver, Andretti, Brack, Solana * Gold Leaf Team Lotus from ZA GP
Rob Walker/Jack Durlacher Racing: Siffert

McLAREN
Bruce McLaren Motor Racing: McLaren, Hulme
Joakim Bonnier Racing Team: Bonnier
Anglo American Racers: Gurney

MATRA
Matra International: Stewart, Servoz-Gavin, Beltoise (E)
Matra Sports: Beltoise, Pescarolo

EAGLE
Anglo American Racers: Gurney
Castrol Oils Ltd: (Pease)

LDS
Team Gunston: Tingle

HONDA
Honda Racing: Surtees, Hobbs
Honda Racing (France): Schlesser
Joakim Bonnier Racing Team: Bonnier

1 Jan 1968 — SOUTH AFRICA: Kyalami (Round: 1) (Race: 162)

80 laps x 4.104 km, 2.550 miles = 328.306 km, 204.000 miles

POS.	NO.	DRIVER	CAR	MODEL	ENGINE		LAPS	TIME/REASON FOR RETIREMENT	GRID:POS	ROW
1	4	J Clark	Lotus	49	Cosworth	V8	80	1h 53m 56.600s	1	1
2	5	G Hill	Lotus	49	Cosworth	V8	80	1h 54m 21.900s	2	1
3	3	J Rindt	Brabham	BT24	Repco	V8	80	1h 54m 27.000s	4	2
4	8	C Amon	Ferrari	312	Ferrari	V12	78		8	3
5	1	D Hulme	McLaren	M5A	BRM	V12	78		9	4
6	21	J-P Beltoise	Matra	MS7	Cosworth	4	77		18	7
7	19	J Siffert	Cooper	T81	Maserati	V12	77		16	7
8	7	J Surtees	Honda	RA300	Honda	V12	75		6	3
9	17	J Love	Brabham	BT20	Repco	V8	75		17	7
nc	23	J Pretorius	Brabham	BT11	Climax	4	70		23	9
r	6	D Gurney	Eagle	T1G	Weslake	V12	58	oil leak/ engine overheating	12	5
r	9	J Ickx	Ferrari	312	Ferrari	V12	51	oil tank burst	11	5
r	20	J Bonnier	Cooper	T81	Maserati	V12	47	rear wheel lost	19	8
r	16	J Stewart	Matra	MS9	Cosworth	V8	43	connecting rod	3	1
r	18	S Tingle	LDS	Mk 3B	Repco	V8	35	engine overheating	22	9
r	25	B van Rooyen	Cooper	T79	Climax	4	22	head gasket	20	8
r	11	P Rodriguez	BRM	P126	BRM	V12	20	ignition/ boiling fuel	10	4
r	2	J Brabham	Brabham	BT24	Repco	V8	17	valve spring	5	2
r	10	A de Adamich	Ferrari	312	Ferrari	V12	13	accident	7	3
r	12	M Spence	BRM	P115	BRM	H16	8	boiling fuel	13	5
r	14	B Redman	Cooper	T81B	Maserati	V12	4	camshaft/ oil leak/ engine	21	9
r	22	D Charlton	Brabham	BT11	Repco	V8	3	crown wheel & pinion	14	6
r	15	L Scarfiotti	Cooper	T86	Maserati	V12	2	brake pipe/ accident	15	6

Winning speed: 172.879 km/h, 107.422 mph
Pole Position speed: 181.051 km/h, 112.500 mph (J Clark, 1 min:21.600 sec)
Fastest Lap speed: 176.509 km/h, 109.677 mph (J Clark, 1 min:23.700 sec on lap 73)
Lap Leaders: J Stewart 1 (1); J Clark 2-80 (79).

12 May 1968 — SPAIN: Járama (Round: 2) (Race: 163)

90 laps x 3.404 km, 2.115 miles = 306.360 km, 190.363 miles

POS.	NO.	DRIVER	CAR	MODEL	ENGINE		LAPS	TIME/REASON FOR RETIREMENT	GRID:POS	ROW
1	10	G Hill	Lotus	49	Cosworth	V8	90	2h 15m 20.100s	6	3
2	1	D Hulme	McLaren	M7A	Cosworth	V8	90	2h 15m 36.000s	3	1
3	14	B Redman	Cooper	T86B	BRM	V12	89		13	5
4	15	L Scarfiotti	Cooper	T86B	BRM	V12	89		12	5
5	6	J-P Beltoise	Matra	MS10	Cosworth	V8	81		5	2
r	2	B McLaren	McLaren	M7A	Cosworth	V8	77	oil loss	4	2
r	7	J Surtees	Honda	RA301	Honda	V12	74	gear linkage	7	3
r	16	J Siffert	Lotus	49	Cosworth	V8	62	transmission	10	4
r	19	C Amon	Ferrari	312	Ferrari	V12	57	fuel pump	1	1
r	5	P Courage	BRM	P126	BRM	V12	52	fuel metering unit	11	5
r	9	P Rodriguez	BRM	P133	BRM	V12	27	accident	2	1
r	21	J Ickx	Ferrari	312	Ferrari	V12	13	ignition	8	3
r	4	J Rindt	Brabham	BT24	Repco	V8	10	oil pressure	9	4
ns	8	J Brabham	Brabham	BT26	Repco	V8		engine		

Winning speed: 135.823 km/h, 84.396 mph
Pole Position speed: 139.413 km/h, 86.627 mph (C Amon, 1 min:27.900 sec)
Fastest Lap speed: 138.781 km/h, 86.235 mph (J-P Beltoise, 1 min:28.300 sec on lap 47)
Lap Leaders: P Rodriguez 1-11 (11); J-P Beltoise 12-15 (4); C Amon 16-57 (42); G Hill 58-90 (33).

26 May 1968 — MONACO: Monte Carlo (Round: 3) (Race: 164)

80 laps x 3.145 km, 1.954 miles = 251.600 km, 156.337 miles

POS.	NO.	DRIVER	CAR	MODEL	ENGINE		LAPS	TIME/REASON FOR RETIREMENT	GRID:POS	ROW
1	9	G Hill	Lotus	49B	Cosworth	V8	80	2h 00m 32.300s	1	1
2	15	D Attwood	BRM	P126	BRM	V12	80	2h 00m 34.500s	6	3
3	7	L Bianchi	Cooper	T86B	BRM	V12	76		14	7
4	6	L Scarfiotti	Cooper	T86B	BRM	V12	76		15	8
5	12	D Hulme	McLaren	M7A	Cosworth	V8	73		10	5
r	8	J Surtees	Honda	RA301	Honda	V12	16	gearbox	4	2
r	4	P Rodriguez	BRM	P133	BRM	V12	16	accident	9	5
r	16	P Courage	BRM	P126	BRM	V12	12	chassis	11	6
r	1	J-P Beltoise	Matra	MS11	Matra	V12	11	accident	8	4
r	17	J Siffert	Lotus	49	Cosworth	V8	11	crown wheel & pinion	3	2
r	19	D Gurney	Eagle	T1G	Weslake	V12	9	ignition	16	8
r	3	J Rindt	Brabham	BT24	Repco	V8	8	accident	5	3
r	2	J Brabham	Brabham	BT26	Repco	V8	7	rear suspension	12	6
r	11	J Servoz-Gavin	Matra	MS10	Cosworth	V8	3	accident/ drive shaft	2	1
r	10	J Oliver	Lotus	49	Cosworth	V8	0	accident	13	7
r	14	B McLaren	McLaren	M7A	Cosworth	V8	0	accident	7	4
nq	18	J Bonnier	McLaren	M5A	BRM	V12				
nq	21	S Moser	Brabham	BT20	Repco	V8				

Winning speed: 125.238 km/h, 77.819 mph
Pole Position speed: 128.367 km/h, 79.764 mph (G Hill, 1 min:28.200 sec)
Fastest Lap speed: 128.513 km/h, 79.854 mph (D Attwood, 1 min:28.100 sec on lap 80)
Lap Leaders: J Servoz-Gavin 1-3 (3); G Hill 4-80 (77).

9 Jun 1968 — BELGIUM: Spa-Francorchamps (Round: 4) (Race: 165)

28 laps x 14.100 km, 8.761 miles = 394.800 km, 245.317 miles

POS.	NO.	DRIVER	CAR	MODEL	ENGINE		LAPS	TIME/REASON FOR RETIREMENT	GRID:POS	ROW
1	5	B McLaren	McLaren	M7A	Cosworth	V8	28	1h 40m 02.100s	6	3
2	11	P Rodriguez	BRM	P133	BRM	V12	28	1h 40m 14.200s	8	3
3	23	J Ickx	Ferrari	312	Ferrari	V12	28	1h 40m 41.700s	3	1
4	7	J Stewart	Matra	MS10	Cosworth	V8	27		2	1
5r	2	J Oliver	Lotus	49B	Cosworth	V8	26	drive shaft	15	6
6	15	L Bianchi	Cooper	T86B	BRM	V12	26		12	5
7r	3	J Siffert	Lotus	49	Cosworth	V8	25	oil pressure	9	4
8	10	J-P Beltoise	Matra	MS11	Matra	V12	25		13	5
r	14	P Courage	BRM	P126	BRM	V12	22	engine	7	3
r	6	D Hulme	McLaren	M7A	Cosworth	V8	18	drive shaft	5	2
r	20	J Surtees	Honda	RA301	Honda	V12	11	suspension	4	2
r	22	C Amon	Ferrari	312	Ferrari	V12	8	radiator	1	1
r	12	D Attwood	BRM	P126	BRM	V12	6	oil line	11	5
r	18	J Brabham	Brabham	BT26	Repco	V8	6	throttle slides	18	7
r	16	B Redman	Cooper	T86B	BRM	V12	6	accident	10	4
r	19	J Rindt	Brabham	BT26	Repco	V8	5	valve insert	17	7
r	1	G Hill	Lotus	49B	Cosworth	V8	5	universal joint	14	6
r	17	J Bonnier	McLaren	M5A	BRM	V12	1	wheel stud	16	7

Winning speed: 236.797 km/h, 147.139 mph
Pole Position speed: 243.337 km/h, 151.202 mph (C Amon, 3 min:28.600 sec)
Fastest Lap speed: 241.140 km/h, 149.838 mph (J Surtees, 3 min:30.500 sec on lap 5)
Lap Leaders: C Amon 1 (1); J Surtees 2-10 (9); D Hulme 11,15 (2); J Stewart 12-14,16-27 (15); B McLaren 28 (1).

23 Jun 1968 — NETHERLANDS: Zandvoort (Round: 5) (Race: 166)

90 laps x 4.193 km, 2.605 miles = 377.370 km, 234.487 miles

POS.	NO.	DRIVER	CAR	MODEL	ENGINE		LAPS	TIME/REASON FOR RETIREMENT	GRID:POS	ROW
1	8	J Stewart	Matra	MS10	Cosworth	V8	90	2h 46m 11.260s	5	2
2	17	J-P Beltoise	Matra	MS11	Matra	V12	90	2h 47m 45.190s	16	7
3	15	P Rodriguez	BRM	P133	BRM	V12	89		11	5
4	10	J Ickx	Ferrari	312	Ferrari	V12	88		6	3
5	22	S Moser	Brabham	BT20	Repco	V8	87		17	7
6	9	C Amon	Ferrari	312	Ferrari	V12	85		1	1
7	16	D Attwood	BRM	P126	BRM	V12	85		15	6
8	19	J Bonnier	McLaren	M5A	BRM	V12	82		19	8
9r	3	G Hill	Lotus	49B	Cosworth	V8	81	spin	3	1
nc	4	J Oliver	Lotus	49B	Cosworth	V8	80		10	4
r	18	D Gurney	Brabham	BT24	Repco	V8	63	throttle slides	12	5
r	21	J Siffert	Lotus	49	Cosworth	V8	55	gear selection	13	5
r	7	J Surtees	Honda	RA301	Honda	V12	50	alternator	9	4
r	20	P Courage	BRM	P126	BRM	V12	50	spin	14	6
r	6	J Rindt	Brabham	BT26	Repco	V8	39	ignition damp	2	1
r	5	J Brabham	Brabham	BT26	Repco	V8	22	spin	4	2
r	2	B McLaren	McLaren	M7A	Cosworth	V8	19	accident	8	3
r	1	D Hulme	McLaren	M7A	Cosworth	V8	10	ignition damp	7	3
r	14	L Bianchi	Cooper	T86B	BRM	V12	9	accident	18	7

Winning speed: 136.245 km/h, 84.659 mph
Pole Position speed: 180.689 km/h, 112.275 mph (C Amon, 1 min:23.540 sec)
Fastest Lap speed: 142.525 km/h, 88.561 mph (J-P Beltoise, 1 min:45.910 sec on lap 6)
Lap Leaders: G Hill 1-3 (3); J Stewart 4-90 (87).

7 Jul 1968 — FRANCE: Rouen-les-Essarts (Round: 6) (Race: 167)

60 laps x 6.542 km, 4.065 miles = 392.520 km, 243.901 miles

POS.	NO.	DRIVER	CAR	MODEL	ENGINE		LAPS	TIME/REASON FOR RETIREMENT	GRID:POS	ROW
1	26	J Ickx	Ferrari	312	Ferrari	V12	60	2h 25m 40.900s	3	1
2	16	J Surtees	Honda	RA301	Honda	V12	60	2h 27m 39.500s	7	3
3	28	J Stewart	Matra	MS10	Cosworth	V8	59		2	1
4	30	V Elford	Cooper	T86B	BRM	V12	58		17	7
5	8	D Hulme	McLaren	M7A	Cosworth	V8	58		4	2
6	36	P Courage	BRM	P126	BRM	V12	57		14	6
7	22	D Attwood	BRM	P126	BRM	V12	57		12	5
8	10	B McLaren	McLaren	M7A	Cosworth	V8	56		6	3
9	6	J-P Beltoise	Matra	MS11	Matra	V12	56		8	3
10	24	C Amon	Ferrari	312	Ferrari	V12	55		5	2
11	34	J Siffert	Lotus	49	Cosworth	V8	54		11	5
nc	20	P Rodriguez	BRM	P133	BRM	V12	53		10	4
r	2	J Rindt	Brabham	BT26	Repco	V8	45	fuel tank	1	1
r	4	J Brabham	Brabham	BT26	Repco	V8	15	fuel pump	13	5
r	32	J Servoz-Gavin	Cooper	T86B	BRM	V12	14	accident	15	6
r	12	G Hill	Lotus	49B	Cosworth	V8	14	drive shaft	9	4
r	18	J Schlesser	Honda	RA302	Honda	V8	2	fatal accident	16	7
ns	14	J Oliver	Lotus	49B	Cosworth	V8		accident		

Winning speed: 161.662 km/h, 100.452 mph
Pole Position speed: 202.853 km/h, 126.047 mph (J Rindt, 1 min:56.100 sec)
Fastest Lap speed: 179.097 km/h, 111.285 mph (P Rodriguez, 2 min:11.500 sec on lap 19)
Lap Leaders: J Ickx 1-18,20-60 (59); P Rodriguez 19 (1).

20 Jul 1968 — BRITAIN: Brands Hatch (Round: 7) (Race: 168)

80 laps x 4.265 km, 2.650 miles = 341.181 km, 212.000 miles

POS.	NO.	DRIVER	CAR	MODEL	ENGINE		LAPS	TIME/REASON FOR RETIREMENT	GRID:POS	ROW
1	22	J Siffert	Lotus	49B	Cosworth	V8	80	2h 01m 20.300s	4	2
2	5	C Amon	Ferrari	312	Ferrari	V12	80	2h 01m 24.700s	3	1
3	6	J Ickx	Ferrari	312	Ferrari	V12	79		12	5
4	1	D Hulme	McLaren	M7A	Cosworth	V8	79		11	5
5	7	J Surtees	Honda	RA301	Honda	V12	78		9	4
6	14	J Stewart	Matra	MS10	Cosworth	V8	78		7	3
7	2	B McLaren	McLaren	M7A	Cosworth	V8	77		10	4
8	20	P Courage	BRM	P126	BRM	V12	72		16	7
r	4	J Rindt	Brabham	BT26	Repco	V8	55	fuel system	5	2
r	10	P Rodriguez	BRM	P133	BRM	V12	52	timing chain	13	5
nc	19	S Moser	Brabham	BT20	Repco	V8	52		19	8
r	9	J Oliver	Lotus	49B	Cosworth	V8	43	crown wheel & pinion	2	1
r	16	R Widdows	Cooper	T86	BRM	V12	34	ignition	18	7
r	15	V Elford	Cooper	T86B	BRM	V12	26	engine	17	7
r	8	G Hill	Lotus	49B	Cosworth	V8	26	universal joint	1	1
r	18	J-P Beltoise	Matra	MS11	Matra	V12	11	oil pressure	14	6
r	11	D Attwood	BRM	P126	BRM	V12	10	radiator	15	6
r	24	D Gurney	Eagle	T1G	Weslake	V12	8	fuel pump	6	3
r	23	J Bonnier	McLaren	M5A	BRM	V12	6	dropped valve	20	8
r	3	J Brabham	Brabham	BT26	Repco	V8	0	camshaft	8	3

Winning speed: 168.709 km/h, 104.831 mph
Pole Position speed: 172.701 km/h, 107.312 mph (G Hill, 1 min:28.900 sec)
Fastest Lap speed: 171.161 km/h, 106.355 mph (J Siffert, 1 min:29.700 sec on lap 42)
Lap Leaders: J Oliver 1-3,27-43 (20); G Hill 4-26 (23); J Siffert 44-80 (37).

4 Aug 1968 — GERMANY: Nürburgring (Round: 8) (Race: 169)

14 laps x 22.835 km, 14.189 miles = 319.690 km, 198.646 miles

POS.	NO.	DRIVER	CAR	MODEL	ENGINE		LAPS	TIME/REASON FOR RETIREMENT	GRID:POS	ROW
1	6	J Stewart	Matra	MS10	Cosworth	V8	14	2h 19m 03.200s	6	3
2	3	G Hill	Lotus	49B	Cosworth	V8	14	2h 23m 06.400s	4	2
3	5	J Rindt	Brabham	BT26	Repco	V8	14	2h 23m 12.600s	3	1
4	9	J Ickx	Ferrari	312	Ferrari	V12	14	2h 24m 58.400s	1	1
5	4	J Brabham	Brabham	BT26	Repco	V8	14	2h 25m 24.300s	15	6
6	10	P Rodriguez	BRM	P133	BRM	V12	14	2h 25m 28.200s	14	6
7	1	D Hulme	McLaren	M7A	Cosworth	V8	14	2h 25m 34.200s	11	5
8	22	P Courage	BRM	P126	BRM	V12	14	2h 26m 59.600s	8	3
9	14	D Gurney	Eagle	T1G	Weslake	V12	14	2h 27m 16.900s	10	4
10	18	H Hahne	Lola	T102	BMW	4	14	2h 29m 14.600s	18	7
11	21	J Oliver	Lotus	49B	Cosworth	V8	13		13	5
12	17	K Ahrens	Brabham	BT24	Repco	V8	13		17	7
13	2	B McLaren	McLaren	M7A	Cosworth	V8	13		16	7
14	11	D Attwood	BRM	P126	BRM	V12	13		20	8
r	8	C Amon	Ferrari	312	Ferrari	V12	11	accident	2	1
r	12	J-P Beltoise	Matra	MS11	Matra	V12	8	accident	12	5
r	19	L Bianchi	Cooper	T86B	BRM	V12	7	fuel tank leak	19	8
r	16	J Siffert	Lotus	49B	Cosworth	V8	6	ignition wet	9	4
r	7	J Surtees	Honda	RA301	Honda	V12	3	ignition	7	3
r	20	V Elford	Cooper	T86B	BRM	V12	0	accident	5	2
ns	23	S Moser	Brabham	BT20	Repco	V8		oil pump		

Winning speed: 137.943 km/h, 85.714 mph
Pole Position speed: 151.114 km/h, 93.898 mph (J Ickx, 9 min: 4.000 sec)
Fastest Lap speed: 142.719 km/h, 88.681 mph (J Stewart, 9 min:36.000 sec on lap 8)
Lap Leaders: J Stewart 1-14 (14).

Also the Grand Prix of Europe.

8 Sep 1968 — ITALY: Monza — (Round: 9) (Race: 170)

68 laps x 5.750 km, 3.573 miles = 391.000 km, 242.956 miles

POS.	NO.	DRIVER	CAR	MODEL	ENGINE		LAPS	TIME/REASON FOR RETIREMENT	GRID:POS	ROW
1	1	D Hulme	McLaren	M7A	Cosworth	V8	68	1h 40m 14.800s	7	3
2	5	J Servoz-Gavin	Matra	MS10	Cosworth	V8	68	1h 41m 43.200s	13	5
3	8	J Ickx	Ferrari	312	Ferrari	V12	68	1h 41m 43.400s	4	2
4	27	P Courage	BRM	P126	BRM	V12	67		17	7
5	6	J-P Beltoise	Matra	MS11	Matra	V12	66		18	7
6	3	J Bonnier	McLaren	M5A	BRM	V12	64		19	8
r	20	J Siffert	Lotus	49B	Cosworth	V8	58	rear suspension	9	4
r	10	J Brabham	Brabham	BT26	Repco	V8	56	oil pressure	16	7
r	15	D Hobbs	Honda	RA301	Honda	V12	42	dropped valve	14	6
r	4	J Stewart	Matra	MS10	Cosworth	V8	42	engine	6	3
r	19	J Oliver	Lotus	49B	Cosworth	V8	38	transmission	11	5
r	2	B McLaren	McLaren	M7A	Cosworth	V8	34	oil loss	2	1
r	11	J Rindt	Brabham	BT26	Repco	V8	33	dropped valve	10	4
r	26	P Rodriguez	BRM	P138	BRM	V12	22	timing chain	15	6
r	21	D Gurney	Eagle	T1G	Weslake	V12	19	engine overheating	12	5
r	16	G Hill	Lotus	49B	Cosworth	V8	10	lost wheel/ accident	5	2
r	14	J Surtees	Honda	RA301	Honda	V12	8	accident	1	1
r	9	C Amon	Ferrari	312	Ferrari	V12	8	accident	3	1
r	7	D Bell	Ferrari	312	Ferrari	V12	4	fuel metering unit	8	3
r	23	V Elford	Cooper	T86B	BRM	V12	2	brakes/ accident	20	8
exc	18	M Andretti	Lotus	49B	Cosworth	V8		raced in USA within 24 hours		
exc	25	B Unser	BRM	P126	BRM	V12		raced in USA within 24 hours		
nq	28	F Gardner	BRM	P261	BRM	V12				
nq	12	S Moser	Brabham	BT20	Repco	V8				

Winning speed: 234.023 km/h, 145.415 mph
Pole Position speed: 240.502 km/h, 149.441 mph (J Surtees, 1 min:26.070 sec)
Fastest Lap speed: 239.306 km/h, 148.698 mph (J Oliver, 1 min:26.500 sec on lap 7) *
Lap Leaders: B McLaren 1-6,8-12,14 (12); J Surtees 7 (1); J Stewart 13,17-18,27,30,33,40 (7); J Siffert 15-16 (2); D Hulme 19-26,28-29,31-32,34-39,41-68 (46).

** Although Oliver was officially credited with fastest lap, it is more likely that J Ickx achieved it in 1 min 26.600s on laps 53 and 63.*

22 Sep 1968 — CANADA: Mont-Tremblant — (Round:10) (Race: 171)

90 laps x 4.265 km, 2.650 miles = 383.829 km, 238.500 miles

POS.	NO.	DRIVER	CAR	MODEL	ENGINE		LAPS	TIME/REASON FOR RETIREMENT	GRID:POS	ROW
1	1	D Hulme	McLaren	M7A	Cosworth	V8	90	2h 27m 11.200s	6	3
2	2	B McLaren	McLaren	M7A	Cosworth	V8	89		8	3
3	16	P Rodriguez	BRM	P133	BRM	V12	88		12	5
4	3	G Hill	Lotus	49B	Cosworth	V8	86		5	2
5	21	V Elford	Cooper	T86B	BRM	V12	86		16	7
6	14	J Stewart	Matra	MS10	Cosworth	V8	83		11	5
r	18	J-P Beltoise	Matra	MS11	Matra	V12	77	gearbox	15	6
r	9	C Amon	Ferrari	312	Ferrari	V12	72	transmission	2	1
r	15	J Servoz-Gavin	Matra	MS10	Cosworth	V8	71	accident	13	5
nc	20	L Bianchi	Cooper	T86B	BRM	V12	56		18	7
r	19	H Pescarolo	Matra	MS11	Matra	V12	54	oil pressure	19	8
r	6	J Rindt	Brabham	BT26	Repco	V8	39	engine overheating	1	1
r	4	J Oliver	Lotus	49B	Cosworth	V8	32	transmission	9	4
r	5	J Brabham	Brabham	BT26	Repco	V8	31	suspension	10	4
r	12	J Siffert	Lotus	49B	Cosworth	V8	29	oil leak	3	1
r	11	D Gurney	McLaren	M7A	Cosworth	V8	29	radiator	4	2
r	24	P Courage	BRM	P126	BRM	V12	22	gearbox	14	6
r	27	B Brack	Lotus	49B	Cosworth	V8	18	drive shaft	20	8
r	8	J Surtees	Honda	RA301	Honda	V12	10	gearbox	7	3
r	22	J Bonnier	McLaren	M5A	BRM	V12	0	fuel metering unit	17	7
ns	10	J Ickx	Ferrari	312	Ferrari	V12		accident/ injury		
ns	25	A Pease	Eagle	T1G	Climax	4		engine		

Winning speed: 156.466 km/h, 97.223 mph
Pole Position speed: 163.680 km/h, 101.706 mph (J Rindt, 1 min:33.800 sec)
Fastest Lap speed: 161.442 km/h, 100.315 mph (J Siffert, 1 min:35.100 sec on lap 22)
Lap Leaders: C Amon 1-72 (72); D Hulme 73-90 (18).

6 Oct 1968 — USA: Watkins Glen (Round:11) (Race: 172)

108 laps x 3.701 km, 2.300 miles = 399.761 km, 248.400 miles

POS.	NO.	DRIVER	CAR	MODEL	ENGINE		LAPS	TIME/REASON FOR RETIREMENT	GRID:POS	ROW
1	15	J Stewart	Matra	MS10	Cosworth	V8	108	1h 59m 20.290s	2	1
2	10	G Hill	Lotus	49B	Cosworth	V8	108	1h 59m 44.970s	3	2
3	5	J Surtees	Honda	RA301	Honda	V12	107		9	5
4	14	D Gurney	McLaren	M7A	Cosworth	V8	107		7	4
5	16	J Siffert	Lotus	49B	Cosworth	V8	105		12	6
6	2	B McLaren	McLaren	M7A	Cosworth	V8	103		10	5
r	22	P Courage	BRM	P126	BRM	V12	93	suspension bolt	14	7
r	1	D Hulme	McLaren	M7A	Cosworth	V8	92	accident	5	3
r	19	L Bianchi	Cooper	T86B	BRM	V12	88	clutch	20	10
r	3	J Brabham	Brabham	BT26	Repco	V8	77	engine	8	4
r	4	J Rindt	Brabham	BT26	Repco	V8	73	engine	6	3
r	18	V Elford	Cooper	T86B	BRM	V12	71	camshaft	17	9
r	8	P Rodriguez	BRM	P133	BRM	V12	66	rear suspension	11	6
r	17	J Bonnier	McLaren	M5A	BRM	V12	62	ignition	18	9
r	6	C Amon	Ferrari	312	Ferrari	V12	59	water pipe	4	2
r	21	J-P Beltoise	Matra	MS11	Matra	V12	44	drive shaft	13	7
r	9	B Unser	BRM	P138	BRM	V12	35	engine	19	10
r	12	M Andretti	Lotus	49B	Cosworth	V8	32	clutch	1	1
r	7	D Bell	Ferrari	312	Ferrari	V12	14	engine	15	8
ns	11	J Oliver	Lotus	49B	Cosworth	V8		accident	16	8
ns	21	H Pescarolo	Matra	MS11	Matra	V12		engine		

Winning speed: 200.989 km/h, 124.889 mph
Pole Position speed: 207.560 km/h, 128.972 mph (M Andretti, 1 min: 4.200 sec)
Fastest Lap speed: 204.314 km/h, 126.955 mph (J Stewart, 1 min: 5.220 sec on lap 52)
Lap Leaders: J Stewart 1-108 (108).

3 Nov 1968 — MEXICO: Mexico City (Round:12) (Race: 173)

65 laps x 5.000 km, 3.107 miles = 325.000 km, 201.946 miles

POS.	NO.	DRIVER	CAR	MODEL	ENGINE		LAPS	TIME/REASON FOR RETIREMENT	GRID:POS	ROW
1	10	G Hill	Lotus	49B	Cosworth	V8	65	1h 56m 43.950s	3	2
2	2	B McLaren	McLaren	M7A	Cosworth	V8	65	1h 58m 03.270s	9	5
3	11	J Oliver	Lotus	49B	Cosworth	V8	65	1h 58m 24.600s	14	7
4	8	P Rodriguez	BRM	P133	BRM	V12	65	1h 58m 25.040s	12	6
5	17	J Bonnier	Honda	RA301	Honda	V12	64		18	9
6	16	J Siffert	Lotus	49B	Cosworth	V8	64		1	1
7	15	J Stewart	Matra	MS10	Cosworth	V8	64		7	4
8	18	V Elford	Cooper	T86B	BRM	V12	63		17	9
9	9	H Pescarolo	Matra	MS11	Matra	V12	62		20	10
10r	3	J Brabham	Brabham	BT26	Repco	V8	59	oil pressure	8	4
r	23	J Servoz-Gavin	Matra	MS10	Cosworth	V8	57	ignition	16	8
r	14	D Gurney	McLaren	M7A	Cosworth	V8	28	rear suspension	5	3
r	22	P Courage	BRM	P126	BRM	V12	25	engine overheating	19	10
r	19	L Bianchi	Cooper	T86B	BRM	V12	21	engine	21	11
r	5	J Surtees	Honda	RA301	Honda	V12	17	engine overheating	6	3
r	6	C Amon	Ferrari	312	Ferrari	V12	16	water pump	2	1
r	12	M Solana	Lotus	49B	Cosworth	V8	14	wing collapsed	11	6
r	21	J-P Beltoise	Matra	MS11	Matra	V12	10	rear suspension	13	7
r	1	D Hulme	McLaren	M7A	Cosworth	V8	10	suspension/ accident	4	2
r	7	J Ickx	Ferrari	312	Ferrari	V12	3	ignition	15	8
r	4	J Rindt	Brabham	BT26	Repco	V8	2	ignition	10	5

Winning speed: 167.049 km/h, 103.799 mph
Pole Position speed: 171.070 km/h, 106.298 mph (J Siffert, 1 min:45.220 sec)
Fastest Lap speed: 172.695 km/h, 107.308 mph (J Siffert, 1 min:44.230 sec on lap 52)
Lap Leaders: G Hill 1-4,9-21,25-65 (58); J Stewart 5-8 (4); J Siffert 22-24 (3).

Lap Leaders 1968

POS	DRIVER	CAR-ENGINE	GPS	LAPS	KM	MILES
1	J Stewart	Matra-Cosworth	7	236	1,360.0	845.1
2	G Hill	Lotus-Cosworth	5	194	755.2	469.2
3	C Amon	Ferrari	3	115	464.1	288.4
4	J Clark	Lotus-Cosworth	1	79	324.2	201.5
5	D Hulme	McLaren-Cosworth	3	66	369.5	229.6
6	J Ickx	Ferrari	1	59	386.0	239.8
7	J Siffert	Lotus-Cosworth	3	42	184.3	114.5
8	J Oliver	Lotus-Cosworth	1	20	85.3	53.0
9	B McLaren	McLaren-Cosworth	2	13	83.1	51.6
10	P Rodriguez	BRM	2	12	44.0	27.3
11	J Surtees	Honda	2	10	132.6	82.4
12	J-P Beltoise	Matra-Cosworth	1	4	13.6	8.5
13	J Servoz-Gavin	Matra-Cosworth	1	3	9.4	5.9
			12	**853**	**4,211.4**	**2,616.9**

Driver Points 1968

		ZA	E	MC	B	NL	F	GB	D	I	CDN	USA	MEX	TOTAL
1	G Hill	6	9	9	-	-	-	-	6	-	3	6	9	48
2	J Stewart	-	-	-	3	9	4	1	9	-	1	9	-	36
3	D Hulme	2	6	2	-	-	2	3	-	9	9	-	-	33
4	J Ickx	-	-	-	4	3	9	4	3	4	-	-	-	27
5	B McLaren	-	-	-	9	-	-	-	-	-	6	1	6	22
6	P Rodriguez	-	-	-	6	4	-	-	1	-	4	-	3	18
7	J Siffert	-	-	-	-	-	-	9	-	-	-	2	1	12
	J Surtees	-	-	-	-	-	6	2	-	-	-	4	-	12
9	J-P Beltoise	1	2	-	-	6	-	-	-	2	-	-	-	11
10	C Amon	3	-	-	-	1	-	6	-	-	-	-	-	10
11	J Clark	9	-	-	-	-	-	-	-	-	-	-	-	9
12	J Rindt	4	-	-	-	-	-	-	4	-	-	-	-	8
13	D Attwood	-	-	6	-	-	-	-	-	-	-	-	-	6
	J Servoz-Gavin	-	-	-	-	-	-	-	-	6	-	-	-	6
	J Oliver	-	-	-	2	-	-	-	-	-	-	-	4	6
	L Scarfiotti	-	3	3	-	-	-	-	-	-	-	-	-	6
17	L Bianchi	-	-	4	1	-	-	-	-	-	-	-	-	5
	V Elford	-	-	-	-	-	3	-	-	-	2	-	-	5
19	B Redman	-	4	-	-	-	-	-	-	-	-	-	-	4
	P Courage	-	-	-	-	-	1	-	-	3	-	-	-	4
21	D Gurney	-	-	-	-	-	-	-	-	-	-	3	-	3
	J Bonnier	-	-	-	-	-	-	-	-	1	-	-	2	3
23	S Moser	-	-	-	-	2	-	-	-	-	-	-	-	2
	J Brabham	-	-	-	-	-	-	-	2	-	-	-	-	2

9, 6, 4, 3, 2 and 1 point awarded to the first six finishers.

Best 5 scores from first 6 races, best 5 from remaining 6 races.

Constructor Points 1968

		ZA	E	MC	B	NL	F	GB	D	I	CDN	USA	MEX	TOTAL
1	Lotus-Cosworth	9	9	9	2	-	-	9	6	-	3	6	9	62
2	McLaren-Cosworth	-	6	2	9	-	2	3	-	9	9	3	6	49
3	Matra-Cosworth	1	2	-	3	9	4	1	9	6	1	9	-	45
4	Ferrari	3	-	-	4	3	9	6	3	4	-	-	-	32
5	BRM	-	-	6	6	4	1	-	1	3	4	-	3	28
6	Honda	-	-	-	-	-	6	2	-	-	-	4	2	14
	Cooper-BRM	-	4	4	1	-	3	-	-	-	2	-	-	14
8	Brabham-Repco	4	-	-	-	2	-	-	4	-	-.	-	-	10
9	Matra	-	-	-	-	6	-	-	-	2	-	-	-	8
10	McLaren-BRM	2	-	-	-	-	-	-	-	1	-	-	-	3

9, 6, 4, 3 ,2 and 1 point awarded to the first six finishers. Points only for highest placed car.

Best 5 scores from first 6 races, best 5 from remaining 6 races.

Cosworth-engined cars were beginning to dominate the grids. Ferrari effectively withdrew at the end of the season, to concentrate on development work. This was the year of the four wheel drive experiments, with Lotus, Matra and McLaren trying out such cars. In June, FIAT bought a 50% stake in Ferrari. Shortly afterwards, Tony Rudd and BRM parted company. Grids fell to their smallest during this season, averaging below 16 starters.

FERRARI
Scuderia Ferrari SpA SEFAC: Amon, Rodriguez, (Brambilla)
North American Racing Team: Rodriguez (CDN,USA,MEX)

BRABHAM
Motor Racing Developments: Brabham, Ickx
Frank Williams Racing Cars: Courage
Silvio Moser Racing Team: Moser
Team Gunston: Tingle
Jack Holme: de Klerk
Paul Seitz: Cordts

BRM
Owen Racing Organisation: Surtees, Oliver, Eaton, Brack
Reg Parnell Racing Ltd: Rodriguez

COOPER
Antique Automobiles: Elford

LOTUS
Gold Leaf Team Lotus: Hill, Rindt, Miles, Andretti, Attwood
Rob Walker/Jack Durlacher Racing: Siffert
Pete Lovely Volkswagen Inc: Lovely
Ecurie Bonnier: Bonnier
Team Gunston: Love

McLAREN
Bruce McLaren Motor Racing: McLaren, Hulme, Bell
Antique Automobiles: Elford
Team Lawson: van Rooyen

MATRA
Matra International: Stewart, Beltoise, Servoz-Gavin

EAGLE
John Maryon: Pease

(Entries for the F2 section are not included)

1 Mar 1969 — SOUTH AFRICA: Kyalami (Round: 1) (Race: 174)
80 laps x 4.104 km, 2.550 miles = 328.306 km, 204.000 miles

POS.	NO.	DRIVER	CAR	MODEL	ENGINE		LAPS	TIME/REASON FOR RETIREMENT	GRID:POS	ROW
1	7	J Stewart	Matra	MS10	Cosworth	V8	80	1h 50m 39.100s	4	2
2	1	G Hill	Lotus	49B	Cosworth	V8	80	1h 50m 57.900s	7	3
3	5	D Hulme	McLaren	M7A	Cosworth	V8	80	1h 51m 10.900s	3	1
4	4	J Siffert	Lotus	49B	Cosworth	V8	80	1h 51m 28.300s	12	5
5	6	B McLaren	McLaren	M7A	Cosworth	V8	79		8	3
6	8	J-P Beltoise	Matra	MS10	Cosworth	V8	78		11	5
7	11	J Oliver	BRM	P133	BRM	V12	77		14	6
8	17	S Tingle	Brabham	BT24	Repco	V8	73		17	7
nc	19	P de Klerk	Brabham	BT20	Repco	V8	67		16	7
r	2	J Rindt	Lotus	49B	Cosworth	V8	44	fuel system	2	1
r	10	J Surtees	BRM	P138	BRM	V12	40	engine	18	7
r	12	P Rodriguez	BRM	P126	BRM	V12	38	water leak	15	6
r	9	C Amon	Ferrari	312	Ferrari	V12	34	engine	5	2
r	14	J Brabham	Brabham	BT26A	Cosworth	V8	32	rear wing lost	1	1
r	3	M Andretti	Lotus	49B	Cosworth	V8	31	gearbox	6	3
r	16	J Love	Lotus	49	Cosworth	V8	31	ignition	10	4
r	15	J Ickx	Brabham	BT26A	Cosworth	V8	20	ignition	13	5
r	18	B van Rooyen	McLaren	M7A	Cosworth	V8	12	brakes	9	4

Winning speed: 178.021 km/h, 110.617 mph
Pole Position speed: 184.672 km/h, 114.750 mph (J Brabham, 1 min:20.000 sec)
Fastest Lap speed: 181.051 km/h, 112.500 mph (J Stewart, 1 min:21.600 sec on lap 50)
Lap Leaders: J Stewart 1-80 (80).

4 May 1969 — SPAIN: Montjuich Park (Round: 2) (Race: 175)
90 laps x 3.791 km, 2.356 miles = 341.190 km, 212.006 miles

POS.	NO.	DRIVER	CAR	MODEL	ENGINE		LAPS	TIME/REASON FOR RETIREMENT	GRID:POS	ROW
1	7	J Stewart	Matra	MS80	Cosworth	V8	90	2h 16m 53.990s	4	2
2	6	B McLaren	McLaren	M7C	Cosworth	V8	88		13	5
3	8	J-P Beltoise	Matra	MS80	Cosworth	V8	87		12	5
4	5	D Hulme	McLaren	M7A	Cosworth	V8	87		8	3
5	14	J Surtees	BRM	P138	BRM	V12	84		9	4
6r	4	J Ickx	Brabham	BT26A	Cosworth	V8	83	rear suspension	7	3
r	9	P Rodriguez	BRM	P126	BRM	V12	73	piston	14	6
r	15	C Amon	Ferrari	312	Ferrari	V12	56	engine	2	1
r	3	J Brabham	Brabham	BT26A	Cosworth	V8	51	engine	5	2
r	10	J Siffert	Lotus	49B	Cosworth	V8	30	oil loss/ engine	6	3
r	2	J Rindt	Lotus	49B	Cosworth	V8	19	accident	1	1
r	11	P Courage	Brabham	BT26A	Cosworth	V8	18	valve spring	11	5
r	1	G Hill	Lotus	49B	Cosworth	V8	8	accident	3	1
r	12	J Oliver	BRM	P133	BRM	V12	1	oil line	10	4

Winning speed: 149.536 km/h, 92.917 mph
Pole Position speed: 159.249 km/h, 98.952 mph (J Rindt, 1 min:25.700 sec)
Fastest Lap speed: 154.559 km/h, 96.039 mph (J Rindt, 1 min:28.300 sec on lap 15)
Lap Leaders: J Rindt 1-19 (19); C Amon 20-56 (37); J Stewart 57-90 (34).

18 May 1969 — MONACO: Monte Carlo — (Round: 3) (Race: 176)

80 laps x 3.145 km, 1.954 miles = 251.600 km, 156.337 miles

POS.	NO.	DRIVER	CAR	MODEL	ENGINE		LAPS	TIME/REASON FOR RETIREMENT	GRID:POS	ROW
1	1	G Hill	Lotus	49B	Cosworth	V8	80	1h 56m 59.400s	4	2
2	16	P Courage	Brabham	BT26A	Cosworth	V8	80	1h 57m 16.700s	9	5
3	9	J Siffert	Lotus	49B	Cosworth	V8	80	1h 57m 34.000s	5	3
4	2	D Attwood	Lotus	49B	Cosworth	V8	80	1h 57m 52.300s	10	5
5	4	B McLaren	McLaren	M7C	Cosworth	V8	79		11	6
6	3	D Hulme	McLaren	M7A	Cosworth	V8	78		12	6
7	12	V Elford	Cooper	T86B	Maserati	V12	74		16	8
r	6	J Ickx	Brabham	BT26A	Cosworth	V8	48	rear suspension	7	4
r	7	J Stewart	Matra	MS80	Cosworth	V8	22	universal joint	1	1
r	8	J-P Beltoise	Matra	MS80	Cosworth	V8	20	universal joint	3	2
r	11	C Amon	Ferrari	312	Ferrari	V12	16	differential	2	1
r	10	P Rodriguez	BRM	P126	BRM	V12	15	engine	14	7
r	17	S Moser	Brabham	BT24	Cosworth	V8	15	universal joint	15	8
r	14	J Surtees	BRM	P138	BRM	V12	9	accident/ gearbox	6	3
r	5	J Brabham	Brabham	BT26A	Cosworth	V8	9	accident	8	4
r	15	J Oliver	BRM	P133	BRM	V12	0	accident	13	7

Winning speed: 129.037 km/h, 80.180 mph
Pole Position speed: 133.830 km/h, 83.158 mph (J Stewart, 1 min:24.600 sec)
Fastest Lap speed: 133.043 km/h, 82.669 mph (J Stewart, 1 min:25.100 sec on lap 16)
Lap Leaders: J Stewart 1-22 (22); G Hill 23-80 (58).

21 Jun 1969 — NETHERLANDS: Zandvoort — (Round: 4) (Race: 177)

90 laps x 4.193 km, 2.605 miles = 377.370 km, 234.487 miles

POS.	NO.	DRIVER	CAR	MODEL	ENGINE		LAPS	TIME/REASON FOR RETIREMENT	GRID:POS	ROW
1	4	J Stewart	Matra	MS80	Cosworth	V8	90	2h 06m 42.080s	2	1
2	10	J Siffert	Lotus	49B	Cosworth	V8	90	2h 07m 06.600s	10	4
3	8	C Amon	Ferrari	312	Ferrari	V12	90	2h 07m 12.590s	4	2
4	7	D Hulme	McLaren	M7A	Cosworth	V8	90	2h 07m 19.240s	7	3
5	12	J Ickx	Brabham	BT26A	Cosworth	V8	90	2h 07m 19.750s	5	2
6	11	J Brabham	Brabham	BT26A	Cosworth	V8	90	2h 07m 52.890s	8	3
7	1	G Hill	Lotus	49B	Cosworth	V8	88		3	1
8	5	J-P Beltoise	Matra	MS80	Cosworth	V8	87		11	5
9	14	J Surtees	BRM	P138	BRM	V12	87		12	5
10	18	V Elford	McLaren	M7A	Cosworth	V8	84		15	6
r	17	S Moser	Brabham	BT24	Cosworth	V8	54	steering/ electrics	14	6
r	6	B McLaren	McLaren	M7C	Cosworth	V8	24	suspension	6	3
r	2	J Rindt	Lotus	49B	Cosworth	V8	16	cv joint	1	1
r	16	P Courage	Brabham	BT26A	Cosworth	V8	12	clutch	9	4
r	15	J Oliver	BRM	P133	BRM	V12	9	gear selection	13	5

Winning speed: 178.705 km/h, 111.042 mph
Pole Position speed: 186.701 km/h, 116.011 mph (J Rindt, 1 min:20.850 sec)
Fastest Lap speed: 181.997 km/h, 113.087 mph (J Stewart, 1 min:22.940 sec on lap 5)
Lap Leaders: G Hill 1-2 (2); J Rindt 3-16 (14); J Stewart 17-90 (74).

6 Jul 1969 — FRANCE: Clermont-Ferrand — (Round: 5) (Race: 178)

38 laps x 8.055 km, 5.005 miles = 306.090 km, 190.196 miles

POS.	NO.	DRIVER	CAR	MODEL	ENGINE		LAPS	TIME/REASON FOR RETIREMENT	GRID:POS	ROW
1	2	J Stewart	Matra	MS80	Cosworth	V8	38	1h 56m 47.400s	1	1
2	7	J-P Beltoise	Matra	MS80	Cosworth	V8	38	1h 57m 44.500s	5	3
3	11	J Ickx	Brabham	BT26A	Cosworth	V8	38	1h 57m 44.700s	4	2
4	5	B McLaren	McLaren	M7C	Cosworth	V8	37		7	4
5	10	V Elford	McLaren	M7A	Cosworth	V8	37		10	5
6	1	G Hill	Lotus	49B	Cosworth	V8	37		8	4
7	12	S Moser	Brabham	BT24	Cosworth	V8	36		13	7
8	4	D Hulme	McLaren	M7A	Cosworth	V8	35		2	1
9	3	J Siffert	Lotus	49B	Cosworth	V8	34		9	5
r	6	C Amon	Ferrari	312	Ferrari	V12	30	engine	6	3
r	15	J Rindt	Lotus	49B	Cosworth	V8	22	driver had double vision	3	2
r	9	P Courage	Brabham	BT26A	Cosworth	V8	21	nose cone mounting	11	6
r	14	J Miles	Lotus	63	Cosworth	V8	1	fuel pump belt	12	6

Winning speed: 157.251 km/h, 97.712 mph
Pole Position speed: 160.565 km/h, 99.770 mph (J Stewart, 3 min: 0.600 sec)
Fastest Lap speed: 158.719 km/h, 98.624 mph (J Stewart, 3 min: 2.700 sec on lap 27)
Lap Leaders: J Stewart 1-38 (38).

19 Jul 1969 — BRITAIN: Silverstone — (Round: 6) (Race: 179)

84 laps x 4.711 km, 2.927 miles = 395.686 km, 245.868 miles

POS.	NO.	DRIVER	CAR	MODEL	ENGINE		LAPS	TIME/REASON FOR RETIREMENT	GRID:POS	ROW
1	3	J Stewart	Matra	MS80	Cosworth	V8	84	1h 55m 55.600s	2	1
2	7	J Ickx	Brabham	BT26A	Cosworth	V8	83		4	2
3	6	B McLaren	McLaren	M7C	Cosworth	V8	83		7	3
4	2	J Rindt	Lotus	49B	Cosworth	V8	83		1	1
5	16	P Courage	Brabham	BT26A	Cosworth	V8	83		10	4

POS.	NO.	DRIVER	CAR	MODEL	ENGINE		LAPS	TIME/REASON FOR RETIREMENT	GRID:POS	ROW
6	19	V Elford	McLaren	M7A	Cosworth	V8	82		11	5
7	1	G Hill	Lotus	49B	Cosworth	V8	82		12	5
8	10	J Siffert	Lotus	49B	Cosworth	V8	81		9	4
9	4	J-P Beltoise	Matra	MS84	Cosworth	V8	78		17	7
r	12	P Rodriguez	Ferrari	312	Ferrari	V12	61	engine	8	3
r	11	C Amon	Ferrari	312	Ferrari	V12	45	gearbox	5	2
r	5	D Hulme	McLaren	M7A	Cosworth	V8	27	camshaft	3	1
r	15	J Oliver	BRM	P133	BRM	V12	19	transmission	13	5
r	18	J Bonnier	Lotus	63	Cosworth	V8	6	engine	16	7
r	20	D Bell	McLaren	M9A	Cosworth	V8	5	rear suspension	15	6
r	14	J Surtees	BRM	P139	BRM	V12	1	front suspension	6	3

Winning speed: 204.795 km/h, 127.254 mph
Pole Position speed: 209.876 km/h, 130.411 mph (J Rindt, 1 min:20.800 sec)
Fastest Lap speed: 208.585 km/h, 129.609 mph (J Stewart, 1 min:21.300 sec on lap 57 & 60)
Lap Leaders: J Rindt 1-5,16-61 (51); J Stewart 6-15,62-84 (33).

3 Aug 1969 — GERMANY: Nürburgring — (Round: 7) (Race: 180)

14 laps x 22.835 km, 14.189 miles = 319.690 km, 198.646 miles

POS.	NO.	DRIVER	CAR	MODEL	ENGINE		LAPS	TIME/REASON FOR RETIREMENT	GRID:POS	ROW
1	6	J Ickx	Brabham	BT26A	Cosworth	V8	14	1h 49m 55.400s	1	1
2	7	J Stewart	Matra	MS80	Cosworth	V8	14	1h 50m 53.100s	2	1
3	10	B McLaren	McLaren	M7C	Cosworth	V8	14	1h 53m 17.000s	8	3
4	1	G Hill	Lotus	49B	Cosworth	V8	14	1h 53m 54.200s	9	4
5	26	H Pescarolo	* Matra	MS7	Cosworth	4	14	1h 58m 06.400s (1st F2 section)	17	7
6	29	D Attwood	* Brabham	BT30	Cosworth	4	13		20	9
7	20	K Ahrens	* Brabham	BT30	Cosworth	4	13		19	8
8	22	R Stommelen	* Lotus	59B	Cosworth	4	13		21	9
9	31	P Westbury	* Brabham	BT30	Cosworth	4	13		18	8
10	30	X Perrot	* Brabham	BT23C	Cosworth	4	13		22	9
11r	11	J Siffert	Lotus	49B	Cosworth	V8	12	suspension (5th F1 section)	4	2
12r	8	J-P Beltoise	Matra	MS80	Cosworth	V8	12	front suspension	10	4
r	15	J Oliver	BRM	P138	BRM	V12	11	oil sump	13	5
r	9	D Hulme	McLaren	M7A	Cosworth	V8	11	transmission	5	2
r	2	J Rindt	Lotus	49B	Cosworth	V8	10	ignition	3	1
r	28	F Cevert	* Tecno	TOO	Cosworth	4	9	crown wheel & pinion	16	7
r	27	J Servoz-Gavin	* Matra	MS7	Cosworth	4	6	engine	15	7
r	16	J Bonnier	Lotus	49B	Cosworth	V8	4	fuel tank leak	14	6
r	17	P Courage	Brabham	BT26A	Cosworth	V8	1	accident	7	3
r	12	V Elford	McLaren	M7A	Cosworth	V8	0	accident	6	3
r	3	M Andretti	Lotus	63	Cosworth	V8	0	accident	12	5
ns	14	J Surtees	BRM	P139	BRM	V12		suspension	11	5
ns	23	H Hahne	* BMW	269	BMW	4		withdrew after Mitter accident		
ns	25	D Quester	* BMW	269	BMW	4		withdrew after Mitter accident		
ns	24	G Mitter	* BMW	269	BMW	4		fatal accident		
ns	21	H Herrmann	* Lotus	59B	Cosworth	4		withdrew after Mitter accident		

Winning speed: 174.498 km/h, 108.428 mph
Pole Position speed: 177.897 km/h, 110.540 mph (J Ickx, 7 min:42.100 sec)
Fastest Lap speed: 177.245 km/h, 110.135 mph (J Ickx, 7 min:43.800 sec on lap 7)
Lap Leaders: J Stewart 1-6 (6); J Ickx 7-14 (8).

*Formula 2 cars raced simultaneously with F1, and are marked thus *.*
H Pescarolo and D Attwood finished 5th and 6th, but were not eligible for points due to being in the F2 section of the race.

7 Sep 1969 — ITALY: Monza — (Round: 8) (Race: 181)

68 laps x 5.750 km, 3.573 miles = 391.000 km, 242.956 miles

POS.	NO.	DRIVER	CAR	MODEL	ENGINE		LAPS	TIME/REASON FOR RETIREMENT	GRID:POS	ROW
1	20	J Stewart	Matra	MS80	Cosworth	V8	68	1h 39m 11.260s	3	2
2	4	J Rindt	Lotus	49B	Cosworth	V8	68	1h 39m 11.340s	1	1
3	22	J-P Beltoise	Matra	MS80	Cosworth	V8	68	1h 39m 11.430s	6	3
4	18	B McLaren	McLaren	M7C	Cosworth	V8	68	1h 39m 11.450s	5	3
5	32	P Courage	Brabham	BT26A	Cosworth	V8	68	1h 39m 44.700s	4	2
6	10	P Rodriguez	Ferrari	312	Ferrari	V12	66		12	6
7	16	D Hulme	McLaren	M7A	Cosworth	V8	66		2	1
8r	30	J Siffert	Lotus	49B	Cosworth	V8	64	piston	8	4
9r	2	G Hill	Lotus	49B	Cosworth	V8	63	drive shaft	9	5
10r	26	J Ickx	Brabham	BT26A	Cosworth	V8	61	oil pressure	15	8
nc	14	J Surtees	BRM	P139	BRM	V12	60		10	5
r	12	J Oliver	BRM	P139	BRM	V12	48	oil pressure	11	6
r	36	S Moser	Brabham	BT24	Cosworth	V8	9	fuel leak	13	7
r	28	J Brabham	Brabham	BT26A	Cosworth	V8	6	fuel line	7	4
r	6	J Miles	Lotus	63	Cosworth	V8	3	engine	14	7
ns	10	T Brambilla	Ferrari	312	Ferrari	V12		car raced by Rodriguez		

Winning speed: 236.521 km/h, 146.968 mph
Pole Position speed: 242.162 km/h, 150.472 mph (J Rindt, 1 min:25.480 sec)
Fastest Lap speed: 242.958 km/h, 150.967 mph (J-P Beltoise, 1 min:25.200 sec on lap 64)
Lap Leaders: J Stewart 1-6,9-17,19-24,28-30,33,35-36,38-68 (58);J Rindt 7,25-27,31,34,37 (7);D Hulme 8 (1);P Courage 18,32 (2).

20 Sep 1969 — CANADA: Mosport Park (Round: 9) (Race: 182)

90 laps x 3.957 km, 2.459 miles = 356.164 km, 221.310 miles

POS.	NO.	DRIVER	CAR	MODEL	ENGINE		LAPS	TIME/REASON FOR RETIREMENT	GRID:POS	ROW
1	11	J Ickx	Brabham	BT26A	Cosworth	V8	90	1h 59m 25.700s	1	1
2	12	J Brabham	Brabham	BT26A	Cosworth	V8	90	2h 00m 11.900s	6	3
3	2	J Rindt	Lotus	49B	Cosworth	V8	90	2h 00m 17.700s	3	1
4	18	J-P Beltoise	Matra	MS80	Cosworth	V8	89		2	1
5	4	B McLaren	McLaren	M7C	Cosworth	V8	87		9	4
6	19	J Servoz-Gavin	Matra	MS84	Cosworth	V8	84		15	6
7	25	P Lovely	Lotus	49B	Cosworth	V8	81		16	7
nc	16	B Brack	BRM	P138	BRM	V12	80		18	7
r	1	G Hill	Lotus	49B	Cosworth	V8	42	camshaft	7	3
r	9	J Siffert	Lotus	49B	Cosworth	V8	40	drive shaft	8	3
r	3	J Miles	Lotus	63	Cosworth	V8	40	gearbox	11	5
r	6	P Rodriguez	Ferrari	312	Ferrari	V12	37	oil pressure	13	5
r	17	J Stewart	Matra	MS80	Cosworth	V8	32	accident	4	2
dq	69	A Pease	Eagle	T1G	Climax	4	22	too slow	17	7
r	14	J Surtees	BRM	P139	BRM	V12	15	engine	14	6
r	21	P Courage	Brabham	BT26A	Cosworth	V8	13	fuel leak	10	4
r	26	J Cordts	Brabham	BT23B	Climax	4	10	oil leak	19	8
r	5	D Hulme	McLaren	M7A	Cosworth	V8	9	distributor	5	2
r	15	J Oliver	BRM	P139	BRM	V12	2	engine	12	5
r	20	S Moser	Brabham	BT24	Cosworth	V8	0	accident	20	8

Winning speed: 178.934 km/h, 111.185 mph
Pole Position speed: 184.064 km/h, 114.372 mph (J Ickx, 1 min:17.400 sec)
Fastest Lap speed: 182.414 km/h, 113.347 mph (J Ickx/ J Brabham, 1 min:18.100 sec on lap 30 / 62)
Lap Leaders: J Rindt 1-5 (5); J Stewart 6-32 (27); J Ickx 33-90 (58).

5 Oct 1969 — USA: Watkins Glen (Round:10) (Race: 183)

108 laps x 3.701 km, 2.300 miles = 399.761 km, 248.400 miles

POS.	NO.	DRIVER	CAR	MODEL	ENGINE		LAPS	TIME/REASON FOR RETIREMENT	GRID:POS	ROW
1	2	J Rindt	Lotus	49B	Cosworth	V8	108	1h 57m 56.840s	1	1
2	18	P Courage	Brabham	BT26A	Cosworth	V8	108	1h 58m 43.830s	9	5
3	14	J Surtees	BRM	P139	BRM	V12	106		11	6
4	8	J Brabham	Brabham	BT26A	Cosworth	V8	106		10	5
5	12	P Rodriguez	Ferrari	312	Ferrari	V12	101		12	6
6	19	S Moser	Brabham	BT24	Cosworth	V8	98		17	9
nc	16	J Servoz-Gavin	Matra	MS84	Cosworth	V8	92		15	8
r	1	G Hill	Lotus	49B	Cosworth	V8	90	accident	4	2
r	7	J Ickx	Brabham	BT26A	Cosworth	V8	77	engine	8	4
r	22	G Eaton	BRM	P138	BRM	V12	76	engine	18	9
r	4	J-P Beltoise	Matra	MS80	Cosworth	V8	72	engine	7	4
r	5	D Hulme	McLaren	M7A	Cosworth	V8	52	gear selection	2	1
r	3	J Stewart	Matra	MS80	Cosworth	V8	35	engine	3	2
r	21	P Lovely	Lotus	49B	Cosworth	V8	25	universal joint	16	8
r	15	J Oliver	BRM	P139	BRM	V12	23	engine	14	7
r	9	M Andretti	Lotus	63	Cosworth	V8	3	rear suspension	13	7
r	10	J Siffert	Lotus	49B	Cosworth	V8	3	fuel metering unit	5	3
ns	6	B McLaren	McLaren	M7C	Cosworth	V8		engine	6	3

Winning speed: 203.359 km/h, 126.361 mph
Pole Position speed: 209.453 km/h, 130.148 mph (J Rindt, 1 min: 3.620 sec)
Fastest Lap speed: 207.109 km/h, 128.691 mph (J Rindt, 1 min: 4.340 sec on lap 69)
Lap Leaders: J Rindt 1-11,21-108 (99); J Stewart 12-20 (9).

19 Oct 1969 — MEXICO: Mexico City (Round:11) (Race: 184)

65 laps x 5.000 km, 3.107 miles = 325.000 km, 201.946 miles

POS.	NO.	DRIVER	CAR	MODEL	ENGINE		LAPS	TIME/REASON FOR RETIREMENT	GRID:POS	ROW
1	5	D Hulme	McLaren	M7A	Cosworth	V8	65	1h 54m 08.800s	4	2
2	7	J Ickx	Brabham	BT26A	Cosworth	V8	65	1h 54m 11.360s	2	1
3	8	J Brabham	Brabham	BT26A	Cosworth	V8	65	1h 54m 47.280s	1	1
4	3	J Stewart	Matra	MS80	Cosworth	V8	65	1h 54m 55.840s	3	2
5	4	J-P Beltoise	Matra	MS80	Cosworth	V8	65	1h 55m 47.320s	8	4
6	15	J Oliver	BRM	P139	BRM	V12	63		12	6
7	12	P Rodriguez	Ferrari	312	Ferrari	V12	63		15	8
8	16	J Servoz-Gavin	Matra	MS84	Cosworth	V8	63		14	7
9	21	P Lovely	Lotus	49B	Cosworth	V8	62		16	8
10	18	P Courage	Brabham	BT26A	Cosworth	V8	61		9	5
11r	19	S Moser	Brabham	BT24	Cosworth	V8	60	fuel leak	13	7
r	14	J Surtees	BRM	P139	BRM	V12	53	gearbox	10	5
r	2	J Rindt	Lotus	49B	Cosworth	V8	21	suspension	6	3
r	22	G Eaton	BRM	P138	BRM	V12	6	gearbox	17	9
r	10	J Siffert	Lotus	49B	Cosworth	V8	4	accident	5	3
r	9	J Miles	Lotus	63	Cosworth	V8	3	fuel pump	11	6
r	6	B McLaren	McLaren	M7C	Cosworth	V8	-1	fuel injection	7	4

Winning speed: 170.833 km/h, 106.151 mph
Pole Position speed: 174.927 km/h, 108.695 mph (J Brabham, 1 min:42.900 sec)
Fastest Lap speed: 174.672 km/h, 108.536 mph (J Ickx, 1 min:43.050 sec on lap 64)
Lap Leaders: J Stewart 1-5 (5); J Ickx 6-9 (4); D Hulme 10-65 (56).

Jo Siffert in the Lotus 49B-Ford Cosworth, 1969.

Lap Leaders 1969

POS	DRIVER	CAR-ENGINE	GPS	LAPS	KM	MILES
1	J Stewart	Matra-Cosworth	11	386	1,933.9	1,201.7
2	J Rindt	Lotus-Cosworth	6	195	797.4	495.5
3	J Ickx	Brabham-Cosworth	3	70	432.2	268.5
4	G Hill	Lotus-Cosworth	2	60	190.8	118.6
5	D Hulme	McLaren-Cosworth	2	57	285.7	177.6
6	C Amon	Ferrari	1	37	140.3	87.2
7	P Courage	Brabham-Cosworth	1	2	11.5	7.1
			11	**807**	**3,791.8**	**2,356.1**

Driver Points 1969

		ZA	E	MC	NL	F	GB	D	I	CDN	USA	MEX	TOTAL
1	J Stewart	9	9	-	9	9	9	6	9	-	-	3	63
2	J Ickx	-	1	-	2	4	6	9	-	9	-	6	37
3	B McLaren	2	6	2	-	3	4	4	3	2	-	-	26
4	J Rindt	-	-	-	-	-	3	-	6	4	9	-	22
5	J-P Beltoise	1	4	-	-	6	-	1	4	3	-	2	21
6	D Hulme	4	3	1	3	-	-	-	-	-	-	9	20
7	G Hill	6	-	9	-	1	-	3	-	-	-	-	19
8	P Courage	-	-	6	-	-	2	-	2	-	6	-	16
9	J Siffert	3	-	4	6	-	-	2	-	-	-	-	15
10	J Brabham	-	-	-	1	-	-	-	-	6	3	4	14
11	J Surtees	-	2	-	-	-	-	-	-	-	4	-	6
12	C Amon	-	-	-	4	-	-	-	-	-	-	-	4
13	D Attwood	-	-	3	-	-	-	-	-	-	-	-	3
	V Elford	-	-	-	-	2	1	-	-	-	-	-	3
	P Rodriguez	-	-	-	-	-	-	-	1	-	2	-	3
16	J Servoz-Gavin	-	-	-	-	-	-	-	-	1	-	-	1
	S Moser	-	-	-	-	-	-	-	-	-	1	-	1
	J Oliver	-	-	-	-	-	-	-	-	-	-	1	1

9, 6, 4, 3, 2 and 1 point awarded to the first six finishers.
Best 5 scores from first 6 races, best 4 from remaining 5 races.

Constructor Points 1969

		ZA	E	MC	NL	F	GB	D	I	CDN	USA	MEX	TOTAL	
1	Matra-Cosworth	9	9	-	9	9	9	6	9	3	-	3	66	
2	Brabham-Cosworth	-	1	6	2	4	6	9	(2)	9	6	6	49	(2)
3	Lotus-Cosworth	6	-	9	6	1	3	3	6	4	9	-	47	
4	McLaren-Cosworth	4	6	(2)	3	3	4	4	3	2	-	9	38	(2)
5	Ferrari	-	-	-	4	-	-	-	1	-	2	-	7	
	BRM	-	2	-	-	-	-	-	-	-	4	1	7	

9, 6, 4, 3, 2 and 1 point awarded to the first six finishers. Points only for highest placed car.
Best 5 scores from first 6 races, best 4 from remaining 5 races.

RACE ENTRANTS & RESULTS 1970

New entrant March helped increase grids by making their car available to customers, the first of which was Ken Tyrrell who had split from his successful partnership with Matra. Lotus again introduced an advancement in design, with the wedge shaped 72 created by radiators alongside the cockpit. Brabham produced its first monocoque, the turquoise BT33, BRM appeared in Yardley cosmetic colours and Dunlop withdrew at the season's end.

FERRARI
Scuderia Ferrari SpA SEFAC: Ickx, Regazzoni, Giunti

BELLASI
Silvio Moser Racing Team: Moser

DE TOMASO
Frank Williams Racing Cars: Courage, Schenken, (Redman)

BRABHAM
Motor Racing Developments: Brabham
Auto Motor Und Sport: Stommelen
Tom Wheatcroft Racing: Bell
Team Gunston: de Klerk
Privateer: Hutchison

BRM
Owen Racing Organisation*: Rodriguez, Oliver, Eaton, (Westbury)
* Yardley Team BRM from E GP

LOTUS
Gold Leaf Team Lotus: Rindt, Miles, Fittipaldi, Wisell
World Wide Racing: (Soler-Roig)
Garvey Team Lotus at E GP
Brooke Bond Oxo Racing/Rob Walker: Hill
Rob Walker Racing Team (first two GPs)
Pete Lovely Volkswagen Inc: Lovely
Team Gunston: Love
Scuderia Scribante: Charlton

MARCH
March Engineering: Amon, Siffert
STP Corporation: Andretti
Tyrrell Racing Organisation: Stewart, Cevert, Servoz-Gavin
Colin Crabbe Racing: Peterson
(Antique Automobiles Racing Team at MC & B GPs)
Privateer: (Hahne)

McLAREN
Bruce McLaren Motor Racing: McLaren, Hulme, Gethin, Gurney, de Adamich, (Galli)
Team Surtees: Surtees
Ecurie Bonnier: Bonnier

SURTEES
Team Surtees: Surtees, Bell

TYRRELL
Tyrrell Racing Organisation: Stewart

MATRA SIMCA
Equipe Matra Elf: Beltoise, Pescarolo

7 Mar 1970 — SOUTH AFRICA: Kyalami — (Round: 1) (Race: 185)
80 laps x 4.104 km, 2.550 miles = 328.306 km, 204.000 miles

POS.	NO.	DRIVER	CAR	MODEL	ENGINE		LAPS	TIME/REASON FOR RETIREMENT	GRID:POS	ROW
1	12	J Brabham	Brabham	BT33	Cosworth	V8	80	1h 49m 34.600s	3	1
2	6	D Hulme	McLaren	M14A	Cosworth	V8	80	1h 49m 42.700s	6	3
3	1	J Stewart	March	701	Cosworth	V8	80	1h 49m 51.700s	1	1
4	3	J-P Beltoise	Matra Simca	MS120	Matra	V12	80	1h 50m 47.700s	8	3
5	10	J Miles	Lotus	49C	Cosworth	V8	79		14	6
6	11	G Hill	Lotus	49C	Cosworth	V8	79		19	8
7	4	H Pescarolo	Matra Simca	MS120	Matra	V12	78		18	7
8	23	J Love	Lotus	49	Cosworth	V8	78		22	9
9	20	P Rodriguez	BRM	P153	BRM	V12	76		16	7
10	16	J Siffert	March	701	Cosworth	V8	75		9	4
11	24	P de Klerk	Brabham	BT26A	Cosworth	V8	75		21	9
12r	25	D Charlton	Lotus	49C	Cosworth	V8	73	puncture/ ignition	13	5
13r	9	J Rindt	Lotus	49C	Cosworth	V8	72	engine	4	2
r	7	J Surtees	McLaren	M7C	Cosworth	V8	60	engine	7	3
r	17	J Ickx	Ferrari	312B	Ferrari	F12	60	engine	5	2
r	21	G Eaton	BRM	P139	BRM	V12	58	engine	23	9
r	2	J Servoz-Gavin	March	701	Cosworth	V8	57	engine	17	7
r	22	P Courage	De Tomaso	505	Cosworth	V8	39	accident/ suspension	20	8
r	5	B McLaren	McLaren	M14A	Cosworth	V8	39	engine	10	4
r	8	M Andretti	March	701	Cosworth	V8	26	engine overheating	11	5
r	14	R Stommelen	Brabham	BT33	Cosworth	V8	23	engine	15	6
r	19	J Oliver	BRM	P153	BRM	V12	22	gear selection	12	5
r	15	C Amon	March	701	Cosworth	V8	14	engine overheating	2	1

Winning speed: 179.768 km/h, 111.703 mph
Pole Position speed: 186.302 km/h, 115.763 mph (J Stewart, 1 min:19.300 sec)
Fastest Lap speed: 182.844 km/h, 113.614 mph (J Surtees/ J Brabham, 1 min:20.800 sec on lap 6 / 71)
Lap Leaders: J Stewart 1-19 (19); J Brabham 20-80 (61).

19 Apr 1970 — SPAIN: Járama — (Round: 2) (Race: 186)
90 laps x 3.404 km, 2.115 miles = 306.360 km, 190.363 miles

POS.	NO.	DRIVER	CAR	MODEL	ENGINE		LAPS	TIME/REASON FOR RETIREMENT	GRID:POS	ROW
1	1	J Stewart	March	701	Cosworth	V8	90	2h 10m 58.200s	3	1
2	11	B McLaren	McLaren	M14A	Cosworth	V8	89		11	5
3	18	M Andretti	March	701	Cosworth	V8	89		16	7
4	6	G Hill	Lotus	49C	Cosworth	V8	89		15	6
5	16	J Servoz-Gavin	March	701	Cosworth	V8	88		14	6
r	8	J Surtees	McLaren	M7C	Cosworth	V8	76	gearbox	12	5
r	7	J Brabham	Brabham	BT33	Cosworth	V8	61	engine	1	1
r	24	R Stommelen	Brabham	BT33	Cosworth	V8	43	valve spring	17	7
r	22	H Pescarolo	Matra Simca	MS120	Matra	V12	33	connecting rod	9	4
r	4	J-P Beltoise	Matra Simca	MS120	Matra	V12	31	engine	4	2
r	9	C Amon	March	701	Cosworth	V8	10	clutch/ engine	6	3
r	5	D Hulme	McLaren	M14A	Cosworth	V8	10	rotor arm shaft	2	1
r	3	J Rindt	Lotus	72	Cosworth	V8	9	ignition	8	3
r	10	P Rodriguez	BRM	P153	BRM	V12	4	withdrew	5	2
r	2	J Ickx	Ferrari	312B	Ferrari	F12	0	accident	7	3
r	15	J Oliver	BRM	P153	BRM	V12	0	accident	10	4
ns	12	P Courage	De Tomaso	505	Cosworth	V8		accident	13	5
nq	20	A de Adamich	McLaren	M7D	Alfa Romeo	V8				
nq	19	J Miles	Lotus	72	Cosworth	V8				

POS.	NO.	DRIVER	CAR	MODEL	ENGINE		LAPS	TIME/REASON FOR RETIREMENT	GRID:POS	ROW
nq	14	J Siffert	March	701	Cosworth	V8				
nq	23	A Soler-Roig	Lotus	49C	Cosworth	V8				
nq	21	G Eaton	BRM	P153	BRM	V12				

Winning speed: 140.350 km/h, 87.209 mph
Pole Position speed: 146.060 km/h, 90.757 mph (J Brabham, 1 min:23.900 sec)
Fastest Lap speed: 145.367 km/h, 90.327 mph (J Brabham, 1 min:24.300 sec on lap 19)
Lap Leaders: J Stewart 1-90 (90).

10 May 1970 — MONACO: Monte Carlo — (Round: 3) (Race: 187)

80 laps x 3.145 km, 1.954 miles = 251.600 km, 156.337 miles

POS.	NO.	DRIVER	CAR	MODEL	ENGINE		LAPS	TIME/REASON FOR RETIREMENT	GRID:POS	ROW
1	3	J Rindt	Lotus	49C	Cosworth	V8	80	1h 54m 36.600s	8	4
2	5	J Brabham	Brabham	BT33	Cosworth	V8	80	1h 54m 59.700s	4	2
3	9	H Pescarolo	Matra Simca	MS120	Matra	V12	80	1h 55m 28.000s	7	4
4	11	D Hulme	McLaren	M14A	Cosworth	V8	80	1h 56m 04.900s	3	2
5	1	G Hill	Lotus	49C	Cosworth	V8	79		16	8
6	17	P Rodriguez	BRM	P153	BRM	V12	78		15	8
7	23	R Peterson	March	701	Cosworth	V8	78		12	6
8r	19	J Siffert	March	701	Cosworth	V8	76	fuel injection	11	6
r	28	C Amon	March	701	Cosworth	V8	60	rear suspension	2	1
nc	24	P Courage	De Tomaso	505	Cosworth	V8	58		9	5
r	21	J Stewart	March	701	Cosworth	V8	57	engine	1	1
r	16	J Oliver	BRM	P153	BRM	V12	42	engine	14	7
r	8	J-P Beltoise	Matra Simca	MS120	Matra	V12	21	crown wheel & pinion	6	3
r	12	B McLaren	McLaren	M14A	Cosworth	V8	19	accident/ suspension	10	5
r	14	J Surtees	McLaren	M7C	Cosworth	V8	14	oil pressure	13	7
r	26	J Ickx	Ferrari	312B	Ferrari	F12	11	universal joint	5	3
nq	6	R Stommelen	Brabham	BT33	Cosworth	V8				
nq	10	A de Adamich	McLaren	M7D	Alfa Romeo	V8				
nq	20	J Servoz-Gavin	March	701	Cosworth	V8				
nq	15	G Eaton	BRM	P153	BRM	V12				
nq	2	J Miles	Lotus	72	Cosworth	V8				

Winning speed: 131.716 km/h, 81.845 mph
Pole Position speed: 134.786 km/h, 83.752 mph (J Stewart, 1 min:24.000 sec)
Fastest Lap speed: 136.082 km/h, 84.557 mph (J Rindt, 1 min:23.200 sec on lap 80)
Lap Leaders: J Stewart 1-27 (27); J Brabham 28-79 (52); J Rindt 80 (1).

7 Jun 1970 — BELGIUM: Spa-Francorchamps — (Round: 4) (Race: 188)

28 laps x 14.100 km, 8.761 miles = 394.800 km, 245.317 miles

POS.	NO.	DRIVER	CAR	MODEL	ENGINE		LAPS	TIME/REASON FOR RETIREMENT	GRID:POS	ROW
1	1	P Rodriguez	BRM	P153	BRM	V12	28	1h 38m 09.900s	6	3
2	10	C Amon	March	701	Cosworth	V8	28	1h 38m 11.000s	3	1
3	25	J-P Beltoise	Matra Simca	MS120	Matra	V12	28	1h 39m 53.600s	11	5
4	28	I Giunti	Ferrari	312B	Ferrari	F12	28	1h 40m 48.400s	8	3
5	19	R Stommelen	Brabham	BT33	Cosworth	V8	28	1h 41m 41.700s	7	3
6r	26	H Pescarolo	Matra Simca	MS120	Matra	V12	27	out of fuel	17	7
7r	9	J Siffert	March	701	Cosworth	V8	26	fuel injection	10	4
8	27	J Ickx	Ferrari	312B	Ferrari	F12	26		4	2
nc	14	R Peterson	March	701	Cosworth	V8	20		9	4
r	18	J Brabham	Brabham	BT33	Cosworth	V8	19	clutch/ flywheel	5	2
r	23	G Hill	Lotus	49C	Cosworth	V8	19	engine	16	7
r	11	J Stewart	March	701	Cosworth	V8	14	engine	1	1
r	21	J Miles	Lotus	72B	Cosworth	V8	13	gear selection	13	5
r	20	J Rindt	Lotus	49C	Cosworth	V8	10	piston	2	1
r	2	J Oliver	BRM	P153	BRM	V12	7	throttle linkage	14	6
r	7	P Courage	De Tomaso	505	Cosworth	V8	4	oil pressure	12	5
r	8	D Bell	Brabham	BT26A	Cosworth	V8	1	gear linkage	15	6
nq	22	A Soler-Roig	Lotus	72	Cosworth	V8				

Winning speed: 241.308 km/h, 149.942 mph
Pole Position speed: 244.038 km/h, 151.638 mph (J Stewart, 3 min:28.000 sec)
Fastest Lap speed: 244.744 km/h, 152.077 mph (C Amon, 3 min:27.400 sec on lap 28)
Lap Leaders: C Amon 1,3-4 (3); J Stewart 2 (1); P Rodriguez 5-28 (24).

21 Jun 1970 — NETHERLANDS: Zandvoort — (Round: 5) (Race: 189)

80 laps x 4.193 km, 2.605 miles = 335.440 km, 208.433 miles

POS.	NO.	DRIVER	CAR	MODEL	ENGINE		LAPS	TIME/REASON FOR RETIREMENT	GRID:POS	ROW
1	10	J Rindt	Lotus	72C	Cosworth	V8	80	1h 50m 43.410s	1	1
2	5	J Stewart	March	701	Cosworth	V8	80	1h 51m 13.410s	2	1
3	25	J Ickx	Ferrari	312B	Ferrari	F12	79		3	1
4	26	C Regazzoni	Ferrari	312B	Ferrari	F12	79		6	3
5	23	J-P Beltoise	Matra Simca	MS120	Matra	V12	79		10	4
6	16	J Surtees	McLaren	M7C	Cosworth	V8	79		14	6
7	12	J Miles	Lotus	72B	Cosworth	V8	78		8	3
8	24	H Pescarolo	Matra Simca	MS120	Matra	V12	78		13	5
9	22	R Peterson	March	701	Cosworth	V8	78		16	7
10	1	P Rodriguez	BRM	P153	BRM	V12	77		7	3
11	18	J Brabham	Brabham	BT33	Cosworth	V8	76		12	5
nc	15	G Hill	Lotus	49C	Cosworth	V8	71		20	8

POS.	NO.	DRIVER	CAR	MODEL	ENGINE		LAPS	TIME/REASON FOR RETIREMENT	GRID:POS	ROW
r	6	F Cevert	March	701	Cosworth	V8	31	connecting rod	15	6
r	3	G Eaton	BRM	P153	BRM	V12	26	oil tank loose	18	7
r	2	J Oliver	BRM	P153	BRM	V12	23	connecting rod	5	2
r	4	P Courage	De Tomaso	505	Cosworth	V8	22	fatal accident	9	4
r	9	J Siffert	March	701	Cosworth	V8	22	engine	17	7
r	20	P Gethin	McLaren	M14A	Cosworth	V8	18	accident	11	5
r	32	D Gurney	McLaren	M14A	Cosworth	V8	2	timing gear	19	8
r	8	C Amon	March	701	Cosworth	V8	1	clutch	4	2
nq	21	A de Adamich	McLaren	M14D	Alfa Romeo	V8				
nq	19	R Stommelen	Brabham	BT33	Cosworth	V8				
nq	31	P Lovely	Lotus	49B	Cosworth	V8				
nq	29	S Moser	Bellasi		Cosworth	V8				

Winning speed: 181.772 km/h, 112.948 mph
Pole Position speed: 192.290 km/h, 119.484 mph (J Rindt, 1 min:18.500 sec)
Fastest Lap speed: 190.519 km/h, 118.383 mph (J Ickx, 1 min:19.230 sec on lap 22)
Lap Leaders: J Ickx 1-2 (2); J Rindt 3-80 (78).

5 Jul 1970 FRANCE: Clermont-Ferrand (Round: 6) (Race: 190)

38 laps x 8.055 km, 5.005 miles = 306.090 km, 190.196 miles

POS.	NO.	DRIVER	CAR	MODEL	ENGINE		LAPS	TIME/REASON FOR RETIREMENT	GRID:POS	ROW
1	6	J Rindt	Lotus	72C	Cosworth	V8	38	1h 55m 57.000s	6	3
2	14	C Amon	March	701	Cosworth	V8	38	1h 56m 04.610s	3	2
3	23	J Brabham	Brabham	BT33	Cosworth	V8	38	1h 56m 41.830s	5	3
4	19	D Hulme	McLaren	M14D	Cosworth	V8	38	1h 56m 42.660s	7	4
5	20	H Pescarolo	Matra Simca	MS120	Matra	V12	38	1h 57m 16.420s	8	4
6	17	D Gurney	McLaren	M14A	Cosworth	V8	38	1h 57m 16.650s	17	9
7	22	R Stommelen	Brabham	BT33	Cosworth	V8	38	1h 58m 17.160s	14	7
8	7	J Miles	Lotus	72B	Cosworth	V8	38	1h 58m 44.170s	18	9
9	1	J Stewart	March	701	Cosworth	V8	38	1h 59m 06.610s	4	2
10	8	G Hill	Lotus	49C	Cosworth	V8	37		20	10
11	2	F Cevert	March	701	Cosworth	V8	37		13	7
12	4	G Eaton	BRM	P153	BRM	V12	36		19	10
13r	21	J-P Beltoise	Matra Simca	MS120	Matra	V12	35	fuel pressure	2	1
14	11	I Giunti	Ferrari	312B	Ferrari	F12	35		11	6
nc	16	A de Adamich	McLaren	M7D	Alfa Romeo	V8	29		15	8
r	12	J Siffert	March	701	Cosworth	V8	23	accident	16	8
r	18	R Peterson	March	701	Cosworth	V8	17	crown wheel & pinion	9	5
r	10	J Ickx	Ferrari	312B	Ferrari	F12	16	valve	1	1
r	3	P Rodriguez	BRM	P153	BRM	V12	6	gearbox	10	5
r	5	J Oliver	BRM	P153	BRM	V12	5	timing	12	6
nq	24	S Moser	Bellasi		Cosworth	V8				
nq	9	A Soler-Roig	Lotus	49C	Cosworth	V8				
nq	35	P Lovely	Lotus	49B	Cosworth	V8				

Winning speed: 158.391 km/h, 98.419 mph
Pole Position speed: 162.709 km/h, 101.103 mph (J Ickx, 2 min:58.220 sec)
Fastest Lap speed: 160.432 km/h, 99.688 mph (J Brabham, 3 min: 0.750 sec on lap 29)
Lap Leaders: J Ickx 1-14 (14); J-P Beltoise 15-25 (11); J Rindt 26-38 (13).

18 Jul 1970 BRITAIN: Brands Hatch (Round: 7) (Race: 191)

80 laps x 4.265 km, 2.650 miles = 341.181 km, 212.000 miles

POS.	NO.	DRIVER	CAR	MODEL	ENGINE		LAPS	TIME/REASON FOR RETIREMENT	GRID:POS	ROW
1	5	J Rindt	Lotus	72C	Cosworth	V8	80	1h 57m 02.000s	1	1
2	17	J Brabham	Brabham	BT33	Cosworth	V8	80	1h 57m 34.900s	2	1
3	9	D Hulme	McLaren	M14D	Cosworth	V8	80	1h 57m 56.400s	5	2
4	4	C Regazzoni	Ferrari	312B	Ferrari	F12	80	1h 57m 56.800s	6	3
5	16	C Amon	March	701	Cosworth	V8	79		17	7
6	14	G Hill	Lotus	49C	Cosworth	V8	79		22	9
7	2	F Cevert	March	701	Cosworth	V8	79		14	6
8	28	E Fittipaldi	Lotus	49C	Cosworth	V8	78		21	9
9	27	R Peterson	March	701	Cosworth	V8	72		13	5
nc	29	P Lovely	Lotus	49B	Cosworth	V8	69		23	9
r	10	D Gurney	McLaren	M14A	Cosworth	V8	60	oil pressure	11	5
r	22	P Rodriguez	BRM	P153	BRM	V12	58	accident	15	6
r	23	J Oliver	BRM	P153	BRM	V12	54	engine	4	2
r	1	J Stewart	March	701	Cosworth	V8	52	clutch/ fire	8	3
r	20	J Surtees	Surtees	TS7	Cosworth	V8	51	oil pressure	19	8
r	8	H Pescarolo	Matra Simca	MS120	Matra	V12	41	accident	12	5
r	7	J-P Beltoise	Matra Simca	MS120	Matra	V12	24	front wheel bearing	10	4
r	26	M Andretti	March	701	Cosworth	V8	21	rear suspension	9	4
r	15	J Siffert	March	701	Cosworth	V8	19	suspension	20	8
r	6	J Miles	Lotus	72B	Cosworth	V8	15	camshaft	7	3
r	24	G Eaton	BRM	P153	BRM	V12	10	oil pressure	16	7
r	3	J Ickx	Ferrari	312B	Ferrari	F12	6	differential	3	1
ns	11	A de Adamich	McLaren	M7D	Alfa Romeo	V8		fuel tank leak	18	7
ns	18	R Stommelen	Brabham	BT33	Cosworth	V8		accident		
ns	25	B Redman	De Tomaso	505	Cosworth	V8		hub		

Winning speed: 174.915 km/h, 108.687 mph
Pole Position speed: 181.051 km/h, 112.500 mph (J Rindt, 1 min:24.800 sec)
Fastest Lap speed: 178.733 km/h, 111.059 mph (J Brabham, 1 min:25.900 sec on lap 70)
Lap Leaders: J Ickx 1-6 (6); J Rindt 7-68,80 (63); J Brabham 69-79 (11).

J Rindt was originally disqualified for wing being too high, but was later reinstated.

2 Aug 1970 — GERMANY: Hockenheim (Round: 8) (Race: 192)

50 laps x 6.789 km, 4.218 miles = 339.450 km, 210.924 miles

POS.	NO.	DRIVER	CAR	MODEL	ENGINE		LAPS	TIME/REASON FOR RETIREMENT	GRID:POS	ROW
1	2	J Rindt	Lotus	72C	Cosworth	V8	50	1h 42m 00.300s	2	1
2	10	J Ickx	Ferrari	312B	Ferrari	F12	50	1h 42m 01.000s	1	1
3	4	D Hulme	McLaren	M14A	Cosworth	V8	50	1h 43m 22.100s	16	8
4	17	E Fittipaldi	Lotus	49C	Cosworth	V8	50	1h 43m 55.400s	13	7
5	21	R Stommelen	Brabham	BT33	Cosworth	V8	49		11	6
6	14	H Pescarolo	Matra Simca	MS120	Matra	V12	49		5	3
7	23	F Cevert	March	701	Cosworth	V8	49		14	7
8r	12	J Siffert	March	701	Cosworth	V8	47	engine	4	2
9r	7	J Surtees	Surtees	TS7	Cosworth	V8	46	engine	15	8
r	9	G Hill	Lotus	49C	Cosworth	V8	37	engine	20	10
r	5	C Amon	March	701	Cosworth	V8	34	engine	6	3
r	15	C Regazzoni	Ferrari	312B	Ferrari	F12	30	engine	3	2
r	16	J Miles	Lotus	72C	Cosworth	V8	24	engine	10	5
r	1	J Stewart	March	701	Cosworth	V8	20	engine	7	4
r	11	M Andretti	March	701	Cosworth	V8	15	gear selection	9	5
r	22	R Peterson	March	701	Cosworth	V8	11	engine	19	10
r	6	P Rodriguez	BRM	P153	BRM	V12	7	ignition	8	4
r	18	J Oliver	BRM	P153	BRM	V12	5	engine	18	9
r	3	J Brabham	Brabham	BT33	Cosworth	V8	4	oil union leak	12	6
r	8	J-P Beltoise	Matra Simca	MS120	Matra	V12	4	front suspension	21	11
r	24	P Gethin	McLaren	M14A	Cosworth	V8	3	throttle slides	17	9
nq	25	B Redman	De Tomaso	505	Cosworth	V8				
nq	20	A de Adamich	McLaren	M14D	Alfa Romeo	V8				
nq	27	S Moser	Bellasi		Cosworth	V8				
nq	26	H Hahne	March	701	Cosworth	V8				

Winning speed: 199.667 km/h, 124.067 mph
Pole Position speed: 204.522 km/h, 127.084 mph (J Ickx, 1 min:59.500 sec)
Fastest Lap speed: 202.825 km/h, 126.030 mph (J Ickx, 2 min: 0.500 sec on lap 49)
Lap Leaders: J Ickx 1-6,10-17,26-31,36-43,45-46,48 (31); J Rindt 7-9,18-21,24-25,32-35,44,47,49-50 (17); C Regazzoni 22-23 (2).

16 Aug 1970 — AUSTRIA: Österreichring (Round: 9) (Race: 193)

60 laps x 5.911 km, 3.673 miles = 354.660 km, 220.376 miles

POS.	NO.	DRIVER	CAR	MODEL	ENGINE		LAPS	TIME/REASON FOR RETIREMENT	GRID:POS	ROW
1	12	J Ickx	Ferrari	312B	Ferrari	F12	60	1h 42m 17.320s	3	2
2	27	C Regazzoni	Ferrari	312B	Ferrari	F12	60	1h 42m 17.930s	2	1
3	11	R Stommelen	Brabham	BT33	Cosworth	V8	60	1h 43m 45.200s	17	9
4	17	P Rodriguez	BRM	P153	BRM	V12	59		22	11
5	16	J Oliver	BRM	P153	BRM	V12	59		14	7
6	19	J-P Beltoise	Matra Simca	MS120	Matra	V12	59		7	4
7	14	I Giunti	Ferrari	312B	Ferrari	F12	59		5	3
8	4	C Amon	March	701	Cosworth	V8	59		6	3
9	3	J Siffert	March	701	Cosworth	V8	59		20	10
10	23	P Gethin	McLaren	M14A	Cosworth	V8	59		21	11
11	18	G Eaton	BRM	P153	BRM	V12	58		23	12
12	22	A de Adamich	McLaren	M14D	Alfa Romeo	V8	57		15	8
13	10	J Brabham	Brabham	BT33	Cosworth	V8	56		8	4
14	20	H Pescarolo	Matra Simca	MS120	Matra	V12	56		13	7
15	8	E Fittipaldi	Lotus	49C	Cosworth	V8	55		16	8
r	21	D Hulme	McLaren	M14A	Cosworth	V8	30	engine	11	6
r	15	J Surtees	Surtees	TS7	Cosworth	V8	27	engine	12	6
r	26	T Schenken	De Tomaso	505	Cosworth	V8	25	engine	19	10
r	6	J Rindt	Lotus	72C	Cosworth	V8	21	engine	1	1
r	24	S Moser	Bellasi		Cosworth	V8	13	radiator	24	12
r	5	M Andretti	March	701	Cosworth	V8	13	throttle jammed/ accident	18	9
r	1	J Stewart	March	701	Cosworth	V8	7	fuel line	4	2
r	7	J Miles	Lotus	72C	Cosworth	V8	4	brake shaft	10	5
r	2	F Cevert	March	701	Cosworth	V8	0	engine	9	5

Winning speed: 208.035 km/h, 129.267 mph
Pole Position speed: 214.447 km/h, 133.251 mph (J Rindt, 1 min:39.230 sec)
Fastest Lap speed: 211.948 km/h, 131.699 mph (J Ickx/ C Regazzoni, 1 min:40.400 sec on lap 45)
Lap Leaders: C Regazzoni 1 (1); J Ickx 2-60 (59).

6 Sep 1970 — ITALY: Monza (Round: 10) (Race: 194)

68 laps x 5.750 km, 3.573 miles = 391.000 km, 242.956 miles

POS.	NO.	DRIVER	CAR	MODEL	ENGINE		LAPS	TIME/REASON FOR RETIREMENT	GRID:POS	ROW
1	4	C Regazzoni	Ferrari	312B	Ferrari	F12	68	1h 39m 06.880s	3	2
2	18	J Stewart	March	701	Cosworth	V8	68	1h 39m 12.610s	4	2
3	40	J-P Beltoise	Matra Simca	MS120	Matra	V12	68	1h 39m 12.680s	14	7
4	30	D Hulme	McLaren	M14A	Cosworth	V8	68	1h 39m 13.030s	9	5
5	46	R Stommelen	Brabham	BT33	Cosworth	V8	68	1h 39m 13.290s	17	9
6	20	F Cevert	March	701	Cosworth	V8	68	1h 40m 10.340s	11	6
7	48	C Amon	March	701	Cosworth	V8	67		18	9
8	34	A de Adamich	McLaren	M14D	Alfa Romeo	V8	61		12	6
nc	32	P Gethin	McLaren	M14A	Cosworth	V8	60		16	8
r	8	J Oliver	BRM	P153	BRM	V12	36	engine	6	3
r	52	R Peterson	March	701	Cosworth	V8	35	engine	13	7
r	44	J Brabham	Brabham	BT33	Cosworth	V8	31	engine/accident	8	4
r	2	J Ickx	Ferrari	312B	Ferrari	F12	25	clutch	1	1

POS.	NO.	DRIVER	CAR	MODEL	ENGINE		LAPS	TIME/REASON FOR RETIREMENT	GRID:POS	ROW
r	12	G Eaton	BRM	P153	BRM	V12	21	engine overheating	20	10
r	54	T Schenken	De Tomaso	505	Cosworth	V8	17	engine	19	10
r	42	H Pescarolo	Matra Simca	MS120	Matra	V12	14	valve spring	15	8
r	6	I Giunti	Ferrari	312B	Ferrari	F12	14	fuel metering unit	5	3
r	10	P Rodriguez	BRM	P153	BRM	V12	12	engine	2	1
r	50	J Siffert	March	701	Cosworth	V8	3	engine	7	4
r	14	J Surtees	Surtees	TS7	Cosworth	V8	0	electrics	10	5
ns	22	J Rindt	Lotus	72C	Cosworth	V8		fatal accident		
ns	28	G Hill	Lotus	72C	Cosworth	V8		withdrew after Rindt accident		
ns	24	J Miles	Lotus	72C	Cosworth	V8		withdrew after Rindt accident		
nq	38	J Bonnier	McLaren	M7C	Cosworth	V8				
ns	26	E Fittipaldi	Lotus	72C	Cosworth	V8		withdrew after Rindt accident		
nq	36	N Galli	McLaren	M7D	Alfa Romeo	V8				
nq	56	S Moser	Bellasi		Cosworth	V8				

Winning speed: 236.696 km/h, 147.076 mph
Pole Position speed: 246.019 km/h, 152.869 mph (J Ickx, 1 min:24.140 sec)
Fastest Lap speed: 242.958 km/h, 150.967 mph (C Regazzoni, 1 min:25.200 sec on lap 65)
Lap Leaders: J Ickx 1-3,19-20 (5); P Rodriguez 4,7-8 (3); J Stewart 5-6,9,11,14-17,26-27,31,35,37,42-43,51,53 (17); C Regazzoni 10,12,32-34,36,38-41,44-50,52,54-68 (33); J Oliver 13,18,21-25,28,30 (9); D Hulme 29 (1).

20 Sep 1970 — CANADA: Mont-Tremblant — (Round:11) (Race: 195)

90 laps x 4.265 km, 2.650 miles = 383.829 km, 238.500 miles

POS.	NO.	DRIVER	CAR	MODEL	ENGINE		LAPS	TIME/REASON FOR RETIREMENT	GRID:POS	ROW
1	18	J Ickx	Ferrari	312B	Ferrari	F12	90	2h 21m 18.400s	2	1
2	19	C Regazzoni	Ferrari	312B	Ferrari	F12	90	2h 21m 33.200s	3	2
3	20	C Amon	March	701	Cosworth	V8	90	2h 22m 16.300s	6	3
4	14	P Rodriguez	BRM	P153	BRM	V12	89		7	4
5	4	J Surtees	Surtees	TS7	Cosworth	V8	89		5	3
6	6	P Gethin	McLaren	M14A	Cosworth	V8	88		11	6
7	24	H Pescarolo	Matra Simca	MS120	Matra	V12	87		8	4
8	23	J-P Beltoise	Matra Simca	MS120	Matra	V12	85		13	7
9	2	F Cevert	March	701	Cosworth	V8	85		4	2
10	16	G Eaton	BRM	P153	BRM	V12	85		9	5
nc	10	T Schenken	De Tomaso	505	Cosworth	V8	79		17	9
nc	9	G Hill	Lotus	72C	Cosworth	V8	77		20	10
r	8	A de Adamich	McLaren	M14D	Alfa Romeo	V8	69	oil pressure	12	6
nc	26	R Peterson	March	701	Cosworth	V8	65		16	8
r	5	D Hulme	McLaren	M14A	Cosworth	V8	59	flywheel	15	8
r	11	J Brabham	Brabham	BT33	Cosworth	V8	57	oil leak	19	10
nc	15	J Oliver	BRM	P153	BRM	V12	52		10	5
r	3	J Stewart	Tyrrell	001	Cosworth	V8	31	stub axle	1	1
r	12	R Stommelen	Brabham	BT33	Cosworth	V8	23	steering	18	9
r	21	J Siffert	March	701	Cosworth	V8	22	engine	14	7

Winning speed: 162.977 km/h, 101.269 mph
Pole Position speed: 167.794 km/h, 104.262 mph (J Stewart, 1 min:31.500 sec)
Fastest Lap speed: 166.520 km/h, 103.471 mph (C Regazzoni, 1 min:32.200 sec on lap 75)
Lap Leaders: J Stewart 1-31 (31); J Ickx 32-90 (59).

4 Oct 1970 — USA: Watkins Glen — (Round:12) (Race: 196)

108 laps x 3.701 km, 2.300 miles = 399.761 km, 248.400 miles

POS.	NO.	DRIVER	CAR	MODEL	ENGINE		LAPS	TIME/REASON FOR RETIREMENT	GRID:POS	ROW
1	24	E Fittipaldi	Lotus	72C	Cosworth	V8	108	1h 57m 32.790s	3	2
2	19	P Rodriguez	BRM	P153	BRM	V12	108	1h 58m 09.180s	4	2
3	23	R Wisell	Lotus	72C	Cosworth	V8	108	1h 58m 17.960s	9	5
4	3	J Ickx	Ferrari	312B	Ferrari	F12	107		1	1
5	12	C Amon	March	701	Cosworth	V8	107		5	3
6	18	D Bell	Surtees	TS7	Cosworth	V8	107		13	7
7	8	D Hulme	McLaren	M14A	Cosworth	V8	106		11	6
8	7	H Pescarolo	Matra Simca	MS120	Matra	V12	105		12	6
9	11	J Siffert	March	701	Cosworth	V8	105		23	12
10	15	J Brabham	Brabham	BT33	Cosworth	V8	105		16	8
11	29	R Peterson	March	701	Cosworth	V8	104		15	8
12	16	R Stommelen	Brabham	BT33	Cosworth	V8	104		19	10
13	4	C Regazzoni	Ferrari	312B	Ferrari	F12	101		6	3
14	9	P Gethin	McLaren	M14A	Cosworth	V8	100		21	11
r	1	J Stewart	Tyrrell	001	Cosworth	V8	82	oil leak	2	1
r	14	G Hill	Lotus	72C	Cosworth	V8	72	clutch	10	5
r	2	F Cevert	March	701	Cosworth	V8	62	rear wheel lost	17	9
r	30	T Schenken	De Tomaso	505	Cosworth	V8	61	rear suspension	20	10
r	27	J Bonnier	McLaren	M7C	Cosworth	V8	50	water pipe	24	12
r	6	J-P Beltoise	Matra Simca	MS120	Matra	V12	27	handling	18	9
r	31	G Hutchison	Brabham	BT26A	Cosworth	V8	21	accident/ fuel tank	22	11
r	20	J Oliver	BRM	P153	BRM	V12	14	engine	7	4
r	21	G Eaton	BRM	P153	BRM	V12	10	engine	14	7
r	17	J Surtees	Surtees	TS7	Cosworth	V8	6	flywheel	8	4
nq	32	P Westbury	BRM	P153	BRM	V12				
nq	28	P Lovely	Lotus	49B	Cosworth	V8				
nq	10	A de Adamich	McLaren	M14D	Alfa Romeo	V8				

Winning speed: 204.053 km/h, 126.792 mph
Pole Position speed: 211.279 km/h, 131.283 mph (J Ickx, 1 min: 3.070 sec)
Fastest Lap speed: 212.390 km/h, 131.973 mph (J Ickx, 1 min: 2.740 sec on lap 105)
Lap Leaders: J Stewart 1-82 (82); P Rodriguez 83-100 (18); E Fittipaldi 101-108 (8).

25 Oct 1970 MEXICO: Mexico City (Round:13) (Race: 197)

65 laps x 5.000 km, 3.107 miles = 325.000 km, 201.946 miles

POS.	NO.	DRIVER	CAR	MODEL	ENGINE		LAPS	TIME/REASON FOR RETIREMENT	GRID:POS	ROW
1	3	J Ickx	Ferrari	312B	Ferrari	F12	65	1h 53m 28.360s	3	2
2	4	C Regazzoni	Ferrari	312B	Ferrari	F12	65	1h 54m 13.820s	1	1
3	8	D Hulme	McLaren	M14A	Cosworth	V8	65	1h 54m 14.330s	14	7
4	12	C Amon	March	701	Cosworth	V8	65	1h 54m 15.410s	5	3
5	6	J-P Beltoise	Matra Simca	MS120	Matra	V12	65	1h 54m 18.470s	6	3
6	19	P Rodriguez	BRM	P153	BRM	V12	65	1h 54m 53.120s	7	4
7	20	J Oliver	BRM	P153	BRM	V12	64		13	7
8	17	J Surtees	Surtees	TS7	Cosworth	V8	64		15	8
9	7	H Pescarolo	Matra Simca	MS120	Matra	V12	61		11	6
nc	23	R Wisell	Lotus	72C	Cosworth	V8	56		12	6
r	15	J Brabham	Brabham	BT33	Cosworth	V8	52	oil pressure	4	2
r	1	J Stewart	Tyrrell	001	Cosworth	V8	33	front suspension	2	1
r	9	P Gethin	McLaren	M14A	Cosworth	V8	27	engine	10	5
r	16	R Stommelen	Brabham	BT33	Cosworth	V8	15	fuel system	17	9
r	2	F Cevert	March	701	Cosworth	V8	8	engine	9	5
r	14	G Hill	Lotus	72C	Cosworth	V8	4	engine overheating	8	4
r	11	J Siffert	March	701	Cosworth	V8	3	engine	16	8
r	24	E Fittipaldi	Lotus	72C	Cosworth	V8	1	engine	18	9

Winning speed: 171.848 km/h, 106.781 mph
Pole Position speed: 176.713 km/h, 109.804 mph (C Regazzoni, 1 min:41.860 sec)
Fastest Lap speed: 174.571 km/h, 108.473 mph (J Ickx, 1 min:43.110 sec on lap 46)
Lap Leaders: C Regazzoni 1 (1); J Ickx 2-65 (64).

P Rodriguez, G Eaton and J Oliver, British Grand Prix 1970

Lap Leaders 1970

POS	DRIVER	CAR-ENGINE	GPS	LAPS	KM	MILES
1	J Stewart	March-Cosworth	5	154	581.1	361.1
		Tyrrell-Cosworth	2	113	435.7	270.7
			7	267	1,016.8	631.8
2	J Ickx	Ferrari	8	240	1,306.3	811.7
3	J Rindt	Lotus-Cosworth	5	172	819.0	508.9
4	J Brabham	Brabham-Cosworth	3	124	460.8	286.3
5	P Rodriguez	BRM	3	45	422.3	262.4
6	C Regazzoni	Ferrari	4	37	214.2	133.1
7	J-P Beltoise	Matra Simca	1	11	88.6	55.1
8	J Oliver	BRM	1	9	51.7	32.2
9	E Fittipaldi	Lotus-Cosworth	1	8	29.6	18.4
10	C Amon	March-Cosworth	1	3	42.3	26.3
11	D Hulme	McLaren-Cosworth	1	1	5.7	3.6
			13	**917**	**4,457.5**	**2,769.7**

Driver Points 1970

		ZA	E	MC	B	NL	F	GB	D	A	I	CDN	USA	MEX	TOTAL
1	J Rindt	-	-	9	-	9	9	9	9	-	-	-	-	-	45
2	J Ickx	-	-	-	-	4	-	-	6	9	-	9	3	9	40
3	C Regazzoni	-	-	-	-	3	-	3	-	6	9	6	-	6	33
4	D Hulme	6	-	3	-	-	3	4	4	-	3	-	-	4	27
5	J Brabham	9	-	6	-	-	4	6	-	-	-	-	-	-	25
	J Stewart	4	9	-	-	6	-	-	-	-	6	-	-	-	25
7	P Rodriguez	-	-	1	9	-	-	-	-	3	-	3	6	1	23
	C Amon	-	-	-	6	-	6	2	-	-	-	4	2	3	23
9	J-P Beltoise	3	-	-	4	2	-	-	-	1	4	-	-	2	16
10	E Fittipaldi	-	-	-	-	-	-	-	3	-	-	-	9	-	12
11	R Stommelen	-	-	-	2	-	-	-	2	4	2	-	-	-	10
12	H Pescarolo	-	-	4	1	-	2	-	1	-	-	-	-	-	8
13	G Hill	1	3	2	-	-	-	1	-	-	-	-	-	-	7
14	B McLaren	-	6	-	-	-	-	-	-	-	-	-	-	-	6
15	M Andretti	-	4	-	-	-	-	-	-	-	-	-	-	-	4
	R Wisell	-	-	-	-	-	-	-	-	-	-	-	4	-	4
17	I Giunti	-	-	-	3	-	-	-	-	-	-	-	-	-	3
	J Surtees	-	-	-	-	1	-	-	-	-	-	2	-	-	3
19	J Miles	2	-	-	-	-	-	-	-	-	-	-	-	-	2
	J Servoz-Gavin	-	2	-	-	-	-	-	-	-	-	-	-	-	2
	J Oliver	-	-	-	-	-	-	-	-	2	-	-	-	-	2
22	D Gurney	-	-	-	-	-	1	-	-	-	-	-	-	-	1
	F Cevert	-	-	-	-	-	-	-	-	-	1	-	-	-	1
	P Gethin	-	-	-	-	-	-	-	-	-	-	1	-	-	1
	D Bell	-	-	-	-	-	-	-	-	-	-	-	1	-	1

9, 6, 4, 3, 2 and 1 point awarded to the first six finishers. Best 6 scores from first 7 races, best 5 from remaining 6 races.

Constructor Points 1970

		ZA	E	MC	B	NL	F	GB	D	A	I	CDN	USA	MEX	TOTAL	
1	Lotus-Cosworth	2	3	9	-	9	9	9	9	-	-	-	9	-	59	
2	Ferrari	-	-	-	3	4	-	3	6	9	9	9	(3)	9	52	(3)
3	March-Cosworth	4	9	-	6	6	6	2	-	-	6	4	2	3	48	
4	Brabham-Cosworth	9	-	6	2	-	4	6	2	4	2	-	-	-	35	
	McLaren-Cosworth	6	6	3	-	1	3	4	4	-	3	1	-	4	35	
6	BRM	-	-	1	9	-	-	-	-	3	-	3	6	1	23	
	Matra Simca	3	-	4	4	2	2	-	1	1	4	-	-	2	23	
8	Surtees-Cosworth	-	-	-	-	-	-	-	-	-	-	2	1	-	3	

9, 6, 4, 3,2 and 1 point awarded to the first six finishers. Points only for highest placed car.
Best 6 scores from first 7 races, best 5 from remaining 6 races.

Progress in tyre design lead to substantial width increases, as well as the introduction of the treadless slicks. Air scoops appeared on some cars and Lotus tried out its turbine car in selected races. The season ended on a sour note when Siffert was killed in a non-championship race at Brands Hatch.

FERRARI
Scuderia Ferrari SpA SEFAC: Ickx, Regazzoni, Andretti

BELLASI
Jolly Club Switzerland: Moser

BRABHAM
Motor Racing Developments: Hill, Schenken, Charlton
Ecurie Evergreen/Alain de Cadenet: Craft
Team Gunston: Pretorius

BRM
Yardley Team BRM: Rodriguez, Siffert, Ganley, Marko, Gethin, Elford, Eaton, Cannon

LOTUS
Gold Leaf Team Lotus: Fittipaldi, Wisell, Charlton, Walker
World Wide Racing: Fittipaldi (I)
Pete Lovely Volkswagen Inc: Lovely

MARCH
STP March Racing Team: Peterson, Galli, de Adamich, Soler-Roig, Lauda, Beuttler (CDN)
Frank Williams Racing Cars: Pescarolo, Max
Gene Mason Racing: Barber
Clarke-Mordaunt-Guthrie Racing: Beuttler
Shell Arnold Team: Jarier
Jo Siffert Automobiles: Mazet
Team Gunston: Love

McLAREN
Bruce McLaren Motor Racing: Hulme, Gethin, Oliver
Ecurie Bonnier: Bonnier, (Marko)
Penske-White Racing: Donohue, Hobbs

SURTEES
Brooke Bond Oxo-Rob Walker Team Surtees: Surtees
Auto Motor Und Sport-Eifelland Team Surtees: Stommelen
Team Surtees: Redman, Hailwood, Bell, Posey
Stichting Autoraces Nederland: van Lennep

TYRRELL
Elf Team Tyrrell: Stewart, Cevert, Revson

MATRA SIMCA
Equipe Matra Sports: Amon, Beltoise

6 Mar 1971 — **SOUTH AFRICA: Kyalami** — **(Round: 1) (Race: 198)**
79 laps x 4.104 km, 2.550 miles = 324.216 km, 201.458 miles

POS.	NO.	DRIVER	CAR	MODEL	ENGINE		LAPS	TIME/REASON FOR RETIREMENT	GRID:POS	ROW
1	6	M Andretti	Ferrari	312B	Ferrari	F12	79	1h 47m 35.500s	4	2
2	9	J Stewart	Tyrrell	001	Cosworth	V8	79	1h 47m 56.400s	1	1
3	5	C Regazzoni	Ferrari	312B	Ferrari	F12	79	1h 48m 06.900s	3	1
4	3	R Wisell	Lotus	72C	Cosworth	V8	79	1h 48m 44.900s	14	6
5	19	C Amon	Matra Simca	MS120B	Matra	V12	78		2	1
6	11	D Hulme	McLaren	M19A	Cosworth	V8	78		7	3
7	28	B Redman	Surtees	TS7	Cosworth	V8	78		17	7
8	4	J Ickx	Ferrari	312B	Ferrari	F12	78		8	3
9	14	G Hill	Brabham	BT33	Cosworth	V8	77		19	8
10	7	R Peterson	March	711	Cosworth	V8	77		13	5
11	22	H Pescarolo	March	701	Cosworth	V8	77		18	7
12	21	R Stommelen	Surtees	TS7	Cosworth	V8	77		15	6
13	8	A de Adamich	March	711	Alfa Romeo	V8	75		22	9
r	2	E Fittipaldi	Lotus	72C	Cosworth	V8	58	engine	5	2
r	20	J Surtees	Surtees	TS9	Cosworth	V8	56	gearbox oil pipe	6	3
r	10	F Cevert	Tyrrell	002	Cosworth	V8	45	accident	9	4
r	27	H Ganley	BRM	P153	BRM	V12	42	driver ill	24	10
r	16	P Rodriguez	BRM	P160	BRM	V12	33	engine overheating	10	4
r	17	J Siffert	BRM	P153	BRM	V12	31	engine overheating	16	7
r	15	D Charlton	Brabham	BT33	Cosworth	V8	31	valve spring	12	5
r	24	J Love	March	701	Cosworth	V8	30	differential	21	9
r	25	J Pretorius	Brabham	BT26A	Cosworth	V8	22	camshaft	20	8
r	12	P Gethin	McLaren	M14A	Cosworth	V8	7	fuel line/ leak	11	5
r	23	J Bonnier	McLaren	M7C	Cosworth	V8	5	suspension	23	9
r	26	A Soler-Roig	March	711	Cosworth	V8	5	engine	25	10

Winning speed: 180.804 km/h, 112.346 mph
Pole Position speed: 189.902 km/h, 118.000 mph (J Stewart, 1 min:17.800 sec)
Fastest Lap speed: 183.990 km/h, 114.326 mph (M Andretti, 1 min:20.300 sec on lap 73)
Lap Leaders: C Regazzoni 1-16 (16); D Hulme 17-75 (59); M Andretti 76-79 (4).

18 Apr 1971 — **SPAIN: Montjuich Park** — **(Round: 2) (Race: 199)**
75 laps x 3.791 km, 2.356 miles = 284.325 km, 176.671 miles

POS.	NO.	DRIVER	CAR	MODEL	ENGINE		LAPS	TIME/REASON FOR RETIREMENT	GRID:POS	ROW
1	11	J Stewart	Tyrrell	003	Cosworth	V8	75	1h 49m 03.400s	4	2
2	4	J Ickx	Ferrari	312B	Ferrari	F12	75	1h 49m 06.800s	1	1
3	20	C Amon	Matra Simca	MS120B	Matra	V12	75	1h 50m 01.500s	3	1
4	14	P Rodriguez	BRM	P160	BRM	V12	75	1h 50m 21.300s	5	2
5	9	D Hulme	McLaren	M19A	Cosworth	V8	75	1h 50m 30.400s	9	4
6	21	J-P Beltoise	Matra Simca	MS120B	Matra	V12	74		6	3
7	12	F Cevert	Tyrrell	002	Cosworth	V8	74		12	5
8	10	P Gethin	McLaren	M14A	Cosworth	V8	73		7	3
9	8	T Schenken	Brabham	BT33	Cosworth	V8	72		21	9
10	16	H Ganley	BRM	P153	BRM	V12	71		17	7
11	24	J Surtees	Surtees	TS9	Cosworth	V8	67		22	9
nc	3	R Wisell	Lotus	72C	Cosworth	V8	58		16	7
r	2	E Fittipaldi	Lotus	72C	Cosworth	V8	54	rear suspension	14	6
r	27	H Pescarolo	March	711	Cosworth	V8	53	engine/ rear wing	11	5
r	6	M Andretti	Ferrari	312B	Ferrari	F12	50	fuel pump/ oil pressure	8	3
r	19	A Soler-Roig	March	711	Cosworth	V8	46	fuel line	20	8
r	17	A de Adamich	March	711	Alfa Romeo	V8	26	transmission	18	7
r	18	R Peterson	March	711	Cosworth	V8	24	ignition	13	5
r	5	C Regazzoni	Ferrari	312B	Ferrari	F12	13	engine	2	1
r	25	R Stommelen	Surtees	TS9	Cosworth	V8	9	fuel pressure	19	8

POS.	NO.	DRIVER	CAR	MODEL	ENGINE		LAPS	TIME/REASON FOR RETIREMENT	GRID:POS	ROW
r	7	G Hill	Brabham	BT34	Cosworth	V8	5	steering	15	6
r	15	J Siffert	BRM	P160	BRM	V12	5	gear linkage	10	4

Winning speed: 156.428 km/h, 97.200 mph
Pole Position speed: 158.878 km/h, 98.722 mph (J Ickx, 1 min:25.900 sec)
Fastest Lap speed: 160.371 km/h, 99.650 mph (J Ickx, 1 min:25.100 sec on lap 69)
Lap Leaders: J Ickx 1-5 (5); J Stewart 6-75 (70).

23 May 1971 — MONACO: Monte Carlo (Round: 3) (Race: 200)

80 laps x 3.145 km, 1.954 miles = 251.600 km, 156.337 miles

POS.	NO.	DRIVER	CAR	MODEL	ENGINE		LAPS	TIME/REASON FOR RETIREMENT	GRID:POS	ROW
1	11	J Stewart	Tyrrell	003	Cosworth	V8	80	1h 52m 21.300s	1	1
2	17	R Peterson	March	711	Cosworth	V8	80	1h 52m 46.900s	8	4
3	4	J Ickx	Ferrari	312B2	Ferrari	F12	80	1h 53m 14.600s	2	1
4	9	D Hulme	McLaren	M19A	Cosworth	V8	80	1h 53m 28.000s	6	3
5	1	E Fittipaldi	Lotus	72D	Cosworth	V8	79		17	9
6	24	R Stommelen	Surtees	TS9	Cosworth	V8	79		16	8
7	22	J Surtees	Surtees	TS9	Cosworth	V8	79		10	5
8	27	H Pescarolo	March	711	Cosworth	V8	77		13	7
9	15	P Rodriguez	BRM	P160	BRM	V12	76		5	3
10	8	T Schenken	Brabham	BT33	Cosworth	V8	76		18	9
r	14	J Siffert	BRM	P160	BRM	V12	58	oil line	3	2
r	21	J-P Beltoise	Matra Simca	MS120B	Matra	V12	47	crown wheel & pinion	7	4
r	20	C Amon	Matra Simca	MS120B	Matra	V12	45	crown wheel & pinion	4	2
r	3	C Regazzoni	Ferrari	312B2	Ferrari	F12	24	accident	11	6
r	10	P Gethin	McLaren	M14A	Cosworth	V8	22	accident	14	7
r	2	R Wisell	Lotus	72C	Cosworth	V8	21	rear hub bearing	12	6
r	12	F Cevert	Tyrrell	002	Cosworth	V8	5	suspension/ accident	15	8
r	7	G Hill	Brabham	BT34	Cosworth	V8	1	accident	9	5
nq	16	H Ganley	BRM	P153	BRM	V12				
nq	6	M Andretti	Ferrari	312B	Ferrari	F12				
nq	19	N Galli	March	711	Alfa Romeo	V8				
nq	18	A Soler-Roig	March	711	Cosworth	V8				
nq	28	S Barber	March	711	Cosworth	V8				

Winning speed: 134.360 km/h, 83.487 mph
Pole Position speed: 136.082 km/h, 84.557 mph (J Stewart, 1 min:23.200 sec)
Fastest Lap speed: 137.737 km/h, 85.586 mph (J Stewart, 1 min:22.200 sec on lap 57)
Lap Leaders: J Stewart 1-80 (80).

20 Jun 1971 — NETHERLANDS: Zandvoort (Round: 4) (Race: 201)

70 laps x 4.193 km, 2.605 miles = 293.510 km, 182.379 miles

POS.	NO.	DRIVER	CAR	MODEL	ENGINE		LAPS	TIME/REASON FOR RETIREMENT	GRID:POS	ROW
1	2	J Ickx	Ferrari	312B2	Ferrari	F12	70	1h 56m 20.090s	1	1
2	8	P Rodriguez	BRM	P160	BRM	V12	70	1h 56m 28.080s	2	1
3	3	C Regazzoni	Ferrari	312B2	Ferrari	F12	69		4	2
4	16	R Peterson	March	711	Cosworth	V8	68		13	5
5	23	J Surtees	Surtees	TS9	Cosworth	V8	68		7	3
6	9	J Siffert	BRM	P160	BRM	V12	68		8	3
7	10	H Ganley	BRM	P153	BRM	V12	66		9	4
8	30	G van Lennep	Surtees	TS7	Cosworth	V8	65		21	9
9	21	J-P Beltoise	Matra Simca	MS120B	Matra	V12	65		11	5
10	24	G Hill	Brabham	BT34	Cosworth	V8	65		16	7
11	5	J Stewart	Tyrrell	003	Cosworth	V8	65		3	1
12	26	D Hulme	McLaren	M19A	Cosworth	V8	63		14	6
nc	31	H Pescarolo	March	711	Cosworth	V8	62		15	6
nc	22	S Barber	March	711	Cosworth	V8	60		24	10
nc	28	P Gethin	McLaren	M19A	Cosworth	V8	60		23	9
r	19	A Soler-Roig	March	711	Cosworth	V8	57	engine	17	7
r	25	T Schenken	Brabham	BT33	Cosworth	V8	39	suspension	19	8
r	6	F Cevert	Tyrrell	002	Cosworth	V8	29	accident	12	5
dq	29	R Stommelen	Surtees	TS9	Cosworth	V8	19	push start after spin	10	4
dq	14	R Wisell	Lotus	72D	Cosworth	V8	17	reversed into pits	6	3
r	18	N Galli	March	711	Alfa Romeo	V8	7	accident	20	8
r	15	D Walker	Lotus	56B	Pratt & Whitney	tbn	6	accident	22	9
r	4	M Andretti	Ferrari	312B	Ferrari	F12	5	fuel pump/ engine	18	7
r	20	C Amon	Matra Simca	MS120B	Matra	V12	2	spin/ radiator	5	2

Winning speed: 151.379 km/h, 94.062 mph
Pole Position speed: 194.973 km/h, 121.151 mph (J Ickx, 1 min:17.420 sec)
Fastest Lap speed: 158.976 km/h, 98.783 mph (J Ickx, 1 min:34.950 sec on lap 49)
Lap Leaders: J Ickx 1-8,30,32-70 (48); P Rodriguez 9-29,31 (22).

4 Jul 1971 — FRANCE: Paul Ricard (Round: 5) (Race: 202)

55 laps x 5.810 km, 3.610 miles = 319.550 km, 198.559 miles

POS.	NO.	DRIVER	CAR	MODEL	ENGINE		LAPS	TIME/REASON FOR RETIREMENT	GRID:POS	ROW
1	11	J Stewart	Tyrrell	003	Cosworth	V8	55	1h 46m 41.680s	1	1
2	12	F Cevert	Tyrrell	002	Cosworth	V8	55	1h 47m 09.800s	7	3
3	1	E Fittipaldi	Lotus	72D	Cosworth	V8	55	1h 47m 15.750s	17	7
4	14	J Siffert	BRM	P160	BRM	V12	55	1h 47m 18.850s	6	3
5	20	C Amon	Matra Simca	MS120B	Matra	V12	55	1h 47m 22.760s	9	4
6	2	R Wisell	Lotus	72D	Cosworth	V8	55	1h 47m 57.700s	15	6
7	21	J-P Beltoise	Matra Simca	MS120B	Matra	V12	55	1h 47m 58.610s	8	3
8	22	J Surtees	Surtees	TS9	Cosworth	V8	55	1h 48m 06.590s	13	5
9	10	P Gethin	McLaren	M19A	Cosworth	V8	54		19	8
10	16	H Ganley	BRM	P153	BRM	V12	54		16	7
11	24	R Stommelen	Surtees	TS9	Cosworth	V8	53		10	4
12r	8	T Schenken	Brabham	BT33	Cosworth	V8	50	oil pressure	14	6
13	34	F Mazet	March	701	Cosworth	V8	50		23	9
nc	28	J Max	March	701	Cosworth	V8	46		22	9
r	27	H Pescarolo	March	711	Cosworth	V8	45	gearbox	18	7
r	7	G Hill	Brabham	BT34	Cosworth	V8	34	oil line	4	2
r	19	A de Adamich	March	711	Alfa Romeo	V8	31	engine	20	8
r	15	P Rodriguez	BRM	P160	BRM	V12	27	coil	5	2
r	5	C Regazzoni	Ferrari	312B2	Ferrari	F12	20	spin/ wheel	2	1
r	17	R Peterson	March	711	Alfa Romeo	V8	19	engine	12	5
r	9	D Hulme	McLaren	M19A	Cosworth	V8	16	ignition	11	5
r	4	J Ickx	Ferrari	312B2	Ferrari	F12	4	engine	3	1
r	18	A Soler-Roig	March	711	Cosworth	V8	4	fuel pump	21	9
ns	33	N Galli	March	711	Cosworth	V8		car raced by Soler-Roig		

Winning speed: 179.700 km/h, 111.660 mph
Pole Position speed: 188.926 km/h, 117.393 mph (J Stewart, 1 min:50.710 sec)
Fastest Lap speed: 183.329 km/h, 113.915 mph (J Stewart, 1 min:54.090 sec on lap 2)
Lap Leaders: J Stewart 1-55 (55).

17 Jul 1971 — BRITAIN: Silverstone (Round: 6) (Race: 203)

68 laps x 4.711 km, 2.927 miles = 320.317 km, 199.036 miles

POS.	NO.	DRIVER	CAR	MODEL	ENGINE		LAPS	TIME/REASON FOR RETIREMENT	GRID:POS	ROW
1	12	J Stewart	Tyrrell	003	Cosworth	V8	68	1h 31m 31.500s	2	1
2	18	R Peterson	March	711	Cosworth	V8	68	1h 32m 07.600s	5	2
3	1	E Fittipaldi	Lotus	72D	Cosworth	V8	68	1h 32m 22.000s	4	2
4	26	H Pescarolo	March	711	Cosworth	V8	67		17	7
5	24	R Stommelen	Surtees	TS9	Cosworth	V8	67		12	5
6	23	J Surtees	Surtees	TS9	Cosworth	V8	67		18	7
7	22	J-P Beltoise	Matra Simca	MS120B	Matra	V12	66		15	6
8	17	H Ganley	BRM	P153	BRM	V12	66		11	5
9	16	J Siffert	BRM	P160	BRM	V12	66		3	1
10	14	F Cevert	Tyrrell	002	Cosworth	V8	65		10	4
11	20	N Galli	March	711	Cosworth	V8	65		21	9
12r	8	T Schenken	Brabham	BT33	Cosworth	V8	63	gearbox	7	3
nc	3	R Wisell	Lotus	56B	Pratt & Whitney	tbn	57		19	8
nc	19	A de Adamich	March	711	Alfa Romeo	V8	56		24	10
r	10	P Gethin	McLaren	M19A	Cosworth	V8	53	engine	14	6
r	4	J Ickx	Ferrari	312B2	Ferrari	F12	51	engine	6	3
r	5	C Regazzoni	Ferrari	312B2	Ferrari	F12	48	oil pressure	1	1
r	21	C Amon	Matra Simca	MS120B	Matra	V12	35	dropped valve	9	4
r	9	D Hulme	McLaren	M19A	Cosworth	V8	32	engine	8	3
r	25	D Bell	Surtees	TS9	Cosworth	V8	23	suspension	23	9
r	6	M Beuttler	March	711	Cosworth	V8	21	oil pressure	20	8
r	2	D Charlton	Lotus	72D	Cosworth	V8	1	engine	13	5
r	11	J Oliver	McLaren	M14A	Cosworth	V8	0	accident	22	9
r	7	G Hill	Brabham	BT34	Cosworth	V8	0	accident	16	7

Winning speed: 209.987 km/h, 130.480 mph
Pole Position speed: 217.132 km/h, 134.919 mph (C Regazzoni, 1 min:18.100 sec)
Fastest Lap speed: 212.240 km/h, 131.880 mph (J Stewart, 1 min:19.900 sec on lap 45)
Lap Leaders: C Regazzoni 1-3 (3); J Stewart 4-68 (65).

1 Aug 1971 — GERMANY: Nürburgring (Round: 7) (Race: 204)

12 laps x 22.835 km, 14.189 miles = 274.020 km, 170.268 miles

POS.	NO.	DRIVER	CAR	MODEL	ENGINE		LAPS	TIME/REASON FOR RETIREMENT	GRID:POS	ROW
1	2	J Stewart	Tyrrell	003	Cosworth	V8	12	1h 29m 15.700s	1	1
2	3	F Cevert	Tyrrell	002	Cosworth	V8	12	1h 29m 45.800s	5	3
3	6	C Regazzoni	Ferrari	312B2	Ferrari	F12	12	1h 29m 52.800s	4	2
4	5	M Andretti	Ferrari	312B2	Ferrari	F12	12	1h 31m 20.700s	11	6
5	15	R Peterson	March	711	Cosworth	V8	12	1h 31m 44.800s	7	4
6	25	T Schenken	Brabham	BT33	Cosworth	V8	12	1h 32m 14.300s	9	5
7	7	J Surtees	Surtees	TS9	Cosworth	V8	12	1h 32m 34.700s	15	8
8	9	R Wisell	Lotus	72D	Cosworth	V8	12	1h 35m 47.400s	17	9
9	24	G Hill	Brabham	BT34	Cosworth	V8	12	1h 35m 52.700s	13	7
10	12	R Stommelen	Surtees	TS9	Cosworth	V8	11		12	6
11	22	V Elford	BRM	P160	BRM	V12	11		18	9
12	17	N Galli	March	711	Alfa Romeo	V8	10		21	11
r	8	E Fittipaldi	Lotus	72D	Cosworth	V8	8	oil leak	8	4
r	21	J Siffert	BRM	P160	BRM	V12	6	coil	3	2

POS.	NO.	DRIVER	CAR	MODEL	ENGINE		LAPS	TIME/REASON FOR RETIREMENT	GRID:POS	ROW
r	10	C Amon	Matra Simca	MS120B	Matra	V12	6	accident	16	8
r	20	P Gethin	McLaren	M19A	Cosworth	V8	5	accident/ suspension	19	10
r	14	H Pescarolo	March	711	Cosworth	V8	5	suspension	10	5
dq	28	M Beuttler	March	711	Cosworth	V8	3	incorrect route into pits	22	11
r	18	D Hulme	McLaren	M19A	Cosworth	V8	3	fuel leak	6	3
r	16	A de Adamich	March	711	Alfa Romeo	V8	2	fuel injection	20	10
r	23	H Ganley	BRM	P153	BRM	V12	2	engine	14	7
r	4	J Ickx	Ferrari	312B2	Ferrari	F12	1	accident	2	1
nq	27	J Bonnier	McLaren	M7C	Cosworth	V8				
nq	27	H Marko	McLaren	M7C	Cosworth	V8		out of fuel/ withdrew		

Winning speed: 184.191 km/h, 114.451 mph
Pole Position speed: 187.257 km/h, 116.356 mph (J Stewart, 7 min:19.000 sec)
Fastest Lap speed: 186.789 km/h, 116.066 mph (F Cevert, 7 min:20.100 sec on lap 10)
Lap Leaders: J Stewart 1-12 (12).

15 Aug 1971 AUSTRIA: Österreichring (Round: 8) (Race: 205)

54 laps x 5.911 km, 3.673 miles = 319.194 km, 198.338 miles

POS.	NO.	DRIVER	CAR	MODEL	ENGINE		LAPS	TIME/REASON FOR RETIREMENT	GRID:POS	ROW
1	14	J Siffert	BRM	P160	BRM	V12	54	1h 30m 23.910s	1	1
2	2	E Fittipaldi	Lotus	72D	Cosworth	V8	54	1h 30m 28.030s	5	3
3	8	T Schenken	Brabham	BT33	Cosworth	V8	54	1h 30m 43.680s	7	4
4	3	R Wisell	Lotus	72D	Cosworth	V8	54	1h 30m 55.780s	10	5
5	7	G Hill	Brabham	BT34	Cosworth	V8	54	1h 31m 12.340s	8	4
6	25	H Pescarolo	March	711	Cosworth	V8	54	1h 31m 48.420s	13	7
7	24	R Stommelen	Surtees	TS9	Cosworth	V8	54	1h 32m 01.330s	12	6
8	17	R Peterson	March	711	Cosworth	V8	53		11	6
9	10	J Oliver	McLaren	M19A	Cosworth	V8	53		22	11
10	23	P Gethin	BRM	P160	BRM	V12	52		16	8
11	16	H Marko	BRM	P153	BRM	V12	52		17	9
12	19	N Galli	March	711	Alfa Romeo	V8	51		15	8
nc	27	M Beuttler	March	711	Cosworth	V8	47		19	10
r	12	F Cevert	Tyrrell	002	Cosworth	V8	42	engine	3	2
r	11	J Stewart	Tyrrell	003	Cosworth	V8	35	drive shaft/ wheel lost	2	1
r	4	J Ickx	Ferrari	312B2	Ferrari	F12	31	spark plug leads	6	3
r	26	N Lauda	March	711	Cosworth	V8	20	handling	21	11
r	22	J Surtees	Surtees	TS9	Cosworth	V8	12	engine	18	9
r	5	C Regazzoni	Ferrari	312B2	Ferrari	F12	8	engine	4	2
r	15	H Ganley	BRM	P160	BRM	V12	6	ignition	14	7
r	9	D Hulme	McLaren	M19A	Cosworth	V8	4	engine	9	5
ns	28	J Bonnier	McLaren	M7C	Cosworth	V8		fuel leak	20	10

Winning speed: 211.858 km/h, 131.642 mph
Pole Position speed: 218.387 km/h, 135.699 mph (J Siffert, 1 min:37.440 sec)
Fastest Lap speed: 216.102 km/h, 134.280 mph (J Siffert, 1 min:38.470 sec on lap 22)
Lap Leaders: J Siffert 1-54 (54).

5 Sep 1971 ITALY: Monza (Round: 9) (Race: 206)

55 laps x 5.750 km, 3.573 miles = 316.250 km, 196.509 miles

POS.	NO.	DRIVER	CAR	MODEL	ENGINE		LAPS	TIME/REASON FOR RETIREMENT	GRID:POS	ROW
1	18	P Gethin	BRM	P160	BRM	V12	55	1h 18m 12.600s	11	6
2	25	R Peterson	March	711	Cosworth	V8	55	1h 18m 12.610s	6	3
3	2	F Cevert	Tyrrell	002	Cosworth	V8	55	1h 18m 12.690s	5	3
4	9	M Hailwood	Surtees	TS9	Cosworth	V8	55	1h 18m 12.780s	17	9
5	19	H Ganley	BRM	P160	BRM	V12	55	1h 18m 13.210s	4	2
6	12	C Amon	Matra Simca	MS120B	Matra	V12	55	1h 18m 44.960s	1	1
7	14	J Oliver	McLaren	M14A	Cosworth	V8	55	1h 19m 37.430s	13	7
8	5	E Fittipaldi	Lotus	56B	Pratt & Whitney	tbn	54		18	9
9	20	J Siffert	BRM	P160	BRM	V12	53		3	2
10	28	J Bonnier	McLaren	M7C	Cosworth	V8	51		21	11
r	10	G Hill	Brabham	BT34	Cosworth	V8	47	gearbox	14	7
nc	26	J-P Jarier	March	701	Cosworth	V8	47		24	12
r	24	M Beuttler	March	711	Cosworth	V8	41	piston/ valves	16	8
r	16	H Pescarolo	March	711	Cosworth	V8	40	rear suspension	10	5
r	23	A de Adamich	March	711	Alfa Romeo	V8	33	engine	20	10
r	4	C Regazzoni	Ferrari	312B2	Ferrari	F12	17	engine	8	4
r	3	J Ickx	Ferrari	312B	Ferrari	F12	15	engine	2	1
r	30	J Stewart	Tyrrell	003	Cosworth	V8	15	connecting rod	7	4
r	22	N Galli	March	711	Cosworth	V8	11	electrics	19	10
r	27	S Moser	Bellasi		Cosworth	V8	5	suspension	22	11
r	11	T Schenken	Brabham	BT33	Cosworth	V8	5	rear suspension	9	5
r	21	H Marko	BRM	P153	BRM	V12	3	engine	12	6
r	7	J Surtees	Surtees	TS9	Cosworth	V8	3	engine	15	8
ns	8	R Stommelen	Surtees	TS9	Cosworth	V8		accident	23	12

Winning speed: 242.616 km/h, 150.755 mph
Pole Position speed: 251.214 km/h, 156.097 mph (C Amon, 1 min:22.400 sec)
Fastest Lap speed: 247.017 km/h, 153.489 mph (H Pescarolo, 1 min:23.800 sec on lap 9)
Lap Leaders: C Regazzoni 1-3,9 (4); R Peterson 4-7,10-14,17-22,24,26,33,47-50,54 (23); J Stewart 8 (1); F Cevert 15-16,23,31-32,34,36 (7); M Hailwood 25,27,35,42,51 (5); J Siffert 28-30 (3); C Amon 37-41,43-46 (9); P Gethin 52-53,55 (3).

19 Sep 1971 — CANADA: Mosport Park (Round:10) (Race: 207)

64 laps x 3.957 km, 2.459 miles = 253.272 km, 157.376 miles

POS.	NO.	DRIVER	CAR	MODEL	ENGINE		LAPS	TIME/REASON FOR RETIREMENT	GRID:POS	ROW
1	11	J Stewart	Tyrrell	003	Cosworth	V8	64	1h 55m 12.900s	1	1
2	17	R Peterson	March	711	Cosworth	V8	64	1h 55m 51.200s	6	3
3	10	M Donohue	McLaren	M19A	Cosworth	V8	64	1h 56m 48.700s	8	3
4	9	D Hulme	McLaren	M19A	Cosworth	V8	63		10	4
5	3	R Wisell	Lotus	72D	Cosworth	V8	63		7	3
6	12	F Cevert	Tyrrell	002	Cosworth	V8	62		3	1
7	2	E Fittipaldi	Lotus	72D	Cosworth	V8	62		4	2
8	4	J Ickx	Ferrari	312B2	Ferrari	F12	62		12	5
9	14	J Siffert	BRM	P160	BRM	V12	61		2	1
10	20	C Amon	Matra Simca	MS120B	Matra	V12	61		5	2
11	22	J Surtees	Surtees	TS9	Cosworth	V8	60		14	6
12	31	H Marko	BRM	P153	BRM	V12	60		19	8
13	6	M Andretti	Ferrari	312B2	Ferrari	F12	60		13	5
14	15	P Gethin	BRM	P160	BRM	V12	59		16	7
15	28	G Eaton	BRM	P160	BRM	V12	59		21	9
16	18	N Galli	March	711	Cosworth	V8	57		20	8
nc	19	M Beuttler	March	711	Cosworth	V8	56		22	9
nc	35	P Lovely	Lotus	69	Cosworth	V8	55		25	10
r	24	R Stommelen	Surtees	TS9	Cosworth	V8	26	oil pressure/ engine overheating	23	9
r	21	J-P Beltoise	Matra Simca	MS120B	Matra	V12	15	accident	11	5
r	33	S Barber	March	711	Cosworth	V8	13	oil pressure	24	10
r	5	C Regazzoni	Ferrari	312B2	Ferrari	F12	7	accident	18	7
r	37	G Hill	Brabham	BT34	Cosworth	V8	2	accident	15	6
r	8	T Schenken	Brabham	BT33	Cosworth	V8	1	ignition	17	7
ns	16	H Ganley	BRM	P160	BRM	V12		accident (familiarisation laps)	9	4
ns	26	C Craft	Brabham	BT33	Cosworth	V8		engine		
ns	27	H Pescarolo	March	711	Cosworth	V8		accident/ injury		

Winning speed: 131.895 km/h, 81.956 mph
Pole Position speed: 189.197 km/h, 117.562 mph (J Stewart, 1 min:15.300 sec)
Fastest Lap speed: 137.648 km/h, 85.530 mph (D Hulme, 1 min:43.500 sec on lap 57)
Lap Leaders: J Stewart 1-17,31-64 (51); R Peterson 18-30 (13).

Scheduled for 80 laps, but stopped early because of rain.

3 Oct 1971 — USA: Watkins Glen (Round:11) (Race: 208)

59 laps x 5.435 km, 3.377 miles = 320.651 km, 199.243 miles

POS.	NO.	DRIVER	CAR	MODEL	ENGINE		LAPS	TIME/REASON FOR RETIREMENT	GRID:POS	ROW
1	9	F Cevert	Tyrrell	002	Cosworth	V8	59	1h 43m 51.991s	5	2
2	14	J Siffert	BRM	P160	BRM	V12	59	1h 44m 32.053s	6	3
3	25	R Peterson	March	711	Cosworth	V8	59	1h 44m 36.061s	11	5
4	16	H Ganley	BRM	P160	BRM	V12	59	1h 44m 48.740s	12	5
5	8	J Stewart	Tyrrell	003	Cosworth	V8	59	1h 44m 51.994s	1	1
6	5	C Regazzoni	Ferrari	312B2	Ferrari	F12	59	1h 45m 08.417s	4	2
7	22	G Hill	Brabham	BT34	Cosworth	V8	58		18	7
8	12	J-P Beltoise	Matra Simca	MS120B	Matra	V12	58		10	4
9	15	P Gethin	BRM	P160	BRM	V12	58		21	9
10	31	D Hobbs	McLaren	M19A	Cosworth	V8	58		22	9
11	27	A de Adamich	March	711	Alfa Romeo	V8	57		26	11
12	11	C Amon	Matra Simca	MS120B	Matra	V12	57		8	3
13	17	H Marko	BRM	P160	BRM	V12	57		16	7
14	28	J Cannon	BRM	P153	BRM	V12	56		24	10
15r	20	M Hailwood	Surtees	TS9	Cosworth	V8	54	puncture/ accident	14	6
16r	29	J Bonnier	McLaren	M7C	Cosworth	V8	54	out of fuel	28	11
17	18	J Surtees	Surtees	TS9	Cosworth	V8	54		13	5
nc	33	S Barber	March	711	Cosworth	V8	52		25	10
nc	2	E Fittipaldi	Lotus	72D	Cosworth	V8	49		2	1
nc	30	P Lovely	Lotus	69	Cosworth	V8	49		29	12
r	4	J Ickx	Ferrari	312B	Ferrari	F12	49	alternator	7	3
r	7	D Hulme	McLaren	M19A	Cosworth	V8	47	accident	3	1
r	23	T Schenken	Brabham	BT33	Cosworth	V8	41	engine	15	6
r	24	C Craft	Brabham	BT33	Cosworth	V8	30	rear suspension	27	11
r	21	H Pescarolo	March	711	Cosworth	V8	23	camshaft	20	8
r	19	S Posey	Surtees	TS9	Cosworth	V8	15	piston	17	7
r	26	N Galli	March	711	Cosworth	V8	11	wheel	23	9
r	3	R Wisell	Lotus	72D	Cosworth	V8	5	brakes/ accident	9	4
r	10	P Revson	Tyrrell	001	Cosworth	V8	1	clutch	19	8
ns	6	M Andretti	Ferrari	312B2	Ferrari	F12		raced elsewhere		
ns	31	M Donohue	McLaren	M19A	Cosworth	V8		raced elsewhere		
ns	19	G van Lennep	Surtees	TS9	Cosworth	V8		car raced by Posey		

Winning speed: 185.228 km/h, 115.096 mph
Pole Position speed: 190.615 km/h, 118.443 mph (J Stewart, 1 min:42.642 sec)
Fastest Lap speed: 189.082 km/h, 117.490 mph (J Ickx, 1 min:43.474 sec on lap 43)
Lap Leaders: J Stewart 1-13 (13); F Cevert 14-59 (46).

Lap Leaders 1971

POS	DRIVER	CAR-ENGINE	GPS	LAPS	KM	MILES
1	J Stewart	Tyrrell-Cosworth	8	347	1,695.0	1,053.2
2	D Hulme	McLaren-Cosworth	1	59	242.1	150.5
3	J Siffert	BRM	2	57	336.4	209.1
4	F Cevert	Tyrrell-Cosworth	2	53	290.3	180.4
	J Ickx	Ferrari	2	53	220.2	136.8
6	R Peterson	March-Cosworth	2	36	183.7	114.1
7	C Regazzoni	Ferrari	3	23	102.8	63.9
8	P Rodriguez	BRM	1	22	92.2	57.3
9	C Amon	Matra Simca	1	9	51.7	32.2
10	M Hailwood	Surtees-Cosworth	1	5	28.7	17.9
11	M Andretti	Ferrari	1	4	16.4	10.2
12	P Gethin	BRM	1	3	17.2	10.7
			11	**671**	**3,276.9**	**2,036.2**

Driver Points 1971

		ZA	E	MC	NL	F	GB	D	A	I	CDN	USA	TOTAL
1	J Stewart	6	9	9	-	9	9	9	-	-	9	2	62
2	R Peterson	-	-	6	3	-	6	2	-	6	6	4	33
3	F Cevert	-	-	-	-	6	-	6	-	4	1	9	26
4	J Ickx	-	6	4	9	-	-	-	-	-	-	-	19
	J Siffert	-	-	-	1	3	-	-	9	-	-	6	19
6	E Fittipaldi	-	-	2	-	4	4	-	6	-	-	-	16
7	C Regazzoni	4	-	-	4	-	-	4	-	-	-	1	13
8	M Andretti	9	-	-	-	-	-	3	-	-	-	-	12
9	P Gethin	-	-	-	-	-	-	-	-	9	-	-	9
	P Rodriguez	-	3	-	6	-	-	-	-	-	-	-	9
	C Amon	2	4	-	-	2	-	-	-	1	-	-	9
	R Wisell	3	-	-	-	1	-	-	3	-	2	-	9
	D Hulme	1	2	3	-	-	-	-	-	-	3	-	9
14	T Schenken	-	-	-	-	-	-	1	4	-	-	-	5
	H Ganley	-	-	-	-	-	-	-	-	2	-	3	5
16	M Donohue	-	-	-	-	-	-	-	-	-	4	-	4
	H Pescarolo	-	-	-	-	-	3	-	1	-	-	-	4
18	M Hailwood	-	-	-	-	-	-	-	-	3	-	-	3
	J Surtees	-	-	-	2	-	1	-	-	-	-	-	3
	R Stommelen	-	-	1	-	-	2	-	-	-	-	-	3
21	G Hill	-	-	-	-	-	-	-	2	-	-	-	2
22	J-P Beltoise	-	1	-	-	-	-	-	-	-	-	-	1

9, 6, 4, 3,2 and 1 point awarded to the first six finishers.
Best 5 scores from first 6 races, best 4 from remaining 5 races.

Constructor Points 1971

		ZA	E	MC	NL	F	GB	D	A	I	CDN	USA	TOTAL	
1	Tyrrell-Cosworth	6	9	9	-	9	9	9	-	4	9	9	73	
2	BRM	-	3	-	6	3	-	-	9	9	-	6	36	
3	Ferrari	9	6	4	9	-	-	4	-	-	-	1	33	
	March-Cosworth	-	-	6	3	-	6	2	(1)	6	6	4	33	(1)
5	Lotus-Cosworth	3	-	2	-	4	4	-	6	-	2	-	21	
6	McLaren-Cosworth	1	2	3	-	-	-	-	-	-	4	-	10	
7	Matra Simca	2	4	-	-	2	-	-	-	1	-	-	9	
8	Surtees-Cosworth	-	-	1	2	-	2	-	-	3	-	-	8	
9	Brabham-Cosworth	-	-	-	-	-	-	1	4	-	-	-	5	

9, 6, 4, 3,2 and 1 point awarded to the first six finishers. Points only for highest placed car.
Best 5 scores from first 6 races, best 4 from remaining 5 races.

The Brabham team was sold to businessman and former entrant Bernie Ecclestone. Sponsorship changes meant that Lotus turned into the black and gold John Player Specials and McLaren inherited Yardley's colours, while BRM created its multiple entry team with Marlboro assistance.

FERRARI
Scuderia Ferrari SpA SEFAC: Ickx, Regazzoni, Andretti, Merzario, Galli

TECNO
Martini Racing Team: Bell, Galli

BRABHAM
Motor Racing Developments: Hill, Reutemann, W Fittipaldi
Team Gunston: (Ferguson)

BRM
Marlboro BRM: Beltoise, Gethin, Ganley, Wisell, Marko, Soler-Roig, Oliver, Redman, Brack, (Schuppan)

CONNEW
Darnval Connew Racing Team: Migault

LOTUS
John Player Team Lotus: E Fittipaldi, Walker, Wisell
World Wide Racing: E Fittipaldi (I)
Scuderia Scribante-Lucky Strike Racing: Charlton

MARCH
STP March Racing Team: Peterson, Lauda
Team Williams-Motul: Pescarolo, Pace
Team Eifelland Caravans: Stommelen
Clarke-Mordaunt-Guthrie Racing: Beuttler
Gene Mason Racing: Barber

McLAREN
Yardley Team McLaren: Hulme, Revson, Redman, Scheckter

SURTEES
Team Surtees: Schenken, Surtees
with Brooke Bond Oxo/Rob Walker: Hailwood, Schenken (RA,ZA,E) with Ceramica Pagnossin: de Adamich
Champcarr Inc: Posey
Team Gunston: Love

TYRRELL
Elf Team Tyrrell: Stewart, Cevert, Depailler

WILLIAMS (POLITOYS)
Team Williams-Motul: Pescarolo

MATRA SIMCA
Equipe Matra: Amon

23 Jan 1972 — ARGENTINA: Buenos Aires No.9 (Round: 1) (Race: 209)

95 laps x 3.345 km, 2.078 miles = 317.775 km, 197.456 miles

POS.	NO.	DRIVER	CAR	MODEL	ENGINE		LAPS	TIME/REASON FOR RETIREMENT	GRID:POS	ROW
1	21	J Stewart	Tyrrell	003	Cosworth	V8	95	1h 57m 58.820s	2	1
2	17	D Hulme	McLaren	M19A	Cosworth	V8	95	1h 58m 24.780s	4	2
3	8	J Ickx	Ferrari	312B2	Ferrari	F12	95	1h 58m 58.210s	8	4
4	9	C Regazzoni	Ferrari	312B2	Ferrari	F12	95	1h 59m 05.540s	6	3
5	19	T Schenken	Surtees	TS9B	Cosworth	V8	95	1h 59m 07.930s	11	6
6	14	R Peterson	March	721	Cosworth	V8	94		10	5
7	2	C Reutemann	Brabham	BT34	Cosworth	V8	93		1	1
8	23	H Pescarolo	March	721	Cosworth	V8	93		15	8
9	3	H Ganley	BRM	P160B	BRM	V12	93		13	7
10	7	H Marko	BRM	P153	BRM	V12	93		19	10
11	15	N Lauda	March	721	Cosworth	V8	93		22	11
r	11	E Fittipaldi	JPS Lotus	72D	Cosworth	V8	61	rear suspension radius rod	5	3
r	4	R Wisell	BRM	P153	BRM	V12	59	water hose	17	9
r	22	F Cevert	Tyrrell	002	Cosworth	V8	59	gearbox oil line	7	4
r	18	P Revson	McLaren	M19A	Cosworth	V8	50	spin/ water pipe/ engine	3	2
r	10	M Andretti	Ferrari	312B2	Ferrari	F12	20	misfire	9	5
r	1	G Hill	Brabham	BT33	Cosworth	V8	11	puncture/ fuel pump	16	8
r	20	A de Adamich	Surtees	TS9B	Cosworth	V8	11	fuel metering unit	14	7
dq	12	D Walker	JPS Lotus	72D	Cosworth	V8	8	used pit tools to repair car	20	10
r	5	P Gethin	BRM	P160B	BRM	V12	1	accident/ oil pipe	18	9
r	6	A Soler-Roig	BRM	P160B	BRM	V12	1	throttle jammed/ accident	21	11
r	16	C Amon	Matra Simca	MS120C	Matra	V12	-1	gearbox	12	6

Winning speed: 161.607 km/h, 100.418 mph
Pole Position speed: 166.188 km/h, 103.265 mph (C Reutemann, 1 min:12.460 sec)
Fastest Lap speed: 163.481 km/h, 101.582 mph (J Stewart, 1 min:13.660 sec on lap 25)
Lap Leaders: J Stewart 1-95 (95).

4 Mar 1972 — SOUTH AFRICA: Kyalami (Round: 2) (Race: 210)

79 laps x 4.104 km, 2.550 miles = 324.216 km, 201.458 miles

POS.	NO.	DRIVER	CAR	MODEL	ENGINE		LAPS	TIME/REASON FOR RETIREMENT	GRID:POS	ROW
1	12	D Hulme	McLaren	M19A	Cosworth	V8	79	1h 45m 49.100s	5	2
2	8	E Fittipaldi	JPS Lotus	72D	Cosworth	V8	79	1h 46m 03.200s	3	1
3	14	P Revson	McLaren	M19A	Cosworth	V8	79	1h 46m 14.900s	12	5
4	7	M Andretti	Ferrari	312B2	Ferrari	F12	79	1h 46m 27.600s	6	3
5	3	R Peterson	March	721	Cosworth	V8	79	1h 46m 38.100s	9	4
6	19	G Hill	Brabham	BT33	Cosworth	V8	78		14	6
7	4	N Lauda	March	721	Cosworth	V8	78		21	9
8	5	J Ickx	Ferrari	312B2	Ferrari	F12	78		7	3
9	2	F Cevert	Tyrrell	002	Cosworth	V8	78		8	3
10	9	D Walker	JPS Lotus	72D	Cosworth	V8	78		19	8
11	21	H Pescarolo	March	721	Cosworth	V8	77		22	9
12	6	C Regazzoni	Ferrari	312B2	Ferrari	F12	77		2	1
13	25	R Stommelen	Eifelland March	721	Cosworth	V8	77		25	10
14	24	H Marko	BRM	P153	BRM	V12	76		23	9
15	15	C Amon	Matra Simca	MS120C	Matra	V12	76		13	5
16r	27	J Love	Surtees	TS9	Cosworth	V8	73	puncture/ accident	26	11
17	22	C Pace	March	711	Cosworth	V8	73		24	10
nc	23	H Ganley	BRM	P160B	BRM	V12	70		16	7
nc	18	A de Adamich	Surtees	TS9B	Cosworth	V8	69		20	8
nc	11	P Gethin	BRM	P160B	BRM	V12	65		18	7
r	10	J-P Beltoise	BRM	P160B	BRM	V12	60	valve springs	11	5
r	1	J Stewart	Tyrrell	003	Cosworth	V8	45	gearbox	1	1
r	17	M Hailwood	Surtees	TS9B	Cosworth	V8	28	rear suspension	4	2
r	20	C Reutemann	Brabham	BT34	Cosworth	V8	27	fuel line	15	6

POS.	NO.	DRIVER	CAR	MODEL	ENGINE		LAPS	TIME/REASON FOR RETIREMENT	GRID:POS	ROW
r	16	T Schenken	Surtees	TS9B	Cosworth	V8	9	cylinder liner/ engine	10	4
r	26	D Charlton	Lotus	72D	Cosworth	V8	2	fuel pump	17	7
ns	28	W Ferguson	Brabham	BT33	Cosworth	V8		engine		

Winning speed: 183.834 km/h, 114.229 mph
Pole Position speed: 191.875 km/h, 119.226 mph (J Stewart, 1 min:17.000 sec)
Fastest Lap speed: 187.255 km/h, 116.355 mph (M Hailwood, 1 min:18.900 sec on lap 20)
Lap Leaders: D Hulme 1,57-79 (24); J Stewart 2-44 (43); E Fittipaldi 45-56 (12).

W Ferguson also practiced in a Surtees TS9-Cosworth V8 (27) which was raced by J Love.

1 May 1972 — SPAIN: Járama (Round: 3) (Race: 211)

90 laps x 3.404 km, 2.115 miles = 306.360 km, 190.363 miles

POS.	NO.	DRIVER	CAR	MODEL	ENGINE		LAPS	TIME/REASON FOR RETIREMENT	GRID:POS	ROW
1	5	E Fittipaldi	JPS Lotus	72D	Cosworth	V8	90	2h 03m 41.230s	3	1
2	4	J Ickx	Ferrari	312B2	Ferrari	F12	90	2h 04m 00.150s	1	1
3	6	C Regazzoni	Ferrari	312B2	Ferrari	F12	89		8	3
4	26	A de Adamich	Surtees	TS9B	Cosworth	V8	89		13	5
5	20	P Revson	McLaren	M19A	Cosworth	V8	89		11	5
6	29	C Pace	March	711	Cosworth	V8	89		16	7
7	22	W Fittipaldi	Brabham	BT33	Cosworth	V8	88		14	6
8	12	T Schenken	Surtees	TS9B	Cosworth	V8	88		18	7
9r	21	D Walker	JPS Lotus	72D	Cosworth	V8	87	out of fuel	24	10
10	18	G Hill	Brabham	BT37	Cosworth	V8	86		23	9
11	14	H Pescarolo	March	721	Cosworth	V8	86		19	8
r	1	J Stewart	Tyrrell	003	Cosworth	V8	69	accident	4	2
r	9	C Amon	Matra Simca	MS120C	Matra	V12	66	gearbox pinion bearing	6	3
r	3	F Cevert	Tyrrell	002	Cosworth	V8	65	ignition	12	5
r	8	P Gethin	BRM	P180	BRM	V12	65	engine	21	9
r	11	D Hulme	McLaren	M19A	Cosworth	V8	48	gearbox pinion bearing	2	1
r	25	H Ganley	BRM	P160B	BRM	V12	38	engine	20	8
r	10	R Wisell	BRM	P160B	BRM	V12	24	accident	10	4
r	7	M Andretti	Ferrari	312B2	Ferrari	F12	23	oil pressure/ engine	5	2
r	15	M Hailwood	Surtees	TS9B	Cosworth	V8	20	starter solenoid	15	6
r	2	R Peterson	March	721X	Cosworth	V8	16	accident/ fuel leak	9	4
r	16	R Stommelen	Eifelland March	721	Cosworth	V8	15	accident	17	7
r	19	J-P Beltoise	BRM	P160B	BRM	V12	9	gear linkage	7	3
r	24	N Lauda	March	721X	Cosworth	V8	7	throttle jammed	25	10
r	28	A Soler-Roig	BRM	P160B	BRM	V12	6	gear selection/ accident	22	9
nq	23	M Beuttler	March	721G	Cosworth	V8				

Winning speed: 148.614 km/h, 92.344 mph
Pole Position speed: 156.246 km/h, 97.087 mph (J Ickx, 1 min:18.430 sec)
Fastest Lap speed: 151.270 km/h, 93.995 mph (J Ickx, 1 min:21.010 sec on lap 52)
Lap Leaders: D Hulme 1-4 (4); J Stewart 5-8 (4); E Fittipaldi 9-90 (82).

14 May 1972 — MONACO: Monte Carlo (Round: 4) (Race: 212)

80 laps x 3.145 km, 1.954 miles = 251.600 km, 156.337 miles

POS.	NO.	DRIVER	CAR	MODEL	ENGINE		LAPS	TIME/REASON FOR RETIREMENT	GRID:POS	ROW
1	17	J-P Beltoise	BRM	P160B	BRM	V12	80	2h 26m 54.700s	4	2
2	6	J Ickx	Ferrari	312B2	Ferrari	F12	80	2h 27m 32.900s	2	1
3	8	E Fittipaldi	JPS Lotus	72D	Cosworth	V8	79		1	1
4	1	J Stewart	Tyrrell	004	Cosworth	V8	78		8	4
5	15	B Redman	McLaren	M19A	Cosworth	V8	77		10	5
6	16	C Amon	Matra Simca	MS120C	Matra	V12	77		6	3
7	12	A de Adamich	Surtees	TS9B	Cosworth	V8	77		18	9
8	26	H Marko	BRM	P153B	BRM	V12	77		17	9
9	21	W Fittipaldi	Brabham	BT33	Cosworth	V8	77		21	11
10	27	R Stommelen	Eifelland March	721	Cosworth	V8	77		25	13
11	3	R Peterson	March	721X	Cosworth	V8	76		15	8
12	20	G Hill	Brabham	BT37	Cosworth	V8	76		19	10
13	5	M Beuttler	March	721G	Cosworth	V8	76		23	12
14	9	D Walker	JPS Lotus	72D	Cosworth	V8	75		14	7
15	14	D Hulme	McLaren	M19C	Cosworth	V8	74		7	4
16	4	N Lauda	March	721X	Cosworth	V8	74		22	11
17	23	C Pace	March	711	Cosworth	V8	72		24	12
nc	2	F Cevert	Tyrrell	002	Cosworth	V8	70		12	6
r	22	H Pescarolo	March	721	Cosworth	V8	58	accident	9	5
r	7	C Regazzoni	Ferrari	312B2	Ferrari	F12	51	accident	3	2
r	11	M Hailwood	Surtees	TS9B	Cosworth	V8	48	accident	11	6
r	19	H Ganley	BRM	P180	BRM	V12	47	accident	20	10
r	10	T Schenken	Surtees	TS9B	Cosworth	V8	31	accident	13	7
dq	18	P Gethin	BRM	P160B	BRM	V12	27	accident/ reversed into pits	5	3
r	28	R Wisell	BRM	P160B	BRM	V12	16	engine	16	8

Winning speed: 102.756 km/h, 63.849 mph
Pole Position speed: 139.091 km/h, 86.427 mph (E Fittipaldi, 1 min:21.400 sec)
Fastest Lap speed: 113.220 km/h, 70.352 mph (J-P Beltoise, 1 min:40.000 sec on lap 9).
Lap Leaders: J-P Beltoise 1-80 (80).

4 Jun 1972 — BELGIUM: Nivelles-Baulers (Round: 5) (Race: 213)

85 laps x 3.724 km, 2.314 miles = 316.540 km, 196.689 miles

POS.	NO.	DRIVER	CAR	MODEL	ENGINE		LAPS	TIME/REASON FOR RETIREMENT	GRID:POS	ROW
1	32	E Fittipaldi	JPS Lotus	72D	Cosworth	V8	85	1h 44m 06.700s	1	1
2	8	F Cevert	Tyrrell	002	Cosworth	V8	85	1h 44m 33.300s	5	2
3	9	D Hulme	McLaren	M19C	Cosworth	V8	85	1h 45m 04.800s	3	1
4	34	M Hailwood	Surtees	TS9B	Cosworth	V8	85	1h 45m 18.700s	8	3
5	16	C Pace	March	711	Cosworth	V8	84		11	5
6	5	C Amon	Matra Simca	MS120C	Matra	V12	84		13	5
7	10	P Revson	McLaren	M19A	Cosworth	V8	83		7	3
8	25	H Ganley	BRM	P160B	BRM	V12	83		15	6
9	11	R Peterson	March	721X	Cosworth	V8	83		14	6
10	27	H Marko	BRM	P153B	BRM	V12	83		23	9
11	6	R Stommelen	Eifelland March	721	Cosworth	V8	83		20	8
12	12	N Lauda	March	721X	Cosworth	V8	82		25	10
13	19	C Reutemann	Brabham	BT37	Cosworth	V8	81		9	4
14	33	D Walker	JPS Lotus	72D	Cosworth	V8	79		12	5
r	17	G Hill	Brabham	BT37	Cosworth	V8	73	rear suspension	16	7
nc	15	H Pescarolo	March	721	Cosworth	V8	59		19	8
r	30	C Regazzoni	Ferrari	312B2	Ferrari	F12	57	accident	2	1
r	36	A de Adamich	Surtees	TS9B	Cosworth	V8	55	connecting rod	10	4
r	22	N Galli	Tecno	PA123	Tecno	F12	54	accident/ suspension	24	10
r	29	J Ickx	Ferrari	312B2	Ferrari	F12	47	fuel injection	4	2
r	14	M Beuttler	March	721G	Cosworth	V8	31	drive shaft	22	9
r	18	W Fittipaldi	Brabham	BT34	Cosworth	V8	28	gearbox	18	7
r	24	P Gethin	BRM	P160B	BRM	V12	27	fuel pump	17	7
r	23	J-P Beltoise	BRM	P160B	BRM	V12	15	engine overheating	6	3
r	35	T Schenken	Surtees	TS9B	Cosworth	V8	11	engine overheating	21	9
ns	26	V Schuppan	BRM	P153B	BRM	V12		car raced by Marko		

Winning speed: 182.423 km/h, 113.353 mph
Pole Position speed: 187.686 km/h, 116.623 mph (E Fittipaldi, 1 min:11.430 sec)
Fastest Lap speed: 185.890 km/h, 115.507 mph (C Amon, 1 min:12.120 sec on lap 66)
Lap Leaders: C Regazzoni 1-8 (8); E Fittipaldi 9-85 (77).

2 Jul 1972 — FRANCE: Clermont-Ferrand (Round: 6) (Race: 214)

38 laps x 8.055 km, 5.005 miles = 306.090 km, 190.196 miles

POS.	NO.	DRIVER	CAR	MODEL	ENGINE		LAPS	TIME/REASON FOR RETIREMENT	GRID:POS	ROW
1	4	J Stewart	Tyrrell	003	Cosworth	V8	38	1h 52m 21.500s	3	2
2	1	E Fittipaldi	JPS Lotus	72D	Cosworth	V8	38	1h 52m 49.200s	8	4
3	9	C Amon	Matra Simca	MS120D	Matra	V12	38	1h 52m 53.400s	1	1
4	7	F Cevert	Tyrrell	002	Cosworth	V8	38	1h 53m 10.800s	7	4
5	12	R Peterson	March	721G	Cosworth	V8	38	1h 53m 18.300s	9	5
6	26	M Hailwood	Surtees	TS9B	Cosworth	V8	38	1h 53m 57.600s	10	5
7	2	D Hulme	McLaren	M19C	Cosworth	V8	38	1h 54m 09.600s	2	1
8	19	W Fittipaldi	Brabham	BT34	Cosworth	V8	38	1h 54m 46.600s	14	7
9	11	B Redman	McLaren	M19A	Cosworth	V8	38	1h 55m 17.000s	13	7
10	18	G Hill	Brabham	BT37	Cosworth	V8	38	1h 55m 21.000s	20	10
11	3	J Ickx	Ferrari	312B2	Ferrari	F12	37		4	2
12	20	C Reutemann	Brabham	BT37	Cosworth	V8	37		17	9
13	30	N Galli	Ferrari	312B2	Ferrari	F12	37		19	10
14	28	A de Adamich	Surtees	TS9B	Cosworth	V8	37		12	6
15	5	J-P Beltoise	BRM	P160B	BRM	V12	37		24	12
16	10	R Stommelen	Eifelland March	721	Cosworth	V8	37		15	8
17	27	T Schenken	Surtees	TS9B	Cosworth	V8	36		5	3
18r	6	D Walker	JPS Lotus	72D	Cosworth	V8	34	crown wheel & pinion	22	11
r	15	M Beuttler	March	721G	Cosworth	V8	33	out of fuel	23	12
nc	8	P Depailler	Tyrrell	004	Cosworth	V8	33		16	8
r	24	R Wisell	BRM	P160B	BRM	V12	25	gear linkage	18	9
r	17	C Pace	March	711	Cosworth	V8	18	connecting rod	11	6
r	25	H Marko	BRM	P160B	BRM	V12	8	eye hit by flying stone	6	3
r	14	N Lauda	March	721G	Cosworth	V8	4	drive shaft	21	11
ns	16	H Pescarolo	March	721	Cosworth	V8		accident		
ns	23	H Ganley	BRM	P160B	BRM	V12		car raced by Beltoise		
ns	22	P Gethin	BRM	P160B	BRM	V12		accident		
ns	21	D Bell	Tecno	PA123	Tecno	F12		chassis		
ns	29	D Charlton	Lotus	72D	Cosworth	V8		car unprepared		

Winning speed: 163.454 km/h, 101.566 mph
Pole Position speed: 167.232 km/h, 103.913 mph (C Amon, 2 min:53.400 sec)
Fastest Lap speed: 166.751 km/h, 103.614 mph (C Amon, 2 min:53.900 sec on lap 32)
Lap Leaders: C Amon 1-19 (19); J Stewart 20-38 (19).

15 Jul 1972 — BRITAIN: Brands Hatch (Round: 7) (Race: 215)

76 laps x 4.265 km, 2.650 miles = 324.122 km, 201.400 miles

POS.	NO.	DRIVER	CAR	MODEL	ENGINE		LAPS	TIME/REASON FOR RETIREMENT	GRID:POS	ROW
1	8	E Fittipaldi	JPS Lotus	72D	Cosworth	V8	76	1h 47m 50.200s	2	1
2	1	J Stewart	Tyrrell	003	Cosworth	V8	76	1h 47m 54.300s	4	2
3	19	P Revson	McLaren	M19A	Cosworth	V8	76	1h 49m 02.700s	3	2
4	17	C Amon	Matra Simca	MS120C	Matra	V12	75		17	9
5	18	D Hulme	McLaren	M19C	Cosworth	V8	75		11	6
6	6	A Merzario	Ferrari	312B2	Ferrari	F12	75		9	5
7r	3	R Peterson	March	721G	Cosworth	V8	74	accident	8	4
8	27	C Reutemann	Brabham	BT37	Cosworth	V8	73		10	5
9	4	N Lauda	March	721G	Cosworth	V8	73		19	10
10	33	R Stommelen	Eifelland March	721	Cosworth	V8	71		25	13
11	11	J-P Beltoise	BRM	P160C	BRM	V12	70		6	3
12r	28	W Fittipaldi	Brabham	BT34	Cosworth	V8	69	rear suspension radius rod	22	11
13	31	M Beuttler	March	721G	Cosworth	V8	69		23	12
r	22	T Schenken	Surtees	TS9B	Cosworth	V8	64	rear suspension	5	3
r	2	F Cevert	Tyrrell	002	Cosworth	V8	60	accident	12	6
r	9	D Walker	JPS Lotus	72D	Cosworth	V8	59	rear suspension radius rod	15	8
r	5	J Ickx	Ferrari	312B2	Ferrari	F12	49	oil radiator leak	1	1
r	26	G Hill	Brabham	BT37	Cosworth	V8	47	accident	21	11
r	25	C Pace	March	711	Cosworth	V8	39	differential	13	7
r	14	J Oliver	BRM	P160B	BRM	V12	36	rear suspension radius rod	14	7
r	21	M Hailwood	Surtees	TS9B	Cosworth	V8	31	gear linkage	7	4
r	29	D Charlton	Lotus	72D	Cosworth	V8	21	gear selection	24	12
r	30	N Galli	Tecno	PA123	Tecno	F12	9	accident	18	9
r	24	H Pescarolo	Politoys	FX3	Cosworth	V8	7	suspension/ accident	26	13
r	12	P Gethin	BRM	P160B	BRM	V12	5	engine	16	8
r	23	A de Adamich	Surtees	TS9B	Cosworth	V8	3	accident	20	10
ns	34	F Migault	Connew	PC1	Cosworth	V8		suspension		

Winning speed: 180.340 km/h, 112.058 mph
Pole Position speed: 186.778 km/h, 116.058 mph (J Ickx, 1 min:22.200 sec)
Fastest Lap speed: 182.775 km/h, 113.571 mph (J Stewart, 1 min:24.000 sec on lap 58 & 60)
Lap Leaders: J Ickx 1-48 (48); E Fittipaldi 49-76 (28).

Also the Grand Prix of Europe.

30 Jul 1972 — GERMANY: Nürburgring (Round: 8) (Race: 216)

14 laps x 22.835 km, 14.189 miles = 319.690 km, 198.646 miles

POS.	NO.	DRIVER	CAR	MODEL	ENGINE		LAPS	TIME/REASON FOR RETIREMENT	GRID:POS	ROW
1	4	J Ickx	Ferrari	312B2	Ferrari	F12	14	1h 42m 12.300s	1	1
2	9	C Regazzoni	Ferrari	312B2	Ferrari	F12	14	1h 43m 00.600s	7	4
3	10	R Peterson	March	721G	Cosworth	V8	14	1h 43m 19.000s	4	2
4	17	H Ganley	BRM	P160C	BRM	V12	14	1h 44m 32.500s	18	9
5	5	B Redman	McLaren	M19A	Cosworth	V8	14	1h 44m 48.000s	19	10
6	11	G Hill	Brabham	BT37	Cosworth	V8	14	1h 45m 11.900s	15	8
7	26	W Fittipaldi	Brabham	BT34	Cosworth	V8	14	1h 45m 12.400s	21	11
8	28	M Beuttler	March	721G	Cosworth	V8	14	1h 47m 23.000s	27	14
9	6	J-P Beltoise	BRM	P160C	BRM	V12	14	1h 47m 32.500s	13	7
10	7	F Cevert	Tyrrell	002	Cosworth	V8	14	1h 47m 56.000s	5	3
11r	1	J Stewart	Tyrrell	003	Cosworth	V8	13	accident	2	1
12	19	A Merzario	Ferrari	312B2	Ferrari	F12	13		22	11
13	16	A de Adamich	Surtees	TS9B	Cosworth	V8	13		20	10
14	15	T Schenken	Surtees	TS9B	Cosworth	V8	13		12	6
15	8	C Amon	Matra Simca	MS120D	Matra	V12	13		8	4
nc	21	C Pace	March	711	Cosworth	V8	11		11	6
r	20	H Pescarolo	March	721	Cosworth	V8	10	accident	9	5
r	2	E Fittipaldi	JPS Lotus	72D	Cosworth	V8	10	gearbox casing/ oil fire	3	2
r	3	D Hulme	McLaren	M19C	Cosworth	V8	8	engine	10	5
r	14	M Hailwood	Surtees	TS9B	Cosworth	V8	8	front suspension	16	8
r	12	C Reutemann	Brabham	BT37	Cosworth	V8	6	crown wheel & pinion	6	3
r	22	R Stommelen	Eifelland March	721	Cosworth	V8	6	electrics	14	7
r	25	D Walker	JPS Lotus	72D	Cosworth	V8	6	oil tank	23	12
r	27	D Bell	Tecno	PA123	Tecno	F12	4	dropped valve	25	13
r	29	D Charlton	Lotus	72D	Cosworth	V8	4	driver ill	26	13
r	23	N Lauda	March	721G	Cosworth	V8	4	oil tank	24	12
r	18	R Wisell	BRM	P160C	BRM	V12	3	engine	17	9

Winning speed: 187.676 km/h, 116.616 mph
Pole Position speed: 192.520 km/h, 119.626 mph (J Ickx, 7 min: 7.000 sec)
Fastest Lap speed: 189.589 km/h, 117.805 mph (J Ickx, 7 min:13.600 sec on lap 10)
Lap Leaders: J Ickx 1-14 (14).

13 Aug 1972 AUSTRIA: Österreichring (Round: 9) (Race: 217)

54 laps x 5.911 km, 3.673 miles = 319.194 km, 198.338 miles

POS.	NO.	DRIVER	CAR	MODEL	ENGINE		LAPS	TIME/REASON FOR RETIREMENT	GRID:POS	ROW
1	31	E Fittipaldi	JPS Lotus	72D	Cosworth	V8	54	1h 29m 16.660s	1	1
2	12	D Hulme	McLaren	M19C	Cosworth	V8	54	1h 29m 17.840s	7	4
3	14	P Revson	McLaren	M19C	Cosworth	V8	54	1h 29m 53.190s	4	2
4	25	M Hailwood	Surtees	TS9B	Cosworth	V8	54	1h 30m 01.420s	12	6
5	10	C Amon	Matra Simca	MS120D	Matra	V12	54	1h 30m 02.300s	6	3
6	9	H Ganley	BRM	P160C	BRM	V12	54	1h 30m 17.850s	10	5
7	1	J Stewart	Tyrrell	005	Cosworth	V8	54	1h 30m 25.750s	3	2
8	7	J-P Beltoise	BRM	P160C	BRM	V12	54	1h 30m 38.110s	21	11
9	2	F Cevert	Tyrrell	002	Cosworth	V8	53		20	10
10	4	N Lauda	March	721G	Cosworth	V8	53		22	11
11	24	T Schenken	Surtees	TS9B	Cosworth	V8	52		8	4
12	5	R Peterson	March	721G	Cosworth	V8	52		11	6
13	6	P Gethin	BRM	P160C	BRM	V12	51		16	8
14	11	A de Adamich	Surtees	TS9B	Cosworth	V8	51		13	7
15	27	R Stommelen	Eifelland March	721	Cosworth	V8	48		17	9
nc	23	C Pace	March	711	Cosworth	V8	46		18	9
nc	15	N Galli	Tecno	PA123	Tecno	F12	45		23	12
r	16	G Hill	Brabham	BT37	Cosworth	V8	36	fuel metering unit	14	7
r	28	W Fittipaldi	Brabham	BT34	Cosworth	V8	31	brake pipe	15	8
r	3	M Beuttler	March	721G	Cosworth	V8	24	fuel metering unit	24	12
r	29	F Migault	Connew	PC1	Cosworth	V8	22	rear suspension	25	13
r	18	J Ickx	Ferrari	312B2	Ferrari	F12	20	fuel vaporisation	9	5
r	17	C Reutemann	Brabham	BT37	Cosworth	V8	14	fuel metering unit	5	3
r	19	C Regazzoni	Ferrari	312B2	Ferrari	F12	13	fuel vaporisation	2	1
r	21	D Walker	JPS Lotus	72D	Cosworth	V8	6	connecting rod	19	10
ns	22	H Pescarolo	March	721	Cosworth	V8		accident		

Winning speed: 214.518 km/h, 133.295 mph
Pole Position speed: 221.732 km/h, 137.778 mph (E Fittipaldi, 1 min:35.970 sec)
Fastest Lap speed: 216.432 km/h, 134.485 mph (D Hulme, 1 min:38.320 sec on lap 47)
Lap Leaders: J Stewart 1-23 (23); E Fittipaldi 24-54 (31).

10 Sep 1972 ITALY: Monza (Round:10) (Race: 218)

55 laps x 5.775 km, 3.588 miles = 317.625 km, 197.363 miles

POS.	NO.	DRIVER	CAR	MODEL	ENGINE		LAPS	TIME/REASON FOR RETIREMENT	GRID:POS	ROW
1	6	E Fittipaldi	JPS Lotus	72D	Cosworth	V8	55	1h 29m 58.400s	6	3
2	10	M Hailwood	Surtees	TS9B	Cosworth	V8	55	1h 30m 12.900s	9	5
3	14	D Hulme	McLaren	M19C	Cosworth	V8	55	1h 30m 22.200s	5	3
4	15	P Revson	McLaren	M19C	Cosworth	V8	55	1h 30m 34.100s	8	4
5	28	G Hill	Brabham	BT37	Cosworth	V8	55	1h 31m 04.000s	13	7
6	23	P Gethin	BRM	P160C	BRM	V12	55	1h 31m 20.300s	12	6
7	3	M Andretti	Ferrari	312B2	Ferrari	F12	54		7	4
8	21	J-P Beltoise	BRM	P180	BRM	V12	54		16	8
9	19	R Peterson	March	721G	Cosworth	V8	54		24	12
10	16	M Beuttler	March	721G	Cosworth	V8	54		25	13
11	22	H Ganley	BRM	P160C	BRM	V12	52		17	9
12	24	R Wisell	BRM	P160C	BRM	V12	51		10	5
13	18	N Lauda	March	721G	Cosworth	V8	50		20	10
r	4	J Ickx	Ferrari	312B2	Ferrari	F12	46	battery	1	1
r	20	C Amon	Matra Simca	MS120D	Matra	V12	38	brake pads	2	1
r	9	A de Adamich	Surtees	TS9B	Cosworth	V8	33	brake calipers	21	11
r	7	J Surtees	Surtees	TS14	Cosworth	V8	20	fuel vaporisation	19	10
r	8	T Schenken	Surtees	TS9B	Cosworth	V8	20	suspension/ accident	22	11
r	29	W Fittipaldi	Brabham	BT34	Cosworth	V8	20	rear suspension	15	8
r	5	C Regazzoni	Ferrari	312B2	Ferrari	F12	16	accident	4	2
r	26	C Pace	March	711	Cosworth	V8	15	accident	18	9
r	30	C Reutemann	Brabham	BT37	Cosworth	V8	14	front suspension	11	6
r	2	F Cevert	Tyrrell	002	Cosworth	V8	14	engine	14	7
r	11	N Galli	Tecno	PA123	Tecno	F12	6	engine	23	12
r	1	J Stewart	Tyrrell	005	Cosworth	V8	0	clutch	3	2
nq	25	H Pescarolo	March	721	Cosworth	V8				
nq	12	D Bell	Tecno	PA123	Tecno	F12				

Winning speed: 211.813 km/h, 131.614 mph
Pole Position speed: 217.355 km/h, 135.058 mph (J Ickx, 1 min:35.650 sec)
Fastest Lap speed: 215.888 km/h, 134.146 mph (J Ickx, 1 min:36.300 sec on lap 44)
Lap Leaders: J Ickx 1-13,17-45 (42); C Regazzoni 14-16 (3); E Fittipaldi 46-55 (10).

24 Sep 1972 — CANADA: Mosport Park (Round:11) (Race: 219)

80 laps x 3.957 km, 2.459 miles = 316.590 km, 196.720 miles

POS.	NO.	DRIVER	CAR	MODEL	ENGINE		LAPS	TIME/REASON FOR RETIREMENT	GRID:POS	ROW
1	1	J Stewart	Tyrrell	005	Cosworth	V8	80	1h 43m 16.900s	5	2
2	19	P Revson	McLaren	M19C	Cosworth	V8	80	1h 44m 05.100s	1	1
3	18	D Hulme	McLaren	M19C	Cosworth	V8	80	1h 44m 11.500s	2	1
4	8	C Reutemann	Brabham	BT37	Cosworth	V8	80	1h 44m 17.600s	9	4
5	11	C Regazzoni	Ferrari	312B2	Ferrari	F12	80	1h 44m 23.900s	7	3
6	4	C Amon	Matra Simca	MS120D	Matra	V12	79		10	4
7	22	T Schenken	Surtees	TS9B	Cosworth	V8	79		13	5
8	7	G Hill	Brabham	BT37	Cosworth	V8	79		17	7
9r	29	C Pace	March	711	Cosworth	V8	78	fuel pressure	18	7
10	15	H Ganley	BRM	P160C	BRM	V12	78		14	6
11	5	E Fittipaldi	JPS Lotus	72D	Cosworth	V8	78		4	2
12	10	J Ickx	Ferrari	312B2	Ferrari	F12	77		8	3
13	28	H Pescarolo	March	721	Cosworth	V8	73		21	9
r	6	R Wisell	JPS Lotus	72D	Cosworth	V8	65	valve spring	16	7
dq	26	N Lauda	March	721G	Cosworth	V8	64	push start after spin	19	8
dq	25	R Peterson	March	721G	Cosworth	V8	61	push start after accident	3	1
nc	27	M Beuttler	March	721G	Cosworth	V8	59		24	10
r	2	F Cevert	Tyrrell	006	Cosworth	V8	51	gearbox	6	3
r	16	P Gethin	BRM	P160C	BRM	V12	25	rear suspension radius rod	12	5
nc	33	S Barber	March	711	Cosworth	V8	24		22	9
r	14	J-P Beltoise	BRM	P180	BRM	V12	21	oil radiator leak	20	8
r	17	B Brack	BRM	P180	BRM	V12	20	spin	23	9
r	9	W Fittipaldi	Brabham	BT34	Cosworth	V8	5	gearbox	11	5
r	23	A de Adamich	Surtees	TS9B	Cosworth	V8	2	gearbox	15	6
ns	31	D Bell	Tecno	PA123	Tecno	F12		accident		

Winning speed: 183.918 km/h, 114.282 mph
Pole Position speed: 193.567 km/h, 120.277 mph (P Revson, 1 min:13.600 sec)
Fastest Lap speed: 188.198 km/h, 116.941 mph (J Stewart, 1 min:15.700 sec on lap 25)
Lap Leaders: R Peterson 1-3 (3); J Stewart 4-80 (77).

8 Oct 1972 — USA: Watkins Glen (Round:12) (Race: 220)

59 laps x 5.435 km, 3.377 miles = 320.651 km, 199.243 miles

POS.	NO.	DRIVER	CAR	MODEL	ENGINE		LAPS	TIME/REASON FOR RETIREMENT	GRID:POS	ROW
1	1	J Stewart	Tyrrell	005	Cosworth	V8	59	1h 41m 45.354s	1	1
2	2	F Cevert	Tyrrell	006	Cosworth	V8	59	1h 42m 17.622s	4	2
3	19	D Hulme	McLaren	M19C	Cosworth	V8	59	1h 42m 22.882s	3	1
4	4	R Peterson	March	721G	Cosworth	V8	59	1h 43m 07.870s	26	11
5	7	J Ickx	Ferrari	312B2	Ferrari	F12	59	1h 43m 08.473s	12	5
6	9	M Andretti	Ferrari	312B2	Ferrari	F12	58		10	4
7	3	P Depailler	Tyrrell	004	Cosworth	V8	58		11	5
8	8	C Regazzoni	Ferrari	312B2	Ferrari	F12	58		6	3
9	21	J Scheckter	McLaren	M19A	Cosworth	V8	58		8	3
10	12	R Wisell	JPS Lotus	72D	Cosworth	V8	57		16	7
11	28	G Hill	Brabham	BT37	Cosworth	V8	57		27	11
12	34	S Posey	Surtees	TS9B	Cosworth	V8	57		23	9
13	6	M Beuttler	March	721G	Cosworth	V8	57		21	9
14	26	H Pescarolo	March	721	Cosworth	V8	57		22	9
15	18	C Amon	Matra Simca	MS120D	Matra	V12	57		7	3
16	33	S Barber	March	711	Cosworth	V8	57		20	8
17r	23	M Hailwood	Surtees	TS9B	Cosworth	V8	56	accident	14	6
18r	20	P Revson	McLaren	M19C	Cosworth	V8	54	ignition	2	1
nc	5	N Lauda	March	721G	Cosworth	V8	49		25	10
r	27	C Pace	March	711	Cosworth	V8	48	fuel injection	15	6
r	14	P Gethin	BRM	P160C	BRM	V12	47	engine	28	11
r	16	H Ganley	BRM	P160C	BRM	V12	44	engine	17	7
r	11	D Walker	JPS Lotus	72D	Cosworth	V8	44	coil	30	12
r	30	W Fittipaldi	Brabham	BT34	Cosworth	V8	43	engine	13	5
r	17	J-P Beltoise	BRM	P180	BRM	V12	40	ignition rotor	18	7
r	15	B Redman	BRM	P180	BRM	V12	34	connecting rod	24	10
r	29	C Reutemann	Brabham	BT37	Cosworth	V8	31	engine	5	2
r	25	A de Adamich	Surtees	TS9B	Cosworth	V8	25	front suspension	19	8
r	22	T Schenken	Surtees	TS14	Cosworth	V8	22	rear suspension	31	13
r	10	E Fittipaldi	JPS Lotus	72D	Cosworth	V8	17	suspension	9	4
r	31	D Bell	Tecno	PA123	Tecno	F12	8	cylinder head gasket	29	12
ns	24	J Surtees	Surtees	TS14	Cosworth	V8		engine shortage		

Winning speed: 189.070 km/h, 117.483 mph
Pole Position speed: 194.715 km/h, 120.990 mph (J Stewart, 1 min:40.481 sec)
Fastest Lap speed: 192.487 km/h, 119.606 mph (J Stewart, 1 min:41.644 sec on lap 33)
Lap Leaders: J Stewart 1-59 (59).

Lap Leaders 1972

POS	DRIVER	CAR-ENGINE	GPS	LAPS	KM	MILES
1	J Stewart	Tyrrell-Cosworth	7	320	1,422.2	883.7
2	E Fittipaldi	Lotus-Cosworth	6	240	975.5	606.2
3	J Ickx	Ferrari	3	104	767.0	476.6
4	J-P Beltoise	BRM	1	80	251.6	156.3
5	D Hulme	McLaren-Cosworth	2	28	112.1	69.7
6	C Amon	Matra Simca	1	19	153.0	95.1
7	C Regazzoni	Ferrari	2	11	47.1	29.3
8	R Peterson	March-Cosworth	1	3	11.9	7.4
			12	**805**	**3,740.5**	**2,324.2**

Driver Points 1972

		RA	ZA	E	MC	B	F	GB	D	A	I	CDN	USA	TOTAL
1	E Fittipaldi	-	6	9	4	9	6	9	-	9	9	-	-	61
2	J Stewart	9	-	-	3	-	9	6	-	-	-	9	9	45
3	D Hulme	6	9	-	-	4	-	2	-	6	4	4	4	39
4	J Ickx	4	-	6	6	-	-	-	9	-	-	-	2	27
5	P Revson	-	4	2	-	-	-	4	-	4	3	6	-	23
6	F Cevert	-	-	-	-	6	3	-	-	-	-	-	6	15
	C Regazzoni	3	-	4	-	-	-	-	6	-	-	2	-	15
8	M Hailwood	-	-	-	-	3	1	-	-	3	6	-	-	13
9	R Peterson	1	2	-	-	-	2	-	4	-	-	-	3	12
	C Amon	-	-	-	1	1	4	3	-	2	-	1	-	12
11	J-P Beltoise	-	-	-	9	-	-	-	-	-	-	-	-	9
12	M Andretti	-	3	-	-	-	-	-	-	-	-	-	1	4
	H Ganley	-	-	-	-	-	-	-	3	1	-	-	-	4
	B Redman	-	-	-	2	-	-	-	2	-	-	-	-	4
	G Hill	-	1	-	-	-	-	-	1	-	2	-	-	4
16	A de Adamich	-	-	3	-	-	-	-	-	-	-	-	-	3
	C Reutemann	-	-	-	-	-	-	-	-	-	-	3	-	3
	C Pace	-	-	1	-	2	-	-	-	-	-	-	-	3
19	T Schenken	2	-	-	-	-	-	-	-	-	-	-	-	2
20	A Merzario	-	-	-	-	-	-	1	-	-	-	-	-	1
	P Gethin	-	-	-	-	-	-	-	-	-	1	-	-	1

9, 6, 4, 3,2 and 1 point awarded to the first six finishers.
Best 5 scores from first 6 races, best 5 from remaining 6 races.

Constructor Points 1972

		RA	ZA	E	MC	B	F	GB	D	A	I	CDN	USA	TOTAL	
1	Lotus-Cosworth	-	6	9	4	9	6	9	-	9	9	-	-	61	
2	Tyrrell-Cosworth	9	-	-	3	6	9	6	-	-	-	9	9	51	
3	McLaren-Cosworth	6	9	2	2	4	-	4	(2)	6	4	6	4	47	(2)
4	Ferrari	4	3	6	6	-	-	1	9	-	-	2	2	33	
5	Surtees-Cosworth	2	-	3	-	3	1	-	-	3	6	-	-	18	
6	March-Cosworth	1	2	1	-	2	2	-	4	-	-	-	3	15	
7	BRM	-	-	-	9	-	-	-	3	1	1	-	-	14	
8	Matra Simca	-	-	-	1	1	4	3	-	2	-	1	-	12	
9	Brabham-Cosworth	-	1	-	-	-	-	-	1	-	2	3	-	7	

9, 6, 4, 3,2 and 1 point awarded to the first six finishers. Points only for highest placed car.
Best 5 scores from first 6 races, best 5 from remaining 6 races.

Mike Hailwood driving the Surtees TS9B-Ford Cosworth

RACE ENTRANTS & RESULTS 1973

The Formula 1 Constructors Association demanded more start and appearance money. Safety became a major issue; deformable structures required from the Spanish race and after the Dutch race all grids would be 2 x 2 formation. Frank Williams had his first full season with the Iso Marlboro and Ferrari produced its first full monocoque

FERRARI
Scuderia Ferrari SpA SEFAC: Ickx, Merzario

TECNO
Martini Racing Team: Amon

BRABHAM
Motor Racing Developments: Reutemann, W Fittipaldi
Ceramica Pagnossin-Team MRD: de Adamich, Stommelen, Watson

BRM
Marlboro BRM: Beltoise, Regazzoni, Lauda, Gethin

ENSIGN
Team Ensign: von Opel

LOTUS
John Player Team Lotus: E Fittipaldi, Peterson
Scuderia Scribante-Lucky Strike Racing: Charlton

MARCH
STP March Racing Team: Jarier, Williamson*, Pescarolo
Clarke-Mordaunt-Guthrie-Durlacher: Beuttler, Wisell (F)
Hesketh Racing: Hunt
Lec Refrigeration Racing: Purley
Team Pierre Robert: (Wisell)
** co-entered by Wheatcroft Racing at GB GP*

McLAREN
Yardley Team McLaren: Hulme, Revson, Scheckter, Ickx

SHADOW
UOP Shadow Racing Team: Oliver, Follmer, Redman
Embassy Racing: Hill

SURTEES
Team Surtees-Brooke Bond Oxo/Rob Walker: Hailwood
Team Surtees-Brooke Bond Oxo: Pace
Ceramica Pagnossin-Team Surtees: de Adamich
Team Surtees: Mass, Bueno

TYRRELL
Elf Team Tyrrell: Stewart, Cevert, Amon
Blignaut-Lucky Strike Racing: Keizan

WILLIAMS (ISO MARLBORO)
Frank Williams Racing Cars: Ganley, Galli, Pescarolo, van Lennep, Pretorius, McRae, Schenken, Ickx, (Belso)

28 Jan 1973 — ARGENTINA: Buenos Aires No.9 (Round: 1) (Race: 221)
96 laps x 3.345 km, 2.078 miles = 321.1280 km, 199.535 miles

POS.	NO.	DRIVER	CAR	MODEL	ENGINE		LAPS	TIME/REASON FOR RETIREMENT	GRID:POS	ROW
1	2	E Fittipaldi	JPS Lotus	72D	Cosworth	V8	96	1h 56m 18.220s	2	1
2	8	F Cevert	Tyrrell	006	Cosworth	V8	96	1h 56m 22.910s	6	3
3	6	J Stewart	Tyrrell	005	Cosworth	V8	96	1h 56m 51.410s	4	2
4	18	J Ickx	Ferrari	312B2	Ferrari	F12	96	1h 57m 00.790s	3	2
5	14	D Hulme	McLaren	M19C	Cosworth	V8	95		8	4
6	12	W Fittipaldi	Brabham	BT37	Cosworth	V8	95		12	6
7	32	C Regazzoni	BRM	P160D	BRM	V12	93		1	1
8	16	P Revson	McLaren	M19C	Cosworth	V8	92		11	6
9	20	A Merzario	Ferrari	312B2	Ferrari	F12	92		14	7
10r	22	M Beuttler	March	721G	Cosworth	V8	90	suspension radius rod	18	9
r	24	J-P Jarier	March	721G	Cosworth	V8	84	gear linkage/ radiator	17	9
r	30	J-P Beltoise	BRM	P160D	BRM	V12	79	engine	7	4
nc	38	H Ganley	Iso Marlboro	FX3B	Cosworth	V8	79		19	10
r	4	R Peterson	JPS Lotus	72D	Cosworth	V8	66	oil pressure	5	3
r	34	N Lauda	BRM	P160C	BRM	V12	66	oil pressure	13	7
r	10	C Reutemann	Brabham	BT37	Cosworth	V8	16	gearbox	9	5
r	28	C Pace	Surtees	TS14A	Cosworth	V8	10	suspension	15	8
r	26	M Hailwood	Surtees	TS14A	Cosworth	V8	10	drive shaft	10	5
r	36	N Galli	Iso Marlboro	FX3B	Cosworth	V8	0	engine	16	8

Winning speed: 165.663 km/h, 102.938 mph
Pole Position speed: 170.712 km/h, 106.075 mph (C Regazzoni, 1 min:10.540 sec)
Fastest Lap speed: 169.082 km/h, 105.063 mph (E Fittipaldi, 1 min:11.220 sec on lap 79)
Lap Leaders: C Regazzoni 1-28 (28); F Cevert 29-85 (57); E Fittipaldi 86-96 (11).

11 Feb 1973 — BRAZIL: Interlagos (Round: 2) (Race: 222)
40 laps x 7.960 km, 4.946 miles = 318.400 km, 197.845 miles

POS.	NO.	DRIVER	CAR	MODEL	ENGINE		LAPS	TIME/REASON FOR RETIREMENT	GRID:POS	ROW
1	1	E Fittipaldi	JPS Lotus	72D	Cosworth	V8	40	1h 43m 55.600s	2	1
2	3	J Stewart	Tyrrell	005	Cosworth	V8	40	1h 44m 09.100s	8	3
3	7	D Hulme	McLaren	M19C	Cosworth	V8	40	1h 45m 42.000s	5	2
4	10	A Merzario	Ferrari	312B2	Ferrari	F12	39		17	7
5	9	J Ickx	Ferrari	312B2	Ferrari	F12	39		3	1
6	14	C Regazzoni	BRM	P160D	BRM	V12	39		4	2
7	19	H Ganley	Iso Marlboro	FX3B	Cosworth	V8	39		16	7
8	16	N Lauda	BRM	P160C	BRM	V12	38		13	5
9	20	N Galli	Iso Marlboro	FX3B	Cosworth	V8	38		18	7
10	4	F Cevert	Tyrrell	006	Cosworth	V8	38		9	4
11	17	C Reutemann	Brabham	BT37	Cosworth	V8	38		7	3
12	23	L Bueno	Surtees	TS9B	Cosworth	V8	36		20	8
r	15	J-P Beltoise	BRM	P160D	BRM	V12	23	electrics	10	4
r	12	M Beuttler	March	721G	Cosworth	V8	18	engine overheating	19	8
r	6	C Pace	Surtees	TS14A	Cosworth	V8	8	suspension	6	3
r	5	M Hailwood	Surtees	TS14A	Cosworth	V8	6	gearbox pinion bearing	14	6
r	11	J-P Jarier	March	721G	Cosworth	V8	5	gearbox	15	6
r	2	R Peterson	JPS Lotus	72D	Cosworth	V8	5	rear wheel	1	1
r	18	W Fittipaldi	Brabham	BT37	Cosworth	V8	5	cylinder head ring	11	5
r	8	P Revson	McLaren	M19C	Cosworth	V8	3	gearbox	12	5

Winning speed: 183.822 km/h, 114.222 mph
Pole Position speed: 190.405 km/h, 118.312 mph (R Peterson, 2 min:30.500 sec)
Fastest Lap speed: 184.877 km/h, 114.878 mph (E Fittipaldi/ D Hulme, 2 min:35.000 sec on lap 14 / 20)
Lap Leaders: E Fittipaldi 1-40 (40).

3 Mar 1973 SOUTH AFRICA: Kyalami (Round: 3) (Race: 223)

79 laps x 4.104 km, 2.550 miles = 324.216 km, 201.458 miles

POS.	NO.	DRIVER	CAR	MODEL	ENGINE		LAPS	TIME/REASON FOR RETIREMENT	GRID:POS	ROW
1	3	J Stewart	Tyrrell	006	Cosworth	V8	79	1h 43m 11.070s	16	7
2	6	P Revson	McLaren	M19C	Cosworth	V8	79	1h 43m 35.620s	6	3
3	1	E Fittipaldi	JPS Lotus	72D	Cosworth	V8	79	1h 43m 36.130s	2	1
4	9	A Merzario	Ferrari	312B2	Ferrari	F12	78		15	6
5	5	D Hulme	McLaren	M23	Cosworth	V8	77		1	1
6	23	G Follmer	Shadow	DN1	Cosworth	V8	77		21	9
7	18	C Reutemann	Brabham	BT37	Cosworth	V8	77		8	3
8	12	A de Adamich	Surtees	TS9B	Cosworth	V8	77		20	8
9r	7	J Scheckter	McLaren	M19C	Cosworth	V8	75	engine	3	1
10	21	H Ganley	Iso Marlboro	FX3B	Cosworth	V8	73		19	8
11	2	R Peterson	JPS Lotus	72D	Cosworth	V8	73		4	2
r	11	C Pace	Surtees	TS14A	Cosworth	V8	69	tyre burst/ accident	9	4
nc	26	E Keizan	Tyrrell	004	Cosworth	V8	67		22	9
nc	14	J-P Jarier	March	721G	Cosworth	V8	66		18	7
nc	4	F Cevert	Tyrrell	005	Cosworth	V8	66		25	10
nc	24	M Beuttler	March	721G	Cosworth	V8	65		23	9
r	19	W Fittipaldi	Brabham	BT37	Cosworth	V8	52	gear selection	17	7
r	20	J Pretorius	Iso Marlboro	FX3B	Cosworth	V8	35	engine overheating	24	10
r	17	N Lauda	BRM	P160D	BRM	V12	26	engine	10	4
r	22	J Oliver	Shadow	DN1	Cosworth	V8	14	engine	14	6
r	16	J-P Beltoise	BRM	P160D	BRM	V12	4	clutch	7	3
r	25	D Charlton	Lotus	72D	Cosworth	V8	3	accident	13	5
r	8	J Ickx	Ferrari	312B2	Ferrari	F12	2	accident	11	5
r	15	C Regazzoni	BRM	P160D	BRM	V12	2	accident/fire	5	2
r	10	M Hailwood	Surtees	TS14A	Cosworth	V8	2	accident	12	5

Winning speed: 188.526 km/h, 117.145 mph
Pole Position speed: 193.686 km/h, 120.351 mph (D Hulme, 1 min:16.280 sec)
Fastest Lap speed: 191.626 km/h, 119.071 mph (E Fittipaldi, 1 min:17.100 sec on lap 76)
Lap Leaders: D Hulme 1-4 (4); J Scheckter 5-6 (2); J Stewart 7-79 (73).

29 Apr 1973 SPAIN: Montjuich Park (Round: 4) (Race: 224)

75 laps x 3.791 km, 2.356 miles = 284.325 km, 176.671 miles

POS.	NO.	DRIVER	CAR	MODEL	ENGINE		LAPS	TIME/REASON FOR RETIREMENT	GRID:POS	ROW
1	1	E Fittipaldi	JPS Lotus	72E	Cosworth	V8	75	1h 48m 18.700s	7	4
2	4	F Cevert	Tyrrell	006	Cosworth	V8	75	1h 49m 01.400s	3	2
3	20	G Follmer	Shadow	DN1	Cosworth	V8	75	1h 49m 31.800s	14	7
4	6	P Revson	McLaren	M23	Cosworth	V8	74		5	3
5	15	J-P Beltoise	BRM	P160E	BRM	V12	74		10	5
6	5	D Hulme	McLaren	M23	Cosworth	V8	74		2	1
7	12	M Beuttler	March	731	Cosworth	V8	74		19	10
8	11	H Pescarolo	March	731	Cosworth	V8	73		18	9
9	14	C Regazzoni	BRM	P160E	BRM	V12	69		8	4
10	17	W Fittipaldi	Brabham	BT42	Cosworth	V8	69		12	6
11	24	N Galli	Iso Marlboro	IR	Cosworth	V8	69		20	10
12	7	J Ickx	Ferrari	312B3	Ferrari	F12	69		6	3
r	18	C Reutemann	Brabham	BT42	Cosworth	V8	66	drive shaft	15	8
r	23	H Ganley	Iso Marlboro	IR	Cosworth	V8	63	out of fuel	21	11
r	2	R Peterson	JPS Lotus	72E	Cosworth	V8	56	gearbox	1	1
r	3	J Stewart	Tyrrell	006	Cosworth	V8	47	brake disc	4	2
r	16	N Lauda	BRM	P160E	BRM	V12	28	tyres	11	6
r	25	G Hill	Shadow	DN1	Cosworth	V8	27	brakes	22	11
r	9	M Hailwood	Surtees	TS14A	Cosworth	V8	25	oil line	9	5
r	19	J Oliver	Shadow	DN1	Cosworth	V8	23	oil loss/ engine	13	7
r	21	A de Adamich	Brabham	BT37	Cosworth	V8	17	hub/ wheel lost	17	9
r	10	C Pace	Surtees	TS14A	Cosworth	V8	13	drive shaft	16	8

Winning speed: 157.504 km/h, 97.868 mph
Pole Position speed: 166.841 km/h, 103.670 mph (R Peterson, 1 min:21.800 sec)
Fastest Lap speed: 162.859 km/h, 101.196 mph (R Peterson, 1 min:23.800 sec on lap 13)
Lap Leaders: R Peterson 1-56 (56); E Fittipaldi 57-75 (19).

20 May 1973 BELGIUM Zolder (Round: 5) (Race: 225)

70 laps x 4.220 km, 2.622 miles = 295.400 km, 183.553 miles

POS.	NO.	DRIVER	CAR	MODEL	ENGINE		LAPS	TIME/REASON FOR RETIREMENT	GRID:POS	ROW
1	5	J Stewart	Tyrrell	006	Cosworth	V8	70	1h 42m 13.430s	6	3
2	6	F Cevert	Tyrrell	006	Cosworth	V8	70	1h 42m 45.270s	4	2
3	1	E Fittipaldi	JPS Lotus	72E	Cosworth	V8	70	1h 44m 16.220s	9	5
4	9	A de Adamich	Brabham	BT37	Cosworth	V8	69		18	9
5	21	N Lauda	BRM	P160E	BRM	V12	69		14	7
6	22	C Amon	Tecno	PA123	Tecno	F12	67		15	8
7	7	D Hulme	McLaren	M23	Cosworth	V8	67		2	1
8	24	C Pace	Surtees	TS14A	Cosworth	V8	66		8	4
9	12	G Hill	Shadow	DN1	Cosworth	V8	65		23	12
10r	19	C Regazzoni	BRM	P160E	BRM	V12	63	accident	12	6
11r	15	M Beuttler	March	731	Cosworth	V8	63	accident	20	10
r	14	J-P Jarier	March	731	Cosworth	V8	60	accident	16	8
r	20	J-P Beltoise	BRM	P160E	BRM	V12	56	engine	5	3
r	11	W Fittipaldi	Brabham	BT42	Cosworth	V8	46	engine	19	10
r	2	R Peterson	JPS Lotus	72E	Cosworth	V8	42	accident	1	1

POS.	NO.	DRIVER	CAR	MODEL	ENGINE		LAPS	TIME/REASON FOR RETIREMENT	GRID:POS	ROW
r	8	P Revson	McLaren	M23	Cosworth	V8	33	accident	10	5
r	25	H Ganley	Iso Marlboro	IR	Cosworth	V8	16	throttle jammed/ accident	21	11
r	10	C Reutemann	Brabham	BT42	Cosworth	V8	14	oil leak/ engine	7	4
r	16	G Follmer	Shadow	DN1	Cosworth	V8	13	throttle slides jammed	11	6
r	17	J Oliver	Shadow	DN1	Cosworth	V8	11	accident	22	11
r	26	N Galli	Iso Marlboro	IR	Cosworth	V8	6	engine	17	9
r	3	J Ickx	Ferrari	312B3	Ferrari	F12	6	oil pump	3	2
r	23	M Hailwood	Surtees	TS14A	Cosworth	V8	4	accident	13	7

Winning speed: 173.384 km/h, 107.736 mph
Pole Position speed: 184.235 km/h, 114.478 mph (R Peterson, 1 min:22.460 sec)
Fastest Lap speed: 177.851 km/h, 110.511 mph (F Cevert, 1 min:25.420 sec on lap 28)
Lap Leaders: R Peterson 1 (1); F Cevert 2-19 (18); E Fittipaldi 20-24 (5); J Stewart 25-70 (46).

3 Jun 1973 MONACO: Monte Carlo (Round: 6) (Race: 226)
78 laps x 3.278 km, 2.037 miles = 255.684 km, 158.875 miles

POS.	NO.	DRIVER	CAR	MODEL	ENGINE		LAPS	TIME/REASON FOR RETIREMENT	GRID:POS	ROW
1	5	J Stewart	Tyrrell	006	Cosworth	V8	78	1h 57m 44.300s	1	1
2	1	E Fittipaldi	JPS Lotus	72E	Cosworth	V8	78	1h 57m 45.600s	5	3
3	2	R Peterson	JPS Lotus	72E	Cosworth	V8	77		2	1
4	6	F Cevert	Tyrrell	006	Cosworth	V8	77		4	2
5	8	P Revson	McLaren	M23	Cosworth	V8	76		15	8
6	7	D Hulme	McLaren	M23	Cosworth	V8	76		3	2
7	9	A de Adamich	Brabham	BT37	Cosworth	V8	75		25	13
8	23	M Hailwood	Surtees	TS14A	Cosworth	V8	75		13	7
9r	27	J Hunt	March	731	Cosworth	V8	73	engine	18	9
10	17	J Oliver	Shadow	DN1	Cosworth	V8	72		22	11
11r	11	W Fittipaldi	Brabham	BT42	Cosworth	V8	71	fuel system	9	5
r	14	J-P Jarier	March	731	Cosworth	V8	67	gearbox	14	7
r	12	G Hill	Shadow	DN1	Cosworth	V8	62	rear suspension	24	12
r	4	A Merzario	Ferrari	312B3	Ferrari	F12	58	oil pressure	16	8
r	10	C Reutemann	Brabham	BT42	Cosworth	V8	46	gearbox	19	10
r	3	J Ickx	Ferrari	312B3	Ferrari	F12	44	drive shaft	7	4
r	25	H Ganley	Iso Marlboro	IR	Cosworth	V8	41	drive shaft	10	5
r	20	J-P Beltoise	BRM	P160E	BRM	V12	39	accident	11	6
r	18	D Purley	March	731	Cosworth	V8	31	fuel system	23	12
r	24	C Pace	Surtees	TS14A	Cosworth	V8	31	drive shaft	17	9
r	26	N Galli	Iso Marlboro	IR	Cosworth	V8	30	drive shaft	21	11
r	21	N Lauda	BRM	P160E	BRM	V12	24	gearbox	6	3
r	22	C Amon	Tecno	PA123	Tecno	F12	22	engine overheating	12	6
r	19	C Regazzoni	BRM	P160E	BRM	V12	15	brake fluid boiling	8	4
r	15	M Beuttler	March	731	Cosworth	V8	3	engine	20	10
ns	16	G Follmer	Shadow	DN1	Cosworth	V8		accident		

Winning speed: 130.298 km/h, 80.963 mph
Pole Position speed: 134.866 km/h, 83.802 mph (J Stewart, 1 min:27.500 sec)
Fastest Lap speed: 133.948 km/h, 83.231 mph (E Fittipaldi, 1 min:28.100 sec on lap 78)
Lap Leaders: F Cevert 1 (1); R Peterson 2-7 (6); J Stewart 8-78 (71).

17 Jun 1973 SWEDEN: Anderstorp (Round: 7) (Race: 227)
80 laps x 4.018 km, 2.497 miles = 321.440 km, 199.734 miles

POS.	NO.	DRIVER	CAR	MODEL	ENGINE		LAPS	TIME/REASON FOR RETIREMENT	GRID:POS	ROW
1	7	D Hulme	McLaren	M23	Cosworth	V8	80	1h 56m 46.049s	6	3
2	2	R Peterson	JPS Lotus	72E	Cosworth	V8	80	1h 56m 50.088s	1	1
3	6	F Cevert	Tyrrell	006	Cosworth	V8	80	1h 57m 00.716s	2	1
4	10	C Reutemann	Brabham	BT42	Cosworth	V8	80	1h 57m 04.117s	5	3
5	5	J Stewart	Tyrrell	006	Cosworth	V8	80	1h 57m 12.047s	3	2
6	3	J Ickx	Ferrari	312B3	Ferrari	F12	79		8	4
7	8	P Revson	McLaren	M23	Cosworth	V8	79		7	4
8	15	M Beuttler	March	731	Cosworth	V8	77		21	11
9	19	C Regazzoni	BRM	P160E	BRM	V12	77		12	6
10	24	C Pace	Surtees	TS14A	Cosworth	V8	77		16	8
11	25	H Ganley	Iso Marlboro	IR	Cosworth	V8	76		11	6
12r	1	E Fittipaldi	JPS Lotus	72E	Cosworth	V8	76	gearbox/ brakes	4	2
13	21	N Lauda	BRM	P160E	BRM	V12	75		15	8
14	16	G Follmer	Shadow	DN1	Cosworth	V8	74		19	10
r	20	J-P Beltoise	BRM	P160E	BRM	V12	57	engine	9	5
r	17	J Oliver	Shadow	DN1	Cosworth	V8	50	suspension/ transmission	17	9
r	23	M Hailwood	Surtees	TS14A	Cosworth	V8	41	tyres/ vibration	10	5
r	14	J-P Jarier	March	731	Cosworth	V8	36	throttle linkage	20	10
r	12	G Hill	Shadow	DN1	Cosworth	V8	16	ignition	18	9
r	11	W Fittipaldi	Brabham	BT42	Cosworth	V8	0	accident	13	7
r	27	R Wisell	March	731	Cosworth	V8	-1	suspension	14	7
ns	26	T Belso	Iso Marlboro	IR	Cosworth	V8		car raced by Ganley		

Winning speed: 165.169 km/h, 102.631 mph
Pole Position speed: 172.590 km/h, 107.243 mph (R Peterson, 1 min:23.810 sec)
Fastest Lap speed: 167.910 km/h, 104.335 mph (D Hulme, 1 min:26.146 sec on lap 7)
Lap Leaders: R Peterson 1-78 (78); D Hulme 79-80 (2).

1 Jul 1973 — FRANCE: Paul Ricard (Round: 8) (Race: 228)

54 laps x 5.810 km, 3.610 miles = 313.740 km, 194.949 miles

POS.	NO.	DRIVER	CAR	MODEL	ENGINE		LAPS	TIME/REASON FOR RETIREMENT	GRID:POS	ROW
1	2	R Peterson	JPS Lotus	72E	Cosworth	V8	54	1h 41m 36.520s	5	2
2	6	F Cevert	Tyrrell	006	Cosworth	V8	54	1h 42m 17.440s	4	2
3	10	C Reutemann	Brabham	BT42	Cosworth	V8	54	1h 42m 23.000s	8	3
4	5	J Stewart	Tyrrell	006	Cosworth	V8	54	1h 42m 23.450s	1	1
5	3	J Ickx	Ferrari	312B3	Ferrari	F12	54	1h 42m 25.420s	12	5
6	27	J Hunt	March	731	Cosworth	V8	54	1h 42m 59.060s	14	6
7	4	A Merzario	Ferrari	312B3	Ferrari	F12	54	1h 43m 05.710s	10	4
8	7	D Hulme	McLaren	M23	Cosworth	V8	54	1h 43m 06.050s	6	3
9	21	N Lauda	BRM	P160E	BRM	V12	54	1h 43m 22.280s	17	7
10	12	G Hill	Shadow	DN1	Cosworth	V8	53		16	7
11	20	J-P Beltoise	BRM	P160E	BRM	V12	53		15	6
12	19	C Regazzoni	BRM	P160E	BRM	V12	53		9	4
13	24	C Pace	Surtees	TS14A	Cosworth	V8	51		18	7
14	25	H Ganley	Iso Marlboro	IR	Cosworth	V8	51		24	10
15	29	R von Opel	Ensign	N173	Cosworth	V8	51		25	10
16r	11	W Fittipaldi	Brabham	BT42	Cosworth	V8	50	fuel metering unit	19	8
r	8	J Scheckter	McLaren	M23	Cosworth	V8	43	accident/ suspension	2	1
r	1	E Fittipaldi	JPS Lotus	72E	Cosworth	V8	41	accident	3	1
r	23	M Hailwood	Surtees	TS14A	Cosworth	V8	30	oil leak	11	5
r	9	A de Adamich	Brabham	BT37	Cosworth	V8	28	drive shaft	13	5
r	15	R Wisell	March	731	Cosworth	V8	20	engine overheating	22	9
r	16	G Follmer	Shadow	DN1	Cosworth	V8	16	fuel vaporisation	20	8
r	26	H Pescarolo	Iso Marlboro	IR	Cosworth	V8	16	engine overheating	23	9
r	14	J-P Jarier	March	731	Cosworth	V8	7	drive shaft	7	3
r	17	J Oliver	Shadow	DN1	Cosworth	V8	0	clutch	21	9

Winning speed: 185.264 km/h, 115.118 mph
Pole Position speed: 193.005 km/h, 119.928 mph (J Stewart, 1 min:48.370 sec)
Fastest Lap speed: 188.449 km/h, 117.097 mph (D Hulme, 1 min:50.990 sec on lap 52)
Lap Leaders: J Scheckter 1-41 (41); R Peterson 42-54 (13).

14 Jul 1973 — BRITAIN: Silverstone (Round: 9) (Race: 229)

67 laps x 4.711 km, 2.927 miles = 315.607 km, 196.109 miles

POS.	NO.	DRIVER	CAR	MODEL	ENGINE		LAPS	TIME/REASON FOR RETIREMENT	GRID:POS	ROW
1	8	P Revson	McLaren	M23	Cosworth	V8	67	1h 29m 18.500s	3	1
2	2	R Peterson	JPS Lotus	72E	Cosworth	V8	67	1h 29m 21.300s	1	1
3	7	D Hulme	McLaren	M23	Cosworth	V8	67	1h 29m 21.500s	2	1
4	27	J Hunt	March	731	Cosworth	V8	67	1h 29m 21.900s	11	5
5	6	F Cevert	Tyrrell	006	Cosworth	V8	67	1h 29m 55.100s	7	3
6	10	C Reutemann	Brabham	BT42	Cosworth	V8	67	1h 30m 03.200s	8	3
7	19	C Regazzoni	BRM	P160E	BRM	V12	67	1h 30m 30.200s	10	4
8	3	J Ickx	Ferrari	312B3	Ferrari	F12	67	1h 30m 35.900s	19	8
9	25	H Ganley	Iso Marlboro	IR	Cosworth	V8	66		18	7
10	5	J Stewart	Tyrrell	006	Cosworth	V8	66		4	2
11	15	M Beuttler	March	731	Cosworth	V8	65		24	10
12	21	N Lauda	BRM	P160E	BRM	V12	63		9	4
13	28	R von Opel	Ensign	N173	Cosworth	V8	61		21	9
r	11	W Fittipaldi	Brabham	BT42	Cosworth	V8	44	oil line	13	5
r	1	E Fittipaldi	JPS Lotus	72E	Cosworth	V8	36	cv joint	5	2
r	29	J Watson	Brabham	BT37	Cosworth	V8	36	fuel metering unit	23	9
r	12	G Hill	Shadow	DN1	Cosworth	V8	24	front sub-frame	27	11
r	22	C Amon	Tecno	PA123	Tecno	F12	6	fuel pressure	29	12
r	26	G McRae	Iso Marlboro	IR	Cosworth	V8	0	throttle slides	28	11
r	20	J-P Beltoise	BRM	P160E	BRM	V12	0	accident *	17	7
r	9	A de Adamich	Brabham	BT42	Cosworth	V8	0	accident *	20	8
r	16	G Follmer	Shadow	DN1	Cosworth	V8	0	accident *	25	10
r	23	M Hailwood	Surtees	TS14A	Cosworth	V8	0	accident *	12	5
r	31	J Mass	Surtees	TS14A	Cosworth	V8	0	accident *	14	6
r	24	C Pace	Surtees	TS14A	Cosworth	V8	0	accident *	15	6
r	30	J Scheckter	McLaren	M23	Cosworth	V8	0	accident *	6	3
r	14	R Williamson	March	731	Cosworth	V8	0	accident *	22	9
r	17	J Oliver	Shadow	DN1	Cosworth	V8	0	accident *	26	11
ns	18	D Purley	March	731	Cosworth	V8		accident	16	7

Winning speed: 212.034 km/h, 131.752 mph
Pole Position speed: 222.254 km/h, 138.102 mph (R Peterson, 1 min:16.300 sec)
Fastest Lap speed: 215.750 km/h, 134.061 mph (J Hunt, 1 min:18.600 sec on lap 63)
Lap Leaders: R Peterson 1-38 (38); P Revson 39-67 (29).

Interrupted after 2nd lap, because of an accident. Restarted for original distance. * *retired after first start.*

29 Jul 1973 — NETHERLANDS: Zandvoort (Round:10) (Race: 230)

72 laps x 4.226 km, 2.626 miles = 304.272 km, 189.066 miles

POS.	NO.	DRIVER	CAR	MODEL	ENGINE		LAPS	TIME/REASON FOR RETIREMENT	GRID:POS	ROW
1	5	J Stewart	Tyrrell	006	Cosworth	V8	72	1h 39m 12.450s	2	1
2	6	F Cevert	Tyrrell	006	Cosworth	V8	72	1h 39m 28.280s	3	1
3	27	J Hunt	March	731	Cosworth	V8	72	1h 40m 15.460s	7	3
4	8	P Revson	McLaren	M23	Cosworth	V8	72	1h 40m 21.580s	6	3
5	20	J-P Beltoise	BRM	P160E	BRM	V12	72	1h 40m 25.820s	9	4
6	26	G van Lennep	Iso Marlboro	IR	Cosworth	V8	70		20	8
7	24	C Pace	Surtees	TS14A	Cosworth	V8	69		8	3
8	19	C Regazzoni	BRM	P160E	BRM	V12	68		12	5
9	25	H Ganley	Iso Marlboro	IR	Cosworth	V8	68		15	6
10	16	G Follmer	Shadow	DN1	Cosworth	V8	67		22	9
11r	2	R Peterson	JPS Lotus	72E	Cosworth	V8	66	gearbox	1	1
nc	12	G Hill	Shadow	DN1	Cosworth	V8	56		17	7
r	23	M Hailwood	Surtees	TS14A	Cosworth	V8	52	electrics	24	10
r	21	N Lauda	BRM	P160E	BRM	V12	51	fuel pump/ tyres	11	5
r	7	D Hulme	McLaren	M23	Cosworth	V8	31	engine	4	2
r	11	W Fittipaldi	Brabham	BT42	Cosworth	V8	27	accident	13	5
r	22	C Amon	Tecno	PA123	Tecno	F12	22	fuel pressure	19	8
r	10	C Reutemann	Brabham	BT42	Cosworth	V8	9	tyre burst	5	2
r	18	D Purley	March	731	Cosworth	V8	8	stopped to help Williamson	21	9
r	14	R Williamson	March	731	Cosworth	V8	7	fatal accident	18	7
r	15	M Beuttler	March	731	Cosworth	V8	2	electrics	23	9
r	1	E Fittipaldi	JPS Lotus	72E	Cosworth	V8	2	driver discomfort	16	7
r	17	J Oliver	Shadow	DN1	Cosworth	V8	1	throttle jammed/ accident	10	4
ns	28	R von Opel	Ensign	N173	Cosworth	V8		suspension	14	6

Winning speed: 184.022 km/h, 114.346 mph
Pole Position speed: 191.438 km/h, 118.954 mph (R Peterson, 1 min:19.470 sec)
Fastest Lap speed: 189.436 km/h, 117.710 mph (R Peterson, 1 min:20.310 sec on lap 42)
Lap Leaders: R Peterson 1-63 (63); J Stewart 64-72 (9).

5 Aug 1973 — GERMANY: Nürburgring (Round:11) (Race: 231)

14 laps x 22.835 km, 14.189 miles = 319.690 km, 198.646 miles

POS.	NO.	DRIVER	CAR	MODEL	ENGINE		LAPS	TIME/REASON FOR RETIREMENT	GRID:POS	ROW
1	5	J Stewart	Tyrrell	006	Cosworth	V8	14	1h 42m 03.000s	1	1
2	6	F Cevert	Tyrrell	006	Cosworth	V8	14	1h 42m 04.600s	3	2
3	30	J Ickx	McLaren	M23	Cosworth	V8	14	1h 42m 44.200s	4	2
4	24	C Pace	Surtees	TS14A	Cosworth	V8	14	1h 42m 56.800s	11	6
5	11	W Fittipaldi	Brabham	BT42	Cosworth	V8	14	1h 43m 22.900s	13	7
6	1	E Fittipaldi	JPS Lotus	72E	Cosworth	V8	14	1h 43m 27.300s	14	7
7	31	J Mass	Surtees	TS14A	Cosworth	V8	14	1h 43m 28.200s	15	8
8	17	J Oliver	Shadow	DN1	Cosworth	V8	14	1h 43m 28.700s	17	9
9	8	P Revson	McLaren	M23	Cosworth	V8	14	1h 44m 14.800s	7	4
10	26	H Pescarolo	Iso Marlboro	IR	Cosworth	V8	14	1h 44m 25.500s	12	6
11	9	R Stommelen	Brabham	BT42	Cosworth	V8	14	1h 45m 30.300s	16	8
12	7	D Hulme	McLaren	M23	Cosworth	V8	14	1h 45m 41.700s	8	4
13	12	G Hill	Shadow	DN1	Cosworth	V8	14	1h 45m 52.000s	20	10
14	23	M Hailwood	Surtees	TS14A	Cosworth	V8	13		18	9
15	18	D Purley	March	731	Cosworth	V8	13		22	11
16	15	M Beuttler	March	731	Cosworth	V8	13		19	10
r	10	C Reutemann	Brabham	BT42	Cosworth	V8	7	engine	6	3
r	19	C Regazzoni	BRM	P160E	BRM	V12	7	engine	10	5
r	16	G Follmer	Shadow	DN1	Cosworth	V8	5	accident	21	11
r	20	J-P Beltoise	BRM	P160E	BRM	V12	4	puncture/ gearbox	9	5
r	21	N Lauda	BRM	P160E	BRM	V12	1	accident	5	3
r	2	R Peterson	JPS Lotus	72E	Cosworth	V8	0	distributor	2	1
ns	25	H Ganley	Iso Marlboro	IR	Cosworth	V8		accident		

Winning speed: 187.961 km/h, 116.793 mph
Pole Position speed: 192.160 km/h, 119.403 mph (J Stewart, 7 min: 7.800 sec)
Fastest Lap speed: 190.556 km/h, 118.406 mph (C Pace, 7 min:11.400 sec on lap 13)
Lap Leaders: J Stewart 1-14 (14).

19 Aug 1973 — AUSTRIA: Österreichring (Round:12) (Race: 232)

54 laps x 5.911 km, 3.673 miles = 319.194 km, 198.338 miles

POS.	NO.	DRIVER	CAR	MODEL	ENGINE		LAPS	TIME/REASON FOR RETIREMENT	GRID:POS	ROW
1	2	R Peterson	JPS Lotus	72E	Cosworth	V8	54	1h 28m 48.780s	2	1
2	5	J Stewart	Tyrrell	006	Cosworth	V8	54	1h 28m 57.790s	7	4
3	24	C Pace	Surtees	TS14A	Cosworth	V8	54	1h 29m 35.420s	8	4
4	10	C Reutemann	Brabham	BT42	Cosworth	V8	54	1h 29m 36.690s	5	3
5	20	J-P Beltoise	BRM	P160E	BRM	V12	54	1h 30m 10.380s	13	7
6	19	C Regazzoni	BRM	P160E	BRM	V12	54	1h 30m 27.180s	14	7
7	4	A Merzario	Ferrari	312B3	Ferrari	F12	53		6	3
8	7	D Hulme	McLaren	M23	Cosworth	V8	53		3	2
9	26	G van Lennep	Iso Marlboro	IR	Cosworth	V8	52		23	12
10	23	M Hailwood	Surtees	TS14A	Cosworth	V8	49		15	8
11r	1	E Fittipaldi	JPS Lotus	72E	Cosworth	V8	48	fuel line	1	1
nc	25	H Ganley	Iso Marlboro	IR	Cosworth	V8	44		21	11
r	18	J-P Jarier	March	731	Cosworth	V8	37	gearbox/ engine	12	6
r	28	R von Opel	Ensign	N173	Cosworth	V8	34	fuel pressure	19	10
r	11	W Fittipaldi	Brabham	BT42	Cosworth	V8	31	fuel metering unit	16	8

POS.	NO.	DRIVER	CAR	MODEL	ENGINE		LAPS	TIME/REASON FOR RETIREMENT	GRID:POS	ROW
r	12	G Hill	Shadow	DN1	Cosworth	V8	28	rear suspension radius rod	22	11
r	16	G Follmer	Shadow	DN1	Cosworth	V8	23	crown wheel & pinion	20	10
r	9	R Stommelen	Brabham	BT42	Cosworth	V8	21	front wheel bearing	17	9
r	17	J Oliver	Shadow	DN1	Cosworth	V8	9	fuel leak	18	9
r	6	F Cevert	Tyrrell	006	Cosworth	V8	6	accident/ suspension	10	5
r	27	J Hunt	March	731	Cosworth	V8	3	fuel metering unit	9	5
r	8	P Revson	McLaren	M23	Cosworth	V8	0	clutch	4	2
r	15	M Beuttler	March	731	Cosworth	V8	0	accident/ oil radiator	11	6
ns	22	C Amon	Tecno	E731	Tecno	F12		engine shortage		
ns	21	N Lauda	BRM	P160E	BRM	V12		driver unfit (Germany injury)		

Winning speed: 215.640 km/h, 133.993 mph
Pole Position speed: 224.043 km/h, 139.214 mph (E Fittipaldi, 1 min:34.980 sec)
Fastest Lap speed: 218.723 km/h, 135.908 mph (C Pace, 1 min:37.290 sec on lap 46)
Lap Leaders: R Peterson 1-16,49-54 (22); E Fittipaldi 17-48 (32).

9 Sep 1973 — ITALY: Monza (Round:13) (Race: 233)

55 laps x 5.775 km, 3.588 miles = 317.625 km, 197.363 miles

POS.	NO.	DRIVER	CAR	MODEL	ENGINE		LAPS	TIME/REASON FOR RETIREMENT	GRID:POS	ROW
1	2	R Peterson	JPS Lotus	72E	Cosworth	V8	55	1h 29m 17.000s	1	1
2	1	E Fittipaldi	JPS Lotus	72E	Cosworth	V8	55	1h 29m 17.800s	4	2
3	8	P Revson	McLaren	M23	Cosworth	V8	55	1h 29m 45.800s	2	1
4	5	J Stewart	Tyrrell	006	Cosworth	V8	55	1h 29m 50.200s	6	3
5	6	F Cevert	Tyrrell	006	Cosworth	V8	55	1h 30m 03.200s	11	6
6	10	C Reutemann	Brabham	BT42	Cosworth	V8	55	1h 30m 16.800s	10	5
7	23	M Hailwood	Surtees	TS14A	Cosworth	V8	55	1h 30m 45.700s	8	4
8	3	J Ickx	Ferrari	312B3	Ferrari	F12	54		14	7
9	29	D Purley	March	731	Cosworth	V8	54		24	12
10	16	G Follmer	Shadow	DN1	Cosworth	V8	54		21	11
11	17	J Oliver	Shadow	DN1	Cosworth	V8	54		19	10
12	9	R Stommelen	Brabham	BT42	Cosworth	V8	54		9	5
13	20	J-P Beltoise	BRM	P160E	BRM	V12	54		13	7
14	12	G Hill	Shadow	DN1	Cosworth	V8	54		22	11
15	7	D Hulme	McLaren	M23	Cosworth	V8	53		3	2
nc	25	H Ganley	Iso Marlboro	IR	Cosworth	V8	44		20	10
r	15	M Beuttler	March	731	Cosworth	V8	34	gear lever	12	6
r	21	N Lauda	BRM	P160E	BRM	V12	33	tyre burst/ accident	15	8
r	19	C Regazzoni	BRM	P160E	BRM	V12	31	coil	18	9
r	24	C Pace	Surtees	TS14A	Cosworth	V8	17	tyre burst	5	3
r	26	G van Lennep	Iso Marlboro	IR	Cosworth	V8	14	engine overheating	23	12
r	28	R von Opel	Ensign	N173	Cosworth	V8	10	engine overheating	17	9
r	11	W Fittipaldi	Brabham	BT42	Cosworth	V8	6	brakes	16	8
r	4	A Merzario	Ferrari	312B3	Ferrari	F12	2	accident/ suspension	7	4
ns	27	J Hunt	March	731	Cosworth	V8		accident		

Winning speed: 213.450 km/h, 132.631 mph
Pole Position speed: 219.304 km/h, 136.269 mph (R Peterson, 1 min:34.800 sec)
Fastest Lap speed: 218.153 km/h, 135.554 mph (J Stewart, 1 min:35.300 sec on lap 51)
Lap Leaders: R Peterson 1-55 (55).

23 Sep 1973 — CANADA: Mosport Park (Round:14) (Race: 234)

80 laps x 3.957 km, 2.459 miles = 316.590 km, 196.720 miles

POS.	NO.	DRIVER	CAR	MODEL	ENGINE		LAPS	TIME/REASON FOR RETIREMENT	GRID:POS	ROW
1	8	P Revson	McLaren	M23	Cosworth	V8	80	1h 59m 04.083s	2	1
2	1	E Fittipaldi	JPS Lotus	72E	Cosworth	V8	80	1h 59m 36.817s	5	3
3	17	J Oliver	Shadow	DN1	Cosworth	V8	80	1h 59m 38.588s	14	7
4	20	J-P Beltoise	BRM	P160E	BRM	V12	80	1h 59m 40.597s	16	8
5	5	J Stewart	Tyrrell	006	Cosworth	V8	79		9	5
6	25	H Ganley	Iso Marlboro	IR	Cosworth	V8	79		22	11
7	27	J Hunt	March	731	Cosworth	V8	78		15	8
8	10	C Reutemann	Brabham	BT42	Cosworth	V8	78		4	2
9	23	M Hailwood	Surtees	TS14A	Cosworth	V8	78		12	6
10	29	C Amon	Tyrrell	005	Cosworth	V8	77		11	6
11	11	W Fittipaldi	Brabham	BT42	Cosworth	V8	77		10	5
12	9	R Stommelen	Brabham	BT42	Cosworth	V8	76		18	9
13	7	D Hulme	McLaren	M23	Cosworth	V8	75		7	4
14	26	T Schenken	Iso Marlboro	IR	Cosworth	V8	75		24	12
15	4	A Merzario	Ferrari	312B3	Ferrari	F12	75		20	10
16	12	G Hill	Shadow	DN1	Cosworth	V8	73		17	9
17	16	G Follmer	Shadow	DN1	Cosworth	V8	73		13	7
18r	24	C Pace	Surtees	TS14A	Cosworth	V8	72	wheel	19	10
nc	18	J-P Jarier	March	731	Cosworth	V8	71		23	12
nc	28	R von Opel	Ensign	N173	Cosworth	V8	68		26	13
r	21	N Lauda	BRM	P160E	BRM	V12	62	transmission	8	4
r	0	J Scheckter	McLaren	M23	Cosworth	V8	32	accident	3	2
r	6	F Cevert	Tyrrell	006	Cosworth	V8	32	accident	6	3
r	15	M Beuttler	March	731	Cosworth	V8	20	engine	21	11
r	2	R Peterson	JPS Lotus	72E	Cosworth	V8	16	puncture/ accident	1	1
r	19	P Gethin	BRM	P160E	BRM	V12	5	oil pump belt	25	13

Winning speed: 159.534 km/h, 99.130 mph
Pole Position speed: 193.313 km/h, 120.119 mph (R Peterson, 1 min:13.697 sec)
Fastest Lap speed: 188.706 km/h, 117.257 mph (E Fittipaldi, 1 min:15.496 sec)
Lap Leaders: R Peterson 1-2 (2); N Lauda 3-19 (17); E Fittipaldi 20-32 (13); J Stewart 33 (1); J-P Beltoise 34-39 (6); J Oliver 40-46 (7); P Revson 47-80 (34).

7 Oct 1973	USA: Watkins Glen	(Round:15) (Race: 235)
	59 laps x 5.435 km, 3.377 miles = 320.651 km, 199.243 miles	

POS.	NO.	DRIVER	CAR	MODEL	ENGINE		LAPS	TIME/REASON FOR RETIREMENT	GRID:POS	ROW
1	2	R Peterson	JPS Lotus	72E	Cosworth	V8	59	1h 41m 15.799s	1	1
2	27	J Hunt	March	731	Cosworth	V8	59	1h 41m 16.467s	4	2
3	10	C Reutemann	Brabham	BT42	Cosworth	V8	59	1h 41m 38.729s	2	1
4	7	D Hulme	McLaren	M23	Cosworth	V8	59	1h 42m 06.025s	8	4
5	8	P Revson	McLaren	M23	Cosworth	V8	59	1h 42m 36.166s	7	4
6	1	E Fittipaldi	JPS Lotus	72E	Cosworth	V8	59	1h 43m 03.744s	3	2
7	26	J Ickx	Iso Marlboro	IR	Cosworth	V8	58		23	12
8	19	C Regazzoni	BRM	P160E	BRM	V12	58		15	8
9	20	J-P Beltoise	BRM	P160E	BRM	V12	58		14	7
10	15	M Beuttler	March	731	Cosworth	V8	58		26	13
11r	18	J-P Jarier	March	731	Cosworth	V8	57	accident	17	9
12	25	H Ganley	Iso Marlboro	IR	Cosworth	V8	57		19	10
13	12	G Hill	Shadow	DN1	Cosworth	V8	57		18	9
14	16	G Follmer	Shadow	DN1	Cosworth	V8	57		20	10
15	17	J Oliver	Shadow	DN1	Cosworth	V8	55		22	11
16	4	A Merzario	Ferrari	312B3	Ferrari	F12	55		11	6
nc	11	W Fittipaldi	Brabham	BT42	Cosworth	V8	52		25	13
r	0	J Scheckter	McLaren	M23	Cosworth	V8	39	suspension	10	5
r	30	J Mass	Surtees	TS14A	Cosworth	V8	35	engine	16	8
r	21	N Lauda	BRM	P160E	BRM	V12	35	fuel pump	21	11
r	23	M Hailwood	Surtees	TS14A	Cosworth	V8	34	suspension	6	3
r	24	C Pace	Surtees	TS14A	Cosworth	V8	32	suspension	9	5
r	9	J Watson	Brabham	BT42	Cosworth	V8	7	engine	24	12
dq	31	B Redman	Shadow	DN1	Cosworth	V8	5	push start after spin	13	7
r	28	R von Opel	Ensign	N173	Cosworth	V8	0	throttle slides jammed	27	14
ns	6	F Cevert	Tyrrell	006	Cosworth	V8		fatal accident		
ns	5	J Stewart	Tyrrell	006	Cosworth	V8		withdrew after Cevert accident	5	3
ns	29	C Amon	Tyrrell	005	Cosworth	V8		withdrew after Cevert accident	12	6

Winning speed: 189.990 km/h, 118.054 mph
Pole Position speed: 196.325 km/h, 121.990 mph (R Peterson, 1 min:39.657 sec)
Fastest Lap speed: 192.472 km/h, 119.596 mph (J Hunt, 1 min:41.652 sec on lap 58)
Lap Leaders: R Peterson 1-59 (59).

Lap Leaders 1973

POS	DRIVER	CAR-ENGINE	GPS	LAPS	KM	MILES
1	R Peterson	Lotus-Cosworth	11	393	1,846.6	1,147.4
2	J Stewart	Tyrrell-Cosworth	6	214	1,088.1	676.1
3	E Fittipaldi	Lotus-Cosworth	6	120	688.9	428.1
4	F Cevert	Tyrrell-Cosworth	3	76	269.9	167.7
5	P Revson	McLaren-Cosworth	2	63	271.2	168.5
6	J Scheckter	McLaren-Cosworth	2	43	246.4	153.1
7	C Regazzoni	BRM	1	28	93.7	58.2
8	N Lauda	BRM	1	17	67.3	41.8
9	J Oliver	Shadow-Cosworth	1	7	27.7	17.2
10	D Hulme	McLaren-Cosworth	2	6	24.5	15.2
	J-P Beltoise	BRM	1	6	23.7	14.8
			15	**973**	**4,648.0**	**2,888.1**

Driver Points 1973

		RA	BR	ZA	E	B	MC	S	F	GB	NL	D	A	I	CDN	USA	TOTAL
1	J Stewart	4	6	9	-	9	9	2	3	-	9	9	6	3	2	-	71
2	E Fittipaldi	9	9	4	9	4	6	-	-	-	-	1	-	6	6	1	55
3	R Peterson	-	-	-	-	-	4	6	9	6	-	-	9	9	-	9	52
4	F Cevert	6	-	-	6	6	3	4	6	2	6	6	-	2	-	-	47
5	P Revson	-	-	6	3	-	2	-	-	9	3	-	-	4	9	2	38
6	D Hulme	2	4	2	1	-	1	9	-	4	-	-	-	-	-	3	26
7	C Reutemann	-	-	-	-	-	-	3	4	1	-	-	3	1	-	4	16
8	J Hunt	-	-	-	-	-	-	-	1	3	4	-	-	-	-	6	14
9	J Ickx	3	2	-	-	-	-	1	2	-	-	4	-	-	-	-	12
10	J-P Beltoise	-	-	-	2	-	-	-	-	-	2	-	2	-	3	-	9
11	C Pace	-	-	-	-	-	-	-	-	-	-	3	4	-	-	-	7
12	A Merzario	-	3	3	-	-	-	-	-	-	-	-	-	-	-	-	6
13	G Follmer	-	-	1	4	-	-	-	-	-	-	-	-	-	-	-	5
14	J Oliver	-	-	-	-	-	-	-	-	-	-	-	-	-	4	-	4
15	A de Adamich	-	-	-	-	3	-	-	-	-	-	-	-	-	-	-	3
	W Fittipaldi	1	-	-	-	-	-	-	-	-	-	2	-	-	-	-	3
17	N Lauda	-	-	-	-	2	-	-	-	-	-	-	-	-	-	-	2
	C Regazzoni	-	1	-	-	-	-	-	-	-	-	-	1	-	-	-	2
19	C Amon	-	-	-	-	1	-	-	-	-	-	-	-	-	-	-	1
	G van Lennep	-	-	-	-	-	-	-	-	-	1	-	-	-	-	-	1
	H Ganley	-	-	-	-	-	-	-	-	-	-	-	-	-	1	-	1

9, 6, 4, 3, 2 and 1 point awarded to the first six finishers.

Best 7 scores from first 8 races, best 6 from 4remaining 7 races.

Constructor Points 1973

		RA	BR	ZA	E	B	MC	S	F	GB	NL	D	A	I	CDN	USA	TOTAL	
1	Lotus-Cosworth	9	9	4	9	(4)	6	6	9	6	-	1	9	9	6	9	92	(4)
2	Tyrrell-Cosworth	6	6	9	6	9	9	(4)	6	2	9	9	6	3	2	-	82	(4)
3	McLaren-Cosworth	2	4	6	3	-	2	9	-	9	3	4	-	4	9	3	58	
4	Brabham-Cosworth	1	-	-	-	3	-	3	4	1	-	2	3	1	-	4	22	
5	March-Cosworth	-	-	-	-	-	-	-	1	3	4	-	-	-	-	6	14	
6	Ferrari	3	3	3	-	-	-	1	2	-	-	-	-	-	-	-	12	
	BRM	-	1	-	2	2	-	-	-	-	2	-	2	-	3	-	12	
8	Shadow-Cosworth	-	-	1	4	-	-	-	-	-	-	-	-	-	4	-	9	
9	Surtees-Cosworth	-	-	-	-	-	-	-	-	-	-	3	4	-	-	-	7	
10	Iso-Cosworth	-	-	-	-	-	-	-	-	-	1	-	-	-	1	-	2	
11	Tecno	-	-	-	-	1	-	-	-	-	-	-	-	-	-	-	1	

9, 6, 4, 3, 2 and 1 point awarded to the first six finishers. Points only for highest placed car.
Best 7 scores from first 8 races, best 6 from remaining 7 races.

Top Left: P Revson, winner of the British Grand Prix 1973, driving the McLaren M23.
Bottom Left: R Peterson

There was an increase in the number of participating teams, most notably from Hesketh, Parnelli and Penske, to make a new record total of 18. This led to further restrictions in qualifying. Ferrari introduced the 312T transverse gearbox and Marlboro began their long association with McLaren. From this year, entrants generally held the same numbers throughout the season, and are listed in numerical order of the works teams.

LOTUS
John Player Team Lotus: Peterson, Ickx, Schenken
Team Gunston: I Scheckter, Driver

TYRRELL
Elf Team Tyrrell: J Scheckter, Depailler
Alex Blignaut/Embassy Racing SA: Keizan

McLAREN
Marlboro Team Texaco: E Fittipaldi, Hulme
Yardley Team McLaren: Hailwood, Hobbs, Mass
Scuderia Scribante-Lucky Strike: Charlton

BRABHAM
Motor Racing Developments: Reutemann, Robarts, von Opel, Pace, Pilette
John Goldie Racing With Hexagon: Watson, (Pace (F))
Scuderia Finotto: Larrousse, (Koinigg, Facetti)
Team Canada F1 Racing: Weitzes
Chequered Flag: (Ashley)
Allied Polymer Group: (Lombardi)

MARCH
March Engineering: Stuck, Wisell, Ganley, Brambilla
Hesketh Racing: Hunt
Dempster International Racing Team: (Wilds)

FERRARI
Scuderia Ferrari SpA SEFAC: Regazzoni, Lauda

BRM
Team Motul BRM: Beltoise, Pescarolo, Migault, Amon

SHADOW
UOP Shadow Racing Team: Revson, Redman, Roos, Pryce, Jarier

SURTEES
Bang & Olufson* Team Surtees: Pace, Dolhem, Bell, Mass, (Jabouille), Koinigg*
ZA-D GPs only
Memphis International Team Surtees: Quester
AAW Racing Team: Kinnunen

WILLIAMS (ISO MARLBORO)
Frank Williams Racing Cars: Merzario, (Robarts), Belso, van Lennep, (Jabouille), Laffite

ENSIGN
Team Ensign: (von Opel), Schuppan, Wilds

TROJAN
Trojan-Tauranac Racing: Schenken

HESKETH
Hesketh Racing: Hunt, (I Scheckter)

MAKI
Maki Engineering: (Ganley)

LOLA
Embassy Racing With Graham Hill: Hill, Edwards, Gethin, Stommelen

AMON
Chris Amon Racing: Amon, (Perkins)

LYNCAR
Pinch (Plant) Ltd: (Nicholson)

TOKEN
Token Racing: Pryce, (Purley), Ashley

PARNELLI
Vel's Parnelli Jones Racing: Andretti

PENSKE
Penske Cars: Donohue

13 Jan 1974 — ARGENTINA: Buenos Aires No.15 (Round: 1) (Race: 236)

53 laps x 5.968 km, 3.708 miles = 316.304 km, 196.542 miles

POS.	NO.	DRIVER	CAR	MODEL	ENGINE		LAPS	TIME/REASON FOR RETIREMENT	GRID:POS	ROW
1	6	D Hulme	McLaren	M23	Cosworth	V8	53	1h 41m 02.010s	10	5
2	12	N Lauda	Ferrari	312B3	Ferrari	F12	53	1h 41m 11.280s	8	4
3	11	C Regazzoni	Ferrari	312B3	Ferrari	F12	53	1h 41m 22.420s	2	1
4	33	M Hailwood	McLaren	M23	Cosworth	V8	53	1h 41m 33.800s	9	5
5	14	J-P Beltoise	BRM	P160E	BRM	V12	53	1h 41m 53.850s	14	7
6	4	P Depailler	Tyrrell	005	Cosworth	V8	53	1h 42m 54.490s	15	8
7r	7	C Reutemann	Brabham	BT44	Cosworth	V8	52	out of fuel	6	3
8r	10	H Ganley	March	741	Cosworth	V8	52	out of fuel	19	10
9	15	H Pescarolo	BRM	P160E	BRM	V12	52		21	11
10	5	E Fittipaldi	McLaren	M23	Cosworth	V8	51		3	2
11	27	G Edwards	Lola	T370	Cosworth	V8	50		25	13
12	28	J Watson	Brabham	BT42	Cosworth	V8	49		20	10
13	1	R Peterson	JPS Lotus	72E	Cosworth	V8	48		1	1
r	26	G Hill	Lola	T370	Cosworth	V8	45	engine overheating	17	9
r	8	R Robarts	Brabham	BT44	Cosworth	V8	35	gearbox	22	11
r	2	J Ickx	JPS Lotus	72E	Cosworth	V8	35	transmission	7	4
r	9	H-J Stuck	March	741	Cosworth	V8	31	clutch	23	12
r	37	F Migault	BRM	P160E	BRM	V12	31	water leak	24	12
r	3	J Scheckter	Tyrrell	006	Cosworth	V8	25	cylinder head gasket	12	6
r	18	C Pace	Surtees	TS16	Cosworth	V8	21	engine	11	6
r	20	A Merzario	Iso Marlboro	FW	Cosworth	V8	19	engine	13	7
r	24	J Hunt	March	731	Cosworth	V8	11	engine overheating	5	3
r	19	J Mass	Surtees	TS16	Cosworth	V8	10	piston	18	9
r	16	P Revson	Shadow	DN3	Cosworth	V8	1	accident	4	2
r	17	J-P Jarier	Shadow	DN1	Cosworth	V8	0	accident	16	8
ns	22	R von Opel	Ensign	N174	Cosworth	V8		handling	26	13

Winning speed: 187.841 km/h, 116.719 mph
Pole Position speed: 193.941 km/h, 120.509 mph (R Peterson, 1 min:50.780 sec)
Fastest Lap speed: 191.657 km/h, 119.090 mph (C Regazzoni, 1 min:52.100 sec on lap 38)
Lap Leaders: R Peterson 1-2 (2); C Reutemann 3-51 (49); D Hulme 52-53 (2).

27 Jan 1974 — BRAZIL: Interlagos (Round: 2) (Race: 237)

32 laps x 7.960 km, 4.946 miles = 254.720 km, 158.276 miles

POS.	NO.	DRIVER	CAR	MODEL	ENGINE		LAPS	TIME/REASON FOR RETIREMENT	GRID:POS	ROW
1	5	E Fittipaldi	McLaren	M23	Cosworth	V8	32	1h 24m 37.060s	1	1
2	11	C Regazzoni	Ferrari	312B3	Ferrari	F12	32	1h 24m 50.630s	8	4
3	2	J Ickx	JPS Lotus	72E	Cosworth	V8	31		5	3
4	18	C Pace	Surtees	TS16	Cosworth	V8	31		12	6
5	33	M Hailwood	McLaren	M23	Cosworth	V8	31		7	4
6	1	R Peterson	JPS Lotus	72E	Cosworth	V8	31		4	2
7	7	C Reutemann	Brabham	BT44	Cosworth	V8	31		2	1
8	4	P Depailler	Tyrrell	005	Cosworth	V8	31		16	8
9	24	J Hunt	March	731	Cosworth	V8	31		18	9
10	14	J-P Beltoise	BRM	P160E	BRM	V12	31		17	9
11	26	G Hill	Lola	T370	Cosworth	V8	31		21	11
12	6	D Hulme	McLaren	M23	Cosworth	V8	31		11	6
13	3	J Scheckter	Tyrrell	006	Cosworth	V8	31		14	7
14	15	H Pescarolo	BRM	P160E	BRM	V12	30		22	11
15	8	R Robarts	Brabham	BT44	Cosworth	V8	30		24	12
16	37	F Migault	BRM	P160E	BRM	V12	30		23	12
17	19	J Mass	Surtees	TS16	Cosworth	V8	30		10	5
r	28	J Watson	Brabham	BT42	Cosworth	V8	27	clutch	15	8
r	9	H-J Stuck	March	741	Cosworth	V8	24	cv joint	13	7
r	17	J-P Jarier	Shadow	DN1	Cosworth	V8	22	brakes	19	10
r	20	A Merzario	Iso Marlboro	FW	Cosworth	V8	20	throttle slides	9	5
r	16	P Revson	Shadow	DN3	Cosworth	V8	11	engine overheating	6	3
r	10	H Ganley	March	741	Cosworth	V8	9	ignition switch	20	10
r	27	G Edwards	Lola	T370	Cosworth	V8	3	rear aerofoil	25	13
r	12	N Lauda	Ferrari	312B3	Ferrari	F12	3	engine	3	2

Winning speed: 180.615 km/h, 112.229 mph
Pole Position speed: 187.331 km/h, 116.402 mph (E Fittipaldi, 2 min:32.970 sec)
Fastest Lap speed: 183.633 km/h, 114.105 mph (C Regazzoni, 2 min:36.050 sec on lap 26)
Lap Leaders: C Reutemann 1-3 (3); R Peterson 4-15 (12); E Fittipaldi 16-32 (17).

Scheduled for 40 laps, but stopped early because of rain.

30 Mar 1974 — SOUTH AFRICA: Kyalami (Round: 3) (Race: 238)

78 laps x 4.104 km, 2.550 miles = 320.112 km, 198.908 miles

POS.	NO.	DRIVER	CAR	MODEL	ENGINE		LAPS	TIME/REASON FOR RETIREMENT	GRID:POS	ROW
1	7	C Reutemann	Brabham	BT44	Cosworth	V8	78	1h 42m 40.960s	4	2
2	14	J-P Beltoise	BRM	P201	BRM	V12	78	1h 43m 14.900s	11	6
3	33	M Hailwood	McLaren	M23	Cosworth	V8	78	1h 43m 23.120s	12	6
4	4	P Depailler	Tyrrell	005	Cosworth	V8	78	1h 43m 25.150s	15	8
5	9	H-J Stuck	March	741	Cosworth	V8	78	1h 43m 27.190s	7	4
6	20	A Merzario	Iso Marlboro	FW	Cosworth	V8	78	1h 43m 37.000s	3	2
7	5	E Fittipaldi	McLaren	M23	Cosworth	V8	78	1h 43m 49.350s	5	3
8	3	J Scheckter	Tyrrell	006	Cosworth	V8	78	1h 43m 51.500s	8	4
9	6	D Hulme	McLaren	M23	Cosworth	V8	77		9	5
10	10	V Brambilla	March	741	Cosworth	V8	77		19	10
11	18	C Pace	Surtees	TS16	Cosworth	V8	77		2	1
12	26	G Hill	Lola	T370	Cosworth	V8	77		18	9
13	29	I Scheckter	Lotus	72E	Cosworth	V8	76		22	11
14	32	E Keizan	Tyrrell	004	Cosworth	V8	76		24	12
15	37	F Migault	BRM	P160E	BRM	V12	75		25	13
16r	12	N Lauda	Ferrari	312B3	Ferrari	F12	74	ignition	1	1
17	8	R Robarts	Brabham	BT44	Cosworth	V8	74		23	12
18	15	H Pescarolo	BRM	P160E	BRM	V12	72		21	11
19	23	D Charlton	McLaren	M23	Cosworth	V8	71		20	10
r	11	C Regazzoni	Ferrari	312B3	Ferrari	F12	65	oil pressure	6	3
r	28	J Watson	Brabham	BT42	Cosworth	V8	56	fuel union	13	7
r	2	J Ickx	JPS Lotus	76	Cosworth	V8	31	brakes	10	5
r	24	J Hunt	Hesketh	308	Cosworth	V8	13	cv joint	14	7
r	19	J Mass	Surtees	TS16	Cosworth	V8	11	accident/ withdrew	17	9
r	30	P Driver	Lotus	72E	Cosworth	V8	6	clutch	26	13
r	1	R Peterson	JPS Lotus	76	Cosworth	V8	2	accident	16	8
r	21	T Belso	Iso Marlboro	FW	Cosworth	V8	0	clutch	27	14

Winning speed: 187.049 km/h, 116.227 mph
Pole Position speed: 192.928 km/h, 119.880 mph (N Lauda, 1 min:16.580 sec)
Fastest Lap speed: 189.028 km/h, 117.456 mph (C Reutemann, 1 min:18.160 sec on lap 58)
Lap Leaders: N Lauda 1-8 (8); C Reutemann 9-78 (70).

28 Apr 1974 — SPAIN: Járama — (Round: 4) (Race: 239)

84 laps x 3.404 km, 2.115 miles = 285.936 km, 177.672 miles

POS.	NO.	DRIVER	CAR	MODEL	ENGINE		LAPS	TIME/REASON FOR RETIREMENT	GRID:POS	ROW
1	12	N Lauda	Ferrari	312B3	Ferrari	F12	84	2h 00m 29.560s	1	1
2	11	C Regazzoni	Ferrari	312B3	Ferrari	F12	84	2h 01m 05.170s	3	2
3	5	E Fittipaldi	McLaren	M23	Cosworth	V8	83		4	2
4	9	H-J Stuck	March	741	Cosworth	V8	82		13	7
5	3	J Scheckter	Tyrrell	007	Cosworth	V8	82		9	5
6	56	D Hulme	McLaren	M23	Cosworth	V8	82		8	4
7	16	B Redman	Shadow	DN3	Cosworth	V8	81		21	11
8	4	P Depailler	Tyrrell	006	Cosworth	V8	81		16	8
9	33	M Hailwood	McLaren	M23	Cosworth	V8	81		17	9
10	24	J Hunt	Hesketh	308	Cosworth	V8	81		10	5
11	28	J Watson	Brabham	BT42	Cosworth	V8	80		15	8
12	15	H Pescarolo	BRM	P160E	BRM	V12	80		20	10
13	18	C Pace	Surtees	TS16	Cosworth	V8	78		14	7
14r	23	T Schenken	Trojan	T103	Cosworth	V8	76	spin	25	13
nc	17	J-P Jarier	Shadow	DN3	Cosworth	V8	73		12	6
r	26	G Hill	Lola	T370	Cosworth	V8	43	engine	19	10
r	20	A Merzario	Iso Marlboro	FW	Cosworth	V8	37	accident	7	4
r	19	J Mass	Surtees	TS16	Cosworth	V8	35	gearbox	18	9
r	37	F Migault	BRM	P160E	BRM	V12	27	engine	22	11
r	2	J Ickx	JPS Lotus	76	Cosworth	V8	26	brake fluid leak	5	3
r	1	R Peterson	JPS Lotus	76	Cosworth	V8	23	engine overheating	2	1
r	30	C Amon	Amon	AF101	Cosworth	V8	22	brake shaft	23	12
r	8	R von Opel	Brabham	BT44	Cosworth	V8	14	oil leak	24	12
r	7	C Reutemann	Brabham	BT44	Cosworth	V8	12	accident	6	3
r	14	J-P Beltoise	BRM	P201	BRM	V12	2	engine	11	6
ns	10	V Brambilla	March	741	Cosworth	V8		accident		
nq	27	G Edwards	Lola	T370	Cosworth	V8				
nq	21	T Belso	Iso Marlboro	FW	Cosworth	V8				

Winning speed: 142.383 km/h, 88.473 mph
Pole Position speed: 156.226 km/h, 97.075 mph (N Lauda, 1 min:18.440 sec)
Fastest Lap speed: 151.607 km/h, 94.204 mph (N Lauda, 1 min:20.830 sec on lap 47)
Lap Leaders: R Peterson 1-20 (20); N Lauda 21-23,25-84 (63); J Ickx 24 (1).

Scheduled for 90 laps, but stopped at 2 hours.

12 May 1974 — BELGIUM: Nivelles-Baulers — (Round: 5) (Race: 240)

85 laps x 3.724 km, 2.314 miles = 316.540 km, 196.689 miles

POS.	NO.	DRIVER	CAR	MODEL	ENGINE		LAPS	TIME/REASON FOR RETIREMENT	GRID:POS	ROW
1	5	E Fittipaldi	McLaren	M23	Cosworth	V8	85	1h 44m 20.570s	4	2
2	12	N Lauda	Ferrari	312B3	Ferrari	F12	85	1h 44m 20.920s	3	2
3	3	J Scheckter	Tyrrell	007	Cosworth	V8	85	1h 45m 06.180s	2	1
4	11	C Regazzoni	Ferrari	312B3	Ferrari	F12	85	1h 45m 12.590s	1	1
5	14	J-P Beltoise	BRM	P201	BRM	V12	85	1h 45m 28.620s	7	4
6	6	D Hulme	McLaren	M23	Cosworth	V8	85	1h 45m 31.110s	12	6
7	33	M Hailwood	McLaren	M23	Cosworth	V8	84		13	7
8	26	G Hill	Lola	T370	Cosworth	V8	83		29	15
9	10	V Brambilla	March	741	Cosworth	V8	83		31	16
10	41	T Schenken	Trojan	T103	Cosworth	V8	83		23	12
11	28	J Watson	Brabham	BT42	Cosworth	V8	83		19	10
12	27	G Edwards	Lola	T370	Cosworth	V8	82		21	11
13	17	J-P Jarier	Shadow	DN3	Cosworth	V8	82		17	9
14	21	G van Lennep	Iso Marlboro	FW	Cosworth	V8	82		30	15
15	22	V Schuppan	Ensign	N174	Cosworth	V8	82		14	7
16	37	F Migault	BRM	P160E	BRM	V12	82		25	13
17	34	T Pilette	Brabham	BT42	Cosworth	V8	81		27	14
18r	16	B Redman	Shadow	DN3	Cosworth	V8	80	engine	18	9
r	2	J Ickx	JPS Lotus	76	Cosworth	V8	72	brakes	16	8
r	42	T Pryce	Token	RJ02	Cosworth	V8	66	fuel pressure/ accident	20	10
r	7	C Reutemann	Brabham	BT44	Cosworth	V8	62	fuel line	24	12
r	1	R Peterson	JPS Lotus	76	Cosworth	V8	56	fuel tank leak	5	3
r	43	G Larrousse	Brabham	BT42	Cosworth	V8	53	tyres	28	14
r	19	J Mass	Surtees	TS16	Cosworth	V8	53	rear suspension	26	13
r	4	P Depailler	Tyrrell	007	Cosworth	V8	53	brake strap	11	6
r	18	C Pace	Surtees	TS16	Cosworth	V8	50	tyres/ vibration	8	4
r	8	R von Opel	Brabham	BT44	Cosworth	V8	49	oil pressure	22	11
r	24	J Hunt	Hesketh	308	Cosworth	V8	45	rear suspension	9	5
r	20	A Merzario	Iso Marlboro	FW	Cosworth	V8	29	drive shaft	6	3
r	15	H Pescarolo	BRM	P160E	BRM	V12	12	accident	15	8
r	9	H-J Stuck	March	741	Cosworth	V8	6	clutch	10	5
nq	44	L Kinnunen	Surtees	TS16	Cosworth	V8				

Winning speed: 182.019 km/h, 113.101 mph
Pole Position speed: 192.014 km/h, 119.312 mph (C Regazzoni, 1 min: 9.820 sec)
Fastest Lap speed: 188.002 km/h, 116.819 mph (D Hulme, 1 min:11.310 sec on lap 37)
Lap Leaders: C Regazzoni 1-38 (38); E Fittipaldi 39-85 (47).

26 May 1974 — MONACO: Monte Carlo (Round: 6) (Race: 241)

78 laps x 3.278 km, 2.037 miles = 255.684 km, 158.875 miles

POS.	NO.	DRIVER	CAR	MODEL	ENGINE		LAPS	TIME/REASON FOR RETIREMENT	GRID:POS	ROW
1	1	R Peterson	JPS Lotus	72E	Cosworth	V8	78	1h 58m 03.700s	3	2
2	3	J Scheckter	Tyrrell	007	Cosworth	V8	78	1h 58m 32.500s	5	3
3	17	J-P Jarier	Shadow	DN3	Cosworth	V8	78	1h 58m 52.600s	6	3
4	11	C Regazzoni	Ferrari	312B3	Ferrari	F12	78	1h 59m 06.800s	2	1
5	5	E Fittipaldi	McLaren	M23	Cosworth	V8	77		13	7
6	28	J Watson	Brabham	BT42	Cosworth	V8	77		23	12
7	26	G Hill	Lola	T370	Cosworth	V8	76		21	11
8	27	G Edwards	Lola	T370	Cosworth	V8	76		26	13
9	4	P Depailler	Tyrrell	006	Cosworth	V8	75		4	2
r	15	H Pescarolo	BRM	P160E	BRM	V12	62	gearbox	27	14
r	2	J Ickx	JPS Lotus	72E	Cosworth	V8	34	engine	19	10
r	12	N Lauda	Ferrari	312B3	Ferrari	F12	32	ignition	1	1
r	24	J Hunt	Hesketh	308	Cosworth	V8	28	drive shaft	7	4
r	33	M Hailwood	McLaren	M23	Cosworth	V8	11	accident	10	5
r	7	C Reutemann	Brabham	BT44	Cosworth	V8	5	accident	8	4
r	37	F Migault	BRM	P160E	BRM	V12	5	brakes/ accident	22	11
r	22	V Schuppan	Ensign	N174	Cosworth	V8	4	accident	25	13
r	9	H-J Stuck	March	741	Cosworth	V8	3	accident	9	5
r	10	V Brambilla	March	741	Cosworth	V8	1	accident	15	8
r	14	J-P Beltoise	BRM	P201	BRM	V12	1	accident	11	6
r	23	T Schenken	Trojan	T103	Cosworth	V8	0	accident	24	12
r	18	C Pace	Surtees	TS16	Cosworth	V8	0	accident	18	9
r	16	B Redman	Shadow	DN3	Cosworth	V8	0	accident	16	8
r	20	A Merzario	Iso Marlboro	FW	Cosworth	V8	0	accident	14	7
r	6	D Hulme	McLaren	M23	Cosworth	V8	0	accident	12	6
ns	19	J Mass	Surtees	TS16	Cosworth	V8		shortage of parts	17	9
ns	30	C Amon	Amon	AF101	Cosworth	V8		hub	20	10
nq	8	R von Opel	Brabham	BT44	Cosworth	V8				

Winning speed: 129.941 km/h, 80.742 mph
Pole Position speed: 136.742 km/h, 84.967 mph (N Lauda, 1 min:26.300 sec)
Fastest Lap speed: 134.253 km/h, 83.421 mph (R Peterson, 1 min:27.900 sec on lap 57)
Lap Leaders: C Regazzoni 1-20 (20); N Lauda 21-32 (12); R Peterson 33-78 (46).

9 Jun 1974 — SWEDEN: Anderstorp (Round: 7) (Race: 242)

80 laps x 4.018 km, 2.497 miles = 321.440 km, 199.734 miles

POS.	NO.	DRIVER	CAR	MODEL	ENGINE		LAPS	TIME/REASON FOR RETIREMENT	GRID:POS	ROW
1	3	J Scheckter	Tyrrell	007	Cosworth	V8	80	1h 58m 31.391s	2	1
2	4	P Depailler	Tyrrell	007	Cosworth	V8	80	1h 58m 31.771s	1	1
3	24	J Hunt	Hesketh	308	Cosworth	V8	80	1h 58m 34.716s	6	3
4	5	E Fittipaldi	McLaren	M23	Cosworth	V8	80	1h 59m 24.898s	9	5
5	17	J-P Jarier	Shadow	DN3	Cosworth	V8	80	1h 59m 47.794s	8	4
6	26	G Hill	Lola	T370	Cosworth	V8	79		15	8
7	27	G Edwards	Lola	T370	Cosworth	V8	79		18	9
8	21	T Belso	Iso Marlboro	FW	Cosworth	V8	79		21	11
9	8	R von Opel	Brabham	BT44	Cosworth	V8	79		20	10
10r	10	V Brambilla	March	741	Cosworth	V8	79	engine	17	9
11	28	J Watson	Brabham	BT42	Cosworth	V8	77		14	7
dq	22	V Schuppan	Ensign	N174	Cosworth	V8	77	started unofficially	26	13
r	12	N Lauda	Ferrari	312B3	Ferrari	F12	70	transmission	3	2
r	9	R Wisell	March	741	Cosworth	V8	59	suspension	16	8
r	6	D Hulme	McLaren	M23	Cosworth	V8	56	suspension	12	6
r	19	J Mass	Surtees	TS16	Cosworth	V8	53	suspension	22	11
r	7	C Reutemann	Brabham	BT44	Cosworth	V8	30	oil leak	10	5
r	2	J Ickx	JPS Lotus	72E	Cosworth	V8	27	oil pressure	7	4
r	11	C Regazzoni	Ferrari	312B3	Ferrari	F12	24	gearbox	4	2
r	18	C Pace	Surtees	TS16	Cosworth	V8	15	handling	24	12
r	23	L Kinnunen	Surtees	TS16	Cosworth	V8	8	electrics	25	13
r	1	R Peterson	JPS Lotus	72E	Cosworth	V8	8	drive shaft	5	3
r	33	M Hailwood	McLaren	M23	Cosworth	V8	5	fuel leak	11	6
r	14	J-P Beltoise	BRM	P201	BRM	V12	3	engine	13	7
r	16	B Roos	Shadow	DN3	Cosworth	V8	2	gearbox	23	12
r	15	H Pescarolo	BRM	P201	BRM	V12	0	fire	19	10
ns	20	R Robarts	Iso Marlboro	FW	Cosworth	V8		car raced by Belso		
ns	20	A Merzario	Iso Marlboro	FW	Cosworth	V8		driver ill		

Winning speed: 162.723 km/h, 101.111 mph
Pole Position speed: 170.660 km/h, 106.043 mph (P Depailler, 1 min:24.758 sec)
Fastest Lap speed: 165.763 km/h, 103.000 mph (P Depailler, 1 min:27.262 sec on lap 72)
Lap Leaders: J Scheckter 1-80 (80).

23 Jun 1974 — NETHERLANDS: Zandvoort — (Round: 8) (Race: 243)

75 laps x 4.226 km, 2.626 miles = 316.950 km, 196.944 miles

POS.	NO.	DRIVER	CAR	MODEL	ENGINE		LAPS	TIME/REASON FOR RETIREMENT	GRID:POS	ROW
1	12	N Lauda	Ferrari	312B3	Ferrari	F12	75	1h 43m 00.350s	1	1
2	11	C Regazzoni	Ferrari	312B3	Ferrari	F12	75	1h 43m 08.600s	2	1
3	5	E Fittipaldi	McLaren	M23	Cosworth	V8	75	1h 43m 30.620s	3	2
4	33	M Hailwood	McLaren	M23	Cosworth	V8	75	1h 43m 31.640s	4	2
5	3	J Scheckter	Tyrrell	007	Cosworth	V8	75	1h 43m 34.630s	5	3
6	4	P Depailler	Tyrrell	007	Cosworth	V8	75	1h 43m 51.870s	8	4
7	28	J Watson	Brabham	BT42	Cosworth	V8	75	1h 44m 14.300s	13	7
8	1	R Peterson	JPS Lotus	72E	Cosworth	V8	73		10	5
9	8	R von Opel	Brabham	BT44	Cosworth	V8	73		23	12
10	10	V Brambilla	March	741	Cosworth	V8	72		15	8
11	2	J Ickx	JPS Lotus	72E	Cosworth	V8	71		18	9
12	7	C Reutemann	Brabham	BT44	Cosworth	V8	71		12	6
dq	22	V Schuppan	Ensign	N174	Cosworth	V8	69	tyre change outside pits	17	9
r	6	D Hulme	McLaren	M23	Cosworth	V8	65	ignition	9	5
r	37	F Migault	BRM	P201	BRM	V12	60	gear linkage	25	13
r	20	A Merzario	Iso Marlboro	FW	Cosworth	V8	54	gearbox	21	11
r	27	G Edwards	Lola	T370	Cosworth	V8	36	fuel system	14	7
r	17	J-P Jarier	Shadow	DN3	Cosworth	V8	27	clutch	7	4
r	14	J-P Beltoise	BRM	P201	BRM	V12	18	gearbox	16	8
r	26	G Hill	Lola	T370	Cosworth	V8	16	clutch	19	10
r	15	H Pescarolo	BRM	P160E	BRM	V12	15	handling	24	12
r	19	J Mass	Surtees	TS16	Cosworth	V8	8	cv joint	20	10
r	24	J Hunt	Hesketh	308	Cosworth	V8	2	accident/ suspension	6	3
r	9	H-J Stuck	March	741	Cosworth	V8	0	accident	22	11
r	16	T Pryce	Shadow	DN3	Cosworth	V8	0	accident	11	6
nq	23	T Schenken	Trojan	T103	Cosworth	V8				
nq	21	G van Lennep	Iso Marlboro	FW	Cosworth	V8				

Winning speed: 184.621 km/h, 114.718 mph
Pole Position speed: 194.274 km/h, 120.716 mph (N Lauda, 1 min:18.310 sec)
Fastest Lap speed: 186.807 km/h, 116.077 mph (R Peterson, 1 min:21.440 sec on lap 63)
Lap Leaders: N Lauda 1-75 (75).

7 Jul 1974 — FRANCE: Dijon-Prenois — (Round: 9) (Race: 244)

80 laps x 3.289 km, 2.044 miles = 263.120 km, 163.495 miles

POS.	NO.	DRIVER	CAR	MODEL	ENGINE		LAPS	TIME/REASON FOR RETIREMENT	GRID:POS	ROW
1	1	R Peterson	JPS Lotus	72E	Cosworth	V8	80	1h 21m 55.020s	2	1
2	12	N Lauda	Ferrari	312B3	Ferrari	F12	80	1h 22m 15.380s	1	1
3	11	C Regazzoni	Ferrari	312B3	Ferrari	F12	80	1h 22m 22.860s	4	2
4	3	J Scheckter	Tyrrell	007	Cosworth	V8	80	1h 22m 23.130s	7	4
5	2	J Ickx	JPS Lotus	72E	Cosworth	V8	80	1h 22m 32.560s	13	7
6	6	D Hulme	McLaren	M23	Cosworth	V8	80	1h 22m 33.160s	11	6
7	33	M Hailwood	McLaren	M23	Cosworth	V8	79		6	3
8	4	P Depailler	Tyrrell	006	Cosworth	V8	79		9	5
9	20	A Merzario	Iso Marlboro	FW	Cosworth	V8	79		15	8
10	14	J-P Beltoise	BRM	P201	BRM	V12	79		17	9
11	10	V Brambilla	March	741	Cosworth	V8	79		16	8
12	17	J-P Jarier	Shadow	DN3	Cosworth	V8	79		12	6
13	26	G Hill	Lola	T370	Cosworth	V8	78		21	11
14	37	F Migault	BRM	P160E	BRM	V12	78		22	11
15	27	G Edwards	Lola	T370	Cosworth	V8	77		20	1
16	28	J Watson	Brabham	BT42	Cosworth	V8	76		14	7
r	5	E Fittipaldi	McLaren	M23	Cosworth	V8	27	engine	5	3
r	7	C Reutemann	Brabham	BT44	Cosworth	V8	24	handling	8	4
r	19	J Mass	Surtees	TS16	Cosworth	V8	4	clutch	18	9
r	15	H Pescarolo	BRM	P201	BRM	V12	1	clutch	19	10
r	16	T Pryce	Shadow	DN3	Cosworth	V8	1	accident	3	2
r	24	J Hunt	Hesketh	308	Cosworth	V8	0	accident	10	5
nq	22	V Schuppan	Ensign	N174	Cosworth	V8				
nq	34	C Pace	Brabham	BT42	Cosworth	V8				
nq	21	J-P Jabouille	Iso Marlboro	FW	Cosworth	V8				
nq	9	H-J Stuck	March	741	Cosworth	V8				
nq	18	J Dolhem	Surtees	TS16	Cosworth	V8				
nq	8	R von Opel	Brabham	BT44	Cosworth	V8				
nq	23	L Kinnunen	Surtees	TS16	Cosworth	V8				
nq	43	G Larrousse	Brabham	BT42	Cosworth	V8				

Winning speed: 192.722 km/h, 119.752 mph
Pole Position speed: 201.402 km/h, 125.145 mph (N Lauda, 0 min:58.790 sec)
Fastest Lap speed: 197.340 km/h, 122.621 mph (J Scheckter, 1 min: 0.000 sec on lap 10)
Lap Leaders: N Lauda 1-16 (16); R Peterson 17-80 (64).

20 Jul 1974 — BRITAIN: Brands Hatch (Round:10) (Race: 245)

75 laps x 4.265 km, 2.650 miles = 319.857 km, 198.750 miles

POS.	NO.	DRIVER	CAR	MODEL	ENGINE		LAPS	TIME/REASON FOR RETIREMENT	GRID:POS	ROW
1	3	J Scheckter	Tyrrell	007	Cosworth	V8	75	1h 43m 02.200s	3	2
2	5	E Fittipaldi	McLaren	M23	Cosworth	V8	75	1h 43m 17.500s	8	4
3	2	J Ickx	JPS Lotus	72E	Cosworth	V8	75	1h 44m 03.700s	12	6
4	11	C Regazzoni	Ferrari	312B3	Ferrari	F12	75	1h 44m 09.400s	7	4
5	12	N Lauda	Ferrari	312B3	Ferrari	F12	74		1	1
6	7	C Reutemann	Brabham	BT44	Cosworth	V8	74		4	2
7	6	D Hulme	McLaren	M23	Cosworth	V8	74		19	10
8	16	T Pryce	Shadow	DN3	Cosworth	V8	74		5	3
9	8	C Pace	Brabham	BT44	Cosworth	V8	74		20	10
10	1	R Peterson	JPS Lotus	72E	Cosworth	V8	73		2	1
11	28	J Watson	Brabham	BT42	Cosworth	V8	73		13	7
12	14	J-P Beltoise	BRM	P201	BRM	V12	72		23	12
13	26	G Hill	Lola	T370	Cosworth	V8	69		22	11
14	19	J Mass	Surtees	TS16	Cosworth	V8	68		17	9
r	15	H Pescarolo	BRM	P201	BRM	V12	64	engine	24	12
nc	37	F Migault	BRM	P160E	BRM	V12	62		14	7
r	33	M Hailwood	McLaren	M23	Cosworth	V8	57	spin	11	6
r	17	J-P Jarier	Shadow	DN3	Cosworth	V8	45	suspension	16	8
r	9	H-J Stuck	March	741	Cosworth	V8	36	accident	9	5
r	4	P Depailler	Tyrrell	007	Cosworth	V8	35	engine	10	5
r	20	A Merzario	Iso Marlboro	FW	Cosworth	V8	25	engine	15	8
r	10	V Brambilla	March	741	Cosworth	V8	17	fuel pressure	18	9
r	23	T Schenken	Trojan	T103	Cosworth	V8	6	suspension	25	13
r	24	J Hunt	Hesketh	308	Cosworth	V8	2	rear suspension/ spin	6	3
r	27	P Gethin	Lola	T370	Cosworth	V8	0	driver discomfort	21	11
nq	42	D Purley	Token	RJ02	Cosworth	V8				
nq	39	D Bell	Surtees	TS16	Cosworth	V8				
nq	21	T Belso	Iso Marlboro	FW	Cosworth	V8				
nq	208	L Lombardi	Brabham	BT42	Cosworth	V8				
nq	22	V Schuppan	Ensign	N174	Cosworth	V8				
nq	29	J Nicholson	Lyncar	006	Cosworth	V8				
nq	25	H Ganley	Maki	F101	Cosworth	V8				
nq	35	M Wilds	March	731	Cosworth	V8				
nq	43	L Kinnunen	Surtees	TS16	Cosworth	V8				
nq	27	G Edwards	Lola	T370	Cosworth	V8		driver unfit (earlier accident)		

Winning speed: 186.258 km/h, 115.735 mph
Pole Position speed: 192.637 km/h, 119.699 mph (N Lauda, 1 min:19.700 sec)
Fastest Lap speed: 189.311 km/h, 117.633 mph (N Lauda, 1 min:21.100 sec on lap 25)
Lap Leaders: N Lauda 1-69 (69); J Scheckter 70-75 (6).

N Lauda completed 73 laps and was initially classified 9th, but awarded an extra lap and 5th place on appeal because his exit from a pit stop was blocked.

4 Aug 1974 — GERMANY: Nürburgring (Round:11) (Race: 246)

14 laps x 22.835 km, 14.189 miles = 319.690 km, 198.646 miles

POS.	NO.	DRIVER	CAR	MODEL	ENGINE		LAPS	TIME/REASON FOR RETIREMENT	GRID:POS	ROW
1	11	C Regazzoni	Ferrari	312B3	Ferrari	F12	14	1h 41m 35.000s	2	1
2	3	J Scheckter	Tyrrell	007	Cosworth	V8	14	1h 42m 25.700s	4	2
3	7	C Reutemann	Brabham	BT44	Cosworth	V8	14	1h 42m 58.300s	6	3
4	1	R Peterson	JPS Lotus	76	Cosworth	V8	14	1h 42m 59.200s	8	4
5	2	J Ickx	JPS Lotus	72E	Cosworth	V8	14	1h 43m 00.000s	9	5
6	16	T Pryce	Shadow	DN3	Cosworth	V8	14	1h 43m 53.100s	11	6
7	9	H-J Stuck	March	741	Cosworth	V8	14	1h 44m 33.700s	20	10
8	17	J-P Jarier	Shadow	DN3	Cosworth	V8	14	1h 45m 00.900s	18	9
9	26	G Hill	Lola	T370	Cosworth	V8	14	1h 45m 01.400s	19	10
10	15	H Pescarolo	BRM	P201	BRM	V12	14	1h 45m 52.700s	24	12
11	18	D Bell	Surtees	TS16	Cosworth	V8	14	1h 46m 52.700s	25	13
12	8	C Pace	Brabham	BT44	Cosworth	V8	14	1h 48m 01.300s	17	9
13	10	V Brambilla	March	741	Cosworth	V8	14	1h 50m 18.100s	23	12
14	32	I Ashley	Token	RJ02	Cosworth	V8	13		26	13
15r	33	M Hailwood	McLaren	M23	Cosworth	V8	12	accident	12	6
r	24	J Hunt	Hesketh	308	Cosworth	V8	11	gearbox	13	7
r	19	J Mass	Surtees	TS16	Cosworth	V8	10	engine	10	5
r	4	P Depailler	Tyrrell	007	Cosworth	V8	5	accident/ suspension	5	3
r	20	A Merzario	Iso Marlboro	FW	Cosworth	V8	5	throttle linkage	16	8
r	14	J-P Beltoise	BRM	P201	BRM	V12	4	transmission	15	8
r	22	V Schuppan	Ensign	N174	Cosworth	V8	4	gearbox	22	11
r	5	E Fittipaldi	McLaren	M23	Cosworth	V8	2	accident/ suspension	3	2
r	21	J Laffite	Iso Marlboro	FW	Cosworth	V8	2	accident/ suspension	21	11
r	28	J Watson	Brabham	BT44	Cosworth	V8	1	accident/ suspension	14	7
r	12	N Lauda	Ferrari	312B3	Ferrari	F12	0	accident	1	1
r/dq	6	D Hulme	McLaren	M23	Cosworth	V8	0	accident/ took over spare car	7	4
nq	37	F Migault	BRM	P160E	BRM	V12				
nq	23	T Schenken	Trojan	T103	Cosworth	V8				
nq	27	G Edwards	Lola	T370	Cosworth	V8				
nq	30	L Perkins	Amon	AF101	Cosworth	V8				
nq	30	C Amon	Amon	AF101	Cosworth	V8		driver ill		
nq	25	H Ganley	Maki	F101	Cosworth	V8		accident/ injury		

Winning speed: 188.824 km/h, 117.330 mph
Pole Position speed: 195.356 km/h, 121.389 mph (N Lauda, 7 min: 0.800 sec)
Fastest Lap speed: 190.689 km/h, 118.489 mph (J Scheckter, 7 min:11.100 sec on lap 11)
Lap Leaders: C Regazzoni 1-14 (14).

Also the Grand Prix of Europe. D Hulme took over the spare car after retiring, only to be disqualified.

18 Aug 1974 — AUSTRIA: Österreichring — (Round:12) (Race: 247)

54 laps x 5.911 km, 3.673 miles = 319.194 km, 198.338 miles

POS.	NO.	DRIVER	CAR	MODEL	ENGINE		LAPS	TIME/REASON FOR RETIREMENT	GRID:POS	ROW
1	7	C Reutemann	Brabham	BT44	Cosworth	V8	54	1h 28m 44.720s	2	1
2	6	D Hulme	McLaren	M23	Cosworth	V8	54	1h 29m 27.640s	10	5
3	24	J Hunt	Hesketh	308	Cosworth	V8	54	1h 29m 46.260s	7	4
4	28	J Watson	Brabham	BT44	Cosworth	V8	54	1h 29m 54.110s	11	6
5	11	C Regazzoni	Ferrari	312B3	Ferrari	F12	54	1h 29m 57.800s	8	4
6	10	V Brambilla	March	741	Cosworth	V8	54	1h 29m 58.540s	20	10
7	33	D Hobbs	McLaren	M23	Cosworth	V8	53		17	9
8	17	J-P Jarier	Shadow	DN3	Cosworth	V8	52		23	12
9	30	D Quester	Surtees	TS16	Cosworth	V8	51		25	13
10	23	T Schenken	Trojan	T103	Cosworth	V8	50		19	10
11r	9	H-J Stuck	March	741	Cosworth	V8	48	suspension/ spin	15	8
12	26	G Hill	Lola	T370	Cosworth	V8	48		21	11
nc	35	I Ashley	Token	RJ02	Cosworth	V8	46		24	12
r	1	R Peterson	JPS Lotus	72E	Cosworth	V8	45	universal joint	6	3
r	2	J Ickx	JPS Lotus	76	Cosworth	V8	43	accident	22	11
r	4	P Depailler	Tyrrell	007	Cosworth	V8	42	accident	14	7
r	8	C Pace	Brabham	BT44	Cosworth	V8	41	fuel leak	4	2
r	5	E Fittipaldi	McLaren	M23	Cosworth	V8	37	engine	3	2
nc	21	J Laffite	Iso Marlboro	FW	Cosworth	V8	37		12	6
r	20	A Merzario	Iso Marlboro	FW	Cosworth	V8	24	fuel pressure	9	5
r	14	J-P Beltoise	BRM	P201	BRM	V12	22	engine	18	9
r	16	T Pryce	Shadow	DN3	Cosworth	V8	22	spin	16	8
r	12	N Lauda	Ferrari	312B3	Ferrari	F12	17	valve	1	1
r	27	R Stommelen	Lola	T370	Cosworth	V8	14	puncture/ accident	13	7
r	3	J Scheckter	Tyrrell	007	Cosworth	V8	8	engine	5	3
nq	31	I Scheckter	Hesketh	308	Cosworth	V8				
nq	43	L Kinnunen	Surtees	TS16	Cosworth	V8				
nq	18	D Bell	Surtees	TS16	Cosworth	V8				
nq	22	M Wilds	Ensign	N174	Cosworth	V8				
nq	19	J-P Jabouille	Surtees	TS16	Cosworth	V8				
nq	32	H Koinigg	Brabham	BT42	Cosworth	V8				

Winning speed: 215.804 km/h, 134.095 mph
Pole Position speed: 223.057 km/h, 138.601 mph (N Lauda, 1 min:35.400 sec)
Fastest Lap speed: 218.881 km/h, 136.006 mph (C Regazzoni, 1 min:37.220 sec on lap 46)
Lap Leaders: C Reutemann 1-54 (54).

8 Sep 1974 — ITALY: Monza — (Round:13) (Race: 248)

52 laps x 5.780 km, 3.592 miles = 300.560 km, 186.759 miles

POS.	NO.	DRIVER	CAR	MODEL	ENGINE		LAPS	TIME/REASON FOR RETIREMENT	GRID:POS	ROW
1	1	R Peterson	JPS Lotus	72E	Cosworth	V8	52	1h 22m 56.600s	7	4
2	5	E Fittipaldi	McLaren	M23	Cosworth	V8	52	1h 22m 57.400s	6	3
3	3	J Scheckter	Tyrrell	007	Cosworth	V8	52	1h 23m 21.300s	12	6
4	20	A Merzario	Iso Marlboro	FW	Cosworth	V8	52	1h 24m 24.300s	15	8
5	8	C Pace	Brabham	BT44	Cosworth	V8	51		3	2
6	6	D Hulme	McLaren	M23	Cosworth	V8	51		19	10
7	28	J Watson	Brabham	BT44	Cosworth	V8	51		4	2
8	26	G Hill	Lola	T370	Cosworth	V8	51		21	11
9	33	D Hobbs	McLaren	M23	Cosworth	V8	51		23	12
10	16	T Pryce	Shadow	DN3	Cosworth	V8	50		22	11
11	4	P Depailler	Tyrrell	007	Cosworth	V8	50		10	5
r	11	C Regazzoni	Ferrari	312B3	Ferrari	F12	40	oil seal	5	3
r	12	N Lauda	Ferrari	312B3	Ferrari	F12	32	water leak	1	1
r	2	J Ickx	JPS Lotus	76	Cosworth	V8	31	throttle linkage	16	8
r	27	R Stommelen	Lola	T370	Cosworth	V8	25	suspension	14	7
r	21	J Laffite	Iso Marlboro	FW	Cosworth	V8	22	engine	17	9
r	17	J-P Jarier	Shadow	DN3	Cosworth	V8	19	engine	9	5
r	10	V Brambilla	March	741	Cosworth	V8	16	accident	13	7
r	29	T Schenken	Trojan	T103	Cosworth	V8	15	gear selection	20	10
r	7	C Reutemann	Brabham	BT44	Cosworth	V8	11	gearbox bearing	2	1
r	9	H-J Stuck	March	741	Cosworth	V8	10	engine mounting bolts	18	9
r	15	H Pescarolo	BRM	P201	BRM	V12	3	engine	25	13
r	24	J Hunt	Hesketh	308	Cosworth	V8	2	engine	8	4
r	37	F Migault	BRM	P201	BRM	V12	1	gearbox	24	12
r	14	J-P Beltoise	BRM	P201	BRM	V12	0	electrics	11	6
nq	19	J Dolhem	Surtees	TS16	Cosworth	V8				
nq	31	C Facetti	Brabham	BT42	Cosworth	V8				
nq	18	D Bell	Surtees	TS16	Cosworth	V8				
nq	25	M Wilds	Ensign	N174	Cosworth	V8				
nq	22	C Amon	Amon	AF101	Cosworth	V8				
nq	23	L Kinnunen	Surtees	TS16	Cosworth	V8				

Winning speed: 217.421 km/h, 135.099 mph
Pole Position speed: 223.358 km/h, 138.788 mph (N Lauda, 1 min:33.160 sec)
Fastest Lap speed: 220.892 km/h, 137.256 mph (C Pace, 1 min:34.200 sec on lap 46)
Lap Leaders: N Lauda 1-29 (29); C Regazzoni 30-40 (11); R Peterson 41-52 (12).

22 Sep 1974 — CANADA: Mosport Park — (Round:14) (Race: 249)

80 laps x 3.957 km, 2.459 miles = 316.590 km, 196.720 miles

POS.	NO.	DRIVER	CAR	MODEL	ENGINE		LAPS	TIME/REASON FOR RETIREMENT	GRID:POS	ROW
1	5	E Fittipaldi	McLaren	M23	Cosworth	V8	80	1h 40m 26.136s	1	1
2	11	C Regazzoni	Ferrari	312B3	Ferrari	F12	80	1h 40m 39.170s	6	3
3	1	R Peterson	JPS Lotus	72E	Cosworth	V8	80	1h 40m 40.630s	10	5
4	24	J Hunt	Hesketh	308	Cosworth	V8	80	1h 40m 41.805s	8	4
5	4	P Depailler	Tyrrell	007	Cosworth	V8	80	1h 41m 21.458s	7	4
6	6	D Hulme	McLaren	M23	Cosworth	V8	79		14	7
7	55	M Andretti	Parnelli	VPJ4	Cosworth	V8	79		16	8
8	8	C Pace	Brabham	BT44	Cosworth	V8	79		9	5
9	7	C Reutemann	Brabham	BT44	Cosworth	V8	79		4	2
10	19	H Koinigg	Surtees	TS16	Cosworth	V8	78		22	11
11	27	R Stommelen	Lola	T370	Cosworth	V8	78		11	6
12	66	M Donohue	Penske	PC1	Cosworth	V8	78		24	12
13	2	J Ickx	JPS Lotus	72E	Cosworth	V8	78		21	11
14	26	G Hill	Lola	T370	Cosworth	V8	77		20	10
15r	21	J Laffite	Iso Marlboro	FW	Cosworth	V8	74	puncture	18	9
16	33	J Mass	McLaren	M23	Cosworth	V8	72		12	6
nc	15	C Amon	BRM	P201	BRM	V12	70		25	13
r	12	N Lauda	Ferrari	312B3	Ferrari	F12	67	accident	2	1
r	16	T Pryce	Shadow	DN3	Cosworth	V8	65	engine	13	7
r	28	J Watson	Brabham	BT44	Cosworth	V8	61	suspension/ accident	15	8
nc	14	J-P Beltoise	BRM	P201	BRM	V12	60		17	9
r	3	J Scheckter	Tyrrell	007	Cosworth	V8	48	brakes/ accident	3	2
r	17	J-P Jarier	Shadow	DN3	Cosworth	V8	46	drive shaft	5	3
r	20	A Merzario	Iso Marlboro	FW	Cosworth	V8	40	handling	19	10
r	50	E Wietzes	Brabham	BT42	Cosworth	V8	33	transmission	26	13
r	9	H-J Stuck	March	741	Cosworth	V8	12	fuel pressure	23	12
nq	18	D Bell	Surtees	TS16	Cosworth	V8				
nq	22	M Wilds	Ensign	N174	Cosworth	V8				
nq	10	V Brambilla	March	741	Cosworth	V8		accident		
nq	42	I Ashley	Brabham	BT42	Cosworth	V8				

Winning speed: 189.130 km/h, 117.520 mph
Pole Position speed: 194.657 km/h, 120.954 mph (E Fittipaldi, 1 min:13.188 sec)
Fastest Lap speed: 193.412 km/h, 120.181 mph (N Lauda, 1 min:13.659 sec on lap 60)
Lap Leaders: N Lauda 1-67 (67); E Fittipaldi 68-80 (13).

6 Oct 1974 — USA: Watkins Glen — (Round:15) (Race: 250)

59 laps x 5.435 km, 3.377 miles = 320.651 km, 199.243 miles

POS.	NO.	DRIVER	CAR	MODEL	ENGINE		LAPS	TIME/REASON FOR RETIREMENT	GRID:POS	ROW
1	7	C Reutemann	Brabham	BT44	Cosworth	V8	59	1h 40m 21.439s	1	1
2	8	C Pace	Brabham	BT44	Cosworth	V8	59	1h 40m 32.174s	4	2
3	24	J Hunt	Hesketh	308	Cosworth	V8	59	1h 41m 31.823s	2	1
4	5	E Fittipaldi	McLaren	M23	Cosworth	V8	59	1h 41m 39.192s	8	4
5	28	J Watson	Brabham	BT44	Cosworth	V8	59	1h 41m 47.243s	7	4
6	4	P Depailler	Tyrrell	007	Cosworth	V8	59	1h 41m 48.945s	13	7
7	33	J Mass	McLaren	M23	Cosworth	V8	59	1h 41m 51.451s	20	10
8	26	G Hill	Lola	T370	Cosworth	V8	58		24	12
9	15	C Amon	BRM	P201	BRM	V12	57		12	6
10	17	J-P Jarier	Shadow	DN3	Cosworth	V8	57		10	5
11	11	C Regazzoni	Ferrari	312B3	Ferrari	F12	55		9	5
12	27	R Stommelen	Lola	T370	Cosworth	V8	54		21	11
r	1	R Peterson	JPS Lotus	72E	Cosworth	V8	52	fuel line	19	10
nc	22	M Wilds	Ensign	N174	Cosworth	V8	50		22	11
nc	16	T Pryce	Shadow	DN3	Cosworth	V8	47		18	9
r	3	J Scheckter	Tyrrell	007	Cosworth	V8	44	fuel line	6	3
r	20	A Merzario	Iso Marlboro	FW	Cosworth	V8	43	fire extinguisher discharge	15	8
r	12	N Lauda	Ferrari	312B3	Ferrari	F12	38	front suspension	5	3
r	21	J Laffite	Iso Marlboro	FW	Cosworth	V8	31	rear wheel centre	11	6
r	66	M Donohue	Penske	PC1	Cosworth	V8	27	rear suspension	14	7
r	18	J Dolhem	Surtees	TS16	Cosworth	V8	25	withdrew (after Koinigg's death)	26	14
r	10	V Brambilla	March	741	Cosworth	V8	21	fuel metering unit	25	13
r	19	H Koinigg	Surtees	TS16	Cosworth	V8	9	fatal accident	23	12
r	2	J Ickx	JPS Lotus	72E	Cosworth	V8	7	suspension/ accident	16	8
dq	31	T Schenken	JPS Lotus	76	Cosworth	V8	6	started unofficially	27	14
r	6	D Hulme	McLaren	M23	Cosworth	V8	4	engine	17	9
dq	55	M Andretti	Parnelli	VPJ4	Cosworth	V8	4	push start on grid	3	2
nq	9	H-J Stuck	March	741	Cosworth	V8				
nq	42	I Ashley	Brabham	BT42	Cosworth	V8				
nq	14	J-P Beltoise	BRM	P201	BRM	V12		accident/ injury		

Winning speed: 191.705 km/h, 119.120 mph
Pole Position speed: 197.671 km/h, 122.827 mph (C Reutemann, 1 min:38.978 sec)
Fastest Lap speed: 194.469 km/h, 120.837 mph (C Pace, 1 min:40.608 sec on lap 54)
Lap Leaders: C Reutemann 1-59 (59).

Lap Leaders 1974

POS	DRIVER	CAR-ENGINE	GPS	LAPS	KM	MILES
1	N Lauda	Ferrari	8	339	1,383.2	859.5
2	C Reutemann	Brabham-Cosworth	5	235	1,243.5	772.6
3	R Peterson	Lotus-Cosworth	6	156	606.2	376.7
4	J Scheckter	Tyrrell-Cosworth	2	86	347.0	215.6
5	C Regazzoni	Ferrari	4	83	590.3	366.8
6	E Fittipaldi	McLaren-Cosworth	3	77	361.8	224.8
7	D Hulme	McLaren-Cosworth	1	2	11.9	7.4
8	J Ickx	Lotus-Cosworth	1	1	3.4	2.1
			15	**979**	**4,547.3**	**2,825.6**

Driver Points 1974

		RA	BR	ZA	E	B	MC	S	NL	F	GB	D	A	I	CDN	USA	TOTAL
1	E Fittipaldi	-	9	-	4	9	2	3	4	-	6	-	-	6	9	3	55
2	C Regazzoni	4	6	-	6	3	3	-	6	4	3	9	2	-	6	-	52
3	J Scheckter	-	-	-	2	4	6	9	2	3	9	6	-	4	-	-	45
4	N Lauda	6	-	-	9	6	-	-	9	6	2	-	-	-	-	-	38
5	R Peterson	-	1	-	-	-	9	-	-	9	-	3	-	9	4	-	35
6	C Reutemann	-	-	9	-	-	-	-	-	-	1	4	9	-	-	9	32
7	D Hulme	9	-	-	1	1	-	-	-	1	-	-	6	1	1	-	20
8	J Hunt	-	-	-	-	-	-	4	-	-	-	-	4	-	3	4	15
9	P Depailler	1	-	3	-	-	-	6	1	-	-	-	-	-	2	1	14
10	J Ickx	-	4	-	-	-	-	-	-	2	4	2	-	-	-	-	12
	M Hailwood	3	2	4	-	-	-	-	3	-	-	-	-	-	-	-	12
12	C Pace	-	3	-	-	-	-	-	-	-	-	-	-	2	-	6	11
13	J-P Beltoise	2	-	6	-	2	-	-	-	-	-	-	-	-	-	-	10
14	J-P Jarier	-	-	-	-	-	4	2	-	-	-	-	-	-	-	-	6
	J Watson	-	-	-	-	-	1	-	-	-	-	-	3	-	-	2	6
16	H-J Stuck	-	-	2	3	-	-	-	-	-	-	-	-	-	-	-	5
17	A Merzario	-	-	1	-	-	-	-	-	-	-	-	-	3	-	-	4
18	G Hill	-	-	-	-	-	-	1	-	-	-	-	-	-	-	-	1
	T Pryce	-	-	-	-	-	-	-	-	-	-	1	-	-	-	-	1
	V Brambilla	-	-	-	-	-	-	-	-	-	-	-	1	-	-	-	1

9, 6, 4, 3, 2 and 1 point awarded to the first six finishers.
Best 7 scores from first 8 races, best 6 from remaining 7 races.

Constructor Points 1974

		RA	BR	ZA	E	B	MC	S	NL	F	GB	D	A	I	CDN	USA	TOTAL	
1	McLaren-Cosworth	9	9	4	4	9	(2)	3	4	1	6	-	6	6	9	3	73	(2)
2	Ferrari	6	6	-	9	6	3	-	9	6	3	9	2	-	6	-	65	
3	Tyrrell-Cosworth	1	-	3	2	4	6	9	2	3	9	6	-	4	2	1	52	
4	Lotus-Cosworth	-	4	-	-	-	9	-	-	9	4	3	-	9	4	-	42	
5	Brabham-Cosworth	-	-	9	-	-	1	-	-	-	1	4	9	2	-	9	35	
6	Hesketh-Cosworth	-	-	-	-	-	-	4	-	-	-	-	4	-	3	4	15	
7	BRM	2	-	6	-	2	-	-	-	-	-	-	-	-	-	-	10	
8	Shadow-Cosworth	-	-	-	-	-	4	2	-	-	-	1	-	-	-	-	7	
9	March-Cosworth	-	-	2	3	-	-	-	-	-	-	-	1	-	-	-	6	
10	Iso-Cosworth	-	-	1	-	-	-	-	-	-	-	-	-	3	-	-	4	
11	Surtees-Cosworth	-	3	-	-	-	-	-	-	-	-	-	-	-	-	-	3	
12	Lola-Cosworth	-	-	-	-	-	-	1	-	-	-	-	-	-	-	-	1	

9, 6, 4, 3, 2 and 1 point awarded to the first six finishers. Points only for highest placed car.
Best 7 scores from first 8 races, best 6 from remaining 7 races.

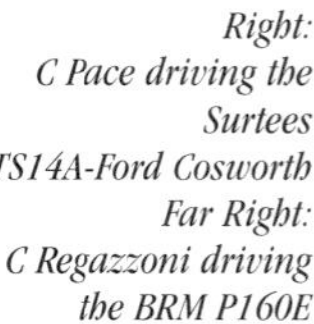

Right: C Pace driving the Surtees TS14A-Ford Cosworth
Far Right: C Regazzoni driving the BRM P160E

Firestone withdrew early in the season, leaving a Goodyear tyre monopoly. BRM restructured as Stanley BRM after the withdrawal of Rubery Owen support. The accident strewn Spanish Grand Prix was prematurely stopped after an accident involving spectators, making it the first event at which half points were awarded.

McLAREN
Marlboro Team McLaren: E Fittipaldi, Mass
Lucky Strike Racing: Charlton

TYRRELL
Elf Team Tyrrell: J Scheckter, Depailler, Jabouille, Leclère
Lexington Racing: I Scheckter

LOTUS
John Player Team Lotus: Peterson, Ickx, Henton, Crawford, Watson
Team Gunston: Keizan, Tunmer

BRABHAM
Martini Racing: Reutemann, Pace

MARCH
Beta Team March: Brambilla
Lavazza March: Lombardi, Stuck
Penske Cars: Donohue

FERRARI
Scuderia Ferrari SpA SEFAC: Regazzoni, Lauda

BRM
Stanley BRM: Wilds, Evans

SHADOW
UOP Shadow Racing Team: Pryce, Jarier

SURTEES
Team Surtees: Watson, Morgan (with National Organs)

WILLIAMS
Frank Williams Racing Cars: Merzario, Magee, (Migault), Vonlanthen, Zorzi, (Lombardi), I Scheckter, Laffite, Brise

LOLA
Embassy Racing with Graham Hill: Hill, Stommelen

HILL
Embassy Racing with Graham Hill: Stommelen, Migault, Schuppan, Jones, (Hill), Brise

HESKETH
Hesketh Racing: Hunt, Lunger
Custom Made Harry Stiller Racing: Jones
Warsteiner Brewery: Ertl
Polar Caravans: Palm

PARNELLI
Vel's Parnelli Jones Racing: Andretti

PENSKE
Penske Cars: Donohue, Watson

FITTIPALDI (COPERSUCAR)
Copersucar-Fittipaldi: W Fittipaldi, Merzario

LYNCAR
Pinch (Plant) Ltd: Nicholson

ENSIGN
HB Bewaking Team Ensign: Wunderink, van Lennep, Amon

MAKI
Maki Engineering: (Fushida, Trimmer)

12 Jan 1975 — ARGENTINA: Buenos Aires No.15 — (Round: 1) (Race: 251)
53 laps x 5.968 km, 3.708 miles = 316.304 km, 196.542 miles

POS.	NO.	DRIVER	CAR	MODEL	ENGINE		LAPS	TIME/REASON FOR RETIREMENT	GRID:POS	ROW
1	1	E Fittipaldi	McLaren	M23	Cosworth	V8	53	1h 39m 26.290s	5	3
2	24	J Hunt	Hesketh	308	Cosworth	V8	53	1h 39m 32.200s	6	3
3	7	C Reutemann	Brabham	BT44B	Cosworth	V8	53	1h 39m 43.350s	3	2
4	11	C Regazzoni	Ferrari	312B3	Ferrari	F12	53	1h 40m 02.080s	7	4
5	4	P Depailler	Tyrrell	007	Cosworth	V8	53	1h 40m 20.540s	8	4
6	12	N Lauda	Ferrari	312B3	Ferrari	F12	53	1h 40m 45.940s	4	2
7	28	M Donohue	Penske	PC1	Cosworth	V8	52		16	8
8	6	J Ickx	JPS Lotus	72E	Cosworth	V8	52		18	9
9	9	V Brambilla	March	741	Cosworth	V8	52		12	6
10	22	G Hill	Lola	T370	Cosworth	V8	52		21	11
11	3	J Scheckter	Tyrrell	007	Cosworth	V8	52		9	5
12r	16	T Pryce	Shadow	DN3B	Cosworth	V8	51	transmission	14	7
13	23	R Stommelen	Lola	T370	Cosworth	V8	51		19	10
14	2	J Mass	McLaren	M23	Cosworth	V8	50		13	7
r	8	C Pace	Brabham	BT44B	Cosworth	V8	46	engine	2	1
nc	20	A Merzario	Williams	FW	Cosworth	V8	44		20	10
r	27	M Andretti	Parnelli	VPJ4	Cosworth	V8	27	cv joint	10	5
r	14	M Wilds	Stanley BRM	P201	BRM	V12	24	oil scavenge pump drive belt	22	11
r	5	R Peterson	JPS Lotus	72E	Cosworth	V8	15	brakes/ gearbox	11	6
r	21	J Laffite	Williams	FW	Cosworth	V8	15	gearbox	17	9
r	30	W Fittipaldi	Copersucar	FD01	Cosworth	V8	12	accident	23	12
dq	18	J Watson	Surtees	TS16	Cosworth	V8	6	repaired outside pits	15	8
ns	17	J-P Jarier	Shadow	DN5	Cosworth	V8		crown wheel & pinion	1	1

Winning speed: 190.855 km/h, 118.592 mph
Pole Position speed: 196.729 km/h, 122.242 mph (J-P Jarier, 1 min:49.210 sec)
Fastest Lap speed: 193.714 km/h, 120.368 mph (J Hunt, 1 min:50.910 sec on lap 34)
Lap Leaders: C Reutemann 1-25 (25); J Hunt 26-34 (9); E Fittipaldi 35-53 (19).

J-P Jarier qualified for pole position, but did not start due to car failure in warm-up. Pole position left vacant.

26 Jan 1975 — BRAZIL: Interlagos — (Round: 2) (Race: 252)

40 laps x 7.960 km, 4.946 miles = 318.400 km, 197.845 miles

POS.	NO.	DRIVER	CAR	MODEL	ENGINE		LAPS	TIME/REASON FOR RETIREMENT	GRID:POS	ROW
1	8	C Pace	Brabham	BT44B	Cosworth	V8	40	1h 44m 41.170s	6	3
2	1	E Fittipaldi	McLaren	M23	Cosworth	V8	40	1h 44m 46.960s	2	1
3	2	J Mass	McLaren	M23	Cosworth	V8	40	1h 45m 17.830s	10	5
4	11	C Regazzoni	Ferrari	312B3	Ferrari	F12	40	1h 45m 24.450s	5	3
5	12	N Lauda	Ferrari	312B3	Ferrari	F12	40	1h 45m 43.050s	4	2
6	24	J Hunt	Hesketh	308	Cosworth	V8	40	1h 45m 46.290s	7	4
7	27	M Andretti	Parnelli	VPJ4	Cosworth	V8	40	1h 45m 47.980s	18	9
8	7	C Reutemann	Brabham	BT44B	Cosworth	V8	40	1h 46m 20.790s	3	2
9	6	J Ickx	JPS Lotus	72E	Cosworth	V8	40	1h 46m 33.010s	12	6
10	18	J Watson	Surtees	TS16	Cosworth	V8	40	1h 47m 10.770s	13	7
11	21	J Laffite	Williams	FW	Cosworth	V8	39		19	10
12	22	G Hill	Lola	T370	Cosworth	V8	39		20	10
13	30	W Fittipaldi	Copersucar	FD02	Cosworth	V8	39		21	11
14	23	R Stommelen	Lola	T370	Cosworth	V8	39		23	12
15	5	R Peterson	JPS Lotus	72E	Cosworth	V8	38		16	8
r	17	J-P Jarier	Shadow	DN5	Cosworth	V8	32	fuel metering unit	1	1
r	4	P Depailler	Tyrrell	007	Cosworth	V8	31	front suspension/ accident	9	5
r	16	T Pryce	Shadow	DN3B	Cosworth	V8	31	accident	14	7
r	20	A Merzario	Williams	FW	Cosworth	V8	24	fuel metering unit	11	6
r	14	M Wilds	Stanley BRM	P201	BRM	V12	22	clutch nut loose/ electrics	22	11
r	28	M Donohue	Penske	PC1	Cosworth	V8	22	handling	15	8
r	3	J Scheckter	Tyrrell	007	Cosworth	V8	18	oil tank	8	4
r	9	V Brambilla	March	741	Cosworth	V8	1	engine	17	9

Winning speed: 182.488 km/h, 113.393 mph
Pole Position speed: 191.193 km/h, 118.802 mph (J-P Jarier, 2 min:29.880 sec)
Fastest Lap speed: 185.885 km/h, 115.503 mph (J-P Jarier, 2 min:34.160 sec on lap 10)
Lap Leaders: C Reutemann 1-4 (4); J-P Jarier 5-32 (28); C Pace 33-40 (8).

1 Mar 1975 — SOUTH AFRICA: Kyalami — (Round: 3) (Race: 253)

78 laps x 4.104 km, 2.550 miles = 320.112 km, 198.908 miles

POS.	NO.	DRIVER	CAR	MODEL	ENGINE		LAPS	TIME/REASON FOR RETIREMENT	GRID:POS	ROW
1	3	J Scheckter	Tyrrell	007	Cosworth	V8	78	1h 43m 16.900s	3	2
2	7	C Reutemann	Brabham	BT44B	Cosworth	V8	78	1h 43m 20.640s	2	1
3	4	P Depailler	Tyrrell	007	Cosworth	V8	78	1h 43m 33.820s	5	3
4	8	C Pace	Brabham	BT44B	Cosworth	V8	78	1h 43m 34.210s	1	1
5	12	N Lauda	Ferrari	312T	Ferrari	F12	78	1h 43m 45.540s	4	2
6	2	J Mass	McLaren	M23	Cosworth	V8	78	1h 44m 20.240s	16	8
7	23	R Stommelen	Lola	T371	Cosworth	V8	78	1h 44m 29.810s	14	7
8	28	M Donohue	Penske	PC1	Cosworth	V8	77		18	9
9	16	T Pryce	Shadow	DN5	Cosworth	V8	77		19	10
10	5	R Peterson	JPS Lotus	72E	Cosworth	V8	77		8	4
11	34	G Tunmer	Lotus	72	Cosworth	V8	76		25	13
12	6	J Ickx	JPS Lotus	72E	Cosworth	V8	76		21	11
13	33	E Keizan	Lotus	72	Cosworth	V8	76		22	11
14	31	D Charlton	McLaren	M23	Cosworth	V8	76		20	10
15	14	B Evans	Stanley BRM	P201	BRM	V12	76		24	12
16r	11	C Regazzoni	Ferrari	312T	Ferrari	F12	71	throttle linkage	9	5
17r	27	M Andretti	Parnelli	VPJ4	Cosworth	V8	70	cv joint	6	3
nc	21	J Laffite	Williams	FW	Cosworth	V8	69		23	12
nc	1	E Fittipaldi	McLaren	M23	Cosworth	V8	65		11	6
r	32	I Scheckter	Tyrrell	007	Cosworth	V8	55	accident	17	9
r	24	J Hunt	Hesketh	308	Cosworth	V8	53	fuel metering unit	12	6
r	17	J-P Jarier	Shadow	DN5	Cosworth	V8	37	engine	13	7
r	10	L Lombardi	March	741	Cosworth	V8	23	engine	26	13
r	20	A Merzario	Williams	FW	Cosworth	V8	22	engine	15	8
r	18	J Watson	Surtees	TS16	Cosworth	V8	19	clutch	10	5
r	9	V Brambilla	March	751	Cosworth	V8	16	oil cooler leak	7	4
r	30	W Fittipaldi	Copersucar	FD02	Cosworth	V8	0	withdrew (reserve entry)	27	14
ns	22	G Hill	Lola	T370	Cosworth	V8		accident		

Winning speed: 185.964 km/h, 115.553 mph
Pole Position speed: 193.357 km/h, 120.146 mph (C Pace, 1 min:16.410 sec)
Fastest Lap speed: 191.378 km/h, 118.917 mph (C Pace, 1 min:17.200 sec on lap 11)
Lap Leaders: C Pace 1-2 (2); J Scheckter 3-78 (76).

27 Apr 1975 — SPAIN: Montjuich Park (Round: 4) (Race: 254)

29 laps x 3.791 km, 2.356 miles = 109.939 km, 68.313 miles

POS.	NO.	DRIVER	CAR	MODEL	ENGINE		LAPS	TIME/REASON FOR RETIREMENT	GRID:POS	ROW
1	2	J Mass	McLaren	M23	Cosworth	V8	29	42m 53.700s	11	6
2	6	J Ickx	JPS Lotus	72E	Cosworth	V8	29	42m 54.800s	16	8
3	7	C Reutemann	Brabham	BT44B	Cosworth	V8	28		15	8
4	17	J-P Jarier	Shadow	DN5	Cosworth	V8	28		10	5
5	9	V Brambilla	March	751	Cosworth	V8	28		5	3
6	10	L Lombardi	March	751	Cosworth	V8	27		24	12
7	21	T Brise	Williams	FW	Cosworth	V8	27		18	9
8	18	J Watson	Surtees	TS16	Cosworth	V8	26		6	3
r	22	R Stommelen	Hill	GH1	Cosworth	V8	25	rear wing/ accident	9	5
r	8	C Pace	Brabham	BT44B	Cosworth	V8	25	accident	14	7
nc	11	C Regazzoni	Ferrari	312T	Ferrari	F12	25		2	1
r	5	R Peterson	JPS Lotus	72E	Cosworth	V8	23	accident	12	6
r	16	T Pryce	Shadow	DN5	Cosworth	V8	23	accident	8	4
r	31	R Wunderink	Ensign	N174	Cosworth	V8	20	cv joint	19	10
nc	23	F Migault	Hill	GH1	Cosworth	V8	18		22	11
r	27	M Andretti	Parnelli	VPJ4	Cosworth	V8	16	accident/ rear suspension	4	2
r	14	B Evans	Stanley BRM	P201	BRM	V12	7	fuel metering unit	23	12
r	24	J Hunt	Hesketh	308	Cosworth	V8	6	accident	3	2
r	3	J Scheckter	Tyrrell	007	Cosworth	V8	3	engine	13	7
r	28	M Donohue	Penske	PC1	Cosworth	V8	3	accident	17	9
r	25	A Jones	Hesketh	308	Cosworth	V8	3	accident	20	10
r	4	P Depailler	Tyrrell	007	Cosworth	V8	1	accident	7	4
r	20	A Merzario	Williams	FW04	Cosworth	V8	1	withdrew (protest)	25	13
r	30	W Fittipaldi	Copersucar	FD02	Cosworth	V8	1	withdrew (protest)	21	11
r	12	N Lauda	Ferrari	312T	Ferrari	F12	0	accident	1	1
ns	1	E Fittipaldi	McLaren	M23	Cosworth	V8		considered track unsafe		

Winning speed: 153.779 km/h, 95.554 mph
Pole Position speed: 163.640 km/h, 101.681 mph (N Lauda, 1 min:23.400 sec)
Fastest Lap speed: 160.371 km/h, 99.650 mph (M Andretti, 1 min:25.100 sec on lap 14)
Lap Leaders: J Hunt 1-6 (6);M Andretti 7-16 (10);R Stommelen 17-21,23-25 (8);C Pace 22 (1);J Mass 26-27,29 (3);J Ickx 28 (1).

Scheduled for 75 laps, but stopped after
R Stommelen's accident which killed 5 spectators. Half points were awarded.
J-P Jarier penalised 1 lap for overtaking under a yellow flag.

11 May 1975 — MONACO: Monte Carlo (Round: 5) (Race: 255)

75 laps x 3.278 km, 2.037 miles = 245.850 km, 152.764 miles

POS.	NO.	DRIVER	CAR	MODEL	ENGINE		LAPS	TIME/REASON FOR RETIREMENT	GRID:POS	ROW
1	12	N Lauda	Ferrari	312T	Ferrari	F12	75	2h 01m 21.310s	1	1
2	1	E Fittipaldi	McLaren	M23	Cosworth	V8	75	2h 01m 24.090s	9	5
3	8	C Pace	Brabham	BT44B	Cosworth	V8	75	2h 01m 39.120s	8	4
4	5	R Peterson	JPS Lotus	72E	Cosworth	V8	75	2h 01m 59.760s	4	2
5	4	P Depailler	Tyrrell	007	Cosworth	V8	75	2h 02m 02.170s	12	6
6	2	J Mass	McLaren	M23	Cosworth	V8	75	2h 02m 03.380s	15	8
7	3	J Scheckter	Tyrrell	007	Cosworth	V8	74		7	4
8	6	J Ickx	JPS Lotus	72E	Cosworth	V8	74		14	7
9	7	C Reutemann	Brabham	BT44B	Cosworth	V8	73		10	5
r	28	M Donohue	Penske	PC1	Cosworth	V8	66	accident	16	8
r	24	J Hunt	Hesketh	308	Cosworth	V8	63	accident	11	6
r	26	A Jones	Hesketh	308	Cosworth	V8	61	wheel lost	18	9
r	9	V Brambilla	March	751	Cosworth	V8	48	accident	5	3
r	16	T Pryce	Shadow	DN5	Cosworth	V8	39	accident	2	1
r	18	J Watson	Surtees	TS16	Cosworth	V8	36	spin	17	9
r	11	C Regazzoni	Ferrari	312T	Ferrari	F12	36	accident	6	3
r	27	M Andretti	Parnelli	VPJ4	Cosworth	V8	9	oil line/ fire	13	7
r	17	J-P Jarier	Shadow	DN5	Cosworth	V8	0	accident	3	2
nq	21	J Laffite	Williams	FW04	Cosworth	V8				
nq	20	A Merzario	Williams	FW	Cosworth	V8				
nq	23	G Hill	Hill	GH1	Cosworth	V8				
nq	14	B Evans	Stanley BRM	P201	BRM	V12				
nq	31	R Wunderink	Ensign	N174	Cosworth	V8				
nq	25	T Palm	Hesketh	308	Cosworth	V8				
nq	10	L Lombardi	March	751	Cosworth	V8				
nq	30	W Fittipaldi	Copersucar	FD02	Cosworth	V8				

Winning speed: 121.552 km/h, 75.529 mph
Pole Position speed: 136.583 km/h, 84.869 mph (N Lauda, 1 min:26.400 sec)
Fastest Lap speed: 133.087 km/h, 82.696 mph (P Depailler, 1 min:28.670 sec on lap 68)
Lap Leaders: N Lauda 1-23,25-75 (74); R Peterson 24 (1).

Scheduled for 78 laps, but stopped at 2 hours. G Hill also practiced in a Lola T370-Cosworth V8 (22).

25 May 1975 — BELGIUM: Zolder — (Round: 6) (Race: 256)

70 laps x 4.262 km, 2.648 miles = 298.340 km, 185.380 miles

POS.	NO.	DRIVER	CAR	MODEL	ENGINE		LAPS	TIME/REASON FOR RETIREMENT	GRID:POS	ROW
1	12	N Lauda	Ferrari	312T	Ferrari	F12	70	1h 43m 53.980s	1	1
2	3	J Scheckter	Tyrrell	007	Cosworth	V8	70	1h 44m 13.200s	9	5
3	7	C Reutemann	Brabham	BT44B	Cosworth	V8	70	1h 44m 35.800s	6	3
4	4	P Depailler	Tyrrell	007	Cosworth	V8	70	1h 44m 54.060s	12	6
5	11	C Regazzoni	Ferrari	312T	Ferrari	F12	70	1h 44m 57.840s	4	2
6	16	T Pryce	Shadow	DN5	Cosworth	V8	70	1h 45m 22.430s	5	3
7	1	E Fittipaldi	McLaren	M23	Cosworth	V8	69		8	4
8	8	C Pace	Brabham	BT44B	Cosworth	V8	69		2	1
9	14	B Evans	Stanley BRM	P201	BRM	V12	68		20	10
10	18	J Watson	Surtees	TS16	Cosworth	V8	68		18	9
11	28	M Donohue	Penske	PC1	Cosworth	V8	67		21	11
12	30	W Fittipaldi	Copersucar	FD02	Cosworth	V8	67		24	12
r	22	F Migault	Hill	GH1	Cosworth	V8	57	rear suspension	22	11
r	9	V Brambilla	March	751	Cosworth	V8	54	brakes	3	2
r	6	J Ickx	JPS Lotus	72E	Cosworth	V8	52	front brake shaft	16	8
r	5	R Peterson	JPS Lotus	72E	Cosworth	V8	36	brakes/ accident	14	7
r	10	L Lombardi	March	751	Cosworth	V8	18	oil cooler leak/ engine	23	12
r	21	J Laffite	Williams	FW04	Cosworth	V8	18	gearbox	17	9
r	23	T Brise	Hill	GH1	Cosworth	V8	17	piston	7	4
r	24	J Hunt	Hesketh	308	Cosworth	V8	15	gear linkage	11	6
r	17	J-P Jarier	Shadow	DN5	Cosworth	V8	13	spin	10	5
r	20	A Merzario	Williams	FW	Cosworth	V8	2	clutch	19	10
r	26	A Jones	Hesketh	308	Cosworth	V8	1	accident	13	7
r	2	J Mass	McLaren	M23	Cosworth	V8	0	accident	15	8

Winning speed: 172.285 km/h, 107.053 mph
Pole Position speed: 179.600 km/h, 111.598 mph (N Lauda, 1 min:25.430 sec)
Fastest Lap speed: 176.846 km/h, 109.887 mph (C Regazzoni, 1 min:26.760 sec on lap 11)
Lap Leaders: C Pace 1-3 (3); V Brambilla 4-5 (2); N Lauda 6-70 (65).

8 Jun 1975 — SWEDEN: Anderstorp — (Round: 7) (Race: 257)

80 laps x 4.018 km, 2.497 miles = 321.440 km, 199.734 miles

POS.	NO.	DRIVER	CAR	MODEL	ENGINE		LAPS	TIME/REASON FOR RETIREMENT	GRID:POS	ROW
1	12	N Lauda	Ferrari	312T	Ferrari	F12	80	1h 59m 18.319s	5	3
2	7	C Reutemann	Brabham	BT44B	Cosworth	V8	80	1h 59m 24.607s	4	2
3	11	C Regazzoni	Ferrari	312T	Ferrari	F12	80	1h 59m 47.414s	12	6
4	27	M Andretti	Parnelli	VPJ4	Cosworth	V8	80	2h 00m 02.699s	15	8
5	28	M Donohue	Penske	PC1	Cosworth	V8	80	2h 00m 49.082s	16	8
6	23	T Brise	Hill	GH1	Cosworth	V8	79		17	9
7	3	J Scheckter	Tyrrell	007	Cosworth	V8	79		8	4
8	1	E Fittipaldi	McLaren	M23	Cosworth	V8	79		11	6
9	5	R Peterson	JPS Lotus	72E	Cosworth	V8	79		9	5
10r	32	T Palm	Hesketh	308	Cosworth	V8	78	out of fuel	21	11
11	26	A Jones	Hesketh	308	Cosworth	V8	79		19	10
12	4	P Depailler	Tyrrell	007	Cosworth	V8	78		2	1
13	14	B Evans	Stanley BRM	P201	BRM	V12	78		23	12
14	20	D Magee	Williams	FW	Cosworth	V8	78		22	11
15	6	J Ickx	JPS Lotus	72E	Cosworth	V8	77		18	9
16	18	J Watson	Surtees	TS16	Cosworth	V8	77		10	5
17	30	W Fittipaldi	Copersucar	FD02	Cosworth	V8	74		25	13
r	16	T Pryce	Shadow	DN5	Cosworth	V8	53	spin	7	4
r	21	I Scheckter	Williams	FW04	Cosworth	V8	49	tyre burst/ accident	20	10
r	22	V Schuppan	Hill	GH1	Cosworth	V8	47	drive shaft	26	13
r	8	C Pace	Brabham	BT44B	Cosworth	V8	41	accident	6	3
r	17	J-P Jarier	Shadow	DN5	Cosworth	V8	38	engine	3	2
r	9	V Brambilla	March	751	Cosworth	V8	36	universal joint	1	1
r	2	J Mass	McLaren	M23	Cosworth	V8	34	water leak	14	7
r	24	J Hunt	Hesketh	308	Cosworth	V8	21	brake fluid leak	13	7
r	10	L Lombardi	March	751	Cosworth	V8	10	fuel metering unit	24	12

Winning speed: 161.656 km/h, 100.448 mph
Pole Position speed: 170.918 km/h, 106.204 mph (V Brambilla, 1 min:24.630 sec)
Fastest Lap speed: 163.876 km/h, 101.828 mph (N Lauda, 1 min:28.267 sec on lap 61)
Lap Leaders: V Brambilla 1-15 (15); C Reutemann 16-69 (54); N Lauda 70-80 (11).

22 Jun 1975 — NETHERLANDS: Zandvoort (Round: 8) (Race: 258)

75 laps x 4.226 km, 2.626 miles = 316.950 km, 196.944 miles

POS.	NO.	DRIVER	CAR	MODEL	ENGINE		LAPS	TIME/REASON FOR RETIREMENT	GRID:POS	ROW
1	24	J Hunt	Hesketh	308	Cosworth	V8	75	1h 46m 57.400s	3	2
2	12	N Lauda	Ferrari	312T	Ferrari	F12	75	1h 46m 58.460s	1	1
3	11	C Regazzoni	Ferrari	312T	Ferrari	F12	75	1h 47m 52.460s	2	1
4	7	C Reutemann	Brabham	BT44B	Cosworth	V8	74		5	3
5	8	C Pace	Brabham	BT44B	Cosworth	V8	74		9	5
6	16	T Pryce	Shadow	DN5	Cosworth	V8	74		12	6
7	23	T Brise	Hill	GH1	Cosworth	V8	74		7	4
8	28	M Donohue	Penske	PC1	Cosworth	V8	74		18	9
9	4	P Depailler	Tyrrell	007	Cosworth	V8	73		13	7
10	31	G van Lennep	Ensign	N174	Cosworth	V8	71		22	11
11	30	W Fittipaldi	Copersucar	FD03	Cosworth	V8	71		24	12
12	20	I Scheckter	Williams	FW	Cosworth	V8	70		19	10
13	22	A Jones	Hill	GH1	Cosworth	V8	70		17	9
14	10	L Lombardi	March	751	Cosworth	V8	70		23	12
15r	5	R Peterson	JPS Lotus	72E	Cosworth	V8	69	out of fuel	16	8
16r	3	J Scheckter	Tyrrell	007	Cosworth	V8	67	engine	4	2
r	21	J Laffite	Williams	FW04	Cosworth	V8	65	engine	15	8
r	2	J Mass	McLaren	M23	Cosworth	V8	61	accident	8	4
r	17	J-P Jarier	Shadow	DN5	Cosworth	V8	44	tyre burst/ accident	10	5
r	18	J Watson	Surtees	TS16	Cosworth	V8	43	vibration	14	7
r	1	E Fittipaldi	McLaren	M23	Cosworth	V8	40	engine	6	3
r	14	B Evans	Stanley BRM	P201	BRM	V12	23	crown wheel & pinion	20	10
r	6	J Ickx	JPS Lotus	72E	Cosworth	V8	6	engine	21	11
r	9	V Brambilla	March	751	Cosworth	V8	0	accident	11	6
ns	35	H Fushida	Maki	F101C	Cosworth	V8		engine		

Winning speed: 177.801 km/h, 110.480 mph
Pole Position speed: 189.483 km/h, 117.739 mph (N Lauda, 1 min:20.290 sec)
Fastest Lap speed: 186.578 km/h, 115.934 mph (N Lauda, 1 min:21.540 sec on lap 55)
Lap Leaders: N Lauda 1-12 (12); C Regazzoni 13-14 (2); J Hunt 15-75 (61).

6 Jul 1975 — FRANCE: Paul Ricard (Round: 9) (Race: 259)

54 laps x 5.810 km, 3.610 miles = 313.740 km, 194.949 miles

POS.	NO.	DRIVER	CAR	MODEL	ENGINE		LAPS	TIME/REASON FOR RETIREMENT	GRID:POS	ROW
1	12	N Lauda	Ferrari	312T	Ferrari	F12	54	1h 40m 18.840s	1	1
2	24	J Hunt	Hesketh	308	Cosworth	V8	54	1h 40m 20.430s	3	2
3	2	J Mass	McLaren	M23	Cosworth	V8	54	1h 40m 21.150s	7	4
4	1	E Fittipaldi	McLaren	M23	Cosworth	V8	54	1h 40m 58.610s	10	5
5	27	M Andretti	Parnelli	VPJ4	Cosworth	V8	54	1h 41m 20.920s	15	8
6	4	P Depailler	Tyrrell	007	Cosworth	V8	54	1h 41m 26.240s	13	7
7	23	T Brise	Hill	GH1	Cosworth	V8	54	1h 41m 28.450s	12	6
8	17	J-P Jarier	Shadow	DN5	Cosworth	V8	54	1h 41m 38.620s	4	2
9	3	J Scheckter	Tyrrell	007	Cosworth	V8	54	1h 41m 50.520s	2	1
10	5	R Peterson	JPS Lotus	72E	Cosworth	V8	54	1h 41m 54.860s	17	9
11	21	J Laffite	Williams	FW04	Cosworth	V8	54	1h 41m 55.610s	16	8
12	15	J-P Jabouille	Tyrrell	007	Cosworth	V8	54	1h 41m 55.970s	21	11
13	18	J Watson	Surtees	TS16	Cosworth	V8	53		14	7
14	7	C Reutemann	Brabham	BT44B	Cosworth	V8	53		11	6
15	31	G van Lennep	Ensign	N175	Cosworth	V8	53		22	11
16	22	A Jones	Hill	GH1	Cosworth	V8	53		20	10
17	14	B Evans	Stanley BRM	P201	BRM	V12	52		25	13
18	10	L Lombardi	March	751	Cosworth	V8	50		26	13
r	8	C Pace	Brabham	BT44B	Cosworth	V8	26	cv joint	5	3
r	6	J Ickx	JPS Lotus	72E	Cosworth	V8	17	cv joint	19	10
r	30	W Fittipaldi	Copersucar	FD03	Cosworth	V8	14	engine	23	12
r	28	M Donohue	Penske	PC1	Cosworth	V8	6	cv joint	18	9
r	9	V Brambilla	March	751	Cosworth	V8	6	rear suspension	8	4
r	11	C Regazzoni	Ferrari	312T	Ferrari	F12	6	engine	9	5
r	16	T Pryce	Shadow	DN5	Cosworth	V8	2	transmission	6	3
ns	20	F Migault	Williams	FW	Cosworth	V8		engine	24	12

Winning speed: 187.655 km/h, 116.603 mph
Pole Position speed: 193.990 km/h, 120.540 mph (N Lauda, 1 min:47.820 sec)
Fastest Lap speed: 189.114 km/h, 117.510 mph (J Mass, 1 min:50.600 sec on lap 38)
Lap Leaders: N Lauda 1-54 (54).

19 Jul 1975 — BRITAIN: Silverstone (Round:10) (Race: 260)

56 laps x 4.719 km, 2.932 miles = 264.241 km, 164.192 miles

POS.	NO.	DRIVER	CAR	MODEL	ENGINE		LAPS	TIME/REASON FOR RETIREMENT	GRID:POS	ROW
1	1	E Fittipaldi	McLaren	M23	Cosworth	V8	56	1h 22m 05.000s	7	4
2r	8	C Pace	Brabham	BT44B	Cosworth	V8	55	accident	2	1
3r	3	J Scheckter	Tyrrell	007	Cosworth	V8	55	accident	6	3
4r	24	J Hunt	Hesketh	308	Cosworth	V8	55	accident	9	5
5r	28	M Donohue	March	751	Cosworth	V8	55	accident	15	8
6	9	V Brambilla	March	751	Cosworth	V8	55		5	3
7r	2	J Mass	McLaren	M23	Cosworth	V8	55	accident	10	5
8	12	N Lauda	Ferrari	312T	Ferrari	F12	54		3	2
9r	4	P Depailler	Tyrrell	007	Cosworth	V8	54	accident	17	9
10	22	A Jones	Hill	GH1	Cosworth	V8	54		20	10
11r	18	J Watson	Surtees	TS16	Cosworth	V8	54	accident	18	9
12	27	M Andretti	Parnelli	VPJ4	Cosworth	V8	54		12	6
13	11	C Regazzoni	Ferrari	312T	Ferrari	F12	54		4	2
14r	17	J-P Jarier	Shadow	DN5	Cosworth	V8	53	accident	11	6
15r	23	T Brise	Hill	GH1	Cosworth	V8	53	accident	13	7
16r	15	B Henton	JPS Lotus	72E	Cosworth	V8	53	accident	21	11
17r	32	J Nicholson	Lyncar	006	Cosworth	V8	51	accident	26	13
18r	19	D Morgan	Surtees	TS16	Cosworth	V8	50	accident	23	12
19r	30	W Fittipaldi	Copersucar	FD03	Cosworth	V8	50	accident	24	12
r	10	H-J Stuck	March	751	Cosworth	V8	45	accident	14	7
r	6	J Crawford	JPS Lotus	72E	Cosworth	V8	28	accident	25	13
r	16	T Pryce	Shadow	DN5	Cosworth	V8	20	accident	1	1
r	29	L Lombardi	March	751	Cosworth	V8	18	ignition	22	11
r	5	R Peterson	JPS Lotus	72E	Cosworth	V8	7	engine	16	8
r	21	J Laffite	Williams	FW04	Cosworth	V8	5	gearbox	19	10
r	7	C Reutemann	Brabham	BT44B	Cosworth	V8	4	engine	8	4
nq	31	R Wunderink	Ensign	N175	Cosworth	V8				
nq	35	H Fushida	Maki	F101C	Cosworth	V8				

Winning speed: 193.151 km/h, 120.019 mph
Pole Position speed: 214.049 km/h, 133.004 mph (T Pryce, 1 min:19.360 sec)
Fastest Lap speed: 209.975 km/h, 130.472 mph (C Regazzoni, 1 min:20.900 sec on lap 16)
Lap Leaders: C Pace 1-12,22-26 (17); C Regazzoni 13-18 (6); T Pryce 19-20 (2); J Scheckter 21,27-32 (7); J-P Jarier 33-34 (2); J Hunt 35-42 (8); E Fittipaldi 43-56 (14).

Scheduled for 67 laps, but stopped early because of rain.

3 Aug 1975 — GERMANY: Nürburgring (Round:11) (Race: 261)

14 laps x 22.835 km, 14.189 miles = 319.690 km, 198.646 miles

POS.	NO.	DRIVER	CAR	MODEL	ENGINE		LAPS	TIME/REASON FOR RETIREMENT	GRID:POS	ROW
1	7	C Reutemann	Brabham	BT44B	Cosworth	V8	14	1h 41m 14.100s	10	5
2	21	J Laffite	Williams	FW04	Cosworth	V8	14	1h 42m 51.800s	15	8
3	12	N Lauda	Ferrari	312T	Ferrari	F12	14	1h 43m 37.400s	1	1
4	16	T Pryce	Shadow	DN5	Cosworth	V8	14	1h 44m 45.500s	16	8
5	22	A Jones	Hill	GH1	Cosworth	V8	14	1h 45m 04.400s	21	11
6	19	G van Lennep	Ensign	N175	Cosworth	V8	14	1h 46m 19.600s	24	12
7	29	L Lombardi	March	751	Cosworth	V8	14	1h 48m 44.500s	25	13
8	25	H Ertl	Hesketh	308	Cosworth	V8	14	1h 48m 55.000s	23	12
9	4	P Depailler	Tyrrell	007	Cosworth	V8	13		4	2
10r	27	M Andretti	Parnelli	VPJ4	Cosworth	V8	12	out of fuel (leak)	13	7
r	24	J Hunt	Hesketh	308	Cosworth	V8	10	rear hub	9	5
r	11	C Regazzoni	Ferrari	312T	Ferrari	F12	9	engine	5	3
r	23	T Brise	Hill	GH1	Cosworth	V8	9	suspension/ accident	17	9
r	3	J Scheckter	Tyrrell	007	Cosworth	V8	7	tyre burst/ accident	3	2
r	17	J-P Jarier	Shadow	DN5	Cosworth	V8	7	puncture	12	6
r	8	C Pace	Brabham	BT44B	Cosworth	V8	5	rear suspension	2	1
r	30	W Fittipaldi	Copersucar	FD03	Cosworth	V8	4	engine	22	11
r	1	E Fittipaldi	McLaren	M23	Cosworth	V8	3	puncture/ rear suspension	8	4
r	10	H-J Stuck	March	751	Cosworth	V8	3	engine	7	4
r	9	V Brambilla	March	751	Cosworth	V8	3	punctures/ suspension	11	6
r	6	J Watson	JPS Lotus	72F	Cosworth	V8	2	front suspension	14	7
r	5	R Peterson	JPS Lotus	72E	Cosworth	V8	1	clutch	18	9
r	28	M Donohue	March	751	Cosworth	V8	1	puncture	19	10
r	2	J Mass	McLaren	M23	Cosworth	V8	0	tyre burst/ accident	6	3
ns	20	I Ashley	Williams	FW	Cosworth	V8		accident/ injury	20	10
nq	35	T Trimmer	Maki	F101C	Cosworth	V8				

Winning speed: 189.474 km/h, 117.734 mph
Pole Position speed: 196.383 km/h, 122.027 mph (N Lauda, 6 min:58.600 sec)
Fastest Lap speed: 192.791 km/h, 119.795 mph (C Regazzoni, 7 min: 6.400 sec on lap 7)
Lap Leaders: N Lauda 1-9 (9); C Reutemann 10-14 (5).

17 Aug 1975 — AUSTRIA: Österreichring (Round:12) (Race: 262)

29 laps x 5.911 km, 3.673 miles = 171.419 km, 106.515 miles

POS.	NO.	DRIVER	CAR	MODEL	ENGINE		LAPS	TIME/REASON FOR RETIREMENT	GRID:POS	ROW
1	9	V Brambilla	March	751	Cosworth	V8	29	57m 56.690s	8	4
2	24	J Hunt	Hesketh	308	Cosworth	V8	29	58m 23.720s	2	1
3	16	T Pryce	Shadow	DN5	Cosworth	V8	29	58m 31.540s	15	8
4	2	J Mass	McLaren	M23	Cosworth	V8	29	59m 09.350s	9	5
5	5	R Peterson	JPS Lotus	72E	Cosworth	V8	29	59m 20.020s	13	7
6	12	N Lauda	Ferrari	312T	Ferrari	F12	29	59m 26.970s	1	1
7	11	C Regazzoni	Ferrari	312T	Ferrari	F12	29	59m 35.760s	5	3
8	3	J Scheckter	Tyrrell	007	Cosworth	V8	28		10	5
9	1	E Fittipaldi	McLaren	M23	Cosworth	V8	28		3	2
10	18	J Watson	Surtees	TS16	Cosworth	V8	28		18	9
11	4	P Depailler	Tyrrell	007	Cosworth	V8	28		7	4
12	31	C Amon	Ensign	N175	Cosworth	V8	28		23	12
13	25	B Lunger	Hesketh	308	Cosworth	V8	28		17	9
14	7	C Reutemann	Brabham	BT44B	Cosworth	V8	28		11	6
15	23	T Brise	Hill	GH1	Cosworth	V8	28		16	8
16	22	R Stommelen	Hill	GH1	Cosworth	V8	27		25	13
17	29	L Lombardi	March	751	Cosworth	V8	26		21	11
nc	33	R Wunderink	Ensign	N174	Cosworth	V8	25		27	14
r	32	H Ertl	Hesketh	308	Cosworth	V8	23	electrics	26	13
r	21	J Laffite	Williams	FW04	Cosworth	V8	21	handling	12	6
r	8	C Pace	Brabham	BT44B	Cosworth	V8	17	engine	6	3
r	20	J Vonlanthen	Williams	FW	Cosworth	V8	14	engine	28	14
r	10	H-J Stuck	March	751	Cosworth	V8	10	accident	4	2
r	17	J-P Jarier	Shadow	DN7	Matra	V12	10	fuel injection	14	7
r	14	B Evans	Stanley BRM	P201	BRM	V12	2	engine	24	12
r	27	M Andretti	Parnelli	VPJ4	Cosworth	V8	1	spin	19	10
ns	30	W Fittipaldi	Copersucar	FD03	Cosworth	V8		accident/ injury		
ns	28	M Donohue	March	751	Cosworth	V8		tyre/ fatal accident	20	10
ns	6	B Henton	JPS Lotus	72F	Cosworth	V8		accident	22	11
nq	35	T Trimmer	Maki	F101C	Cosworth	V8				

Winning speed: 177.499 km/h, 110.293 mph
Pole Position speed: 224.350 km/h, 139.405 mph (N Lauda, 1 min:34.850 sec)
Fastest Lap speed: 186.827 km/h, 116.089 mph (V Brambilla, 1 min:53.900 sec)
Lap Leaders: N Lauda 1-14 (14); J Hunt 15-18 (4); V Brambilla 19-29 (11).

Scheduled for 54 laps, but stopped early because of rain. Half points were awarded. Also the Grand Prix of Europe.

7 Sep 1975 — ITALY: Monza (Round:13) (Race: 263)

52 laps x 5.780 km, 3.592 miles = 300.560 km, 186.759 miles

POS.	NO.	DRIVER	CAR	MODEL	ENGINE		LAPS	TIME/REASON FOR RETIREMENT	GRID:POS	ROW
1	11	C Regazzoni	Ferrari	312T	Ferrari	F12	52	1h 22m 42.600s	2	1
2	1	E Fittipaldi	McLaren	M23	Cosworth	V8	52	1h 22m 59.200s	3	2
3	12	N Lauda	Ferrari	312T	Ferrari	F12	52	1h 23m 05.800s	1	1
4	7	C Reutemann	Brabham	BT44B	Cosworth	V8	52	1h 23m 37.700s	7	4
5	24	J Hunt	Hesketh	308C	Cosworth	V8	52	1h 23m 39.700s	8	4
6	16	T Pryce	Shadow	DN5	Cosworth	V8	52	1h 23m 58.500s	14	7
7	4	P Depailler	Tyrrell	007	Cosworth	V8	51		12	6
8	3	J Scheckter	Tyrrell	007	Cosworth	V8	51		4	2
9	34	H Ertl	Hesketh	308	Cosworth	V8	51		17	9
10	25	B Lunger	Hesketh	308	Cosworth	V8	50		21	11
11	30	A Merzario	Copersucar	FD03	Cosworth	V8	48		26	13
12	32	C Amon	Ensign	N175	Cosworth	V8	48		19	10
13	6	J Crawford	JPS Lotus	72F	Cosworth	V8	46		25	13
14	20	R Zorzi	Williams	FW	Cosworth	V8	46		22	11
r	17	J-P Jarier	Shadow	DN7	Matra	V12	32	fuel pump	13	7
r	29	L Lombardi	March	751	Cosworth	V8	21	accident	24	12
r	10	H-J Stuck	March	751	Cosworth	V8	15	accident	16	8
r	21	J Laffite	Williams	FW04	Cosworth	V8	7	gearbox	18	9
r	8	C Pace	Brabham	BT44B	Cosworth	V8	6	throttle linkage	10	5
r	22	R Stommelen	Hill	GH1	Cosworth	V8	3	accident	23	12
r	2	J Mass	McLaren	M23	Cosworth	V8	2	accident	5	3
r	9	V Brambilla	March	751	Cosworth	V8	1	clutch	9	5
r	27	M Andretti	Parnelli	VPJ4	Cosworth	V8	1	accident	15	8
r	23	T Brise	Hill	GH1	Cosworth	V8	1	accident	6	3
r	5	R Peterson	JPS Lotus	72E	Cosworth	V8	1	engine	11	6
r	14	B Evans	Stanley BRM	P201	BRM	V12	0	clutch nut loose/ electrics	20	10
nq	31	R Wunderink	Ensign	N174	Cosworth	V8				
nq	35	T Trimmer	Maki	F101C	Cosworth	V8				

Winning speed: 218.034 km/h, 135.480 mph
Pole Position speed: 225.585 km/h, 140.172 mph (N Lauda, 1 min:32.240 sec)
Fastest Lap speed: 223.502 km/h, 138.877 mph (C Regazzoni, 1 min:33.100 sec on lap 47)
Lap Leaders: C Regazzoni 1-52 (52).

5 Oct 1975 — USA: Watkins Glen — (Round:14) (Race: 264)

59 laps x 5.435 km, 3.377 miles = 320.651 km, 199.243 miles

POS.	NO.	DRIVER	CAR	MODEL	ENGINE		LAPS	TIME/REASON FOR RETIREMENT	GRID:POS	ROW
1	12	N Lauda	Ferrari	312T	Ferrari	F12	59	1h 42m 58.175s	1	1
2	1	E Fittipaldi	McLaren	M23	Cosworth	V8	59	1h 43m 03.118s	2	1
3	2	J Mass	McLaren	M23	Cosworth	V8	59	1h 43m 45.812s	9	5
4	24	J Hunt	Hesketh	308C	Cosworth	V8	59	1h 43m 47.650s	15	8
5	5	R Peterson	JPS Lotus	72E	Cosworth	V8	59	1h 43m 48.161s	14	7
6	3	J Scheckter	Tyrrell	007	Cosworth	V8	59	1h 43m 48.496s	10	5
7	9	V Brambilla	March	751	Cosworth	V8	59	1h 44m 42.206s	6	3
8	10	H-J Stuck	March	751	Cosworth	V8	58		13	7
9	28	J Watson	Penske	PC1	Cosworth	V8	57		12	6
10	30	W Fittipaldi	Copersucar	FD03	Cosworth	V8	55		23	12
nc	16	T Pryce	Shadow	DN5	Cosworth	V8	52		7	4
nc	6	B Henton	JPS Lotus	72F	Cosworth	V8	49		19	10
r	25	B Lunger	Hesketh	308	Cosworth	V8	46	accident	18	9
r	31	R Wunderink	Ensign	N175	Cosworth	V8	41	gearbox	22	11
r	11	C Regazzoni	Ferrari	312T	Ferrari	F12	28	withdrew (protest)	11	6
r	17	J-P Jarier	Shadow	DN5	Cosworth	V8	19	wheel bearing	4	2
r	7	C Reutemann	Brabham	BT44B	Cosworth	V8	9	engine	3	2
r	27	M Andretti	Parnelli	VPJ4	Cosworth	V8	9	suspension	5	3
r	23	T Brise	Hill	GH1	Cosworth	V8	5	accident	17	9
r	15	M Leclère	Tyrrell	007	Cosworth	V8	5	engine	20	10
r	4	P Depailler	Tyrrell	007	Cosworth	V8	2	accident	8	4
r	8	C Pace	Brabham	BT44B	Cosworth	V8	2	accident	16	8
ns	21	J Laffite	Williams	FW04	Cosworth	V8		visor cleaning fluid in eyes	21	11
ns	20	L Lombardi	Williams	FW04	Cosworth	V8		ignition	24	12

Winning speed: 186.842 km/h, 116.098 mph
Pole Position speed: 191.809 km/h, 119.185 mph (N Lauda, 1 min:42.003 sec)
Fastest Lap speed: 189.265 km/h, 117.604 mph (E Fittipaldi, 1 min:43.374 sec on lap 43)
Lap Leaders: N Lauda 1-59 (59).

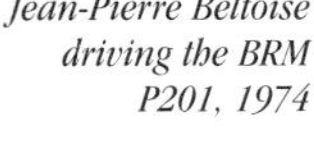
Jean-Pierre Beltoise driving the BRM P201, 1974

Lap Leaders 1975

POS	DRIVER	CAR-ENGINE	GPS	LAPS	KM	MILES
1	N Lauda	Ferrari	8	298	1,537.2	955.2
2	J Hunt	Hesketh-Cosworth	5	88	395.6	245.8
	C Reutemann	Brabham-Cosworth	4	88	512.2	318.3
4	J Scheckter	Tyrrell-Cosworth	2	83	344.9	214.3
5	C Regazzoni	Ferrari	3	60	337.3	209.6
6	E Fittipaldi	McLaren-Cosworth	2	33	179.5	111.5
7	C Pace	Brabham-Cosworth	5	31	168.7	104.8
8	J-P Jarier	Shadow-Cosworth	2	30	232.3	144.4
9	V Brambilla	March-Cosworth	3	28	133.8	83.1
10	M Andretti	Parnelli-Cosworth	1	10	37.9	23.6
11	R Stommelen	Hill-Cosworth	1	8	30.3	18.8
12	J Mass	McLaren-Cosworth	1	3	11.4	7.1
13	T Pryce	Shadow-Cosworth	1	2	9.4	5.9
14	J Ickx	Lotus-Cosworth	1	1	3.8	2.4
	R Peterson	Lotus-Cosworth	1	1	3.3	2.0
			14	**764**	**3,937.7**	**2,446.8**

Driver Points 1975

		RA	BR	ZA	E	MC	B	S	NL	F	GB	D	A	I	USA	TOTAL
1	N Lauda	1	2	2	-	9	9	9	6	9	-	4	0.5	4	9	64.5
2	E Fittipaldi	9	6	-	-	6	-	-	-	3	9	-	-	6	6	45
3	C Reutemann	4	-	6	2	-	4	6	3	-	-	9	-	3	-	37
4	J Hunt	6	1	-	-	-	-	-	9	6	3	-	3	2	3	33
5	C Regazzoni	3	3	-	-	-	2	4	4	-	-	-	-	9	-	25
6	C Pace	-	9	3	-	4	-	-	2	-	6	-	-	-	-	24
7	J Scheckter	-	-	9	-	-	6	-	-	-	4	-	-	-	1	20
	J Mass	-	4	1	4.5	1	-	-	-	4	-	-	1.5	-	4	20
9	P Depailler	2	-	4	-	2	3	-	-	1	-	-	-	-	-	12
10	T Pryce	-	-	-	-	-	1	-	1	-	-	3	2	1	-	8
11	V Brambilla	-	-	-	1	-	-	-	-	-	1	-	4.5	-	-	6.5
12	J Laffite	-	-	-	-	-	-	-	-	-	-	6	-	-	-	6
	R Peterson	-	-	-	-	3	-	-	-	-	-	-	1	-	2	6
14	M Andretti	-	-	-	-	-	-	3	-	2	-	-	-	-	-	5
15	M Donohue	-	-	-	-	-	-	2	-	-	2	-	-	-	-	4
16	J Ickx	-	-	-	3	-	-	-	-	-	-	-	-	-	-	3
17	A Jones	-	-	-	-	-	-	-	-	-	-	2	-	-	-	2
18	J-P Jarier	-	-	-	1.5	-	-	-	-	-	-	-	-	-	-	1.5
19	T Brise	-	-	-	-	-	-	1	-	-	-	-	-	-	-	1
	G van Lennep	-	-	-	-	-	-	-	-	-	-	1	-	-	-	1
21	L Lombardi	-	-	-	0.5	-	-	-	-	-	-	-	-	-	-	0.5

9, 6, 4, 3,2 and 1 point awarded to the first six finishers. Best 7 scores from first 8 races, best 5 from remaining 6 races.
Half points awarded in Spain and Austria where race was stopped early.

Constructor Points 1975

		RA	BR	ZA	E	MC	B	S	NL	F	GB	D	A	I	USA	TOTAL	
1	Ferrari	3	3	2	-	9	9	9	6	9	-	4	0.5	9	9	72.5	
2	Brabham-Cosworth	4	9	6	(2)	4	4	6	3	-	6	9	-	3	-	54	(2)
3	McLaren-Cosworth	9	6	1	4.5	6	-	-	-	4	9	-	1.5	6	6	53	
4	Hesketh-Cosworth	6	1	-	-	-	-	-	9	6	3	-	3	2	3	33	
5	Tyrrell-Cosworth	2	-	9	-	2	6	-	-	1	4	-	-	-	1	25	
6	Shadow-Cosworth	-	-	-	1.5	-	1	-	1	-	-	3	2	1	-	9.5	
7	Lotus-Cosworth	-	-	-	3	3	-	-	-	-	-	-	1	-	2	9	
8	March-Cosworth	-	-	-	1	-	-	-	-	-	2	-	4.5	-	-	7.5	
9	Williams-Cosworth	-	-	-	-	-	-	-	-	-	-	6	-	-	-	6	
10	Parnelli-Cosworth	-	-	-	-	-	-	3	-	2	-	-	-	-	-	5	
11	Hill-Cosworth	-	-	-	-	-	-	1	-	-	-	2	-	-	-	3	
12	Penske-Cosworth	-	-	-	-	-	-	2	-	-	-	-	-	-	-	2	
13	Ensign-Cosworth	-	-	-	-	-	-	-	-	-	-	1	-	-	-	1	

9, 6, 4, 3,2 and 1 point awarded to the first six finishers. Points only for highest placed car.
Best 7 scores from first 8 races, best 5 from remaining 6 races.

RACE ENTRANTS & RESULTS 1976

At the end of the previous season, the sports world was devastated by the air crash that killed Graham Hill, Tony Brise and four members of the racing team. Emerson Fittipaldi's sudden switch to the family team, left a vacancy at McLaren, quickly filled by Hunt after the works Hesketh closure. Alfa and Matra engines made their full return and Tyrrell unveiled its unique 6-wheeler. Lauda was lucky to survive a fiery crash at the Nürburgring, but made an incredibly swift return to the tracks.

FERRARI
Scuderia Ferrari SpA SEFAC: Lauda, Regazzoni, Reutemann

TYRRELL
Elf Team Tyrrell: J Scheckter, Depailler
Scuderia Gulf Rondini: Pesenti-Rossi
Lexington Racing: I Scheckter
Heros Racing: Hoshino
OASC Racing Team: (Stuppacher)

LOTUS
John Player Team Lotus: Peterson, Evans, Andretti, Nilsson

BRABHAM
Martini Racing: Reutemann, Stommelen, Perkins, Pace
RAM Racing: Kessel, Evans, Neve, Lombardi, (de Villota, Nelleman, Magee)

MARCH
Beta Team March: Brambilla
March Engineering: Peterson, Stuck
Ovoro Team March: Merzario
Lavazza March: Lombardi

McLAREN
Marlboro Team McLaren: Hunt, Mass

BRM
Stanley BRM: Ashley

SHADOW
Shadow Racing Team: Pryce, Jarier
Team P R Reilly: (Wilds)

SURTEES
Team Surtees: Jones, Lunger, Andersson, Takahara
Team Norev Racing/BS Fabrications: Pescarolo
Shellsport: (Galica)

WILLIAMS
Walter Wolf Racing*: Ickx, Merzario, Zorzi, Leclère, Brown, Binder (Amon, Kuwashima)
** known as Frank Williams Racing Cars for first 3 GPs* Mapfre-Williams: (Zapico)

ENSIGN
Team Ensign: Amon, Neve, Binder, Ickx
HB Bewaking Alarm Systems: Perkins (BORO)

HESKETH
Hesketh Racing: Ertl
Penthouse Rizla Racing with Hesketh: Edwards, Stommelen, Riberio

LIGIER
Ligier Gitanes: Laffite

PARNELLI
Vel's Parnelli Jones Racing: Andretti

PENSKE
Citibank Team Penske: Watson

FITTIPALDI (COPERSUCAR)
Copersucar-Fittipaldi: Fittipaldi, Hoffman

KOJIMA
Kojima Engineering: Hasemi

MAKI
Maki Engineering: (Trimmer)

25 Jan 1976 — BRAZIL: Interlagos — (Round: 1) (Race: 265)
40 laps x 7.960 km, 4.946 miles = 318.400 km, 197.845 miles

POS.	NO.	DRIVER	CAR	MODEL	ENGINE		LAPS	TIME/REASON FOR RETIREMENT	GRID:POS	ROW
1	1	N Lauda	Ferrari	312T	Ferrari	F12	40	1h 45m 16.780s	2	1
2	4	P Depailler	Tyrrell	007	Cosworth	V8	40	1h 45m 38.250s	9	5
3	16	T Pryce	Shadow	DN5B	Cosworth	V8	40	1h 45m 40.620s	12	6
4	34	H-J Stuck	March	761	Cosworth	V8	40	1h 46m 44.950s	14	7
5	3	J Scheckter	Tyrrell	007	Cosworth	V8	40	1h 47m 13.240s	13	7
6	12	J Mass	McLaren	M23	Cosworth	V8	40	1h 47m 15.050s	6	3
7	2	C Regazzoni	Ferrari	312T	Ferrari	F12	40	1h 47m 32.020s	4	2
8	20	J Ickx	Wolf Williams	FW05	Cosworth	V8	39		19	10
9	21	R Zorzi	Wolf Williams	FW04	Cosworth	V8	39		17	9
10	8	C Pace	Brabham	BT45	Alfa Romeo	F12	39		10	5
11	31	I Hoffman	Copersucar	FD03	Cosworth	V8	39		20	10
12r	7	C Reutemann	Brabham	BT45	Alfa Romeo	F12	37	out of fuel	15	8
13	30	E Fittipaldi	Copersucar	FD04	Cosworth	V8	37		5	3
14	10	L Lombardi	March	761	Cosworth	V8	36		22	11
r	17	J-P Jarier	Shadow	DN5B	Cosworth	V8	33	accident	3	2
r	11	J Hunt	McLaren	M23	Cosworth	V8	32	accident	1	1
r	9	V Brambilla	March	761	Cosworth	V8	15	oil leak	7	4
r	26	J Laffite	Ligier	JS5	Matra	V12	14	gear linkage	11	6
r	5	R Peterson	JPS Lotus	77	Cosworth	V8	10	accident	18	9
r	6	M Andretti	JPS Lotus	77	Cosworth	V8	6	accident	16	8
r	28	J Watson	Penske	PC3	Cosworth	V8	2	fuel line/ fire	8	4
r	14	I Ashley	Stanley BRM	P201B	BRM	V12	2	oil pump	21	11

Winning speed: 181.460 km/h, 112.754 mph
Pole Position speed: 187.908 km/h, 116.761 mph (J Hunt, 2 min:32.500 sec)
Fastest Lap speed: 184.794 km/h, 114.826 mph (J-P Jarier, 2 min:35.070 sec on lap 31)
Lap Leaders: C Regazzoni 1-8 (8); N Lauda 9-40 (32).

6 Mar 1976 — SOUTH AFRICA: Kyalami — (Round: 2) (Race: 266)
78 laps x 4.104 km, 2.550 miles = 320.112 km, 198.908 miles

POS.	NO.	DRIVER	CAR	MODEL	ENGINE		LAPS	TIME/REASON FOR RETIREMENT	GRID:POS	ROW
1	1	N Lauda	Ferrari	312T	Ferrari	F12	78	1h 42m 18.400s	2	1
2	11	J Hunt	McLaren	M23	Cosworth	V8	78	1h 42m 19.700s	1	1
3	12	J Mass	McLaren	M23	Cosworth	V8	78	1h 43m 04.300s	4	2
4	3	J Scheckter	Tyrrell	007	Cosworth	V8	78	1h 43m 26.800s	12	6
5	28	J Watson	Penske	PC3	Cosworth	V8	77		3	2
6	27	M Andretti	Parnelli	VPJ4B	Cosworth	V8	77		13	7
7	16	T Pryce	Shadow	DN5B	Cosworth	V8	77		7	4
8	9	V Brambilla	March	761	Cosworth	V8	77		5	3
9	4	P Depailler	Tyrrell	007	Cosworth	V8	77		6	3
10	5	B Evans	JPS Lotus	77	Cosworth	V8	77		23	12
11	18	B Lunger	Surtees	TS19	Cosworth	V8	77		20	10
12	34	H-J Stuck	March	761	Cosworth	V8	76		17	9
13	21	M Leclère	Wolf Williams	FW05	Cosworth	V8	76		22	11
14	22	C Amon	Ensign	N174	Cosworth	V8	76		18	9

POS.	NO.	DRIVER	CAR	MODEL	ENGINE		LAPS	TIME/REASON FOR RETIREMENT	GRID:POS	ROW
15	24	H Ertl	Hesketh	308D	Cosworth	V8	74		24	12
16	20	J Ickx	Wolf Williams	FW05	Cosworth	V8	73		19	10
17r	30	E Fittipaldi	Copersucar	FD04	Cosworth	V8	70	engine	21	11
r	2	C Regazzoni	Ferrari	312T	Ferrari	F12	52	engine	9	5
r	26	J Laffite	Ligier	JS5	Matra	V12	49	engine	8	4
r	17	J-P Jarier	Shadow	DN5B	Cosworth	V8	28	radiator	15	8
r	8	C Pace	Brabham	BT45	Alfa Romeo	F12	22	engine	14	7
r	6	G Nilsson	JPS Lotus	77	Cosworth	V8	18	clutch	25	13
r	7	C Reutemann	Brabham	BT45	Alfa Romeo	F12	16	engine	11	6
r	10	R Peterson	March	761	Cosworth	V8	15	accident	10	5
r	15	I Scheckter	Tyrrell	007	Cosworth	V8	0	accident	16	8

Winning speed: 187.737 km/h, 116.654 mph
Pole Position speed: 194.145 km/h, 120.636 mph (J Hunt, 1 min:16.100 sec)
Fastest Lap speed: 189.488 km/h, 117.743 mph (N Lauda, 1 min:17.970 sec on lap 6)
Lap Leaders: N Lauda 1-78 (78).

First 2 rows of the grid, chose to line up on the other side.

28 Mar 1976 — USA West: Long Beach (Round: 3) (Race: 267)
80 laps x 3.251 km, 2.020 miles = 260.070 km, 161.600 miles

POS.	NO.	DRIVER	CAR	MODEL	ENGINE		LAPS	TIME/REASON FOR RETIREMENT	GRID:POS	ROW
1	2	C Regazzoni	Ferrari	312T	Ferrari	F12	80	1h 53m 18.471s	1	1
2	1	N Lauda	Ferrari	312T	Ferrari	F12	80	1h 54m 00.885s	4	2
3	4	P Depailler	Tyrrell	007	Cosworth	V8	80	1h 54m 08.443s	2	1
4	26	J Laffite	Ligier	JS5	Matra	V12	80	1h 54m 31.299s	12	6
5	12	J Mass	McLaren	M23	Cosworth	V8	80	1h 54m 40.763s	14	7
6	30	E Fittipaldi	Copersucar	FD04	Cosworth	V8	79		16	8
7	17	J-P Jarier	Shadow	DN5B	Cosworth	V8	79		7	4
8	22	C Amon	Ensign	N174	Cosworth	V8	78		17	9
9	8	C Pace	Brabham	BT45	Alfa Romeo	F12	77		13	7
10	10	R Peterson	March	761	Cosworth	V8	77		6	3
nc	19	A Jones	Surtees	TS19	Cosworth	V8	70		19	10
nc	28	J Watson	Penske	PC3	Cosworth	V8	69		9	5
r	3	J Scheckter	Tyrrell	007	Cosworth	V8	34	suspension	11	6
r	16	T Pryce	Shadow	DN5B	Cosworth	V8	32	drive shaft	5	3
r	27	M Andretti	Parnelli	VPJ4B	Cosworth	V8	15	water leak	15	8
r	11	J Hunt	McLaren	M23	Cosworth	V8	3	accident	3	2
r	34	H-J Stuck	March	761	Cosworth	V8	2	accident	18	9
r	6	G Nilsson	JPS Lotus	77	Cosworth	V8	0	suspension/ accident	20	10
r	7	C Reutemann	Brabham	BT45	Alfa Romeo	F12	0	accident	10	5
r	9	V Brambilla	March	761	Cosworth	V8	0	accident	8	4
nq	21	M Leclère	Wolf Williams	FW05	Cosworth	V8				
nq	31	I Hoffman	Copersucar	FD04	Cosworth	V8				
nq	35	A Merzario	March	761	Cosworth	V8				
nq	5	B Evans	JPS Lotus	77	Cosworth	V8				
nq	20	J Ickx	Wolf Williams	FW05	Cosworth	V8				
nq	24	H Ertl	Hesketh	308D	Cosworth	V8				
nq	18	B Lunger	Surtees	TS19	Cosworth	V8				

Winning speed: 137.715 km/h, 85.572 mph
Pole Position speed: 140.834 km/h, 87.510 mph (C Regazzoni, 1 min:23.099 sec)
Fastest Lap speed: 140.873 km/h, 87.534 mph (C Regazzoni, 1 min:23.076 sec on lap 61)
Lap Leaders: C Regazzoni 1-80 (80).

2 May 1976 — SPAIN: Járama (Round: 4) (Race: 268)
75 laps x 3.404 km, 2.115 miles = 255.300 km, 158.636 miles

POS.	NO.	DRIVER	CAR	MODEL	ENGINE		LAPS	TIME/REASON FOR RETIREMENT	GRID:POS	ROW
1	11	J Hunt	McLaren	M23	Cosworth	V8	75	1h 42m 20.430s	1	1
2	1	N Lauda	Ferrari	312T2	Ferrari	F12	75	1h 42m 51.400s	2	1
3	6	G Nilsson	JPS Lotus	77	Cosworth	V8	75	1h 43m 08.450s	7	4
4	7	C Reutemann	Brabham	BT45	Alfa Romeo	F12	74		12	6
5	22	C Amon	Ensign	N176	Cosworth	V8	74		10	5
6	8	C Pace	Brabham	BT45	Alfa Romeo	F12	74		11	6
7	20	J Ickx	Wolf Williams	FW05	Cosworth	V8	74		21	11
8	16	T Pryce	Shadow	DN5B	Cosworth	V8	74		22	11
9	19	A Jones	Surtees	TS19	Cosworth	V8	74		20	10
10	21	M Leclère	Wolf Williams	FW05	Cosworth	V8	73		23	12
11	2	C Regazzoni	Ferrari	312T2	Ferrari	F12	72		5	3
12	26	J Laffite	Ligier	JS5	Matra	V12	72		8	4
13	37	L Perkins	Boro	N175	Cosworth	V8	72		24	12
r	12	J Mass	McLaren	M23	Cosworth	V8	65	engine	4	2
r	17	J-P Jarier	Shadow	DN5B	Cosworth	V8	61	electrics	15	8
r	3	J Scheckter	Tyrrell	007	Cosworth	V8	53	oil pump drive	14	7
r	28	J Watson	Penske	PC3	Cosworth	V8	51	engine	13	7
r	35	A Merzario	March	761	Cosworth	V8	36	gear linkage	18	9
r	5	M Andretti	JPS Lotus	77	Cosworth	V8	34	gear selection	9	5
r	4	P Depailler	Tyrrell	P34	Cosworth	V8	25	brakes/ accident	3	2
r	9	V Brambilla	March	761	Cosworth	V8	21	accident	6	3
r	34	H-J Stuck	March	761	Cosworth	V8	16	gearbox	17	9
r	10	R Peterson	March	761	Cosworth	V8	11	transmission	16	8
r	30	E Fittipaldi	Copersucar	FD04	Cosworth	V8	3	gear linkage	19	10
nq	18	B Lunger	Surtees	TS19	Cosworth	V8				
nq	32	L Kessel	Brabham	BT44B	Cosworth	V8				

POS.	NO.	DRIVER	CAR	MODEL	ENGINE		LAPS	TIME/REASON FOR RETIREMENT	GRID:POS	ROW
nq	25	E Zapico	Williams	FW04	Cosworth	V8				
nq	33	E de Villota	Brabham	BT44B	Cosworth	V8				
nq	24	H Ertl	Hesketh	308D	Cosworth	V8				
nq	31	I Hoffman	Copersucar	FD04	Cosworth	V8				

Winning speed: 149.677 km/h, 93.005 mph
Pole Position speed: 156.067 km/h, 96.976 mph (J Hunt, 1 min:18.520 sec)
Fastest Lap speed: 151.420 km/h, 94.088 mph (J Mass, 1 min:20.930 sec on lap 52)
Lap Leaders: N Lauda 1-31 (31); J Hunt 32-75 (44).

J Hunt originally disqualified for car being too wide, but reinstated after appeal.
J Laffite originally disqualified for rear aerofoil irregularities, but reinstated after appeal.

16 May 1976 — BELGIUM: Zolder (Round: 5) (Race: 269)

70 laps x 4.262 km, 2.648 miles = 298.340 km, 185.380 miles

POS.	NO.	DRIVER	CAR	MODEL	ENGINE		LAPS	TIME/REASON FOR RETIREMENT	GRID:POS	ROW
1	1	N Lauda	Ferrari	312T2	Ferrari	F12	70	1h 42m 53.230s	1	1
2	2	C Regazzoni	Ferrari	312T2	Ferrari	F12	70	1h 42m 56.690s	2	1
3	26	J Laffite	Ligier	JS5	Matra	V12	70	1h 43m 28.610s	6	3
4	3	J Scheckter	Tyrrell	P34	Cosworth	V8	70	1h 44m 24.310s	7	4
5	19	A Jones	Surtees	TS19	Cosworth	V8	69		16	8
6	12	J Mass	McLaren	M23	Cosworth	V8	69		18	9
7	28	J Watson	Penske	PC3	Cosworth	V8	69		17	9
8	37	L Perkins	Boro	N175	Cosworth	V8	69		20	10
9	17	J-P Jarier	Shadow	DN5B	Cosworth	V8	69		14	7
10	16	T Pryce	Shadow	DN5B	Cosworth	V8	68		13	7
11	21	M Leclère	Wolf Williams	FW05	Cosworth	V8	68		25	13
12	32	L Kessel	Brabham	BT44B	Cosworth	V8	63		23	12
r	18	B Lunger	Surtees	TS19	Cosworth	V8	62	electrics	26	13
r	8	C Pace	Brabham	BT45	Alfa Romeo	F12	58	electrics	9	5
r	22	C Amon	Ensign	N176	Cosworth	V8	51	wheel lost/ accident	8	4
r	11	J Hunt	McLaren	M23	Cosworth	V8	35	transmission	3	2
r	34	H-J Stuck	March	761	Cosworth	V8	33	suspension	15	8
r	24	H Ertl	Hesketh	308D	Cosworth	V8	31	engine	24	12
r	4	P Depailler	Tyrrell	P34	Cosworth	V8	29	engine	4	2
r	5	M Andretti	JPS Lotus	77	Cosworth	V8	28	cv joint	11	6
r	33	P Neve	Brabham	BT44B	Cosworth	V8	24	cv joint	19	10
r	35	A Merzario	March	761	Cosworth	V8	21	engine	21	11
r	7	C Reutemann	Brabham	BT45	Alfa Romeo	F12	17	engine	12	6
r	10	R Peterson	March	761	Cosworth	V8	16	accident	10	5
r	6	G Nilsson	JPS Lotus	77	Cosworth	V8	7	accident	22	11
r	9	V Brambilla	March	761	Cosworth	V8	6	drive shaft	5	3
nq	30	E Fittipaldi	Copersucar	FD04	Cosworth	V8				
nq	20	J Ickx	Wolf Williams	FW05	Cosworth	V8				
nq	25	G Edwards	Hesketh	308D	Cosworth	V8				

Winning speed: 173.981 km/h, 108.107 mph
Pole Position speed: 177.276 km/h, 110.154 mph (N Lauda, 1 min:26.550 sec)
Fastest Lap speed: 178.451 km/h, 110.884 mph (N Lauda, 1 min:25.980 sec)
Lap Leaders: N Lauda 1-70 (70).

30 May 1976 — MONACO: Monte Carlo (Round: 6) (Race: 270)

78 laps x 3.312 km, 2.058 miles = 258.336 km, 160.523 miles

POS.	NO.	DRIVER	CAR	MODEL	ENGINE		LAPS	TIME/REASON FOR RETIREMENT	GRID:POS	ROW
1	1	N Lauda	Ferrari	312T2	Ferrari	F12	78	1h 59m 51.470s	1	1
2	3	J Scheckter	Tyrrell	P34	Cosworth	V8	78	2h 00m 02.600s	5	3
3	4	P Depailler	Tyrrell	P34	Cosworth	V8	78	2h 00m 56.310s	4	2
4	34	H-J Stuck	March	761	Cosworth	V8	77		6	3
5	12	J Mass	McLaren	M23	Cosworth	V8	77		11	6
6	30	E Fittipaldi	Copersucar	FD04	Cosworth	V8	77		7	4
7	16	T Pryce	Shadow	DN5B	Cosworth	V8	77		15	8
8	17	J-P Jarier	Shadow	DN5B	Cosworth	V8	76		10	5
9	8	C Pace	Brabham	BT45	Alfa Romeo	F12	76		13	7
10	28	J Watson	Penske	PC3	Cosworth	V8	76		17	9
11	21	M Leclère	Wolf Williams	FW05	Cosworth	V8	76		18	9
12r	26	J Laffite	Ligier	JS5	Matra	V12	75	accident	8	4
13	22	C Amon	Ensign	N176	Cosworth	V8	74		12	6
14r	2	C Regazzoni	Ferrari	312T2	Ferrari	F12	73	accident	2	1
r	6	G Nilsson	JPS Lotus	77	Cosworth	V8	39	engine	16	8
r	10	R Peterson	March	761	Cosworth	V8	26	accident	3	2
r	11	J Hunt	McLaren	M23	Cosworth	V8	24	engine	14	7
r	9	V Brambilla	March	761	Cosworth	V8	9	suspension	9	5
r	19	A Jones	Surtees	TS19	Cosworth	V8	1	accident	19	10
r	7	C Reutemann	Brabham	BT45	Alfa Romeo	F12	0	accident	20	10
nq	20	J Ickx	Wolf Williams	FW05	Cosworth	V8				
nq	38	H Pescarolo	Surtees	TS19	Cosworth	V8				
nq	37	L Perkins	Boro	N175	Cosworth	V8				
nq	24	H Ertl	Hesketh	308D	Cosworth	V8				
nq	35	A Merzario	March	761	Cosworth	V8				

Winning speed: 129.321 km/h, 80.356 mph
Pole Position speed: 132.997 km/h, 82.641 mph (N Lauda, 1 min:29.650 sec)
Fastest Lap speed: 132.069 km/h, 82.064 mph (C Regazzoni, 1 min:30.280 sec on lap 60)
Lap Leaders: N Lauda 1-78 (78).

13 Jun 1976 — SWEDEN: Anderstorp — (Round: 7) (Race: 271)

72 laps x 4.018 km, 2.497 miles = 289.296 km, 179.760 miles

POS.	NO.	DRIVER	CAR	MODEL	ENGINE		LAPS	TIME/REASON FOR RETIREMENT	GRID:POS	ROW
1	3	J Scheckter	Tyrrell	P34	Cosworth	V8	72	1h 46m 53.729s	1	1
2	4	P Depailler	Tyrrell	P34	Cosworth	V8	72	1h 47m 13.495s	4	2
3	1	N Lauda	Ferrari	312T2	Ferrari	F12	72	1h 47m 27.595s	5	3
4	26	J Laffite	Ligier	JS5	Matra	V12	72	1h 47m 49.548s	7	4
5	11	J Hunt	McLaren	M23	Cosworth	V8	72	1h 47m 53.212s	8	4
6	2	C Regazzoni	Ferrari	312T2	Ferrari	F12	72	1h 47m 54.095s	11	6
7	10	R Peterson	March	761	Cosworth	V8	72	1h 47m 57.222s	9	5
8	8	C Pace	Brabham	BT45	Alfa Romeo	F12	72	1h 48m 05.342s	10	5
9	16	T Pryce	Shadow	DN5B	Cosworth	V8	71		12	6
10	9	V Brambilla	March	761	Cosworth	V8	71		15	8
11	12	J Mass	McLaren	M23	Cosworth	V8	71		13	7
12	17	J-P Jarier	Shadow	DN5B	Cosworth	V8	71		14	7
13	19	A Jones	Surtees	TS19	Cosworth	V8	71		18	9
14r	35	A Merzario	March	761	Cosworth	V8	70	engine	19	10
15	18	B Lunger	Surtees	TS19	Cosworth	V8	70		24	12
r	24	H Ertl	Hesketh	308D	Cosworth	V8	54	spin	23	12
r	34	H-J Stuck	March	761	Cosworth	V8	52	engine	20	10
r	5	M Andretti	JPS Lotus	77	Cosworth	V8	45	engine	2	1
r	22	C Amon	Ensign	N176	Cosworth	V8	38	suspension/ accident	3	2
r	21	M Leclère	Wolf Williams	FW05	Cosworth	V8	20	engine	25	13
r	37	L Perkins	Boro	N175	Cosworth	V8	18	engine	22	11
r	30	E Fittipaldi	Copersucar	FD04	Cosworth	V8	10	handling	21	11
r	32	L Kessel	Brabham	BT44B	Cosworth	V8	5	accident	26	13
r	6	G Nilsson	JPS Lotus	77	Cosworth	V8	2	accident	6	3
r	7	C Reutemann	Brabham	BT45	Alfa Romeo	F12	2	engine	16	8
r	28	J Watson	Penske	PC4	Cosworth	V8	0	throttle jammed/ accident	17	9
nq	33	J Nelleman	Brabham	BT44B	Cosworth	V8				

Winning speed: 162.381 km/h, 100.899 mph
Pole Position speed: 168.865 km/h, 104.928 mph (J Scheckter, 1 min:25.659 sec)
Fastest Lap speed: 164.369 km/h, 102.134 mph (M Andretti, 1 min:28.002 sec on lap 11)
Lap Leaders: M Andretti 1-45 (45); J Scheckter 46-72 (27).

M Andretti was given a 1 min penalty for jumping the start but led until lap 45. He is shown as a lap leader 'on the road'.

4 Jul 1976 — FRANCE: Paul Ricard — (Round: 8) (Race: 272)

54 laps x 5.810 km, 3.610 miles = 313.740 km, 194.949 miles

POS.	NO.	DRIVER	CAR	MODEL	ENGINE		LAPS	TIME/REASON FOR RETIREMENT	GRID:POS	ROW
1	11	J Hunt	McLaren	M23	Cosworth	V8	54	1h 40m 58.600s	1	1
2	4	P Depailler	Tyrrell	P34	Cosworth	V8	54	1h 41m 11.300s	3	2
3	28	J Watson	Penske	PC4	Cosworth	V8	54	1h 41m 22.150s	8	4
4	8	C Pace	Brabham	BT45	Alfa Romeo	F12	54	1h 41m 23.420s	5	3
5	5	M Andretti	JPS Lotus	77	Cosworth	V8	54	1h 41m 42.520s	7	4
6	3	J Scheckter	Tyrrell	P34	Cosworth	V8	54	1h 41m 53.670s	9	5
7	34	H-J Stuck	March	761	Cosworth	V8	54	1h 42m 20.150s	17	9
8	16	T Pryce	Shadow	DN5B	Cosworth	V8	54	1h 42m 29.270s	16	8
9	35	A Merzario	March	761	Cosworth	V8	54	1h 42m 52.170s	20	10
10	20	J Ickx	Wolf Williams	FW05	Cosworth	V8	53		19	10
11	7	C Reutemann	Brabham	BT45	Alfa Romeo	F12	53		10	5
12	17	J-P Jarier	Shadow	DN5B	Cosworth	V8	53		15	8
13	21	M Leclère	Wolf Williams	FW05	Cosworth	V8	53		22	11
14	26	J Laffite	Ligier	JS5	Matra	V12	53		13	7
15	12	J Mass	McLaren	M23	Cosworth	V8	53		14	7
16	18	B Lunger	Surtees	TS19	Cosworth	V8	53		23	12
17	25	G Edwards	Hesketh	308D	Cosworth	V8	53		25	13
18	22	P Neve	Ensign	N176	Cosworth	V8	53		26	13
19r	10	R Peterson	March	761	Cosworth	V8	51	fuel metering unit	6	3
r	19	A Jones	Surtees	TS19	Cosworth	V8	44	rear suspension	18	9
r	9	V Brambilla	March	761	Cosworth	V8	28	oil pressure	11	6
r	30	E Fittipaldi	Copersucar	FD04	Cosworth	V8	21	oil pressure	21	11
r	38	H Pescarolo	Surtees	TS19	Cosworth	V8	19	rear suspension	24	12
r	2	C Regazzoni	Ferrari	312T2	Ferrari	F12	17	crankshaft/ spin	4	2
r	1	N Lauda	Ferrari	312T2	Ferrari	F12	8	crankshaft	2	1
r	6	G Nilsson	JPS Lotus	77	Cosworth	V8	8	transmission	12	6
r	24	H Ertl	Hesketh	308D	Cosworth	V8	4	drive shaft (unofficial starter)	27	14
nq	33	D Magee	Brabham	BT44B	Cosworth	V8				
nq	31	I Hoffman	Copersucar	FD04	Cosworth	V8				
nq	32	L Kessel	Brabham	BT44B	Cosworth	V8				

Winning speed: 186.423 km/h, 115.838 mph
Pole Position speed: 193.864 km/h, 120.462 mph (J Hunt, 1 min:47.890 sec)
Fastest Lap speed: 188.432 km/h, 117.086 mph (N Lauda, 1 min:51.000 sec on lap 4)
Lap Leaders: N Lauda 1-8 (8); J Hunt 9-54 (46).

J Watson originally disqualified for rear aerofoil irregularities, but reinstated after appeal

18 Jul 1976 — BRITAIN: Brands Hatch (Round: 9) (Race: 273)

76 laps x 4.207 km, 2.614 miles = 319.719 km, 198.664 miles

POS.	NO.	DRIVER	CAR	MODEL	ENGINE		LAPS	TIME/REASON FOR RETIREMENT	GRID:POS	ROW
dq	11	J Hunt	McLaren	M23	Cosworth	V8	76	used spare car in restart	2	1
1	1	N Lauda	Ferrari	312T2	Ferrari	F12	76	1h 44m 19.660s	1	1
2	3	J Scheckter	Tyrrell	P34	Cosworth	V8	76	1h 44m 35.840s	8	4
3	28	J Watson	Penske	PC4	Cosworth	V8	75		11	6
4	16	T Pryce	Shadow	DN5B	Cosworth	V8	75		20	10
5	19	A Jones	Surtees	TS19	Cosworth	V8	75		19	10
6	30	E Fittipaldi	Copersucar	FD04	Cosworth	V8	74		21	11
7	24	H Ertl	Hesketh	308D	Cosworth	V8	73		23	12
8	8	C Pace	Brabham	BT45	Alfa Romeo	F12	73		16	8
9	17	J-P Jarier	Shadow	DN5B	Cosworth	V8	70		24	12
r	6	G Nilsson	JPS Lotus	77	Cosworth	V8	67	engine	14	7
r	10	R Peterson	March	761	Cosworth	V8	60	fuel pressure	7	4
r	18	B Lunger	Surtees	TS19	Cosworth	V8	55	gearbox	18	9
r	4	P Depailler	Tyrrell	P34	Cosworth	V8	47	engine	5	3
r	7	C Reutemann	Brabham	BT45	Alfa Romeo	F12	46	oil pressure	15	8
r	35	A Merzario	March	761	Cosworth	V8	39	engine	9	5
r/dq	2	C Regazzoni	Ferrari	312T2	Ferrari	F12	36	engine *	4	2
r/dq	26	J Laffite	Ligier	JS5	Matra	V12	31	suspension *	13	7
r	32	B Evans	Brabham	BT44B	Cosworth	V8	24	gearbox	22	11
r	9	V Brambilla	March	761	Cosworth	V8	22	accident/ suspension	10	5
r	38	H Pescarolo	Surtees	TS19	Cosworth	V8	16	fuel pressure	26	13
r	22	C Amon	Ensign	N176	Cosworth	V8	8	water leak	6	3
r	5	M Andretti	JPS Lotus	77	Cosworth	V8	4	engine	3	2
r	12	J Mass	McLaren	M23	Cosworth	V8	1	clutch	12	6
r	34	H-J Stuck	March	761	Cosworth	V8	0	accident	17	9
r	25	G Edwards	Hesketh	308D	Cosworth	V8	0	accident	25	13
nq	20	J Ickx	Wolf Williams	FW05	Cosworth	V8				
nq	13	D Galica	Surtees	TS16	Cosworth	V8				
nq	40	M Wilds	Shadow	DN3	Cosworth	V8				
nq	33	L Lombardi	Brabham	BT44B	Cosworth	V8				

Winning speed: 183.874 km/h, 114.254 mph
Pole Position speed: 190.858 km/h, 118.594 mph (N Lauda, 1 min:19.350 sec)
Fastest Lap speed: 189.520 km/h, 117.762 mph (N Lauda, 1 min:19.910 sec on lap 41)
Lap Leaders: N Lauda 1-44 (44); J Hunt 45-76 (32).

Interrupted after 1st lap accident. Restarted for original distance. J Hunt finished 1st in 1h 43m 27.61s (185.416 km/h, 115.212 mph) and recorded the fastest lap in 1m 19.82s (189.734 km/h, 117.895 mph).

** C Regazzoni and J Laffite disqualified (after their retirement), for restarting in spare cars.*

J-P Jarier and H Ertl qualified 23rd and 24th, but lined up on the grid in reverse order.

1 Aug 1976 — GERMANY: Nürburgring (Round:10) (Race: 274)

14 laps x 22.835 km, 14.189 miles = 319.690 km, 198.646 miles

POS.	NO.	DRIVER	CAR	MODEL	ENGINE		LAPS	TIME/REASON FOR RETIREMENT	GRID:POS	ROW
1	11	J Hunt	McLaren	M23	Cosworth	V8	14	1h 41m 42.700s	1	1
2	3	J Scheckter	Tyrrell	P34	Cosworth	V8	14	1h 42m 10.400s	8	4
3	12	J Mass	McLaren	M23	Cosworth	V8	14	1h 42m 35.100s	9	5
4	8	C Pace	Brabham	BT45	Alfa Romeo	F12	14	1h 42m 36.900s	7	4
5	6	G Nilsson	JPS Lotus	77	Cosworth	V8	14	1h 43m 40.000s	16	8
6	77	R Stommelen	Brabham	BT45	Alfa Romeo	F12	14	1h 44m 13.000s	15	8
7	28	J Watson	Penske	PC4	Cosworth	V8	14	1h 44m 16.600s	19	10
8	16	T Pryce	Shadow	DN5B	Cosworth	V8	14	1h 44m 30.900s	18	9
9	2	C Regazzoni	Ferrari	312T2	Ferrari	F12	14	1h 45m 28.700s	5	3
10	19	A Jones	Surtees	TS19	Cosworth	V8	14	1h 45m 30.000s	14	7
11	17	J-P Jarier	Shadow	DN5B	Cosworth	V8	14	1h 46m 34.400s	23	12
12	5	M Andretti	JPS Lotus	77	Cosworth	V8	14	1h 46m 40.800s	12	6
13	30	E Fittipaldi	Copersucar	FD04	Cosworth	V8	14	1h 47m 07.900s	20	10
14	40	S Pesenti-Rossi	Tyrrell	007	Cosworth	V8	13		26	13
15	25	G Edwards	Hesketh	308D	Cosworth	V8	13		25	13
r	20	A Merzario	Wolf Williams	FW05	Cosworth	V8	3	brakes	21	11
r	9	V Brambilla	March	761	Cosworth	V8	1	brakes/ accident	13	7
r	4	P Depailler	Tyrrell	P34	Cosworth	V8	0	accident	3	2
r	7	C Reutemann	Brabham	BT45	Alfa Romeo	F12	0	engine	10	5
r	10	R Peterson	March	761	Cosworth	V8	0	accident	11	6
r	34	H-J Stuck	March	761	Cosworth	V8	0	clutch *	4	2
r	26	J Laffite	Ligier	JS5	Matra	V12	0	gearbox *	6	3
r	22	C Amon	Ensign	N176	Cosworth	V8	0	withdrew *	17	9
r	1	N Lauda	Ferrari	312T2	Ferrari	F12	0	accident *	2	1
r	18	B Lunger	Surtees	TS19	Cosworth	V8	0	accident *	24	12
r	24	H Ertl	Hesketh	308D	Cosworth	V8	0	accident *	22	11
nq	33	L Lombardi	Brabham	BT44B	Cosworth	V8		car impounded by police		
nq	38	H Pescarolo	Surtees	TS19	Cosworth	V8				

Winning speed: 188.586 km/h, 117.182 mph
Pole Position speed: 192.746 km/h, 119.767 mph (J Hunt, 7 min: 6.500 sec)
Fastest Lap speed: 190.822 km/h, 118.571 mph (J Scheckter, 7 min:10.800 sec on lap 13)
Lap Leaders: J Hunt 1-14 (14).

*Interrupted after 1st lap accident. Restarted for original distance. * retired after first start.*

15 Aug 1976 — AUSTRIA: Österreichring (Round:11) (Race: 275)

54 laps x 5.910 km, 3.672 miles = 319.140 km, 198.304 miles

POS.	NO.	DRIVER	CAR	MODEL	ENGINE		LAPS	TIME/REASON FOR RETIREMENT	GRID:POS	ROW
1	28	J Watson	Penske	PC4	Cosworth	V8	54	1h 30m 07.860s	2	1
2	26	J Laffite	Ligier	JS5	Matra	V12	54	1h 30m 18.650s	5	3
3	6	G Nilsson	JPS Lotus	77	Cosworth	V8	54	1h 30m 19.840s	4	2
4	11	J Hunt	McLaren	M23	Cosworth	V8	54	1h 30m 20.300s	1	1
5	5	M Andretti	JPS Lotus	77	Cosworth	V8	54	1h 30m 29.350s	9	5
6	10	R Peterson	March	761	Cosworth	V8	54	1h 30m 42.200s	3	2
7	12	J Mass	McLaren	M23	Cosworth	V8	54	1h 31m 07.310s	12	6
8	24	H Ertl	Hesketh	308D	Cosworth	V8	53		20	10
9	38	H Pescarolo	Surtees	TS19	Cosworth	V8	52		22	11
10r	18	B Lunger	Surtees	TS19	Cosworth	V8	51	brakes/ accident	16	8
11	39	S Pesenti-Rossi	Tyrrell	007	Cosworth	V8	51		23	12
12	33	L Lombardi	Brabham	BT44B	Cosworth	V8	50		24	12
r	22	H Binder	Ensign	N176	Cosworth	V8	47	throttle linkage	19	10
nc	32	L Kessel	Brabham	BT44B	Cosworth	V8	44		25	13
r	9	V Brambilla	March	761	Cosworth	V8	43	accident	7	4
r	30	E Fittipaldi	Copersucar	FD04	Cosworth	V8	43	accident	17	9
r	17	J-P Jarier	Shadow	DN5B	Cosworth	V8	40	fuel pump	18	9
r	8	C Pace	Brabham	BT45	Alfa Romeo	F12	40	brakes/ accident	8	4
r	19	A Jones	Surtees	TS19	Cosworth	V8	40	engine/ accident	15	8
r	34	H-J Stuck	March	761	Cosworth	V8	26	fuel pressure	11	6
r	4	P Depailler	Tyrrell	P34	Cosworth	V8	24	suspension	13	7
r	20	A Merzario	Wolf Williams	FW05	Cosworth	V8	17	accident	21	11
r	16	T Pryce	Shadow	DN5B	Cosworth	V8	14	brakes	6	3
r	3	J Scheckter	Tyrrell	P34	Cosworth	V8	14	front suspension/ accident	10	5
r	7	C Reutemann	Brabham	BT45	Alfa Romeo	F12	0	clutch	14	7

Winning speed: 212.451 km/h, 132.011 mph
Pole Position speed: 223.911 km/h, 139.132 mph (J Hunt, 1 min:35.020 sec)
Fastest Lap speed: 221.833 km/h, 137.841 mph (J Hunt, 1 min:35.910 sec)
Lap Leaders: J Watson 1-2,12-54 (45); R Peterson 3-9,11 (8); J Scheckter 10 (1).

29 Aug 1976 — NETHERLANDS: Zandvoort (Round:12) (Race: 276)

75 laps x 4.226 km, 2.626 miles = 316.950 km, 196.944 miles

POS.	NO.	DRIVER	CAR	MODEL	ENGINE		LAPS	TIME/REASON FOR RETIREMENT	GRID:POS	ROW
1	11	J Hunt	McLaren	M23	Cosworth	V8	75	1h 44m 52.090s	2	1
2	2	C Regazzoni	Ferrari	312T2	Ferrari	F12	75	1h 44m 53.010s	5	3
3	5	M Andretti	JPS Lotus	77	Cosworth	V8	75	1h 44m 54.180s	6	3
4	16	T Pryce	Shadow	DN8	Cosworth	V8	75	1h 44m 59.030s	3	2
5	3	J Scheckter	Tyrrell	P34	Cosworth	V8	75	1h 45m 14.550s	8	4
6	9	V Brambilla	March	761	Cosworth	V8	75	1h 45m 37.120s	7	4
7	4	P Depailler	Tyrrell	P34	Cosworth	V8	75	1h 45m 48.370s	14	7
8	19	A Jones	Surtees	TS19	Cosworth	V8	74		16	8
9	12	J Mass	McLaren	M26	Cosworth	V8	74		15	8
10	17	J-P Jarier	Shadow	DN5B	Cosworth	V8	74		20	10
11	38	H Pescarolo	Surtees	TS19	Cosworth	V8	74		22	11
12	25	R Stommelen	Hesketh	308D	Cosworth	V8	72		25	13
r	22	J Ickx	Ensign	N176	Cosworth	V8	66	electrics	11	6
r	39	B Hayje	Penske	PC3	Cosworth	V8	63	drive shaft	21	11
r	8	C Pace	Brabham	BT45	Alfa Romeo	F12	53	oil leak	9	5
r	26	J Laffite	Ligier	JS5	Matra	V12	53	oil pressure	10	5
r	10	R Peterson	March	761	Cosworth	V8	52	oil pressure	1	1
r	24	H Ertl	Hesketh	308D	Cosworth	V8	49	spin/ gearbox	24	12
r	28	J Watson	Penske	PC4	Cosworth	V8	47	gearbox	4	2
r	37	L Perkins	Boro	N175	Cosworth	V8	44	accident	19	10
r	30	E Fittipaldi	Copersucar	FD04	Cosworth	V8	40	electrics	17	9
r	7	C Reutemann	Brabham	BT45	Alfa Romeo	F12	11	clutch fluid loss	12	6
r	6	G Nilsson	JPS Lotus	77	Cosworth	V8	10	accident	13	7
r	18	C Andersson	Surtees	TS19	Cosworth	V8	9	engine	26	13
r	34	H-J Stuck	March	761	Cosworth	V8	9	engine	18	9
r	20	A Merzario	Wolf Williams	FW05	Cosworth	V8	5	accident	23	12
nq	40	S Pesenti-Rossi	Tyrrell	007	Cosworth	V8				

Winning speed: 181.342 km/h, 112.681 mph
Pole Position speed: 187.106 km/h, 116.262 mph (R Peterson, 1 min:21.310 sec)
Fastest Lap speed: 184.206 km/h, 114.461 mph (C Regazzoni, 1 min:22.590 sec on lap 49)
Lap Leaders: R Peterson 1-11 (11); J Hunt 12-75 (64).

Also the Grand Prix of Europe.

12 Sep 1976 — ITALY: Monza (Round:13) (Race: 277)

52 laps x 5.800 km, 3.604 miles = 301.600 km, 187.406 miles

POS.	NO.	DRIVER	CAR	MODEL	ENGINE		LAPS	TIME/REASON FOR RETIREMENT	GRID:POS	ROW
1	10	R Peterson	March	761	Cosworth	V8	52	1h 30m 35.600s	8	4
2	2	C Regazzoni	Ferrari	312T2	Ferrari	F12	52	1h 30m 37.900s	9	5
3	26	J Laffite	Ligier	JS5	Matra	V12	52	1h 30m 38.600s	1	1
4	1	N Lauda	Ferrari	312T2	Ferrari	F12	52	1h 30m 55.000s	5	3
5	3	J Scheckter	Tyrrell	P34	Cosworth	V8	52	1h 30m 55.100s	2	1
6	4	P Depailler	Tyrrell	P34	Cosworth	V8	52	1h 31m 11.300s	4	2
7	9	V Brambilla	March	761	Cosworth	V8	52	1h 31m 19.500s	16	8
8	16	T Pryce	Shadow	DN8	Cosworth	V8	52	1h 31m 28.500s	15	8
9	35	C Reutemann	Ferrari	312T2	Ferrari	F12	52	1h 31m 33.100s	7	4
10	22	J Ickx	Ensign	N176	Cosworth	V8	52	1h 31m 48.000s	10	5
11	28	J Watson	Penske	PC4	Cosworth	V8	52	1h 32m 17.800s	27	14
12	19	A Jones	Surtees	TS19	Cosworth	V8	51		18	9
13	6	G Nilsson	JPS Lotus	77	Cosworth	V8	51		12	6
14	18	B Lunger	Surtees	TS19	Cosworth	V8	50		24	12
15	30	E Fittipaldi	Copersucar	FD04	Cosworth	V8	50		20	10
16r	24	H Ertl	Hesketh	308D	Cosworth	V8	49	drive shaft	19	10
17	38	H Pescarolo	Surtees	TS19	Cosworth	V8	49		22	11
18	37	S Pesenti-Rossi	Tyrrell	007	Cosworth	V8	49		21	11
19	17	J-P Jarier	Shadow	DN5B	Cosworth	V8	47		17	9
r	7	R Stommelen	Brabham	BT45	Alfa Romeo	F12	41	fuel system	11	6
r	34	H-J Stuck	March	761	Cosworth	V8	23	accident	6	3
r	5	M Andretti	JPS Lotus	77	Cosworth	V8	23	accident	14	7
r	11	J Hunt	McLaren	M23	Cosworth	V8	11	spin	25	13
r	40	L Perkins	Boro	N175	Cosworth	V8	8	connecting rod	13	7
r	8	C Pace	Brabham	BT45	Alfa Romeo	F12	4	piston	3	2
r	12	J Mass	McLaren	M23	Cosworth	V8	2	ignition	26	13
ns	25	G Edwards	Hesketh	308D	Cosworth	V8		allowed Watson to race	23	12
ns	20	A Merzario	Wolf Williams	FW05	Cosworth	V8		withdrew		
ns	39	O Stuppacher	Tyrrell	007	Cosworth	V8		believed he hadn't qualified		

Winning speed: 199.750 km/h, 124.119 mph
Pole Position speed: 206.019 km/h, 128.014 mph (J Laffite, 1 min:41.350 sec)
Fastest Lap speed: 206.120 km/h, 128.077 mph (R Peterson, 1 min:41.300 sec on lap 50)
Lap Leaders: J Scheckter 1-10 (10); R Peterson 11-52 (42).

3 Oct 1976 — CANADA: Mosport Park (Round:14) (Race: 278)

80 laps x 3.957 km, 2.459 miles = 316.590 km, 196.720 miles

POS.	NO.	DRIVER	CAR	MODEL	ENGINE		LAPS	TIME/REASON FOR RETIREMENT	GRID:POS	ROW
1	11	J Hunt	McLaren	M23	Cosworth	V8	80	1h 40m 09.626s	1	1
2	4	P Depailler	Tyrrell	P34	Cosworth	V8	80	1h 40m 15.957s	4	2
3	5	M Andretti	JPS Lotus	77	Cosworth	V8	80	1h 40m 19.992s	5	3
4	3	J Scheckter	Tyrrell	P34	Cosworth	V8	80	1h 40m 29.371s	7	4
5	12	J Mass	McLaren	M23	Cosworth	V8	80	1h 40m 51.437s	11	6
6	2	C Regazzoni	Ferrari	312T2	Ferrari	F12	80	1h 40m 55.882s	12	6
7	8	C Pace	Brabham	BT45	Alfa Romeo	F12	80	1h 40m 56.098s	10	5
8	1	N Lauda	Ferrari	312T2	Ferrari	F12	80	1h 41m 22.583s	6	3
9	10	R Peterson	March	761	Cosworth	V8	79		2	1
10	28	J Watson	Penske	PC4	Cosworth	V8	79		14	7
11	16	T Pryce	Shadow	DN8	Cosworth	V8	79		13	7
12	6	G Nilsson	JPS Lotus	77	Cosworth	V8	79		15	8
13	22	J Ickx	Ensign	N176	Cosworth	V8	79		16	8
14	9	V Brambilla	March	761	Cosworth	V8	79		3	2
15	18	B Lunger	Surtees	TS19	Cosworth	V8	78		22	11
16	19	A Jones	Surtees	TS19	Cosworth	V8	78		20	10
17	7	L Perkins	Brabham	BT45	Alfa Romeo	F12	78		19	10
18	17	J-P Jarier	Shadow	DN5B	Cosworth	V8	77		18	9
19	38	H Pescarolo	Surtees	TS19	Cosworth	V8	77		21	11
20	25	G Edwards	Hesketh	308D	Cosworth	V8	75		23	12
r	26	J Laffite	Ligier	JS5	Matra	V12	43	oil pressure	9	5
r	30	E Fittipaldi	Copersucar	FD04	Cosworth	V8	41	exhaust/ wing bracket	17	9
r	34	H-J Stuck	March	761	Cosworth	V8	36	handling	8	4
r	20	A Merzario	Wolf Williams	FW05	Cosworth	V8	11	spin	24	12
ns	24	H Ertl	Hesketh	308D	Cosworth	V8		accident		
ns	21	C Amon	Wolf Williams	FW05	Cosworth	V8		accident		
nq	39	O Stuppacher	Tyrrell	007	Cosworth	V8				

Winning speed: 189.650 km/h, 117.843 mph
Pole Position speed: 196.806 km/h, 122.289 mph (J Hunt, 1 min:12.389 sec)
Fastest Lap speed: 192.998 km/h, 119.924 mph (P Depailler, 1 min:13.817 sec on lap 60)
Lap Leaders: R Peterson 1-8 (8); J Hunt 9-80 (72).

10 Oct 1976 USA East: Watkins Glen (Round:15) (Race: 279)

59 laps x 5.435 km, 3.377 miles = 320.651 km, 199.243 miles

POS.	NO.	DRIVER	CAR	MODEL	ENGINE		LAPS	TIME/REASON FOR RETIREMENT	GRID:POS	ROW
1	11	J Hunt	McLaren	M23	Cosworth	V8	59	1h 42m 40.741s	1	1
2	3	J Scheckter	Tyrrell	P34	Cosworth	V8	59	1h 42m 48.771s	2	1
3	1	N Lauda	Ferrari	312T2	Ferrari	F12	59	1h 43m 43.065s	5	3
4	12	J Mass	McLaren	M23	Cosworth	V8	59	1h 43m 43.199s	17	9
5	34	H-J Stuck	March	761	Cosworth	V8	59	1h 43m 48.719s	6	3
6	28	J Watson	Penske	PC4	Cosworth	V8	59	1h 43m 48.931s	8	4
7	2	C Regazzoni	Ferrari	312T2	Ferrari	F12	58		14	7
8	19	A Jones	Surtees	TS19	Cosworth	V8	58		18	9
9	30	E Fittipaldi	Copersucar	FD04	Cosworth	V8	57		15	8
10	17	J-P Jarier	Shadow	DN5B	Cosworth	V8	57		16	8
11	18	B Lunger	Surtees	TS19	Cosworth	V8	57		24	12
12	25	A-D Ribeiro	Hesketh	308D	Cosworth	V8	57		22	11
13	24	H Ertl	Hesketh	308D	Cosworth	V8	54		21	11
14	21	W Brown	Wolf Williams	FW05	Cosworth	V8	54		23	12
nc	38	H Pescarolo	Surtees	TS19	Cosworth	V8	48		26	13
r	16	T Pryce	Shadow	DN8	Cosworth	V8	45	engine	9	5
r	26	J Laffite	Ligier	JS5	Matra	V12	34	tyre burst/ suspension	12	6
r	9	V Brambilla	March	761	Cosworth	V8	34	tyre burst	4	2
r	8	C Pace	Brabham	BT45	Alfa Romeo	F12	31	accident	10	5
r	7	L Perkins	Brabham	BT45	Alfa Romeo	F12	30	front suspension	13	7
r	5	M Andretti	JPS Lotus	77	Cosworth	V8	23	suspension	11	6
r	22	J Ickx	Ensign	N176	Cosworth	V8	14	accident	19	10
r	6	G Nilsson	JPS Lotus	77	Cosworth	V8	13	engine	20	10
r	10	R Peterson	March	761	Cosworth	V8	12	front suspension	3	2
r	20	A Merzario	Wolf Williams	FW05	Cosworth	V8	9	spin	25	13
r	4	P Depailler	Tyrrell	P34	Cosworth	V8	7	fuel line	7	4
nq	39	O Stuppacher	Tyrrell	007	Cosworth	V8				

Winning speed: 187.371 km/h, 116.427 mph
Pole Position speed: 188.812 km/h, 117.323 mph (J Hunt, 1 min:43.622 sec)
Fastest Lap speed: 190.228 km/h, 118.202 mph (J Hunt, 1 min:42.851 sec on lap 53)
Lap Leaders: J Scheckter 1-36,41-45 (41); J Hunt 37-40,46-59 (18).

24 Oct 1976 JAPAN: Fuji (Round:16) (Race: 280)

73 laps x 4.359 km, 2.709 miles = 318.207 km, 197.725 miles

POS.	NO.	DRIVER	CAR	MODEL	ENGINE		LAPS	TIME/REASON FOR RETIREMENT	GRID:POS	ROW
1	5	M Andretti	JPS Lotus	77	Cosworth	V8	73	1h 43m 58.860s	1	1
2	4	P Depailler	Tyrrell	P34	Cosworth	V8	72		13	7
3	11	J Hunt	McLaren	M23	Cosworth	V8	72		2	1
4	19	A Jones	Surtees	TS19	Cosworth	V8	72		20	10
5	2	C Regazzoni	Ferrari	312T2	Ferrari	F12	72		7	4
6	6	G Nilsson	JPS Lotus	77	Cosworth	V8	72		16	8
7	26	J Laffite	Ligier	JS5	Matra	V12	72		11	6
8	24	H Ertl	Hesketh	308D	Cosworth	V8	72		22	11
9	18	N Takahara	Surtees	TS19	Cosworth	V8	70		24	12
10	17	J-P Jarier	Shadow	DN5B	Cosworth	V8	69		15	8
11	51	M Hasemi	Kojima	KE007	Cosworth	V8	66		10	5
r	3	J Scheckter	Tyrrell	P34	Cosworth	V8	58	engine overheating	5	3
r	21	H Binder	Wolf Williams	FW05	Cosworth	V8	49	wheel bearing	25	13
r	16	T Pryce	Shadow	DN8	Cosworth	V8	46	engine	14	7
r	9	V Brambilla	March	761	Cosworth	V8	38	engine	8	4
r	34	H-J Stuck	March	761	Cosworth	V8	37	electrics	18	9
r	12	J Mass	McLaren	M23	Cosworth	V8	35	accident	12	6
r	28	J Watson	Penske	PC4	Cosworth	V8	33	engine	4	2
r	52	K Hoshino	Tyrrell	007	Cosworth	V8	27	tyres	21	11
r	20	A Merzario	Wolf Williams	FW05	Cosworth	V8	23	gearbox	19	10
r	30	E Fittipaldi	Copersucar	FD04	Cosworth	V8	9	withdrew	23	12
r	8	C Pace	Brabham	BT45	Alfa Romeo	F12	7	withdrew	6	3
r	1	N Lauda	Ferrari	312T2	Ferrari	F12	2	withdrew	3	2
r	7	L Perkins	Brabham	BT45	Alfa Romeo	F12	1	withdrew	17	9
r	10	R Peterson	March	761	Cosworth	V8	0	engine	9	5
ns	21	M Kuwashima	Wolf Williams	FW05	Cosworth	V8		sponsors withdrew		
nq	54	T Trimmer	Maki	F102A	Cosworth	V8				

Winning speed: 183.615 km/h, 114.093 mph
Pole Position speed: 215.644 km/h, 133.995 mph (M Andretti, 1 min:12.770 sec)
Fastest Lap speed: 200.593 km/h, 124.643 mph (M Hasemi, 1 min:18.230 sec on lap 25)
Lap Leaders: J Hunt 1-61 (61); P Depailler 62-63 (2); M Andretti 64-73 (10).

Lap Leaders 1976

POS	DRIVER	CAR-ENGINE	GPS	LAPS	KM	MILES
1	J Hunt	McLaren-Cosworth	8	351	1,790.4	1,112.5
2	N Lauda	Ferrari	7	341	1,468.6	912.6
3	C Regazzoni	Ferrari	2	88	323.8	201.2
4	J Scheckter	Tyrrell-Cosworth	4	79	395.2	245.6
5	R Peterson	March-Cosworth	4	69	369.0	229.3
6	M Andretti	Lotus-Cosworth	2	55	224.4	139.4
7	J Watson	Penske-Cosworth	1	45	265.9	165.3
8	P Depailler	Tyrrell-Cosworth	1	2	8.7	5.4
			16	**1,030**	**4,846.1**	**3,011.3**

Driver Points 1976

		BR	ZA	USAW	E	B	MC	S	F	GB	D	A	NL	I	CDN	USAE	J	TOTAL
1	J Hunt	-	6	-	9	-	-	2	9	-	9	3	9	-	9	9	4	69
2	N Lauda	9	9	6	6	9	9	4	-	9	-	-	-	3	-	4	-	68
3	J Scheckter	2	3	-	-	3	6	9	1	6	6	-	2	2	3	6	-	49
4	P Depailler	6	-	4	-	-	4	6	6	-	-	-	-	1	6	-	6	39
5	C Regazzoni	-	-	9	-	6	-	1	-	-	-	-	6	6	1	-	2	31
6	M Andretti	-	1	-	-	-	-	-	2	-	-	2	4	-	4	-	9	22
7	J Watson	-	2	-	-	-	-	-	4	4	-	9	-	-	-	1	-	20
	J Laffite	-	-	3	-	4	-	3	-	-	-	6	-	4	-	-	-	20
9	J Mass	1	4	2	-	1	2	-	-	-	4	-	-	-	2	3	-	19
10	G Nilsson	-	-	-	4	-	-	-	-	-	2	4	-	-	-	-	1	11
11	R Peterson	-	-	-	-	-	-	-	-	-	-	1	-	9	-	-	-	10
	T Pryce	4	-	-	-	-	-	-	-	3	-	-	3	-	-	-	-	10
13	H-J Stuck	3	-	-	-	-	3	-	-	-	-	-	-	-	-	2	-	8
14	C Pace	-	-	-	1	-	-	-	3	-	3	-	-	-	-	-	-	7
	A Jones	-	-	-	-	2	-	-	-	2	-	-	-	-	-	-	3	7
16	C Reutemann	-	-	-	3	-	-	-	-	-	-	-	-	-	-	-	-	3
	E Fittipaldi	-	-	1	-	-	1	-	-	1	-	-	-	-	-	-	-	3
18	C Amon	-	-	-	2	-	-	-	-	-	-	-	-	-	-	-	-	2
19	R Stommelen	-	-	-	-	-	-	-	-	-	1	-	-	-	-	-	-	1
	V Brambilla	-	-	-	-	-	-	-	-	-	-	-	1	-	-	-	-	1

9, 6, 4, 3,2 and 1 point awarded to the first six finishers.
Best 7 scores from first 8 races, best 7 from remaining 8 races.

Constructor Points 1976

		BR	ZA	USAW	E	B	MC	S	F	GB	D	A	NL	I	CDN	USAE	J	TOTAL	
1	Ferrari	9	9	9	6	9	9	4	-	9	-	-	6	6	1	4	2	83	
2	McLaren-Cosworth	1	6	2	9	(1)	2	2	9	-	9	3	9	-	9	9	4	74	(1)
3	Tyrrell-Cosworth	6	3	4	-	3	6	9	6	6	6	-	2	2	6	6	6	71	
4	Lotus-Cosworth	-	-	-	4	-	-	-	2	-	2	4	4	-	4	-	9	29	
5	Penske-Cosworth	-	2	-	-	-	-	-	4	4	-	9	-	-	-	1	-	20	
	Ligier-Matra	-	-	3	-	4	-	3	-	-	-	6	-	4	-	-	-	20	
7	March-Cosworth	3	-	-	-	-	3	-	-	-	-	1	1	9	-	2	-	19	
8	Shadow-Cosworth	4	-	-	-	-	-	-	-	3	-	-	3	-	-	-	-	10	
9	Brabham-Alfa Romeo	-	-	-	3	-	-	-	3	-	3	-	-	-	-	-	-	9	
10	Surtees-Cosworth	-	-	-	-	2	-	-	-	2	-	-	-	-	-	-	3	7	
11	Copersucar-Cosworth	-	-	1	-	-	1	-	-	1	-	-	-	-	-	-	-	3	
12	Ensign-Cosworth	-	-	-	2	-	-	-	-	-	-	-	-	-	-	-	-	2	
13	Parnelli-Cosworth	-	1	-	-	-	-	-	-	-	-	-	-	-	-	-	-	1	

9, 6, 4, 3,2 and 1 point awarded to the first six finishers. Points only for highest placed car.
Best 7 scores from first 8 races, best 7 from remaining 8 races.

Lotus made another significant step forward, with the 78 wing car, the first successful attempt at ground effects. Renault also introduced the first turbo to World Championship racing, complying with the equivalent formula of 1.5 litres. Ferrari appeared with FIAT advertising for the first time and Wolf introduced their new car, enticing Scheckter away from Tyrrell. BRM finally ran out of steam and Tom Pryce was killed in a bizarre accident, colliding with a marshal crossing the track at Kyalami.

McLAREN
Marlboro Team McLaren: Hunt, Mass, Villeneuve, Giacomelli
Chesterfield Racing: Lunger
Iberia Airlines: de Villota

TYRRELL
Elf Team Tyrrell: Peterson, Depailler
Meritsu Racing Team: Takahashi

LOTUS
John Player Team Lotus: Andretti, Nilsson

BRABHAM
Martini Racing: Watson, Pace, Stuck, (Francia)

MARCH
Hollywood March Racing: Riberio
Team Rothmans International: I Scheckter, Stuck, Henton (USAW)
Williams Grand Prix Engineering: Neve
Chesterfield Racing: Lunger
Team Merzario: Merzario
Ram Racing F & S Properties: Hayje, (Sutcliffe, Kozarowitsky, Bleekemolen)
British Formula 1 Racing: (Henton, de Dryver)

FERRARI
Scuderia Ferrari SpA SEFAC: Lauda, Villeneuve, Reutemann

BRM
Rotary Watches-Stanley BRM: Perkins, (Andersson, Edwards, Pilette)

RENAULT
Equipe Renault Elf: Jabouille

SHADOW
Shadow Racing Team: Pryce, Jones, Zorzi, Patrese,
Oliver, Merzario, Jarier

SURTEES
Team Surtees: Binder, Brambilla, Perkins, Schuppan, (Tambay, Leoni)
Melchester Racing: (Trimmer)

WOLF
Walter Wolf Racing: J Scheckter

ENSIGN
Team Tissot Ensign with Castrol: Regazzoni, Ickx
Theodore Racing Hong Kong: Tambay
HB Bewaking Alarm Systems: Henton (BORO)

HESKETH
Hesketh Racing: Ertl, Rebaque, Ashley
Penthouse Rizla Racing: Keegan

LIGIER
Ligier Gitanes: Laffite, Jarier

FITTIPALDI (COPERSUCAR)
Copersucar-Fittipaldi: Fittipaldi, Hoffman

LEC
Lec Refrigeration Racing: Purley

PENSKE
ATS Racing Team: Jarier, Heyer, Binder
Interscope Racing: Ongais

KOJIMA
Kojima Engineering: Takahara
Heros Racing: Hoshino

WILLIAMS
Jolly Club of Switzerland: (Kessel)
Privateer: (McGuire)

9 Jan 1977 — ARGENTINA: Buenos Aires No.15 (Round: 1) (Race: 281)

53 laps x 5.968 km, 3.708 miles = 316.304 km, 196.542 miles

POS.	NO.	DRIVER	CAR	MODEL	ENGINE		LAPS	TIME/REASON FOR RETIREMENT	GRID:POS	ROW
1	20	J Scheckter	Wolf	WR1	Cosworth	V8	53	1h 40m 11.190s	11	6
2	8	C Pace	Brabham	BT45	Alfa Romeo	F12	53	1h 40m 54.430s	6	3
3	12	C Reutemann	Ferrari	312T2	Ferrari	F12	53	1h 40m 57.210s	7	4
4	28	E Fittipaldi	Copersucar	FD04	Cosworth	V8	53	1h 41m 06.670s	16	8
5r	5	M Andretti	JPS Lotus	78	Cosworth	V8	51	rear wheel bearing	8	4
6	22	C Regazzoni	Ensign	N177	Cosworth	V8	51		12	6
7r	19	V Brambilla	Surtees	TS19	Cosworth	V8	48	fuel injection	13	7
r	10	I Scheckter	March	761B	Cosworth	V8	45	battery terminal	17	9
nc	16	T Pryce	Shadow	DN8	Cosworth	V8	45		9	5
r	7	J Watson	Brabham	BT45	Alfa Romeo	F12	41	suspension/ handling	2	1
r	9	A-D Ribeiro	March	761B	Cosworth	V8	39	gear lever	20	10
nc	26	J Laffite	Ligier	JS7	Matra	V12	37		15	8
r	4	P Depailler	Tyrrell	P34	Cosworth	V8	32	engine overheating	3	2
r	1	J Hunt	McLaren	M23	Cosworth	V8	31	suspension	1	1
r	2	J Mass	McLaren	M23	Cosworth	V8	28	engine/ spin	5	3
r	3	R Peterson	Tyrrell	P34	Cosworth	V8	28	spin	14	7
r	29	I Hoffmann	Copersucar	FD04	Cosworth	V8	22	engine	19	10
r	11	N Lauda	Ferrari	312T2	Ferrari	F12	20	fuel metering unit	4	2
r	18	H Binder	Surtees	TS19	Cosworth	V8	18	nose section	18	9
r	17	R Zorzi	Shadow	DN5B	Cosworth	V8	2	gearbox	21	11
ns	6	G Nilsson	JPS Lotus	78	Cosworth	V8		car raced by Andretti	10	5

Winning speed: 189.429 km/h, 117.706 mph
Pole Position speed: 197.689 km/h, 122.838 mph (J Hunt, 1 min:48.680 sec)
Fastest Lap speed: 193.452 km/h, 120.206 mph (J Hunt, 1 min:51.060 sec on lap 21)
Lap Leaders: J Watson 1-10,32-34 (13); J Hunt 11-31 (21); C Pace 35-47 (13); J Scheckter 48-53 (6).

23 Jan 1977 — BRAZIL: Interlagos (Round: 2) (Race: 282)

40 laps x 7.960 km, 4.946 miles = 318.400 km, 197.845 miles

POS.	NO.	DRIVER	CAR	MODEL	ENGINE		LAPS	TIME/REASON FOR RETIREMENT	GRID:POS	ROW
1	12	C Reutemann	Ferrari	312T2	Ferrari	F12	40	1h 45m 07.720s	2	1
2	1	J Hunt	McLaren	M23	Cosworth	V8	40	1h 45m 18.430s	1	1
3	11	N Lauda	Ferrari	312T2	Ferrari	F12	40	1h 46m 55.230s	13	7
4	28	E Fittipaldi	Copersucar	FD04	Cosworth	V8	39		16	8
5	6	G Nilsson	JPS Lotus	78	Cosworth	V8	39		10	5
6	17	R Zorzi	Shadow	DN5B	Cosworth	V8	39		18	9
7	29	I Hoffmann	Copersucar	FD04	Cosworth	V8	38		19	10
r	16	T Pryce	Shadow	DN8	Cosworth	V8	33	engine	12	6
r	8	C Pace	Brabham	BT45	Alfa Romeo	F12	33	accident	5	3
r	18	H Binder	Surtees	TS19	Cosworth	V8	32	suspension	20	10
r	7	J Watson	Brabham	BT45	Alfa Romeo	F12	30	accident	7	4
r	26	J Laffite	Ligier	JS7	Matra	V12	26	accident	14	7

POS.	NO.	DRIVER	CAR	MODEL	ENGINE		LAPS	TIME/REASON FOR RETIREMENT	GRID:POS	ROW
r	4	P Depailler	Tyrrell	P34	Cosworth	V8	23	accident	6	3
r	5	M Andretti	JPS Lotus	78	Cosworth	V8	19	ignition	3	2
r	9	A-D Ribeiro	March	761B	Cosworth	V8	16	dropped valve	21	11
r	2	J Mass	McLaren	M23	Cosworth	V8	12	accident	4	2
r	22	C Regazzoni	Ensign	N177	Cosworth	V8	12	accident	9	5
r	3	R Peterson	Tyrrell	P34	Cosworth	V8	12	accident	8	4
r	20	J Scheckter	Wolf	WR1	Cosworth	V8	11	engine	15	8
r	19	V Brambilla	Surtees	TS19	Cosworth	V8	11	radiator	11	6
r	10	I Scheckter	March	761B	Cosworth	V8	1	transmission	17	9
r	14	L Perkins	Stanley BRM	P207	BRM	V12	1	water loss/ engine	22	11

Winning speed: 181.720 km/h, 112.916 mph
Pole Position speed: 190.900 km/h, 118.620 mph (J Hunt, 2 min:30.110 sec)
Fastest Lap speed: 185.416 km/h, 115.212 mph (J Hunt, 2 min:34.550 sec on lap 33)
Lap Leaders: C Pace 1-6 (6); J Hunt 7-22 (16); C Reutemann 23-40 (18).

5 Mar 1977 — SOUTH AFRICA: Kyalami — (Round: 3) (Race: 283)

78 laps x 4.104 km, 2.550 miles = 320.112 km, 198.908 miles

POS.	NO.	DRIVER	CAR	MODEL	ENGINE		LAPS	TIME/REASON FOR RETIREMENT	GRID:POS	ROW
1	11	N Lauda	Ferrari	312T2	Ferrari	F12	78	1h 42m 21.600s	3	2
2	20	J Scheckter	Wolf	WR1	Cosworth	V8	78	1h 42m 26.800s	5	3
3	4	P Depailler	Tyrrell	P34	Cosworth	V8	78	1h 42m 27.300s	4	2
4	1	J Hunt	McLaren	M23	Cosworth	V8	78	1h 42m 31.100s	1	1
5	2	J Mass	McLaren	M23	Cosworth	V8	78	1h 42m 41.500s	13	7
6	7	J Watson	Brabham	BT45	Alfa Romeo	F12	78	1h 42m 41.800s	11	6
7	19	V Brambilla	Surtees	TS19	Cosworth	V8	78	1h 42m 45.200s	14	7
8	12	C Reutemann	Ferrari	312T2	Ferrari	F12	78	1h 42m 48.300s	8	4
9	22	C Regazzoni	Ensign	N177	Cosworth	V8	78	1h 43m 07.800s	16	8
10	28	E Fittipaldi	Copersucar	FD04	Cosworth	V8	78	1h 43m 33.300s	9	5
11	18	H Binder	Surtees	TS19	Cosworth	V8	77		19	10
12	6	G Nilsson	JPS Lotus	78	Cosworth	V8	77		10	5
13	8	C Pace	Brabham	BT45B	Alfa Romeo	F12	76		2	1
14	30	B Lunger	March	761	Cosworth	V8	76		23	12
15	14	L Perkins	Stanley BRM	P201B	BRM	V12	73		22	11
r	9	A-D Ribeiro	March	761B	Cosworth	V8	66	engine	17	9
r	10	H-J Stuck	March	761B	Cosworth	V8	55	engine	18	9
r	5	M Andretti	JPS Lotus	78	Cosworth	V8	43	accident/ front suspension	6	3
r	33	B Hayje	March	761	Cosworth	V8	33	gearbox	21	11
r	16	T Pryce	Shadow	DN8	Cosworth	V8	22	fatal accident	15	8
r	26	J Laffite	Ligier	JS7	Matra	V12	22	accident	12	6
r	17	R Zorzi	Shadow	DN8	Cosworth	V8	21	engine	20	10
r	3	R Peterson	Tyrrell	P34	Cosworth	V8	5	fuel pressure	7	4

Winning speed: 187.639 km/h, 116.593 mph
Pole Position speed: 194.502 km/h, 120.858 mph (J Hunt, 1 min:15.960 sec)
Fastest Lap speed: 190.318 km/h, 118.258 mph (J Watson, 1 min:17.630 sec on lap 7)
Lap Leaders: J Hunt 1-6 (6); N Lauda 7-78 (72).

3 Apr 1977 — USA West: Long Beach — (Round: 4) (Race: 284)

80 laps x 3.251 km, 2.020 miles = 260.070 km, 161.600 miles

POS.	NO.	DRIVER	CAR	MODEL	ENGINE		LAPS	TIME/REASON FOR RETIREMENT	GRID:POS	ROW
1	5	M Andretti	JPS Lotus	78	Cosworth	V8	80	1h 51m 35.470s	2	1
2	11	N Lauda	Ferrari	312T2	Ferrari	F12	80	1h 51m 36.243s	1	1
3	20	J Scheckter	Wolf	WR1	Cosworth	V8	80	1h 51m 40.327s	3	2
4	4	P Depailler	Tyrrell	P34	Cosworth	V8	80	1h 52m 49.957s	12	6
5	28	E Fittipaldi	Copersucar	FD04	Cosworth	V8	80	1h 52m 56.378s	7	4
6	34	J-P Jarier	Penske	PC4	Cosworth	V8	79		9	5
7	1	J Hunt	McLaren	M23	Cosworth	V8	79		8	4
8	6	G Nilsson	JPS Lotus	78	Cosworth	V8	79		16	8
9r	26	J Laffite	Ligier	JS7	Matra	V12	78	electrics	5	3
10	10	B Henton	March	761	Cosworth	V8	77		18	9
11	18	H Binder	Surtees	TS19	Cosworth	V8	77		19	10
r	3	R Peterson	Tyrrell	P34	Cosworth	V8	62	fuel line	10	5
r	22	C Regazzoni	Ensign	N177	Cosworth	V8	57	gearbox	13	7
r	8	H-J Stuck	Brabham	BT45B	Alfa Romeo	F12	53	brakes	17	9
r	17	A Jones	Shadow	DN8	Cosworth	V8	40	gearbox	14	7
r	2	J Mass	McLaren	M23	Cosworth	V8	39	vibration	15	8
dq	7	J Watson	Brabham	BT45B	Alfa Romeo	F12	33	push start after engine cut	6	3
r	16	R Zorzi	Shadow	DN8	Cosworth	V8	27	gearbox	20	10
r	9	A-D Ribeiro	March	761B	Cosworth	V8	15	gearbox oil leak	22	11
r	12	C Reutemann	Ferrari	312T2	Ferrari	F12	5	accident	4	2
r	30	B Lunger	March	761	Cosworth	V8	4	accident	21	11
r	19	V Brambilla	Surtees	TS19	Cosworth	V8	0	accident	11	6

Winning speed: 139.834 km/h, 86.889 mph
Pole Position speed: 143.333 km/h, 89.063 mph (N Lauda, 1 min:21.650 sec)
Fastest Lap speed: 141.423 km/h, 87.876 mph (N Lauda, 1 min:22.753 sec on lap 62)
Lap Leaders: J Scheckter 1-76 (76); M Andretti 77-80 (4).

8 May 1977 SPAIN: Járama (Round: 5) (Race: 285)

75 laps x 3.404 km, 2.115 miles = 255.300 km, 158.636 miles

POS.	NO.	DRIVER	CAR	MODEL	ENGINE		LAPS	TIME/REASON FOR RETIREMENT	GRID:POS	ROW
1	5	M Andretti	JPS Lotus	78	Cosworth	V8	75	1h 42m 52.220s	1	1
2	12	C Reutemann	Ferrari	312T2	Ferrari	F12	75	1h 43m 08.070s	4	2
3	20	J Scheckter	Wolf	WR2	Cosworth	V8	75	1h 43m 16.730s	5	3
4	2	J Mass	McLaren	M23	Cosworth	V8	75	1h 43m 17.090s	9	5
5	6	G Nilsson	JPS Lotus	78	Cosworth	V8	75	1h 43m 58.050s	12	6
6	8	H-J Stuck	Brabham	BT45B	Alfa Romeo	F12	74		13	7
7	26	J Laffite	Ligier	JS7	Matra	V12	74		2	1
8	3	R Peterson	Tyrrell	P34	Cosworth	V8	74		15	8
9	18	H Binder	Surtees	TS19	Cosworth	V8	73		20	10
10	30	B Lunger	March	761	Cosworth	V8	72		25	13
11	10	I Scheckter	March	761B	Cosworth	V8	72		17	9
12	27	P Neve	March	761	Cosworth	V8	71		22	11
13	36	E de Villota	McLaren	M23	Cosworth	V8	70		23	12
14	28	E Fittipaldi	Copersucar	FD04	Cosworth	V8	70		19	10
r	7	J Watson	Brabham	BT45B	Alfa Romeo	F12	64	fuel metering unit	6	3
r	17	A Jones	Shadow	DN8	Cosworth	V8	56	accident	14	7
r	24	R Keegan	Hesketh	308E	Cosworth	V8	32	accident	16	8
r	25	H Ertl	Hesketh	308E	Cosworth	V8	29	radiator	18	9
r	16	R Zorzi	Shadow	DN8	Cosworth	V8	25	engine	24	12
r	37	A Merzario	March	761B	Cosworth	V8	16	suspension	21	11
r	4	P Depailler	Tyrrell	P34	Cosworth	V8	12	engine	10	5
r	1	J Hunt	McLaren	M26	Cosworth	V8	10	engine	7	4
r	22	C Regazzoni	Ensign	N177	Cosworth	V8	9	accident	8	4
r	19	V Brambilla	Surtees	TS19	Cosworth	V8	9	accident	11	6
ns	11	N Lauda	Ferrari	312T2	Ferrari	F12		accident/ injury	3	2
nq	34	J-P Jarier	Penske	PC4	Cosworth	V8				
nq	9	A-D Ribeiro	March	761B	Cosworth	V8				
nq	33	B Hayje	March	761	Cosworth	V8				
nq	38	B Henton	March	761	Cosworth	V8				
nq	31	D Purley	Lec	CRP1	Cosworth	V8				
nq	35	C Andersson	Stanley BRM	P207	BRM	V12				

Winning speed: 148.906 km/h, 92.526 mph
Pole Position speed: 155.710 km/h, 96.754 mph (M Andretti, 1 min:18.700 sec)
Fastest Lap speed: 151.645 km/h, 94.228 mph (J Laffite, 1 min:20.810 sec on lap 5)
Lap Leaders: M Andretti 1-75 (75).

22 May 1977 MONACO: Monte Carlo (Round: 6) (Race: 286)

76 laps x 3.312 km, 2.058 miles = 251.712 km, 156.407 miles

POS.	NO.	DRIVER	CAR	MODEL	ENGINE		LAPS	TIME/REASON FOR RETIREMENT	GRID:POS	ROW
1	20	J Scheckter	Wolf	WR1	Cosworth	V8	76	1h 57m 52.770s	2	1
2	11	N Lauda	Ferrari	312T2	Ferrari	F12	76	1h 57m 53.660s	6	3
3	12	C Reutemann	Ferrari	312T2	Ferrari	F12	76	1h 58m 25.570s	3	2
4	2	J Mass	McLaren	M23	Cosworth	V8	76	1h 58m 27.370s	9	5
5	5	M Andretti	JPS Lotus	78	Cosworth	V8	76	1h 58m 28.320s	10	5
6	17	A Jones	Shadow	DN8	Cosworth	V8	76	1h 58m 29.380s	11	6
7	26	J Laffite	Ligier	JS7	Matra	V12	76	1h 58m 57.210s	16	8
8	19	V Brambilla	Surtees	TS19	Cosworth	V8	76	1h 59m 01.410s	14	7
9	16	R Patrese	Shadow	DN8	Cosworth	V8	75		15	8
10	22	J Ickx	Ensign	N177	Cosworth	V8	75		17	9
11	34	J-P Jarier	Penske	PC4	Cosworth	V8	74		12	6
12	24	R Keegan	Hesketh	308E	Cosworth	V8	73		20	10
r	6	G Nilsson	JPS Lotus	78	Cosworth	V8	51	gearbox	13	7
r	7	J Watson	Brabham	BT45B	Alfa Romeo	F12	48	gearbox	1	1
r	4	P Depailler	Tyrrell	P34	Cosworth	V8	46	brakes/ gearbox	8	4
r	18	H Binder	Surtees	TS19	Cosworth	V8	41	fuel injection	19	10
r	28	E Fittipaldi	Copersucar	FD04	Cosworth	V8	37	engine	18	9
r	1	J Hunt	McLaren	M23	Cosworth	V8	25	dropped valve	7	4
r	8	H-J Stuck	Brabham	BT45B	Alfa Romeo	F12	19	electrics/ fire	5	3
r	3	R Peterson	Tyrrell	P34	Cosworth	V8	10	brakes	4	2
nq	37	A Merzario	March	761B	Cosworth	V8				
nq	33	B Hayje	March	761	Cosworth	V8				
nq	25	H Ertl	Hesketh	308E	Cosworth	V8				
nq	22	C Regazzoni	Ensign	N177	Cosworth	V8				
nq	9	A-D Ribeiro	March	761B	Cosworth	V8				
nq	10	I Scheckter	March	761B	Cosworth	V8				

Winning speed: 128.120 km/h, 79.610 mph
Pole Position speed: 132.686 km/h, 82.448 mph (J Watson, 1 min:29.860 sec)
Fastest Lap speed: 130.923 km/h, 81.352 mph (J Scheckter, 1 min:31.070 sec on lap 35)
Lap Leaders: J Scheckter 1-76 (76).

5 Jun 1977 BELGIUM: Zolder (Round: 7) (Race: 287)

70 laps x 4.262 km, 2.648 miles = 298.340 km, 185.380 miles

POS.	NO.	DRIVER	CAR	MODEL	ENGINE		LAPS	TIME/REASON FOR RETIREMENT	GRID:POS	ROW
1	6	G Nilsson	JPS Lotus	78	Cosworth	V8	70	1h 55m 05.710s	3	2
2	11	N Lauda	Ferrari	312T2	Ferrari	F12	70	1h 55m 19.900s	11	6
3	3	R Peterson	Tyrrell	P34	Cosworth	V8	70	1h 55m 25.660s	8	4
4	19	V Brambilla	Surtees	TS19	Cosworth	V8	70	1h 55m 30.690s	12	6
5	17	A Jones	Shadow	DN8	Cosworth	V8	70	1h 56m 21.180s	17	9

POS.	NO.	DRIVER	CAR	MODEL	ENGINE		LAPS	TIME/REASON FOR RETIREMENT	GRID:POS	ROW
6	8	H-J Stuck	Brabham	BT45B	Alfa Romeo	F12	69		18	9
7	1	J Hunt	McLaren	M26	Cosworth	V8	69		9	5
8	4	P Depailler	Tyrrell	P34	Cosworth	V8	69		5	3
9	25	H Ertl	Hesketh	308E	Cosworth	V8	69		25	13
10	27	P Neve	March	761	Cosworth	V8	68		24	12
11	34	J-P Jarier	Penske	PC4	Cosworth	V8	68		26	13
12	18	L Perkins	Surtees	TS19	Cosworth	V8	67		23	12
13	31	D Purley	Lec	CRP1	Cosworth	V8	67		20	10
14	37	A Merzario	March	761B	Cosworth	V8	65		14	7
15	33	B Hayje	March	761	Cosworth	V8	63		27	14
r	20	J Scheckter	Wolf	WR3	Cosworth	V8	62	engine	4	2
r	2	J Mass	McLaren	M23	Cosworth	V8	39	accident	6	3
r	26	J Laffite	Ligier	JS7	Matra	V12	32	engine	10	5
r	22	C Regazzoni	Ensign	N177	Cosworth	V8	29	engine	13	7
r	24	R Keegan	Hesketh	308E	Cosworth	V8	14	accident	19	10
r	12	C Reutemann	Ferrari	312T2	Ferrari	F12	14	accident	7	4
r	16	R Patrese	Shadow	DN8	Cosworth	V8	12	accident	15	8
r	10	I Scheckter	March	761B	Cosworth	V8	8	accident	21	11
r	28	E Fittipaldi	Copersucar	F5	Cosworth	V8	2	water in electrics	16	8
r	5	M Andretti	JPS Lotus	78	Cosworth	V8	0	accident	1	1
r	7	J Watson	Brabham	BT45B	Alfa Romeo	F12	0	accident	2	1
ns	30	B Lunger	McLaren	M23	Cosworth	V8		car not ready	22	11
nq	36	E de Villota	McLaren	M23	Cosworth	V8				
nq	35	C Andersson	Stanley BRM	P207	BRM	V12				
nq	9	A-D Ribeiro	March	761B	Cosworth	V8				
nq	38	B de Dryver	March	761	Cosworth	V8				
nq	39	H Rebaque	Hesketh	308E	Cosworth	V8				

Winning speed: 155.527 km/h, 96.640 mph
Pole Position speed: 181.276 km/h, 112.640 mph (M Andretti, 1 min:24.640 sec)
Fastest Lap speed: 175.271 km/h, 108.908 mph (G Nilsson, 1 min:27.540 sec on lap 53)
Lap Leaders: J Scheckter 1-16 (16); J Mass 17-18 (2); N Lauda 23-49 (27); V Brambilla 19-22 (4); G Nilsson 50-70 (21).

19 Jun 1977 — SWEDEN: Anderstorp (Round: 8) (Race: 288)

72 laps x 4.018 km, 2.497 miles = 289.296 km, 179.760 miles

POS.	NO.	DRIVER	CAR	MODEL	ENGINE		LAPS	TIME/REASON FOR RETIREMENT	GRID:POS	ROW
1	26	J Laffite	Ligier	JS7	Matra	V12	72	1h 46m 55.520s	8	4
2	2	J Mass	McLaren	M23	Cosworth	V8	72	1h 47m 03.969s	9	5
3	12	C Reutemann	Ferrari	312T2	Ferrari	F12	72	1h 47m 09.889s	12	6
4	4	P Depailler	Tyrrell	P34	Cosworth	V8	72	1h 47m 11.828s	6	3
5	7	J Watson	Brabham	BT45B	Alfa Romeo	F12	72	1h 47m 14.255s	2	1
6	5	M Andretti	JPS Lotus	78	Cosworth	V8	72	1h 47m 20.797s	1	1
7	22	C Regazzoni	Ensign	N177	Cosworth	V8	72	1h 47m 26.786s	14	7
8	34	J-P Jarier	Penske	PC4	Cosworth	V8	72	1h 48m 00.087s	17	9
9	16	J Oliver	Shadow	DN8	Cosworth	V8	72	1h 48m 17.999s	16	8
10	8	H-J Stuck	Brabham	BT45B	Alfa Romeo	F12	71		5	3
11	30	B Lunger	McLaren	M23	Cosworth	V8	71		22	11
12	1	J Hunt	McLaren	M26	Cosworth	V8	71		3	2
13	24	R Keegan	Hesketh	308E	Cosworth	V8	71		24	12
14	31	D Purley	Lec	CRP1	Cosworth	V8	70		19	10
15	27	P Neve	March	761	Cosworth	V8	69		20	10
16	25	H Ertl	Hesketh	308E	Cosworth	V8	68		23	12
17	17	A Jones	Shadow	DN8	Cosworth	V8	67		11	6
18	28	E Fittipaldi	Copersucar	FD04	Cosworth	V8	66		18	9
19r	6	G Nilsson	JPS Lotus	78	Cosworth	V8	64	wheel bearing	7	4
r	10	I Scheckter	March	761B	Cosworth	V8	61	cv joint	21	11
r	19	V Brambilla	Surtees	TS19	Cosworth	V8	52	fuel pressure	13	7
r	11	N Lauda	Ferrari	312T2	Ferrari	F12	47	handling	15	8
r	20	J Scheckter	Wolf	WR1	Cosworth	V8	29	accident	4	2
r	3	R Peterson	Tyrrell	P34	Cosworth	V8	7	ignition	10	5
nq	9	A-D Ribeiro	March	761B	Cosworth	V8				
nq	36	E de Villota	McLaren	M23	Cosworth	V8				
nq	18	L Perkins	Surtees	TS19	Cosworth	V8				
nq	33	B Hayje	March	761	Cosworth	V8				
nq	39	H Rebaque	Hesketh	308E	Cosworth	V8				
nq	35	C Andersson	Stanley BRM	P207	BRM	V12				
nq	32	M Kozarowitsky	March	761	Cosworth	V8				

Winning speed: 162.335 km/h, 100.871 mph
Pole Position speed: 169.369 km/h, 105.241 mph (M Andretti, 1 min:25.404 sec)
Fastest Lap speed: 165.110 km/h, 102.595 mph (M Andretti, 1 min:27.607 sec)
Lap Leaders: J Watson 1 (1); M Andretti 2-69 (68); J Laffite 70-72 (3).

3 Jul 1977 — FRANCE: Dijon-Prenois (Round: 9) (Race: 289)

80 laps x 3.800 km, 2.361 miles = 304.000 km, 188.897 miles

POS.	NO.	DRIVER	CAR	MODEL	ENGINE		LAPS	TIME/REASON FOR RETIREMENT	GRID:POS	ROW
1	5	M Andretti	JPS Lotus	78	Cosworth	V8	80	1h 39m 40.130s	1	1
2	7	J Watson	Brabham	BT45B	Alfa Romeo	F12	80	1h 39m 41.680s	4	2
3	1	J Hunt	McLaren	M26	Cosworth	V8	80	1h 40m 14.000s	2	1
4	6	G Nilsson	JPS Lotus	78	Cosworth	V8	80	1h 40m 51.210s	3	2
5	11	N Lauda	Ferrari	312T2	Ferrari	F12	80	1h 40m 54.580s	9	5
6	12	C Reutemann	Ferrari	312T2	Ferrari	F12	79		6	3
7	22	C Regazzoni	Ensign	N177	Cosworth	V8	79		16	8
8	26	J Laffite	Ligier	JS7	Matra	V12	78		5	3
9	2	J Mass	McLaren	M23	Cosworth	V8	78		7	4

POS.	NO.	DRIVER	CAR	MODEL	ENGINE		LAPS	TIME/REASON FOR RETIREMENT	GRID:POS	ROW
10	24	R Keegan	Hesketh	308E	Cosworth	V8	78		14	7
11	28	E Fittipaldi	Copersucar	F5	Cosworth	V8	77		22	11
12	3	R Peterson	Tyrrell	P34	Cosworth	V8	77		17	9
13	19	V Brambilla	Surtees	TS19	Cosworth	V8	77		11	6
nc	10	I Scheckter	March	761B	Cosworth	V8	69		20	10
r	20	J Scheckter	Wolf	WR3	Cosworth	V8	66	accident	8	4
r	8	H-J Stuck	Brabham	BT45B	Alfa Romeo	F12	64	accident	13	7
r	17	A Jones	Shadow	DN8	Cosworth	V8	60	drive shaft	10	5
r	37	A Merzario	March	761B	Cosworth	V8	27	gearbox	18	9
r	4	P Depailler	Tyrrell	P34	Cosworth	V8	21	accident	12	6
r	16	R Patrese	Shadow	DN8	Cosworth	V8	6	clutch/ engine	15	8
r	31	D Purley	Lec	CRP1	Cosworth	V8	5	brakes/ accident	21	11
r	34	J-P Jarier	Penske	PC4	Cosworth	V8	4	gearbox/ accident	19	10
nq	9	A-D Ribeiro	March	761B	Cosworth	V8				
nq	27	P Neve	March	761	Cosworth	V8				
nq	30	B Lunger	McLaren	M23	Cosworth	V8				
nq	25	H Ertl	Hesketh	308E	Cosworth	V8				
nq	18	L Perkins	Surtees	TS19	Cosworth	V8				
nq	39	H Rebaque	Hesketh	308E	Cosworth	V8				
nq	18	P Tambay	Surtees	TS19	Cosworth	V8				
nq	35	C Andersson	Stanley BRM	P207	BRM	V12				

Winning speed: 183.006 km/h, 113.715 mph
Pole Position speed: 189.447 km/h, 117.717 mph (M Andretti, 1 min:12.210 sec)
Fastest Lap speed: 185.492 km/h, 115.259 mph (M Andretti, 1 min:13.750 sec on lap 76)
Lap Leaders: J Hunt 1-4 (4); J Watson 5-79 (75); M Andretti 80 (1).

16 Jul 1977 — BRITAIN: Silverstone — (Round:10) (Race: 290)

68 laps x 4.719 km, 2.932 miles = 320.865 km, 199.376 miles

POS.	NO.	DRIVER	CAR	MODEL	ENGINE		LAPS	TIME/REASON FOR RETIREMENT	GRID:POS	ROW
1	1	J Hunt	McLaren	M26	Cosworth	V8	68	1h 31m 46.060s	1	1
2	11	N Lauda	Ferrari	312T2	Ferrari	F12	68	1h 32m 04.370s	3	2
3	6	G Nilsson	JPS Lotus	78	Cosworth	V8	68	1h 32m 05.630s	5	3
4	2	J Mass	McLaren	M26	Cosworth	V8	68	1h 32m 33.820s	11	6
5	8	H-J Stuck	Brabham	BT45B	Alfa Romeo	F12	68	1h 32m 57.790s	7	4
6	26	J Laffite	Ligier	JS7	Matra	V12	67		15	8
7	17	A Jones	Shadow	DN8	Cosworth	V8	67		12	6
8	19	V Brambilla	Surtees	TS19	Cosworth	V8	67		8	4
9	34	J-P Jarier	Penske	PC4	Cosworth	V8	67		20	10
10	27	P Neve	March	761	Cosworth	V8	66		26	13
11	40	G Villeneuve	McLaren	M23	Cosworth	V8	66		9	5
12	18	V Schuppan	Surtees	TS19	Cosworth	V8	66		23	12
13	30	B Lunger	McLaren	M23	Cosworth	V8	64		19	10
14r	5	M Andretti	JPS Lotus	78	Cosworth	V8	62	engine	6	3
15	12	C Reutemann	Ferrari	312T2	Ferrari	F12	62		14	7
r	7	J Watson	Brabham	BT45B	Alfa Romeo	F12	60	fuel injection	2	1
r	20	J Scheckter	Wolf	WR1	Cosworth	V8	59	engine	4	2
r	28	E Fittipaldi	Copersucar	F5	Cosworth	V8	42	engine	22	11
r	37	A Merzario	March	761B	Cosworth	V8	28	drive shaft	17	9
r	16	R Patrese	Shadow	DN8	Cosworth	V8	20	fuel pressure	25	13
r	4	P Depailler	Tyrrell	P34	Cosworth	V8	16	brakes/ accident	18	9
r	15	J-P Jabouille	Renault	RS01	Renault	V6t	16	turbo	21	11
r	10	I Scheckter	March	761B	Cosworth	V8	6	accident	24	12
r	23	P Tambay	Ensign	N177	Cosworth	V8	3	electrics	16	8
r	3	R Peterson	Tyrrell	P34	Cosworth	V8	3	engine	10	5
r	24	R Keegan	Hesketh	308E	Cosworth	V8	0	accident	13	7
nq	9	A-D Ribeiro	March	761B	Cosworth	V8				
nq	22	C Regazzoni	Ensign	N177	Cosworth	V8				
nq	38	B Henton	March	761	Cosworth	V8				
nq	36	E de Villota	McLaren	M23	Cosworth	V8				
npq	31	D Purley	Lec	CRP1	Cosworth	V8		accident/ injury		
npq	33	A Sutcliffe	March	761	Cosworth	V8				
npq	35	G Edwards	Stanley BRM	P207	BRM	V12				
npq	44	T Trimmer	Surtees	TS19	Cosworth	V8				
npq	45	B McGuire	McGuire	BM1	Cosworth	V8				
npq	32	M Kozarowitsky	March	761	Cosworth	V8				

Winning speed: 209.789 km/h, 130.357 mph
Pole Position speed: 216.422 km/h, 134.478 mph (J Hunt, 1 min:18.490 sec)
Fastest Lap speed: 213.404 km/h, 132.603 mph (J Hunt, 1 min:19.600 sec on lap 48)
Lap Leaders: J Watson 1-49 (49); J Hunt 50-68 (19).

Also the Grand Prix of Europe.

31 Jul 1977 — GERMANY: Hockenheim — (Round:11) (Race: 291)

47 laps x 6.789 km, 4.218 miles = 319.083 km, 198.269 miles

POS.	NO.	DRIVER	CAR	MODEL	ENGINE		LAPS	TIME/REASON FOR RETIREMENT	GRID:POS	ROW
1	11	N Lauda	Ferrari	312T2	Ferrari	F12	47	1h 31m 48.620s	3	2
2	20	J Scheckter	Wolf	WR2	Cosworth	V8	47	1h 32m 02.950s	1	1
3	8	H-J Stuck	Brabham	BT45B	Alfa Romeo	F12	47	1h 32m 09.520s	5	3
4	12	C Reutemann	Ferrari	312T2	Ferrari	F12	47	1h 32m 48.890s	8	4
5	19	V Brambilla	Surtees	TS19	Cosworth	V8	47	1h 33m 15.990s	10	5
6	23	P Tambay	Ensign	N177	Cosworth	V8	47	1h 33m 18.430s	11	6
7	18	V Schuppan	Surtees	TS19	Cosworth	V8	46		19	10
8	9	A-D Ribeiro	March	761B	Cosworth	V8	46		20	10

POS.	NO.	DRIVER	CAR	MODEL	ENGINE		LAPS	TIME/REASON FOR RETIREMENT	GRID:POS	ROW
9r	3	R Peterson	Tyrrell	P34	Cosworth	V8	42	engine	14	7
10r	16	R Patrese	Shadow	DN8	Cosworth	V8	42	wheel lost	16	8
r	24	R Keegan	Hesketh	308E	Cosworth	V8	40	accident	23	12
r	5	M Andretti	JPS Lotus	78	Cosworth	V8	34	engine	7	4
r	1	J Hunt	McLaren	M26	Cosworth	V8	32	fuel pump	4	2
r	6	G Nilsson	JPS Lotus	78	Cosworth	V8	31	engine	9	5
r	2	J Mass	McLaren	M26	Cosworth	V8	26	gearbox	13	7
r	4	P Depailler	Tyrrell	P34	Cosworth	V8	22	engine	15	8
r	26	J Laffite	Ligier	JS7	Matra	V12	21	engine	6	3
r	25	H Rebaque	Hesketh	308E	Cosworth	V8	20	battery	24	12
r	30	B Lunger	McLaren	M23	Cosworth	V8	14	accident	21	11
r	10	I Scheckter	March	761B	Cosworth	V8	9	clutch	18	9
r	35	H Heyer	Penske	PC4	Cosworth	V8	9	gear linkage (unofficial starter)	25	13
r	7	J Watson	Brabham	BT45B	Alfa Romeo	F12	8	engine	2	1
r	34	J-P Jarier	Penske	PC4	Cosworth	V8	5	accident	12	6
r	17	A Jones	Shadow	DN8	Cosworth	V8	0	accident	17	9
r	22	C Regazzoni	Ensign	N177	Cosworth	V8	0	accident	22	11
nq	27	P Neve	March	761	Cosworth	V8				
nq	36	E de Villota	McLaren	M23	Cosworth	V8				
nq	28	E Fittipaldi	Copersucar	F5	Cosworth	V8				
nq	37	A Merzario	March	761B	Cosworth	V8				
nq	40	T Pilette	Stanley BRM	P207	BRM	V12				

Winning speed: 208.528 km/h, 129.573 mph
Pole Position speed: 216.153 km/h, 134.311 mph (J Scheckter, 1 min:53.070 sec)
Fastest Lap speed: 210.711 km/h, 130.930 mph (N Lauda, 1 min:55.990 sec on lap 28)
Lap Leaders: J Scheckter 1-12 (12); N Lauda 13-47 (35).

14 Aug 1977 — AUSTRIA: Österreichring (Round:12) (Race: 292)

54 laps x 5.942 km, 3.692 miles = 320.868 km, 199.378 miles

POS.	NO.	DRIVER	CAR	MODEL	ENGINE		LAPS	TIME/REASON FOR RETIREMENT	GRID:POS	ROW
1	17	A Jones	Shadow	DN8	Cosworth	V8	54	1h 37m 16.490s	14	7
2	11	N Lauda	Ferrari	312T2	Ferrari	F12	54	1h 37m 36.620s	1	1
3	8	H-J Stuck	Brabham	BT45B	Alfa Romeo	F12	54	1h 37m 50.990s	4	2
4	12	C Reutemann	Ferrari	312T2	Ferrari	F12	54	1h 37m 51.240s	5	3
5	3	R Peterson	Tyrrell	P34	Cosworth	V8	54	1h 38m 18.580s	15	8
6	2	J Mass	McLaren	M26	Cosworth	V8	53		9	5
7	24	R Keegan	Hesketh	308E	Cosworth	V8	53		20	10
8	7	J Watson	Brabham	BT45B	Alfa Romeo	F12	53		12	6
9	27	P Neve	March	761	Cosworth	V8	53		22	11
10	30	B Lunger	McLaren	M23	Cosworth	V8	53		17	9
11	28	E Fittipaldi	Copersucar	F5	Cosworth	V8	53		23	12
12	33	H Binder	Penske	PC4	Cosworth	V8	53		19	10
13	4	P Depailler	Tyrrell	P34	Cosworth	V8	53		10	5
14	34	J-P Jarier	Penske	PC4	Cosworth	V8	52		18	9
15	19	V Brambilla	Surtees	TS19	Cosworth	V8	52		13	7
16	18	V Schuppan	Surtees	TS19	Cosworth	V8	52		25	13
17r	36	E de Villota	McLaren	M23	Cosworth	V8	50	accident	26	13
r	20	J Scheckter	Wolf	WR3	Cosworth	V8	45	spin	8	4
r	1	J Hunt	McLaren	M26	Cosworth	V8	43	engine	2	1
r	23	P Tambay	Ensign	N177	Cosworth	V8	41	engine	7	4
r	6	G Nilsson	JPS Lotus	78	Cosworth	V8	38	engine	16	8
r	16	A Merzario	Shadow	DN8	Cosworth	V8	29	gear linkage	21	11
r	26	J Laffite	Ligier	JS7	Matra	V12	21	oil leak onto tyre/ handling	6	3
r	5	M Andretti	JPS Lotus	78	Cosworth	V8	11	engine	3	2
r	10	I Scheckter	March	761B	Cosworth	V8	2	accident	24	12
r	22	C Regazzoni	Ensign	N177	Cosworth	V8	0	accident	11	6
nq	38	B Henton	March	761	Cosworth	V8				
nq	39	I Ashley	Hesketh	308E	Cosworth	V8				
nq	25	H Rebaque	Hesketh	308E	Cosworth	V8				
nq	9	A-D Ribeiro	March	761B	Cosworth	V8				

Winning speed: 197.914 km/h, 122.978 mph
Pole Position speed: 215.377 km/h, 133.829 mph (N Lauda, 1 min:39.320 sec)
Fastest Lap speed: 211.878 km/h, 131.655 mph (J Watson, 1 min:40.960 sec on lap 52)
Lap Leaders: M Andretti 1-11 (11); J Hunt 12-43 (32); A Jones 44-54 (11).

28 Aug 1977 — NETHERLANDS: Zandvoort (Round:13) (Race: 293)

75 laps x 4.226 km, 2.626 miles = 316.950 km, 196.944 miles

POS.	NO.	DRIVER	CAR	MODEL	ENGINE		LAPS	TIME/REASON FOR RETIREMENT	GRID:POS	ROW
1	11	N Lauda	Ferrari	312T2	Ferrari	F12	75	1h 41m 45.930s	4	2
2	26	J Laffite	Ligier	JS7	Matra	V12	75	1h 41m 47.820s	2	1
3	20	J Scheckter	Wolf	WR2	Cosworth	V8	74		15	8
4	28	E Fittipaldi	Copersucar	F5	Cosworth	V8	74		17	9
5r	23	P Tambay	Ensign	N177	Cosworth	V8	73	out of fuel	12	6
6	12	C Reutemann	Ferrari	312T2	Ferrari	F12	73		6	3
7	8	H-J Stuck	Brabham	BT45B	Alfa Romeo	F12	73		19	10
8	35	H Binder	Penske	PC4	Cosworth	V8	73		18	9
9	30	B Lunger	McLaren	M23	Cosworth	V8	73		20	10
10	10	I Scheckter	March	771	Cosworth	V8	73		25	13
11	9	A-D Ribeiro	March	761B	Cosworth	V8	72		24	12
12r	19	V Brambilla	Surtees	TS19	Cosworth	V8	67	accident	22	11
13	16	R Patrese	Shadow	DN8	Cosworth	V8	67		16	8
dq	38	B Henton	Boro	N175	Cosworth	V8	52	push start after spin	23	12
r	15	J-P Jabouille	Renault	RS01	Renault	V6t	39	rear suspension	10	5

POS.	NO.	DRIVER	CAR	MODEL	ENGINE		LAPS	TIME/REASON FOR RETIREMENT	GRID:POS	ROW
r	6	G Nilsson	JPS Lotus	78	Cosworth	V8	34	accident	5	3
r	17	A Jones	Shadow	DN8	Cosworth	V8	32	engine	13	7
r	4	P Depailler	Tyrrell	P34	Cosworth	V8	31	engine	11	6
r	3	R Peterson	Tyrrell	P34	Cosworth	V8	18	ignition	7	4
r	22	C Regazzoni	Ensign	N177	Cosworth	V8	17	throttle linkage	9	5
r	5	M Andretti	JPS Lotus	78	Cosworth	V8	14	engine	1	1
r	24	R Keegan	Hesketh	308E	Cosworth	V8	8	accident	26	13
r	1	J Hunt	McLaren	M26	Cosworth	V8	5	accident	3	2
r	34	J-P Jarier	Penske	PC4	Cosworth	V8	4	engine	21	11
r	7	J Watson	Brabham	BT45B	Alfa Romeo	F12	2	oil sump/ engine	8	4
r	2	J Mass	McLaren	M26	Cosworth	V8	0	accident	14	7
nq	27	P Neve	March	761	Cosworth	V8				
nq	37	A Merzario	March	761B	Cosworth	V8				
nq	18	V Schuppan	Surtees	TS19	Cosworth	V8				
nq	39	I Ashley	Hesketh	308E	Cosworth	V8				
nq	33	B Hayje	March	761	Cosworth	V8				
nq	25	H Rebaque	Hesketh	308E	Cosworth	V8				
nq	29	T Pilette	Stanley BRM	P207	BRM	V12				
nq	32	M Bleekemolen	March	761	Cosworth	V8				

Winning speed: 186.871 km/h, 116.116 mph
Pole Position speed: 193.434 km/h, 120.194 mph (M Andretti, 1 min:18.650 sec)
Fastest Lap speed: 190.194 km/h, 118.181 mph (N Lauda, 1 min:19.990 sec on lap 72)
Lap Leaders: J Hunt 1-5 (5); J Laffite 6-19 (14); N Lauda 20-75 (56).

11 Sep 1977 ITALY: Monza (Round:14) (Race: 294)
52 laps x 5.800 km, 3.604 miles = 301.600 km, 187.406 miles

POS.	NO.	DRIVER	CAR	MODEL	ENGINE		LAPS	TIME/REASON FOR RETIREMENT	GRID:POS	ROW
1	5	M Andretti	JPS Lotus	78	Cosworth	V8	52	1h 27m 50.300s	4	2
2	11	N Lauda	Ferrari	312T2	Ferrari	F12	52	1h 28m 07.260s	5	3
3	17	A Jones	Shadow	DN8	Cosworth	V8	52	1h 28m 13.930s	16	8
4	2	J Mass	McLaren	M26	Cosworth	V8	52	1h 28m 18.780s	9	5
5	22	C Regazzoni	Ensign	N177	Cosworth	V8	52	1h 28m 21.410s	7	4
6	3	R Peterson	Tyrrell	P34	Cosworth	V8	52	1h 29m 09.520s	12	6
7	27	P Neve	March	761	Cosworth	V8	50		24	12
8	26	J Laffite	Ligier	JS7	Matra	V12	50		8	4
9	24	R Keegan	Hesketh	308E	Cosworth	V8	48		23	12
r	10	I Scheckter	March	771	Cosworth	V8	41	transmission	17	9
r	12	C Reutemann	Ferrari	312T2	Ferrari	F12	39	accident	2	1
r	14	B Giacomelli	McLaren	M23	Cosworth	V8	38	engine	15	8
r	16	R Patrese	Shadow	DN8	Cosworth	V8	38	accident	6	3
r	8	H-J Stuck	Brabham	BT45B	Alfa Romeo	F12	31	engine	11	6
r	1	J Hunt	McLaren	M26	Cosworth	V8	26	brakes/ spin	1	1
r	4	P Depailler	Tyrrell	P34	Cosworth	V8	24	engine	13	7
r	20	J Scheckter	Wolf	WR1	Cosworth	V8	23	engine	3	2
r	15	J-P Jabouille	Renault	RS01	Renault	V6t	23	engine	20	10
r	34	J-P Jarier	Penske	PC4	Cosworth	V8	19	engine	18	9
r	23	P Tambay	Ensign	N177	Cosworth	V8	8	engine	21	11
r	19	V Brambilla	Surtees	TS19	Cosworth	V8	5	accident/ radiator	10	5
r	30	B Lunger	McLaren	M23	Cosworth	V8	4	engine	22	11
r	6	G Nilsson	JPS Lotus	78	Cosworth	V8	4	front suspension	19	10
r	7	J Watson	Brabham	BT45B	Alfa Romeo	F12	3	accident	14	7
nq	9	A-D Ribeiro	March	761B	Cosworth	V8				
nq	28	E Fittipaldi	Copersucar	F5	Cosworth	V8				
nq	18	L Leoni	Surtees	TS19	Cosworth	V8				
nq	38	B Henton	Boro	N175	Cosworth	V8				
nq	36	E de Villota	McLaren	M23	Cosworth	V8				
nq	25	I Ashley	Hesketh	308E	Cosworth	V8				
nq	29	T Pilette	Stanley BRM	P207	BRM	V12				
nq	33	H Binder	Penske	PC4	Cosworth	V8				
nq	41	L Kessel	Williams	FW	Cosworth	V8				
nq	21	G Francia	Brabham	BT45B	Alfa Romeo	F12				

Winning speed: 206.015 km/h, 128.012 mph
Pole Position speed: 212.887 km/h, 132.282 mph (J Hunt, 1 min:38.080 sec)
Fastest Lap speed: 210.696 km/h, 130.921 mph (M Andretti, 1 min:39.100 sec on lap 31)
Lap Leaders: J Scheckter 1-9 (9); M Andretti 10-52 (43).

2 Oct 1977 USA East: Watkins Glen (Round:15) (Race: 295)
59 laps x 5.435 km, 3.377 miles = 320.651 km, 199.243 miles

POS.	NO.	DRIVER	CAR	MODEL	ENGINE		LAPS	TIME/REASON FOR RETIREMENT	GRID:POS	ROW
1	1	J Hunt	McLaren	M26	Cosworth	V8	59	1h 58m 23.267s	1	1
2	5	M Andretti	JPS Lotus	78	Cosworth	V8	59	1h 58m 25.293s	4	2
3	20	J Scheckter	Wolf	WR2	Cosworth	V8	59	1h 59m 42.146s	9	5
4	11	N Lauda	Ferrari	312T2	Ferrari	F12	59	2h 00m 03.882s	7	4
5	22	C Regazzoni	Ensign	N177	Cosworth	V8	59	2h 00m 11.405s	19	10
6	12	C Reutemann	Ferrari	312T2	Ferrari	F12	58		6	3
7	26	J Laffite	Ligier	JS7	Matra	V12	58		10	5
8	24	R Keegan	Hesketh	308E	Cosworth	V8	58		20	10
9	16	J-P Jarier	Shadow	DN8	Cosworth	V8	58		16	8
10	30	B Lunger	McLaren	M23	Cosworth	V8	57		17	9
11	18	H Binder	Surtees	TS19	Cosworth	V8	57		25	13
12	7	J Watson	Brabham	BT45B	Alfa Romeo	F12	57		3	2
13	28	E Fittipaldi	Copersucar	F5	Cosworth	V8	57		18	9
14	4	P Depailler	Tyrrell	P34	Cosworth	V8	56		8	4
15	9	A-D Ribeiro	March	761B	Cosworth	V8	56		23	12

POS.	NO.	DRIVER	CAR	MODEL	ENGINE		LAPS	TIME/REASON FOR RETIREMENT	GRID:POS	ROW
16	3	R Peterson	Tyrrell	P34	Cosworth	V8	56		5	3
17	25	I Ashley	Hesketh	308E	Cosworth	V8	55		22	11
18	27	P Neve	March	761	Cosworth	V8	55		24	12
19	19	V Brambilla	Surtees	TS19	Cosworth	V8	54		11	6
r	15	J-P Jabouille	Renault	RS01	Renault	V6t	30	alternator	14	7
r	6	G Nilsson	JPS Lotus	78	Cosworth	V8	17	accident	12	6
r	8	H-J Stuck	Brabham	BT45B	Alfa Romeo	F12	14	accident	2	1
r	10	I Scheckter	March	771	Cosworth	V8	10	accident	21	11
r	2	J Mass	McLaren	M26	Cosworth	V8	8	fuel pump belt	15	8
r	14	D Ongais	Penske	PC4	Cosworth	V8	6	accident	26	13
r	17	A Jones	Shadow	DN8	Cosworth	V8	3	accident	13	7
nq	23	P Tambay	Ensign	N177	Cosworth	V8				

Winning speed: 162.509 km/h, 100.978 mph
Pole Position speed: 193.977 km/h, 120.532 mph (J Hunt, 1 min:40.863 sec)
Fastest Lap speed: 174.917 km/h, 108.688 mph (R Peterson, 1 min:51.854 sec on lap 56)
Lap Leaders: H-J Stuck 1-14 (14); J Hunt 15-59 (45).

9 Oct 1977 CANADA: Mosport Park (Round:16) (Race: 296)

80 laps x 3.957 km, 2.459 miles = 316.590 km, 196.720 miles

POS.	NO.	DRIVER	CAR	MODEL	ENGINE		LAPS	TIME/REASON FOR RETIREMENT	GRID:POS	ROW
1	20	J Scheckter	Wolf	WR1	Cosworth	V8	80	1h 40m 00.000s	9	5
2	4	P Depailler	Tyrrell	P34	Cosworth	V8	80	1h 40m 06.770s	6	3
3	2	J Mass	McLaren	M26	Cosworth	V8	80	1h 40m 15.760s	5	3
4	17	A Jones	Shadow	DN8	Cosworth	V8	80	1h 40m 46.690s	7	4
5	23	P Tambay	Ensign	N177	Cosworth	V8	80	1h 41m 03.260s	16	8
6r	19	V Brambilla	Surtees	TS19	Cosworth	V8	78	accident	15	8
7	14	D Ongais	Penske	PC4	Cosworth	V8	78		22	11
8	9	A-D Ribeiro	March	761B	Cosworth	V8	78		23	12
9r	5	M Andretti	JPS Lotus	78	Cosworth	V8	77	engine	1	1
10r	16	R Patrese	Shadow	DN8	Cosworth	V8	76	accident	8	4
11r	30	B Lunger	McLaren	M23	Cosworth	V8	76	engine	20	10
12r	21	G Villeneuve	Ferrari	312T2	Ferrari	F12	76	drive shaft	17	9
r	1	J Hunt	McLaren	M26	Cosworth	V8	61	accident	2	1
r	27	P Neve	March	761	Cosworth	V8	56	oil pressure	21	11
r	3	R Peterson	Tyrrell	P34	Cosworth	V8	34	fuel leak	3	2
r	24	R Keegan	Hesketh	308E	Cosworth	V8	32	accident	25	13
r	18	H Binder	Surtees	TS19	Cosworth	V8	31	accident	24	12
r	28	E Fittipaldi	Copersucar	F5	Cosworth	V8	29	engine	19	10
r	10	I Scheckter	March	771	Cosworth	V8	29	engine	18	9
r	12	C Reutemann	Ferrari	312T2	Ferrari	F12	20	fuel pressure	12	6
r	8	H-J Stuck	Brabham	BT45B	Alfa Romeo	F12	19	engine	13	7
r	6	G Nilsson	JPS Lotus	78	Cosworth	V8	17	throttle jammed/ accident	4	2
r	26	J Laffite	Ligier	JS7	Matra	V12	12	drive shaft	11	6
r	7	J Watson	Brabham	BT45B	Alfa Romeo	F12	1	accident	10	5
r	22	C Regazzoni	Ensign	N177	Cosworth	V8	0	accident	14	7
ns	25	I Ashley	Hesketh	308E	Cosworth	V8		accident/ injury		
nq	15	J-P Jabouille	Renault	RS01	Renault	V6t				

Winning speed: 189.954 km/h, 118.032 mph
Pole Position speed: 199.574 km/h, 124.009 mph (M Andretti, 1 min:11.385 sec)
Fastest Lap speed: 194.362 km/h, 120.771 mph (M Andretti, 1 min:13.299 sec on lap 56)
Lap Leaders: M Andretti 1-60,62-78 (77); J Hunt 61 (1); J Scheckter 79-80 (2).

23 Oct 1977 JAPAN: Fuji (Round:17) (Race: 297)

73 laps x 4.359 km, 2.709 miles = 318.207 km, 197.725 miles

POS.	NO.	DRIVER	CAR	MODEL	ENGINE		LAPS	TIME/REASON FOR RETIREMENT	GRID:POS	ROW
1	1	J Hunt	McLaren	M26	Cosworth	V8	73	1h 31m 51.680s	2	1
2	12	C Reutemann	Ferrari	312T2	Ferrari	F12	73	1h 32m 54.130s	7	4
3	4	P Depailler	Tyrrell	P34	Cosworth	V8	73	1h 32m 58.070s	15	8
4	17	A Jones	Shadow	DN8	Cosworth	V8	73	1h 32m 58.290s	12	6
5r	26	J Laffite	Ligier	JS7	Matra	V12	72	out of fuel	5	3
6	16	R Patrese	Shadow	DN8	Cosworth	V8	72		13	7
7	8	H-J Stuck	Brabham	BT45B	Alfa Romeo	F12	72		4	2
8	19	V Brambilla	Surtees	TS19	Cosworth	V8	71		9	5
9	50	K Takahashi	Tyrrell	007	Cosworth	V8	71		22	11
10	20	J Scheckter	Wolf	WR3	Cosworth	V8	71		6	3
11	52	K Hoshino	Kojima	KE009	Cosworth	V8	71		11	6
12	9	A-D Ribeiro	March	761B	Cosworth	V8	69		23	12
r	6	G Nilsson	JPS Lotus	78	Cosworth	V8	63	gearbox	14	7
r	22	C Regazzoni	Ensign	N177	Cosworth	V8	43	engine	10	5
r	7	J Watson	Brabham	BT45B	Alfa Romeo	F12	29	gearbox	3	2
r	2	J Mass	McLaren	M26	Cosworth	V8	28	engine	8	4
r	23	P Tambay	Ensign	N177	Cosworth	V8	14	engine	16	8
r	3	R Peterson	Tyrrell	P34	Cosworth	V8	5	accident	18	9
r	11	G Villeneuve	Ferrari	312T2	Ferrari	F12	5	accident	20	10
r	27	J-P Jarier	Ligier	JS7	Matra	V12	3	engine	17	9
r	18	H Binder	Surtees	TS19	Cosworth	V8	1	accident	21	11
r	51	N Takahara	Kojima	KE009	Cosworth	V8	1	accident	19	10
r	5	M Andretti	JPS Lotus	78	Cosworth	V8	1	accident	1	1

Winning speed: 207.840 km/h, 129.146 mph
Pole Position speed: 217.256 km/h, 134.997 mph (M Andretti, 1 min:12.230 sec)
Fastest Lap speed: 211.203 km/h, 131.236 mph (J Scheckter, 1 min:14.300 sec on lap 72)
Lap Leaders: J Hunt 1-73 (73).

Lap Leaders 1977

POS	DRIVER	CAR-ENGINE	GPS	LAPS	KM	MILES
1	M Andretti	Lotus-Cosworth	7	279	1,164.8	723.8
2	J Hunt	McLaren-Cosworth	10	222	1,160.2	720.9
3	J Scheckter	Wolf-Cosworth	7	197	744.4	462.5
4	N Lauda	Ferrari	4	190	884.8	549.8
5	J Watson	Brabham-Alfa Romeo	4	138	597.8	371.5
6	G Nilsson	Lotus-Cosworth	1	21	89.5	55.6
7	C Pace	Brabham-Alfa Romeo	2	19	125.3	77.9
8	C Reutemann	Ferrari	1	18	143.3	89.0
9	J Laffite	Ligier-Matra	2	17	71.2	44.3
10	H-J Stuck	Brabham-Alfa Romeo	1	14	76.1	47.3
11	A Jones	Shadow-Cosworth	1	11	65.4	40.6
12	V Brambilla	Surtees-Cosworth	1	4	17.0	10.6
13	J Mass	McLaren-Cosworth	1	2	8.5	5.3
			17	**1,132**	**5,148.4**	**3,199.0**

Driver Points 1977

		RA	BR	ZA	USAW	E	MC	B	S	F	GB	D	A	NL	I	USAE	CDN	J	TOTAL
1	N Lauda	-	4	9	6	-	6	6	-	2	6	9	6	9	6	3	-	-	72
2	J Scheckter	9	-	6	4	4	9	-	-	-	-	6	-	4	-	4	9	-	55
3	M Andretti	2	-	-	9	9	2	-	1	9	-	-	-	-	9	6	-	-	47
4	C Reutemann	4	9	-	-	6	4	-	4	1	-	3	3	1	-	1	-	6	42
5	J Hunt	-	6	3	-	-	-	-	-	4	9	-	-	-	-	9	-	9	40
6	J Mass	-	-	2	-	3	3	-	6	-	3	-	1	-	3	-	4	-	25
7	A Jones	-	-	-	-	-	1	2	-	-	-	-	9	-	4	-	3	3	22
8	G Nilsson	-	2	-	-	2	-	9	-	3	4	-	-	-	-	-	-	-	20
	P Depailler	-	-	4	3	-	-	-	3	-	-	-	-	-	-	-	6	4	20
10	J Laffite	-	-	-	-	-	-	-	9	-	1	-	-	6	-	-	-	2	18
11	H-J Stuck	-	-	-	-	1	-	1	-	-	2	4	4	-	-	-	-	-	12
12	E Fittipaldi	3	3	-	2	-	-	-	-	-	-	-	-	3	-	-	-	-	11
13	J Watson	-	-	1	-	-	-	-	2	6	-	-	-	-	-	-	-	-	9
14	R Peterson	-	-	-	-	-	-	4	-	-	-	-	2	-	1	-	-	-	7
15	C Pace	6	-	-	-	-	-	-	-	-	-	-	-	-	-	-	-	-	6
	V Brambilla	-	-	-	-	-	-	3	-	-	-	2	-	-	-	-	1	-	6
17	P Tambay	-	-	-	-	-	-	-	-	-	-	1	-	2	-	-	2	-	5
	C Regazzoni	1	-	-	-	-	-	-	-	-	-	-	-	-	2	2	-	-	5
19	R Zorzi	-	1	-	-	-	-	-	-	-	-	-	-	-	-	-	-	-	1
	J-P Jarier	-	-	-	1	-	-	-	-	-	-	-	-	-	-	-	-	-	1
	R Patrese	-	-	-	-	-	-	-	-	-	-	-	-	-	-	-	-	1	1

9, 6, 4, 3,2 and 1 point awarded to the first six finishers.

Best 8 scores from first 9 races, best 7 from remaining 8 races.

Constructor Points 1977

		RA	BR	ZA	USAW	E	MC	B	S	F	GB	D	A	NL	I	USAE	CDN	J	TOTAL	
1	Ferrari	4	9	9	6	6	6	6	4	(2)	6	9	6	9	6	3	-	6	95	(2)
2	Lotus-Cosworth	2	2	-	9	9	2	9	1	9	4	-	-	-	9	6	-	-	62	
3	McLaren-Cosworth	-	6	3	-	3	3	-	6	4	9	-	1	-	3	9	4	9	60	
4	Wolf-Cosworth	9	-	6	4	4	9	-	-	-	-	6	-	4	-	4	9	-	55	
5	Brabham-Alfa Romeo	6	-	1	-	1	-	1	2	6	2	4	4	-	-	-	-	-	27	
	Tyrrell-Cosworth	-	-	4	3	-	-	4	3	-	-	-	2	-	1	-	6	4	27	
7	Shadow-Cosworth	-	1	-	-	-	1	2	-	-	-	-	9	-	4	-	3	3	23	
8	Ligier-Matra	-	-	-	-	-	-	-	9	-	1	-	-	6	-	-	-	2	18	
9	Copersucar-Cosworth	3	3	-	2	-	-	-	-	-	-	-	-	3	-	-	-	-	11	
10	Ensign-Cosworth	1	-	-	-	-	-	-	-	-	-	1	-	2	2	2	2	-	10	
11	Surtees-Cosworth	-	-	-	-	-	-	3	-	-	-	2	-	-	-	-	1	-	6	
12	Penske-Cosworth	-	-	-	1	-	-	-	-	-	-	-	-	-	-	-	-	-	1	

9, 6, 4, 3,2 and 1 point awarded to the first six finishers. Points only for highest placed car.

Best 8 scores from first 9 races, best 7 from remaining 8 races.

RACE ENTRANTS & RESULTS 1978

Ferrari turned to Michelin radial tyres as used by Renault, while Goodyear produced the soft qualifying rubber. Lotus developed the wing car, with skirts along the sidepods to avoid escaping air. The Brabham fan-car was created in the same vein but was made illegal after its first win. A new team, Arrows was created by a splinter group from the ailing Shadow operation.

BRABHAM
Parmalat Racing Team: Lauda, Watson, Piquet

TYRRELL
Elf Team Tyrrell: Pironi, Depailler

LOTUS
John Player Team Lotus: Andretti, Peterson, Jarier
Team Rebaque: Rebaque

McLAREN
Marlboro Team McLaren: Hunt, Tambay, Giacomelli
B & S Fabrications: Lunger, Piquet
Melchester Racing: (Trimmer)
Centro Aseguredor F1: (de Villota)

ATS
ATS Racing Team: Mass, Bleekemolen, Jarier, (Colombo), Rosberg, (Binder, Ertl)

FERRARI
Scuderia Ferrari SpA SEFAC: Reutemann, Villeneuve

FITTIPALDI (COPERSUCAR)
Fittipaldi Automotive: Fittipaldi

RENAULT
Equipe Renault Elf: Jabouille

SHADOW
Shadow Racing Team: Stuck, Regazzoni
Interscope Racing: (Ongais)

SURTEES
Team Surtees: Keegan, Brambilla, (Gimax, Henton), Arnoux, (Gabbiani)

WOLF
Walter Wolf Racing: Scheckter, Rahal
Theodore Racing Hong Kong: Rosberg

ENSIGN
Team Tissot Ensign: Ongais, Ickx, Daly, Piquet, Leoni, Lunger
Sachs Racing: Ertl
Privateer: (de Dryver)

HESKETH
Olympus Cameras/Hesketh Racing: (Galica), Cheever, (Daly)

LIGIER
Ligier Gitanes: Laffite

WILLIAMS
Williams Grand Prix Engineering: Jones

MARTINI
Automobiles Martini: Arnoux

THEODORE
Theodore Racing Hong Kong: (Cheever), Rosberg

ARROWS
Arrows Racing Team: Patrese, Stommelen

MERZARIO
Team Merzario: Merzario, (Colombo)

MARCH
Privateer: (Neve)

15 Jan 1978 — ARGENTINA: Buenos Aires No.15 — (Round: 1) (Race: 298)
52 laps x 5.968 km, 3.708 miles = 310.336 km, 192.834 miles

POS.	NO.	DRIVER	CAR	MODEL	ENGINE		LAPS	TIME/REASON FOR RETIREMENT	GRID:POS	ROW
1	5	M Andretti	JPS Lotus	78	Cosworth	V8	52	1h 37m 04.470s	1	1
2	1	N Lauda	Brabham	BT45C	Alfa Romeo	F12	52	1h 37m 17.680s	5	3
3	4	P Depailler	Tyrrell	008	Cosworth	V8	52	1h 37m 18.110s	10	5
4	7	J Hunt	McLaren	M26	Cosworth	V8	52	1h 37m 20.520s	6	3
5	6	R Peterson	JPS Lotus	78	Cosworth	V8	52	1h 38m 19.320s	3	2
6	8	P Tambay	McLaren	M26	Cosworth	V8	52	1h 38m 24.370s	9	5
7	11	C Reutemann	Ferrari	312T2	Ferrari	F12	52	1h 38m 27.070s	2	1
8	12	G Villeneuve	Ferrari	312T2	Ferrari	F12	52	1h 38m 43.350s	7	4
9	14	E Fittipaldi	Copersucar	F5A	Cosworth	V8	52	1h 38m 45.070s	17	9
10	20	J Scheckter	Wolf	WR4	Cosworth	V8	52	1h 38m 47.970s	15	8
11	9	J Mass	ATS	HS1	Cosworth	V8	52	1h 38m 53.540s	13	7
12	10	J-P Jarier	ATS	HS1	Cosworth	V8	51		11	6
13	30	B Lunger	McLaren	M23	Cosworth	V8	51		24	12
14	3	D Pironi	Tyrrell	008	Cosworth	V8	51		23	12
15	17	C Regazzoni	Shadow	DN8	Cosworth	V8	51		16	8
16r	26	J Laffite	Ligier	JS7	Matra	V12	50	engine	8	4
17	16	H-J Stuck	Shadow	DN8	Cosworth	V8	50		18	9
18	19	V Brambilla	Surtees	TS19	Cosworth	V8	50		12	6
r	2	J Watson	Brabham	BT45C	Alfa Romeo	F12	41	engine	4	2
r	27	A Jones	Williams	FW06	Cosworth	V8	36	fuel vaporisation	14	7
r	22	D Ongais	Ensign	N177	Cosworth	V8	35	distributor rotor arm	21	11
r	23	L Leoni	Ensign	N177	Cosworth	V8	28	engine	22	11
r	37	A Merzario	Merzario	A1	Cosworth	V8	9	differential	20	10
r	18	R Keegan	Surtees	TS19	Cosworth	V8	4	engine overheating	19	10
nq	25	H Rebaque	Lotus	78	Cosworth	V8				
nq	32	E Cheever	Theodore	TR1	Cosworth	V8				
nq	24	D Galica	Hesketh	308E	Cosworth	V8				

Winning speed: 191.813 km/h, 119.187 mph
Pole Position speed: 199.395 km/h, 123.898 mph (M Andretti, 1 min:47.750 sec)
Fastest Lap speed: 195.743 km/h, 121.629 mph (G Villeneuve, 1 min:49.760 sec on lap 3)
Lap Leaders: M Andretti 1-52 (52).

29 Jan 1978 — BRAZIL: Rio de Janeiro — (Round: 2) (Race: 299)
63 laps x 5.031 km, 3.126 miles = 316.953 km, 196.945 miles

POS.	NO.	DRIVER	CAR	MODEL	ENGINE		LAPS	TIME/REASON FOR RETIREMENT	GRID:POS	ROW
1	11	C Reutemann	Ferrari	312T2	Ferrari	F12	63	1h 49m 59.860s	4	2
2	14	E Fittipaldi	Copersucar	F5A	Cosworth	V8	63	1h 50m 48.990s	7	4
3	1	N Lauda	Brabham	BT45C	Alfa Romeo	F12	63	1h 50m 56.880s	10	5
4	5	M Andretti	JPS Lotus	78	Cosworth	V8	63	1h 51m 32.980s	3	2
5	17	C Regazzoni	Shadow	DN8	Cosworth	V8	62		15	8
6	3	D Pironi	Tyrrell	008	Cosworth	V8	62		19	10
7	9	J Mass	ATS	HS1	Cosworth	V8	62		20	10
8	2	J Watson	Brabham	BT45C	Alfa Romeo	F12	61		21	11
9	26	J Laffite	Ligier	JS7	Matra	V12	61		14	7
10	36	R Patrese	Arrows	FA1	Cosworth	V8	59		18	9

POS.	NO.	DRIVER	CAR	MODEL	ENGINE		LAPS	TIME/REASON FOR RETIREMENT	GRID:POS	ROW
11	27	A Jones	Williams	FW06	Cosworth	V8	58		8	4
r	25	H Rebaque	Lotus	78	Cosworth	V8	40	driver exhausted	22	11
r	12	G Villeneuve	Ferrari	312T2	Ferrari	F12	35	accident	6	3
r	8	P Tambay	McLaren	M26	Cosworth	V8	34	accident	5	3
r	16	H-J Stuck	Shadow	DN8	Cosworth	V8	25	fuel pump	9	5
r	7	J Hunt	McLaren	M26	Cosworth	V8	25	accident	2	1
r	20	J Scheckter	Wolf	WR1	Cosworth	V8	16	accident/ suspension	12	6
r	6	R Peterson	JPS Lotus	78	Cosworth	V8	15	accident/ suspension	1	1
r	22	D Ongais	Ensign	N177	Cosworth	V8	13	brake disc	23	12
r	30	B Lunger	McLaren	M23	Cosworth	V8	11	engine overheating	13	7
r	4	P Depailler	Tyrrell	008	Cosworth	V8	8	spin/ brake master cylinder	11	6
r	18	R Keegan	Surtees	TS19	Cosworth	V8	5	accident	24	12
r	23	L Leoni	Ensign	N177	Cosworth	V8	-1	drive shaft	17	9
ns	10	J-P Jarier	ATS	HS1	Cosworth	V8		car raced by Mass	16	8
nq	37	A Merzario	Merzario	A1	Cosworth	V8				
nq	32	E Cheever	Theodore	TR1	Cosworth	V8				
nq	19	V Brambilla	Surtees	TS19	Cosworth	V8				
nq	24	D Galica	Hesketh	308E	Cosworth	V8				

Winning speed: 172.887 km/h, 107.427 mph
Pole Position speed: 180.305 km/h, 112.036 mph (R Peterson, 1 min:40.450 sec)
Fastest Lap speed: 175.721 km/h, 109.188 mph (C Reutemann, 1 min:43.070 sec on lap 35)
Lap Leaders: C Reutemann 1-63 (63).

4 Mar 1978 — SOUTH AFRICA: Kyalami (Round: 3) (Race: 300)
78 laps x 4.104 km, 2.550 miles = 320.112 km, 198.908 miles

POS.	NO.	DRIVER	CAR	MODEL	ENGINE		LAPS	TIME/REASON FOR RETIREMENT	GRID:POS	ROW
1	6	R Peterson	JPS Lotus	78	Cosworth	V8	78	1h 42m 15.767s	12	6
2	4	P Depailler	Tyrrell	008	Cosworth	V8	78	1h 42m 16.233s	11	6
3	2	J Watson	Brabham	BT46	Alfa Romeo	F12	78	1h 42m 20.209s	10	5
4	27	A Jones	Williams	FW06	Cosworth	V8	78	1h 42m 54.753s	18	9
5	26	J Laffite	Ligier	JS7	Matra	V12	78	1h 43m 24.985s	13	7
6	3	D Pironi	Tyrrell	008	Cosworth	V8	77		14	7
7	5	M Andretti	JPS Lotus	78	Cosworth	V8	77		2	1
8	10	J-P Jarier	ATS	HS1	Cosworth	V8	77		17	9
9	36	R Stommelen	Arrows	FA1	Cosworth	V8	77		22	11
10	25	H Rebaque	Lotus	78	Cosworth	V8	77		21	11
11	30	B Lunger	McLaren	M23	Cosworth	V8	76		20	10
12	19	V Brambilla	Surtees	TS19	Cosworth	V8	76		19	10
r	35	R Patrese	Arrows	FA1	Cosworth	V8	63	engine	7	4
r	20	J Scheckter	Wolf	WR1	Cosworth	V8	59	accident	5	3
r	8	P Tambay	McLaren	M26	Cosworth	V8	56	accident	4	2
r	11	C Reutemann	Ferrari	312T3	Ferrari	F12	55	accident	9	5
r	12	G Villeneuve	Ferrari	312T3	Ferrari	F12	55	oil leak	8	4
r	18	R Keegan	Surtees	TS19	Cosworth	V8	52	oil line	23	12
r	1	N Lauda	Brabham	BT46	Alfa Romeo	F12	52	engine	1	1
r	9	J Mass	ATS	HS1	Cosworth	V8	43	engine	15	8
r	37	A Merzario	Merzario	A1	Cosworth	V8	39	suspension radius rod	26	13
r	15	J-P Jabouille	Renault	RS01	Renault	V6t	38	misfire	6	3
r	32	K Rosberg	Theodore	TR1	Cosworth	V8	14	clutch/ engine/ fuel leak	24	12
r	14	E Fittipaldi	Copersucar	F5A	Cosworth	V8	8	drive shaft	16	8
r	24	E Cheever	Hesketh	308E	Cosworth	V8	8	oil line/ engine	25	13
r	7	J Hunt	McLaren	M26	Cosworth	V8	5	engine	3	2
nq	31	R Arnoux	Martini	MK23	Cosworth	V8				
nq	17	C Regazzoni	Shadow	DN8	Cosworth	V8				
nq	22	L Leoni	Ensign	N177	Cosworth	V8				
nq	16	H-J Stuck	Shadow	DN8	Cosworth	V8				

Winning speed: 187.817 km/h, 116.704 mph
Pole Position speed: 197.916 km/h, 122.979 mph (N Lauda, 1 min:14.650 sec)
Fastest Lap speed: 191.651 km/h, 119.087 mph (M Andretti, 1 min:17.090 sec on lap 2)
Lap Leaders: M Andretti 1-20 (20); J Scheckter 21-26 (6); R Patrese 27-63 (37); P Depailler 64-77 (14); R Peterson 78 (1).

Cars on rows 6,7,8,10 and 11 lined up on the grid in reverse order (as listed above), due to N Lauda choosing, at a late stage, to line up on the other side and causing confusion.

2 Apr 1978 — USA West: Long Beach (Round: 4) (Race: 301)
80.5 laps x 3.251 km, 2.020 miles = 261.706 km, 162.616 miles

POS.	NO.	DRIVER	CAR	MODEL	ENGINE		LAPS	TIME/REASON FOR RETIREMENT	GRID:POS	ROW
1	11	C Reutemann	Ferrari	312T3	Ferrari	F12	80	1h 52m 01.301s	1	1
2	5	M Andretti	JPS Lotus	78	Cosworth	V8	80	1h 52m 12.362s	4	2
3	4	P Depailler	Tyrrell	008	Cosworth	V8	80	1h 52m 30.252s	12	6
4	6	R Peterson	JPS Lotus	78	Cosworth	V8	80	1h 52m 46.904s	6	3
5	26	J Laffite	Ligier	JS7	Matra	V12	80	1h 53m 24.185s	14	7
6	35	R Patrese	Arrows	FA1	Cosworth	V8	79		9	5
7	27	A Jones	Williams	FW06	Cosworth	V8	79		8	4
8	14	E Fittipaldi	Copersucar	F5A	Cosworth	V8	79		15	8
9	36	R Stommelen	Arrows	FA1	Cosworth	V8	79		18	9
10	17	C Regazzoni	Shadow	DN8	Cosworth	V8	79		20	10
11	10	J-P Jarier	ATS	HS1	Cosworth	V8	75		19	10
12r	8	P Tambay	McLaren	M26	Cosworth	V8	74	accident	11	6
r	20	J Scheckter	Wolf	WR3	Cosworth	V8	59	accident	10	5
r	19	V Brambilla	Surtees	TS19	Cosworth	V8	50	crown wheel & pinion	17	9
r	15	J-P Jabouille	Renault	RS01	Renault	V6t	43	turbo	13	7
r	12	G Villeneuve	Ferrari	312T3	Ferrari	F12	38	accident	2	1
r	1	N Lauda	Brabham	BT46	Alfa Romeo	F12	27	ignition	3	2
r	3	D Pironi	Tyrrell	008	Cosworth	V8	25	gearbox	22	11
r	37	A Merzario	Merzario	A1	Cosworth	V8	17	gearbox	21	11

POS.	NO.	DRIVER	CAR	MODEL	ENGINE		LAPS	TIME/REASON FOR RETIREMENT	GRID:POS	ROW
r	9	J Mass	ATS	HS1	Cosworth	V8	11	brake master cylinder	16	8
r	2	J Watson	Brabham	BT46	Alfa Romeo	F12	9	oil tank	5	3
r	7	J Hunt	McLaren	M26	Cosworth	V8	5	accident	7	4
ns	18	R Keegan	Surtees	TS19	Cosworth	V8		accident		
ns	16	H-J Stuck	Shadow	DN9	Cosworth	V8		accident		
nq	30	B Lunger	McLaren	M23	Cosworth	V8				
nq	22	L Leoni	Ensign	N177	Cosworth	V8				
npq	32	K Rosberg	Theodore	TR1	Cosworth	V8				
npq	25	H Rebaque	Lotus	78	Cosworth	V8				
npq	39	D Ongais	Shadow	DN9	Cosworth	V8				
npq	24	D Daly	Hesketh	308E	Cosworth	V8				

Winning speed: 140.172 km/h, 87.099 mph
Pole Position speed: 145.141 km/h, 90.187 mph (C Reutemann, 1 min:20.636 sec)
Fastest Lap speed: 142.354 km/h, 88.454 mph (A Jones, 1 min:22.215 sec on lap 27)
Lap Leaders: G Villeneuve 1-38 (38.5); C Reutemann 39-80 (42).

The start and finish lines were at different positions on the circuit. The fraction of a lap is credited to the first lap leader.

7 May 1978 — MONACO: Monte Carlo (Round: 5) (Race: 302)

75 laps x 3.312 km, 2.058 miles = 248.400 km, 154.349 miles

POS.	NO.	DRIVER	CAR	MODEL	ENGINE		LAPS	TIME/REASON FOR RETIREMENT	GRID:POS	ROW
1	4	P Depailler	Tyrrell	008	Cosworth	V8	75	1h 55m 14.660s	5	3
2	1	N Lauda	Brabham	BT46	Alfa Romeo	F12	75	1h 55m 37.110s	3	2
3	20	J Scheckter	Wolf	WR1	Cosworth	V8	75	1h 55m 46.950s	9	5
4	2	J Watson	Brabham	BT46	Alfa Romeo	F12	75	1h 55m 48.190s	2	1
5	3	D Pironi	Tyrrell	008	Cosworth	V8	75	1h 56m 22.720s	13	7
6	35	R Patrese	Arrows	FA1	Cosworth	V8	75	1h 56m 23.430s	14	7
7	8	P Tambay	McLaren	M26	Cosworth	V8	74		11	6
8	11	C Reutemann	Ferrari	312T3	Ferrari	F12	74		1	1
9	14	E Fittipaldi	Copersucar	F5A	Cosworth	V8	74		20	10
10	15	J-P Jabouille	Renault	RS01	Renault	V6t	71		12	6
11	5	M Andretti	JPS Lotus	78	Cosworth	V8	69		4	2
r	12	G Villeneuve	Ferrari	312T3	Ferrari	F12	62	tyre burst/ accident	8	4
r	6	R Peterson	JPS Lotus	78	Cosworth	V8	56	gearbox	7	4
r	7	J Hunt	McLaren	M26	Cosworth	V8	43	anti-roll bar	6	3
r	36	R Stommelen	Arrows	FA1	Cosworth	V8	38	driver ill	19	10
r	27	A Jones	Williams	FW06	Cosworth	V8	29	oil leak	10	5
r	22	J Ickx	Ensign	N177	Cosworth	V8	27	brakes	16	8
r	16	H-J Stuck	Shadow	DN9	Cosworth	V8	24	accident/ steering	17	9
r	26	J Laffite	Ligier	JS9	Matra	V12	13	gearbox	15	8
r	18	R Keegan	Surtees	TS19	Cosworth	V8	8	crown wheel & pinion	18	9
nq	9	J Mass	ATS	HS1	Cosworth	V8				
nq	17	C Regazzoni	Shadow	DN9	Cosworth	V8				
nq	10	J-P Jarier	ATS	HS1	Cosworth	V8				
nq	19	V Brambilla	Surtees	TS20	Cosworth	V8				
npq	32	K Rosberg	Theodore	TR1	Cosworth	V8				
npq	24	D Daly	Hesketh	308E	Cosworth	V8				
npq	31	R Arnoux	Martini	MK23	Cosworth	V8				
npq	25	H Rebaque	Lotus	78	Cosworth	V8				
npq	30	B Lunger	McLaren	M26	Cosworth	V8				
npq	37	A Merzario	Merzario	A1	Cosworth	V8				

Winning speed: 129.325 km/h, 80.359 mph
Pole Position speed: 134.969 km/h, 83.866 mph (C Reutemann, 1 min:28.340 sec)
Fastest Lap speed: 134.497 km/h, 83.573 mph (N Lauda, 1 min:28.650 sec on lap 72)
Lap Leaders: J Watson 1-37 (37); P Depailler 38-75 (38).

21 May 1978 — BELGIUM: Zolder (Round: 6) (Race: 303)

70 laps x 4.262 km, 2.648 miles = 298.340 km, 185.380 miles

POS.	NO.	DRIVER	CAR	MODEL	ENGINE		LAPS	TIME/REASON FOR RETIREMENT	GRID:POS	ROW
1	5	M Andretti	JPS Lotus	79	Cosworth	V8	70	1h 39m 52.020s	1	1
2	6	R Peterson	JPS Lotus	78	Cosworth	V8	70	1h 40m 01.920s	7	4
3	11	C Reutemann	Ferrari	312T3	Ferrari	F12	70	1h 40m 16.360s	2	1
4	12	G Villeneuve	Ferrari	312T3	Ferrari	F12	70	1h 40m 39.060s	4	2
5r	26	J Laffite	Ligier	JS7	Matra	V12	69	accident	14	7
6	3	D Pironi	Tyrrell	008	Cosworth	V8	69		23	12
7	30	B Lunger	McLaren	M26	Cosworth	V8	69		24	12
8	33	B Giacomelli	McLaren	M26	Cosworth	V8	69		21	11
9	31	R Arnoux	Martini	MK23	Cosworth	V8	68		19	10
10	27	A Jones	Williams	FW06	Cosworth	V8	68		11	6
11	9	J Mass	ATS	HS1	Cosworth	V8	68		16	8
12	22	J Ickx	Ensign	N177	Cosworth	V8	64		22	11
13r	19	V Brambilla	Surtees	TS20	Cosworth	V8	63	engine	12	6
r	16	H-J Stuck	Shadow	DN9	Cosworth	V8	56	spin	20	10
nc	15	J-P Jabouille	Renault	RS01	Renault	V6t	56		10	5
r	20	J Scheckter	Wolf	WR1	Cosworth	V8	53	accident	5	3
r	4	P Depailler	Tyrrell	008	Cosworth	V8	51	gearbox	13	7
r	17	C Regazzoni	Shadow	DN9	Cosworth	V8	40	differential	18	9
r	35	R Patrese	Arrows	FA1	Cosworth	V8	31	rear suspension	8	4
r	36	R Stommelen	Arrows	FA1	Cosworth	V8	26	accident	17	9
r	2	J Watson	Brabham	BT46	Alfa Romeo	F12	18	accident	9	5
r	14	E Fittipaldi	Copersucar	F5A	Cosworth	V8	0	accident	15	8
r	7	J Hunt	McLaren	M26	Cosworth	V8	0	accident	6	3

POS.	NO.	DRIVER	CAR	MODEL	ENGINE		LAPS	TIME/REASON FOR RETIREMENT	GRID:POS	ROW
r	1	N Lauda	Brabham	BT46	Alfa Romeo	F12	0	accident	3	2
nq	18	R Keegan	Surtees	TS20	Cosworth	V8				
nq	24	D Daly	Hesketh	308E	Cosworth	V8				
nq	32	K Rosberg	Theodore	TR1	Cosworth	V8				
nq	10	A Colombo	ATS	HS1	Cosworth	V8				
npq	25	H Rebaque	Lotus	78	Cosworth	V8				
npq	37	A Merzario	Merzario	A1	Cosworth	V8				
npq	-	P Neve	March	781S	Cosworth	V8				
npq	-	B de Dryver	Ensign	N177	Cosworth	V8				

Winning speed: 179.242 km/h, 111.376 mph
Pole Position speed: 189.656 km/h, 117.847 mph (M Andretti, 1 min:20.900 sec)
Fastest Lap speed: 184.569 km/h, 114.686 mph (R Peterson, 1 min:23.130 sec on lap 66)
Lap Leaders: M Andretti 1-70 (70).

4 Jun 1978 SPAIN: Járama (Round: 7) (Race: 304)

75 laps x 3.404 km, 2.115 miles = 255.300 km, 158.636 miles

POS.	NO.	DRIVER	CAR	MODEL	ENGINE		LAPS	TIME/REASON FOR RETIREMENT	GRID:POS	ROW
1	5	M Andretti	JPS Lotus	79	Cosworth	V8	75	1h 41m 47.060s	1	1
2	6	R Peterson	JPS Lotus	79	Cosworth	V8	75	1h 42m 06.620s	2	1
3	26	J Laffite	Ligier	JS9	Matra	V12	75	1h 42m 24.300s	10	5
4	20	J Scheckter	Wolf	WR5	Cosworth	V8	75	1h 42m 47.120s	9	5
5	2	J Watson	Brabham	BT46	Alfa Romeo	F12	75	1h 42m 52.980s	7	4
6	7	J Hunt	McLaren	M26	Cosworth	V8	74		4	2
7	19	V Brambilla	Surtees	TS20	Cosworth	V8	74		16	8
8	27	A Jones	Williams	FW06	Cosworth	V8	74		18	9
9	9	J Mass	ATS	HS1	Cosworth	V8	74		17	9
10	12	G Villeneuve	Ferrari	312T3	Ferrari	F12	74		5	3
11	18	R Keegan	Surtees	TS20	Cosworth	V8	73		23	12
12	3	D Pironi	Tyrrell	008	Cosworth	V8	71		13	7
13	15	J-P Jabouille	Renault	RS01	Renault	V6t	71		11	6
14	36	R Stommelen	Arrows	FA1	Cosworth	V8	71		19	10
15r	17	C Regazzoni	Shadow	DN9	Cosworth	V8	67	fuel union	22	11
r	22	J Ickx	Ensign	N177	Cosworth	V8	64	engine	21	11
r	14	E Fittipaldi	Copersucar	F5A	Cosworth	V8	62	throttle linkage	15	8
r	11	C Reutemann	Ferrari	312T3	Ferrari	F12	57	drive shaft/ accident	3	2
r	1	N Lauda	Brabham	BT46	Alfa Romeo	F12	56	engine	6	3
r	4	P Depailler	Tyrrell	008	Cosworth	V8	51	engine	12	6
r	16	H-J Stuck	Shadow	DN9	Cosworth	V8	45	rear suspension radius rod	24	12
r	25	H Rebaque	Lotus	78	Cosworth	V8	21	exhaust	20	10
r	35	R Patrese	Arrows	FA1	Cosworth	V8	21	engine	8	4
r	8	P Tambay	McLaren	M26	Cosworth	V8	16	spin/ clutch	14	7
nq	37	A Merzario	Merzario	A1	Cosworth	V8				
nq	30	B Lunger	McLaren	M26	Cosworth	V8				
nq	36	E de Villota	McLaren	M23	Cosworth	V8				
nq	10	A Colombo	ATS	HS1	Cosworth	V8				
npq	32	K Rosberg	Theodore	TR1	Cosworth	V8				

Winning speed: 150.495 km/h, 93.513 mph
Pole Position speed: 160.419 km/h, 99.680 mph (M Andretti, 1 min:16.390 sec)
Fastest Lap speed: 153.065 km/h, 95.110 mph (M Andretti, 1 min:20.060 sec on lap 5)
Lap Leaders: J Hunt 1-5 (5); M Andretti 6-75 (70).

17 Jun 1978 SWEDEN: Anderstorp (Round: 8) (Race: 305)

70 laps x 4.031 km, 2.505 miles = 282.170 km, 175.332 miles

POS.	NO.	DRIVER	CAR	MODEL	ENGINE		LAPS	TIME/REASON FOR RETIREMENT	GRID:POS	ROW
1	1	N Lauda	Brabham	BT46B	Alfa Romeo	F12	70	1h 41m 00.606s	3	2
2	35	R Patrese	Arrows	FA1	Cosworth	V8	70	1h 41m 34.625s	5	3
3	6	R Peterson	JPS Lotus	79	Cosworth	V8	70	1h 41m 34.711s	4	2
4	8	P Tambay	McLaren	M26	Cosworth	V8	69		15	8
5	17	C Regazzoni	Shadow	DN9	Cosworth	V8	69		16	8
6	14	E Fittipaldi	Copersucar	F5A	Cosworth	V8	69		13	7
7	26	J Laffite	Ligier	JS9	Matra	V12	69		11	6
8	7	J Hunt	McLaren	M26	Cosworth	V8	69		14	7
9	12	G Villeneuve	Ferrari	312T3	Ferrari	F12	69		7	4
10	11	C Reutemann	Ferrari	312T3	Ferrari	F12	69		8	4
11	16	H-J Stuck	Shadow	DN9	Cosworth	V8	68		20	10
12	25	H Rebaque	Lotus	78	Cosworth	V8	68		21	11
13	9	J Mass	ATS	HS1	Cosworth	V8	68		19	10
14	36	R Stommelen	Arrows	FA1	Cosworth	V8	67		24	12
15	10	K Rosberg	ATS	HS1	Cosworth	V8	63		23	12
nc	37	A Merzario	Merzario	A1	Cosworth	V8	62		22	11
r	5	M Andretti	JPS Lotus	79	Cosworth	V8	46	piston	1	1
r	27	A Jones	Williams	FW06	Cosworth	V8	46	front wheel bearing	9	5
r	4	P Depailler	Tyrrell	008	Cosworth	V8	42	suspension	12	6
r	15	J-P Jabouille	Renault	RS01	Renault	V6t	28	piston	10	5
r	2	J Watson	Brabham	BT46B	Alfa Romeo	F12	19	spin/ throttle jammed	2	1
r	20	J Scheckter	Wolf	WR5	Cosworth	V8	16	water pipe	6	3
r	3	D Pironi	Tyrrell	008	Cosworth	V8	8	accident/ puncture/ suspension	17	9
r	19	V Brambilla	Surtees	TS20	Cosworth	V8	7	accident	18	9
nq	18	R Keegan	Surtees	TS20	Cosworth	V8				
nq	30	B Lunger	McLaren	M26	Cosworth	V8				
nq	22	J Ickx	Ensign	N177	Cosworth	V8				

Winning speed: 167.609 km/h, 104.147 mph
Pole Position speed: 176.846 km/h, 109.887 mph (M Andretti, 1 min:22.058 sec)
Fastest Lap speed: 171.055 km/h, 106.288 mph (N Lauda, 1 min:24.836 sec on lap 33)
Lap Leaders: M Andretti 1-38 (38); N Lauda 39-70 (32).

2 Jul 1978 — FRANCE: Paul Ricard (Round: 9) (Race: 306)

54 laps x 5.810 km, 3.610 miles = 313.740 km, 194.949 miles

POS.	NO.	DRIVER	CAR	MODEL	ENGINE		LAPS	TIME/REASON FOR RETIREMENT	GRID:POS	ROW
1	5	M Andretti	JPS Lotus	79	Cosworth	V8	54	1h 38m 51.920s	2	1
2	6	R Peterson	JPS Lotus	79	Cosworth	V8	54	1h 38m 54.850s	5	3
3	7	J Hunt	McLaren	M26	Cosworth	V8	54	1h 39m 11.720s	4	2
4	2	J Watson	Brabham	BT46	Alfa Romeo	F12	54	1h 39m 28.800s	1	1
5	27	A Jones	Williams	FW06	Cosworth	V8	54	1h 39m 33.730s	14	7
6	20	J Scheckter	Wolf	WR5	Cosworth	V8	54	1h 39m 46.450s	7	4
7	26	J Laffite	Ligier	JS9	Matra	V12	54	1h 39m 46.660s	10	5
8	35	R Patrese	Arrows	FA1	Cosworth	V8	54	1h 40m 16.800s	12	6
9	8	P Tambay	McLaren	M26	Cosworth	V8	54	1h 40m 18.980s	6	3
10	3	D Pironi	Tyrrell	008	Cosworth	V8	54	1h 40m 21.900s	16	8
11	16	H-J Stuck	Shadow	DN9	Cosworth	V8	53		20	10
12	12	G Villeneuve	Ferrari	312T3	Ferrari	F12	53		9	5
13	9	J Mass	ATS	HS1	Cosworth	V8	53		25	13
14	31	R Arnoux	Martini	MK23	Cosworth	V8	53		18	9
15	36	R Stommelen	Arrows	FA1	Cosworth	V8	53		21	11
16	10	K Rosberg	ATS	HS1	Cosworth	V8	52		26	13
17	19	V Brambilla	Surtees	TS20	Cosworth	V8	52		19	10
18	11	C Reutemann	Ferrari	312T3	Ferrari	F12	49		8	4
r	30	B Lunger	McLaren	M26	Cosworth	V8	45	engine	24	12
r	14	E Fittipaldi	Copersucar	F5A	Cosworth	V8	43	rear suspension	15	8
r	18	R Keegan	Surtees	TS20	Cosworth	V8	40	engine	23	12
r	33	B Giacomelli	McLaren	M26	Cosworth	V8	28	engine	22	11
r	4	P Depailler	Tyrrell	008	Cosworth	V8	10	engine	13	7
r	1	N Lauda	Brabham	BT46	Alfa Romeo	F12	10	engine	3	2
r	17	C Regazzoni	Shadow	DN9	Cosworth	V8	4	electrics	17	9
r	15	J-P Jabouille	Renault	RS01	Renault	V6t	1	engine	11	6
nq	37	A Merzario	Merzario	A1	Cosworth	V8				
nq	22	D Daly	Ensign	N177	Cosworth	V8				
nq	25	H Rebaque	Lotus	78	Cosworth	V8				

Winning speed: 190.404 km/h, 118.312 mph
Pole Position speed: 200.326 km/h, 124.477 mph (J Watson, 1 min:44.410 sec)
Fastest Lap speed: 192.668 km/h, 119.718 mph (C Reutemann, 1 min:48.560 sec on lap 48)
Lap Leaders: M Andretti 1-54 (54).

16 Jul 1978 — BRITAIN: Brands Hatch (Round:10) (Race: 307)

76 laps x 4.207 km, 2.614 miles = 319.719 km, 198.664 miles

POS.	NO.	DRIVER	CAR	MODEL	ENGINE		LAPS	TIME/REASON FOR RETIREMENT	GRID:POS	ROW
1	11	C Reutemann	Ferrari	312T3	Ferrari	F12	76	1h 42m 12.390s	8	4
2	1	N Lauda	Brabham	BT46	Alfa Romeo	F12	76	1h 42m 13.620s	4	2
3	2	J Watson	Brabham	BT46	Alfa Romeo	F12	76	1h 42m 49.640s	9	5
4	4	P Depailler	Tyrrell	008	Cosworth	V8	76	1h 43m 25.660s	10	5
5	16	H-J Stuck	Shadow	DN9	Cosworth	V8	75		18	9
6	8	P Tambay	McLaren	M26	Cosworth	V8	75		20	10
7	33	B Giacomelli	McLaren	M26	Cosworth	V8	75		16	8
8	30	B Lunger	McLaren	M26	Cosworth	V8	75		24	12
9	19	V Brambilla	Surtees	TS20	Cosworth	V8	75		25	13
10	26	J Laffite	Ligier	JS9	Matra	V12	73		7	4
nc	9	J Mass	ATS	HS1	Cosworth	V8	66		26	13
r	10	K Rosberg	ATS	HS1	Cosworth	V8	59	front suspension	22	11
r	17	C Regazzoni	Shadow	DN9	Cosworth	V8	49	gearbox	17	9
r	15	J-P Jabouille	Renault	RS01	Renault	V6t	46	engine	12	6
r	35	R Patrese	Arrows	FA1	Cosworth	V8	40	puncture/ rear suspension	5	3
r	3	D Pironi	Tyrrell	008	Cosworth	V8	40	gearbox mounting	19	10
r	20	J Scheckter	Wolf	WR5	Cosworth	V8	36	gearbox	3	2
r	14	E Fittipaldi	Copersucar	F5A	Cosworth	V8	32	engine	11	6
r	37	A Merzario	Merzario	A1	Cosworth	V8	32	fuel pump	23	12
r	22	D Daly	Ensign	N177	Cosworth	V8	30	wheel lost/ accident	15	8
r	5	M Andretti	JPS Lotus	79	Cosworth	V8	28	engine	2	1
r	27	A Jones	Williams	FW06	Cosworth	V8	26	drive shaft	6	3
r	12	G Villeneuve	Ferrari	312T3	Ferrari	F12	19	drive shaft	13	7
r	25	H Rebaque	Lotus	78	Cosworth	V8	15	gearbox	21	11
r	7	J Hunt	McLaren	M26	Cosworth	V8	7	accident	14	7
r	6	R Peterson	JPS Lotus	79	Cosworth	V8	6	fuel leak	1	1
nq	36	R Stommelen	Arrows	FA1	Cosworth	V8				
nq	23	G Lees	Ensign	N175	Cosworth	V8				
nq	18	R Keegan	Surtees	TS20	Cosworth	V8				
nq	40	T Trimmer	McLaren	M23	Cosworth	V8				

Winning speed: 187.690 km/h, 116.625 mph
Pole Position speed: 197.195 km/h, 122.531 mph (R Peterson, 1 min:16.800 sec)
Fastest Lap speed: 192.679 km/h, 119.725 mph (N Lauda, 1 min:18.600 sec on lap 72)
Lap Leaders: M Andretti 1-23 (23); J Scheckter 24-33 (10); N Lauda 34-59 (26); C Reutemann 60-76 (17).

30 Jul 1978 — GERMANY: Hockenheim (Round:11) (Race: 308)

45 laps x 6.789 km, 4.218 miles = 305.505 km, 189.832 miles

POS.	NO.	DRIVER	CAR	MODEL	ENGINE		LAPS	TIME/REASON FOR RETIREMENT	GRID:POS	ROW
1	5	M Andretti	JPS Lotus	79	Cosworth	V8	45	1h 28m 00.900s	1	1
2	20	J Scheckter	Wolf	WR5	Cosworth	V8	45	1h 28m 16.250s	4	2
3	26	J Laffite	Ligier	JS9	Matra	V12	45	1h 28m 28.910s	7	4
4	14	E Fittipaldi	Copersucar	F5A	Cosworth	V8	45	1h 28m 37.780s	10	5
5	3	D Pironi	Tyrrell	008	Cosworth	V8	45	1h 28m 58.160s	16	8
6	25	H Rebaque	Lotus	78	Cosworth	V8	45	1h 29m 38.760s	18	9
7	2	J Watson	Brabham	BT46	Alfa Romeo	F12	45	1h 29m 40.430s	5	3
8	12	G Villeneuve	Ferrari	312T3	Ferrari	F12	45	1h 29m 57.770s	15	8
9	35	R Patrese	Arrows	FA1	Cosworth	V8	44		14	7
10	32	K Rosberg	Wolf	WR3	Cosworth	V8	42		19	10
dq	36	R Stommelen	Arrows	FA1	Cosworth	V8	42	incorrect route into pits	17	9
11r	23	H Ertl	Ensign	N177	Cosworth	V8	41	engine	23	12
r	6	R Peterson	JPS Lotus	79	Cosworth	V8	36	gearbox	2	1
dq	7	J Hunt	McLaren	M26	Cosworth	V8	34	incorrect route into pits	8	4
r	27	A Jones	Williams	FW06	Cosworth	V8	31	fuel vaporisation	6	3
r	22	N Piquet	Ensign	N177	Cosworth	V8	31	engine	21	11
r	19	V Brambilla	Surtees	TS20	Cosworth	V8	24	fuel vaporisation	20	10
r	8	P Tambay	McLaren	M26	Cosworth	V8	16	puncture/ suspension/ accident	11	6
r	11	C Reutemann	Ferrari	312T3	Ferrari	F12	14	fuel vaporisation	12	6
r	1	N Lauda	Brabham	BT46	Alfa Romeo	F12	11	engine	3	2
r	15	J-P Jabouille	Renault	RS01	Renault	V6t	5	engine	9	5
r	16	H-J Stuck	Shadow	DN9	Cosworth	V8	1	accident	24	12
r	9	J Mass	ATS	HS1	Cosworth	V8	1	accident/ suspension	22	11
r	4	P Depailler	Tyrrell	008	Cosworth	V8	0	accident	13	7
nq	17	C Regazzoni	Shadow	DN9	Cosworth	V8				
nq	10	J-P Jarier	ATS	HS1	Cosworth	V8				
nq	18	R Keegan	Surtees	TS20	Cosworth	V8				
nq	37	A Merzario	Merzario	A1	Cosworth	V8				
npq	31	R Arnoux	Martini	MK23	Cosworth	V8				
npq	30	B Lunger	McLaren	M26	Cosworth	V8				

Winning speed: 208.263 km/h, 129.409 mph
Pole Position speed: 218.413 km/h, 135.715 mph (M Andretti, 1 min:51.900 sec)
Fastest Lap speed: 211.386 km/h, 131.349 mph (R Peterson, 1 min:55.620 sec on lap 26)
Lap Leaders: R Peterson 1-4 (4); M Andretti 5-45 (41).

13 Aug 1978 — AUSTRIA: Österreichring (Round:12) (Race: 309)

54 laps x 5.942 km, 3.692 miles = 320.868 km, 199.378 miles

POS.	NO.	DRIVER	CAR	MODEL	ENGINE		LAPS	TIME/REASON FOR RETIREMENT	GRID:POS	ROW
1	6	R Peterson	JPS Lotus	79	Cosworth	V8	54	1h 41m 21.570s	1	1
2	4	P Depailler	Tyrrell	008	Cosworth	V8	54	1h 42m 09.010s	13	7
3	12	G Villeneuve	Ferrari	312T3	Ferrari	F12	54	1h 43m 01.330s	11	6
4	14	E Fittipaldi	Copersucar	F5A	Cosworth	V8	53		6	3
5	26	J Laffite	Ligier	JS9	Matra	V12	53		5	3
6	19	V Brambilla	Surtees	TS20	Cosworth	V8	53		21	11
7	2	J Watson	Brabham	BT46	Alfa Romeo	F12	53		10	5
8	30	B Lunger	McLaren	M26	Cosworth	V8	52		17	9
9	31	R Arnoux	Martini	MK23	Cosworth	V8	52		26	13
nc	17	C Regazzoni	Shadow	DN9	Cosworth	V8	50		22	11
nc	32	K Rosberg	Wolf	WR3	Cosworth	V8	49		25	13
dq	22	D Daly	Ensign	N177	Cosworth	V8	43	push start after spin	19	10
r	8	P Tambay	McLaren	M26	Cosworth	V8	40	accident	14	7
r	16	H-J Stuck	Shadow	DN9	Cosworth	V8	33	accident	23	12
r	15	J-P Jabouille	Renault	RS01	Renault	V6t	31	gearbox	3	2
r	1	N Lauda	Brabham	BT46	Alfa Romeo	F12	28	accident	12	6
dq	11	C Reutemann	Ferrari	312T3	Ferrari	F12	27	push start after spin	4	2
r	3	D Pironi	Tyrrell	008	Cosworth	V8	20	accident	9	5
r	7	J Hunt	McLaren	M26	Cosworth	V8	8	accident	8	4
r	27	A Jones	Williams	FW06	Cosworth	V8	7	accident	15	8
r	23	H Ertl	Ensign	N177	Cosworth	V8	6	accident	24	12
r	35	R Patrese	Arrows	A1	Cosworth	V8	6	accident	16	8
r	20	J Scheckter	Wolf	WR5	Cosworth	V8	3	accident	7	4
r	29	N Piquet	McLaren	M23	Cosworth	V8	2	accident	20	10
r	25	H Rebaque	Lotus	78	Cosworth	V8	1	clutch	18	9
r	5	M Andretti	JPS Lotus	79	Cosworth	V8	0	accident	2	1
nq	37	A Merzario	Merzario	A1	Cosworth	V8				
nq	9	J Mass	ATS	HS1	Cosworth	V8				
nq	18	R Keegan	Surtees	TS20	Cosworth	V8				
nq	10	H Binder	ATS	HS1	Cosworth	V8				
nq	18	B Henton	Surtees	TS20	Cosworth	V8		tested only/ car raced by Keegan		
npq	36	R Stommelen	Arrows	A1	Cosworth	V8				

Winning speed: 189.939 km/h, 118.022 mph
Pole Position speed: 218.925 km/h, 136.034 mph (R Peterson, 1 min:37.710 sec)
Fastest Lap speed: 207.440 km/h, 128.897 mph (R Peterson, 1 min:43.120 sec)
Lap Leaders: R Peterson 1-18,29-54 (44); C Reutemann 19-22 (4); G Villeneuve 23-28 (6).

Interrupted after 7 laps, because of an accident. Restarted for the remaining 47 laps, with results being on aggregate. Lap leaders are given 'on the road'.

27 Aug 1978 — NETHERLANDS: Zandvoort — (Round:13) (Race: 310)

75 laps x 4.226 km, 2.626 miles = 316.950 km, 196.944 miles

POS.	NO.	DRIVER	CAR	MODEL	ENGINE		LAPS	TIME/REASON FOR RETIREMENT	GRID:POS	ROW
1	5	M Andretti	JPS Lotus	79	Cosworth	V8	75	1h 41m 04.230s	1	1
2	6	R Peterson	JPS Lotus	79	Cosworth	V8	75	1h 41m 04.550s	2	1
3	1	N Lauda	Brabham	BT46	Alfa Romeo	F12	75	1h 41m 16.440s	3	2
4	2	J Watson	Brabham	BT46	Alfa Romeo	F12	75	1h 41m 25.150s	8	4
5	14	E Fittipaldi	Copersucar	F5A	Cosworth	V8	75	1h 41m 25.730s	10	5
6	12	G Villeneuve	Ferrari	312T3	Ferrari	F12	75	1h 41m 50.180s	5	3
7	11	C Reutemann	Ferrari	312T3	Ferrari	F12	75	1h 42m 04.730s	4	2
8	26	J Laffite	Ligier	JS9	Matra	V12	74		6	3
9	8	P Tambay	McLaren	M26	Cosworth	V8	74		14	7
10	7	J Hunt	McLaren	M26	Cosworth	V8	74		7	4
11	25	H Rebaque	Lotus	78	Cosworth	V8	74		20	10
12	20	J Scheckter	Wolf	WR6	Cosworth	V8	73		15	8
r	33	B Giacomelli	McLaren	M26	Cosworth	V8	60	spin	19	10
r	16	H-J Stuck	Shadow	DN9	Cosworth	V8	56	differential	18	9
r	31	R Arnoux	Martini	MK23	Cosworth	V8	40	rear wing mounting	23	12
r	37	A Merzario	Merzario	A1	Cosworth	V8	40	engine	27	14
dq	19	V Brambilla	Surtees	TS20	Cosworth	V8	37	push start after spin	22	11
r	15	J-P Jabouille	Renault	RS01	Renault	V6t	35	piston	9	5
r	30	B Lunger	McLaren	M26	Cosworth	V8	35	engine	21	11
r	32	K Rosberg	Wolf	WR4	Cosworth	V8	21	throttle jammed/ accident	24	12
r	27	A Jones	Williams	FW06	Cosworth	V8	17	throttle linkage	11	6
r	29	N Piquet	McLaren	M23	Cosworth	V8	16	drive shaft	26	13
r	4	P Depailler	Tyrrell	008	Cosworth	V8	13	engine	12	6
r	22	D Daly	Ensign	N177	Cosworth	V8	10	drive shaft	16	8
r	35	R Patrese	Arrows	A1	Cosworth	V8	0	accident	13	7
r	3	D Pironi	Tyrrell	008	Cosworth	V8	0	accident	17	9
ns	18	R Keegan	Surtees	TS20	Cosworth	V8		accident/ injury	25	13
nq	17	C Regazzoni	Shadow	DN9	Cosworth	V8				
nq	10	M Bleekemolen	ATS	HS1	Cosworth	V8				
nq	9	J Mass	ATS	HS1	Cosworth	V8				
npq	23	H Ertl	Ensign	N177	Cosworth	V8				
npq	39	D Ongais	Shadow	DN9	Cosworth	V8				
npq	36	R Stommelen	Arrows	A1	Cosworth	V8				

Winning speed: 188.156 km/h, 116.915 mph
Pole Position speed: 199.235 km/h, 123.799 mph (M Andretti, 1 min:16.360 sec)
Fastest Lap speed: 191.198 km/h, 118.805 mph (N Lauda, 1 min:19.570 sec on lap 57)
Lap Leaders: M Andretti 1-75 (75).

10 Sep 1978 — ITALY: Monza — (Round:14) (Race: 311)

40 laps x 5.800 km, 3.604 miles = 232.000 km, 144.158 miles

POS.	NO.	DRIVER	CAR	MODEL	ENGINE		LAPS	TIME/REASON FOR RETIREMENT	GRID:POS	ROW
1	1	N Lauda	Brabham	BT46	Alfa Romeo	F12	40	1h 07m 04.540s	4	2
2	2	J Watson	Brabham	BT46	Alfa Romeo	F12	40	1h 07m 06.020s	7	4
3	11	C Reutemann	Ferrari	312T3	Ferrari	F12	40	1h 07m 25.010s	11	6
4	26	J Laffite	Ligier	JS9	Matra	V12	40	1h 07m 42.070s	8	4
5	8	P Tambay	McLaren	M26	Cosworth	V8	40	1h 07m 44.930s	19	10
6	5	M Andretti	JPS Lotus	79	Cosworth	V8	40	1h 07m 50.870s	1	1
7	12	G Villeneuve	Ferrari	312T3	Ferrari	F12	40	1h 07m 53.020s	2	1
8	14	E Fittipaldi	Copersucar	F5A	Cosworth	V8	40	1h 07m 59.780s	13	7
9	29	N Piquet	McLaren	M23	Cosworth	V8	40	1h 08m 11.370s	24	12
10	22	D Daly	Ensign	N177	Cosworth	V8	40	1h 08m 13.650s	18	9
11	4	P Depailler	Tyrrell	008	Cosworth	V8	40	1h 08m 21.110s	16	8
12	20	J Scheckter	Wolf	WR5	Cosworth	V8	39		9	5
13	27	A Jones	Williams	FW06	Cosworth	V8	39		6	3
14	33	B Giacomelli	McLaren	M26	Cosworth	V8	39		20	10
nc	17	C Regazzoni	Shadow	DN9	Cosworth	V8	33		15	8
r	35	R Patrese	Arrows	A1	Cosworth	V8	29	engine	12	6
r	7	J Hunt	McLaren	M26	Cosworth	V8	19	distributor	10	5
r	37	A Merzario	Merzario	A1	Cosworth	V8	14	engine	22	11
r	15	J-P Jabouille	Renault	RS01	Renault	V6t	6	dropped valve	3	2
r	6	R Peterson	JPS Lotus	78	Cosworth	V8	0	fatal accident *	5	3
r	19	V Brambilla	Surtees	TS20	Cosworth	V8	0	accident *	23	12
r	30	B Lunger	McLaren	M26	Cosworth	V8	0	accident *	21	11
r	3	D Pironi	Tyrrell	008	Cosworth	V8	0	accident *	14	7
r	16	H-J Stuck	Shadow	DN9	Cosworth	V8	0	accident *	17	9
nq	25	H Rebaque	Lotus	78	Cosworth	V8				
nq	10	H Ertl	ATS	HS1	Cosworth	V8				
nq	9	M Bleekemolen	ATS	HS1	Cosworth	V8				
nq	18	Gimax	Surtees	TS20	Cosworth	V8				
npq	32	K Rosberg	Wolf	WR4	Cosworth	V8				
npq	36	R Stommelen	Arrows	A1	Cosworth	V8				
npq	34	A Colombo	Merzario	A1	Cosworth	V8				

Winning speed: 207.527 km/h, 128.951 mph
Pole Position speed: 214.110 km/h, 133.042 mph (M Andretti, 1 min:37.520 sec)
Fastest Lap speed: 212.562 km/h, 132.080 mph (M Andretti, 1 min:38.230 sec on lap 33)
Lap Leaders: G Villeneuve 1-34 (34); M Andretti 35-40 (6).

Scheduled for 52 laps, but interrupted after 1st lap accident. Restarted race was shortened. M Andretti finished 1st in 1h 06m 40.39s (208.780 km/h, 129.730 mph), but penalised 1 minute for jumping the start and classified 6th. G Villeneuve finished 2nd, but penalised 1 minute for jumping the start and classified 7th. These drivers are shown as leaders 'on the road'. H Ertl also practiced in an Ensign N177-Cosworth V8 (23) but failed to pre-qualify.

1 Oct 1978 — USA East: Watkins Glen (Round:15) (Race: 312)

59 laps x 5.435 km, 3.377 miles = 320.651 km, 199.243 miles

POS.	NO.	DRIVER	CAR	MODEL	ENGINE		LAPS	TIME/REASON FOR RETIREMENT	GRID:POS	ROW
1	11	C Reutemann	Ferrari	312T3	Ferrari	F12	59	1h 40m 48.800s	2	1
2	27	A Jones	Williams	FW06	Cosworth	V8	59	1h 41m 08.539s	3	2
3	20	J Scheckter	Wolf	WR6	Cosworth	V8	59	1h 41m 34.501s	11	6
4	15	J-P Jabouille	Renault	RS01	Renault	V6t	59	1h 42m 13.807s	9	5
5	14	E Fittipaldi	Copersucar	F5A	Cosworth	V8	59	1h 42m 16.889s	13	7
6	8	P Tambay	McLaren	M26	Cosworth	V8	59	1h 42m 39.010s	18	9
7	7	J Hunt	McLaren	M26	Cosworth	V8	58		6	3
8	22	D Daly	Ensign	N177	Cosworth	V8	58		19	10
9	18	R Arnoux	Surtees	TS20	Cosworth	V8	58		21	11
10	3	D Pironi	Tyrrell	008	Cosworth	V8	58		16	8
11	26	J Laffite	Ligier	JS9	Matra	V12	58		10	5
12	21	B Rahal	Wolf	WR5	Cosworth	V8	58		20	10
13	23	B Lunger	Ensign	N177	Cosworth	V8	58		24	12
14	17	C Regazzoni	Shadow	DN9	Cosworth	V8	56		17	9
15r	55	J-P Jarier	JPS Lotus	79	Cosworth	V8	55	out of fuel	8	4
16	36	R Stommelen	Arrows	A1	Cosworth	V8	54		22	11
r	37	A Merzario	Merzario	A1	Cosworth	V8	46	gearbox oil leak	26	13
r	9	M Bleekemolen	ATS	HS1	Cosworth	V8	43	oil pump leak	25	13
r	1	N Lauda	Brabham	BT46	Alfa Romeo	F12	28	engine	5	3
r	5	M Andretti	JPS Lotus	79	Cosworth	V8	27	engine	1	1
r	2	J Watson	Brabham	BT46	Alfa Romeo	F12	25	engine	7	4
r	4	P Depailler	Tyrrell	008	Cosworth	V8	23	rear hub	12	6
r	12	G Villeneuve	Ferrari	312T3	Ferrari	F12	22	engine	4	2
r	32	K Rosberg	ATS	D1	Cosworth	V8	21	gear linkage	15	8
r	16	H-J Stuck	Shadow	DN9	Cosworth	V8	1	fuel pump	14	7
r	25	H Rebaque	Lotus	78	Cosworth	V8	0	clutch	23	12
nq	19	B Gabbiani	Surtees	TS20	Cosworth	V8				

Winning speed: 190.838 km/h, 118.581 mph
Pole Position speed: 199.412 km/h, 123.909 mph (M Andretti, 1 min:38.114 sec)
Fastest Lap speed: 196.522 km/h, 122.113 mph (J-P Jarier, 1 min:39.557 sec on lap 55)
Lap Leaders: M Andretti 1-2 (2); C Reutemann 3-59 (57).

8 Oct 1978 — CANADA: Montréal (Round: 16) (Race: 313)

70 laps x 4.500 km, 2.796 miles = 315.000 km, 195.732 miles

POS.	NO.	DRIVER	CAR	MODEL	ENGINE		LAPS	TIME/REASON FOR RETIREMENT	GRID:POS	ROW
1	12	G Villeneuve	Ferrari	312T3	Ferrari	F12	70	1h 57m 49.196s	3	2
2	20	J Scheckter	Wolf	WR6	Cosworth	V8	70	1h 58m 02.568s	2	1
3	11	C Reutemann	Ferrari	312T3	Ferrari	F12	70	1h 58m 08.604s	11	6
4	35	R Patrese	Arrows	A1	Cosworth	V8	70	1h 58m 13.863s	12	6
5	4	P Depailler	Tyrrell	008	Cosworth	V8	70	1h 58m 17.754s	13	7
6	22	D Daly	Ensign	N177	Cosworth	V8	70	1h 58m 43.672s	15	8
7	3	D Pironi	Tyrrell	008	Cosworth	V8	70	1h 59m 10.446s	18	9
8	8	P Tambay	McLaren	M26	Cosworth	V8	70	1h 59m 15.756s	17	9
9	27	A Jones	Williams	FW06	Cosworth	V8	70	1h 59m 18.138s	5	3
10	5	M Andretti	JPS Lotus	79	Cosworth	V8	69		9	5
11	66	N Piquet	Brabham	BT46	Alfa Romeo	F12	69		14	7
12	15	J-P Jabouille	Renault	RS01	Renault	V6t	65		22	11
nc	32	K Rosberg	ATS	D1	Cosworth	V8	58		21	11
r	26	J Laffite	Ligier	JS9	Matra	V12	52	transmission	10	5
r	7	J Hunt	McLaren	M26	Cosworth	V8	51	accident	19	10
r	55	J-P Jarier	JPS Lotus	79	Cosworth	V8	49	oil radiator leak	1	1
r	18	R Arnoux	Surtees	TS20	Cosworth	V8	37	oil pressure	16	8
r	21	B Rahal	Wolf	WR1	Cosworth	V8	16	fuel system	20	10
r	2	J Watson	Brabham	BT46	Alfa Romeo	F12	8	accident	4	2
r	1	N Lauda	Brabham	BT46	Alfa Romeo	F12	5	brakes/ accident	7	4
r	16	H-J Stuck	Shadow	DN9	Cosworth	V8	1	accident	8	4
r	14	E Fittipaldi	Copersucar	F5A	Cosworth	V8	0	accident	6	3
nq	17	C Regazzoni	Shadow	DN9	Cosworth	V8				
nq	19	B Gabbiani	Surtees	TS20	Cosworth	V8				
nq	37	A Merzario	Merzario	A1	Cosworth	V8				
nq	25	H Rebaque	Lotus	78	Cosworth	V8				
nq	36	R Stommelen	Arrows	A1	Cosworth	V8				
nq	9	M Bleekemolen	ATS	HS1	Cosworth	V8				

Winning speed: 160.414 km/h, 99.677 mph
Pole Position speed: 165.281 km/h, 102.701 mph (J-P Jarier, 1 min:38.015 sec)
Fastest Lap speed: 165.185 km/h, 102.641 mph (A Jones, 1 min:38.072 sec on lap 70)
Lap Leaders:J-P Jarier 1-49 (49); G Villeneuve 50-70 (21).

Lap Leaders 1978

POS	DRIVER	CAR-ENGINE	GPS	LAPS	KM	MILES
1	M Andretti	Lotus-Cosworth	11	451	2,133.7	1,325.8
2	C Reutemann	Ferrari	5	183	858.6	533.5
3	G Villeneuve	Ferrari	4	99.5	452.5	281.2
4	N Lauda	Brabham-Alfa Romeo	2	58	238.4	148.1
5	P Depailler	Tyrrell-Cosworth	2	52	183.3	113.9
6	R Peterson	Lotus-Cosworth	3	49	292.7	181.9
	J-P Jarier	Lotus-Cosworth	1	49	220.5	137.0
8	R Patrese	Arrows-Cosworth	1	37	151.8	94.4
	J Watson	Brabham-Alfa Romeo	1	37	122.5	76.1
10	J Scheckter	Wolf-Cosworth	2	16	66.7	41.4
11	J Hunt	McLaren-Cosworth	1	5	17.0	10.6
			16	**1,036.5**	**4,737.8**	**2,943.9**

Driver Points 1978

		RA	BR	ZA	USAW	MC	B	E	S	F	GB	D	A	NL	I	USAE	CDN	TOTAL
1	M Andretti	9	3	-	6	-	9	9	-	9	-	9	-	9	1	-	-	64
2	R Peterson	2	-	9	3	-	6	6	4	6	-	-	9	6	-	-	-	51
3	C Reutemann	-	9	-	9	-	4	-	-	-	9	-	-	-	4	9	4	48
4	N Lauda	6	4	-	-	6	-	-	9	-	6	-	-	4	9	-	-	44
5	P Depailler	4	-	6	4	9	-	-	-	-	3	-	6	-	-	-	2	34
6	J Watson	-	-	4	-	3	-	2	-	3	4	-	-	3	6	-	-	25
7	J Scheckter	-	-	-	-	4	-	3	-	1	-	6	-	-	-	4	6	24
8	J Laffite	-	-	2	2	-	2	4	-	-	-	4	2	-	3	-	-	19
9	G Villeneuve	-	-	-	-	-	3	-	-	-	-	-	4	1	-	-	9	17
	E Fittipaldi	-	6	-	-	-	-	-	1	-	-	3	3	2	-	2	-	17
11	A Jones	-	-	3	-	-	-	-	-	2	-	-	-	-	-	6	-	11
	R Patrese	-	-	-	1	1	-	-	6	-	-	-	-	-	-	-	3	11
13	J Hunt	3	-	-	-	-	-	1	-	4	-	-	-	-	-	-	-	8
	P Tambay	1	-	-	-	-	-	-	3	-	1	-	-	-	2	1	-	8
15	D Pironi	-	1	1	-	2	1	-	-	-	-	2	-	-	-	-	-	7
16	C Regazzoni	-	2	-	-	-	-	-	2	-	-	-	-	-	-	-	-	4
17	J-P Jabouille	-	-	-	-	-	-	-	-	-	-	-	-	-	-	3	-	3
18	H-J Stuck	-	-	-	-	-	-	-	-	-	2	-	-	-	-	-	-	2
19	H Rebaque	-	-	-	-	-	-	-	-	-	-	1	-	-	-	-	-	1
	V Brambilla	-	-	-	-	-	-	-	-	-	-	-	1	-	-	-	-	1
	D Daly	-	-	-	-	-	-	-	-	-	-	-	-	-	-	-	1	1

9, 6, 4, 3,2 and 1 point awarded to the first six finishers.
Best 7 scores from first 8 races, best 7 from remaining 8 races.

Constructor Points 1978

		RA	BR	ZA	USAW	MC	B	E	S	F	GB	D	A	NL	I	USAE	CDN	TOTAL
1	Lotus-Cosworth	9	3	9	6	-	9	9	4	9	-	9	9	9	1	-	-	86
2	Ferrari	-	9	-	9	-	4	-	-	-	9	-	4	1	4	9	9	58
3	Brabham-Alfa Romeo	6	4	4	-	6	-	2	9	3	6	-	-	4	9	-	-	53
4	Tyrrell-Cosworth	4	1	6	4	9	1	-	-	-	3	2	6	-	-	-	2	38
5	Wolf-Cosworth	-	-	-	-	4	-	3	-	1	-	6	-	-	-	4	6	24
6	Ligier-Matra	-	-	2	2	-	2	4	-	-	-	4	2	-	3	-	-	19
7	Copersucar-Cosworth	-	6	-	-	-	-	-	1	-	-	3	3	2	-	2	-	17
8	McLaren-Cosworth	3	-	-	-	-	-	1	3	4	1	-	-	-	2	1	-	15
9	Williams-Cosworth	-	-	3	-	-	-	-	-	2	-	-	-	-	-	6	-	11
	Arrows-Cosworth	-	-	-	1	1	-	-	6	-	-	-	-	-	-	-	3	11
11	Shadow-Cosworth	-	2	-	-	-	-	-	2	-	2	-	-	-	-	-	-	6
12	Renault	-	-	-	-	-	-	-	-	-	-	-	-	-	-	3	-	3
13	Surtees-Cosworth	-	-	-	-	-	-	-	-	-	-	-	1	-	-	-	-	1
	Ensign-Cosworth	-	-	-	-	-	-	-	-	-	-	-	-	-	-	-	1	1

9, 6, 4, 3,2 and 1 point awarded to the first six finishers. Points only for highest placed car.
Best 7 scores from first 8 races, best 7 from remaining 8 races.

JPS left as Lotus sponsors and the new model was too advanced to tame. Alfa Romeo returned as a constructor in its own right. The CSI was replaced by la Fédération Internationale du Sport Automobile (FISA) headed by Jean-Marie Balestre. A turbo won for the first time and carbon-fibre formed part of the new Brabham chassis.

LOTUS
Martini Racing Team Lotus: Andretti, Reutemann
Team Rebaque: Rebaque

TYRRELL
Team Tyrrell: Pironi, Jarier, Lees, Daly
Candy Team Tyrrell from B GP

BRABHAM
Parmalat Racing Team: Lauda, Zunino, Piquet

McLAREN
Marlboro Team McLaren: Watson, Tambay

ATS
ATS Wheels: Stuck

FERRARI
Scuderia Ferrari SpA SEFAC: Scheckter, Villeneuve

FITTIPALDI (COPERSUCAR)
Fittipaldi Automotive: Fittipaldi, (Ribeiro)

RENAULT
Equipe Renault Elf: Jabouille, Arnoux

SHADOW
Samson Shadow Racing Team: Lammers
Interscope Shadow Racing Team: de Angelis

WOLF
Olympus Cameras Wolf Racing: Hunt, Rosberg

ENSIGN
Team Ensign: Daly, Gaillard, Surer

MERZARIO
Team Merzario: Merzario, (Brancatelli)

LIGIER
Ligier Gitanes: Depailler, Ickx, Laffite

WILLIAMS
Albilad-Saudia Racing Team: Jones, Regazzoni

ARROWS
Warsteiner Arrows Racing Team: Patrese, Mass

REBAQUE
Team Rebaque: Rebaque

ALFA ROMEO
Autodelta: Giacomelli, Brambilla

KAUHSEN
Willi Kauhsen Racing Team: (Brancatelli)

21 Jan 1979 — ARGENTINA: Buenos Aires No.15 (Round: 1) (Race: 314)

53 laps x 5.968 km, 3.708 miles = 316.304 km, 196.542 miles

POS.	NO.	DRIVER	CAR	MODEL	ENGINE		LAPS	TIME/REASON FOR RETIREMENT	GRID:POS	ROW
1	26	J Laffite	Ligier	JS11	Cosworth	V8	53	1h 36m 03.210s	1	1
2	2	C Reutemann	Lotus	79	Cosworth	V8	53	1h 36m 18.150s	3	2
3	7	J Watson	McLaren	M28	Cosworth	V8	53	1h 37m 32.020s	6	3
4	25	P Depailler	Ligier	JS11	Cosworth	V8	53	1h 37m 44.930s	2	1
5	1	M Andretti	Lotus	79	Cosworth	V8	52		7	4
6	14	E Fittipaldi	Copersucar	F5A	Cosworth	V8	52		11	6
7	18	E de Angelis	Shadow	DN9	Cosworth	V8	52		16	8
8	30	J Mass	Arrows	A1B	Cosworth	V8	51		14	7
9	27	A Jones	Williams	FW06	Cosworth	V8	51		15	8
10	28	C Regazzoni	Williams	FW06	Cosworth	V8	51		17	9
11	22	D Daly	Ensign	N177	Cosworth	V8	51		24	12
12r	12	G Villeneuve	Ferrari	312T3	Ferrari	F12	48	engine	10	5
r	31	H Rebaque	Lotus	79	Cosworth	V8	46	suspension bracket	19	10
r	17	J Lammers	Shadow	DN9	Cosworth	V8	42	cv joint	21	11
r	20	J Hunt	Wolf	WR7	Cosworth	V8	41	electrics	18	9
r	4	J-P Jarier	Tyrrell	009	Cosworth	V8	15	engine	4	2
r	15	J-P Jabouille	Renault	RS01	Renault	V6t	15	engine	12	6
r	5	N Lauda	Brabham	BT48	Alfa Romeo	V12	8	fuel pressure	23	12
r	16	R Arnoux	Renault	RS01	Renault	V6t	6	engine	25	13
r	11	J Scheckter	Ferrari	312T3	Ferrari	F12	0	accident *	5	3
r	3	D Pironi	Tyrrell	009	Cosworth	V8	0	accident *	8	4
r	8	P Tambay	McLaren	M28	Cosworth	V8	0	accident *	9	5
r	6	N Piquet	Brabham	BT46	Alfa Romeo	F12	0	accident *	20	10
r	24	A Merzario	Merzario	A1B	Cosworth	V8	0	accident *	22	11
ns	29	R Patrese	Arrows	A1B	Cosworth	V8		accident	13	7
ns	9	H-J Stuck	ATS	D2	Cosworth	V8		car unprepared		

Winning speed: 197.580 km/h, 122.770 mph
Pole Position speed: 206.188 km/h, 128.119 mph (J Laffite, 1 min:44.200 sec)
Fastest Lap speed: 200.962 km/h, 124.872 mph (J Laffite, 1 min:46.910 sec on lap 42)
Lap Leaders: P Depailler 1-10 (10); J Laffite 11-53 (43).

*Interrupted after 1st lap accident. Restarted for original distance. * retired after first start.*

4 Feb 1979 — BRAZIL: Interlagos (Round: 2) (Race: 315)

40 laps x 7.874 km, 4.893 miles = 314.960 km, 195.707 miles

POS.	NO.	DRIVER	CAR	MODEL	ENGINE		LAPS	TIME/REASON FOR RETIREMENT	GRID:POS	ROW
1	26	J Laffite	Ligier	JS11	Cosworth	V8	40	1h 40m 09.640s	1	1
2	25	P Depailler	Ligier	JS11	Cosworth	V8	40	1h 40m 14.920s	2	1
3	2	C Reutemann	Lotus	79	Cosworth	V8	40	1h 40m 53.780s	3	2
4	3	D Pironi	Tyrrell	009	Cosworth	V8	40	1h 41m 35.520s	8	4
5	12	G Villeneuve	Ferrari	312T3	Ferrari	F12	39		5	3
6	11	J Scheckter	Ferrari	312T3	Ferrari	F12	39		6	3
7	30	J Mass	Arrows	A1B	Cosworth	V8	39		19	10
8	7	J Watson	McLaren	M28	Cosworth	V8	39		14	7
9	29	R Patrese	Arrows	A1B	Cosworth	V8	39		16	8
10	15	J-P Jabouille	Renault	RS01	Renault	V6t	39		7	4
11	14	E Fittipaldi	Copersucar	F5A	Cosworth	V8	39		9	5
12	18	E de Angelis	Shadow	DN9	Cosworth	V8	39		20	10
13	22	D Daly	Ensign	N177	Cosworth	V8	39		23	12
14	17	J Lammers	Shadow	DN9	Cosworth	V8	39		21	11
15	28	C Regazzoni	Williams	FW06	Cosworth	V8	38		17	9
r	27	A Jones	Williams	FW06	Cosworth	V8	33	fuel pressure	13	7

POS.	NO.	DRIVER	CAR	MODEL	ENGINE		LAPS	TIME/REASON FOR RETIREMENT	GRID:POS	ROW
r	9	H-J Stuck	ATS	D2	Cosworth	V8	31	steering wheel	24	12
r	16	R Arnoux	Renault	RS01	Renault	V6t	28	spin	11	6
r	8	P Tambay	McLaren	M26	Cosworth	V8	7	accident	18	9
r	20	J Hunt	Wolf	WR7	Cosworth	V8	7	steering rack	10	5
r	6	N Piquet	Brabham	BT48	Alfa Romeo	V12	5	accident	22	11
r	5	N Lauda	Brabham	BT48	Alfa Romeo	V12	5	gear linkage	12	6
r	1	M Andretti	Lotus	79	Cosworth	V8	2	misfire/ fuel leak/ fire	4	2
r	4	J-P Jarier	Tyrrell	009	Cosworth	V8	-1	electrics	15	8
nq	31	H Rebaque	Lotus	79	Cosworth	V8				
nq	24	A Merzario	Merzario	A1B	Cosworth	V8				

Winning speed: 188.673 km/h, 117.236 mph
Pole Position speed: 198.130 km/h, 123.112 mph (J Laffite, 2 min:23.070 sec)
Fastest Lap speed: 190.551 km/h, 118.403 mph (J Laffite, 2 min:28.760 sec on lap 23)
Lap Leaders: J Laffite 1-40 (40).

3 Mar 1979 SOUTH AFRICA: Kyalami (Round: 3) (Race: 316)

78 laps x 4.104 km, 2.550 miles = 320.112 km, 198.908 miles

POS.	NO.	DRIVER	CAR	MODEL	ENGINE		LAPS	TIME/REASON FOR RETIREMENT	GRID:POS	ROW
1	12	G Villeneuve	Ferrari	312T4	Ferrari	F12	78	1h 41m 49.960s	3	2
2	11	J Scheckter	Ferrari	312T4	Ferrari	F12	78	1h 41m 53.380s	2	1
3	4	J-P Jarier	Tyrrell	009	Cosworth	V8	78	1h 42m 12.070s	9	5
4	1	M Andretti	Lotus	79	Cosworth	V8	78	1h 42m 17.840s	8	4
5	2	C Reutemann	Lotus	79	Cosworth	V8	78	1h 42m 56.930s	11	6
6	5	N Lauda	Brabham	BT48	Alfa Romeo	V12	77		4	2
7	6	N Piquet	Brabham	BT48	Alfa Romeo	V12	77		12	6
8	20	J Hunt	Wolf	WR7	Cosworth	V8	77		13	7
9	28	C Regazzoni	Williams	FW06	Cosworth	V8	76		22	11
10	8	P Tambay	McLaren	M28	Cosworth	V8	75		17	9
11	29	R Patrese	Arrows	A1B	Cosworth	V8	75		16	8
12	30	J Mass	Arrows	A1B	Cosworth	V8	74		20	10
13	14	E Fittipaldi	Copersucar	F6	Cosworth	V8	74		18	9
14r	31	H Rebaque	Lotus	79	Cosworth	V8	71	engine	23	12
r	16	R Arnoux	Renault	RS01	Renault	V6t	67	puncture	10	5
r	27	A Jones	Williams	FW06	Cosworth	V8	63	rear suspension	19	10
r	7	J Watson	McLaren	M28	Cosworth	V8	61	ignition	14	7
r	9	H-J Stuck	ATS	D2	Cosworth	V8	57	accident	24	12
r	15	J-P Jabouille	Renault	RS01	Renault	V6t	47	valve spring	1	1
r	26	J Laffite	Ligier	JS11	Cosworth	V8	45	accident	6	3
r	3	D Pironi	Tyrrell	009	Cosworth	V8	25	throttle linkage	7	4
r	18	E de Angelis	Shadow	DN9	Cosworth	V8	16	accident	15	8
r	25	P Depailler	Ligier	JS11	Cosworth	V8	4	accident	5	3
r	17	J Lammers	Shadow	DN9	Cosworth	V8	2	accident	21	11
nq	22	D Daly	Ensign	N179	Cosworth	V8				
nq	24	A Merzario	Merzario	A1B	Cosworth	V8				

Winning speed: 188.611 km/h, 117.197 mph
Pole Position speed: 205.772 km/h, 127.861 mph (J-P Jabouille, 1 min:11.800 sec)
Fastest Lap speed: 198.549 km/h, 123.372 mph (G Villeneuve, 1 min:14.412 sec on lap 23)
Lap Leaders: J-P Jabouille 1 (1); G Villeneuve 2-14,53-78 (39); J Scheckter 15-52 (38).

Interrupted after 2 laps, because of heavy rain. Restarted for remaining 76 laps, with results being on aggregate. Lap leaders are given 'on the road'.

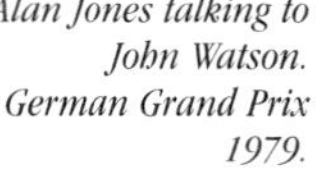

Alan Jones talking to John Watson. German Grand Prix 1979.

8 Apr 1979 — USA West: Long Beach (Round: 4) (Race: 317)

80.5 laps x 3.251 km, 2.020 miles = 261.706 km, 162.616 miles

POS.	NO.	DRIVER	CAR	MODEL	ENGINE		LAPS	TIME/REASON FOR RETIREMENT	GRID:POS	ROW
1	12	G Villeneuve	Ferrari	312T4	Ferrari	F12	80	1h 50m 25.400s	1	1
2	11	J Scheckter	Ferrari	312T4	Ferrari	F12	80	1h 50m 54.780s	3	2
3	27	A Jones	Williams	FW06	Cosworth	V8	80	1h 51m 25.090s	10	5
4	1	M Andretti	Lotus	79	Cosworth	V8	80	1h 51m 29.730s	6	3
5	25	P Depailler	Ligier	JS11	Cosworth	V8	80	1h 51m 48.920s	4	2
6	4	J-P Jarier	Tyrrell	009	Cosworth	V8	79		7	4
7	18	E de Angelis	Shadow	DN9	Cosworth	V8	78		20	10
8	6	N Piquet	Brabham	BT48	Alfa Romeo	V12	78		12	6
9	30	J Mass	Arrows	A1B	Cosworth	V8	78		13	7
dq	3	D Pironi	Tyrrell	009	Cosworth	V8	72	push start after spin	17	9
r	31	H Rebaque	Lotus	79	Cosworth	V8	71	accident	23	12
r	22	D Daly	Ensign	N179	Cosworth	V8	69	accident	24	12
r	7	J Watson	McLaren	M28	Cosworth	V8	62	fuel injection	18	9
dq	9	H-J Stuck	ATS	D2	Cosworth	V8	49	push start after spin	21	11
r	28	C Regazzoni	Williams	FW06	Cosworth	V8	48	engine	15	8
r	17	J Lammers	Shadow	DN9	Cosworth	V8	47	suspension	14	7
r	29	R Patrese	Arrows	A1B	Cosworth	V8	40	brake master cylinder	9	5
r	2	C Reutemann	Lotus	79	Cosworth	V8	21	drive shaft	2	1
r	14	E Fittipaldi	Copersucar	F5A	Cosworth	V8	19	drive shaft	16	8
r	24	A Merzario	Merzario	A1B	Cosworth	V8	13	engine	22	11
r	26	J Laffite	Ligier	JS11	Cosworth	V8	8	brakes	5	3
r	20	J Hunt	Wolf	WR8	Cosworth	V8	0	drive shaft joint	8	4
r	5	N Lauda	Brabham	BT48	Alfa Romeo	V12	0	accident	11	6
r	8	P Tambay	McLaren	M28	Cosworth	V8	0	accident	19	10
ns	15	J-P Jabouille	Renault	RS01	Renault	V6t		accident/ injury		
ns	16	R Arnoux	Renault	RS01	Renault	V6t		universal joint		

Winning speed: 141.313 km/h, 87.808 mph (based on time taken to complete 80 laps)
Pole Position speed: 148.476 km/h, 92.259 mph (G Villeneuve, 1 min:18.825 sec)
Fastest Lap speed: 144.133 km/h, 89.560 mph (G Villeneuve, 1 min:21.200 sec)
Lap Leaders: G Villeneuve 1-80 (80.5).

The start and finish lines were at different positions on the circuit.
The fraction of a lap is credited to the first lap leader.

29 Apr 1979 — SPAIN: Járama (Round: 5) (Race: 318)

75 laps x 3.404 km, 2.115 miles = 255.300 km, 158.636 miles

POS.	NO.	DRIVER	CAR	MODEL	ENGINE		LAPS	TIME/REASON FOR RETIREMENT	GRID:POS	ROW
1	25	P Depailler	Ligier	JS11	Cosworth	V8	75	1h 39m 11.840s	2	1
2	2	C Reutemann	Lotus	79	Cosworth	V8	75	1h 39m 32.780s	8	4
3	1	M Andretti	Lotus	80	Cosworth	V8	75	1h 39m 39.150s	4	2
4	11	J Scheckter	Ferrari	312T4	Ferrari	F12	75	1h 39m 40.520s	5	3
5	4	J-P Jarier	Tyrrell	009	Cosworth	V8	75	1h 39m 42.230s	12	6
6	3	D Pironi	Tyrrell	009	Cosworth	V8	75	1h 40m 00.270s	10	5
7	12	G Villeneuve	Ferrari	312T4	Ferrari	F12	75	1h 40m 04.150s	3	2
8	30	J Mass	Arrows	A1B	Cosworth	V8	75	1h 40m 26.680s	17	9
9	16	R Arnoux	Renault	RS01	Renault	V6t	74		11	6
10	29	R Patrese	Arrows	A1B	Cosworth	V8	74		16	8
11	14	E Fittipaldi	Copersucar	F5A	Cosworth	V8	74		19	10
12	17	J Lammers	Shadow	DN9	Cosworth	V8	73		24	12
13	8	P Tambay	McLaren	M28	Cosworth	V8	72		20	10
14	9	H-J Stuck	ATS	D2	Cosworth	V8	69		21	11
r	5	N Lauda	Brabham	BT48	Alfa Romeo	V12	63	water leak	6	3
r	31	H Rebaque	Lotus	79	Cosworth	V8	58	engine	23	12
r	27	A Jones	Williams	FW07	Cosworth	V8	54	gear selection	13	7
r	18	E de Angelis	Shadow	DN9	Cosworth	V8	52	engine	22	11
r	28	C Regazzoni	Williams	FW07	Cosworth	V8	32	engine	14	7
r	20	J Hunt	Wolf	WR7	Cosworth	V8	26	brakes	15	8
r	7	J Watson	McLaren	M28	Cosworth	V8	21	engine	18	9
r	15	J-P Jabouille	Renault	RS10	Renault	V6t	21	turbo leak	9	5
r	26	J Laffite	Ligier	JS11	Cosworth	V8	15	engine	1	1
r	6	N Piquet	Brabham	BT48	Alfa Romeo	V12	15	fuel metering unit	7	4
nq	22	D Daly	Ensign	N177	Cosworth	V8				
nq	24	A Merzario	Merzario	A2	Cosworth	V8				
nq	36	G Brancatelli	Kauhsen	WK	Cosworth	V8				

Winning speed: 154.419 km/h, 95.952 mph
Pole Position speed: 164.489 km/h, 102.208 mph (J Laffite, 1 min:14.500 sec)
Fastest Lap speed: 160.314 km/h, 99.614 mph (G Villeneuve, 1 min:16.440 sec on lap 72)
Lap Leaders: P Depailler 1-75 (75).

13 May 1979 BELGIUM: Zolder (Round: 6) (Race: 319)

70 laps x 4.262 km, 2.648 miles = 298.340 km, 185.380 miles

POS.	NO.	DRIVER	CAR	MODEL	ENGINE		LAPS	TIME/REASON FOR RETIREMENT	GRID:POS	ROW
1	11	J Scheckter	Ferrari	312T4	Ferrari	F12	70	1h 39m 59.530s	7	4
2	26	J Laffite	Ligier	JS11	Cosworth	V8	70	1h 40m 14.890s	1	1
3	3	D Pironi	Tyrrell	009	Cosworth	V8	70	1h 40m 34.700s	12	6
4	2	C Reutemann	Lotus	79	Cosworth	V8	70	1h 40m 46.020s	10	5
5	29	R Patrese	Arrows	A1B	Cosworth	V8	70	1h 41m 03.840s	16	8
6	7	J Watson	McLaren	M28	Cosworth	V8	70	1h 41m 05.380s	19	10
7r	12	G Villeneuve	Ferrari	312T4	Ferrari	F12	69	out of fuel	6	3
8	9	H-J Stuck	ATS	D2	Cosworth	V8	69		20	10
9	14	E Fittipaldi	Copersucar	F5A	Cosworth	V8	68		23	12
10	17	J Lammers	Shadow	DN9	Cosworth	V8	68		21	11
11	4	J-P Jarier	Tyrrell	009	Cosworth	V8	67		11	6
r	25	P Depailler	Ligier	JS11	Cosworth	V8	46	accident	2	1
r	20	J Hunt	Wolf	WR8	Cosworth	V8	40	accident	9	5
r	27	A Jones	Williams	FW07	Cosworth	V8	39	electrics	4	2
r	1	M Andretti	Lotus	79	Cosworth	V8	27	brakes	5	3
r	6	N Piquet	Brabham	BT48	Alfa Romeo	V12	23	engine	3	2
r	5	N Lauda	Brabham	BT48	Alfa Romeo	V12	23	engine	13	7
r	16	R Arnoux	Renault	RS01	Renault	V6t	22	turbo boost pressure	18	9
r	35	B Giacomelli	Alfa Romeo	177	Alfa Romeo	F12	21	accident	14	7
r	18	E de Angelis	Shadow	DN9	Cosworth	V8	21	accident	24	12
r	30	J Mass	Arrows	A1B	Cosworth	V8	17	spin	22	11
r	31	H Rebaque	Lotus	79	Cosworth	V8	13	drive shaft	15	8
r	15	J-P Jabouille	Renault	RS10	Renault	V6t	13	turbo	17	9
r	28	C Regazzoni	Williams	FW07	Cosworth	V8	1	accident	8	4
nq	8	P Tambay	McLaren	M26	Cosworth	V8				
nq	24	A Merzario	Merzario	A2	Cosworth	V8				
nq	22	D Daly	Ensign	N177	Cosworth	V8				
nq	36	G Brancatelli	Kauhsen	WK	Cosworth	V8				

Winning speed: 179.018 km/h, 111.237 mph
Pole Position speed: 189.119 km/h, 117.513 mph (J Laffite, 1 min:21.130 sec)
Fastest Lap speed: 184.658 km/h, 114.741 mph (G Villeneuve, 1 min:23.090 sec on lap 63)
Lap Leaders: P Depailler 1-18,40-46 (25); J Laffite 19-23,47-53 (12); A Jones 24-39 (16); J Scheckter 54-70 (17).

J Scheckter originally credited with fastest lap, but this was later amended.

27 May 1979 MONACO: Monte Carlo (Round: 7) (Race: 320)

76 laps x 3.312 km, 2.058 miles = 251.712 km, 156.407 miles

POS.	NO.	DRIVER	CAR	MODEL	ENGINE		LAPS	TIME/REASON FOR RETIREMENT	GRID:POS	ROW
1	11	J Scheckter	Ferrari	312T4	Ferrari	F12	76	1h 55m 22.480s	1	1
2	28	C Regazzoni	Williams	FW07	Cosworth	V8	76	1h 55m 22.920s	16	8
3	2	C Reutemann	Lotus	79	Cosworth	V8	76	1h 55m 31.050s	11	6
4	7	J Watson	McLaren	M28	Cosworth	V8	76	1h 56m 03.790s	14	7
5r	25	P Depailler	Ligier	JS11	Cosworth	V8	74	engine	3	2
6	30	J Mass	Arrows	A1B	Cosworth	V8	69		8	4
7r	6	N Piquet	Brabham	BT48	Alfa Romeo	V12	68	drive shaft	18	9
8	15	J-P Jabouille	Renault	RS10	Renault	V6t	68		20	10
r	26	J Laffite	Ligier	JS11	Cosworth	V8	55	gearbox	5	3
r	12	G Villeneuve	Ferrari	312T4	Ferrari	F12	54	transmission	2	1
r	27	A Jones	Williams	FW07	Cosworth	V8	43	accident	9	5
r	4	J-P Jarier	Tyrrell	009	Cosworth	V8	34	rear suspension	6	3
r	9	H-J Stuck	ATS	D2	Cosworth	V8	30	wheel lost	12	6
r	5	N Lauda	Brabham	BT48	Alfa Romeo	V12	21	accident	4	2
r	3	D Pironi	Tyrrell	009	Cosworth	V8	21	accident	7	4
r	1	M Andretti	Lotus	80	Cosworth	V8	21	rear suspension	13	7
r	14	E Fittipaldi	Copersucar	F5A	Cosworth	V8	17	engine	17	9
r	16	R Arnoux	Renault	RS10	Renault	V6t	8	accident	19	10
r	20	J Hunt	Wolf	WR7	Cosworth	V8	4	cv joint	10	5
r	29	R Patrese	Arrows	A1B	Cosworth	V8	4	suspension	15	8
nq	18	E de Angelis	Shadow	DN9	Cosworth	V8				
nq	8	P Tambay	McLaren	M28	Cosworth	V8				
nq	17	J Lammers	Shadow	DN9	Cosworth	V8				
nq	22	D Daly	Ensign	N179	Cosworth	V8				
npq	24	G Brancatelli	Merzario	A2	Cosworth	V8				

Winning speed: 130.902 km/h, 81.338 mph
Pole Position speed: 137.920 km/h, 85.700 mph (J Scheckter, 1 min:26.450 sec)
Fastest Lap speed: 134.240 km/h, 83.413 mph (P Depailler, 1 min:28.820 sec on lap 69)
Lap Leaders: J Scheckter 1-76 (76).

1 Jul 1979 FRANCE: Dijon-Prenois (Round: 8) (Race: 321)

80 laps x 3.800 km, 2.361 miles = 304.000 km, 188.897 miles

POS.	NO.	DRIVER	CAR	MODEL	ENGINE		LAPS	TIME/REASON FOR RETIREMENT	GRID:POS	ROW
1	15	J-P Jabouille	Renault	RS10	Renault	V6t	80	1h 35m 20.420s	1	1
2	12	G Villeneuve	Ferrari	312T4	Ferrari	F12	80	1h 35m 35.010s	3	2
3	16	R Arnoux	Renault	RS10	Renault	V6t	80	1h 35m 35.250s	2	1
4	27	A Jones	Williams	FW07	Cosworth	V8	80	1h 35m 57.030s	7	4
5	4	J-P Jarier	Tyrrell	009	Cosworth	V8	80	1h 36m 24.930s	10	5
6	28	C Regazzoni	Williams	FW07	Cosworth	V8	80	1h 36m 25.930s	9	5
7	11	J Scheckter	Ferrari	312T4	Ferrari	F12	79		5	3
8	26	J Laffite	Ligier	JS11	Cosworth	V8	79		8	4
9	20	K Rosberg	Wolf	WR8	Cosworth	V8	79		16	8
10	8	P Tambay	McLaren	M28	Cosworth	V8	78		20	10
11	7	J Watson	McLaren	M28	Cosworth	V8	78		15	8
12	31	H Rebaque	Lotus	79	Cosworth	V8	78		23	12
13r	2	C Reutemann	Lotus	79	Cosworth	V8	77	accident	13	7
14	29	R Patrese	Arrows	A2	Cosworth	V8	77		19	10
15	30	J Mass	Arrows	A2	Cosworth	V8	75		22	11
16	18	E de Angelis	Shadow	DN9	Cosworth	V8	75		24	12
17	35	B Giacomelli	Alfa Romeo	177	Alfa Romeo	F12	75		17	9
18	17	J Lammers	Shadow	DN9	Cosworth	V8	73		21	11
r	3	D Pironi	Tyrrell	009	Cosworth	V8	71	suspension	11	6
r	14	E Fittipaldi	Copersucar	F5A	Cosworth	V8	53	oil loss/ engine	18	9
r	6	N Piquet	Brabham	BT48	Alfa Romeo	V12	52	accident	4	2
r	1	M Andretti	Lotus	80	Cosworth	V8	51	brakes/ suspension/ puncture	12	6
r	25	J Ickx	Ligier	JS11	Cosworth	V8	45	engine	14	7
r	5	N Lauda	Brabham	BT48	Alfa Romeo	V12	23	spin	6	3
ns	9	H-J Stuck	ATS	D2	Cosworth	V8		tyre dispute		
nq	22	P Gaillard	Ensign	N179	Cosworth	V8				
nq	24	A Merzario	Merzario	A2	Cosworth	V8				

Winning speed: 191.315 km/h, 118.877 mph
Pole Position speed: 203.602 km/h, 126.512 mph (J-P Jabouille, 1 min: 7.190 sec)
Fastest Lap speed: 197.802 km/h, 122.909 mph (R Arnoux, 1 min: 9.160 sec on lap 71)
Lap Leaders: G Villeneuve 1-46 (46); J-P Jabouille 47-80 (34).

14 Jul 1979 BRITAIN: Silverstone (Round: 9) (Race: 322)

68 laps x 4.719 km, 2.932 miles = 320.865 km, 199.376 miles

POS.	NO.	DRIVER	CAR	MODEL	ENGINE		LAPS	TIME/REASON FOR RETIREMENT	GRID:POS	ROW
1	28	C Regazzoni	Williams	FW07	Cosworth	V8	68	1h 26m 11.170s	4	2
2	16	R Arnoux	Renault	RS10	Renault	V6t	68	1h 26m 35.450s	5	3
3	4	J-P Jarier	Tyrrell	009	Cosworth	V8	67		16	8
4	7	J Watson	McLaren	M29	Cosworth	V8	67		7	4
5	11	J Scheckter	Ferrari	312T4	Ferrari	F12	67		11	6
6	25	J Ickx	Ligier	JS11	Cosworth	V8	67		17	9
7r	8	P Tambay	McLaren	M28	Cosworth	V8	66	out of fuel	18	9
8	2	C Reutemann	Lotus	79	Cosworth	V8	66		8	4
9	31	H Rebaque	Lotus	79	Cosworth	V8	66		24	12
10	3	D Pironi	Tyrrell	009	Cosworth	V8	66		15	8
11	17	J Lammers	Shadow	DN9	Cosworth	V8	65		21	11
12	18	E de Angelis	Shadow	DN9	Cosworth	V8	65		12	6
13	22	P Gaillard	Ensign	N179	Cosworth	V8	65		23	12
14r	12	G Villeneuve	Ferrari	312T4	Ferrari	F12	63	fuel vaporisation	13	7
r	29	R Patrese	Arrows	A2	Cosworth	V8	45	gearbox	19	10
r	20	K Rosberg	Wolf	WR7	Cosworth	V8	44	fuel system	14	7
r	26	J Laffite	Ligier	JS11	Cosworth	V8	44	spark plug	10	5
r	27	A Jones	Williams	FW07	Cosworth	V8	38	water pump	1	1
r	30	J Mass	Arrows	A2	Cosworth	V8	37	gearbox	20	10
r	14	E Fittipaldi	Copersucar	F5A	Cosworth	V8	25	engine	22	11
r	15	J-P Jabouille	Renault	RS10	Renault	V6t	21	engine	2	1
r	5	N Lauda	Brabham	BT48	Alfa Romeo	V12	12	brakes	6	3
r	1	M Andretti	Lotus	79	Cosworth	V8	3	wheel bearing	9	5
r	6	N Piquet	Brabham	BT48	Alfa Romeo	V12	1	spin	3	2
nq	9	H-J Stuck	ATS	D2	Cosworth	V8				
nq	24	A Merzario	Merzario	A4	Cosworth	V8				

Winning speed: 223.375 km/h, 138.799 mph
Pole Position speed: 236.324 km/h, 146.845 mph (A Jones, 1 min:11.880 sec)
Fastest Lap speed: 228.319 km/h, 141.871 mph (C Regazzoni, 1 min:14.400 sec on lap 39)
Lap Leaders: A Jones 1-38 (38); C Regazzoni 39-68 (30).

E de Angelis penalised 1 minute for jumping the start.

29 Jul 1979 — GERMANY: Hockenheim (Round:10) (Race: 323)

45 laps x 6.789 km, 4.218 miles = 305.505 km, 189.832 miles

POS.	NO.	DRIVER	CAR	MODEL	ENGINE		LAPS	TIME/REASON FOR RETIREMENT	GRID:POS	ROW
1	27	A Jones	Williams	FW07	Cosworth	V8	45	1h 24m 48.830s	2	1
2	28	C Regazzoni	Williams	FW07	Cosworth	V8	45	1h 24m 51.740s	6	3
3	26	J Laffite	Ligier	JS11	Cosworth	V8	45	1h 25m 07.220s	3	2
4	11	J Scheckter	Ferrari	312T4	Ferrari	F12	45	1h 25m 20.030s	5	3
5	7	J Watson	McLaren	M29	Cosworth	V8	45	1h 26m 26.630s	12	6
6	30	J Mass	Arrows	A2	Cosworth	V8	44		18	9
7	4	G Lees	Tyrrell	009	Cosworth	V8	44		16	8
8	12	G Villeneuve	Ferrari	312T4	Ferrari	F12	44		9	5
9	3	D Pironi	Tyrrell	009	Cosworth	V8	44		8	4
10	17	J Lammers	Shadow	DN9	Cosworth	V8	44		20	10
11	18	E de Angelis	Shadow	DN9	Cosworth	V8	43		21	11
12r	6	N Piquet	Brabham	BT48	Alfa Romeo	V12	42	engine	4	2
r	29	R Patrese	Arrows	A2	Cosworth	V8	34	puncture	19	10
r	8	P Tambay	McLaren	M29	Cosworth	V8	30	rear suspension	15	8
r	20	K Rosberg	Wolf	WR8	Cosworth	V8	29	engine	17	9
r	5	N Lauda	Brabham	BT48	Alfa Romeo	V12	27	engine	7	4
r	25	J Ickx	Ligier	JS11	Cosworth	V8	24	puncture	14	7
r	31	H Rebaque	Lotus	79	Cosworth	V8	22	handling	24	12
r	1	M Andretti	Lotus	79	Cosworth	V8	16	cv joint	11	6
r	16	R Arnoux	Renault	RS10	Renault	V6t	9	puncture	10	5
r	15	J-P Jabouille	Renault	RS10	Renault	V6t	7	spin	1	1
r	14	E Fittipaldi	Copersucar	F6A	Cosworth	V8	4	electrics	22	11
r	2	C Reutemann	Lotus	79	Cosworth	V8	1	accident	13	7
r	9	H-J Stuck	ATS	D2	Cosworth	V8	0	suspension	23	12
nq	22	P Gaillard	Ensign	N179	Cosworth	V8				
nq	24	A Merzario	Merzario	A4	Cosworth	V8				

Winning speed: 216.124 km/h, 134.293 mph
Pole Position speed: 225.299 km/h, 139.994 mph (J-P Jabouille, 1 min:48.480 sec)
Fastest Lap speed: 218.432 km/h, 135.728 mph (G Villeneuve, 1 min:51.890 sec on lap 40)
Lap Leaders: A Jones 1-45 (45).

12 Aug 1979 — AUSTRIA: Österreichring (Round:11) (Race: 324)

54 laps x 5.942 km, 3.692 miles = 320.868 km, 199.378 miles

POS.	NO.	DRIVER	CAR	MODEL	ENGINE		LAPS	TIME/REASON FOR RETIREMENT	GRID:POS	ROW
1	27	A Jones	Williams	FW07	Cosworth	V8	54	1h 27m 38.010s	2	1
2	12	G Villeneuve	Ferrari	312T4	Ferrari	F12	54	1h 28m 14.060s	5	3
3	26	J Laffite	Ligier	JS11	Cosworth	V8	54	1h 28m 24.780s	8	4
4	11	J Scheckter	Ferrari	312T4	Ferrari	F12	54	1h 28m 25.220s	9	5
5	28	C Regazzoni	Williams	FW07	Cosworth	V8	54	1h 28m 26.930s	6	3
6	16	R Arnoux	Renault	RS10	Renault	V6t	53		1	1
7	3	D Pironi	Tyrrell	009	Cosworth	V8	53		10	5
8	4	D Daly	Tyrrell	009	Cosworth	V8	53		11	6
9	7	J Watson	McLaren	M29	Cosworth	V8	53		16	8
10	8	P Tambay	McLaren	M29	Cosworth	V8	53		14	7
r	5	N Lauda	Brabham	BT48	Alfa Romeo	V12	45	oil pressure	4	2
r	22	P Gaillard	Ensign	N179	Cosworth	V8	42	front suspension	24	12
r	18	E de Angelis	Shadow	DN9	Cosworth	V8	34	engine	22	11
r	29	R Patrese	Arrows	A2	Cosworth	V8	34	rear suspension	13	7
r	6	N Piquet	Brabham	BT48	Alfa Romeo	V12	32	engine	7	4
r	9	H-J Stuck	ATS	D3	Cosworth	V8	28	engine	18	9
r	25	J Ickx	Ligier	JS11	Cosworth	V8	26	engine	21	11
r	2	C Reutemann	Lotus	79	Cosworth	V8	22	handling	17	9
r	15	J-P Jabouille	Renault	RS10	Renault	V6t	16	clutch/ transmission	3	2
r	14	E Fittipaldi	Copersucar	F6A	Cosworth	V8	15	brakes	19	10
r	20	K Rosberg	Wolf	WR9	Cosworth	V8	15	electrics	12	6
r	17	J Lammers	Shadow	DN9	Cosworth	V8	3	accident	23	12
r	30	J Mass	Arrows	A2	Cosworth	V8	1	engine	20	10
r	1	M Andretti	Lotus	79	Cosworth	V8	0	clutch	15	8
nq	31	H Rebaque	Lotus	79	Cosworth	V8				
nq	24	A Merzario	Merzario	A4	Cosworth	V8				

Winning speed: 219.689 km/h, 136.508 mph
Pole Position speed: 227.397 km/h, 141.298 mph (R Arnoux, 1 min:34.070 sec)
Fastest Lap speed: 223.360 km/h, 138.790 mph (R Arnoux, 1 min:35.770 sec on lap 40)
Lap Leaders: G Villeneuve 1-3 (3); A Jones 4-54 (51).

26 Aug 1979 — NETHERLANDS: Zandvoort (Round:12) (Race: 325)

75 laps x 4.226 km, 2.626 miles = 316.950 km, 196.944 miles

POS.	NO.	DRIVER	CAR	MODEL	ENGINE		LAPS	TIME/REASON FOR RETIREMENT	GRID:POS	ROW
1	27	A Jones	Williams	FW07	Cosworth	V8	75	1h 41m 19.775s	2	1
2	11	J Scheckter	Ferrari	312T4	Ferrari	F12	75	1h 41m 41.558s	5	3
3	26	J Laffite	Ligier	JS11	Cosworth	V8	75	1h 42m 23.028s	7	4
4	6	N Piquet	Brabham	BT48	Alfa Romeo	V12	74		11	6
5	25	J Ickx	Ligier	JS11	Cosworth	V8	74		20	10
6	30	J Mass	Arrows	A2	Cosworth	V8	73		18	9
7	31	H Rebaque	Lotus	79	Cosworth	V8	73		24	12
r	3	D Pironi	Tyrrell	009	Cosworth	V8	51	rear suspension	10	5
r	12	G Villeneuve	Ferrari	312T4	Ferrari	F12	49	puncture/ suspension	6	3
r	18	E de Angelis	Shadow	DN9	Cosworth	V8	40	drive shaft	22	11
r	20	K Rosberg	Wolf	WR9	Cosworth	V8	33	engine	8	4
r	15	J-P Jabouille	Renault	RS10	Renault	V6t	26	clutch	4	2
r	7	J Watson	McLaren	M29	Cosworth	V8	22	engine	12	6
r	4	J-P Jarier	Tyrrell	009	Cosworth	V8	20	throttle slides jammed/ spin	16	8
r	9	H-J Stuck	ATS	D3	Cosworth	V8	19	drive shaft	15	8
r	17	J Lammers	Shadow	DN9	Cosworth	V8	12	gearbox	23	12
r	1	M Andretti	Lotus	79	Cosworth	V8	9	rear suspension	17	9
r	29	R Patrese	Arrows	A2	Cosworth	V8	7	brakes/ accident	19	10
r	8	P Tambay	McLaren	M29	Cosworth	V8	6	engine	14	7
r	5	N Lauda	Brabham	BT48	Alfa Romeo	V12	4	driver unfit (wrist injury)	9	5
r	14	E Fittipaldi	Copersucar	F6A	Cosworth	V8	2	electrics	21	11
r	2	C Reutemann	Lotus	79	Cosworth	V8	1	accident	13	7
r	16	R Arnoux	Renault	RS10	Renault	V6t	1	accident	1	1
r	28	C Regazzoni	Williams	FW07	Cosworth	V8	0	accident	3	2
nq	22	P Gaillard	Ensign	N179	Cosworth	V8				
nq	24	A Merzario	Merzario	A4	Cosworth	V8				

Winning speed: 187.675 km/h, 116.616 mph
Pole Position speed: 201.609 km/h, 125.274 mph (R Arnoux, 1 min:15.461 sec)
Fastest Lap speed: 191.515 km/h, 119.002 mph (G Villeneuve, 1 min:19.438 sec on lap 39)
Lap Leaders: A Jones 1-10,47-75 (39); G Villeneuve 11-46 (36).

9 Sep 1979 — ITALY: Monza (Round:13) (Race: 326)

50 laps x 5.800 km, 3.604 miles = 290.000 km, 180.198 miles

POS.	NO.	DRIVER	CAR	MODEL	ENGINE		LAPS	TIME/REASON FOR RETIREMENT	GRID:POS	ROW
1	11	J Scheckter	Ferrari	312T4	Ferrari	F12	50	1h 22m 00.220s	3	2
2	12	G Villeneuve	Ferrari	312T4	Ferrari	F12	50	1h 22m 00.680s	5	3
3	28	C Regazzoni	Williams	FW07	Cosworth	V8	50	1h 22m 05.000s	6	3
4	5	N Lauda	Brabham	BT48	Alfa Romeo	V12	50	1h 22m 54.620s	9	5
5	1	M Andretti	Lotus	79	Cosworth	V8	50	1h 22m 59.920s	10	5
6	4	J-P Jarier	Tyrrell	009	Cosworth	V8	50	1h 23m 01.770s	16	8
7	2	C Reutemann	Lotus	79	Cosworth	V8	50	1h 23m 24.360s	13	7
8	14	E Fittipaldi	Copersucar	F6A	Cosworth	V8	49		20	10
9	27	A Jones	Williams	FW07	Cosworth	V8	49		4	2
10	3	D Pironi	Tyrrell	009	Cosworth	V8	49		12	6
11	9	H-J Stuck	ATS	D3	Cosworth	V8	49		15	8
12	36	V Brambilla	Alfa Romeo	177	Alfa Romeo	F12	49		22	11
13	29	R Patrese	Arrows	A2	Cosworth	V8	47		17	9
14r	15	J-P Jabouille	Renault	RS10	Renault	V6t	45	engine	1	1
r	26	J Laffite	Ligier	JS11	Cosworth	V8	41	engine	7	4
r	20	K Rosberg	Wolf	WR8	Cosworth	V8	41	engine	23	12
r	25	J Ickx	Ligier	JS11	Cosworth	V8	40	engine	11	6
r	18	E de Angelis	Shadow	DN9	Cosworth	V8	33	clutch	24	12
r	35	B Giacomelli	Alfa Romeo	179	Alfa Romeo	V12	28	spin	18	9
r	7	J Watson	McLaren	M29	Cosworth	V8	13	accident	19	10
r	16	R Arnoux	Renault	RS10	Renault	V6t	13	misfire	2	1
r	8	P Tambay	McLaren	M29	Cosworth	V8	3	engine	14	7
r	30	J Mass	Arrows	A2	Cosworth	V8	3	suspension	21	11
r	6	N Piquet	Brabham	BT48	Alfa Romeo	V12	1	accident	8	4
nq	17	J Lammers	Shadow	DN9	Cosworth	V8				
nq	22	M Surer	Ensign	N179	Cosworth	V8				
nq	24	A Merzario	Merzario	A4	Cosworth	V8				
nq	31	H Rebaque	Rebaque	HR100	Cosworth	V8				

Winning speed: 212.186 km/h, 131.846 mph
Pole Position speed: 220.765 km/h, 137.177 mph (J-P Jabouille, 1 min:34.580 sec)
Fastest Lap speed: 218.410 km/h, 135.714 mph (C Regazzoni, 1 min:35.600 sec on lap 46)
Lap Leaders: J Scheckter 1,13-50 (39); R Arnoux 2-12 (11).

30 Sep 1979 — CANADA: Montréal (Round:14) (Race: 327)

72 laps x 4.410 km, 2.740 miles = 317.520 km, 197.298 miles

POS.	NO.	DRIVER	CAR	MODEL	ENGINE		LAPS	TIME/REASON FOR RETIREMENT	GRID:POS	ROW
1	27	A Jones	Williams	FW07	Cosworth	V8	72	1h 52m 06.892s	1	1
2	12	G Villeneuve	Ferrari	312T4	Ferrari	F12	72	1h 52m 07.972s	2	1
3	28	C Regazzoni	Williams	FW07	Cosworth	V8	72	1h 53m 20.548s	3	2
4	11	J Scheckter	Ferrari	312T4	Ferrari	F12	71		9	5
5	3	D Pironi	Tyrrell	009	Cosworth	V8	71		6	3
6	7	J Watson	McLaren	M29	Cosworth	V8	70		17	9
7	5	R Zunino	Brabham	BT49	Cosworth	V8	68		19	10
8	14	E Fittipaldi	Copersucar	F6A	Cosworth	V8	67		15	8
9	17	J Lammers	Shadow	DN9	Cosworth	V8	67		21	11
10r	1	M Andretti	Lotus	79	Cosworth	V8	66	out of fuel	10	5
r	6	N Piquet	Brabham	BT49	Cosworth	V8	61	gearbox	4	2
r	36	V Brambilla	Alfa Romeo	179	Alfa Romeo	V12	52	fuel metering unit	18	9
r	25	J Ickx	Ligier	JS11	Cosworth	V8	47	gearbox	16	8
r	4	J-P Jarier	Tyrrell	009	Cosworth	V8	33	engine	13	7
r	33	D Daly	Tyrrell	009	Cosworth	V8	28	engine	24	12
r	31	H Rebaque	Rebaque	HR100	Cosworth	V8	26	engine mounting	22	11
r	18	E de Angelis	Shadow	DN9	Cosworth	V8	24	distributor rotor arm	23	12
r	15	J-P Jabouille	Renault	RS10	Renault	V6t	24	brakes	7	4
r	2	C Reutemann	Lotus	79	Cosworth	V8	23	rear suspension	11	6
r	29	R Patrese	Arrows	A1B	Cosworth	V8	20	spin	14	7
r	8	P Tambay	McLaren	M29	Cosworth	V8	19	engine	20	10
r	16	R Arnoux	Renault	RS10	Renault	V6t	14	accident	8	4
r	9	H-J Stuck	ATS	D3	Cosworth	V8	14	accident	12	6
r	26	J Laffite	Ligier	JS11	Cosworth	V8	10	engine	5	3
nq	30	J Mass	Arrows	A2	Cosworth	V8				
nq	22	M Surer	Ensign	N179	Cosworth	V8				
nq	20	K Rosberg	Wolf	WR9	Cosworth	V8				
nq	19	A-D Ribeiro	Copersucar	F6A	Cosworth	V8				
nq	24	A Merzario	Merzario	A4	Cosworth	V8				
ew	5	N Lauda	Brabham	BT49	Cosworth	V8		sudden retirement from the sport		

Winning speed: 169.926 km/h, 105.587 mph
Pole Position speed: 176.612 km/h, 109.742 mph (A Jones, 1 min:29.892 sec)
Fastest Lap speed: 173.942 km/h, 108.082 mph (A Jones, 1 min:31.272 sec on lap 65)
Lap Leaders: G Villeneuve 1-50 (50); A Jones 51-72 (22).

7 Oct 1979 — USA East: Watkins Glen (Round:15) (Race: 328)

59 laps x 5.435 km, 3.377 miles = 320.651 km, 199.243 miles

POS.	NO.	DRIVER	CAR	MODEL	ENGINE		LAPS	TIME/REASON FOR RETIREMENT	GRID:POS	ROW
1	12	G Villeneuve	Ferrari	312T4	Ferrari	F12	59	1h 52m 17.734s	3	2
2	16	R Arnoux	Renault	RS10	Renault	V6t	59	1h 53m 06.521s	7	4
3	3	D Pironi	Tyrrell	009	Cosworth	V8	59	1h 53m 10.933s	10	5
4	18	E de Angelis	Shadow	DN9	Cosworth	V8	59	1h 53m 48.246s	20	10
5	9	H-J Stuck	ATS	D3	Cosworth	V8	59	1h 53m 58.993s	14	7
6	7	J Watson	McLaren	M29	Cosworth	V8	58		13	7
7	14	E Fittipaldi	Copersucar	F6A	Cosworth	V8	54		23	12
8r	6	N Piquet	Brabham	BT49	Cosworth	V8	53	drive shaft	2	1
r	33	D Daly	Tyrrell	009	Cosworth	V8	52	accident	15	8
r	11	J Scheckter	Ferrari	312T4	Ferrari	F12	48	tyre burst/ suspension	16	8
r	29	R Patrese	Arrows	A2	Cosworth	V8	44	rear suspension	19	10
r	27	A Jones	Williams	FW07	Cosworth	V8	36	wheel lost	1	1
r	22	M Surer	Ensign	N179	Cosworth	V8	32	engine	21	11
r	28	C Regazzoni	Williams	FW07	Cosworth	V8	29	accident	5	3
r	5	R Zunino	Brabham	BT49	Cosworth	V8	25	accident	9	5
r	15	J-P Jabouille	Renault	RS10	Renault	V6t	24	camshaft belt	8	4
r	8	P Tambay	McLaren	M29	Cosworth	V8	20	engine	22	11
r	20	K Rosberg	Wolf	WR8/9	Cosworth	V8	20	accident	12	6
r	4	J-P Jarier	Tyrrell	009	Cosworth	V8	18	accident	11	6
r	1	M Andretti	Lotus	79	Cosworth	V8	16	gearbox	17	9
r	2	C Reutemann	Lotus	79	Cosworth	V8	6	accident	6	3
r	26	J Laffite	Ligier	JS11	Cosworth	V8	3	accident	4	2
r	25	J Ickx	Ligier	JS11	Cosworth	V8	2	accident	24	12
r	35	B Giacomelli	Alfa Romeo	179	Alfa Romeo	V12	0	accident	18	9
nq	36	V Brambilla	Alfa Romeo	179	Alfa Romeo	V12				
nq	30	J Mass	Arrows	A2	Cosworth	V8				
nq	17	J Lammers	Shadow	DN9	Cosworth	V8				
nq	31	H Rebaque	Rebaque	HR100	Cosworth	V8				
nq	19	A-D Ribeiro	Copersucar	F6A	Cosworth	V8				
nq	24	A Merzario	Merzario	A4	Cosworth	V8				

Winning speed: 171.325 km/h, 106.456 mph
Pole Position speed: 204.624 km/h, 127.147 mph (A Jones, 1 min:35.615 sec)
Fastest Lap speed: 195.546 km/h, 121.506 mph (N Piquet, 1 min:40.054 sec on lap 51)
Lap Leaders: G Villeneuve 1-31,37-59 (54); A Jones 32-36 (5).

Lap Leaders 1979

POS	DRIVER	CAR-ENGINE	GPS	LAPS	KM	MILES
1	G Villeneuve	Ferrari	7	308.5	1,280.5	795.7
2	A Jones	Williams-Cosworth	7	216	1,145.1	711.5
3	J Scheckter	Ferrari	4	170	706.3	438.9
4	P Depailler	Ligier-Cosworth	3	110	421.5	261.9
5	J Laffite	Ligier-Cosworth	3	95	622.7	386.9
6	J-P Jabouille	Renault	2	35	133.3	82.8
7	C Regazzoni	Williams-Cosworth	1	30	141.6	88.0
8	R Arnoux	Renault	1	11	63.8	39.6
			15	**975.5**	**4,514.8**	**2,805.4**

Driver Points 1979

		RA	BR	ZA	USAW	E	B	MC	F	GB	D	A	NL	I	CDN	USAE	TOTAL	
1	J Scheckter	-	(1)	6	6	(3)	9	9	-	(2)	3	3	6	9	(3)	-	51	(9)
2	G Villeneuve	-	2	9	9	-	-	-	6	-	-	6	-	6	(6)	9	47	(6)
3	A Jones	-	-	-	4	-	-	-	(3)	-	9	9	9	-	9	-	40	(3)
4	J Laffite	9	9	-	-	-	6	-	-	-	4	4	4	-	-	-	36	
5	C Regazzoni	-	-	-	-	-	-	6	(1)	9	6	(2)	-	4	4	-	29	(3)
6	P Depailler	3	6	-	2	9	-	(2)	-	-	-	-	-	-	-	-	20	(2)
	C Reutemann	6	4	(2)	-	6	(3)	4	-	-	-	-	-	-	-	-	20	(5)
8	R Arnoux	-	-	-	-	-	-	-	4	6	-	1	-	-	-	6	17	
9	J Watson	4	-	-	-	-	1	3	-	3	2	-	-	-	1	1	15	
10	D Pironi	-	3	-	-	1	4	-	-	-	-	-	-	-	2	4	14	
	J-P Jarier	-	-	4	1	2	-	-	2	4	-	-	-	1	-	-	14	
	M Andretti	2	-	3	3	4	-	-	-	-	-	-	-	2	-	-	14	
13	J-P Jabouille	-	-	-	-	-	-	-	9	-	-	-	-	-	-	-	9	
14	N Lauda	-	-	1	-	-	-	-	-	-	-	-	-	3	-	-	4	
15	N Piquet	-	-	-	-	-	-	-	-	-	-	-	3	-	-	-	3	
	E de Angelis	-	-	-	-	-	-	-	-	-	-	-	-	-	-	3	3	
	J Ickx	-	-	-	-	-	-	-	-	1	-	-	2	-	-	-	3	
	J Mass	-	-	-	-	-	-	1	-	-	1	-	1	-	-	-	3	
19	R Patrese	-	-	-	-	-	2	-	-	-	-	-	-	-	-	-	2	
	H-J Stuck	-	-	-	-	-	-	-	-	-	-	-	-	-	-	2	2	
21	E Fittipaldi	1	-	-	-	-	-	-	-	-	-	-	-	-	-	-	1	

9, 6, 4, 3 ,2 and 1 point awarded to the first six finishers. Best 4 scores from first 7 races, best 4 from remaining 8 races.

Constructor Points 1979

		RA	BR	ZA	USAW	E	B	MC	F	GB	D	A	NL	I	CDN	USAE	TOTAL
1	Ferrari	-	3	15	15	3	9	9	6	2	3	9	6	15	9	9	113
2	Williams-Cosworth	-	-	-	4	-	-	6	4	9	15	11	9	4	13	-	75
3	Ligier-Cosworth	12	15	-	2	9	6	2	-	1	4	4	6	-	-	-	61
4	Lotus-Cosworth	8	4	5	3	10	3	4	-	-	-	-	-	2	-	-	39
5	Tyrrell-Cosworth	-	3	4	1	3	4	-	2	4	-	-	-	1	2	4	28
6	Renault	-	-	-	-	-	-	-	13	6	-	1	-	-	-	6	26
7	McLaren-Cosworth	4	-	-	-	-	1	3	-	3	2	-	-	-	1	1	15
8	Brabham-Alfa Romeo	-	-	1	-	-	-	-	-	-	-	-	3	3	-	-	7
9	Arrows-Cosworth	-	-	-	-	-	2	1	-	-	1	-	1	-	-	-	5
10	Shadow-Cosworth	-	-	-	-	-	-	-	-	-	-	-	-	-	-	3	3
11	ATS-Cosworth	-	-	-	-	-	-	-	-	-	-	-	-	-	-	2	2
12	Copersucar-Cosworth	1	-	-	-	-	-	-	-	-	-	-	-	-	-	-	1

9, 6, 4, 3, 2 and 1 point awarded to the first six finishers.

RACE ENTRANTS & RESULTS 1980

A power struggle emerged between FISA and FOCA (the constructors association headed by Bernie Ecclestone). McLaren merged with Ron Dennis's Project 4 team to produce McLaren International, while Shadow was sold to Teddy Yip.

Cornering speeds were causing concern with huge G-Forces imposed on the drivers. Williams emerged as the favourites, as Ferrari and Alfa worked on turbo engines.

FERRARI
Scuderia Ferrari SpA SEFAC: Scheckter, Villeneuve

TYRRELL
Candy Team Tyrrell: Jarier, Daly, Thackwell

BRABHAM
Parmalat Racing Team: Piquet, Zunino, Rebaque

McLAREN
Marlboro Team McLaren: Watson, Prost, (South)

ATS
Team ATS: Surer, Lammers, (Ertl)

LOTUS
Team Essex Lotus: Andretti, de Angelis, Mansell

ENSIGN
Unipart Racing Team: Regazzoni, Needell, Lammers, Lees

RENAULT
Equipe Renault Elf: Jabouille, Arnoux

SHADOW
Shadow Cars: (Johansson), Lees, (Kennedy)
Theodore Shadow from MC GP

FITTIPALDI
Skol Fittipaldi Team: Fittipaldi, Rosberg

ALFA ROMEO
Marlboro Team Alfa Romeo: Depailler, Brambilla, de Cesaris, Giacomelli

LIGIER
Equipe Ligier Gitanes: Pironi, Laffite

WILLIAMS
Albilad Williams Racing Team: Jones, Reutemann
RAM/Penthouse Rizla Racing: Keegan
RAM/Rainbow Jeans Racing: (Cogan, Lees)
Brands Hatch Racing: Wilson

ARROWS
Warsteiner Arrows Racing Team: Patrese, Mass, (Thackwell, Winkelhock)

OSELLA
Osella Squadra Corse: Cheever

13 Jan 1980 — ARGENTINA: Buenos Aires No.15 — (Round: 1) (Race: 329)
53 laps x 5.968 km, 3.708 miles = 316.304 km, 196.542 miles

POS.	NO.	DRIVER	CAR	MODEL	ENGINE		LAPS	TIME/REASON FOR RETIREMENT	GRID:POS	ROW
1	27	A Jones	Williams	FW07	Cosworth	V8	53	1h 43m 24.380s	1	1
2	5	N Piquet	Brabham	BT49	Cosworth	V8	53	1h 43m 48.970s	4	2
3	21	K Rosberg	Fittipaldi	F7	Cosworth	V8	53	1h 44m 43.020s	13	7
4	4	D Daly	Tyrrell	009	Cosworth	V8	53	1h 44m 47.860s	22	11
5	23	B Giacomelli	Alfa Romeo	179	Alfa Romeo	V12	52		20	10
6	8	A Prost	McLaren	M29	Cosworth	V8	52		12	6
7	6	R Zunino	Brabham	BT49	Cosworth	V8	51		16	8
r	22	P Depailler	Alfa Romeo	179	Alfa Romeo	V12	46	engine	23	12
r	1	J Scheckter	Ferrari	312T5	Ferrari	F12	45	engine	11	6
nc	14	C Regazzoni	Ensign	N180	Cosworth	V8	44		15	8
nc	20	E Fittipaldi	Fittipaldi	F7	Cosworth	V8	37		24	12
r	2	G Villeneuve	Ferrari	312T5	Ferrari	F12	36	steering/ accident	8	4
r	26	J Laffite	Ligier	JS11/15	Cosworth	V8	30	engine	2	1
r	9	M Surer	ATS	D3	Cosworth	V8	27	brake fluid on disc/ fire	21	11
r	29	R Patrese	Arrows	A3	Cosworth	V8	27	engine	7	4
r	30	J Mass	Arrows	A3	Cosworth	V8	20	gearbox	14	7
r	11	M Andretti	Lotus	81	Cosworth	V8	20	fuel metering unit	6	3
r	28	C Reutemann	Williams	FW07B	Cosworth	V8	12	engine	10	5
r	12	E de Angelis	Lotus	81	Cosworth	V8	7	suspension	5	3
r	7	J Watson	McLaren	M29	Cosworth	V8	5	gearbox oil leak	17	9
r	15	J-P Jabouille	Renault	RE20	Renault	V6t	3	clutch/ gearbox	9	5
r	16	R Arnoux	Renault	RE20	Renault	V6t	2	suspension	19	10
r	25	D Pironi	Ligier	JS11/15	Cosworth	V8	1	engine	3	2
r	3	J-P Jarier	Tyrrell	009	Cosworth	V8	1	accident	18	9
nq	18	D Kennedy	Shadow	DN11	Cosworth	V8				
nq	10	J Lammers	ATS	D3	Cosworth	V8				
nq	17	S Johansson	Shadow	DN11	Cosworth	V8				
nq	31	E Cheever	Osella	FA1	Cosworth	V8				

Winning speed: 183.531 km/h, 114.041 mph
Pole Position speed: 206.247 km/h, 128.156 mph (A Jones, 1 min:44.170 sec)
Fastest Lap speed: 194.521 km/h, 120.869 mph (A Jones, 1 min:50.450 sec on lap 5)
Lap Leaders: A Jones 1-17,30-53 (41); J Laffite 18-29 (12).

27 Jan 1980 — BRAZIL: Interlagos — (Round: 2) (Race: 330)

40 laps x 7.874 km, 4.893 miles = 314.960 km, 195.707 miles

POS.	NO.	DRIVER	CAR	MODEL	ENGINE		LAPS	TIME/REASON FOR RETIREMENT	GRID:POS	ROW
1	16	R Arnoux	Renault	RE20	Renault	V6t	40	1h 40m 01.330s	6	3
2	12	E de Angelis	Lotus	81	Cosworth	V8	40	1h 40m 23.190s	7	4
3	27	A Jones	Williams	FW07B	Cosworth	V8	40	1h 41m 07.440s	10	5
4	25	D Pironi	Ligier	JS11/15	Cosworth	V8	40	1h 41m 41.460s	2	1
5	8	A Prost	McLaren	M29	Cosworth	V8	40	1h 42m 26.740s	13	7
6	29	R Patrese	Arrows	A3	Cosworth	V8	39		14	7
7	9	M Surer	ATS	D3	Cosworth	V8	39		20	10
8	6	R Zunino	Brabham	BT49	Cosworth	V8	39		18	9
9	21	K Rosberg	Fittipaldi	F7	Cosworth	V8	39		15	8
10	30	J Mass	Arrows	A3	Cosworth	V8	39		16	8
11	7	J Watson	McLaren	M29	Cosworth	V8	39		23	12
12	3	J-P Jarier	Tyrrell	009	Cosworth	V8	39		22	11
13	23	B Giacomelli	Alfa Romeo	179	Alfa Romeo	V12	39		17	9
14	4	D Daly	Tyrrell	009	Cosworth	V8	38		24	12
15	20	E Fittipaldi	Fittipaldi	F7	Cosworth	V8	38		19	10
16r	2	G Villeneuve	Ferrari	312T5	Ferrari	F12	36	throttle jammed/ spin	3	2
r	22	P Depailler	Alfa Romeo	179	Alfa Romeo	V12	33	electrics	21	11
r	15	J-P Jabouille	Renault	RE20	Renault	V6t	25	turbo	1	1
r	5	N Piquet	Brabham	BT49	Cosworth	V8	14	suspension/ accident	9	5
r	14	C Regazzoni	Ensign	N180	Cosworth	V8	13	handling	12	6
r	26	J Laffite	Ligier	JS11/15	Cosworth	V8	13	electrics	5	3
r	1	J Scheckter	Ferrari	312T5	Ferrari	F12	10	engine	8	4
r	28	C Reutemann	Williams	FW07B	Cosworth	V8	1	drive shaft	4	2
r	11	M Andretti	Lotus	81	Cosworth	V8	1	spin	11	6
nq	10	J Lammers	ATS	D3	Cosworth	V8				
nq	18	D Kennedy	Shadow	DN11	Cosworth	V8				
nq	17	S Johansson	Shadow	DN11	Cosworth	V8				
nq	31	E Cheever	Osella	FA1	Cosworth	V8				

Winning speed: 188.934 km/h, 117.398 mph
Pole Position speed: 200.470 km/h, 124.566 mph (J-P Jabouille, 2 min:21.400 sec)
Fastest Lap speed: 192.427 km/h, 119.569 mph (R Arnoux, 2 min:27.310 sec on lap 22)
Lap Leaders: G Villeneuve 1 (1); J-P Jabouille 2-24 (23); R Arnoux 25-40 (16).

1 Mar 1980 — SOUTH AFRICA: Kyalami — (Round: 3) (Race: 331)

78 laps x 4.104 km, 2.550 miles = 320.112 km, 198.908 miles

POS.	NO.	DRIVER	CAR	MODEL	ENGINE		LAPS	TIME/REASON FOR RETIREMENT	GRID:POS	ROW
1	16	R Arnoux	Renault	RE20	Renault	V6t	78	1h 36m 52.540s	2	1
2	26	J Laffite	Ligier	JS11/15	Cosworth	V8	78	1h 37m 26.610s	4	2
3	25	D Pironi	Ligier	JS11/15	Cosworth	V8	78	1h 37m 45.030s	5	3
4	5	N Piquet	Brabham	BT49	Cosworth	V8	78	1h 37m 53.560s	3	2
5	28	C Reutemann	Williams	FW07B	Cosworth	V8	77		6	3
6	30	J Mass	Arrows	A3	Cosworth	V8	77		19	10
7	3	J-P Jarier	Tyrrell	010	Cosworth	V8	77		13	7
8	20	E Fittipaldi	Fittipaldi	F7	Cosworth	V8	77		18	9
9	14	C Regazzoni	Ensign	N180	Cosworth	V8	77		20	10
10	6	R Zunino	Brabham	BT49	Cosworth	V8	77		17	9
11	7	J Watson	McLaren	M29	Cosworth	V8	76		21	11
12	11	M Andretti	Lotus	81	Cosworth	V8	76		15	8
13r	17	G Lees	Shadow	DN11	Cosworth	V8	70	suspension/ accident	24	12
r	23	B Giacomelli	Alfa Romeo	179	Alfa Romeo	V12	69	engine	12	6
r	15	J-P Jabouille	Renault	RE20	Renault	V6t	61	puncture	1	1
r	4	D Daly	Tyrrell	010	Cosworth	V8	61	puncture	16	8
r	21	K Rosberg	Fittipaldi	F7	Cosworth	V8	58	accident	23	12
nc	22	P Depailler	Alfa Romeo	179	Alfa Romeo	V12	53		7	4
r	27	A Jones	Williams	FW07B	Cosworth	V8	34	gearbox oil cooler	8	4
r	2	G Villeneuve	Ferrari	312T5	Ferrari	F12	31	transmission	10	5
r	1	J Scheckter	Ferrari	312T5	Ferrari	F12	14	engine/ electrics	9	5
r	29	R Patrese	Arrows	A3	Cosworth	V8	10	accident	11	6
r	31	E Cheever	Osella	FA1	Cosworth	V8	8	accident	22	11
r	12	E de Angelis	Lotus	81	Cosworth	V8	1	accident	14	7
ns	8	A Prost	McLaren	M29	Cosworth	V8		accident/ injury		
nq	9	M Surer	ATS	D4	Cosworth	V8		accident/ injury		
nq	18	D Kennedy	Shadow	DN11	Cosworth	V8				
nq	9	J Lammers	ATS	D3	Cosworth	V8				

Winning speed: 198.262 km/h, 123.194 mph
Pole Position speed: 211.063 km/h, 131.148 mph (J-P Jabouille, 1 min:10.000 sec)
Fastest Lap speed: 201.974 km/h, 125.501 mph (R Arnoux, 1 min:13.150 sec on lap 51)
Lap Leaders: J-P Jabouille 1-61 (61); R Arnoux 62-78 (17).

30 Mar 1980 — USA West: Long Beach (Round: 4) (Race: 332)

80.5 laps x 3.251 km, 2.020 miles = 261.706 km, 162.616 miles

POS.	NO.	DRIVER	CAR	MODEL	ENGINE		LAPS	TIME/REASON FOR RETIREMENT	GRID:POS	ROW
1	5	N Piquet	Brabham	BT49	Cosworth	V8	80	1h 50m 18.550s	1	1
2	29	R Patrese	Arrows	A3	Cosworth	V8	80	1h 51m 07.762s	8	4
3	20	E Fittipaldi	Fittipaldi	F7	Cosworth	V8	80	1h 51m 37.113s	24	12
4	7	J Watson	McLaren	M29	Cosworth	V8	79		21	11
5	1	J Scheckter	Ferrari	312T5	Ferrari	F12	79		16	8
6	25	D Pironi	Ligier	JS11/15	Cosworth	V8	79		9	5
7	30	J Mass	Arrows	A3	Cosworth	V8	79		17	9
8	4	D Daly	Tyrrell	010	Cosworth	V8	79		14	7
9	16	R Arnoux	Renault	RE20	Renault	V6t	78		2	1
10	15	J-P Jabouille	Renault	RE20	Renault	V6t	71		11	6
r	21	K Rosberg	Fittipaldi	F7	Cosworth	V8	58	engine overheating	22	11
r	14	C Regazzoni	Ensign	N180	Cosworth	V8	50	accident	23	12
r	23	B Giacomelli	Alfa Romeo	179	Alfa Romeo	V12	49	accident	6	3
r	27	A Jones	Williams	FW07B	Cosworth	V8	47	accident	5	3
r	2	G Villeneuve	Ferrari	312T5	Ferrari	F12	46	drive shaft	10	5
r	22	P Depailler	Alfa Romeo	179	Alfa Romeo	V12	40	rear suspension	3	2
r	26	J Laffite	Ligier	JS11/15	Cosworth	V8	36	puncture/ suspension	13	7
r	31	E Cheever	Osella	FA1	Cosworth	V8	11	drive shaft	19	10
r	28	C Reutemann	Williams	FW07B	Cosworth	V8	3	drive shaft	7	4
r	3	J-P Jarier	Tyrrell	010	Cosworth	V8	3	accident	12	6
r	12	E de Angelis	Lotus	81	Cosworth	V8	3	accident	20	10
r	6	R Zunino	Brabham	BT49	Cosworth	V8	0	accident	18	9
r	11	M Andretti	Lotus	81	Cosworth	V8	0	accident	15	8
r	9	J Lammers	ATS	D4	Cosworth	V8	0	drive shaft	4	2
nq	18	D Kennedy	Shadow	DN11	Cosworth	V8				
nq	17	G Lees	Shadow	DN11	Cosworth	V8		driver ill		
nq	8	S South	McLaren	M29	Cosworth	V8				

Winning speed: 142.348 km/h, 88.451 mph
Pole Position speed: 150.637 km/h, 93.602 mph (N Piquet, 1 min:17.694 sec)
Fastest Lap speed: 146.607 km/h, 91.097 mph (N Piquet, 1 min:19.830 sec on lap 38)
Lap Leaders: N Piquet 1-80 (80.5).

The start and finish lines were at different positions on the circuit. The fraction of a lap is credited to the first lap leader.

4 May 1980 — BELGIUM: Zolder (Round: 5) (Race: 333)

72 laps x 4.262 km, 2.648 miles = 306.8864 km, 190.676 miles

POS.	NO.	DRIVER	CAR	MODEL	ENGINE		LAPS	TIME/REASON FOR RETIREMENT	GRID:POS	ROW
1	25	D Pironi	Ligier	JS11/15	Cosworth	V8	72	1h 38m 46.510s	2	1
2	27	A Jones	Williams	FW07B	Cosworth	V8	72	1h 39m 33.880s	1	1
3	28	C Reutemann	Williams	FW07B	Cosworth	V8	72	1h 40m 10.630s	4	2
4	16	R Arnoux	Renault	RE20	Renault	V6t	71		6	3
5	3	J-P Jarier	Tyrrell	010	Cosworth	V8	71		9	5
6	2	G Villeneuve	Ferrari	312T5	Ferrari	F12	71		12	6
7	21	K Rosberg	Fittipaldi	F7	Cosworth	V8	71		21	11
8	1	J Scheckter	Ferrari	312T5	Ferrari	F12	70		14	7
9	4	D Daly	Tyrrell	010	Cosworth	V8	70		11	6
10r	12	E de Angelis	Lotus	81	Cosworth	V8	69	accident	8	4
11	26	J Laffite	Ligier	JS11/15	Cosworth	V8	68		3	2
12r	9	J Lammers	ATS	D4	Cosworth	V8	64	engine	15	8
nc	7	J Watson	McLaren	M29	Cosworth	V8	61		20	10
r	29	R Patrese	Arrows	A3	Cosworth	V8	58	accident	16	8
r	11	M Andretti	Lotus	81	Cosworth	V8	41	gear linkage	17	9
r	22	P Depailler	Alfa Romeo	179	Alfa Romeo	V12	38	exhaust	10	5
r	5	N Piquet	Brabham	BT49	Cosworth	V8	32	accident	7	4
r	8	A Prost	McLaren	M29	Cosworth	V8	29	transmission	19	10
r	20	E Fittipaldi	Fittipaldi	F7	Cosworth	V8	16	electrics	24	12
r	14	T Needell	Ensign	N180	Cosworth	V8	12	engine	23	12
r	23	B Giacomelli	Alfa Romeo	179	Alfa Romeo	V12	11	suspension	18	9
r	6	R Zunino	Brabham	BT49	Cosworth	V8	5	clutch/ gearbox	22	11
r	15	J-P Jabouille	Renault	RE20	Renault	V6t	1	clutch	5	3
r	30	J Mass	Arrows	A3	Cosworth	V8	1	accident	13	7
nq	17	G Lees	Shadow	DN12	Cosworth	V8				
nq	18	D Kennedy	Shadow	DN11	Cosworth	V8				
nq	31	E Cheever	Osella	FA1	Cosworth	V8				

Winning speed: 186.402 km/h, 115.825 mph
Pole Position speed: 193.923 km/h, 120.498 mph (A Jones, 1 min:19.120 sec)
Fastest Lap speed: 189.703 km/h, 117.876 mph (J Laffite, 1 min:20.880 sec on lap 57)
Lap Leaders: D Pironi 1-72 (72).

18 May 1980 — MONACO: Monte Carlo (Round: 6) (Race: 334)

76 laps x 3.312 km, 2.058 miles = 251.712 km, 156.407 miles

POS.	NO.	DRIVER	CAR	MODEL	ENGINE		LAPS	TIME/REASON FOR RETIREMENT	GRID:POS	ROW
1	28	C Reutemann	Williams	FW07B	Cosworth	V8	76	1h 55m 34.365s	2	1
2	26	J Laffite	Ligier	JS11/15	Cosworth	V8	76	1h 56m 47.994s	5	3
3	5	N Piquet	Brabham	BT49	Cosworth	V8	76	1h 56m 52.091s	4	2
4	30	J Mass	Arrows	A3	Cosworth	V8	75		15	8
5	2	G Villeneuve	Ferrari	312T5	Ferrari	F12	75		6	3
6	20	E Fittipaldi	Fittipaldi	F7	Cosworth	V8	74		18	9
7	11	M Andretti	Lotus	81	Cosworth	V8	73		19	10
8	29	R Patrese	Arrows	A3	Cosworth	V8	73		11	6
9r	12	E de Angelis	Lotus	81	Cosworth	V8	68	accident	14	7
nc	9	J Lammers	ATS	D4	Cosworth	V8	64		13	7
r	25	D Pironi	Ligier	JS11/15	Cosworth	V8	54	accident	1	1
r	16	R Arnoux	Renault	RE20	Renault	V6t	53	accident	20	10
r	22	P Depailler	Alfa Romeo	179	Alfa Romeo	V12	50	engine	7	4
r	1	J Scheckter	Ferrari	312T5	Ferrari	F12	27	handling	17	9
r	15	J-P Jabouille	Renault	RE20	Renault	V6t	25	gearbox	16	8
r	27	A Jones	Williams	FW07B	Cosworth	V8	24	differential	3	2
r	3	J-P Jarier	Tyrrell	010	Cosworth	V8	0	accident	9	5
r	23	B Giacomelli	Alfa Romeo	179	Alfa Romeo	V12	0	accident	8	4
r	8	A Prost	McLaren	M29	Cosworth	V8	0	accident	10	5
r	4	D Daly	Tyrrell	010	Cosworth	V8	0	accident	12	6
nq	7	J Watson	McLaren	M29	Cosworth	V8				
nq	31	E Cheever	Osella	FA1	Cosworth	V8				
nq	17	G Lees	Shadow	DN12	Cosworth	V8				
nq	21	K Rosberg	Fittipaldi	F7	Cosworth	V8				
nq	6	R Zunino	Brabham	BT49	Cosworth	V8				
nq	14	T Needell	Ensign	N180	Cosworth	V8				
nq	18	D Kennedy	Shadow	DN11	Cosworth	V8				

Winning speed: 130.677 km/h, 81.199 mph
Pole Position speed: 140.582 km/h, 87.354 mph (D Pironi, 1 min:24.813 sec)
Fastest Lap speed: 136.393 km/h, 84.751 mph (C Reutemann, 1 min:27.418 sec on lap 40)
Lap Leaders: D Pironi 1-54 (54); C Reutemann 55-76 (22).

R Patrese was officially credited with fastest lap in 1m 26.058s (138.548 km/h, 86.090 mph), but this is considered impossible, because of wet conditions on that particular lap.

29 Jun 1980 — FRANCE: Paul Ricard (Round: 7) (Race: 335)

54 laps x 5.810 km, 3.610 miles = 313.740 km, 194.949 miles

POS.	NO.	DRIVER	CAR	MODEL	ENGINE		LAPS	TIME/REASON FOR RETIREMENT	GRID:POS	ROW
1	27	A Jones	Williams	FW07B	Cosworth	V8	54	1h 32m 43.420s	4	2
2	25	D Pironi	Ligier	JS11/15	Cosworth	V8	54	1h 32m 47.940s	3	2
3	26	J Laffite	Ligier	JS11/15	Cosworth	V8	54	1h 33m 13.680s	1	1
4	5	N Piquet	Brabham	BT49	Cosworth	V8	54	1h 33m 58.300s	8	4
5	16	R Arnoux	Renault	RE20	Renault	V6t	54	1h 33m 59.570s	2	1
6	28	C Reutemann	Williams	FW07B	Cosworth	V8	54	1h 34m 00.160s	5	3
7	7	J Watson	McLaren	M29	Cosworth	V8	53		13	7
8	2	G Villeneuve	Ferrari	312T5	Ferrari	F12	53		17	9
9	29	R Patrese	Arrows	A3	Cosworth	V8	53		18	9
10	30	J Mass	Arrows	A3	Cosworth	V8	53		15	8
11	4	D Daly	Tyrrell	010	Cosworth	V8	52		20	10
12	1	J Scheckter	Ferrari	312T5	Ferrari	F12	52		19	10
13r	20	E Fittipaldi	Fittipaldi	F7	Cosworth	V8	50	engine	24	12
14	3	Jarier	Tyrrell	010	Cosworth	V8	50		16	8
r	31	E Cheever	Osella	FA1	Cosworth	V8	43	engine	21	11
r	9	M Surer	ATS	D4	Cosworth	V8	26	gearbox	11	6
r	22	P Depailler	Alfa Romeo	179	Alfa Romeo	V12	25	handling	10	5
r	11	M Andretti	Lotus	81	Cosworth	V8	18	gearbox	12	6
r	21	K Rosberg	Fittipaldi	F7	Cosworth	V8	8	accident	23	12
r	23	B Giacomelli	Alfa Romeo	179	Alfa Romeo	V12	8	handling	9	5
r	8	A Prost	McLaren	M29	Cosworth	V8	6	transmission	7	4
r	12	E de Angelis	Lotus	81	Cosworth	V8	3	clutch	14	7
r	6	R Zunino	Brabham	BT49	Cosworth	V8	0	clutch	22	11
r	15	J-P Jabouille	Renault	RE20	Renault	V6t	0	transmission	6	3
nq	17	G Lees	Shadow	DN12	Cosworth	V8				
nq	14	J Lammers	Ensign	N180	Cosworth	V8				
nq	18	D Kennedy	Shadow	DN12	Cosworth	V8				

Winning speed: 203.016 km/h, 126.148 mph
Pole Position speed: 211.529 km/h, 131.438 mph (J Laffite, 1 min:38.880 sec)
Fastest Lap speed: 206.171 km/h, 128.108 mph (A Jones, 1 min:41.450 sec on lap 48)
Lap Leaders: J Laffite 1-34 (34); A Jones 35-54 (20).

13 Jul 1980 — BRITAIN: Brands Hatch (Round: 8) (Race: 336)

76 laps x 4.207 km, 2.614 miles = 319.719 km, 198.664 miles

POS.	NO.	DRIVER	CAR	MODEL	ENGINE		LAPS	TIME/REASON FOR RETIREMENT	GRID:POS	ROW
1	27	A Jones	Williams	FW07B	Cosworth	V8	76	1h 34m 49.228s	3	2
2	5	N Piquet	Brabham	BT49	Cosworth	V8	76	1h 35m 00.235s	5	3
3	28	C Reutemann	Williams	FW07B	Cosworth	V8	76	1h 35m 02.513s	4	2
4	4	D Daly	Tyrrell	010	Cosworth	V8	75		10	5
5	3	J-P Jarier	Tyrrell	010	Cosworth	V8	75		11	6
6	8	A Prost	McLaren	M29	Cosworth	V8	75		7	4
7	6	H Rebaque	Brabham	BT49	Cosworth	V8	74		17	9
8	7	J Watson	McLaren	M29	Cosworth	V8	74		12	6
9	29	R Patrese	Arrows	A3	Cosworth	V8	73		21	11
10	1	J Scheckter	Ferrari	312T5	Ferrari	F12	73		23	12
11	50	R Keegan	Williams	FW07	Cosworth	V8	73		18	9
12	20	E Fittipaldi	Fittipaldi	F8	Cosworth	V8	72		22	11
13	30	J Mass	Arrows	A3	Cosworth	V8	69		24	12
nc	16	R Arnoux	Renault	RE20	Renault	V6t	67		16	8
r	25	D Pironi	Ligier	JS11/15	Cosworth	V8	63	wheel/ tyre	1	1
r	9	M Surer	ATS	D4	Cosworth	V8	59	engine	15	8
r	11	M Andretti	Lotus	81	Cosworth	V8	57	gearbox	9	5
r	23	B Giacomelli	Alfa Romeo	179	Alfa Romeo	V12	42	accident	6	3
r	2	G Villeneuve	Ferrari	312T5	Ferrari	F12	35	engine	19	10
r	26	J Laffite	Ligier	JS11/15	Cosworth	V8	30	wheel/ puncture/ accident	2	1
r	22	P Depailler	Alfa Romeo	179	Alfa Romeo	V12	27	engine	8	4
r	31	E Cheever	Osella	FA1	Cosworth	V8	17	rear suspension	20	10
r	12	E de Angelis	Lotus	81	Cosworth	V8	16	rear suspension	14	7
r	15	J-P Jabouille	Renault	RE20	Renault	V6t	6	engine	13	7
nq	14	J Lammers	Ensign	N180	Cosworth	V8				
nq	21	K Rosberg	Fittipaldi	F7	Cosworth	V8				
nq	43	D Wilson	Williams	FW07	Cosworth	V8				

Winning speed: 202.310 km/h, 125.710 mph
Pole Position speed: 213.292 km/h, 132.533 mph (D Pironi, 1 min:11.004 sec)
Fastest Lap speed: 209.272 km/h, 130.035 mph (D Pironi, 1 min:12.368 sec on lap 54)
Lap Leaders: D Pironi 1-18 (18); J Laffite 19-30 (12); A Jones 31-76 (46).

10 Aug 1980 — GERMANY: Hockenheim (Round: 9) (Race: 337)

45 laps x 6.789 km, 4.218 miles = 305.505 km, 189.832 miles

POS.	NO.	DRIVER	CAR6	MODEL	ENGINE		LAPS	TIME/REASON FOR RETIREMENT	GRID:POS	ROW
1	26	J Laffite	Ligier	JS11/15	Cosworth	V8	45	1h 22m 59.730s	5	3
2	28	C Reutemann	Williams	FW07B	Cosworth	V8	45	1h 23m 02.920s	4	2
3	27	A Jones	Williams	FW07B	Cosworth	V8	45	1h 23m 43.260s	1	1
4	5	N Piquet	Brabham	BT49	Cosworth	V8	45	1h 23m 44.210s	6	3
5	23	B Giacomelli	Alfa Romeo	179	Alfa Romeo	V12	45	1h 24m 16.220s	19	10
6	2	G Villeneuve	Ferrari	312T5	Ferrari	F12	45	1h 24m 28.450s	16	8
7	11	M Andretti	Lotus	81	Cosworth	V8	45	1h 24m 32.740s	9	5
8	30	J Mass	Arrows	A3	Cosworth	V8	45	1h 24m 47.480s	17	9
9	29	R Patrese	Arrows	A3	Cosworth	V8	44		10	5
10	4	D Daly	Tyrrell	010	Cosworth	V8	44		22	11
11	8	A Prost	McLaren	M29	Cosworth	V8	44		14	7
12	9	M Surer	ATS	D4	Cosworth	V8	44		13	7
13	1	J Scheckter	Ferrari	312T5	Ferrari	F12	44		21	11
14	14	J Lammers	Ensign	N180	Cosworth	V8	44		24	12
15	3	J-P Jarier	Tyrrell	010	Cosworth	V8	44		23	12
16r	12	E de Angelis	Lotus	81	Cosworth	V8	43	wheel bearing	11	6
r	7	J Watson	McLaren	M29	Cosworth	V8	39	engine	20	10
r	15	J-P Jabouille	Renault	RE20	Renault	V6t	27	valve spring	2	1
r	16	R Arnoux	Renault	RE20	Renault	V6t	26	valve spring	3	2
r	31	E Cheever	Osella	FA1	Cosworth	V8	23	gearbox	18	9
r	25	D Pironi	Ligier	JS11/15	Cosworth	V8	18	drive shaft	7	4
r	20	E Fittipaldi	Fittipaldi	F8	Cosworth	V8	18	skirt	12	6
r	21	K Rosberg	Fittipaldi	F8	Cosworth	V8	8	wheel bearing	8	4
r	6	H Rebaque	Brabham	BT49	Cosworth	V8	4	gearbox	15	8
nq	50	R Keegan	Williams	FW07B	Cosworth	V8				
nq	10	H Ertl	ATS	D4	Cosworth	V8				

Winning speed: 220.859 km/h, 137.235 mph
Pole Position speed: 230.897 km/h, 143.472 mph (A Jones, 1 min:45.850 sec)
Fastest Lap speed: 225.278 km/h, 139.981 mph (A Jones, 1 min:48.490 sec on lap 43)
Lap Leaders: J-P Jabouille 1-26 (26); A Jones 27-40 (14); J Laffite 41-45 (5).

17 Aug 1980 — AUSTRIA: Österreichring (Round:10) (Race: 338)

54 laps x 5.942 km, 3.692 miles = 320.868 km, 199.378 miles

POS.	NO.	DRIVER	CAR	MODEL	ENGINE		LAPS	TIME/REASON FOR RETIREMENT	GRID:POS	ROW
1	15	J-P Jabouille	Renault	RE20	Renault	V6t	54	1h 26m 15.730s	2	1
2	27	A Jones	Williams	FW07B	Cosworth	V8	54	1h 26m 16.550s	3	2
3	28	C Reutemann	Williams	FW07B	Cosworth	V8	54	1h 26m 35.090s	4	2
4	26	J Laffite	Ligier	JS11/15	Cosworth	V8	54	1h 26m 57.750s	5	3
5	5	N Piquet	Brabham	BT49	Cosworth	V8	54	1h 27m 18.540s	7	4
6	12	E de Angelis	Lotus	81	Cosworth	V8	54	1h 27m 30.700s	9	5
7	8	A Prost	McLaren	M29	Cosworth	V8	54	1h 27m 49.140s	12	6
8	2	G Villeneuve	Ferrari	312T5	Ferrari	F12	53		15	8
9	16	R Arnoux	Renault	RE20	Renault	V6t	53		1	1

POS.	NO.	DRIVER	CAR	MODEL	ENGINE		LAPS	TIME/REASON FOR RETIREMENT	GRID:POS	ROW
10	6	H Rebaque	Brabham	BT49	Cosworth	V8	53		14	7
11	20	E Fittipaldi	Fittipaldi	F8	Cosworth	V8	53		23	12
12	9	M Surer	ATS	D4	Cosworth	V8	53		16	8
13	1	J Scheckter	Ferrari	312T5	Ferrari	F12	53		22	11
14	29	R Patrese	Arrows	A3	Cosworth	V8	53		18	9
15	50	R Keegan	Williams	FW07B	Cosworth	V8	52		20	10
16	21	K Rosberg	Fittipaldi	F8	Cosworth	V8	52		11	6
r	43	N Mansell	Lotus	81B	Cosworth	V8	40	engine	24	12
r	7	J Watson	McLaren	M29	Cosworth	V8	34	engine	21	11
r	23	B Giacomelli	Alfa Romeo	179	Alfa Romeo	V12	28	rear suspension	8	4
r	3	J-P Jarier	Tyrrell	010	Cosworth	V8	25	engine	13	7
r	25	D Pironi	Ligier	JS11/15	Cosworth	V8	25	handling	6	3
r	31	E Cheever	Osella	FA1	Cosworth	V8	23	wheel bearing	19	10
r	4	D Daly	Tyrrell	010	Cosworth	V8	12	brake disc/ accident	10	5
r	11	M Andretti	Lotus	81	Cosworth	V8	6	engine	17	9
nq	14	J Lammers	Ensign	N180	Cosworth	V8				
nq	30	J Mass	Arrows	A3	Cosworth	V8		accident/ injury		

Winning speed: 223.181 km/h, 138.678 mph
Pole Position speed: 236.969 km/h, 147.246 mph (R Arnoux, 1 min:30.270 sec)
Fastest Lap speed: 231.181 km/h, 143.649 mph (R Arnoux, 1 min:32.530 sec on lap 50)
Lap Leaders: A Jones 1-2 (2); R Arnoux 3-21 (19); J-P Jabouille 22-54 (33).

31 Aug 1980 NETHERLANDS: Zandvoort (Round:11) (Race: 339)

72 laps x 4.252 km, 2.642 miles = 306.144 km, 190.229 miles

POS.	NO.	DRIVER	CAR	MODEL	ENGINE		LAPS	TIME/REASON FOR RETIREMENT	GRID:POS	ROW
1	5	N Piquet	Brabham	BT49	Cosworth	V8	72	1h 38m 13.830s	5	3
2	16	R Arnoux	Renault	RE20	Renault	V6t	72	1h 38m 26.760s	1	1
3	26	J Laffite	Ligier	JS11/15	Cosworth	V8	72	1h 38m 27.260s	6	3
4	28	C Reutemann	Williams	FW07B	Cosworth	V8	72	1h 38m 29.120s	3	2
5	3	J-P Jarier	Tyrrell	010	Cosworth	V8	72	1h 39m 13.850s	17	9
6	8	A Prost	McLaren	M30	Cosworth	V8	72	1h 39m 36.450s	18	9
7	2	G Villeneuve	Ferrari	312T5	Ferrari	F12	71		7	4
8r	11	M Andretti	Lotus	81	Cosworth	V8	70	out of fuel	10	5
9	1	J Scheckter	Ferrari	312T5	Ferrari	F12	70		12	6
10	9	M Surer	ATS	D4	Cosworth	V8	69		20	10
11	27	A Jones	Williams	FW07B	Cosworth	V8	69		4	
r	4	D Daly	Tyrrell	010	Cosworth	V8	60	brake disc/ accident	23	12
r	23	B Giacomelli	Alfa Romeo	179	Alfa Romeo	V12	58	skirt	8	4
r	31	E Cheever	Osella	FA1	Cosworth	V8	38	engine	19	10
r	29	R Patrese	Arrows	A3	Cosworth	V8	29	engine	14	7
r	15	J-P Jabouille	Renault	RE20	Renault	V6t	23	differential/ handling	2	1
r	41	G Lees	Ensign	N180	Cosworth	V8	21	accident	24	12
r	22	V Brambilla	Alfa Romeo	179	Alfa Romeo	V12	21	accident	22	11
r	7	J Watson	McLaren	M29	Cosworth	V8	18	engine	9	5
r	20	E Fittipaldi	Fittipaldi	F8	Cosworth	V8	16	brakes	21	11
r	43	N Mansell	Lotus	81B	Cosworth	V8	15	brakes/ accident	16	8
r	25	D Pironi	Ligier	JS11/15	Cosworth	V8	2	accident	15	8
r	12	E de Angelis	Lotus	81	Cosworth	V8	2	accident	11	6
r	6	H Rebaque	Brabham	BT49	Cosworth	V8	1	gearbox	13	7
nq	50	R Keegan	Williams	FW07B	Cosworth	V8				
nq	14	J Lammers	Ensign	N180	Cosworth	V8				
nq	30	M Thackwell	Arrows	A3	Cosworth	V8				
nq	21	K Rosberg	Fittipaldi	F8	Cosworth	V8				
ew	30	J Mass	Arrows	A3	Cosworth	V8		driver unfit (Austria injury)		

Winning speed: 186.995 km/h, 116.193 mph
Pole Position speed: 197.665 km/h, 122.824 mph (R Arnoux, 1 min:17.440 sec)
Fastest Lap speed: 192.907 km/h, 119.867 mph (R Arnoux, 1 min:19.350 sec on lap 67)
Lap Leaders: A Jones 1 (1); R Arnoux 2 (1); J Laffite 3-12 (10); N Piquet 13-72 (60).

14 Sep 1980 ITALY: Imola (Round:12) (Race: 340)

60 laps x 5.000 km, 3.107 miles = 300.000 km, 186.411 miles

POS.	NO.	DRIVER	CAR	MODEL	ENGINE		LAPS	TIME/REASON FOR RETIREMENT	GRID:POS	ROW
1	5	N Piquet	Brabham	BT49	Cosworth	V8	60	1h 38m 07.520s	5	3
2	27	A Jones	Williams	FW07B	Cosworth	V8	60	1h 38m 36.450s	6	3
3	28	C Reutemann	Williams	FW07B	Cosworth	V8	60	1h 39m 21.190s	3	2
4	12	E de Angelis	Lotus	81	Cosworth	V8	59		18	9
5	21	K Rosberg	Fittipaldi	F8	Cosworth	V8	59		11	6
6	25	D Pironi	Ligier	JS11/15	Cosworth	V8	59		13	7
7	8	A Prost	McLaren	M30	Cosworth	V8	59		24	12
8	1	J Scheckter	Ferrari	312T5	Ferrari	F12	59		16	8
9	26	J Laffite	Ligier	JS11/15	Cosworth	V8	59		20	10
10	16	R Arnoux	Renault	RE20	Renault	V6t	58		1	1
11	50	R Keegan	Williams	FW07B	Cosworth	V8	58		21	11
12	31	E Cheever	Osella	FA1	Cosworth	V8	57		17	9
13r	3	J-P Jarier	Tyrrell	010	Cosworth	V8	54	brakes	12	6
r	15	J-P Jabouille	Renault	RE20	Renault	V6t	53	gearbox	2	1
r	9	M Surer	ATS	D4	Cosworth	V8	45	engine	23	12
r	11	M Andretti	Lotus	81	Cosworth	V8	40	engine	10	5
r	29	R Patrese	Arrows	A3	Cosworth	V8	38	engine	7	4
r	4	D Daly	Tyrrell	010	Cosworth	V8	33	accident	22	11
r	7	J Watson	McLaren	M29	Cosworth	V8	20	brakes/ wheel bearing	14	7
r	6	H Rebaque	Brabham	BT49	Cosworth	V8	18	rear suspension	9	5
r	20	E Fittipaldi	Fittipaldi	F8	Cosworth	V8	17	accident	15	8

POS.	NO.	DRIVER	CAR	MODEL	ENGINE		LAPS	TIME/REASON FOR RETIREMENT	GRID:POS	ROW
r	2	G Villeneuve	Ferrari	312T5	Ferrari	F12	5	puncture/ accident	8	4
r	23	B Giacomelli	Alfa Romeo	179	Alfa Romeo	V12	5	puncture/ accident	4	2
r	22	V Brambilla	Alfa Romeo	179	Alfa Romeo	V12	4	accident	19	10
nq	43	N Mansell	Lotus	81B	Cosworth	V8				
nq	30	M Winkelhock	Arrows	A3	Cosworth	V8				
nq	14	J Lammers	Ensign	N180	Cosworth	V8				
nq	41	G Lees	Ensign	N180	Cosworth	V8				

Winning speed: 183.439 km/h, 113.984 mph
Pole Position speed: 191.514 km/h, 119.001 mph (R Arnoux, 1 min:33.988 sec)
Fastest Lap speed: 187.326 km/h, 116.399 mph (A Jones, 1 min:36.089 sec on lap 47)
Lap Leaders: R Arnoux 1-2 (2); J-P Jabouille 3 (1); N Piquet 4-60 (57).

28 Sep 1980 — CANADA: Montréal (Round:13) (Race: 341)

70 laps x 4.410 km, 2.740 miles = 308.700 km, 191.817 miles

POS.	NO.	DRIVER	CAR	MODEL	ENGINE		LAPS	TIME/REASON FOR RETIREMENT	GRID:POS	ROW
1	27	A Jones	Williams	FW07B	Cosworth	V8	70	1h 46m 45.530s	2	1
2	28	C Reutemann	Williams	FW07B	Cosworth	V8	70	1h 47m 01.070s	5	3
3	25	D Pironi	Ligier	JS11/15	Cosworth	V8	70	1h 47m 04.660s	3	2
4	7	J Watson	McLaren	M29	Cosworth	V8	70	1h 47m 16.510s	7	4
5	2	G Villeneuve	Ferrari	312T5	Ferrari	F12	70	1h 47m 40.760s	22	11
6	6	H Rebaque	Brabham	BT49	Cosworth	V8	69		10	5
7	3	J-P Jarier	Tyrrell	010	Cosworth	V8	69		15	8
8r	26	J Laffite	Ligier	JS11/15	Cosworth	V8	68	out of fuel	9	5
9	21	K Rosberg	Fittipaldi	F8	Cosworth	V8	68		6	3
10	12	E de Angelis	Lotus	81	Cosworth	V8	68		17	9
11	30	J Mass	Arrows	A3	Cosworth	V8	67		21	11
12	14	J Lammers	Ensign	N180	Cosworth	V8	66		19	10
r	8	A Prost	McLaren	M30	Cosworth	V8	41	suspension/ accident	12	6
r	16	R Arnoux	Renault	RE20	Renault	V6t	39	brakes/ gearbox	23	12
r	15	J-P Jabouille	Renault	RE20	Renault	V6t	25	suspension/ accident	13	7
r	5	N Piquet	Brabham	BT49	Cosworth	V8	23	engine	1	1
r	11	M Andretti	Lotus	81	Cosworth	V8	11	engine	18	9
r	22	A de Cesaris	Alfa Romeo	179	Alfa Romeo	V12	8	engine	8	4
r	31	E Cheever	Osella	FA1	Cosworth	V8	8	fuel pressure	14	7
r	20	E Fittipaldi	Fittipaldi	F8	Cosworth	V8	8	gearbox	16	8
r	23	B Giacomelli	Alfa Romeo	179	Alfa Romeo	V12	7	skirt	4	2
r	29	R Patrese	Arrows	A3	Cosworth	V8	6	accident	11	6
r	4	D Daly	Tyrrell	010	Cosworth	V8	0	accident *	20	10
r	43	M Thackwell	Tyrrell	010	Cosworth	V8	0	accident *	24	12
nq	9	M Surer	ATS	D4	Cosworth	V8				
nq	1	J Scheckter	Ferrari	312T5	Ferrari	F12				
nq	50	R Keegan	Williams	FW07B	Cosworth	V8				
nq	51	K Cogan	Williams	FW07B	Cosworth	V8				

Winning speed: 173.494 km/h, 107.804 mph
Pole Position speed: 181.797 km/h, 112.964 mph (N Piquet, 1 min:27.328 sec)
Fastest Lap speed: 178.846 km/h, 111.130 mph (D Pironi, 1 min:28.769 sec on lap 62)
Lap Leaders: A Jones 1-2,24-43 (22); N Piquet 3-23 (21); D Pironi 44-70 (27).

*Interrupted after 1st lap accident. Restarted for original distance. * retired after first start. D Pironi finished 1st in 1h 45m 19.06s (175.868 km/h, 109.279 mph), but penalised 1 minute for jumping the second start and classified 3rd. He is shown as leader 'on the road' but on corrected time, A Jones led laps 44-70.*

5 Oct 1980 — USA East: Watkins Glen (Round:14) (Race: 342)

59 laps x 5.435 km, 3.377 miles = 320.651 km, 199.243 miles

POS.	NO.	DRIVER	CAR	MODEL	ENGINE		LAPS	TIME/REASON FOR RETIREMENT	GRID:POS	ROW
1	27	A Jones	Williams	FW07B	Cosworth	V8	59	1h 34m 36.050s	5	3
2	28	C Reutemann	Williams	FW07B	Cosworth	V8	59	1h 34m 40.260s	3	2
3	25	D Pironi	Ligier	JS11/15	Cosworth	V8	59	1h 34m 48.620s	7	4
4	12	E de Angelis	Lotus	81	Cosworth	V8	59	1h 35m 05.740s	4	2
5	26	J Laffite	Ligier	JS11/15	Cosworth	V8	58		12	6
6	11	M Andretti	Lotus	81	Cosworth	V8	58		11	6
7	16	R Arnoux	Renault	RE20	Renault	V6t	58		6	3
8	9	M Surer	ATS	D4	Cosworth	V8	57		17	9
9	50	R Keegan	Williams	FW07B	Cosworth	V8	57		15	8
10	21	K Rosberg	Fittipaldi	F8	Cosworth	V8	57		14	7
11	1	J Scheckter	Ferrari	312T5	Ferrari	F12	56		23	12
nc	7	J Watson	McLaren	M29	Cosworth	V8	50		9	5
r	2	G Villeneuve	Ferrari	312T5	Ferrari	F12	49	accident	18	9
nc	3	J-P Jarier	Tyrrell	010	Cosworth	V8	40		22	11
r	30	J Mass	Arrows	A3	Cosworth	V8	36	drive shaft	24	12
r	23	B Giacomelli	Alfa Romeo	179	Alfa Romeo	V12	31	electrics	1	1
r	5	N Piquet	Brabham	BT49	Cosworth	V8	25	spin	2	1
r	31	E Cheever	Osella	FA1	Cosworth	V8	21	suspension	16	8
r	6	H Rebaque	Brabham	BT49	Cosworth	V8	20	engine	8	4
r	29	R Patrese	Arrows	A3	Cosworth	V8	16	accident	20	10
r	14	J Lammers	Ensign	N180	Cosworth	V8	16	steering mount	25	13
r	20	E Fittipaldi	Fittipaldi	F8	Cosworth	V8	15	rear suspension	19	10
r	4	D Daly	Tyrrell	010	Cosworth	V8	3	accident/ suspension	21	11
r	22	A de Cesaris	Alfa Romeo	179	Alfa Romeo	V12	2	accident	10	5
ns	8	A Prost	McLaren	M30	Cosworth	V8		accident/ injury	13	7
nq	43	M Thackwell	Tyrrell	010	Cosworth	V8				
nq	51	G Lees	Williams	FW07B	Cosworth	V8				

Winning speed: 203.371 km/h, 126.369 mph
Pole Position speed: 209.721 km/h, 130.315 mph (B Giacomelli, 1 min:33.291 sec)
Fastest Lap speed: 207.989 km/h, 129.238 mph (A Jones, 1 min:34.068 sec on lap 44)
Lap Leaders: B Giacomelli 1-31 (31); A Jones 32-59 (28).

Lap Leaders 1980

POS	DRIVER	CAR-ENGINE	GPS	LAPS	KM	MILES
1	N Piquet	Brabham-Cosworth	4	218.5	894.4	555.8
2	A Jones	Williams-Cosworth	8	174	914.8	568.4
3	D Pironi	Ligier-Cosworth	4	171	680.5	422.8
4	J-P Jabouille	Renault	5	144	809.0	502.7
5	J Laffite	Ligier-Cosworth	5	73	396.1	246.1
6	R Arnoux	Renault	5	55	322.9	200.6
7	B Giacomelli	Alfa Romeo	1	31	168.5	104.7
8	C Reutemann	Williams-Cosworth	1	22	72.9	45.3
9	G Villeneuve	Ferrari	1	1	7.9	4.9
			14	**889.5**	**4,267.0**	**2,651.4**

Driver Points 1980

		RA	BR	ZA	USAW	B	MC	F	GB	D	A	NL	I	CDN	USAE	TOTAL	
1	A Jones	9	4	-	-	6	-	9	9	(4)	6	-	6	9	9	67	(4)
2	N Piquet	6	-	3	9	-	4	3	6	3	2	9	9	-	-	54	
3	C Reutemann	-	-	2	-	4	9	1	4	6	4	(3)	(4)	6	6	42	(7)
4	J Laffite	-	-	6	-	-	6	4	-	9	3	4	-	-	2	34	
5	D Pironi	-	3	4	1	9	-	6	-	-	-	-	1	4	4	32	
6	R Arnoux	-	9	9	-	3	-	2	-	-	-	6	-	-	-	29	
7	E de Angelis	-	6	-	-	-	-	-	-	-	1	-	3	-	3	13	
8	J-P Jabouille	-	-	-	-	-	-	-	-	-	9	-	-	-	-	9	
9	R Patrese	-	1	-	6	-	-	-	-	-	-	-	-	-	-	7	
10	K Rosberg	4	-	-	-	-	-	-	-	-	-	-	2	-	-	6	
	D Daly	3	-	-	-	-	-	-	3	-	-	-	-	-	-	6	
	J Watson	-	-	-	3	-	-	-	-	-	-	-	-	3	-	6	
	J-P Jarier	-	-	-	-	2	-	-	2	-	-	2	-	-	-	6	
	G Villeneuve	-	-	-	-	1	2	-	-	1	-	-	-	2	-	6	
15	E Fittipaldi	-	-	-	4	-	1	-	-	-	-	-	-	-	-	5	
	A Prost	1	2	-	-	-	-	-	1	-	-	1	-	-	-	5	
17	J Mass	-	-	1	-	-	3	-	-	-	-	-	-	-	-	4	
	B Giacomelli	2	-	-	-	-	-	-	-	2	-	-	-	-	-	4	
19	J Scheckter	-	-	-	2	-	-	-	-	-	-	-	-	-	-	2	
20	H Rebaque	-	-	-	-	-	-	-	-	-	-	-	-	1	-	1	
	M Andretti	-	-	-	-	-	-	-	-	-	-	-	-	-	1	1	

9, 6, 4, 3, 2 and 1 point awarded to the first six finishers.

Best 5 scores from first 7 races, best 5 from remaining 7 races.

Constructor Points 1980

		RA	BR	ZA	USAW	B	MC	F	GB	D	A	NL	I	CDN	USAE	TOTAL
1	Williams-Cosworth	9	4	2	-	10	9	10	13	10	10	3	10	15	15	120
2	Ligier-Cosworth	-	3	10	1	9	6	10	-	9	3	4	1	4	6	66
3	Brabham-Cosworth	6	-	3	9	-	4	3	6	3	2	9	9	1	-	55
4	Renault	-	9	9	-	3	-	2	-	-	9	6	-	-	-	38
5	Lotus-Cosworth	-	6	-	-	-	-	-	-	-	1	-	3	-	4	14
6	Tyrrell-Cosworth	3	-	-	-	2	-	-	5	-	-	2	-	-	-	12
7	Arrows-Cosworth	-	1	1	6	-	3	-	-	-	-	-	-	-	-	11
	Fittipaldi-Cosworth	4	-	-	4	-	1	-	-	-	-	-	2	-	-	11
	McLaren-Cosworth	1	2	-	3	-	-	-	1	-	-	1	-	3	-	11
10	Ferrari	-	-	-	2	1	2	-	-	1	-	-	-	2	-	8
11	Alfa Romeo	2	-	-	-	-	-	-	-	2	-	-	-	-	-	4

9, 6, 4, 3, 2 and 1 point awarded to the first six finishers.

Politics stole the headlines with threats of a breakaway series, until all parties talked through their differences to arrive at what was known as the Concorde Agreement. A ban on skirts was eventually agreed, as well as a 6cm ground clearance: which was soon overcome with various hydraulic devices. In view of the goings on, Goodyear withdrew only to come back later after Pirelli and Avon re-entered Formula 1. McLaren and Lotus both built carbon-fibre chassis.

WILLIAMS
Albilad Williams Racing Team: Jones, Reutemann
TAG Williams Team from E GP
Equipe Banco Occidental: (de Villota)

TYRRELL
Team Tyrrell: Cheever, (Cogan), Zunino, Alboreto

BRABHAM
Parmalat Racing Team: Piquet, Rebaque

McLAREN
McLaren International: Watson, de Cesaris

ATS
Team ATS: Lammers, Borgudd

LOTUS
Team Essex Lotus: de Angelis, Mansell
John Player Team Lotus from E GP

ENSIGN
Ensign Racing: Surer, Salazar

RENAULT
Equipe Renault Elf: Prost, Arnoux

MARCH
March Grand Prix Team: Daly, Salazar

FITTIPALDI
Fittipaldi Automotive: Rosberg, Serra

ALFA ROMEO
Marlboro Team Alfa Romeo: Andretti, Giacomelli

LIGIER
Equipe Talbot Gitanes: Jarier, Jabouille, Tambay, Laffite

FERRARI
Scuderia Ferrari SpA SEFAC: G Villeneuve, Pironi

ARROWS
Arrows Racing Team: Patrese, Stohr, (J Villeneuve)

OSELLA
Osella Squadra Corse: Gabbiani, Guerra, Ghinzani, (Francia), Jarier

THEODORE
Theodore Racing Team: Tambay, Surer

TOLEMAN
Candy Toleman Motorsport: Henton, Warwick

15 Mar 1981 — USA West: Long Beach (Round: 1) (Race: 343)

80.5 laps x 3.251 km, 2.020 miles = 261.706 km, 162.616 miles

POS.	NO.	DRIVER	CAR	MODEL	ENGINE		LAPS	TIME/REASON FOR RETIREMENT	GRID:POS	ROW
1	1	A Jones	Williams	FW07C	Cosworth	V8	80	1h 50m 41.330s	2	1
2	2	C Reutemann	Williams	FW07C	Cosworth	V8	80	1h 50m 50.520s	3	2
3	5	N Piquet	Brabham	BT49C	Cosworth	V8	80	1h 51m 16.250s	4	2
4	22	M Andretti	Alfa Romeo	179C	Alfa Romeo	V12	80	1h 51m 30.640s	6	3
5	3	E Cheever	Tyrrell	010	Cosworth	V8	80	1h 51m 48.030s	8	4
6	33	P Tambay	Theodore	TY01	Cosworth	V8	79		17	9
7	21	C Serra	Fittipaldi	F8C	Cosworth	V8	78		18	9
8	16	R Arnoux	Renault	RE20B	Renault	V6t	77		20	10
r	14	M Surer	Ensign	N180B	Cosworth	V8	70	electrics	19	10
r	28	D Pironi	Ferrari	126CK	Ferrari	V6t	67	engine	11	6
r	25	J-P Jarier	Talbot Ligier	JS17	Matra	V12	64	fuel pump	10	5
r	6	H Rebaque	Brabham	BT49C	Cosworth	V8	49	accident	15	8
r	26	J Laffite	Talbot Ligier	JS17	Matra	V12	41	accident	12	6
r	23	B Giacomelli	Alfa Romeo	179C	Alfa Romeo	V12	41	accident	9	5
r	9	J Lammers	ATS	D4	Cosworth	V8	41	accident	21	11
r	20	K Rosberg	Fittipaldi	F8C	Cosworth	V8	41	distributor rotor arm	16	8
r	29	R Patrese	Arrows	A3	Cosworth	V8	33	fuel filter	1	1
r	32	B Gabbiani	Osella	FA1B	Cosworth	V8	26	accident	24	12
r	12	N Mansell	Lotus	81B	Cosworth	V8	25	accident	7	4
r	27	G Villeneuve	Ferrari	126CK	Ferrari	V6t	17	drive shaft	5	3
r	7	J Watson	McLaren	M29F	Cosworth	V8	16	engine	23	12
r	11	E de Angelis	Lotus	81B	Cosworth	V8	13	accident	13	7
r	15	A Prost	Renault	RE20B	Renault	V6t	0	accident	14	7
r	8	A de Cesaris	McLaren	M29F	Cosworth	V8	0	accident	22	11
nq	4	K Cogan	Tyrrell	010	Cosworth	V8				
nq	17	D Daly	March	811	Cosworth	V8				
nq	31	M-A Guerra	Osella	FA1B	Cosworth	V8				
nq	30	S Stohr	Arrows	A3	Cosworth	V8				
nq	18	E Salazar	March	811	Cosworth	V8				

Winning speed: 140.974 km/h, 87.597 mph (based on time taken to complete 80 laps)
Pole Position speed: 147.402 km/h, 91.592 mph (R Patrese, 1 min:19.399 sec)
Fastest Lap speed: 144.666 km/h, 89.891 mph (A Jones, 1 min:20.901 sec on lap 31)
Lap Leaders: R Patrese 1-24 (24.5); C Reutemann 25-31 (7); A Jones 32-80 (49).

The start and finish lines were at different positions on the circuit.
The fraction of a lap is credited to the first lap leader.

29 Mar 1981 — BRAZIL: Rio de Janeiro (Round: 2) (Race: 344)

62 laps x 5.031 km, 3.126 miles = 311.922 km, 193.819 miles

POS.	NO.	DRIVER	CAR	MODEL	ENGINE		LAPS	TIME/REASON FOR RETIREMENT	GRID:POS	ROW
1	2	C Reutemann	Williams	FW07C	Cosworth	V8	62	2h 00m 23.660s	2	1
2	1	A Jones	Williams	FW07C	Cosworth	V8	62	2h 00m 28.100s	3	2
3	29	R Patrese	Arrows	A3	Cosworth	V8	62	2h 01m 26.740s	4	2
4	14	M Surer	Ensign	N180B	Cosworth	V8	62	2h 01m 40.690s	18	9
5	11	E de Angelis	Lotus	81B	Cosworth	V8	62	2h 01m 50.080s	10	5
6	26	J Laffite	Talbot Ligier	JS17	Matra	V12	62	2h 01m 50.490s	16	8
7	25	J-P Jarier	Talbot Ligier	JS17	Matra	V12	62	2h 01m 53.910s	23	12
8	7	J Watson	McLaren	M29F	Cosworth	V8	61		15	8
9	20	K Rosberg	Fittipaldi	F8C	Cosworth	V8	61		12	6
10	33	P Tambay	Theodore	TY01	Cosworth	V8	61		19	10
11	12	N Mansell	Lotus	81B	Cosworth	V8	61		13	7
12	5	N Piquet	Brabham	BT49C	Cosworth	V8	60		1	1
13	4	R Zunino	Tyrrell	010	Cosworth	V8	57		24	12
nc	3	E Cheever	Tyrrell	010	Cosworth	V8	49		14	7
nc	23	B Giacomelli	Alfa Romeo	179C	Alfa Romeo	V12	40		6	3
r	27	G Villeneuve	Ferrari	126CK	Ferrari	V6t	25	turbo wastegate	7	4
r	6	H Rebaque	Brabham	BT49C	Cosworth	V8	22	rear suspension	11	6
r	30	S Stohr	Arrows	A3	Cosworth	V8	20	accident	21	11
r	15	A Prost	Renault	RE20B	Renault	V6t	20	accident	5	3
r	28	D Pironi	Ferrari	126CK	Ferrari	V6t	19	accident	17	9
r	8	A de Cesaris	McLaren	M29F	Cosworth	V8	9	electrics	20	10
r	21	C Serra	Fittipaldi	F8C	Cosworth	V8	0	accident	22	11
r	16	R Arnoux	Renault	RE20B	Renault	V6t	0	accident	8	4
r	22	M Andretti	Alfa Romeo	179C	Alfa Romeo	V12	0	accident	9	5
nq	9	J Lammers	ATS	D4	Cosworth	V8				
nq	25	J-P Jabouille	Talbot Ligier	JS17	Matra	V12		car raced by Jarier		
nq	32	B Gabbiani	Osella	FA1B	Cosworth	V8				
nq	31	M-A Guerra	Osella	FA1B	Cosworth	V8				
nq	18	E Salazar	March	811	Cosworth	V8				
nq	17	D Daly	March	811	Cosworth	V8				

Winning speed: 155.450 km/h, 96.592 mph
Pole Position speed: 190.490 km/h, 118.365 mph (N Piquet, 1 min:35.079 sec)
Fastest Lap speed: 158.454 km/h, 98.459 mph (M Surer, 1 min:54.302 sec on lap 36)
Lap Leaders: C Reutemann 1-62 (62).

Scheduled for 63 laps, but stopped at 2 hours.

12 Apr 1981 — ARGENTINA: Buenos Aires No.15 (Round: 3) (Race: 345)

53 laps x 5.968 km, 3.708 miles = 316.304 km, 196.542 miles

POS.	NO.	DRIVER	CAR	MODEL	ENGINE		LAPS	TIME/REASON FOR RETIREMENT	GRID:POS	ROW
1	5	N Piquet	Brabham	BT49C	Cosworth	V8	53	1h 34m 32.740s	1	1
2	2	C Reutemann	Williams	FW07C	Cosworth	V8	53	1h 34m 59.350s	4	2
3	15	A Prost	Renault	RE20B	Renault	V6t	53	1h 35m 22.720s	2	1
4	1	A Jones	Williams	FW07C	Cosworth	V8	53	1h 35m 40.620s	3	2
5	16	R Arnoux	Renault	RE20B	Renault	V6t	53	1h 36m 04.590s	5	3
6	11	E de Angelis	Lotus	81B	Cosworth	V8	52		10	5
7	29	R Patrese	Arrows	A3	Cosworth	V8	52		9	5
8	22	M Andretti	Alfa Romeo	179C	Alfa Romeo	V12	52		17	9
9	30	S Stohr	Arrows	A3	Cosworth	V8	52		19	10
10r	23	B Giacomelli	Alfa Romeo	179C	Alfa Romeo	V12	51	out of fuel	22	11
11	8	A de Cesaris	McLaren	M29F	Cosworth	V8	51		18	9
12	9	J Lammers	ATS	D4	Cosworth	V8	51		23	12
13	4	R Zunino	Tyrrell	010	Cosworth	V8	51	1 lap penalty (missed chicane)	24	12
r	27	G Villeneuve	Ferrari	126CK	Ferrari	V6t	40	drive shaft	7	4
r	33	P Tambay	Theodore	TY01	Cosworth	V8	36	oil loss/ engine	14	7
r	7	J Watson	McLaren	MP4	Cosworth	V8	36	crown wheel & pinion	11	6
r	6	H Rebaque	Brabham	BT49C	Cosworth	V8	32	distributor rotor arm	6	3
r	21	C Serra	Fittipaldi	F8C	Cosworth	V8	28	gearbox	20	10
r	26	J Laffite	Talbot Ligier	JS17	Matra	V12	19	vibration/ handling	21	11
r	14	M Surer	Ensign	N180B	Cosworth	V8	14	engine	16	8
r	20	K Rosberg	Fittipaldi	F8C	Cosworth	V8	4	fuel pump belt	8	4
r	12	N Mansell	Lotus	81B	Cosworth	V8	3	engine	15	8
r	28	D Pironi	Ferrari	126CK	Ferrari	V6t	3	engine	12	6
r	3	E Cheever	Tyrrell	010	Cosworth	V8	1	clutch	13	7
nq	31	M-A Guerra	Osella	FA1B	Cosworth	V8				
nq	32	B Gabbiani	Osella	FA1B	Cosworth	V8				
nq	17	D Daly	March	811	Cosworth	V8				
nq	25	J-P Jabouille	Talbot Ligier	JS17	Matra	V12				
nq	18	E Salazar	March	811	Cosworth	V8				

Winning speed: 200.731 km/h, 124.728 mph
Pole Position speed: 209.271 km/h, 130.035 mph (N Piquet, 1 min:42.665 sec)
Fastest Lap speed: 204.059 km/h, 126.797 mph (N Piquet, 1 min:45.287 sec on lap 6)
Lap Leaders: N Piquet 1-53 (53).

R Zunino penalised 1 lap for taking a short cut.

3 May 1981 — SAN MARINO: Imola — (Round: 4) (Race: 346)

60 laps x 5.040 km, 3.132 miles = 302.400 km, 187.903 miles

POS.	NO.	DRIVER	CAR	MODEL	ENGINE		LAPS	TIME/REASON FOR RETIREMENT	GRID:POS	ROW
1	5	N Piquet	Brabham	BT49C	Cosworth	V8	60	1h 51m 23.970s	5	3
2	29	R Patrese	Arrows	A3	Cosworth	V8	60	1h 51m 28.550s	9	5
3	2	C Reutemann	Williams	FW07C	Cosworth	V8	60	1h 51m 30.310s	2	1
4	6	H Rebaque	Brabham	BT49C	Cosworth	V8	60	1h 51m 46.860s	13	7
5	28	D Pironi	Ferrari	126CK	Ferrari	V6t	60	1h 51m 49.840s	6	3
6	8	A de Cesaris	McLaren	M29F	Cosworth	V8	60	1h 52m 30.580s	14	7
7	27	G Villeneuve	Ferrari	126CK	Ferrari	V6t	60	1h 53m 05.940s	1	1
8	16	R Arnoux	Renault	RE20B	Renault	V6t	59		3	2
9	14	M Surer	Ensign	N180B	Cosworth	V8	59		21	11
10	7	J Watson	McLaren	MP4	Cosworth	V8	58		7	4
11	33	P Tambay	Theodore	TY01	Cosworth	V8	58		16	8
12	1	A Jones	Williams	FW07C	Cosworth	V8	58		8	4
13	10	S Borgudd	ATS	D4	Cosworth	V8	57		24	12
nc	25	J-P Jabouille	Talbot Ligier	JS17	Matra	V12	45		18	9
r	17	E Salazar	March	811	Cosworth	V8	38	oil pressure	23	12
r	4	M Alboreto	Tyrrell	010	Cosworth	V8	31	accident	17	9
r	32	B Gabbiani	Osella	FA1B	Cosworth	V8	31	accident	20	10
r	23	B Giacomelli	Alfa Romeo	179C	Alfa Romeo	V12	28	accident	11	6
r	3	E Cheever	Tyrrell	010	Cosworth	V8	28	accident	19	10
r	22	M Andretti	Alfa Romeo	179C	Alfa Romeo	V12	26	gearbox	12	6
r	20	K Rosberg	Fittipaldi	F8C	Cosworth	V8	14	engine	15	8
r	26	J Laffite	Talbot Ligier	JS17	Matra	V12	7	accident	10	5
r	15	A Prost	Renault	RE20B	Renault	V6t	3	gearbox	4	2
r	31	M-A Guerra	Osella	FA1B	Cosworth	V8	0	accident	22	11
nq	30	S Stohr	Arrows	A3	Cosworth	V8				
nq	18	D Daly	March	811	Cosworth	V8				
nq	9	J Lammers	ATS	D4	Cosworth	V8				
nq	21	C Serra	Fittipaldi	F8C	Cosworth	V8				
nq	36	D Warwick	Toleman	TG181	Hart	4t				
nq	35	B Henton	Toleman	TG181	Hart	4t				

Winning speed: 162.873 km/h, 101.205 mph
Pole Position speed: 191.953 km/h, 119.274 mph (G Villeneuve, 1 min:34.523 sec)
Fastest Lap speed: 167.901 km/h, 104.329 mph (G Villeneuve, 1 min:48.064 sec on lap 46)
Lap Leaders: G Villeneuve 1-14 (14); D Pironi 15-46 (32); N Piquet 47-60 (14).

17 May 1981 — BELGIUM: Zolder — (Round: 5) (Race: 347)

54 laps x 4.262 km, 2.648 miles = 230.148 km, 143.007 miles

POS.	NO.	DRIVER	CAR	MODEL	ENGINE		LAPS	TIME/REASON FOR RETIREMENT	GRID:POS	ROW
1	2	C Reutemann	Williams	FW07C	Cosworth	V8	54	1h 16m 31.610s	1	1
2	26	J Laffite	Talbot Ligier	JS17	Matra	V12	54	1h 17m 07.670s	9	5
3	12	N Mansell	Lotus	81B	Cosworth	V8	54	1h 17m 15.300s	10	5
4	27	G Villeneuve	Ferrari	126CK	Ferrari	V6t	54	1h 17m 19.250s	7	4
5	11	E de Angelis	Lotus	81B	Cosworth	V8	54	1h 17m 20.810s	14	7
6	3	E Cheever	Tyrrell	010	Cosworth	V8	54	1h 17m 24.120s	8	4
7	7	J Watson	McLaren	MP4	Cosworth	V8	54	1h 17m 33.270s	5	3
8	28	D Pironi	Ferrari	126CK	Ferrari	V6t	54	1h 18m 03.650s	3	2
9	23	B Giacomelli	Alfa Romeo	179C	Alfa Romeo	V12	54	1h 18m 07.190s	17	9
10	22	M Andretti	Alfa Romeo	179C	Alfa Romeo	V12	53		18	9
11	14	M Surer	Ensign	N180B	Cosworth	V8	52		15	8
12	4	M Alboreto	Tyrrell	010	Cosworth	V8	52		19	10
13	31	P Ghinzani	Osella	FA1B	Cosworth	V8	50		24	12
r	6	H Rebaque	Brabham	BT49C	Cosworth	V8	39	accident	21	11
r	25	J-P Jabouille	Talbot Ligier	JS17	Matra	V12	35	transmission	16	8
r	21	C Serra	Fittipaldi	F8C	Cosworth	V8	29	engine	20	10
r	32	B Gabbiani	Osella	FA1B	Cosworth	V8	22	engine	22	11
r	1	A Jones	Williams	FW07C	Cosworth	V8	19	accident	6	3
r	8	A de Cesaris	McLaren	M29F	Cosworth	V8	11	gearbox	23	12
r	5	N Piquet	Brabham	BT49C	Cosworth	V8	10	accident	2	1
r	20	K Rosberg	Fittipaldi	F8C	Cosworth	V8	10	gear lever	11	6
r	15	A Prost	Renault	RE20B	Renault	V6t	2	clutch	12	6
r	30	S Stohr	Arrows	A3	Cosworth	V8	0	accident *	13	7
r	29	R Patrese	Arrows	A3	Cosworth	V8	0	stalled on grid/ accident *	4	2
nq	16	R Arnoux	Renault	RE30	Renault	V6t				
nq	17	E Salazar	March	811	Cosworth	V8				
nq	10	S Borgudd	ATS	HGS1	Cosworth	V8				
nq	33	P Tambay	Theodore	TY01	Cosworth	V8				
nq	36	D Warwick	Toleman	TG181	Hart	4t				
nq	35	B Henton	Toleman	TG181	Hart	4t				
nq	18	D Daly	March	811	Cosworth	V8				

Winning speed: 180.445 km/h, 112.123 mph
Pole Position speed: 186.475 km/h, 115.870 mph (C Reutemann, 1 min:22.280 sec)
Fastest Lap speed: 184.192 km/h, 114.452 mph (C Reutemann, 1 min:23.300 sec on lap 37)
Lap Leaders: D Pironi 1-12 (12); A Jones 13-19 (7); C Reutemann 20-54 (35).

Scheduled for 70 laps, but interrupted after 1st lap accident.
*Restarted for original distance, but stopped early because of rain. * retired after first start.*

31 May 1981 — MONACO: Monte Carlo (Round: 6) (Race: 348)

76 laps x 3.312 km, 2.058 miles = 251.712 km, 156.407 miles

POS.	NO.	DRIVER	CAR	MODEL	ENGINE		LAPS	TIME/REASON FOR RETIREMENT	GRID:POS	ROW
1	27	G Villeneuve	Ferrari	126CK	Ferrari	V6t	76	1h 54m 23.380s	2	1
2	1	A Jones	Williams	FW07C	Cosworth	V8	76	1h 55m 03.290s	7	4
3	26	J Laffite	Talbot Ligier	JS17	Matra	V12	76	1h 55m 52.620s	8	4
4	28	D Pironi	Ferrari	126CK	Ferrari	V6t	75		17	9
5	3	E Cheever	Tyrrell	010	Cosworth	V8	74		15	8
6	14	M Surer	Ensign	N180B	Cosworth	V8	74		19	10
7	33	P Tambay	Theodore	TY01	Cosworth	V8	72		16	8
r	5	N Piquet	Brabham	BT49C	Cosworth	V8	53	accident	1	1
r	7	J Watson	McLaren	MP4	Cosworth	V8	53	engine	10	5
r	4	M Alboreto	Tyrrell	010	Cosworth	V8	50	accident	20	10
r	23	B Giacomelli	Alfa Romeo	179C	Alfa Romeo	V12	50	accident	18	9
r	15	A Prost	Renault	RE30	Renault	V6t	45	engine	9	5
r	2	C Reutemann	Williams	FW07C	Cosworth	V8	34	gearbox	4	2
r	16	R Arnoux	Renault	RE20B	Renault	V6t	32	accident	13	7
r	11	E de Angelis	Lotus	87	Cosworth	V8	32	engine	6	3
r	29	R Patrese	Arrows	A3	Cosworth	V8	29	gearbox	5	3
r	12	N Mansell	Lotus	87	Cosworth	V8	16	rear suspension	3	2
r	30	S Stohr	Arrows	A3	Cosworth	V8	15	electrical misfire	14	7
r	8	A de Cesaris	McLaren	MP4	Cosworth	V8	0	accident	11	6
r	22	M Andretti	Alfa Romeo	179C	Alfa Romeo	V12	0	accident	12	6
nq	20	K Rosberg	Fittipaldi	F8C	Cosworth	V8				
nq	25	J-P Jabouille	Talbot Ligier	JS17	Matra	V12				
nq	6	H Rebaque	Brabham	BT49C	Cosworth	V8				
nq	21	C Serra	Fittipaldi	F8C	Cosworth	V8				
nq	32	P Ghinzani	Osella	FA1B	Cosworth	V8				
nq	31	B Gabbiani	Osella	FA1B	Cosworth	V8				
npq	10	S Borgudd	ATS	D4	Cosworth	V8				
npq	18	D Daly	March	811	Cosworth	V8				
npq	17	E Salazar	March	811	Cosworth	V8				
npq	35	B Henton	Toleman	TG181	Hart	4t				
npq	36	D Warwick	Toleman	TG181	Hart	4t				

Winning speed: 132.029 km/h, 82.039 mph
Pole Position speed: 139.111 km/h, 86.440 mph (N Piquet, 1 min:25.710 sec)
Fastest Lap speed: 136.312 km/h, 84.700 mph (A Jones, 1 min:27.470 sec on lap 48)
Lap Leaders: N Piquet 1-53 (53); A Jones 54-72 (19); G Villeneuve 73-76 (4).

21 Jun 1981 — SPAIN: Járama (Round: 7) (Race: 349)

80 laps x 3.312 km, 2.058 miles = 264.960 km, 164.639 miles

POS.	NO.	DRIVER	CAR	MODEL	ENGINE		LAPS	TIME/REASON FOR RETIREMENT	GRID:POS	ROW
1	27	G Villeneuve	Ferrari	126CK	Ferrari	V6t	80	1h 46m 35.019s	7	4
2	26	J Laffite	Talbot Ligier	JS17	Matra	V12	80	1h 46m 35.230s	1	1
3	7	J Watson	McLaren	MP4	Cosworth	V8	80	1h 46m 35.590s	4	2
4	2	C Reutemann	Williams	FW07C	Cosworth	V8	80	1h 46m 36.020s	3	2
5	11	E de Angelis	Lotus	87	Cosworth	V8	80	1h 46m 36.250s	10	5
6	12	N Mansell	Lotus	87	Cosworth	V8	80	1h 47m 03.590s	11	6
7	1	A Jones	Williams	FW07C	Cosworth	V8	80	1h 47m 31.590s	2	1
8	22	M Andretti	Alfa Romeo	179C	Alfa Romeo	V12	80	1h 47m 35.810s	8	4
9	16	R Arnoux	Renault	RE30	Renault	V6t	80	1h 47m 42.090s	17	9
10	23	B Giacomelli	Alfa Romeo	179C	Alfa Romeo	V12	80	1h 47m 48.660s	6	3
11	21	C Serra	Fittipaldi	F8C	Cosworth	V8	79		21	11
12	20	K Rosberg	Fittipaldi	F8C	Cosworth	V8	78		15	8
13	33	P Tambay	Theodore	TY01	Cosworth	V8	78		16	8
14	14	E Salazar	Ensign	N180B	Cosworth	V8	77		24	12
15	28	D Pironi	Ferrari	126CK	Ferrari	V6t	76		13	7
16	17	D Daly	March	811	Cosworth	V8	75		22	11
nc	3	E Cheever	Tyrrell	010	Cosworth	V8	61		20	10
r	25	J-P Jabouille	Talbot Ligier	JS17	Matra	V12	52	brakes	19	10
r	6	H Rebaque	Brabham	BT49C	Cosworth	V8	46	gearbox	18	9
r	5	N Piquet	Brabham	BT49C	Cosworth	V8	43	accident	9	5
r	30	S Stohr	Arrows	A3	Cosworth	V8	43	engine	23	12
r	15	A Prost	Renault	RE30	Renault	V6t	28	accident	5	3
r	29	R Patrese	Arrows	A3	Cosworth	V8	21	engine	12	6
r	8	A de Cesaris	McLaren	MP4	Cosworth	V8	9	accident	14	7
nq	4	M Alboreto	Tyrrell	010	Cosworth	V8				
nq	31	B Gabbiani	Osella	FA1B	Cosworth	V8				
nq	10	S Borgudd	ATS	HGS1	Cosworth	V8				
nq	35	B Henton	Toleman	TG181	Hart	4t				
nq	36	D Warwick	Toleman	TG181	Hart	4t				
nq	32	G Francia	Osella	FA1B	Cosworth	V8				
exc	37	E de Villota	Williams	FW07	Cosworth	V8		not allowed to practice		

Winning speed: 149.156 km/h, 92.681 mph
Pole Position speed: 161.662 km/h, 100.452 mph (J Laffite, 1 min:13.754 sec)
Fastest Lap speed: 153.219 km/h, 95.206 mph (A Jones, 1 min:17.818 sec on lap 5)
Lap Leaders: A Jones 1-13 (13); G Villeneuve 14-80 (67).

5 Jul 1981 — FRANCE: Dijon-Prenois — (Round: 8) (Race: 350)

80 laps x 3.800 km, 2.361 miles = 304.000 km, 188.897 miles

POS.	NO.	DRIVER	CAR	MODEL	ENGINE		LAPS	TIME/REASON FOR RETIREMENT	GRID:POS	ROW
1	15	A Prost	Renault	RE30	Renault	V6t	80	1h 35m 48.130s	3	2
2	7	J Watson	McLaren	MP4	Cosworth	V8	80	1h 35m 50.420s	2	1
3	5	N Piquet	Brabham	BT49C	Cosworth	V8	80	1h 36m 12.350s	4	2
4	16	R Arnoux	Renault	RE30	Renault	V6t	80	1h 36m 30.430s	1	1
5	28	D Pironi	Ferrari	126CK	Ferrari	V6t	79		14	7
6	11	E de Angelis	Lotus	87	Cosworth	V8	79		8	4
7	12	N Mansell	Lotus	87	Cosworth	V8	79		13	7
8	22	M Andretti	Alfa Romeo	179C	Alfa Romeo	V12	79		10	5
9	6	H Rebaque	Brabham	BT49C	Cosworth	V8	78		15	8
10	2	C Reutemann	Williams	FW07C	Cosworth	V8	78		7	4
11	8	A de Cesaris	McLaren	MP4	Cosworth	V8	78		5	3
12	33	M Surer	Theodore	TY01	Cosworth	V8	78		21	11
13	3	E Cheever	Tyrrell	010	Cosworth	V8	77		19	10
14	29	R Patrese	Arrows	A3	Cosworth	V8	77		18	9
15	23	B Giacomelli	Alfa Romeo	179C	Alfa Romeo	V12	77		12	6
16	4	M Alboreto	Tyrrell	010	Cosworth	V8	77		23	12
17	1	A Jones	Williams	FW07C	Cosworth	V8	76		9	5
r	26	J Laffite	Talbot Ligier	JS17	Matra	V12	57	front suspension	6	3
r	17	D Daly	March	811	Cosworth	V8	55	engine	20	10
r	27	G Villeneuve	Ferrari	126CK	Ferrari	V6t	41	electrics	11	6
r	25	P Tambay	Talbot Ligier	JS17	Matra	V12	30	wheel bearing	16	8
r	20	K Rosberg	Fittipaldi	F8C	Cosworth	V8	11	rear suspension	17	9
r	14	E Salazar	Ensign	N180B	Cosworth	V8	6	rear suspension	22	11
ns	21	C Serra	Fittipaldi	F8C	Cosworth	V8		accident	24	12
nq	30	S Stohr	Arrows	A3	Cosworth	V8				
nq	35	B Henton	Toleman	TG181	Hart	4t				
nq	10	S Borgudd	ATS	HGS1	Cosworth	V8				
nq	31	B Gabbiani	Osella	FA1B	Cosworth	V8				
nq	36	D Warwick	Toleman	TG181	Hart	4t				

Winning speed: 190.392 km/h, 118.304 mph
Pole Position speed: 207.430 km/h, 128.891 mph (R Arnoux, 1 min: 5.950 sec)
Fastest Lap speed: 197.859 km/h, 122.944 mph (A Prost, 1 min: 9.140 sec on lap 64)
Lap Leaders: N Piquet 1-58 (58); A Prost 59-80 (22).

Interrupted after 58 laps, because of rain. Restarted for remaining 22 laps, with results being on aggregate. Lap leaders are given 'on the road'.

18 Jul 1981 — BRITAIN: Silverstone — (Round: 9) (Race: 351)

68 laps x 4.719 km, 2.932 miles = 320.865 km, 199.376 miles

POS.	NO.	DRIVER	CAR	MODEL	ENGINE		LAPS	TIME/REASON FOR RETIREMENT	GRID:POS	ROW
1	7	J Watson	McLaren	MP4	Cosworth	V8	68	1h 26m 54.800s	5	3
2	2	C Reutemann	Williams	FW07C	Cosworth	V8	68	1h 27m 35.450s	9	5
3	26	J Laffite	Talbot Ligier	JS17	Matra	V12	67		14	7
4	3	E Cheever	Tyrrell	010	Cosworth	V8	67		23	12
5	6	H Rebaque	Brabham	BT49C	Cosworth	V8	67		13	7
6	10	S Borgudd	ATS	HGS1	Cosworth	V8	67		21	11
7	17	D Daly	March	811	Cosworth	V8	66		17	9
8	32	J-P Jarier	Osella	FA1B	Cosworth	V8	65		20	10
9r	16	R Arnoux	Renault	RE30	Renault	V6t	64	engine	1	1
10r	29	R Patrese	Arrows	A3	Cosworth	V8	64	engine	10	5
11r	33	M Surer	Theodore	TY01	Cosworth	V8	61	out of fuel	24	12
r	22	M Andretti	Alfa Romeo	179D	Alfa Romeo	V12	59	throttle linkage	11	6
r	20	K Rosberg	Fittipaldi	F8C	Cosworth	V8	56	rear suspension	16	8
r	11	E de Angelis	Lotus	87	Cosworth	V8	25	black-flagged/ withdrew	22	11
r	15	A Prost	Renault	RE30	Renault	V6t	17	engine	2	1
r	25	P Tambay	Talbot Ligier	JS17	Matra	V12	15	ignition	15	8
r	28	D Pironi	Ferrari	126CK	Ferrari	V6t	13	engine	4	2
r	5	N Piquet	Brabham	BT49C	Cosworth	V8	11	tyre burst/ accident	3	2
r	23	B Giacomelli	Alfa Romeo	179D	Alfa Romeo	V12	5	gearbox	12	6
r	27	G Villeneuve	Ferrari	126CK	Ferrari	V6t	4	accident	8	4
r	1	A Jones	Williams	FW07C	Cosworth	V8	3	accident	7	4
r	8	A de Cesaris	McLaren	MP4	Cosworth	V8	3	accident	6	3
r	4	M Alboreto	Tyrrell	010	Cosworth	V8	0	clutch	19	10
r	30	S Stohr	Arrows	A3	Cosworth	V8	0	accident	18	9
nq	21	C Serra	Fittipaldi	F8C	Cosworth	V8				
nq	35	B Henton	Toleman	TG181	Hart	4t				
nq	12	N Mansell	Lotus	87	Cosworth	V8				
nq	14	E Salazar	Ensign	N180B	Cosworth	V8				
nq	36	D Warwick	Toleman	TG181	Hart	4t				
nq	31	B Gabbiani	Osella	FA1B	Cosworth	V8				

Winning speed: 221.507 km/h, 137.638 mph
Pole Position speed: 239.253 km/h, 148.665 mph (R Arnoux, 1 min:11.000 sec)
Fastest Lap speed: 226.290 km/h, 140.610 mph (R Arnoux, 1 min:15.067 sec on lap 50)
Lap Leaders: A Prost 1-16 (16); R Arnoux 17-60 (44); J Watson 61-68 (8).

2 Aug 1981 — GERMANY: Hockenheim (Round:10) (Race: 352)

45 laps x 6.789 km, 4.218 miles = 305.505 km, 189.832 miles

POS.	NO.	DRIVER	CAR	MODEL	ENGINE		LAPS	TIME/REASON FOR RETIREMENT	GRID:POS	ROW
1	5	N Piquet	Brabham	BT49C	Cosworth	V8	45	1h 25m 55.600s	6	3
2	15	A Prost	Renault	RE30	Renault	V6t	45	1h 26m 07.120s	1	1
3	26	J Laffite	Talbot Ligier	JS17	Matra	V12	45	1h 27m 00.200s	7	4
4	6	H Rebaque	Brabham	BT49C	Cosworth	V8	45	1h 27m 35.290s	16	8
5	3	E Cheever	Tyrrell	011	Cosworth	V8	45	1h 27m 46.120s	18	9
6	7	J Watson	McLaren	MP4	Cosworth	V8	44		9	5
7	11	E de Angelis	Lotus	87	Cosworth	V8	44		14	7
8	32	J-P Jarier	Osella	FA1B	Cosworth	V8	44		17	9
9	22	M Andretti	Alfa Romeo	179E	Alfa Romeo	V12	44		12	6
10	27	G Villeneuve	Ferrari	126CK	Ferrari	V6t	44		8	4
11	1	A Jones	Williams	FW07C	Cosworth	V8	44		4	2
12	30	S Stohr	Arrows	A3	Cosworth	V8	44		24	12
13	16	R Arnoux	Renault	RE30	Renault	V6t	44		2	1
14r	33	M Surer	Theodore	TY01	Cosworth	V8	43	suspension/ accident	22	11
15	23	B Giacomelli	Alfa Romeo	179D	Alfa Romeo	V12	43		19	10
nc	14	E Salazar	Ensign	N180B	Cosworth	V8	39		23	12
r	10	S Borgudd	ATS	HGS1	Cosworth	V8	35	engine	20	10
r	2	C Reutemann	Williams	FW07C	Cosworth	V8	27	engine	3	2
r	29	R Patrese	Arrows	A3	Cosworth	V8	27	engine	13	7
r	25	P Tambay	Talbot Ligier	JS17	Matra	V12	27	rear wheel bearing	11	6
r	17	D Daly	March	811	Cosworth	V8	15	steering tie rod	21	11
r	12	N Mansell	Lotus	87	Cosworth	V8	12	fuel leak	15	8
r	8	A de Cesaris	McLaren	MP4	Cosworth	V8	4	spin	10	5
r	28	D Pironi	Ferrari	126CK	Ferrari	V6t	1	engine	5	3
nq	20	K Rosberg	Fittipaldi	F8C	Cosworth	V8				
nq	35	B Henton	Toleman	TG181	Hart	4t				
nq	31	B Gabbiani	Osella	FA1B	Cosworth	V8				
nq	36	D Warwick	Toleman	TG181	Hart	4t				
nq	4	M Alboreto	Tyrrell	010	Cosworth	V8				
nq	21	C Serra	Fittipaldi	F8C	Cosworth	V8				

Winning speed: 213.325 km/h, 132.554 mph
Pole Position speed: 227.353 km/h, 141.270 mph (A Prost, 1 min:47.500 sec)
Fastest Lap speed: 217.403 km/h, 135.088 mph (A Jones, 1 min:52.420 sec on lap 4)
Lap Leaders: A Prost 1-20 (20); A Jones 21-38 (18); N Piquet 39-45 (7).

16 Aug 1981 — AUSTRIA: Österreichring (Round:11) (Race: 353)

53 laps x 5.942 km, 3.692 miles = 314.926 km, 195.686 miles

POS.	NO.	DRIVER	CAR	MODEL	ENGINE		LAPS	TIME/REASON FOR RETIREMENT	GRID:POS	ROW
1	26	J Laffite	Talbot Ligier	JS17	Matra	V12	53	1h 27m 36.470s	4	2
2	16	R Arnoux	Renault	RE30	Renault	V6t	53	1h 27m 41.640s	1	1
3	5	N Piquet	Brabham	BT49C	Cosworth	V8	53	1h 27m 43.810s	7	4
4	1	A Jones	Williams	FW07C	Cosworth	V8	53	1h 27m 48.510s	6	3
5	2	C Reutemann	Williams	FW07C	Cosworth	V8	53	1h 28m 08.320s	5	3
6	7	J Watson	McLaren	MP4	Cosworth	V8	53	1h 29m 07.610s	12	6
7	11	E de Angelis	Lotus	87	Cosworth	V8	52		9	5
8	8	A de Cesaris	McLaren	MP4	Cosworth	V8	52		18	9
9	28	D Pironi	Ferrari	126CK	Ferrari	V6t	52		8	4
10	32	J-P Jarier	Osella	FA1B	Cosworth	V8	51		14	7
11	17	D Daly	March	811	Cosworth	V8	47		19	10
r	22	M Andretti	Alfa Romeo	179E	Alfa Romeo	V12	46	engine	13	7
r	10	S Borgudd	ATS	HGS1	Cosworth	V8	44	brakes	21	11
r	29	R Patrese	Arrows	A3	Cosworth	V8	43	engine	10	5
r	14	E Salazar	Ensign	N180B	Cosworth	V8	43	engine	20	10
r	4	M Alboreto	Tyrrell	010	Cosworth	V8	40	engine	22	11
r	23	B Giacomelli	Alfa Romeo	179D	Alfa Romeo	V12	35	engine/ fire	16	8
r	6	H Rebaque	Brabham	BT49C	Cosworth	V8	31	clutch	15	8
r	30	S Stohr	Arrows	A3	Cosworth	V8	27	spin	24	12
r	15	A Prost	Renault	RE30	Renault	V6t	26	front suspension	2	1
r	25	P Tambay	Talbot Ligier	JS17	Matra	V12	26	engine	17	9
r	12	N Mansell	Lotus	87	Cosworth	V8	23	engine	11	6
r	27	G Villeneuve	Ferrari	126CK	Ferrari	V6t	11	accident	3	2
r	33	M Surer	Theodore	TY01	Cosworth	V8	0	distributor	23	12
nq	3	E Cheever	Tyrrell	011	Cosworth	V8				
nq	36	D Warwick	Toleman	TG181	Hart	4t				
nq	35	B Henton	Toleman	TG181	Hart	4t				
nq	31	B Gabbiani	Osella	FA1B	Cosworth	V8				

Winning speed: 215.683 km/h, 134.019 mph
Pole Position speed: 232.468 km/h, 144.449 mph (R Arnoux, 1 min:32.018 sec)
Fastest Lap speed: 219.127 km/h, 136.159 mph (J Laffite, 1 min:37.620 sec on lap 47)
Lap Leaders: G Villeneuve 1 (1); A Prost 2-26 (25); R Arnoux 27-38 (12); J Laffite 39-53 (15).

30 Aug 1981 — NETHERLANDS: Zandvoort — (Round:12) (Race: 354)

72 laps x 4.252 km, 2.642 miles = 306.144 km, 190.229 miles

POS.	NO.	DRIVER	CAR	MODEL	ENGINE		LAPS	TIME/REASON FOR RETIREMENT	GRID:POS	ROW
1	15	A Prost	Renault	RE30	Renault	V6t	72	1h 40m 22.430s	1	1
2	5	N Piquet	Brabham	BT49C	Cosworth	V8	72	1h 40m 30.670s	3	2
3	1	A Jones	Williams	FW07C	Cosworth	V8	72	1h 40m 57.930s	4	2
4	6	H Rebaque	Brabham	BT49C	Cosworth	V8	71		15	8
5	11	E de Angelis	Lotus	87	Cosworth	V8	71		9	5
6	14	E Salazar	Ensign	N180B	Cosworth	V8	70		24	12
7	30	S Stohr	Arrows	A3	Cosworth	V8	69		21	11
8	33	M Surer	Theodore	TY01	Cosworth	V8	69		20	10
9r	4	M Alboreto	Tyrrell	011	Cosworth	V8	68	engine	25	13
10	10	S Borgudd	ATS	HGS1	Cosworth	V8	68		23	12
r	22	M Andretti	Alfa Romeo	179D	Alfa Romeo	V12	62	tyre burst/ accident	7	4
r	7	J Watson	McLaren	MP4	Cosworth	V8	50	electrics	8	4
r	3	E Cheever	Tyrrell	011	Cosworth	V8	46	suspension/ accident	22	11
r	32	J-P Jarier	Osella	FA1B	Cosworth	V8	29	gearbox	18	9
r	16	R Arnoux	Renault	RE30	Renault	V6t	21	accident	2	1
r	23	B Giacomelli	Alfa Romeo	179C	Alfa Romeo	V12	19	accident	14	7
r	26	J Laffite	Talbot Ligier	JS17	Matra	V12	18	accident	6	3
r	2	C Reutemann	Williams	FW07C	Cosworth	V8	18	accident	5	3
r	29	R Patrese	Arrows	A3	Cosworth	V8	16	suspension	10	5
r	17	D Daly	March	811	Cosworth	V8	5	suspension	19	10
r	28	D Pironi	Ferrari	126CK	Ferrari	V6t	4	accident	12	6
r	12	N Mansell	Lotus	87	Cosworth	V8	1	electrics	17	9
r	25	P Tambay	Talbot Ligier	JS17	Matra	V12	0	accident	11	6
r	27	G Villeneuve	Ferrari	126CK	Ferrari	V6t	0	accident	16	8
ns	8	A de Cesaris	McLaren	MP4	Cosworth	V8		withdrawn by team (accidents)	13	7
nq	35	B Henton	Toleman	TG181	Hart	4t				
nq	20	K Rosberg	Fittipaldi	F8C	Cosworth	V8				
nq	21	C Serra	Fittipaldi	F8C	Cosworth	V8				
nq	31	B Gabbiani	Osella	FA1B	Cosworth	V8				
nq	36	D Warwick	Toleman	TG181	Hart	4t				

Winning speed: 183.002 km/h, 113.712 mph
Pole Position speed: 195.804 km/h, 121.667 mph (A Prost, 1 min:18.176 sec)
Fastest Lap speed: 187.061 km/h, 116.234 mph (A Jones, 1 min:21.830 sec on lap 15)
Lap Leaders: A Prost 1-22,24-72 (71); A Jones 23 (1).

13 Sep 1981 — ITALY: Monza — (Round:13) (Race: 355)

52 laps x 5.800 km, 3.604 miles = 301.600 km, 187.406 miles

POS.	NO.	DRIVER	CAR	MODEL	ENGINE		LAPS	TIME/REASON FOR RETIREMENT	GRID:POS	ROW
1	15	A Prost	Renault	RE30	Renault	V6t	52	1h 26m 33.897s	3	2
2	1	A Jones	Williams	FW07C	Cosworth	V8	52	1h 26m 56.072s	5	3
3	2	C Reutemann	Williams	FW07C	Cosworth	V8	52	1h 27m 24.484s	2	1
4	11	E de Angelis	Lotus	87	Cosworth	V8	52	1h 28m 06.799s	11	6
5	28	D Pironi	Ferrari	126CK	Ferrari	V6t	52	1h 28m 08.419s	8	4
6r	5	N Piquet	Brabham	BT49C	Cosworth	V8	51	engine	6	3
7r	8	A de Cesaris	McLaren	MP4	Cosworth	V8	51	tyre burst/ accident	16	8
8	23	B Giacomelli	Alfa Romeo	179C	Alfa Romeo	V12	50		10	5
9	32	J-P Jarier	Osella	FA1C	Cosworth	V8	50		18	9
10	35	B Henton	Toleman	TG181	Hart	4t	49		23	12
r	22	M Andretti	Alfa Romeo	179D	Alfa Romeo	V12	41	flywheel coupling	13	7
r	17	D Daly	March	811	Cosworth	V8	37	gearbox	19	10
r	25	P Tambay	Talbot Ligier	JS17	Matra	V12	22	puncture	15	8
r	12	N Mansell	Lotus	87	Cosworth	V8	21	handling	12	6
r	7	J Watson	McLaren	MP4	Cosworth	V8	19	accident	7	4
r	29	R Patrese	Arrows	A3	Cosworth	V8	19	gearbox	20	10
r	4	M Alboreto	Tyrrell	011	Cosworth	V8	16	accident	22	11
r	14	E Salazar	Ensign	N180B	Cosworth	V8	13	tyre burst	24	12
r	16	R Arnoux	Renault	RE30	Renault	V6t	12	accident	1	1
r	3	E Cheever	Tyrrell	011	Cosworth	V8	11	spin	17	9
r	26	J Laffite	Talbot Ligier	JS17	Matra	V12	11	puncture	4	2
r	10	S Borgudd	ATS	HGS1	Cosworth	V8	10	spin	21	11
r	27	G Villeneuve	Ferrari	126CK	Ferrari	V6t	6	turbo	9	5
r	6	H Rebaque	Brabham	BT49C	Cosworth	V8	0	electrics	14	7
nq	33	M Surer	Theodore	TY01	Cosworth	V8				
nq	31	B Gabbiani	Osella	FA1B	Cosworth	V8				
nq	36	D Warwick	Toleman	TG181	Hart	4t				
nq	30	S Stohr	Arrows	A3	Cosworth	V8				
nq	20	K Rosberg	Fittipaldi	F8C	Cosworth	V8				
nq	21	C Serra	Fittipaldi	F8C	Cosworth	V8				

Winning speed: 209.045 km/h, 129.895 mph
Pole Position speed: 223.394 km/h, 138.811 mph (R Arnoux, 1 min:33.467 sec)
Fastest Lap speed: 214.092 km/h, 133.031 mph (C Reutemann, 1 min:37.528 sec on lap 48)
Lap Leaders: A Prost 1-52 (52).

27 Sep 1981 — CANADA: Montréal (Round:14) (Race: 356)

63 laps x 4.410 km, 2.740 miles = 277.830 km, 172.636 miles

POS.	NO.	DRIVER	CAR	MODEL	ENGINE		LAPS	TIME/REASON FOR RETIREMENT	GRID:POS	ROW
1	26	J Laffite	Talbot Ligier	JS17	Matra	V12	63	2h 01m 25.205s	10	5
2	7	J Watson	McLaren	MP4	Cosworth	V8	63	2h 01m 31.438s	9	5
3	27	G Villeneuve	Ferrari	126CK	Ferrari	V6t	63	2h 03m 15.480s	11	6
4	23	B Giacomelli	Alfa Romeo	179C	Alfa Romeo	V12	62		15	8
5	5	N Piquet	Brabham	BT49C	Cosworth	V8	62		1	1
6	11	E de Angelis	Lotus	87	Cosworth	V8	62		7	4
7	22	M Andretti	Alfa Romeo	179D	Alfa Romeo	V12	62		16	8
8	17	D Daly	March	811	Cosworth	V8	61		20	10
9	33	M Surer	Theodore	TY01	Cosworth	V8	61		19	10
10	2	C Reutemann	Williams	FW07C	Cosworth	V8	60		2	1
11	4	M Alboreto	Tyrrell	011	Cosworth	V8	59		22	11
12r	3	E Cheever	Tyrrell	011	Cosworth	V8	56	engine	14	7
r	8	A de Cesaris	McLaren	MP4	Cosworth	V8	51	spin	13	7
r	15	A Prost	Renault	RE30	Renault	V6t	48	accident	4	2
r	12	N Mansell	Lotus	87	Cosworth	V8	45	accident	5	3
r	10	S Borgudd	ATS	HGS1	Cosworth	V8	39	spin	21	11
r	6	H Rebaque	Brabham	BT49C	Cosworth	V8	35	spin	6	3
r	32	J-P Jarier	Osella	FA1C	Cosworth	V8	26	accident	23	12
r	28	D Pironi	Ferrari	126CK	Ferrari	V6t	24	engine	12	6
r	1	A Jones	Williams	FW07C	Cosworth	V8	24	handling	3	2
r	14	E Salazar	Ensign	N180B	Cosworth	V8	8	spin	24	12
r	25	P Tambay	Talbot Ligier	JS17	Matra	V12	6	spin	17	9
r	29	R Patrese	Arrows	A3	Cosworth	V8	6	spin	18	9
r	16	R Arnoux	Renault	RE30	Renault	V6t	0	accident	8	4
nq	20	K Rosberg	Fittipaldi	F8C	Cosworth	V8				
nq	21	C Serra	Fittipaldi	F8C	Cosworth	V8				
nq	35	B Henton	Toleman	TG181	Hart	4t				
nq	30	J Villeneuve	Arrows	A3	Cosworth	V8				
nq	36	D Warwick	Toleman	TG181	Hart	4t				
nq	31	B Gabbiani	Osella	FA1B	Cosworth	V8				

Winning speed: 137.290 km/h, 85.308 mph
Pole Position speed: 177.960 km/h, 110.579 mph (N Piquet, 1 min:29.211 sec)
Fastest Lap speed: 145.019 km/h, 90.111 mph (J Watson, 1 min:49.475 sec on lap 43)
Lap Leaders: A Jones 1-6 (6); A Prost 7-12 (6); J Laffite 13-63 (51).

Scheduled for 70 laps, but stopped at 2 hours.

17 Oct 1981 — CAESARS PALACE: Las Vegas (Round:15) (Race: 357)

75 laps x 3.650 km, 2.268 miles = 273.749 km, 170.100 miles

POS.	NO.	DRIVER	CAR	MODEL	ENGINE		LAPS	TIME/REASON FOR RETIREMENT	GRID:POS	ROW
1	1	A Jones	Williams	FW07C	Cosworth	V8	75	1h 44m 09.077s	2	1
2	15	A Prost	Renault	RE30	Renault	V6t	75	1h 44m 29.125s	5	3
3	23	B Giacomelli	Alfa Romeo	179C	Alfa Romeo	V12	75	1h 44m 29.505s	8	4
4	12	N Mansell	Lotus	87	Cosworth	V8	75	1h 44m 56.550s	9	5
5	5	N Piquet	Brabham	BT49C	Cosworth	V8	75	1h 45m 25.515s	4	2
6	26	J Laffite	Talbot Ligier	JS17	Matra	V12	75	1h 45m 27.252s	12	6
7	7	J Watson	McLaren	MP4	Cosworth	V8	75	1h 45m 27.574s	6	3
8	2	C Reutemann	Williams	FW07C	Cosworth	V8	74		1	1
9	28	D Pironi	Ferrari	126CK	Ferrari	V6t	73		18	9
10	20	K Rosberg	Fittipaldi	F8C	Cosworth	V8	73		20	10
11	29	R Patrese	Arrows	A3	Cosworth	V8	71		11	6
12	8	A de Cesaris	McLaren	MP4	Cosworth	V8	69		14	7
13r	4	M Alboreto	Tyrrell	011	Cosworth	V8	67	engine	17	9
nc	14	E Salazar	Ensign	N180B	Cosworth	V8	61		24	12
r	36	D Warwick	Toleman	TG181	Hart	4t	43	gearbox	22	11
r	22	M Andretti	Alfa Romeo	179D	Alfa Romeo	V12	29	rear suspension	10	5
dq	27	G Villeneuve	Ferrari	126CK	Ferrari	V6t	22	started from wrong grid position	3	2
r	6	H Rebaque	Brabham	BT49C	Cosworth	V8	20	spin	16	8
r	33	M Surer	Theodore	TY01	Cosworth	V8	19	rear suspension	23	12
r	3	E Cheever	Tyrrell	011	Cosworth	V8	10	engine	19	10
r	16	R Arnoux	Renault	RE30	Renault	V6t	10	electrics	13	7
r	25	P Tambay	Talbot Ligier	JS17	Matra	V12	2	accident	7	4
r	11	E de Angelis	Lotus	87	Cosworth	V8	2	water leak	15	8
r	32	J-P Jarier	Osella	FA1C	Cosworth	V8	0	transmission	21	11
nq	10	S Borgudd	ATS	HGS1	Cosworth	V8				
nq	21	C Serra	Fittipaldi	F8C	Cosworth	V8				
nq	17	D Daly	March	811	Cosworth	V8				
nq	30	J Villeneuve	Arrows	A3	Cosworth	V8				
nq	35	B Henton	Toleman	TG181	Hart	4t				
nq	31	B Gabbiani	Osella	FA1B	Cosworth	V8				

Winning speed: 157.703 km/h, 97.992 mph
Pole Position speed: 168.849 km/h, 104.918 mph (C Reutemann, 1 min:17.821 sec)
Fastest Lap speed: 163.930 km/h, 101.861 mph (D Pironi, 1 min:20.156 sec on lap 49)
Lap Leaders: A Jones 1-75 (75).

Lap Leaders 1981

POS	DRIVER	CAR-ENGINE	GPS	LAPS	KM	MILES
1	A Prost	Renault	7	212	1,073.4	667.0
2	A Jones	Williams-Cosworth	8	188	721.8	448.5
3	N Piquet	Brabham-Cosworth	5	185	830.3	515.9
4	C Reutemann	Williams-Cosworth	3	104	483.8	300.6
5	G Villeneuve	Ferrari	4	86	311.7	193.7
6	J Laffite	Talbot Ligier-Matra	2	66	314.0	195.1
7	R Arnoux	Renault	2	56	278.9	173.3
8	D Pironi	Ferrari	2	44	212.4	132.0
9	R Patrese	Arrows-Cosworth	1	24.5	79.6	49.5
10	J Watson	McLaren-Cosworth	1	8	37.8	23.5
			15	**973.5**	**4,343.8**	**2,699.1**

Driver Points 1981

		USAW	BR	RA	RSM	B	MC	E	F	GB	D	A	NL	I	CDN	LV	TOTAL
1	N Piquet	4	-	9	9	-	-	-	4	-	9	4	6	1	2	2	50
2	C Reutemann	6	9	6	4	9	-	3	-	6	-	2	-	4	-	-	49
3	A Jones	9	6	3	-	-	6	-	-	-	-	3	4	6	-	9	46
4	J Laffite	-	1	-	-	6	4	6	-	4	4	9	-	-	9	1	44
5	A Prost	-	-	4	-	-	-	-	9	-	6	-	9	9	-	6	43
6	J Watson	-	-	-	-	-	-	4	6	9	1	1	-	-	6	-	27
7	G Villeneuve	-	-	-	-	3	9	9	-	-	-	-	-	-	4	-	25
8	E de Angelis	-	2	1	-	2	-	2	1	-	-	-	2	3	1	-	14
9	R Arnoux	-	-	2	-	-	-	-	3	-	-	6	-	-	-	-	11
	H Rebaque	-	-	-	3	-	-	-	-	2	3	-	3	-	-	-	11
11	R Patrese	-	4	-	6	-	-	-	-	-	-	-	-	-	-	-	10
	E Cheever	2	-	-	-	1	2	-	-	3	2	-	-	-	-	-	10
13	D Pironi	-	-	-	2	-	3	-	2	-	-	-	-	2	-	-	9
14	N Mansell	-	-	-	-	4	-	1	-	-	-	-	-	-	-	3	8
15	B Giacomelli	-	-	-	-	-	-	-	-	-	-	-	-	-	3	4	7
16	M Surer	-	3	-	-	-	1	-	-	-	-	-	-	-	-	-	4
17	M Andretti	3	-	-	-	-	-	-	-	-	-	-	-	-	-	-	3
18	P Tambay	1	-	-	-	-	-	-	-	-	-	-	-	-	-	-	1
	A de Cesaris	-	-	-	1	-	-	-	-	-	-	-	-	-	-	-	1
	S Borgudd	-	-	-	-	-	-	-	-	1	-	-	-	-	-	-	1
	E Salazar	-	-	-	-	-	-	-	-	-	-	-	1	-	-	-	1

9, 6, 4, 3, 2 and 1 point awarded to the first six finishers. Best 11 scores.

Constructor Points 1981

		USAW	BR	RA	RSM	B	MC	E	F	GB	D	A	NL	I	CDN	LV	TOTAL
1	Williams-Cosworth	15	15	9	4	9	6	3	-	6	-	5	4	10	-	9	95
2	Brabham-Cosworth	4	-	9	12	-	-	-	4	2	12	4	9	1	2	2	61
3	Renault	-	-	6	-	-	-	-	12	-	6	6	9	9	-	6	54
4	Talbot Ligier-Matra	-	1	-	-	6	4	6	-	4	4	9	-	-	9	1	44
5	Ferrari	-	-	-	2	3	12	9	2	-	-	-	-	2	4	-	34
6	McLaren-Cosworth	-	-	-	1	-	-	4	6	9	1	1	-	-	6	-	28
7	Lotus-Cosworth	-	2	1	-	6	-	3	1	-	-	-	2	3	1	3	22
8	Arrows-Cosworth	-	4	-	6	-	-	-	-	-	-	-	-	-	-	-	10
	Alfa Romeo	3	-	-	-	-	-	-	-	-	-	-	-	-	3	4	10
	Tyrrell-Cosworth	2	-	-	-	1	2	-	-	3	2	-	-	-	-	-	10
11	Ensign-Cosworth	-	3	-	-	-	1	-	-	-	-	-	1	-	-	-	5
12	Theodore-Cosworth	1	-	-	-	-	-	-	-	-	-	-	-	-	-	-	1
	ATS-Cosworth	-	-	-	-	-	-	-	-	1	-	-	-	-	-	-	1

9, 6, 4, 3, 2 and 1 point awarded to the first six finishers.

Lauda returned after his sudden retirement and promptly organised a drivers strike over licences, at the first race. By now, cars had rigid suspension and were subjected to even higher G forces, the aluminium chassis was a thing of the past. The lighter Cosworth-engined cars got round the weight limit by topping up water tanks, apparently needed for water cooled brakes. Ferrari had a distraught year with appalling accidents to both Villeneuve and Pironi.

BRABHAM
Parmalat Racing Team: Piquet, Patrese

TYRRELL
Team Tyrrell: Alboreto, Borgudd, Henton

WILLIAMS
TAG Williams Team: Reutemann, Andretti, Daly, Rosberg

McLAREN
Marlboro McLaren International: Watson, Lauda

ATS
Team ATS: Winkelhock, Salazar

LOTUS
John Player Team Lotus: de Angelis, Mansell, (Moreno), Lees

ENSIGN
Ensign Racing: Guerrero

RENAULT
Equipe Renault Elf: Prost, Arnoux

MARCH
Rothmans March Grand Prix Team: Mass, Keegan, Boesel
LBT Team March: (de Villota)

FITTIPALDI
Fittipaldi Automotive: Serra

ALFA ROMEO
Marlboro Team Alfa Romeo: de Cesaris, Giacomelli

LIGIER
Equipe Talbot Gitanes: Cheever, Laffite

FERRARI
Scuderia Ferrari SpA SEFAC: Villeneuve, Tambay Pironi, Andretti

ARROWS
Arrows Racing Team: Henton, Surer, Baldi

OSELLA
Osella Squadra Corse: Jarier, Paletti

THEODORE
Theodore Racing Team: Daly, Lammers, Lees, Byrne

TOLEMAN
Candy Toleman Motorsport: Warwick, Fabi
Toleman Group Motorsport from RSM GP

23 Jan 1982 — SOUTH AFRICA: Kyalami (Round: 1) (Race: 358)

77 laps x 4.104 km, 2.550 miles = 316.008 km, 196.358 miles

POS.	NO.	DRIVER	CAR	MODEL	ENGINE		LAPS	TIME/REASON FOR RETIREMENT	GRID:POS	ROW
1	15	A Prost	Renault	RE30B	Renault	V6t	77	1h 32m 08.401s	5	3
2	5	C Reutemann	Williams	FW07C	Cosworth	V8	77	1h 32m 23.347s	8	4
3	16	R Arnoux	Renault	RE30B	Renault	V6t	77	1h 32m 36.301s	1	1
4	8	N Lauda	McLaren	MP4	Cosworth	V8	77	1h 32m 40.514s	13	7
5	6	K Rosberg	Williams	FW07C	Cosworth	V8	77	1h 32m 54.540s	7	4
6	7	J Watson	McLaren	MP4B	Cosworth	V8	77	1h 32m 59.394s	9	5
7	3	M Alboreto	Tyrrell	011	Cosworth	V8	76		10	5
8	11	E de Angelis	Lotus	87B	Cosworth	V8	76		15	8
9	10	E Salazar	ATS	D5	Cosworth	V8	75		12	6
10	9	M Winkelhock	ATS	D5	Cosworth	V8	75		20	10
11	23	B Giacomelli	Alfa Romeo	179D	Alfa Romeo	V12	74		19	10
12	17	J Mass	March	821	Cosworth	V8	74		22	11
13	22	A de Cesaris	Alfa Romeo	179D	Alfa Romeo	V12	73		16	8
14	33	D Daly	Theodore	TY01	Cosworth	V8	73		24	12
15	18	R Boesel	March	821	Cosworth	V8	72		21	11
16	4	S Borgudd	Tyrrell	011	Cosworth	V8	72		23	12
17	20	C Serra	Fittipaldi	F8D	Cosworth	V8	72		25	13
18	28	D Pironi	Ferrari	126C2	Ferrari	V6t	71		6	3
r	26	J Laffite	Talbot Ligier	JS17	Matra	V12	54	fuel vaporisation	11	6
r	35	D Warwick	Toleman	TG181C	Hart	4t	43	accident	14	7
r	2	R Patrese	Brabham	BT50	BMW	4t	18	turbo bearing	4	2
r	25	E Cheever	Talbot Ligier	JS17	Matra	V12	11	fuel vaporisation	17	9
r	27	G Villeneuve	Ferrari	126C2	Ferrari	V6t	6	turbo	3	2
r	1	N Piquet	Brabham	BT50	BMW	4t	3	accident	2	1
r	12	N Mansell	Lotus	87B	Cosworth	V8	0	electrics	18	9
r	31	J-P Jarier	Osella	FA1C	Cosworth	V8	0	accident	26	13
nq	30	M Baldi	Arrows	A4	Cosworth	V8				
nq	32	R Paletti	Osella	FA1C	Cosworth	V8				
nq	29	B Henton	Arrows	A4	Cosworth	V8				
nq	36	T Fabi	Toleman	TG181B	Hart	4t				

Winning speed: 205.779 km/h, 127.865 mph
Pole Position speed: 222.670 km/h, 138.361 mph (R Arnoux, 1 min: 6.351 sec)
Fastest Lap speed: 216.386 km/h, 134.456 mph (A Prost, 1 min: 8.278 sec on lap 49)
Lap Leaders: R Arnoux 1-13,41-67 (40); A Prost 14-40,68-77 (37).

21 Mar 1982 — BRAZIL: Rio de Janeiro (Round: 2) (Race: 359)

63 laps x 5.031 km, 3.126 miles = 316.953 km, 196.945 miles

POS.	NO.	DRIVER	CAR	MODEL	ENGINE		LAPS	TIME/REASON FOR RETIREMENT	GRID:POS	ROW
dq	1	N Piquet	Brabham	BT49D	Cosworth	V8	63	car under weight	7	4
dq	6	K Rosberg	Williams	FW07C	Cosworth	V8	63	car under weight	3	2
1	15	A Prost	Renault	RE30B	Renault	V6t	63	1h 44m 33.134s	1	1
2	7	J Watson	McLaren	MP4B	Cosworth	V8	63	1h 44m 36.124s	12	6
3	12	N Mansell	Lotus	91	Cosworth	V8	63	1h 45m 09.993s	14	7
4	3	M Alboreto	Tyrrell	011	Cosworth	V8	63	1h 45m 23.895s	13	7
5	9	M Winkelhock	ATS	D5	Cosworth	V8	62		15	8
6	28	D Pironi	Ferrari	126C2	Ferrari	V6t	62		8	4
7	4	S Borgudd	Tyrrell	011	Cosworth	V8	61		21	11
8	17	J Mass	March	821	Cosworth	V8	61		22	11
9	31	J-P Jarier	Osella	FA1C	Cosworth	V8	60		23	12
10	30	M Baldi	Arrows	A4	Cosworth	V8	57		19	10
r	10	E Salazar	ATS	D5	Cosworth	V8	38	engine	18	9
r	20	C Serra	Fittipaldi	F8D	Cosworth	V8	36	accident	25	13

POS.	NO.	DRIVER	CAR	MODEL	ENGINE		LAPS	TIME/REASON FOR RETIREMENT	GRID:POS	ROW
r	2	R Patrese	Brabham	BT49D	Cosworth	V8	34	driver exhausted	9	5
r	27	G Villeneuve	Ferrari	126C2	Ferrari	V6t	29	accident	2	1
r	8	N Lauda	McLaren	MP4B	Cosworth	V8	22	accident	5	3
r	16	R Arnoux	Renault	RE30B	Renault	V6t	21	accident	4	2
r	5	C Reutemann	Williams	FW07C	Cosworth	V8	21	accident	6	3
r	11	E de Angelis	Lotus	91	Cosworth	V8	21	accident	11	6
r	25	E Cheever	Talbot Ligier	JS17	Matra	V12	19	water leak	26	13
r	23	B Giacomelli	Alfa Romeo	182	Alfa Romeo	V12	16	engine	16	8
r	26	J Laffite	Talbot Ligier	JS17	Matra	V12	15	misfire/ handling	24	12
r	22	A de Cesaris	Alfa Romeo	182	Alfa Romeo	V12	14	undertray	10	5
r	33	D Daly	Theodore	TY02	Cosworth	V8	12	puncture/ spin	20	10
r	18	R Boesel	March	821	Cosworth	V8	11	puncture/ spin	17	9
nq	36	T Fabi	Toleman	TG181B	Hart	4t				
nq	14	R Guerrero	Ensign	N181	Cosworth	V8				
nq	29	B Henton	Arrows	A4	Cosworth	V8				
nq	35	D Warwick	Toleman	TG181C	Hart	4t				
npq	32	R Paletti	Osella	FA1C	Cosworth	V8				

Winning speed: 181.892 km/h, 113.022 mph
Pole Position speed: 203.941 km/h, 126.723 mph (A Prost, 1 min:28.808 sec)
Fastest Lap speed: 186.687 km/h, 116.002 mph (A Prost, 1 min:37.016 sec on lap 36)
Lap Leaders: G Villeneuve 1-29 (29); N Piquet 30-63 (34).

N Piquet finished 1st in 1m 43m 53.760s (183.041 km/h, 113.736 mph), and recorded the fastest lap in 1m 36.582s (187.526 km/h, 116.523 mph). K Rosberg finished 2nd in 1h 44m 05.737s.

4 Apr 1982 — USA West: Long Beach — (Round: 3) (Race: 360)

75.5 laps x 3.428 km, 2.130 miles = 258.807 km, 160.815 miles

POS.	NO.	DRIVER	CAR	MODEL	ENGINE		LAPS	TIME/REASON FOR RETIREMENT	GRID:POS	ROW
1	8	N Lauda	McLaren	MP4B	Cosworth	V8	75	1h 58m 25.318s	2	1
2	6	K Rosberg	Williams	FW07C	Cosworth	V8	75	1h 58m 39.978s	8	4
dq	27	G Villeneuve	Ferrari	126C2	Ferrari	V6t	75	irregular wing	7	4
3	2	R Patrese	Brabham	BT49C	Cosworth	V8	75	1h 59m 44.461s	18	9
4	3	M Alboreto	Tyrrell	011	Cosworth	V8	75	1h 59m 46.265s	12	6
5	11	E de Angelis	Lotus	91	Cosworth	V8	74		16	8
6	7	J Watson	McLaren	MP4B	Cosworth	V8	74		11	6
7	12	N Mansell	Lotus	91	Cosworth	V8	73		17	9
8	17	J Mass	March	821	Cosworth	V8	73		21	11
9	18	R Boesel	March	821	Cosworth	V8	70		23	12
10	4	S Borgudd	Tyrrell	011	Cosworth	V8	68		24	12
r	25	E Cheever	Talbot Ligier	JS17B	Matra	V12	59	gearbox	13	7
r	22	A de Cesaris	Alfa Romeo	182	Alfa Romeo	V12	33	accident	1	1
r	29	B Henton	Arrows	A4	Cosworth	V8	32	accident	20	10
r	14	R Guerrero	Ensign	N181	Cosworth	V8	27	accident	19	10
r	26	J Laffite	Talbot Ligier	JS17B	Matra	V12	26	spin	15	8
r	31	J-P Jarier	Osella	FA1C	Cosworth	V8	26	gearbox	10	5
r	1	N Piquet	Brabham	BT49D	Cosworth	V8	25	accident	6	3
r	33	D Daly	Theodore	TY02	Cosworth	V8	23	accident	22	11
r	5	M Andretti	Williams	FW07C	Cosworth	V8	19	accident/ rear suspension	14	7
r	15	A Prost	Renault	RE30B	Renault	V6t	10	brakes/ accident	4	2
r	28	D Pironi	Ferrari	126C2	Ferrari	V6t	6	accident	9	5
r	16	R Arnoux	Renault	RE30B	Renault	V6t	5	accident	3	2
r	23	B Giacomelli	Alfa Romeo	182	Alfa Romeo	V12	5	accident	5	3
r	10	E Salazar	ATS	D5	Cosworth	V8	3	accident	26	13
r	9	M Winkelhock	ATS	D5	Cosworth	V8	1	accident	25	13
nq	36	T Fabi	Toleman	TG181C	Hart	4t				
nq	32	R Paletti	Osella	FA1C	Cosworth	V8				
nq	20	C Serra	Fittipaldi	F8D	Cosworth	V8				
nq	30	M Baldi	Arrows	A4	Cosworth	V8				
npq	35	D Warwick	Toleman	TG181C	Hart	4t				

Winning speed: 131.128 km/h, 81.479 mph
Pole Position speed: 141.331 km/h, 87.819 mph (A de Cesaris, 1 min:27.316 sec)
Fastest Lap speed: 135.862 km/h, 84.421 mph (N Lauda, 1 min:30.831 sec on lap 12)
Lap Leaders: A de Cesaris 1-14 (14.5); N Lauda 15-75 (61).

The start and finish lines were at different positions on the circuit.
The fraction of a lap is credited to the first lap leader. G Villeneuve finished 3rd in 1h 59m 29.606s.

25 Apr 1982 — SAN MARINO: Imola — (Round: 4) (Race: 361)

60 laps x 5.040 km, 3.132 miles = 302.400 km, 187.903 miles

POS.	NO.	DRIVER	CAR	MODEL	ENGINE		LAPS	TIME/REASON FOR RETIREMENT	GRID:POS	ROW
1	28	D Pironi	Ferrari	126C2	Ferrari	V6t	60	1h 36m 38.887s	4	2
2	27	G Villeneuve	Ferrari	126C2	Ferrari	V6t	60	1h 36m 39.253s	3	2
3	3	M Alboreto	Tyrrell	011	Cosworth	V8	60	1h 37m 46.571s	5	3
4	31	J-P Jarier	Osella	FA1C	Cosworth	V8	59		9	5
5	10	E Salazar	ATS	D5	Cosworth	V8	57		14	7
dq	9	M Winkelhock	ATS	D5	Cosworth	V8	54	car under weight	12	6
nc	36	T Fabi	Toleman	TG181C	Hart	4t	52		10	5
r	16	R Arnoux	Renault	RE30B	Renault	V6t	44	engine	1	1
r	23	B Giacomelli	Alfa Romeo	182	Alfa Romeo	V12	24	engine	6	3
r	32	R Paletti	Osella	FA1C	Cosworth	V8	7	suspension	13	7
r	15	A Prost	Renault	RE30B	Renault	V6t	6	engine	2	1
r	22	A de Cesaris	Alfa Romeo	182	Alfa Romeo	V12	4	fuel pump	7	4

POS.	NO.	DRIVER	CAR	MODEL	ENGINE		LAPS	TIME/REASON FOR RETIREMENT	GRID:POS	ROW
r	4	B Henton	Tyrrell	011	Cosworth	V8	0	clutch	11	6
r	35	D Warwick	Toleman	TG181C	Hart	4t	-1	electrics	8	4

Winning speed: 187.733 km/h, 116.652 mph
Pole Position speed: 202.128 km/h, 125.596 mph (R Arnoux, 1 min:29.765 sec)
Fastest Lap speed: 190.917 km/h, 118.630 mph (D Pironi, 1 min:35.036 sec on lap 44)
Lap Leaders: R Arnoux 1-26,31-43 (39); G Villeneuve 27-30,44-45,49-52,59 (11); D Pironi 46-48,53-58,60 (10).

9 May 1982 — BELGIUM: Zolder (Round: 5) (Race: 362)

70 laps x 4.262 km, 2.648 miles = 298.340 km, 185.380 miles

POS.	NO.	DRIVER	CAR	MODEL	ENGINE		LAPS	TIME/REASON FOR RETIREMENT	GRID:POS	ROW
1	7	J Watson	McLaren	MP4B	Cosworth	V8	70	1h 35m 41.995s	10	5
2	6	K Rosberg	Williams	FW08	Cosworth	V8	70	1h 35m 49.263s	3	2
dq	8	N Lauda	McLaren	MP4B	Cosworth	V8	70	car under weight	4	2
3	25	E Cheever	Talbot Ligier	JS17B	Matra	V12	69		14	7
4	11	E de Angelis	Lotus	91	Cosworth	V8	68		11	6
5	1	N Piquet	Brabham	BT50	BMW	4t	67		8	4
6	20	C Serra	Fittipaldi	F8D	Cosworth	V8	67		23	12
7	29	M Surer	Arrows	A4	Cosworth	V8	66		22	11
8	18	R Boesel	March	821	Cosworth	V8	66		24	12
9	26	J Laffite	Talbot Ligier	JS17B	Matra	V12	66		17	9
r	5	D Daly	Williams	FW08	Cosworth	V8	60	accident	13	7
r	17	J Mass	March	821	Cosworth	V8	60	engine	25	13
r	15	A Prost	Renault	RE30B	Renault	V6t	59	spin	1	1
r	2	R Patrese	Brabham	BT50	BMW	4t	52	accident	9	5
r	30	M Baldi	Arrows	A4	Cosworth	V8	51	throttle/ spin	26	13
r	31	J-P Jarier	Osella	FA1C	Cosworth	V8	37	rear aerofoil	16	8
r	22	A de Cesaris	Alfa Romeo	182	Alfa Romeo	V12	34	gear linkage	6	3
r	4	B Henton	Tyrrell	011	Cosworth	V8	33	engine	20	10
r	3	M Alboreto	Tyrrell	011	Cosworth	V8	29	engine	5	3
r	35	D Warwick	Toleman	TG181C	Hart	4t	29	drive shaft	19	10
r	36	T Fabi	Toleman	TG181C	Hart	4t	13	brakes	21	11
r	12	N Mansell	Lotus	91	Cosworth	V8	9	clutch	7	4
r	16	R Arnoux	Renault	RE30B	Renault	V6t	7	turbo compressor	2	1
r	9	M Winkelhock	ATS	D5	Cosworth	V8	0	clutch	12	6
r	10	E Salazar	ATS	D5	Cosworth	V8	0	accident	18	9
r	23	B Giacomelli	Alfa Romeo	182	Alfa Romeo	V12	0	accident	15	8
ns	28	D Pironi	Ferrari	126C2	Ferrari	V6t		withdrew after Villeneuve accid.		
ns	27	G Villeneuve	Ferrari	126C2	Ferrari	V6t		fatal accident		
nq	14	R Guerrero	Ensign	N181	Cosworth	V8				
nq	33	J Lammers	Theodore	TY02	Cosworth	V8				
npq	32	R Paletti	Osella	FA1C	Cosworth	V8				
npq	19	E de Villota	March	821	Cosworth	V8				

Winning speed: 187.047 km/h, 116.226 mph
Pole Position speed: 202.682 km/h, 125.941 mph (A Prost, 1 min:15.701 sec)
Fastest Lap speed: 191.278 km/h, 118.855 mph (J Watson, 1 min:20.214 sec on lap 67)
Lap Leaders: R Arnoux 1-4 (4); K Rosberg 5-68 (64); J Watson 69-70 (2).

N Lauda finished 3rd in 1h 36m 50.132s.

23 May 1982 — MONACO: Monte Carlo (Round: 6) (Race: 363)

76 laps x 3.312 km, 2.058 miles = 251.712 km, 156.407 miles

POS.	NO.	DRIVER	CAR	MODEL	ENGINE		LAPS	TIME/REASON FOR RETIREMENT	GRID:POS	ROW
1	2	R Patrese	Brabham	BT49D	Cosworth	V8	76	1h 54m 11.259s	2	1
2r	28	D Pironi	Ferrari	126C2	Ferrari	V6t	75	electrics	5	3
3r	22	A de Cesaris	Alfa Romeo	182	Alfa Romeo	V12	75	out of fuel	7	4
4	12	N Mansell	Lotus	91	Cosworth	V8	75		11	6
5	11	E de Angelis	Lotus	91	Cosworth	V8	75		15	8
6r	5	D Daly	Williams	FW08	Cosworth	V8	74	accident/ gearbox	8	4
7r	15	A Prost	Renault	RE30B	Renault	V6t	73	accident	4	2
8	4	B Henton	Tyrrell	011	Cosworth	V8	72		17	9
9	29	M Surer	Arrows	A4	Cosworth	V8	70		19	10
10r	3	M Alboreto	Tyrrell	011	Cosworth	V8	69	front suspension	9	5
r	6	K Rosberg	Williams	FW08	Cosworth	V8	64	front suspension	6	3
r	8	N Lauda	McLaren	MP4B	Cosworth	V8	56	engine	12	6
r	1	N Piquet	Brabham	BT50	BMW	4t	49	gearbox	13	7
r	7	J Watson	McLaren	MP4B	Cosworth	V8	35	oil leak/ battery	10	5
r	9	M Winkelhock	ATS	D5	Cosworth	V8	31	differential	14	7
r	26	J Laffite	Talbot Ligier	JS19	Matra	V12	29	handling	18	9
r	25	E Cheever	Talbot Ligier	JS19	Matra	V12	27	engine	16	8
r	10	E Salazar	ATS	D5	Cosworth	V8	22	fire extinguisher	20	10
r	16	R Arnoux	Renault	RE30B	Renault	V6t	14	spin	1	1
r	23	B Giacomelli	Alfa Romeo	182	Alfa Romeo	V12	4	transmission	3	2
nq	30	M Baldi	Arrows	A4	Cosworth	V8				
nq	33	J Lammers	Theodore	TY02	Cosworth	V8				
nq	17	J Mass	March	821	Cosworth	V8				
nq	35	D Warwick	Toleman	TG181C	Hart	4t				
nq	31	J-P Jarier	Osella	FA1C	Cosworth	V8				
nq	14	R Guerrero	Ensign	N181	Cosworth	V8				
npq	36	T Fabi	Toleman	TG181C	Hart	4t				
npq	32	R Paletti	Osella	FA1C	Cosworth	V8				
npq	18	R Boesel	March	821	Cosworth	V8				

POS.	NO.	DRIVER	CAR	MODEL	ENGINE		LAPS	TIME/REASON FOR RETIREMENT	GRID:POS	ROW
npq	20	C Serra	Fittipaldi	F8D	Cosworth	V8				
npq	19	E de Villota	March	821	Cosworth	V8				

Winning speed: 132.262 km/h, 82.184 mph
Pole Position speed: 143.168 km/h, 88.961 mph (R Arnoux, 1 min:23.281 sec)
Fastest Lap speed: 138.074 km/h, 85.795 mph (R Patrese, 1 min:26.354 sec on lap 69)
Lap Leaders: R Arnoux 1-14 (14); A Prost 15-73 (59); R Patrese 74,76 (2); D Pironi 75 (1).

6 Jun 1982 — USA: Detroit — (Round: 7) (Race: 364)

62 laps x 4.012 km, 2.493 miles = 248.750 km, 154.566 miles

POS.	NO.	DRIVER	CAR	MODEL	ENGINE		LAPS	TIME/REASON FOR RETIREMENT	GRID:POS	ROW
1	7	J Watson	McLaren	MP4B	Cosworth	V8	62	1h 58m 41.043s	17	9
2	25	E Cheever	Talbot Ligier	JS17B	Matra	V12	62	1h 58m 56.769s	9	5
3	28	D Pironi	Ferrari	126C2	Ferrari	V6t	62	1h 59m 09.120s	4	2
4	6	K Rosberg	Williams	FW08	Cosworth	V8	62	1h 59m 53.019s	3	2
5	5	D Daly	Williams	FW08	Cosworth	V8	62	2h 00m 04.800s	12	6
6	26	J Laffite	Talbot Ligier	JS17B	Matra	V12	61		13	7
7	17	J Mass	March	821	Cosworth	V8	61		18	9
8	29	M Surer	Arrows	A4	Cosworth	V8	61		19	10
9	4	B Henton	Tyrrell	011	Cosworth	V8	60		20	10
10	16	R Arnoux	Renault	RE30B	Renault	V6t	59		15	8
11	20	C Serra	Fittipaldi	F8D	Cosworth	V8	59		26	13
nc	15	A Prost	Renault	RE30B	Renault	V6t	54		1	1
r	12	N Mansell	Lotus	91	Cosworth	V8	44	engine	7	4
r	8	N Lauda	McLaren	MP4B	Cosworth	V8	40	accident	10	5
r	3	M Alboreto	Tyrrell	011	Cosworth	V8	40	accident	16	8
r	23	B Giacomelli	Alfa Romeo	182	Alfa Romeo	V12	30	accident	6	3
r	11	E de Angelis	Lotus	91	Cosworth	V8	17	gearbox	8	4
r	10	E Salazar	ATS	D5	Cosworth	V8	13	accident	25	13
r	14	R Guerrero	Ensign	N181	Cosworth	V8	6	accident	11	6
r	2	R Patrese	Brabham	BT49D	Cosworth	V8	6	accident/ fire	14	7
r	22	A de Cesaris	Alfa Romeo	182	Alfa Romeo	V12	2	transmission	2	1
r	31	J-P Jarier	Osella	FA1C	Cosworth	V8	2	electrics	22	11
r	9	M Winkelhock	ATS	D5	Cosworth	V8	1	accident	5	3
r	18	R Boesel	March	821	Cosworth	V8	0	accident	21	11
r	30	M Baldi	Arrows	A4	Cosworth	V8	0	accident	24	12
ns	32	R Paletti	Osella	FA1C	Cosworth	V8		accident	23	12
nq	19	E de Villota	March	821	Cosworth	V8				
nq	1	N Piquet	Brabham	BT50	BMW	4t				
nq	33	J Lammers	Theodore	TY02	Cosworth	V8		accident/ injury		

Winning speed: 125.754 km/h, 78.140 mph
Pole Position speed: 133.075 km/h, 82.689 mph (A Prost, 1 min:48.537 sec)
Fastest Lap speed: 130.784 km/h, 81.266 mph (A Prost, 1 min:50.438 sec on lap 45)
Lap Leaders: A Prost 1-22 (22); K Rosberg 23-36 (14); J Watson 37-62 (26).

Scheduled for 70 laps but interrupted after 6 laps, because of an accident.
Restart scheduled for a further 64 laps, but stopped at 2 hours, with results being an aggregate of 6 and 56 laps. Lap leaders are given 'on the road'.

13 Jun 1982 — CANADA: Montréal — (Round: 8) (Race: 365)

70 laps x 4.410 km, 2.740 miles = 308.700 km, 191.817 miles

POS.	NO.	DRIVER	CAR	MODEL	ENGINE		LAPS	TIME/REASON FOR RETIREMENT	GRID:POS	ROW
1	1	N Piquet	Brabham	BT50	BMW	4t	70	1h 46m 39.577s	4	2
2	2	R Patrese	Brabham	BT49D	Cosworth	V8	70	1h 46m 53.376s	8	4
3	7	J Watson	McLaren	MP4B	Cosworth	V8	70	1h 47m 41.413s	6	3
4	11	E de Angelis	Lotus	91	Cosworth	V8	69		10	5
5	29	M Surer	Arrows	A4	Cosworth	V8	69		16	8
6r	22	A de Cesaris	Alfa Romeo	182	Alfa Romeo	V12	68	out of fuel	9	5
7r	5	D Daly	Williams	FW08	Cosworth	V8	68	out of fuel	13	7
8	30	M Baldi	Arrows	A4	Cosworth	V8	68		17	9
9	28	D Pironi	Ferrari	126C2	Ferrari	V6t	67		1	1
10r	25	E Cheever	Talbot Ligier	JS17B	Matra	V12	66	out of fuel	12	6
11	17	J Mass	March	821	Cosworth	V8	66		22	11
nc	4	B Henton	Tyrrell	011	Cosworth	V8	59		26	13
r	6	K Rosberg	Williams	FW08	Cosworth	V8	52	gearbox	7	4
r	18	R Boesel	March	821	Cosworth	V8	47	engine	21	11
r	3	M Alboreto	Tyrrell	011	Cosworth	V8	41	gearbox/ fuel pressure	15	8
r	15	A Prost	Renault	RE30B	Renault	V6t	30	engine	3	2
r	16	R Arnoux	Renault	RE30B	Renault	V6t	28	spin	2	1
r	10	E Salazar	ATS	D5	Cosworth	V8	20	transmission	24	12
r	8	N Lauda	McLaren	MP4B	Cosworth	V8	17	clutch	11	6
r	26	J Laffite	Talbot Ligier	JS17B	Matra	V12	8	handling	19	10
r	14	R Guerrero	Ensign	N181	Cosworth	V8	2	clutch	20	10
r	23	B Giacomelli	Alfa Romeo	182	Alfa Romeo	V12	1	accident	5	3
r	12	N Mansell	Lotus	91	Cosworth	V8	1	accident	14	7
r	33	G Lees	Theodore	TY02	Cosworth	V8	0	accident *	25	13
r	31	J-P Jarier	Osella	FA1C	Cosworth	V8	0	withdrew after Paletti accident*	18	9
r	32	R Paletti	Osella	FA1C	Cosworth	V8	0	fatal accident *	23	12
nq	9	M Winkelhock	ATS	D5	Cosworth	V8				
nq	19	E de Villota	March	821	Cosworth	V8				
nq	20	C Serra	Fittipaldi	F8D	Cosworth	V8				

Winning speed: 173.655 km/h, 107.904 mph
Pole Position speed: 181.421 km/h, 112.730 mph (D Pironi, 1 min:27.509 sec)
Fastest Lap speed: 179.749 km/h, 111.691 mph (D Pironi, 1 min:28.323 sec on lap 66)
Lap Leaders: D Pironi 1 (1); R Arnoux 2-8 (7); N Piquet 9-70 (62).

Interrupted after 1st lap accident. Restarted for original distance.   ** retired after first start.*

3 Jul 1982 NETHERLANDS: Zandvoort (Round: 9) (Race: 366)

72 laps x 4.252 km, 2.642 miles = 306.144 km, 190.229 miles

POS.	NO.	DRIVER	CAR	MODEL	ENGINE		LAPS	TIME/REASON FOR RETIREMENT	GRID:POS	ROW
1	28	D Pironi	Ferrari	126C2	Ferrari	V6t	72	1h 38m 03.254s	4	2
2	1	N Piquet	Brabham	BT50	BMW	4t	72	1h 38m 24.903s	3	2
3	6	K Rosberg	Williams	FW08	Cosworth	V8	72	1h 38m 25.619s	7	4
4	8	N Lauda	McLaren	MP4B	Cosworth	V8	72	1h 39m 26.974s	5	3
5	5	D Daly	Williams	FW08	Cosworth	V8	71		12	6
6	30	M Baldi	Arrows	A4	Cosworth	V8	71		16	8
7	3	M Alboreto	Tyrrell	011	Cosworth	V8	71		14	7
8	27	P Tambay	Ferrari	126C2	Ferrari	V6t	71		6	3
9	7	J Watson	McLaren	MP4B	Cosworth	V8	71		11	6
10	29	M Surer	Arrows	A4	Cosworth	V8	71		17	9
11	23	B Giacomelli	Alfa Romeo	182	Alfa Romeo	V12	70		8	4
12	9	M Winkelhock	ATS	D5	Cosworth	V8	70		18	9
13	10	E Salazar	ATS	D5	Cosworth	V8	70		25	13
14	31	J-P Jarier	Osella	FA1C	Cosworth	V8	69		23	12
15	2	R Patrese	Brabham	BT50	BMW	4t	69		10	5
r	17	J Mass	March	821	Cosworth	V8	60	engine	24	12
r	33	J Lammers	Theodore	TY02	Cosworth	V8	41	engine	26	13
r	11	E de Angelis	Lotus	91	Cosworth	V8	40	handling	15	8
r	22	A de Cesaris	Alfa Romeo	182	Alfa Romeo	V12	35	electrics	9	5
r	15	A Prost	Renault	RE30B	Renault	V6t	33	engine	2	1
r	16	R Arnoux	Renault	RE30B	Renault	V6t	21	suspension/ accident	1	1
r	4	B Henton	Tyrrell	011	Cosworth	V8	21	throttle linkage	20	10
r	18	R Boesel	March	821	Cosworth	V8	21	engine	22	11
r	20	C Serra	Fittipaldi	F8D	Cosworth	V8	18	fuel pump	19	10
r	35	D Warwick	Toleman	TG181C	Hart	4t	15	oil union leak	13	7
r	26	J Laffite	Talbot Ligier	JS19	Matra	V12	4	handling	21	11
nq	14	R Guerrero	Ensign	N181	Cosworth	V8				
nq	36	T Fabi	Toleman	TG181C	Hart	4t				
nq	25	E Cheever	Talbot Ligier	JS19	Matra	V12				
nq	12	R Moreno	Lotus	91	Cosworth	V8				
npq	19	E de Villota	March	821	Cosworth	V8				

Winning speed: 187.331 km/h, 116.402 mph
Pole Position speed: 206.205 km/h, 128.130 mph (R Arnoux, 1 min:14.233 sec)
Fastest Lap speed: 191.868 km/h, 119.221 mph (D Warwick, 1 min:19.780 sec on lap 13)
Lap Leaders: A Prost 1-4 (4); D Pironi 5-72 (68).

18 Jul 1982 BRITAIN: Brands Hatch (Round:10) (Race: 367)

76 laps x 4.207 km, 2.614 miles = 319.719 km, 198.664 miles

POS.	NO.	DRIVER	CAR	MODEL	ENGINE		LAPS	TIME/REASON FOR RETIREMENT	GRID:POS	ROW
1	8	N Lauda	McLaren	MP4B	Cosworth	V8	76	1h 35m 33.812s	5	3
2	28	D Pironi	Ferrari	126C2	Ferrari	V6t	76	1h 35m 59.538s	4	2
3	27	P Tambay	Ferrari	126C2	Ferrari	V6t	76	1h 36m 12.248s	13	7
4	11	E de Angelis	Lotus	91	Cosworth	V8	76	1h 36m 15.054s	7	4
5	5	D Daly	Williams	FW08	Cosworth	V8	76	1h 36m 15.242s	10	5
6	15	A Prost	Renault	RE30B	Renault	V6t	76	1h 36m 15.448s	8	4
7	23	B Giacomelli	Alfa Romeo	182	Alfa Romeo	V12	75		14	7
8	4	B Henton	Tyrrell	011	Cosworth	V8	75		17	9
9	30	M Baldi	Arrows	A4	Cosworth	V8	74		26	13
10	17	J Mass	March	821	Cosworth	V8	73		25	13
r	22	A de Cesaris	Alfa Romeo	182	Alfa Romeo	V12	66	electrics	11	6
r	25	E Cheever	Talbot Ligier	JS19	Matra	V12	60	engine	24	12
r	29	M Surer	Arrows	A4	Cosworth	V8	59	engine	22	11
r	6	K Rosberg	Williams	FW08	Cosworth	V8	50	fuel pressure	1	1
nc	3	M Alboreto	Tyrrell	011	Cosworth	V8	44		9	5
r	26	J Laffite	Talbot Ligier	JS19	Matra	V12	41	gearbox	20	10
r	35	D Warwick	Toleman	TG181C	Hart	4t	40	cv joint	16	8
r	12	N Mansell	Lotus	91	Cosworth	V8	29	broken skirt/ driver discomfort	23	12
r	1	N Piquet	Brabham	BT50	BMW	4t	9	fuel injection pump belt	3	2
r	14	R Guerrero	Ensign	N181	Cosworth	V8	3	accident/ oil pipe/ engine	19	10
r	31	J-P Jarier	Osella	FA1C	Cosworth	V8	2	accident	18	9
r	20	C Serra	Fittipaldi	F8D	Cosworth	V8	2	accident/ fire	21	11
r	7	J Watson	McLaren	MP4B	Cosworth	V8	2	spin	12	6
r	36	T Fabi	Toleman	TG181C	Hart	4t	0	accident	15	8
r	16	R Arnoux	Renault	RE30B	Renault	V6t	0	accident	6	3
r	2	R Patrese	Brabham	BT50	BMW	4t	0	stalled on grid/ accident	2	1
nq	9	M Winkelhock	ATS	D5	Cosworth	V8				
nq	33	J Lammers	Theodore	TY02	Cosworth	V8				
nq	10	E Salazar	ATS	D5	Cosworth	V8				
nq	18	R Boesel	March	821	Cosworth	V8				

Winning speed: 200.737 km/h, 124.732 mph
Pole Position speed: 217.782 km/h, 135.324 mph (K Rosberg, 1 min: 9.540 sec)
Fastest Lap speed: 207.380 km/h, 128.860 mph (B Henton, 1 min:13.028 sec on lap 63)
Lap Leaders: N Piquet 1-9 (9); N Lauda 10-76 (67).

25 Jul 1982 FRANCE: Paul Ricard (Round:11) (Race: 368)

54 laps x 5.810 km, 3.610 miles = 313.740 km, 194.949 miles

POS.	NO.	DRIVER	CAR	MODEL	ENGINE		LAPS	TIME/REASON FOR RETIREMENT	GRID:POS	ROW
1	16	R Arnoux	Renault	RE30B	Renault	V6t	54	1h 33m 33.217s	1	1
2	15	A Prost	Renault	RE30B	Renault	V6t	54	1h 33m 50.525s	2	1
3	28	D Pironi	Ferrari	126C2	Ferrari	V6t	54	1h 34m 15.345s	3	2
4	27	P Tambay	Ferrari	126C2	Ferrari	V6t	54	1h 34m 49.458s	5	3
5	6	K Rosberg	Williams	FW08	Cosworth	V8	54	1h 35m 04.211s	10	5
6	3	M Alboreto	Tyrrell	011	Cosworth	V8	54	1h 35m 05.556s	15	8
7	5	D Daly	Williams	FW08	Cosworth	V8	53		11	6
8	8	N Lauda	McLaren	MP4B	Cosworth	V8	53		9	5
9	23	B Giacomelli	Alfa Romeo	182	Alfa Romeo	V12	53		8	4
10	4	B Henton	Tyrrell	011	Cosworth	V8	53		23	12
11	9	M Winkelhock	ATS	D5	Cosworth	V8	52		18	9
12	12	G Lees	Lotus	91	Cosworth	V8	52		24	12
13	29	M Surer	Arrows	A4	Cosworth	V8	52		20	10
14	26	J Laffite	Talbot Ligier	JS19	Matra	V12	51		16	8
15	35	D Warwick	Toleman	TG181C	Hart	4t	50		14	7
16	25	E Cheever	Talbot Ligier	JS19	Matra	V12	49		19	10
r	22	A de Cesaris	Alfa Romeo	182	Alfa Romeo	V12	25	puncture/ accident	7	4
r	1	N Piquet	Brabham	BT50	BMW	4t	23	engine	6	3
r	11	E de Angelis	Lotus	91	Cosworth	V8	17	fuel pressure	13	7
r	7	J Watson	McLaren	MP4B	Cosworth	V8	13	battery lead	12	6
r	17	J Mass	March	821	Cosworth	V8	10	accident	26	13
r	30	M Baldi	Arrows	A4	Cosworth	V8	10	accident	25	13
r	2	R Patrese	Brabham	BT50	BMW	4t	8	engine/ fire	4	2
r	10	E Salazar	ATS	D5	Cosworth	V8	2	accident	22	11
r	36	T Fabi	Toleman	TG181C	Hart	4t	0	oil pump drive	21	11
r	31	J-P Jarier	Osella	FA1C	Cosworth	V8	0	drive shaft	17	9
nq	33	J Lammers	Theodore	TY02	Cosworth	V8				
nq	14	R Guerrero	Ensign	N181	Cosworth	V8				
nq	20	C Serra	Fittipaldi	F9	Cosworth	V8				
nq	18	R Boesel	March	821	Cosworth	V8				

Winning speed: 201.215 km/h, 125.029 mph
Pole Position speed: 221.554 km/h, 137.667 mph (R Arnoux, 1 min:34.406 sec)
Fastest Lap speed: 209.003 km/h, 129.869 mph (R Patrese, 1 min:40.075 sec on lap 4)
Lap Leaders: R Arnoux 1-2,24-54 (33); R Patrese 3-7 (5); N Piquet 8-23 (16).

8 Aug 1982 GERMANY: Hockenheim (Round:12) (Race: 369)

45 laps x 6.797 km, 4.223 miles = 305.865 km, 190.056 miles

POS.	NO.	DRIVER	CAR	MODEL	ENGINE		LAPS	TIME/REASON FOR RETIREMENT	GRID:POS	ROW
1	27	P Tambay	Ferrari	126C2	Ferrari	V6t	45	1h 27m 25.178s	5	3
2	16	R Arnoux	Renault	RE30B	Renault	V6t	45	1h 27m 41.557s	3	2
3	6	K Rosberg	Williams	FW08	Cosworth	V8	44		9	5
4	3	M Alboreto	Tyrrell	011	Cosworth	V8	44		7	4
5	23	B Giacomelli	Alfa Romeo	182	Alfa Romeo	V12	44		11	6
6	29	M Surer	Arrows	A4	Cosworth	V8	44		26	13
7	4	B Henton	Tyrrell	011	Cosworth	V8	44		17	9
8	14	R Guerrero	Ensign	N181	Cosworth	V8	44		21	11
9	12	N Mansell	Lotus	91	Cosworth	V8	43		18	9
10	35	D Warwick	Toleman	TG181C	Hart	4t	43		14	7
11	20	C Serra	Fittipaldi	F9	Cosworth	V8	43		25	13
r	7	J Watson	McLaren	MP4B	Cosworth	V8	36	front suspension	10	5
r	26	J Laffite	Talbot Ligier	JS19	Matra	V12	36	handling	15	8
r	5	D Daly	Williams	FW08	Cosworth	V8	25	engine	19	10
r	18	R Boesel	March	821	Cosworth	V8	22	puncture	24	12
r	11	E de Angelis	Lotus	91	Cosworth	V8	21	transmission	13	7
r	1	N Piquet	Brabham	BT50	BMW	4t	18	accident	4	2
r	10	E Salazar	ATS	D5	Cosworth	V8	17	accident	22	11
r	15	A Prost	Renault	RE30B	Renault	V6t	14	electrics	2	1
r	2	R Patrese	Brabham	BT50	BMW	4t	13	piston	6	3
r	22	A de Cesaris	Alfa Romeo	182	Alfa Romeo	V12	9	accident	8	4
r	25	E Cheever	Talbot Ligier	JS19	Matra	V12	8	handling	12	6
r	30	M Baldi	Arrows	A4	Cosworth	V8	6	misfire	23	12
r	31	J-P Jarier	Osella	FA1D	Cosworth	V8	3	steering	20	10
r	9	M Winkelhock	ATS	D5	Cosworth	V8	3	clutch/ gearbox	16	8
ns	28	D Pironi	Ferrari	126C2	Ferrari	V6t		accident/ injury	1	1
ns	8	N Lauda	McLaren	MP4B	Cosworth	V8		accident/ injury		
nq	33	T Byrne	Theodore	TY02	Cosworth	V8				
nq	17	R Keegan	March	821	Cosworth	V8				
nq	36	T Fabi	Toleman	TG181C	Hart	4t				

Winning speed: 209.929 km/h, 130.444 mph
Pole Position speed: 226.678 km/h, 140.851 mph (D Pironi, 1 min:47.947 sec)
Fastest Lap speed: 214.576 km/h, 133.331 mph (N Piquet, 1 min:54.035 sec on lap 7)
Lap Leaders: R Arnoux 1 (1); N Piquet 2-18 (17); P Tambay 19-45 (27).

D Pironi qualified for pole position, but did not start, because of an accident in qualifying. Pole position left vacant.

15 Aug 1982 — AUSTRIA: Österreichring (Round:13) (Race: 370)

53 laps x 5.942 km, 3.692 miles = 314.926 km, 195.686 miles

POS.	NO.	DRIVER	CAR	MODEL	ENGINE		LAPS	TIME/REASON FOR RETIREMENT	GRID:POS	ROW
1	11	E de Angelis	Lotus	91	Cosworth	V8	53	1h 25m 02.212s	7	4
2	6	K Rosberg	Williams	FW08	Cosworth	V8	53	1h 25m 02.262s	6	3
3	26	J Laffite	Talbot Ligier	JS19	Matra	V12	52		14	7
4	27	P Tambay	Ferrari	126C2	Ferrari	V6t	52		4	2
5	8	N Lauda	McLaren	MP4B	Cosworth	V8	52		10	5
6	30	M Baldi	Arrows	A4	Cosworth	V8	52		23	12
7	20	C Serra	Fittipaldi	F9	Cosworth	V8	51		20	10
8r	15	A Prost	Renault	RE30B	Renault	V6t	48	fuel injection	3	2
r	7	J Watson	McLaren	MP4B	Cosworth	V8	44	water pipe	18	9
r	4	B Henton	Tyrrell	011	Cosworth	V8	32	valve spring	19	10
r	1	N Piquet	Brabham	BT50	BMW	4t	31	camshaft drive	1	1
r	33	T Byrne	Theodore	TY02	Cosworth	V8	28	spin	26	13
r	29	M Surer	Arrows	A4	Cosworth	V8	28	fuel system	21	11
r	2	R Patrese	Brabham	BT50	BMW	4t	27	engine gudgeon pin/ spin	2	1
r	25	E Cheever	Talbot Ligier	JS19	Matra	V12	22	valve	22	11
r	12	N Mansell	Lotus	91	Cosworth	V8	17	engine	12	6
r	16	R Arnoux	Renault	RE30B	Renault	V6t	16	turbo	5	3
r	9	M Winkelhock	ATS	D5	Cosworth	V8	15	spin	25	13
r	35	D Warwick	Toleman	TG181C	Hart	4t	7	rear suspension	15	8
r	36	T Fabi	Toleman	TG181C	Hart	4t	7	drive shaft	17	9
r	14	R Guerrero	Ensign	N181	Cosworth	V8	6	drive shaft	16	8
r	3	M Alboreto	Tyrrell	011	Cosworth	V8	1	accident	8	4
r	17	R Keegan	March	821	Cosworth	V8	1	accident	24	12
r	22	A de Cesaris	Alfa Romeo	182	Alfa Romeo	V12	0	accident	11	6
r	5	D Daly	Williams	FW08	Cosworth	V8	0	accident	9	5
r	23	B Giacomelli	Alfa Romeo	182	Alfa Romeo	V12	0	accident	13	7
nq	18	R Boesel	March	821	Cosworth	V8				
nq	31	J-P Jarier	Osella	FA1D	Cosworth	V8				
nq	10	E Salazar	ATS	D5	Cosworth	V8				

Winning speed: 222.204 km/h, 138.071 mph
Pole Position speed: 244.158 km/h, 151.713 mph (N Piquet, 1 min:27.612 sec)
Fastest Lap speed: 228.297 km/h, 141.857 mph (N Piquet, 1 min:33.699 sec on lap 5)
Lap Leaders: N Piquet 1 (1); R Patrese 2-27 (26); A Prost 28-48 (21); E de Angelis 49-53 (5).

29 Aug 1982 — SWITZERLAND: Dijon-Prenois (Round:14) (Race: 371)

80 laps x 3.800 km, 2.361 miles = 304.000 km, 188.897 miles

POS.	NO.	DRIVER	CAR	MODEL	ENGINE		LAPS	TIME/REASON FOR RETIREMENT	GRID:POS	ROW
1	6	K Rosberg	Williams	FW08	Cosworth	V8	80	1h 32m 41.087s	8	4
2	15	A Prost	Renault	RE30B	Renault	V6t	80	1h 32m 45.529s	1	1
3	8	N Lauda	McLaren	MP4B	Cosworth	V8	80	1h 33m 41.430s	4	2
4	1	N Piquet	Brabham	BT50	BMW	4t	79		6	3
5	2	R Patrese	Brabham	BT50	BMW	4t	79		3	2
6	11	E de Angelis	Lotus	91	Cosworth	V8	79		15	8
7	3	M Alboreto	Tyrrell	011	Cosworth	V8	79		12	6
8	12	N Mansell	Lotus	91	Cosworth	V8	79		26	13
9	5	D Daly	Williams	FW08	Cosworth	V8	79		7	4
10	22	A de Cesaris	Alfa Romeo	182	Alfa Romeo	V12	78		5	3
11	4	B Henton	Tyrrell	011	Cosworth	V8	78		18	9
12	23	B Giacomelli	Alfa Romeo	182	Alfa Romeo	V12	78		9	5
13	7	J Watson	McLaren	MP4B	Cosworth	V8	77		11	6
14	10	E Salazar	ATS	D5	Cosworth	V8	77		25	13
15	29	M Surer	Arrows	A5	Cosworth	V8	76		14	7
16r	16	R Arnoux	Renault	RE30B	Renault	V6t	75	fuel injection	2	1
nc	25	E Cheever	Talbot Ligier	JS19	Matra	V12	70		16	8
r	9	M Winkelhock	ATS	D5	Cosworth	V8	55	engine mounting	20	10
r	31	J-P Jarier	Osella	FA1D	Cosworth	V8	44	engine	17	9
r	26	J Laffite	Talbot Ligier	JS19	Matra	V12	33	skirts/ handling	13	7
r	36	T Fabi	Toleman	TG181C	Hart	4t	31	engine overheating	23	12
r	18	R Boesel	March	821	Cosworth	V8	31	gearbox oil leak	24	12
r	17	R Keegan	March	821	Cosworth	V8	25	spin	22	11
r	35	D Warwick	Toleman	TG181C	Hart	4t	24	engine	21	11
r	14	R Guerrero	Ensign	N181	Cosworth	V8	4	engine	19	10
ns	27	P Tambay	Ferrari	126C2	Ferrari	V6t		driver unfit (neck injury)	10	5
nq	20	C Serra	Fittipaldi	F9	Cosworth	V8				
nq	33	T Byrne	Theodore	TY02	Cosworth	V8				
nq	30	M Baldi	Arrows	A4	Cosworth	V8				

Winning speed: 196.796 km/h, 122.283 mph
Pole Position speed: 222.874 km/h, 138.487 mph (A Prost, 1 min: 1.380 sec)
Fastest Lap speed: 202.736 km/h, 125.974 mph (A Prost, 1 min: 7.477 sec on lap 2)
Lap Leaders: R Arnoux 1 (1); A Prost 2-78 (77); K Rosberg 79-80 (2).

12 Sep 1982 ITALY: Monza (Round:15) (Race: 372)

52 laps x 5.800 km, 3.604 miles = 301.600 km, 187.406 miles

POS.	NO.	DRIVER	CAR	MODEL	ENGINE		LAPS	TIME/REASON FOR RETIREMENT	GRID:POS	ROW
1	16	R Arnoux	Renault	RE30B	Renault	V6t	52	1h 22m 25.734s	6	3
2	27	P Tambay	Ferrari	126C2	Ferrari	V6t	52	1h 22m 39.798s	3	2
3	28	M Andretti	Ferrari	126C2	Ferrari	V6t	52	1h 23m 14.186s	1	1
4	7	J Watson	McLaren	MP4B	Cosworth	V8	52	1h 23m 53.579s	12	6
5	3	M Alboreto	Tyrrell	011	Cosworth	V8	51		11	6
6	25	E Cheever	Talbot Ligier	JS19	Matra	V12	51		14	7
7	12	N Mansell	Lotus	91	Cosworth	V8	51		23	12
8	6	K Rosberg	Williams	FW08	Cosworth	V8	50		7	4
9	10	E Salazar	ATS	D5	Cosworth	V8	50		25	13
10	22	A de Cesaris	Alfa Romeo	182	Alfa Romeo	V12	50		9	5
11	20	C Serra	Fittipaldi	F9	Cosworth	V8	49		26	13
12	30	M Baldi	Arrows	A5	Cosworth	V8	49		24	12
nc	14	R Guerrero	Ensign	N181	Cosworth	V8	40		18	9
r	11	E de Angelis	Lotus	91	Cosworth	V8	33	throttle jammed	17	9
r	23	B Giacomelli	Alfa Romeo	182	Alfa Romeo	V12	32	side-pod/ handling	8	4
r	29	M Surer	Arrows	A4	Cosworth	V8	28	ignition	19	10
r	15	A Prost	Renault	RE30B	Renault	V6t	27	fuel injection	5	3
r	8	N Lauda	McLaren	MP4B	Cosworth	V8	21	brakes/ handling	10	5
r	31	J-P Jarier	Osella	FA1D	Cosworth	V8	10	rear wheel lost	15	8
r	1	N Piquet	Brabham	BT50	BMW	4t	7	clutch	2	1
r	2	R Patrese	Brabham	BT50	BMW	4t	6	clutch	4	2
r	26	J Laffite	Talbot Ligier	JS19	Matra	V12	5	gearbox	21	11
r	36	T Fabi	Toleman	TG181C	Hart	4t	2	engine	22	11
r	5	D Daly	Williams	FW08	Cosworth	V8	0	accident/ rear suspension	13	7
r	35	D Warwick	Toleman	TG183	Hart	4t	0	accident	16	8
r	4	B Henton	Tyrrell	011	Cosworth	V8	0	accident	20	10
nq	17	R Keegan	March	821	Cosworth	V8				
nq	9	M Winkelhock	ATS	D5	Cosworth	V8				
nq	18	R Boesel	March	821	Cosworth	V8				
nq	33	T Byrne	Theodore	TY02	Cosworth	V8				

Winning speed: 219.535 km/h, 136.413 mph
Pole Position speed: 236.004 km/h, 146.646 mph (M Andretti, 1 min:28.473 sec)
Fastest Lap speed: 223.032 km/h, 138.585 mph (R Arnoux, 1 min:33.619 sec on lap 25)
Lap Leaders: R Arnoux 1-52 (52).

25 Sep 1982 CAESARS PALACE: Las Vegas (Round:16) (Race: 373)

75 laps x 3.650 km, 2.268 miles = 273.749 km, 170.100 miles

POS.	NO.	DRIVER	CAR	MODEL	ENGINE		LAPS	TIME/REASON FOR RETIREMENT	GRID:POS	ROW
1	3	M Alboreto	Tyrrell	011	Cosworth	V8	75	1h 41m 56.888s	3	2
2	7	J Watson	McLaren	MP4B	Cosworth	V8	75	1h 42m 24.180s	9	5
3	25	E Cheever	Talbot Ligier	JS19	Matra	V12	75	1h 42m 53.338s	4	2
4	15	A Prost	Renault	RE30B	Renault	V6t	75	1h 43m 05.536s	1	1
5	6	K Rosberg	Williams	FW08	Cosworth	V8	75	1h 43m 08.263s	6	3
6	5	D Daly	Williams	FW08	Cosworth	V8	74		14	7
7	29	M Surer	Arrows	A5	Cosworth	V8	74		17	9
8	4	B Henton	Tyrrell	011	Cosworth	V8	74		19	10
9	22	A de Cesaris	Alfa Romeo	182	Alfa Romeo	V12	73		18	9
10	23	B Giacomelli	Alfa Romeo	182	Alfa Romeo	V12	73		16	8
11	30	M Baldi	Arrows	A4	Cosworth	V8	73		23	12
12	17	R Keegan	March	821	Cosworth	V8	73		25	13
13	18	R Boesel	March	821	Cosworth	V8	69		24	12
nc	9	M Winkelhock	ATS	D5	Cosworth	V8	62		22	11
r	8	N Lauda	McLaren	MP4B	Cosworth	V8	53	engine	13	7
r	33	T Byrne	Theodore	TY02	Cosworth	V8	39	spin	26	13
r	35	D Warwick	Toleman	TG183	Hart	4t	32	spark plugs	10	5
r	11	E de Angelis	Lotus	91	Cosworth	V8	28	engine	20	10
r	28	M Andretti	Ferrari	126C2	Ferrari	V6t	26	rear suspension	7	4
r	1	N Piquet	Brabham	BT50	BMW	4t	26	spark plug	12	6
r	16	R Arnoux	Renault	RE30B	Renault	V6t	20	engine	2	1
r	2	R Patrese	Brabham	BT50	BMW	4t	17	clutch	5	3
r	12	N Mansell	Lotus	91	Cosworth	V8	8	accident	21	11
r	26	J Laffite	Talbot Ligier	JS19	Matra	V12	5	ignition	11	6
ns	27	P Tambay	Ferrari	126C2	Ferrari	V6t		driver unfit	8	4
ns	14	R Guerrero	Ensign	N181	Cosworth	V8		engine	15	8
ns	31	J-P Jarier	Osella	FA1D	Cosworth	V8		accident		
nq	36	T Fabi	Toleman	TG181C	Hart	4t				
nq	10	E Salazar	ATS	D5	Cosworth	V8				
nq	20	C Serra	Fittipaldi	F9	Cosworth	V8				

Winning speed: 161.111 km/h, 100.110 mph
Pole Position speed: 172.088 km/h, 106.931 mph (A Prost, 1 min:16.356 sec)
Fastest Lap speed: 164.994 km/h, 102.523 mph (M Alboreto, 1 min:19.639 sec on lap 59)
Lap Leaders: A Prost 1,15-51 (38); R Arnoux 2-14 (13); M Alboreto 52-75 (24).

Lap Leaders 1982

POS	DRIVER	CAR-ENGINE	GPS	LAPS	KM	MILES
1	A Prost	Renault	7	258	1,008.6	626.7
2	R Arnoux	Renault	10	204	1,006.4	625.3
3	N Piquet	Brabham-BMW	5	105	525.7	*326.7*
		Brabham-Cosworth	1	34	171.1	*106.3*
			6	139	696.8	433.0
4	N Lauda	McLaren-Cosworth	2	128	491.0	305.1
5	D Pironi	Ferrari	4	80	347.3	215.8
	K Rosberg	Williams-Cosworth	3	80	336.5	209.1
7	G Villeneuve	Ferrari	2	40	201.3	125.1
8	R Patrese	Brabham-BMW	2	31	183.5	*114.0*
		Brabham-Cosworth	1	2	6.6	*4.1*
			3	33	190.2	118.2
9	J Watson	McLaren-Cosworth	2	28	112.8	70.1
10	P Tambay	Ferrari	1	27	183.5	114.0
11	M Alboreto	Tyrrell-Cosworth	1	24	87.6	54.4
12	A de Cesaris	Alfa Romeo	1	14.5	49.7	30.9
13	E de Angelis	Lotus-Cosworth	1	5	29.7	18.5
			16	**1,060.5**	**4,741.4**	**2,946.2**

Driver Points 1982

		ZA	BR	USAW	RSM	B	MC	DET	CDN	NL	GB	F	D	A	CH	I	LV	TOTAL
1	K Rosberg	2	-	6	-	6	-	3	-	4	-	2	4	6	9	-	2	44
2	D Pironi	-	1	-	9	-	6	4	-	9	6	4	-	-	-	-	-	39
	J Watson	1	6	1	-	9	-	9	4	-	-	-	-	-	-	3	6	39
4	A Prost	9	9	-	-	-	-	-	-	-	1	6	-	-	6	-	3	34
5	N Lauda	3	-	9	-	-	-	-	-	3	9	-	-	2	4	-	-	30
6	R Arnoux	4	-	-	-	-	-	-	-	-	-	9	6	-	-	9	-	28
7	P Tambay	-	-	-	-	-	-	-	-	-	4	3	9	3	-	6	-	25
	M Alboreto	-	3	3	4	-	-	-	-	-	-	1	3	-	-	2	9	25
9	E de Angelis	-	-	2	-	3	2	-	3	-	3	-	-	9	1	-	-	23
10	R Patrese	-	-	4	-	-	9	-	6	-	-	-	-	-	2	-	-	21
11	N Piquet	-	-	-	-	2	-	-	9	6	-	-	-	-	3	-	-	20
12	E Cheever	-	-	-	-	4	-	6	-	-	-	-	-	-	-	1	4	15
13	D Daly	-	-	-	-	-	1	2	-	2	2	-	-	-	-	-	1	8
14	N Mansell	-	4	-	-	-	3	-	-	-	-	-	-	-	-	-	-	7
15	C Reutemann	6	-	-	-	-	-	-	-	-	-	-	-	-	-	-	-	6
	G Villeneuve	-	-	-	6	-	-	-	-	-	-	-	-	-	-	-	-	6
17	A de Cesaris	-	-	-	-	-	4	-	1	-	-	-	-	-	-	-	-	5
	J Laffite	-	-	-	-	-	-	1	-	-	-	-	-	4	-	-	-	5
19	M Andretti	-	-	-	-	-	-	-	-	-	-	-	-	-	-	4	-	4
20	J-P Jarier	-	-	-	3	-	-	-	-	-	-	-	-	-	-	-	-	3
	M Surer	-	-	-	-	-	-	-	2	-	-	-	1	-	-	-	-	3
22	M Winkelhock	-	2	-	-	-	-	-	-	-	-	-	-	-	-	-	-	2
	E Salazar	-	-	-	2	-	-	-	-	-	-	-	-	-	-	-	-	2
	B Giacomelli	-	-	-	-	-	-	-	-	-	-	-	2	-	-	-	-	2
	M Baldi	-	-	-	-	-	-	-	-	1	-	-	-	1	-	-	-	2
26	C Serra	-	-	-	-	1	-	-	-	-	-	-	-	-	-	-	-	1

9, 6, 4, 3, 2 and 1 point awarded to the first six finishers. Best 11 scores.

Constructor Points 1982

		ZA	BR	USAW	RSM	B	MC	DET	CDN	NL	GB	F	D	A	CH	I	LV	TOTAL
1	Ferrari	-	1	-	15	-	6	4	-	9	10	7	9	3	-	10	-	74
2	McLaren-Cosworth	4	6	10	-	9	-	9	4	3	9	-	-	2	4	3	6	69
3	Renault	13	9	-	-	-	-	-	-	-	1	15	6	-	6	9	3	62
4	Williams-Cosworth	8	-	6	-	6	1	5	-	6	2	2	4	6	9	-	3	58
5	Lotus-Cosworth	-	4	2	-	3	5	-	3	-	3	-	-	9	1	-	-	30
6	Tyrrell-Cosworth	-	3	3	4	-	-	-	-	-	-	1	3	-	-	2	9	25
7	Brabham-BMW	-	-	-	-	2	-	-	9	6	-	-	-	-	5	-	-	22
8	Talbot Ligier-Matra	-	-	-	-	4	-	7	-	-	-	-	-	4	-	1	4	20
9	Brabham-Cosworth	-	-	4	-	-	9	-	6	-	-	-	-	-	-	-	-	19
10	Alfa Romeo	-	-	-	-	-	4	-	1	-	-	-	2	-	-	-	-	7
11	Arrows-Cosworth	-	-	-	-	-	-	-	2	1	-	-	1	1	-	-	-	5
12	ATS-Cosworth	-	2	-	2	-	-	-	-	-	-	-	-	-	-	-	-	4
13	Osella-Cosworth	-	-	-	3	-	-	-	-	-	-	-	-	-	-	-	-	3
14	Fittipaldi-Cosworth	-	-	-	-	1	-	-	-	-	-	-	-	-	-	-	-	1

9, 6, 4, 3, 2 and 1 point awarded to the first six finishers.

Colin Chapman, the genius behind Lotus, died suddenly at the end of 1982. New rules insisted on flat bottomed cars with no skirts. Fuel stops, tried out by Brabham in 1992, were a major new strategy tried by all teams. Alfa Romeo transferred its racing operation to Euroracing.

WILLIAMS
TAG Williams Team: Rosberg, Laffite, Palmer

TYRRELL
Benetton Tyrrell Team: Alboreto, Sullivan

BRABHAM
Fila Sport: Piquet, Patrese

McLAREN
Marlboro McLaren International: Watson, Lauda

ATS
Team ATS: Winkelhock

LOTUS
John Player Team Lotus: de Angelis, Mansell

RENAULT
Equipe Renault Elf: Prost, Cheever

RAM
RAM Automotive Team March: Salazar, (Villeneuve), Acheson, (Schlesser)

ALFA ROMEO
Marlboro Team Alfa Romeo: de Cesaris, Baldi

LIGIER
Equipe Ligier Gitanes: Jarier, Boesel

FERRARI
Scuderia Ferrari SpA SEFAC: Tambay, Arnoux

ARROWS
Arrows Racing Team: Surer, Serra, Jones, Boutsen

OSELLA
Osella Squadra Corse: Fabi, Ghinzani

THEODORE
Theodore Racing Team: Guerrero, Cecotto

TOLEMAN
Candy Toleman Motorsport: Warwick, Giacomelli

SPIRIT
Spirit Racing: Johansson

13 Mar 1983 BRAZIL: Rio de Janeiro (Round: 1) (Race: 374)
63 laps x 5.031 km, 3.126 miles = 316.953 km, 196.945 miles

POS.	NO.	DRIVER	CAR	MODEL	ENGINE		LAPS	TIME/REASON FOR RETIREMENT	GRID:POS	ROW
1	5	N Piquet	Brabham	BT52	BMW	4t	63	1h 48m 27.731s	4	2
dq	1	K Rosberg	Williams	FW08C	Cosworth	V8	63	push start in pits	1	1
3	8	N Lauda	McLaren	MP4/1C	Cosworth	V8	63	1h 49m 19.614s	9	5
4	2	J Laffite	Williams	FW08C	Cosworth	V8	63	1h 49m 41.682s	18	9
5	27	P Tambay	Ferrari	126C2B	Ferrari	V6t	63	1h 49m 45.848s	3	2
6	29	M Surer	Arrows	A6	Cosworth	V8	63	1h 49m 45.938s	20	10
7	15	A Prost	Renault	RE30C	Renault	V6t	62		2	1
8	35	D Warwick	Toleman	TG183B	Hart	4t	62		5	3
9	30	C Serra	Arrows	A6	Cosworth	V8	62		23	12
10	28	R Arnoux	Ferrari	126C2B	Ferrari	V6t	62		6	3
11	4	D Sullivan	Tyrrell	011	Cosworth	V8	62		21	11
12	12	N Mansell	Lotus	92	Cosworth	V8	61		22	11
dq	11	E de Angelis	Lotus	91	Cosworth	V8	60	changed car after parade lap	13	7
14	34	J Cecotto	Theodore	N183	Cosworth	V8	60		19	10
15	17	E Salazar	RAM March	01	Cosworth	V8	59		26	13
16	9	M Winkelhock	ATS	D6	BMW	4t	59		25	13
nc	33	R Guerrero	Theodore	N183	Cosworth	V8	53		14	7
r	16	E Cheever	Renault	RE30C	Renault	V6t	41	turbo	8	4
r	7	J Watson	McLaren	MP4/1C	Cosworth	V8	34	engine	16	8
r	26	R Boesel	Ligier	JS21	Cosworth	V8	25	electrics	17	9
r	23	M Baldi	Alfa Romeo	183T	Alfa Romeo	V8t	23	accident/ front suspension	10	5
r	25	J-P Jarier	Ligier	JS21	Cosworth	V8	22	rear suspension	12	6
r	6	R Patrese	Brabham	BT52	BMW	4t	19	exhaust	7	4
r	31	C Fabi	Osella	FA1D	Cosworth	V8	17	engine	24	12
r	36	B Giacomelli	Toleman	TG183B	Hart	4t	16	spin	15	8
r	3	M Alboreto	Tyrrell	011	Cosworth	V8	7	accident	11	6
nq	32	P Ghinzani	Osella	FA1D	Cosworth	V8				
exc	22	A de Cesaris	Alfa Romeo	183T	Alfa Romeo	V8t		missed weight check		

Winning speed: 175.335 km/h, 108.948 mph
Pole Position speed: 191.604 km/h, 119.057 mph (K Rosberg, 1 min:34.526 sec)
Fastest Lap speed: 181.426 km/h, 112.733 mph (N Piquet, 1 min:39.829 sec on lap 4)
Lap Leaders: K Rosberg 1-6 (6); N Piquet 7-63 (57).

K Rosberg finished 2nd in 1h 48m 48.362s. E de Angelis retired his Lotus 93T-Renault V6t on the parade lap with a turbo failure and proceeded to race in the Cosworth powered car, being consequently disqualified.

27 Mar 1983 — USA West: Long Beach (Round: 2) (Race: 375)

75 laps x 3.275 km, 2.035 miles = 245.626 km, 152.625 miles

POS.	NO.	DRIVER	CAR	MODEL	ENGINE		LAPS	TIME/REASON FOR RETIREMENT	GRID:POS	ROW
1	7	J Watson	McLaren	MP4/1C	Cosworth	V8	75	1h 53m 34.889s	22	11
2	8	N Lauda	McLaren	MP4/1C	Cosworth	V8	75	1h 54m 02.882s	23	12
3	28	R Arnoux	Ferrari	126C2B	Ferrari	V6t	75	1h 54m 48.527s	2	1
4	2	J Laffite	Williams	FW08C	Cosworth	V8	74		4	2
5	29	M Surer	Arrows	A6	Cosworth	V8	74		16	8
6	34	J Cecotto	Theodore	N183	Cosworth	V8	74		17	9
7	26	R Boesel	Ligier	JS21	Cosworth	V8	73		26	13
8	4	D Sullivan	Tyrrell	011	Cosworth	V8	73		9	5
9	3	M Alboreto	Tyrrell	011	Cosworth	V8	73		7	4
10r	6	R Patrese	Brabham	BT52	BMW	4t	72	distributor	11	6
11	15	A Prost	Renault	RE40	Renault	V6t	72		8	4
12	12	N Mansell	Lotus	92	Cosworth	V8	72		13	7
13r	16	E Cheever	Renault	RE30C	Renault	V6t	67	gearbox	15	8
r	30	A Jones	Arrows	A6	Cosworth	V8	58	driver discomfort	12	6
r	5	N Piquet	Brabham	BT52	BMW	4t	51	throttle jammed	20	10
r	22	A de Cesaris	Alfa Romeo	183T	Alfa Romeo	V8t	48	gearbox	19	10
r	11	E de Angelis	Lotus	93T	Renault	V6t	29	tyres	5	3
r	33	R Guerrero	Theodore	N183	Cosworth	V8	27	gearbox	18	9
r	25	J-P Jarier	Ligier	JS21	Cosworth	V8	26	accident	10	5
r	36	B Giacomelli	Toleman	TG183B	Hart	4t	26	battery	14	7
r	23	M Baldi	Alfa Romeo	183T	Alfa Romeo	V8t	26	accident	21	11
r	27	P Tambay	Ferrari	126C2B	Ferrari	V6t	25	accident	1	1
r	1	K Rosberg	Williams	FW08C	Cosworth	V8	25	accident	3	2
r	17	E Salazar	RAM March	01	Cosworth	V8	25	gear linkage	25	13
r	35	D Warwick	Toleman	TG183B	Hart	4t	11	tyre burst/ accident	6	3
r	9	M Winkelhock	ATS	D6	BMW	4t	3	accident	24	12
nq	31	C Fabi	Osella	FA1D	Cosworth	V8				
nq	32	P Ghinzani	Osella	FA1D	Cosworth	V8				

Winning speed: 129.753 km/h, 80.625 mph
Pole Position speed: 136.907 km/h, 85.070 mph (P Tambay, 1 min:26.117 sec)
Fastest Lap speed: 133.477 km/h, 82.939 mph (N Lauda, 1 min:28.330 sec on lap 42)
Lap Leaders: P Tambay 1-25 (25); J Laffite 26-44 (19); J Watson 45-75 (31).

17 Apr 1983 — FRANCE: Paul Ricard (Round: 3) (Race: 376)

54 laps x 5.810 km, 3.610 miles = 313.740 km, 194.949 miles

POS.	NO.	DRIVER	CAR	MODEL	ENGINE		LAPS	TIME/REASON FOR RETIREMENT	GRID:POS	ROW
1	15	A Prost	Renault	RE40	Renault	V6t	54	1h 34m 13.913s	1	1
2	5	N Piquet	Brabham	BT52	BMW	4t	54	1h 34m 43.633s	6	3
3	16	E Cheever	Renault	RE40	Renault	V6t	54	1h 34m 54.145s	2	1
4	27	P Tambay	Ferrari	126C2B	Ferrari	V6t	54	1h 35m 20.793s	11	6
5	1	K Rosberg	Williams	FW08C	Cosworth	V8	53		16	8
6	2	J Laffite	Williams	FW08C	Cosworth	V8	53		19	10
7	28	R Arnoux	Ferrari	126C2B	Ferrari	V6t	53		4	2
8	3	M Alboreto	Tyrrell	011	Cosworth	V8	53		15	8
9	25	J-P Jarier	Ligier	JS21	Cosworth	V8	53		20	10
10	29	M Surer	Arrows	A6	Cosworth	V8	53		21	11
11	34	J Cecotto	Theodore	N183	Cosworth	V8	52		17	9
12	22	A de Cesaris	Alfa Romeo	183T	Alfa Romeo	V8t	50		7	4
13r	36	B Giacomelli	Toleman	TG183B	Hart	4t	49	gearbox	13	7
r	26	R Boesel	Ligier	JS21	Cosworth	V8	47	engine	25	13
r	31	C Fabi	Osella	FA1D	Cosworth	V8	36	engine	23	12
r	9	M Winkelhock	ATS	D6	BMW	4t	36	engine/ exhaust	10	5
r	8	N Lauda	McLaren	MP4/1C	Cosworth	V8	29	wheel bearing	12	6
r	23	M Baldi	Alfa Romeo	183T	Alfa Romeo	V8t	28	accident	8	4
r	30	C Serra	Arrows	A6	Cosworth	V8	26	gearbox	26	13
r	33	R Guerrero	Theodore	N183	Cosworth	V8	23	engine	22	11
r	4	D Sullivan	Tyrrell	011	Cosworth	V8	21	clutch	24	12
r	11	E de Angelis	Lotus	93T	Renault	V6t	20	electrics	5	3
r	6	R Patrese	Brabham	BT52	BMW	4t	19	engine overheating	3	2
r	35	D Warwick	Toleman	TG183B	Hart	4t	14	water pipe/ engine	9	5
r	12	N Mansell	Lotus	92	Cosworth	V8	6	driver discomfort	18	9
r	7	J Watson	McLaren	MP4/1C	Cosworth	V8	3	throttle linkage	14	7
nq	17	E Salazar	RAM March	01	Cosworth	V8				
nq	32	P Ghinzani	Osella	FA1D	Cosworth	V8				
nq	18	J-L Schlesser	RAM March	01	Cosworth	V8				

Winning speed: 199.767 km/h, 124.129 mph
Pole Position speed: 216.360 km/h, 134.440 mph (A Prost, 1 min:36.672 sec)
Fastest Lap speed: 203.671 km/h, 126.555 mph (A Prost, 1 min:42.695 sec on lap 34)
Lap Leaders: A Prost 1-29,33-54 (51); N Piquet 30-32 (3).

1 May 1983 — SAN MARINO: Imola (Round: 4) (Race: 377)

60 laps x 5.040 km, 3.132 miles = 302.400 km, 187.903 miles

POS.	NO.	DRIVER	CAR	MODEL	ENGINE		LAPS	TIME/REASON FOR RETIREMENT	GRID:POS	ROW
1	27	P Tambay	Ferrari	126C2B	Ferrari	V6t	60	1h 37m 52.460s	3	2
2	15	A Prost	Renault	RE40	Renault	V6t	60	1h 38m 41.241s	4	2
3	28	R Arnoux	Ferrari	126C2B	Ferrari	V6t	59		1	1
4	1	K Rosberg	Williams	FW08C	Cosworth	V8	59		11	6
5	7	J Watson	McLaren	MP4/1C	Cosworth	V8	59		24	12
6	29	M Surer	Arrows	A6	Cosworth	V8	59		12	6
7	2	J Laffite	Williams	FW08C	Cosworth	V8	59		16	8
8	30	C Serra	Arrows	A6	Cosworth	V8	58		20	10
9	26	R Boesel	Ligier	JS21	Cosworth	V8	58		25	13
10r	23	M Baldi	Alfa Romeo	183T	Alfa Romeo	V8t	57	engine	10	5
11	9	M Winkelhock	ATS	D6	BMW	4t	57		7	4
12r	12	N Mansell	Lotus	92	Cosworth	V8	56	rear wing/ accident	15	8
13r	6	R Patrese	Brabham	BT52	BMW	4t	54	accident	5	3
r	22	A de Cesaris	Alfa Romeo	183T	Alfa Romeo	V8t	45	distributor	8	4
r	11	E de Angelis	Lotus	93T	Renault	V6t	43	handling	9	5
r	5	N Piquet	Brabham	BT52	BMW	4t	41	engine	2	1
r	25	J-P Jarier	Ligier	JS21	Cosworth	V8	39	radiator	19	10
r	4	D Sullivan	Tyrrell	011	Cosworth	V8	37	accident	22	11
r	35	D Warwick	Toleman	TG183B	Hart	4t	27	accident	14	7
r	31	C Fabi	Osella	FA1D	Cosworth	V8	20	accident	26	13
r	36	B Giacomelli	Toleman	TG183B	Hart	4t	20	rear suspension	17	9
r	8	N Lauda	McLaren	MP4/1C	Cosworth	V8	11	accident	18	9
r	34	J Cecotto	Theodore	N183	Cosworth	V8	11	accident	23	12
r	3	M Alboreto	Tyrrell	011	Cosworth	V8	10	accident/ rear suspension	13	7
r	33	R Guerrero	Theodore	N183	Cosworth	V8	3	accident	21	11
r	16	E Cheever	Renault	RE40	Renault	V6t	2	turbo	6	3
nq	17	E Salazar	RAM March	01	Cosworth	V8				
nq	32	P Ghinzani	Osella	FA1E	Alfa Romeo	V12				

Winning speed: 185.381 km/h, 115.190 mph
Pole Position speed: 198.865 km/h, 123.569 mph (R Arnoux, 1 min:31.238 sec)
Fastest Lap speed: 192.128 km/h, 119.383 mph (R Patrese, 1 min:34.437 sec on lap 47)
Lap Leaders: R Arnoux 1-5 (5); R Patrese 6-33 (28); P Tambay 34-60 (27).

15 May 1983 — MONACO: Monte Carlo (Round: 5) (Race: 378)

76 laps x 3.312 km, 2.058 miles = 251.712 km, 156.407 miles

POS.	NO.	DRIVER	CAR	MODEL	ENGINE		LAPS	TIME/REASON FOR RETIREMENT	GRID:POS	ROW
1	1	K Rosberg	Williams	FW08C	Cosworth	V8	76	1h 56m 38.121s	5	3
2	5	N Piquet	Brabham	BT52	BMW	4t	76	1h 56m 56.596s	6	3
3	15	A Prost	Renault	RE40	Renault	V6t	76	1h 57m 09.487s	1	1
4	27	P Tambay	Ferrari	126C2B	Ferrari	V6t	76	1h 57m 42.418s	4	2
5	4	D Sullivan	Tyrrell	011	Cosworth	V8	74		20	10
6	23	M Baldi	Alfa Romeo	183T	Alfa Romeo	V8t	74		13	7
7	30	C Serra	Arrows	A6	Cosworth	V8	74		15	8
r	6	R Patrese	Brabham	BT52	BMW	4t	64	electrics	17	9
r	2	J Laffite	Williams	FW08C	Cosworth	V8	53	gearbox	8	4
r	29	M Surer	Arrows	A6	Cosworth	V8	49	accident	12	6
r	35	D Warwick	Toleman	TG183B	Hart	4t	49	accident	10	5
r	11	E de Angelis	Lotus	93T	Renault	V6t	49	drive shaft	19	10
r	25	J-P Jarier	Ligier	JS21	Cosworth	V8	32	suspension hydraulics	9	5
r	16	E Cheever	Renault	RE40	Renault	V6t	30	electrics	3	2
r	22	A de Cesaris	Alfa Romeo	183T	Alfa Romeo	V8t	13	gearbox	7	4
r	28	R Arnoux	Ferrari	126C2B	Ferrari	V6t	6	accident	2	1
r	26	R Boesel	Ligier	JS21	Cosworth	V8	3	accident	18	9
r	9	M Winkelhock	ATS	D6	BMW	4t	3	accident	16	8
r	3	M Alboreto	Tyrrell	011	Cosworth	V8	0	accident	11	6
r	12	N Mansell	Lotus	92	Cosworth	V8	0	accident	14	7
nq	36	B Giacomelli	Toleman	TG183B	Hart	4t				
nq	8	N Lauda	McLaren	MP4/1C	Cosworth	V8				
nq	7	J Watson	McLaren	MP4/1C	Cosworth	V8				
nq	31	C Fabi	Osella	FA1D	Cosworth	V8				
nq	17	E Salazar	RAM March	01	Cosworth	V8				
nq	32	P Ghinzani	Osella	FA1E	Alfa Romeo	V12				
npq	34	J Cecotto	Theodore	N183	Cosworth	V8				
npq	33	R Guerrero	Theodore	N183	Cosworth	V8				

Winning speed: 129.487 km/h, 80.459 mph
Pole Position speed: 140.537 km/h, 87.326 mph (A Prost, 1 min:24.840 sec)
Fastest Lap speed: 136.604 km/h, 84.882 mph (N Piquet, 1 min:27.283 sec on lap 69)
Lap Leaders: K Rosberg 1-76 (76).

2 May 1983 — BELGIUM: Spa-Francorchamps — (Round: 6) (Race: 379)

40.0953 laps x 6.949 km, 4.318 miles = 278.620 km, 173.126 miles

POS.	NO.	DRIVER	CAR	MODEL	ENGINE		LAPS	TIME/REASON FOR RETIREMENT	GRID:POS	ROW
1	15	A Prost	Renault	RE40	Renault	V6t	40	1h 27m 11.502s	1	1
2	27	P Tambay	Ferrari	126C2B	Ferrari	V6t	40	1h 27m 34.684s	2	1
3	16	E Cheever	Renault	RE40	Renault	V6t	40	1h 27m 51.371s	8	4
4	5	N Piquet	Brabham	BT52	BMW	4t	40	1h 27m 53.797s	4	2
5	1	K Rosberg	Williams	FW08C	Cosworth	V8	40	1h 28m 01.982s	9	5
6	2	J Laffite	Williams	FW08C	Cosworth	V8	40	1h 28m 44.609s	11	6
7	35	D Warwick	Toleman	TG183B	Hart	4t	40	1h 29m 10.041s	22	11
8	36	B Giacomelli	Toleman	TG183B	Hart	4t	40	1h 29m 49.775s	16	8
9	11	E de Angelis	Lotus	93T	Renault	V6t	39		13	7
10	34	J Cecotto	Theodore	N183	Cosworth	V8	39		25	13
11	29	M Surer	Arrows	A6	Cosworth	V8	39		10	5
12	4	D Sullivan	Tyrrell	011	Cosworth	V8	39		23	12
13	26	R Boesel	Ligier	JS21	Cosworth	V8	39		26	13
14	3	M Alboreto	Tyrrell	011	Cosworth	V8	38		17	9
r	8	N Lauda	McLaren	MP4/1C	Cosworth	V8	33	engine	15	8
r	12	N Mansell	Lotus	92	Cosworth	V8	30	gearbox	19	10
r	22	A de Cesaris	Alfa Romeo	183T	Alfa Romeo	V8t	25	engine	3	2
r	33	R Guerrero	Theodore	N183	Cosworth	V8	23	engine	14	7
r	28	R Arnoux	Ferrari	126C2B	Ferrari	V6t	22	engine	5	3
r	31	C Fabi	Osella	FA1D	Cosworth	V8	19	rear suspension	24	12
r	9	M Winkelhock	ATS	D6	BMW	4t	18	rear wheel lost/accident	7	4
r	7	J Watson	McLaren	MP4/1C	Cosworth	V8	8	accident	20	10
r	25	J-P Jarier	Ligier	JS21	Cosworth	V8	8	accident	21	11
r	30	T Boutsen	Arrows	A6	Cosworth	V8	4	rear suspension	18	9
r	23	M Baldi	Alfa Romeo	183T	Alfa Romeo	V8t	3	throttle linkage	12	6
r	6	R Patrese	Brabham	BT52	BMW	4t	0	engine	6	3
nq	32	P Ghinzani	Osella	FA1E	Alfa Romeo	V12				
nq	17	E Salazar	RAM March	01	Cosworth	V8				

Winning speed: 191.729 km/h, 119.135 mph
Pole Position speed: 200.750 km/h, 124.740 mph (A Prost, 2 min: 4.615 sec)
Fastest Lap speed: 196.218 km/h, 121.924 mph (A de Cesaris, 2 min: 7.493 sec on lap 17)
Lap Leaders: A de Cesaris 1-18 (18.1); A Prost 19-22,24-40 (21); N Piquet 23 (1).

The start and finish lines were at different positions on the circuit. The fraction of a lap is credited to the first lap leader.

5 Jun 1983 — USA: Detroit — (Round: 7) (Race: 380)

60 laps x 4.023 km, 2.500 miles = 241.402 km, 150.000 miles

POS.	NO.	DRIVER	CAR	MODEL	ENGINE		LAPS	TIME/REASON FOR RETIREMENT	GRID:POS	ROW
1	3	M Alboreto	Tyrrell	011	Cosworth	V8	60	1h 50m 53.669s	6	3
2	1	K Rosberg	Williams	FW08C	Cosworth	V8	60	1h 51m 01.371s	12	6
3	7	J Watson	McLaren	MP4/1C	Cosworth	V8	60	1h 51m 02.952s	21	11
4	5	N Piquet	Brabham	BT52	BMW	4t	60	1h 52m 05.854s	2	1
5	2	J Laffite	Williams	FW08C	Cosworth	V8	60	1h 52m 26.272s	20	10
6	12	N Mansell	Lotus	92	Cosworth	V8	59		14	7
7	30	T Boutsen	Arrows	A6	Cosworth	V8	59		10	5
8	15	A Prost	Renault	RE40	Renault	V6t	59		13	7
9	36	B Giacomelli	Toleman	TG183B	Hart	4t	59		17	9
10	26	R Boesel	Ligier	JS21	Cosworth	V8	58		23	12
11	29	M Surer	Arrows	A6	Cosworth	V8	58		5	3
12	23	M Baldi	Alfa Romeo	183T	Alfa Romeo	V8t	56		25	13
r	8	N Lauda	McLaren	MP4/1C	Cosworth	V8	49	suspension	18	9
nc	33	R Guerrero	Theodore	N183	Cosworth	V8	38		11	6
r	34	J Cecotto	Theodore	N183	Cosworth	V8	34	gear linkage	26	13
r	22	A de Cesaris	Alfa Romeo	183T	Alfa Romeo	V8t	33	turbo	8	4
r	28	R Arnoux	Ferrari	126C2B	Ferrari	V6t	31	electrics	1	1
r	4	D Sullivan	Tyrrell	011	Cosworth	V8	30	electrics	16	8
r	25	J-P Jarier	Ligier	JS21	Cosworth	V8	29	wheel nut	19	10
r	9	M Winkelhock	ATS	D6	BMW	4t	26	accident	22	11
r	35	D Warwick	Toleman	TG183B	Hart	4t	25	water leak/ engine	9	5
r	6	R Patrese	Brabham	BT52	BMW	4t	24	brakes	15	8
r	11	E de Angelis	Lotus	93T	Renault	V6t	5	transmission	4	2
r	16	E Cheever	Renault	RE40	Renault	V6t	4	distributor	7	4
r	32	P Ghinzani	Osella	FA1E	Alfa Romeo	V12	4	engine overheating	24	12
r	27	P Tambay	Ferrari	126C2B	Ferrari	V6t	0	stalled on grid	3	2
nq	31	C Fabi	Osella	FA1D	Cosworth	V8				

Winning speed: 130.612 km/h, 81.158 mph
Pole Position speed: 138.294 km/h, 85.932 mph (R Arnoux, 1 min:44.734 sec)
Fastest Lap speed: 134.526 km/h, 83.590 mph (J Watson, 1 min:47.668 sec on lap 55)
Lap Leaders: N Piquet 1-9,32-50 (28); R Arnoux 10-31 (22); M Alboreto 51-60 (10).

12 Jun 1983 — CANADA: Montréal (Round: 8) (Race: 381)

70 laps x 4.410 km, 2.740 miles = 308.700 km, 191.817 miles

POS.	NO.	DRIVER	CAR	MODEL	ENGINE		LAPS	TIME/REASON FOR RETIREMENT	GRID:POS	ROW
1	28	R Arnoux	Ferrari	126C2B	Ferrari	V6t	70	1h 48m 31.838s	1	1
2	16	E Cheever	Renault	RE40	Renault	V6t	70	1h 49m 13.867s	6	3
3	27	P Tambay	Ferrari	126C2B	Ferrari	V6t	70	1h 49m 24.448s	4	2
4	1	K Rosberg	Williams	FW08C	Cosworth	V8	70	1h 49m 48.886s	9	5
5	15	A Prost	Renault	RE40	Renault	V6t	69		2	1
6	7	J Watson	McLaren	MP4/1C	Cosworth	V8	69		20	10
7	30	T Boutsen	Arrows	A6	Cosworth	V8	69		15	8
8	3	M Alboreto	Tyrrell	011	Cosworth	V8	68		17	9
dq	4	D Sullivan	Tyrrell	011	Cosworth	V8	68	car under weight	22	11
9r	9	M Winkelhock	ATS	D6	BMW	4t	67	fuel system	7	4
10	23	M Baldi	Alfa Romeo	183T	Alfa Romeo	V8t	67		26	13
r	6	R Patrese	Brabham	BT52	BMW	4t	56	gearbox	5	3
r	35	D Warwick	Toleman	TG183B	Hart	4t	47	turbo	12	6
r	36	B Giacomelli	Toleman	TG183B	Hart	4t	43	engine	10	5
r	12	N Mansell	Lotus	92	Cosworth	V8	43	handling/ tyres	18	9
r	22	A de Cesaris	Alfa Romeo	183T	Alfa Romeo	V8t	42	engine	8	4
r	2	J Laffite	Williams	FW08C	Cosworth	V8	37	gearbox	13	7
r	26	R Boesel	Ligier	JS21	Cosworth	V8	32	wheel bearing	24	12
r	33	R Guerrero	Theodore	N183	Cosworth	V8	27	engine	21	11
r	31	C Fabi	Osella	FA1D	Cosworth	V8	26	engine	25	13
r	34	J Cecotto	Theodore	N183	Cosworth	V8	17	crown wheel & pinion	23	12
r	5	N Piquet	Brabham	BT52	BMW	4t	15	throttle linkage	3	2
r	8	N Lauda	McLaren	MP4/1C	Cosworth	V8	11	spin	19	10
r	11	E de Angelis	Lotus	93T	Renault	V6t	1	throttle linkage	11	6
r	25	J-P Jarier	Ligier	JS21	Cosworth	V8	0	gearbox	16	8
r	29	M Surer	Arrows	A6	Cosworth	V8	0	transmission	14	7
nq	17	J Villeneuve	RAM March	01	Cosworth	V8				
nq	32	P Ghinzani	Osella	FA1E	Alfa Romeo	V12				

Winning speed: 170.661 km/h, 106.044 mph
Pole Position speed: 178.927 km/h, 111.180 mph (R Arnoux, 1 min:28.729 sec)
Fastest Lap speed: 174.748 km/h, 108.583 mph (P Tambay, 1 min:30.851 sec on lap 42)
Lap Leaders: R Arnoux 1-34,39-70 (66); R Patrese 35-37 (3); P Tambay 38 (1).

16 Jul 1983 — BRITAIN: Silverstone (Round: 9) (Race: 382)

67 laps x 4.719 km, 2.932 miles = 316.146 km, 196.444 miles

POS.	NO.	DRIVER	CAR	MODEL	ENGINE		LAPS	TIME/REASON FOR RETIREMENT	GRID:POS	ROW
1	15	A Prost	Renault	RE40	Renault	V6t	67	1h 24m 39.780s	3	2
2	5	N Piquet	Brabham	BT52B	BMW	4t	67	1h 24m 58.941s	6	3
3	27	P Tambay	Ferrari	126C3	Ferrari	V6t	67	1h 25m 06.026s	2	1
4	12	N Mansell	Lotus	94T	Renault	V6t	67	1h 25m 18.732s	18	9
5	28	R Arnoux	Ferrari	126C3	Ferrari	V6t	67	1h 25m 38.654s	1	1
6	8	N Lauda	McLaren	MP4/1C	Cosworth	V8	66		15	8
7	23	M Baldi	Alfa Romeo	183T	Alfa Romeo	V8t	66		11	6
8	22	A de Cesaris	Alfa Romeo	183T	Alfa Romeo	V8t	66		9	5
9	7	J Watson	McLaren	MP4/1C	Cosworth	V8	66		24	12
10	25	J-P Jarier	Ligier	JS21	Cosworth	V8	65		25	13
11	1	K Rosberg	Williams	FW08C	Cosworth	V8	65		13	7
12	2	J Laffite	Williams	FW08C	Cosworth	V8	65		20	10
13	3	M Alboreto	Tyrrell	011	Cosworth	V8	65		16	8
14	4	D Sullivan	Tyrrell	011	Cosworth	V8	65		23	12
15	30	T Boutsen	Arrows	A6	Cosworth	V8	65		17	9
16	33	R Guerrero	Theodore	N183	Cosworth	V8	64		21	11
17	29	M Surer	Arrows	A6	Cosworth	V8	64		19	10
r	9	M Winkelhock	ATS	D6	BMW	4t	49	engine overheating	8	4
r	26	R Boesel	Ligier	JS21	Cosworth	V8	48	suspension hydraulic leak	22	11
r	32	P Ghinzani	Osella	FA1E	Alfa Romeo	V12	46	fuel pressure	26	13
r	35	D Warwick	Toleman	TG183B	Hart	4t	27	gearbox	10	5
r	6	R Patrese	Brabham	BT52B	BMW	4t	9	turbo	5	3
r	40	S Johansson	Spirit	201	Honda	V6t	5	fuel pump belt	14	7
r	16	E Cheever	Renault	RE40	Renault	V6t	3	cylinder head gasket	7	4
r	36	B Giacomelli	Toleman	TG183B	Hart	4t	3	turbo	12	6
r	11	E de Angelis	Lotus	94T	Renault	V6t	1	distributor	4	2
nq	34	J Cecotto	Theodore	N183	Cosworth	V8				
nq	31	C Fabi	Osella	FA1E	Alfa Romeo	V12				
nq	17	K Acheson	RAM March	01	Cosworth	V8				

Winning speed: 224.050 km/h, 139.218 mph
Pole Position speed: 244.550 km/h, 151.956 mph (R Arnoux, 1 min: 9.462 sec)
Fastest Lap speed: 228.898 km/h, 142.230 mph (A Prost, 1 min:14.212 sec on lap 32)
Lap Leaders: P Tambay 1-19 (19); A Prost 20-36,42-67 (43); N Piquet 37-41 (5).

7 Aug 1983 — GERMANY: Hockenheim (Round:10) (Race: 383)

45 laps x 6.797 km, 4.223 miles = 305.865 km, 190.056 miles

POS.	NO.	DRIVER	CAR	MODEL	ENGINE		LAPS	TIME/REASON FOR RETIREMENT	GRID:POS	ROW
1	28	R Arnoux	Ferrari	126C3	Ferrari	V6t	45	1h 27m 10.319s	2	1
2	22	A de Cesaris	Alfa Romeo	183T	Alfa Romeo	V8t	45	1h 28m 20.971s	3	2
3	6	R Patrese	Brabham	BT52B	BMW	4t	45	1h 28m 54.412s	8	4
4	15	A Prost	Renault	RE40	Renault	V6t	45	1h 29m 11.069s	5	3
dq	8	N Lauda	McLaren	MP4/1C	Cosworth	V8	44	reversed in pits	18	9
5	7	J Watson	McLaren	MP4/1C	Cosworth	V8	44		23	12
6	2	J Laffite	Williams	FW08C	Cosworth	V8	44		15	8
7	29	M Surer	Arrows	A6	Cosworth	V8	44		20	10
8	25	J-P Jarier	Ligier	JS21	Cosworth	V8	44		19	10
9	30	T Boutsen	Arrows	A6	Cosworth	V8	44		14	7
10	1	K Rosberg	Williams	FW08C	Cosworth	V8	44		12	6
11	34	J Cecotto	Theodore	N183	Cosworth	V8	44		22	11
12	4	D Sullivan	Tyrrell	011	Cosworth	V8	43		21	11
13r	5	N Piquet	Brabham	BT52B	BMW	4t	42	fuel filter leak/ fire	4	2
r	16	E Cheever	Renault	RE40	Renault	V6t	38	fuel injection pump	6	3
r	32	P Ghinzani	Osella	FA1E	Alfa Romeo	V12	34	engine	26	13
r	26	R Boesel	Ligier	JS21	Cosworth	V8	27	engine	25	13
r	23	M Baldi	Alfa Romeo	183T	Alfa Romeo	V8t	24	engine	7	4
r	36	B Giacomelli	Toleman	TG183B	Hart	4t	19	turbo	10	5
r	35	D Warwick	Toleman	TG183B	Hart	4t	17	engine	9	5
r	40	S Johansson	Spirit	201C	Honda	V6t	11	engine	13	7
r	27	P Tambay	Ferrari	126C3	Ferrari	V6t	11	engine	1	1
r	11	E de Angelis	Lotus	94T	Renault	V6t	10	engine overheating	11	6
r	3	M Alboreto	Tyrrell	011	Cosworth	V8	4	fuel pump drive	16	8
r	12	N Mansell	Lotus	94T	Renault	V6t	1	engine	17	9
r	33	R Guerrero	Theodore	N183	Cosworth	V8	0	engine	24	12
nq	17	K Acheson	RAM March	01	Cosworth	V8				
nq	31	C Fabi	Osella	FA1E	Alfa Romeo	V12				
nq	9	M Winkelhock	ATS	D6	BMW	4t				

Winning speed: 210.525 km/h, 130.814 mph
Pole Position speed: 223.815 km/h, 139.072 mph (P Tambay, 1 min:49.328 sec)
Fastest Lap speed: 214.759 km/h, 133.445 mph (R Arnoux, 1 min:53.938 sec on lap 12)
Lap Leaders: P Tambay 1 (1); R Arnoux 2-23,31-45 (37); N Piquet 24-30 (7).

14 Aug 1983 — AUSTRIA: Österreichring (Round:11) (Race: 384)

53 laps x 5.942 km, 3.692 miles = 314.926 km, 195.686 miles

POS.	NO.	DRIVER	CAR	MODEL	ENGINE		LAPS	TIME/REASON FOR RETIREMENT	GRID:POS	ROW
1	15	A Prost	Renault	RE40	Renault	V6t	53	1h 24m 32.745s	5	3
2	28	R Arnoux	Ferrari	126C3	Ferrari	V6t	53	1h 24m 39.580s	2	1
3	5	N Piquet	Brabham	BT52B	BMW	4t	53	1h 25m 00.404s	4	2
4	16	E Cheever	Renault	RE40	Renault	V6t	53	1h 25m 01.140s	8	4
5	12	N Mansell	Lotus	94T	Renault	V6t	52		3	2
6	8	N Lauda	McLaren	MP4/1C	Cosworth	V8	51		14	7
7	25	J-P Jarier	Ligier	JS21	Cosworth	V8	51		20	10
8	1	K Rosberg	Williams	FW08C	Cosworth	V8	51		15	8
9	7	J Watson	McLaren	MP4/1C	Cosworth	V8	51		17	9
10	31	C Fabi	Osella	FA1E	Alfa Romeo	V12	50		26	13
11	32	P Ghinzani	Osella	FA1E	Alfa Romeo	V12	49		25	13
12	40	S Johansson	Spirit	201	Honda	V6t	48		16	8
13	30	T Boutsen	Arrows	A6	Cosworth	V8	48		19	10
r	9	M Winkelhock	ATS	D6	BMW	4t	33	engine overheating	13	7
r	22	A de Cesaris	Alfa Romeo	183T	Alfa Romeo	V8t	31	out of fuel	11	6
r	27	P Tambay	Ferrari	126C3	Ferrari	V6t	30	oil union/ engine	1	1
r	6	R Patrese	Brabham	BT52B	BMW	4t	29	engine overheating	6	3
r	33	R Guerrero	Theodore	N183	Cosworth	V8	25	gearbox	21	11
r	2	J Laffite	Williams	FW08C	Cosworth	V8	21	accident damage/ handling	24	12
r	23	M Baldi	Alfa Romeo	183T	Alfa Romeo	V8t	13	engine	9	5
r	3	M Alboreto	Tyrrell	012	Cosworth	V8	8	accident	18	9
r	35	D Warwick	Toleman	TG183B	Hart	4t	2	turbo	10	5
r	36	B Giacomelli	Toleman	TG183B	Hart	4t	1	accident	7	4
r	4	D Sullivan	Tyrrell	011	Cosworth	V8	0	accident	23	12
r	29	M Surer	Arrows	A6	Cosworth	V8	0	accident	22	11
r	11	E de Angelis	Lotus	94T	Renault	V6t	0	accident	12	6
nq	26	R Boesel	Ligier	JS21	Cosworth	V8				
nq	34	J Cecotto	Theodore	N183	Cosworth	V8				
nq	17	K Acheson	RAM March	01	Cosworth	V8				

Winning speed: 223.495 km/h, 138.873 mph
Pole Position speed: 238.021 km/h, 147.899 mph (P Tambay, 1 min:29.871 sec)
Fastest Lap speed: 227.660 km/h, 141.462 mph (A Prost, 1 min:33.961 sec on lap 20)
Lap Leaders: P Tambay 1-21 (21); R Arnoux 22-27,38-47 (16); N Piquet 28-37 (10); A Prost 48-53 (6).

28 Aug 1983 — NETHERLANDS: Zandvoort (Round:12) (Race: 385)

72 laps x 4.252 km, 2.642 miles = 306.144 km, 190.229 miles

POS.	NO.	DRIVER	CAR	MODEL	ENGINE		LAPS	TIME/REASON FOR RETIREMENT	GRID:POS	ROW
1	28	R Arnoux	Ferrari	126C3	Ferrari	V6t	72	1h 38m 41.950s	10	5
2	27	P Tambay	Ferrari	126C3	Ferrari	V6t	72	1h 39m 02.789s	2	1
3	7	J Watson	McLaren	MP4/1C	Cosworth	V8	72	1h 39m 25.691s	15	8
4	35	D Warwick	Toleman	TG183B	Hart	4t	72	1h 39m 58.789s	7	4
5	23	M Baldi	Alfa Romeo	183T	Alfa Romeo	V8t	72	1h 40m 06.242s	12	6
6	3	M Alboreto	Tyrrell	012	Cosworth	V8	71		18	9
7	40	S Johansson	Spirit	201C	Honda	V6t	70		16	8
8	29	M Surer	Arrows	A6	Cosworth	V8	70		14	7
9	6	R Patrese	Brabham	BT52B	BMW	4t	70		6	3
10	26	R Boesel	Ligier	JS21	Cosworth	V8	70		24	12
11r	31	C Fabi	Osella	FA1E	Alfa Romeo	V12	68	engine	25	13
12	33	R Guerrero	Theodore	N183	Cosworth	V8	68		20	10
13	36	B Giacomelli	Toleman	TG183B	Hart	4t	68		13	7
14r	30	T Boutsen	Arrows	A6	Cosworth	V8	65	engine	21	11
r	1	K Rosberg	Williams	FW08C	Cosworth	V8	53	misfire	23	12
dq	9	M Winkelhock	ATS	D6	BMW	4t	50	overtook on parade lap	9	5
r	5	N Piquet	Brabham	BT52B	BMW	4t	41	accident	1	1
r	15	A Prost	Renault	RE40	Renault	V6t	41	accident	4	2
r	16	E Cheever	Renault	RE40	Renault	V6t	39	electrics	11	6
r	2	J Laffite	Williams	FW08C	Cosworth	V8	37	tyres	17	9
r	12	N Mansell	Lotus	94T	Renault	V6t	26	spin	5	3
r	8	N Lauda	McLaren	MP4/1E	TAG Porsche	V6t	25	brakes	19	10
r	4	D Sullivan	Tyrrell	011	Cosworth	V8	20	engine	26	13
r	11	E de Angelis	Lotus	94T	Renault	V6t	12	fuel metering unit	3	2
r	22	A de Cesaris	Alfa Romeo	183T	Alfa Romeo	V8t	5	engine	8	4
r	25	J-P Jarier	Ligier	JS21	Cosworth	V8	3	suspension	22	11
nq	32	P Ghinzani	Osella	FA1E	Alfa Romeo	V12				
nq	34	J Cecotto	Theodore	N183	Cosworth	V8				
nq	17	K Acheson	RAM March	01	Cosworth	V8				

Winning speed: 186.107 km/h, 115.642 mph
Pole Position speed: 202.396 km/h, 125.763 mph (N Piquet, 1 min:15.630 sec)
Fastest Lap speed: 191.668 km/h, 119.097 mph (R Arnoux, 1 min:19.863 sec on lap 33)
Lap Leaders: N Piquet 1-41 (41); R Arnoux 42-72 (31).

11 Sep 1983 — ITALY: Monza (Round:13) (Race: 386)

52 laps x 5.800 km, 3.604 miles = 301.600 km, 187.406 miles

POS.	NO.	DRIVER	CAR	MODEL	ENGINE		LAPS	TIME/REASON FOR RETIREMENT	GRID:POS	ROW
1	5	N Piquet	Brabham	BT52B	BMW	4t	52	1h 23m 10.880s	4	2
2	28	R Arnoux	Ferrari	126C3	Ferrari	V6t	52	1h 23m 21.092s	3	2
3	16	E Cheever	Renault	RE40	Renault	V6t	52	1h 23m 29.492s	7	4
4	27	P Tambay	Ferrari	126C3	Ferrari	V6t	52	1h 23m 39.903s	2	1
5	11	E de Angelis	Lotus	94T	Renault	V6t	52	1h 24m 04.560s	8	4
6	35	D Warwick	Toleman	TG183B	Hart	4t	52	1h 24m 24.228s	12	6
7	36	B Giacomelli	Toleman	TG183B	Hart	4t	52	1h 24m 44.802s	14	7
8	12	N Mansell	Lotus	94T	Renault	V6t	52	1h 24m 46.915s	11	6
9	25	J-P Jarier	Ligier	JS21	Cosworth	V8	51		19	10
10	29	M Surer	Arrows	A6	Cosworth	V8	51		20	10
11	1	K Rosberg	Williams	FW08C	Cosworth	V8	51		16	8
12	34	J Cecotto	Theodore	N183	Cosworth	V8	50		26	13
13	33	R Guerrero	Theodore	N183	Cosworth	V8	50		21	11
r	31	C Fabi	Osella	FA1E	Alfa Romeo	V12	45	oil union	25	13
r	4	D Sullivan	Tyrrell	011	Cosworth	V8	44	fuel pump drive	22	11
r	30	T Boutsen	Arrows	A6	Cosworth	V8	41	engine	18	9
r	9	M Winkelhock	ATS	D6	BMW	4t	35	exhaust	9	5
r	3	M Alboreto	Tyrrell	012	Cosworth	V8	28	clutch	24	12
r	15	A Prost	Renault	RE40	Renault	V6t	26	turbo	5	3
r	8	N Lauda	McLaren	MP4/1E	TAG Porsche	V6t	24	electrics	13	7
r	7	J Watson	McLaren	MP4/1E	TAG Porsche	V6t	13	engine	15	8
r	32	P Ghinzani	Osella	FA1E	Alfa Romeo	V12	10	gearbox	23	12
r	23	M Baldi	Alfa Romeo	183T	Alfa Romeo	V8t	4	turbo	10	5
r	40	S Johansson	Spirit	201	Honda	V6t	4	distributor	17	9
r	6	R Patrese	Brabham	BT52B	BMW	4t	2	electrics	1	1
r	22	A de Cesaris	Alfa Romeo	183T	Alfa Romeo	V8t	2	spin	6	3
nq	26	R Boesel	Ligier	JS21	Cosworth	V8				
nq	2	J Laffite	Williams	FW08C	Cosworth	V8				
nq	17	K Acheson	RAM March	01	Cosworth	V8				

Winning speed: 217.549 km/h, 135.179 mph
Pole Position speed: 234.286 km/h, 145.578 mph (R Patrese, 1 min:29.122 sec)
Fastest Lap speed: 221.114 km/h, 137.394 mph (N Piquet, 1 min:34.431 sec on lap 20)
Lap Leaders: R Patrese 1-2 (2); N Piquet 3-52 (50).

K Rosberg finished 9th, but penalised 1 minute for infringement at start.

25 Sep 1983 — EUROPE: Brands Hatch (Round:14) (Race: 387)

76 laps x 4.207 km, 2.614 miles = 319.719 km, 198.664 miles

POS.	NO.	DRIVER	CAR	MODEL	ENGINE		LAPS	TIME/REASON FOR RETIREMENT	GRID:POS	ROW
1	5	N Piquet	Brabham	BT52B	BMW	4t	76	1h 36m 45.865s	4	2
2	15	A Prost	Renault	RE40	Renault	V6t	76	1h 36m 52.436s	8	4
3	12	N Mansell	Lotus	94T	Renault	V6t	76	1h 37m 16.180s	3	2
4	22	A de Cesaris	Alfa Romeo	183T	Alfa Romeo	V8t	76	1h 37m 20.261s	14	7
5	35	D Warwick	Toleman	TG183B	Hart	4t	76	1h 37m 30.780s	11	6
6	36	B Giacomelli	Toleman	TG183B	Hart	4t	76	1h 37m 38.055s	12	6
7	6	R Patrese	Brabham	BT52B	BMW	4t	76	1h 37m 58.549s	2	1
8	9	M Winkelhock	ATS	D6	BMW	4t	75		9	5
9	28	R Arnoux	Ferrari	126C3	Ferrari	V6t	75		5	3
10	16	E Cheever	Renault	RE40	Renault	V6t	75		7	4
11	30	T Boutsen	Arrows	A6	Cosworth	V8	75		18	9
12	33	R Guerrero	Theodore	N183	Cosworth	V8	75		21	11
13	42	J Palmer	Williams	FW08C	Cosworth	V8	74		25	13
14	40	S Johansson	Spirit	201	Honda	V6t	74		19	10
15	26	R Boesel	Ligier	JS21	Cosworth	V8	73		23	12
r	27	P Tambay	Ferrari	126C3	Ferrari	V6t	67	accident/ brake fluid lost	6	3
r	3	M Alboreto	Tyrrell	012	Cosworth	V8	64	engine	26	13
nc	32	P Ghinzani	Osella	FA1E	Alfa Romeo	V12	63		24	12
r	29	M Surer	Arrows	A6	Cosworth	V8	50	engine	17	9
r	1	K Rosberg	Williams	FW08C	Cosworth	V8	43	engine	16	8
r	23	M Baldi	Alfa Romeo	183T	Alfa Romeo	V8t	39	clutch	15	8
r	7	J Watson	McLaren	MP4/1E	TAG Porsche	V6t	36	accident	10	5
r	4	D Sullivan	Tyrrell	012	Cosworth	V8	27	oil line/ fire	20	10
r	8	N Lauda	McLaren	MP4/1E	TAG Porsche	V6t	25	engine	13	7
r	11	E de Angelis	Lotus	94T	Renault	V6t	12	engine	1	1
r	25	J-P Jarier	Ligier	JS21	Cosworth	V8	0	gearbox	22	11
nq	17	K Acheson	RAM March	01	Cosworth	V8				
nq	31	C Fabi	Osella	FA1E	Alfa Romeo	V12				
nq	2	J Laffite	Williams	FW08C	Cosworth	V8				

Winning speed: 198.246 km/h, 123.184 mph
Pole Position speed: 210.073 km/h, 130.533 mph (E de Angelis, 1 min:12.092 sec)
Fastest Lap speed: 203.715 km/h, 126.583 mph (N Mansell, 1 min:14.342 sec on lap 70)
Lap Leaders: R Patrese 1-10 (10); N Piquet 11-76 (66).

15 Oct 1983 — SOUTH AFRICA: Kyalami (Round:15) (Race: 388)

77 laps x 4.104 km, 2.550 miles = 316.008 km, 196.358 miles

POS.	NO.	DRIVER	CAR	MODEL	ENGINE		LAPS	TIME/REASON FOR RETIREMENT	GRID:POS	ROW
1	6	R Patrese	Brabham	BT52B	BMW	4t	77	1h 33m 25.708s	3	2
2	22	A de Cesaris	Alfa Romeo	183T	Alfa Romeo	V8t	77	1h 33m 35.027s	9	5
3	5	N Piquet	Brabham	BT52B	BMW	4t	77	1h 33m 47.677s	2	1
4	35	D Warwick	Toleman	TG183B	Hart	4t	76		13	7
5	1	K Rosberg	Williams	FW09	Honda	V6t	76		6	3
6	16	E Cheever	Renault	RE40	Renault	V6t	76		14	7
7	4	D Sullivan	Tyrrell	012	Cosworth	V8	75		19	10
8	29	M Surer	Arrows	A6	Cosworth	V8	75		22	11
9	30	T Boutsen	Arrows	A6	Cosworth	V8	74		20	10
10	25	J-P Jarier	Ligier	JS21	Cosworth	V8	73		21	11
11r	8	N Lauda	McLaren	MP4/1E	TAG Porsche	V6t	71	electrics	12	6
12	17	K Acheson	RAM March	01	Cosworth	V8	71		24	12
nc	12	N Mansell	Lotus	94T	Renault	V6t	68		7	4
nc	26	R Boesel	Ligier	JS21	Cosworth	V8	66		23	12
r	3	M Alboreto	Tyrrell	012	Cosworth	V8	60	engine	18	9
r	27	P Tambay	Ferrari	126C3	Ferrari	V6t	56	turbo	1	1
r	36	B Giacomelli	Toleman	TG183B	Hart	4t	56	turbo/ fire	16	8
r	15	A Prost	Renault	RE40	Renault	V6t	35	turbo	5	3
r	31	C Fabi	Osella	FA1E	Alfa Romeo	V12	28	engine	25	13
r	11	E de Angelis	Lotus	94T	Renault	V6t	20	misfire	11	6
dq	7	J Watson	McLaren	MP4/1E	TAG Porsche	V6t	18	overtook on parade lap	15	8
r	28	R Arnoux	Ferrari	126C3	Ferrari	V6t	9	engine	4	2
r	23	M Baldi	Alfa Romeo	183T	Alfa Romeo	V8t	5	engine	17	9
r	9	M Winkelhock	ATS	D6	BMW	4t	1	engine	8	4
r	2	J Laffite	Williams	FW09	Honda	V6t	1	accident	10	5
r	32	P Ghinzani	Osella	FA1E	Alfa Romeo	V12	1	engine	26	13

Winning speed: 202.941 km/h, 126.102 mph
Pole Position speed: 221.991 km/h, 137.939 mph (P Tambay, 1 min: 6.554 sec)
Fastest Lap speed: 211.220 km/h, 131.246 mph (N Piquet, 1 min: 9.948 sec on lap 6)
Lap Leaders: N Piquet 1-59 (59); R Patrese 60-77 (18).

Lap Leaders 1983

POS	DRIVER	CAR-ENGINE	GPS	LAPS	KM	MILES
1	N Piquet	Brabham-BMW	11	327	1,538.5	956.0
2	R Arnoux	Ferrari	6	177	883.1	548.8
3	A Prost	Renault	4	121	680.8	423.0
4	P Tambay	Ferrari	6	94	443.6	275.6
5	K Rosberg	Williams-Cosworth	2	82	281.9	175.2
6	R Patrese	Brabham-BMW	5	61	281.9	175.2
7	J Watson	McLaren-Cosworth	1	31	101.5	63.1
8	J Laffite	Williams-Cosworth	1	19	62.2	38.7
9	A de Cesaris	Alfa Romeo	1	18.1	125.7	78.1
10	M Alboreto	Tyrrell-Cosworth	1	10	40.2	25.0
			15	**940.1**	**4,439.6**	**2,758.6**

Driver Points 1983

		BR	USAW	F	RSM	MC	B	DET	CDN	GB	D	A	NL	I	EUR	ZA	TOTAL
1	N Piquet	9	-	6	-	6	3	3	-	6	-	4	-	9	9	4	59
2	A Prost	-	-	9	6	4	9	-	2	9	3	9	-	-	6	-	57
3	R Arnoux	-	4	-	4	-	-	-	9	2	9	6	9	6	-	-	49
4	P Tambay	2	-	3	9	3	6	-	4	4	-	-	6	3	-	-	40
5	K Rosberg	-	-	2	3	9	2	6	3	-	-	-	-	-	-	2	27
6	J Watson	-	9	-	2	-	-	4	1	-	2	-	4	-	-	-	22
	E Cheever	-	-	4	-	-	4	-	6	-	-	3	-	4	-	1	22
8	A de Cesaris	-	-	-	-	-	-	-	-	-	6	-	-	-	3	6	15
9	R Patrese	-	-	-	-	-	-	-	-	-	4	-	-	-	-	9	13
10	N Lauda	4	6	-	-	-	-	-	-	1	-	1	-	-	-	-	12
11	J Laffite	3	3	1	-	-	1	2	-	-	1	-	-	-	-	-	11
12	M Alboreto	-	-	-	-	-	-	9	-	-	-	-	1	-	-	-	10
	N Mansell	-	-	-	-	-	-	1	-	3	-	2	-	-	4	-	10
14	D Warwick	-	-	-	-	-	-	-	-	-	-	-	3	1	2	3	9
15	M Surer	1	2	-	1	-	-	-	-	-	-	-	-	-	-	-	4
16	M Baldi	-	-	-	-	1	-	-	-	-	-	-	2	-	-	-	3
17	D Sullivan	-	-	-	-	2	-	-	-	-	-	-	-	-	-	-	2
	E de Angelis	-	-	-	-	-	-	-	-	-	-	-	-	2	-	-	2
19	J Cecotto	-	1	-	-	-	-	-	-	-	-	-	-	-	-	-	1
	B Giacomelli	-	-	-	-	-	-	-	-	-	-	-	-	-	1	-	1

9, 6, 4, 3, 2 and 1 point awarded to the first six finishers. Best 11 scores.

Constructor Points 1983

		BR	USAW	F	RSM	MC	B	DET	CDN	GB	D	A	NL	I	EUR	ZA	TOTAL
1	Ferrari	2	4	3	13	3	6	-	13	6	9	6	15	9	-	-	89
2	Renault	-	-	13	6	4	13	-	8	9	3	12	-	4	6	1	79
3	Brabham-BMW	9	-	6	-	6	3	3	-	6	4	4	-	9	9	13	72
4	Williams-Cosworth	3	3	3	3	9	3	8	3	-	1	-	-	-	-	-	36
5	McLaren-Cosworth	4	15	-	2	-	-	4	1	1	2	1	4	-	-	-	34
6	Alfa Romeo	-	-	-	-	1	-	-	-	-	6	-	2	-	3	6	18
7	Tyrrell-Cosworth	-	-	-	-	2	-	9	-	-	-	-	1	-	-	-	12
8	Lotus-Renault	-	-	-	-	-	-	-	-	3	-	2	-	2	4	-	11
9	Toleman-Hart	-	-	-	-	-	-	-	-	-	-	-	3	1	3	3	10
10	Arrows-Cosworth	1	2	-	1	-	-	-	-	-	-	-	-	-	-	-	4
11	Williams-Honda	-	-	-	-	-	-	-	-	-	-	-	-	-	-	2	2
12	Theodore-Cosworth	-	1	-	-	-	-	-	-	-	-	-	-	-	-	-	1
	Lotus-Cosworth	-	-	-	-	-	-	1	-	-	-	-	-	-	-	-	1

9, 6, 4, 3, 2 and 1 point awarded to the first six finishers.

Safety issues forced a refuelling ban as teams now had a fuel limit of 220 litres. After the first turbo champion, virtually all entries followed this route, with the TAG Porsche powered McLaren emerging dominant. Tyrrell was the only normally aspirated car but they found themselves banned for weight deception after, among other infringements, ball bearings were found in tanks at post race scrutineering.

BRABHAM
MRD International: Piquet, T Fabi, C Fabi, Winkelhock

TYRRELL
Tyrrell Racing Organisation: Brundle, Johansson, Bellof, (Thackwell)

WILLIAMS
Williams Grand Prix Engineering: Laffite, Rosberg

McLAREN
Marlboro McLaren International: Prost, Lauda

RAM
Skoal Bandit Formula 1 Team: Alliot, Palmer, Thackwell

LOTUS
John Player Team Lotus: de Angelis, Mansell

ATS
Team ATS: Winkelhock, Berger

RENAULT
Equipe Renault Elf: Tambay, Warwick, Streiff

ARROWS
Barclay Nordica Arrows BMW: Surer, Boutsen

TOLEMAN
Toleman Group Motorsport: Senna, (Martini), Cecotto, Johansson

SPIRIT
Spirit Racing: Baldi, Rothengatter

ALFA ROMEO
Benetton Team Alfa Romeo: Patrese, Cheever

OSELLA
Osella Squadra Corse: Ghinzani, Gartner

LIGIER
Ligier Loto: Hesnault, de Cesaris

FERRARI
Scuderia Ferrari SpA SEFAC: Alboreto, Arnoux

25 Mar 1984 — BRAZIL: Rio de Janeiro (Round: 1) (Race: 389)

61 laps x 5.031 km, 3.126 miles = 306.891 km, 190.693 miles

POS.	NO.	DRIVER	CAR	MODEL	ENGINE		LAPS	TIME/REASON FOR RETIREMENT	GRID:POS	ROW
1	7	A Prost	McLaren	MP4/2	TAG Porsche	V6t	61	1h 42m 34.492s	4	2
2	6	K Rosberg	Williams	FW09	Honda	V6t	61	1h 43m 15.006s	9	5
3	11	E de Angelis	Lotus	95T	Renault	V6t	61	1h 43m 33.620s	1	1
4	23	E Cheever	Alfa Romeo	184T	Alfa Romeo	V8t	60		12	6
dq	3	M Brundle	Tyrrell	012	Cosworth	V8	60	(1)	18	9
5r	15	P Tambay	Renault	RE50	Renault	V6t	59	out of fuel	8	4
6	18	T Boutsen	Arrows	A6	Cosworth	V8	59		20	10
7	17	M Surer	Arrows	A6	Cosworth	V8	59		24	12
8	10	J Palmer	RAM	01	Hart	4t	58		26	13
r	16	D Warwick	Renault	RE50	Renault	V6t	51	front suspension	3	2
r	26	A de Cesaris	Ligier	JS23	Renault	V6t	42	gearbox	14	7
r	22	R Patrese	Alfa Romeo	184T	Alfa Romeo	V8t	41	gearbox	11	6
r	8	N Lauda	McLaren	MP4/2	TAG Porsche	V6t	38	electrics	6	3
r	12	N Mansell	Lotus	95T	Renault	V6t	35	accident	5	3
r	1	N Piquet	Brabham	BT53	BMW	4t	32	engine	7	4
r	2	T Fabi	Brabham	BT53	BMW	4t	32	turbo	15	8
r	28	R Arnoux	Ferrari	126C4	Ferrari	V6t	30	battery	10	5
r	24	P Ghinzani	Osella	FA1F	Alfa Romeo	V8t	28	gearbox	21	11
r	25	F Hesnault	Ligier	JS23	Renault	V6t	25	engine overheating	19	10
r	9	P Alliot	RAM	02	Hart	4t	24	battery mounting	25	13
r	20	J Cecotto	Toleman	TG183B	Hart	4t	18	turbo boost pressure	17	9
r	5	J Laffite	Williams	FW09	Honda	V6t	15	electrics	13	7
r	27	M Alboreto	Ferrari	126C4	Ferrari	V6t	14	brake caliper	2	1
r	21	M Baldi	Spirit	101	Hart	4t	12	distributor	23	12
dq	4	S Bellof	Tyrrell	012	Cosworth	V8	11	throttle linkage/ (1)	22	11
r	19	A Senna	Toleman	TG183B	Hart	4t	8	turbo boost pressure	16	8
exc	14	M Winkelhock	ATS	D7	BMW	4t		mechanics pushed car into pits		

Winning speed: 179.512 km/h, 111.544 mph
Pole Position speed: 204.901 km/h, 127.320 mph (E de Angelis, 1 min:28.392 sec)
Fastest Lap speed: 187.687 km/h, 116.623 mph (A Prost, 1 min:36.499 sec on lap 42)
Lap Leaders: M Alboreto 1-11 (11); N Lauda 12-37 (26); A Prost 38,51-61 (12); D Warwick 39-50 (12).

(1) On 18 July 1984, due to infringing the rules, Tyrrell were disqualified from all the races they had competed in during the season, and refused entry to all remaining races, although the team was allowed to continue until their appeal was heard.

7 Apr 1984 — SOUTH AFRICA: Kyalami (Round: 2) (Race: 390)

75 laps x 4.104 km, 2.550 miles = 307.800 km, 191.258 miles

POS.	NO.	DRIVER	CAR	MODEL	ENGINE		LAPS	TIME/REASON FOR RETIREMENT	GRID:POS	ROW
1	8	N Lauda	McLaren	MP4/2	TAG Porsche	V6t	75	1h 29m 23.430s	8	4
2	7	A Prost	McLaren	MP4/2	TAG Porsche	V6t	75	1h 30m 29.380s	5	3
3	16	D Warwick	Renault	RE50	Renault	V6t	74		9	5
4	22	R Patrese	Alfa Romeo	184T	Alfa Romeo	V8t	73		18	9
5	26	A de Cesaris	Ligier	JS23	Renault	V6t	73		14	7
6	19	A Senna	Toleman	TG183B	Hart	4t	72		13	7
7	11	E de Angelis	Lotus	95T	Renault	V6t	71		7	4
8	21	M Baldi	Spirit	101	Hart	4t	71		20	10
9	17	M Surer	Arrows	A6	Cosworth	V8	71		23	12
10	25	F Hesnault	Ligier	JS23	Renault	V6t	71		17	9
dq	3	M Brundle	Tyrrell	012	Cosworth	V8	71	(1)	25	13
11r	27	M Alboreto	Ferrari	126C4	Ferrari	V6t	70	ignition	10	5
12	18	T Boutsen	Arrows	A6	Cosworth	V8	70		26	13
r	15	P Tambay	Renault	RE50	Renault	V6t	66	fuel metering unit	4	2
r	5	J Laffite	Williams	FW09	Honda	V6t	60	cv joint	11	6
dq	4	S Bellof	Tyrrell	012	Cosworth	V8	60	hub/ (1)	24	12
r	14	M Winkelhock	ATS	D7	BMW	4t	53	battery/ engine	12	6
r	6	K Rosberg	Williams	FW09	Honda	V6t	51	wheel nut/ wheel lost	2	1
r	12	N Mansell	Lotus	95T	Renault	V6t	51	turbo inlet duct	3	2
r	28	R Arnoux	Ferrari	126C4	Ferrari	V6t	40	fuel injection	15	8
r	1	N Piquet	Brabham	BT53	BMW	4t	29	turbo compressor	1	1
r	20	J Cecotto	Toleman	TG183B	Hart	4t	26	tyre burst/ suspension	19	10
r	9	P Alliot	RAM	02	Hart	4t	24	water leak/ engine	22	11
r	10	J Palmer	RAM	01	Hart	4t	22	gearbox/ electrics	21	11
r	2	T Fabi	Brabham	BT53	BMW	4t	18	turbo compressor	6	3
r	23	E Cheever	Alfa Romeo	184T	Alfa Romeo	V8t	4	radiator	16	8
ns	24	P Ghinzani	Osella	FA1F	Alfa Romeo	V8t		accident/ injury		

Winning speed: 206.599 km/h, 128.375 mph
Pole Position speed: 227.750 km/h, 141.518 mph (N Piquet, 1 min: 4.871 sec)
Fastest Lap speed: 214.504 km/h, 133.287 mph (P Tambay, 1 min: 8.877 sec on lap 64)
Lap Leaders: K Rosberg 1 (1); N Piquet 2-20 (19); N Lauda 21-75 (55).

T Boutsen should have been placed 9th (71 laps) but a lap charting error cost him a lap. Protest by team was too late to correct the error.

29 Apr 1984 — BELGIUM: Zolder (Round: 3) (Race: 391)

70 laps x 4.262 km, 2.648 miles = 298.340 km, 185.380 miles

POS.	NO.	DRIVER	CAR	MODEL	ENGINE		LAPS	TIME/REASON FOR RETIREMENT	GRID:POS	ROW
1	27	M Alboreto	Ferrari	126C4	Ferrari	V6t	70	1h 36m 32.048s	1	1
2	16	D Warwick	Renault	RE50	Renault	V6t	70	1h 37m 14.434s	4	2
3	28	R Arnoux	Ferrari	126C4	Ferrari	V6t	70	1h 37m 41.851s	2	1
4r	6	K Rosberg	Williams	FW09	Honda	V6t	69	out of fuel	3	2
5	11	E de Angelis	Lotus	95T	Renault	V6t	69		5	3
dq	4	S Bellof	Tyrrell	012	Cosworth	V8	69	(1)	21	11
6	19	A Senna	Toleman	TG183B	Hart	4t	68		19	10
7	15	P Tambay	Renault	RE50	Renault	V6t	68		12	6
8	17	M Surer	Arrows	A6	Cosworth	V8	68		24	12
9r	1	N Piquet	Brabham	BT53	BMW	4t	66	engine	9	5
10	10	J Palmer	RAM	02	Hart	4t	64		26	13
r	21	M Baldi	Spirit	101	Hart	4t	53	suspension	25	13
dq	3	M Brundle	Tyrrell	012	Cosworth	V8	51	wheel lost/ (1)	22	11
r	2	T Fabi	Brabham	BT53	BMW	4t	42	spin	18	9
r	26	A de Cesaris	Ligier	JS23	Renault	V6t	42	accident	13	7
r	14	M Winkelhock	ATS	D7	BMW	4t	39	exhaust/ electrics	6	3
r	8	N Lauda	McLaren	MP4/2	TAG Porsche	V6t	35	water pump	14	7
r	23	E Cheever	Alfa Romeo	184T	Alfa Romeo	V8t	28	engine	11	6
r	5	J Laffite	Williams	FW09	Honda	V6t	15	electrics	15	8
r	25	F Hesnault	Ligier	JS23	Renault	V6t	15	radiator	23	12
r	18	T Boutsen	Arrows	A7	BMW	4t	15	wire loose/ misfire	17	9
r	24	P Ghinzani	Osella	FA1F	Alfa Romeo	V8t	14	transmission	20	10
r	12	N Mansell	Lotus	95T	Renault	V6t	14	clutch	10	5
r	7	A Prost	McLaren	MP4/2	TAG Porsche	V6t	5	distributor	8	4
r	22	R Patrese	Alfa Romeo	184T	Alfa Romeo	V8t	2	ignition	7	4
r	20	J Cecotto	Toleman	TG183B	Hart	4t	1	clutch	16	8
nq	9	P Alliot	RAM	02	Hart	4t				

Winning speed: 185.431 km/h, 115.221 mph
Pole Position speed: 204.997 km/h, 127.379 mph (M Alboreto, 1 min:14.846 sec)
Fastest Lap speed: 193.498 km/h, 120.234 mph (R Arnoux, 1 min:19.294 sec on lap 64)
Lap Leaders: M Alboreto 1-70 (70).

6 May 1984 — SAN MARINO: Imola — (Round: 4) (Race: 392)

60 laps x 5.040 km, 3.132 miles = 302.400 km, 187.903 miles

POS.	NO.	DRIVER	CAR	MODEL	ENGINE		LAPS	TIME/REASON FOR RETIREMENT	GRID:POS	ROW
1	7	A Prost	McLaren	MP4/2	TAG Porsche	V6t	60	1h 36m 53.679s	2	1
2	28	R Arnoux	Ferrari	126C4	Ferrari	V6t	60	1h 37m 07.095s	6	3
3r	11	E de Angelis	Lotus	95T	Renault	V6t	59	out of fuel	11	6
4	16	D Warwick	Renault	RE50	Renault	V6t	59		4	2
dq	4	S Bellof	Tyrrell	012	Cosworth	V8	59	(1)	21	11
5	18	T Boutsen	Arrows	A6	Cosworth	V8	59		20	10
6r	26	A de Cesaris	Ligier	JS23	Renault	V6t	58	out of fuel	12	6
7r	23	E Cheever	Alfa Romeo	184T	Alfa Romeo	V8t	58	out of fuel	8	4
8	21	M Baldi	Spirit	101	Hart	4t	58		24	12
9	10	J Palmer	RAM	02	Hart	4t	57		25	13
dq	3	M Brundle	Tyrrell	012	Cosworth	V8	55	fuel injection/ (1)	22	11
r	9	P Alliot	RAM	02	Hart	4t	53	engine	23	12
nc	20	J Cecotto	Toleman	TG183B	Hart	4t	52		19	10
r	1	N Piquet	Brabham	BT53	BMW	4t	48	turbo	1	1
r	2	T Fabi	Brabham	BT53	BMW	4t	48	turbo	9	5
r	30	J Gartner	Osella	FA1E	Alfa Romeo	V12	46	engine	26	13
r	17	M Surer	Arrows	A7	BMW	4t	40	turbo	16	8
r	14	M Winkelhock	ATS	D7	BMW	4t	31	turbo	7	4
r	27	M Alboreto	Ferrari	126C4	Ferrari	V6t	23	exhaust	13	7
r	8	N Lauda	McLaren	MP4/2	TAG Porsche	V6t	15	engine	5	3
r	5	J Laffite	Williams	FW09	Honda	V6t	11	engine	15	8
r	22	R Patrese	Alfa Romeo	184T	Alfa Romeo	V8t	6	electrics	10	5
r	12	N Mansell	Lotus	95T	Renault	V6t	2	brakes/ spin	18	9
r	6	K Rosberg	Williams	FW09	Honda	V6t	2	electrics	3	2
r	15	P Tambay	Renault	RE50	Renault	V6t	0	accident	14	7
r	25	F Hesnault	Ligier	JS23	Renault	V6t	0	accident	17	9
nq	24	P Ghinzani	Osella	FA1F	Alfa Romeo	V8t				
nq	19	A Senna	Toleman	TG183B	Hart	4t				

Winning speed: 187.255 km/h, 116.355 mph
Pole Position speed: 204.978 km/h, 127.367 mph (N Piquet, 1 min:28.517 sec)
Fastest Lap speed: 194.522 km/h, 120.870 mph (N Piquet, 1 min:33.275 sec on lap 48)
Lap Leaders: A Prost 1-60 (60).

20 May 1984 — FRANCE: Dijon-Prenois — (Round: 5) (Race: 393)

79 laps x 3.887 km, 2.415 miles = 307.073 km, 190.806 miles

POS.	NO.	DRIVER	CAR	MODEL	ENGINE		LAPS	TIME/REASON FOR RETIREMENT	GRID:POS	ROW
1	8	N Lauda	McLaren	MP4/2	TAG Porsche	V6t	79	1h 31m 11.951s	9	5
2	15	P Tambay	Renault	RE50	Renault	V6t	79	1h 31m 19.105s	1	1
3	12	N Mansell	Lotus	95T	Renault	V6t	79	1h 31m 35.920s	6	3
4	28	R Arnoux	Ferrari	126C4	Ferrari	V6t	79	1h 31m 55.657s	11	6
5	11	E de Angelis	Lotus	95T	Renault	V6t	79	1h 32m 18.076s	2	1
6	6	K Rosberg	Williams	FW09	Honda	V6t	78		4	2
7	7	A Prost	McLaren	MP4/2	TAG Porsche	V6t	78		5	3
8	5	J Laffite	Williams	FW09	Honda	V6t	78		12	6
9	2	T Fabi	Brabham	BT53	BMW	4t	78		17	9
10	26	A de Cesaris	Ligier	JS23	Renault	V6t	77		26	13
11	18	T Boutsen	Arrows	A7	BMW	4t	77		14	7
dq	3	M Brundle	Tyrrell	012	Cosworth	V8	76	(1)	23	12
12	24	P Ghinzani	Osella	FA1F	Alfa Romeo	V8t	74		25	13
13	10	J Palmer	RAM	02	Hart	4t	72		21	11
r	21	M Baldi	Spirit	101	Hart	4t	61	engine	24	12
r	16	D Warwick	Renault	RE50	Renault	V6t	53	accident	7	4
r	17	M Surer	Arrows	A6	Cosworth	V8	51	accident	19	10
r	23	E Cheever	Alfa Romeo	184T	Alfa Romeo	V8t	51	engine	16	8
r	19	A Senna	Toleman	TG184	Hart	4t	35	turbo	13	7
r	27	M Alboreto	Ferrari	126C4	Ferrari	V6t	33	engine	10	5
r	20	J Cecotto	Toleman	TG184	Hart	4t	22	turbo	18	9
r	22	R Patrese	Alfa Romeo	184T	Alfa Romeo	V8t	15	engine	15	8
r	1	N Piquet	Brabham	BT53	BMW	4t	11	turbo	3	2
dq	4	S Bellof	Tyrrell	012	Cosworth	V8	11	thought engine had failed/ (1)	20	10
r	14	M Winkelhock	ATS	D7	BMW	4t	5	clutch	8	4
r	9	P Alliot	RAM	02	Hart	4t	4	electrics	22	11
ns	25	F Hesnault	Ligier	JS23	Renault	V6t		car raced by de Cesaris		

Winning speed: 202.024 km/h, 125.532 mph
Pole Position speed: 224.971 km/h, 139.791 mph (P Tambay, 1 min: 2.200 sec)
Fastest Lap speed: 214.432 km/h, 133.242 mph (A Prost, 1 min: 5.257 sec on lap 59)
Lap Leaders: P Tambay 1-40,54-62 (49); N Lauda 41-53,63-79 (30).

3 Jun 1984 — MONACO: Monte Carlo — (Round: 6) (Race: 394)

31 laps x 3.312 km, 2.058 miles = 102.672 km, 63.797 miles

POS.	NO.	DRIVER	CAR	MODEL	ENGINE		LAPS	TIME/REASON FOR RETIREMENT	GRID:POS	ROW
1	7	A Prost	McLaren	MP4/2	TAG Porsche	V6t	31	1h 01m 07.740s	1	1
2	19	A Senna	Toleman	TG184	Hart	4t	31	1h 01m 15.186s	13	7
dq	4	S Bellof	Tyrrell	012	Cosworth	V8	31	1h 01m 28.881s/ (1)	20	10
3	28	R Arnoux	Ferrari	126C4	Ferrari	V6t	31	1h 01m 36.817s	3	2
4	6	K Rosberg	Williams	FW09	Honda	V6t	31	1h 01m 42.986s	10	5
5	11	E de Angelis	Lotus	95T	Renault	V6t	31	1h 01m 52.179s	11	6
6	27	M Alboreto	Ferrari	126C4	Ferrari	V6t	30		4	2
7	24	P Ghinzani	Osella	FA1F	Alfa Romeo	V8t	30		19	10
8	5	J Laffite	Williams	FW09	Honda	V6t	30		16	8
r	22	R Patrese	Alfa Romeo	184T	Alfa Romeo	V8t	24	steering	14	7
r	8	N Lauda	McLaren	MP4/2	TAG Porsche	V6t	23	spin	8	4
r	14	M Winkelhock	ATS	D7	BMW	4t	22	spin	12	6
r	12	N Mansell	Lotus	95T	Renault	V6t	15	accident	2	1
r	1	N Piquet	Brabham	BT53	BMW	4t	14	electrics	9	5
r	25	F Hesnault	Ligier	JS23	Renault	V6t	12	electrics	17	9
r	2	C Fabi	Brabham	BT53	BMW	4t	9	spin	15	8
r	20	J Cecotto	Toleman	TG184	Hart	4t	1	spin	18	9
r	26	A de Cesaris	Ligier	JS23	Renault	V6t	1	accident damage	7	4
r	16	D Warwick	Renault	RE50	Renault	V6t	0	accident	5	3
r	15	P Tambay	Renault	RE50	Renault	V6t	0	accident	6	3
nq	17	M Surer	Arrows	A6	Cosworth	V8				
nq	3	M Brundle	Tyrrell	012	Cosworth	V8				
nq	23	E Cheever	Alfa Romeo	184T	Alfa Romeo	V8t				
nq	18	T Boutsen	Arrows	A7	BMW	4t				
nq	10	J Palmer	RAM	02	Hart	4t				
nq	21	M Baldi	Spirit	101	Hart	4t				
nq	9	P Alliot	RAM	02	Hart	4t				

Winning speed: 100.776 km/h, 62.619 mph
Pole Position speed: 144.242 km/h, 89.628 mph (A Prost, 1 min:22.661 sec)
Fastest Lap speed: 104.284 km/h, 64.799 mph (A Senna, 1 min:54.334 sec on lap 24)
Lap Leaders: A Prost 1-10,16-31 (26); N Mansell 11-15 (5).

Scheduled for 77 laps, but stopped early because of rain. Half points were awarded.

17 Jun 1984 — CANADA: Montréal — (Round: 7) (Race: 395)

70 laps x 4.410 km, 2.740 miles = 308.700 km, 191.817 miles

POS.	NO.	DRIVER	CAR	MODEL	ENGINE		LAPS	TIME/REASON FOR RETIREMENT	GRID:POS	ROW
1	1	N Piquet	Brabham	BT53	BMW	4t	70	1h 46m 23.748s	1	1
2	8	N Lauda	McLaren	MP4/2	TAG Porsche	V6t	70	1h 46m 26.360s	8	4
3	7	A Prost	McLaren	MP4/2	TAG Porsche	V6t	70	1h 47m 51.780s	2	1
4	11	E de Angelis	Lotus	95T	Renault	V6t	69		3	2
5	28	R Arnoux	Ferrari	126C4	Ferrari	V6t	68		5	3
6	12	N Mansell	Lotus	95T	Renault	V6t	68		7	4
7	19	A Senna	Toleman	TG184	Hart	4t	68		9	5
8	14	M Winkelhock	ATS	D7	BMW	4t	68		12	6
dq	3	M Brundle	Tyrrell	012	Cosworth	V8	68	(1)	21	11
9	20	J Cecotto	Toleman	TG184	Hart	4t	68		20	10
10	9	P Alliot	RAM	02	Hart	4t	65		26	13
11r	23	E Cheever	Alfa Romeo	184T	Alfa Romeo	V8t	63	out of fuel	11	6
r	17	M Surer	Arrows	A6	Cosworth	V8	59	engine	23	12
r	16	D Warwick	Renault	RE50	Renault	V6t	57	undertray	4	2
nc	21	H Rothengatter	Spirit	101	Hart	4t	56		24	12
dq	4	S Bellof	Tyrrell	012	Cosworth	V8	52	drive shaft/ (1)	22	11
r	26	A de Cesaris	Ligier	JS23	Renault	V6t	40	brakes	10	5
r	2	C Fabi	Brabham	BT53	BMW	4t	39	turbo boost pressure	16	8
r	18	T Boutsen	Arrows	A7	BMW	4t	38	engine	18	9
r	22	R Patrese	Alfa Romeo	184T	Alfa Romeo	V8t	37	accident	14	7
r	6	K Rosberg	Williams	FW09	Honda	V6t	32	fuel system	15	8
r	5	J Laffite	Williams	FW09	Honda	V6t	31	turbo boost pressure	17	9
r	10	M Thackwell	RAM	02	Hart	4t	29	turbo wastegate	25	13
r	24	P Ghinzani	Osella	FA1F	Alfa Romeo	V8t	11	gearbox	19	10
r	27	M Alboreto	Ferrari	126C4	Ferrari	V6t	10	engine	6	3
r	25	F Hesnault	Ligier	JS23	Renault	V6t	7	turbo	13	7
ew	15	P Tambay	Renault	RE50	Renault	V6t		driver unfit (Monaco injury)		

Winning speed: 174.086 km/h, 108.172 mph
Pole Position speed: 185.810 km/h, 115.457 mph (N Piquet, 1 min:25.442 sec)
Fastest Lap speed: 178.858 km/h, 111.137 mph (N Piquet, 1 min:28.763 sec on lap 55)
Lap Leaders: N Piquet 1-70 (70).

24 Jun 1984 — USA: Detroit — (Round: 8) (Race: 396)

63 laps x 4.023 km, 2.500 miles = 253.472 km, 157.500 miles

POS.	NO.	DRIVER	CAR	MODEL	ENGINE		LAPS	TIME/REASON FOR RETIREMENT	GRID:POS	ROW
1	1	N Piquet	Brabham	BT53	BMW	4t	63	1h 55m 41.842s	1	1
dq	3	M Brundle	Tyrrell	012	Cosworth	V8	63	1h 55m 42.679s/ (1)	11	6
2	11	E de Angelis	Lotus	95T	Renault	V6t	63	1h 56m 14.480s	5	3
3	2	T Fabi	Brabham	BT53	BMW	4t	63	1h 57m 08.370s	23	12
4	7	A Prost	McLaren	MP4/2	TAG Porsche	V6t	63	1h 57m 37.100s	2	1
5	5	J Laffite	Williams	FW09	Honda	V6t	62		19	10
r	27	M Alboreto	Ferrari	126C4	Ferrari	V6t	49	engine	4	2
r	6	K Rosberg	Williams	FW09	Honda	V6t	47	exhaust/ turbo	21	11
r	16	D Warwick	Renault	RE50	Renault	V6t	40	gearbox	6	3
dq	4	S Bellof	Tyrrell	012	Cosworth	V8	33	accident/ (1)	16	8
r	15	P Tambay	Renault	RE50	Renault	V6t	33	transmission	9	5
r	9	P Alliot	RAM	02	Hart	4t	33	brakes/ accident	20	10
r	8	N Lauda	McLaren	MP4/2	TAG Porsche	V6t	33	electronics	10	5
r	12	N Mansell	Lotus	95T	Renault	V6t	27	gearbox	3	2
r	18	T Boutsen	Arrows	A7	BMW	4t	27	engine	13	7
r	26	A de Cesaris	Ligier	JS23	Renault	V6t	24	engine overheating	12	6
r	20	J Cecotto	Toleman	TG184	Hart	4t	23	clutch	17	9
r	23	E Cheever	Alfa Romeo	184T	Alfa Romeo	V8t	21	engine	8	4
r	19	A Senna	Toleman	TG184	Hart	4t	21	accident	7	4
r	22	R Patrese	Alfa Romeo	184T	Alfa Romeo	V8t	20	spin	25	13
r	25	F Hesnault	Ligier	JS23	Renault	V6t	3	accident	18	9
r	24	P Ghinzani	Osella	FA1F	Alfa Romeo	V8t	3	accident	26	13
r	28	R Arnoux	Ferrari	126C4	Ferrari	V6t	2	accident	15	8
r	10	J Palmer	RAM	02	Hart	4t	2	tyre burst/ accident	24	12
r	14	M Winkelhock	ATS	D7	BMW	4t	0	accident	14	7
r	17	M Surer	Arrows	A6	Cosworth	V8	0	accident *	22	11
nq	21	H Rothengatter	Spirit	101	Cosworth	V8				

Winning speed: 131.449 km/h, 81.679 mph
Pole Position speed: 143.435 km/h, 89.127 mph (N Piquet, 1 min:40.980 sec)
Fastest Lap speed: 136.358 km/h, 84.729 mph (D Warwick, 1 min:46.221 sec on lap 32)
Lap Leaders: N Piquet 1-63 (63).

*Interrupted after 1st lap accident. Restarted for original distance. * retired after first start.*
It was at this race that a water sample from M Brundle's car was found to infringe the regulations, resulting in Tyrrell's disqualification from the season.

8 Jul 1984 — USA: Dallas — (Round: 9) (Race: 397)

67 laps x 3.901 km, 2.424 miles = 261.370 km, 162.408 miles

POS.	NO.	DRIVER	CAR	MODEL	ENGINE		LAPS	TIME/REASON FOR RETIREMENT	GRID:POS	ROW
1	6	K Rosberg	Williams	FW09	Honda	V6t	67	2h 01m 22.617s	8	4
2	28	R Arnoux	Ferrari	126C4	Ferrari	V6t	67	2h 01m 45.081s	4	2
3	11	E de Angelis	Lotus	95T	Renault	V6t	66		2	1
4	5	J Laffite	Williams	FW09	Honda	V6t	65		24	12
5	24	P Ghinzani	Osella	FA1F	Alfa Romeo	V8t	65		18	9
6r	12	N Mansell	Lotus	95T	Renault	V6t	64	gearbox	1	1
7	2	C Fabi	Brabham	BT53	BMW	4t	64		11	6
8	14	M Winkelhock	ATS	D7	BMW	4t	64		13	7
9r	8	N Lauda	McLaren	MP4/2	TAG Porsche	V6t	60	accident	5	3
r	7	A Prost	McLaren	MP4/2	TAG Porsche	V6t	56	accident	7	4
r	18	T Boutsen	Arrows	A7	BMW	4t	55	accident	20	10
r	27	M Alboreto	Ferrari	126C4	Ferrari	V6t	54	accident	9	5
r	17	M Surer	Arrows	A7	BMW	4t	54	accident	22	11
r	19	A Senna	Toleman	TG184	Hart	4t	47	drive shaft	6	3
r	10	J Palmer	RAM	02	Hart	4t	46	electrics	25	13
r	1	N Piquet	Brabham	BT53	BMW	4t	45	throttle jammed/ accident	12	6
r	20	J Cecotto	Toleman	TG184	Hart	4t	25	accident	15	8
r	15	P Tambay	Renault	RE50	Renault	V6t	25	accident	10	5
r	26	A de Cesaris	Ligier	JS23	Renault	V6t	15	accident	16	8
r	21	H Rothengatter	Spirit	101	Hart	4t	15	fuel leak in cockpit	23	12
r	22	R Patrese	Alfa Romeo	184T	Alfa Romeo	V8t	12	accident	21	11
r	16	D Warwick	Renault	RE50	Renault	V6t	10	spin	3	2
dq	4	S Bellof	Tyrrell	012	Cosworth	V8	9	accident/ (1)	17	9
r	23	E Cheever	Alfa Romeo	184T	Alfa Romeo	V8t	8	accident	14	7
r	25	F Hesnault	Ligier	JS23	Renault	V6t	0	accident	19	10
ns	9	P Alliot	RAM	02	Hart	4t		accident		
nq	3	M Brundle	Tyrrell	012	Cosworth	V8		accident/ injury		

Winning speed: 129.203 km/h, 80.283 mph
Pole Position speed: 144.720 km/h, 89.925 mph (N Mansell, 1 min:37.041 sec)
Fastest Lap speed: 133.302 km/h, 82.830 mph (N Lauda, 1 min:45.353 sec on lap 22)
Lap Leaders: N Mansell 1-35 (35); K Rosberg 36-48,57-67 (24); A Prost 49-56 (8).

Scheduled for 78 laps, but stopped at 2 hours.

22 Jul 1984 BRITAIN: Brands Hatch (Round:10) (Race: 398)

71 laps x 4.207 km, 2.614 miles = 298.685 km, 185.594 miles

POS.	NO.	DRIVER	CAR	MODEL	ENGINE		LAPS	TIME/REASON FOR RETIREMENT	GRID:POS	ROW
1	8	N Lauda	McLaren	MP4/2	TAG Porsche	V6t	71	1h 29m 28.532s	3	2
2	16	D Warwick	Renault	RE50	Renault	V6t	71	1h 30m 10.655s	6	3
3	19	A Senna	Toleman	TG184	Hart	4t	71	1h 30m 31.860s	7	4
4	11	E de Angelis	Lotus	95T	Renault	V6t	70		4	2
5	27	M Alboreto	Ferrari	126C4	Ferrari	V6t	70		9	5
6	28	R Arnoux	Ferrari	126C4	Ferrari	V6t	70		13	7
7	1	N Piquet	Brabham	BT53	BMW	4t	70		1	1
8r	15	P Tambay	Renault	RE50	Renault	V6t	69	turbo	10	5
9	24	P Ghinzani	Osella	FA1F	Alfa Romeo	V8t	68		21	11
10	26	A de Cesaris	Ligier	JS23	Renault	V6t	68		19	10
dq	4	S Bellof	Tyrrell	012	Cosworth	V8	68	(1)	26	13
11	17	M Surer	Arrows	A7	BMW	4t	67		15	8
12r	22	R Patrese	Alfa Romeo	184T	Alfa Romeo	V8t	66	out of fuel	17	9
nc	21	H Rothengatter	Spirit	101	Hart	4t	62		22	11
r	25	F Hesnault	Ligier	JS23	Renault	V6t	43	electrics	20	10
r	7	A Prost	McLaren	MP4/2	TAG Porsche	V6t	37	gearbox pinion	2	1
r	12	N Mansell	Lotus	95T	Renault	V6t	24	gearbox	8	4
r	18	T Boutsen	Arrows	A7	BMW	4t	24	electrics	12	6
r	5	J Laffite	Williams	FW09B	Honda	V6t	14	water pump	16	8
r	10	J Palmer	RAM	02	Hart	4t	10	steering/ accident	23	12
r	2	T Fabi	Brabham	BT53	BMW	4t	9	electrics	14	7
r	14	M Winkelhock	ATS	D7	BMW	4t	8	spin	11	6
r	6	K Rosberg	Williams	FW09B	Honda	V6t	5	engine	5	3
r	23	E Cheever	Alfa Romeo	184T	Alfa Romeo	V8t	1	accident	18	9
dq	3	S Johansson	Tyrrell	012	Cosworth	V8	1	accident/ (1)	25	13
r	9	P Alliot	RAM	02	Hart	4t	0	accident	24	12
r	30	J Gartner	Osella	FA1F	Alfa Romeo	V8t	0	accident	27	14
nq	20	J Cecotto	Toleman	TG184	Hart	4t		accident/ injury		

Winning speed: 200.290 km/h, 124.455 mph
Pole Position speed: 213.698 km/h, 132.786 mph (N Piquet, 1 min:10.869 sec)
Fastest Lap speed: 206.918 km/h, 128.573 mph (N Lauda, 1 min:13.191 sec on lap 57)
Lap Leaders: N Piquet 1-11 (11); A Prost 12-37 (26); N Lauda 38-71 (34).

Scheduled for 75 laps, but interrupted after 11 laps, because of an accident. Restarted for a further 60 laps, with results being on aggregate. Lap leaders are given 'on the road'.

5 Aug 1984 GERMANY: Hockenheim (Round:11) (Race: 399)

44 laps x 6.797 km, 4.223 miles = 299.068 km, 185.832 miles

POS.	NO.	DRIVER	CAR	MODEL	ENGINE		LAPS	TIME/REASON FOR RETIREMENT	GRID:POS	ROW
1	7	A Prost	McLaren	MP4/2	TAG Porsche	V6t	44	1h 24m 43.210s	1	1
2	8	N Lauda	McLaren	MP4/2	TAG Porsche	V6t	44	1h 24m 46.359s	7	4
3	16	D Warwick	Renault	RE50	Renault	V6t	44	1h 25m 19.633s	3	2
4	12	N Mansell	Lotus	95T	Renault	V6t	44	1h 25m 34.873s	16	8
5	15	P Tambay	Renault	RE50	Renault	V6t	44	1h 25m 55.159s	4	2
6	28	R Arnoux	Ferrari	126C4	Ferrari	V6t	43		10	5
7	26	A de Cesaris	Ligier	JS23	Renault	V6t	43		11	6
8	25	F Hesnault	Ligier	JS23	Renault	V6t	43		17	9
dq	3	S Johansson	Tyrrell	012	Cosworth	V8	42	(1)	26	13
9	21	H Rothengatter	Spirit	101	Hart	4t	40		24	12
r	14	M Winkelhock	ATS	D7	BMW	4t	31	turbo boost pressure/gearbox	13	7
r	23	E Cheever	Alfa Romeo	184T	Alfa Romeo	V8t	29	engine	18	9
r	2	T Fabi	Brabham	BT53	BMW	4t	28	turbo boost pressure	8	4
r	1	N Piquet	Brabham	BT53	BMW	4t	23	gearbox pinion	5	3
r	22	R Patrese	Alfa Romeo	184T	Alfa Romeo	V8t	16	fuel metering unit	20	10
r	24	P Ghinzani	Osella	FA1F	Alfa Romeo	V8t	14	electrics	21	11
r	30	J Gartner	Osella	FA1F	Alfa Romeo	V8t	13	turbo	23	12
r	27	M Alboreto	Ferrari	126C4	Ferrari	V6t	13	misfire	6	3
r	10	J Palmer	RAM	02	Hart	4t	11	turbo	25	13
r	6	K Rosberg	Williams	FW09B	Honda	V6t	10	electrics	19	10
r	5	J Laffite	Williams	FW09B	Honda	V6t	10	engine	12	6
r	18	T Boutsen	Arrows	A7	BMW	4t	8	oil pressure	15	8
r	11	E de Angelis	Lotus	95T	Renault	V6t	8	turbo	2	1
r	9	P Alliot	RAM	02	Hart	4t	7	engine overheating	22	11
r	19	A Senna	Toleman	TG184	Hart	4t	4	rear wing failure/ accident	9	5
r	17	M Surer	Arrows	A7	BMW	4t	1	turbo	14	7
nq	4	M Thackwell	Tyrrell	012	Cosworth	V8				

Winning speed: 211.804 km/h, 131.609 mph
Pole Position speed: 228.658 km/h, 142.082 mph (A Prost, 1 min:47.012 sec)
Fastest Lap speed: 215.516 km/h, 133.915 mph (A Prost, 1 min:53.538 sec on lap 31)
Lap Leaders: E de Angelis 1-7 (7); N Piquet 8-21 (14); A Prost 22-44 (23).

19 Aug 1984 — AUSTRIA: Österreichring — (Round:12) (Race: 400)

51 laps x 5.942 km, 3.692 miles = 303.042 km, 188.302 miles

POS.	NO.	DRIVER	CAR	MODEL	ENGINE		LAPS	TIME/REASON FOR RETIREMENT	GRID:POS	ROW
1	8	N Lauda	McLaren	MP4/2	TAG Porsche	V6t	51	1h 21m 12.851s	4	2
2	1	N Piquet	Brabham	BT53	BMW	4t	51	1h 21m 36.376s	1	1
3	27	M Alboreto	Ferrari	126C4	Ferrari	V6t	51	1h 22m 01.849s	12	6
4	2	T Fabi	Brabham	BT53	BMW	4t	51	1h 22m 09.163s	7	4
5	18	T Boutsen	Arrows	A7	BMW	4t	50		17	9
6	17	M Surer	Arrows	A7	BMW	4t	50		19	10
7	28	R Arnoux	Ferrari	126C4	Ferrari	V6t	50		15	8
8	25	F Hesnault	Ligier	JS23	Renault	V6t	49		21	11
9	10	J Palmer	RAM	02	Hart	4t	49		24	12
10r	22	R Patrese	Alfa Romeo	184T	Alfa Romeo	V8t	48	out of fuel	13	7
11	9	P Alliot	RAM	02	Hart	4t	48		25	13
12r	31	G Berger	ATS	D7	BMW	4t	48	gearbox	20	10
r	15	P Tambay	Renault	RE50	Renault	V6t	42	engine	5	3
r	19	A Senna	Toleman	TG184	Hart	4t	35	oil pressure	10	5
r	12	N Mansell	Lotus	95T	Renault	V6t	32	engine	8	4
r	7	A Prost	McLaren	MP4/2	TAG Porsche	V6t	28	spin	2	1
r	11	E de Angelis	Lotus	95T	Renault	V6t	28	engine	3	2
nc	21	H Rothengatter	Spirit	101	Hart	4t	23		26	13
r	23	E Cheever	Alfa Romeo	184T	Alfa Romeo	V8t	18	engine	16	8
r	16	D Warwick	Renault	RE50	Renault	V6t	17	engine	6	3
r	26	A de Cesaris	Ligier	JS23	Renault	V6t	15	fuel injection	18	9
r	6	K Rosberg	Williams	FW09B	Honda	V6t	15	handling	9	5
r	5	J Laffite	Williams	FW09B	Honda	V6t	12	engine	11	6
r	30	J Gartner	Osella	FA1F	Alfa Romeo	V8t	6	engine	22	11
r	24	P Ghinzani	Osella	FA1F	Alfa Romeo	V8t	4	gearbox	23	12
ns	14	M Winkelhock	ATS	D7	BMW	4t		gearbox	14	7
nq	3	S Johansson	Tyrrell	012	Cosworth	V8				
nq	4	S Bellof	Tyrrell	012	Cosworth	V8				

Winning speed: 223.884 km/h, 139.115 mph
Pole Position speed: 248.236 km/h, 154.246 mph (N Piquet, 1 min:26.173 sec)
Fastest Lap speed: 230.305 km/h, 143.105 mph (N Lauda, 1 min:32.882 sec on lap 23)
Lap Leaders: N Piquet 1-39 (39); N Lauda 40-51 (12).

Interrupted after 1st lap, because of a mis-start. Restarted for original distance.

26 Aug 1984 — NETHERLANDS: Zandvoort — (Round:13) (Race: 401)

71 laps x 4.252 km, 2.642 miles = 301.892 km, 187.587 miles

POS.	NO.	DRIVER	CAR	MODEL	ENGINE		LAPS	TIME/REASON FOR RETIREMENT	GRID:POS	ROW
1	7	A Prost	McLaren	MP4/2	TAG Porsche	V6t	71	1h 37m 21.468s	1	1
2	8	N Lauda	McLaren	MP4/2	TAG Porsche	V6t	71	1h 37m 31.751s	6	3
3	12	N Mansell	Lotus	95T	Renault	V6t	71	1h 38m 41.012s	12	6
4	11	E de Angelis	Lotus	95T	Renault	V6t	70		3	2
5	2	T Fabi	Brabham	BT53	BMW	4t	70		10	5
6	15	P Tambay	Renault	RE50	Renault	V6t	70		5	3
7	25	F Hesnault	Ligier	JS23	Renault	V6t	69		20	10
dq	3	S Johansson	Tyrrell	012	Cosworth	V8	69	(1)	25	13
dq	4	S Bellof	Tyrrell	012	Cosworth	V8	69	(1)	24	12
8r	6	K Rosberg	Williams	FW09B	Honda	V6t	68	out of fuel	7	4
9	10	J Palmer	RAM	02	Hart	4t	67		22	11
10	9	P Alliot	RAM	02	Hart	4t	67		26	13
11r	28	R Arnoux	Ferrari	126C4	Ferrari	V6t	66	electrics	15	8
12	30	J Gartner	Osella	FA1F	Alfa Romeo	V8t	66		23	12
13r	23	E Cheever	Alfa Romeo	184T	Alfa Romeo	V8t	65	out of fuel	17	9
r	18	T Boutsen	Arrows	A7	BMW	4t	59	accident	11	6
r	21	H Rothengatter	Spirit	101	Hart	4t	53	throttle linkage	27	14
r	22	R Patrese	Alfa Romeo	184T	Alfa Romeo	V8t	51	engine	18	9
r	26	A de Cesaris	Ligier	JS23	Renault	V6t	31	engine	14	7
r	5	J Laffite	Williams	FW09B	Honda	V6t	23	engine	8	4
r	16	D Warwick	Renault	RE50	Renault	V6t	23	spin	4	2
r	14	M Winkelhock	ATS	D7	BMW	4t	22	spin	16	8
r	19	A Senna	Toleman	TG184	Hart	4t	19	engine	13	7
r	17	M Surer	Arrows	A7	BMW	4t	17	wheel bearing	19	10
r	1	N Piquet	Brabham	BT53	BMW	4t	10	oil union	2	1
r	24	P Ghinzani	Osella	FA1F	Alfa Romeo	V8t	8	fuel pump	21	11
r	27	M Alboreto	Ferrari	126C4	Ferrari	V6t	7	engine	9	5

Winning speed: 186.051 km/h, 115.607 mph
Pole Position speed: 208.072 km/h, 129.290 mph (A Prost, 1 min:13.567 sec)
Fastest Lap speed: 192.628 km/h, 119.694 mph (R Arnoux, 1 min:19.465 sec on lap 64)
Lap Leaders: N Piquet 1-10 (10); A Prost 11-71 (61).

9 Sep 1984 — ITALY: Monza (Round:14) (Race: 402)

51 laps x 5.800 km, 3.604 miles = 295.800 km, 183.802 miles

POS.	NO.	DRIVER	CAR	MODEL	ENGINE		LAPS	TIME/REASON FOR RETIREMENT	GRID:POS	ROW
1	8	N Lauda	McLaren	MP4/2	TAG Porsche	V6t	51	1h 20m 29.065s	4	2
2	27	M Alboreto	Ferrari	126C4	Ferrari	V6t	51	1h 20m 53.314s	11	6
3	22	R Patrese	Alfa Romeo	184T	Alfa Romeo	V8t	50		9	5
4	19	S Johansson	Toleman	TG184	Hart	4t	49		17	9
5	30	J Gartner	Osella	FA1F	Alfa Romeo	V8t	49		24	12
6	31	G Berger	ATS	D7	BMW	4t	49		20	10
7r	24	P Ghinzani	Osella	FA1F	Alfa Romeo	V8t	48	out of fuel	22	11
8	21	H Rothengatter	Spirit	101	Hart	4t	48		25	13
9r	23	E Cheever	Alfa Romeo	184T	Alfa Romeo	V8t	45	out of fuel	10	5
10	18	T Boutsen	Arrows	A7	BMW	4t	45		19	10
r	15	P Tambay	Renault	RE50	Renault	V6t	43	throttle linkage	8	4
r	2	T Fabi	Brabham	BT53	BMW	4t	43	oil union/ engine	5	3
r	17	M Surer	Arrows	A7	BMW	4t	43	engine	15	8
r	16	D Warwick	Renault	RE50	Renault	V6t	31	oil pressure	12	6
r	10	J Palmer	RAM	02	Hart	4t	20	oil pressure	26	13
r	1	N Piquet	Brabham	BT53	BMW	4t	15	radiator/ engine	1	1
r	11	E de Angelis	Lotus	95T	Renault	V6t	14	gearbox	3	2
r	12	N Mansell	Lotus	95T	Renault	V6t	13	spin	7	4
r	5	J Laffite	Williams	FW09B	Honda	V6t	10	turbo	13	7
r	6	K Rosberg	Williams	FW09B	Honda	V6t	8	engine	6	3
r	26	A de Cesaris	Ligier	JS23	Renault	V6t	7	engine	16	8
r	25	F Hesnault	Ligier	JS23	Renault	V6t	7	spin	18	9
r	9	P Alliot	RAM	02	Hart	4t	6	electrics	23	12
r	28	R Arnoux	Ferrari	126C4	Ferrari	V6t	5	gearbox	14	7
r	7	A Prost	McLaren	MP4/2	TAG Porsche	V6t	3	engine	2	1
r	14	M Winkelhock	ATS	D7	BMW	4t	-1	gearbox	21	11
nq	20	P Martini	Toleman	TG184	Hart	4t				

Winning speed: 220.515 km/h, 137.022 mph
Pole Position speed: 241.153 km/h, 149.846 mph (N Piquet, 1 min:26.584 sec)
Fastest Lap speed: 227.174 km/h, 141.159 mph (N Lauda, 1 min:31.912 sec on lap 42)
Lap Leaders: N Piquet 1-15 (15); P Tambay 16-42 (27); N Lauda 43-51 (9).

7 Oct 1984 — EUROPE: Nürburgring (Round:15) (Race: 403)

67 laps x 4.542 km, 2.822 miles = 304.314 km, 189.092 miles

POS.	NO.	DRIVER	CAR	MODEL	ENGINE		LAPS	TIME/REASON FOR RETIREMENT	GRID:POS	ROW
1	7	A Prost	McLaren	MP4/2	TAG Porsche	V6t	67	1h 35m 13.284s	2	1
2	27	M Alboreto	Ferrari	126C4	Ferrari	V6t	67	1h 35m 37.195s	5	3
3	1	N Piquet	Brabham	BT53	BMW	4t	67	1h 35m 38.206s	1	1
4	8	N Lauda	McLaren	MP4/2	TAG Porsche	V6t	67	1h 35m 56.370s	15	8
5	28	R Arnoux	Ferrari	126C4	Ferrari	V6t	67	1h 36m 14.714s	6	3
6	22	R Patrese	Alfa Romeo	184T	Alfa Romeo	V8t	66		9	5
7	26	A de Cesaris	Ligier	JS23	Renault	V6t	65		17	9
8	21	M Baldi	Spirit	101	Hart	4t	65		24	12
9r	18	T Boutsen	Arrows	A7	BMW	4t	64	electrics/ ignition	11	6
10	25	F Hesnault	Ligier	JS23	Renault	V6t	64		19	10
11r	16	D Warwick	Renault	RE50	Renault	V6t	61	valve/ engine overheating	7	4
12r	30	J Gartner	Osella	FA1F	Alfa Romeo	V8t	60	fuel injection	22	11
r	2	T Fabi	Brabham	BT53	BMW	4t	57	gearbox	10	5
r	12	N Mansell	Lotus	95T	Renault	V6t	51	engine	8	4
r	15	P Tambay	Renault	RE50	Renault	V6t	47	fuel injection	3	2
r	23	E Cheever	Alfa Romeo	184T	Alfa Romeo	V8t	37	fuel pump	13	7
r	9	P Alliot	RAM	02	Hart	4t	37	turbo	25	13
r	10	J Palmer	RAM	02	Hart	4t	35	turbo	21	11
r	5	J Laffite	Williams	FW09B	Honda	V6t	27	engine	14	7
r	11	E de Angelis	Lotus	95T	Renault	V6t	25	turbo	23	12
r	20	S Johansson	Toleman	TG184	Hart	4t	17	engine overheating	26	13
r	6	K Rosberg	Williams	FW09B	Honda	V6t	0	accident	4	2
r	31	G Berger	ATS	D7	BMW	4t	0	accident	18	9
r	17	M Surer	Arrows	A7	BMW	4t	0	accident	16	8
r	24	P Ghinzani	Osella	FA1F	Alfa Romeo	V8t	0	accident	20	10
r	19	A Senna	Toleman	TG184	Hart	4t	0	accident	12	6

Winning speed: 191.751 km/h, 119.149 mph
Pole Position speed: 207.316 km/h, 128.820 mph (N Piquet, 1 min:18.871 sec)
Fastest Lap speed: 196.656 km/h, 122.197 mph (M Alboreto/ N Piquet, 1 min:23.146 sec on lap 62)
Lap Leaders: A Prost 1-67 (67).

21 Oct 1984 — PORTUGAL: Estoril (Round:16) (Race: 404)

70 laps x 4.350 km, 2.703 miles = 304.500 km, 189.208 miles

POS.	NO.	DRIVER	CAR	MODEL	ENGINE		LAPS	TIME/REASON FOR RETIREMENT	GRID:POS	ROW
1	7	A Prost	McLaren	MP4/2	TAG Porsche	V6t	70	1h 41m 11.753s	2	1
2	8	N Lauda	McLaren	MP4/2	TAG Porsche	V6t	70	1h 41m 25.178s	11	6
3	19	A Senna	Toleman	TG184	Hart	4t	70	1h 41m 31.795s	3	2
4	27	M Alboreto	Ferrari	126C4	Ferrari	V6t	70	1h 41m 32.070s	8	4
5	11	E de Angelis	Lotus	95T	Renault	V6t	70	1h 42m 43.922s	5	3
6	1	N Piquet	Brabham	BT53	BMW	4t	69		1	1
7	15	P Tambay	Renault	RE50	Renault	V6t	69		7	4
8	22	R Patrese	Alfa Romeo	184T	Alfa Romeo	V8t	69		12	6
9	28	R Arnoux	Ferrari	126C4	Ferrari	V6t	69		17	9
10	2	M Winkelhock	Brabham	BT53	BMW	4t	69		19	10
11	20	S Johansson	Toleman	TG184	Hart	4t	69		10	5
12	26	A de Cesaris	Ligier	JS23	Renault	V6t	69		20	10
13	31	G Berger	ATS	D7	BMW	4t	68		23	12
14	5	J Laffite	Williams	FW09B	Honda	V6t	67		15	8
15	21	M Baldi	Spirit	101	Hart	4t	66		25	13
16r	30	J Gartner	Osella	FA1F	Alfa Romeo	V8t	65	out of fuel	24	12
17	23	E Cheever	Alfa Romeo	184T	Alfa Romeo	V8t	64		14	7
r	24	P Ghinzani	Osella	FA1F	Alfa Romeo	V8t	60	engine	22	11
r	12	N Mansell	Lotus	95T	Renault	V6t	52	brake fluid loss/ spin	6	3
r	16	D Warwick	Renault	RE50	Renault	V6t	51	gearbox	9	5
r	33	P Streiff	Renault	RE50	Renault	V6t	48	drive shaft	13	7
r	6	K Rosberg	Williams	FW09B	Honda	V6t	39	engine	4	2
r	25	F Hesnault	Ligier	JS23	Renault	V6t	31	electrics	21	11
r	18	T Boutsen	Arrows	A7	BMW	4t	24	drive shaft	18	9
r	10	J Palmer	RAM	02	Hart	4t	19	gearbox	26	13
r	17	M Surer	Arrows	A7	BMW	4t	8	electrics	16	8
r	9	P Alliot	RAM	02	Hart	4t	2	engine	27	14

Winning speed: 180.541 km/h, 112.183 mph
Pole Position speed: 191.670 km/h, 119.098 mph (N Piquet, 1 min:21.703 sec)
Fastest Lap speed: 188.684 km/h, 117.243 mph (N Lauda, 1 min:22.996 sec on lap 51)
Lap Leaders: K Rosberg 1-8 (8); A Prost 9-70 (62).

Lap Leaders 1984

POS	DRIVER	CAR-ENGINE	GPS	LAPS	KM	MILES
1	A Prost	McLaren-TAG Porsche	9	345	1,579.2	981.3
2	N Piquet	Brabham-BMW	8	241	1,142.8	710.1
3	N Lauda	McLaren-TAG Porsche	6	166	739.7	459.6
4	M Alboreto	Ferrari	2	81	353.7	219.8
5	P Tambay	Renault	2	76	347.1	215.7
6	N Mansell	Lotus-Renault	2	40	153.1	95.1
7	K Rosberg	Williams-Honda	3	33	132.5	82.3
8	D Warwick	Renault	1	12	60.4	37.5
9	E de Angelis	Lotus-Renault	1	7	47.6	29.6
			16	**1,001**	**4,556.0**	**2,831.0**

Driver Points 1984

		BR	ZA	B	RSM	F	MC	CDN	DET	DAL	GB	D	A	NL	I	EUR	P	TOTAL	
1	N Lauda	-	9	-	-	9	-	6	-	-	9	6	9	6	9	3	6	72	
2	A Prost	9	6	-	9	-	4.5	4	3	-	-	9	-	9	-	9	9	71.5	
3	E de Angelis	4	-	2	4	2	1	3	6	4	3	-	-	3	-	-	2	34	
4	M Alboreto	-	-	9	-	-	0.5	-	-	-	2	-	4	-	6	6	3	30.5	
5	N Piquet	-	-	-	-	-	-	9	9	-	-	-	6	-	-	4	1	29	
6	R Arnoux	-	-	4	6	3	2	2	-	6	1	1	-	-	-	2	-	27	
7	D Warwick	-	4	6	3	-	-	-	-	-	6	4	-	-	-	-	-	23	
8	K Rosberg	6	-	3	-	1	1.5	-	-	9	-	-	-	-	-	-	-	20.5	
9	N Mansell	-	-	-	-	4	-	1	-	1	-	3	-	4	-	-	-	13	
	A Senna	-	1	1	-	-	3	-	-	-	4	-	-	-	-	-	4	13	
11	P Tambay	2	-	-	-	6	-	-	-	-	-	2	-	1	-	-	-	11	
12	T Fabi	-	-	-	-	-	-	-	4	-	-	-	3	2	-	-	-	9	
13	R Patrese	-	3	-	-	-	-	-	-	-	-	-	-	-	4	1	-	8	
14	J Laffite	-	-	-	-	-	-	-	2	3	-	-	-	-	-	-	-	5	
	T Boutsen	1	-	-	2	-	-	-	-	-	-	-	2	-	-	-	-	5	
16	E Cheever	3	-	-	-	-	-	-	-	-	-	-	-	-	-	-	-	3	
	S Johansson	-	-	-	-	-	-	-	-	-	-	-	-	-	3	-	-	3	
	A de Cesaris	-	2	-	1	-	-	-	-	-	-	-	-	-	-	-	-	3	
19	P Ghinzani	-	-	-	-	-	-	-	-	2	-	-	-	-	-	-	-	2	
20	M Surer	-	-	-	-	-	-	-	-	-	-	-	1	-	-	-	-	1	
21	J Gartner	-	-	-	-	-	-	-	-	-	-	-	-	-	(2)	-	-	-	(2)
	G Berger	-	-	-	-	-	-	-	-	-	-	-	-	-	(1)	-	-	-	(1)

9, 6, 4, 3,2 and 1 point awarded to the first six finishers. Best 11 scores. Half points awarded in Monaco where race was stopped early. J Gartner (Osella-Alfa Romeo) andG Berger (ATS-BMW) finished 5th and 6th respectively in Italy, but points not valid for Championship because these Constructors had only entered one car for the season. All points scored by Tyrrell were redistributed due infringing the rules. Points originally scored were Brundle 8, Bellof, 7, Tyrrell-Cosworth 15.

Constructor Points 1984

		BR	ZA	B	RSM	F	MC	CDN	DET	DAL	GB	D	A	NL	I	EUR	P	TOTAL	
1	McLaren-TAG Porsche	9	15	-	9	9	4.5	10	3	-	9	15	9	15	9	12	15	143.5	
2	Ferrari	-	-	13	6	3	2.5	2	-	6	3	1	4	-	6	8	3	57.5	
3	Lotus-Renault	4	-	2	4	6	1	4	6	5	3	3	-	7	-	-	2	47	
4	Brabham-BMW	-	-	-	-	-	-	9	13	-	-	-	9	2	-	4	1	38	
5	Renault	2	4	6	3	6	-	-	-	-	6	6	-	1	-	-	-	34	
6	Williams-Honda	6	-	3	-	1	1.5	-	2	12	-	-	-	-	-	-	-	25.5	
7	Toleman-Hart	-	1	1	-	-	3	-	-	-	4	-	-	-	3	-	4	16	
8	Alfa Romeo	3	3	-	-	-	-	-	-	-	-	-	-	-	4	1	-	11	
9	Arrows-BMW	-	-	-	-	-	-	-	-	-	-	-	3	-	-	-	-	3	
	Ligier-Renault	-	2	-	1	-	-	-	-	-	-	-	-	-	-	-	-	3	
	Arrows-Cosworth	1	-	-	2	-	-	-	-	-	-	-	-	-	-	-	-	3	
12	Osella-Alfa Romeo	-	-	-	-	-	-	-	-	2	-	-	-	-	(2)	-	-	2	(2)
13	ATS-BMW	-	-	-	-	-	-	-	-	-	-	-	-	-	(1)	-	-	-	(1)

9, 6, 4, 3, 2 and 1 point awarded to the first six finishers.

Michelin withdrew at the end of 1984. McLaren merged with the TAG group. The ever increasing power from the turbo brigade, at the time, appeared to signal the end of the most successful Formula 1 engine: the Cosworth V8. At season's end, Renault announced its intentions to withdraw.

McLAREN
Marlboro McLaren International: Lauda, Watson, Prost

TYRRELL
Tyrrell Racing Organisation: Brundle, Johansson, Bellof, Capelli, Streiff

WILLIAMS
Canon Williams Team: Mansell, Rosberg

BRABHAM
Motor Racing Developments: Piquet, Hesnault, Surer

RAM
Skoal Bandit Formula 1 Team: Winkelhock, Acheson, Alliot

LOTUS
John Player Special Team Lotus: de Angelis, Senna

RENAULT
Equipe Renault Elf: Tambay, Warwick, Hesnault

ARROWS
Barclay Arrows BMW: Berger, Boutsen

TOLEMAN
Toleman Group Motorsport: Fabi, Ghinzani

SPIRIT
Spirit Enterprises Ltd: Baldi

ALFA ROMEO
Benetton Team Alfa Romeo: Patrese, Cheever

OSELLA
Osella Squadra Corse: Ghinzani, /Rothengatter

LIGIER
Equipe Ligier Gitanes: de Cesaris, Streiff, Laffite

FERRARI
Scuderia Ferrari SpA SEFAC: Alboreto, Arnoux, Johansson

MINARDI
Minardi Team: Martini

ZAKSPEED
West Zakspeed Racing: Palmer, Danner

LOLA
Team Haas (USA) Ltd: Jones

7 Apr 1985 BRAZIL: Rio de Janeiro (Round: 1) (Race: 405)
61 laps x 5.031 km, 3.126 miles = 306.891 km, 190.693 miles

POS.	NO.	DRIVER	CAR	MODEL	ENGINE		LAPS	TIME/REASON FOR RETIREMENT	GRID:POS	ROW
1	2	A Prost	McLaren	MP4/2B	TAG Porsche	V6t	61	1h 41m 26.115s	6	3
2	27	M Alboreto	Ferrari	156/85	Ferrari	V6t	61	1h 41m 29.374s	1	1
3	11	E de Angelis	Lotus	97T	Renault	V6t	60		3	2
4	28	R Arnoux	Ferrari	156/85	Ferrari	V6t	59		7	4
5	15	P Tambay	Renault	RE60	Renault	V6t	59		11	6
6	26	J Laffite	Ligier	JS25	Renault	V6t	59		15	8
7	4	S Johansson	Tyrrell	012	Cosworth	V8	58		23	12
8	3	M Brundle	Tyrrell	012	Cosworth	V8	58		21	11
9	10	P Alliot	RAM	03	Hart	4t	58		20	10
10	16	D Warwick	Renault	RE60	Renault	V6t	57		10	5
11	18	T Boutsen	Arrows	A8	BMW	4t	57		12	6
12	24	P Ghinzani	Osella	FA1F	Alfa Romeo	V8t	57		22	11
13	9	M Winkelhock	RAM	03	Hart	4t	57		16	8
r	17	G Berger	Arrows	A8	BMW	4t	51	suspension	19	10
r	12	A Senna	Lotus	97T	Renault	V6t	48	electrics	4	2
r	23	E Cheever	Alfa Romeo	185T	Alfa Romeo	V8t	42	engine	18	9
r	29	P Martini	Minardi	M185	Cosworth	V8	41	engine	25	13
r	1	N Lauda	McLaren	MP4/2B	TAG Porsche	V6t	27	fuel metering unit	9	5
r	25	A de Cesaris	Ligier	JS25	Renault	V6t	26	accident damage	13	7
r	22	R Patrese	Alfa Romeo	185T	Alfa Romeo	V8t	20	puncture	14	7
r	6	K Rosberg	Williams	FW10	Honda	V6t	10	turbo	2	1
r	8	F Hesnault	Brabham	BT54	BMW	4t	9	accident damage	17	9
r	5	N Mansell	Williams	FW10	Honda	V6t	8	accident/ exhaust	5	3
r	21	M Baldi	Spirit	101D	Hart	4t	7	turbo/ misfire	24	12
r	7	N Piquet	Brabham	BT54	BMW	4t	2	accident	8	4

Winning speed: 181.529 km/h, 112.797 mph
Pole Position speed: 206.358 km/h, 128.225 mph (M Alboreto, 1 min:27.768 sec)
Fastest Lap speed: 187.293 km/h, 116.378 mph (A Prost, 1 min:36.702 sec on lap 34)
Lap Leaders: K Rosberg 1-9 (9); M Alboreto 10-17 (8); A Prost 18-61 (44).

21 Apr 1985 PORTUGAL: Estoril (Round: 2) (Race: 406)
67 laps x 4.350 km, 2.703 miles = 291.450 km, 181.099 miles

POS.	NO.	DRIVER	CAR	MODEL	ENGINE		LAPS	TIME/REASON FOR RETIREMENT	GRID:POS	ROW
1	12	A Senna	Lotus	97T	Renault	V6t	67	2h 00m 28.006s	1	1
2	27	M Alboreto	Ferrari	156/85	Ferrari	V6t	67	2h 01m 30.984s	5	3
3	15	P Tambay	Renault	RE60	Renault	V6t	66		12	6
4	11	E de Angelis	Lotus	97T	Renault	V6t	66		4	2
5	5	N Mansell	Williams	FW10	Honda	V6t	65		9	5
6	4	S Bellof	Tyrrell	012	Cosworth	V8	65		21	11
7	16	D Warwick	Renault	RE60	Renault	V6t	65		6	3
8	28	S Johansson	Ferrari	156/85	Ferrari	V6t	62		11	6
9	24	P Ghinzani	Osella	FA1F	Alfa Romeo	V8t	61		26	13
nc	9	M Winkelhock	RAM	03	Hart	4t	50		15	8
r	1	N Lauda	McLaren	MP4/2B	TAG Porsche	V6t	49	piston	7	4
r	23	E Cheever	Alfa Romeo	185T	Alfa Romeo	V8t	36	misfire	14	7
r	2	A Prost	McLaren	MP4/2B	TAG Porsche	V6t	30	spin	2	1
r	25	A de Cesaris	Ligier	JS25	Renault	V6t	29	tyres/ handling	8	4
r	18	T Boutsen	Arrows	A8	BMW	4t	28	electrics	16	8
r	7	N Piquet	Brabham	BT54	BMW	4t	28	tyres/ handling	10	5
r	3	M Brundle	Tyrrell	012	Cosworth	V8	20	gear linkage	22	11
r	21	M Baldi	Spirit	101D	Hart	4t	19	spin	24	12
r	6	K Rosberg	Williams	FW10	Honda	V6t	16	spin	3	2

POS.	NO.	DRIVER	CAR	MODEL	ENGINE		LAPS	TIME/REASON FOR RETIREMENT	GRID:POS	ROW
r	26	J Laffite	Ligier	JS25	Renault	V6t	15	tyres/ handling	18	9
r	17	G Berger	Arrows	A8	BMW	4t	12	spin	17	9
r	29	P Martini	Minardi	M185	Cosworth	V8	12	spin	25	13
r	22	R Patrese	Alfa Romeo	185T	Alfa Romeo	V8t	4	spin	13	7
r	10	P Alliot	RAM	03	Hart	4t	3	spin	20	10
r	8	F Hesnault	Brabham	BT54	BMW	4t	3	electrics	19	10
r	30	J Palmer	Zakspeed	841	Zakspeed	4t	2	accident/ front suspension	23	12

Winning speed: 145.160 km/h, 90.198 mph
Pole Position speed: 193.317 km/h, 120.121 mph (A Senna, 1 min:21.007 sec)
Fastest Lap speed: 150.402 km/h, 93.455 mph (A Senna, 1 min:44.121 sec on lap 15)
Lap Leaders: A Senna 1-67 (67).

Scheduled for 69 laps, but stopped at 2 hours.

5 May 1985 — SAN MARINO: Imola — (Round: 3) (Race: 407)

60 laps x 5.040 km, 3.132 miles = 302.400 km, 187.903 miles

POS.	NO.	DRIVER	CAR	MODEL	ENGINE		LAPS	TIME/REASON FOR RETIREMENT	GRID:POS	ROW
dq	2	A Prost	McLaren	MP4/2B	TAG Porsche	V6t	60	car under weight	6	3
1	11	E de Angelis	Lotus	97T	Renault	V6t	60	1h 34m 35.955s	3	2
2	18	T Boutsen	Arrows	A8	BMW	4t	59		5	3
3	15	P Tambay	Renault	RE60	Renault	V6t	59		11	6
4	1	N Lauda	McLaren	MP4/2B	TAG Porsche	V6t	59		8	4
5	5	N Mansell	Williams	FW10	Honda	V6t	58		7	4
6r	28	S Johansson	Ferrari	156/85	Ferrari	V6t	57	out of fuel	15	8
7r	12	A Senna	Lotus	97T	Renault	V6t	57	out of fuel	1	1
8r	7	N Piquet	Brabham	BT54	BMW	4t	57	out of fuel	9	5
9	3	M Brundle	Tyrrell	012	Cosworth	V8	56		25	13
10	16	D Warwick	Renault	RE60	Renault	V6t	56		14	7
r	23	E Cheever	Alfa Romeo	185T	Alfa Romeo	V8t	50	engine	12	6
nc	24	P Ghinzani	Osella	FA1G	Alfa Romeo	V8t	46		22	11
r	27	M Alboreto	Ferrari	156/85	Ferrari	V6t	29	electrics	4	2
r	9	M Winkelhock	RAM	03	Hart	4t	27	engine	23	12
r	10	P Alliot	RAM	03	Hart	4t	24	turbo	21	11
r	6	K Rosberg	Williams	FW10	Honda	V6t	23	throttle linkage/ brakes	2	1
r	26	J Laffite	Ligier	JS25	Renault	V6t	22	turbo	16	8
r	29	P Martini	Minardi	M185	Motori Moderni	V6t	14	turbo	19	10
r	25	A de Cesaris	Ligier	JS25	Renault	V6t	11	spin	13	7
r	21	M Baldi	Spirit	101D	Hart	4t	9	electrics	26	13
r	8	F Hesnault	Brabham	BT54	BMW	4t	5	engine	20	10
r	4	S Bellof	Tyrrell	012	Cosworth	V8	5	engine	24	12
r	17	G Berger	Arrows	A8	BMW	4t	4	electrics	10	5
r	22	R Patrese	Alfa Romeo	185T	Alfa Romeo	V8t	4	turbo	18	9
r	30	J Palmer	Zakspeed	841	Zakspeed	4t	-1	misfire	17	9

Winning speed: 191.799 km/h, 119.178 mph
Pole Position speed: 207.771 km/h, 129.103 mph (A Senna, 1 min:27.327 sec)
Fastest Lap speed: 199.470 km/h, 123.945 mph (M Alboreto, 1 min:30.961 sec on lap 29)
Lap Leaders: A Senna 1-56 (56); S Johansson 57 (1); A Prost 58-60 (3).

A Prost finished 1st in 1h 33m 57.118s (193.120 km/h, 119.999 mph).

19 May 1985 — MONACO: Monte Carlo — (Round: 4) (Race: 408)

78 laps x 3.312 km, 2.058 miles = 258.336 km, 160.523 miles

POS.	NO.	DRIVER	CAR	MODEL	ENGINE		LAPS	TIME/REASON FOR RETIREMENT	GRID:POS	ROW
1	2	A Prost	McLaren	MP4/2B	TAG Porsche	V6t	78	1h 51m 58.034s	5	3
2	27	M Alboreto	Ferrari	156/85	Ferrari	V6t	78	1h 52m 05.575s	3	2
3	11	E de Angelis	Lotus	97T	Renault	V6t	78	1h 53m 25.205s	9	5
4	25	A de Cesaris	Ligier	JS25	Renault	V6t	77		8	4
5	16	D Warwick	Renault	RE60	Renault	V6t	77		10	5
6	26	J Laffite	Ligier	JS25	Renault	V6t	77		16	8
7	5	N Mansell	Williams	FW10	Honda	V6t	77		2	1
8	6	K Rosberg	Williams	FW10	Honda	V6t	76		7	4
9	18	T Boutsen	Arrows	A8	BMW	4t	76		6	3
10	3	M Brundle	Tyrrell	012	Cosworth	V8	74		18	9
11	30	J Palmer	Zakspeed	841	Zakspeed	4t	74		19	10
r	1	N Lauda	McLaren	MP4/2B	TAG Porsche	V6t	17	spin	14	7
r	22	R Patrese	Alfa Romeo	185T	Alfa Romeo	V8t	16	accident	12	6
r	7	N Piquet	Brabham	BT54	BMW	4t	16	accident	13	7
r	19	T Fabi	Toleman	TG185	Hart	4t	16	turbo	20	10
r	12	A Senna	Lotus	97T	Renault	V6t	13	engine	1	1
r	23	E Cheever	Alfa Romeo	185T	Alfa Romeo	V8t	10	alternator	4	2
r	28	S Johansson	Ferrari	156/85	Ferrari	V6t	1	accident/ rear suspension	15	8
r	15	P Tambay	Renault	RE60	Renault	V6t	0	accident	17	9
r	17	G Berger	Arrows	A8	BMW	4t	0	accident	11	6
nq	24	P Ghinzani	Osella	FA1G	Alfa Romeo	V8t				
nq	4	S Bellof	Tyrrell	012	Cosworth	V8				
nq	10	P Alliot	RAM	03	Hart	4t				
nq	9	M Winkelhock	RAM	03	Hart	4t				
nq	8	F Hesnault	Brabham	BT54	BMW	4t				
nq	29	P Martini	Minardi	M185	Motori Moderni	V6t		accident/ injury		

Winning speed: 138.435 km/h, 86.019 mph
Pole Position speed: 148.206 km/h, 92.091 mph (A Senna, 1 min:20.450 sec)
Fastest Lap speed: 144.284 km/h, 89.654 mph (M Alboreto, 1 min:22.637 sec on lap 60)
Lap Leaders: A Senna 1-13 (13); M Alboreto 14-17,24-31 (12); A Prost 18-23,32-78 (53).

16 Jun 1985 — CANADA: Montréal (Round: 5) (Race: 409)

70 laps x 4.410 km, 2.740 miles = 308.700 km, 191.817 miles

POS.	NO.	DRIVER	CAR	MODEL	ENGINE		LAPS	TIME/REASON FOR RETIREMENT	GRID:POS	ROW
1	27	M Alboreto	Ferrari	156/85	Ferrari	V6t	70	1h 46m 01.813s	3	2
2	28	S Johansson	Ferrari	156/85	Ferrari	V6t	70	1h 46m 03.770s	4	2
3	2	A Prost	McLaren	MP4/2B	TAG Porsche	V6t	70	1h 46m 06.154s	5	3
4	6	K Rosberg	Williams	FW10	Honda	V6t	70	1h 46m 29.634s	8	4
5	11	E de Angelis	Lotus	97T	Renault	V6t	70	1h 46m 45.162s	1	1
6	5	N Mansell	Williams	FW10	Honda	V6t	70	1h 47m 19.691s	16	8
7	15	P Tambay	Renault	RE60	Renault	V6t	69		10	5
8	26	J Laffite *	Ligier	JS25	Renault	V6t	69		19	10
9	18	T Boutsen	Arrows	A8	BMW	4t	68		7	4
10	22	R Patrese	Alfa Romeo	185T	Alfa Romeo	V8t	68		13	7
11	4	S Bellof	Tyrrell	012	Cosworth	V8	68		23	12
12	3	M Brundle	Tyrrell	012	Cosworth	V8	68		24	12
13	17	G Berger	Arrows	A8	BMW	4t	67		12	6
14	25	A de Cesaris	Ligier	JS25	Renault	V6t	67		15	8
15	8	M Surer	Brabham	BT54	BMW	4t	67		20	10
16	12	A Senna	Lotus	97T	Renault	V6t	65		2	1
17	23	E Cheever	Alfa Romeo	185T	Alfa Romeo	V8t	64		11	6
r	29	P Martini	Minardi	M185	Motori Moderni	V6t	57	accident	25	13
r	1	N Lauda	McLaren	MP4/2B	TAG Porsche	V6t	37	engine	17	9
r	24	P Ghinzani	Osella	FA1G	Alfa Romeo	V8t	35	engine	22	11
r	10	P Alliot	RAM	03	Hart	4t	28	accident	21	11
r	16	D Warwick	Renault	RE60	Renault	V6t	25	accident	6	3
r	9	M Winkelhock	RAM	03	Hart	4t	5	accident	14	7
r	19	T Fabi	Toleman	TG185	Hart	4t	3	turbo	18	9
r	7	N Piquet	Brabham	BT54	BMW	4t	0	transmission	9	5

Winning speed: 174.686 km/h, 108.545 mph
Pole Position speed: 187.733 km/h, 116.652 mph (E de Angelis, 1 min:24.567 sec)
Fastest Lap speed: 181.554 km/h, 112.812 mph (A Senna, 1 min:27.445 sec on lap 45)
Lap Leaders: E de Angelis 1-15 (15); M Alboreto 16-70 (55).

** includes 1 minute penalty for jumping the start.*

23 Jun 1985 — USA: Detroit (Round: 6) (Race: 410)

63 laps x 4.023 km, 2.500 miles = 253.472 km, 157.500 miles

POS.	NO.	DRIVER	CAR	MODEL	ENGINE		LAPS	TIME/REASON FOR RETIREMENT	GRID:POS	ROW
1	6	K Rosberg	Williams	FW10	Honda	V6t	63	1h 55m 39.851s	5	3
2	28	S Johansson	Ferrari	156/85	Ferrari	V6t	63	1h 56m 37.400s	9	5
3	27	M Alboreto	Ferrari	156/85	Ferrari	V6t	63	1h 56m 43.021s	3	2
4	4	S Bellof	Tyrrell	012	Cosworth	V8	63	1h 56m 46.076s	19	10
5	11	E de Angelis	Lotus	97T	Renault	V6t	63	1h 57m 06.817s	8	4
6	7	N Piquet	Brabham	BT54	BMW	4t	62		10	5
7	18	T Boutsen	Arrows	A8	BMW	4t	62		21	11
8	8	M Surer	Brabham	BT54	BMW	4t	62		11	6
9	23	E Cheever	Alfa Romeo	185T	Alfa Romeo	V8t	61		7	4
10	25	A de Cesaris	Ligier	JS25	Renault	V6t	61		17	9
11	17	G Berger	Arrows	A8	BMW	4t	60		24	12
12	26	J Laffite	Ligier	JS25	Renault	V6t	58		16	8
r	12	A Senna	Lotus	97T	Renault	V6t	51	accident	1	1
r	3	M Brundle	Tyrrell	012	Cosworth	V8	30	accident	18	9
r	10	P Alliot	RAM	03	Hart	4t	27	accident	23	12
r	5	N Mansell	Williams	FW10	Honda	V6t	26	accident	2	1
r	2	A Prost	McLaren	MP4/2B	TAG Porsche	V6t	19	brakes/ accident	4	2
r	22	R Patrese	Alfa Romeo	185T	Alfa Romeo	V8t	19	electrics	14	7
r	16	D Warwick	Renault	RE60	Renault	V6t	18	transmission	6	3
r	15	P Tambay	Renault	RE60	Renault	V6t	15	accident	15	8
r	29	P Martini	Minardi	M185	Motori Moderni	V6t	11	turbo	25	13
r	1	N Lauda	McLaren	MP4/2B	TAG Porsche	V6t	10	brakes	12	6
r	19	T Fabi	Toleman	TG185	Hart	4t	4	clutch	13	7
r	9	M Winkelhock	RAM	03	Hart	4t	3	turbo	20	10
r	24	P Ghinzani	Osella	FA1G	Alfa Romeo	V8t	0	accident	22	11

Winning speed: 131.487 km/h, 81.702 mph
Pole Position speed: 141.930 km/h, 88.191 mph (A Senna, 1 min:42.051 sec)
Fastest Lap speed: 137.144 km/h, 85.218 mph (A Senna, 1 min:45.612 sec on lap 51)
Lap Leaders: A Senna 1-7 (7); K Rosberg 8-63 (56).

7 Jul 1985 — FRANCE: Paul Ricard (Round: 7) (Race: 411)

53 laps x 5.810 km, 3.610 miles = 307.930 km, 191.339 miles

POS.	NO.	DRIVER	CAR	MODEL	ENGINE		LAPS	TIME/REASON FOR RETIREMENT	GRID:POS	ROW
1	7	N Piquet	Brabham	BT54	BMW	4t	53	1h 31m 46.266s	5	3
2	6	K Rosberg	Williams	FW10	Honda	V6t	53	1h 31m 52.926s	1	1
3	2	A Prost	McLaren	MP4/2B	TAG Porsche	V6t	53	1h 31m 55.551s	4	2
4	28	S Johansson	Ferrari	156/85	Ferrari	V6t	53	1h 32m 39.757s	15	8
5	11	E de Angelis	Lotus	97T	Renault	V6t	53	1h 32m 39.956s	7	4
6	15	P Tambay	Renault	RE60B	Renault	V6t	53	1h 33m 01.433s	9	5
7	16	D Warwick	Renault	RE60	Renault	V6t	53	1h 33m 30.478s	10	5
8	8	M Surer	Brabham	BT54	BMW	4t	52		13	7
9	18	T Boutsen	Arrows	A8	BMW	4t	52		11	6

POS.	NO.	DRIVER	CAR	MODEL	ENGINE		LAPS	TIME/REASON FOR RETIREMENT	GRID:POS	ROW
10	23	E Cheever	Alfa Romeo	185T	Alfa Romeo	V8t	52		17	9
11	22	R Patrese	Alfa Romeo	185T	Alfa Romeo	V8t	52		16	8
12	9	M Winkelhock	RAM	03	Hart	4t	50		19	10
13	4	S Bellof	Tyrrell	012	Cosworth	V8	50		25	13
14r	19	T Fabi	Toleman	TG185	Hart	4t	49	fuel pressure	18	9
15	24	P Ghinzani	Osella	FA1G	Alfa Romeo	V8t	49		23	12
r	3	M Brundle	Tyrrell	014	Renault	V6t	32	gearbox	20	10
r	1	N Lauda	McLaren	MP4/2B	TAG Porsche	V6t	30	gearbox	6	3
r	12	A Senna	Lotus	97T	Renault	V6t	26	engine/ accident	2	1
r	17	G Berger	Arrows	A8	BMW	4t	20	accident	8	4
r	29	P Martini	Minardi	M185	Motori Moderni	V6t	19	accident	24	12
r	10	P Alliot	RAM	03	Hart	4t	8	fuel pressure	22	11
r	30	J Palmer	Zakspeed	841	Zakspeed	4t	6	engine	21	11
r	27	M Alboreto	Ferrari	156/85	Ferrari	V6t	5	turbo	3	2
r	25	A de Cesaris	Ligier	JS25	Renault	V6t	4	drive shaft	12	6
r	26	J Laffite	Ligier	JS25	Renault	V6t	2	turbo	14	7
ns	5	N Mansell	Williams	FW10	Honda	V6t		accident/ injury		

Winning speed: 201.325 km/h, 125.097 mph
Pole Position speed: 226.212 km/h, 140.562 mph (K Rosberg, 1 min:32.462 sec)
Fastest Lap speed: 209.340 km/h, 130.078 mph (K Rosberg, 1 min:39.914 sec on lap 46)
Lap Leaders: K Rosberg 1-10 (10); N Piquet 11-53 (43).

21 Jul 1985 — BRITAIN: Silverstone (Round: 8) (Race: 412)

65 laps x 4.719 km, 2.932 miles = 306.709 km, 190.580 miles

POS.	NO.	DRIVER	CAR	MODEL	ENGINE		LAPS	TIME/REASON FOR RETIREMENT	GRID:POS	ROW
1	2	A Prost	McLaren	MP4/2B	TAG Porsche	V6t	65	1h 18m 10.436s	3	2
2	27	M Alboreto	Ferrari	156/85	Ferrari	V6t	64		6	3
3	26	J Laffite	Ligier	JS25	Renault	V6t	64		16	8
4	7	N Piquet	Brabham	BT54	BMW	4t	64		2	1
5	16	D Warwick	Renault	RE60B	Renault	V6t	64		12	6
6	8	M Surer	Brabham	BT54	BMW	4t	63		15	8
7	3	M Brundle	Tyrrell	014	Renault	V6t	63		20	10
8	17	G Berger	Arrows	A8	BMW	4t	63		17	9
9	22	R Patrese	Alfa Romeo	185T	Alfa Romeo	V8t	62		14	7
10r	12	A Senna	Lotus	97T	Renault	V6t	60	fuel injection	4	2
11	4	S Bellof	Tyrrell	012	Cosworth	V8	59		26	13
r	1	N Lauda	McLaren	MP4/2B	TAG Porsche	V6t	57	electrics	10	5
r	18	T Boutsen	Arrows	A8	BMW	4t	57	spin	19	10
r	25	A de Cesaris	Ligier	JS25	Renault	V6t	41	clutch	7	4
r	29	P Martini	Minardi	M185	Motori Moderni	V6t	38	transmission	23	12
nc	11	E de Angelis	Lotus	97T	Renault	V6t	37		8	4
r	9	M Winkelhock	RAM	03	Hart	4t	28	turbo	18	9
r	6	K Rosberg	Williams	FW10	Honda	V6t	21	exhaust	1	1
r	5	N Mansell	Williams	FW10	Honda	V6t	17	clutch	5	3
r	23	E Cheever	Alfa Romeo	185T	Alfa Romeo	V8t	17	turbo	22	11
r	30	J Palmer	Zakspeed	841	Zakspeed	4t	6	camshaft drive pinion	24	12
r	19	T Fabi	Toleman	TG185	Hart	4t	4	crown wheel & pinion	9	5
r	28	S Johansson	Ferrari	156/85	Ferrari	V6t	1	accident/ intercooler	11	6
r	15	P Tambay	Renault	RE60B	Renault	V6t	0	accident	13	7
r	10	P Alliot	RAM	03	Hart	4t	0	accident	21	11
r	24	P Ghinzani	Osella	FA1G	Alfa Romeo	V8t	0	accident	25	13

Winning speed: 235.405 km/h, 146.274 mph
Pole Position speed: 258.983 km/h, 160.925 mph (K Rosberg, 1 min: 5.591 sec)
Fastest Lap speed: 243.067 km/h, 151.035 mph (A Prost, 1 min: 9.886 sec on lap 43)
Lap Leaders: A Senna 1-57,59 (58); A Prost 58,60-65 (7).

Scheduled for 66 laps, but stopped 1 lap early in error.

4 Aug 1985 — GERMANY: Nürburgring (Round: 9) (Race: 413)

67 laps x 4.542 km, 2.822 miles = 304.314 km, 189.092 miles

POS.	NO.	DRIVER	CAR	MODEL	ENGINE		LAPS	TIME/REASON FOR RETIREMENT	GRID:POS	ROW
1	27	M Alboreto	Ferrari	156/85	Ferrari	V6t	67	1h 35m 31.337s	8	4
2	2	A Prost	McLaren	MP4/2B	TAG Porsche	V6t	67	1h 35m 42.998s	3	2
3	26	J Laffite	Ligier	JS25	Renault	V6t	67	1h 36m 22.491s	13	7
4	18	T Boutsen	Arrows	A8	BMW	4t	67	1h 36m 26.616s	15	8
5	1	N Lauda	McLaren	MP4/2B	TAG Porsche	V6t	67	1h 36m 45.309s	12	6
6	5	N Mansell	Williams	FW10	Honda	V6t	67	1h 36m 48.157s	10	5
7	17	G Berger	Arrows	A8	BMW	4t	66		17	9
8	3	S Bellof	Tyrrell	014	Renault	V6t	66		19	10
9	28	S Johansson	Ferrari	156/85	Ferrari	V6t	66		2	1
10	4	M Brundle	Tyrrell	012	Cosworth	V8	63		26	13
11r	29	P Martini	Minardi	M185	Motori Moderni	V6t	62	engine	27	14
12r	6	K Rosberg	Williams	FW10	Honda	V6t	61	brake caliper	4	2
r	23	E Cheever	Alfa Romeo	184T	Alfa Romeo	V8t	45	turbo	18	9
r	11	E de Angelis	Lotus	97T	Renault	V6t	40	engine	7	4
r	24	H Rothengatter	Osella	FA1G	Alfa Romeo	V8t	32	gearbox	25	13
r	19	T Fabi	Toleman	TG185	Hart	4t	29	clutch	1	1
r	12	A Senna	Lotus	97T	Renault	V6t	27	cv joint	5	3
r	16	D Warwick	Renault	RE60B	Renault	V6t	25	ignition	20	10
r	7	N Piquet	Brabham	BT54	BMW	4t	23	turbo	6	3
r	15	P Tambay	Renault	RE60B	Renault	V6t	19	spin	16	8
r	8	M Surer	Brabham	BT54	BMW	4t	15	engine	11	6

POS.	NO.	DRIVER	CAR	MODEL	ENGINE		LAPS	TIME/REASON FOR RETIREMENT	GRID:POS	ROW
r	9	M Winkelhock	RAM	03	Hart	4t	8	engine	22	11
r	22	R Patrese	Alfa Romeo	184T	Alfa Romeo	V8t	8	gearbox	9	5
r	14	F Hesnault	Renault	RE60	Renault	V6t	8	clutch	23	12
r	10	P Alliot	RAM	03	Hart	4t	8	oil pressure	21	11
r	30	J Palmer	Zakspeed	841	Zakspeed	4t	7	alternator belt	24	12
r	25	A de Cesaris	Ligier	JS25	Renault	V6t	0	accident/ steering arm	14	7

Winning speed: 191.147 km/h, 118.774 mph
Pole Position speed: 211.177 km/h, 131.219 mph (T Fabi, 1 min:17.429 sec)
Fastest Lap speed: 197.464 km/h, 122.698 mph (N Lauda, 1 min:22.806 sec on lap 53)
Lap Leaders: K Rosberg 1-15,27-44 (33); A Senna 16-26 (11); M Alboreto 45-67 (23).

18 Aug 1985 — AUSTRIA: Österreichring (Round:10) (Race: 414)
52 laps x 5.942 km, 3.692 miles = 308.984 km, 191.994 miles

POS.	NO.	DRIVER	CAR	MODEL	ENGINE		LAPS	TIME/REASON FOR RETIREMENT	GRID:POS	ROW
1	2	A Prost	McLaren	MP4/2B	TAG Porsche	V6t	52	1h 20m 12.583s	1	1
2	12	A Senna	Lotus	97T	Renault	V6t	52	1h 20m 42.585s	14	7
3	27	M Alboreto	Ferrari	156/85	Ferrari	V6t	52	1h 20m 46.939s	9	5
4	28	S Johansson	Ferrari	156/85	Ferrari	V6t	52	1h 20m 51.656s	12	6
5	11	E de Angelis	Lotus	97T	Renault	V6t	52	1h 21m 34.675s	7	4
6	8	M Surer	Brabham	BT54	BMW	4t	51		11	6
7r	3	S Bellof	Tyrrell	014	Renault	V6t	49	out of fuel	22	11
8	18	T Boutsen	Arrows	A8	BMW	4t	49		16	8
9	24	H Rothengatter	Osella	FA1G	Alfa Romeo	V8t	48		24	12
10r	15	P Tambay	Renault	RE60B	Renault	V6t	46	engine	8	4
r	26	J Laffite	Ligier	JS25	Renault	V6t	43	accident	15	8
r	29	P Martini	Minardi	M185	Motori Moderni	V6t	40	suspension	26	13
r	1	N Lauda	McLaren	MP4/2B	TAG Porsche	V6t	39	turbo	3	2
r	17	G Berger	Arrows	A8	BMW	4t	33	turbo	17	9
r	19	T Fabi	Toleman	TG185	Hart	4t	31	electrics	6	3
r	16	D Warwick	Renault	RE60B	Renault	V6t	29	engine	13	7
r	10	K Acheson	RAM	03	Hart	4t	28	engine	23	12
r	7	N Piquet	Brabham	BT54	BMW	4t	26	turbo	5	3
r	5	N Mansell	Williams	FW10	Honda	V6t	25	engine	2	1
r	22	R Patrese	Alfa Romeo	184T	Alfa Romeo	V8t	25	turbo	10	5
r	30	J Palmer	Zakspeed	841	Zakspeed	4t	17	engine	25	13
r	9	P Alliot	RAM	03	Hart	4t	16	turbo	21	11
r	25	A de Cesaris	Ligier	JS25	Renault	V6t	13	accident	18	9
r	23	E Cheever	Alfa Romeo	184T	Alfa Romeo	V8t	6	turbo	20	10
r	6	K Rosberg	Williams	FW10	Honda	V6t	4	engine	4	2
r	20	P Ghinzani	Toleman	TG185	Hart	4t	0	engine *	19	10
nq	4	M Brundle	Tyrrell	012	Cosworth	V8				

Winning speed: 231.132 km/h, 143.619 mph
Pole Position speed: 250.219 km/h, 155.479 mph (A Prost, 1 min:25.490 sec)
Fastest Lap speed: 239.701 km/h, 148.944 mph (A Prost, 1 min:29.241 sec on lap 39)
Lap Leaders: A Prost 1-25,40-52 (38); N Lauda 26-39 (14).

*Interrupted after 1st lap accident. Restarted for original distance. * retired after first start.*

25 Aug 1985 — NETHERLANDS: Zandvoort (Round:11) (Race: 415)
70 laps x 4.252 km, 2.642 miles = 297.640 km, 184.945 miles

POS.	NO.	DRIVER	CAR	MODEL	ENGINE		LAPS	TIME/REASON FOR RETIREMENT	GRID:POS	ROW
1	1	N Lauda	McLaren	MP4/2B	TAG Porsche	V6t	70	1h 32m 29.263s	10	5
2	2	A Prost	McLaren	MP4/2B	TAG Porsche	V6t	70	1h 32m 29.495s	3	2
3	12	A Senna	Lotus	97T	Renault	V6t	70	1h 33m 17.754s	4	2
4	27	M Alboreto	Ferrari	156/85	Ferrari	V6t	70	1h 33m 18.100s	16	8
5	11	E de Angelis	Lotus	97T	Renault	V6t	69		11	6
6	5	N Mansell	Williams	FW10	Honda	V6t	69		7	4
7	3	M Brundle	Tyrrell	014	Renault	V6t	69		21	11
8	7	N Piquet	Brabham	BT54	BMW	4t	69		1	1
9	17	G Berger	Arrows	A8	BMW	4t	68		14	7
10r	8	M Surer	Brabham	BT54	BMW	4t	65	exhaust	9	5
nc	24	H Rothengatter	Osella	FA1G	Alfa Romeo	V8t	56		26	13
r	18	T Boutsen	Arrows	A8	BMW	4t	54	suspension	8	4
r	9	P Alliot	RAM	03	Hart	4t	52	engine	25	13
r	4	S Bellof	Tyrrell	014	Renault	V6t	39	engine	22	11
r	16	D Warwick	Renault	RE60B	Renault	V6t	27	gearbox	12	6
r	25	A de Cesaris	Ligier	JS25	Renault	V6t	25	turbo	18	9
r	15	P Tambay	Renault	RE60B	Renault	V6t	22	transmission	6	3
r	6	K Rosberg	Williams	FW10	Honda	V6t	20	engine	2	1
r	19	T Fabi	Toleman	TG185	Hart	4t	18	wheel bearing	5	3
r	26	J Laffite	Ligier	JS25	Renault	V6t	17	electrics	13	7
r	30	J Palmer	Zakspeed	841	Zakspeed	4t	13	oil pressure	23	12
r	20	P Ghinzani	Toleman	TG185	Hart	4t	12	engine	15	8
r	28	S Johansson	Ferrari	156/85	Ferrari	V6t	9	engine	17	9
r	29	P Martini	Minardi	M185	Motori Moderni	V6t	1	accident	24	12
r	23	E Cheever	Alfa Romeo	184T	Alfa Romeo	V8t	1	turbo	20	10
r	22	R Patrese	Alfa Romeo	184T	Alfa Romeo	V8t	1	turbo	19	10
nq	10	K Acheson	RAM	03	Hart	4t				

Winning speed: 193.089 km/h, 119.980 mph
Pole Position speed: 215.370 km/h, 133.825 mph (N Piquet, 1 min:11.074 sec)
Fastest Lap speed: 199.995 km/h, 124.271 mph (A Prost, 1 min:16.538 sec on lap 57)
Lap Leaders: K Rosberg 1-19 (19); A Prost 20-33 (14); N Lauda 34-70 (37).

8 Sep 1985 — ITALY: Monza — (Round:12) (Race: 416)

51 laps x 5.800 km, 3.604 miles = 295.800 km, 183.802 miles

POS.	NO.	DRIVER	CAR	MODEL	ENGINE		LAPS	TIME/REASON FOR RETIREMENT	GRID:POS	ROW
1	2	A Prost	McLaren	MP4/2B	TAG Porsche	V6t	51	1h 17m 59.451s	5	3
2	7	N Piquet	Brabham	BT54	BMW	4t	51	1h 18m 51.086s	4	2
3	12	A Senna	Lotus	97T	Renault	V6t	51	1h 18m 59.841s	1	1
4	8	M Surer	Brabham	BT54	BMW	4t	51	1h 19m 00.060s	9	5
5r	28	S Johansson	Ferrari	156/85	Ferrari	V6t	50	out of fuel	10	5
6	11	E de Angelis	Lotus	97T	Renault	V6t	50		6	3
7	15	P Tambay	Renault	RE60B	Renault	V6t	50		8	4
8	3	M Brundle	Tyrrell	014	Renault	V6t	50		18	9
9	18	T Boutsen	Arrows	A8	BMW	4t	50		14	7
10	25	P Streiff	Ligier	JS25	Renault	V6t	49		19	10
11r	5	N Mansell	Williams	FW10	Honda	V6t	47	engine	3	2
12	19	T Fabi	Toleman	TG185	Hart	4t	47		15	8
13r	27	M Alboreto	Ferrari	156/85	Ferrari	V6t	45	engine	7	4
r	6	K Rosberg	Williams	FW10	Honda	V6t	44	engine	2	1
r	26	J Laffite	Ligier	JS25	Renault	V6t	40	engine	20	10
r	1	N Lauda	McLaren	MP4/2B	TAG Porsche	V6t	33	transmission	16	8
r	22	R Patrese	Alfa Romeo	184T	Alfa Romeo	V8t	31	exhaust	13	7
r	24	H Rothengatter	Osella	FA1G	Alfa Romeo	V8t	26	engine	22	11
r	9	P Alliot	RAM	03	Hart	4t	19	turbo	26	13
r	17	G Berger	Arrows	A8	BMW	4t	13	engine	11	6
r	16	D Warwick	Renault	RE60B	Renault	V6t	9	transmission	12	6
r	33	A Jones	Lola	THL1	Hart	4t	6	distributor	25	13
r	23	E Cheever	Alfa Romeo	184T	Alfa Romeo	V8t	3	engine	17	9
r	10	K Acheson	RAM	03	Hart	4t	2	clutch	24	12
r	29	P Martini	Minardi	M185	Motori Moderni	V6t	0	fuel pump	23	12
r	20	P Ghinzani	Toleman	TG185	Hart	4t	0	stalled on grid	21	11

Winning speed: 227.565 km/h, 141.402 mph
Pole Position speed: 245.405 km/h, 152.487 mph (A Senna, 1 min:25.084 sec)
Fastest Lap speed: 236.512 km/h, 146.962 mph (N Mansell, 1 min:28.283 sec on lap 38)
Lap Leaders: K Rosberg 1-27,40-44 (32); A Prost 28-39,45-51 (19).

15 Sep 1985 — BELGIUM: Spa-Francorchamps — (Round:13) (Race: 417)

43 laps x 6.940 km, 4.312 miles = 298.420 km, 185.430 miles

POS.	NO.	DRIVER	CAR	MODEL	ENGINE		LAPS	TIME/REASON FOR RETIREMENT	GRID:POS	ROW
1	12	A Senna	Lotus	97T	Renault	V6t	43	1h 34m 19.893s	2	1
2	5	N Mansell	Williams	FW10	Honda	V6t	43	1h 34m 48.315s	7	4
3	2	A Prost	McLaren	MP4/2B	TAG Porsche	V6t	43	1h 35m 15.002s	1	1
4	6	K Rosberg	Williams	FW10	Honda	V6t	43	1h 35m 35.183s	10	5
5	7	N Piquet	Brabham	BT54	BMW	4t	42		3	2
6	16	D Warwick	Renault	RE60B	Renault	V6t	42		14	7
7	17	G Berger	Arrows	A8	BMW	4t	42		8	4
8	8	M Surer	Brabham	BT54	BMW	4t	42		12	6
9	25	P Streiff	Ligier	JS25	Renault	V6t	42		18	9
10r	18	T Boutsen	Arrows	A8	BMW	4t	40	gearbox	6	3
11r	26	J Laffite	Ligier	JS25	Renault	V6t	38	accident	17	9
12	29	P Martini	Minardi	M185	Motori Moderni	V6t	38		24	12
13	3	M Brundle	Tyrrell	014	Renault	V6t	38		21	11
nc	24	H Rothengatter	Osella	FA1G	Alfa Romeo	V8t	37		23	12
r	22	R Patrese	Alfa Romeo	184T	Alfa Romeo	V8t	31	engine	15	8
r	23	E Cheever	Alfa Romeo	184T	Alfa Romeo	V8t	26	gearbox	19	10
r	15	P Tambay	Renault	RE60B	Renault	V6t	24	gearbox	13	7
r	19	T Fabi	Toleman	TG185	Hart	4t	23	throttle linkage	11	6
r	11	E de Angelis	Lotus	97T	Renault	V6t	17	turbo	9	5
r	30	C Danner	Zakspeed	841	Zakspeed	4t	16	gearbox	22	11
r	9	P Alliot	RAM	03	Hart	4t	10	accident	20	10
r	28	S Johansson	Ferrari	156/85	Ferrari	V6t	7	engine/ spin	5	3
r	20	P Ghinzani	Toleman	TG185	Hart	4t	7	accident	16	8
r	27	M Alboreto	Ferrari	156/85	Ferrari	V6t	3	clutch	4	2
ns	1	N Lauda	McLaren	MP4/2B	TAG Porsche	V8		accident/ injury		

Winning speed: 189.811 km/h, 117.943 mph
Pole Position speed: 216.676 km/h, 134.636 mph (A Prost, 1 min:55.306 sec)
Fastest Lap speed: 205.241 km/h, 127.531 mph (A Prost, 2 min: 1.730 sec on lap 38)
Lap Leaders: A Senna 1-8,10-43 (42); E de Angelis 9 (1).

Race originally scheduled for 2 June but postponed after Friday's qualifying due to track surface disintegration.

6 Oct 1985 — EUROPE: Brands Hatch — (Round:14) (Race: 418)

75 laps x 4.207 km, 2.614 miles = 315.512 km, 196.050 miles

POS.	NO.	DRIVER	CAR	MODEL	ENGINE		LAPS	TIME/REASON FOR RETIREMENT	GRID:POS	ROW
1	5	N Mansell	Williams	FW10	Honda	V6t	75	1h 32m 58.109s	3	2
2	12	A Senna	Lotus	97T	Renault	V6t	75	1h 33m 19.505s	1	1
3	6	K Rosberg	Williams	FW10	Honda	V6t	75	1h 33m 56.642s	4	2
4	2	A Prost	McLaren	MP4/2B	TAG Porsche	V6t	75	1h 34m 04.230s	6	3
5	11	E de Angelis	Lotus	97T	Renault	V6t	74		9	5
6	18	T Boutsen	Arrows	A8	BMW	4t	73		12	6
7	1	J Watson	McLaren	MP4/2B	TAG Porsche	V6t	73		21	11
8	25	P Streiff	Ligier	JS25	Renault	V6t	73		5	3

POS.	NO.	DRIVER	CAR	MODEL	ENGINE		LAPS	TIME/REASON FOR RETIREMENT	GRID:POS	ROW
9	22	R Patrese	Alfa Romeo	184T	Alfa Romeo	V8t	73		11	6
10	17	G Berger	Arrows	A8	BMW	4t	73		19	10
11	23	E Cheever	Alfa Romeo	184T	Alfa Romeo	V8t	73		18	9
12	15	P Tambay	Renault	RE60B	Renault	V6t	72		17	9
r	8	M Surer	Brabham	BT54	BMW	4t	62	turbo/ fire	7	4
r	28	S Johansson	Ferrari	156/85	Ferrari	V6t	59	alternator	13	7
r	26	J Laffite	Ligier	JS25	Renault	V6t	58	engine	10	5
r	30	C Danner	Zakspeed	841	Zakspeed	4t	55	turbo	25	13
r	4	I Capelli	Tyrrell	014	Renault	V6t	44	accident	24	12
r	3	M Brundle	Tyrrell	014	Renault	V6t	40	water pipe	16	8
r	19	T Fabi	Toleman	TG185	Hart	4t	33	engine	20	10
r	9	P Alliot	RAM	03	Hart	4t	31	engine overheating	23	12
r	20	P Ghinzani	Toleman	TG185	Hart	4t	16	engine	14	7
r	33	A Jones	Lola	THL1	Hart	4t	13	radiator/ engine overheating	22	11
r	27	M Alboreto	Ferrari	156/85	Ferrari	V6t	13	turbo/ fire	15	8
r	7	N Piquet	Brabham	BT54	BMW	4t	6	accident	2	1
r	16	D Warwick	Renault	RE60B	Renault	V6t	4	fuel injection	8	4
r	29	P Martini	Minardi	M185	Motori Moderni	V6t	3	accident	26	13
nq	24	H Rothengatter	Osella	FA1G	Alfa Romeo	V8t				

Winning speed: 203.625 km/h, 126.527 mph
Pole Position speed: 225.470 km/h, 140.100 mph (A Senna, 1 min: 7.169 sec)
Fastest Lap speed: 211.735 km/h, 131.566 mph (J Laffite, 1 min:11.526 sec on lap 55)
Lap Leaders: A Senna 1-8 (8); N Mansell 9-75 (67).

19 Oct 1985 SOUTH AFRICA: Kyalami (Round:15) (Race: 419)

75 laps x 4.104 km, 2.550 miles = 307.800 km, 191.258 miles

POS.	NO.	DRIVER	CAR	MODEL	ENGINE		LAPS	TIME/REASON FOR RETIREMENT	GRID:POS	ROW
1	5	N Mansell	Williams	FW10	Honda	V6t	75	1h 28m 22.866s	1	1
2	6	K Rosberg	Williams	FW10	Honda	V6t	75	1h 28m 30.438s	3	2
3	2	A Prost	McLaren	MP4/2B	TAG Porsche	V6t	74		9	5
4	28	S Johansson	Ferrari	156/85	Ferrari	V6t	74		16	8
5	17	G Berger	Arrows	A8	BMW	4t	74		11	6
6	18	T Boutsen	Arrows	A8	BMW	4t	74		10	5
7	3	M Brundle	Tyrrell	014	Renault	V6t	73		17	9
r	11	E de Angelis	Lotus	97T	Renault	V6t	52	engine	6	3
r	29	P Martini	Minardi	M185	Motori Moderni	V6t	45	radiator	19	10
r	1	N Lauda	McLaren	MP4/2B	TAG Porsche	V6t	37	turbo	8	4
r	4	P Streiff	Tyrrell	014	Renault	V6t	16	accident	18	9
r	12	A Senna	Lotus	97T	Renault	V6t	8	engine	4	2
r	27	M Alboreto	Ferrari	156/85	Ferrari	V6t	8	turbo	15	8
r	7	N Piquet	Brabham	BT54	BMW	4t	6	engine	2	1
r	20	P Ghinzani	Toleman	TG185	Hart	4t	4	engine	13	7
r	19	T Fabi	Toleman	TG185	Hart	4t	3	engine	7	4
r	8	M Surer	Brabham	BT54	BMW	4t	3	engine	5	3
r	24	H Rothengatter	Osella	FA1G	Alfa Romeo	V8t	1	electrics	20	10
r	23	E Cheever	Alfa Romeo	184T	Alfa Romeo	V8t	0	accident	14	7
r	22	R Patrese	Alfa Romeo	184T	Alfa Romeo	V8t	0	accident	12	6
ns	33	A Jones	Lola	THL1	Hart	4t		driver ill		

Winning speed: 208.959 km/h, 129.841 mph
Pole Position speed: 236.898 km/h, 147.202 mph (N Mansell, 1 min: 2.366 sec)
Fastest Lap speed: 216.796 km/h, 134.711 mph (K Rosberg, 1 min: 8.149 sec on lap 74)
Lap Leaders: N Mansell 1-7,9-75 (74); K Rosberg 8 (1).

A Prost's final lap (75) was too slow and disallowed for the classification.

3 Nov 1985 AUSTRALIA: Adelaide (Round:16) (Race: 420)

82 laps x 3.778 km, 2.348 miles = 309.796 km, 192.498 miles

POS.	NO.	DRIVER	CAR	MODEL	ENGINE		LAPS	TIME/REASON FOR RETIREMENT	GRID:POS	ROW
1	6	K Rosberg	Williams	FW10	Honda	V6t	82	2h 00m 40.473s	3	2
2	26	J Laffite	Ligier	JS25	Renault	V6t	82	2h 01m 26.603s	20	10
3	25	P Streiff	Ligier	JS25	Renault	V6t	82	2h 02m 09.009s	18	9
4	4	I Capelli	Tyrrell	014	Renault	V6t	81		22	11
5	28	S Johansson	Ferrari	156/85	Ferrari	V6t	81		15	8
6	17	G Berger	Arrows	A8	BMW	4t	81		7	4
7	24	H Rothengatter	Osella	FA1G	Alfa Romeo	V8t	78		25	13
8	29	P Martini	Minardi	M185	Motori Moderni	V6t	78		23	12
r	12	A Senna	Lotus	97T	Renault	V6t	62	engine	1	1
r	27	M Alboreto	Ferrari	156/85	Ferrari	V6t	61	gear linkage	5	3
r	1	N Lauda	McLaren	MP4/2B	TAG Porsche	V6t	57	brakes/ accident	16	8
r	16	D Warwick	Renault	RE60B	Renault	V6t	57	transmission	12	6
nc	3	M Brundle	Tyrrell	014	Renault	V6t	49		17	9
r	8	M Surer	Brabham	BT54	BMW	4t	42	engine	6	3
r	22	R Patrese	Alfa Romeo	184T	Alfa Romeo	V8t	42	exhaust	14	7
r	19	T Fabi	Toleman	TG185	Hart	4t	40	engine	24	12
r	18	T Boutsen	Arrows	A8	BMW	4t	37	oil leak/ spin	11	6
r	20	P Ghinzani	Toleman	TG185	Hart	4t	28	clutch	21	11
r	2	A Prost	McLaren	MP4/2B	TAG Porsche	V6t	26	engine	4	2
r	15	P Tambay	Renault	RE60B	Renault	V6t	20	transmission	8	4
r	33	A Jones	Lola	THL1	Hart	4t	20	electrics	19	10
dq	11	E de Angelis	Lotus	97T	Renault	V6t	19	started from wrong grid position	10	5
r	7	N Piquet	Brabham	BT54	BMW	4t	14	electrics/ fire	9	5
r	23	E Cheever	Alfa Romeo	184T	Alfa Romeo	V8t	5	engine	13	7
r	5	N Mansell	Williams	FW10	Honda	V6t	1	transmission	2	1

Winning speed: 154.032 km/h, 95.711 mph
Pole Position speed: 170.344 km/h, 105.847 mph (A Senna, 1 min:19.843 sec)
Fastest Lap speed: 162.382 km/h, 100.900 mph (K Rosberg, 1 min:23.758 sec on lap 57)
Lap Leaders: K Rosberg 1-41,44-52,62-82 (71); A Senna 42-43,53-55,58-61 (9); N Lauda 56-57 (2).

Lap Leaders 1985

POS	DRIVER	CAR-ENGINE	GPS	LAPS	KM	MILES
1	A Senna	Lotus-Renault	9	271	1,327.7	825.0
2	K Rosberg	Williams-Honda	8	231	1,017.3	632.1
3	A Prost	McLaren-TAG Porsche	7	178	841.5	522.9
4	N Mansell	Williams-Honda	2	141	585.6	363.9
5	M Alboreto	Ferrari	4	98	427.0	265.3
6	N Lauda	McLaren-TAG Porsche	3	53	248.1	154.1
7	N Piquet	Brabham-BMW	1	43	249.8	155.2
8	E de Angelis	Lotus-Renault	2	16	73.1	45.4
9	S Johansson	Ferrari	1	1	5.0	3.1
			16	**1,032**	**4,774.2**	**2,966.5**

Driver Points 1985

		BR	P	RSM	MC	CDN	USA	F	GB	D	A	NL	I	B	EUR	ZA	AUS	TOTAL	
1	A Prost	9	-	-	9	4	-	4	9	6	9	6	9	4	(3)	4	-	73	(3)
2	M Alboreto	6	6	-	6	9	4	-	6	9	4	3	-	-	-	-	-	53	
3	K Rosberg	-	-	-	-	3	9	6	-	-	-	-	-	3	4	6	9	40	
4	A Senna	-	9	-	-	-	-	-	-	-	6	4	4	9	6	-	-	38	
5	E de Angelis	4	3	9	4	2	2	2	-	-	2	2	1	-	2	-	-	33	
6	N Mansell	-	2	2	-	1	-	-	-	1	-	1	-	6	9	9	-	31	
7	S Johansson	-	-	1	-	6	6	3	-	-	3	-	2	-	-	3	2	26	
8	N Piquet	-	-	-	-	-	1	9	3	-	-	-	6	2	-	-	-	21	
9	J Laffite	1	-	-	1	-	-	-	4	4	-	-	-	-	-	-	6	16	
10	N Lauda	-	-	3	-	-	-	-	-	2	-	9	-	-	-	-	-	14	
11	T Boutsen	-	-	6	-	-	-	-	-	3	-	-	-	-	1	1	-	11	
	P Tambay	2	4	4	-	-	-	1	-	-	-	-	-	-	-	-	-	11	
13	M Surer	-	-	-	-	-	-	-	1	-	1	-	3	-	-	-	-	5	
	D Warwick	-	-	-	2	-	-	-	2	-	-	-	-	1	-	-	-	5	
15	P Streiff	-	-	-	-	-	-	-	-	-	-	-	-	-	-	-	4	4	
	S Bellof	-	1	-	-	-	3	-	-	-	-	-	-	-	-	-	-	4	
17	R Arnoux	3	-	-	-	-	-	-	-	-	-	-	-	-	-	-	-	3	
	A de Cesaris	-	-	-	3	-	-	-	-	-	-	-	-	-	-	-	-	3	
	I Capelli	-	-	-	-	-	-	-	-	-	-	-	-	-	-	-	3	3	
	G Berger	-	-	-	-	-	-	-	-	-	-	-	-	-	-	2	1	3	

9, 6, 4, 3, 2 and 1 point awarded to the first six finishers. Best 11 scores.

Constructor Points 1985

		BR	P	RSM	MC	CDN	USA	F	GB	D	A	NL	I	B	EUR	ZA	AUS	TOTAL
1	McLaren-TAG Porsche	9	-	3	9	4	-	4	9	8	9	15	9	4	3	4	-	90
2	Ferrari	9	6	1	6	15	10	3	6	9	7	3	2	-	-	3	2	82
3	Williams-Honda	-	2	2	-	4	9	6	-	1	-	1	-	9	13	15	9	71
	Lotus-Renault	4	12	9	4	2	2	2	-	-	8	6	5	9	8	-	-	71
5	Brabham-BMW	-	-	-	-	-	1	9	4	-	1	-	9	2	-	-	-	26
6	Ligier-Renault	1	-	-	4	-	-	-	4	4	-	-	-	-	-	-	10	23
7	Renault	2	4	4	2	-	-	1	2	-	-	-	-	1	-	-	-	16
8	Arrows-BMW	-	-	6	-	-	-	-	-	3	-	-	-	-	1	3	1	14
9	Tyrrell-Cosworth	-	1	-	-	-	3	-	-	-	-	-	-	-	-	-	-	4
10	Tyrrell-Renault	-	-	-	-	-	-	-	-	-	-	-	-	-	-	-	3	3

9, 6, 4, 3, 2 and 1 point awarded to the first six finishers.

Colour Plate Illustrations by Alain Baudouin

Ferrari 375
1951

Maserati A6GCM
1953

Mercedes-Benz W196 str.
1954-1955

Lancia Ferrari D50
1956

Vanwall
1957

Ferrari D246
1958-1960

BRM P25
1959

Cooper T53-Climax
1960

Ferrari 156
1961

Porsche 804
1962

Brabham BT7-Climax
1964

Ferrari 312
1966

Honda RA300
1967

Lotus 49B-Ford Cosworth
1968

BRM P153
1970

Lotus 72D-Ford Cosworth
1972

Ferrari 312B3
1974

Hesketh 308-Ford Cosworth
1975

Tyrrell P34-Ford Cosworth
1976

Wolf WR1-Ford Cosworth
1977

Brabham BT46-Alfa Romeo
1978

Ligier JS11-Ford Cosworth
1979-1980

Renault RE30
1981

Ferrari 126C2
1982

Tyrrell Oll-Ford Cosworth
1983

McLaren MP4/2-TAG/Porsche
1984

Brabham BT54-BMW
1985

Benetton B186-BMW
1986

Williams FW15C-Renault
1993

Ferrari 412T1B
1994

Benetton B195-Renault
1995

Williams FW17-Renault
1995

Only turbos (1.5 litre) were permitted with a new fuel allowance of 195 litres. The Williams FW11 was the car to have, but the team had a dreadful setback when Frank Williams was paralysed in a road accident after pre-season testing in the South of France. Toleman was purchased and re-named by Benetton. Gordon Murray produced the ultra low-line BT55 only to leave at the end of the year, as did Pirelli.

McLAREN
Marlboro McLaren International: Prost, Rosberg

TYRRELL
Data General Team Tyrrell: Brundle, Streiff

WILLIAMS
Canon Williams Team: Mansell, Piquet

BRABHAM
Motor Racing Developments: Patrese, de Angelis, Warwick

LOTUS
John Player Special Team Lotus: Dumfries, Senna

ZAKSPEED
West Zakspeed Racing: Palmer, Rothengatter

LOLA
Team Haas (USA) Ltd: Jones, Tambay, Cheever

ARROWS
Barclay Arrows BMW: Surer, Danner, Boutsen

BENETTON
Benetton Formula: Fabi, Berger

OSELLA
Osella Squadra Corse: Ghinzani, Danner, Berg, Caffi

MINARDI
Minardi Team: de Cesaris, Nannini

LIGIER
Equipe Ligier: Arnoux, Laffite, Alliot

FERRARI
Scuderia Ferrari SpA SEFAC: Alboreto, Johansson

AGS
Jolly Club SpA: Capelli

23 Mar 1986 — BRAZIL: Rio de Janeiro (Round: 1) (Race: 421)

61 laps x 5.031 km, 3.126 miles = 306.891 km, 190.693 miles

POS.	NO.	DRIVER	CAR	MODEL	ENGINE		LAPS	TIME/REASON FOR RETIREMENT	GRID:POS	ROW
1	6	N Piquet	Williams	FW11	Honda	V6t	61	1h 39m 32.583s	2	1
2	12	A Senna	Lotus	98T	Renault	V6t	61	1h 40m 07.410s	1	1
3	26	J Laffite	Ligier	JS27	Renault	V6t	61	1h 40m 32.342s	5	3
4	25	R Arnoux	Ligier	JS27	Renault	V6t	61	1h 41m 01.012s	4	2
5	3	M Brundle	Tyrrell	014	Renault	V6t	60		17	9
6	20	G Berger	Benetton	B186	BMW	4t	59		16	8
7	4	P Streiff	Tyrrell	014	Renault	V6t	59		18	9
8	8	E de Angelis	Brabham	BT55	BMW	4t	58		14	7
9	11	J Dumfries	Lotus	98T	Renault	V6t	58		11	6
10	19	T Fabi	Benetton	B186	BMW	4t	56		12	6
r	18	T Boutsen	Arrows	A8	BMW	4t	37	turbo wastegate	15	8
r	27	M Alboreto	Ferrari	F186	Ferrari	V6t	35	fuel pump drive	6	3
r	1	A Prost	McLaren	MP4/2C	TAG Porsche	V6t	30	engine	9	5
r	22	C Danner	Osella	FA1F	Alfa Romeo	V8t	29	engine	24	12
r	28	S Johansson	Ferrari	F186	Ferrari	V6t	26	brakes/ spin	8	4
r	16	P Tambay	Lola	THL1	Hart	4t	24	alternator	13	7
r	7	R Patrese	Brabham	BT55	BMW	4t	21	water pipe	10	5
r	14	J Palmer	Zakspeed	861	Zakspeed	4t	20	airbox	21	11
r	17	M Surer	Arrows	A8	BMW	4t	19	engine overheating	20	10
r	24	A Nannini	Minardi	M185B	Motori Moderni	V6t	18	clutch	25	13
r	23	A de Cesaris	Minardi	M185B	Motori Moderni	V6t	16	turbo	22	11
r	21	P Ghinzani	Osella	FA1G	Alfa Romeo	V8t	16	engine	23	12
r	2	K Rosberg	McLaren	MP4/2C	TAG Porsche	V6t	6	engine	7	4
r	15	A Jones	Lola	THL1	Hart	4t	5	distributor rotor arm	19	10
r	5	N Mansell	Williams	FW11	Honda	V6t	0	accident	3	2

Winning speed: 184.980 km/h, 114.941 mph
Pole Position speed: 211.829 km/h, 131.625 mph (A Senna, 1 min:25.501 sec)
Fastest Lap speed: 193.612 km/h, 120.305 mph (N Piquet, 1 min:33.546 sec on lap 46)
Lap Leaders: A Senna 1-2,19,41 (4); N Piquet 3-18,27-40,42-61 (50); A Prost 20-26 (7).

13 Apr 1986 — SPAIN: Jerez de la Frontera (Round: 2) (Race: 422)

72 laps x 4.218 km, 2.621 miles = 303.696 km, 188.708 miles

POS.	NO.	DRIVER	CAR	MODEL	ENGINE		LAPS	TIME/REASON FOR RETIREMENT	GRID:POS	ROW
1	12	A Senna	Lotus	98T	Renault	V6t	72	1h 48m 47.735s	1	1
2	5	N Mansell	Williams	FW11	Honda	V6t	72	1h 48m 47.749s	3	2
3	1	A Prost	McLaren	MP4/2C	TAG Porsche	V6t	72	1h 49m 09.287s	4	2
4	2	K Rosberg	McLaren	MP4/2C	TAG Porsche	V6t	71		5	3
5	19	T Fabi	Benetton	B186	BMW	4t	71		9	5
6	20	G Berger	Benetton	B186	BMW	4t	71		7	4
7	18	T Boutsen	Arrows	A8	BMW	4t	68		19	10
8	16	P Tambay	Lola	THL1	Hart	4t	66		18	9
r	11	J Dumfries	Lotus	98T	Renault	V6t	52	gearbox	10	5
r	3	M Brundle	Tyrrell	014	Renault	V6t	41	oil loss	12	6
r	26	J Laffite	Ligier	JS27	Renault	V6t	40	drive shaft	8	4
r	6	N Piquet	Williams	FW11	Honda	V6t	39	engine overheating	2	1
r	17	M Surer	Arrows	A8	BMW	4t	39	fuel leak	22	11
r	8	E de Angelis	Brabham	BT55	BMW	4t	29	gearbox	15	8
r	25	R Arnoux	Ligier	JS27	Renault	V6t	29	drive shaft	6	3
r	27	M Alboreto	Ferrari	F186	Ferrari	V6t	22	wheel bearing	13	7
r	4	P Streiff	Tyrrell	014	Renault	V6t	22	oil loss	20	10
r	22	C Danner	Osella	FA1F	Alfa Romeo	V8t	14	engine	23	12
r	28	S Johansson	Ferrari	F186	Ferrari	V6t	11	brakes/ accident	11	6
r	21	P Ghinzani	Osella	FA1G	Alfa Romeo	V8t	10	engine	21	11
r	7	R Patrese	Brabham	BT55	BMW	4t	8	gearbox	14	7
r	23	A de Cesaris	Minardi	M185B	Motori Moderni	V6t	1	differential	24	12
r	14	J Palmer	Zakspeed	861	Zakspeed	4t	0	accident	16	8
r	15	A Jones	Lola	THL1	Hart	4t	0	accident	17	9
r	24	A Nannini	Minardi	M185B	Motori Moderni	V6t	-1	differential	25	13

Winning speed: 167.486 km/h, 104.071 mph
Pole Position speed: 186.077 km/h, 115.623 mph (A Senna, 1 min:21.605 sec)
Fastest Lap speed: 174.186 km/h, 108.234 mph (N Mansell, 1 min:27.176 sec on lap 65)
Lap Leaders: A Senna 1-39,63-72 (49); N Mansell 40-62 (23).

27 Apr 1986 — SAN MARINO: Imola (Round: 3) (Race: 423)

60 laps x 5.040 km, 3.132 miles = 302.400 km, 187.903 miles

POS.	NO.	DRIVER	CAR	MODEL	ENGINE		LAPS	TIME/REASON FOR RETIREMENT	GRID:POS	ROW
1	1	A Prost	McLaren	MP4/2C	TAG Porsche	V6t	60	1h 32m 28.408s	4	2
2	6	N Piquet	Williams	FW11	Honda	V6t	60	1h 32m 36.053s	2	1
3	20	G Berger	Benetton	B186	BMW	4t	59		9	5
4	28	S Johansson	Ferrari	F186	Ferrari	V6t	59		7	4
5r	2	K Rosberg	McLaren	MP4/2C	TAG Porsche	V6t	58	out of fuel	6	3
6r	7	R Patrese	Brabham	BT55	BMW	4t	58	out of fuel	16	8
7	18	T Boutsen	Arrows	A8	BMW	4t	58		12	6
8	3	M Brundle	Tyrrell	014	Renault	V6t	58		13	7
9r	17	M Surer	Arrows	A8	BMW	4t	57	out of fuel	15	8
10r	27	M Alboreto	Ferrari	F186	Ferrari	V6t	56	turbo boost pressure	5	3
r	21	P Ghinzani	Osella	FA1G	Alfa Romeo	V8t	52	out of fuel	26	13
r	25	R Arnoux	Ligier	JS27	Renault	V6t	46	wheel lost	8	4
r	4	P Streiff	Tyrrell	014	Renault	V6t	41	transmission	22	11
r	19	T Fabi	Benetton	B186	BMW	4t	39	engine	10	5
r	14	J Palmer	Zakspeed	861	Zakspeed	4t	38	brakes	20	10
r	22	C Danner	Osella	FA1F	Alfa Romeo	V8t	31	electrics	25	13
r	15	A Jones	Lola	THL2	Cosworth	V6t	28	radiator/ engine overheating	21	11
r	23	A de Cesaris	Minardi	M185B	Motori Moderni	V6t	20	engine	23	12
r	8	E de Angelis	Brabham	BT55	BMW	4t	19	engine	19	10
r	26	J Laffite	Ligier	JS27	Renault	V6t	14	turbo boost pressure	14	7
r	12	A Senna	Lotus	98T	Renault	V6t	11	wheel bearing	1	1
r	5	N Mansell	Williams	FW11	Honda	V6t	8	engine	3	2
r	11	J Dumfries	Lotus	98T	Renault	V6t	8	wheel bearing	17	9
r	29	H Rothengatter	Zakspeed	861	Zakspeed	4t	7	turbo boost pressure	24	12
r	16	P Tambay	Lola	THL1	Hart	4t	5	engine	11	6
r	24	A Nannini	Minardi	M185B	Motori Moderni	V6t	0	accident	18	9

Winning speed: 196.208 km/h, 121.918 mph
Pole Position speed: 213.333 km/h, 132.559 mph (A Senna, 1 min:25.050 sec)
Fastest Lap speed: 204.631 km/h, 127.152 mph (N Piquet, 1 min:28.667 sec on lap 57)
Lap Leaders: N Piquet 1-28 (28); K Rosberg 29-32 (4); A Prost 33-60 (28).

11 May 1986 — MONACO: Monte Carlo (Round: 4) (Race: 424)

78 laps x 3.328 km, 2.068 miles = 259.584 km, 161.298 miles

POS.	NO.	DRIVER	CAR	MODEL	ENGINE		LAPS	TIME/REASON FOR RETIREMENT	GRID:POS	ROW
1	1	A Prost	McLaren	MP4/2C	TAG Porsche	V6t	78	1h 55m 41.060s	1	1
2	2	K Rosberg	McLaren	MP4/2C	TAG Porsche	V6t	78	1h 56m 06.082s	9	5
3	12	A Senna	Lotus	98T	Renault	V6t	78	1h 56m 34.706s	3	2
4	5	N Mansell	Williams	FW11	Honda	V6t	78	1h 56m 52.462s	2	1
5	25	R Arnoux	Ligier	JS27	Renault	V6t	77		12	6
6	26	J Laffite	Ligier	JS27	Renault	V6t	77		7	4
7	6	N Piquet	Williams	FW11	Honda	V6t	77		11	6
8	18	T Boutsen	Arrows	A8	BMW	4t	75		14	7
9	17	M Surer	Arrows	A8	BMW	4t	75		17	9
10	28	S Johansson	Ferrari	F186	Ferrari	V6t	75		15	8
11	4	P Streiff	Tyrrell	015	Renault	V6t	74		13	7
12	14	J Palmer	Zakspeed	861	Zakspeed	4t	74		19	10

POS.	NO.	DRIVER	CAR	MODEL	ENGINE		LAPS	TIME/REASON FOR RETIREMENT	GRID:POS	ROW
r	3	M Brundle	Tyrrell	015	Renault	V6t	67	accident	10	5
r	16	P Tambay	Lola	THL2	Cosworth	V6t	67	accident	8	4
r	20	G Berger	Benetton	B186	BMW	4t	42	wheel drive pegs	5	3
r	27	M Alboreto	Ferrari	F186	Ferrari	V6t	38	turbo	4	2
r	7	R Patrese	Brabham	BT55	BMW	4t	38	fuel pump	6	3
r	8	E de Angelis	Brabham	BT55	BMW	4t	31	turbo boost pressure	20	10
r	19	T Fabi	Benetton	B186	BMW	4t	17	brakes	16	8
r	15	A Jones	Lola	THL2	Cosworth	V6t	2	accident	18	9
nq	21	P Ghinzani	Osella	FA1G	Alfa Romeo	V8t				
nq	11	J Dumfries	Lotus	98T	Renault	V6t				
nq	29	H Rothengatter	Zakspeed	861	Zakspeed	4t				
nq	22	C Danner	Osella	FA1F	Alfa Romeo	V8t				
nq	23	A de Cesaris	Minardi	M185B	Motori Moderni	V6t				
nq	24	A Nannini	Minardi	M185B	Motori Moderni	V6t				

Winning speed: 134.634 km/h, 83.658 mph
Pole Position speed: 144.999 km/h, 90.098 mph (A Prost, 1 min:22.627 sec)
Fastest Lap speed: 138.335 km/h, 85.958 mph (A Prost, 1 min:26.607 sec on lap 51)
Lap Leaders: A Prost 1-34,42-78 (71); A Senna 35-41 (7).

25 May 1986 — BELGIUM: Spa-Francorchamps (Round: 5) (Race: 425)

43 laps x 6.940 km, 4.312 miles = 298.420 km, 185.430 miles

POS.	NO.	DRIVER	CAR	MODEL	ENGINE		LAPS	TIME/REASON FOR RETIREMENT	GRID:POS	ROW
1	5	N Mansell	Williams	FW11	Honda	V6t	43	1h 27m 57.925s	5	3
2	12	A Senna	Lotus	98T	Renault	V6t	43	1h 28m 17.752s	4	2
3	28	S Johansson	Ferrari	F186	Ferrari	V6t	43	1h 28m 24.517s	11	6
4	27	M Alboreto	Ferrari	F186	Ferrari	V6t	43	1h 28m 27.559s	9	5
5	26	J Laffite	Ligier	JS27	Renault	V6t	43	1h 29m 08.615s	17	9
6	1	A Prost	McLaren	MP4/2C	TAG Porsche	V6t	43	1h 30m 15.697s	3	2
7	19	T Fabi	Benetton	B186	BMW	4t	42		6	3
8	7	R Patrese	Brabham	BT55	BMW	4t	42		15	8
9	17	M Surer	Arrows	A8	BMW	4t	41		21	11
10	20	G Berger	Benetton	B186	BMW	4t	41		2	1
11r	15	A Jones	Lola	THL2	Cosworth	V6t	40	out of fuel	16	8
12	4	P Streiff	Tyrrell	015	Renault	V6t	40		18	9
nc	14	J Palmer	Zakspeed	861	Zakspeed	4t	37		20	10
r	23	A de Cesaris	Minardi	M185B	Motori Moderni	V6t	35	out of fuel	19	10
r	3	M Brundle	Tyrrell	015	Renault	V6t	25	gearbox	12	6
r	29	H Rothengatter	Zakspeed	861	Zakspeed	4t	25	alternator	23	12
r	24	A Nannini	Minardi	M185B	Motori Moderni	V6t	24	gearbox	22	11
r	25	R Arnoux	Ligier	JS27	Renault	V6t	23	engine	7	4
r	6	N Piquet	Williams	FW11	Honda	V6t	16	turbo boost control	1	1
r	18	T Boutsen	Arrows	A8	BMW	4t	7	electrics	14	7
r	11	J Dumfries	Lotus	98T	Renault	V6t	7	spin/ radiator	13	7
r	2	K Rosberg	McLaren	MP4/2C	TAG Porsche	V6t	6	engine	8	4
r	21	P Ghinzani	Osella	FA1G	Alfa Romeo	V8t	3	engine	24	12
r	22	C Danner	Osella	FA1F	Alfa Romeo	V8t	2	engine	25	13
r	16	P Tambay	Lola	THL2	Cosworth	V6t	0	accident	10	5

Winning speed: 203.548 km/h, 126.479 mph
Pole Position speed: 218.523 km/h, 135.784 mph (N Piquet, 1 min:54.331 sec)
Fastest Lap speed: 209.453 km/h, 130.148 mph (A Prost, 1 min:59.282 sec on lap 31)
Lap Leaders: N Piquet 1-16 (16); A Senna 17-21 (5); S Johansson 22-23 (2); N Mansell 24-43 (20).

15 Jun 1986 — CANADA: Montréal (Round: 6) (Race: 426)

69 laps x 4.410 km, 2.740 miles = 304.290 km, 189.077 miles

POS.	NO.	DRIVER	CAR	MODEL	ENGINE		LAPS	TIME/REASON FOR RETIREMENT	GRID:POS	ROW
1	5	N Mansell	Williams	FW11	Honda	V6t	69	1h 42m 26.415s	1	1
2	1	A Prost	McLaren	MP4/2C	TAG Porsche	V6t	69	1h 42m 47.074s	4	2
3	6	N Piquet	Williams	FW11	Honda	V6t	69	1h 43m 02.677s	3	2
4	2	K Rosberg	McLaren	MP4/2C	TAG Porsche	V6t	69	1h 44m 02.088s	6	3
5	12	A Senna	Lotus	98T	Renault	V6t	68		2	1
6	25	R Arnoux	Ligier	JS27	Renault	V6t	68		5	3
7	26	J Laffite	Ligier	JS27	Renault	V6t	68		8	4
8	27	M Alboreto	Ferrari	F186	Ferrari	V6t	68		11	6
9	3	M Brundle	Tyrrell	015	Renault	V6t	67		18	9
10	15	A Jones	Lola	THL2	Cosworth	V6t	66		13	7
11	4	P Streiff	Tyrrell	014	Renault	V6t	65		16	8
12	29	H Rothengatter	Zakspeed	861	Zakspeed	4t	63		23	12
r	7	R Patrese	Brabham	BT55	BMW	4t	44	turbo	9	5
r	21	P Ghinzani	Osella	FA1G	Alfa Romeo	V8t	43	gearbox	22	11
r	23	A de Cesaris	Minardi	M185B	Motori Moderni	V6t	40	gearbox	20	10
r	18	T Boutsen	Arrows	A8	BMW	4t	38	electrics	12	6
r	20	G Berger	Benetton	B186	BMW	4t	34	turbo boost pressure	7	4
r	28	S Johansson	Ferrari	F186	Ferrari	V6t	29	accident	17	9
r	11	J Dumfries	Lotus	98T	Renault	V6t	28	accident	15	8
r	14	J Palmer	Zakspeed	861	Zakspeed	4t	24	engine	21	11
r	8	D Warwick	Brabham	BT55	BMW	4t	20	engine	10	5
r	24	A Nannini	Minardi	M185B	Motori Moderni	V6t	17	turbo	19	10
r	19	T Fabi	Benetton	B186	BMW	4t	13	battery	14	7
r	22	C Danner	Osella	FA1F	Alfa Romeo	V8t	6	turbo	24	12
ns	16	P Tambay	Lola	THL2	Cosworth	V6t		accident/ injury		

Winning speed: 178.225 km/h, 110.744 mph
Pole Position speed: 188.735 km/h, 117.274 mph (N Mansell, 1 min:24.118 sec)
Fastest Lap speed: 185.808 km/h, 115.456 mph (N Piquet, 1 min:25.443 sec on lap 63)
Lap Leaders: N Mansell 1-16,22-30,32-69 (63); K Rosberg 17-21 (5); A Prost 31 (1).

22 Jun 1986 — USA: Detroit — (Round: 7) (Race: 427)

63 laps x 4.023 km, 2.500 miles = 253.472 km, 157.500 miles

POS.	NO.	DRIVER	CAR	MODEL	ENGINE		LAPS	TIME/REASON FOR RETIREMENT	GRID:POS	ROW
1	12	A Senna	Lotus	98T	Renault	V6t	63	1h 51m 12.847s	1	1
2	26	J Laffite	Ligier	JS27	Renault	V6t	63	1h 51m 43.864s	6	3
3	1	A Prost	McLaren	MP4/2C	TAG Porsche	V6t	63	1h 51m 44.671s	7	4
4	27	M Alboreto	Ferrari	F186	Ferrari	V6t	63	1h 52m 43.783s	11	6
5	5	N Mansell	Williams	FW11	Honda	V6t	62		2	1
6	7	R Patrese	Brabham	BT55	BMW	4t	62		8	4
7	11	J Dumfries	Lotus	98T	Renault	V6t	61		14	7
8	14	J Palmer	Zakspeed	861	Zakspeed	4t	61		20	10
9	4	P Streiff	Tyrrell	015	Renault	V6t	61		18	9
10	8	D Warwick	Brabham	BT55	BMW	4t	60		15	8
r	17	C Danner	Arrows	A8	BMW	4t	51	fuel metering unit	19	10
r	25	R Arnoux	Ligier	JS27	Renault	V6t	46	accident	4	2
r	18	T Boutsen	Arrows	A8	BMW	4t	44	accident	13	7
r	23	A de Cesaris	Minardi	M185B	Motori Moderni	V6t	43	differential	23	12
r	6	N Piquet	Williams	FW11	Honda	V6t	41	accident	3	2
r	28	S Johansson	Ferrari	F186	Ferrari	V6t	40	alternator	5	3
r	19	T Fabi	Benetton	B186	BMW	4t	38	gearbox	17	9
r	16	E Cheever	Lola	THL2	Cosworth	V6t	37	drive pegs	10	5
r	15	A Jones	Lola	THL2	Cosworth	V6t	33	drive pegs	21	11
r	22	A Berg	Osella	FA1F	Alfa Romeo	V8t	28	electrics	25	13
r	3	M Brundle	Tyrrell	015	Renault	V6t	15	electrics	16	8
r	21	P Ghinzani	Osella	FA1G	Alfa Romeo	V8t	14	turbo	22	11
r	2	K Rosberg	McLaren	MP4/2C	TAG Porsche	V6t	12	gearbox	9	5
r	20	G Berger	Benetton	B186	BMW	4t	8	ignition	12	6
r	24	A Nannini	Minardi	M185B	Motori Moderni	V6t	3	turbo	24	12
r	29	H Rothengatter	Zakspeed	861	Zakspeed	4t	-1	electrics	26	13

Winning speed: 136.748 km/h, 84.971 mph
Pole Position speed: 147.344 km/h, 91.556 mph (A Senna, 1 min:38.301 sec)
Fastest Lap speed: 143.077 km/h, 88.904 mph (N Piquet, 1 min:41.233 sec on lap 41)
Lap Leaders: A Senna 1,8-13,39-63 (32); N Mansell 2-7 (6); R Arnoux 14-17 (4); J Laffite 18-30 (13); N Piquet 31-38 (8).

6 Jul 1986 — FRANCE: Paul Ricard — (Round: 8) (Race: 428)

80 laps x 3.813 km, 2.369 miles = 305.040 km, 189.543 miles

POS.	NO.	DRIVER	CAR	MODEL	ENGINE		LAPS	TIME/REASON FOR RETIREMENT	GRID:POS	ROW
1	5	N Mansell	Williams	FW11	Honda	V6t	80	1h 37m 19.272s	2	1
2	1	A Prost	McLaren	MP4/2C	TAG Porsche	V6t	80	1h 37m 36.400s	5	3
3	6	N Piquet	Williams	FW11	Honda	V6t	80	1h 37m 56.817s	3	2
4	2	K Rosberg	McLaren	MP4/2C	TAG Porsche	V6t	80	1h 38m 07.975s	7	4
5	25	R Arnoux	Ligier	JS27	Renault	V6t	79		4	2
6	26	J Laffite	Ligier	JS27	Renault	V6t	79		11	6
7	7	R Patrese	Brabham	BT55	BMW	4t	78		16	8
8	27	M Alboreto	Ferrari	F186	Ferrari	V6t	78		6	3
9	8	D Warwick	Brabham	BT55	BMW	4t	77		14	7
10	3	M Brundle	Tyrrell	015	Renault	V6t	77		15	8
11	17	C Danner	Arrows	A8	BMW	4t	76		18	9
nc	18	T Boutsen	Arrows	A8	BMW	4t	67		21	11
r	16	P Tambay	Lola	THL2	Cosworth	V6t	64	brake caliper	13	7
r	11	J Dumfries	Lotus	98T	Renault	V6t	56	engine	12	6
r	14	J Palmer	Zakspeed	861	Zakspeed	4t	46	engine	22	11
r	4	P Streiff	Tyrrell	015	Renault	V6t	43	fuel injection/ fire	17	9
r	29	H Rothengatter	Zakspeed	861	Zakspeed	4t	32	accident	24	12
r	22	A Berg	Osella	FA1G	Alfa Romeo	V8t	25	turbo	26	13
r	20	G Berger	Benetton	B186	BMW	4t	22	accident/ gear selector	8	4
r	19	T Fabi	Benetton	B186	BMW	4t	7	misfire	9	5
r	28	S Johansson	Ferrari	F186	Ferrari	V6t	5	turbo	10	5
r	12	A Senna	Lotus	98T	Renault	V6t	3	accident	1	1
r	21	P Ghinzani	Osella	FA1H	Alfa Romeo	V8t	3	accident	25	13
r	24	A Nannini	Minardi	M185B	Motori Moderni	V6t	3	accident	19	10
r	23	A de Cesaris	Minardi	M185B	Motori Moderni	V6t	3	turbo	23	12
r	15	A Jones	Lola	THL2	Cosworth	V6t	2	accident	20	10

Winning speed: 188.062 km/h, 116.856 mph
Pole Position speed: 206.337 km/h, 128.212 mph (A Senna, 1 min: 6.526 sec)
Fastest Lap speed: 196.117 km/h, 121.861 mph (N Mansell, 1 min: 9.993 sec on lap 57)
Lap Leaders: N Mansell 1-25,37-53,59-80 (64); A Prost 26-36,54-58 (16).

13 Jul 1986 — BRITAIN: Brands Hatch (Round: 9) (Race: 429)

75 laps x 4.207 km, 2.614 miles = 315.512 km, 196.050 miles

POS.	NO.	DRIVER	CAR	MODEL	ENGINE		LAPS	TIME/REASON FOR RETIREMENT	GRID:POS	ROW
1	5	N Mansell	Williams	FW11	Honda	V6t	75	1h 30m 38.471s	2	1
2	6	N Piquet	Williams	FW11	Honda	V6t	75	1h 30m 44.045s	1	1
3	1	A Prost	McLaren	MP4/2C	TAG Porsche	V6t	74		6	3
4	25	R Arnoux	Ligier	JS27	Renault	V6t	73		8	4
5	3	M Brundle	Tyrrell	015	Renault	V6t	72		11	6
6	4	P Streiff	Tyrrell	015	Renault	V6t	72		16	8
7	11	J Dumfries	Lotus	98T	Renault	V6t	72		10	5
8	8	D Warwick	Brabham	BT55	BMW	4t	72		9	5
9	14	J Palmer	Zakspeed	861	Zakspeed	4t	69		22	11
nc	18	T Boutsen	Arrows	A8	BMW	4t	62		13	7
r	16	P Tambay	Lola	THL2	Cosworth	V6t	60	gearbox pinion bearing	17	9
r	27	M Alboreto	Ferrari	F186	Ferrari	V6t	51	turbo	12	6
r	24	A Nannini	Minardi	M185B	Motori Moderni	V6t	50	cv joint	20	10
r	19	T Fabi	Benetton	B186	BMW	4t	45	fuel pump	7	4
r	7	R Patrese	Brabham	BT54	BMW	4t	39	engine	15	8
r	12	A Senna	Lotus	98T	Renault	V6t	27	gearbox	3	2
r	29	H Rothengatter	Zakspeed	861	Zakspeed	4t	24	engine	25	13
r	23	A de Cesaris	Minardi	M185B	Motori Moderni	V6t	23	alternator	21	11
r	20	G Berger	Benetton	B186	BMW	4t	22	electrics	4	2
r	15	A Jones	Lola	THL2	Cosworth	V6t	22	throttle linkage	14	7
r	28	S Johansson	Ferrari	F186	Ferrari	V6t	20	radiator	18	9
r	2	K Rosberg	McLaren	MP4/2C	TAG Porsche	V6t	7	gearbox	5	3
r	26	J Laffite	Ligier	JS27	Renault	V6t	0	accident *	19	10
r	17	C Danner	Arrows	A8	BMW	4t	0	accident *	23	12
r	21	P Ghinzani	Osella	FA1G	Alfa Romeo	V8t	0	accident *	24	12
r	22	A Berg	Osella	FA1H	Alfa Romeo	V8t	0	accident *	26	13

Winning speed: 208.853 km/h, 129.775 mph
Pole Position speed: 226.170 km/h, 140.536 mph (N Piquet, 1 min: 6.961 sec)
Fastest Lap speed: 217.616 km/h, 135.220 mph (N Mansell, 1 min: 9.593 sec on lap 69)
Lap Leaders: N Piquet 1-22 (22); N Mansell 23-75 (53).

*Interrupted after 1st lap accident. Restarted for original distance. * retired after first start.*

27 Jul 1986 — GERMANY: Hockenheim (Round:10) (Race: 430)

44 laps x 6.797 km, 4.223 miles = 299.068 km, 185.832 miles

POS.	NO.	DRIVER	CAR	MODEL	ENGINE		LAPS	TIME/REASON FOR RETIREMENT	GRID:POS	ROW
1	6	N Piquet	Williams	FW11	Honda	V6t	44	1h 22m 08.263s	5	3
2	12	A Senna	Lotus	98T	Renault	V6t	44	1h 22m 23.700s	3	2
3	5	N Mansell	Williams	FW11	Honda	V6t	44	1h 22m 52.843s	6	3
4	25	R Arnoux	Ligier	JS27	Renault	V6t	44	1h 23m 23.439s	8	4
5r	2	K Rosberg	McLaren	MP4/2C	TAG Porsche	V6t	43	out of fuel	1	1
6r	1	A Prost	McLaren	MP4/2C	TAG Porsche	V6t	43	out of fuel	2	1
7	8	D Warwick	Brabham	BT55	BMW	4t	43		20	10
8	16	P Tambay	Lola	THL2	Cosworth	V6t	43		13	7
9	15	A Jones	Lola	THL2	Cosworth	V6t	42		19	10
10	20	G Berger	Benetton	B186	BMW	4t	42		4	2
11r	28	S Johansson	Ferrari	F186	Ferrari	V6t	41	rear wing	11	6
12	22	A Berg	Osella	FA1F	Alfa Romeo	V8t	40		26	13
r	17	C Danner	Arrows	A8	BMW	4t	38	turbo	17	9
r	29	H Rothengatter	Zakspeed	861	Zakspeed	4t	38	gearbox	24	12
r	14	J Palmer	Zakspeed	861	Zakspeed	4t	37	engine	16	8
r	3	M Brundle	Tyrrell	015	Renault	V6t	34	electrics/ fire	15	8
r	7	R Patrese	Brabham	BT55	BMW	4t	22	spark plug	7	4
r	23	A de Cesaris	Minardi	M185B	Motori Moderni	V6t	20	gearbox	23	12
r	24	A Nannini	Minardi	M185B	Motori Moderni	V6t	19	engine overheating	22	11
r	11	J Dumfries	Lotus	98T	Renault	V6t	17	radiator leak	12	6
r	18	T Boutsen	Arrows	A9	BMW	4t	13	turbo/ fire	21	11
r	26	P Alliot	Ligier	JS27	Renault	V6t	11	engine	14	7
r	21	P Ghinzani	Osella	FA1G	Alfa Romeo	V8t	10	clutch	25	13
r	4	P Streiff	Tyrrell	015	Renault	V6t	7	engine	18	9
r	27	M Alboreto	Ferrari	F186	Ferrari	V6t	6	transmission	10	5
r	19	T Fabi	Benetton	B186	BMW	4t	0	accident	9	5

Winning speed: 218.463 km/h, 135.747 mph
Pole Position speed: 239.864 km/h, 149.044 mph (K Rosberg, 1 min:42.013 sec)
Fastest Lap speed: 229.534 km/h, 142.626 mph (G Berger, 1 min:46.604 sec on lap 35)
Lap Leaders: A Senna 1 (1); K Rosberg 2-5,15-19, 27-38 (21); N Piquet 6-14,21-26,39-44 (21); A Prost 20 (1).

10 Aug 1986 — HUNGARY: Hungaroring (Round:11) (Race: 431)

76 laps x 4.014 km, 2.494 miles = 305.064 km, 189.558 miles

POS.	NO.	DRIVER	CAR	MODEL	ENGINE		LAPS	TIME/REASON FOR RETIREMENT	GRID:POS	ROW
1	6	N Piquet	Williams	FW11	Honda	V6t	76	2h 00m 34.508s	2	1
2	12	A Senna	Lotus	98T	Renault	V6t	76	2h 00m 52.181s	1	1
3	5	N Mansell	Williams	FW11	Honda	V6t	75		4	2
4	28	S Johansson	Ferrari	F186	Ferrari	V6t	75		7	4
5	11	J Dumfries	Lotus	98T	Renault	V6t	74		8	4
6	3	M Brundle	Tyrrell	015	Renault	V6t	74		16	8
7	16	P Tambay	Lola	THL2	Cosworth	V6t	74		6	3
8	4	P Streiff	Tyrrell	015	Renault	V6t	74		18	9
9	26	P Alliot	Ligier	JS27	Renault	V6t	73		12	6
10	14	J Palmer	Zakspeed	861	Zakspeed	4t	70		24	12
r	25	R Arnoux	Ligier	JS27	Renault	V6t	48	engine	9	5
r	15	A Jones	Lola	THL2	Cosworth	V6t	46	differential	10	5
r	20	G Berger	Benetton	B186	BMW	4t	44	fuel leak/ transmission	11	6
r	18	T Boutsen	Arrows	A8	BMW	4t	40	fuel metering unit	22	11
r	2	K Rosberg	McLaren	MP4/2C	TAG Porsche	V6t	34	rear suspension	5	3
r	19	T Fabi	Benetton	B186	BMW	4t	32	spin/ clutch	13	7
r	24	A Nannini	Minardi	M185B	Motori Moderni	V6t	30	engine	17	9
r	27	M Alboreto	Ferrari	F186	Ferrari	V6t	29	accident	15	8
r	8	D Warwick	Brabham	BT55	BMW	4t	28	accident	19	10
r	1	A Prost	McLaren	MP4/2C	TAG Porsche	V6t	23	accident/ suspension	3	2
r	21	P Ghinzani	Osella	FA1G	Alfa Romeo	V8t	15	rear suspension	23	12
r	17	C Danner	Arrows	A9	BMW	4t	7	rear suspension	21	11
r	7	R Patrese	Brabham	BT55	BMW	4t	5	accident	14	7
r	23	A de Cesaris	Minardi	M186	Motori Moderni	V6t	5	engine	20	10
r	29	H Rothengatter	Zakspeed	861	Zakspeed	4t	2	oil cooler	25	13
r	22	A Berg	Osella	FA1F	Alfa Romeo	V8t	1	turbo	26	13

Winning speed: 151.804 km/h, 94.327 mph
Pole Position speed: 161.547 km/h, 100.381 mph (A Senna, 1 min:29.450 sec)
Fastest Lap speed: 158.794 km/h, 98.670 mph (N Piquet, 1 min:31.001 sec on lap 73)
Lap Leaders: A Senna 1-11,36-56 (32); N Piquet 12-35,57-76 (44).

Scheduled for 77 laps, but stopped at 2 hours.

17 Aug 1986 — AUSTRIA: Österreichring (Round:12) (Race: 432)

52 laps x 5.942 km, 3.692 miles = 308.984 km, 191.994 miles

POS.	NO.	DRIVER	CAR	MODEL	ENGINE		LAPS	TIME/REASON FOR RETIREMENT	GRID:POS	ROW
1	1	A Prost	McLaren	MP4/2C	TAG Porsche	V6t	52	1h 21m 22.531s	5	3
2	27	M Alboreto	Ferrari	F186	Ferrari	V6t	51		9	5
3	28	S Johansson	Ferrari	F186	Ferrari	V6t	50		14	7
4	15	A Jones	Lola	THL2	Cosworth	V6t	50		16	8
5	16	P Tambay	Lola	THL2	Cosworth	V6t	50		13	7
6	17	C Danner	Arrows	A8	BMW	4t	49		22	11
7	20	G Berger	Benetton	B186	BMW	4t	49		2	1
8	29	H Rothengatter	Zakspeed	861	Zakspeed	4t	48		24	12
9r	2	K Rosberg	McLaren	MP4/2C	TAG Porsche	V6t	47	electrics	3	2
10	25	R Arnoux	Ligier	JS27	Renault	V6t	47		12	6
11	21	P Ghinzani	Osella	FA1G	Alfa Romeo	V8t	46		25	13
r	5	N Mansell	Williams	FW11	Honda	V6t	32	cv joint	6	3
r	6	N Piquet	Williams	FW11	Honda	V6t	29	engine overheating	7	4
r	18	T Boutsen	Arrows	A9	BMW	4t	25	turbo	18	9
r	19	T Fabi	Benetton	B186	BMW	4t	17	engine	1	1
r	26	P Alliot	Ligier	JS27	Renault	V6t	16	engine	11	6
r	24	A Nannini	Minardi	M185B	Motori Moderni	V6t	13	rear suspension/ spin	19	10
r	23	A de Cesaris	Minardi	M186	Motori Moderni	V6t	13	drive shaft	23	12
r	12	A Senna	Lotus	98T	Renault	V6t	13	misfire	8	4
r	3	M Brundle	Tyrrell	015	Renault	V6t	12	turbo	17	9
r	4	P Streiff	Tyrrell	015	Renault	V6t	10	engine	20	10
r	11	J Dumfries	Lotus	98T	Renault	V6t	9	spark plug	15	8
r	14	J Palmer	Zakspeed	861	Zakspeed	4t	8	engine	21	11
r	22	A Berg	Osella	FA1F	Alfa Romeo	V8t	6	electrics	26	13
r	7	R Patrese	Brabham	BT55	BMW	4t	2	engine	4	2
ns	8	D Warwick	Brabham	BT55	BMW	4t		car raced by Patrese	10	5

Winning speed: 227.821 km/h, 141.561 mph
Pole Position speed: 256.032 km/h, 159.091 mph (T Fabi, 1 min:23.549 sec)
Fastest Lap speed: 239.157 km/h, 148.606 mph (G Berger, 1 min:29.444 sec on lap 49)
Lap Leaders: G Berger 1-25 (25); N Mansell 26-28 (3); A Prost 29-52 (24).

7 Sep 1986 ITALY: Monza (Round:13) (Race: 433)

51 laps x 5.800 km, 3.604 miles = 295.800 km, 183.802 miles

POS.	NO.	DRIVER	CAR	MODEL	ENGINE		LAPS	TIME/REASON FOR RETIREMENT	GRID:POS	ROW
1	6	N Piquet	Williams	FW11	Honda	V6t	51	1h 17m 42.889s	6	3
2	5	N Mansell	Williams	FW11	Honda	V6t	51	1h 17m 52.717s	3	2
3	28	S Johansson	Ferrari	F186	Ferrari	V6t	51	1h 18m 05.804s	12	6
4	2	K Rosberg	McLaren	MP4/2C	TAG Porsche	V6t	51	1h 18m 36.698s	8	4
5	20	G Berger	Benetton	B186	BMW	4t	50		4	2
6	15	A Jones	Lola	THL2	Cosworth	V6t	49		18	9
7	18	T Boutsen	Arrows	A8	BMW	4t	49		13	7
8	17	C Danner	Arrows	A8	BMW	4t	49		16	8
9	4	P Streiff	Tyrrell	015	Renault	V6t	49		23	12
10	3	M Brundle	Tyrrell	015	Renault	V6t	49		20	10
11	22	A Caffi	Osella	FA1F	Alfa Romeo	V8t	45		27	14
r	19	T Fabi	Benetton	B186	BMW	4t	44	puncture/ spin	1	1
r	27	M Alboreto	Ferrari	F186	Ferrari	V6t	33	engine	9	5
r	23	A de Cesaris	Minardi	M186	Motori Moderni	V6t	33	engine	21	11
r	31	I Capelli	AGS	JH21C	Motori Moderni	V6t	31	puncture	25	13
r	25	R Arnoux	Ligier	JS27	Renault	V6t	30	gearbox	11	6
r/dq	1	A Prost	McLaren	MP4/2C	TAG Porsche	V6t	27	engine *	2	1
r	14	J Palmer	Zakspeed	861	Zakspeed	4t	27	alternator	22	11
r	26	P Alliot	Ligier	JS27	Renault	V6t	22	engine	14	7
r	11	J Dumfries	Lotus	98T	Renault	V6t	18	gearbox	17	9
r	8	D Warwick	Brabham	BT55	BMW	4t	16	brakes/ spin	7	4
r	24	A Nannini	Minardi	M185B	Motori Moderni	V6t	15	alternator belt	19	10
r	21	P Ghinzani	Osella	FA1G	Alfa Romeo	V8t	12	rear suspension/ spin	26	13
r	16	P Tambay	Lola	THL2	Cosworth	V6t	2	accident	15	8
r	7	R Patrese	Brabham	BT55	BMW	4t	2	accident	10	5
r	29	H Rothengatter	Zakspeed	861	Zakspeed	4t	1	electrics	24	12
r	12	A Senna	Lotus	98T	Renault	V6t	0	clutch	5	3

Winning speed: 228.373 km/h, 141.905 mph
Pole Position speed: 248.341 km/h, 154.312 mph (T Fabi, 1 min:24.078 sec)
Fastest Lap speed: 237.006 km/h, 147.269 mph (T Fabi, 1 min:28.099 sec on lap 35)
Lap Leaders: G Berger 1-6,25-26 (8); N Mansell 7-24,27-37 (29); N Piquet 38-51 (14).

** A Prost was belatedly disqualified for changing to the spare car after the start of the parade lap.*

21 Sep 1986 PORTUGAL: Estoril (Round:14) (Race: 434)

70 laps x 4.350 km, 2.703 miles = 304.500 km, 189.208 miles

POS.	NO.	DRIVER	CAR	MODEL	ENGINE		LAPS	TIME/REASON FOR RETIREMENT	GRID:POS	ROW
1	5	N Mansell	Williams	FW11	Honda	V6t	70	1h 37m 21.900s	2	1
2	1	A Prost	McLaren	MP4/2C	TAG Porsche	V6t	70	1h 37m 40.672s	3	2
3	6	N Piquet	Williams	FW11	Honda	V6t	70	1h 38m 11.174s	6	3
4r	12	A Senna	Lotus	98T	Renault	V6t	69	out of fuel	1	1
5	27	M Alboreto	Ferrari	F186	Ferrari	V6t	69		13	7
6	28	S Johansson	Ferrari	F186	Ferrari	V6t	69		8	4
7	25	R Arnoux	Ligier	JS27	Renault	V6t	69		10	5
8	19	T Fabi	Benetton	B186	BMW	4t	68		5	3
9	11	J Dumfries	Lotus	98T	Renault	V6t	68		15	8
10	18	T Boutsen	Arrows	A8	BMW	4t	67		21	11
11	17	C Danner	Arrows	A8	BMW	4t	67		22	11
12	14	J Palmer	Zakspeed	861	Zakspeed	4t	67		20	10
13	22	A Berg	Osella	FA1F	Alfa Romeo	V8t	63		27	14
r	7	R Patrese	Brabham	BT55	BMW	4t	62	engine	9	5
nc	16	P Tambay	Lola	THL2	Cosworth	V6t	62		14	7
r	24	A Nannini	Minardi	M185B	Motori Moderni	V6t	60	gearbox	18	9
r	20	G Berger	Benetton	B186	BMW	4t	44	accident	4	2
r	23	A de Cesaris	Minardi	M186	Motori Moderni	V6t	43	accident	16	8
r	2	K Rosberg	McLaren	MP4/2C	TAG Porsche	V6t	41	engine	7	4
r	8	D Warwick	Brabham	BT55	BMW	4t	41	electrics	12	6
r	26	P Alliot	Ligier	JS27	Renault	V6t	39	engine	11	6
r	4	P Streiff	Tyrrell	015	Renault	V6t	28	engine	23	12
r	3	M Brundle	Tyrrell	015	Renault	V6t	18	engine	19	10
r	15	A Jones	Lola	THL2	Cosworth	V6t	10	brakes/ spin	17	9
r	29	H Rothengatter	Zakspeed	861	Zakspeed	4t	9	crown wheel & pinion	26	13
r	21	P Ghinzani	Osella	FA1G	Alfa Romeo	V8t	8	electrics	24	12
r	31	I Capelli	AGS	JH21C	Motori Moderni	V6t	6	gearbox	25	13

Winning speed: 187.644 km/h, 116.597 mph
Pole Position speed: 204.244 km/h, 126.911 mph (A Senna, 1 min:16.673 sec)
Fastest Lap speed: 193.469 km/h, 120.216 mph (N Mansell, 1 min:20.943 sec on lap 53)
Lap Leaders: N Mansell 1-70 (70).

12 Oct 1986 — MEXICO: Mexico City (Round:15) (Race: 435)

68 laps x 4.421 km, 2.747 miles = 300.628 km, 186.802 miles

POS.	NO.	DRIVER	CAR	MODEL	ENGINE		LAPS	TIME/REASON FOR RETIREMENT	GRID:POS	ROW
1	20	G Berger	Benetton	B186	BMW	4t	68	1h 33m 18.700s	4	2
2	1	A Prost	McLaren	MP4/2C	TAG Porsche	V6t	68	1h 33m 44.138s	6	3
3	12	A Senna	Lotus	98T	Renault	V6t	68	1h 34m 11.213s	1	1
4	6	N Piquet	Williams	FW11	Honda	V6t	67		2	1
5	5	N Mansell	Williams	FW11	Honda	V6t	67		3	2
6	26	P Alliot	Ligier	JS27	Renault	V6t	67		10	5
7	18	T Boutsen	Arrows	A8	BMW	4t	66		21	11
8	23	A de Cesaris	Minardi	M186	Motori Moderni	V6t	66		22	11
9	17	C Danner	Arrows	A8	BMW	4t	66		20	10
10r	14	J Palmer	Zakspeed	861	Zakspeed	4t	65	out of fuel	18	9
11	3	M Brundle	Tyrrell	015	Renault	V6t	65		16	8
12r	28	S Johansson	Ferrari	F186	Ferrari	V6t	64	turbo	14	7
13r	7	R Patrese	Brabham	BT55	BMW	4t	64	accident	5	3
14	24	A Nannini	Minardi	M185B	Motori Moderni	V6t	64		24	12
15r	25	R Arnoux	Ligier	JS27	Renault	V6t	63	engine	13	7
16	22	A Berg	Osella	FA1F	Alfa Romeo	V8t	61		26	13
r	11	J Dumfries	Lotus	98T	Renault	V6t	53	battery	17	9
r	8	D Warwick	Brabham	BT55	BMW	4t	37	engine	7	4
r	15	A Jones	Lola	THL2	Cosworth	V6t	35	gear selection/ radiator	15	8
r	2	K Rosberg	McLaren	MP4/2C	TAG Porsche	V6t	32	puncture/ suspension	11	6
r	27	M Alboreto	Ferrari	F186	Ferrari	V6t	10	turbo	12	6
r	4	P Streiff	Tyrrell	015	Renault	V6t	8	turbo	19	10
r	21	P Ghinzani	Osella	FA1G	Alfa Romeo	V8t	8	turbo	25	13
r	19	T Fabi	Benetton	B186	BMW	4t	4	engine	9	5
r	16	P Tambay	Lola	THL2	Cosworth	V6t	0	accident	8	4
ns	29	H Rothengatter	Zakspeed	861	Zakspeed	4t		accident	23	12

Winning speed: 193.306 km/h, 120.115 mph
Pole Position speed: 206.723 km/h, 128.452 mph (A Senna, 1 min:16.990 sec)
Fastest Lap speed: 200.549 km/h, 124.616 mph (N Piquet, 1 min:19.360 sec on lap 64)
Lap Leaders: N Piquet 1-31 (31); A Senna 32-35 (4); G Berger 36-68 (33).

26 Oct 1986 — AUSTRALIA: Adelaide (Round:16) (Race: 436)

82 laps x 3.779 km, 2.348 miles = 309.878 km, 192.549 miles

POS.	NO.	DRIVER	CAR	MODEL	ENGINE		LAPS	TIME/REASON FOR RETIREMENT	GRID:POS	ROW
1	1	A Prost	McLaren	MP4/2C	TAG Porsche	V6t	82	1h 54m 20.388s	4	2
2	6	N Piquet	Williams	FW11	Honda	V6t	82	1h 54m 24.593s	2	1
3	28	S Johansson	Ferrari	F186	Ferrari	V6t	81		12	6
4	3	M Brundle	Tyrrell	015	Renault	V6t	81		16	8
5r	4	P Streiff	Tyrrell	015	Renault	V6t	80	out of fuel	10	5
6	11	J Dumfries	Lotus	98T	Renault	V6t	80		14	7
7	25	R Arnoux	Ligier	JS27	Renault	V6t	79		5	3
8	26	P Alliot	Ligier	JS27	Renault	V6t	79		8	4
9	14	J Palmer	Zakspeed	861	Zakspeed	4t	77		21	11
10	19	T Fabi	Benetton	B186	BMW	4t	77		13	7
nc	16	P Tambay	Lola	THL2	Cosworth	V6t	70		17	9
r	5	N Mansell	Williams	FW11	Honda	V6t	63	tyre burst/ accident	1	1
r	7	R Patrese	Brabham	BT55	BMW	4t	63	electrics	19	10
r	2	K Rosberg	McLaren	MP4/2C	TAG Porsche	V6t	62	tyre burst	7	4
nc	22	A Berg	Osella	FA1F	Alfa Romeo	V8t	61		26	13
r	8	D Warwick	Brabham	BT55	BMW	4t	57	brakes	20	10
r	17	C Danner	Arrows	A8	BMW	4t	52	engine	24	12
r	18	T Boutsen	Arrows	A8	BMW	4t	50	throttle spring	22	11
r	12	A Senna	Lotus	98T	Renault	V6t	43	engine	3	2
r	20	G Berger	Benetton	B186	BMW	4t	40	clutch/ engine	6	3
r	23	A de Cesaris	Minardi	M186	Motori Moderni	V6t	40	fire extinguisher	11	6
r	29	H Rothengatter	Zakspeed	861	Zakspeed	4t	29	rear suspension	23	12
r	15	A Jones	Lola	THL2	Cosworth	V6t	16	engine	15	8
r	24	A Nannini	Minardi	M185B	Motori Moderni	V6t	10	accident	18	9
r	21	P Ghinzani	Osella	FA1G	Alfa Romeo	V8t	2	crown wheel & pinion	25	13
r	27	M Alboreto	Ferrari	F186	Ferrari	V6t	0	accident/ rear suspension	9	5

Winning speed: 162.609 km/h, 101.041 mph
Pole Position speed: 173.519 km/h, 107.820 mph (N Mansell, 1 min:18.403 sec)
Fastest Lap speed: 168.398 km/h, 104.638 mph (N Piquet, 1 min:20.787 sec on lap 82)
Lap Leaders: N Piquet 1-6,63-64 (8); K Rosberg 7-62 (56); A Prost 65-82 (18).

Lap Leaders 1986

POS	DRIVER	CAR-ENGINE	GPS	LAPS	KM	MILES
1	N Mansell	Williams-Honda	9	331	1,495.3	929.1
2	N Piquet	Williams-Honda	10	242	1,196.3	743.3
3	A Prost	McLaren-TAG Porsche	8	166	695.5	432.1
4	A Senna	Lotus-Renault	8	134	566.5	352.0
5	K Rosberg	McLaren-TAG Porsche	4	86	396.6	246.4
6	G Berger	Benetton-BMW	3	66	340.8	211.8
7	J Laffite	Ligier-Renault	1	13	52.3	32.5
8	R Arnoux	Ligier-Renault	1	4	16.1	10.0
9	S Johansson	Ferrari	1	2	13.9	8.6
			16	**1,044**	**4,773.2**	**2,965.9**

Driver Points 1986

		BR	E	RSM	MC	B	CDN	USA	F	GB	D	H	A	I	P	MEX	AUS	TOTAL	
1	A Prost	-	4	9	9	(1)	6	4	6	4	(1)	-	9	-	6	6	9	72	(2)
2	N Mansell	-	6	-	3	9	9	2	9	9	4	4	-	6	9	(2)	-	70	(2)
3	N Piquet	9	-	6	-	-	4	-	4	6	9	9	-	9	4	3	6	69	
4	A Senna	6	9	-	4	6	2	9	-	-	6	6	-	-	3	4	-	55	
5	S Johansson	-	-	3	-	4	-	-	-	-	-	3	4	4	1	-	4	23	
6	K Rosberg	-	3	2	6	-	3	-	3	-	2	-	-	3	-	-	-	22	
7	G Berger	1	1	4	-	-	-	-	-	-	-	-	-	2	-	9	-	17	
8	J Laffite	4	-	-	1	2	-	6	1	-	-	-	-	-	-	-	-	14	
	M Alboreto	-	-	-	-	3	-	3	-	-	-	-	6	-	2	-	-	14	
	R Arnoux	3	-	-	2	-	1	-	2	3	3	-	-	-	-	-	-	14	
11	M Brundle	2	-	-	-	-	-	-	-	2	-	1	-	-	-	-	3	8	
12	A Jones	-	-	-	-	-	-	-	-	-	-	-	3	1	-	-	-	4	
13	P Streiff	-	-	-	-	-	-	-	-	1	-	-	-	-	-	-	2	3	
	J Dumfries	-	-	-	-	-	-	-	-	-	-	2	-	-	-	-	1	3	
15	T Fabi	-	2	-	-	-	-	-	-	-	-	-	-	-	-	-	-	2	
	P Tambay	-	-	-	-	-	-	-	-	-	-	-	2	-	-	-	-	2	
	R Patrese	-	-	1	-	-	-	1	-	-	-	-	-	-	-	-	-	2	
18	P Alliot	-	-	-	-	-	-	-	-	-	-	-	-	-	-	1	-	1	
	C Danner	-	-	-	-	-	-	-	-	-	-	-	1	-	-	-	-	1	

9, 6, 4, 3, 2 and 1 point awarded to the first six finishers. Best 11 scores.

Constructor Points 1986

		BR	E	RSM	MC	B	CDN	USA	F	GB	D	H	A	I	P	MEX	AUS	TOTAL
1	Williams-Honda	9	6	6	3	9	13	2	13	15	13	13	-	15	13	5	6	141
2	McLaren-TAG Porsche	-	7	11	15	1	9	4	9	4	3	-	9	3	6	6	9	96
3	Lotus-Renault	6	9	-	4	6	2	9	-	-	6	8	-	-	3	4	1	58
4	Ferrari	-	-	3	-	7	-	3	-	-	-	3	10	4	3	-	4	37
5	Ligier-Renault	7	-	-	3	2	1	6	3	3	3	-	-	-	-	1	-	29
6	Benetton-BMW	1	3	4	-	-	-	-	-	-	-	-	-	2	-	9	-	19
7	Tyrrell-Renault	2	-	-	-	-	-	-	-	3	-	1	-	-	-	-	5	11
8	Lola-Cosworth	-	-	-	-	-	-	-	-	-	-	-	5	1	-	-	-	6
9	Brabham-BMW	-	-	1	-	-	-	1	-	-	-	-	-	-	-	-	-	2
10	Arrows-BMW	-	-	-	-	-	-	-	-	-	-	-	1	-	-	-	-	1

9, 6, 4, 3, 2 and 1 point awarded to the first six finishers.

March returned to compete in the newly created 3.5 litre normally aspirated division. Turbos would be limited to a maximum boost to 4.0 bar by compulsory pop-off valves. Lotus raced its active suspension system utilising computer controlled hydraulics. Ligier was left without a suitable engine when the new Alfa unit was suddenly withdrawn.

McLAREN
Marlboro McLaren International: Prost, Johansson

TYRRELL
Data General Team Tyrrell: Palmer, Streiff

WILLIAMS
Canon Williams Team: Mansell, Patrese, Piquet

BRABHAM
Motor Racing Developments: Patrese, Modena, de Cesaris

ZAKSPEED
West Zakspeed Racing: Brundle, Danner

LOTUS
Camel Team Lotus Honda: Nakajima, Senna

AGS
Team El Charro AGS: Fabre, Moreno

MARCH
Leyton House March Racing Team: Capelli

ARROWS
USF&G Arrows Megatron: Warwick, Cheever

BENETTON
Benetton Formula: Fabi, Boutsen

OSELLA
Osella Squadra Corse: Caffi, Tarquini, Forini

MINARDI
Minardi Team: Campos, Nannini

LIGIER
Ligier Loto: Arnoux, Ghinzani

FERRARI
Scuderia Ferrari SpA SEFAC: Alboreto, Berger

LOLA
Larrousse Calmels: Dalmas, Alliot

COLONI
Enzo Coloni Racing Car System: Larini

12 Apr 1987 — BRAZIL: Rio de Janeiro (Round: 1) (Race: 437)

61 laps x 5.031 km, 3.126 miles = 306.891 km, 190.693 miles

POS.	NO.	DRIVER	CAR	MODEL	ENGINE		LAPS	TIME/REASON FOR RETIREMENT	GRID:POS	ROW
1	1	A Prost	McLaren	MP4/3	TAG Porsche	V6t	61	1h 39m 45.141s	5	3
2	6	N Piquet	Williams	FW11B	Honda	V6t	61	1h 40m 25.688s	2	1
3	2	S Johansson	McLaren	MP4/3	TAG Porsche	V6t	61	1h 40m 41.899s	10	5
4	28	G Berger	Ferrari	F187	Ferrari	V6t	61	1h 41m 24.376s	7	4
5	20	T Boutsen	Benetton	B187	Cosworth	V6t	60		6	3
6	5	N Mansell	Williams	FW11B	Honda	V6t	60		1	1
7	11	S Nakajima	Lotus	99T	Honda	V6t	59		12	6
8r	27	M Alboreto	Ferrari	F187	Ferrari	V6t	58	spin	9	5
9	10	C Danner	Zakspeed	861	Zakspeed	4t	58		17	9
10	3	J Palmer	Tyrrell	DG016	Cosworth	V8	58		18	9
11	4	P Streiff	Tyrrell	DG016	Cosworth	V8	57		20	10
12	14	P Fabre	AGS	JH22	Cosworth	V8	55		22	11
r	18	E Cheever	Arrows	A10	Megatron	4t	52	engine	14	7
r	12	A Senna	Lotus	99T	Honda	V6t	50	engine	3	2
r	7	R Patrese	Brabham	BT56	BMW	4t	48	battery loose	11	6
r	8	A de Cesaris	Brabham	BT56	BMW	4t	21	differential	13	7
r	17	D Warwick	Arrows	A10	Megatron	4t	20	engine overheating	8	4
r	21	A Caffi	Osella	FA11	Alfa Romeo	V8t	20	driver exhausted	21	11
r	24	A Nannini	Minardi	M187	Motori Moderni	V6t	17	suspension	15	8
r	9	M Brundle	Zakspeed	861	Zakspeed	4t	15	turbo	19	10
r	19	T Fabi	Benetton	B187	Cosworth	V6t	9	turbo	4	2
dq	23	A Campos	Minardi	M187	Motori Moderni	V6t	3	incorrect starting procedure	16	8
ns	16	I Capelli	March	87P	Cosworth	V8		no engine	23	12

Winning speed: 184.592 km/h, 114.700 mph
Pole Position speed: 210.287 km/h, 130.666 mph (N Mansell, 1 min:26.128 sec)
Fastest Lap speed: 192.962 km/h, 119.901 mph (N Piquet, 1 min:33.861 sec on lap 42)
Lap Leaders: N Piquet 1-7,17-20 (11); A Senna 8-12 (5); A Prost 13-16,21-61 (45).

3 May 1987 — SAN MARINO: Imola (Round: 2) (Race: 438)

59 laps x 5.040 km, 3.132 miles = 297.360 km, 184.771 miles

POS.	NO.	DRIVER	CAR	MODEL	ENGINE		LAPS	TIME/REASON FOR RETIREMENT	GRID:POS	ROW
1	5	N Mansell	Williams	FW11B	Honda	V6t	59	1h 31m 24.076s	2	1
2	12	A Senna	Lotus	99T	Honda	V6t	59	1h 31m 51.621s	1	1
3	27	M Alboreto	Ferrari	F187	Ferrari	V6t	59	1h 32m 03.220s	6	3
4	2	S Johansson	McLaren	MP4/3	TAG Porsche	V6t	59	1h 32m 24.664s	8	4
5	9	M Brundle	Zakspeed	871	Zakspeed	4t	57		14	7
6	11	S Nakajima	Lotus	99T	Honda	V6t	57		12	6
7	10	C Danner	Zakspeed	861	Zakspeed	4t	57		17	9
8	4	P Streiff	Tyrrell	DG016	Cosworth	V8	57		20	10
9	7	R Patrese	Brabham	BT56	BMW	4t	57		7	4
10	30	P Alliot	Lola	LC87	Cosworth	V8	56		21	11
11r	17	D Warwick	Arrows	A10	Megatron	4t	55	out of fuel	10	5
12r	21	A Caffi	Osella	FA11	Alfa Romeo	V8t	54	out of fuel	19	10
13	14	P Fabre	AGS	JH22	Cosworth	V8	53		24	12
r	19	T Fabi	Benetton	B187	Cosworth	V6t	51	turbo	4	2
r	20	T Boutsen	Benetton	B187	Cosworth	V6t	48	engine	11	6
r	18	E Cheever	Arrows	A10	Megatron	4t	48	engine overheating	9	5
r	3	J Palmer	Tyrrell	DG016	Cosworth	V8	48	clutch	23	12
r	8	A de Cesaris	Brabham	BT56	BMW	4t	39	spin	13	7
r	23	A Campos	Minardi	M187	Motori Moderni	V6t	30	gearbox	16	8
r	22	G Tarquini	Osella	FA1G	Alfa Romeo	V8t	26	gearbox	25	13
r	24	A Nannini	Minardi	M187	Motori Moderni	V6t	25	engine	15	8
r	16	I Capelli	March	871	Cosworth	V8	18	distributor rotor arm	22	11
r	28	G Berger	Ferrari	F187	Ferrari	V6t	16	electronics	5	3
r	1	A Prost	McLaren	MP4/3	TAG Porsche	V6t	14	alternator belt	3	2

POS.	NO.	DRIVER	CAR	MODEL	ENGINE		LAPS	TIME/REASON FOR RETIREMENT	GRID:POS	ROW
r	26	P Ghinzani	Ligier	JS29B	Megatron	4t	7	handling	18	9
ns	6	N Piquet	Williams	FW11B	Honda	V6t		accident/ injury		
ns	25	R Arnoux	Ligier	JS29B	Megatron	4t		suspension		

Winning speed: 195.201 km/h, 121.292 mph
Pole Position speed: 211.404 km/h, 131.361 mph (A Senna, 1 min:25.826 sec)
Fastest Lap speed: 203.303 km/h, 126.327 mph (T Fabi, 1 min:29.246 sec on lap 51)
Lap Leaders: A Senna 1,25-26 (3); N Mansell 2-21,27-59 (53); M Alboreto 22-24 (3).

17 May 1987 BELGIUM: Spa-Francorchamps (Round: 3) (Race: 439)

43 laps x 6.940 km, 4.312 miles = 298.420 km, 185.430 miles

POS.	NO.	DRIVER	CAR	MODEL	ENGINE		LAPS	TIME/REASON FOR RETIREMENT	GRID:POS	ROW
1	1	A Prost	McLaren	MP4/3	TAG Porsche	V6t	43	1h 27m 03.217s	6	3
2	2	S Johansson	McLaren	MP4/3	TAG Porsche	V6t	43	1h 27m 27.981s	10	5
3r	8	A de Cesaris	Brabham	BT56	BMW	4t	42	out of fuel	13	7
4	18	E Cheever	Arrows	A10	Megatron	4t	42		11	6
5	11	S Nakajima	Lotus	99T	Honda	V6t	42		15	8
6	25	R Arnoux	Ligier	JS29B	Megatron	4t	41		16	8
7r	26	P Ghinzani	Ligier	JS29B	Megatron	4t	40	out of fuel	17	9
8	30	P Alliot	Lola	LC87	Cosworth	V8	40		22	11
9	4	P Streiff	Tyrrell	DG016	Cosworth	V8	39		23	12
10r	14	P Fabre	AGS	JH22	Cosworth	V8	38	electrics	25	13
r	19	T Fabi	Benetton	B187	Cosworth	V6t	34	oil pump drive	9	5
r	9	M Brundle	Zakspeed	871	Zakspeed	4t	19	engine	18	9
r	20	T Boutsen	Benetton	B187	Cosworth	V6t	18	cv joint	7	4
r	5	N Mansell	Williams	FW11B	Honda	V6t	17	accident/ undertray	1	1
r	16	I Capelli	March	871	Cosworth	V8	14	oil pressure	21	11
r	6	N Piquet	Williams	FW11B	Honda	V6t	11	turbo sensor	2	1
r	21	A Caffi	Osella	FA1I	Alfa Romeo	V8t	11	engine	26	13
r	27	M Alboreto	Ferrari	F187	Ferrari	V6t	9	wheel bearing	5	3
r	10	C Danner	Zakspeed	871	Zakspeed	4t	9	brakes/ spin	20	10
r	17	D Warwick	Arrows	A10	Megatron	4t	8	water hose/ engine overheating	12	6
r	7	R Patrese	Brabham	BT56	BMW	4t	5	clutch	8	4
r	28	G Berger	Ferrari	F187	Ferrari	V6t	2	turbo	4	2
r	24	A Nannini	Minardi	M187	Motori Moderni	V6t	1	turbo	14	7
r	12	A Senna	Lotus	99T	Honda	V6t	0	accident	3	2
r	23	A Campos	Minardi	M187	Motori Moderni	V6t	0	clutch	19	10
r	3	J Palmer	Tyrrell	DG016	Cosworth	V8	1	accident *	24	12

Winning speed: 205.680 km/h, 127.804 mph
Pole Position speed: 223.020 km/h, 138.578 mph (N Mansell, 1 min:52.026 sec)
Fastest Lap speed: 213.260 km/h, 132.513 mph (A Prost, 1 min:57.153 sec on lap 26)
Lap Leaders: N Piquet 1-9 (9); A Prost 10-43 (34).

*Interrupted after 2nd lap accident. Restarted for original distance. * retired after first start.*

René Arnoux in the Ligier JS29B-Megatron at Monaco 1987.

31 May 1987 — MONACO: Monte Carlo (Round: 4) (Race: 440)

78 laps x 3.328 km, 2.068 miles = 259.584 km, 161.298 miles

POS.	NO.	DRIVER	CAR	MODEL	ENGINE		LAPS	TIME/REASON FOR RETIREMENT	GRID:POS	ROW
1	12	A Senna	Lotus	99T	Honda	V6t	78	1h 57m 54.085s	2	1
2	6	N Piquet	Williams	FW11B	Honda	V6t	78	1h 58m 27.297s	3	2
3	27	M Alboreto	Ferrari	F187	Ferrari	V6t	78	1h 59m 06.924s	5	3
4	28	G Berger	Ferrari	F187	Ferrari	V6t	77		8	4
5	3	J Palmer	Tyrrell	DG016	Cosworth	V8	76		15	8
6	16	I Capelli	March	871	Cosworth	V8	76		19	10
7	9	M Brundle	Zakspeed	871	Zakspeed	4t	76		14	7
8	19	T Fabi	Benetton	B187	Cosworth	V6t	76		12	6
9r	1	A Prost	McLaren	MP4/3	TAG Porsche	V6t	75	engine	4	2
10	11	S Nakajima	Lotus	99T	Honda	V6t	75		17	9
11	25	R Arnoux	Ligier	JS29B	Megatron	4t	74		22	11
12	26	P Ghinzani	Ligier	JS29B	Megatron	4t	74		20	10
13	14	P Fabre	AGS	JH22	Cosworth	V8	71		24	12
r	18	E Cheever	Arrows	A10	Megatron	4t	59	cylinder head gasket	6	3
r	17	D Warwick	Arrows	A10	Megatron	4t	58	gear linkage	11	6
r	2	S Johansson	McLaren	MP4/3	TAG Porsche	V6t	57	engine	7	4
r	30	P Alliot	Lola	LC87	Cosworth	V8	42	engine	18	9
r	7	R Patrese	Brabham	BT56	BMW	4t	41	electronics	10	5
r	21	A Caffi	Osella	FA11	Alfa Romeo	V8t	39	electrics	16	8
r	8	A de Cesaris	Brabham	BT56	BMW	4t	38	suspension	21	11
r	5	N Mansell	Williams	FW11B	Honda	V6t	29	turbo wastegate	1	1
r	24	A Nannini	Minardi	M187	Motori Moderni	V6t	21	electrics	13	7
r	4	P Streiff	Tyrrell	DG016	Cosworth	V8	9	accident	23	12
r	20	T Boutsen	Benetton	B187	Cosworth	V6t	5	cv joint	9	5
ns	23	A Campos	Minardi	M187	Motori Moderni	V6t		accident/ injury		
exc	10	C Danner	Zakspeed	871	Zakspeed	4t		dangerous driving		

Winning speed: 132.102 km/h, 82.085 mph
Pole Position speed: 144.279 km/h, 89.651 mph (N Mansell, 1 min:23.039 sec)
Fastest Lap speed: 136.635 km/h, 84.901 mph (A Senna, 1 min:27.685 sec on lap 72)
Lap Leaders: N Mansell 1-29 (29); A Senna 30-78 (49).

21 Jun 1987 — USA: Detroit (Round: 5) (Race: 441)

63 laps x 4.023 km, 2.500 miles = 253.472 km, 157.500 miles

POS.	NO.	DRIVER	CAR	MODEL	ENGINE		LAPS	TIME/REASON FOR RETIREMENT	GRID:POS	ROW
1	12	A Senna	Lotus	99T	Honda	V6t	63	1h 50m 16.358s	2	1
2	6	N Piquet	Williams	FW11B	Honda	V6t	63	1h 50m 50.177s	3	2
3	1	A Prost	McLaren	MP4/3	TAG Porsche	V6t	63	1h 51m 01.685s	5	3
4	28	G Berger	Ferrari	F187	Ferrari	V6t	63	1h 51m 18.959s	12	6
5	5	N Mansell	Williams	FW11B	Honda	V6t	62		1	1
6r	18	E Cheever	Arrows	A10	Megatron	4t	60	out of fuel	6	3
7	2	S Johansson	McLaren	MP4/3	TAG Porsche	V6t	60		11	6
8	10	C Danner	Zakspeed	871	Zakspeed	4t	60		16	8
9	7	R Patrese	Brabham	BT56	BMW	4t	60		9	5
10	25	R Arnoux	Ligier	JS29B	Megatron	4t	60		21	11
11	3	J Palmer	Tyrrell	DG016	Cosworth	V8	60		13	7
12	14	P Fabre	AGS	JH22	Cosworth	V8	58		26	13
r	20	T Boutsen	Benetton	B187	Cosworth	V6t	52	brake disc	4	2
r	26	P Ghinzani	Ligier	JS29B	Megatron	4t	51	clutch	23	12
r	4	P Streiff	Tyrrell	DG016	Cosworth	V8	44	accident	14	7
r	30	P Alliot	Lola	LC87	Cosworth	V8	38	accident	20	10
r	27	M Alboreto	Ferrari	F187	Ferrari	V6t	25	gearbox	7	4
r	24	A Nannini	Minardi	M187	Motori Moderni	V6t	22	gearbox	18	9
r	9	M Brundle	Zakspeed	871	Zakspeed	4t	16	turbo/ fire	15	8
r	17	D Warwick	Arrows	A10	Megatron	4t	12	accident	10	5
r	16	I Capelli	March	871	Cosworth	V8	9	battery	22	11
r	19	T Fabi	Benetton	B187	Cosworth	V6t	6	accident	8	4
r	21	A Caffi	Osella	FA11	Alfa Romeo	V8t	3	gear lever	19	10
r	8	A de Cesaris	Brabham	BT56	BMW	4t	2	gearbox	17	9
r	23	A Campos	Minardi	M187	Motori Moderni	V6t	1	accident	25	13
r	11	S Nakajima	Lotus	99T	Honda	V6t	0	accident	24	12

Winning speed: 137.915 km/h, 85.697 mph
Pole Position speed: 145.388 km/h, 90.340 mph (N Mansell, 1 min:39.264 sec)
Fastest Lap speed: 145.915 km/h, 90.667 mph (A Senna, 1 min:40.464 sec on lap 39)
Lap Leaders: N Mansell 1-33 (33); A Senna 34-63 (30).

5 Jul 1987 — FRANCE: Paul Ricard (Round: 6) (Race: 442)

80 laps x 3.813 km, 2.369 miles = 305.040 km, 189.543 miles

POS.	NO.	DRIVER	CAR	MODEL	ENGINE		LAPS	TIME/REASON FOR RETIREMENT	GRID:POS	ROW
1	5	N Mansell	Williams	FW11B	Honda	V6t	80	1h 37m 03.839s	1	1
2	6	N Piquet	Williams	FW11B	Honda	V6t	80	1h 37m 11.550s	4	2
3	1	A Prost	McLaren	MP4/3	TAG Porsche	V6t	80	1h 37m 59.094s	2	1
4	12	A Senna	Lotus	99T	Honda	V6t	79		3	2
5r	19	T Fabi	Benetton	B187	Cosworth	V6t	77	drive shaft	7	4
6	4	P Streiff	Tyrrell	DG016	Cosworth	V8	76		25	13
7	3	J Palmer	Tyrrell	DG016	Cosworth	V8	76		24	12
8r	2	S Johansson	McLaren	MP4/3	TAG Porsche	V6t	74	alternator belt	9	5
9	14	P Fabre	AGS	JH22	Cosworth	V8	74		26	13
r	28	G Berger	Ferrari	F187	Ferrari	V6t	71	suspension/ spin	6	3

POS.	NO.	DRIVER	CAR	MODEL	ENGINE		LAPS	TIME/REASON FOR RETIREMENT	GRID:POS	ROW
nc	11	S Nakajima	Lotus	99T	Honda	V6t	71		16	8
r	27	M Alboreto	Ferrari	F187	Ferrari	V6t	64	engine	8	4
r	17	D Warwick	Arrows	A10	Megatron	4t	62	turbo	10	5
r	30	P Alliot	Lola	LC87	Cosworth	V8	57	transmission	23	12
r	16	I Capelli	March	871	Cosworth	V8	52	engine	22	11
r	23	A Campos	Minardi	M187	Motori Moderni	V6t	52	turbo	21	11
r	25	R Arnoux	Ligier	JS29C	Megatron	4t	33	exhaust	13	7
r	20	T Boutsen	Benetton	B187	Cosworth	V6t	31	distributor	5	3
r	10	C Danner	Zakspeed	871	Zakspeed	4t	26	engine overheating	19	10
r	26	P Ghinzani	Ligier	JS29C	Megatron	4t	24	engine	17	9
r	24	A Nannini	Minardi	M187	Motori Moderni	V6t	23	turbo	15	8
r	7	R Patrese	Brabham	BT56	BMW	4t	19	crown wheel & pinion	12	6
r	9	M Brundle	Zakspeed	871	Zakspeed	4t	18	rear wheel lost	18	9
r	21	A Caffi	Osella	FA1I	Alfa Romeo	V8t	11	gearbox	20	10
r	8	A de Cesaris	Brabham	BT56	BMW	4t	2	turbo/ fire	11	6
r	18	E Cheever	Arrows	A10	Megatron	4t	0	driver turned off ignition	14	7

Winning speed: 188.560 km/h, 117.166 mph
Pole Position speed: 206.561 km/h, 128.351 mph (N Mansell, 1 min: 6.454 sec)
Fastest Lap speed: 197.372 km/h, 122.641 mph (N Piquet, 1 min: 9.548 sec on lap 68)
Lap Leaders: N Mansell 1-35,46-80 (70); N Piquet 36-45 (10).

12 Jul 1987 — BRITAIN: Silverstone (Round: 7) (Race: 443)

65 laps x 4.778 km, 2.969 miles = 310.579 km, 192.985 miles

POS.	NO.	DRIVER	CAR	MODEL	ENGINE		LAPS	TIME/REASON FOR RETIREMENT	GRID:POS	ROW
1	5	N Mansell	Williams	FW11B	Honda	V6t	65	1h 19m 11.780s	2	1
2	6	N Piquet	Williams	FW11B	Honda	V6t	65	1h 19m 13.698s	1	1
3	12	A Senna	Lotus	99T	Honda	V6t	64		3	2
4	11	S Nakajima	Lotus	99T	Honda	V6t	63		12	6
5	17	D Warwick	Arrows	A10	Megatron	4t	63		13	7
6	19	T Fabi	Benetton	B187	Cosworth	V6t	63		6	3
7	20	T Boutsen	Benetton	B187	Cosworth	V6t	62		5	3
8	3	J Palmer	Tyrrell	DG016	Cosworth	V8	60		23	12
9	14	P Fabre	AGS	JH22	Cosworth	V8	59		25	13
r	4	P Streiff	Tyrrell	DG016	Cosworth	V8	57	engine	22	11
nc	9	M Brundle	Zakspeed	871	Zakspeed	4t	54		17	9
r	1	A Prost	McLaren	MP4/3	TAG Porsche	V6t	53	clutch bearing/ engine	4	2
r	27	M Alboreto	Ferrari	F187	Ferrari	V6t	52	rear suspension	7	4
r	18	E Cheever	Arrows	A10	Megatron	4t	45	engine overheating	14	7
r	23	A Campos	Minardi	M187	Motori Moderni	V6t	34	fuel pump	19	10
r	21	A Caffi	Osella	FA1I	Alfa Romeo	V8t	32	turbo	20	10
r	10	C Danner	Zakspeed	871	Zakspeed	4t	32	gearbox	18	9
r	7	R Patrese	Brabham	BT56	BMW	4t	28	fuel metering unit	11	6
r	2	S Johansson	McLaren	MP4/3	TAG Porsche	V6t	18	engine	10	5
r	24	A Nannini	Minardi	M187	Motori Moderni	V6t	10	engine	15	8
r	8	A de Cesaris	Brabham	BT56	BMW	4t	8	fuel line/ fire	9	5
r	28	G Berger	Ferrari	F187	Ferrari	V6t	7	accident	8	4
r	30	P Alliot	Lola	LC87	Cosworth	V8	7	gearbox	21	11
r	25	R Arnoux	Ligier	JS29C	Megatron	4t	3	electrics	16	8
r	16	I Capelli	March	871	Cosworth	V8	3	gearbox	24	12
exc	26	P Ghinzani	Ligier	JS29C	Megatron	4t		refuelled on circuit		

Winning speed: 235.298 km/h, 146.208 mph
Pole Position speed: 256.315 km/h, 159.267 mph (N Piquet, 1 min: 7.110 sec)
Fastest Lap speed: 246.324 km/h, 153.059 mph (N Mansell, 1 min: 9.832 sec on lap 58)
Lap Leaders: N Piquet 1-62 (62); N Mansell 63-65 (3).

26 Jul 1987 — GERMANY: Hockenheim (Round: 8) (Race: 444)

44 laps x 6.797 km, 4.223 miles = 299.068 km, 185.832 miles

POS.	NO.	DRIVER	CAR	MODEL	ENGINE		LAPS	TIME/REASON FOR RETIREMENT	GRID:POS	ROW
1	6	N Piquet	Williams	FW11B	Honda	V6t	44	1h 21m 25.091s	4	2
2	2	S Johansson	McLaren	MP4/3	TAG Porsche	V6t	44	1h 23m 04.682s	8	4
3	12	A Senna	Lotus	99T	Honda	V6t	43		2	1
4	4	P Streiff	Tyrrell	DG016	Cosworth	V8	43		22	11
5	3	J Palmer	Tyrrell	DG016	Cosworth	V8	43		23	12
6	30	P Alliot	Lola	LC87	Cosworth	V8	42		21	11
7r	1	A Prost	McLaren	MP4/3	TAG Porsche	V6t	39	alternator belt	3	2
nc	9	M Brundle	Zakspeed	871	Zakspeed	4t	34		19	10
r	26	P Ghinzani	Ligier	JS29C	Megatron	4t	32	engine	17	9
r	23	A Campos	Minardi	M187	Motori Moderni	V6t	28	engine	18	9
r	20	T Boutsen	Benetton	B187	Cosworth	V6t	26	engine	6	3
r	5	N Mansell	Williams	FW11B	Honda	V6t	25	engine	1	1
r	24	A Nannini	Minardi	M187	Motori Moderni	V6t	25	engine	16	8
r	17	D Warwick	Arrows	A10	Megatron	4t	23	turbo	13	7
r	10	C Danner	Zakspeed	871	Zakspeed	4t	21	input shaft	20	10
r	28	G Berger	Ferrari	F187	Ferrari	V6t	19	turbo	10	5
r	19	T Fabi	Benetton	B187	Cosworth	V6t	18	engine	9	5
r	21	A Caffi	Osella	FA1I	Alfa Romeo	V8t	17	engine	26	13
r	8	A de Cesaris	Brabham	BT56	BMW	4t	12	engine	7	4
r	27	M Alboreto	Ferrari	F187	Ferrari	V6t	10	turbo	5	3
r	14	P Fabre	AGS	JH22	Cosworth	V8	10	valve	25	13
r	18	E Cheever	Arrows	A10	Megatron	4t	9	throttle linkage	15	8
r	11	S Nakajima	Lotus	99T	Honda	V6t	9	suspension	14	7

POS.	NO.	DRIVER	CAR	MODEL	ENGINE		LAPS	TIME/REASON FOR RETIREMENT	GRID:POS	ROW
r	16	I Capelli	March	871	Cosworth	V8	7	distributor rotor arm	24	12
r	25	R Arnoux	Ligier	JS29C	Megatron	4t	6	electrics	12	6
r	7	R Patrese	Brabham	BT56	BMW	4t	5	engine	11	6

Winning speed: 220.394 km/h, 136.946 mph
Pole Position speed: 238.454 km/h, 148.168 mph (N Mansell, 1 min:42.616 sec)
Fastest Lap speed: 231.462 km/h, 143.824 mph (N Mansell, 1 min:45.716 sec on lap 24)
Lap Leaders: A Senna 1 (1); N Mansell 2-7,19-22 (10); A Prost 8-18,23-39 (28); N Piquet 40-44 (5).

9 Aug 1987 — HUNGARY: Hungaroring (Round: 9) (Race: 445)

76 laps x 4.014 km, 2.494 miles = 305.064 km, 189.558 miles

POS.	NO.	DRIVER	CAR	MODEL	ENGINE		LAPS	TIME/REASON FOR RETIREMENT	GRID:POS	ROW
1	6	N Piquet	Williams	FW11B	Honda	V6t	76	1h 59m 26.793s	3	2
2	12	A Senna	Lotus	99T	Honda	V6t	76	2h 00m 04.520s	6	3
3	1	A Prost	McLaren	MP4/3	TAG Porsche	V6t	76	2h 00m 54.249s	4	2
4	20	T Boutsen	Benetton	B187	Cosworth	V6t	75		7	4
5	7	R Patrese	Brabham	BT56	BMW	4t	75		10	5
6	17	D Warwick	Arrows	A10	Megatron	4t	74		9	5
7	3	J Palmer	Tyrrell	DG016	Cosworth	V8	74		16	8
8	18	E Cheever	Arrows	A10	Megatron	4t	74		11	6
9	4	P Streiff	Tyrrell	DG016	Cosworth	V8	74		14	7
10	16	I Capelli	March	871	Cosworth	V8	74		18	9
11	24	A Nannini	Minardi	M187	Motori Moderni	V6t	73		20	10
12	26	P Ghinzani	Ligier	JS29C	Megatron	4t	73		25	13
13	14	P Fabre	AGS	JH22	Cosworth	V8	71		26	13
14r	5	N Mansell	Williams	FW11B	Honda	V6t	70	wheel nut lost	1	1
r	21	A Caffi	Osella	FA1I	Alfa Romeo	V8t	64	out of fuel	21	11
r	25	R Arnoux	Ligier	JS29C	Megatron	4t	57	electrics	19	10
r	30	P Alliot	Lola	LC87	Cosworth	V8	48	accident	15	8
r	9	M Brundle	Zakspeed	871	Zakspeed	4t	45	turbo	22	11
r	27	M Alboreto	Ferrari	F187	Ferrari	V6t	43	engine	5	3
r	8	A de Cesaris	Brabham	BT56	BMW	4t	43	gearbox	13	7
r	2	S Johansson	McLaren	MP4/3	TAG Porsche	V6t	14	gearbox	8	4
r	19	T Fabi	Benetton	B187	Cosworth	V6t	14	gearbox	12	6
r	23	A Campos	Minardi	M187	Motori Moderni	V6t	14	accident	24	12
r	28	G Berger	Ferrari	F187	Ferrari	V6t	13	cv joint	2	1
r	10	C Danner	Zakspeed	871	Zakspeed	4t	3	electrics	23	12
r	11	S Nakajima	Lotus	99T	Honda	V6t	1	drive shaft	17	9

Winning speed: 153.239 km/h, 95.218 mph
Pole Position speed: 164.121 km/h, 101.980 mph (N Mansell, 1 min:28.047 sec)
Fastest Lap speed: 160.295 km/h, 99.602 mph (N Piquet, 1 min:30.149 sec on lap 63)
Lap Leaders: N Mansell 1-70 (70); N Piquet 71-76 (6).

16 Aug 1987 — AUSTRIA: Österreichring (Round:10) (Race: 446)

52 laps x 5.942 km, 3.692 miles = 308.984 km, 191.994 miles

POS.	NO.	DRIVER	CAR	MODEL	ENGINE		LAPS	TIME/REASON FOR RETIREMENT	GRID:POS	ROW
1	5	N Mansell	Williams	FW11B	Honda	V6t	52	1h 18m 44.898s	2	1
2	6	N Piquet	Williams	FW11B	Honda	V6t	52	1h 19m 40.602s	1	1
3	19	T Fabi	Benetton	B187	Cosworth	V6t	51		5	3
4	20	T Boutsen	Benetton	B187	Cosworth	V6t	51		4	2
5	12	A Senna	Lotus	99T	Honda	V6t	50		7	4
6	1	A Prost	McLaren	MP4/3	TAG Porsche	V6t	50		9	5
7	2	S Johansson	McLaren	MP4/3	TAG Porsche	V6t	50		14	7
8	26	P Ghinzani	Ligier	JS29C	Megatron	4t	50		18	9
9	10	C Danner	Zakspeed	871	Zakspeed	4t	49		20	10
10	25	R Arnoux	Ligier	JS29C	Megatron	4t	49		16	8
11	16	I Capelli	March	871	Cosworth	V8	49		23	12
12	30	P Alliot	Lola	LC87	Cosworth	V8	49		22	11
13	11	S Nakajima	Lotus	99T	Honda	V6t	49		13	7
dq	9	M Brundle	Zakspeed	871	Zakspeed	4t	48	bodywork infringement	17	9
14	3	J Palmer	Tyrrell	DG016	Cosworth	V8	47		24	12
nc	14	P Fabre	AGS	JH22	Cosworth	V8	45		26	13
r	7	R Patrese	Brabham	BT56	BMW	4t	43	engine	8	4
r	27	M Alboreto	Ferrari	F187	Ferrari	V6t	42	exhaust	6	3
r	8	A de Cesaris	Brabham	BT56	BMW	4t	35	turbo	10	5
r	17	D Warwick	Arrows	A10	Megatron	4t	35	engine	11	6
r	18	E Cheever	Arrows	A10	Megatron	4t	31	puncture	12	6
r	28	G Berger	Ferrari	F187	Ferrari	V6t	5	turbo	3	2
r	23	A Campos	Minardi	M187	Motori Moderni	V6t	3	distributor belt	19	10
r	24	A Nannini	Minardi	M187	Motori Moderni	V6t	1	engine	15	8
r	21	A Caffi	Osella	FA1I	Alfa Romeo	V8t	0	electrics	21	11
r	4	P Streiff	Tyrrell	DG016	Cosworth	V8	0	accident *	25	13

Winning speed: 235.421 km/h, 146.284 mph
Pole Position speed: 256.622 km/h, 159.457 mph (N Piquet, 1 min:23.357 sec)
Fastest Lap speed: 242.207 km/h, 150.500 mph (N Mansell, 1 min:28.318 sec on lap 31)
Lap Leaders: N Piquet 1-20 (20); N Mansell 21-52 (32).

*Interrupted twice after 1st lap accidents. Restarted for original distance. * retired after second start.*

6 Sep 1987 — ITALY: Monza (Round:11) (Race: 447)

50 laps x 5.800 km, 3.604 miles = 290.000 km, 180.198 miles

POS.	NO.	DRIVER	CAR	MODEL	ENGINE		LAPS	TIME/REASON FOR RETIREMENT	GRID:POS	ROW
1	6	N Piquet	Williams	FW11B	Honda	V6t	50	1h 14m 47.707s	1	1
2	12	A Senna	Lotus	99T	Honda	V6t	50	1h 14m 49.513s	4	2
3	5	N Mansell	Williams	FW11B	Honda	V6t	50	1h 15m 36.743s	2	1
4	28	G Berger	Ferrari	F187	Ferrari	V6t	50	1h 15m 45.686s	3	2
5	20	T Boutsen	Benetton	B187	Cosworth	V6t	50	1h 16m 09.026s	6	3
6	2	S Johansson	McLaren	MP4/3	TAG Porsche	V6t	50	1h 16m 16.494s	11	6
7	19	T Fabi	Benetton	B187	Cosworth	V6t	49		7	4
8	26	P Ghinzani	Ligier	JS29C	Megatron	4t	48		19	10
9	10	C Danner	Zakspeed	871	Zakspeed	4t	48		16	8
10	25	R Arnoux	Ligier	JS29C	Megatron	4t	48		15	8
11	11	S Nakajima	Lotus	99T	Honda	V6t	47		14	7
12	4	P Streiff	Tyrrell	DG016	Cosworth	V8	47		24	12
13	16	I Capelli	March	871	Cosworth	V8	47		25	13
14	3	J Palmer	Tyrrell	DG016	Cosworth	V8	47		22	11
15	1	A Prost	McLaren	MP4/3	TAG Porsche	V6t	46		5	3
16r	24	A Nannini	Minardi	M187	Motori Moderni	V6t	45	out of fuel	18	9
r	9	M Brundle	Zakspeed	871	Zakspeed	4t	43	gearbox	17	9
r	30	P Alliot	Lola	LC87	Cosworth	V8	37	accident	23	12
r	23	A Campos	Minardi	M187	Motori Moderni	V6t	34	fuel filter/ fire	20	10
r	18	E Cheever	Arrows	A10	Megatron	4t	27	cv joint	13	7
r	22	F Forini	Osella	FA1I	Alfa Romeo	V8t	27	turbo	26	13
r	21	A Caffi	Osella	FA1I	Alfa Romeo	V8t	16	suspension	21	11
r	27	M Alboreto	Ferrari	F187	Ferrari	V6t	13	turbo	8	4
r	17	D Warwick	Arrows	A10	Megatron	4t	9	fuel metering unit	12	6
r	8	A de Cesaris	Brabham	BT56	BMW	4t	7	suspension	10	5
r	7	R Patrese	Brabham	BT56	BMW	4t	5	engine	9	5
nq	32	N Larini	Coloni	FC187	Cosworth	V8				
nq	14	P Fabre	AGS	JH22	Cosworth	V8				

Winning speed: 232.636 km/h, 144.553 mph
Pole Position speed: 250.180 km/h, 155.454 mph (N Piquet, 1 min:23.460 sec)
Fastest Lap speed: 240.564 km/h, 149.480 mph (A Senna, 1 min:26.796 sec on lap 49)
Lap Leaders: N Piquet 1-23,43-50 (31); A Senna 24-42 (19).

20 Sep 1987 — PORTUGAL: Estoril (Round:12) (Race: 448)

70 laps x 4.350 km, 2.703 miles = 304.500 km, 189.208 miles

POS.	NO.	DRIVER	CAR	MODEL	ENGINE		LAPS	TIME/REASON FOR RETIREMENT	GRID:POS	ROW
1	1	A Prost	McLaren	MP4/3	TAG Porsche	V6t	70	1h 37m 03.906s	3	2
2	28	G Berger	Ferrari	F187	Ferrari	V6t	70	1h 37m 24.399s	1	1
3	6	N Piquet	Williams	FW11B	Honda	V6t	70	1h 38m 07.201s	4	2
4r	19	T Fabi	Benetton	B187	Cosworth	V6t	69	out of fuel	10	5
5	2	S Johansson	McLaren	MP4/3	TAG Porsche	V6t	69		8	4
6	18	E Cheever	Arrows	A10	Megatron	4t	68		11	6
7	12	A Senna	Lotus	99T	Honda	V6t	68		5	3
8	11	S Nakajima	Lotus	99T	Honda	V6t	68		15	8
9	16	I Capelli	March	871	Cosworth	V8	67		22	11
10	3	J Palmer	Tyrrell	DG016	Cosworth	V8	67		24	12
11r	24	A Nannini	Minardi	M187	Motori Moderni	V6t	66	out of fuel	14	7
12	4	P Streiff	Tyrrell	DG016	Cosworth	V8	66		21	11
13	17	D Warwick	Arrows	A10	Megatron	4t	66		12	6
14	20	T Boutsen	Benetton	B187	Cosworth	V6t	64		9	5
r	8	A de Cesaris	Brabham	BT56	BMW	4t	54	injector pipe	13	7
r	27	M Alboreto	Ferrari	F187	Ferrari	V6t	38	gear linkage	6	3
r	9	M Brundle	Zakspeed	871	Zakspeed	4t	35	gearbox	17	9
r	22	F Forini	Osella	FA1I	Alfa Romeo	V8t	32	rear wheel bearing	26	13
r	30	P Alliot	Lola	LC87	Cosworth	V8	31	fuel pump	19	10
r	25	R Arnoux	Ligier	JS29C	Megatron	4t	29	intercooler	18	9
r	21	A Caffi	Osella	FA1I	Alfa Romeo	V8t	27	turbo	25	13
r	26	P Ghinzani	Ligier	JS29C	Megatron	4t	24	clutch/ ignition	23	12
r	23	A Campos	Minardi	M187	Motori Moderni	V6t	24	intercooler	20	10
r	5	N Mansell	Williams	FW11B	Honda	V6t	13	electrics	2	1
r	7	R Patrese	Brabham	BT56	BMW	4t	13	engine	7	4
r	10	C Danner	Zakspeed	871	Zakspeed	4t	0	accident *	16	8
nq	14	P Fabre	AGS	JH22	Cosworth	V8				

Winning speed: 188.224 km/h, 116.957 mph
Pole Position speed: 201.752 km/h, 125.363 mph (G Berger, 1 min:17.620 sec)
Fastest Lap speed: 197.523 km/h, 122.735 mph (G Berger, 1 min:19.282 sec on lap 66)
Lap Leaders: N Mansell 1 (1); G Berger 2-33,36-67 (64); M Alboreto 34-35 (2); A Prost 68-70 (3).

*Interrupted after 2nd lap, because of an accident. Restarted for original distance.   * retired after first start.*

27 Sep 1987 — SPAIN: Jerez de la Frontera (Round:13) (Race: 449)

72 laps x 4.218 km, 2.621 miles = 303.696 km, 188.708 miles

POS.	NO.	DRIVER	CAR	MODEL	ENGINE		LAPS	TIME/REASON FOR RETIREMENT	GRID:POS	ROW
1	5	N Mansell	Williams	FW11B	Honda	V6t	72	1h 49m 12.692s	2	1
2	1	A Prost	McLaren	MP4/3	TAG Porsche	V6t	72	1h 49m 34.917s	7	4
3	2	S Johansson	McLaren	MP4/3	TAG Porsche	V6t	72	1h 49m 43.510s	11	6
4	6	N Piquet	Williams	FW11B	Honda	V6t	72	1h 49m 44.142s	1	1

POS.	NO.	DRIVER	CAR	MODEL	ENGINE		LAPS	TIME/REASON FOR RETIREMENT	GRID:POS	ROW
5	12	A Senna	Lotus	99T	Honda	V6t	72	1h 50m 26.199s	5	3
6	30	P Alliot	Lola	LC87	Cosworth	V8	71		17	9
7	4	P Streiff	Tyrrell	DG016	Cosworth	V8	71		15	8
8r	18	E Cheever	Arrows	A10	Megatron	4t	70	out of fuel	13	7
9	11	S Nakajima	Lotus	99T	Honda	V6t	70		18	9
10	17	D Warwick	Arrows	A10	Megatron	4t	70		12	6
11	9	M Brundle	Zakspeed	871	Zakspeed	4t	70		20	10
12	16	I Capelli	March	871	Cosworth	V8	70		19	10
13	7	R Patrese	Brabham	BT56	BMW	4t	68		9	5
14	23	A Campos	Minardi	M187	Motori Moderni	V6t	68		24	12
15r	27	M Alboreto	Ferrari	F187	Ferrari	V6t	67	engine	4	2
16r	20	T Boutsen	Benetton	B187	Cosworth	V6t	66	brakes/ spin	8	4
r	28	G Berger	Ferrari	F187	Ferrari	V6t	62	oil radiator/ engine	3	2
r	3	J Palmer	Tyrrell	DG016	Cosworth	V8	55	accident	16	8
r	25	R Arnoux	Ligier	JS29C	Megatron	4t	55	engine	14	7
r	10	C Danner	Zakspeed	871	Zakspeed	4t	50	gearbox	22	11
r	24	A Nannini	Minardi	M187	Motori Moderni	V6t	45	turbo	21	11
r	19	T Fabi	Benetton	B187	Cosworth	V6t	40	engine	6	3
r	8	A de Cesaris	Brabham	BT56	BMW	4t	26	gearbox	10	5
r	26	P Ghinzani	Ligier	JS29C	Megatron	4t	24	ignition	23	12
r	14	P Fabre	AGS	JH22	Cosworth	V8	10	clutch	25	13
r	32	N Larini	Coloni	FC187	Cosworth	V8	8	suspension	26	13
nq	21	A Caffi	Osella	FA1I	Alfa Romeo	V8t				
nq	22	F Forini	Osella	FA1I	Alfa Romeo	V8t				

Winning speed: 166.848 km/h, 103.675 mph
Pole Position speed: 184.145 km/h, 114.423 mph (N Piquet, 1 min:22.461 sec)
Fastest Lap speed: 174.566 km/h, 108.470 mph (G Berger, 1 min:26.986 sec on lap 49)
Lap Leaders: N Mansell 1-72 (72).

18 Oct 1987 — MEXICO: Mexico City (Round:14) (Race: 450)
63 laps x 4.421 km, 2.747 miles = 278.523 km, 173.066 miles

POS.	NO.	DRIVER	CAR	MODEL	ENGINE		LAPS	TIME/REASON FOR RETIREMENT	GRID:POS	ROW
1	5	N Mansell	Williams	FW11B	Honda	V6t	63	1h 26m 24.207s	1	1
2	6	N Piquet	Williams	FW11B	Honda	V6t	63	1h 26m 50.383s	3	2
3	7	R Patrese	Brabham	BT56	BMW	4t	63	1h 27m 51.086s	8	4
4	18	E Cheever	Arrows	A10	Megatron	4t	63	1h 28m 05.559s	12	6
5	19	T Fabi	Benetton	B187	Cosworth	V6t	61		6	3
6	30	P Alliot	Lola	LC87	Cosworth	V8	60		24	12
7	3	J Palmer	Tyrrell	DG016	Cosworth	V8	60		22	11
8	4	P Streiff	Tyrrell	DG016	Cosworth	V8	60		25	13
9	29	Y Dalmas	Lola	LC87	Cosworth	V8	59		23	12
r	12	A Senna	Lotus	99T	Honda	V6t	54	spin	7	4
r	16	I Capelli	March	871	Cosworth	V8	51	engine	20	10
r	21	A Caffi	Osella	FA1I	Alfa Romeo	V8t	50	engine	26	13
r	26	P Ghinzani	Ligier	JS29C	Megatron	4t	43	engine overheating	21	11
r	23	A Campos	Minardi	M187	Motori Moderni	V6t	32	gear linkage	19	10
r	25	R Arnoux	Ligier	JS29C	Megatron	4t	29	ignition	18	9
r	17	D Warwick	Arrows	A10	Megatron	4t	26	accident	11	6
r	8	A de Cesaris	Brabham	BT56	BMW	4t	22	spin	10	5
r	28	G Berger	Ferrari	F187	Ferrari	V6t	20	engine	2	1
r	20	T Boutsen	Benetton	B187	Cosworth	V6t	15	electronics	4	2
r	24	A Nannini	Minardi	M187	Motori Moderni	V6t	13	turbo	14	7
r	27	M Alboreto	Ferrari	F187	Ferrari	V6t	12	engine	9	5
r	9	M Brundle	Zakspeed	871	Zakspeed	4t	3	turbo	13	7
r	2	S Johansson	McLaren	MP4/3	TAG Porsche	V6t	1	accident	15	8
r	11	S Nakajima	Lotus	99T	Honda	V6t	1	accident	16	8
r	10	C Danner	Zakspeed	871	Zakspeed	4t	1	accident	17	9
r	1	A Prost	McLaren	MP4/3	TAG Porsche	V6t	0	accident	5	3
nq	14	P Fabre	AGS	JH22	Cosworth	V8				

Winning speed: 193.411 km/h, 120.180 mph
Pole Position speed: 203.049 km/h, 126.169 mph (N Mansell, 1 min:18.383 sec)
Fastest Lap speed: 201.127 km/h, 124.975 mph (N Piquet, 1 min:19.132 sec on lap 57)
Lap Leaders: G Berger 1,15-20 (7); T Boutsen 2-14 (13); N Mansell 21-30 (10); N Piquet 31-63 (33).

Scheduled for 68 laps, but interrupted after 30 laps, because of an accident. Restarted for a further 33 laps, with results being on aggregate and lap leaders 'on the road'.

1 Nov 1987 — JAPAN: Suzuka (Round:15) (Race: 451)
51 laps x 5.859 km, 3.641 miles = 298.809 km, 185.671 miles

POS.	NO.	DRIVER	CAR	MODEL	ENGINE		LAPS	TIME/REASON FOR RETIREMENT	GRID:POS	ROW
1	28	G Berger	Ferrari	F187	Ferrari	V6t	51	1h 32m 58.072s	1	1
2	12	A Senna	Lotus	99T	Honda	V6t	51	1h 33m 15.456s	7	4
3	2	S Johansson	McLaren	MP4/3	TAG Porsche	V6t	51	1h 33m 15.766s	9	5
4	27	M Alboreto	Ferrari	F187	Ferrari	V6t	51	1h 34m 18.513s	4	2
5	20	T Boutsen	Benetton	B187	Cosworth	V6t	51	1h 34m 23.648s	3	2
6	11	S Nakajima	Lotus	99T	Honda	V6t	51	1h 34m 34.551s	11	6
7	1	A Prost	McLaren	MP4/3	TAG Porsche	V6t	50		2	1
8	3	J Palmer	Tyrrell	DG016	Cosworth	V8	50		19	10
9	18	E Cheever	Arrows	A10	Megatron	4t	50		12	6
10	17	D Warwick	Arrows	A10	Megatron	4t	50		13	7
11r	7	R Patrese	Brabham	BT56	BMW	4t	49	engine	8	4
12	4	P Streiff	Tyrrell	DG016	Cosworth	V8	49		25	13
13r	26	P Ghinzani	Ligier	JS29C	Megatron	4t	48	out of fuel	24	12

POS.	NO.	DRIVER	CAR	MODEL	ENGINE	LAPS	TIME/REASON FOR RETIREMENT	GRID:POS	ROW
14r	29	Y Dalmas	Lola	LC87	Cosworth V8	47	electrics	22	11
15r	6	N Piquet	Williams	FW11B	Honda V6t	46	engine	5	3
r	25	R Arnoux	Ligier	JS29C	Megatron 4t	44	out of fuel	17	9
r	21	A Caffi	Osella	FA1I	Alfa Romeo V8t	43	out of fuel	23	12
r	14	R Moreno	AGS	JH22	Cosworth V8	38	fuel injection	26	13
r	24	A Nannini	Minardi	M187	Motori Moderni V6t	35	engine	14	7
r	9	M Brundle	Zakspeed	871	Zakspeed 4t	32	engine overheating	15	8
r	8	A de Cesaris	Brabham	BT56	BMW 4t	26	turbo	10	5
r	19	T Fabi	Benetton	B187	Cosworth V6t	16	engine	6	3
r	10	C Danner	Zakspeed	871	Zakspeed 4t	13	engine/ oil on tyres/ accident	16	8
r	16	I Capelli	March	871	Cosworth V8	13	accident	20	10
r	23	A Campos	Minardi	M187	Motori Moderni V6t	2	engine	21	11
r	30	P Alliot	Lola	LC87	Cosworth V8	0	accident	18	9
ns	5	N Mansell	Williams	FW11B	Honda V6t		accident/ injury		

Winning speed: 192.847 km/h, 119.829 mph
Pole Position speed: 210.835 km/h, 131.007 mph (G Berger, 1 min:40.042 sec)
Fastest Lap speed: 203.116 km/h, 126.211 mph (A Prost, 1 min:43.844 sec on lap 35)
Lap Leaders: G Berger 1-24,26-51 (50); A Senna 25 (1).

15 Nov 1987 — AUSTRALIA: Adelaide (Round:16) (Race: 452)

82 laps x 3.779 km, 2.348 miles = 309.878 km, 192.549 miles

POS.	NO.	DRIVER	CAR	MODEL	ENGINE	LAPS	TIME/REASON FOR RETIREMENT	GRID:POS	ROW
1	28	G Berger	Ferrari	F187	Ferrari V6t	82	1h 52m 56.144s	1	1
dq	12	A Senna	Lotus	99T	Honda V6t	82	brake duct irregularities	4	2
2	27	M Alboreto	Ferrari	F187	Ferrari V6t	82	1h 54m 04.028s	6	3
3	20	T Boutsen	Benetton	B187	Cosworth V6t	81		5	3
4	3	J Palmer	Tyrrell	DG016	Cosworth V8	80		19	10
5	29	Y Dalmas	Lola	LC87	Cosworth V8	79		21	11
6	14	R Moreno	AGS	JH22	Cosworth V8	79		25	13
7	10	C Danner	Zakspeed	871	Zakspeed 4t	79		24	12
8r	8	A de Cesaris	Brabham	BT56	BMW 4t	78	spin	10	5
9r	5	R Patrese	Williams	FW11B	Honda V6t	76	engine	7	4
r	6	N Piquet	Williams	FW11B	Honda V6t	58	brakes/ gear linkage	3	2
r	16	I Capelli	March	871	Cosworth V8	58	spin	23	12
r	1	A Prost	McLaren	MP4/3	TAG Porsche V6t	53	brakes/ accident	2	1
r	18	E Cheever	Arrows	A10	Megatron 4t	53	engine overheating	11	6
r	2	S Johansson	McLaren	MP4/3	TAG Porsche V6t	48	brakes	8	4
r	19	T Fabi	Benetton	B187	Cosworth V6t	46	brakes	9	5
r	23	A Campos	Minardi	M187	Motori Moderni V6t	46	gearbox	26	13
r	30	P Alliot	Lola	LC87	Cosworth V8	45	electrics	17	9
r	25	R Arnoux	Ligier	JS29C	Megatron 4t	41	electrics	20	10
r	7	S Modena	Brabham	BT56	BMW 4t	31	driver exhausted	15	8
r	26	P Ghinzani	Ligier	JS29C	Megatron 4t	26	engine	22	11
r	11	S Nakajima	Lotus	99T	Honda V6t	22	suspension hydraulics	14	7
r	17	D Warwick	Arrows	A10	Megatron 4t	19	transmission	12	6
r	9	M Brundle	Zakspeed	871	Zakspeed 4t	18	gear selection/ turbo	16	8
r	4	P Streiff	Tyrrell	DG016	Cosworth V8	6	spin	18	9
r	24	A Nannini	Minardi	M187	Motori Moderni V6t	0	accident	13	7
nq	21	A Caffi	Osella	FA1I	Alfa Romeo V8t				

Winning speed: 164.631 km/h, 102.297 mph
Pole Position speed: 176.070 km/h, 109.405 mph (G Berger, 1 min:17.267 sec)
Fastest Lap speed: 169.175 km/h, 105.121 mph (G Berger, 1 min:20.416 sec on lap 72)
Lap Leaders: G Berger 1-82 (82).

A Senna finished 2nd in 1h 53m 30.989s.

Martin Brundle at Imola in 1987, in the Zakspeed 871.

Lap Leaders 1987

POS		CAR-ENGINE	GPS	LAPS	KM	MILES
1	N Mansell	Williams-Honda	11	383	1,669.0	1,037.1
2	G Berger	Ferrari	4	203	912.2	566.8
3	N Piquet	Williams-Honda	9	187	954.8	593.3
4	A Prost	McLaren-TAG Porsche	4	110	665.7	413.7
5	A Senna	Lotus-Honda	7	108	446.9	277.7
6	T Boutsen	Benetton-Cosworth	1	13	57.5	35.7
7	M Alboreto	Ferrari	2	5	23.8	14.8
			16	**1,009**	**4,729.8**	**2,939.0**

Driver Points 1987

		BR	RSM	B	MC	USA	F	GB	D	H	A	I	P	E	MEX	J	AUS	TOTAL	
1	N Piquet	6	-	-	6	6	6	6	9	9	6	9	4	(3)	6	-	-	73	(3)
2	N Mansell	1	9	-	-	2	9	9	-	-	9	4	-	9	9	-	-	61	
3	A Senna	-	6	-	9	9	3	4	4	6	2	6	-	2	-	6	-	57	
4	A Prost	9	-	9	-	4	4	-	-	4	1	-	9	6	-	-	-	46	
5	G Berger	3	-	-	3	3	-	-	-	-	-	3	6	-	-	9	9	36	
6	S Johansson	4	3	6	-	-	-	-	6	-	-	1	2	4	-	4	-	30	
7	M Alboreto	-	4	-	4	-	-	-	-	-	-	-	-	-	-	3	6	17	
8	T Boutsen	2	-	-	-	-	-	-	-	3	3	2	-	-	-	2	4	16	
9	T Fabi	-	-	-	-	-	2	1	-	-	4	-	3	-	2	-	-	12	
10	E Cheever	-	-	3	-	1	-	-	-	-	-	-	1	-	3	-	-	8	
11	J Palmer	-	-	-	2	-	-	-	2	-	-	-	-	-	-	-	3	7	
	S Nakajima	-	1	2	-	-	-	3	-	-	-	-	-	-	-	1	-	7	
13	R Patrese	-	-	-	-	-	-	-	-	2	-	-	-	-	4	-	-	6	
14	A de Cesaris	-	-	4	-	-	-	-	-	-	-	-	-	-	-	-	-	4	
	P Streiff	-	-	-	-	-	1	-	3	-	-	-	-	-	-	-	-	4	
16	D Warwick	-	-	-	-	-	-	2	-	1	-	-	-	-	-	-	-	3	
	P Alliot	-	-	-	-	-	-	-	1	-	-	-	-	1	1	-	-	3	
18	M Brundle	-	2	-	-	-	-	-	-	-	-	-	-	-	-	-	-	2	
19	R Arnoux	-	-	1	-	-	-	-	-	-	-	-	-	-	-	-	-	1	
	I Capelli	-	-	-	1	-	-	-	-	-	-	-	-	-	-	-	-	1	
	R Moreno	-	-	-	-	-	-	-	-	-	-	-	-	-	-	-	1	1	
22	Y Dalmas	-	-	-	-	-	-	-	-	-	-	-	-	-	-	-	(2)	-	(2)

JIM CLARK TROPHY

		BR	RSM	B	MC	USA	F	GB	D	H	A	I	P	E	MEX	J	AUS	TOTAL	
1	J Palmer	9	-	-	9	9	6	9	6	9	(4)	(4)	6	-	6	9	9	87	(8)
2	P Streiff	6	9	6	-	-	9	-	9	6	-	9	4	6	4	6	-	74	
3	P Alliot	-	6	9	-	-	-	-	4	-	6	-	-	9	9	-	-	43	
4	I Capelli	-	-	-	6	-	-	-	-	4	9	6	9	4	-	-	-	38	
5	P Fabre	-	4	4	4	4	6	4	6	-	3	-	-	-	-	-	-	35	
6	R Moreno	-	-	-	-	-	-	-	-	-	-	-	-	-	-	-	4	4	
7	Y Dalmas	-	-	-	-	-	-	-	-	-	-	-	-	-	-	-	(6)	-	(6)

9, 6, 4, 3, 2 and 1 point awarded to the first six finishers. Best 11 scores. Y Dalmas (Lola-Cosworth) finished 5th in Australia, but points not valid for Championship because Constructor had only entered one car for the season.

In an effort to promote interest in the power disadvantaged normally aspirated cars, separate Championships were created (Jim Clark and Colin Chapman Trophies) and points distributed in the usual manner. Drivers were eligible for World Championship points, if they finished in the top six overall.

Constructor Points 1987

		BR	RSM	B	MC	USA	F	GB	D	H	A	I	P	E	MEX	J	AUS	TOTAL	
1	Williams-Honda	7	9	-	6	8	15	15	9	9	15	13	4	12	15	-	-	137	
2	McLaren-TAG Porsche	13	3	15	-	4	4	-	6	4	1	1	11	10	-	4	-	76	
3	Lotus-Honda	-	7	2	9	9	3	7	4	6	2	6	-	2	-	7	-	64	
4	Ferrari	3	4	-	7	3	-	-	-	-	-	3	6	-	-	12	15	53	
5	Benetton-Cosworth	2	-	-	-	-	2	1	-	3	7	2	3	-	2	2	4	28	
6	Tyrrell-Cosworth	-	-	-	2	-	1	-	5	-	-	-	-	-	-	-	3	11	
	Arrows-Megatron	-	-	3	-	1	-	2	-	1	-	-	1	-	3	-	-	11	
8	Brabham-BMW	-	-	4	-	-	-	-	-	2	-	-	-	-	4	-	-	10	
9	Lola-Cosworth	-	-	-	-	-	-	-	1	-	-	-	-	1	1	-	(2)	3	(2)
10	Zakspeed	-	2	-	-	-	-	-	-	-	-	-	-	-	-	-	-	2	
11	Ligier-Megatron	-	-	1	-	-	-	-	-	-	-	-	-	-	-	-	-	1	
	March-Cosworth	-	-	-	1	-	-	-	-	-	-	-	-	-	-	-	-	1	
	AGS-Cosworth	-	-	-	-	-	-	-	-	-	-	-	-	-	-	-	1	1	

COLIN CHAPMAN TROPHY

		BR	RSM	B	MC	USA	F	GB	D	H	A	I	P	E	MEX	J	AUS	TOTAL	
1	Tyrrell-Cosworth	15	9	(6)	9	9	15	(9)	15	15	(4)	13	10	(6)	10	10	(9)	130	(34)
2	Lola-Cosworth	-	6	9	-	-	-	-	4	-	6	-	-	9	9	9	(6)	52	(6)
3	AGS-Cosworth	4	4	4	4	6	4	6	-	3	-	-	-	-	-	-	4	39	
4	March-Cosworth	-	-	-	6	-	-	-	-	4	9	6	6	4	-	-	-	35	

9, 6, 4, 3, 2 and 1 point awarded to the first six finishers.

The turbos were further regulated with 2.5 bar pressure and only 150 litres of fuel. Honda took their engine from Williams to McLaren. Enzo Ferrari died in August of this year at the age of 90. Pre-qualifying re-emerged in a small way and it was to become an early morning ritual for some teams in years to come.

LOTUS
Camel Team Lotus Honda: Piquet, Nakajima

TYRRELL
Tyrrell Racing Organisation: Palmer, Bailey

WILLIAMS
Canon Williams Team: Mansell, Brundle, Schlesser, Patrese

ZAKSPEED
West Zakspeed Racing: Ghinzani, Schneider

McLAREN
Honda Marlboro McLaren: Prost, Senna

AGS
Automobiles Gonfaronaises Sportives: Streiff

MARCH
Leyton House March Racing Team: Gugelmin, Capelli

ARROWS
USF&G Arrows Megatron: Warwick, Cheever

BENETTON
Benetton Formula: Nannini, Boutsen

OSELLA
Osella Squadra Corse: Larini

RIAL
Rial Racing: de Cesaris

MINARDI
Lois Minardi Team: Campos, Martini, Sala

LIGIER
Ligier Loto: Arnoux, Johansson

FERRARI
Scuderia Ferrari SpA SEFAC: Alboreto, Berger

LOLA
Larrousse Calmels: Dalmas, Suzuki, (Raphanel), Alliot

COLONI
Coloni SpA: Tarquini

EUROBRUN
EuroBrun Racing: Larrauri, Modena

DALLARA
Scuderia Italia: Caffi

3 Apr 1988 — BRAZIL: Rio de Janeiro (Round: 1) (Race: 453)

60 laps x 5.031 km, 3.126 miles = 301.860 km, 187.567 miles

POS.	NO.	DRIVER	CAR	MODEL	ENGINE		LAPS	TIME/REASON FOR RETIREMENT	GRID:POS	ROW
1	11	A Prost	McLaren	MP4/4	Honda	V6t	60	1h 36m 06.857s	3	2
2	28	G Berger	Ferrari	F187/88C	Ferrari	V6t	60	1h 36m 16.730s	4	2
3	1	N Piquet	Lotus	100T	Honda	V6t	60	1h 37m 15.438s	5	3
4	17	D Warwick	Arrows	A10B	Megatron	4t	60	1h 37m 20.205s	11	6
5	27	M Alboreto	Ferrari	F187/88C	Ferrari	V6t	60	1h 37m 21.413s	6	3
6	2	S Nakajima	Lotus	100T	Honda	V6t	59		10	5
7	20	T Boutsen	Benetton	B188	Cosworth	V8	59		7	4
8	18	E Cheever	Arrows	A10B	Megatron	4t	59		15	8
9	26	S Johansson	Ligier	JS31	Judd	V8	57		21	11
r	22	A de Cesaris	Rial	ARC1	Cosworth	V8	53	engine	14	7
r	3	J Palmer	Tyrrell	017	Cosworth	V8	47	drive shaft	22	11
r	24	L Sala	Minardi	M188	Cosworth	V8	46	rear aerofoil	20	10
r	30	P Alliot	Lola	LC88	Cosworth	V8	40	rear suspension/ accident	16	8
r	31	G Tarquini	Coloni	FC188	Cosworth	V8	35	suspension	25	13
r	14	P Streiff	AGS	JH23	Cosworth	V8	35	brakes/ spin	19	10
r	29	Y Dalmas	Lola	LC88	Cosworth	V8	32	engine	17	9
dq	12	A Senna	McLaren	MP4/4	Honda	V6t	31	changed car after parade lap	1	1
r	25	R Arnoux	Ligier	JS31	Judd	V8	23	clutch	18	9
r	33	S Modena	EuroBrun	ER188	Cosworth	V8	20	fuel pump/ engine	24	12
r	5	N Mansell	Williams	FW12	Judd	V8	18	electrics/ engine overheating	2	1
r	19	A Nannini	Benetton	B188	Cosworth	V8	7	engine overheating	12	6
r	6	R Patrese	Williams	FW12	Judd	V8	6	engine overheating	8	4
r	16	I Capelli	March	881	Judd	V8	6	engine overheating	9	5
r	23	A Campos	Minardi	M188	Cosworth	V8	5	rear aerofoil	23	12
r	15	M Gugelmin	March	881	Judd	V8	0	transmission	13	7
r	32	O Larrauri	EuroBrun	ER188	Cosworth	V8	-1	electrics	26	13
nq	4	J Bailey	Tyrrell	017	Cosworth	V8				
nq	9	P Ghinzani	Zakspeed	881	Zakspeed	4t				
nq	21	N Larini	Osella	FA11	Alfa Romeo	V8t				
nq	10	B Schneider	Zakspeed	881	Zakspeed	4t				
npq	36	A Caffi	Dallara	3087	Cosworth	V8				

Winning speed: 188.438 km/h, 117.090 mph
Pole Position speed: 205.589 km/h, 127.747 mph (A Senna, 1 min:28.096 sec)
Fastest Lap speed: 194.868 km/h, 121.085 mph (G Berger, 1 min:32.943 sec on lap 45)
Lap Leaders: A Prost 1-60 (60).

Scheduled for 61 laps but reduced after second parade lap, due to gearbox problems on Senna's car.

1 May 1988 — SAN MARINO: Imola (Round: 2) (Race: 454)

60 laps x 5.040 km, 3.132 miles = 302.400 km, 187.903 miles

POS.	NO.	DRIVER	CAR	MODEL	ENGINE		LAPS	TIME/REASON FOR RETIREMENT	GRID:POS	ROW
1	12	A Senna	McLaren	MP4/4	Honda	V6t	60	1h 32m 41.264s	1	1
2	11	A Prost	McLaren	MP4/4	Honda	V6t	60	1h 32m 43.598s	2	1
3	1	N Piquet	Lotus	100T	Honda	V6t	59		3	2
4	20	T Boutsen	Benetton	B188	Cosworth	V8	59		8	4
5	28	G Berger	Ferrari	F187/88C	Ferrari	V6t	59		5	3
6	19	A Nannini	Benetton	B188	Cosworth	V8	59		4	2
7	18	E Cheever	Arrows	A10B	Megatron	4t	59		7	4
8	2	S Nakajima	Lotus	100T	Honda	V6t	59		12	6
9	17	D Warwick	Arrows	A10B	Megatron	4t	58		14	7
10	14	P Streiff	AGS	JH23	Cosworth	V8	58		13	7
11	24	L Sala	Minardi	M188	Cosworth	V8	58		18	9
12	29	Y Dalmas	Lola	LC88	Cosworth	V8	58		19	10
13	6	R Patrese	Williams	FW12	Judd	V8	58		6	3
14	3	J Palmer	Tyrrell	017	Cosworth	V8	58		23	12
15	15	M Gugelmin	March	881	Judd	V8	58		20	10
16	23	A Campos	Minardi	M188	Cosworth	V8	57		22	11
17	30	P Alliot	Lola	LC88	Cosworth	V8	57		15	8
18r	27	M Alboreto	Ferrari	F187/88C	Ferrari	V6t	54	engine	10	5
nc	33	S Modena	EuroBrun	ER188	Cosworth	V8	52		26	13
r	4	J Bailey	Tyrrell	017	Cosworth	V8	48	gearbox	21	11
r	5	N Mansell	Williams	FW12	Judd	V8	42	electrics	11	6
r	31	G Tarquini	Coloni	FC188	Cosworth	V8	40	throttle linkage	17	9
r	36	A Caffi	Dallara	188	Cosworth	V8	18	gearbox	24	12
r	9	P Ghinzani	Zakspeed	881	Zakspeed	4t	16	electrics	25	13
r	16	I Capelli	March	881	Judd	V8	2	gearbox	9	5
r	22	A de Cesaris	Rial	ARC1	Cosworth	V8	0	front suspension	16	8
nq	32	O Larrauri	EuroBrun	ER188	Cosworth	V8				
nq	26	S Johansson	Ligier	JS31	Judd	V8				
nq	25	R Arnoux	Ligier	JS31	Judd	V8				
nq	10	B Schneider	Zakspeed	881	Zakspeed	4t				
exc	21	N Larini	Osella	FA1L	Alfa Romeo	V8t		failed scrutineering		

Winning speed: 195.754 km/h, 121.636 mph
Pole Position speed: 208.198 km/h, 129.368 mph (A Senna, 1 min:27.148 sec)
Fastest Lap speed: 202.308 km/h, 125.708 mph (A Prost, 1 min:29.685 sec on lap 53)
Lap Leaders: A Senna 1-60 (60).

15 May 1988 — MONACO: Monte Carlo (Round: 3) (Race: 455)

78 laps x 3.328 km, 2.068 miles = 259.584 km, 161.298 miles

POS.	NO.	DRIVER	CAR	MODEL	ENGINE		LAPS	TIME/REASON FOR RETIREMENT	GRID:POS	ROW
1	11	A Prost	McLaren	MP4/4	Honda	V6t	78	1h 57m 17.077s	2	1
2	28	G Berger	Ferrari	F187/88C	Ferrari	V6t	78	1h 57m 37.530s	3	2
3	27	M Alboreto	Ferrari	F187/88C	Ferrari	V6t	78	1h 57m 58.306s	4	2
4	17	D Warwick	Arrows	A10B	Megatron	4t	77		7	4
5	3	J Palmer	Tyrrell	017	Cosworth	V8	77		10	5
6	6	R Patrese	Williams	FW12	Judd	V8	77		8	4
7	29	Y Dalmas	Lola	LC88	Cosworth	V8	77		21	11
8	20	T Boutsen	Benetton	B188	Cosworth	V8	76		16	8
9	21	N Larini	Osella	FA1L	Alfa Romeo	V8t	75		25	13
10	16	I Capelli	March	881	Judd	V8	72		22	11
r	12	A Senna	McLaren	MP4/4	Honda	V6t	66	accident	1	1
r	30	P Alliot	Lola	LC88	Cosworth	V8	50	accident	13	7
r	15	M Gugelmin	March	881	Judd	V8	45	fuel pump	14	7
r	9	P Ghinzani	Zakspeed	881	Zakspeed	4t	43	gearbox	23	12
r	19	A Nannini	Benetton	B188	Cosworth	V8	38	gearbox/ clutch	6	3
r	24	L Sala	Minardi	M188	Cosworth	V8	36	drive shafts	15	8
r	5	N Mansell	Williams	FW12	Judd	V8	32	accident	5	3
r	22	A de Cesaris	Rial	ARC1	Cosworth	V8	28	oil pressure	19	10
r	25	R Arnoux	Ligier	JS31	Judd	V8	17	electrics	20	10
r	32	O Larrauri	EuroBrun	ER188	Cosworth	V8	14	accident	18	9
r	18	E Cheever	Arrows	A10B	Megatron	4t	8	electronics	9	5
r	26	S Johansson	Ligier	JS31	Judd	V8	6	electrics	26	13
r	31	G Tarquini	Coloni	FC188	Cosworth	V8	5	suspension	24	12
r	1	N Piquet	Lotus	100T	Honda	V6t	0	accident	11	6
r	36	A Caffi	Dallara	188	Cosworth	V8	0	accident	17	9
r	14	P Streiff	AGS	JH23	Cosworth	V8	-1	throttle linkage	12	6
nq	2	S Nakajima	Lotus	100T	Honda	V6t				
nq	10	B Schneider	Zakspeed	881	Zakspeed	4t				
nq	23	A Campos	Minardi	M188	Cosworth	V8				
nq	4	J Bailey	Tyrrell	017	Cosworth	V8				
exc	33	S Modena	EuroBrun	ER188	Cosworth	V8		missed weight check		

Winning speed: 132.797 km/h, 82.516 mph
Pole Position speed: 142.632 km/h, 88.627 mph (A Senna, 1 min:23.998 sec)
Fastest Lap speed: 138.794 km/h, 86.242 mph (A Senna, 1 min:26.321 sec on lap 59)
Lap Leaders: A Senna 1-66 (66); A Prost 67-78 (12).

29 May 1988 — MEXICO: Mexico City (Round: 4) (Race: 456)

67 laps x 4.421 km, 2.747 miles = 296.207 km, 184.054 miles

POS.	NO.	DRIVER	CAR	MODEL	ENGINE		LAPS	TIME/REASON FOR RETIREMENT	GRID:POS	ROW
1	11	A Prost	McLaren	MP4/4	Honda	V6t	67	1h 30m 15.737s	2	1
2	12	A Senna	McLaren	MP4/4	Honda	V6t	67	1h 30m 22.841s	1	1
3	28	G Berger	Ferrari	F187/88C	Ferrari	V6t	67	1h 31m 13.051s	3	2
4	27	M Alboreto	Ferrari	F187/88C	Ferrari	V6t	66		5	3
5	17	D Warwick	Arrows	A10B	Megatron	4t	66		9	5
6	18	E Cheever	Arrows	A10B	Megatron	4t	66		7	4
7	19	A Nannini	Benetton	B188	Cosworth	V8	65		8	4
8	20	T Boutsen	Benetton	B188	Cosworth	V8	64		11	6
9	29	Y Dalmas	Lola	LC88	Cosworth	V8	64		22	11
10	26	S Johansson	Ligier	JS31	Judd	V8	63		24	12
11	24	L Sala	Minardi	M188	Cosworth	V8	63		25	13
12	14	P Streiff	AGS	JH23	Cosworth	V8	63		19	10
13	32	O Larrauri	EuroBrun	ER188	Cosworth	V8	63		26	13
14	31	G Tarquini	Coloni	FC188	Cosworth	V8	62		21	11
15	9	P Ghinzani	Zakspeed	881	Zakspeed	4t	61		18	9
16	16	I Capelli	March	881	Judd	V8	61		10	5
r	1	N Piquet	Lotus	100T	Honda	V6t	58	engine	4	2
r	22	A de Cesaris	Rial	ARC1	Cosworth	V8	52	clutch	12	6
r	2	S Nakajima	Lotus	100T	Honda	V6t	27	turbo	6	3
r	5	N Mansell	Williams	FW12	Judd	V8	20	engine	14	7
r	10	B Schneider	Zakspeed	881	Zakspeed	4t	16	engine overheating	15	8
r	6	R Patrese	Williams	FW12	Judd	V8	16	engine	17	9
r	25	R Arnoux	Ligier	JS31	Judd	V8	13	accident/ rear wing	20	10
r	36	A Caffi	Dallara	188	Cosworth	V8	13	brakes/ accident	23	12
r	15	M Gugelmin	March	881	Judd	V8	10	electrics	16	8
r	30	P Alliot	Lola	LC88	Cosworth	V8	0	rear suspension/ handling	13	7
nq	3	J Palmer	Tyrrell	017	Cosworth	V8				
nq	21	N Larini	Osella	FA1L	Alfa Romeo	V8t				
nq	4	J Bailey	Tyrrell	017	Cosworth	V8				
nq	23	A Campos	Minardi	M188	Cosworth	V8				
exc	33	S Modena	EuroBrun	ER188	Cosworth	V8		rear wing infringement		

Winning speed: 196.898 km/h, 122.346 mph
Pole Position speed: 205.447 km/h, 127.659 mph (A Senna, 1 min:17.468 sec)
Fastest Lap speed: 202.468 km/h, 125.808 mph (A Prost, 1 min:18.608 sec on lap 52)
Lap Leaders: A Prost 1-67 (67).

12 Jun 1988 — CANADA: Montréal (Round: 5) (Race: 457)

69 laps x 4.390 km, 2.728 miles = 302.910 km, 188.220 miles

POS.	NO.	DRIVER	CAR	MODEL	ENGINE		LAPS	TIME/REASON FOR RETIREMENT	GRID:POS	ROW
1	12	A Senna	McLaren	MP4/4	Honda	V6t	69	1h 39m 46.618s	1	1
2	11	A Prost	McLaren	MP4/4	Honda	V6t	69	1h 39m 52.552s	2	1
3	20	T Boutsen	Benetton	B188	Cosworth	V8	69	1h 40m 38.027s	7	4
4	1	N Piquet	Lotus	100T	Honda	V6t	68		6	3
5	16	I Capelli	March	881	Judd	V8	68		14	7
6	3	J Palmer	Tyrrell	017	Cosworth	V8	67		19	10
7	17	D Warwick	Arrows	A10B	Megatron	4t	67		16	8
8	31	G Tarquini	Coloni	FC188	Cosworth	V8	67		26	13
9r	22	A de Cesaris	Rial	ARC1	Cosworth	V8	66	out of fuel	12	6
10r	30	P Alliot	Lola	LC88	Cosworth	V8	66	engine	17	9
11	2	S Nakajima	Lotus	100T	Honda	V6t	66		13	7
12	33	S Modena	EuroBrun	ER188	Cosworth	V8	66		15	8
13	24	L Sala	Minardi	M188	Cosworth	V8	64		21	11
14r	9	P Ghinzani	Zakspeed	881	Zakspeed	4t	63	engine	22	11
r	15	M Gugelmin	March	881	Judd	V8	54	gearbox	18	9
r	14	P Streiff	AGS	JH23	Cosworth	V8	41	rear suspension	10	5
r	25	R Arnoux	Ligier	JS31	Judd	V8	36	gearbox	20	10
r	27	M Alboreto	Ferrari	F187/88C	Ferrari	V6t	33	engine	4	2
r	6	R Patrese	Williams	FW12	Judd	V8	32	engine	11	6
r	18	E Cheever	Arrows	A10B	Megatron	4t	31	throttle spring	8	4
r	5	N Mansell	Williams	FW12	Judd	V8	28	engine	9	5
r	26	S Johansson	Ligier	JS31	Judd	V8	24	engine	25	13
r	28	G Berger	Ferrari	F187/88C	Ferrari	V6t	22	ignition	3	2
r	19	A Nannini	Benetton	B188	Cosworth	V8	15	water leak/ electrics	5	3
r	32	O Larrauri	EuroBrun	ER188	Cosworth	V8	8	accident/ nose mounting	24	12
r	4	J Bailey	Tyrrell	017	Cosworth	V8	0	accident/ front susp. wishbone	23	12
nq	23	A Campos	Minardi	M188	Cosworth	V8				
nq	21	N Larini	Osella	FA1L	Alfa Romeo	V8t				
nq	29	Y Dalmas	Lola	LC88	Cosworth	V8				
nq	10	B Schneider	Zakspeed	881	Zakspeed	4t				
npq	36	A Caffi	Dallara	188	Cosworth	V8				

Winning speed: 182.152 km/h, 113.184 mph
Pole Position speed: 193.484 km/h, 120.226 mph (A Senna, 1 min:21.681 sec)
Fastest Lap speed: 185.988 km/h, 115.568 mph (A Senna, 1 min:24.973 sec on lap 53)
Lap Leaders: A Prost 1-18 (18); A Senna 19-69 (51).

19 Jun 1988 — USA: Detroit (Round: 6) (Race: 458)

63 laps x 4.023 km, 2.500 miles = 253.472 km, 157.500 miles

POS.	NO.	DRIVER	CAR	MODEL	ENGINE		LAPS	TIME/REASON FOR RETIREMENT	GRID:POS	ROW
1	12	A Senna	McLaren	MP4/4	Honda	V6t	63	1h 54m 56.035s	1	1
2	11	A Prost	McLaren	MP4/4	Honda	V6t	63	1h 55m 34.748s	4	2
3	20	T Boutsen	Benetton	B188	Cosworth	V8	62		5	3
4	22	A de Cesaris	Rial	ARC1	Cosworth	V8	62		12	6
5	3	J Palmer	Tyrrell	017	Cosworth	V8	62		17	9
6	23	P Martini	Minardi	M188	Cosworth	V8	62		16	8
7	29	Y Dalmas	Lola	LC88	Cosworth	V8	61		24	12
8	36	A Caffi	Dallara	188	Cosworth	V8	61		21	11
9r	4	J Bailey	Tyrrell	017	Cosworth	V8	59	accident	22	11
r	24	L Sala	Minardi	M188	Cosworth	V8	54	clutch	25	13
r	30	P Alliot	Lola	LC88	Cosworth	V8	46	gearbox	14	7
r	33	S Modena	EuroBrun	ER188	Cosworth	V8	46	accident	19	10
r	27	M Alboreto	Ferrari	F187/88C	Ferrari	V6t	45	engine/ spin	3	2
r	25	R Arnoux	Ligier	JS31	Judd	V8	45	engine	20	10
r	15	M Gugelmin	March	881	Judd	V8	34	engine	13	7
r	6	R Patrese	Williams	FW12	Judd	V8	26	electrics	10	5
r	1	N Piquet	Lotus	100T	Honda	V6t	26	accident	8	4
r	32	O Larrauri	EuroBrun	ER188	Cosworth	V8	26	gearbox	23	12
r	17	D Warwick	Arrows	A10B	Megatron	4t	24	accident	9	5
r	5	N Mansell	Williams	FW12	Judd	V8	18	electrics	6	3
r	14	P Streiff	AGS	JH23	Cosworth	V8	15	suspension	11	6
r	19	A Nannini	Benetton	B188	Cosworth	V8	14	suspension	7	4
r	18	E Cheever	Arrows	A10B	Megatron	4t	14	electrics	15	8
r	21	N Larini	Osella	FA1L	Alfa Romeo	V8t	7	engine	26	13
r	28	G Berger	Ferrari	F187/88C	Ferrari	V6t	6	puncture	2	1
r	26	S Johansson	Ligier	JS31	Judd	V8	2	engine overheating	18	9
ns	16	I Capelli	March	881	Judd	V8		accident/ injury		
nq	2	S Nakajima	Lotus	100T	Honda	V6t				
nq	10	B Schneider	Zakspeed	881	Zakspeed	4t				
nq	9	P Ghinzani	Zakspeed	881	Zakspeed	4t				
npq	31	G Tarquini	Coloni	FC188	Cosworth	V8				

Winning speed: 132.322 km/h, 82.221 mph
Pole Position speed: 143.969 km/h, 89.458 mph (A Senna, 1 min:40.606 sec)
Fastest Lap speed: 138.160 km/h, 85.848 mph (A Prost, 1 min:44.836 sec on lap 4)
Lap Leaders: A Senna 1-63 (63).

3 Jul 1988 — FRANCE: Paul Ricard (Round: 7) (Race: 459)

80 laps x 3.813 km, 2.369 miles = 305.040 km, 189.543 miles

POS.	NO.	DRIVER	CAR	MODEL	ENGINE		LAPS	TIME/REASON FOR RETIREMENT	GRID:POS	ROW
1	11	A Prost	McLaren	MP4/4	Honda	V6t	80	1h 37m 37.328s	1	1
2	12	A Senna	McLaren	MP4/4	Honda	V6t	80	1h 38m 09.080s	2	1
3	27	M Alboreto	Ferrari	F187/88C	Ferrari	V6t	80	1h 38m 43.833s	4	2
4	28	G Berger	Ferrari	F187/88C	Ferrari	V6t	79		3	2
5	1	N Piquet	Lotus	100T	Honda	V6t	79		7	4
6	19	A Nannini	Benetton	B188	Cosworth	V8	79		6	3
7	2	S Nakajima	Lotus	100T	Honda	V6t	79		8	4
8	15	M Gugelmin	March	881	Judd	V8	79		16	8
9	16	I Capelli	March	881	Judd	V8	79		10	5
10	22	A de Cesaris	Rial	ARC1	Cosworth	V8	78		12	6
11	18	E Cheever	Arrows	A10B	Megatron	4t	78		13	7
12	36	A Caffi	Dallara	188	Cosworth	V8	78		14	7
13	29	Y Dalmas	Lola	LC88	Cosworth	V8	78		19	10
14	33	S Modena	EuroBrun	ER188	Cosworth	V8	77		20	10
15	23	P Martini	Minardi	M188	Cosworth	V8	77		22	11
nc	24	L Sala	Minardi	M188	Cosworth	V8	70		25	13
r	32	O Larrauri	EuroBrun	ER188	Cosworth	V8	64	clutch	26	13
r	21	N Larini	Osella	FA1L	Alfa Romeo	V8t	56	drive shaft	24	12
r	10	B Schneider	Zakspeed	881	Zakspeed	4t	55	gearbox	21	11
r	5	N Mansell	Williams	FW12	Judd	V8	48	suspension	9	5
r	30	P Alliot	Lola	LC88	Cosworth	V8	46	electrics	18	9
r	3	J Palmer	Tyrrell	017	Cosworth	V8	40	engine	23	12
r	6	R Patrese	Williams	FW12	Judd	V8	35	brakes	15	8
r	20	T Boutsen	Benetton	B188	Cosworth	V8	28	electrics	5	3
r	14	P Streiff	AGS	JH23	Cosworth	V8	20	fuel leak	17	9
r	17	D Warwick	Arrows	A10B	Megatron	4t	11	spin	11	6
exc	9	P Ghinzani	Zakspeed	881	Zakspeed	4t		missed weight check		
nq	25	R Arnoux	Ligier	JS31	Judd	V8				
nq	4	J Bailey	Tyrrell	017	Cosworth	V8				
nq	26	S Johansson	Ligier	JS31	Judd	V8				
npq	31	G Tarquini	Coloni	FC188	Cosworth	V8				

Winning speed: 187.482 km/h, 116.496 mph
Pole Position speed: 203.092 km/h, 126.196 mph (A Prost, 1 min: 7.589 sec)
Fastest Lap speed: 191.349 km/h, 118.899 mph (A Prost, 1 min:11.737 sec on lap 45)
Lap Leaders: A Prost 1-36,61-80 (56); A Senna 37-60 (24).

10 Jul 1988 BRITAIN: Silverstone (Round: 8) (Race: 460)

65 laps x 4.778 km, 2.969 miles = 310.579 km, 192.985 miles

POS.	NO.	DRIVER	CAR	MODEL	ENGINE		LAPS	TIME/REASON FOR RETIREMENT	GRID:POS	ROW
1	12	A Senna	McLaren	MP4/4	Honda	V6t	65	1h 33m 16.367s	3	2
2	5	N Mansell	Williams	FW12	Judd	V8	65	1h 33m 39.711s	11	6
3	19	A Nannini	Benetton	B188	Cosworth	V8	65	1h 34m 07.581s	8	4
4	15	M Gugelmin	March	881	Judd	V8	65	1h 34m 27.745s	5	3
5	1	N Piquet	Lotus	100T	Honda	V6t	65	1h 34m 37.202s	7	4
6	17	D Warwick	Arrows	A10B	Megatron	4t	64		9	5
7	18	E Cheever	Arrows	A10B	Megatron	4t	64		13	7
8	6	R Patrese	Williams	FW12	Judd	V8	64		15	8
9	28	G Berger	Ferrari	F187/88C	Ferrari	V6t	64		1	1
10	2	S Nakajima	Lotus	100T	Honda	V6t	64		10	5
11	36	A Caffi	Dallara	188	Cosworth	V8	64		21	11
12	33	S Modena	EuroBrun	ER188	Cosworth	V8	64		20	10
13	29	Y Dalmas	Lola	LC88	Cosworth	V8	63		23	12
14	30	P Alliot	Lola	LC88	Cosworth	V8	63		22	11
15	23	P Martini	Minardi	M188	Cosworth	V8	63		19	10
16	4	J Bailey	Tyrrell	017	Cosworth	V8	63		24	12
17r	27	M Alboreto	Ferrari	F187/88C	Ferrari	V6t	62	out of fuel	2	1
18	25	R Arnoux	Ligier	JS31	Judd	V8	62		25	13
19r	21	N Larini	Osella	FA1L	Alfa Romeo	V8t	60	out of fuel	26	13
r	20	T Boutsen	Benetton	B188	Cosworth	V8	38	cv joint	12	6
r	16	I Capelli	March	881	Judd	V8	34	alternator	6	3
r	11	A Prost	McLaren	MP4/4	Honda	V6t	24	handling	4	2
r	3	J Palmer	Tyrrell	017	Cosworth	V8	14	transmission	17	9
r	22	A de Cesaris	Rial	ARC1	Cosworth	V8	9	clutch	14	7
r	14	P Streiff	AGS	JH23	Cosworth	V8	8	accident/ rear wing	16	8
r	24	L Sala	Minardi	M188	Cosworth	V8	0	accident	18	9
nq	32	O Larrauri	EuroBrun	ER188	Cosworth	V8				
nq	9	P Ghinzani	Zakspeed	881	Zakspeed	4t				
nq	26	S Johansson	Ligier	JS31	Judd	V8				
nq	10	B Schneider	Zakspeed	881	Zakspeed	4t				
npq	31	G Tarquini	Coloni	FC188	Cosworth	V8				

Winning speed: 199.788 km/h, 124.142 mph
Pole Position speed: 245.267 km/h, 152.402 mph (G Berger, 1 min:10.133 sec)
Fastest Lap speed: 206.479 km/h, 128.300 mph (N Mansell, 1 min:23.308 sec on lap 48)
Lap Leaders: G Berger 1-13 (13); A Senna 14-65 (52).

24 Jul 1988 GERMANY: Hockenheim (Round: 9) (Race: 461)

44 laps x 6.797 km, 4.223 miles = 299.068 km, 185.832 miles

POS.	NO.	DRIVER	CAR	MODEL	ENGINE		LAPS	TIME/REASON FOR RETIREMENT	GRID:POS	ROW
1	12	A Senna	McLaren	MP4/4	Honda	V6t	44	1h 32m 54.188s	1	1
2	11	A Prost	McLaren	MP4/4	Honda	V6t	44	1h 33m 07.797s	2	1
3	28	G Berger	Ferrari	F187/88C	Ferrari	V6t	44	1h 33m 46.283s	3	2
4	27	M Alboreto	Ferrari	F187/88C	Ferrari	V6t	44	1h 34m 35.100s	4	2
5	16	I Capelli	March	881	Judd	V8	44	1h 34m 43.794s	7	4
6	20	T Boutsen	Benetton	B188	Cosworth	V8	43		9	5
7	17	D Warwick	Arrows	A10B	Megatron	4t	43		12	6
8	15	M Gugelmin	March	881	Judd	V8	43		10	5
9	2	S Nakajima	Lotus	100T	Honda	V6t	43		8	4
10	18	E Cheever	Arrows	A10B	Megatron	4t	43		15	8
11	3	J Palmer	Tyrrell	017	Cosworth	V8	43		24	12
12	10	B Schneider	Zakspeed	881	Zakspeed	4t	43		22	11
13	22	A de Cesaris	Rial	ARC1	Cosworth	V8	42		14	7
14	9	P Ghinzani	Zakspeed	881	Zakspeed	4t	42		23	12
15	36	A Caffi	Dallara	188	Cosworth	V8	42		19	10
16	32	O Larrauri	EuroBrun	ER188	Cosworth	V8	42		26	13
17	25	R Arnoux	Ligier	JS31	Judd	V8	41		17	9
18	19	A Nannini	Benetton	B188	Cosworth	V8	40		6	3
19r	29	Y Dalmas	Lola	LC88	Cosworth	V8	39	clutch	21	11
r	14	P Streiff	AGS	JH23	Cosworth	V8	38	throttle linkage	16	8
r	6	R Patrese	Williams	FW12	Judd	V8	34	accident	13	7
r	21	N Larini	Osella	FA1L	Alfa Romeo	V8t	27	electronic ignition	18	9
r	5	N Mansell	Williams	FW12	Judd	V8	16	accident	11	6
r	33	S Modena	EuroBrun	ER188	Cosworth	V8	15	electrics	25	13
r	30	P Alliot	Lola	LC88	Cosworth	V8	8	accident	20	10
r	1	N Piquet	Lotus	100T	Honda	V6t	1	accident	5	3
nq	24	L Sala	Minardi	M188	Cosworth	V8				
nq	26	S Johansson	Ligier	JS31	Judd	V8				
nq	4	J Bailey	Tyrrell	017	Cosworth	V8				
nq	23	P Martini	Minardi	M188	Cosworth	V8				
npq	31	G Tarquini	Coloni	FC188	Cosworth	V8				

Winning speed: 193.148 km/h, 120.017 mph
Pole Position speed: 233.940 km/h, 145.364 mph (A Senna, 1 min:44.596 sec)
Fastest Lap speed: 198.885 km/h, 123.581 mph (A Nannini, 2 min: 3.032 sec on lap 40)
Lap Leaders: A Senna 1-44 (44).

7 Aug 1988 — HUNGARY: Hungaroring (Round:10) (Race: 462)

76 laps x 4.014 km, 2.494 miles = 305.064 km, 189.558 miles

POS.	NO.	DRIVER	CAR	MODEL	ENGINE		LAPS	TIME/REASON FOR RETIREMENT	GRID:POS	ROW
1	12	A Senna	McLaren	MP4/4	Honda	V6t	76	1h 57m 47.081s	1	1
2	11	A Prost	McLaren	MP4/4	Honda	V6t	76	1h 57m 47.610s	7	4
3	20	T Boutsen	Benetton	B188	Cosworth	V8	76	1h 58m 18.491s	3	2
4	28	G Berger	Ferrari	F187/88C	Ferrari	V6t	76	1h 59m 15.751s	9	5
5	15	M Gugelmin	March	881	Judd	V8	75		8	4
6	6	R Patrese	Williams	FW12	Judd	V8	75		6	3
7	2	S Nakajima	Lotus	100T	Honda	V6t	73		19	10
8	1	N Piquet	Lotus	100T	Honda	V6t	73		13	7
9	29	Y Dalmas	Lola	LC88	Cosworth	V8	73		17	9
10	24	L Sala	Minardi	M188	Cosworth	V8	72		11	6
11	33	S Modena	EuroBrun	ER188	Cosworth	V8	72		26	13
12	30	P Alliot	Lola	LC88	Cosworth	V8	72		20	10
13	31	G Tarquini	Coloni	FC188	Cosworth	V8	71		22	11
r	17	D Warwick	Arrows	A10B	Megatron	4t	65	brakes	12	6
r	5	N Mansell	Williams	FW12	Judd	V8	60	driver exhausted	2	1
r	18	E Cheever	Arrows	A10B	Megatron	4t	55	brakes	14	7
r	27	M Alboreto	Ferrari	F187/88C	Ferrari	V6t	40	engine	15	8
r	25	R Arnoux	Ligier	JS31	Judd	V8	32	engine	25	13
r	22	A de Cesaris	Rial	ARC1	Cosworth	V8	28	cv joint	18	9
r	19	A Nannini	Benetton	B188	Cosworth	V8	24	water pipe	5	3
r	36	A Caffi	Dallara	188	Cosworth	V8	22	engine	10	5
r	26	S Johansson	Ligier	JS31	Judd	V8	19	throttle jammed	24	12
r	23	P Martini	Minardi	M188	Cosworth	V8	8	accident	16	8
r	14	P Streiff	AGS	JH23	Cosworth	V8	8	suspension	23	12
r	16	I Capelli	March	881	Judd	V8	5	misfire	4	2
r	3	J Palmer	Tyrrell	017	Cosworth	V8	3	engine	21	11
nq	32	O Larrauri	EuroBrun	ER188	Cosworth	V8				
nq	10	B Schneider	Zakspeed	881	Zakspeed	4t				
nq	4	J Bailey	Tyrrell	017	Cosworth	V8				
nq	9	P Ghinzani	Zakspeed	881	Zakspeed	4t				
npq	21	N Larini	Osella	FA1L	Alfa Romeo	V8t				

Winning speed: 155.401 km/h, 96.562 mph
Pole Position speed: 164.893 km/h, 102.460 mph (A Senna, 1 min:27.635 sec)
Fastest Lap speed: 159.428 km/h, 99.064 mph (A Prost, 1 min:30.639 sec on lap 51)
Lap Leaders: A Senna 1-76 (76).

28 Aug 1988 — BELGIUM: Spa-Francorchamps (Round:11) (Race: 463)

43 laps x 6.940 km, 4.312 miles = 298.420 km, 185.430 miles

POS.	NO.	DRIVER	CAR	MODEL	ENGINE		LAPS	TIME/REASON FOR RETIREMENT	GRID:POS	ROW
1	12	A Senna	McLaren	MP4/4	Honda	V6t	43	1h 28m 00.549s	1	1
2	11	A Prost	McLaren	MP4/4	Honda	V6t	43	1h 28m 31.019s	2	1
dq	20	T Boutsen	Benetton	B188	Cosworth	V8	43	fuel irregularities	6	3
dq	19	A Nannini	Benetton	B188	Cosworth	V8	43	fuel irregularities	7	4
3	16	I Capelli	March	881	Judd	V8	43	1h 29m 16.317s	14	7
4	1	N Piquet	Lotus	100T	Honda	V6t	43	1h 29m 24.177s	9	5
5	17	D Warwick	Arrows	A10B	Megatron	4t	43	1h 29m 25.904s	10	5
6	18	E Cheever	Arrows	A10B	Megatron	4t	42		11	6
7	5	M Brundle	Williams	FW12	Judd	V8	42		12	6
8	36	A Caffi	Dallara	188	Cosworth	V8	42		15	8
9	30	P Alliot	Lola	LC88	Cosworth	V8	42		16	8
10	14	P Streiff	AGS	JH23	Cosworth	V8	42		18	9
11r	26	S Johansson	Ligier	JS31	Judd	V8	39	crown wheel & pinion	20	10
12r	3	J Palmer	Tyrrell	017	Cosworth	V8	39	throttle linkage	21	11
13r	10	B Schneider	Zakspeed	881	Zakspeed	4t	38	gearbox	25	13
nc	31	G Tarquini	Coloni	FC188	Cosworth	V8	36		22	11
r	27	M Alboreto	Ferrari	F187/88C	Ferrari	V6t	35	engine	4	2
r	6	R Patrese	Williams	FW12	Judd	V8	30	engine	5	3
r	15	M Gugelmin	March	881	Judd	V8	29	clutch/ accident	13	7
r	9	P Ghinzani	Zakspeed	881	Zakspeed	4t	25	oil leak	24	12
r	2	S Nakajima	Lotus	100T	Honda	V6t	22	engine	8	4
r	21	N Larini	Osella	FA1L	Alfa Romeo	V8t	14	fuel pump	26	13
r	28	G Berger	Ferrari	F187/88C	Ferrari	V6t	11	electronics	3	2
r	29	Y Dalmas	Lola	LC88	Cosworth	V8	9	engine	23	12
r	22	A de Cesaris	Rial	ARC1	Cosworth	V8	2	accident	19	10
r	25	R Arnoux	Ligier	JS31	Judd	V8	2	accident	17	9
nq	24	L Sala	Minardi	M188	Cosworth	V8				
nq	23	P Martini	Minardi	M188	Cosworth	V8				
nq	33	S Modena	EuroBrun	ER188	Cosworth	V8				
nq	4	J Bailey	Tyrrell	017	Cosworth	V8				
npq	32	O Larrauri	EuroBrun	ER188	Cosworth	V8				

Winning speed: 203.447 km/h, 126.416 mph
Pole Position speed: 219.701 km/h, 136.516 mph (A Senna, 1 min:53.718 sec)
Fastest Lap speed: 206.869 km/h, 128.543 mph (G Berger, 2 min: 0.772 sec on lap 10)
Lap Leaders: A Senna 1-43 (43).

T Boutsen finished 3rd in 1h 29m 00.230s and A Nannini finished 4th in 1h 29m 09.143s but both were disqualified after analysis of fuel later in the year.

11 Sep 1988 — ITALY: Monza (Round:12) (Race: 464)

51 laps x 5.800 km, 3.604 miles = 295.800 km, 183.802 miles

POS.	NO.	DRIVER	CAR	MODEL	ENGINE		LAPS	TIME/REASON FOR RETIREMENT	GRID:POS	ROW
1	28	G Berger	Ferrari	F187/88C	Ferrari	V6t	51	1h 17m 39.744s	3	2
2	27	M Alboreto	Ferrari	F187/88C	Ferrari	V6t	51	1h 17m 40.246s	4	2
3	18	E Cheever	Arrows	A10B	Megatron	4t	51	1h 18m 15.276s	5	3
4	17	D Warwick	Arrows	A10B	Megatron	4t	51	1h 18m 15.858s	6	3
5	16	I Capelli	March	881	Judd	V8	51	1h 18m 32.266s	11	6
6	20	T Boutsen	Benetton	B188	Cosworth	V8	51	1h 18m 39.622s	8	4
7	6	R Patrese	Williams	FW12	Judd	V8	51	1h 18m 54.487s	10	5
8	15	M Gugelmin	March	881	Judd	V8	51	1h 19m 12.310s	13	7
9	19	A Nannini	Benetton	B188	Cosworth	V8	50		9	5
10r	12	A Senna	McLaren	MP4/4	Honda	V6t	49	accident	1	1
11	5	J-L Schlesser	Williams	FW12	Judd	V8	49		22	11
12	4	J Bailey	Tyrrell	017	Cosworth	V8	49		26	13
13	25	R Arnoux	Ligier	JS31	Judd	V8	49		24	12
r	11	A Prost	McLaren	MP4/4	Honda	V6t	34	engine	2	1
r	30	P Alliot	Lola	LC88	Cosworth	V8	33	engine	20	10
r	14	P Streiff	AGS	JH23	Cosworth	V8	31	gear linkage	23	12
r	10	B Schneider	Zakspeed	881	Zakspeed	4t	28	engine	15	8
r	22	A de Cesaris	Rial	ARC1	Cosworth	V8	27	accident/ front suspension	18	9
r	9	P Ghinzani	Zakspeed	881	Zakspeed	4t	25	engine	16	8
r	36	A Caffi	Dallara	188	Cosworth	V8	24	electrics	21	11
r	29	Y Dalmas	Lola	LC88	Cosworth	V8	17	spin/ radiator	25	13
r	23	P Martini	Minardi	M188	Cosworth	V8	15	engine	14	7
r	2	S Nakajima	Lotus	100T	Honda	V6t	14	engine	12	6
r	24	L Sala	Minardi	M188	Cosworth	V8	12	gearbox	19	10
r	1	N Piquet	Lotus	100T	Honda	V6t	11	clutch/ spin	7	4
r	21	N Larini	Osella	FA1L	Alfa Romeo	V8t	2	engine	17	9
nq	3	J Palmer	Tyrrell	017	Cosworth	V8				
nq	26	S Johansson	Ligier	JS31	Judd	V8				
nq	31	G Tarquini	Coloni	FC188B	Cosworth	V8				
nq	33	S Modena	EuroBrun	ER188	Cosworth	V8				
npq	32	O Larrauri	EuroBrun	ER188	Cosworth	V8				

Winning speed: 228.528 km/h, 142.000 mph
Pole Position speed: 242.864 km/h, 150.909 mph (A Senna, 1 min:25.974 sec)
Fastest Lap speed: 234.422 km/h, 145.663 mph (M Alboreto, 1 min:29.070 sec on lap 44)
Lap Leaders: A Senna 1-49 (49); G Berger 50-51 (2).

25 Sep 1988 — PORTUGAL: Estoril (Round:13) (Race: 465)

70 laps x 4.350 km, 2.703 miles = 304.500 km, 189.208 miles

POS.	NO.	DRIVER	CAR	MODEL	ENGINE		LAPS	TIME/REASON FOR RETIREMENT	GRID:POS	ROW
1	11	A Prost	McLaren	MP4/4	Honda	V6t	70	1h 37m 40.958s	1	1
2	16	I Capelli	March	881	Judd	V8	70	1h 37m 50.511s	3	2
3	20	T Boutsen	Benetton	B188	Cosworth	V8	70	1h 38m 25.577s	13	7
4	17	D Warwick	Arrows	A10B	Megatron	4t	70	1h 38m 48.377s	10	5
5	27	M Alboreto	Ferrari	F187/88C	Ferrari	V6t	70	1h 38m 52.842s	7	4
6	12	A Senna	McLaren	MP4/4	Honda	V6t	70	1h 38m 59.227s	2	1
7	36	A Caffi	Dallara	188	Cosworth	V8	69		17	9
8	24	L Sala	Minardi	M188	Cosworth	V8	68		19	10
9	14	P Streiff	AGS	JH23	Cosworth	V8	68		21	11
10	25	R Arnoux	Ligier	JS31	Judd	V8	68		23	12
11	31	G Tarquini	Coloni	FC188B	Cosworth	V8	65		26	13
12	21	N Larini	Osella	FA1L	Alfa Romeo	V8t	63		25	13
r	15	M Gugelmin	March	881	Judd	V8	59	engine	5	3
r	5	N Mansell	Williams	FW12	Judd	V8	54	accident	6	3
r	3	J Palmer	Tyrrell	017	Cosworth	V8	53	engine overheating	22	11
r	19	A Nannini	Benetton	B188	Cosworth	V8	52	vibration/ driver exhausted	9	5
r	28	G Berger	Ferrari	F187/88C	Ferrari	V6t	35	fire extinguisher/ accident	4	2
r	1	N Piquet	Lotus	100T	Honda	V6t	34	clutch	8	4
r	6	R Patrese	Williams	FW12	Judd	V8	29	radiator	11	6
r	23	P Martini	Minardi	M188	Cosworth	V8	27	engine	14	7
r	29	Y Dalmas	Lola	LC88	Cosworth	V8	20	alternator belt	15	8
r	2	S Nakajima	Lotus	100T	Honda	V6t	16	accident	16	8
r	22	A de Cesaris	Rial	ARC1	Cosworth	V8	11	drive shaft	12	6
r	18	E Cheever	Arrows	A10B	Megatron	4t	10	turbo	18	9
r	30	P Alliot	Lola	LC88	Cosworth	V8	7	engine	20	10
r	26	S Johansson	Ligier	JS31	Judd	V8	4	engine	24	12
nq	4	J Bailey	Tyrrell	017	Cosworth	V8				
nq	9	P Ghinzani	Zakspeed	881	Zakspeed	4t				
nq	33	S Modena	EuroBrun	ER188	Cosworth	V8				
nq	10	B Schneider	Zakspeed	881	Zakspeed	4t				
npq	32	O Larrauri	EuroBrun	ER188	Cosworth	V8				

Winning speed: 187.034 km/h, 116.218 mph
Pole Position speed: 202.297 km/h, 125.701 mph (A Prost, 1 min:17.411 sec)
Fastest Lap speed: 191.066 km/h, 118.723 mph (G Berger, 1 min:21.961 sec on lap 31)
Lap Leaders: A Senna 1 (1); A Prost 2-70 (69).

2 Oct 1988 — SPAIN: Jerez de la Frontera (Round:14) (Race: 466)

72 laps x 4.218 km, 2.621 miles = 303.696 km, 188.708 miles

POS.	NO.	DRIVER	CAR	MODEL	ENGINE		LAPS	TIME/REASON FOR RETIREMENT	GRID:POS	ROW
1	11	A Prost	McLaren	MP4/4	Honda	V6t	72	1h 48m 43.851s	2	1
2	5	N Mansell	Williams	FW12	Judd	V8	72	1h 49m 10.083s	3	2
3	19	A Nannini	Benetton	B188	Cosworth	V8	72	1h 49m 19.297s	5	3
4	12	A Senna	McLaren	MP4/4	Honda	V6t	72	1h 49m 30.561s	1	1
5	6	R Patrese	Williams	FW12	Judd	V8	72	1h 49m 31.281s	7	4
6	28	G Berger	Ferrari	F187/88C	Ferrari	V6t	72	1h 49m 35.664s	8	4
7	15	M Gugelmin	March	881	Judd	V8	72	1h 49m 59.815s	11	6
8	1	N Piquet	Lotus	100T	Honda	V6t	72	1h 50m 01.160s	9	5
9	20	T Boutsen	Benetton	B188	Cosworth	V8	72	1h 50m 01.506s	4	2
10	36	A Caffi	Dallara	188	Cosworth	V8	71		18	9
11	29	Y Dalmas	Lola	LC88	Cosworth	V8	71		16	8
12	24	L Sala	Minardi	M188	Cosworth	V8	70		24	12
13	33	S Modena	EuroBrun	ER188	Cosworth	V8	70		26	13
14	30	P Alliot	Lola	LC88	Cosworth	V8	69		12	6
r	26	S Johansson	Ligier	JS31	Judd	V8	62	wheel lost	21	11
r	18	E Cheever	Arrows	A10B	Megatron	4t	60	handling	25	13
r	16	I Capelli	March	881	Judd	V8	45	engine	6	3
r	17	D Warwick	Arrows	A10B	Megatron	4t	41	accident/ chassis	17	9
r	22	A de Cesaris	Rial	ARC1	Cosworth	V8	37	engine	23	12
r	14	P Streiff	AGS	JH23	Cosworth	V8	16	engine	13	7
r	27	M Alboreto	Ferrari	F187/88C	Ferrari	V6t	15	engine	10	5
r	23	P Martini	Minardi	M188	Cosworth	V8	15	gearbox	20	10
r	2	S Nakajima	Lotus	100T	Honda	V6t	14	spin	15	8
r	21	N Larini	Osella	FA1L	Alfa Romeo	V8t	9	suspension	14	7
r	3	J Palmer	Tyrrell	017	Cosworth	V8	4	accident/ radiator	22	11
r	25	R Arnoux	Ligier	JS31	Judd	V8	0	throttle jammed	19	10
nq	10	B Schneider	Zakspeed	881	Zakspeed	4t				
nq	32	O Larrauri	EuroBrun	ER188	Cosworth	V8				
nq	4	J Bailey	Tyrrell	017	Cosworth	V8				
nq	9	P Ghinzani	Zakspeed	881	Zakspeed	4t				
npq	31	G Tarquini	Coloni	FC188B	Cosworth	V8				

Winning speed: 167.586 km/h, 104.133 mph
Pole Position speed: 180.627 km/h, 112.237 mph (A Senna, 1 min:24.067 sec)
Fastest Lap speed: 172.859 km/h, 107.410 mph (A Prost, 1 min:27.845 sec on lap 60)
Lap Leaders: A Prost 1-72 (72).

30 Oct 1988 — JAPAN: Suzuka (Round:15) (Race: 467)

51 laps x 5.859 km, 3.641 miles = 298.809 km, 185.671 miles

POS.	NO.	DRIVER	CAR	MODEL	ENGINE		LAPS	TIME/REASON FOR RETIREMENT	GRID:POS	ROW
1	12	A Senna	McLaren	MP4/4	Honda	V6t	51	1h 33m 26.173s	1	1
2	11	A Prost	McLaren	MP4/4	Honda	V6t	51	1h 33m 39.536s	2	1
3	20	T Boutsen	Benetton	B188	Cosworth	V8	51	1h 34m 02.282s	10	5
4	28	G Berger	Ferrari	F187/88C	Ferrari	V6t	51	1h 34m 52.887s	3	2
5	19	A Nannini	Benetton	B188	Cosworth	V8	51	1h 34m 56.776s	12	6
6	6	R Patrese	Williams	FW12	Judd	V8	51	1h 35m 03.788s	11	6
7	2	S Nakajima	Lotus	100T	Honda	V6t	50		6	3
8	14	P Streiff	AGS	JH23	Cosworth	V8	50		18	9
9	30	P Alliot	Lola	LC88	Cosworth	V8	50		19	10
10	15	M Gugelmin	March	881	Judd	V8	50		13	7
11	27	M Alboreto	Ferrari	F187/88C	Ferrari	V6t	50		9	5
12	3	J Palmer	Tyrrell	017	Cosworth	V8	50		16	8
13	23	P Martini	Minardi	M188	Cosworth	V8	49		17	9
14	4	J Bailey	Tyrrell	017	Cosworth	V8	49		26	13
15	24	L Sala	Minardi	M188	Cosworth	V8	49		22	11
16	29	A Suzuki	Lola	LC88	Cosworth	V8	48		20	10
17	25	R Arnoux	Ligier	JS31	Judd	V8	48		23	12
r	22	A de Cesaris	Rial	ARC1	Cosworth	V8	36	engine overheating	14	7
r	18	E Cheever	Arrows	A10B	Megatron	4t	35	turbo	15	8
r	21	N Larini	Osella	FA1L	Alfa Romeo	V8t	34	wheel nut loose	24	12
r	1	N Piquet	Lotus	100T	Honda	V6t	34	driver ill	5	3
r	5	N Mansell	Williams	FW12	Judd	V8	24	accident	8	4
r	36	A Caffi	Dallara	188	Cosworth	V8	22	accident	21	11
r	16	I Capelli	March	881	Judd	V8	19	electrics	4	2
r	17	D Warwick	Arrows	A10B	Megatron	4t	16	spin	7	4
r	10	B Schneider	Zakspeed	881	Zakspeed	4t	14	driver unfit (practice accident)	25	13
nq	26	S Johansson	Ligier	JS31	Judd	V8				
nq	32	O Larrauri	EuroBrun	ER188	Cosworth	V8				
nq	9	P Ghinzani	Zakspeed	881	Zakspeed	4t				
nq	33	S Modena	EuroBrun	ER188	Cosworth	V8				
npq	31	G Tarquini	Coloni	FC188B	Cosworth	V8				

Winning speed: 191.880 km/h, 119.229 mph
Pole Position speed: 207.087 km/h, 128.678 mph (A Senna, 1 min:41.853 sec)
Fastest Lap speed: 198.375 km/h, 123.264 mph (A Senna, 1 min:46.326 sec on lap 33)
Lap Leaders: A Prost 1-15,17-27 (26); I Capelli 16 (1); A Senna 28-51 (24).

13 Nov 1988 AUSTRALIA: Adelaide (Round:16) (Race: 468)

82 laps x 3.780 km, 2.349 miles = 309.960 km, 192.600 miles

POS.	NO.	DRIVER	CAR	MODEL	ENGINE		LAPS	TIME/REASON FOR RETIREMENT	GRID:POS	ROW
1	11	A Prost	McLaren	MP4/4	Honda	V6t	82	1h 53m 14.676s	2	1
2	12	A Senna	McLaren	MP4/4	Honda	V6t	82	1h 53m 51.463s	1	1
3	1	N Piquet	Lotus	100T	Honda	V6t	82	1h 54m 02.222s	5	3
4	6	R Patrese	Williams	FW12	Judd	V8	82	1h 54m 34.764s	6	3
5	20	T Boutsen	Benetton	B188	Cosworth	V8	81		10	5
6	16	I Capelli	March	881	Judd	V8	81		9	5
7	23	P Martini	Minardi	M188	Cosworth	V8	80		14	7
8r	22	A de Cesaris	Rial	ARC1	Cosworth	V8	77	out of fuel	15	8
9r	26	S Johansson	Ligier	JS31	Judd	V8	76	out of fuel	22	11
10r	30	P Alliot	Lola	LC88	Cosworth	V8	75	out of fuel	24	12
11r	14	P Streiff	AGS	JH23	Cosworth	V8	73	electrics	16	8
r	9	P Ghinzani	Zakspeed	881	Zakspeed	4t	69	fuel pump	26	13
r	5	N Mansell	Williams	FW12	Judd	V8	65	brakes/ accident	3	2
r	19	A Nannini	Benetton	B188	Cosworth	V8	63	handling/ spin	8	4
r	33	S Modena	EuroBrun	ER188	Cosworth	V8	63	half shaft	20	10
r	17	D Warwick	Arrows	A10B	Megatron	4t	52	throttle	7	4
r	18	E Cheever	Arrows	A10B	Megatron	4t	51	engine	18	9
r	15	M Gugelmin	March	881	Judd	V8	46	accident	19	10
r	2	S Nakajima	Lotus	100T	Honda	V6t	45	accident	13	7
r	24	L Sala	Minardi	M188	Cosworth	V8	41	electrics	21	11
r	36	A Caffi	Dallara	188	Cosworth	V8	32	clutch	11	6
r	28	G Berger	Ferrari	F187/88C	Ferrari	V6t	25	accident	4	2
r	25	R Arnoux	Ligier	JS31	Judd	V8	24	accident	23	12
r	3	J Palmer	Tyrrell	017	Cosworth	V8	16	crown wheel & pinion	17	9
r	32	O Larrauri	EuroBrun	ER188	Cosworth	V8	12	half shaft/ accident	25	13
r	27	M Alboreto	Ferrari	F187/88C	Ferrari	V6t	0	accident	12	6
nq	31	G Tarquini	Coloni	FC188B	Cosworth	V8				
nq	4	J Bailey	Tyrrell	017	Cosworth	V8				
nq	29	P-H Raphanel	Lola	LC88	Cosworth	V8				
nq	10	B Schneider	Zakspeed	881	Zakspeed	4t				
npq	21	N Larini	Osella	FA1L	Alfa Romeo	V8t				

Winning speed: 164.225 km/h, 102.045 mph
Pole Position speed: 175.027 km/h, 108.757 mph (A Senna, 1 min:17.748 sec)
Fastest Lap speed: 167.553 km/h, 104.113 mph (A Prost, 1 min:21.216 sec on lap 59)
Lap Leaders: A Prost 1-13,26-82 (70); G Berger 14-25 (12).

Thierry Boutsen, and the Benetton B188 at Silverstone in 1988

Lap Leaders 1988

POS	DRIVER	CAR-ENGINE	GPS	LAPS	KM	MILES
1	A Senna	McLaren-Honda	12	553	2,671.1	1,659.7
2	A Prost	McLaren-Honda	9	450	1,951.3	1,212.5
3	G Berger	Ferrari	3	27	119.1	74.0
4	I Capelli	March-Judd	1	1	5.9	3.6
			16	**1,031**	**4,747.3**	**2,949.9**

Driver Points 1988

		BR	RSM	MC	MEX	CDN	USA	F	GB	D	H	B	I	P	E	J	AUS	TOTAL	
1	A Senna	-	9	-	6	9	9	6	9	9	9	9	-	(1)	(3)	9	6	90	(4)
2	A Prost	9	6	9	9	6	6	9	-	6	(6)	(6)	-	9	9	(6)	9	87	(18)
3	G Berger	6	2	6	4	-	-	3	-	4	3	-	9	-	1	3	-	41	
4	T Boutsen	-	3	-	-	4	4	-	-	1	4	-	1	4	-	4	2	27	
5	M Alboreto	2	-	4	3	-	-	4	-	3	-	-	6	2	-	-	-	24	
6	N Piquet	4	4	-	-	3	-	2	2	-	-	3	-	-	-	-	4	22	
7	I Capelli	-	-	-	-	2	-	-	-	2	-	4	2	6	-	-	1	17	
	D Warwick	3	-	3	2	-	-	-	1	-	-	2	3	3	-	-	-	17	
9	N Mansell	-	-	-	-	-	-	-	6	-	-	-	-	-	6	-	-	12	
	A Nannini	-	1	-	-	-	-	1	4	-	-	-	-	-	4	2	-	12	
11	R Patrese	-	-	1	-	-	-	-	-	-	1	-	-	-	2	1	3	8	
12	E Cheever	-	-	-	1	-	-	-	-	-	-	1	4	-	-	-	-	6	
13	M Gugelmin	-	-	-	-	-	-	-	3	-	2	-	-	-	-	-	-	5	
	J Palmer	-	-	2	-	1	2	-	-	-	-	-	-	-	-	-	-	5	
15	A de Cesaris	-	-	-	-	-	3	-	-	-	-	-	-	-	-	-	-	3	
16	S Nakajima	1	-	-	-	-	-	-	-	-	-	-	-	-	-	-	-	1	
	P Martini	-	-	-	-	-	1	-	-	-	-	-	-	-	-	-	-	1	

9, 6, 4, 3, 2 and 1 point awarded to the first six finishers. Best 11 scores.

Constructor Points 1988

		BR	RSM	MC	MEX	CDN	USA	F	GB	D	H	B	I	P	E	J	AUS	TOTAL
1	McLaren-Honda	9	15	9	15	15	15	15	9	15	15	15	-	10	12	15	15	199
2	Ferrari	8	2	10	7	-	-	7	-	7	3	-	15	2	1	3	-	65
3	Benetton-Cosworth	-	4	-	-	4	4	1	4	1	4	-	1	4	4	6	2	39
4	Arrows-Megatron	3	-	3	3	-	-	-	1	-	-	3	7	3	-	-	-	23
	Lotus-Honda	5	4	-	-	3	-	2	2	-	-	3	-	-	-	-	4	23
6	March-Judd	-	-	-	2	-	-	-	3	2	2	4	2	6	-	-	1	22
7	Williams-Judd	-	-	1	-	-	-	-	6	-	1	-	-	-	8	1	3	20
8	Tyrrell-Cosworth	-	-	2	-	1	2	-	-	-	-	-	-	-	-	-	-	5
9	Rial-Cosworth	-	-	-	-	-	3	-	-	-	-	-	-	-	-	-	-	3
10	Minardi-Cosworth	-	-	-	-	-	1	-	-	-	-	-	-	-	-	-	-	1

9, 6, 4, 3, 2 and 1 point awarded to the first six finishers.

Turbo engines were banned, with only 3.5 litre atmospheric engines being permitted. There was a record entry of 20 teams with new engines from Lamborghini and Yamaha as well as a return for Pirelli. Brabham also returned after a year away, now owned by Joachim Luhti. Ferrari produced the revolutionary semi-automatic gearbox, controlled by switches on the steering wheel.

McLAREN
Honda Marlboro McLaren: Senna, Prost

TYRRELL
Tyrrell Racing Organisation: Palmer, Alboreto, Alesi, Herbert

WILLIAMS
Canon Williams Team: Boutsen, Patrese

BRABHAM
Motor Racing Developments: Brundle, Modena

ARROWS
USF&G Arrows: Warwick, Donnelly, Cheever

LOTUS
Camel Team Lotus: Piquet, Nakajima

MARCH
Leyton House March Racing Team: Gugelmin, Capelli

OSELLA
Osella Squadra Corse: Larini, Ghinzani

BENETTON
Benetton Formula: Nannini, Herbert, Pirro

DALLARA
Scuderia Italia: Caffi, de Cesaris

MINARDI
Lois Minardi Team: Martini, Barilla, Sala

LIGIER
Ligier Loto: Arnoux, Grouillard

FERRARI
Scuderia Ferrari SpA SEFAC: Mansell, Berger

LOLA
Equipe Larrousse: Dalmas, Bernard, Alboreto, Alliot

COLONI
Coloni SpA: Moreno, Raphanel, (Bertaggia)

EUROBRUN
EuroBrun Racing: (Foitek, Larrauri)

ZAKSPEED
West Zakspeed Racing: Schneider, (Suzuki)

ONYX
Moneytron Onyx: Johansson, Gachot, Lehto

RIAL
Rial Racing: Danner, (Foitek, Gachot, Weidler, Raphanel)

AGS
Automobiles Gonfaronaises Sportives: Tarquini, (Winkelhock, Dalmas)

26 Mar 1989 — BRAZIL: Rio de Janeiro (Round: 1) (Race: 469)

61 laps x 5.031 km, 3.126 miles = 306.891 km, 190.693 miles

POS.	NO.	DRIVER	CAR	MODEL	ENGINE		LAPS	TIME/REASON FOR RETIREMENT	GRID:POS	ROW
1	27	N Mansell	Ferrari	640	Ferrari	V12	61	1h 38m 58.744s	6	3
2	2	A Prost	McLaren	MP4/5	Honda	V10	61	1h 39m 06.553s	5	3
3	15	M Gugelmin	March	881	Judd	V8	61	1h 39m 08.114s	12	6
4	20	J Herbert	Benetton	B188	Cosworth	V8	61	1h 39m 09.237s	10	5
5	9	D Warwick	Arrows	A11	Cosworth	V8	61	1h 39m 16.610s	8	4
6	19	A Nannini	Benetton	B188	Cosworth	V8	61	1h 39m 16.985s	11	6
7	3	J Palmer	Tyrrell	017B	Cosworth	V8	60		18	9
8	12	S Nakajima	Lotus	101	Judd	V8	60		21	11
9	26	O Grouillard	Ligier	JS33	Cosworth	V8	60		22	11
10	4	M Alboreto	Tyrrell	017B	Cosworth	V8	59		20	10
11	1	A Senna	McLaren	MP4/5	Honda	V10	59		1	1
12	30	P Alliot	Lola	LC88B	Lamborghini	V12	58		26	13
13r	22	A de Cesaris	Dallara	189	Cosworth	V8	57	engine	15	8
14r	38	C Danner	Rial	ARC2	Cosworth	V8	56	gearbox	17	9
r	6	R Patrese	Williams	FW12C	Renault	V10	51	camshaft pulley	2	1
r	10	E Cheever	Arrows	A11	Cosworth	V8	37	accident	24	12
r	34	B Schneider	Zakspeed	891	Yamaha	V8	36	suspension/ accident	25	13
r	7	M Brundle	Brabham	BT58	Judd	V8	27	wiring loom	13	7
r	16	I Capelli	March	881	Judd	V8	22	rear suspension	7	4
r	11	N Piquet	Lotus	101	Judd	V8	10	fuel pump	9	5
dq	17	N Larini	Osella	FA1M	Cosworth	V8	10	started from wrong grid position	19	10
r	8	S Modena	Brabham	BT58	Judd	V8	9	cv joint	14	7
r	5	T Boutsen	Williams	FW12C	Renault	V10	3	engine	4	2
r	23	P Martini	Minardi	M188B	Cosworth	V8	2	engine mounting	16	8
r	24	L Sala	Minardi	M188B	Cosworth	V8	0	accident	23	12
r	28	G Berger	Ferrari	640	Ferrari	V12	0	accident	3	2
nq	29	Y Dalmas	Lola	LC88B	Lamborghini	V12				
nq	25	R Arnoux	Ligier	JS33	Cosworth	V8				
nq	33	G Foitek	EuroBrun	ER188B	Judd	V8				
nq	31	R Moreno	Coloni	FC188B	Cosworth	V8				
npq	21	A Caffi	Dallara	189	Cosworth	V8				
npq	18	P Ghinzani	Osella	FA1M	Cosworth	V8				
npq	39	V Weidler	Rial	ARC2	Cosworth	V8				
npq	32	P-H Raphanel	Coloni	FC188B	Cosworth	V8				
npq	41	J Winkelhock	AGS	JH23B	Cosworth	V8				
npq	35	A Suzuki	Zakspeed	891	Yamaha	V8				
npq	36	S Johansson	Onyx	ORE-1	Cosworth	V8				
npq	37	B Gachot	Onyx	ORE-1	Cosworth	V8				

Winning speed: 186.034 km/h, 115.596 mph
Pole Position speed: 212.323 km/h, 131.932 mph (A Senna, 1 min:25.302 sec)
Fastest Lap speed: 195.786 km/h, 121.656 mph (R Patrese, 1 min:32.507 sec on lap 47)
Lap Leaders: R Patrese 1-15,21-22 (17); N Mansell 16-20,28-44,47-61 (37); A Prost 23-27,45-46 (7).

23 Apr 1989 — SAN MARINO: Imola (Round: 2) (Race: 470)

58 laps x 5.040 km, 3.132 miles = 292.320 km, 181.639 miles

POS.	NO.	DRIVER	CAR	MODEL	ENGINE		LAPS	TIME/REASON FOR RETIREMENT	GRID:POS	ROW
1	1	A Senna	McLaren	MP4/5	Honda	V10	58	1h 26m 51.245s	1	1
2	2	A Prost	McLaren	MP4/5	Honda	V10	58	1h 27m 31.470s	2	1
3	19	A Nannini	Benetton	B188	Cosworth	V8	57		7	4
4	5	T Boutsen	Williams	FW12C	Renault	V10	57		6	3

POS.	NO.	DRIVER	CAR	MODEL	ENGINE		LAPS	TIME/REASON FOR RETIREMENT	GRID:POS	ROW
5	9	D Warwick	Arrows	A11	Cosworth	V8	57		12	6
6	3	J Palmer	Tyrrell	018	Cosworth	V8	57		25	13
7	21	A Caffi	Dallara	189	Cosworth	V8	57		9	5
8	40	G Tarquini	AGS	JH23B	Cosworth	V8	57		18	9
9	10	E Cheever	Arrows	A11	Cosworth	V8	56		21	11
10	22	A de Cesaris	Dallara	189	Cosworth	V8	56		16	8
11	20	J Herbert	Benetton	B188	Cosworth	V8	56		23	12
12r	17	N Larini	Osella	FA1M	Cosworth	V8	52	hub/ accident	14	7
r	7	M Brundle	Brabham	BT58	Judd	V8	51	fuel pressure	22	11
nc	12	S Nakajima	Lotus	101	Judd	V8	46		24	12
r	24	L Sala	Minardi	M188B	Cosworth	V8	43	accident	15	8
r	15	M Gugelmin	March	881	Judd	V8	39	clutch	19	10
r	11	N Piquet	Lotus	101	Judd	V8	29	engine	8	4
r	27	N Mansell	Ferrari	640	Ferrari	V12	23	gearbox	3	2
r	6	R Patrese	Williams	FW12C	Renault	V10	21	camshaft belt	4	2
r	8	S Modena	Brabham	BT58	Judd	V8	19	accident	17	9
r	23	P Martini	Minardi	M188B	Cosworth	V8	6	gearbox	11	6
dq	26	O Grouillard	Ligier	JS33	Cosworth	V8	4	car worked on between starts	10	5
r	28	G Berger	Ferrari	640	Ferrari	V12	3	accident/ fire	5	3
r	16	I Capelli	March	881	Judd	V8	1	accident	13	7
r	30	P Alliot	Lola	LC89	Lamborghini	V12	0	fuel injection	20	10
ns	29	Y Dalmas	Lola	LC89	Lamborghini	V12		stalled on dummy grid	26	13
nq	4	M Alboreto	Tyrrell	018	Cosworth	V8				
nq	25	R Arnoux	Ligier	JS33	Cosworth	V8				
nq	38	C Danner	Rial	ARC2	Cosworth	V8				
nq	31	R Moreno	Coloni	FC188B	Cosworth	V8				
npq	37	B Gachot	Onyx	ORE-1	Cosworth	V8				
npq	33	G Foitek	EuroBrun	ER188B	Judd	V8				
npq	18	P Ghinzani	Osella	FA1M	Cosworth	V8				
npq	36	S Johansson	Onyx	ORE-1	Cosworth	V8				
npq	41	J Winkelhock	AGS	JH23B	Cosworth	V8				
npq	32	P-H Raphanel	Coloni	FC188B	Cosworth	V8				
npq	35	A Suzuki	Zakspeed	891	Yamaha	V8				
npq	34	B Schneider	Zakspeed	891	Yamaha	V8				
npq	39	V Weidler	Rial	ARC2	Cosworth	V8				

Winning speed: 201.939 km/h, 125.479 mph
Pole Position speed: 210.952 km/h, 131.080 mph (A Senna, 1 min:26.010 sec)
Fastest Lap speed: 209.044 km/h, 129.894 mph (A Prost, 1 min:26.795 sec on lap 45)
Lap Leaders: A Senna 1-58 (58).

Scheduled for 61 laps, but interrupted after 3 laps, because of an accident. Restarted for a further 55 laps, with results being on aggregate.

7 May 1989 — MONACO: Monte Carlo (Round: 3) (Race: 471)

77 laps x 3.328 km, 2.068 miles = 256.256 km, 159.230 miles

POS.	NO.	DRIVER	CAR	MODEL	ENGINE		LAPS	TIME/REASON FOR RETIREMENT	GRID:POS	ROW
1	1	A Senna	McLaren	MP4/5	Honda	V10	77	1h 53m 33.251s	1	1
2	2	A Prost	McLaren	MP4/5	Honda	V10	77	1h 54m 25.780s	2	1
3	8	S Modena	Brabham	BT58	Judd	V8	76		8	4
4	21	A Caffi	Dallara	189	Cosworth	V8	75		9	5
5	4	M Alboreto	Tyrrell	018	Cosworth	V8	75		12	6
6	7	M Brundle	Brabham	BT58	Judd	V8	75		4	2
7	10	E Cheever	Arrows	A11	Cosworth	V8	75		20	10
8	19	A Nannini	Benetton	B188	Cosworth	V8	74		15	8
9	3	J Palmer	Tyrrell	018	Cosworth	V8	74		23	12
10	5	T Boutsen	Williams	FW12C	Renault	V10	74		3	2
11r	16	I Capelli	March	CG891	Judd	V8	73	electrics/ fire	22	11
12	25	R Arnoux	Ligier	JS33	Cosworth	V8	73		21	11
13	22	A de Cesaris	Dallara	189	Cosworth	V8	73		10	5
14	20	J Herbert	Benetton	B188	Cosworth	V8	73		24	12
15	6	R Patrese	Williams	FW12C	Renault	V10	73		7	4
r	24	L Sala	Minardi	M188B	Cosworth	V8	48	engine/ fire	26	13
r	40	G Tarquini	AGS	JH23B	Cosworth	V8	46	electrics	13	7
r	31	R Moreno	Coloni	FC188B	Cosworth	V8	44	gearbox pinion	25	13
r	30	P Alliot	Lola	LC89	Lamborghini	V12	38	engine	17	9
r	15	M Gugelmin	March	CG891	Judd	V8	36	engine	14	7
r	11	N Piquet	Lotus	101	Judd	V8	32	accident	19	10
r	27	N Mansell	Ferrari	640	Ferrari	V12	30	gearbox	5	3
r	32	P-H Raphanel	Coloni	FC188B	Cosworth	V8	19	gearbox	18	9
r	26	O Grouillard	Ligier	JS33	Cosworth	V8	4	gearbox	16	8
r	23	P Martini	Minardi	M188B	Cosworth	V8	3	clutch	11	6
r	9	D Warwick	Arrows	A11	Cosworth	V8	2	electrics/ fire	6	3
nq	38	C Danner	Rial	ARC2	Cosworth	V8				
nq	29	Y Dalmas	Lola	LC89	Lamborghini	V12				
nq	12	S Nakajima	Lotus	101	Judd	V8				
npq	18	P Ghinzani	Osella	FA1M	Cosworth	V8				
npq	36	S Johansson	Onyx	ORE-1	Cosworth	V8				
npq	17	N Larini	Osella	FA1M	Cosworth	V8				
npq	34	B Schneider	Zakspeed	891	Yamaha	V8				
npq	37	B Gachot	Onyx	ORE-1	Cosworth	V8				
npq	33	G Foitek	EuroBrun	ER188B	Judd	V8				
npq	39	V Weidler	Rial	ARC2	Cosworth	V8				
npq	35	A Suzuki	Zakspeed	891	Yamaha	V8				
npq	41	J Winkelhock	AGS	JH23B	Cosworth	V8				

Winning speed: 135.401 km/h, 84.134 mph
Pole Position speed: 145.561 km/h, 90.447 mph (A Senna, 1 min:22.308 sec)
Fastest Lap speed: 140.125 km/h, 87.069 mph (A Prost, 1 min:25.501 sec on lap 59)
Lap Leaders: A Senna 1-77 (77).

28 May 1989 — MEXICO: Mexico City (Round: 4) (Race: 472)

69 laps x 4.421 km, 2.747 miles = 305.049 km, 189.549 miles

POS.	NO.	DRIVER	CAR	MODEL	ENGINE		LAPS	TIME/REASON FOR RETIREMENT	GRID:POS	ROW
1	1	A Senna	McLaren	MP4/5	Honda	V10	69	1h 35m 21.431s	1	1
2	6	R Patrese	Williams	FW12C	Renault	V10	69	1h 35m 36.991s	5	3
3	4	M Alboreto	Tyrrell	018	Cosworth	V8	69	1h 35m 52.685s	7	4
4	19	A Nannini	Benetton	B188	Cosworth	V8	69	1h 36m 06.926s	13	7
5	2	A Prost	McLaren	MP4/5	Honda	V10	69	1h 36m 17.544s	2	1
6	40	G Tarquini	AGS	JH23B	Cosworth	V8	68		17	9
7	10	E Cheever	Arrows	A11	Cosworth	V8	68		24	12
8	26	O Grouillard	Ligier	JS33	Cosworth	V8	68		11	6
9	7	M Brundle	Brabham	BT58	Judd	V8	68		20	10
10	8	S Modena	Brabham	BT58	Judd	V8	68		9	5
11	11	N Piquet	Lotus	101	Judd	V8	68		26	13
12	38	C Danner	Rial	ARC2	Cosworth	V8	67		23	12
13	21	A Caffi	Dallara	189	Cosworth	V8	67		19	10
14	25	R Arnoux	Ligier	JS33	Cosworth	V8	66		25	13
15	20	J Herbert	Benetton	B188	Cosworth	V8	66		18	9
r	23	P Martini	Minardi	M189	Cosworth	V8	53	engine	22	11
r	27	N Mansell	Ferrari	640	Ferrari	V12	43	gearbox hydraulic fluid loss	3	2
r	9	D Warwick	Arrows	A11	Cosworth	V8	35	electrics	10	5
r	12	S Nakajima	Lotus	101	Judd	V8	35	gearbox/ spin	15	8
nc	30	P Alliot	Lola	LC89	Lamborghini	V12	28		16	8
r	22	A de Cesaris	Dallara	189	Cosworth	V8	20	fuel pump	12	6
r	28	G Berger	Ferrari	640	Ferrari	V12	16	gearbox hydraulic fluid loss	6	3
r	36	S Johansson	Onyx	ORE-1	Cosworth	V8	16	clutch	21	11
r	5	T Boutsen	Williams	FW12C	Renault	V10	15	electrics	8	4
r	3	J Palmer	Tyrrell	018	Cosworth	V8	9	throttle linkage	14	7
r	16	I Capelli	March	CG891	Judd	V8	1	cv joint	4	2
nq	24	L Sala	Minardi	M189	Cosworth	V8				
nq	15	M Gugelmin	March	CG891	Judd	V8				
nq	29	Y Dalmas	Lola	LC89	Lamborghini	V12				
nq	31	R Moreno	Coloni	FC188B	Cosworth	V8				
npq	37	B Gachot	Onyx	ORE-1	Cosworth	V8				
npq	33	G Foitek	EuroBrun	ER188B	Judd	V8				
npq	17	N Larini	Osella	FA1M	Cosworth	V8				
npq	39	V Weidler	Rial	ARC2	Cosworth	V8				
npq	34	B Schneider	Zakspeed	891	Yamaha	V8				
npq	35	A Suzuki	Zakspeed	891	Yamaha	V8				
exc	18	P Ghinzani	Osella	FA1M	Cosworth	V8		missed weight check		
npq	41	J Winkelhock	AGS	JH23B	Cosworth	V8				
npq	32	P-H Raphanel	Coloni	FC188B	Cosworth	V8				

Winning speed: 191.941 km/h, 119.267 mph
Pole Position speed: 204.371 km/h, 126.990 mph (A Senna, 1 min:17.876 sec)
Fastest Lap speed: 197.906 km/h, 122.973 mph (N Mansell, 1 min:20.420 sec on lap 41)
Lap Leaders: A Senna 1-69 (69).

Interrupted after 2nd lap, because of an accident. Restarted for original distance.

4 Jun 1989 — USA: Phoenix (Round: 5) (Race: 473)

75 laps x 3.798 km, 2.360 miles = 284.854 km, 177.000 miles

POS.	NO.	DRIVER	CAR	MODEL	ENGINE		LAPS	TIME/REASON FOR RETIREMENT	GRID:POS	ROW
1	2	A Prost	McLaren	MP4/5	Honda	V10	75	2h 01m 33.133s	2	1
2	6	R Patrese	Williams	FW12C	Renault	V10	75	2h 02m 12.829s	14	7
3	10	E Cheever	Arrows	A11	Cosworth	V8	75	2h 02m 16.343s	17	9
4	38	C Danner	Rial	ARC2	Cosworth	V8	74		26	13
5	20	J Herbert	Benetton	B188	Cosworth	V8	74		25	13
6	5	T Boutsen	Williams	FW12C	Renault	V10	74		16	8
7r	40	G Tarquini	AGS	JH23B	Cosworth	V8	73	engine	24	12
8r	22	A de Cesaris	Dallara	189	Cosworth	V8	70	fuel pump	13	7
9r	3	J Palmer	Tyrrell	018	Cosworth	V8	69	fuel injection	21	11
r	28	G Berger	Ferrari	640	Ferrari	V12	61	alternator	8	4
r	21	A Caffi	Dallara	189	Cosworth	V8	52	accident	6	3
r	11	N Piquet	Lotus	101	Judd	V8	52	suspension/ accident	22	11
r	36	S Johansson	Onyx	ORE-1	Cosworth	V8	50	puncture/ suspension	19	10
r	24	L Sala	Minardi	M189	Cosworth	V8	46	engine overheating	20	10
r	1	A Senna	McLaren	MP4/5	Honda	V10	44	electronics	1	1
r	7	M Brundle	Brabham	BT58	Judd	V8	43	brakes	5	3
r	8	S Modena	Brabham	BT58	Judd	V8	37	brakes	7	4
r	27	N Mansell	Ferrari	640	Ferrari	V12	31	gearbox	4	2
r	23	P Martini	Minardi	M189	Cosworth	V8	26	engine overheating	15	8
r	12	S Nakajima	Lotus	101	Judd	V8	24	throttle linkage	23	12
r	16	I Capelli	March	CG891	Judd	V8	22	gearbox	11	6
dq	15	M Gugelmin	March	CG891	Judd	V8	20	brake fluid refilled during race	18	9
r	4	M Alboreto	Tyrrell	018	Cosworth	V8	17	gearbox	9	5
r	19	A Nannini	Benetton	B188	Cosworth	V8	10	driver exhausted	3	2
r	9	D Warwick	Arrows	A11	Cosworth	V8	7	accident	10	5
r	30	P Alliot	Lola	LC89	Lamborghini	V12	3	spin	12	6
nq	26	O Grouillard	Ligier	JS33	Cosworth	V8				
nq	31	R Moreno	Coloni	FC188B	Cosworth	V8				
nq	25	R Arnoux	Ligier	JS33	Cosworth	V8				
nq	29	Y Dalmas	Lola	LC89	Lamborghini	V12				
npq	18	P Ghinzani	Osella	FA1M	Cosworth	V8				
npq	32	P-H Raphanel	Coloni	FC188B	Cosworth	V8				
npq	33	G Foitek	EuroBrun	ER188B	Judd	V8				

POS.	NO.	DRIVER	CAR	MODEL	ENGINE		LAPS	TIME/REASON FOR RETIREMENT	GRID:POS	ROW
npq	17	N Larini	Osella	FA1M	Cosworth	V8				
npq	41	J Winkelhock	AGS	JH23B	Cosworth	V8				
npq	39	V Weidler	Rial	ARC2	Cosworth	V8				
npq	34	B Schneider	Zakspeed	891	Yamaha	V8				
npq	35	A Suzuki	Zakspeed	891	Yamaha	V8				
npq	37	B Gachot	Onyx	ORE-1	Cosworth	V8				

Winning speed: 140.608 km/h, 87.370 mph
Pole Position speed: 151.740 km/h, 94.287 mph (A Senna, 1 min:30.108 sec)
Fastest Lap speed: 145.505 km/h, 90.413 mph (A Senna, 1 min:33.969 sec on lap 38)
Lap Leaders: A Senna 1-33 (33); A Prost 34-75 (42).

Scheduled for 81 laps, but stopped at 2 hours.

18 Jun 1989 — CANADA: Montréal (Round: 6) (Race: 474)

69 laps x 4.390 km, 2.728 miles = 302.910 km, 188.220 miles

POS.	NO.	DRIVER	CAR	MODEL	ENGINE		LAPS	TIME/REASON FOR RETIREMENT	GRID:POS	ROW
1	5	T Boutsen	Williams	FW12C	Renault	V10	69	2h 01m 24.073s	6	3
2	6	R Patrese	Williams	FW12C	Renault	V10	69	2h 01m 54.080s	3	2
3	22	A de Cesaris	Dallara	189	Cosworth	V8	69	2h 03m 00.722s	9	5
4	11	N Piquet	Lotus	101	Judd	V8	69	2h 03m 05.557s	19	10
5	25	R Arnoux	Ligier	JS33	Cosworth	V8	68		22	11
6	21	A Caffi	Dallara	189	Cosworth	V8	67		8	4
7r	1	A Senna	McLaren	MP4/5	Honda	V10	66	engine	2	1
8	38	C Danner	Rial	ARC2	Cosworth	V8	66		23	12
r	31	R Moreno	Coloni	FC189	Cosworth	V8	57	gearbox	26	13
r	9	D Warwick	Arrows	A11	Cosworth	V8	40	engine	12	6
r	3	J Palmer	Tyrrell	018	Cosworth	V8	35	accident	14	7
r	17	N Larini	Osella	FA1M	Cosworth	V8	33	electrics	15	8
r	16	I Capelli	March	CG891	Judd	V8	28	accident	21	11
r	30	P Alliot	Lola	LC89	Lamborghini	V12	26	accident	10	5
r	15	M Gugelmin	March	CG891	Judd	V8	11	electrics	17	9
dq	36	S Johansson	Onyx	ORE-1	Cosworth	V8	13	ignored black flag	18	9
r	24	L Sala	Minardi	M189	Cosworth	V8	11	accident	24	12
r	28	G Berger	Ferrari	640	Ferrari	V12	6	alternator belt	4	2
r	40	G Tarquini	AGS	JH23B	Cosworth	V8	6	accident	25	13
r	10	E Cheever	Arrows	A11	Cosworth	V8	3	electrics	16	8
r	2	A Prost	McLaren	MP4/5	Honda	V10	2	suspension	1	1
r	4	M Alboreto	Tyrrell	018	Cosworth	V8	0	electrics	20	10
r	8	S Modena	Brabham	BT58	Judd	V8	0	accident	7	4
r	23	P Martini	Minardi	M189	Cosworth	V8	0	accident	11	6
dq	27	N Mansell	Ferrari	640	Ferrari	V12	0	started from pits too soon	5	3
dq	19	A Nannini	Benetton	B188	Cosworth	V8	0	started from pits too soon	13	7
nq	12	S Nakajima	Lotus	101	Judd	V8				
nq	29	Y Dalmas	Lola	LC89	Lamborghini	V12				
nq	20	J Herbert	Benetton	B188	Cosworth	V8				
nq	26	O Grouillard	Ligier	JS33	Cosworth	V8				
npq	7	M Brundle	Brabham	BT58	Judd	V8				
npq	37	B Gachot	Onyx	ORE-1	Cosworth	V8				
npq	33	G Foitek	EuroBrun	ER188B	Judd	V8				
npq	18	P Ghinzani	Osella	FA1M	Cosworth	V8				
npq	34	B Schneider	Zakspeed	891	Yamaha	V8				
npq	41	J Winkelhock	AGS	JH23B	Cosworth	V8				
npq	39	V Weidler	Rial	ARC2	Cosworth	V8				
npq	35	A Suzuki	Zakspeed	891	Yamaha	V8				
npq	32	P-H Raphanel	Coloni	FC189	Cosworth	V8				

Winning speed: 149.707 km/h, 93.024 mph
Pole Position speed: 195.176 km/h, 121.277 mph (A Prost, 1 min:20.973 sec)
Fastest Lap speed: 171.923 km/h, 106.828 mph (J Palmer, 1 min:31.925 sec on lap 11)
Lap Leaders: A Prost 1 (1); A Senna 2-3,39-66 (30); R Patrese 4-34 (31); D Warwick 35-38 (4); T Boutsen 67-69 (3).

9 Jul 1989 — FRANCE: Paul Ricard (Round: 7) (Race: 475)

80 laps x 3.813 km, 2.369 miles = 305.040 km, 189.543 miles

POS.	NO.	DRIVER	CAR	MODEL	ENGINE		LAPS	TIME/REASON FOR RETIREMENT	GRID:POS	ROW
1	2	A Prost	McLaren	MP4/5	Honda	V10	80	1h 38m 29.411s	1	1
2	27	N Mansell	Ferrari	640	Ferrari	V12	80	1h 39m 13.428s	3	2
3	6	R Patrese	Williams	FW12C	Renault	V10	80	1h 39m 36.332s	8	4
4	4	J Alesi	Tyrrell	018	Cosworth	V8	80	1h 39m 42.643s	16	8
5	36	S Johansson	Onyx	ORE-1	Cosworth	V8	79		13	7
6	26	O Grouillard	Ligier	JS33	Cosworth	V8	79		17	9
7	10	E Cheever	Arrows	A11	Cosworth	V8	79		25	13
8	11	N Piquet	Lotus	101	Judd	V8	78		20	10
9	20	E Pirro	Benetton	B188	Cosworth	V8	78		24	12
10	3	J Palmer	Tyrrell	018	Cosworth	V8	78		9	5
11r	29	É Bernard	Lola	LC89	Lamborghini	V12	77	engine	15	8
12	9	M Donnelly	Arrows	A11	Cosworth	V8	77		14	7
13	37	B Gachot	Onyx	ORE-1	Cosworth	V8	76		11	6
nc	15	M Gugelmin	March	CG891	Judd	V8	71		10	5
r	8	S Modena	Brabham	BT58	Judd	V8	67	engine	22	11
r	5	T Boutsen	Williams	FW12C	Renault	V10	50	gearbox	5	3
r	12	S Nakajima	Lotus	101	Judd	V8	49	electrics	19	10
r	16	I Capelli	March	CG891	Judd	V8	43	engine	12	6
r	19	A Nannini	Benetton	B189	Cosworth	V8	40	rear suspension	4	2

POS.	NO.	DRIVER	CAR	MODEL	ENGINE		LAPS	TIME/REASON FOR RETIREMENT	GRID:POS	ROW
r	23	P Martini	Minardi	M189	Cosworth	V8	31	oil pressure	23	12
r	30	P Alliot	Lola	LC89	Lamborghini	V12	30	engine	7	4
r	40	G Tarquini	AGS	JH23B	Cosworth	V8	30	engine	21	11
r	28	G Berger	Ferrari	640	Ferrari	V12	29	gearbox oil leak	6	3
r	21	A Caffi	Dallara	189	Cosworth	V8	27	accident/ clutch master cylinder	26	13
r	25	R Arnoux	Ligier	JS33	Cosworth	V8	14	gearbox	18	9
r	1	A Senna	McLaren	MP4/5	Honda	V10	0	differential	2	1
nq	22	A de Cesaris	Dallara	189	Cosworth	V8				
nq	24	L Sala	Minardi	M189	Cosworth	V8				
nq	38	C Danner	Rial	ARC2	Cosworth	V8				
nq	31	R Moreno	Coloni	FC189	Cosworth	V8				
npq	17	N Larini	Osella	FA1M	Cosworth	V8				
npq	7	M Brundle	Brabham	BT58	Judd	V8				
npq	39	V Weidler	Rial	ARC2	Cosworth	V8				
npq	34	B Schneider	Zakspeed	891	Yamaha	V8				
npq	18	P Ghinzani	Osella	FA1M	Cosworth	V8				
npq	32	P-H Raphanel	Coloni	FC189	Cosworth	V8				
npq	35	A Suzuki	Zakspeed	891	Yamaha	V8				
npq	33	G Foitek	EuroBrun	ER188B	Judd	V8				
npq	41	J Winkelhock	AGS	JH23B	Cosworth	V8				

Winning speed: 185.830 km/h, 115.469 mph
Pole Position speed: 204.259 km/h, 126.920 mph (A Prost, 1 min: 7.203 sec)
Fastest Lap speed: 190.412 km/h, 118.317 mph (M Gugelmin, 1 min:12.090 sec on lap 29)
Lap Leaders: A Prost 1-80 (80).

Interrupted after 1st lap accident. Restarted for original distance.

16 Jul 1989 BRITAIN: Silverstone (Round: 8) (Race: 476)
64 laps x 4.780 km, 2.970 miles = 305.904 km, 190.080 miles

POS.	NO.	DRIVER	CAR	MODEL	ENGINE		LAPS	TIME/REASON FOR RETIREMENT	GRID:POS	ROW
1	2	A Prost	McLaren	MP4/5	Honda	V10	64	1h 19m 22.131s	2	1
2	27	N Mansell	Ferrari	640	Ferrari	V12	64	1h 19m 41.500s	3	2
3	19	A Nannini	Benetton	B189	Cosworth	V8	64	1h 20m 10.150s	9	5
4	11	N Piquet	Lotus	101	Judd	V8	64	1h 20m 28.866s	10	5
5	23	P Martini	Minardi	M189	Cosworth	V8	63		11	6
6	24	L Sala	Minardi	M189	Cosworth	V8	63		15	8
7	26	O Grouillard	Ligier	JS33	Cosworth	V8	63		24	12
8	12	S Nakajima	Lotus	101	Judd	V8	63		16	8
9	9	D Warwick	Arrows	A11	Cosworth	V8	62		19	10
10	5	T Boutsen	Williams	FW12C	Renault	V10	62		7	4
11	20	E Pirro	Benetton	B188	Cosworth	V8	62		26	13
12	37	B Gachot	Onyx	ORE-1	Cosworth	V8	62		21	11
r	15	M Gugelmin	March	CG891	Judd	V8	54	gearbox	6	3
r	7	M Brundle	Brabham	BT58	Judd	V8	49	engine	20	10
r	28	G Berger	Ferrari	640	Ferrari	V12	49	gearbox	4	2
r	29	É Bernard	Lola	LC89	Lamborghini	V12	46	gearbox	13	7
r	30	P Alliot	Lola	LC89	Lamborghini	V12	39	engine	12	6
r	3	J Palmer	Tyrrell	018	Cosworth	V8	32	accident	18	9
r	8	S Modena	Brabham	BT58	Judd	V8	31	engine	14	7
r	4	J Alesi	Tyrrell	018	Cosworth	V8	28	accident	22	11
r	17	N Larini	Osella	FA1M	Cosworth	V8	23	handling	17	9
r	6	R Patrese	Williams	FW12C	Renault	V10	19	water leak/ accident	5	3
r	16	I Capelli	March	CG891	Judd	V8	15	differential	8	4
r	22	A de Cesaris	Dallara	189	Cosworth	V8	14	gearbox	25	13
r	1	A Senna	McLaren	MP4/5	Honda	V10	11	gearbox/ spin	1	1
r	31	R Moreno	Coloni	FC189	Cosworth	V8	2	gearbox	23	12
nq	25	R Arnoux	Ligier	JS33	Cosworth	V8				
nq	10	E Cheever	Arrows	A11	Cosworth	V8				
nq	40	G Tarquini	AGS	JH24	Cosworth	V8				
nq	38	C Danner	Rial	ARC2	Cosworth	V8				
npq	36	S Johansson	Onyx	ORE-1	Cosworth	V8				
npq	21	A Caffi	Dallara	189	Cosworth	V8				
npq	33	G Foitek	EuroBrun	ER188B	Judd	V8				
npq	18	P Ghinzani	Osella	FA1M	Cosworth	V8				
npq	41	Y Dalmas	AGS	JH23B	Cosworth	V8				
npq	34	B Schneider	Zakspeed	891	Yamaha	V8				
npq	32	P-H Raphanel	Coloni	FC189	Cosworth	V8				
npq	35	A Suzuki	Zakspeed	891	Yamaha	V8				
npq	39	V Weidler	Rial	ARC2	Cosworth	V8				

Winning speed: 231.253 km/h, 143.694 mph
Pole Position speed: 249.021 km/h, 154.735 mph (A Senna, 1 min: 9.099 sec)
Fastest Lap speed: 238.931 km/h, 148.465 mph (N Mansell, 1 min:12.017 sec on lap 57)
Lap Leaders: A Senna 1-11 (11); A Prost 10-64 (53).

30 Jul 1989 GERMANY: Hockenheim (Round: 9) (Race: 477)
45 laps x 6.797 km, 4.223 miles = 305.865 km, 190.056 miles

POS.	NO.	DRIVER	CAR	MODEL	ENGINE		LAPS	TIME/REASON FOR RETIREMENT	GRID:POS	ROW
1	1	A Senna	McLaren	MP4/5	Honda	V10	45	1h 21m 43.302s	1	1
2	2	A Prost	McLaren	MP4/5	Honda	V10	45	1h 22m 01.453s	2	1
3	27	N Mansell	Ferrari	640	Ferrari	V12	45	1h 23m 06.556s	3	2
4	6	R Patrese	Williams	FW12C	Renault	V10	44		5	3
5	11	N Piquet	Lotus	101	Judd	V8	44		8	4

POS.	NO.	DRIVER	CAR	MODEL	ENGINE		LAPS	TIME/REASON FOR RETIREMENT	GRID:POS	ROW
6	9	D Warwick	Arrows	A11	Cosworth	V8	44		17	9
7	22	A de Cesaris	Dallara	189	Cosworth	V8	44		21	11
8	7	M Brundle	Brabham	BT58	Judd	V8	44		12	6
9	23	P Martini	Minardi	M189	Cosworth	V8	44		13	7
10	4	J Alesi	Tyrrell	018	Cosworth	V8	43		10	5
11	25	R Arnoux	Ligier	JS33	Cosworth	V8	42		23	12
12r	10	E Cheever	Arrows	A11	Cosworth	V8	40	fuel pick-up	25	13
r	8	S Modena	Brabham	BT58	Judd	V8	37	engine	16	8
r	12	S Nakajima	Lotus	101	Judd	V8	36	spin	18	9
r	16	I Capelli	March	CG891	Judd	V8	32	electronics	22	11
r	15	M Gugelmin	March	CG891	Judd	V8	28	gearbox	14	7
r	20	E Pirro	Benetton	B189	Cosworth	V8	26	accident	9	5
r	30	P Alliot	Lola	LC89	Lamborghini	V12	20	oil leak/ fire	15	8
r	3	J Palmer	Tyrrell	018	Cosworth	V8	16	throttle linkage	19	10
r	28	G Berger	Ferrari	640	Ferrari	V12	13	puncture/ accident	4	2
r	36	S Johansson	Onyx	ORE-1	Cosworth	V8	8	rear wheel bearing	24	12
r	19	A Nannini	Benetton	B189	Cosworth	V8	6	electrical sensor	7	4
r	5	T Boutsen	Williams	FW12C	Renault	V10	4	accident	6	3
r	21	A Caffi	Dallara	189	Cosworth	V8	2	electrics	20	10
r	29	M Alboreto	Lola	LC89	Lamborghini	V12	1	electrics	26	13
r	26	O Grouillard	Ligier	JS33	Cosworth	V8	0	input shaft	11	6
nq	24	L Sala	Minardi	M189	Cosworth	V8				
nq	37	B Gachot	Onyx	ORE-1	Cosworth	V8				
nq	38	C Danner	Rial	ARC2	Cosworth	V8				
exc	39	V Weidler	Rial	ARC2	Cosworth	V8		push start after spin		
npq	41	Y Dalmas	AGS	JH24	Cosworth	V8				
npq	17	N Larini	Osella	FA1M	Cosworth	V8				
npq	40	G Tarquini	AGS	JH23B	Cosworth	V8				
npq	18	P Ghinzani	Osella	FA1M	Cosworth	V8				
npq	31	R Moreno	Coloni	FC189	Cosworth	V8				
npq	32	P-H Raphanel	Coloni	FC189	Cosworth	V8				
npq	33	G Foitek	EuroBrun	ER189	Judd	V8				
npq	35	A Suzuki	Zakspeed	891	Yamaha	V8				
npq	34	B Schneider	Zakspeed	891	Yamaha	V8				

Winning speed: 224.566 km/h, 139.539 mph
Pole Position speed: 239.191 km/h, 148.626 mph (A Senna, 1 min:42.300 sec)
Fastest Lap speed: 231.094 km/h, 143.595 mph (A Senna, 1 min:45.884 sec on lap 43)
Lap Leaders: A Senna 1-19,43-45 (22); A Prost 20-42 (23).

13 Aug 1989 — HUNGARY: Hungaroring — (Round:10) (Race: 478)

77 laps x 3.968 km, 2.466 miles = 305.536 km, 189.851 miles

POS.	NO.	DRIVER	CAR	MODEL	ENGINE		LAPS	TIME/REASON FOR RETIREMENT	GRID:POS	ROW
1	27	N Mansell	Ferrari	640	Ferrari	V12	77	1h 49m 38.650s	12	6
2	1	A Senna	McLaren	MP4/5	Honda	V10	77	1h 50m 04.617s	2	1
3	5	T Boutsen	Williams	FW12C	Renault	V10	77	1h 50m 17.004s	4	2
4	2	A Prost	McLaren	MP4/5	Honda	V10	77	1h 50m 22.827s	5	3
5	10	E Cheever	Arrows	A11	Cosworth	V8	77	1h 50m 23.756s	16	8
6	11	N Piquet	Lotus	101	Judd	V8	77	1h 50m 50.689s	17	9
7	21	A Caffi	Dallara	189	Cosworth	V8	77	1h 51m 02.875s	3	2
8	20	E Pirro	Benetton	B189	Cosworth	V8	76		25	13
9	4	J Alesi	Tyrrell	018	Cosworth	V8	76		11	6
10	9	D Warwick	Arrows	A11	Cosworth	V8	76		9	5
11	8	S Modena	Brabham	BT58	Judd	V8	76		8	4
12	7	M Brundle	Brabham	BT58	Judd	V8	75		15	8
13	3	J Palmer	Tyrrell	018	Cosworth	V8	73		19	10
r	24	L Sala	Minardi	M189	Cosworth	V8	57	accident	23	12
r	28	G Berger	Ferrari	640	Ferrari	V12	56	gearbox	6	3
r	6	R Patrese	Williams	FW12C	Renault	V10	54	radiator	1	1
r	36	S Johansson	Onyx	ORE-1	Cosworth	V8	48	gear linkage	24	12
r	19	A Nannini	Benetton	B189	Cosworth	V8	46	gear linkage	7	4
r	37	B Gachot	Onyx	ORE-1	Cosworth	V8	38	gear linkage	21	11
r	12	S Nakajima	Lotus	101	Judd	V8	33	accident	20	10
r	15	M Gugelmin	March	CG891	Judd	V8	27	electrics	13	7
r	16	I Capelli	March	CG891	Judd	V8	26	wheel drive pegs	14	7
r	29	M Alboreto	Lola	LC89	Lamborghini	V12	26	engine	26	13
r	18	P Ghinzani	Osella	FA1M	Cosworth	V8	20	electrics	22	11
r	23	P Martini	Minardi	M189	Cosworth	V8	19	wheel bearings/ brake fire	10	5
r	22	A de Cesaris	Dallara	189	Cosworth	V8	0	clutch	18	9
nq	25	R Arnoux	Ligier	JS33	Cosworth	V8				
nq	26	O Grouillard	Ligier	JS33	Cosworth	V8				
nq	38	C Danner	Rial	ARC2	Cosworth	V8				
nq	39	V Weidler	Rial	ARC2	Cosworth	V8				
npq	17	N Larini	Osella	FA1M	Cosworth	V8				
npq	30	P Alliot	Lola	LC89	Lamborghini	V12				
npq	41	Y Dalmas	AGS	JH23B	Cosworth	V8				
npq	34	B Schneider	Zakspeed	891	Yamaha	V8				
npq	40	G Tarquini	AGS	JH24	Cosworth	V8				
npq	31	R Moreno	Coloni	FC189	Cosworth	V8				
npq	33	G Foitek	EuroBrun	ER189	Judd	V8				
npq	35	A Suzuki	Zakspeed	891	Yamaha	V8				
npq	32	P-H Raphanel	Coloni	FC189	Cosworth	V8				

Winning speed: 167.197 km/h, 103.891 mph
Pole Position speed: 179.174 km/h, 111.333 mph (R Patrese, 1 min:19.726 sec)
Fastest Lap speed: 172.862 km/h, 107.411 mph (N Mansell, 1 min:22.637 sec on lap 66)
Lap Leaders: R Patrese 1-52 (52); A Senna 53-57 (5); N Mansell 58-77 (20).

27 Aug 1989 — BELGIUM: Spa-Francorchamps (Round:11) (Race: 479)

44 laps x 6.940 km, 4.312 miles = 305.360 km, 189.742 miles

POS.	NO.	DRIVER	CAR	MODEL	ENGINE		LAPS	TIME/REASON FOR RETIREMENT	GRID:POS	ROW
1	1	A Senna	McLaren	MP4/5	Honda	V10	44	1h 40m 54.196s	1	1
2	2	A Prost	McLaren	MP4/5	Honda	V10	44	1h 40m 55.500s	2	1
3	27	N Mansell	Ferrari	640	Ferrari	V12	44	1h 40m 56.020s	6	3
4	5	T Boutsen	Williams	FW12C	Renault	V10	44	1h 41m 48.614s	4	2
5	19	A Nannini	Benetton	B189	Cosworth	V8	44	1h 42m 03.001s	7	4
6	9	D Warwick	Arrows	A11	Cosworth	V8	44	1h 42m 12.512s	10	5
7	15	M Gugelmin	March	CG891	Judd	V8	43		9	5
8	36	S Johansson	Onyx	ORE-1	Cosworth	V8	43		15	8
9	23	P Martini	Minardi	M189	Cosworth	V8	43		14	7
10	20	E Pirro	Benetton	B189	Cosworth	V8	43		13	7
11	22	A de Cesaris	Dallara	189	Cosworth	V8	43		18	9
12	16	I Capelli	March	CG891	Judd	V8	43		19	10
13	26	O Grouillard	Ligier	JS33	Cosworth	V8	43		26	13
14	3	J Palmer	Tyrrell	018	Cosworth	V8	42		21	11
15	24	L Sala	Minardi	M189	Cosworth	V8	41		25	13
16r	30	P Alliot	Lola	LC89	Lamborghini	V12	39	oil pressure	11	6
r	10	E Cheever	Arrows	A11	Cosworth	V8	38	wheel nut	24	12
r	37	B Gachot	Onyx	ORE-1	Cosworth	V8	21	wheel bearing/ accident	23	12
r	6	R Patrese	Williams	FW12C	Renault	V10	20	accident	5	3
r	29	M Alboreto	Lola	LC89	Lamborghini	V12	19	accident	22	11
r	21	A Caffi	Dallara	189	Cosworth	V8	13	spin	12	6
r	7	M Brundle	Brabham	BT58	Judd	V8	12	brakes	20	10
r	28	G Berger	Ferrari	640	Ferrari	V12	9	spin	3	2
r	8	S Modena	Brabham	BT58	Judd	V8	9	handling	8	4
r	25	R Arnoux	Ligier	JS33	Cosworth	V8	4	accident	17	9
r	4	J Herbert	Tyrrell	018	Cosworth	V8	3	spin	16	8
nq	12	S Nakajima	Lotus	101	Judd	V8				
nq	11	N Piquet	Lotus	101	Judd	V8				
nq	38	C Danner	Rial	ARC2	Cosworth	V8				
nq	39	P-H Raphanel	Rial	ARC2	Cosworth	V8				
npq	17	N Larini	Osella	FA1M	Cosworth	V8				
npq	18	P Ghinzani	Osella	FA1M	Cosworth	V8				
npq	31	R Moreno	Coloni	FC189	Cosworth	V8				
npq	40	G Tarquini	AGS	JH24	Cosworth	V8				
npq	34	B Schneider	Zakspeed	891	Yamaha	V8				
npq	35	A Suzuki	Zakspeed	891	Yamaha	V8				
npq	41	Y Dalmas	AGS	JH23B	Cosworth	V8				
npq	33	G Foitek	EuroBrun	ER188B	Judd	V8				
npq	32	E Bertaggia	Coloni	FC189	Cosworth	V8				

Winning speed: 181.576 km/h, 112.826 mph
Pole Position speed: 225.351 km/h, 140.027 mph (A Senna, 1 min:50.867 sec)
Fastest Lap speed: 189.890 km/h, 117.992 mph (A Prost, 2 min:11.571 sec on lap 44)
Lap Leaders: A Senna 1-44 (44).

10 Sep 1989 — ITALY: Monza (Round:12) (Race: 480)

53 laps x 5.800 km, 3.604 miles = 307.400 km, 191.010 miles

POS.	NO.	DRIVER	CAR	MODEL	ENGINE		LAPS	TIME/REASON FOR RETIREMENT	GRID:POS	ROW
1	2	A Prost	McLaren	MP4/5	Honda	V10	53	1h 19m 27.550s	4	2
2	28	G Berger	Ferrari	640	Ferrari	V12	53	1h 19m 34.876s	2	1
3	5	T Boutsen	Williams	FW12C	Renault	V10	53	1h 19m 42.525s	6	3
4	6	R Patrese	Williams	FW12C	Renault	V10	53	1h 20m 06.272s	5	3
5	4	J Alesi	Tyrrell	018	Cosworth	V8	52		10	5
6	7	M Brundle	Brabham	BT58	Judd	V8	52		12	6
7	23	P Martini	Minardi	M189	Cosworth	V8	52		15	8
8	24	L Sala	Minardi	M189	Cosworth	V8	51		26	13
9	25	R Arnoux	Ligier	JS33	Cosworth	V8	51		23	12
10	12	S Nakajima	Lotus	101	Judd	V8	51		19	10
11r	21	A Caffi	Dallara	189	Cosworth	V8	47	engine	20	10
r	22	A de Cesaris	Dallara	189	Cosworth	V8	45	engine	17	9
r	1	A Senna	McLaren	MP4/5	Honda	V10	44	engine/ spin	1	1
r	27	N Mansell	Ferrari	640	Ferrari	V12	41	gearbox	3	2
r	37	B Gachot	Onyx	ORE-1	Cosworth	V8	38	engine overheating/ spin	22	11
r	19	A Nannini	Benetton	B189	Cosworth	V8	33	brakes	8	4
r	16	I Capelli	March	CG891	Judd	V8	30	engine	18	9
r	26	O Grouillard	Ligier	JS33	Cosworth	V8	30	exhaust	21	11
r	11	N Piquet	Lotus	101	Judd	V8	23	spin	11	6
r	3	J Palmer	Tyrrell	018	Cosworth	V8	18	engine	14	7
r	9	D Warwick	Arrows	A11	Cosworth	V8	18	engine	16	8
r	17	N Larini	Osella	FA1M	Cosworth	V8	16	gearbox	24	12
r	29	M Alboreto	Lola	LC89	Lamborghini	V12	14	electrics	13	7
r	15	M Gugelmin	March	CG891	Judd	V8	14	throttle jammed	25	13
r	30	P Alliot	Lola	LC89	Lamborghini	V12	1	throttle jammed/ spin	7	4
r	20	E Pirro	Benetton	B189	Cosworth	V8	0	gearbox	9	5
nq	10	E Cheever	Arrows	A11	Cosworth	V8				
nq	38	C Danner	Rial	ARC2	Cosworth	V8				
nq	39	P-H Raphanel	Rial	ARC2	Cosworth	V8				
exc	8	S Modena	Brabham	BT58	Judd	V8		missed weight check		
npq	36	S Johansson	Onyx	ORE-1	Cosworth	V8				
npq	40	G Tarquini	AGS	JH24	Cosworth	V8				
npq	31	R Moreno	Coloni	FC189	Cosworth	V8				
npq	18	P Ghinzani	Osella	FA1M	Cosworth	V8				
npq	34	B Schneider	Zakspeed	891	Yamaha	V8				

POS.	NO.	DRIVER	CAR	MODEL	ENGINE		LAPS	TIME/REASON FOR RETIREMENT	GRID:POS	ROW
npq	35	A Suzuki	Zakspeed	891	Yamaha	V8				
npq	33	O Larrauri	EuroBrun	ER189	Judd	V8				
npq	41	Y Dalmas	AGS	JH24	Cosworth	V8				
npq	32	E Bertaggia	Coloni	FC189	Cosworth	V8				

Winning speed: 232.119 km/h, 144.232 mph
Pole Position speed: 249.403 km/h, 154.972 mph (A Senna, 1 min:23.720 sec)
Fastest Lap speed: 236.985 km/h, 147.255 mph (A Prost, 1 min:28.107 sec on lap 43)
Lap Leaders: A Senna 1-44 (44); A Prost 45-53 (9).

24 Sep 1989 — PORTUGAL: Estoril (Round:13) (Race: 481)

71 laps x 4.350 km, 2.703 miles = 308.850 km, 191.910 miles

POS.	NO.	DRIVER	CAR	MODEL	ENGINE		LAPS	TIME/REASON FOR RETIREMENT	GRID:POS	ROW
1	28	G Berger	Ferrari	640	Ferrari	V12	71	1h 36m 48.546s	2	1
2	2	A Prost	McLaren	MP4/5	Honda	V10	71	1h 37m 21.183s	4	2
3	36	S Johansson	Onyx	ORE-1	Cosworth	V8	71	1h 37m 43.871s	12	6
4	19	A Nannini	Benetton	B189	Cosworth	V8	71	1h 38m 10.915s	13	7
5	23	P Martini	Minardi	M189	Cosworth	V8	70		5	3
6	3	J Palmer	Tyrrell	018	Cosworth	V8	70		18	9
7	12	S Nakajima	Lotus	101	Judd	V8	70		25	13
8	7	M Brundle	Brabham	BT58	Judd	V8	70		10	5
9	30	P Alliot	Lola	LC89	Lamborghini	V12	70		17	9
10	15	M Gugelmin	March	CG891	Judd	V8	69		14	7
11	29	M Alboreto	Lola	LC89	Lamborghini	V12	69		21	11
12	24	L Sala	Minardi	M189	Cosworth	V8	69		9	5
13	25	R Arnoux	Ligier	JS33	Cosworth	V8	69		23	12
14	8	S Modena	Brabham	BT58	Judd	V8	69		11	6
r	6	R Patrese	Williams	FW13	Renault	V10	60	radiator	6	3
r	5	T Boutsen	Williams	FW13	Renault	V10	60	radiator	8	4
r	1	A Senna	McLaren	MP4/5	Honda	V10	48	accident	1	1
r/dq	27	N Mansell	Ferrari	640	Ferrari	V12	48	accident (disqualified for push)	3	2
r	9	D Warwick	Arrows	A11	Cosworth	V8	37	accident	22	11
r	11	N Piquet	Lotus	101	Judd	V8	33	accident	20	10
r	21	A Caffi	Dallara	189	Cosworth	V8	33	accident	7	4
r	20	E Pirro	Benetton	B189	Cosworth	V8	29	suspension	16	8
r	16	I Capelli	March	CG891	Judd	V8	25	engine	24	12
r	10	E Cheever	Arrows	A11	Cosworth	V8	24	engine/ spin	26	13
r	22	A de Cesaris	Dallara	189	Cosworth	V8	17	electronics	19	10
r	31	R Moreno	Coloni	FC189	Cosworth	V8	11	electrics	15	8
nq	4	J Herbert	Tyrrell	018	Cosworth	V8				
nq	26	O Grouillard	Ligier	JS33	Cosworth	V8				
nq	39	P-H Raphanel	Rial	ARC2	Cosworth	V8				
nq	38	C Danner	Rial	ARC2	Cosworth	V8				
npq	37	J J Lehto	Onyx	ORE-1	Cosworth	V8				
npq	18	P Ghinzani	Osella	FA1M	Cosworth	V8				
npq	33	O Larrauri	EuroBrun	ER189	Judd	V8				
npq	40	G Tarquini	AGS	JH24	Cosworth	V8				
npq	35	A Suzuki	Zakspeed	891	Yamaha	V8				
npq	34	B Schneider	Zakspeed	891	Yamaha	V8				
npq	32	E Bertaggia	Coloni	FC189	Cosworth	V8				
exc	41	Y Dalmas	AGS	JH24	Cosworth	V8		tyre infringement		
exc	17	N Larini	Osella	FA1M	Cosworth	V8		missed weight check		

Winning speed: 191.418 km/h, 118.942 mph
Pole Position speed: 207.505 km/h, 128.938 mph (A Senna, 1 min:15.468 sec)
Fastest Lap speed: 198.263 km/h, 123.195 mph (G Berger, 1 min:18.986 sec on lap 49)
Lap Leaders: G Berger 1-23,41-71 (54); N Mansell 24-39 (16); P Martini 40 (1).

1 Oct 1989 — SPAIN: Jerez de la Frontera (Round:14) (Race: 482)

73 laps x 4.218 km, 2.621 miles = 307.914 km, 191.329 miles

POS.	NO.	DRIVER	CAR	MODEL	ENGINE		LAPS	TIME/REASON FOR RETIREMENT	GRID:POS	ROW
1	1	A Senna	McLaren	MP4/5	Honda	V10	73	1h 47m 48.264s	1	1
2	28	G Berger	Ferrari	640	Ferrari	V12	73	1h 48m 15.315s	2	1
3	2	A Prost	McLaren	MP4/5	Honda	V10	73	1h 48m 42.052s	3	2
4	4	J Alesi	Tyrrell	018	Cosworth	V8	72		9	5
5	6	R Patrese	Williams	FW12C	Renault	V10	72		6	3
6	30	P Alliot	Lola	LC89	Lamborghini	V12	72		5	3
7	22	A de Cesaris	Dallara	189	Cosworth	V8	72		15	8
8	11	N Piquet	Lotus	101	Judd	V8	71		7	4
9	9	D Warwick	Arrows	A11	Cosworth	V8	71		16	8
10	3	J Palmer	Tyrrell	018	Cosworth	V8	71		13	7
r	10	E Cheever	Arrows	A11	Cosworth	V8	61	engine	22	11
r	20	E Pirro	Benetton	B189	Cosworth	V8	59	driver discomfort (cramp)/ spin	10	5
r	21	A Caffi	Dallara	189	Cosworth	V8	55	engine	23	12
r	7	M Brundle	Brabham	BT58	Judd	V8	51	rear suspension/ spin	8	4
r	15	M Gugelmin	March	CG891	Judd	V8	47	accident	26	13
r	24	L Sala	Minardi	M189	Cosworth	V8	47	accident	20	10
r	5	T Boutsen	Williams	FW13	Renault	V10	40	fuel pump	21	11
r	26	O Grouillard	Ligier	JS33	Cosworth	V8	34	engine	24	12
r	23	P Martini	Minardi	M189	Cosworth	V8	27	spin	4	2
r	16	I Capelli	March	CG891	Judd	V8	23	differential	19	10
r	37	J J Lehto	Onyx	ORE-1	Cosworth	V8	20	gearbox	17	9
r	18	P Ghinzani	Osella	FA1M	Cosworth	V8	17	gearbox	25	13
r	19	A Nannini	Benetton	B189	Cosworth	V8	14	spin	14	7
r	8	S Modena	Brabham	BT58	Judd	V8	11	electrics	12	6

POS.	NO.	DRIVER	CAR	MODEL	ENGINE		LAPS	TIME/REASON FOR RETIREMENT	GRID:POS	ROW
r	17	N Larini	Osella	FA1M	Cosworth	V8	6	suspension/ accident	11	6
r	12	S Nakajima	Lotus	101	Judd	V8	0	accident	18	9
nq	25	R Arnoux	Ligier	JS33	Cosworth	V8				
nq	39	P-H Raphanel	Rial	ARC2	Cosworth	V8				
nq	38	G Foitek	Rial	ARC2	Cosworth	V8				
npq	40	G Tarquini	AGS	JH24	Cosworth	V8				
npq	36	S Johansson	Onyx	ORE-1	Cosworth	V8				
npq	31	R Moreno	Coloni	FC189	Cosworth	V8				
npq	29	M Alboreto	Lola	LC89	Lamborghini	V12				
npq	34	B Schneider	Zakspeed	891	Yamaha	V8				
npq	41	Y Dalmas	AGS	JH24	Cosworth	V8				
npq	35	A Suzuki	Zakspeed	891	Yamaha	V8				
npq	33	O Larrauri	EuroBrun	ER189	Judd	V8				
npq	32	E Bertaggia	Coloni	FC189	Cosworth	V8				

Winning speed: 171.374 km/h, 106.487 mph
Pole Position speed: 189.122 km/h, 117.515 mph (A Senna, 1 min:20.291 sec)
Fastest Lap speed: 177.022 km/h, 109.997 mph (A Senna, 1 min:25.779 sec on lap 55)
Lap Leaders: A Senna 1-73 (73).

22 Oct 1989 JAPAN: Suzuka (Round:15) (Race: 483)

53 laps x 5.859 km, 3.641 miles = 310.527 km, 192.953 miles

POS.	NO.	DRIVER	CAR	MODEL	ENGINE		LAPS	TIME/REASON FOR RETIREMENT	GRID:POS	ROW
dq	1	A Senna	McLaren	MP4/5	Honda	V10	53	push start after accident	1	1
1	19	A Nannini	Benetton	B189	Cosworth	V8	53	1h 35m 06.277s	6	3
2	6	R Patrese	Williams	FW13	Renault	V10	53	1h 35m 18.181s	5	3
3	5	T Boutsen	Williams	FW13	Renault	V10	53	1h 35m 19.723s	7	4
4	11	N Piquet	Lotus	101	Judd	V8	53	1h 36m 50.502s	11	6
5	7	M Brundle	Brabham	BT58	Judd	V8	52		13	7
6	9	D Warwick	Arrows	A11	Cosworth	V8	52		25	13
7	15	M Gugelmin	March	CG891	Judd	V8	52		20	10
8	10	E Cheever	Arrows	A11	Cosworth	V8	52		24	12
9	21	A Caffi	Dallara	189	Cosworth	V8	52		15	8
10	22	A de Cesaris	Dallara	189	Cosworth	V8	51		16	8
r	2	A Prost	McLaren	MP4/5	Honda	V10	46	accident	2	1
r	8	S Modena	Brabham	BT58	Judd	V8	46	alternator	9	5
r	27	N Mansell	Ferrari	640	Ferrari	V12	43	engine	4	2
r	12	S Nakajima	Lotus	101	Judd	V8	41	engine	12	6
r	4	J Alesi	Tyrrell	018	Cosworth	V8	37	gearbox	18	9
r	30	P Alliot	Lola	LC89	Lamborghini	V12	36	engine	8	4
r	28	G Berger	Ferrari	640	Ferrari	V12	34	transmission	3	2
r	20	E Pirro	Benetton	B189	Cosworth	V8	33	accident	22	11
r	26	O Grouillard	Ligier	JS33	Cosworth	V8	31	engine	23	12
r	16	I Capelli	March	CG891	Judd	V8	27	front suspension	17	9
r	17	N Larini	Osella	FA1M	Cosworth	V8	21	brakes	10	5
r	3	J Palmer	Tyrrell	018	Cosworth	V8	20	fuel leak	26	13
r	34	B Schneider	Zakspeed	891	Yamaha	V8	1	drive shaft	21	11
r	23	P Barilla	Minardi	M189	Cosworth	V8	0	clutch	19	10
r	24	L Sala	Minardi	M189	Cosworth	V8	0	accident	14	7
nq	25	R Arnoux	Ligier	JS33	Cosworth	V8				
nq	29	M Alboreto	Lola	LC89	Lamborghini	V12				
nq	38	P-H Raphanel	Rial	ARC2	Cosworth	V8				
nq	39	B Gachot	Rial	ARC2	Cosworth	V8				
npq	18	P Ghinzani	Osella	FA1M	Cosworth	V8				
npq	31	R Moreno	Coloni	FC189	Cosworth	V8				
npq	36	S Johansson	Onyx	ORE-1	Cosworth	V8				
npq	35	A Suzuki	Zakspeed	891	Yamaha	V8				
npq	33	O Larrauri	EuroBrun	ER189	Judd	V8				
npq	37	J J Lehto	Onyx	ORE-1	Cosworth	V8				
npq	40	G Tarquini	AGS	JH24	Cosworth	V8				
npq	41	Y Dalmas	AGS	JH24	Cosworth	V8				
npq	32	E Bertaggia	Coloni	FC189	Cosworth	V8				

Winning speed: 195.907 km/h, 121.731 mph
Pole Position speed: 215.139 km/h, 133.681 mph (A Senna, 1 min:38.041 sec)
Fastest Lap speed: 203.779 km/h, 126.623 mph (A Prost, 1 min:43.506 sec on lap 43)
Lap Leaders: A Prost 1-20,24-46 (43); A Senna 21-23,47-48,51-53 (8); A Nannini 49-50 (2).

A Senna finished 1st in 1h 35m 03.980s (195.985 km/h,121.780 mph) and recorded the fastest lap in 1m 43.025s (204.731 km/h,127.214 mph).

5 Nov 1989 — AUSTRALIA: Adelaide (Round:16) (Race: 484)

70 laps x 3.780 km, 2.349 miles = 264.600 km, 164.415 miles

POS.	NO.	DRIVER	CAR	MODEL	ENGINE		LAPS	TIME/REASON FOR RETIREMENT	GRID:POS	ROW
1	5	T Boutsen	Williams	FW13	Renault	V10	70	2h 00m 17.421s	5	3
2	19	A Nannini	Benetton	B189	Cosworth	V8	70	2h 00m 46.079s	4	2
3	6	R Patrese	Williams	FW13	Renault	V10	70	2h 00m 55.104s	6	3
4	12	S Nakajima	Lotus	101	Judd	V8	70	2h 00m 59.752s	23	12
5	20	E Pirro	Benetton	B189	Cosworth	V8	68		13	7
6	23	P Martini	Minardi	M189	Cosworth	V8	67		3	2
7	15	M Gugelmin	March	CG891	Judd	V8	66		25	13
8	8	S Modena	Brabham	BT58	Judd	V8	64		8	4
r	10	E Cheever	Arrows	A11	Cosworth	V8	42	misfire/ spin	22	11
r	37	J J Lehto	Onyx	ORE-1	Cosworth	V8	27	electrics/ spin	17	9
r	26	O Grouillard	Ligier	JS33	Cosworth	V8	22	accident	24	12
r	11	N Piquet	Lotus	101	Judd	V8	19	accident	18	9
r	18	P Ghinzani	Osella	FA1M	Cosworth	V8	18	accident damage	21	11
r	27	N Mansell	Ferrari	640	Ferrari	V12	17	accident	7	4
r	1	A Senna	McLaren	MP4/5	Honda	V10	13	accident	1	1
r	21	A Caffi	Dallara	189	Cosworth	V8	13	spin	10	5
r	16	I Capelli	March	CG891	Judd	V8	13	radiator	16	8
r	22	A de Cesaris	Dallara	189	Cosworth	V8	12	accident	9	5
r	7	M Brundle	Brabham	BT58	Judd	V8	12	accident	12	6
r	9	D Warwick	Arrows	A11	Cosworth	V8	7	engine/ accident	20	10
r	28	G Berger	Ferrari	640	Ferrari	V12	6	accident	14	7
r	30	P Alliot	Lola	LC89	Lamborghini	V12	6	accident	19	10
r	4	J Alesi	Tyrrell	018	Cosworth	V8	5	electrics	15	8
r	25	R Arnoux	Ligier	JS33	Cosworth	V8	4	spin	26	13
r	17	N Larini	Osella	FA1M	Cosworth	V8	0	engine cut out	11	6
r	2	A Prost	McLaren	MP4/5	Honda	V10	0	withdrew *	2	1
nq	3	J Palmer	Tyrrell	018	Cosworth	V8				
nq	24	L Sala	Minardi	M189	Cosworth	V8				
nq	39	B Gachot	Rial	ARC2	Cosworth	V8				
nq	38	P-H Raphanel	Rial	ARC2	Cosworth	V8				
npq	36	S Johansson	Onyx	ORE-1	Cosworth	V8				
npq	29	M Alboreto	Lola	LC89	Lamborghini	V12				
npq	34	B Schneider	Zakspeed	891	Yamaha	V8				
npq	31	R Moreno	Coloni	FC189	Cosworth	V8				
npq	33	O Larrauri	EuroBrun	ER189	Judd	V8				
npq	35	A Suzuki	Zakspeed	891	Yamaha	V8				
npq	41	Y Dalmas	AGS	JH24	Cosworth	V8				
npq	40	G Tarquini	AGS	JH24	Cosworth	V8				
npq	32	E Bertaggia	Coloni	FC189	Cosworth	V8				

Winning speed: 131.981 km/h, 82.009 mph
Pole Position speed: 177.500 km/h, 110.293 mph (A Senna, 1 min:16.665 sec)
Fastest Lap speed: 138.180 km/h, 85.861 mph (S Nakajima, 1 min:38.480 sec on lap 64)
Lap Leaders: A Senna 1-13 (13); T Boutsen 14-70 (57).

Scheduled for 81 laps, but interrupted after 1st lap, because of rain.
*Restarted for original distance, but stopped at 2 hours. * retired after first start.*

Lap Leaders 1989

POS	DRIVER	CAR-ENGINE	GPS	LAPS	KM	MILES
1	A Senna	McLaren-Honda	13	487	2,297.1	1,427.4
2	A Prost	McLaren-Honda	8	258	1,218.8	756.8
3	R Patrese	Williams-Renault	3	100	428.0	265.9
4	N Mansell	Ferrari	3	73	335.1	208.2
5	T Boutsen	Williams-Renault	2	60	228.6	142.1
6	G Berger	Ferrari	1	54	234.9	146.0
7	D Warwick	Arrows-Cosworth	1	4	17.6	10.9
8	A Nannini	Benetton-Cosworth	1	2	11.7	7.3
9	P Martini	Minardi-Cosworth	1	1	4.3	2.7
			16	**1,039**	**4,775.3**	**2,967.2**

Driver Points 1989

		BR	RSM	MC	MEX	USA	CDN	F	GB	D	H	B	I	P	E	J	AUS	TOTAL	
1	A Prost	6	6	6	(2)	9	-	9	9	6	(3)	6	9	6	4	-	-	76	(5)
2	A Senna	-	9	9	9	-	-	-	-	9	6	9	-	-	9	-	-	60	
3	R Patrese	-	-	-	6	6	6	4	-	3	-	-	3	-	2	6	4	40	
4	N Mansell	9	-	-	-	-	-	6	6	4	9	4	-	-	-	-	-	38	
5	T Boutsen	-	3	-	-	1	9	-	-	-	4	3	4	-	-	4	9	37	
6	A Nannini	1	4	-	3	-	-	-	4	-	-	2	-	3	-	9	6	32	
7	G Berger	-	-	-	-	-	-	-	-	-	-	-	6	9	6	-	-	21	
8	N Piquet	-	-	-	-	-	3	-	3	2	1	-	-	-	-	3	-	12	
9	J Alesi	-	-	-	-	-	-	3	-	-	-	-	2	-	3	-	-	8	
10	D Warwick	2	2	-	-	-	-	-	-	1	-	1	-	-	-	1	-	7	
11	M Alboreto	-	-	2	4	-	-	-	-	-	-	-	-	-	-	-	-	6	
	E Cheever	-	-	-	-	4	-	-	-	-	2	-	-	-	-	-	-	6	
	S Johansson	-	-	-	-	-	-	2	-	-	-	-	-	4	-	-	-	6	
14	J Herbert	3	-	-	-	2	-	-	-	-	-	-	-	-	-	-	-	5	
	P Martini	-	-	-	-	-	-	-	2	-	-	-	-	2	-	-	1	5	
16	M Gugelmin	4	-	-	-	-	-	-	-	-	-	-	-	-	-	-	-	4	
	S Modena	-	-	4	-	-	-	-	-	-	-	-	-	-	-	-	-	4	
	A de Cesaris	-	-	-	-	-	4	-	-	-	-	-	-	-	-	-	-	4	
	A Caffi	-	-	3	-	-	1	-	-	-	-	-	-	-	-	-	-	4	
	M Brundle	-	-	1	-	-	-	-	-	-	-	-	1	-	-	2	-	4	
21	C Danner	-	-	-	-	3	-	-	-	-	-	-	-	-	-	-	-	3	
	S Nakajima	-	-	-	-	-	-	-	-	-	-	-	-	-	-	-	3	3	
23	R Arnoux	-	-	-	-	-	2	-	-	-	-	-	-	-	-	-	-	2	
	E Pirro	-	-	-	-	-	-	-	-	-	-	-	-	-	-	-	2	2	
	J Palmer	-	1	-	-	-	-	-	-	-	-	-	-	1	-	-	-	2	
26	G Tarquini	-	-	-	1	-	-	-	-	-	-	-	-	-	-	-	-	1	
	O Grouillard	-	-	-	-	-	-	1	-	-	-	-	-	-	-	-	-	1	
	L Sala	-	-	-	-	-	-	-	1	-	-	-	-	-	-	-	-	1	
	P Alliot	-	-	-	-	-	-	-	-	-	-	-	-	-	1	-	-	1	

9, 6, 4, 3, 2 and 1 point awarded to the first six finishers. Best 11 scores.

Constructor Points 1989

		BR	RSM	MC	MEX	USA	CDN	F	GB	D	H	B	I	P	E	J	AUS	TOTAL
1	McLaren-Honda	6	15	15	11	9	-	9	9	15	9	15	9	6	13	-	-	141
2	Williams-Renault	-	3	-	6	7	15	4	-	3	4	3	7	-	2	10	13	77
3	Ferrari	9	-	-	-	-	-	6	6	4	9	4	6	9	6	-	-	59
4	Benetton-Cosworth	4	4	-	3	2	-	-	4	-	-	2	-	3	-	9	8	39
5	Tyrrell-Cosworth	-	1	2	4	-	-	3	-	-	-	-	2	1	3	-	-	16
6	Lotus-Judd	-	-	-	-	-	3	-	3	2	1	-	-	-	-	3	3	15
7	Arrows-Cosworth	2	2	-	-	4	-	-	-	1	2	1	-	-	-	1	-	13
8	Dallara-Cosworth	-	-	3	-	-	5	-	-	-	-	-	-	-	-	-	-	8
	Brabham-Judd	-	-	5	-	-	-	-	-	-	-	-	1	-	-	2	-	8
10	Onyx-Cosworth	-	-	-	-	-	-	2	-	-	-	-	-	4	-	-	-	6
	Minardi-Cosworth	-	-	-	-	-	-	-	3	-	-	-	-	2	-	-	1	6
12	March-Judd	4	-	-	-	-	-	-	-	-	-	-	-	-	-	-	-	4
13	Rial-Cosworth	-	-	-	-	3	-	-	-	-	-	-	-	-	-	-	-	3
	Ligier-Cosworth	-	-	-	-	-	2	1	-	-	-	-	-	-	-	-	-	3
15	AGS-Cosworth	-	-	-	1	-	-	-	-	-	-	-	-	-	-	-	-	1
	Lola-Lamborghini	-	-	-	-	-	-	-	-	-	-	-	-	-	1	-	-	1

9, 6, 4, 3, 2 and 1 point awarded to the first six finishers.

Senna and FISA were still in dispute over the crash at Suzuka and this would rumble on for the early part of the year. The AGS driver Philippe Streiff was paralysed after a pre-season testing crash at Rio. Subaru entered with its Flat 12 engine while Life introduced their unusual W12 engine (neither would qualify).

FERRARI
Scuderia Ferrari SpA: Prost, Mansell

TYRRELL
Tyrrell Racing Organisation: Nakajima, Alesi

WILLIAMS
Canon Williams Team: Boutsen, Patrese

BRABHAM
Motor Racing Developments: Foitek, D Brabham, Modena

ARROWS
Footwork Arrows Racing: Alboreto, Caffi, Schneider

LOTUS
Camel Team Lotus: Warwick, Donnelly, Herbert

OSELLA
Fondmetal Osella: Grouillard

LEYTON HOUSE
Leyton House Racing: Gugelmin, Capelli

AGS
Automobiles Gonfaronaises Sportives: Tarquini, Dalmas

BENETTON
Benetton Formula: Nannini, Moreno, Piquet

DALLARA
Scuderia Italia SpA: Pirro, Morbidelli, de Cesaris

MINARDI
SCM Minardi Team: Martini, Barilla, Morbidelli

LIGIER
Ligier Gitanes: Larini, Alliot

McLAREN
Honda Marlboro McLaren: Senna, Berger

LOLA
Espo Larrousse F1: Bernard, Suzuki

COLONI
Coloni Racing: (Gachot)

EUROBRUN
EuroBrun Racing: Moreno, (Langes)

ONYX
Monteverdi Onyx Formula One: (Johansson), Foitek, Lehto

LIFE
Life Racing Engines: (G Brabham, Giacomelli)

11 Mar 1990 — USA: Phoenix — (Round: 1) (Race: 485)
72 laps x 3.798 km, 2.360 miles = 273.460 km, 169.920 miles

POS.	NO.	DRIVER	CAR	MODEL	ENGINE		LAPS	TIME/REASON FOR RETIREMENT	GRID:POS	ROW
1	27	A Senna	McLaren	MP4/5B	Honda	V10	72	1h 52m 32.829s	5	3
2	4	J Alesi	Tyrrell	018	Cosworth	V8	72	1h 52m 41.514s	4	2
3	5	T Boutsen	Williams	FW13B	Renault	V10	72	1h 53m 26.909s	9	5
4	20	N Piquet	Benetton	B189B	Cosworth	V8	72	1h 53m 41.187s	6	3
5	8	S Modena	Brabham	BT58	Judd	V8	72	1h 53m 42.332s	10	5
6	3	S Nakajima	Tyrrell	018	Cosworth	V8	71		11	6
7	23	P Martini	Minardi	M189	Cosworth	V8	71		2	1
8	29	É Bernard	Lola	LC89	Lamborghini	V12	71		15	8
9	6	R Patrese	Williams	FW13B	Renault	V10	71		12	6
10	9	M Alboreto	Arrows	A11B	Cosworth	V8	70		21	11
11	19	A Nannini	Benetton	B189B	Cosworth	V8	70		22	11
12	10	B Schneider	Arrows	A11	Cosworth	V8	70		20	10
13	33	R Moreno	EuroBrun	ER189	Judd	V8	67		16	8
14	15	M Gugelmin	Leyton House	CG901	Judd	V8	66		25	13
r	24	P Barilla	Minardi	M189	Cosworth	V8	54	driver discomfort (arm cramp)	14	7
r	30	A Suzuki	Lola	LC89	Lamborghini	V12	53	brakes	18	9
r	2	N Mansell	Ferrari	641	Ferrari	V12	49	clutch/ spin/ fire	17	9
r	28	G Berger	McLaren	MP4/5B	Honda	V10	44	clutch	1	1
r	7	G Foitek	Brabham	BT58	Judd	V8	39	accident	23	12
r	14	O Grouillard	Osella	FA1M	Cosworth	V8	39	accident/ front suspension	8	4
r	22	A de Cesaris	Dallara	190	Cosworth	V8	25	brakes/ engine	3	2
r	1	A Prost	Ferrari	641	Ferrari	V12	21	oil leak	7	4
r	16	I Capelli	Leyton House	CG901	Judd	V8	20	electrics/ suspension	26	13
r	11	D Warwick	Lotus	102	Lamborghini	V12	6	rear suspension	24	12
r	25	N Larini	Ligier	JS33B	Cosworth	V8	4	throttle jammed	13	7
ns	12	M Donnelly	Lotus	102	Lamborghini	V12		ignition on dummy grid	19	10
nq	35	S Johansson	Onyx	ORE-1	Cosworth	V8				
nq	21	G Morbidelli	Dallara	190	Cosworth	V8				
nq	36	J J Lehto	Onyx	ORE-1	Cosworth	V8				
exc	26	P Alliot	Ligier	JS33B	Cosworth	V8		push start during practice		
npq	17	G Tarquini	AGS	JH24	Cosworth	V8				
npq	18	Y Dalmas	AGS	JH24	Cosworth	V8				
npq	34	C Langes	EuroBrun	ER189	Judd	V8				
npq	39	G Brabham	Life	L190	Life	W12				
npq	31	B Gachot	Coloni	FC189B	Subaru	F12				

Winning speed: 145.784 km/h, 90.586 mph
Pole Position speed: 154.211 km/h, 95.822 mph (G Berger, 1 min:28.664 sec)
Fastest Lap speed: 150.170 km/h, 93.311 mph (G Berger, 1 min:31.050 sec on lap 34)
Lap Leaders: J Alesi 1-34 (34); A Senna 35-72 (38).

25 Mar 1990 — BRAZIL: Interlagos — (Round: 2) (Race: 486)
71 laps x 4.325 km, 2.687 miles = 307.075 km, 190.808 miles

POS.	NO.	DRIVER	CAR	MODEL	ENGINE		LAPS	TIME/REASON FOR RETIREMENT	GRID:POS	ROW
1	1	A Prost	Ferrari	641	Ferrari	V12	71	1h 37m 21.258s	6	3
2	28	G Berger	McLaren	MP4/5B	Honda	V10	71	1h 37m 34.822s	2	1
3	27	A Senna	McLaren	MP4/5B	Honda	V10	71	1h 37m 58.980s	1	1
4	2	N Mansell	Ferrari	641	Ferrari	V12	71	1h 38m 08.524s	5	3
5	5	T Boutsen	Williams	FW13B	Renault	V10	70		3	2
6	20	N Piquet	Benetton	B189B	Cosworth	V8	70		13	7
7	4	J Alesi	Tyrrell	018	Cosworth	V8	70		7	4
8	3	S Nakajima	Tyrrell	018	Cosworth	V8	70		19	10
9	23	P Martini	Minardi	M189	Cosworth	V8	69		8	4

POS.	NO.	DRIVER	CAR	MODEL	ENGINE		LAPS	TIME/REASON FOR RETIREMENT	GRID:POS	ROW
10r	19	A Nannini	Benetton	B189B	Cosworth	V8	68	puncture	15	8
11	25	N Larini	Ligier	JS33B	Cosworth	V8	68		20	10
12	26	P Alliot	Ligier	JS33B	Cosworth	V8	68		10	5
13r	6	R Patrese	Williams	FW13B	Renault	V10	65	oil radiator leak	4	2
14	21	G Morbidelli	Dallara	190	Cosworth	V8	64		16	8
r	10	A Caffi	Arrows	A11B	Cosworth	V8	49	driver exhausted	25	13
r	12	M Donnelly	Lotus	102	Lamborghini	V12	43	spin	14	7
r	8	S Modena	Brabham	BT58	Judd	V8	39	spin	12	6
r	24	P Barilla	Minardi	M189	Cosworth	V8	38	valve	17	9
r	18	Y Dalmas	AGS	JH24	Cosworth	V8	28	front suspension	26	13
r	11	D Warwick	Lotus	102	Lamborghini	V12	25	electrics	24	12
r	30	A Suzuki	Lola	LC89	Lamborghini	V12	24	suspension	18	9
r	9	M Alboreto	Arrows	A11B	Cosworth	V8	24	suspension	23	12
r	7	G Foitek	Brabham	BT58	Judd	V8	14	gear selection	22	11
r	29	É Bernard	Lola	LC89	Lamborghini	V12	13	gearbox	11	6
r	14	O Grouillard	Osella	FA1M	Cosworth	V8	8	accident/ steering/ suspension	21	11
r	22	A de Cesaris	Dallara	190	Cosworth	V8	0	throttle jammed/ accident	9	5
nq	35	S Johansson	Onyx	ORE-1	Cosworth	V8				
nq	36	J J Lehto	Onyx	ORE-1	Cosworth	V8				
nq	16	I Capelli	Leyton House	CG901	Judd	V8				
nq	15	M Gugelmin	Leyton House	CG901	Judd	V8				
npq	17	G Tarquini	AGS	JH24	Cosworth	V8				
npq	33	R Moreno	EuroBrun	ER189	Judd	V8				
npq	31	B Gachot	Coloni	FC189B	Subaru	F12				
npq	34	C Langes	EuroBrun	ER189	Judd	V8				
npq	39	G Brabham	Life	L190	Life	W12				

Winning speed: 189.252 km/h, 117.596 mph
Pole Position speed: 201.483 km/h, 125.196 mph (A Senna, 1 min:17.277 sec)
Fastest Lap speed: 194.871 km/h, 121.087 mph (G Berger, 1 min:19.899 sec on lap 55)
Lap Leaders: A Senna 1-32,35-40 (38); G Berger 33-34 (2); A Prost 41-71 (31).

I Capelli also practiced in a March CG891-Judd V8 (16).

13 May 1990 — SAN MARINO: Imola — (Round: 3) (Race: 487)

61 laps x 5.040 km, 3.132 miles = 307.440 km, 191.034 miles

POS.	NO.	DRIVER	CAR	MODEL	ENGINE		LAPS	TIME/REASON FOR RETIREMENT	GRID:POS	ROW
1	6	R Patrese	Williams	FW13B	Renault	V10	61	1h 30m 55.478s	3	2
2	28	G Berger	McLaren	MP4/5B	Honda	V10	61	1h 31m 00.595s	2	1
3	19	A Nannini	Benetton	B190	Cosworth	V8	61	1h 31m 01.718s	9	5
4	1	A Prost	Ferrari	641	Ferrari	V12	61	1h 31m 02.321s	6	3
5	20	N Piquet	Benetton	B190	Cosworth	V8	61	1h 31m 48.590s	8	4
6	4	J Alesi	Tyrrell	019	Cosworth	V8	60		7	4
7	11	D Warwick	Lotus	102	Lamborghini	V12	60		10	5
8	12	M Donnelly	Lotus	102	Lamborghini	V12	60		11	6
9	26	P Alliot	Ligier	JS33B	Cosworth	V8	60		16	8
10	25	N Larini	Ligier	JS33B	Cosworth	V8	59		20	10
11	24	P Barilla	Minardi	M190	Cosworth	V8	59		26	13
12	36	J J Lehto	Onyx	ORE-2	Cosworth	V8	59		25	13
13r	29	É Bernard	Lola	90	Lamborghini	V12	56	gearbox	13	7
r	14	O Grouillard	Osella	FA1M-E	Cosworth	V8	52	wheel bearing	22	11
r	2	N Mansell	Ferrari	641	Ferrari	V12	38	engine	5	3
r	35	G Foitek	Onyx	ORE-2	Cosworth	V8	35	engine	23	12
r	8	S Modena	Brabham	BT59	Judd	V8	31	brakes/ spin	14	7
r	22	A de Cesaris	Dallara	190	Cosworth	V8	29	wheel bearing	17	9
r	15	M Gugelmin	Leyton House	CG901	Judd	V8	24	electrics	12	6
r	5	T Boutsen	Williams	FW13B	Renault	V10	17	engine	4	2
r	30	A Suzuki	Lola	90	Lamborghini	V12	17	clutch	15	8
r	27	A Senna	McLaren	MP4/5B	Honda	V10	3	wheel rim/ spin	1	1
r	21	E Pirro	Dallara	190	Cosworth	V8	2	spin	21	11
r	16	I Capelli	Leyton House	CG901	Judd	V8	0	accident	18	9
r	3	S Nakajima	Tyrrell	019	Cosworth	V8	0	accident	19	10
r	33	R Moreno	EuroBrun	ER189	Judd	V8	0	throttle slides	24	12
ns	23	P Martini	Minardi	M190	Cosworth	V8		accident/ injury		
nq	10	A Caffi	Arrows	A11B	Cosworth	V8				
nq	9	M Alboreto	Arrows	A11B	Cosworth	V8				
nq	7	D Brabham	Brabham	BT59	Judd	V8				
npq	31	B Gachot	Coloni	FC189B	Subaru	F12				
npq	34	C Langes	EuroBrun	ER189B	Judd	V8				
npq	39	B Giacomelli	Life	L190	Life	W12				
npq	17	G Tarquini	AGS	JH25	Cosworth	V8				

Winning speed: 202.876 km/h, 126.061 mph
Pole Position speed: 218.025 km/h, 135.474 mph (A Senna, 1 min:23.220 sec)
Fastest Lap speed: 208.178 km/h, 129.356 mph (A Nannini, 1 min:27.156 sec on lap 60)
Lap Leaders: A Senna 1-3 (3); T Boutsen 4-17 (14); G Berger 18-50 (33); R Patrese 51-61 (11).

27 May 1990 — MONACO: Monte Carlo — (Round: 4) (Race: 488)

78 laps x 3.328 km, 2.068 miles = 259.584 km, 161.298 miles

POS.	NO.	DRIVER	CAR	MODEL	ENGINE		LAPS	TIME/REASON FOR RETIREMENT	GRID:POS	ROW
1	27	A Senna	McLaren	MP4/5B	Honda	V10	78	1h 52m 46.982s	1	1
2	4	J Alesi	Tyrrell	019	Cosworth	V8	78	1h 52m 48.069s	3	2
3	28	G Berger	McLaren	MP4/5B	Honda	V10	78	1h 52m 49.055s	5	3
4	5	T Boutsen	Williams	FW13B	Renault	V10	77		6	3

POS.	NO.	DRIVER	CAR	MODEL	ENGINE		LAPS	TIME/REASON FOR RETIREMENT	GRID:POS	ROW
5	10	A Caffi	Arrows	A11B	Cosworth	V8	76		22	11
6	29	É Bernard	Lola	90	Lamborghini	V12	76		24	12
7r	35	G Foitek	Onyx	ORE-2	Cosworth	V8	72	accident	20	10
r	11	D Warwick	Lotus	102	Lamborghini	V12	66	brakes/ spin	13	7
r	2	N Mansell	Ferrari	641	Ferrari	V12	63	battery/ gearbox electronics	7	4
r	24	P Barilla	Minardi	M190	Cosworth	V8	52	gearbox	19	10
r	36	J J Lehto	Onyx	ORE-2	Cosworth	V8	52	gearbox	26	13
r	26	P Alliot	Ligier	JS33B	Cosworth	V8	47	gearbox	18	9
r	6	R Patrese	Williams	FW13B	Renault	V10	41	valve gear	4	2
r	22	A de Cesaris	Dallara	190	Cosworth	V8	38	throttle linkage	12	6
r	3	S Nakajima	Tyrrell	019	Cosworth	V8	36	spin	21	11
dq	20	N Piquet	Benetton	B190	Cosworth	V8	35	push start after spin	10	5
r	1	A Prost	Ferrari	641	Ferrari	V12	30	battery	2	1
r	19	A Nannini	Benetton	B190	Cosworth	V8	20	oil pressure/ engine	16	8
r	7	D Brabham	Brabham	BT59	Judd	V8	16	cv joint	25	13
r	16	I Capelli	Leyton House	CG901	Judd	V8	13	brakes	23	12
r	25	N Larini	Ligier	JS33B	Cosworth	V8	12	differential	17	9
r	30	A Suzuki	Lola	90	Lamborghini	V12	11	electrics	15	8
r	23	P Martini	Minardi	M190	Cosworth	V8	7	ignition	8	4
r	12	M Donnelly	Lotus	102	Lamborghini	V12	6	transmission	11	6
r	8	S Modena	Brabham	BT59	Judd	V8	3	differential	14	7
r	21	E Pirro	Dallara	190	Cosworth	V8	0	fuel vaporisation *	9	5
nq	9	M Alboreto	Arrows	A11B	Cosworth	V8				
nq	14	O Grouillard	Osella	FA1M-E	Cosworth	V8				
nq	15	M Gugelmin	Leyton House	CG901	Judd	V8				
nq	33	R Moreno	EuroBrun	ER189	Judd	V8				
npq	17	G Tarquini	AGS	JH25	Cosworth	V8				
npq	18	Y Dalmas	AGS	JH25	Cosworth	V8				
npq	34	C Langes	EuroBrun	ER189B	Judd	V8				
npq	31	B Gachot	Coloni	FC189B	Subaru	F12				
npq	39	B Giacomelli	Life	L190	Life	W12				

Winning speed: 138.097 km/h, 85.810 mph
Pole Position speed: 147.340 km/h, 91.553 mph (A Senna, 1 min:21.314 sec)
Fastest Lap speed: 141.838 km/h, 88.134 mph (A Senna, 1 min:24.468 sec on lap 59)
Lap Leaders: A Senna 1-78 (78).

*Interrupted after 1st lap accident. Restarted for original distance. * retired after first start.*

10 Jun 1990 — CANADA: Montréal — (Round: 5) (Race: 489)

70 laps x 4.390 km, 2.728 miles = 307.300 km, 190.947 miles

POS.	NO.	DRIVER	CAR	MODEL	ENGINE		LAPS	TIME/REASON FOR RETIREMENT	GRID:POS	ROW
1	27	A Senna	McLaren	MP4/5B	Honda	V10	70	1h 42m 56.400s	1	1
2	20	N Piquet	Benetton	B190	Cosworth	V8	70	1h 43m 06.897s	5	3
3	2	N Mansell	Ferrari	641	Ferrari	V12	70	1h 43m 09.785s	7	4
4	28	G Berger *	McLaren	MP4/5B	Honda	V10	70	1h 43m 11.254s	2	1
5	1	A Prost	Ferrari	641	Ferrari	V12	70	1h 43m 12.220s	3	2
6	11	D Warwick	Lotus	102	Lamborghini	V12	68		11	6
7	8	S Modena	Brabham	BT59	Judd	V8	68		10	5
8	10	A Caffi	Arrows	A11B	Cosworth	V8	68		26	13
9	29	É Bernard	Lola	90	Lamborghini	V12	67		23	12
10	16	I Capelli	Leyton House	CG901	Judd	V8	67		24	12
11	3	S Nakajima	Tyrrell	019	Cosworth	V8	67		13	7
12	30	A Suzuki	Lola	90	Lamborghini	V12	66		18	9
13	14	O Grouillard	Osella	FA1M-E	Cosworth	V8	65		15	8
r	12	M Donnelly	Lotus	102	Lamborghini	V12	57	dropped valve	12	6
r	35	G Foitek	Onyx	ORE-2	Cosworth	V8	53	valve	21	11
r	22	A de Cesaris	Dallara	190	Cosworth	V8	50	input shaft	25	13
r	36	J J Lehto	Onyx	ORE-2	Cosworth	V8	46	misfire	22	11
r	6	R Patrese	Williams	FW13B	Renault	V10	44	brakes	9	5
r	26	P Alliot	Ligier	JS33B	Cosworth	V8	34	engine	17	9
r	4	J Alesi	Tyrrell	019	Cosworth	V8	26	accident	8	4
r	19	A Nannini	Benetton	B190	Cosworth	V8	21	accident	4	2
r	5	T Boutsen	Williams	FW13B	Renault	V10	19	accident	6	3
r	25	N Larini	Ligier	JS33B	Cosworth	V8	18	accident	20	10
r	21	E Pirro	Dallara	190	Cosworth	V8	11	accident	19	10
r	9	M Alboreto	Arrows	A11B	Cosworth	V8	11	accident	14	7
r	23	P Martini	Minardi	M190	Cosworth	V8	0	spin	16	8
nq	33	R Moreno	EuroBrun	ER189	Judd	V8				
nq	15	M Gugelmin	Leyton House	CG901	Judd	V8				
nq	24	P Barilla	Minardi	M190	Cosworth	V8				
nq	7	D Brabham	Brabham	BT59	Judd	V8				
npq	17	G Tarquini	AGS	JH25	Cosworth	V8				
npq	18	Y Dalmas	AGS	JH25	Cosworth	V8				
npq	31	B Gachot	Coloni	FC189B	Subaru	F12				
npq	34	C Langes	EuroBrun	ER189B	Judd	V8				
npq	39	B Giacomelli	Life	L190	Life	W12				

Winning speed: 179.114 km/h, 111.296 mph
Pole Position speed: 196.570 km/h, 122.143 mph (A Senna, 1 min:20.399 sec)
Fastest Lap speed: 192.551 km/h, 119.646 mph (G Berger, 1 min:22.077 sec on lap 70)
Lap Leaders: A Senna 1-11 (11); A Nannini 12-14 (3); G Berger 15-70 (56)

** G Berger finished 1st but was classified 4th, after 1 minute penalty for jumping the start. Lap leaders are shown 'on the road', but on corrected time, A Senna led laps 15-70.*

24 Jun 1990 — MEXICO: Mexico City (Round: 6) (Race: 490)

69 laps x 4.421 km, 2.747 miles = 305.049 km, 189.549 miles

POS.	NO.	DRIVER	CAR	MODEL	ENGINE		LAPS	TIME/REASON FOR RETIREMENT	GRID:POS	ROW
1	1	A Prost	Ferrari	641	Ferrari	V12	69	1h 32m 35.783s	13	7
2	2	N Mansell	Ferrari	641	Ferrari	V12	69	1h 33m 01.134s	4	2
3	28	G Berger	McLaren	MP4/5B	Honda	V10	69	1h 33m 01.313s	1	1
4	19	A Nannini	Benetton	B190	Cosworth	V8	69	1h 33m 16.882s	14	7
5	5	T Boutsen	Williams	FW13B	Renault	V10	69	1h 33m 22.452s	5	3
6	20	N Piquet	Benetton	B190	Cosworth	V8	69	1h 33m 22.726s	8	4
7	4	J Alesi	Tyrrell	019	Cosworth	V8	69	1h 33m 24.860s	6	3
8	12	M Donnelly	Lotus	102	Lamborghini	V12	69	1h 33m 41.925s	12	6
9	6	R Patrese	Williams	FW13B	Renault	V10	69	1h 33m 45.701s	2	1
10	11	D Warwick	Lotus	102	Lamborghini	V12	68		11	6
11	8	S Modena	Brabham	BT59	Judd	V8	68		10	5
12	23	P Martini	Minardi	M190	Cosworth	V8	68		7	4
13	22	A de Cesaris	Dallara	190	Cosworth	V8	68		15	8
14	24	P Barilla	Minardi	M190	Cosworth	V8	67		16	8
15	35	G Foitek	Onyx	ORE-2	Cosworth	V8	67		23	12
16	25	N Larini	Ligier	JS33B	Cosworth	V8	67		24	12
17	9	M Alboreto	Arrows	A11B	Cosworth	V8	66		17	9
18	26	P Alliot	Ligier	JS33B	Cosworth	V8	66		22	11
19	14	O Grouillard	Osella	FA1M-E	Cosworth	V8	65		20	10
20r	27	A Senna	McLaren	MP4/5B	Honda	V10	63	puncture	3	2
r	36	J J Lehto	Onyx	ORE-2	Cosworth	V8	26	engine	26	13
r	29	É Bernard	Lola	90	Lamborghini	V12	12	brakes/ spin	25	13
r	30	A Suzuki	Lola	90	Lamborghini	V12	11	accident	19	10
r	3	S Nakajima	Tyrrell	019	Cosworth	V8	11	accident	9	5
r	7	D Brabham	Brabham	BT59	Judd	V8	11	electrics	21	11
r	21	E Pirro	Dallara	190	Cosworth	V8	10	engine	18	9
exc	33	R Moreno	EuroBrun	ER189B	Judd	V8		push start after spin		
nq	16	I Capelli	Leyton House	CG901	Judd	V8				
nq	15	M Gugelmin	Leyton House	CG901	Judd	V8				
nq	10	A Caffi	Arrows	A11B	Cosworth	V8				
npq	18	Y Dalmas	AGS	JH25	Cosworth	V8				
npq	17	G Tarquini	AGS	JH25	Cosworth	V8				
npq	31	B Gachot	Coloni	FC189B	Subaru	F12				
npq	34	C Langes	EuroBrun	ER189B	Judd	V8				
npq	39	B Giacomelli	Life	L190	Life	W12				

Winning speed: 197.664 km/h, 122.823 mph
Pole Position speed: 206.089 km/h, 128.057 mph (G Berger, 1 min:17.227 sec)
Fastest Lap speed: 204.156 km/h, 126.857 mph (A Prost, 1 min:17.958 sec on lap 58)
Lap Leaders: A Senna 1-60 (60); A Prost 61-69 (9).

8 Jul 1990 — FRANCE: Paul Ricard (Round: 7) (Race: 491)

80 laps x 3.813 km, 2.369 miles = 305.040 km, 189.543 miles

POS.	NO.	DRIVER	CAR	MODEL	ENGINE		LAPS	TIME/REASON FOR RETIREMENT	GRID:POS	ROW
1	1	A Prost	Ferrari	641	Ferrari	V12	80	1h 33m 29.606s	4	2
2	16	I Capelli	Leyton House	CG901	Judd	V8	80	1h 33m 38.232s	7	4
3	27	A Senna	McLaren	MP4/5B	Honda	V10	80	1h 33m 41.212s	3	2
4	20	N Piquet	Benetton	B190	Cosworth	V8	80	1h 34m 10.813s	9	5
5	28	G Berger	McLaren	MP4/5B	Honda	V10	80	1h 34m 11.825s	2	1
6	6	R Patrese	Williams	FW13B	Renault	V10	80	1h 34m 38.957s	6	3
7	30	A Suzuki	Lola	90	Lamborghini	V12	79		14	7
8	29	É Bernard	Lola	90	Lamborghini	V12	79		11	6
9	26	P Alliot	Ligier	JS33B	Cosworth	V8	79		12	6
10	9	M Alboreto	Arrows	A11B	Cosworth	V8	79		18	9
11	11	D Warwick	Lotus	102	Lamborghini	V12	79		16	8
12	12	M Donnelly	Lotus	102	Lamborghini	V12	79		17	9
13	8	S Modena	Brabham	BT59	Judd	V8	78		20	10
14	25	N Larini	Ligier	JS33B	Cosworth	V8	78		19	10
dq	22	A de Cesaris	Dallara	190	Cosworth	V8	78	car under weight	21	11
15	7	D Brabham	Brabham	BT59	Judd	V8	77		25	13
16r	19	A Nannini	Benetton	B190	Cosworth	V8	75	electrics	5	3
17	18	Y Dalmas	AGS	JH25	Cosworth	V8	75		26	13
18r	2	N Mansell	Ferrari	641	Ferrari	V12	72	engine	1	1
r	3	S Nakajima	Tyrrell	019	Cosworth	V8	63	gear linkage	15	8
r	15	M Gugelmin	Leyton House	CG901	Judd	V8	58	engine	10	5
r	23	P Martini	Minardi	M190	Cosworth	V8	40	electrics	23	12
r	4	J Alesi	Tyrrell	019	Cosworth	V8	23	differential	13	7
r	10	A Caffi	Arrows	A11B	Cosworth	V8	22	rear suspension	22	11
r	5	T Boutsen	Williams	FW13B	Renault	V10	7	engine	8	4
r	21	E Pirro	Dallara	190	Cosworth	V8	7	brake disc/ spin	24	12
nq	24	P Barilla	Minardi	M190	Cosworth	V8				
nq	17	G Tarquini	AGS	JH25	Cosworth	V8				
nq	35	G Foitek	Onyx	ORE-2	Cosworth	V8				
nq	36	J J Lehto	Onyx	ORE-2	Cosworth	V8				
npq	14	O Grouillard	Osella	FA1M-E	Cosworth	V8				
npq	33	R Moreno	EuroBrun	ER189B	Judd	V8				
npq	34	C Langes	EuroBrun	ER189B	Judd	V8				
npq	31	B Gachot	Coloni	FC189B	Subaru	F12				
npq	39	B Giacomelli	Life	L190	Life	W12				

Winning speed: 195.761 km/h, 121.640 mph
Pole Position speed: 213.142 km/h, 132.441 mph (N Mansell, 1 min: 4.402 sec)
Fastest Lap speed: 201.829 km/h, 125.411 mph (N Mansell, 1 min: 8.012 sec on lap 64)
Lap Leaders: G Berger 1-27 (27); A Senna 28-29 (2); N Mansell 30-31 (2); R Patrese 32 (1); I Capelli 33-77 (45);A Prost 78-80 (3).

15 Jul 1990 — BRITAIN: Silverstone (Round: 8) (Race: 492)

64 laps x 4.780 km, 2.970 miles = 305.904 km, 190.080 miles

POS.	NO.	DRIVER	CAR	MODEL	ENGINE		LAPS	TIME/REASON FOR RETIREMENT	GRID:POS	ROW
1	1	A Prost	Ferrari	641	Ferrari	V12	64	1h 18m 30.999s	5	3
2	5	T Boutsen	Williams	FW13B	Renault	V10	64	1h 19m 10.091s	4	2
3	27	A Senna	McLaren	MP4/5B	Honda	V10	64	1h 19m 14.087s	2	1
4	29	É Bernard	Lola	90	Lamborghini	V12	64	1h 19m 46.301s	8	4
5	20	N Piquet	Benetton	B190	Cosworth	V8	64	1h 19m 55.002s	11	6
6	30	A Suzuki	Lola	90	Lamborghini	V12	63		9	5
7	10	A Caffi	Arrows	A11B	Cosworth	V8	63		17	9
8	4	J Alesi	Tyrrell	019	Cosworth	V8	63		6	3
9	8	S Modena	Brabham	BT59	Judd	V8	62		20	10
10	25	N Larini	Ligier	JS33B	Cosworth	V8	62		21	11
11	21	E Pirro	Dallara	190	Cosworth	V8	62		19	10
12	24	P Barilla	Minardi	M190	Cosworth	V8	62		24	12
13	26	P Alliot	Ligier	JS33B	Cosworth	V8	61		22	11
14r	28	G Berger	McLaren	MP4/5B	Honda	V10	60	throttle linkage	3	2
r	2	N Mansell	Ferrari	641	Ferrari	V12	55	gearbox	1	1
r	16	I Capelli	Leyton House	CG901	Judd	V8	48	fuel line	10	5
r	12	M Donnelly	Lotus	102	Lamborghini	V12	48	engine	14	7
r	11	D Warwick	Lotus	102	Lamborghini	V12	46	engine	16	8
r	17	G Tarquini	AGS	JH25	Cosworth	V8	41	engine	26	13
r	9	M Alboreto	Arrows	A11B	Cosworth	V8	37	electrics	25	13
r	6	R Patrese	Williams	FW13B	Renault	V10	26	accident/ undertray	7	4
r	3	S Nakajima	Tyrrell	019	Cosworth	V8	20	electrics	12	6
r	19	A Nannini	Benetton	B190	Cosworth	V8	15	accident	13	7
r	22	A de Cesaris	Dallara	190	Cosworth	V8	12	gearbox	23	12
r	23	P Martini	Minardi	M190	Cosworth	V8	3	alternator	18	9
ns	15	M Gugelmin	Leyton House	CG901	Judd	V8		fuel pump on dummy grid	15	8
nq	14	O Grouillard	Osella	FA1M-E	Cosworth	V8				
nq	7	D Brabham	Brabham	BT59	Judd	V8				
nq	36	J J Lehto	Onyx	ORE-2	Cosworth	V8				
nq	35	G Foitek	Onyx	ORE-2	Cosworth	V8				
npq	33	R Moreno	EuroBrun	ER189B	Judd	V8				
npq	18	Y Dalmas	AGS	JH25	Cosworth	V8				
npq	34	C Langes	EuroBrun	ER189B	Judd	V8				
npq	31	B Gachot	Coloni	FC189B	Subaru	F12				
npq	39	B Giacomelli	Life	L190	Life	W12				

Winning speed: 233.762 km/h, 145.253 mph
Pole Position speed: 255.192 km/h, 158.569 mph (N Mansell, 1 min: 7.428 sec)
Fastest Lap speed: 241.364 km/h, 149.977 mph (N Mansell, 1 min:11.291 sec on lap 51)
Lap Leaders: A Senna 1-11 (11); N Mansell 12-21,28-42 (25); G Berger 22-27 (6); A Prost 43-64 (22).

29 Jul 1990 — GERMANY: Hockenheim (Round: 9) (Race: 493)

45 laps x 6.802 km, 4.227 miles = 306.090 km, 190.196 miles

POS.	NO.	DRIVER	CAR	MODEL	ENGINE		LAPS	TIME/REASON FOR RETIREMENT	GRID:POS	ROW
1	27	A Senna	McLaren	MP4/5B	Honda	V10	45	1h 20m 47.164s	1	1
2	19	A Nannini	Benetton	B190	Cosworth	V8	45	1h 20m 53.684s	9	5
3	28	G Berger	McLaren	MP4/5B	Honda	V10	45	1h 20m 55.717s	2	1
4	1	A Prost	Ferrari	641	Ferrari	V12	45	1h 21m 32.434s	3	2
5	6	R Patrese	Williams	FW13B	Renault	V10	45	1h 21m 35.192s	5	3
6	5	T Boutsen	Williams	FW13B	Renault	V10	45	1h 22m 08.655s	6	3
7	16	I Capelli	Leyton House	CG901	Judd	V8	44		10	5
8	11	D Warwick	Lotus	102	Lamborghini	V12	44		16	8
9	10	A Caffi	Arrows	A11B	Cosworth	V8	44		18	9
10	25	N Larini	Ligier	JS33B	Cosworth	V8	43		22	11
11r	4	J Alesi	Tyrrell	019	Cosworth	V8	40	cv joint	8	4
nc	36	J J Lehto	Monteverdi	ORE-2	Cosworth	V8	39		25	13
r	29	É Bernard	Lola	90	Lamborghini	V12	35	fuel pressure	12	6
r	30	A Suzuki	Lola	90	Lamborghini	V12	33	clutch	11	6
r	3	S Nakajima	Tyrrell	019	Cosworth	V8	24	electrics	13	7
r	20	N Piquet	Benetton	B190	Cosworth	V8	23	engine	7	4
r	23	P Martini	Minardi	M190	Cosworth	V8	20	engine	15	8
r	35	G Foitek	Monteverdi	ORE-2	Cosworth	V8	19	spin	26	13
r	2	N Mansell	Ferrari	641	Ferrari	V12	15	undertray damage	4	2
r	15	M Gugelmin	Leyton House	CG901	Judd	V8	12	dropped valve	14	7
r	7	D Brabham	Brabham	BT59	Judd	V8	12	valve	21	11
dq	26	P Alliot	Ligier	JS33B	Cosworth	V8	12	push start after accident	24	12
r	9	M Alboreto	Arrows	A11B	Cosworth	V8	10	engine	19	10
r	12	M Donnelly	Lotus	102	Lamborghini	V12	1	clutch	20	10
r	21	E Pirro	Dallara	190	Cosworth	V8	0	accident	23	12
r	8	S Modena	Brabham	BT59	Judd	V8	0	clutch	17	9
nq	14	O Grouillard	Osella	FA1M-E	Cosworth	V8				
nq	24	P Barilla	Minardi	M190	Cosworth	V8				
nq	18	Y Dalmas	AGS	JH25	Cosworth	V8				
nq	22	A de Cesaris	Dallara	190	Cosworth	V8				
npq	17	G Tarquini	AGS	JH25	Cosworth	V8				
npq	33	R Moreno	EuroBrun	ER189B	Judd	V8				
npq	31	B Gachot	Coloni	FC189C	Cosworth	V8				
npq	34	C Langes	EuroBrun	ER189B	Judd	V8				
npq	39	B Giacomelli	Life	L190	Life	W12				

Winning speed: 227.334 km/h, 141.259 mph
Pole Position speed: 244.388 km/h, 151.856 mph (A Senna, 1 min:40.198 sec)
Fastest Lap speed: 231.882 km/h, 144.085 mph (T Boutsen, 1 min:45.602 sec on lap 31)
Lap Leaders: A Senna 1-17,34-45 (29); A Nannini 18-33 (16).

12 Aug 1990 — HUNGARY: Hungaroring (Round:10) (Race: 494)

77 laps x 3.968 km, 2.466 miles = 305.536 km, 189.851 miles

POS.	NO.	DRIVER	CAR	MODEL	ENGINE		LAPS	TIME/REASON FOR RETIREMENT	GRID:POS	ROW
1	5	T Boutsen	Williams	FW13B	Renault	V10	77	1h 49m 30.597s	1	1
2	27	A Senna	McLaren	MP4/5B	Honda	V10	77	1h 49m 30.885s	4	2
3	20	N Piquet	Benetton	B190	Cosworth	V8	77	1h 49m 58.490s	9	5
4	6	R Patrese	Williams	FW13B	Renault	V10	77	1h 50m 02.430s	2	1
5	11	D Warwick	Lotus	102	Lamborghini	V12	77	1h 50m 44.841s	11	6
6	29	É Bernard	Lola	90	Lamborghini	V12	77	1h 50m 54.905s	12	6
7	12	M Donnelly	Lotus	102	Lamborghini	V12	76		18	9
8	15	M Gugelmin	Leyton House	CG901	Judd	V8	76		17	9
9	10	A Caffi	Arrows	A11B	Cosworth	V8	76		26	13
10	21	E Pirro	Dallara	190	Cosworth	V8	76		13	7
11	25	N Larini	Ligier	JS33B	Cosworth	V8	76		25	13
12	9	M Alboreto	Arrows	A11B	Cosworth	V8	75		22	11
13	17	G Tarquini	AGS	JH25	Cosworth	V8	74		24	12
14	26	P Alliot	Ligier	JS33B	Cosworth	V8	74		21	11
15	24	P Barilla	Minardi	M190	Cosworth	V8	74		23	12
16r	28	G Berger	McLaren	MP4/5B	Honda	V10	72	accident	3	2
17r	2	N Mansell	Ferrari	641	Ferrari	V12	71	accident	5	3
r	19	A Nannini	Benetton	B190	Cosworth	V8	64	accident	7	4
r	16	I Capelli	Leyton House	CG901	Judd	V8	56	gearbox	16	8
r	30	A Suzuki	Lola	90	Lamborghini	V12	37	oil filter/ engine	19	10
r	1	A Prost	Ferrari	641	Ferrari	V12	36	gearbox/ spin	8	4
r	4	J Alesi	Tyrrell	019	Cosworth	V8	36	accident	6	3
r	8	S Modena	Brabham	BT59	Judd	V8	35	engine	20	10
r	23	P Martini	Minardi	M190	Cosworth	V8	35	accident	14	7
r	22	A de Cesaris	Dallara	190	Cosworth	V8	22	engine	10	5
r	3	S Nakajima	Tyrrell	019	Cosworth	V8	9	brakes/ accident	15	8
nq	18	Y Dalmas	AGS	JH25	Cosworth	V8				
nq	7	D Brabham	Brabham	BT59	Judd	V8				
nq	36	J J Lehto	Monteverdi	ORE-2	Cosworth	V8				
nq	35	G Foitek	Monteverdi	ORE-2	Cosworth	V8				
npq	14	O Grouillard	Osella	FA1M-E	Cosworth	V8				
npq	31	B Gachot	Coloni	FC189C	Cosworth	V8				
npq	33	R Moreno	EuroBrun	ER189B	Judd	V8				
npq	34	C Langes	EuroBrun	ER189B	Judd	V8				
npq	39	B Giacomelli	Life	L190	Life	W12				

Winning speed: 167.402 km/h, 104.019 mph
Pole Position speed: 183.329 km/h, 113.915 mph (T Boutsen, 1 min:17.919 sec)
Fastest Lap speed: 174.082 km/h, 108.169 mph (R Patrese, 1 min:22.058 sec on lap 63)
Lap Leaders: T Boutsen 1-77 (77).

26 Aug 1990 — BELGIUM: Spa-Francorchamps (Round:11) (Race: 495)

44 laps x 6.940 km, 4.312 miles = 305.360 km, 189.742 miles

POS.	NO.	DRIVER	CAR	MODEL	ENGINE		LAPS	TIME/REASON FOR RETIREMENT	GRID:POS	ROW
1	27	A Senna	McLaren	MP4/5B	Honda	V10	44	1h 26m 31.997s	1	1
2	1	A Prost	Ferrari	641	Ferrari	V12	44	1h 26m 35.547s	3	2
3	28	G Berger	McLaren	MP4/5B	Honda	V10	44	1h 27m 00.459s	2	1
4	19	A Nannini	Benetton	B190	Cosworth	V8	44	1h 27m 21.334s	6	3
5	20	N Piquet	Benetton	B190	Cosworth	V8	44	1h 28m 01.647s	8	4
6	15	M Gugelmin	Leyton House	CG901	Judd	V8	44	1h 28m 20.848s	14	7
7	16	I Capelli	Leyton House	CG901	Judd	V8	43		12	6
8	4	J Alesi	Tyrrell	019	Cosworth	V8	43		9	5
9	29	É Bernard	Lola	90	Lamborghini	V12	43		15	8
10	10	A Caffi	Arrows	A11B	Cosworth	V8	43		19	10
11	11	D Warwick	Lotus	102	Lamborghini	V12	43		18	9
12	12	M Donnelly	Lotus	102	Lamborghini	V12	43		22	11
13	9	M Alboreto	Arrows	A11B	Cosworth	V8	43		26	13
14	25	N Larini	Ligier	JS33B	Cosworth	V8	42		21	11
15	23	P Martini	Minardi	M190	Cosworth	V8	42		16	8
16	14	O Grouillard	Osella	FA1M-E	Cosworth	V8	42		23	12
17r	8	S Modena	Brabham	BT59	Judd	V8	39	engine	13	7
r	7	D Brabham	Brabham	BT59	Judd	V8	36	electrics	24	12
r	22	A de Cesaris	Dallara	190	Cosworth	V8	27	oil leak/ engine	20	10
r	5	T Boutsen	Williams	FW13B	Renault	V10	21	cv joint	4	2
r	2	N Mansell	Ferrari	641	Ferrari	V12	19	handling	5	3
r	6	R Patrese	Williams	FW13B	Renault	V10	18	gearbox	7	4
r	21	E Pirro	Dallara	190	Cosworth	V8	5	water pipe	17	9
r	3	S Nakajima	Tyrrell	019	Cosworth	V8	4	engine	10	5
r	24	P Barilla	Minardi	M190	Cosworth	V8	0	accident **	25	13
r	30	A Suzuki	Lola	90	Lamborghini	V12	0	accident *	11	6
nq	26	P Alliot	Ligier	JS33B	Cosworth	V8				
nq	17	G Tarquini	AGS	JH25	Cosworth	V8				
nq	18	Y Dalmas	AGS	JH25	Cosworth	V8				
nq	31	B Gachot	Coloni	FC189C	Cosworth	V8				
npq	33	R Moreno	EuroBrun	ER189B	Judd	V8				
npq	34	C Langes	EuroBrun	ER189B	Judd	V8				
npq	39	B Giacomelli	Life	L190	Life	W12				

Winning speed: 211.729 km/h, 131.562 mph
Pole Position speed: 226.376 km/h, 140.664 mph (A Senna, 1 min:50.365 sec)
Fastest Lap speed: 217.088 km/h, 134.892 mph (A Prost, 1 min:55.087 sec on lap 38)
Lap Leaders: A Senna 1-44 (44).

*Interrupted twice after 1st lap accidents. Restarted for original distance. * retired after first start. ** retired after second start.*

9 Sep 1990 — ITALY: Monza — (Round:12) (Race: 496)

53 laps x 5.800 km, 3.604 miles = 307.400 km, 191.010 miles

POS.	NO.	DRIVER	CAR	MODEL	ENGINE		LAPS	TIME/REASON FOR RETIREMENT	GRID:POS	ROW
1	27	A Senna	McLaren	MP4/5B	Honda	V10	53	1h 17m 57.878s	1	1
2	1	A Prost	Ferrari	641	Ferrari	V12	53	1h 18m 03.932s	2	1
3	28	G Berger	McLaren	MP4/5B	Honda	V10	53	1h 18m 05.282s	3	2
4	2	N Mansell	Ferrari	641	Ferrari	V12	53	1h 18m 54.097s	4	2
5	6	R Patrese	Williams	FW13B	Renault	V10	53	1h 19m 23.152s	7	4
6	3	S Nakajima	Tyrrell	019	Cosworth	V8	52		14	7
7	20	N Piquet	Benetton	B190	Cosworth	V8	52		9	5
8	19	A Nannini	Benetton	B190	Cosworth	V8	52		8	4
9	10	A Caffi	Arrows	A11B	Cosworth	V8	51		21	11
10	22	A de Cesaris	Dallara	190	Cosworth	V8	51		25	13
11	25	N Larini	Ligier	JS33B	Cosworth	V8	51		26	13
12r	9	M Alboreto	Arrows	A11B	Cosworth	V8	50	spin	22	11
13	26	P Alliot	Ligier	JS33B	Cosworth	V8	50		20	10
nc	18	Y Dalmas	AGS	JH25	Cosworth	V8	45		24	12
r	16	I Capelli	Leyton House	CG901	Judd	V8	36	fuel pump	16	8
r	30	A Suzuki	Lola	90	Lamborghini	V12	36	electrics	18	9
r	14	O Grouillard	Osella	FA1M-E	Cosworth	V8	27	wheel bearing	23	12
r	15	M Gugelmin	Leyton House	CG901	Judd	V8	24	engine	10	5
r	8	S Modena	Brabham	BT59	Judd	V8	21	valve	17	9
r	5	T Boutsen	Williams	FW13B	Renault	V10	18	suspension	6	3
r	11	D Warwick	Lotus	102	Lamborghini	V12	15	clutch	12	6
r	21	E Pirro	Dallara	190	Cosworth	V8	14	gearbox/ spin	19	10
r	12	M Donnelly	Lotus	102	Lamborghini	V12	13	engine	11	6
r	29	É Bernard	Lola	90	Lamborghini	V12	10	clutch	13	7
r	23	P Martini	Minardi	M190	Cosworth	V8	7	spin/ rear suspension	15	8
r	4	J Alesi	Tyrrell	019	Cosworth	V8	4	spin	5	3
nq	17	G Tarquini	AGS	JH25	Cosworth	V8				
nq	24	P Barilla	Minardi	M190	Cosworth	V8				
nq	7	D Brabham	Brabham	BT59	Judd	V8				
nq	31	B Gachot	Coloni	FC189C	Cosworth	V8				
npq	33	R Moreno	EuroBrun	ER189B	Judd	V8				
npq	34	C Langes	EuroBrun	ER189B	Judd	V8				
npq	39	B Giacomelli	Life	L190	Life	W12				

Winning speed: 236.569 km/h, 146.997 mph
Pole Position speed: 252.990 km/h, 157.201 mph (A Senna, 1 min:22.533 sec)
Fastest Lap speed: 242.076 km/h, 150.419 mph (A Senna, 1 min:26.254 sec on lap 46)
Lap Leaders: A Senna 1-53 (53).

Interrupted after 1st lap accident. Restarted for original distance.

23 Sep 1990 — PORTUGAL: Estoril — (Round:13) (Race: 497)

61 laps x 4.350 km, 2.703 miles = 265.350 km, 164.881 miles

POS.	NO.	DRIVER	CAR	MODEL	ENGINE		LAPS	TIME/REASON FOR RETIREMENT	GRID:POS	ROW
1	2	N Mansell	Ferrari	641	Ferrari	V12	61	1h 22m 11.014s	1	1
2	27	A Senna	McLaren	MP4/5B	Honda	V10	61	1h 22m 13.822s	3	2
3	1	A Prost	Ferrari	641	Ferrari	V12	61	1h 22m 15.203s	2	1
4	28	G Berger	McLaren	MP4/5B	Honda	V10	61	1h 22m 16.910s	4	2
5	20	N Piquet	Benetton	B190	Cosworth	V8	61	1h 23m 08.432s	6	3
6	19	A Nannini	Benetton	B190	Cosworth	V8	61	1h 23m 09.263s	9	5
7	6	R Patrese	Williams	FW13B	Renault	V10	60		5	3
8	4	J Alesi	Tyrrell	019	Cosworth	V8	60		8	4
9	9	M Alboreto	Arrows	A11B	Cosworth	V8	60		19	10
10	25	N Larini	Ligier	JS33B	Cosworth	V8	59		22	11
11	23	P Martini	Minardi	M190	Cosworth	V8	59		16	8
12	15	M Gugelmin	Leyton House	CG901	Judd	V8	59		14	7
13r	10	A Caffi	Arrows	A11B	Cosworth	V8	58	accident	17	9
14r	30	A Suzuki	Lola	90	Lamborghini	V12	58	accident	11	6
15	21	E Pirro	Dallara	190	Cosworth	V8	58		13	7
r	26	P Alliot	Ligier	JS33B	Cosworth	V8	52	accident	20	10
r	7	D Brabham	Brabham	BT59	Judd	V8	52	gearbox	25	13
r	16	I Capelli	Leyton House	CG901	Judd	V8	51	engine	12	6
r	5	T Boutsen	Williams	FW13B	Renault	V10	30	gearbox	7	4
r	29	É Bernard	Lola	90	Lamborghini	V12	24	gearbox	10	5
r	8	S Modena	Brabham	BT59	Judd	V8	21	gearbox	23	12
r	12	M Donnelly	Lotus	102	Lamborghini	V12	14	alternator	15	8
r	11	D Warwick	Lotus	102	Lamborghini	V12	5	throttle slides jammed	21	11
r	18	Y Dalmas	AGS	JH25	Cosworth	V8	3	drive shaft	24	12
r	22	A de Cesaris	Dallara	190	Cosworth	V8	0	throttle jammed/ spin	18	9
ns	3	S Nakajima	Tyrrell	019	Cosworth	V8		driver ill (earlier accident)		
nq	14	O Grouillard	Osella	FA1M-E	Cosworth	V8				
nq	24	P Barilla	Minardi	M190	Cosworth	V8				
nq	17	G Tarquini	AGS	JH25	Cosworth	V8				
nq	31	B Gachot	Coloni	FC189C	Cosworth	V8				
npq	33	R Moreno	EuroBrun	ER189B	Judd	V8				
npq	34	C Langes	EuroBrun	ER189B	Judd	V8				
npq	39	B Giacomelli	Life	L190	Judd	V8				

Winning speed: 193.725 km/h, 120.375 mph
Pole Position speed: 212.896 km/h, 132.288 mph (N Mansell, 1 min:13.557 sec)
Fastest Lap speed: 199.985 km/h, 124.265 mph (R Patrese, 1 min:18.306 sec on lap 56)
Lap Leaders: A Senna 1-28,32-49 (46); G Berger 29-31 (3); N Mansell 50-61 (12).

Scheduled for 71 laps, but stopped early, because of an accident.

30 Sep 1990 — SPAIN: Jerez de la Frontera (Round:14) (Race: 498)

73 laps x 4.218 km, 2.621 miles = 307.914 km, 191.329 miles

POS.	NO.	DRIVER	CAR	MODEL	ENGINE		LAPS	TIME/REASON FOR RETIREMENT	GRID:POS	ROW
1	1	A Prost	Ferrari	641	Ferrari	V12	73	1h 48m 01.461s	2	1
2	2	N Mansell	Ferrari	641	Ferrari	V12	73	1h 48m 23.525s	3	2
3	19	A Nannini	Benetton	B190	Cosworth	V8	73	1h 48m 36.335s	9	5
4	5	T Boutsen	Williams	FW13B	Renault	V10	73	1h 48m 44.757s	7	4
5	6	R Patrese	Williams	FW13B	Renault	V10	73	1h 48m 58.991s	6	3
6	30	A Suzuki	Lola	90	Lamborghini	V12	73	1h 49m 05.189s	15	8
7	25	N Larini	Ligier	JS33B	Cosworth	V8	72		20	10
8	15	M Gugelmin	Leyton House	CG901	Judd	V8	72		12	6
9	18	Y Dalmas	AGS	JH25	Cosworth	V8	72		23	12
10	9	M Alboreto	Arrows	A11B	Cosworth	V8	71		25	13
r	11	D Warwick	Lotus	102	Lamborghini	V12	63	gearbox	10	5
r	16	I Capelli	Leyton House	CG901	Judd	V8	59	driver discomfort (leg cramp)	19	10
r	28	G Berger	McLaren	MP4/5B	Honda	V10	56	accident	5	3
r	27	A Senna	McLaren	MP4/5B	Honda	V10	53	radiator	1	1
r	20	N Piquet	Benetton	B190	Cosworth	V8	47	alternator	8	4
r	22	A de Cesaris	Dallara	190	Cosworth	V8	47	dropped valve	17	9
r	14	O Grouillard	Osella	FA1M-E	Cosworth	V8	45	wheel bearing	21	11
r	23	P Martini	Minardi	M190	Cosworth	V8	41	wheel nut loose/ spin	11	6
r	26	P Alliot	Ligier	JS33B	Cosworth	V8	22	spin	13	7
r	29	É Bernard	Lola	90	Lamborghini	V12	20	gearbox	18	9
r	3	S Nakajima	Tyrrell	019	Cosworth	V8	13	spin	14	7
r	17	G Tarquini	AGS	JH25	Cosworth	V8	5	electrics	22	11
r	8	S Modena	Brabham	BT59	Judd	V8	5	accident	24	12
r	21	E Pirro	Dallara	190	Cosworth	V8	0	throttle slides/ spin	16	8
r	4	J Alesi	Tyrrell	019	Cosworth	V8	0	accident	4	2
ns	12	M Donnelly	Lotus	102	Lamborghini	V12		accident/ injury		
nq	7	D Brabham	Brabham	BT59	Judd	V8				
nq	24	P Barilla	Minardi	M190	Cosworth	V8				
nq	10	B Schneider	Arrows	A11B	Cosworth	V8				
nq	31	B Gachot	Coloni	FC189C	Cosworth	V8				
npq	33	R Moreno	EuroBrun	ER189B	Judd	V8				
npq	34	C Langes	EuroBrun	ER189B	Judd	V8				
npq	39	B Giacomelli	Life	L190	Judd	V8				

Winning speed: 171.025 km/h, 106.270 mph
Pole Position speed: 193.716 km/h, 120.369 mph (A Senna, 1 min:18.387 sec)
Fastest Lap speed: 179.674 km/h, 111.644 mph (R Patrese, 1 min:24.513 sec on lap 53)
Lap Leaders: A Senna 1-26 (26); N Piquet 27-28 (2); A Prost 29-73 (45).

21 Oct 1990 — JAPAN: Suzuka (Round:15) (Race: 499)

53 laps x 5.859 km, 3.641 miles = 310.527 km, 192.953 miles

POS.	NO.	DRIVER	CAR	MODEL	ENGINE		LAPS	TIME/REASON FOR RETIREMENT	GRID:POS	ROW
1	20	N Piquet	Benetton	B190	Cosworth	V8	53	1h 34m 36.824s	6	3
2	19	R Moreno	Benetton	B190	Cosworth	V8	53	1h 34m 44.047s	8	4
3	30	A Suzuki	Lola	90	Lamborghini	V12	53	1h 34m 59.293s	9	5
4	6	R Patrese	Williams	FW13B	Renault	V10	53	1h 35m 13.082s	7	4
5	5	T Boutsen	Williams	FW13B	Renault	V10	53	1h 35m 23.708s	5	3
6	3	S Nakajima	Tyrrell	019	Cosworth	V8	53	1h 35m 49.174s	13	7
7	25	N Larini	Ligier	JS33B	Cosworth	V8	52		17	9
8	23	P Martini	Minardi	M190	Cosworth	V8	52		10	5
9	10	A Caffi	Arrows	A11B	Cosworth	V8	52		23	12
10	26	P Alliot	Ligier	JS33B	Cosworth	V8	52		20	10
r	11	D Warwick	Lotus	102	Lamborghini	V12	38	gearbox	11	6
r	12	J Herbert	Lotus	102	Lamborghini	V12	31	engine	14	7
r	9	M Alboreto	Arrows	A11B	Cosworth	V8	28	engine	24	12
r	2	N Mansell	Ferrari	641	Ferrari	V12	26	drive shaft	3	2
r	21	E Pirro	Dallara	190	Cosworth	V8	24	alternator	18	9
r	29	É Bernard	Lola	90	Lamborghini	V12	24	oil leak/ fire	16	8
r	24	G Morbidelli	Minardi	M190	Cosworth	V8	18	spin	19	10
r	16	I Capelli	Leyton House	CG901	Judd	V8	16	electrics	12	6
r	22	A de Cesaris	Dallara	190	Cosworth	V8	13	spin	25	13
r	15	M Gugelmin	Leyton House	CG901	Judd	V8	5	engine	15	8
r	7	D Brabham	Brabham	BT59	Judd	V8	2	clutch	22	11
r	28	G Berger	McLaren	MP4/5B	Honda	V10	1	spin	4	2
r	8	S Modena	Brabham	BT59	Judd	V8	0	accident	21	11
r	1	A Prost	Ferrari	641	Ferrari	V12	0	accident	2	1
r	27	A Senna	McLaren	MP4/5B	Honda	V10	0	accident	1	1
ns	4	J Alesi	Tyrrell	019	Cosworth	V8		driver unfit (earlier accident)		
nq	14	O Grouillard	Osella	FA1M-E	Cosworth	V8				
nq	17	G Tarquini	AGS	JH25	Cosworth	V8				
nq	18	Y Dalmas	AGS	JH25	Cosworth	V8				
nq	31	B Gachot	Coloni	FC189C	Cosworth	V8				

Winning speed: 196.923 km/h, 122.362 mph
Pole Position speed: 217.456 km/h, 135.121 mph (A Senna, 1 min:36.996 sec)
Fastest Lap speed: 202.358 km/h, 125.740 mph (R Patrese, 1 min:44.233 sec on lap 40)
Lap Leaders: G Berger 1 (1); N Mansell 2-26 (25); N Piquet 27-53 (27).

4 Nov 1990 — AUSTRALIA: Adelaide (Round:16) (Race: 500)

81 laps x 3.780 km, 2.349 miles = 306.180 km, 190.251 miles

POS.	NO.	DRIVER	CAR	MODEL	ENGINE		LAPS	TIME/REASON FOR RETIREMENT	GRID:POS	ROW
1	20	N Piquet	Benetton	B190	Cosworth	V8	81	1h 49m 44.570s	7	4
2	2	N Mansell	Ferrari	641	Ferrari	V12	81	1h 49m 47.699s	3	2
3	1	A Prost	Ferrari	641	Ferrari	V12	81	1h 50m 21.829s	4	2
4	28	G Berger	McLaren	MP4/5B	Honda	V10	81	1h 50m 31.432s	2	1
5	5	T Boutsen	Williams	FW13B	Renault	V10	81	1h 51m 35.730s	9	5
6	6	R Patrese	Williams	FW13B	Renault	V10	80		6	3
7	19	R Moreno	Benetton	B190	Cosworth	V8	80		8	4
8	4	J Alesi	Tyrrell	019	Cosworth	V8	80		5	3
9	23	P Martini	Minardi	M190	Cosworth	V8	79		10	5
10	25	N Larini	Ligier	JS33B	Cosworth	V8	79		12	6
11	26	P Alliot	Ligier	JS33B	Cosworth	V8	78		19	10
12	8	S Modena	Brabham	BT59	Judd	V8	77		17	9
13	14	O Grouillard	Osella	FA1M-E	Cosworth	V8	74		22	11
r	21	E Pirro	Dallara	190	Cosworth	V8	68	electrics	21	11
r	27	A Senna	McLaren	MP4/5B	Honda	V10	61	accident	1	1
r	17	G Tarquini	AGS	JH25	Cosworth	V8	58	engine/ oil fire	26	13
r	12	J Herbert	Lotus	102	Lamborghini	V12	57	clutch	18	9
r	3	S Nakajima	Tyrrell	019	Cosworth	V8	53	accident	13	7
r	16	I Capelli	Leyton House	CG901	Judd	V8	46	throttle jammed	14	7
r	11	D Warwick	Lotus	102	Lamborghini	V12	43	gearbox	11	6
r	15	M Gugelmin	Leyton House	CG901	Judd	V8	27	brakes/ spin	16	8
r	22	A de Cesaris	Dallara	190	Cosworth	V8	23	electrics	15	8
r	29	É Bernard	Lola	90	Lamborghini	V12	21	gear selection	23	12
r	24	G Morbidelli	Minardi	M190	Cosworth	V8	20	gearbox	20	10
r	7	D Brabham	Brabham	BT59	Judd	V8	18	spin	25	13
r	30	A Suzuki	Lola	90	Lamborghini	V12	6	differential	24	12
nq	9	M Alboreto	Arrows	A11B	Cosworth	V8				
nq	18	Y Dalmas	AGS	JH25	Cosworth	V8				
nq	10	A Caffi	Arrows	A11B	Cosworth	V8				
nq	31	B Gachot	Coloni	FC189C	Cosworth	V8				

Winning speed: 167.399 km/h, 104.017 mph
Pole Position speed: 179.831 km/h, 111.742 mph (A Senna, 1 min:15.671 sec)
Fastest Lap speed: 174.009 km/h, 108.124 mph (N Mansell, 1 min:18.203 sec on lap 75)
Lap Leaders: A Senna 1-61 (61); N Piquet 62-81 (20).

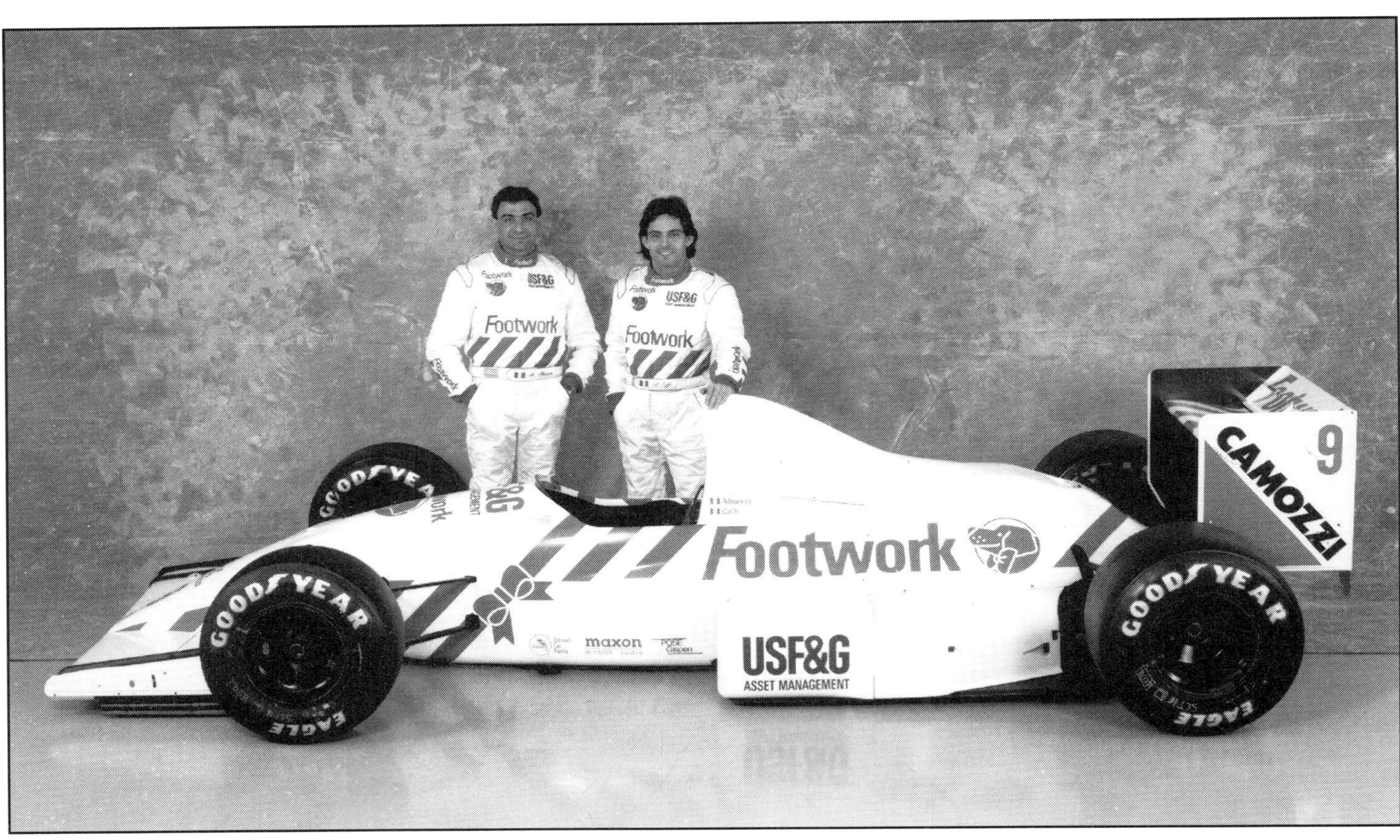

Michele Albereto & Alex Caffi and the Arrows A11B, 1990.

Lap Leaders 1990

POS	DRIVER	CAR-ENGINE	GPS	LAPS	KM	MILES
1	A Senna	McLaren-Honda	14	500	2,307.5	1,433.8
2	G Berger	McLaren-Honda	7	128	571.3	355.0
3	A Prost	Ferrari	5	110	480.3	298.4
4	T Boutsen	Williams-Renault	2	91	376.1	233.7
5	N Mansell	Ferrari	4	64	325.8	202.4
6	N Piquet	Benetton-Cosworth	3	49	242.2	150.5
7	I Capelli	Leyton House-Judd	1	45	171.6	106.6
8	J Alesi	Tyrrell-Cosworth	1	34	129.1	80.2
9	A Nannini	Benetton-Cosworth	2	19	122.0	75.8
10	R Patrese	Williams-Renault	2	12	59.3	36.8
			16	**1,052**	**4,785.2**	**2,973.4**

Driver Points 1990

		USA	BR	RSM	MC	CDN	MEX	F	GB	D	H	B	I	P	E	J	AUS	TOTAL	
1	A Senna	9	4	-	9	9	-	4	4	9	6	9	9	6	-	-	-	78	
2	A Prost	-	9	3	-	(2)	9	9	9	3	-	6	6	4	9	-	4	71	(2)
3	N Piquet	3	1	2	-	6	(1)	3	2	-	4	2	-	2	-	9	9	43	(1)
	G Berger	-	6	6	4	3	4	2	-	4	-	4	4	3	-	-	3	43	
5	N Mansell	-	3	-	-	4	6	-	-	-	-	-	3	9	6	-	6	37	
6	T Boutsen	4	2	-	3	-	2	-	6	1	9	-	-	-	3	2	2	34	
7	R Patrese	-	-	9	-	-	-	1	-	2	3	-	2	-	2	3	1	23	
8	A Nannini	-	-	4	-	-	3	-	-	6	-	3	-	1	4	-	-	21	
9	J Alesi	6	-	1	6	-	-	-	-	-	-	-	-	-	-	-	-	13	
10	I Capelli	-	-	-	-	-	-	6	-	-	-	-	-	-	-	-	-	6	
	R Moreno	-	-	-	-	-	-	-	-	-	-	-	-	-	-	6	-	6	
	A Suzuki	-	-	-	-	-	-	-	1	-	-	-	-	-	1	4	-	6	
13	É Bernard	-	-	-	1	-	-	-	3	-	1	-	-	-	-	-	-	5	
14	D Warwick	-	-	-	-	1	-	-	-	-	2	-	-	-	-	-	-	3	
	S Nakajima	1	-	-	-	-	-	-	-	-	-	-	1	-	-	1	-	3	
16	S Modena	2	-	-	-	-	-	-	-	-	-	-	-	-	-	-	-	2	
	A Caffi	-	-	-	2	-	-	-	-	-	-	-	-	-	-	-	-	2	
18	M Gugelmin	-	-	-	-	-	-	-	-	-	-	1	-	-	-	-	-	1	

9, 6, 4, 3, 2 and 1 point awarded to the first six finishers. Best 11 scores.

Constructor Points 1990

		USA	BR	RSM	MC	CDN	MEX	F	GB	D	H	B	I	P	E	J	AUS	TOTAL
1	McLaren-Honda	9	10	6	13	12	4	6	4	13	6	13	13	9	-	-	3	121
2	Ferrari	-	12	3	-	6	15	9	9	3	-	6	9	13	15	-	10	110
3	Benetton-Cosworth	3	1	6	-	6	4	3	2	6	4	5	-	3	4	15	9	71
4	Williams-Renault	4	2	9	3	-	2	1	6	3	12	-	2	-	5	5	3	57
5	Tyrrell-Cosworth	7	-	1	6	-	-	-	-	-	-	-	1	-	-	1	-	16
6	Lola-Lamborghini	-	-	-	1	-	-	-	4	-	1	-	-	-	1	4	-	11 *
7	Leyton House-Judd	-	-	-	-	-	-	6	-	-	-	1	-	-	-	-	-	7
8	Lotus-Lamborghini	-	-	-	-	1	-	-	-	-	2	-	-	-	-	-	-	3
9	Brabham-Judd	2	-	-	-	-	-	-	-	-	-	-	-	-	-	-	-	2
	Arrows-Cosworth	-	-	-	2	-	-	-	-	-	-	-	-	-	-	-	-	2

*9, 6, 4, 3, 2 and 1 point awarded to the first six finishers. * Points disallowed by FISA at end of season, due to entry irregularity.*

Honda raced its new V12 engine and Porsche returned with the Footwork Arrows team. Jordan made an impressive debut although Gachot found himself in a British jail after a traffic argument. Tom Walkinshaw purchased a share of the Benetton operation. 10 points now awarded to race winners.

McLAREN
Honda Marlboro McLaren: Senna, Berger

TYRRELL
Braun Tyrrell Honda: Nakajima, Modena

WILLIAMS
Canon Williams Team: Mansell, Patrese

BRABHAM
Motor Racing Developments: Brundle, Blundell

FOOTWORK
Footwork (Porsche): Alboreto, Caffi, Johansson

LOTUS
Team Lotus: Häkkinen, Bailey, Herbert, (Bartels)

FOMET
Fondmetal F1 SpA: Grouillard, Tarquini

LEYTON HOUSE
Leyton House Racing: Gugelmin, Capelli, Wendlinger

AGS
Automobiles Gonfaronaises Sportives: Tarquini, (Grouillard, Johansson, Barbazza)

BENETTON
Camel Benetton Ford: Moreno, Schumacher, Piquet

DALLARA
Scuderia Italia SpA: Pirro, Lehto

MINARDI
SCM Minardi Team: Martini, Morbidelli, Moreno

LIGIER
Ligier Gitanes: Boutsen, Comas

FERRARI
Scuderia Ferrari SpA: Prost, Morbidelli, Alesi

LOLA
Larrousse: Bernard, (Gachot), Suzuki

COLONI
Coloni Racing Srl: (Chaves, Hattori)

JORDAN
Team 7UP Jordan: Gachot, Schumacher, Moreno, Zanardi, de Cesaris

LAMBORGHINI
Modena Team SpA: Larini, van de Poele

10 Mar 1991 — USA: Phoenix — (Round: 1) (Race: 501)

81 laps x 3.721 km, 2.312 miles = 301.385 km, 187.272 miles

POS.	NO.	DRIVER	CAR	MODEL	ENGINE		LAPS	TIME/REASON FOR RETIREMENT	GRID:POS	ROW
1	1	A Senna	McLaren	MP4/6	Honda	V12	81	2h 00m 47.828s	1	1
2	27	A Prost	Ferrari	642	Ferrari	V12	81	2h 01m 04.150s	2	1
3	20	N Piquet	Benetton	B190B	Cosworth	V8	81	2h 01m 05.204s	5	3
4	4	S Modena	Tyrrell	020	Honda	V10	81	2h 01m 13.237s	11	6
5	3	S Nakajima	Tyrrell	020	Honda	V10	80		16	8
6	30	A Suzuki	Lola	L91	Cosworth	V8	79		21	11
7	34	N Larini	Lamborghini	291	Lamborghini	V12	78		17	9
8	17	G Tarquini	AGS	JH25	Cosworth	V8	77		22	11
9r	23	P Martini	Minardi	M191	Ferrari	V12	75	engine	15	8
10r	32	B Gachot	Jordan	191	Cosworth	V8	75	engine	14	7
11	7	M Brundle	Brabham	BT59Y	Yamaha	V12	73		12	6
12r	28	J Alesi	Ferrari	642	Ferrari	V12	72	gearbox	6	3
r	11	M Häkkinen	Lotus	102B	Judd	V8	59	oil union/ fire	13	7
r	6	R Patrese	Williams	FW14	Renault	V10	49	gearbox/ accident	3	2
r	19	R Moreno	Benetton	B190B	Cosworth	V8	49	accident	8	4
r	9	M Alboreto	Footwork	A11C	Porsche	V12	41	gearbox	25	13
r	16	I Capelli	Leyton House	CG911	Ilmor	V10	40	gearbox oil pump	18	9
r	25	T Boutsen	Ligier	JS35	Lamborghini	V12	40	electronics	20	10
r	2	G Berger	McLaren	MP4/6	Honda	V12	36	fuel pump	7	4
r	5	N Mansell	Williams	FW14	Renault	V10	35	gearbox	4	2
r	15	M Gugelmin	Leyton House	CG911	Ilmor	V10	34	gearbox	23	12
r	8	M Blundell	Brabham	BT59Y	Yamaha	V12	32	accident	24	12
r	21	E Pirro	Dallara	191	Judd	V10	16	gearbox	9	5
r	24	G Morbidelli	Minardi	M191	Ferrari	V12	15	gearbox	26	13
r	22	J J Lehto	Dallara	191	Judd	V10	12	clutch	10	5
r	29	É Bernard	Lola	L91	Cosworth	V8	4	engine	19	10
nq	26	E Comas	Ligier	JS35	Lamborghini	V12				
nq	10	A Caffi	Footwork	A11C	Porsche	V12				
nq	18	S Johansson	AGS	JH25	Cosworth	V8				
nq	12	J Bailey	Lotus	102B	Judd	V8				
npq	33	A de Cesaris	Jordan	191	Cosworth	V8				
npq	31	P Chaves	Coloni	C4	Cosworth	V8				
npq	14	O Grouillard	Fomet	FA1M-E	Cosworth	V8				
npq	35	E van de Poele	Lamborghini	291	Lamborghini	V12				

Winning speed: 149.698 km/h, 93.018 mph
Pole Position speed: 164.488 km/h, 102.208 mph (A Senna, 1 min:21.434 sec)
Fastest Lap speed: 154.394 km/h, 95.936 mph (J Alesi, 1 min:26.758 sec on lap 49)
Lap Leaders: A Senna 1-81 (81).

Scheduled for 82 laps, but stopped at 2 hours.

24 Mar 1991 — BRAZIL: Interlagos (Round: 2) (Race: 502)

71 laps x 4.325 km, 2.687 miles = 307.075 km, 190.808 miles

POS.	NO.	DRIVER	CAR	MODEL	ENGINE		LAPS	TIME/REASON FOR RETIREMENT	GRID:POS	ROW
1	1	A Senna	McLaren	MP4/6	Honda	V12	71	1h 38m 28.128s	1	1
2	6	R Patrese	Williams	FW14	Renault	V10	71	1h 38m 31.119s	2	1
3	2	G Berger	McLaren	MP4/6	Honda	V12	71	1h 38m 33.544s	4	2
4	27	A Prost	Ferrari	642	Ferrari	V12	71	1h 38m 47.497s	6	3
5	20	N Piquet	Benetton	B190B	Cosworth	V8	71	1h 38m 50.088s	7	4
6	28	J Alesi	Ferrari	642	Ferrari	V12	71	1h 38m 51.769s	5	3
7	19	R Moreno	Benetton	B190B	Cosworth	V8	70		14	7
8	24	G Morbidelli	Minardi	M191	Ferrari	V12	69		21	11
9	11	M Häkkinen	Lotus	102B	Judd	V8	68		22	11
10	25	T Boutsen	Ligier	JS35	Lamborghini	V12	68		18	9
11	21	E Pirro	Dallara	191	Judd	V10	68		12	6
12	7	M Brundle	Brabham	BT59Y	Yamaha	V12	67		26	13
13r	32	B Gachot	Jordan	191	Cosworth	V8	63	exhaust/ fuel pick-up	10	5
r	5	N Mansell	Williams	FW14	Renault	V10	59	gearbox	3	2
r	26	E Comas	Ligier	JS35	Lamborghini	V12	50	oil radiator fire/ spin	23	12
r	23	P Martini	Minardi	M191	Ferrari	V12	47	spin	20	10
r	8	M Blundell	Brabham	BT59Y	Yamaha	V12	34	engine	25	13
r	29	É Bernard	Lola	L91	Cosworth	V8	33	clutch hydraulic pipe	11	6
r	22	J J Lehto	Dallara	191	Judd	V10	22	alternator	19	10
r	33	A de Cesaris	Jordan	191	Cosworth	V8	20	electronics/ accident	13	7
r	4	S Modena	Tyrrell	020	Honda	V10	19	gear linkage	9	5
r	16	I Capelli	Leyton House	CG911	Ilmor	V10	16	engine	15	8
r	3	S Nakajima	Tyrrell	020	Honda	V10	12	spin	16	8
r	15	M Gugelmin	Leyton House	CG911	Ilmor	V10	9	driver unfit (burnt in warm-up)	8	4
r	17	G Tarquini	AGS	JH25	Cosworth	V8	0	accident	24	12
ns	30	A Suzuki	Lola	L91	Cosworth	V8		fuel pump on dummy grid	17	9
nq	10	A Caffi	Footwork	A11C	Porsche	V12				
nq	18	S Johansson	AGS	JH25	Cosworth	V8				
nq	9	M Alboreto	Footwork	A11C	Porsche	V12				
nq	12	J Bailey	Lotus	102B	Judd	V8				
npq	35	E van de Poele	Lamborghini	291	Lamborghini	V12				
npq	34	N Larini	Lamborghini	291	Lamborghini	V12				
npq	31	P Chaves	Coloni	C4	Cosworth	V8				
npq	14	O Grouillard	Fomet	FA1M-E	Cosworth	V8				

Winning speed: 187.110 km/h, 116.265 mph
Pole Position speed: 203.817 km/h, 126.646 mph (A Senna, 1 min:16.392 sec)
Fastest Lap speed: 193.570 km/h, 120.279 mph (N Mansell, 1 min:20.436 sec on lap 35)
Lap Leaders: A Senna 1-71 (71).

28 Apr 1991 — SAN MARINO: Imola (Round: 3) (Race: 503)

61 laps x 5.040 km, 3.132 miles = 307.440 km, 191.034 miles

POS.	NO.	DRIVER	CAR	MODEL	ENGINE		LAPS	TIME/REASON FOR RETIREMENT	GRID:POS	ROW
1	1	A Senna	McLaren	MP4/6	Honda	V12	61	1h 35m 14.750s	1	1
2	2	G Berger	McLaren	MP4/6	Honda	V12	61	1h 35m 16.425s	5	3
3	22	J J Lehto	Dallara	191	Judd	V10	60		16	8
4	23	P Martini	Minardi	M191	Ferrari	V12	59		9	5
5	11	M Häkkinen	Lotus	102B	Judd	V8	58		25	13
6	12	J Bailey	Lotus	102B	Judd	V8	58		26	13
7	25	T Boutsen	Ligier	JS35	Lamborghini	V12	58		24	12
8	8	M Blundell	Brabham	BT60Y	Yamaha	V12	58		23	12
9r	35	E van de Poele	Lamborghini	291	Lamborghini	V12	57	fuel pump	21	11
10	26	E Comas	Ligier	JS35	Lamborghini	V12	57		19	10
11	7	M Brundle	Brabham	BT60Y	Yamaha	V12	57		18	9
12r	15	M Gugelmin	Leyton House	CG911	Ilmor	V10	55	engine	15	8
13r	19	R Moreno	Benetton	B191	Cosworth	V8	54	gearbox/ engine	13	7
r	4	S Modena	Tyrrell	020	Honda	V10	41	transmission	6	3
r	33	A de Cesaris	Jordan	191	Cosworth	V8	37	gear linkage	11	6
r	32	B Gachot	Jordan	191	Cosworth	V8	37	spin/ suspension	12	6
r	16	I Capelli	Leyton House	CG911	Ilmor	V10	24	puncture/ spin	22	11
r	29	É Bernard	Lola	L91	Cosworth	V8	17	camshaft sensor/ engine	17	9
r	6	R Patrese	Williams	FW14	Renault	V10	17	electrics/ engine	2	1
r	3	S Nakajima	Tyrrell	020	Honda	V10	15	transmission	10	5
r	24	G Morbidelli	Minardi	M191	Ferrari	V12	10	gearbox	8	4
r	28	J Alesi	Ferrari	642	Ferrari	V12	2	spin	7	4
r	30	A Suzuki	Lola	L91	Cosworth	V8	2	spin	20	10
r	20	N Piquet	Benetton	B191	Cosworth	V8	1	spin	14	7
r	5	N Mansell	Williams	FW14	Renault	V10	0	gearbox/ accident	4	2
r	27	A Prost	Ferrari	642	Ferrari	V12	-1	spin	3	2
nq	17	G Tarquini	AGS	JH25	Cosworth	V8				
nq	18	F Barbazza	AGS	JH25	Cosworth	V8				
nq	10	A Caffi	Footwork	FA12	Porsche	V12				
nq	9	M Alboreto	Footwork	A11C	Porsche	V12				
npq	21	E Pirro	Dallara	191	Judd	V10				
npq	14	O Grouillard	Fomet	F1	Cosworth	V8				
npq	34	N Larini	Lamborghini	291	Lamborghini	V12				
npq	31	P Chaves	Coloni	C4	Cosworth	V8				

Winning speed: 193.671 km/h, 120.342 mph
Pole Position speed: 221.601 km/h, 137.696 mph (A Senna, 1 min:21.877 sec)
Fastest Lap speed: 209.682 km/h, 130.290 mph (G Berger, 1 min:26.531 sec on lap 55)
Lap Leaders: R Patrese 1-9 (9); A Senna 10-61 (52).

12 May 1991 MONACO: Monte Carlo (Round: 4) (Race: 504)

78 laps x 3.328 km, 2.068 miles = 259.584 km, 161.298 miles

POS.	NO.	DRIVER	CAR	MODEL	ENGINE		LAPS	TIME/REASON FOR RETIREMENT	GRID:POS	ROW
1	1	A Senna	McLaren	MP4/6	Honda	V12	78	1h 53m 02.334s	1	1
2	5	N Mansell	Williams	FW14	Renault	V10	78	1h 53m 20.682s	5	3
3	28	J Alesi	Ferrari	642	Ferrari	V12	78	1h 53m 49.789s	9	5
4	19	R Moreno	Benetton	B191	Cosworth	V8	77		8	4
5	27	A Prost	Ferrari	642	Ferrari	V12	77		7	4
6	21	E Pirro	Dallara	191	Judd	V10	77		12	6
7	25	T Boutsen	Ligier	JS35	Lamborghini	V12	76		16	8
8	32	B Gachot	Jordan	191	Cosworth	V8	76		24	12
9	29	É Bernard	Lola	L91	Cosworth	V8	76		21	11
10	26	E Comas	Ligier	JS35	Lamborghini	V12	76		23	12
11	22	J J Lehto	Dallara	191	Judd	V10	75		13	7
12	23	P Martini	Minardi	M191	Ferrari	V12	72		14	7
r	11	M Häkkinen	Lotus	102B	Judd	V8	64	oil leak/ fire	26	13
r	24	G Morbidelli	Minardi	M191	Ferrari	V12	49	gearbox	17	9
r	15	M Gugelmin	Leyton House	CG911	Ilmor	V10	43	throttle linkage	15	8
r	4	S Modena	Tyrrell	020	Honda	V10	42	engine	2	1
r	6	R Patrese	Williams	FW14	Renault	V10	42	accident	3	2
r	8	M Blundell	Brabham	BT60Y	Yamaha	V12	41	accident	22	11
r	9	M Alboreto	Footwork	FA12	Porsche	V12	39	engine	25	13
r	3	S Nakajima	Tyrrell	020	Honda	V10	35	spin	11	6
r	30	A Suzuki	Lola	L91	Cosworth	V8	24	brakes/ accident	19	10
r	33	A de Cesaris	Jordan	191	Cosworth	V8	21	throttle linkage	10	5
r	16	I Capelli	Leyton House	CG911	Ilmor	V10	12	brake fluid loss	18	9
r	17	G Tarquini	AGS	JH25	Cosworth	V8	9	gearbox	20	10
r	2	G Berger	McLaren	MP4/6	Honda	V12	9	accident	6	3
r	20	N Piquet	Benetton	B191	Cosworth	V8	0	accident/ rear suspension	4	2
nq	12	J Bailey	Lotus	102B	Judd	V8				
nq	18	F Barbazza	AGS	JH25	Cosworth	V8				
nq	10	A Caffi	Footwork	FA12	Porsche	V12		accident/ injury		
npq	34	N Larini	Lamborghini	291	Lamborghini	V12				
npq	35	E van de Poele	Lamborghini	291	Lamborghini	V12				
npq	31	P Chaves	Coloni	C4	Cosworth	V8				
npq	14	O Grouillard	Fomet	F1	Cosworth	V8				
exc	7	M Brundle	Brabham	BT60Y	Yamaha	V12		missed weight check		

Winning speed: 137.785 km/h, 85.615 mph
Pole Position speed: 149.119 km/h, 92.658 mph (A Senna, 1 min:20.344 sec)
Fastest Lap speed: 142.006 km/h, 88.239 mph (A Prost, 1 min:24.368 sec on lap 77)
Lap Leaders: A Senna 1-78 (78).

2 Jun 1991 CANADA: Montréal (Round: 5) (Race: 505)

69 laps x 4.430 km, 2.753 miles = 305.670 km, 189.935 miles

POS.	NO.	DRIVER	CAR	MODEL	ENGINE		LAPS	TIME/REASON FOR RETIREMENT	GRID:POS	ROW
1	20	N Piquet	Benetton	B191	Cosworth	V8	69	1h 38m 51.490s	8	4
2	4	S Modena	Tyrrell	020	Honda	V10	69	1h 39m 23.322s	9	5
3	6	R Patrese	Williams	FW14	Renault	V10	69	1h 39m 33.707s	1	1
4	33	A de Cesaris	Jordan	191	Cosworth	V8	69	1h 40m 11.700s	11	6
5	32	B Gachot	Jordan	191	Cosworth	V8	69	1h 40m 13.841s	14	7
6r	5	N Mansell	Williams	FW14	Renault	V10	68	gearbox/ engine	2	1
7	23	P Martini	Minardi	M191	Ferrari	V12	68		18	9
8	26	E Comas	Ligier	JS35	Lamborghini	V12	68		26	13
9	21	E Pirro	Dallara	191	Judd	V10	68		10	5
10	3	S Nakajima	Tyrrell	020	Honda	V10	67		12	6
r	15	M Gugelmin	Leyton House	CG911	Ilmor	V10	61	engine	23	12
r	22	J J Lehto	Dallara	191	Judd	V10	50	engine	17	9
r	10	S Johansson	Footwork	FA12	Porsche	V12	48	gearbox/ engine	25	13
r	16	I Capelli	Leyton House	CG911	Ilmor	V10	42	engine	13	7
r	28	J Alesi	Ferrari	642	Ferrari	V12	34	engine	7	4
r	29	É Bernard	Lola	L91	Cosworth	V8	29	transmission	19	10
r	27	A Prost	Ferrari	642	Ferrari	V12	27	gearbox	4	2
r	25	T Boutsen	Ligier	JS35	Lamborghini	V12	27	engine	16	8
r	1	A Senna	McLaren	MP4/6	Honda	V12	25	alternator	3	2
r	11	M Häkkinen	Lotus	102B	Judd	V8	21	spin	24	12
r	7	M Brundle	Brabham	BT60Y	Yamaha	V12	21	engine	20	10
r	24	G Morbidelli	Minardi	M191	Ferrari	V12	20	spin	15	8
r	19	R Moreno	Benetton	B191	Cosworth	V8	10	spin/ suspension	5	3
r	2	G Berger	McLaren	MP4/6	Honda	V12	4	electronics	6	3
r	30	A Suzuki	Lola	L91	Cosworth	V8	3	fuel line/ fire	22	11
r	9	M Alboreto	Footwork	FA12	Porsche	V12	2	throttle jammed/ engine	21	11
nq	18	F Barbazza	AGS	JH25	Cosworth	V8				
nq	17	G Tarquini	AGS	JH25	Cosworth	V8				
nq	8	M Blundell	Brabham	BT60Y	Yamaha	V12				
nq	12	J Herbert	Lotus	102B	Judd	V8				
npq	14	O Grouillard	Fomet	F1	Cosworth	V8				
npq	34	N Larini	Lamborghini	291	Lamborghini	V12				
npq	35	E van de Poele	Lamborghini	291	Lamborghini	V12				
npq	31	P Chaves	Coloni	C4	Cosworth	V8				

Winning speed: 185.520 km/h, 115.277 mph
Pole Position speed: 199.757 km/h, 124.123 mph (R Patrese, 1 min:19.837 sec)
Fastest Lap speed: 193.579 km/h, 120.284 mph (N Mansell, 1 min:22.385 sec on lap 65)
Lap Leaders: N Mansell 1-68 (68); N Piquet 69 (1).

16 Jun 1991 — MEXICO: Mexico City (Round: 6) (Race: 506)

67 laps x 4.421 km, 2.747 miles = 296.207 km, 184.054 miles

POS.	NO.	DRIVER	CAR	MODEL	ENGINE		LAPS	TIME/REASON FOR RETIREMENT	GRID:POS	ROW
1	6	R Patrese	Williams	FW14	Renault	V10	67	1h 29m 52.205s	1	1
2	5	N Mansell	Williams	FW14	Renault	V10	67	1h 29m 53.541s	2	1
3	1	A Senna	McLaren	MP4/6	Honda	V12	67	1h 30m 49.561s	3	2
4r	33	A de Cesaris	Jordan	191	Cosworth	V8	66	throttle potentiometer	11	6
5	19	R Moreno	Benetton	B191	Cosworth	V8	66		9	5
6	29	É Bernard	Lola	L91	Cosworth	V8	66		18	9
7	24	G Morbidelli	Minardi	M191	Ferrari	V12	66		23	12
8	25	T Boutsen	Ligier	JS35	Lamborghini	V12	65		14	7
9	11	M Häkkinen	Lotus	102B	Judd	V8	65		24	12
10	12	J Herbert	Lotus	102B	Judd	V8	65		25	13
11	4	S Modena	Tyrrell	020	Honda	V10	64		8	4
12	3	S Nakajima	Tyrrell	020	Honda	V10	64		13	7
r	8	M Blundell	Brabham	BT60Y	Yamaha	V12	54	engine	12	6
r	32	B Gachot	Jordan	191	Cosworth	V8	51	spin	20	10
r	30	A Suzuki	Lola	L91	Cosworth	V8	48	gearbox	19	10
r	20	N Piquet	Benetton	B191	Cosworth	V8	44	wheel bearing	6	3
r	28	J Alesi	Ferrari	642	Ferrari	V12	42	clutch	4	2
r	22	J J Lehto	Dallara	191	Judd	V10	30	engine	16	8
r	9	M Alboreto	Footwork	FA12	Porsche	V12	24	oil pressure	26	13
r	7	M Brundle	Brabham	BT60Y	Yamaha	V12	20	rear wheel lost	17	9
r	16	I Capelli	Leyton House	CG911	Ilmor	V10	19	engine	22	11
r	27	A Prost	Ferrari	642	Ferrari	V12	16	alternator	7	4
r	15	M Gugelmin	Leyton House	CG911	Ilmor	V10	15	engine	21	11
r	14	O Grouillard	Fomet	F1	Cosworth	V8	13	oil leak	10	5
r	2	G Berger	McLaren	MP4/6	Honda	V12	5	radiator/ engine	5	3
r	23	P Martini	Minardi	M191	Ferrari	V12	4	spin	15	8
nq	26	E Comas	Ligier	JS35	Lamborghini	V12				
nq	17	G Tarquini	AGS	JH25	Cosworth	V8				
nq	10	S Johansson	Footwork	FA12	Porsche	V12				
nq	18	F Barbazza	AGS	JH25	Cosworth	V8				
exc	34	N Larini	Lamborghini	291	Lamborghini	V12		rear wing infringement		
npq	35	E van de Poele	Lamborghini	291	Lamborghini	V12				
npq	31	P Chaves	Coloni	C4	Cosworth	V8				
npq	21	E Pirro	Dallara	191	Judd	V10				

Winning speed: 197.757 km/h, 122.880 mph
Pole Position speed: 207.515 km/h, 128.944 mph (R Patrese, 1 min:16.696 sec)
Fastest Lap speed: 207.267 km/h, 128.790 mph (N Mansell, 1 min:16.788 sec on lap 61)
Lap Leaders: N Mansell 1-14 (14); R Patrese 15-67 (53).

7 Jul 1991 — FRANCE: Magny-Cours (Round: 7) (Race: 507)

72 laps x 4.271 km, 2.654 miles = 307.512 km, 191.079 miles

POS.	NO.	DRIVER	CAR	MODEL	ENGINE		LAPS	TIME/REASON FOR RETIREMENT	GRID:POS	ROW
1	5	N Mansell	Williams	FW14	Renault	V10	72	1h 38m 00.056s	4	2
2	27	A Prost	Ferrari	643	Ferrari	V12	72	1h 38m 05.059s	2	1
3	1	A Senna	McLaren	MP4/6	Honda	V12	72	1h 38m 34.990s	3	2
4	28	J Alesi	Ferrari	643	Ferrari	V12	72	1h 38m 35.976s	6	3
5	6	R Patrese	Williams	FW14	Renault	V10	71		1	1
6	33	A de Cesaris	Jordan	191	Cosworth	V8	71		13	7
7	15	M Gugelmin	Leyton House	CG911	Ilmor	V10	70		9	5
8	20	N Piquet	Benetton	B191	Cosworth	V8	70		7	4
9	23	P Martini	Minardi	M191	Ferrari	V12	70		12	6
10	12	J Herbert	Lotus	102B	Judd	V8	70		20	10
11	26	E Comas	Ligier	JS35B	Lamborghini	V12	70		14	7
12	25	T Boutsen	Ligier	JS35B	Lamborghini	V12	69		16	8
r	19	R Moreno	Benetton	B191	Cosworth	V8	63	driver ill	8	4
r	4	S Modena	Tyrrell	020	Honda	V10	57	gearbox	11	6
r	14	O Grouillard	Fomet	F1	Cosworth	V8	47	oil leak	21	11
r	29	É Bernard	Lola	L91	Cosworth	V8	43	puncture	23	12
r	22	J J Lehto	Dallara	191	Judd	V10	39	puncture	26	13
r	8	M Blundell	Brabham	BT60Y	Yamaha	V12	36	accident	17	9
r	30	A Suzuki	Lola	L91	Cosworth	V8	32	clutch	22	11
r	9	M Alboreto	Footwork	FA12	Cosworth	V8	31	gearbox	25	13
r	7	M Brundle	Brabham	BT60Y	Yamaha	V12	21	gearbox	24	12
r	3	S Nakajima	Tyrrell	020	Honda	V10	12	spin	18	9
r	24	G Morbidelli	Minardi	M191	Ferrari	V12	8	accident	10	5
r	16	I Capelli	Leyton House	CG911	Ilmor	V10	7	spin	15	8
r	2	G Berger	McLaren	MP4/6	Honda	V12	6	engine	5	3
r	32	B Gachot	Jordan	191	Cosworth	V8	0	spin	19	10
nq	11	M Häkkinen	Lotus	102B	Judd	V8				
nq	18	F Barbazza	AGS	JH25B	Cosworth	V8				
nq	17	G Tarquini	AGS	JH25B	Cosworth	V8				
nq	10	S Johansson	Footwork	FA12	Cosworth	V8				
npq	21	E Pirro	Dallara	191	Judd	V10				
npq	34	N Larini	Lamborghini	291	Lamborghini	V12				
npq	35	E van de Poele	Lamborghini	291	Lamborghini	V12				
npq	31	P Chaves	Coloni	C4	Cosworth	V8				

Winning speed: 188.271 km/h, 116.986 mph
Pole Position speed: 206.221 km/h, 128.140 mph (R Patrese, 1 min:14.559 sec)
Fastest Lap speed: 194.215 km/h, 120.680 mph (N Mansell, 1 min:19.168 sec on lap 49)
Lap Leaders: A Prost 1-21,32-54 (44); N Mansell 22-31,55-72 (28).

14 Jul 1991 — BRITAIN: Silverstone (Round: 8) (Race: 508)

59 laps x 5.226 km, 3.247 miles = 308.334 km, 191.590 miles

POS.	NO.	DRIVER	CAR	MODEL	ENGINE		LAPS	TIME/REASON FOR RETIREMENT	GRID:POS	ROW
1	5	N Mansell	Williams	FW14	Renault	V10	59	1h 27m 35.479s	1	1
2	2	G Berger	McLaren	MP4/6	Honda	V12	59	1h 28m 17.772s	4	2
3	27	A Prost	Ferrari	643	Ferrari	V12	59	1h 28m 35.629s	5	3
4r	1	A Senna	McLaren	MP4/6	Honda	V12	58	out of fuel	2	1
5	20	N Piquet	Benetton	B191	Cosworth	V8	58		8	4
6	32	B Gachot	Jordan	191	Cosworth	V8	58		17	9
7	4	S Modena	Tyrrell	020	Honda	V10	58		10	5
8	3	S Nakajima	Tyrrell	020	Honda	V10	58		15	8
9	23	P Martini	Minardi	M191	Ferrari	V12	58		23	12
10	21	E Pirro	Dallara	191	Judd	V10	57		18	9
11	24	G Morbidelli	Minardi	M191	Ferrari	V12	57		20	10
12	11	M Häkkinen	Lotus	102B	Judd	V8	57		25	13
13	22	J J Lehto	Dallara	191	Judd	V10	56		11	6
14r	12	J Herbert	Lotus	102B	Judd	V8	55	engine	24	12
r	8	M Blundell	Brabham	BT60Y	Yamaha	V12	52	engine	12	6
r	33	A de Cesaris	Jordan	191	Cosworth	V8	41	suspension/ accident	13	7
r	28	J Alesi	Ferrari	643	Ferrari	V12	31	accident	6	3
r	30	A Suzuki	Lola	L91	Cosworth	V8	29	accident	22	11
r	25	T Boutsen	Ligier	JS35B	Lamborghini	V12	29	engine	19	10
r	7	M Brundle	Brabham	BT60Y	Yamaha	V12	28	throttle linkage	14	7
r	9	M Alboreto	Footwork	FA12	Cosworth	V8	25	gearbox	26	13
r	15	M Gugelmin	Leyton House	CG911	Ilmor	V10	24	chassis vibration/ driver cramp	9	5
r	19	R Moreno	Benetton	B191	Cosworth	V8	21	gearbox	7	4
r	29	É Bernard	Lola	L91	Cosworth	V8	21	crown wheel & pinion	21	11
r	16	I Capelli	Leyton House	CG911	Ilmor	V10	16	spin	16	8
r	6	R Patrese	Williams	FW14	Renault	V10	1	accident	3	2
nq	26	E Comas	Ligier	JS35B	Lamborghini	V12				
nq	10	S Johansson	Footwork	FA12	Cosworth	V8				
nq	18	F Barbazza	AGS	JH25B	Cosworth	V8				
nq	17	G Tarquini	AGS	JH25B	Cosworth	V8				
npq	14	O Grouillard	Fomet	F1	Cosworth	V8				
npq	34	N Larini	Lamborghini	291	Lamborghini	V12				
npq	35	E van de Poele	Lamborghini	291	Lamborghini	V12				
npq	31	P Chaves	Coloni	C4	Cosworth	V8				

Winning speed: 211.209 km/h, 131.239 mph
Pole Position speed: 232.442 km/h, 144.433 mph (N Mansell, 1 min:20.939 sec)
Fastest Lap speed: 217.803 km/h, 135.336 mph (N Mansell, 1 min:26.379 sec on lap 43)
Lap Leaders: N Mansell 1-59 (59).

28 Jul 1991 — GERMANY: Hockenheim (Round: 9) (Race: 509)

45 laps x 6.802 km, 4.227 miles = 306.090 km, 190.196 miles

POS.	NO.	DRIVER	CAR	MODEL	ENGINE		LAPS	TIME/REASON FOR RETIREMENT	GRID:POS	ROW
1	5	N Mansell	Williams	FW14	Renault	V10	45	1h 19m 29.661s	1	1
2	6	R Patrese	Williams	FW14	Renault	V10	45	1h 19m 43.440s	4	2
3	28	J Alesi	Ferrari	643	Ferrari	V12	45	1h 19m 47.279s	6	3
4	2	G Berger	McLaren	MP4/6	Honda	V12	45	1h 20m 02.312s	3	2
5	33	A de Cesaris	Jordan	191	Cosworth	V8	45	1h 20m 47.198s	7	4
6	32	B Gachot	Jordan	191	Cosworth	V8	45	1h 21m 10.266s	11	6
7r	1	A Senna	McLaren	MP4/6	Honda	V12	44	out of fuel	2	1
8	19	R Moreno	Benetton	B191	Cosworth	V8	44		9	5
9	25	T Boutsen	Ligier	JS35B	Lamborghini	V12	44		17	9
10	21	E Pirro	Dallara	191	Judd	V10	44		18	9
11	7	M Brundle	Brabham	BT60Y	Yamaha	V12	43		15	8
12	8	M Blundell	Brabham	BT60Y	Yamaha	V12	43		21	11
13	4	S Modena	Tyrrell	020	Honda	V10	41		14	7
r	27	A Prost	Ferrari	643	Ferrari	V12	37	accident	5	3
r	16	I Capelli	Leyton House	CG911	Ilmor	V10	36	misfire	12	6
r	22	J J Lehto	Dallara	191	Judd	V10	35	engine	20	10
r	20	N Piquet	Benetton	B191	Cosworth	V8	27	gearbox	8	4
r	3	S Nakajima	Tyrrell	020	Honda	V10	26	gearbox	13	7
r	26	E Comas	Ligier	JS35B	Lamborghini	V12	22	oil pressure	26	13
r	15	M Gugelmin	Leyton House	CG911	Ilmor	V10	21	gearbox	16	8
r	11	M Häkkinen	Lotus	102B	Judd	V8	19	engine	23	12
r	30	A Suzuki	Lola	L91	Cosworth	V8	15	engine	22	11
r	24	G Morbidelli	Minardi	M191	Ferrari	V12	14	differential	19	10
r	23	P Martini	Minardi	M191	Ferrari	V12	11	engine/ spin	10	5
r	29	É Bernard	Lola	L91	Cosworth	V8	9	crown wheel & pinion	25	13
r	34	N Larini	Lamborghini	291	Lamborghini	V12	0	spin	24	12
nq	9	M Alboreto	Footwork	FA12	Cosworth	V8				
nq	12	M Bartels	Lotus	102B	Judd	V8				
nq	17	G Tarquini	AGS	JH25B	Cosworth	V8				
nq	35	E van de Poele	Lamborghini	291	Lamborghini	V12				
npq	14	O Grouillard	Fomet	F1	Cosworth	V8				
npq	10	A Caffi	Footwork	FA12	Cosworth	V8				
npq	18	F Barbazza	AGS	JH25B	Cosworth	V8				
npq	31	P Chaves	Coloni	C4	Cosworth	V8				

Winning speed: 231.028 km/h, 143.554 mph
Pole Position speed: 252.219 km/h, 156.722 mph (N Mansell, 1 min:37.087 sec)
Fastest Lap speed: 236.434 km/h, 146.913 mph (R Patrese, 1 min:43.569 sec on lap 35)
Lap Leaders: N Mansell 1-18,21-45 (43); J Alesi 19-20 (2).

11 Aug 1991 — HUNGARY: Hungaroring (Round:10) (Race: 510)

77 laps x 3.968 km, 2.466 miles = 305.536 km, 189.851 miles

POS.	NO.	DRIVER	CAR	MODEL	ENGINE		LAPS	TIME/REASON FOR RETIREMENT	GRID:POS	ROW
1	1	A Senna	McLaren	MP4/6	Honda	V12	77	1h 49m 12.796s	1	1
2	5	N Mansell	Williams	FW14	Renault	V10	77	1h 49m 17.395s	3	2
3	6	R Patrese	Williams	FW14	Renault	V10	77	1h 49m 28.390s	2	1
4	2	G Berger	McLaren	MP4/6	Honda	V12	77	1h 49m 34.652s	5	3
5	28	J Alesi	Ferrari	643	Ferrari	V12	77	1h 49m 44.185s	6	3
6	16	I Capelli	Leyton House	CG911	Ilmor	V10	76		9	5
7	33	A de Cesaris	Jordan	191	Cosworth	V8	76		17	9
8	19	R Moreno	Benetton	B191	Cosworth	V8	76		15	8
9	32	B Gachot	Jordan	191	Cosworth	V8	75		16	8
10	26	E Comas	Ligier	JS35B	Lamborghini	V12	75		25	13
11	15	M Gugelmin	Leyton House	CG911	Ilmor	V10	75		13	7
12	4	S Modena	Tyrrell	020	Honda	V10	75		8	4
13	24	G Morbidelli	Minardi	M191	Ferrari	V12	75		23	12
14	11	M Häkkinen	Lotus	102B	Judd	V8	74		26	13
15	3	S Nakajima	Tyrrell	020	Honda	V10	74		14	7
16	34	N Larini	Lamborghini	291	Lamborghini	V12	74		24	12
17r	25	T Boutsen	Ligier	JS35B	Lamborghini	V12	71	engine	19	10
r	23	P Martini	Minardi	M191	Ferrari	V12	65	engine	18	9
r	8	M Blundell	Brabham	BT60Y	Yamaha	V12	62	spin	20	10
r	7	M Brundle	Brabham	BT60Y	Yamaha	V12	59	driver discomfort (cramp)	10	5
r	22	J J Lehto	Dallara	191	Judd	V10	49	oil pressure	12	6
r	20	N Piquet	Benetton	B191	Cosworth	V8	38	gearbox	11	6
r	29	É Bernard	Lola	L91	Cosworth	V8	38	engine	21	11
r	30	A Suzuki	Lola	L91	Cosworth	V8	38	engine	22	11
r	21	E Pirro	Dallara	191	Judd	V10	37	oil pressure	7	4
r	27	A Prost	Ferrari	643	Ferrari	V12	28	engine	4	2
nq	14	O Grouillard	Fomet	F1	Cosworth	V8				
nq	9	M Alboreto	Footwork	FA12	Cosworth	V8				
nq	35	E van de Poele	Lamborghini	291	Lamborghini	V12				
nq	12	M Bartels	Lotus	102B	Judd	V8				
npq	17	G Tarquini	AGS	JH25B	Cosworth	V8				
npq	10	A Caffi	Footwork	FA12	Cosworth	V8				
npq	18	F Barbazza	AGS	JH25B	Cosworth	V8				
npq	31	P Chaves	Coloni	C4	Cosworth	V8				

Winning speed: 167.857 km/h, 104.301 mph
Pole Position speed: 187.595 km/h, 116.566 mph (A Senna, 1 min:16.147 sec)
Fastest Lap speed: 175.173 km/h, 108.847 mph (B Gachot, 1 min:21.547 sec on lap 71)
Lap Leaders: A Senna 1-77 (77).

25 Aug 1991 — BELGIUM: Spa-Francorchamps (Round:11) (Race: 511)

44 laps x 6.940 km, 4.312 miles = 305.360 km, 189.742 miles

POS.	NO.	DRIVER	CAR	MODEL	ENGINE		LAPS	TIME/REASON FOR RETIREMENT	GRID:POS	ROW
1	1	A Senna	McLaren	MP4/6	Honda	V12	44	1h 27m 17.669s	1	1
2	2	G Berger	McLaren	MP4/6	Honda	V12	44	1h 27m 19.570s	4	2
3	20	N Piquet	Benetton	B191	Cosworth	V8	44	1h 27m 49.845s	6	3
4	19	R Moreno	Benetton	B191	Cosworth	V8	44	1h 27m 54.979s	8	4
5	6	R Patrese	Williams	FW14	Renault	V10	44	1h 28m 14.856s	17	9
6	8	M Blundell	Brabham	BT60Y	Yamaha	V12	44	1h 28m 57.704s	13	7
7	12	J Herbert	Lotus	102B	Judd	V8	44	1h 29m 02.268s	21	11
8	21	E Pirro	Dallara	191	Judd	V10	43		25	13
9	7	M Brundle	Brabham	BT60Y	Yamaha	V12	43		16	8
10	14	O Grouillard	Fomet	F1	Cosworth	V8	43		23	12
11	25	T Boutsen	Ligier	JS35B	Lamborghini	V12	43		18	9
12	23	P Martini	Minardi	M191	Ferrari	V12	42		9	5
13r	33	A de Cesaris	Jordan	191	Cosworth	V8	41	radiator/ engine	11	6
r	4	S Modena	Tyrrell	020	Honda	V10	33	oil leak/ fire	10	5
r	22	J J Lehto	Dallara	191	Judd	V10	33	engine	14	7
r	28	J Alesi	Ferrari	643	Ferrari	V12	30	engine	5	3
r	24	G Morbidelli	Minardi	M191	Ferrari	V12	29	clutch	19	10
r	11	M Häkkinen	Lotus	102B	Judd	V8	25	engine	24	12
r	26	E Comas	Ligier	JS35B	Lamborghini	V12	25	engine	26	13
r	5	N Mansell	Williams	FW14	Renault	V10	22	voltage regulator	3	2
r	29	É Bernard	Lola	L91	Cosworth	V8	21	gearbox	20	10
r	16	I Capelli	Leyton House	CG911	Ilmor	V10	13	engine	12	6
r	3	S Nakajima	Tyrrell	020	Honda	V10	7	accident	22	11
r	27	A Prost	Ferrari	643	Ferrari	V12	2	engine	2	1
r	15	M Gugelmin	Leyton House	CG911	Ilmor	V10	1	engine	15	8
r	32	M Schumacher	Jordan	191	Cosworth	V8	0	clutch	7	4
nq	30	A Suzuki	Lola	L91	Cosworth	V8				
nq	34	N Larini	Lamborghini	291	Lamborghini	V12				
nq	10	A Caffi	Footwork	FA12	Cosworth	V8				
nq	35	E van de Poele	Lamborghini	291	Lamborghini	V12				
npq	9	M Alboreto	Footwork	FA12	Cosworth	V8				
npq	17	G Tarquini	AGS	JH25B	Cosworth	V8				
npq	31	P Chaves	Coloni	C4	Cosworth	V8				
npq	18	F Barbazza	AGS	JH25B	Cosworth	V8				

Winning speed: 209.883 km/h, 130.415 mph
Pole Position speed: 231.739 km/h, 143.996 mph (A Senna, 1 min:47.811 sec)
Fastest Lap speed: 216.948 km/h, 134.806 mph (R Moreno, 1 min:55.161 sec on lap 40)
Lap Leaders: A Senna 1-14,31-44 (28); N Mansell 15-16,18-21 (6); N Piquet 17 (1); J Alesi 22-30 (9).

8 Sep 1991 — ITALY: Monza (Round:12) (Race: 512)

53 laps x 5.800 km, 3.604 miles = 307.400 km, 191.010 miles

POS.	NO.	DRIVER	CAR	MODEL	ENGINE		LAPS	TIME/REASON FOR RETIREMENT	GRID:POS	ROW
1	5	N Mansell	Williams	FW14	Renault	V10	53	1h 17m 54.319s	2	1
2	1	A Senna	McLaren	MP4/6	Honda	V12	53	1h 18m 10.581s	1	1
3	27	A Prost	Ferrari	643	Ferrari	V12	53	1h 18m 11.148s	5	3
4	2	G Berger	McLaren	MP4/6	Honda	V12	53	1h 18m 22.038s	3	2
5	19	M Schumacher	Benetton	B191	Cosworth	V8	53	1h 18m 28.782s	7	4
6	20	N Piquet	Benetton	B191	Cosworth	V8	53	1h 18m 39.919s	8	4
7	33	A de Cesaris	Jordan	191	Cosworth	V8	53	1h 18m 45.455s	14	7
8	16	I Capelli	Leyton House	CG911	Ilmor	V10	53	1h 19m 09.338s	12	6
9	24	G Morbidelli	Minardi	M191	Ferrari	V12	52		17	9
10	21	E Pirro	Dallara	191	Judd	V10	52		16	8
11	26	E Comas	Ligier	JS35B	Lamborghini	V12	52		22	11
12	8	M Blundell	Brabham	BT60Y	Yamaha	V12	52		11	6
13	7	M Brundle	Brabham	BT60Y	Yamaha	V12	52		19	10
14	11	M Häkkinen	Lotus	102B	Judd	V8	49		25	13
15	15	M Gugelmin	Leyton House	CG911	Ilmor	V10	49		18	9
16	34	N Larini	Lamborghini	291	Lamborghini	V12	48		23	12
r	14	O Grouillard	Fomet	F1	Cosworth	V8	46	gearbox/ engine	26	13
r	22	J J Lehto	Dallara	191	Judd	V10	35	puncture/ suspension	20	10
r	4	S Modena	Tyrrell	020	Honda	V10	32	engine	13	7
r	28	J Alesi	Ferrari	643	Ferrari	V12	29	engine	6	3
r	6	R Patrese	Williams	FW14	Renault	V10	27	gearbox/ clutch	4	2
r	3	S Nakajima	Tyrrell	020	Honda	V10	24	throttle jammed	15	8
r	29	É Bernard	Lola	L91	Cosworth	V8	21	engine	24	12
r	23	P Martini	Minardi	M191	Ferrari	V12	8	brakes/ spin	10	5
r	32	R Moreno	Jordan	191	Cosworth	V8	2	brakes/ spin	9	5
r	25	T Boutsen	Ligier	JS35B	Lamborghini	V12	1	spin	21	11
nq	9	M Alboreto	Footwork	FA12	Cosworth	V8				
nq	12	M Bartels	Lotus	102B	Judd	V8				
nq	35	E van de Poele	Lamborghini	291	Lamborghini	V12				
nq	30	A Suzuki	Lola	L91	Cosworth	V8				
npq	18	F Barbazza	AGS	JH25B	Cosworth	V8				
npq	17	G Tarquini	AGS	JH27	Cosworth	V8				
npq	10	A Caffi	Footwork	FA12	Cosworth	V8				
npq	31	P Chaves	Coloni	C4	Cosworth	V8				

Winning speed: 236.749 km/h, 147.109 mph
Pole Position speed: 257.415 km/h, 159.951 mph (A Senna, 1 min:21.114 sec)
Fastest Lap speed: 242.619 km/h, 150.756 mph (A Senna, 1 min:26.061 sec on lap 41)
Lap Leaders: A Senna 1-25,27-33 (32); R Patrese 26 (1); N Mansell 34-53 (20).

22 Sep 1991 — PORTUGAL: Estoril (Round:13) (Race: 513)

71 laps x 4.350 km, 2.703 miles = 308.850 km, 191.910 miles

POS.	NO.	DRIVER	CAR	MODEL	ENGINE		LAPS	TIME/REASON FOR RETIREMENT	GRID:POS	ROW
1	6	R Patrese	Williams	FW14	Renault	V10	71	1h 35m 42.304s	1	1
2	1	A Senna	McLaren	MP4/6	Honda	V12	71	1h 36m 03.245s	3	2
3	28	J Alesi	Ferrari	643	Ferrari	V12	71	1h 36m 35.858s	6	3
4	23	P Martini	Minardi	M191	Ferrari	V12	71	1h 36m 45.802s	8	4
5	20	N Piquet	Benetton	B191	Cosworth	V8	71	1h 36m 52.337s	11	6
6	19	M Schumacher	Benetton	B191	Cosworth	V8	71	1h 36m 58.886s	10	5
7	15	M Gugelmin	Leyton House	CG911	Ilmor	V10	70		7	4
8	33	A de Cesaris	Jordan	191	Cosworth	V8	70		14	7
9	24	G Morbidelli	Minardi	M191	Ferrari	V12	70		13	7
10	32	R Moreno	Jordan	191	Cosworth	V8	70		16	8
11	26	E Comas	Ligier	JS35B	Lamborghini	V12	70		23	12
12	7	M Brundle	Brabham	BT60Y	Yamaha	V12	69		19	10
13	3	S Nakajima	Tyrrell	020	Honda	V10	68		21	11
14	11	M Häkkinen	Lotus	102B	Judd	V8	68		26	13
15	9	M Alboreto	Footwork	FA12	Cosworth	V8	68		24	12
16	25	T Boutsen	Ligier	JS35B	Lamborghini	V12	68		20	10
17r	16	I Capelli	Leyton House	CG911	Ilmor	V10	64	nose cone	9	5
r	4	S Modena	Tyrrell	020	Honda	V10	56	visor into air intake/ engine	12	6
r/dq	5	N Mansell	Williams	FW14	Renault	V10	51	wheel change outside pit/ accid.	4	2
r	30	A Suzuki	Lola	L91	Cosworth	V8	40	gearbox	25	13
r	27	A Prost	Ferrari	643	Ferrari	V12	39	engine	5	3
r	2	G Berger	McLaren	MP4/6	Honda	V12	37	engine	2	1
r	21	E Pirro	Dallara	191	Judd	V10	18	engine	17	9
r	22	J J Lehto	Dallara	191	Judd	V10	14	gear linkage	18	9
r	8	M Blundell	Brabham	BT60Y	Yamaha	V12	12	rear suspension	15	8
r	12	J Herbert	Lotus	102B	Judd	V8	1	engine/ clutch	22	11
nq	29	É Bernard	Lola	L91	Cosworth	V8				
nq	17	G Tarquini	AGS	JH27	Cosworth	V8				
nq	34	N Larini	Lamborghini	291	Lamborghini	V12				
nq	35	E van de Poele	Lamborghini	291	Lamborghini	V12				
npq	18	F Barbazza	AGS	JH27	Cosworth	V8				
npq	14	O Grouillard	Fomet	F1	Cosworth	V8				
npq	10	A Caffi	Footwork	FA12	Cosworth	V8				
npq	31	P Chaves	Coloni	C4	Cosworth	V8				

Winning speed: 193.626 km/h, 120.314 mph
Pole Position speed: 214.518 km/h, 133.295 mph (R Patrese, 1 min:13.001 sec)
Fastest Lap speed: 200.310 km/h, 124.467 mph (N Mansell, 1 min:18.179 sec on lap 36)
Lap Leaders: R Patrese 1-17,30-71 (59); N Mansell 18-29 (12).

Although N Mansell was disqualified, the authorities appeared to forget to withdraw his fastest lap. Second fastest was set by R Patrese on lap 38 (1m 18.350s, 199.872 km/h, 124.195 mph).

29 Sep 1991 — SPAIN: Montmeló — (Round:14) (Race: 514)

65 laps x 4.747 km, 2.950 miles = 308.555 km, 191.727 miles

POS.	NO.	DRIVER	CAR	MODEL	ENGINE		LAPS	TIME/REASON FOR RETIREMENT	GRID:POS	ROW
1	5	N Mansell	Williams	FW14	Renault	V10	65	1h 38m 41.541s	2	1
2	27	A Prost	Ferrari	643	Ferrari	V12	65	1h 38m 52.872s	6	3
3	6	R Patrese	Williams	FW14	Renault	V10	65	1h 38m 57.450s	4	2
4	28	J Alesi	Ferrari	643	Ferrari	V12	65	1h 39m 04.313s	7	4
5	1	A Senna	McLaren	MP4/6	Honda	V12	65	1h 39m 43.943s	3	2
6	19	M Schumacher	Benetton	B191	Cosworth	V8	65	1h 40m 01.009s	5	3
7	15	M Gugelmin	Leyton House	CG911	Ilmor	V10	64		13	7
8	22	J J Lehto	Dallara	191	Judd	V10	64		15	8
9	32	A Zanardi	Jordan	191	Cosworth	V8	64		20	10
10	7	M Brundle	Brabham	BT60Y	Yamaha	V12	63		11	6
11	20	N Piquet	Benetton	B191	Cosworth	V8	63		10	5
12	14	G Tarquini	Fomet	F1	Cosworth	V8	63		22	11
13	23	P Martini	Minardi	M191	Ferrari	V12	63		19	10
14r	24	G Morbidelli	Minardi	M191	Ferrari	V12	62	accident	16	8
15	21	E Pirro	Dallara	191	Judd	V10	62		9	5
16	4	S Modena	Tyrrell	020	Honda	V10	62		14	7
17	3	S Nakajima	Tyrrell	020	Honda	V10	62		18	9
r	8	M Blundell	Brabham	BT60Y	Yamaha	V12	49	engine	12	6
r	26	E Comas	Ligier	JS35B	Lamborghini	V12	36	electronics	25	13
r	2	G Berger	McLaren	MP4/6	Honda	V12	33	electrics	1	1
r	9	M Alboreto	Footwork	FA12	Cosworth	V8	23	engine	24	12
r	33	A de Cesaris	Jordan	191	Cosworth	V8	22	electrics	17	9
r	11	M Häkkinen	Lotus	102B	Judd	V8	5	accident	21	11
r	16	I Capelli	Leyton House	CG911	Ilmor	V10	1	accident	8	4
r	29	É Bernard	Lola	L91	Cosworth	V8	0	accident	23	12
r	25	T Boutsen	Ligier	JS35B	Lamborghini	V12	0	accident	26	13
nq	30	A Suzuki	Lola	L91	Cosworth	V8				
nq	34	N Larini	Lamborghini	291	Lamborghini	V12				
nq	12	M Bartels	Lotus	102B	Judd	V8				
nq	35	E van de Poele	Lamborghini	291	Lamborghini	V12				
npq	10	A Caffi	Footwork	FA12	Cosworth	V8				
npq	18	F Barbazza	AGS	JH27	Cosworth	V8				
npq	17	O Grouillard	AGS	JH27	Cosworth	V8				

Winning speed: 187.586 km/h, 116.561 mph
Pole Position speed: 217.003 km/h, 134.839 mph (G Berger, 1 min:18.751 sec)
Fastest Lap speed: 206.299 km/h, 128.188 mph (R Patrese, 1 min:22.837 sec on lap 63)
Lap Leaders: G Berger 1-8,12-20 (17); N Mansell 9,21-65 (46); R Patrese 10 (1); A Senna 11 (1).

20 Oct 1991 — JAPAN: Suzuka — (Round:15) (Race: 515)

53 laps x 5.864 km, 3.644 miles = 310.792 km, 193.117 miles

POS.	NO.	DRIVER	CAR	MODEL	ENGINE		LAPS	TIME/REASON FOR RETIREMENT	GRID:POS	ROW
1	2	G Berger	McLaren	MP4/6	Honda	V12	53	1h 32m 10.695s	1	1
2	1	A Senna	McLaren	MP4/6	Honda	V12	53	1h 32m 11.039s	2	1
3	6	R Patrese	Williams	FW14	Renault	V10	53	1h 33m 07.426s	5	3
4	27	A Prost	Ferrari	643	Ferrari	V12	53	1h 33m 31.456s	4	2
5	7	M Brundle	Brabham	BT60Y	Yamaha	V12	52		19	10
6	4	S Modena	Tyrrell	020	Honda	V10	52		14	7
7	20	N Piquet	Benetton	B191	Cosworth	V8	52		10	5
8	15	M Gugelmin	Leyton House	CG911	Ilmor	V10	52		18	9
9	25	T Boutsen	Ligier	JS35B	Lamborghini	V12	52		17	9
10	10	A Caffi	Footwork	FA12	Cosworth	V8	51		26	13
11	14	G Tarquini	Fomet	F1	Cosworth	V8	50		24	12
r	26	E Comas	Ligier	JS35B	Lamborghini	V12	41	alternator	20	10
r	23	P Martini	Minardi	M191	Ferrari	V12	39	clutch	7	4
r	19	M Schumacher	Benetton	B191	Cosworth	V8	34	engine	9	5
r	12	J Herbert	Lotus	102B	Judd	V8	31	earth wire/ engine	23	12
r	3	S Nakajima	Tyrrell	020	Honda	V10	30	suspension/ accident	15	8
r	30	A Suzuki	Lola	L91	Cosworth	V8	26	electrics	25	13
r	24	G Morbidelli	Minardi	M191	Ferrari	V12	15	wheel bearing	8	4
r	5	N Mansell	Williams	FW14	Renault	V10	9	brakes/ spin	3	2
r	32	A Zanardi	Jordan	191	Cosworth	V8	7	gearbox	13	7
r	11	M Häkkinen	Lotus	102B	Judd	V8	4	spin	21	11
r	33	A de Cesaris	Jordan	191	Cosworth	V8	1	accident	11	6
r	22	J J Lehto	Dallara	191	Judd	V10	1	accident	12	6
r	21	E Pirro	Dallara	191	Judd	V10	1	accident	16	8
r	16	K Wendlinger	Leyton House	CG911	Ilmor	V10	1	accident	22	11
r	28	J Alesi	Ferrari	643	Ferrari	V12	0	engine	6	3
nq	9	M Alboreto	Footwork	FA12	Cosworth	V8				
nq	34	N Larini	Lamborghini	291	Lamborghini	V12				
nq	35	E van de Poele	Lamborghini	291	Lamborghini	V12				
nq	29	É Bernard	Lola	L91	Cosworth	V8		accident/ injury		
npq	8	M Blundell	Brabham	BT60Y	Yamaha	V12				
npq	31	N Hattori	Coloni	C4	Cosworth	V8				

Winning speed: 202.298 km/h, 125.702 mph
Pole Position speed: 222.919 km/h, 138.515 mph (G Berger, 1 min:34.700 sec)
Fastest Lap speed: 207.919 km/h, 129.195 mph (A Senna, 1 min:41.532 sec on lap 39)
Lap Leaders: G Berger 1-17,53 (18); A Senna 18-21,24-52 (33); R Patrese 22-23 (2).

3 Nov 1991 | **AUSTRALIA: Adelaide** | **(Round:16) (Race: 516)**

14 laps x 3.780 km, 2.349 miles = 52.920 km, 32.883 miles

POS.	NO.	DRIVER	CAR	MODEL	ENGINE		LAPS	TIME/REASON FOR RETIREMENT	GRID:POS	ROW
1	1	A Senna	McLaren	MP4/6	Honda	V12	14	24m 34.899s	1	1
2	5	N Mansell	Williams	FW14	Renault	V10	14	24m 36.158s	3	2
3	2	G Berger	McLaren	MP4/6	Honda	V12	14	24m 40.019s	2	1
4	20	N Piquet	Benetton	B191	Cosworth	V8	14	25m 05.002s	5	3
5	6	R Patrese	Williams	FW14	Renault	V10	14	25m 25.436s	4	2
6	27	G Morbidelli	Ferrari	643	Ferrari	V12	14	25m 25.968s	8	4
7	21	E Pirro	Dallara	191	Judd	V10	14	25m 27.260s	13	7
8	33	A de Cesaris	Jordan	191	Cosworth	V8	14	25m 35.330s	12	6
9	32	A Zanardi	Jordan	191	Cosworth	V8	14	25m 50.466s	16	8
10	4	S Modena	Tyrrell	020	Honda	V10	14	25m 55.269s	9	5
11	12	J Herbert	Lotus	102B	Judd	V8	14	25m 56.972s	21	11
12	22	J J Lehto	Dallara	191	Judd	V10	14	26m 13.418s	11	6
13	9	M Alboreto	Footwork	FA12	Cosworth	V8	14	26m 14.202s	15	8
14r	15	M Gugelmin	Leyton House	CG911	Ilmor	V10	13	accident in pit lane	14	7
15	10	A Caffi	Footwork	FA12	Cosworth	V8	13		23	12
16	24	R Moreno	Minardi	M191	Ferrari	V12	13		18	9
17	8	M Blundell	Brabham	BT60Y	Yamaha	V12	13		17	9
18	26	E Comas	Ligier	JS35B	Lamborghini	V12	13		22	11
19	11	M Häkkinen	Lotus	102B	Judd	V8	13		25	13
20	16	K Wendlinger	Leyton House	CG911	Ilmor	V10	12		26	13
r	23	P Martini	Minardi	M191	Ferrari	V12	8	accident	10	5
r	19	M Schumacher	Benetton	B191	Cosworth	V8	5	accident	6	3
r	28	J Alesi	Ferrari	643	Ferrari	V12	5	accident	7	4
r	34	N Larini	Lamborghini	291	Lamborghini	V12	5	accident	19	10
r	25	T Boutsen	Ligier	JS35B	Lamborghini	V12	5	accident	20	10
r	3	S Nakajima	Tyrrell	020	Honda	V10	4	accident	24	12
nq	30	A Suzuki	Lola	L91	Cosworth	V8				
nq	7	M Brundle	Brabham	BT60Y	Yamaha	V12				
nq	35	E van de Poele	Lamborghini	291	Lamborghini	V12				
nq	29	B Gachot	Lola	L91	Cosworth	V8				
npq	14	G Tarquini	Fomet	F1	Cosworth	V8				
npq	31	N Hattori	Coloni	C4	Cosworth	V8				

Winning speed: 129.170 km/h, 80.262 mph
Pole Position speed: 183.790 km/h, 114.202 mph (A Senna, 1 min:14.041 sec)
Fastest Lap speed: 134.545 km/h, 83.602 mph (G Berger, 1 min:41.141 sec on lap 14)
Lap Leaders: A Senna 1-14 (14).

Scheduled for 81 laps, but stopped early, because of rain. Half points awarded.

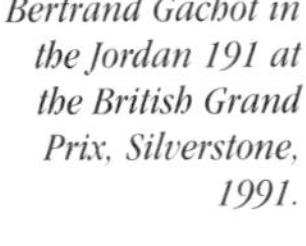

Bertrand Gachot in the Jordan 191 at the British Grand Prix, Silverstone, 1991.

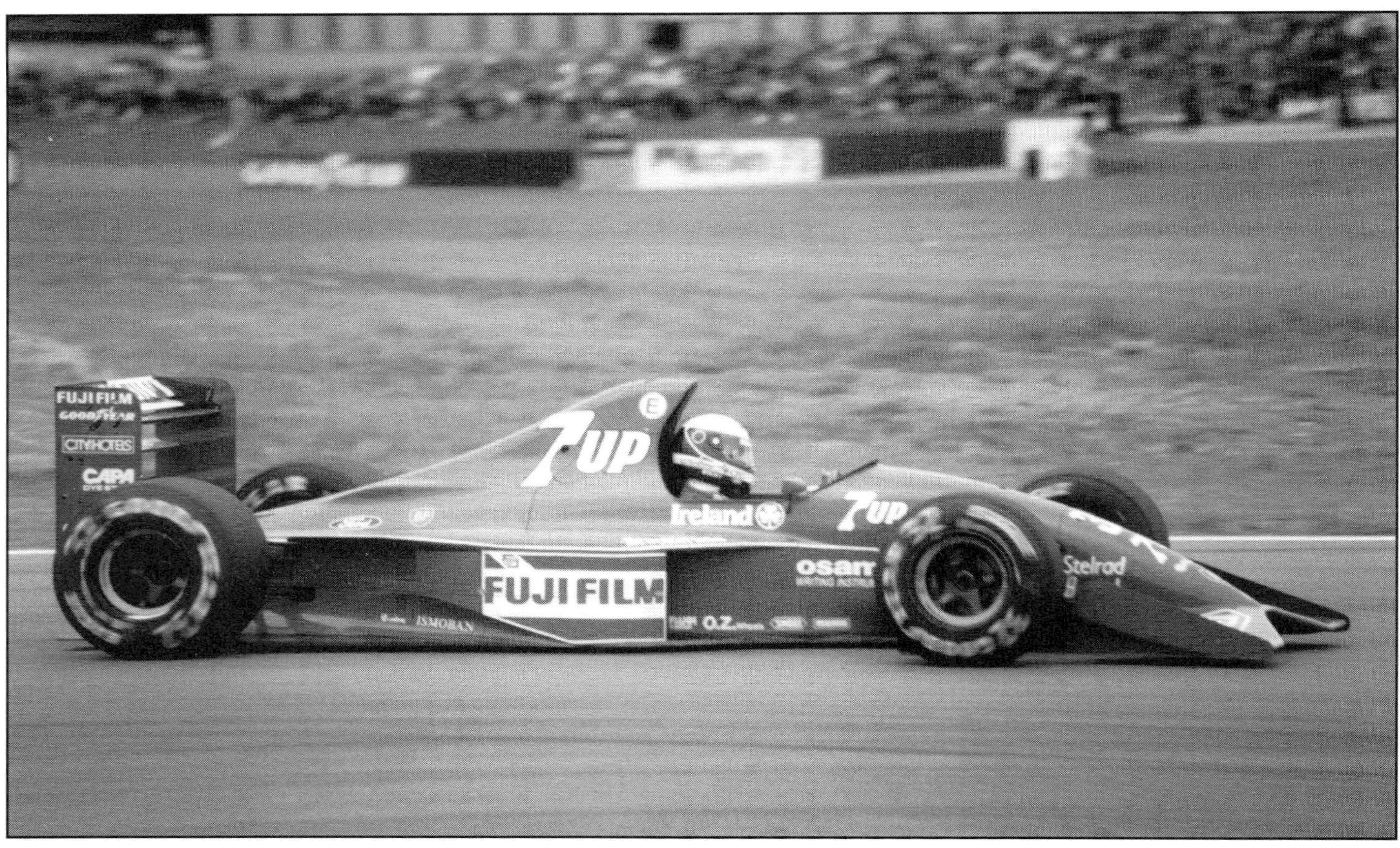

Lap Leaders 1991

POS	DRIVER	CAR-ENGINE	GPS	LAPS	KM	MILES
1	A Senna	McLaren-Honda	10	467	2,066.8	1,284.2
2	N Mansell	Williams-Renault	9	296	1,511.7	939.4
3	R Patrese	Williams-Renault	6	125	558.6	347.1
4	A Prost	Ferrari	1	44	187.9	116.8
5	G Berger	McLaren-Honda	2	35	186.3	115.7
6	J Alesi	Ferrari	2	11	76.1	47.3
7	N Piquet	Benetton-Cosworth	2	2	11.4	7.1
			16	**980**	**4,598.7**	**2,857.5**

Driver Points 1991

		USA	BR	RSM	MC	CDN	MEX	F	GB	D	H	B	I	P	E	J	AUS	TOTAL
1	A Senna	10	10	10	10	-	4	4	3	-	10	10	6	6	2	6	5	96
2	N Mansell	-	-	-	6	1	6	10	10	10	6	-	10	-	10	-	3	72
3	R Patrese	-	6	-	-	4	10	2	-	6	4	2	-	10	4	4	1	53
4	G Berger	-	4	6	-	-	-	-	6	3	3	6	3	-	-	10	2	43
5	A Prost	6	3	-	2	-	-	6	4	-	-	-	4	-	6	3	-	34
6	N Piquet	4	2	-	-	10	-	-	2	-	-	4	1	2	-	-	1.5	26.5
7	J Alesi	-	1	-	4	-	-	3	-	4	2	-	-	4	3	-	-	21
8	S Modena	3	-	-	-	6	-	-	-	-	-	-	-	-	-	1	-	10
9	A de Cesaris	-	-	-	-	3	3	1	-	2	-	-	-	-	-	-	-	9
10	R Moreno	-	-	-	3	-	2	-	-	-	-	3	-	-	-	-	-	8
11	P Martini	-	-	3	-	-	-	-	-	-	-	-	-	3	-	-	-	6
12	J J Lehto	-	-	4	-	-	-	-	-	-	-	-	-	-	-	-	-	4
	B Gachot	-	-	-	-	2	-	-	1	1	-	-	-	-	-	-	-	4
	M Schumacher	-	-	-	-	-	-	-	-	-	-	-	2	1	1	-	-	4
15	S Nakajima	2	-	-	-	-	-	-	-	-	-	-	-	-	-	-	-	2
	M Häkkinen	-	-	2	-	-	-	-	-	-	-	-	-	-	-	-	-	2
	M Brundle	-	-	-	-	-	-	-	-	-	-	-	-	-	-	2	-	2
18	A Suzuki	1	-	-	-	-	-	-	-	-	-	-	-	-	-	-	-	1
	J Bailey	-	-	1	-	-	-	-	-	-	-	-	-	-	-	-	-	1
	E Pirro	-	-	-	1	-	-	-	-	-	-	-	-	-	-	-	-	1
	É Bernard	-	-	-	-	-	1	-	-	-	-	-	-	-	-	-	-	1
	I Capelli	-	-	-	-	-	-	-	-	-	1	-	-	-	-	-	-	1
	M Blundell	-	-	-	-	-	-	-	-	-	-	1	-	-	-	-	-	1
24	G Morbidelli	-	-	-	-	-	-	-	-	-	-	-	-	-	-	-	0.5	0.5

10, 6, 4, 3, 2 and 1 point awarded to the first six finishers. Half points awarded in Australia where race was stopped early.

Constructor Points 1991

		USA	BR	RSM	MC	CDN	MEX	F	GB	D	H	B	I	P	E	J	AUS	TOTAL
1	McLaren-Honda	10	14	16	10	-	4	4	9	3	13	16	9	6	2	16	7	139
2	Williams-Renault	-	6	-	6	5	16	12	10	16	10	2	10	10	14	4	4	125
3	Ferrari	6	4	-	6	-	-	9	4	4	2	-	4	4	9	3	0.5	55.5
4	Benetton-Cosworth	4	2	-	3	10	2	-	2	-	-	7	3	3	1	-	1.5	38.5
5	Jordan-Cosworth	-	-	-	-	5	3	1	1	3	-	-	-	-	-	-	-	13
6	Tyrrell-Honda	5	-	-	-	6	-	-	-	-	-	-	-	-	-	1	-	12
7	Minardi-Ferrari	-	-	3	-	-	-	-	-	-	-	-	-	3	-	-	-	6
8	Dallara-Judd	-	-	4	1	-	-	-	-	-	-	-	-	-	-	-	-	5
9	Lotus-Judd	-	-	3	-	-	-	-	-	-	-	-	-	-	-	-	-	3
	Brabham-Yamaha	-	-	-	-	-	-	-	-	-	-	1	-	-	-	2	-	3
11	Lola-Cosworth	1	-	-	-	-	1	-	-	-	-	-	-	-	-	-	-	2
12	Leyton House-Ilmor	-	-	-	-	-	-	-	-	-	1	-	-	-	-	-	-	1

10, 6, 4, 3, 2 and 1 point awarded to the first six finishers.

Max Mosley became the new president of FISA. Giovanna Amati caused a lot of the pre-season interest as there hadn't been a lady in Formula 1 since 1980. Honda withdrew at season's end, but retained a presence with their related company Mugen. March returned to its original name and Larrousse built its own car with help from the Venturi concern. Pirelli left Formula 1 again. Denny Hulme became the first world champion to die of natural causes.

McLAREN
Honda Marlboro McLaren: Senna, Berger

TYRRELL
Tyrrell Racing Organisation: Grouillard, de Cesaris

WILLIAMS
Canon Williams Team: Mansell, Patrese

BRABHAM
Motor Racing Developments: van de Poele, (Amati), Hill

FOOTWORK
Footwork Mugen Honda: Alboreto, Suzuki

LOTUS
Team Lotus: Häkkinen, Herbert

FONDMETAL
Fondmetal: Chiesa, van de Poele, Tarquini

MARCH
March F1: Wendlinger, Lammers, Belmondo, Naspetti

BENETTON
Camel Benetton Ford: Schumacher, Brundle

DALLARA
Scuderia Italia SpA: Lehto, Martini

MINARDI
Minardi Team: Fittipaldi, Zanardi, Morbidelli

LIGIER
Ligier Gitanes Blondes: Boutsen, Comas

FERRARI
Scuderia Ferrari SpA: Alesi, Capelli, Larini

VENTURI LARROUSSE
Central Park Venturi Larrousse: Gachot, Katayama

JORDAN
Sasol Jordan Yamaha: Modena, Gugelmin

ANDREA MODA
Andrea Moda Formula: Moreno, (McCarthy)

1 Mar 1992 — SOUTH AFRICA: Kyalami (Round: 1) (Race: 517)

72 laps x 4.261 km, 2.648 miles = 306.792 km, 190.632 miles

POS.	NO.	DRIVER	CAR	MODEL	ENGINE		LAPS	TIME/REASON FOR RETIREMENT	GRID:POS	ROW
1	5	N Mansell	Williams	FW14B	Renault	V10	72	1h 36m 45.320s	1	1
2	6	R Patrese	Williams	FW14B	Renault	V10	72	1h 37m 09.680s	4	2
3	1	A Senna	McLaren	MP4/6B	Honda	V12	72	1h 37m 19.995s	2	1
4	19	M Schumacher	Benetton	B191B	Cosworth	V8	72	1h 37m 33.183s	6	3
5	2	G Berger	McLaren	MP4/6B	Honda	V12	72	1h 37m 58.954s	3	2
6	12	J Herbert	Lotus	102D	Cosworth	V8	71		11	6
7	26	E Comas	Ligier	JS37	Renault	V10	71		13	7
8	10	A Suzuki	Footwork	FA13	Mugen Honda	V10	70		16	8
9	11	M Häkkinen	Lotus	102D	Cosworth	V8	70		21	11
10	9	M Alboreto	Footwork	FA13	Mugen Honda	V10	70		17	9
11	33	M Gugelmin	Jordan	192	Yamaha	V12	70		23	12
12	30	U Katayama	Venturi Larrousse	LC92	Lamborghini	V12	68		18	9
13	7	E van de Poele	Brabham	BT60B	Judd	V10	68		26	13
r	3	O Grouillard	Tyrrell	020B	Ilmor	V10	62	clutch	12	6
r	25	T Boutsen	Ligier	JS37	Renault	V10	60	engine	14	7
r	22	P Martini	Dallara	192	Ferrari	V12	56	clutch	25	13
r	24	G Morbidelli	Minardi	M191B	Lamborghini	V12	55	engine	19	10
r	21	J J Lehto	Dallara	192	Ferrari	V12	46	crown wheel	24	12
r	23	C Fittipaldi	Minardi	M191B	Lamborghini	V12	43	electrics	20	10
r	4	A de Cesaris	Tyrrell	020B	Ilmor	V10	41	engine	10	5
r	27	J Alesi	Ferrari	F92A	Ferrari	V12	40	engine	5	3
r	28	I Capelli	Ferrari	F92A	Ferrari	V12	28	engine	9	5
r	15	G Tarquini	Fondmetal	GR01	Cosworth	V8	23	engine	15	8
r	16	K Wendlinger	March	CG911	Ilmor	V10	13	engine overheating	7	4
r	29	B Gachot	Venturi Larrousse	LC92	Lamborghini	V12	8	accident/ suspension	22	11
r	20	M Brundle	Benetton	B191B	Cosworth	V8	1	accident/ clutch	8	4
nq	17	P Belmondo	March	CG911	Ilmor	V10				
nq	14	A Chiesa	Fondmetal	GR01	Cosworth	V8				
nq	32	S Modena	Jordan	192	Yamaha	V12				
nq	8	G Amati	Brabham	BT60B	Judd	V10				

Winning speed: 190.248 km/h, 118.215 mph
Pole Position speed: 203.211 km/h, 126.270 mph (N Mansell, 1 min:15.486 sec)
Fastest Lap speed: 197.731 km/h, 122.865 mph (N Mansell, 1 min:17.578 sec on lap 70)
Lap Leaders: N Mansell 1-72 (72).

22 Mar 1992 — MEXICO: Mexico City (Round: 2) (Race: 518)

69 laps x 4.421 km, 2.747 miles = 305.049 km, 189.549 miles

POS.	NO.	DRIVER	CAR	MODEL	ENGINE		LAPS	TIME/REASON FOR RETIREMENT	GRID:POS	ROW
1	5	N Mansell	Williams	FW14B	Renault	V10	69	1h 31m 53.587s	1	1
2	6	R Patrese	Williams	FW14B	Renault	V10	69	1h 32m 06.558s	2	1
3	19	M Schumacher	Benetton	B191B	Cosworth	V8	69	1h 32m 15.016s	3	2
4	2	G Berger	McLaren	MP4/6B	Honda	V12	69	1h 32m 26.934s	5	3
5	4	A de Cesaris	Tyrrell	020B	Ilmor	V10	68		11	6
6	11	M Häkkinen	Lotus	102D	Cosworth	V8	68		18	9
7	12	J Herbert	Lotus	102D	Cosworth	V8	68		12	6
8	21	J J Lehto	Dallara	192	Ferrari	V12	68		7	4
9	26	E Comas	Ligier	JS37	Renault	V10	67		26	13
10	25	T Boutsen	Ligier	JS37	Renault	V10	67		22	11
11	29	B Gachot	Venturi Larrousse	LC92	Lamborghini	V12	66		13	7
12	30	U Katayama	Venturi Larrousse	LC92	Lamborghini	V12	66		24	12
13	9	M Alboreto	Footwork	FA13	Mugen Honda	V10	65		25	13
r	20	M Brundle	Benetton	B191B	Cosworth	V8	47	engine overheating	4	2
r	15	G Tarquini	Fondmetal	GR01	Cosworth	V8	45	clutch	14	7

POS.	NO.	DRIVER	CAR	MODEL	ENGINE		LAPS	TIME/REASON FOR RETIREMENT	GRID:POS	ROW
r	14	A Chiesa	Fondmetal	GR01	Cosworth	V8	37	spin	23	12
r	22	P Martini	Dallara	192	Ferrari	V12	36	handling	9	5
r	27	J Alesi	Ferrari	F92A	Ferrari	V12	31	engine	10	5
r	24	G Morbidelli	Minardi	M191B	Lamborghini	V12	29	spin	21	11
r	32	S Modena	Jordan	192	Yamaha	V12	17	gearbox	15	8
r	3	O Grouillard	Tyrrell	020B	Ilmor	V10	12	engine	16	8
r	1	A Senna	McLaren	MP4/6B	Honda	V12	11	transmission	6	3
r	23	C Fittipaldi	Minardi	M191B	Lamborghini	V12	2	spin	17	9
r	33	M Gugelmin	Jordan	192	Yamaha	V12	0	engine	8	4
r	28	I Capelli	Ferrari	F92A	Ferrari	V12	0	accident	20	10
r	16	K Wendlinger	March	CG911	Ilmor	V10	0	accident	19	10
nq	10	A Suzuki	Footwork	FA13	Mugen Honda	V10				
nq	17	P Belmondo	March	CG911	Ilmor	V10				
nq	7	E van de Poele	Brabham	BT60B	Judd	V10				
nq	8	G Amati	Brabham	BT60B	Judd	V10				

Winning speed: 199.176 km/h, 123.762 mph
Pole Position speed: 208.467 km/h, 129.535 mph (N Mansell, 1 min:16.346 sec)
Fastest Lap speed: 204.805 km/h, 127.260 mph (G Berger, 1 min:17.711 sec on lap 60)
Lap Leaders: N Mansell 1-69 (69).

5 Apr 1992 — BRAZIL: Interlagos — (Round: 3) (Race: 519)

71 laps x 4.325 km, 2.687 miles = 307.075 km, 190.808 miles

POS.	NO.	DRIVER	CAR	MODEL	ENGINE		LAPS	TIME/REASON FOR RETIREMENT	GRID:POS	ROW
1	5	N Mansell	Williams	FW14B	Renault	V10	71	1h 36m 51.856s	1	1
2	6	R Patrese	Williams	FW14B	Renault	V10	71	1h 37m 21.186s	2	1
3	19	M Schumacher	Benetton	B191B	Cosworth	V8	70		5	3
4	27	J Alesi	Ferrari	F92A	Ferrari	V12	70		6	3
5	28	I Capelli	Ferrari	F92A	Ferrari	V12	70		11	6
6	9	M Alboreto	Footwork	FA13	Mugen Honda	V10	70		14	7
7	24	G Morbidelli	Minardi	M191B	Lamborghini	V12	69		23	12
8	21	J J Lehto	Dallara	192	Ferrari	V12	69		16	8
9	30	U Katayama	Venturi Larrousse	LC92	Lamborghini	V12	68		25	13
10	11	M Häkkinen	Lotus	102D	Cosworth	V8	67		24	12
r	15	G Tarquini	Fondmetal	GR01	Cosworth	V8	62	radiator	19	10
r	16	K Wendlinger	March	CG911	Ilmor	V10	55	clutch	9	5
r	23	C Fittipaldi	Minardi	M191B	Lamborghini	V12	54	gearbox	20	10
r	3	O Grouillard	Tyrrell	020B	Ilmor	V10	52	engine	17	9
r	26	E Comas	Ligier	JS37	Renault	V10	42	engine	15	8
r	12	J Herbert	Lotus	102D	Cosworth	V8	36	accident	26	13
r	25	T Boutsen	Ligier	JS37	Renault	V10	36	accident	10	5
r	33	M Gugelmin	Jordan	192	Yamaha	V12	36	gearbox	21	11
r	20	M Brundle	Benetton	B191B	Cosworth	V8	30	accident	7	4
r	22	P Martini	Dallara	192	Ferrari	V12	24	clutch	8	4
r	29	B Gachot	Venturi Larrousse	LC92	Lamborghini	V12	23	rear suspension	18	9
r	4	A de Cesaris	Tyrrell	020B	Ilmor	V10	21	electrics	13	7
r	1	A Senna	McLaren	MP4/7A	Honda	V12	17	electrics	3	2
r	2	G Berger	McLaren	MP4/7A	Honda	V12	4	engine overheating	4	2
r	10	A Suzuki	Footwork	FA13	Mugen Honda	V10	2	oil system	22	11
r	32	S Modena	Jordan	192	Yamaha	V12	1	gearbox	12	6
nq	14	A Chiesa	Fondmetal	GR01	Cosworth	V8				
nq	17	P Belmondo	March	CG911	Ilmor	V10				
nq	7	E van de Poele	Brabham	BT60B	Judd	V10				
nq	8	G Amati	Brabham	BT60B	Judd	V10				
npq	34	R Moreno	Andrea Moda	S921	Judd	V10				

Winning speed: 190.209 km/h, 118.191 mph
Pole Position speed: 205.672 km/h, 127.799 mph (N Mansell, 1 min:15.703 sec)
Fastest Lap speed: 195.874 km/h, 121.710 mph (R Patrese, 1 min:19.490 sec on lap 34)
Lap Leaders: R Patrese 1-31 (31); N Mansell 32-71 (40).

3 May 1992 — SPAIN: Montmeló — (Round: 4) (Race: 520)

65 laps x 4.747 km, 2.950 miles = 308.555 km, 191.727 miles

POS.	NO.	DRIVER	CAR	MODEL	ENGINE		LAPS	TIME/REASON FOR RETIREMENT	GRID:POS	ROW
1	5	N Mansell	Williams	FW14B	Renault	V10	65	1h 56m 10.674s	1	1
2	19	M Schumacher	Benetton	B192	Cosworth	V8	65	1h 56m 34.588s	2	1
3	27	J Alesi	Ferrari	F92A	Ferrari	V12	65	1h 56m 37.136s	8	4
4	2	G Berger	McLaren	MP4/7A	Honda	V12	65	1h 57m 31.321s	7	4
5	9	M Alboreto	Footwork	FA13	Mugen Honda	V10	64		16	8
6	22	P Martini	Dallara	192	Ferrari	V12	63		13	7
7	10	A Suzuki	Footwork	FA13	Mugen Honda	V10	63		19	10
8	16	K Wendlinger	March	CG911	Ilmor	V10	63		9	5
9r	1	A Senna	McLaren	MP4/7A	Honda	V12	62	spin	3	2
10r	28	I Capelli	Ferrari	F92A	Ferrari	V12	62	spin	5	3
11	23	C Fittipaldi	Minardi	M191B	Lamborghini	V12	61		22	11
12	17	P Belmondo	March	CG911	Ilmor	V10	61		23	12
r	21	J J Lehto	Dallara	192	Ferrari	V12	56	spin	12	6
r	15	G Tarquini	Fondmetal	GR01	Cosworth	V8	56	spin	18	9
r	11	M Häkkinen	Lotus	102D	Cosworth	V8	56	spin	21	11
r	26	E Comas	Ligier	JS37	Renault	V10	55	spin	10	5
r	29	B Gachot	Venturi Larrousse	LC92	Lamborghini	V12	35	engine	24	12
r	3	O Grouillard	Tyrrell	020B	Ilmor	V10	30	spin	15	8
r	24	G Morbidelli	Minardi	M191B	Lamborghini	V12	26	handling	25	13
r	33	M Gugelmin	Jordan	192	Yamaha	V12	24	spin	17	9
r	14	A Chiesa	Fondmetal	GR01	Cosworth	V8	22	spin	20	10

POS.	NO.	DRIVER	CAR	MODEL	ENGINE		LAPS	TIME/REASON FOR RETIREMENT	GRID:POS	ROW
r	6	R Patrese	Williams	FW14B	Renault	V10	19	spin	4	2
r	12	J Herbert	Lotus	102D	Cosworth	V8	13	spin	26	13
r	25	T Boutsen	Ligier	JS37	Renault	V10	11	engine	14	7
r	20	M Brundle	Benetton	B192	Cosworth	V8	4	spin	6	3
r	4	A de Cesaris	Tyrrell	020B	Ilmor	V10	2	oil pressure/ spin	11	6
nq	30	U Katayama	Venturi Larrousse	LC92	Lamborghini	V12				
nq	7	E van de Poele	Brabham	BT60B	Judd	V10				
nq	32	S Modena	Jordan	192	Yamaha	V12				
nq	8	D Hill	Brabham	BT60B	Judd	V10				
npq	34	R Moreno	Andrea Moda	S921	Judd	V10				
npq	35	P McCarthy	Andrea Moda	S921	Judd	V10				

Winning speed: 159.353 km/h, 99.017 mph
Pole Position speed: 213.109 km/h, 132.420 mph (N Mansell, 1 min:20.190 sec)
Fastest Lap speed: 166.719 km/h, 103.594 mph (N Mansell, 1 min:42.503 sec on lap 10)
Lap Leaders: N Mansell 1-65 (65).

17 May 1992 — SAN MARINO: Imola (Round: 5) (Race: 521)

60 laps x 5.040 km, 3.132 miles = 302.400 km, 187.903 miles

POS.	NO.	DRIVER	CAR	MODEL	ENGINE		LAPS	TIME/REASON FOR RETIREMENT	GRID:POS	ROW
1	5	N Mansell	Williams	FW14B	Renault	V10	60	1h 28m 40.927s	1	1
2	6	R Patrese	Williams	FW14B	Renault	V10	60	1h 28m 50.378s	2	1
3	1	A Senna	McLaren	MP4/7A	Honda	V12	60	1h 29m 29.911s	3	2
4	20	M Brundle	Benetton	B192	Cosworth	V8	60	1h 29m 33.934s	6	3
5	9	M Alboreto	Footwork	FA13	Mugen Honda	V10	59		9	5
6	22	P Martini	Dallara	192	Ferrari	V12	59		15	8
7	33	M Gugelmin	Jordan	192	Yamaha	V12	58		18	9
8	3	O Grouillard	Tyrrell	020B	Ilmor	V10	58		20	10
9	26	E Comas	Ligier	JS37	Renault	V10	58		13	7
10	10	A Suzuki	Footwork	FA13	Mugen Honda	V10	58		11	6
11r	21	J J Lehto	Dallara	192	Ferrari	V12	57	engine overheating	16	8
12	16	K Wendlinger	March	CG911	Ilmor	V10	57		12	6
13	17	P Belmondo	March	CG911	Ilmor	V10	57		24	12
14r	4	A de Cesaris	Tyrrell	020B	Ilmor	V10	55	fuel pressure	14	7
r	30	U Katayama	Venturi Larrousse	LC92	Lamborghini	V12	40	spin	17	9
r	27	J Alesi	Ferrari	F92A	Ferrari	V12	39	accident	7	4
r	2	G Berger	McLaren	MP4/7A	Honda	V12	39	accident	4	2
r	29	B Gachot	Venturi Larrousse	LC92	Lamborghini	V12	32	spin	19	10
r	25	T Boutsen	Ligier	JS37	Renault	V10	29	fuel pump	10	5
r	32	S Modena	Jordan	192	Yamaha	V12	25	gearbox	23	12
r	24	G Morbidelli	Minardi	M192	Lamborghini	V12	24	transmission	21	11
r	15	G Tarquini	Fondmetal	GR01	Cosworth	V8	24	engine overheating	22	11
r	19	M Schumacher	Benetton	B192	Cosworth	V8	20	spin/ suspension	5	3
r	28	I Capelli	Ferrari	F92A	Ferrari	V12	11	spin	8	4
r	23	C Fittipaldi	Minardi	M192	Lamborghini	V12	8	transmission	25	13
r	12	J Herbert	Lotus	107	Cosworth	V8	8	gearbox	26	13
nq	11	M Häkkinen	Lotus	102D	Cosworth	V8				
nq	14	A Chiesa	Fondmetal	GR01	Cosworth	V8				
nq	8	D Hill	Brabham	BT60B	Judd	V10				
nq	7	E van de Poele	Brabham	BT60B	Judd	V10				
npq	34	R Moreno	Andrea Moda	S921	Judd	V10				
npq	35	P McCarthy	Andrea Moda	S921	Judd	V10				

Winning speed: 204.596 km/h, 127.130 mph
Pole Position speed: 221.695 km/h, 137.755 mph (N Mansell, 1 min:21.842 sec)
Fastest Lap speed: 210.732 km/h, 130.943 mph (R Patrese, 1 min:26.100 sec on lap 60)
Lap Leaders: N Mansell 1-60 (60).

31 May 1992 — MONACO: Monte Carlo (Round: 6) (Race: 522)

78 laps x 3.328 km, 2.068 miles = 259.584 km, 161.298 miles

POS.	NO.	DRIVER	CAR	MODEL	ENGINE		LAPS	TIME/REASON FOR RETIREMENT	GRID:POS	ROW
1	1	A Senna	McLaren	MP4/7A	Honda	V12	78	1h 50m 59.372s	3	2
2	5	N Mansell	Williams	FW14B	Renault	V10	78	1h 50m 59.587s	1	1
3	6	R Patrese	Williams	FW14B	Renault	V10	78	1h 51m 31.215s	2	1
4	19	M Schumacher	Benetton	B192	Cosworth	V8	78	1h 51m 38.666s	6	3
5	20	M Brundle	Benetton	B192	Cosworth	V8	78	1h 52m 20.719s	7	4
6	29	B Gachot	Venturi Larrousse	LC92	Lamborghini	V12	77		15	8
7	9	M Alboreto	Footwork	FA13	Mugen Honda	V10	77		11	6
8	23	C Fittipaldi	Minardi	M192	Lamborghini	V12	77		17	9
9	21	J J Lehto	Dallara	192	Ferrari	V12	76		20	10
10	26	E Comas	Ligier	JS37	Renault	V10	76		23	12
11	10	A Suzuki	Footwork	FA13	Mugen Honda	V10	76		19	10
12	25	T Boutsen	Ligier	JS37	Renault	V10	75		22	11
r	28	I Capelli	Ferrari	F92A	Ferrari	V12	60	accident/ steering arm	8	4
r	2	G Berger	McLaren	MP4/7A	Honda	V12	32	gearbox	5	3
r	11	M Häkkinen	Lotus	107	Cosworth	V8	30	clutch/ gearbox	14	7
r	27	J Alesi	Ferrari	F92A	Ferrari	V12	28	gearbox	4	2
r	33	M Gugelmin	Jordan	192	Yamaha	V12	18	transmission	13	7
r	12	J Herbert	Lotus	107	Cosworth	V8	17	accident	9	5
r	34	R Moreno	Andrea Moda	S921	Judd	V10	11	engine	26	13
r	4	A de Cesaris	Tyrrell	020B	Ilmor	V10	9	gearbox	10	5
r	15	G Tarquini	Fondmetal	GR01	Cosworth	V8	9	engine overheating	25	13
r	32	S Modena	Jordan	192	Yamaha	V12	6	accident	21	11
r	3	O Grouillard	Tyrrell	020B	Ilmor	V10	4	transmission	24	12
r	16	K Wendlinger	March	CG911	Ilmor	V10	1	gearbox	16	8

POS.	NO.	DRIVER	CAR	MODEL	ENGINE		LAPS	TIME/REASON FOR RETIREMENT	GRID:POS	ROW
r	24	G Morbidelli	Minardi	M192	Lamborghini	V12	1	battery	12	6
r	22	P Martini	Dallara	192	Ferrari	V12	0	accident	18	9
nq	7	E van de Poele	Brabham	BT60B	Judd	V10				
nq	8	D Hill	Brabham	BT60B	Judd	V10				
nq	14	A Chiesa	Fondmetal	GR01	Cosworth	V8				
nq	17	P Belmondo	March	CG911	Ilmor	V10				
npq	30	U Katayama	Venturi Larrousse	LC92	Lamborghini	V12				
npq	35	P McCarthy	Andrea Moda	S921	Judd	V10				

Winning speed: 140.329 km/h, 87.196 mph
Pole Position speed: 150.711 km/h, 93.648 mph (N Mansell, 1 min:19.495 sec)
Fastest Lap speed: 146.827 km/h, 91.234 mph (N Mansell, 1 min:21.598 sec on lap 74)
Lap Leaders: N Mansell 1-70 (70); A Senna 71-78 (8).

14 Jun 1992 — CANADA: Montréal (Round: 7) (Race: 523)

69 laps x 4.430 km, 2.753 miles = 305.670 km, 189.935 miles

POS.	NO.	DRIVER	CAR	MODEL	ENGINE		LAPS	TIME/REASON FOR RETIREMENT	GRID:POS	ROW
1	2	G Berger	McLaren	MP4/7A	Honda	V12	69	1h 37m 08.299s	4	2
2	19	M Schumacher	Benetton	B192	Cosworth	V8	69	1h 37m 20.700s	5	3
3	27	J Alesi	Ferrari	F92A	Ferrari	V12	69	1h 38m 15.626s	8	4
4	16	K Wendlinger	March	CG911	Ilmor	V10	68		12	6
5	4	A de Cesaris	Tyrrell	020B	Ilmor	V10	68		14	7
6	26	E Comas	Ligier	JS37	Renault	V10	68		22	11
7	9	M Alboreto	Footwork	FA13	Mugen Honda	V10	68		16	8
8	22	P Martini	Dallara	192	Ferrari	V12	68		15	8
9	21	J J Lehto	Dallara	192	Ferrari	V12	68		23	12
10	25	T Boutsen	Ligier	JS37	Renault	V10	67		21	11
11	24	G Morbidelli	Minardi	M192	Lamborghini	V12	67		13	7
12	3	O Grouillard	Tyrrell	020B	Ilmor	V10	67		26	13
13r	23	C Fittipaldi	Minardi	M192	Lamborghini	V12	65	gearbox oil fire	25	13
14	17	P Belmondo	March	CG911	Ilmor	V10	64		20	10
r	30	U Katayama	Venturi Larrousse	LC92	Lamborghini	V12	61	engine	11	6
r	20	M Brundle	Benetton	B192	Cosworth	V8	45	transmission	7	4
r	6	R Patrese	Williams	FW14B	Renault	V10	43	gearbox	2	1
r	1	A Senna	McLaren	MP4/7A	Honda	V12	37	electrics	1	1
r	32	S Modena	Jordan	192	Yamaha	V12	36	transmission	17	9
r	11	M Häkkinen	Lotus	107	Cosworth	V8	35	gearbox	10	5
r	12	J Herbert	Lotus	107	Cosworth	V8	34	clutch	6	3
r	28	I Capelli	Ferrari	F92A	Ferrari	V12	18	accident	9	5
r	5	N Mansell	Williams	FW14B	Renault	V10	14	accident	3	2
r	33	M Gugelmin	Jordan	192	Yamaha	V12	14	transmission	24	12
dq	29	B Gachot	Venturi Larrousse	LC92	Lamborghini	V12	14	push start after accident	19	10
r	15	G Tarquini	Fondmetal	GR02	Cosworth	V8	0	gearbox	18	9
nq	10	A Suzuki	Footwork	FA13	Mugen Honda	V10				
nq	7	E van de Poele	Brabham	BT60B	Judd	V10				
nq	14	A Chiesa	Fondmetal	GR01	Cosworth	V8				
nq	8	D Hill	Brabham	BT60B	Judd	V10				
npq	34	R Moreno	Andrea Moda	S921	Judd	V10				

Winning speed: 188.805 km/h, 117.318 mph
Pole Position speed: 199.912 km/h, 124.220 mph (A Senna, 1 min:19.775 sec)
Fastest Lap speed: 193.720 km/h, 120.372 mph (G Berger, 1 min:22.325 sec on lap 61)
Lap Leaders: A Senna 1-37 (37); G Berger 38-69 (32).

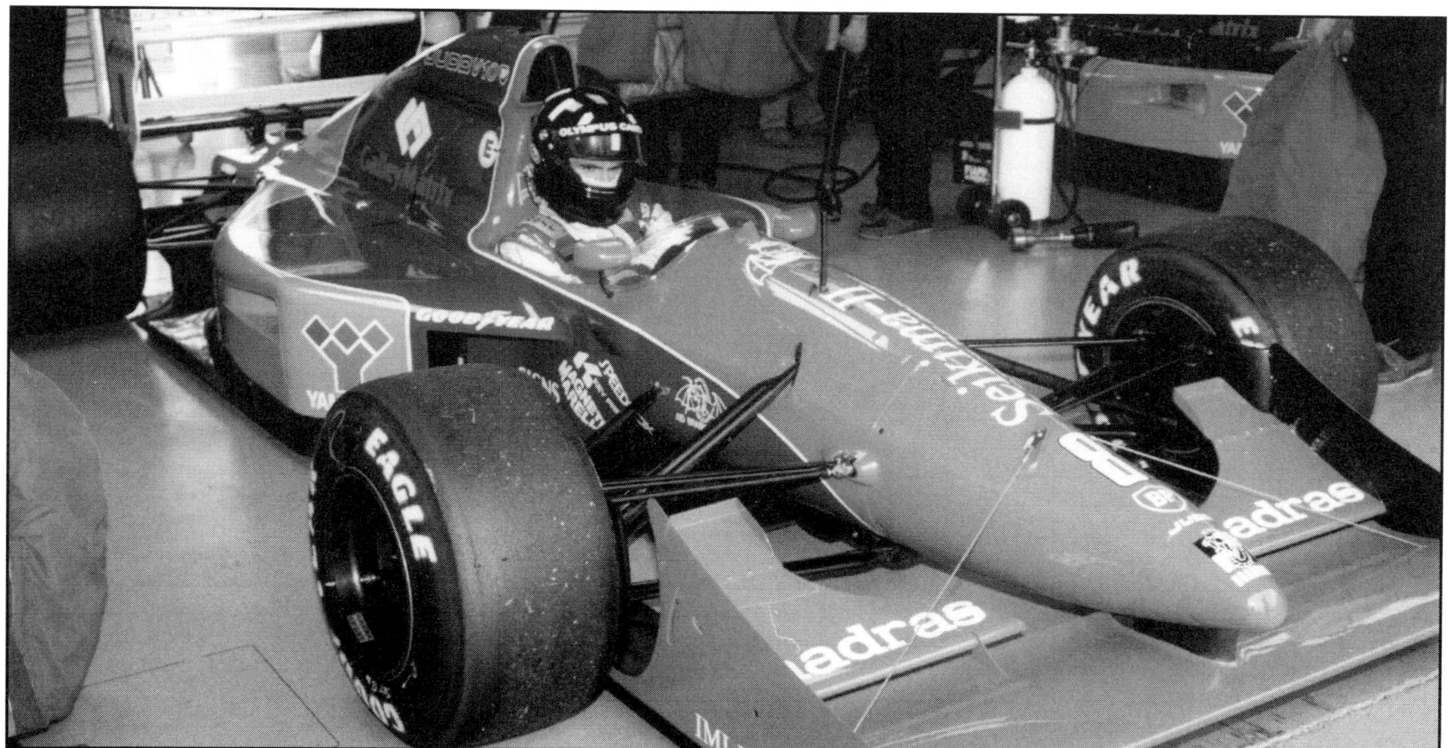

Damon Hill at the wheel of the Bradham BT60B-Judd, at Silverstone, 1992.

5 Jul 1992 FRANCE: Magny-Cours (Round: 8) (Race: 524)

69 laps x 4.250 km, 2.641 miles = 293.250 km, 182.217 miles

POS.	NO.	DRIVER	CAR	MODEL	ENGINE		LAPS	TIME/REASON FOR RETIREMENT	GRID:POS	ROW
1	5	N Mansell	Williams	FW14B	Renault	V10	69	1h 38m 08.459s	1	1
2	6	R Patrese	Williams	FW14B	Renault	V10	69	1h 38m 54.906s	2	1
3	20	M Brundle	Benetton	B192	Cosworth	V8	69	1h 39m 21.038s	7	4
4	11	M Häkkinen	Lotus	107	Cosworth	V8	68		11	6
5	26	E Comas	Ligier	JS37	Renault	V10	68		10	5
6	12	J Herbert	Lotus	107	Cosworth	V8	68		12	6
7	9	M Alboreto	Footwork	FA13	Mugen Honda	V10	68		14	7
8	24	G Morbidelli	Minardi	M192	Lamborghini	V12	68		16	8
9	21	J J Lehto	Dallara	192	Ferrari	V12	67		17	9
10	22	P Martini	Dallara	192	Ferrari	V12	67		25	13
11	3	O Grouillard	Tyrrell	020B	Ilmor	V10	66		22	11
r	27	J Alesi	Ferrari	F92A	Ferrari	V12	61	engine	6	3
r	4	A de Cesaris	Tyrrell	020B	Ilmor	V10	51	spin	19	10
r	30	U Katayama	Venturi Larrousse	LC92	Lamborghini	V12	49	engine	18	9
r	25	T Boutsen	Ligier	JS37	Renault	V10	46	spin	9	5
r	28	I Capelli	Ferrari	F92A	Ferrari	V12	38	electrics	8	4
r	16	K Wendlinger	March	CG911	Ilmor	V10	33	gearbox	21	11
r	32	S Modena	Jordan	192	Yamaha	V12	25	engine	20	10
r	10	A Suzuki	Footwork	FA13	Mugen Honda	V10	20	spin	15	8
r	19	M Schumacher	Benetton	B192	Cosworth	V8	17	accident	5	3
r	2	G Berger	McLaren	MP4/7A	Honda	V12	10	engine	4	2
r	15	G Tarquini	Fondmetal	GR02	Cosworth	V8	6	throttle linkage	23	12
r	29	B Gachot	Venturi Larrousse	LC92	Lamborghini	V12	0	accident	13	7
r	33	M Gugelmin	Jordan	192	Yamaha	V12	0	accident	24	12
r	14	A Chiesa	Fondmetal	GR02	Cosworth	V8	0	accident	26	13
r	1	A Senna	McLaren	MP4/7A	Honda	V12	0	accident	3	2
nq	17	P Belmondo	March	CG911	Ilmor	V10				
nq	23	C Fittipaldi	Minardi	M192	Lamborghini	V12		accident/ injury		
nq	7	E van de Poele	Brabham	BT60B	Judd	V10				
nq	8	D Hill	Brabham	BT60B	Judd	V10				

Winning speed: 179.283 km/h, 111.401 mph
Pole Position speed: 207.137 km/h, 128.709 mph (N Mansell, 1 min:13.864 sec)
Fastest Lap speed: 198.521 km/h, 123.355 mph (N Mansell, 1 min:17.070 sec on lap 37)
Lap Leaders: R Patrese 1-18 (18); N Mansell 19-69 (51).

Scheduled for 72 laps, but interrupted after 18 laps, because of rain. Restarted for a further 51 laps. Lap leaders are shown 'on the road'.

12 Jul 1992 BRITAIN: Silverstone (Round: 9) (Race: 525)

59 laps x 5.226 km, 3.247 miles = 308.334 km, 191.590 miles

POS.	NO.	DRIVER	CAR	MODEL	ENGINE		LAPS	TIME/REASON FOR RETIREMENT	GRID:POS	ROW
1	5	N Mansell	Williams	FW14B	Renault	V10	59	1h 25m 42.991s	1	1
2	6	R Patrese	Williams	FW14B	Renault	V10	59	1h 26m 22.085s	2	1
3	20	M Brundle	Benetton	B192	Cosworth	V8	59	1h 26m 31.386s	6	3
4	19	M Schumacher	Benetton	B192	Cosworth	V8	59	1h 26m 36.258s	4	2
5	2	G Berger	McLaren	MP4/7A	Honda	V12	59	1h 26m 38.786s	5	3
6	11	M Häkkinen	Lotus	107	Cosworth	V8	59	1h 27m 03.129s	9	5
7	9	M Alboreto	Footwork	FA13	Mugen Honda	V10	58		12	6
8	26	E Comas	Ligier	JS37	Renault	V10	58		10	5
9	28	I Capelli	Ferrari	F92A	Ferrari	V12	58		14	7
10	25	T Boutsen	Ligier	JS37	Renault	V10	57		13	7
11	3	O Grouillard	Tyrrell	020B	Ilmor	V10	57		20	10
12	10	A Suzuki	Footwork	FA13	Mugen Honda	V10	57		17	9
13	21	J J Lehto	Dallara	192	Ferrari	V12	57		19	10
14	15	G Tarquini	Fondmetal	GR02	Cosworth	V8	57		15	8
15	22	P Martini	Dallara	192	Ferrari	V12	56		22	11
16	8	D Hill	Brabham	BT60B	Judd	V10	55		26	13
17r	24	G Morbidelli	Minardi	M192	Lamborghini	V12	53	oil pressure	25	13
r	1	A Senna	McLaren	MP4/7A	Honda	V12	52	gearbox	3	2
r	4	A de Cesaris	Tyrrell	020B	Ilmor	V10	46	suspension/ spin	18	9
r	27	J Alesi	Ferrari	F92A	Ferrari	V12	43	fire extinguisher	8	4
r	32	S Modena	Jordan	192	Yamaha	V12	43	engine	23	12
r	33	M Gugelmin	Jordan	192	Yamaha	V12	37	engine	24	12
r	29	B Gachot	Venturi Larrousse	LC92	Lamborghini	V12	32	rear wheel bearing	11	6
r	12	J Herbert	Lotus	107	Cosworth	V8	31	gearbox	7	4
r	16	K Wendlinger	March	CG911	Ilmor	V10	27	gearbox	21	11
r	30	U Katayama	Venturi Larrousse	LC92	Lamborghini	V12	27	gear linkage	16	8
nq	23	A Zanardi	Minardi	M192	Lamborghini	V12				
nq	17	P Belmondo	March	CG911	Ilmor	V10				
nq	14	A Chiesa	Fondmetal	GR01	Cosworth	V8				
nq	7	E van de Poele	Brabham	BT60B	Judd	V10				
npq	34	R Moreno	Andrea Moda	S921	Judd	V10				
npq	35	P McCarthy	Andrea Moda	S921	Judd	V10				

Winning speed: 215.828 km/h, 134.109 mph
Pole Position speed: 238.252 km/h, 148.043 mph (N Mansell, 1 min:18.965 sec)
Fastest Lap speed: 227.936 km/h, 141.633 mph (N Mansell, 1 min:22.539 sec on lap 57)
Lap Leaders: N Mansell 1-59 (59).

26 Jul 1992 — GERMANY: Hockenheim (Round:10) (Race: 526)

45 laps x 6.815 km, 4.235 miles = 306.675 km, 190.559 miles

POS.	NO.	DRIVER	CAR	MODEL	ENGINE		LAPS	TIME/REASON FOR RETIREMENT	GRID:POS	ROW
1	5	N Mansell	Williams	FW14B	Renault	V10	45	1h 18m 22.032s	1	1
2	1	A Senna	McLaren	MP4/7A	Honda	V12	45	1h 18m 26.532s	3	2
3	19	M Schumacher	Benetton	B192	Cosworth	V8	45	1h 18m 56.494s	6	3
4	20	M Brundle	Benetton	B192	Cosworth	V8	45	1h 18m 58.991s	9	5
5	27	J Alesi	Ferrari	F92A	Ferrari	V12	45	1h 19m 34.639s	5	3
6	26	E Comas	Ligier	JS37	Renault	V10	45	1h 19m 58.530s	7	4
7	25	T Boutsen	Ligier	JS37	Renault	V10	45	1h 19m 59.212s	8	4
8r	6	R Patrese	Williams	FW14B	Renault	V10	44	spin	2	1
9	9	M Alboreto	Footwork	FA13	Mugen Honda	V10	44		17	9
10	21	J J Lehto	Dallara	192	Ferrari	V12	44		21	11
11	22	P Martini	Dallara	192	Ferrari	V12	44		18	9
12	24	G Morbidelli	Minardi	M192	Lamborghini	V12	44		26	13
13	17	P Belmondo	March	CG911	Ilmor	V10	44		22	11
14	29	B Gachot	Venturi Larrousse	LC92	Lamborghini	V12	44		25	13
15	33	M Gugelmin	Jordan	192	Yamaha	V12	43		23	12
16	16	K Wendlinger	March	CG911	Ilmor	V10	42		10	5
r	15	G Tarquini	Fondmetal	GR02	Cosworth	V8	33	engine	19	10
r	4	A de Cesaris	Tyrrell	020B	Ilmor	V10	25	engine	20	10
r	12	J Herbert	Lotus	107	Cosworth	V8	23	engine	11	6
r	28	I Capelli	Ferrari	F92A	Ferrari	V12	21	engine	12	6
r	11	M Häkkinen	Lotus	107	Cosworth	V8	21	engine	13	7
r	2	G Berger	McLaren	MP4/7A	Honda	V12	16	misfire	4	2
r	3	O Grouillard	Tyrrell	020B	Ilmor	V10	8	engine overheating	14	7
r	30	U Katayama	Venturi Larrousse	LC92	Lamborghini	V12	8	accident	16	8
r	10	A Suzuki	Footwork	FA13	Mugen Honda	V10	1	spin	15	8
r	23	A Zanardi	Minardi	M192	Lamborghini	V12	1	clutch	24	12
nq	32	S Modena	Jordan	192	Yamaha	V12				
nq	7	E van de Poele	Brabham	BT60B	Judd	V10				
nq	14	A Chiesa	Fondmetal	GR02	Cosworth	V8				
nq	8	D Hill	Brabham	BT60B	Judd	V10				
npq	34	R Moreno	Andrea Moda	S921	Judd	V10				
exc	35	P McCarthy	Andrea Moda	S921	Judd	V10		missed weight check		

Winning speed: 234.798 km/h, 145.897 mph
Pole Position speed: 250.449 km/h, 155.622 mph (N Mansell, 1 min:37.960 sec)
Fastest Lap speed: 241.498 km/h, 150.060 mph (R Patrese, 1 min:41.591 sec on lap 36)
Lap Leaders: N Mansell 1-14,20-45 (40); R Patrese 15-19 (5).

16 Aug 1992 — HUNGARY: Hungaroring (Round:11) (Race: 527)

77 laps x 3.968 km, 2.466 miles = 305.536 km, 189.851 miles

POS.	NO.	DRIVER	CAR	MODEL	ENGINE		LAPS	TIME/REASON FOR RETIREMENT	GRID:POS	ROW
1	1	A Senna	McLaren	MP4/7A	Honda	V12	77	1h 46m 19.216s	3	2
2	5	N Mansell	Williams	FW14B	Renault	V10	77	1h 46m 59.355s	2	1
3	2	G Berger	McLaren	MP4/7A	Honda	V12	77	1h 47m 09.998s	5	3
4	11	M Häkkinen	Lotus	107	Cosworth	V8	77	1h 47m 13.529s	16	8
5	20	M Brundle	Benetton	B192	Cosworth	V8	77	1h 47m 16.714s	6	3
6	28	I Capelli	Ferrari	F92A	Ferrari	V12	76		10	5
7	9	M Alboreto	Footwork	FA13	Mugen Honda	V10	75		7	4
8	4	A de Cesaris	Tyrrell	020B	Ilmor	V10	75		19	10
9	17	P Belmondo	March	CG911	Ilmor	V10	74		17	9
10	33	M Gugelmin	Jordan	192	Yamaha	V12	73		21	11
11	8	D Hill	Brabham	BT60B	Judd	V10	73		25	13
r	19	M Schumacher	Benetton	B192	Cosworth	V8	63	spin/ rear wing lost	4	2
r	6	R Patrese	Williams	FW14B	Renault	V10	55	engine	1	1
r	22	P Martini	Dallara	192	Ferrari	V12	40	gearbox	26	13
r	30	U Katayama	Venturi Larrousse	LC92	Lamborghini	V12	35	engine	20	10
r	27	J Alesi	Ferrari	F92A	Ferrari	V12	14	spin	9	5
r	29	B Gachot	Venturi Larrousse	LC92	Lamborghini	V12	13	accident	15	8
r	10	A Suzuki	Footwork	FA13	Mugen Honda	V10	13	accident	14	7
r	3	O Grouillard	Tyrrell	020B	Ilmor	V10	13	accident	22	11
r	16	K Wendlinger	March	CG911	Ilmor	V10	13	accident	23	12
r	32	S Modena	Jordan	192	Yamaha	V12	13	accident	24	12
r	14	E van de Poele	Fondmetal	GR02	Cosworth	V8	2	spin	18	9
r	26	E Comas	Ligier	JS37	Renault	V10	0	accident	11	6
r	25	T Boutsen	Ligier	JS37	Renault	V10	0	accident	8	4
r	12	J Herbert	Lotus	107	Cosworth	V8	0	accident	13	7
r	15	G Tarquini	Fondmetal	GR02	Cosworth	V8	0	accident	12	6
nq	24	G Morbidelli	Minardi	M192	Lamborghini	V12				
nq	21	J J Lehto	Dallara	192	Ferrari	V12				
nq	23	A Zanardi	Minardi	M192	Lamborghini	V12				
nq	34	R Moreno	Andrea Moda	S921	Judd	V10				
npq	35	P McCarthy	Andrea Moda	S921	Judd	V10				

Winning speed: 172.424 km/h, 107.139 mph
Pole Position speed: 189.263 km/h, 117.602 mph (R Patrese, 1 min:15.476 sec)
Fastest Lap speed: 182.418 km/h, 113.349 mph (N Mansell, 1 min:18.308 sec on lap 63)
Lap Leaders: R Patrese 1-38 (38); A Senna 39-77 (39).

30 Aug 1992 — BELGIUM: Spa-Francorchamps — (Round:12) (Race: 528)

44 laps x 6.974 km, 4.333 miles = 306.856 km, 190.671 miles

POS.	NO.	DRIVER	CAR	MODEL	ENGINE		LAPS	TIME/REASON FOR RETIREMENT	GRID:POS	ROW
1	19	M Schumacher	Benetton	B192	Cosworth	V8	44	1h 36m 10.721s	3	2
2	5	N Mansell	Williams	FW14B	Renault	V10	44	1h 36m 47.316s	1	1
3	6	R Patrese	Williams	FW14B	Renault	V10	44	1h 36m 54.618s	4	2
4	20	M Brundle	Benetton	B192	Cosworth	V8	44	1h 36m 56.780s	9	5
5	1	A Senna	McLaren	MP4/7A	Honda	V12	44	1h 37m 19.090s	2	1
6	11	M Häkkinen	Lotus	107	Cosworth	V8	44	1h 37m 20.751s	8	4
7	21	J J Lehto	Dallara	192	Ferrari	V12	44	1h 37m 48.958s	16	8
8	4	A de Cesaris	Tyrrell	020B	Ilmor	V10	43		13	7
9	10	A Suzuki	Footwork	FA13	Mugen Honda	V10	43		25	13
10	14	E van de Poele	Fondmetal	GR02	Cosworth	V8	43		15	8
11	16	K Wendlinger	March	CG911	Ilmor	V10	43		18	9
12	17	E Naspetti	March	CG911	Ilmor	V10	43		21	11
13r	12	J Herbert	Lotus	107	Cosworth	V8	42	engine	10	5
14	33	M Gugelmin	Jordan	192	Yamaha	V12	42		24	12
15	32	S Modena	Jordan	192	Yamaha	V12	42		17	9
16	24	G Morbidelli	Minardi	M192	Lamborghini	V12	42		23	12
17	30	U Katayama	Venturi Larrousse	LC92	Lamborghini	V12	42		26	13
18r	29	B Gachot	Venturi Larrousse	LC92	Lamborghini	V12	40	spin	20	10
r	25	T Boutsen	Ligier	JS37	Renault	V10	27	accident	7	4
r	28	I Capelli	Ferrari	F92A	Ferrari	V12	25	engine	12	6
r	15	G Tarquini	Fondmetal	GR02	Cosworth	V8	25	engine	11	6
r	9	M Alboreto	Footwork	FA13	Mugen Honda	V10	20	gearbox	14	7
r	27	J Alesi	Ferrari	F92AT	Ferrari	V12	7	spin	5	3
r	3	O Grouillard	Tyrrell	020B	Ilmor	V10	1	accident	22	11
r	22	P Martini	Dallara	192	Ferrari	V12	0	spin	19	10
r	2	G Berger	McLaren	MP4/7A	Honda	V12	0	transmission	6	3
nq	23	C Fittipaldi	Minardi	M192	Lamborghini	V12				
nq	34	R Moreno	Andrea Moda	S921	Judd	V10				
nq	35	P McCarthy	Andrea Moda	S921	Judd	V10				
nq	26	E Comas	Ligier	JS37	Renault	V10		accident/ injury		

Winning speed: 191.429 km/h, 118.948 mph
Pole Position speed: 227.115 km/h, 141.123 mph (N Mansell, 1 min:50.545 sec)
Fastest Lap speed: 220.636 km/h, 137.097 mph (M Schumacher, 1 min:53.791 sec on lap 39)
Lap Leaders: A Senna 1,7-10 (5); N Mansell 2-3,11-33 (25); R Patrese 4-6 (3); M Schumacher 34-44 (11).

13 Sep 1992 — ITALY: Monza — (Round:13) (Race: 529)

53 laps x 5.800 km, 3.604 miles = 307.400 km, 191.010 miles

POS.	NO.	DRIVER	CAR	MODEL	ENGINE		LAPS	TIME/REASON FOR RETIREMENT	GRID:POS	ROW
1	1	A Senna	McLaren	MP4/7A	Honda	V12	53	1h 18m 15.349s	2	1
2	20	M Brundle	Benetton	B192	Cosworth	V8	53	1h 18m 32.399s	9	5
3	19	M Schumacher	Benetton	B192	Cosworth	V8	53	1h 18m 39.722s	6	3
4	2	G Berger	McLaren	MP4/7A	Honda	V12	53	1h 19m 40.839s	5	3
5	6	R Patrese	Williams	FW14B	Renault	V10	53	1h 19m 48.507s	4	2
6	4	A de Cesaris	Tyrrell	020B	Ilmor	V10	52		21	11
7	9	M Alboreto	Footwork	FA13	Mugen Honda	V10	52		16	8
8	22	P Martini	Dallara	192	Ferrari	V12	52		22	11
9r	30	U Katayama	Venturi Larrousse	LC92	Lamborghini	V12	50	transmission/ spin	23	12
10	16	K Wendlinger	March	CG911	Ilmor	V10	50		17	9
11r	21	J J Lehto	Dallara	192	Ferrari	V12	47	electrics	14	7
r	33	M Gugelmin	Jordan	192	Yamaha	V12	46	transmission	26	13
r	5	N Mansell	Williams	FW14B	Renault	V10	41	gearbox hydraulic pump	1	1
r	25	T Boutsen	Ligier	JS37	Renault	V10	41	electronics	8	4
r	26	E Comas	Ligier	JS37	Renault	V10	35	accident	15	8
r	15	G Tarquini	Fondmetal	GR02	Cosworth	V8	30	gearbox	20	10
r	3	O Grouillard	Tyrrell	020B	Ilmor	V10	26	engine	18	9
r	12	J Herbert	Lotus	107	Cosworth	V8	18	engine	13	7
r	17	E Naspetti	March	CG911	Ilmor	V10	17	accident	24	12
r	27	J Alesi	Ferrari	F92AT	Ferrari	V12	12	fuel pressure	3	2
r	28	I Capelli	Ferrari	F92AT	Ferrari	V12	12	spin	7	4
r	24	G Morbidelli	Minardi	M192	Lamborghini	V12	12	engine	12	6
r	29	B Gachot	Venturi Larrousse	LC92	Lamborghini	V12	11	engine	10	5
r	11	M Häkkinen	Lotus	107	Cosworth	V8	5	electrics	11	6
r	10	A Suzuki	Footwork	FA13	Mugen Honda	V10	2	puncture/ accident	19	10
r	14	E van de Poele	Fondmetal	GR02	Cosworth	V8	0	clutch	25	13
nq	23	C Fittipaldi	Minardi	M192	Lamborghini	V12				
nq	32	S Modena	Jordan	192	Yamaha	V12				

Winning speed: 235.689 km/h, 146.450 mph
Pole Position speed: 253.950 km/h, 157.797 mph (N Mansell, 1 min:22.221 sec)
Fastest Lap speed: 242.455 km/h, 150.655 mph (N Mansell, 1 min:26.119 sec on lap 39)
Lap Leaders: N Mansell 1-19 (19); R Patrese 20-47 (28); A Senna 48-53 (6).

27 Sep 1992 — PORTUGAL: Estoril — (Round:14) (Race: 530)

71 laps x 4.350 km, 2.703 miles = 308.850 km, 191.910 miles

POS.	NO.	DRIVER	CAR	MODEL	ENGINE		LAPS	TIME/REASON FOR RETIREMENT	GRID:POS	ROW
1	5	N Mansell	Williams	FW14B	Renault	V10	71	1h 34m 46.659s	1	1
2	2	G Berger	McLaren	MP4/7A	Honda	V12	71	1h 35m 24.192s	4	2
3	1	A Senna	McLaren	MP4/7A	Honda	V12	70		3	2
4	20	M Brundle	Benetton	B192	Cosworth	V8	70		6	3

POS.	NO.	DRIVER	CAR	MODEL	ENGINE		LAPS	TIME/REASON FOR RETIREMENT	GRID:POS	ROW
5	11	M Häkkinen	Lotus	107	Cosworth	V8	70		7	4
6	9	M Alboreto	Footwork	FA13	Mugen Honda	V10	70		8	4
7	19	M Schumacher	Benetton	B192	Cosworth	V8	69		5	3
8	25	T Boutsen	Ligier	JS37	Renault	V10	69		11	6
9	4	A de Cesaris	Tyrrell	020B	Ilmor	V10	69		12	6
10	10	A Suzuki	Footwork	FA13	Mugen Honda	V10	68		17	9
11	17	E Naspetti	March	CG911	Ilmor	V10	68		23	12
12	23	C Fittipaldi	Minardi	M192	Lamborghini	V12	68		26	13
13	32	S Modena	Jordan	192	Yamaha	V12	68		24	12
14	24	G Morbidelli	Minardi	M192	Lamborghini	V12	68		18	9
r	21	J J Lehto	Dallara	192	Ferrari	V12	51	accident/ chassis	19	10
r	16	K Wendlinger	March	CG911	Ilmor	V10	48	oil radiator/ gearbox	22	11
r	26	E Comas	Ligier	JS37	Renault	V10	47	engine	14	7
r	30	U Katayama	Venturi Larrousse	LC92	Lamborghini	V12	46	spin	25	13
r	6	R Patrese	Williams	FW14B	Renault	V10	43	accident	2	1
r	22	P Martini	Dallara	192	Ferrari	V12	43	puncture	21	11
r	28	I Capelli	Ferrari	F92AT	Ferrari	V12	34	engine	16	8
r	3	O Grouillard	Tyrrell	020B	Ilmor	V10	27	gearbox	15	8
r	29	B Gachot	Venturi Larrousse	LC92	Lamborghini	V12	25	fuel pressure	13	7
r	33	M Gugelmin	Jordan	192	Yamaha	V12	19	electrics	20	10
r	27	J Alesi	Ferrari	F92AT	Ferrari	V12	12	spin	10	5
r	12	J Herbert	Lotus	107	Cosworth	V8	2	accident/ steering arm	9	5

Winning speed: 195.521 km/h, 121.491 mph
Pole Position speed: 214.400 km/h, 133.222 mph (N Mansell, 1 min:13.041 sec)
Fastest Lap speed: 205.318 km/h, 127.579 mph (A Senna, 1 min:16.272 sec on lap 66)
Lap Leaders: N Mansell 1-71 (71).

25 Oct 1992 — JAPAN: Suzuka (Round:15) (Race: 531)

53 laps x 5.864 km, 3.644 miles = 310.792 km, 193.117 miles

POS.	NO.	DRIVER	CAR	MODEL	ENGINE		LAPS	TIME/REASON FOR RETIREMENT	GRID:POS	ROW
1	6	R Patrese	Williams	FW14B	Renault	V10	53	1h 33m 09.553s	2	1
2	2	G Berger	McLaren	MP4/7A	Honda	V12	53	1h 33m 23.282s	4	2
3	20	M Brundle	Benetton	B192	Cosworth	V8	53	1h 34m 25.056s	13	7
4	4	A de Cesaris	Tyrrell	020B	Ilmor	V10	52		9	5
5	27	J Alesi	Ferrari	F92AT	Ferrari	V12	52		15	8
6	23	C Fittipaldi	Minardi	M192	Lamborghini	V12	52		12	6
7	32	S Modena	Jordan	192	Yamaha	V12	52		17	9
8	10	A Suzuki	Footwork	FA13	Mugen Honda	V10	52		16	8
9	21	J J Lehto	Dallara	192	Ferrari	V12	52		22	11
10	22	P Martini	Dallara	192	Ferrari	V12	52		19	10
11	30	U Katayama	Venturi Larrousse	LC92	Lamborghini	V12	52		20	10
12	28	N Larini	Ferrari	F9200	Ferrari	V12	52		11	6
13	17	E Naspetti	March	CG911	Ilmor	V10	51		26	13
14	24	G Morbidelli	Minardi	M192	Lamborghini	V12	51		14	7
15	9	M Alboreto	Footwork	FA13	Mugen Honda	V10	51		24	12
r	5	N Mansell	Williams	FW14B	Renault	V10	44	engine	1	1
r	11	M Häkkinen	Lotus	107	Cosworth	V8	44	engine	7	4
r	29	B Gachot	Venturi Larrousse	LC92	Lamborghini	V12	39	accident	18	9
r	26	E Comas	Ligier	JS37	Renault	V10	36	oil pressure	8	4
r	16	J Lammers	March	CG911	Ilmor	V10	27	clutch	23	12
r	33	M Gugelmin	Jordan	192	Yamaha	V12	22	accident	25	13
r	12	J Herbert	Lotus	107	Cosworth	V8	15	gearbox	6	3
r	19	M Schumacher	Benetton	B192	Cosworth	V8	13	gearbox	5	3
r	3	O Grouillard	Tyrrell	020B	Ilmor	V10	6	accident	21	11
r	25	T Boutsen	Ligier	JS37	Renault	V10	3	gearbox	10	5
r	1	A Senna	McLaren	MP4/7A	Honda	V12	2	engine	3	2

Winning speed: 200.168 km/h, 124.379 mph
Pole Position speed: 216.828 km/h, 134.731 mph (N Mansell, 1 min:37.360 sec)
Fastest Lap speed: 209.749 km/h, 130.332 mph (N Mansell, 1 min:40.646 sec on lap 44)
Lap Leaders: N Mansell 1-35 (35); R Patrese 36-53 (18).

8 Nov 1992 — AUSTRALIA: Adelaide (Round:16) (Race: 532)

81 laps x 3.780 km, 2.349 miles = 306.180 km, 190.251 miles

POS.	NO.	DRIVER	CAR	MODEL	ENGINE		LAPS	TIME/REASON FOR RETIREMENT	GRID:POS	ROW
1	2	G Berger	McLaren	MP4/7A	Honda	V12	81	1h 46m 54.786s	4	2
2	19	M Schumacher	Benetton	B192	Cosworth	V8	81	1h 46m 55.527s	5	3
3	20	M Brundle	Benetton	B192	Cosworth	V8	81	1h 47m 48.942s	8	4
4	27	J Alesi	Ferrari	F92AT	Ferrari	V12	80		6	3
5	25	T Boutsen	Ligier	JS37	Renault	V10	80		22	11
6	32	S Modena	Jordan	192	Yamaha	V12	80		15	8
7	11	M Häkkinen	Lotus	107	Cosworth	V8	80		10	5
8	10	A Suzuki	Footwork	FA13	Mugen Honda	V10	79		18	9
9	23	C Fittipaldi	Minardi	M192	Lamborghini	V12	79		17	9
10	24	G Morbidelli	Minardi	M192	Lamborghini	V12	79		16	8
11	28	N Larini	Ferrari	F9200	Ferrari	V12	79		19	10
12	16	J Lammers	March	CG911	Ilmor	V10	78		25	13
13	12	J Herbert	Lotus	107	Cosworth	V8	77		12	6
r	21	J J Lehto	Dallara	192	Ferrari	V12	70	gearbox	24	12
r	17	E Naspetti	March	CG911	Ilmor	V10	55	gearbox	23	12
r	29	B Gachot	Venturi Larrousse	LC92	Lamborghini	V12	51	engine	21	11
r	6	R Patrese	Williams	FW14B	Renault	V10	50	fuel pressure	3	2
r	30	U Katayama	Venturi Larrousse	LC92	Lamborghini	V12	35	differential	26	13
r	4	A de Cesaris	Tyrrell	020B	Ilmor	V10	29	fuel pressure/ fire	7	4

POS.	NO.	DRIVER	CAR	MODEL	ENGINE		LAPS	TIME/REASON FOR RETIREMENT	GRID:POS	ROW
r	5	N Mansell	Williams	FW14B	Renault	V10	18	accident	1	1
r	1	A Senna	McLaren	MP4/7A	Honda	V12	18	accident	2	1
r	33	M Gugelmin	Jordan	192	Yamaha	V12	7	brakes/ accident	20	10
r	26	E Comas	Ligier	JS37	Renault	V10	4	engine	9	5
r	9	M Alboreto	Footwork	FA13	Mugen Honda	V10	0	accident	11	6
r	22	P Martini	Dallara	192	Ferrari	V12	0	accident	14	7
r	3	O Grouillard	Tyrrell	020B	Ilmor	V10	0	accident	13	7

Winning speed: 171.829 km/h, 106.770 mph
Pole Position speed: 184.560 km/h, 114.680 mph (N Mansell, 1 min:13.732 sec)
Fastest Lap speed: 178.869 km/h, 111.144 mph (M Schumacher, 1 min:16.078 sec on lap 68)
Lap Leaders: N Mansell 1-18 (18); R Patrese 19-50 (32); G Berger 51-81 (31).

Lap Leaders 1992

POS	DRIVER	CAR-ENGINE	GPS	LAPS	KM	MILES
1	N Mansell	Williams-Renault	14	694	3,293.1	2,046.2
2	R Patrese	Williams-Renault	8	173	805.3	500.4
3	A Senna	McLaren-Honda	5	95	415.0	257.8
4	G Berger	McLaren-Honda	2	63	258.9	160.9
5	M Schumacher	Benetton-Cosworth	1	11	76.7	47.7
			16	**1,036**	**4,849.0**	**3,013.0**

Driver Points 1992

		ZA	MEX	BR	E	RSM	MC	CDN	F	GB	D	H	B	I	P	J	AUS	TOTAL
1	N Mansell	10	10	10	10	10	6	-	10	10	10	6	6	-	10	-	-	108
2	R Patrese	6	6	6	-	6	4	-	6	6	-	-	4	2	-	10	-	56
3	M Schumacher	3	4	4	6	-	3	6	-	3	4	-	10	4	-	-	6	53
4	A Senna	4	-	-	-	4	10	-	-	-	6	10	2	10	4	-	-	50
5	G Berger	2	3	-	3	-	-	10	-	2	-	4	-	3	6	6	10	49
6	M Brundle	-	-	-	-	3	2	-	4	4	3	2	3	6	3	4	4	38
7	J Alesi	-	-	3	4	-	-	4	-	-	2	-	-	-	-	2	3	18
8	M Häkkinen	-	1	-	-	-	-	-	3	1	-	3	1	-	2	-	-	11
9	A de Cesaris	-	2	-	-	-	-	2	-	-	-	-	-	1	-	3	-	8
10	M Alboreto	-	-	1	2	2	-	-	-	-	-	-	-	-	1	-	-	6
11	E Comas	-	-	-	-	-	-	1	2	-	1	-	-	-	-	-	-	4
12	K Wendlinger	-	-	-	-	-	-	3	-	-	-	-	-	-	-	-	-	3
	I Capelli	-	-	2	-	-	-	-	-	-	-	1	-	-	-	-	-	3
14	T Boutsen	-	-	-	-	-	-	-	-	-	-	-	-	-	-	-	2	2
	J Herbert	1	-	-	-	-	-	-	1	-	-	-	-	-	-	-	-	2
	P Martini	-	-	-	1	1	-	-	-	-	-	-	-	-	-	-	-	2
17	B Gachot	-	-	-	-	-	1	-	-	-	-	-	-	-	-	-	-	1
	C Fittipaldi	-	-	-	-	-	-	-	-	-	-	-	-	-	-	1	-	1
	S Modena	-	-	-	-	-	-	-	-	-	-	-	-	-	-	-	1	1

10, 6 ,4, 3, 2 and 1 point awarded to the first six finishers.

Constructor Points 1992

		ZA	MEX	BR	E	RSM	MC	CDN	F	GB	D	H	B	I	P	J	AUS	TOTAL
1	Williams-Renault	16	16	16	10	16	10	-	16	16	10	6	10	2	10	10	-	164
2	McLaren-Honda	6	3	-	3	4	10	10	-	2	6	14	2	13	10	6	10	99
3	Benetton-Cosworth	3	4	4	6	3	5	6	4	7	7	2	13	10	3	4	10	91
4	Ferrari	-	-	5	4	-	-	4	-	-	2	1	-	-	-	2	3	21
5	Lotus-Cosworth	1	1	-	-	-	-	-	4	1	-	3	1	-	2	-	-	13
6	Tyrrell-Ilmor	-	2	-	-	-	-	2	-	-	-	-	-	1	-	3	-	8
7	Footwork-Mugen	-	-	1	2	2	-	-	-	-	-	-	-	-	1	-	-	6
	Ligier-Renault	-	-	-	-	-	-	1	2	-	1	-	-	-	-	-	2	6
9	March-Ilmor	-	-	-	-	-	-	3	-	-	-	-	-	-	-	-	-	3
10	Dallara-Ferrari	-	-	-	1	1	-	-	-	-	-	-	-	-	-	-	-	2
11	Venturi Larrousse-Lamborghini	-	-	-	-	-	1	-	-	-	-	-	-	-	-	-	-	1
	Minardi-Lamborghini	-	-	-	-	-	-	-	-	-	-	-	-	-	-	1	-	1
	Jordan-Yamaha	-	-	-	-	-	-	-	-	-	-	-	-	-	-	-	1	1

10, 6, 4, 3, 2 and 1 point awarded to the first six finishers.

The new World Champion left after a team dispute to race in the American IndyCar series. A safety and cost reduction package called for narrower tyres, smaller wings and tyre and spare car restrictions. Safety cars were re introduced in an effort to improve the movement of damaged cars from dangerous positions. Traction control and other computer aids were the major technical progression. Sauber entered with backing from Mercedes-Benz. The racing world was stunned by the sudden death of James Hunt from a heart attack at the early age of 45.

WILLIAMS
Canon Williams Team: Hill, Prost

TYRRELL
Tyrrell Racing Organisation: Katayama, de Cesaris

BENETTON
Camel Benetton Ford: Schumacher, Patrese

McLAREN
Marlboro McLaren: Andretti, Häkkinen, Senna

FOOTWORK
Footwork Mugen Honda: Warwick, A Suzuki

LOTUS
Team Lotus: Zanardi, Lamy, Herbert

JORDAN
Sasol Jordan: Barrichello, Capelli, Boutsen, Apicella, Naspetti, Irvine

LARROUSSE
Larrousse F1: Alliot, T Suzuki, Comas

LOLA
Lola BMS Scuderia Italia: Alboreto, Badoer

MINARDI
Minardi Team: Fittipaldi, Gounon, Barbazza, Martini

LIGIER
Ligier Gitanes Blondes: Brundle, Blundell

FERRARI
Scuderia Ferrari SpA: Alesi, Berger

SAUBER
Sauber: Wendlinger, Lehto

14 Mar 1993 — SOUTH AFRICA: Kyalami (Round: 1) (Race: 533)

72 laps x 4.261 km, 2.648 miles = 306.792 km, 190.632 miles

POS.	NO.	DRIVER	CAR	MODEL	ENGINE		LAPS	TIME/REASON FOR RETIREMENT	GRID:POS	ROW
1	2	A Prost	Williams	FW15C	Renault	V10	72	1h 38m 45.082s	1	1
2	8	A Senna	McLaren	MP4/8	Cosworth	V8	72	1h 40m 04.906s	2	1
3	26	M Blundell	Ligier	JS39	Renault	V10	71		8	4
4	23	C Fittipaldi	Minardi	M193	Cosworth	V8	71		13	7
5	30	J J Lehto	Sauber	C12	Ilmor	V10	70		6	3
6r	28	G Berger	Ferrari	F93A	Ferrari	V12	69	engine	15	8
7r	9	D Warwick	Footwork	FA13B	Mugen Honda	V10	69	spin	22	11
r	25	M Brundle	Ligier	JS39	Renault	V10	57	spin	12	6
r	21	M Alboreto	Lola	T93/30	Ferrari	V12	55	engine	25	13
r	20	E Comas	Larrousse	LH93	Lamborghini	V12	51	engine	19	10
r	6	R Patrese	Benetton	B192B	Cosworth	V8	46	spin	7	4
r	5	M Schumacher	Benetton	B192B	Cosworth	V8	39	accident	3	2
r	12	J Herbert	Lotus	107B	Cosworth	V8	38	fuel pressure	17	9
r	29	K Wendlinger	Sauber	C12	Ilmor	V10	33	electrics	10	5
r	14	R Barrichello	Jordan	193	Hart	V10	31	gearbox	14	7
r	27	J Alesi	Ferrari	F93A	Ferrari	V12	30	hydraulics belt	5	3
r	19	P Alliot	Larrousse	LH93	Lamborghini	V12	27	spin	11	6
r	24	F Barbazza	Minardi	M193	Cosworth	V8	21	accident	24	12
r	10	A Suzuki	Footwork	FA13B	Mugen Honda	V10	21	accident	20	10
r	22	L Badoer	Lola	T93/30	Ferrari	V12	20	gearbox	26	13
r	0	D Hill	Williams	FW15C	Renault	V10	16	accident	4	2
r	11	A Zanardi	Lotus	107B	Cosworth	V8	16	accident	16	8
r	7	M Andretti	McLaren	MP4/8	Cosworth	V8	4	accident	9	5
r	15	I Capelli	Jordan	193	Hart	V10	2	accident	18	9
r	3	U Katayama	Tyrrell	020C	Yamaha	V10	1	transmission	21	11
r	4	A de Cesaris	Tyrrell	020C	Yamaha	V10	0	transmission	23	12

Winning speed: 186.403 km/h, 115.825 mph
Pole Position speed: 202.647 km/h, 125.919 mph (A Prost, 1 min:15.696 sec)
Fastest Lap speed: 192.970 km/h, 119.906 mph (A Prost, 1 min:19.492 sec on lap 40)
Lap Leaders: A Senna 1-23 (23); A Prost 24-72 (49).

28 Mar 1993 — BRAZIL: Interlagos (Round: 2) (Race: 534)

71 laps x 4.325 km, 2.687 miles = 307.075 km, 190.808 miles

POS.	NO.	DRIVER	CAR	MODEL	ENGINE		LAPS	TIME/REASON FOR RETIREMENT	GRID:POS	ROW
1	8	A Senna	McLaren	MP4/8	Cosworth	V8	71	1h 51m 15.485s	3	2
2	0	D Hill	Williams	FW15C	Renault	V10	71	1h 51m 32.110s	2	1
3	5	M Schumacher	Benetton	B192B	Cosworth	V8	71	1h 52m 00.921s	4	2
4	12	J Herbert	Lotus	107B	Cosworth	V8	71	1h 52m 02.042s	12	6
5	26	M Blundell	Ligier	JS39	Renault	V10	71	1h 52m 07.612s	10	5
6	11	A Zanardi	Lotus	107B	Cosworth	V8	70		15	8
7	19	P Alliot	Larrousse	LH93	Lamborghini	V12	70		11	6
8	27	J Alesi	Ferrari	F93A	Ferrari	V12	70		9	5
9	9	D Warwick	Footwork	FA13B	Mugen Honda	V10	69		18	9
10	20	E Comas	Larrousse	LH93	Lamborghini	V12	69		17	9
11	21	M Alboreto	Lola	T93/30	Ferrari	V12	68		25	13
12	22	L Badoer	Lola	T93/30	Ferrari	V12	68		21	11
r	29	K Wendlinger	Sauber	C12	Ilmor	V10	61	engine overheating	8	4
r	30	J J Lehto	Sauber	C12	Ilmor	V10	52	electrics	7	4
r	4	A de Cesaris	Tyrrell	020C	Yamaha	V10	48	electrics	23	12
r	2	A Prost	Williams	FW15C	Renault	V10	29	accident	1	1
r	23	C Fittipaldi	Minardi	M193	Cosworth	V8	28	accident	20	10
r	10	A Suzuki	Footwork	FA13B	Mugen Honda	V10	27	accident	19	10
r	3	U Katayama	Tyrrell	020C	Yamaha	V10	26	accident	22	11
r	14	R Barrichello	Jordan	193	Hart	V10	13	gearbox hydraulics	14	7
r	6	R Patrese	Benetton	B192B	Cosworth	V8	3	suspension	6	3
r	25	M Brundle	Ligier	JS39	Renault	V10	0	accident	16	8

POS.	NO.	DRIVER	CAR	MODEL	ENGINE		LAPS	TIME/REASON FOR RETIREMENT	GRID:POS	ROW
r	24	F Barbazza	Minardi	M193	Cosworth	V8	0	accident	24	12
r	7	M Andretti	McLaren	MP4/8	Cosworth	V8	0	accident	5	3
r	28	G Berger	Ferrari	F93A	Ferrari	V12	0	accident	13	7
nq	15	I Capelli	Jordan	193	Hart	V10				

Winning speed: 165.601 km/h, 102.900 mph
Pole Position speed: 205.230 km/h, 127.524 mph (A Prost, 1 min:15.866 sec)
Fastest Lap speed: 194.567 km/h, 120.898 mph (M Schumacher, 1 min:20.024 sec on lap 61)
Lap Leaders: A Prost 1-29 (29); D Hill 30-41 (12); A Senna 42-71 (30).

11 Apr 1993 — EUROPE: Donington Park — (Round: 3) (Race: 535)

76 laps x 4.023 km, 2.500 miles = 305.748 km, 189.983 miles

POS.	NO.	DRIVER	CAR	MODEL	ENGINE		LAPS	TIME/REASON FOR RETIREMENT	GRID:POS	ROW
1	8	A Senna	McLaren	MP4/8	Cosworth	V8	76	1h 50m 46.570s	4	2
2	0	D Hill	Williams	FW15C	Renault	V10	76	1h 52m 09.769s	2	1
3	2	A Prost	Williams	FW15C	Renault	V10	75		1	1
4	12	J Herbert	Lotus	107B	Cosworth	V8	75		11	6
5	6	R Patrese	Benetton	B193B	Cosworth	V8	74		10	5
6	24	F Barbazza	Minardi	M193	Cosworth	V8	74		20	10
7	23	C Fittipaldi	Minardi	M193	Cosworth	V8	73		16	8
8	11	A Zanardi	Lotus	107B	Cosworth	V8	72		13	7
9	20	E Comas	Larrousse	LH93	Lamborghini	V12	72		17	9
10r	14	R Barrichello	Jordan	193	Hart	V10	70	fuel pressure	12	6
11	21	M Alboreto	Lola	T93/30	Ferrari	V12	70		24	12
r	9	D Warwick	Footwork	FA14	Mugen Honda	V10	66	gearbox	14	7
r	15	T Boutsen	Jordan	193	Hart	V10	61	throttle jammed	19	10
r	4	A de Cesaris	Tyrrell	020C	Yamaha	V10	55	gearbox	25	13
r	27	J Alesi	Ferrari	F93A	Ferrari	V12	36	suspension hydraulics	9	5
r	10	A Suzuki	Footwork	FA14	Mugen Honda	V10	29	gearbox	23	12
r	19	P Alliot	Larrousse	LH93	Lamborghini	V12	27	accident	15	8
r	5	M Schumacher	Benetton	B193B	Cosworth	V8	22	accident	3	2
r	26	M Blundell	Ligier	JS39	Renault	V10	20	accident	21	11
r	28	G Berger	Ferrari	F93A	Ferrari	V12	19	suspension hydraulics	8	4
r	30	J J Lehto	Sauber	C12	Ilmor	V10	13	handling	7	4
r	3	U Katayama	Tyrrell	020C	Yamaha	V10	11	clutch	18	9
r	25	M Brundle	Ligier	JS39	Renault	V10	7	accident	22	11
r	7	M Andretti	McLaren	MP4/8	Cosworth	V8	0	accident	6	3
r	29	K Wendlinger	Sauber	C12	Ilmor	V10	0	accident	5	3
nq	22	L Badoer	Lola	T93/30	Ferrari	V12				

Winning speed: 165.603 km/h, 102.901 mph
Pole Position speed: 205.552 km/h, 127.724 mph (A Prost, 1 min:10.458 sec)
Fastest Lap speed: 185.608 km/h, 115.331 mph (A Senna, 1 min:18.029 sec on lap 57)
Lap Leaders: A Senna 1-18,20-34,39-76 (71); A Prost 19,35-38 (5).

The official fastest lap credited to A Senna was set via the pit lane. The fastest complete lap was set by D Hill on lap 55 (1m 19.379s, 182.451 km/h, 113.370 mph).

25 Apr 1993 — SAN MARINO: Imola — (Round: 4) (Race: 536)

61 laps x 5.040 km, 3.132 miles = 307.440 km, 191.034 miles

POS.	NO.	DRIVER	CAR	MODEL	ENGINE		LAPS	TIME/REASON FOR RETIREMENT	GRID:POS	ROW
1	2	A Prost	Williams	FW15C	Renault	V10	61	1h 33m 20.413s	1	1
2	5	M Schumacher	Benetton	B193B	Cosworth	V8	61	1h 33m 52.823s	3	2
3	25	M Brundle	Ligier	JS39	Renault	V10	60		10	5
4r	30	J J Lehto	Sauber	C12	Ilmor	V10	59	engine	16	8
5	19	P Alliot	Larrousse	LH93	Lamborghini	V12	59		14	7
6	24	F Barbazza	Minardi	M193	Cosworth	V8	59		25	13
7	22	L Badoer	Lola	T93/30	Ferrari	V12	58		24	12
8r	12	J Herbert	Lotus	107B	Cosworth	V8	57	engine	12	6
9	10	A Suzuki	Footwork	FA14	Mugen Honda	V10	54		21	11
r	11	A Zanardi	Lotus	107B	Cosworth	V8	53	accident	20	10
r	29	K Wendlinger	Sauber	C12	Ilmor	V10	48	engine	5	3
r	8	A Senna	McLaren	MP4/8	Cosworth	V8	42	hydraulics	4	2
r	27	J Alesi	Ferrari	F93A	Ferrari	V12	40	clutch	9	5
r	23	C Fittipaldi	Minardi	M193	Cosworth	V8	36	steering	23	12
r	7	M Andretti	McLaren	MP4/8	Cosworth	V8	32	brakes/ spin	6	3
r	9	D Warwick	Footwork	FA14	Mugen Honda	V10	29	spin	15	8
r	3	U Katayama	Tyrrell	020C	Yamaha	V10	22	engine	22	11
r	0	D Hill	Williams	FW15C	Renault	V10	20	spin	2	1
r	20	E Comas	Larrousse	LH93	Lamborghini	V12	18	oil pressure	17	9
r	4	A de Cesaris	Tyrrell	020C	Yamaha	V10	18	gearbox	18	9
r	14	R Barrichello	Jordan	193	Hart	V10	17	spin	13	7
r	28	G Berger	Ferrari	F93A	Ferrari	V12	8	gearbox	8	4
r	15	T Boutsen	Jordan	193	Hart	V10	1	gearbox	19	10
r	6	R Patrese	Benetton	B193B	Cosworth	V8	0	accident	11	6
r	26	M Blundell	Ligier	JS39	Renault	V10	0	accident	7	4
nq	21	M Alboreto	Lola	T93/30	Ferrari	V12				

Winning speed: 197.625 km/h, 122.799 mph
Pole Position speed: 221.080 km/h, 137.372 mph (A Prost, 1 min:22.070 sec)
Fastest Lap speed: 210.663 km/h, 130.900 mph (A Prost, 1 min:26.128 sec on lap 42)
Lap Leaders: D Hill 1-11 (11); A Prost 12-61 (50).

9 May 1993 — SPAIN: Montmeló (Round: 5) (Race: 537)

65 laps x 4.747 km, 2.950 miles = 308.555 km, 191.727 miles

POS.	NO.	DRIVER	CAR	MODEL	ENGINE		LAPS	TIME/REASON FOR RETIREMENT	GRID:POS	ROW
1	2	A Prost	Williams	FW15C	Renault	V10	65	1h 32m 27.685s	1	1
2	8	A Senna	McLaren	MP4/8	Cosworth	V8	65	1h 32m 44.558s	3	2
3	5	M Schumacher	Benetton	B193B	Cosworth	V8	65	1h 32m 54.810s	4	2
4	6	R Patrese	Benetton	B193B	Cosworth	V8	64		5	3
5	7	M Andretti	McLaren	MP4/8	Cosworth	V8	64		7	4
6	28	G Berger	Ferrari	F93A	Ferrari	V12	63		11	6
7	26	M Blundell	Ligier	JS39	Renault	V10	63		12	6
8	23	C Fittipaldi	Minardi	M193	Cosworth	V8	63		20	10
9	20	E Comas	Larrousse	LH93	Lamborghini	V12	63		14	7
10	10	A Suzuki	Footwork	FA14	Mugen Honda	V10	63		19	10
11	15	T Boutsen	Jordan	193	Hart	V10	62		21	11
12	14	R Barrichello	Jordan	193	Hart	V10	62		17	9
13	9	D Warwick	Footwork	FA14	Mugen Honda	V10	62		16	8
14r	11	A Zanardi	Lotus	107B	Cosworth	V8	60	engine	15	8
r	30	J J Lehto	Sauber	C12	Ilmor	V10	53	engine	9	5
r	22	L Badoer	Lola	T93/30	Ferrari	V12	43	clutch	22	11
r	29	K Wendlinger	Sauber	C12	Ilmor	V10	42	fuel pressure	6	3
dq	4	A de Cesaris	Tyrrell	020C	Yamaha	V10	42	push start after engine cut	24	12
r	0	D Hill	Williams	FW15C	Renault	V10	41	engine	2	1
r	27	J Alesi	Ferrari	F93A	Ferrari	V12	40	engine	8	4
r	24	F Barbazza	Minardi	M193	Cosworth	V8	37	accident	25	13
r	19	P Alliot	Larrousse	LH93	Lamborghini	V12	26	gearbox	13	7
r	25	M Brundle	Ligier	JS39	Renault	V10	11	accident	18	9
r	3	U Katayama	Tyrrell	020C	Yamaha	V10	11	accident	23	12
r	12	J Herbert	Lotus	107B	Cosworth	V8	2	suspension	10	5
nq	21	M Alboreto	Lola	T93/30	Ferrari	V12				

Winning speed: 200.227 km/h, 124.415 mph
Pole Position speed: 219.630 km/h, 136.472 mph (A Prost, 1 min:17.809 sec)
Fastest Lap speed: 211.006 km/h, 131.113 mph (M Schumacher, 1 min:20.989 sec on lap 61)
Lap Leaders: D Hill 1-10 (10); A Prost 11-65 (55).

23 May 1993 — MONACO: Monte Carlo (Round: 6) (Race: 538)

78 laps x 3.328 km, 2.068 miles = 259.584 km, 161.298 miles

POS.	NO.	DRIVER	CAR	MODEL	ENGINE		LAPS	TIME/REASON FOR RETIREMENT	GRID:POS	ROW
1	8	A Senna	McLaren	MP4/8	Cosworth	V8	78	1h 52m 10.947s	3	2
2	0	D Hill	Williams	FW15C	Renault	V10	78	1h 53m 03.065s	4	2
3	27	J Alesi	Ferrari	F93A	Ferrari	V12	78	1h 53m 14.309s	5	3
4	2	A Prost	Williams	FW15C	Renault	V10	77		1	1
5	23	C Fittipaldi	Minardi	M193	Cosworth	V8	76		17	9
6	25	M Brundle	Ligier	JS39	Renault	V10	76		13	7
7	11	A Zanardi	Lotus	107B	Cosworth	V8	76		20	10
8	7	M Andretti	McLaren	MP4/8	Cosworth	V8	76		9	5
9	14	R Barrichello	Jordan	193	Hart	V10	76		16	8
10	4	A de Cesaris	Tyrrell	020C	Yamaha	V10	76		19	10
11	24	F Barbazza	Minardi	M193	Cosworth	V8	75		25	13
12	19	P Alliot	Larrousse	LH93	Lamborghini	V12	75		15	8
13	29	K Wendlinger	Sauber	C12	Ilmor	V10	74		8	4
14r	28	G Berger	Ferrari	F93A	Ferrari	V12	70	accident	7	4
r	12	J Herbert	Lotus	107B	Cosworth	V8	61	accident	14	7
r	6	R Patrese	Benetton	B193B	Cosworth	V8	53	engine	6	3
r	20	E Comas	Larrousse	LH93	Lamborghini	V12	51	accident	10	5
r	10	A Suzuki	Footwork	FA14	Mugen Honda	V10	46	accident	18	9
r	9	D Warwick	Footwork	FA14	Mugen Honda	V10	43	throttle	12	6
r	5	M Schumacher	Benetton	B193B	Cosworth	V8	32	suspension hydraulics	2	1
r	3	U Katayama	Tyrrell	020C	Yamaha	V10	31	oil leak	22	11
r	21	M Alboreto	Lola	T93/30	Ferrari	V12	28	gearbox	24	12
r	30	J J Lehto	Sauber	C12	Ilmor	V10	23	accident	11	6
r	15	T Boutsen	Jordan	193	Hart	V10	12	suspension	23	12
r	26	M Blundell	Ligier	JS39	Renault	V10	3	suspension	21	11
nq	22	L Badoer	Lola	T93/30	Ferrari	V12				

Winning speed: 138.837 km/h, 86.269 mph
Pole Position speed: 148.725 km/h, 92.413 mph (A Prost, 1 min:20.557 sec)
Fastest Lap speed: 143.304 km/h, 89.045 mph (A Prost, 1 min:23.604 sec on lap 52)
Lap Leaders: A Prost 1-11 (11); M Schumacher 12-32 (21); A Senna 33-78 (46).

13 Jun 1993 — CANADA: Montréal (Round: 7) (Race: 539)

69 laps x 4.430 km, 2.753 miles = 305.670 km, 189.935 miles

POS.	NO.	DRIVER	CAR	MODEL	ENGINE		LAPS	TIME/REASON FOR RETIREMENT	GRID:POS	ROW
1	2	A Prost	Williams	FW15C	Renault	V10	69	1h 36m 41.822s	1	1
2	5	M Schumacher	Benetton	B193B	Cosworth	V8	69	1h 36m 56.349s	3	2
3	0	D Hill	Williams	FW15C	Renault	V10	69	1h 37m 34.507s	2	1
4	28	G Berger	Ferrari	F93A	Ferrari	V12	68		5	3
5	25	M Brundle	Ligier	JS39	Renault	V10	68		7	4
6	29	K Wendlinger	Sauber	C12	Ilmor	V10	68		9	5
7	30	J J Lehto	Sauber	C12	Ilmor	V10	68		11	6
8	20	E Comas	Larrousse	LH93	Lamborghini	V12	68		13	7
9	23	C Fittipaldi	Minardi	M193	Cosworth	V8	67		17	9
10	12	J Herbert	Lotus	107B	Cosworth	V8	67		20	10

POS.	NO.	DRIVER	CAR	MODEL	ENGINE		LAPS	TIME/REASON FOR RETIREMENT	GRID:POS	ROW
11	11	A Zanardi	Lotus	107B	Cosworth	V8	67		21	11
12	15	T Boutsen	Jordan	193	Hart	V10	67		24	12
13	10	A Suzuki	Footwork	FA14	Mugen Honda	V10	66		16	8
14	7	M Andretti	McLaren	MP4/8	Cosworth	V8	66		12	6
15	22	L Badoer	Lola	T93/30	Ferrari	V12	65		25	13
16	9	D Warwick	Footwork	FA14	Mugen Honda	V10	65		18	9
17	3	U Katayama	Tyrrell	020C	Yamaha	V10	64		22	11
18r	8	A Senna	McLaren	MP4/8	Cosworth	V8	62	alternator	8	4
r	6	R Patrese	Benetton	B193B	Cosworth	V8	52	driver discomfort	4	2
r	4	A de Cesaris	Tyrrell	020C	Yamaha	V10	45	accident	19	10
r	24	F Barbazza	Minardi	M193	Cosworth	V8	33	gearbox	23	12
r	27	J Alesi	Ferrari	F93A	Ferrari	V12	23	engine	6	3
r	26	M Blundell	Ligier	JS39	Renault	V10	13	accident	10	5
r	14	R Barrichello	Jordan	193	Hart	V10	10	electrics	14	7
r	19	P Alliot	Larrousse	LH93	Lamborghini	V12	8	gear lever	15	8
nq	21	M Alboreto	Lola	T93/30	Ferrari	V12				

Winning speed: 189.667 km/h, 117.853 mph
Pole Position speed: 201.907 km/h, 125.459 mph (A Prost, 1 min:18.987 sec)
Fastest Lap speed: 195.681 km/h, 121.591 mph (M Schumacher, 1 min:21.500 sec on lap 57)
Lap Leaders: D Hill 1-5 (5); A Prost 6-69 (64).

4 Jul 1993 — FRANCE: Magny-Cours — (Round: 8) (Race: 540)

72 laps x 4.250 km, 2.641 miles = 306.000 km, 190.140 miles

POS.	NO.	DRIVER	CAR	MODEL	ENGINE		LAPS	TIME/REASON FOR RETIREMENT	GRID:POS	ROW
1	2	A Prost	Williams	FW15C	Renault	V10	72	1h 38m 35.241s	2	1
2	0	D Hill	Williams	FW15C	Renault	V10	72	1h 38m 35.583s	1	1
3	5	M Schumacher	Benetton	B193B	Cosworth	V8	72	1h 38m 56.450s	7	4
4	8	A Senna	McLaren	MP4/8	Cosworth	V8	72	1h 39m 07.646s	5	3
5	25	M Brundle	Ligier	JS39	Renault	V10	72	1h 39m 09.036s	3	2
6	7	M Andretti	McLaren	MP4/8	Cosworth	V8	71		16	8
7	14	R Barrichello	Jordan	193	Hart	V10	71		8	4
8	23	C Fittipaldi	Minardi	M193	Cosworth	V8	71		23	12
9	19	P Alliot	Larrousse	LH93	Lamborghini	V12	70		10	5
10	6	R Patrese	Benetton	B193B	Cosworth	V8	70		12	6
11	15	T Boutsen	Jordan	193	Hart	V10	70		20	10
12	10	A Suzuki	Footwork	FA14	Mugen Honda	V10	70		13	7
13	9	D Warwick	Footwork	FA14	Mugen Honda	V10	70		15	8
14	28	G Berger	Ferrari	F93A	Ferrari	V12	70		14	7
15	4	A de Cesaris	Tyrrell	020C	Yamaha	V10	68		25	13
16r	20	E Comas	Larrousse	LH93	Lamborghini	V12	66	gearbox	9	5
r	27	J Alesi	Ferrari	F93A	Ferrari	V12	47	engine	6	3
r	22	L Badoer	Lola	T93/30	Ferrari	V12	28	suspension	22	11
r	29	K Wendlinger	Sauber	C12	Ilmor	V10	25	gearbox	11	6
r	30	J J Lehto	Sauber	C12	Ilmor	V10	22	gearbox	18	9
r	26	M Blundell	Ligier	JS39	Renault	V10	20	spin	4	2
r	12	J Herbert	Lotus	107B	Cosworth	V8	16	spin	19	10
r	24	F Barbazza	Minardi	M193	Cosworth	V8	16	gearbox	24	12
r	3	U Katayama	Tyrrell	020C	Yamaha	V10	9	oil leak	21	11
r	11	A Zanardi	Lotus	107B	Cosworth	V8	3	suspension	17	9
nq	21	M Alboreto	Lola	T93/30	Ferrari	V12				

Winning speed: 186.231 km/h, 115.718 mph
Pole Position speed: 205.695 km/h, 127.813 mph (D Hill, 1 min:14.382 sec)
Fastest Lap speed: 193.045 km/h, 119.953 mph (M Schumacher, 1 min:19.256 sec on lap 47)
Lap Leaders: D Hill 1-26 (26); A Prost 27-72 (46).

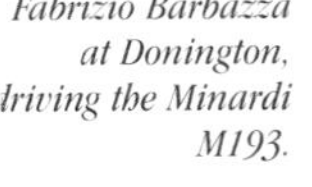
Fabrizio Barbazza at Donington, driving the Minardi M193.

11 Jul 1993 BRITAIN: Silverstone (Round: 9) (Race: 541)

59 laps x 5.226 km, 3.247 miles = 308.334 km, 191.590 miles

POS.	NO.	DRIVER	CAR	MODEL	ENGINE		LAPS	TIME/REASON FOR RETIREMENT	GRID:POS	ROW
1	2	A Prost	Williams	FW15C	Renault	V10	59	1h 25m 38.189s	1	1
2	5	M Schumacher	Benetton	B193B	Cosworth	V8	59	1h 25m 45.849s	3	2
3	6	R Patrese	Benetton	B193B	Cosworth	V8	59	1h 26m 55.671s	5	3
4	12	J Herbert	Lotus	107B	Cosworth	V8	59	1h 26m 56.596s	7	4
5r	8	A Senna	McLaren	MP4/8	Cosworth	V8	58	out of fuel	4	2
6	9	D Warwick	Footwork	FA14	Mugen Honda	V10	58		8	4
7	26	M Blundell	Ligier	JS39	Renault	V10	58		9	5
8	30	J J Lehto	Sauber	C12	Ilmor	V10	58		16	8
9	27	J Alesi	Ferrari	F93A	Ferrari	V12	58		12	6
10	14	R Barrichello	Jordan	193	Hart	V10	58		15	8
11	19	P Alliot	Larrousse	LH93	Lamborghini	V12	57		24	12
12r	23	C Fittipaldi	Minardi	M193	Cosworth	V8	56	gearbox	19	10
13	3	U Katayama	Tyrrell	020C	Yamaha	V10	55		22	11
14r	25	M Brundle	Ligier	JS39	Renault	V10	53	gearbox	6	3
nc	4	A de Cesaris	Tyrrell	021	Yamaha	V10	43		21	11
r	0	D Hill	Williams	FW15C	Renault	V10	41	engine	2	1
r	11	A Zanardi	Lotus	107B	Cosworth	V8	41	spin	14	7
r	15	T Boutsen	Jordan	193	Hart	V10	41	wheel bearing	23	12
r	22	L Badoer	Lola	T93/30	Ferrari	V12	32	electrics	25	13
r	24	P Martini	Minardi	M193	Cosworth	V8	31	driver discomfort	20	10
r	29	K Wendlinger	Sauber	C12	Ilmor	V10	24	accident	18	9
r	28	G Berger	Ferrari	F93A	Ferrari	V12	10	suspension	13	7
r	10	A Suzuki	Footwork	FA14	Mugen Honda	V10	8	spin	10	5
r	7	M Andretti	McLaren	MP4/8	Cosworth	V8	0	spin	11	6
r	20	E Comas	Larrousse	LH93	Lamborghini	V12	0	drive shaft	17	9
nq	21	M Alboreto	Lola	T93/30	Ferrari	V12				

Winning speed: 216.030 km/h, 134.235 mph
Pole Position speed: 238.129 km/h, 147.966 mph (A Prost, 1 min:19.006 sec)
Fastest Lap speed: 228.002 km/h, 141.674 mph (D Hill, 1 min:22.515 sec on lap 41)
Lap Leaders: D Hill 1-41 (41); A Prost 42-59 (18).

25 Jul 1993 GERMANY: Hockenheim (Round:10) (Race: 542)

45 laps x 6.815 km, 4.235 miles = 306.675 km, 190.559 miles

POS.	NO.	DRIVER	CAR	MODEL	ENGINE		LAPS	TIME/REASON FOR RETIREMENT	GRID:POS	ROW
1	2	A Prost	Williams	FW15C	Renault	V10	45	1h 18m 40.885s	1	1
2	5	M Schumacher	Benetton	B193B	Cosworth	V8	45	1h 18m 57.549s	3	2
3	26	M Blundell	Ligier	JS39	Renault	V10	45	1h 19m 40.234s	5	3
4	8	A Senna	McLaren	MP4/8	Cosworth	V8	45	1h 19m 49.114s	4	2
5	6	R Patrese	Benetton	B193B	Cosworth	V8	45	1h 20m 12.401s	7	4
6	28	G Berger	Ferrari	F93A	Ferrari	V12	45	1h 20m 15.639s	9	5
7	27	J Alesi	Ferrari	F93A	Ferrari	V12	45	1h 20m 16.726s	10	5
8	25	M Brundle	Ligier	JS39	Renault	V10	44		6	3
9	29	K Wendlinger	Sauber	C12	Ilmor	V10	44		14	7
10	12	J Herbert	Lotus	107B	Cosworth	V8	44		13	7
11	23	C Fittipaldi	Minardi	M193	Cosworth	V8	44		20	10
12	19	P Alliot	Larrousse	LH93	Lamborghini	V12	44		23	12
13	15	T Boutsen	Jordan	193	Hart	V10	44		24	12
14	24	P Martini	Minardi	M193	Cosworth	V8	44		22	11
15r	0	D Hill	Williams	FW15C	Renault	V10	43	puncture	2	1
16	21	M Alboreto	Lola	T93/30	Ferrari	V12	43		26	13
17	9	D Warwick	Footwork	FA14	Mugen Honda	V10	42		11	6
r	14	R Barrichello	Jordan	193	Hart	V10	34	wheel bearing	17	9
r	3	U Katayama	Tyrrell	021	Yamaha	V10	28	spin/ drive shaft	21	11
r	30	J J Lehto	Sauber	C12	Ilmor	V10	22	throttle jammed/ spin	18	9
r	11	A Zanardi	Lotus	107B	Cosworth	V8	19	spin	15	8
r	10	A Suzuki	Footwork	FA14	Mugen Honda	V10	9	gearbox	8	4
r	7	M Andretti	McLaren	MP4/8	Cosworth	V8	4	accident/ steering	12	6
r	22	L Badoer	Lola	T93/30	Ferrari	V12	4	suspension	25	13
r	4	A de Cesaris	Tyrrell	021	Yamaha	V10	1	gearbox	19	10
r	20	E Comas	Larrousse	LH93	Lamborghini	V12	0	clutch	16	8

Winning speed: 233.861 km/h, 145.314 mph
Pole Position speed: 248.451 km/h, 154.380 mph (A Prost, 1 min:38.748 sec)
Fastest Lap speed: 240.862 km/h, 149.665 mph (M Schumacher, 1 min:41.859 sec on lap 40)
Lap Leaders: D Hill 1-7,10-43 (41); A Prost 8-9,44-45 (4).

15 Aug 1993 HUNGARY: Hungaroring (Round:11) (Race: 543)

77 laps x 3.968 km, 2.466 miles = 305.536 km, 189.851 miles

POS.	NO.	DRIVER	CAR	MODEL	ENGINE		LAPS	TIME/REASON FOR RETIREMENT	GRID:POS	ROW
1	0	D Hill	Williams	FW15C	Renault	V10	77	1h 47m 39.098s	2	1
2	6	R Patrese	Benetton	B193B	Cosworth	V8	77	1h 48m 51.013s	5	3
3	28	G Berger	Ferrari	F93A	Ferrari	V12	77	1h 48m 57.140s	6	3
4	9	D Warwick	Footwork	FA14	Mugen Honda	V10	76		9	5
5	25	M Brundle	Ligier	JS39	Renault	V10	76		13	7
6	29	K Wendlinger	Sauber	C12	Ilmor	V10	76		17	9
7	26	M Blundell	Ligier	JS39	Renault	V10	76		12	6
8	19	P Alliot	Larrousse	LH93	Lamborghini	V12	75		19	10
9	15	T Boutsen	Jordan	193	Hart	V10	75		24	12
10	3	U Katayama	Tyrrell	021	Yamaha	V10	73		23	12

POS.	NO.	DRIVER	CAR	MODEL	ENGINE		LAPS	TIME/REASON FOR RETIREMENT	GRID:POS	ROW
11	4	A de Cesaris	Tyrrell	021	Yamaha	V10	72		22	11
12	2	A Prost	Williams	FW15C	Renault	V10	70		1	1
r	24	P Martini	Minardi	M193	Cosworth	V8	59	accident	7	4
r	20	E Comas	Larrousse	LH93	Lamborghini	V12	54	oil leak	18	9
r	11	A Zanardi	Lotus	107B	Cosworth	V8	45	gearbox	21	11
r	10	A Suzuki	Footwork	FA14	Mugen Honda	V10	41	spin	10	5
r	21	M Alboreto	Lola	T93/30	Ferrari	V12	39	engine overheating	25	13
r	12	J Herbert	Lotus	107B	Cosworth	V8	38	spin	20	10
r	22	L Badoer	Lola	T93/30	Ferrari	V12	37	spin	26	13
r	5	M Schumacher	Benetton	B193B	Cosworth	V8	26	spin	3	2
r	23	C Fittipaldi	Minardi	M193	Cosworth	V8	22	accident	14	7
r	27	J Alesi	Ferrari	F93A	Ferrari	V12	22	accident	8	4
r	30	J J Lehto	Sauber	C12	Ilmor	V10	18	engine	15	8
r	8	A Senna	McLaren	MP4/8	Cosworth	V8	17	throttle	4	2
r	7	M Andretti	McLaren	MP4/8	Cosworth	V8	15	throttle	11	6
r	14	R Barrichello	Jordan	193	Hart	V10	0	accident	16	8

Winning speed: 170.292 km/h, 105.814 mph
Pole Position speed: 191.406 km/h, 118.934 mph (A Prost, 1 min:14.631 sec)
Fastest Lap speed: 179.383 km/h, 111.463 mph (A Prost, 1 min:19.633 sec on lap 52)
Lap Leaders: D Hill 1-77 (77).

29 Aug 1993 BELGIUM: Spa-Francorchamps (Round:12) (Race: 544)

44 laps x 6.974 km, 4.333 miles = 306.856 km, 190.671 miles

POS.	NO.	DRIVER	CAR	MODEL	ENGINE		LAPS	TIME/REASON FOR RETIREMENT	GRID:POS	ROW
1	0	D Hill	Williams	FW15C	Renault	V10	44	1h 24m 32.124s	2	1
2	5	M Schumacher	Benetton	B193B	Cosworth	V8	44	1h 24m 35.792s	3	2
3	2	A Prost	Williams	FW15C	Renault	V10	44	1h 24m 47.112s	1	1
4	8	A Senna	McLaren	MP4/8	Cosworth	V8	44	1h 26m 11.887s	5	3
5	12	J Herbert	Lotus	107B	Cosworth	V8	43		10	5
6	6	R Patrese	Benetton	B193B	Cosworth	V8	43		8	4
7	25	M Brundle	Ligier	JS39	Renault	V10	43		11	6
8	7	M Andretti	McLaren	MP4/8	Cosworth	V8	43		14	7
9	30	J J Lehto	Sauber	C12	Ilmor	V10	43		9	5
10r	28	G Berger	Ferrari	F93A	Ferrari	V12	42	accident	16	8
11r	26	M Blundell	Ligier	JS39	Renault	V10	42	accident	15	8
12	19	P Alliot	Larrousse	LH93	Lamborghini	V12	42		18	9
13	22	L Badoer	Lola	T93/30	Ferrari	V12	42		24	12
14	21	M Alboreto	Lola	T93/30	Ferrari	V12	41		25	13
15	3	U Katayama	Tyrrell	021	Yamaha	V10	40		23	12
r	20	E Comas	Larrousse	LH93	Lamborghini	V12	37	fuel pump	19	10
r	9	D Warwick	Footwork	FA14	Mugen Honda	V10	28	electrics	7	4
r	29	K Wendlinger	Sauber	C12	Ilmor	V10	27	engine	12	6
r	4	A de Cesaris	Tyrrell	021	Yamaha	V10	24	engine	17	9
r	23	C Fittipaldi	Minardi	M193	Cosworth	V8	15	accident	22	11
r	24	P Martini	Minardi	M193	Cosworth	V8	15	spin	21	11
r	10	A Suzuki	Footwork	FA14	Mugen Honda	V10	14	suspension hydraulics	6	3
r	14	R Barrichello	Jordan	193	Hart	V10	11	wheel bearing	13	7
r	27	J Alesi	Ferrari	F93A	Ferrari	V12	4	suspension	4	2
r	15	T Boutsen	Jordan	193	Hart	V10	0	gearbox	20	10
ns	11	A Zanardi	Lotus	107B	Cosworth	V8		accident/ injury		

Winning speed: 217.795 km/h, 135.331 mph
Pole Position speed: 233.394 km/h, 145.024 mph (A Prost, 1 min:47.571 sec)
Fastest Lap speed: 225.990 km/h, 140.424 mph (A Prost, 1 min:51.095 sec on lap 41)
Lap Leaders: A Prost 1-30 (30); D Hill 31-44 (14).

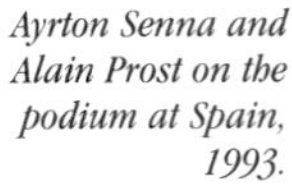

Ayrton Senna and Alain Prost on the podium at Spain, 1993.

12 Sep 1993 — ITALY: Monza — (Round:13) (Race: 545)

53 laps x 5.800 km, 3.604 miles = 307.400 km, 191.010 miles

POS.	NO.	DRIVER	CAR	MODEL	ENGINE		LAPS	TIME/REASON FOR RETIREMENT	GRID:POS	ROW
1	0	D Hill	Williams	FW15C	Renault	V10	53	1h 17m 07.509s	2	1
2	27	J Alesi	Ferrari	F93A	Ferrari	V12	53	1h 17m 47.521s	3	2
3	7	M Andretti	McLaren	MP4/8	Cosworth	V8	52		9	5
4	29	K Wendlinger	Sauber	C12	Ilmor	V10	52		15	8
5	6	R Patrese	Benetton	B193B	Cosworth	V8	52		10	5
6	20	E Comas	Larrousse	LH93	Lamborghini	V12	51		20	10
7r	24	P Martini	Minardi	M193	Cosworth	V8	51	accident	22	11
8r	23	C Fittipaldi	Minardi	M193	Cosworth	V8	51	accident	24	12
9	19	P Alliot	Larrousse	LH93	Lamborghini	V12	51		16	8
10	22	L Badoer	Lola	T93/30	Ferrari	V12	51		25	13
11r	11	P Lamy	Lotus	107B	Cosworth	V8	49	engine	26	13
12r	2	A Prost	Williams	FW15C	Renault	V10	48	engine	1	1
13r	4	A de Cesaris	Tyrrell	021	Yamaha	V10	47	oil pressure	18	9
14	3	U Katayama	Tyrrell	021	Yamaha	V10	47		17	9
r	21	M Alboreto	Lola	T93/30	Ferrari	V12	23	suspension	21	11
r	5	M Schumacher	Benetton	B193B	Cosworth	V8	21	engine	5	3
r	26	M Blundell	Ligier	JS39	Renault	V10	20	accident	14	7
r	28	G Berger	Ferrari	F93A	Ferrari	V12	15	suspension	6	3
r	12	J Herbert	Lotus	107B	Cosworth	V8	14	accident	7	4
r	25	M Brundle	Ligier	JS39	Renault	V10	8	accident	12	6
r	8	A Senna	McLaren	MP4/8	Cosworth	V8	8	accident	4	2
r	10	A Suzuki	Footwork	FA14	Mugen Honda	V10	0	accident	8	4
r	9	D Warwick	Footwork	FA14	Mugen Honda	V10	0	accident	11	6
r	30	J J Lehto	Sauber	C12	Ilmor	V10	0	accident	13	7
r	14	R Barrichello	Jordan	193	Hart	V10	0	accident	19	10
r	15	M Apicella	Jordan	193	Hart	V10	0	accident	23	12

Winning speed: 239.144 km/h, 148.597 mph
Pole Position speed: 257.209 km/h, 159.822 mph (A Prost, 1 min:21.179 sec)
Fastest Lap speed: 249.835 km/h, 155.241 mph (D Hill, 1 min:23.575 sec on lap 45)
Lap Leaders: A Prost 1-48 (48); D Hill 49-53 (5).

26 Sep 1993 — PORTUGAL: Estoril — (Round:14) (Race: 546)

71 laps x 4.350 km, 2.703 miles = 308.850 km, 191.910 miles

POS.	NO.	DRIVER	CAR	MODEL	ENGINE		LAPS	TIME/REASON FOR RETIREMENT	GRID:POS	ROW
1	5	M Schumacher	Benetton	B193B	Cosworth	V8	71	1h 32m 46.309s	6	3
2	2	A Prost	Williams	FW15C	Renault	V10	71	1h 32m 47.291s	2	1
3	0	D Hill	Williams	FW15C	Renault	V10	71	1h 32m 54.515s	1	1
4	27	J Alesi	Ferrari	F93A	Ferrari	V12	71	1h 33m 53.914s	5	3
5	29	K Wendlinger	Sauber	C12	Ilmor	V10	70		13	7
6	25	M Brundle	Ligier	JS39	Renault	V10	70		11	6
7	30	J J Lehto	Sauber	C12	Ilmor	V10	69		12	6
8	24	P Martini	Minardi	M193	Cosworth	V8	69		19	10
9	23	C Fittipaldi	Minardi	M193	Cosworth	V8	69		24	12
10	19	P Alliot	Larrousse	LH93	Lamborghini	V12	69		20	10
11	20	E Comas	Larrousse	LH93	Lamborghini	V12	68		22	11
12	4	A de Cesaris	Tyrrell	021	Yamaha	V10	68		17	9
13	14	R Barrichello	Jordan	193	Hart	V10	68		15	8
14	22	L Badoer	Lola	T93/30	Ferrari	V12	68		26	13
15r	9	D Warwick	Footwork	FA14	Mugen Honda	V10	63	accident	9	5
16r	6	R Patrese	Benetton	B193B	Cosworth	V8	63	accident	7	4
r	11	P Lamy	Lotus	107B	Cosworth	V8	61	accident	18	9
r	12	J Herbert	Lotus	107B	Cosworth	V8	60	accident	14	7
r	26	M Blundell	Ligier	JS39	Renault	V10	51	accident	10	5
r	21	M Alboreto	Lola	T93/30	Ferrari	V12	38	gearbox/ accident	25	13
r	28	G Berger	Ferrari	F93A	Ferrari	V12	35	suspension/ accident	8	4
r	7	M Häkkinen	McLaren	MP4/8	Cosworth	V8	32	accident	3	2
r	10	A Suzuki	Footwork	FA14	Mugen Honda	V10	27	gearbox	16	8
r	8	A Senna	McLaren	MP4/8	Cosworth	V8	19	engine	4	2
r	3	U Katayama	Tyrrell	021	Yamaha	V10	12	accident	21	11
r	15	E Naspetti	Jordan	193	Hart	V10	8	engine	23	12

Winning speed: 199.748 km/h, 124.118 mph
Pole Position speed: 219.039 km/h, 136.105 mph (D Hill, 1 min:11.494 sec)
Fastest Lap speed: 209.193 km/h, 129.987 mph (D Hill, 1 min:14.859 sec on lap 68)
Lap Leaders: J Alesi 1-19 (19); A Prost 20-29 (10); M Schumacher 30-71 (42).

24 Oct 1993 — JAPAN: Suzuka (Round:15) (Race: 547)

53 laps x 5.864 km, 3.644 miles = 310.792 km, 193.117 miles

POS.	NO.	DRIVER	CAR	MODEL	ENGINE		LAPS	TIME/REASON FOR RETIREMENT	GRID:POS	ROW
1	8	A Senna	McLaren	MP4/8	Cosworth	V8	53	1h 40m 27.912s	2	1
2	2	A Prost	Williams	FW15C	Renault	V10	53	1h 40m 39.347s	1	1
3	7	M Häkkinen	McLaren	MP4/8	Cosworth	V8	53	1h 40m 54.041s	3	2
4	0	D Hill	Williams	FW15C	Renault	V10	53	1h 41m 51.450s	6	3
5	14	R Barrichello	Jordan	193	Hart	V10	53	1h 42m 03.013s	12	6
6	15	E Irvine	Jordan	193	Hart	V10	53	1h 42m 14.333s	8	4
7	26	M Blundell	Ligier	JS39	Renault	V10	52		17	9
8	30	J J Lehto	Sauber	C12	Ilmor	V10	52		11	6
9r	25	M Brundle	Ligier	JS39	Renault	V10	51	accident	15	8
10	24	P Martini	Minardi	M193	Cosworth	V8	51		22	11
11	12	J Herbert	Lotus	107B	Cosworth	V8	51		19	10
12	19	T Suzuki	Larrousse	LH93	Lamborghini	V12	51		23	12
13r	11	P Lamy	Lotus	107B	Cosworth	V8	49	accident	20	10
14r	9	D Warwick	Footwork	FA14	Mugen Honda	V10	48	accident	7	4
r	6	R Patrese	Benetton	B193B	Cosworth	V8	45	accident	10	5
r	28	G Berger	Ferrari	F93A	Ferrari	V12	40	engine	5	3
r	10	A Suzuki	Footwork	FA14	Mugen Honda	V10	28	spin	9	5
r	3	U Katayama	Tyrrell	021	Yamaha	V10	26	engine	13	7
r	23	J-M Gounon	Minardi	M193	Cosworth	V8	26	withdrawn by team	24	12
r	29	K Wendlinger	Sauber	C12	Ilmor	V10	25	throttle jammed	16	8
r	20	E Comas	Larrousse	LH93	Lamborghini	V12	17	engine	21	11
r	5	M Schumacher	Benetton	B193B	Cosworth	V8	10	accident	4	2
r	27	J Alesi	Ferrari	F93A	Ferrari	V12	7	electrics	14	7
r	4	A de Cesaris	Tyrrell	021	Yamaha	V10	0	accident/ puncture	18	9

Winning speed: 185.612 km/h, 115.334 mph
Pole Position speed: 217.288 km/h, 135.017 mph (A Prost, 1 min:37.154 sec)
Fastest Lap speed: 208.650 km/h, 129.649 mph (A Prost, 1 min:41.176 sec on lap 53)
Lap Leaders: A Senna 1-13,21-53 (46); A Prost 14-20 (7).

7 Nov 1993 — AUSTRALIA: Adelaide (Round:16) (Race: 548)

79 laps x 3.780 km, 2.349 miles = 298.620 km, 185.554 miles

POS.	NO.	DRIVER	CAR	MODEL	ENGINE		LAPS	TIME/REASON FOR RETIREMENT	GRID:POS	ROW
1	8	A Senna	McLaren	MP4/8	Cosworth	V8	79	1h 43m 27.476s	1	1
2	2	A Prost	Williams	FW15C	Renault	V10	79	1h 43m 36.735s	2	1
3	0	D Hill	Williams	FW15C	Renault	V10	79	1h 44m 01.378s	3	2
4	27	J Alesi	Ferrari	F93A	Ferrari	V12	78		7	4
5	28	G Berger	Ferrari	F93A	Ferrari	V12	78		6	3
6	25	M Brundle	Ligier	JS39	Renault	V10	78		8	4
7	10	A Suzuki	Footwork	FA14	Mugen Honda	V10	78		10	5
8r	6	R Patrese	Benetton	B193B	Cosworth	V8	77	fuel pressure	9	5
9	26	M Blundell	Ligier	JS39	Renault	V10	77		14	7
10	9	D Warwick	Footwork	FA14	Mugen Honda	V10	77		17	9
11	14	R Barrichello	Jordan	193	Hart	V10	76		13	7
12	20	E Comas	Larrousse	LH93	Lamborghini	V12	76		21	11
13	4	A de Cesaris	Tyrrell	021	Yamaha	V10	75		15	8
14	19	T Suzuki	Larrousse	LH93	Lamborghini	V12	74		24	12
15r	29	K Wendlinger	Sauber	C12	Ilmor	V10	73	brake disc/ accident	11	6
r	30	J J Lehto	Sauber	C12	Ilmor	V10	56	throttle jammed/ accident	12	6
r	23	J-M Gounon	Minardi	M193	Cosworth	V8	34	spin	22	11
r	7	M Häkkinen	McLaren	MP4/8	Cosworth	V8	28	brake pipe	5	3
r	5	M Schumacher	Benetton	B193B	Cosworth	V8	19	engine	4	2
r	3	U Katayama	Tyrrell	021	Yamaha	V10	11	accident	18	9
r	15	E Irvine	Jordan	193	Hart	V10	10	accident/ suspension	19	10
r	12	J Herbert	Lotus	107B	Cosworth	V8	9	suspension hydraulics	20	10
r	24	P Martini	Minardi	M193	Cosworth	V8	5	gearbox	16	8
r	11	P Lamy	Lotus	107B	Cosworth	V8	0	accident	23	12

Winning speed: 173.183 km/h, 107.611 mph
Pole Position speed: 185.468 km/h, 115.245 mph (A Senna, 1 min:13.371 sec)
Fastest Lap speed: 180.523 km/h, 112.172 mph (D Hill, 1 min:15.381 sec on lap 64)
Lap Leaders: A Senna 1-23,29-79 (74); A Prost 24-28 (5).

Lap Leaders 1993

POS	DRIVER	CAR-ENGINE	GPS	LAPS	KM	MILES
1	A Prost	Williams-Renault	15	431	2,095.4	1,302.0
2	A Senna	McLaren-Cosworth	6	290	1,215.9	755.5
3	D Hill	Williams-Renault	10	242	1,213.3	753.9
4	M Schumacher	Benetton-Cosworth	2	63	252.6	157.0
5	J Alesi	Ferrari	1	19	82.6	51.4
			16	**1,045**	**4,859.9**	**3,019.8**

Driver Points 1993

		ZA	BR	EUR	RSM	E	MC	CDN	F	GB	D	H	B	I	P	J	AUS	TOTAL
1	A Prost	10	-	4	10	10	3	10	10	10	10	-	4	-	6	6	6	99
2	A Senna	6	10	10	-	6	10	-	3	2	3	-	3	-	-	10	10	73
3	D Hill	-	6	6	-	-	6	4	6	-	-	10	10	10	4	3	4	69
4	M Schumacher	-	4	-	6	4	-	6	4	6	6	-	6	-	10	-	-	52
5	R Patrese	-	-	2	-	3	-	-	-	4	2	6	1	2	-	-	-	20
6	J Alesi	-	-	-	-	-	4	-	-	-	-	-	-	6	3	-	3	16
7	M Brundle	-	-	-	4	-	1	2	2	-	-	2	-	-	1	-	1	13
8	G Berger	1	-	-	-	1	-	3	-	-	1	4	-	-	-	-	2	12
9	J Herbert	-	3	3	-	-	-	-	-	3	-	-	2	-	-	-	-	11
10	M Blundell	4	2	-	-	-	-	-	-	-	4	-	-	-	-	-	-	10
11	M Andretti	-	-	-	-	2	-	-	1	-	-	-	-	4	-	-	-	7
	K Wendlinger	-	-	-	-	-	-	1	-	-	-	1	-	3	2	-	-	7
13	C Fittipaldi	3	-	-	-	-	2	-	-	-	-	-	-	-	-	-	-	5
	J J Lehto	2	-	-	3	-	-	-	-	-	-	-	-	-	-	-	-	5
15	M Häkkinen	-	-	-	-	-	-	-	-	-	-	-	-	-	-	4	-	4
	D Warwick	-	-	-	-	-	-	-	-	1	-	3	-	-	-	-	-	4
17	P Alliot	-	-	-	2	-	-	-	-	-	-	-	-	-	-	-	-	2
	R Barrichello	-	-	-	-	-	-	-	-	-	-	-	-	-	-	2	-	2
	F Barbazza	-	-	1	1	-	-	-	-	-	-	-	-	-	-	-	-	2
20	A Zanardi	-	1	-	-	-	-	-	-	-	-	-	-	-	-	-	-	1
	E Comas	-	-	-	-	-	-	-	-	-	-	-	-	1	-	-	-	1
	E Irvine	-	-	-	-	-	-	-	-	-	-	-	-	-	-	1	-	1

10, 6, 4, 3, 2 and 1 point awarded to the first six finishers.

Constructor Points 1993

		ZA	BR	EUR	RSM	E	MC	CDN	F	GB	D	H	B	I	P	J	AUS	TOTAL
1	Williams-Renault	10	6	10	10	10	9	14	16	10	10	10	14	10	10	9	10	168
2	McLaren-Cosworth	6	10	10	-	8	10	-	4	2	3	-	3	4	-	14	10	84
3	Benetton-Cosworth	-	4	2	6	7	-	6	4	10	8	6	7	2	10	-	-	72
4	Ferrari	1	-	-	-	1	4	3	-	-	1	4	-	6	3	-	5	28
5	Ligier-Renault	4	2	-	4	-	1	2	2	-	4	2	-	-	1	-	1	23
6	Lotus-Cosworth	-	4	3	-	-	-	-	-	3	-	-	2	-	-	-	-	12
	Sauber-Ilmor	2	-	-	3	-	-	1	-	-	-	1	-	3	2	-	-	12
8	Minardi-Cosworth	3	-	1	1	-	2	-	-	-	-	-	-	-	-	-	-	7
9	Footwork-Mugen	-	-	-	-	-	-	-	-	1	-	3	-	-	-	-	-	4
10	Jordan-Hart	-	-	-	-	-	-	-	-	-	-	-	-	-	-	3	-	3
	Larrousse-Lamborghini	-	-	-	2	-	-	-	-	-	-	-	-	1	-	-	-	3

10, 6, 4, 3, 2 and 1 point awarded to the first six finishers.

RACE ENTRANTS & RESULTS 1994

Traction control and other driver aids were banned in an attempt to emphasise the driver's input. Re-fuelling returned, to increase the strategic aspect of racing. Camel and Canon left Formula 1 as high profile sponsors. Once again the World Champion departed, this time to retirement. Frank Williams finally got his man, only for Ayrton Senna to die on the traumatic weekend of Imola, a day after Roland Ratzenberger.

WILLIAMS
Rothmans Williams Renault: Hill, Senna, Coulthard, Mansell

TYRRELL
Tyrrell Racing Organisation: Katayama, Blundell

BENETTON
Mild Seven Benetton Ford: Schumacher, Lehto, Verstappen, Herbert

McLAREN
Marlboro McLaren Peugeot: Häkkinen, Alliot, Brundle

FOOTWORK
Arrows Grand Prix International: Fittipaldi, Morbidelli

LOTUS
Team Lotus: Lamy, Zanardi, Adams, Herbert, Bernard, Salo

JORDAN
Sasol Jordan: Barrichello, Irvine, Suzuki, de Cesaris

LARROUSSE
Tourtel Larrousse F1: Beretta, Alliot, Dalmas, Noda, Comas, Deletraz

MINARDI
Minardi Scuderia Italia: Martini, Alboreto

LIGIER
Ligier Gitanes Blondes: Bernard, Herbert, Lagorce, Panis

FERRARI
Scuderia Ferrari SpA: Alesi, Larini, Berger

SAUBER
PP Sauber AG: Wendlinger, de Cesaris, Lehto, Frentzen

SIMTEK
MTV Simtek Ford: Brabham, Ratzenberger, (Montermini), Gounon, Schiattarella, Inoue

PACIFIC
Pacific Grand Prix: Belmondo, Gachot

27 Mar 1994 — BRAZIL: Interlagos (Round: 1) (Race: 549)

71 laps x 4.325 km, 2.687 miles = 307.075 km, 190.808 miles

POS.	NO.	DRIVER	CAR	MODEL	ENGINE		LAPS	TIME/REASON FOR RETIREMENT	GRID:POS	ROW
1	5	M Schumacher	Benetton	B194	Cosworth	V8	71	1h 35m 38.759s	2	1
2	0	D Hill	Williams	FW16	Renault	V10	70		4	2
3	27	J Alesi	Ferrari	412T1	Ferrari	V12	70		3	2
4	14	R Barrichello	Jordan	194	Hart	V10	70		14	7
5	3	U Katayama	Tyrrell	022	Yamaha	V10	69		10	5
6	29	K Wendlinger	Sauber	C13	Mercedes	V10	69		7	4
7	12	J Herbert	Lotus	107C	Mugen Honda	V10	69		21	11
8	23	P Martini	Minardi	M193B	Cosworth	V8	69		15	8
9	20	E Comas	Larrousse	LH94	Cosworth	V8	68		13	7
10	11	P Lamy	Lotus	107C	Mugen Honda	V10	68		24	12
11	26	O Panis	Ligier	JS39B	Renault	V10	68		19	10
12	31	D Brabham	Simtek	S941	Cosworth	V8	67		26	13
r	2	A Senna	Williams	FW16	Renault	V10	55	spin	1	1
r	8	M Brundle	McLaren	MP4/9	Peugeot	V10	34	accident	18	9
r	15	E Irvine	Jordan	194	Hart	V10	34	accident	16	8
r	6	J Verstappen	Benetton	B194	Cosworth	V8	34	accident	9	5
r	25	É Bernard	Ligier	JS39B	Renault	V10	33	accident	20	10
r	4	M Blundell	Tyrrell	022	Yamaha	V10	21	accident	12	6
r	9	C Fittipaldi	Footwork	FA15	Cosworth	V8	21	gearbox	11	6
r	30	H-H Frentzen	Sauber	C13	Mercedes	V10	15	spin	5	3
r	7	M Häkkinen	McLaren	MP4/9	Peugeot	V10	13	airbox fire/ electrics	8	4
r	24	M Alboreto	Minardi	M193B	Cosworth	V8	7	electrics	22	11
r	10	G Morbidelli	Footwork	FA15	Cosworth	V8	5	gearbox	6	3
r	28	G Berger	Ferrari	412T1	Ferrari	V12	5	engine	17	9
r	19	O Beretta	Larrousse	LH94	Cosworth	V8	2	accident	23	12
r	34	B Gachot	Pacific	PR01	Ilmor	V10	1	accident	25	13
nq	32	R Ratzenberger	Simtek	S941	Cosworth	V8				
nq	33	P Belmondo	Pacific	PR01	Ilmor	V10				

Winning speed: 192.632 km/h, 119.696 mph
Pole Position speed: 204.971 km/h, 127.363 mph (A Senna, 1 min:15.962 sec)
Fastest Lap speed: 198.458 km/h, 123.316 mph (M Schumacher, 1 min:18.455 sec on lap 7)
Lap Leaders: A Senna 1-21 (21); M Schumacher 22-71 (50).

17 Apr 1994 — PACIFIC: Aida (Round: 2) (Race: 550)

83 laps x 3.703 km, 2.301 miles = 307.349 km, 190.978 miles

POS.	NO.	DRIVER	CAR	MODEL	ENGINE		LAPS	TIME/REASON FOR RETIREMENT	GRID:POS	ROW
1	5	M Schumacher	Benetton	B194	Cosworth	V8	83	1h 46m 01.693s	2	1
2	28	G Berger	Ferrari	412T1	Ferrari	V12	83	1h 47m 16.993s	5	3
3	14	R Barrichello	Jordan	194	Hart	V10	82		8	4
4	9	C Fittipaldi	Footwork	FA15	Cosworth	V8	82		9	5
5	30	H-H Frentzen	Sauber	C13	Mercedes	V10	82		11	6
6	20	E Comas	Larrousse	LH94	Cosworth	V8	80		16	8
7	12	J Herbert	Lotus	107C	Mugen Honda	V10	80		23	12
8	11	P Lamy	Lotus	107C	Mugen Honda	V10	79		24	12
9	26	O Panis	Ligier	JS39B	Renault	V10	78		22	11
10	25	É Bernard	Ligier	JS39B	Renault	V10	78		18	9
11	32	R Ratzenberger	Simtek	S941	Cosworth	V8	78		26	13
r	10	G Morbidelli	Footwork	FA15	Cosworth	V8	69	engine	13	7
r	29	K Wendlinger	Sauber	C13	Mercedes	V10	69	accident	19	10
r	24	M Alboreto	Minardi	M193B	Cosworth	V8	69	accident	15	8
r	8	M Brundle	McLaren	MP4/9	Peugeot	V10	67	engine overheating	6	3
r	23	P Martini	Minardi	M193B	Cosworth	V8	63	brakes/ spin	17	9

POS.	NO.	DRIVER	CAR	MODEL	ENGINE		LAPS	TIME/REASON FOR RETIREMENT	GRID:POS	ROW
r	6	J Verstappen	Benetton	B194	Cosworth	V8	54	spin	10	5
r	0	D Hill	Williams	FW16	Renault	V10	49	transmission	3	2
r	15	A Suzuki	Jordan	194	Hart	V10	44	steering upright/ accident	20	10
r	3	U Katayama	Tyrrell	022	Yamaha	V10	42	engine	14	7
r	7	M Häkkinen	McLaren	MP4/9	Peugeot	V10	19	gearbox hydraulics	4	2
r	19	O Beretta	Larrousse	LH94	Cosworth	V8	14	electrics	21	11
r	31	D Brabham	Simtek	S941	Cosworth	V8	2	engine	25	13
r	2	A Senna	Williams	FW16	Renault	V10	0	accident	1	1
r	4	M Blundell	Tyrrell	022	Yamaha	V10	0	accident	12	6
r	27	N Larini	Ferrari	412T1	Ferrari	V12	0	accident	7	4
nq	34	B Gachot	Pacific	PR01	Ilmor	V10				
nq	33	P Belmondo	Pacific	PR01	Ilmor	V10				

Winning speed: 173.925 km/h, 108.072 mph
Pole Position speed: 189.849 km/h, 117.967 mph (A Senna, 1 min:10.218 sec)
Fastest Lap speed: 180.090 km/h, 111.903 mph (M Schumacher, 1 min:14.023 sec on lap 10)
Lap Leaders: M Schumacher 1-83 (83).

1 May 1994 — SAN MARINO: Imola — (Round: 3) (Race: 551)

58 laps x 5.040 km, 3.132 miles = 292.320 km, 181.639 miles

POS.	NO.	DRIVER	CAR	MODEL	ENGINE		LAPS	TIME/REASON FOR RETIREMENT	GRID:POS	ROW
1	5	M Schumacher	Benetton	B194	Cosworth	V8	58	1h 28m 28.642s	2	1
2	27	N Larini	Ferrari	412T1	Ferrari	V12	58	1h 29m 23.584s	6	3
3	7	M Häkkinen	McLaren	MP4/9	Peugeot	V10	58	1h 29m 39.321s	8	4
4	29	K Wendlinger	Sauber	C13	Mercedes	V10	58	1h 29m 42.300s	10	5
5	3	U Katayama	Tyrrell	022	Yamaha	V10	57		9	5
6	0	D Hill	Williams	FW16	Renault	V10	57		4	2
7	30	H-H Frentzen	Sauber	C13	Mercedes	V10	57		7	4
8	8	M Brundle	McLaren	MP4/9	Peugeot	V10	57		13	7
9	4	M Blundell	Tyrrell	022	Yamaha	V10	56		12	6
10	12	J Herbert	Lotus	107C	Mugen Honda	V10	56		20	10
11	26	O Panis	Ligier	JS39B	Renault	V10	56		19	10
12	25	É Bernard	Ligier	JS39B	Renault	V10	56		17	9
13r	9	C Fittipaldi	Footwork	FA15	Cosworth	V8	54	brakes/ spin	16	8
r	15	A de Cesaris	Jordan	194	Hart	V10	49	accident	21	11
r	24	M Alboreto	Minardi	M193B	Cosworth	V8	44	wheel lost	15	8
r	10	G Morbidelli	Footwork	FA15	Cosworth	V8	40	engine	11	6
r	23	P Martini	Minardi	M193B	Cosworth	V8	37	spin	14	7
r	31	D Brabham	Simtek	S941	Cosworth	V8	27	puncture/ accident	24	12
r	34	B Gachot	Pacific	PR01	Ilmor	V10	23	oil pressure	25	13
r	19	O Beretta	Larrousse	LH94	Cosworth	V8	17	engine	23	12
r	28	G Berger	Ferrari	412T1	Ferrari	V12	16	handling	3	2
r	2	A Senna	Williams	FW16	Renault	V10	5	steering column/ fatal accident	1	1
r	20	E Comas	Larrousse	LH94	Cosworth	V8	5	accident/ under-wing	18	9
r	6	J J Lehto	Benetton	B194	Cosworth	V8	0	accident	5	3
r	11	P Lamy	Lotus	107C	Mugen Honda	V10	0	accident	22	11
ns	32	R Ratzenberger	Simtek	S941	Cosworth	V8		fatal accident	26	13
nq	33	P Belmondo	Pacific	PR01	Ilmor	V10				
nq	14	R Barrichello	Jordan	194	Hart	V10		accident/ injury		

Winning speed: 198.234 km/h, 123.177 mph
Pole Position speed: 222.495 km/h, 138.252 mph (A Senna, 1 min:21.548 sec)
Fastest Lap speed: 215.142 km/h, 133.683 mph (D Hill, 1 min:24.335 sec on lap 10)
Lap Leaders: A Senna 1-5 (5); G Berger 6-14 (9); M Häkkinen 15-18 (4); N Larini 19-23 (5); M Schumacher 24-58 (35).

Scheduled for 61 laps, but interrupted after 5 laps, because of an accident. Restarted for a further 53 laps, with results being on aggregate. Lap leaders are given 'on the road'

15 May 1994 — MONACO: Monte Carlo (Round: 4) (Race: 552)

78 laps x 3.328 km, 2.068 miles = 259.584 km, 161.298 miles

POS.	NO.	DRIVER	CAR	MODEL	ENGINE		LAPS	TIME/REASON FOR RETIREMENT	GRID:POS	ROW
1	5	M Schumacher	Benetton	B194	Cosworth	V8	78	1h 49m 55.372s	1	1
2	8	M Brundle	McLaren	MP4/9	Peugeot	V10	78	1h 50m 32.650s	8	4
3	28	G Berger	Ferrari	412T1	Ferrari	V12	78	1h 51m 12.196s	3	2
4	15	A de Cesaris	Jordan	194	Hart	V10	77		14	7
5	27	J Alesi	Ferrari	412T1	Ferrari	V12	77		5	3
6	24	M Alboreto	Minardi	M193B	Cosworth	V8	77		12	6
7	6	J J Lehto	Benetton	B194	Cosworth	V8	77		17	9
8	19	O Beretta	Larrousse	LH94	Cosworth	V8	76		18	9
9	26	O Panis	Ligier	JS39B	Renault	V10	76		20	10
10	20	E Comas	Larrousse	LH94	Cosworth	V8	75		13	7
11	11	P Lamy	Lotus	107C	Mugen Honda	V10	73		19	10
r	12	J Herbert	Lotus	107C	Mugen Honda	V10	68	gearbox	16	8
r	33	P Belmondo	Pacific	PR01	Ilmor	V10	53	driver discomfort	24	12
r	34	B Gachot	Pacific	PR01	Ilmor	V10	49	gearbox	23	12
r	9	C Fittipaldi	Footwork	FA15	Cosworth	V8	47	gearbox	6	3
r	31	D Brabham	Simtek	S941	Cosworth	V8	45	accident/ front suspension	22	11
r	4	M Blundell	Tyrrell	022	Yamaha	V10	40	engine	10	5
r	3	U Katayama	Tyrrell	022	Yamaha	V10	38	gearbox	11	6
r	25	É Bernard	Ligier	JS39B	Renault	V10	34	spin	21	11
r	14	R Barrichello	Jordan	194	Hart	V10	27	electrics	15	8
r	0	D Hill	Williams	FW16	Renault	V10	0	accident	4	2
r	7	M Häkkinen	McLaren	MP4/9	Peugeot	V10	0	accident	2	1
r	10	G Morbidelli	Footwork	FA15	Cosworth	V8	0	accident	7	4
r	23	P Martini	Minardi	M193B	Cosworth	V8	0	accident	9	5
ns	30	H-H Frentzen	Sauber	C13	Mercedes	V10		withdrew after Wendlinger accid.		
ns	29	K Wendlinger	Sauber	C13	Mercedes	V10		accident/ injury		

Winning speed: 141.691 km/h, 88.042 mph
Pole Position speed: 152.505 km/h, 94.762 mph (M Schumacher, 1 min:18.560 sec)
Fastest Lap speed: 147.772 km/h, 91.822 mph (M Schumacher, 1 min:21.076 sec on lap 35)
Lap Leaders: M Schumacher 1-78 (78).

The usual front row of the grid was left vacant, in memory of Ayrton Senna and Roland Ratzenberger.

29 May 1994 — SPAIN: Montmeló (Round: 5) (Race: 553)

65 laps x 4.747 km, 2.950 miles = 308.555 km, 191.727 miles

POS.	NO.	DRIVER	CAR	MODEL	ENGINE		LAPS	TIME/REASON FOR RETIREMENT	GRID:POS	ROW
1	0	D Hill	Williams	FW16	Renault	V10	65	1h 36m 14.374s	2	1
2	5	M Schumacher	Benetton	B194	Cosworth	V8	65	1h 36m 38.540s	1	1
3	4	M Blundell	Tyrrell	022	Yamaha	V10	65	1h 37m 41.343s	11	6
4	27	J Alesi	Ferrari	412T1	Ferrari	V12	64		6	3
5	23	P Martini	Minardi	M193B	Cosworth	V8	64		18	9
6	15	E Irvine	Jordan	194	Hart	V10	64		13	7
7	26	O Panis	Ligier	JS39B	Renault	V10	63		19	10
8	25	É Bernard	Ligier	JS39B	Renault	V10	62		20	10
9	11	A Zanardi	Lotus	107C	Mugen Honda	V10	62		23	12
10	31	D Brabham	Simtek	S941	Cosworth	V8	61		24	12
11r	8	M Brundle	McLaren	MP4/9	Peugeot	V10	59	transmission	8	4
r	6	J J Lehto	Benetton	B194	Cosworth	V8	53	engine	4	2
r	7	M Häkkinen	McLaren	MP4/9	Peugeot	V10	48	engine	3	2
r	12	J Herbert	Lotus	109	Mugen Honda	V10	41	spin	22	11
r	14	R Barrichello	Jordan	194	Hart	V10	39	gearbox	5	3
r	9	C Fittipaldi	Footwork	FA15	Cosworth	V8	35	engine	21	11
r	2	D Coulthard	Williams	FW16	Renault	V10	32	electronics	9	5
r	34	B Gachot	Pacific	PR01	Ilmor	V10	32	rear wing	25	13
r	28	G Berger	Ferrari	412T1	Ferrari	V12	27	gearbox	7	4
r	10	G Morbidelli	Footwork	FA15	Cosworth	V8	24	fuel valve fell into tank	15	8
r	30	H-H Frentzen	Sauber	C13	Mercedes	V10	21	gearbox	12	6
r	20	E Comas	Larrousse	LH94	Cosworth	V8	19	water leak	16	8
r	3	U Katayama	Tyrrell	022	Yamaha	V10	16	engine	10	5
r	24	M Alboreto	Minardi	M193B	Cosworth	V8	4	engine	14	7
r	33	P Belmondo	Pacific	PR01	Ilmor	V10	2	spin	26	13
r	19	O Beretta	Larrousse	LH94	Cosworth	V8	-1	engine	17	9
nq	32	A Montermini	Simtek	S941	Cosworth	V8		accident/ injury		

Winning speed: 192.367 km/h, 119.531 mph
Pole Position speed: 208.639 km/h, 129.642 mph (M Schumacher, 1 min:21.908 sec)
Fastest Lap speed: 200.683 km/h, 124.699 mph (M Schumacher, 1 min:25.155 sec on lap 18)
Lap Leaders: M Schumacher 1-22,41-45 (27); M Häkkinen 23-30 (8); D Hill 31-40,46-65 (30).

12 Jun 1994 — CANADA: Montréal (Round: 6) (Race: 554)

69 laps x 4.450 km, 2.765 miles = 307.050 km, 190.792 miles

POS.	NO.	DRIVER	CAR	MODEL	ENGINE		LAPS	TIME/REASON FOR RETIREMENT	GRID:POS	ROW
1	5	M Schumacher	Benetton	B194	Cosworth	V8	69	1h 44m 31.887s	1	1
2	0	D Hill	Williams	FW16	Renault	V10	69	1h 45m 11.547s	4	2
3	27	J Alesi	Ferrari	412T1	Ferrari	V12	69	1h 45m 45.275s	2	1
4	28	G Berger	Ferrari	412T1	Ferrari	V12	69	1h 45m 47.496s	3	2
5	2	D Coulthard	Williams	FW16	Renault	V10	68		5	3
dq	9	C Fittipaldi	Footwork	FA15	Cosworth	V8	68	car under weight	16	8

POS.	NO.	DRIVER	CAR	MODEL	ENGINE		LAPS	TIME/REASON FOR RETIREMENT	GRID:POS	ROW
6	6	J J Lehto	Benetton	B194	Cosworth	V8	68		20	10
7	14	R Barrichello	Jordan	194	Hart	V10	68		6	3
8	12	J Herbert	Lotus	109	Mugen Honda	V10	68		17	9
9	23	P Martini	Minardi	M194	Cosworth	V8	68		15	8
10r	4	M Blundell	Tyrrell	022	Yamaha	V10	67	accident	13	7
11	24	M Alboreto	Minardi	M194	Cosworth	V8	67		18	9
12	26	O Panis	Ligier	JS39B	Renault	V10	67		19	10
13	25	É Bernard	Ligier	JS39B	Renault	V10	66		24	12
14	31	D Brabham	Simtek	S941	Cosworth	V8	65		25	13
15r	11	A Zanardi	Lotus	107C	Mugen Honda	V10	62	engine	23	12
r	7	M Häkkinen	McLaren	MP4/9	Peugeot	V10	61	engine	7	4
r	19	O Beretta	Larrousse	LH94	Cosworth	V8	57	engine	22	11
r	10	G Morbidelli	Footwork	FA15	Cosworth	V8	50	gearbox hydraulics	11	6
r	34	B Gachot	Pacific	PR01	Ilmor	V10	47	oil pressure	26	13
r	20	E Comas	Larrousse	LH94	Cosworth	V8	45	clutch	21	11
r	3	U Katayama	Tyrrell	022	Yamaha	V10	44	spin	9	5
r	15	E Irvine	Jordan	194	Hart	V10	40	accident	8	4
r	29	A de Cesaris	Sauber	C13	Mercedes	V10	24	oil leak	14	7
r	30	H-H Frentzen	Sauber	C13	Mercedes	V10	5	accident	10	5
r	8	M Brundle	McLaren	MP4/9	Peugeot	V10	3	electrics	12	6
nq	33	P Belmondo	Pacific	PR01	Ilmor	V10				

Winning speed: 176.244 km/h, 109.513 mph
Pole Position speed: 185.894 km/h, 115.509 mph (M Schumacher, 1 min:26.178 sec)
Fastest Lap speed: 180.148 km/h, 111.939 mph (M Schumacher, 1 min:28.927 sec on lap 31)
Lap Leaders: M Schumacher 1-69 (69).

3 Jul 1994 — FRANCE: Magny-Cours (Round: 7) (Race: 555)

72 laps x 4.250 km, 2.641 miles = 306.000 km, 190.140 miles

POS.	NO.	DRIVER	CAR	MODEL	ENGINE		LAPS	TIME/REASON FOR RETIREMENT	GRID:POS	ROW
1	5	M Schumacher	Benetton	B194	Cosworth	V8	72	1h 38m 35.704s	3	2
2	0	D Hill	Williams	FW16	Renault	V10	72	1h 38m 48.346s	1	1
3	28	G Berger	Ferrari	412T1B	Ferrari	V12	72	1h 39m 28.469s	5	3
4	30	H-H Frentzen	Sauber	C13	Mercedes	V10	71		10	5
5	23	P Martini	Minardi	M194	Cosworth	V8	70		16	8
6	29	A de Cesaris	Sauber	C13	Mercedes	V10	70		11	6
7	12	J Herbert	Lotus	109	Mugen Honda	V10	70		19	10
8	9	C Fittipaldi	Footwork	FA15	Cosworth	V8	70		18	9
9	32	J-M Gounon	Simtek	S941	Cosworth	V8	68		26	13
10	4	M Blundell	Tyrrell	022	Yamaha	V10	67		17	9
11r	20	E Comas	Larrousse	LH94	Cosworth	V8	66	engine	20	10
r	3	U Katayama	Tyrrell	022	Yamaha	V10	53	spin	14	7
r	7	M Häkkinen	McLaren	MP4/9	Peugeot	V10	48	engine	9	5
r	2	N Mansell	Williams	FW16	Renault	V10	45	transmission	2	1
r	27	J Alesi	Ferrari	412T1B	Ferrari	V12	41	accident	4	2
r	14	R Barrichello	Jordan	194	Hart	V10	41	accident	7	4
r	25	É Bernard	Ligier	JS39B	Renault	V10	40	gearbox	15	8
r	19	O Beretta	Larrousse	LH94	Cosworth	V8	36	engine	25	13
r	8	M Brundle	McLaren	MP4/9	Peugeot	V10	29	engine	12	6
r	10	G Morbidelli	Footwork	FA15	Cosworth	V8	28	accident	22	11
r	26	O Panis	Ligier	JS39B	Renault	V10	28	accident	13	7
r	31	D Brabham	Simtek	S941	Cosworth	V8	28	gearbox	24	12
r	6	J Verstappen	Benetton	B194	Cosworth	V8	25	spin	8	4
r	15	E Irvine	Jordan	194	Hart	V10	24	gearbox	6	3
r	24	M Alboreto	Minardi	M194	Cosworth	V8	21	engine	21	11
r	11	A Zanardi	Lotus	109	Mugen Honda	V10	20	engine/ fire	23	12
nq	34	B Gachot	Pacific	PR01	Ilmor	V10				
nq	33	P Belmondo	Pacific	PR01	Ilmor	V10				

Winning speed: 186.216 km/h, 115.709 mph
Pole Position speed: 200.572 km/h, 124.629 mph (D Hill, 1 min:16.282 sec)
Fastest Lap speed: 192.023 km/h, 119.317 mph (D Hill, 1 min:19.678 sec on lap 4)
Lap Leaders: M Schumacher 1-37,45-72 (65); D Hill 38-44 (7).

10 Jul 1994 — BRITAIN: Silverstone (Round: 8) (Race: 556)

60 laps x 5.057 km, 3.142 miles = 303.420 km, 188.536 miles

POS.	NO.	DRIVER	CAR	MODEL	ENGINE		LAPS	TIME/REASON FOR RETIREMENT	GRID:POS	ROW
1	0	D Hill	Williams	FW16	Renault	V10	60	1h 30m 03.640s	1	1
dq	5	M Schumacher	Benetton	B194	Cosworth	V8	60	overtook on parade lap	2	1
2	27	J Alesi	Ferrari	412T1B	Ferrari	V12	60	1h 31m 11.768s	4	2
3	7	M Häkkinen	McLaren	MP4/9	Peugeot	V10	60	1h 31m 44.299s	5	3
4	14	R Barrichello	Jordan	194	Hart	V10	60	1h 31m 45.391s	6	3
5	2	D Coulthard	Williams	FW16	Renault	V10	59		7	4
6	3	U Katayama	Tyrrell	022	Yamaha	V10	59		8	4
7	30	H-H Frentzen	Sauber	C13	Mercedes	V10	59		13	7
8	6	J Verstappen	Benetton	B194	Cosworth	V8	59		10	5
9	9	C Fittipaldi	Footwork	FA15	Cosworth	V8	58		20	10
10	23	P Martini	Minardi	M194	Cosworth	V8	58		14	7
11	12	J Herbert	Lotus	109	Mugen Honda	V10	58		21	11
12	26	O Panis	Ligier	JS39B	Renault	V10	58		15	8
13	25	É Bernard	Ligier	JS39B	Renault	V10	58		23	12
14	19	O Beretta	Larrousse	LH94	Cosworth	V8	58		24	12
15	31	D Brabham	Simtek	S941	Cosworth	V8	57		25	13
16	32	J-M Gounon	Simtek	S941	Cosworth	V8	57		26	13
r	24	M Alboreto	Minardi	M194	Cosworth	V8	48	engine	17	9

POS.	NO.	DRIVER	CAR	MODEL	ENGINE		LAPS	TIME/REASON FOR RETIREMENT	GRID:POS	ROW
r	28	G Berger	Ferrari	412T1B	Ferrari	V12	32	engine	3	2
r	4	M Blundell	Tyrrell	022	Yamaha	V10	20	gearbox	11	6
r	20	E Comas	Larrousse	LH94	Cosworth	V8	12	engine	22	11
r	29	A de Cesaris	Sauber	C13	Mercedes	V10	11	engine	18	9
r	10	G Morbidelli	Footwork	FA15	Cosworth	V8	5	fuel line	16	8
r	11	A Zanardi	Lotus	109	Mugen Honda	V10	4	engine	19	10
r	8	M Brundle	McLaren	MP4/9	Peugeot	V10	0	engine	9	5
r	15	E Irvine	Jordan	194	Hart	V10	-1	engine	12	6
nq	34	B Gachot	Pacific	PR01	Ilmor	V10				
nq	33	P Belmondo	Pacific	PR01	Ilmor	V10				

Winning speed: 202.144 km/h, 125.606 mph
Pole Position speed: 214.280 km/h, 133.147 mph (D Hill, 1 min:24.960 sec)
Fastest Lap speed: 209.015 km/h, 129.876 mph (D Hill, 1 min:27.100 sec on lap 11)
Lap Leaders: D Hill 1-14,27-60 (48); M Schumacher 15-17,22-26 (8); G Berger 18-21 (4).

M Schumacher finished 2nd in 1h 30m 22.418s.

31 Jul 1994 — GERMANY: Hockenheim (Round: 9) (Race: 557)

45 laps x 6.823 km, 4.240 miles = 307.035 km, 190.783 miles

POS.	NO.	DRIVER	CAR	MODEL	ENGINE		LAPS	TIME/REASON FOR RETIREMENT	GRID:POS	ROW
1	28	G Berger	Ferrari	412T1B	Ferrari	V12	45	1h 22m 37.272s	1	1
2	26	O Panis	Ligier	JS39B	Renault	V10	45	1h 23m 32.051s	12	6
3	25	É Bernard	Ligier	JS39B	Renault	V10	45	1h 23m 42.314s	14	7
4	9	C Fittipaldi	Footwork	FA15	Cosworth	V8	45	1h 23m 58.881s	17	9
5	10	G Morbidelli	Footwork	FA15	Cosworth	V8	45	1h 24m 07.816s	16	8
6	20	E Comas	Larrousse	LH94	Cosworth	V8	45	1h 24m 22.717s	22	11
7	19	O Beretta	Larrousse	LH94	Cosworth	V8	44		24	12
8	0	D Hill	Williams	FW16B	Renault	V10	44		3	2
r	32	J-M Gounon	Simtek	S941	Cosworth	V8	39	gearbox	26	13
r	31	D Brabham	Simtek	S941	Cosworth	V8	37	clutch	25	13
r	5	M Schumacher	Benetton	B194	Cosworth	V8	20	engine	4	2
r	8	M Brundle	McLaren	MP4/9	Peugeot	V10	19	engine	13	7
r	2	D Coulthard	Williams	FW16B	Renault	V10	17	electrics	6	3
r	6	J Verstappen	Benetton	B194	Cosworth	V8	15	refuelling fire	19	10
r	3	U Katayama	Tyrrell	022	Yamaha	V10	6	throttle jammed	5	3
r	27	J Alesi	Ferrari	412T1B	Ferrari	V12	0	electrics	2	1
r	30	H-H Frentzen	Sauber	C13	Mercedes	V10	0	accident	9	5
r	12	J Herbert	Lotus	109	Mugen Honda	V10	0	accident	15	8
r	14	R Barrichello	Jordan	194	Hart	V10	0	accident	11	6
r	15	E Irvine	Jordan	194	Hart	V10	0	accident	10	5
r	4	M Blundell	Tyrrell	022	Yamaha	V10	0	accident	7	4
r	7	M Häkkinen	McLaren	MP4/9	Peugeot	V10	0	accident	8	4
r	11	A Zanardi	Lotus	109	Mugen Honda	V10	0	accident	21	11
r	23	P Martini	Minardi	M194	Cosworth	V8	0	accident	20	10
r	24	M Alboreto	Minardi	M194	Cosworth	V8	0	accident	23	12
r	29	A de Cesaris	Sauber	C13	Mercedes	V10	0	accident	18	9
nq	33	P Belmondo	Pacific	PR01	Ilmor	V10				
nq	34	B Gachot	Pacific	PR01	Ilmor	V10				

Winning speed: 222.971 km/h, 138.548 mph
Pole Position speed: 237.134 km/h, 147.348 mph (G Berger, 1 min:43.582 sec)
Fastest Lap speed: 231.264 km/h, 143.701 mph (D Coulthard, 1 min:46.211 sec on lap 11)
Lap Leaders: G Berger 1-45 (45).

14 Aug 1994 — HUNGARY: Hungaroring (Round:10) (Race: 558)

77 laps x 3.968 km, 2.466 miles = 305.536 km, 189.851 miles

POS.	NO.	DRIVER	CAR	MODEL	ENGINE		LAPS	TIME/REASON FOR RETIREMENT	GRID:POS	ROW
1	5	M Schumacher	Benetton	B194	Cosworth	V8	77	1h 48m 00.185s	1	1
2	0	D Hill	Williams	FW16B	Renault	V10	77	1h 48m 21.012s	2	1
3	6	J Verstappen	Benetton	B194	Cosworth	V8	77	1h 49m 10.514s	12	6
4r	8	M Brundle	McLaren	MP4/9	Peugeot	V10	76	alternator	6	3
5	4	M Blundell	Tyrrell	022	Yamaha	V10	76		11	6
6	26	O Panis	Ligier	JS39B	Renault	V10	76		9	5
7	24	M Alboreto	Minardi	M194	Cosworth	V8	75		20	10
8	20	E Comas	Larrousse	LH94	Cosworth	V8	75		21	11
9	19	O Beretta	Larrousse	LH94	Cosworth	V8	75		25	13
10	25	É Bernard	Ligier	JS39B	Renault	V10	75		18	9
11	31	D Brabham	Simtek	S941	Cosworth	V8	74		23	12
12r	28	G Berger	Ferrari	412T1B	Ferrari	V12	72	pneumatic valve air pressure	4	2
13	11	A Zanardi	Lotus	109	Mugen Honda	V10	72		22	11
14r	9	C Fittipaldi	Footwork	FA15	Cosworth	V8	69	gearbox	16	8
r	2	D Coulthard	Williams	FW16B	Renault	V10	59	accident	3	2
r	27	J Alesi	Ferrari	412T1B	Ferrari	V12	58	gearbox	13	7
r	23	P Martini	Minardi	M194	Cosworth	V8	58	spin	15	8
r	30	H-H Frentzen	Sauber	C13	Mercedes	V10	39	gearbox	8	4
r	12	J Herbert	Lotus	109	Mugen Honda	V10	34	electrics	24	12
r	29	A de Cesaris	Sauber	C13	Mercedes	V10	30	accident	17	9
r	10	G Morbidelli	Footwork	FA15	Cosworth	V8	30	accident	19	10
r	7	P Alliot	McLaren	MP4/9	Peugeot	V10	21	water leak	14	7
r	32	J-M Gounon	Simtek	S941	Cosworth	V8	9	handling	26	13
r	3	U Katayama	Tyrrell	022	Yamaha	V10	0	accident	5	3
r	14	R Barrichello	Jordan	194	Hart	V10	0	accident	10	5
r	15	E Irvine	Jordan	194	Hart	V10	0	accident	7	4
nq	34	B Gachot	Pacific	PR01	Ilmor	V10				
nq	33	P Belmondo	Pacific	PR01	Ilmor	V10				

Winning speed: 169.737 km/h, 105.470 mph
Pole Position speed: 182.535 km/h, 113.422 mph (M Schumacher, 1 min:18.258 sec)
Fastest Lap speed: 176.615 km/h, 109.743 mph (M Schumacher, 1 min:20.881 sec on lap 5)
Lap Leaders: M Schumacher 1-16,26-77 (68); D Hill 17-25 (9).

28 Aug 1994 — BELGIUM: Spa-Francorchamps (Round:11) (Race: 559)

44 laps x 7.001 km, 4.350 miles = 308.044 km, 191.410 miles

POS.	NO.	DRIVER	CAR	MODEL	ENGINE		LAPS	TIME/REASON FOR RETIREMENT	GRID:POS	ROW
dq	5	M Schumacher	Benetton	B194	Cosworth	V8	44	illegal skidblock wear	2	1
1	0	D Hill	Williams	FW16B	Renault	V10	44	1h 28m 47.170s	3	2
2	7	M Häkkinen	McLaren	MP4/9	Peugeot	V10	44	1h 29m 38.551s	8	4
3	6	J Verstappen	Benetton	B194	Cosworth	V8	44	1h 29m 57.623s	6	3
4	2	D Coulthard	Williams	FW16B	Renault	V10	44	1h 30m 32.957s	7	4
5	4	M Blundell	Tyrrell	022	Yamaha	V10	43		12	6
6	10	G Morbidelli	Footwork	FA15	Cosworth	V8	43		14	7
7	26	O Panis	Ligier	JS39B	Renault	V10	43		17	9
8	23	P Martini	Minardi	M194	Cosworth	V8	43		10	5
9	24	M Alboreto	Minardi	M194	Cosworth	V8	43		18	9
10	25	É Bernard	Ligier	JS39B	Renault	V10	42		16	8
11	32	J-M Gounon	Simtek	S941	Cosworth	V8	42		25	13
12	12	J Herbert	Lotus	109	Mugen Honda	V10	41		20	10
13r	15	E Irvine	Jordan	194	Hart	V10	40	alternator	4	2
r	9	C Fittipaldi	Footwork	FA15	Cosworth	V8	33	engine	24	12
r	31	D Brabham	Simtek	S941	Cosworth	V8	29	wheel lost	21	11
r	29	A de Cesaris	Sauber	C13	Mercedes	V10	27	throttle jammed/ accident	15	8
r	8	M Brundle	McLaren	MP4/9	Peugeot	V10	24	spin	13	7
r	14	R Barrichello	Jordan	194	Hart	V10	19	spin	1	1
r	3	U Katayama	Tyrrell	022	Yamaha	V10	18	engine/ spin	23	12
r	11	P Adams	Lotus	109	Mugen Honda	V10	15	spin	26	13
r	28	G Berger	Ferrari	412T1B	Ferrari	V12	11	engine	11	6
r	19	P Alliot	Larrousse	LH94	Cosworth	V8	11	engine	19	10
r	30	H-H Frentzen	Sauber	C13	Mercedes	V10	10	spin	9	5
r	20	E Comas	Larrousse	LH94	Cosworth	V8	3	engine	22	11
r	27	J Alesi	Ferrari	412T1B	Ferrari	V12	2	engine	5	3
nq	34	B Gachot	Pacific	PR01	Ilmor	V10				
nq	33	P Belmondo	Pacific	PR01	Ilmor	V10				

Winning speed: 208.170 km/h, 129.351 mph
Pole Position speed: 178.543 km/h, 110.941 mph (R Barrichello, 2 min:21.163 sec)
Fastest Lap speed: 215.200 km/h, 133.719 mph (D Hill, 1 min:57.117 sec on lap 41)
Lap Leaders: M Schumacher 1-28,30-44 (43); D Coulthard 29 (1).

M Schumacher finished 1st in 1h 28m 33.508s (208.706 km/h, 129.684 mph).

11 Sep 1994 — ITALY: Monza (Round:12) (Race: 560)

53 laps x 5.800 km, 3.604 miles = 307.400 km, 191.010 miles

POS.	NO.	DRIVER	CAR	MODEL	ENGINE		LAPS	TIME/REASON FOR RETIREMENT	GRID:POS	ROW
1	0	D Hill	Williams	FW16B	Renault	V10	53	1h 18m 02.754s	3	2
2	28	G Berger	Ferrari	412T1B	Ferrari	V12	53	1h 18m 07.684s	2	1
3	7	M Häkkinen	McLaren	MP4/9	Peugeot	V10	53	1h 18m 28.394s	7	4
4	14	R Barrichello	Jordan	194	Hart	V10	53	1h 18m 53.388s	16	8
5	8	M Brundle	McLaren	MP4/9	Peugeot	V10	53	1h 19m 28.329s	15	8
6r	2	D Coulthard	Williams	FW16B	Renault	V10	52	out of fuel	5	3
7	25	É Bernard	Ligier	JS39B	Renault	V10	52		12	6
8	20	E Comas	Larrousse	LH94	Cosworth	V8	52		24	12
9	5	J J Lehto	Benetton	B194	Cosworth	V8	52		20	10
10	26	O Panis	Ligier	JS39B	Renault	V10	51		6	3
r	31	D Brabham	Simtek	S941	Cosworth	V8	46	brakes	26	13
r	3	U Katayama	Tyrrell	022	Yamaha	V10	45	brake disc/ accident	14	7
r	9	C Fittipaldi	Footwork	FA15	Cosworth	V8	43	engine	19	10
r	15	E Irvine	Jordan	194	Hart	V10	41	engine	9	5
r	4	M Blundell	Tyrrell	022	Yamaha	V10	39	brake disc/ accident	21	11
r	23	P Martini	Minardi	M194	Cosworth	V8	30	spin	18	9
r	24	M Alboreto	Minardi	M194	Cosworth	V8	28	gearbox	22	11
r	30	H-H Frentzen	Sauber	C13	Mercedes	V10	22	engine	11	6
r	29	A de Cesaris	Sauber	C13	Mercedes	V10	20	engine	8	4
r	32	J-M Gounon	Simtek	S941	Cosworth	V8	20	transmission	25	13
r	19	Y Dalmas	Larrousse	LH94	Cosworth	V8	18	spin	23	12
r	27	J Alesi	Ferrari	412T1B	Ferrari	V12	14	gearbox	1	1
r	12	J Herbert	Lotus	109	Mugen Honda	V10	13	engine	4	2
r	6	J Verstappen	Benetton	B194	Cosworth	V8	0	puncture	10	5
r	11	A Zanardi	Lotus	109	Mugen Honda	V10	0	accident	13	7
r	10	G Morbidelli	Footwork	FA15	Cosworth	V8	0	tyre blow-out/ accident	17	9
nq	34	B Gachot	Pacific	PR01	Ilmor	V10				
nq	33	P Belmondo	Pacific	PR01	Ilmor	V10				

Winning speed: 236.322 km/h, 146.844 mph
Pole Position speed: 249.034 km/h, 154.743 mph (J Alesi, 1 min:23.844 sec)
Fastest Lap speed: 242.988 km/h, 150.986 mph (D Hill, 1 min:25.930 sec on lap 24)
Lap Leaders: J Alesi 1-14 (14); G Berger 15-23 (9); D Hill 24,29-53 (26); D Coulthard 25,27-28 (3); M Häkkinen 26 (1).

25 Sep 1994 — PORTUGAL: Estoril (Round:13) (Race: 561)

71 laps x 4.360 km, 2.709 miles = 309.560 km, 192.352 miles

POS.	NO.	DRIVER	CAR	MODEL	ENGINE		LAPS	TIME/REASON FOR RETIREMENT	GRID:POS	ROW
1	0	D Hill	Williams	FW16B	Renault	V10	71	1h 41m 10.165s	2	1
2	2	D Coulthard	Williams	FW16B	Renault	V10	71	1h 41m 10.768s	3	2
3	7	M Häkkinen	McLaren	MP4/9	Peugeot	V10	71	1h 41m 30.358s	4	2
4	14	R Barrichello	Jordan	194	Hart	V10	71	1h 41m 38.168s	8	4
5	6	J Verstappen	Benetton	B194	Cosworth	V8	71	1h 41m 39.550s	10	5
6	8	M Brundle	McLaren	MP4/9	Peugeot	V10	71	1h 42m 02.867s	7	4
7	15	E Irvine	Jordan	194	Hart	V10	70		13	7
8	9	C Fittipaldi	Footwork	FA15	Cosworth	V8	70		11	6
dq	26	O Panis	Ligier	JS39B	Renault	V10	70	illegal skidblock wear	15	8
9	10	G Morbidelli	Footwork	FA15	Cosworth	V8	70		16	8
10	25	É Bernard	Ligier	JS39B	Renault	V10	70		21	11
11	12	J Herbert	Lotus	109	Mugen Honda	V10	70		20	10
12	23	P Martini	Minardi	M194	Cosworth	V8	69		18	9
13	24	M Alboreto	Minardi	M194	Cosworth	V8	69		19	10
14	19	Y Dalmas	Larrousse	LH94	Cosworth	V8	69		23	12
15	32	J-M Gounon	Simtek	S941	Cosworth	V8	67		26	13
16	11	P Adams	Lotus	109	Mugen Honda	V10	67		25	13
r	4	M Blundell	Tyrrell	022	Yamaha	V10	61	engine	12	6
r	5	J J Lehto	Benetton	B194	Cosworth	V8	60	spin	14	7
r	29	A de Cesaris	Sauber	C13	Mercedes	V10	54	spin	17	9
r	27	J Alesi	Ferrari	412T1B	Ferrari	V12	38	accident	5	3
r	31	D Brabham	Simtek	S941	Cosworth	V8	36	accident	24	12
r	30	H-H Frentzen	Sauber	C13	Mercedes	V10	31	transmission	9	5
r	20	E Comas	Larrousse	LH94	Cosworth	V8	27	accident	22	11
r	3	U Katayama	Tyrrell	022	Yamaha	V10	26	gearbox	6	3
r	28	G Berger	Ferrari	412T1B	Ferrari	V12	7	gearbox hydraulics	1	1
nq	34	B Gachot	Pacific	PR01	Ilmor	V10				
nq	33	P Belmondo	Pacific	PR01	Ilmor	V10				

Winning speed: 183.589 km/h, 114.077 mph
Pole Position speed: 194.720 km/h, 120.993 mph (G Berger, 1 min:20.608 sec)
Fastest Lap speed: 190.379 km/h, 118.296 mph (D Coulthard, 1 min:22.446 sec on lap 12)
Lap Leaders: G Berger 1-7 (7); D Coulthard 8-17,26-27 (12); D Hill 18,28-71 (45); J Alesi 19-22 (4); R Barrichello 23-25 (3).

16 Oct 1994 — EUROPE: Jerez de la Frontera (Round:14) (Race: 562)

69 laps x 4.428 km, 2.751 miles = 305.532 km, 189.849 miles

POS.	NO.	DRIVER	CAR	MODEL	ENGINE		LAPS	TIME/REASON FOR RETIREMENT	GRID:POS	ROW
1	5	M Schumacher	Benetton	B194	Cosworth	V8	69	1h 40m 26.689s	1	1
2	0	D Hill	Williams	FW16B	Renault	V10	69	1h 40m 51.378s	2	1
3	7	M Häkkinen	McLaren	MP4/9	Peugeot	V10	69	1h 41m 36.337s	9	5
4	15	E Irvine	Jordan	194	Hart	V10	69	1h 41m 45.135s	10	5
5	28	G Berger	Ferrari	412T1B	Ferrari	V12	68		6	3
6	30	H-H Frentzen	Sauber	C13	Mercedes	V10	68		4	2

POS.	NO.	DRIVER	CAR	MODEL	ENGINE		LAPS	TIME/REASON FOR RETIREMENT	GRID:POS	ROW
7	3	U Katayama	Tyrrell	022	Yamaha	V10	68		13	7
8	25	J Herbert	Ligier	JS39B	Renault	V10	68		7	4
9	26	O Panis	Ligier	JS39B	Renault	V10	68		11	6
10	27	J Alesi	Ferrari	412T1B	Ferrari	V12	68		16	8
11	10	G Morbidelli	Footwork	FA15	Cosworth	V8	68		8	4
12	14	R Barrichello	Jordan	194	Hart	V10	68		5	3
13	4	M Blundell	Tyrrell	022	Yamaha	V10	68		14	7
14	24	M Alboreto	Minardi	M194	Cosworth	V8	67		20	10
15	23	P Martini	Minardi	M194	Cosworth	V8	67		17	9
16	12	A Zanardi	Lotus	109	Mugen Honda	V10	67		21	11
17	9	C Fittipaldi	Footwork	FA15	Cosworth	V8	66		19	10
18	11	É Bernard	Lotus	109	Mugen Honda	V10	66		22	11
19	32	M Schiattarella	Simtek	S941	Cosworth	V8	64		26	13
r	2	N Mansell	Williams	FW16B	Renault	V10	47	spin	3	2
r	31	D Brabham	Simtek	S941	Cosworth	V8	42	engine	25	13
r	29	A de Cesaris	Sauber	C13	Mercedes	V10	37	throttle	18	9
r	20	E Comas	Larrousse	LH94	Cosworth	V8	37	electrics	23	12
r	6	J Verstappen	Benetton	B194	Cosworth	V8	15	spin	12	6
r	19	H Noda	Larrousse	LH94	Cosworth	V8	10	gearbox	24	12
r	8	M Brundle	McLaren	MP4/9	Peugeot	V10	8	engine	15	8
nq	34	B Gachot	Pacific	PR01	Ilmor	V10				
nq	33	P Belmondo	Pacific	PR01	Ilmor	V10				

Winning speed: 182.507 km/h, 113.405 mph
Pole Position speed: 192.610 km/h, 119.682 mph (M Schumacher, 1 min:22.762 sec)
Fastest Lap speed: 187.451 km/h, 116.476 mph (M Schumacher, 1 min:25.040 sec on lap 17)
Lap Leaders: D Hill 1-17,33-34 (19); M Schumacher 18-32,35-69 (50).

6 Nov 1994 — JAPAN: Suzuka — (Round:15) (Race: 563)

50 laps x 5.864 km, 3.644 miles = 293.200 km, 182.186 miles

POS.	NO.	DRIVER	CAR	MODEL	ENGINE		LAPS	TIME/REASON FOR RETIREMENT	GRID:POS	ROW
1	0	D Hill	Williams	FW16B	Renault	V10	50	1h 55m 53.532s	2	1
2	5	M Schumacher	Benetton	B194	Cosworth	V8	50	1h 55m 56.897s	1	1
3	27	J Alesi	Ferrari	412T1B	Ferrari	V12	50	1h 56m 45.577s	7	4
4	2	N Mansell	Williams	FW16B	Renault	V10	50	1h 56m 49.606s	4	2
5	15	E Irvine	Jordan	194	Hart	V10	50	1h 57m 35.639s	6	3
6	30	H-H Frentzen	Sauber	C13	Mercedes	V10	50	1h 57m 53.395s	3	2
7	7	M Häkkinen	McLaren	MP4/9	Peugeot	V10	50	1h 57m 56.517s	8	4
8	9	C Fittipaldi	Footwork	FA15	Cosworth	V8	49		18	9
9	20	E Comas	Larrousse	LH94	Cosworth	V8	49		22	11
10	11	M Salo	Lotus	109	Mugen Honda	V10	49		25	13
11	26	O Panis	Ligier	JS39B	Renault	V10	49		19	10
12	31	D Brabham	Simtek	S941	Cosworth	V8	48		24	12
13	12	A Zanardi	Lotus	109	Mugen Honda	V10	48		17	9
r	4	M Blundell	Tyrrell	022	Yamaha	V10	26	engine	13	7
r	14	R Barrichello	Jordan	194	Hart	V10	16	gearbox	10	5
r	8	M Brundle	McLaren	MP4/9	Peugeot	V10	13	accident	9	5
r	10	G Morbidelli	Footwork	FA15	Cosworth	V8	13	accident	12	6
r	28	G Berger	Ferrari	412T1B	Ferrari	V12	10	coil	11	6
r	25	F Lagorce	Ligier	JS39B	Renault	V10	10	accident	20	10
r	23	P Martini	Minardi	M194	Cosworth	V8	10	accident	16	8
r	24	M Alboreto	Minardi	M194	Cosworth	V8	10	spin	21	11
r	6	J Herbert	Benetton	B194	Cosworth	V8	3	spin	5	3
r	3	U Katayama	Tyrrell	022	Yamaha	V10	3	accident	14	7
r	32	T Inoue	Simtek	S941	Cosworth	V8	3	accident	26	13
r	19	H Noda	Larrousse	LH94	Cosworth	V8	0	fuel injection	23	12
r	29	J J Lehto	Sauber	C13	Mercedes	V10	0	engine	15	8
nq	34	B Gachot	Pacific	PR01	Ilmor	V10				
nq	33	P Belmondo	Pacific	PR01	Ilmor	V10				

Winning speed: 151.796 km/h, 94.322 mph
Pole Position speed: 217.165 km/h, 134.940 mph (M Schumacher, 1 min:37.209 sec)
Fastest Lap speed: 181.054 km/h, 112.502 mph (D Hill, 1 min:56.597 sec on lap 24)
Lap Leaders: M Schumacher 1-18 (18); D Hill 19-50 (32).

Scheduled for 53 laps, but interrupted after 13 laps, because of an accident. Restarted for a further 37 laps, with results being given on aggregate. Lap leaders are given 'on the road', although on aggregated time, the lead alternated between Hill and Schumacher.

13 Nov 1994 — AUSTRALIA: Adelaide — (Round:16) (Race: 564)

81 laps x 3.780 km, 2.349 miles = 306.180 km, 190.251 miles

POS.	NO.	DRIVER	CAR	MODEL	ENGINE		LAPS	TIME/REASON FOR RETIREMENT	GRID:POS	ROW
1	2	N Mansell	Williams	FW16B	Renault	V10	81	1h 47m 51.480s	1	1
2	28	G Berger	Ferrari	412T1B	Ferrari	V12	81	1h 47m 53.991s	11	6
3	8	M Brundle	McLaren	MP4/9	Peugeot	V10	81	1h 48m 43.967s	9	5
4	14	R Barrichello	Jordan	194	Hart	V10	81	1h 49m 02.010s	5	3
5	26	O Panis	Ligier	JS39B	Renault	V10	80		12	6
6	27	J Alesi	Ferrari	412T1B	Ferrari	V12	80		8	4
7	30	H-H Frentzen	Sauber	C13	Mercedes	V10	80		10	5
8	9	C Fittipaldi	Footwork	FA15	Cosworth	V8	80		19	10
9	23	P Martini	Minardi	M194	Cosworth	V8	79		18	9
10	29	J J Lehto	Sauber	C13	Mercedes	V10	79		17	9
11	25	F Lagorce	Ligier	JS39B	Renault	V10	79		20	10
12r	7	M Häkkinen	McLaren	MP4/9	Peugeot	V10	76	brakes/ accident	4	2
r	24	M Alboreto	Minardi	M194	Cosworth	V8	69	accident/ suspension	16	8

POS.	NO.	DRIVER	CAR	MODEL	ENGINE		LAPS	TIME/REASON FOR RETIREMENT	GRID:POS	ROW
r	4	M Blundell	Tyrrell	022	Yamaha	V10	66	accident	13	7
r	20	J-D Deletraz	Larrousse	LH94	Cosworth	V8	56	gearbox	25	13
r	11	M Salo	Lotus	109	Mugen Honda	V10	49	electrics	22	11
r	31	D Brabham	Simtek	S941	Cosworth	V8	49	engine	24	12
r	12	A Zanardi	Lotus	109	Mugen Honda	V10	40	throttle	14	7
r	0	D Hill	Williams	FW16B	Renault	V10	35	accident/ front suspension	3	2
r	5	M Schumacher	Benetton	B194	Cosworth	V8	35	accident	2	1
r	32	M Schiattarella	Simtek	S941	Cosworth	V8	21	gear lever	26	13
r	3	U Katayama	Tyrrell	022	Yamaha	V10	19	spin	15	8
r	19	H Noda	Larrousse	LH94	Cosworth	V8	18	oil leak	23	12
r	10	G Morbidelli	Footwork	FA15	Cosworth	V8	17	oil scavenge pump	21	11
r	15	E Irvine	Jordan	194	Hart	V10	15	spin	6	3
r	6	J Herbert	Benetton	B194	Cosworth	V8	13	gearbox	7	4
nq	33	P Belmondo	Pacific	PR01	Ilmor	V10				
nq	34	B Gachot	Pacific	PR01	Ilmor	V10				

Winning speed: 170.324 km/h, 105.834 mph
Pole Position speed: 178.632 km/h, 110.997 mph (N Mansell, 1 min:16.179 sec)
Fastest Lap speed: 176.407 km/h, 109.614 mph (M Schumacher, 1 min:17.140 sec on lap 29)
Lap Leaders: M Schumacher 1-35 (35); N Mansell 36-53,64-81 (36); G Berger 54-63 (10).

Lap Leaders 1994

POS	DRIVER	CAR-ENGINE	GPS	LAPS	KM	MILES
1	M Schumacher	Benetton-Cosworth	13	629	2,741.5	1,703.5
2	D Hill	Williams-Renault	8	216	1,069.4	664.5
3	G Berger	Ferrari	6	84	493.1	306.4
4	N Mansell	Williams-Renault	1	36	136.1	84.6
5	A Senna	Williams-Renault	2	26	116.0	72.1
6	J Alesi	Ferrari	2	18	98.6	61.3
7	D Coulthard	Williams-Renault	3	16	76.7	47.7
8	M Häkkinen	McLaren-Peugeot	3	13	63.9	39.7
9	N Larini	Ferrari	1	5	25.2	15.7
10	R Barrichello	Jordan-Hart	1	3	13.1	8.1
			16	**1,046**	**4,833.8**	**3,003.6**

Driver Points 1994

		BR	PAC	RSM	MC	E	CDN	F	GB	D	H	B	I	P	EUR	J	AUS	TOTAL
1	M Schumacher	10	10	10	10	6	10	10	-	-	10	-	-	-	10	6	-	92
2	D Hill	6	-	1	-	10	6	6	10	-	6	10	10	10	6	10	-	91
3	G Berger	-	6	-	4	-	3	4	-	10	-	-	6	-	2	-	6	41
4	M Häkkinen	-	-	4	-	-	-	-	4	-	-	6	4	4	4	-	-	26
5	J Alesi	4	-	-	2	3	4	-	6	-	-	-	-	-	-	4	1	24
6	R Barrichello	3	4	-	-	-	-	-	3	-	-	-	3	3	-	-	3	19
7	M Brundle	-	-	-	6	-	-	-	-	-	3	-	2	1	-	-	4	16
8	D Coulthard	-	-	-	-	-	2	-	2	-	-	3	1	6	-	-	-	14
9	N Mansell	-	-	-	-	-	-	-	-	-	-	-	-	-	-	3	10	13
10	J Verstappen	-	-	-	-	-	-	-	-	-	4	4	-	2	-	-	-	10
11	O Panis	-	-	-	-	-	-	-	-	6	1	-	-	-	-	-	2	9
12	M Blundell	-	-	-	-	4	-	-	-	-	2	2	-	-	-	-	-	8
13	H-H Frentzen	-	2	-	-	-	-	3	-	-	-	-	-	-	1	1	-	7
14	N Larini	-	-	6	-	-	-	-	-	-	-	-	-	-	-	-	-	6
	C Fittipaldi	-	3	-	-	-	-	-	-	3	-	-	-	-	-	-	-	6
	E Irvine	-	-	-	-	1	-	-	-	-	-	-	-	-	3	2	-	6
17	U Katayama	2	-	2	-	-	-	-	1	-	-	-	-	-	-	-	-	5
18	É Bernard	-	-	-	-	-	-	-	-	4	-	-	-	-	-	-	-	4
	K Wendlinger	1	-	3	-	-	-	-	-	-	-	-	-	-	-	-	-	4
	A de Cesaris	-	-	-	3	-	-	1	-	-	-	-	-	-	-	-	-	4
	P Martini	-	-	-	-	2	-	2	-	-	-	-	-	-	-	-	-	4
22	G Morbidelli	-	-	-	-	-	-	-	-	2	-	1	-	-	-	-	-	3
23	E Comas	-	1	-	-	-	-	-	-	1	-	-	-	-	-	-	-	2
24	M Alboreto	-	-	-	1	-	-	-	-	-	-	-	-	-	-	-	-	1
	J J Lehto	-	-	-	-	-	1	-	-	-	-	-	-	-	-	-	-	1

10, 6, 4, 3, 2 and 1 point awarded to the first six finishers.

Constructor Points 1994

		BR	PAC	RSM	MC	E	CDN	F	GB	D	H	B	I	P	EUR	J	AUS	TOTAL
1	Williams-Renault	6	-	1	-	10	8	6	12	-	6	13	11	16	6	13	10	118
2	Benetton-Cosworth	10	10	10	10	6	11	10	-	-	14	4	-	2	10	6	-	103
3	Ferrari	4	6	6	6	3	7	4	6	10	-	-	6	-	2	4	7	71
4	McLaren-Peugeot	-	-	4	6	-	-	-	4	-	3	6	6	5	4	-	4	42
5	Jordan-Hart	3	4	-	3	1	-	-	3	-	-	-	3	3	3	2	3	28
6	Ligier-Renault	-	-	-	-	-	-	-	-	10	1	-	-	-	-	-	2	13
	Tyrrell-Yamaha	2	-	2	-	4	-	-	1	-	2	2	-	-	-	-	-	13
8	Sauber-Mercedes	1	2	3	-	-	-	4	-	-	-	-	-	-	1	1	-	12
9	Footwork-Cosworth	-	3	-	-	-	-	-	-	5	-	1	-	-	-	-	-	9
10	Minardi-Cosworth	-	-	-	1	2	-	2	-	-	-	-	-	-	-	-	-	5
11	Larrousse-Cosworth	-	1	-	-	-	-	-	-	1	-	-	-	-	-	-	-	2

10, 6, 4, 3, 2 and 1 point awarded to the first six finishers.

The final safety measures came into effect with the reduction in engine size to 3 litres and a fully stepped chassis bottom to help reduce speeds. Benetton moved from Ford to Renault with McLaren, Jordan and Sauber all negotiating new engine deals. With the addition of Argentina, there would be 17 races for only the second time ever although the motor racing world mourned the death of the man who epitomised all that was good in motor sport - the great Juan Manuel Fangio.

BENETTON
Mild Seven Benetton Renault: Schumacher, Herbert

TYRRELL
Nokia Tyrrell Yamaha: Katayama, Tarquini, Salo

WILLIAMS
Rothmans Williams Renault: Hill, Coulthard

McLAREN
Marlboro McLaren Mercedes: Blundell, Mansell, Häkkinen, Magnussen

FOOTWORK
Footwork Hart: Morbidelli, Papis, Inoue

SIMTEK
MTV Simtek Ford: Schiattarella, Verstappen

JORDAN
Total Jordan Peugeot: Barrichello, Irvine

PACIFIC
Pacific Grand Prix: Gachot, Lavaggi, Deletraz, Montermini

FORTI
Parmalat Forti Ford: Diniz, Moreno

MINARDI
Minardi-Scuderia Italia: Martini, Lamy, Badoer

LIGIER
Ligier Gitanes Blondes: Suzuki, Brundle, Panis

FERRARI
Scuderia Ferrari SpA: Alesi, Berger

SAUBER
Red Bull Sauber Ford: Wendlinger, Boullion, Frentzen

26 Mar 1995 — BRAZIL: Interlagos (Round: 1) (Race: 565)

71 laps x 4.325 km, 2.687 miles = 307.075 km, 190.808 miles

POS.	NO.	DRIVER	CAR	MODEL	ENGINE		LAPS	TIME/REASON FOR RETIREMENT	GRID:POS	ROW
1	1	M Schumacher	Benetton	B195	Renault	V10	71	1h 38m 34.154s	2	1
2	6	D Coulthard	Williams	FW17	Renault	V10	71	1h 38m 42.214s	3	2
3	28	G Berger	Ferrari	412T2	Ferrari	V12	70		5	3
4	8	M Häkkinen	McLaren	MP4/10	Mercedes	V10	70		7	4
5	27	J Alesi	Ferrari	412T2	Ferrari	V12	70		6	3
6	7	M Blundell	McLaren	MP4/10	Mercedes	V10	70		9	5
7	4	M Salo	Tyrrell	023	Yamaha	V10	69		12	6
8	25	A Suzuki	Ligier	JS41	Mugen Honda	V10	69		15	8
9	17	A Montermini	Pacific	PR02	Cosworth	V8	65		22	11
10	21	P Diniz	Forti	FG01-95	Cosworth	V8	64		25	13
r	9	G Morbidelli	Footwork	FA16	Hart	V8	62	fuel pressure valve	13	7
r	10	T Inoue	Footwork	FA16	Hart	V8	48	fuel leak/ engine fire	21	11
r	24	L Badoer	Minardi	M195	Cosworth	V8	47	gearbox	18	9
r	22	R Moreno	Forti	FG01-95	Cosworth	V8	47	spin	23	12
r	29	K Wendlinger	Sauber	C14	Cosworth	V8	41	heat shield loss/ battery wire	19	10
r	5	D Hill	Williams	FW17	Renault	V10	30	rear suspension/ spin	1	1
r	2	J Herbert	Benetton	B195	Renault	V10	30	accident	4	2
r	16	B Gachot	Pacific	PR02	Cosworth	V8	23	gearbox	20	10
r	14	R Barrichello	Jordan	195	Peugeot	V10	16	gearbox actuator	16	8
r	12	J Verstappen	Simtek	S951	Cosworth	V8	16	clutch	24	12
r	3	U Katayama	Tyrrell	023	Yamaha	V10	15	spin	11	6
r	15	E Irvine	Jordan	195	Peugeot	V10	15	gearbox hydraulics	8	4
r	11	M Schiattarella	Simtek	S951	Cosworth	V8	12	steering box loose	26	13
r	30	H-H Frentzen	Sauber	C14	Cosworth	V8	10	electrics	14	7
r	26	O Panis	Ligier	JS41	Mugen Honda	V10	0	accident	10	5
r	23	P Martini	Minardi	M195	Cosworth	V8	-1	gearbox	17	9

Winning speed: 186.919 km/h, 116.146 mph
Pole Position speed: 194.428 km/h, 120.812 mph (D Hill, 1 min:20.081 sec)
Fastest Lap speed: 192.410 km/h, 119.558 mph (M Schumacher, 1 min:20.921 sec on lap 51)
Lap Leaders: M Schumacher 1-17,31-35,47-71 (47); D Hill 18-21,23-30 (12); D Coulthard 22,36-46 (12).

Benetton (finishing 1st) and Williams (finishing 2nd) received no points towards the Constructors' Championship, due to fuel irregularities.

9 Apr 1995 — ARGENTINA: Buenos Aires (Round: 2) (Race: 566)

72 laps x 4.259 km, 2.646 miles = 306.481 km, 190.438 miles

POS.	NO.	DRIVER	CAR	MODEL	ENGINE		LAPS	TIME/REASON FOR RETIREMENT	GRID:POS	ROW
1	5	D Hill	Williams	FW17	Renault	V10	72	1h 53m 14.532s	2	1
2	27	J Alesi	Ferrari	412T2	Ferrari	V12	72	1h 53m 20.939s	6	3
3	1	M Schumacher	Benetton	B195	Renault	V10	72	1h 53m 47.908s	3	2
4	2	J Herbert	Benetton	B195	Renault	V10	71		11	6
5	30	H-H Frentzen	Sauber	C14	Cosworth	V8	70		9	5
6	28	G Berger	Ferrari	412T2	Ferrari	V12	70		8	4
7	26	O Panis	Ligier	JS41	Mugen Honda	V10	70		18	9
8	3	U Katayama	Tyrrell	023	Yamaha	V10	69		15	8
9	11	M Schiattarella	Simtek	S951	Cosworth	V8	68		20	10
nc	21	P Diniz	Forti	FG01-95	Cosworth	V8	63		25	13
nc	22	R Moreno	Forti	FG01-95	Cosworth	V8	63		24	12
r	4	M Salo	Tyrrell	023	Yamaha	V10	48	accident	7	4
r	25	A Suzuki	Ligier	JS41	Mugen Honda	V10	47	accident	19	10
r	23	P Martini	Minardi	M195	Cosworth	V8	44	spin	16	8
r	9	G Morbidelli	Footwork	FA16	Hart	V8	43	electrics	12	6
r	10	T Inoue	Footwork	FA16	Hart	V8	40	spin	26	13
r	14	R Barrichello	Jordan	195	Peugeot	V10	33	oil leak/ engine	10	5
r	12	J Verstappen	Simtek	S951	Cosworth	V8	23	gearbox	14	7
r	6	D Coulthard	Williams	FW17	Renault	V10	16	throttle	1	1
r	7	M Blundell	McLaren	MP4/10	Mercedes	V10	9	gearbox casing/ oil loss	17	9
r	15	E Irvine	Jordan	195	Peugeot	V10	6	engine	4	2

POS.	NO.	DRIVER	CAR	MODEL	ENGINE		LAPS	TIME/REASON FOR RETIREMENT	GRID:POS	ROW
r	17	A Montermini	Pacific	PR02	Cosworth	V8	1	accident/ suspension	22	11
r	8	M Häkkinen	McLaren	MP4/10	Mercedes-	V10	0	accident	5	3
r	16	B Gachot	Pacific	PR02	Cosworth	V8	0	accident	23	12
r	29	K Wendlinger	Sauber	C14	Cosworth	V8	0	accident	21	11
r	24	L Badoer	Minardi	M195	Cosworth	V8	0	accident *	13	7

Winning speed: 162.385 km/h, 100.902 mph
Pole Position speed: 135.396 km/h, 84.131 mph (D Coulthard, 1 min:53.241 sec)
Fastest Lap speed: 169.378 km/h, 105.246 mph (M Schumacher, 1 min:30.522 sec on lap 55)
Lap Leaders: D Coulthard 1-5 (5); M Schumacher 6-10,17 (6); D Hill 11-16,26-72 (53); J Alesi 18-25 (8).

*Interrupted after 1st lap accident. Restarted for original distance. * retired after first start.*

30 Apr 1995 — SAN MARINO: Imola — (Round: 3) (Race: 567)
63 laps x 4.895 km, 3.042 miles = 308.385 km, 191.622 miles

POS.	NO.	DRIVER	CAR	MODEL	ENGINE		LAPS	TIME/REASON FOR RETIREMENT	GRID:POS	ROW
1	5	D Hill	Williams	FW17	Renault	V10	63	1h 41m 42.552s	4	2
2	27	J Alesi	Ferrari	412T2	Ferrari	V12	63	1h 42m 01.062s	5	3
3	28	G Berger	Ferrari	412T2	Ferrari	V12	63	1h 42m 25.668s	2	1
4	6	D Coulthard	Williams	FW17	Renault	V10	63	1h 42m 34.442s	3	2
5	8	M Häkkinen	McLaren	MP4/10	Mercedes	V10	62		6	3
6	30	H-H Frentzen	Sauber	C14	Cosworth	V8	62		14	7
7	2	J Herbert	Benetton	B195	Renault	V10	61		8	4
8	15	E Irvine	Jordan	195	Peugeot	V10	61		7	4
9	26	O Panis	Ligier	JS41	Mugen Honda	V10	61		12	6
10	7	N Mansell	McLaren	MP4/10B	Mercedes	V10	61		9	5
11	25	A Suzuki	Ligier	JS41	Mugen Honda	V10	60		16	8
12	23	P Martini	Minardi	M195	Cosworth	V8	59		18	9
13	9	G Morbidelli	Footwork	FA16	Hart	V8	59		11	6
14	24	L Badoer	Minardi	M195	Cosworth	V8	59		20	10
15	21	P Diniz	Forti	FG01-95	Cosworth	V8	56		26	13
16	22	R Moreno	Forti	FG01-95	Cosworth	V8	56		25	13
r	29	K Wendlinger	Sauber	C14	Cosworth	V8	43	rear wheel nut jammed	21	11
r	16	B Gachot	Pacific	PR02	Cosworth	V8	36	gearbox hydraulic leak	22	11
r	11	M Schiattarella	Simtek	S951	Cosworth	V8	35	accident/ rear suspension	23	12
r	14	R Barrichello	Jordan	195	Peugeot	V10	31	gearbox	10	5
r	3	U Katayama	Tyrrell	023	Yamaha	V10	23	spin	15	8
r	4	M Salo	Tyrrell	023	Yamaha	V10	19	engine	13	7
r	17	A Montermini	Pacific	PR02	Cosworth	V8	15	gearbox hydraulics	24	12
r	12	J Verstappen	Simtek	S951	Cosworth	V8	14	gearbox	17	9
r	10	T Inoue	Footwork	FA16	Hart	V8	12	spin	19	10
r	1	M Schumacher	Benetton	B195	Renault	V10	10	accident	1	1

Winning speed: 181.922 km/h, 113.041 mph
Pole Position speed: 201.916 km/h, 125.465 mph (M Schumacher, 1 min:27.274 sec)
Fastest Lap speed: 196.744 km/h, 122.251 mph (G Berger, 1 min:29.568 sec on lap 57)
Lap Leaders: M Schumacher 1-9 (9); D Coulthard 10 (1); G Berger 11-21 (11); D Hill 22-63 (42).

14 May 1995 — SPAIN: Montmeló — (Round: 4) (Race: 568)
65 laps x 4.727 km, 2.937 miles = 307.114 km, 190.832 miles

POS.	NO.	DRIVER	CAR	MODEL	ENGINE		LAPS	TIME/REASON FOR RETIREMENT	GRID:POS	ROW
1	1	M Schumacher	Benetton	B195	Renault	V10	65	1h 34m 20.507s	1	1
2	2	J Herbert	Benetton	B195	Renault	V10	65	1h 35m 12.495s	7	4
3	28	G Berger	Ferrari	412T2	Ferrari	V12	65	1h 35m 25.744s	3	2
4	5	D Hill	Williams	FW17	Renault	V10	65	1h 36m 22.256s	5	3
5	15	E Irvine	Jordan	195	Peugeot	V10	64		6	3
6	26	O Panis	Ligier	JS41	Mugen Honda	V10	64		15	8
7	14	R Barrichello	Jordan	195	Peugeot	V10	64		8	4
8	30	H-H Frentzen	Sauber	C14	Cosworth	V8	64		12	6
9	25	M Brundle	Ligier	JS41	Mugen Honda	V10	64		11	6
10	4	M Salo	Tyrrell	023	Yamaha	V10	64		13	7
11	9	G Morbidelli	Footwork	FA16	Hart	V8	63		14	7
12	12	J Verstappen	Simtek	S951	Cosworth	V8	63		16	8
13	29	K Wendlinger	Sauber	C14	Cosworth	V8	63		20	10
14	23	P Martini	Minardi	M195	Cosworth	V8	62		19	10
15	11	M Schiattarella	Simtek	S951	Cosworth	V8	61		22	11
r	3	U Katayama	Tyrrell	023	Yamaha	V10	56	engine pneumatic valve system	17	9
r	6	D Coulthard	Williams	FW17	Renault	V10	54	gearbox	4	2
r	8	M Häkkinen	McLaren	MP4/10	Mercedes	V10	53	fuel pressure	9	5
r	10	T Inoue	Footwork	FA16	Hart	V8	43	engine hydraulic fire	18	9
r	16	B Gachot	Pacific	PR02	Cosworth	V8	43	refuelling valve/ fire	24	12
r	22	R Moreno	Forti	FG01-95	Cosworth	V8	39	water pump	25	13
r	27	J Alesi	Ferrari	412T2	Ferrari	V12	25	engine	2	1
r	24	L Badoer	Minardi	M195	Cosworth	V8	21	gearbox hydraulics	21	11
r	7	N Mansell	McLaren	MP4/10B	Mercedes	V10	18	handling	10	5
r	21	P Diniz	Forti	FG01-95	Cosworth	V8	17	exhaust/ gearbox cable	26	13
r	17	A Montermini	Pacific	PR02	Cosworth	V8	-1	gearbox hydraulics	23	12

Winning speed: 195.320 km/h, 121.367 mph
Pole Position speed: 208.923 km/h, 129.819 mph (M Schumacher, 1 min:21.452 sec)
Fastest Lap speed: 201.313 km/h, 125.090 mph (D Hill, 1 min:24.531 sec on lap 46)
Lap Leaders: M Schumacher 1-65 (65).

28 May 1995 — MONACO: Monte Carlo (Round: 5) (Race: 569)

78 laps x 3.328 km, 2.068 miles = 259.584 km, 161.298 miles

POS.	NO.	DRIVER	CAR	MODEL	ENGINE		LAPS	TIME/REASON FOR RETIREMENT	GRID:POS	ROW
1	1	M Schumacher	Benetton	B195	Renault	V10	78	1h 53m 11.258s	2	1
2	5	D Hill	Williams	FW17	Renault	V10	78	1h 53m 46.075s	1	1
3	28	G Berger	Ferrari	412T2	Ferrari	V12	78	1h 54m 22.705s	4	2
4	2	J Herbert	Benetton	B195	Renault	V10	77		7	4
5	7	M Blundell	McLaren	MP4/10B	Mercedes	V10	77		10	5
6	30	H-H Frentzen	Sauber	C14	Cosworth	V8	76		14	7
7	23	P Martini	Minardi	M195	Cosworth	V8	76		18	9
8r	29	J-C Boullion	Sauber	C14	Cosworth	V8	74	accident	19	10
9	9	G Morbidelli	Footwork	FA16	Hart	V8	74		13	7
10	21	P Diniz	Forti	FG01-95	Cosworth	V8	72		22	11
r	24	L Badoer	Minardi	M195	Cosworth	V8	68	accident/ suspension arm	16	8
r	26	O Panis	Ligier	JS41	Mugen Honda	V10	65	accident	12	6
r	4	M Salo	Tyrrell	023	Yamaha	V10	63	engine	17	9
r	14	R Barrichello	Jordan	195	Peugeot	V10	60	throttle jammed open	11	6
r	16	B Gachot	Pacific	PR02	Cosworth	V8	42	gearbox hydraulics	21	11
r	27	J Alesi	Ferrari	412T2	Ferrari	V12	41	accident	5	3
r	25	M Brundle	Ligier	JS41	Mugen Honda	V10	40	accident	8	4
r	10	T Inoue	Footwork	FA16	Hart	V8	27	gearbox	26	13
r	3	U Katayama	Tyrrell	023	Yamaha	V10	26	accident	15	8
dq	17	A Montermini	Pacific	PR02	Cosworth	V8	23	late for stop-go penalty	25	13
r	15	E Irvine	Jordan	195	Peugeot	V10	22	wheel collapsed	9	5
r	6	D Coulthard	Williams	FW17	Renault	V10	16	throttle/ gearbox	3	2
r	22	R Moreno	Forti	FG01-95	Cosworth	V8	9	brakes/ accident	24	12
r	8	M Häkkinen	McLaren	MP4/10B	Mercedes	V10	8	engine	6	3
r	11	M Schiattarella	Simtek	S951	Cosworth	V8	0	accident *	20	10
r	12	J Verstappen	Simtek	S951	Cosworth	V8	0	gearbox *	23	12

Winning speed: 137.604 km/h, 85.503 mph
Pole Position speed: 146.193 km/h, 90.840 mph (D Hill, 1 min:21.952 sec)
Fastest Lap speed: 141.582 km/h, 87.975 mph (J Alesi, 1 min:24.621 sec on lap 36)
Lap Leaders: D Hill 1-23 (23); M Schumacher 24-35,37-78 (54); J Alesi 36 (1).

*Interrupted after 1st lap accident. Restarted for original distance. * retired after first start.*

11 Jun 1995 — CANADA: Montréal (Round: 6) (Race: 570)

68 laps x 4.430 km, 2.753 miles = 301.240 km, 187.182 miles

POS.	NO.	DRIVER	CAR	MODEL	ENGINE		LAPS	TIME/REASON FOR RETIREMENT	GRID:POS	ROW
1	27	J Alesi	Ferrari	412T2	Ferrari	V12	68	1h 46m 31.333s	5	3
2	14	R Barrichello	Jordan	195	Peugeot	V10	68	1h 47m 03.020s	9	5
3	15	E Irvine	Jordan	195	Peugeot	V10	68	1h 47m 04.603s	8	4
4	26	O Panis	Ligier	JS41	Mugen Honda	V10	68	1h 47m 07.839s	11	6
5	1	M Schumacher	Benetton	B195	Renault	V10	68	1h 47m 08.393s	1	1
6	9	G Morbidelli	Footwork	FA16	Hart	V8	67		13	7
7	4	M Salo	Tyrrell	023	Yamaha	V10	67		15	8
8	24	L Badoer	Minardi	M195	Cosworth	V8	67		19	10
9	10	T Inoue	Footwork	FA16	Hart	V8	66		22	11
10r	25	M Brundle	Ligier	JS41	Mugen Honda	V10	61	accident	14	7
11r	28	G Berger	Ferrari	412T2	Ferrari	V12	61	accident	4	2
r	23	P Martini	Minardi	M195	Cosworth	V8	60	throttle cable	17	9
r	22	R Moreno	Forti	FG01-95	Cosworth	V8	54	out of fuel (refuelling failure)	23	12
r	5	D Hill	Williams	FW17	Renault	V10	50	gearbox hydraulic pump	2	1
r	7	M Blundell	McLaren	MP4/10B	Mercedes	V10	47	engine	10	5
r	3	U Katayama	Tyrrell	023	Yamaha	V10	42	engine air pressure	16	8
r	16	B Gachot	Pacific	PR02	Cosworth	V8	36	battery	20	10
r	30	H-H Frentzen	Sauber	C14	Cosworth	V8	26	engine	12	6
r	21	P Diniz	Forti	FG01-95	Cosworth	V8	26	gearbox	24	12
r	29	J-C Boullion	Sauber	C14	Cosworth	V8	19	spin	18	9
r	17	A Montermini	Pacific	PR02	Cosworth	V8	5	gearbox hydraulics	21	11
r	6	D Coulthard	Williams	FW17	Renault	V10	1	spin	3	2
r	2	J Herbert	Benetton	B195	Renault	V10	0	accident	6	3
r	8	M Häkkinen	McLaren	MP4/10B	Mercedes	V10	0	accident	7	4

Winning speed: 172.297 km/h, 107.060 mph
Pole Position speed: 181.928 km/h, 113.045 mph (M Schumacher, 1 min:27.661 sec)
Fastest Lap speed: 178.841 km/h, 111.127 mph (M Schumacher, 1 min:29.174 sec on lap 67)
Lap Leaders: M Schumacher 1-57 (57); J Alesi 58-68 (11).

Scheduled for 69 laps but results declared after 68 laps due to a crowd invasion of the track.

2 Jul 1995 — FRANCE: Magny-Cours (Round: 7) (Race: 571)

72 laps x 4.250 km, 2.641 miles = 305.814 km, 190.024 miles

POS.	NO.	DRIVER	CAR	MODEL	ENGINE		LAPS	TIME/REASON FOR RETIREMENT	GRID:POS	ROW
1	1	M Schumacher	Benetton	B195	Renault	V10	72	1h 38m 28.429s	2	1
2	5	D Hill	Williams	FW17	Renault	V10	72	1h 38m 59.738s	1	1
3	6	D Coulthard	Williams	FW17	Renault	V10	72	1h 39m 31.255s	3	2
4	25	M Brundle	Ligier	JS41	Mugen Honda	V10	72	1h 39m 31.722s	9	5
5	27	J Alesi	Ferrari	412T2	Ferrari	V12	72	1h 39m 46.298s	4	2
6	14	R Barrichello	Jordan	195	Peugeot	V10	71		5	3
7	8	M Häkkinen	McLaren	MP4/10B	Mercedes	V10	71		8	4

POS.	NO.	DRIVER	CAR	MODEL	ENGINE		LAPS	TIME/REASON FOR RETIREMENT	GRID:POS	ROW
8	26	O Panis	Ligier	JS41	Mugen Honda	V10	71		6	3
9	15	E Irvine	Jordan	195	Peugeot	V10	71		11	6
10	30	H-H Frentzen	Sauber	C14	Cosworth	V8	71		12	6
11	7	M Blundell	McLaren	MP4/10B	Mercedes	V10	70		13	7
12	28	G Berger	Ferrari	412T2	Ferrari	V12	70		7	4
13	24	L Badoer	Minardi	M195	Cosworth	V8	69		17	9
14	9	G Morbidelli	Footwork	FA16	Hart	V8	69		16	8
15	4	M Salo	Tyrrell	023	Yamaha	V10	69		14	7
16	22	R Moreno	Forti	FG01-95	Cosworth	V8	66		24	12
nc	17	A Montermini	Pacific	PR02	Cosworth	V8	62		21	11
r	29	J-C Boullion	Sauber	C14	Cosworth	V8	48	transmission	15	8
r	16	B Gachot	Pacific	PR02	Cosworth	V8	24	gearbox	22	11
r	23	P Martini	Minardi	M195	Cosworth	V8	23	gear selection	20	10
r	2	J Herbert	Benetton	B195	Renault	V10	2	accident	10	5
r	3	U Katayama	Tyrrell	023	Yamaha	V10	0	accident	19	10
r	10	T Inoue	Footwork	FA16	Hart	V8	0	accident	18	9
r	21	P Diniz	Forti	FG01-95	Cosworth	V8	0	accident	23	12

Winning speed: 186.332 km/h, 115.781 mph
Pole Position speed: 198.122 km/h, 123.108 mph (D Hill, 1 min:17.225 sec)
Fastest Lap speed: 190.730 km/h, 118.514 mph (M Schumacher, 1 min:20.218 sec on lap 51)
Lap Leaders: D Hill 1-21 (21); M Schumacher 22-72 (51).

16 Jul 1995 BRITAIN: Silverstone (Round: 8) (Race: 572)

61 laps x 5.057 km, 3.142 miles = 308.477 km, 191.679 miles

POS.	NO.	DRIVER	CAR	MODEL	ENGINE		LAPS	TIME/REASON FOR RETIREMENT	GRID:POS	ROW
1	2	J Herbert	Benetton	B195	Renault	V10	61	1h 34m 35.093s	5	3
2	27	J Alesi	Ferrari	412T2	Ferrari	V12	61	1h 34m 51.572s	6	3
3	6	D Coulthard	Williams	FW17	Renault	V10	61	1h 34m 58.981s	3	2
4	26	O Panis	Ligier	JS41	Mugen Honda	V10	61	1h 36m 08.261s	13	7
5	7	M Blundell	McLaren	MP4/10B	Mercedes	V10	61	1h 36m 23.265s	10	5
6	30	H-H Frentzen	Sauber	C14	Cosworth	V8	60		12	6
7	23	P Martini	Minardi	M195	Cosworth	V8	60		15	8
8	4	M Salo	Tyrrell	023	Yamaha	V10	60		23	12
9	29	J-C Boullion	Sauber	C14	Cosworth	V8	60		16	8
10	24	L Badoer	Minardi	M195	Cosworth	V8	60		18	9
11r	14	R Barrichello	Jordan	195	Peugeot	V10	59	accident/ front suspension	9	5
12	16	B Gachot	Pacific	PR02	Cosworth	V8	58		21	11
r	22	R Moreno	Forti	FG01-95	Cosworth	V8	48	pneumatic valve fluid pressure	22	11
r	1	M Schumacher	Benetton	B195	Renault	V10	45	accident	2	1
r	5	D Hill	Williams	FW17	Renault	V10	45	accident	1	1
r	9	M Papis	Footwork	FA16	Hart	V8	28	accident/ front suspension	17	9
r	3	U Katayama	Tyrrell	023	Yamaha	V10	22	fuel starvation	14	7
r	17	A Montermini	Pacific	PR02	Cosworth	V8	21	spin	24	12
r	8	M Häkkinen	McLaren	MP4/10B	Mercedes	V10	20	gearbox electronic control unit	8	4
r	28	G Berger	Ferrari	412T2	Ferrari	V12	20	front left wheel loose	4	2
r	25	M Brundle	Ligier	JS41	Mugen Honda	V10	16	spin	11	6
r	10	T Inoue	Footwork	FA16	Hart	V8	16	spin	19	10
r	21	P Diniz	Forti	FG01-95	Cosworth	V8	13	gear selection	20	10
r	15	E Irvine	Jordan	195	Peugeot	V10	2	crankshaft se	nsor	7
4										

Winning speed: 195.683 km/h, 121.592 mph
Pole Position speed: 206.586 km/h, 128.367 mph (D Hill, 1 min:28.124 sec)
Fastest Lap speed: 202.839 km/h, 126.038 mph (D Hill, 1 min:29.752 sec on lap 37)
Lap Leaders: D Hill 1-22,32-41 (32); M Schumacher 23-31,42-45 (13); J Herbert 46-48,51-61 (14); D Coulthard 49-50 (2).

30 Jul 1995 — GERMANY: Hockenheim (Round: 9) (Race: 573)

45 laps x 6.823 km, 4.240 miles = 307.022 km, 190.775 miles

POS.	NO.	DRIVER	CAR	MODEL	ENGINE		LAPS	TIME/REASON FOR RETIREMENT	GRID:POS	ROW
1	1	M Schumacher	Benetton	B195	Renault	V10	45	1h 22m 56.043s	2	1
2	6	D Coulthard	Williams	FW17	Renault	V10	45	1h 23m 02.031s	3	2
3	28	G Berger	Ferrari	412T2	Ferrari	V12	45	1h 24m 04.140s	4	2
4	2	J Herbert	Benetton	B195	Renault	V10	45	1h 24m 19.479s	9	5
5	29	J-C Boullion	Sauber	C14	Cosworth	V8	44		14	7
6	25	A Suzuki	Ligier	JS41	Mugen Honda	V10	44		18	9
7	3	U Katayama	Tyrrell	023	Yamaha	V10	44		17	9
8	17	A Montermini	Pacific	PR02	Cosworth	V8	42		23	12
9r	15	E Irvine	Jordan	195	Peugeot	V10	41	throttle potentiometer	6	3
r	8	M Häkkinen	McLaren	MP4/10B	Mercedes	V10	33	pneumatic pressure/ engine	7	4
r	30	H-H Frentzen	Sauber	C14	Cosworth	V8	32	engine	11	6
r	24	L Badoer	Minardi	M195	Cosworth	V8	28	gearbox actuator oil leak	16	8
r	16	G Lavaggi	Pacific	PR02	Cosworth	V8	27	gearbox	24	12
r	22	R Moreno	Forti	FG01-95	Cosworth	V8	27	drive shaft	22	11
r	14	R Barrichello	Jordan	195	Peugeot	V10	20	pneumatic pressure/ engine	5	3
r	7	M Blundell	McLaren	MP4/10B	Mercedes	V10	17	engine	8	4
r	26	O Panis	Ligier	JS41	Mugen Honda	V10	13	water pipe split	12	6
r	27	J Alesi	Ferrari	412T2	Ferrari	V12	12	engine	10	5
r	23	P Martini	Minardi	M195	Cosworth	V8	11	engine	20	10
r	10	T Inoue	Footwork	FA16	Hart	V8	9	gearbox	19	10
r	21	P Diniz	Forti	FG01-95	Cosworth	V8	8	brakes	21	11
r	5	D Hill	Williams	FW17	Renault	V10	1	accident	1	1
r	4	M Salo	Tyrrell	023	Yamaha	V10	0	drive shaft	13	7
r	9	M Papis	Footwork	FA16	Hart	V8	0	gearbox electrics	15	8

Winning speed: 222.120 km/h, 138.019 mph
Pole Position speed: 235.310 km/h, 146.215 mph (D Hill, 1 min:44.385 sec)
Fastest Lap speed: 225.711 km/h, 140.250 mph (M Schumacher, 1 min:48.824 sec on lap 22)
Lap Leaders: D Hill 1 (1); M Schumacher 2-19,24-45 (40); D Coulthard 20-23 (4).

13 Aug 1995 — HUNGARY: Hungaroring (Round:10) (Race: 574)

77 laps x 3.968 km, 2.466 miles = 305.536 km, 189.851 miles

POS.	NO.	DRIVER	CAR	MODEL	ENGINE		LAPS	TIME/REASON FOR RETIREMENT	GRID:POS	ROW
1	5	D Hill	Williams	FW17	Renault	V10	77	1h 46m 25.721s	1	1
2	6	D Coulthard	Williams	FW17	Renault	V10	77	1h 46m 59.119s	2	1
3	28	G Berger	Ferrari	412T2	Ferrari	V12	76		4	2
4	2	J Herbert	Benetton	B195	Renault	V10	76		9	5
5	30	H-H Frentzen	Sauber	C14	Cosworth	V8	76		11	6
6	26	O Panis	Ligier	JS41	Mugen Honda	V10	76		10	5
7	14	R Barrichello	Jordan	195	Peugeot	V10	76		14	7
8	24	L Badoer	Minardi	M195	Cosworth	V8	75		12	6
9	23	P Lamy	Minardi	M195	Cosworth	V8	74		15	8
10	29	J-C Boullion	Sauber	C14	Cosworth	V8	74		19	10
11r	1	M Schumacher	Benetton	B195	Renault	V10	73	fuel pump	3	2
12	17	A Montermini	Pacific	PR02	Cosworth	V8	73		22	11
13r	15	E Irvine	Jordan	195	Peugeot	V10	70	clutch	7	4
r	25	M Brundle	Ligier	JS41	Mugen Honda	V10	67	engine	8	4
r	4	M Salo	Tyrrell	023	Yamaha	V10	58	throttle potentiometer	16	8
r	7	M Blundell	McLaren	MP4/10B	Mercedes	V10	54	engine	13	7
r	3	U Katayama	Tyrrell	023	Yamaha	V10	46	accident	17	9
r	9	M Papis	Footwork	FA16	Hart	V8	45	brake fluid loss	20	10
r	27	J Alesi	Ferrari	412T2	Ferrari	V12	42	spark plug dropped/ piston	6	3
r	21	P Diniz	Forti	FG01-95	Cosworth	V8	32	oil pressure/ engine	23	12
r	10	T Inoue	Footwork	FA16	Hart	V8	13	oil pressure loss/ fire	18	9
r	22	R Moreno	Forti	FG01-95	Cosworth	V8	8	gear lever	21	11
r	16	G Lavaggi	Pacific	PR02	Cosworth	V8	5	spin	24	12
r	8	M Häkkinen	McLaren	MP4/10B	Mercedes	V10	3	engine	5	3

Winning speed: 172.248 km/h, 107.030 mph
Pole Position speed: 185.560 km/h, 115.302 mph (D Hill, 1 min:16.982 sec)
Fastest Lap speed: 178.010 km/h, 110.611 mph (D Hill, 1 min:20.247 sec on lap 34)
Lap Leaders: D Hill 1-77 (77).

27 Aug 1995 — BELGIUM: Spa-Francorchamps (Round:11) (Race: 575)

44 laps x 6.974 km, 4.333 miles = 306.856 km, 190.671 miles

POS.	NO.	DRIVER	CAR	MODEL	ENGINE		LAPS	TIME/REASON FOR RETIREMENT	GRID:POS	ROW
1	1	M Schumacher	Benetton	B195	Renault	V10	44	1h 36m 47.875s	16	8
2	5	D Hill	Williams	FW17	Renault	V10	44	1h 37m 07.368s	8	4
3	25	M Brundle	Ligier	JS41	Mugen Honda	V10	44	1h 37m 12.873s	13	7
4	30	H-H Frentzen	Sauber	C14	Cosworth	V8	44	1h 37m 14.847s	10	5
5	7	M Blundell	McLaren	MP4/10B	Mercedes	V10	44	1h 37m 21.647s	6	3
6	14	R Barrichello	Jordan	195	Peugeot	V10	44	1h 37m 27.549s	12	6
7	2	J Herbert	Benetton	B195	Renault	V10	44	1h 37m 41.923s	4	2
8	4	M Salo	Tyrrell	023	Yamaha	V10	44	1h 37m 42.423s	11	6
9	26	O Panis	Ligier	JS41	Mugen Honda	V10	44	1h 37m 54.045s	9	5
10	23	P Lamy	Minardi	M195	Cosworth	V8	44	1h 38m 07.664s	17	9
11	29	J-C Boullion	Sauber	C14	Cosworth	V8	43		14	7
12	10	T Inoue	Footwork	FA16	Hart	V8	43		18	9
13	21	P Diniz	Forti	FG01-95	Cosworth	V8	42		24	12
14	22	R Moreno	Forti	FG01-95	Cosworth	V8	42		22	11

POS.	NO.	DRIVER	CAR	MODEL	ENGINE		LAPS	TIME/REASON FOR RETIREMENT	GRID:POS	ROW
r	3	U Katayama	Tyrrell	023	Yamaha	V10	28	spin	15	8
r	16	G Lavaggi	Pacific	PR02	Cosworth	V8	27	gearbox	23	12
r	24	L Badoer	Minardi	M195	Cosworth	V8	23	accident	19	10
r	28	G Berger	Ferrari	412T2	Ferrari	V12	22	electrics	1	1
r	15	E Irvine	Jordan	195	Peugeot	V10	21	refuelling fire	7	4
r	9	M Papis	Footwork	FA16	Hart	V8	20	spin	20	10
r	17	A Montermini	Pacific	PR02	Cosworth	V8	18	fuel pressure	21	11
r	6	D Coulthard	Williams	FW17	Renault	V10	13	gearbox oil loss	5	3
r	27	J Alesi	Ferrari	412T2	Ferrari	V12	4	rear suspension	2	1
r	8	M Häkkinen	McLaren	MP4/10B	Mercedes	V10	1	spin	3	2

Winning speed: 190.204 km/h, 118.187 mph
Pole Position speed: 219.477 km/h, 136.377 mph (G Berger, 1 min:54.392 sec)
Fastest Lap speed: 221.373 km/h, 137.555 mph (D Coulthard, 1 min:53.412 sec on lap 11)
Lap Leaders: J Herbert 1,4-5 (3); J Alesi 2-3 (2); D Coulthard 6-13 (8); D Hill 14-15,19-21,24 (6); M Schumacher 16-18,22-23,25-44 (25).

10 Sep 1995 — ITALY: Monza (Round:12) (Race: 576)

53 laps x 5.770 km, 3.585 miles = 305.771 km, 189.997 miles

POS.	NO.	DRIVER	CAR	MODEL	ENGINE		LAPS	TIME/REASON FOR RETIREMENT	GRID:POS	ROW
1	2	J Herbert	Benetton	B195	Renault	V10	53	1h 18m 27.916s	8	4
2	8	M Häkkinen	McLaren	MP4/10B	Mercedes	V10	53	1h 18m 45.695s	7	4
3	30	H-H Frentzen	Sauber	C14	Cosworth	V8	53	1h 18m 52.237s	10	5
4	7	M Blundell	McLaren	MP4/10B	Mercedes	V10	53	1h 18m 56.139s	9	5
5	4	M Salo	Tyrrell	023	Yamaha	V10	52		16	8
6	29	J-C Boullion	Sauber	C14	Cosworth	V8	52		14	7
7	9	M Papis	Footwork	FA16	Hart	V8	52		15	8
8	10	T Inoue	Footwork	FA16	Hart	V8	52		20	10
9	21	P Diniz	Forti	FG01-95	Cosworth	V8	50		23	12
10	3	U Katayama	Tyrrell	023	Yamaha	V10	47		17	9
r	27	J Alesi	Ferrari	412T2	Ferrari	V12	45	rear wheel bearing	5	3
r	14	R Barrichello	Jordan	195	Peugeot	V10	43	hydraulics	6	3
r	15	E Irvine	Jordan	195	Peugeot	V10	40	oil pressure/ engine	12	6
r	28	G Berger	Ferrari	412T2	Ferrari	V12	32	front suspension(Alesi's camera)	3	2
r	24	L Badoer	Minardi	M195	Cosworth	V8	26	accident	18	9
r	1	M Schumacher	Benetton	B195	Renault	V10	23	accident	2	1
r	5	D Hill	Williams	FW17	Renault	V10	23	accident	4	2
r	26	O Panis	Ligier	JS41	Mugen Honda	V10	20	spin	13	7
r	6	D Coulthard	Williams	FW17	Renault	V10	13	front wheel bearing/ spin	1	1
r	25	M Brundle	Ligier	JS41	Mugen Honda	V10	10	puncture	11	6
r	16	G Lavaggi	Pacific	PR02	Cosworth	V8	6	spin	24	12
r	23	P Lamy	Minardi	M195	Cosworth	V8	0	differential	19	10
r	22	R Moreno	Forti	FG01-95	Cosworth	V8	0	accident *	22	11
r	17	A Montermini	Pacific	PR02	Cosworth	V8	0	accident *	21	11

Winning speed: 233.814 km/h, 145.285 mph
Pole Position speed: 245.933 km/h, 152.816 mph (D Coulthard, 1 min:24.462 sec)
Fastest Lap speed: 240.364 km/h, 149.355 mph (G Berger, 1 min:26.419 sec on lap 24)
Lap Leaders: D Coulthard 1-13 (13); G Berger 14-24 (11); J Alesi 25,30-45 (17); R Barrichello 26 (1); M Häkkinen 27 (1); J Herbert 28-29,46-53 (10).

*Interrupted after 1st lap accident. Restarted for original distance. * retired after first start.*

24 Sep 1995 — PORTUGAL: Estoril (Round:13) (Race: 577)

71 laps x 4.360 km, 2.709 miles = 309.544 km, 192.342 miles

POS.	NO.	DRIVER	CAR	MODEL	ENGINE		LAPS	TIME/REASON FOR RETIREMENT	GRID:POS	ROW
1	6	D Coulthard	Williams	FW17	Renault	V10	71	1h 41m 52.145s	1	1
2	1	M Schumacher	Benetton	B195	Renault	V10	71	1h 41m 59.393s	3	2
3	5	D Hill	Williams	FW17	Renault	V10	71	1h 42m 14.266s	2	1
4	28	G Berger	Ferrari	412T2	Ferrari	V12	71	1h 43m 17.024s	4	2
5	27	J Alesi	Ferrari	412T2	Ferrari	V12	71	1h 43m 17.574s	7	4
6	30	H-H Frentzen	Sauber	C14	Cosworth	V8	70		5	3
7	2	J Herbert	Benetton	B195	Renault	V10	70		6	3
8	25	M Brundle	Ligier	JS41	Mugen Honda	V10	70		9	5
9	7	M Blundell	McLaren	MP4/10C	Mercedes	V10	70		12	6
10	15	E Irvine	Jordan	195	Peugeot	V10	70		10	5
11	14	R Barrichello	Jordan	195	Peugeot	V10	70		8	4
12	29	J-C Boullion	Sauber	C14	Cosworth	V8	70		14	7
13	4	M Salo	Tyrrell	023	Yamaha	V10	69		15	8
14	24	L Badoer	Minardi	M195	Cosworth	V8	68		18	9
15	10	T Inoue	Footwork	FA16	Hart	V8	68		19	10
16	21	P Diniz	Forti	FG01-95	Cosworth	V8	66		22	11
17	22	R Moreno	Forti	FG01-95	Cosworth	V8	64		23	12
r	17	A Montermini	Pacific	PR02	Cosworth	V8	53	gear selection	21	11
r	8	M Häkkinen	McLaren	MP4/10B	Mercedes	V10	44	engine	13	7
r	16	J-D Deletraz	Pacific	PR02	Cosworth	V8	14	driver discomfort (cramp)	24	12
r	26	O Panis	Ligier	JS41	Mugen Honda	V10	10	spin	11	6
r	23	P Lamy	Minardi	M195	Cosworth	V8	7	gearbox hydraulics	17	9
r	3	U Katayama	Tyrrell	023	Yamaha	V10	0	accident *	16	8
r	9	M Papis	Footwork	FA16	Hart	V8	0	gearbox *	20	10

Winning speed: 182.319 km/h, 113.288 mph
Pole Position speed: 194.892 km/h, 121.100 mph (D Coulthard, 1 min:20.537 sec)
Fastest Lap speed: 188.609 km/h, 117.196 mph (D Coulthard, 1 min:23.220 sec on lap 2)
Lap Leaders: D Coulthard 1-38,44-71 (66); D Hill 39-43 (5).

*Interrupted after 1st lap accident. Restarted for original distance. * retired after first start.*

1 Oct 1995 EUROPE: Nürburgring (Round:14) (Race: 578)

67 laps x 4.556 km, 2.831 miles = 305.252 km, 189.675 miles

POS.	NO.	DRIVER	CAR	MODEL	ENGINE		LAPS	TIME/REASON FOR RETIREMENT	GRID:POS	ROW
1	1	M Schumacher	Benetton	B195	Renault	V10	67	1h 39m 59.044s	3	2
2	27	J Alesi	Ferrari	412T2	Ferrari	V12	67	1h 40m 01.728s	6	3
3	6	D Coulthard	Williams	FW17B	Renault	V10	67	1h 40m 34.426s	1	1
4	14	R Barrichello	Jordan	195	Peugeot	V10	66		11	6
5	2	J Herbert	Benetton	B195	Renault	V10	66		7	4
6	15	E Irvine	Jordan	195	Peugeot	V10	66		5	3
7	25	M Brundle	Ligier	JS41	Mugen Honda	V10	66		12	6
8	8	M Häkkinen	McLaren	MP4/10C	Mercedes	V10	65		9	5
9	23	P Lamy	Minardi	M195	Cosworth	V8	64		16	8
10	4	M Salo	Tyrrell	023	Yamaha	V10	64		15	8
11	24	L Badoer	Minardi	M195	Cosworth	V8	64		18	9
12	9	M Papis	Footwork	FA16	Hart	V8	64		17	9
13	21	P Diniz	Forti	FG01-95	Cosworth	V8	62		22	11
14	3	G Tarquini	Tyrrell	023	Yamaha	V10	61		19	10
15	16	J-D Deletraz	Pacific	PR02	Cosworth	V8	60		24	12
r	5	D Hill	Williams	FW17B	Renault	V10	58	accident	2	1
r	17	A Montermini	Pacific	PR02	Cosworth	V8	45	out of fuel	20	10
r	29	J-C Boullion	Sauber	C14	Cosworth	V8	44	accident	13	7
r	28	G Berger	Ferrari	412T2	Ferrari	V12	40	electronics	4	2
r	22	R Moreno	Forti	FG01-95	Cosworth	V8	22	gearbox	23	12
r	30	H-H Frentzen	Sauber	C14	Cosworth	V8	17	accident	8	4
r	26	O Panis	Ligier	JS41	Mugen Honda	V10	14	spin	14	7
r	7	M Blundell	McLaren	MP4/10C	Mercedes	V10	14	spin	10	5
r	10	T Inoue	Footwork	FA16	Hart	V8	0	electronic control system	21	11

Winning speed: 183.180 km/h, 113.823 mph
Pole Position speed: 208.306 km/h, 129.435 mph (D Coulthard, 1 min:18.738 sec)
Fastest Lap speed: 202.040 km/h, 125.542 mph (M Schumacher, 1 min:21.180 sec on lap 57)
Lap Leaders: D Coulthard 1-12 (12); J Alesi 13-64 (52); M Schumacher 65-67 (3).

Scheduled for 68 laps but reduced to 67 due to aborted start and extra parade lap.

22 Oct 1995 PACIFIC: Aida (Round:15) (Race: 579)

83 laps x 3.703 km, 2.301 miles = 307.349 km, 190.978 miles

POS.	NO.	DRIVER	CAR	MODEL	ENGINE		LAPS	TIME/REASON FOR RETIREMENT	GRID:POS	ROW
1	1	M Schumacher	Benetton	B195	Renault	V10	83	1h 48m 49.972s	3	2
2	6	D Coulthard	Williams	FW17B	Renault	V10	83	1h 49m 04.892s	1	1
3	5	D Hill	Williams	FW17B	Renault	V10	83	1h 49m 38.305s	2	1
4	28	G Berger	Ferrari	412T2	Ferrari	V12	82		5	3
5	27	J Alesi	Ferrari	412T2	Ferrari	V12	82		4	2
6	2	J Herbert	Benetton	B195	Renault	V10	82		7	4
7	30	H-H Frentzen	Sauber	C14	Cosworth	V8	82		8	4
8	26	O Panis	Ligier	JS41	Mugen Honda	V10	81		9	5
9	7	M Blundell	McLaren	MP4/10B	Mercedes	V10	81		10	5
10	8	J Magnussen	McLaren	MP4/10B	Mercedes	V10	81		12	6
11	15	E Irvine	Jordan	195	Peugeot	V10	81		6	3
12	4	M Salo	Tyrrell	023	Yamaha	V10	80		18	9
13	23	P Lamy	Minardi	M195	Cosworth	V8	80		14	7
14	3	U Katayama	Tyrrell	023	Yamaha	V10	80		17	9
15	24	L Badoer	Minardi	M195	Cosworth	V8	80		16	8
16	22	R Moreno	Forti	FG01-95	Cosworth	V8	78		22	11
17	21	P Diniz	Forti	FG01-95	Cosworth	V8	77		21	11
r	14	R Barrichello	Jordan	195	Peugeot	V10	67	electronics	11	6
r	9	G Morbidelli	Footwork	FA16	Hart	V8	53	engine	19	10
r	10	T Inoue	Footwork	FA16	Hart	V8	38	engine	20	10
r	17	A Montermini	Pacific	PR02	Cosworth	V8	14	gearbox	23	12
r	25	A Suzuki	Ligier	JS41	Mugen Honda	V10	10	spin	13	7
r	29	J-C Boullion	Sauber	C14	Cosworth	V8	7	spin	15	8
r	16	B Gachot	Pacific	PR02	Cosworth	V8	2	gearbox hydraulics	24	12

Winning speed: 169.443 km/h, 105.287 mph
Pole Position speed: 180.114 km/h, 111.918 mph (D Coulthard, 1 min:14.013 sec)
Fastest Lap speed: 174.546 km/h, 108.458 mph (M Schumacher, 1 min:16.374 sec on lap 40)
Lap Leaders: D Coulthard 1-49 (49); M Schumacher 50-83 (34).

29 Oct 1995 — JAPAN: Suzuka (Round:16) (Race: 580)

53 laps x 5.864 km, 3.644 miles = 310.588 km, 192.989 miles

POS.	NO.	DRIVER	CAR	MODEL	ENGINE		LAPS	TIME/REASON FOR RETIREMENT	GRID:POS	ROW
1	1	M Schumacher	Benetton	B195	Renault	V10	53	1h 36m 52.930s	1	1
2	8	M Häkkinen	McLaren	MP4/10B	Mercedes	V10	53	1h 37m 12.267s	3	2
3	2	J Herbert	Benetton	B195	Renault	V10	53	1h 38m 16.734s	9	5
4	15	E Irvine	Jordan	195	Peugeot	V10	53	1h 38m 35.066s	7	4
5	26	O Panis	Ligier	JS41	Mugen Honda	V10	52		11	6
6	4	M Salo	Tyrrell	023	Yamaha	V10	52		12	6
7	7	M Blundell	McLaren	MP4/10B	Mercedes	V10	52		23	12
8	30	H-H Frentzen	Sauber	C14	Cosworth	V8	52		8	4
9	24	L Badoer	Minardi	M195	Cosworth	V8	51		17	9
10	29	K Wendlinger	Sauber	C14	Cosworth	V8	51		15	8
11	23	P Lamy	Minardi	M195	Cosworth	V8	51		16	8
12	10	T Inoue	Footwork	FA16	Hart	V8	51		18	9
r	5	D Hill	Williams	FW17B	Renault	V10	40	spin	4	2
r	6	D Coulthard	Williams	FW17B	Renault	V10	39	accident	6	3
r	21	P Diniz	Forti	FG01-95	Cosworth	V8	32	spin	20	10
r	27	J Alesi	Ferrari	412T2	Ferrari	V12	24	differential	2	1
r	17	A Montermini	Pacific	PR02	Cosworth	V8	23	spin	19	10
r	28	G Berger	Ferrari	412T2	Ferrari	V12	16	electronics sensor	5	3
r	14	R Barrichello	Jordan	195	Peugeot	V10	15	accident	10	5
r	3	U Katayama	Tyrrell	023	Yamaha	V10	12	accident	13	7
r	16	B Gachot	Pacific	PR02	Cosworth	V8	6	drive shaft bearing	22	11
r	22	R Moreno	Forti	FG01-95	Cosworth	V8	1	gearbox	21	11
r	9	G Morbidelli	Footwork	FA16	Hart	V8	0	spin	14	7
ns	25	A Suzuki	Ligier	JS41	Mugen Honda	V10		accident/ injury		

Winning speed: 192.350 km/h, 119.521 mph
Pole Position speed: 215.362 km/h, 133.820 mph (M Schumacher, 1 min:38.023 sec)
Fastest Lap speed: 205.003 km/h, 127.383 mph (M Schumacher, 1 min:42.976 sec on lap 33)
Lap Leaders: M Schumacher 1-10,12-31;36-53 (48); M Häkkinen 11 (1); D Hill 32-35 (4).

12 Nov 1995 — AUSTRALIA: Adelaide (Round:17) (Race: 581)

81 laps x 3.780 km, 2.349 miles = 306.180 km, 190.251 miles

POS.	NO.	DRIVER	CAR	MODEL	ENGINE		LAPS	TIME/REASON FOR RETIREMENT	GRID:POS	ROW
1	5	D Hill	Williams	FW17B	Renault	V10	81	1h 49m 15.946s	1	1
2	26	O Panis	Ligier	JS41	Mugen Honda	V10	79		12	6
3	9	G Morbidelli	Footwork	FA16	Hart	V8	79		13	7
4	7	M Blundell	McLaren	MP4/10B	Mercedes	V10	79		10	5
5	4	M Salo	Tyrrell	023	Yamaha	V10	78		14	7
6	23	P Lamy	Minardi	M195	Cosworth	V8	78		17	9
7	21	P Diniz	Forti	FG01-95	Cosworth	V8	77		21	11
8	16	B Gachot	Pacific	PR02	Cosworth	V8	76		23	12
r	3	U Katayama	Tyrrell	023	Yamaha	V10	70	oil pressure/ engine	16	8
r	2	J Herbert	Benetton	B195	Renault	V10	69	drive shaft	8	4
r	15	E Irvine	Jordan	195	Peugeot	V10	62	engine hydraulic pressure	9	5
r	30	H-H Frentzen	Sauber	C14	Cosworth	V8	39	gearbox	6	3
r	28	G Berger	Ferrari	412T2	Ferrari	V12	34	engine	4	2
r	25	M Brundle	Ligier	JS41	Mugen Honda	V10	29	accident	11	6
r	1	M Schumacher	Benetton	B195	Renault	V10	25	accident/ rear suspension	3	2
r	27	J Alesi	Ferrari	412T2	Ferrari	V12	23	accident/ front suspension	5	3
r	22	R Moreno	Forti	FG01-95	Cosworth	V8	21	accident	20	10
r	14	R Barrichello	Jordan	195	Peugeot	V10	20	accident	7	4
r	6	D Coulthard	Williams	FW17B	Renault	V10	19	accident	2	1
r	10	T Inoue	Footwork	FA16	Hart	V8	15	accident	19	10
r	29	K Wendlinger	Sauber	C14	Cosworth	V8	8	withdrew (neck injury)	18	9
r	17	A Montermini	Pacific	PR02	Cosworth	V8	2	gearbox/ spin	22	11
ns	24	L Badoer	Minardi	M195	Cosworth	V8		electronics on dummy grid	15	8
ns	8	M Häkkinen	McLaren	MP4/10B	Mercedes	V10		tyre/ accident/ injury		

Winning speed: 168.130 km/h, 104.471 mph
Pole Position speed: 180.226 km/h, 111.988 mph (D Hill, 1 min:15.505 sec)
Fastest Lap speed: 174.589 km/h, 108.485 mph (D Hill, 1 min:17.943 sec on lap 16)
Lap Leaders: D Coulthard 1-19 (19); M Schumacher 20-21 (2); D Hill 22-81 (60).

Lap Leaders 1995

POS	DRIVER	CAR-ENGINE	GPS	LAPS	KM	MILES
1	M Schumacher	Benetton-Renault	14	454	2,170.7	1,348.8
2	D Hill	Williams-Renault	12	336	1,437.1	893.0
3	D Coulthard	Williams-Renault	11	191	842.0	523.2
4	J Alesi	Ferrari	6	91	435.1	270.3
5	J Herbert	Benetton-Renault	3	27	149.4	92.8
6	G Berger	Ferrari	2	22	117.3	72.9
7	M Häkkinen	McLaren-Mercedes Benz	2	2	11.6	7.2
8	R Barrichello	Jordan-Peugeot	1	1	5.8	3.6
			17	**1,124**	**5,169.0**	**3,211.9**

Driver Points 1995

		BR	RA	RSM	E	MC	CDN	F	GB	D	H	B	I	P	EUR	PAC	J	AUS	TOTAL
1	M Schumacher	10	4	-	10	10	2	10	-	10	-	10	-	6	10	10	10	-	102
2	D Hill	-	10	10	3	6	-	6	-	-	10	6	-	4	-	4	-	10	69
3	D Coulthard	6	-	3	-	-	-	4	4	6	6	-	-	10	4	6	-	-	49
4	J Herbert	-	3	-	6	3	-	-	10	3	3	-	10	-	2	1	4	-	45
5	J Alesi	2	6	6	-	-	10	2	6	-	-	-	-	2	6	2	-	-	42
6	G Berger	4	1	4	4	4	-	-	-	4	4	-	-	3	-	3	-	-	31
7	M Häkkinen	3	-	2	-	-	-	-	-	-	-	-	6	-	-	-	6	-	17
8	O Panis	-	-	-	1	-	3	-	3	-	1	-	-	-	-	-	2	6	16
9	H-H Frentzen	-	2	1	-	1	-	-	1	-	2	3	4	1	-	-	-	-	15
10	M Blundell	1	-	-	-	2	-	-	2	-	-	2	3	-	-	-	-	3	13
11	R Barrichello	-	-	-	-	-	6	1	-	-	-	1	-	-	3	-	-	-	11
12	E Irvine	-	-	-	2	-	4	-	-	-	-	-	-	-	1	-	3	-	10
13	M Brundle	-	-	-	-	-	-	3	-	-	-	4	-	-	-	-	-	-	7
14	M Salo	-	-	-	-	-	-	-	-	-	-	-	2	-	-	-	1	2	5
	G Morbidelli	-	-	-	-	-	1	-	-	-	-	-	-	-	-	-	-	4	5
16	J-C Boullion	-	-	-	-	-	-	-	-	2	-	-	1	-	-	-	-	-	3
17	A Suzuki	-	-	-	-	-	-	-	-	1	-	-	-	-	-	-	-	-	1
	P Lamy	-	-	-	-	-	-	-	-	-	-	-	-	-	-	-	-	1	1

10, 6, 4, 3, 2 and 1 point awarded to the first six finishers.

Constructor Points 1995

		BR	RA	RSM	E	MC	CDN	F	GB	D	H	B	I	P	EUR	PAC	J	AUS	TOTAL
1	Benetton-Renault	-	7	-	16	13	2	10	10	13	3	10	10	6	12	11	14	-	137
2	Williams-Renault	-	10	13	3	6	-	10	4	6	16	6	-	14	4	10	-	10	112
3	Ferrari	6	7	10	4	4	10	2	6	4	4	-	-	5	6	5	-	-	73
4	McLaren-Mercedes	4	-	2	-	2	-	-	2	-	-	2	9	-	-	-	6	3	30
5	Ligier-Mugen Honda	-	-	-	1	-	3	3	3	1	1	4	-	-	-	-	2	6	24
6	Jordan-Peugeot	-	-	-	2	-	10	1	-	-	-	1	-	-	4	-	3	-	21
7	Sauber-Cosworth	-	2	1	-	1	-	-	1	2	2	3	5	1	-	-	-	-	18
8	Footwork-Hart	-	-	-	-	-	1	-	-	-	-	-	-	-	-	-	-	4	5
	Tyrrell-Yamaha	-	-	-	-	-	-	-	-	-	-	-	2	-	-	-	1	2	5
10	Minardi-Cosworth	-	-	-	-	-	-	-	-	-	-	-	-	-	-	-	-	1	1

10, 6, 4, 3, 2 and 1 point awarded to the first six finishers.

Safety was still very high on the priority list and driver protection continued with higher cockpit sides and removable padding around the drivers' heads. Jacques Villeneuve, the reigning IndyCar champion landed a plum drive with the best team and his results were eagerly anticipated. The World Champion switched teams and joined Ferrari, knowing this first season would be spent developing the new V10 engine into a potential championship winning car. The entry list was down to eleven teams and some races started with less than 20 cars on the grid.

FERRARI
Scuderia Ferrari SpA: Schumacher, Irvine

BENETTON
Mild Seven Benetton Renault: Alesi, Berger

WILLIAMS
Rothmans Williams Renault: Hill, Villeneuve

McLAREN
Marlboro McLaren Mercedes: Häkkinen, Coulthard

LIGIER
Equipe Ligier Gauloises Blondes: Panis, Diniz

JORDAN
Benson & Hedges Jordan Peugeot: Barrichello, Brundle

SAUBER
Red Bull Sauber Ford: Herbert, Frentzen

FOOTWORK/TWR ARROWS
Footwork Hart: Rosset, Verstappen

TYRRELL
Tyrrell Yamaha: Katayama, Salo

MINARDI
Minardi Team S.p.A.: Lamy, Fisichella, Marques, Lavaggi

FORTI
Forti Grand Prix: Badoer, Montermini

10 Mar 1996 — AUSTRALIA: Melbourne (Round: 1) (Race: 582)

58 laps x 5.302 km, 3.295 miles = 307.516 km, 191.082 miles

POS.	NO.	DRIVER	CAR	MODEL	ENGINE		LAPS	TIME/REASON FOR RETIREMENT	GRID:POS	ROW
1	5	D Hill	Williams	FW18	Renault	V10	58	1h 32m 50.491s	2	1
2	6	J Villeneuve	Williams	FW18	Renault	V10	58	1h 33m 28.511s	1	1
3	2	E Irvine	Ferrari	F310	Ferrari	V10	58	1h 33m 53.062s	3	2
4	4	G Berger	Benetton	B196	Renault	V10	58	1h 34m 07.528s	7	4
5	7	M Häkkinen	McLaren	MP4/11	Mercedes	V10	58	1h 34m 25.562s	5	3
6	19	M Salo	Tyrrell	024	Yamaha	V10	57		10	5
7	9	O Panis	Ligier	JS43	Mugen Honda	V10	57		11	6
8	15	H-H Frentzen	Sauber	C15	Cosworth	V10	57		9	5
9	16	R Rosset	Footwork	FA17	Hart	V8	56		18	9
10	10	P Diniz	Ligier	JS43	Mugen Honda	V10	56		20	10
11	18	U Katayama	Tyrrell	024	Yamaha	V10	55		15	8
r	20	P Lamy	Minardi	M195B	Cosworth	V8	42	accident/ loose seat belts	17	9
r	1	M Schumacher	Ferrari	F310	Ferrari	V10	32	brake fluid loss	4	2
r	21	G Fisichella	Minardi	M195B	Cosworth	V8	32	clutch	16	8
r	11	R Barrichello	Jordan	196	Peugeot	V10	29	engine	8	4
r	8	D Coulthard	McLaren	MP4/11	Mercedes	V10	24	throttle jammed	13	7
r	17	J Verstappen	Footwork	FA17	Hart	V8	15	engine	12	6
r	3	J Alesi	Benetton	B196	Renault	V10	9	accident	6	3
r	12	M Brundle	Jordan	196	Peugeot	V10	1	spin	19	10
r	14	J Herbert	Sauber	C15	Cosworth	V10	0	accident *	14	7
nq	22	L Badoer	Forti	FG01-95B	Cosworth	V8				
nq	23	A Montermini	Forti	FG01-95B	Cosworth	V8				

Winning speed: 198.736 km/h, 123.489 mph
Pole Position speed: 206.636 km/h, 128.398 mph (J Villeneuve, 1 min:32.371 sec)
Fastest Lap speed: 204.314 km/h, 126.955 mph (J Villeneuve, 1 min:33.421 sec on lap 27)
Lap Leaders: J Villeneuve 1-29,33-53 (50); D Hill 30-32,54-58 (8).

*Interrupted after 1st lap accident. Restarted for original distance. * retired after first start.*

31 Mar 1996 — BRAZIL: Interlagos (Round: 2) (Race: 583)

71 laps x 4.325 km, 2.687 miles = 307.075 km, 190.808 miles

POS.	NO.	DRIVER	CAR	MODEL	ENGINE		LAPS	TIME/REASON FOR RETIREMENT	GRID:POS	ROW
1	5	D Hill	Williams	FW18	Renault	V10	71	1h 49m 52.976s	1	1
2	3	J Alesi	Benetton	B196	Renault	V10	71	1h 50m 10.958s	5	3
3	1	M Schumacher	Ferrari	F310	Ferrari	V10	70		4	2
4	7	M Häkkinen	McLaren	MP4/11	Mercedes	V10	70		7	4
5	19	M Salo	Tyrrell	024	Yamaha	V10	70		11	6
6	9	O Panis	Ligier	JS43	Mugen Honda	V10	70		15	8
7	2	E Irvine	Ferrari	F310	Ferrari	V10	70		10	5
8	10	P Diniz	Ligier	JS43	Mugen Honda	V10	69		22	11
9	18	U Katayama	Tyrrell	024	Yamaha	V10	69		16	8
10	20	P Lamy	Minardi	M195B	Cosworth	V8	68		18	9
11	22	L Badoer	Forti	FG01-95B	Cosworth	V8	67		19	10
12r	12	M Brundle	Jordan	196	Peugeot	V10	64	spin	6	3
r	11	R Barrichello	Jordan	196	Peugeot	V10	59	spin	2	1
r	15	H-H Frentzen	Sauber	C15	Cosworth	V10	36	engine	9	5
r	8	D Coulthard	McLaren	MP4/11	Mercedes	V10	29	spin	14	7
r	14	J Herbert	Sauber	C15	Cosworth	V10	28	engine	12	6
r	6	J Villeneuve	Williams	FW18	Renault	V10	26	spin	3	2
r	4	G Berger	Benetton	B196	Renault	V10	26	hydraulic pressure	8	4
r	23	A Montermini	Forti	FG01-95B	Cosworth	V8	26	spin	20	10
r	16	R Rosset	Footwork	FA17	Hart	V8	24	accident	17	9
r	17	J Verstappen	Footwork	FA17	Hart	V8	19	engine	13	7
r	21	T Marques	Minardi	M195B	Cosworth	V8	0	spin	21	11

Winning speed: 167.674 km/h, 104.188 mph
Pole Position speed: 199.332 km/h, 123.859 mph (D Hill, 1 min:18.111 sec)
Fastest Lap speed: 190.933 km/h, 118.640 mph (D Hill, 1 min:21.547 sec on lap 65)
Lap Leaders: D Hill 1-39,43-71 (68); J Alesi 40-42 (3).

P Diniz (qualified 18th) and T Marques (qualified 19th) were penalised for qualifying irregularities and demoted to the back row of the grid.

7 Apr 1996 — ARGENTINA: Buenos Aires (Round: 3) (Race: 584)

72 laps x 4.259 km, 2.646 miles = 306.484 km, 190.440 miles

POS.	NO.	DRIVER	CAR	MODEL	ENGINE		LAPS	TIME/REASON FOR RETIREMENT	GRID:POS	ROW
1	5	D Hill	Williams	FW18	Renault	V10	72	1h 54m 55.322s	1	1
2	6	J Villeneuve	Williams	FW18	Renault	V10	72	1h 55m 07.489s	3	2
3	3	J Alesi	Benetton	B196	Renault	V10	72	1h 55m 10.076s	4	2
4	11	R Barrichello	Jordan	196	Peugeot	V10	72	1h 55m 50.453s	6	3
5	2	E Irvine	Ferrari	F310	Ferrari	V10	72	1h 56m 00.313s	10	5
6	17	J Verstappen	Footwork	FA17	Hart	V8	72	1h 56m 04.235s	7	4
7	8	D Coulthard	McLaren	MP4/11	Mercedes	V10	72	1h 56m 08.722s	9	5
8	9	O Panis	Ligier	JS43	Mugen Honda	V10	72	1h 56m 09.617s	12	6
9	14	J Herbert	Sauber	C15	Cosworth	V10	71		17	9
10	23	A Montermini	Forti	FG01-95B	Cosworth	V8	69		22	11
r	4	G Berger	Benetton	B196	Renault	V10	56	rear suspension	5	3
r	1	M Schumacher	Ferrari	F310	Ferrari	V10	46	rear wing/ handling	2	1
r	20	P Lamy	Minardi	M195B	Cosworth	V8	39	cv joint	19	10
r	19	M Salo	Tyrrell	024	Yamaha	V10	36	throttle jammed	16	8
r	12	M Brundle	Jordan	196	Peugeot	V10	34	accident/ rear wing	15	8
r	21	T Marques	Minardi	M195B	Cosworth	V8	33	accident	14	7
r	15	H-H Frentzen	Sauber	C15	Cosworth	V10	32	spin	11	6
r	10	P Diniz	Ligier	JS43	Mugen Honda	V10	29	fuel leak/ fire	18	9
r	18	U Katayama	Tyrrell	024	Yamaha	V10	28	transmission	13	7
r	16	R Rosset	Footwork	FA17	Hart	V8	24	fuel pump	20	10
r	22	L Badoer	Forti	FG01-95B	Cosworth	V8	24	accident	21	11
r	7	M Häkkinen	McLaren	MP4/11	Mercedes	V10	19	throttle valve	8	4

Winning speed: 160.013 km/h, 99.428 mph
Pole Position speed: 169.708 km/h, 105.451 mph (D Hill, 1 min:30.346 sec)
Fastest Lap speed: 171.478 km/h, 106.552 mph (J Alesi, 1 min:29.413 sec on lap 66)
Lap Leaders: D Hill 1-72 (72).

28 Apr 1996 — EUROPE: Nürburgring (Round: 4) (Race: 585)

67 laps x 4.556 km, 2.831 miles = 305.252 km, 189.675 miles

POS.	NO.	DRIVER	CAR	MODEL	ENGINE		LAPS	TIME/REASON FOR RETIREMENT	GRID:POS	ROW
1	6	J Villeneuve	Williams	FW18	Renault	V10	67	1h 33m 26.473s	2	1
2	1	M Schumacher	Ferrari	F310	Ferrari	V10	67	1h 33m 27.235s	3	2
3	8	D Coulthard	McLaren	MP4/11	Mercedes	V10	67	1h 33m 59.307s	6	3
4	5	D Hill	Williams	FW18	Renault	V10	67	1h 33m 59.984s	1	1
5	11	R Barrichello	Jordan	196	Peugeot	V10	67	1h 34m 00.186s	5	3
6	12	M Brundle	Jordan	196	Peugeot	V10	67	1h 34m 22.040s	11	6
7	14	J Herbert	Sauber	C15	Cosworth	V10	67	1h 34m 44.500s	12	6
8	7	M Häkkinen	McLaren	MP4/11	Mercedes	V10	67	1h 34m 44.911s	9	5
9	4	G Berger	Benetton	B196	Renault	V10	67	1h 34m 47.534s	8	4
dq	19	M Salo	Tyrrell	024	Yamaha	V10	66	car under weight	14	7
10	10	P Diniz	Ligier	JS43	Mugen Honda	V10	66		17	9
dq	18	U Katayama	Tyrrell	024	Yamaha	V10	65	push start on grid	16	8
11	16	R Rosset	Footwork	FA17	Hart	V8	65		20	10
12	20	P Lamy	Minardi	M195B	Cosworth	V8	65		19	10
13	21	G Fisichella	Minardi	M195B	Cosworth	V8	65		18	9
r	15	H-H Frentzen	Sauber	C15	Cosworth	V10	59	handling/ spin	10	5
r	17	J Verstappen	Footwork	FA17	Hart	V8	38	gearbox	13	7
r	9	O Panis	Ligier	JS43	Mugen Honda	V10	6	accident	15	8
r	2	E Irvine	Ferrari	F310	Ferrari	V10	6	spin	7	4
r	3	J Alesi	Benetton	B196	Renault	V10	1	accident	4	2
nq	23	A Montermini	Forti	FG03-96	Cosworth	V8				
nq	22	L Badoer	Forti	FG03-96	Cosworth	V8				

Winning speed: 196.007 km/h, 121.793 mph
Pole Position speed: 207.770 km/h, 129.103 mph (D Hill, 1 min:18.941 sec)
Fastest Lap speed: 201.585 km/h, 125.259 mph (D Hill, 1 min:21.363 sec on lap 55)
Lap Leaders: J Villeneuve 1-67 (67).

5 May 1996 — SAN MARINO: Imola (Round: 5) (Race: 586)

63 laps x 4.892 km, 3.040 miles = 308.196 km, 191.504 miles

POS.	NO.	DRIVER	CAR	MODEL	ENGINE		LAPS	TIME/REASON FOR RETIREMENT	GRID:POS	ROW
1	5	D Hill	Williams	FW18	Renault	V10	63	1h 35m 26.156s	2	1
2	1	M Schumacher	Ferrari	F310	Ferrari	V10	63	1h 35m 42.616s	1	1
3	4	G Berger	Benetton	B196	Renault	V10	63	1h 36m 13.047s	7	4
4	2	E Irvine	Ferrari	F310	Ferrari	V10	63	1h 36m 27.739s	6	3
5	11	R Barrichello	Jordan	196	Peugeot	V10	63	1h 36m 44.646s	9	5
6	3	J Alesi	Benetton	B196	Renault	V10	62		5	3
7	10	P Diniz	Ligier	JS43	Mugen Honda	V10	62		17	9
8r	7	M Häkkinen	McLaren	MP4/11	Mercedes	V10	61	engine	11	6
9	20	P Lamy	Minardi	M195B	Cosworth	V8	61		18	9
10	22	L Badoer	Forti	FG03-96	Cosworth	V8	59		21	11
11r	6	J Villeneuve	Williams	FW18	Renault	V10	57	rear suspension	3	2
r	9	O Panis	Ligier	JS43	Mugen Honda	V10	54	gearbox	13	7
r	18	U Katayama	Tyrrell	024	Yamaha	V10	45	transmission	16	8
r	8	D Coulthard	McLaren	MP4/11	Mercedes	V10	44	gearbox hydraulics	4	2
r	16	R Rosset	Footwork	FA17	Hart	V8	40	engine	20	10
r	17	J Verstappen	Footwork	FA17	Hart	V8	38	refuelling hose attached	14	7
r	12	M Brundle	Jordan	196	Peugeot	V10	36	spin	12	6
r	15	H-H Frentzen	Sauber	C15	Cosworth	V10	32	brakes	10	5

POS.	NO.	DRIVER	CAR	MODEL	ENGINE		LAPS	TIME/REASON FOR RETIREMENT	GRID:POS	ROW
r	21	G Fisichella	Minardi	M195B	Cosworth	V8	30	engine	19	10
r	14	J Herbert	Sauber	C15	Cosworth	V10	25	electronics/ misfire	15	8
r	19	M Salo	Tyrrell	024	Yamaha	V10	23	engine	8	4
nq	23	A Montermini	Forti	FG01-95B	Cosworth	V8				

Winning speed: 193.761 km/h, 120.397 mph
Pole Position speed: 202.684 km/h, 125.942 mph (M Schumacher, 1 min:26.890 sec)
Fastest Lap speed: 198.032 km/h, 123.051 mph (D Hill, 1 min:28.931 sec on lap 49)
Lap Leaders: D Coulthard 1-19 (19); M Schumacher 20 (1); D Hill 21-63 (43).

19 May 1996 — MONACO: Monte Carlo (Round: 6) (Race: 587)

75 laps x 3.328 km, 2.068 miles = 249.600 km, 155.094 miles

POS.	NO.	DRIVER	CAR	MODEL	ENGINE		LAPS	TIME/REASON FOR RETIREMENT	GRID:POS	ROW
1	9	O Panis	Ligier	JS43	Mugen Honda	V10	75	2h 00m 45.629s	14	7
2	8	D Coulthard	McLaren	MP4/11B	Mercedes	V10	75	2h 00m 50.457s	5	3
3	14	J Herbert	Sauber	C15	Cosworth	V10	75	2h 01m 23.132s	13	7
4	15	H-H Frentzen	Sauber	C15	Cosworth	V10	74	in pits at chequered flag	9	5
5r	19	M Salo	Tyrrell	024	Yamaha	V10	70	accident	11	6
6r	7	M Häkkinen	McLaren	MP4/11B	Mercedes	V10	70	accident	8	4
7r	2	E Irvine	Ferrari	F310	Ferrari	V10	68	accident	7	4
r	6	J Villeneuve	Williams	FW18	Renault	V10	66	accident	10	5
r	3	J Alesi	Benetton	B196	Renault	V10	60	rear suspension	3	2
r	22	L Badoer	Forti	FG03-96	Cosworth	V8	60	accident	21	11
r	5	D Hill	Williams	FW18	Renault	V10	40	oil pump/ engine	2	1
r	12	M Brundle	Jordan	196	Peugeot	V10	30	accident	16	8
r	4	G Berger	Benetton	B196	Renault	V10	9	gearbox sensor	4	2
r	10	P Diniz	Ligier	JS43	Mugen Honda	V10	5	transmission/ spin	17	9
r	16	R Rosset	Footwork	FA17	Hart	V8	3	accident	20	10
r	18	U Katayama	Tyrrell	024	Yamaha	V10	2	throttle jammed/ accident	15	8
r	1	M Schumacher	Ferrari	F310	Ferrari	V10	0	accident	1	1
r	11	R Barrichello	Jordan	196	Peugeot	V10	0	accident	6	3
r	17	J Verstappen	Footwork	FA17	Hart	V8	0	spin	12	6
r	20	P Lamy	Minardi	M195B	Cosworth	V8	0	accident	19	10
r	21	G Fisichella	Minardi	M195B	Cosworth	V8	0	accident	18	9
ns	23	A Montermini	Forti	FG03-96	Cosworth	V8		accident	22	11

Winning speed: 124.014 km/h, 77.059 mph
Pole Position speed: 149.097 km/h, 92.644 mph (M Schumacher, 1 min:20.356 sec)
Fastest Lap speed: 140.611 km/h, 87.372 mph (J Alesi, 1 min:25.205 sec on lap 59)
Lap Leaders: D Hill 1-27,30-40 (38); J Alesi 28-29,41-59 (21); O Panis 60-75 (16).

Scheduled for 78 laps, but stopped at 2 hours.

2 Jun 1996 — SPAIN: Montmeló (Round: 7) (Race: 588)

65 laps x 4.727 km, 2.937 miles = 307.114 km, 190.832 miles

POS.	NO.	DRIVER	CAR	MODEL	ENGINE		LAPS	TIME/REASON FOR RETIREMENT	GRID:POS	ROW
1	1	M Schumacher	Ferrari	F310	Ferrari	V10	65	1h 59m 49.307s	3	2
2	3	J Alesi	Benetton	B196	Renault	V10	65	2h 00m 34.609s	4	2
3	6	J Villeneuve	Williams	FW18	Renault	V10	65	2h 00m 37.695s	2	1
4	15	H-H Frentzen	Sauber	C15	Cosworth	V10	64		11	6
5	7	M Häkkinen	McLaren	MP4/11	Mercedes	V10	64		10	5
6	10	P Diniz	Ligier	JS43	Mugen Honda	V10	63		17	9
r	17	J Verstappen	Footwork	FA17	Hart	V8	47	spin	13	7
r	11	R Barrichello	Jordan	196	Peugeot	V10	45	differential	7	4
r	4	G Berger	Benetton	B196	Renault	V10	44	spin	5	3
r	14	J Herbert	Sauber	C15	Cosworth	V10	20	spin	9	5
r	12	M Brundle	Jordan	196	Peugeot	V10	17	differential	15	8
dq	19	M Salo	Tyrrell	024	Yamaha	V10	16	changed car after parade lap	12	6
r	5	D Hill	Williams	FW18	Renault	V10	10	spin	1	1
r	18	U Katayama	Tyrrell	024	Yamaha	V10	8	electrics	16	8
r	2	E Irvine	Ferrari	F310	Ferrari	V10	1	spin	6	3
r	9	O Panis	Ligier	JS43	Mugen Honda	V10	1	accident damage	8	4
r	21	G Fisichella	Minardi	M195B	Cosworth	V8	1	accident damage	19	10
r	8	D Coulthard	McLaren	MP4/11	Mercedes	V10	0	accident	14	7
r	16	R Rosset	Footwork	FA17	Hart	V8	0	accident	20	10
r	20	P Lamy	Minardi	M195B	Cosworth	V8	0	accident	18	9
nq	22	L Badoer	Forti	FG01-95B	Cosworth	V8				
nq	23	A Montermini	Forti	FG01-95B	Cosworth	V8				

Winning speed: 153.785 km/h, 95.558 mph
Pole Position speed: 211.001 km/h, 131.110 mph (D Hill, 1 min:20.650 sec)
Fastest Lap speed: 161.274 km/h, 100.211 mph (M Schumacher, 1 min:45.517 sec on lap 14)
Lap Leaders: J Villeneuve 1-11 (11); M Schumacher 12-65 (54).

16 Jun 1996 — CANADA: Montréal (Round: 8) (Race: 589)

69 laps x 4.421 km, 2.747 miles = 305.049 km, 189.549 miles

POS.	NO.	DRIVER	CAR	MODEL	ENGINE		LAPS	TIME/REASON FOR RETIREMENT	GRID:POS	ROW
1	5	D Hill	Williams	FW18	Renault	V10	69	1h 36m 03.465s	1	1
2	6	J Villeneuve	Williams	FW18	Renault	V10	69	1h 36m 07.648s	2	1
3	3	J Alesi	Benetton	B196	Renault	V10	69	1h 36m 58.121s	4	2
4	8	D Coulthard	McLaren	MP4/11	Mercedes	V10	69	1h 37m 07.138s	10	5
5	7	M Häkkinen	McLaren	MP4/11	Mercedes	V10	68		6	3
6	12	M Brundle	Jordan	196	Peugeot	V10	68		9	5
7	14	J Herbert	Sauber	C15	Cosworth	V10	68		15	8
8	21	G Fisichella	Minardi	M195B	Cosworth	V8	67		16	8
r	20	P Lamy	Minardi	M195B	Cosworth	V8	44	accident	19	10
r	22	L Badoer	Forti	FG03-96	Cosworth	V8	44	gearbox	20	10
r	4	G Berger	Benetton	B196	Renault	V10	42	spin	7	4
r	1	M Schumacher	Ferrari	F310	Ferrari	V10	41	driveshaft	3	2
r	9	O Panis	Ligier	JS43	Mugen Honda	V10	39	electrics	11	6
r	19	M Salo	Tyrrell	024	Yamaha	V10	39	engine	14	7
r	10	P Diniz	Ligier	JS43	Mugen Honda	V10	38	engine	18	9
r	11	R Barrichello	Jordan	196	Peugeot	V10	22	clutch	8	4
r	23	A Montermini	Forti	FG03-96	Cosworth	V8	22	loose ballast	22	11
r	15	H-H Frentzen	Sauber	C15	Cosworth	V10	19	gearbox	12	6
r	17	J Verstappen	Footwork	FA17	Hart	V8	10	engine	13	7
r	16	R Rosset	Footwork	FA17	Hart	V8	6	accident	21	11
r	18	U Katayama	Tyrrell	024	Yamaha	V10	6	accident	17	9
r	2	E Irvine	Ferrari	F310	Ferrari	V10	1	right steering push-rod	5	3

Winning speed: 190.541 km/h, 118.397 mph
Pole Position speed: 196.346 km/h, 122.004 mph (D Hill, 1 min:21.059 sec)
Fastest Lap speed: 194.292 km/h, 120.727 mph (J Villeneuve, 1 min:21.916 sec on lap 67)
Lap Leaders: D Hill 1-27,36-69 (61); J Villeneuve 28-35 (8).

30 Jun 1996 — FRANCE: Magny-Cours (Round: 9) (Race: 590)

72 laps x 4.250 km, 2.641 miles = 305.814 km, 190.024 miles

POS.	NO.	DRIVER	CAR	MODEL	ENGINE		LAPS	TIME/REASON FOR RETIREMENT	GRID:POS	ROW
1	5	D Hill	Williams	FW18	Renault	V10	72	1h 36m 28.795s	2	1
2	6	J Villeneuve	Williams	FW18	Renault	V10	72	1h 36m 36.922s	6	3
3	3	J Alesi	Benetton	B196	Renault	V10	72	1h 37m 15.237s	3	2
4	4	G Berger	Benetton	B196	Renault	V10	72	1h 37m 15.654s	4	2
5	7	M Häkkinen	McLaren	MP4/11	Mercedes	V10	72	1h 37m 31.569s	5	3
6	8	D Coulthard	McLaren	MP4/11	Mercedes	V10	71		7	4
7	9	O Panis	Ligier	JS43	Mugen Honda	V10	71		9	5
8	12	M Brundle	Jordan	196	Peugeot	V10	71		8	4
9	11	R Barrichello	Jordan	196	Peugeot	V10	71		10	5
10	19	M Salo	Tyrrell	024	Yamaha	V10	70		13	7
dq	14	J Herbert	Sauber	C15	Cosworth	V10	70	bodywork infringement	16	8
11	16	R Rosset	Footwork	FA17	Hart	V8	69		19	10
12	20	P Lamy	Minardi	M195B	Cosworth	V8	69		18	9
r	15	H-H Frentzen	Sauber	C15	Cosworth	V10	56	throttle jammed/ spin	12	6
r	18	U Katayama	Tyrrell	024	Yamaha	V10	33	engine	14	7
r	22	L Badoer	Forti	FG03-96	Cosworth	V8	29	fuel feed	20	10
r	10	P Diniz	Ligier	JS43	Mugen Honda	V10	28	engine pneumatic valve system	11	6
r	17	J Verstappen	Footwork	FA17	Hart	V8	10	front steering arm/ accident	15	8
r	2	E Irvine	Ferrari	F310	Ferrari	V10	5	gearbox	22	11
r	21	G Fisichella	Minardi	M195B	Cosworth	V8	2	fuel pump	17	9
r	23	A Montermini	Forti	FG03-96	Cosworth	V8	2	electrics	21	11
r	1	M Schumacher	Ferrari	F310	Ferrari	V10	-1	engine	1	1

Winning speed: 190.183 km/h, 118.174 mph
Pole Position speed: 201.345 km/h, 125.110 mph (M Schumacher, 1 min:15.989 sec)
Fastest Lap speed: 194.632 km/h, 120.939 mph (J Villeneuve, 1 min:18.610 sec on lap 48)
Lap Leaders: D Hill 1-27,31-72 (69); J Villeneuve 28-30 (3).

E Irvine qualified 10th, but was placed at the back of the grid, due to bodywork infringement

14 Jul 1996 — BRITAIN: Silverstone (Round:10) (Race: 591)

61 laps x 5.072 km, 3.152 miles = 309.392 km, 192.247 miles

POS.	NO.	DRIVER	CAR	MODEL	ENGINE		LAPS	TIME/REASON FOR RETIREMENT	GRID:POS	ROW
1	6	J Villeneuve	Williams	FW18	Renault	V10	61	1h 33m 00.874s	2	1
2	4	G Berger	Benetton	B196	Renault	V10	61	1h 33m 19.900s	7	4
3	7	M Häkkinen	McLaren	MP4/11B	Mercedes	V10	61	1h 33m 51.704s	4	2
4	11	R Barrichello	Jordan	196	Peugeot	V10	61	1h 34m 07.590s	6	3
5	8	D Coulthard	McLaren	MP4/11B	Mercedes	V10	61	1h 34m 23.381s	9	5
6	12	M Brundle	Jordan	196	Peugeot	V10	60		8	4
7	19	M Salo	Tyrrell	024	Yamaha	V10	60		14	7
8	15	H-H Frentzen	Sauber	C15	Cosworth	V10	60		11	6
9	14	J Herbert	Sauber	C15	Cosworth	V10	60		13	7
10	17	J Verstappen	Footwork	FA17	Hart	V8	60		15	8
11	21	G Fisichella	Minardi	M195B	Cosworth	V8	59		18	9
r	3	J Alesi	Benetton	B196	Renault	V10	44	right rear wheel bearing	5	3
r	9	O Panis	Ligier	JS43	Mugen Honda	V10	40	handling	16	8
r	10	P Diniz	Ligier	JS43	Mugen Honda	V10	38	engine	17	9
r	5	D Hill	Williams	FW18	Renault	V10	26	front wheel nut loose/ spin	1	1

POS.	NO.	DRIVER	CAR	MODEL	ENGINE		LAPS	TIME/REASON FOR RETIREMENT	GRID:POS	ROW
r	20	P Lamy	Minardi	M195B	Cosworth	V8	21	gearbox hydraulics	19	10
r	16	R Rosset	Footwork	FA17	Hart	V8	13	alternator	20	10
r	18	U Katayama	Tyrrell	024	Yamaha	V10	12	engine overheating	12	6
r	2	E Irvine	Ferrari	F310	Ferrari	V10	5	differential bearing	10	5
r	1	M Schumacher	Ferrari	F310	Ferrari	V10	3	gearbox hydraulic valve	3	2
nq	23	A Montermini	Forti	FG03-96	Cosworth	V8				
nq	22	L Badoer	Forti	FG03-96	Cosworth	V8				

Winning speed: 199.576 km/h, 124.011 mph
Pole Position speed: 210.178 km/h, 130.598 mph (D Hill, 1 min:26.875 sec)
Fastest Lap speed: 204.498 km/h, 127.069 mph (J Villeneuve, 1 min:29.288 sec on lap 21)
Lap Leaders: J Villeneuve 1-23,31-61 (54); J Alesi 24-30 (7).

R Rosset qualified 17th, but was placed at the back of the grid, for failing to stop for scrutineering.

28 Jul 1996 — GERMANY: Hockenheim (Round:11) (Race: 592)

45 laps x 6.823 km, 4.240 miles = 307.022 km, 190.775 miles

POS.	NO.	DRIVER	CAR	MODEL	ENGINE		LAPS	TIME/REASON FOR RETIREMENT	GRID:POS	ROW
1	5	D Hill	Williams	FW18	Renault	V10	45	1h 21m 43.417s	1	1
2	3	J Alesi	Benetton	B196	Renault	V10	45	1h 21m 54.869s	5	3
3	6	J Villeneuve	Williams	FW18	Renault	V10	45	1h 22m 17.343s	6	3
4	1	M Schumacher	Ferrari	F310	Ferrari	V10	45	1h 22m 24.934s	3	2
5	8	D Coulthard	McLaren	MP4/11B	Mercedes	V10	45	1h 22m 25.613s	7	4
6	11	R Barrichello	Jordan	196	Peugeot	V10	45	1h 23m 25.516s	9	5
7	9	O Panis	Ligier	JS43	Mugen Honda	V10	45	1h 23m 27.329s	12	6
8	15	H-H Frentzen	Sauber	C15	Cosworth	V10	44		13	7
9	19	M Salo	Tyrrell	024	Yamaha	V10	44		15	8
10	12	M Brundle	Jordan	196	Peugeot	V10	44		10	5
11	16	R Rosset	Footwork	FA17	Hart	V8	44		19	10
12	20	P Lamy	Minardi	M195B	Cosworth	V8	43		18	9
13r	4	G Berger	Benetton	B196	Renault	V10	42	engine	2	1
r	2	E Irvine	Ferrari	F310	Ferrari	V10	34	gearbox oil lost	8	4
r	14	J Herbert	Sauber	C15	Cosworth	V10	25	gearbox electronics	14	7
r	10	P Diniz	Ligier	JS43	Mugen Honda	V10	19	throttle	11	6
r	18	U Katayama	Tyrrell	024	Yamaha	V10	19	accident	16	8
r	7	M Häkkinen	McLaren	MP4/11B	Mercedes	V10	13	gearbox	4	2
r	17	J Verstappen	Footwork	FA17	Hart	V8	0	accident	17	9
nq	21	G Lavaggi	Minardi	M195B	Cosworth	V8				

Winning speed: 225.410 km/h, 140.063 mph
Pole Position speed: 236.381 km/h, 146.880 mph (D Hill, 1 min:43.912 sec)
Fastest Lap speed: 230.628 km/h, 143.306 mph (D Hill, 1 min:46.504 sec on lap 26)
Lap Leaders: G Berger 1-23,35-42 (31); D Hill 24-34, 43-45 (14).

11 Aug 1996 — HUNGARY: Hungaroring (Round:12) (Race: 593)

77 laps x 3.968 km, 2.466 miles = 305.536 km, 189.851 miles

POS.	NO.	DRIVER	CAR	MODEL	ENGINE		LAPS	TIME/REASON FOR RETIREMENT	GRID:POS	ROW
1	6	J Villeneuve	Williams	FW18	Renault	V10	77	1h 46m 21.134s	3	2
2	5	D Hill	Williams	FW18	Renault	V10	77	1h 46m 21.905s	2	1
3	3	J Alesi	Benetton	B196	Renault	V10	77	1h 47m 45.346s	5	3
4	7	M Häkkinen	McLaren	MP4/11B	Mercedes	V10	76		7	4
5	9	O Panis	Ligier	JS43	Mugen Honda	V10	76		11	6
6	11	R Barrichello	Jordan	196	Peugeot	V10	75		13	7
7	18	U Katayama	Tyrrell	024	Yamaha	V10	74		14	7
8	16	R Rosset	Footwork	FA17	Hart	V8	74		18	9
9r	1	M Schumacher	Ferrari	F310	Ferrari	V10	70	throttle control unit	1	1
10r	21	G Lavaggi	Minardi	M195B	Cosworth	V8	69	spin	20	10
r	4	G Berger	Benetton	B196	Renault	V10	64	engine	6	3
r	15	H-H Frentzen	Sauber	C15	Cosworth	V10	50	electronics	10	5
r	14	J Herbert	Sauber	C15	Cosworth	V10	35	engine	8	4
r	2	E Irvine	Ferrari	F310	Ferrari	V10	31	gearbox oil temperature	4	2
r	20	P Lamy	Minardi	M195B	Cosworth	V8	24	accident/ rear suspension	19	10
r	8	D Coulthard	McLaren	MP4/11B	Mercedes	V10	23	water pump drive/ spin	9	5
r	17	J Verstappen	Footwork	FA17	Hart	V8	10	spin	17	9
r	12	M Brundle	Jordan	196	Peugeot	V10	5	accident	12	6
r	10	P Diniz	Ligier	JS43	Mugen Honda	V10	1	accident/ suspension	15	8
r	19	M Salo	Tyrrell	024	Yamaha	V10	0	accident	16	8

Winning speed: 172.372 km/h, 107.107 mph
Pole Position speed: 185.207 km/h, 115.082 mph (M Schumacher, 1 min:17.129 sec)
Fastest Lap speed: 178.353 km/h, 110.823 mph (D Hill, 1 min:20.093 sec on lap 67)
Lap Leaders: M Schumacher 1-18 (18); J Villeneuve 19-21,25-58,64-77 (51); D Hill 22-24,59-63 (8).

25 Aug 1996 — BELGIUM: Spa-Francorchamps (Round:13) (Race: 594)

44 laps x 6.968 km, 4.330 miles = 306.592 km, 190.507 miles

POS.	NO.	DRIVER	CAR	MODEL	ENGINE		LAPS	TIME/REASON FOR RETIREMENT	GRID:POS	ROW
1	1	M Schumacher	Ferrari	F310	Ferrari	V10	44	1h 28m 15.125s	3	2
2	6	J Villeneuve	Williams	FW18	Renault	V10	44	1h 28m 20.727s	1	1
3	7	M Häkkinen	McLaren	MP4/11B	Mercedes	V10	44	1h 28m 30.835s	6	3
4	3	J Alesi	Benetton	B196	Renault	V10	44	1h 28m 34.250s	7	4
5	5	D Hill	Williams	FW18	Renault	V10	44	1h 28m 44.304s	2	1
6	4	G Berger	Benetton	B196	Renault	V10	44	1h 28m 45.021s	5	3
7	19	M Salo	Tyrrell	024	Yamaha	V10	44	1h 29m 15.879s	13	7
8	18	U Katayama	Tyrrell	024	Yamaha	V10	44	1h 29m 55.352s	17	9
9	16	R Rosset	Footwork	FA17	Hart	V8	43		18	9
10	20	P Lamy	Minardi	M195B	Cosworth	V8	43		19	10
r	8	D Coulthard	McLaren	MP4/11B	Mercedes	V10	37	spin	4	2
r	12	M Brundle	Jordan	196	Peugeot	V10	34	engine	8	4
r	2	E Irvine	Ferrari	F310	Ferrari	V10	29	gearbox	9	5
r	11	R Barrichello	Jordan	196	Peugeot	V10	29	accident/ front suspension	10	5
r	10	P Diniz	Ligier	JS43	Mugen Honda	V10	22	engine misfire	15	8
r	17	J Verstappen	Footwork	FA17	Hart	V8	11	stub axle/ accident	16	8
r	9	O Panis	Ligier	JS43	Mugen Honda	V10	0	accident	14	7
r	14	J Herbert	Sauber	C15	Cosworth	V10	0	accident	12	6
r	15	H-H Frentzen	Sauber	C15	Cosworth	V10	0	accident	11	6
nq	21	G Lavaggi	Minardi	M195B	Cosworth	V8				

Winning speed: 208.443 km/h, 129.520 mph
Pole Position speed: 226.860 km/h, 140.964 mph (J Villeneuve, 1 min:50.574 sec)
Fastest Lap speed: 221.858 km/h, 137.856 mph (G Berger, 1 min:53.067 sec on lap 42)
Lap Leaders: J Villeneuve 1-14,30-32 (17); D Coulthard 15-21 (7); M Häkkinen 22-23 (2); M Schumacher 24-29,33-44 (18).

8 Sep 1996 — ITALY: Monza (Round:14) (Race: 595)

53 laps x 5.770 km, 3.585 miles = 305.771 km, 189.998 miles

POS.	NO.	DRIVER	CAR	MODEL	ENGINE		LAPS	TIME/REASON FOR RETIREMENT	GRID:POS	ROW
1	1	M Schumacher	Ferrari	F310	Ferrari	V10	53	1h 17m 43.632s	3	2
2	3	J Alesi	Benetton	B196	Renault	V10	53	1h 18m 01.897s	6	3
3	7	M Häkkinen	McLaren	MP4/11B	Mercedes	V10	53	1h 18m 50.267s	4	2
4	12	M Brundle	Jordan	196	Peugeot	V10	53	1h 19m 08.849s	9	5
5	11	R Barrichello	Jordan	196	Peugeot	V10	53	1h 19m 09.107s	10	5
6	10	P Diniz	Ligier	JS43	Mugen Honda	V10	52		14	7
7	6	J Villeneuve	Williams	FW18	Renault	V10	52		2	1
8	17	J Verstappen	Footwork	FA17	Hart	V8	52		15	8
9r	14	J Herbert	Sauber	C15	Cosworth	V10	51	engine	12	6
10	18	U Katayama	Tyrrell	024	Yamaha	V10	51		16	8
r	16	R Rosset	Footwork	FA17	Hart	V8	36	accident	19	10
r	2	E Irvine	Ferrari	F310	Ferrari	V10	23	accident	7	4
r	20	P Lamy	Minardi	M195B	Cosworth	V8	12	engine	18	9
r	19	M Salo	Tyrrell	024	Yamaha	V10	9	engine	17	9
r	15	H-H Frentzen	Sauber	C15	Cosworth	V10	7	accident	13	7
r	5	D Hill	Williams	FW18	Renault	V10	5	accident	1	1
r	21	G Lavaggi	Minardi	M195B	Cosworth	V8	5	engine	20	10
r	4	G Berger	Benetton	B196	Renault	V10	4	gearbox hydraulics	8	4
r	9	O Panis	Ligier	JS43	Mugen Honda	V10	2	accident	11	6
r	8	D Coulthard	McLaren	MP4/11B	Mercedes	V10	1	accident	5	3

Winning speed: 236.034 km/h, 146.665 mph
Pole Position speed: 246.687 km/h, 153.284 mph (D Hill, 1 min:24.204 sec)
Fastest Lap speed: 241.226 km/h, 149.891 mph (M Schumacher, 1 min:26.110 sec on lap 50)
Lap Leaders: D Hill 1-5 (5); J Alesi 6-30 (25); M Schumacher 31-53 (23).

22 Sep 1996 — PORTUGAL: Estoril (Round:15) (Race: 596)

70 laps x 4.360 km, 2.709 miles = 305.200 km, 189.642 miles

POS.	NO.	DRIVER	CAR	MODEL	ENGINE		LAPS	TIME/REASON FOR RETIREMENT	GRID:POS	ROW
1	6	J Villeneuve	Williams	FW18	Renault	V10	70	1h 40m 22.915s	2	1
2	5	D Hill	Williams	FW18	Renault	V10	70	1h 40m 42.881s	1	1
3	1	M Schumacher	Ferrari	F310	Ferrari	V10	70	1h 41m 16.680s	4	2
4	3	J Alesi	Benetton	B196	Renault	V10	70	1h 41m 18.024s	3	2
5	2	E Irvine	Ferrari	F310	Ferrari	V10	70	1h 41m 50.304s	6	3
6	4	G Berger	Benetton	B196	Renault	V10	70	1h 41m 56.056s	5	3
7	15	H Frentzen	Sauber	C15	Cosworth	V10	69		11	6
8	14	J Herbert	Sauber	C15	Cosworth	V10	69		12	6
9	12	M Brundle	Jordan	196	Peugeot	V10	69		10	5
10	9	O Panis	Ligier	JS43	Mugen Honda	V10	69		15	8
11	19	M Salo	Tyrrell	024	Yamaha	V10	69		13	7
12	18	U Katayama	Tyrrell	024	Yamaha	V10	68		14	7
13	8	D Coulthard	McLaren	MP4/11B	Mercedes	V10	68		8	4
14	16	R Rosset	Footwork	FA17	Hart	V8	67		17	9
15	21	G Lavaggi	Minardi	M195B	Cosworth	V8	65		20	10
16	20	P Lamy	Minardi	M195B	Cosworth	V8	65		19	10
r	7	M Häkkinen	McLaren	MP4/11B	Mercedes	V10	52	accident/ handling	7	4
r	17	J Verstappen	Footwork	FA17	Hart	V8	47	engine	16	8
r	10	P Diniz	Ligier	JS43	Mugen Honda	V10	46	spin	18	9
r	11	R Barrichello	Jordan	196	Peugeot	V10	41	spin	9	5

Winning speed: 182.423 km/h, 113.353 mph
Pole Position speed: 195.394 km/h, 121.412 mph (D Hill, 1 min:20.330 sec)
Fastest Lap speed: 189.398 km/h, 117.687 mph (J Villeneuve, 1 min:22.873 sec on lap 37)
Lap Leaders: D Hill 1-17,22-33,36-48 (42); J Alesi 18-21 (4); J Villeneuve 34-35,49-70 (24).

13 Oct 1996 — JAPAN : Suzuka — (Round:16) (Race: 597)

52 laps x 5.864 km, 3.644 miles = 304.718 km, 189.343 miles

POS.	NO.	DRIVER	CAR	MODEL	ENGINE		LAPS	TIME/REASON FOR RETIREMENT	GRID:POS	ROW
1	5	D Hill	Williams	FW18	Renault	V10	52	1h 32m 33.791s	2	1
2	1	M Schumacher	Ferrari	F310	Ferrari	V10	52	1h 32m 35.674s	3	2
3	7	M Häkkinen	McLaren	MP4/11B	Mercedes	V10	52	1h 32m 37.003s	5	3
4	4	G Berger	Benetton	B196	Renault	V10	52	1h 33m 00.317s	4	2
5	12	M Brundle	Jordan	196	Peugeot	V10	52	1h 33m 40.911s	10	5
6	15	H Frentzen	Sauber	C15	Cosworth	V10	52	1h 33m 54.977s	7	4
7	9	O Panis	Ligier	JS43	Mugen Honda	V10	52	1h 33m 58.301s	12	6
8	8	D Coulthard	McLaren	MP4/11B	Mercedes	V10	52	1h 33m 59.024s	8	4
9	11	R Barrichello	Jordan	196	Peugeot	V10	52	1h 34m 14.856s	11	6
10	14	J Herbert	Sauber	C15	Cosworth	V10	52	1h 34m 15.590s	13	7
11	17	J Verstappen	Footwork	FA17	Hart	V8	51		17	9
12	20	P Lamy	Minardi	M195B	Cosworth	V8	50		18	9
13	16	R Rosset	Footwork	FA17	Hart	V8	50		19	10
r	2	E Irvine	Ferrari	F310	Ferrari	V10	39	accident	6	3
r	18	U Katayama	Tyrrell	024	Yamaha	V10	37	engine	14	7
r	6	J Villeneuve	Williams	FW18	Renault	V10	36	wheel lost/ accident	1	1
r	19	M Salo	Tyrrell	024	Yamaha	V10	20	engine	15	8
r	10	P Diniz	Ligier	JS43	Mugen Honda	V10	13	spin	16	8
r	3	J Alesi	Benetton	B196	Renault	V10	0	accident	9	5
nq	21	G Lavaggi	Minardi	M195B	Cosworth	V8				

Winning speed: 197.520 km/h, 122.733 mph
Pole Position speed: 213.433 km/h, 132.621 mph (J Villeneuve, 1 min:38.909 sec)
Fastest Lap speed: 202.901 km/h, 126.077 mph (J Villeneuve, 1 min:44.043 sec on lap 34)
Lap Leaders: D Hill 1-52 (52).

Lap Leaders 1996

POS	DRIVER	CAR-ENGINE	GPS	LAPS	KM	MILES
1	D Hill	Williams-Renault	12	480	2,187.1	1,359.0
2	J Villeneuve	Williams-Renault	9	285	1,369.8	851.2
3	M Schumacher	Ferrari	5	114	589.7	366.4
4	J Alesi	Benetton-Renault	5	60	280.1	174.0
5	G Berger	Benetton-Renault	1	31	211.5	131.4
6	D Coulthard	McLaren-Mercedes Benz	2	26	141.7	88.1
7	O Panis	Ligier-Mugen Honda	1	16	53.2	33.1
8	M Häkkinen	McLaren-Mercedes Benz	1	2	13.9	8.7
			16	**1,014**	**4,847.1**	**3,011.8**

Driver Points 1996

		AUS	BR	RA	EUR	RSM	MC	E	CDN	F	GB	D	H	B	I	P	J	TOTAL
1	D Hill	10	10	10	3	10	-	-	10	10	-	10	6	2	-	6	10	97
2	J Villeneuve	6	-	6	10	-	-	4	6	6	10	4	10	6	-	10	-	78
3	M Schumacher	-	4	-	6	6	-	10	-	-	-	3	-	10	10	4	6	59
4	J Alesi	-	6	4	-	1	-	6	4	4	-	6	4	3	6	3	-	47
5	M Häkkinen	2	3	-	-	-	1	2	2	2	4	-	3	4	4	-	4	31
6	G Berger	3	-	-	-	4	-	-	-	3	6	-	-	1	-	1	3	21
	D Coulthard	-	-	-	4	-	6	-	3	1	2	2	-	-	-	-	-	18
8	R Barrichello	-	-	3	2	2	-	-	-	-	3	1	1	-	2	-	-	14
9	O Panis	-	1	-	-	-	10	-	-	-	-	-	2	-	-	-	-	13
10	E Irvine	4	-	2	-	3	-	-	-	-	-	-	-	-	-	2	-	11
11	H-H Frentzen	-	-	-	-	-	3	3	-	-	-	-	-	-	-	-	2	8
	M Brundle	-	-	-	1	-	-	-	1	-	1	-	-	-	3	-	1	7
13	M Salo	1	2	-	-	-	2	-	-	-	-	-	-	-	-	-	-	5
14	J Herbert	-	-	-	-	-	4	-	-	-	-	-	-	-	-	-	-	4
15	P Diniz	-	-	-	-	-	-	1	-	-	-	-	-	-	1	-	-	2
16	J Verstappen	-	-	1	-	-	-	-	-	-	-	-	-	-	-	-	-	1

10, 6, 4, 3, 2 and 1 point awarded to the first six finishers.

Constructor Points 1996

		AUS	BR	RA	EUR	RSM	MC	E	CDN	F	GB	D	H	B	I	P	J	TOTAL
1	Williams-Renault	16	10	16	13	10	-	4	16	16	10	14	16	8	-	16	10	175
3	Ferrari	4	4	2	6	9	-	10	-	-	-	3	-	10	10	6	6	70
2	Benetton-Renault	3	6	4	-	5	-	6	4	7	6	6	4	4	6	4	3	68
4	McLaren-Mercedes	2	3	-	4	-	7	2	5	3	6	2	3	4	4	-	4	49
5	Jordan-Peugeot	-	-	3	3	2	-	-	1	-	4	1	1	-	5	-	2	22
6	Ligier-Mugen Honda	-	1	-	-	-	10	1	-	-	-	-	2	-	1	-	-	15
7	Sauber-Cosworth	-	-	-	-	-	7	3	-	-	-	-	-	-	-	-	1	11
8	Tyrrell-Yamaha	1	2	-	-	-	2	-	-	-	-	-	-	-	-	-	-	5
9	Footwork-Hart	-	-	1	-	-	-	-	-	-	-	-	-	-	-	-	-	1

10, 6, 4, 3, 2 and 1 point awarded to the first six finishers.

2

SEASON SUMMARY

GRANDS PRIX 1950 - 1996

RACE RESULTS & GRID POSITIONS

1950 RACE RESULTS & GRID POSITIONS

	GB	MC	CH	B	F	I
Alberto ASCARI	-	2	r	5	-	r/2=
(Ferrari)	-	7	5	6	ns	2
Clemente BIONDETTI	-	-	-	-	-	r
(Ferrari-Jaguar)	-	-	-	-	-	25
B BIRA	r	5	4	-	-	r
(Maserati)	5	15	8	-	-	15
Felice BONETTO	-	-	5	-	r	-
(Maserati Milano)	-	-	12	-	11	-
(Milano-Maserati)	-	-	-	-	-	23ns
Toni BRANCA	-	-	11	10	-	-
(Maserati)	-	-	17	11	-	-
Eugène CHABOUD	-	-	-	r	5=	-
(Talbot Lago)	-	-	-	13	10ns	-
Louis CHIRON	r	3	9	-	r	r
(Maserati)	11	8	16	-	14	19
Johnny CLAES	11	7	10	8	r	r
(Talbot Lago)	21	19	14	14	15	22
Franco COMOTTI	-	-	-	-	-	r
(Maserati Milano)	-	-	-	-	-	26
Geoffrey CROSSLEY	r	-	-	9	-	-
(Alta)	17	-	-	12	-	-
Emmanuel de GRAFFENRIED	r	r	6	-	-	6
(Maserati)	8	12	11	-	-	17
Philippe ÉTANÇELIN	8	r	r	r	5=	5
(Talbot Lago)	14	4	6	7	4	16
Luigi FAGIOLI	2	r	2	2	2	3
(Alfa Romeo)	2	5	3	3	3	5
Juan Manuel FANGIO	r	1f	r	1	1f	rf/r=
(Alfa Romeo)	3	1	1	2	1	1
Giuseppe FARINA	1f	r	1f	4f	7r	1
(Alfa Romeo)	1	2	2	1	2	3
Joe FRY +	10=	-	-	-	-	-
(Maserati)	20	-	-	-	-	-
Bob GERARD	6	6	-	-	-	-
(ERA)	13	16	-	-	-	-
Yves GIRAUD-CABANTOUS	4	-	r	r	8	-
(Talbot Lago)	6	-	7	9	5	-
Froilán GONZÁLEZ	-	r	-	-	r	-
(Maserati)	-	3	-	-	8	-
David HAMPSHIRE	9	-	-	-	r	-
(Maserati)	16	-	-	-	18	-
Cuth HARRISON	7	r	-	-	-	r
(ERA)	15	14	-	-	-	21
Leslie JOHNSON	r	-	-	-	-	-
(ERA)	12	-	-	-	-	-
Joe KELLY	nc	-	-	-	-	-
(Alta)	19	-	-	-	-	-
Pierre LEVEGH	-	-	-	7	r	r
(Talbot Lago)	-	-	-	10	9	20
Henri LOUVEAU	-	-	-	-	-	r
(Talbot Lago)	-	-	-	-	-	14
Guy MAIRESSE	-	-	-	-	-	r
(Talbot Lago)	-	-	-	-	-	11
Robert MANZON	-	r	-	-	4	r
(Simca Gordini)	-	11	-	-	13	10
Eugène MARTIN	r	-	r	-	-	-
(Talbot Lago)	7	-	9	-	-	-
David MURRAY	r	-	-	-	-	r
(Maserati)	18	-	-	-	-	24
Nello PAGANI	-	-	7	-	-	-
(Maserati)	-	-	15	-	-	-
Reg PARNELL	3	-	-	-	r	-
(Alfa Romeo)	4	-	-	-	-	-
(Maserati)	-	-	-	-	12	-
Alfredo PIÀN	-	-	-	-	-	-
(Maserati)	-	18ns	-	-	-	-
Paul PIETSCH	-	-	-	-	-	r
(Maserati)	-	-	-	-	-	27
Charles POZZI	-	-	-	-	6=	-
(Talbot Lago)	-	-	-	-	16	-
Franco ROL	-	r	-	-	r	r
(Maserati)	-	17	-	-	7	9
Tony ROLT	r=	-	-	-	-	-
(ERA)	-	-	-	-	-	-
Louis ROSIER	5	r	3	3	r/6=	4
(Talbot Lago)	9	10	10	8	6	13
Consalvo SANESI	-	-	-	-	-	r
(Alfa Romeo)	-	-	-	-	-	4
Harry SCHELL	-	r	8	-	-	-
(Cooper-JAP)	-	20	-	-	-	-
(Talbot Lago)	-	-	18	-	-	-
Dorino SERAFINI	-	-	-	-	-	2=
(Ferrari)	-	-	-	-	-	6
Brian SHAWE-TAYLOR	10=	-	-	-	-	-
(Maserati)	-	-	-	-	-	-
Raymond SOMMER +	-	4	r	r	r	r
(Ferrari)	-	9	13	-	-	-
(Talbot Lago)	-	-	-	5	17	8
Piero TARUFFI	-	-	-	-	-	r=
(Alfa Romeo)	-	-	-	-	-	7
Maurice TRINTIGNANT	-	r	-	-	-	r
(Simca Gordini)	-	13	-	-	-	12
Luigi VILLORESI	-	r	r	6	-	-
(Ferrari)	-	6	4	4	ns	-
Peter WALKER	r=	-	-	-	-	-
(ERA)	10	-	-	-	-	-
Peter WHITEHEAD	-	-	-	-	3	7
(Ferrari)	-	ns	-	-	19	18

1951 RACE RESULTS & GRID POSITIONS

	CH	B	F	GB	D	I	E
George ABECASSIS	r	-	-	-	-	-	-
(HWM)	20	-	-	-	-	-	-
Alberto ASCARI	6	2	r/2=	r	1	1	4
(Ferrari)	7	4	3	4	1	3	1
B BIRA	-	-	-	-	-	-	r
(Maserati-OSCA)	-	-	-	-	-	-	19
Felice BONETTO	-	-	-	4	r	3=	5
(Alfa Romeo)	-	-	-	7	10	7	8
Toni BRANCA	-	-	-	-	r	-	-
(Maserati)	-	-	-	-	17	-	-
Eugène CHABOUD	-	-	8	-	-	-	-
(Talbot Lago)	-	-	14	-	-	-	-
Louis CHIRON	7	r	6	r	r	r	r
(Maserati)	19	-	-	-	-	-	-
(Talbot Lago)	-	9	8	13	13	17	12
Johnny CLAES	13	7	r	13	11	r	r
(Talbot Lago)	18	11	12	14	18	21	15
Emmanuel de GRAFFENRIED	5	-	r	-	r	r	6
(Alfa Romeo)	5	-	-	-	-	9	6
(Maserati)	-	-	16	-	16	-	-
Philippe ÉTANÇELIN	10	r	r	-	r	-	8
(Talbot Lago)	12	10	10	-	21	-	13
Luigi FAGIOLI	-	-	1=/11=	-	-	-	-
(Alfa Romeo)	-	-	7	-	-	-	-
Juan Manuel FANGIO	1f	9f	11=/1=f	2	2f	r	1f
(Alfa Romeo)	1	1	1	2	3	1	2
Giuseppe FARINA	3	1	5	rf	r	r/3=f	3
(Alfa Romeo)	2	2	2	3	4	2	4
Rudi FISCHER	11	-	-	-	6	-	-
(Ferrari)	10	-	-	-	8	ns	-
Philip FOTHERINGHAM-PARKER	-	-	-	r	-	-	-
(Maserati)	-	-	-	16	-	-	-
Bob GERARD	-	-	-	11	-	-	-
(ERA)	-	-	-	10	-	-	-
Yves GIRAUD-CABANTOUS	r	5	7	-	r	8	r
(Talbot Lago)	15	8	11	-	11	14	14
Chico GODIA	-	-	-	-	-	-	10
(Maserati)	-	-	-	-	-	-	17
Froilán GONZÁLEZ	r	-	2=	1	3	2	2
(Talbot Lago)	13	-	-	-	-	-	-
(Ferrari)	-	-	6	1	2	4	3
Aldo GORDINI	-	-	r	-	-	-	-
(Simca Gordini)	-	-	17	-	-	-	-
Georges GRIGNARD	-	-	-	-	-	-	r
(Talbot Lago)	-	-	-	-	-	-	16
Duncan HAMILTON	-	-	-	12	r	-	-
(Talbot Lago)	-	-	-	11	20	-	-
Peter HIRT	r	-	-	-	-	-	-
(Veritas)	16	-	-	-	-	-	-
John JAMES	-	-	-	r	-	-	-
(Maserati)	-	-	-	17	-	-	-
Juan JOVER	-	-	-	-	-	-	-
(Maserati)	-	-	-	-	-	-	18ns
Joe KELLY	-	-	-	nc	-	-	-
(Alta)	-	-	-	18	-	-	-
Chico LANDI	-	-	-	-	-	r	-
(Ferrari)	-	-	-	-	-	16	-
Pierre LEVEGH	-	8	-	-	9	r	-
(Talbot Lago)	-	13	-	-	19	20	-
Henri LOUVEAU	r	-	-	-	-	-	-
(Talbot Lago)	11	-	-	-	-	-	-
Guy MAIRESSE	14	-	9	-	-	-	-
(Talbot Lago)	21	-	19	-	-	-	-
Robert MANZON	-	-	r	-	7	r	9
(Simca Gordini)	-	-	23	-	9	13	9
Onofré MARIMON	-	-	r	-	-	-	-
(Maserati Milano)	-	-	15	-	-	-	-
Stirling MOSS	8	-	-	-	-	-	-
(HWM)	14	-	-	-	-	-	-
David MURRAY	-	-	-	r	-	-	-
(Maserati)	-	-	-	15	ns	-	-
Reg PARNELL	-	-	4	5	-	-	-
(Thin Wall Ferrari)	-	-	9	-	-	-	-
(BRM)	-	-	-	20	-	8ns	-
Paul PIETSCH	-	-	-	-	r	-	-
(Alfa Romeo)	-	-	-	-	7	-	-
André PILETTE	-	6	-	-	-	-	-
(Talbot Lago)	-	12	-	-	-	-	-
Ken RICHARDSON	-	-	-	-	-	-	-
(BRM)	-	-	-	-	-	10ns	-
Franco ROL	-	-	-	-	-	9	-
(OSCA)	-	-	-	-	-	18	-
Louis ROSIER	9	4	r	10	8	7	7
(Talbot Lago)	8	7	13	9	15	15	20
Consalvo SANESI	4	r	10	6	-	-	-
(Alfa Romeo)	4	6	5	6	-	-	-
Harry SCHELL	12	-	r	-	-	-	-
(Maserati)	17	-	22	-	-	-	-
Brian SHAWE-TAYLOR	-	-	-	8	-	-	-
(Thin Wall Ferrari)	-	-	ns	-	-	-	-
(ERA)	-	-	-	12	-	-	-
André SIMON	-	-	r	-	r	6	r
(Simca Gordini)	-	-	21	-	12	11	10
Hans STUCK	-	-	-	-	-	-	-
(BRM)	-	-	ns	-	-	-	-
Jacques SWATERS	-	-	-	-	10	r	-
(Talbot Lago)	-	-	-	-	22	22	-
Piero TARUFFI	2	r	-	-	5	5	r
(Ferrari)	6	5	-	-	6	6	7
Maurice TRINTIGNANT	-	-	r	-	r	r	r
(Simca Gordini)	-	-	18	-	14	12	11
Luigi VILLORESI	r	3	3	3	4	4	r
(Ferrari)	3	3	4	5	5	5	5
Peter WALKER	-	-	-	7	-	-	-
(BRM)	-	-	-	19	-	-	-
Peter WHITEHEAD	r	-	r	9	-	r	-
(Ferrari)	9	-	20	-	-	19	-
(Thin Wall Ferrari)	-	-	-	8	-	-	-

1952 RACE RESULTS & GRID POSITIONS

Driver	CH	B	F	GB	D	NL	I
George ABECASSIS	r	-	-	-	-	-	-
(HWM)	10	-	-	-	-	-	-
Alberto ASCARI	-	1f	1f	1f	1f	1f	1f=
(Ferrari)	-	1	1	2	1	1	1
Bill ASTON	-	-	-	-	r	-	-
(Aston-Butterworth)	-	-	-	30ns	21	-	nq
Marcel BALSA	-	-	-	-	r	-	-
(BMW)	-	-	-	-	25	-	-
Elie BAYOL	-	-	-	-	-	-	r
(OSCA)	-	-	-	-	-	-	10
Jean BEHRA	3	r	7	-	5	r	r
(Gordini)	7	5	4	-	11	6	11
Gino BIANCO	-	-	-	18	r	r	r
(Maserati)	-	-	-	28	16	12	24
B BIRA	r	10	r	11	-	-	-
(Gordini) *	11	18	7	10	-	-	-
Felice BONETTO	-	-	-	-	dq	-	5
(Maserati)	-	-	-	-	10	-	13
Eric BRANDON	8	9	-	20	-	-	13
(Cooper-Bristol)	17	12	-	18	-	-	20
Alan BROWN	5	6	-	22	-	-	15
(Cooper-Bristol)	15	9	-	13	-	-	21
Adolf BRUDES	-	-	-	-	r	-	-
(Veritas)	-	-	-	-	19	-	-
Eitel CANTONI	-	-	-	r	r	-	11
(Maserati)	-	-	-	27	26	-	23
Piero CARINI	-	-	r	-	r	-	-
(Ferrari)	-	-	19	-	27	-	-
Johnny CLAES	-	8	r	14	10	-	-
(Gordini) *	-	19	20	23	-	-	nq
(HWM)	-	-	-	-	32	-	-
Peter COLLINS	r	r	6	r	-	-	-
(HWM)	6	11	8	14	ns	-	nq
Franco COMOTTI	-	-	12	-	-	-	-
(Ferrari)	-	-	16	-	-	-	-
Alberto CRESPO	-	-	-	-	-	-	-
(Maserati Platé)	-	-	-	-	-	-	nq
Tony CROOK	-	-	-	21	-	-	-
(Frazer Nash-Bristol)	-	-	-	25	-	-	-
Emmanuel de GRAFFENRIED	6	-	r=	19	-	-	-
(Maserati Platé)	8	-	12	31	-	-	nq
Max de TERRA	r	-	-	-	-	-	-
(Simca Gordini)	21	-	-	-	-	-	-
Charles de TORNACO	-	7	-	-	-	r	-
(Ferrari)	-	13	-	-	-	17	nq
Ken DOWNING	-	-	-	9	-	r	-
(Connaught)	-	-	-	5	-	13	-
Piero DUSIO	-	-	-	-	-	-	-
(Cisitalia-BPM)	-	-	-	-	-	-	nq
Philippe ÉTANÇELIN	-	-	8	-	-	-	-
(Maserati)	-	-	18	-	-	-	-
Giuseppe FARINA	r/r=	2	2	6	2	2	4
(Ferrari)	1	2	2	1	2	2	3
Ludwig FISCHER	-	-	-	-	-	-	-
(AFM-BMW)	-	-	-	-	31ns	-	-
Rudi FISCHER	2	-	11=	13	3	-	r
(Ferrari)	5	-	17	15	6	-	14
Jan FLINTERMAN	-	-	-	-	-	r/9=	-
(Maserati)	-	-	-	-	-	15	-
Paul FRÈRE	-	5	-	-	r	r	-
(HWM)	-	8	-	-	13	-	-
(Simca Gordini)	-	-	-	-	-	11	-
Tony GAZE	-	15	-	r	r	-	-
(HWM)	-	16	-	26	14	-	nq
Yves GIRAUD-CABANTOUS	-	-	10	-	-	-	-
(HWM)	-	-	10	-	-	-	-
Froilán GONZÀLEZ	-	-	-	-	-	-	2f=
(Maserati)	-	-	-	-	-	-	5
Duncan HAMILTON	-	-	-	r	-	7	-
(HWM)	-	-	-	11	-	10	-
Mike HAWTHORN	-	4	r	3	-	4	nc
(Cooper-Bristol)	-	6	15	7	-	3	12
Willi HEEKS	-	-	-	-	r	-	-
(AFM-BMW)	-	-	-	-	9	-	-
Theo HELFRICH	-	-	-	-	r	-	-
(Veritas)	-	-	-	-	18	-	-
Peter HIRT	7	-	11=	r	-	-	-
(Ferrari)	19	-	-	24	-	-	-
Hans KLENK	-	-	-	-	11	-	-
(Veritas)	-	-	-	-	8	-	-
Ernst KLODWIG	-	-	-	-	12	-	-
(BMW)	-	-	-	-	29	-	-
Willi KRAKAU	-	-	-	-	-	-	-
(AFM-BMW)	-	-	-	-	28ns	-	-
Rudolf KRAUSE	-	-	-	-	r	-	-
(BMW)	-	-	-	-	23	-	-
Chico LANDI	-	-	-	-	-	9=	8
(Maserati)	-	-	-	-	-	16	18
Roger LAURENT	-	12	-	-	6	-	-
(HWM)	-	20	-	-	-	-	-
(Ferrari)	-	-	-	-	17	-	-
Arthur LEGAT	-	13	-	-	-	-	-
(Veritas)	-	21	-	-	-	-	-
Lance MACKLIN	r	11	9	15	-	8	-
(HWM)	12	14	14	29	-	9	nq
Robert MANZON	r	3	4	r	r	5	14
(Gordini)	3	4	5	4	4	8	7
Ken McALPINE	-	-	-	16	-	-	r
(Connaught)	-	-	-	17	-	-	22
Harry MERKEL	-	-	-	-	-	-	-
(BMW)	-	-	-	-	ns	-	-
Robin MONTGOMERIE -CHARRINGTON	-	r	-	-	-	-	-
(Aston-Butterworth)	-	15	-	-	-	-	-
Stirling MOSS	r	r	-	r	-	r	r
(HWM)	9	-	-	-	-	-	-
(ERA-Bristol)	-	10	-	16	-	18	-
(Connaught)	-	-	-	-	-	-	9
David MURRAY	-	-	-	r	-	-	-
(Cooper-Bristol)	-	-	-	22	-	-	-
Bernd NACKE #	-	-	-	-	r	-	-
(BMW)	-	-	-	-	30	-	-
Helmut NIEDERMAYR	-	-	-	-	9	-	-
(AFM-BMW)	-	-	-	-	22	-	-
Robert O'BRIEN	-	14	-	-	-	-	-
(Simca Gordini)	-	22	-	-	-	-	-
Reg PARNELL	-	-	-	7	-	-	-
(Cooper-Bristol)	-	-	-	6	-	-	-
Josef PETERS	-	-	-	-	r	-	-
(Veritas)	-	-	-	-	20	-	-
Paul PIETSCH	-	-	-	-	r	-	-
(Veritas)	-	-	-	-	7	-	-
Dennis POORE	-	-	-	4	-	-	12
(Connaught)	-	-	-	8	-	-	19
Fritz RIESS	-	-	-	-	7	-	-
(Veritas)	-	-	-	-	12	-	-
Franco ROL	-	-	-	-	-	-	r
(Maserati)	-	-	-	-	-	-	16
Louis ROSIER	r	r	r	-	-	-	10
(Ferrari)	20	17	9	-	-	-	17
Roy SALVADORI	-	-	-	8	-	-	-
(Ferrari)	-	-	-	19	-	-	-
Harry SCHELL	r	-	r/r=	17	-	-	-
(Maserati Platé)	18	-	11	32	-	-	-
Rudolf SCHOELLER	-	-	-	-	r	-	-
(Ferrari)	-	-	-	-	24	-	-
André SIMON	r=	-	-	-	-	-	6
(Ferrari)	4	-	-	-	-	-	8
Hans STUCK	r	-	-	-	-	-	-
(AFM-Küchen)	14	-	-	-	-	-	-
(Ferrari)	-	-	-	-	-	-	nq
Piero TARUFFI	1f	r	3	2	4	-	7
(Ferrari)	2	3	3	3	5	-	6
Eric THOMPSON	-	-	-	5	-	-	-
(Connaught)	-	-	-	9	-	-	-
Maurice TRINTIGNANT	-	-	5	r	r	6	r
(Ferrari)	ns	-	-	-	-	-	-
(Gordini) *	-	-	6	21	3	5	4
Toni ULMEN	r	-	-	-	8	-	-
(Veritas)	16	-	-	-	15	-	-
Dries van der LOF	-	-	-	-	-	nc	-
(HWM)	-	-	-	-	-	14	-
Luigi VILLORESI	-	-	-	-	-	3	3
(Ferrari)	-	-	-	-	-	4	2
Ken WHARTON	4	r	-	-	-	r	9
(Frazer Nash-Bristol)	13	7	-	-	-	7	-
(Cooper-Bristol)	-	-	-	-	-	-	15
Graham WHITEHEAD	-	-	-	12	-	-	-
(Alta)	-	-	-	12	-	-	-
Peter WHITEHEAD	-	-	r	10	-	-	-
(Alta)	-	-	13	-	-	-	-
(Ferrari)	-	-	-	20	-	-	nq

pseudonym of Günther BECHEM who also raced in 1953.

* *Although the Simca Gordini partnership was dissolved in 1951, B Bira, J Claes and M Trintignant drove one or more of those cars in 1952. The car was a Gordini for the remainder of the season.*

1953 RACE RESULTS & GRID POSITIONS

Driver	RA	NL	B	F	GB	D	CH	I
Kurt ADOLFF	-	-	-	-	-	r	-	-
(Ferrari)	-	-	-	-	-	27	-	-
Alberto ASCARI	1f	1	1	4f=	1f=	8=/r=f	1f	r
(Ferrari)	1	1	2	1	1	1	2	1
John BARBER	8	-	-	-	-	-	-	-
(Cooper-Bristol)	16	-	-	-	-	-	-	-
Edgar BARTH	-	-	-	-	-	r	-	-
(EMW)	-	-	-	-	-	24	-	-
Erwin BAUER	-	-	-	-	-	r	-	-
(Veritas)	-	-	-	-	-	33	-	-
Elie BAYOL	-	-	-	r	-	-	-	r
(OSCA)	-	-	-	15	-	-	ns	13
Günther BECHEM	-	-	-	-	-	r	-	-
(AFM-BMW)	-	-	-	-	-	30	-	-
Jean BEHRA	6	-	r	10	r	r	r	-
(Gordini)	11	-	14	22	22	9	12	-
Georges BERGER	-	-	r	-	-	-	-	-
(Simca Gordini)	-	-	20	-	-	-	-	-
B BIRA	-	-	-	r	7	r	-	11
(Connaught)	-	-	-	11	19	15	-	-
(Maserati)	-	-	-	-	-	-	-	23
Pablo BIRGER	r	-	-	-	-	-	-	-
(Simca Gordini)	14	-	-	-	-	-	-	-
Felice BONETTO +	r	3=	-	r	6	4	r=/4=	r
(Maserati)	15	13	-	2	16	7	10	7
Alan BROWN	9	-	-	-	r	r	-	12
(Cooper-Bristol)	12	-	-	-	21	17	-	24
Piero CARINI	-	-	-	-	-	-	-	r
(Ferrari)	-	-	-	-	-	-	-	20

	RA	NL	B	F	GB	D	CH	I
Louis CHIRON	-	-	-	**15**	-	-	-	**10**
(OSCA)	-	-	-	25	ns	-	ns	25
Johnny CLAES	-	**nc**	**r=**	**12**	-	**r**	-	**r**
(Connaught)	-	17	-	21	-	25	-	30
(Maserati)	-	-	10	-	-	-	-	-
Peter COLLINS	-	**8**	**r**	**13**	**r**	-	-	-
(HWM)	-	16	16	17	23	-	-	-
Tony CROOK	-	-	-	-	**r**	-	-	-
(Cooper-Bristol)	-	-	-	-	25	-	-	-
Emmanuel de GRAFFENRIED	-	**5**	**4**	**7**	**r**	**5**	**r**	**r**
(Maserati)	-	7	9	9	26	11	8	9
Max de TERRA	-	-	-	-	-	-	**8**	-
(Ferrari)	-	-	-	-	-	-	19	-
Charles de TORNACO	-	-	-	-	-	-	-	-
(Ferrari)	-	-	ns	-	-	-	-	-
Jack FAIRMAN	-	-	-	-	**r**	-	-	**nc**
(HWM)	-	-	-	-	27	-	-	-
(Connaught)	-	-	-	-	-	-	-	22
Juan Manuel FANGIO	**r**	**r**	**r/r=**	**2f=**	**2**	**2**	**4=/r=**	**1f**
(Maserati)	2	2	1	4	4	2	1	2
Giuseppe FARINA	**r**	**2**	**r**	**5**	**3**	**1**	**2**	**2**
(Ferrari)	4	3	4	6	5	3	3	3
John FITCH	-	-	-	-	-	-	-	**r**
(HWM)	-	-	-	-	-	-	-	26
Theo FITZAU	-	-	-	-	-	**r**	-	-
(AFM-BMW)	-	-	-	-	-	21	-	-
Paul FRÈRE	-	-	**10**	-	-	-	**r**	-
(HWM)	-	-	11	-	-	-	16	-
Oscar GÂLVEZ	**5**	-	-	-	-	-	-	-
(Maserati)	9	-	-	-	-	-	-	-
Bob GERARD	-	-	-	**11**	**r**	-	-	-
(Cooper-Bristol)	-	-	-	12	18	-	-	-
Yves GIRAUD-CABANTOUS	-	-	-	**14**	-	-	-	**15**
(HWM)	-	-	-	18	-	-	-	28
Helm GLÖCKLER	-	-	-	-	-	-	-	-
(Cooper-Bristol)	-	-	-	-	-	ns	-	-
Froilán GONZÁLEZ	**3**	**r/3=**	**rf**	**3**	**4f=**	-	-	-
(Maserati)	5	5	3	5	2	-	-	-
Duncan HAMILTON	-	-	-	-	**r**	-	-	-
(HWM)	-	-	-	-	17	-	-	-
Mike HAWTHORN	**4**	**4**	**6**	**1**	**5**	**3**	**3**	**4**
(Ferrari)	6	6	7	7	3	4	7	6
Willi HEEKS	-	-	-	-	-	**r**	-	-
(Veritas)	-	-	-	-	-	18	-	-
Theo HELFRICH	-	-	-	-	-	**12**	-	-
(Veritas)	-	-	-	-	-	28	-	-
Hans HERRMANN	-	-	-	-	-	**9**	-	-
(Veritas)	-	-	-	-	-	14	-	-
Peter HIRT	-	-	-	-	-	-	**r**	-
(Ferrari)	-	-	-	-	-	-	17	-
Oswald KARCH	-	-	-	-	-	**r**	-	-
(Veritas)	-	-	-	-	-	34	-	-
Ernst KLODWIG	-	-	-	-	-	**15**	-	-
(BMW)	-	-	-	-	-	32	-	-
Rudolf KRAUSE	-	-	-	-	-	**14**	-	-
(BMW)	-	-	-	-	-	26	-	-
Chico LANDI	-	-	-	-	-	-	**r**	**r**
(Maserati)	-	-	-	-	-	-	20	21
Hermann LANG	-	-	-	-	-	-	**5**	-
(Maserati)	-	-	-	-	-	-	11	-
Arthur LEGAT	-	-	**r**	-	-	-	-	-
(Veritas)	-	-	19	-	-	-	-	-
Ernst LOOF	-	-	-	-	-	**r**	-	-
(Veritas)	-	-	-	-	-	31	-	-
Lance MACKLIN	-	**r**	**r**	**r**	**r**	-	**r**	**r**
(HWM)	-	15	17	16	12	-	15	27
Umberto MAGLIOLI	-	-	-	-	-	-	-	**8**
(Ferrari)	-	-	-	-	-	-	-	11
Sergio MANTOVANI	-	-	-	-	-	-	-	**7=**
(Maserati)	-	-	-	-	-	-	-	12
Robert MANZON	**r**	-	-	-	-	-	-	-
(Gordini)	8	-	-	-	-	-	-	-
Onofré MARIMON	-	-	**3**	**9**	**r**	**r**	**r**	**r**
(Maserati)	-	-	6	8	7	8	5	4
Ken McALPINE	-	**r**	-	-	**r**	**13**	-	**nc**
(Connaught)	-	14	-	-	13	16	-	18
Carlos MENDITÉGUY	**r**	-	-	-	-	-	-	-
(Gordini)	10	-	-	-	-	-	-	-
Roberto MIÈRES	-	**r**	-	**r**	-	-	-	**6**
(Gordini)	-	19	-	24	-	-	-	16
Stirling MOSS	-	**9**	-	**r**	-	**6**	-	**13**
(Connaught)	-	9	-	-	-	-	-	-
(Cooper-Alta)	-	-	-	13	-	12	-	10
Luigi MUSSO	-	-	-	-	-	-	-	**7=**
(Maserati)	-	-	-	-	-	-	-	-
Rodney NUCKEY	-	-	-	-	-	**11**	-	-
(Cooper-Bristol)	-	-	-	-	-	20	-	-
André PILETTE	-	-	**11**	-	-	-	-	-
(Connaught)	-	-	18	-	-	-	-	-
Tony ROLT	-	-	-	-	**r**	-	-	-
(Connaught)	-	-	-	-	10	-	-	-
Louis ROSIER	-	**7**	**8**	**8**	**10**	**10**	**r**	**16**
(Ferrari)	-	8	13	10	24	22	14	17
Roy SALVADORI	-	**r**	-	**r**	**r**	**r**	-	**r**
(Connaught)	-	11	-	19	28	13	-	14
Harry SCHELL	**7=**	**r**	**7**	**r**	**r**	**r**	-	**9**
(Gordini)	-	10	12	20	9	10	-	15
Albert SCHERRER	-	-	-	-	-	-	**9**	-
(HWM)	-	-	-	-	-	-	18	-
Adolfo SCHWELM CRUZ	**r**	-	-	-	-	-	-	-
(Cooper-Bristol)	13	-	-	-	-	-	-	-
Wolfgang SEIDEL	-	-	-	-	-	**16**	-	-
(Veritas)	-	-	-	-	-	29	-	-
Ian STEWART	-	-	-	-	**r**	-	-	-
(Connaught)	-	-	-	-	20	-	-	-
Jimmy STEWART	-	-	-	-	**r**	-	-	-
(Cooper-Bristol)	-	-	-	-	15	-	-	-
Hans STUCK	-	-	-	-	-	**r**	-	**14**
(AFM-Bristol)	-	-	-	-	-	23	-	29
Jacques SWATERS	-	-	-	-	-	**7**	**r**	-
(Ferrari)	-	-	ns	-	-	19	13	-
Maurice TRINTIGNANT	**7=**	**6**	**5**	**r**	**r**	**r**	**r**	**5**
(Gordini)	7	12	8	23	8	5	4	8
Luigi VILLORESI	**2**	**rf**	**2**	**6**	**r**	**r=/8=**	**6**	**3**
(Ferrari)	3	4	5	3	6	6	6	5
Fred WACKER	-	-	**9**	-	-	-	-	-
(Gordini)	-	ns	15	-	-	-	ns	-
Ken WHARTON	-	**r**	-	**r**	**8**	-	**7**	**nc**
(Cooper-Bristol)	-	18	-	14	11	-	9	19
Peter WHITEHEAD	-	-	-	-	**9**	-	-	-
(Cooper-Alta)	-	-	-	-	14	-	-	-

1954 RACE RESULTS & GRID POSITIONS

	RA	B	F	GB	D	CH	I	E
Alberto ASCARI	-	-	**r**	**r/r=f=**	-	-	**r**	**rf**
(Maserati)	-	-	3	30	-	-	-	-
(Ferrari)	-	-	-	-	-	-	2	-
(Lancia)	-	-	-	-	-	-	-	1
Elie BAYOL	**5**	-	-	-	-	-	-	-
(Gordini)	14	-	-	-	-	-	-	-
Don BEAUMAN	-	-	-	**11**	-	-	-	-
(Connaught)	-	-	-	17	-	-	-	-
Jean BEHRA	**dq**	**r**	**6**	**rf=**	**10**	**r**	**r**	**r**
(Gordini)	16	7	17	5	9	14	12	18
Georges BERGER	-	-	**r**	-	-	-	-	-
(Gordini)	-	-	20	-	-	-	-	-
B BIRA	**7**	**6**	**4**	**r=**	**r**	-	-	**9**
(Maserati)	9	13	6	10	19	-	-	15
Eric BRANDON	-	-	-	**r**	-	-	-	-
(Cooper-Bristol)	-	-	-	25	-	-	-	-
Alan BROWN	-	-	-	-	-	-	-	-
(Cooper-Bristol)	-	-	-	26ns	-	-	-	-
Clemar BUCCI	-	-	-	**r**	**r**	**r**	**r**	-
(Gordini)	-	-	-	13	16	10	17	-
Peter COLLINS	-	-	-	**r**	-	-	**7**	-
(Vanwall)	-	-	-	11	-	-	16	ns
Jorge DAPONTE	**r**	-	-	-	-	-	**11**	-
(Maserati)	17	-	-	-	-	-	19	-
Emmanuel de GRAFFENRIED	**8**	-	-	-	-	-	-	**r=**
(Maserati)	12	-	-	-	-	-	-	21
Giovanni de RIU	-	-	-	-	-	-	-	-
(Maserati)	-	-	-	-	-	-	ns	-
Juan Manuel FANGIO	**1**	**1f**	**1**	**4f=**	**1**	**1f**	**1**	**3**
(Maserati)	3	1	-	-	-	-	-	-
(Mercedes-Benz)	-	-	1	1	1	2	1	2
Giuseppe FARINA	**2**	**r**	-	-	-	-	-	-
(Ferrari)	1	3	-	-	-	-	-	-
Ron FLOCKHART	-	-	-	**r=**	-	-	-	-
(Maserati)	-	-	-	-	-	-	-	-
Paul FRÈRE	-	**r**	**r**	-	**r**	-	-	-
(Gordini)	-	10	19	-	6	-	-	-
Bob GERARD	-	-	-	**10**	-	-	-	-
(Cooper-Bristol)	-	-	-	18	-	-	-	-
Chico GODIA	-	-	-	-	-	-	-	**6**
(Maserati)	-	-	-	-	-	-	-	13
Froilán GONZÁLEZ	**3f**	**r/4=**	**r**	**1f=**	**2=**	**2**	**r/3=f**	-
(Ferrari)	2	2	4	2	5	1	5	-
Horace GOULD	-	-	-	**15**	-	-	-	-
(Cooper-Bristol)	-	-	-	20	-	-	-	-
Mike HAWTHORN	**dq**	**4=**	**r**	**2f=**	**r/2=**	**r**	**2**	**1**
(Ferrari)	4	5	8	3	2	6	7	3
Theo HELFRICH	-	-	-	-	**r**	-	-	-
(Klenk-BMW)	-	-	-	-	21	-	-	-
Hans HERRMANN	-	-	**rf**	-	**r**	**3**	**4**	**r**
(Mercedes-Benz)	-	-	7	-	4	7	8	9
Karl KLING	-	-	**2**	**7**	**4f**	**r**	**r**	**5**
(Mercedes-Benz)	-	-	2	6	23	5	4	12
Hermann LANG	-	-	-	-	**r**	-	-	-
(Mercedes-Benz)	-	-	-	-	11	-	-	-
Roger LOYER	**r**	-	-	-	-	-	-	-
(Gordini)	15	-	-	-	-	-	-	-
Lance MACKLIN	-	-	**r**	-	-	-	-	-
(HWM)	-	-	15	-	-	-	-	-
Umberto MAGLIOLI	**9**	-	-	-	-	**7**	**3=**	-
(Ferrari)	11	-	-	-	-	11	13	-
Sergio MANTOVANI	-	**7**	-	-	**5**	**5**	**9**	**r**
(Maserati)	-	11	ns	-	15	9	9	10
Robert MANZON	-	-	**3**	**r**	**9**	-	**r**	**r**
(Ferrari)	-	-	12	15	12	ns	15	17
Onofré MARIMON +	**r**	**r**	**r**	**3f=**	-	-	-	-
(Maserati)	6	4	5	28	8ns	-	-	-
Leslie MARR	-	-	-	**13**	-	-	-	-
(Connaught)	-	-	-	22	-	-	-	-
Carlos MENDITÉGUY	-	-	-	-	-	-	-	-
(Maserati)	ns	-	-	-	-	-	-	-
Roberto MIÈRES	**r**	**r**	**r**	**6**	**r**	**4**	**r**	**4**
(Maserati)	8	12	11	32	17	12	10	11
Stirling MOSS	-	**3**	-	**rf=**	**r**	**r**	**10**	**r**
(Maserati)	-	9	-	4	3	3	3	6
Luigi MUSSO	-	-	-	-	-	-	**r**	**2**
(Maserati)	7ns	-	-	-	-	-	14	7
Rodney NUCKEY	-	-	-	-	-	-	-	-
(Cooper-Bristol)	-	-	-	29ns	-	-	-	-
Reg PARNELL	-	-	-	**r**	-	-	-	-
(Ferrari)	-	-	-	14	-	-	-	-
André PILETTE	-	**5**	-	**9**	**r**	-	-	-
(Gordini)	-	8	-	12	20	-	-	-
Jacques POLLET	-	-	**r**	-	-	-	-	**r**
(Gordini)	-	-	18	-	-	-	-	16
John RISELEY-PRICHARD	-	-	-	**r**	-	-	-	-
(Connaught)	-	-	-	21	-	-	-	-
Louis ROSIER	**r**	-	**r**	**r**	**8**	-	**8**	**7**
(Ferrari)	13	-	13	31	18	-	-	-
(Maserati)	-	-	-	-	-	-	20	20

	RA	B	F	GB	D	CH	I	E
Roy SALVADORI	-	-	r	r	-	-	-	-
(Maserati)	-	-	10	7	-	-	-	-
Harry SCHELL	6	-	r	12	7	r	-	r
(Maserati)	10	-	21	16	14	13	-	4
Jacques SWATERS	-	r	-	-	-	8	-	r
(Ferrari)	-	14	-	-	-	16	-	19
Piero TARUFFI	-	-	-	-	6	-	-	-
(Ferrari)	-	-	-	-	13	-	-	-
Leslie THORNE	-	-	-	14	-	-	-	-
(Connaught)	-	-	-	23	-	-	-	-
Maurice TRINTIGNANT	4	2	r	5	3	r	5	r
(Ferrari)	5	6	9	8	7	4	11	8
Luigi VILLORESI	-	-	5	r=	-	-	r	r
(Maserati)	-	-	14	27	10ns	-	6	-
(Lancia)	-	-	-	-	-	-	-	5
Ottorino VOLONTERIO	-	-	-	-	-	-	-	r=
(Maserati)	-	-	-	-	-	-	-	-
Fred WACKER	-	-	-	-	-	r	6	-
(Gordini)	-	-	-	-	-	15	18	-
Ken WHARTON	-	-	r	8	-	6	-	8
(Maserati)	-	-	16	9	22ns	8	-	14
Peter WHITEHEAD	-	-	-	r	-	-	-	-
(Cooper-Alta)	-	-	-	24	-	-	-	-
Bill WHITEHOUSE	-	-	-	r	-	-	-	-
(Connaught)	-	-	-	19	-	-	-	-

1955 RACE RESULTS & GRID POSITIONS

	RA	MC	B	NL	GB	I
Alberto ASCARI +	r	r	-	-	-	-
(Lancia)	2	2	-	-	-	-
Elie BAYOL	r	r	-	-	-	-
(Gordini)	15	16	-	-	-	-
Jean BEHRA	r/r=/6=	3=/r=	r/5=	6	r	4
(Maserati)	4	5	5	6	3	6
Pablo BIRGER	r	-	-	-	-	-
(Gordini)	9	-	-	-	-	-
Jack BRABHAM	-	-	-	-	r	-
(Cooper-Bristol)	-	-	-	-	25	-
Clemar BUCCI	r=	-	-	-	-	-
(Maserati)	20	-	-	-	-	-
Eugenio CASTELLOTTI	r=	2	r	5	r/6=	3
(Lancia)	12	4	1	-	-	-
(Ferrari)	-	-	-	9	10	4
Louis CHIRON	-	6	-	-	-	-
(Lancia)	-	19	-	-	-	-
Johnny CLAES	-	-	-	11	-	-
(Maserati)	-	-	ns	-	-	-
(Ferrari)	-	-	-	16	-	-
Peter COLLINS	-	-	-	-	r	r
(Maserati)	-	-	-	-	24	11
Nano da SILVA RAMOS	-	-	-	8	r	r
(Gordini)	-	-	-	14	18	18
Jack FAIRMAN	-	-	-	-	-	-
(Connaught)	-	-	-	-	21ns	-
Juan Manuel FANGIO	1f	rf	1f	1	2	1
(Mercedes-Benz)	3	1	2	1	2	1
Giuseppe FARINA	3=/2=	4	3	-	-	-
(Ferrari)	5	14	4	-	-	-
(Lancia)	-	-	-	-	-	5ns
John FITCH	-	-	-	-	-	9
(Maserati)	-	-	-	-	-	20
Paul FRÈRE	-	8=	4	-	-	-
(Ferrari)	-	-	8	-	-	-
Froilán GONZÁLEZ	2=	-	-	-	-	-
(Ferrari)	1	-	-	-	-	-
Horace GOULD	-	-	-	r	r	r
(Maserati)	-	-	-	15	22	21
Mike HAWTHORN	-	r	r	7	6=	r
(Vanwall)	-	12	9	-	-	-
(Ferrari)	-	-	-	5	12	14
Hans HERRMANN	4=	-	-	-	-	-
(Mercedes-Benz)	10	ns	-	-	-	-
Jesus IGLESIAS	r	-	-	-	-	-
(Gordini)	17	-	-	-	-	-
Karl KLING	r/4=	-	r	r	3	r
(Mercedes-Benz)	6	-	6	3	4	3
Jean LUCAS	-	-	-	-	-	r
(Gordini)	-	-	-	-	-	22
Lance MACKLIN	-	-	-	-	8	-
(Maserati)	-	nq	-	-	16	-
Umberto MAGLIOLI	3=	-	-	-	-	6
(Ferrari)	-	-	-	-	-	12
Sergio MANTOVANI	r=/7=	-	-	-	-	-
(Maserati)	19	-	-	-	-	-
Robert MANZON	-	r	-	r	r	-
(Gordini)	-	13	-	11	11	-
Leslie MARR	-	-	-	-	r	-
(Connaught)	-	-	-	-	19	-
Ken McALPINE	-	-	-	-	r	-
(Connaught)	-	-	-	-	17	-
Carlos MENDITÉGUY	r/r=	-	-	-	-	5
(Maserati)	13	-	-	-	-	16
Roberto MIÈRES	5	r	5=	4f	r	7
(Maserati)	16	6	13	7	6	7
Stirling MOSS	r/4=	9	2	2	1f	rf
(Mercedes-Benz)	8	3	3	2	1	2
Luigi MUSSO	7=/r=	r	7	3	5	r
(Maserati)	18	8	7	4	9	10
Cesare PERDISA	-	r=/3=	8	-	-	-
(Maserati)	-	11	11	-	-	-
Luigi PIOTTI	-	-	-	-	-	-
(Arzani Volpini-Maserati)	-	-	-	-	-	ns
Jacques POLLET	-	7	-	10	-	r
(Gordini)	-	20	-	12	-	19
Tony ROLT	-	-	-	-	r=	-
(Connaught)	-	-	-	-	14	-
Louis ROSIER	-	r	9	9	-	-
(Maserati)	-	17	12	13	-	-
Roy SALVADORI	-	-	-	-	r	-
(Maserati)	-	-	-	-	20	-
Harry SCHELL	6=/r=/7=	r	-	-	r/9=	r
(Maserati)	7	-	-	-	-	-
(Ferrari)	-	18	-	-	-	-
(Vanwall)	-	-	-	-	7	13
André SIMON	-	r	-	-	r	-
(Mercedes-Benz)	-	10	-	-	-	-
(Maserati)	-	-	-	-	8	-
Mike SPARKEN	-	-	-	-	7	-
(Gordini)	-	-	-	-	23	-
Piero TARUFFI	-	8=	-	-	4	2
(Ferrari)	-	15	-	-	-	-
(Mercedes-Benz)	-	-	-	-	5	9
Maurice TRINTIGNANT	r/2=/3=	1	6	r	r	8
(Ferrari)	14	9	10	8	13	15
Alfredo URIA	r	-	-	-	-	-
(Maserati)	21	-	-	-	-	-
Luigi VILLORESI	r/r=	5	-	-	-	-
(Lancia)	11	7	-	-	-	8ns
Peter WALKER	-	-	-	r	r=	-
(Maserati)	-	-	-	10	-	-
(Connaught)	-	-	-	-	Ø	-
Ken WHARTON	-	-	-	-	9=	r
(Vanwall)	-	-	-	-	15	17
Ted WHITEAWAY	-	-	-	-	-	-
(HWM)	-	nq	-	-	-	-

Ø Took over in a shared drive and was not on the grid

1956 RACE RESULTS & GRID POSITIONS

	RA	MC	B	F	GB	D	I
Elie BAYOL	-	6=	-	-	-	-	-
(Gordini)	-	11	-	-	-	-	-
Jean BEHRA	2	3	7	3	3	3	r/r=
(Maserati)	4	4	4	7	13	8	5
Jo BONNIER	-	-	-	-	-	-	r=
(Maserati)	-	-	-	-	-	-	-
Jack BRABHAM	-	-	-	-	r	-	-
(Maserati)	-	-	-	-	28	-	-
Tony BROOKS	-	-	-	-	r	-	-
(BRM)	-	13ns	-	-	9	-	-
Eugenio CASTELLOTTI	r	r/4=	r	2	10=	r/r=	r/8=
(Lancia Ferrari)	2	3	5	2	8	3	2
Colin CHAPMAN	-	-	-	-	-	-	-
(Vanwall)	-	-	-	5ns	-	-	-
Louis CHIRON	-	-	-	-	-	-	-
(Maserati)	-	ns	-	-	-	-	-
Peter COLLINS	r	2=	1	1	r/2=	r/r=	2=
(Ferrari)	9	-	-	-	-	-	-
(Lancia Ferrari)	-	9	3	3	4	2	7
Nano da SILVA RAMOS	-	5	-	8	r	-	r
(Gordini)	-	14	-	14	26	-	20
Emmanuel de GRAFFENRIED	-	-	-	-	-	-	7
(Maserati)	-	-	-	-	-	-	18
Alfonso de PORTAGO	-	-	-	r	2=/10=	r=	r
(Lancia Ferrari)	-	-	-	9	12	10	9
Paul EMERY	-	-	-	-	r	-	-
(Emeryson-Alta)	-	-	-	-	23	-	-
Jack FAIRMAN	-	-	-	-	4	-	5
(Connaught)	-	-	-	-	21	-	15
Juan Manuel FANGIO	r/1=f	4=/2=f	r	4f	1	1f	8=/2=
(Lancia Ferrari)	1	1	1	1	2	1	1
Ron FLOCKHART	-	-	-	-	r	-	3
(BRM)	-	-	-	-	17	-	-
(Connaught)	-	-	-	-	-	-	23
Paul FRÈRE	-	-	2	-	-	-	-
(Lancia Ferrari)	-	-	8	-	-	-	-
Olivier GENDEBIEN	5	-	-	r	-	-	-
(Ferrari-Lancia)	10	-	-	-	-	-	-
(Lancia Ferrari)	-	-	-	11	-	-	-
Bob GERARD	-	-	-	-	11	-	-
(Cooper-Bristol)	-	-	-	-	22	-	-
Gerino GERINI	4=	-	-	-	-	-	10
(Maserati)	-	-	-	-	-	-	16
Chico GODIA	-	-	r	7	8	4	4
(Maserati)	-	-	13	17	25	16	17
Froilán GONZÁLEZ	r	-	-	-	r	-	-
(Maserati)	5	-	-	-	-	-	-
(Vanwall)	-	-	-	-	6	-	-
Oscar GONZÁLEZ	6=	-	-	-	-	-	-
(Maserati)	-	-	-	-	-	-	-
Horace GOULD	-	8	r	-	5	r	-
(Maserati)	-	16	14	-	14	13	-
Bruce HALFORD	-	-	-	-	r	dq	r
(Maserati)	-	-	-	-	20	11	21
Mike HAWTHORN	3	-	-	10=	r	-	-
(Maserati)	8	-	ns	-	-	-	-
(BRM)	-	10ns	-	-	3	-	-
(Vanwall)	-	-	-	6	-	-	-

	RA	MC	B	F	GB	D	I
Chico LANDI	**4=**	**-**	**-**	**-**	**-**	**-**	**-**
(Maserati)	11	-	-	-	-	-	-
Les LESTON	**-**	**-**	**-**	**-**	**-**	**-**	**r**
(Connaught)	-	-	-	-	-	-	19
Umberto MAGLIOLI	**-**	**-**	**-**	**-**	**r**	**r**	**r=**
(Maserati)	-	-	-	-	24	7	12
Robert MANZON	**-**	**r**	**-**	**9**	**9**	**r**	**r**
(Gordini)	-	12	-	15	18	15	22
Carlos MENDITÉGUY	**r**	**-**	**-**	**-**	**-**	**-**	**-**
(Maserati)	6	-	-	-	-	-	-
André MILHOUX	**-**	**-**	**-**	**-**	**-**	**r**	**-**
(Gordini)	-	-	-	-	-	21	-
Stirling MOSS	**r**	**1**	**r/3=f**	**r/5=**	**rf**	**2**	**1f**
(Maserati)	7	2	2	8	1	4	6
Luigi MUSSO	**1=**	**r**	**-**	**-**	**-**	**r=**	**r**
(Lancia Ferrari)	3	8	-	-	-	5	3
Cesare PERDISA	**-**	**7**	**3=**	**5=**	**7**	**-**	**-**
(Maserati)	-	7	9	13	15	6ns	-
André PILETTE	**-**	**6=**	**6**	**11**	**-**	**-**	**-**
(Gordini)	-	Ø	-	19	-	18ns	-
(Lancia Ferrari)	-	-	15	-	-	-	-
Luigi PIOTTI	**r**	**-**	**-**	**-**	**-**	**-**	**6**
(Maserati)	12	-	-	-	-	ns	14
Louis ROSIER +	**-**	**r**	**8**	**6**	**r**	**5**	**-**
(Maserati)	-	15	10	12	27	14	-
Roy SALVADORI	**-**	**-**	**-**	**-**	**r**	**r**	**11**
(Maserati)	-	-	-	-	7	9	13
Giorgio SCARLATTI	**-**	**-**	**-**	**-**	**-**	**r**	**-**
(Ferrari)	-	nq	-	-	-	17	-
Harry SCHELL	**-**	**r**	**4**	**r/10=**	**r**	**r**	**r**
(Vanwall)	-	5	6	4	5	-	10
(Maserati)	-	-	-	-	-	12	-
Archie SCOTT-BROWN	**-**	**-**	**-**	**-**	**r**	**-**	**-**
(Connaught)	-	-	-	-	10	-	ns
Piero SCOTTI	**-**	**-**	**r**	**-**	**-**	**-**	**-**
(Connaught)	-	-	12	-	-	-	-
André SIMON	**-**	**-**	**-**	**r**	**-**	**-**	**9**
(Maserati)	-	-	-	20	-	-	-
(Gordini)	-	-	-	-	-	-	24
Piero TARUFFI	**-**	**-**	**-**	**r**	**-**	**-**	**r**
(Maserati)	-	-	-	16	-	-	-
(Vanwall)	-	-	-	-	-	-	4
Desmond TITTERINGTON	**-**	**-**	**-**	**-**	**r**	**-**	**-**
(Connaught)	-	-	-	-	11	-	-
Maurice TRINTIGNANT	**-**	**r**	**r**	**r**	**r**	**-**	**r**
(Vanwall)	-	6	7	-	16	-	11
(Bugatti)	-	-	-	18	-	-	-
Alfredo URIA	**6=**	**-**	**-**	**-**	**-**	**-**	**-**
(Maserati)	13	-	-	-	-	-	-
Luigi VILLORESI	**-**	**-**	**5**	**r**	**6**	**r**	**r=**
(Maserati)	-	-	11	10	19	20	8
Ottorino VOLONTERIO	**-**	**-**	**-**	**-**	**-**	**nc**	**-**
(Maserati)	-	-	-	-	-	19	-
Wolfgang von TRIPS	**-**	**-**	**-**	**-**	**-**	**-**	**-**
(Lancia Ferrari)	-	-	-	-	-	-	ns

Ø Took over in a shared drive and was not on the grid

1957 RACE RESULTS & GRID POSITIONS

	RA	MC	F	GB	D	PES	I
Edgar BARTH	**-**	**-**	**-**	**-**	**12**	**-**	**-**
(Porsche)	-	-	-	-	12	-	-
Jean BEHRA	**2**	**-**	**5**	**r**	**6**	**r**	**r**
(Maserati)	3	-	2	2	3	4	5
Jo BONNIER	**7**	**-**	**-**	**r**	**-**	**r**	**r**
(Maserati)	13	-	-	17	-	9	13
Jack BRABHAM	**-**	**6**	**r/7=**	**r**	**r**	**7**	**-**
(Cooper-Climax)	-	15	13	13	18	16	-
Tony BROOKS	**-**	**2**	**-**	**1=/r=**	**9**	**r**	**7f**
(Vanwall)	-	4	-	3	5	6	3
Ivor BUEB	**-**	**r**	**-**	**8**	**-**	**-**	**-**
(Connaught)	-	16	-	-	-	-	-
(Maserati)	-	-	-	19	-	-	-
Eugenio CASTELLOTTI +	**r**	**-**	**-**	**-**	**-**	**-**	**-**
(Lancia Ferrari)	4	-	-	-	-	-	-
Peter COLLINS	**r/6=**	**r**	**3**	**r/4=**	**3**	**-**	**r**
(Lancia Ferrari)	5	2	5	8	4	-	7
Carel Godin de BEAUFORT	**-**	**-**	**-**	**-**	**14**	**-**	**-**
(Porsche)	-	-	-	-	20	-	-
Alfonso de PORTAGO +	**5=**	**-**	**-**	**-**	**-**	**-**	**-**
(Lancia Ferrari)	-	-	-	-	-	-	-
Alessandro de TOMASO	**9**	**-**	**-**	**-**	**-**	**-**	**-**
(Ferrari)	12	-	-	-	-	-	-
Paul ENGLAND	**-**	**-**	**-**	**-**	**r**	**-**	**-**
(Cooper-Climax)	-	-	-	-	23	-	-
Jack FAIRMAN	**-**	**-**	**-**	**r**	**-**	**-**	**-**
(BRM)	-	-	-	16	-	-	-
Juan Manuel FANGIO	**1**	**1f**	**1**	**r**	**1f**	**2**	**2**
(Maserati)	2	1	1	4	1	1	4
Ron FLOCKHART	**-**	**r**	**r**	**-**	**-**	**-**	**-**
(BRM)	-	11	11	-	-	-	-
Bob GERARD	**-**	**-**	**-**	**6**	**-**	**-**	**-**
(Cooper-Bristol)	-	-	-	18	-	-	-
Dick GIBSON	**-**	**-**	**-**	**-**	**r**	**-**	**-**
(Cooper-Climax)	-	-	-	-	24	-	-
Chico GODIA	**-**	**-**	**-**	**-**	**r**	**r**	**9**
(Maserati)	-	-	-	-	21	12	15
Froilán GONZÁLEZ	**5=**	**-**	**-**	**-**	**-**	**-**	**-**
(Lancia Ferrari)	10	-	-	-	-	-	-
Horace GOULD	**-**	**r**	**r**	**-**	**r**	**r**	**10**
(Maserati)	-	12	14	14ns	19	11	18
Masten GREGORY	**-**	**3**	**-**	**-**	**8**	**4**	**4**
(Maserati)	-	10	-	-	10	7	11
Bruce HALFORD	**-**	**-**	**-**	**-**	**11**	**r**	**r**
(Maserati)	-	-	-	-	16	14	14
Mike HAWTHORN	**r**	**r/7r=**	**4**	**3**	**2**	**-**	**6**
(Lancia Ferrari)	7	5	7	5	2	-	10
Hans HERRMANN	**-**	**-**	**-**	**-**	**r**	**-**	**-**
(Maserati)	-	nq	-	-	11	-	-
Les LESTON	**-**	**-**	**-**	**r**	**-**	**-**	**-**
(Cooper-Climax)	-	nq	-	-	-	-	-
(BRM)	-	-	-	12	-	-	-
Stuart LEWIS-EVANS	**-**	**4**	**r**	**7**	**r**	**5**	**r**
(Connaught)	-	13	-	-	-	-	-
(Vanwall)	-	-	10	6	9	8	1
Mike MacDOWEL	**-**	**-**	**7=**	**-**	**-**	**-**	**-**
(Cooper-Climax)	-	-	15	-	-	-	-
Herbert MacKAY-FRASER +	**-**	**-**	**r**	**-**	**-**	**-**	**-**
(BRM)	-	-	12	-	-	-	-
Umberto MAGLIOLI	**-**	**-**	**-**	**-**	**r**	**-**	**-**
(Porsche)	-	-	-	-	15	-	-
Tony MARSH	**-**	**-**	**-**	**-**	**15**	**-**	**-**
(Cooper-Climax)	-	-	-	-	22	-	-
Carlos MENDITÉGUY	**3**	**r**	**r**	**r**	**-**	**-**	**-**
(Maserati)	8	7	9	11	-	-	-
Stirling MOSS	**8f**	**r**	**-**	**r=/1=f**	**5**	**1f**	**1**
(Maserati)	1	-	-	-	-	-	-
(Vanwall)	-	3	-	1	7	2	2
Luigi MUSSO	**r**	**-**	**2f**	**2**	**4**	**r**	**8**
(Lancia-Ferrari)	6	-	3	10	8	3	9
Brian NAYLOR	**-**	**-**	**-**	**-**	**13**	**-**	**-**
(Cooper-Climax)	-	-	-	-	17	-	-
Cesare PERDISA	**6=**	**-**	**-**	**-**	**-**	**-**	**-**
(Lancia-Ferrari)	11	-	-	-	-	-	-
Luigi PIOTTI	**10**	**-**	**-**	**-**	**-**	**r**	**r**
(Maserati)	14	nq	-	-	-	13	17
Roy SALVADORI	**-**	**-**	**r**	**5**	**r**	**r**	**-**
(BRM)	-	nq	-	-	-	-	-
(Vanwall)	-	-	6	-	-	-	-
(Cooper-Climax)	-	-	-	15	14	15	-
Giorgio SCARLATTI	**-**	**r=**	**-**	**-**	**10**	**6**	**5=**
(Maserati)	-	14	-	-	13	10	12
Harry SCHELL	**4**	**r/r=**	**6**	**r**	**7**	**3**	**r/5=**
(Maserati)	9	8	4	7	6	5	6
André SIMON	**-**	**-**	**-**	**-**	**-**	**-**	**11=**
(Maserati)	-	nq	-	-	-	-	16
Maurice TRINTIGNANT	**-**	**5**	**r**	**4=**	**-**	**-**	**-**
(Lancia-Ferrari)	-	6	8	9	-	-	-
Ottorino VOLONTERIO	**-**	**-**	**-**	**-**	**-**	**-**	**11=**
(Maserati)	-	-	-	-	-	-	-
Wolfgang von TRIPS	**6=**	**7r=**	**-**	**-**	**-**	**-**	**3**
(Lancia-Ferrari)	-	9	-	-	-	-	8

1958 RACE RESULTS & GRID POSITIONS

	RA	MC	NL	B	F	GB	D	P	I	MA
Cliff ALLISON	**-**	**6**	**6**	**4**	**r**	**r**	**10**	**r**	**7**	**10**
(Lotus-Climax)	-	13	11	12	20	5	24	-	16	16
(Maserati)	-	-	-	-	-	-	-	13	-	-
Edgar BARTH	**-**	**-**	**-**	**-**	**-**	**-**	**6**	**-**	**-**	**-**
(Porsche)	-	-	-	-	-	-	13	-	-	-
Jean BEHRA	**5**	**r**	**3**	**r**	**r**	**r**	**r**	**4**	**r**	**r**
(Maserati)	4	-	-	-	-	-	-	-	-	-
(BRM)	-	2	4	10	9	8	9	4	8	4
Jo BONNIER	**-**	**r**	**10**	**9**	**8**	**r**	**r**	**r**	**r**	**4**
(Maserati)	-	16	15	14	16	13	21	14	-	-
(BRM)	-	-	-	-	-	-	-	-	10	8
Jack BRABHAM	**-**	**4**	**8**	**r**	**6**	**6**	**r**	**7**	**r**	**11**
(Cooper-Climax)	-	3	5	8	12	10	19	8	15	19
Tom BRIDGER	**-**	**-**	**-**	**-**	**-**	**-**	**-**	**-**	**-**	**r**
(Cooper-Climax)	-	-	-	-	-	-	-	-	-	22
Tony BROOKS	**-**	**r**	**r**	**1**	**r/r=**	**7**	**1**	**r**	**1**	**r**
(Vanwall)	-	1	3	5	5	9	2	5	2	7
Ivor BUEB	**-**	**-**	**-**	**-**	**-**	**r**	**11**	**-**	**-**	**-**
(Connaught)	-	-	-	-	-	17	-	-	-	-
(Lotus-Climax)	-	-	-	-	-	-	16	-	-	-

	RA	MC	NL	B	F	GB	D	P	I	MA
Ian BURGESS	**-**	**-**	**-**	**-**	**-**	**r**	**7**	**-**	**-**	**-**
(Cooper-Climax)	-	-	-	-	-	16	11	-	-	-
Giulio CABIANCA	**-**	**-**	**-**	**-**	**-**	**-**	**-**	**-**	**r**	**-**
(OSCA)	-	nq	-	-	-	-	-	-	-	-
(Maserati)	-	-	-	-	-	-	-	-	20	-
Louis CHIRON	**-**	**-**	**-**	**-**	**-**	**-**	**-**	**-**	**-**	**-**
(Maserati)	-	nq	-	-	-	-	-	-	-	-
Peter COLLINS +	**r**	**3**	**r**	**r**	**5**	**1**	**r**	**-**	**-**	**-**
(Ferrari)	3	9	10	4	4	6	4	-	-	-
Carel Godin de BEAUFORT	**-**	**-**	**11**	**-**	**-**	**-**	**r**	**-**	**-**	**-**
(Porsche)	-	-	17	-	-	-	15	-	-	-
Maria Teresa de FILIPPIS	**-**	**-**	**-**	**10**	**-**	**-**	**-**	**r**	**r**	**-**
(Maserati)	-	nq	-	19	-	-	-	15	21	-
Bernie ECCLESTONE	**-**	**-**	**-**	**-**	**-**	**-**	**-**	**-**	**-**	**-**
(Connaught)	-	nq	-	-	-	-	-	-	-	-
Paul EMERY	**-**	**-**	**-**	**-**	**-**	**-**	**-**	**-**	**-**	**-**
(Connaught)	-	nq	-	-	-	-	-	-	-	-
Jack FAIRMAN	**-**	**-**	**-**	**-**	**-**	**r**	**-**	**-**	**-**	**8**
(Connaught)	-	-	-	-	-	19	-	-	-	-
(Cooper-Climax)	-	-	-	-	-	-	-	-	-	11
Juan Manuel FANGIO	**4f**	**-**	**-**	**-**	**4**	**-**	**-**	**-**	**-**	**-**
(Maserati)	1	-	-	-	8	-	-	-	-	-
Ron FLOCKHART	**-**	**-**	**-**	**-**	**-**	**-**	**-**	**-**	**-**	**r**
(Cooper-Climax)	-	nq	-	-	-	-	-	-	-	-
(BRM)	-	-	-	-	-	-	-	-	-	15
Olivier GENDEBIEN	**-**	**-**	**-**	**6**	**-**	**-**	**-**	**-**	**r**	**r**
(Ferrari)	-	-	-	6	-	-	-	-	5	6
Gerino GERINI	**-**	**-**	**-**	**-**	**9**	**r**	**-**	**-**	**r**	**12**
(Maserati)	-	nq	-	-	15	18	-	-	19	17
Dick GIBSON	**-**	**-**	**-**	**-**	**-**	**-**	**r**	**-**	**-**	**-**
(Cooper-Climax)	-	-	-	-	-	-	18	-	-	-
Chico GODIA	**8**	**-**	**-**	**r**	**r**	**-**	**-**	**-**	**-**	**-**
(Maserati)	9	nq	-	18	11	-	-	-	-	-
Christian GOETHALS	**-**	**-**	**-**	**-**	**-**	**-**	**r**	**-**	**-**	**-**
(Cooper-Climax)	-	-	-	-	-	-	23	-	-	-
Horace GOULD	**9**	**-**	**-**	**-**	**-**	**-**	**-**	**-**	**-**	**-**
(Maserati)	10	nq	ns	-	-	-	-	-	-	-
Masten GREGORY	**-**	**-**	**r**	**r**	**-**	**-**	**-**	**-**	**4=**	**6**
(Maserati)	-	-	14	9	-	-	-	-	11	13
André GUELFI	**-**	**-**	**-**	**-**	**-**	**-**	**-**	**-**	**-**	**15**
(Cooper-Climax)	-	-	-	-	-	-	-	-	-	25
Mike HAWTHORN	**3**	**rf**	**5**	**2f**	**1f**	**2f**	**r**	**2f**	**2**	**2**
(Ferrari)	2	6	6	1	1	4	1	2	3	1
Hans HERRMANN	**-**	**-**	**-**	**-**	**-**	**-**	**r**	**-**	**r**	**9**
(Maserati)	-	-	-	-	-	-	20	-	18	18
Graham HILL	**-**	**r**	**r**	**r**	**r**	**r**	**r**	**r**	**6**	**16**
(Lotus-Climax)	-	15	13	15	19	14	22	12	12	12
Phil HILL	**-**	**-**	**-**	**-**	**7**	**-**	**9**	**-**	**3f**	**3**
(Maserati)	-	-	-	-	13	-	-	-	-	-
(Ferrari)	-	-	-	-	-	-	10	-	7	5
Ken KAVANAGH	**-**	**-**	**-**	**-**	**-**	**-**	**-**	**-**	**-**	**-**
(Maserati)	-	nq	-	ns	-	-	-	-	-	-
Bruce KESSLER	**-**	**-**	**-**	**-**	**-**	**-**	**-**	**-**	**-**	**-**
(Connaught)	-	nq	-	-	-	-	-	-	-	-
Robert La CAZE	**-**	**-**	**-**	**-**	**-**	**-**	**-**	**-**	**-**	**14**
(Cooper-Climax)	-	-	-	-	-	-	-	-	-	23
Stuart LEWIS-EVANS +	**-**	**r**	**r**	**3**	**r=**	**4**	**-**	**3**	**r**	**r**
(Vanwall)	-	7	1	11	10	7	-	3	4	3
Tony MARSH	**-**	**-**	**-**	**-**	**-**	**-**	**8**	**-**	**-**	**-**
(Cooper-Climax)	-	-	-	-	-	-	14	-	-	-
Bruce McLAREN	**-**	**-**	**-**	**-**	**-**	**-**	**5**	**-**	**-**	**13**
(Cooper-Climax)	-	-	-	-	-	-	12	-	-	21
Carlos MENDITÉGUY	**7**	**-**	**-**	**-**	**-**	**-**	**-**	**-**	**-**	**-**
(Maserati)	6	-	-	-	-	-	-	-	-	-
Stirling MOSS	**1**	**r**	**1f**	**r**	**2**	**r**	**rf**	**1**	**r**	**1f**
(Cooper-Climax)	7	-	-	-	-	-	-	-	-	-
(Vanwall)	-	8	2	3	6	1	3	1	1	2
Luigi MUSSO +	**2**	**2**	**7**	**r**	**r**	**-**	**-**	**-**	**-**	**-**
(Ferrari)	5	10	12	2	2	-	-	-	-	-
Brian NAYLOR	**-**	**-**	**-**	**-**	**-**	**-**	**r**	**-**	**-**	**-**
(Cooper-Climax)	-	-	-	-	-	-	25	-	-	-
François PICARD	**-**	**-**	**-**	**-**	**-**	**-**	**-**	**-**	**-**	**r**
(Cooper-Climax)	-	-	-	-	-	-	-	-	-	24
Luigi PIOTTI	**-**	**-**	**-**	**-**	**-**	**-**	**-**	**-**	**-**	**-**
(OSCA)	-	nq	-	-	-	-	-	-	-	-
Troy RUTTMAN	**-**	**-**	**-**	**-**	**10**	**-**	**-**	**-**	**-**	**-**
(Maserati)	-	-	-	-	18	-	ns	-	-	-
Roy SALVADORI	**-**	**r**	**4**	**8**	**11**	**3**	**2**	**9**	**5**	**7**
(Cooper-Climax)	-	4	9	13	14	3	6	11	14	14
Giorgio SCARLATTI	**-**	**r**	**r**	**-**	**-**	**-**	**-**	**-**	**-**	**-**
(Maserati)	-	14	16	-	-	-	-	-	-	-
Harry SCHELL	**6**	**5**	**2**	**5**	**r**	**5**	**r**	**6**	**r**	**5**
(Maserati)	8	-	-	-	-	-	-	-	-	-
(BRM)	-	12	7	7	3	2	8	7	9	10
Wolfgang SEIDEL	**-**	**-**	**-**	**r**	**-**	**-**	**r**	**-**	**-**	**r**
(Maserati)	-	-	-	17	-	-	-	-	-	20
(Cooper-Climax)	-	-	-	-	-	-	17	-	-	-
Carroll SHELBY	**-**	**-**	**-**	**-**	**r**	**9**	**-**	**r**	**r/4=**	**-**
(Maserati)	-	-	-	-	17	15	-	10	17	-
Alan STACEY	**-**	**-**	**-**	**-**	**-**	**r**	**-**	**-**	**-**	**-**
(Lotus-Climax)	-	-	-	-	-	20	-	-	-	-
Luigi TARAMAZZO	**-**	**-**	**-**	**-**	**-**	**-**	**-**	**-**	**-**	**-**
(Maserati)	-	nq	-	-	-	-	-	-	-	-
André TESTUT	**-**	**-**	**-**	**-**	**-**	**-**	**-**	**-**	**-**	**-**
(Maserati)	-	nq	-	-	-	-	-	-	-	-
Maurice TRINTIGNANT	**-**	**1**	**9**	**7**	**r**	**8**	**3**	**8**	**r**	**r**
(Cooper-Climax)	-	5	8	-	-	12	7	9	13	9
(Maserati)	-	-	-	16	-	-	-	-	-	-
(BRM)	-	-	-	-	7	-	-	-	-	-
Wolfgang von TRIPS	**-**	**r**	**-**	**-**	**3**	**r**	**4**	**5**	**r**	**-**
(Ferrari)	-	11	-	-	21	11	5	6	6	-

1959 RACE RESULTS & GRID POSITIONS

	MC	NL	F	GB	D	P	I	USA
Cliff ALLISON	**r**	**9**	-	-	**r**	-	**5**	**r**
(Ferrari)	15	15	-	-	14	-	8	7
Peter ASHDOWN	-	-	-	**12**	-	-	-	-
(Cooper-Climax)	-	-	-	23	-	-	-	-
Astrubel BAYARDO	-	-	-	-	-	-	-	-
(Maserati)	-	-	nq	-	-	-	-	-
Jean BEHRA +	**r**	**5**	**r**	-	-	-	-	-
(Ferrari)	2	4	5	-	-	-	-	-
(Behra Porsche)	-	-	-	-	ns	-	-	-
Lucien BIANCHI	-	-	-	-	-	-	-	-
(Cooper-Climax)	nq	-	-	-	-	-	-	-
Harry BLANCHARD	-	-	-	-	-	-	-	**7**
(Porsche)	-	-	-	-	-	-	-	16
Jo BONNIER	**r**	**1**	**r**	**r**	**5**	**r**	**8**	-
(BRM)	7	1	6	10	7	5	11	-
Jack BRABHAM	**1f**	**2**	**3**	**1**	**r**	**r**	**3**	**4**
(Cooper-Climax)	3	2	2	1	4	2	3	2
Chris BRISTOW	-	-	-	**10**	-	-	-	-
(Cooper-Borgward)	-	-	-	16	-	-	-	-
Tony BROOKS	**2**	**r**	**1**	**r**	**1f**	**9**	**r**	**3**
(Ferrari)	4	8	1	-	1	10	2	4
(Vanwall)	-	-	-	17	-	-	-	-
Ivor BUEB +	-	-	-	**13**	-	-	-	-
(Cooper-Climax)	nq	-	-	-	-	-	-	-
(Cooper-Borgward)	-	-	-	18	-	-	-	-
Ian BURGESS	-	-	**r**	**r**	**6**	-	**14**	-
(Cooper-Maserati)	-	-	19	13	15	-	16	-
Giulio CABIANCA	-	-	-	-	-	-	**15**	-
(Maserati)	-	-	-	-	-	-	21	-
Phil CADE	-	-	-	-	-	-	-	-
(Maserati)	-	-	-	-	-	-	-	18ns
George CONSTANTINE	-	-	-	-	-	-	-	**r**
(Cooper-Climax)	-	-	-	-	-	-	-	15
Fritz d'OREY	-	-	**10**	**r**	-	-	-	**r**
(Maserati)	-	-	18	20	-	-	-	-
(Tec Mec)	-	-	-	-	-	-	-	17
Colin DAVIS	-	-	**r**	-	-	-	**11**	-
(Cooper-Maserati)	-	-	17	-	-	-	18	-
Carel Godin de BEAUFORT	-	**10**	**9**	-	-	-	-	-
(Porsche)	-	14	-	-	-	-	-	-
(Maserati)	-	-	20	-	-	-	-	-
Mario de CABRAL	-	-	-	-	-	**10**	-	-
(Cooper-Maserati)	-	-	-	-	-	14	-	-
Alain de CHANGY	-	-	-	-	-	-	-	-
(Cooper-Climax)	nq	-	-	-	-	-	-	-
Maria Teresa de FILIPPIS	-	-	-	-	-	-	-	-
(Behra Porsche)	nq	-	-	-	-	-	-	-
Alessandro de TOMASO	-	-	-	-	-	-	-	**r**
(Cooper-OSCA)	-	-	-	-	-	-	-	14
Jack FAIRMAN	-	-	-	**r**	-	-	**r**	-
(Cooper-Climax)	-	-	-	15	-	-	-	-
(Cooper-Maserati)	-	-	-	-	-	-	20	-
Ron FLOCKHART	**r**	-	**6**	**r**	-	**7**	**13**	-
(BRM)	10	-	13	11	-	11	15	-
Olivier GENDEBIEN	-	-	**4**	-	-	-	**6**	-
(Ferrari)	-	-	11	-	-	-	6	-
Keith GREENE	-	-	-	-	-	-	-	-
(Cooper-Climax)	-	-	-	nq	-	-	-	-
Masten GREGORY	**r**	**3**	**r**	**7**	**r**	**2**	-	-
(Cooper-Climax)	11	7	7	5	5	3	-	-
Dan GURNEY	-	-	**r**	-	**2**	**3**	**4**	-
(Ferrari)	-	-	12	-	3	6	4	-
Bruce HALFORD	**r**	-	-	-	-	-	-	-
(Lotus-Climax)	16	-	-	-	-	-	-	-
Hans HERRMANN	-	-	-	**r**	**r**	-	-	-
(Cooper-Maserati)	-	-	-	19	-	-	-	-
(BRM)	-	-	-	-	11	-	-	-
Graham HILL	**r**	**7**	**r**	**9**	**r**	**r**	**r**	-
(Lotus-Climax)	14	5	14	9	10	15	10	-
Phil HILL	**4**	**6**	**2**	-	**3**	**r**	**2f**	**r**
(Ferrari)	5	12	3	-	6	7	5	8
Innes IRELAND	-	**4**	**r**	-	**r**	**r**	**r**	**5**
(Lotus-Climax)	-	9	15	ns	13	16	14	9
Pete LOVELY	-	-	-	-	-	-	-	-
(Lotus-Climax)	nq	-	-	-	-	-	-	-
Jean LUCIENBONNET	-	-	-	-	-	-	-	-
(Cooper-Climax)	nq	-	-	-	-	-	-	-
Bruce McLAREN	**5**	-	**5**	**3f=**	**r**	**r**	**r**	**1**
(Cooper-Climax)	13	-	10	8	9	8	9	10
Bill MOSS	-	-	-	-	-	-	-	-
(Cooper-Climax)	-	-	-	nq	-	-	-	-
Stirling MOSS	**r**	**rf**	**dqf**	**2f=**	**r**	**1f**	**1**	**r**
(Cooper-Climax)	1	3	-	-	2	1	1	1
(BRM)	-	-	4	7	-	-	-	-
Brian NAYLOR	-	-	-	**r**	-	-	-	-
(JBW-Maserati)	-	-	-	14	-	-	-	-
Mike PARKES	-	-	-	-	-	-	-	-
(Fry-Climax)	-	-	-	nq	-	-	-	-
Tim PARNELL	-	-	-	-	-	-	-	-
(Cooper-Climax)	-	-	-	nq	-	-	-	-
David PIPER	-	-	-	**r**	-	-	-	-
(Lotus-Climax)	-	-	-	22	-	-	-	-
Bob SAID	-	-	-	-	-	-	-	**r**
(Connaught)	-	-	-	-	-	-	-	13
Roy SALVADORI	**6r**	**r**	**r**	**6**	-	**6**	**r**	**r**
(Cooper-Maserati)	8	-	16	-	-	-	-	11
(Aston Martin)	-	13	-	2	-	12	17	-
Giorgio SCARLATTI	-	-	**8**	-	-	-	**12**	-
(Maserati) nq	-	21	-	-	-	-	-	
(Cooper-Climax)	-	-	-	-	-	-	12	-
Harry SCHELL	**r**	**r**	**7**	**4**	**7r**	**5**	**7**	**r**
(BRM)	9	6	9	3	8	9	7	-
(Cooper-Climax)	-	-	-	-	-	-	-	3
Carroll SHELBY	-	**r**	-	**r**	-	**8**	**10**	-
(Aston Martin)	-	10	-	6	-	13	19	-
Alan STACEY	-	-	-	**8**	-	-	-	**r**
(Lotus-Climax)	-	-	-	12	-	-	-	12
Dennis TAYLOR	-	-	-	-	-	-	-	-
(Lotus-Climax)	-	-	-	nq	-	-	-	-
Henry TAYLOR	-	-	-	**11**	-	-	-	-
(Cooper-Climax)	-	-	-	21	-	-	-	-
Mike TAYLOR	-	-	-	**r**	-	-	-	-
(Cooper-Climax)	-	-	-	24	-	-	-	-
Trevor TAYLOR	-	-	-	-	-	-	-	-
(Cooper-Climax)	-	-	-	nq	-	-	-	-
André TESTUT	-	-	-	-	-	-	-	-
(Maserati) nq	-	-	-	-	-	-	-	
Maurice TRINTIGNANT	**3**	**8**	**11**	**5**	**4**	**4**	**9**	**2f**
(Cooper-Climax)	6	11	8	4	12	4	13	5
Wolfgang von TRIPS	**r**	-	-	-	-	-	-	**6**
(Porsche)	12	-	-	-	ns	-	-	-
(Ferrari)	-	-	-	-	-	-	-	6
Rodger WARD	-	-	-	-	-	-	-	**r**
(Kurtis Kraft-Offenhauser)	-	-	-	-	-	-	-	19

1960 RACE RESULTS & GRID POSITIONS

	RA	MC	NL	B	F	GB	P	I	USA
Cliff ALLISON	**2**	-	-	-	-	-	-	-	-
(Ferrari)	7	nq	-	-	-	-	-	-	-
Edgar BARTH	-	-	-	-	-	-	-	**7**	-
(Porsche)	-	-	-	-	-	-	-	12	-
Lucien BIANCHI	-	-	-	**6**	**r**	**r**	-	-	-
(Cooper-Climax)	-	-	-	14	15	17	-	-	-
Jo BONNIER	**7**	**5**	**r**	**r**	**r**	**r**	**r**	-	**5**
(BRM)	4	5	4	6	10	4	13	-	4
Roberto BONOMI	**11**	-	-	-	-	-	-	-	-
(Cooper-Maserati)	17	-	-	-	-	-	-	-	-
Jack BRABHAM	**r**	**dq**	**1**	**1f=**	**1f**	**1**	**1**	-	**4f**
(Cooper-Climax)	10	2	2	1	1	1	3	-	2
Chris BRISTOW +	-	**r**	**r**	**r**	-	-	-	-	-
(Cooper-Climax)	-	4	7	8	-	-	-	-	-
Tony BROOKS	-	**4**	**r**	**r**	**r**	**5**	**5**	-	**r**
(Cooper-Climax)	-	3	10	2	-	9	12	-	9
(Vanwall)	-	-	-	-	14	-	-	-	-
Ian BURGESS	-	-	-	-	**10**	**r**	-	-	**r**
(Cooper-Climax)	-	nq	-	-	-	-	-	-	-
(Cooper-Maserati)	-	-	-	-	20	20	-	-	23
Giulio CABIANCA	-	-	-	-	-	-	-	**4**	-
(Cooper-Castellotti)	-	-	-	-	-	-	-	4	-
Ettore CHIMERI +	**r**	-	-	-	-	-	-	-	-
(Maserati)	21	-	-	-	-	-	-	-	-
Jim CLARK	-	-	**r**	**5**	**5**	**16**	**3**	-	**16**
(Lotus-Climax)	-	-	11	9	12	8	8	-	5
Antonio CREUS	**r**	-	-	-	-	-	-	-	-
(Maserati)	22	-	-	-	-	-	-	-	-
Chuck DAIGH	-	-	-	**r**	-	**r**	-	-	**10**
(Scarab)	-	nq	ns	17	ns	-	-	-	18
(Cooper-Climax)	-	-	-	-	-	19	-	-	-
Carel Godin de BEAUFORT	-	-	**8**	-	-	-	-	-	-
(Cooper-Climax)	-	-	17	-	-	-	-	-	-
Mario de CABRAL	-	-	-	-	-	-	**r**	-	-
(Cooper-Maserati)	-	-	-	-	-	-	15	-	-
Bob DRAKE	-	-	-	-	-	-	-	-	**13**
(Maserati)	-	-	-	-	-	-	-	-	22
Piero DROGO	-	-	-	-	-	-	-	**8**	-
(Cooper-Climax)	-	-	-	-	-	-	-	15	-

	RA	MC	NL	B	F	GB	P	I	USA
Nasif ESTEFANO	14	-	-	-	-	-	-	-	-
(Maserati)	20	-	-	-	-	-	-	-	-
Jack FAIRMAN	-	-	-	-	-	r	-	-	-
(Cooper-Climax)	-	-	-	-	-	15	-	-	-
Ron FLOCKHART	-	-	-	-	6	-	-	-	r
(Lotus-Climax)	-	-	-	-	8	-	-	-	-
(Cooper-Climax)	-	-	-	-	-	-	-	-	21
Fred GAMBLE	-	-	-	-	-	-	-	10	-
(Behra Porsche)	-	-	-	-	-	-	-	14	-
Olivier GENDEBIEN	-	-	-	3	2	9	7	-	12
(Cooper-Climax)	-	-	-	4	11	12	14	-	8
Richie GINTHER	-	6	6	-	-	-	-	2	-
(Ferrari)	-	9	12	-	-	-	-	2	-
(Scarab)	-	-	-	-	ns	-	-	-	-
Froilán GONZÀLEZ	10	-	-	-	-	-	-	-	-
(Ferrari)	11	-	-	-	-	-	-	-	-
Horace GOULD	-	-	-	-	-	-	-	-	-
(Maserati)	-	-	-	-	-	-	-	ns	-
Keith GREENE	-	-	-	-	-	r	-	-	-
(Cooper-Maserati)	-	-	-	-	-	22	-	-	-
Masten GREGORY	12	-	-	-	9	14	r	-	-
(Behra Porsche)	16	-	-	-	-	-	-	-	-
(Cooper-Maserati)	-	nq	ns	-	17	14	11	-	-
Dan GURNEY	-	r	r	r	r	10	r	-	r
(BRM)	-	14	6	11	7	6	2	-	3
Bruce HALFORD	-	-	-	-	8r	-	-	-	-
(Cooper-Climax)	-	nq	-	-	16	-	-	-	-
Jim HALL	-	-	-	-	-	-	-	-	7
(Lotus-Climax)	-	-	-	-	-	-	-	-	12
Hans HERRMANN	-	-	-	-	-	-	-	6	-
(Porsche)	-	-	-	-	-	-	-	10	-
Graham HILL	r	7r	3	r	r	rf	r	-	r
(BRM)	3	6	5	5	3	2	5	-	11
Phil HILL	8	3	r	4f=	12r	7	r	1f	6
(Ferrari)	6	10	13	3	2	10	10	1	-
(Cooper-Climax)	-	-	-	-	-	-	-	-	13
Innes IRELAND	6	9	2	rf=	7	3	6	-	2
(Lotus-Climax)	2	7	3	7	4	5	7	-	7
Rodriguez LARRETA	9	-	-	-	-	-	-	-	-
(Lotus-Climax)	15	-	-	-	-	-	-	-	-
Pete LOVELY	-	-	-	-	-	-	-	-	11
(Cooper-Castellotti)	-	-	-	-	-	-	-	-	20
Willy MAIRESSE	-	-	-	r	r	-	-	3	-
(Ferrari)	-	-	-	12	5	-	-	3	-
Bruce McLAREN	1	2f	r	2	3	4	2	-	3
(Cooper-Climax)	13	11	9	13	9	3	6	-	10
Carlos MENDITÉGUY	4	-	-	-	-	-	-	-	-
(Cooper-Maserati)	12	-	-	-	-	-	-	-	-
Stirling MOSS	r/3=f	1	4f	-	-	-	dq	-	1
(Cooper-Climax)	1	-	-	-	-	-	-	-	-
(Lotus-Climax)	-	1	1	ns	-	-	4	-	1
Gino MUNARON	13	-	-	-	r	15	-	r	-
(Maserati)	19	-	-	-	-	-	-	-	-
(Cooper-Castellotti)	-	nq	-	-	19	24	-	8	-
Brian NAYLOR	-	-	-	-	-	13	-	r	r
(JBW-Maserati)	-	nq	-	-	-	18	-	7	17
Arthur OWEN	-	-	-	-	-	-	-	r	-
(Cooper-Climax)	-	-	-	-	-	-	-	11	-
David PIPER	-	-	-	-	-	12	-	-	-
(Lotus-Climax)	-	-	-	-	ns	23	-	-	-
Lance REVENTLOW	-	-	-	r	-	-	-	-	-
(Scarab)	-	nq	ns	15	-	-	-	-	-
(Cooper-Climax)	-	-	-	-	-	ns	-	-	-
Roy SALVADORI	-	r	-	-	-	r	-	-	8
(Cooper-Climax)	-	12	-	-	-	-	-	-	15
(Aston Martin)	-	-	ns	-	-	13	-	-	-
Giorgio SCARLATTI	r	-	-	-	-	-	-	r	-
(Maserati)	18	-	-	-	-	-	-	-	-
(Cooper-Castellotti)	-	nq	-	-	-	-	-	-	-
(Cooper-Maserati)	-	-	-	-	-	-	-	5	-
Harry SCHELL +	r	-	-	-	-	-	-	-	-
(Cooper-Climax)	9	-	-	-	-	-	-	-	-
Wolfgang SEIDEL	-	-	-	-	-	-	-	9	-
(Cooper-Climax)	-	-	-	-	-	-	-	13	-
Alan STACEY +	r	r	r	r	-	-	-	-	-
(Lotus-Climax)	14	13	8	16	-	-	-	-	-
John SURTEES	-	r	-	-	-	2	rf	-	r
(Lotus-Climax)	-	15	-	-	-	11	1	-	6
Henry TAYLOR	-	-	7	-	4	8	-	-	14
(Cooper-Climax)	-	-	14	-	13	16	ns	-	14
Mike TAYLOR	-	-	-	-	-	-	-	-	-
(Lotus-Climax)	-	-	-	ns	-	-	-	-	-
Alfonse THIELE	-	-	-	-	-	-	-	r	-
(Cooper-Maserati)	-	-	-	-	-	-	-	9	-
Maurice TRINTIGNANT	3=	r	r	-	r	11	-	-	15
(Cooper-Climax)	8	-	-	-	-	-	-	-	-
(Cooper-Maserati)	-	16	16	-	18	-	-	-	19
(Aston Martin)	-	-	-	-	-	21	-	-	-
Wolfgang von TRIPS	5	8r	5	r	11r	6	4	5	9
(Ferrari)	5	8	15	10	6	7	9	6	-
(Cooper-Maserati)	-	-	-	-	-	-	-	-	16
Vic WILSON	-	-	-	-	-	-	-	r	-
(Cooper-Climax)	-	-	-	-	-	-	-	16	-

1961 RACE RESULTS & GRID POSITIONS

	MC	NL	B	F	GB	D	I	USA
Cliff ALLISON	8	-	-	-	-	-	-	-
(Lotus-Climax)	14	-	ns	-	-	-	-	-
Gerry ASHMORE	-	-	-	-	r	16	r	-
(Lotus-Climax)	-	-	-	-	26	25	25	-
Giancarlo BAGHETTI	-	-	-	1	r	-	rf	-
(Ferrari)	-	-	-	12	19	-	6	-
Lorenzo BANDINI	-	-	r	-	12	r	8	-
(Cooper-Maserati)	-	-	17	-	21	19	21	-
Lucien BIANCHI	-	-	r	r	r	-	-	-
(Emeryson-Maserati)	nq	-	-	-	-	-	-	-
(Lotus-Climax)	-	-	21	19	30	-	-	-
Jo BONNIER	12r	11	7	7	5	r	r	6
(Porsche)	9	11	9	13	3	4	8	10

	MC	NL	B	F	GB	D	I	USA
Juan-Manuel BORDEU	**-**	**-**	**-**	**-**	**-**	**-**	**-**	**-**
(Lotus-Climax)	-	-	-	ns	-	-	-	-
Jack BRABHAM	**r**	**6**	**r**	**r**	**4**	**r**	**r**	**rf**
(Cooper-Climax)	16	7	11	14	9	2	10	1
Tony BROOKS	**13r**	**9**	**13**	**r**	**9f**	**r**	**5**	**3**
(BRM-Climax)	8	8	7	11	6	9	13	6
Ian BURGESS	**-**	**-**	**-**	**14**	**14**	**12**	**-**	**-**
(Lotus-Climax)	-	ns	ns	24	25	-	-	-
(Cooper-Climax)	-	-	-	-	-	24	-	-
Roberto BUSSINELLO	**-**	**-**	**-**	**-**	**-**	**-**	**r**	**-**
(De Tomaso-Conrero)	-	-	-	-	-	-	24	-
Jim CLARK	**10**	**3f**	**12**	**3**	**r**	**4**	**r**	**7**
(Lotus-Climax)	3	10	18	5	8	8	7	5
Bernard COLLOMB	**-**	**-**	**-**	**r**	**-**	**r**	**-**	**-**
(Cooper-Climax)	-	-	-	21	-	26	-	-
Carel Godin de BEAUFORT	**-**	**14**	**11**	**r**	**16**	**14**	**7**	**-**
(Porsche)	-	15	14	17	18	17	15	-
Jack FAIRMAN	**-**	**-**	**-**	**-**	**dq=**	**-**	**r**	**-**
(Ferguson-Climax)	-	-	-	-	20	-	-	-
(Cooper-Climax)	-	-	-	-	-	-	26	-
Olivier GENDEBIEN	**-**	**-**	**4**	**-**	**-**	**-**	**-**	**11=**
(Emeryson-Maserati)	nq	-	-	-	-	-	-	-
(Ferrari)	-	-	3	-	-	-	-	-
(Lotus-Climax)	-	-	-	-	-	-	-	15
Richie GINTHER	**2f=**	**5**	**3f**	**15r**	**3**	**8**	**r**	**-**
(Ferrari)	2	3	5	3	2	14	3	-
Keith GREENE	**-**	**-**	**-**	**-**	**15**	**-**	**-**	**-**
(Gilby-Climax)	-	-	-	-	23	-	-	-
Masten GREGORY	**-**	**-**	**10**	**12**	**11**	**-**	**r**	**r/11=**
(Cooper-Climax)	nq	ns	12	16	16	-	-	-
(Lotus-Climax)	-	-	-	-	-	-	17	11
Dan GURNEY	**5**	**10**	**6**	**2**	**7**	**7**	**2**	**2**
(Porsche)	10	6	10	9	12	7	12	7
Jim HALL	**-**	**-**	**-**	**-**	**-**	**-**	**-**	**r**
(Lotus-Climax)	-	-	-	-	-	-	-	18
Walt HANSGEN	**-**	**-**	**-**	**-**	**-**	**-**	**-**	**r**
(Cooper-Climax)	-	-	-	-	-	-	-	14
Hans HERRMANN	**9**	**15**	**-**	**-**	**-**	**13**	**-**	**-**
(Porsche)	12	12	-	-	-	11	-	-
Graham HILL	**r**	**8**	**r**	**6**	**r**	**r**	**r**	**5**
(BRM-Climax)	4	5	6	6	11	6	5	2
Phil HILL	**3**	**2**	**1**	**9f**	**2**	**3f**	**1**	**-**
(Ferrari)	5	1	1	1	1	1	4	-
Innes IRELAND	**-**	**-**	**r**	**4**	**10**	**r**	**r**	**1**
(Lotus-Climax)	ns	-	16	10	7	16	9	8
Jack LEWIS	**-**	**-**	**9**	**r**	**r**	**9**	**4**	**-**
(Cooper-Climax)	-	-	13	18	15	18	16	-
Roberto LIPPI	**-**	**-**	**-**	**-**	**-**	**-**	**r**	**-**
(De Tomaso-OSCA)	-	-	-	-	-	-	32	-
Tony MAGGS	**-**	**-**	**-**	**-**	**13**	**11**	**-**	**-**
(Lotus-Climax)	-	-	-	-	24	22	-	-
Willy MAIRESSE	**-**	**-**	**r**	**r**	**-**	**r**	**-**	**-**
(Lotus-Climax)	-	-	19	20	-	-	-	-
(Ferrari)	-	-	-	-	-	13	-	-
Tony MARSH	**-**	**-**	**-**	**-**	**r**	**15**	**-**	**-**
(Lotus-Climax)	-	-	ns	-	27	20	-	-
Michael MAY	**r**	**-**	**-**	**11**	**-**	**-**	**-**	**-**
(Lotus-Climax)	13	-	-	22	-	ns	-	-
Bruce McLAREN	**6**	**12**	**r**	**5**	**8**	**6**	**3**	**4**
(Cooper-Climax)	7	13	15	8	14	12	14	4
Stirling MOSS	**1f=**	**4**	**8**	**r**	**r/dq=**	**1**	**r**	**r**
(Lotus-Climax)	1	4	8	4	5/-	3	11	3
(Ferguson-Climax)	-	-	-	-	-/Ø	-	-	-
Massimo NATILI	**-**	**-**	**-**	**-**	**r**	**-**	**-**	**-**
(Cooper-Maserati)	-	-	-	-	28	-	ns	-
Brian NAYLOR	**-**	**-**	**-**	**-**	**-**	**-**	**r**	**-**
(JBW-Climax)	-	-	-	-	-	-	31	-
Tim PARNELL	**-**	**-**	**-**	**-**	**r**	**-**	**10**	**-**
(Lotus-Climax)	-	-	-	-	29	-	27	-
Roger PENSKE	**-**	**-**	**-**	**-**	**-**	**-**	**-**	**8**
(Cooper-Climax)	-	-	-	-	-	-	-	16
André PILETTE	**-**	**-**	**-**	**-**	**-**	**-**	**-**	**-**
(Emeryson-Climax)	-	-	-	-	-	-	nq	-
Renato PIROCCHI	**-**	**-**	**-**	**-**	**-**	**-**	**12**	**-**
(Cooper-Maserati)	-	-	-	-	-	-	29	-
Ricardo RODRIGUEZ	**-**	**-**	**-**	**-**	**-**	**-**	**r**	**-**
(Ferrari)	-	-	-	-	-	-	2	-
Lloyd RUBY	**-**	**-**	**-**	**-**	**-**	**-**	**-**	**r**
(Lotus-Climax)	-	-	-	-	-	-	-	19
Peter RYAN	**-**	**-**	**-**	**-**	**-**	**-**	**-**	**9**
(Lotus-Climax)	-	-	-	-	-	-	-	13
Roy SALVADORI	**-**	**-**	**-**	**8**	**6**	**10**	**6**	**r**
(Cooper-Climax)	-	-	-	15	13	15	18	12
Giorgio SCARLATTI	**-**	**-**	**-**	**r**	**-**	**-**	**-**	**-**
(De Tomaso-OSCA)	-	-	-	26	-	-	-	-
Wolfgang SEIDEL	**-**	**-**	**-**	**-**	**17**	**r**	**r**	**-**
(Lotus-Climax)	-	-	ns	-	22	23	28	-
Hap SHARP	**-**	**-**	**-**	**-**	**-**	**-**	**-**	**10**
(Cooper-Climax)	-	-	-	-	-	-	-	17
Gaetano STARRABBA	**-**	**-**	**-**	**-**	**-**	**-**	**r**	**-**
(Lotus-Maserati)	-	-	-	-	-	-	30	-
John SURTEES	**11r**	**7**	**5**	**r**	**r**	**5**	**r**	**r**
(Cooper-Climax)	11	9	4	7	10	10	19	9
Henry TAYLOR	**-**	**-**	**-**	**10**	**r**	**-**	**11**	**-**
(Lotus-Climax)	nq	-	-	25	17	-	23	-
Trevor TAYLOR	**-**	**13**	**-**	**-**	**-**	**-**	**-**	**-**
(Lotus-Climax)	-	14	-	-	-	-	-	-
Maurice TRINTIGNANT	**7**	**-**	**r**	**13**	**-**	**r**	**9**	**-**
(Cooper-Maserati)	15	-	20	23	-	21	22	-
Nino VACCARELLA	**-**	**-**	**-**	**-**	**-**	**-**	**r**	**-**
(De Tomaso-Conrero)	-	-	-	-	-	-	20	-
Wolfgang von TRIPS +	**4r**	**1**	**2**	**r**	**1**	**2**	**r**	**-**
(Ferrari)	6	2	2	2	4	5	1	-

Ø Took over in a shared drive and was not on the grid in this car

1962 RACE RESULTS & GRID POSITIONS

	NL	MC	B	F	GB	D	I	USA	ZA
Gerry ASHMORE	-	-	-	-	-	-	-	-	-
(Lotus-Climax)	-	-	-	-	-	-	nq	-	-
Giancario BAGHETTI	**4**	-	**r**	-	-	**10**	**5**	-	-
(Ferrari)	12	-	14	-	-	13	18	-	-
Lorenzo BANDINI	-	**5**	-	-	-	**r**	**8**	-	-
(Ferrari)	-	10	-	-	-	18	17	-	-
Luclen BIANCHI	-	-	**9**	-	-	**10**	-	-	-
(Lotus-Climax)	-	-	18	-	-	-	-	-	-
(ENB-Maseratti)	-	-	-	-	-	25	-	-	-
Jo BONNER	**7**	**5**	-	**10r**	**r**	**7**	**6**	**13**	-
(Porsche)	13	15	-	9	7	6	9	9	-
Jack BRABHAM	**r**	**8r**	**6**	**r**	**5**	**r**	-	**4**	**4**
(Lotus-Climax)	4	6	15	4	9	-	-	-	-
(Brabham-Climax)	-	-	-	-	-	24	-	5	3
Ian BURGESS	-	-	-	-	**12**	**11**	-	-	-
(Cooper-Climax)	-	-	-	-	16	16	nq	-	-
John CAMPBELL-JONES	-	-	**11**	-	-	-	-	-	-
(Lotus-Climax)	-	-	19	-	-	-	-	-	-
Jay CHAMBERLAIN	-	-	-	-	**15**	-	-	-	-
(Lotus-Climax)	-	-	-	-	20	nq	nq	-	-
Jim CLARK	**9**	**rf**	**1f**	**r**	**1f**	**4**	**r**	**1f**	**rf**
(Lotus-Climax)	3	1	12	1	1	3	1	1	1
Bernard COLLOMB	-	-	-	-	-	**r**	-	-	-
(Cooper-Climax)	-	-	-	-	-	22	-	-	-
Carel Godin de BEAUFORT	**6**	-	**7**	**6**	**14**	**13**	**10**	**r**	**11r**
(Porsche)	14	nq	13	17	17	8	20	13	16
Nasif ESTEFANO	-	-	-	-	-	-	-	-	-
(De Tomaso)	-	-	-	-	-	-	nq	-	-
Richie GINTHER	**r**	**r**	**r**	**3**	**13**	**8**	**2**	**r**	**7**
(BRM)	7	13	9	10	8	7	3	2	7
Keith GREENE	-	-	-	-	-	**r**	-	-	-
(Lotus-Climax)	-	-	-	-	ns	-	-	-	-
(Gilby-BRM)	-	-	-	-	-	19	nq	-	-
Masten GREGORY	**r**	-	**r**	**r**	**7**	-	**12**	**6**	-
(Lotus-Climax)	16	-	-	-	14	-	-	-	-
(Lotus-BRM)	-	nq	8	7	-	-	6	7	-
Dan GURNEY	**r**	**r**	-	**1**	**9**	**3**	**13r**	**5**	-
(Porsche)	8	5	-	6	6	1	7	4	-
(Lotus-BRM)	-	-	ns	-	-	-	-	-	-
Jim HALL	-	-	-	-	-	-	-	-	-
(Lotus-Climax)	-	-	-	-	-	-	-	ns	-
Mike HARRIS	-	-	-	-	-	-	-	-	**r**
(Cooper-Alfa Romeo)	-	-	-	-	-	-	-	-	15
Graham HILL	**1**	**6r**	**2**	**9rf**	**4**	**1f**	**1f**	**2**	**1**
(BRM)	2	2	1	2	5	2	2	3	2
Phil HILL	**3**	**2**	**3**	-	**r**	**r**	**11**	-	-
(Ferrari)	9	9	4	-	12	12	15	-	-
(Porsche)	-	-	-	-	-	-	-	ns	-
Innes IRELAND	**r**	**r**	**r**	**r**	**16**	-	**r**	**8**	**5**
(Lotus-Climax)	6	8	5	8	3	-	5	15	4
Bruce JOHNSTONE	-	-	-	-	-	-	-	-	**9**
(BRM)	-	-	-	-	-	-	-	-	17
Neville LEDERLE	-	-	-	-	-	-	-	-	**6**
(Lotus-Climax)	-	-	-	-	-	-	-	-	10
Jack LEWIS	**8**	-	-	**r**	**10**	**17r**	-	-	-
(Cooper-Climax)	19	-	-	16	15	21	-	-	-
(BRM)	-	nq	-	-	-	-	-	-	-
Roberto LIPPI	-	-	-	-	-	-	-	-	-
(De Tomaso-OSCA)	-	-	-	-	-	-	nq	-	-
John LOVE	-	-	-	-	-	-	-	-	**8**
(Cooper-Climax)	-	-	-	-	-	-	-	-	12
Tony MAGGS	**5**	**r**	**r**	**2**	**6**	**9**	**7**	**7**	**3**
(Cooper-Climax)	15	16	10	11	13	23	12	10	6
Willy MAIRESSE	-	**7r**	**r**	-	-	-	**4**	-	-
(Ferrari)	-	4	6	-	-	-	10	-	-
Timmy MAYER	-	-	-	-	-	-	-	**r**	-
(Cooper-Climax)	-	-	-	-	-	-	-	11	-
Bruce McLAREN	**rf**	**1**	**r**	**4**	**3**	**5**	**3**	**3**	**2**
(Cooper-Climax)	5	3	2	3	4	5	4	6	8
Roger PENSKE	-	-	-	-	-	-	-	**9**	-
(Lotus-Climax)	-	-	-	-	-	-	-	12	-
Ernie PIETERSE	-	-	-	-	-	-	-	-	**10**
(Lotus-Climax)	-	-	-	-	-	-	-	-	13
Ben PON	**r**	-	-	-	-	-	-	-	-
(Porsche)	18	-	-	-	-	-	-	-	-
Ernesto PRINOTH	-	-	-	-	-	-	-	-	-
(Lotus-Climax)	-	-	-	-	-	-	nq	-	-
Ricardo RODRIGUEZ +	**r**	-	**4**	-	-	**6**	**14r**	-	-
(Ferrari)	11	ns	7	-	-	10	11	-	-
Roy SALVADORI	**r**	**r**	-	**r**	**r**	**r**	**r**	-	**r**
(Lola-Climax)	17	12	-	14	11	9	13	ns	11
Heinz SCHILLER	-	-	-	-	-	**r**	-	-	-
(Lotus-BRM)	-	-	-	-	-	20	-	-	-
Rob SCHROEDER	-	-	-	-	-	-	-	**10**	-
(Lotus-Climax)	-	-	-	-	-	-	-	16	-
Wolfgang SEIDEL	**nc**	-	-	-	**r**	-	-	-	-
(Emeryson-Climax)	20	-	-	-	-	-	-	-	-
(Lotus-BRM)	-	-	-	-	21	nq	-	-	-
Günther SEIFFERT	-	-	-	-	-	-	-	-	-
(Lotus-BRM)	-	-	-	-	-	nq	-	-	-
Doug SERRURIER	-	-	-	-	-	-	-	-	**r**
(LDS-Alfa Romeo)	-	-	-	-	-	-	-	-	14
Tony SETTEMBER	-	-	-	-	**11**	-	**r**	-	-
(Emeryson-Climax)	-	-	-	-	19	-	21	-	-
Hap SHARP	-	-	-	-	-	-	-	**11**	-
(Cooper-Climax)	-	-	-	-	-	-	-	14	-
Tony SHELLY	-	-	-	-	**r**	-	-	-	-
(Lotus-Climax)	-	-	-	-	18	nq	-	-	-
(Lotus-BRM)	-	-	-	-	-	-	nq	-	-
Jo SIFFERT	-	-	**10**	**r**	-	**12**	-	-	-
(Lotus-Climax)	-	nq	17	-	-	17	-	-	-
(Lotus-BRM)	-	-	-	15	-	-	nq	-	-
John SURTEES	**r**	**4**	**5**	**5**	**2**	**2**	**r**	**r**	**r**
(Lola-Climax)	1	11	11	5	2	4	8	18	5
Trevor TAYLOR	**2**	**r**	**r**	**8**	**8**	**r**	**r**	**12**	**r**
(Lotus-Climax)	10	14	3	12	10	26	16	8	9
Maurice TRINTIGNANT	-	**r**	**8**	**7**	-	**r**	**r**	**r**	-
(Lotus-Climax)	-	7	16	13	-	11	19	17	-
Nino VACCARELLA	-	-	-	-	-	**15**	**9**	-	-
(Lotus-Climax)	-	nq	-	-	-	-	14	-	-
(Porsche)	-	-	-	-	-	15	-	-	-
Heini WALTER	-	-	-	-	-	**14**	-	-	-
(Porsche)	-	-	-	-	-	14	-	-	-

1963 RACE RESULTS & GRID POSITIONS

	MC	B	NL	F	GB	D	I	USA	MEX	ZA
Chris AMON	-	r	r	7	7	r	-	-	r	-
(Lola-Climax)	ns	15	12	15	14	14	ns	-	-	-
(Lotus-BRM)	-	-	-	-	-	-	-	-	19	-
Bob ANDERSON	-	-	-	-	12	-	12	-	-	-
(Lola-Climax)	-	-	-	-	16	-	18	-	-	-
Peter ARUNDELL	-	-	-	-	-	-	-	-	-	-
(Lotus-Climax)	-	-	-	ns	-	-	-	-	-	-
Giancarlo BAGHETTI	-	r	r	-	-	-	15	r	r	-
(ATS)	-	20	15	-	-	-	20	20	21	-
Lorenzo BANDINI	-	-	-	10	5	r	r	5	r	5
(BRM)	-	-	-	19	8	3	-	-	-	-
(Ferrari)	-	-	-	-	-	-	6	9	7	5
Lucien BIANCHI	-	r	-	-	-	-	-	-	-	-
(Lola-Climax)	-	16	-	-	-	-	-	-	-	-
Trevor BLOKDYK	-	-	-	-	-	-	-	-	-	12
(Cooper-Maserati)	-	-	-	-	-	-	-	-	-	19
Jo BONNIER	7	5	11	r	r	6	7	8	5	6
(Cooper-Climax)	11	13	8	11	12	12	11	12	8	11
Jack BRABHAM	9r	r	r	4	r	7	5	4	2	13r
(Lotus-Climax)	15	-	-	-	-	-	-	-	-	-
(Brabham-Climax)	-	6	4	5	4	8	7	5	10	2
Tino BRAMBILLA	-	-	-	-	-	-	-	-	-	-
(Cooper-Maserati)	-	-	-	-	-	-	nq	-	-	-
Peter BROEKER	-	-	-	-	-	-	-	7	-	-
(Stebro-Ford)	-	-	-	-	-	-	-	21	-	-
Ian BURGESS	-	-	-	-	r	r	-	-	-	-
(Scirocco-BRM)	-	-	-	-	20	19	-	-	-	-
John CAMPBELL-JONES	-	-	-	-	13	-	-	-	-	-
(Lola-Climax)	-	-	-	-	23	-	-	-	-	-
Jim CLARK	8r	1f	1f	1f	1	2	1f	3f	1f	1
(Lotus-Climax)	1	8	1	1	1	1	3	2	1	1
Bernard COLLOMB	-	-	-	-	-	10	-	-	-	-
(Lotus-Climax)	nq	-	-	-	-	21	-	-	-	-
Carel Godin de BEAUFORT	-	6	9	-	10	r	-	6	10	10
(Porsche)	-	18	19	-	21	17	nq	19	18	20
Mario de CABRAL	-	-	-	-	-	r	-	-	-	-
(Cooper-Climax)	-	-	-	-	-	20	nq	-	-	-
Peter de KLERK	-	-	-	-	-	-	-	-	-	r
(Alfa Special)	-	-	-	-	-	-	-	-	-	16
Frank DOCHNAL	-	-	-	-	-	-	-	-	-	-
(Cooper-Climax)	-	-	-	-	-	-	-	-	ns	-
Paddy DRIVER	-	-	-	-	-	-	-	-	-	-
(Lotus-BRM)	-	-	-	-	-	-	-	-	-	ns
Richie GINTHER	2	4	5	r	4	3	2	2	3	r
(BRM)	4	9	6	12	9	6	4	4	5	7
Masten GREGORY	-	-	-	r	11	-	r	r	r	-
(Lotus-BRM)	-	-	-	17	22	-	12	-	-	-
(Lola-Climax)	-	-	-	-	-	-	-	8	14	-
Dan GURNEY	r	3	2	5	r	r	14r	r	6	2f
(Brabham-Climax)	6	2	14	3	2	13	5	6	4	3
Mike HAILWOOD	-	-	-	-	8	-	10	-	-	-
(Lotus-Climax)	-	-	-	-	17	-	-	-	-	-
(Lola-Climax)	-	-	-	-	-	-	17	-	-	-
Jim HALL	r	r	8	11	6	5	8	10r	8	-
(Lotus-BRM)	13	12	18	16	13	16	16	16	15	-
Graham HILL	1	r	r	3	3	r	16r	1	4	3
(BRM)	2	1	2	2	3	4	2	1	3	6
Phil HILL	-	r	r	r	-	-	11	r	r	-
(ATS)	-	17	13	-	-	-	14	15	17	-
(Lotus-BRM)	-	-	-	13	-	-	-	-	-	-
Innes IRELAND	r	r	4	9	dq	r	4r	-	-	-
(Lotus-BRM)	5	-	-	-	-	11	-	-	-	-
(BRP-BRM)	-	7	7	9	11	-	10	-	-	-
Kurt KUHNKE	-	-	-	-	-	-	-	-	-	-
(Lotus-Borgward)	-	-	-	-	-	nq	-	-	-	-
Roberto LIPPI	-	-	-	-	-	-	-	-	-	-
(De Tomaso-Ferrari)	-	-	-	-	-	-	nq	-	-	-
John LOVE	-	-	-	-	-	-	-	-	-	9
(Cooper-Climax)	-	-	-	-	-	-	-	-	-	13
Tony MAGGS	5	7r	r	2	9	r	6	r	r	7
(Cooper-Climax)	10	4	9	8	7	10	13	10	13	10
Willy MAIRESSE	r	r	-	-	-	r	-	-	-	-
(Ferrari)	7	3	-	-	-	7	-	-	-	-
Bruce McLAREN	3	2	r	12r	r	r	3	11r	r	4
(Cooper-Climax)	8	5	3	6	6	5	8	11	6	9
Gerhard MITTER	-	-	r	-	-	4	-	-	-	-
(Porsche)	-	-	16	-	-	15	-	-	-	-
Brausch NIEMANN	-	-	-	-	-	-	-	-	-	14
(Lotus-Ford)	-	-	-	-	-	-	-	-	-	15
Tim PARNELL	-	-	-	-	-	-	-	-	-	-
(Lotus-Climax)	-	-	-	-	-	nq	-	-	-	-
Ernie PIETERSE	-	-	-	-	-	-	-	-	-	r
(Lotus-Climax)	-	-	-	-	-	-	-	-	-	12
André PILETTE	-	-	-	-	-	-	-	-	-	-
(Lotus-Climax)	-	-	-	-	-	nq	nq	-	-	-
David PROPHET	-	-	-	-	-	-	-	-	-	r
(Brabham-Ford)	-	-	-	-	-	-	-	-	-	14
Ian RABY	-	-	-	-	r	-	-	-	-	-
(Gilby-BRM)	-	-	-	-	19	nq	nq	-	-	-
Pedro RODRIGUEZ	-	-	-	-	-	-	-	r	r	-
(Lotus-Climax)	-	-	-	-	-	-	-	13	20	-
Ludovico SCARFIOTTI	-	-	6	-	-	-	-	-	-	-
(Ferrari)	-	-	11	ns	-	-	-	-	-	-
Doug SERRURIER	-	-	-	-	-	-	-	-	-	11
(LDS-Alfa Romeo)	-	-	-	-	-	-	-	-	-	18
Tony SETTEMBER	-	8r	-	r	r	r	-	-	-	-
(Scirocco-BRM)	-	19	-	18	18	22	nq	-	-	-
Hap SHARP	-	-	-	-	-	-	-	r	7	-
(Lotus-BRM)	-	-	-	-	-	-	-	18	16	-
Jo SIFFERT	r	r	7	6	r	9r	r	r	9	-
(Lotus-BRM)	12	14	17	10	15	9	15	14	9	-
Moises SOLANA	-	-	-	-	-	-	-	-	11r	-
(BRM)	-	-	-	-	-	-	-	-	11	-
Mike SPENCE	-	-	-	-	-	-	13r	-	-	-
(Lotus-Climax)	-	-	-	-	-	-	9	-	-	-
John SURTEES	4f	r	3	r	2f	1f	r	9r	dq	r
(Ferrari)	3	10	5	4	5	2	1	3	2	4
Trevor TAYLOR	6	r	10	13r	dq	8	-	r	r	8
(Lotus-Climax)	9	11	10	7	10	18	-	7	12	8

	MC	B	NL	F	GB	D	I	USA	MEX	ZA
Sam TINGLE	-	-	-	-	-	-	-	-	-	r
(LDS-Alfa Romeo)	-	-	-	-	-	-	-	-	-	17
Maurice TRINTIGNANT	r	-	-	8	-	-	9	-	-	-
(Lola-Climax)	14	-	-	-	-	-	-	-	-	-
(Lotus-Climax)	-	-	-	14	-	-	-	-	-	-
(BRM)	-	-	-	-	-	-	19	-	-	-
Rodger WARD	-	-	-	-	-	-	-	r	-	-
(Lotus-BRM)	-	-	-	-	-	-	-	17	-	-

1964 RACE RESULTS & GRID POSITIONS

	MC	NL	B	F	GB	D	A	I	USA	MEX
Chris AMON	-	5	r	10	r	11r	r	-	r	r
(Lotus-BRM)	nq	13	11	14	11	9	-	-	11	12
(Lotus-Climax)	-	-	-	-	-	-	17	-	-	-
Bob ANDERSON	7r	6	-	12	7	r	3	11	-	-
(Brabham-Climax)	12	11	ns	15	7	15	14	14	-	-
Peter ARUNDELL	3	3	9	4	-	-	-	-	-	-
(Lotus-Climax)	6	6	4	4	-	-	-	-	-	-
Dickie ATTWOOD	-	-	-	-	-	-	-	-	-	-
(BRM)	-	-	-	-	ns	-	-	-	-	-
Giancarlo BAGHETTI	-	10	8	-	12	r	7	8	-	-
(BRM)	-	16	17	-	21	21	15	15	-	-
Lorenzo BANDINI	10r	r	r	9	5	3	1	3	r	3
(Ferrari)	7	10	9	8	8	4	7	7	8	3
Edgar BARTH	-	-	-	-	-	r	-	-	-	-
(Cooper-Climax)	-	-	-	-	-	20	-	-	-	-
Jo BONNIER	5	9	r	-	r	r	6	12	r	r
(Cooper-Climax)	11	-	-	-	-	-	-	-	-	-
(Brabham-BRM)	-	12	14	-	9	12	-	-	-	-
(Brabham-Climax)	-	-	-	-	-	-	10	12	9	8
Jack BRABHAM	r	r	3	3f	4	12r	9	14r	r	r
(Brabham-Climax)	2	7	3	5	4	6	6	11	7	7
Ronnie BUCKNUM	-	-	-	-	-	13r	-	r	r	-
(Honda)	-	-	-	-	-	22	-	10	14	-
Jim CLARK	4r	1f	1	r	1f	r	r	r	r=/7r=f	5rf
(Lotus-Climax)	1	2	6	1	1	2	3	4	1	1
Bernard COLLOMB	-	-	-	-	-	-	-	-	-	-
(Lotus-Climax)	nq	-	-	-	-	-	-	-	-	-
Carel Godin de BEAUFORT +	-	r	-	-	-	-	-	-	-	-
(Porsche)	-	17	-	-	-	ns	-	-	-	-
Mario de CABRAL	-	-	-	-	-	-	-	r	-	-
(Derrington Francis-ATS)	-	-	-	-	-	-	-	19	-	-
Frank GARDNER	-	-	-	-	r	-	-	-	-	-
(Brabham-Ford)	-	-	-	-	19	-	-	-	-	-
GEKI	-	-	-	-	-	-	-	-	-	-
(Brabham-BRM)	-	-	-	-	-	-	-	nq	-	-
Richie GINTHER	2	11	4	5	8	7	2	4	4	8
(BRM)	8	8	8	9	14	11	5	9	13	11
Dan GURNEY	r	r	6rf	1	13	10	rf	10	r	1
(Brabham-Climax)	5	1	1	2	3	3	4	2	3	2
Mike HAILWOOD	6	12r	-	8	r	r	8	r	8r	r
(Lotus-BRM)	15	14	-	13	12	13	18	17	16	17
Walt HANSGEN	-	-	-	-	-	-	-	-	5	-
(Lotus-Climax)	-	-	-	-	-	-	-	-	17	-
Graham HILL	1f	4	5r	2	2	2	r	r	1	11
(BRM)	3	3	2	6	2	5	1	3	4	6
Phil HILL	9r	8	r	7	6	r	r	-	r	9r
(Cooper-Climax)	9	9	15	10	15	8	20	-	19	15
Innes IRELAND	-	-	10	r	10	-	5	5	r	12
(Lotus-BRM)	ns	-	-	-	-	-	-	-	-	-
(BRP-BRM)	-	-	16	11	10	-	11	13	10	16
John LOVE	-	-	-	-	-	-	-	-	-	-
(Cooper-Climax)	-	-	-	-	-	-	-	nq	-	-
Tony MAGGS	-	-	-	-	r	6	4	-	-	-
(BRM)	-	15ns	ns	-	23	16	19	-	-	-
Bruce McLAREN	r	7	2	6	r	r	r	2	r	7
(Cooper-Climax)	10	5	7	7	6	7	9	5	5	10
Gerhard MITTER	-	-	-	-	-	9	-	-	-	-
(Lotus-Climax)	-	-	-	-	-	19	-	-	-	-
André PILETTE	-	-	r	-	-	-	-	-	-	-
(Scirocco-Climax)	-	-	18	-	-	nq	-	-	-	-
Ian RABY	-	-	-	-	r	-	-	-	-	-
(Brabham-BRM)	-	-	-	-	17	-	-	nq	-	-
Peter REVSON	-	-	dq	-	r	14r	-	13	-	-
(Lotus-BRM)	nq	-	10	ns	22	18	-	18	-	-
Jochen RINDT	-	-	-	-	-	-	r	-	-	-
(Brabham-BRM)	-	-	-	-	-	-	13	-	-	-
Pedro RODRIGUEZ	-	-	-	-	-	-	-	-	-	6
(Ferrari)	-	-	-	-	-	-	-	-	-	9
Jean-Claude RUDAZ	-	-	-	-	-	-	-	-	-	-
(Cooper-Climax)	-	-	-	-	-	-	-	ns	-	-
Ludovico SCARFIOTTI	-	-	-	-	-	-	-	9	-	-
(Ferrari)	-	-	-	-	-	-	-	16	-	-
Hap SHARP	-	-	-	-	-	-	-	-	nc	13
(Brabham-BRM)	-	-	-	-	-	-	-	-	18	19
Jo SIFFERT	8	13	r	r	11	4	r	7	3	r
(Lotus-BRM)	16	-	-	-	-	-	-	-	-	-
(Brabham-BRM)	-	18	13	17	16	10	12	6	12	13
Moises SOLANA	-	-	-	-	-	-	-	-	-	10
(Lotus-Climax)	-	-	-	-	-	-	-	-	-	14
Mike SPENCE	-	-	-	-	9	8	r	6	7r=/r=	4
(Lotus-Climax)	-	-	-	-	13	17	8	8	6	5
John SURTEES	r	2	r	r	3	1f	r	1f	2	2
(Ferrari)	4	4	5	3	5	1	2	1	2	4
John TAYLOR	-	-	-	-	14	-	-	-	-	-
(Cooper-Ford)	-	-	-	-	20	-	-	-	-	-
Trevor TAYLOR	r	-	7	r	r	-	r	-	6	r
(BRP-BRM)	14	-	12	12	-	-	16	nq	15	18
(Lotus-BRM)	-	-	-	-	18	-	-	-	-	-
Maurice TRINTIGNANT	r	-	-	11	-	5r	-	r	-	-
(BRM)	13	-	-	16	nq	14	-	20	-	-

1965 RACE RESULTS & GRID POSITIONS

	ZA	MC	B	F	GB	NL	D	I	USA	MEX
Chris AMON	**-**	**-**	**-**	**r**	**-**	**-**	**r**	**-**	**-**	**-**
(Lotus-BRM)	-	-	-	8	-	-	15	-	-	-
(Brabham-BRM)	-	-	-	-	ns	-	-	-	-	-
Bob ANDERSON	**nc**	**9**	**-**	**9r**	**r**	**r**	**-**	**-**	**-**	**-**
(Brabham-Climax)	12	9	ns	15	17	16	ns	-	-	-
Dickie ATTWOOD	**-**	**r**	**14r**	**-**	**13**	**12**	**r**	**6**	**10**	**6**
(Lotus-BRM)	-	6	13	-	16	17	16	13	16	16
Giancarlo BAGHETTI	**-**	**-**	**-**	**-**	**-**	**-**	**-**	**r**	**-**	**-**
(Brabham-Climax)	-	-	-	-	-	-	-	19	-	-
Lorenzo BANDINI	**15r**	**2**	**9**	**8r**	**r**	**9**	**6**	**4**	**4**	**8**
(Ferrari)	6	4	15	3	9	12	7	5	5	7
Giorgio BASSI	**-**	**-**	**-**	**-**	**-**	**-**	**-**	**r**	**-**	**-**
(BRM)	-	-	-	-	-	-	-	22	-	-
Lucien BIANCHI	**-**	**-**	**12**	**-**	**-**	**-**	**-**	**-**	**-**	**-**
(BRM)	-	-	17	-	-	-	-	-	-	-
Trevor BLOKDYK	**-**	**-**	**-**	**-**	**-**	**-**	**-**	**-**	**-**	**-**
(Cooper-Ford)	nq	-	-	-	-	-	-	-	-	-
Bob BONDURANT	**-**	**-**	**-**	**-**	**-**	**-**	**-**	**-**	**9**	**r**
(Ferrari)	-	-	-	-	-	-	-	-	14	-
(Lotus-BRM)	-	-	-	-	-	-	-	-	-	17
Jo BONNIER	**r**	**7**	**r**	**r**	**7**	**r**	**7**	**7**	**8**	**r**
(Brabham-Climax)	7	13	7	11	14	15	9	14	10	12
Jack BRABHAM	**8**	**r**	**4**	**-**	**-**	**-**	**5**	**-**	**3**	**r**
(Brabham-Climax)	3	2	10	-	8ns	-	14	-	7	4
Ronnie BUCKNUM	**-**	**r**	**r**	**r**	**-**	**-**	**-**	**r**	**13**	**5**
(Honda)	-	15	11	16	-	-	-	6	12	10
Roberto BUSSINELLO	**-**	**-**	**-**	**-**	**-**	**-**	**-**	**13r**	**-**	**-**
(BRM)	-	-	-	-	-	-	nq	21	-	-
Dave CHARLTON	**-**	**-**	**-**	**-**	**-**	**-**	**-**	**-**	**-**	**-**
(Lotus-Ford)	npq	-	-	-	-	-	-	-	-	-
Jim CLARK	**1f**	**-**	**1f**	**1f**	**1**	**1f**	**1f**	**10rf**	**r**	**r**
(Lotus-Climax)	1	-	2	1	1	2	1	1	2	1
Peter de KLERK	**10**	**-**	**-**	**-**	**-**	**-**	**-**	**-**	**-**	**-**
(Alfa Special)	17	-	-	-	-	-	-	-	-	-
Frank GARDNER	**12**	**r**	**r**	**-**	**8**	**11**	**r**	**r**	**-**	**-**
(Brabham-BRM)	15	11	18	-	13	11	17	16	-	-
GEKI	**-**	**-**	**-**	**-**	**-**	**-**	**-**	**r**	**-**	**-**
(Lotus-Climax)	-	-	-	-	-	-	-	20	-	-
Richie GINTHER	**-**	**r**	**6**	**r**	**r**	**6**	**-**	**14r**	**7**	**1**
(Honda)	-	16	4	7	3	3	-	17	3	3
Masten GREGORY	**-**	**-**	**r**	**-**	**12**	**-**	**8**	**r**	**-**	**-**
(BRM)	-	-	19	-	19	-	18	23	-	-
Brian GUBBY	**-**	**-**	**-**	**-**	**-**	**-**	**-**	**-**	**-**	**-**
(Lotus-Climax)	-	-	-	-	nq	-	-	-	-	-
Dan GURNEY	**r**	**-**	**10**	**r**	**6**	**3**	**3**	**3**	**2**	**2f**
(Brabham-Climax)	9	-	5	5	7	5	5	9	8	2
Mike HAILWOOD	**-**	**r**	**-**	**-**	**-**	**-**	**-**	**-**	**-**	**-**
(Lotus-BRM)	-	12	-	-	-	-	-	-	-	-
Paul HAWKINS	**9**	**10r**	**-**	**-**	**-**	**-**	**r**	**-**	**-**	**-**
(Brabham-Ford)	16	-	-	-	-	-	-	-	-	-
(Lotus-Climax)	-	14	-	-	-	-	19	-	-	-
Graham HILL	**3**	**1f**	**5**	**5**	**2f**	**4**	**2**	**2**	**1f**	**r**
(BRM)	5	1	1	13	2	1	3	4	1	5
Denny HULME	**-**	**8**	**-**	**4**	**r**	**5**	**r**	**r**	**-**	**-**
(Brabham-Climax)	-	8	-	6	10	7	13	12	-	-
Innes IRELAND	**-**	**-**	**13**	**r**	**r**	**10**	**-**	**9**	**r**	**-**
(Lotus-BRM)	-	-	16	17	15	13	-	18	18	ns
Neville LEDERLE	**-**	**-**	**-**	**-**	**-**	**-**	**-**	**-**	**-**	**-**
(Lotus-Climax)	nq	-	-	-	-	-	-	-	-	-
John LOVE	**r**	**-**	**-**	**-**	**-**	**-**	**-**	**-**	**-**	**-**
(Cooper-Climax)	18	-	-	-	-	-	-	-	-	-
Tony MAGGS	**11**	**-**	**-**	**-**	**-**	**-**	**-**	**-**	**-**	**-**
(Lotus-BRM)	13	-	-	-	-	-	-	-	-	-
Willy MAIRESSE	**-**	**-**	**-**	**-**	**-**	**-**	**-**	**-**	**-**	**-**
(BRM)	-	-	ns	-	-	-	-	-	-	-
Bruce McLAREN	**5**	**5**	**3**	**r**	**10**	**r**	**r**	**5**	**r**	**r**
(Cooper-Climax)	8	7	9	9	11	9	10	11	9	14
Gerhard MITTER	**-**	**-**	**-**	**-**	**-**	**-**	**r**	**-**	**-**	**-**
(Lotus-Climax)	-	-	-	-	-	-	12	-	-	-
Brausch NIEMANN	**-**	**-**	**-**	**-**	**-**	**-**	**-**	**-**	**-**	**-**
(Lotus-Ford)	nq	-	-	-	-	-	-	-	-	-
Ernie PIETERSE	**-**	**-**	**-**	**-**	**-**	**-**	**-**	**-**	**-**	**-**
(Lotus-Climax)	nq	-	-	-	-	-	-	-	-	-
Jackie PRETORIUS	**-**	**-**	**-**	**-**	**-**	**-**	**-**	**-**	**-**	**-**
(LDS-Alfa Romeo)	npq	-	-	-	-	-	-	-	-	-
David PROPHET	**14**	**-**	**-**	**-**	**-**	**-**	**-**	**-**	**-**	**-**
(Brabham-Ford)	19	-	-	-	-	-	-	-	-	-
Clive PUZEY	**-**	**-**	**-**	**-**	**-**	**-**	**-**	**-**	**-**	**-**
(Lotus-Climax)	npq	-	-	-	-	-	-	-	-	-
Ian RABY	**-**	**-**	**-**	**-**	**11**	**-**	**-**	**-**	**-**	**-**
(Brabham-BRM)	-	-	-	-	20	-	nq	-	-	-
John RHODES	**-**	**-**	**-**	**-**	**r**	**-**	**-**	**-**	**-**	**-**
(Cooper-Climax)	-	-	-	-	21	-	-	-	-	-
Jochen RINDT	**r**	**-**	**11**	**r**	**14r**	**r**	**4**	**8**	**6**	**r**
(Cooper-Climax)	10	nq	14	12	12	14	8	7	13	15
Pedro RODRIGUEZ	**-**	**-**	**-**	**-**	**-**	**-**	**-**	**-**	**5**	**7**
(Ferrari)	-	-	-	-	-	-	-	-	15	13
Alan ROLLINSON	**-**	**-**	**-**	**-**	**-**	**-**	**-**	**-**	**-**	**-**
(Cooper-Ford)	-	-	-	-	nq	-	-	-	-	-
Ludovico SCARFIOTTI	**-**	**-**	**-**	**-**	**-**	**-**	**-**	**-**	**-**	**-**
(Ferrari)	-	-	-	-	-	-	-	-	-	ns
Doug SERRURIER	**-**	**-**	**-**	**-**	**-**	**-**	**-**	**-**	**-**	**-**
(LDS-Climax)	nq	-	-	-	-	-	-	-	-	-
Jo SIFFERT	**7**	**6**	**8**	**6**	**9**	**13**	**r**	**r**	**11**	**4**
(Brabham-BRM)	14	10	8	14	18	10	11	10	11	11
Moises SOLANA	**-**	**-**	**-**	**-**	**-**	**-**	**-**	**-**	**12**	**r**
(Lotus-Climax)	-	-	-	-	-	-	-	-	17	9
Mike SPENCE	**4**	**-**	**7**	**7**	**4**	**8**	**r**	**11r**	**r**	**3**
(Lotus-Climax)	4	-	12	10	6	8	6	8	4	6
Jackie STEWART	**6**	**3**	**2**	**2**	**5**	**2**	**r**	**1**	**r**	**r**
(BRM)	11	3	3	2	4	6	2	3	6	8
John SURTEES	**2**	**4r**	**r**	**3**	**3**	**7**	**r**	**r**	**-**	**-**
(Ferrari)	2	5	6	4	5	4	4	2	-	-
Sam TINGLE	**13**	**-**	**-**	**-**	**-**	**-**	**-**	**-**	**-**	**-**
(LDS-Alfa Romeo)	20	-	-	-	-	-	-	-	-	-
Nino VACCARELLA	**-**	**-**	**-**	**-**	**-**	**-**	**-**	**12r**	**-**	**-**
(Ferrari)	-	-	-	-	-	-	-	15	-	-

1966 RACE RESULTS & GRID POSITIONS

	MC	B	F	GB	NL	D	I	USA	MEX
Kurt AHRENS	-	-	-	-	-	r	-	-	-
(Brabham-Ford Cosworth)	-	-	-	-	-	21	-	-	-
Chris AMON	-	-	8	-	-	-	-	-	-
(Cooper-Maserati)	-	-	7	-	-	-	-	-	-
(Brabham-BRM)	-	-	-	-	-	-	nq	-	-
Bob ANDERSON	r	-	7	nc	r	r	6	-	-
(Brabham-Climax)	8	-	12	10	14	14	15	-	-
Peter ARUNDELL	-	-	r	r	r	12	8r	6	7
(Lotus-BRM)	-	ns	16	20	15	17	13	-	17
(Lotus-Climax)	-	-	-	-	-	-	-	19	-
Giancarlo BAGHETTI	-	-	-	-	-	-	nc	-	-
(Ferrari)	-	-	-	-	-	-	16	-	-
Lorenzo BANDINI	2f	3	ncf	-	6	6	r	r	-
(Ferrari)	5	5	1	-	9	6	5	3	-
Jean-Pierre BELTOISE	-	-	-	-	-	8	-	-	-
(Matra-Ford Cosworth)	-	-	-	-	-	18	-	-	-
Bob BONDURANT	4	r	-	9	-	r	7	dq	r
(BRM)	16	11	-	14	-	11	18	-	-
(Eagle-Climax)	-	-	-	-	-	-	-	16	-
(Eagle-Weslake)	-	-	-	-	-	-	-	-	18
Jo BONNIER	nc	r	nc	r	7	r	r	nc	6
(Cooper-Maserati)	14	6	-	-	13	12	12	15	12
(Brabham-Climax)	-	-	17	15	-	-	-	-	-
Jack BRABHAM	r	4	1	1f	1	1	r	r	2
(Brabham-Repco)	11	4	4	1	1	5	6	1	4
Ronnie BUCKNUM	-	-	-	-	-	-	-	r	8
(Honda)	-	-	-	-	-	-	-	18	13
Jim CLARK	r	r	-	4	3	r	r	1	r
(Lotus-Climax)	1	10	ns	5	3	1	-	-	-
(Lotus-BRM)	-	-	-	-	-	-	3	2	2
Piers COURAGE	-	-	-	-	-	r	-	-	-
(Lotus-Ford Cosworth)	-	-	-	-	-	23	-	-	-
GEKI	-	-	-	-	-	-	9	-	-
(Lotus-Climax)	-	-	-	-	-	-	20	-	-
Richie GINTHER	r	5	-	-	-	-	r	nc	4f
(Cooper-Maserati)	9	8	-	-	-	-	-	-	-
(Honda)	-	-	-	-	-	-	7	8	3
Dan GURNEY	-	nc	5	r	r	7	r	r	5
(Eagle-Climax)	-	15	14	3	4	8	-	-	9
(Eagle-Weslake)	-	-	-	-	-	-	19	14	-
Hubert HAHNE	-	-	-	-	-	9	-	-	-
(Matra-BRM)	-	-	-	-	-	27	-	-	-
Hans HERRMANN	-	-	-	-	-	11	-	-	-
(Brabham-Ford Cosworth)	-	-	-	-	-	22	-	-	-
Graham HILL	3	r	r	3	2	4	r	r	r
(BRM)	4	9	8	4	7	10	11	5	7
Phil HILL	-	-	-	-	-	-	-	-	-
(Eagle-Climax)	-	-	-	-	-	-	nq	-	-
Denny HULME	r	r	3	2	rf	r	3	r	3
(Brabham-Climax)	6	13	-	-	-	-	-	-	-
(Brabham-Repco)	-	-	9	2	2	15	10	7	6
Jacky ICKX	-	-	-	-	-	r	-	-	-
(Matra-Ford Cosworth)	-	-	-	-	-	16	-	-	-
Innes IRELAND	-	-	-	-	-	-	-	r	r
(BRM)	-	-	-	-	-	-	-	17	16
Chris IRWIN	-	-	-	7	-	-	-	-	-
(Brabham-Climax)	-	-	-	12	-	-	-	-	-
Chris LAWRENCE	-	-	-	11	-	r	-	-	-
(Cooper-Ferrari)	-	-	-	19	-	26	-	-	-
Guy LIGIER	nc	nc	nc	10	9	-	-	-	-
(Cooper-Maserati)	15	12	11	17	16	ns	-	-	-
Bruce McLAREN	r	-	-	6	-	-	-	5	r
(McLaren-Ford)	10	-	-	-	-	-	-	11	14
(McLaren-Serenissima)	-	ns	-	13	ns	-	-	-	-
Gerhard MITTER	-	-	-	-	-	-	-	-	-
(Lotus-Ford Cosworth)	-	-	-	-	-	ns	-	-	-
Silvio MOSER	-	-	-	-	-	-	-	-	-
(Brabham-Ford Cosworth)	-	-	-	-	-	ns	-	-	-
Mike PARKES	-	-	2	-	r	r	2	-	-
(Ferrari)	-	-	3	-	5	7	1	-	-
Alan REES	-	-	-	-	-	r	-	-	-
(Brabham-Ford Cosworth)	-	-	-	-	-	24	-	-	-
Jochen RINDT	r	2	4	5	r	3	4	2	r
(Cooper-Maserati)	7	2	5	7	6	9	8	9	5
Pedro RODRIGUEZ	-	-	r	-	-	r	-	r	r
(Lotus-Climax)	-	-	13	-	-	-	-	-	8
(Lotus-Ford Cosworth)	-	-	-	-	-	20	-	-	-
(Lotus-BRM)	-	-	-	-	-	-	-	10	-
Ludovico SCARFIOTTI	-	-	-	-	-	r	1f	-	-
(Ferrari)	-	-	-	-	-	4	2	-	-
Jo SCHLESSER	-	-	-	-	-	10	-	-	-
(Matra-Ford Cosworth)	-	-	-	-	-	19	-	-	-
Jo SIFFERT	r	r	r	nc	r	-	r	4	r
(Brabham-BRM)	13	-	-	-	-	-	-	-	-
(Cooper-Maserati)	-	14	6	11	11	-	17	13	11
Moises SOLANA	-	-	-	-	-	-	-	-	r
(Cooper-Maserati)	-	-	-	-	-	-	-	-	15
Mike SPENCE	r	r	r	r	5	r	5	r	-
(Lotus-BRM)	12	7	10	9	12	13	14	12	ns
Jackie STEWART	1	r	-	r	4	5	r	r	r
(BRM)	3	3	-	8	8	3	9	6	10
John SURTEES	r	1f	r	r	r	2f	r	3f	1
(Ferrari)	2	1	-	-	-	-	-	-	-
(Cooper-Maserati)	-	-	2	6	10	2	4	4	1
John TAYLOR +	-	-	6	8	8	r	-	-	-
(Brabham-BRM)	-	-	15	16	17	25	-	-	-
Trevor TAYLOR	-	-	-	r	-	-	-	-	-
(Shannon-Climax)	-	-	-	18	-	-	-	-	-
Vic WILSON	-	-	-	-	-	-	-	-	-
(BRM)	-	ns	-	-	-	-	-	-	-

1967 RACE RESULTS & GRID POSITIONS

	ZA	MC	NL	B	F	GB	D	CDN	I	USA	MEX
Kurt AHRENS	**-**	**-**	**-**	**-**	**-**	**-**	**r**	**-**	**-**	**-**	**-**
(Protos-Ford Cosworth)	-	-	-	-	-	-	23	-	-	-	-
Chris AMON	**-**	**3**	**4**	**3**	**r**	**3**	**3**	**6**	**7**	**r**	**9**
(Ferrari)	-	14	9	5	7	6	8	4	4	4	2
Bob ANDERSON +	**5**	**-**	**9**	**8**	**r**	**r**	**-**	**-**	**-**	**-**	**-**
(Brabham-Climax)	10	nq	17	17	14	17	-	-	-	-	-
Dickie ATTWOOD	**-**	**-**	**-**	**-**	**-**	**-**	**-**	**10**	**-**	**-**	**-**
(Cooper-Maserati)	-	-	-	-	-	-	-	13	-	-	-
Giancarlo BAGHETTI	**-**	**-**	**-**	**-**	**-**	**-**	**-**	**-**	**r**	**-**	**-**
(Lotus-Ford Cosworth)	-	-	-	-	-	-	-	-	17	-	-
Lorenzo BANDINI +	**-**	**r**	**-**	**-**	**-**	**-**	**-**	**-**	**-**	**-**	**-**
(Ferrari)	-	2	-	-	-	-	-	-	-	-	-
Jean-Pierre BELTOISE	**-**	**-**	**-**	**-**	**-**	**-**	**-**	**-**	**-**	**7**	**7**
(Matra-Ford Cosworth)	-	nq	-	-	-	-	-	-	-	18	14
Jo BONNIER	**r**	**-**	**-**	**r**	**-**	**r**	**6**	**8**	**r**	**6**	**10**
(Cooper-Maserati)	12	-	-	12	-	19	16	14	14	15	17
Luki BOTHA	**nc**	**-**	**-**	**-**	**-**	**-**	**-**	**-**	**-**	**-**	**-**
(Brabham-Climax)	17	-	-	-	-	-	-	-	-	-	-
Jack BRABHAM	**6**	**r**	**2**	**r**	**1**	**4**	**2**	**1**	**2**	**5**	**2**
(Brabham-Repco)	1	1	3	7	2	3	7	7	2	5	5
Dave CHARLTON	**nc**	**-**	**-**	**-**	**-**	**-**	**-**	**-**	**-**	**-**	**-**
(Brabham-Climax)	8	-	-	-	-	-	-	-	-	-	-
Jim CLARK	**r**	**rf**	**1f**	**6**	**r**	**1**	**r**	**rf**	**3f**	**1**	**1f**
(Lotus-BRM)	3	-	-	-	-	-	-	-	-	-	-
(Lotus-Climax)	-	5	-	-	-	-	-	-	-	-	-
(Lotus-Ford Cosworth)	-	-	8	1	4	1	1	1	1	2	1
Piers COURAGE	**r**	**r**	**-**	**-**	**-**	**-**	**-**	**-**	**-**	**-**	**-**
(Lotus-BRM)	18	-	-	-	-	-	-	-	-	-	-
(BRM)	-	13	-	-	-	16ns	-	-	-	-	-
Mike FISHER	**-**	**-**	**-**	**-**	**-**	**-**	**-**	**11**	**-**	**-**	**r**
(Lotus-BRM)	-	-	-	-	-	-	-	17	-	-	18
Richie GINTHER	**-**	**-**	**-**	**-**	**-**	**-**	**-**	**-**	**-**	**-**	**-**
(Eagle-Weslake)	-	nq	-	-	-	-	-	-	-	-	-
Dan GURNEY	**r**	**r**	**r**	**1f**	**r**	**r**	**rf**	**3**	**r**	**r**	**r**
(Eagle-Climax)	11	-	-	-	-	-	-	-	-	-	-
(Eagle-Weslake)	-	7	2	2	3	5	4	5	5	3	3
Hubert HAHNE	**-**	**-**	**-**	**-**	**-**	**-**	**r**	**-**	**-**	**-**	**-**
(Lola-BMW)	-	-	-	-	-	-	14	-	-	-	-
Brian HART	**-**	**-**	**-**	**-**	**-**	**-**	**nc**	**-**	**-**	**-**	**-**
(Protos-Ford Cosworth)	-	-	-	-	-	-	25	-	-	-	-
Graham HILL	**r**	**2**	**r**	**r**	**rf**	**r**	**r**	**4**	**r**	**2f**	**r**
(Lotus-BRM)	15	8	-	-	-	-	-	-	-	-	-
(Lotus-Ford Cosworth)	-	-	1	3	1	2	13	2	8	1	4
David HOBBS	**-**	**-**	**-**	**-**	**-**	**8**	**10**	**9**	**-**	**-**	**-**
(BRM)	-	-	-	-	-	14	-	12	-	-	-
(Lola-BMW)	-	-	-	-	-	-	22	-	-	-	-
Denny HULME	**4f**	**1**	**3**	**r**	**2**	**2f**	**1**	**2**	**r**	**3**	**3**
(Brabham-Repco)	2	4	7	14	6	4	2	3	6	6	6
Jacky ICKX	**-**	**-**	**-**	**-**	**-**	**-**	**r**	**-**	**6**	**r**	**-**
(Matra-Ford Cosworth)	-	-	-	-	-	-	18	-	-	-	-
(Cooper-Maserati)	-	-	-	-	-	-	-	-	15	16	-
Chris IRWIN	**-**	**-**	**7**	**r**	**5r**	**7**	**9**	**r**	**r**	**r**	**r**
(Lotus-BRM)	-	-	13	-	-	-	-	-	-	-	-
(BRM)	-	-	-	15	9	13	15	11	16	14	15
Tom JONES	**-**	**-**	**-**	**-**	**-**	**-**	**-**	**-**	**-**	**-**	**-**
(Cooper-Climax)	-	-	-	-	-	-	-	nq	-	-	-
Guy LIGIER	**-**	**-**	**-**	**10**	**nc**	**10**	**8**	**-**	**r**	**r**	**11**
(Cooper-Maserati)	-	-	-	18	15	-	-	-	-	-	-
(Brabham-Repco)	-	-	-	-	-	21	17	-	18	17	19
John LOVE	**2**	**-**	**-**	**-**	**-**	**-**	**-**	**-**	**-**	**-**	**-**
(Cooper-Climax)	5	-	-	-	-	-	-	-	-	-	-
Bruce McLAREN	**-**	**4**	**r**	**-**	**r**	**r**	**r**	**7**	**r**	**r**	**r**
(McLaren-BRM)	-	10	14	-	-	-	-	6	3	9	8
(Eagle-Weslake)	-	-	-	-	5	10	5	-	-	-	-
Gerhard MITTER	**-**	**-**	**-**	**-**	**-**	**-**	**r**	**-**	**-**	**-**	**-**
(Brabham-Ford Cosworth)	-	-	-	-	-	-	24	-	-	-	-
Silvio MOSER	**-**	**-**	**-**	**-**	**-**	**r**	**-**	**-**	**-**	**-**	**-**
(Cooper-ATS)	-	-	-	-	-	20	-	-	-	-	-
Jackie OLIVER	**-**	**-**	**-**	**-**	**-**	**-**	**5**	**-**	**-**	**-**	**-**
(Lotus-Ford Cosworth)	-	-	-	-	-	-	19	-	-	-	-
Mike PARKES	**-**	**-**	**5**	**r**	**-**	**-**	**-**	**-**	**-**	**-**	**-**
(Ferrari)	-	-	10	8	-	-	-	-	-	-	-
Al PEASE -	**-**	**-**	**-**	**-**	**-**	**-**	**nc**	**-**	**-**	**-**	
(Eagle-Climax)	-	-	-	-	-	-	-	15	-	-	-
Brian REDMAN	**-**	**-**	**-**	**-**	**-**	**-**	**-**	**-**	**-**	**-**	**-**
(Lola-Ford Cosworth)	-	-	-	-	-	-	ns	-	-	-	-
Alan REES	**-**	**-**	**-**	**-**	**-**	**9**	**7**	**-**	**-**	**-**	**-**
(Cooper-Maserati)	-	-	-	-	-	15	-	-	-	-	-
(Brabham-Ford Cosworth)	-	-	-	-	-	-	20	-	-	-	-
Jochen RINDT	**r**	**r**	**r**	**4**	**r**	**r**	**r**	**r**	**4**	**r**	**-**
(Cooper-Maserati)	7	15	4	4	8	8	9	8	11	8	-
Pedro RODRIGUEZ	**1**	**5**	**r**	**9r**	**6**	**5**	**11**	**-**	**-**	**-**	**6**
(Cooper-Maserati)	4	16	5	13	13	9	10	-	-	-	13
Ludovico SCARFIOTTI	**-**	**-**	**6**	**nc**	**-**	**-**	**-**	**-**	**r**	**-**	**-**
(Ferrari)	-	-	15	9	-	-	-	-	-	-	-
(Eagle-Weslake)	-	-	-	-	-	-	-	-	10	-	-
Jo SCHLESSER	**-**	**-**	**-**	**-**	**-**	**-**	**r**	**-**	**-**	**-**	**-**
(Matra-Ford Cosworth)	-	-	-	-	-	-	21	-	-	-	-
Johnny SERVOZ-GAVIN	**-**	**r**	**-**	**-**	**-**	**-**	**-**	**-**	**-**	**-**	**-**
(Matra-Ford Cosworth)	-	11	-	-	-	-	-	-	-	-	-
Jo SIFFERT	**r**	**r**	**10**	**7**	**4**	**r**	**r**	**-**	**r**	**4**	**12r**
(Cooper-Maserati)	16	9	16	16	11	18	12	ns	13	12	10
Moises SOLANA	**-**	**-**	**-**	**-**	**-**	**-**	**-**	**-**	**-**	**r**	**r**
(Lotus-Ford Cosworth)	-	-	-	-	-	-	-	-	-	7	9
Mike SPENCE	**r**	**6**	**8**	**5**	**r**	**r**	**r**	**5**	**5**	**r**	**5**
(BRM)	13	12	12	11	12	11	11	10	12	13	11
Jackie STEWART	**r**	**r**	**r**	**2**	**3**	**r**	**r**	**r**	**r**	**r**	**r**
(BRM)	9	6	11	6	10	12	3	9	7	10	12
John SURTEES	**3**	**r**	**r**	**r**	**-**	**6**	**4**	**-**	**1**	**r**	**4**
(Honda)	6	3	6	10	-	7	6	-	9	11	7
Sam TINGLE	**r**	**-**	**-**	**-**	**-**	**-**	**-**	**-**	**-**	**-**	**-**
(LDS-Climax)	14	-	-	-	-	-	-	-	-	-	-
Eppie WIETZES	**-**	**-**	**-**	**-**	**-**	**-**	**-**	**r**	**-**	**-**	**-**
(Lotus-Ford Cosworth)	-	-	-	-	-	-	-	16	-	-	-
Jonathan WILLIAMS	**-**	**-**	**-**	**-**	**-**	**-**	**-**	**-**	**-**	**-**	**8**
(Ferrari)	-	-	-	-	-	-	-	-	-	-	16

1968 RACE RESULTS & GRID POSITIONS

	ZA	E	MC	B	NL	F	GB	D	I	CDN	USA	MEX
Kurt AHRENS	-	-	-	-	-	-	-	12	-	-	-	-
(Brabham-Repco)	-	-	-	-	-	-	-	17	-	-	-	-
Chris AMON	4	r	-	r	6	10	2	r	r	r	r	r
(Ferrari)	8	1	-	1	1	5	3	2	3	2	4	2
Mario ANDRETTI	-	-	-	-	-	-	-	-	-	-	r	-
(Lotus-Ford Cosworth)	-	-	-	-	-	-	-	-	exc	-	1	-
Dickie ATTWOOD	-	-	2f	r	7	7	r	14	-	-	-	-
(BRM)	-	-	6	11	15	12	15	20	-	-	-	-
Derek BELL	-	-	-	-	-	-	-	-	r	-	r	-
(Ferrari)	-	-	-	-	-	-	-	-	8	-	15	-
Jean-Pierre BELTOISE	6	5f	r	8	2f	9	r	r	5	r	r	r
(Matra-Ford Cosworth)	18	5	-	-	-	-	-	-	-	-	-	-
(Matra)	-	-	8	13	16	8	14	12	18	15	13	13
Lucien BIANCHI	-	-	3	6	r	-	-	r	-	nc	r	r
(Cooper-BRM)	-	-	14	12	18	-	-	19	-	18	20	21
Jo BONNIER	r	-	-	r	8	-	r	-	6	r	r	5
(Cooper-Maserati)	19	-	-	-	-	-	-	-	-	-	-	-
(McLaren-BRM)	-	-	nq	16	19	-	20	-	19	17	18	-
(Honda)	-	-	-	-	-	-	-	-	-	-	-	18
Jack BRABHAM	r	-	r	r	r	r	r	5	r	r	r	10r
(Brabham-Repco)	5	ns	12	18	4	13	8	15	16	10	8	8
Bill BRACK	-	-	-	-	-	-	-	-	-	r	-	-
(Lotus-Ford Cosworth)	-	-	-	-	-	-	-	-	-	20	-	-
Dave CHARLTON	r	-	-	-	-	-	-	-	-	-	-	-
(Brabham-Repco)	14	-	-	-	-	-	-	-	-	-	-	-
Jim CLARK +	1f	-	-	-	-	-	-	-	-	-	-	-
(Lotus-Ford Cosworth)	1	-	-	-	-	-	-	-	-	-	-	-
Piers COURAGE	-	r	r	r	r	6	8	8	4	r	r	r
(BRM)	-	11	11	7	14	14	16	8	17	14	14	19
Andrea de ADAMICH	r	-	-	-	-	-	-	-	-	-	-	-
(Ferrari)	7	-	-	-	-	-	-	-	-	-	-	-
Vic ELFORD	-	-	-	-	-	4	r	r	r	5	r	8
(Cooper-BRM)	-	-	-	-	-	17	17	5	20	16	17	17
Frank GARDNER	-	-	-	-	-	-	-	-	-	-	-	-
(BRM)	-	-	-	-	-	-	-	-	nq	-	-	-
Dan GURNEY	r	-	r	-	r	-	r	9	r	r	4	r
(Eagle-Weslake)	12	-	16	-	-	-	6	10	12	-	-	-
(Brabham-Repco)	-	-	-	-	12	-	-	-	-	-	-	-
(McLaren-Ford Cosworth)	-	-	-	-	-	-	-	-	-	4	7	5
Hubert HAHNE	-	-	-	-	-	-	-	10	-	-	-	-
(Lola-BMW)	-	-	-	-	-	-	-	18	-	-	-	-
Graham HILL	2	1	1	r	9r	r	r	2	r	4	2	1
(Lotus-Ford Cosworth)	2	6	1	14	3	9	1	4	5	5	3	3
David HOBBS	-	-	-	-	-	-	-	-	r	-	-	-
(Honda)	-	-	-	-	-	-	-	-	14	-	-	-
Denny HULME	5	2	5	r	r	5	4	7	1	1	r	r
(McLaren-BRM)	9	-	-	-	-	-	-	-	-	-	-	-
(McLaren-Ford Cosworth)	-	3	10	5	7	4	11	11	7	6	5	4
Jacky ICKX	r	r	-	3	4	1	3	4	3	-	-	r
(Ferrari)	11	8	-	3	6	3	12	1	4	ns	-	15
John LOVE	9	-	-	-	-	-	-	-	-	-	-	-
(Brabham-Repco)	17	-	-	-	-	-	-	-	-	-	-	-
Bruce McLAREN	-	r	r	1	r	8	7	13	r	2	6	2
(McLaren-Ford Cosworth)	-	4	7	6	8	6	10	16	2	8	10	9
Silvio MOSER	-	-	-	-	5	-	nc	-	-	-	-	-
(Brabham-Repco)	-	-	nq	-	17	-	19	ns	nq	-	-	-
Jackie OLIVER	-	-	r	5r	nc	-	r	11	rf	r	-	3
(Lotus-Ford Cosworth)	-	-	13	15	10	ns	2	13	11	9	16ns	14
Al PEASE	-	-	-	-	-	-	-	-	-	-	-	-
(Eagle-Climax)	-	-	-	-	-	-	-	-	-	ns	-	-
Henri PESCAROLO	-	-	-	-	-	-	-	-	-	r	-	9
(Matra)	-	-	-	-	-	-	-	-	-	19	ns	20
Jackie PRETORIUS	nc	-	-	-	-	-	-	-	-	-	-	-
(Brabham-Climax)	23	-	-	-	-	-	-	-	-	-	-	-
Brian REDMAN	r	3	-	r	-	-	-	-	-	-	-	-
(Cooper-Maserati)	21	-	-	-	-	-	-	-	-	-	-	-
(Cooper-BRM)	-	13	-	10	-	-	-	-	-	-	-	-
Jochen RINDT	3	r	r	r	r	r	r	3	r	r	r	r
(Brabham-Repco)	4	9	5	17	2	1	5	3	10	1	6	10
Pedro RODRIGUEZ	r	r	r	2	3	ncf	r	6	r	3	r	4
(BRM)	10	2	9	8	11	10	13	14	15	12	11	12
Ludovico SCARFIOTTI +	r	4	4	-	-	-	-	-	-	-	-	-
(Cooper-Maserati)	15	-	-	-	-	-	-	-	-	-	-	-
(Cooper-BRM)	-	12	15	-	-	-	-	-	-	-	-	-
Jo SCHLESSER +	-	-	-	-	-	r	-	-	-	-	-	-
(Honda)	-	-	-	-	-	16	-	-	-	-	-	-
Johnny SERVOZ-GAVIN	-	-	r	-	-	r	-	-	2	r	-	11r
(Matra-Ford Cosworth)	-	-	2	-	-	-	-	-	13	13	-	16
(Cooper-BRM)	-	-	-	-	-	15	-	-	-	-	-	-
Jo SIFFERT	7	r	r	7r	r	11	1f	r	r	rf	5	6f
(Cooper-Maserati)	16	-	-	-	-	-	-	-	-	-	-	-
(Lotus-Ford Cosworth)	-	10	3	9	13	11	4	9	9	3	12	1
Moises SOLANA	-	-	-	-	-	-	-	-	-	-	-	r
(Lotus-Ford Cosworth)	-	-	-	-	-	-	-	-	-	-	-	11
Mike SPENCE +	r	-	-	-	-	-	-	-	-	-	-	-
(BRM)	13	-	-	-	-	-	-	-	-	-	-	-
Jackie STEWART	r	-	-	4	1	3	6	1f	r	6	1f	7
(Matra-Ford Cosworth)	3	-	-	2	5	2	7	6	6	11	2	7
John SURTEES	8	r	r	rf	r	2	5	r	r	r	3	r
(Honda)	6	7	4	4	9	7	9	7	1	7	9	6
Sam TINGLE	r	-	-	-	-	-	-	-	-	-	-	-
(LDS-Repco)	22	-	-	-	-	-	-	-	-	-	-	-
Bobby UNSER	-	-	-	-	-	-	-	-	-	-	r	-
(BRM)	-	-	-	-	-	-	-	-	exc	-	19	-
Basil van ROOYEN	r	-	-	-	-	-	-	-	-	-	-	-
(Cooper-Climax)	20	-	-	-	-	-	-	-	-	-	-	-
Robin WIDDOWS	-	-	-	-	-	-	r	-	-	-	-	-
(Cooper-BRM)	-	-	-	-	-	-	18	-	-	-	-	-

1969 RACE RESULTS & GRID POSITIONS

	ZA	E	MC	NL	F	GB	D	I	CDN	USA	MEX
Kurt AHRENS	-	-	-	-	-	-	7	-	-	-	-
(Brabham-Ford Cosworth)	-	-	-	-	-	-	19	-	-	-	-
Chris AMON	r	r	r	3	r	r	-	-	-	-	-
(Ferrari)	5	2	2	4	6	5	-	-	-	-	-
Mario ANDRETTI	r	-	-	-	-	-	r	-	-	r	-
(Lotus-Ford Cosworth)	6	-	-	-	-	-	12	-	-	13	-
Dickie ATTWOOD	-	-	4	-	-	-	6	-	-	-	-
(Lotus-Ford Cosworth)	-	-	10	-	-	-	-	-	-	-	-
(Brabham-Ford Cosworth)	-	-	-	-	-	-	20	-	-	-	-
Derek BELL	-	-	-	-	-	r	-	-	-	-	-
(McLaren-Ford Cosworth)	-	-	-	-	-	15	-	-	-	-	-
Jean-Pierre BELTOISE	6	3	r	8	2	9	12r	3f	4	r	5
(Matra-Ford Cosworth)	11	12	3	11	5	17	10	6	2	7	8
Jo BONNIER	-	-	-	-	-	r	r	-	-	-	-
(Lotus-Ford Cosworth)	-	-	-	-	-	16	14	-	-	-	-
Jack BRABHAM	r	r	r	6	-	-	-	r	2f=	4	3
(Brabham-Ford Cosworth)	1	5	8	8	-	-	-	7	6	10	1
Bill BRACK	-	-	-	-	-	-	-	-	nc	-	-
(BRM)	-	-	-	-	-	-	-	-	18	-	-
Tino BRAMBILLA	-	-	-	-	-	-	-	-	-	-	-
(Ferrari)	-	-	-	-	-	-	-	ns	-	-	-
François CEVERT	-	-	-	-	-	-	r	-	-	-	-
(Tecno-Ford Cosworth)	-	-	-	-	-	-	16	-	-	-	-
John CORDTS	-	-	-	-	-	-	-	-	r	-	-
(Brabham-Climax)	-	-	-	-	-	-	-	-	19	-	-
Piers COURAGE	-	r	2	r	r	5	r	5	r	2	10
(Brabham-Ford Cosworth)	-	11	9	9	11	10	7	4	10	9	9
Peter de KLERK	nc	-	-	-	-	-	-	-	-	-	-
(Brabham-Repco)	16	-	-	-	-	-	-	-	-	-	-
George EATON	-	-	-	-	-	-	-	-	-	r	r
(BRM)	-	-	-	-	-	-	-	-	-	18	17
Vic ELFORD	-	-	7	10	5	6	r	-	-	-	-
(Cooper-Maserati)	-	-	16	-	-	-	-	-	-	-	-
(McLaren-Ford Cosworth)	-	-	-	15	10	11	6	-	-	-	-
Hubert HAHNE	-	-	-	-	-	-	-	-	-	-	-
(BMW)	-	-	-	-	-	-	ns	-	-	-	-
Hans HERRMANN	-	-	-	-	-	-	-	-	-	-	-
(Lotus-Ford Cosworth)	-	-	-	-	-	-	ns	-	-	-	-
Graham HILL	2	r	1	7	6	7	4	9r	r	r	-
(Lotus-Ford Cosworth)	7	3	4	3	8	12	9	9	7	4	-
Denny HULME	3	4	6	4	8	r	r	7	r	r	1
(McLaren-Ford Cosworth)	3	8	12	7	2	3	5	2	5	2	4
Jacky ICKX	r	6r	r	5	3	2	1f	10r	1f=	r	2f
(Brabham-Ford Cosworth)	13	7	7	5	4	4	1	15	1	8	2
John LOVE	r	-	-	-	-	-	-	-	-	-	-
(Lotus-Ford Cosworth)	10	-	-	-	-	-	-	-	-	-	-
Pete LOVELY	-	-	-	-	-	-	-	-	7	r	9
(Lotus-Ford Cosworth)	-	-	-	-	-	-	-	-	16	16	16
Bruce McLAREN	5	2	5	r	4	3	3	4	5	-	r
(McLaren-Ford Cosworth)	8	13	11	6	7	7	8	5	9	6ns	7
John MILES	-	-	-	-	r	10	-	r	r	-	r
(Lotus-Ford Cosworth)	-	-	-	-	12	14	-	14	11	-	11
Gerhard MITTER +	-	-	-	-	-	-	-	-	-	-	-
(BMW)	-	-	-	-	-	-	ns	-	-	-	-
Silvio MOSER	-	-	r	r	7	-	-	r	r	6	11r
(Brabham-Ford Cosworth)	-	-	15	14	13	-	-	13	20	17	13
Jackie OLIVER	7	r	r	r	-	r	r	r	r	r	6
(BRM)	14	10	13	13	-	13	13	11	12	14	12
Al PEASE	-	-	-	-	-	-	-	-	dq	-	-
(Eagle-Climax)	-	-	-	-	-	-	-	-	17	-	-
Xavier PERROT	-	-	-	-	-	-	10	-	-	-	-
(Brabham-Ford Cosworth)	-	-	-	-	-	-	22	-	-	-	-
Henri PESCAROLO	-	-	-	-	-	-	5	-	-	-	-
(Matra-Ford Cosworth)	-	-	-	-	-	-	17	-	-	-	-
Dieter QUESTER	-	-	-	-	-	-	-	-	-	-	-
(BMW)	-	-	-	-	-	-	ns	-	-	-	-
Jochen RINDT	r	rf	-	r	r	4	r	2	3	1f	r
(Lotus-Ford Cosworth)	2	1	-	1	3	1	3	1	3	1	6
Pedro RODRIGUEZ	r	r	r	-	-	r	-	6	r	5	7
(BRM)	15	14	14	-	-	-	-	-	-	-	-
(Ferrari)	-	-	-	-	-	8	-	12	13	12	15
Johnny SERVOZ-GAVIN	-	-	-	-	-	-	r	-	6	nc	8
(Matra-Ford Cosworth)	-	-	-	-	-	-	15	-	15	15	14
Jo SIFFERT	4	r	3	2	9	8	11r	8r	r	r	r
(Lotus-Ford Cosworth)	12	6	5	10	9	9	4	8	8	5	5
Jackie STEWART	1f	1	rf	1f	1f	1f	2	1	r	r	4
(Matra-Ford Cosworth)	4	4	1	2	1	2	2	3	4	3	3
Rolf STOMMELEN	-	-	-	-	-	-	8	-	-	-	-
(Lotus-Ford Cosworth)	-	-	-	-	-	-	21	-	-	-	-
John SURTEES	r	5	r	9	-	r	-	nc	r	3	r
(BRM)	18	9	6	12	-	6	11ns	10	14	11	10
Sam TINGLE	8	-	-	-	-	-	-	-	-	-	-
(Brabham-Repco)	17	-	-	-	-	-	-	-	-	-	-
Basil van ROOYEN	r	-	-	-	-	-	-	-	-	-	-
(McLaren-Ford Cosworth)	9	-	-	-	-	-	-	-	-	-	-
Peter WESTBURY	-	-	-	-	-	-	9	-	-	-	-
(Brabham-Ford Cosworth)	-	-	-	-	-	-	18	-	-	-	-

1970 RACE RESULTS & GRID POSITIONS

Driver	ZA	E	MC	B	NL	F	GB	D	A	I	CDN	USA	MEX
Chris AMON	r	r	r	2f	r	2	5	r	8	7	3	5	4
(March-Ford Cosworth)	2	6	2	3	4	3	17	6	6	18	6	5	5
Mario ANDRETTI	r	3	-	-	-	-	r	r	r	-	-	-	-
(March-Ford Cosworth)	11	16	-	-	-	-	9	9	18	-	-	-	-
Derek BELL	-	-	-	r	-	-	-	-	-	-	-	6	-
(Brabham-Ford Cosworth)	-	-	-	15	-	-	-	-	-	-	-	-	-
(Surtees-Ford Cosworth)	-	-	-	-	-	-	-	-	-	-	-	13	-
Jean-Pierre BELTOISE	4	r	r	3	5	13r	r	r	6	3	8	r	5
(Matra Simca)	8	4	6	11	10	2	10	21	7	14	13	18	6
Jo BONNIER	-	-	-	-	-	-	-	-	-	-	-	r	-
(McLaren-Ford Cosworth)	-	-	-	-	-	-	-	-	-	nq	-	24	-
Jack BRABHAM	1f=	rf	2	r	11	3f	2f	r	13	r	r	10	r
(Brabham-Ford Cosworth)	3	1	4	5	12	5	2	12	8	8	19	16	4
François CEVERT	-	-	-	-	r	11	7	7	r	6	9	r	r
(March-Ford Cosworth)	-	-	-	-	15	13	14	14	9	11	4	17	9
Dave CHARLTON	12r	-	-	-	-	-	-	-	-	-	-	-	-
(Lotus-Ford Cosworth)	13	-	-	-	-	-	-	-	-	-	-	-	-
Piers COURAGE +	r	-	nc	r	r	-	-	-	-	-	-	-	-
(De Tomaso-Ford Cosworth)	20	13ns	9	12	9	-	-	-	-	-	-	-	-
Andrea de ADAMICH	-	-	-	-	-	nc	-	-	12	8	r	-	-
(McLaren-Alfa Romeo)	-	nq	nq	-	nq	15	18ns	nq	15	12	12	nq	-
Peter de KLERK	11	-	-	-	-	-	-	-	-	-	-	-	-
(Brabham-Ford Cosworth)	21	-	-	-	-	-	-	-	-	-	-	-	-
George EATON	r	-	-	-	r	12	r	-	11	r	10	r	-
(BRM)	23	nq	nq	-	18	19	16	-	23	20	9	14	-
Emerson FITTIPALDI	-	-	-	-	-	-	8	4	15	-	-	1	r
(Lotus-Ford Cosworth)	-	-	-	-	-	-	21	13	16	ns	-	3	18
Nanni GALLI	-	-	-	-	-	-	-	-	-	-	-	-	-
(McLaren-Alfa Romeo)	-	-	-	-	-	-	-	-	-	nq	-	-	-
Peter GETHIN	-	-	-	-	r	-	-	r	10	nc	6	14	r
(McLaren-Ford Cosworth)	-	-	-	-	11	-	-	17	21	16	11	21	10
Ignazio GIUNTI	-	-	-	4	-	14	-	-	7	r	-	-	-
(Ferrari)	-	-	-	8	-	11	-	-	5	5	-	-	-
Dan GURNEY	-	-	-	-	r	6	r	-	-	-	-	-	-
(McLaren-Ford Cosworth)	-	-	-	-	19	17	11	-	-	-	-	-	-
Hubert HAHNE	-	-	-	-	-	-	-	-	-	-	-	-	-
(March-Ford Cosworth)	-	-	-	-	-	-	-	nq	-	-	-	-	-
Graham HILL	6	4	5	r	nc	10	6	r	-	-	nc	r	r
(Lotus-Ford Cosworth)	19	15	16	16	20	20	22	20	-	ns	20	10	8
Denny HULME	2	r	4	-	-	4	3	3	r	4	r	7	3
(McLaren-Ford Cosworth)	6	2	3	-	-	7	5	16	11	9	15	11	14
Gus HUTCHISON	-	-	-	-	-	-	-	-	-	-	-	r	-
(Brabham-Ford Cosworth)	-	-	-	-	-	-	-	-	-	-	-	22	-
Jacky ICKX	r	r	r	8	3f	r	r	2f	1f=	r	1	4f	1f
(Ferrari)	5	7	5	4	3	1	3	1	3	1	2	1	3
John LOVE	8	-	-	-	-	-	-	-	-	-	-	-	-
(Lotus-Ford Cosworth)	22	-	-	-	-	-	-	-	-	-	-	-	-
Pete LOVELY	-	-	-	-	-	-	nc	-	-	-	-	-	-
(Lotus-Ford Cosworth)	-	-	-	-	nq	nq	23	-	-	-	-	nq	-
Bruce McLAREN +	r	2	r	-	-	-	-	-	-	-	-	-	-
(McLaren-Ford Cosworth)	10	11	10	-	-	-	-	-	-	-	-	-	-
John MILES	5	-	-	r	7	8	r	r	r	-	-	-	-
(Lotus-Ford Cosworth)	14	nq	nq	13	8	18	7	10	10	ns	-	-	-
Silvio MOSER	-	-	-	-	-	-	-	-	r	-	-	-	-
(Bellasi-Ford Cosworth)	-	-	-	-	nq	nq	-	nq	24	nq	-	-	-
Jackie OLIVER	r	r	r	r	r	r	r	r	5	r	nc	r	7
(BRM)	12	10	14	14	5	12	4	18	14	6	10	7	13
Henri PESCAROLO	7	r	3	6r	8	5	r	6	14	r	7	8	9
(Matra Simca)	18	9	7	17	13	8	12	5	13	15	8	12	11
Ronnie PETERSON	-	-	7	nc	9	r	9	r	-	r	nc	11	-
(March-Ford Cosworth)	-	-	12	9	16	9	13	19	-	13	16	15	-
Brian REDMAN	-	-	-	-	-	-	-	-	-	-	-	-	-
(De Tomaso-Ford Cosworth)	-	-	-	-	-	-	ns	nq	-	-	-	-	-
Clay REGAZZONI	-	-	-	-	4	-	4	r	2f=	1f	2f	13	2
(Ferrari)	-	-	-	-	6	-	6	3	2	3	3	6	1
Jochen RINDT +	13r	r	1f	r	1	1	1	1	r	-	-	-	-
(Lotus-Ford Cosworth)	4	8	8	2	1	6	1	2	1	ns	-	-	-
Pedro RODRIGUEZ	9	r	6	1	10	r	r	r	4	r	4	2	6
(BRM)	16	5	15	6	7	10	15	8	22	2	7	4	7
Tim SCHENKEN	-	-	-	-	-	-	-	-	r	r	nc	r	-
(De Tomaso-Ford Cosworth)	-	-	-	-	-	-	-	-	19	19	17	20	-
Johnny SERVOZ-GAVIN	r	5	-	-	-	-	-	-	-	-	-	-	-
(March-Ford Cosworth)	17	14	nq	-	-	-	-	-	-	-	-	-	-
Jo SIFFERT	10	-	8r	7r	r	r	r	8r	9	r	r	9	r
(March-Ford Cosworth)	9	nq	11	10	17	16	20	4	20	7	14	23	16
Alex SOLER-ROIG	-	-	-	-	-	-	-	-	-	-	-	-	-
(Lotus-Ford Cosworth)	-	nq	-	nq	-	nq	-	-	-	-	-	-	-
Jackie STEWART	3	1	r	r	2	9	r	r	r	2	r	r	r
(March-Ford Cosworth)	1	3	1	1	2	4	8	7	4	4	-	-	-
(Tyrrell-Ford Cosworth)	-	-	-	-	-	-	-	-	-	-	1	2	2
Rolf STOMMELEN	r	r	-	5	-	7	-	5	3	5	r	12	r
(Brabham-Ford Cosworth)	15	17	nq	7	nq	14	ns	11	17	17	18	19	17
John SURTEES	rf=	r	r	-	6	-	r	9r	r	r	5	r	8
(McLaren-Ford Cosworth)	7	12	13	-	14	-	-	-	-	-	-	-	-
(Surtees-Ford Cosworth)	-	-	-	-	-	-	19	15	12	10	5	8	15
Peter WESTBURY	-	-	-	-	-	-	-	-	-	-	-	-	-
(BRM)	-	-	-	-	-	-	-	-	-	-	-	nq	-
Reine WISELL	-	-	-	-	-	-	-	-	-	-	-	3	nc
(Lotus-Ford Cosworth)	-	-	-	-	-	-	-	-	-	-	-	9	12

1971 RACE RESULTS & GRID POSITIONS

	ZA	E	MC	NL	F	GB	D	A	I	CDN	USA
Chris AMON	**5**	**3**	**r**	**r**	**5**	**r**	**r**	-	**6**	**10**	**12**
(Matra Simca)	2	3	4	5	9	9	16	-	1	5	8
Mario ANDRETTI	**1f**	**r**	-	**r**	-	-	**4**	-	-	**13**	-
(Ferrari)	4	8	nq	18	-	-	11	-	-	13	ns
Skip BARBER	-	-	-	**nc**	-	-	-	-	-	**r**	**nc**
(March-Ford Cosworth)	-	-	nq	24	-	-	-	-	-	24	25
Derek BELL	-	-	-	-	-	**r**	-	-	-	-	-
(Surtees-Ford Cosworth)	-	-	-	-	-	23	-	-	-	-	-
Jean-Pierre BELTOISE	-	**6**	**r**	**9**	**7**	**7**	-	-	-	**r**	**8**
(Matra Simca)	-	6	7	11	8	15	-	-	-	11	10
Mike BEUTTLER	-	-	-	-	-	**r**	**dq**	**nc**	**r**	**nc**	-
(March-Ford Cosworth)	-	-	-	-	-	20	22	19	16	22	-
Jo BONNIER	**r**	-	-	-	-	-	-	-	**10**	-	**16r**
(McLaren-Ford Cosworth)	23	-	-	-	-	-	nq	20ns	21	-	28
John CANNON	-	-	-	-	-	-	-	-	-	-	**14**
(BRM)	-	-	-	-	-	-	-	-	-	-	24
François CEVERT	**r**	**7**	**r**	**r**	**2**	**10**	**2f**	**r**	**3**	**6**	**1**
(Tyrrell-Ford Cosworth)	9	12	15	12	7	10	5	3	5	3	5
Dave CHARLTON	**r**	-	-	-	-	**r**	-	-	-	-	-
(Brabham-Ford Cosworth)	12	-	-	-	-	-	-	-	-	-	-
(Lotus-Ford Cosworth)	-	-	-	-	-	13	-	-	-	-	-
Chris CRAFT	-	-	-	-	-	-	-	-	-	-	**r**
(Brabham-Ford Cosworth)	-	-	-	-	-	-	-	-	-	ns	27
Andrea de ADAMICH	**13**	**r**	-	-	**r**	**nc**	**r**	-	**r**	-	**11**
(March-Alfa Romeo)	22	18	-	-	20	24	20	-	20	-	26
Mark DONOHUE	-	-	-	-	-	-	-	-	-	**3**	-
(McLaren-Ford Cosworth)	-	-	-	-	-	-	-	-	-	8	ns
George EATON	-	-	-	-	-	-	-	-	-	**15**	-
(BRM)	-	-	-	-	-	-	-	-	-	21	-
Vic ELFORD	-	-	-	-	-	-	**11**	-	-	-	-
(BRM)	-	-	-	-	-	-	18	-	-	-	-
Emerson FITTIPALDI	**r**	**r**	**5**	-	**3**	**3**	**r**	**2**	**8**	**7**	**nc**
(Lotus-Ford Cosworth)	5	14	17	-	17	4	8	5	-	4	2
(Lotus-Pratt & Whitney)	-	-	-	-	-	-	-	-	18	-	-
Nanni GALLI	-	-	-	**r**	-	**11**	**12**	**12**	**r**	**16**	**r**
(March-Alfa Romeo)	-	-	nq	20	-	-	21	15	-	-	-
(March-Ford Cosworth)	-	-	-	-	ns	21	-	-	19	20	23
Howden GANLEY	**r**	**10**	-	**7**	**10**	**8**	**r**	**r**	**5**	-	**4**
(BRM)	24	17	nq	9	16	11	14	14	4	9ns	12
Peter GETHIN	**r**	**8**	**r**	**nc**	**9**	**r**	**r**	**10**	**1**	**14**	**9**
(McLaren-Ford Cosworth)	11	7	14	23	19	14	19	-	-	-	-
(BRM)	-	-	-	-	-	-	-	16	11	16	21
Mike HAILWOOD	-	-	-	-	-	-	-	-	**4**	-	**15r**
(Surtees-Ford Cosworth)	-	-	-	-	-	-	-	-	17	-	14
Graham HILL	**9**	**r**	**r**	**10**	**r**	**r**	**9**	**5**	**r**	**r**	**7**
(Brabham-Ford Cosworth)	19	15	9	16	4	16	13	8	14	15	18
David HOBBS	-	-	-	-	-	-	-	-	-	-	**10**
(McLaren-Ford Cosworth)	-	-	-	-	-	-	-	-	-	-	22
Denny HULME	**6**	**5**	**4**	**12**	**r**	**r**	**r**	**r**	-	**4f**	**r**
(McLaren-Ford Cosworth)	7	9	6	14	11	8	6	9	-	10	3
Jacky ICKX	**8**	**2f**	**3**	**1f**	**r**	**r**	**r**	**r**	**r**	**8**	**rf**
(Ferrari)	8	1	2	1	3	6	2	6	2	12	7
Jean-Pierre JARIER	-	-	-	-	-	-	-	-	**nc**	-	-
(March-Ford Cosworth)	-	-	-	-	-	-	-	-	24	-	-
Niki LAUDA	-	-	-	-	-	-	-	**r**	-	-	-
(March-Ford Cosworth)	-	-	-	-	-	-	-	21	-	-	-
John LOVE	**r**	-	-	-	-	-	-	-	-	-	-
(March-Ford Cosworth)	21	-	-	-	-	-	-	-	-	-	-
Pete LOVELY	-	-	-	-	-	-	-	-	-	**nc**	**nc**
(Lotus-Ford Cosworth)	-	-	-	-	-	-	-	-	-	25	29
Helmut MARKO	-	-	-	-	-	-	-	**11**	**r**	**12**	**13**
(McLaren-Ford Cosworth)	-	-	-	-	-	-	nq	-	-	-	-
(BRM)	-	-	-	-	-	-	-	17	12	19	16
Jean MAX	-	-	-	-	**nc**	-	-	-	-	-	-
(March-Ford Cosworth)	-	-	-	-	22	-	-	-	-	-	-
François MAZET	-	-	-	-	**13**	-	-	-	-	-	-
(March-Ford Cosworth)	-	-	-	-	23	-	-	-	-	-	-
Silvio MOSER	-	-	-	-	-	-	-	-	**r**	-	-
(Bellasi-Ford Cosworth)	-	-	-	-	-	-	-	-	22	-	-
Jackie OLIVER	-	-	-	-	-	**r**	-	**9**	**7**	-	-
(McLaren-Ford Cosworth)	-	-	-	-	-	22	-	22	13	-	-
Henri PESCAROLO	**11**	**r**	**8**	**nc**	**r**	**4**	**r**	**6**	**rf**	-	**r**
(March-Ford Cosworth)	18	11	13	15	18	17	10	13	10	ns	20
Ronnie PETERSON	**10**	**r**	**2**	**4**	**r**	**2**	**5**	**8**	**2**	**2**	**3**
(March-Ford Cosworth)	13	13	8	13	-	5	7	11	6	6	11
(March-Alfa Romeo)	-	-	-	-	12	-	-	-	-	-	-
Sam POSEY	-	-	-	-	-	-	-	-	-	-	**r**
(Surtees-Ford Cosworth)	-	-	-	-	-	-	-	-	-	-	17
Jackie PRETORIUS	**r**	-	-	-	-	-	-	-	-	-	-
(Brabham-Ford Cosworth)	20	-	-	-	-	-	-	-	-	-	-
Brian REDMAN	**7**	-	-	-	-	-	-	-	-	-	-
(Surtees-Ford Cosworth)	17	-	-	-	-	-	-	-	-	-	-
Clay REGAZZONI	**3**	**r**	**r**	**3**	**r**	**r**	**3**	**r**	**r**	**r**	**6**
(Ferrari)	3	2	11	4	2	1	4	4	8	18	4
Peter REVSON	-	-	-	-	-	-	-	-	-	-	**r**
(Tyrrell-Ford Cosworth)	-	-	-	-	-	-	-	-	-	-	19
Pedro RODRIGUEZ +	**r**	**4**	**9**	**2**	**r**	-	-	-	-	-	-
(BRM)	10	5	5	2	5	-	-	-	-	-	-
Tim SCHENKEN	-	**9**	**10**	**r**	**12r**	**12r**	**6**	**3**	**r**	**r**	**r**
(Brabham-Ford Cosworth)	-	21	18	19	14	7	9	7	9	17	15
Jo SIFFERT +	**r**	**r**	**r**	**6**	**4**	**9**	**r**	**1f**	**9**	**9**	**2**
(BRM)	16	10	3	8	6	3	3	1	3	2	6
Alex SOLER-ROIG	**r**	**r**	-	**r**	**r**	-	-	-	-	-	-
(March-Ford Cosworth)	25	20	nq	17	21	-	-	-	-	-	-
Jackie STEWART	**2**	**1**	**1f**	**11**	**1f**	**1f**	**1**	**r**	**r**	**1**	**5**
(Tyrrell-Ford Cosworth)	1	4	1	3	1	2	1	2	7	1	1
Rolf STOMMELEN	**12**	**r**	**6**	**dq**	**11**	**5**	**10**	**7**	-	**r**	-
(Surtees-Ford Cosworth)	15	19	16	10	10	12	12	12	23ns	23	-
John SURTEES	**r**	**11**	**7**	**5**	**8**	**6**	**7**	**r**	**r**	**11**	**17**
(Surtees-Ford Cosworth)	6	22	10	7	13	18	15	18	15	14	13
Gijs van LENNEP	-	-	-	**8**	-	-	-	-	-	-	-
(Surtees-Ford Cosworth)	-	-	-	21	-	-	-	-	-	-	ns
Dave WALKER	-	-	-	**r**	-	-	-	-	-	-	-
(Lotus-Pratt & Whitney)	-	-	-	22	-	-	-	-	-	-	-
Reine WISELL	**4**	**nc**	**r**	**dq**	**6**	**nc**	**8**	**4**	-	**5**	**r**
(Lotus-Ford Cosworth)	14	16	12	6	15	-	17	10	-	7	9
(Lotus-Pratt & Whitney)	-	-	-	-	-	19	-	-	-	-	-

1972 RACE RESULTS & GRID POSITIONS

	RA	ZA	E	MC	B	F	GB	D	A	I	CDN	USA
Chris AMON	**r**	**15**	**r**	**6**	**6f**	**3f**	**4**	**15**	**5**	**r**	**6**	**15**
(Matra Simca)	12	13	6	6	13	1	17	8	6	2	10	7
Mario ANDRETTI	**r**	**4**	**r**	-	-	-	-	-	-	**7**	-	**6**
(Ferrari)	9	6	5	-	-	-	-	-	-	7	-	10
Skip BARBER	-	-	-	-	-	-	-	-	-	-	**nc**	**16**
(March-Ford Cosworth)	-	-	-	-	-	-	-	-	-	-	22	20
Derek BELL	-	-	-	-	-	-	-	**r**	-	-	-	**r**
(Tecno)	-	-	-	-	-	ns	-	25	-	nq	ns	29
Jean-Pierre BELTOISE	-	**r**	**r**	**1f**	**r**	**15**	**11**	**9**	**8**	**8**	**r**	**r**
(BRM)	-	11	7	4	6	24	6	13	21	16	20	18
Mike BEUTTLER	-	-	-	**13**	**r**	**r**	**13**	**8**	**r**	**10**	**nc**	**13**
(March-Ford Cosworth)	-	-	nq	23	22	23	23	27	24	25	24	21
Bill BRACK	-	-	-	-	-	-	-	-	-	-	**r**	-
(BRM)	-	-	-	-	-	-	-	-	-	-	23	-
François CEVERT	**r**	**9**	**r**	**nc**	**2**	**4**	**r**	**10**	**9**	**r**	**r**	**2**
(Tyrrell-Ford Cosworth)	7	8	12	12	5	7	12	5	20	14	6	4
Dave CHARLTON	-	**r**	-	-	-	-	**r**	**r**	-	-	-	-
(Lotus-Ford Cosworth)	-	17	-	-	-	ns	24	26	-	-	-	-
Andrea de ADAMICH	**r**	**nc**	**4**	**7**	**r**	**14**	**r**	**13**	**14**	**r**	**r**	**r**
(Surtees-Ford Cosworth)	14	20	13	18	10	12	20	20	13	21	15	19
Patrick DEPAILLER	-	-	-	-	-	**nc**	-	-	-	-	-	**7**
(Tyrrell-Ford Cosworth)	-	-	-	-	-	16	-	-	-	-	-	11
Willie FERGUSON	-	-	-	-	-	-	-	-	-	-	-	-
(Brabham-Ford Cosworth)	-	ns	-	-	-	-	-	-	-	-	-	-
Emerson FITTIPALDI	**r**	**2**	**1**	**3**	**1**	**2**	**1**	**r**	**1**	**1**	**11**	**r**
(JPS Lotus-Ford Cosworth)	5	3	3	1	1	8	2	3	1	6	4	9
Wilson FITTIPALDI	-	-	**7**	**9**	**r**	**8**	**12r**	**7**	**r**	**r**	**r**	**r**
(Brabham-Ford Cosworth)	-	-	14	21	18	14	22	21	15	15	11	13
Nanni GALLI	-	-	-	-	**r**	**13**	**r**	-	**nc**	**r**	-	-
(Tecno)	-	-	-	-	24	-	18	-	23	23	-	-
(Ferrari)	-	-	-	-	-	19	-	-	-	-	-	-
Howden GANLEY	**9**	**nc**	**r**	**r**	**8**	-	-	**4**	**6**	**11**	**10**	**r**
(BRM)	13	16	20	20	15	ns	-	18	10	17	14	17
Peter GETHIN	**r**	**nc**	**r**	**dq**	**r**	-	**r**	-	**13**	**6**	**r**	**r**
(BRM)	18	18	21	5	17	ns	16	-	16	12	12	28
Mike HAILWOOD	-	**rf**	**r**	**r**	**4**	**6**	**r**	**r**	**4**	**2**	-	**17r**
(Surtees-Ford Cosworth)	-	4	15	11	8	10	7	16	12	9	-	14
Graham HILL	**r**	**6**	**10**	**12**	**r**	**10**	**r**	**6**	**r**	**5**	**8**	**11**
(Brabham-Ford Cosworth)	16	14	23	19	16	20	21	15	14	13	17	27
Denny HULME	**2**	**1**	**r**	**15**	**3**	**7**	**5**	**r**	**2f**	**3**	**3**	**3**
(McLaren-Ford Cosworth)	4	5	2	7	3	2	11	10	7	5	2	3
Jacky ICKX	**3**	**8**	**2f**	**2**	**r**	**11**	**r**	**1f**	**r**	**rf**	**12**	**5**
(Ferrari)	8	7	1	2	4	4	1	1	9	1	8	12
Niki LAUDA	**11**	**7**	**r**	**16**	**12**	**r**	**9**	**r**	**10**	**13**	**dq**	**nc**
(March-Ford Cosworth)	22	21	25	22	25	21	19	24	22	20	19	25
John LOVE	-	**16r**	-	-	-	-	-	-	-	-	-	-
(Surtees-Ford Cosworth)	-	26	-	-	-	-	-	-	-	-	-	-
Helmut MARKO	**10**	**14**	-	**8**	**10**	**r**	-	-	-	-	-	-
(BRM)	19	23	-	17	23	6	-	-	-	-	-	-
Arturo MERZARIO	-	-	-	-	-	-	**6**	**12**	-	-	-	-
(Ferrari)	-	-	-	-	-	-	9	22	-	-	-	-
François MIGAULT	-	-	-	-	-	-	-	-	**r**	-	-	-
(Connew-Ford Cosworth)	-	-	-	-	-	-	ns	-	25	-	-	-
Jackie OLIVER	-	-	-	-	-	-	**r**	-	-	-	-	-
(BRM)	-	-	-	-	-	-	14	-	-	-	-	-
Carlos PACE	-	**17**	**6**	**17**	**5**	**r**	**r**	**nc**	**nc**	**r**	**9r**	**r**
(March-Ford Cosworth)	-	24	16	24	11	11	13	11	18	18	18	15
Henri PESCAROLO	**8**	**11**	**11**	**r**	**nc**	-	**r**	**r**	-	-	**13**	**14**
(March-Ford Cosworth)	15	22	19	9	19	ns	-	9	ns	nq	21	22
(Politoys-Ford Cosworth)	-	-	-	-	-	-	26	-	-	-	-	-
Ronnie PETERSON	**6**	**5**	**r**	**11**	**9**	**5**	**7r**	**3**	**12**	**9**	**dq**	**4**
(March-Ford Cosworth)	10	9	9	15	14	9	8	4	11	24	3	26
Sam POSEY	-	-	-	-	-	-	-	-	-	-	-	**12**
(Surtees-Ford Cosworth)	-	-	-	-	-	-	-	-	-	-	-	23
Brian REDMAN	-	-	-	**5**	-	**9**	-	**5**	-	-	-	**r**
(McLaren-Ford Cosworth)	-	-	-	10	-	13	-	19	-	-	-	-
(BRM)	-	-	-	-	-	-	-	-	-	-	-	24
Clay REGAZZONI	**4**	**12**	**3**	**r**	**r**	-	-	**2**	**r**	**r**	**5**	**8**
(Ferrari)	6	2	8	3	2	-	-	7	2	4	7	6
Carlos REUTEMANN	**7**	**r**	-	-	**13**	**12**	**8**	**r**	**r**	**r**	**4**	**r**
(Brabham-Ford Cosworth)	1	15	-	-	9	17	10	6	5	11	9	5
Peter REVSON	**r**	**3**	**5**	-	**7**	-	**3**	-	**3**	**4**	**2**	**18r**
(McLaren-Ford Cosworth)	3	12	11	-	7	-	3	-	4	8	1	2
Jody SCHECKTER	-	-	-	-	-	-	-	-	-	-	-	**9**
(McLaren-Ford Cosworth)	-	-	-	-	-	-	-	-	-	-	-	8
Tim SCHENKEN	**5**	**r**	**8**	**r**	**r**	**17**	**r**	**14**	**11**	**r**	**7**	**r**
(Surtees-Ford Cosworth)	11	10	18	13	21	5	5	12	8	22	13	31
Vern SCHUPPAN	-	-	-	-	-	-	-	-	-	-	-	-
(BRM)	-	-	-	-	ns	-	-	-	-	-	-	-
Alex SOLER-ROIG	**r**	-	**r**	-	-	-	-	-	-	-	-	-
(BRM)	21	-	22	-	-	-	-	-	-	-	-	-
Jackie STEWART	**1f**	**r**	**r**	**4**	-	**1**	**2f**	**11r**	**7**	**r**	**1f**	**1f**
(Tyrrell-Ford Cosworth)	2	1	4	8	-	3	4	2	3	3	5	1
Rolf STOMMELEN	-	**13**	**r**	**10**	**11**	**16**	**10**	**r**	**15**	-	-	-
(Eiffeland March-Cosworth)	-	25	17	25	20	15	25	14	17	-	-	-
John SURTEES	-	-	-	-	-	-	-	-	-	**r**	-	-
(Surtees-Ford Cosworth)	-	-	-	-	-	-	-	-	-	19	-	ns
Dave WALKER	**dq**	**10**	**9r**	**14**	**14**	**18r**	**r**	**r**	**r**	-	-	**r**
(JPS Lotus-Ford Cosworth)	20	19	24	14	12	22	15	23	19	-	-	30
Reine WISELL	**r**	-	**r**	**r**	-	**r**	-	**r**	-	**12**	**r**	**10**
(BRM)	17	-	10	16	-	18	-	17	-	10	-	-
(JPS Lotus-Ford Cosworth)	-	-	-	-	-	-	-	-	-	-	16	16

1973 RACE RESULTS & GRID POSITIONS

	RA	BR	ZA	E	B	MC	S	F	GB	NL	D	A	I	CDN	USA
Chris AMON	**-**	**-**	**-**	**-**	**6**	**r**	**-**	**-**	**r**	**r**	**-**	**-**	**-**	**10**	**-**
(Tecno)	-	-	-	-	15	12	-	-	29	19	-	ns	-	-	-
(Tyrrell-Ford Cosworth)	-	-	-	-	-	-	-	-	-	-	-	-	-	11	12ns
Tom BELSO	**-**	**-**	**-**	**-**	**-**	**-**	**-**	**-**	**-**	**-**	**-**	**-**	**-**	**-**	**-**
(Iso Marlboro-Ford Cosworth)	-	-	-	-	-	-	ns	-	-	-	-	-	-	-	-
Jean-Pierre BELTOISE	**r**	**r**	**r**	**5**	**r**	**r**	**r**	**11**	**r**	**5**	**r**	**5**	**13**	**4**	**9**
(BRM)	7	10	7	10	5	11	9	15	17	9	9	13	13	16	14
Mike BEUTTLER	**10r**	**r**	**nc**	**7**	**11r**	**r**	**8**	**-**	**11**	**r**	**16**	**r**	**r**	**r**	**10**
(March-Ford Cosworth)	18	19	23	19	20	20	21	-	24	23	19	11	12	21	26
Luiz BUENO	**-**	**12**	**-**	**-**	**-**	**-**	**-**	**-**	**-**	**-**	**-**	**-**	**-**	**-**	**-**
(Surtees-Ford Cosworth)	-	20	-	-	-	-	-	-	-	-	-	-	-	-	-
François CEVERT +	**2**	**10**	**nc**	**2**	**2f**	**4**	**3**	**2**	**5**	**2**	**2**	**r**	**5**	**r**	**-**
(Tyrrell-Ford Cosworth)	6	9	25	3	4	4	2	4	7	3	3	10	11	6	ns
Dave CHARLTON	**-**	**-**	**r**	**-**	**-**	**-**	**-**	**-**	**-**	**-**	**-**	**-**	**-**	**-**	**-**
(Lotus-Ford Cosworth)	-	-	13	-	-	-	-	-	-	-	-	-	-	-	-
Andrea de ADAMICH	**-**	**-**	**8**	**r**	**4**	**7**	**-**	**r**	**r**	**-**	**-**	**-**	**-**	**-**	**-**
(Surtees-Ford Cosworth)	-	-	20	-	-	-	-	-	-	-	-	-	-	-	-
(Brabham-Ford Cosworth)	-	-	-	17	18	25	-	13	20	-	-	-	-	-	-
Emerson FITTIPALDI	**1f**	**1f=**	**3f**	**1**	**3**	**2f**	**12r**	**r**	**r**	**r**	**6**	**11r**	**2**	**2f**	**6**
(JPS Lotus-Ford Cosworth)	2	2	2	7	9	5	4	3	5	16	14	1	4	5	3
Wilson FITTIPALDI	**6**	**r**	**r**	**10**	**r**	**11r**	**r**	**16r**	**r**	**r**	**5**	**r**	**r**	**11**	**nc**
(Brabham-Ford Cosworth)	12	11	17	12	19	9	13	19	13	13	13	16	16	10	25
George FOLLMER	**-**	**-**	**6**	**3**	**r**	**-**	**14**	**r**	**r**	**10**	**r**	**r**	**10**	**17**	**14**
(Shadow-Ford Cosworth)	-	-	21	14	11	ns	19	20	25	22	21	20	21	13	20
Nanni GALLI	**r**	**9**	**-**	**11**	**r**	**r**	**-**	**-**	**-**	**-**	**-**	**-**	**-**	**-**	**-**
(Iso Marlboro-Ford Cosworth)	16	18	-	20	17	21	-	-	-	-	-	-	-	-	-
Howden GANLEY	**nc**	**7**	**10**	**r**	**r**	**r**	**11**	**14**	**9**	**9**	**-**	**nc**	**nc**	**6**	**12**
(Iso Marlboro-Ford Cosworth)	19	16	19	21	21	10	11	24	18	15	ns	21	20	22	19
Peter GETHIN	**-**	**-**	**-**	**-**	**-**	**-**	**-**	**-**	**-**	**-**	**-**	**-**	**-**	**r**	**-**
(BRM)	-	-	-	-	-	-	-	-	-	-	-	-	-	25	-
Mike HAILWOOD	**r**	**r**	**r**	**r**	**r**	**8**	**r**	**r**	**r**	**r**	**14**	**10**	**7**	**9**	**r**
(Surtees-Ford Cosworth)	10	14	12	9	13	13	10	11	12	24	18	15	8	12	6
Graham HILL	**-**	**-**	**-**	**r**	**9**	**r**	**r**	**10**	**r**	**nc**	**13**	**r**	**14**	**16**	**13**
(Shadow-Ford Cosworth)	-	-	-	22	23	24	18	16	27	17	20	22	22	17	18
Denny HULME	**5**	**3f=**	**5**	**6**	**7**	**6**	**1f**	**8f**	**3**	**r**	**12**	**8**	**15**	**13**	**4**
(McLaren-Ford Cosworth)	8	5	1	2	2	3	6	6	2	4	8	3	3	7	8
James HUNT	**-**	**-**	**-**	**-**	**-**	**9r**	**-**	**6**	**4f**	**3**	**-**	**r**	**-**	**7**	**2f**
(March-Ford Cosworth)	-	-	-	-	-	18	-	14	11	7	-	9	ns	15	4
Jacky ICKX	**4**	**5**	**r**	**12**	**r**	**r**	**6**	**5**	**8**	**-**	**3**	**-**	**8**	**-**	**7**
(Ferrari)	3	3	11	6	3	7	8	12	19	-	-	-	14	-	-
(McLaren-Ford Cosworth)	-	-	-	-	-	-	-	-	-	-	4	-	-	-	-
(Iso Marlboro-Ford Cosworth)	-	-	-	-	-	-	-	-	-	-	-	-	-	-	23
Jean-Pierre JARIER	**r**	**r**	**nc**	**-**	**r**	**r**	**r**	**r**	**-**	**-**	**-**	**r**	**-**	**nc**	**11r**
(March-Ford Cosworth)	17	15	18	-	16	14	20	7	-	-	-	12	-	23	17
Eddie KEIZAN	**-**	**-**	**nc**	**-**	**-**	**-**	**-**	**-**	**-**	**-**	**-**	**-**	**-**	**-**	**-**
(Tyrrell-Ford Cosworth)	-	-	22	-	-	-	-	-	-	-	-	-	-	-	-
Niki LAUDA	**r**	**8**	**r**	**r**	**5**	**r**	**13**	**9**	**12**	**r**	**r**	**-**	**r**	**r**	**r**
(BRM)	13	13	10	11	14	6	15	17	9	11	5	ns	15	8	21
Jochen MASS	**-**	**-**	**-**	**-**	**-**	**-**	**-**	**-**	**r**	**-**	**7**	**-**	**-**	**-**	**r**
(Surtees-Ford Cosworth)	-	-	-	-	-	-	-	-	14	-	15	-	-	-	16
Graham McRAE	**-**	**-**	**-**	**-**	**-**	**-**	**-**	**-**	**r**	**-**	**-**	**-**	**-**	**-**	**-**
(Iso Marlboro-Ford Cosworth)	-	-	-	-	-	-	-	-	28	-	-	-	-	-	-
Arturo MERZARIO	**9**	**4**	**4**	**-**	**-**	**r**	**-**	**7**	**-**	**-**	**-**	**7**	**r**	**15**	**16**
(Ferrari)	14	17	15	-	-	16	-	10	-	-	-	6	7	20	11
Jackie OLIVER	**-**	**-**	**r**	**r**	**r**	**10**	**r**	**r**	**r**	**r**	**8**	**r**	**11**	**3**	**15**
(Shadow-Ford Cosworth)	-	-	14	13	22	22	17	21	26	10	17	18	19	14	22
Carlos PACE	**r**	**r**	**r**	**r**	**8**	**r**	**10**	**13**	**r**	**7**	**4f**	**3f**	**r**	**18r**	**r**
(Surtees-Ford Cosworth)	15	6	9	16	8	17	16	18	15	8	11	8	5	19	9
Henri PESCAROLO	**-**	**-**	**-**	**8**	**-**	**-**	**-**	**r**	**-**	**-**	**10**	**-**	**-**	**-**	**-**
(March-Ford Cosworth)	-	-	-	18	-	-	-	-	-	-	-	-	-	-	-
(Iso Marlboro-Ford Cosworth)	-	-	-	-	-	-	-	23	-	-	12	-	-	-	-
Ronnie PETERSON	**r**	**r**	**11**	**rf**	**r**	**3**	**2**	**1**	**2**	**11rf**	**r**	**1**	**1**	**r**	**1**
(JPS Lotus-Ford Cosworth)	5	1	4	1	1	2	1	5	1	1	2	2	1	1	1
Jackie PRETORIUS	**-**	**-**	**r**	**-**	**-**	**-**	**-**	**-**	**-**	**-**	**-**	**-**	**-**	**-**	**-**
(Iso Marlboro-Ford Cosworth)	-	-	24	-	-	-	-	-	-	-	-	-	-	-	-
David PURLEY	**-**	**-**	**-**	**-**	**-**	**r**	**-**	**-**	**-**	**r**	**15**	**-**	**9**	**-**	**-**
(March-Ford Cosworth)	-	-	-	-	-	23	-	-	16ns	21	22	-	24	-	-
Brian REDMAN	**-**	**-**	**-**	**-**	**-**	**-**	**-**	**-**	**-**	**-**	**-**	**-**	**-**	**-**	**dq**
(Shadow-Ford Cosworth)	-	-	-	-	-	-	-	-	-	-	-	-	-	-	13
Clay REGAZZONI	**7**	**6**	**r**	**9**	**10r**	**r**	**9**	**12**	**7**	**8**	**r**	**6**	**r**	**-**	**8**
(BRM)	1	4	5	8	12	8	12	9	10	12	10	14	18	-	15
Carlos REUTEMANN	**r**	**11**	**7**	**r**	**r**	**r**	**4**	**3**	**6**	**r**	**r**	**4**	**6**	**8**	**3**
(Brabham-Ford Cosworth)	9	7	8	15	7	19	5	8	8	5	6	5	10	4	2
Peter REVSON	**8**	**r**	**2**	**4**	**r**	**5**	**7**	**-**	**1**	**4**	**9**	**r**	**3**	**1**	**5**
(McLaren-Ford Cosworth)	11	12	6	5	10	15	7	-	3	6	7	4	2	2	7
Jody SCHECKTER	**-**	**-**	**9r**	**-**	**-**	**-**	**-**	**r**	**r**	**-**	**-**	**-**	**-**	**r**	**r**
(McLaren-Ford Cosworth)	-	-	3	-	-	-	-	2	6	-	-	-	-	3	10
Tim SCHENKEN	**-**	**-**	**-**	**-**	**-**	**-**	**-**	**-**	**-**	**-**	**-**	**-**	**-**	**14**	**-**
(Iso Marlboro-Ford Cosworth)	-	-	-	-	-	-	-	-	-	-	-	-	-	24	-
Jackie STEWART	**3**	**2**	**1**	**r**	**1**	**1**	**5**	**4**	**10**	**1**	**1**	**2**	**4f**	**5**	**-**
(Tyrrell-Ford Cosworth)	4	8	16	4	6	1	3	1	4	2	1	7	6	9	5ns
Rolf STOMMELEN	**-**	**-**	**-**	**-**	**-**	**-**	**-**	**-**	**-**	**-**	**11**	**r**	**12**	**12**	**-**
(Brabham-Ford Cosworth)	-	-	-	-	-	-	-	-	-	-	16	17	9	18	-
Gijs van LENNEP	**-**	**-**	**-**	**-**	**-**	**-**	**-**	**-**	**-**	**6**	**-**	**9**	**r**	**-**	**-**
(Iso Marlboro-Ford Cosworth)	-	-	-	-	-	-	-	-	-	20	-	23	23	-	-
Rikky von OPEL	**-**	**-**	**-**	**-**	**-**	**-**	**-**	**15**	**13**	**-**	**-**	**r**	**r**	**nc**	**r**
(Ensign-Ford Cosworth)	-	-	-	-	-	-	-	25	21	14ns	-	19	17	26	27
John WATSON	**-**	**-**	**-**	**-**	**-**	**-**	**-**	**-**	**r**	**-**	**-**	**-**	**-**	**-**	**r**
(Brabham-Ford Cosworth)	-	-	-	-	-	-	-	-	23	-	-	-	-	-	24
Roger WILLIAMSON +	**-**	**-**	**-**	**-**	**-**	**-**	**-**	**-**	**r**	**r**	**-**	**-**	**-**	**-**	**-**
(March-Ford Cosworth)	-	-	-	-	-	-	-	-	22	18	-	-	-	-	-
Reine WISELL	**-**	**-**	**-**	**-**	**-**	**-**	**r**	**r**	**-**	**-**	**-**	**-**	**-**	**-**	**-**
(March-Ford Cosworth)	-	-	-	-	-	-	14	22	-	-	-	-	-	-	-

1974 RACE RESULTS & GRID POSITIONS

	RA	BR	ZA	E	B	MC	S	NL	F	GB	D	A	I	CDN	USA
Chris AMON	-	-	-	r	-	-	-	-	-	-	-	-	-	nc	9
(Amon-Ford Cosworth)	-	-	-	23	-	20ns	-	-	-	-	nq	-	nq	-	-
(BRM)	-	-	-	-	-	-	-	-	-	-	-	-	-	25	12
Mario ANDRETTI	-	-	-	-	-	-	-	-	-	-	-	-	-	7	dq
(Parnelli-Ford Cosworth)	-	-	-	-	-	-	-	-	-	-	-	-	-	16	3
Ian ASHLEY	-	-	-	-	-	-	-	-	-	-	14	nc	-	-	-
(Token-Ford Cosworth)	-	-	-	-	-	-	-	-	-	-	26	24	-	-	-
(Brabham-Ford Cosworth)	-	-	-	-	-	-	-	-	-	-	-	-	-	nq	nq
Derek BELL	-	-	-	-	-	-	-	-	-	-	11	-	-	-	-
(Surtees-Ford Cosworth)	-	-	-	-	-	-	-	-	-	nq	25	nq	nq	nq	-
Tom BELSO	-	-	r	-	-	-	8	-	-	-	-	-	-	-	-
(Iso Marlboro-Ford Cosworth)	-	-	27	nq	-	-	21	-	-	nq	-	-	-	-	-
Jean-Pierre BELTOISE	5	10	2	r	5	r	r	r	10	12	r	r	r	nc	-
(BRM)	14	17	11	11	7	11	13	16	17	23	15	18	11	17	nq
Vittorio BRAMBILLA	-	-	10	-	9	r	10r	10	11	r	13	6	r	-	r
(March-Ford Cosworth)	-	-	19	ns	31	15	17	15	16	18	23	20	13	nq	25
Dave CHARLTON	-	-	19	-	-	-	-	-	-	-	-	-	-	-	-
(McLaren-Ford Cosworth)	-	-	20	-	-	-	-	-	-	-	-	-	-	-	-
Patrick DEPAILLER	6	8	4	8	r	9	2f	6	8	r	r	r	11	5	6
(Tyrrell-Ford Cosworth)	15	16	15	16	11	4	1	8	9	10	5	14	10	7	13
José DOLHEM	-	-	-	-	-	-	-	-	-	-	-	-	-	-	r
(Surtees-Ford Cosworth)	-	-	-	-	-	-	-	-	nq	-	-	-	nq	-	26
Mark DONOHUE	-	-	-	-	-	-	-	-	-	-	-	-	-	12	r
(Penske-Ford Cosworth)	-	-	-	-	-	-	-	-	-	-	-	-	-	24	14
Paddy DRIVER	-	-	r	-	-	-	-	-	-	-	-	-	-	-	-
(Lotus-Ford Cosworth)	-	-	26	-	-	-	-	-	-	-	-	-	-	-	-
Guy EDWARDS	11	r	-	-	12	8	7	r	15	-	-	-	-	-	-
(Lola-Ford Cosworth)	25	25	-	nq	21	26	18	14	20	nq	nq	-	-	-	-
Carlo FACETTI	-	-	-	-	-	-	-	-	-	-	-	-	-	-	-
(Brabham-Ford Cosworth)	-	-	-	-	-	-	-	-	-	-	-	-	nq	-	-
Emerson FITTIPALDI	10	1	7	3	1	5	4	3	r	2	r	r	2	1	4
(McLaren-Ford Cosworth)	3	1	5	4	4	13	9	3	5	8	3	3	6	1	8
Howden GANLEY	8r	r	-	-	-	-	-	-	-	-	-	-	-	-	-
(March-Ford Cosworth)	19	20	-	-	-	-	-	-	-	-	-	-	-	-	-
(Maki-Ford Cosworth)	-	-	-	-	-	-	-	-	-	nq	nq	-	-	-	-
Peter GETHIN	-	-	-	-	-	-	-	-	-	r	-	-	-	-	-
(Lola-Ford Cosworth)	-	-	-	-	-	-	-	-	-	21	-	-	-	-	-
Mike HAILWOOD	4	5	3	9	7	r	r	4	7	r	15r	-	-	-	-
(McLaren-Ford Cosworth)	9	7	12	17	13	10	11	4	6	11	12	-	-	-	-
Graham HILL	r	11	12	r	8	7	6	r	13	13	9	12	8	14	8
(Lola-Ford Cosworth)	17	21	18	19	29	21	15	19	21	22	19	21	21	20	24
David HOBBS	-	-	-	-	-	-	-	-	-	-	-	7	9	-	-
(McLaren-Ford Cosworth)	-	-	-	-	-	-	-	-	-	-	-	17	23	-	-
Denny HULME	1	12	9	6	6f	r	r	r	6	7	r/dq	2	6	6	r
(McLaren-Ford Cosworth)	10	11	9	8	12	12	12	9	11	19	7	10	19	14	17
James HUNT	r	9	r	10	r	r	3	r	r	r	r	3	r	4	3
(March-Ford Cosworth)	5	18	-	-	-	-	-	-	-	-	-	-	-	-	-
(Hesketh-Ford Cosworth)	-	-	14	10	9	7	6	6	10	6	13	7	8	8	2
Jacky ICKX	r	3	r	r	r	r	r	11	5	3	5	r	r	13	r
(JPS Lotus-Ford Cosworth)	7	5	10	5	16	19	7	18	13	12	9	22	16	21	16
Jean-Pierre JABOUILLE	-	-	-	-	-	-	-	-	-	-	-	-	-	-	-
(Iso Marlboro-Ford Cosworth)	-	-	-	-	-	-	-	-	nq	-	-	-	-	-	-
(Surtees-Ford Cosworth)	-	-	-	-	-	-	-	-	-	-	-	nq	-	-	-
Jean-Pierre JARIER	r	r	-	nc	13	3	5	r	12	r	8	8	r	r	10
(Shadow-Ford Cosworth)	16	19	-	12	17	6	8	7	12	16	18	23	9	5	10
Eddie KEIZAN	-	-	14	-	-	-	-	-	-	-	-	-	-	-	-
(Tyrrell-Ford Cosworth)	-	-	24	-	-	-	-	-	-	-	-	-	-	-	-
Leo KINNUNEN	-	-	-	-	-	-	r	-	-	-	-	-	-	-	-
(Surtees-Ford Cosworth)	-	-	-	-	nq	-	25	-	nq	nq	-	nq	nq	-	-
Helmut KOINIGG +	-	-	-	-	-	-	-	-	-	-	-	-	-	10	r
(Brabham-Ford Cosworth)	-	-	-	-	-	-	-	-	-	-	-	nq	-	-	-
(Surtees-Ford Cosworth)	-	-	-	-	-	-	-	-	-	-	-	-	-	22	23
Jacques LAFFITE	-	-	-	-	-	-	-	-	-	-	r	nc	r	15r	r
(Iso Marlboro-Ford Cosworth)	-	-	-	-	-	-	-	-	-	-	21	12	17	18	11
Gérard LARROUSSE	-	-	-	-	r	-	-	-	-	-	-	-	-	-	-
(Brabham-Ford Cosworth)	-	-	-	-	28	-	-	-	nq	-	-	-	-	-	-
Niki LAUDA	2	r	16r	1f	2	r	r	1	2	5f	r	r	r	rf	r
(Ferrari)	8	3	1	1	3	1	3	1	1	1	1	1	1	2	5
Lella LOMBARDI	-	-	-	-	-	-	-	-	-	-	-	-	-	-	-
(Brabham-Ford Cosworth)	-	-	-	-	-	-	-	-	-	nq	-	-	-	-	-
Jochen MASS	r	17	r	r	r	-	r	r	r	14	r	-	-	16	7
(Surtees-Ford Cosworth)	18	10	17	18	26	17ns	22	20	18	17	10	-	-	-	-
(McLaren-Ford Cosworth)	-	-	-	-	-	-	-	-	-	-	-	-	-	12	20
Arturo MERZARIO	r	r	6	r	r	r	-	r	9	r	r	r	4	r	r
(Iso Marlboro-Ford Cosworth)	13	9	3	7	6	14	ns	21	15	15	16	9	15	19	15
François MIGAULT	r	16	15	r	16	r	-	r	14	nc	-	-	r	-	-
(BRM)	24	23	25	22	25	22	-	25	22	14	nq	-	24	-	-
John NICHOLSON	-	-	-	-	-	-	-	-	-	-	-	-	-	-	-
(Lyncar-Ford Cosworth)	-	-	-	-	-	-	-	-	-	nq	-	-	-	-	-
Carlos PACE	r	4	11	13	r	r	r	-	-	9	12	r	5f	8	2f
(Surtees-Ford Cosworth)	11	12	2	14	8	18	24	-	-	-	-	-	-	-	-
(Brabham-Ford Cosworth)	-	-	-	-	-	-	-	-	nq	20	17	4	3	9	4
Larry PERKINS	-	-	-	-	-	-	-	-	-	-	-	-	-	-	-
(Amon-Ford Cosworth)	-	-	-	-	-	-	-	-	-	-	nq	-	-	-	-
Henri PESCAROLO	9	14	18	12	r	r	r	r	r	r	10	-	r	-	-
(BRM)	21	22	21	20	15	27	19	24	19	24	24	-	25	-	-
Ronnie PETERSON	13	6	r	r	r	1f	r	8f	1	10	4	r	1	3	r
(JPS Lotus-Ford Cosworth)	1	4	16	2	5	3	5	10	2	2	8	6	7	10	19
Teddy PILETTE	-	-	-	-	17	-	-	-	-	-	-	-	-	-	-
(Brabham-Ford Cosworth)	-	-	-	-	27	-	-	-	-	-	-	-	-	-	-
Tom PRYCE	-	-	-	-	r	-	-	r	r	8	6	r	10	r	nc
(Token-Ford Cosworth)	-	-	-	-	20	-	-	-	-	-	-	-	-	-	-
(Shadow-Ford Cosworth)	-	-	-	-	-	-	-	11	3	5	11	16	22	13	18
David PURLEY	-	-	-	-	-	-	-	-	-	-	-	-	-	-	-
(Token-Ford Cosworth)	-	-	-	-	-	-	-	-	-	nq	-	-	-	-	-
Dieter QUESTER	-	-	-	-	-	-	-	-	-	-	-	9	-	-	-
(Surtees-Ford Cosworth)	-	-	-	-	-	-	-	-	-	-	-	25	-	-	-
Brian REDMAN	-	-	-	7	18r	r	-	-	-	-	-	-	-	-	-
(Shadow-Ford Cosworth)	-	-	-	21	18	16	-	-	-	-	-	-	-	-	-
Clay REGAZZONI	3f	2f	r	2	4	4	r	2	3	4	1	5f	r	2	11
(Ferrari)	2	8	6	3	1	2	4	2	4	7	2	8	5	6	9
Carlos REUTEMANN	7r	7	1f	r	r	r	r	12	r	6	3	1	r	9	1
(Brabham-Ford Cosworth)	6	2	4	6	24	8	10	12	8	4	6	2	2	4	1
Peter REVSON +	r	r	-	-	-	-	-	-	-	-	-	-	-	-	-
(Shadow-Ford Cosworth)	4	6	-	-	-	-	-	-	-	-	-	-	-	-	-
Richard ROBARTS	r	15	17	-	-	-	-	-	-	-	-	-	-	-	-
(Brabham-Ford Cosworth)	22	24	23	-	-	-	-	-	-	-	-	-	-	-	-
(Iso Marlboro-Ford Cosworth)	-	-	-	-	-	-	ns	-	-	-	-	-	-	-	-
Bertil ROOS	-	-	-	-	-	-	r	-	-	-	-	-	-	-	-
(Shadow-Ford Cosworth)	-	-	-	-	-	-	23	-	-	-	-	-	-	-	-

	RA	BR	ZA	E	B	MC	S	NL	F	GB	D	A	I	CDN	USA
Ian SCHECKTER	-	-	13	-	-	-	-	-	-	-	-	-	-	-	-
(Lotus-Ford Cosworth)	-	-	22	-	-	-	-	-	-	-	-	-	-	-	-
(Hesketh-Ford Cosworth)	-	-	-	-	-	-	-	-	-	-	-	nq	-	-	-
Jody SCHECKTER	r	13	8	5	3	2	1	5	4f	1	2f	r	3	r	r
(Tyrrell-Ford Cosworth)	12	14	8	9	2	5	2	5	7	3	4	5	12	3	6
Tim SCHENKEN	-	-	-	14r	10	r	-	-	-	r	-	10	r	-	dq
(Trojan-Ford Cosworth)	-	-	-	25	23	24	-	nq	-	25	nq	19	20	-	-
(JPS Lotus-Ford Cosworth)	-	-	-	-	-	-	-	-	-	-	-	-	-	-	27
Vern SCHUPPAN	-	-	-	-	15	r	dq	dq	-	-	r	-	-	-	-
(Ensign-Ford Cosworth)	-	-	-	-	14	25	26	17	nq	nq	22	-	-	-	-
Rolf STOMMELEN	-	-	-	-	-	-	-	-	-	-	-	r	r	11	12
(Lola-Ford Cosworth)	-	-	-	-	-	-	-	-	-	-	-	13	14	11	21
Hans-Joachim STUCK	r	r	5	4	r	r	-	r	-	r	7	11r	r	r	-
(March-Ford Cosworth)	23	13	7	13	10	9	-	22	nq	9	20	15	18	23	nq
Gijs van LENNEP	-	-	-	-	14	-	-	-	-	-	-	-	-	-	-
(Iso Marlboro-Ford Cosworth)	-	-	-	-	30	-	-	nq	-	-	-	-	-	-	-
Rikky von OPEL	-	-	-	r	r	-	9	9	-	-	-	-	-	-	-
(Ensign-Ford Cosworth)	26ns	-	-	-	-	-	-	-	-	-	-	-	-	-	-
(Brabham-Ford Cosworth)	-	-	-	24	22	nq	20	23	nq	-	-	-	-	-	-
John WATSON	12	r	r	11	11	6	11	7	16	11	r	4	7	r	5
(Brabham-Ford Cosworth)	20	15	13	15	19	23	14	13	14	13	14	11	4	15	7
Eppie WIETZES	-	-	-	-	-	-	-	-	-	-	-	-	-	r	-
(Brabham-Ford Cosworth)	-	-	-	-	-	-	-	-	-	-	-	-	-	26	-
Mike WILDS	-	-	-	-	-	-	-	-	-	-	-	-	-	-	nc
(March-Ford Cosworth)	-	-	-	-	-	-	-	-	-	nq	-	-	-	-	-
(Ensign-Ford Cosworth)	-	-	-	-	-	-	-	-	-	-	-	nq	nq	nq	22
Reine WISELL	-	-	-	-	-	-	r	-	-	-	-	-	-	-	-
(March-Ford Cosworth)	-	-	-	-	-	-	16	-	-	-	-	-	-	-	-

1975 RACE RESULTS & GRID POSITIONS

	RA	BR	ZA	E	MC	B	S	NL	F	GB	D	A	I	USA
Chris AMON	-	-	-	-	-	-	-	-	-	-	-	12	12	-
(Ensign-Ford Cosworth)	-	-	-	-	-	-	-	-	-	-	-	23	19	-
Mario ANDRETTI	r	7	17r	rf	r	-	4	-	5	12	10r	r	r	r
(Parnelli-Ford Cosworth)	10	18	6	4	13	-	15	-	15	12	13	19	15	5
Ian ASHLEY	-	-	-	-	-	-	-	-	-	-	-	-	-	-
(Williams-Ford Cosworth)	-	-	-	-	-	-	-	-	-	-	20ns	-	-	-
Vittorio BRAMBILLA	9	r	r	5	r	r	r	r	r	6	r	1f	r	7
(March-Ford Cosworth)	12	17	7	5	5	3	1	11	8	5	11	8	9	6
Tony BRISE +	-	-	-	7	-	r	6	7	7	15r	r	15	r	r
(Williams-Ford Cosworth)	-	-	-	18	-	-	-	-	-	-	-	-	-	-
(Hill-Ford Cosworth)	-	-	-	-	-	7	17	7	12	13	17	16	6	17
Dave CHARLTON	-	-	14	-	-	-	-	-	-	-	-	-	-	-
(McLaren-Ford Cosworth)	-	-	20	-	-	-	-	-	-	-	-	-	-	-
Jim CRAWFORD	-	-	-	-	-	-	-	-	-	r	-	-	13	-
(JPS Lotus-Ford Cosworth)	-	-	-	-	-	-	-	-	-	25	-	-	25	-
Patrick DEPAILLER	5	r	3	r	5f	4	12	9	6	9r	9	11	7	r
(Tyrrell-Ford Cosworth)	8	9	5	7	12	12	2	13	13	17	4	7	12	8
Mark DONOHUE +	7	r	8	r	r	11	5	8	r	5r	r	-	-	-
(Penske-Ford Cosworth)	16	15	18	17	16	21	16	18	18	-	-	-	-	-
(March-Ford Cosworth)	-	-	-	-	-	-	-	-	-	15	19	20ns	-	-
Harald ERTL	-	-	-	-	-	-	-	-	-	-	8	r	9	-
(Hesketh-Ford Cosworth)	-	-	-	-	-	-	-	-	-	-	23	26	17	-
Bob EVANS	-	-	15	r	-	9	13	r	17	-	-	r	r	-
(Stanley BRM)	-	-	24	23	nq	20	23	20	25	-	-	24	20	-
Emerson FITTIPALDI	1	2	nc	-	2	7	8	r	4	1	r	9	2	2f
(McLaren-Ford Cosworth)	5	2	11	ns	9	8	11	6	10	7	8	3	3	2
Wilson FITTIPALDI	r	13	r	r	-	12	17	11	r	19r	r	-	-	10
(Copersucar-Ford Cosworth)	23	21	27	21	nq	24	25	24	23	24	22	ns	-	23
Hiroshi FUSHIDA	-	-	-	-	-	-	-	-	-	-	-	-	-	-
(Maki-Ford Cosworth)	-	-	-	-	-	-	-	ns	-	nq	-	-	-	-
Brian HENTON	-	-	-	-	-	-	-	-	-	16r	-	-	-	nc
(JPS Lotus-Ford Cosworth)	-	-	-	-	-	-	-	-	-	21	-	22ns	-	19
Graham HILL	10	12	-	-	-	-	-	-	-	-	-	-	-	-
(Lola-Ford Cosworth)	21	20	ns	-	-	-	-	-	-	-	-	-	-	-
(Hill-Ford Cosworth)	-	-	-	-	nq	-	-	-	-	-	-	-	-	-
James HUNT	2f	6	r	r	r	r	r	1	2	4r	r	2	5	4
(Hesketh-Ford Cosworth)	6	7	12	3	11	11	13	3	3	9	9	2	8	15
Jacky ICKX	8	9	12	2	8	r	15	r	r	-	-	-	-	-
(JPS Lotus-Ford Cosworth)	18	12	21	16	14	16	18	21	19	-	-	-	-	-
Jean-Pierre JABOUILLE	-	-	-	-	-	-	-	-	12	-	-	-	-	-
(Tyrrell-Ford Cosworth)	-	-	-	-	-	-	-	-	21	-	-	-	-	-
Jean-Pierre JARIER	-	rf	r	4	r	r	r	r	8	14r	r	r	r	r
(Shadow-Ford Cosworth)	1ns	1	13	10	3	10	3	10	4	11	12	-	-	4
(Shadow-Matra)	-	-	-	-	-	-	-	-	-	-	-	14	13	-
Alan JONES	-	-	-	r	r	r	11	13	16	10	5	-	-	-
(Hesketh-Ford Cosworth)	-	-	-	20	18	13	19	-	-	-	-	-	-	-
(Hill-Ford Cosworth)	-	-	-	-	-	-	-	17	20	20	21	-	-	-
Eddie KEIZAN	-	-	13	-	-	-	-	-	-	-	-	-	-	-
(Lotus-Ford Cosworth)	-	-	22	-	-	-	-	-	-	-	-	-	-	-
Jacques LAFFITE	r	11	nc	-	-	r	-	r	11	r	2	r	r	-
(Williams-Ford Cosworth)	17	19	23	-	nq	17	-	15	16	19	15	12	18	21ns
Niki LAUDA	6	5	5	r	1	1	1f	2f	1	8	3	6	3	1
(Ferrari)	4	4	4	1	1	1	5	1	1	3	1	1	1	1
Michel LECLERE	-	-	-	-	-	-	-	-	-	-	-	-	-	r
(Tyrrell-Ford Cosworth)	-	-	-	-	-	-	-	-	-	-	-	-	-	20
Lella LOMBARDI	-	-	r	6	-	r	r	14	18	r	7	17	r	-
(March-Ford Cosworth)	-	-	26	24	nq	23	24	23	26	22	25	21	24	-
(Williams-Ford Cosworth)	-	-	-	-	-	-	-	-	-	-	-	-	-	24ns
Brett LUNGER	-	-	-	-	-	-	-	-	-	-	-	13	10	r
(Hesketh-Ford Cosworth)	-	-	-	-	-	-	-	-	-	-	-	17	21	18
Damien MAGEE	-	-	-	-	-	-	14	-	-	-	-	-	-	-
(Williams-Ford Cosworth)	-	-	-	-	-	-	22	-	-	-	-	-	-	-
Jochen MASS	14	3	6	1	6	r	r	r	3f	7r	r	4	r	3
(McLaren-Ford Cosworth)	13	10	16	11	15	15	14	8	7	10	6	9	5	9
Arturo MERZARIO	nc	r	r	r	-	r	-	-	-	-	-	-	11	-
(Williams-Ford Cosworth)	20	11	15	25	nq	19	-	-	-	-	-	-	-	-
(Copersucar-Ford Cosworth)	-	-	-	-	-	-	-	-	-	-	-	-	26	-
François MIGAULT	-	-	-	nc	-	r	-	-	-	-	-	-	-	-
(Hill-Ford Cosworth)	-	-	-	22	-	22	-	-	-	-	-	-	-	-
(Williams-Ford Cosworth)	-	-	-	-	-	-	-	-	24ns	-	-	-	-	-
Dave MORGAN	-	-	-	-	-	-	-	-	-	18r	-	-	-	-
(Surtees-Ford Cosworth)	-	-	-	-	-	-	-	-	-	23	-	-	-	-
John NICHOLSON	-	-	-	-	-	-	-	-	-	17r	-	-	-	-
(Lyncar-Ford Cosworth)	-	-	-	-	-	-	-	-	-	26	-	-	-	-
Carlos PACE	r	1	4f	r	3	8	r	5	r	2r	r	r	r	r
(Brabham-Ford Cosworth)	2	6	1	14	8	2	6	9	5	2	2	6	10	16
Torsten PALM	-	-	-	-	-	-	10r	-	-	-	-	-	-	-
(Hesketh-Ford Cosworth)	-	-	-	-	nq	-	21	-	-	-	-	-	-	-
Ronnie PETERSON	r	15	10	r	4	r	9	15r	10	r	r	5	r	5
(JPS Lotus-Ford Cosworth)	11	16	8	12	4	14	9	16	17	16	18	13	11	14

	RA	BR	ZA	E	MC	B	S	NL	F	GB	D	A	I	USA
Tom PRYCE	**12r**	**r**	**9**	**r**	**r**	**6**	**r**	**6**	**r**	**r**	**4**	**3**	**6**	**nc**
(Shadow-Ford Cosworth)	14	14	19	8	2	5	7	12	6	1	16	15	14	7
Clay REGAZZONI	**4**	**4**	**16r**	**nc**	**r**	**5f**	**3**	**3**	**r**	**13f**	**rf**	**7**	**1f**	**r**
(Ferrari)	7	5	9	2	6	4	12	2	9	4	5	5	2	11
Carlos REUTEMANN	**3**	**8**	**2**	**3**	**9**	**3**	**2**	**4**	**14**	**r**	**1**	**14**	**4**	**r**
(Brabham-Ford Cosworth)	3	3	2	15	10	6	4	5	11	8	10	11	7	3
Ian SCHECKTER	-	-	**r**	-	-	-	**r**	**12**	-	-	-	-	-	-
(Tyrrell-Ford Cosworth)	-	-	17	-	-	-	-	-	-	-	-	-	-	-
(Williams-Ford Cosworth)	-	-	-	-	-	-	20	19	-	-	-	-	-	-
Jody SCHECKTER	**11**	**r**	**1**	**r**	**7**	**2**	**7**	**16r**	**9**	**3r**	**r**	**8**	**8**	**6**
(Tyrrell-Ford Cosworth)	9	8	3	13	7	9	8	4	2	6	3	10	4	10
Vern SCHUPPAN	-	-	-	-	-	-	**r**	-	-	-	-	-	-	-
(Hill-Ford Cosworth)	-	-	-	-	-	-	26	-	-	-	-	-	-	-
Rolf STOMMELEN	**13**	**14**	**7**	**r**	-	-	-	-	-	-	-	**16**	**r**	-
(Lola-Ford Cosworth)	19	23	14	-	-	-	-	-	-	-	-	-	-	-
(Hill-Ford Cosworth)	-	-	-	9	-	-	-	-	-	-	-	25	23	-
Hans-Joachim STUCK	-	-	-	-	-	-	-	-	-	**r**	**r**	**r**	**r**	**8**
(March-Ford Cosworth)	-	-	-	-	-	-	-	-	-	14	7	4	16	13
Tony TRIMMER	-	-	-	-	-	-	-	-	-	-	-	-	-	-
(Maki-Ford Cosworth)	-	-	-	-	-	-	-	-	-	-	nq	nq	nq	-
Guy TUNMER	-	-	**11**	-	-	-	-	-	-	-	-	-	-	-
(Lotus-Ford Cosworth)	-	-	25	-	-	-	-	-	-	-	-	-	-	-
Gijs van LENNEP	-	-	-	-	-	-	-	**10**	**15**	-	**6**	-	-	-
(Ensign-Ford Cosworth)	-	-	-	-	-	-	-	22	22	-	24	-	-	-
Jo VONLANTHEN	-	-	-	-	-	-	-	-	-	-	-	**r**	-	-
(Williams-Ford Cosworth)	-	-	-	-	-	-	-	-	-	-	-	28	-	-
John WATSON	**dq**	**10**	**r**	**8**	**r**	**10**	**16**	**r**	**13**	**11r**	**r**	**10**	-	**9**
(Surtees-Ford Cosworth)	15	13	10	6	17	18	10	14	14	18	-	18	-	-
(JPS Lotus-Ford Cosworth)	-	-	-	-	-	-	-	-	-	-	14	-	-	-
(Penske-Ford Cosworth)	-	-	-	-	-	-	-	-	-	-	-	-	-	12
Mike WILDS	**r**	**r**	-	-	-	-	-	-	-	-	-	-	-	-
(Stanley BRM)	22	22	-	-	-	-	-	-	-	-	-	-	-	-
Roelof WUNDERINK	-	-	-	**r**	-	-	-	-	-	-	-	**nc**	-	**r**
(Ensign-Ford Cosworth)	-	-	-	19	nq	-	-	-	-	nq	-	27	nq	22
Renzo ZORZI	-	-	-	-	-	-	-	-	-	-	-	-	**14**	-
(Williams-Ford Cosworth)	-	-	-	-	-	-	-	-	-	-	-	-	22	-

1976 RACE RESULTS & GRID POSITIONS

	BR	ZA	USAW	E	B	MC	S	F	GB	D	A	NL	I	CDN	USAE	J
Chris AMON	-	**14**	**8**	**5**	**r**	**13**	**r**	-	**r**	**r**	-	-	-	-	-	-
(Ensign-Ford Cosworth)	-	18	17	10	8	12	3	-	6	17	-	-	-	-	-	-
(Wolf Williams-Ford Cosworth)	-	-	-	-	-	-	-	-	-	-	-	-	-	ns	-	-
Conny ANDERSSON	-	-	-	-	-	-	-	-	-	-	-	**r**	-	-	-	-
(Surtees-Ford Cosworth)	-	-	-	-	-	-	-	-	-	-	-	26	-	-	-	-
Mario ANDRETTI	**r**	**6**	**r**	**r**	**r**	-	**rf**	**5**	**r**	**12**	**5**	**3**	**r**	**3**	**r**	**1**
(JPS Lotus-Ford Cosworth)	16	-	-	9	11	-	2	7	3	12	9	6	14	5	11	1
(Parnelli-Ford Cosworth)	-	13	15	-	-	-	-	-	-	-	-	-	-	-	-	-
Ian ASHLEY	**r**	-	-	-	-	-	-	-	-	-	-	-	-	-	-	-
(Stanley BRM)	21	-	-	-	-	-	-	-	-	-	-	-	-	-	-	-
Hans BINDER	-	-	-	-	-	-	-	-	-	-	**r**	-	-	-	-	**r**
(Ensign-Ford Cosworth)	-	-	-	-	-	-	-	-	-	-	19	-	-	-	-	-
(Wolf Williams-Ford Cosworth)	-	-	-	-	-	-	-	-	-	-	-	-	-	-	-	25
Vittorio BRAMBILLA	**r**	**8**	**r**	**r**	**r**	**r**	**10**	**r**	**r**	**r**	**r**	**6**	**7**	**14**	**r**	**r**
(March-Ford Cosworth)	7	5	8	6	5	9	15	11	10	13	7	7	16	3	4	8
Warwick BROWN	-	-	-	-	-	-	-	-	-	-	-	-	-	-	**14**	-
(Wolf Williams-Ford Cosworth)	-	-	-	-	-	-	-	-	-	-	-	-	-	-	23	-
Emilio de VILLOTA	-	-	-	-	-	-	-	-	-	-	-	-	-	-	-	-
(Brabham-Ford Cosworth)	-	-	-	nq	-	-	-	-	-	-	-	-	-	-	-	-
Patrick DEPAILLER	**2**	**9**	**3**	**r**	**r**	**3**	**2**	**2**	**r**	**r**	**r**	**7**	**6**	**2f**	**r**	**2**
(Tyrrell-Ford Cosworth)	9	6	2	3	4	4	4	3	5	3	13	14	4	4	7	13
Guy EDWARDS	-	-	-	-	-	-	-	**17**	**r**	**15**	-	-	-	**20**	-	-
(Hesketh-Ford Cosworth)	-	-	-	-	nq	-	-	25	25	25	-	-	23ns	23	-	-
Harald ERTL	-	**15**	-	-	**r**	-	**r**	**r**	**7**	**r**	**8**	**r**	**16r**	-	**13**	**8**
(Hesketh-Ford Cosworth)	-	24	nq	nq	24	nq	23	27	23	22	20	24	19	ns	21	22
Bob EVANS	-	**10**	-	-	-	-	-	-	**r**	-	-	-	-	-	-	-
(JPS Lotus-Ford Cosworth)	-	23	nq	-	-	-	-	-	-	-	-	-	-	-	-	-
(Brabham-Ford Cosworth)	-	-	-	-	-	-	-	-	22	-	-	-	-	-	-	-
Emerson FITTIPALDI	**13**	**17r**	**6**	**r**	-	**6**	**r**	**r**	**6**	**13**	**r**	**r**	**15**	**r**	**9**	**r**
(Copersucar-Ford Cosworth)	5	21	16	19	nq	7	21	21	21	20	17	17	20	17	15	23
Divina GALICA	-	-	-	-	-	-	-	-	-	-	-	-	-	-	-	-
(Surtees-Ford Cosworth)	-	-	-	-	-	-	-	-	nq	-	-	-	-	-	-	-
Masahiro HASEMI	-	-	-	-	-	-	-	-	-	-	-	-	-	-	-	**11f**
(Kojima-Ford Cosworth)	-	-	-	-	-	-	-	-	-	-	-	-	-	-	-	10
Boy HAYJE	-	-	-	-	-	-	-	-	-	-	-	**r**	-	-	-	-
(Penske-Ford Cosworth)	-	-	-	-	-	-	-	-	-	-	-	21	-	-	-	-
Ingo HOFFMAN	**11**	-	-	-	-	-	-	-	-	-	-	-	-	-	-	-
(Copersucar-Ford Cosworth)	20	-	nq	nq	-	-	-	nq	-	-	-	-	-	-	-	-
Kazuyoshi HOSHINO	-	-	-	-	-	-	-	-	-	-	-	-	-	-	-	**r**
(Tyrrell-Ford Cosworth)	-	-	-	-	-	-	-	-	-	-	-	-	-	-	-	21
James HUNT	**r**	**2**	**r**	**1**	**r**	**r**	**5**	**1**	**dq**	**1**	**4f**	**1**	**r**	**1**	**1f**	**3**
(McLaren-Ford Cosworth)	1	1	3	1	3	14	8	1	2	1	1	2	25	1	1	2
Jacky ICKX	**8**	**16**	-	**7**	-	-	-	**10**	-	-	-	**r**	**10**	**13**	**r**	-
(Wolf Williams-Ford Cosworth)	19	19	nq	21	nq	nq	-	19	nq	-	-	-	-	-	-	-
(Ensign-Ford Cosworth)	-	-	-	-	-	-	-	-	-	-	-	11	10	16	19	-
Jean-Pierre JARIER	**rf**	**r**	**7**	**r**	**9**	**8**	**12**	**12**	**9**	**11**	**r**	**10**	**19**	**18**	**10**	**10**
(Shadow-Ford Cosworth)	3	15	7	15	14	10	14	15	24	23	18	20	17	18	16	15
Alan JONES	-	-	**nc**	**9**	**5**	**r**	**13**	**r**	**5**	**10**	**r**	**8**	**12**	**16**	**8**	**4**
(Surtees-Ford Cosworth)	-	-	19	20	16	19	18	18	19	14	15	16	18	20	18	20
Loris KESSEL	-	-	-	-	**12**	-	**r**	-	-	-	**nc**	-	-	-	-	-
(Brabham-Ford Cosworth)	-	-	-	nq	23	-	26	nq	-	-	25	-	-	-	-	-
Masami KUWASHIMA	-	-	-	-	-	-	-	-	-	-	-	-	-	-	-	-
(Wolf Williams-Ford Cosworth)	-	-	-	-	-	-	-	-	-	-	-	-	-	-	-	ns
Jacques LAFFITE	**r**	**r**	**4**	**12**	**3**	**12r**	**4**	**14**	**r/dq**	**r**	**2**	**r**	**3**	**r**	**r**	**7**
(Ligier-Matra)	11	8	12	8	6	8	7	13	13	6	5	10	1	9	12	11
Niki LAUDA	**1**	**1f**	**2**	**2**	**1f**	**1**	**3**	**rf**	**1f**	**r**	-	-	**4**	**8**	**3**	**r**
(Ferrari)	2	2	4	2	1	1	5	2	1	2	-	-	5	6	5	3
Michel LECLERE	-	**13**	-	**10**	**11**	**11**	**r**	**13**	-	-	-	-	-	-	-	-
(Wolf Williams-Ford Cosworth)	-	22	nq	23	25	18	25	22	-	-	-	-	-	-	-	-
Lella LOMBARDI	**14**	-	-	-	-	-	-	-	-	-	**12**	-	-	-	-	-
(March-Ford Cosworth)	22	-	-	-	-	-	-	-	-	-	-	-	-	-	-	-
(Brabham-Ford Cosworth)	-	-	-	-	-	-	-	-	nq	nq	24	-	-	-	-	-
Brett LUNGER	-	**11**	-	-	**r**	-	**15**	**16**	**r**	**r**	**10r**	-	**14**	**15**	**11**	-
(Surtees-Ford Cosworth)	-	20	nq	nq	26	-	24	23	18	24	16	-	24	22	24	-
Damien MAGEE	-	-	-	-	-	-	-	-	-	-	-	-	-	-	-	-
(Brabham-Ford Cosworth)	-	-	-	-	-	-	-	nq	-	-	-	-	-	-	-	-
Jochen MASS	**6**	**3**	**5**	**rf**	**6**	**5**	**11**	**15**	**r**	**3**	**7**	**9**	**r**	**5**	**4**	**r**
(McLaren-Ford Cosworth)	6	4	14	4	18	11	13	14	12	9	12	15	26	11	17	12
Arturo MERZARIO	-	-	-	**r**	**r**	-	**14r**	**9**	**r**	**r**	**r**	**r**	-	**r**	**r**	**r**
(March-Ford Cosworth)	-	-	nq	18	21	nq	19	20	9	-	-	-	-	-	-	-
(Wolf Williams-Ford Cosworth)	-	-	-	-	-	-	-	-	-	21	21	23	ns	24	25	19

	BR	ZA	USAW	E	B	MC	S	F	GB	D	A	NL	I	CDN	USAE	J
Jac NELLEMAN	-	-	-	-	-	-	-	-	-	-	-	-	-	-	-	-
(Brabham-Ford Cosworth)	-	-	-	-	-	-	nq	-	-	-	-	-	-	-	-	-
Patrick NEVE	-	-	-	-	r	-	-	18	-	-	-	-	-	-	-	-
(Brabham-Ford Cosworth)	-	-	-	-	19	-	-	-	-	-	-	-	-	-	-	-
(Ensign-Ford Cosworth)	-	-	-	-	-	-	-	26	-	-	-	-	-	-	-	-
Gunnar NILSSON	-	r	r	3	r	r	r	r	r	5	3	r	13	12	r	6
(JPS Lotus-Ford Cosworth)	-	25	20	7	22	16	6	12	14	16	4	13	12	15	20	16
Carlos PACE	10	r	9	6	r	9	8	4	8	4	r	r	r	7	r	r
(Brabham-Alfa Romeo)	10	14	13	11	9	13	10	5	16	7	8	9	3	10	10	6
Larry PERKINS	-	-	-	13	8	-	r	-	-	-	-	r	r	17	r	r
(Boro-Ford Cosworth)	-	-	-	24	20	nq	22	-	-	-	-	19	13	-	-	-
(Brabham-Alfa Romeo)	-	-	-	-	-	-	-	-	-	-	-	-	-	19	13	17
Henri PESCAROLO	-	-	-	-	-	-	-	r	r	-	9	11	17	19	nc	-
(Surtees-Ford Cosworth)	-	-	-	-	-	nq	-	24	26	nq	22	22	22	21	26	-
Sandro PESENTI-ROSSI	-	-	-	-	-	-	-	-	-	14	11	-	18	-	-	-
(Tyrrell-Ford Cosworth)	-	-	-	-	-	-	-	-	-	26	23	nq	21	-	-	-
Ronnie PETERSON	r	r	10	r	r	r	7	19r	r	r	6	r	1f	9	r	r
(JPS Lotus-Ford Cosworth)	18	-	-	-	-	-	-	-	-	-	-	-	-	-	-	-
(March-Ford Cosworth)	-	10	6	16	10	3	9	6	7	11	3	1	8	2	3	9
Tom PRYCE	3	7	r	8	10	7	9	8	4	8	r	4	8	11	r	r
(Shadow-Ford Cosworth)	12	7	5	22	13	15	12	16	20	18	6	3	15	13	9	14
Clay REGAZZONI	7	r	1f	11	2	14rf	6	r	r/dq	9	-	2f	2	6	7	5
(Ferrari)	4	9	1	5	2	2	11	4	4	5	-	5	9	12	14	7
Carlos REUTEMANN	12r	r	r	4	r	r	r	11	r	r	r	r	9	-	-	-
(Brabham-Alfa Romeo)	15	11	10	12	12	20	16	10	15	10	14	12	-	-	-	-
(Ferrari)	-	-	-	-	-	-	-	-	-	-	-	-	7	-	-	-
Alex-Dias RIBEIRO	-	-	-	-	-	-	-	-	-	-	-	-	-	-	12	-
(Hesketh-Ford Cosworth)	-	-	-	-	-	-	-	-	-	-	-	-	-	-	22	-
Ian SCHECKTER	-	r	-	-	-	-	-	-	-	-	-	-	-	-	-	-
(Tyrrell-Ford Cosworth)	-	16	-	-	-	-	-	-	-	-	-	-	-	-	-	-
Jody SCHECKTER	5	4	r	r	4	2	1	6	2	2f	r	5	5	4	2	r
(Tyrrell-Ford Cosworth)	13	12	11	14	7	5	1	9	8	8	10	8	2	7	2	5
Rolf STOMMELEN	-	-	-	-	-	-	-	-	-	6	-	12	r	-	-	-
(Brabham-Alfa Romeo)	-	-	-	-	-	-	-	-	-	15	-	-	11	-	-	-
(Hesketh-Ford Cosworth)	-	-	-	-	-	-	-	-	-	-	-	25	-	-	-	-
Hans-Joachim STUCK	4	12	r	r	r	4	r	7	r	r	r	r	r	r	5	r
(March-Ford Cosworth)	14	17	18	17	15	6	20	17	17	4	11	18	6	8	6	18
Otto STUPPACHER	-	-	-	-	-	-	-	-	-	-	-	-	-	-	-	-
(Tyrrell-Ford Cosworth)	-	-	-	-	-	-	-	-	-	-	-	-	ns	nq	nq	-
Noritake TAKAHARA	-	-	-	-	-	-	-	-	-	-	-	-	-	-	-	9
(Surtees-Ford Cosworth)	-	-	-	-	-	-	-	-	-	-	-	-	-	-	-	24
Tony TRIMMER	-	-	-	-	-	-	-	-	-	-	-	-	-	-	-	-
(Maki-Ford Cosworth)	-	-	-	-	-	-	-	-	-	-	-	-	-	-	-	nq
John WATSON	r	5	nc	r	7	10	r	3	3	7	1	r	11	10	6	r
(Penske-Ford Cosworth)	8	3	9	13	17	17	17	8	11	19	2	4	27	14	8	4
Mike WILDS	-	-	-	-	-	-	-	-	-	-	-	-	-	-	-	-
(Shadow-Ford Cosworth)	-	-	-	-	-	-	-	-	nq	-	-	-	-	-	-	-
Emilio ZAPICO	-	-	-	-	-	-	-	-	-	-	-	-	-	-	-	-
(Williams-Ford Cosworth)	-	-	-	nq	-	-	-	-	-	-	-	-	-	-	-	-
Renzo ZORZI	9	-	-	-	-	-	-	-	-	-	-	-	-	-	-	-
(Wolf Williams-Ford Cosworth)	17	-	-	-	-	-	-	-	-	-	-	-	-	-	-	-

1977 RACE RESULTS & GRID POSITIONS

	RA	BR	ZA	USAW	E	MC	B	S	F	GB	D	A	NL	I	USAE	CDN	J
Conny ANDERSSON	-	-	-	-	-	-	-	-	-	-	-	-	-	-	-	-	-
(Stanley BRM)	-	-	-	-	nq	-	nq	nq	nq	-	-	-	-	-	-	-	-
Mario ANDRETTI	5r	r	r	1	1	5	r	6f	1f	14r	r	r	r	1f	2	9rf	r
(JPS Lotus-Ford Cosworth)	8	3	6	2	1	10	1	1	1	6	7	3	1	4	4	1	1
Ian ASHLEY	-	-	-	-	-	-	-	-	-	-	-	-	-	-	17	-	-
(Hesketh-Ford Cosworth)	-	-	-	-	-	-	-	-	-	-	-	nq	nq	nq	22	ns	-
Hans BINDER	r	r	11	11	9	r	-	-	-	-	-	12	8	-	11	r	r
(Surtees-Ford Cosworth)	18	20	19	19	20	19	-	-	-	-	-	-	-	-	25	24	21
(Penske-Ford Cosworth)	-	-	-	-	-	-	-	-	-	-	-	19	18	nq	-	-	-
Michael BLEEKEMOLEN	-	-	-	-	-	-	-	-	-	-	-	-	-	-	-	-	-
(March-Ford Cosworth)	-	-	-	-	-	-	-	-	-	-	-	-	nq	-	-	-	-
Vittorio BRAMBILLA	7r	r	7	r	r	8	4	r	13	8	5	15	12r	r	19	6r	8
(Surtees-Ford Cosworth)	13	11	14	11	11	14	12	13	11	8	10	13	22	10	11	15	9
Bernard de DRYVER	-	-	-	-	-	-	-	-	-	-	-	-	-	-	-	-	-
(March-Ford Cosworth)	-	-	-	-	-	-	nq	-	-	-	-	-	-	-	-	-	-
Emilio de VILLOTA	-	-	-	-	13	-	-	-	-	-	-	17r	-	-	-	-	-
(McLaren-Ford Cosworth)	-	-	-	-	23	-	nq	nq	-	nq	nq	26	-	nq	-	-	-
Patrick DEPAILLER	r	r	3	4	r	r	8	4	r	r	r	13	r	r	14	2	3
(Tyrrell-Ford Cosworth)	3	6	4	12	10	8	5	6	12	18	15	10	11	13	8	6	15
Guy EDWARDS	-	-	-	-	-	-	-	-	-	-	-	-	-	-	-	-	-
(Stanley BRM)	-	-	-	-	-	-	-	-	-	npq	-	-	-	-	-	-	-
Harald ERTL	-	-	-	-	r	-	9	16	-	-	-	-	-	-	-	-	-
(Hesketh-Ford Cosworth)	-	-	-	-	18	nq	25	23	nq	-	-	-	-	-	-	-	-
Emerson FITTIPALDI	4	4	10	5	14	r	r	18	11	r	-	11	4	-	13	r	-
(Copersucar-Ford Cosworth)	16	16	9	7	19	18	16	18	22	22	nq	23	17	nq	18	19	-
Giorgio FRANCIA	-	-	-	-	-	-	-	-	-	-	-	-	-	-	-	-	-
(Brabham-Alfa Romeo)	-	-	-	-	-	-	-	-	-	-	-	-	-	nq	-	-	-
Bruno GIACOMELLI	-	-	-	-	-	-	-	-	-	-	-	-	-	r	-	-	-
(McLaren-Ford Cosworth)	-	-	-	-	-	-	-	-	-	-	-	-	-	15	-	-	-
Boy HAYJE	-	-	r	-	-	-	15	-	-	-	-	-	-	-	-	-	-
(March-Ford Cosworth)	-	-	21	-	nq	nq	27	nq	-	-	-	-	nq	-	-	-	-
Brian HENTON	-	-	-	10	-	-	-	-	-	-	-	-	dq	-	-	-	-
(March-Ford Cosworth)	-	-	-	18	nq	-	-	-	-	nq	-	nq	-	-	-	-	-
(Boro-Ford Cosworth)	-	-	-	-	-	-	-	-	-	-	-	-	23	nq	-	-	-
Hans HEYER	-	-	-	-	-	-	-	-	-	-	r	-	-	-	-	-	-
(Penske-Ford Cosworth)	-	-	-	-	-	-	-	-	-	-	25	-	-	-	-	-	-
Ingo HOFFMAN	r	7	-	-	-	-	-	-	-	-	-	-	-	-	-	-	-
(Copersucar-Ford Cosworth)	19	19	-	-	-	-	-	-	-	-	-	-	-	-	-	-	-
Kazuyoshi HOSHINO	-	-	-	-	-	-	-	-	-	-	-	-	-	-	-	-	11
(Kojima-Ford Cosworth)	-	-	-	-	-	-	-	-	-	-	-	-	-	-	-	-	11
James HUNT	rf	2f	4	7	r	r	7	12	3	1f	r	r	r	r	1	r	1
(McLaren-Ford Cosworth)	1	1	1	8	7	7	9	3	2	1	4	2	3	1	1	2	2
Jacky ICKX	-	-	-	-	-	10	-	-	-	-	-	-	-	-	-	-	-
(Ensign-Ford Cosworth)	-	-	-	-	-	17	-	-	-	-	-	-	-	-	-	-	-
Jean-Pierre JABOUILLE	-	-	-	-	-	-	-	-	-	r	-	-	r	r	r	-	-
(Renault)	-	-	-	-	-	-	-	-	-	21	-	-	10	20	14	nq	-
Jean-Pierre JARIER	-	-	-	6	-	11	11	8	r	9	r	14	r	r	9	-	r
(Penske-Ford Cosworth)	-	-	-	9	nq	12	26	17	19	20	12	18	21	18	-	-	-
(Shadow-Ford Cosworth)	-	-	-	-	-	-	-	-	-	-	-	-	-	-	16	-	-
(Ligier-Matra)	-	-	-	-	-	-	-	-	-	-	-	-	-	-	-	-	17
Alan JONES	-	-	-	r	r	6	5	17	r	7	r	1	r	3	r	4	4
(Shadow-Ford Cosworth)	-	-	-	14	14	11	17	11	10	12	17	14	13	16	13	7	12
Rupert KEEGAN	-	-	-	-	r	12	r	13	10	r	r	7	r	9	8	r	-
(Hesketh-Ford Cosworth)	-	-	-	-	16	20	19	24	14	13	23	20	26	23	20	25	-

Loris KESSEL (Williams-Ford Cosworth)	- -	- -	- -	- -	- -	- -	- -	- -	- -	- -	- -	- -	- -	- nq	- -	- -	- -
Mikko KOZAROWITSKY (March-Ford Cosworth)	- -	- -	- -	- -	- -	- -	- -	- nq	- -	- npq	- -	- -	- -	- -	- -	- -	- -
Jacques LAFFITE (Ligier-Matra)	nc 15	r 14	r 12	9r 5	7f 2	7 16	r 10	1 8	8 5	6 15	r 6	r 6	2 2	8 8	7 10	r 11	5r 5
Niki LAUDA (Ferrari)	r 4	3 13	1 3	2f 1	- 3ns	2 6	2 11	r 15	5 9	2 3	1f 3	2 1	1f 4	2 5	4 7	- -	- -
Lamberto LEONI (Surtees-Ford Cosworth)	- -	- -	- -	- -	- -	- -	- -	- -	- -	- -	- -	- -	- -	- -	- -	- -	- -
Brett LUNGER (March-Ford Cosworth) (McLaren-Ford Cosworth)	- - -	- - -	14 23 -	r 21 -	10 25 -	- - -	- - 22ns	11 - 22	- - nq	13 - 19	r - 21	10 - 17	9 - 20	nq r - 22	10 - 17	11r - 20	- - -
Jochen MASS (McLaren-Ford Cosworth)	r 5	r 4	5 13	r 15	4 9	4 9	r 6	2 9	9 7	4 11	r 13	6 9	r 14	4 9	r 15	3 5	r 8
Brian McGUIRE (McGuire-Ford Cosworth)	- -	- -	- -	- -	- -	- -	- -	- -	- -	- npq	- -	- -	- -	- -	- -	- -	- -
Arturo MERZARIO (March-Ford Cosworth) (Shadow-Ford Cosworth)	- - -	- - -	- - -	- - -	r 21 -	- nq -	14 14 -	- - -	r 18 -	r 17 -	- nq -	r - 21	- nq -	- - -	- - -	- - -	- - -
Patrick NEVE (March-Ford Cosworth)	- -	- -	- -	- -	12 22	- -	10 24	15 20	- nq	10 26	- nq	9 22	- nq	7 24	18 24	r 21	- -
Gunnar NILSSON (JPS Lotus-Ford Cosworth)	- 10ns	5 10	12 10	8 16	5 12	r 13	1f 3	19r 7	4 3	3 5	r 9	r 16	r 5	r 19	r 12	r 4	r 14
Jackie OLIVER (Shadow-Ford Cosworth)	- -	- -	- -	- -	- -	- -	- -	9 16	- -	- -	- -	- -	- -	- -	- -	- -	- -
Danny ONGAIS (Penske-Ford Cosworth)	- -	- -	- -	- -	- -	- -	- -	- -	- -	- -	- -	- -	- -	- -	r 26	7 22	- -
Carlos PACE + (Brabham-Alfa Romeo)	2 6	r 5	13 2	- -	- -	- -	- -	- -	- -	- -	- -	- -	- -	- -	- -	- -	- -
Riccardo PATRESE (Shadow-Ford Cosworth)	- -	- -	- -	- -	- -	9 15	r 15	- -	r 15	r 25	10r 16	- -	13 16	r 6	- -	10r 8	6 13
Larry PERKINS (Stanley BRM) (Surtees-Ford Cosworth)	- - -	r 22 -	15 22 -	- - -	- - -	- - -	12 - 23	- - nq	- - nq	- - -	- - -	- - -	- - -	- - -	- - -	- - -	- - -
Ronnie PETERSON (Tyrrell-Ford Cosworth)	r 14	r 8	r 7	r 10	8 15	r 4	3 8	r 10	12 17	r 10	9r 14	5 15	r 7	6 12	16f 5	r 3	r 18
Teddy PILETTE (Stanley BRM)	- -	- -	- -	- -	- -	- -	- -	- -	- -	- -	- nq	- -	- nq	- nq	- -	- -	- -
Tom PRYCE + (Shadow-Ford Cosworth)	nc 9	r 12	r 15	- -	- -	- -	- -	- -	- -	- -	- -	- -	- -	- -	- -	- -	- -
David PURLEY (Lec-Ford Cosworth)	- -	- -	- -	- -	- nq	- -	13 20	14 19	r 21	- npq	- -	- -	- -	- -	- -	- -	- -
Hector REBAQUE (Hesketh-Ford Cosworth)	- -	- -	- -	- -	- -	- -	- nq	- nq	- nq	- -	r 24	- nq	- nq	- -	- -	- -	- -
Clay REGAZZONI (Ensign-Ford Cosworth)	6 12	r 9	9 16	r 13	r 8	- nq	r 13	7 14	7 16	- nq	r 22	r 11	r 9	5 7	5 19	r 14	r 10
Carlos REUTEMANN (Ferrari)	3 7	1 2	8 8	r 4	2 4	3 3	r 7	3 12	6 6	15 14	4 8	4 5	6 6	r 2	6 6	r 12	2 7
Alex-Dias RIBEIRO (March-Ford Cosworth)	r 20	r 21	r 17	r 22	- nq	- nq	- nq	- nq	- nq	- nq	8 20	- nq	11 24	- nq	15 23	8 23	12 23
Ian SCHECKTER (March-Ford Cosworth)	r 17	r 17	- -	- -	11 17	- nq	r 21	r 21	nc 20	r 24	r 18	r 24	10 25	r 17	r 21	r 18	- -
Jody SCHECKTER (Wolf-Ford Cosworth)	1 11	r 15	2 5	3 3	3 5	1f 2	r 4	r 4	r 8	r 4	2 1	r 8	3 15	r 3	3 9	1 9	10f 6
Vern SCHUPPAN (Surtees-Ford Cosworth)	- -	- -	- -	- -	- -	- -	- -	- -	- -	12 23	7 19	16 25	- nq	- -	- -	- -	- -
Hans-Joachim STUCK (March-Ford Cosworth) (Brabham-Alfa Romeo)	- - -	- - -	r 18 -	r - 17	6 - 13	r - 5	6 - 18	10 - 5	r - 13	5 - 7	3 - 5	3 - 4	7 - 19	r - 11	r - 2	r - 13	7 - 4
Andy SUTCLIFFE (March-Ford Cosworth)	- -	- -	- -	- -	- -	- -	- -	- -	- -	- npq	- -	- -	- -	- -	- -	- -	- -
Noritake TAKAHARA (Kojima-Ford Cosworth)	- -	- -	- -	- -	- -	- -	- -	- -	- -	- -	- -	- -	- -	- -	- -	- -	r 19
Kunimitsu TAKAHASHI (Tyrrell-Ford Cosworth)	- -	- -	- -	- -	- -	- -	- -	- -	- -	- -	- -	- -	- -	- -	- -	- -	9 22
Patrick TAMBAY (Surtees-Ford Cosworth) (Ensign-Ford Cosworth)	- - -	- - -	- - -	- - -	- - -	- - -	- - -	- - -	- nq -	r - 16	6 - 11	r - 7	5r - 12	r - 21	- - nq	5 - 16	r - 16
Tony TRIMMER (Surtees-Ford Cosworth)	- -	- -	- -	- -	- -	- -	- -	- -	- -	- npq	- -	- -	- -	- -	- -	- -	- -
Gilles VILLENEUVE (McLaren-Ford Cosworth) (Ferrari)	- - -	- - -	- - -	- - -	- - -	- - -	- - -	- - -	- - -	11 9 -	- - -	- - -	- - -	- - -	- - -	12r - 17	r - 20
John WATSON (Brabham-Alfa Romeo)	r 2	r 7	6f 11	dq 6	r 6	r 2	r 2	5 2	2 4	r 2	r 2	8f 12	r 8	r 14	12 3	r 10	r 3
Renzo ZORZI (Shadow-Ford Cosworth)	r 21	6 18	r 20	r 20	r 24	- -	- -	- -	- -	- -	- -	- -	- -	- -	- -	- -	- -

1978 RACE RESULTS & GRID POSITIONS

	RA	BR	ZA	USAW	MC	B	E	S	F	GB	D	A	NL	I	USAE	CDN
Mario ANDRETTI (JPS Lotus-Ford Cosworth)	1 1	4 3	7f 2	2 4	11 4	1 1	1f 1	r 1	1 2	r 2	1 1	r 2	1 1	6f 1	r 1	10 9
René ARNOUX (Martini-Ford Cosworth) (Surtees-Ford Cosworth)	- - -	- - -	- nq -	- - -	- npq -	9 19 -	- - -	- - -	14 18 -	- - -	- npq -	9 26 -	r 23 -	- - -	9 - 21	r - 16
Hans BINDER (ATS-Ford Cosworth)	- -	- -	- -	- -	- -	- -	- -	- -	- -	- -	- -	- nq	- -	- -	- -	- -
Michael BLEEKEMOLEN (ATS-Ford Cosworth)	- -	- -	- -	- -	- -	- -	- -	- -	- -	- -	- -	- -	- nq	- nq	r 25	- nq
Vittorio BRAMBILLA (Surtees-Ford Cosworth)	18 12	- nq	12 19	r 17	- nq	13r 12	7 16	r 18	17 19	9 25	r 20	6 21	dq 22	r 23	- -	- -
Eddie CHEEVER (Theodore-Ford Cosworth) (Hesketh-Ford Cosworth)	- nq -	- nq -	r - 25	- - -	- - -	- - -	- - -	- - -	- - -	- - -	- - -	- - -	- - -	- - -	- - -	- - -
Alberto COLOMBO (ATS-Ford Cosworth) (Merzario-Ford Cosworth)	- - -	- - -	- - -	- - -	- - -	- nq -	- nq -	- - -	- - -	- - -	- - -	- - -	- - -	- - npq	- - -	- - -
Derek DALY (Hesketh-Ford Cosworth) (Ensign-Ford Cosworth)	- - -	- - -	- - -	- npq -	- npq -	- nq -	- - -	- - -	- - nq	r - 15	- - -	dq - 19	r - 16	10 - 18	8 - 19	6 - 15
Bernard de DRYVER (Ensign-Ford Cosworth)	- -	- -	- -	- -	- -	- npq	- -	- -	- -	- -	- -	- -	- -	- -	- -	- -
Emilio de VILLOTA (McLaren-Ford Cosworth)	- -	- -	- -	- -	- -	- -	- nq	- -	- -	- -	- -	- -	- -	- -	- -	- -
Patrick DEPAILLER (Tyrrell-Ford Cosworth)	3 10	r 11	2 11	3 12	1 5	r 13	r 12	r 12	r 13	4 10	r 13	2 13	r 12	11 16	r 12	5 13
Harald ERTL (Ensign-Ford Cosworth) (ATS-Ford Cosworth)	- - -	- - -	- - -	- - -	- - -	- - -	- - -	- - -	- - -	- - -	11r 23 -	r 24 -	- npq -	- - nq	- - -	- - -

	RA	BR	ZA	USAW	MC	B	E	S	F	GB	D	A	NL	I	USAE	CDN
Emerson FITTIPALDI	**9**	**2**	**r**	**8**	**9**	**r**	**r**	**6**	**r**	**r**	**4**	**4**	**5**	**8**	**5**	**r**
(Copersucar-Ford Cosworth)	17	7	16	15	20	15	15	13	15	11	10	6	10	13	13	6
Beppe GABBIANI	-	-	-	-	-	-	-	-	-	-	-	-	-	-	-	-
(Surtees-Ford Cosworth)	-	-	-	-	-	-	-	-	-	-	-	-	-	-	nq	nq
Divina GALICA	-	-	-	-	-	-	-	-	-	-	-	-	-	-	-	-
(Hesketh-Ford Cosworth)	nq	nq	-	-	-	-	-	-	-	-	-	-	-	-	-	-
Bruno GIACOMELLI	-	-	-	-	-	**8**	-	-	**r**	**7**	-	-	**r**	**14**	-	-
(McLaren-Ford Cosworth)	-	-	-	-	-	21	-	-	22	16	-	-	19	20	-	-
GIMAX	-	-	-	-	-	-	-	-	-	-	-	-	-	-	-	-
(Surtees-Ford Cosworth)	-	-	-	-	-	-	-	-	-	-	-	-	-	nq	-	-
Brian HENTON	-	-	-	-	-	-	-	-	-	-	-	-	-	-	-	-
(Surtees-Ford Cosworth)	-	-	-	-	-	-	-	-	-	-	-	nq	-	-	-	-
James HUNT	**4**	**r**	**r**	**r**	**r**	**r**	**6**	**8**	**3**	**r**	**dq**	**r**	**10**	**r**	**7**	**r**
(McLaren-Ford Cosworth)	6	2	3	7	6	6	4	14	4	14	8	8	7	10	6	19
Jacky ICKX	-	-	-	-	**r**	**12**	**r**	-	-	-	-	-	-	-	-	-
(Ensign-Ford Cosworth)	-	-	-	-	16	22	21	nq	-	-	-	-	-	-	-	-
Jean-Pierre JABOUILLE	-	-	**r**	**r**	**10**	**nc**	**13**	**r**	**r**	**r**	**r**	**r**	**r**	**r**	**4**	**12**
(Renault)	-	-	6	13	12	10	11	10	11	12	9	3	9	3	9	22
Jean-Pierre JARIER	**12**	-	**8**	**11**	-	-	-	-	-	-	-	-	-	-	**15rf**	**r**
(ATS-Ford Cosworth)	11	16ns	17	19	nq	-	-	-	-	-	nq	-	-	-	-	-
(JPS Lotus-Ford Cosworth)	-	-	-	-	-	-	-	-	-	-	-	-	-	-	8	1
Alan JONES	**r**	**11**	**4**	**7f**	**r**	**10**	**8**	**r**	**5**	**r**	**r**	**r**	**r**	**13**	**2**	**9f**
(Williams-Ford Cosworth)	14	8	18	8	10	11	18	9	14	6	6	15	11	6	3	5
Rupert KEEGAN	**r**	**r**	**r**	-	**r**	-	**11**	-	**r**	-	-	-	-	-	-	-
(Surtees-Ford Cosworth)	19	24	23	ns	18	nq	23	nq	23	nq	nq	nq	25ns	-	-	-
Jacques LAFFITE	**16r**	**9**	**5**	**5**	**r**	**5r**	**3**	**7**	**7**	**10**	**3**	**5**	**8**	**4**	**11**	**r**
(Ligier-Matra)	8	14	13	14	15	14	10	11	10	7	7	5	6	8	10	10
Niki LAUDA	**2**	**3**	**r**	**r**	**2f**	**r**	**r**	**1f**	**r**	**2f**	**r**	**r**	**3f**	**1**	**r**	**r**
(Brabham-Alfa Romeo)	5	10	1	3	3	3	6	3	3	4	3	12	3	4	5	7
Geoff LEES	-	-	-	-	-	-	-	-	-	-	-	-	-	-	-	-
(Ensign-Ford Cosworth)	-	-	-	-	-	-	-	-	-	nq	-	-	-	-	-	-
Lamberto LEONI	**r**	**r**	-	-	-	-	-	-	-	-	-	-	-	-	-	-
(Ensign-Ford Cosworth)	22	17	nq	nq	-	-	-	-	-	-	-	-	-	-	-	-
Brett LUNGER	**13**	**r**	**11**	-	-	**7**	-	-	**r**	**8**	-	**8**	**r**	**r**	**13**	-
(McLaren-Ford Cosworth)	24	13	20	nq	npq	24	nq	nq	24	24	npq	17	21	21	-	-
(Ensign-Ford Cosworth)	-	-	-	-	-	-	-	-	-	-	-	-	-	-	24	-
Jochen MASS	**11**	**7**	**r**	**r**	-	**11**	**9**	**13**	**13**	**nc**	**r**	-	-	-	-	-
(ATS-Ford Cosworth)	13	20	15	16	nq	16	17	19	25	26	22	nq	nq	-	-	-
Arturo MERZARIO	**r**	-	**r**	**r**	-	-	-	**nc**	-	**r**	-	-	**r**	**r**	**r**	-
(Merzario-Ford Cosworth)	20	nq	26	21	npq	npq	nq	22	nq	23	nq	nq	27	22	26	nq
Patrick NEVE	-	-	-	-	-	-	-	-	-	-	-	-	-	-	-	-
(March-Ford Cosworth)	-	-	-	-	-	npq	-	-	-	-	-	-	-	-	-	-
Danny ONGAIS	**r**	**r**	-	-	-	-	-	-	-	-	-	-	-	-	-	-
(Ensign-Ford Cosworth)	21	23	-	-	-	-	-	-	-	-	-	-	-	-	-	-
(Shadow-Ford Cosworth)	-	-	-	npq	-	-	-	-	-	-	-	-	npq	-	-	-
Riccardo PATRESE	-	**10**	**r**	**6**	**6**	**r**	**r**	**2**	**8**	**r**	**9**	**r**	**r**	**r**	-	**4**
(Arrows-Ford Cosworth)	-	18	7	9	14	8	8	5	12	5	14	16	13	12	-	12
Ronnie PETERSON +	**5**	**r**	**1**	**4**	**r**	**2f**	**2**	**3**	**2**	**r**	**rf**	**1f**	**2**	**r**	-	-
(Lotus-Ford Cosworth)	3	1	12	6	7	7	2	4	5	1	2	1	2	5	-	-
Nelson PIQUET	-	-	-	-	-	-	-	-	-	-	**r**	**r**	**r**	**9**	-	**11**
(Ensign-Ford Cosworth)	-	-	-	-	-	-	-	-	-	-	21	-	-	-	-	-
(McLaren-Ford Cosworth)	-	-	-	-	-	-	-	-	-	-	-	20	26	24	-	-
(Brabham-Alfa Romeo)	-	-	-	-	-	-	-	-	-	-	-	-	-	-	-	14
Didier PIRONI	**14**	**6**	**6**	**r**	**5**	**6**	**12**	**r**	**10**	**r**	**5**	**r**	**r**	**r**	**10**	**7**
(Tyrrell-Ford Cosworth)	23	19	14	22	13	23	13	17	16	19	16	9	17	14	16	18
Bobby RAHAL	-	-	-	-	-	-	-	-	-	-	-	-	-	-	**12**	**r**
(Wolf-Ford Cosworth)	-	-	-	-	-	-	-	-	-	-	-	-	-	-	20	20
Hector REBAQUE	-	**r**	**10**	-	-	-	**r**	**12**	-	**r**	**6**	**r**	**11**	-	**r**	-
(Lotus-Ford Cosworth)	nq	22	21	npq	npq	npq	20	21	nq	21	18	18	20	nq	23	nq
Clay REGAZZONI	**15**	**5**	-	**10**	-	**r**	**15r**	**5**	**r**	**r**	-	**nc**	-	**nc**	**14**	-
(Shadow-Ford Cosworth)	16	15	nq	20	nq	18	22	16	17	17	nq	22	nq	15	17	nq
Carlos REUTEMANN	**7**	**1f**	**r**	**1**	**8**	**3**	**r**	**10**	**18f**	**1**	**r**	**dq**	**7**	**3**	**1**	**3**
(Ferrari)	2	4	9	1	1	2	3	8	8	8	12	4	4	11	2	11
Keke ROSBERG	-	-	**r**	-	-	-	-	**15**	**16**	**r**	**10**	**nc**	**r**	-	**r**	**nc**
(Theodore-Ford Cosworth)	-	-	24	npq	npq	nq	npq	-	-	-	-	-	-	-	-	-
(ATS-Ford Cosworth)	-	-	-	-	-	-	-	23	26	22	-	-	-	-	15	21
(Wolf-Ford Cosworth)	-	-	-	-	-	-	-	-	-	-	19	25	24	npq	-	-
Jody SCHECKTER	**10**	**r**	**r**	**r**	**3**	**r**	**4**	**r**	**6**	**r**	**2**	**r**	**12**	**12**	**3**	**2**
(Wolf-Ford Cosworth)	15	12	5	10	9	5	9	6	7	3	4	7	15	9	11	2
Rolf STOMMELEN	-	-	**9**	**9**	**r**	**r**	**14**	**14**	**15**	-	**dq**	-	-	-	**16**	-
(Arrows-Ford Cosworth)	-	-	22	18	19	17	19	24	21	nq	17	npq	npq	npq	22	nq
Hans-Joachim STUCK	**17**	**r**	-	-	**r**	**r**	**r**	**11**	**11**	**5**	**r**	**r**	**r**	**r**	**r**	**r**
(Shadow-Ford Cosworth)	18	9	nq	ns	17	20	24	20	20	18	24	23	18	17	14	8
Patrick TAMBAY	**6**	**r**	**r**	**12r**	**7**	-	**r**	**4**	**9**	**6**	**r**	**r**	**9**	**5**	**6**	**8**
(McLaren-Ford Cosworth)	9	5	4	11	11	-	14	15	6	20	11	14	14	19	18	17
Tony TRIMMER	-	-	-	-	-	-	-	-	-	-	-	-	-	-	-	-
(McLaren-Ford Cosworth)	-	-	-	-	-	-	-	-	-	nq	-	-	-	-	-	-
Gilles VILLENEUVE	**8f**	**r**	**r**	**r**	**r**	**4**	**10**	**9**	**12**	**r**	**8**	**3**	**6**	**7**	**r**	**1**
(Ferrari)	7	6	8	2	8	4	5	7	9	13	15	11	5	2	4	3
John WATSON	**r**	**8**	**3**	**r**	**4**	**r**	**5**	**r**	**4**	**3**	**7**	**7**	**4**	**2**	**r**	**r**
(Brabham-Alfa Romeo)	4	21	10	5	2	9	7	2	1	9	5	10	8	7	7	4

1979 RACE RESULTS & GRID POSITIONS

	RA	BR	ZA	USAW	E	B	MC	F	GB	D	A	NL	I	CDN	USAE
Mario ANDRETTI	**5**	**r**	**4**	**4**	**3**	**r**	**r**	**r**	**r**	**r**	**r**	**r**	**5**	**10r**	**r**
(Lotus-Ford Cosworth)	7	4	8	6	4	5	13	12	9	11	15	17	10	10	17
René ARNOUX	**r**	**r**	**r**	-	**9**	**r**	**r**	**3f**	**2**	**r**	**6f**	**r**	**r**	**r**	**2**
(Renault)	25	11	10	ns	11	18	19	2	5	10	1	1	2	8	7
Vittorio BRAMBILLA	-	-	-	-	-	-	-	-	-	-	-	-	**12**	**r**	-
(Alfa Romeo)	-	-	-	-	-	-	-	-	-	-	-	-	22	18	nq
Gianfranco BRANCATELLI	-	-	-	-	-	-	-	-	-	-	-	-	-	-	-
(Kauhsen-Ford Cosworth)	-	-	-	-	nq	nq	-	-	-	-	-	-	-	-	-
(Merzario-Ford Cosworth)	-	-	-	-	-	-	npq	-	-	-	-	-	-	-	-
Derek DALY	**11**	**13**	-	**r**	-	-	-	-	-	-	**8**	-	-	**r**	**r**
(Ensign-Ford Cosworth)	24	23	nq	24	nq	nq	nq	-	-	-	-	-	-	-	-
(Tyrrell-Ford Cosworth)	-	-	-	-	-	-	-	-	-	-	11	-	-	24	15
Elio de ANGELIS	**7**	**12**	**r**	**7**	**r**	**r**	-	**16**	**12**	**11**	**r**	**r**	**r**	**r**	**4**
(Shadow-Ford Cosworth)	16	20	15	20	22	24	nq	24	12	21	22	22	24	23	20
Patrick DEPAILLER	**4**	**2**	**r**	**5**	**1**	**r**	**5rf**	-	-	-	-	-	-	-	-
(Ligier-Ford Cosworth)	2	2	5	4	2	2	3	-	-	-	-	-	-	-	-
Emerson FITTIPALDI	**6**	**11**	**13**	**r**	**11**	**9**	**r**	**r**	**r**	**r**	**r**	**r**	**8**	**8**	**7**
(Copersucar-Ford Cosworth)	11	9	18	16	19	23	17	18	22	22	19	21	20	15	23
Patrick GAILLARD	-	-	-	-	-	-	-	-	**13**	-	**r**	-	-	-	-
(Ensign-Ford Cosworth)	-	-	-	-	-	-	-	nq	23	nq	24	nq	-	-	-
Bruno GIACOMELLI	-	-	-	-	-	**r**	-	**17**	-	-	-	-	**r**	-	**r**
(Alfa Romeo)	-	-	-	-	-	14	-	17	-	-	-	-	18	-	18
James HUNT	**r**	**r**	**8**	**r**	**r**	**r**	**r**	-	-	-	-	-	-	-	-
(Wolf-Ford Cosworth)	18	10	13	8	15	9	10	-	-	-	-	-	-	-	-
Jacky ICKX	-	-	-	-	-	-	-	**r**	**6**	**r**	**r**	**5**	**r**	**r**	**r**
(Ligier-Ford Cosworth)	-	-	-	-	-	-	-	14	17	14	21	20	11	16	24

Driver	RA	BR	ZA	USAW	E	B	MC	F	GB	D	A	NL	I	CDN	USAE
Jean-Pierre JABOUILLE	**r**	**10**	**r**	**-**	**r**	**r**	**8**	**1**	**r**	**r**	**r**	**r**	**14r**	**r**	**r**
(Renault)	12	7	1	ns	9	17	20	1	2	1	3	4	1	7	8
Jean-Pierre JARIER	**r**	**r**	**3**	**6**	**5**	**11**	**r**	**5**	**3**	**-**	**-**	**r**	**6**	**r**	**r**
(Tyrrell-Ford Cosworth)	4	15	9	7	12	11	6	10	16	-	-	16	16	13	11
Alan JONES	**9**	**r**	**r**	**3**	**r**	**r**	**r**	**4**	**r**	**1**	**1**	**1**	**9**	**1f**	**r**
(Williams-Ford Cosworth)	15	13	19	10	13	4	9	7	1	2	2	2	4	1	1
Jacques LAFFITE	**1f**	**1f**	**r**	**r**	**r**	**2**	**r**	**8**	**r**	**3**	**3**	**3**	**r**	**r**	**r**
(Ligier-Ford Cosworth)	1	1	6	5	1	1	5	8	10	3	8	7	7	5	4
Jan LAMMERS	**r**	**14**	**r**	**r**	**12**	**10**	**-**	**18**	**11**	**10**	**r**	**r**	**-**	**9**	**-**
(Shadow-Ford Cosworth)	21	21	21	14	24	21	nq	21	21	20	23	23	nq	21	nq
Niki LAUDA	**r**	**r**	**6**	**r**	**r**	**r**	**r**	**r**	**r**	**r**	**r**	**r**	**4**	**-**	**-**
(Brabham-Alfa Romeo)	23	12	4	11	6	13	4	6	6	7	4	9	9	-	-
(Brabham-Ford Cosworth)	-	-	-	-	-	-	-	-	-	-	-	-	-	ew	-
Geoff LEES	**-**	**-**	**-**	**-**	**-**	**-**	**-**	**-**	**-**	**7**	**-**	**-**	**-**	**-**	**-**
(Tyrrell-Ford Cosworth)	-	-	-	-	-	-	-	-	-	16	-	-	-	-	-
Jochen MASS	**8**	**7**	**12**	**9**	**8**	**r**	**6**	**15**	**r**	**6**	**r**	**6**	**r**	**-**	**-**
(Arrows-Ford Cosworth)	14	19	20	13	17	22	8	22	20	18	20	18	21	nq	nq
Arturo MERZARIO	**r**	**-**	**-**	**r**	**-**	**-**	**-**	**-**	**-**	**-**	**-**	**-**	**-**	**-**	**-**
(Merzario-Ford Cosworth)	22	nq	nq	22	nq	nq	-	nq	nq	nq	nq	nq	nq	nq	nq
Riccardo PATRESE	**-**	**9**	**11**	**r**	**10**	**5**	**r**	**14**	**r**	**r**	**r**	**r**	**13**	**r**	**r**
(Arrows-Ford Cosworth)	13ns	16	16	9	16	16	15	19	19	19	13	19	17	14	19
Nelson PIQUET	**r**	**r**	**7**	**8**	**r**	**r**	**7r**	**r**	**r**	**12r**	**r**	**4**	**r**	**r**	**8rf**
(Brabham-Alfa Romeo)	20	22	12	12	7	3	18	4	3	4	7	11	8	-	-
(Brabham-Ford Cosworth)	-	-	-	-	-	-	-	-	-	-	-	-	-	4	2
Didier PIRONI	**r**	**4**	**r**	**dq**	**6**	**3**	**r**	**r**	**10**	**9**	**7**	**r**	**10**	**5**	**3**
(Tyrrell-Ford Cosworth)	8	8	7	17	10	12	7	11	15	8	10	10	12	6	10
Hector REBAQUE	**r**	**-**	**14r**	**r**	**r**	**r**	**-**	**12**	**9**	**r**	**-**	**7**	**-**	**r**	**-**
(Lotus-Ford Cosworth)	19	nq	23	23	23	15	-	23	24	24	nq	24	-	-	-
(Rebaque-Ford Cosworth)	-	-	-	-	-	-	-	-	-	-	-	-	nq	22	nq
Clay REGAZZONI	**10**	**15**	**9**	**r**	**r**	**r**	**2**	**6**	**1f**	**2**	**5**	**r**	**3f**	**3**	**r**
(Williams-Ford Cosworth)	17	17	22	15	14	8	16	9	4	6	6	3	6	3	5
Carlos REUTEMANN	**2**	**3**	**5**	**r**	**2**	**4**	**3**	**13r**	**8**	**r**	**r**	**r**	**7**	**r**	**r**
(Lotus-Ford Cosworth)	3	3	11	2	8	10	11	13	8	13	17	13	13	11	6
Alex RIBEIRO	**-**	**-**	**-**	**-**	**-**	**-**	**-**	**-**	**-**	**-**	**-**	**-**	**-**	**-**	**-**
(Copersucar-Ford Cosworth)	-	-	-	-	-	-	-	-	-	-	-	-	-	nq	nq
Keke ROSBERG	**-**	**-**	**-**	**-**	**-**	**-**	**-**	**9**	**r**	**r**	**r**	**r**	**r**	**-**	**r**
(Wolf-Ford Cosworth)	-	-	-	-	-	-	-	16	14	17	12	8	23	nq	12
Jody SCHECKTER	**r**	**6**	**2**	**2**	**4**	**1**	**1**	**7**	**5**	**4**	**4**	**2**	**1**	**4**	**r**
(Ferrari)	5	6	2	3	5	7	1	5	11	5	9	5	3	9	16
Hans-Joachim STUCK	**-**	**r**	**r**	**dq**	**14**	**8**	**r**	**-**	**-**	**r**	**r**	**r**	**11**	**r**	**5**
(ATS-Ford Cosworth)	ns	24	24	21	21	20	12	ns	nq	23	18	15	15	12	14
Marc SURER	**-**	**-**	**-**	**-**	**-**	**-**	**-**	**-**	**-**	**-**	**-**	**-**	**-**	**-**	**r**
(Ensign-Ford Cosworth)	-	-	-	-	-	-	-	-	-	-	-	-	nq	nq	21
Patrick TAMBAY	**r**	**r**	**10**	**r**	**13**	**-**	**-**	**10**	**7r**	**r**	**10**	**r**	**r**	**r**	**r**
(McLaren-Ford Cosworth)	9	18	17	19	20	nq	nq	20	18	15	14	14	14	20	22
Gilles VILLENEUVE	**12r**	**5**	**1f**	**1f**	**7f**	**7rf**	**r**	**2**	**14r**	**8f**	**2**	**rf**	**2**	**2**	**1**
(Ferrari)	10	5	3	1	3	6	2	3	13	9	5	6	5	2	3
John WATSON	**3**	**8**	**r**	**r**	**r**	**6**	**4**	**11**	**4**	**5**	**9**	**r**	**r**	**6**	**6**
(McLaren-Ford Cosworth)	6	14	14	18	18	19	14	15	7	12	16	12	19	17	13
Ricardo ZUNINO	**-**	**-**	**-**	**-**	**-**	**-**	**-**	**-**	**-**	**-**	**-**	**-**	**-**	**7**	**r**
(Brabham-Ford Cosworth)	-	-	-	-	-	-	-	-	-	-	-	-	-	19	9

1980 RACE RESULTS & GRID POSITIONS

Driver	RA	BR	ZA	USAW	B	MC	F	GB	D	A	NL	I	CDN	USAE
Mario ANDRETTI	**r**	**r**	**12**	**r**	**r**	**7**	**r**	**r**	**7**	**r**	**8r**	**r**	**r**	**6**
(Lotus-Ford Cosworth)	6	11	15	15	17	19	12	9	9	17	10	10	18	11
René ARNOUX	**r**	**1f**	**1f**	**9**	**4**	**r**	**5**	**nc**	**r**	**9f**	**2f**	**10**	**r**	**7**
(Renault)	19	6	2	2	6	20	2	16	3	1	1	1	23	6
Vittorio BRAMBILLA	**-**	**-**	**-**	**-**	**-**	**-**	**-**	**-**	**-**	**-**	**r**	**r**	**-**	**-**
(Alfa Romeo)	-	-	-	-	-	-	-	-	-	-	22	19	-	-
Eddie CHEEVER	**-**	**-**	**r**	**r**	**-**	**-**	**r**	**r**	**r**	**r**	**r**	**12**	**r**	**r**
(Osella-Ford Cosworth)	nq	nq	22	19	nq	nq	21	20	18	19	19	17	14	16
Kevin COGAN	**-**	**-**	**-**	**-**	**-**	**-**	**-**	**-**	**-**	**-**	**-**	**-**	**-**	**-**
(Williams-Ford Cosworth)	-	-	-	-	-	-	-	-	-	-	-	-	nq	-
Derek DALY	**4**	**14**	**r**	**8**	**9**	**r**	**11**	**4**	**10**	**r**	**r**	**r**	**r**	**r**
(Tyrrell-Ford Cosworth)	22	24	16	14	11	12	20	10	22	10	23	22	20	21
Elio de ANGELIS	**r**	**2**	**r**	**r**	**10r**	**9r**	**r**	**r**	**16r**	**6**	**r**	**4**	**10**	**4**
(Lotus-Ford Cosworth)	5	7	14	20	8	14	14	14	11	9	11	18	17	4
Andrea de CESARIS	**-**	**-**	**-**	**-**	**-**	**-**	**-**	**-**	**-**	**-**	**-**	**-**	**r**	**r**
(Alfa Romeo)	-	-	-	-	-	-	-	-	-	-	-	-	8	10
Patrick DEPAILLER +	**r**	**r**	**nc**	**r**	**r**	**r**	**r**	**r**	**-**	**-**	**-**	**-**	**-**	**-**
(Alfa Romeo)	23	21	7	3	10	7	10	8	-	-	-	-	-	-
Harald ERTL	**-**	**-**	**-**	**-**	**-**	**-**	**-**	**-**	**-**	**-**	**-**	**-**	**-**	**-**
(ATS-Ford Cosworth)	-	-	-	-	-	-	-	-	nq	-	-	-	-	-
Emerson FITTIPALDI	**nc**	**15**	**8**	**3**	**r**	**6**	**13r**	**12**	**r**	**11**	**r**	**r**	**r**	**r**
(Fittipaldi-Ford Cosworth)	24	19	18	24	24	18	24	22	12	23	21	15	16	19
Bruno GIACOMELLI	**5**	**13**	**r**	**r**	**r**	**r**	**r**	**r**	**5**	**r**	**r**	**r**	**r**	**r**
(Alfa Romeo)	20	17	12	6	18	8	9	6	19	8	8	4	4	1
Jean-Pierre JABOUILLE	**r**	**r**	**r**	**10**	**r**	**r**	**r**	**r**	**r**	**1**	**r**	**r**	**r**	**-**
(Renault)	9	1	1	11	5	16	6	13	2	2	2	2	13	-
Jean-Pierre JARIER	**r**	**12**	**7**	**r**	**5**	**r**	**14**	**5**	**15**	**r**	**5**	**13r**	**7**	**nc**
(Tyrrell-Ford Cosworth)	18	22	13	12	9	9	16	11	23	13	17	12	15	22
Stefan JOHANSSON	**-**	**-**	**-**	**-**	**-**	**-**	**-**	**-**	**-**	**-**	**-**	**-**	**-**	**-**
(Shadow-Ford Cosworth)	nq	nq	-	-	-	-	-	-	-	-	-	-	-	-
Alan JONES	**1f**	**3**	**r**	**r**	**2**	**r**	**1f**	**1**	**3f**	**2**	**11**	**2f**	**1**	**1f**
(Williams-Ford Cosworth)	1	10	8	5	1	3	4	3	1	3	4	6	2	5
Rupert KEEGAN	**-**	**-**	**-**	**-**	**-**	**-**	**-**	**11**	**-**	**15**	**-**	**11**	**-**	**9**
(Williams-Ford Cosworth)	-	-	-	-	-	-	-	18	nq	20	nq	21	nq	15
David KENNEDY	**-**	**-**	**-**	**-**	**-**	**-**	**-**	**-**	**-**	**-**	**-**	**-**	**-**	**-**
(Shadow-Ford Cosworth)	nq	nq	nq	nq	nq	nq	nq	-	-	-	-	-	-	-
Jacques LAFFITE	**r**	**r**	**2**	**r**	**11f**	**2**	**3**	**r**	**1**	**4**	**3**	**9**	**8r**	**5**
(Ligier-Ford Cosworth)	2	5	4	13	3	5	1	2	5	5	6	20	9	12
Jan LAMMERS	**-**	**-**	**-**	**r**	**12r**	**nc**	**-**	**-**	**14**	**-**	**-**	**-**	**12**	**r**
(ATS-Ford Cosworth)	nq	nq	nq	4	15	13	-	-	-	-	-	-	-	-
(Ensign-Ford Cosworth)	-	-	-	-	-	-	nq	nq	24	nq	nq	nq	19	25
Geoff LEES	**-**	**-**	**13r**	**-**	**-**	**-**	**-**	**-**	**-**	**-**	**r**	**-**	**-**	**-**
(Shadow-Ford Cosworth)	-	-	24	nq	nq	nq	nq	-	-	-	-	-	-	-
(Ensign-Ford Cosworth)	-	-	-	-	-	-	-	-	-	-	24	nq	-	-
(Williams-Ford Cosworth)	-	-	-	-	-	-	-	-	-	-	-	-	-	nq
Nigel MANSELL	**-**	**-**	**-**	**-**	**-**	**-**	**-**	**-**	**-**	**r**	**r**	**-**	**-**	**-**
(Lotus-Ford Cosworth)	-	-	-	-	-	-	-	-	-	24	16	nq	-	-
Jochen MASS	**r**	**10**	**6**	**7**	**r**	**4**	**10**	**13**	**8**	**-**	**-**	**-**	**11**	**r**
(Arrows-Ford Cosworth)	14	16	19	17	13	15	15	24	17	nq	ew	-	21	24
Tiff NEEDELL	**-**	**-**	**-**	**-**	**r**	**-**	**-**	**-**	**-**	**-**	**-**	**-**	**-**	**-**
(Ensign-Ford Cosworth)	-	-	-	-	23	nq	-	-	-	-	-	-	-	-
Riccardo PATRESE	**r**	**6**	**r**	**2**	**r**	**8**	**9**	**9**	**9**	**14**	**r**	**r**	**r**	**r**
(Arrows-Ford Cosworth)	7	14	11	8	16	11	18	21	10	18	14	7	11	20
Nelson PIQUET	**2**	**r**	**4**	**1f**	**r**	**3**	**4**	**2**	**4**	**5**	**1**	**1**	**r**	**r**
(Brabham-Ford Cosworth)	4	9	3	1	7	4	8	5	6	7	5	5	1	2
Didier PIRONI	**r**	**4**	**3**	**6**	**1**	**r**	**2**	**rf**	**r**	**r**	**r**	**6**	**3f**	**3**
(Ligier-Ford Cosworth)	3	2	5	9	2	1	3	1	7	6	15	13	3	7

	RA	BR	ZA	USAW	B	MC	F	GB	D	A	NL	I	CDN	USAE
Alain PROST	6	5	-	-	r	r	r	6	11	7	6	7	r	-
(McLaren-Ford Cosworth)	12	13	ns	-	19	10	7	7	14	12	18	24	12	13ns
Hector REBAQUE	-	-	-	-	-	-	-	7	r	10	r	r	6	r
(Brabham-Ford Cosworth)	-	-	-	-	-	-	-	17	15	14	13	9	10	8
Clay REGAZZONI	nc	r	9	r	-	-	-	-	-	-	-	-	-	-
(Ensign-Ford Cosworth)	15	12	20	23	-	-	-	-	-	-	-	-	-	-
Carlos REUTEMANN	r	r	5	r	3	1f	6	3	2	3	4	3	2	2
(Williams-Ford Cosworth)	10	4	6	7	4	2	5	4	4	4	3	3	5	3
Keke ROSBERG	3	9	r	r	7	-	r	-	r	16	-	5	9	10
(Fittipaldi-Ford Cosworth)	13	15	23	22	21	nq	23	nq	8	11	nq	11	6	14
Jody SCHECKTER	r	r	r	5	8	r	12	10	13	13	9	8	-	11
(Ferrari)	11	8	9	16	14	17	19	23	21	22	12	16	nq	23
Stephen SOUTH	-	-	-	-	-	-	-	-	-	-	-	-	-	-
(McLaren-Ford Cosworth)	-	-	-	nq	-	-	-	-	-	-	-	-	-	-
Marc SURER	r	7	-	-	-	-	r	r	12	12	10	r	-	8
(ATS-Ford Cosworth)	21	20	nq	-	-	-	11	15	13	16	20	23	nq	17
Mike THACKWELL	-	-	-	-	-	-	-	-	-	-	-	-	r	-
(Arrows-Ford Cosworth)	-	-	-	-	-	-	-	-	-	-	nq	-	-	-
(Tyrrell-Ford Cosworth)	-	-	-	-	-	-	-	-	-	-	-	-	24	nq
Gilles VILLENEUVE	r	16r	r	r	6	5	8	r	6	8	7	r	5	r
(Ferrari)	8	3	10	10	12	6	17	19	16	15	7	8	22	18
John WATSON	r	11	11	4	nc	-	7	8	r	r	r	r	4	nc
(McLaren-Ford Cosworth)	17	23	21	21	20	nq	13	12	20	21	9	14	7	9
Desiré WILSON	-	-	-	-	-	-	-	-	-	-	-	-	-	-
(Williams-Ford Cosworth)	-	-	-	-	-	-	-	nq	-	-	-	-	-	-
Manfred WINKELHOCK	-	-	-	-	-	-	-	-	-	-	-	-	-	-
(Arrows-Ford Cosworth)	-	-	-	-	-	-	-	-	-	-	-	nq	-	-
Ricardo ZUNINO	7	8	10	r	r	-	r	-	-	-	-	-	-	-
(Brabham-Ford Cosworth)	16	18	17	18	22	nq	22	-	-	-	-	-	-	-

1981 RACE RESULTS & GRID POSITIONS

	USAW	BR	RA	RSM	B	MC	E	F	GB	D	A	NL	I	CDN	LV
Michele ALBORETO	-	-	-	r	12	r	-	16	r	-	r	9r	r	11	13r
(Tyrrell-Ford Cosworth)	-	-	-	17	19	20	nq	23	19	nq	22	25	22	22	17
Mario ANDRETTI	4	r	8	r	10	r	8	8	r	9	r	r	r	7	r
(Alfa Romeo)	6	9	17	12	18	12	8	10	11	12	13	7	13	16	10
René ARNOUX	8	r	5	8	-	r	9	4	9rf	13	2	r	r	r	r
(Renault)	20	8	5	3	nq	13	17	1	1	2	1	2	1	8	13
Slim BORGUDD	-	-	-	13	-	-	-	-	6	r	r	10	r	r	-
(ATS-Ford Cosworth)	-	-	-	24	nq	npq	nq	nq	21	20	21	23	21	21	nq
Eddie CHEEVER	5	nc	r	r	6	5	nc	13	4	5	-	r	r	12r	r
(Tyrrell-Ford Cosworth)	8	14	13	19	8	15	20	19	23	18	nq	22	17	14	19
Kevin COGAN	-	-	-	-	-	-	-	-	-	-	-	-	-	-	-
(Tyrrell-Ford Cosworth)	nq	-	-	-	-	-	-	-	-	-	-	-	-	-	-
Derek DALY	-	-	-	-	-	-	16	r	7	r	11	r	r	8	-
(March-Ford Cosworth)	nq	nq	nq	nq	nq	npq	22	20	17	21	19	19	19	20	nq
Elio de ANGELIS	r	5	6	-	5	r	5	6	r	7	7	5	4	6	r
(Lotus-Ford Cosworth)	13	10	10	-	14	6	10	8	22	14	9	9	11	7	15
Andrea de CESARIS	r	r	11	6	r	r	r	11	r	r	8	-	7r	r	12
(McLaren-Ford Cosworth)	22	20	18	14	23	11	14	5	6	10	18	13ns	16	13	14
Emilio de VILLOTA	-	-	-	-	-	-	-	-	-	-	-	-	-	-	-
(Williams-Ford Cosworth)	-	-	-	-	-	-	exc	-	-	-	-	-	-	-	-
Giorgio FRANCIA	-	-	-	-	-	-	-	-	-	-	-	-	-	-	-
(Osella-Ford Cosworth)	-	-	-	-	-	-	nq	-	-	-	-	-	-	-	-
Beppe GABBIANI	r	-	-	r	r	-	-	-	-	-	-	-	-	-	-
(Osella-Ford Cosworth)	24	nq	nq	20	22	nq	nq	nq	nq	nq	nq	nq	nq	nq	nq
Piercarlo GHINZANI	-	-	-	-	13	-	-	-	-	-	-	-	-	-	-
(Osella-Ford Cosworth)	-	-	-	-	24	nq	-	-	-	-	-	-	-	-	-
Bruno GIACOMELLI	r	nc	10r	r	9	r	10	15	r	15	r	r	8	4	3
(Alfa Romeo)	9	6	22	11	17	18	6	12	12	19	16	14	10	15	8
Miguel-Angel GUERRA	-	-	-	r	-	-	-	-	-	-	-	-	-	-	-
(Osella-Ford Cosworth)	nq	nq	nq	22	-	-	-	-	-	-	-	-	-	-	-
Brian HENTON	-	-	-	-	-	-	-	-	-	-	-	-	10	-	-
(Toleman-Hart)	-	-	-	nq	nq	npq	nq	nq	nq	nq	nq	nq	23	nq	nq
Jean-Pierre JABOUILLE	-	-	-	nc	r	-	r	-	-	-	-	-	-	-	-
(Talbot Ligier-Matra)	-	nq	nq	18	16	nq	19	-	-	-	-	-	-	-	-
Jean-Pierre JARIER	r	7	-	-	-	-	-	-	8	8	10	r	9	r	r
(Talbot Ligier-Matra)	10	23	-	-	-	-	-	-	-	-	-	-	-	-	-
(Osella-Ford Cosworth)	-	-	-	-	-	-	-	-	20	17	14	18	18	23	21
Alan JONES	1f	2	4	12	r	2f	7f	17	r	11f	4	3f	2	r	1
(Williams-Ford Cosworth)	2	3	3	8	6	7	2	9	7	4	6	4	5	3	2
Jacques LAFFITE	r	6	r	r	2	3	2	r	3	3	1f	r	r	1	6
(Talbot Ligier-Matra)	12	16	21	10	9	8	1	6	14	7	4	6	4	10	12
Jan LAMMERS	r	-	12	-	-	-	-	-	-	-	-	-	-	-	-
(ATS-Ford Cosworth)	21	nq	23	nq	-	-	-	-	-	-	-	-	-	-	-
Nigel MANSELL	r	11	r	-	3	r	6	7	-	r	r	r	r	r	4
(Lotus-Ford Cosworth)	7	13	15	-	10	3	11	13	nq	15	11	17	12	5	9
Riccardo PATRESE	r	3	7	2	r	r	r	14	10r	r	r	r	r	r	11
(Arrows-Ford Cosworth)	1	4	9	9	4	5	12	18	10	13	10	10	20	18	11
Nelson PIQUET	3	12	1f	1	r	r	r	3	r	1	3	2	6r	5	5
(Brabham-Ford Cosworth)	4	1	1	5	2	1	9	4	3	6	7	3	6	1	4
Didier PIRONI	r	r	r	5	8	4	15	5	r	r	9	r	5	r	9f
(Ferrari)	11	17	12	6	3	17	13	14	4	5	8	12	8	12	18
Alain PROST	r	r	3	r	r	r	r	1f	r	2	r	1	1	r	2
(Renault)	14	5	2	4	12	9	5	3	2	1	2	1	3	4	5
Hector REBAQUE	r	r	r	4	r	-	r	9	5	4	r	4	r	r	r
(Brabham-Ford Cosworth)	15	11	6	13	21	nq	18	15	13	16	15	15	14	6	16
Carlos REUTEMANN	2	1	2	3	1f	r	4	10	2	r	5	r	3f	10	8
(Williams-Ford Cosworth)	3	2	4	2	1	4	3	7	9	3	5	5	2	2	1
Keke ROSBERG	r	9	r	r	r	-	12	r	r	-	-	-	-	-	10
(Fittipaldi-Ford Cosworth)	16	12	8	15	11	nq	15	17	16	nq	-	nq	nq	nq	20
Eliseo SALAZAR	-	-	-	r	-	-	14	r	-	nc	r	6	r	r	nc
(March-Ford Cosworth)	nq	nq	nq	23	nq	npq	-	-	-	-	-	-	-	-	-
(Ensign-Ford Cosworth)	-	-	-	-	-	-	24	22	nq	23	20	24	24	24	24
Chico SERRA	7	r	r	-	r	-	11	-	-	-	-	-	-	-	-
(Fittipaldi-Ford Cosworth)	18	22	20	nq	20	nq	21	24ns	nq	nq	-	nq	nq	nq	nq
Siegfried STOHR	-	r	9	-	r	r	r	-	r	12	r	7	-	-	-
(Arrows-Ford Cosworth)	nq	21	19	nq	13	14	23	nq	18	24	24	21	nq	-	-
Marc SURER	r	4f	r	9	11	6	-	12	11r	14r	r	8	-	9	r
(Ensign-Ford Cosworth)	19	18	16	21	15	19	-	-	-	-	-	-	-	-	-
(Theodore-Ford Cosworth)	-	-	-	-	-	-	-	21	24	22	23	20	nq	19	23
Patrick TAMBAY	6	10	r	11	-	7	13	r	r	r	r	r	r	r	r
(Theodore-Ford Cosworth)	17	19	14	16	nq	16	16	-	-	-	-	-	-	-	-
(Talbot Ligier-Matra)	-	-	-	-	-	-	-	16	15	11	17	11	15	17	7
Gilles VILLENEUVE	r	r	r	7f	4	1	1	r	r	10	r	r	r	3	dq
(Ferrari)	5	7	7	1	7	2	7	11	8	8	3	16	9	11	3
Jacques VILLENEUVE	-	-	-	-	-	-	-	-	-	-	-	-	-	-	-
(Arrows-Ford Cosworth)	-	-	-	-	-	-	-	-	-	-	-	-	-	nq	nq
Derek WARWICK	-	-	-	-	-	-	-	-	-	-	-	-	-	-	r
(Toleman-Hart)	-	-	-	nq	nq	npq	nq	nq	nq	nq	nq	nq	nq	nq	22

	USAW	BR	RA	RSM	B	MC	E	F	GB	D	A	NL	I	CDN	LV
John WATSON	r	8	r	10	7	r	3	2	1	6	6	r	r	2f	7
(McLaren-Ford Cosworth)	23	15	11	7	5	10	4	2	5	9	12	8	7	9	6
Ricardo ZUNINO	-	13	13	-	-	-	-	-	-	-	-	-	-	-	-
(Tyrrell-Ford Cosworth)	-	24	24	-	-	-	-	-	-	-	-	-	-	-	-

1982 RACE RESULTS & GRID POSITIONS

	ZA	BR	USAW	RSM	B	MC	DET	CDN	NL	GB	F	D	A	CH	I	LV
Michele ALBORETO	7	4	4	3	r	10r	r	r	7	nc	6	4	r	7	5	1f
(Tyrrell-Ford Cosworth)	10	13	12	5	5	9	16	15	14	9	15	7	8	12	11	3
Mario ANDRETTI	-	-	r	-	-	-	-	-	-	-	-	-	-	-	3	r
(Williams-Ford Cosworth)	-	-	14	-	-	-	-	-	-	-	-	-	-	-	-	-
(Ferrari)	-	-	-	-	-	-	-	-	-	-	-	-	-	-	1	7
René ARNOUX	3	r	r	r	r	r	10	r	r	r	1	2	r	16r	1f	r
(Renault)	1	4	3	1	2	1	15	2	1	6	1	3	5	2	6	2
Mauro BALDI	-	10	-	-	r	-	r	8	6	9	r	r	6	-	12	11
(Arrows-Ford Cosworth)	nq	19	nq	-	26	nq	24	17	16	26	25	23	23	nq	24	23
Raul BOESEL	15	r	9	-	8	-	r	r	r	-	-	r	-	r	-	13
(March-Ford Cosworth)	21	17	23	-	24	npq	21	21	22	nq	nq	24	nq	24	nq	24
Slim BORGUDD	16	7	10	-	-	-	-	-	-	-	-	-	-	-	-	-
(Tyrrell-Ford Cosworth)	23	21	24	-	-	-	-	-	-	-	-	-	-	-	-	-
Tommy BYRNE	-	-	-	-	-	-	-	-	-	-	-	-	r	-	-	r
(Theodore-Ford Cosworth)	-	-	-	-	-	-	-	-	-	-	-	nq	26	nq	nq	26
Eddie CHEEVER	r	r	r	-	3	r	2	10r	-	r	16	r	r	nc	6	3
(Talbot Ligier-Matra)	17	26	13	-	14	16	9	12	nq	24	19	12	22	16	14	4
Derek DALY	14	r	r	-	r	6r	5	7r	5	5	7	r	r	9	r	6
(Theodore-Ford Cosworth)	24	20	22	-	-	-	-	-	-	-	-	-	-	-	-	-
(Williams-Ford Cosworth)	-	-	-	-	13	8	12	13	12	10	11	19	9	7	13	14
Elio de ANGELIS	8	r	5	-	4	5	r	4	r	4	r	r	1	6	r	r
(Lotus-Ford Cosworth)	15	11	16	-	11	15	8	10	15	7	13	13	7	15	17	20
Andrea de CESARIS	13	r	r	r	r	3r	r	6r	r	r	r	r	r	10	10	9
(Alfa Romeo)	16	10	1	7	6	7	2	9	9	11	7	8	11	5	9	18
Emilio de VILLOTA	-	-	-	-	-	-	-	-	-	-	-	-	-	-	-	-
(March-Ford Cosworth)	-	-	-	-	npq	npq	nq	nq	npq	-	-	-	-	-	-	-
Teo FABI	-	-	-	nc	r	-	-	-	-	r	r	-	r	r	r	-
(Toleman-Hart)	nq	nq	nq	10	21	npq	-	-	nq	15	21	nq	17	23	22	nq
Bruno GIACOMELLI	11	r	r	r	r	r	r	r	11	7	9	5	r	12	r	10
(Alfa Romeo)	19	16	5	6	15	3	6	5	8	14	8	11	13	9	8	16
Roberto GUERRERO	-	-	r	-	-	-	r	r	-	r	-	8	r	r	nc	-
(Ensign-Ford Cosworth)	-	nq	19	-	nq	nq	11	20	nq	19	nq	21	16	19	18	15ns
Brian HENTON	-	-	r	r	r	8	9	nc	r	8f	10	7	r	11	r	8
(Arrows-Ford Cosworth)	nq	nq	20	-	-	-	-	-	-	-	-	-	-	-	-	-
(Tyrrell-Ford Cosworth)	-	-	-	11	20	17	20	26	20	17	23	17	19	18	20	19
Jean-Pierre JARIER	r	9	r	4	r	-	r	r	14	r	r	r	-	r	r	-
(Osella-Ford Cosworth)	26	23	10	9	16	nq	22	18	23	18	17	20	nq	17	15	ns
Rupert KEEGAN	-	-	-	-	-	-	-	-	-	-	-	-	r	r	-	12
(March-Ford Cosworth)	-	-	-	-	-	-	-	-	-	-	-	nq	24	22	nq	25
Jacques LAFFITE	r	r	r	-	9	r	6	r	r	r	14	r	3	r	r	r
(Talbot Ligier-Matra)	11	24	15	-	17	18	13	19	21	20	16	15	14	13	21	11
Jan LAMMERS	-	-	-	-	-	-	-	-	r	-	-	-	-	-	-	-
(Theodore-Ford Cosworth)	-	-	-	-	nq	nq	nq	-	26	nq	nq	-	-	-	-	-
Niki LAUDA	4	r	1f	-	dq	r	r	r	4	1	8	-	5	3	r	r
(McLaren-Ford Cosworth)	13	5	2	-	4	12	10	11	5	5	9	ns	10	4	10	13
Geoff LEES	-	-	-	-	-	-	-	r	-	-	12	-	-	-	-	-
(Theodore-Ford Cosworth)	-	-	-	-	-	-	-	25	-	-	-	-	-	-	-	-
(Lotus-Ford Cosworth)	-	-	-	-	-	-	-	-	-	-	24	-	-	-	-	-
Nigel MANSELL	r	3	7	-	r	4	r	r	-	r	-	9	r	8	7	r
(Lotus-Ford Cosworth)	18	14	17	-	7	11	7	14	-	23	-	18	12	26	23	21
Jochen MASS	12	8	8	-	r	-	7	11	r	10	r	-	-	-	-	-
(March-Ford Cosworth)	22	22	21	-	25	nq	18	22	24	25	26	-	-	-	-	-
Roberto MORENO	-	-	-	-	-	-	-	-	-	-	-	-	-	-	-	-
(Lotus-Ford Cosworth)	-	-	-	-	-	-	-	-	nq	-	-	-	-	-	-	-
Riccardo PALETTI +	-	-	-	r	-	-	-	r	-	-	-	-	-	-	-	-
(Osella-Ford Cosworth)	nq	npq	nq	13	npq	npq	23ns	23	-	-	-	-	-	-	-	-
Riccardo PATRESE	r	r	3	-	r	1f	r	2	15	r	rf	r	r	5	r	r
(Brabham-BMW)	4	-	-	-	9	-	-	-	10	2	4	6	2	3	4	5
(Brabham-Ford Cosworth)	-	9	18	-	-	2	14	8	-	-	-	-	-	-	-	-
Nelson PIQUET	r	dq	r	-	5	r	-	1	2	r	r	rf	rf	4	r	r
(Brabham-BMW)	2	-	-	-	8	13	nq	4	3	3	6	4	1	6	2	12
(Brabham-Ford Cosworth)	-	7	6	-	-	-	-	-	-	-	-	-	-	-	-	-
Didier PIRONI	18	6	r	1f	-	2r	3	9f	1	2	3	-	-	-	-	-
(Ferrari)	6	8	9	4	ns	5	4	1	4	4	3	1ns	-	-	-	-
Alain PROST	1f	1f	r	r	r	7r	ncf	r	r	6	2	r	8r	2f	r	4
(Renault)	5	1	4	2	1	4	1	3	2	8	2	2	3	1	5	1
Carlos REUTEMANN	2	r	-	-	-	-	-	-	-	-	-	-	-	-	-	-
(Williams-Ford Cosworth)	8	6	-	-	-	-	-	-	-	-	-	-	-	-	-	-
Keke ROSBERG	5	dq	2	-	2	r	4	r	3	r	5	3	2	1	8	5
(Williams-Ford Cosworth)	7	3	8	-	3	6	3	7	7	1	10	9	6	8	7	6
Eliseo SALAZAR	9	r	r	5	r	r	r	r	13	-	r	r	-	14	9	-
(ATS-Ford Cosworth)	12	18	26	14	18	20	25	24	25	nq	22	22	nq	25	25	nq
Chico SERRA	17	r	-	-	6	-	11	-	r	r	-	11	7	-	11	-
(Fittipaldi-Ford Cosworth)	25	25	nq	-	23	npq	26	nq	19	21	nq	25	20	nq	26	nq
Marc SURER	-	-	-	-	7	9	8	5	10	r	13	6	r	15	r	7
(Arrows-Ford Cosworth)	-	-	-	-	22	19	19	16	17	22	20	26	21	14	19	17
Patrick TAMBAY	-	-	-	-	-	-	-	-	8	3	4	1	4	-	2	-
(Ferrari)	-	-	-	-	-	-	-	-	6	13	5	5	4	10ns	3	8ns
Gilles VILLENEUVE +	r	r	dq	2	-	-	-	-	-	-	-	-	-	-	-	-
(Ferrari)	3	2	7	3	ns	-	-	-	-	-	-	-	-	-	-	-
Derek WARWICK	r	-	-	r	r	-	-	-	rf	r	15	10	r	r	r	r
(Toleman-Hart)	14	nq	npq	8	19	nq	-	-	13	16	14	14	15	21	16	10
John WATSON	6	2	6	-	1f	r	1	3	9	r	r	r	r	13	4	2
(McLaren-Ford Cosworth)	9	12	11	-	10	10	17	6	11	12	12	10	18	11	12	9
Manfred WINKELHOCK	10	5	r	dq	r	r	r	-	12	-	11	r	r	r	-	nc
(ATS-Ford Cosworth)	20	15	25	12	12	14	5	nq	18	nq	18	16	25	20	nq	22

1983 RACE RESULTS & GRID POSITIONS

	BR	USAW	F	RSM	MC	B	DET	CDN	GB	D	A	NL	I	EUR	ZA
Kenny ACHESON	-	-	-	-	-	-	-	-	-	-	-	-	-	-	12
(RAM March-Ford Cosworth)	-	-	-	-	-	-	-	-	nq	nq	nq	nq	nq	nq	24
Michele ALBORETO	r	9	8	r	r	14	1	8	13	r	r	6	r	r	r
(Tyrrell-Ford Cosworth)	11	7	15	13	11	17	6	17	16	16	18	18	24	26	18
René ARNOUX	10	3	7	3	r	r	r	1	5	1f	2	1f	2	9	r
(Ferrari)	6	2	4	1	2	5	1	1	1	2	2	10	3	5	4
Mauro BALDI	r	r	r	10r	6	r	12	10	7	r	r	5	r	r	r
(Alfa Romeo)	10	21	8	10	13	12	25	26	11	7	9	12	10	15	17

	BR	USAW	F	RSM	MC	B	DET	CDN	GB	D	A	NL	I	EUR	ZA
Raul BOESEL	**r**	**7**	**r**	**9**	**r**	**13**	**10**	**r**	**r**	**r**	**-**	**10**	**-**	**15**	**nc**
(Ligier-Ford Cosworth)	17	26	25	25	18	26	23	24	22	25	nq	24	nq	23	23
Thierry BOUTSEN	**-**	**-**	**-**	**-**	**-**	**r**	**7**	**7**	**15**	**9**	**13**	**14r**	**r**	**11**	**9**
(Arrows-Ford Cosworth)	-	-	-	-	-	18	10	15	17	14	19	21	18	18	20
Johnny CECOTTO	**14**	**6**	**11**	**r**	**-**	**10**	**r**	**r**	**-**	**11**	**-**	**-**	**12**	**-**	**-**
(Theodore-Ford Cosworth)	19	17	17	23	npq	25	26	23	nq	22	nq	nq	26	-	-
Eddie CHEEVER	**r**	**13r**	**3**	**r**	**r**	**3**	**r**	**2**	**r**	**r**	**4**	**r**	**3**	**10**	**6**
(Renault)	8	15	2	6	3	8	7	6	7	6	8	11	7	7	14
Elio de ANGELIS	**dq**	**r**	**r**	**r**	**r**	**9**	**r**	**r**	**r**	**r**	**r**	**r**	**5**	**r**	**r**
(Lotus-Ford Cosworth)	13	-	-	-	-	-	-	-	-	-	-	-	-	-	-
(Lotus-Renault)	-	5	5	9	19	13	4	11	4	11	12	3	8	1	11
Andrea de CESARIS	**-**	**r**	**12**	**r**	**r**	**rf**	**r**	**r**	**8**	**2**	**r**	**r**	**r**	**4**	**2**
(Alfa Romeo)	exc	19	7	8	7	3	8	8	9	3	11	8	6	14	9
Corrado FABI	**r**	**-**	**r**	**r**	**-**	**r**	**-**	**r**	**-**	**-**	**10**	**11r**	**r**	**-**	**r**
(Osella-Ford Cosworth)	24	nq	23	26	nq	24	nq	25	-	-	-	-	-	-	-
(Osella-Alfa Romeo)	-	-	-	-	-	-	-	-	nq	nq	26	25	25	nq	25
Piercarlo GHINZANI	**-**	**-**	**-**	**-**	**-**	**-**	**r**	**-**	**r**	**r**	**11**	**-**	**r**	**nc**	**r**
(Osella-Ford Cosworth)	nq	nq	nq	-	-	-	-	-	-	-	-	-	-	-	-
(Osella-Alfa Romeo)	-	-	-	nq	nq	nq	24	nq	26	26	25	nq	23	24	26
Bruno GIACOMELLI	**r**	**r**	**13r**	**r**	**-**	**8**	**9**	**r**	**r**	**r**	**r**	**13**	**7**	**6**	**r**
(Toleman-Hart)	15	14	13	17	nq	16	17	10	12	10	7	13	14	12	16
Roberto GUERRERO	**nc**	**r**	**r**	**r**	**-**	**r**	**nc**	**r**	**16**	**r**	**r**	**12**	**13**	**12**	**-**
(Theodore-Ford Cosworth)	14	18	22	21	npq	14	11	21	21	24	21	20	21	21	-
Jean-Pierre JARIER	**r**	**r**	**9**	**r**	**r**	**r**	**r**	**r**	**10**	**8**	**7**	**r**	**9**	**r**	**10**
(Ligier-Ford Cosworth)	12	10	20	19	9	21	19	16	25	19	20	22	19	22	21
Stefan JOHANSSON	**-**	**-**	**-**	**-**	**-**	**-**	**-**	**-**	**r**	**r**	**12**	**7**	**r**	**14**	**-**
(Spirit-Honda)	-	-	-	-	-	-	-	-	14	13	16	16	17	19	-
Alan JONES	**-**	**r**	**-**	**-**	**-**	**-**	**-**	**-**	**-**	**-**	**-**	**-**	**-**	**-**	**-**
(Arrows-Ford Cosworth)	-	12	-	-	-	-	-	-	-	-	-	-	-	-	-
Jacques LAFFITE	**4**	**4**	**6**	**7**	**r**	**6**	**5**	**r**	**12**	**6**	**r**	**r**	**-**	**-**	**r**
(Williams-Ford Cosworth)	18	4	19	16	8	11	20	13	20	15	24	17	nq	nq	-
(Williams-Honda)	-	-	-	-	-	-	-	-	-	-	-	-	-	-	10
Niki LAUDA	**3**	**2f**	**r**	**r**	**-**	**r**	**r**	**r**	**6**	**dq**	**6**	**r**	**r**	**r**	**11r**
(McLaren-Ford Cosworth)	9	23	12	18	nq	15	18	19	15	18	14	-	-	-	-
(McLaren-TAG Porsche)	-	-	-	-	-	-	-	-	-	-	-	19	13	13	12
Nigel MANSELL	**12**	**12**	**r**	**12r**	**r**	**r**	**6**	**r**	**4**	**r**	**5**	**r**	**8**	**3f**	**nc**
(Lotus-Ford Cosworth)	22	13	18	15	14	19	14	18	-	-	-	-	-	-	-
(Lotus-Renault)	-	-	-	-	-	-	-	-	18	17	3	5	11	3	7
Jonathan PALMER	**-**	**-**	**-**	**-**	**-**	**-**	**-**	**-**	**-**	**-**	**-**	**-**	**-**	**13**	**-**
(Williams-Ford Cosworth)	-	-	-	-	-	-	-	-	-	-	-	-	-	25	-
Riccardo PATRESE	**r**	**10r**	**r**	**13rf**	**r**	**r**	**r**	**r**	**r**	**3**	**r**	**9**	**r**	**7**	**1**
(Brabham-BMW)	7	11	3	5	17	6	15	5	5	8	6	6	1	2	3
Nelson PIQUET	**1f**	**r**	**2**	**r**	**2f**	**4**	**4**	**r**	**2**	**13r**	**3**	**r**	**1f**	**1**	**3f**
(Brabham-BMW)	4	20	6	2	6	4	2	3	6	4	4	1	4	4	2
Alain PROST	**7**	**11**	**1f**	**2**	**3**	**1**	**8**	**5**	**1f**	**4**	**1f**	**r**	**r**	**2**	**r**
(Renault)	2	8	1	4	1	1	13	2	3	5	5	4	5	8	5
Keke ROSBERG	**dq**	**r**	**5**	**4**	**1**	**5**	**2**	**4**	**11**	**10**	**8**	**r**	**11**	**r**	**5**
(Williams-Ford Cosworth)	1	3	16	11	5	9	12	9	13	12	15	23	16	16	-
(Williams-Honda)	-	-	-	-	-	-	-	-	-	-	-	-	-	-	6
Eliseo SALAZAR	**15**	**r**	**-**	**-**	**-**	**-**	**-**	**-**	**-**	**-**	**-**	**-**	**-**	**-**	**-**
(RAM March-Ford Cosworth)	26	25	nq	nq	nq	nq	-	-	-	-	-	-	-	-	-
Jean-Louis SCHLESSER	**-**	**-**	**-**	**-**	**-**	**-**	**-**	**-**	**-**	**-**	**-**	**-**	**-**	**-**	**-**
(RAM March-Ford Cosworth)	-	-	nq	-	-	-	-	-	-	-	-	-	-	-	-
Chico SERRA	**9**	**-**	**r**	**8**	**7**	**-**	**-**	**-**	**-**	**-**	**-**	**-**	**-**	**-**	**-**
(Arrows-Ford Cosworth)	23	-	26	20	15	-	-	-	-	-	-	-	-	-	-
Danny SULLIVAN	**11**	**8**	**r**	**r**	**5**	**12**	**r**	**dq**	**14**	**12**	**r**	**r**	**r**	**r**	**7**
(Tyrrell-Ford Cosworth)	21	9	24	22	20	23	16	22	23	21	23	26	22	20	19
Marc SURER	**6**	**5**	**10**	**6**	**r**	**11**	**11**	**r**	**17**	**7**	**r**	**8**	**10**	**r**	**8**
(Arrows-Ford Cosworth)	20	16	21	12	12	10	5	14	19	20	22	14	20	17	22
Patrick TAMBAY	**5**	**r**	**4**	**1**	**4**	**2**	**r**	**3f**	**3**	**r**	**r**	**2**	**4**	**r**	**r**
(Ferrari)	3	1	11	3	4	2	3	4	2	1	1	2	2	6	1
Jacques VILLENEUVE	**-**	**-**	**-**	**-**	**-**	**-**	**-**	**-**	**-**	**-**	**-**	**-**	**-**	**-**	**-**
(RAM March-Ford Cosworth)	-	-	-	-	-	-	-	nq	-	-	-	-	-	-	-
Derek WARWICK	**8**	**r**	**r**	**r**	**r**	**7**	**r**	**r**	**r**	**r**	**r**	**4**	**6**	**5**	**4**
(Toleman-Hart)	5	6	9	14	10	22	9	12	10	9	10	7	12	11	13
John WATSON	**r**	**1**	**r**	**5**	**-**	**r**	**3f**	**6**	**9**	**5**	**9**	**3**	**r**	**r**	**dq**
(McLaren-Ford Cosworth)	16	22	14	24	nq	20	21	20	24	23	17	15	-	-	-
(McLaren-TAG Porsche)	-	-	-	-	-	-	-	-	-	-	-	-	15	10	15
Manfred WINKELHOCK	**16**	**r**	**r**	**11**	**r**	**r**	**r**	**9r**	**r**	**-**	**r**	**dq**	**r**	**8**	**r**
(ATS-BMW)	25	24	10	7	16	7	22	7	8	nq	13	9	9	9	8

1984 RACE RESULTS & GRID POSITIONS

	BR	ZA	B	RSM	F	MC	CDN	DET	DAL	GB	D	A	NL	I	EUR	P
Michele ALBORETO	**r**	**11r**	**1**	**r**	**r**	**6**	**r**	**r**	**r**	**5**	**r**	**3**	**r**	**2**	**2f=**	**4**
(Ferrari)	2	10	1	13	10	4	6	4	9	9	6	12	9	11	5	8
Philippe ALLIOT	**r**	**r**	**-**	**r**	**r**	**-**	**10**	**r**	**-**	**r**	**r**	**11**	**10**	**r**	**r**	**r**
(RAM-Hart)	25	22	nq	23	22	nq	26	20	ns	24	22	25	26	23	25	27
René ARNOUX	**r**	**r**	**3f**	**2**	**4**	**3**	**5**	**r**	**2**	**6**	**6**	**7**	**11rf**	**r**	**5**	**9**
(Ferrari)	10	15	2	6	11	3	5	15	4	13	10	15	15	14	6	17
Mauro BALDI	**r**	**8**	**r**	**8**	**r**	**-**	**-**	**-**	**-**	**-**	**-**	**-**	**-**	**-**	**8**	**15**
(Spirit-Hart)	23	20	25	24	24	nq	-	-	-	-	-	-	-	-	24	25
Stefan BELLOF	**dq**	**dq**	**dq**	**dq**	**dq**	**dq**	**dq**	**dq**	**dq**	**dq**	**-**	**-**	**dq**	**-**	**-**	**-**
(Tyrrell-Ford Cosworth)	22	24	21	21	20	20	22	16	17	26	-	nq	24	-	-	-
Gerhard BERGER	**-**	**-**	**-**	**-**	**-**	**-**	**-**	**-**	**-**	**-**	**-**	**12r**	**-**	**6**	**r**	**13**
(ATS-BMW)	-	-	-	-	-	-	-	-	-	-	-	20	-	20	18	23
Thierry BOUTSEN	**6**	**12**	**r**	**5**	**11**	**-**	**r**	**r**	**r**	**r**	**r**	**5**	**r**	**10**	**9r**	**r**
(Arrows-Ford Cosworth)	20	26	-	20	-	-	-	-	-	-	-	-	-	-	-	-
(Arrows-BMW)	-	-	17	-	14	nq	18	13	20	12	15	17	11	19	11	18
Martin BRUNDLE	**dq**	**dq**	**dq**	**dq**	**dq**	**-**	**dq**	**dq**	**-**	**-**	**-**	**-**	**-**	**-**	**-**	**-**
(Tyrrell-Ford Cosworth)	18	25	22	22	23	nq	21	11	nq	-	-	-	-	-	-	-
Johnny CECOTTO	**r**	**r**	**r**	**nc**	**r**	**r**	**9**	**r**	**r**	**-**	**-**	**-**	**-**	**-**	**-**	**-**
(Toleman-Hart)	17	19	16	19	18	18	20	17	15	nq	-	-	-	-	-	-
Eddie CHEEVER	**4**	**r**	**r**	**7r**	**r**	**-**	**11r**	**r**	**r**	**r**	**r**	**r**	**13r**	**9r**	**r**	**17**
(Alfa Romeo)	12	16	11	8	16	nq	11	8	14	18	18	16	17	10	13	14
Elio de ANGELIS	**3**	**7**	**5**	**3r**	**5**	**5**	**4**	**2**	**3**	**4**	**r**	**r**	**4**	**r**	**r**	**5**
(Lotus-Renault)	1	7	5	11	2	11	3	5	2	4	2	3	3	3	23	5
Andrea de CESARIS	**r**	**5**	**r**	**6r**	**10**	**r**	**r**	**r**	**r**	**10**	**7**	**r**	**r**	**r**	**7**	**12**
(Ligier-Renault)	14	14	13	12	26	7	10	12	16	19	11	18	14	16	17	20
Corrado FABI	**-**	**-**	**-**	**-**	**-**	**r**	**r**	**-**	**7**	**-**	**-**	**-**	**-**	**-**	**-**	**-**
(Brabham-BMW)	-	-	-	-	-	15	16	-	11	-	-	-	-	-	-	-
Teo FABI	**r**	**r**	**r**	**r**	**9**	**-**	**-**	**3**	**-**	**r**	**r**	**4**	**5**	**r**	**r**	**-**
(Brabham-BMW)	15	6	18	9	17	-	-	23	-	14	8	7	10	5	10	-
Jo GARTNER	**-**	**-**	**-**	**r**	**-**	**-**	**-**	**-**	**-**	**r**	**r**	**r**	**12**	**5**	**12r**	**16r**
(Osella-Alfa Romeo)	-	-	-	26	-	-	-	-	-	27	23	22	23	24	22	24
Piercarlo GHINZANI	**r**	**-**	**r**	**-**	**12**	**7**	**r**	**r**	**5**	**9**	**r**	**r**	**r**	**7r**	**r**	**r**
(Osella-Alfa Romeo)	21	ns	20	nq	25	19	19	26	18	21	21	23	21	22	20	22
François HESNAULT	**r**	**10**	**r**	**r**	**-**	**r**	**r**	**r**	**r**	**r**	**8**	**8**	**7**	**r**	**10**	**r**
(Ligier-Renault)	19	17	23	17	ns	17	13	18	19	20	17	21	20	18	19	21

	BR	ZA	B	RSM	F	MC	CDN	DET	DAL	GB	D	A	NL	I	EUR	P
Stefan JOHANSSON	**-**	**-**	**-**	**-**	**-**	**-**	**-**	**-**	**-**	**dq**	**dq**	**-**	**dq**	**4**	**r**	**11**
(Tyrrell-Ford Cosworth)	-	-	-	-	-	-	-	-	-	25	26	nq	25	-	-	-
(Toleman-Hart)	-	-	-	-	-	-	-	-	-	-	-	-	-	17	26	10
Jacques LAFFITE	**r**	**r**	**r**	**r**	**8**	**8**	**r**	**5**	**4**	**r**	**r**	**r**	**r**	**r**	**r**	**14**
(Williams-Honda)	13	11	15	15	12	16	17	19	24	16	12	11	8	13	14	15
Niki LAUDA	**r**	**1**	**r**	**r**	**1**	**r**	**2**	**r**	**9rf**	**1f**	**2**	**1f**	**2**	**1f**	**4**	**2f**
(McLaren-TAG Porsche)	6	8	14	5	9	8	8	10	5	3	7	4	6	4	15	11
Nigel MANSELL	**r**	**r**	**r**	**r**	**3**	**r**	**6**	**r**	**6r**	**r**	**4**	**r**	**3**	**r**	**r**	**r**
(Lotus-Renault)	5	3	10	18	6	2	7	3	1	8	16	8	12	7	8	6
Pierluigi MARTINI	**-**	**-**	**-**	**-**	**-**	**-**	**-**	**-**	**-**	**-**	**-**	**-**	**-**	**-**	**-**	**-**
(Toleman-Hart)	-	-	-	-	-	-	-	-	-	-	-	-	-	nq	-	-
Jonathan PALMER	**8**	**r**	**10**	**9**	**13**	**-**	**-**	**r**	**r**	**r**	**r**	**9**	**9**	**r**	**r**	**r**
(RAM-Hart)	26	21	26	25	21	nq	-	24	25	23	25	24	22	26	21	26
Riccardo PATRESE	**r**	**4**	**r**	**r**	**r**	**r**	**r**	**r**	**r**	**12r**	**r**	**10r**	**r**	**3**	**6**	**8**
(Alfa Romeo)	11	18	7	10	15	14	14	25	21	17	20	13	18	9	9	12
Nelson PIQUET	**r**	**r**	**9r**	**rf**	**r**	**r**	**1f**	**1**	**r**	**7**	**r**	**2**	**r**	**r**	**3f=**	**6**
(Brabham-BMW)	7	1	9	1	3	9	1	1	12	1	5	1	2	1	1	1
Alain PROST	**1f**	**2**	**r**	**1**	**7f**	**1**	**3**	**4**	**r**	**r**	**1f**	**r**	**1**	**r**	**1**	**1**
(McLaren-TAG Porsche)	4	5	8	2	5	1	2	2	7	2	1	2	1	2	2	2
Keke ROSBERG	**2**	**r**	**4r**	**r**	**6**	**4**	**r**	**r**	**1**	**r**	**r**	**r**	**8r**	**r**	**r**	**r**
(Williams-Honda)	9	2	3	3	4	10	15	21	8	5	19	9	7	6	4	4
Huub ROTHENGATTER	**-**	**-**	**-**	**-**	**-**	**-**	**nc**	**-**	**r**	**nc**	**9**	**nc**	**r**	**8**	**-**	**-**
(Spirit-Hart)	-	-	-	-	-	-	24	-	23	22	24	26	27	25	-	-
(Spirit-Ford Cosworth)	-	-	-	-	-	-	-	nq	-	-	-	-	-	-	-	-
Ayrton SENNA	**r**	**6**	**6**	**-**	**r**	**2f**	**7**	**r**	**r**	**3**	**r**	**r**	**r**	**-**	**r**	**3**
(Toleman-Hart)	16	13	19	nq	13	13	9	7	6	7	9	10	13	-	12	3
Philippe STREIFF	**-**	**-**	**-**	**-**	**-**	**-**	**-**	**-**	**-**	**-**	**-**	**-**	**-**	**-**	**-**	**r**
(Renault)	-	-	-	-	-	-	-	-	-	-	-	-	-	-	-	13
Marc SURER	**7**	**9**	**8**	**r**	**r**	**-**	**r**	**r**	**r**	**11**	**r**	**6**	**r**	**r**	**r**	**r**
(Arrows-Ford Cosworth)	24	23	24	-	19	nq	23	22	-	-	-	-	-	-	-	-
(Arrows-BMW)	-	-	-	16	-	-	-	-	22	15	14	19	19	15	16	16
Patrick TAMBAY	**5r**	**rf**	**7**	**r**	**2**	**r**	**-**	**r**	**r**	**8r**	**5**	**r**	**6**	**r**	**r**	**7**
(Renault)	8	4	12	14	1	6	ew	9	10	10	4	5	5	8	3	7
Mike THACKWELL	**-**	**-**	**-**	**-**	**-**	**-**	**r**	**-**	**-**	**-**	**-**	**-**	**-**	**-**	**-**	**-**
(RAM-Hart)	-	-	-	-	-	-	25	-	-	-	-	-	-	-	-	-
(Tyrrell-Ford Cosworth)	-	-	-	-	-	-	-	-	-	-	nq	-	-	-	-	-
Derek WARWICK	**r**	**3**	**2**	**4**	**r**	**r**	**r**	**rf**	**r**	**2**	**3**	**r**	**r**	**r**	**11r**	**r**
(Renault)	3	9	4	4	7	5	4	6	3	6	3	6	4	12	7	9
Manfred WINKELHOCK	**-**	**r**	**r**	**r**	**r**	**r**	**8**	**r**	**8**	**r**	**r**	**-**	**r**	**r**	**-**	**10**
(ATS-BMW)	exc	12	6	7	8	12	12	14	13	11	13	14ns	16	21	-	-
(Brabham-BMW)	-	-	-	-	-	-	-	-	-	-	-	-	-	-	-	19

1985 RACE RESULTS & GRID POSITIONS

	BR	P	RSM	MC	CDN	USA	F	GB	D	A	NL	I	B	EUR	ZA	AUS
Kenny ACHESON	**-**	**-**	**-**	**-**	**-**	**-**	**-**	**-**	**-**	**r**	**-**	**r**	**-**	**-**	**-**	**-**
(RAM-Hart)	-	-	-	-	-	-	-	-	-	23	nq	24	-	-	-	-
Michele ALBORETO	**2**	**2**	**rf**	**2f**	**1**	**3**	**r**	**2**	**1**	**3**	**4**	**13r**	**r**	**r**	**r**	**r**
(Ferrari)	1	5	4	3	3	3	3	6	8	9	16	7	4	15	15	5
Philippe ALLIOT	**9**	**r**	**r**	**-**	**r**	**r**	**r**	**r**	**r**	**r**	**r**	**r**	**r**	**r**	**-**	**-**
(RAM-Hart)	20	20	21	nq	21	23	22	21	21	21	25	26	20	23	-	-
René ARNOUX	**4**	**-**	**-**	**-**	**-**	**-**	**-**	**-**	**-**	**-**	**-**	**-**	**-**	**-**	**-**	**-**
(Ferrari)	7	-	-	-	-	-	-	-	-	-	-	-	-	-	-	-
Mauro BALDI	**r**	**r**	**r**	**-**	**-**	**-**	**-**	**-**	**-**	**-**	**-**	**-**	**-**	**-**	**-**	**-**
(Spirit-Hart)	24	24	26	-	-	-	-	-	-	-	-	-	-	-	-	-
Stefan BELLOF +	**-**	**6**	**r**	**-**	**11**	**4**	**13**	**11**	**8**	**7r**	**r**	**-**	**-**	**-**	**-**	**-**
(Tyrrell-Ford Cosworth)	-	21	24	nq	23	19	25	26	-	-	-	-	-	-	-	-
(Tyrrell-Renault)	-	-	-	-	-	-	-	-	19	22	22	-	-	-	-	-
Gerhard BERGER	**r**	**r**	**r**	**r**	**13**	**11**	**r**	**8**	**7**	**r**	**9**	**r**	**7**	**10**	**5**	**6**
(Arrows-BMW)	19	17	10	11	12	24	8	17	17	17	14	11	8	19	11	7
Thierry BOUTSEN	**11**	**r**	**2**	**9**	**9**	**7**	**9**	**r**	**4**	**8**	**r**	**9**	**10r**	**6**	**6**	**r**
(Arrows-BMW)	12	16	5	6	7	21	11	19	15	16	8	14	6	12	10	11
Martin BRUNDLE	**8**	**r**	**9**	**10**	**12**	**r**	**r**	**7**	**10**	**-**	**7**	**8**	**13**	**r**	**7**	**nc**
(Tyrrell-Ford Cosworth)	21	22	25	18	24	18	-	-	26	nq	-	-	-	-	-	-
(Tyrrell-Renault)	-	-	-	-	-	-	20	20	-	-	21	18	21	16	17	17
Ivan CAPELLI	**-**	**-**	**-**	**-**	**-**	**-**	**-**	**-**	**-**	**-**	**-**	**-**	**-**	**r**	**-**	**4**
(Tyrrell-Renault)	-	-	-	-	-	-	-	-	-	-	-	-	-	24	-	22
Eddie CHEEVER	**r**	**r**	**r**	**r**	**17**	**9**	**10**	**r**	**r**	**r**	**r**	**r**	**r**	**11**	**r**	**r**
(Alfa Romeo)	18	14	12	4	11	7	17	22	18	20	20	17	19	18	14	13
Christian DANNER	**-**	**-**	**-**	**-**	**-**	**-**	**-**	**-**	**-**	**-**	**-**	**-**	**r**	**r**	**-**	**-**
(Zakspeed)	-	-	-	-	-	-	-	-	-	-	-	-	22	25	-	-
Elio de ANGELIS	**3**	**4**	**1**	**3**	**5**	**5**	**5**	**nc**	**r**	**5**	**5**	**6**	**r**	**5**	**r**	**dq**
(Lotus-Renault)	3	4	3	9	1	8	7	8	7	7	11	6	9	9	6	10
Andrea de CESARIS	**r**	**r**	**r**	**4**	**14**	**10**	**r**	**r**	**r**	**r**	**r**	**-**	**-**	**-**	**-**	**-**
(Ligier-Renault)	13	8	13	8	15	17	12	7	14	18	18	-	-	-	-	-
Teo FABI	**-**	**-**	**-**	**r**	**r**	**r**	**14r**	**r**	**r**	**r**	**r**	**12**	**r**	**r**	**r**	**r**
(Toleman-Hart)	-	-	-	20	18	13	18	9	1	6	5	15	11	20	7	24
Piercarlo GHINZANI	**12**	**9**	**nc**	**-**	**r**	**r**	**15**	**r**	**-**	**r**	**r**	**r**	**r**	**r**	**r**	**r**
(Osella-Alfa Romeo)	22	26	22	nq	22	22	23	25	-	-	-	-	-	-	-	-
(Toleman-Hart)	-	-	-	-	-	-	-	-	-	19	15	21	16	14	13	21
François HESNAULT	**r**	**r**	**r**	**-**	**-**	**-**	**-**	**-**	**r**	**-**	**-**	**-**	**-**	**-**	**-**	**-**
(Brabham-BMW)	17	19	20	nq	-	-	-	-	-	-	-	-	-	-	-	-
(Renault)	-	-	-	-	-	-	-	-	23	-	-	-	-	-	-	-
Stefan JOHANSSON	**7**	**8**	**6r**	**r**	**2**	**2**	**4**	**r**	**9**	**4**	**r**	**5r**	**r**	**r**	**4**	**5**
(Tyrrell-Ford Cosworth)	23	-	-	-	-	-	-	-	-	-	-	-	-	-	-	-
(Ferrari)	-	11	15	15	4	9	15	11	2	12	17	10	5	13	16	15
Alan JONES	**-**	**-**	**-**	**-**	**-**	**-**	**-**	**-**	**-**	**-**	**-**	**r**	**-**	**r**	**-**	**r**
(Lola-Hart)	-	-	-	-	-	-	-	-	-	-	-	25	-	22	ns	19
Jacques LAFFITE	**6**	**r**	**r**	**6**	**8**	**12**	**r**	**3**	**3**	**r**	**r**	**r**	**11r**	**rf**	**-**	**2**
(Ligier-Renault)	15	18	16	16	19	16	14	16	13	15	13	20	17	10	-	20
Niki LAUDA	**r**	**r**	**4**	**r**	**r**	**r**	**r**	**r**	**5f**	**r**	**1**	**r**	**-**	**-**	**r**	**r**
(McLaren-TAG Porsche)	9	7	8	14	17	12	6	10	12	3	10	16	ns	-	8	16
Nigel MANSELL	**r**	**5**	**5**	**7**	**6**	**r**	**-**	**r**	**6**	**r**	**6**	**11rf**	**2**	**1**	**1**	**r**
(Williams-Honda)	5	9	7	2	16	2	ns	5	10	2	7	3	7	3	1	2
Pierluigi MARTINI	**r**	**r**	**r**	**-**	**r**	**r**	**r**	**r**	**11r**	**r**	**r**	**r**	**12**	**r**	**r**	**8**
(Minardi-Ford Cosworth)	25	25	-	-	-	-	-	-	-	-	-	-	-	-	-	-
(Minardi-Motori Moderni)	-	-	19	nq	25	25	24	23	27	26	24	23	24	26	19	23
Jonathan PALMER	**-**	**r**	**r**	**11**	**-**	**-**	**r**	**r**	**r**	**r**	**r**	**-**	**-**	**-**	**-**	**-**
(Zakspeed)	-	23	17	19	-	-	21	24	24	25	23	-	-	-	-	-
Riccardo PATRESE	**r**	**r**	**r**	**r**	**10**	**r**	**11**	**9**	**r**	**r**	**r**	**r**	**r**	**9**	**r**	**r**
(Alfa Romeo)	14	13	18	12	13	14	16	14	9	10	19	13	15	11	12	14
Nelson PIQUET	**r**	**r**	**8r**	**r**	**r**	**6**	**1**	**4**	**r**	**r**	**8**	**2**	**5**	**r**	**r**	**r**
(Brabham-BMW)	8	10	9	13	9	10	5	2	6	5	1	4	3	2	2	9
Alain PROST	**1f**	**r**	**dq**	**1**	**3**	**r**	**3**	**1f**	**2**	**1f**	**2f**	**1**	**3f**	**4**	**3**	**r**
(McLaren-TAG Porsche)	6	2	6	5	5	4	4	3	3	1	3	5	1	6	9	4
Keke ROSBERG	**r**	**r**	**r**	**8**	**4**	**1**	**2f**	**r**	**12r**	**r**	**r**	**r**	**4**	**3**	**2f**	**1f**
(Williams-Honda)	2	3	2	7	8	5	1	1	4	4	2	2	10	4	3	3
Huub ROTHENGATTER	**-**	**-**	**-**	**-**	**-**	**-**	**-**	**-**	**r**	**9**	**nc**	**r**	**nc**	**-**	**r**	**7**
(Osella-Alfa Romeo)	-	-	-	-	-	-	-	-	25	24	26	22	23	nq	20	25
Ayrton SENNA	**r**	**1f**	**7r**	**r**	**16f**	**rf**	**r**	**10r**	**r**	**2**	**3**	**3**	**1**	**2**	**r**	**r**
(Lotus-Renault)	4	1	1	1	2	1	2	4	5	14	4	1	2	1	4	1

	BR	P	RSM	MC	CDN	USA	F	GB	D	A	NL	I	B	EUR	ZA	AUS
Philippe STREIFF	-	-	-	-	-	-	-	-	-	-	-	**10**	**9**	**8**	**r**	**3**
(Ligier-Renault)	-	-	-	-	-	-	-	-	-	-	-	19	18	5	-	18
(Tyrrell-Renault)	-	-	-	-	-	-	-	-	-	-	-	-	-	-	18	-
Marc SURER	-	-	-	-	**15**	**8**	**8**	**6**	**r**	**6**	**10r**	**4**	**8**	**r**	**r**	**r**
(Brabham-BMW)	-	-	-	-	20	11	13	15	11	11	9	9	12	7	5	6
Patrick TAMBAY	**5**	**3**	**3**	**r**	**7**	**r**	**6**	**r**	**r**	**10r**	**r**	**7**	**r**	**12**	-	**r**
(Renault)	11	12	11	17	10	15	9	13	16	8	6	8	13	17	-	8
Derek WARWICK	**10**	**7**	**10**	**5**	**r**	**r**	**7**	**5**	**r**	**r**	**r**	**r**	**6**	**r**	-	**r**
(Renault)	10	6	14	10	6	6	10	12	20	13	12	12	14	8	-	12
John WATSON	-	-	-	-	-	-	-	-	-	-	-	-	-	**7**	-	-
(McLaren-TAG Porsche)	-	-	-	-	-	-	-	-	-	-	-	-	-	21	-	-
Manfred WINKELHOCK +	**13**	**nc**	**r**	-	**r**	**r**	**12**	**r**	**r**	-	-	-	-	-	-	-
(RAM-Hart)	16	15	23	nq	14	20	19	18	22	-	-	-	-	-	-	-

1986 RACE RESULTS & GRID POSITIONS

	BR	E	RSM	MC	B	CDN	USA	F	GB	D	H	A	I	P	MEX	AUS
Michele ALBORETO	**r**	**r**	**10r**	**r**	**4**	**8**	**4**	**8**	**r**	**r**	**r**	**2**	**r**	**5**	**r**	**r**
(Ferrari)	6	13	5	4	9	11	11	6	12	10	15	9	9	13	12	9
Philippe ALLIOT	-	-	-	-	-	-	-	-	-	**r**	**9**	**r**	**r**	**r**	**6**	**8**
(Ligier-Renault)	-	-	-	-	-	-	-	-	-	14	12	11	14	11	10	8
René ARNOUX	**4**	**r**	**r**	**5**	**r**	**6**	**r**	**5**	**4**	**4**	**r**	**10**	**r**	**7**	**15r**	**7**
(Ligier-Renault)	4	6	8	12	7	5	4	4	8	8	9	12	11	10	13	5
Allen BERG	-	-	-	-	-	-	**r**	**r**	**r**	**12**	**r**	**r**	-	**13**	**16**	**nc**
(Osella-Alfa Romeo)	-	-	-	-	-	-	25	26	26	26	26	26	-	27	26	26
Gerhard BERGER	**6**	**6**	**3**	**r**	**10**	**r**	**r**	**r**	**r**	**10f**	**r**	**7f**	**5**	**r**	**1**	**r**
(Benetton-BMW)	16	7	9	5	2	7	12	8	4	4	11	2	4	4	4	6
Thierry BOUTSEN	**r**	**7**	**7**	**8**	**r**	**r**	**r**	**nc**	**nc**	**r**	**r**	**r**	**7**	**10**	**7**	**r**
(Arrows-BMW)	15	19	12	14	14	12	13	21	13	21	22	18	13	21	21	22
Martin BRUNDLE	**5**	**r**	**8**	**r**	**r**	**9**	**r**	**10**	**5**	**r**	**6**	**r**	**10**	**r**	**11**	**4**
(Tyrrell-Renault)	17	12	13	10	12	18	16	15	11	15	16	17	20	19	16	16
Alex CAFFI	-	-	-	-	-	-	-	-	-	-	-	-	**11**	-	-	-
(Osella-Alfa Romeo)	-	-	-	-	-	-	-	-	-	-	-	-	27	-	-	-
Ivan CAPELLI	-	-	-	-	-	-	-	-	-	-	-	-	**r**	**r**	-	-
(AGS-Motori Moderni)	-	-	-	-	-	-	-	-	-	-	-	-	25	25	-	-
Eddie CHEEVER	-	-	-	-	-	-	**r**	-	-	-	-	-	-	-	-	-
(Lola-Ford Cosworth)	-	-	-	-	-	-	10	-	-	-	-	-	-	-	-	-
Christian DANNER	**r**	**r**	**r**	-	**r**	**r**	**r**	**11**	**r**	**r**	**r**	**6**	**8**	**11**	**9**	**r**
(Osella-Alfa Romeo)	24	23	25	nq	25	24	-	-	-	-	-	-	-	-	-	-
(Arrows-BMW)	-	-	-	-	-	-	19	18	23	17	21	22	16	22	20	24
Elio de ANGELIS +	**8**	**r**	**r**	**r**	-	-	-	-	-	-	-	-	-	-	-	-
(Brabham-BMW)	14	15	19	20	-	-	-	-	-	-	-	-	-	-	-	-
Andrea de CESARIS	**r**	**r**	**r**	-	**r**	**r**	**r**	**r**	**r**	**r**	**r**	**r**	**r**	**r**	**8**	**r**
(Minardi-Motori Moderni)	22	24	23	nq	19	20	23	23	21	23	20	23	21	16	22	11
Johnny DUMFRIES	**9**	**r**	**r**	-	**r**	**r**	**7**	**r**	**7**	**r**	**5**	**r**	**r**	**9**	**r**	**6**
(Lotus-Renault)	11	10	17	nq	13	15	14	12	10	12	8	15	17	15	17	14
Teo FABI 10	**5**	**r**	**r**	**7**	**r**	**r**	**r**	**r**	**r**	**r**	**r**	**rf**	**8**	**r**	**10**	
(Benetton-BMW)	12	9	10	16	6	14	17	9	7	9	13	1	1	5	9	13
Piercarlo GHINZANI	**r**	**r**	**r**	-	**r**	**r**	**r**	**r**	**r**	**r**	**r**	**11**	**r**	**r**	**r**	**r**
(Osella-Alfa Romeo)	23	21	26	nq	24	22	22	25	24	25	23	25	26	24	25	25
Stefan JOHANSSON	**r**	**r**	**4**	**10**	**3**	**r**	**r**	**r**	**r**	**11r**	**4**	**3**	**3**	**6**	**12r**	**3**
(Ferrari)	8	11	7	15	11	17	5	10	18	11	7	14	12	8	14	12
Alan JONES	**r**	**r**	**r**	**r**	**11r**	**10**	**r**	**r**	**r**	**9**	**r**	**4**	**6**	**r**	**r**	**r**
(Lola-Hart)	19	17	-	-	-	-	-	-	-	-	-	-	-	-	-	-
(Lola-Ford Cosworth)	-	-	21	18	16	13	21	20	14	19	10	16	18	17	15	15
Jacques LAFFITE	**3**	**r**	**r**	**6**	**5**	**7**	**2**	**6**	**r**	-	-	-	-	-	-	-
(Ligier-Renault)	5	8	14	7	17	8	6	11	19	-	-	-	-	-	-	-
Nigel MANSELL	**r**	**2f**	**r**	**4**	**1**	**1**	**5**	**1f**	**1f**	**3**	**3**	**r**	**2**	**1f**	**5**	**r**
(Williams-Honda)	3	3	3	2	5	1	2	2	2	6	4	6	3	2	3	1
Alessandro NANNINI	**r**	**r**	**r**	-	**r**	**r**	**r**	**r**	**r**	**r**	**r**	**r**	**r**	**r**	**14**	**r**
(Minardi-Motori Moderni)	25	25	18	nq	22	19	24	19	20	22	17	19	19	18	24	18
Jonathan PALMER	**r**	**r**	**r**	**12**	**nc**	**r**	**8**	**r**	**9**	**r**	**10**	**r**	**r**	**12**	**10r**	**9**
(Zakspeed)	21	16	20	19	20	21	20	22	22	16	24	21	22	20	18	21
Riccardo PATRESE	**r**	**r**	**6r**	**r**	**8**	**r**	**6**	**7**	**r**	**r**	**r**	**r**	**r**	**r**	**13r**	**r**
(Brabham-BMW)	10	14	16	6	15	9	8	16	15	7	14	4	10	9	5	19
Nelson PIQUET	**1f**	**r**	**2f**	**7**	**r**	**3f**	**rf**	**3**	**2**	**1**	**1f**	**r**	**1**	**3**	**4f**	**2f**
(Williams-Honda)	2	2	2	11	1	3	3	3	1	5	2	7	6	6	2	2
Alain PROST	**r**	**3**	**1**	**1f**	**6f**	**2**	**3**	**2**	**3**	**6r**	**r**	**1**	**r/dq**	**2**	**2**	**1**
(McLaren-TAG Porsche)	9	4	4	1	3	4	7	5	6	2	3	5	2	3	6	4
Keke ROSBERG	**r**	**4**	**5r**	**2**	**r**	**4**	**r**	**4**	**r**	**5r**	**r**	**9r**	**4**	**r**	**r**	**r**
(McLaren-TAG Porsche)	7	5	6	9	8	6	9	7	5	1	5	3	8	7	11	7
Huub ROTHENGATTER	-	-	**r**	-	**r**	**12**	**r**	**r**	**r**	**r**	**r**	**8**	**r**	**r**	-	**r**
(Zakspeed)	-	-	24	nq	23	23	26	24	25	24	25	24	24	26	23ns	23
Ayrton SENNA	**2**	**1**	**r**	**3**	**2**	**5**	**1**	**r**	**r**	**2**	**2**	**r**	**r**	**4r**	**3**	**r**
(Lotus-Renault)	1	1	1	3	4	2	1	1	3	3	1	8	5	1	1	3
Philippe STREIFF	**7**	**r**	**r**	**11**	**12**	**11**	**9**	**r**	**6**	**r**	**8**	**r**	**9**	**r**	**r**	**5r**
(Tyrrell-Renault)	18	20	22	13	18	16	18	17	16	18	18	20	23	23	19	10
Marc SURER	**r**	**r**	**9r**	**9**	**9**	-	-	-	-	-	-	-	-	-	-	-
(Arrows-BMW)	20	22	15	17	21	-	-	-	-	-	-	-	-	-	-	-
Patrick TAMBAY	**r**	**8**	**r**	**r**	**r**	-	-	**r**	**r**	**8**	**7**	**5**	**r**	**nc**	**r**	**nc**
(Lola-Hart)	13	18	11	-	-	-	-	-	-	-	-	-	-	-	-	-
(Lola-Ford Cosworth)	-	-	-	8	10	ns	-	13	17	13	6	13	15	14	8	17
Derek WARWICK	-	-	-	-	-	**r**	**10**	**9**	**8**	**7**	**r**	-	**r**	**r**	**r**	**r**
(Brabham-BMW)	-	-	-	-	-	10	15	14	9	20	19	10ns	7	12	7	20

1987 RACE RESULTS & GRID POSITIONS

	BR	RSM	B	MC	USA	F	GB	D	H	A	I	P	E	MEX	J	AUS
Michele ALBORETO	**8r**	**3**	**r**	**3**	**r**	**r**	**r**	**r**	**r**	**r**	**r**	**r**	**15r**	**r**	**4**	**2**
(Ferrari)	9	6	5	5	7	8	7	5	5	6	8	6	4	9	4	6
Philippe ALLIOT	-	**10**	**8**	**r**	**r**	**r**	**r**	**6**	**r**	**12**	**r**	**r**	**6**	**6**	**r**	**r**
(Lola-Ford Cosworth)	-	21	22	18	20	23	21	21	15	22	23	19	17	24	18	17
René ARNOUX	-	-	**6**	**11**	**10**	**r**	**r**	**r**	**r**	**10**	**10**	**r**	**r**	**r**	**r**	**r**
(Ligier-Megatron)	-	ns	16	22	21	13	16	12	19	16	15	18	14	18	17	20
Gerhard BERGER	**4**	**r**	**r**	**4**	**4**	**r**	**r**	**r**	**r**	**r**	**4**	**2f**	**rf**	**r**	**1**	**1f**
(Ferrari)	7	5	4	8	12	6	8	10	2	3	3	1	3	2	1	1
Thierry BOUTSEN	**5**	**r**	**r**	**r**	**r**	**r**	**7**	**r**	**4**	**4**	**5**	**14**	**16r**	**r**	**5**	**3**
(Benetton-Ford Cosworth)	6	11	7	9	4	5	5	6	7	4	6	9	8	4	3	5
Martin BRUNDLE	**r**	**5**	**r**	**7**	**r**	**r**	**nc**	**nc**	**r**	**dq**	**r**	**r**	**11**	**r**	**r**	**r**
(Zakspeed)	19	14	18	14	15	18	17	19	22	17	17	17	20	13	15	16
Alex CAFFI	**r**	**12r**	**r**	**r**	**r**	**r**	**r**	**r**	**r**	**r**	**r**	**r**	-	**r**	**r**	-
(Osella-Alfa Romeo)	21	19	26	16	19	20	20	26	21	21	21	25	nq	26	23	nq
Adrian CAMPOS	**dq**	**r**	**r**	-	**r**	**r**	**r**	**r**	**r**	**r**	**r**	**r**	**14**	**r**	**r**	**r**
(Minardi-Motori Moderni)	16	16	19	ns	25	21	19	18	24	19	20	20	24	19	21	26
Ivan CAPELLI	-	**r**	**r**	**6**	**r**	**r**	**r**	**r**	**10**	**11**	**13**	**9**	**12**	**r**	**r**	**r**
(March-Ford Cosworth)	23ns	22	21	19	22	22	24	24	18	23	25	22	19	20	20	23
Eddie CHEEVER	**r**	**r**	**4**	**r**	**6r**	**r**	**r**	**r**	**8**	**r**	**r**	**6**	**8r**	**4**	**9**	**r**
(Arrows-Megatron)	14	9	11	6	6	14	14	15	11	12	13	11	13	12	12	11
Yannick DALMAS	-	-	-	-	-	-	-	-	-	-	-	-	-	**9**	**14r**	**5**
(Lola-Ford Cosworth)	-	-	-	-	-	-	-	-	-	-	-	-	-	23	22	21

	BR	RSM	B	MC	USA	F	GB	D	H	A	I	P	E	MEX	J	AUS
Christian DANNER	**9**	**7**	**r**	**-**	**8**	**r**	**r**	**r**	**r**	**9**	**9**	**r**	**r**	**r**	**r**	**7**
(Zakspeed)	17	17	20	exc	16	19	18	20	23	20	16	16	22	17	16	24
Andrea de CESARIS	**r**	**r**	**3r**	**r**	**r**	**r**	**r**	**r**	**r**	**r**	**r**	**r**	**r**	**r**	**r**	**8r**
(Brabham-BMW)	13	13	13	21	17	11	9	7	13	10	10	13	10	10	10	10
Teo FABI	**r**	**rf**	**r**	**8**	**r**	**5r**	**6**	**r**	**r**	**3**	**7**	**4r**	**r**	**5**	**r**	**r**
(Benetton-Ford Cosworth)	4	4	9	12	8	7	6	9	12	5	7	10	6	6	6	9
Pascal FABRE	**12**	**13**	**10r**	**13**	**12**	**9**	**9**	**r**	**13**	**nc**	**-**	**-**	**r**	**-**	**-**	**-**
(AGS-Ford Cosworth)	22	24	25	24	26	26	25	25	26	26	nq	nq	25	nq	-	-
Franco FORINI	**-**	**-**	**-**	**-**	**-**	**-**	**-**	**-**	**-**	**-**	**r**	**r**	**-**	**-**	**-**	**-**
(Osella-Alfa Romeo)	-	-	-	-	-	-	-	-	-	-	26	26	nq	-	-	-
Piercarlo GHINZANI	**-**	**r**	**7r**	**12**	**r**	**r**	**-**	**r**	**12**	**8**	**8**	**r**	**r**	**r**	**13r**	**r**
(Ligier-Megatron)	-	18	17	20	23	17	exc	17	25	18	19	23	23	21	24	22
Stefan JOHANSSON	**3**	**4**	**2**	**r**	**7**	**8r**	**r**	**2**	**r**	**7**	**6**	**5**	**3**	**r**	**3**	**r**
(McLaren-TAG Porsche)	10	8	10	7	11	9	10	8	8	14	11	8	11	15	9	8
Nicola LARINI	**-**	**-**	**-**	**-**	**-**	**-**	**-**	**-**	**-**	**-**	**-**	**-**	**r**	**-**	**-**	**-**
(Coloni-Ford Cosworth)	-	-	-	-	-	-	-	-	-	-	nq	-	26	-	-	-
Nigel MANSELL	**6**	**1**	**r**	**r**	**5**	**1**	**1f**	**rf**	**14r**	**1f**	**3**	**r**	**1**	**1**	**-**	**-**
(Williams-Honda)	1	2	1	1	1	1	2	1	1	2	2	2	2	1	ns	-
Stefano MODENA	**-**	**-**	**-**	**-**	**-**	**-**	**-**	**-**	**-**	**-**	**-**	**-**	**-**	**-**	**-**	**r**
(Brabham-BMW)	-	-	-	-	-	-	-	-	-	-	-	-	-	-	-	15
Roberto MORENO	**-**	**-**	**-**	**-**	**-**	**-**	**-**	**-**	**-**	**-**	**-**	**-**	**-**	**-**	**r**	**6**
(AGS-Ford Cosworth)	-	-	-	-	-	-	-	-	-	-	-	-	-	-	26	25
Satoru NAKAJIMA	**7**	**6**	**5**	**10**	**r**	**nc**	**4**	**r**	**r**	**13**	**11**	**8**	**9**	**r**	**6**	**r**
(Lotus-Honda)	12	12	15	17	24	16	12	14	17	13	14	15	18	16	11	14
Alessandro NANNINI	**r**	**r**	**r**	**r**	**r**	**r**	**r**	**r**	**11**	**r**	**16r**	**11r**	**r**	**r**	**r**	**r**
(Minardi-Motori Moderni)	15	15	14	13	18	15	15	16	20	15	18	14	21	14	14	13
Jonathan PALMER	**10**	**r**	**r**	**5**	**11**	**7**	**8**	**5**	**7**	**14**	**14**	**10**	**r**	**7**	**8**	**4**
(Tyrrell-Ford Cosworth)	18	23	24	15	13	24	23	23	16	24	22	24	16	22	19	19
Riccardo PATRESE	**r**	**9**	**r**	**r**	**9**	**r**	**r**	**r**	**5**	**r**	**r**	**r**	**13**	**3**	**11r**	**9r**
(Brabham-BMW)	11	7	8	10	9	12	11	11	10	8	9	7	9	8	8	-
(Williams-Honda)	-	-	-	-	-	-	-	-	-	-	-	-	-	-	-	7
Nelson PIQUET	**2f**	**-**	**r**	**2**	**2**	**2f**	**2**	**1**	**1f**	**2**	**1**	**3**	**4**	**2f**	**15r**	**r**
(Williams-Honda)	2	ns	2	3	3	4	1	4	3	1	1	4	1	3	5	3
Alain PROST	**1**	**r**	**1f**	**9r**	**3**	**3**	**r**	**7r**	**3**	**6**	**15**	**1**	**2**	**r**	**7f**	**r**
(McLaren-TAG Porsche)	5	3	6	4	5	2	4	3	4	9	5	3	7	5	2	2
Ayrton SENNA	**r**	**2**	**r**	**1f**	**1f**	**4**	**3**	**3**	**2**	**5**	**2f**	**7**	**5**	**r**	**2**	**dq**
(Lotus-Honda)	3	1	3	2	2	3	3	2	6	7	4	5	5	7	7	4
Philippe STREIFF	**11**	**8**	**9**	**r**	**r**	**6**	**r**	**4**	**9**	**r**	**12**	**12**	**7**	**8**	**12**	**r**
(Tyrrell-Ford Cosworth)	20	20	23	23	14	25	22	22	14	25	24	21	15	25	25	18
Gabriele TARQUINI	**-**	**r**	**-**	**-**	**-**	**-**	**-**	**-**	**-**	**-**	**-**	**-**	**-**	**-**	**-**	**-**
(Osella-Alfa Romeo)	-	25	-	-	-	-	-	-	-	-	-	-	-	-	-	-
Derek WARWICK	**r**	**11r**	**r**	**r**	**r**	**r**	**5**	**r**	**6**	**r**	**r**	**13**	**10**	**r**	**10**	**r**
(Arrows-Megatron)	8	10	12	11	10	10	13	13	9	11	12	12	12	11	13	12

1988 RACE RESULTS & GRID POSITIONS

	BR	RSM	MC	MEX	CDN	USA	F	GB	D	H	B	I	P	E	J	AUS
Michele ALBORETO	**5**	**18r**	**3**	**4**	**r**	**r**	**3**	**17r**	**4**	**r**	**r**	**2f**	**5**	**r**	**11**	**r**
(Ferrari)	6	10	4	5	4	3	4	2	4	15	4	4	7	10	9	12
Philippe ALLIOT	**r**	**17**	**r**	**r**	**10r**	**r**	**r**	**14**	**r**	**12**	**9**	**r**	**r**	**14**	**9**	**10r**
(Lola-Ford Cosworth)	16	15	13	13	17	14	18	22	20	20	16	20	20	12	19	24
René ARNOUX	**r**	**-**	**r**	**r**	**r**	**r**	**-**	**18**	**17**	**r**	**r**	**13**	**10**	**r**	**17**	**r**
(Ligier-Judd)	18	nq	20	20	20	20	nq	25	17	25	17	24	23	19	23	23
Julian BAILEY	**-**	**r**	**-**	**-**	**r**	**9r**	**-**	**16**	**-**	**-**	**-**	**12**	**-**	**-**	**14**	**-**
(Tyrrell-Ford Cosworth)	nq	21	nq	nq	23	22	nq	24	nq	nq	nq	26	nq	nq	26	nq
Gerhard BERGER	**2f**	**5**	**2**	**3**	**r**	**r**	**4**	**9**	**3**	**4**	**rf**	**1**	**rf**	**6**	**4**	**r**
(Ferrari)	4	5	3	3	3	2	3	1	3	9	3	3	4	8	3	4
Thierry BOUTSEN	**7**	**4**	**8**	**8**	**3**	**3**	**r**	**r**	**6**	**3**	**dq**	**6**	**3**	**9**	**3**	**5**
(Benetton-Ford Cosworth)	7	8	16	11	7	5	5	12	9	3	6	8	13	4	10	10
Martin BRUNDLE	**-**	**-**	**-**	**-**	**-**	**-**	**-**	**-**	**-**	**-**	**7**	**-**	**-**	**-**	**-**	**-**
(Williams-Judd)	-	-	-	-	-	-	-	-	-	-	12	-	-	-	-	-
Alex CAFFI	**-**	**r**	**r**	**r**	**-**	**8**	**12**	**11**	**15**	**r**	**8**	**r**	**7**	**10**	**r**	**r**
(Dallara-Ford Cosworth)	npq	24	17	23	npq	21	14	21	19	10	15	21	17	18	21	11
Adrian CAMPOS	**r**	**16**	**-**	**-**	**-**	**-**	**-**	**-**	**-**	**-**	**-**	**-**	**-**	**-**	**-**	**-**
(Minardi-Ford Cosworth)	23	22	nq	nq	nq	-	-	-	-	-	-	-	-	-	-	-
Ivan CAPELLI	**r**	**r**	**10**	**16**	**5**	**-**	**9**	**r**	**5**	**r**	**3**	**5**	**2**	**r**	**r**	**6**
(March-Judd)	9	9	22	10	14	ns	10	6	7	4	14	11	3	6	4	9
Eddie CHEEVER	**8**	**7**	**r**	**6**	**r**	**r**	**11**	**7**	**10**	**r**	**6**	**3**	**r**	**r**	**r**	**r**
(Arrows-Megatron)	15	7	9	7	8	15	13	13	15	14	11	5	18	25	15	18
Yannick DALMAS	**r**	**12**	**7**	**9**	**-**	**7**	**13**	**13**	**19r**	**9**	**r**	**r**	**r**	**11**	**-**	**-**
(Lola-Ford Cosworth)	17	19	21	22	nq	24	19	23	21	17	23	25	15	16	-	-
Andrea de CESARIS	**r**	**r**	**r**	**r**	**9r**	**4**	**10**	**r**	**13**	**r**	**r**	**r**	**r**	**r**	**r**	**8r**
(Rial-Ford Cosworth)	14	16	19	12	12	12	12	14	14	18	19	18	12	23	14	15
Piercarlo GHINZANI	**-**	**r**	**r**	**15**	**14r**	**-**	**-**	**-**	**14**	**-**	**r**	**r**	**-**	**-**	**-**	**r**
(Zakspeed)	nq	25	23	18	22	nq	exc	nq	23	nq	24	16	nq	nq	nq	26
Mauricio GUGELMIN	**r**	**15**	**r**	**r**	**r**	**r**	**8**	**4**	**8**	**5**	**r**	**8**	**r**	**7**	**10**	**r**
(March-Judd)	13	20	14	16	18	13	16	5	10	8	13	13	5	11	13	19
Stefan JOHANSSON	**9**	**-**	**r**	**10**	**r**	**r**	**-**	**-**	**-**	**r**	**11r**	**-**	**r**	**r**	**-**	**9r**
(Ligier-Judd)	21	nq	26	24	25	18	nq	nq	nq	24	20	nq	24	21	nq	22
Nicola LARINI	**-**	**-**	**9**	**-**	**-**	**r**	**r**	**19r**	**r**	**-**	**r**	**r**	**12**	**r**	**r**	**-**
(Osella-Alfa Romeo)	nq	exc	25	nq	nq	26	24	26	18	npq	26	17	25	14	24	npq
Oscar LARRAURI	**r**	**-**	**r**	**13**	**r**	**r**	**r**	**-**	**16**	**-**	**-**	**-**	**-**	**-**	**-**	**r**
(EuroBrun-Ford Cosworth)	26	nq	18	26	24	23	26	nq	26	nq	npq	npq	npq	nq	nq	25
Nigel MANSELL	**r**	**r**	**r**	**r**	**r**	**r**	**r**	**2f**	**r**	**r**	**-**	**-**	**r**	**2**	**r**	**r**
(Williams-Judd)	2	11	5	14	9	6	9	11	11	2	-	-	6	3	8	3
Pierluigi MARTINI	**-**	**-**	**-**	**-**	**-**	**6**	**15**	**15**	**-**	**r**	**-**	**r**	**r**	**r**	**13**	**7**
(Minardi-Ford Cosworth)	-	-	-	-	-	16	22	19	nq	16	nq	14	14	20	17	14
Stefano MODENA	**r**	**nc**	**-**	**-**	**12**	**r**	**14**	**12**	**r**	**11**	**-**	**-**	**-**	**13**	**-**	**r**
(EuroBrun-Ford Cosworth)	24	26	exc	exc	15	19	20	20	25	26	nq	nq	nq	26	nq	20
Satoru NAKAJIMA	**6**	**8**	**-**	**r**	**11**	**-**	**7**	**10**	**9**	**7**	**r**	**r**	**r**	**r**	**7**	**r**
(Lotus-Honda)	10	12	nq	6	13	nq	8	10	8	19	8	12	16	15	6	13
Alessandro NANNINI	**r**	**6**	**r**	**7**	**r**	**r**	**6**	**3**	**18f**	**r**	**dq**	**9**	**r**	**3**	**5**	**r**
(Benetton-Ford Cosworth)	12	4	6	8	5	7	6	8	6	5	7	9	9	5	12	8
Jonathan PALMER	**r**	**14**	**5**	**-**	**6**	**5**	**r**	**r**	**11**	**r**	**12r**	**-**	**r**	**r**	**12**	**r**
(Tyrrell-Ford Cosworth)	22	23	10	nq	19	17	23	17	24	21	21	nq	22	22	16	17
Riccardo PATRESE	**r**	**13**	**6**	**r**	**r**	**r**	**r**	**8**	**r**	**6**	**r**	**7**	**r**	**5**	**6**	**4**
(Williams-Judd)	8	6	8	17	11	10	15	15	13	6	5	10	11	7	11	6
Nelson PIQUET	**3**	**3**	**r**	**r**	**4**	**r**	**5**	**5**	**r**	**8**	**4**	**r**	**r**	**8**	**r**	**3**
(Lotus-Honda)	5	3	11	4	6	8	7	7	5	13	9	7	8	9	5	5
Alain PROST	**1**	**2f**	**1**	**1f**	**2**	**2f**	**1f**	**r**	**2**	**2f**	**2**	**r**	**1**	**1f**	**2**	**1f**
(McLaren-Honda)	3	2	2	2	2	4	1	4	2	7	2	2	1	2	2	2
Pierre-Henri RAPHANEL	**-**	**-**	**-**	**-**	**-**	**-**	**-**	**-**	**-**	**-**	**-**	**-**	**-**	**-**	**-**	**-**
(Lola-Ford Cosworth)	-	-	-	-	-	-	-	-	-	-	-	-	-	-	-	nq
Luis SALA	**r**	**11**	**r**	**11**	**13**	**r**	**nc**	**r**	**-**	**10**	**-**	**r**	**8**	**12**	**15**	**r**
(Minardi-Ford Cosworth)	20	18	15	25	21	25	25	18	nq	11	nq	19	19	24	22	21
Jean-Louis SCHLESSER	**-**	**-**	**-**	**-**	**-**	**-**	**-**	**-**	**-**	**-**	**-**	**11**	**-**	**-**	**-**	**-**
(Williams-Judd)	-	-	-	-	-	-	-	-	-	-	-	22	-	-	-	-
Bernd SCHNEIDER	**-**	**-**	**-**	**r**	**-**	**-**	**r**	**-**	**12**	**-**	**13r**	**r**	**-**	**-**	**r**	**-**
(Zakspeed)	nq	nq	nq	15	nq	nq	21	nq	22	nq	25	15	nq	nq	25	nq
Ayrton SENNA	**dq**	**1**	**rf**	**2**	**1f**	**1**	**2**	**1**	**1**	**1**	**1**	**10r**	**6**	**4**	**1f**	**2**
(McLaren-Honda)	1	1	1	1	1	1	2	3	1	1	1	1	2	1	1	1

	BR	RSM	B	MC	USA	F	GB	D	H	A	I	P	E	MEX	J	AUS
Philippe STREIFF	**r**	**10**	**r**	**12**	**r**	**r**	**r**	**r**	**r**	**r**	**10**	**r**	**9**	**r**	**8**	**11r**
(AGS-Ford Cosworth)	19	13	12	19	10	11	17	16	16	23	18	23	21	13	18	16
Aguri SUZUKI	-	-	-	-	-	-	-	-	-	-	-	-	-	-	**16**	-
(Lola-Ford Cosworth)	-	-	-	-	-	-	-	-	-	-	-	-	-	-	20	-
Gabriele TARQUINI	**r**	**r**	**r**	**14**	**8**	-	-	-	-	**13**	**nc**	-	**11**	-	-	-
(Coloni-Ford Cosworth)	25	17	24	21	26	npq	npq	npq	npq	22	22	nq	26	npq	npq	nq
Derek WARWICK	**4**	**9**	**4**	**5**	**7**	**r**	**r**	**6**	**7**	**r**	**5**	**4**	**4**	**r**	**r**	**r**
(Arrows-Megatron)	11	14	7	9	16	9	11	9	12	12	10	6	10	17	7	7

1989 RACE RESULTS & GRID POSITIONS

	BR	RSM	MC	MEX	USA	CDN	F	GB	D	H	B	I	P	E	J	AUS
Michele ALBORETO	**10**	-	**5**	**3**	**r**	**r**	-	-	**r**	**r**	**r**	**r**	**11**	-	-	-
(Tyrrell-Ford Cosworth)	20	nq	12	7	9	20	-	-	-	-	-	-	-	-	-	-
(Lola-Lamborghini)	-	-	-	-	-	-	-	-	26	26	22	13	21	npq	nq	npq
Jean ALESI	-	-	-	-	-	-	**4**	**r**	**10**	**9**	-	**5**	-	**4**	**r**	**r**
(Tyrrell-Ford Cosworth)	-	-	-	-	-	-	16	22	10	11	-	10	-	9	18	15
Philippe ALLIOT	**12**	**r**	**r**	**nc**	**r**	**r**	**r**	**r**	**r**	-	**16r**	**r**	**9**	**6**	**r**	**r**
(Lola-Lamborghini)	26	20	17	16	12	10	7	12	15	npq	11	7	17	5	8	19
René ARNOUX	-	-	**12**	**14**	-	**5**	**r**	-	**11**	-	**r**	**9**	**13**	-	-	**r**
(Ligier-Ford Cosworth)	nq	nq	21	25	nq	22	18	nq	23	nq	17	23	23	nq	nq	26
Paulo BARILLA	-	-	-	-	-	-	-	-	-	-	-	-	-	-	**r**	-
(Minardi-Ford Cosworth)	-	-	-	-	-	-	-	-	-	-	-	-	-	-	19	-
Gerhard BERGER	**r**	**r**	-	**r**	**r**	**r**	**r**	**r**	**r**	**r**	**r**	**2**	**1f**	**2**	**r**	**r**
(Ferrari)	3	5	-	6	8	4	6	4	4	6	3	2	2	2	3	14
Éric BERNARD	-	-	-	-	-	-	**11r**	**r**	-	-	-	-	-	-	-	-
(Lola-Lamborghini)	-	-	-	-	-	-	15	13	-	-	-	-	-	-	-	-
Enrico BERTAGGIA	-	-	-	-	-	-	-	-	-	-	-	-	-	-	-	-
(Coloni-Ford Cosworth)	-	-	-	-	-	-	-	-	-	-	npq	npq	npq	npq	npq	npq
Thierry BOUTSEN	**r**	**4**	**10**	**r**	**6**	**1**	**r**	**10**	**r**	**3**	**4**	**3**	**r**	**r**	**3**	**1**
(Williams-Renault)	4	6	3	8	16	6	5	7	6	4	4	6	8	21	7	5
Martin BRUNDLE	**r**	**r**	**6**	**9**	**r**	-	-	**r**	**8**	**12**	**r**	**6**	**8**	**r**	**5**	**r**
(Brabham-Judd)	13	22	4	20	5	npq	npq	20	12	15	20	12	10	8	13	12
Alex CAFFI	-	**7**	**4**	**13**	**r**	**6**	**r**	-	**r**	**7**	**r**	**11r**	**r**	**r**	**9**	**r**
(Dallara-Ford Cosworth)	npq	9	9	19	6	8	26	npq	20	3	12	20	7	23	15	10
Ivan CAPELLI	**r**	**r**	**11r**	**r**	**r**	**r**	**r**	**r**	**r**	**r**	**12**	**r**	**r**	**r**	**r**	**r**
(March-Judd)	7	13	22	4	11	21	12	8	22	14	19	18	24	19	17	16
Eddie CHEEVER	**r**	**9**	**7**	**7**	**3**	**r**	**7**	-	**12r**	**5**	**r**	-	**r**	**r**	**8**	**r**
(Arrows-Ford Cosworth)	24	21	20	24	17	16	25	nq	25	16	24	nq	26	22	24	22
Yannick DALMAS	-	-	-	-	-	-	-	-	-	-	-	-	-	-	-	-
(Lola-Lamborghini)	nq	26ns	nq	nq	nq	nq	-	-	-	-	-	-	-	-	-	-
(AGS-Ford Cosworth)	-	-	-	-	-	-	-	npq	npq	npq	npq	npq	exc	npq	npq	npq
Christian DANNER	**14r**	-	-	**12**	**4**	**8**	-	-	-	-	-	-	-	-	-	-
(Rial-Ford Cosworth)	17	nq	nq	23	26	23	nq	nq	nq	nq	nq	nq	nq	-	-	-
Andrea de CESARIS	**13r**	**10**	**13**	**r**	**8r**	**3**	-	**r**	**7**	**r**	**11**	**r**	**r**	**7**	**10**	**r**
(Dallara-Ford Cosworth)	15	16	10	12	13	9	nq	25	21	18	18	17	19	15	16	9
Martin DONNELLY	-	-	-	-	-	-	**12**	-	-	-	-	-	-	-	-	-
(Arrows-Ford Cosworth)	-	-	-	-	-	-	14	-	-	-	-	-	-	-	-	-
Gregor FOITEK	-	-	-	-	-	-	-	-	-	-	-	-	-	-	-	-
(EuroBrun-Judd)	nq	npq	npq	npq	npq	npq	npq	npq	npq	npq	npq	-	-	-	-	-
(Rial-Ford Cosworth)	-	-	-	-	-	-	-	-	-	-	-	-	-	nq	-	-
Bertrand GACHOT	-	-	-	-	-	-	**13**	**12**	-	**r**	**r**	**r**	-	-	-	-
(Onyx-Ford Cosworth)	npq	npq	npq	npq	npq	npq	11	21	nq	21	23	22	-	-	-	-
(Rial-Ford Cosworth)	-	-	-	-	-	-	-	-	-	-	-	-	-	-	nq	nq
Piercarlo GHINZANI	-	-	-	-	-	-	-	-	-	**r**	-	-	-	**r**	-	**r**
(Osella-Ford Cosworth)	npq	npq	npq	exc	npq	npq	npq	npq	npq	22	npq	npq	npq	25	npq	21
Olivier GROUILLARD	**9**	**dq**	**r**	**8**	-	-	**6**	**7**	**r**	-	**13**	**r**	-	**r**	**r**	**r**
(Ligier-Ford Cosworth)	22	10	16	11	nq	nq	17	24	11	nq	26	21	nq	24	23	24
Mauricio GUGELMIN	**3**	**r**	**r**	-	**dq**	**r**	**ncf**	**r**	**r**	**r**	**7**	**r**	**10**	**r**	**7**	**7**
(March-Judd)	12	19	14	nq	18	17	10	6	14	13	9	25	14	26	20	25
Johnny HERBERT	**4**	**11**	**14**	**15**	**5**	-	-	-	-	-	**r**	-	-	-	-	-
(Benetton-Ford Cosworth)	10	23	24	18	25	nq	-	-	-	-	-	-	-	-	-	-
(Tyrrell-Ford Cosworth)	-	-	-	-	-	-	-	-	-	-	16	-	nq	-	-	-
Stefan JOHANSSON	-	-	-	**r**	**r**	**dq**	**5**	-	**r**	**r**	**8**	-	**3**	-	-	-
(Onyx-Ford Cosworth)	npq	npq	npq	21	19	18	13	npq	24	24	15	npq	12	npq	npq	npq
Nicola LARINI	**dq**	**12r**	-	-	-	**r**	-	**r**	-	-	-	**r**	-	**r**	**r**	**r**
(Osella-Ford Cosworth)	19	14	npq	npq	npq	15	npq	17	npq	npq	npq	24	exc	11	10	11
Oscar LARRAURI	-	-	-	-	-	-	-	-	-	-	-	-	-	-	-	-
(EuroBrun-Judd)	-	-	-	-	-	-	-	-	-	-	-	npq	npq	npq	npq	npq
J J LEHTO	-	-	-	-	-	-	-	-	-	-	-	-	-	**r**	-	**r**
(Onyx-Ford Cosworth)	-	-	-	-	-	-	-	-	-	-	-	-	npq	17	npq	17
Nigel MANSELL	**1**	**r**	**r**	**rf**	**r**	**dq**	**2**	**2f**	**3**	**1f**	**3**	**r**	**r/dq**	-	**r**	**r**
(Ferrari)	6	3	5	3	4	5	3	3	3	12	6	3	3	-	4	7
Pierluigi MARTINI	**r**	**r**	**r**	**r**	**r**	**r**	**r**	**5**	**9**	**r**	**9**	**7**	**5**	**r**	-	**6**
(Minardi-Ford Cosworth)	16	11	11	22	15	11	23	11	13	10	14	15	5	4	-	3
Stefano MODENA	**r**	**r**	**3**	**10**	**r**	**r**	**r**	**r**	**r**	**11**	**r**	-	**14**	**r**	**r**	**8**
(Brabham-Judd)	14	17	8	9	7	7	22	14	16	8	8	exc	11	12	9	8
Roberto MORENO	-	-	**r**	-	-	**r**	-	**r**	-	-	-	-	**r**	-	-	-
(Coloni-Ford Cosworth)	nq	nq	25	nq	nq	26	nq	23	npq	npq	npq	npq	15	npq	npq	npq
Satoru NAKAJIMA	**8**	**nc**	-	**r**	**r**	-	**r**	**8**	**r**	**r**	-	**10**	**7**	**r**	**r**	**4f**
(Lotus-Judd)	21	24	nq	15	23	nq	19	16	18	20	nq	19	25	18	12	23
Alessandro NANNINI	**6**	**3**	**8**	**4**	**r**	**dq**	**r**	**3**	**r**	**r**	**5**	**r**	**4**	**r**	**1**	**2**
(Benetton-Ford Cosworth)	11	7	15	13	3	13	4	9	7	7	7	8	13	14	6	4
Jonathan PALMER	**7**	**6**	**9**	**r**	**9r**	**rf**	**10**	**r**	**r**	**13**	**14**	**r**	**6**	**10**	**r**	-
(Tyrrell-Ford Cosworth)	18	25	23	14	21	14	9	18	19	19	21	14	18	13	26	nq
Riccardo PATRESE	**rf**	**r**	**15**	**2**	**2**	**2**	**3**	**r**	**4**	**r**	**r**	**4**	**r**	**5**	**2**	**3**
(Williams-Renault)	2	4	7	5	14	3	8	5	5	1	5	5	6	6	5	6
Nelson PIQUET	**r**	**r**	**r**	**11**	**r**	**4**	**8**	**4**	**5**	**6**	-	**r**	**r**	**8**	**4**	**r**
(Lotus-Judd)	9	8	19	26	22	19	20	10	8	17	nq	11	20	7	11	18
Emanuele PIRRO	-	-	-	-	-	-	**9**	**11**	**r**	**8**	**10**	**r**	**r**	**r**	**r**	**5**
(Benetton-Ford Cosworth)	-	-	-	-	-	-	24	26	9	25	13	9	16	10	22	13
Alain PROST	**2**	**2f**	**2f**	**5**	**1**	**r**	**1**	**1**	**2**	**4**	**2f**	**1f**	**2**	**3**	**rf**	**r**
(McLaren-Honda)	5	2	2	2	2	1	1	2	2	5	2	4	4	3	2	2
Pierre-Henri RAPHANEL	-	-	**r**	-	-	-	-	-	-	-	-	-	-	-	-	-
(Coloni-Ford Cosworth)	npq	npq	18	npq	npq	npq	npq	npq	npq	npq	-	-	-	-	-	-
(Rial-Ford Cosworth)	-	-	-	-	-	-	-	-	-	-	nq	nq	nq	nq	nq	nq
Luis SALA	**r**	**r**	**r**	-	**r**	**r**	-	**6**	-	**r**	**15**	**8**	**12**	**r**	**r**	-
(Minardi-Ford Cosworth)	23	15	26	nq	20	24	nq	15	nq	23	25	26	9	20	14	nq
Bernd SCHNEIDER	**r**	-	-	-	-	-	-	-	-	-	-	-	-	-	**r**	-
(Zakspeed-Yamaha)	25	npq	npq	npq	npq	npq	npq	npq	npq	npq	npq	npq	npq	npq	21	npq
Ayrton SENNA	**11**	**1**	**1**	**1**	**rf**	**7r**	**r**	**r**	**1f**	**2**	**1**	**r**	**r**	**1f**	**dq**	**r**
(McLaren-Honda)	1	1	1	1	1	2	2	1	1	2	1	1	1	1	1	1
Aguri SUZUKI	-	-	-	-	-	-	-	-	-	-	-	-	-	-	-	-
(Zakspeed-Yamaha)	npq	npq	npq	npq	npq	npq	npq	npq	npq	npq	npq	npq	npq	npq	npq	npq
Gabriele TARQUINI	-	**8**	**r**	**6**	**7r**	**r**	**r**	-	-	-	-	-	-	-	-	-
(AGS-Ford Cosworth)	-	18	13	17	24	25	21	nq	npq	npq	npq	npq	npq	npq	npq	npq
Derek WARWICK	**5**	**5**	**r**	**r**	**r**	**r**	-	**9**	**6**	**10**	**6**	**r**	**r**	**9**	**6**	**r**
(Arrows-Ford Cosworth)	8	12	6	10	10	12	-	19	17	9	10	16	22	16	25	20
Volker WEIDLER	-	-	-	-	-	-	-	-	-	-	-	-	-	-	-	-
(Rial-Ford Cosworth)	npq	npq	npq	npq	npq	npq	npq	npq	exc	nq	-	-	-	-	-	-
Joachim WINKELHOCK	-	-	-	-	-	-	-	-	-	-	-	-	-	-	-	-
(AGS-Ford Cosworth)	npq	npq	npq	npq	npq	npq	npq	-	-	-	-	-	-	-	-	-

1990 RACE RESULTS & GRID POSITIONS

	USA	BR	RSM	MC	CDN	MEX	F	GB	D	H	B	I	P	E	J	AUS
Michele ALBORETO	10	r	-	-	r	17	10	r	r	12	13	12r	9	10	r	-
(Arrows-Ford Cosworth)	21	23	nq	nq	14	17	18	25	19	22	26	22	19	25	24	nq
Jean ALESI	2	7	6	2	r	7	r	8	11r	r	8	r	8	r	-	8
(Tyrrell-Ford Cosworth)	4	7	7	3	8	6	13	6	8	6	9	5	8	4	ns	5
Philippe ALLIOT	-	12	9	r	r	18	9	13	dq	14	-	13	r	r	10	11
(Ligier-Ford Cosworth)	exc	10	16	18	17	22	12	22	24	21	nq	20	20	13	20	19
Paulo BARILLA	r	r	11	r	-	14	-	12	-	15	r	-	-	-	-	-
(Minardi-Ford Cosworth)	14	17	26	19	nq	16	nq	24	nq	23	25	nq	nq	nq	-	-
Gerhard BERGER	rf	2f	2	3	4f	3	5	14r	3	16r	3	3	4	r	r	4
(McLaren-Honda)	1	2	2	5	2	1	2	3	2	3	2	3	4	5	4	2
Éric BERNARD	8	r	13r	6	9	r	8	4	r	6	9	r	r	r	r	r
(Lola-Lamborghini)	15	11	13	24	23	25	11	8	12	12	15	13	10	18	16	23
Thierry BOUTSEN	3	5	r	4	r	5	r	2	6f	1	r	r	r	4	5	5
(Williams-Renault)	9	3	4	6	6	5	8	4	6	1	4	6	7	7	5	9
David BRABHAM	-	-	-	r	-	r	15	-	r	-	r	-	r	-	r	r
(Brabham-Judd)	-	-	nq	25	nq	21	25	nq	21	nq	24	nq	25	nq	22	25
Gary BRABHAM	-	-	-	-	-	-	-	-	-	-	-	-	-	-	-	-
(Life)	npq	npq	-	-	-	-	-	-	-	-	-	-	-	-	-	-
Alex CAFFI	-	r	-	5	8	-	r	7	9	9	10	9	13r	-	9	-
(Arrows-Ford Cosworth)	-	25	nq	22	26	nq	22	17	18	26	19	21	17	-	23	nq
Ivan CAPELLI	r	-	r	r	10	-	2	r	7	r	7	r	r	r	r	r
(Leyton House-Judd)	26	nq	18	23	24	nq	7	10	10	16	12	16	12	19	12	14
Yannick DALMAS	-	r	-	-	-	-	17	-	-	-	-	nc	r	9	-	-
(AGS-Ford Cosworth)	npq	26	-	npq	npq	npq	26	npq	nq	nq	nq	24	24	23	nq	nq
Andrea de CESARIS	r	r	r	r	r	13	dq	r	-	r	r	10	r	r	r	r
(Dallara-Ford Cosworth)	3	9	17	12	25	15	21	23	nq	10	20	25	18	17	25	15
Martin DONNELLY	-	r	8	r	r	8	12	r	r	7	12	r	r	-	-	-
(Lotus-Lamborghini)	19ns	14	11	11	12	12	17	14	20	18	22	11	15	ns	-	-
Gregor FOITEK	r	r	r	7r	r	15	-	-	r	-	-	-	-	-	-	-
(Brabham-Judd)	23	22	-	-	-	-	-	-	-	-	-	-	-	-	-	-
(Onyx-Ford Cosworth)	-	-	23	20	21	23	nq	nq	26	nq	-	-	-	-	-	-
Bertrand GACHOT	-	-	-	-	-	-	-	-	-	-	-	-	-	-	-	-
(Coloni-Subaru)	npq	npq	npq	npq	npq	npq	npq	npq	-	-	-	-	-	-	-	-
(Coloni-Ford Cosworth)	-	-	-	-	-	-	-	-	npq	npq	nq	nq	nq	nq	nq	nq
Bruno GIACOMELLI	-	-	-	-	-	-	-	-	-	-	-	-	-	-	-	-
(Life)	-	-	npq	npq	npq	npq	npq	npq	npq	npq	npq	npq	-	-	-	-
(Life-Judd)	-	-	-	-	-	-	-	-	-	-	-	-	npq	npq	-	-
Olivier GROUILLARD	r	r	r	-	13	19	-	-	-	-	16	r	-	r	-	13
(Osella-Ford Cosworth)	8	21	22	nq	15	20	npq	nq	nq	npq	23	23	nq	21	nq	22
Mauricio GUGELMIN	14	-	r	-	-	-	r	-	r	8	6	r	12	8	r	r
(Leyton House-Judd)	25	nq	12	nq	nq	nq	10	15ns	14	17	14	10	14	12	15	16
Johnny HERBERT	-	-	-	-	-	-	-	-	-	-	-	-	-	-	r	r
(Lotus-Lamborghini)	-	-	-	-	-	-	-	-	-	-	-	-	-	-	14	18
Stefan JOHANSSON	-	-	-	-	-	-	-	-	-	-	-	-	-	-	-	-
(Onyx-Ford Cosworth)	nq	nq	-	-	-	-	-	-	-	-	-	-	-	-	-	-
Claudio LANGES	-	-	-	-	-	-	-	-	-	-	-	-	-	-	-	-
(EuroBrun-Judd)	npq	npq	npq	npq	npq	npq	npq	npq	npq	npq	npq	npq	npq	npq	-	-
Nicola LARINI	r	11	10	r	r	16	14	10	10	11	14	11	10	7	7	10
(Ligier-Ford Cosworth)	13	20	20	17	20	24	19	21	22	25	21	26	22	20	17	12
J J LEHTO	-	-	12	r	r	r	-	-	nc	-	-	-	-	-	-	-
(Onyx-Ford Cosworth)	nq	nq	25	26	22	26	nq	nq	25	nq	-	-	-	-	-	-
Nigel MANSELL	r	4	r	r	3	2	18rf	rf	r	17r	r	4	1	2	r	2f
(Ferrari)	17	5	5	7	7	4	1	1	4	5	5	4	1	3	3	3
Pierluigi MARTINI	7	9	-	r	r	12	r	r	r	r	15	r	11	r	8	9
(Minardi-Ford Cosworth)	2	8	ns	8	16	7	23	18	15	14	16	15	16	11	10	10
Stefano MODENA	5	r	r	r	7	11	13	9	r	r	17r	r	r	r	r	12
(Brabham-Judd)	10	12	14	14	10	10	20	20	17	20	13	17	23	24	21	17
Gianni MORBIDELLI	-	14	-	-	-	-	-	-	-	-	-	-	-	-	r	r
(Dallara-Ford Cosworth)	nq	16	-	-	-	-	-	-	-	-	-	-	-	-	-	-
(Minardi-Ford Cosworth)	-	-	-	-	-	-	-	-	-	-	-	-	-	-	19	20
Roberto MORENO	13	-	r	-	-	-	-	-	-	-	-	-	-	-	2	7
(EuroBrun-Judd)	16	npq	24	nq	nq	exc	npq	npq	npq	npq	npq	npq	npq	npq	-	-
(Benetton-Ford Cosworth)	-	-	-	-	-	-	-	-	-	-	-	-	-	-	8	8
Satoru NAKAJIMA	6	8	r	r	11	r	r	r	r	r	r	6	-	r	6	r
(Tyrrell-Ford Cosworth)	11	19	19	21	13	9	15	12	13	15	10	14	ns	14	13	13
Alessandro NANNINI	11	10r	3f	r	r	4	16r	r	2	r	4	8	6	3	-	-
(Benetton-Ford Cosworth)	22	15	9	16	4	14	5	13	9	7	6	8	9	9	-	-
Riccardo PATRESE	9	13r	1	r	r	9	6	r	5	4f	r	5	7f	5f	4f	6
(Williams-Renault)	12	4	3	4	9	2	6	7	5	2	7	7	5	6	7	6
Nelson PIQUET	4	6	5	dq	2	6	4	5	r	3	5	7	5	r	1	1
(Benetton-Ford Cosworth)	6	13	8	10	5	8	9	11	7	9	8	9	6	8	6	7
Emanuele PIRRO	-	-	r	r	r	r	r	11	r	10	r	r	15	r	r	r
(Dallara-Ford Cosworth)	-	-	21	9	19	18	24	19	23	13	17	19	13	16	18	21
Alain PROST	r	1	4	r	5	1f	1	1	4	r	2f	2	3	1	r	3
(Ferrari)	7	6	6	2	3	13	4	5	3	8	3	2	2	2	2	4
Bernd SCHNEIDER	12	-	-	-	-	-	-	-	-	-	-	-	-	-	-	-
(Arrows-Ford Cosworth)	20	-	-	-	-	-	-	-	-	-	-	-	-	nq	-	-
Ayrton SENNA	1	3	r	1f	1	20r	3	3	1	2	1	1f	2	r	r	r
(McLaren-Honda)	5	1	1	1	1	3	3	2	1	4	1	1	3	1	1	1
Aguri SUZUKI	r	r	r	r	12	r	7	6	r	r	r	r	14r	6	3	r
(Lola-Lamborghini)	18	18	15	15	18	19	14	9	11	19	11	18	11	15	9	24
Gabriele TARQUINI	-	-	-	-	-	-	-	r	-	13	-	-	-	r	-	r
(AGS-Ford Cosworth)	npq	npq	npq	npq	npq	npq	nq	26	npq	24	nq	nq	nq	22	nq	26
Derek WARWICK	r	r	7	r	6	10	11	r	8	5	11	r	r	r	r	r
(Lotus-Lamborghini)	24	24	10	13	11	11	16	16	16	11	18	12	21	10	11	11

Onyx renamed Monteverdi for Germany and Hungary

1991 RACE RESULTS & GRID POSITIONS

	USA	BR	RSM	MC	CDN	MEX	F	GB	D	H	B	I	P	E	J	AUS
Michele ALBORETO	r	-	-	r	r	r	r	r	-	-	-	-	15	r	-	13
(Footwork-Porsche)	25	nq	nq	25	21	26	-	-	-	-	-	-	-	-	-	-
(Footwork-Ford Cosworth)	-	-	-	-	-	-	25	26	nq	nq	npq	nq	24	24	nq	15
Jean ALESI	12rf	6	r	3	r	r	4	r	3	5	r	r	3	4	r	r
(Ferrari)	6	5	7	9	7	4	6	6	6	6	5	6	6	7	6	7
Julian BAILEY	-	-	6	-	-	-	-	-	-	-	-	-	-	-	-	-
(Lotus-Judd)	nq	nq	26	nq	-	-	-	-	-	-	-	-	-	-	-	-
Fabrizio BARBAZZA	-	-	-	-	-	-	-	-	-	-	-	-	-	-	-	-
(AGS-Ford Cosworth)	-	-	nq	nq	nq	nq	nq	nq	npq	npq	npq	npq	npq	npq	-	-
Michael BARTELS	-	-	-	-	-	-	-	-	-	-	-	-	-	-	-	-
(Lotus-Judd)	-	-	-	-	-	-	-	-	nq	nq	-	nq	-	nq	-	-
Gerhard BERGER	r	3	2f	r	r	r	r	2	4	4	2	4	r	r	1	3f
(McLaren-Honda)	7	4	5	6	6	5	5	4	3	5	4	3	2	1	1	2
Éric BERNARD	r	r	r	9	r	6	r	r	r	r	r	r	-	r	-	-
(Lola-Ford Cosworth)	19	11	17	21	19	18	23	21	25	21	20	24	nq	23	nq	-

	USA	BR	RSM	MC	CDN	MEX	F	GB	D	H	B	I	P	E	J	AUS
Mark BLUNDELL	r	r	8	r	-	r	r	r	12	r	6	12	r	r	-	17
(Brabham-Yamaha)	24	25	23	22	nq	12	17	12	21	20	13	11	15	12	npq	17
Thierry BOUTSEN	r	10	7	7	r	8	12	r	9	17r	11	r	16	r	9	r
(Ligier-Lamborghini)	20	18	24	16	16	14	16	19	17	19	18	21	20	26	17	20
Martin BRUNDLE	11	12	11	-	r	r	r	r	11	r	9	13	12	10	5	-
(Brabham-Yamaha)	12	26	18	exc	20	17	24	14	15	10	16	19	19	11	19	nq
Alex CAFFI	-	-	-	-	-	-	-	-	-	-	-	-	-	-	10	15
(Footwork-Porsche)	nq	nq	nq	nq	-	-	-	-	-	-	-	-	-	-	-	-
(Footwork-Ford Cosworth)	-	-	-	-	-	-	-	-	npq	npq	nq	npq	npq	npq	26	23
Ivan CAPELLI	r	r	r	r	r	r	r	r	r	6	r	8	17r	r	-	-
(Leyton House-Ilmor)	18	15	22	18	13	22	15	16	12	9	12	12	9	8	-	-
Pedro CHAVES	-	-	-	-	-	-	-	-	-	-	-	-	-	-	-	-
(Coloni-Ford Cosworth)	npq	npq	npq	npq	npq	npq	npq	npq	npq	npq	npq	npq	npq	-	-	-
Erik COMAS	-	r	10	10	8	-	11	-	r	10	r	11	11	r	r	18
(Ligier-Lamborghini)	nq	23	19	23	26	nq	14	nq	26	25	26	22	23	25	20	22
Andrea de CESARIS	-	r	r	r	4	4r	6	r	5	7	13r	7	8	r	r	8
(Jordan-Ford Cosworth)	npq	13	11	10	11	11	13	13	7	17	11	14	14	17	11	12
Bertrand GACHOT	10r	13r	r	8	5	r	r	6	6	9f	-	-	-	-	-	-
(Jordan-Ford Cosworth)	14	10	12	24	14	20	19	17	11	16	-	-	-	-	-	-
(Lola-Ford Cosworth)	-	-	-	-	-	-	-	-	-	-	-	-	-	-	-	nq
Olivier GROUILLARD	-	-	-	-	-	r	r	-	-	-	10	r	-	-	-	-
(Fomet-Ford Cosworth)	npq	npq	npq	npq	npq	10	21	npq	npq	nq	23	26	npq	-	-	-
(AGS-Ford Cosworth)	-	-	-	-	-	-	-	-	-	-	-	-	-	npq	-	-
Mauricio GUGELMIN	r	r	12r	r	r	r	7	r	r	11	r	15	7	7	8	14r
(Leyton House-Ilmor)	23	8	15	15	23	21	9	9	16	13	15	18	7	13	18	14
Mika HÄKKINEN	r	9	5	r	r	9	-	12	r	14	r	14	14	r	r	19
(Lotus-Judd)	13	22	25	26	24	24	nq	25	23	26	24	25	26	21	21	25
Naoki HATTORI	-	-	-	-	-	-	-	-	-	-	-	-	-	-	-	-
(Coloni-Ford Cosworth)	-	-	-	-	-	-	-	-	-	-	-	-	-	-	npq	npq
Johnny HERBERT	-	-	-	-	-	10	10	14r	-	-	7	-	r	-	r	11
(Lotus-Judd)	-	-	-	-	nq	25	20	24	-	-	21	-	22	-	23	21
Stefan JOHANSSON	-	-	-	-	r	-	-	-	-	-	-	-	-	-	-	-
(AGS-Ford Cosworth)	nq	nq	-	-	-	-	-	-	-	-	-	-	-	-	-	-
(Footwork-Porsche)	-	-	-	-	25	nq	-	-	-	-	-	-	-	-	-	-
(Footwork-Ford Cosworth)	-	-	-	-	-	-	nq	nq	-	-	-	-	-	-	-	-
Nicola LARINI	7	-	-	-	-	-	-	-	r	16	-	16	-	-	-	r
(Lamborghini)	17	npq	npq	npq	npq	exc	npq	npq	24	24	nq	23	nq	nq	nq	19
J J LEHTO	r	r	3	11	r	r	r	13	r	r	r	r	r	8	r	12
(Dallara-Judd)	10	19	16	13	17	16	26	11	20	12	14	20	18	15	12	11
Nigel MANSELL	r	rf	r	2	6rf	2f	1f	1f	1	2	r	1	dqf	1	r	2
(Williams-Renault)	4	3	4	5	2	2	4	1	1	3	3	2	4	2	3	3
Pierluigi MARTINI	9r	r	4	12	7	r	9	9	r	r	12	r	4	13	r	r
(Minardi-Ferrari)	15	20	9	14	18	15	12	23	10	18	9	10	8	19	7	10
Stefano MODENA	4	r	r	r	2	11	r	7	13	12	r	r	r	16	6	10
(Tyrrell-Honda)	11	9	6	2	9	8	11	10	14	8	10	13	12	14	14	9
Gianni MORBIDELLI	r	8	r	r	r	7	r	11	r	13	r	9	9	14r	r	6
(Minardi-Ferrari)	26	21	8	17	15	23	10	20	19	23	19	17	13	16	8	-
(Ferrari)	-	-	-	-	-	-	-	-	-	-	-	-	-	-	-	8
Roberto MORENO	r	7	13r	4	r	5	r	r	8	8	4f	r	10	-	-	16
(Benetton-Ford Cosworth)	8	14	13	8	5	9	8	7	9	15	8	-	-	-	-	-
(Jordan-Ford Cosworth)	-	-	-	-	-	-	-	-	-	-	-	9	16	-	-	-
(Minardi-Ferrari)	-	-	-	-	-	-	-	-	-	-	-	-	-	-	-	18
Satoru NAKAJIMA	5	r	r	r	10	12	r	8	r	15	r	r	13	17	r	r
(Tyrrell-Honda)	16	16	10	11	12	13	18	15	13	14	22	15	21	18	15	24
Riccardo PATRESE	r	2	r	r	3	1	5	r	2f	3	5	r	1	3f	3	5
(Williams-Renault)	3	2	2	3	1	1	1	3	4	2	17	4	1	4	5	4
Nelson PIQUET	3	5	r	r	1	r	8	5	r	r	3	6	5	11	7	4
(Benetton-Ford Cosworth)	5	7	14	4	8	6	7	8	8	11	6	8	11	10	10	5
Emanuele PIRRO	r	11	-	6	9	-	-	10	10	r	8	10	r	15	r	7
(Dallara-Judd)	9	12	npq	12	10	npq	npq	18	18	7	25	16	17	9	16	13
Alain PROST	2	4	r	5f	r	r	2	3	r	r	r	3	r	2	4	-
(Ferrari)	2	6	3	7	4	7	2	5	5	4	2	5	5	6	4	-
Michael SCHUMACHER	-	-	-	-	-	-	-	-	-	-	r	5	6	6	r	r
(Jordan-Ford Cosworth)	-	-	-	-	-	-	-	-	-	-	7	-	-	-	-	-
(Benetton-Ford Cosworth)	-	-	-	-	-	-	-	-	-	-	-	7	10	5	9	6
Ayrton SENNA	1	1	1	1	r	3	3	4r	7r	1	1	2f	2	5	2f	1
(McLaren-Honda)	1	1	1	1	3	3	3	2	2	1	1	1	3	3	2	1
Aguri SUZUKI	6	-	r	r	r	r	r	r	r	r	-	-	r	-	r	-
(Lola-Ford Cosworth)	21	17ns	20	19	22	19	22	22	22	22	nq	nq	25	nq	25	nq
Gabriele TARQUINI	8	r	-	r	-	-	-	-	-	-	-	-	-	12	11	-
(AGS-Ford Cosworth)	22	24	nq	20	nq	nq	nq	nq	nq	npq	npq	npq	nq	-	-	-
(Fomet-Ford Cosworth)	-	-	-	-	-	-	-	-	-	-	-	-	-	22	24	npq
Eric van de POELE	-	-	9r	-	-	-	-	-	-	-	-	-	-	-	-	-
(Lamborghini)	npq	npq	21	npq	npq	npq	npq	npq	nq	nq	nq	nq	nq	nq	nq	nq
Karl WENDLINGER	-	-	-	-	-	-	-	-	-	-	-	-	-	-	r	20
(Leyton House-Ilmor)	-	-	-	-	-	-	-	-	-	-	-	-	-	-	22	26
Alessandro ZANARDI	-	-	-	-	-	-	-	-	-	-	-	-	-	9	r	9
(Jordan-Ford Cosworth)	-	-	-	-	-	-	-	-	-	-	-	-	-	20	13	16

1992 RACE RESULTS & GRID POSITIONS

	ZA	MEX	BR	E	RSM	MC	CDN	F	GB	D	H	B	I	P	J	AUS
Michele ALBORETO	10	13	6	5	5	7	7	7	7	9	7	r	7	6	15	r
(Footwork-Mugen Honda)	17	25	14	16	9	11	16	14	12	17	7	14	16	8	24	11
Jean ALESI	r	r	4	3	r	r	3	r	r	5	r	r	r	r	5	4
(Ferrari)	5	10	6	8	7	4	8	6	8	5	9	5	3	10	15	6
Giovanna AMATI	-	-	-	-	-	-	-	-	-	-	-	-	-	-	-	-
(Brabham-Judd)	nq	nq	nq	-	-	-	-	-	-	-	-	-	-	-	-	-
Paul BELMONDO	-	-	-	12	13	-	14	-	-	13	9	-	-	-	-	-
(March-Ilmor)	nq	nq	nq	23	24	nq	20	nq	nq	22	17	-	-	-	-	-
Gerhard BERGER	5	4f	r	4	r	r	1f	r	5	r	3	r	4	2	2	1
(McLaren-Honda)	3	5	4	7	4	5	4	4	5	4	5	6	5	4	4	4
Thierry BOUTSEN	r	10	r	r	r	12	10	r	10	7	r	r	r	8	r	5
(Ligier-Renault)	14	22	10	14	10	22	21	9	13	8	8	7	8	11	10	22
Martin BRUNDLE	r	r	r	r	4	5	r	3	3	4	5	4	2	4	3	3
(Benetton-Ford Cosworth)	8	4	7	6	6	7	7	7	6	9	6	9	9	6	13	8
Ivan CAPELLI	r	r	r	10r	r	r	r	r	9	r	6	r	r	r	-	-
(Ferrari)	9	20	11	5	8	8	9	8	14	12	10	12	7	16	-	-
Andrea CHIESA	-	r	-	r	-	-	-	r	-	-	-	-	-	-	-	-
(Fondmetal-Ford Cosworth)	nq	23	nq	20	nq	nq	nq	26	nq	nq	-	-	-	-	-	-
Erik COMAS	7	9	r	r	9	10	6	5	8	6	r	-	r	r	r	r
(Ligier-Renault)	13	26	15	10	13	23	22	10	10	7	11	nq	15	14	8	9
Andrea de CESARIS	r	5	r	r	14r	r	5	r	r	r	8	8	6	9	4	r
(Tyrrell-Ilmor)	10	11	13	11	14	10	14	19	18	20	19	13	21	12	9	7
Christian FITTIPALDI	r	r	r	11	r	8	13r	-	-	-	-	-	-	12	6	9
(Minardi-Lamborghini)	20	17	20	22	25	17	25	nq	-	-	-	nq	nq	26	12	17
Bertrand GACHOT	r	11	r	r	r	6	dq	r	r	14	r	18r	r	r	r	r
(Venturi Larrousse-Lamborghini)	22	13	18	24	19	15	19	13	11	25	15	20	10	13	18	21
Olivier GROUILLARD	r	r	r	r	8	r	12	11	11	r	r	r	r	r	r	r
(Tyrrell-Ilmor)	12	16	17	15	20	24	26	22	20	14	22	22	18	15	21	13
Mauricio GUGELMIN	11	r	r	r	7	r	r	r	r	15	10	14	r	r	r	r
(Jordan-Yamaha)	23	8	21	17	18	13	24	24	24	23	21	24	26	20	25	20

	ZA	MEX	BR	E	RSM	MC	CDN	F	GB	D	H	B	I	P	J	AUS
Mika HÄKKINEN	**9**	**6**	**10**	**r**	-	**r**	**r**	**4**	**6**	**r**	**4**	**6**	**r**	**5**	**r**	**7**
(Lotus-Ford Cosworth)	21	18	24	21	nq	14	10	11	9	13	16	8	11	7	7	10
Johnny HERBERT	**6**	**7**	**r**	**r**	**r**	**r**	**r**	**6**	**r**	**r**	**r**	**13r**	**r**	**r**	**r**	**13**
(Lotus-Ford Cosworth)	11	12	26	26	26	9	6	12	7	11	13	10	13	9	6	12
Damon HILL	-	-	-	-	-	-	-	-	**16**	-	**11**	-	-	-	-	-
(Brabham-Judd)	-	-	-	nq	nq	nq	nq	nq	26	nq	25	-	-	-	-	-
Ukyo KATAYAMA	**12**	**12**	**9**	-	**r**	-	**r**	**r**	**r**	**r**	**r**	**17**	**9r**	**r**	**11**	**r**
(Venturi Larrousse-Lamborghini)	18	24	25	nq	17	npq	11	18	16	16	20	26	23	25	20	26
Jan LAMMERS	-	-	-	-	-	-	-	-	-	-	-	-	-	-	**r**	**12**
(March-Ilmor)	-	-	-	-	-	-	-	-	-	-	-	-	-	-	23	25
Nicola LARINI	-	-	-	-	-	-	-	-	-	-	-	-	-	-	**12**	**11**
(Ferrari)	-	-	-	-	-	-	-	-	-	-	-	-	-	-	11	19
J J LEHTO	**r**	**8**	**8**	**r**	**11r**	**9**	**9**	**9**	**13**	**10**	-	**7**	**11r**	**r**	**9**	**r**
(Dallara-Ferrari)	24	7	16	12	16	20	23	17	19	21	nq	16	14	19	22	24
Nigel MANSELL	**1f**	**1**	**1**	**1f**	**1**	**2f**	**r**	**1f**	**1f**	**1**	**2f**	**2**	**rf**	**1**	**rf**	**r**
(Williams-Renault)	1	1	1	1	1	1	3	1	1	1	2	1	1	1	1	1
Pierluigi MARTINI	**r**	**r**	**r**	**6**	**6**	**r**	**8**	**10**	**15**	**11**	**r**	**r**	**8**	**r**	**10**	**r**
(Dallara-Ferrari)	25	9	8	13	15	18	15	25	22	18	26	19	22	21	19	14
Perry McCARTHY	-	-	-	-	-	-	-	-	-	-	-	-	-	-	-	-
(Andrea Moda-Judd)	-	-	-	npq	npq	npq	-	-	npq	exc	npq	nq	-	-	-	-
Stefano MODENA	-	**r**	**r**	-	**r**	**r**	**r**	**r**	**r**	-	**r**	**15**	-	**13**	**7**	**6**
(Jordan-Yamaha)	nq	15	12	nq	23	21	17	20	23	nq	24	17	nq	24	17	15
Gianni MORBIDELLI	**r**	**r**	**7**	**r**	**r**	**r**	**11**	**8**	**17r**	**12**	-	**16**	**r**	**14**	**14**	**10**
(Minardi-Lamborghini)	19	21	23	25	21	12	13	16	25	26	nq	23	12	18	14	16
Roberto MORENO	-	-	-	-	-	**r**	-	-	-	-	-	-	-	-	-	-
(Andrea Moda-Judd)	-	-	npq	npq	npq	26	npq	-	npq	npq	nq	nq	-	-	-	-
Emanuele NASPETTI	-	-	-	-	-	-	-	-	-	-	-	**12**	**r**	**11**	**13**	**r**
(March-Ilmor)	-	-	-	-	-	-	-	-	-	-	-	21	24	23	26	23
Riccardo PATRESE	**2**	**2**	**2f**	**r**	**2f**	**3**	**r**	**2**	**2**	**8rf**	**r**	**3**	**5**	**r**	**1**	**r**
(Williams-Renault)	4	2	2	4	2	2	2	2	2	2	1	4	4	2	2	3
Michael SCHUMACHER	**4**	**3**	**3**	**2**	**r**	**4**	**2**	**r**	**4**	**3**	**r**	**1f**	**3**	**7**	**r**	**2f**
(Benetton-Ford Cosworth)	6	3	5	2	5	6	5	5	4	6	4	3	6	5	5	5
Ayrton SENNA	**3**	**r**	**r**	**9r**	**3**	**1**	**r**	**r**	**r**	**2**	**1**	**5**	**1**	**3f**	**r**	**r**
(McLaren-Honda)	2	6	3	3	3	3	1	3	3	3	3	2	2	3	3	2
Aguri SUZUKI	**8**	-	**r**	**7**	**10**	**11**	-	**r**	**12**	**r**	**r**	**9**	**r**	**10**	**8**	**8**
(Footwork-Mugen Honda)	16	nq	22	19	11	19	nq	15	17	15	14	25	19	17	16	18
Gabriele TARQUINI	**r**	**r**	**r**	**r**	**r**	**r**	**r**	**r**	**14**	**r**	**r**	**r**	**r**	-	-	-
(Fondmetal-Ford Cosworth)	15	14	19	18	22	25	18	23	15	19	12	11	20	-	-	-
Eric van de POELE	**13**	-	-	-	-	-	-	-	-	-	**r**	**10**	**r**	-	-	-
(Brabham-Judd)	26	nq	nq	nq	nq	nq	nq	nq	nq	nq	-	-	-	-	-	-
(Fondmetal-Ford Cosworth)	-	-	-	-	-	-	-	-	-	-	18	15	25	-	-	-
Karl WENDLINGER	**r**	**r**	**r**	**8**	**12**	**r**	**4**	**r**	**r**	**16**	**r**	**11**	**10**	**r**	-	-
(March-Ilmor)	7	19	9	9	12	16	12	21	21	10	23	18	17	22	-	-
Alessandro ZANARDI	-	-	-	-	-	-	-	-	-	**r**	-	-	-	-	-	-
(Minardi-Lamborghini)	-	-	-	-	-	-	-	-	nq	24	nq	-	-	-	-	-

1993 RACE RESULTS & GRID POSITIONS

	ZA	BR	EUR	RSM	E	MC	CDN	F	GB	D	H	B	I	P	J	AUS
Michele ALBORETO	**r**	**11**	**11**	-	-	**r**	-	-	-	**16**	**r**	**14**	**r**	**r**	-	-
(Lola-Ferrari)	25	25	24	nq	nq	24	nq	nq	nq	26	25	25	21	25	-	-
Jean ALESI	**r**	**8**	**r**	**r**	**r**	**3**	**r**	**r**	**9**	**7**	**r**	**r**	**2**	**4**	**r**	**4**
(Ferrari)	5	9	9	9	8	5	6	6	12	10	8	4	3	5	14	7
Philippe ALLIOT	**r**	**7**	**r**	**5**	**r**	**12**	**r**	**9**	**11**	**12**	**8**	**12**	**9**	**10**	-	-
(Larrousse-Lamborghini)	11	11	15	14	13	15	15	10	24	23	19	18	16	20	-	-
Michael ANDRETTI	**r**	**r**	**r**	**r**	**5**	**8**	**14**	**6**	**r**	**r**	**r**	**8**	**3**	-	-	-
(McLaren-Ford Cosworth)	9	5	6	6	7	9	12	16	11	12	11	14	9	-	-	-
Marco APICELLA	-	-	-	-	-	-	-	-	-	-	-	-	**r**	-	-	-
(Jordan-Hart)	-	-	-	-	-	-	-	-	-	-	-	-	23	-	-	-
Luca BADOER	**r**	**12**	-	**7**	**r**	-	**15**	**r**	**r**	**r**	**r**	**13**	**10**	**14**	-	-
(Lola-Ferrari)	26	21	nq	24	22	nq	25	22	25	25	26	24	25	26	-	-
Fabrizio BARBAZZA	**r**	**r**	**6**	**6**	**r**	**11**	**r**	**r**	-	-	-	-	-	-	-	-
(Minardi-Ford Cosworth)	24	24	20	25	25	25	23	24	-	-	-	-	-	-	-	-
Rubens BARRICHELLO	**r**	**r**	**10r**	**r**	**12**	**9**	**r**	**7**	**10**	**r**	**r**	**r**	**r**	**13**	**5**	**11**
(Jordan-Hart)	14	14	12	13	17	16	14	8	15	17	16	13	19	15	12	13
Gerhard BERGER	**6r**	**r**	**r**	**r**	**6**	**14r**	**4**	**14**	**r**	**6**	**3**	**10r**	**r**	**r**	**r**	**5**
(Ferrari)	15	13	8	8	11	7	5	14	13	9	6	16	6	8	5	6
Mark BLUNDELL	**3**	**5**	**r**	**r**	**7**	**r**	**r**	**r**	**7**	**3**	**7**	**11r**	**r**	**r**	**7**	**9**
(Ligier-Renault)	8	10	21	7	12	21	10	4	9	5	12	15	14	10	17	14
Thierry BOUTSEN	-	-	**r**	**r**	**11**	**r**	**12**	**11**	**r**	**13**	**9**	**r**	-	-	-	-
(Jordan-Hart)	-	-	19	19	21	23	24	20	23	24	24	20	-	-	-	-
Martin BRUNDLE	**r**	**r**	**r**	**3**	**r**	**6**	**5**	**5**	**14r**	**8**	**5**	**7**	**r**	**6**	**9r**	**6**
(Ligier-Renault)	12	16	22	10	18	13	7	3	6	6	13	11	12	11	15	8
Ivan CAPELLI	**r**	-	-	-	-	-	-	-	-	-	-	-	-	-	-	-
(Jordan-Hart)	18	nq	-	-	-	-	-	-	-	-	-	-	-	-	-	-
Erik COMAS	**r**	**10**	**9**	**r**	**9**	**r**	**8**	**16r**	**r**	**r**	**r**	**r**	**6**	**11**	**r**	**12**
(Larrousse-Lamborghini)	19	17	17	17	14	10	13	9	17	16	18	19	20	22	21	21
Andrea de CESARIS	**r**	**r**	**r**	**r**	**dq**	**10**	**r**	**15**	**nc**	**r**	**11**	**r**	**13r**	**12**	**r**	**13**
(Tyrrell-Yamaha)	23	23	25	18	24	19	19	25	21	19	22	17	18	17	18	15
Christian FITTIPALDI	**4**	**r**	**7**	**r**	**8**	**5**	**9**	**8**	**12r**	**11**	**r**	**r**	**8r**	**9**	-	-
(Minardi-Ford Cosworth)	13	20	16	23	20	17	17	23	19	20	14	22	24	24	-	-
Jean-Marc GOUNON	-	-	-	-	-	-	-	-	-	-	-	-	-	-	**r**	**r**
(Minardi-Ford Cosworth)	-	-	-	-	-	-	-	-	-	-	-	-	-	-	24	22
Mika HÄKKINEN	-	-	-	-	-	-	-	-	-	-	-	-	-	**r**	**3**	**r**
(McLaren-Ford Cosworth)	-	-	-	-	-	-	-	-	-	-	-	-	-	3	3	5
Johnny HERBERT	**r**	**4**	**4**	**8r**	**r**	**r**	**10**	**r**	**4**	**10**	**r**	**5**	**r**	**r**	**11**	**r**
(Lotus-Ford Cosworth)	17	12	11	12	10	14	20	19	7	13	20	10	7	14	19	20
Damon HILL	**r**	**2**	**2**	**r**	**r**	**2**	**3**	**2**	**rf**	**15r**	**1**	**1**	**1f**	**3f**	**4**	**3f**
(Williams-Renault)	4	2	2	2	2	4	2	1	2	2	2	2	2	1	6	3
Eddie IRVINE	-	-	-	-	-	-	-	-	-	-	-	-	-	-	**6**	**r**
(Jordan-Hart)	-	-	-	-	-	-	-	-	-	-	-	-	-	-	8	19
Ukyo KATAYAMA	**r**	**r**	**r**	**r**	**r**	**r**	**17**	**r**	**13**	**r**	**10**	**15**	**14**	**r**	**r**	**r**
(Tyrrell-Yamaha)	21	22	18	22	23	22	22	21	22	21	23	23	17	21	13	18
Pedro LAMY	-	-	-	-	-	-	-	-	-	-	-	-	**11r**	**r**	**13r**	**r**
(Lotus-Ford Cosworth)	-	-	-	-	-	-	-	-	-	-	-	-	26	18	20	23
J J LEHTO	**5**	**r**	**r**	**4r**	**r**	**r**	**7**	**r**	**8**	**r**	**r**	**9**	**r**	**7**	**8**	**r**
(Sauber-Ilmor)	6	7	7	16	9	11	11	18	16	18	15	9	13	12	11	12
Pierluigi MARTINI	-	-	-	-	-	-	-	-	**r**	**14**	**r**	**r**	**7r**	**8**	**10**	**r**
(Minardi-Ford Cosworth)	-	-	-	-	-	-	-	-	20	22	7	21	22	19	22	16
Emanuele NASPETTI	-	-	-	-	-	-	-	-	-	-	-	-	-	**r**	-	-
(Jordan-Hart)	-	-	-	-	-	-	-	-	-	-	-	-	-	23	-	-
Riccardo PATRESE	**r**	**r**	**5**	**r**	**4**	**r**	**r**	**10**	**3**	**5**	**2**	**6**	**5**	**16r**	**r**	**8r**
(Benetton-Ford Cosworth)	7	6	10	11	5	6	4	12	5	7	5	8	10	7	10	9
Alain PROST	**1f**	**r**	**3**	**1f**	**1**	**4f**	**1**	**1**	**1**	**1**	**12f**	**3f**	**12r**	**2**	**2f**	**2**
(Williams-Renault)	1	1	1	1	1	1	1	2	1	1	1	1	1	2	1	2
Michael SCHUMACHER	**r**	**3f**	**r**	**2**	**3f**	**r**	**2f**	**3f**	**2**	**2f**	**r**	**2**	**r**	**1**	**r**	**r**
(Benetton-Ford Cosworth)	3	4	3	3	4	2	3	7	3	3	3	3	5	6	4	4
Ayrton SENNA	**2**	**1**	**1f**	**r**	**2**	**1**	**18r**	**4**	**5r**	**4**	**r**	**4**	**r**	**r**	**1**	**1**
(McLaren-Ford Cosworth)	2	3	4	4	3	3	8	5	4	4	4	5	4	4	2	1
Aguri SUZUKI	**r**	**r**	**r**	**9**	**10**	**r**	**13**	**12**	**r**	**r**	**r**	**r**	**r**	**r**	**r**	**7**
(Footwork-Mugen Honda)	20	19	23	21	19	18	16	13	10	8	10	6	8	16	9	10

	ZA	BR	EUR	RSM	E	MC	CDN	F	GB	D	H	B	I	P	J	AUS
Toshio SUZUKI	**-**	**-**	**-**	**-**	**-**	**-**	**-**	**-**	**-**	**-**	**-**	**-**	**-**	**-**	**12**	**14**
(Larrousse-Lamborghini)	-	-	-	-	-	-	-	-	-	-	-	-	-	-	23	24
Derek WARWICK	**7r**	**9**	**r**	**r**	**13**	**r**	**16**	**13**	**6**	**17**	**4**	**r**	**r**	**15r**	**14r**	**10**
(Footwork-Mugen Honda)	22	18	14	15	16	12	18	15	8	11	9	7	11	9	7	17
Karl WENDLINGER	**r**	**r**	**r**	**r**	**r**	**13**	**6**	**r**	**r**	**9**	**6**	**r**	**4**	**5**	**r**	**15r**
(Sauber-Ilmor)	10	8	5	5	6	8	9	11	18	14	17	12	15	13	16	11
Alessandro ZANARDI	**r**	**6**	**8**	**r**	**14r**	**7**	**11**	**r**	**r**	**r**	**r**	**-**	**-**	**-**	**-**	**-**
(Lotus-Ford Cosworth)	16	15	13	20	15	20	21	17	14	15	21	ns	-	-	-	-

1994 RACE RESULTS & GRID POSITIONS

	BR	PAC	RSM	MC	E	CDN	F	GB	D	H	B	I	P	EUR	J	AUS
Philippe ADAMS	**-**	**-**	**-**	**-**	**-**	**-**	**-**	**-**	**-**	**-**	**r**	**-**	**16**	**-**	**-**	**-**
(Lotus-Mugen Honda)	-	-	-	-	-	-	-	-	-	-	26	-	25	-	-	-
Michele ALBORETO	**r**	**r**	**r**	**6**	**r**	**11**	**r**	**r**	**r**	**7**	**9**	**r**	**13**	**14**	**r**	**r**
(Minardi-Ford Cosworth)	22	15	15	12	14	18	21	17	23	20	18	22	19	20	21	16
Jean ALESI	**3**	**-**	**-**	**5**	**4**	**3**	**r**	**2**	**r**	**r**	**r**	**r**	**r**	**10**	**3**	**6**
(Ferrari)	3	-	-	5	6	2	4	4	2	13	5	1	5	16	7	8
Philippe ALLIOT	**-**	**-**	**-**	**-**	**-**	**-**	**-**	**-**	**-**	**r**	**r**	**-**	**-**	**-**	**-**	**-**
(McLaren-Peugeot)	-	-	-	-	-	-	-	-	-	14	-	-	-	-	-	-
(Larrousse-Ford Cosworth)	-	-	-	-	-	-	-	-	-	-	19	-	-	-	-	-
Rubens BARRICHELLO	**4**	**3**	**-**	**r**	**r**	**7**	**r**	**4**	**r**	**r**	**r**	**4**	**4**	**12**	**r**	**4**
(Jordan-Hart)	14	8	nq	15	5	6	7	6	11	10	1	16	8	5	10	5
Paul BELMONDO	**-**	**-**	**-**	**r**	**r**	**-**	**-**	**-**	**-**	**-**	**-**	**-**	**-**	**-**	**-**	**-**
(Pacific-Ilmor)	nq	nq	nq	24	26	nq	nq	nq	nq	nq	nq	nq	nq	nq	nq	nq
Olivier BERETTA	**r**	**r**	**r**	**8**	**r**	**r**	**r**	**14**	**7**	**9**	**-**	**-**	**-**	**-**	**-**	**-**
(Larrousse-Ford Cosworth)	23	21	23	18	17	22	25	24	24	25	-	-	-	-	-	-
Gerhard BERGER	**r**	**2**	**r**	**3**	**r**	**4**	**3**	**r**	**1**	**12r**	**r**	**2**	**r**	**5**	**r**	**2**
(Ferrari)	17	5	3	3	7	3	5	3	1	4	11	2	1	6	11	11
Éric BERNARD	**r**	**10**	**12**	**r**	**8**	**13**	**r**	**13**	**3**	**10**	**10**	**7**	**10**	**18**	**-**	**-**
(Ligier-Renault)	20	18	17	21	20	24	15	23	14	18	16	12	21	-	-	-
(Lotus-Mugen Honda)	-	-	-	-	-	-	-	-	-	-	-	-	-	22	-	-
Mark BLUNDELL	**r**	**r**	**9**	**r**	**3**	**10r**	**10**	**r**	**r**	**5**	**5**	**r**	**r**	**13**	**r**	**r**
(Tyrrell-Yamaha)	12	12	12	10	11	13	17	11	7	11	12	21	12	14	13	13
David BRABHAM	**12**	**r**	**r**	**r**	**10**	**14**	**r**	**15**	**r**	**11**	**r**	**r**	**r**	**r**	**12**	**r**
(Simtek-Ford Cosworth)	26	25	24	22	24	25	24	25	25	23	21	26	24	25	24	24
Martin BRUNDLE	**r**	**r**	**8**	**2**	**11r**	**r**	**r**	**r**	**r**	**4r**	**r**	**5**	**6**	**r**	**r**	**3**
(McLaren-Peugeot)	18	6	13	8	8	12	12	9	13	6	13	15	7	15	9	9
Erik COMAS	**9**	**6**	**r**	**10**	**r**	**r**	**11r**	**r**	**6**	**8**	**r**	**8**	**r**	**r**	**9**	**-**
(Larrousse-Ford Cosworth)	13	16	18	13	16	21	20	22	22	21	22	24	22	23	22	-
David COULTHARD	**-**	**-**	**-**	**-**	**r**	**5**	**-**	**5**	**rf**	**r**	**4**	**6r**	**2f**	**-**	**-**	**-**
(Williams-Renault)	-	-	-	-	9	5	-	7	6	3	7	5	3	-	-	-
Yannick DALMAS	**-**	**-**	**-**	**-**	**-**	**-**	**-**	**-**	**-**	**-**	**-**	**r**	**14**	**-**	**-**	**-**
(Larrousse-Ford Cosworth)	-	-	-	-	-	-	-	-	-	-	-	23	23	-	-	-
Andrea de CESARIS	**-**	**-**	**r**	**4**	**-**	**r**	**6**	**r**	**r**	**r**	**r**	**r**	**r**	**r**	**-**	**-**
(Jordan-Hart)	-	-	21	14	-	-	-	-	-	-	-	-	-	-	-	-
(Sauber-Mercedes Benz)	-	-	-	-	-	14	11	18	18	17	15	8	17	18	-	-
Jean-Denis DELETRAZ	**-**	**-**	**-**	**-**	**-**	**-**	**-**	**-**	**-**	**-**	**-**	**-**	**-**	**-**	**-**	**r**
(Larrousse-Ford Cosworth)	-	-	-	-	-	-	-	-	-	-	-	-	-	-	-	25
Christian FITTIPALDI	**r**	**4**	**13r**	**r**	**r**	**dq**	**8**	**9**	**4**	**14r**	**r**	**r**	**8**	**17**	**8**	**8**
(Footwork-Ford Cosworth)	11	9	16	6	21	16	18	20	17	16	24	19	11	19	18	19
Heinz-Harald FRENTZEN	**r**	**5**	**7**	**-**	**r**	**r**	**4**	**7**	**r**	**r**	**r**	**r**	**r**	**6**	**6**	**7**
(Sauber-Mercedes Benz)	5	11	7	ns	12	10	10	13	9	8	9	11	9	4	3	10
Bertrand GACHOT	**r**	**-**	**r**	**r**	**r**	**r**	**-**	**-**	**-**	**-**	**-**	**-**	**-**	**-**	**-**	**-**
(Pacific-Ilmor)	25	nq	25	23	25	26	nq	nq	nq	nq	nq	nq	nq	nq	nq	nq
Jean-Marc GOUNON	**-**	**-**	**-**	**-**	**-**	**-**	**9**	**16**	**r**	**r**	**11**	**r**	**15**	**-**	**-**	**-**
(Simtek-Ford Cosworth)	-	-	-	-	-	-	26	26	26	26	25	25	26	-	-	-
Mika HÄKKINEN	**r**	**r**	**3**	**r**	**r**	**r**	**r**	**3**	**r**	**-**	**2**	**3**	**3**	**3**	**7**	**12r**
(McLaren-Peugeot)	8	4	8	2	3	7	9	5	8	-	8	7	4	9	8	4
Johnny HERBERT	**7**	**7**	**10**	**r**	**r**	**8**	**7**	**11**	**r**	**r**	**12**	**r**	**11**	**8**	**r**	**r**
(Lotus-Mugen Honda)	21	23	20	16	22	17	19	21	15	24	20	4	20	-	-	-
(Ligier-Renault)	-	-	-	-	-	-	-	-	-	-	-	-	-	7	-	-
(Benetton-Ford Cosworth)	-	-	-	-	-	-	-	-	-	-	-	-	-	-	5	7
Damon HILL	**2**	**r**	**6f**	**r**	**1**	**2**	**2f**	**1f**	**8**	**2**	**1f**	**1f**	**1**	**2**	**1f**	**r**
(Williams-Renault)	4	3	4	4	2	4	1	1	3	2	3	3	2	2	2	3
Taki INOUE	**-**	**-**	**-**	**-**	**-**	**-**	**-**	**-**	**-**	**-**	**-**	**-**	**-**	**-**	**r**	**-**
(Simtek-Ford Cosworth)	-	-	-	-	-	-	-	-	-	-	-	-	-	-	26	-
Eddie IRVINE	**r**	**-**	**-**	**-**	**6**	**r**	**r**	**r**	**r**	**r**	**13r**	**r**	**7**	**4**	**5**	**r**
(Jordan-Hart)	16	-	-	-	13	8	6	12	10	7	4	9	13	10	6	6
Ukyo KATAYAMA	**5**	**r**	**5**	**r**	**r**	**r**	**r**	**6**	**r**	**r**	**r**	**r**	**r**	**7**	**r**	**r**
(Tyrrell-Yamaha)	10	14	9	11	10	9	14	8	5	5	23	14	6	13	14	15
Franck LAGORCE	**-**	**-**	**-**	**-**	**-**	**-**	**-**	**-**	**-**	**-**	**-**	**-**	**-**	**-**	**r**	**11**
(Ligier-Renault)	-	-	-	-	-	-	-	-	-	-	-	-	-	-	20	20
Pedro LAMY	**10**	**8**	**r**	**11**	**-**	**-**	**-**	**-**	**-**	**-**	**-**	**-**	**-**	**-**	**-**	**-**
(Lotus-Mugen Honda)	24	24	22	19	-	-	-	-	-	-	-	-	-	-	-	-
Nicola LARINI	**-**	**r**	**2**	**-**	**-**	**-**	**-**	**-**	**-**	**-**	**-**	**-**	**-**	**-**	**-**	**-**
(Ferrari)	-	7	6	-	-	-	-	-	-	-	-	-	-	-	-	-
J J LEHTO	**-**	**-**	**r**	**7**	**r**	**6**	**-**	**-**	**-**	**-**	**-**	**9**	**r**	**-**	**r**	**10**
(Benetton-Ford Cosworth)	-	-	5	17	4	20	-	-	-	-	-	20	14	-	-	-
(Sauber-Mercedes Benz)	-	-	-	-	-	-	-	-	-	-	-	-	-	-	15	17
Nigel MANSELL	**-**	**-**	**-**	**-**	**-**	**-**	**r**	**-**	**-**	**-**	**-**	**-**	**-**	**r**	**4**	**1**
(Williams-Renault)	-	-	-	-	-	-	2	-	-	-	-	-	-	3	4	1
Pierluigi MARTINI	**8**	**r**	**r**	**r**	**5**	**9**	**5**	**10**	**r**	**r**	**8**	**r**	**12**	**15**	**r**	**9**
(Minardi-Ford Cosworth)	15	17	14	9	18	15	16	14	20	15	10	18	18	17	16	18
Andrea MONTERMINI	**-**	**-**	**-**	**-**	**-**	**-**	**-**	**-**	**-**	**-**	**-**	**-**	**-**	**-**	**-**	**-**
(Simtek-Ford Cosworth)	-	-	-	-	nq	-	-	-	-	-	-	-	-	-	-	-
Gianni MORBIDELLI	**r**	**r**	**r**	**r**	**r**	**r**	**r**	**r**	**5**	**r**	**6**	**r**	**9**	**11**	**r**	**r**
(Footwork-Ford Cosworth)	6	13	11	7	15	11	22	16	16	19	14	17	16	8	12	21
Hideki NODA	**-**	**-**	**-**	**-**	**-**	**-**	**-**	**-**	**-**	**-**	**-**	**-**	**-**	**r**	**r**	**r**
(Larrousse-Ford Cosworth)	-	-	-	-	-	-	-	-	-	-	-	-	-	24	23	23
Olivier PANIS	**11**	**9**	**11**	**9**	**7**	**12**	**r**	**12**	**2**	**6**	**7**	**10**	**dq**	**9**	**11**	**5**
(Ligier-Renault)	19	22	19	20	19	19	13	15	12	9	17	6	15	11	19	12
Roland RATZENBERGER +	**-**	**11**	**-**	**-**	**-**	**-**	**-**	**-**	**-**	**-**	**-**	**-**	**-**	**-**	**-**	**-**
(Simtek-Ford Cosworth)	nq	26	26ns	-	-	-	-	-	-	-	-	-	-	-	-	-
Mika SALO	**-**	**-**	**-**	**-**	**-**	**-**	**-**	**-**	**-**	**-**	**-**	**-**	**-**	**-**	**10**	**r**
(Lotus-Mugen Honda)	-	-	-	-	-	-	-	-	-	-	-	-	-	-	25	22
Mimmo SCHIATTARELLA	**-**	**-**	**-**	**-**	**-**	**-**	**-**	**-**	**-**	**-**	**-**	**-**	**-**	**19**	**-**	**r**
(Simtek-Ford Cosworth)	-	-	-	-	-	-	-	-	-	-	-	-	-	26	-	26
Michael SCHUMACHER	**1f**	**1f**	**1**	**1f**	**2f**	**1f**	**1**	**dq**	**r**	**1f**	**dq**	**-**	**-**	**1f**	**2**	**rf**
(Benetton-Ford Cosworth)	2	2	2	1	1	1	3	2	4	1	2	-	-	1	1	2
Ayrton SENNA +	**r**	**r**	**r**	**-**	**-**	**-**	**-**	**-**	**-**	**-**	**-**	**-**	**-**	**-**	**-**	**-**
(Williams-Renault)	1	1	1	-	-	-	-	-	-	-	-	-	-	-	-	-
Aguri SUZUKI	**-**	**r**	**-**	**-**	**-**	**-**	**-**	**-**	**-**	**-**	**-**	**-**	**-**	**-**	**-**	**-**
(Jordan-Hart)	-	20	-	-	-	-	-	-	-	-	-	-	-	-	-	-
Jos VERSTAPPEN	**r**	**r**	**-**	**-**	**-**	**-**	**r**	**8**	**r**	**3**	**3**	**r**	**5**	**r**	**-**	**-**
(Benetton-Ford Cosworth)	9	10	-	-	-	-	8	10	19	12	6	10	10	12	-	-
Karl WENDLINGER	**6**	**r**	**4**	**-**	**-**	**-**	**-**	**-**	**-**	**-**	**-**	**-**	**-**	**-**	**-**	**-**
(Sauber-Mercedes Benz)	7	19	10	ns	-	-	-	-	-	-	-	-	-	-	-	-
Alessandro ZANARDI	**-**	**-**	**-**	**-**	**9**	**15r**	**r**	**r**	**r**	**13**	**-**	**r**	**-**	**16**	**13**	**r**
(Lotus-Mugen Honda)	-	-	-	-	23	23	23	19	21	22	-	13	-	21	17	14

1995 RACE RESULTS & GRID POSITIONS

	BR	RA	RSM	E	MC	CDN	F	GB	D	H	B	I	P	EUR	PAC	J	AUS
Jean ALESI	**5**	**2**	**2**	**r**	**rf**	**1**	**5**	**2**	**r**	**r**	**r**	**r**	**5**	**2**	**5**	**r**	**r**
(Ferrari)	6	6	5	2	5	5	4	6	10	6	2	5	7	6	4	2	5
Luca BADOER	**r**	**r**	**14**	**r**	**r**	**8**	**13**	**10**	**r**	**8**	**r**	**r**	**14**	**11**	**15**	**9**	**-**
(Minardi-Ford Cosworth)	18	13	20	21	16	19	17	18	16	12	19	18	18	18	16	17	15ns
Rubens BARRICHELLO	**r**	**r**	**r**	**7**	**r**	**2**	**6**	**11r**	**r**	**7**	**6**	**r**	**11**	**4**	**r**	**r**	**r**
(Jordan-Peugeot)	16	10	10	8	11	9	5	9	5	14	12	6	8	11	11	10	7
Gerhard BERGER	**3**	**6**	**3f**	**3**	**3**	**11r**	**12**	**r**	**3**	**3**	**r**	**rf**	**4**	**r**	**4**	**r**	**r**
(Ferrari)	5	8	2	3	4	4	7	4	4	4	1	3	4	4	5	5	4
Mark BLUNDELL	**6**	**r**	**-**	**-**	**5**	**r**	**11**	**5**	**r**	**r**	**5**	**4**	**9**	**r**	**9**	**7**	**4**
(McLaren-Mercedes Benz)	9	17	-	-	10	10	13	10	8	13	6	9	12	10	10	23	10
Jean-Christophe BOULLION	**-**	**-**	**-**	**-**	**8r**	**r**	**r**	**9**	**5**	**10**	**11**	**6**	**12**	**r**	**r**	**-**	**-**
(Sauber-Ford Cosworth)	-	-	-	-	19	18	15	16	14	19	14	14	14	13	15	-	-
Martin BRUNDLE	**-**	**-**	**-**	**9**	**r**	**10r**	**4**	**r**	**-**	**r**	**3**	**r**	**8**	**7**	**-**	**-**	**r**
(Ligier-Mugen Honda)	-	-	-	11	8	14	9	11	-	8	13	11	9	12	-	-	11
David COULTHARD	**2**	**r**	**4**	**r**	**r**	**r**	**3**	**3**	**2**	**2**	**rf**	**r**	**1f**	**3**	**2**	**r**	**r**
(Williams-Renault)	3	1	3	4	3	3	3	3	3	2	5	1	1	1	1	6	2
Jean-Denis DELETRAZ	**-**	**-**	**-**	**-**	**-**	**-**	**-**	**-**	**-**	**-**	**-**	**-**	**r**	**15**	**-**	**-**	**-**
(Pacific-Ford Cosworth)	-	-	-	-	-	-	-	-	-	-	-	-	24	24	-	-	-
Pedro DINIZ	**10**	**nc**	**15**	**r**	**10**	**r**	**r**	**r**	**r**	**r**	**13**	**9**	**16**	**13**	**17**	**r**	**7**
(Forti-Ford Cosworth)	25	25	26	26	22	24	23	20	21	23	24	23	22	22	21	20	21
Heinz-Harald FRENTZEN	**r**	**5**	**6**	**8**	**6**	**r**	**10**	**6**	**r**	**5**	**4**	**3**	**6**	**r**	**7**	**8**	**r**
(Sauber-Ford Cosworth)	14	9	14	12	14	12	12	12	11	11	10	10	5	8	8	8	6
Bertrand GACHOT	**r**	**r**	**r**	**r**	**r**	**r**	**r**	**12**	**-**	**-**	**-**	**-**	**-**	**-**	**r**	**r**	**8**
(Pacific-Ford Cosworth)	20	23	22	24	21	20	22	21	-	-	-	-	-	-	24	22	23
Mika HÄKKINEN	**4**	**r**	**5**	**r**	**r**	**r**	**7**	**r**	**r**	**r**	**r**	**2**	**r**	**8**	**-**	**2**	**-**
(McLaren-Mercedes Benz)	7	5	6	9	6	7	8	8	7	5	3	7	13	9	-	3	ns
Johnny HERBERT	**r**	**4**	**7**	**2**	**4**	**r**	**r**	**1**	**4**	**4**	**7**	**1**	**7**	**5**	**6**	**3**	**r**
(Benetton-Renault)	4	11	8	7	7	6	10	5	9	9	4	8	6	7	7	9	8
Damon HILL	**r**	**1**	**1**	**4f**	**2**	**r**	**2**	**rf**	**r**	**1f**	**2**	**r**	**3**	**r**	**3**	**r**	**1f**
(Williams-Renault)	1	2	4	5	1	2	1	1	1	1	8	4	2	2	2	4	1
Taki INOUE	**r**	**r**	**r**	**r**	**r**	**9**	**r**	**r**	**r**	**r**	**12**	**8**	**15**	**r**	**r**	**12**	**r**
(Footwork-Hart)	21	26	19	18	26	22	18	19	19	18	18	20	19	21	20	18	19
Eddie IRVINE	**r**	**r**	**8**	**5**	**r**	**3**	**9**	**r**	**9r**	**13r**	**r**	**r**	**10**	**6**	**11**	**4**	**r**
(Jordan-Peugeot)	8	4	7	6	9	8	11	7	6	7	7	12	10	5	6	7	9
Ukyo KATAYAMA	**r**	**8**	**r**	**r**	**r**	**r**	**r**	**r**	**7**	**r**	**r**	**10**	**r**	**-**	**14**	**r**	**r**
(Tyrrell-Yamaha)	11	15	15	17	15	16	19	14	17	17	15	17	16	-	17	13	16
Pedro LAMY	**-**	**-**	**-**	**-**	**-**	**-**	**-**	**-**	**-**	**9**	**10**	**r**	**r**	**9**	**13**	**11**	**6**
(Minardi-Ford Cosworth)	-	-	-	-	-	-	-	-	-	15	17	19	17	16	14	16	17
Giovanni LAVAGGI	**-**	**-**	**-**	**-**	**-**	**-**	**-**	**-**	**r**	**r**	**r**	**r**	**-**	**-**	**-**	**-**	**-**
(Pacific-Ford Cosworth)	-	-	-	-	-	-	-	-	24	24	23	24	-	-	-	-	-
Jan MAGNUSSEN	**-**	**-**	**-**	**-**	**-**	**-**	**-**	**-**	**-**	**-**	**-**	**-**	**-**	**-**	**10**	**-**	**-**
(McLaren-Mercedes Benz)	-	-	-	-	-	-	-	-	-	-	-	-	-	-	12	-	-
Nigel MANSELL	**-**	**-**	**10**	**r**	**-**	**-**	**-**	**-**	**-**	**-**	**-**	**-**	**-**	**-**	**-**	**-**	**-**
(McLaren-Mercedes Benz)	-	-	9	10	-	-	-	-	-	-	-	-	-	-	-	-	-
Pierluigi MARTINI	**r**	**r**	**12**	**14**	**7**	**r**	**r**	**7**	**r**	**-**	**-**	**-**	**-**	**-**	**-**	**-**	**-**
(Minardi-Ford Cosworth)	17	16	18	19	18	17	20	15	20	-	-	-	-	-	-	-	-
Andrea MONTERMINI	**9**	**r**	**r**	**r**	**dq**	**r**	**nc**	**r**	**8**	**12**	**r**	**r**	**r**	**r**	**r**	**r**	**r**
(Pacific-Ford Cosworth)	22	22	24	23	25	21	21	24	23	22	21	21	21	20	23	19	22
Gianni MORBIDELLI	**r**	**r**	**13**	**11**	**9**	**6**	**14**	**-**	**-**	**-**	**-**	**-**	**-**	**-**	**r**	**r**	**3**
(Footwork-Hart)	13	12	11	14	13	13	16	-	-	-	-	-	-	-	19	14	13
Roberto MORENO	**r**	**nc**	**16**	**r**	**r**	**r**	**16**	**r**	**r**	**r**	**14**	**r**	**17**	**r**	**16**	**r**	**r**
(Forti-Ford Cosworth)	23	24	25	25	24	23	24	22	22	21	22	22	23	23	22	21	20
Olivier PANIS	**r**	**7**	**9**	**6**	**r**	**4**	**8**	**4**	**r**	**6**	**9**	**r**	**r**	**r**	**8**	**5**	**2**
(Ligier-Mugen Honda)	10	18	12	15	12	11	6	13	12	10	9	13	11	14	9	11	12
Max PAPIS	**-**	**-**	**-**	**-**	**-**	**-**	**-**	**r**	**r**	**r**	**r**	**7**	**r**	**12**	**-**	**-**	**-**
(Footwork-Hart)	-	-	-	-	-	-	-	17	15	20	20	15	20	17	-	-	-
Mika SALO	**7**	**r**	**r**	**10**	**r**	**7**	**15**	**8**	**r**	**r**	**8**	**5**	**13**	**10**	**12**	**6**	**5**
(Tyrrell-Yamaha)	12	7	13	13	17	15	14	23	13	16	11	16	15	15	18	12	14
Mimmo SCHIATTARELLA	**r**	**9**	**r**	**15**	**r**	**-**	**-**	**-**	**-**	**-**	**-**	**-**	**-**	**-**	**-**	**-**	**-**
(Simtek-Ford Cosworth)	26	20	23	22	20	-	-	-	-	-	-	-	-	-	-	-	-
Michael SCHUMACHER	**1f**	**3f**	**r**	**1**	**1**	**5f**	**1f**	**r**	**1f**	**11r**	**1**	**r**	**2**	**1f**	**1f**	**1f**	**r**
(Benetton-Renault)	2	3	1	1	2	1	2	2	2	3	16	2	3	3	3	1	3
Aguri SUZUKI	**8**	**r**	**11**	**-**	**-**	**-**	**-**	**-**	**6**	**-**	**-**	**-**	**-**	**-**	**r**	**-**	**-**
(Ligier-Mugen Honda)	15	19	16	-	-	-	-	-	18	-	-	-	-	-	13	ns	-
Gabriele TARQUINI	**-**	**-**	**-**	**-**	**-**	**-**	**-**	**-**	**-**	**-**	**-**	**-**	**-**	**14**	**-**	**-**	**-**
(Tyrrell-Yamaha)	-	-	-	-	-	-	-	-	-	-	-	-	-	19	-	-	-
Jos VERSTAPPEN	**r**	**r**	**r**	**12**	**r**	**-**	**-**	**-**	**-**	**-**	**-**	**-**	**-**	**-**	**-**	**-**	**-**
(Simtek-Ford Cosworth)	24	14	17	16	23	-	-	-	-	-	-	-	-	-	-	-	-
Karl WENDLINGER	**r**	**r**	**r**	**13**	**-**	**-**	**-**	**-**	**-**	**-**	**-**	**-**	**-**	**-**	**-**	**10**	**r**
(Sauber-Ford Cosworth)	19	21	21	20	-	-	-	-	-	-	-	-	-	-	-	15	18

1996 RACE RESULTS & GRID POSITIONS

	AUS	BR	RA	EUR	RSM	MC	E	CDN	F	GB	D	H	B	I	P	J
Jean ALESI	**r**	**2**	**3f**	**r**	**6**	**rf**	**2**	**3**	**3**	**r**	**2**	**3**	**4**	**2**	**4**	**r**
(Benetton-Renault)	6	5	4	4	5	3	4	4	3	5	5	5	7	6	3	9
Luca BADOER	**-**	**11**	**r**	**-**	**10**	**r**	**-**	**r**	**r**	**-**	**-**	**-**	**-**	**-**	**-**	**-**
(Forti-Ford Cosworth)	nq	19	21	nq	21	21	nq	20	20	nq	-	-	-	-	-	-
Rubens BARRICHELLO	**r**	**r**	**4**	**5**	**5**	**r**	**r**	**r**	**9**	**4**	**6**	**6**	**r**	**5**	**r**	**9**
(Jordan-Peugeot)	8	2	6	5	9	6	7	8	10	6	9	13	10	10	9	11
Gerhard BERGER	**4**	**r**	**r**	**9**	**3**	**r**	**r**	**r**	**4**	**2**	**13r**	**r**	**6f**	**r**	**6**	**4**
(Benetton-Renault)	7	8	5	8	7	4	5	7	4	7	2	6	5	8	5	4
Martin BRUNDLE	**r**	**12r**	**r**	**6**	**r**	**r**	**r**	**6**	**8**	**6**	**10**	**r**	**r**	**4**	**9**	**5**
(Jordan-Peugeot)	19	6	15	11	12	16	15	9	8	8	10	12	8	9	10	10
David COULTHARD	**r**	**r**	**7**	**3**	**r**	**2**	**r**	**4**	**6**	**5**	**5**	**r**	**r**	**r**	**13**	**8**
(McLaren-Mercedes Benz)	13	14	9	6	4	5	14	10	7	9	7	9	4	5	8	8
Pedro DINIZ	**10**	**8**	**r**	**10**	**7**	**r**	**6**	**r**	**r**	**r**	**r**	**r**	**r**	**6**	**r**	**r**
(Ligier-Mugen Honda)	20	22	18	17	17	17	17	18	11	17	11	15	15	14	18	16
Giancarlo FISICHELLA	**r**	**-**	**-**	**13**	**r**	**r**	**r**	**8**	**r**	**11**	**-**	**-**	**-**	**-**	**-**	**-**
(Minardi-Ford Cosworth)	16	-	-	18	19	18	19	16	17	18	-	-	-	-	-	-
Heinz-Harald FRENTZEN	**8**	**r**	**r**	**r**	**r**	**4**	**4**	**r**	**r**	**8**	**8**	**r**	**r**	**r**	**7**	**6**
(Sauber-Ford Cosworth)	9	9	11	10	10	9	11	12	12	11	13	10	11	13	11	7
Mika HÄKKINEN	**5**	**4**	**r**	**8**	**8r**	**6r**	**5**	**5**	**5**	**3**	**r**	**4**	**3**	**3**	**r**	**3**
(McLaren-Mercedes Benz)	5	7	8	9	11	8	10	6	5	4	4	7	6	4	7	5
Johnny HERBERT	**r**	**r**	**9**	**7**	**r**	**3**	**r**	**7**	**dq**	**9**	**r**	**r**	**r**	**9r**	**8**	**10**
(Sauber-Ford Cosworth)	14	12	17	12	15	13	9	15	16	13	14	8	12	12	12	13
Damon HILL	**1**	**1f**	**1**	**4f**	**1f**	**r**	**r**	**1**	**1**	**r**	**1f**	**2f**	**5**	**r**	**2**	**1**
(Williams-Renault)	2	1	1	1	2	2	1	1	2	1	1	2	2	1	1	2
Eddie IRVINE	**3**	**7**	**5**	**r**	**4**	**7r**	**r**	**r**	**r**	**r**	**r**	**r**	**r**	**r**	**5**	**r**
(Ferrari)	3	10	10	7	6	7	6	5	22	10	8	4	9	7	6	6
Ukyo KATAYAMA	**11**	**9**	**r**	**dq**	**r**	**r**	**r**	**r**	**r**	**r**	**r**	**7**	**8**	**10**	**12**	**r**
(Tyrrell-Yamaha)	15	16	13	16	16	15	16	17	14	12	16	14	17	16	14	14
Pedro LAMY	**r**	**10**	**r**	**12**	**9**	**r**	**r**	**r**	**12**	**r**	**12**	**r**	**10**	**r**	**16**	**12**
(Minardi-Ford Cosworth)	17	18	19	19	18	19	18	19	18	19	18	19	19	18	19	18
Giovanni LAVAGGI	**-**	**-**	**-**	**-**	**-**	**-**	**-**	**-**	**-**	**-**	**-**	**10r**	**-**	**r**	**15**	**-**
(Minardi-Ford Cosworth)	-	-	-	-	-	-	-	-	-	-	nq	20	nq	20	20	nq
Tarso MARQUES	**-**	**r**	**r**	**-**	**-**	**-**	**-**	**-**	**-**	**-**	**-**	**-**	**-**	**-**	**-**	**-**
(Minardi-Ford Cosworth)	-	21	14	-	-	-	-	-	-	-	-	-	-	-	-	-
Andrea MONTERMINI	**-**	**r**	**10**	**-**	**-**	**-**	**-**	**r**	**r**	**-**	**-**	**-**	**-**	**-**	**-**	**-**
(Forti-Ford Cosworth)	nq	20	22	nq	nq	22ns	nq	22	21	nq	-	-	-	-	-	-
Olivier PANIS	**7**	**6**	**8**	**r**	**r**	**1**	**r**	**r**	**7**	**r**	**7**	**5**	**r**	**r**	**10**	**7**
(Ligier-Mugen Honda)	11	15	12	15	13	14	8	11	9	16	12	11	14	11	15	12
Ricardo ROSSET	**9**	**r**	**r**	**11**	**r**	**r**	**r**	**r**	**11**	**r**	**11**	**8**	**9**	**r**	**14**	**13**
(Footwork-Hart)	18	17	20	20	20	20	20	21	19	20	19	18	18	19	17	19
Mika SALO	**6**	**5**	**r**	**dq**	**r**	**5r**	**dq**	**r**	**10**	**7**	**9**	**r**	**7**	**r**	**11**	**r**
(Tyrrell-Yamaha)	10	11	16	14	8	11	12	14	13	14	15	16	13	17	13	15
Michael SCHUMACHER	**r**	**3**	**r**	**2**	**2**	**r**	**1f**	**r**	**r**	**r**	**4**	**9r**	**1**	**1f**	**3**	**2**
(Ferrari)	4	4	2	3	1	1	3	3	1	3	3	1	3	3	4	3
Jos VERSTAPPEN	**r**	**r**	**6**	**r**	**r**	**r**	**r**	**r**	**r**	**10**	**r**	**r**	**r**	**8**	**r**	**11**
(Footwork-Hart)	12	13	7	13	14	12	13	13	15	15	17	17	16	15	16	17
Jacques VILLENEUVE	**2f**	**r**	**2**	**1**	**11r**	**r**	**3**	**2f**	**2f**	**1f**	**3**	**1**	**2**	**7**	**1f**	**rf**
(Williams-Renault)	1	3	3	2	3	10	2	2	6	2	6	3	1	2	2	1

3

Grand Prix Starters
Grand Prix Non-Starters
Indianapolis 500 Starters
Indianapolis 500 Non-Starters
Drivers often not known by their real name

DRIVERS

For shared drives, only the best position has been counted in the table, so that the total placings and non-classifications tallies with the number of starts.

Drivers in the Formula 2 section of races who finished in the top 6 'on the road', have been credited in the other placings column, as they were not eligible for championship points.

KEY TO COLUMN HEADINGS

GPs	Race starts
PP	Pole Positions
FL	Fastest Laps
OP	Total Other Placings
NC etc	Total DQ + NC + R
NS etc	Total EW + EXC + NPQ + NQ + NS
R	Retirements (Indy 500 drivers only)

Grand Prix Starters

	Nat	Born Died	Place of Birth Place of Death	Years Entered	No. of Years	GPs	Points	PP	FL	Win	2nd	3rd	4th	5th	6th	OP	NC etc	NS etc
ABECASSIS, George	GB	21 Mar 1913 18 Dec 1991	Chertsey, Surrey Ibstone, Buckinghamshire	1951-52	2	2	-	-	-	-	-	-	-	-	-	-	2	-
ACHESON, Kenny	GB	27 Nov 1957	Cookstown, Tyrone, N Ireland	1983-85	2	3	-	-	-	-	-	-	-	-	-	1	2	7
ADAMS, Philippe	B	19 Nov 1969	Mouscron	1994	1	2	-	-	-	-	-	-	-	-	-	1	1	-
ADOLFF, Kurt	D	5 Nov 1921	Stuttgart	1953	1	1	-	-	-	-	-	-	-	-	-	-	1	-
AHRENS, Kurt	D	19 Apr 1940	Braunschweig, nr Hanover	1966-69	4	4	-	-	-	-	-	-	-	-	-	2	2	-
ALBORETO, Michele	I	23 Dec 1956	Milan	1981-94	14	194	186.50	2	5	5	9	9	10	8	6	55	92	21
ALESI, Jean	F	11 Jun 1964	Montfavet, nr Avignon	1989-96	8	118	189	1	4	1	12	13	11	9	4	14	54	1
ALLIOT, Philippe	F	27 Jul 1954	Voves Eure et Loir	1984-94	9	109	7	-	-	-	-	-	-	1	5	38	65	7
ALLISON, Cliff	GB	8 Feb 1932	Brough, Westmorland	1958-61	4	16	11	-	-	-	1	-	1	2	2	4	6	2
AMON, Chris	NZ	20 Jul 1943	Bulls	1963-76	14	97	83	5	3	-	3	8	4	7	7	22	46	11
ANDERSON, Bob	GB	19 May 1931 14 Aug 1967	Hendon, London Northampton	1963-67	5	25	8	-	-	-	-	1	-	1	2	11	10	4
ANDERSSON, Conny	S	28 Dec 1939	Alingsås	1976-77	2	1	-	-	-	-	-	-	-	-	-	-	1	4
ANDRETTI, Mario	USA	28 Feb 1940	Montona, Italy	1968-82	14	128	180	18	10	12	2	5	7	7	5	24	66	3
ANDRETTI, Michael	USA	5 Oct 1962	Bethlehem, Pennsylvania	1993	1	13	7	-	-	-	-	1	-	1	1	3	7	-
APICELLA, Marco	I	7 Oct 1965	Bologna	1993	1	1	-	-	-	-	-	-	-	-	-	-	1	-
ARNOUX, René	F	4 Jul 1948	Pontcharra, nr Grenoble	1978-89	12	149	181	18	12	7	9	6	7	8	5	40	67	15
ARUNDELL, Peter	GB	8 Nov 1933	Ilford, Essex	1963-66	3	11	12	-	-	-	-	2	1	-	1	4	3	2
ASCARI, Alberto	I	13 Jul 1918 26 May 1955	Milan Monza	1950-55	6	31	140.64	14	13	13	4	-	2	1	1	1	9	1
ASHDOWN, Peter	GB	16 Oct 1934	Danbury, Essex	1959	1	1	-	-	-	-	-	-	-	-	-	1	-	-
ASHLEY, Ian	GB	26 Oct 1947	Wuppertal, Germany	1974-77	4	4	-	-	-	-	-	-	-	-	-	2	2	7
ASHMORE, Gerry	GB	25 Jul 1936	West Bromwich, Staffordshire	1961-62	2	3	-	-	-	-	-	-	-	-	-	1	2	1
ASTON, Bill	GB	29 Mar 1900 4 Mar 1974	Stafford Lingfield, Surrey	1952	1	1	-	-	-	-	-	-	-	-	-	-	1	2
ATTWOOD, Dickie	GB	4 Apr 1940	Wolverhampton, Staffordshire	1964-69	5	17	11	-	1	-	1	-	1	-	2	9	4	1
BADOER, Luca	I	25 Jan 1971	Montebelluna, Treviso	1993-96	3	34	-	-	-	-	-	-	-	-	-	17	17	7
BAGHETTI, Giancarlo	I	25 Dec 1934 27 Nov 1995	Milan Milan	1961-67	7	21	14	-	1	1	-	-	1	1	-	7	11	-
BAILEY, Julian	GB	9 Oct 1961	Woolwich, London	1988-91	2	7	1	-	-	-	-	-	-	-	1	4	2	13
BALDI, Mauro	I	31 Jan 1954	Reggio-Emilia	1982-85	4	36	5	-	-	-	-	-	-	1	3	13	19	5
BALSA, Marcel	F	1 Jan 1909 11 Aug 1984	Saint Frion	1952	1	1	-	-	-	-	-	-	-	-	-	-	1	-
BANDINI, Lorenzo	I	21 Dec 1935 10 May 1967	Barce, Cyrenaica (Libya) Monte Carlo, Monaco	1961-67	7	42	58	1	2	1	2	5	2	4	3	11	14	-
BARBAZZA, Fabrizio	I	2 Apr 1963	Monza	1991-93	2	8	2	-	-	-	-	-	-	-	2	1	5	12

	Nat	Born Died	Place of Birth Place of Death	Years Entered	No. of Years	GPs	Points	PP	FL	Win	2nd	3rd	4th	5th	6th	OP	NC etc	NS etc
BARBER, John	GB	1929/30		1953	1	1	-	-	-	-	-	-	-	-	-	1	-	-
BARBER, Skip	USA	16 Nov 1936	Philadelphia, Pennsylvania	1971-72	2	5	-	-	-	-	-	-	-	-	-	1	4	1
BARILLA, Paolo	I	20 Apr 1961	Milan	1989-90	2	9	-	-	-	-	-	-	-	-	-	4	5	6
BARRICHELLO, Rubens	BR	23 May 1972	São Paulo	1993-96	4	64	46	1	-	-	1	1	8	4	4	15	31	1
BARTH, Edgar	D	26 Jan 1917 20 May 1965	Herold-Erzegeberge Ludwigsburg, nr Stuttgart	1953-64	5	5	-	-	-	-	-	-	-	-	-	3	2	-
BASSI, Giorgio	I	20 Jan 1934	Milan	1965	1	1	-	-	-	-	-	-	-	-	-	-	1	-
BAUER, Erwin	D	17 Jul 1912 3 Jun 1958	(from Stuttgart) Cologne	1953	1	1	-	-	-	-	-	-	-	-	-	-	1	-
BAYOL, Élie	F	28 Feb 1914 25 May 1995	Marseille La Ciotat	1952-56	5	7	2	-	-	-	-	-	-	1	1	-	5	1
BEAUMAN, Don	GB	26 Jul 1928 9 Jul 1955	 Rathnew, Co Wicklow, Ireland	1954	1	1	-	-	-	-	-	-	-	-	-	1	-	-
BECHEM, Günther *(also known as Bernd NACKE)*	D	21 Dec 1921		1952-53	2	2	-	-	-	-	-	-	-	-	-	-	2	-
BEHRA, Jean	F	16 Feb 1921 1 Aug 1959	Nice AVUS, Berlin, Germany	1952-59	8	52	53.14	-	1	-	2	7	2	5	5	4	27	1
BELL, Derek	GB	31 Oct 1941	Pinner, Middlesex	1968-74	6	9	1	-	-	-	-	-	-	-	1	1	7	7
BELLOF, Stefan	D	20 Nov 1957 1 Sep 1985	Giessen Spa-Francorchamps, Belgium	1984-85	2	20	4	-	-	-	-	-	1	-	1	5	13	2
BELMONDO, Paul	F	23 Apr 1963	Boulogne-Billancourt	1992-94	2	7	-	-	-	-	-	-	-	-	-	5	2	20
BELSO, Tom	DK	27 Aug 1942	Copenhagen	1973-74	2	2	-	-	-	-	-	-	-	-	-	1	1	3
BELTOISE, Jean-Pierre	F	26 Apr 1937	Paris	1966-74	9	86	77	-	4	1	3	4	3	10	5	24	36	2
BERETTA, Olivier	MC	23 Nov 1969	Monte Carlo	1994	1	10	-	-	-	-	-	-	-	-	-	4	6	-
BERG, Allen	CDN	1 Aug 1961	Calgary, Alberta	1986	1	9	-	-	-	-	-	-	-	-	-	3	6	-
BERGER, Georges	B	14 Sep 1918 23 Aug 1967	Brussels Nürburgring, Germany	1953-54	2	2	-	-	-	-	-	-	-	-	-	-	2	-
BERGER, Gerhard	A	27 Aug 1959	Wörgl, nr Innsbruck	1984-96	13	196	359	11	19	9	16	21	23	8	11	23	85	-
BERNARD, Éric	F	24 Aug 1964	Istres	1989-94	4	45	10	-	-	-	-	1	1	-	3	17	23	2
BEUTTLER, Mike	GB	13 Apr 1940 29 Dec 1988	Cairo, Egypt San Francisco, CA, USA	1971-73	3	28	-	-	-	-	-	-	-	-	-	12	16	1
BIANCHI, Lucien	B	10 Nov 1934 30 Mar 1969	Milan, Italy Le Mans, France	1959-68	7	17	6	-	-	-	-	1	-	-	2	3	11	2
BIANCO, Gino	BR		Italy	1952	1	4	-	-	-	-	-	-	-	-	-	1	3	-
BINDER, Hans	A	12 Jun 1948	Zell am Ziller, nr Innsbruck	1976-78	3	13	-	-	-	-	-	-	-	-	-	6	7	2
BIONDETTI, Clemente	I	18 Aug 1898 24 Feb 1955	Buddusó, Sardinia Florence	1950	1	1	-	-	-	-	-	-	-	-	-	-	1	-
BIRA, B	T	15 Jul 1914 23 Dec 1985	Bangkok Baron's Court,London,England	1950-54	5	19	8	-	-	-	-	-	2	1	1	6	9	-
BIRGER, Pablo	RA	6 Jan 1924 9 Mar 1966	Buenos Aires Buenos Aires	1953-55	2	2	-	-	-	-	-	-	-	-	-	-	2	-
BLANCHARD, Harry	USA	 31 Jan 1960	 Buenos Aires, Argentina	1959	1	1	-	-	-	-	-	-	-	-	-	1	-	-
BLEEKEMOLEN, Michael	NL	2 Oct 1949	Amsterdam	1977-78	2	1	-	-	-	-	-	-	-	-	-	-	1	4
BLOKDYK, Trevor	ZA	30 Nov 1935 19 Mar 1995	Krugersdorp, Transvaal Hekpoort, nr Krugersdorp	1963-65	2	1	-	-	-	-	-	-	-	-	-	1	-	1

	Nat	Born Died	Place of Birth Place of Death	Years Entered	No. of Years	GPs	Points	PP	FL	Win	2nd	3rd	4th	5th	6th	OP	NC etc	NS etc
BLUNDELL, Mark	GB	8 Apr 1966	Barnet, Hertfordshire	1991-95	4	61	32	-	-	-	-	3	2	6	2	18	30	2
BOESEL, Raul	BR	4 Dec 1957	Curitiba	1982-83	2	23	-	-	-	-	-	-	-	-	-	10	13	7
BONDURANT, Bob	USA	27 Apr 1933	Evanston, Illinois	1965-66	2	9	3	-	-	-	-	-	1	-	-	3	5	-
BONETTO, Felice	I	9 Jun 1903 21 Nov 1953	Brescia Silao, Mexico	1950-53	4	15	17.50	-	-	-	-	2	3	3	1	-	6	1
BONNIER, Jo	S	31 Jan 1930 11 Jun 1972	Stockholm Le Mans, France	1956-71	16	104	39	1	-	1	-	-	1	10	8	31	53	4
BONOMI, Roberto	RA	30 Sep 1919	Buenos Aires	1960	1	1	-	-	-	-	-	-	-	-	-	1	-	-
BORGUDD, Slim	S	25 Nov 1946	Borgholm, nr Kalmar	1981-82	2	10	1	-	-	-	-	-	-	-	1	5	4	5
BOTHA, Luki	ZA	16 Jan 1930		1967	1	1	-	-	-	-	-	-	-	-	-	-	1	-
BOULLION, Jean-Christophe	F	27 Dec 1969	St. Brieuc, nr Côte d'Amor	1995	1	11	3	-	-	-	-	-	-	1	1	5	4	-
BOUTSEN, Thierry	B	13 Jul 1957	Brussels	1983-93	11	163	132	1	1	3	2	10	8	11	7	56	66	1
BRABHAM, David	AUS	5 Sep 1965	Wimbledon, London, England	1990-94	2	24	-	-	-	-	-	-	-	-	-	7	17	6
BRABHAM, Jack	AUS	2 Apr 1926	Hurstville, nr Sydney	1955-70	16	126	261	13	12	14	10	7	13	5	7	17	53	2
BRACK, Bill	CDN	26 Dec 1935	Toronto, Ontario	1968-72	3	3	-	-	-	-	-	-	-	-	-	-	3	-
BRAMBILLA, Vittorio	I	11 Nov 1937	Monza	1974-80	7	74	15.50	1	1	1	-	-	1	2	5	28	37	5
BRANCA, Toni	CH	15 Sep 1916 10 May 1985	 Sierre	1950-51	2	3	-	-	-	-	-	-	-	-	-	2	1	-
BRANDON, Eric	GB	18 Jul 1920 8 Aug 1982	East London Hampshire	1952-54	2	5	-	-	-	-	-	-	-	-	-	4	1	-
BRIDGER, Tom	GB	24 Jun 1934 30 Jul 1991	Welwyn, Hertfordshire Aboyne, Aberdeens., Scotland	1958	1	1	-	-	-	-	-	-	-	-	-	-	1	-
BRISE, Tony	GB	28 Mar 1952 29 Nov 1975	Dartford, Kent Arkley, nr Barnet, Herts	1975	1	10	1	-	-	-	-	-	-	-	1	5	4	-
BRISTOW, Chris	GB	2 Dec 1937 19 Jun 1960	South London Spa-Francorchamps, Belgium	1959-60	2	4	-	-	-	-	-	-	-	-	-	1	3	-
BROEKER, Peter	CDN	15 May 1929		1963	1	1	-	-	-	-	-	-	-	-	-	1	-	-
BROOKS, Tony	GB	25 Feb 1932	Dukinfield, Cheshire	1956-61	6	38	75	3	3	6	2	2	1	3	-	8	16	1
BROWN, Alan	GB	20 Nov 1919	Malton, Yorkshire	1952-54	3	8	2	-	-	-	-	-	-	1	1	4	2	1
BROWN, Warwick	AUS	24 Dec 1949	Sydney, New South Wales	1976	1	1	-	-	-	-	-	-	-	-	-	1	-	-
BRUDES, Adolf	D	15 Oct 1899 5 Nov 1986		1952	1	1	-	-	-	-	-	-	-	-	-	-	1	-
BRUNDLE, Martin	GB	1 Jun 1959	King's Lynn, Norfolk	1984-96	12	158	98	-	-	-	2	7	8	12	10	44	75	7
BUCCI, Clemar	RA	4 Sep 1920	Zenon Pereyra, Santa Fé	1954-55	2	5	-	-	-	-	-	-	-	-	-	-	5	-
BUCKNUM, Ronnie	USA	5 Apr 1936 14 Apr 1992	Alhambra, California	1964-66	3	11	2	-	-	-	-	-	-	1	-	3	7	-
BUEB, Ivor	GB	6 Jun 1923 1 Aug 1959	Dulwich, London Clermont-Ferrand, France	1957-59	3	5	-	-	-	-	-	-	-	-	-	3	2	1
BUENO, Luiz	BR	c1939		1973	1	1	-	-	-	-	-	-	-	-	-	1	-	-
BURGESS, Ian	GB	6 Jul 1930	London	1958-63	6	16	-	-	-	-	-	-	-	-	1	8	7	4
BUSSINELLO, Roberto	I	4 Oct 1927	Pistoïa	1961-65	2	2	-	-	-	-	-	-	-	-	-	1	1	1

	Nat	Born Died	Place of Birth Place of Death	Years Entered	No. of Years	GPs	Points	PP	FL	Win	2nd	3rd	4th	5th	6th	OP	NC etc	NS etc
BYRNE, Tommy	IRL	6 May 1958	Drogheda, Co. Louth	1982	1	2	-	-	-	-	-	-	-	-	-	-	2	3
CABIANCA, Giulio	I	19 Feb 1923 15 Jun 1961	Verona Modena Aerautodromo	1958-60	3	3	3	-	-	-	-	-	1	-	-	1	1	1
CAFFI, Alex	I	18 Mar 1964	Rovato, Brescia	1986-92	7	56	6	-	-	-	-	-	1	1	1	24	29	19
CAMPBELL-JONES, John	GB	21 Jan 1930	Epsom, Surrey	1962-63	2	2	-	-	-	-	-	-	-	-	-	2	-	-
CAMPOS, Adrian	E	17 Jun 1960	Alcira, nr Valencia	1987-88	2	17	-	-	-	-	-	-	-	-	-	2	15	4
CANNON, John	CDN	21 Jun 1937	London, England	1971	1	1	-	-	-	-	-	-	-	-	-	1	-	-
CANTONI, Eitel	U	1896		1952	1	3	-	-	-	-	-	-	-	-	-	1	2	-
CAPELLI, Ivan	I	24 May 1963	Milan	1985-93	9	93	31	-	-	-	2	1	1	4	4	17	64	5
CARINI, Piero	I	6 Mar 1921 30 May 1957	Genova St. Etienne, France	1952-53	2	3	-	-	-	-	-	-	-	-	-	-	3	-
CASTELLOTTI, Eugenio	I	10 Oct 1930 14 Mar 1957	Lodi, Milan Modena Aerautodromo	1955-57	3	14	19.50	1	-	-	2	1	1	1	1	2	6	-
CECOTTO, Johnny	YV	25 Jan 1956	Caracas	1983-84	2	18	1	-	-	-	-	-	-	-	1	6	11	5
CEVERT, François	F	25 Feb 1944 6 Oct 1973	Paris Watkins Glen, NY, USA	1969-73	5	47	89	-	2	1	10	2	2	2	2	10	18	1
CHABOUD, Eugène	F	12 Apr 1907 28 Dec 1983	Lyon Montfermeil	1950-51	2	3	1	-	-	-	-	-	-	1	-	1	1	-
CHAMBERLAIN, Jay	USA	29 Dec 1925		1962	1	1	-	-	-	-	-	-	-	-	-	1	-	2
CHARLTON, Dave	ZA	27 Oct 1936	Brotton, nr Redcar, Yorks	1965-75	9	11	-	-	-	-	-	-	-	-	-	3	8	2
CHEEVER, Eddie	USA	10 Jan 1958	Phoenix, Arizona	1978-89	11	132	70	-	-	-	2	7	5	4	7	30	77	11
CHIESA, Andrea	CH	6 May 1964	Milan	1992	1	3	-	-	-	-	-	-	-	-	-	-	3	7
CHIMERI, Ettore	I	4 Jun 1921 27 Feb 1960	 Cuba	1960	1	1	-	-	-	-	-	-	-	-	-	-	1	-
CHIRON, Louis	MC	3 Aug 1899 22 Jun 1979	Monaco Monaco	1950-58	6	15	4	-	-	-	-	1	-	-	2	4	8	4
CLAES, Johnny	B	11 Aug 1916 3 Feb 1956	London, England Brussels	1950-55	5	23	-	-	-	-	-	-	-	-	-	13	10	2
CLARK, Jim	GB	4 Mar 1936 7 Apr 1968	Kilmany, Fifeshire, Scotland Hockenheim, Germany	1960-68	9	72	274	33	28	25	1	6	4	3	1	9	23	1
COLLINS, Peter	GB	6 Nov 1931 3 Aug 1958	Kidderminster, Worcs Bonn, Germany	1952-58	7	32	47	-	-	3	3	3	1	1	2	3	16	3
COLLOMB, Bernard	F	7 Oct 1930		1961-64	4	4	-	-	-	-	-	-	-	-	-	1	3	2
COMAS, Erik	F	28 Sep 1963	Romans, nr Valence	1991-94	4	59	7	-	-	-	-	-	-	1	5	26	27	4
COMOTTI, Franco	I	24 Jul 1906 10 May 1963	Brescia Bergamo	1950-52	2	2	-	-	-	-	-	-	-	-	-	1	1	-
CONSTANTINE, George	USA	22 Feb 1918		1959	1	1	-	-	-	-	-	-	-	-	-	-	1	-
CORDTS, John	CDN	23 Jul 1935		1969	1	1	-	-	-	-	-	-	-	-	-	-	1	-
COULTHARD, David	GB	27 Mar 1971	Twynholm, Dumfries., Scotland	1994-96	3	41	81	5	4	1	6	4	3	4	2	3	18	-
COURAGE, Piers	GB	27 May 1942 21 Jun 1970	Colchester, Essex Zandvoort, Netherlands	1966-70	5	28	20	-	-	-	2	-	1	2	1	3	19	2
CRAFT, Chris	GB	17 Nov 1939	Porthleven, Cornwall	1971	1	1	-	-	-	-	-	-	-	-	-	-	1	1
CRAWFORD, Jim	GB	13 Feb 1948	Dunfermline, Scotland	1975	1	2	-	-	-	-	-	-	-	-	-	1	1	-

	Nat	Born Died	Place of Birth Place of Death	Years Entered	No. of Years	GPs	Points	PP	FL	Win	2nd	3rd	4th	5th	6th	OP	NC etc	NS etc
CREUS, Antonio	E	1922		1960	1	1	-	-	-	-	-	-	-	-	-	-	1	-
CROOK, Tony	GB	16 Feb 1920	Manchester	1952-53	2	2	-	-	-	-	-	-	-	-	-	1	1	-
CROSSLEY, Geoffrey	GB	11 May 1921	Baslow, nr Bakewell, Derbys	1950	1	2	-	-	-	-	-	-	-	-	-	1	1	-
d'OREY, Fritz	BR	25 Mar 1938 1961	Sân Paulo	1959	1	3	-	-	-	-	-	-	-	-	-	1	2	-
da SILVA RAMOS, Nano	F/BR	7 Dec 1925	Paris	1955-56	2	7	2	-	-	-	-	-	-	1	-	2	4	-
DAIGH, Chuck	USA	29 Nov 1923	Long Beach, California	1960	1	3	-	-	-	-	-	-	-	-	-	1	2	3
DALMAS, Yannick	F	28 Jul 1961	Le Beausset, nr Toulon	1987-94	5	23	2	-	-	-	-	-	-	1	-	14	8	26
DALY, Derek	IRL	11 Mar 1953	Dundrum, Dublin	1978-82	5	49	15	-	-	-	-	-	2	3	3	18	23	15
DANNER, Christian	D	4 Apr 1958	Munich	1985-89	4	36	4	-	-	-	-	-	1	-	1	13	21	11
DAPONTE, Jorge	RA	5 Jun 1923 9 Mar 1963	Buenos Aires Buenos Aires	1954	1	2	-	-	-	-	-	-	-	-	-	1	1	-
DAVIS, Colin	GB	29 Jul 1933	London	1959	1	2	-	-	-	-	-	-	-	-	-	1	1	-
de ADAMICH, Andrea	I	3 Oct 1941	Trieste	1968-73	5	30	6	-	-	-	-	-	2	-	-	10	18	6
de ANGELIS, Elio	I	26 Mar 1958 15 May 1986	Rome Marseille, France	1979-86	8	108	122	3	-	2	2	5	11	17	6	16	49	1
de BEAUFORT, Carel Godin	NL	10 Apr 1934 3 Aug 1964	Maarsbergen Castle Düsseldorf, Germany	1957-64	8	28	4	-	-	-	-	-	-	-	4	19	5	3
de CABRAL, Mario	P	15 Jan 1934		1959-64	4	4	-	-	-	-	-	-	-	-	-	1	3	1
de CESARIS, Andrea	I	31 May 1959	Rome	1980-94	15	208	59	1	1	-	2	3	7	4	6	49	137	6
de FILIPPIS, Maria Teresa	I	11 Nov 1926	Naples	1958-59	2	3	-	-	-	-	-	-	-	-	-	1	2	2
de GRAFFENRIED, Emmanuel	CH	18 May 1914	Paris, France	1950-56	6	22	9	-	-	-	-	-	1	3	4	4	10	1
de KLERK, Peter	ZA	16 Mar 1935	Pilgrims Rest, Transvaal	1963-70	4	4	-	-	-	-	-	-	-	-	-	2	2	-
de PORTAGO, Alfonso	E	11 Oct 1928 12 May 1957	London, England Goito to Guidizzolo, Italy	1956-57	2	5	4	-	-	-	1	-	-	1	-	-	3	-
de TERRA, Max	CH	6 Oct 1918 29 Dec 1982		1952-53	2	2	-	-	-	-	-	-	-	-	-	1	1	-
de TOMASO, Alessandro	RA	10 Jul 1928	Buenos Aires	1957-59	2	2	-	-	-	-	-	-	-	-	-	1	1	-
de TORNACO, Charles	B	7 Jun 1927 18 Sep 1953	Brussels Modena Aerautodromo, Italy	1952-53	2	2	-	-	-	-	-	-	-	-	-	1	1	2
de VILLOTA, Emilio	E	26 Jul 1946	Madrid	1976-82	5	2	-	-	-	-	-	-	-	-	-	2	-	13
DELETRAZ, Jean-Denis	CH	1 Oct 1963	Geneva	1994-95	2	3	-	-	-	-	-	-	-	-	-	1	2	-
DEPAILLER, Patrick	F	9 Aug 1944 1 Aug 1980	Clermont-Ferrand Hockenheim, Germany	1972-80	8	95	141	1	4	2	10	7	6	6	5	18	41	-
DINIZ, Pedro	BR	22 May 1970	São Paulo	1995-96	2	33	2	-	-	-	-	-	-	-	2	13	18	-
DOLHEM, José	F	26 Apr 1944 16 Apr 1988	Paris nr St. Etienne	1974	1	1	-	-	-	-	-	-	-	-	-	-	1	2
DONNELLY, Martin	GB	26 Mar 1964	Belfast, Northern Ireland	1989-90	2	13	-	-	-	-	-	-	-	-	-	6	7	2
DONOHUE, Mark	USA	18 Mar 1937 19 Aug 1975	Summit, New Jersey Graz, Austria	1971-75	3	14	8	-	-	-	-	1	-	2	-	5	6	2
DOWNING, Ken	GB	5 Dec 1917	Chesterton, Staffordshire	1952	1	2	-	-	-	-	-	-	-	-	-	1	1	-

	Nat	Born Died	Place of Birth Place of Death	Years Entered	No. of Years	GPs	Points	PP	FL	Win	2nd	3rd	4th	5th	6th	OP	NC etc	NS etc
DRAKE, Bob	USA	14 Dec 1919 18 Apr 1990		1960	1	1	-	-	-	-	-	-	-	-	-	1	-	-
DRIVER, Paddy	ZA	13 May 1934	Johannesburg	1963-74	2	1	-	-	-	-	-	-	-	-	-	-	1	1
DROGO, Piero	I	8 Aug 1926 28 Apr 1973	Vignale Monferrato Bologna	1960	1	1	-	-	-	-	-	-	-	-	-	1	-	-
DUMFRIES, Johnny	GB	26 Apr 1958	Rothesay, Bute, Scotland	1986	1	15	3	-	-	-	-	-	-	1	1	4	9	1
EATON, George	CDN	12 Nov 1945	Toronto, Ontario	1969-71	3	11	-	-	-	-	-	-	-	-	-	4	7	2
EDWARDS, Guy	GB	30 Dec 1942	Macclesfield, Cheshire	1974-77	3	11	-	-	-	-	-	-	-	-	-	8	3	6
ELFORD, Vic	GB	10 Jun 1935	Peckham, London	1968-71	3	13	8	-	-	-	-	-	1	2	1	4	5	-
EMERY, Paul	GB	12 Nov 1916 3 Feb 1993	Chiswick, London Epsom, Surrey	1956-58	2	1	-	-	-	-	-	-	-	-	-	-	1	1
ENGLAND, Paul	AUS	28 Mar 1929		1957	1	1	-	-	-	-	-	-	-	-	-	-	1	-
ERTL, Harald	A	31 Aug 1948 7 Apr 1982	Zell am See nr Giessen, Germany	1975-80	5	19	-	-	-	-	-	-	-	-	-	11	8	9
ESTEFANO, Nasif	RA	18 Nov 1932 21 Oct 1973	Concepción-Tucumán South America	1960-62	2	1	-	-	-	-	-	-	-	-	-	1	-	1
ÉTANÇELIN, Philippe	F	28 Dec 1896 13 Oct 1981	Rouen Neuilly sur Seine, nr Paris	1950-52	3	12	3	-	-	-	-	-	-	2	-	4	6	-
EVANS, Bob	GB	11 Jun 1947	Waddington, Lincolnshire	1975-76	2	10	-	-	-	-	-	-	-	-	-	5	5	2
FABI, Corrado	I	12 Apr 1961	Milan	1983-84	2	12	-	-	-	-	-	-	-	-	-	3	9	6
FABI, Teo	I	9 Mar 1955	Milan	1982-87	5	64	23	3	2	-	-	2	2	4	1	9	46	7
FABRE, Pascal	F	9 Jan 1960	Lyon	1987	1	11	-	-	-	-	-	-	-	-	-	8	3	3
FAGIOLI, Luigi	I	9 Jun 1898 20 Jun 1952	Osimo, nr Ancona Monte Carlo, Monaco	1950-51	2	7	32	-	-	1	4	1	-	-	-	-	1	-
FAIRMAN, Jack	GB	15 Mar 1913	Smallfield, Surrey	1953-61	8	12	5	-	-	-	-	-	1	1	-	1	9	1
FANGIO, Juan Manuel	RA	24 Jun 1911 17 Jul 1995	Balcarce, Buenos Aires Balcarce, Buenos Aires	1950-58	8	51	277.14	29	23	24	10	1	5	-	-	1	10	-
FARINA, Giuseppe	I	30 Oct 1906 30 Jun 1966	Turin Aiguebelle, France	1950-55	6	33	127.33	5	5	5	9	5	3	2	1	1	7	1
FISCHER, Rudi	CH	19 Apr 1912 30 Dec 1976	Stuttgart, Germany Luzern	1951-52	2	7	10	-	-	-	1	1	-	-	1	3	1	1
FISHER, Mike	USA	13 Mar 1943	Hollywood, California	1967	1	2	-	-	-	-	-	-	-	-	-	1	1	-
FISICHELLA, Giancarlo	I	14 Jan 1973	Rome	1996	1	8	-	-	-	-	-	-	-	-	-	3	5	-
FITCH, John	USA	4 Aug 1917	Indianapolis, Indiana	1953-55	2	2	-	-	-	-	-	-	-	-	-	1	1	-
FITTIPALDI, Christian	BR	18 Jan 1971	São Paulo	1992-94	3	40	12	-	-	-	-	-	3	1	1	21	14	3
FITTIPALDI, Emerson	BR	12 Dec 1946	São Paulo	1970-80	11	144	281	6	6	14	13	8	9	5	8	39	48	5
FITTIPALDI, Wilson	BR	25 Dec 1943	São Paulo	1972-75	3	36	3	-	-	-	-	-	-	1	1	15	19	2
FITZAU, Theo	D	10 Feb 1923 18 Mar 1982		1953	1	1	-	-	-	-	-	-	-	-	-	-	1	-
FLINTERMAN, Jan	NL	2 Oct 1919 26 Dec 1992	 Leiden	1952	1	1	-	-	-	-	-	-	-	-	-	1	-	-
FLOCKHART, Ron	GB	16 Jun 1923 12 Apr 1962	Edinburgh, Scotland Dandenong Ranges, Australia	1954-60	6	13	5	-	-	-	-	1	-	-	2	2	8	1
FOITEK, Gregor	CH	27 Mar 1965	Zurich	1989-90	2	7	-	-	-	-	-	-	-	-	-	2	5	15

	Nat	Born Died	Place of Birth Place of Death	Years Entered	No. of Years	GPs	Points	PP	FL	Win	2nd	3rd	4th	5th	6th	OP	NC etc	NS etc
FOLLMER, George	USA	27 Jan 1934	Phoenix, Arizona	1973	1	12	5	-	-	-	-	1	-	-	1	5	5	1
FORINI, Franco	CH	22 Sep 1958	Muralto, nr Locarno	1987	1	2	-	-	-	-	-	-	-	-	-	-	2	1
FOTHENNGHAM -PARKER, Philip	GB	22 Sep 1907 15 Oct 1981	Beckenham, Kent Beckley, nr Rye, East Sussex	1951	1	1	-	-	-	-	-	-	-	-	-	-	1	-
FRENTZEN, Heinz-Harald	D	18 May 1967	Mönchengladbach	1994-96	3	48	29	-	-	-	-	1	4	3	7	11	22	1
FRÈRE, Paul	B	30 Jan 1917	Le Havre, France	1952-56	5	11	11	-	-	-	1	-	1	1	-	2	6	-
FRY, Joe	GB	26 Oct 1915 29 Jul 1950	Chipping Sodbury, Glos Blandford Camp, Dorset	1950	1	1	-	-	-	-	-	-	-	-	-	1	-	-
GABBIANI, Beppe	I	2 Jan 1957	Piacenza	1978-81	2	3	-	-	-	-	-	-	-	-	-	-	3	14
GACHOT, Bertrand	F	23 Dec 1962	Luxembourg	1989-95	6	47	5	-	1	-	-	-	-	1	3	11	32	37
GAILLARD, Patrick	F	12 Feb 1952	Paris	1979	1	2	-	-	-	-	-	-	-	-	-	1	1	3
GALLI, Nanni	I	2 Oct 1940	Bologna	1970-73	4	17	-	-	-	-	-	-	-	-	-	7	10	3
GÁLVEZ, Oscar	RA	17 Aug 1913 16 Dec 1989	Buenos Aires Buenos Aires	1953	1	1	2	-	-	-	-	-	-	1	-	-	-	-
GAMBLE, Fred	USA	17 Mar 1932	Pittsburg, Pennsylvania	1960	1	1	-	-	-	-	-	-	-	-	-	1	-	-
GANLEY, Howden	NZ	24 Dec 1941	Hamilton	1971-74	4	35	10	-	-	-	-	-	2	1	2	16	14	6
GARDNER, Frank	AUS	1 Oct 1930	Sydney, New South Wales	1964-68	3	8	-	-	-	-	-	-	-	-	-	3	5	1
GARTNER, Jo	A	4 Jan 1954 1 Jun 1986	Vienna Le Mans, France	1984	1	8	2	-	-	-	-	-	-	1	-	3	4	-
GAZE, Tony	AUS	3 Feb 1920	Melbourne, Victoria	1952	1	3	-	-	-	-	-	-	-	-	-	1	2	1
GEKI	I	23 Oct 1937 18 Jun 1967	Milan Caserta, nr Naples	1964-66	3	2	-	-	-	-	-	-	-	-	-	1	1	1
GENDEBIEN, Olivier	B	12 Jan 1924	Brussels	1956-61	5	14	18	-	-	-	1	1	2	1	2	4	3	1
GERARD, Bob	GB	19 Jan 1914 26 Jan 1990	Leicester South Croxton, Leicester	1950-57	6	8	-	-	-	-	-	-	-	-	3	4	1	-
GERINI, Gerino	I	10 Aug 1928	Rome	1956-58	2	6	1.50	-	-	-	-	-	1	-	-	3	2	1
GETHIN, Peter	GB	21 Feb 1940	Ewell, Surrey	1970-74	5	30	11	-	-	1	-	-	-	-	2	8	19	1
GHINZANI, Piercarlo	I	16 Jan 1952	Riviera d'Adda, Bergamo	1981-89	8	76	2	-	-	-	-	-	-	1	-	19	56	35
GIACOMELLI, Bruno	I	10 Sep 1952	Borgo Poncarale, Brescia	1977-90	8	69	14	1	-	-	-	1	1	3	1	22	41	13
GIBSON, Dick	GB	16 Apr 1918	Bourne, Lincolnshire	1957-58	2	2	-	-	-	-	-	-	-	-	-	-	2	-
GINTHER, Richie	USA	5 Aug 1930 20 Sep 1989	Hollywood, California France	1960-67	8	52	107	-	3	1	8	5	6	4	4	11	13	2
GIRAUD-CABANTOUS, Yves	F	8 Oct 1904 30 Mar 1973	St-Gaudens	1950-53	4	13	5	-	-	-	-	-	1	1	-	6	5	-
GIUNTI, Ignazio	I	30 Aug 1941 10 Jan 1971	Rome Buenos Aires, Argentina	1970	1	4	3	-	-	-	-	-	1	-	-	2	1	-
GODIA, Chico	E	21 Mar 1921 28 Nov 1990	Barcelona Barcelona	1951-58	5	13	6	-	-	-	-	-	2	-	1	5	5	1
GOETHALS, Christian	B	4 Aug 1928		1958	1	1	-	-	-	-	-	-	-	-	-	-	1	-
GONZÁLEZ, Froilán	RA	5 Oct 1922	Arrecifes	1950-60	9	26	77.64	3	6	2	7	6	2	1	-	1	7	-
GONZÁLEZ, Oscar	U			1956	1	1	-	-	-	-	-	-	-	-	1	-	-	-

	Nat	Born Died	Place of Birth Place of Death	Years Entered	No. of Years	GPs	Points	PP	FL	Win	2nd	3rd	4th	5th	6th	OP	NC etc	NS etc
GORDINI, Aldo	F	20 May 1921 28 Jan 1995	Bologna, Italy Paris	1951	1	1	-	-	-	-	-	-	-	-	-	-	1	-
GOULD, Horace	GB	20 Sep 1921 4 Nov 1968	Southmead, Bristol Southmead, Bristol	1954-60	6	14	2	-	-	-	-	-	-	1	-	4	9	4
GOUNON, Jean-Marc	F	1 Jan 1963	Aubenas	1993-94	2	9	-	-	-	-	-	-	-	-	-	4	5	-
GREENE, Keith	GB	5 Jan 1938	Leytonstone, London	1959-62	4	3	-	-	-	-	-	-	-	-	-	1	2	3
GREGORY, Masten	USA	29 Feb 1932 8 Nov 1985	Kansas City, Missouri Porto Ecole, nr Rome, Italy	1957-65	8	38	21	-	-	-	1	2	3	-	2	14	16	5
GRIGNARD, Georges	F	25 Jul 1905 7 Dec 1977	Villeneuve-St-Georges, Paris	1951	1	1	-	-	-	-	-	-	-	-	-	-	1	-
GROUILLARD, Olivier	F	2 Sep 1958	Fenouillet, Toulouse	1989-92	4	41	1	-	-	-	-	-	-	-	1	13	27	21
GUELFI, André	MA	6 May 1919		1958	1	1	-	-	-	-	-	-	-	-	-	1	-	-
GUERRA, Miguel-Angel	RA	31 Aug 1953	Buenos Aires	1981	1	1	-	-	-	-	-	-	-	-	-	-	1	3
GUERRERO, Roberto	CO	16 Nov 1958	Medellin	1982-83	2	21	-	-	-	-	-	-	-	-	-	5	16	7
GUGELMIN, Mauricio	BR	20 Apr 1963	Joinville	1988-92	5	74	10	-	1	-	-	1	1	1	1	27	43	6
GURNEY, Dan	USA	13 Apr 1931	Port Jefferson, Long Is., NY	1959-70	11	86	133	3	6	4	8	7	2	5	5	13	42	1
HAHNE, Hubert	D	28 Mar 1935	Moers	1966-70	5	3	-	-	-	-	-	-	-	-	-	2	1	2
HAILWOOD, Mike	GB	2 Apr 1940 23 Mar 1981	Great Milton, Oxford Portway Hospital, Birmingham	1963-74	7	50	29	-	1	-	1	1	5	1	2	17	23	-
HÄKKINEN, Mika	FIN	28 Sep 1968	Helsinki	1991-96	6	79	91	-	-	-	3	10	5	7	4	16	34	3
HALFORD, Bruce	GB	18 May 1931	Hampton-in-Arden, Warwicks	1956-60	4	8	-	-	-	-	-	-	-	-	-	2	6	1
HALL, Jim	USA	23 Jul 1935	Abilene, Texas	1960-63	4	11	3	-	-	-	-	-	-	1	1	6	3	1
HAMILTON, Duncan	GB	30 Apr 1920 13 May 1994	Cork, Ireland Sherbourne, Dorset	1951-53	3	5	-	-	-	-	-	-	-	-	-	2	3	-
HAMPSHIRE, David	GB	29 Dec 1917 25 Aug 1990	Mickleover, nr Derby Newton Solney, Derbyshire	1950	1	2	-	-	-	-	-	-	-	-	-	1	1	-
HANSGEN, Walt	USA	28 Oct 1919 7 Apr 1966	Westfield, New Jersey Orléans, France	1961-64	2	2	2	-	-	-	-	-	-	1	-	-	1	-
HARRIS, Mike	RSR	25 May 1939	Mufulira, N. Rhodesia	1962	1	1	-	-	-	-	-	-	-	-	-	-	1	-
HARRISON, Cuth	GB	6 Jul 1906 21 Jan 1981	Ecclesall, Sheffield Sheffield	1950	1	3	-	-	-	-	-	-	-	-	-	1	2	-
HART, Brian	GB	7 Sep 1936	Enfield, Middlesex	1967	1	1	-	-	-	-	-	-	-	-	-	-	1	-
HASEMI, Masahiro	J	13 Nov 1945	Tokyo	1976	1	1	-	-	1	-	-	-	-	-	-	1	-	-
HAWKINS, Paul	AUS	12 Oct 1937 26 May 1969	Melbourne, Victoria Oulton Park, England	1965	1	3	-	-	-	-	-	-	-	-	-	2	1	-
HAWTHORN, Mike	GB	10 Apr 1929 22 Jan 1959	Mexborough, Yorkshire Guildford-by-pass, Surrey	1952-58	7	45	127.64	4	6	3	9	6	7	2	3	3	12	2
HAYJE, Boy	NL	3 May 1949	Amsterdam	1976-77	2	3	-	-	-	-	-	-	-	-	-	1	2	4
HEEKS, Willi	D	13 Feb 1922	Moorlage	1952-53	2	2	-	-	-	-	-	-	-	-	-	-	2	-
HELFRICH, Theo	D	13 May 1913 28 Apr 1978	Frankfurt-am-Main	1952-54	3	3	-	-	-	-	-	-	-	-	-	1	2	-
HENTON, Brian	GB	19 Sep 1946	Derby	1975-82	5	19	-	-	1	-	-	-	-	-	-	10	9	19
HERBERT, Johnny	GB	25 Jun 1964	Brentwood, Essex	1989-96	8	96	67	-	-	2	1	2	8	3	3	34	43	3

	Nat	Born Died	Place of Birth Place of Death	Years Entered	No. of Years	GPs	Points	PP	FL	Win	2nd	3rd	4th	5th	6th	OP	NC etc	NS etc
HERRMANN, Hans	D	23 Feb 1928	Stuttgart	1953-69	10	18	10	-	1	-	-	1	2	-	1	6	8	3
HESNAULT, François	F	30 Dec 1956	Neuilly sur Seine, nr Paris	1984-85	2	19	-	-	-	-	-	-	-	-	-	5	14	2
HEYER, Hans	D	16 Mar 1943	Mönchengladbach	1977	1	1	-	-	-	-	-	-	-	-	-	-	1	-
HILL, Damon	GB	17 Sep 1960	Hampstead, London	1992-96	5	67	326	20	19	21	14	5	3	1	1	4	18	6
HILL, Graham	GB	15 Feb 1929 29 Nov 1975	Hampstead, London Arkley, nr Barnet, Herts	1958-75	18	176	289	13	10	14	15	7	9	7	9	41	74	3
HILL, Phil	USA	20 Apr 1927	Miami, Florida	1958-66	8	48	98	6	6	3	5	8	2	-	3	12	15	2
HIRT, Peter	CH	30 Mar 1910 28 Jun 1992	Lenzburg Zurich	1951-53	3	5	-	-	-	-	-	-	-	-	-	2	3	-
HOBBS, David	GB	9 Jun 1939	Leamington Spa, Warwickshire	1967-74	4	7	-	-	-	-	-	-	-	-	-	6	1	-
HOFFMAN, Ingo	BR	18 Feb 1953	São Paulo	1976-77	2	3	-	-	-	-	-	-	-	-	-	2	1	3
HOSHINO, Kazuyoshi	J	1 Jul 1947	Shizuoka Prefecture	1976-77	2	2	-	-	-	-	-	-	-	-	-	1	1	-
HULME, Denny	NZ	18 Jun 1936 4 Oct 1992	Nelson Bathurst, NSW, Australia	1965-74	10	112	248	1	9	8	9	16	11	8	9	17	34	-
HUNT, James	GB	29 Aug 1947 15 Jun 1993	Belmont, nr Epsom, Surrey Wimbledon, London	1973-79	7	92	179	14	8	10	6	7	7	2	3	11	46	1
HUTCHISON, Gus	USA	26 Apr 1937	Atlanta, Georgia	1970	1	1	-	-	-	-	-	-	-	-	-	-	1	-
ICKX, Jacky	B	1 Jan 1945	Ixelles, Brussels	1966-79	14	116	181	13	14	8	7	10	4	7	4	26	50	6
IGLESIAS, Jésus	RA	22 Feb 1922	Pergamino, nr Buenos Aires	1955	1	1	-	-	-	-	-	-	-	-	-	-	1	-
INOUE, Taki	J	5 Sep 1963	Kobe	1994-95	2	18	-	-	-	-	-	-	-	-	-	5	13	-
IRELAND, Innes	GB	12 Jun 1930 22 Oct 1993	Mytholmroyd, Yorkshire Reading, Berkshire	1959-66	8	50	47	-	1	1	2	1	4	4	2	12	24	4
IRVINE, Eddie	GB	10 Nov 1965	Conlig, Co. Down, N Ireland	1993-96	4	48	28	-	-	-	-	2	3	4	3	10	26	-
IRWIN, Chris	GB	27 Jun 1942	Wandsworth, London	1966-67	2	10	2	-	-	-	-	-	-	1	-	4	5	-
JABOUILLE, Jean-Pierre	F	1 Oct 1942	Paris	1974-81	7	49	21	6	-	2	-	-	1	-	-	8	38	7
JAMES, John	GB	10 May 1914	Packwood, Warwickshire	1951	1	1	-	-	-	-	-	-	-	-	-	-	1	-
JARIER, Jean-Pierre	F	10 Jul 1946	Charenton, nr Paris	1971-83	12	135	31.50	3	3	-	-	3	2	6	3	50	71	8
JOHANSSON, Stefan	S	8 Sep 1956	Växjö	1983-91	10	79	88	-	-	-	4	8	7	4	3	18	35	24
JOHNSON, Leslie	GB	22 Mar 1912 8 Jun 1959	 Withington, Gloucestershire	1950	1	1	-	-	-	-	-	-	-	-	-	-	1	-
JOHNSTONE, Bruce	ZA	30 Jan 1937	Durban	1962	1	1	-	-	-	-	-	-	-	-	-	1	-	-
JONES, Alan	AUS	2 Nov 1946	Melbourne, Victoria	1975-86	10	116	206	6	13	12	7	5	8	5	2	29	48	1
KARCH, Oswald	D	6 Mar 1917	Ludwigshafen	1953	1	1	-	-	-	-	-	-	-	-	-	-	1	-
KATAYAMA, Ukyo	J	29 May 1963	Tokyo	1992-96	5	78	5	-	-	-	-	-	-	2	1	22	53	2
KEEGAN, Rupert	GB	26 Feb 1955	Westcliff-on-Sea, Essex	1977-82	4	25	-	-	-	-	-	-	-	-	-	12	13	12
KEIZAN, Eddie	ZA	12 Sep 1944	Johannesburg	1973-75	3	3	-	-	-	-	-	-	-	-	-	2	1	-
KELLY, Joe	IRL	13 Mar 1913 28 Nov 1993	Dublin Neston, Cheshire, England	1950-51	2	2	-	-	-	-	-	-	-	-	-	-	2	-

	Nat	Born Died	Place of Birth Place of Death	Years Entered	No. of Years	GPs	Points	PP	FL	Win	2nd	3rd	4th	5th	6th	OP	NC etc	NS etc
KESSEL, Loris	CH	1 Apr 1950	Lugano	1976-77	2	3	-	-	-	-	-	-	-	-	-	1	2	3
KINNUNEN, Leo	FIN	5 Aug 1943	Tampere	1974	1	1	-	-	-	-	-	-	-	-	-	-	1	5
KLENK, Hans	D	28 Oct 1919	Künzelsau	1952	1	1	-	-	-	-	-	-	-	-	-	1	-	-
KLING, Karl	D	16 Sep 1910	Giessen	1954-55	2	11	17	-	1	-	1	1	2	1	-	1	5	-
KLODWIG, Ernst	D	23 May 1903 15 Apr 1973	(from East Berlin)	1952-53	2	2	-	-	-	-	-	-	-	-	-	2	-	-
KOINIGG, Helmut	A	3 Nov 1948 6 Oct 1974	Vienna Watkins Glen, NY, USA	1974	1	2	-	-	-	-	-	-	-	-	-	1	1	1
KRAUSE, Rudolf	D	30 Mar 1907 11 Apr 1987		1952-53	2	2	-	-	-	-	-	-	-	-	-	1	1	-
La CAZE, Robert	MA	26 Feb 1917	Paris, France	1958	1	1	-	-	-	-	-	-	-	-	-	1	-	-
LAFFITE, Jacques	F	21 Nov 1943	Paris	1974-86	13	176	228	7	6	6	10	16	7	9	11	35	82	4
LAGORCE, Franck	F	1 Sep 1968 l'	Hay-Les-Roses, nr Paris	1994	1	2	-	-	-	-	-	-	-	-	-	1	1	-
LAMMERS, Jan	NL	2 Jun 1956	Zandvoort	1979-92	5	23	-	-	-	-	-	-	-	-	-	12	11	18
LAMY, Pedro	P	20 Mar 1972	Aldeia Galega	1993-96	4	32	1	-	-	-	-	-	-	-	1	18	13	-
LANDI, Chico	BR	14 Jul 1907 7 Jun 1989	São Paulo	1951-56	4	6	1.50	-	-	-	-	-	1	-	-	2	3	-
LANG, Hermann	D	6 Apr 1909 19 Oct 1987	Bad Cannstatt, nr Stuttgart Bad Cannstatt, nr Stuttgart	1953-54	2	2	2	-	-	-	-	-	-	1	-	-	1	-
LARINI, Nicola	I	19 Mar 1964	Lido di Camaiore	1987-94	7	44	6	-	-	-	1	-	-	-	-	22	21	26
LARRAURI, Oscar	RA	19 Aug 1954	Rosario	1988-89	2	8	-	-	-	-	-	-	-	-	-	2	6	13
LARRETA, Rodriguez	RA	14 Jan 1934 11 Mar 1977	Buenos Aires	1960	1	1	-	-	-	-	-	-	-	-	-	1	-	-
LARROUSSE, Gérard	F	23 May 1940	Lyon	1974	1	1	-	-	-	-	-	-	-	-	-	-	1	1
LAUDA, Niki	A	22 Feb 1949	Vienna	1971-85	13	171	420.50	24	24	25	20	9	7	7	5	17	81	6
LAURENT, Roger	B	21 Feb 1913	Liège	1952	1	2	-	-	-	-	-	-	-	-	1	1	-	-
LAVAGGI, Giovanni	I	18 Feb 1958	Augusta, Sicily	1995-96	2	7	-	-	-	-	-	-	-	-	-	2	5	3
LAWRENCE, Chris	GB	27 Jul 1933	Ealing, London	1966	1	2	-	-	-	-	-	-	-	-	-	1	1	-
LECLÈRE, Michel	F	18 Mar 1946	Mantes la Jolie, nr Paris	1975-76	2	7	-	-	-	-	-	-	-	-	-	5	2	1
LEDERLE, Neville	ZA	25 Sep 1938	Theunissen, Winburg	1962-65	2	1	1	-	-	-	-	-	-	-	1	-	-	1
LEES, Geoff	GB	1 May 1951	Atherstone, Warwickshire	1978-82	4	5	-	-	-	-	-	-	-	-	-	3	2	7
LEGAT, Arthur	B	1 Nov 1898 23 Feb 1960	Haine-Saint-Paul Haine-Saint-Pierre	1952-53	2	2	-	-	-	-	-	-	-	-	-	1	1	-
LEHTO, J J	FIN	31 Jan 1966	Espoo	1989-94	6	62	10	-	-	-	-	1	1	1	1	24	34	8
LEONI, Lamberto	I	24 May 1953	Argenta, Ferrara	1977-78	2	2	-	-	-	-	-	-	-	-	-	-	2	3
LESTON, Les	GB	16 Dec 1920	Nottingham	1956-57	2	2	-	-	-	-	-	-	-	-	-	-	2	1
LEVEGH, Pierre	F	22 Dec 1905 11 Jun 1955	Paris Le Mans	1950-51	2	6	-	-	-	-	-	-	-	-	-	3	3	-
LEWIS, Jackie	GB	1 Nov 1936	Stroud, Gloucestershire	1961-62	2	9	3	-	-	-	-	-	1	-	-	5	3	1

	Nat	Born Died	Place of Birth Place of Death	Years Entered	No. of Years	GPs	Points	PP	FL	Win	2nd	3rd	4th	5th	6th	OP	NC etc	NS etc
LEWIS-EVANS, Stuart	GB	20 Apr 1930 25 Oct 1958	Luton, Bedfordshire East Grinstead, Sussex	1957-58	2	14	16	2	-	-	-	2	2	1	-	1	8	-
LIGIER, Guy	F	12 Jul 1930	Vichy	1966-67	2	12	1	-	-	-	-	-	-	-	1	5	6	1
LIPPI, Roberto	I	17 Oct 1926	Rome	1961-63	3	1	-	-	-	-	-	-	-	-	-	-	1	2
LOMBARDI, Lella	I	26 Mar 1941 3 Mar 1992	Frugarolo, nr Alessándria Milan	1974-76	3	12	0.50	-	-	-	-	-	-	-	1	6	5	5
LOOF, Ernst	D	4 Jul 1907 3 Mar 1956	Neindorf Bonn	1953	1	1	-	-	-	-	-	-	-	-	-	-	1	-
LOUVEAU, Henri	F	25 Jan 1910 7 Jan 1991		1950-51	2	2	-	-	-	-	-	-	-	-	-	-	2	-
LOVE, John	RSR	7 Dec 1924	Bulawayo	1962-72	10	9	6	-	-	-	1	-	-	-	-	5	3	1
LOVELY, Pete	USA	11 Apr 1926	Livingston, Montana	1959-71	5	7	-	-	-	-	-	-	-	-	-	3	4	4
LOYER, Roger	F	5 Aug 1907 24 Mar 1988		1954	1	1	-	-	-	-	-	-	-	-	-	-	1	-
LUCAS, Jean	F	25 Apr 1917	Le Mans	1955	1	1	-	-	-	-	-	-	-	-	-	-	1	-
LUNGER, Brett	USA	14 Nov 1945	Wilmington, Delaware	1975-78	4	34	-	-	-	-	-	-	-	-	-	23	11	9
MacDOWEL, Mike	GB	13 Sep 1932	Great Yarmouth, Norfolk	1957	1	1	-	-	-	-	-	-	-	-	-	1	-	-
MacKAY-FRASER, Herbert	USA	23 Jun 1927 14 Jul 1957	Connecticut Reims-Gueux, France	1957	1	1	-	-	-	-	-	-	-	-	-	-	1	-
MACKLIN, Lance	GB	2 Sep 1919	Kensington, London	1952-55	4	13	-	-	-	-	-	-	-	-	-	5	8	2
MAGEE, Damien	GB	17 Nov 1945	Belfast, Northern Ireland	1975-76	2	1	-	-	-	-	-	-	-	-	-	1	-	1
MAGGS, Tony	ZA	9 Feb 1937	Pretoria	1961-65	5	25	26	-	-	-	2	1	1	2	3	9	7	2
MAGLIOLI, Umberto	I	5 Jun 1928	Bioglio, Vercelli	1953-57	5	10	3.33	-	-	-	-	2	-	-	1	3	4	-
MAGNUSSEN, Jan	DK	4 Jul 1973	Roskilde	1995	1	1	-	-	-	-	-	-	-	-	-	1	-	-
MAIRESSE, Guy	F	10 Aug 1910 24 Apr 1954	La Capelle, l'Aisne Monthléry, nr Paris	1950-51	2	3	-	-	-	-	-	-	-	-	-	2	1	-
MAIRESSE, Willy	B	1 Oct 1928 2 Sep 1969	Momminges Ostend	1960-65	5	12	7	-	-	-	-	1	1	-	-	1	9	1
MANSELL, Nigel	GB	8 Aug 1953	Baughton, Worcestershire	1980-95	15	187	482	32	30	31	17	11	8	6	9	16	89	4
MANTOVANI, Sergio '	I	22 May 1929	Cusano Milanino, Milan	1953-55	3	7	4	-	-	-	-	-	-	2	-	4	1	1
MANZON, Robert	F	12 Apr 1917	Marseille	1950-56	7	28	16	-	-	-	-	2	2	1	-	6	17	1
MARIMON, Onofré	RA	19 Dec 1923 31 Jul 1954	Cordoba, Buenos Aires Nürburgring, Germany	1951-54	3	11	8.14	-	1	-	-	2	-	-	-	1	8	1
MARKO, Helmut	A	27 Apr 1943	Graz	1971-72	2	9	-	-	-	-	-	-	-	-	-	7	2	1
MARQUES, Tarso	BR	19 Jan 1976	Curitiba (Paranà)	1996	1	2	-	-	-	-	-	-	-	-	-	-	2	-
MARR, Leslie	GB	14 Aug 1922	Durham	1954-55	2	2	-	-	-	-	-	-	-	-	-	1	1	-
MARSH, Tony	GB	20 Jul 1931	Stourbridge, Worcestershire	1957-61	3	4	-	-	-	-	-	-	-	-	-	3	1	1
MARTIN, Eugène	F	24 Mar 1915	Suresnes	1950	1	2	-	-	-	-	-	-	-	-	-	-	2	-
MARTINI, Pierluigi	I	23 Apr 1961	Lugo di Romagna, nr Ravenna	1984-95	10	119	18	-	-	-	-	-	2	4	4	45	64	5
MASS, Jochen	D	30 Sep 1946	Dorfen, nr Munich	1973-82	9	105	71	-	2	1	1	6	7	4	9	36	41	9

	Nat	Born Died	Place of Birth Place of Death	Years Entered	No. of Years	GPs	Points	PP	FL	Win	2nd	3rd	4th	5th	6th	OP	NC etc	NS etc
MAX, Jean	F	27 Jul 1943	Marseille	1971	1	1	-	-	-	-	-	-	-	-	-	-	1	-
MAY, Michael	CH	18 Aug 1934	Stuttgart, Germany	1961	1	2	-	-	-	-	-	-	-	-	-	1	1	1
MAYER, Timmy	USA	22 Feb 1938 28 Feb 1964	Dalton, Pennsylvania Longford,Tasmania,Australia	1962	1	1	-	-	-	-	-	-	-	-	-	-	1	-
MAZET, François	F	26 Feb 1943	Paris	1971	1	1	-	-	-	-	-	-	-	-	-	1	-	-
McALPINE, Ken	GB	21 Sep 1920	Chobham, Surrey	1952-55	3	7	-	-	-	-	-	-	-	-	-	2	5	-
McLAREN, Bruce	NZ	30 Aug 1937 2 Jun 1970	Auckland Goodwood, Sussex, England	1958-70	13	101	196.50	-	3	4	11	12	7	11	5	13	38	3
McRAE, Graham	NZ	5 Mar 1940	Wellington	1973	1	1	-	-	-	-	-	-	-	-	-	-	1	-
MENDITÉGUY, Carlos	RA	10 Aug 1915 28 Apr 1973	Buenos Aires	1953-60	7	10	9	-	-	-	-	1	1	1	-	1	6	1
MERZARIO, Arturo	I	11 Mar 1943	Civenna, Como	1972-79	8	57	11	-	-	-	-	-	3	-	2	11	41	28
MIÈRES, Roberto	RA	3 Dec 1924	Mar del Plata	1953-55	3	17	13	-	1	-	-	-	3	2	2	1	9	-
MIGAULT, François	F	4 Dec 1944	Le Mans	1972-75	3	13	-	-	-	-	-	-	-	-	-	4	9	3
MILES, John	GB	14 Jun 1943	Islington, London	1969-70	2	12	2	-	-	-	-	-	-	1	-	3	8	3
MILHOUX, André	B	9 Dec 1928	Bressoux	1956	1	1	-	-	-	-	-	-	-	-	-	-	1	-
MITTER, Gerhard	D	30 Aug 1935 1 Aug 1969	Schönlinde Nürburgring	1963-69	6	5	3	-	-	-	-	-	1	-	-	1	3	2
MODENA, Stefano	I	12 May 1963	Modena	1987-92	6	70	17	-	-	-	1	1	1	1	2	24	40	11
MONTERMINI, Andrea	I	30 May 1964	Sassuolo, Modena	1994-96	3	21	-	-	-	-	-	-	-	-	-	4	17	7
MONTGOMERIE-CHARRINGTON, Robin	GB	23 Jun 1915	London	1952	1	1	-	-	-	-	-	-	-	-	-	-	1	-
MORBIDELLI, Gianni	I	13 Jan 1968	Pesaro, nr Rimini	1990-95	5	60	8.50	-	-	-	-	1	-	1	3	23	32	2
MORENO, Roberto	BR	11 Feb 1959	Rio de Janeiro	1982-95	7	42	15	-	1	-	1	-	2	1	1	13	24	33
MORGAN, Dave	GB	7 Aug 1944	Shepton Mallet, Somerset	1975	1	1	-	-	-	-	-	-	-	-	-	1	-	-
MOSER, Silvio	CH	24 Apr 1941 26 May 1974	Zurich Locarno	1966-71	6	12	3	-	-	-	-	-	-	1	1	2	8	8
MOSS, Stirling	GB	17 Sep 1929	West Kensington, London	1951-61	11	66	186.64	16	19	16	5	3	3	2	1	7	29	1
MUNARON, Gino	I	2 Apr 1928	Turin	1960	1	4	-	-	-	-	-	-	-	-	-	2	2	1
MURRAY, David	GB	28 Dec 1909 5 Apr 1973	Edinburgh, Scotland Las Palmas, Canary Is, Spain	1950-52	3	4	-	-	-	-	-	-	-	-	-	-	4	1
MUSSO, Luigi	I	28 Jul 1924 6 Jul 1958	Rome Reims, France	1953-58	6	24	44	-	1	1	5	1	1	1	-	5	10	1
NACKE, Bernd *pseudonym of Günther BECHEM*																		
NAKAJIMA, Satoru	J	23 Feb 1953	Okazaki City	1987-91	5	74	16	-	1	-	-	-	2	2	6	25	39	6
NANNINI, Alessandro	I	7 Jul 1959	Siena	1986-90	5	77	65	-	2	1	2	6	4	2	4	12	46	1
NASPETTI, Emanuele	I	24 Feb 1968	Ancona	1992-93	2	6	-	-	-	-	-	-	-	-	-	3	3	-
NATILI, Massimo	I	28 Jul 1935	Ronciglione, Viterbo	1961	1	1	-	-	-	-	-	-	-	-	-	-	1	1
NAYLOR, Brian	GB	24 Mar 1923 8 Aug 1989	Salford, Manchester Marbella, Spain	1957-61	5	7	-	-	-	-	-	-	-	-	-	2	5	1

	Nat	Born Died	Place of Birth Place of Death	Years Entered	No. of Years	GPs	Points	PP	FL	Win	2nd	3rd	4th	5th	6th	OP	NC etc	NS etc
NEEDELL, Tiff	GB	29 Oct 1951	Havant, Hampshire	1980	1	1	-	-	-	-	-	-	-	-	-	-	1	1
NEVE, Patrick	B	13 Oct 1949	Liège	1976-78	3	10	-	-	-	-	-	-	-	-	-	8	2	4
NICHOLSON, John	NZ	6 Oct 1941	Auckland	1974-75	2	1	-	-	-	-	-	-	-	-	-	1	-	1
NIEDERMAYR, Helmut	D	29 Nov 1915 3 Apr 1985	(from Berlin)	1952	1	1	-	-	-	-	-	-	-	-	-	1	-	-
NIEMANN, Brausch	ZA	7 Jan 1939	Durban	1963-65	2	1	-	-	-	-	-	-	-	-	-	1	-	1
NILSSON, Gunnar	S	20 Nov 1948 20 Oct 1978	Helsingborg Hammersmith, London, England	1976-77	2	31	31	-	1	1	-	3	1	3	1	5	17	1
NODA, Hideki	J	7 Mar 1969	Osaka	1994	1	3	-	-	-	-	-	-	-	-	-	-	3	-
NUCKEY, Rodney	GB	26 Jun 1929	Wood Green, London	1953-54	2	1	-	-	-	-	-	-	-	-	-	1	-	1
O'BRIEN, Robert	USA			1952	1	1	-	-	-	-	-	-	-	-	-	1	-	-
OLIVER, Jackie	GB	14 Aug 1942	Chadwell Heath, Essex	1967-77	8	50	13	-	1	-	-	2	-	2	1	11	34	2
ONGAIS, Danny	USA	21 May 1942	Honolulu, Hawaii	1977-78	2	4	-	-	-	-	-	-	-	-	-	1	3	2
OWEN, Arthur	GB	23 Mar 1915	London	1960	1	1	-	-	-	-	-	-	-	-	-	-	1	-
PACE, Carlos	BR	6 Oct 1944 18 Mar 1977	São Paulo nr São Paulo	1972-77	6	72	58	1	5	1	3	2	5	3	2	21	35	1
PAGANI, Nello	I	11 Oct 1911	Milan	1950	1	1	-	-	-	-	-	-	-	-	-	1	-	-
PALETTI, Riccardo	I	15 Jun 1958 13 Jun 1982	Milan Montréal, Canada	1982	1	2	-	-	-	-	-	-	-	-	-	-	2	6
PALM, Torsten	S	23 Jul 1947	Kristinehamn	1975	1	1	-	-	-	-	-	-	-	-	-	1	-	1
PALMER, Jonathan	GB	7 Nov 1956	Lewisham, London	1983-89	7	84	14	-	1	-	-	-	1	4	3	36	40	4
PANIS, Olivier	F	2 Sep 1966	Lyon	1994-96	3	49	38	-	-	1	2	-	2	3	4	22	15	-
PAPIS, Max	I	3 Oct 1969	Como	1995	1	7	-	-	-	-	-	-	-	-	-	2	5	-
PARKES, Mike	GB	24 Sep 1931 28 Aug 1977	Richmond, Surrey nr Turin, Italy	1959-67	3	6	14	1	-	-	2	-	-	1	-	-	3	1
PARNELL, Reg	GB	2 Jul 1911 7 Jan 1964	Derby Derby	1950-54	4	6	9	-	-	-	-	1	1	1	-	1	2	1
PARNELL, Tim	GB	25 Jun 1932	Derby	1959-63	3	2	-	-	-	-	-	-	-	-	-	1	1	2
PATRESE, Riccardo	I	17 Apr 1954	Padua	1977-93	17	256	281	8	13	6	17	14	8	15	13	53	130	1
PEASE, Al	CDN	15 Oct 1921	Darlington, England	1967-69	3	2	-	-	-	-	-	-	-	-	-	-	2	1
PENSKE, Roger	USA	20 Feb 1937	Shaker Heights, Ohio	1961-62	2	2	-	-	-	-	-	-	-	-	-	2	-	-
PERDISA, Cesare	I	21 Oct 1932	Bologna	1955-57	3	7	5	-	-	-	-	2	-	1	1	3	-	1
PERKINS, Larry	AUS	18 Mar 1950	Murrayville, Victoria	1974-77	3	11	-	-	-	-	-	-	-	-	-	5	6	4
PERROT, Xavier	CH	1 Feb 1932	Zurich	1969	1	1	-	-	-	-	-	-	-	-	-	1	-	-
PESCAROLO, Henri	F	25 Sep 1942	Paris	1968-76	8	57	12	-	1	-	-	1	1	1	3	26	25	7
PESENTI-ROSSI, Sandro	I	31 Aug 1942	Bergamo	1976	1	3	-	-	-	-	-	-	-	-	-	3	-	1
PETERS, Josef	D	16 Sep 1914	Düsseldorf	1952	1	1	-	-	-	-	-	-	-	-	-	-	1	-

	Nat	Born Died	Place of Birth Place of Death	Years Entered	No. of Years	GPs	Points	PP	FL	Win	2nd	3rd	4th	5th	6th	OP	NC etc	NS etc
PETERSON, Ronnie	S	14 Feb 1944 11 Sep 1978	Örebro Milan, Italy	1970-78	9	123	206	14	9	10	10	6	5	7	4	29	52	-
PICARD, François	F	26 Apr 1921 Jun 1996	Villefranche sur Saône Monte Carlo, Monaco	1958	1	1	-	-	-	-	-	-	-	-	-	-	1	-
PIETERSE, Ernie	ZA	4 Jul 1938	Parow-Bellville	1962-65	3	2	-	-	-	-	-	-	-	-	-	1	1	1
PIETSCH, Paul	D	20 Jun 1911	Freiburg im Breisgau	1950-52	3	3	-	-	-	-	-	-	-	-	-	-	3	-
PILETTE, André	B	6 Oct 1918 27 Dec 1993	Paris, France	1951-64	7	9	2	-	-	-	-	-	-	1	3	3	2	5
PILETTE, Teddy	B	26 Jul 1942	Brussels	1974-77	2	1	-	-	-	-	-	-	-	-	-	1	-	3
PIOTTI, Luigi	I	27 Oct 1913 19 Apr 1971		1955-58	4	5	-	-	-	-	-	-	-	-	1	1	3	4
PIPER, David	GB	2 Dec 1930	Edgware, Middlesex	1959-60	2	2	-	-	-	-	-	-	-	-	-	1	1	1
PIQUET, Nelson	BR	17 Aug 1952	Rio de Janeiro	1978-91	14	204	485.50	24	23	23	20	17	18	15	7	24	80	3
PIROCCHI, Renato	I	23 Jun 1933	Notaresco, Teramo	1961	1	1	-	-	-	-	-	-	-	-	-	1	-	-
PIRONI, Didier	F	26 Mar 1952 23 Aug 1987	Villecresnes, nr Paris off Isle of Wight, England	1978-82	5	70	101	4	5	3	3	7	3	6	7	15	26	2
PIRRO, Emanuele	I	12 Jan 1962	Rome	1989-91	3	37	3	-	-	-	-	-	-	1	1	15	20	3
POLLET, Jacques	F	28 Jul 1922		1954-55	2	5	-	-	-	-	-	-	-	-	-	2	3	-
PON, Ben	NL	9 Dec 1936	Leiden	1962	1	1	-	-	-	-	-	-	-	-	-	-	1	-
POORE, Dennis	GB	19 Aug 1916 12 Feb 1987	West London Kensington, London	1952	1	2	3	-	-	-	-	-	1	-	-	1	-	-
POSEY, Sam	USA	26 May 1944	New York City, New York	1971-72	2	2	-	-	-	-	-	-	-	-	-	1	1	-
POZZI, Charles	F	27 Aug 1909	Paris	1950	1	1	-	-	-	-	-	-	-	-	1	-	-	-
PRETORIUS, Jackie	ZA	22 Nov 1934	Potchefstroom, Transvaal	1965-73	4	3	-	-	-	-	-	-	-	-	-	-	3	1
PROPHET, David	GB	9 Oct 1937 29 Mar 1981	Hong Kong Silverstone, Northants	1963-65	2	2	-	-	-	-	-	-	-	-	-	1	1	-
PROST, Alain	F	24 Feb 1955	Lorette, Saint-Chamond	1980-93	13	200	798.50	33	41	51	35	20	10	5	7	15	57	2
PRYCE, Tom	GB	11 Jun 1949 5 Mar 1977	Ruthin, Denbighshire, Wales Kyalami, South Africa	1974-77	4	42	19	1	-	-	-	2	3	-	4	13	20	-
PURLEY, David	GB	26 Jan 1945 2 Jul 1985	Bognor Regis, Sussex off Bognor Regis, Sussex	1973-77	3	7	-	-	-	-	-	-	-	-	-	4	3	4
QUESTER, Dieter	A	30 May 1939	Vienna	1969-74	2	1	-	-	-	-	-	-	-	-	-	1	-	1
RABY, Ian	GB	22 Sep 1921 7 Nov 1967	London Waterloo, London	1963-65	3	3	-	-	-	-	-	-	-	-	-	1	2	4
RAHAL, Bobby	USA	10 Jan 1953	Medina, Ohio	1978	1	2	-	-	-	-	-	-	-	-	-	1	1	-
RAPHANEL, Pierre-Henri	F	27 May 1961	Algiers, Algeria	1988-89	2	1	-	-	-	-	-	-	-	-	-	-	1	16
RATZENBERGER, Roland	A	4 Jul 1962 30 Apr 1994	Salzburg Bologna, Italy	1994	1	1	-	-	-	-	-	-	-	-	-	1	-	2
REBAQUE, Hector	MEX	5 Feb 1956	Mexico City	1977-81	5	41	13	-	-	-	-	-	3	1	2	10	25	17
REDMAN, Brian	GB	9 Mar 1937	Colne, Lancashire	1967-74	7	12	8	-	-	-	-	1	-	2	-	4	5	3
REES, Alan	GB	12 Jan 1938	Langstone, Monmouthshire	1966-67	2	3	-	-	-	-	-	-	-	-	-	2	1	-
REGAZZONI, Clay	CH	5 Sep 1939	Mendrisio, nr Lugano	1970-80	11	132	212	5	15	5	13	10	8	9	7	31	49	7

	Nat	Born Died	Place of Birth Place of Death	Years Entered	No. of Years	GPs	Points	PP	FL	Win	2nd	3rd	4th	5th	6th	OP	NC etc	NS etc
REUTEMANN, Carlos	RA	12 Apr 1942	Santa Fé	1972-82	11	146	310	6	6	12	13	20	11	3	7	31	49	-
REVENTLOW, Lance	USA	24 Feb 1936 24 Jul 1972	London, England Colorado	1960	1	1	-	-	-	-	-	-	-	-	-	-	1	3
REVSON, Peter	USA	27 Feb 1939 22 Mar 1974	New York City, New York Kyalami, South Africa	1964-74	5	30	61	1	-	2	2	4	3	3	-	7	9	2
RHODES, John	GB	18 Aug 1927	Wolverhampton, Staffordshire	1965	1	1	-	-	-	-	-	-	-	-	-	-	1	-
RIBEIRO, Alex-Dias	BR	7 Nov 1948	Belo Horizonte	1976-79	3	10	-	-	-	-	-	-	-	-	-	6	4	10
RIESS, Fritz	D	11 Jul 1922 May 1991	Nuremburg	1952	1	1	-	-	-	-	-	-	-	-	-	1	-	-
RINDT, Jochen	A	18 Apr 1942 5 Sep 1970	Mainz-am-Rhein, Germany Milan, Italy	1964-70	7	60	109	10	3	6	3	4	6	1	1	4	35	2
RISELEY-PRICHARD, John	GB	17 Jan 1924	Hereford	1954	1	1	-	-	-	-	-	-	-	-	-	-	1	-
ROBARTS, Richard	GB	22 Sep 1944	Bicknacre, Essex	1974	1	3	-	-	-	-	-	-	-	-	-	2	1	1
RODRIGUEZ, Pedro	MEX	18 Jan 1940 11 Jul 1971	Mexico City Norisring, Germany	1963-71	9	55	71	-	1	2	3	2	4	4	7	7	26	-
RODRIGUEZ, Ricardo	MEX	14 Feb 1942 1 Nov 1962	Mexico City Mexico City	1961-62	2	5	4	-	-	-	-	-	1	-	1	1	2	1
ROL, Franco	I	5 Jun 1908 18 Jun 1977		1950-52	3	5	-	-	-	-	-	-	-	-	-	1	4	-
ROLT, Tony	GB	16 Oct 1918	Bordon, Hampshire	1950-55	3	3	-	-	-	-	-	-	-	-	-	-	3	-
ROOS, Bertil	S	12 Oct 1943	Gothenburg	1974	1	1	-	-	-	-	-	-	-	-	-	-	1	-
ROSBERG, Keke	FIN	6 Dec 1948	Stockholm, Sweden	1978-86	9	114	159.50	5	3	5	8	4	11	9	1	21	55	14
ROSIER, Louis	F	5 Nov 1905 29 Oct 1956	Chapdes-Beaufort Montlhéry, nr Paris	1950-56	7	38	18	-	-	-	-	2	2	2	2	18	12	-
ROSSET, Ricardo	BR	27 Jul 1968	São Paulo	1996	1	16	-	-	-	-	-	-	-	-	-	8	8	-
ROTHENGATTER, Huub	NL	8 Oct 1954	Bussum, nr Hilversum	1984-86	3	26	-	-	-	-	-	-	-	-	-	6	20	4
RUBY, Lloyd	USA	12 Jan 1928	Wichita Falls, Texas	1961	1	1	-	-	-	-	-	-	-	-	-	-	1	-
RUSSO, Giacomo *see GEKI*																		
RUTTMAN, Troy	USA	11 Mar 1930	Mooreland, Oklahoma	1958	1	1	-	-	-	-	-	-	-	-	-	1	-	1
RYAN, Peter	CDN	10 Jun 1940 2 Jul 1962	 Paris, France	1961	1	1	-	-	-	-	-	-	-	-	-	1	-	-
SAID, Bob	USA	5 May 1932	New York City, New York	1959	1	1	-	-	-	-	-	-	-	-	-	-	1	-
SALA, Luis	E	15 May 1959	Barcelona	1988-89	2	26	1	-	-	-	-	-	-	-	1	10	15	6
SALAZAR, Eliseo	RCH	14 Nov 1954	Santiago	1981-83	3	24	3	-	-	-	-	-	-	1	1	6	16	13
SALO, Mika	FIN	30 Nov 1966	Helsinki	1994-96	3	35	10	-	-	-	-	-	-	4	2	15	14	-
SALVADORI, Roy	GB	12 May 1922	Dovercourt, Essex	1952-62	11	47	19	-	-	-	1	1	1	2	5	9	28	3
SANESI, Consalvo	I	28 Mar 1911	Terranuova Bracciolini	1950-51	2	5	3	-	-	-	-	-	1	-	1	1	2	-
SCARFIOTTI, Ludovico	I	18 Oct 1933 8 Jun 1968	Turin Rossfeld, Germany	1963-68	6	10	17	-	1	1	-	-	2	-	2	1	4	2
SCARLATTI, Giorgio	I	2 Oct 1921	Rome	1956-61	6	12	1	-	-	-	-	-	-	1	1	3	7	3
SCHECKTER, Ian	ZA	22 Aug 1947	East London	1974-77	4	18	-	-	-	-	-	-	-	-	-	4	14	2

	Nat	Born Died	Place of Birth Place of Death	Years Entered	No. of Years	GPs	Points	PP	FL	Win	2nd	3rd	4th	5th	6th	OP	NC etc	NS etc
SCHECKTER, Jody	ZA	29 Jan 1950	East London	1972-80	9	112	255	3	5	10	14	9	9	7	4	24	35	1
SCHELL, Harry	USA	29 Jun 1921 13 May 1960	Paris, France Silverstone, England	1950-60	11	56	30	-	-	-	1	1	3	6	5	14	26	-
SCHENKEN, Tim	AUS	26 Sep 1943	Gordon, Sydney, NSW	1970-74	5	34	7	-	-	-	-	1	-	1	1	13	18	2
SCHERRER, Albert	CH	28 Feb 1908 5 Jul 1986		1953	1	1	-	-	-	-	-	-	-	-	-	1	-	-
SCHIATTARELLA, Mimmo	I	17 Nov 1967	Milan	1994-95	2	7	-	-	-	-	-	-	-	-	-	3	4	-
SCHILLER, Heinz	CH	25 Jan 1930	Frauenfeld	1962	1	1	-	-	-	-	-	-	-	-	-	-	1	-
SCHLESSER, Jean-Louis	F	12 Sep 1948	Nancy	1983-88	2	1	-	-	-	-	-	-	-	-	-	1	-	1
SCHLESSER, Jo	F	18 May 1928 7 Jul 1968	Liouville Rouen	1966-68	3	3	-	-	-	-	-	-	-	-	-	1	2	-
SCHNEIDER, Bernd	D	20 Jul 1964	Saarbrücken	1988-90	3	9	-	-	-	-	-	-	-	-	-	3	6	25
SCHOELLER, Rudolf	CH	27 Apr 1902 7 Mar 1978		1952	1	1	-	-	-	-	-	-	-	-	-	-	1	-
SCHROEDER, Rob	USA	11 May 1926		1962	1	1	-	-	-	-	-	-	-	-	-	1	-	-
SCHUMACHER, Michael	D	3 Jan 1969	Hürth-Hermühlheim	1991-96	6	85	362	14	25	22	14	10	4	2	2	3	28	-
SCHUPPAN, Vern	AUS	19 Mar 1943	Booleroo Whyalla, SA	1972-77	4	9	-	-	-	-	-	-	-	-	-	4	5	4
SCHWELM CRUZ, Adolfo	RA	28 Jun 1923	Buenos Aires	1953	1	1	-	-	-	-	-	-	-	-	-	-	1	-
SCOTT-BROWN, Archie	GB	13 May 1927 19 May 1958	Paisley, Renfrews., Scotland Spa-Francorchamps, Belgium	1956	1	1	-	-	-	-	-	-	-	-	-	-	1	1
SCOTTI, Piero	I	11 Nov 1909 14 Feb 1976	Florence	1956	1	1	-	-	-	-	-	-	-	-	-	-	1	-
SEIDEL, Wolfgang	D	4 Jul 1926 1 Mar 1987	(from Düsseldorf)	1953-62	5	10	-	-	-	-	-	-	-	-	-	3	7	2
SENNA, Ayrton	BR	21 Mar 1960 1 May 1994	São Paulo Bologna, Italy	1984-94	11	161	614	65	19	41	23	16	7	6	3	12	53	1
SERAFINI, Dorino	I	22 Jul 1909	Pesaro	1950	1	1	3	-	-	-	1	-	-	-	-	-	-	-
SERRA, Chico	BR	3 Feb 1957	São Paulo	1981-83	3	18	1	-	-	-	-	-	-	-	1	10	7	15
SERRURIER, Doug	ZA	9 Dec 1920	Germiston, Transvaal	1962-65	3	2	-	-	-	-	-	-	-	-	-	1	1	1
SERVOZ-GAVIN, Johnny	F	18 Jan 1942	Grenoble	1967-70	4	12	9	-	-	-	1	-	-	1	1	1	8	1
SETTEMBER, Tony	USA	1930	California	1962-63	2	6	-	-	-	-	-	-	-	-	-	2	4	1
SHARP, Hap	USA	1 Jan 1928 7 May 1993	Tulsa, Oklahoma	1961-64	4	6	-	-	-	-	-	-	-	-	-	4	2	-
SHAWE-TAYLOR, Brian	GB	29 Jan 1915	Dublin, Ireland	1950-51	2	2	-	-	-	-	-	-	-	-	-	2	-	1
SHELBY, Carroll	USA	11 Jan 1923	Leesburg, Texas	1958-59	2	8	-	-	-	-	-	-	1	-	-	3	4	-
SHELLY, Tony	NZ	2 Feb 1937	Wellington	1962	1	1	-	-	-	-	-	-	-	-	-	-	1	2
SIFFERT, Jo	CH	7 Jul 1936 24 Oct 1971	Fribourg Brands Hatch, Kent, England	1962-71	10	96	68	2	4	2	2	2	7	2	5	32	44	4
SIMON, André	F	5 Jan 1920	Paris	1951-57	5	11	-	-	-	-	-	-	-	-	2	2	7	1
SOLANA, Moises	MEX	1936 27 Jul 1969	 Valle de Bravo, nr Mexico City	1963-68	6	8	-	-	-	-	-	-	-	-	-	3	5	-
SOLER-ROIG, Alex	E	29 Oct 1932	Barcelona	1970-72	3	6	-	-	-	-	-	-	-	-	-	-	6	4

	Nat	Born Died	Place of Birth Place of Death	Years Entered	No. of Years	GPs	Points	PP	FL	Win	2nd	3rd	4th	5th	6th	OP	NC etc	NS etc
SOMMER, Raymond	F	31 Aug 1906 10 Sep 1950	Paris Cadours, nr Toulouse	1950	1	5	3	-	-	-	-	-	1	-	-	-	4	-
SPARKEN, Mike	F	16 Jun 1930	Neuilly sur Seine, nr Paris	1955	1	1	-	-	-	-	-	-	-	-	-	1	-	-
SPENCE, Mike	GB	30 Dec 1936 7 May 1968	Croydon, Surrey Indianapolis, Indiana, USA	1963-68	6	36	27	-	-	-	-	1	3	6	2	9	15	1
STACEY, Alan	GB	29 Aug 1933 19 Jun 1960	Broomfield, Essex Spa-Francorchamps, Belgium	1958-60	3	7	-	-	-	-	-	-	-	-	-	1	6	-
STARRABBA, Gaetano	I	3 Dec 1932	Palermo, Sicily	1961	1	1	-	-	-	-	-	-	-	-	-	-	1	-
STEWART, Ian	GB	15 Jul 1929	Edinburgh, Scotland	1953	1	1	-	-	-	-	-	-	-	-	-	-	1	-
STEWART, Jackie	GB	11 Jun 1939	Milton,Dumbarton,Scotland	1965-73	9	99	360	17	15	27	11	5	6	5	3	6	36	1
STEWART, Jimmy	GB	6 Mar 1931	Bowling,Dumbarton,Scotland	1953	1	1	-	-	-	-	-	-	-	-	-	-	1	-
STOHR, Siegfried	I	10 Oct 1952	Rimini	1981	1	9	-	-	-	-	-	-	-	-	-	3	6	4
STOMMELEN, Rolf	D	11 Jul 1943 24 Apr 1983	Siegen Riverside, California, USA	1969-78	9	54	14	-	-	-	-	1	-	4	2	29	18	9
STREIFF, Philippe	F	26 Jun 1955	La Tronche, nr Grenoble	1984-88	5	54	11	-	-	-	-	1	1	1	2	25	24	-
STUCK, Hans	D/A	27 Dec 1900 8 Feb 1978	Warsaw, Poland Grainau	1951-53	3	3	-	-	-	-	-	-	-	-	-	1	2	2
STUCK, Hans-Joachim	D	1 Jan 1951	Grainau	1974-79	6	74	29	-	-	-	-	2	3	5	2	14	48	7
SULLIVAN, Danny	USA	9 Mar 1950	Louisville, Kentucky	1983	1	15	2	-	-	-	-	-	-	1	-	6	8	-
SURER, Marc	CH	18 Sep 1951	Aresdorf	1979-86	8	82	17	-	1	-	-	-	2	2	7	39	32	6
SURTEES, John	GB	11 Feb 1934	Tatsfield, Surrey	1960-72	13	111	180	8	11	6	10	8	5	8	3	14	57	2
SUZUKI, Aguri	J	8 Sep 1960	Tokyo	1988-95	8	64	8	-	-	-	-	1	-	-	4	20	39	24
SUZUKI, Toshio	J	10 Mar 1955	Saitama	1993	1	2	-	-	-	-	-	-	-	-	-	2	-	1
SWATERS, Jacques	B	30 Oct 1926	Woluwe-St.-Lambert, Brussels	1951-54	3	7	-	-	-	-	-	-	-	-	-	3	4	-
TAKAHARA, Noritake	J	6 Jun 1951	Tokyo	1976-77	2	2	-	-	-	-	-	-	-	-	-	1	1	-
TAKAHASHI, Kunimitsu	J	29 Jan 1940	Tokyo	1977	1	1	-	-	-	-	-	-	-	-	-	1	-	-
TAMBAY, Patrick	F	25 Jun 1949	Paris	1977-86	9	114	103	5	2	2	4	5	6	8	7	25	57	9
TARQUINI, Gabriele	I	2 Mar 1962	Guilianova Lido, nr Pescara	1987-95	7	38	1	-	-	-	-	-	-	-	1	12	25	40
TARUFFI, Piero	I	12 Oct 1906 12 Jan 1988	Albano Laziale, Rome Rome	1950-56	6	18	41	-	1	1	3	1	2	2	1	2	6	-
TAYLOR, Henry	GB	16 Dec 1932	Shefford, Bedfordshire	1959-61	3	8	3	-	-	-	-	-	1	-	-	6	1	2
TAYLOR, John	GB	23 Mar 1933 8 Sep 1966	Leicester Koblenz, Germany	1964-66	2	5	1	-	-	-	-	-	-	-	1	3	1	-
TAYLOR, Mike	GB	24 Apr 1934	London	1959-60	2	1	-	-	-	-	-	-	-	-	-	-	1	1
TAYLOR, Trevor	GB	26 Dec 1936	Gleadless, Sheffield, Yorks	1959-66	6	27	8	-	-	-	1	-	-	-	2	9	15	2
THACKWELL, Mike	NZ	30 Mar 1961	Auckland	1980-84	2	2	-	-	-	-	-	-	-	-	-	-	2	3
THIELE, Alfonse	USA/I	1922		1960	1	1	-	-	-	-	-	-	-	-	-	-	1	-
THOMPSON, Eric	GB	4 Nov 1919	Ditton Hill, Surrey	1952	1	1	2	-	-	-	-	-	-	1	-	-	-	-

	Nat	Born Died	Place of Birth Place of Death	Years Entered	No. of Years	GPs	Points	PP	FL	Win	2nd	3rd	4th	5th	6th	OP	NC etc	NS etc
THORNE, Leslie	GB	23 Jun 1916 13 Jul 1993	Greenock,Renfrews.,Scotland Troon, Ayrshire, Scotland	1954	1	1	-	-	-	-	-	-	-	-	-	1	-	-
TINGLE, Sam	RSR	24 Aug 1921	Manchester, England	1963-69	5	5	-	-	-	-	-	-	-	-	-	2	3	-
TITTERINGTON, Desmond	GB	1 May 1928	Cultra, Co. Down, N Ireland	1956	1	1	-	-	-	-	-	-	-	-	-	-	1	-
TRINTIGNANT, Maurice	F	30 Oct 1917	Sainte-Cécile-les-Vignes	1950-64	15	82	72.33	-	1	2	3	4	4	8	3	19	39	2
TUNMER, Guy	ZA	1 Dec 1948	Ficksburg, Transvaal	1975	1	1	-	-	-	-	-	-	-	-	-	1	-	-
ULMEN, Toni	D	25 Jan 1906 4 Nov 1976	Düsseldorf Düsseldorf	1952	1	2	-	-	-	-	-	-	-	-	-	1	1	-
UNSER, Bobby	USA	20 Feb 1934	Colorado Springs, Colorado	1968	1	1	-	-	-	-	-	-	-	-	-	-	1	1
URIA, Alfredo	U			1955-56	2	2	-	-	-	-	-	-	-	-	1	-	1	-
VACCARELLA, Nino	I	4 Mar 1933	Palermo, Sicily	1961-65	3	4	-	-	-	-	-	-	-	-	-	3	1	1
van de POELE, Eric	B	30 Sep 1961	Verviers, nr Spa	1991-92	2	5	-	-	-	-	-	-	-	-	-	3	2	24
van der LOF, Dries	NL	23 Aug 1919 24 May 1990	Emmen Enschede	1952	1	1	-	-	-	-	-	-	-	-	-	-	1	-
van LENNEP, Gijs	NL	16 Mar 1942	Bloemendaal	1971-75	4	8	2	-	-	-	-	-	-	-	2	5	1	2
van ROOYEN, Basil	ZA	19 Apr 1939	Johannesburg	1968-69	2	2	-	-	-	-	-	-	-	-	-	-	2	-
VERSTAPPEN, Jos	NL	4 Mar 1972	Montfort	1994-96	3	31	11	-	-	-	-	2	-	1	1	5	22	-
VILLENEUVE, Gilles	CDN	18 Jan 1950 8 May 1982	Saint-Jean-sur-Richelieu, Quebec Zolder, Belgium	1977-82	6	67	107	2	8	6	5	2	2	3	3	19	27	1
VILLENEUVE, Jacques	CDN	9 Apr 1971	Saint-Jean-sur-Richelieu, Quebec	1996	1	16	78	3	6	4	5	2	-	-	-	2	3	-
VILLORESI, Luigi	I	16 May 1909	Milan	1950-56	7	31	49	-	1	-	2	6	2	3	4	1	13	3
VOLONTERIO, Ottorino	CH	7 Dec 1917	Orselina	1954-57	3	3	-	-	-	-	-	-	-	-	-	1	2	-
von OPEL, Rikky	FL	14 Oct 1947	New York, USA	1973-74	2	10	-	-	-	-	-	-	-	-	-	4	6	4
von TRIPS, Wolfgang	D	4 May 1928 10 Sep 1961	Horrem, nr Cologne Monza, Italy	1956-61	6	27	56	1	-	2	2	2	3	4	3	4	7	2
VONLANTHEN, Jo	CH	31 May 1942	St Ursen	1975	1	1	-	-	-	-	-	-	-	-	-	-	1	-
WACKER, Fred	USA	10 Jul 1918	Chicago, Illinois	1953-54	2	3	-	-	-	-	-	-	-	-	1	1	1	2
WALKER, Dave	AUS	10 Jun 1941	Sydney, New South Wales	1971-72	2	11	-	-	-	-	-	-	-	-	-	5	6	-
WALKER, Peter	GB	7 Oct 1912 1 Mar 1984	Leeds, Yorkshire Newtown	1950-55	3	4	-	-	-	-	-	-	-	-	-	1	3	-
WALTER, Heini	CH	28 Jul 1927	Rüti	1962	1	1	-	-	-	-	-	-	-	-	-	1	-	-
WARD, Rodger	USA	10 Jan 1921	Beloit, Kansas	1959-63	2	2	-	-	-	-	-	-	-	-	-	-	2	-
WARWICK, Derek	GB	27 Aug 1954	Alresford, Hampshire	1981-93	11	147	71	-	2	-	2	2	8	9	9	37	80	15
WATSON, John	GB	4 May 1946	Belfast, Northern Ireland	1973-85	12	152	169	2	5	5	6	9	9	7	11	42	63	2
WENDLINGER, Karl	A	20 Dec 1968	Kufstein	1991-95	5	41	14	-	-	-	-	-	3	1	3	11	23	1
WESTBURY, Peter	GB	26 May 1938	South London	1969-70	2	1	-	-	-	-	-	-	-	-	-	1	-	1
WHARTON, Ken	GB	21 Mar 1916 12 Jan 1957	Smethwick, Worcestershire Ardmore, New Zealand	1952-55	4	15	3	-	-	-	-	-	1	-	1	6	7	1

	Nat	Born Died	Place of Birth Place of Death	Years Entered	No. of Years	GPs	Points	PP	FL	Win	2nd	3rd	4th	5th	6th	OP	NC etc	NS etc
WHITEHEAD, Graham	GB	15 Apr 1922 15 Jan 1981	Harrogate, Yorkshire Lower Basildon, Berkshire	1952	1	1	-	-	-	-	-	-	-	-	-	1	-	-
WHITEHEAD, Peter	GB	12 Nov 1914 20 Sep 1958	Menston, nr Ikley, Yorkshire Lasalle, nr Nîmes, France	1950-54	5	10	4	-	-	-	-	1	-	-	-	4	5	2
WHITEHOUSE, Bill	GB	1 Apr 1909 14 Jul 1957	London Reims-Gueux, France	1954	1	1	-	-	-	-	-	-	-	-	-	-	1	-
WIDDOWS, Robin	GB	27 May 1942	Cowley, nr Uxbridge, Middx	1968	1	1	-	-	-	-	-	-	-	-	-	-	1	-
WIETZES, Eppie	CDN	28 May 1938		1967-74	2	2	-	-	-	-	-	-	-	-	-	-	2	-
WILDS, Mike	GB	7 Jan 1946	Chiswick, London	1974-76	3	3	-	-	-	-	-	-	-	-	-	-	3	5
WILLIAMS, Jonathan	GB	26 Oct 1942	Cairo, Egypt	1967	1	1	-	-	-	-	-	-	-	-	-	1	-	-
WILLIAMSON, Roger	GB	4 Feb 1949 29 Jul 1973	Leicester Zandvoort, Netherlands	1973	1	2	-	-	-	-	-	-	-	-	-	-	2	-
WILSON, Vic	GB	14 Apr 1931	Drypool, Kingston-upon-Hull	1960-66	2	1	-	-	-	-	-	-	-	-	-	-	1	1
WINKELHOCK, Manfred	D	6 Oct 1951 12 Aug 1985	Waiblingen, nr Stuttgart Toronto, Canada	1980-85	5	48	2	-	-	-	-	-	-	1	-	12	35	8
WISELL, Reine	S	30 Sep 1941	Motala, nr Linköping	1970-74	5	23	13	-	-	-	-	1	2	1	1	3	15	-
WUNDERINK, Roelof	NL	12 Dec 1948	Eindhoven	1975	1	3	-	-	-	-	-	-	-	-	-	-	3	3
ZANARDI, Alessandro	I	23 Oct 1966	Bologna	1991-94	4	25	1	-	-	-	-	-	-	-	1	11	13	3
ZORZI, Renzo	I	12 Dec 1946	Ziano di Fiemme, nr Turin	1975-77	3	7	1	-	-	-	-	-	-	-	1	2	4	-
ZUNINO, Ricardo	RA	13 Apr 1949	Buenos Aires	1979-81	3	10	-	-	-	-	-	-	-	-	-	6	4	1

Six Formula 2 races were held simultaneously with Grands Prix (D 57, 58, 66, 67 & 69, and MA 58), in which drivers were classified separately and were ineligible for points. These starts are included in 'GPs' column.

The total points shown, includes those scored but not taken into account for the Championship.

Grand Prix Non-Starters

	Nat	Born	Died	Place of Birth	Place of Death	Years Entered	No. of Years	NS etc
AMATI, Giovanna	I	20 Jul 1962		Rome		1992	1	3
BARTELS, Michael	D	8 Mar 1968		Plettenberg		1991	1	4
BAYARDO, Astrubel	U	1922				1959	1	1
BERTAGGIA, Enrico	I	19 Sep 1964		Noale, nr Venice		1989-92	2	6
BORDEU, Juan-Manuel	RA	1934	24 Nov 1990		Buenos Aires	1961	1	1
BRABHAM, Gary	AUS	29 Mar 1961		Wimbledon, London, England		1990	1	2
BRAMBILLA, Tino	I	31 Jan 1934		Monza		1963-69	2	2
BRANCATELLI, Gianfranco	I	18 Jan 1950				1979	1	3
CADE, Phil	USA	12 Jun 1916		Charles City, Iowa		1959	1	1
CHAPMAN, Colin	GB	19 May 1928	16 Dec 1982	Richmond, Surrey	East Carleton, Norfolk	1956	1	1
CHAVES, Pedro	P	27 Feb 1965		Porto		1991	1	13
COGAN, Kevin	USA	31 Mar 1956		Culver City, California		1980-81	2	2
COLOMBO, Alberto	I	23 Feb 1946		Veredo, nr Milan		1978	1	3
CRESPO, Alberto	I	16 Jan 1930	14 Aug 1991		Buenos Aires, Argentina	1952	1	1
de CHANGY, Alain	B					1959	1	1
de DRYVER, Bernard	B	19 Sep 1952		Brussels		1977-78	2	2
de RIU, Giovanni	I					1954	1	1
DOCHNAL, Frank	USA					1963	1	1
DUSIO, Piero	I	13 Oct 1899	7 Nov 1975	Scurzolengo d'Asti	Buenos Aires, Argentina	1952	1	1
ECCLESTONE, Bernie	GB	28 Oct 1930		St. Peters, Suffolk		1958	1	1
FACETTI, Carlo	I	26 Jun 1935		Cormano, Milan		1974	1	1
FERGUSON, Willie	ZA	6 Mar 1940		Johannesburg		1972	1	1
FISCHER, Ludwig	D					1952	1	1
FRANCIA, Giorgio	I	8 Nov 1947		Bologna		1977-81	2	2
FUSHIDA, Hiroshi	J	10 Mar 1946		Kyoto		1975	1	2
GALICA, Divina	GB	13 Aug 1946		Bushey Heath, Hertfordshire		1976-78	2	3
GIMAX,	I	1938				1978	1	1
GLÖCKLER, Helm	D		1993			1953	1	1
GUBBY, Brian	GB	17 Apr 1934		Epsom, Surrey		1965	1	1
HATTORI, Naoki	J	13 Jun 1966		Yokkaichi, Mie		1991	1	2
JONES, Tom	USA					1967	1	1
JOVER, Juan	E	1903	1960			1951	1	1
KAVANAGH, Ken	AUS	1922				1958	1	2
KENNEDY, David	IRL	15 Jan 1953		Sligo		1980	1	7
KESSLER, Bruce	USA					1958	1	1
KOZAROWITSKY, Mikko	FIN	17 May 1948		Helsinki		1977	1	2
KRAKAU, Willi	D		1995	(from Steuderdorf)		1952	1	1
KUHNKE, Kurt	D					1963	1	1
KUWASHIMA, Masami	J	14 Sep 1950				1976	1	1
LANGES, Claudio	I	20 Jul 1960		Brescia		1990	1	14
LUCIENBONNET, Jean	F		19 Aug 1962	Nice	Sicily, Italy	1959	1	1
McCARTHY, Perry	GB	3 Mar 1963		Stepney, London		1992	1	7
McGUIRE, Brian	AUS	13 Dec 1945	29 Aug 1977	Melbourne, Victoria	Brands Hatch, England	1977	1	1
MERKEL, Harry	D					1952	1	1
MOSS, Bill	GB	1933				1959	1	1
NELLEMAN, Jac	DK	19 Apr 1944		Copenhagen		1976	1	1
PIAN, Alfredo	RA	1912				1950	1	1
PRINOTH, Ernesto	I	1923	1981			1962	1	1
PUZEY, Clive	RSR	11 Jul 1941		Bulawayo		1965	1	1
RICHARDSON, Ken	GB	21 Aug 1911		Bourne, Lincolnshire		1951	1	1
ROLLINSON, Alan	GB	15 May 1943		Walsall, Staffordshire		1965	1	1
RUDAZ, Jean-Claude	CH	7 Jul 1943		Sion		1964	1	1
SEIFFERT, Günther	D					1962	1	1
SOUTH, Stephen	GB	19 Feb 1952		Harrow, Middlesex		1980	1	1
STUPPACHER, Otto	A	3 Mar 1947		Vienna		1976	1	3
SUTCLIFFE, Andy	GB	9 May 1947		Mildenhall, Suffolk		1977	1	1
TARAMAZZO, Luigi	I	1932				1958	1	1
TAYLOR, Dennis	GB	12 Jun 1921	2 Jun 1962	Sidcup, Kent	Monte Carlo, Monaco	1959	1	1
TESTUT, André	MC	13 Apr 1926		France		1958-59	2	2
TRIMMER, Tony	GB	24 Jan 1943		Maidenhead, Berkshire		1975-78	4	6

	Nat	Born / Died	Place of Birth / Place of Death	Years Entered	No. of Years	NS etc
VILLENEUVE Sr., Jacques	CDN	4 Nov 1953	Saint-Jean-sur-Richelieu, Quebec	1981-83	2	3
WEIDLER, Volker	D	18 Mar 1962	Weinheim, nr Mannheim	1989	1	10
WHITEAWAY, Ted	GB	1 Nov 1928	Feltham, Middlesex	1955	1	1
WILSON, Desiré	ZA	26 Nov 1953	Johannesburg	1980	1	1
WINKELHOCK, Joachim	D	24 Oct 1960	Waiblingen, nr Stuttgart	1989	1	7
ZAPICO, Emilio	E			1976	1	1

Indianapolis 500 Starters

	Nat	Born / Died	Place of Birth / Place of Death	Years Entered	No. of Years	Races	Points	PP	FL	Win	2nd	3rd	4th	5th	6th	OP	R	NS etc
ADER, Walt	USA	15 Dec 1913 25 Nov 1982	Long Valley, New Jersey Califon, New Jersey	1950	1	1	-	-	-	-	-	-	-	-	-	1	-	-
AGABASHIAN, Freddie	USA	21 Aug 1913 13 Oct 1989	Modesto, California Alamo, California	1950-58	9	8	1.50	1	-	-	-	-	1	-	1	1	5	1
AMICK, George	USA	24 Oct 1924 9 Apr 1959	Vernonia, Oregon Daytona Beach, Florida	1957-58	2	1	6	-	-	-	1	-	-	-	-	-	-	1
AMICK, Red	USA	19 Jan 1929	Kansas City, Missouri	1959-60	2	2	-	-	-	-	-	-	-	-	-	1	1	-
ANDREWS, Keith	USA	15 Jun 1920 15 May 1957	Denver, Colorado Indianapolis, Indiana	1955-57	3	2	-	-	-	-	-	-	-	-	-	-	2	1
ARMI, Frank	USA	12 Oct 1918 28 Nov 1992	Portland, Oregon Hanford, California	1951-54	3	1	-	-	-	-	-	-	-	-	-	1	-	2
ARNOLD, Chuck	USA	30 May 1926	Stamford, Connecticut	1959-60	2	1	-	-	-	-	-	-	-	-	-	1	-	1
ASCARI, Alberto	I	13 Jul 1918 26 May 1955	Milan Monza	1952	1	1	-	-	-	-	-	-	-	-	-	-	1	-
AYULO, Manny	USA	20 Oct 1921 16 May 1955	Los Angeles, California Indianapolis, Indiana	1950-55	6	4	2	-	-	-	-	1	-	-	-	2	1	2
BALL, Bobby	USA	26 Aug 1925 27 Feb 1954	Phoenix, Arizona Phoenix, Arizona	1951-52	2	2	2	-	-	-	-	-	-	1	-	-	1	-
BANKS, Henry	USA	14 Jun 1913	Surrey, England	1950-54	5	3	-	-	-	-	-	-	-	-	1	1	1	2
BETTENHAUSEN, Tony	USA	12 Sep 1916 12 May 1961	Tinley Park, Illinois Indianapolis, Indiana	1950-60	11	11	11	-	1	-	1	-	2	1	-	2	5	-
BISCH, Art	USA	10 Nov 1926 4 Jul 1958	Mesa, Arizona Lakewood Speedway, Georgia	1958	1	1	-	-	-	-	-	-	-	-	-	-	1	-
BOYD, Johnny	USA	19 Aug 1926	Fresno, California	1955-60	6	6	4	-	-	-	-	1	-	-	2	-	3	-
BRANSON, Don	USA	2 Jun 1920 12 Nov 1966	Rantoul, Illinois Gardena, California	1959-60	2	2	3	-	-	-	-	-	1	-	-	-	1	-
BROWN, Walt	USA	30 Dec 1911 29 Jul 1951	Springfield, New York Williams Grove, Pennsylvania	1950-51	2	2	-	-	-	-	-	-	-	-	-	1	1	-
BRYAN, Jimmy	USA	28 Jan 1927 19 Jun 1960	Phoenix, Arizona Langhorne, Pennsylvania	1951-60	10	9	18	-	-	1	1	1	-	-	1	2	3	1
CANTRELL, Bill	USA	31 Jan 1908	Hardin County, Kentucky	1950-52	3	1	-	-	-	-	-	-	-	-	-	-	1	2
CARTER, Duane	USA	5 May 1913 8 Mar 1993	Fresno, California Indianapolis, Indiana	1950-60	8	8	6.50	-	-	-	-	1	2	-	-	5	-	-
CHEESBOURG, Bill	USA	12 Jun 1927	Tucson, Arizona	1956-60	5	3	-	-	-	-	-	-	-	-	-	1	2	2
CHITWOOD, Joie	USA	14 Apr 1912 3 Jan 1988	Denison, Texas Tampa, Florida	1950	1	1	1	-	-	-	-	-	-	1	-	-	-	-
CHRISTIE, Bob	USA	4 Apr 1924	Grants Pass, Oregon	1954-60	7	5	-	-	-	-	-	-	-	-	-	3	2	2
CONNOR, George	USA	16 Aug 1908	San Bernardino, California	1950-53	4	3	-	-	-	-	-	-	-	-	-	2	1	1
CRAWFORD, Ray	USA	26 Oct 1915	Roswell, New Mexico	1955-59	5	3	-	-	-	-	-	-	-	-	-	-	3	2

	Nat	Born Died	Place of Birth Place of Death	Years Entered	No. of Years	Races	Points	PP	FL	Win	2nd	3rd	4th	5th	6th	OP	R	NS etc
CROCKETT, Larry	USA	23 Oct 1926 20 Mar 1955	Cambridge City, Indiana Langhorne, Pennsylvania	1954	1	1	-	-	-	-	-	-	-	-	-	1	-	-
CROSS, Art	USA	24 Jan 1918	Jersey City, New Jersey	1952-55-	4	4	8	-	-	-	1	-	-	1	-	1	1	-
DAVIES, Jimmy	USA	18 Aug 1929 11 Jun 1966	Glendale, California Chicago, Illinois	1950-60	9	5	4	-	-	-	-	1	-	-	-	3	1	4
DAYWALT, Jimmy	USA	28 Aug 1924 4 Apr 1966	Wabash, Indiana Indianapolis, Indiana	1951-59	9	6	-	-	-	-	-	-	-	-	1	2	3	3
DINSMORE, Duke	USA	10 Apr 1913 12 Oct 1985	Williamstown, West Virgina Daytona Beach, Florida	1950-60	7	4	-	-	-	-	-	-	-	-	-	1	3	3
DUNCAN, Len	USA	25 Jul 1911	New York City, New York	1953-56	4	1	-	-	-	-	-	-	-	-	-	-	1	3
EDMUNDS, Don	USA	23 Sep 1930	Santa Ana, California	1957-59	2	1	-	-	-	-	-	-	-	-	-	-	1	1
ELISIAN, Ed	USA	9 Dec 1926 30 Aug 1959	Oakland, California Milwaukee, Wisconsin	1954-58	5	5	-	-	-	-	-	-	-	-	-	1	4	-
FAULKNER, Walt	USA	16 Feb 1920 22 Apr 1956	Tell, Texas Valleso, California	1950-55	6	5	1	1	-	-	-	-	-	1	-	3	1	1
FLAHERTY, Pat	USA	6 Jan 1926	Glendale, California	1950-59	6	6	8	1	-	1	-	-	-	-	-	2	3	-
FOHR, Myron	USA	17 Jun 1912 14 Jan 1994	Milwaukee, Wisconsin Milwaukee, Wisconsin	1950-51	2	1	-	-	-	-	-	-	-	-	-	1	-	1
FONDER, George	USA	22 Jun 1917 14 Jun 1958	Elmhurst, Pennsylvania Hartfield, Pennsylvania	1950-54	5	2	-	-	-	-	-	-	-	-	-	2	-	3
FORBERG, Carl	USA	4 Mar 1911	Omaha, Nebraska	1950-52	3	1	-	-	-	-	-	-	-	-	-	1	-	2
FORCE, Gene	USA	15 Jun 1916 21 Aug 1983	New Madison, Ohio Richmond, Indiana	1951-60	5	2	-	-	-	-	-	-	-	-	-	-	2	3
FOYT, A J	USA	16 Jan 1935	Houston, Texas	1958-60	3	3	-	-	-	-	-	-	-	-	-	1	2	-
FREELAND, Don	USA	25 Mar 1925	Los Angeles, California	1953-60	8	8	4	-	-	-	-	1	-	-	-	3	4	-
GARRETT, Billy	USA	24 Apr 1933	Princeton, Illinois	1956-58	3	2	-	-	-	-	-	-	-	-	-	1	1	1
GEORGE, Elmer	USA	5 Jul 1928 30 May 1976	Hockerville, Oklahoma Terre Haute, Indiana	1955-57	2	1	-	-	-	-	-	-	-	-	-	-	1	1
GOLDSMITH, Paul	USA	2 Oct 1927	Parkersburg, West Virginia	1958-60	3	3	6	-	-	-	-	1	-	1	-	-	1	-
GREEN, Cecil	USA	30 Sep 1919 29 Jul 1951	Dallas, Texas Winchester, Indiana	1950-51	2	2	3	-	-	-	-	-	1	-	-	-	1	-
GRIFFITH, Cliff	USA	6 Feb 1916	Nineveh, Indiana	1951-60	7	3	-	-	-	-	-	-	-	-	-	2	1	4
GRIM, Bobby	USA	4 Sep 1924 14 Jun 1995	Coal City, Indiana Indianapolis, Indiana	1959-60	2	2	-	-	-	-	-	-	-	-	-	1	1	-
HANKS, Sam	USA	13 Jul 1914 27 Jun 1994	Columbus, Ohio Pacific Palisades,California	1950-57	8	8	20	-	-	1	1	2	-	-	-	1	3	-
HARTLEY, Gene	USA	28 Jan 1926	Roanoke, Indiana	1950-60	10	8	-	-	-	-	-	-	-	-	-	5	3	2
HELLINGS, Mack	USA	14 Sep 1917 11 Nov 1951	Fort Dodge, Iowa California	1950-51	2	2	-	-	-	-	-	-	-	-	-	1	1	-
HERMAN, Al	USA	15 Mar 1927 18 Jun 1960	Topton, Pennsylvania West Haven, Connecticut	1953-60	8	5	-	-	-	-	-	-	-	-	-	2	3	3
HOLLAND, Bill	USA	18 Dec 1907 20 May 1984	Philadelphia, Pennsylvania Tucson, Arizona	1950-53	2	2	6	-	-	-	1	-	-	-	-	-	1	-
HOLMES, Jackie	USA	4 Sep 1920	Indianapolis, Indiana	1950-53	4	2	-	-	-	-	-	-	-	-	-	-	2	2
HOMEIER, Bill	USA	31 Aug 1918	Rock Island, Texas	1953-60	6	3	1	-	-	-	-	-	-	1	-	1	1	3

	Nat	Born Died	Place of Birth Place of Death	Years Entered	No. of Years	Races	Points	PP	FL	Win	2nd	3rd	4th	5th	6th	OP	R	NS etc
HOYT, Jerry	USA	29 Jan 1929 10 Jul 1955	Chicago, Illinois Oklahoma City, Oklahoma	1950-55	5	4	-	1	-	-	-	-	-	-	-	2	2	1
HURTUBISE, Jim	USA	5 Dec 1932 6 Jan 1989	North Tonawanda, New York Port Arthur, Texas	1960	1	1	-	-	-	-	-	-	-	-	-	-	1	-
JACKSON, Jimmy	USA	25 Jul 1910 25 Nov 1984	Indianapolis, Indiana Desert Hot Springs, CA	1950-54	3	2	-	-	-	-	-	-	-	-	-	1	1	1
JAMES, Joe	USA	23 May 1925 5 Nov 1952	Saucier, Mississippi San Jose, California	1950-52	3	2	-	-	-	-	-	-	-	-	-	1	1	1
JOHNSON, Eddie	USA	10 Feb 1919 30 Jun 1974	Richmond, Virginia Cleveland, Ohio	1952-60	9	9	1	-	-	-	-	-	-	-	1	6	2	-
KELLER, Al	USA	11 Apr 1920 19 Nov 1961	Alexander, New York Phoenix, Arizona	1955-60	6	5	-	-	-	-	-	-	-	-	-	2	3	1
KLADIS, Danny	USA	10 Feb 1917	Crystal City, Missouri	1950-57	6	1	-	-	-	-	-	-	-	-	-	-	1	5
LARSON, Jud	USA	21 Jan 1923 11 Jun 1966	Grand Prairie, Texas Reading, Pennsylvania	1952-59	5	2	-	-	-	-	-	-	-	-	-	1	1	3
LEVRETT, Bayliss	USA	14 Feb 1913	Jacksonville, Florida	1950-52	3	1	-	-	-	-	-	-	-	-	-	-	1	2
LINDEN, Andy	USA	5 Apr 1922 10 Feb 1987	Brownsvlle, Pennsylvania Torrance, California	1950-57	8	7	5	-	-	-	-	-	1	1	1	1	3	1
MACKEY, Bill	USA	15 Dec 1927 29 Jul 1951	Dayton, Ohio Winchester, Indiana	1951	1	1	-	-	-	-	-	-	-	-	-	-	1	-
MAGILL, Mike	USA	8 Feb 1920	Haddonfield, New Jersey	1956-60	5	3	-	-	-	-	-	-	-	-	-	-	3	2
MANTZ, Johnny	USA	18 Sep 1918 25 Oct 1972	Hebron, Indiana	1953	1	1	-	-	-	-	-	-	-	-	-	1	-	-
McCOY, Ernie	USA	19 Feb 1921	Reading, Pennsylvania	1953-55	3	2	-	-	-	-	-	-	-	-	-	2	-	1
McDOWELL, Johnny	USA	29 Jan 1915 8 Jun 1952	Delavan, Illinois Milwaukee, Wisconsin	1950-52	3	3	-	-	-	-	-	-	-	-	-	2	1	-
McGRATH, Jack	USA	8 Oct 1919 6 Nov 1955	Los Angeles, California Phoenix, Arizona	1950-55	6	6	9	1	1	-	-	2	-	1	-	1	2	-
McWITHEY, Jim	USA	4 Jul 1927	Grammar, Indiana	1956-60	5	2	-	-	-	-	-	-	-	-	-	1	1	3
MILLER, Chet	USA	19 Jul 1902 15 May 1953	Detroit, Michigan Indianapolis, Indiana	1950-53	4	2	-	-	-	-	-	-	-	-	-	-	2	2
NALON, Duke	USA	12 Mar 1913	Chicago, Illinois	1950-54	5	3	-	1	-	-	-	-	-	-	-	-	3	2
NAZARUK, Mike	USA	2 Oct 1921 1 May 1955	Newark, New Jersey Langhorne, Pennsylvania	1951-54	4	3	8	-	-	-	1	-	-	1	-	-	1	1
NIDAY, Cal	USA	29 Apr 1916 14 Feb 1988	Turlock, California Willow Springs, California	1953-55	3	3	-	-	-	-	-	-	-	-	-	1	2	-
O'CONNOR, Pat	USA	9 Oct 1928 30 May 1958	North Vernon, Indiana Indianapolis, Indiana	1953-58	6	5	-	1	-	-	-	-	-	-	-	3	2	1
PARSONS, Johnnie	USA	4 Jul 1918 8 Sep 1984	Los Angeles, California Van Nuys, California	1950-58	9	9	12	-	1	1	-	-	1	-	-	4	3	-
RATHMANN, Dick	USA	6 Jan 1926	Los Angeles, California	1950-60	5	5	2	1	-	-	-	-	-	1	-	-	4	-
RATHMANN, Jim	USA	16 Jul 1928	Valparaiso, Indiana	1950-60	10	10	29	-	2	1	3	-	-	1	-	3	2	-
REECE, Jimmy	USA	17 Nov 1929 22 Sep 1958	Oklahoma City, Oklahoma Trenton, New Jersey	1952-58	6	6	-	-	-	-	-	-	-	-	1	3	2	-
RIGSBY, Jim	USA	6 Jun 1923 31 Aug 1952	Spadry, Arkansas Dayton, Ohio	1950-52	2	1	-	-	-	-	-	-	-	-	-	1	-	1
ROSE, Mauri	USA	26 May 1906 1 Jan 1981	Columbus, Ohio Royal Oak, Michigan	1950-51	2	2	4	-	-	-	-	1	-	-	-	-	1	-
RUBY, Lloyd	USA	12 Jan 1928	Wichita Falls, Texas	1960	1	1	-	-	-	-	-	-	-	-	-	1	-	-

	Nat	Born Died	Place of Birth Place of Death	Years Entered	No. of Years	Races	Points	PP	FL	Win	2nd	3rd	4th	5th	6th	OP	R	NS etc
RUSSO, Eddie	USA	19 Nov 1925	Chicago, Illinois	1954-60	7	4	-	-	-	-	-	-	-	-	-	-	4	3
RUSSO, Paul	USA	10 Apr 1914 13 Feb 1976	Kenosha, Wisconsin Daytona Beach, Florida	1950-60	11	8	8.50	-	1	-	1	-	2	-	-	3	2	3
RUTTMAN, Troy	USA	11 Mar 1930	Mooreland, Oklahoma	1950-60	9	7	9.50	-	-	1	-	-	1	-	-	1	4	2
SACHS, Eddie	USA	28 May 1927 30 May 1964	Bethlehem, Pennsylvania Indianapolis, Indiana	1953-60	7	4	-	1	-	-	-	-	-	-	-	-	4	3
SCARBOROUGH, Carl	USA	3 Jul 1914 30 May 1953	Benton, Illinois Indianapolis, Indiana	1951-53	2	2	-	-	-	-	-	-	-	-	-	1	1	-
SCHINDLER, Bill	USA	6 Mar 1909 20 Sep 1952	Middletown, New York Allentown, Pennsylvania	1950-52	3	3	-	-	-	-	-	-	-	-	-	1	2	-
SCOTT, Bob	USA	4 Oct 1928 5 Jul 1954	Watsonville, California Darlington, South Carolina	1951-54	4	3	-	-	-	-	-	-	-	-	-	2	1	1
STEVENSON, Chuck	USA	15 Oct 1919	Sidney, Montana	1951-60	5	5	-	-	-	-	-	-	-	-	-	3	2	-
SUTTON, Len	USA	9 Aug 1925	Aims, Oregon	1956-60	4	3	-	-	-	-	-	-	-	-	-	-	3	1
SWEIKERT, Bob	USA	20 May 1926 17 Jun 1956	Los Angeles, California Salem, Indiana	1950-56	7	5	8	-	-	1	-	-	-	-	1	1	2	2
TEAGUE, Marshall	USA	22 May 1921 11 Feb 1959	Daytona Beach, Florida Daytona Beach, Florida	1953-58	5	3	-	-	-	-	-	-	-	-	-	2	1	2
TEMPLEMAN, Shorty	USA	12 Aug 1919 24 Aug 1962	Pueblo, Colorado Marion, Ohio	1955-60	5	3	-	-	-	-	-	-	-	-	-	1	2	2
THOMSON, Johnny	USA	9 Apr 1922 24 Sep 1960	Lowell, Massachusetts Allentown, Pennsylvania	1953-60	8	8	10	1	1	-	-	1	1	1	-	1	4	-
TINGELSTAD, Bud	USA	4 Apr 1928 30 Jul 1981	Frazee, Minnesota Indianapolis, Indiana	1960	1	1	-	-	-	-	-	-	-	-	-	1	-	-
TOLAN, Johnnie	USA	22 Oct 1918 2 Jun 1986	Victor, Colorado Redondo Beach, California	1951-60	8	3	-	-	-	-	-	-	-	-	-	1	2	5
TURNER, Jack	USA	12 Feb 1920	Seattle, Washington	1956-60	5	4	-	-	-	-	-	-	-	-	-	1	3	1
UNSER, Jerry	USA	15 Nov 1932 17 May 1959	Colorado Springs, Colorado Indianapolis, Indiana	1958-59	2	1	-	-	-	-	-	-	-	-	-	-	1	1
VEITH, Bob	USA	1 Nov 1926	Tulare, California	1956-60	5	5	-	-	-	-	-	-	-	-	-	4	1	-
VUKOVICH, Bill	USA	13 Dec 1918 30 May 1955	Fresno, California Indianapolis, Indiana	1950-55	6	5	19	1	3	2	-	-	-	-	-	-	3	1
WALLARD, Lee	USA	7 Sep 1910 28 Nov 1963	Schenectady, New York St. Petersburg, Florida	1950-51	2	2	9	-	1	1	-	-	-	-	1	-	-	-
WARD, Rodger	USA	10 Jan 1921	Beloit, Kansas	1951-60	10	10	14	-	-	1	1	-	-	-	-	1	7	-
WEBB, Spider	USA	8 Oct 1910 29 Jan 1990	Joplin, Missouri McMinnville, Oregon	1950-55	5	4	-	-	-	-	-	-	-	-	-	1	3	1
WEILER, Wayne	USA	9 Dec 1934	Phoenix, Arizona	1960	1	1	-	-	-	-	-	-	-	-	-	-	1	-
WEYANT, Chuck	USA	3 Apr 1923	St. Marys, nr Lima, Ohio	1952-60	7	4	-	-	-	-	-	-	-	-	-	2	2	3
WILSON, Dempsey	USA	11 Mar 1927 23 Apr 1971	Los Angeles, California Los Angeles, California	1956-60	5	2	-	-	-	-	-	-	-	-	-	-	2	3

Indianapolis 500 Non-Starters

Driver	Year(s)
Emil ANDRES	1950
Johnny BALDWIN	1956
Buzz BARTON	1952,53
Joe BARZDA	1951,52,53
Tony BONADIES	1955,56,57
Bill BOYD	1951,53
Mike BURCH	1950
Marvin BURKE	1950
Willard CANTRELL	1953
Bob CLEBERG	1960
Bud CLEMONS	1957
Hal COLE	1950
Russ CONGDON	1960
Bob CORTNER	1958,59
Chuck DAIGH	1959
Jorge DAPONTE	1953
Billy DEVORE	1950,54
Lee DROLLINGER	1960
Ted DUNCAN	1950
Rex EASTON	1958,59
Kenny EATON	1950,51
Jack ENSLEY	1958,59
Milt FANKHOUSER	1950
Giuseppe FARINA	1956
Cotton FARMER	1960
Johnny FEDRICKS	1950,53,57
John FITCH	1953
Dick FRAZIER	1950,52
Andy FURCI	1957
Joe GIBA	1958
Potsy GOACHER	1953,54
Bob GREGG	1950
Norm HALL	1960
Red HAMILTON	1953
Allen HEATH	1952,53
Norm HOUSER	1950,51
Chuck HULSE	1960
Peter J. HAHN	1952
Van JOHNSON	1958
Johnny KAY	1953,55,56,59
Russ KLAR	1955
Ray KNEPPER	1951
Chuck LEIGHTON	1950
Mark LIGHT	1950
Ralph LIGUORI	1959
George LYNCH	1950,51
Frank LUPTOW	1952
Cy MARSHALL	1950
Johnny MAURO	1950,52
Al MILLER	1950
John MOORHOUSE	1959
Earl MOTTER	1959
Frank MUNDY	1954
Roy NEUMAN	1953
Danny OAKES	1953,54
Jim PACKARD	1959,60
Jiggs PETERS	1955
Marvin PIFER	1956
Ralph PRATT	1950
Dick REESE	1956
Gordon REID	1951
Johnny ROBERTS	1953
Hal ROBSON	1953
Chuck RODEE	1959,60
Bud ROSE	1950
Ebb ROSE	1960
Jack ROUNDS	1960
Mike SALAY	1951
Rob SCHROEDER	1959
Wayne SELSER	1953
Bud SENNETT	1951
Doc SHANEBROOK	1951,52
Joe SOSTILLO	1953
Gig STEPHENS	1956
Otis STINE	1952
Bill TAYLOR	1952,53
Joel THORNE	1950,51
George TICHENOR	1952,54,55
Chas. Van ACKER	1950
LeRoy WARRINER	1951,53,55,56,57

Drivers often not known by their real name (Grand Prix and Indianapolis 500 drivers)

Alias	**Real Name**
Kenny ACHESON -	Kenneth ACHESON
Walt ADER -	Walter ADER
Freddie AGABASHIAN -	Frederick AGABASHIAN
Kurt AHRENS -	Kurt AHRENS Jnr.
Jean ALESI -	Giovanni ALESI
Cliff ALLISON -	Henry Clifford ALLISON
Red AMICK -	Richard AMICK
Chris AMON -	Christopher AMON
Bob ANDERSON -	Robert ANDERSON
Gerry ASHMORE -	Gerald ASHMORE
Bill ASTON -	William ASTON
Dickie ATTWOOD -	Richard ATTWOOD
Manny AYULO -	Manuel AYULO
Bobby BALL -	Robert BALL
Skip BARBER -	John BARBER
Astrubel BAYARDO -	Astrubel FONTES-BAYARDO
Don BEAUMAN -	Donald BEAUMAN
Günther BECHEM -	Karl-Günther BECHEM
Jean BEHRA -	Jean Marie BEHRA
Tony BETTENHAUSEN -	Melvin E. BETTENHAUSEN
Mike BEUTTLER -	Michael BEUTTLER
Lucien BIANCHI -	Luciano BIANCHI
B BIRA -	Prince BIRABONGSE BHANUDEJ BHANUBANDH OF SIAM
Art BISCH -	Arthur BISCH
Trevor BLOKDYK -	John Trevor BLOKDYK
Raul BOESEL -	Raul de MESQUITA BOESEL
Bob BONDURANT -	Robert BONDURANT
Jo BONNIER -	Joakim BONNIER
Slim BORGUDD -	Karl Edward Tommy BORGUDD
Johnny BOYD -	John BOYD
Jack BRABHAM -	John BRABHAM
Bill BRACK -	William BRACK
Tino BRAMBILLA -	Ernesto BRAMBILLA
Toni BRANCA -	Antonio BRANCA
Don BRANSON -	Donald BRANSON
Tom BRIDGER -	Thomas BRIDGER
Tony BRISE -	Anthony BRISE
Chris BRISTOW -	Christopher BRISTOW
Tony BROOKS -	Charles Anthony Standish BROOKS
Walt BROWN -	Walter BROWN
Adolf BRUDES -	Adolf BRUDES Von BRESLAU
Jimmy BRYAN -	James BRYAN
Ronnie BUCKNUM -	Ronald BUCKNUM
Luiz BUENO-	Luiz-Pereira BUENO
Tommy BYRNE -	Thomas BYRNE
Phil CADE -	Philip CADE
Alex CAFFI -	Alessandro CAFFI
John CAMPBELL-JONES -	Michael John CAMPBELL-JONES
Bill CANTRELL -	William CANTRELL
Piero CARINI -	Pietro CARINI
Johnny CECOTTO -	Alberton CECOTTO
François CEVERT -	Albert François CEVERT
Colin CHAPMAN -	Anthony Colin Bruce CHAPMAN
Dave CHARLTON -	David CHARLTON
Pedro CHAVES-	Pedro MATOS-CHAVES
Bill CHEESBOURG -	William CHEESBOURG
Eddie CHEEVER -	Edward McKay CHEEVER Jr.
Joie CHITWOOD -	George CHITWOOD
Bob CHRISTIE -	Robert CHRISTIE
Johnny CLAES -	John CLAES
Jim CLARK -	James CLARK
Bernard COLLOMB -	Nicois Bernard COLLOMB-CLERC
Franco COMOTTI -	Gianfranco COMOTTI
Chris CRAFT -	Christopher CRAFT
Jim CRAWFORD -	James CRAWFORD
Ray CRAWFORD -	Raymond CRAWFORD
Tony CROOK -	Thomas Anthony CROOK
Art CROSS -	Arthur CROSS
Nano da SILVA RAMOS -	Hermano da SILVA RAMOS
Chuck DAIGH -	Charles DAIGH
Jimmy DAVIES -	James DAVIES
Jimmy DAYWALT -	James DAYWALT
Carel Godin de BEAUFORT -	Count Jonkheer Carel Pieter Anthonie Jan Hubertus Godin de BEAUFORT
Mario de CABRAL -	Mario Araujo de CABRAL
Alain de CHANGY -	Alain CARPENTIER de CHANGY
Toulo de GRAFFENRIED -	Baron Emmanuel de GRAFFENRIED
Peter de KLERK-	Piet de KLERK
Fon de PORTAGO -	Don Alfonso Cabeza de Vacade y Leighton, Carvajal y Are, 13th Conde de la Majorada, 17th Marquis de PORTAGO
Charles de TORNACO -	Baron Charles de TORNACO
Duke DINSMORE -	J. Carlyle DINSMORE
Martin DONNELLY -	Hugh Martin DONNELLY
Ken DOWNING -	Kenneth DOWNING
Bob DRAKE -	Robert DRAKE
Paddy DRIVER -	Ernest Gould DRIVER
Johnny DUMFRIES -	John Colum CRICHTON-STUART, the Earl of Dumfries
Len DUNCAN -	Leonard DUNCAN
Bernie ECCLESTONE -	Bernard ECCLESTONE
Don EDMUNDS -	Donald EDMUNDS
Vic ELFORD -	Victor ELFORD
Bob EVANS -	Robert EVANS
Teo FABI -	Teodorico FABI
Jack FAIRMAN -	John FAIRMAN
Nino FARINA-	Dr. Giuseppe FARINA
Walt FAULKNER -	Walter FAULKNER
Willie FERGUSON -	William FERGUSON
Rudi FISCHER -	Rudolf FISCHER
Mike FISHER -	Michael FISHER
Theo FITZAU -	Theodor FITZAU
Pat FLAHERTY -	George Francis Patrick FLAHERTY
Jan FLINTERMAN -	Johannes FLINTERMAN
Ron FLOCKHART -	William Ronald FLOCKHART
Philip FOTHERINGHAM-PARKER -	-Philip Fotheringham PARKER
A J FOYT -	Anthony Joseph FOYT Jr.
Don FREELAND -	Donald FREELAND
Beppe GABBIANI -	Giuseppe GABBIANI
Nanni GALLI -	Giovanni Giuseppe Gilberto GALLI
Fred GAMBLE -	Frederick GAMBLE
Howden GANLEY -	James Howden GANLEY
Billy GARRETT -	William GARRETT
Jo GARTNER -	Josef GARTNER
Tony GAZE -	Frederick Anthony Owen GAZE
GEKI -	Giacomo RUSSO
Bob GERARD -	Frederick Robert GERARD
Dick GIBSON -	Richard GIBSON
GIMAX -	Carlo FRANCHI
Richie GINTHER -	Paul Richard GINTHER
Helm GLOCKLER -	Helmut GLOCKLER
Chico GODIA -	Francesco GODIA-SALES
Froilán GONZALEZ -	José Froilán GONZALEZ
Cliff GRIFFITH -	Clifford GRIFFITH
Bobby GRIM -	Robert GRIM
Roberto GUERRERO -	Roberto GUERRERO ISAZA
Dan GURNEY -	Daniel GURNEY
Mike HAILWOOD -	Stanley Michael Bailey HAILWOOD
Jim HALL -	James HALL
Duncan HAMILTON -	James Duncan HAMILTON
Sam HANKS -	Samuel HANKS
Walt HANSGEN -	Walter HANSGEN
Mike HARRIS -	Michael HARRIS
Cuth HARRISON -	Thomas Cuthbert HARRISON
Gene HARTLEY -	Leslie HARTLEY
Paul HAWKINS -	Robert Paul HAWKINS
Mike HAWTHORN -	John Michael HAWTHORN

CONSTRUCTORS

Total points scored relates to those scored by drivers and not by constructors for their championship.

Indianapolis 500 entrants are excluded. Note that Maserati made 3 starts at Indy and Ferrari started on 1 occasion, whilst Kurtis Kraft was a regular entrant.

AFM
AGS
ALFA ROMEO
ALFA SPECIAL
ALTA
AMON
ANDREA MODA
ARROWS
ARZANI VOLPINI see MASERATI
ASTON
ASTON MARTIN
ATS (Germany)
ATS (Italy)
BEHRA PORSCHE see PORSCHE
BELLASI
BENETTON
BMW
BORO see ENSIGN
BRABHAM
BRM
BRP
BUGATTI
CISITALIA
COLONI
CONNAUGHT
CONNEW
COOPER
COPERSUCAR see FITTIPALDI
DALLARA
DE TOMASO
DERRINGTON-FRANCIS see ATS (Italy)
EAGLE
EIFELLAND MARCH see MARCH
EMERYSON
EMW
ENB
ENSIGN
ERA
EUROBRUN
FERGUSON
FERRARI
FITTIPALDI
FOMET see OSELLA
FONDMETAL see OSELLA
FOOTWORK see ARROWS
FORTI
FRAZER NASH
FRY
GILBY
GORDINI
HESKETH
HILL
HONDA
HWM
ISO MARLBORO see WILLIAMS
JBW
JORDAN
JPS LOTUS see LOTUS
KAUHSEN
KLENK
KOJIMA
KURTIS KRAFT
LAMBORGHINI
LANCIA
LANCIA FERRARI see FERRARI
LARROUSSE
LDS
LEC LEYTON HOUSE see MARCH
LIFE
LIGIER
LOLA
LOTUS
LYNCAR
MAKI
MARCH
MARTINI
MASERATI
MATRA
MATRA SIMCA see MATRA
McGUIRE see WILLIAMS
McLAREN
MERCEDES-BENZ
MERZARIO
MILANO see MASERATI
MINARDI
MONTEVERDI see ONYX
ONYX
OSCA
OSELLA
PACIFIC
PARNELLI
PENSKE
POLITOYS see WILLIAMS
PORSCHE
PROTOS
RAM
RAM MARCH see RAM
REBAQUE
RENAULT
RIAL
SAUBER
SCARAB
SCIROCCO
SHADOW
SHANNON
SIMCA GORDINI see GORDINI
SIMTEK
SPIRIT
STANLEY BRM see BRM
STEBRO
SURTEES
TALBOT LAGO
TALBOT LIGIER see LIGIER
TEC MEC
TECNO
THEODORE
THIN WALL FERRARI see FERRARI
TOKEN
TOLEMAN see BENETTON
TROJAN
TYRRELL
VANWALL
VENTURI LARROUSSE see LARROUSSE
VERITAS
WILLIAMS
WOLF
WOLF WILLIAMS see WILLIAMS
ZAKSPEED

AFM (D)

Principal: Alex von Falkenhausen. **Base:** Munich. **Founded:** 1948.
Falkenhausen's connections with BMW, led to the foundation of Alex von Falkenhausen Motorenbau soon after the World War II, basing his developments on the 328 sports car. He built single seaters from 1949, although by 1950 he was virtually working full time for BMW once again. From 1951 his cars used the new Küchen V8 engine, although active support was withdrawn soon after, when the workshop closed and the owner returned to BMW.

TOTALS	GPs	STARTS	POINTS	POLES	F.LAPS	WINS			
	4	7	-	-	-	-			
SEASONS							**COLOUR**	**MAIN DRIVER(S)**	
1952	2	3	-	-	-	-	silver	Stuck	
1953	2	4	-	-	-	-	silver	Stuck	
MODELS							**YEAR(S)**	**CHIEF DESIGNER**	**ENGINE**
—	4	7	-	-	-	-	52-53	A von Falkenhausen	BMW, Küchen, Bristol

AGS (F)

Principal: Henri Julien. **Base:** Gonfaron, nr Toulon/ Le Luc-en-Provence (1990). **Founded:** 1970.
Automobiles Gonfaronaises Sportives was founded by Henri Julien, a driver and car-builder during the 60s. The first AGS (JH1) was built in 1970 for Formula France, the team progressing through other formulae until their Formula 1 debut in 1986 using a revamped Renault chassis. In 1988 most of the team defected to Coloni and in 1990 it was restructured under the direction of Hughes de Chaunac and relocated from the original Gonfaron base to the Var circuit near Le Luc-en-Provence. June 1990 saw another change - de Chaunac left the team and ownership passed to Cyril de Rouvre who in turn, sold the majority shareholdings to Italians Gabriele Rafanelli and Patrizio Cantu in April 1991, only to see the team close before the end of that year.

TOTALS	GPs	STARTS	POINTS	POLES	F.LAPS	WINS			
	48	49	2	-	-	-			
SEASONS							**SPONSOR(S)**	**MAIN DRIVER(S)**	
1986	2	2	-	-	-	-	Charro	Capelli	
1987	13	13	1	-	-	-	Charro	Fabre/Moreno	
1988	16	16	-	-	-	-	Bouygues	Streiff	
1989	6	6	1	-	-	-	Faure	Tarquini, Dalmas	
1990	8	9	-	-	-	-	Lapidus	Tarquini, Dalmas	
1991	3	3	-	-	-	-	Filling	Tarquini, Barbazza	
MODELS							**YEAR(S)**	**CHIEF DESIGNER**	**ENGINE**
JH21C	2	2	-	-	-	-	86	C Vanderpleyn	Motori Moderni
JH22	13	13	1	-	-	-	87	C Vanderpleyn	Ford Cosworth
JH23-B	22	22	1	-	-	-	88-89	C Vanderpleyn	Ford Cosworth
JH24	1	1	-	-	-	-	90	C Galopin	Ford Cosworth
JH25-B	10	11	-	-	-	-	90-91	M Costa	Ford Cosworth

The JH26 was never completed and the JH27 never qualified in 1991.

ALFA ROMEO (I)

Principals: Alfa Corse, Autodelta & Euroracing. **Base:** Portello, Milan. **Founded:** 1918.
Societa Anonima Lombarda Fabbrica Automobili (ALFA) was formed in 1909. Nicola Romeo later took over the factory and the company finally became known as Alfa Romeo in 1918. From its earliest days, Alfa Romeo has celebrated many years of successful racing - Enzo Ferrari ran the racing team in the 30s. The first championship car began life in 1938 as a Voiturette (Formula 2) and was stored during the war to be developed over the years, to become virtually unbeatable. The team withdrew as the first Grand Prix formula came to an end, and after a period of engine supply returned as a fully fledged team in the late 70s. Its racing concern passed from Carlo Chiti's Autodelta operation to Paolo Pavanello's Euroracing team in 1983, before the now FIAT owned group finally wound down its Formula1 activity.

TOTALS	GPs	STARTS	POINTS	POLES	F.LAPS	WINS		
	110	234	214	12	14	10		
SEASONS							**SPONSOR(S)**	**MAIN DRIVER(S)**
1950	6	21	89	6	6	6	(red)	Farina*, Fangio, Fagioli
1951	7	27	75	4	7	4	(red)	Farina, Fangio*, Sanesi, Bonetto
1952-1978 *did not participate*								
1979	5	6	-	-	-	-	Scaini	Giacomelli, Brambilla
1980	14	26	41	-	-		Marlboro Scaini	Depailler, Giacomelli
1981	15	30	10	-	-	-	Marlboro Scaini	Andretti, Giacomelli
1982	16	32	7	1	-	-	Marlboro	de Cesaris, Giacomelli
1983	15	29	18	-	1	-	Marlboro Nordica	de Cesaris, Baldi
1984	16	31	11	-	-	-	Benetton	Patrese, Cheever
1985	16	32	-	-	-	-	Benetton	Patrese, Cheever

* Champion

MODELS	GPs	STARTS	POINTS	POLES	F.LAPS	WINS	YEAR(S)	CHIEF DESIGNER	ENGINE
158-9	13	48	164	10	13	10	50-51	G Colombo	8s
177	3	3	-	-	-	-	79	C Chiti	F12
179-C, D, E	33	61	14	1	-	-	79-82	C Chiti	V12
182	15	30	7	1	-	-	82	G Ducarouge	V12
183T	15	29	18	-	1	-	83	G Ducarouge	V8t
184T	24	47	11	-	-	-	84-85	L Marmiroli	V8t
185T	8	16	-	-	-	-	85	L Marmiroli	V8t

ALFA SPECIAL (ZA)

Principal: Peter de Klerk. **Base:** South Africa. **Founded:** 1962.
Not an Alfa Romeo at all other than the use of the old Alfa 4 cylinder engine mated to a home built chassis. Created by former Lotus mechanic Peter de Klerk for local races, these cars nevertheless performed well against more contemporary cars in two South African Grands Prix during the 1.5 litre formula.

TOTALS	GPs	STARTS	POINTS	POLES	F.LAPS	WINS			
	2	2	-	-	-	-			
SEASONS							**COLOUR**	**MAIN DRIVER(S)**	
1963	1	1	-	-	-	-		de Klerk	
1965	1	1	-	-	-	-		de Klerk	
MODELS							**YEAR(S)**	**CHIEF DESIGNER**	**ENGINE**
—	2	2	-	-	-	-	63-65	P de Klerk	Alfa Romeo

ALTA (GB)

Principal: Geoffrey Taylor. **Base:** Tolworth, Surrey. **Founded:** 1928.
Initially formed as an engineering concern, Alta began by building sports cars before moving on to single seaters in the 30s. After the war, Taylor built one off chassis to order for both Formula 1 and later Formula 2. The company also sold its 4 cylinder, 2 litre engine to the likes of HWM, Cooper and Connaught. After Connaught's demise, there was no call for the engines and the company was wound up. Geoffrey Taylor died in 1966.

TOTALS	GPs	STARTS	POINTS	POLES	F.LAPS	WINS			
	5	6	-	-	-	-			
SEASONS							**COLOUR**	**MAIN DRIVER(S)**	
1950	2	3	-	-	-	-	green	Kelly, Crossley	
1951	1	1	-	-	-	-	green	Kelly	
1952	2	2	-	-	-	-	green	P & G Whitehead	
MODELS							**YEAR(S)**	**CHIEF DESIGNER**	**ENGINE**
GP	3	4	-	-	-	-	50-51	G Taylor	4s
F2	2	2	-	-	-	-	52	G Taylor	4

AMON (GB)

Principal: Chris Amon. **Base:** Reading. **Founded:** 1974.
Amon ventured into the world of driver-constructors with this kit car based around the Ford Cosworth and Hewland gearbox package, financed by John Dalton. The car had unusual features such as titanium suspension and the fuel tank between driver and engine, but unfortunately proved difficult to drive - it only qualified once.

TOTALS	GPs	STARTS	POINTS	POLES	F.LAPS	WINS			
	1	1	-	-	-	-			
SEASONS							**COLOUR**	**MAIN DRIVER(S)**	
1974	1	1	-	-	-	-	light blue	Amon	
MODELS							**YEAR(S)**	**CHIEF DESIGNER**	**ENGINE**
AF101	1	1	-	-	-	-	74	G Fowell	Ford Cosworth

ANDREA MODA (I)

Principal: Andrea Sassetti. **Base:** Trodica di Morovalle, Perugia. **Founded:** 1991.
Created from the ashes of Coloni whose assets were purchased by shoe magnate Andrea Sassetti. The team tried to use the previous year's Coloni chassis but as it was entered as a new team it could only race its own design. This was rushed through but inevitably it failed to qualify apart from a fine effort by Moreno at Monaco. The team suffered the indignity of being expelled from the championship after Sassetti was arrested at Spa for financial irregularities.

TOTALS	GPs	STARTS	POINTS	POLES	F.LAPS	WINS
	1	1	-	-	-	-

SEASONS	GPs	STARTS	POINTS	POLES	F.LAPS	WINS	SPONSOR(S)	MAIN DRIVER(S)
1992	1	1	-	-	-	-	Ellesse	Moreno

MODELS	GPs	STARTS	POINTS	POLES	F.LAPS	WINS	YEAR(S)	CHIEF DESIGNER	ENGINE
S921	1	1	-	-	-	-	92	N Wirth	Judd

ARROWS (GB)

Principals: Jackie Oliver, Alan Rees. **Base:** Bletchley, Milton Keynes/ Leafield, Oxfordshire. **Founded:** 1977.
Created as a breakaway from the Shadow team which later contested the design of the first Arrows FA1. The outfit took its name from the instigators - Franco Ambrosio, Alan Rees, Jack Oliver, Dave Wass and Tony Southgate. The team promised much, but has so far failed to notch up that all important first win after a record number of attempts. In1990 Wataru Ohashi's Japanese Footwork corporation tookover, renaming the cars Footwork from the beginning of the1991 season and effectively reducing the remaining Rees and Oliver to employees. For the 1994 season Oliver and Rees were back in control and the old Arrows name returned to the team although the cars still raced as Footworks in the new livery. 1996 saw another change in ownership as Tom Walkinshaw took over the team in the early part of the season and began the move to a new headquarters in Leafield. From 1997 the car will revert to the original name with Damon Hill as main driver together with Yamaha and Bridgestone Tyres.

TOTALS	GPs	STARTS	POINTS	POLES	F.LAPS	WINS
	288	537	141	1	-	-

SEASONS	GPs	STARTS	POINTS	POLES	F.LAPS	WINS	SPONSOR(S)	MAIN DRIVER(S)
1978	15	23	11	-	-	-	Warsteiner	Patrese, Stommelen
1979	15	27	5	-	-	-	Warsteiner	Patrese, Mass
1980	14	25	11	-	-	-	Warsteiner	Patrese, Mass
1981	15	24	10	1	-	-	Ragno, Penthouse	Patrese, Stohr
1982	14	24	5	-	-	-	Ragno, Nordica	Baldi, Surer
1983	15	30	4	-	-	-	Barclay, Rizla	Surer, Boutsen
1984	15	30	6	-	-	-	Barclay	Surer, Boutsen
1985	16	32	14	-	-	-	Barclay	Berger, Boutsen
1986	16	31	1	-	-	-	USF&G, Barclay	Surer/Danner, Boutsen
1987	16	32	11	-	-	-	USF&G	Warwick, Cheever
1988	16	32	23	-	-	-	USF&G	Warwick, Cheever
1989	16	30	13	-	-	-	USF&G	Warwick, Cheever
1990	14	25	2	-	-	-	Footwork, USF&G	Alboreto, Caffi
1991	10	12	-	-	-	-	Footwork	Alboreto, Caffi
1992	16	30	6	-	-	-	Footwork, Hamacher	Alboreto, Suzuki
1993	16	32	4	-	-	-	Footwork, Japan	Warwick, Suzuki
1994	16	32	9	-	-	-	Uliveto	Fittipaldi, Morbidelli
1995	17	34	5	-	-	-	Sasol, Unimat	Morbidelli, Inoue
1996	16	32	1	-	-	-	Power Horse, Philips	Rosset, Verstappen

MODELS	GPs	STARTS	POINTS	POLES	F.LAPS	WINS	YEAR(S)	CHIEF DESIGNER	ENGINE
FA1	10	18	8	-	-	-	78	T Southgate	Ford Cosworth
A1-B	13	19	6	-	-	-	78-79	T Southgate	Ford Cosworth
A2	7	13	2	-	-	-	79	T Southgate	Ford Cosworth
A3	29	49	21	1	-	-	80-81	T Southgate	Ford Cosworth
A4	13	21	5	-	-	-	82	D Wass	Ford Cosworth
A5	3	3	-	-	-	-	82	D Wass	Ford Cosworth
A6	22	39	7	-	-	-	83-84	D Wass	Ford Cosworth
A7	13	21	3	-	-	-	84	D Wass	BMW
A8	32	60	15	-	-	-	85-86	D Wass	BMW
A9	3	3	-	-	-	-	86	D Wass	BMW
A10-B	32	64	34	-	-	-	87-88	R Brawn	Megatron
A11-B, C	31	56	15	-	-	-	89-91	R Brawn	Ford Cosworth, Porsche
FA12	9	11	-	-	-	-	91	A Jenkins	Porsche, Ford Cosworth
FA13-B	18	34	6	-	-	-	92-93	A Jenkins	Mugen Honda
FA14	14	28	4	-	-	-	93	A Jenkins	Mugen Honda
FA15	16	32	9	-	-	-	94	A Jenkins	Ford Cosworth
FA16	17	34	5	-	-	-	95	A Jenkins	Hart
FA17	16	32	1	-	-	-	96	A Jenkins	Hart

ASTON (GB)

Principal: Bill Aston. **Base:** Frimley, Surrey. **Founded:** 1952.
The Aston Butterworth cars were a combination of Bill Aston's, Cooper-inspired chassis with Archie Butterworth's flat 4 air-cooled engine, more accurately refered to as an AJB unit. Two were built, the first for Aston himself and both were raced privately.

TOTALS	GPs	STARTS	POINTS	POLES	F.LAPS	WINS			
	2	2	-	-	-	-			
SEASONS							**COLOUR**	**MAIN DRIVER(S)**	
1952	2	2	-	-	-	-	green	Aston, Montgomerie-Charrington	
MODELS							**YEAR(S)**	**CHIEF DESIGNER**	**ENGINE**
NB	2	2	-	-	-	-	52	B Aston	Butterworth

ASTON MARTIN (GB)

Principal: David Brown. **Base:** Feltham, Middlesex. **Founded:** 1914.
Founder Lionel Martin built sports cars for the Aston Clinton hill-climb which gave this new marque its name. The company changed ownership many times before David Brown bought the company in 1947. The team re-entered Grand Prix racing in 1959, with the project delayed due to the company's sports car race successes, which unfortunately meant these front-emgined cars were outdated before they had a chance to prove themselves.

TOTALS	GPs	STARTS	POINTS	POLES	F.LAPS	WINS			
	5	10	-	-	-	-			
SEASONS							**COLOUR**	**MAIN DRIVER(S)**	
1959	4	8	-	-	-	-	green	Salvadori, Shelby	
1960	1	2	-	-	-	-	green	Salvadori, Trintignant	
MODELS							**YEAR(S)**	**CHIEF DESIGNER**	**ENGINE**
DBR4	4	8	-	-	-	-	59	T Cutting	6
DBR5	1	2	-	-	-	-	60	T Cutting	6

ATS (D)

Principal: Hans Gunter Schmid. **Base:** Bicester, Oxfordshire, UK. **Founded:** 1972.
Auto Technisches Spezialzubehör was the company name of German wheel magnate Schmid who entered Formula 1 with the Penske PC4 in 1977. This was later developed into the first proper ATS entry and the team took over the facilities of the departing March operation in Bicester. ATS struggled at this level, with a succession of different designers and team managers before Schmid called it a day only to return with his new Rial outfit four years later.

TOTALS	GPs	STARTS	POINTS	POLES	F.LAPS	WINS			
	89	108	8	-	-	-			
SEASONS							**SPONSOR(S)**	**MAIN DRIVER(S)**	
1978	12	19	-	-	-	-	ATS, Fina	Mass, Jarier/Rosberg	
1979	12	12	2	-	-	-	ATS, Hotel Arawak	Stuck	
1980	12	12	-	-	-	-	ATS, Hotel Arawak	Surer	
1981	9	9	1	-	-	-	ATS, ABBA	Borgudd	
1982	15	26	4	-	-	-	ATS, Liqui Moly	Winkelhock, Salazar	
1983	14	14	-	-	-	-	ATS, Steinbock	Winkelhock	
1984	15	16	1	-	-	-	ATS	Winkelhock	
MODELS							**YEAR(S)**	**CHIEF DESIGNER**	**ENGINE**
HS1	11	17	-	-	-	-	78	R Herd	Ford Cosworth
D1	2	2	-	-	-	-	78	J Gentry	Ford Cosworth
D2	7	7	-	-	-	-	79	G Caliri	Ford Cosworth
D3	7	7	2	-	-	-	79-80	N Stroud	Ford Cosworth
D4	13	13	-	-	-	-	80-81	G Brunner	Ford Cosworth
D5(HGS1)	21	32	5	-	-	-	81-82	H Guilpin	Ford Cosworth
D6	14	14	-	-	-	-	83	G Brunner	BMW t
D7	15	16	1	-	-	-	84	G Brunner	BMW t

ATS (I)

Principal: Carlo Chiti. **Base:** Bologna. **Founded:** 1961.
Automobili Turismo e Sport was formed by ex-Ferrari personnel, led by Carlo Chiti (who died in 1994) and Romolo Tavoni, with the backing of Jaime Ortiz Patino, Giorgio Billi and Count Giovanni Volpi (who left early on to form Scuderia Serenissima). The team based itself at Sasso Marconi, Bologna and appeared unprepared for the vigours of Formula 1 racing and effectively finished after the 1963 season, although it continued as an engineering concern.

TOTALS	GPs	STARTS	POINTS	POLES	F.LAPS	WINS			
	6	11	-	-	-	-			
SEASONS							**COLOUR**	**MAIN DRIVER(S)**	
1963	5	10	-	-	-	-	red	P Hill, Baghetti	
1964	1	1	-	-	-	-		de Cabral	
MODELS							**YEAR(S)**	**CHIEF DESIGNER**	**ENGINE**
100	5	10	-	-	-	-	63	C Chiti	V8
(D-F)*	1	1	-	-	-	-	64	V Derrington	V8

** Derrington-Francis -a development of the early chassis by Vic Derrington and Alf Francis*

BELLASI (I)

Principal: Vittorio Bellasi. **Base:** Italy. **Founded:** 1966.
Bellasi designs were created for the domestic Italian market, the first of many designs being an Formula 3 car. The only Formula 1 design was commissioned by Silvio Moser and was not a great success.

TOTALS	GPs	STARTS	POINTS	POLES	F.LAPS	WINS			
	2	2	-	-	-	-			
SEASONS							**COLOUR**	**MAIN DRIVER(S)**	
1970	1	1	-	-	-	-	red	Moser	
1971	1	1	-	-	-	-	red	Moser	
MODELS							**YEAR(S)**	**CHIEF DESIGNER**	**ENGINE**
—	2	2	-	-	-	-	70-71	V Bellasi	Ford Cosworth

BENETTON (GB/I) formerly Toleman (1981 to 1985)

Principals: Ted Toleman/ Alessandro Benetton. **Base:** Witney/ Enstone, Chipping Norton (1993). **Founded:** 1970.
Ted Toleman and his company took part in British club motorsport, building their first car for Formula 2 in 1980 and entering the big time in the following year. In 1985, the Witney based team ran into difficulties and was rescued by Benetton sponsorship which resulted in a full takeover by the Italian company the following season. A succession of team managers has seen Peter Collins, Davide Paolini and Flavio Briatore take control of the racing operations. In 1993 the team moved to new Oxfordshire premises and became the team to beat, the following year. The combination of Schumacher and intelligent team strategy paid off with both titles in 1995, although they seemed to miss their superstar the following season when the team officially changed their nationality to Italian.

CONSTRUCTORS' CHAMPIONSHIPS: 1 (1995)

TOTALS	GPs	STARTS	POINTS	POLES	F.LAPS	WINS		
	234	448	741.5	13	35	26		
SEASONS							**SPONSOR(S)**	**MAIN DRIVER(S)**
1981	2	2	-	-	-	-	Candy	Henton, Warwick
1982	11	18	-	-	1	-	Cougar	Warwick, Fabi
1983	15	29	10	-	-	-	Candy, Magirus	Warwick, Giacomelli
1984	16	26	16	-	1	-	Segafredo, Magirus	Senna, Cecotto
1985	13	20	-	1	-	-	Benetton	Fabi, Ghinzani
1986	16	32	19	2	3	1	Benetton, Sisley	Fabi, Berger
1987	16	32	28	-	1	-	Benetton, Riello	Fabi, Boutsen
1988	16	32	39	-	1	-	Benetton, Riello	Nannini, Boutsen
1989	16	31	39	-	-	1	Benetton, Riello	Nannini, Herbert/Pirro
1990	16	32	71	-	1	2	Benetton, Riello	Nannini, Piquet
1991	16	32	38.5	-	1	1	Camel, Autopolis	Moreno/Schumacher, Piquet
1992	16	32	91	-	2	1	Camel, Benetton	Schumacher, Brundle
1993	16	32	72	-	5	1	Camel, Benetton	Schumacher, Patrese
1994	16	32	103	6	8	8	Mild Seven, Benetton	Schumacher*, Verstappen
1995	17	34	147	4	8	11	Mild Seven, Bitburger	Schumacher*, Herbert
1996	16	32	68	-	3	-	Mild Seven, Benetton	Alesi, Berger

*Champion

MODELS	GPs	STARTS	POINTS	POLES	F.LAPS	WINS	YEAR(S)	CHIEF DESIGNER	ENGINE
TG181-B, C	12	18	-	-	1	-	81-82	R Byrne	Hart t
TG183-B	21	38	12	-	-	-	82-84	R Byrne	Hart t
TG184	12	19	14	-	1	-	84	R Byrne	Hart t
TG185	13	20	-	1	-	-	85	R Byrne	Hart t
B186	16	32	19	2	3	1	86	R Byrne	BMW t
B187	16	32	28	-	1	-	87	R Byrne	Ford Cosworth t
B188	24	45	52	-	1	-	88-89	R Byrne	Ford Cosworth
B189-B	12	22	30	-	-	1	89-90	R Byrne	Ford Cosworth
B190-B	16	32	73	-	1	2	90-91	R Byrne	Ford Cosworth
B191-B	17	34	43.5	-	1	1	91-92	J Barnard	Ford Cosworth
B192-B	15	30	84	-	3	1	92-93	R Brawn	Ford Cosworth
B193B	14	28	68	-	4	1	93	R Brawn	Ford Cosworth
B194	16	32	103	6	8	8	94	R Brawn	Ford Cosworth
B195	17	34	147	4	8	11	95	R Brawn	Renault
B196	16	32	68	-	3	-	96	R Byrne	Renault

BMW (D)

Principal: no works involvement. **Base:** Munich. **Founded:** 1916 (aero engines).
Bayerische Motoren Werke of Munich never entered Formula 1 in their own right, although there were entries for the various home-built specials which raced in Germany in the early fifties.

TOTALS	GPs	STARTS	POINTS	POLES	F.LAPS	WINS			
	2	6	-	-	-	-			
SEASONS							**COLOUR**	**MAIN DRIVER(S)**	
1952	1	4	-	-	-	-	silver	Krause, Klodwig	
1953	1	2	-	-	-	-	silver	Krause, Klodwig	
MODELS							**YEAR(S)**	**CHIEF DESIGNER**	**ENGINE**
Greifzu	2	2	-	-	-	-	52-53	P Greifzu	4
Heck	2	2	-	-	-	-	52-53	E Klodwig	4 *(rear engine)*
Eigenbau	1	1	-	-	-	-	52	G Bechem	4
Speciale	1	1	-	-	-	-	52	M Balsa	4 *(Gordini type body)*

The Len Terry designed 269 failed to start in the Formula 2 class of the 1969 German Grand Prix

BRABHAM (GB)

Principals: Jack Brabham, Ron Tauranac/ Bernie Ecclestone.
Base: Guildford/ New Haw, Weybridge/Chessington/ Tilbrook, Milton Keynes. **Founded:** 1961.
The first car, known as MRD, appeared in 1961 and the early years up until 1970 saw Brabham and Tauranac produce a succession of winners in Formula 1 and lower formulae, as well as providing customer cars from the New Haw factory. Ecclestone purchased the team in 1972 and from new premises continued the team's winning ways, building Formula 1 team cars only. After a year out of the championship (1988), the team was sold to the Swiss financier Joachim Luhti and the marque began its slow decline until closing in late 1992 when owned by the Middlebridge group.

CONSTRUCTORS' CHAMPIONSHIPS: 2 (1966, 67)

TOTALS	GPs	STARTS	POINTS	POLES	F.LAPS	WINS		
	394	932	983	39	42	35		
SEASONS							**SPONSOR(S)**	**MAIN DRIVER(S)**
1962	3	3	6	-	-	-	(green)	Brabham
1963	10	20	33	-	1	-	(green)	Brabham, Gurney
1964	10	49	43	2	3	2	(green)	Brabham, Gurney
1965	10	57	44	-	1	-	(green)	Brabham, Gurney, Hulme
1966	9	35	65	3	2	4	(green)	Brabham*, Hulme
1967	11	36	102	2	2	4	(green)	Brabham, Hulme*
1968	12	30	12	2	-	-	(green)	Brabham, Rindt
1969	11	43	68	4	4	2	(green)	Brabham, Ickx
1970	13	26	35	1	4	1	(turquoise)	Brabham, Stommelen
1971	11	24	7	-	-	-	(white)	Hill, Schenken
1972	12	32	7	1	-	-	YPF, Bardahl	Hill, Reutemann, W Fittipaldi
1973	15	41	22	-	-	-	YPF, Bardahl	Reutemann, W Fittipaldi
1974	15	46	46	1	3	3	Elan, Stroh	Reutemann, von Opel/Pace
1975	14	28	61	1	1	2	Martini	Reutemann, Pace
1976	16	39	11	-	-	-	Martini	Reutemann, Pace
1977	17	34	27	1	2	-	Martini	Watson, Pace/Stuck

*Champion

SEASONS	GPs	STARTS	POINTS	POLES	F.LAPS	WINS	SPONSOR(S)	MAIN DRIVER(S)
1978	16	33	69	2	4	2	Parmalat	Lauda, Watson
1979	15	30	7	-	1	-	Parmalat	Lauda, Piquet
1980	14	27	55	2	1	3	Parmalat	Piquet, Zunino/Rebaque
1981	15	29	61	4	1	3	Parmalat	Piquet*, Rebaque
1982	15	29	41	1	4	2	Parmalat	Piquet, Patrese
1983	15	30	72	2	5	4	Parmalat	Piquet*, Patrese
1984	16	32	38	9	3	2	Parmalat	Piquet, T & C Fabi
1985	16	31	26	1	-	1	Olivetti	Piquet, Surer
1986	16	30	2	-	-	-	Olivetti	Patrese, de Angelis/Warwick
1987	16	32	10	-	-	-	Olivetti	Patrese, de Cesaris
1988 *did not participate*								
1989	16	29	8	-	-	-	Bioptron	Brundle, Modena
1990	16	26	2	-	-	-	Carvico	Brabham, Modena
1991	16	28	3	-	-	-	Mitsukoshi	Brundle, Blundell
1992	3	3	-	-	-	-	Yamazen	van de Poele, Hill

*Champion

MODELS							YEAR(S)	CHIEF DESIGNER	ENGINE
BT3	77	8	-	-	-		62-65	R Tauranac	Climax, BRM
BT6	11	-	-	-	-		63	R Tauranac	Ford
BT7	32	51	62	2	4	2	63-66	R Tauranac	Climax
BT10	2	3	-	-	-	-	64-65	R Tauranac	Ford
BT11	32	88	60	-	1	-	64-68	R Tauranac	Climax, BRM, Repco
BT18	1	3	-	-	-	-	66	R Tauranac	Ford Cosworth
BT19	11	11	45	3	1	4	66-67	R Tauranac	Repco
BT20	19	21	44	2	2	1	66-69	R Tauranac	Repco
BT22	4	4	-	-	-	-	66	R Tauranac	Climax
BT23-B, C	3	4	-	-	-	-	67-69	R Tauranac	Ford Cosworth, Climax
BT24	21	29	81	-	1	3	67-69	R Tauranac	Repco, Ford Cosworth
BT26-A	25	52	73	6	4	2	68-71	R Tauranac	Repco, Ford Cosworth
BT30	13	-	-	-	-		69	R Tauranac	Ford Cosworth
BT33	28	40	41	1	4	1	70-72	R Tauranac	Ford Cosworth
BT34	20	20	2	1	-	-	71-72	R Tauranac	Ford Cosworth
BT37	18	29	10	-	-	-	72-73	R Bellamy	Ford Cosworth
BT42	23	43	19	-	-	-	73-74	G Murray	Ford Cosworth
BT44-B	33	67	106	2	4	5	74-76	G Murray	Ford Cosworth
BT45-B, C	35	71	48	1	2	-	76-78	G Murray	Alfa Romeo F12
BT46-B	15	30	59	2	4	2	78-79	G Murray	Alfa Romeo F12
BT48	13	25	7	-	-	-	79	G Murray	Alfa Romeo V12
BT49-C, D	36	67	135	6	4	7	79-82	G Murray	Ford Cosworth
BT50	12	22	22	1	3	1	82	G Murray	BMW t
BT52-B	15	30	72	2	5	4	83	G Murray	BMW t
BT53	16	32	38	9	3	2	84	G Murray	BMW t
BT54	17	32	26	1	-	1	85-86	G Murray	BMW t
BT55	16	29	2	-	-	-	86	G Murray	BMW t
BT56	16	32	10	-	-	-	87	D North	BMW t
BT58	18	33	10	-	-	-	89-90	S Rinland	Judd
BT59-Y	16	26	-	-	-	-	90-91	S Rinland	Judd, Yamaha
BT60Y, B	17	27	3	-	-	-	91-92	S Rinland	Yamaha, Judd

The BT16-Ford Cosworth did not start in 1966

BRM (GB)

Principals: Raymond Mays, Alfred Owen, Louis Stanley. **Base:** Bourne, Lincolnshire. **Founded:** 1945.
British Racing Motors was founded as a trust by Raymond Mays to help establish Britain as a major force in motor racing - a follow up to his earlier ERA set-up. The first V16 supercharged car was over ambitious and didn't appear at the circuits until 1950. The trust was taken over by Alfred Owen (of Rubery Owen) in 1952, and success gradually came, culminating in winning the drivers' and constructors championships in 1962. Louis Stanley took control in the later years as BRM slowly ceased to exist as a racing operation, finally closing its doors in the late 70s.

CONSTRUCTORS' CHAMPIONSHIPS: 1 (1962)

TOTALS	GPs	STARTS	POINTS	POLES	F.LAPS	WINS
	197	522	537.5	11	15	17

SEASONS							SPONSOR(S)	MAIN DRIVER(S)
1951	1	2	2	-	-	-	(green)	Parnell, Walker
1952-55 *did not participate*								
1956	1	3	-	-	-	-	(green)	Hawthorn, Brooks, Flockhart

SEASONS	GPs	STARTS	POINTS	POLES	F.LAPS	WINS	SPONSOR(S)	MAIN DRIVERS
1957	3	5	-	-	-	-	(green)	Flockhart, MacKay-Fraser
1958	9	22	24	-	-	-	(green)	Schell, Behra
1959	7	22	22.5	1	2	1	(green)	Schell, Bonnier, Flockhart
1960	8	23	8	-	1	-	(green)	G Hill, Bonnier, Gurney
1961	8	16	9	-	1	-	(green)	G Hill, Brooks
1962	9	19	62	1	3	4	(green)	G Hill*, Ginther
1963	10	25	65	2	-	2	(green)	G Hill, Ginther
1964	10	33	70	1	1	2	(green)	G Hill, Ginther
1965	10	27	81	4	3	3	(green)	G Hill, Stewart
1966	9	24	34	-	-	1	(green)	G Hill, Stewart
1967	11	33	21	-	-	-	(green)	Stewart, Spence
1968	12	31	28	-	2	-	(green)	Rodriguez, Attwood
1969	10	25	7	-	-	-	(green)	Surtees, Oliver
1970	13	34	25	-	-	1	Yardley	Rodriguez, Oliver, Eaton
1971	11	36	42	1	1	2	Yardley	Rodriguez, Siffert, Ganley
1972	12	47	14	-	1	1	Marlboro	Beltoise, Gethin, Ganley, Wisell
1973	15	44	13	1	-	-	Marlboro	Beltoise, Regazzoni, Lauda
1974	15	38	10	-	-	-	Motul	Beltoise, Pescarolo, Migault
1975	10	10	-	-	-	-	-	Evans
1976	1	1	-	-	-	-	-	Ashley
1977	2	2	-	-	-	-	Rotary	Perkins

*Champion

MODELS							YEAR(S)	CHIEF DESIGNER	ENGINE
P15	1	2	2	-	-	-	51	P Berthon	V16s
P25	21	54	46.5	1	2	1	56-60	P Berthon	4
P48	7	21	8	-	1	-	60	P Berthon	4
P48/57	11	19	9	-	1	-	61-62	P Berthon	4, Climax
P57	31	59	133	3	3	6	62-65	T Rudd	V8
P61	2	2	-	-	-	-	63	T Rudd	V8
P261	34	65	183	5	4	6	64-67	T Rudd	V8
P83	14	27	17	-	-	-	66-67	T Rudd	H16
P115	6	6	-	-	-	-	67-68	T Rudd	H16
P126	15	21	10	-	1	-	68-69	L Terry	V12
P133	15	15	18	-	1	-	68-69	T Rudd	V12
P138	10	10	2	-	-	-	68-69	T Rudd	V12
P139	6	10	5	-	-	-	69-70	A Osborne	V12
P153-B	27	49	25	-	-	1	70-72	T Southgate	V12
P160-B, C, D, E	47	121	71	2	2	3	71-74	T Southgate	V12
P180	5	7	-	-	-	-	72	T Southgate	V12
P201-B	25	33	8	-	-	-	74-77	M Pilbeam	V12
P207	1	1	-	-	-	-	77	L Terry	V12

The P67 did not start in 1964

BRP (GB)

Principals: Alfred Moss, Ken Gregory. **Base:** Highgate, London. **Founded:** 1959.
British Racing Partnership was formed by Stirling Moss's father and manager. It initially ran a BRM P25 until destroyed at AVUS in 1959. After running customer cars with help from Yeoman Credit/ UDT-Laystall, an Formula 1 car appeared in 1963. The outfit folded in 1966 after attempts at the Indianapolis 500.

TOTALS	GPs	STARTS	POINTS	POLES	F.LAPS	WINS
	13	18	11	-	-	-

SEASONS							COLOUR	MAIN DRIVER(S)
1963	5	5	6	-	-	-	green	Ireland
1964	8	13	5	-	-	-	green	Ireland, T Taylor

MODELS							YEAR(S)	CHIEF DESIGNER	ENGINE
Mk 1	9	9	6	-	-	-	63-64	T Robinson	BRM
Mk 2	7	9	5	-	-	-	64	T Robinson	BRM

BUGATTI (F)

Principal: Roland Bugatti. **Base:** Molsheim, nr Strasbourg. **Founded:** 1909.
This legendary marque made one last attempt at Grand Prix racing with Ettore's son Roland, now in control. Two cars were built with the unusual transverse engine layout and one made an isolated appearance at the French GP.

TOTALS	GPs	STARTS	POINTS	POLES	F.LAPS	WINS
	1	1	-	-	-	-

SEASONS	GPs	STARTS	POINTS	POLES	F.LAPS	WINS	COLOUR	MAIN DRIVER(S)
1956	1	1	-	-	-	-	blue	Trintignant

MODELS	GPs	STARTS	POINTS	POLES	F.LAPS	WINS	YEAR(S)	CHIEF DESIGNER	ENGINE
T251	1	1	-	-	-	-	56	G Colombo	8

CISITALIA (I)

Compagnia Industriale Sportiva Italia was founded by Piero Dusio and Piero Taruffi who created a simple small car for an early forerunner of one-make racing, immediately after the war. Over thirty of these Giacosa designed chassis were built at the Turin workshops, one of which (the BPM-powered D46) suffered engine failure during practice for the 1952 Italian Grand Prix.

COLONI (I)

Principal: Enzo Coloni. **Base:** Passignano sul Trasimeno, Perugia. **Founded:** 1983.
This little team from Perugia initially ran Formula 3 Ralts and built its first car for F1. Always struggling the team was acquired by the Andrea Moda concern after Subaru had purchased a stake in the team and then promptly sold it back again during the 1991 season.

TOTALS	GPs	STARTS	POINTS	POLES	F.LAPS	WINS
	13	14	-	-	-	-

SEASONS	GPs	STARTS	POINTS	POLES	F.LAPS	WINS	SPONSOR(S)	MAIN DRIVER(S)
1987	1	1	-	-	-	-	Himont, Renzacci	Larini
1988	8	8	-	-	-	-	Himont	Tarquini
1989	4	5	-	-	-	-	Himont	Moreno, Raphanel
1990	-	-	-	-	-	-	Agip, Magnabosco	Gachot
1991	-	-	-	-	-	-	Mateus	Chaves

MODELS	GPs	STARTS	POINTS	POLES	F.LAPS	WINS	YEAR(S)	CHIEF DESIGNER	ENGINE
FC187	1	1	-	-	-	-	87	R Ori	Ford Cosworth
FC188-B	9	10	-	-	-	-	88-89	R Ori	Ford Cosworth
FC189	3	3	-	-	-	-	89	C Vanderpleyn	Ford Cosworth

Models also known as C1, C2, C3. The FC189B (Subaru engine) and FC189C (Ford Cosworth engine) did not qualify in 1990, as was the fate of the C4 in 1991

CONNAUGHT (GB)

Principals: Rodney Clarke, Mike Oliver. **Base:** Send, nr Guildford, Surrey. **Founded:** 1948.
Financed by Kenneth McAlpine, the Surrey concern built successful designs for both Formula 2 and later Formula 1 which included the unusual streamlined 'B' version. Connaught were renowned for their engineering excellence and it is quite correct to refer to the modified engines as Lea Francis or Alta based Connaught engines. The team came so close to real success but reluctantly closed after Monaco 1957 and the cars were sold off in September of that year, Bernie Ecclestone purchasing some of the proceeds.

TOTALS	GPs	STARTS	POINTS	POLES	F.LAPS	WINS
	17	49	17	-	-	-

SEASONS	GPs	STARTS	POINTS	POLES	F.LAPS	WINS	COLOUR	MAIN DRIVER(S)
1952	3	8	5	-	-	-	green	McAlpine, Poore, Thompson
1953	6	21	-	-	-	-	green	McAlpine, Salvadori, Bira
1954	1	5	-	-	-	-	green	Marr, Whitehouse *(privateers)*
1955	1	3	-	-	-	-	green	McAlpine
1956	3	7	9	-	-	-	green	Fairman, Flockhart
1957	1	2	3	-	-	-	green	Lewis-Evans, Bueb
1958	1	2	-	-	-	-	green	Bueb, Fairman *(B Ecclestone)*
1959	1	1	-	-	-	-	green	Said *(P Emery)*

MODELS	GPs	STARTS	POINTS	POLES	F.LAPS	WINS	YEAR(S)	CHIEF DESIGNER	ENGINE
A	10	34	5	-	-	-	52-54	R Clarke	Lea Francis
B	6	14	12	-	-	-	55-58	R Clarke	Alta
C	1	1	-	-	-	-	59	R Clarke	Alta

CONNEW (GB)

Principal: Peter Connew. **Base:** Chadwell Heath, Essex. **Founded:** 1971.
Former Surtees draughtsman Peter Connew took on the might of Formula 1 with what was basically a lock-up special. Although only qualifying for one race it remains a remarkable achievement on what was such a financial shoestring.

TOTALS	GPs	STARTS	POINTS	POLES	F.LAPS	WINS
	1	1	-	-	-	-

SEASONS	GPs	STARTS	POINTS	POLES	F.LAPS	WINS	SPONSOR(S)	MAIN DRIVER(S)
1972	1	1	-	-	-	-	Capricorn	Migault

MODELS	GPs	STARTS	POINTS	POLES	F.LAPS	WINS	YEAR(S)	CHIEF DESIGNER	ENGINE
PC1	1	1	-	-	-	-	72	P Connew	Ford Cosworth

COOPER (GB)

Principals: Charles & John Cooper. **Base:** Surbiton/ Byfleet, Surrey. **Founded:** 1946.
In the immediate post war years, Charles Cooper and his son John were supporters of the burgeoning Formula 3 500cc racing. They built small rear-engined cars (one of which appeared at Monaco in 1950), that set a trend for the Formula 2 models of the late fifties, although the first Formula 2 Coopers were conventional front-engined cars. Their pinnacle came with back to back championships in 1959-60. Charles died in 1964 and with John suffering from the effects of a serious road accident, the team was sold to the Chipstead Group and later relocated to Canada Road, Byfleet. In the final years Cooper reintroduced the V12 Maserati engine but the writing was on the wall and they closed soon after.

CONSTRUCTORS' CHAMPIONSHIPS: 2 (1959, 60)

TOTALS	GPs	STARTS	POINTS	POLES	F.LAPS	WINS
	129	499	484.5	11	14	16

SEASONS	GPs	STARTS	POINTS	POLES	F.LAPS	WINS	COLOUR	MAIN DRIVER(S)
1950	1	1	-	-	-	-	blue/white	Schell *(privateer)*
1952	6	16	12	-	-	-	green	Hawthorn, Brown *(privateers)*
1953	7	20	-	-	-	-	green	Moss, Wharton, Brown
1954	1	4	-	-	-	-	green	Gerard *(privateer)*
1955	1	1	-	-	-	-	green	Brabham
1956	1	1	-	-	-	-	green	Gerard *(privateer)*
1957	5	14	2	-	-	-	green	Brabham, Salvadori, MacDowel
1958	10	40	38	-	-	2	green	Brabham, Salvadori, Fairman
1959	8	57	97.5	5	5	5	green	Brabham*, McLaren, Gregory
1960	9	74	108	4	5	6	green	Brabham*, McLaren
1961	8	55	24	1	1	-	green	Brabham, McLaren
1962	9	29	45	-	1	1	green	McLaren, Maggs
1963	10	33	32	-	-	-	green	McLaren, Maggs
1964	10	22	16	-	-	-	green	McLaren, P Hill
1965	10	21	14	-	-	-	green	McLaren, Rindt
1966	9	41	39	1	2	1	green	Rindt, Surtees, Ginther
1967	11	44	37	-	-	1	green	Rindt, Rodriguez, Ickx
1968	12	25	20	-	-	-	green	Bianchi, Elford
1969	1	1	-	-	-	-	maroon	Elford *(Antique Automobiles)*

*Champion

MODELS	GPs	STARTS	POINTS	POLES	F.LAPS	WINS	YEAR(S)	CHIEF DESIGNER	ENGINE
T12	1	1	-	-	-	-	50	O Maddock	JAP
T20	8	20	12	-	-	-	52-53	O Maddock	Bristol
T23	9	18	-	-	-	-	53-56	O Maddock	Bristol, Alta
Spl.	1	1	-	-	-	-	53	R Martin	Alta
T24	2	2	-	-	-	-	53-54	O Maddock	Alta
T40	1	1	-	-	-	-	55	J Brabham	Bristol
T41	1	1	-	-	-	-	57	O Maddock	Climax
T43	12	23	10	-	-	1	57-60	O Maddock	Climax, OSCA
T44	1	1	-	-	-	-	57	B Gerard	Bristol
T45	18	45	30	-	-	1	58-61	O Maddock	Climax, Maserati, Castellotti
T51	24	110	133.5	6	6	6	59-63	O Maddock	Climax, Maserati, Borgward, Castellotti

MODELS	GPs	STARTS	POINTS	POLES	F.LAPS	WINS	YEAR(S)	CHIEF DESIGNER	ENGINE
T53	21	55	81	3	4	5	60-62	O Maddock	Climax, Maserati, Alfa Romeo
T55	14	19	17	-	-	-	61-65	O Maddock	Climax
T58	3	3	-	1	1	-	61	O Maddock	Climax
T60	15	21	45	-	1	1	62-65	O Maddock	Climax
T66	13	30	32	-	-	-	63-64	O Maddock	Climax
T73	13	21	16	-	-	-	64-66	E Stait	Climax, Ford, Ferrari
T77	11	19	12	-	-	-	65-67	E Stait	Climax, ATS
T79	2	2	6	-	-	-	67-68	E Stait	Climax
T81-B	21	82	67	1	2	2	66-68	D White	Maserati
T86-B	17	24	23	-	-	-	67-69	D White	Maserati, BRM

The T59-Ford (1965), T76-Ford (1965) and T82-Climax (1967) did not start

DALLARA (I)

Principal: Gianpaolo Dallara. **Base:** Parma. **Founded:** 1972.
Commissioned by Beppe Lucchini's Brescia Motor Sport operation to build a chassis for his Scuderia Italia team. Dallara's first car was the Wolf-Dallara Formula 3 car of 1978 but prior to this, he was a successful consultant designer, his work incuding the de Tomaso Formula 1 car and various road cars. Gianpaolo Dallara retains an active role in chassis design and assisted in all the following Grand Prix designs. Dallara chassis are still widely used in European lower formula racing and have the contract to build cars for the Indy Racing League.

TOTALS	GPs	STARTS	POINTS	POLES	F.LAPS	WINS
	78	133	15	-	-	-

SEASONS	GPs	STARTS	POINTS	POLES	F.LAPS	WINS	SPONSOR(S)	MAIN DRIVER(S)
1988	14	14	-	-	-	-	Marlboro	Caffi
1989	16	29	8	-	-	-	Marlboro	Caffi, de Cesaris
1990	16	30	-	-	-	-	Marlboro	Pirro, de Cesaris
1991	16	29	5	-	-	-	Marlboro, Lucchini	Pirro, Lehto
1992	16	31	2	-	-	-	Lucchini, Marlboro	Martini, Lehto

MODELS	GPs	STARTS	POINTS	POLES	F.LAPS	WINS	YEAR(S)	CHIEF DESIGNER	ENGINE
188	14	14	-	-	-	-	88	S Rinland	Ford Cosworth
189	16	29	8	-	-	-	89	M Tolentino	Ford Cosworth
190	16	30	-	-	-	-	90	C Vanderpleyn	Ford Cosworth
191	16	29	5	-	-	-	91	N Couperthwaite	Judd
192	16	31	2	-	-	-	92	N Couperthwaite	Ferrari

The 3087 Formula 3000 car did not pre-qualify for the first race of 1988

DE TOMASO (I)

Principal: Alessandro de Tomaso. **Base:** Modena. **Founded:** 1959.
De Tomaso Automobili began in October 1959 building Formula Junior and Formula 2 cars at its Modena base. Argentinian racing driver, Alessandro de Tomaso commissioned Gianpaolo Dallara to build an F2 design in 1969 which formed the basis of the Frank Williams entered Formula 1 car the following year. The company went on to produce exotic Ford engined road cars, before amalgamating with Maserati.

TOTALS	GPs	STARTS	POINTS	POLES	F.LAPS	WINS
	10	12	-	-	-	-

SEASONS	GPs	STARTS	POINTS	POLES	F.LAPS	WINS	SPONSOR(S)	MAIN DRIVER(S)
1961	2	4	-	-	-	-	(red)	Bussinello, Lippi
1962	-	-	-	-	-	-		Estefano
1963	-	-	-	-	-	-		Lippi *(privateer)*
1964-69 *did not participate*								
1970	8	8	-	-	-	-	Ward	Courage/Schenken *(Williams)*

MODELS	GPs	STARTS	POINTS	POLES	F.LAPS	WINS	YEAR(S)	CHIEF DESIGNER	ENGINE
F1	2	4	-	-	-	-	61	A Massimino	OSCA, Conrero
505	8	8	-	-	-	-	70	G Dallara	Ford Cosworth

The De Tomaso-powered 801 did not qualify in 1962

EAGLE (USA)

Principal: Dan Gurney. **Base:** Santa Ana, California (UK Base: Rye, Sussex). **Founded:** 1964.
Initially formed with Carroll Shelby to attack Indianapolis and known as All American Racers. Gurney still had ambitions in Grand Prix and formed Anglo American Racers on the other side of the Atlantic at Weslake's engine workshop. In 1968 Gurney severed his links with the engine builders and moved to a new workshop in Ashford, Kent to develop his own engines. Funds became very tight and Gurney abandoned his Formula 1 aspirations and returned to America where he has achieved many successes most notably with Toyota.

TOTALS	**GPs**	**STARTS**	**POINTS**	**POLES**	**F.LAPS**	**WINS**			
	25	32	17	-	2	1			
SEASONS							**SPONSOR(S)**	**MAIN DRIVER(S)**	
1966	8	10	4	-	-	-	(blue)	Gurney, Bondurant	
1967	11	16	13	-	2	1	(blue)	Gurney, McLaren	
1968	5	5	-	-	-	-	Harvey Titanium	Gurney	
1969	1	1	-	-	-	-		Pease *(privateer)*	
MODELS							**YEAR(S)**	**CHIEF DESIGNER**	**ENGINE**
T1G	25	32	17	-	2	1	66-69	L Terry	Climax, Weslake

The models are sometimes known by their chassis numbers 101 - 104

EMERYSON (GB)

Principal: Paul Emery. **Base:** Send, Surrey/ Fulham, London. **Founded:** 1949.
Paul Emery was a typical 'specials' builder of his era, moving from front-engined 500cc cars to build his first front-line racer in 1953. Using the old Connaught works, a batch of rear-engined cars were created. These in turn were used by others such as ENB and later Scirocco, who took over the Emeryson project in 1962. Paul Emery went on to many more projects including a successful series of oval track midget cars.

TOTALS	**GPs**	**STARTS**	**POINTS**	**POLES**	**F.LAPS**	**WINS**			
	4	4	-	-	-	-			
SEASONS							**COLOUR**	**MAIN DRIVER(S)**	
1956	1	1	-	-	-	-	green	Emery	
1961	-	-	-	-	-	-	yellow	*ENB team*	
1962	3	3	-	-	-	-	green	Settember	
MODELS							**YEAR(S)**	**CHIEF DESIGNER**	**ENGINE**
(56)	1	1	-	-	-	-	56	P Emery	Alta
(61)	3	3	-	-	-	-	62	P Emery	Climax

EMW (D)

Principal: no factory involvement. **Base:** Eisenach, Thuringen, East Germany. **Founded:** 1945.
Eisenacher Motoren Werke began after World War II at Eisenach in the Russian zone of the BMW group. Production cars were built from 1947, with a name change to AWE in 1956. Competition cars were soon forgotten and the company concentrated on producing Wartburg saloons.

TOTALS	**GPs**	**STARTS**	**POINTS**	**POLES**	**F.LAPS**	**WINS**		
	1	1	-	-	-	-		
SEASONS							**COLOUR**	**MAIN DRIVER(S)**
1953	1	1	-	-	-	-	silver	Barth
MODELS							**YEAR(S)**	**ENGINE**
—	1	1	-	-	-	-	53	EMW

ENB (B)

Principal: Jacques Swaters. **Base:** Brussels. **Founded:** 1950s.
Equipe Nationale Belge was a racing organisation for home drivers and was an entrant for many years. In 1961 the team raced Emeryson cars and after various mishaps decided to rebuild one chassis as the one-off ENB-Maserati.

TOTALS	**GPs**	**STARTS**	**POINTS**	**POLES**	**F.LAPS**	**WINS**			
	1	1	-	-	-	-			
SEASONS							**COLOUR**	**MAIN DRIVER(S)**	
1962	1	1	-	-	-	-	yellow	Bianchi	
MODELS							**YEAR(S)**	**CHIEF DESIGNER**	**ENGINE**
	1	1	-	-	-	-	62	P Emery	Maserati

ENSIGN (GB)

Principal: Morris Nunn. **Base:** Chasetown, Staffordshire/ Lichfield, Staffordshire (1981). **Founded:** 1970.
Former racer Nunn started building Formula 3 cars with considerable success and from this, Rikky von Opel commissioned Nunn to build an Formula 1 car for 1973. Nunn stayed with F1 when Opel moved on, but money was always going to be tight. After falling out with his Dutch sponsor, HB Bewaking took the N175 and entered it as a Boro for a couple of seasons. With a shortage of funds, Nunn welcomed a merger with Teddy Yip's Theodore concern and the recently acquired Shadow cars.

TOTALS	GPs	STARTS	POINTS	POLES	F.LAPS	WINS
	99	117	19	-	1	-

SEASONS							SPONSOR(S)	MAIN DRIVER(S)
1973	6	6	-	-	-	-	(green)	von Opel
1974	6	6	-	-	-	-	Dempster	Schuppan
1975	7	8	1	-	-	-	HB Alarmsystemen	Wunderink/van Lennep
1976	14	19	2	-	-	-	F&S Properties, Valvoline	Amon
1977	17	24	10	-	-	-	Tissot, Castrol	Regazzoni, Tambay
1978	12	17	1	-	-	-	Tissot	Ickx/Daly, Ertl
1979	6	6	-	-	-	-	Hi-Line	Daly/Gaillard
1980	9	9	-	-	-	-	Unipart	Regazzoni/Lammers
1981	14	14	5	-	1	-	Din, Toyota	Surer/Salazar
1982	8	8	-	-	-	-	Cafe de Colombia	Guerrero

MODELS							YEAR(S)	CHIEF DESIGNER	ENGINE
N173	6	6	-	-	-	-	73	M Nunn	Ford Cosworth
N174	11	11	-	-	-	-	74-76	M Nunn	Ford Cosworth
N175	11	11	1	-	-	-	75-77	D Baldwin	Ford Cosworth
N176	12	12	2	-	-	-	76	D Baldwin	Ford Cosworth
N177	31	42	11	-	-	-	77-79	D Baldwin	Ford Cosworth
N179	4	4	-	-	-	-	79	M Nunn	Ford Cosworth
N180-B	23	23	5	-	1	-	80-81	R Bellamy	Ford Cosworth
N181	8	8	-	-	-	-	82	N Bennett	Ford Cosworth

Models were sometimes known by their chassis numbers, ie MN01

ERA (GB)

Principal: Leslie Johnson. **Base:** Dunstable, Bedfordshire. **Founded:** 1934.
English Racing Automobiles was originated by Raymond Mays at his Bourne home in Lincolnshire, with the help of his friend, Peter Berthon. The outfit was sold and relocated pre-war, before being purchased by Leslie Johnson in November 1947. Johnson was only interested in the E type cars and later models whilst many of the earlier chassis carried on in private hands.

TOTALS	GPs	STARTS	POINTS	POLES	F.LAPS	WINS
	7	12	-	-	-	-

SEASONS							COLOUR	MAIN DRIVER(S)
1950	3	7	-	-	-	-	green	Johnson
1951	1	2	-	-	-	-	green	Gerard *(privateer)*
1952	3	3	-	-	-	-	green	Moss

MODELS							YEAR(S)	CHIEF DESIGNER	ENGINE
A	1	1	-	-	-	-	50	R Railton	6s
B, B/C	4	6	-	-	-	-	50-51	R Railton	6s
E	1	2	-	-	-	-	50	A Barratt	6s
G	3	3	-	-	-	-	52	D Hodkin	Bristol

EUROBRUN (I)

Principal: Walter Brun. **Base:** Senago, Milan. **Founded:** 1987.
Successful sports car driver and entrant Walter Brun teamed up with Paolo Pavanello's Euroracing operation and built the cars at the latter's workshops. The team struggled in its first year but things didn't get any better, the orange cars failing to qualify the next year, finally winding up before the end of the 1990 season.

TOTALS	GPs	STARTS	POINTS	POLES	F.LAPS	WINS
	14	20	-	-	-	-

SEASONS							SPONSOR(S)	MAIN DRIVER(S)
1988	12	18	-	-	-	-	Tommasini	Modena, Larrauri
1989	-	-	-	-	-	-	Jagermeister	Foitek/Larrauri
1990	2	2	-	-	-	-	JSK	Moreno, Langes

MODELS							YEAR(S)	CHIEF DESIGNER	ENGINE
ER188	12	18	-	-	-	-	88	M Tolentino	Ford Cosworth
ER189	2	2	-	-	-	-	90	G Ryton	Judd

The ER188B-Judd (1989) and ER189B-Judd (1990) did not qualify

FERGUSON (GB)

Principal: Harry Ferguson. **Base:** Coventry. **Founded:** 1950.
After financial success with his tractors and devices, Harry Ferguson Research experimented with a 4 wheel-drive racing car helped by former racer, Major Tony Rolt. It raced only once at championship level and became the last front-engined car in the World Championship. Its traction was useful in its next career step as a hill-climb car.

TOTALS	GPs	STARTS	POINTS	POLES	F.LAPS	WINS			
	1	1	-	-	-	-			
SEASONS							**COLOUR**	**MAIN DRIVER(S)**	
1961	1	1	-	-	-	-	blue	Fairman, Moss	
MODELS							**YEAR(S)**	**CHIEF DESIGNER**	**ENGINE**
P99	1	1	-	-	-	-	61	C Hill	Climax

FERRARI (I)

Principal: Enzo Ferrari. **Base:** Maranello, Modena. **Founded:** 1946.
The most evocative name in Grand Prix, and the only team to have contested every year of the championship, always in the traditional red colour. Enzo Ferrari was a former racer and manager of Alfa Romeo's racing team from 1930-37 but a disagreement saw him leave in 1938. Although he built his first car in 1940, this wasn't known as a Ferrari, as Enzo had agreed not to race under his own name for a further five years, so the first true Ferrari didn't appear until 1946. Early models were known by the displacement size of each cylinder and it is fair to say that Ferrari's priority lay with engine first and chassis second. The Prancing Horse adapted to each formula change quickly and has been a pace setter throughout most of its lifespan, teaming up with FIAT in 1969. Enzo Ferrari died in August 1988 and apart from a close championship call with Prost, Ferrari have not been regular winners since. With Luca di Montezemolo now in charge and a design base in England, Ferrari are now pointing in the right direction. FIAT and Marlboro have bought in the double world champion as they developed their very first V10 Grand Prix engine.

CONSTRUCTORS' CHAMPIONSHIPS: 8 (1961, 64, 75, 76, 77, 79, 82, 83)

TOTALS	GPs	STARTS	POINTS	POLES	F.LAPS	WINS		
	569	1330	2896.8	118	127	108		
SEASONS							**SPONSOR(S)**	**MAIN DRIVER(S)**
1950	5	13	21	-	-	-	(red)	Ascari, Villoresi, Sommer
1951	7	32	86	3	-	3	(red)	Ascari, Villoresi, González
1952	7	43	120.5	7	7	7	(red)	Ascari*, Farina, Taruffi
1953	8	46	122.5	6	6	7	(red)	Ascari*, Farina, Hawthorn, Villoresi
1954	8	43	80.3	2	4	2	(red)	González, Hawthorn, Trintignant
1955	6	21	34	1	-	1	(red)	Trintignant, Farina, Castellotti
1956	7	34	82	6	4	5	(red)	Fangio*, Collins, Castellotti
1957	7	27	48	-	1	-	(red)	Hawthorn, Collins, Musso
1958	10	34	93	4	6	2	(red)	Hawthorn*, Collins, Musso
1959	7	29	67	2	2	2	(red)	Brooks, P Hill, Allison
1960	8	24	43	1	2	1	(red)	P Hill, von Trips
1961	7	27	99	6	5	5	(red)	P Hill*, von Trips, Ginther
1962	6	20	30	-	-	-	(red)	P Hill, Baghetti, R Rodriguez
1963	10	18	27	1	3	1	(red)	Surtees, Bandini
1964	10	22	64	2	2	3	(red)	Surtees*, Bandini
1965	10	22	32	-	-	-	(red)	Surtees, Bandini
1966	7	16	42	3	4	2	(red)	Bandini, Parkes
1967	10	16	23	-	-	-	Shell	Amon, Parkes
1968	11	23	37	4	-	1	Shell	Amon, Ickx
1969	10	11	7	-	-	-	Shell	Amon/P Rodriguez
1970	13	25	76	5	8	4	Shell	Ickx, Regazzoni
1971	11	27	44	3	4	2	Shell	Ickx, Regazzoni
1972	12	30	47	4	3	1	Heuer, FIAT	Ickx, Regazzoni
1973	13	19	14	-	-	-	Ferodo	Ickx, Merzario
1974	15	30	90	10	6	3	Agip	Lauda, Regazzoni
1975	14	28	89.5	9	6	6	Agip, Heuer	Lauda*, Regazzoni
1976	15	30	99	4	7	6	Agip, Heuer	Lauda, Regazzoni
1977	17	33	114	2	3	4	FIAT, Agip	Lauda*, Reutemann
1978	16	32	65	2	3	5	FIAT, Agip	Reutemann, Villeneuve

*Champion

SEASONS	GPs	STARTS	POINTS	POLES	F.LAPS	WINS	SPONSOR(S)	MAIN DRIVERS
1979	15	30	113	2	6	6	FIAT, Agip	Scheckter*, Villeneuve
1980	14	27	8	-	-	-	FIAT, Agip	Scheckter, Villeneuve
1981	15	30	34	1	2	2	FIAT, Agip	Villeneuve, Pironi
1982	14	22	74	3	2	3	FIAT, Agip	Villeneuve/Tambay, Pironi
1983	15	30	89	8	3	4	FIAT, Agip	Tambay, Arnoux
1984	16	32	57.5	1	3	1	FIAT, Agip	Alboreto, Arnoux
1985	16	32	82	1	2	2	FIAT, Agip	Alboreto, Johansson
1986	16	32	37	-	-	-	FIAT, Agip	Alboreto, Johansson
1987	16	32	53	3	3	2	FIAT, Agip	Alboreto, Berger
1988	16	32	65	1	4	1	FIAT, Agip	Alboreto, Berger
1989	16	30	59	-	4	3	FIAT, Agip	Mansell, Berger
1990	16	32	110	3	5	6	FIAT, Agip	Prost, Mansell
1991	16	32	55.5	-	2	-	FIAT, Agip	Prost, Alesi
1992	16	32	21	-	-	-	FIAT, Agip	Alesi, Capelli
1993	16	32	28	-	-	-	FIAT, Agip	Alesi, Berger
1994	16	32	71	3	-	1	Agip	Alesi, Berger
1995	17	34	73	1	3	1	Marlboro	Alesi, Berger
1996	16	32	70	4	2	3	Marlboro	Schumacher, Irvine

*Champion

MODELS							YEAR(S)	CHIEF DESIGNER	ENGINE
125	9	12	13	-	-	-	50-52	G Colombo	V12s
275, 375	9	30	94	3	-	3	50-51	A Lampredi	V12
212	6	6	-	-	-	-	51-52	A Lampredi	V12
500	26	88	243	13	13	14	52-57	A Lampredi	4
166-S	6	7	-	-	-	-	50-53	A Lampredi	V12, Jaguar
553	6	9	9	-	-	1	53-54	A Lampredi	4
625	11	36	92.3	3	4	2	54-55	A Lampredi	4
555	5	14	15	-	-	-	55-56	A Lampredi	4, Lancia-Ferrari
801 & D50	14	57	128	6	5	5	56-57	V Jano	Lancia-Ferrari
D246-P	25	85	203	7	10	5	58-60	V Jano	V6
D156	2	2	-	-	-	-	58-59	V Jano	V6
156	29	71	172	7	8	7	61-64	C Chiti	V6
158	19	23	58	2	2	2	64-65	M Forghieri	V8
1512	12	15	22	-	-	-	64-65	M Forghieri	F12
246	4	4	10	-	1	-	66	M Forghieri	V6
312	38	62	99	7	3	3	66-69	M Forghieri	V12
312B	18	34	95	6	11	5	70-71	M Forghieri	F12
312B2	24	54	83	6	4	2	71-73	M Forghieri	F12
312B3	27	47	102	10	6	3	73-75	M Forghieri	F12
312T	15	30	113.5	10	8	9	75-76	M Forghieri	F12
312T2	31	61	189	5	10	8	76-78	M Forghieri	F12
312T3	16	32	59	2	1	4	78-79	M Forghieri	F12
312T4	13	26	110	2	6	6	79	M Forghieri	F12
312T5	14	27	8	-	-	-	80	M Forghieri	F12
126CK	15	30	34	1	2	2	81	M Forghieri	V6t
126C2-B	22	38	118	7	3	5	82-83	H Postlethwaite	V6t
126C3	7	14	45	4	2	2	83	H Postlethwaite	V6t
126C4	16	32	57.5	1	3	1	84	H Postlethwaite	V6t
156/85	16	32	82	1	2	2	85	H Postlethwaite	V6t
F186	16	32	37	-	-	-	86	H Postlethwaite	V6t
F187	16	32	53	3	3	2	87	J Barnard	V6t
F187/88C	16	32	65	1	4	1	88	J Barnard	V6t
640	16	30	59	-	4	3	89	J Barnard	V12
641	16	32	110	3	5	6	90	J Barnard	V12
642	6	12	16	-	2	-	91	S Nichols	V12
643	10	20	39.5	-	-	-	91	S Nichols	V12
F92A, AT, 00	16	32	21	-	-	-	92	S Nichols	V12
F93A	16	32	28	-	-	-	93	J Barnard	V12
412T1-B	16	32	71	3	-	1	94	J Barnard	V12
412T2	17	34	73	1	3	1	95	J Barnard	V12
F310	16	32	70	4	2	3	96	J Barnard	V10

The modified Thin Wall Ferrari appears under the model number 375, referred to in the RACES chapter as 375tw

FITTIPALDI (BR/GB) formerly Copersucar 1975 to 1979

Principals: Wilson & Emerson Fittipaldi. **Base:** São Paulo (UK Base: Caversham/ Slough/ Reading). **Founded:** 1973.
Set up by Wilson Fittipaldi, with backing from the Brazilian Copersucar sugar organisation, it gained momentum when brother Emerson joined as driver. In 1980, Copersucar had gone and Fittipaldi merged with Wolf, using their third series models (WR7-9) as the Fittipaldi F7s. As the turbo era approached, lack of sponsorship meant the end of this ambitious and colourful project.

TOTALS	GPs	STARTS	POINTS	POLES	F.LAPS	WINS		
	104	123	44	-	-	-		
SEASONS							**SPONSOR(S)**	**MAIN DRIVER(S)**
1975	12	12	-	-	-	-	Copersucar	W Fittipaldi
1976	15	16	3	-	-	-	Copersucar	E Fittipaldi
1977	14	16	11	-	-	-	Copersucar	E Fittipaldi
1978	16	16	17	-	-	-	Copersucar	E Fittipaldi
1979	15	15	1	-	-	-	Copersucar	E Fittipaldi
1980	14	25	11	-	-	-	Skol	Rosberg, Fittipaldi
1981	9	14	-	-	-	-	Pasta Matic	Rosberg, Serra
1982	9	9	1	-	-	-	Brasilinvest	Serra

MODELS	GPs	STARTS	POINTS	POLES	F.LAPS	WINS	YEAR(S)	CHIEF DESIGNER	ENGINE
FD01-03	13	13	-	-	-	-	75-76	R Divila	Ford Cosworth
FD04	22	24	11	-	-	-	76-77	R Divila	Ford Cosworth
F5-A	31	31	21	-	-	-	77-79	D Baldwin	Ford Cosworth
F6-A	7	7	-	-	-	-	79	G Caliri	Ford Cosworth
F7	7	13	9	-	-	-	80	H Postlethwaite	Ford Cosworth
F8-C, D	22	32	3	-	-	-	80-82	H Postlethwaite	Ford Cosworth
F9	3	3	-	-	-	-	82	R Divila	Ford Cosworth

FORTI (I)

Principal: Guido Forti. **Base:** Alessandria. **Founded:** 1975.
A team with an impeccable reputation in Formula 3 and Formula 3000, found its first season very hard going and after back of grid and non-qualifying performances, together with sponsor and ownership disputes, the Italian courts finally wound the team up in August 1996.

TOTALS	GPs	STARTS	POINTS	POLES	F.LAPS	WINS		
	23	44	-	-	-	-		
SEASONS							**SPONSOR(S)**	**MAIN DRIVER(S)**
1995	17	34	-	-	-	-	Parmalut, Arisco	Diniz, Moreno
1996	6	10	-	-	-	-	Hudson, Shannon	Badoer, Montermini

MODELS	GPs	STARTS	POINTS	POLES	F.LAPS	WINS	YEAR(S)	CHIEF DESIGNER	ENGINE
FG01-95, B	19	38	-	-	-	-	95-96	G Stirano	Ford Cosworth
FG03-96	4	6	-	-	-	-	96	P Guerci	Ford Cosworth

FRAZER NASH (GB)

Principal: Archie Frazer-Nash. **Base:** Isleworth, Middlesex. **Founded:** 1922.
Archie Frazer-Nash began production of his own cars in the 1920s as a development of the GN cars he helped to create. Taken over by H J Aldington in 1929, the firm moved to London Road, Isleworth where mainly sports cars were produced, although six single seaters were made, including Wharton's car in 1952. The last Frazer Nash was built in 1957 and the firm went on to be the British concessionaires for Porsche.

TOTALS	GPs	STARTS	POINTS	POLES	F.LAPS	WINS		
	4	4	3	-	-	-		
SEASONS							**COLOUR**	**MAIN DRIVER(S)**
1952	4	4	3	-	-	-	green	Wharton

MODELS	GPs	STARTS	POINTS	POLES	F.LAPS	WINS	YEAR(S)	CHIEF DESIGNER	ENGINE
FN48	2	2	3	-	-	-	52	H Aldington	Bristol
421*	2	2	-	-	-	-	52	H Aldington	Bristol

* *This model was in fact a stripped down Sports car, the Le Mans Replica Mark II*

FRY (GB)

David Fry created this unusual rear-engined design in the late 50s but it failed to qualify for the British Grand Prix in 1959.

GILBY (GB)

Principal: Syd Greene. **Base:** Ongar, Essex. **Founded:** 1953.
Syd Greene and his Gilby Engineering Company from Ongar entered and raced many cars in the 50s. From 1960 the company decided to build its own single seaters with son Keith as the main driver. A Climax-engined car was built in 1960, followed by a BRM V8 version in 1962, the year in which the firm wound up.

TOTALS	GPs	STARTS	POINTS	POLES	F.LAPS	WINS			
	3	3	-	-	-	-			
SEASONS							**COLOUR**	**MAIN DRIVER(S)**	
1961	1	1	-	-	-	-	green	Greene	
1962	1	1	-	-	-	-	green	Greene	
1963	1	1	-	-	-	-	green	Raby *(privateer)*	
MODELS							**YEAR(S)**	**CHIEF DESIGNER**	**ENGINE**
(61)	1	1	-	-	-	-	61	L Terry	Climax
(62)	2	2	-	-	-	-	62-63	L Terry	BRM

GORDINI (F)

Principal: Amédée Gordini. **Base:** Paris. **Founded:** 1945.
Amédée Gordini built his first Simca-FIAT based single seater in 1946 at his Boulevard Victor workshop. These were developed into 1.5 litre versions, known as Simca-Gordinis. This collaboration ended in 1951 and from then on, the Paris-based concern dropped the Simca connection from its cars. Always struggling financially, the team faded away in the late fifties, whilst Amédée began experimental work for Renault.

TOTALS	GPs	STARTS	POINTS	POLES	F.LAPS	WINS			
	40	127	30.1	-	1	-			
SEASONS							**COLOUR**	**MAIN DRIVER(S)**	
1950	3	5	3	-	-	-	blue	Manzon, Trintignant	
1951	4	13	-	-	-	-	blue	Manzon, Trintignant, Simon	
1952	7	28	17	-	-	-	blue	Manzon, Trintignant, Behra	
1953	8	28	4	-	-	-	blue	Trintignant, Behra, Schell	
1954	8	25	4.1	-	1	-	blue	Behra, Bucci, Pilette	
1955	5	15	-	-	-	-	blue	Manzon, Pollet, da Silva Ramos	
1956	5	13	2	-	-	-	blue	Manzon, da Silva Ramos, Pilette	
MODELS							**YEAR(S)**	**CHIEF DESIGNER**	**ENGINE**
T11	2	2	-	-	-	-	51-52	A Gordini	4s
T15	14	26	5	-	-	-	50-53	A Gordini	4s
T16	31	88	25.1	-	1	-	52-56	A Gordini	6
T16S	1	1	-	-	-	-	52	A Gordini	6
T32	6	10	-	-	-	-	55-56	A Gordini	8

HESKETH (GB)

Principal: Lord Alexander Hesketh. **Base:** Easton Neston, nr Towcester, Northamptonshire. **Founded:** 1972.
Lord Alexander Hesketh set up the team in 1972 from his stately home Easton Neston. Quickly rising from Formula 3 to an Formula 1 March in 1973, the team entered as a constructor the following year. At the end of 1975, struggling without sponsorship, Lord Hesketh called a halt, although Anthony Horsley the former team manager, continued a few years more on a rent-a-drive basis.

TOTALS	GPs	STARTS	POINTS	POLES	F.LAPS	WINS		
	52	73	48	-	1	1		
SEASONS							**SPONSOR(S)**	**MAIN DRIVER(S)**
1974	13	13	15	-	-	-	(white)	Hunt
1975	14	25	33	-	1	1	(white)	Hunt, Lunger
1976	12	17	-	-	-	-	Rizla, Penthouse	Ertl, Edwards
1977	12	17	-	-	-	-	Rizla, Penthouse	Ertl, Keegan
1978	1	1	-	-	-	-	Olympus	Cheever

MODELS	GPs	STARTS	POINTS	POLES	F.LAPS	WINS	YEAR(S)	CHIEF DESIGNER	ENGINE
308	27	36	43	-	1	1	74-75	H Postlethwaite	Ford Cosworth
308C	2	2	5	-	-	-	75	H Postlethwaite	Ford Cosworth
308D	12	17	-	-	-	-	76	H Postlethwaite	Ford Cosworth
308E	13	18	-	-	-	-	77-78	F Dernie	Ford Cosworth

HILL (GB)

Principal: Graham Hill. **Base:** Feltham, Middlesex. **Founded:** 1972.
Graham Hill started his own team from a Feltham factory unit in 1973. Initially using a Shadow chassis, the team moved on to build Lola chassis in 1974. By the following year, the Lola T370 had evolved into the T371 and further modifications justified the car to be renamed the first Hill - GH1. The following year's GH2 model was undergoing winter testing at Paul Ricard when on the return to England, the plane which Graham Hill was piloting, crashed on Arkley Golf Course, killing all six team members on board, including his promising young driver, Tony Brise.

TOTALS	GPs	STARTS	POINTS	POLES	F.LAPS	WINS			
	10	19	3	-	-	-			
SEASONS							**SPONSOR(S)**	**MAIN DRIVER(S)**	
1975	10	19	3	-	-	-	Embassy	Brise, Jones	
MODELS							**YEAR(S)**	**CHIEF DESIGNER**	**ENGINE**
GH1	10	19	3	-	-	-	75	A Smallman	Ford Cosworth

HONDA (J)

Principal: Soichiro Honda. **Base:** Tokyo (European Base: Amsterdam/ Slough). **Founded:** 1948.
Honda became world leaders in motorcycle production and racing and by 1962 their attention had turned to cars. A low profile entrance was arranged with engineer Yoshio Nakamura and a new base in Amsterdam. From 1967, John Surtees assumed responsibility for the racing side and moved the team base to Slough, enlisting the help of Lola's Eric Broadley. The new RA300 (dubbed Hondola) won first time out, but tragedy struck the following year when Jo Schlesser was killed in the air-cooled V8 model. Honda's first Formula 1 entry came to a sad end but it would return in glory during the 80s, supplying engines in the turbo years.

TOTALS	GPs	STARTS	POINTS	POLES	F.LAPS	WINS			
	35	46	50	1	2	2			
SEASONS							**COLOUR**	**MAIN DRIVER(S)**	
1964	3	3	-	-	-	-	white	Bucknum	
1965	8	14	13	-	-	1	white	Ginther, Bucknum	
1966	3	5	3	-	1	-	white	Ginther, Bucknum	
1967	9	9	20	-	-	1	white	Surtees	
1968	12	15	14	1	1	-	white	Surtees, Schlesser	
MODELS							**YEAR(S)**	**CHIEF DESIGNER**	**ENGINE**
RA271	3	3	-	-	-	-	64	Y Nakamura	V12
RA272	8	14	13	-	-	1	65	Y Nakamura	V12
RA273	9	11	11	-	1	-	66-67	Y Nakamura	V12
RA300	4	4	12	-	-	1	67-68	E Broadley	V12
RA301	11	13	14	1	1	-	68	Y Nakamura	V12
RA302	1	1	-	-	-	-	68	Y Nakamura	V8

HWM (GB)

Principals: John Heath, George Abecassis. **Base:** Walton-on-Thames, Surrey. **Founded:** 1948.
In 1946 George Abecassis and John Heath bought a garage together and went racing with Alta-engined offset cars as HWM (Hersham & Walton Motors). Single seaters were produced from 1951 and this small team travelled Europe entering as many races as they could. For 1953, the car was lower, causing a different appearance in the once upright front grille. From the start of the 2.5 litre formula, the team began to concentrate on sports car racing but John Heath was killed in the 1956 Mille Miglia and George Abecassis ended the operation soon after.

TOTALS	GPs	STARTS	POINTS	POLES	F.LAPS	WINS		
	14	43	2	-	-	-		
SEASONS							**COLOUR**	**MAIN DRIVER(S)**
1951	1	2	-	-	-	-	green	Abecassis, Moss
1952	6	22	2	-	-	-	green	Macklin, Collins, Frère
1953	6	18	-	-	-	-	green	Macklin, Collins, Frère
1954	1	1	-	-	-	-	green	Macklin
1955	-	-	-	-	-	-	green	Whiteaway *(privateer)*

MODELS	GPs	STARTS	POINTS	POLES	F.LAPS	WINS	YEAR(S)	CHIEF DESIGNER	ENGINE
(51)	2	3	-	-	-	-	51-52	J Heath	Alta
(52)	6	21	2	-	-	-	52	J Heath	Alta
(53)	7	19	-	-	-	-	53-54	J Heath	Alta

JBW (GB)

Principal: Brian Naylor. **Base:** Stockport, Cheshire. **Founded:** 1957.
Stockport motor dealer Brian Naylor, arranged for his chief mechanic Fred Wilkinson to build a Lotus-based sports car in the late 50s, moving on to a Cooper-based single seater in 1959, which was succeeded by a further model in1961. The name was a combination of Naylor's initials J B and Wilkinson's surname.

TOTALS	GPs	STARTS	POINTS	POLES	F.LAPS	WINS			
	5	5	-	-	-	-			
SEASONS							**COLOUR**	**MAIN DRIVER(S)**	
1959	1	1	-	-	-	-	green	Naylor	
1960	3	3	-	-	-	-	green	Naylor	
1961	1	1	-	-	-	-	green	Naylor	
MODELS							**YEAR(S)**	**CHIEF DESIGNER**	**ENGINE**
(59)	4	4	-	-	-	-	59-60	F Wilkinson	Maserati
(61)	1	1	-	-	-	-	61	F Wilkinson	Climax

JORDAN (IRL/GB)

Principal: Eddie Jordan. **Base:** Silverstone, Northamptonshire. **Founded:** 1983.
Irishman Eddie Jordan, followed up a successful racing career as an entrant, to become a manager of promising talent. After Formula 3 from 1983 to 1987 the team progressed swiftly through Formula 3000 in 1988-90, to make an impressive impact on Formula 1 in 1991. Based at Silverstone, the team moved into its new factory just across the road from the circuit gates at the begining of 1992.

TOTALS	GPs	STARTS	POINTS	POLES	F.LAPS	WINS			
	81	155	66	1	1	-			
SEASONS							**SPONSOR(S)**	**MAIN DRIVER(S)**	
1991	16	31	13	-	1	-	7UP, Fuji Film	de Cesaris, Gachot	
1992	16	28	1	-	-	-	Sasol, Barclay	Modena, Gugelmin	
1993	16	31	3	-	-	-	Sasol, Barclay	Barrichello, Boutsen	
1994	16	31	28	1	-	-	Sasol, Arisco	Barrichello, Irvine	
1995	17	34	21	-	-	-	Total, Peugeot	Barrichello, Irvine	
1996				-	-	-	B & H, Total	Barrichello, Brundle	
MODELS							**YEAR(S)**	**CHIEF DESIGNER**	**ENGINE**
191	16	31	13	-	1	-	91	G Anderson	Ford Cosworth
192	16	28	1	-	-	-	92	G Anderson	Yamaha
193	16	31	3	-	-	-	93	G Anderson	Hart
194	16	31	28	1	-	-	94	G Anderson	Hart
195	17	34	21	-	-	-	95	G Anderson	Peugeot
196				-	-	-	96	G Anderson	Peugeot

B & H = Benson & Hedges

KAUHSEN (D)

Willi Kauhsen built Formula 2 cars in 1977 and went on to create five Formula 1 chassis (the WK), designed by Klaus Kapitza which passed onto the Merzario team after unsuccessful attempts to qualify in the early part of the 1979 season.

KLENK (D)

Principal: Hans Klenk. **Base:** Stuttgart. **Founded:** 1953.
One time Mercedes test driver and talented engineer, Hans Klenk produced his own special along Veritas lines. It was a typical BMW-based single seater, with a noticeably large intake bulge in the bonnet.

TOTALS	GPs	STARTS	POINTS	POLES	F.LAPS	WINS			
	1	1	-	-	-	-			
SEASONS							**COLOUR**	**MAIN DRIVER(S)**	
1954	1	1	-	-	-	-	silver	Helfrich	
MODELS							**YEAR(S)**	**CHIEF DESIGNER**	**ENGINE**
Meteor	1	1	-	-	-	-	54	H Klenk	BMW

KOJIMA (J)

Principal: Matsuhisa Kojima. **Base:** Kyoto.
Matsuhisa Kojima, banana importer and moto-cross rider, ran this engineering firm concentrating on Japanese motorsport events. Two versions of an Formula 1 design were produced for the Japanese Grands Prix of the mid-seventies.

TOTALS	GPs	STARTS	POINTS	POLES	F.LAPS	WINS			
	2	3	-	-	1	-			
SEASONS							**SPONSOR(S)**	**MAIN DRIVER(S)**	
1976	1	1	-	-	1	-	(black)	Hasemi	
1977	1	2	-	-	-	-	Uni-Pex	Hoshino, Takahara	
MODELS							**YEAR(S)**	**CHIEF DESIGNER**	**ENGINE**
KE007	1	1	-	-	1	-	76	M Ono	Ford Cosworth
KE009	1	2	-	-	-	-	77	M Ono	Ford Cosworth

KURTIS KRAFT (USA)

Principal: Frank Kurtis. **Base:** Glendale, California. **Founded:** 1941 (first Indy entry).
Californian, Frank Kurtis built front-engined roadsters for Indianapolis and midgets for US-style oval racing. One such design was entered for the first World Championship USA GP in an attempt at an early Grand Prix versus IndyCar showdown.

TOTALS	GPs	STARTS	POINTS	POLES	F.LAPS	WINS			
	1	1	-	-	-	-			
SEASONS							**SPONSOR(S)**	**MAIN DRIVER(S)**	
1959	1	1	-	-	-	-	Leader Cards	Ward	
MODELS							**YEAR(S)**	**CHIEF DESIGNER**	**ENGINE**
Midget	1	1	-	-	-	-	59	F Kurtis	Offenhauser

LAMBORGHINI (I)

Principal: Carlo Patrucco. **Base:** Modena. **Founded:** 1963 (car manufacturer).
Originally tractor manufacturers, Lamborghini built road going sports cars in 1963 and were taken over by Chrysler in 1987. After supplying engines to Larrousse, Lola and Lotus, president Carlo Patrucco decided to create a complete package with the remains of the abandoned Glas project. Modena Team was formed in 1990, with Mauro Forghieri as co-ordinator and the chassis renamed as Lambo.

TOTALS	GPs	STARTS	POINTS	POLES	F.LAPS	WINS			
	6	6	-	-	-	-			
SEASONS							**SPONSOR(S)**	**MAIN DRIVER(S)**	
1991	6	6	-	-	-	-	Central Park	Larini, van de Poele	
MODELS							**YEAR(S)**	**CHIEF DESIGNER**	**ENGINE**
291	6	6	-	-	-	-	91	M Forghieri	V12

LANCIA (I)

Principal: Gianni Lancia. **Base:** Turin. **Founded:** 1906.
Upon the death of Vincenzo Lancia, his son Gianni formed plans for a racing programme, initially with sports cars. Financial problems led to FIAT taking over the company in 1955 and handing the cars to Ferrari, which continued to modify and race them as the 801. Lancia went on to represent FIAT in rally and sports cars.

TOTALS	GPs	STARTS	POINTS	POLES	F.LAPS	WINS			
	4	10	9	2	1	-			
SEASONS							**COLOUR**	**MAIN DRIVER(S)**	
1954	1	2	1	1	1	-	red	Ascari, Villoresi	
1955	3	8	8	1	-	-	red	Ascari, Villoresi, Castellotti	
MODELS							**YEAR(S)**	**CHIEF DESIGNER**	**ENGINE**
D50	4	10	9	2	1	-	54-55	V Jano	V8

LARROUSSE (F)

Principal: Gérard Larrousse. **Base:** Toulon. **Founded:** 1986.
After five years as an entrant of Lola chassis, former racer Gérard Larrousse took the plunge into Formula 1 as a constructor, with a brand new chassis designed by Robin Herd's team in the UK. Funded by Venturi Industrie of France, the new cars were known as Venturi-Larrousse during the debut year. Venturi withdrew its financial support at the end of 1992 and the cars were then known simply as Larrousse. Although entered for 1995 with nominated drivers Bouchut and Hélary, the team never showed and quietly faded away.

TOTALS	GPs	STARTS	POINTS	POLES	F.LAPS	WINS			
	48	94	6	-	-	-			
SEASONS							**SPONSOR(S)**	**MAIN DRIVER(S)**	
1992	16	30	1	-	-	-	Cabin, Central Park	Gachot, Katayama	
1993	16	32	3	-	-	-	Central Park, Charro	Comas, Alliot	
1994	16	32	2	-	-	-	Tourtel, Kronenbourg	Comas, Beretta	
MODELS							**YEAR(S)**	**CHIEF DESIGNER**	**ENGINE**
LC92	16	30	1	-	-	-	92	T Belli	Lamborghini
LH93	16	32	3	-	-	-	93	T Belli	Lamborghini
LH94	16	32	2	-	-	-	94	T Belli	Ford Cosworth

LDS (ZA)

Principal: Doug Serrurier. **Base:** Alberton, Transvaal, South Africa. **Founded:** 1960.
LDS was named after its South African founder, speedway rider, Louis Douglas Serrurier who built his first car (Speedy Engineering Special) in 1956. Various LDS models were built for local races - Mk 1 and 2 were based on Cooper designs, whilst the Mk 3B was based on the Brabham BT11.

TOTALS	GPs	STARTS	POINTS	POLES	F.LAPS	WINS			
	5	6	-	-	-	-			
SEASONS							**COLOUR**	**MAIN DRIVER(S)**	
1962	1	1	-	-	-	-	blue	Serrurier	
1963	1	2	-	-	-	-	blue	Serrurier, Tingle	
1965	1	1	-	-	-	-		Tingle	
1967	1	1	-	-	-	-	green	Tingle	
1968	1	1	-	-	-	-	green	Tingle	
MODELS							**YEAR(S)**	**CHIEF DESIGNER**	**ENGINE**
Mk 1	2	2	-	-	-	-	63-65	D Serrurier	Alfa Romeo
Mk 2	2	2	-	-	-	-	62-63	D Serrurier	Alfa Romeo
Mk 3B	2	2	-	-	-	-	67-68	D Serrurier	Climax, Repco

LEC (GB)

Principal: David Purley. **Base:** Bognor Regis, West Sussex. **Founded:** 1973.
David Purley commissioned Mike Pilbeam to design a new Grand Prix car which was built at his father's Lec refrigeration firm. The project came to an abrupt end when Purley was lucky to survive a massive practice accident at Silverstone. When fully recovered a further car was used in domestic racing.

TOTALS	GPs	STARTS	POINTS	POLES	F.LAPS	WINS			
	3	3	-	-	-	-			
SEASONS							**SPONSOR(S)**	**MAIN DRIVER(S)**	
1977	3	3	-	-	-	-	Lec	Purley	
MODELS							**YEAR(S)**	**CHIEF DESIGNER**	**ENGINE**
CRP1	3	3	-	-	-	-	77	M Pilbeam	Ford Cosworth

LIFE (I)

Ernesto Vita's unique W12 engine was mated to the abandoned First chassis, to create this 1990 entrant (the L190) which never managed to pass through pre-qualifying, before trying out a Judd engine with equally poor results.

LIGIER (F)

Principal: Guy Ligier. **Base:** Abrest-Vichy/ Magny-Cours (1989). **Founded:** 1969.
Successful businessman and sportsman, Guy Ligier initially built electric road cars until the JS3 became the first racing car in 1971. The model number JS is used in memory of Guy Ligier's good friend Jo Schlesser. The company was taken over by Cyril de Rouvre in 1993 but after his arrest, Benetton's Flavio Briatore took control during 1994 finally buying out Guy Ligier's remaining 15% stake in August 1996.

TOTALS	GPs	STARTS	POINTS	POLES	F.LAPS	WINS		
	326	578	388	9	9	9		
SEASONS							**SPONSOR(S)**	**MAIN DRIVER(S)**
1976	16	16	20	1	-	-	Gitanes	Laffite
1977	17	18	18	-	1	1	Gitanes	Laffite
1978	16	16	19	-	-	-	Gitanes	Laffite
1979	15	30	61	4	3	3	Gitanes	Laffite, Depailler/Ickx
1980	14	28	66	3	3	2	Gitanes	Laffite, Pironi
1981	15	28	44	1	1	2	Gitanes, Talbot	Laffite, Tambay
1982	15	29	20	-	-	-	Gitanes, Talbot	Laffite, Cheever
1983	15	28	-	-	-	-	Gitanes, Loto	Jarier, Boesel
1984	16	31	3	-	-	-	Gitanes, Loto	Hesnault, de Cesaris
1985	15	30	23	-	1	-	Gitanes, Candy	Laffite, de Cesaris
1986	16	32	29	-	-	-	Gitanes, Loto	Laffite, Arnoux
1987	15	28	1	-	-	-	Gitanes, Loto	Arnoux, Ghinzani
1988	14	24	-	-	-	-	Gitanes, Loto	Arnoux, Johansson
1989	14	21	3	-	-	-	Gitanes, Loto	Arnoux, Grouillard
1990	16	30	-	-	-	-	Gitanes, Loto	Alliot, Larini
1991	16	29	-	-	-	-	Gitanes	Boutsen, Comas
1992	16	31	6	-	-	-	Gitanes	Boutsen, Comas
1993	16	32	23	-	-	-	Gitanes	Brundle, Blundell
1994	16	32	13	-	-	-	Gitanes	Bernard, Panis
1995	17	33	24	-	-	-	Gitanes	Brundle, Panis
1996	16	32	15	-	-	1	Gauloises, Parmalat	Panis, Diniz

MODELS	GPs	STARTS	POINTS	POLES	F.LAPS	WINS	YEAR(S)	CHIEF DESIGNER	ENGINE
JS5	16	16	20	1	-	-	76	G Ducarouge	Matra
JS7, 7/9	22	23	24	-	1	1	77-78	G Ducarouge	Matra
JS9	11	11	13	-	-	-	79	G Ducarouge	Matra
JS11	15	30	61	4	3	3	79	G Ducarouge	Ford Cosworth
JS11/15	14	28	66	3	3	2	80	G Ducarouge	Ford Cosworth
JS17-B	21	40	55	1	1	2	81-82	G Ducarouge	Matra
JS19	9	17	9	-	-	-	82	M Beaujon	Matra
JS21	15	28	-	-	-	-	83	M Beaujon	Ford Cosworth
JS23	16	31	3	-	-	-	84	M Beaujon	Renault t
JS25	15	30	23	-	1	-	85	M Beaujon	Renault t
JS27	16	32	29	-	-	-	86	M Têtu	Renault t
JS29B, C	15	28	1	-	-	-	87	M Têtu	Megatron t
JS31	14	24	-	-	-	-	88	M Têtu	Judd
JS33-B	30	51	3	-	-	-	89-90	M Beaujon	Ford Cosworth
JS35-B	16	29	-	-	-	-	91	M Beaujon	Lamborghini
JS37	16	31	6	-	-	-	92	F Dernie	Renault
JS39-B	32	64	36	-	-	-	93-94	G Ducarouge	Renault
JS41	17	33	24	-	-	-	95	F Dernie	Mugen Honda
JS43	16	32	15	-	-	1	96	A de Cortanze	Mugen Honda

LOLA (GB)

Principal: Eric Broadley. **Base:** Bromley/ Slough/ Huntingdon. **Founded:** 1957.
Eric Broadley built his own sports car in 1957 and the model was so quick, he was soon in demand to build copies. The company went on to produce cars for many categories of racing, its most well known successes being in IndyCar and sports car racing. Very probably the most successful racing car manufacturer ever, Lola have never tackled Formula 1 full on. The first foray came at the instigation of the Yeoman Credit team and later that decade, BMW commissioned a chassis that was mainly used in Formula 2. Graham Hill used Lola as a base for his own model in the 70s and Carl Haas named his own Force built cars in deference to his American Lola import agency. The Larrousse team used a Lola design for five seasons with limited success while the Scuderia Italia venture of 1993 petered out before the year's end. In spite of this, Lola have plans to enter their own factory team for 1997 in conjunction with Mastercard, under a unique sponsorship deal.

TOTALS	GPs	STARTS	POINTS	POLES	F.LAPS	WINS
	149	245	45	1	-	-

SEASONS							SPONSOR	MAIN DRIVER(S)
1962	9	16	19	1	-	-	(green)	Surtees, Salvadori
1963	9	13	-	-	-	-	(green)	Amon, Anderson
1964-66 *did not participate*								
1967	1	2	-	-	-	-	(white)	Hahne
1968	1	1	-	-	-	-	(white)	Hahne
1969-73 *did not participate*								
1974	15	27	1	-	-	-	Embassy	Hill, Edwards
1975	3	5	-	-	-	-	Embassy	Hill, Stommelen
1976-84 *did not participate*								
1985	3	3	-	-	-	-	Beatrice	Jones
1986	16	31	6	-	-	-	Beatrice	Jones, Tambay
1987	15	18	5	-	-	-	Elkron	Alliot, Dalmas
1988	16	30	-	-	-	-	Elkron	Alliot, Dalmas
1989	16	22	1	-	-	-	BP, Rhône-Poulenc	Alliot, Alboreto
1990	16	32	11	-	-	-	Espo	Bernard, Suzuki
1991	15	24	2	-	-	-	Toshiba	Bernard, Suzuki
1992 *did not participate*								
1993	14	21	-	-	-	-	Chesterfield	Alboreto, Badoer

MODELS							YEAR(S)	CHIEF DESIGNER	ENGINE
Mk 4-A	18	29	19	1	-	-	62-63	E Broadley	Climax
T100	1	2	-	-	-	-	67	E Broadley	BMW
T102	1	1	-	-	-	-	68	E Broadley	BMW
T370, 371	18	32	1	-	-	-	74-75	E Broadley	Ford Cosworth
THL1	6	8	-	-	-	-	85-86	N Oatley	Hart †
THL2	14	26	6	-	-	-	86	N Oatley	Ford Cosworth †
LC87	15	18	5	-	-	-	87	R Bellamy	Ford Cosworth
LC88-B	17	31	-	-	-	-	88-89	C Murphy	Ford Cosworth, Lamborghini
LC89	17	25	1	-	-	-	89-90	G Ducarouge	Lamborghini
90	14	28	11	-	-	-	90	C Murphy	Lamborghini
L91	15	24	2	-	-	-	91	E Broadley	Ford Cosworth
T93/30	14	21	-	-	-	-	93	E Broadley	Ferrari

LOTUS (GB)

Principal: Colin Chapman. **Base:** Hornsey, London/Cheshunt, Hertfordshire/Ketteringham Hall, Norfolk. **Founded:** 1952.
Colin Chapman created Lotus Engineering, later forming Team Lotus in 1954, building sports cars from a small workshop at 7 Tottenham Lane, Hornsey, North London. After design work for Vanwall, Chapman produced his own single- seaters that soon revolutionised Grand Prix racing. On the back of Cooper's rear engine designs, Chapman re- introduced the monocoque chassis with the 25, as well as introducing Ford Cosworth to power the all conquering Lotus 49. The 72 emphasised a new era in lay down designs, removing the bulky radiators to side pods and in doing so produced the streamlined chisel nose. Ground Effects was the next big break through with the first real effective designs in the 78 and 79. Unfortunately the twin chassis 88 got no further than practice, falling foul of technical regulations. Colin Chapman died suddenly in December 1982 and under the guidance of Peter Warr, the team carried on, but apart from the input of Ayrton Senna, never looked like regular winners again. Peter Collins led a buy-out of the famous marque in 1991 but at the end of 1994 the receivers were called in and the team folded in January 1995

CONSTRUCTORS' CHAMPIONSHIPS: 7 (1963, 65, 68, 70, 72, 73, 78)

TOTALS	GPs	STARTS	POINTS	POLES	F.LAPS	WINS
	491	1238	1514	107	71	79

SEASONS							SPONSOR(S)	MAIN DRIVER(S)
1958	9	19	3	-	-	-	(green)	Allison, G Hill
1959	8	17	5	-	-	-	(green)	G Hill, Ireland
1960	8	30	52	4	3	2	(green)	Ireland, Clark, Stacey
1961	8	55	44	1	2	3	(green)	Clark, Ireland
1962	9	57	43	6	5	3	(green)	Clark, T Taylor
1963	10	56	78	7	6	7	(green)	Clark*, T Taylor
1964	10	46	52	5	4	3	(green)	Clark, Arundell/Spence
1965	10	43	66	6	6	6	(green)	Clark*, Spence
1966	9	29	21	2	-	1	(green)	Clark, Arundell
1967	11	31	56	9	7	4	(green)	Clark, G Hill
1968	12	35	75	5	5	5	Gold Leaf	G Hill*, Oliver*

* Champion

SEASONS	GPs	STARTS	POINTS	POLES	F.LAPS	WINS	SPONSOR	MAIN DRIVER(S)
1969	11	47	59	5	2	2	Gold Leaf	G Hill, Rindt
1970	12	37	70	3	1	6	Gold Leaf	Rindt*, Miles
1971	11	24	25	-	-	-	Gold Leaf	Fittipaldi, Wisell
1972	12	27	61	3	-	5	JPS	Fittipaldi*, Walker
1973	15	31	107	10	7	7	JPS	Fittipaldi, Peterson
1974	15	33	47	1	2	3	JPS	Peterson, Ickx
1975	14	30	9	-	-	-	JPS	Peterson, Ickx
1976	16	30	32	1	1	1	JPS	Andretti, Nilsson
1977	17	33	67	7	5	5	JPS	Andretti, Nilsson
1978	16	41	116	12	7	8	JPS	Andretti*, Peterson
1979	15	39	39	-	-	-	Martini, Essex	Andretti, Reutemann
1980	14	30	14	-	-	-	Essex, Tissot	Andretti, de Angelis
1981	14	27	22	-	-	-	JPS, Essex	de Angelis, Mansell
1982	15	29	30	-	-	1	JPS	de Angelis, Mansell
1983	15	30	12	1	1	-	JPS	de Angelis, Mansell
1984	16	32	47	2	-	-	JPS, Elf	de Angelis, Mansell
1985	16	32	71	8	3	3	JPS, Olympus	Senna, de Angelis
1986	16	31	58	8	-	2	JPS, De Longhi	Senna, Dumfries
1987	16	32	64	1	3	2	Camel, De Longhi	Senna, Nakajima
1988	16	30	23	-	-	-	Camel	Piquet, Nakajima
1989	15	28	15	-	1	-	Camel, Epson	Piquet, Nakajima
1990	16	30	3	-	-	-	Camel	Warwick, Donnelly
1991	16	23	3	-	-	-	Tamiya, Komatsu	Häkkinen, Bailey/Herbert
1992	16	31	13	-	-	-	Castrol, Komatsu	Häkkinen, Herbert
1993	16	31	12	-	-	-	Castrol, Hitachi	Zanardi, Herbert
1994	16	32	-	-	-	-	Loctite, Shionogi	Lamy/Zanardi, Herbert

JPS = John Player Special

* Champion

MODELS							YEAR(S)	CHIEF DESIGNER	ENGINE
12	8	11	3	-	-	-	58	C Chapman	Climax
16	16	28	5	-	-	-	58-60	C Chapman	Climax
18, 18/21	19	72	73	5	4	4	60-62	C Chapman	Climax, Maserati
21	12	20	24	-	1	1	61-63	C Chapman	Climax
22	1	1	-	-	-	-	63-65	C Chapman	Ford
24	23	72	16	-	-	-	62-64	C Chapman	Climax, BRM
25	49	101	156	18	14	14	62-67	C Chapman	Climax, BRM
33	27	47	84	8	8	5	64-67	C Chapman	Climax, BRM
43	5	6	9	-	-	1	66-67	C Chapman	BRM
44	1	2	-	-	-	-	66	C Chapman	Ford Cosworth
48	1	1	-	-	-	-	67	C Chapman	Ford Cosworth
49-B, C	41	113	205	19	14	12	67-70	M Phillippe	Ford Cosworth
56B	3	3	-	-	-	-	71	M Phillippe	Pratt & Whitney
59B	1	1	-	-	-	-	69	M Phillippe	Ford Cosworth
63	7	8	-	-	-	-	69	M Phillippe	Ford Cosworth
69	2	2	-	-	-	-	71	M Phillippe	Ford Cosworth
72-B-F	74	149	295	17	9	20	70-75	M Phillippe	Ford Cosworth
76	7	10	3	-	-	-	74	R Bellamy	Ford Cosworth
77	16	30	32	1	1	1	76	R Bellamy	Ford Cosworth
78	31	54	106	9	7	7	77-78	R Bellamy	Ford Cosworth
79	26	56	112	10	5	6	78-79	M Ogilvie	Ford Cosworth
80	3	3	4	-	-	-	79	M Ogilvie	Ford Cosworth
81-B	18	38	23	-	-	-	80-81	M Ogilvie	Ford Cosworth
87-B	11	21	13	-	-	-	81-82	M Ogilvie	Ford Cosworth
91	15	28	30	-	-	1	82-83	M Ogilvie	Ford Cosworth
92	8	8	1	-	-	-	83	M Ogilvie	Ford Cosworth
93T	7	7	-	-	-	-	83	M Ogilvie	Renault t
94T	7	14	11	1	1	-	83	G Ducarouge	Renault t
95T	16	32	47	2	-	-	84	G Ducarouge	Renault t
97T	16	32	71	8	3	3	85	G Ducarouge	Renault t
98T	16	31	58	8	-	2	86	G Ducarouge	Renault t
99T	16	32	64	1	3	2	87	G Ducarouge	Honda t
100T	16	30	23	-	-	-	88	G Ducarouge	Honda t
101	15	28	15	-	1	-	89	F Dernie	Judd
102-B, D	36	61	8	-	-	-	90-92	F Dernie	Lamborghini, Judd, Ford Cosworth
107-B, C	34	64	23	-	-	-	92-94	C Murphy	Ford Cosworth, Mugen Honda
109	12	22	-	-	-	-	94	C Murphy	Mugen Honda

The Lotus 20-Ford did not pre-qualify in South Africa 1965

LYNCAR (GB)

Principal: Martin Slater. **Base:** Slough. **Founded:** 1971.
Martin Slater built his first Lyncar for Formula Atlantic in 1971 and successful customer John Nicholson commissioned an Formula 1 car for the 1974 season. After the 1975 season, the car passed into other hands and Nicholson concentrated on his engine business.

TOTALS	GPs	STARTS	POINTS	POLES	F.LAPS	WINS			
	1	1	-	-	-	-			
SEASONS							**SPONSOR(S)**		**MAIN DRIVER(S)**
1974	-	-	-	-	-	-	Pinch		Nicholson
1975	1	1	-	-	-	-	Pinch		Nicholson
MODELS							**YEAR(S)**	**CHIEF DESIGNER**	**ENGINE**
006	1	1	-	-	-	-	75	M Slater	Ford Cosworth

MAKI (J)

The F101 and F102-A models designed by Kenji Mimura, never managed to start a race despite noble efforts in 1974, 75 and 76.

MARCH (GB)

Principals: Robin Herd, Max Mosley. **Base:** Bicester, Oxfordshire. **Founded:** 1969.
Created as an assault on the Formula 1 establishment by a quartet that gave the car its name; Max Mosley, Alan Rees, Graham Coaker and Robin Herd. They established a works team in F1 and produced customer cars for most of the top single seater formulae. Mosley left the team at the end of 1977, while Herd continued alone, building customer cars including a very productive period in IndyCar Racing. March became a public limited company at the time of its third F1 entry and sold the F1 operation to the sponsors Leyton House in 1989, with new owner Akira Akagi assuming control. After a financial scandal in Japan, the team resumed the familar March name once again in 1992 and under the guidence of Ken Marrable struggled through one final season.

TOTALS	GPs	STARTS	POINTS	POLES	F.LAPS	WINS			
	227	558	193	5	7	3			
SEASONS							**SPONSOR(S)**		**MAIN DRIVER(S)**
1970	13	60	55	3	1	1	STP		Amon, Siffert
1971	11	52	37	-	1	-	STP		Peterson, Soler-Roig
1972	12	62	15	-	-	-	STP		Peterson, Lauda
1973	15	40	14	-	2	-	STP		Jarier, Williamson
1974	15	28	6	-	-	-	Beta		Stuck, Brambilla
1975	14	31	9	1	1	1	Beta		Brambilla, Lombardi
1976	16	53	19	1	1	1	Beta		Brambilla, Peterson, Stuck
1977	16	41	-	-	-	-	Rothmans		Ribeiro, I Scheckter
1978	-	-	-	-	-	-			Neve *(privateer)*
1979-80 *did not participate*									
1981	9	9	-	-	-	-	Guinness		Daly, Salazar *(RAM)*
1982	13	22	-	-	-	-	Rothmans		Mass, Boesel *(RAM)*
1983-86 *did not participate*									
1987	15	15	1	-	-	-	Leyton House		Capelli
1988	16	31	22	-	-	-	Leyton House		Capelli, Gugelmin
1989	16	31	4	-	1	-	Leyton House		Capelli, Gugelmin
1990	14	25	7	-	-	-	Leyton House		Capelli, Gugelmin
1991	16	32	1	-	-	-	Leyton House		Capelli, Gugelmin
1992	16	26	3	-	-	-	Uliveto, Rial		Wendlinger, Belmondo
MODELS							**YEAR(S)**	**CHIEF DESIGNER**	**ENGINE**
701	16	65	55	3	1	1	70-71	R Herd	Ford Cosworth
711	22	60	40	-	1	-	71-72	R Herd	Ford Cosworth, Alfa Romeo
721-X, G	15	55	12	-	-	-	72-73	R Herd	Ford Cosworth
731	14	36	14	-	2	-	73-74	R Herd	Ford Cosworth
741	18	29	6	-	-	-	74-75	R Herd	Ford Cosworth
751	12	28	9	1	1	1	75	R Herd	Ford Cosworth
761-B	32	90	19	1	1	1	76-77	R Herd	Ford Cosworth
771	4	4	-	-	-	-	77	R Herd	Ford Cosworth
811	9	9	-	-	-	-	81	A Reynard	Ford Cosworth
821	13	22	-	-	-	-	82	A Reynard	Ford Cosworth
871	15	15	1	-	-	-	87	G Coppuck	Ford Cosworth
881	18	35	26	-	-	-	88-89	A Newey	Judd

MODELS	GPs	STARTS	POINTS	POLES	F.LAPS	WINS	YEAR(S)	CHIEF DESIGNER	ENGINE
CG891	14	27	-	-	1	-	89	A Newey	Judd
CG901	14	25	7	-	-	-	90	A Newey	Judd
CG911	32	58	4	-	-	-	91-92	C Murphy	Ilmor

The 781S (1978) and 87P (1987) with Ford Cosworth engines, did not start.

MARTINI (F)

Principal: Tico Martini. **Base:** Magny-Cours. **Founded:** 1962.
The first car was built in 1963 for the race track base of the Knight brothers' Winfield racing school. The cars designation MK refers to the collaboration between the two businesses. Most French formulae were successfully catered for including Formula 2, until the venture in Formula 1 in 1978. Martini pulled out at year's end and returned to build cars for the French domestic market.

TOTALS	GPs	STARTS	POINTS	POLES	F.LAPS	WINS		
	4	4	-	-	-	-		
SEASONS							**SPONSOR(S)**	**MAIN DRIVER(S)**
1978	4	4	-	-	-	-	Silver Match, RMO	Arnoux

MODELS	GPs	STARTS	POINTS	POLES	F.LAPS	WINS	YEAR(S)	CHIEF DESIGNER	ENGINE
MK23	4	4	-	-	-	-	78	T Martini	Ford Cosworth

MASERATI (I)

Principal: Adolfo and Omer Orsi. **Base:** Modena. **Founded:** 1914.
Alfieri Maserati (1887-1932) started building cars at his Bologna engineering firm back in 1926; the business also included his brothers Bindo, Ettore and Ernesto. In 1937, Maserati was sold to the Orsi family, and the remaining brothers stayed in a consulting role until returning to Bologna to form OSCA. Maserati was a leading light in the 50s scene and produced one of the greatest cars of the era in the 250F. The factory team withdrew at the end of 1957, but the name returned later as an engine supplier to the Cooper team. The Milano and Platé cars were early refinements of Maserati chassis (4CLT), separate from the factory. Now a part of the Citroen group and still building classic road cars.

TOTALS	GPs	STARTS	POINTS	POLES	F.LAPS	WINS		
	68	368	313.4	10	17	9		
SEASONS							**COLOUR**	**MAIN DRIVER(S)**
1950	6	31	11	-	-	-	red	Chiron, Rol
1951	5	12	-	-	-	-	red	de Graffenried, Schell *(Platé)*
1952	6	21	8.5	-	1	-	red	Bonetto, Rol, González
1953	8	40	65.5	2	4	1	red	Fangio, Bonetto, González, Marimón
1954	8	57	46.4	1	4	2	red	Fangio*, Marimón, Mantovani, Miäres
1955	6	39	23	-	1	-	red	Behra, Musso, Miäres, Perdisa
1956	7	60	72	1	3	2	red	Moss, Behra, Perdisa, Godia
1957	7	54	78	5	3	4	red	Fangio*, Behra, Schell, Menditéguy
1958	10	43	9	1	1	-	red	Gregory, Shelby *(Centro Sud)*
1959	3	5	-	-	-	-	red	d'Orey *(Centro Sud)*
1960	2	6	-	-	-	-	red	Drake *(privateer)*

*Champion

MODELS	GPs	STARTS	POINTS	POLES	F.LAPS	WINS	YEAR(S)	CHIEF DESIGNER	ENGINE
4CL	4	4	-	-	-	-	50-51	E Maserati	4s
4CLT	10	35	9	-	-	-	50-51	A Massimino	4s, OSCA
Milano	4	4	2	-	-	-	50-51	Ruggeri bros.	4s
Platé	3	6	-	-	-	-	52	E Platé	4
A6GCM	23	71	74	2	5	1	52-56	A Massimino	6
250F	43	248	228.4	8	12	8	54-60	G Colombo	6, V12

The Arzani Volpini was a further refinement of the Milano chassis and failed to start the 1955 Italian GP.

MATRA (F)

Principal: Jean-Luc Lagardäre. **Base:** Vichy. **Founded:** 1942.
Mécanique Aviation Traction were originally a military hardware company which acquired the René Bonnet car company in 1964. Under the Matra Sports subsidiary, they contested Formula 3 in 1965, Formula 2 in 1966, until entering Grand Prix via the back door of the F2 class. A two pronged attack on the championship was established with Ken Tyrrell's team, using a chassis mated to the Ford Cosworth DFV and the factory producing a variation to take its own V12 engine. Victory eluded the factory operation but the howling V12 engine continued for some time with Shadow and Ligier. Matra withdrew from Formula 1 to continue with its sports car successes.

CONSTRUCTORS' CHAMPIONSHIPS: 1 (1969)

TOTALS	**GPs**	**STARTS**	**POINTS**	**POLES**	**F.LAPS**	**WINS**		
	63	119	184	41	2	9		
SEASONS							**SPONSOR(S)**	**MAIN DRIVER(S)**
1966	1	4	-	-	-	-	(blue)	*(F2 class entry only)*
1967	4	5	-	-	-	-	Elf	Beltoise
1968	12	28	53	-	4	3	Elf	Beltoise, Pescarolo
1969	11	27	85	2	6	6	Elf	Stewart*, Beltoise *(Tyrrell)*
1970	13	26	24	-	-	-	Elf	Beltoise, Pescarolo
1971	10	17	10	1	-	-	Elf	Amon, Beltoise
1972	12	12	12	1	2	-	Shell	Amon

*Champion

MODELS							**YEAR(S)**	**CHIEF DESIGNER**	**ENGINE**
MS5	2	5	-	-	-	-	66-67	B Boyer	Ford Cosworth, BRM
MS7	6	7	1	-	-	-	67-69	B Boyer	Ford Cosworth
MS9	1	1	-	-	-	-	68	B Boyer	Ford Cosworth
MS10	12	16	54	-	4	4	68-69	B Boyer	Ford Cosworth
MS11	10	12	8	-	1	-	68	B Boyer	V12
MS80	10	19	74	2	5	5	69	B Boyer	Ford Cosworth
MS84	4	4	1	-	-	-	69	B Boyer	Ford Cosworth
MS120, B-D	35	55	46	2	2	-	70-72	B Boyer	V12

McLAREN (GB)

Principals: Bruce McLaren, Teddy Mayer, Ron Dennis. **Base:** Colnbrook, nr Slough/ Woking, Surrey. **Founded:** 1963 .
Formed initially for Tasman racing, the team built its first sports cars in 1964 and 1965 before Bruce left Cooper to tackle Formula 1 on his own. Initial success turned to tragedy when Bruce was killed testing a Can-Am car at Goodwood in 1970. With the help of Denny Hulme the team struggled on and established itself at the top during the mid 70s. A steady decline left the team floundering as the decade turned to a close and sponsors Marlboro instigated a merger with Ron Dennis's Project Four Formula 2 operation. Teddy Mayer left soon after, whilst with the help of John Barnard's revolutionary carbon-fibre monocoque, McLaren not only returned to the very top, but led the next major innovation in chassis design. With the departure of Prost and Senna, who scored six championships between them, the team entered a barren period culminating in the loss of the longest running sponsorship deal in Formula 1, switching from Marlboro to West for 1997.

CONSTRUCTORS' CHAMPIONSHIPS: 7 (1974, 84, 85, 88, 89, 90, 91)

TOTALS	**GPs**	**STARTS**	**POINTS**	**POLES**	**F.LAPS**	**WINS**		
	443	941	2084.5	79	69	104		
SEASONS							**SPONSOR(S)**	**MAIN DRIVER(S)**
1966	4	4	3	-	-	-	(white)	McLaren
1967	6	6	3	-	-	-	(red)	McLaren
1968	12	32	59	-	-	3	(orange)	McLaren, Hulme
1969	11	27	49	-	-	1	(orange)	McLaren, Hulme
1970	12	33	36	-	1	-	(orange)	McLaren, Hulme
1971	11	25	13	-	1	-	(orange)	Hulme, Gethin
1972	12	25	66	1	1	1	Yardley	Hulme, Revson
1973	15	35	68	1	3	3	Yardley	Hulme, Revson
1974	15	46	87	2	1	4	Marlboro	Hulme, Fittipaldi*
1975	14	28	65	-	2	3	Marlboro	Fittipaldi, Mass
1976	16	32	88	8	3	6	Marlboro	Hunt*, Mass
1977	17	46	65	6	3	3	Marlboro	Hunt, Mass
1978	16	48	16	-	-	-	Marlboro	Hunt, Tambay
1979	15	28	15	-	-	-	Marlboro	Watson, Tambay
1980	14	24	11	-	-	-	Marlboro	Watson, Prost
1981	15	29	28	-	1	1	Marlboro	Watson, de Cesaris

*Champion

SEASONS	GPs	STARTS	POINTS	POLES	F.LAPS	WINS	SPONSOR(S)	MAIN DRIVER(S)
1982	15	29	69	-	2	4	Marlboro	Watson, Lauda
1983	14	28	34	-	2	1	Marlboro	Watson, Lauda
1984	16	32	143.5	3	8	12	Marlboro	Prost, Lauda*
1985	16	31	90	2	6	6	Marlboro	Prost*, Lauda
1986	16	32	96	2	2	4	Marlboro	Prost*, Rosberg
1987	16	32	76	-	2	3	Marlboro	Prost, Johansson
1988	16	32	199	15	10	15	Marlboro	Prost, Senna*
1989	16	32	141	15	8	10	Marlboro	Prost*, Senna
1990	16	32	121	12	5	6	Marlboro	Senna*, Berger
1991	16	32	139	10	4	8	Marlboro	Senna*, Berger
1992	16	32	99	1	3	5	Marlboro	Senna, Berger
1993	16	32	84	1	1	5	Marlboro	Senna, Andretti
1994	16	32	42	-	-	-	Marlboro	Häkkinen, Brundle
1995	17	33	30	-	-	-	Marlboro	Häkkinen, Blundell
1996	16	32	49	-	-	-	Marlboro	Häkkinen, Coulthard

*Champion

MODELS	GPs	STARTS	POINTS	POLES	F.LAPS	WINS	YEAR(S)	CHIEF DESIGNER	ENGINE
M2B	4	4	3	-	-	-	66	R Herd	Ford, Serenissima
M4B	2	2	3	-	-	-	67	R Herd	BRM
M5A	11	11	3	-	-	-	67-68	R Herd	BRM
M7A, C, D	31	60	106	-	1	4	68-71	R Herd	Ford Cosworth, Alfa Romeo
M9A	1	1	-	-	-	-	69	J Marquart	Ford Cosworth
M14A, D	17	32	35	-	-	-	70-71	J Marquart	Ford Cosworth, Alfa Romeo
M19A, C	25	48	91	1	3	1	71-73	R Bellamy	Ford Cosworth
M23	80	166	319	14	10	16	73-78	G Coppuck	Ford Cosworth
M26	30	64	58	3	1	3	76-79	G Coppuck	Ford Cosworth
M28	9	14	8	-	-	-	79	G Coppuck	Ford Cosworth
M29-F	26	41	17	-	-	-	79-81	G Coppuck	Ford Cosworth
M30	3	3	1	-	-	-	80	G Coppuck	Ford Cosworth
MP4-B, /1C, /1E	42	79	131	-	5	6	81-83	J Barnard	Ford Cosworth, TAG Porsche t
MP4/2-B, C	48	95	329.5	7	16	22	84-86	J Barnard	TAG Porsche t
MP4/3	16	32	76	-	2	3	87	S Nichols	TAG Porsche t
MP4/4	16	32	199	15	10	15	88	S Nichols	Honda t
MP4/5-B	16	64	262	27	13	16	89-90	N Oatley	Honda
MP4/6-B	18	36	148	10	5	8	91-92	N Oatley	Honda
MP4/7A	14	28	90	1	2	5	92	N Oatley	Honda
MP4/8	16	32	84	1	1	5	93	N Oatley	Ford Cosworth
MP4/9	16	32	42	-	-	-	94	N Oatley	Peugeot
MP4/10-B, C	17	33	30	-	-	-	95	N Oatley	Mercedes-Benz
MP4/11-B	16	32	49	-	-	-	96	N Oatley	Mercedes-Benz

MERCEDES-BENZ (D)

Principal: Walter Kostelezky. **Base:** Stuttgart-Unterturkheim. **Re-formed:** 1926 (as Mercedes-Benz).
Mercedes, initially founded in 1901, was one of the great racing car constructors of the early part of the century, their 1930s cars dominating many Grands Prix. After a low key entry post-war, the three-pointed star reappeared on the grid in its startling stromlinienwagen (streamlined) form. A combination of a revolutionary design, Alfred Neubauer's team management and the talents of the current world champion, meant Mercedes started where they left off. With nothing further to prove and the Le Mans disaster very much in the public eye, the team made a tearful exit at the end of 1955. Mercedes returned to sports car racing with Peter Sauber and featured in the engine development on their Formula 1 debut before forming a partnership with McLaren.

TOTALS	GPs	STARTS	POINTS	POLES	F.LAPS	WINS
	12	39	139.1	8	9	9

SEASONS	GPs	STARTS	POINTS	POLES	F.LAPS	WINS	COLOUR	MAIN DRIVER(S)
1954	6	18	60.1	4	4	4	silver	Fangio*, Kling, Herrmann
1955	6	21	79	4	5	5	silver	Fangio*, Moss, Kling

MODELS	GPs	STARTS	POINTS	POLES	F.LAPS	WINS	YEAR(S)	CHIEF DESIGNER	ENGINE
W196	12	39	139.1	8	9	9	54-55	R Uhlenhaut	8

*Champion

MERZARIO (I)

Principal: Arturo Merzario. **Base:** Milan. **Founded:** 1977.
Former driver, Merzario turned his hand as a constructor when his Grand Prix career waned, but these cars proved ineffective. A merger with the Kauhsen operation was equally unsuccessful and the A2 and A4 designs never made the grid. Merzario turned his attention to Formula 2 and continued with this series until it became the Formula 3000 championship.

TOTALS	GPs	STARTS	POINTS	POLES	F.LAPS	WINS			
	10	10	-	-	-	-			
SEASONS							**SPONSOR(S)**	**MAIN DRIVER(S)**	
1978	8	8	-	-	-	-	Flor Bath	Merzario	
1979	2	2	-	-	-	-	Flor Bath	Merzario	
MODELS							**YEAR(S)**	**CHIEF DESIGNER**	**ENGINE**
A1-B	10	10	-	-	-	-	78-79	A Merzario	Ford Cosworth

The A2 and the A4 never qualified in 1979

MINARDI (I)

Principal: Giancarlo Minardi. **Base:** Faenza, Ravenna. **Founded:** 1972.
Based near his FIAT dealership, Minardi entered Italian Formula 3 and Formula 2, building his first Formula 2 car in 1980. Entering with the Carlo Chiti Motori Moderni engine, the team found Formula 1 a struggle. Minardi persevered with very few highs, before merging with Scuderia Italia for the 1994 season.

TOTALS	GPs	STARTS	POINTS	POLES	F.LAPS	WINS			
	188	338	27	-	-	-			
SEASONS							**SPONSOR(S)**	**MAIN DRIVER(S)**	
1985	15	15	-	-	-	-	Simod	Martini	
1986	15	30	-	-	-	-	Simod	de Cesaris, Nannini	
1987	16	31	-	-	-	-	Lois, Simod	Campos, Nannini	
1988	14	25	1	-	-	-	Lois, Cimarron	Martini, Sala	
1989	16	28	6	-	-	-	SCM, Lois	Martini, Sala	
1990	16	25	-	-	-	-	SCM	Martini, Barilla	
1991	16	32	6	-	-	-	SCM	Martini, Morbidelli	
1992	15	26	1	-	-	-	Sabiem, Mercatone Uno	Fittipaldi, Morbidelli	
1993	16	32	7	-	-	-	Beta, Cocif	Fittipaldi, Barbazza/Martini	
1994	16	32	5	-	-	-	Lucchini, Beta	Martini, Alboreto	
1995	17	33	1	-	-	-	Doimo, Valleverde	Martini/Lamy, Badoer	
1996	16	29	-	-	-	-	Doimo, Bossini	Lamy, Fisichella	
MODELS							**YEAR(S)**	**CHIEF DESIGNER**	**ENGINE**
M185-B	30	39	-	-	-	-	85-86	G Caliri	Ford Cosworth, Motori Moderni
M186	6	6	-	-	-	-	86	G Caliri	Motori Moderni
M187	16	31	-	-	-	-	87	G Caliri	Motori Moderni
M188-B	17	31	1	-	-	-	88-89	G Caliri	Ford Cosworth
M189	15	26	6	-	-	-	89-90	A Costa	Ford Cosworth
M190	14	21	-	-	-	-	90	A Costa	Ford Cosworth
M191-B	20	40	6	-	-	-	91-92	A Costa	Ferrari, Lamborghini
M192	11	18	1	-	-	-	92	A Costa	Lamborghini
M193-B	21	42	10	-	-	-	93-94	A Costa	Ford Cosworth
M194	11	22	2	-	-	-	94	A Costa	Ford Cosworth
M195-B	33	62	1	-	-	-	95-96	A Costa	Ford Cosworth

ONYX (GB)

Principal: Mike Earle. **Base:** Fontwell, nr Arundel, West Sussex. **Founded:** 1979.
This operation began as Onyx Engineering at Littlehampton and achieved many successful years in Formula 3000. An eventful Formula 1 baptism saw the team initially failing to qualify and then ending with a podium finish. The colourful Jean-Pierre van Rossem (of sponsor's Moneytron) bought out Mike Earle in December 1989, but sold the team to Peter Monteverdi early the next year. He relocated to Switzerland in July and renamed the cars Monteverdi, before folding altogether in August of that year.

TOTALS	GPs	STARTS	POINTS	POLES	F.LAPS	WINS			
	17	25	6	-	-	-			
SEASONS							**SPONSOR(S)**	**MAIN DRIVER(S)**	
1989	12	15	6	-	-	-	Moneytron	Johansson, Gachot	
1990	5	10	-	-	-	-	Marlboro	Foitek, Lehto	
MODELS							**YEAR(S)**	**CHIEF DESIGNER**	**ENGINE**
ORE-1	12	15	6	-	-	-	89	A Jenkins	Ford Cosworth
ORE-2	5	10	-	-	-	-	90	A Jenkins	Ford Cosworth

OSCA (I)

Principals: Ernesto, Ettore & Bindo Maserati. **Base:** Bologna. **Founded:** 1947.
Officine Specializate Costruzione Automobili Fratelli Maserati. The three Maserati brothers left Maserati after their ten year contract with Orsi, to reform their car construction business. They specialised in sports cars but built three types of single seaters; the last of which, an Formula 2 design failed to qualify at Monaco in 1957. The company was sold to MV in 1962.

TOTALS	GPs	STARTS	POINTS	POLES	F.LAPS	WINS			
	4	6	-	-	-	-			
SEASONS							**COLOUR**	**MAIN DRIVER(S)**	
1951	1	1	-	-	-	-	red	Rol	
1952	1	1	-	-	-	-	red	Bayol	
1953	2	4	-	-	-	-	red	Bayol, Chiron	
MODELS							**YEAR(S)**	**CHIEF DESIGNER**	**ENGINE**
4500G	1	1	-	-	-	-	51	Maserati bros.	V12
20	3	5	-	-	-	-	52-53	Maserati bros.	6

The 1958 model entered by Cabianca and Piotto, did not start in Monaco.

OSELLA (I)

Principal: Enzo Osella. **Base:** Volpiano, Turin/ Palosco, Bergamo (1990). **Founded:** 1972.
Initially running Abarth sports cars, Osella built its first car for Formula 2 in 1974. Ever the enthusiast, Osella mainly ran a one car team usually found at the back of the grid. Taken over by Gabriele Rumi's Fondmetal in 1990 and renamed the following year, the team finally closed after the Italian Grand Prix in 1992.

TOTALS	GPs	STARTS	POINTS	POLES	F.LAPS	WINS		
	151	191	7	-	-	-		
SEASONS							**SPONSOR(S)**	**MAIN DRIVER(S)**
1980	10	10	-	-	-	-	Denim	Cheever
1981	10	12	-	-	-	-	Denim	Gabbiani, Jarier
1982	13	15	3	-	-	-	Denim	Jarier, Paletti
1983	13	16	-	-	-	-	Kelemata	Ghinzani, C Fabi
1984	15	22	4	-	-	-	Kelemata	Ghinzani, Gartner
1985	14	14	-	-	-	-	Kelemata	Ghinzani, Rothengatter
1986	15	30	-	-	-	-	Landis & Gyr	Ghinzani, Berg
1987	14	17	-	-	-	-	Landis & Gyr	Caffi
1988	10	10	-	-	-	-	Stievani	Larini
1989	9	11	-	-	-	-	Fondmetal	Larini, Ghinzani
1990	9	9	-	-	-	-	Fondmetal, Spal	Grouillard
1991	6	6	-	-	-	-	Fondmetal	Grouillard
1992	13	19	-	-	-	-	Fondmetal, Sgomma Tutto	Tarquini, Chiesa

MODELS	GPs	STARTS	POINTS	POLES	F.LAPS	WINS	YEAR(S)	CHIEF DESIGNER	ENGINE
FA1	10	10	-	-	-	-	80	E Osella	Ford Cosworth
FA1B	7	9	-	-	-	-	81	G Valentin	Ford Cosworth
FA1C	13	15	3	-	-	-	81-82	G Valentin	Ford Cosworth
FA1D	8	8	-	-	-	-	82-83	G Petrotta	Ford Cosworth
FA1E	9	12	-	-	-	-	83-84	T Southgate	Alfa Romeo
FA1F	29	36	4	-	-	-	84-86	G Petrotta	Alfa Romeo t
FA1G	28	28	-	-	-	-	85-87	G Petrotta	Alfa Romeo t
FA1H	2	2	-	-	-	-	86	G Petrotta	Alfa Romeo t
FA1I	14	16	-	-	-	-	87	G Petrotta	Alfa Romeo t
FA1L	10	10	-	-	-	-	88	A Tomaini	Alfa Romeo t
FA1M-E	18	20	-	-	-	-	89-90	A Tomaini	Ford Cosworth
F1 & GRO1	12	14	-	-	-	-	91-92	T Belli	Ford Cosworth
GRO2	7	11	-	-	-	-	92	S Rinland	Ford Cosworth

In 1988, the Alfa Romeo engines had Osella name on the cam covers

PACIFIC (GB)

Principal: Keith Wiggins. **Base:** Thetford, Norfolk. **Founded:** 1984.
Pacific achieved major success in all levels the team entered, although it suffered from the outdated chassis that was originally part of the abortive Reynard Formula 1 entry. Pacific joined with the moribund Team Lotus for 1995 but its lack of success sealed its fate as a Grand Prix concern during the winter.

TOTALS	GPs	STARTS	POINTS	POLES	F.LAPS	WINS			
	22	41	-	-	-	-	-		
SEASONS							**SPONSOR(S)**	**MAIN DRIVER(S)**	
1994	5	7	-	-	-	-	Ursus	Gachot, Belmondo	
1995	17	34	-	-	-	-	Ursus	Gachot, Montermini	
MODELS							**YEAR(S)**	**CHIEF DESIGNER**	**ENGINE**
PRO1	5	7	-	-	-	-	94	R Byrne	Ilmor
PRO2	17	34	-	-	-	-	95	F Coppuck	Ford Cosworth

PARNELLI (USA)

Principals: Velco Miletich, Rufus Parnelli Jones. **Base:** Torrance, California (UK **Base:** Griston, Norfolk). **Founded:** 1969.
With backing from Firestone, Parnelli entered the Formula 1 fray but it was soon apparent that American racing was their priority and when Firestone withdrew, the team soon followed back to the United States.

TOTALS	GPs	STARTS	POINTS	POLES	F.LAPS	WINS			
	16	16	6	-	1	-			
SEASONS							**SPONSOR(S)**	**MAIN DRIVER(S)**	
1974	2	2	-	-	-	-	Viceroy, Firestone	Andretti	
1975	12	12	5	-	1	-	Viceroy	Andretti	
1976	2	2	1	-	-	-	American Wheels	Andretti	
MODELS							**YEAR(S)**	**CHIEF DESIGNER**	**ENGINE**
VPJ4-B	16	16	6	-	1	-	74-76	M Phillippe	Ford Cosworth

PENSKE (USA)

Principal: Roger Penske. **Base:** Reading, Pennsylvania (UK Base: Poole, Dorset). **Founded:** 1966 .
After a career as driver and entrant in America, wealthy businessman Roger Penske decided to tackle Formula 1, using Graham McRae's old workshop as his base. After a successful but tragic period, in which his friend and regular driver Mark Donohue was killed, Penske sold his cars to the ATS team and returned to the US racing scene. He has since become a mainstay of the IndyCar movement, owning various circuits and going on to be the most successful IndyCar entrant of all time.

TOTALS	GPs	STARTS	POINTS	POLES	F.LAPS	WINS		
	40	44	23	-	-	1		
SEASONS							**SPONSOR(S)**	**MAIN DRIVER(S)**
1974	2	2	-	-	-	-	First National City	Donohue
1975	10	10	2	-	-	-	First National City	Donohue
1976	16	17	20	-	-	1	First National City	Watson
1977	12	15	1	-	-	-	ATS	Jarier *(ATS)*

MODELS	GPs	STARTS	POINTS	POLES	F.LAPS	WINS	YEAR(S)	CHIEF DESIGNER	ENGINE
PC1	12	12	2	-	-	-	74-75	G Ferris	Ford Cosworth
PC3	7	7	2	-	-	-	76	G Ferris	Ford Cosworth
PC4	22	25	19	-	-	1	76-77	G Ferris	Ford Cosworth

PORSCHE (D)

Principal: Ferry Porsche. **Base:** Stuttgart-Zuffenhausen. **Founded:** 1948.
The company's vast racing success has been built upon sports car racing and it was through this medium that the Porsche name appeared as modified two seaters in Formula 2 racing. A true Formula 1 entry didn't materialise until 1961 and the team soon withdrew and concentrated on the racing it knew best. The TAG-backed turbo engine of the mid eighties was a great success but this was tempered by the disastrous V12 produced for Footwork in 1991.

TOTALS	GPs	STARTS	POINTS	POLES	F.LAPS	WINS
	33	73	50	1	-	1

SEASONS							COLOUR	MAIN DRIVER(S)
1957	1	3	-	-	-	-	silver	*(F2 class entry only)*
1958	2	3	-	-	-	-	silver	de Beaufort *(Maarsbergen)*
1959	3	3	-	-	-	-	silver	von Trips
1960	2	4	1	-	-	-	silver	Barth, Herrmann
1961	8	25	24	-	-	-	silver	Gurney, Bonnier
1962	9	25	20	1	-	1	silver	Gurney, Bonnier
1963	7	9	5	-	-	-	orange	de Beaufort *(Maarsbergen)*
1964	1	1	-	-	-	-	orange	de Beaufort *(Maarsbergen)*

MODELS							YEAR(S)	CHIEF DESIGNER	ENGINE
RS550	2	4	-	-	-	-	57-58	W Hild	F4
RSK	4	4	-	-	-	-	58-59	W Hild	F4
Behra	2	2	-	-	-	-	59-60	V Colloti	F4
718	27	46	34	-	-	-	59-64	W Hild	F4
787	3	4	-	-	-	-	61-62	W Hild	F4
804	7	13	16	1	-	1	62	H Bott	F8

PROTOS (GB)

Not really a Formula 1 car at all, this unusual design took part in the Formula 2 class of the German Grand Prix.

TOTALS	GPs	STARTS	POINTS	POLES	F.LAPS	WINS
	1	2	-	-	-	-

SEASONS							COLOUR	MAIN DRIVER(S)
1967	1	2	-	-	-	-	green	*(F2 class entry only)*

MODELS							YEAR(S)	CHIEF DESIGNER	ENGINE
—	1	2	-	-	-	-	67	F Costin	Ford Cosworth

RAM (GB)

Principals: John MacDonald, Mick Ralph. **Base:** Bicester, Oxfordshire. **Founded:** 1975.
One time Formula 1 entrants with March and Williams chassis, the team had strong March connections and brought the constuctor back into Grand Prix in 1981-82. The March name was retained the following year but these were the first true RAM cars. An unsuccessful period followed and although Mike Thackwell tested in Rio prior to the 1986 season, the team folded through lack of funds.

TOTALS	GPs	STARTS	POINTS	POLES	F.LAPS	WINS
	31	54	-	-	-	-

SEASONS							SPONSOR(S)	MAIN DRIVER(S)
1983	3	3	-	-	-	-	Rizla	Salazar, Acheson
1984	15	28	-	-	-	-	Skoal Bandit	Palmer, Alliot
1985	13	23	-	-	-	-	Skoal Bandit	Alliot, Winkelhock

MODELS							YEAR(S)	CHIEF DESIGNER	ENGINE
01	5	5	-	-	-	-	83-84	D Kelly	Ford Cosworth, Hart t
02	15	26	-	-	-	-	84	D Kelly	Hart t
03	13	23	-	-	-	-	85	G Brunner	Hart t

REBAQUE (MEX/GB)

Principal: Hector Rebaque. **Base:** Leamington Spa, Warwickshire. **Founded:** 1977.
Built at Penske in Poole and based on the Lotus he previously entered. The car was soon discarded when the wealthy Mexican managed a works Brabham drive the following year.

TOTALS	GPs	STARTS	POINTS	POLES	F.LAPS	WINS			
	1	1	-	-	-	-			
SEASONS							**SPONSOR(S)**	**MAIN DRIVER(S)**	
1979	1	1	-	-	-	-	Carta Blanca	Rebaque	
MODELS							**YEAR(S)**	**CHIEF DESIGNER**	**ENGINE**
HR100	1	1	-	-	-	-	79	G Ferris	Ford Cosworth

RENAULT (F)

Principal: Bernard Dudot. **Base:** Viry-Châtillon, nr Paris. **Founded:** 1898.
Renault began manufacturing racing cars back in 1899 and went on to win the first ever Grand Prix in 1906. After establishing itself as France's leading motor manufacturer a sporting division was created for sports car racing with the Alpine-Renault. After Formula 2 success Renault went on to introduce one of the major Formula 1 innovations - the turbo engine, based on a Renault-Gordini design. Following their failure to win the World Championship, after coming so close, the Regie concentrated on engine supply which came to fruition with the Williams partnership of the 1990s.

TOTALS	GPs	STARTS	POINTS	POLES	F.LAPS	WINS			
	123	227	312	31	18	15			
SEASONS							**SPONSOR(S)**	**MAIN DRIVER(S)**	
1977	4	4	-	-	-	-	Elf	Jabouille	
1978	14	14	3	-	-	-	Elf	Jabouille	
1979	14	28	26	6	2	1	Elf	Jabouille, Arnoux	
1980	14	27	38	5	4	3	Elf	Jabouille, Arnoux	
1981	15	29	54	6	2	3	Elf	Prost, Arnoux	
1982	16	32	62	10	5	4	Elf	Prost, Arnoux	
1983	15	30	79	3	3	4	Elf	Prost, Cheever	
1984	16	32	34	1	2	-	Elf	Tambay, Warwick	
1985	15	31	16	-	-	-	Elf	Tambay, Warwick	
MODELS							**YEAR(S)**	**CHIEF DESIGNER**	**ENGINE**
RS01	23	26	3	1	-	-	77-79	F Castaing	V6t
RS10	11	20	26	5	2	1	79	F Castaing	V6t
RE20-B	20	37	44	5	4	3	80-81	M Têtu	V6t
RE30-B, C	28	54	110	16	7	7	81-83	M Têtu	V6t
RE40	14	27	79	3	3	4	83	M Têtu	V6t
RE50	16	32	34	1	2	-	84	M Têtu	V6t
RE60-B	15	31	16	-	-	-	85	M Têtu	V6t

The cars are often referred to by their chassis numbers incorporated into the model number, ie RE23.

RIAL (D)

Principal: Hans Günter Schmid. **Base:** Fussgönheim, nr Ludwigshafen. **Founded:** 1987.
The founder of ATS returned to Formula 1 with his team renamed after his wheel company. Schmid withdrew yet again at the end of his second season.

TOTALS	GPs	STARTS	POINTS	POLES	F.LAPS	WINS			
	20	20	6	-	-	-			
SEASONS							**SPONSOR(S)**	**MAIN DRIVER(S)**	
1988	16	16	3	-	-	-	Rial	de Cesaris	
1989	4	4	3	-	-	-	Rial	Danner, Weidler	
MODELS							**YEAR(S)**	**CHIEF DESIGNER**	**ENGINE**
ARC1	16	16	3	-	-	-	88	G Brunner	Ford Cosworth
ARC2	4	4	3	-	-	-	89	R Bell	Ford Cosworth

SAUBER (CH)

Principal: Peter Sauber. **Base:** Hinwil. **Founded:** 1970.
Former racer, Peter Sauber built his first car in 1970 and continued with sports cars, achieving many successes including Le Mans and Sportscar World Championships in 1989-90. He helped bring Mercedes back to front line motorsport with the C8 sports car in 1984 although their relationship finished at the end of the 1994 season. A Ford works deal was snatched away by the new Stewart Grand Prix team and it appears that Sauber have not matched their expected promise.

TOTALS	GPs	STARTS	POINTS	POLES	F.LAPS	WINS		
	64	127	53	-	-	-		
SEASONS							**SPONSOR(S)**	**MAIN DRIVER(S)**
1993	16	32	12	-	-	-	Lighthouse, Liqui Moly	Wendlinger, Lehto
1994	15	29	12	-	-	-	Tissot	Wendlinger/de Cesaris, Frentzen
1995	17	34	18	-	-	-	Red Bull, Petronas	Wendlinger/Boullion, Frentzen
1996	16	32	11	-		-	Red Bull, Petronas	Herbert, Frentzen

MODELS							YEAR(S)	CHIEF DESIGNER	ENGINE
C12	16	32	12	-	-	-	93	L Ress	Ilmor
C13	15	29	12	-	-	-	94	L Ress	Mercedes-Benz
C14	17	34	18	-	-	-	95	L Ress	Ford Cosworth
C15	16	32	11	-	-	-	96	L Ress	Ford Cosworth

SCARAB (USA)

Principal: Lance Reventlow. **Base:** Culver City, California. **Founded:** 1957.
Multi-millionaire and heir to the Woolworth empire, Reventlow decided to take on the might of Europe with a front-engined car based on his successful sports car design. Basing itself in Kingston-upon-Thames the team soon realised their Goodyear shod cars were outdated and returned to America, closing down in 1962.

TOTALS	GPs	STARTS	POINTS	POLES	F.LAPS	WINS		
	2	3	-	-	-	-		
SEASONS							**COLOUR**	**MAIN DRIVER(S)**
1960	2	3	-	-	-	-	blue/white	Daigh, Reventlow

MODELS							YEAR(S)	CHIEF DESIGNER	ENGINE
—	2	3	-	-	-	-	60	M Whitfield	4

SCIROCCO (USA)

Principal: Hugh Powell. **Base:** Shepherds Bush, London, UK. **Founded:** 1962.
American enthusiast Hugh Powell acquired the assets of the Emeryson Company in 1962. After racing with these chassis it was decided to build new cars for the 1963 season. They raced in American blue and white colours, although based in Goldhawk Road, Shepherds Bush, London.

TOTALS	GPs	STARTS	POINTS	POLES	F.LAPS	WINS		
	5	7	-	-	-	-		
SEASONS							**COLOUR**	**MAIN DRIVER(S)**
1963	4	6	-	-	-	-	blue/white	Settember, Burgess
1964	1	1	-	-	-	-	yellow	Pilette

MODELS							YEAR(S)	CHIEF DESIGNER	ENGINE
SP	5	7	-	-	-	-	63-64	H Aiden-Jones	BRM, Climax

SHADOW (USA)

Principal: Don Nicholls. **UK Base:** Northampton. **Founded:** 1968 .
Don Nicholls, the founder of Advanced Vehicle Systems built his first car for CanAm racing in 1970 and whilst continuing to race back home, set up an English establishment for a serious and occasionally successful Formula 1 venture. In 1980, Teddy Yip's Theodore operation took over the Shadow team.

TOTALS	GPs	STARTS	POINTS	POLES	F.LAPS	WINS		
	104	211	68.5	3	2	1		
SEASONS							**SPONSOR(S)**	**MAIN DRIVER(S)**
1973	13	38	9	-	-	-	UOP	Follmer, Oliver
1974	14	28	7	-	-	-	UOP	Revson/Pryce, Jarier
1975	14	27	9.5	3	1	-	UOP	Pryce, Jarier
1976	16	32	10	-	1	-	Tabatip, Valvoline	Pryce, Jarier
1977	17	34	24	-	-	1	Ambrosio, Tabatip	Pryce/Jones, Patrese
1978	15	25	6	-	-	-	Villiger, Tabatip	Stuck, Regazzoni
1979	14	26	3	-	-	-	Samson	Lammers, de Angelis
1980	1	1	-	-	-	-	Interlekt	Lees, Kennedy

MODELS							YEAR(S)	CHIEF DESIGNER	ENGINE
DN1	15	40	9	-	-	-	73-74	T Southgate	Ford Cosworth
DN3-B	16	28	7	-	-	-	74-75	T Southgate	Ford Cosworth
DN5-B	31	52	17.5	3	2	-	75-77	T Southgate	Ford Cosworth
DN7	2	2	-	-	-	-	75	T Southgate	Matra
DN8	25	42	28	-	-	1	76-78	T Southgate	Ford Cosworth
DN9	26	46	7	-	-	-	78-79	T Southgate	Ford Cosworth
DN11	1	1	-	-	-	-	80	J Gentry	Ford Cosworth

The DN12-Ford Cosworth (1980) did not start in the World Championship and became the Theodore TR2

SHANNON (GB)

Principals: Hugh Aiden-Jones, Paul Emery.
This one-off design used the un-raced Climax FPE V8 engine. It retired after a quarter of a lap of its only race at Brands Hatch which gives it the record of the shortest Grand Prix race career.

TOTALS	GPs	STARTS	POINTS	POLES	F.LAPS	WINS		
	1	1	-	-	-	-		
SEASONS							**COLOUR**	**MAIN DRIVER(S)**
1966	1	1	-	-	-	-	green	T Taylor

MODELS							YEAR(S)	CHIEF DESIGNER	ENGINE
Mk 1	1	1	-	-	-	-	66	H Aiden-Jones	Climax

SIMTEK (GB)

Principal: Nick Wirth. **Base:** Banbury, Oxfordshire. **Founded:** 1989.
Nick Wirth had undertaken design work on many recent Formula 1 cars when Max Mosley was a part owner of Simtek Research. With the backing of the Brabham family their debut year was especially fraught with the death of newcomer Roland Ratzenberger. The team pushed on but found themselves without the funds to continue during the 1995 season and sold its assets at auction.

TOTALS	GPs	STARTS	POINTS	POLES	F.LAPS	WINS		
	21	37	-	-	-	-		
SEASONS							**SPONSOR(S)**	**MAIN DRIVER(S)**
1994	16	27	-	-	-	-	MTV, Barbara MC	Brabham, Ratzenberger/Gounon
1995	5	10	-	-	-	-	MTV, Barbara MC	Schiattarella, Verstappen

MODELS							YEAR(S)	CHIEF DESIGNER	ENGINE
S941	16	27	-	-	-	-	94	N Wirth	Ford Cosworth
S951	5	10	-	-	-	-	95	P Crooks	Ford Cosworth

SPIRIT (GB)

Principals: John Wickham, Gordon Coppuck. **Base:** Slough. **Founded:** 1981.
The first Formula 2 car was built in 1982 and the following year they reintroduced Honda to Formula 1 in a hybrid chassis. Honda soon took their engines to Williams and the team struggled without them, withdrawing during the 1985 season.

TOTALS	GPs	STARTS	POINTS	POLES	F.LAPS	WINS			
	23	23	-	-	-	-			
SEASONS							**SPONSOR(S)**	**MAIN DRIVER(S)**	
1983	6	6	-	-	-	-	Honda	Johansson	
1984	14	14	-	-	-	-	Australian	Baldi, Rothengatter	
1985	3	3	-	-	-	-	Australian	Baldi	
MODELS							**YEAR(S)**	**CHIEF DESIGNER**	**ENGINE**
201-C	6	6	-	-	-	-	83	G Coppuck	Honda t
101-D	17	17	-	-	-	-	84-85	G Coppuck	Hart t

STEBRO (CDN)

This Canadian Formula Junior constructor managed to reach the grid in the United States Grand Prix, but was hopelessly off the pace.

TOTALS	GPs	STARTS	POINTS	POLES	F.LAPS	WINS		
	1	1	-	-	-	-		
SEASONS							**COLOUR**	**MAIN DRIVER(S)**
1963	1	1	-	-	-	-	blue/white	Broeker
MODELS							**YEAR(S)**	**ENGINE**
Mk IV	1	1	-	-	-	-	63	Ford

SURTEES (GB)

Principal: John Surtees. **Base:** Edenbridge, Kent. **Founded:** 1966.
The first car was a Formula 5000 design originating from the Leda project which formed the basis of the first proper Formula 1 car. Although successful in F5000 and Formula 2, Grand Prix glory eluded the team. Somewhat disillusioned, the operation closed at the end of 1978.

TOTALS	GPs	STARTS	POINTS	POLES	F.LAPS	WINS			
	118	224	54	-	3	-			
SEASONS							**SPONSOR(S)**	**MAIN DRIVER(S)**	
1970	7	8	3	-	-	-	-	Surtees	
1971	11	26	9	-	-	-	Brooke Bond Oxo	Surtees, Stommelen	
1972	12	37	18	-	1	-	Brooke Bond Oxo	Hailwood, Schenken, de Adamich	
1973	15	35	7	-	2	-	Brooke Bond Oxo	Hailwood, Pace	
1974	14	23	3	-	-	-	Fina	Pace, Mass	
1975	11	12	-	-	-	-	Matchbox	Watson	
1976	15	33	7	-	-	-	Durex, Chesterfield	Jones, Lunger	
1977	17	30	6	-	-	-	Durex, Beta	Binder, Brambilla	
1978	16	20	1	-	-	-	Durex, Beta, BAF	Keegan, Brambilla	
MODELS							**YEAR(S)**	**CHIEF DESIGNER**	**ENGINE**
TS79	1	1	3	-	-	-	70-71	J Surtees	Ford Cosworth
TS9-B	25	60	27	-	1	-	71-73	J Surtees	Ford Cosworth
TS14-A	17	35	7	-	2	-	72-73	J Surtees	Ford Cosworth
TS16	25	35	3	-	-	-	74-75	J Surtees	Ford Cosworth
TS19	37	70	13	-	-	-	76-78	K Sears	Ford Cosworth
TS20	11	13	1	-	-	-	78	K Sears	Ford Cosworth

TALBOT LAGO (F)

Principal: Anthony Lago. **Base:** Suresnes, Paris. **Founded:** 1935.
After taking over the Sunbeam-Talbot-Darracq concern, Lago developed the sports cars and produced their first single seater in 1939. The works operation withdrew in early 1951 but cars raced on in private hands.

TOTALS	GPs	STARTS	POINTS	POLES	F.LAPS	WINS			
	13	80	25	-	-	-			
SEASONS							**COLOUR**	**MAIN DRIVER(S)**	
1950	6	35	20	-	-	-	blue	Giraud-Cabantous, Martin	
1951	7	45	5	-	-	-	blue	Rosier, Claes (privateers)	
MODELS							**YEAR(S)**	**CHIEF DESIGNER**	**ENGINE**
T26C-DA, GS	13	80	25	-	-	-	50-51	A Lago	6

TEC MEC (I)

Principal: Valerio Colotti. **Base:** Modena. **Founded:** 1958.
Tecnica Mecanica, derived from the Maserati 250F, was a one-off evolution of that famous marque. Originated by Valerio Colotti at his Modena studio, the design passed into the hands of a syndicate led by Gordon Pennington, after Giorgio Scarlatti lost interest in the project. It raced only once.

TOTALS	GPs	STARTS	POINTS	POLES	F.LAPS	WINS			
	1	1	-	-	-	-			
SEASONS							**COLOUR**	**MAIN DRIVER(S)**	
1959	1	1	-	-	-	-	red	d'Orey	
MODELS							**YEAR(S)**	**CHIEF DESIGNER**	**ENGINE**
F415	1	1	-	-	-	-	59	V Colotti	'Maserati'

TECNO (I)

Principals: Luciano & Gianfranco Pederzani. **Base:** Bologna. **Founded:** 1962.
The Pederzani brothers created Tecnokart, initially building karts until their first Formula 4 car in 1964. They progressed through the lower formulae, until finance by Martini drinks enabled them to enter the top flight.

TOTALS	GPs	STARTS	POINTS	POLES	F.LAPS	WINS			
	11	11	1	-	-	-			
SEASONS							**SPONSOR(S)**	**MAIN DRIVER(S)**	
1969	1	1	-	-	-	-	—	*(F2 class entry only)*	
1972	6	6	-	-	-	-	Martini	Galli, Bell	
1973	4	4	1	-	-	-	Martini	Amon	
MODELS							**YEAR(S)**	**CHIEF DESIGNER**	**ENGINE**
TOO	1	1	-	-	-	-	69	L&G Pederzani	Ford Cosworth
PA123	6	6	-	-	-	-	72	L&G Pederzani	F12
PA123	4	4	1	-	-	-	73	A McCall	F12

Although carrying the same name, the latest two models were different chassis designs, a third, the E731 (1973) never raced

THEODORE (GB)

Principal: Teddy Yip. **Base:** Woking, Surrey. **Founded:** 1978.
Founded by millionaire businessman Teddy Yip and based at Ralt's old works at Woking. Yip had previously backed drivers such as Tambay and Jones and decided to enter his own design. A second attempt with the Shadow design didn't fair much better and neither did a final attempt with an amalgamation of the struggling Ensign team, after which this Macau based entrepeneur turned his attention to the IndyCar scene.

TOTALS	GPs	STARTS	POINTS	POLES	F.LAPS	WINS		
	34	43	2	-	-	-		
SEASONS							**SPONSOR(S)**	**MAIN DRIVER(S)**
1978	1	1	-	-	-	-	Hi-Line	Rosberg
1979-80 *did not participate*								
1981	13	13	1	-	-	-	Moulin Rouge, Penthouse	Tambay/Surer
1982	7	7	-	-	-	-	Rizla	Daly/Byrne
1983	13	22	1	-	-	-	Cafe de Colombia	Guerrero, Cecotto

MODELS	GPs	STARTS	POINTS	POLES	F.LAPS	WINS	YEAR(S)	CHIEF DESIGNER	ENGINE
TR1	1	1	-	-	-	-	78	R Tauranac	Ford Cosworth
TY01	14	14	1	-	-	-	81-82	T Southgate	Ford Cosworth
TY02	6	6	-	-	-	-	82	T Southgate	Ford Cosworth
N183	13	22	1	-	-	-	83	N Bennett	Ford Cosworth

TOKEN (GB)

Principals: Tony Vlassopoulo, Ken Grob. **Base:** Woking, Surrey. **Founded:** 1973.
Originally built for Rondel Racing run by Ron Dennis and Neil Trundle. Finance problems resulted in this being taken over by Tony Vlassopoulo and Ken Grob who gave their name to the team. This car became the Safir in 1975 UK domestic racing.

TOTALS	GPs	STARTS	POINTS	POLES	F.LAPS	WINS			
	3	3	-	-	-	-			
SEASONS							**SPONSOR(S)**	**MAIN DRIVER(S)**	
1974	3	3	-	-	-	-	Shell	Pryce/Ashley	
MODELS							**YEAR(S)**	**CHIEF DESIGNER**	**ENGINE**
RJ02	3	3	-	-	-	-	74	R Jessop	Ford Cosworth

TROJAN (GB)

Principal: Peter Agg. **Base:** Croydon, Surrey. **Founded:** 1964 .
After taking over the Elva concern, the Beddington Lane based company forged a deal to reconstruct McLaren sports cars during the 60s and early 70s. From this they established their own Formula 5000 designs in 1973 before venturing into Formula 1.

TOTALS	GPs	STARTS	POINTS	POLES	F.LAPS	WINS			
	6	6	-	-	-	-			
SEASONS							**SPONSOR(S)**	**MAIN DRIVER(S)**	
1974	6	6	-	-	-	-	Suzuki, Homelite	Schenken	
MODELS							**YEAR(S)**	**CHIEF DESIGNER**	**ENGINE**
T103	6	6	-	-	-	-	74	R Tauranac	Ford Cosworth

TYRRELL (GB)

Principal: Ken Tyrrell. **Base:** Ockham, Woking, Surrey. **Founded:** 1960.
Former wood merchant and one time Formula 3 racer, Ken Tyrrell moved towards team management, first with a Cooper Formula 2 and then with his own team. Successful years with Matra in F2/F3 led to a Grand Prix entry in 1968 with Matra's first Formula 1 chassis. Reacquainted with Jackie Stewart, the team had two successful years with the Matra-Cosworth DFV combination including a debut World Championship in 1969. With Matra using its own engine, Tyrrell stayed with Ford Cosworth power and needed a new chassis for 1970. The new March organisation became the stop-gap until the first Tyrrell, built in utmost secrecy, was ready to race late that season. The passing years haven't been kind to the Tyrrell organisation. After such a high flying start, the team's results declined with its nadir being the disqualification from the World Championship in 1984 for alleged fuel irregularities.

CONSTRUCTORS' CHAMPIONSHIPS: 1 (1971)

TOTALS	GPs	STARTS	POINTS	POLES	F.LAPS	WINS		
	397	782	709	14	20	23		
SEASONS							**SPONSOR(S)**	**MAIN DRIVER(S)**
1970	3	3	-	1	-	-	Elf	Stewart
1971	11	23	88	6	4	7	Elf	Stewart*, Cevert
1972	12	25	60	2	4	4	Elf	Stewart, Cevert
1973	14	30	118	3	2	5	Elf	Stewart*, Cevert
1974	15	31	59	1	3	2	Elf	J Scheckter, Depailler
1975	14	31	32	-	1	1	Elf	J Scheckter, Depailler
1976	16	37	88	1	2	1	Elf	J Scheckter, Depailler
1977	17	35	27	-	1	-	Elf, First Nat City	Peterson, Depailler
1978	16	32	41	-	-	1	Elf, First Nat City	Pironi, Depailler
1979	15	32	28	-	-	-	Candy	Pironi, Jarier
1980	14	29	12	-	-	-	Candy	Jarier, Daly
1981	15	26	10	-	-	-	Ceramica Imola	Cheever, Alboreto
1982	16	32	25	-	2	1	Denim, Candy	Alboreto, Henton
1983	15	30	12	-	-	1	Benetton	Alboreto, Sullivan
1984	12	21	0*	-	-	-	Systime, De Longhi	Brundle, Bellof

* Champion

SEASONS	GPs	STARTS	POINTS	POLES	F.LAPS	WINS	SPONSOR(S)	MAIN DRIVER(S)
1985	16	28	7	-	-	-	Maredo, Porchester	Brundle, Bellof
1986	16	32	11	-	-	-	Data General	Brundle, Streiff
1987	16	32	11	-	-	-	Data General	Palmer, Streiff
1988	15	20	5	-	-	-	Courtaulds	Palmer, Bailey
1989	16	29	16	-	1	-	Camel	Palmer, Alboreto
1990	16	30	16	-	-	-	Epson	Nakajima, Alesi
1991	16	32	12	-	-	-	Braun, Epson	Nakajima, Modena
1992	16	32	8	-	-	-	Calbee, Club Angle	Grouillard, de Cesaris
1993	16	32	-	-	-	-	Cabin, Calbee	Katayama, de Cesaris
1994	16	32	13	-	-	-	Mild Seven, Calbee	Katayama, Blundell
1995	17	34	5	-	-	-	Nokia, Mild Seven	Katayama, Salo
1996	16	32	5	-	-	-	Mild Seven, Korean Air	Katayama, Salo

MODELS	GPs	STARTS	POINTS	POLES	F.LAPS	WINS	YEAR(S)	CHIEF DESIGNER	ENGINE
001-4	27	47	124	8	6	9	70-74	D Gardner	Ford Cosworth
005-6	24	44	146	4	4	7	72-74	D Gardner	Ford Cosworth
007	35	65	102	1	4	3	74-77	D Gardner	Ford Cosworth
P34	30	59	100	1	3	1	76-77	D Gardner	Ford Cosworth
008	16	32	41	-	-	1	78	M Phillippe	Ford Cosworth
009	17	36	31	-	-	-	79-80	M Phillippe	Ford Cosworth
010	22	42	17	-	-	-	80-81	M Phillippe	Ford Cosworth
011	34	64	38	-	2	2	81-83	M Phillippe	Ford Cosworth
012	26	42	5	-	-	-	83-85	M Phillippe	Ford Cosworth
014	14	21	5	-	-	-	85-86	M Phillippe	Renault t
015	13	25	9	-	-	-	86	M Phillippe	Renault t
DG016	16	32	11	-	-	-	87	M Phillippe	Ford Cosworth
017-B	16	22	5	-	-	-	88-89	B Lisles	Ford Cosworth
018	17	31	23	-	1	-	89-90	H Postlethwaite	Ford Cosworth
019	14	26	9	-	-	-	90	H Postlethwaite	Ford Cosworth
020-B, C	41	81	20	-	-	-	91-93	G Ryton	Honda, Ilmor, Yamaha
021	8	15	-	-	-	-	93	M Coughlan	Yamaha
022	16	32	13	-	-	-	94	H Postlethwaite	Yamaha
023	17	34	5	-	-	-	95	H Postlethwaite	Yamaha
024	16	32	5	-	-	-	96	H Postlethwaite	Yamaha

** Team disqualified in 1984 and all points from that season removed. It wasn't until the 007, that the model number was attributed to a type of car. Prior to this, they related to chassis numbers over two distinct types of model.*

VANWALL (GB)

Principal: Tony Vandervell. **Base:** Acton, London. **Founded:** 1949.
Guy Anthony Vandervell, owner of VP bearings, began racing with the Thin Wall Ferrari, but soon moved on to his own designs. A very thorough organisation, each year the cars were dismantled and completely revised and rebuilt (hence the difficulty with model numbers, as all cars were known by the chassis number). Upset by the death of Stuart Lewis-Evans, the team withdrew from extensive racing and finally closed due to ill health of the owner.

CONSTRUCTORS' CHAMPIONSHIPS: 1 (1958)

TOTALS	GPs	STARTS	POINTS	POLES	F.LAPS	WINS
	28	64	108	7	6	9

SEASONS	GPs	STARTS	POINTS	POLES	F.LAPS	WINS	COLOUR	MAIN DRIVER(S)
1954	2	2	-	-	-	-	green	Collins
1955	4	6	-	-	-	-	green	Hawthorn, Wharton, Schell
1956	5	12	3	-	-	-	green	Schell, Trintignant
1957	6	16	37	2	3	3	green	Moss, Brooks, Lewis-Evans
1958	9	26	68	5	3	6	green	Moss, Brooks, Lewis-Evans
1959	1	1	-	-	-	-	green	Brooks
1960	1	1	-	-	-	-	green	Brooks

MODELS	GPs	STARTS	POINTS	POLES	F.LAPS	WINS	YEAR(S)	CHIEF DESIGNER	ENGINE
Spl.	2	2	-	-	-	-	54	O Maddock	4
VW (55)	4	6	-	-	-	-	55	O Maddock	4
VW (56)	5	12	3	-	-	-	56	C Chapman	4
VW (57)	15	42	105	7	6	9	57-58	F Costin	4
VW (59)	1	1	-	-	-	-	59	F Costin	4
VW11	1	1	-	-	-	-	60	F Costin	4

Prior, to the VW11, the cars were referred to by chassis numbers only, although each year's model was a slight variation on the predecessor.

VERITAS (D)

Principal: Ernst Loof. **Base:** Nürburgring. **Founded:** 1948.
Formed by BMW engineers Ernst Loof and Lorenz Dietrich to build BMW-based sports cars (RS) and later single seaters (Meteor). Financial problems in 1950 moved the firm to a small workshop at the Nürburgring but it finally closed in 1953 when Loof returned to BMW.

TOTALS	GPs	STARTS	POINTS	POLES	F.LAPS	WINS		
	6	18	-	-	-	-		
SEASONS							**COLOUR**	**MAIN DRIVER(S)**
1951	1	1	-	-	-	-	silver	Hirt
1952	3	9	-	-	-	-	silver	Ulmen, Legat, Riess
1953	2	8	-	-	-	-	silver	Herrmann, Helfrich

MODELS	GPs	STARTS	POINTS	POLES	F.LAPS	WINS	YEAR(S)	CHIEF DESIGNER	ENGINE
Meteor	6	10	-	-	-	-	51-53	E Loof	6
RS	2	8	-	-	-	-	52-53	E Loof	6

WILLIAMS (GB)

Principal: Frank Williams. **Base:** Reading, Berkshire/ Didcot, Oxfordshire (1976)/ Grove, Wantage, Oxfordshire (1996). **Founded:** 1968.
Frank Williams, one time racer and racing car dealer, took the step up to Formula 1 with his good friend Piers Courage. Racing a Brabham very successfully in 1969 turned to disaster when Piers perished in a de Tomaso car the following year. The team struggled on using March chassis, until the finance was available for their own car. The first true Williams appeared in 1972 and was known as a Politoys in deference to the sponsors. Future cars would follow this trend as with the Iso-Marlboros the following year. After a split from team sponsor Wolf in 1976, Williams virtually started again. Moving from the Reading base, a new factory was found and Williams Grand Prix Engineering came into being. After a first season with the March chassis once again, the team has never looked back with the Patrick Head designed cars winning driver and constructor championships on a regular basis. Frank Williams was paralysed in a road accident while returning from a test session at the Paul Ricard circuit in March 1986. The combination of Renault engines and Adrian Newey's design expertise has made the 90's cars virtually unstoppable although this partnership ends at the end of 1997. Damon Hill has become the fourth World Champion to vacate the number one seat in the wake of Prost, Mansell and Piquet.

CONSTRUCTORS' CHAMPIONSHIPS: 8 (1980, 81, 86, 87, 92, 93, 94, 96)

TOTALS	GPs	STARTS	POINTS	POLES	F.LAPS	WINS		
	355	672	1805.5	97	101	95		
SEASONS							**SPONSOR(S)**	**MAIN DRIVER(S)**
1972	1	1	-	-	-	-	Politoys	Pescarolo
1973	15	28	2	-	-	-	Iso, Marlboro	Ganley, Galli
1974	15	22	4	-	-	-	Iso, Marlboro	Merzario, Laffite
1975	12	21	6	-	-	-	Fina, Ambrozium	Laffite, Merzario
1976	13	19	-	-	-	-	Marlboro	Ickx, Leclére/Merzario
1977 *used March chassis*								
1978	16	16	11	-	2	-	Saudia, Albilad	Jones
1979	15	30	75	3	3	5	Saudia, Albilad	Jones, Regazzoni
1980	14	32	120	3	6	6	Saudia, Leyland	Jones*, Reutemann
1981	15	30	95	2	7	4	Saudia, Leyland	Jones, Reutemann
1982	15	30	58	1	-	1	Saudia, TAG	Rosberg*, Daly
1983	15	29	38	1	-	1	Denim, Saudia	Rosberg, Laffite
1984	16	32	25.5	-	-	1	Saudia, Denim	Rosberg, Laffite
1985	16	31	71	3	4	4	Canon, Denim	Rosberg, Mansell
1986	16	32	141	4	11	9	Canon, Mobil	Piquet, Mansell
1987	16	30	137	12	7	9	Canon	Piquet*, Mansell
1988	16	32	20	-	1	-	Canon	Mansell, Patrese
1989	16	32	77	1	1	2	Canon	Boutsen, Patrese
1990	16	32	57	1	5	2	Canon	Boutsen, Patrese
1991	16	32	125	6	8	7	Canon, Labatt's	Mansell, Patrese
1992	16	32	164	15	11	10	Canon, Labatt's	Mansell*, Patrese
1993	16	32	168	15	10	10	Canon, Camel	Prost*, Hill
1994	16	31	118	6	8	7	Rothmans	Hill, Senna/Coulthard
1995	17	34	118	12	6	5	Rothmans	Hill, Coulthard
1996	16	32	175	12	11	12	Rothmans	Hill*, Villeneuve

*Champion

MODELS	GPs	STARTS	POINTS	POLES	F.LAPS	WINS	YEAR(S)	CHIEF DESIGNER	ENGINE
FX3-B	4	7	-	-	-	-	72-73	L Bailey	Ford Cosworth
IR	12	22	2	-	-	-	73	J Clarke	Ford Cosworth
FW	24	34	4	-	-	-	74-75	J Clarke	Ford Cosworth
FW04	10	10	6	-	-	-	75-76	R Stokoe	Ford Cosworth
FW05	13	18	-	-	-	-	76	H Postlethwaite	Ford Cosworth
FW06	20	24	15	-	2	-	78-79	P Head	Ford Cosworth
FW07-B, C	43	90	300	8	16	15	79-82	P Head	Ford Cosworth
FW08-C	26	51	80	2	-	2	82-83	P Head	Ford Cosworth
FW09-B	17	34	27.5	-	-	1	83-84	P Head	Honda t
FW10	16	31	71	3	4	4	85	P Head	Honda t
FW11-B	32	62	278	16	18	18	86-87	P Head	Honda t
FW12-C	29	57	74	1	2	1	88-89	P Head	Judd, Renault
FW13-B	20	39	80	1	5	3	89-90	P Head	Renault
FW14-B	32	64	289	21	19	17	91-92	P Head	Renault
FW15C	16	32	168	15	10	10	93	P Head	Renault
FW16-B	16	31	118	6	8	7	94	P Head	Renault
FW17-B	17	34	118	12	6	5	95	P Head	Renault
FW18	16	32	175	12	11	12	96	P Head	Renault

The McGuire BM1 which was a modification of the FW04 failed to pre-qualify in 1977. It wasn't until the FW04, that the model number was attributed to a type of car. Prior to this, they were related to different chassis.

WOLF (CDN/GB)

Principal: Walter Wolf. **Base:** Reading, Berkshire. **Founded:** 1975.
Canadian oil businessman, Walter Wolf financed the Williams Formula 1 operation in 1976. Disappointed, he bought out Williams and set up his own Walter Wolf Racing. The new car was an instant success, winning first time out. After a great first season, the team faded quickly and by the end of 1979 had withdrawn from racing completely.

TOTALS	GPs	STARTS	POINTS	POLES	F.LAPS	WINS			
	47	52	79	1	2	3			
SEASONS							**SPONSOR(S)**	**MAIN DRIVER(S)**	
1977	17	17	55	1	2	3	Castrol, Fina	J Scheckter	
1978	16	21	24	-	-	-	Castrol	J Scheckter, Rahal	
1979	14	14	-	-	-	-	Olympus	Hunt, Rosberg	
MODELS							**YEAR(S)**	**CHIEF DESIGNER**	**ENGINE**
WR1-4	27	27	59	1	2	3	77-78	H Postlethwaite	Ford Cosworth
WR5-6	10	11	20	-	-	-	78	H Postlethwaite	Ford Cosworth
WR7-9	14	14	-	-	-	-	79	H Postlethwaite	Ford Cosworth

Cars were not given separate model numbers and were known by chassis numbers. They are grouped here in their three distinct model variations.

ZAKSPEED (D)

Principal: Erich Zakowski. **Base:** Niederzissen, nr Koblenz. **Founded:** 1968.
Formed from a saloon car team from which Zakowski helped develop the Ford Capri and Escort, after taking over the factory team in 1976. In a bold move, this ambitious team built both chassis and turbo engine, with the car completed late in 1984. After no real results with either its own turbo or the Yamaha unit it introduced to Grands Prix, Zakowski returned to the German Touring Car series.

TOTALS	GPs	STARTS	POINTS	POLES	F.LAPS	WINS			
	54	85	2	-	-	-			
SEASONS							**SPONSOR(S)**	**MAIN DRIVER(S)**	
1985	10	10	-	-	-	-	West	Palmer	
1986	16	28	-	-	-	-	West	Palmer, Rothengatter	
1987	16	31	2	-	-	-	West	Brundle, Danner	
1988	10	14	-	-	-	-	West	Schneider, Ghinzani	
1989	2	2	-	-	-	-	West	Schneider, Suzuki	
MODELS							**YEAR(S)**	**CHIEF DESIGNER**	**ENGINE**
841	10	10	-	-	-	-	85	P Brown	4t
861	18	31	-	-	-	-	86-87	P Brown	4t
871	15	28	2	-	-	-	87	H Zollinir	4t
881	10	14	-	-	-	-	88	H Zollinir	4t
891	2	2	-	-	-	-	89	G Brunner	Yamaha

5

CIRCUIT HISTORY

COUNTRIES

ARGENTINA
AUSTRALIA
AUSTRIA
BELGIUM
BRAZIL
CANADA
FRANCE
GERMANY
GREAT BRITAIN
HUNGARY
ITALY
JAPAN
MEXICO
MONACO
MOROCCO
NETHERLANDS
PORTUGAL
SOUTH AFRICA
SPAIN
SWEDEN
SWITZERLAND
UNITED STATES OF AMERICA

The sketches in this chapter are intended as a guide to circuit layouts and appear as you would expect to find them on a map, with nearly all drawn vertically North. They are also to approximately the same scale, the exceptions being the old Nürburgring and Pescara, which due to their size, are half scale.

CIRCUITS

CIRCUITS

ADELAIDE
AIDA
AIN-DIAB
AINTREE
ANDERSTORP
AVUS
BRANDS HATCH
BREMGARTEN
BUENOS AIRES
BUGATTI AU MANS
CLERMONT-FERRAND
DALLAS
DETROIT
DIJON-PRENOIS
DONINGTON PARK
EAST LONDON
ESTORIL
FUJI
HOCKENHEIM
HUNGARORING
IMOLA
INDIANAPOLIS
INTERLAGOS
JARAMA
JEREZ de la FRONTERA
KYALAMI
LAS VEGAS
LONG BEACH
MAGNY-COURS
MELBOURNE
MEXICO CITY
MONSANTO PARK
MONT-TREMBLANT
MONTE CARLO
MONTJUICH PARK
MONTMELO
MONTRÉAL
MONZA
MOSPORT PARK
NIVELLES-BAULERS
NÜRBURGRING
ÖSTERREICHRING
PAUL RICARD
PEDRALBES
PESCARA
PHOENIX
PORTO
REIMS & REIMS-GUEUX
RIO de JANEIRO
RIVERSIDE
ROUEN-les-ESSARTS
SEBRING
SILVERSTONE
SPA-FRANCORCHAMPS
SUZUKA
WATKINS GLEN
ZANDVOORT
ZELTWEG
ZOLDER

Argentina (RA)

BUENOS AIRES

Location: Buenos Aires (outskirts). **First Used:** 1952.
Overseen by President Juan Domingo Peron and named El Autodromo 17 de Octobre (date of Peron's accession), the circuit included various permutations. A much faster extension was later added on swamp land around the lake, when the circuit was known as the Autodromo Almirante (Admiral) Brown. Further redevelopment in the 1990s and another new name, Autodromo Oscar Alfredo Gálvez, after the Argentinian driver, has seen the circuit emerge as a Championship venue once again. The lake extension has been lost to a power station, but the track now uses the existing infield and the new Senna 'S' section.

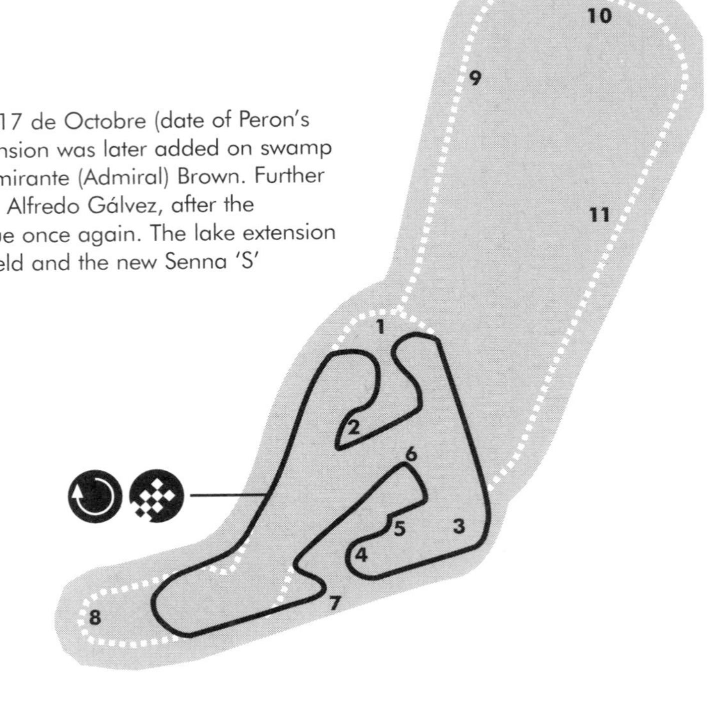

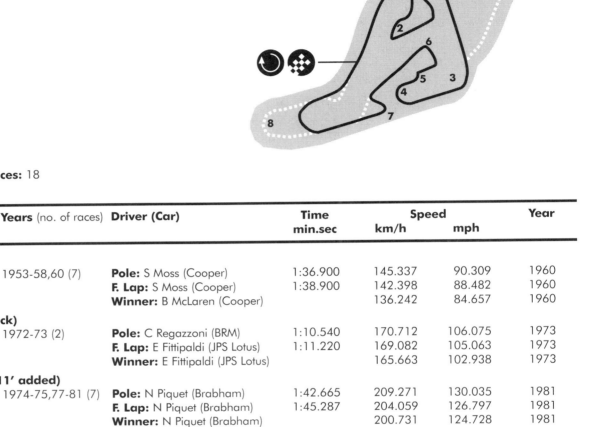

Key to the circuit:
1=Curva Numero Uno
2=Curva de la Confiteria
3=Curva de Ascari
4=Entrata a los Mixtos
5=Viborita
6=Curva del Ombú
7=Senna 'S'
8=Tobogán-Horquilla
9=Recta del Fondo
10=Curvón
11=Recta del Lago

World Championship races: 18

	Length km	miles	Years (no. of races)	Driver (Car)	Time min.sec	Speed km/h	mph	Year
No. 2								
a)	3.912	2.431	1953-58,60 (7)	**Pole:** S Moss (Cooper)	1:36.900	145.337	90.309	1960
				F. Lap: S Moss (Cooper)	1:38.900	142.398	88.482	1960
				Winner: B McLaren (Cooper)		136.242	84.657	1960
No. 9 (section '8' cut back)								
b)	3.345	2.078	1972-73 (2)	**Pole:** C Regazzoni (BRM)	1:10.540	170.712	106.075	1973
				F. Lap: E Fittipaldi (JPS Lotus)	1:11.220	169.082	105.063	1973
				Winner: E Fittipaldi (JPS Lotus)		165.663	102.938	1973
No. 15 (sections '9' to '11' added)								
c)	5.968	3.708	1974-75,77-81 (7)	**Pole:** N Piquet (Brabham)	1:42.665	209.271	130.035	1981
				F. Lap: N Piquet (Brabham)	1:45.287	204.059	126.797	1981
				Winner: N Piquet (Brabham)		200.731	124.728	1981
No. 6 (existing infield section added)								
c)	4.259	2.646	1995-96 (2)	**Pole:** D Hill (Williams)	1:30.346	169.708	105.451	1996
				F. Lap: J Alesi (Benetton)	1:29.413	171.478	106.552	1996
				Winner: D Hill (Williams)		162.385	100.902	1995

Australia (AUS)

ADELAIDE

Location: Adelaide (city centre), South Australia. **First Used:** 1985.
One of the best street circuits and a firm favourite with the Grand Prix fraternity. The wide track works its way around the city parkland and even includes part of the Victoria Park racecourse. The main straight is unusually long for a street circuit and is often remembered for the spectacular blow-out suffered by Mansell in the 1986 title decider. There were many sad faces in the Formula 1 world when the venue was switched to Melbourne.

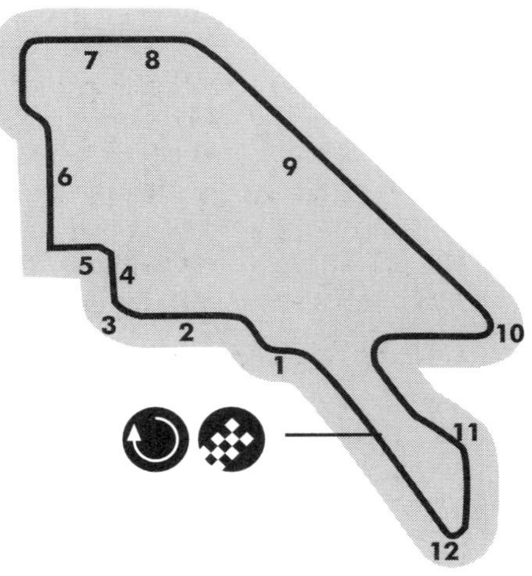

Key to the circuit:
1=Senna Chicane *(named from 1994)*
2=Wakefield Road
3=Wakefield Corner
4=East Terrace
5=Flinders Street
6=Hutt Street
7=Rundle Road/ Jones Straight
8=Malthouse Corner
9=Dequetteville Terrace/ Brabham Straight
10=Roundabout/ Dequetteville Hairpin
11=Race Course
12=Foster's Corner/ Adelaide Hairpin

World Championship races: 11

	Length km	miles	Years (no. of races)	Driver (Car)	Time min:sec	Speed km/h	mph	Year
a)	3.778	2.348	1985 (1)					
b)	3.779	2.348	1986 (1)					
c)	3.780	2.349	1987-96 (9)	**Pole:** A Senna (McLaren)	1:13.371	185.468	115.245	1993
				F. Lap: D Hill (Williams)	1:15.381	180.523	112.172	1993
				Winner: A Senna (McLaren)		173.183	107.611	1993

MELBOURNE

Location: Melbourne (Albert Park, city centre), Victoria. **First Used:** 1953.
Albert Park was used for the non-championship Australian Grand Prix as early as 1953 and GP racing has now returned to the sporting capital of Australia. The circuit is remarkably unchanged, still weaving around the park lake, although now in a clock-wise direction with the old circuit running along the back of the pit area.

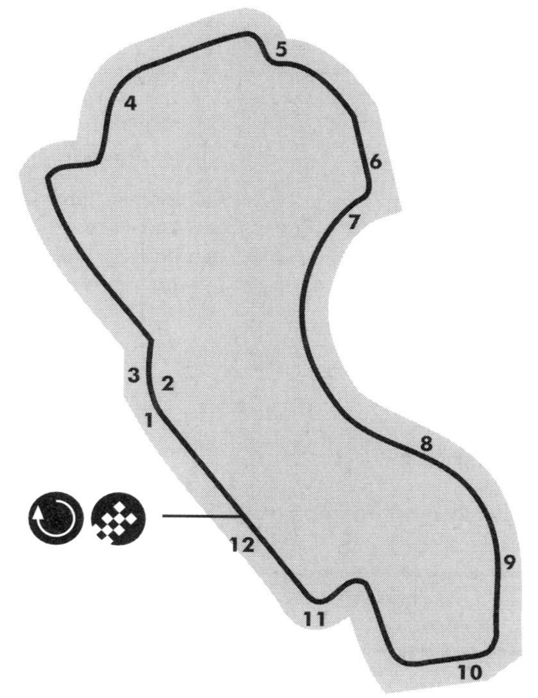

Key to the circuit:

1= Fangio Stand
2= Brabham Stand
3= Jones Stand
4= Whitford Stand
5= Lauda Stand
6= Clark Stand
7= Fittipaldi Stand
8= Waite Stand
9= Hill Stand
10= Stewart Stand
11= Prost Stand
12= Senna Stand

Key refers to names of spectator stands only

World Championship races: 1

	Length km	miles	Years (no. of races)	Driver (Car)	Time min:sec	Speed km/h	mph	Year
a)	5.302	2.349	1996 (1)	**Pole:** J Villeneuve (Williams)	1:32.371	206.636	128.398	1996
				F. Lap: J Villeneuve (Williams)	1:33.421	204.314	126.955	1996
				Winner: D Hill (Williams)		198.736	123.489	1996

Austria (A)

ÖSTERREICHRING

Location: 6 km (4 miles) west of Knittelfeld. **First Used:** 1969.
Built as a replacement for Zeltweg in the wooded Styrian hills, above the airfield circuit. Renowned for its beauty, the track rises and falls in a natural hillside bowl. A chicane was added where Mark Donohue was killed and problems with the narrow startline and deer wandering onto the track, led to its eventual disuse. A shortened and much modified version, now renamed the A-1 Ring, has been included as a provisional new Grand Prix venue for 1997.

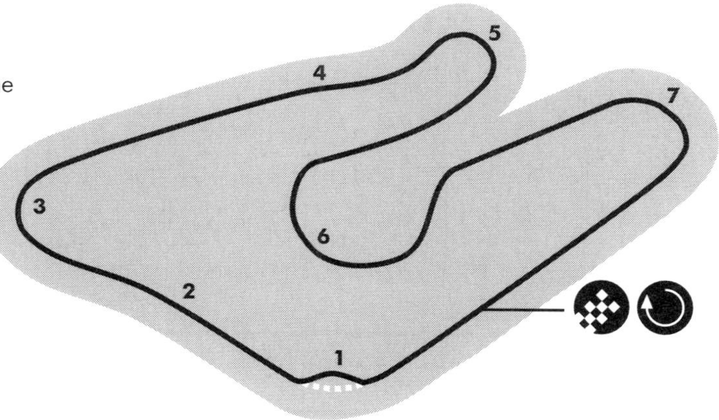

Key to the circuit:

1=Vöest-Hügel/ Hella-Licht 'S'/ Niki-Schikane
2=Flatschach
3=Sebring-Auspuffkurve/ Dr. Tiroch-Kurve/Glatz-Kurve
4=Valvoline-Gerade
5=Bosch-Kurve/ Krainer-Kurve
6=Texaco-Schikane/ Panorama-Kurve
7=Jochen-Rindt-Kurve

World Championship races: 18

	Length km	miles	Years (no. of races)	Driver (Car)	Time min:sec	Speed km/h	mph	Year
a)	5.911	3.673	1970-75 (6)	**Pole:** N Lauda (Ferrari)	1:34.850	224.350	139.405	1975
				F. Lap: C Regazzoni (Ferrari)	1:37.220	218.881	136.006	1974
				Winner: C Reutemann (Brabham)		215.804	134.095	1974
First corner eased								
b)	5.910	3.672	1976 (1)	**Pole:** J Hunt (McLaren)	1:35.020	223.911	139.132	1976
				F. Lap: J Hunt (McLaren)	1:35.910	221.833	137.841	1976
				Winner: J Watson (Penske)		212.451	132.011	1976
Hella-Licht 'S'								
c)	5.942	3.692	1977-87 (11)	**Pole:** N Piquet (Williams)	1:23.357	256.622	159.457	1987
				F. Lap: N Mansell (Williams)	1:28.318	242.207	150.500	1987
				Winner: N Mansell (Williams)		235.421	146.284	1987

ZELTWEG

Location: 6 km (4 miles) west of Knittelfeld. **First Used:** 1958.
A simple circuit, laid out along runways of a military airfield north of Graz. Situated in the River Mur valley, its bumpy surface meant that the track was redundant as soon as the new 'Zeltweg' appeared.

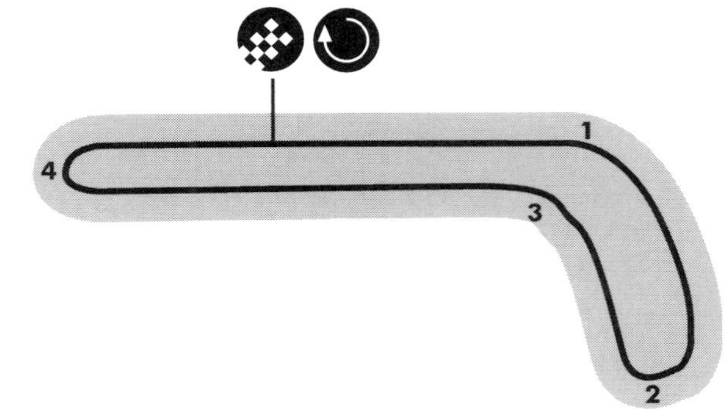

Key to the circuit:
1=Flatschacher-Kurve
2=Hangar-Kurve
3=Inner-Kurve
4=Südenburg-Kurve

World Championship races: 1

	Length km	miles	Years (no. of races)	Driver (Car)	Time min:sec	Speed km/h	mph	Year
a)	3.200	1.988	1964 (1)	**Pole:** G Hill (BRM)	1: 9.840	164.948	102.494	1964
				F. Lap: D Gurney (Brabham)	1:10.560	163.265	101.448	1964
				Winner: L Bandini (Ferrari)		159.615	99.180	1964

Belgium (B)

NIVELLES-BAULERS

Location: 30 km (20 miles) south of Brussels. **First Used:** 1971.
This flat and unpopular purpose-built circuit came into Grand Prix use after the loss of Spa and suffered by comparison. A typical modern facility, it had good safety provisions and was extended to full Grand Prix length in 1972.

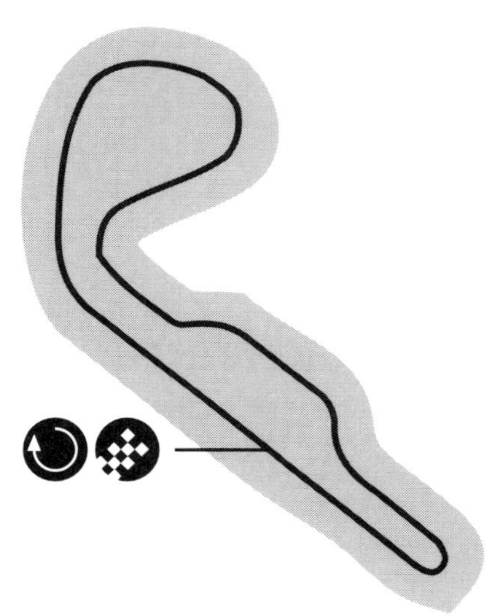

Key to the circuit:
Corners were not named

World Championship races: 2

	Length km	miles	Years (no. of races)	Driver (Car)	Time min:sec	Speed km/h	mph	Year
a)	3.724	2.314	1972,74 (2)	**Pole:** C Regazzoni (Ferrari)	1: 9.820	192.014	119.312	1974
				F. Lap: D Hulme (McLaren)	1:11.310	188.002	116.819	1974
				Winner: E Fittipaldi (JPS Lotus)		182.423	113.353	1972

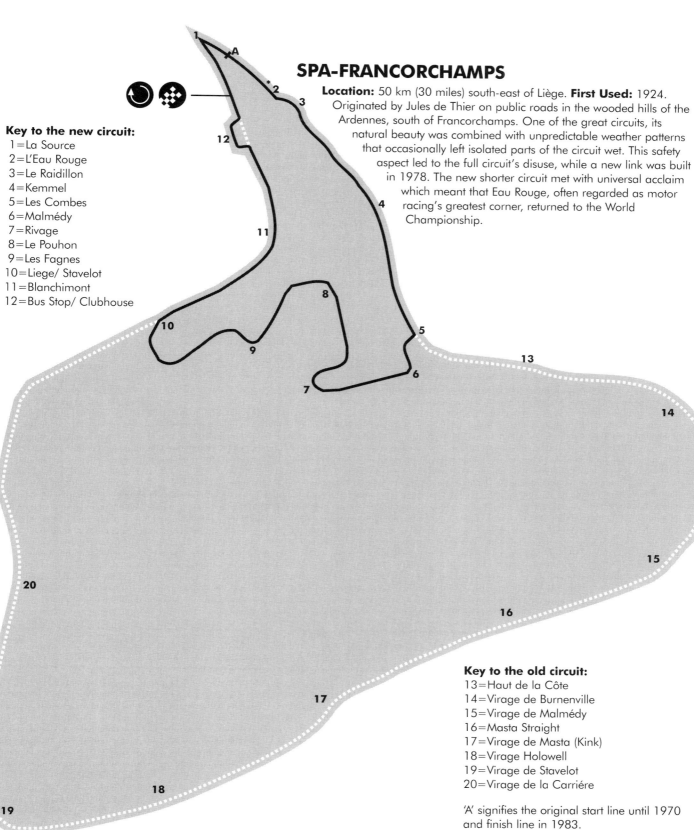

SPA-FRANCORCHAMPS

Location: 50 km (30 miles) south-east of Liège. **First Used:** 1924. Originated by Jules de Thier on public roads in the wooded hills of the Ardennes, south of Francorchamps. One of the great circuits, its natural beauty was combined with unpredictable weather patterns that occasionally left isolated parts of the circuit wet. This safety aspect led to the full circuit's disuse, while a new link was built in 1978. The new shorter circuit met with universal acclaim which meant that Eau Rouge, often regarded as motor racing's greatest corner, returned to the World Championship.

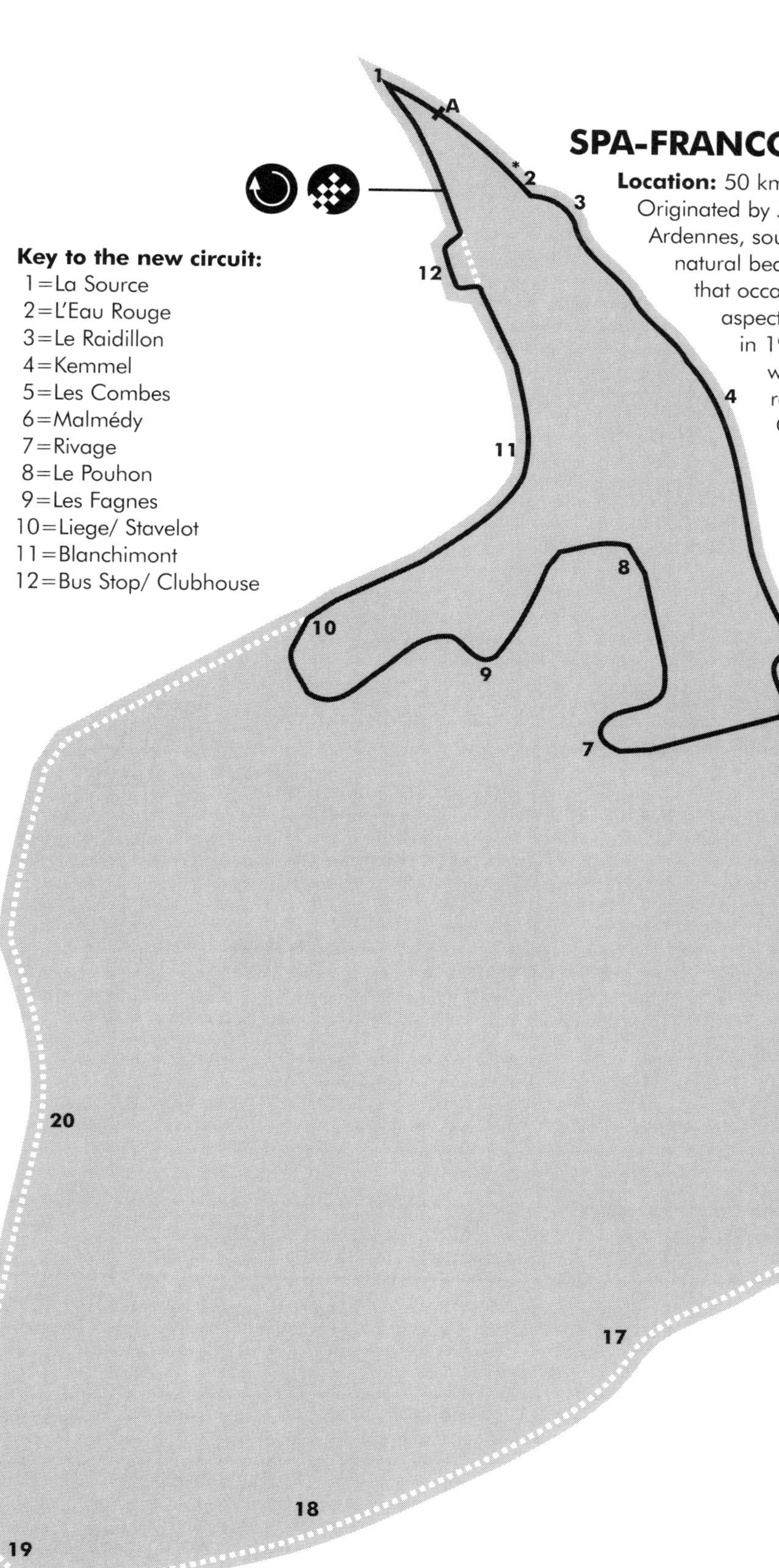

Key to the new circuit:
1=La Source
2=L'Eau Rouge
3=Le Raidillon
4=Kemmel
5=Les Combes
6=Malmédy
7=Rivage
8=Le Pouhon
9=Les Fagnes
10=Liege/ Stavelot
11=Blanchimont
12=Bus Stop/ Clubhouse

Key to the old circuit:
13=Haut de la Côte
14=Virage de Burnenville
15=Virage de Malmédy
16=Masta Straight
17=Virage de Masta (Kink)
18=Virage Holowell
19=Virage de Stavelot
20=Virage de la Carriére

'A' signifies the original start line until 1970 and finish line in 1983.

* chicane in 1994

World Championship races: 31

	Length km	miles	**Years** (no. of races)	**Driver (Car)**	**Time** min:sec	**Speed** km/h	mph	**Year**
a)	14.120	8.774	1950-56 (7)	**Pole:** J M Fangio (Lancia Ferrari)	4: 9.800	203.491	126.443	1956
				F. Lap: S Moss (Maserati)	4:14.700	199.576	124.011	1956
				Winner: J M Fangio (Mercedes-Benz)		191.238	118.829	1955
Corners eased								
b)	14.100	8.761	1958,60-68,70 (11)	**Pole:** J Stewart (March)	3:28.000	244.038	151.638	1970
				F. Lap: C Amon (March)	3:27.400	244.744	152.077	1970
				Winner: P Rodriguez (BRM)		241.308	149.942	1970
Shorter circuit								
c)	6.949	4.318	1983 (1)	**Pole:** A Prost (Renault)	2:4.615	200.750	124.740	1983
				F. Lap: A de Cesaris (Alfa Romeo)	2:7.493	196.218	121.924	1983
				Winner: A Prost (Renault)		191.729	119.135	1983

	km	miles	Years (no. of races)	Driver (Car)	Time min:sec	km/h	mph	Year
(Circuit length recalculated)								
d)	6.940	4.312	1985-91 (7)	**Pole:** A Senna (McLaren)	1:47.811	231.739	143.996	1991
				F. Lap: A Prost (Ferrari)	1:55.087	217.088	134.892	1990
				Winner: A Senna (McLaren)		211.729	131.562	1990
e)	6.974	4.333	1992-93,95 (3)	**Pole:** A Prost (Williams)	1:47.571	233.394	145.024	1993
				F. Lap: A Prost (Williams)	1:51.095	225.990	140.424	1993
				Winner: D Hill (Williams)		217.795	135.331	1993
Eau Rouge diverted								
f)	7.001	4.350	1994 (1)	**Pole:** R Barrichello (Jordan)	2:21.163	178.543	110.941	1994
				F. Lap: D Hill (Williams)	1:57.117	215.200	133.719	1994
				Winner: D Hill (Williams)		208.170	129.351	1994
La Source eased								
g)	6.968	4.330	1996 (1)	**Pole:** J Villeneuve (Williams)	1:50.574	226.860	140.964	1996
				F. Lap: G Berger (Benetton)	1:53.067	221.858	137.856	1996
				Winner: M Schumacher (Ferrari)		208.443	129.520	1996

ZOLDER

Location: 10 km (6 miles) north of Hasselt. **First Used:** 1965.
Another of the purpose-built circuits of the time, Zolder was situated in sandy woodland hills of Flemish speaking Belgium. As a circuit, it came to be infested with numerous chicanes and is sadly associated with the fatal accident of Gilles Villeneuve at the approach to Terlamenbocht. A memorial to this popular driver can be found near the pit entrance.

Key to the circuit:
1=Eerste Linkse
2=Sterrewachtbocht
3=Kanaalbocht
4=Lucien Bianchibocht
5=Kleine Chicane
6=Butte
7=Terlamenbocht
8=Bolderberghaarspeldbocht
9=Jochen Rindtbocht
10=Jacky Ickxbocht

World Championship races: 10

	Length km	miles	Years (no. of races)	Driver (Car)	Time min:sec	Speed km/h	mph	Year
a)	4.220	2.622	1973 (1)	**Pole:** R Peterson (JPS Lotus)	1:22.460	184.235	114.478	1973
				F. Lap: F Cevert (Tyrrell)	1:25.420	177.851	110.511	1973
				Winner: J Stewart (Tyrrell)		173.384	107.736	1973
New chicane at '10'								
b)	4.262	2.648	1975-82,84 (9)	**Pole:** M Alboreto (Ferrari)	1:14.846	204.997	127.379	1984
				F. Lap: R Arnoux (Ferrari)	1:19.294	193.498	120.234	1984
				Winner: J Watson (McLaren)		187.047	116.226	1982

Brazil (BR)

INTERLAGOS

Location: Sao Paulo suburb, 16 km (10 miles) south of city centre. **First Used:** 1940.
The Autodromo José Carlos Pace was built in a natural bowl that has gradually been absorbed by this sprawling city. The original track twisted around itself between two lakes, giving the circuit its name. A new shorter version, missed out much of the old track, but maintained the steep startline straight.

Key to the circuit:
1=Curva 1
2=Curva 2
3=Retao
4=Curva 3
5=Junçáo
6=Curva da Ferradura
7=Subida do Lago/ Descida do Lago
8=Reta Oposta
9=Curva do Sol
10=Curva do Sargento
11=Estacionamento
12=Curva do Laranja
13=Curva do Pinheirinho
14=Curva do Cotovêlo/ Bico de Pato
15=Mergulho
16=Curva 4/ Junçáo
17=Subida
18=Arquibancadas
19='S' do Senna

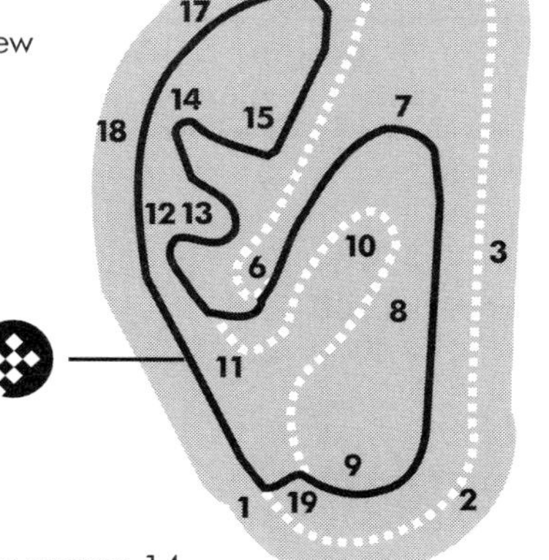

World Championship races: 14

	Length km	miles	Years (no. of races)	Driver (Car)	Time min:sec	Speed km/h	mph	Year
a)	7.960	4.946	1973-77 (5)	**Pole:** J-P Jarier (Shadow)	2:29.880	191.193	118.802	1975
				F. Lap: J-P Jarier (Shadow)	2:34.160	185.885	115.503	1975
				Winner: E Fittipaldi (JPS Lotus)		183.822	114.222	1973
Corners eased								
b)	7.874	4.893	1979-80 (2)	**Pole:** J-P Jabouille (Renault)	2:21.400	200.470	124.566	1980
				F. Lap: R Arnoux (Renault)	2:27.310	192.427	119.569	1980
				Winner: R Arnoux (Renault)		188.934	117.398	1980
Shortened								
c)	4.325	2.687	1990-96 (7)	**Pole:** N Mansell (Williams)	1:15.703	205.672	127.799	1992
				F. Lap: M Schumacher (Benetton)	1:18.455	198.458	123.316	1994
				Winner: M Schumacher (Benetton)		192.632	119.696	1994

RIO de JANEIRO

Location: 30 km (19 miles) south-west of Rio de Janeiro city centre. **First Used:** 1978.
The Jacarepagua circuit was built in the late 1970s, on reclaimed marshland near the sea. The Autodromo International do Rio has a flat, but bumpy surface and rests in a backdrop of impressive mountains. Often used in winter testing, it was renamed in honour of Nelson Piquet in 1988.

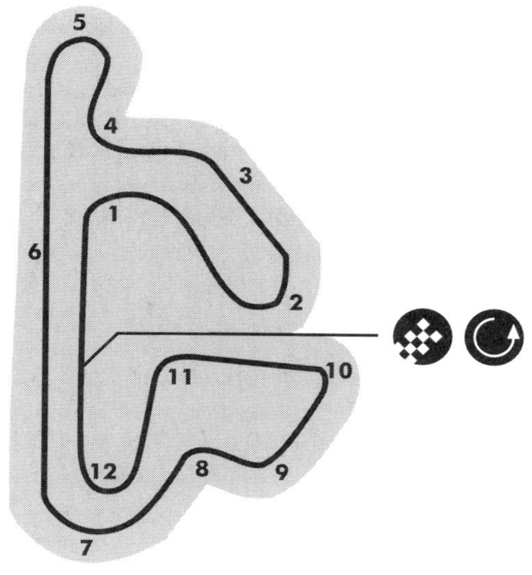

Key to the circuit:
1=Molykote
2=Carlos Pace
3=Kartodromo
4=Nonato
5=Norte
6=Juncao
7=Sul
8=Girao
9=Morette
10=Lagoa
11=Box
12=Vitoria

World Championship races: 10

	Length km	miles	Years (no. of races)	Driver (Car)	Time min:sec	Speed km/h	mph	Year
a)	5.031	3.126	1978,81-89 (10)	**Pole:** A Senna (McLaren)	1:25.302	212.323	131.932	1989
				F. Lap: R Patrese (Williams)	1:32.507	195.786	121.656	1989
				Winner: A Prost (McLaren)		188.438	117.090	1988

Canada (CDN)

MONT-TREMBLANT

Location: 145 km (90 miles) north of Montréal, Québec. **First Used:** 1964.
Mont-Tremblant or St.-Jovite is situated in the scenic woodland of the Laurentian Mountains. The short circuit was lengthened to Grand Prix standards in 1966 but was regarded as too narrow and bumpy for regular use.

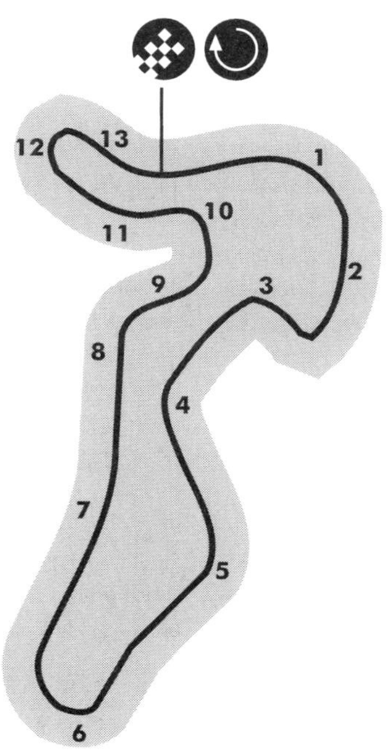

Key to the circuit:
1=Conner Corner
2=Le Diable
3=The Esses
4=Corner 6
5=Corner 7
6=Corner 8
7=Hump
8=Corner 10
9=The Gulch
10=Bridge Turn
11=Kink
12=Namerow Corner
13=Paddock Bend

World Championship races: 2

	Length km	miles	Years (no. of races)	Driver (Car)	Time min:sec	Speed km/h	mph	Year
a)	4.265	2.650	1968,70 (2)	**Pole:** J Stewart (Tyrrell)	1:31.500	167.794	104.262	1970
				F. Lap: C Regazzoni (Ferrari)	1:32.200	166.520	103.471	1970
				Winner: J Ickx (Ferrari)		162.977	101.269	1970

MONTRÉAL

Location: Montréal (east of city centre), Québec. **First Used:** 1978.
Now named after the late Gilles Villeneuve, the Ile Notre Dame circuit is built on a man-made island in the St. Lawrence Seaway. Its tight and narrow track is laid out among lakes and parkland pavilions, used in the Expo 67 exhibition. The pits were relocated along with other changes, after the race was cancelled in 1987, due to a sponsorship dispute between beer giants Labatt's and Molson.

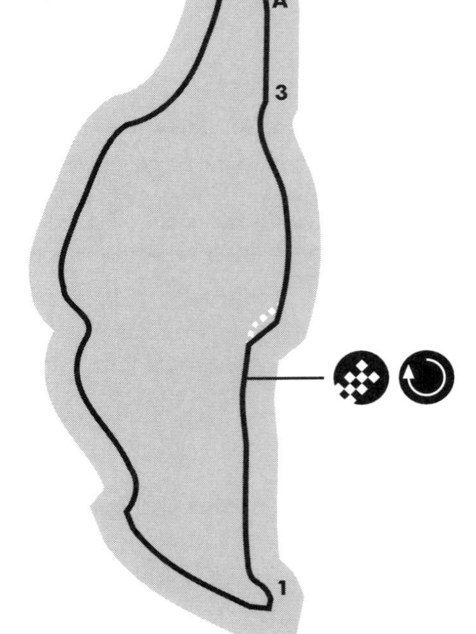

Key to the circuit:
Corners are simply known numerically (turns 1 to 13), apart from:
1=Island Hairpin/ Épingle de L'ile/ Virage Senna
2=Pits Hairpin/ Épingle des Stands
3=Casino Corner/ Virage du Casino

'A' signifies the original startline until 1986.

World Championship races: 18

	Length km	miles	Years (no. of races)	Driver (Car)	Time min:sec	Speed km/h	mph	Year
a)	4.500	2.796	1978 (1)	**Pole:** J-P Jarier (JPS Lotus)	1:38.015	165.281	102.701	1978
				F. Lap: A Jones (Williams)	1:38.072	165.185	102.641	1978
				Winner: G Villeneuve (Ferrari)		160.414	99.677	1978
Corners eased								
b)	4.410	2.740	1979-86 (8)	**Pole:** N Mansell (Williams)	1:24.118	188.735	117.274	1986
				F. Lap: N Piquet (Williams)	1:25.443	185.808	115.456	1986
				Winner: N Mansell (Williams)		178.225	110.744	1986
Pits/corner change								
c)	4.390	2.728	1988-90 (3)	**Pole:** A Senna (McLaren)	1:20.399	196.570	122.143	1990
				F. Lap: G Berger (McLaren)	1:22.077	192.551	119.646	1990
				Winner: A Senna (McLaren)		182.152	113.184	1988
New corner before pits								
d)	4.430	2.753	1991-93 (3)	**Pole:** A Prost (Williams)	1:18.987	201.907	125.459	1993
				F. Lap: M Schumacher (Benetton)	1:21.500	195.681	121.591	1993
				Winner: A Prost (Williams)		189.667	117.853	1993
Chicane (after old pits)(at '3')								
e)	4.450	2.765	1994 (1)	**Pole:** M Schumacher (Benetton)	1:26.178	185.894	115.509	1994
				F. Lap: M Schumacher (Benetton)	1:28.927	180.148	111.939	1994
				Winner: M Schumacher (Benetton)		176.244	109.513	1994
f)	4.430	2.753	1995 (1)	**Pole:** M Schumacher (Benetton)	1:27.661	181.928	113.045	1995
				F. Lap: M Schumacher (Benetton)	1:29.174	178.841	111.127	1995
				Winner: J Alesi (Ferrari)		172.297	107.060	1995
g)	4.421	2.747	1996 (1)	**Pole:** D Hill (Williams)	1:21.059	196.346	122.004	1996
				F. Lap: J Villeneuve (Williams)	1:21.916	194.292	120.727	1996
				Winner: D Hill (Williams)		190.541	118.397	1996

MOSPORT PARK

Location: 100 km (60 miles) north-east of Toronto, Ontario. **First Used:** 1961.
Mosport Park is located in wooded hills, close to Lake Ontario. Characterised by sweeping bends, it is regarded as too dangerous for modern Grand Prix cars. Manfred Winkelhock was killed at turn two (sports cars) and serious accidents have befallen John Surtees (Can-Am) and Ian Ashley (GP practice).

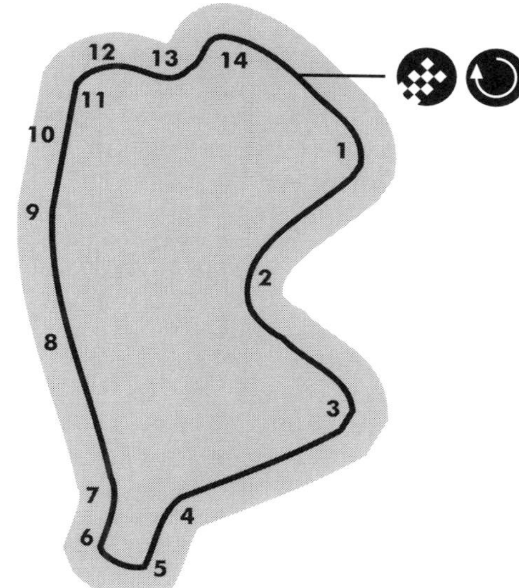

Key to the circuit:
1=Corner One
2=Corner Two
3=Three
4=Four
5=Five A
6=Five B/ Moss
7=Five C
8=Six
9=Seven
10=Mario Andretti Straightaway
11=Eight
12=The Esses
13=Nine
14=Whites Corner/ Corner Ten

World Championship races: 8

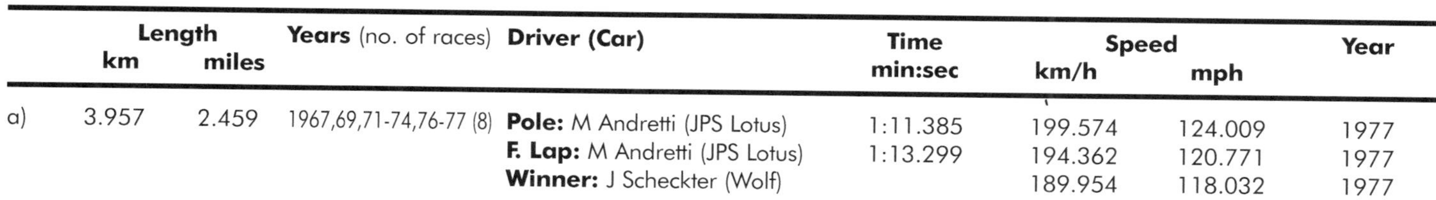

	Length km	Length miles	**Years** (no. of races)	**Driver (Car)**	Time min:sec	Speed km/h	Speed mph	Year
a)	3.957	2.459	1967,69,71-74,76-77 (8)	**Pole:** M Andretti (JPS Lotus)	1:11.385	199.574	124.009	1977
				F. Lap: M Andretti (JPS Lotus)	1:13.299	194.362	120.771	1977
				Winner: J Scheckter (Wolf)		189.954	118.032	1977

France (F)

BUGATTI AU MANS

Location: Le Mans. **First Used:** 1966.
There has been motor racing around Le Mans since the first Grand Prix in 1906, and the famous Sarthe circuit has been used for the 24-hour race since 1923. The Bugatti track incorporated part of the Le Mans start-finish straight, before turning infield and weaving through the car parking area. This twisty circuit didn't prove to be popular with drivers or spectators and was used just once in the World Championship.

Key to the circuit:
1=Courbe Dunlop
2=Virage de la Chapelle
3=Virage du Le Musée
4=Virage du Garage Vert
5=Chemin aux Boeufs
6=les 'S' du Garage Bleu
7=Virage du Raccordement

World Championship races: 1

	Length km	Length miles	**Years** (no. of races)	**Driver (Car)**	Time min:sec	Speed km/h	Speed mph	Year
a)	4.422	2.748	1967 (1)	**Pole:** G Hill (Lotus)	1:36.200	165.480	102.825	1967
				F. Lap: G Hill (Lotus)	1:36.700	164.625	102.293	1967
				Winner: J Brabham (Brabham)		159.166	98.901	1967

F

CLERMONT-FERRAND

Location: 10 km (6 miles) south-west of Clermont-Ferrand, Montagne d'Auvergne.
First Used: 1958.

Otherwise known as the Louis Rosier circuit or Charade, this mini Nürburgring was situated south-west of the town itself. In planning for many years and eventually built around volcanic plugs in this mountainous region, it was developed from public roads and was notorious for its up and down layout. The circuit finally closed in 1988.

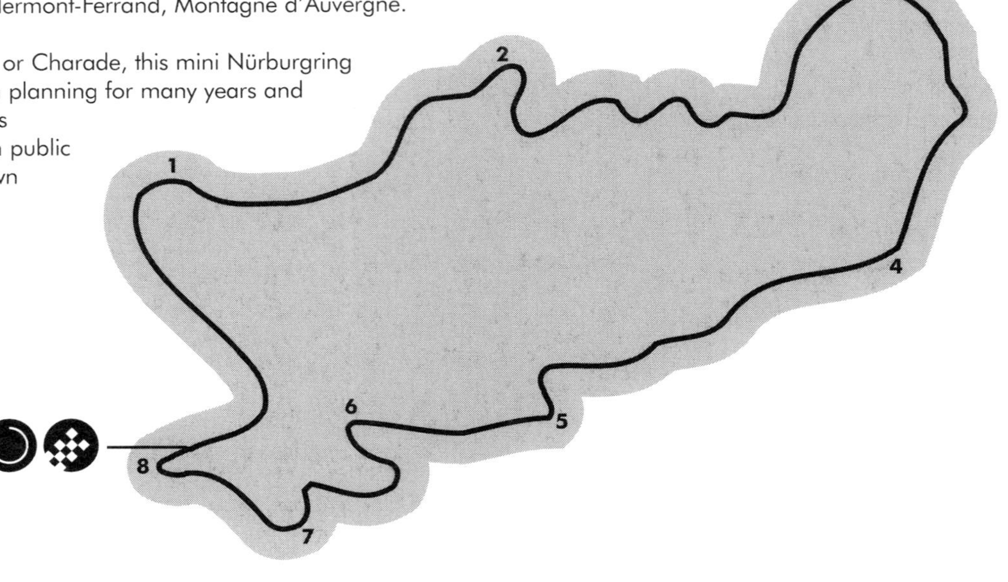

Key to the circuit:
1=Charade
2=Le Belvedere
3=Carrefour de Gravenoire
4=La Carrière
5=Carrefour de Champeaux
6=Terte de Charade
7=Terte de Thedes
8=Virage Rosier

World Championship races: 4

	Length km	miles	**Years** (no. of races)	**Driver (Car)**	**Time** min:sec	**Speed** km/h	mph	**Year**
a)	8.055	5.005	1965,69-70,72 (4)	**Pole:** C Amon (Matra Simca)	2:53.400	167.232	103.913	1972
				F. Lap: C Amon (Matra Simca)	2:53.900	166.751	103.614	1972
				Winner: J Stewart (Tyrrell)		163.454	101.566	1972

DIJON-PRENOIS

Location: 15 km (9 miles) north-west of Dijon. **First Used:** 1972.

Situated deep in the Burgundy region and built in the early 70s, it suffered from being too short. This was overcome with the addition of the Parabolique loop in 1976. This undulating track proved popular with the infield spectators, but never more so than in 1979, when they witnessed the first turbo win and the dramatic Arnoux-Villeneuve fight for second place.

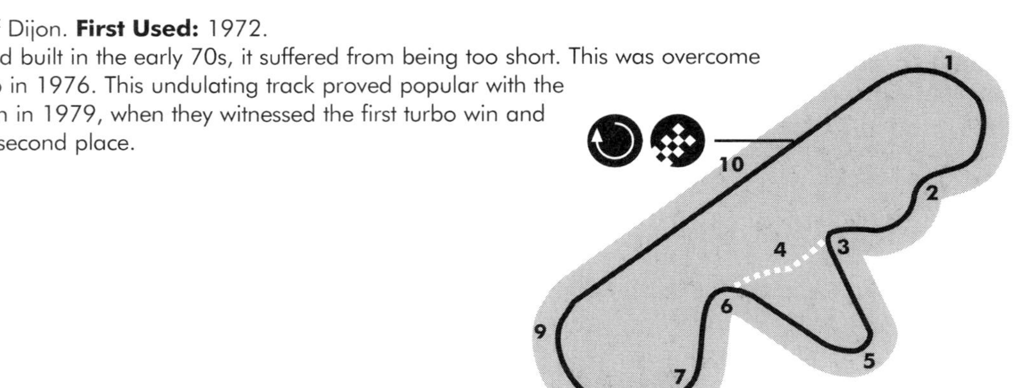

Key to the circuit:
1=Double-Droite de Villeroy
2='S' des Sablières
3=Gauche de la Bretelle
4='S' de la Bretelle
5=Parabolique
6=Double-Gauche de la Bretelle
7=Courbe des Gorgeolles
8=Virage de la Combe
9=Courbe de Pouas
10=Ligne Droite de la Fouine

World Championship races: 6 (including Swiss Grand Prix in 1982)

	Length km	miles	**Years** (no. of races)	**Driver (Car)**	**Time** min:sec	**Speed** km/h	mph	**Year**
a)	3.289	2.044	1974 (1)	**Pole:** N Lauda (Ferrari)	0:58.790	201.402	125.145	1974
				F. Lap: J Scheckter (Tyrrell)	1: 0.000	197.340	122.621	1974
				Winner: R Peterson (JPS Lotus)		192.722	119.752	1974
Parabolique								
b)	3.800	2.361	1977,79,81-82 (4)	**Pole:** A Prost (Renault)	1: 1.380	222.874	138.487	1982
				F. Lap: A Prost (Renault)	1: 7.477	202.736	125.974	1982
				Winner: K Rosberg (Williams)		196.796	122.283	1982
c)	3.887	2.415	1984 (1)	**Pole:** P Tambay (Renault)	1: 2.200	224.971	139.791	1984
				F. Lap: A Prost (McLaren)	1: 5.257	214.432	133.242	1984
				Winner: N Lauda (McLaren)		202.024	125.532	1984

MAGNY-COURS

Location: 12 km (7 miles) south of Nevers. **First Used:** 1961.
The circuit de Nevers Magny-Cours was recently redeveloped and has one of the flattest and smoothest surfaces in the business. It is the home of the Knight brothers' Winfield racing school and Ligier later moved its factory to the circuit. Its compact layout makes for good viewing, but access is very poor, being served by only one major road.

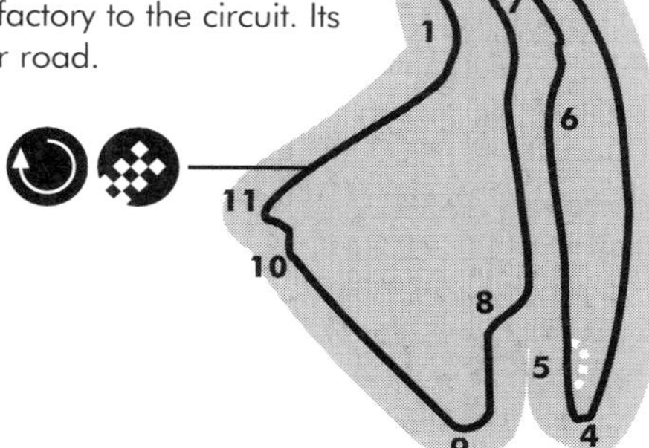

Key to the circuit:

1=Grande Courbe
2=Estoril
3=Golf
4=Adelaide
5=Esse
6=Nürburgring
7=180°
8=Imola
9=Châteaux d'Eau
10=Chicane
11=Lycée

World Championship races: 6

	Length km	miles	**Years** (no. of races)	**Driver (Car)**	**Time** min:sec	**Speed** km/h	mph	**Year**
a)	4.271	2.654	1991 (1)	**Pole:** R Patrese (Williams)	1:14.559	206.221	128.140	1991
				F. Lap: N Mansell (Williams)	1:19.168	194.215	120.680	1991
				Winner: N Mansell (Williams)		188.271	116.986	1991
Straightening at 'Esse'								
b)	4.250	2.641	1992-96 (5)	**Pole:** N Mansell (Williams)	1:13.864	207.137	128.709	1992
				F. Lap: N Mansell (Williams)	1:17.070	198.521	123.355	1992
				Winner: D Hill (Williams)		190.183	118.174	1996

PAUL RICARD

Location: Le Castellet, 34 km (21 miles) east of Marseille. **First Used:** 1970.
Inspired and financed by drinks magnate Paul Ricard, this modern complex had a combination of various circuits. Built on a windy plateau and containing the long Mistral Straight, it was radically shortened after Elio de Angelis' testing accident at the ess bend after the pits in 1986. Nowadays, a favourite circuit for winter testing. It still has ambitions to reclaim a part in the World Championship.

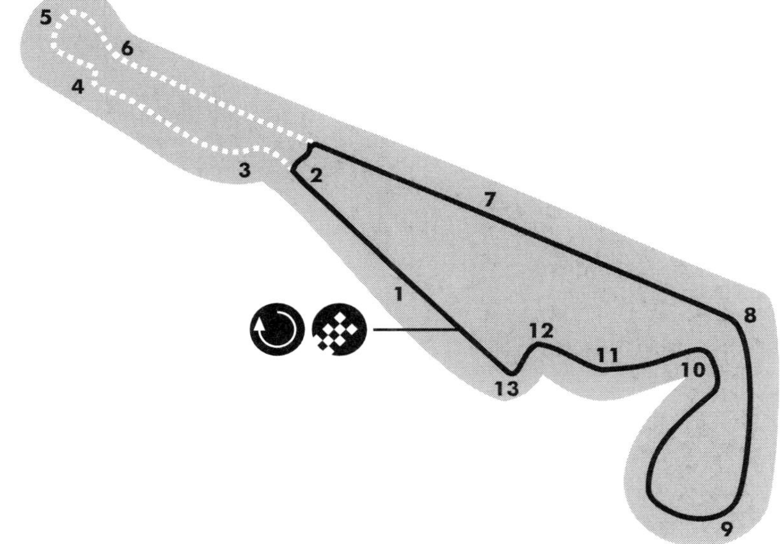

Key to the circuit:

1=La Bretelle
2=S de l'école
3=S de la Verriere
4=La Chicane
5=Virage de la Sainte-Beaume
6=Virage de l'école
7=Ligne droite du Mistral
8=Courbe de Signes
9=Double Droite du Beausset
10=L'Épingle de Bendor
11=S de Bendor/ S du Village
12=Virage de la Tour
13=Virage du Pont

World Championship races: 14

	Length km	miles	**Years** (no. of races)	**Driver (Car)**	**Time** min:sec	**Speed** km/h	mph	**Year**
a)	5.810	3.610	1971,73,75-76,78,80,	**Pole:** K Rosberg (Williams)	1:32.462	226.212	140.562	1985
			82-83,85 (9)	**F. Lap:** K Rosberg (Williams)	1:39.914	209.340	130.078	1985
				Winner: A Jones (Williams)		203.016	126.148	1980
Shortened circuit								
b)	3.813	2.369	1986-90 (5)	**Pole:** N Mansell (Ferrari)	1: 4.402	213.142	132.441	1990
				F. Lap: N Mansell (Ferrari)	1: 8.012	201.829	125.411	1990
				Winner: A Prost (Ferrari)		195.761	121.640	1990

REIMS & REIMS-GUEUX

Location: 7 km (4 miles) west of Reims. **First Used:** 1925.
A real classic circuit, using public roads around the fields of this Champagne region. Originally called Reims-Gueux, after the village that the cars passed through. This was diverted for safety reasons, but Luigi Musso was killed on the sweeping bend that replaced it. Closed in 1970, but not forgotten, as the old pits complex can still been seen at the roadside.

Key to the circuit:
1=Gueux
2=Virage de la Garenne
3=Route Nationale 31
4=Virage de Thillois
5=Bretelle Sud
6=Bretelle Nord
7=Virage de la Hovette
8=Muizon

World Championship races: 11

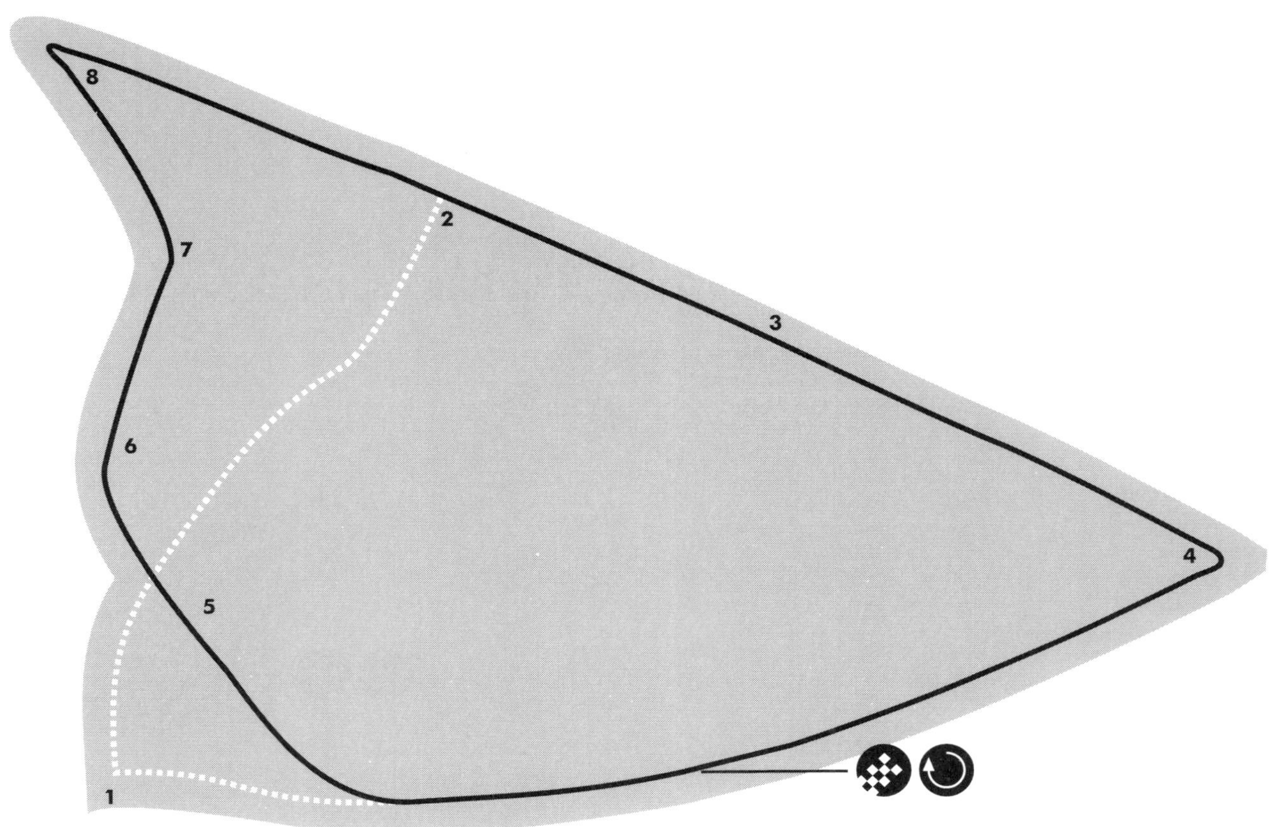

	Length km	miles	Years (no. of races)	Driver (Car)	Time min:sec	Speed km/h	mph	Year
a)	7.816	4.857	1950-51 (2)	**Pole:** J M Fangio (Alfa Romeo)	2:25.700	193.120	119.999	1951
				F. Lap: J M Fangio (Alfa Romeo)	2:27.800	190.376	118.294	1951
				Winner: L Fagioli/ J M Fangio (Alfa Romeo)		178.600	110.977	1951
Gueux by-pass								
b)	8.347	5.187	1953 (1)	**Pole:** A Ascari (Ferrari)	2:41.200	186.409	115.829	1953
				F. Lap: J M Fangio (Maserati)/ A Ascari (Ferrari)	2:41.100	186.525	115.901	1953
				Winner: M Hawthorn (Ferrari)		182.881	113.637	1953
Thillois eased								
c)	8.302	5.159	1954,56,58-61,63,66 (8)	**Pole:** L Bandini (Ferrari)	2:07.800	233.859	145.313	1966
				F. Lap: L Bandini (Ferrari)	2:11.300	227.625	141.440	1966
				Winner: J Brabham (Brabham)		220.322	136.902	1966

ROUEN-les-ESSARTS

Location: 12 km (7 miles) south-west of Rouen. **First Used:** 1950. Situated in the wooded valley of les-Essarts, it utilises public roads that wind downhill to the hairpin, a favourite viewing place. The circuit was extended in 1955, but has since been interrupted by a new motorway. No longer in use, it is sadly remembered for Jo Schlesser's fiery crash on the daunting downhill section.

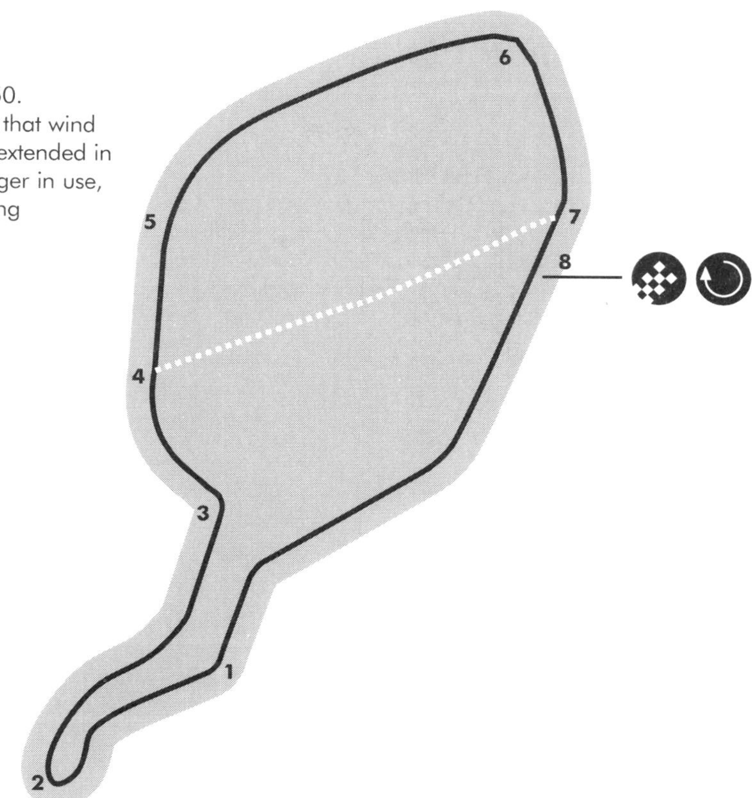

Key to the circuit:
1=Virages des Six Frères
2=Virage du Nouveau Monde
3=Virage Sanson
4=(Virage de) Beauval
5=Virage du Gresil
6=Virage de la Scierie
7=Virage de l'Etoile
8=Virage du Paradis

World Championship races: 5

	Length km	miles	**Years** (no. of races)	**Driver (Car)**	Time min:sec	Speed km/h	mph	Year
a)	5.100	3.169	1952 (1)	**Pole:** A Ascari (Ferrari)	2:14.800	136.202	84.632	1952
				F. Lap: A Ascari (Ferrari)	2:17.300	133.722	83.091	1952
				Winner: A Ascari (Ferrari)		128.958	80.131	1952
Extended								
b)	6.542	4.065	1957,62,64,68 (4)	**Pole:** J Rindt (Brabham)	1:56.100	202.853	126.047	1968
				F. Lap: J Brabham (Brabham)	2:11.400	179.233	111.370	1964
				Winner: D Gurney (Brabham)		175.042	108.766	1964

Germany (D)

AVUS

Location: Western Berlin. **First Used:** 1921.
The Automobil Verkehrs und Ubungs Strasse was constructed as a dual carriageway in the Grünewald area of the city. Unimaginative in its layout, the addition of a 43 degree banking in 1937 led to extremely fast times. The circuit had to be shortened, with a new south curve in 1954, as the original was in the Soviet sector. Jean Behra perished in his sports car on the banking during the Grand Prix meeting and this was later demolished in 1967. After a period of disuse, a shorter circuit appeared for domestic racing.

Key to the circuit:
1=Südschleife
2=Nordschleife

World Championship races: 1

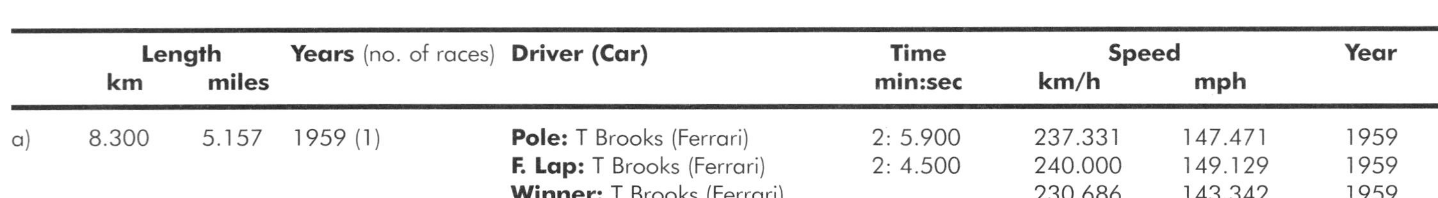

	Length km	Length miles	Years (no. of races)	Driver (Car)	Time min:sec	Speed km/h	Speed mph	Year
a)	8.300	5.157	1959 (1)	**Pole:** T Brooks (Ferrari)	2: 5.900	237.331	147.471	1959
				F. Lap: T Brooks (Ferrari)	2: 4.500	240.000	149.129	1959
				Winner: T Brooks (Ferrari)		230.686	143.342	1959

HOCKENHEIM

Location: 25 km (16 miles) south-west of Heidelberg. **First Used:** 1939.
Reopened in 1966, after the original oval was cut in two by the construction of an autobahn. This left the circuit in two distinct parts, the winding stadium section and the long blast and return into the thick pine forest. Hockenheim is also remembered for the death of Jim Clark on the outward kink of the forest section, a stone cross marking the spot where he perished.

Key to the circuit:
1=Nordkurve
2=Schikane 1/ Jim Clarkkurve
3=Östkurve
4=Schikane 1/ Ayrton Sennakurve
5=Onkokurve/ Agipkurve
6=Sachskurve
7=Elfkurve/ FIAMMkurve
8=Südkurve/ Opelkurve

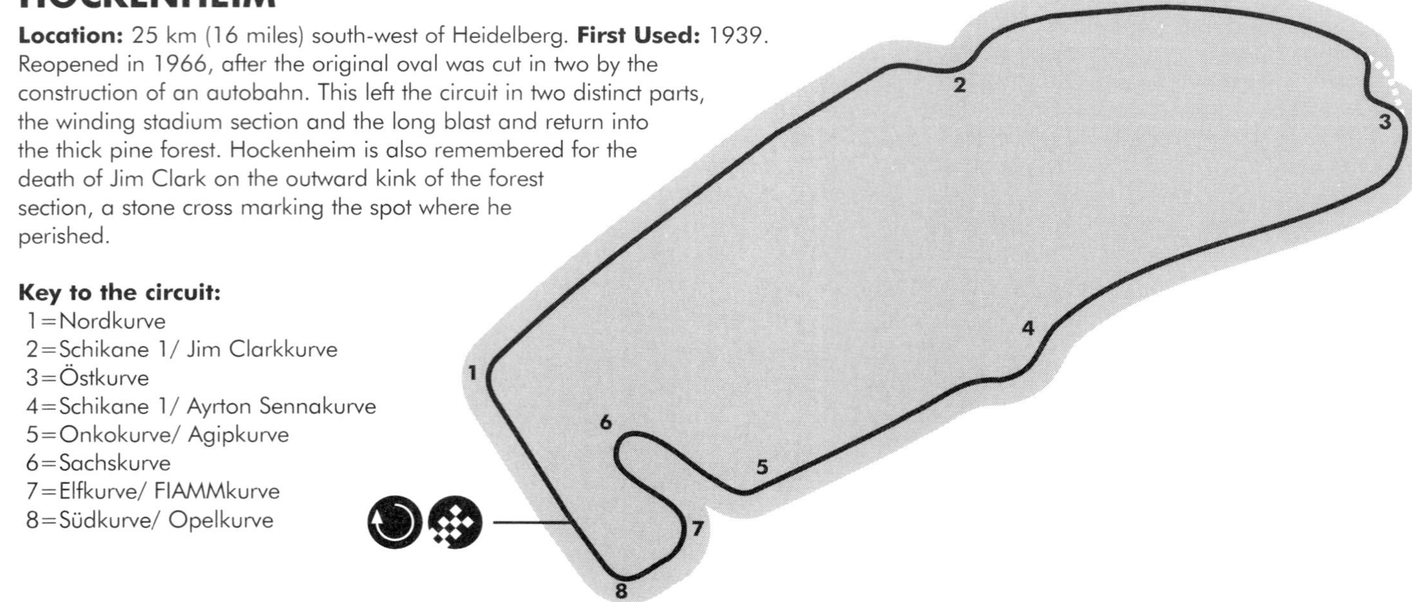

World Championship races: 20

	Length km	miles	**Years** (no. of races)	**Driver (Car)**	**Time** min:sec	**Speed** km/h	mph	**Year**
a)	6.789	4.218	1970,77-81 (6)	**Pole:** A Jones (Williams)	1:45.850	230.897	143.472	1980
				F. Lap: A Jones (Williams)	1:48.490	225.278	139.981	1980
				Winner: J Laffite (Ligier)		220.859	137.235	1980
Östkurve								
b)	6.797	4.223	1982-84,86-89 (7)	**Pole:** K Rosberg (McLaren)	1:42.013	239.864	149.044	1986
				F. Lap: N Mansell (Williams)	1:45.716	231.462	143.824	1987
				Winner: A Senna (McLaren)		224.566	139.539	1989
Östkurve altered								
c)	6.802	4.227	1990-91 (2)	**Pole:** N Mansell (Williams)	1:37.087	252.219	156.722	1991
				F. Lap: R Patrese (Williams)	1:43.569	236.434	146.913	1991
				Winner: N Mansell (Williams)		231.028	143.554	1991
Tighter Östkurve								
d)	6.815	4.235	1992-93 (2)	**Pole:** N Mansell (Williams)	1:37.960	250.449	155.622	1992
				F. Lap: R Patrese (Williams)	1:41.591	241.498	150.060	1992
				Winner: N Mansell (Williams)		234.798	145.897	1992
Senna Schikane tighter								
e)	6.823	4.240	1994-96 (3)	**Pole:** G Berger (Ferrari)	1:43.582	237.134	147.348	1994
				F. Lap: D Coulthard (Williams)	1:46.211	231.264	143.701	1994
				Winner: D Hill (Williams)		225.410	140.063	1996

NÜRBURGRING

Location: 60 km (37 miles) west of Koblenz.
First Used: 1927.
This giant of a track was built as a government employment programme, around the village of Nürburg, deep in the Eifel mountains. Officially consisting of 174 corners and a shorter separate south circuit, the Nürburgring was a supreme challenge to man and machine. Its length meant that it faded from major international racing on safety grounds. The Nürburgring has caught out more Grand Prix drivers than any other track, amongst them Onofre Marimón, killed at the Wehrseifen bridge, Peter Collins at the Pflanzgarten and Niki Lauda's near fatal accident at Bergwerk which meant the end of this circuit for GP racing. A new shorter and safer circuit was opened in May 1984 that incorporated part of the original startline.

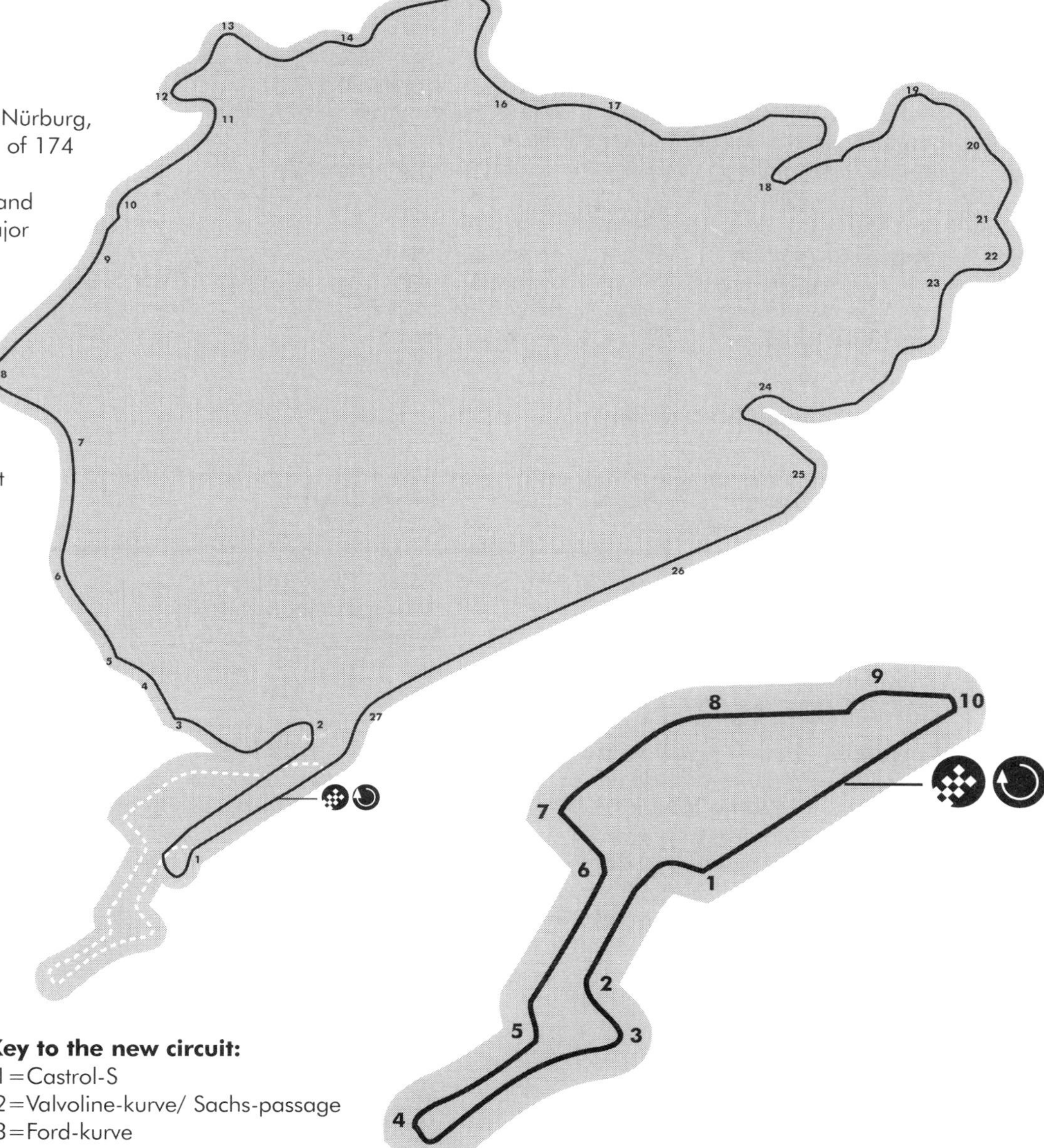

Key to the old circuit:
1=Südkehre
2=Nordkehre
3=Hatzenbach
4=Hocheichen
5=Quiddelbacher-Höhe
6=Flugplatz
7=Schwedenkreuz
8=Aremberg
9=Fuchsröhre
10=Adenauer-Forst
11=Metzgesfeld
12=Kallenhard
13=Wehrseifen
14=Ex-Mühle
15=Bergwerk
16=Breitscheid
17=Kesselchen
18=Karussell
19=Höhe-Acht
20=Wippermann
21=Eschbach
22=Brünnchen
23=Pflanzgarten
24=Schwalbenschwanz
25=Döttinger Höhe
26=Antoniusbuche
27=Tiergarten (Bremskurve)

Key to the new circuit:
1=Castrol-S
2=Valvoline-kurve/ Sachs-passage
3=Ford-kurve
4=Dunlop-kehre
5=Shell-kurve
6=RTL-kurve (named 1995)
7=Bit-kurve
8=Hatzenbach-bogen/ ITT-bogen
9=Veedol-schikane
10=Romer-kurve/ Coca-Cola kurve

World Championship races: 26 (including Grand Prix of Europe in 1984, 95 and 96)

	Length km	Length miles	Years (no. of races)	Driver (Car)	Time min:sec	Speed km/h	Speed mph	Year
a)	22.810	14.173	1951-54,56-58 61-66 (13)	**Pole:** J Clark (Lotus)	8:16.500	165.390	102.768	1966
				F. Lap: J Clark (Lotus)	8:24.100	162.896	101.219	1965
				Winner: J Clark (Lotus)		160.542	99.756	1965
Bremskurve added								
b)	22.835	14.189	1967-69,71-76 (9)	**Pole:** N Lauda (Ferrari)	6:58.600	196.383	122.027	1975
				F. Lap: C Regazzoni (Ferrari)	7: 6.400	192.791	119.795	1975
				Winner: C Reutemann (Brabham)		189.474	117.734	1975
New circuit								
c)	4.542	2.822	1984-85 (2)	**Pole:** T Fabi (Toleman)	1:17.429	211.177	131.219	1985
				F. Lap: N Lauda (McLaren)	1:22.806	197.464	122.698	1985
				Winner: A Prost (McLaren)		191.751	119.149	1984
Schikane altered								
d)	4.556	2.831	1995-96 (2)	**Pole:** D Coulthard (Williams)	1:18.738	208.306	129.435	1995
				F. Lap: M Schumacher (Benetton)	1:21.180	202.040	125.542	1995
				Winner: J Villeneuve (Williams)		196.007	121.793	1996

Great Britain (GB)

AINTREE

Location: Liverpool, 9 km (6 miles) north-east of city centre, England.
First Used: May 1954.
A flat and featureless track that ran alongside the famous Grand National steeplechase course and shared many of its facilities. It initially ran anti-clockwise, but reverted after the first meeting. With the owner Mirabelle Topham keen to sell the land, it fell out of favour, but the shorter, triangular club circuit was revived for local sprint meetings.

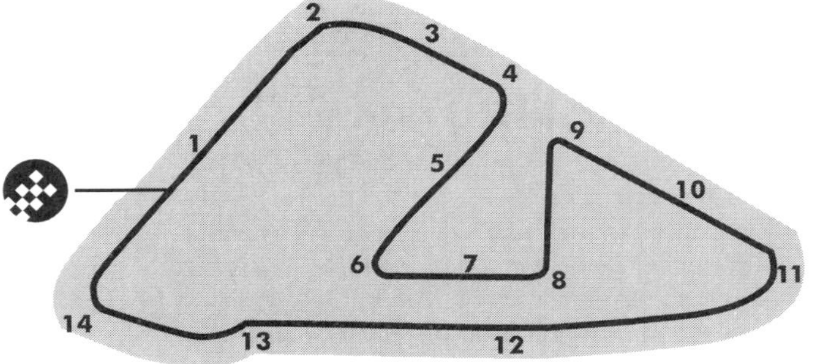

Key to the circuit:
1=Finishing Straight
2=Waterway Corner
3=Canal Straight
4=Anchor Crossing
5=Sefton Straight
6=Cottage Corner
7=Country Loop
8=Country Corner
9=Village Corner
10=Valentine's Way
11=Bechers Bend
12=Railway Straight
13=Melling Road Crossing
14=Tatts Corner

World Championship races: 5

	Length km	Length miles	Years (no. of races)	Driver (Car)	Time min:sec	Speed km/h	Speed mph	Year
a)	4.828	3.000	1955,57,59,61,62 (5)	**Pole:** J Clark (Lotus)	1:53.600	153.001	95.070	1962
				F. Lap: J Clark (Lotus)	1:55.000	151.138	93.913	1962
				Winner: J Clark (Lotus)		148.457	92.247	1962

BRANDS HATCH

Location: 12 km (7 miles) south of Dartford, Kent, England. **First Used:** 1949.
Originally a cycle/ motorcycle dirt track pre-war, it was surfaced for the first car races which took place anti-clockwise around the natural bowl, later named the Indy circuit. 1954 saw the addition of the Druids section and all racing continued clockwise. John Webb, a major force behind the circuit, instigated a new loop into the woodland to bring it up to Grand Prix length (2.65 miles) in 1960. Alterations to the south bank and pits complex slightly reduced the circuit length in 1976. With Silverstone reaching a deal to stage the British Grand Prix annually, this meant the end of this very popular track as far as the World Championship is concerned.

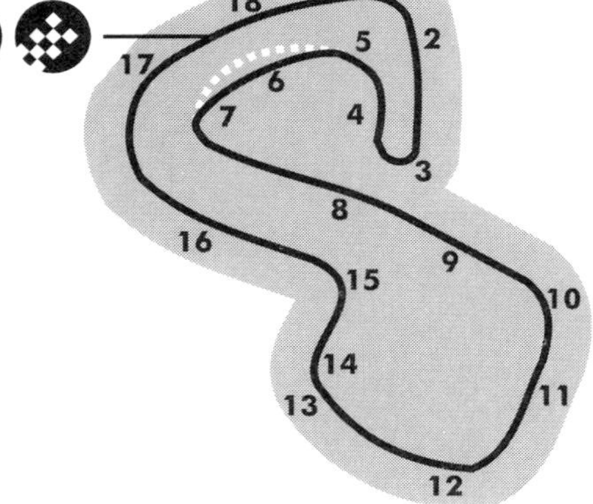

Key to the circuit:
1=Paddock Hill Bend
2=Pilgrim's Rise/ Hailwood Hill
3=Druids Bend
4=Graham Hill
5=Bottom Bend/ Graham Hill Bend
6=Bottom Straight/ Cooper Straight
7=South Bank Bend/ Surtees
8=Pilgrim's Drop
9=Hawthorn Hill
10=Hawthorn Bend
11=Portobello Straight/ Derek Minter Straight
12=Westfield Bend
13=Dingle Dell
14=Dingle Dell Corner
15=Stirling's Bend
16=Clearways
17=Clark Curve
18=Brabham Straight

Most of the renaming took place in 1976

World Championship races: 14 (including Grand Prix of Europe in 1983 and 1985)

	Length km	miles	Years (no. of races)	Driver (Car)	Time min:sec	Speed km/h	mph	Year
a)	4.265	2.650	1964,66,68, 70,72,74 (6)	**Pole:** N Lauda (Ferrari)	1:19.700	192.637	119.699	1974
				F. Lap: N Lauda (Ferrari)	1:21.100	189.311	117.633	1974
				Winner: J Scheckter (Tyrrell)		186.258	115.735	1974
South Bank Alterations								
b)	4.207	2.614	1976,78,80,82,83, 84,85,86 (8)	**Pole:** N Piquet (Williams)	1: 6.961	226.170	140.536	1986
				F. Lap: N Mansell (Williams)	1: 9.593	217.616	135.220	1986
				Winner: N Mansell (Williams)		208.853	129.775	1986

DONINGTON PARK

Location: Castle Donington, 13 km (8 miles) south-east of Derby, England.
First Used: March 1933.

Situated in the grounds of 17th century Donington Hall, it became Britain's premier circuit, but fell into disrepair during the war years. Builder Tom Wheatcroft bought the circuit in 1971, adding the magnificent 'Donington Collection' Grand Prix car museum in 1973 and reopening the circuit for racing in 1977. The track followed the lines of the old circuit and even added a new loop in 1985, to mirror the original Melbourne Hairpin, now outside the circuit. After many years of applications, Tom Wheatcroft finally realised his dream of hosting a Grand Prix, with the 1993 Grand Prix of Europe.

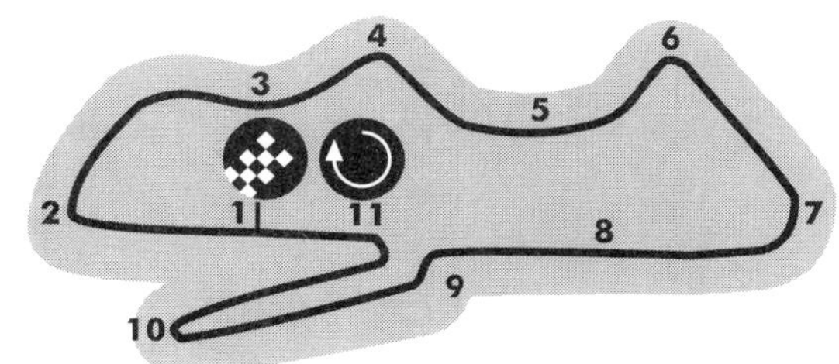

World Championship races: 1 (Grand Prix of Europe)

Key to the circuit:
1=Wheatcroft Straight
2=Redgate Corner
3=Craner Curves
4=Old Hairpin
5=Starkey's Bridge
6=McLean's Corner
7=Coppice Corner
8=Starkey's Straight
9=The Esses
10=Melbourne Hairpin
11=Goddard Corner

	Length km	miles	Years (no. of races)	Driver (Car)	Time min:sec	Speed km/h	mph	Year
a)	4.023	2.500	1993 (1)	**Pole:** A Prost (Williams)	1:10.458	205.552	127.724	1993
				F. Lap: A Senna (McLaren)	1:18.029	185.608	115.331	1993
				Winner: A Senna (McLaren)		165.603	102.901	1993

SILVERSTONE

Location: 5 km (3 miles) south of Towcester, Northamptonshire, England.
First Used: October 1948.

Incorporated from the runways and perimeter roads of a wartime bomber base, the first permutation formed a dangerous x shape. The following year, the familiar perimeter roads were laid out. Jimmy Brown was the first track manager and the British Racing Drivers' Club (BRDC) bought the circuit in 1961 and steadily developed it into Britain's premier circuit. For many years, the infield was active farmland and the buildings can be seen at Abbey. Although not changing its fundamental shape, Silverstone has undergone many changes in its years, most notably at Woodcote, the sweeping right-hander that holds the distinction of being the first corner faced in the World Championship.

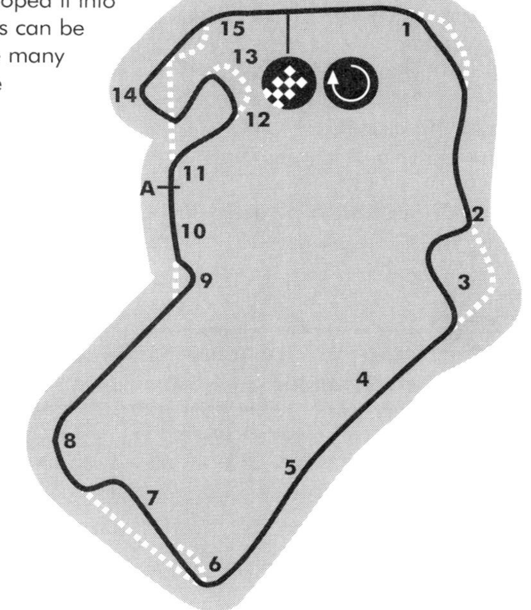

Key to the circuit:
1=Copse Corner
2=Maggotts Curve
3=Becketts Corner
4=Chapel Curve
5=Hangar Straight
6=Stowe Corner
7=Vale
8=Club Corner
9=Abbey Curve
10=Farm Straight
11=Bridge
12=Priory
13=Brooklands
14=Luffield
15=Woodcote Corner/ Chicane

'A' signifies the original startline until 1951.

World Championship races: 30

	Length km	miles	Years (no. of races)	Driver (Car)	Time min:sec	Speed km/h	mph	Year
a)	4.649	2.889	1950,51 (2)	**Pole:** F González (Ferrari)	1:43.400	161.874	100.584	1951
				F. Lap: G Farina (Alfa Romeo)	1:44.000	160.941	100.004	1951
				Winner: F González (Ferrari)		154.690	96.120	1951
New Woodcote/ Pits								
b)	4.711	2.927	1952-54,56,58,60,63 65,67,69,71,73 (12)	**Pole:** R Peterson (Lotus)	1:16.300	222.254	138.102	1973
				F. Lap: J Hunt (March)	1:18.600	215.750	134.061	1973
				Winner: P Revson (McLaren)		212.034	131.752	1973
Woodcote Chicane								
c)	4.719	2.932	1975,77,79,81,83,85 (6)	**Pole:** K Rosberg (Williams)	1: 5.591	258.983	160.925	1985
				F. Lap: A Prost (McLaren)	1: 9.886	243.067	151.035	1985
				Winner: A Prost (McLaren)		235.405	146.274	1985
New Woodcote Corner								
d)	4.778	2.969	1987-88 (2)					
e)	4.780	2.970	1989-90 (2)	**Pole:** N Piquet (Williams)	1: 7.110	256.315	159.267	1987
				F. Lap: N Mansell (Williams)	1: 9.832	246.324	153.059	1987
				Winner: N Mansell (Williams)		235.298	146.208	1987
New Complex								
f)	5.226	3.247	1991-93 (3)	**Pole:** N Mansell (Williams)	1:18.965	238.252	148.043	1992
				F. Lap: D Hill (Williams)	1:22.515	228.002	141.674	1993
				Winner: A Prost (Williams)		216.030	134.235	1993
Safety Revisions								
g)	5.057	3.142	1994-95 (2)	**Pole:** D Hill (Williams)	1:24.960	214.280	133.147	1994
				F. Lap: D Hill (Williams)	1:27.100	209.015	129.876	1994
				Winner: D Hill (Williams)		202.144	125.606	1994
Stowe reprofiled								
h)	5.072	3.152	1996 (1)	**Pole:** D Hill (Williams)	1:26.875	210.178	130.598	1996
				F. Lap: J Villeneuve (Williams)	1:29.288	204.498	127.069	1996
				Winner: J Villeneuve (Williams)		199.576	124.011	1996

Hungary (H)

HUNGARORING

Location: near Mogyoród, 20 km (12 miles) north-east of Budapest.
First Used: 1986.
Hungary has a good racing pedigree; the first Grand Prix in 1906 was won by the Hungarian Ferenc Szisz, and racing in Budapest goes back to 1926. This first Eastern Bloc venue was built with the help of a state loan, and the natural amphitheatre attracted vast crowds to its early races. Initial construction problems with an underground spring meant the track was rather too twisty, but thankfully, this was later overcome.

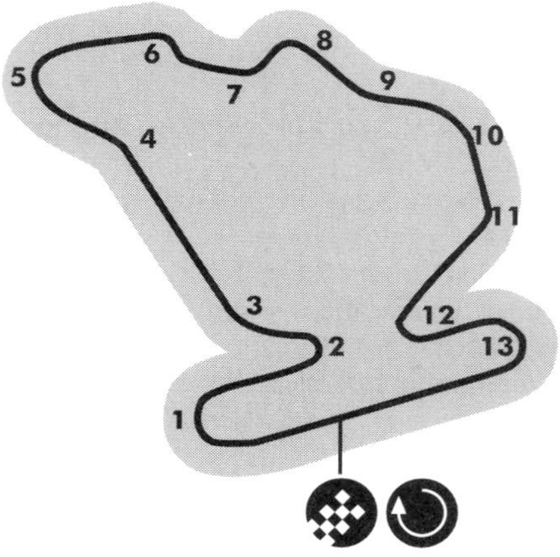

Key to the circuit:
Corners are simply known numerically.

World Championship races: 11

	Length km	miles	Years (no. of races)	Driver (Car)	Time min:sec	Speed km/h	mph	Year
a)	4.014	2.494	1986-88 (3)	**Pole:** A Senna (McLaren)	1:27.635	164.893	102.460	1988
				F. Lap: N Piquet (Williams)	1:30.149	160.295	99.602	1987
				Winner: A Senna (McLaren)		155.401	96.562	1988
Spring diverted								
b)	3.968	2.466	1989-96 (8)	**Pole:** A Prost (Williams)	1:14.631	191.406	118.934	1993
				F. Lap: N Mansell (Williams)	1:18.308	182.418	113.349	1992
				Winner: A Senna (McLaren)		172.424	107.139	1992

Italy (I)

IMOLA

Location: 33 km (20 miles) south-east of Bologna. **First Used:** 1950.
The Autodromo Enzo e Dino Ferrari is situated in woodland and runs alongside the Santerno river. A circuit of contrasts with the sweeps of the river side and the twists and gradients of the southern side. Sadly, Imola will always be remembered for the double tragedy during the 1994 San Marino Grand Prix meeting.

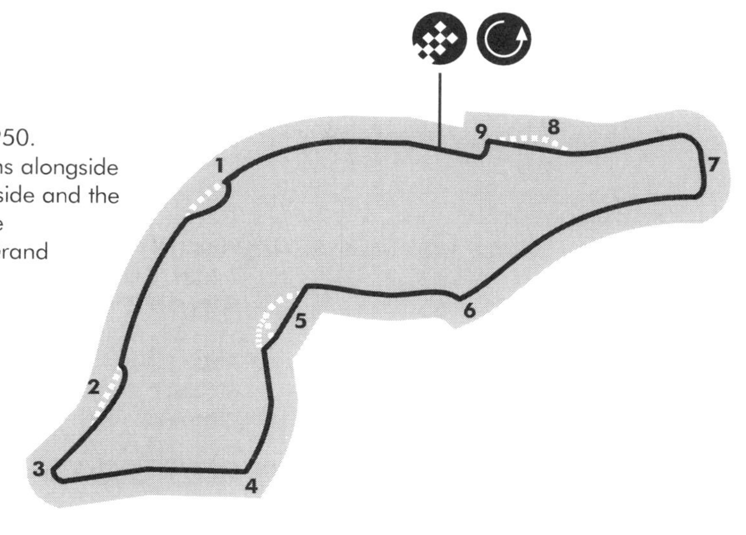

Key to the circuit:
1=Tamburello
2=Villeneuve
3=Tosa
4=Piratella
5=Acque Minerale
6=Variante Alta
7=Rivazza
8=Variante Marlboro/ Bassa
9=Traguardo

World Championship races: 17 (Italian GP 1980/ San Marino GP from 1981)

	Length km	Length miles	Years (no. of races)	Driver (Car)	Time min:sec	Speed km/h	Speed mph	Year
a)	5.000	3.107	1980 (1)	**Pole:** R Arnoux (Renault)	1:33.988	191.514	119.001	1980
				F. Lap: A Jones (Williams)	1:36.089	187.326	116.399	1980
				Winner: N Piquet (Brabham)		183.439	113.984	1980
Acque Minerale chicane								
b)	5.040	3.132	1981-94 (14)	**Pole:** A Senna (Williams)	1:21.548	222.495	138.252	1994
				F. Lap: D Hill (Williams)	1:24.335	215.142	133.683	1994
				Winner: N Mansell (Williams)		204.596	127.130	1992
New chicane and other variations								
c)	4.895	3.042	1995 (1)					
d)	4.892	3.040	1996 (1)	**Pole:** M Schumacher (Ferrari)	1:26.890	202.684	125.942	1996
				F. Lap: D Hill (Williams)	1:28.931	198.032	123.051	1996
				Winner: D Hill (Williams)		193.761	120.397	1996

MONZA

Location: 15 km (9 miles) north-east of Milan. **First Used:** 1922.
A circuit steeped in history, built in the grounds of the wooded Monza royal park. The road circuit was rebuilt in 1948 and a new banked speedway section, half sunk in the ground, was constructed in 1955. This section fell into general disuse from 1968, when Monza established itself as the fastest Grand Prix track, with its slipstreaming battles. The introduction of chicanes, ensured that the previous race (1971) still holds the distinction of being the fastest, as well as the closest finish.

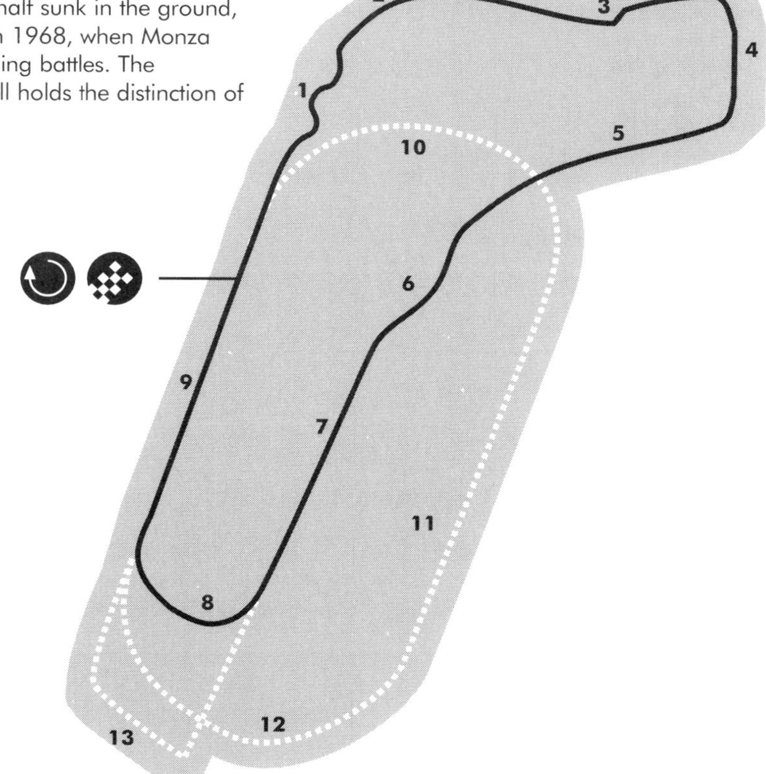

Key to the circuit:
1=Variante Goodyear/ del Rettifilo
2=Curva Grande
3=Curva/ Variante della Roggia
4=Curve di Lesmo
5=Curva del Serraglio
6=Curva del Vialone/ Variante Ascari
7=Rettifilo Centrale
8=Curva Parabolica/ Curvetta Sud
9=Rettifilo Tribune
10=Curva Nord alta velocità
11=Rettifilo Levante/ Est
12=Curva Sud alta velocità
13=Curva di Vedano

World Championship races: 46

	Length km	miles	Years (no. of races)	Driver (Car)	Time min:sec	Speed km/h	mph	Year
a)	6.300	3.915	1950-54 (5)	**Pole:** J M Fangio (Alfa Romeo)	1:53.200	200.353	124.494	1951
				F. Lap: G Farina (Alfa Romeo)	1:56.500	194.678	120.967	1951
				Winner: A Ascari (Ferrari)		185.915	115.522	1951
Banked circuit								
b)	10.000	6.214	1955-56,60-61 (4)	**Pole:** P Hill (Ferrari)	2:41.400	223.048	138.596	1960
				F. Lap: P Hill (Ferrari)	2:43.600	220.049	136.732	1960
				Winner: P Hill (Ferrari)		212.535	132.063	1960
Parabolica								
c)	5.750	3.573	1957-59,62-71 (13)	**Pole:** C Amon (Matra Simca)	1:22.400	251.214	156.097	1971
				F. Lap: H Pescarolo (March)	1:23.800	247.017	153.489	1971
				Winner: P Gethin (BRM)		242.616	150.755	1971
Two chicanes								
d)	5.775	3.588	1972-73 (2)	**Pole:** R Peterson (JPS Lotus)	1:34.800	219.304	136.269	1973
				F. Lap: J Stewart (Tyrrell)	1:35.300	218.153	135.554	1973
				Winner: R Peterson (JPS Lotus)		213.450	132.631	1973
Vialone eased								
e)	5.780	3.592	1974-75 (2)	**Pole:** N Lauda (Ferrari)	1:32.240	225.585	140.172	1975
				F. Lap: C Regazzoni (Ferrari)	1:33.100	223.502	138.877	1975
				Winner: C Regazzoni (Ferrari)		218.034	135.480	1975
Two more chicanes								
f)	5.800	3.604	1976-79,81-94 (18)	**Pole:** A Senna (McLaren)	1:21.114	257.415	159.951	1991
				F. Lap: D Hill (Williams)	1:23.575	249.835	155.241	1993
				Winner: D Hill (Williams)		239.144	148.597	1993
Curva Grande and Curve di Lesmo altered								
g)	5.770	3.585	1995-96 (2)	**Pole:** D Hill (Williams)	1:24.204	246.687	153.284	1996
				F. Lap: M Schumacher (Ferrari)	1:26.110	241.226	149.891	1996
				Winner: M Schumacher (Ferrari)		236.034	146.665	1996

PESCARA

Location: Adriatic Coast. **First Used:** 1924.

The longest track in the World Championship consisted of roads linking villages around the coastal town of Pescara. It ran along the edge of the sea, towards the 1934 chicane, before turning inland along the winding Abruzzi mountain track. The inherent dangers meant that the Pescara Grand Prix (later non-championship) ended in the early 60s.

Key to the circuit:
1=Pescara
2=Montani
3=Villa Raspa
4=Spoltore
5=Pornace
6=Villa St. Maria
7=Cappelle
8=Mulino
9=Monte-Silvano
10=Madonna

World Championship races: 1

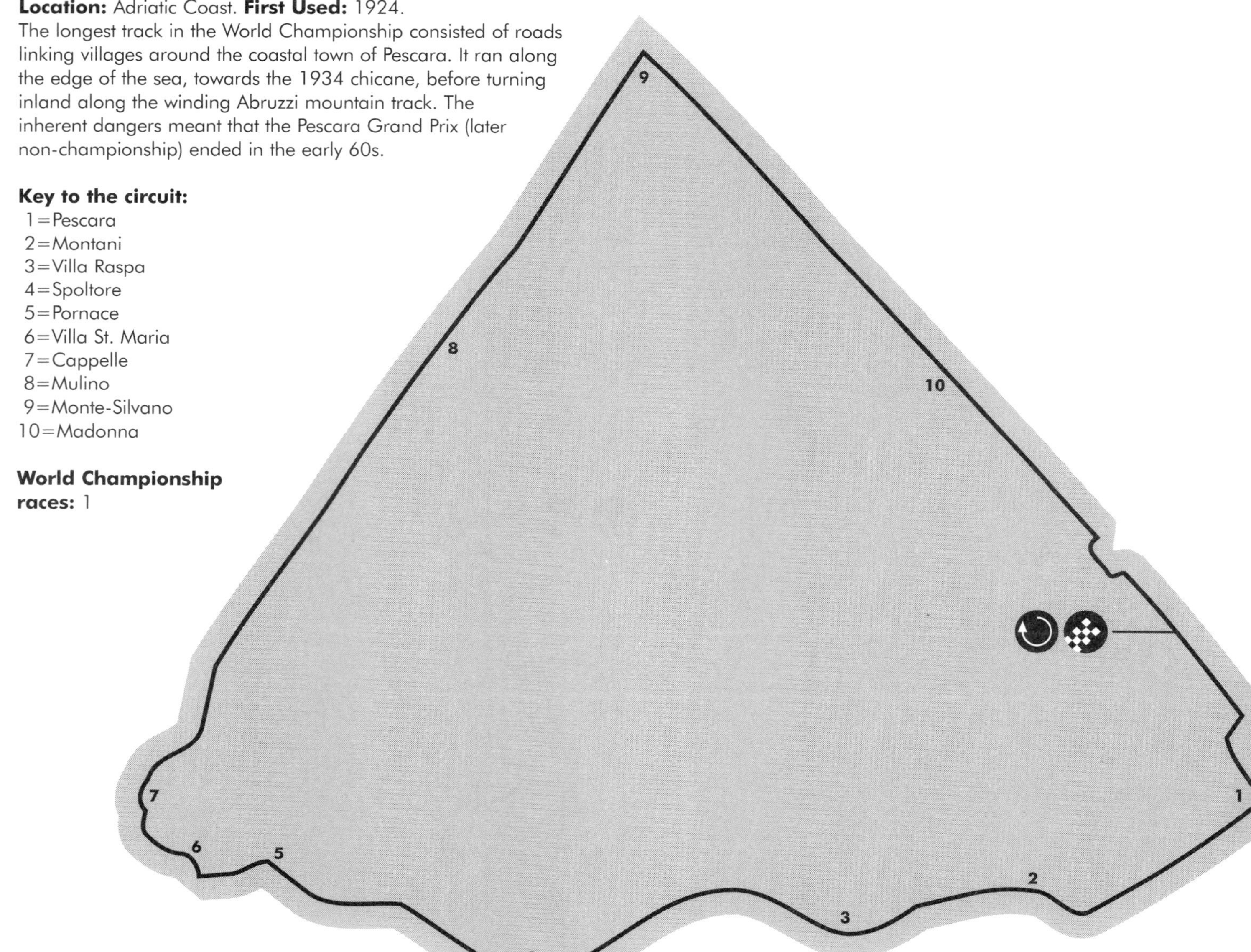

	Length km	miles	Years (no. of races)	Driver (Car)	Time min:sec	Speed km/h	mph	Year
a)	25.579	15.894	1957 (1)	**Pole:** J M Fangio (Maserati)	9:44.600	157.517	97.876	1957
				F. Lap: S Moss (Vanwall)	9:44.600	157.517	97.876	1957
				Winner: S Moss (Vanwall)		154.006	95.695	1957

Japan (J)

AIDA

Location: 70 km (44 miles) north-east of Okayama City. **First Used:** 1990.
Hajime Tanaka created the Tanaka International Circuit (TI) as a private club racetrack. The inaugural race was for invited English drivers and their historic sports cars, hence the names given to some of the corners. Situated in an isolated, mountainous region, the circuit does have access problems, but coped well with its first big international event.

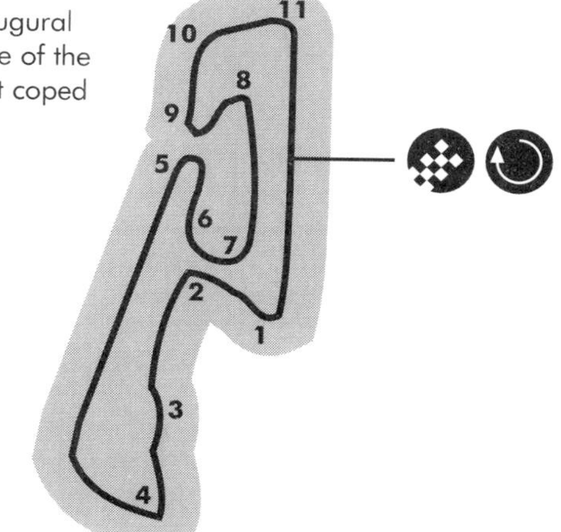

Key to the circuit:
1=First corner
2=Williams corner
3=Moss 'S'
4=Attwood curve
5=Hair Pin corner
6=Revolver corner
7=Piper corner
8=Redman corner
9=Hobbs corner
10=Mike Knight corner
11=Last corner

World Championship races: 2 (Pacific Grand Prix)

	Length km	miles	Years (no. of races)	Driver (Car)	Time min:sec	Speed km/h	mph	Year
a)	3.703	2.301	1994-95 (2)	**Pole:** A Senna (Williams)	1:10.218	189.849	117.967	1994
				F. Lap: M Schumacher (Benetton)	1:14.023	180.090	111.903	1994
				Winner: M Schumacher (Benetton)		173.925	108.072	1994

FUJI

Location: 70 km (44 miles) west of Yokohama. **First Used:** 1965.
Fuji International Speedway lies in the shadow of the imposing Mount Fuji, a dormant volcano usually hidden in mist. As the name suggests, it was intended as an American style speedway track, but the banked section wasn't used for F1 and was rarely utilised after. Due to its mountainous location, rain is often a factor, as in the 1976 championship decider, when Lauda withdrew due to the appalling conditions.

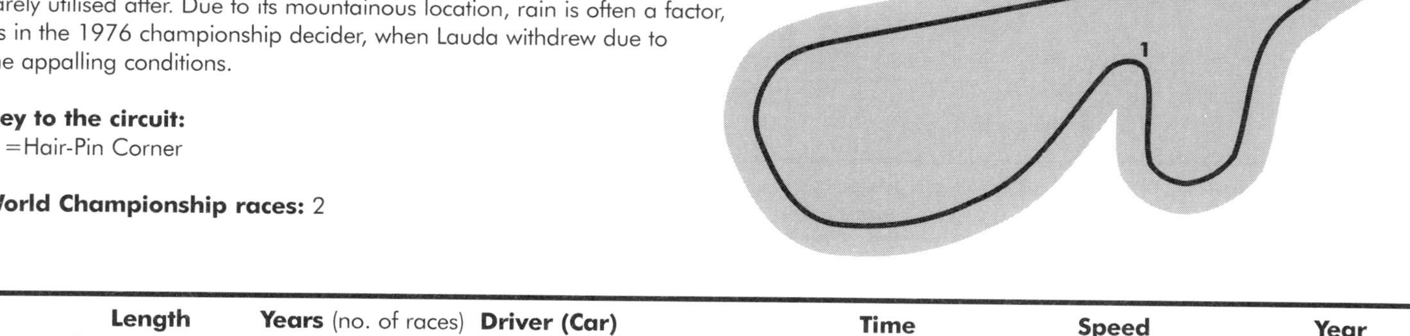

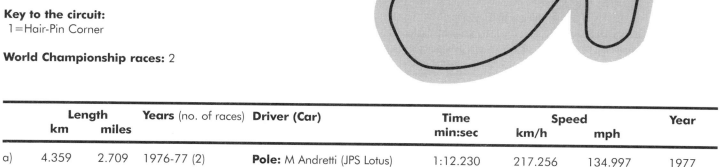

Key to the circuit:
1=Hair-Pin Corner

World Championship races: 2

	Length km	miles	Years (no. of races)	Driver (Car)	Time min:sec	Speed km/h	mph	Year
a)	4.359	2.709	1976-77 (2)	**Pole:** M Andretti (JPS Lotus)	1:12.230	217.256	134.997	1977
				F. Lap: J Scheckter (Wolf)	1:14.300	211.203	131.236	1977
				Winner: J Hunt (McLaren)		207.840	129.146	1977

SUZUKA

Location: 50 km (31 miles) south-west of Nagoya.
First Used: 1961.

Built as a test track for Honda and designed by John Hugenholtz, incorporating a very unusual crossover section. Suzuka is a self contained theme park with a funfair, golf and other facilities, including the Honda racing museum. The track has a variety of corners and cambers, as well as a second fully operational pit area at the other side of the circuit.

Key to the circuit:

1=First Curve
2=Second Curve
3=S Curves
4=Dunlop Curve
5=Degner Curve
6=Hairpin
7=Spoon Curve
8=Crossing/ Underpass
9='130 R'
10=Chicane/ Casio Triangle

World Championship races: 10

	Length km	miles	Years (no. of races)	Driver (Car)	Time min:sec	Speed km/h	mph	Year
a)	5.859	3.641	1987-90 (4)	**Pole:** A Senna (McLaren)	1:36.996	217.456	135.121	1990
				F. Lap: A Prost (McLaren)	1:43.506	203.779	126.623	1989
				Winner: N Piquet (Benetton)		196.923	122.362	1990
Chicane moved								
b)	5.864	3.644	1991-96 (6)	**Pole:** G Berger (McLaren)	1:34.700	222.919	138.515	1991
				F. Lap: N Mansell (Williams	1:40.646	209.749	130.332	1992
				Winner: G Berger (McLaren)		202.298	125.702	1991

Mexico (MEX)

MEXICO CITY

Location: Mexico City (eastern suburb). **First Used:** 1962.
The Magdalena Mixhuca circuit is situated in a municipal sports park, built on a dried up lake bed and at an altitude of 7,500 feet. In early days, there were always crowd problems and with the very bumpy surface, its days were numbered. The circuit was later renamed Autodromo Hermanos Ricardo y Pedro Rodriguez, in memory of the Rodriguez brothers. After a facelift and revised layout, the track returned, although the magnificent banked Peralta curve was flattened out in 1992.

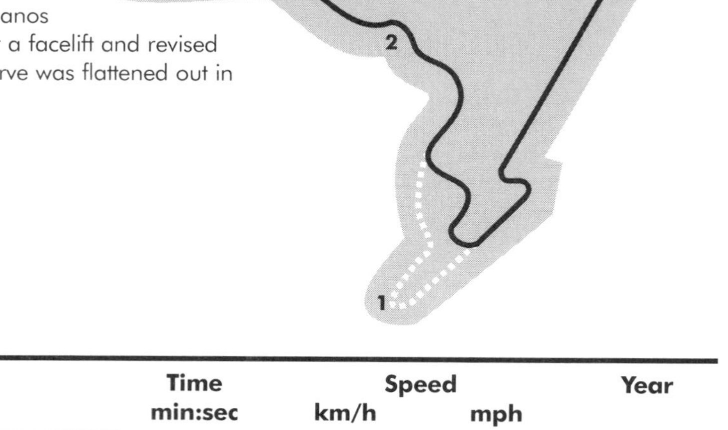

Key to the circuit:

1=Hairpin
2=The Esses
3=Peralta

World Championship races: 15

	Length km	miles	Years (no. of races)	Driver (Car)	Time min:sec	Speed km/h	mph	Year
a)	5.000	3.107	1963-70 (8)	**Pole:** C Regazzoni (Ferrari)	1:41.860	176.713	109.804	1970
				F. Lap: J Ickx (Brabham)	1:43.050	174.672	108.536	1969
				Winner: J Ickx (Ferrari)		171.848	106.781	1970
Revised/ shorter								
b)	4.421	2.747	1986-92 (7)	**Pole:** N Mansell (Williams)	1:16.346	208.467	129.535	1992
				F. Lap: N Mansell (Williams)	1:16.788	207.267	128.790	1991
				Winner: N Mansell (Williams)		199.176	123.762	1992

Monaco (MC)

MONTE CARLO

Location: Monte Carlo (around the harbour of the Principality). **First Used:** 1929.
Conceived by Antony Noghes, the Monaco race is the most famous on the Grand Prix calendar. An anachronism for modern machines that gasp and crawl around the tight corners, buildings and harbour front. It is no longer a pure race, given the difficulty in overtaking, but television and the sponsors love it. Its basic layout remained much the same over the years, with the only real change introduced around the waterside swimming pool complex.

Key to the circuit:
1=Virage de Sainte Dévote
2=Montée du Beau Rivage
3=Virage Massenet
4=Virage Casino
5=Virage Mirabeau
6=Virage de la (Ancienne) Gare/ Loews
7=Virage du Portier
8=Tunnel
9=Chicane/ Nouvelle Chicane
10=Virage du Bureau de Tabac
11=Virages Piscine
12=Virage La Rascasse
13=Virage Anthony Noghès
14=Courbe des Gazométres

'A' signifies the startline from 1955-62.

World Championship races: 43

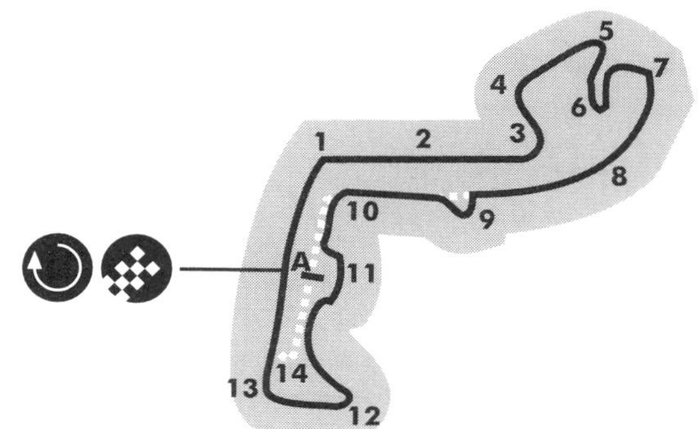

	Length km	Length miles	**Years** (no. of races)	**Driver (Car)**	**Time** min:sec	**Speed** km/h	**Speed** mph	**Year**
a)	3.180	1.976	1950 (1)	**Pole:** J M Fangio (Alfa Romeo)	1:50.200	103.884	64.550	1950
				F. Lap: J M Fangio (Alfa Romeo)	1:51.000	103.135	64.085	1950
				Winner: J M Fangio (Alfa Romeo)		98.701	61.330	1950
b)	3.145	1.954	1955-72 (18)	**Pole:** E Fittipaldi (JPS Lotus)	1:21.400	139.091	86.427	1972
				F. Lap: J Stewart (Tyrrell)	1:22.200	137.737	85.586	1971
				Winner: J Stewart (Tyrrell)		134.360	83.487	1971
New layout								
c)	3.278	2.037	1973-75 (3)	**Pole:** N Lauda (Ferrari)	1:26.300	136.742	84.967	1974
				F. Lap: R Peterson (JPS Lotus)	1:27.900	134.253	83.421	1974
				Winner: J Stewart (Tyrrell)		130.298	80.963	1973
Tighter Dévote/ Rascasse								
d)	3.312	2.058	1976-85 (10)	**Pole:** A Senna (Lotus)	1:20.450	148.206	92.091	1985
				F. Lap: M Alboreto (Ferrari)	1:22.637	144.284	89.654	1985
				Winner: A Prost (McLaren)		138.435	86.019	1985
New Chicane								
e)	3.328	2.068	1986-96 (11)	**Pole:** M Schumacher (Benetton)	1:18.560	152.505	94.762	1994
				F. Lap: M Schumacher (Benetton)	1:21.076	147.772	91.822	1994
				Winner: M Schumacher (Benetton)		141.691	88.042	1994

Morocco (MA)

AIN-DIAB

Location: Casablanca. **First Used:** 1957.
Utilising public roads, by the Atlantic coast on the outskirts of Casablanca, Ain-Diab was the scene of the 1958 championship decider. Sometimes dusty and covered by sea mist, its fast layout caused high speed accidents and Stuart Lewis-Evans suffered fatal burns at this race.

Key to the circuit:
1=Ain-Diab
2=Boulevard Panoramique
3=Boulevard Alexandre
4=Azemmour-Casablanca Road
5=Azemmour
6=Sidi Abderhaman
7=Coast Road

World Championship races: 1

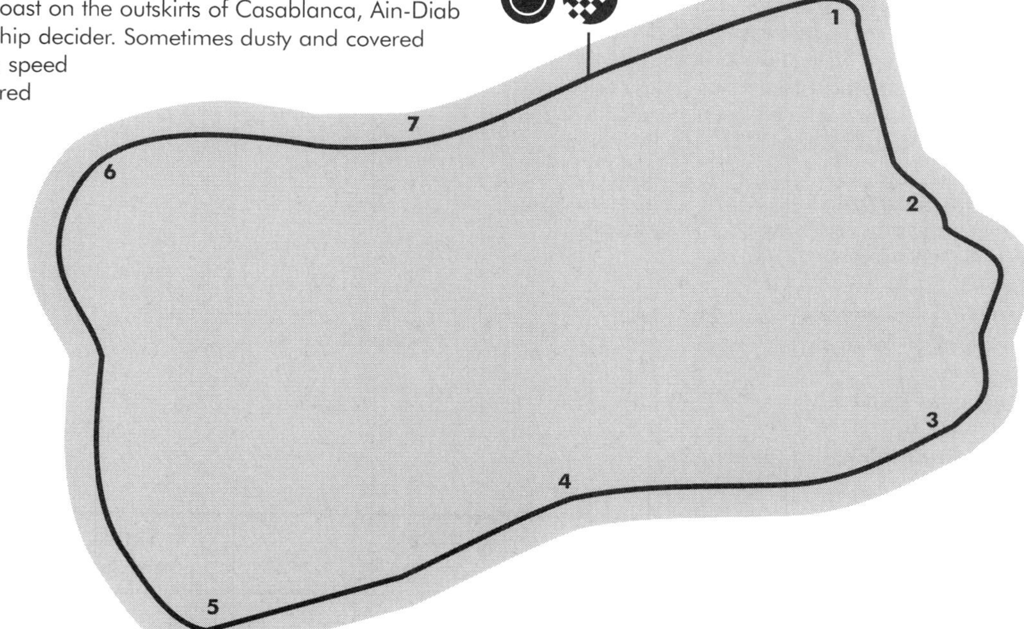

	Length km	Length miles	**Years** (no. of races)	**Driver (Car)**	**Time** min:sec	**Speed** km/h	**Speed** mph	**Year**
a)	7.618	4.734	1958 (1)	**Pole:** M Hawthorn (Ferrari)	2:23.100	191.648	119.084	1958
				F. Lap: S Moss (Vanwall)	2:22.500	192.455	119.586	1958
				Winner: S Moss (Vanwall)		187.427	116.462	1958

Netherlands (NL)

ZANDVOORT

Location: 9 km (6 miles) west of Haarlem. **First Used:** 1948.
Designed by John Hugenholtz, linking new track with existing wartime service roads through the seaside sand dunes. The main straight runs parallel to the North Sea and strong winds often blew sand over the track. The facilities became outdated and with noise pollution problems, the track fell from major use and was drastically remodelled in the late 80s.

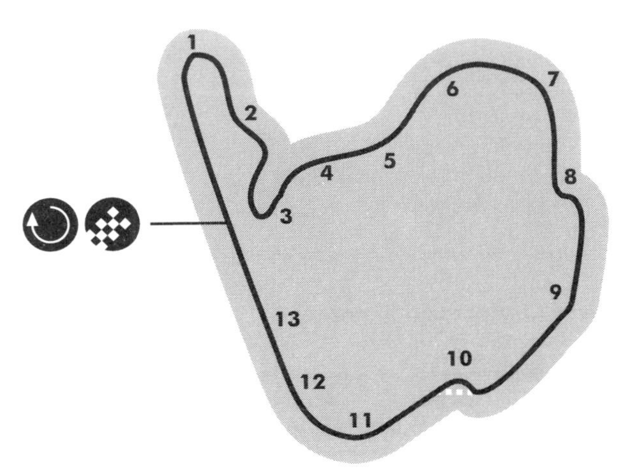

Key to the circuit:
1=Tarzanbocht
2=Gerlachbocht
3=Hugenholtzbocht
4=Hunserug
5=Zijn Veld
6=Jan de Wyker/ Rob Slotenmakerbocht
7=Scheivlak
8=Hondenvlak/ Marlborobocht
9=Tunnel Oost
10=Panoramabocht
11=Pulleveld
12=Bos Uit
13=Huzaren Vlak

World Championship races: 30

	Length km	miles	Years (no. of races)	Driver (Car)	Time min:sec	Speed km/h	mph	Year
a)	4.193	2.605	1952-53,55,58-71 (17)	**Pole:** J Ickx (Ferrari)	1:17.420	194.973	121.151	1971
				F. Lap: J Ickx (Ferrari)	1:19.230	190.519	118.383	1970
				Winner: J Rindt (Lotus)		181.772	112.948	1970
New corner at Panoramabocht								
b)	4.226	2.626	1973-79 (7)	**Pole:** R Arnoux (Renault)	1:15.461	201.609	125.274	1979
				F. Lap: G Villeneuve (Ferrari)	1:19.438	191.515	119.002	1979
				Winner: M Andretti (JPS Lotus)		188.156	116.915	1978
Marlborobocht								
c)	4.252	2.642	1980-85 (6)	**Pole:** N Piquet (Brabham)	1:11.074	215.370	133.825	1985
				F. Lap: A Prost (McLaren)	1:16.538	199.995	124.271	1985
				Winner: N Lauda (McLaren)		193.089	119.980	1985

Portugal (P)

ESTORIL

Location: 6.5 km (4 miles) north of Estoril. **First Used:** 1972.
Built on a barren, rocky plateau, inland from the popular beach resort. Used for local racing in its early years before falling into disrepair, it was redeveloped in the early 80s ready for a return to international racing. Due to the increase in safety measures, following Imola 1994, a new slower link was added before turn 8, soon nicknamed Cadwell Park, by Damon Hill, after the twisty narrow circuit in Lincolnshire.

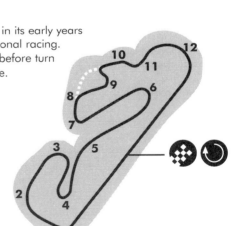

Key to the circuit:
Corners are simply known numerically, apart from the following:
4=VIP
6=Parabolica Interior
8=Curva do Tanque
11=Esses
12=Senna/ Parabolica

World Championship races: 13

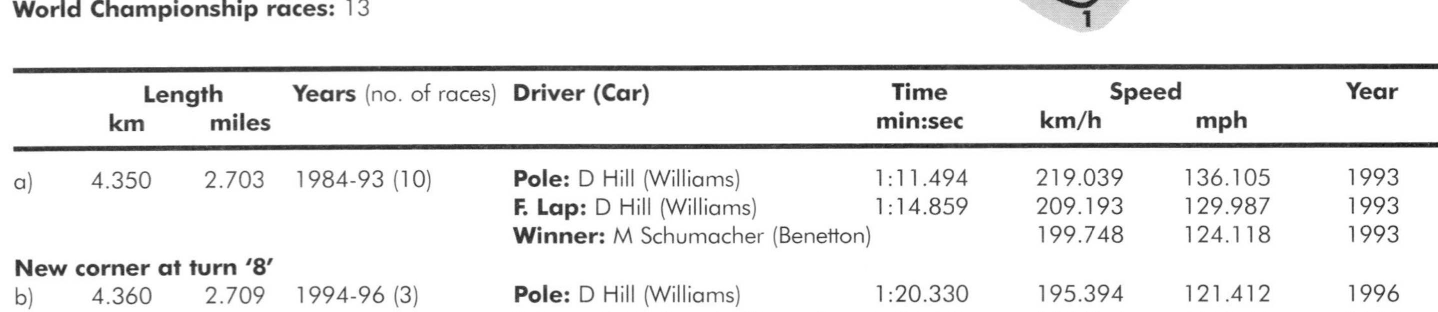

	Length km	miles	Years (no. of races)	Driver (Car)	Time min:sec	Speed km/h	mph	Year
a)	4.350	2.703	1984-93 (10)	**Pole:** D Hill (Williams)	1:11.494	219.039	136.105	1993
				F. Lap: D Hill (Williams)	1:14.859	209.193	129.987	1993
				Winner: M Schumacher (Benetton)		199.748	124.118	1993
New corner at turn '8'								
b)	4.360	2.709	1994-96 (3)	**Pole:** D Hill (Williams)	1:20.330	195.394	121.412	1996
				F. Lap: D Coulthard (Williams)	1:22.446	190.379	118.296	1994
				Winner: D Hill (Williams)		183.589	114.077	1994

MONSANTO PARK

Location: Lisbon, 5 km (3 miles) west of city centre.
First Used: 1954.
A natural circuit, built around the roads of the picturesque Monsanto Park. Its main straight was the dual carriageway of the main Lisbon to Estoril road. Generally used for sportscar racing, the circuit quickly faded from international racing.

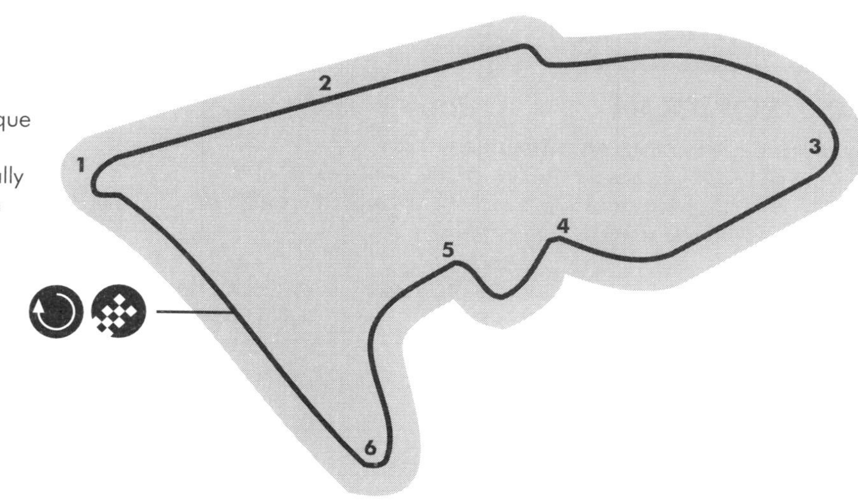

Key to the circuit:
1=Clover Leaf Hairpin
2=Autostrada
3=Lake Hairpin
4=Riding School Corner
5=Windmill Bend
6=Pits Hairpin

World Championship races: 1

	Length km	Length miles	Years (no. of races)	Driver (Car)	Time min:sec	Speed km/h	Speed mph	Year
a)	5.440	3.380	1959 (1)	**Pole:** S Moss (Cooper)	2: 2.890	159.362	99.023	1959
				F. Lap: S Moss (Cooper)	2: 5.070	156.584	97.297	1959
				Winner: S Moss (Cooper)		153.398	95.317	1959

PORTO

Location: Porto (outskirts of city centre). **First Used:** 1950.
A true street circuit, situated close to the harbour front and incorporating part of a dual carriageway. It included all manner of hazards with houses, shops, lamp posts, cobbles and even tram lines. Mainly used for sportscar racing, it was regarded as too dangerous, the last event being staged in 1960.

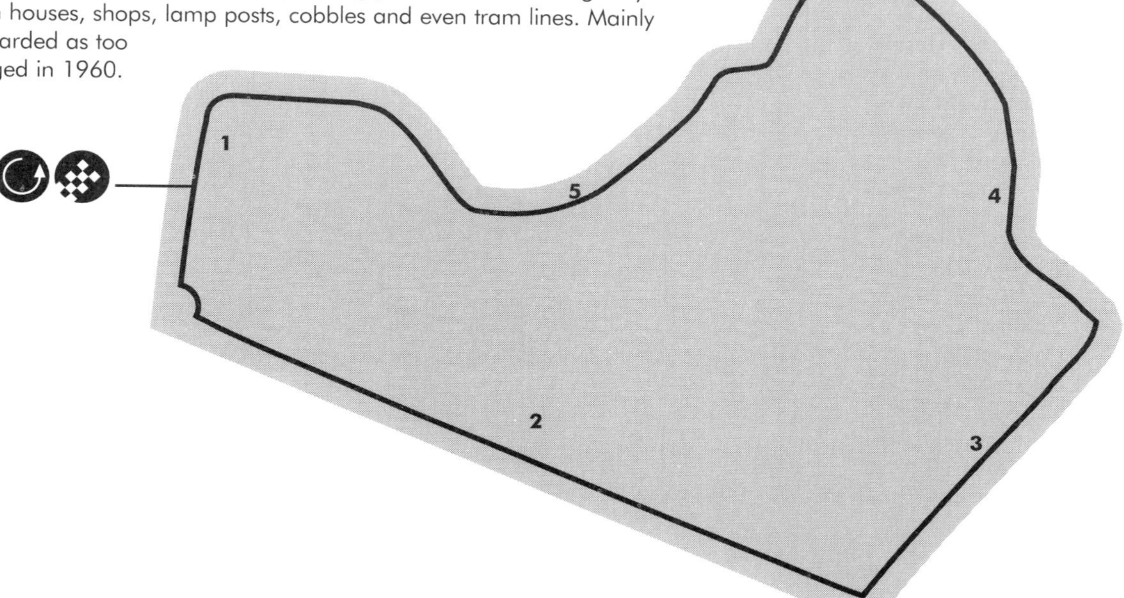

Key to the circuit:
1=Esplanade do Rio de Janeiro
2=Avenida da Boavista
3=Avenida de Atunes Guimaraes
4=Rua do Lidador
5=Estrada da Circunvalagäo

World Championship races: 2

	Length km	Length miles	Years (no. of races)	Driver (Car)	Time min:sec	Speed km/h	Speed mph	Year
a)	7.407	4.602	1958,60 (2)	**Pole:** J Surtees (Lotus)	2:25.560	183.190	113.829	1960
				F. Lap: J Surtees (Lotus)	2:27.530	180.744	112.309	1960
				Winner: J Brabham (Cooper)		175.849	109.268	1960

South Africa (ZA)

EAST LONDON

Location: Cape Province. **First Used:** July 1959.
Back in the 1930s, races were run around the public roads of this resort. A new circuit was built into a natural hollow by the coastline, which included a rifle range in part of the complex.

Key to the circuit:
1=Main Straight
2=Potters Pass Curve
3=Rifle Bend
4=Cocabana Corner
5=Beach Straight
6=Butts Bend
7=The Esses
8=Cox's Corner
9=The Sweep
10=Back Straight
11=Beacon Bend

World Championship races: 3

	Length km	Length miles	Years (no. of races)	Driver (Car)	Time min:sec	Speed km/h	Speed mph	Year
a)	3.920	2.436	1962-63,65 (3)	**Pole:** J Clark (Lotus)	1:27.200	161.850	100.569	1965
				F. Lap: J Clark (Lotus)	1:27.600	161.111	100.110	1965
				Winner: J Clark (Lotus)		157.722	98.004	1965

KYALAMI

Location: 24 km (15 miles) north of Johannesburg. **First Used:** December 1961.
Kyalami, meaning 'my house' in the Sesotro language, is built on a plateau, 5,000 feet above sea level. Its first rate facilities were popular with drivers, however South African politics caused the venue to be dropped from the schedule and part of the circuit was sold to developers. In 1987, work began on a total revamp of the circuit, using part of the old track, although the new tighter version was dropped after just two events.

Key to the circuit:
1=Crowthorne Corner
2=Barbeque Bend
3=Jukskei Sweep
4=Sunset Bend
5=Clubhouse Bend
6=The Esses
7=Leeukop Bend
8=The Kink
9=Brilliant Straight
10=Total Curve
11=Nashua
12=Budget Corner
13=Yellow Pages
14=Topsport Esses
15=Winfield
16=Wesbank
17=Mineshaft
18=Continental

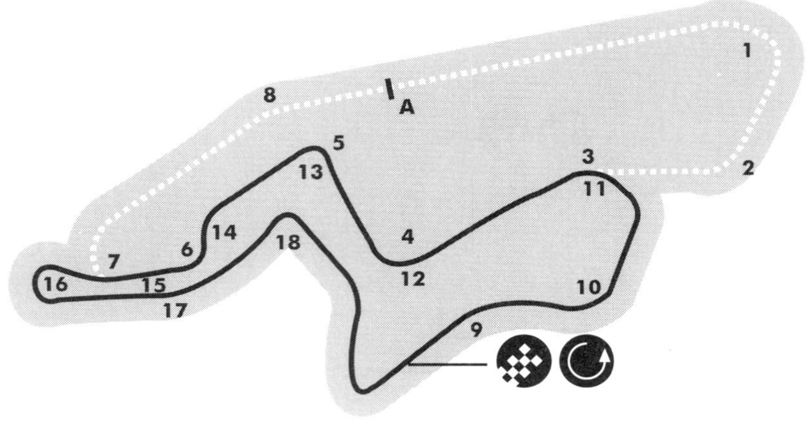

'A' signifies the original start line until 1985.

World Championship races: 20

	Length km	Length miles	Years (no. of races)	Driver (Car)	Time min:sec	Speed km/h	Speed mph	Year
a)	4.094	2.544	1967 (1)	**Pole:** J Brabham (Brabham)	1:28.300	166.920	103.719	1967
				F. Lap: D Hulme (Brabham)	1:29.900	163.949	101.873	1967
				Winner: P Rodriguez (Cooper)		156.260	97.095	1967
Widened								
b)	4.104	2.550	1968-80,82-85 (17)	**Pole:** N Mansell (Williams)	1: 2.366	236.898	147.202	1985
				F. Lap: K Rosberg (Williams)	1: 8.149	216.796	134.711	1985
				Winner: N Mansell (Williams)		208.959	129.841	1985
New circuit								
c)	4.261	2.648	1992-93 (2)	**Pole:** N Mansell (Williams)	1:15.486	203.211	126.270	1992
				F. Lap: N Mansell (Williams)	1:17.578	197.731	122.865	1992
				Winner: N Mansell (Williams)		190.248	118.215	1992

Spain (E)

JÁRAMA

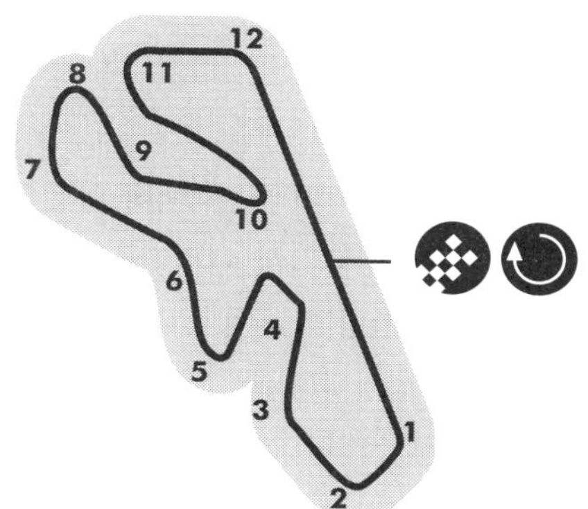

Location: 28 km (17 miles) north of Madrid. **First Used:** July 1967.
Designed by John Hugenholtz to fit into a small pocket of land in the arid and hilly scrubland north of Madrid. It was considered by many to be too cramped for car racing although it is still used in motorcycling and has developed as a golfing centre.

Key to the circuit:

1=Viraje Nuvolari
2=Viraje Fangio
3=Viraje Varzi
4=Virajes de Le Mans
5=Viraje Farina
6=Rampa Pegaso
7=Viraje Ascari
8=Virajes Portago
9=Eses de Bugatti
10=Viraje Pegio
11=Virajes de Monza
12=Viraje del Tunel

World Championship races: 9

	Length km	miles	Years (no. of races)	Driver (Car)	Time min:sec	Speed km/h	mph	Year
a)	3.404	2.115	1968,70,72,74,76-79 (8)	**Pole:** J Laffite (Ligier)	1:14.500	164.489	102.208	1979
				F. Lap: G Villeneuve (Ferrari)	1:16.440	160.314	99.614	1979
				Winner: P Depailler (Ligier)		154.419	95.952	1979
b)	3.312	2.058	1981 (1)	**Pole:** J Laffite (Ligier)	1:13.754	161.662	100.452	1981
				F. Lap: A Jones (Williams)	1:17.818	153.219	95.206	1981
				Winner: G Villeneuve (Ferrari)		149.156	92.681	1981

JEREZ de la FRONTERA

Location: North-east of Jerez de la Frontera, 35 km (22 miles) north-east of Cadiz. **First Used:** 1986.
Jerez reintroduced F1 in Spain, but due to its isolated location, deep in the sherry producing region of the southern plains, it has never attracted large crowds. It was dropped from the calender after Martin Donnelly's dreadful practice accident in 1990, but returned after a chicane was added prior to that corner, to become a last minute addition to the 1994 calendar.

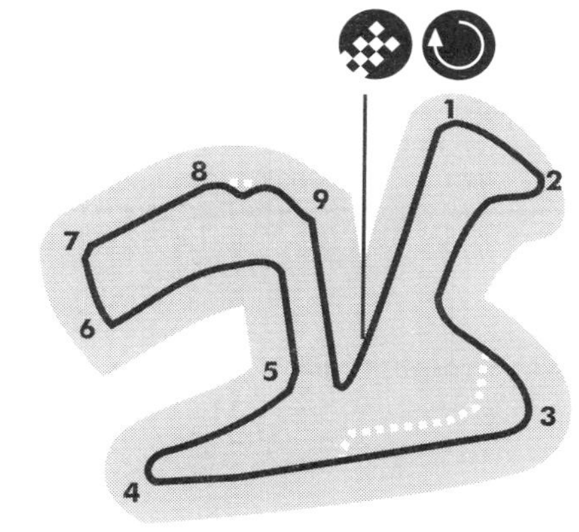

Key to the circuit:

1=Curva Expo 92
2=Curva Michelin
3=Curva Sito Pons
4=Curva Dry Sac
5=Curva Ducados
6=Curva Angel Nieto
7=Curva Peluqui
8=Curva Ayrton Senna
9=Curva Ferrari

World Championship races: 6 (including Grand Prix of Europe in 1994)

	Length km	miles	Years (no. of races)	Driver (Car)	Time min:sec	Speed km/h	mph	Year
a)	4.218	2.621	1986-90 (5)	**Pole:** A Senna (McLaren)	1:18.387	193.716	120.369	1990
				F. Lap: R Patrese (Williams)	1:24.513	179.674	111.644	1990
				Winner: A Senna (McLaren)		171.374	106.487	1989
New corner at '3' & chicane at '8'								
b)	4.428	2.751	1994 (1)	**Pole:** M Schumacher (Benetton)	1:22.762	192.610	119.682	1994
				F. Lap: M Schumacher (Benetton)	1:25.040	187.451	116.476	1994
				Winner: M Schumacher (Benetton)		182.507	113.405	1994

MONTJUICH PARK

Location: Barcelona (city centre). **First Used:** 1933.

Situated within the undulating roads of a public park, near Barcelona's Olympic stadium. The circuit was revived in 1966, but saw dreadful accidents in its time. The wings failed on both Lotus cars in 1969 and Rolf Stommelen suffered a similar problem in 1975, crashing over the barriers and killing four spectators. Montjuich was not used again.

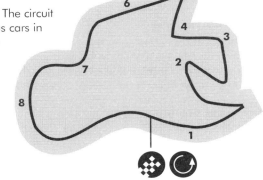

Key to the circuit:

1=Estadilo
2=Tecnica
3=Palico Agricultura
4=Riug y Taulet
5=Viraje
6=La Pergola
7=Peublo Español
8=San Jordi

World Championship races: 4

	Length km	miles	Years (no. of races)	Driver (Car)	Time min:sec	Speed km/h	mph	Year
a)	3.791	2.356	1969,71,73,75 (4)	**Pole:** R Peterson (JPS Lotus)	1:21.800	166.841	103.670	1973
				F. Lap: R Peterson (JPS Lotus)	1:23.800	162.859	101.196	1973
				Winner: E Fittipaldi (JPS Lotus)		157.504	97.868	1973

MONTMELO

Location: 20 km (12 miles) north of Barcelona. **First Used:** 1991.

Built on land purchased by the Real Automovil Club de Catalunya, who hoped to bring F1 back to Spain's spiritual home of motorsport on a permanent basis. Completed just in time for the first Grand Prix, it was well laid out for easy access and incorporated good viewing positions. Driver Luis Perez Sala advised on the layout which follows the principles of many modern day circuits.

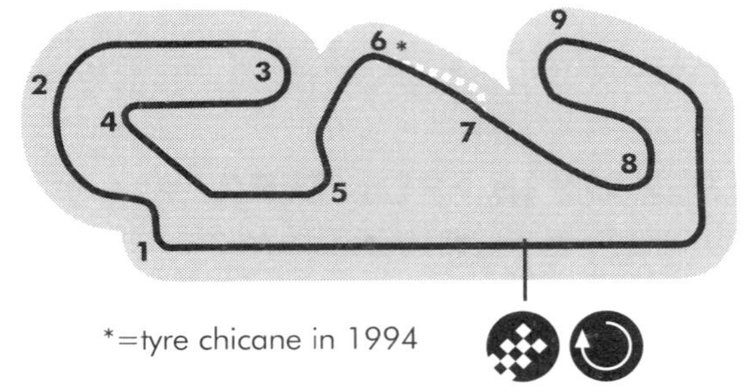

*=tyre chicane in 1994

Key to the circuit:

1=Curvone Elf
2=Revolt Renault
3=Revolt Repsol
4=Revolt Seat
5=Revolt Würth
6=Revolt Campsa
7=Nissan
8=Revolt La Caixa
9=Banc de Sabadell

World Championship races: 6

	Length km	miles	Years (no. of races)	Driver (Car)	Time min:sec	Speed km/h	mph	Year
a)	4.747	2.950	1991-94 (4)	**Pole:** A Prost (Williams)	1:17.809	219.630	136.472	1993
				F. Lap: M Schumacher (Benetton)	1:20.989	211.006	131.113	1993
				Winner: A Prost (Williams)		200.227	124.415	1993
Nissan straightened								
b)	4.727	2.937	1995-96 (2)	**Pole:** D Hill (Williams)	1:20.650	211.001	131.110	1996
				F. Lap: D Hill (Williams)	1:24.531	201.313	125.090	1995
				Winner: M Schumacher (Benetton)		195.320	121.367	1995

PEDRALBES

Location: Barcelona, 7 km (4 miles) north-west of city centre. **First Used:** 1946.

The circuit incorporated the wide avenues of the outskirts of the city, in the shadow of the Pedralbes Monastery. It was one of the first major venues after the war, when it hosted the Penya Rhin Grand Prix, but soon faded from the international calendar.

Key to the circuit:

1=Avenida del Generalisimo Franco
2=Carretera de Cornella a Fogas de Tordera
3=Avenida de la Victoria
4=Paseo de Manuel Girona
5=Calle de Numancia

World Championship races: 2

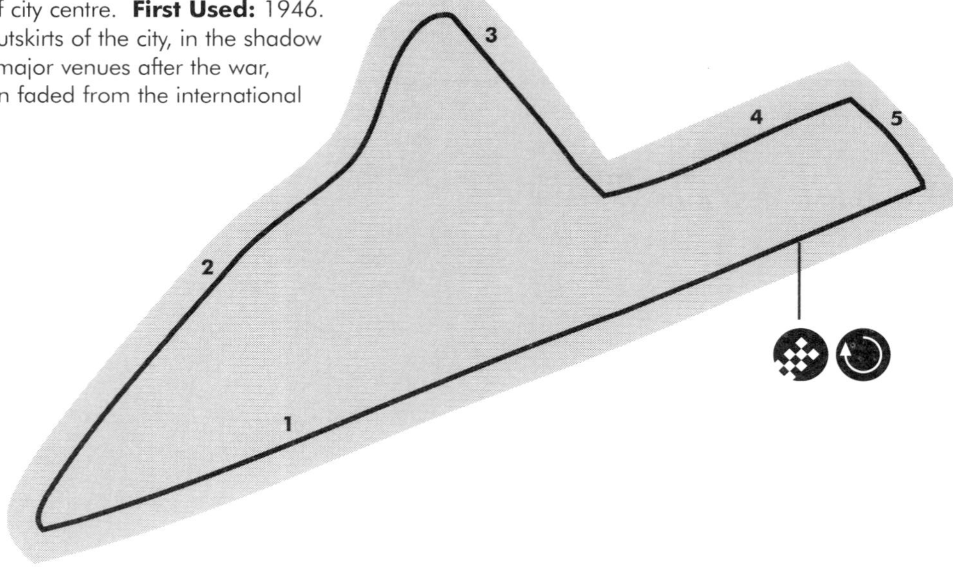

	Length km	miles	Years (no. of races)	Driver (Car)	Time min:sec	Speed km/h	mph	Year
a)	6.316	3.925	1951,54 (2)	**Pole:** A Ascari (Ferrari)	2:10.590	174.114	108.190	1951
				F. Lap: J M Fangio (Alfa Romeo)	2:16.930	166.053	103.180	1951
				Winner: J M Fangio (Alfa Romeo)		158.939	98.760	1951

Sweden (S)

ANDERSTORP

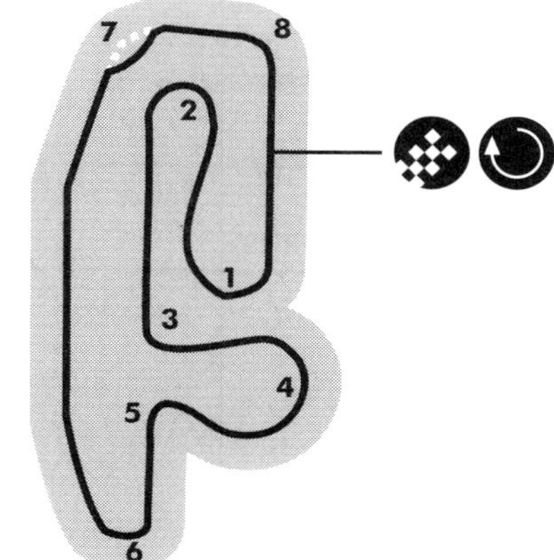

Location: 80 km (50 miles) south of Jönköping. **First Used:** 1968.
Conceived by Sven Asberg and built on flat marshland forest with a runway forming part of the back straight. Also known as the Scandinavian Raceway, Anderstorp was renowned for unpredictable race results.

Key to the circuit:
1=Startkurvan
2=Opelkurvan
3=Hansenkurvan
4=Karusellkurvan
5=Gislavedkurvan
6=Sodrakurvan
7=Norrakurvan
8=Läktarkurvan

World Championship races: 6

	Length km	miles	Years (no. of races)	Driver (Car)	Time min:sec	Speed km/h	mph	Year
a)	4.018	2.497	1973-77 (5)	**Pole:** R Peterson (JPS Lotus)	1:23.810	172.590	107.243	1973
				F. Lap: D Hulme (McLaren)	1:26.146	167.910	104.335	1973
				Winner: D Hulme (McLaren)		165.169	102.631	1973
Chicane at '7'								
b)	4.031	2.505	1978 (1)	**Pole:** M Andretti (JPS Lotus)	1:22.058	176.846	109.887	1978
				F. Lap: N Lauda (Brabham)	1:24.836	171.055	106.288	1978
				Winner: N Lauda (Brabham)		167.609	104.147	1978

Switzerland (CH)

BREMGARTEN

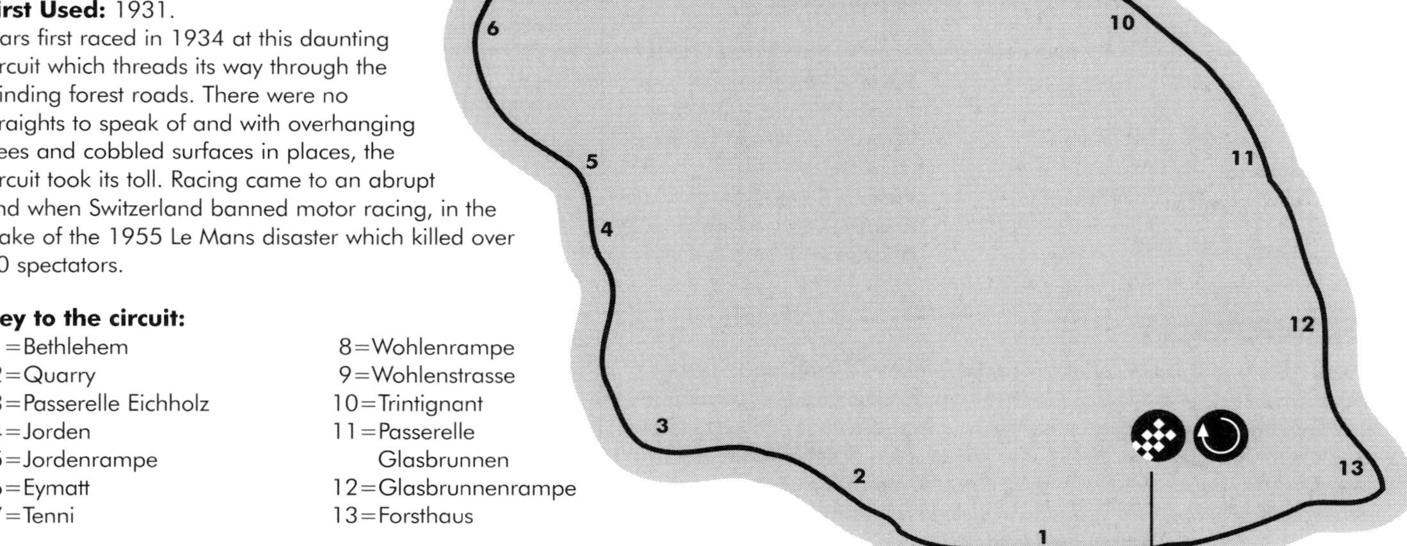

Location: North-west of Bern.
First Used: 1931.
Cars first raced in 1934 at this daunting circuit which threads its way through the winding forest roads. There were no straights to speak of and with overhanging trees and cobbled surfaces in places, the circuit took its toll. Racing came to an abrupt end when Switzerland banned motor racing, in the wake of the 1955 Le Mans disaster which killed over 80 spectators.

Key to the circuit:
1=Bethlehem
2=Quarry
3=Passerelle Eichholz
4=Jorden
5=Jordenrampe
6=Eymatt
7=Tenni
8=Wohlenrampe
9=Wohlenstrasse
10=Trintignant
11=Passerelle Glasbrunnen
12=Glasbrunnenrampe
13=Forsthaus

World Championship races: 5

	Length km	miles	Years (no. of races)	Driver (Car)	Time min:sec	Speed km/h	mph	Year
a)	7.280	4.524	1950-54 (5)	**Pole:** J M Fangio (Alfa Romeo)	2:35.900	168.108	104.457	1951
				F. Lap: J M Fangio (Mercedes)	2:39.700	164.108	101.972	1954
				Winner: J M Fangio (Mercedes-Benz)		159.650	99.202	1954

United States of America (USA)

DALLAS

Location: Dallas (city centre), Texas. **First Used:** 1984.
Located in the Fair Park area of the city, this was a fairly typical angular street circuit. Used only once, it is best remembered for the poor surface that crumbled during racing, catching out many of the drivers.

Key to the circuit:
Corners were not named

World Championship races: 1

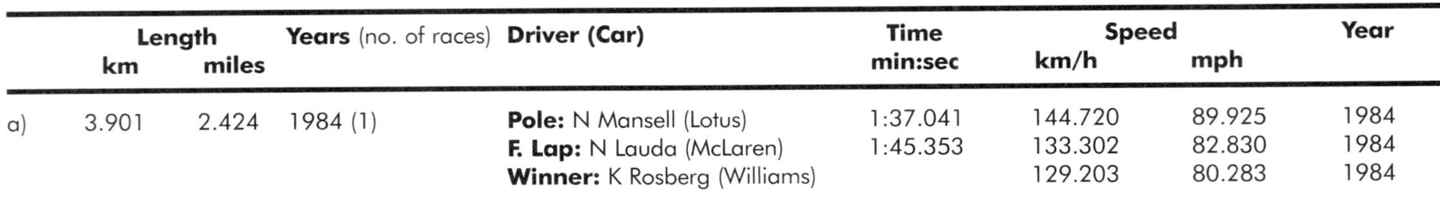

	Length km	Length miles	Years (no. of races)	Driver (Car)	Time min:sec	Speed km/h	Speed mph	Year
a)	3.901	2.424	1984 (1)	**Pole:** N Mansell (Lotus)	1:37.041	144.720	89.925	1984
				F. Lap: N Lauda (McLaren)	1:45.353	133.302	82.830	1984
				Winner: K Rosberg (Williams)		129.203	80.283	1984

DETROIT

Location: Detroit (city centre), Michigan. **First Used:** 1982.
A street circuit in Motown is a good marketing idea, but the right-angle nature of the course, didn't show F1 cars in their true light. A tunnel and the nearby water, didn't make for another Monaco and the race transferred to the IndyCar series in 1989, before they switched their venue to nearby Belle Isle.

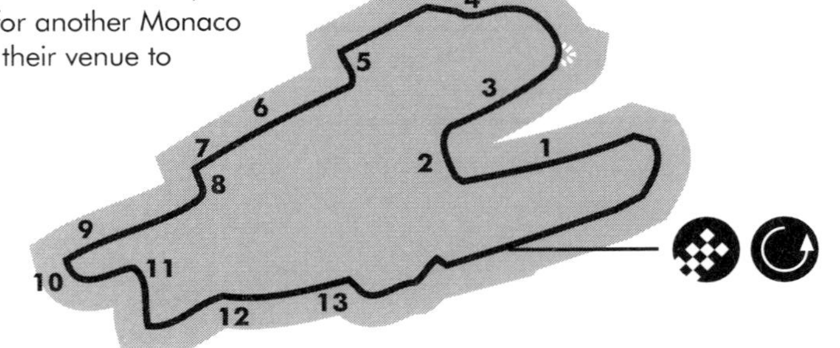

Key to the circuit:
1=Atwater Street
2=St. Antoine Street
3=Woodbridge Street
4=Congress
5=Beaubien
6=Larned Street
7=Larned Tunnel
8=Woodward Avenue
9=Jefferson Avenue
10=Washington Boulevard
11=Kodak Camera Corner
12=Goodyear Tunnel
13=Ford Corner

World Championship races: 7

	Length km	Length miles	Years (no. of races)	Driver (Car)	Time min:sec	Speed km/h	Speed mph	Year
a)	4.012	2.493	1982 (1)	**Pole:** A Prost (Renault)	1:48.537	133.075	82.689	1982
				F. Lap: A Prost (Renault)	1:50.438	130.784	81.266	1982
				Winner: J Watson (McLaren)		125.754	78.140	1982
Corners eased								
b)	4.023	2.500	1983-88 (6)	**Pole:** A Senna (Lotus)	1:38.301	147.344	91.556	1986
				F. Lap: A Senna (Lotus)	1:40.464	144.172	89.584	1987
				Winner: A Senna (Lotus)		137.915	85.697	1987

INDIANAPOLIS

Location: 10 km (6 miles) west of city centre, Indiana. **First Used:** 1909.
The oldest race track in the world. Carl Fisher organised construction of this world famous circuit, perfectly rectangular with 9 degree banked corners, eventually paved with over 3 million bricks (these were replaced with asphalt in 1961). The Indianapolis 500 began in 1911 and became the largest attended, one day sports event with over 400,000 spectators. After the war it was purchased by Anton Hulman who redeveloped the grounds to include a museum and a golf course, amongst other attractions. Included as a part of the world championship to attract American drivers for a brief period, it has confused historians ever since.

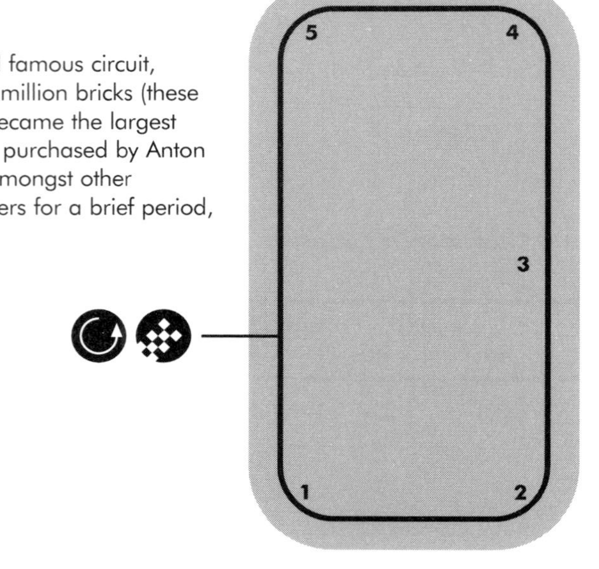

Key to the circuit:
1=South-west
2=South-east
3=Backstretch
4=North-east
5=North-west

World Championship races: 11

	Length km	miles	Years (no. of races)	Driver (Car)	Time min:sec	Speed km/h	mph	Year
a)	4.023	2.500	1950-60 (11)	**Pole:** E Sachs (Ewing)	1: 1.395	235.917	146.592	1960
				F. Lap: J Rathmann (Watson)	1: 1.590	235.170	146.128	1960
				Winner: J Rathmann (Watson)		223.324	138.767	1960

LAS VEGAS

Location: Las Vegas, Nevada. **First Used:** 1981.
Built within the confines of Caesars Palace Hotel car park, with the use of interlocking concrete barriers. A true temporary circuit, it ran anti-clockwise and witnessed the championship showdown in both years.

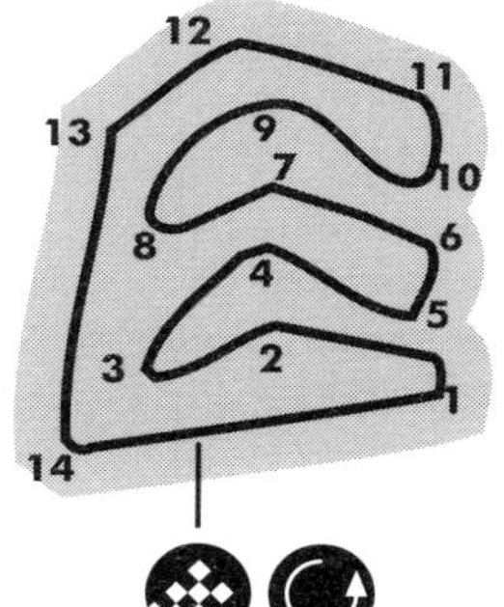

Key to the circuit:
Corners were simply known numerically

World Championship races: 2

	Length km	miles	Years (no. of races)	Driver (Car)	Time min:sec	Speed km/h	mph	Year
a)	3.650	2.268	1981-82 (2)	**Pole:** A Prost (Renault)	1:16.356	172.088	106.931	1982
				F. Lap: M Alboreto (Tyrrell)	1:19.639	164.994	102.523	1982
				Winner: M Alboreto (Tyrrell)		161.111	100.110	1982

LONG BEACH

Location: Long Beach (waterfront), southern Los Angeles, California. **First Used:** 1975.
Originated by Chris Pook, who arranged for this street race around the sea's edge under the shadow of the Queen Mary ship. It achieved its objective of adding glamour to this part of Los Angeles, but after substantial circuit route changes, the race transferred to IndyCars.

Key to the circuit:

1=Shoreline Drive
2=Bridgestone Bend
3=Queen's Hairpin
4=Pine Avenue
5=Toyota Corner
6=Ocean Boulevard
7=Cook's Corner
8=Linden Avenue
9=Penthouse Corner
10=Les Esses du Clos
11=Indy Left
12=Le Gasomet
13=Toyota Corner (new)
14=Michelob Corner
15=Hyatt Garage
16=Seaside Way

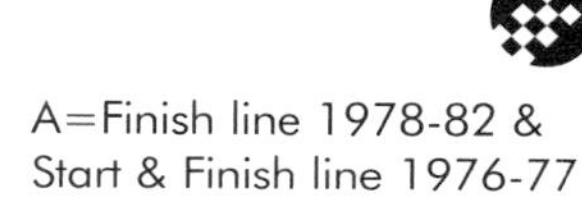

A=Finish line 1978-82 &
Start & Finish line 1976-77

World Championship races: 8

	Length km	miles	Years (no. of races)	Driver (Car)	Time min:sec	Speed km/h	mph	Year
a)	3.251	2.020	1976-81 (6)	**Pole:** N Piquet (Brabham)	1:17.694	150.637	93.602	1980
				F. Lap: N Piquet (Brabham)	1:19.830	146.607	91.097	1980
				Winner: N Piquet (Brabham)		142.348	88.451	1980
New route (Michelob at '14')								
b)	3.428	2.130	1982 (1)	**Pole:** A de Cesaris (Alfa Romeo)	1:27.316	141.331	87.819	1982
				F. Lap: N Lauda (McLaren)	1:30.831	135.862	84.421	1982
				Winner: N Lauda (McLaren)		131.128	81.479	1982
Shortened (Seaside Way at '16')								
c)	3.275	2.035	1983 (1)	**Pole:** P Tambay (Ferrari)	1:26.117	136.907	85.070	1983
				F. Lap: N Lauda (McLaren)	1:28.330	133.477	82.939	1983
				Winner: J Watson (McLaren)		129.753	80.625	1983

PHOENIX

Location: Phoenix (west of city centre), Arizona. **First Used:** 1989.
Another point and squirt, 90 degree street circuit, laid out amongst concrete barriers. Phoenix never proved to be popular with drivers or spectators, and after an attempt to rearrange the circuit with less right angle bends, it was never used again.

Key to the circuit:
1=Jefferson Street
2=1st Street
3=Madison Street
4=Jackson Street
5=5th Street
6=Munroe Street
7=3rd Street
8=Washington Street
9=3rd Avenue
10=Adams Street
11=5th Avenue

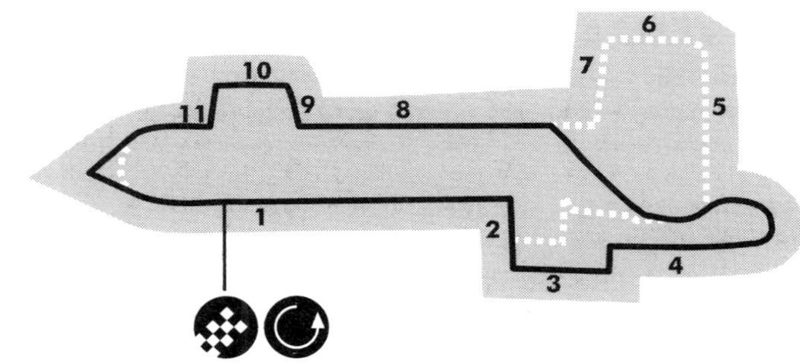

World Championship races: 3

	Length km	miles	**Years** (no. of races)	**Driver (Car)**	**Time** min:sec	**Speed** km/h	mph	**Year**
a)	3.798	2.360	1989-90 (2)	**Pole:** G Berger (McLaren)	1:28.664	154.211	95.822	1990
				F. Lap: G Berger (McLaren)	1:31.050	150.170	93.311	1990
				Winner: A Senna (McLaren)		145.784	90.586	1990
Munroe Street by-pass								
b)	3.721	2.312	1991 (1)	**Pole:** A Senna (McLaren)	1:21.434	164.488	102.208	1991
				F. Lap: J Alesi (Ferrari)	1:26.758	154.394	95.936	1991
				Winner: A Senna (McLaren)		149.698	93.018	1991

RIVERSIDE

Location: 100 km (60 miles) east of Los Angeles, California. **First Used:** 1957.
A purpose-built circuit with various combinations, including a drag strip. It was deep in the hilly desert country which made corner marking difficult. It fell into disrepair and was closed in 1988.

Key to the circuit:
Corners were simply known numerically.
Corners 2 to 5 were also known as 'Esses'.

World Championship races: 1

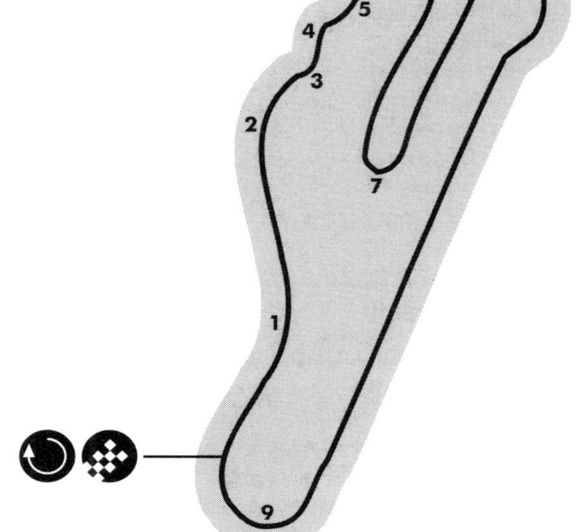

	Length km	miles	**Years** (no. of races)	**Driver (Car)**	**Time** min:sec	**Speed** km/h	mph	**Year**
a)	5.271	3.275	1960 (1)	**Pole:** S Moss (Lotus)	1:54.400	165.858	103.059	1960
				F. Lap: J Brabham (Cooper)	1:56.300	163.148	101.376	1960
				Winner: S Moss (Lotus)		159.318	98.996	1960

SEBRING

Location: 137 km (85 miles) south of Oralndo, Florida. **First Used:** 1950.
Conceived by Alex Ulmann, who created the circuit from a combination of concrete runway and tarmac roads of the disused wartime Hendrick Field airbase. It has become an important venue for sports car racing and due to its nature has had various permutations, most notably in 1966 and 1987.

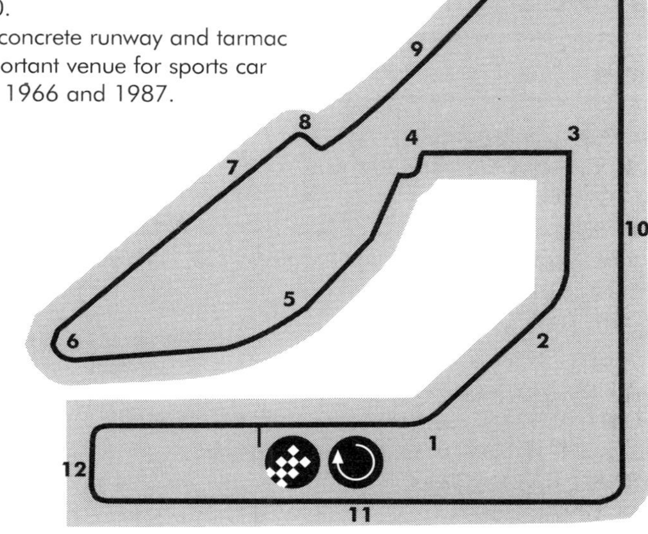

Key to the circuit:
1=First Bend
2=Second Bend
3=Tower Turn
4=The Esses
5=Big Bend
6=Hairpin Turn
7=Warehouse Straight
8=Webster Turn
9=Green Park Boulevard
10=The Straight (North South Runway)
11=Backstretch (East West Runway)
12=U Turn

World Championship races: 1

	Length km	Length miles	Years (no. of races)	Driver (Car)	Time min:sec	Speed km/h	Speed mph	Year
a)	8.369	5.200	1959 (1)	**Pole:** S Moss (Cooper)	3: 0.000	167.372	104.000	1959
				F. Lap: M Trintignant (Cooper)	3: 5.000	162.848	101.189	1959
				Winner: B McLaren (Cooper)		159.047	98.827	1959

WATKINS GLEN

Location: 30 km (18 miles) north of Elmira, New York State. **First Used:** 1956.
After races in the village and on surrounding public roads, a new track, designed by Bill Milliken, was built in the wooded hill tops of the Lake Seneca area. The summer of 1971 saw a radical redesign of the circuit, again with the help of Cornell University. The twisting undulations of the track caught out many drivers including François Cevert, who was killed in practice for what would have been team-mate Jackie Stewart's last race before his retirement.

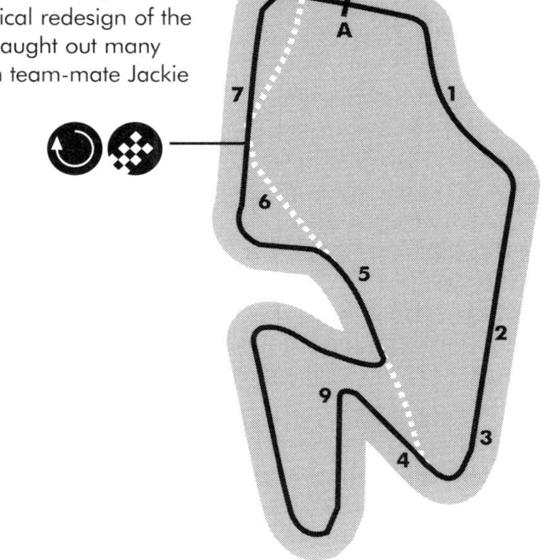

Key to the circuit:
1=The Esses
2=Wedgewood/ Front Straight
3=The Loop
4=The Dip/ Chute
5=The Fast/ Back Straight
6=The Speed Trap
7=Big/ Fast Bend
8=The Hard Right/ The 90°
9=The Anvil

'A' signifies the original startline until 1971.

World Championship races: 20

	Length km	Length miles	Years (no. of races)	Driver (Car)	Time min:sec	Speed km/h	Speed mph	Year
a)	3.701	2.300	1961-70 (10)	**Pole:** J Ickx (Ferrari)	1: 3.070	211.279	131.283	1970
				F. Lap: J Ickx (Ferrari)	1: 2.740	212.390	131.973	1970
				Winner: E Fittipaldi (Lotus)		204.053	126.792	1970
Revised (including 'The Anvil')								
b)	5.435	3.377	1971-80 (10)	**Pole:** B Giacomelli (Alfa Romeo)	1:33.291	209.721	130.315	1980
				F. Lap: A Jones (Williams)	1:34.068	207.989	129.238	1980
				Winner: A Jones (Williams)		203.371	126.369	1980

Circuit Summary

CIRCUIT	COUNTRY	NO. OF RACES	YEARS
ADELAIDE, South Australia	AUSTRALIA	11	1985-95
AIDA/ TI, near Okayama City	JAPAN	2	1994-95
AIN-DIAB, Casablanca	MOROCCO	1	1958
AINTREE, Liverpool	BRITAIN	5	1955-62
ANDERSTORP/ SCANDINAVIAN RACEWAY, near Jönköping	SWEDEN	6	1973-78
AVUS, Berlin	GERMANY	1	1959
BRANDS HATCH, near Dartford, Kent	BRITAIN	14	1964-86
BREMGARTEN, near Bern	SWITZERLAND	5	1950-54
BUENOS AIRES/ ALMIRANTE BROWN no.2,6,9,15	ARGENTINA	18	1953-96
BUGATTI AU MANS, Le Mans	FRANCE	1	1967
CLERMONT-FERRAND, Montagne d'Auvergne	FRANCE	4	1965-72
DALLAS/ FAIR PARK, Texas	USA	1	1984
DETROIT, Michigan	USA	7	1982-88
DIJON-PRENOIS, near Dijon	FRANCE	6	1974-84
DONINGTON PARK, near Derby	BRITAIN	1	1993
EAST LONDON, Cape Province	SOUTH AFRICA	3	1962-65
ESTORIL, near Lisbon	PORTUGAL	13	1984-96
FUJI, near Yokohama/ Tokyo	JAPAN	2	1976-77
HOCKENHEIM, near Heidelberg	GERMANY	20	1970-96
HUNGARORING, Mogyorod, Budapest	HUNGARY	11	1986-96
IMOLA/ ENZO & DINO-FERRARI, near Bologna	ITALY	17	1980-96
INDIANAPOLIS, Indiana	USA	11	1950-60
INTERLAGOS, Sao Paulo	BRAZIL	14	1973-96
JARAMA, near Madrid	SPAIN	9	1968-81
JEREZ de la FRONTERA, near Cadiz	SPAIN	6	1986-94
KYALAMI, near Johannesburg	SOUTH AFRICA	20	1967-93
LAS VEGAS/ CAESARS PALACE, Nevada	USA	2	1981-82
LONG BEACH, Los Angeles, California	USA	8	1976-83
MAGNY-COURS, near Nevers	FRANCE	6	1991-96
MELBOURNE/ ALBERT PARK	AUSTRALIA	1	1996
MEXICO CITY/ HERMANOS R & P RODRIGUEZ/ MAGDALENA MIXHUCA	MEXICO	15	1963-92
MONSANTO PARK, Lisbon	PORTUGAL	1	1959
MONT-TREMBLANT/ ST.-JOVITE, near Montréal, Québec	CANADA	2	1968-70
MONTE CARLO	MONACO	43	1950-96
MONTJUICH PARK, Barcelona	SPAIN	4	1969-75
MONTMELO/ CATALUNYA, near Barcelona	SPAIN	6	1991-96
MONTRÉAL/ GILLES VILLENEUVE/ ILE NOTRE DAME	CANADA	18	1978-96
MONZA, near Milan	ITALY	46	1950-96
MOSPORT PARK, near Bowmanville, Ontario	CANADA	8	1967-77
NIVELLES-BAULERS, near Brussels	BELGIUM	2	1972-74
NÜRBURGRING, near Koblenz	GERMANY	26	1951-96
ÖSTERREICHRING, near Knittelfeld	AUSTRIA	18	1970-87
PAUL RICARD/ LE CASTELLET, near Marseille	FRANCE	14	1971-90
PEDRALBES, Barcelona	SPAIN	2	1951-54
PESCARA	ITALY	1	1957
PHOENIX	USA	3	1989-91
PORTO	PORTUGAL	2	1958-60
REIMS & REIMS-GUEUX	FRANCE	11	1950-66
RIO de JANEIRO/ NELSON PIQUET/ JACAREPAGUA	BRAZIL	10	1978-89
RIVERSIDE, near Los Angeles, California	USA	1	1960
ROUEN-les-ESSARTS	FRANCE	5	1952-68
SEBRING, Florida	USA	1	1959
SILVERSTONE, near Towcester, Northamptonshire	BRITAIN	30	1950-96
SPA-FRANCORCHAMPS, near Liège	BELGIUM	31	1950-96
SUZUKA, near Nagoya	JAPAN	10	1987-96
WATKINS GLEN, near Elmira, New York State	USA	20	1961-80
ZANDVOORT, near Haarlem	NETHERLANDS	30	1952-85
ZELTWEG, near Knittelfeld	AUSTRIA	1	1964
ZOLDER, near Hasselt	BELGIUM	10	1973-84

TOTAL RACES:
597
(inc. 11 at Indianapolis)

TOTAL VENUES:
59
(inc. Indianapolis)

TOTAL COUNTRIES TO HOST A RACE:
22

TOTAL LAPS IN THE WORLD CHAMPIONSHIP1950-1996:
40,506.6
(inc. 2,138.0 at Indy)

TOTAL DISTANCE: 200,314 km
(inc. 8,602 km at Indy)

TOTAL DRIVERS ENTRANTS IN THE WORLD CHAMPIONSHIP:
814
(inc. 178 only at Indy)

TOTAL STARTING DRIVERS:
673
(inc. 103 only at Indy)
(inc. 4 who started an F1 and Indy race)

TOTAL NON-STARTERS:
66 plus an additional 75 Indy

TOTAL RACE STARTERS IN THE WORLD CHAMPIONSHIP:
13,874

RECORDS & TRIVIA

SEASONS

SEASON LENGTH

Longest	MONTHS	DAYS
1968	10	2
1965	9	23
1967	9	20
1977	9	14
1960	9	13
Shortest		
1952	3	20
1950	3	21
1961	4	24
1951	5	1
1966	5	1

CLOSED SEASON

Longest	MONTHS	DAYS
1950/51	8	24
1961/62	7	12
1958/59	6	31
1965/66	6	28
1951/52	6	20
Shortest		
1959/60	1	26
1964/65	2	7
1966/67	2	10
1967/68	2	10
1976/77	2	16

SEASON OPENER

Earliest

1 January 1965
" 1968
2 January 1967

Latest

27 May 1951
26 May 1963
22 May 1960

SEASON CLOSER

Earliest

2 September 1956
3 September 1950
7 September 1952

Latest

29 December 1962
28 December 1963
12 December 1959

The last time that a Grand Prix was run on a Saturday was 3 Nov 1985 in South Africa.

VENUES

COUNTRIES STAGING A CHAMPIONSHIP RACE

Italy	64(a)
United States	54(b)
Great Britain	50(c)
Germany	47(c)
France	47(d)
Belgium	43
Monaco	43
Netherlands	30
Canada	28
Spain	27(e)
Brazil	24
South Africa	23
Austria	19
Argentina	18
Mexico	15
Portugal	16
Japan	14(f)
Australia	12
Hungary	11
Sweden	6
Switzerland	5
Morocco	1

(a) includes 1 Pescara & 16 San Marino GPs
(b) includes 11 Indianapolis 500 races
(c) includes 3 European GPs
(d) includes 1 Swiss GP
(e) includes 1 European GP
(f) includes 2 Pacific GPs

The only countries to produce a race winner and yet never host a Grand Prix are Finland and New Zealand

COUNTRIES STAGING ANOTHER COUNTRY'S GP

Dijon-Prenois (France)	Swiss GP 1982
Imola (Italy)	San Marino GP 1981-94 (14 races)

RACES IN ONE COUNTRY IN A SEASON (Most)

USA 82 — 3 (Long Beach, Detroit & Las Vegas)

CIRCUITS USED (Most races at)

Monza, I *(every year exc. 1980)*	46
Monte Carlo, MC	43
Spa-Francorchamps, B	31
Silverstone, GB	30
Zandvoort, NL	30

OPENING VENUE (Most races at)

Buenos Aires, RA	15 (1953-80)
Kyalami, ZA	8 (1967-93)
Rio de Janeiro, BR	7 (1983-89)
Monte Carlo, MC	5 (1959-66)

CLOSING VENUE (Most races at)

Adelaide, AUS	11 (1985-95)
Watkins Glen, USA	8 (1961-80)
Mexico City, MEX	7 (1964-70)
Monza, I	6 (1950-57)

LANDMARKS

100th World Championship race	D 61
200th	MC 71
250th	USA 74
300th	ZA 78
400th	A 84
500th	AUS 90

RACES IN A SEASON

Most

17 — 1977 & 1995

Fewest

7 — 1950 & 1955*

** includes 1 Indianapolis 500 in each year*

CIRCUITS WHICH HAVE MOVED THEIR STARTLINE

Kyalami	Spa-Francorchamps
Monaco	Watkins Glen
Montréal	Silverstone

RACE LENGTH (Time)

Longest	
D 54	3h 45m 45.800s
D 56	3h 38m 43.700s
D 57	3h 30m 38.300s
D 51	3h 23m 03.300s
F 51	3h 22m 11.000s
Indy	
INDY 51	3h 57m 38.050s

Shortest (all shortened races)	
AUS 91	24m 34.899s
E 75	42m 53.700s
A 75	57m 56.690s
MC 84	1h 01m 07.740s
I 78	1h 07m 04.540s

The shortest full distance race was Italy 1987 at 1h 14m 47.707s

RACE LENGTH (Distance)

Longest	KM	MILES
INDY 51-60	804.672	500.000
F 51	601.832	373.961
INDY 50	555.224	345.000
B 51-56	508.320	315.855
B 60	507.600	315.408
F 54,56	506.422	314.676
Shortest		
AUS 91	52.920	32.883
MC 84	102.672	63.797
E 75	109.939	68.313
A 75	171.419	106.515
B 81	230.148	143.007

CIRCUIT LENGTH

Longest	KM	MILES
Pescara 57	25.579	15.894
Nürburgring 67-76	22.835	14.189
Nürburgring 51-66	22.810	14.173
Spa 50-56	14.120	8.774
Spa 58-70	14.100	8.761
Shortest		
Monte Carlo 55-72	3.145	1.954
Monte Carlo 50	3.180	1.976
Zeltweg 64	3.200	1.988
Long Beach 76-81	3.251	2.020
Long Beach 83	3.275	2.035

LAPS IN A RACE

Most

110	USA 63-65
108	USA 66-70
105	MC 57
105	A 64
101	GB 56

The Indy 500 ran a full distance of 200 laps from 1951 to 1960

Fewest

12	D 71
14	D 68-69, 72-76
14	AUS 91
15	D 58, 61-67

LAPS RACED IN A SEASON

Most

1,132	1977
1,124	1995
1,060.5	1982

Fewest

391	1950
415	1951
447	1952

excludes Indy

RACES IN TWO PARTS, WITH TIMES AGGREGATED

D 59 *	A 78	ZA 79
F 81	DET 82	GB 84
MEX 87	RSM 89	F 92
RSM 94	J 94	

** intentionally a 2-part race*

RACES STOPPED AND RESTARTED AS A NEW RACE

GB 73	GB 76	D 76
I 78	RA 79	CDN 80
B 81	CDN 82	DET 84
A 84	A 85	GB 86
B 87	A 87 *	P 87
MEX 89	F 89	AUS 89
MC 90	B 90 *	I 90
RA 95	MC 95	I 95
P 95	AUS 96	

** 3 starts*

The most entrants in a race was 39. This occurred for the majority of the races during the 1989 season.

TOTAL DRIVER ENTRANTS

Most

76 - 1952	(71 starters)
73 - 1953	(71)
62 - 1974	(56)
61 - 1977	(49)

Fewest

24 - 1996
32 - 1986 & 87
35 - 1983, 84 & 93

NATIONALITIES IN A SEASON

Most

19 - 1974
18 - 1977* & 78*
16 - 1976**
17 - 1971 & 79
16 - 1973*, 80* & 82*

Fewest

10 - 1954, 55 & 91*
11 - 1950, 53, 57, 92, 93 & 96

** plus 1 nq/ns ** plus 2 nq/ns*

STARTERS

Most

34	D 53
32	I 61
31	GB 52
31	USA 72
31	B 74

(exc INDY races which had 33 on each grid)

Fewest

10	RA 58
13	B 51
13	B 55
13	RA 56
13	E 68
13	F 69

CLASSIFIED FINISHERS

Most

22	INDY 50
22	GB 52
20	INDY 52
20	CDN 76
19	INDY 56
19	USAE 77
19	MEX 90
19	AUS 91
19	EUR 94

Fewest

4	MC 66
4*	MC 96
5	D 56
5	B 66
5	E 68
5	MC 68
5	E 70
5	RSM 82
5	DET 84

** including one driver in the pits at the chequered flag*

RETIREMENTS

Most

21	ZA 93
20	I 61
20	GB 75
20	RSM 86

excludes Indy

Fewest

0	NL 61
1	RA 58

Not only were there no retirements at NL 61 but there is no record of any pit stops either.

CARS RETIRED BEFORE END OF FIRST LAP

Most

11	D 94
10	GB 73
9	MC 50
9	D 76
8	B 66

J Oliver was the only driver to be the first retirement in four successive races, from F to NL 1973. He was also the first retirement in three successive races from E to NL 1969.

RETIREMENTS IN A SEASON BY DRIVER

Most

A de Cesaris	16 *(every race)*	(1987)
A Nannini	15	(1987)
I Capelli	15	(1989)

RETIREMENTS BEFORE THE END OF LAP 1 BY DRIVER

Most

A de Cesaris	11
P Tambay	10
J-P Jarier	9
P Martini	9

DRIVERS

Starts

R Patrese	256
A de Cesaris	208
N Piquet	204
A Prost	200
G Berger	196
M Alboreto	194
N Mansell	187
G Hill	176
J Laffite	176
N Lauda	171
T Boutsen	163
A Senna	161
M Brundle	158
J Watson	152
R Arnoux	149
D Warwick	147
C Reutemann	146
E Fittipaldi	144
J-P Jarier	135
E Cheever	132
C Regazzoni	132
M Andretti	128
J Brabham	126
R Peterson	123
P Martini	119
J Alesi	118

J Ickx	116
A Jones	116
K Rosberg	114
P Tambay	114
D Hulme	112
J Scheckter	112
J Surtees	111
P Alliot	109
E de Angelis	108
J Mass	105
J Bonnier	104
B McLaren	101
J Stewart	99
C Amon	97
J Herbert	96
J Siffert	96
P Depailler	95
I Capelli	93
J Hunt	92
J-P Beltoise	86
D Gurney	86
M Schumacher	85
J Palmer	84
M Surer	82
M Trintignant	82
M Häkkinen	79
S Johansson	79
U Katayama	78
A Nannini	77
P Ghinzani	76
V Brambilla	74
M Gugelmin	74
S Nakajima	74
H-J Stuck	74
J Clark	72
C Pace	72
S Modena	70
D Pironi	70
B Giacomelli	69
D Hill	67
G Villeneuve	67
S Moss	66
R Barrichello	64
T Fabi	64
A Suzuki	64
J J Lehto	62
M Blundell	61
G Morbidelli	60
J Rindt	60
P Alliot	109
J Palmer	84
M Surer	82

The following drivers only ever started in the F2 section of a Grand Prix: T Bridger, P England, D Gibson, C Goethals, A Guelfi, B Hart, R La Caze, X Perrot, F Picard, P Westbury

ACTIVE SEASONS

G Hill	18 (1958-75)
R Patrese	17 (1977-93)
J Bonnier	16 (1956-71)
J Brabham	16 (1955-70)

Drivers who achieved more than one top six placing by car sharing in the same race were J M Fangio in MC 56 and G Farina & M Trintignant both in RA 55

The last time a car was shared in a race was at USA 64 between M Spence and J Clark

STARTER AGE

Youngest

M Thackwell	19y 5m 29d
R Rodriguez	19y 6m 27d
C Amon	19y10m 20d
E Cheever	20y 1m 22d
T Marques	20y 2m 12d
P Collins	21y 6m 12d

Indy

T Ruttman	20y 2m 19d

Oldest

L Chiron	55y 9m 19d
P Étançelin	55y 6m 8d
A Legat	54y 7m 20d
L Fagioli	53y 0m 22d
A Brudes	52y 9m 19d

It is probable that E Cantoni was about 56 years old when he raced in 1952. Exact date of birth not known

SUCCESSIVE STARTS (Most)

R Patrese	186	B 82-AUS 93
A Prost	173	USAW 81-J 91
A Senna	149	EUR 84-RSM 94
T Boutsen	138	CDN 84-AUS 92
G Berger	126	MEX 89-J 96
M Alboreto	117	A 81-BR 89
R Peterson	114	ZA 71-I 78
J Scheckter	107	CDN 73-I 80
J Laffite	96	BR 76-USAW 82
G Hill	90	USA 60-USA 69
M Andretti	87	S 76-LV 81
J Hunt	87	CDN 73-MC 79
P Depailler	85	RA 74-MC 79
J Herbert	83	J 91-J 96

STARTS WITHOUT A WIN (Most)

A de Cesaris	208
M Brundle	158
D Warwick	147
J-P Jarier	135
E Cheever	132
P Martini	119
P Alliot	109

STARTS WITHOUT A POLE POSITION (Most)

M Brundle	158
D Warwick	147
E Cheever	132
P Martini	119
P Alliot	109

STARTS WITHOUT A FASTEST LAP (Most)

M Brundle	158
E Cheever	132
P Martini	119
P Alliot	109
E de Angelis	108

STARTS WITHOUT A POINT (Most)

L Badoer	34
B Lunger	34
M Beuttler	28
H Rothengatter	26
R Keegan	25
D Brabham	24

STARTS WITHOUT LEADING (Most)

M Brundle	158
E Cheever	132

STARTS WITH SAME CONSTRUCTOR (Most)

J Laffite	132	Ligier
A Prost	107	McLaren
N Piquet	106	Brabham
P Martini	103	Minardi
G Berger	96	Ferrari
A Senna	96	McLaren
N Mansell	95	Williams
E de Angelis	90	Lotus
D Hulme	86	McLaren
R Patrese	81	Williams
M Alboreto	80	Ferrari
J Brabham	80	Brabham
P Depailler	80	Tyrrell

J Clark started the most races exclusively for one constructor, with 72 for Lotus.

SUCCESSIVE STARTS WITH SAME CONSTRUCTOR (Most)

J Laffite	96	(Ligier, 1976-82)
A Prost	96	(McLaren, 1984-89)
A Senna	96	(McLaren, 1988-93)
R Patrese	81	(Williams, 1987-92)
M Alboreto	80	(Ferrari, 1984-88)
P Depailler	78	(Tyrrell, 1974-78)
M Andretti	72	(Lotus, 1976-80)
J Alesi	66	(Ferrari, 1991-95)
G Villeneuve	66	(Ferrari, 1977-82)
D Hill	65	(Williams, 1993-96)
C Reutemann	64	(Brabham, 1972-76)
A Jones	60	(Williams, 1978-81)

STARTS WITH SAME ENGINE MAKE (Most)

E Fittipaldi	143	Ford Cosworth
J-P Jarier	130	Ford Cosworth
R Peterson	122	Ford Cosworth
J Watson	115	Ford Cosworth
A Jones	111	Ford Cosworth
J Mass	105	Ford Cosworth
M Andretti	101	Ford Cosworth
C Reutemann	100	Ford Cosworth
G Berger	96	Ferrari
A Senna	96	Honda
G Hill	94	Ford Cosworth
J Hunt	92	Ford Cosworth
M Alboreto	89	Ferrari

STARTS WITH TURBOCHARGED ENGINE (Most)

A Prost	126
R Arnoux	120
N Piquet	106
D Warwick	100
R Patrese	89
M Alboreto	80
E Cheever	79
A Senna	78
A de Cesaris	72

STARTS AS TEAM-MATES (Most)

J Alesi/ G Berger	63	1993-96
N Mansell/ E de Angelis	59 (2)	1980-84
N Lauda/ C Regazzoni	56 (1)	1973-76
I Capelli/ M Gugelmin	55 (7)	1988-91
G Berger/ A Senna	48	1990-92
N Mansell/ R Patrese	46	1988-92
D Warwick/ E Cheever	45 (2)	1987-89
J Stewart/ F Cevert	45 (1)	1970-73
J Scheckter/ P Depailler	45	1974-76
N Lauda/ J Watson	44 (2)	1978-83

The number of races refers to races which both started. Numbers in brackets refer to races which one or both did not start.

DRIVER ACHIEVEMENTS PER COUNTRY
(Number of drivers)

	starters	point scorers	winners	champions
Great Britain GB	137	54	16	8
Italy I	79	44	13	2
France F	63	33	12	1
United States USA	47	16	5	2
Germany D	37	13	3	1
Switzerland CH	22	6	2	-
Brazil BR	20	12	4	3
Argentina RA	19	7	3	1
Belgium B	19	7	2	-
South Africa ZA	17	3	1	1
Australia AUS	12	3	2	2
Austria A	11	5	3	2
Netherlands NL	11	3	-	-
Canada CDN	11	2	2	-
Japan J	10	3	-	-
Sweden S	9	6	3	-
New Zealand NZ	8	4	2	1
Spain E	7	3	-	-
Finland FIN	5	4	1	1
Mexico MEX	4	3	1	-
Ireland IRL	3	1	-	-
S Rhodesia RSR	3	1	-	-
Uruguay U	3	-	-	-
Monaco MC	2	1	-	-
Portugal P	2	1	-	-
Denmark DK	2	-	-	-
Morocco MA	2	-	-	-
Chile RCH	1	1	-	-
Thailand T	1	1	-	-
Venezuela YV	1	1	-	-
Colombia CO	1	-	-	-
Liechtenstein FL	1	-	-	-
TOTAL	**570**	**238**	**75**	**25**

Three drivers used dual nationality: H da Silva Ramos is regarded as French, H Stuck regarded as German and A Thiele regarded as American in the above table (excludes 103 Indy only drivers)

GAP BETWEEN STARTS (Longest)

	YRS	MONTHS	
J Lammers	10	3	F 82-J 92
P Lovely	8	10	USA 60-CDN 69
A Pilette	7	11	F 56-B 64
P Revson	7	1	I 64-USA 71
E Wietzes	7	1	CDN 67-CDN 71
M Hailwood	6	3	MC 65-I 71

RACES WITHOUT A WORLD CHAMPION ON THE GRID

1950: GB-I
1958: MC-B,GB-MA
1959: MC-USA
1960: I
1975: E
1982: RSM
1994: MC-CDN,GB-P

All of these races were run with drivers who would later become World Champion

SUCCESSIVE FINISHES IN THE SAME POSITION (excluding wins) (Most)

4 x 2nd: N Piquet	MC-GB 87
4 x 7th: M Alboreto	MC-GB 92
3 x 2nd: L Fagioli	CH-F 50
3 x 2nd: J M Fangio	F-D 53
3 x 2nd: G Farina	CH 53-RA 54
3 x 2nd: M Hawthorn	P-MA 58
3 x 2nd: G Hill	F-D 64
3 x 2nd: J Surtees	USA 64-ZA 65
3 x 2nd: C Reutemann	CDN 80-USAW 81
3 x 2nd: A Prost	D-B 88, BR-MC 89,P-AUS 93
3 x 2nd: R Patrese	MEX-CDN 89,ZA-BR 92
3 x 3rd: L Villoresi	B-GB 51
3 x 3rd: J Behra	F-D 56
3 x 3rd: G Berger	RSM-MC 95
3 x 3rd: D Gurney	NL-I 65
3 x 3rd: M Häkkinen	I-EUR 94
3 x 3rd: D Hulme	I-USA 72
3 x 3rd: J Laffite	D-NL 79
3 x 5th: E de Angelis	CDN-F 85
3 x 5th: M Häkkinen	E-F 96
3 x 6th: G Berger	AUS 85-E 86
3 x 9th: R Patrese	F-D 80
3 x 9th: J J Lehto	MC-F 92

CLASSIFIED RETIREMENTS (Highest)

2nd	C Pace	GB 75
	D Pironi	MC 82
3rd	J Scheckter	GB 75
	A de Cesaris	MC 82
	E de Angelis	RSM 84
	A de Cesaris	B 87

DUMMY GRID RETIREMENTS

Y Dalmas	RSM 89
M Donnelly	USA 90
M Gugelmin	GB 90
A Suzuki	BR 91
L Badoer	AUS 95

PARADE LAP RETIREMENTS

M Fisher	MEX 67
B McLaren	MEX 69
C Amon	RA 72
R Wisell	S 73
L Leoni	BR 78
J-P Jarier	BR 79
D Warwick	RSM 82
M Winkelhock	I 84
J Palmer	RSM 85
A Nannini	E 86
H Rothengatter	USA 86
O Larrauri	BR 88
P Streiff	MC 88
A Prost	RSM 91
O Beretta	E 94
E Irvine	GB 94
P Martini	BR 95
A Montermini	E 95
M Schumacher	F 96

WINS

		%
A Prost	51	25.50
A Senna	41	25.47
N Mansell	31	16.58
J Stewart	27	27.27
J Clark	25	34.72
N Lauda	25	14.62
J M Fangio	24**	47.06
N Piquet	23	11.27
M Schumacher	22	25.88
D Hill	21	31.34
S Moss	16*	24.24
J Brabham	14	11.11
E Fittipaldi	14	9.72
G Hill	14	7.95
A Ascari	13	41.94
A Jones	12	10.34
M Andretti	12	9.38
C Reutemann	12	8.22
J Hunt	10	10.87
J Scheckter	10	8.93
R Peterson	10	8.13
G Berger	9	4.59
D Hulme	8	7.14
J Ickx	8	6.90
R Arnoux	7	4.70
J Rindt	6	10.00
G Villeneuve	6	8.96
J Surtees	6	5.41
J Laffite	6	3.41
R Patrese	6	2.34
T Brooks	6*	15.79
G Farina	5	15.15
K Rosberg	5	4.39
C Regazzoni	5	3.79
J Watson	5	3.29
M Alboreto	5	2.58
J Villeneuve	4	25.00
D Gurney	4	4.65
B McLaren	4	3.96
P Collins	3	9.38
M Hawthorn	3	6.67
P Hill	3	6.25
D Pironi	3	4.29
T Boutsen	3	1.84
F González	2	7.69
W von Trips	2	7.41
P Revson	2	6.67
J-P Jabouille	2	4.08
P Rodriguez	2	3.64
M Trintignant	2	2.44
P Depailler	2	2.11
J Herbert	2	2.08
J Siffert	2	2.08
E de Angelis	2	1.85
P Tambay	2	1.75
L Scarfiotti	1	10.00
P Taruffi	1	5.56
G Baghetti	1	4.76
P Gethin	1	3.33
G Nilsson	1	3.23
D Coulthard	1	2.44
L Bandini	1	2.38

F Cevert	1	2.13
O Panis	1	2.04
I Ireland	1	2.00
R Ginther	1	1.92
C Pace	1	1.39
V Brambilla	1	1.35
A Nannini	1	1.30
J-P Beltoise	1	1.16
J Bonnier	1	0.96
J Mass	1	0.95
J Alesi	1	0.85
L Fagioli	1*	14.29
L Musso	1*	4.17

Indy

B Vukovich	2	40.00
L Wallard	1	50.00
B Sweikert	1	20.00
P Flaherty	1	16.67
T Ruttman	1	14.29
S Hanks	1	12.50
J Bryan	1	11.11
J Parsons	1	11.11
J Rathmann	1	10.00
R Ward	1	10.00

** including shared win(s)*

WINNING DRIVER AGE

Youngest

B McLaren	22y 3m 12d
J Ickx	23y 6m 6d
M Schumacher	23y 7m 27d
E Fittipaldi	23y 9m 22d
M Hawthorn	24y 2m 25d

Indy

T Ruttman	22y 2m 19d

Oldest

L Fagioli	53y 0m 22d
G Farina	46y 9m 3d
J M Fangio	46y 1m 11d
P Taruffi	45y 7m 6d
J Brabham	43y 11m 5d

There most different winners in successive races was nine from F 61 to F 62. There were occasions of eight different successive winners during the 1982 and 83 seasons

WINS IN A SEASON (Most)

N Mansell	9	1992
M Schumacher	9	1995
D Hill	8	1996
A Senna	8	1988
M Schumacher	8	1994
J Clark	7	1963
A Prost	7	1984, 88, 93
A Senna	7	1991

The driver to win most races in a season without becoming Champion, was A Prost with 7 wins in both 1984 and 1988

SUCCESSIVE WINS FROM THE START OF A SEASON (Most)

N Mansell	5	1992
A Senna	4	1991
M Schumacher	4	1994

SUCCESSIVE SEASONS OF WINNING (Most)

A Prost	10	1981-90
A Senna	9	1985-93
N Piquet	8	1962-68
S Moss	7	1955-61
J Stewart	6	1968-73
J M Fangio	5	1953-57
J Ickx	5	1968-72
N Lauda	5	1974-78
M Schumacher	5	1992-96

SUCCESSIVE GP WINS (Most)

A Ascari	9	B 52-B 53
J Brabham	5	NL-P 60
J Clark	5	B-D 65
N Mansell	5	ZA-RSM 92

WINS AT SAME CIRCUIT (Most)

A Senna	6	Monte Carlo	1987-93
G Hill	5	Monte Carlo	1963-69
A Prost	5	Rio de Janeiro	1982-88
A Prost	5	Silverstone	1983-93
A Senna	5	Spa-Francorchamps	1985-91

WINS IN SAME GRAND PRIX (Most)

A Prost	6	BR 82-90
A Prost	6	F 81-93
A Senna	6	MC 87-93
J Clark	5	GB 62-67
G Hill	5	MC 63-69
A Prost	5	GB 83-93
A Senna	5	B 85-91

SUCCESSIVE WINS AT SAME CIRCUIT (Most)

A Senna	5	Monte Carlo	1989-93
J Clark	4	Spa-Francorchamps	1962-65
A Senna	4	Spa-Francorchamps	1988-91

SUCCESSIVE WINS IN SAME GRAND PRIX (Most)

A Senna	5	MC 89-93
J Clark	4	GB 62-65 & B 62-65
J M Fangio	4	RA 54-57
A Senna	4	B 88-91

RACES TAKEN TO ACHIEVE FIRST WIN

Fewest

G Farina	1
G Baghetti	1
J M Fangio	2
T Brooks	3
E Fittipaldi	4
L Scarfiotti	4
J Villeneuve	4
F Gonzalez	5
C Regazzoni	5
L Fagioli	7
P Taruffi	7
J Stewart	8
A Ascari	9
M Hawthorn	9
J Ickx	9
B McLaren	9

Most

T Boutsen	95
J Alesi	91
N Mansell	72
J Herbert	71
R Patrese	71
P Depailler	69
A Nannini	62
J Siffert	57
E de Angelis	54
P Tambay	53
J Rindt	50

DEBUT WIN IMMEDIATELY FOLLOWED 3 BY FURTHER WIN(S)

3 Wins

D Hill	H-B-I 93

2 Wins

A Ascari	D-I 51
P Collins	B-F 56
B McLaren	USA 59-RA 60
R Arnoux	BR-ZA 80
N Mansell	EUR-ZA 85

SHARED WINS

F 51	L Fagioli/ J M Fangio
RA 56	L Musso/ J M Fangio
GB 57	T Brooks/ S Moss

WON THEIR FINAL RACE

L Fagioli	F 51
J Clark	ZA 68

WINNER & SECOND BY TEAM-MATES (Most)

A Senna/ A Prost	14	RSM 88-B 89
N Mansell/ R Patrese	8	MEX 91-GB 92
J Stewart/ F Cevert	6	F 71-D 73
N Mansell/ N Piquet	6	GB 86-MEX 87
D Hill/ J Villeneuve	6	AUS-P 96

WINNER OF OWN NATIONAL GRAND PRIX (Most)

A Prost	6	F 81-93
J Clark	5	GB 62-67
J M Fangio	4	RA 54-57
N Mansell	4	GB 86-92

WINNER FROM LOWEST GRID POSITION (Most)

J Watson	22nd	USAW 83
J Watson	17th	DET 82
M Schumacher	16th	B 95
J Stewart	16th	ZA 73
A Jones	14th	A 77
B McLaren	13th	RA 60
A Prost	13th	MEX 90

Indy

B Vukovich	19th	INDY 54
B Sweikert	14th	INDY 55

WINNING CAR NUMBER (Most)

No. 5	92*
No. 1	86*
No. 2	53
No. 6	39*
No.12	36
No.11	35

** Including Indy 500 races*

WINNING MARGIN

1 lap or more

2 laps: E 69 (J Stewart), AUS 95 (D Hill)
1 lap: MC 50, F 52, GB 52, RA 53, I 54, GB 56, P 59, F 62, NL 63, MC 64, NL 66, USA 66, MC 67, CDN 68, GB 69, E 70, GB 75, J 76, MC 82, RSM 85, GB 85, A 86, BR 94

Smallest

0.010s:	I 71
0.014s:	E- 86
0.020s:	NL 76
0.050s:	A 82
0.080s:	I 69
0.100s:	F 54, F 61
0.200s:	GB 55, I 67
0.211s:	E 81
0.215s:	MC 92
0.232s:	NL 85

PODIUM DOMINATION - ALL OF SAME NATIONALITY

I 50	I	G Farina,D Serafini/ A Ascari, L Fagioli
B 51	I	G Farina, A Ascari, L Villoresi
F 52	I	A Ascari, G Farina, P Taruffi
NL 52	I	A Ascari, G Farina, L Villoresi
B 58	GB	T Brooks, M Hawthorn, S Lewis-Evans
GB 58	GB	P Collins, M Hawthorn, R Salvadori
P 58	GB	S Moss, M Hawthorn, S Lewis-Evans
GB 63	GB	J Clark, J Surtees, G Hill
NL 64	GB	J Clark, J Surtees, P Arundell
GB 64	GB	J Clark, G Hill, J Surtees
ZA 65	GB	J Clark, J Surtees, G Hill
F 65	GB	J Clark, J Stewart, J Surtees
GB 65	GB	J Clark, G Hill, J Surtees
USA 68	GB	J Stewart, G Hill, J Surtees
ZA 80	F	R Arnoux, J Laffite, D Pironi
F 82	F	R Arnoux, A Prost, D Pironi
RSM 83	F	P Tambay, A Prost, R Arnoux

Totals: GB = 10, I = 4, F = 3

WITHIN 1 MINUTE OF WINNER (Most drivers)

9: I 76, ZA 77
8: I 78, B 95
7: A 76, NL 76, CDN 76, S 77, F 78, E 79, E 81, MEX 90, I 91, AUS 91

WITHIN 1 SECOND OF WINNER (Most drivers)

5: I 71
4: D 69
3: E 81

WIN IN DEBUT RACE

G Farina	GB 50
G Baghetti	F 61

2ND IN DEBUT RACE

A Ascari	MC 50
L Fagioli	GB 50
D Serafini	I 50
K Kling	F 54
M Parkes	F 66
J Villeneuve	AUS 96

3RD IN DEBUT RACE

J Behra	CH 52
G Perdisa	MC 55
M Gregory	MC 57
P Arundell	MC 64
R Wisell	USA 70
M Donohue	CDN 71

WIN IN DEBUT SEASON

J Villeneuve	4 in 1996
G Farina	3 in 1950
J M Fangio	3 in 1950
G Baghetti	1 in 1961
J Stewart	1 in 1965
C Regazzoni	1 in 1970
E Fittipaldi	1 in 1970

WINS WITHOUT A WORLD CHAMPIONSHIP (Most)

S Moss	16
C Reutemann	12
R Peterson	10
G Berger	9
J Ickx	8

S Moss finished runner-up in the Championship on four successive occasions (1955-58).

WINS WITHOUT A POLE POSITION (Most)

B McLaren	4
P Collins	3
J Herbert	2
P Rodriguez	2
M Trintignant	2

WINS WITHOUT A FASTEST LAP (Most)

P Collins	3
E de Angelis	2
J Herbert	2
J-P Jabouille	2
P Revson	2
W von Trips	2

RACE WINNING SPEEDS

Fastest: P Gethin

	KM/H	MPH
I 71	242.616	150.755
B 70	241.308	149.942
I 93	239.144	148.597
B 68	236.797	147.139
I 91	236.749	147.109
I 70	236.696	147.076

Slowest: J M Fangio

	KM/H	MPH
MC 50	98.701	61.330
MC 84	100.776	62.619
MC 72	102.756	63.849
MC 57	104.165	64.725
MC 56	104.515	64.943
MC 55	105.915	65.813

POLE POSITIONS

		%
A Senna	65	40.37
J Clark	33	45.83
A Prost	33	16.50
N Mansell	32	17.11
J M Fangio	29	56.86
N Lauda	24	14.04
N Piquet	24	11.76
D Hill	20	29.85
M Andretti	18	14.06
R Arnoux	18	12.08
J Stewart	17	17.17
S Moss	16	24.24
A Ascari	14	45.16
M Schumacher	14	16.47
J Hunt	14	15.22
R Peterson	14	11.38
J Ickx	13	11.21
J Brabham	13	10.32
G Hill	13	7.39
G Berger	11	5.61
J Rindt	10	16.67
J Surtees	8	7.21
R Patrese	8	3.13
J Laffite	7	3.98
P Hill	6	12.50
J-P Jabouille	6	12.24
A Jones	6	5.17
E Fittipaldi	6	4.17
C Reutemann	6	4.11
G Farina	5	15.15
D Coulthard	5	12.20
C Amon	5	5.15
K Rosberg	5	4.39
P Tambay	5	4.39
C Regazzoni	5	3.79
M Hawthorn	4	8.89
D Pironi	4	5.71
J Villeneuve	3	18.75
F González	3	11.54
T Brooks	3	7.89
T Fabi	3	4.69
D Gurney	3	3.49
J Scheckter	3	2.68
E de Angelis	3	2.78
J-P Jarier	3	2.22
S Lewis-Evans	2	14.29
G Villeneuve	2	2.99
J Siffert	2	2.08
J Watson	2	1.32
M Alboreto	2	1.03
M Parkes	1	16.67

E Castellotti	1	7.14
W von Trips	1	3.70
P Revson	1	3.33
L Bandini	1	2.38
T Pryce	1	2.38
R Barrichello	1	1.56
B Giacomelli	1	1.45
C Pace	1	1.39
V Brambilla	1	1.35
P Depailler	1	1.05
J Bonnier	1	0.96
D Hulme	1	0.89
J Alesi	1	0.85
T Boutsen	1	0.61
A de Cesaris	1	0.48

Indy

D Nalon	1	33.33
J Hoyt	1	25.00
E Sachs	1	25.00
W Faulkner	1	20.00
P O'Connor	1	20.00
D Rathmann	1	20.00
B Vukovich	1	20.00
P Flaherty	1	16.67
J McGrath	1	16.67
F Agabashian	1	12.50
J Thomson	1	12.50

POLE POSITION DRIVER AGE

Youngest

R Barrichello	22y 3m 5d
A de Cesaris	22y 10m 4d
J Ickx	23y 7m 3d
E Castellotti	24y 7m 26d
C Amon	24y 9m 22d

Oldest

G Farina	47y 2m 18d
J M Fangio	46y 6m 26d
J Brabham	44y 0m 17d
M Andretti	42y 6m 15d
N Mansell	41y 3m 5d

POLE POSITIONS IN A SEASON (Most)

N Mansell	14	1992
A Senna	13	1988,89
A Prost	13	1993
A Senna	10	1990

SUCCESSIVE POLE POSITIONS (Most)

A Senna	8	E 88-USA 89
A Prost	7	ZA-CDN 93
A Senna	7	E 90-MC 91

POLE POSITION IN DEBUT RACE

G Farina	GB 50
M Andretti	USA 68
C Reutemann	RA 72
J Villeneuve	AUS 96

POLE POSITIONS AT SAME CIRCUIT (Most)

A Senna	8	Imola	1985-94
"	6	Adelaide	1985-94
"	6	Monte Carlo	1985-91

SUCCESSIVE POLE POSITIONS AT SAME CIRCUIT (Most)

A Senna	7	Imola	1985-91
J Clark	4	Nürburgring	1965-67
J M Fangio	4	Monte Carlo	1950-57
A Senna	4	Adelaide	1988-91
"	4	Monte Carlo	1988-91
"	4	Monza	1988-91
"	4	Spa	1988-91

RACES TAKEN TO ACHIEVE FIRST POLE

Fewest

M Andretti	1
G Farina	1
C Reutemann	1
J Villeneuve	1
J M Fangio	2
E Castellotti	3
J Surtees	3
M Parkes	4
F González	5
S Lewis-Evans	6
T Brooks	7
C Regazzoni	8
A Ascari	9
P Depailler	9
D Coulthard	10
D Hill	10

Most

T Boutsen	115
D Hulme	85
J Alesi	81
J Siffert	62
A Jones	61

POLE POSITION NON-STARTERS

J-P Jarier	RA 75
D Pironi	D 82

POLE POSITION TO RETIREMENT WITHIN 1 LAP

D Rathmann	INDY 58
J Brabham	MC 67
N Lauda	D 74
N Lauda	E 75
J Watson	B 77
A Senna	J 90
A Senna	PAC 94

POLE POSITIONS WITHOUT A WIN (Most)

C Amon	5
T Fabi	3
J-P Jarier	3
S Lewis-Evans	2

POLE POSITIONS WITHOUT A CHAMPIONSHIP (Most)

R Arnoux	18
S Moss	16
R Peterson	14
J Ickx	13
G Berger	11

POLE POSITIONS WITHOUT A FASTEST LAP (Most)

J-P Jabouille	6
E de Angelis	3
S Lewis-Evans	2

POLE POSITIONS WITHOUT LEADING (Most)

T Fabi	3

POLE POSITION SPEED

Fastest: K Rosberg

	KM/H	MPH
GB 85	258.983	160.925
I 91	257.415	159.951
I 93	257.209	159.822
A 87	256.622	159.457
GB 87	256.315	159.267

Slowest: J M Fangio

MC 50	103.884	64.550
MC 56	108.865	67.646
MC 57	110.243	68.502
MC 55	111.988	69.586
MC 58	113.447	70.493

POLE POSITION CAR NUMBER (Most)

No. 5	91
No. 1	74
No. 2	66*
No.12	59*
No. 6	38*

** Including Indy 500 races*

FRONT ROWS (Most)

A Senna	87
A Prost	86
N Mansell	56
J Clark	48
J M Fangio	48
N Piquet	44
G Hill	42
J Stewart	42

FRONT ROWS WITHOUT A POLE (Most)

J Behra	10
P Collins	8
R Ginther	8
B McLaren	7
L Musso	6

FRONT ROWS WITHOUT A WIN (Most)

C Amon	19
J Behra	10
E Castellotti	7

FASTEST LAPS

		%
A Prost	41	20.50
N Mansell	30	16.04
J Clark	28	38.89
M Schumacher	25	29.41
N Lauda	24	14.04
J M Fangio	23*	45.10
N Piquet	23*	11.27
S Moss	19*	28.79
D Hill	19	28.36
A Senna	19	11.80
G Berger	19	9.69
J Stewart	15	15.15
C Regazzoni	15*	11.36
J Ickx	14*	12.07
A Ascari	13*	41.94
A Jones	13	11.21
R Patrese	13	5.08
J Brabham	12*	9.52
R Arnoux	12	8.05
J Surtees	11*	9.91
M Andretti	10	7.81
G Hill	10	5.68
D Hulme	9*	8.04
R Peterson	9	7.32
G Villeneuve	8	11.94
J Hunt	8	8.70
J Villeneuve	6	37.50
F González	6*	23.08
M Hawthorn	6*	13.33
P Hill	6*	12.50
D Gurney	6	6.98
E Fittipaldi	6*	4.17
C Reutemann	6	4.11
J Laffite	6	3.41
G Farina	5	15.15
D Pironi	5	7.14
C Pace	5	6.94
J Scheckter	5	4.46
J Watson	5	3.29
M Alboreto	5*	2.58
D Coulthard	4	9.76
J-P Beltoise	4	4.65
P Depailler	4	4.21
J Siffert	4	4.17
J Alesi	4	3.39
T Brooks	3	7.89
R Ginther	3*	5.77
J Rindt	3	5.00
C Amon	3	3.09
B McLaren	3*	2.97
K Rosberg	3	2.63
J-P Jarier	3	2.22
L Bandini	2	4.76
F Cevert	2	4.26
T Fabi	2	3.13
A Nannini	2	2.60
J Mass	2	1.90
P Tambay	2	1.75
D Warwick	2	1.36
M Hasemi	1	100.00
P Russo	1	12.50
L Scarfiotti	1	10.00
K Kling	1	9.09
O Marimón	1*	9.09
D Attwood	1	5.88
R Mières	1	5.88
H Herrmann	1	5.56
P Taruffi	1	5.56
B Henton	1	5.26
G Baghetti	1	4.76
L Musso	1	4.17
R Moreno	1	4.00
G Nilsson	1	3.23
L Villoresi	1	3.23
B Gachot	1	2.78
M Hailwood	1	2.00
I Ireland	1*	2.00
J Oliver	1	2.00
J Behra	1*	1.92
P Rodriguez	1	1.82
H Pescarolo	1	1.75
V Brambilla	1	1.35
M Gugelmin	1	1.35
S Nakajima	1	1.35
M Surer	1	1.22
M Trintignant	1	1.22
J Palmer	1	1.19
T Boutsen	1	0.61
A de Cesaris	1	0.48
Indy		
B Vukovich	3	60.00
J Rathmann	2	20.00
T Bettenhausen	1	9.09
J McGrath	1	16.67
J Parsons	1	11.11
J Thomson	1	12.50
L Wallard	1	50.00

** includes one or more shared fastest laps*

Fastest Lap times and speeds for the Indianapolis 500 races (1950 to 1960) are based on times recorded on the drivers' fastest leading lap.

FASTEST LAP DRIVER AGE

Youngest

B McLaren	21y 10m 18d
D Coulthard	23y 4m 4d
M Schumacher	23y 7m 27d
A de Cesaris	23y 11m 21d
A Senna	24y 2m 13d

Oldest

J M Fangio	46y 6m 26d
P Taruffi	45y 7m 6d
G Farina	44y 10m 17d
J Brabham	44y 3m 16d
L Villoresi	44y 0m 22d

FASTEST LAPS IN A SEASON (Most)

N Mansell	8	1992
M Schumacher	8	1994, 95
N Piquet	7	1986
A Prost	7	1988
A Ascari	6	1952
J Clark	6	1963, 65
D Hill	6	1994
N Mansell	6	1991
A Prost	6	1993
G Villeneuve	6	1979
J Villeneuve	6	1996

SUCCESSIVE FASTEST LAPS (Most)

A Ascari	7	B 52-RA 53
J M Fangio	5	F 50-F 51 *
A Ascari	4	F-CH 53
J Stewart	4	MC-GB 69
G Villeneuve	4	ZA-B 79
N Mansell	4	CDN-GB 91

** excluding INDY*

FASTEST LAP IN DEBUT RACE

G Farina	GB 50
M Hasemi	J 76
J Villeneuve	AUS 96

FASTEST LAPS AT SAME CIRCUIT (Most)

N Mansell	6	Silverstone	1987-92
A Prost	6	Spas	1985-93
J Clark	5	Zandvoort	1961-67
J M Fangio	4	Monte Carlo	1950-57
N Lauda	4	Brands Hatch	1974-84
A Prost	4	Monte Carlo	1986-93
A Senna	4	Monte Carlo	1984-90

SUCCESSIVE FASTEST LAPS AT SAME CIRCUIT (Most)

N Mansell	6	Silverstone	1987-92
J M Fangio	4	Monte Carlo	1950-57

RACES TAKEN TO ACHIEVE FIRST FASTEST LAP (Fewest)

G Farina	1
M Hasemi	1
J Villeneuve	1
J M Fangio	2
H Herrmann	2
G Baghetti	3
P Hill	3
J Hunt	3
K Kling	3
J Surtees	3
D Coulthard	4
R Ginther	4
C Regazzoni	4
L Scarfiotti	4
G Villeneuve	4

FASTEST LAP ON HOME SOIL (Most)

N Mansell	8	EUR 83, GB 86-92
S Moss	5	GB 54-59
A Prost	5	F 81-88, CH 82
J M Fangio	3	RA 55-58
D Hill	3	GB 93-95
J Stewart	3	GB 69-72
N Piquet	3	BR 83-87

SHARED FASTEST LAPS IN A RACE (Most)

GB 54	7	B 60	3

The last time a fastest lap was shared was at EUR 84

FASTEST LAPS WITHOUT A POLE (Most)

J-P Beltoise	4
R Ginther	3
B McLaren	3

FASTEST LAPS WITHOUT A WIN (Most)

C Amon	3
J-P Jarier	3
D Coulthard	2
T Fabi	2
D Warwick	2

FASTEST LAPS WITHOUT A POINT

M Hasemi	1
B Henton	1

FASTEST LAP SPEED

Fastest: D Hill

	KM/H	MPH
I 93	249.835	155.241
I 71	247.017	153.489
GB 87	246.324	153.059
B 70	244.744	152.077
GB 85	243.067	151.035

Slowest: J M Fangio

	KM/H	MPH
MC 50	103.135	64.085
MC 84	104.284	64.799
MC 57	107.216	66.621
MC 56	108.448	67.387
MC 55	110.566	68.703

The last time that there were 4 cars in a row on a grid was in D 1967. The last time that there were 3 cars in a row on a grid wasin NL 1973. All grids were 2 x 2 from D 1973. The first 2 x 2 grid was however in I 1961.

POLE POSITION/ FASTEST LAP DOUBLES (Most)

J Clark	18	MC 62-ZA 68
A Prost	15	BR 82-J 93
J M Fangio	15	MC 50-RA 58
N Mansell	11	D 87-J 92
A Senna	11	P 85-I 91
A Ascari	10	B 52-E 54

SUCCESSIVE POLE POSITION/ FASTEST LAP DOUBLES (Most)

J M Fangio	5	F 50-F 51 *
A Ascari	4	D 52-RA 53

** excluding INDY*

WIN/POLE POSITION DOUBLES (Most)

A Senna	29	P 85-AUS 93
A Prost	18	NL 81-D 93
N Mansell	16	ZA 85-P 92
J Clark	15	GB 62-ZA 68
J M Fangio	13	MC 50-D 57
N Lauda	10	E 74-GB 76

SUCCESSIVE WIN/ POLE POSITION DOUBLES (Most)

A Ascari	5	D 52-NL 53 *
N Mansell	5	ZA-RSM 92
A Senna	4	USA-MC 91

** excluding INDY*

WIN/ POLE POSITION/FASTEST LAP TREBLES (Most)

J Clark	11	GB 62-ZA 68
J M Fangio	9	MC 50-D 57
A Prost	8	BR 82-RSM 93
A Ascari	7	B 52-GB 53
A Senna	7	P 85-I 90
D Hill	5	GB 94-D 96
N Mansell	5	GB 91-GB 92
M Schumacher	5	MC 94-J 95

SUCCESSIVE WIN/ POLE POSITION/FASTEST LAP TREBLES (Most)

A Ascari	4	D-RA 52
A Ascari	2	B-F 52
J Brabham	2	B-F 60
J Clark	2	NL-F 63 & MEX 67-ZA 68
J Laffite	2	RA-BR 79
N Mansell	2	F-GB 92

WIN/ POLE POSITION/FASTEST LAP TREBLES AND ALSO LED EVERY LAP (Most)

J Clark	8	GB 62-D 65
A Ascari	5	F 52-GB 53
N Mansell	4	GB 91-GB 92
A Senna	4	P 85-I 90
J Stewart	4	F 69-USA 72

WIN/ FASTEST LAP DOUBLES (Most)

A Prost	21	F 81-RSM 93
J Clark	18	B 62-ZA 68
M Schumacher	15	B 92-I 96
J M Fangio	14	MC 50-D 57
N Lauda	12	E 74-I 84
N Mansell	12	F 86-GB 92
J Stewart	12	D 68-USA 72

SUCCESSIVE WIN/FASTEST LAP DOUBLES (Most)

A Ascari	7	B 52-RA 53
J Clark	3	B-F 63
M Schumacher	3	EUR-J 95
J Stewart	3	NL-GB 69

POINTS

		ratio
A Prost	798.50	3.99
A Senna	614.00	3.81
N Piquet	485.50	2.38
N Mansell	482.00	2.58
N Lauda	420.50	2.46
M Schumacher	362.00	4.26
J Stewart	360.00	3.64
G Berger	359.00	1.83
D Hill	326.00	4.87
C Reutemann	310.00	2.12
G Hill	289.00	1.64
E Fittipaldi	281.00	1.95
R Patrese	281.00	1.10
J M Fangio	277.14	5.43
J Clark	274.00	3.81
J Brabham	261.00	2.07
J Scheckter	255.00	2.28
D Hulme	248.00	2.21
J Laffite	228.00	1.30
C Regazzoni	212.00	1.61
A Jones	206.00	1.78
R Peterson	206.00	1.67
B McLaren	196.50	1.95
J Alesi	189.00	1.60
S Moss	186.64	2.83
M Alboreto	186.50	0.96
J Ickx	181.00	1.56
R Arnoux	181.00	1.21
J Surtees	180.00	1.62
M Andretti	180.00	1.41
J Hunt	179.00	1.95
J Watson	169.00	1.11
K Rosberg	159.50	1.40
P Depailler	141.00	1.48
A Ascari	140.64	4.54
D Gurney	133.00	1.55
T Boutsen	132.00	0.81
M Hawthorn	127.64	2.84
G Farina	127.33	3.86
E de Angelis	122.00	1.13
J Rindt	109.00	1.82
R Ginther	107.00	2.06
G Villeneuve	107.00	1.60
P Tambay	103.00	0.90
D Pironi	101.00	1.44
P Hill	98.00	2.04
M Brundle	98.00	0.62
M Häkkinen	91.00	1.15
F Cevert	89.00	1.89
S Johansson	88.00	1.11
C Amon	83.00	0.86
D Coulthard	81.00	1.98
J Villeneuve	78.00	4.88
F González	77.64	2.99
J-P Beltoise	77.00	0.90
T Brooks	75.00	1.97
M Trintignant	72.33	0.88
P Rodriguez	71.00	1.29
J Mass	71.00	0.68
D Warwick	71.00	0.48
E Cheever	70.00	0.53
J Siffert	68.00	0.71
J Herbert	67.00	0.70
A Nannini	65.00	0.84
P Revson	61.00	2.03
A de Cesaris	59.00	0.28
L Bandini	58.00	1.38
C Pace	58.00	0.81
W von Trips	56.00	2.07
J Behra	53.14	1.02
L Villoresi	49.00	1.58
P Collins	47.00	1.47
I Ireland	47.00	0.94
R Barrichello	46.00	0.72
L Musso	44.00	1.83
P Taruffi	41.00	2.28
J Bonnier	39.00	0.38
O Panis	38.00	0.78
L Fagioli	32.00	4.57
M Blundell	32.00	0.52
J-P Jarier	31.50	0.23
G Nilsson	31.00	1.00
I Capelli	31.00	0.33
H Schell	30.00	0.54

Y Dalmas and J Gartner were the only drivers, whose only points did not count towards the Championship (see 1984 & 87)

POINT SCORER AGE

Youngest

R Rodriguez	20y 4m 3d
C Amon	20y 10m 4d
R Barrichello	21y 5m 1d
E de Angelis	21y 6m 11d
B McLaren	21y 8m 10d

Oldest

P Étançelin	53y 8m 6d
L Fagioli	53y 0m 22d
L Chiron	50y 9m 18d
L Rosier	50y 9m 0d
F Bonetto	50y 2m 14d

POINTS IN A SEASON (Most)

N Mansell	108	1992
A Prost	105	1988*
M Schumacher	102	1995
A Prost	99	1993
D Hill	97	1996
A Senna	96	1991
A Senna	94	1988
A Prost	81	1989

** not World Champion*

SUCCESSIVE RACES IN THE POINTS (Most)

J M Fangio	21	F 53-MC 56
C Reutemann	15	B 80-B 81
A Ascari	13	B 52-CH 53
J Clark	12	B 63-B 64
N Lauda	11	D 75-S 76
N Piquet	11	MC-MEX 87

POINTS SCORED IN EACH OF A DRIVER'S FIRST TWO (OR MORE) RACES

	RACES	POINTS
J Stewart	6	25
P Arundell	2	8
C Regazzoni	2	6
G Follmer	2	5
A Prost	2	3
R Ginther	2	2

HALF POINTS AWARDED (Shortened races)

E 75, A 75, MC 84, AUS 91

POINTS WITHOUT A WIN (MOST)

M Brundle	98
M Häkkinen	91
S Johansson	88
C Amon	83
D Warwick	71

POINTS WITHOUT A WORLD CHAMPIONSHIP (Most)

G Berger	359
C Reutemann	310
R Patrese	281
J Laffite	228
C Regazzoni	212

POINTS WITHOUT A POLE (Most)

B McLaren	196.5
R Ginther	107
M Brundle	98
M Häkkinen	91
F Cevert	89

POINTS WITHOUT A FASTEST LAP (Most)

E de Angelis	122
M Brundle	98
M Häkkinen	91
S Johansson	88
E Cheever	70

TOP 3 FROM LOWEST GRID POSITION

	RESULT	GRID	
O Marimón	3rd	27th	GB 54
E Fittipaldi	3rd	24th	USAW 80
R Flockhart	3rd	23rd	I 56
N Lauda	2nd	23rd	USAW 83
T Fabi	3rd	23rd	DET 84
J Watson	1st	22nd	USAW 83
W von Trips	3rd	21st	F 58
J Watson	3rd	21st	DET 83
J Laffite	2nd	20th	AUS 85
Indy			
J Rathmann	2nd	32nd	INDY 57
D Freeland	3rd	26th	INDY 56
P Goldsmith	3rd	26th	INDY 60
G Amick	2nd	25th	INDY 58

WORLD CHAMPIONS

YEAR	DRIVER	NAT	CARS DRIVEN	DECIDED
1950	G Farina	I	Alfa Romeo	I, 3 Sep
1951	J M Fangio	RA	Alfa Romeo	E, 28 Oct
1952	A Ascari	I	Ferrari	D, 3 Aug
1953	A Ascari	I	Ferrari	CH, 23 Aug
1954	J M Fangio	RA	Maserati & Mercedes	CH, 22 Aug
1955	J M Fangio	RA	Mercedes-Benz	I, 11 Sep
1956	J M Fangio	RA	Ferrari	I, 2 Sep
1957	J M Fangio	RA	Maserati	D, 4 Aug
1958	M Hawthorn	GB	Ferrari	MA, 19 Oct
1959	J Brabham	AUS	Cooper-Climax	USA, 12 Dec
1960	J Brabham	AUS	Cooper-Climax	P, 14 Aug
1961	P Hill	USA	Ferrari	I, 10 Sep
1962	G Hill	GB	BRM	ZA, 29 Dec
1963	J Clark	GB	Lotus-Climax	I, 8 Sep
1964	J Surtees	GB	Ferrari	MEX, 25 Oct
1965	J Clark	GB	Lotus-Climax	D, 1 Aug
1966	J Brabham	AUS	Brabham-Repco	I, 4 Sep
1967	D Hulme	NZ	Brabham-Repco	MEX, 22 Oct
1968	G Hill	GB	Lotus-Ford	MEX, 3 Nov
1969	J Stewart	GB	Matra-Ford	I, 7 Sep
1970	J Rindt	A	Lotus-Ford	USA, 4 Oct
1971	J Stewart	GB	Tyrrell-Ford	A, 15 Aug
1972	E Fittipaldi	BR	Lotus-Ford	I, 10 Sep
1973	J Stewart	GB	Tyrrell-Ford	I, 9 Sep
1974	E Fittipaldi	BR	McLaren-Ford	USA, 6 Oct
1975	N Lauda	A	Ferrari	I, 7 Sep
1976	J Hunt	GB	McLaren-Ford	J, 24 Oct
1977	N Lauda	A	Ferrari	USAE, 2 Oct
1978	M Andretti	USA	Lotus-Ford	I, 10 Sep
1979	J Scheckter	ZA	Ferrari	I, 9 Sep
1980	A Jones	AUS	Williams-Ford	CDN, 28 Sep
1981	N Piquet	BR	Brabham-Ford	LV, 17 Oct
1982	K Rosberg	SF	Williams-Ford	LV, 25 Sep
1983	N Piquet	BR	Brabham-BMW	ZA, 15 Oct
1984	N Lauda	A	McLaren-TAG Porsche	P, 21 Oct
1985	A Prost	F	McLaren-TAG Porsche	EUR, 6 Oct
1986	A Prost	F	McLaren-TAG Porsche	AUS, 26 Oct
1987	N Piquet	BR	Williams-Honda	J, 31 Oct*
1988	A Senna	BR	McLaren-Honda	J, 30 Oct
1989	A Prost	F	McLaren-Honda	J, 22 Oct**
1990	A Senna	BR	McLaren-Honda	J, 21 Oct
1991	A Senna	BR	McLaren-Honda	J, 20 Oct
1992	N Mansell	GB	Williams-Renault	H, 16 Aug
1993	A Prost	F	Williams-Renault	P, 26 Sep
1994	M Schumacher	D	Benetton-Ford	AUS, 13 Nov
1995	M Schumacher	D	Benetton-Renault	PAC, 22 Oct
1996	D Hill	GB	Williams-Renault	J, 13 Oct

Ford = Ford Cosworth

* the day before the J GP when Mansell flew home

** confirmed on day of appeal (31 Oct)

WORLD CHAMPIONSHIPS

J M Fangio	5
A Prost	4
J Brabham	3
N Lauda	3
N Piquet	3
A Senna	3
J Stewart	3
A Ascari	2
J Clark	2
E Fittipaldi	2
G Hill	2
M Schumacher	2
M Andretti	1
G Farina	1
M Hawthorn	1
D Hill	1
P Hill	1
D Hulme	1
J Hunt	1
A Jones	1
N Mansell	1
J Rindt	1
K Rosberg	1
J Scheckter	1
J Surtees	1

No driver has ever failed to qualify for a GP during his World Championship winning season

Monaco 1973 was the only race in which the top six finishers were placed in the same order as the eventual Championship table for the year

WORLD CHAMPION AGE

Youngest

E Fittipaldi	25y 8m 29d	(1972)
M Schumacher	25y 10m 10d	(1994)
N Lauda	26y 6m 16d	(1975)
J Clark	27y 6m 4d	(1963)

Oldest

J M Fangio	46y 1m 11d	(1957)
G Farina	43y 10m 3d	(1950)
J Brabham	40y 5m 2d	(1966)
G Hill	39y 8m 19d	(1968)
N Mansell	39y 0m 8d	(1992)

Jochen Rindt who died at age 28, was the only posthumous World Champion

COUNTRY HOSTING CHAMPIONSHIP DECIDER

Italy	12
Japan	8
United States	6
Germany	3
Mexico	3

CHAMPIONSHIP DECIDED IN FINAL ROUND

1950 I, 1951 E, 1956 I, 1958 MA 1959 USA, 1962 ZA, 1964 MEX, 1967 MEX, 1968 MEX, 1974 USA, 1976 J, 1981 LV, 1982 LV, 1983 ZA, 1984 P, 1986 AUS, 1994 AUS, 1996 J

DATE CROWNED CHAMPION

Earliest

1 Aug 1965	J Clark
3 Aug 1952	A Ascari
4 Aug 1957	J M Fangio
14 Aug 1960	J Brabham

Latest

29 Dec 1962	G Hill
12 Dec 1959	J Brabham
13 Nov 1994	M Schumacher
3 Nov 1968	G Hill

RACES REMAINING AFTER CHAMPIONSHIP DECIDED (Most)

1992 H (N Mansell)	5
1963 I	3
1965 D	3
1969 I	3
1971 A	3

WORLD CHAMPIONS NOT PARTICIPATING IN THE FOLLOWING SEASON

M Hawthorn	1958
J Rindt	1970
J Stewart	1973
A Prost	1993
N Mansell	1992*

** returned in 1994*

OTHER WORLD CHAMPIONS WHO FAILED TO WIN THE SEASON AFTER BEING WORLD CHAMPION

A Ascari	1954
J M Fangio	1958
J Brabham	1961
P Hill	1962
J Surtees	1965
M Andretti	1979
J Scheckter	1980
N Piquet	1988

REIGNING WORLD CHAMPION WHO FAILED TO QUALIFY FOR AT LEAST ONE RACE IN THE FOLLOWING SEASON

N Piquet	DET 82 (1981 Champion)
J Scheckter	CDN 80 (1979 Champion)

TOTAL CAREER REIGN AS CHAMPION

Longest

	DAYS
J M Fangio	1,799
A Prost	1,532
J Stewart	1,176
N Lauda	1,106
N Piquet	1,080
J Brabham	1,051
A Senna	1,022

Shortest

J Surtees	280
J Rindt	315*
J Hunt	343
M Andretti	364
D Hulme	378

** died before he became World Champion*

CONTINUOUS REIGN AS CHAMPION

Longest

	YRS:M:D	WINNING SEASONS
J M Fangio	4:1:27	1954-55-56-57
A Prost	2:0:25	1985-86
A Ascari	2:0:19	1952-53
M Schumacher	1:11:0	1994-96
A Senna	1:9:26	1990-91
J Brabham	1:8:29	1959-60

Shortest

G Hill	8:10	1962
J M Fangio	9:6	1951
J Surtees	9:7	1964

Jackie Stewart, the master of consistent lap times, also carried this over to his Championship seasons — each of his three championships lasted exactly 392 days!

SPAN BETWEEN CHAMPIONSHIP DECIDERS

Longest	DAYS	SEASONS
P Hill	475	1961-62
J M Fangio	441	1957-58
G Farina	420	1950-51
M Hawthorn	419	1958-59
Shortest		
J Brabham	246	1959-60
G Hill	253	1962-63
J M Fangio	280	1951-52
J Surtees	280	1964-65

CHAMPIONSHIP WINNING MARGIN Narrowest (Net points)

	POINTS	WINNER
1984	0.5	N Lauda
1958	1	M Hawthorn
1961	1	P Hill
1964	1	J Surtees
1976	1	J Hunt
1981	1	N Piquet
1994	1	M Schumacher
Widest (net points)		
1992	52	N Mansell
1995	33	M Schumacher
1971	29	J Stewart
1969	26	J Stewart
1993	26	A Prost
1963	25	J Clark
1991	24	A Senna

WINS IN CHAMPIONSHIP SEASON

Fewest

M Hawthorn	1	1958
K Rosberg	1	1982

LAP LEADERS

Laps Led (Most)

	LAPS	RACES	KM	MILES
A Senna	2,931	86	13,430.4	8,345.3
A Prost	2,683	84	12,476.7	7,752.7
N Mansell	2,058	55	9,504.8	5,906.0
J Clark	1,942	43	10,121.1	6,288.9
J Stewart	1,918	51	9,173.4	5,700.1
N Piquet	1,633.5	59	7,757.4	4,820.2
N Lauda	1,590	41	7,058.2	4,385.8
J M Fangio	1,347	38	9,316.0	5,788.7
D Hill	1,274	42	5,906.8	3,670.3
M Schumacher	1,271	35	5,831.3	3,623.4
S Moss	1,181	31	6,369.0	3,957.5
G Hill	1,105	32	4,763.9	2,960.2
A Ascari	927	21	5,902.0	3,677.3
J Brabham	825	28	4,540.1	2,821.1
M Andretti	799	22	3,577.2	2,222.8
G Berger	713	31	3,445.5	2,140.9
R Peterson	707	28	3,313.4	2,058.8
J Scheckter	674	23	2,851.0	1,771.5
J Hunt	666	24	3,363.3	2,089.9
C Reutemann	650	19	3,314.2	2,059.4
A Jones	589	24	2,847.0	1,769.0
R Patrese	565.5	29	2,554.6	1,587.4
G Villeneuve	535	18	2,253.9	1,400.5
J Ickx	528	19	3,118.9	1,938.0
K Rosberg	512	20	2,164.8	1,345.2
R Arnoux	507	25	2,571.3	1,597.7
E Fittipaldi	478	18	2,235.3	1,389.0
D Hulme	436	18	1,920.0	1,193.0

All distances completed as lap leaders are calculated as complete laps (actual distances in the lead are never recorded for the official results).

RACES LED (Most)

A Senna	86
A Prost	84
N Piquet	59
N Mansell	55
J Stewart	51
J Clark	43
D Hill	42
N Lauda	41

DISTANCE LED (Most km)

A Senna	13,430.4
A Prost	12,476.7
J Clark	10,121.1
N Mansell	9,504.8
J M Fangio	9,316.0
J Stewart	9,173.4

LAPS LED IN CHAMPIONSHIP SEASON

Fewest (% of total)

K Rosberg	1982	7.5%	80 out of 1,060.5
E Fittipaldi	1974	7.9%	77 out of 979
J Surtees	1964	12.3%	89 out of 722

Most (% of total)

A Ascari	1953	78.0%	418 out of 536
A Ascari	1952	77.9%	348 out of 447
J Clark	1963	71.5%	506 out of 708
N Mansell	1992	67.0%	694 out of 1,036
J M Fangio	1955	65.5%	309 out of 472

LAPS LED IN A SEASON (Most)

N Mansell	692	1992
M Schumacher	629	1994
A Senna	556	1990
A Senna	553	1988
J Clark	506	1963
A Senna	486	1989 *
D Hill	480	1996
A Senna	467	1991
M Schumacher	454	1995
M Andretti	451	1978
A Prost	450	1988 *

** not World Champion*

GPs LED IN A SEASON (Most)

A Prost	15	1993
N Mansell	14	1992
M Schumacher	14	1995
A Senna	14	1990

LED EVERY GP IN A SEASON

J M Fangio	1951 (6 GPs)
J M Fangio	1955 (6 GPs)
J Stewart	1969 (11 GPs)

LAP LEADERS IN A GP (Most)

8 - I 71
7 - CDN 73, GB 75
6 - F 61, I 66, I 67, I 70, E 75, F 90, I 95

LAP LEADERS IN A SEASON

Most

15 - 1975
13 - 1968, 77, 82
12 - 1971

Fewest

4 - 1988
5 - 1950, 52, 53, 64, 92, 93

LED THROUGHOUT THE GP (Most)

A Senna	19	P 85-AUS 91
J Clark	13	GB 62-D 65
J Stewart	11	D 68-D 73
N Mansell	9	P 86-P 92
A Prost	7	I 81-F 89
A Ascari	7	F 52-GB 53
N Lauda	6	NL 74-MC 76

CARS ON LEADING LAP AT FINISH (Most)

13 - D 62, D 73, D 74, D 76, AUS 91
12 - F 75

LEAD CHANGES IN A RACE (Most)

I 65	41
I 70	28
I 64	27
I 63	25
I 71	25
D 59	22

LED ONLY THE FINAL LAP (To win the race)

B McLaren	USA 59
J Clark	B 64
J Surtees	I 67
B McLaren	B 68
J Rindt	MC 70
M Andretti	F 77
R Peterson	ZA 78
N Piquet	CDN 91

The only driver to lead every lap of a race except the final one was N Mansell in CDN 1991

WON WITHOUT LEADING A LAP

L Fagioli F 51
(shared drive in which Fangio took over the car)
L Musso RA 56
(shared drive in which Fangio took over the car)
T Brooks GB 57
(shared drive in which Moss took over the car)
N Lauda I 78
(due to Andretti/ Villeneuve penalty)
A Prost BR 82
(due to Piquet/ Rosberg disqualification)
E de Angelis RSM 85
(due to Prost disqualification)
D Hill B 94
(due to Schumacher disqualification)

L Fagioli and L Musso have been credited with a win each although neither actually took the chequered flag in their World Championship careers

LEAD LAPS WITHOUT A CHAMPIONSHIP (Most)

S Moss	1181
G Berger	713
R Peterson	707
C Reutemann	650
R Patrese	565.5
G Villeneuve	535

LEAD LAPS WITHOUT A WIN (Most)

C Amon	183
J Behra	107
J-P Jarier	79
I Capelli	46
J Oliver	36

LEAD LAPS WITHOUT A POLE (Most)

F Cevert	129
P Collins	127
R Ginther	116
J Behra	107
J-P Beltoise	101

LEAD LAPS WITHOUT A FASTEST LAP (Most)

J-P Jabouille	179
W von Trips	156
J Bonnier	139
P Collins	127
P Revson	63

ONE LAP WONDERS (World Championship Career Less Than 1 Lap Duration)

J Peters	D 52
E Loof	D 53
B Said	USA 59
A Owen	I 60
M Natili	GB 61
G McRae	GB 73
M-A Guerra	RSM 81
M Apicella	I 93

RACES WITHOUT EVER FINISHING (Most)

A Soler-Roig	6
C Bucci	5
D Murray	4

LADY DRIVERS

Maria-Teresa de Filippis		1958-59
Lella Lombardi		1974-76
Divina Galica	(nq)	1976-78
Desire Wilson	(nq)	1980
Giovanna Amati	(nq)	1992

RELATIVES IN GRANDS PRIX

Father/ Son

Mario/ Michael Andretti
Jack/ David & *Gary* Brabham
Wilson/ Christian Fittipaldi
Graham/ Damon Hill
Reg/ Tim Parnell
André/ Teddy Pilette
Hans/ Hans-Joachim Stuck
Gilles/ Jacques Villeneuve

Brothers

David/ *Gary* Brabham
Tino/ Vittorio Brambilla
Corrado/ Teo Fabi
Emerson/ Wilson Fittipaldi
Pedro/ Ricardo Rodriguez
Ian/ Jody Scheckter
Jackie/ Jimmy Stewart
Gilles/ *Jacques (Sr.)* Villeneuve
Graham/ Peter Whitehead (half)
Joachim/ Manfred Winkelhock

Uncle/ Nephew

Emerson/ Christian Fittipaldi
Jo/ Jean-Louis Schlesser
Jacques (Sr.)/ Jacques Villeneuve

Cousins

José Dolhem/ Didier Pironi

Brothers-in-law

Jean-Pierre Beltoise/ François Cevert
David Brabham/ Mike Thackwell
Jean-Pierre Jabouille/ Jacques Laffite

Italicised drivers did not start

The most drivers with the same surname to enter a Grand Prix, was 4 at Britain 1959. Dennis, Henry, Mike & Trevor Taylor, none of whom were related to each other, all made their debut at this race.

NON-ENGLISH GB DRIVERS

Northern Ireland

K Acheson, M Donnelly, E Irvine
D Magee, D Titterington, J Watson

Scotland

J Clark, D Coulthard, J Crawford
J Dumfries, R Flockhart, I Ireland
D Murray, A Scott-Brown, I Stewart
Jackie Stewart, Jimmy Stewart, L Thorne

Wales

J Lewis, T Pryce, A Rees

Jersey

A Owen

BANNED FROM ENTERING

N Mansell	P 89 (1)
E Irvine	PAC, RSM, MC 94 (3)
M Häkkinen	H 94 (1)
M Schumacher	I, P 94 (2)

DISQUALIFIED (MOST)

S Bellof	11	BR 84-NL 84 *
M Brundle	7	BR 84-DET 84 *
S Johansson	4	GB 84-CDN 89 *

** includes Tyrrell team disqualifications*

DISQUALIFIED FROM TOP 3

J Hunt	1st	GB 76
N Piquet	1st	BR 82
K Rosberg	2nd	BR 82
G Villeneuve	3rd	USAW 82
N Lauda	3rd	B 82
K Rosberg	2nd	BR 83
S Bellof	3rd	MC 84
M Brundle	2nd	DET 84
A Prost	1st	RSM 85
A Senna	2nd	AUS 87
T Boutsen	3rd	B 88
A Senna	1st	J 89
M Schumacher	2nd	GB 94
M Schumacher	1st	B 94

The most disqualifications in one race occurred in CDN 1989 (3)

DRIVERS WITH DIFFERENT CONSTRUCTORS IN A SEASON (Most)

S Moss	3	1952	HWM/ ERA/ Connaught
A Ascari	3	1954	Maserati/ Ferrari/ Lancia
H Schell	3	1955	Maserati/ Ferrari/ Vanwall
M Hawthorn	3	1956	Maserati/ BRM/ Vanwall
R Salvadori	3	1957	BRM (nq)/ Vanwall/ Cooper
D Gurney	3	1968	Eagle/ Brabham/ McLaren
J Bonnier	3	1968	Cooper/ McLaren/ Honda
J Ickx	3	1973	Ferrari/ McLaren/ Iso Marlboro
J Watson	3	1975	Surtees/ Lotus/ Penske
J-P Jarier	3	1977	Penske/ Shadow/ Ligier
N Piquet	3	1978	Ensign/ McLaren/ Brabham
K Rosberg	3	1978	Theodore/ ATS/ Wolf
G Lees	3	1980	Shadow/ Ensign/ Williams (nq)
R Moreno	3	1991	Benetton/ Jordan/ Minardi
J Herbert	3	1994	Lotus/ Ligier/ Benetton

RACED IN CAR OF THEIR SURNAME

C Amon	1974
B Aston	1952
D Brabham	1990
J Brabham	1962,63,64,65,66,67,68,69,70
E Fittipaldi	(1976,77,78,79)*,80
W Fittipaldi	1975*
A Gordini	1951**
G Hill	1975
B McLaren	1966,67,68,69,70
A Merzario	1978,79
H Rebaque	1979
J Surtees	1970,71,72

** drove a Copersucar (Fittipaldi)*
*** drove a Simca Gordini*

WORLD CHAMPION IN OWN CAR

J Brabham	1966

RACE WINNER IN OWN CAR

J Brabham	1966,67,70
D Gurney (Eagle)	1967
B McLaren	1968

DIFFERENT MAKES OF CAR DRIVEN DURING WORLD CHAMPIONSHIP CAREER

C Amon	13
A de Cesaris	10
S Johansson	10
S Moss	10
M Trintignant	10
E Cheever	9
J Ickx	9
R Moreno	9

Stirling Moss was the only driver to race two different makes of car in a Grand Prix: a Lotus and a Ferguson in GB 1961

Two cars have gone into the harbour at Monte Carlo: A Ascari in 1955 and P Hawkins in 1965. Neither were fatal, although Ascari died 4 days later at Monza on 26 May, and Hawkins died 4 years after his Monaco accident, at Oulton Park, coincidentally also on 26 May

The only time that car number 13 has been in a Grand Prix, was in Mexico 1963, driven by M Solana. D Galica did not qualify in car 13 in Britain 1976

Car number 0 has only been used by two drivers: J Scheckter in Canada and USA 1973, and by D Hill throughout 1993 and 1994

The highest car number was 208 (sponsored by Radio Luxembourg) and driven by L Lombardi in Britain 1974 (non-qualified)

The highest car number to start a race was 136, driven by R Krause in Germany 1952

The lowest number never to be used is 63

Apart from 13, the lowest number never to win is 29

NON-QUALIFICATIONS (Most)

G Tarquini	40
B Gachot	37
R Moreno	32
P Ghinzani	31
A Merzario	26
B Schneider	25
Y Dalmas	24
N Larini	23

A Suzuki was the only driver to non pre-qualify in every race during a season (1989)

UNSUCCESSFUL QUALIFYING ATTEMPTS FOR DRIVERS WHO NEVER STARTED A RACE (Most)

C Langes	14
P Chaves	13
V Weidler	10
D Kennedy	7
P McCarthy	7
J Winkelhock	7
E Bertaggia	6
T Trimmer	6

SUCCESSES OUTSIDE THE F1 WORLD CHAMPIONSHIP

EUROPEAN FORMULA 3000

Winners

	F3000 WINS	BEST F3000 CHAMPIONSHIP SEASON	BEST GP RESULT
E Comas	6	1/ 1990	5/ 1992
R Moreno	5	1/ 1988	2/ 1990
E Naspetti	5	3/ 1991	11/ 1992
L Badoer	4	1/ 1992	7/ 1993
C Danner	4	1/ 1985	4/ 1989
F Lagorce	4	2/ 1994	11/ 1994
P Martini	4	2/ 1986	4/ 1991
L Sala	4	2/ 1987	6/ 1989
M Thackwell	4	2/ 1985	r/1980,84
J Alesi	3	1/ 1989	1/ 1995
J Boullion	3	1/ 1994	5/ 1995
I Capelli	3	1/ 1986	2/ 1990
M Donnelly	3	3/ 1988	7/ 1990
S Modena	3	1/ 1987	2/ 1991
A Montermini	3	2/ 1992	8/1995
O Panis	3	1/ 1993	1/ 1996
E Pirro	3	3/ 1985,86	5/ 1989
E v de Poele	3	2/ 1990	9/ 1991
Y Dalmas	2	5/ 1987	5/ 1987
C Fittipaldi	2	1/ 1991	4/ 1993,94
J-M Gounon	2	6/ 1991,92	9/ 1994
O Grouillard	2	2/ 1988	6/ 1989
F Lagorce	2	2/ 1994	11/ 1994
R Rosset	2	2/ 1995	8/ 1996
A Zanardi	2	2/ 1991	6/ 1993
P Alliot	1	9/ 1986	5/ 1993
J Bailey	1	7/ 1987	6/ 1991
O Beretta	1	6/ 1993	7/ 1994
É Bernard	1	3/ 1989	3/ 1994
A Chiesa	1	6/ 1989	r/ 1992
D Coulthard	1	3/ 1993	1/ 1995
P Fabre	1	7/ 1986	9/ 1987
G Foitek	1	7/ 1988	7/ 1990
M Gugelmin	1	4/ 1987	3/ 1989
J Herbert	1	8/ 1988	1/ 1995
E Irvine	1	3/ 1990	3/ 1995,96
P Lamy	1	2/ 1993	6/ 1995
T Marques	1	5/ 1995	r/ 1996
G Morbidelli	1	5/ 1990	3/ 1995
M Papis	1	5/ 1994	7/ 1995

EUROPEAN F3000 NON-WINNERS WHO HAVE ACHIEVED A TOP 6 GP PLACING

	F3000 WINS	BEST F3000 CHAMPIONSHIP SEASON	BEST GP RESULT
D Hill	2nd	7/ 1991	1/1993-96
R Barrichello	2nd	3/ 1992	3/1994
M Blundell	2nd	6/ 1988	3/1993,94
J J Lehto	4th	13/ 1989	3/ 1991
P Streiff	3rd	8/ 1985	3/ 1985
A Suzuki	11th	—	3/ 1990
H-H Frentzen	5th	14/ 1991	4/ 1994
S Nakajima	4th	10/ 1986	4/1987,89
K Wendlinger	3rd	11/ 1991	4/1993,94
J Dumfries	6th	16/ 1985	5/ 1986
B Gachot	2nd	5/ 1988	5/ 1991
U Katayama	18th	—	5/ 1994
P Diniz	4th	12/ 1994	6/ 1996
G Tarquini	3rd	6/ 1985	6/ 1989

EUROPEAN F2 CHAMPIONS (1967-84)

R Arnoux	1977
J P Beltoise	1968
P Depailler	1974
C Fabi	1982
B Giacomelli	1978
M Hailwood	1972
B Henton	1980
J Ickx	1967
J-P Jabouille	1976
J-P Jarier	1973
J Laffite	1975
G Lees	1981
J Palmer	1983
R Peterson	1971
C Regazzoni	1970
J Servoz-Gavin	1969
M Surer	1979
M Thackwell	1984

EUROPEAN F3 CHAMPIONS (1975-84)

M Alboreto	1980
M Baldi	1981
I Capelli	1984
P Ghinzani	1977
J Lammers	1978
O Larrauri	1982
P Martini	1983
R Patrese	1976
L Perkins	1975
A Prost	1979

ALL-JAPAN F2, F3000 CHAMPIONS

M Apicella	1994
M Hasemi	1980
K Hoshino	1978,87,90,93
U Katayama	1991
G Lees	1983
S Nakajima	1981,82,84,85,86
A Suzuki	1988

PRE-CHAMPIONSHIP MAJOR SINGLE-SEATER GRAND PRIX WINNERS

A Ascari	1949
L Chiron	1928-49
E de Graffenried	1949
L Fagioli	1933-35
G Farina	1940-48
H Lang	1937-39
L Rosier	1949
H Stuck	1934-35
L Villoresi	1948
P Whitehead	1949

INDYCAR DRIVERS IN THE FORMULA 1 WORLD CHAMPIONSHIP

Indianapolis 500 Drivers (1950-60) Who Won the Race in Other Years

A J Foyt	1961,64,67,77
B Holland	1949
M Rose	1941,47,48
R Ward	1962

Indianapolis 500 Winners

Mario Andretti *	1969
J Clark *	1965
M Donohue	1972
E Fittipaldi *	1989,93
G Hill *	1966
B Rahal	1986
T Ruttman	1952
D Sullivan	1985
B Unser	1968,75,81
J Villeneuve	1995
R Ward	1959,62

** also an F1 World Champion*

F1 AND INDYCAR RACE WINNERS

	F1	IndyCar
Mario Andretti	1971-78	1965-93
E Fittipaldi	1970-75	1985-95
D Gurney	1962-67	1967-70
J Clark	1962-68	1963-65
N Mansell	1985-94	1993
G Hill	1962-69	1966
P Revson	1973	1969
J Villeneuve	1996	1994-95

F1 NON-WINNERS WHO WON AN INDYCAR RACE

Michael Andretti	1986-96
R Bucknum	1968
M Donohue	1971-72
T Fabi	1983-89
G Follmer	1969

R Guerrero	1987
D Ongais	1977-78
B Rahal	1982-92
H Rebaque	1982
L Ruby	1961-70
T Ruttman	1952
D Sullivan	1984-93
B Unser	1966-81
R Ward	1953-66
A Zanardi	1996

F1 DRIVERS WHO WON THE INDYCAR WORLD SERIES*

Mario Andretti	1965,66,69,84
Michael Andretti	1991
E Fittipaldi	1989
N Mansell	1993
B Rahal	1986,87,92
D Sullivan	1988
B Unser	1968,74
J Villeneuve	1995
R Ward	1959,62

** USAC National Championship until 1979, CART IndyCar World Series 1979-91*

F1 AND INDYCAR WORLD CHAMPIONS

	F1	INDYCAR
M Andretti	1978	1965,66,69,84
E Fittipaldi	1972,74	1989
N Mansell	1992	1993

Nigel Mansell was the only driver to hold the F1 and IndyCar Championships simultaneously

F1 DRIVERS WHO STARTED AT INDY (1950-60)

A Ascari, L Ruby, T Ruttman, R Ward

LE MANS 24-HOURS RACE WINNERS

C Amon	1966
D Attwood	1970
M Baldi	1994
L Bandini	1963
P Barilla	1985
D Bell	1975,81,82,86,87
L Bianchi	1968
M Blundell	1992
M Brundle	1990
I Bueb	1955,57
E Chaboud	1938
Y Dalmas	1992,94,95
J Dumfries	1988
P Étançelin	1934
R Flockhart	1956,57
A J Foyt	1967
P Frère	1960
B Gachot	1991
O Gendebien	1958,60,61,62
F González	1954
M Gregory	1965
D Gurney	1967
D Hamilton	1953
M Hawthorn	1955
J Herbert	1991
H Herrmann	1970
G Hill	1972
P Hill	1958,61,62
J Ickx	1969,75,76,77,81,82
J Lammers	1988
H Lang	1952
G Larrousse	1973,74
J J Lehto	1995
H Marko	1971
J Mass	1989
B McLaren	1966
J Oliver	1969
H Pescarolo	1972,73,74,84
D Pironi	1978
F Riess	1952
J Rindt	1965
P Rodriguez	1968
T Rolt	1953
L Rosier	1950
R Salvadori	1959
L Scarfiotti	1963
V Schuppan	1983
C Shelby	1959
R Sommer	1932,33
H-J Stuck	1986,87
M Trintignant	1954
N Vaccarella	1964
G Van Lennep	1971,76
P Walker	1951
D Warwick	1992
P Whitehead	1951

WORLD SPORTSCAR CHAMPIONS

M Baldi	1990 *
D Bell	1985*,86
S Bellof	1984
R Boesel	1987
M Brundle	1988
Y Dalmas	1992 *
T Fabi	1991
J Ickx	1982,3
J L Schlesser	1989,90 *
H-J Stuck	1985 *
D Warwick	1992 *

** shared championship*

MOTORCYCLE 500CC WORLD CHAMPIONSHIP POINT SCORERS

B Anderson	1958-59
J Cecotto *	1976-80
P Driver	1959-65
M Hailwood *	1960-67
N Pagani *	1949-55
J Surtees *	1952-60

** race winners*

John Surtees is the only man to become F1 car and 500cc Motorcycle World Champion

CONSTRUCTORS

STARTS

Grands Prix (Most)

Ferrari	569
Lotus	491
McLaren	443
Tyrrell	397
Brabham	394
Williams	355
Ligier	326
Arrows	288
Benetton	234
March	227
BRM	197
Minardi	188
Osella	151
Lola	149
Cooper	129
Renault	123
Surtees	118
Alfa Romeo	110
Fittipaldi	104
Shadow	104

TOTAL RACE STARTS (Most)

(Number of cars to start)

Ferrari	1330
Lotus	1238
Brabham	932
McLaren	941
Tyrrell	782
Williams	672
Ligier	578
March	558
Arrows	537
BRM	522
Cooper	499
Benetton	448
Maserati	368
Minardi	338
Lola	245
Alfa Romeo	234
Renault	227
Surtees	224
Shadow	211

WORLD CHAMPIONS

YEAR		NAT
1958	Vanwall	GB
1959	Cooper-Climax	GB
1960	Cooper-Climax	GB
1961	Ferrari	I
1962	BRM	GB
1963	Lotus-Climax	GB
1964	Ferrari	I
1965	Lotus-Climax	GB
1966	Brabham-Repco	GB/AUS
1967	Brabham-Repco	GB/AUS
1968	Lotus-Ford Cosworth	GB
1969	Matra-Ford Cosworth	F/GB
1970	Lotus-Ford Cosworth	GB
1971	Tyrrell-Ford Cosworth	GB
1972	Lotus-Ford Cosworth	GB
1973	Lotus-Ford Cosworth	GB
1974	McLaren-Ford Cosworth	GB
1975	Ferrari	I
1976	Ferrari	I
1977	Ferrari	I
1978	Lotus-Ford Cosworth	GB
1979	Ferrari	I
1980	Williams-Ford Cosworth	GB
1981	Williams-Ford Cosworth	GB
1982	Ferrari	I
1983	Ferrari	I
1984	McLaren-TAG Porsche	GB/D
1985	McLaren-TAG Porsche	GB/D
1986	Williams-Honda	GB/J
1987	Williams-Honda	GB/J
1988	McLaren-Honda	GB/J
1989	McLaren-Honda	GB/J
1990	McLaren-Honda	GB/J
1991	McLaren-Honda	GB/J
1992	Williams-Renault	GB/F
1993	Williams-Renault	GB/F
1994	Williams-Renault	GB/F
1995	Benetton-Renault	GB/F
1996	Williams-Renault	GB/F

CONSTRUCTORS' WORLD CHAMPIONSHIPS

Ferrari	8
Williams	8
Lotus	7
McLaren	7
Brabham	2
Cooper	2
Benetton	1
BRM	1
Matra	1
Tyrrell	1
Vanwall	1

DRIVERS' CHAMPIONSHIPS

Ferrari	9
McLaren	9
Lotus	6
Williams	6
Brabham	4
Alfa Romeo	2
Benetton	2
Cooper	2
Maserati	2
Mercedes-Benz	2
Tyrrell	2
BRM	1
Matra	1

WINS

Ferrari	108
McLaren	104
Williams	95
Lotus	79
Brabham	35
Benetton	26
Tyrrell	23
BRM	17
Cooper	16
Renault	15
Alfa Romeo	10
Ligier	9
Maserati	9
Matra	9
Mercedes-Benz	9
Vanwall	9
March	3
Wolf	3
Honda	2
Eagle	1
Hesketh	1
Penske	1
Porsche	1
Shadow	1

WINS IN A SEASON (Most)

McLaren	15	1988
McLaren	12	1984
Benetton	11	1995
Williams	11	1996
McLaren	10	1989
Williams	10	1992, 93
Williams	9	1986, 87
Benetton	8	1994 *
Lotus	8	1978
McLaren	8	1991

** not Constructors' World Champion*

SUCCESSIVE WINS (Most)

Ferrari	14	CH 52-CH 53
McLaren	11	BR-B 88
Alfa Romeo	9	GB 50-F 51
McLaren	8	GB 84-BR 85
Williams	7	CDN-I 93

SUCCESSIVE SEASONS OF WINNING (Most)

McLaren	13	(1981-93)
Lotus	11	(1960-70)
Williams	9	(1979-87)

WIN IN DEBUT RACE

Alfa Romeo	GB 50
Mercedes-Benz	F 54
Wolf	RA 77

TOP FOUR CARS OF SAME CONSTRUCTOR

D 52	Ferrari
GB 55	Mercedes-Benz
RA 57	Maserati
F 60	Cooper
B 61	Ferrari

(excludes Indy)

In GB 81, the top 14 cars were of different makes

FIRST WIN FOR NATIONALITY

Italy	GB 50	Alfa Romeo
Germany	F 54	Mercedes
Great Britain	GB 57	Vanwall
United States	B 67	Eagle
Japan	I 67	Honda
France	NL 68	Matra
Canada	RA 77	Wolf

POLE POSITIONS

Ferrari	118
Lotus	107
Williams	97
McLaren	79
Brabham	39
Renault	31
Tyrrell	14
Benetton	13
Alfa Romeo	12
BRM	11
Cooper	11
Maserati	10
Ligier	9
Mercedes-Benz	8
Vanwall	7
March	5
Matra	4
Shadow	3
Lancia	2
Arrows	1
Honda	1
Jordan	1
Lola	1
Porsche	1
Wolf	1

POLE POSITIONS IN A SEASON (Most)

McLaren	15	1988, 89
Williams	15	1992, 93
Lotus	12	1978
McLaren	12	1990
Williams	12	1987, 95, 96

SUCCESSIVE POLE POSITIONS (Most)

Williams	24	F 92-J 93
McLaren	17	D 88-D 89
McLaren	12	B 89-MEX 90
Ferrari	10	E 51-NL 53
Lotus	10	NL 67-ZA 68

POLE POSITION IN DEBUT RACE

Alfa Romeo	GB 50
Lancia	E 54
Lola	NL 62
March	ZA 70
Mercedes-Benz	F 54
Tyrrell	CDN 70

FASTEST LAPS

Ferrari	127
Williams	101
Lotus	71
McLaren	69
Brabham	42
Benetton	35
Tyrrell	20
Renault	18
Maserati	17
BRM	15
Alfa Romeo	14
Cooper	14
Matra	12
Ligier	9
Mercedes-Benz	9
March	7
Vanwall	6
Surtees	3
Eagle	2
Honda	2
Shadow	2
Wolf	2
Ensign	1
Gordini	1
Jordan	1
Kojima	1
Lancia	1
Parnelli	1

FASTEST LAPS IN A SEASON (Most)

Williams	11	1986, 92, 96
McLaren	10	1988
Williams	10	1993

SUCCESSIVE FASTEST LAPS (Most)

Alfa Romeo	13	GB 50-E 51
Ferrari	9	CH 52-NL 53
Ferrari	8	D 70-E 71
McLaren	6	RSM-F 88
Williams	6	H-AUS 93

POINTS (Most)

Gross points scored

Ferrari	2896.8
McLaren	2084.5
Williams	1805.5
Lotus	1514
Brabham	983
Benetton	741.5
Tyrrell	709
BRM	537.5
Cooper	484.5
Ligier	388
Maserati	313.4
Renault	312
Alfa Romeo	214
March	193
Matra	184

POINTS IN A SEASON (Gross / Most)

McLaren	199	1988
Williams	175	1996
Williams	168	1993
Williams	164	1992
McLaren	143.5	1984
McLaren	141	1989
Williams	141	1986

POINTS IN DEBUT RACE

Alfa Romeo	GB 50
Talbot Lago	GB 50
Ferrari	MC 50
BRM	GB 51
Mercedes-Benz	F 54
March	ZA 70
Shadow	ZA 73
Wolf	RA 77
ATS	USAW 77
Sauber	ZA 93

LAP LEADERS

Laps Led (Most)

	LAPS	KM	MILES
Ferrari	7,203	39,613.9	24,614.9
Williams	6,274	29,021.7	18,033.3
McLaren	5,698	26,473.1	16,449.6
Lotus	5,498	26,183.8	16,269.9
Brabham	2,721	13,239.8	8,226.8
Tyrrell	1,493	6,737.4	4,186.4
Benetton	1,426	6,668.2	4,143.4
BRM	1,347	6,099.4	3,790.0
Renault	1,184	5,784.6	3,594.4
Cooper	829	4,537.4	2,819.4
Maserati	826	4,720.7	2,933.3
Alfa Romeo	702	4,793.1	2,978.3
Matra	668	3,610.4	2,243.4
Mercedes	589	3,976.4	2,470.8
Ligier	565	2,627.8	1,632.8

Led Whole Race (Most races)

Williams	44	GB 79-J 96
Ferrari	40	CH 52-D 94
McLaren	36	D 76-CDN 92
Lotus	30	D 61-B 85
Brabham	11	GB 66-DET 84
Tyrrell	8	MC 71-S 74
Mercedes-Benz	7	F 54-I 55

FASTEST LAPS

Ferrari	127
Williams	101
Lotus	71

GRANDS PRIX WITHOUT POINTS (Most)

RAM	31
Forti	23
Spirit	23
Pacific	22
Simtek	21

MISCELLANEOUS

DIFFERENT CONSTRUCTORS IN ONE RACE (Most)

MC 88	18
CDN 89	18

FOUR-WHEEL DRIVE ENTRIES

First:

GB 61	Ferguson P99-Climax S Moss/J Fairman

Last:

I 71	Lotus 56B-Pratt & Whitney E Fittipaldi

MODELS

Grands Prix (Most)

McLaren M23	80
Lotus 72	74
Lotus 25	49

Total Race Starts (Most)

Maserati 250F	248
McLaren M23	166
Lotus 72	149

Wins (Most)

McLaren MP4/2	22
Lotus 72	20
Williams FW11	18

Pole Positions (Most)

McLaren MP4/5	27
Williams FW14	21
Lotus 49	19

Fastest Laps (Most)

Williams FW14	19
Williams FW11	18
McLaren MP4/2	16
Williams FW07	16

Points (Most)

McLaren MP4/2	329.5
McLaren M23	319
Williams FW07	300

ENGINES

GP Starts

Ferrari	570
Ford Cosworth	434
Renault	269
Alfa Romeo	222
BRM	197
Honda	186
Hart	128
Matra	125
Maserati	109
Climax	96

Wins

Ford Cosworth	174
Ferrari	108
Renault	86
Honda	71
Climax	40
TAG Porsche	25
BRM	18
Alfa Romeo	12
Maserati	11
Mercedes-Benz	9
Vanwall	9
BMW	9
Repco	8
Matra	3
Mugen Honda	1
Porsche	1
Weslake	1

excludes Indy

POLE POSITIONS

Ford Cosworth	138
Renault	122
Ferrari	118
Honda	74
Climax	44
Alfa Romeo	15
BMW	15
Maserati	11
BRM	11
Mercedes-Benz	8
Repco	7
TAG Porsche	7
Vanwall	7
Matra	4
Lancia	2
Hart	2
Porsche	1

exc Indy

From Belgium in 1973, as is common practice today, teams generally held the same numbers throughout the season, with the reigning World Champion holding no.1

The only time a Constructor had the same name as the Grand Prix, was Pacific in 1994

The first race for a rear-engined car was Monaco 1950

The first win for a rear-engined car was Argentina 1958

The last race for a front-engined car was Britain 1961 (Ferguson)

The last win for a front-engined car was Italy 1960

The first race where all the starters were powered by turbo engines was Austria 1984 (the 400th Championship race)

The last time a constructor had three cars in a Grand Prix was at Germany 1985 (Renault)

Turbo engined cars won 109 Grands Prix, from France 1979 (J-P Jabouille) to Australia 1988 (A Prost)

The oldest car to race in the Championship was a 1935 ERA type A in Monaco 1950 (chassis number 4A)

DRIVERS WHO HAVE DIED FROM MOTOR RACING INJURIES

It is an overused phrase in journalism, that sportsmen have 'given their all'. It can be said of the drivers listed below, that they have truly given their all, in the name of motor racing, and it is in their memory that the following tables appear.

Grand Prix Drivers

	DRIVER	NAT	CAR	RACE FORMULA	EVENT	PLACE
1950						
	J Fry	GB	Freikaiserwagen	Non Formula 1	Hill-climb	Blandford Camp, Dorset, England
	R Sommer	F	Cooper	Non Formula 1	Haute Garonne Grand Prix F3 race	Cadours, nr Toulouse, France
1952						
	L Fagioli	I	Lancia	Non Formula 1	Monaco sportscar Grand Prix	Monte Carlo, Monaco
1953						
	C de Tornaco	B	Ferrari	Non Formula 1	Modena Grand Prix (F2)	Modena Aerautodrome, Italy
	F Bonetto	I	Lancia	Non Formula 1	Carrera Panamericana race	Silao, Mexico
1954						
	G Mairesse	F	Talbot Lago	Non Formula 1	Coupe de Paris practice	Montlhéry, nr Paris, France
	O Marimon	RA	Maserati	Grand Prix Practice	German Grand Prix	Nürburgring, Germany
1955						
	A Ascari	I	Ferrari	Non Formula 1	Sportscar testing	Monza, Italy
	P Levegh	F	Mercedes-Benz	Non Formula 1	Le Mans 24 Hours race	Le Mans, France
	D Beauman	GB	Connaught	Non Formula 1	Leinster trophy sportscar race	Rathnew, County Wicklow, Ireland
1956						
	L Rosier	F	Ferrari	Non Formula 1	Coupe de Salon sportscar race	Montlhéry, nr Paris, France
1957						
	K Wharton	GB	Ferrari	Non Formula 1	Sportscar race	Ardmore, New Zealand
	E Castellotti	I	Ferrari	Grand Prix Testing		Modena Aerautodrome, Italy
	A de Portago	E	Ferrari	Non Formula 1	Mille Miglia sports car race	between Goito and Guidizzolo, Italy
	P Carini	I	Ferrari	Non Formula 1	Sportscar race	St. Etienne, France
	B Whitehouse	GB	Cooper	Non Formula 1	Coupe de Vitesse F2 race	Reims, France
	H MacKay-Fraser	USA	Lotus	Non Formula 1	Coupe de Vitesse F2 race	Reims, France
1958						
	A Scott-Brown	GB	Lister	Non Formula 1	Sportscar race	Spa-Francorchamps, Belgium
	E Bauer	D	Ferrari	Non Formula 1	1,000 km sportscar race	Nürburgring, Germany
	L Musso	I	Ferrari	Grand Prix Race	French Grand Prix	Reims, France
	P Collins	GB	Ferrari	Grand Prix Race	German Grand Prix	Nürburgring, Germany
	P Whitehead	GB	Jaguar	Non Formula 1	Tour de France Automobile	Lasalle, nr Nîmes, France
	S Lewis-Evans	GB	Vanwall	Grand Prix Race	Moroccan Grand Prix	Casablanca, Morocco
1959						
	J Behra	F	Porsche	Non Formula 1	Berlin sportscar Grand Prix race	AVUS, Berlin, Germany
	I Bueb	GB	Cooper	Non Formula 1	Auvergne Trophy F2 race	Clermont-Ferrand, France
1960						
	H Blanchard	USA	Porsche	Non Formula 1	1,000 km sportscar race	Buenos Aires, Argentina
	E Chimeri	I	Ferrari	Non Formula 1	Sportscar practice	Cuba
	H Schell	USA	Cooper	Other Formula 1	International trophy practice	Silverstone, England
	C Bristow	GB	Cooper	Grand Prix Race	Belgian Grand Prix	Spa-Francorchamps, Belgium
	A Stacey	GB	Lotus	Grand Prix Race	Belgian Grand Prix	Spa-Francorchamps, Belgium
1961						
	G Cabianca	I	Cooper	Grand Prix Testing		Modena Aerautodrome, Italy
	W von Trips	D	Ferrari	Grand Prix Race	Italian Grand Prix	Monza, Italy
1962						
	P Ryan	CDN	Lotus	Non Formula 1	Coupe de Vitesse des Juniors race	Reims, France
	R Rodriguez	MEX	Lotus	Other Formula 1	Mexican Grand Prix practice	Mexico City, Mexico
1964						
	T Mayer	USA	Cooper	Non Formula 1	Tasman Championship race practice	Longford, Tasmania, Australia
	C de Beaufort	NL	Porsche	Grand Prix Practice	German Grand Prix	Nürburgring, Germany
1966						
	W Hansgen	USA	Ford	Non Formula 1	Le Mans 24 Hours testing	Le Mans, France
	J Taylor	GB	Brabham	Grand Prix Race	German Grand Prix	Nürburgring, Germany
1967						
	L Bandini	I	Ferrari	Grand Prix Race	Monaco Grand Prix	Monte Carlo, Monaco
	"Geki"	I	Matra	Non Formula 1	Italian F3 race	Caserta, nr Naples, Italy
	B Anderson	GB	Brabham	Grand Prix Testing		Silverstone, England
	G Berger	B	Porsche	Non Formula 1	Endurance race	Nürburgring, Germany
	I Raby	GB	Brabham	Non Formula 1	Formula 2 race	Zandvoort, Netherlands

Year	Driver	Nat.	Car	Type	Event	Location
1968						
	J Clark	GB	Lotus	Non Formula 1	European Formula 2 race	Hockenheim, Germany
	M Spence	GB	Lotus	Non Formula 1	Indianapolis 500 practice	Indianapolis, USA
	L Scarfiotti	I	Porsche	Non Formula 1	Mountain climb	Rossfeld, Germany
	J Schlesser	F	Honda	Grand Prix Race	French Grand Prix	Rouen, France
1969						
	L Bianchi	B	Alfa Romeo	Non Formula 1	Le Mans 24 Hours testing	Le Mans, France
	P Hawkins	AUS	Lola	Non Formula 1	Tourist Trophy race	Oulton Park, England
	M Solana	MEX	McLaren	Non Formula 1	Hill-climb	Valle de Bravo, Mexico
	G Mitter	D	BMW	Grand Prix Practice	German Grand Prix	Nürburgring, Germany
1970						
	B McLaren	NZ	McLaren	Non Formula 1	Can-Am car testing	Goodwood, England
	P Courage	GB	de Tomaso	Grand Prix Race	Dutch Grand Prix	Zandvoort, Netherlands
	J Rindt	A	Lotus	Grand Prix Practice	Italian Grand Prix	Monza, Italy
1971						
	I Giunti	I	Ferrari	Non Formula 1	1,000 km sportscar race	Buenos Aires, Argentina
	P Rodriguez	MEX	Ferrari	Non Formula 1	Interserie sportscar race	Norisring, Germany
	J Siffert	CH	BRM	Other Formula 1	Rothmans Victory Race	Brands Hatch, England
1972						
	J Bonnier	S	Lola	Non Formula 1	Le Mans 24 Hours race	Le Mans, France
1973						
	R Williamson	GB	March	Grand Prix Race	Dutch Grand Prix	Zandvoort, Netherlands
	F Cevert	F	Tyrrell	Grand Prix Practice	USA Grand Prix	Watkins Glen, USA
	N Estefano	RA		Non Formula 1	Turismo Carretara	South America
1974						
	P Revson	USA	Shadow	Grand Prix Testing		Kyalami, South Africa
	S Moser	CH	Lola	Non Formula 1	Monza 1,000 km sportscar race	Monza, Italy
	H Koinigg	A	Surtees	Grand Prix Race	USA Grand Prix	Watkins Glen, USA
1975						
	M Donohue	USA	March	Grand Prix Practice	Austrian Grand Prix	Österreichring, Austria
1977						
	T Pryce	GB	Shadow	Grand Prix Race	South African Grand Prix	Kyalami, South Africa
1978						
	R Peterson	S	Lotus	Grand Prix Race	Italian Grand Prix	Monza, Italy
1980						
	P Depailler	F	Alfa Romeo	Grand Prix Testing		Hockenheim, Germany
1982						
	G Villeneuve	CDN	Ferrari	Grand Prix Practice	Belgian Grand Prix	Zolder, Belgium
	R Paletti	I	Osella	Grand Prix Race	Canadian Grand Prix	Montreal, Canada
1983						
	R Stommelen	D	Porsche	Non Formula 1	IMSA sportscar race	Riverside, California, USA
1985						
	M Winkelhock	D	Porsche	Non Formula 1	Sportscar race	Mosport, Ontario, Canada
	S Bellof	D	Porsche	Non Formula 1	Sportscar race	Spa-Francorchamps, Belgium
1986						
	E de Angelis	I	Brabham	Grand Prix Testing		Paul Ricard, France
	J Gartner	A	Porsche	Non Formula 1	Le Mans 24 Hours race	Le Mans, France
1994						
	R Ratzenberger	A	Simtek	Grand Prix Practice	San Marino Grand Prix	Imola, Italy
	A Senna	BR	Williams	Grand Prix Race	San Marino Grand Prix	Imola, Italy

Additionally the following Grand Prix non-starters died from racing injuries:

Brian McGuire at Brands Hatch in 1977 during practice for a Shellsport Championship race and Dennis Taylor at Monte Carlo in 1962 during the Grand Prix Monaco-Junior race.

Ricardo Rodriguez was the youngest World Championship driver to be killed racing, at the age of 20.

A total of 16 drivers have lost their lives in World Championship Grand Prix races, whilst a further 8 have died during practice sessions.

The Nürburgring claimed the most lives among Grand Prix drivers with a total of seven (two more than Le Mans and Monza).

Indianapolis 500 Drivers

	DRIVER	NAT EVENT	PLACE
1951			
	W Brown	USA Sprint car race	Williams Grove, Pennsylvania
	C Green	USA Sprint car qualifying	Winchester, Indiana
	B Mackey	USA Sprint car qualifying	Winchester, Indiana
1952			
	J McDowell	USA Championship car race	Milwaukee, Wisconsin
	J Rigsby	USA Sprint car race	Dayton, Ohio
	B Schindler	USA Sprint car race	Allentown, Pennsylvania
	J James	USA Championship car race	San Jose, California
1953			
	C Miller	USA Indianapolis 500 practice	Indianapolis, Indiana
	C Scarborough	USA Indianapolis 500 race	Indianapolis, Indiana
1954			
	B Ball	USA Midget car race	Gardena, California
	B Scott	USA Championship car race	Darlington, South Carolina
1955			
	L Crockett	USA Sprint car race	Langhorne, Pennsylvania
	M Nazaruk	USA Sprint car race	Langhorne, Pennsylvania
	M Ayulo	USA Indianapolis 500 practice	Indianapolis, Indiana
	B Vukovich	USA Indianapolis 500 race	Indianapolis, Indiana
	J Hoyt	USA Sprint car race	Oklahoma City, Oklahoma
	J McGrath	USA Championship car race on dirt track	Phoenix, Arizona
1956			
	W Faulkner	USA Stock car qualifying	Valleso, California
	B Sweikert	USA Sprint car race	Salem, Indiana
1957			
	K Andrews	USA Indianapolis 500 practice	Indianapolis, Indiana
1958			
	P O'Connor	USA Indianapolis 500 race	Indianapolis, Indiana
	G Fonder	USA Midget car race	Hartfield, Pennsylvania
	A Bisch	USA Lakewood Speedway,	Atlanta, Georgia
	J Reece	USA Championship car race	Trenton, New Jersey
1959			
	M Teague	USA Championship car testing	Daytona Beach, Florida
	G Amick	USA Championship car race	Daytona Beach, Florida
	J Unser	USA Indianapolis 500 practice	Indianapolis, Indiana
	E Elisian	USA Championship car race	Milwaukee, Wisconsin
1960			
	A Herman	USA Midget car race	West Haven, Connecticut
	J Bryan	USA Championship car race	Langhorne, Pennsylvania
	J Thomson	USA Sprint car race	Allentown, Pennsylvania
1961			
	T Bettenhausen	USA Indianapolis 500 practice	Indianapolis, Indiana
	A Keller	USA Championship car race	Phoenix, Arizona
1962			
	S Templeman	USA Midget car race	Marion, Ohio
1964			
	E Sachs	USA Indianapolis 500 race	Indianapolis, Indiana
1966			
	J Davies	USA Midget car race	Santa Fe, Illinois
	J Larson	USA Sprint car race	Reading, Pennsylvania
	D Branson	USA Ascot Park Sprint car race	Gardena, California
1988			
	C Niday	USA Antique Car race	Willow Springs, California

7

ANNIVERSARIES

1 Jan 1909 Marcel Balsa born
1 Jan 1963 Jean-Marc Gounon born
1 Jan 1945 Jacky Ickx born
1 Jan 1951 Hans-Joachim Stuck born
1 Jan 1928 Hap Sharp born
1 Jan 1951 Leo Ress born
1 Jan 1981 Mauri Rose died
1 Jan 1968 Jim Clark last win
1 Jan 1965 Jackie Stewart first start
1 Jan 1968 Jim Clark last start
1 Jan 1965 Last GP at East London

2 Jan 1957 Beppe Gabbiani born
2 Jan 1967 Cooper last win
2 Jan 1967 First GP at Kyalami

3 Jan 1969 Michael Schumacher born
3 Jan 1988 Joie Chitwood died

4 Jan 1954 Jo Gartner born

5 Jan 1938 Keith Greene born
5 Jan 1920 André Simon born

6 Jan 1924 Pablo Birger born
6 Jan 1926 Pat Flaherty born
6 Jan 1926 Dick Rathmann born
6 Jan 1989 Jim Hurtubise died

7 Jan 1939 Brausch Niemann born
7 Jan 1946 Mike Wilds born
7 Jan 1991 Henri Louveau died
7 Jan 1964 Reg Parnell died

9 Jan 1960 Pascal Fabre born
9 Jan 1977 Wolf first start & win

10 Jan 1958 Eddie Cheever born
10 Jan 1953 Bobby Rahal born
10 Jan 1921 Rodger Ward born
10 Jan 1971 Ignazio Giunti died
10 Jan 1944 Rory Byrne born

11 Jan 1923 Carroll Shelby born

12 Jan 1924 Olivier Gendebien born
12 Jan 1962 Emanuele Pirro born
12 Jan 1938 Alan Rees born
12 Jan 1928 Lloyd Ruby born
12 Jan 1988 Piero Taruffi died
12 Jan 1957 Ken Wharton died
12 Jan 1975 Fittipaldi first start

13 Jan 1968 Gianni Morbidelli born
13 Jan 1935 Mauro Forghieri born
13 Jan 1925 Ron Tauranac born
13 Jan 1974 Denny Hulme last win
13 Jan 1980 Alain Prost first start

14 Jan 1973 Giancarlo Fisichella born
14 Jan 1934 Rodriguez Larreta born
14 Jan 1994 Myron Fohr died

15 Jan 1934 Mario de Cabral born
15 Jan 1953 David Kennedy born
15 Jan 1981 Graham Whitehead died

16 Jan 1930 Luki Botha born
16 Jan 1930 Alberto Crespo born
16 Jan 1935 A J Foyt born
16 Jan 1952 Piercarlo Ghinzani born

17 Jan 1924 John Riseley-Prichard born

18 Jan 1950 Gianfranco Brancatelli born
18 Jan 1971 Christian Fittipaldi born
18 Jan 1940 Pedro Rodriguez born
18 Jan 1942 Johnny Servoz-Gavin born
18 Jan 1950 Gilles Villeneuve born

19 Jan 1929 Red Amick born
19 Jan 1914 Bob Gerard born
19 Jan 1976 Tarso Marques born
19 Jan 1958 Cooper first win
19 Jan 1958 Climax engine first win

20 Jan 1934 Giorgio Bassi born
20 Jan 1993 Feruccio Lamborghini died

21 Jan 1930 John Campbell-Jones born
21 Jan 1923 Jud Larson born
21 Jan 1981 Cuth Harrison died
21 Jan 1979 Elio de Angelis first start

22 Jan 1959 Mike Hawthorn died

23 Jan 1972 Carlos Reutemann first start

24 Jan 1918 Art Cross born
24 Jan 1943 Tony Trimmer born
24 Jan 1925 Owen Maddock born

25 Jan 1971 Luca Badoer born
25 Jan 1956 Johnny Cecotto born
25 Jan 1910 Henri Louveau born
25 Jan 1930 Heinz Schiller born
25 Jan 1906 Toni Ulmen born
25 Jan 1976 Ligier first start

26 Jan 1917 Edgar Barth born
26 Jan 1945 David Purley born
26 Jan 1990 Bob Gerard died
26 Jan 1975 Graham Hill last start

27 Jan 1934 George Follmer born
27 Jan 1980 René Arnoux first win

28 Jan 1927 Jimmy Bryan born
28 Jan 1926 Gene Hartley born
28 Jan 1995 Aldo Gordini died

29 Jan 1929 Jerry Hoyt born
29 Jan 1915 Johnny McDowell born
29 Jan 1950 Jody Scheckter born
29 Jan 1915 Brian Shawe-Taylor born
29 Jan 1940 Kunimitsu Takahashi born
29 Jan 1990 Spider Webb died
29 Jan 1978 Arrows first start

30 Jan 1917 Paul Frère born
30 Jan 1937 Bruce Johnstone born
30 Jan 1939 Bernard Dudot born

31 Jan 1954 Mauro Baldi born
31 Jan 1930 Jo Bonnier born
31 Jan 1934 Tino Brambilla born
31 Jan 1908 Bill Cantrell born
31 Jan 1966 J J Lehto born
31 Jan 1960 Harry Blanchard died

1 Feb 1932 Xavier Perrot born

2 Feb 1937 Tony Shelly born

3 Feb 1920 Tony Gaze born
3 Feb 1957 Chico Serra born
3 Feb 1956 Johnny Claes died
3 Feb 1993 Paul Emery died

4 Feb 1949 Roger Williamson born
4 Feb 1938 Ralph Bellamy born

5 Feb 1956 Hector Rebaque born

6 Feb 1916 Cliff Griffith born

8 Feb 1932 Cliff Allison born
8 Feb 1920 Mike Magill born
8 Feb 1978 Hans Stuck died

9 Feb 1937 Tony Maggs born
9 Feb 1951 Ian Phillips born

10 Feb 1923 Theo Fitzau born
10 Feb 1919 Eddie Johnson born
10 Feb 1917 Danny Kladis born
10 Feb 1987 Andy Linden died

11 Feb 1959 Roberto Moreno born
11 Feb 1934 John Surtees born
11 Feb 1959 Marshall Teague died
11 Feb 1973 First GP at Interlagos

12 Feb 1952 Patrick Gaillard born
12 Feb 1920 Jack Turner born
12 Feb 1987 Dennis Poore died

13 Feb 1948 Jim Crawford born
13 Feb 1922 Willi Heeks born
13 Feb 1976 Paul Russo died

14 Feb 1913 Bayliss Levrett born
14 Feb 1944 Ronnie Peterson born
14 Feb 1942 Ricardo Rodriguez born
14 Feb 1988 Cal Niday died
14 Feb 1976 Piero Scotti died

15 Feb 1929 Graham Hill born
15 Feb 1937 Vincenzo Lancia died

16 Feb 1921 Jean Behra born
16 Feb 1920 Tony Crook born
16 Feb 1920 Walt Faulkner born

17 Feb 1959 Mike Coughlan born

18 Feb 1953 Ingo Hoffman born
18 Feb 1958 Giovanni Lavaggi born
18 Feb 1898 Enzo Ferrari born

19 Feb 1923 Giulio Cabianca born
19 Feb 1921 Ernie McCoy born
19 Feb 1952 Stephen South born

20 Feb 1937 Roger Penske born
20 Feb 1934 Bobby Unser born
20 Feb 1947 Steve Nichols born

21 Feb 1940 Peter Gethin born
21 Feb 1913 Roger Laurent born

22 Feb 1918 George Constantine born
22 Feb 1922 Jesus Iglesias born
22 Feb 1949 Niki Lauda born
22 Feb 1938 Timmy Mayer born

23 Feb 1946 Alberto Colombo born
23 Feb 1928 Hans Herrmann born
23 Feb 1953 Satoru Nakajima born
23 Feb 1960 Arthur Legat died

24 Feb 1968 Emanuele Naspetti born
24 Feb 1955 Alain Prost born
24 Feb 1936 Lance Reventlow born
24 Feb 1955 Clemente Biondetti died

25 Feb 1932 Tony Brooks born
25 Feb 1944 François Cevert born
25 Feb 1946 Jean Todt born

26 Feb 1955 Rupert Keegan born
26 Feb 1917 Robert La Caze born
26 Feb 1943 François Mazet born

27 Feb 1965 Pedro Chaves born
27 Feb 1939 Peter Revson born
27 Feb 1954 Bobby Ball died
27 Feb 1960 Ettore Chimeri died

28 Feb 1940 Mario Andretti born
28 Feb 1914 Élie Bayol born
28 Feb 1908 Albert Scherrer born
28 Feb 1964 Timmy Mayer died

29 Feb 1932 Masten Gregory born

1 Mar 1987 Wolfgang Seidel died
1 Mar 1984 Peter Walker died
1 Mar 1980 Osella first start
1 Mar 1980 Shadow last start
1 Mar 1992 Mugen Honda first start
1 Mar 1969 Repco engine last start

2 Mar 1962 Gabriele Tarquini born

3 Mar 1963 Perry McCarthy born
3 Mar 1947 Otto Stuppacher born
3 Mar 1992 Lella Lombardi died
3 Mar 1956 Ernst Loof died
3 Mar 1973 Shadow first start

4 Mar 1936 Jim Clark born
4 Mar 1911 Carl Forberg born
4 Mar 1933 Nino Vaccarella born
4 Mar 1972 Jos Verstappen born
4 Mar 1944 Harvey Postlethwaite born
4 Mar 1974 Bill Aston died
4 Mar 1978 Eddie Cheever first start
4 Mar 1978 Keke Rosberg first start
4 Mar 1978 Hesketh last start

5 Mar 1940 Graham McRae born
5 Mar 1977 Tom Pryce died
5 Mar 1977 BRM last start

6 Mar 1921 Piero Carini born
6 Mar 1940 Willie Ferguson born
6 Mar 1917 Oswald Karch born
6 Mar 1909 Bill Schindler born
6 Mar 1931 Jimmy Stewart born
6 Mar 1971 Mario Andretti first win

7 Mar 1969 Hideki Noda born
7 Mar 1978 Rudolf Schoeller died
7 Mar 1970 Jack Brabham last win
7 Mar 1970 March first start

8 Mar 1968 Michael Bartels born
8 Mar 1993 Duane Carter died
9 Mar 1955 Teo Fabi born
9 Mar 1937 Brian Redman born
9 Mar 1950 Danny Sullivan born
9 Mar 1951 Gary Anderson born
9 Mar 1966 Pablo Birger died
9 Mar 1963 Jorge Daponte died

10 Mar 1946 Hiroshi Fushida born
10 Mar 1955 Toshio Suzuki born
10 Mar 1967 Tony Vandervell died
10 Mar 1991 Jordan first start
10 Mar 1996 Jacques Villeneuve first start
10 Mar 1991 Ilmor engine first start
10 Mar 1996 First GP at Melbourne
10 Mar 1991 Last GP at Phoenix

11 Mar 1953 Derek Daly born
11 Mar 1943 Arturo Merzario born
11 Mar 1930 Troy Ruttman born
11 Mar 1927 Dempsey Wilson born
11 Mar 1977 Rodriguez Larreta died
11 Mar 1992 Christian Vanderpleyn died

12 Mar 1913 Duke Nalon born

13 Mar 1943 Mike Fisher born
13 Mar 1913 Joe Kelly born

14 Mar 1957 Eugenio Castellotti died
14 Mar 1993 Last GP at Kyalami

15 Mar 1913 Jack Fairman born
15 Mar 1927 Al Herman born

16 Mar 1935 Peter de Klerk born
16 Mar 1943 Hans Heyer born
16 Mar 1942 Gijs van Lennep born

17 Mar 1932 Fred Gamble born
17 Mar 1952 Sergio Rinland born

18 Mar 1964 Alex Caffi born
18 Mar 1937 Mark Donohue born
18 Mar 1946 Michel Leclère born
18 Mar 1950 Larry Perkins born
18 Mar 1962 Volker Weidler born
18 Mar 1954 David Hayhoe born
18 Mar 1982 Theo Fitzau died
18 Mar 1977 Carlos Pace died

19 Mar 1964 Nicola Larini born
19 Mar 1943 Vern Schuppan born
19 Mar 1937 Mike Pilbeam born
19 Mar 1995 Trevor Blokdyk died

20 Mar 1972 Pedro Lamy born
20 Mar 1955 Larry Crockett died

21 Mar 1913 George Abecassis born
21 Mar 1921 Chico Godia born
21 Mar 1960 Ayrton Senna born
21 Mar 1916 Ken Wharton born
21 Mar 1982 Carlos Reutemann last start

22 Mar 1912 Leslie Johnson born
22 Mar 1974 Peter Revson died
22 Mar 1992 Last GP at Mexico City

23 Mar 1915 Arthur Owen born
23 Mar 1933 John Taylor born
23 Mar 1939 Robin Herd born
23 Mar 1951 Adrian Reynard born
23 Mar 1981 Mike Hailwood died

24 Mar 1915 Eugène Martin born
24 Mar 1923 Brian Naylor born
24 Mar 1988 Roger Loyer died

25 Mar 1938 Fritz d'Orey born
25 Mar 1925 Don Freeland born
25 Mar 1995 John Hugenholtz died
25 Mar 1984 Philippe Alliot first start
25 Mar 1984 Martin Brundle first start
25 Mar 1984 Ayrton Senna first start
25 Mar 1984 TAG Porsche engine first win

26 Mar 1958 Elio de Angelis born
26 Mar 1964 Martin Donnelly born
26 Mar 1941 Lella Lombardi born
26 Mar 1952 Didier Pironi born
26 Mar 1966 Nick Wirth born
26 Mar 1989 Lamborghini engine first start
26 Mar 1989 Yamaha engine first start
26 Mar 1989 Last GP at Rio de Janeiro

27 Mar 1971 David Coulthard born
27 Mar 1965 Gregor Foitek born
27 Mar 1934 Giampaolo Pavanello born
27 Mar 1983 John Watson last win
27 Mar 1994 Heinz-Harald Frentzen 1st start
27 Mar 1994 Olivier Panis first start
27 Mar 1994 Peugeot engine first start
27 Mar 1983 Last GP at Long Beach

28 Mar 1952 Tony Brise born
28 Mar 1929 Paul England born
28 Mar 1935 Hubert Hahne born
28 Mar 1911 Consalvo Sanesi born

29 Mar 1900 Bill Aston born
29 Mar 1961 Gary Brabham born
29 Mar 1891 Alfred Neubauer born
29 Mar 1981 David Prophet died

30 Mar 1910 Peter Hirt born
30 Mar 1907 Rudolf Krause born
30 Mar 1961 Mike Thackwell born
30 Mar 1969 Lucien Bianchi died
30 Mar 1973 Yves Giraud-Cabantous died
30 Mar 1941 André De Cortanze born
30 Mar 1948 Eddie Jordan born
30 Mar 1980 Nelson Piquet first win
30 Mar 1974 Carlos Reutemann first win
30 Mar 1980 Clay Regazzoni last start
30 Mar 1974 Hesketh first start

31 Mar 1956 Kevin Cogan born

1 Apr 1950 Loris Kessel born
1 Apr 1909 Bill Whitehouse born

2 Apr 1963 Fabrizio Barbazza born
2 Apr 1926 Jack Brabham born
2 Apr 1940 Mike Hailwood born
2 Apr 1928 Gino Munaron born
2 Apr 1963 Mike Gascoyne born

3 Apr 1923 Chuck Weyant born
3 Apr 1950 Frank Dernie born
3 Apr 1985 Helmut Niedermayr died
3 Apr 1988 Judd engine first start

4 Apr 1940 Dickie Attwood born
4 Apr 1924 Bob Christie born
4 Apr 1958 Christian Danner born
4 Apr 1928 Bud Tingelstad born
4 Apr 1966 Jimmy Daywalt died

5 Apr 1936 Ronnie Bucknum born
5 Apr 1922 Andy Linden born
5 Apr 1973 David Murray died

6 Apr 1909 Hermann Lang born

7 Apr 1968 Jim Clark died
7 Apr 1982 Harald Ertl died
7 Apr 1966 Walt Hansgen died
7 Apr 1985 Pierluigi Martini first start
7 Apr 1985 Minardi first start

8 Apr 1966 Mark Blundell born

9 Apr 1922 Johnny Thomson born
9 Apr 1971 Jacques Villeneuve born
9 Apr 1959 George Amick died
9 Apr 1921 Jean-Marie Balestre born
9 Apr 1942 John Judd born

10 Apr 1913 Duke Dinsmore born
10 Apr 1934 Carel Godin de Beaufort born
10 Apr 1929 Mike Hawthorn born
10 Apr 1914 Paul Russo born

11 Apr 1920 Al Keller born
11 Apr 1926 Pete Lovely born
11 Apr 1987 Rudolf Krause died
11 Apr 1993 GP at Donington

12 Apr 1907 Eugène Chaboud born
12 Apr 1961 Corrado Fabi born
12 Apr 1917 Robert Manzon born
12 Apr 1942 Carlos Reutemann born
12 Apr 1950 Flavio Briatore born
12 Apr 1962 Ron Flockhart died

13 Apr 1940 Mike Beuttler born
13 Apr 1931 Dan Gurney born
13 Apr 1926 André Testut born
13 Apr 1949 Ricardo Zunino born
13 Apr 1940 Max Mosley born
13 Apr 1986 First GP at Jerez

14 Apr 1912 Joie Chitwood born
14 Apr 1931 Vic Wilson born
14 Apr 1992 Ronnie Bucknum died

15 Apr 1922 Graham Whitehead born
15 Apr 1957 Chris Murphy born
15 Apr 1947 Dave Wass born
15 Apr 1973 Ernst Klodwig died

16 Apr 1918 Dick Gibson born
16 Apr 1942 Frank Williams born
16 Apr 1988 José Dolhem died

17 Apr 1934 Brian Gubby born
17 Apr 1954 Riccardo Patrese born
17 Apr 1994 First GP at Aida

18 Apr 1942 Jochen Rindt born
18 Apr 1990 Bob Drake died
18 Apr 1971 Tyrrell first win

19 Apr 1940 Kurt Ahrens born
19 Apr 1912 Rudi Fischer born
19 Apr 1944 Jac Nelleman born
19 Apr 1939 Basil van Rooyen born
19 Apr 1971 Luigi Piotti died
19 Apr 1970 March first win

20 Apr 1961 Paolo Barilla born
20 Apr 1963 Mauricio Gugelmin born
20 Apr 1927 Phil Hill born
20 Apr 1930 Stuart Lewis-Evans born

21 Apr 1985 Ayrton Senna first win

22 Apr 1956 Walt Faulkner died

23 Apr 1963 Paul Belmondo born
23 Apr 1961 Pierluigi Martini born
23 Apr 1971 Dempsey Wilson died

24 Apr 1933 Billy Garrett born
24 Apr 1941 Silvio Moser born
24 Apr 1934 Mike Taylor born
24 Apr 1954 Guy Mairesse died
24 Apr 1983 Rolf Stommelen died

25 Apr 1917 Jean Lucas born
25 Apr 1982 Gilles Villeneuve last start

26 Apr 1937 Jean-Pierre Beltoise born
26 Apr 1944 José Dolhem born
26 Apr 1958 Johnny Dumfries born
26 Apr 1937 Gus Hutchison born
26 Apr 1921 François Picard born

27 Apr 1933 Bob Bondurant born
27 Apr 1943 Helmut Marko born
27 Apr 1902 Rudolf Schoeller born
27 Apr 1975 Alan Jones first start
27 Apr 1975 Last GP at Montjuich Park

28 Apr 1973 Piero Drogo died
28 Apr 1978 Theo Helfrich died
28 Apr 1973 Carlos Menditéguy died
28 Apr 1974 Niki Lauda first win
28 Apr 1996 Jacques Villeneuve first win

29 Apr 1916 Cal Niday born
29 Apr 1984 Last GP at Zolder

30 Apr 1920 Duncan Hamilton born
30 Apr 1946 Hughes de Chaunac born
30 Apr 1994 Roland Ratzenberger died

1 May 1951 Geoff Lees born
1 May 1928 Desmond Titterington born
1 May 1955 Mike Nazaruk died
1 May 1994 Ayrton Senna died
1 May 1994 Ayrton Senna last start

3 May 1949 Boy Hayje born
3 May 1924 Ken Tyrrell born
3 May 1981 Michele Alboreto first start

4 May 1928 Wolfgang von Trips born
4 May 1946 John Watson born
4 May 1946 John Barnard born

5 May 1913 Duane Carter born
5 May 1932 Bob Said born
5 May 1985 Mot. Moderni engine first start

6 May 1958 Tommy Byrne born
6 May 1964 Andrea Chiesa born
6 May 1919 André Guelfi born

7 May 1993 Hap Sharp died
7 May 1968 Mike Spence died
7 May 1967 Denny Hulme first win

8 May 1982 Gilles Villeneuve died

9 May 1947 Andy Sutcliffe born

10 May 1914 John James born
10 May 1967 Lorenzo Bandini died
10 May 1985 Toni Branca died
10 May 1963 Franco Comotti died
10 May 1959 Jack Brabham first win
10 May 1970 Ronnie Peterson first start
10 May 1970 Bruce McLaren last start

11 May 1921 Geoffrey Crossley born
11 May 1926 Rob Schroeder born
11 May 1986 Elio de Angelis last start

12 May 1963 Stefano Modena born
12 May 1922 Roy Salvadori born
12 May 1961 Tony Bettenhausen died
12 May 1957 Alfonso de Portago died
12 May 1974 Last GP at Nivelles-Baulers

13 May 1934 Paddy Driver born
13 May 1913 Theo Helfrich born
13 May 1927 Archie Scott-Brown born
13 May 1994 Duncan Hamilton died
13 May 1960 Harry Schell died
13 May 1950 First World Championship GP
13 May 1950 Giuseppe Farina first win
13 May 1950 Giuseppe Farina first start
13 May 1950 Juan M. Fangio first start
13 May 1950 Alfa Romeo first win
13 May 1950 Maserati first start
13 May 1950 Alfa Romeo first start
13 May 1950 Alfa Romeo engine first start
13 May 1950 Alfa Romeo engine first win

14 May 1995 Nigel Mansell last start
14 May 1972 BRM last win

15 May 1929 Peter Broeker born
15 May 1943 Alan Rollinson born
15 May 1959 Luis Sala born
15 May 1957 Keith Andrews died
15 May 1986 Elio de Angelis died
15 May 1953 Chet Miller died

16 May 1909 Luigi Villoresi born
16 May 1955 Manny Ayulo died

17 May 1948 Mikko Kozarowitsky born
17 May 1959 Jerry Unser died
17 May 1981 Carlos Reutemann last win

18 May 1914 E. de Graffenried born
18 May 1931 Bruce Halford born
18 May 1967 Heinz-Harald Frentzen born
18 May 1928 Jo Schlesser born
18 May 1969 Graham Hill last win
18 May 1958 Graham Hill first start
18 May 1958 Lotus first start
18 May 1969 Cooper last start

19 May 1931 Bob Anderson born
19 May 1928 Colin Chapman born
19 May 1958 Archie Scott-Brown died
19 May 1996 Olivier Panis first win
19 May 1996 Ligier last win
19 May 1996 Mugen Honda first win
19 May 1957 Climax engine first start

20 May 1921 Aldo Gordini born
20 May 1926 Bob Sweikert born
20 May 1965 Edgar Barth died
20 May 1984 Bill Holland died
20 May 1962 Graham Hill first win
20 May 1962 Lola first start
20 May 1984 Last GP at Dijon-Prenois

21 May 1942 Danny Ongais born
21 May 1950 Juan Manuel Fangio first win
21 May 1978 René Arnoux first start
21 May 1950 Alberto Ascari first start
21 May 1950 Cooper first start
21 May 1950 Ferrari first start

22 May 1970 Pedro Diniz born
22 May 1929 Sergio Mantovani born
22 May 1921 Marshall Teague born
22 May 1983 Thierry Boutsen first start
22 May 1977 Riccardo Patrese first start
22 May 1955 Alberto Ascari last start
22 May 1966 McLaren first start
22 May 1966 Repco engine first start
22 May 1983 First GP at Spa (new)

23 May 1972 Rubens Barrichello born
23 May 1925 Joe James born
23 May 1903 Ernst Klodwig born
23 May 1940 Gérard Larrousse born
23 May 1982 Riccardo Patrese first win

24 May 1963 Ivan Capelli born
24 May 1953 Lamberto Leoni born
24 May 1990 Dries van der Lof died
24 May 1964 Porsche last start

25 May 1939 Mike Harris born
25 May 1940 Tony Southgate born
25 May 1995 Élie Bayol died

26 May 1944 Sam Posey born
26 May 1906 Mauri Rose born
26 May 1938 Peter Westbury born
26 May 1939 Cesare Fiorio born
26 May 1955 Alberto Ascari died
26 May 1969 Paul Hawkins died
26 May 1974 Silvio Moser died
26 May 1903 Marcel Renault died
26 May 1968 Matra engine first start

27 May 1942 Piers Courage born
27 May 1961 Pierre-Henri Raphanel born
27 May 1942 Robin Widdows born
27 May 1946 Peter Wright born
27 May 1951 Stirling Moss first start
27 May 1979 James Hunt last start

28 May 1927 Eddie Sachs born
28 May 1938 Eppie Wietzes born

29 May 1963 Ukyo Katayama born
29 May 1994 David Coulthard first start
29 May 1960 John Surtees first start
29 May 1949 Bob Tyrrell born
29 May 1960 Lotus first win

30 May 1926 Chuck Arnold born
30 May 1964 Andrea Montermini born
30 May 1939 Dieter Quester born
30 May 1957 Piero Carini died
30 May 1976 Elmer George died
30 May 1958 Pat O'Connor died
30 May 1964 Eddie Sachs died
30 May 1953 Carl Scarborough died
30 May 1955 Bill Vukovich died
30 May 1965 Denny Hulme first start

31 May 1959 Andrea de Cesaris born
31 May 1942 Jo Vonlanthen born
31 May 1959 BRM first win

1 Jun 1959 Martin Brundle born
1 Jun 1947 Ron Dennis born
1 Jun 1986 Jo Gartner died

2 Jun 1920 Don Branson born
2 Jun 1956 Jan Lammers born
2 Jun 1970 Bruce McLaren died
2 Jun 1962 Dennis Taylor died
2 Jun 1986 Johnnie Tolan died
2 Jun 1991 Nelson Piquet last win

3 Jun 1958 Erwin Bauer died
3 Jun 1973 James Hunt first start

4 Jun 1921 Ettore Chimeri born
4 Jun 1967 Ford Cosworth DFV engine first start & win

5 Jun 1923 Jorge Daponte born
5 Jun 1928 Umberto Maglioli born
5 Jun 1908 Franco Rol born
5 Jun 1961 Aldo Costa born
5 Jun 1946 Patrick Head born
5 Jun 1955 Giuseppe Farina last start
5 Jun 1983 Tyrrell last win

6 Jun 1923 Ivor Bueb born
6 Jun 1923 Jim Rigsby born
6 Jun 1951 Noritake Takahara born
6 Jun 1960 Jim Clark first start

7 Jun 1927 Charles de Tornaco born
7 Jun 1989 Chico Landi died
7 Jun 1970 Last GP at Spa (old)

8 Jun 1959 Leslie Johnson died
8 Jun 1952 Johnny McDowell died
8 Jun 1968 Ludovico Scarfiotti died

9 Jun 1903 Felice Bonetto born
9 Jun 1898 Luigi Fagioli born
9 Jun 1939 David Hobbs born
9 Jun 1974 Jody Scheckter first win
9 Jun 1968 Bruce McLaren last win
9 Jun 1968 McLaren first win

10 Jun 1935 Vic Elford born
10 Jun 1940 Peter Ryan born
10 Jun 1941 Dave Walker born

11 Jun 1964 Jean Alesi born
11 Jun 1947 Bob Evans born
11 Jun 1949 Tom Pryce born
11 Jun 1939 Jackie Stewart born
11 Jun 1953 Pat Symonds born
11 Jun 1972 Jo Bonnier died
11 Jun 1966 Jimmy Davies died
11 Jun 1966 Jud Larson died
11 Jun 1955 Pierre Levegh died
11 Jun 1995 Jean Alesi first win

12 Jun 1948 Hans Binder born
12 Jun 1916 Phil Cade born
12 Jun 1927 Bill Cheesbourg born
12 Jun 1930 Innes Ireland born
12 Jun 1921 Dennis Taylor born
12 Jun 1954 Neil Oatley born
12 Jun 1966 Eagle first start
12 Jun 1994 Ilmor engine last start

13 Jun 1966 Naoki Hattori born
13 Jun 1982 Riccardo Paletti died
13 Jun 1982 BMW engine first win

14 Jun 1913 Henry Banks born
14 Jun 1943 John Miles born
14 Jun 1958 George Fonder died
14 Jun 1995 Bobby Grim died

15 Jun 1920 Keith Andrews born
15 Jun 1916 Gene Force born
15 Jun 1958 Riccardo Paletti born
15 Jun 1961 Giulio Cabianca died
15 Jun 1993 James Hunt died

16 Jun 1923 Ron Flockhart born
16 Jun 1930 Mike Sparken born

17 Jun 1960 Adrian Campos born
17 Jun 1912 Myron Fohr born
17 Jun 1956 Bob Sweikert died
17 Jun 1962 Jim Clark first win
17 Jun 1978 Last GP at Anderstorp

18 Jun 1936 Denny Hulme born
18 Jun 1967 Geki died
18 Jun 1960 Al Herman died
18 Jun 1977 Franco Rol died
18 Jun 1967 Dan Gurney last win
18 Jun 1967 Eagle first win
18 Jun 1967 Weslake engine win

19 Jun 1960 Chris Bristow died
19 Jun 1960 Jimmy Bryan died
19 Jun 1960 Alan Stacey died
19 Jun 1977 Jacques Laffite first win
19 Jun 1977 Ligier first win
19 Jun 1977 Matra engine first win
19 Jun 1988 Last GP at Detroit

20 Jun 1911 Paul Pietsch born
20 Jun 1952 Luigi Fagioli died

21 Jun 1937 John Cannon born
21 Jun 1970 Piers Courage died
21 Jun 1981 Gilles Villeneuve last win
21 Jun 1970 Clay Regazzoni first start
21 Jun 1987 Lotus last win
21 Jun 1981 Last GP at Járama

22 Jun 1917 George Fonder born
22 Jun 1979 Louis Chiron died
22 Jun 1975 James Hunt first win
22 Jun 1952 Mike Hawthorn first start
22 Jun 1975 Hesketh first win

23 Jun 1927 Herbert MacKay-Fraser born
23 Jun 1915 R Montgomerie-Charrington born
23 Jun 1933 Renato Pirocchi born
23 Jun 1916 Leslie Thorne born
23 Jun 1899 Amédée Gordini born
23 Jun 1968 Matra car first win

24 Jun 1934 Tom Bridger born
24 Jun 1911 Juan Manuel Fangio born

25 Jun 1964 Johnny Herbert born
25 Jun 1932 Tim Parnell born
25 Jun 1949 Patrick Tambay born

26 Jun 1935 Carlo Facetti born
26 Jun 1929 Rodney Nuckey born
26 Jun 1955 Philippe Streiff born

27 Jun 1942 Chris Irwin born
27 Jun 1994 Sam Hanks died

28 Jun 1923 Adolfo Schwelm Cruz born
28 Jun 1992 Peter Hirt died
28 Jun 1964 Brabham first win

29 Jun 1921 Harry Schell born

30 Jun 1975 Ralf Schumacher born
30 Jun 1966 Giuseppe Farina died
30 Jun 1974 Eddie Johnson died

1 Jul 1947 Kazuyoshi Hoshino born
1 Jul 1958 Keith Wiggins born
1 Jul 1973 Ronnie Peterson first win
1 Jul 1973 Ensign first start
1 Jul 1979 Renault first win
1 Jul 1979 turbo first win

2 Jul 1911 Reg Parnell born
2 Jul 1952 Beppe Lucchini born
2 Jul 1985 David Purley died
2 Jul 1962 Peter Ryan died
2 Jul 1964 Steve Nielsen born
2 Jul 1967 GP at Bugatti au Mans
2 Jul 1972 Last GP at Clermont-Ferrand

3 Jul 1914 Carl Scarborough born
3 Jul 1960 Vanwall last start
3 Jul 1966 Repco engine first win
3 Jul 1966 Last GP at Reims

4 Jul 1948 René Arnoux born
4 Jul 1907 Ernst Loof born
4 Jul 1973 Jan Magnussen born
4 Jul 1927 Jim McWithey born
4 Jul 1918 Johnnie Parsons born
4 Jul 1938 Ernie Pieterse born
4 Jul 1962 Roland Ratzenberger born
4 Jul 1926 Wolfgang Seidel born
4 Jul 1958 Art Bisch died
4 Jul 1954 Mercedes-Benz first win
4 Jul 1954 Mercedes-Benz first start

5 Jul 1928 Elmer George born
5 Jul 1986 Albert Scherrer died
5 Jul 1954 Bob Scott died
5 Jul 1953 Mike Hawthorn first win
5 Jul 1981 Alain Prost first win
5 Jul 1959 Dan Gurney first start

6 Jul 1930 Ian Burgess born
6 Jul 1906 Cuth Harrison born
6 Jul 1958 Luigi Musso died
6 Jul 1958 Mike Hawthorn last win
6 Jul 1958 Phil Hill first start
6 Jul 1958 Juan M Fangio last start

7 Jul 1959 Alessandro Nannini born
7 Jul 1943 Jean-Claude Rudaz born
7 Jul 1936 Jo Siffert born
7 Jul 1968 Jo Schlesser died
7 Jul 1968 Jacky Ickx first win
7 Jul 1985 Brabham last win
7 Jul 1991 First GP at Magny-Cours
7 Jul 1968 Last GP at Rouen-les-Essarts

8 Jul 1962 Dan Gurney first win
8 Jul 1962 Porsche first win
8 Jul 1984 GP at Dallas
8 Jul 1990 Last GP at Paul Ricard

9 Jul 1955 Don Beauman died

10 Jul 1928 Alessandro de Tomaso born
10 Jul 1946 Jean-Pierre Jarier born
10 Jul 1918 Fred Wacker born
10 Jul 1940 Guido Forti born
10 Jul 1955 Jerry Hoyt died

11 Jul 1941 Clive Puzey born
11 Jul 1922 Fritz Riess born
11 Jul 1943 Rolf Stommelen born
11 Jul 1964 First GP at Brands Hatch
11 Jul 1971 Pedro Rodriguez died

12 Jul 1930 Guy Ligier born

13 Jul 1918 Alberto Ascari born
13 Jul 1957 Thierry Boutsen born
13 Jul 1914 Sam Hanks born
13 Jul 1993 Leslie Thorne died
13 Jul 1986 Jacques Laffite last start
13 Jul 1986 Last GP at Brands Hatch

14 Jul 1907 Chico Landi born
14 Jul 1957 Herbert MacKay-Fraser died
14 Jul 1957 Bill Whitehouse died
14 Jul 1979 Clay Regazzoni last win
14 Jul 1956 Tony Brooks first start
14 Jul 1973 Jochen Mass first start
14 Jul 1973 John Watson first start
14 Jul 1951 Ferrari first win
14 Jul 1979 Williams first win
14 Jul 1951 BRM first start

15 Jul 1914 B Bira born
15 Jul 1929 Ian Stewart born
15 Jul 1972 Williams (Politoys) first start

16 Jul 1928 Jim Rathmann born
16 Jul 1995 Johnny Herbert first win
16 Jul 1955 Stirling Moss first win
16 Jul 1955 Jack Brabham first start
16 Jul 1977 Patrick Tambay first start
16 Jul 1977 Gilles Villeneuve first start
16 Jul 1977 Renault first start
16 Jul 1977 turbo first start

17 Jul 1912 Erwin Bauer born
17 Jul 1923 John Cooper born
17 Jul 1995 Juan-Manuel Fangio died
17 Jul 1954 Vanwall first start

18 Jul 1920 Eric Brandon born
18 Jul 1970 Emerson Fittipaldi first start
18 Jul 1970 Dan Gurney last start
18 Jul 1970 Surtees first start

19 Jul 1902 Chet Miller born
19 Jul 1975 Emerson Fittipaldi last win

20 Jul 1962 Giovanna Amati born
20 Jul 1943 Chris Amon born
20 Jul 1960 Claudio Langes born
20 Jul 1931 Tony Marsh born
20 Jul 1964 Bernd Schneider born
20 Jul 1957 Tony Brooks first win
20 Jul 1957 Vanwall first win

21 Jul 1962 Last GP at Aintree

22 Jul 1909 Dorino Serafini born

23 Jul 1935 John Cordts born
23 Jul 1935 Jim Hall born
23 Jul 1947 Torsten Palm born

24 Jul 1906 Franco Comotti born
24 Jul 1947 Alan Jenkins born
24 Jul 1972 Lance Reventlow died

25 Jul 1936 Gerry Ashmore born
25 Jul 1911 Len Duncan born
25 Jul 1905 Georges Grignard born
25 Jul 1910 Jimmy Jackson born
25 Jul 1993 Alain Prost last win
25 Jul 1982 Jochen Mass last start

26 Jul 1928 Don Beauman born
26 Jul 1946 Emilio de Villota born
26 Jul 1942 Teddy Pilette born

27 Jul 1954 Philippe Alliot born
27 Jul 1933 Chris Lawrence born
27 Jul 1943 Jean Max born
27 Jul 1968 Ricardo Rosset born
27 Jul 1961 David Holland born
27 Jul 1969 Moises Solana died

28 Jul 1961 Yannick Dalmas born
28 Jul 1924 Luigi Musso born
28 Jul 1935 Massimo Natili born
28 Jul 1922 Jacques Pollet born
28 Jul 1927 Heini Walter born

29 Jul 1933 Colin Davis born
29 Jul 1951 Walt Brown died
29 Jul 1950 Joe Fry died
29 Jul 1951 Cecil Green died
29 Jul 1951 Bill Mackey died
29 Jul 1973 Roger Williamson died
29 Jul 1951 Alberto Ascari first win

30 Jul 1991 Tom Bridger died
30 Jul 1940 Giacomo Caliri born
30 Jul 1981 Bud Tingelstad died
30 Jul 1972 Jacky Ickx last win
30 Jul 1978 Nelson Piquet first start

31 Jul 1954 Onofré Marimón died
31 Jul 1994 Gerhard Berger last win

1 Aug 1961 Allen Berg born
1 Aug 1959 Jean Behra died
1 Aug 1959 Ivor Bueb died
1 Aug 1980 Patrick Depailler died
1 Aug 1969 Gerhard Mitter died
1 Aug 1899 Raymond Mays born
1 Aug 1965 Jim Clark clinched last Championship
1 Aug 1965 Climax engine last win
1 Aug 1976 Last GP at Nürburgring (old)

2 Aug 1959 Tony Brooks last win
2 Aug 1953 Giuseppe Farina last win
2 Aug 1970 Jochen Rindt last win
2 Aug 1964 Honda first start
2 Aug 1959 GP at AVUS
2 Aug 1970 First GP at Hockenheim

3 Aug 1899 Louis Chiron born
3 Aug 1958 Peter Collins died
3 Aug 1964 Carel Godin de Beaufort died
3 Aug 1958 Bruce McLaren first start
3 Aug 1952 Alberto Ascari clinched first Championship
3 Aug 1952 BMW engine first start

4 Aug 1917 John Fitch born
4 Aug 1928 Christian Goethals born

4 Aug 1957 Juan Manuel Fangio last win
4 Aug 1963 John Surtees first win
4 Aug 1985 Michele Alboreto last win
4 Aug 1974 Jacques Laffite first start
4 Aug 1957 Maserati last win
4 Aug 1957 Porsche first start
4 Aug 1957 Juan Manuel Fangio clinched last Championship

5 Aug 1930 Richie Ginther born
5 Aug 1943 Leo Kinnunen born
5 Aug 1907 Roger Loyer born
5 Aug 1991 Soichiro Honda died
5 Aug 1973 Jackie Stewart last win
5 Aug 1962 Brabham first start

6 Aug 1941 Michel Têtu born
6 Aug 1961 Stirling Moss last win

7 Aug 1944 Dave Morgan born
7 Aug 1966 Jacky Ickx first start
7 Aug 1966 Matra car first start
7 Aug 1966 Ford Cosworth (F2) engine first start

8 Aug 1926 Piero Drogo born
8 Aug 1953 Nigel Mansell born
8 Aug 1982 Eric Brandon died
8 Aug 1989 Brian Naylor died

9 Aug 1944 Patrick Depailler born
9 Aug 1925 Len Sutton born

10 Aug 1928 Gerino Gerini born
10 Aug 1910 Guy Mairesse born
10 Aug 1915 Carlos Menditéguy born
10 Aug 1986 First GP at Hungaroring

11 Aug 1916 Johnny Claes born
11 Aug 1984 Marcel Balsa died

12 Aug 1919 Shorty Templeman born
12 Aug 1933 Parnelli Jones born
12 Aug 1985 Manfred Winkelhock died

13 Aug 1946 Divina Galica born
13 Aug 1978 Ronnie Peterson last win

14 Aug 1922 Leslie Marr born
14 Aug 1942 Jackie Oliver born
14 Aug 1917 Rob Walker born
14 Aug 1967 Bob Anderson died
14 Aug 1991 Alberto Crespo died
14 Aug 1988 Enzo Ferrari died
14 Aug 1977 Alan Jones first win
14 Aug 1960 Jack Brabham clinched second Championship
14 Aug 1977 Shadow first win
14 Aug 1983 Renault last win
14 Aug 1960 Last GP at Porto

15 Aug 1948 George Ryton born
15 Aug 1993 Damon Hill first win
15 Aug 1976 John Watson first win
15 Aug 1971 Niki Lauda first start
15 Aug 1976 Penske first win
15 Aug 1971 Jackie Stewart clinched second Championship

16 Aug 1908 George Connor born
16 Aug 1970 Jochen Rindt last start
16 Aug 1992 Nigel Mansell clinched Championship
16 Aug 1992 Brabham last start
16 Aug 1992 Judd engine last start
16 Aug 1987 Last GP at Österreichring

17 Aug 1913 Oscar Gálvez born
17 Aug 1952 Nelson Piquet born
17 Aug 1980 Nigel Mansell first start

18 Aug 1898 Clemente Biondetti born
18 Aug 1929 Jimmy Davies born
18 Aug 1934 Michael May born
18 Aug 1927 John Rhodes born
18 Aug 1957 GP at Pescara

19 Aug 1926 Johnny Boyd born
19 Aug 1954 Oscar Larrauri born
19 Aug 1916 Dennis Poore born
19 Aug 1946 Tom Walkinshaw born
19 Aug 1975 Mark Donohue died
19 Aug 1962 Jean Lucienbonnet died
19 Aug 1984 Gerhard Berger first start

20 Aug 1941 Jo Ramirez born
20 Aug 1980 Alfred Neubauer died

21 Aug 1913 Freddie Agabashian born
21 Aug 1911 Ken Richardson born
21 Aug 1983 Gene Force died
21 Aug 1947 Ettore Bugatti died
21 Aug 1980 Alfred Neubauer died

22 Aug 1947 Ian Scheckter born
22 Aug 1950 Peter Collins (Lotus) born
22 Aug 1954 Juan Manuel Fangio clinched second Championship
22 Aug 1954 Last GP at Bremgarten

23 Aug 1919 Dries van der Lof born
23 Aug 1967 Georges Berger died
23 Aug 1987 Didier Pironi died
23 Aug 1953 Alberto Ascari last win
23 Aug 1964 Jochen Rindt first start
23 Aug 1953 Alberto Ascari clinched last Championship
23 Aug 1959 GP at Monsanto Park
23 Aug 1964 GP at Zeltweg

24 Aug 1964 Éric Bernard born
24 Aug 1921 Sam Tingle born
24 Aug 1962 Shorty Templeman died
24 Aug 1881 Vincenzo Lancia born

25 Aug 1990 David Hampshire died
25 Aug 1985 Niki Lauda last win
25 Aug 1991 Michael Schumacher first start
25 Aug 1985 Last GP at Zandvoort

26 Aug 1925 Bobby Ball born

27 Aug 1942 Tom Belso born
27 Aug 1959 Gerhard Berger born
27 Aug 1909 Charles Pozzi born
27 Aug 1954 Derek Warwick born
27 Aug 1978 Mario Andretti last win
27 Aug 1967 Repco engine last win

28 Aug 1924 Jimmy Daywalt born
28 Aug 1977 Mike Parkes died
28 Aug 1983 René Arnoux last win
28 Aug 1994 Philippe Alliot last start
28 Aug 1983 TAG Porsche engine first start

29 Aug 1947 James Hunt born
29 Aug 1933 Alan Stacey born
29 Aug 1977 Brian McGuire died
29 Aug 1982 Keke Rosberg first win
29 Aug 1993 Thiery Boutsen last start

30 Aug 1941 Ignazio Giunti born
30 Aug 1937 Bruce McLaren born
30 Aug 1935 Gerhard Mitter born
30 Aug 1959 Ed Elisian died
30 Aug 1992 Michael Schumacher first win

31 Aug 1953 Miguel-Angel Guerra born
31 Aug 1948 Harald Ertl born
31 Aug 1918 Bill Homeier born
31 Aug 1942 Sandro Pesenti-Rossi born
31 Aug 1906 Raymond Sommer born
31 Aug 1952 Jim Rigsby died
31 Aug 1947 Luca di Montezemolo born

1 Sep 1968 Franck Lagorce born
1 Sep 1985 Stefan Bellof died

2 Sep 1958 Olivier Grouillard born
2 Sep 1919 Lance Macklin born
2 Sep 1966 Olivier Panis born
2 Sep 1969 Willy Mairesse died
2 Sep 1956 Jo Bonnier first start
2 Sep 1956 Juan Manuel Fangio clinched fourth Championship

3 Sep 1950 Giuseppe Farina clinched Championship

4 Sep 1920 Clemar Bucci born
4 Sep 1924 Bobby Grim born
4 Sep 1920 Jackie Holmes born
4 Sep 1960 Phil Hill first win
4 Sep 1966 Weslake engine first start
4 Sep 1966 Jack Brabham clinched last Championship

5 Sep 1965 David Brabham born
5 Sep 1963 Taki Inoue born
5 Sep 1939 Clay Regazzoni born
5 Sep 1970 Jochen Rindt died
5 Sep 1971 Jean-Pierre Jarier first start

6 Sep 1970 Clay Regazzoni first win
6 Sep 1952 Max Welti born

7 Sep 1936 Brian Hart born
7 Sep 1910 Lee Wallard born
7 Sep 1975 Niki Lauda clinched first Championship
7 Sep 1969 Jackie Stewart clinched first Championship
7 Sep 1969 Matra car last win

8 Sep 1956 Stefan Johansson born
8 Sep 1960 Aguri Suzuki born
8 Sep 1984 Johnnie Parsons died
8 Sep 1966 John Taylor died
8 Sep 1898 Tony Vandervell born
8 Sep 1963 Jim Clark clinched first Championship
8 Sep 1968 Weslake engine last start

9 Sep 1979 Jody Scheckter last win
9 Sep 1979 Jody Scheckter clinched Championship

9 Sep 1973 Jackie Stewart clinched last Championship

10 Sep 1952 Bruno Giacomelli born
10 Sep 1950 Raymond Sommer died
10 Sep 1961 Wolfgang von Trips died
10 Sep 1995 Johnny Herbert last win
10 Sep 1961 Phil Hill last win
10 Sep 1967 John Surtees last win
10 Sep 1978 Ronnie Peterson last start
10 Sep 1972 John Surtees last start
10 Sep 1978 Mario Andretti clinched Championship
10 Sep 1972 Emerson Fittipaldi clinched first Championship
10 Sep 1961 Phil Hill clinched Championship
10 Sep 1978 Alfa Romeo engine last win

11 Sep 1946 Martin Ogilvie born
11 Sep 1978 Ronnie Peterson died
11 Sep 1955 Juan Manuel Fangio clinched third Championship
11 Sep 1955 Mercedes-Benz last win
11 Sep 1955 Mercedes-Benz last start

12 Sep 1916 Tony Bettenhausen born
12 Sep 1944 Eddie Keizan born
12 Sep 1948 Jean-Louis Schlesser born
12 Sep 1950 Gustav Brunner born
12 Sep 1965 Jackie Stewart first win
12 Sep 1976 March last win
12 Sep 1982 Ensign last start
12 Sep 1982 Fittipaldi last start

13 Sep 1932 Mike MacDowel born
13 Sep 1953 Maserati first win
13 Sep 1981 Toleman (Benetton) first start
13 Sep 1992 Fondmetal (Osella) last start
13 Sep 1981 Hart engine first start

14 Sep 1918 Georges Berger born
14 Sep 1917 Mack Hellings born
14 Sep 1950 Masami Kuwashima born
14 Sep 1980 First GP at Imola

15 Sep 1916 Toni Branca born
15 Sep 1881 Ettore Bugatti born

16 Sep 1910 Karl Kling born
16 Sep 1914 Josef Peters born

17 Sep 1960 Damon Hill born
17 Sep 1929 Stirling Moss born

18 Sep 1918 Johnny Mantz born
18 Sep 1951 Marc Surer born
18 Sep 1947 Giancarlo Minardi born
18 Sep 1953 Charles de Tornaco died

19 Sep 1964 Enrico Bertaggia born
19 Sep 1952 Bernard de Dryver born
19 Sep 1946 Brian Henton born

20 Sep 1921 Horace Gould born
20 Sep 1989 Richie Ginther died
20 Sep 1952 Bill Schindler died
20 Sep 1958 Peter Whitehead died
20 Sep 1969 Eagle last start
20 Sep 1970 Tyrrell first start
20 Sep 1969 Climax engine last start
20 Sep 1987 TAG Porsche engine last win
20 Sep 1970 Last GP at Mont-Tremblant

21 Sep 1920 Ken McAlpine born

22 Sep 1958 Franco Forini born
22 Sep 1907 P Fotheringham-Parker born
22 Sep 1921 Ian Raby born
22 Sep 1944 Richard Robarts born
22 Sep 1928 Eric Broadley born
22 Sep 1958 Jimmy Reece died
22 Sep 1974 Penkse first start

23 Sep 1930 Don Edmunds born
23 Sep 1973 Jackie Stewart last start

24 Sep 1931 Mike Parkes born
24 Sep 1960 Johnny Thomson died
24 Sep 1995 David Coulthard first win

25 Sep 1938 Neville Lederle born
25 Sep 1942 Henri Pescarolo born
25 Sep 1982 Michele Alboreto first win
25 Sep 1982 Mario Andretti last start
25 Sep 1982 Keke Rosberg clinched Championship
25 Sep 1982 Matra engine last start
25 Sep 1982 Last GP at Las Vegas

26 Sep 1943 Tim Schenken born
26 Sep 1993 Alain Prost clinched last Championship
26 Sep 1993 Lola last start

27 Sep 1981 Jacques Laffite last win
27 Sep 1981 Matra engine last win

28 Sep 1963 Erik Comas born
28 Sep 1968 Mika Häkkinen born
28 Sep 1980 Andrea de Cesaris first start
28 Sep 1980 Alan Jones clinched Championship

29 Sep 1991 First GP at Montmeló

30 Sep 1919 Roberto Bonomi born
30 Sep 1919 Cecil Green born
30 Sep 1946 Jochen Mass born
30 Sep 1961 Eric van de Poele born
30 Sep 1941 Reine Wisell born

1 Oct 1963 Jean-Denis Deletraz born
1 Oct 1930 Frank Gardner born
1 Oct 1928 Willy Mairesse born
1 Oct 1942 Jean-Pierre Jabouille born

2 Oct 1949 Michael Bleekemolen born
2 Oct 1919 Jan Flinterman born
2 Oct 1940 Nanni Galli born
2 Oct 1927 Paul Goldsmith born
2 Oct 1921 Mike Nazaruk born
2 Oct 1921 Giorgio Scarlatti born
2 Oct 1964 Charles Cooper died
2 Oct 1977 Niki Lauda clinched second Championship

3 Oct 1941 Andrea de Adamich born
3 Oct 1969 Max Papis born
3 Oct 1971 Jo Bonnier last start

4 Oct 1927 Roberto Bussinello born
4 Oct 1928 Bob Scott born
4 Oct 1992 Denny Hulme died
4 Oct 1970 Emerson Fittipaldi first win
4 Oct 1970 Jochen Rindt clinched Championship

5 Oct 1962 Michael Andretti born
5 Oct 1922 Froilán González born
5 Oct 1969 Jochen Rindt first win
5 Oct 1980 Emerson Fittipaldi last start
5 Oct 1980 Jody Scheckter last start

6 Oct 1918 Max de Terra born
6 Oct 1941 John Nicholson born
6 Oct 1944 Carlos Pace born
6 Oct 1918 André Pilette born
6 Oct 1951 Manfred Winkelhock born
6 Oct 1973 François Cevert died
6 Oct 1974 Helmut Koinigg died
6 Oct 1985 Nigel Mansell first win
6 Oct 1968 Mario Andretti first start
6 Oct 1974 Denny Hulme last start
6 Oct 1985 John Watson last start
6 Oct 1963 Ford engine first start
6 Oct 1974 Emerson Fittipaldi clinched last Championship
6 Oct 1985 Alain Prost clinched first Championship

7 Oct 1965 Marco Apicella born
7 Oct 1930 Bernard Collomb born
7 Oct 1912 Peter Walker born
7 Oct 1979 Jacky Ickx last start
7 Oct 1979 Wolf last start
7 Oct 1984 First GP at new Nürburgring

8 Oct 1904 Yves Giraud-Cabantous born
8 Oct 1919 Jack McGrath born
8 Oct 1954 Huub Rothengatter born
8 Oct 1910 Spider Webb born
8 Oct 1978 Gilles Villeneuve first win
8 Oct 1972 Jody Scheckter first start
8 Oct 1961 Tony Brooks last start
8 Oct 1961 Stirling Moss last start
8 Oct 1972 Matra last start
8 Oct 1978 Surtees last start
8 Oct 1978 First GP at Montreal

9 Oct 1961 Julian Bailey born
9 Oct 1928 Pat O'Connor born
9 Oct 1937 David Prophet born
9 Oct 1977 Penske last start
9 Oct 1977 Wolf last win
9 Oct 1977 Last GP at Mosport Park

10 Oct 1930 Eugenio Castellotti born
10 Oct 1952 Siegfried Stohr born
10 Oct 1923 Murray Walker born

11 Oct 1928 Alfonso de Portago born
11 Oct 1911 Nello Pagani born

12 Oct 1918 Frank Armi born
12 Oct 1937 Paul Hawkins born
12 Oct 1943 Bertil Roos born
12 Oct 1906 Piero Taruffi born
12 Oct 1985 Duke Dinsmore died
12 Oct 1986 Gerhard Berger first win
12 Oct 1986 Benetton first win
12 Oct 1986 BMW engine last win

13 Oct 1899 Piero Dusio born
13 Oct 1949 Patrick Neve born
13 Oct 1989 Freddie Agabashian died
13 Oct 1981 Philippe Étançelin died
13 Oct 1943 Peter Sauber born
13 Oct 1996 Damon Hill clinched Championship

14 Oct 1947 Rikky von Opel born
14 Oct 1893 Charles Cooper born

15 Oct 1899 Adolf Brudes born
15 Oct 1921 Al Pease born
15 Oct 1919 Chuck Stevenson born
15 Oct 1981 P Fotheringham-Parker died
15 Oct 1983 Jean-Pierre Jarier last start
15 Oct 1983 Nelson Piquet clinched second Championship

16 Oct 1934 Peter Ashdown born
16 Oct 1918 Tony Rolt born
16 Oct 1994 Andrea de Cesaris last start
16 Oct 1994 Ford Cosworth engine last win
16 Oct 1994 Last GP at Jerez

17 Oct 1926 Roberto Lippi born
17 Oct 1946 Enzo Coloni born
17 Oct 1981 Alan Jones last win
17 Oct 1981 Derek Warwick first start
17 Oct 1981 Nelson Piquet clinched first Championship

18 Oct 1933 Ludovico Scarfiotti born

19 Oct 1987 Hermann Lang died
19 Oct 1958 Mike Hawthorn last start
19 Oct 1958 Mike Hawthorn clinched Championship
19 Oct 1958 Vanwall last win
19 Oct 1958 GP at Ain-Diab

20 Oct 1921 Manny Ayulo born
20 Oct 1942 Walter Brun born
20 Oct 1978 Gunnar Nilsson died
20 Oct 1991 Ayrton Senna clinched last Championship

21 Oct 1932 Cesare Perdisa born
21 Oct 1973 Nasif Estefano died
21 Oct 1984 Niki Lauda clinched last Championship
21 Oct 1990 Ayrton Senna clinched second Championship
21 Oct 1984 First GP at Estoril

22 Oct 1918 Johnnie Tolan born
22 Oct 1993 Innes Ireland died
22 Oct 1967 Denny Hulme clinched Championship
22 Oct 1989 Alain Prost clinched third Championship
22 Oct 1995 Michael Schumacher clinched second Championship
22 Oct 1995 Last GP at Aida

23 Oct 1937 Geki born
23 Oct 1926 Larry Crockett born
23 Oct 1966 Alessandro Zanardi born
23 Oct 1941 Gérard Ducarouge born
23 Oct 1977 James Hunt last win
23 Oct 1977 Last GP at Fuji

24 Oct 1924 George Amick born
24 Oct 1960 Joachim Winkelhock born
24 Oct 1971 Jo Siffert died
24 Oct 1976 James Hunt clinched Championship
24 Oct 1965 Honda first win
24 Oct 1954 Last GP at Pedralbes

25 Oct 1958 Stuart Lewis-Evans died
25 Oct 1972 Johnny Mantz died
25 Oct 1992 Riccardo Patrese last win
25 Oct 1970 Jack Brabham last start
25 Oct 1964 Phil Hill last start
25 Oct 1964 John Surtees clinched Championship
25 Oct 1980 Last GP at Watkins Glen

26 Oct 1947 Ian Ashley born
26 Oct 1915 Ray Crawford born
26 Oct 1915 Joe Fry born
26 Oct 1942 Jonathan Williams born
26 Oct 1986 Alan Jones last start
26 Oct 1986 Keke Rosberg last start
26 Oct 1986 Patrick Tambay last start
26 Oct 1986 Alain Prost clinched second Championship

27 Oct 1936 Dave Charlton born
27 Oct 1913 Luigi Piotti born

28 Oct 1930 Bernie Ecclestone born
28 Oct 1919 Walt Hansgen born
28 Oct 1919 Hans Klenk born
28 Oct 1950 Lord A Hesketh born
28 Oct 1951 Juan Manuel Fangio clinched first Championship
28 Oct 1951 Alfa Romeo last win

29 Oct 1951 Tiff Needell born
29 Oct 1932 Alex Soler-Roig born
29 Oct 1956 Louis Rosier died
29 Oct 1995 Benetton last win

30 Oct 1906 Giuseppe Farina born
30 Oct 1926 Jacques Swaters born
30 Oct 1917 Maurice Trintignant born
30 Oct 1988 Ayrton Senna clinched first Championship
30 Oct 1988 Alfa Romeo engine last start

31 Oct 1941 Derek Bell born
31 Oct 1987 Nelson Piquet clinched last Championship

1 Nov 1898 Arthur Legat born
1 Nov 1936 Jackie Lewis born
1 Nov 1926 Bob Veith born
1 Nov 1928 Ted Whiteaway born
1 Nov 1962 Ricardo Rodriguez died
1 Nov 1987 First GP at Suzuka

2 Nov 1946 Alan Jones born

3 Nov 1948 Helmut Koinigg born
3 Nov 1985 Keke Rosberg last win
3 Nov 1985 Niki Lauda last start
3 Nov 1991 Nelson Piquet last start
3 Nov 1968 Graham Hill clinched last Championship
3 Nov 1968 Honda car last start
3 Nov 1985 Renault last start
3 Nov 1985 Alfa Romeo last start
3 Nov 1985 First GP at Adelaide

4 Nov 1919 Eric Thompson born
4 Nov 1953 Jacques Villeneuve Sr. born
4 Nov 1968 Horace Gould died
4 Nov 1976 Toni Ulmen died
4 Nov 1884 Harry Ferguson born

5 Nov 1921 Kurt Adolff born
5 Nov 1905 Louis Rosier born
5 Nov 1986 Adolf Brudes died
5 Nov 1952 Joe James died
5 Nov 1989 René Arnoux last start
5 Nov 1989 Eddie Cheever last start

6 Nov 1931 Peter Collins born
6 Nov 1955 Jack McGrath died

7 Nov 1948 Alex-Dias Ribeiro born
7 Nov 1956 Jonathan Palmer born
7 Nov 1975 Piero Dusio died
7 Nov 1967 Ian Raby died
7 Nov 1993 Ayrton Senna last win
7 Nov 1993 Riccardo Patrese last start
7 Nov 1993 Alain Prost last start
7 Nov 1993 Derek Warwick last start
7 Nov 1993 McLaren last win
7 Nov 1993 Lamborghini engine last start

8 Nov 1933 Peter Arundell born
8 Nov 1947 Giorgio Francia born
8 Nov 1985 Masten Gregory died
8 Nov 1992 March last start
8 Nov 1992 Honda engine last start & win

10 Nov 1934 Lucien Bianchi born
10 Nov 1926 Art Bisch born
10 Nov 1965 Eddie Irvine born
10 Nov 1915 Rodney Clarke born

11 Nov 1937 Vittorio Brambilla born
11 Nov 1909 Piero Scotti born
11 Nov 1926 Maria Teresa de Filippis born
11 Nov 1951 Mack Hellings died

12 Nov 1945 George Eaton born
12 Nov 1916 Paul Emery born
12 Nov 1914 Peter Whitehead born
12 Nov 1966 Don Branson died
12 Nov 1995 Last GP at Adelaide

13 Nov 1945 Masahiro Hasemi born
13 Nov 1994 Nigel Mansell last win
13 Nov 1994 Michele Alboreto last start
13 Nov 1994 Michael Schumacher clinched first Championship
13 Nov 1994 Lotus last start
13 Nov 1988 turbo last start & win

14 Nov 1945 Brett Lunger born
14 Nov 1954 Eliseo Salazar born

15 Nov 1932 Jerry Unser born
15 Nov 1987 BMW engine last start
15 Nov 1987 Mot. Moderni engine last start
15 Nov 1987 TAG Porsche engine last start

16 Nov 1936 Skip Barber born
16 Nov 1958 Roberto Guerrero born
16 Nov 1936 Gianpaolo Dallara born

17 Nov 1939 Chris Craft born
17 Nov 1945 Damien Magee born
17 Nov 1929 Jimmy Reece born
17 Nov 1967 Mimmo Schiattarella born
17 Nov 1906 Soichiro Honda born

18 Nov 1932 Nasif Estefano born

19 Nov 1969 Philippe Adams born

19 Nov 1925 Eddie Russo born
19 Nov 1961 Al Keller died

20 Nov 1957 Stefan Bellof born
20 Nov 1919 Alan Brown born
20 Nov 1948 Gunnar Nilsson born
20 Nov 1960 Maserati last start
20 Nov 1960 GP at Riverside

21 Nov 1943 Jacques Laffite born
21 Nov 1953 Felice Bonetto died

22 Nov 1934 Jackie Pretorius born

23 Nov 1969 Olivier Beretta born
23 Nov 1954 Ross Brawn born

24 Nov 1949 John Wickham born
24 Nov 1990 Juan-Manuel Bordeu died

25 Nov 1946 Slim Borgudd born
25 Nov 1982 Walt Ader died
25 Nov 1984 Jimmy Jackson died

26 Nov 1953 Desiré Wilson born

27 Nov 1957 Kenny Acheson born
27 Nov 1995 Gincarlo Baghetti died

28 Nov 1992 Frank Armi died
28 Nov 1990 Chico Godia died
28 Nov 1993 Joe Kelly died
28 Nov 1963 Lee Wallard died

29 Nov 1923 Chuck Daigh born
29 Nov 1915 Helmut Niedermayr born
29 Nov 1975 Tony Brise died
29 Nov 1975 Graham Hill died

30 Nov 1935 Trevor Blokdyk born
30 Nov 1966 Mika Salo born
30 Nov 1961 René Hilhorst born

1 Dec 1948 Guy Tunmer born

2 Dec 1937 Chris Bristow born
2 Dec 1930 David Piper born

3 Dec 1924 Roberto Mières born
3 Dec 1932 Gaetano Starrabba born

4 Dec 1957 Raul Boesel born
4 Dec 1944 François Migault born

5 Dec 1917 Ken Downing born
5 Dec 1932 Jim Hurtubise born

6 Dec 1948 Keke Rosberg born

7 Dec 1925 Nano da Silva Ramos born
7 Dec 1924 John Love born
7 Dec 1917 Ottorino Volonterio born
7 Dec 1977 Georges Grignard died

8 Dec 1955 Paul Crooks born

9 Dec 1926 Ed Elisian born
9 Dec 1928 André Milhoux born
9 Dec 1936 Ben Pon born
9 Dec 1920 Doug Serrurier born
9 Dec 1934 Wayne Weiler born

12 Dec 1946 Emerson Fittipaldi born
12 Dec 1948 Roelof Wunderink born
12 Dec 1946 Renzo Zorzi born
12 Dec 1959 Bruce McLaren first win
12 Dec 1959 Jack Brabham clinched first Championship
12 Dec 1959 GP at Sebring

13 Dec 1945 Brian McGuire born
13 Dec 1918 Bill Vukovich born

14 Dec 1919 Bob Drake born

15 Dec 1913 Walt Ader born
15 Dec 1927 Bill Mackey born

16 Dec 1920 Les Leston born
16 Dec 1932 Henry Taylor born
16 Dec 1982 Colin Chapman died
16 Dec 1989 Oscar Gálvez died

18 Dec 1907 Bill Holland born
18 Dec 1991 George Abecassis died

19 Dec 1923 Onofré Marimón born

20 Dec 1968 Karl Wendlinger born

21 Dec 1935 Lorenzo Bandini born
21 Dec 1921 Günther Bechem born

22 Dec 1905 Pierre Levegh born

23 Dec 1956 Michele Alboreto born
23 Dec 1962 Bertrand Gachot born
23 Dec 1985 B Bira died

24 Dec 1949 Warwick Brown born
24 Dec 1941 Howden Ganley born

25 Dec 1934 Giancarlo Baghetti born
25 Dec 1943 Wilson Fittipaldi born

26 Dec 1935 Bill Brack born
26 Dec 1936 Trevor Taylor born
26 Dec 1958 Adrian Newey born
26 Dec 1992 Jan Flinterman died

27 Dec 1969 Jean-Christophe Boullion born
27 Dec 1900 Hans Stuck born
27 Dec 1993 André Pilette died

28 Dec 1939 Conny Andersson born
28 Dec 1896 Philippe Étançelin born
28 Dec 1909 David Murray born
28 Dec 1983 Eugène Chaboud died

29 Dec 1925 Jay Chamberlain born
29 Dec 1917 David Hampshire born
29 Dec 1924 Carlo Chiti born
29 Dec 1988 Mike Beuttler died
29 Dec 1982 Max de Terra died
29 Dec 1962 Graham Hill clinched first Championship

30 Dec 1911 Walt Brown born
30 Dec 1942 Guy Edwards born
30 Dec 1956 François Hesnault born
30 Dec 1936 Mike Spence born
30 Dec 1976 Rudi Fischer died

BIBLIOGRAPHY

During compilation of this book, we referred to numerous publications, the most useful of which were:

MAGAZINES

Autosport
F1 News
Motoring News

BOOKS

33 Anni Di Gran Premio Iridati F.1 (1950-82)
Autosprint, Italy

A Record of Grand Prix and Voiturette Racing (1950-64)
Sheldon

A-Z of Formula Racing Cars
Hodges

Autocourse (from 1961/62)
Hazleton Publishing

Benetton-Ford A Racing Partnership
Drackett

Brabham The Grand Prix Cars
Henry

BRM The Saga of British Racing Motors Vol.1 (1945-60)
Nye

Champion Book of World Championship Motor Racing Facts & Figures
Kettlewell

Cooper Cars
Nye

Directory of Formula One Cars (1966-86)
Pritchard

Ferrari The Grand Prix Cars
Henry

FIA Yearbook of Automobile Sport (from 1969)
FIA, France

Formula One Championship Computerised Results & Timing Service (1982-1993)
Longines, Olivetti & TAG/Heuer

Formula 3000 Yearbook (1987-1992)
Barbe etc, France

Grand Prix Cars (1945-65)
Lawrence

Grand Prix! (1950-84)
Lang

Grand Prix Who's Who
Small

Guide to Formula 1 (1994-1996)
ICN

Guinness Guide to International Motor Racing
Higham

Handbook of Grand Prix Cars Post-War to Present
Tanner, USA

History of the Grand Prix Car (1945-91)
Nye

Illustrated History of the Indianapolis 500 (1911-1994)
Fox, USA

IndyCar/ CART Media Guides (1988-1996)
IndyCar/ CART, USA

Jacques Villeneuve In His Own Right
Hilton

Kimberley's Team and Driver Guides
Various

McLaren The Grand Prix, Can-Am & Indy Cars
Nye

Motor Racing and Motor Rally Directory (1957)
Motor Racing staff

The Motor Racing Register (1961/62-1966)
Dempsey

The Formula One Record Book (1961-1965)
Thomson

The Motor Racing Directory
Kettlewell

The Concise Dictionary of Motorsport
Bishop

The Encyclopedia of Motorsport
Georgano

Theme Lotus From Chapman To Ducarouge (1956-1986)
Nye